Official 1989
National Footba

Record
& Fact Book

A National Football League Book.
Workman Publishing Co., New York.

National Football League, 1989

410 Park Avenue, New York, N.Y. 10022 (212) 758-1500

Commissioner: Pete Rozelle
Executive Vice President & League Counsel: Jay Moyer
Acting Treasurer: Tom Sullivan
Executive Director: Don Weiss
Director of Administration: Joe Rhein
Director of Communications: Joe Browne
Director of Operations: Jan Van Duser
Director of Broadcasting: Val Pinchbeck, Jr.
Assistant Director of Broadcasting: Nancy Behar
Director of Public Relations: Jim Heffernan
Director of Security: Warren Welsh
Assistant Director of Security: Charles R. Jackson
Director of Player Personnel: Joel Bussert
Supervisor of Officials: Art McNally
Assistant Supervisors of Officials: Jack Reader, Joe Gardi, Tony Veteri
Director of Special Events: Jim Steeg
Assistant Director of Special Events: Susan McCann Minogue
Director of Equal Employment & Assistant Counsel: David Cornwell
Director of Personnel: John Buzzeo
Director of Special Projects: Bill Granholm
Operations Coordinator: Frank Cuce
Director of Player Relations: Mel Blount

American Football Conference

President: Lamar Hunt, Kansas City Chiefs
Assistant to President: Roger Goodell
Director of Information: Pete Abitante

National Football Conference

President: Wellington Mara, New York Giants
Assistant to President: Jim Noel
Director of Information: Dick Maxwell

Cover Photograph by Mike Powell, Allsport.

Printed in the United States of America.

A National Football League Book.
Compiled by the NFL Public Relations Department and Seymour Siwoff, Elias Sports Bureau.
Edited by Pete Abitante, NFL Public Relations and Chuck Garrity, Jr., NFLP Creative Services.
Statistics by Elias Sports Bureau.
Produced by NFL Properties, Inc., Creative Services Division.

Workman Publishing Co.
708 Broadway, New York, N.Y. 10003
Manufactured in the United States of America.
First printing, July 1989.
10 9 8 7 6 5 4 3 2 1

Contents

1989 SCHEDULE AND NOTE CALENDAR

All times P.M. local daylight.
Nationally televised games in parentheses. CBS and NBC television doubleheader games in the regular season to be announced.

Preseason/First Week

Saturday, August 5	Hall of Fame Game at Canton, Ohio Buffalo ___ vs. Washington ___	(ABC) 1:30
	American Bowl '89 at Tokyo, Japan Los Angeles Rams ___ vs. San Francisco ___	(ESPN) 10:00*
Sunday, August 6	American Bowl '89 at London, England Cleveland ___ vs. Philadelphia ___	(NBC) 1:00*
Friday, August 11	Seattle ___ at Phoenix ___	7:30
Saturday, August 12	Atlanta ___ at Philadelphia ___	7:30
	Cleveland ___ at Detroit ___	7:30
	Houston ___ at Tampa Bay ___	7:00
	Indianapolis ___ at New Orleans ___	7:00
	Kansas City ___ vs. Minnesota ___ at Memphis, Tenn.	7:30
	Los Angeles Rams ___ at Denver ___	7:00
	New York Giants ___ at New England ___	7:00
	New York Jets ___ vs. Green Bay ___ at Milwaukee	1:00
	San Francisco ___ at Los Angeles Raiders ___	6:00
	Washington ___ at Pittsburgh ___	8:00
Sunday, August 13	Buffalo ___ at Cincinnati ___	(ESPN) 8:00
	Dallas ___ at San Diego ___	(CBS) 12:00
Monday, August 14	Chicago ___ at Miami ___	(ABC) 8:00

*Eastern Time.
(Tokyo game actual kickoff 11:00 a.m. August 6; London game actual kickoff 6:00 p.m. August 6)

Preseason/Second Week

Saturday, August 19	Atlanta ___ at Tampa Bay ___	7:00
	Cincinnati ___ at Detroit ___	7:30
	Dallas ___ at Los Angeles Raiders ___	6:00
	Denver ___ at San Francisco ___	(CBS) 6:00
	Indianapolis ___ at Green Bay ___	1:00
	Miami ___ vs. Houston ___ at Jacksonville, Fla.	7:30
	New Orleans ___ at Buffalo ___	7:30
	Pittsburgh ___ at Cleveland ___	7:30
	San Diego ___ at Chicago ___	6:00
	Seattle ___ vs. New England ___ at St. Louis, Mo.	8:00
Sunday, August 20	New York Giants ___ at Kansas City ___	7:00
	New York Jets ___ vs. Philadelphia ___ at Raleigh, N.C.	(ESPN) 8:00
Monday, August 21	Phoenix ___ at Los Angeles Rams ___	8:00
	Washington ___ at Minnesota ___	(ABC) 7:00

Preseason/Third Week

Wednesday, August 23	San Diego ___ at San Francisco ___	6:00
Friday, August 25	Detroit ___ at Seattle ___	7:30
	Miami ___ at Washington ___	(NBC) 8:00
Saturday, August 26	Buffalo ___ vs. Green Bay ___ at Madison, Wis.	1:00
	Cleveland ___ at Phoenix ___	6:00
	Dallas ___ at Denver ___	7:00
	Houston ___ vs. Los Angeles Raiders ___ at Oakland	7:00
	Minnesota ___ at Los Angeles Rams ___	6:00
	New England ___ at Atlanta ___	7:30
	New York Jets ___ at New York Giants ___	8:00
	Pittsburgh ___ at Philadelphia ___	7:30
	Tampa Bay ___ at Indianapolis ___	7:30
Sunday, August 27	Kansas City ___ at Chicago ___	(ESPN) 7:00
Monday, August 28	Cincinnati ___ at New Orleans ___	(ABC) 7:00

Preseason/Fourth Week

Friday, September 1	Atlanta ___ vs. Buffalo ___ at Jacksonville, Fla.	8:00
	Cincinnati ___ at Minnesota ___	7:00
	Green Bay ___ at New England ___	7:00
	New York Jets ___ at Kansas City ___	7:30
	Phoenix ___ at San Diego ___	7:00
	San Francisco ___ at Seattle ___	(NBC) 6:00
	Washington ___ at New Orleans ___	7:00
Saturday, September 2	Chicago ___ at Los Angeles Raiders ___	1:00
	Denver ___ at Indianapolis ___	7:30
	Detroit ___ at Los Angeles Rams ___	6:00
	Houston ___ at Dallas ___	8:00
	Philadelphia ___ at Miami ___	(CBS) 9:00
	Pittsburgh ___ at New York Giants ___	8:00
	Tampa Bay ___ at Cleveland ___	7:00

First Week

Sunday, September 10 (NBC-TV doubleheader)	Buffalo ___ at Miami ___	4:00
	Cincinnati ___ at Chicago ___	12:00
	Cleveland ___ at Pittsburgh ___	4:00
	Dallas ___ at New Orleans ___	12:00
	Houston ___ at Minnesota ___	3:00
	Kansas City ___ at Denver ___	2:00
	Los Angeles Rams ___ at Atlanta ___	1:00
	New England ___ at New York Jets ___	4:00
	Phoenix ___ at Detroit ___	1:00
	San Diego ___ at Los Angeles Raiders ___	1:00
	San Francisco ___ at Indianapolis ___	12:00
	Seattle ___ at Philadelphia ___	4:00
	Tampa Bay ___ at Green Bay ___	12:00
Monday, September 11	New York Giants ___ at Washington ___	(ABC) 9:00

Second Week

Sunday, September 17 (CBS-TV doubleheader)	Dallas ___ at Atlanta ___	1:00
	Detroit ___ at New York Giants ___	4:00
	Houston ___ at San Diego ___	1:00
	Indianapolis ___ at Los Angeles Rams ___	1:00
	Los Angeles Raiders ___ at Kansas City ___	12:00
	Miami ___ at New England ___	1:00
	Minnesota ___ at Chicago ___	3:00
	New Orleans ___ at Green Bay ___	12:00
	New York Jets ___ at Cleveland ___	1:00
	Philadelphia ___ at Washington ___	1:00
	Phoenix ___ at Seattle ___	1:00
	Pittsburgh ___ at Cincinnati ___	1:00
	San Francisco ___ at Tampa Bay ___	4:00
Monday, September 18	Denver ___ at Buffalo ___	(ABC) 9:00

Third Week

Sunday, September 24 (NBC-TV doubleheader)	Atlanta ___ at Indianapolis ___	12:00
	Buffalo ___ at Houston ___	12:00
	Chicago ___ at Detroit ___	1:00
	Green Bay ___ at Los Angeles Rams ___	1:00
	Kansas City ___ at San Diego ___	1:00
	Los Angeles Raiders ___ at Denver ___	2:00
	Minnesota ___ at Pittsburgh ___	1:00
	New Orleans ___ at Tampa Bay ___	1:00
	New York Jets ___ at Miami ___	4:00
	Phoenix ___ at New York Giants ___	1:00
	San Francisco ___ at Philadelphia ___	1:00
	Seattle ___ at New England ___	1:00
	Washington ___ at Dallas ___	12:00
Monday, September 25	Cleveland ___ at Cincinnati ___	(ABC) 9:00

Fourth Week

Sunday, October 1 (CBS-TV doubleheader)	Atlanta ___ vs. Green Bay ___ at Milwaukee		12:00
	Cincinnati ___ at Kansas City ___		12:00
	Denver ___ at Cleveland ___		1:00
	Indianapolis ___ at New York Jets ___		1:00
	Los Angeles Rams ___ at San Francisco ___		1:00
	Miami ___ at Houston ___		12:00
	New England ___ at Buffalo ___		1:00
	New York Giants ___ at Dallas ___		3:00
	Pittsburgh ___ at Detroit ___		1:00
	San Diego ___ at Phoenix ___		1:00
	Seattle ___ at Los Angeles Raiders ___		1:00
	Tampa Bay ___ at Minnesota ___		12:00
	Washington ___ at New Orleans ___		12:00
Monday, October 2	Philadelphia ___ at Chicago ___	(ABC)	8:00

Fifth Week

Sunday, October 8 (CBS-TV doubleheader)	Atlanta ___ at Los Angeles Rams ___		1:00
	Buffalo ___ at Indianapolis ___		12:00
	Chicago ___ at Tampa Bay ___		1:00
	Cincinnati ___ at Pittsburgh ___		1:00
	Cleveland ___ at Miami ___		1:00
	Dallas ___ at Green Bay ___		12:00
	Detroit ___ at Minnesota ___		12:00
	Houston ___ at New England ___		1:00
	Kansas City ___ at Seattle ___		1:00
	New Orleans ___ at San Francisco ___		1:00
	New York Giants ___ at Philadelphia ___		1:00
	Phoenix ___ at Washington ___		4:00
	San Diego ___ at Denver ___		2:00
Monday, October 9	L.A. Raiders ___ at New York Jets ___	(ABC)	9:00

Sixth Week

Sunday, October 15 (NBC-TV doubleheader)	Detroit ___ at Tampa Bay ___		1:00
	Green Bay ___ at Minnesota ___		12:00
	Houston ___ at Chicago ___		12:00
	Indianapolis ___ at Denver ___		2:00
	Kansas City ___ at Los Angeles Raiders ___		1:00
	Miami ___ at Cincinnati ___		1:00
	New England ___ at Atlanta ___		1:00
	New York Jets ___ at New Orleans ___		3:00
	Philadelphia ___ at Phoenix ___		1:00
	Pittsburgh ___ at Cleveland ___		4:00
	San Francisco ___ at Dallas ___		12:00
	Seattle ___ at San Diego ___		1:00
	Washington ___ at New York Giants ___		1:00
Monday, October 16	Los Angeles Rams ___ at Buffalo ___	(ABC)	9:00

Seventh Week

Sunday, October 22 (NBC-TV doubleheader)	Atlanta ___ at Phoenix ___		1:00
	Dallas ___ at Kansas City ___		12:00
	Denver ___ at Seattle ___		1:00
	Green Bay ___ at Miami ___		1:00
	Indianapolis ___ at Cincinnati ___		1:00
	Los Angeles Raiders ___ at Philadelphia ___		1:00
	Minnesota ___ at Detroit ___		1:00
	New England ___ at San Francisco ___		1:00
	New Orleans ___ at Los Angeles Rams ___		1:00
	New York Giants ___ at San Diego ___		1:00
	New York Jets ___ at Buffalo ___		1:00
	Pittsburgh ___ at Houston ___		12:00
	Tampa Bay ___ at Washington ___		1:00
Monday, October 23	Chicago ___ at Cleveland ___	(ABC)	9:00

Eighth Week

Sunday, October 29	Atlanta ___ at New Orleans ___		12:00
(CBS-TV doubleheader)	Detroit ___ vs. Green Bay ___ at Milwaukee		12:00
	Houston ___ at Cleveland ___		1:00
	Kansas City ___ at Pittsburgh ___		1:00
	Los Angeles Rams ___ at Chicago ___		12:00
	Miami ___ at Buffalo ___		1:00
	New England ___ at Indianapolis ___		1:00
	Philadelphia ___ at Denver ___		2:00
	Phoenix ___ at Dallas ___		12:00
	San Diego ___ at Seattle ___		1:00
	San Francisco ___ at New York Jets ___		4:00
	Tampa Bay ___ at Cincinnati ___		1:00
	Washington ___ at Los Angeles Raiders ___		1:00
Monday, October 30	Minnesota ___ at New York Giants ___	(ABC)	9:00

Ninth Week

Sunday, November 5	Buffalo ___ at Atlanta ___		1:00
(NBC-TV doubleheader)	Chicago ___ at Green Bay ___		12:00
	Cincinnati ___ at Los Angeles Raiders ___		1:00
	Cleveland ___ at Tampa Bay ___		1:00
	Detroit ___ at Houston ___		12:00
	Indianapolis ___ at Miami ___		1:00
	Los Angeles Rams ___ at Minnesota ___		12:00
	New York Giants ___ at Phoenix ___		2:00
	New York Jets ___ at New England ___		1:00
	Philadelphia ___ at San Diego ___		1:00
	Pittsburgh ___ at Denver ___		2:00
	Seattle ___ at Kansas City ___		12:00
Sunday Night	Dallas ___ at Washington ___	(ESPN)	8:00
Monday, November 6	San Francisco ___ at New Orleans ___	(ABC)	8:00

Tenth Week

Sunday, November 12	Atlanta ___ at San Francisco ___		1:00
(CBS-TV doubleheader)	Chicago ___ at Pittsburgh ___		1:00
	Cleveland ___ at Seattle ___		1:00
	Dallas ___ at Phoenix ___		2:00
	Denver ___ at Kansas City ___		12:00
	Green Bay ___ at Detroit ___		1:00
	Indianapolis ___ at Buffalo ___		1:00
	Miami ___ at New York Jets ___		1:00
	Minnesota ___ at Tampa Bay ___		1:00
	New Orleans ___ at New England ___		1:00
	New York Giants ___ at Los Angeles Rams ___		1:00
	Washington ___ at Philadelphia ___		1:00
Sunday Night	Los Angeles Raiders ___ at San Diego ___	(ESPN)	5:00
Monday, November 13	Cincinnati ___ at Houston ___	(ABC)	8:00

Eleventh Week

Sunday, November 19	Buffalo ___ at New England ___		1:00
(NBC-TV doubleheader)	Detroit ___ at Cincinnati ___		1:00
	Green Bay ___ at San Francisco ___		1:00
	Kansas City ___ at Cleveland ___		1:00
	Los Angeles Raiders ___ at Houston ___		3:00
	Miami ___ at Dallas ___		12:00
	Minnesota ___ at Philadelphia ___		1:00
	New Orleans ___ at Atlanta ___		1:00
	Phoenix ___ at Los Angeles Rams ___		1:00
	San Diego ___ at Pittsburgh ___		1:00
	Seattle ___ at New York Giants ___		4:00
	Tampa Bay ___ at Chicago ___		12:00
Sunday Night	New York Jets ___ at Indianapolis ___	(ESPN)	8:00
Monday, November 20	Denver ___ at Washington ___	(ABC)	9:00

Twelfth Week

Thursday, November 23 **Thanksgiving Day**	Cleveland ___ at Detroit ___	(NBC)	12:30
	Philadelphia ___ at Dallas ___	(CBS)	3:00
Sunday, November 26 **(CBS-TV doubleheader)**	Atlanta ___ at New York Jets ___		1:00
	Chicago ___ at Washington ___		4:00
	Cincinnati ___ at Buffalo ___		1:00
	Houston ___ at Kansas City ___		12:00
	Minnesota ___ vs. Green Bay ___ at Milwaukee		12:00
	New England ___ at Los Angeles Raiders ___		1:00
	Pittsburgh ___ at Miami ___		1:00
	San Diego ___ at Indianapolis ___		1:00
	Seattle ___ at Denver ___		2:00
	Tampa Bay ___ at Phoenix ___		2:00
Sunday Night	Los Angeles Rams ___ at New Orleans ___	(ESPN)	7:00
Monday, November 27	New York Giants ___ at San Francisco ___	(ABC)	6:00

Thirteenth Week

Sunday, December 3 **(NBC-TV doubleheader)**	Cincinnati ___ at Cleveland ___		1:00
	Denver ___ at Los Angeles Raiders ___		1:00
	Green Bay ___ at Tampa Bay ___		1:00
	Houston ___ at Pittsburgh ___		1:00
	Indianapolis ___ at New England ___		1:00
	Los Angeles Rams ___ at Dallas ___		12:00
	Miami ___ at Kansas City ___		12:00
	New Orleans ___ at Detroit ___		1:00
	New York Jets ___ at San Diego ___		1:00
	Philadelphia ___ at New York Giants ___		1:00
	San Francisco ___ at Atlanta ___		1:00
	Washington ___ at Phoenix ___		2:00
Sunday Night	Chicago ___ at Minnesota ___	(ESPN)	7:00
Monday, December 4	Buffalo ___ at Seattle ___	(ABC)	6:00

Fourteenth Week

Sunday, December 10 **(CBS-TV doubleheader)**	Atlanta ___ at Minnesota ___		12:00
	Cleveland ___ at Indianapolis ___		4:00
	Dallas ___ at Philadelphia ___		1:00
	Detroit ___ at Chicago ___		12:00
	Kansas City ___ at Green Bay ___		12:00
	New Orleans ___ at Buffalo ___		1:00
	New York Giants ___ at Denver ___		2:00
	Phoenix ___ at Los Angeles Raiders ___		1:00
	Pittsburgh ___ at New York Jets ___		1:00
	San Diego ___ at Washington ___		1:00
	Seattle ___ at Cincinnati ___		1:00
	Tampa Bay ___ at Houston ___		12:00
Sunday Night	New England ___ at Miami ___	(ESPN)	8:00
Monday, December 11	San Francisco ___ at Los Angeles Rams ___	(ABC)	6:00

Fifteenth Week

Saturday, December 16	Dallas ___ at New York Giants ___	(CBS)	12:30
	Denver ___ at Phoenix ___	(NBC)	2:00
Sunday, December 17 **(NBC-TV doubleheader)**	Buffalo ___ at San Francisco ___		1:00
	Green Bay ___ at Chicago ___		12:00
	Houston ___ at Cincinnati ___		1:00
	Miami ___ at Indianapolis ___		1:00
	Minnesota ___ at Cleveland ___		1:00
	New England ___ at Pittsburgh ___		1:00
	New York Jets ___ at Los Angeles Rams ___		1:00
	San Diego ___ at Kansas City ___		12:00
	Tampa Bay ___ at Detroit ___		1:00
	Washington ___ at Atlanta ___		4:00
Sunday Night	Los Angeles Raiders ___ at Seattle ___	(ESPN)	5:00
Monday, December 18	Philadelphia ___ at New Orleans ___	(ABC)	8:00

Sixteenth Week

Saturday, December 23	Buffalo ___ at New York Jets ___	(NBC)	12:30
	Washington ___ at Seattle ___	(CBS)	1:00
Saturday Night	Cleveland ___ at Houston ___	(ESPN)	7:00
Sunday, December 24 (CBS-TV doubleheader)	Chicago ___ at San Francisco ___		1:00
	Denver ___ at San Diego ___		1:00
	Detroit ___ at Atlanta ___		1:00
	Green Bay ___ at Dallas ___		12:00
	Indianapolis ___ at New Orleans ___		12:00
	Kansas City ___ at Miami ___		1:00
	Los Angeles Raiders ___ at New York Giants ___		1:00
	Los Angeles Rams ___ at New England ___		1:00
	Phoenix ___ at Philadelphia ___		1:00
	Pittsburgh ___ at Tampa Bay ___		1:00
Monday, December 25	Cincinnati ___ at Minnesota ___	(ABC)	8:00

First-Round Playoff Games

Site Priorities

Two wild card teams (fourth- and fifth-best records) from each conference will enter the first round of the playoffs. The wild cards from the same conference will play each other. Home clubs will be the clubs with the best won-lost-tied percentage in the regular season. If tied in record, the tie will be broken by the tie-breaking procedures already in effect.

Sunday, December 31, 1989

American Football Conference

___ at ___ (NBC)

National Football Conference

___ at ___ (CBS)

Divisional Playoff Games

Site Priorities

In each conference, the two division winners with the highest won-lost-tied percentage during the regular season will be the home teams. The division winner with the best percentage will be host to the wild card winner from the first-round playoff, and the division winner with the second-best percentage will be host to the third division winner, unless the wild card team is from the same division as the winner with the highest percentage. In that case, the division winner with the best percentage will be host to the third division winner and the second highest division winner will be host to the wild card.

Saturday, January 6, 1990

American Football Conference

___ at ___ (NBC)

National Football Conference

___ at ___ (CBS)

Sunday, January 7, 1990

American Football Conference

___ at ___ (NBC)

National Football Conference

___ at ___ (CBS)

Conference Championship Games, Super Bowl XXIV, and AFC-NFC Pro Bowl

Site Priorities for Championship Games

The home teams will be the surviving divisional playoff winners with the best won-lost-tied percentage during the regular season. The wild card team will never be the home team, in either the divisional playoffs or the championship games. Any ties in won-lost-tied percentage will be broken by the tie-breaking procedures already in effect.

Sunday, January 14, 1990

American Football Conference Championship Game

___ at ___ (NBC)

National Football Conference Championship Game

___ at ___ (CBS)

Sunday, January 28, 1990

Super Bowl XXIV at Louisiana Superdome, New Orleans

___ vs. ___ (CBS)

Sunday, February 4, 1990

AFC-NFC Pro Bowl at Honolulu, Hawaii

AFC ___ vs. NFC ___ (ESPN)

Postseason Games

Sunday, December 31	AFC and NFC First-Round Playoffs (NBC and CBS)
Saturday, January 6	AFC and NFC Divisional Playoffs (NBC and CBS)
Sunday, January 7	AFC and NFC Divisional Playoffs (NBC and CBS)
Sunday, January 14	AFC and NFC Championship Games (NBC and CBS)
Sunday, January 28	Super Bowl XXIV at the Louisiana Superdome, New Orleans, Louisiana (CBS)
Sunday, February 4	AFC-NFC Pro Bowl at Honolulu, Hawaii (ESPN)

1989 Nationally Televised Games

(All games carried on CBS Radio Network.)

Regular Season

Monday, September 11	New York Giants at Washington (night, ABC)
Monday, September 18	Denver at Buffalo (night, ABC)
Monday, September 25	Cleveland at Cincinnati (night, ABC)
Monday, October 2	Philadelphia at Chicago (night, ABC)
Monday, October 9	Los Angeles Raiders at New York Jets (night, ABC)
Monday, October 16	Los Angeles Rams at Buffalo (night, ABC)
Monday, October 23	Chicago at Cleveland (night, ABC)
Monday, October 30	Minnesota at New York Giants (night, ABC)
Sunday, November 5	Dallas at Washington (night, ESPN)
Monday, November 6	San Francisco at New Orleans (night, ABC)
Sunday, November 12	Los Angeles Raiders at San Diego (night, ESPN)
Monday, November 13	Cincinnati at Houston (night, ABC)
Sunday, November 19	New York Jets at Indianapolis (night, ESPN)
Monday, November 20	Denver at Washington (night, ABC)
Thursday, November 23	Cleveland at Detroit (day, NBC)
	Philadelphia at Dallas (day, CBS)
Sunday, November 26	Los Angeles Rams at New Orleans (night, ESPN)
Monday, November 27	New York Giants at San Francisco (night, ABC)
Sunday, December 3	Chicago at Minnesota (night, ESPN)
Monday, December 4	Buffalo at Seattle (night, ABC)
Sunday, December 10	New England at Miami (night, ESPN)
Monday, December 11	San Francisco at Los Angeles Rams (night, ABC)
Saturday, December 16	Dallas at New York Giants (day, CBS)
	Denver at Phoenix (day, NBC)
Sunday, December 17	Los Angeles Raiders at Seattle (night, ESPN)
Monday, December 18	Philadelphia at New Orleans (night, ABC)
Saturday, December 23	Buffalo at New York Jets (day, NBC)
	Washington at Seattle (day, CBS)
	Cleveland at Houston (night, ESPN)
Monday, December 25	Cincinnati at Minnesota (night, ABC)

1989 AFC-NFC Interconference Games

(Sunday unless noted; all times local.)

September 10	Cincinnati at Chicago	4:00
	Houston at Minnesota	3:00
	San Francisco at Indianapolis	12:00
	Seattle at Philadelphia	4:00
September 17	Indianapolis at Los Angeles Rams	1:00
	Phoenix at Seattle	1:00
September 24	Atlanta at Indianapolis	12:00
	Minnesota at Pittsburgh	1:00
October 1	Pittsburgh at Detroit	1:00
	San Diego at Phoenix	1:00
October 15	Houston at Chicago	12:00
	New England at Atlanta	1:00
	New York Jets at New Orleans	3:00
October 16	Los Angeles Rams at Buffalo	9:00
October 22	Dallas at Kansas City	12:00
	Green Bay at Miami	1:00
	Los Angeles Raiders at Philadelphia	1:00
	New England at San Francisco	1:00
	New York Giants at San Diego	1:00
October 23	Chicago at Cleveland	9:00
October 29	Philadelphia at Denver	2:00
	San Francisco at New York Jets	4:00
	Tampa Bay at Cincinnati	1:00
	Washington at Los Angeles Raiders	1:00
November 5	Buffalo at Atlanta	1:00
	Cleveland at Tampa Bay	1:00
	Detroit at Houston	12:00
	Philadelphia at San Diego	1:00
November 12	Chicago at Pittsburgh	1:00
	New Orleans at New England	1:00
November 19	Detroit at Cincinnati	1:00
	Miami at Dallas	12:00
	Seattle at New York Giants	4:00
November 20	Denver at Washington	9:00
November 23	Cleveland at Detroit	12:30
November 26	Atlanta at New York Jets	1:00
December 10	Kansas City at Green Bay	12:00
	New Orleans at Buffalo	1:00
	New York Giants at Denver	2:00
	Phoenix at Los Angeles Raiders	1:00
	San Diego at Washington	1:00
	Tampa Bay at Houston	12:00
December 16	Denver at Phoenix	2:00
December 17	Buffalo at San Francisco	1:00
	Minnesota at Cleveland	1:00
	New York Jets at Los Angeles Rams	1:00
December 23	Washington at Seattle	1:00
December 24	Indianapolis at New Orleans	12:00
	L.A. Raiders at N.Y. Giants	1:00
	Los Angeles Rams at New England	1:00
	Pittsburgh at Tampa Bay	1:00
December 25	Cincinnati at Minnesota	8:00

Saturday, Sunday, and Monday Night Games at a Glance

(All times local; Saturday and Sunday on ESPN; Monday on ABC-TV; all on CBS Radio Network.)

Monday, September 11	New York Giants at Washington (ABC)	9:00
Monday, September 18	Denver at Buffalo (ABC)	9:00
Monday, September 25	Cleveland at Cincinnati (ABC)	9:00
Monday, October 2	Philadelphia at Chicago (ABC)	8:00
Monday, October 9	L.A. Raiders at N.Y. Jets (ABC)	9:00
Monday, October 16	Los Angeles Rams at Buffalo (ABC)	9:00
Monday, October 23	Chicago at Cleveland (ABC)	9:00
Monday, October 30	Minnesota at New York Giants (ABC)	9:00
Sunday, November 5	Dallas at Washington (ESPN)	8:00
Monday, November 6	San Francisco at New Orleans (ABC)	8:00
Sunday, November 12	L.A. Raiders at San Diego (ESPN)	5:00
Monday, November 13	Cincinnati at Houston (ABC)	8:00
Sunday, November 19	New York Jets at Indianapolis (ESPN)	8:00
Monday, November 20	Denver at Washington (ABC)	9:00
Sunday, November 26	L.A. Rams at New Orleans (ESPN)	7:00
Monday, November 27	N.Y. Giants at San Francisco (ABC)	6:00
Sunday, December 3	Chicago at Minnesota (ESPN)	7:00
Monday, December 4	Buffalo at Seattle (ABC)	6:00
Sunday, December 10	New England at Miami (ESPN)	8:00
Monday, December 11	San Francisco at L.A. Rams (ABC)	6:00
Sunday, December 17	Los Angeles Raiders at Seattle (ESPN)	5:00
Monday, December 18	Philadelphia at New Orleans (ABC)	8:00
Saturday, December 23	Cleveland at Houston (ESPN)	7:00
Monday, December 25	Cincinnati at Minnesota (ABC)	8:00

Important Dates

1989

July 5	Claiming period of 24 hours begins in waiver system. All waivers for the year are no-recall and no-withdrawal.
Mid-July	Team training camps open.
August 5	Hall of Fame Game, Canton, Ohio: Buffalo vs. Washington.
August 5	American Bowl '89, Tokyo, Japan: Los Angeles Rams vs. San Francisco.
August 6	American Bowl '89, London, England: Cleveland vs. Philadelphia.
August 11-14	First preseason weekend.
August 19-21	Second preseason weekend.
August 23-28	Third preseason weekend.
August 29	Roster cutdown to maximum of 60 players.
September 1-2	Fourth preseason weekend.
September 4	Roster cutdown to maximum of 47 players. Clubs may dress 45 players for each game. No later than one hour prior to kickoff of each game, clubs must establish an Inactive List of two players.
September 5	After 4 P.M. New York Time, clubs may establish a Developmental Squad of six players.
September 10-11	Regular season opens.
September 26	Priority on multiple waiver claims is now based on the current season's standings.
October 17	Trading of player contracts/rights ends at 4 P.M., New York Time.
October 24-25	NFL Meeting, Cleveland, Ohio.
November 25	Deadline for reinstatement of players in Reserve List categories of Retired, Did Not Report, and Veteran Free Agents Asked to Re-sign.
December 18-19	Balloting for AFC-NFC Pro Bowl.
December 22	Deadline for waiver requests in 1989.
December 27	Deadline for postseason participants to sign free agents for playoffs, except punters or kickers.
December 31	AFC and NFC First-Round Playoff Games.

1990

January 6-7	AFC and NFC Divisional Playoff Games.
January 14	AFC and NFC Championship Games.
January 28	Super Bowl XXIV at Louisiana Superdome, New Orleans, Louisiana.
January 31-February 4	Combine timing and testing of college players, Hoosier Dome, Indianapolis, Indiana.
February 1	Deadline for establishing Protected List of 37 players. All players who are not on Protected List will be eligible to sign as free agents with any other club through April 1.
February 4	AFC-NFC Pro Bowl at Aloha Stadium, Honolulu, Hawaii.
February 5	Waiver system begins for 1990.
February 5	Trading period begins.
March 12-16	NFL Annual Meeting, Orlando, Florida.
April 1	Deadline for signing of offer sheets by veteran free agents and new clubs.
April 1	Expiration of free agency for unprotected players.
April 22-23	55th Annual NFL Selection Meeting, New York, New York.
May 23-24	NFL Spring Meeting, Dallas, Texas.
August 4	Hall of Fame Game, Canton, Ohio: Denver vs. Chicago.
August 10-12	First preseason weekend.
September 9-10	Regular season opens.
December 23	Regular season closes.
December 30	AFC and NFC First-Round Playoff Games.

1991

January 5-6	AFC and NFC Divisional Playoff Games.
January 13	AFC and NFC Championship Games.
January 27	Super Bowl XXV at Tampa Stadium, Tampa, Florida.
February 3	AFC-NFC Pro Bowl.
March 17-22	NFL Annual Meeting, Kona, Hawaii.
April 21-22	56th Annual NFL Selection Meeting, New York, New York.
August 3	Hall of Fame Game, Canton, Ohio: Miami vs. Detroit.
August 9-11	First preseason weekend.
September 8-9	Regular season opens.
December 22	Regular season closes.
December 29	AFC and NFC First-Round Playoff Games.

1992

January 4-5	AFC and NFC Divisional Playoff Games.
January 12	AFC and NFC Championship Games.
January 26	Super Bowl XXVI at Hubert H. Humphrey Metrodome, Minneapolis, Minnesota.
February 2	AFC-NFC Pro Bowl.
March 16-20	NFL Annual Meeting, Phoenix, Arizona.
April 26-27	57th Annual NFL Selection Meeting, New York, New York.
August 8	Hall of Fame Game, Canton, Ohio: New York Jets vs. Philadelphia.
August 14-16	First preseason weekend.
September 13-14	Regular season opens.
December 28-29	Regular season closes.

1993

January 3	AFC and NFC First-Round Playoff Games.
January 9-10	AFC and NFC Divisional Playoff Games.
January 17	AFC and NFC Championship Games.
January 31	Super Bowl XXVII (site to be determined).
February 7	AFC-NFC Pro Bowl.
March	NFL Annual Meeting, Palm Springs, California.

Future Pro Football Hall of Fame Games

1993	Los Angeles Raiders (AFC) vs. Green Bay Packers (NFC)
1994	Cleveland Browns (AFC) vs. Dallas Cowboys (NFC)
1995	San Diego Chargers (AFC) vs. Atlanta Falcons (NFC)
1996	Indianapolis Colts (AFC) vs. New Orleans Saints (NFC)
1997	Seattle Seahawks (AFC) vs. Minnesota Vikings (NFC)
1998	Pittsburgh Steelers (AFC) vs. Tampa Bay Buccaneers (NFC)

Waivers

The waiver system is a procedure by which player contracts or NFL rights to players are made available by a club to other clubs in the League. During the procedure the 27 other clubs either file claims to obtain the players or waive the opportunity to do so—thus the term "waiver." Claiming clubs are assigned players on a priority based on the inverse of won-and-lost standing. The claiming period normally is 10 days during the offseason and 24 hours from early July through December. In some circumstances another 24 hours is added on to allow the original club to rescind its action (known as a recall of a waiver request) and/or the claiming club to do the same (known as withdrawal of a claim). If a player passes through waivers unclaimed and is not recalled by the original club, he becomes a free agent. All waivers from July through December are no recall and no withdrawal. Under the Collective Bargaining Agreement, from February 1 through October 17, any veteran who has acquired four years of pension credit may, if about to be assigned to another club through the waiver system, reject such assignment and become a free agent.

Active List

The Active List is the principal status for players participating for a club. It consists of all players under contract, including option, who are eligible for preseason, regular season, and postseason games. In 1989, teams will be permitted to open training camp with no more than 80 players under contract and thereafter must meet a series of mandatory roster reductions prior to the season opener. Teams will be permitted to dress up to 45 players for each regular season and postseason game during the 1989 season; in addition, each club will have an Inactive List of two players. Maximum roster limits and dates for 1989 are:

Through May 31, 1989	maximum 90 players under contract
June 1......................	maximum 80 players under contract
August 29...................	active list of 60 players
September 4	active list of 45 players (plus two-player Inactive List)

In addition to the Active List limits described above, there also is an overall roster limit of 90 players through May 31, 1989, and 80 players thereafter that is applicable to all players on a club's Active, Inactive, or Exempt Lists and Developmental Squad, and any players on Reserve as Injured, Physically Unable to Perform, Non-Football Illness/Injury, and Suspended.

Reserve List

The Reserve List is a status for players who, for reasons of injury, retirement, military service, or other circumstances, are not immediately available for participation with a club. Those players in the category of Reserve/Injured who were physically unable to play football for a minimum of four weeks from the date of going onto Reserve would fall under two practice options:

Option 1: After four weeks on Reserve/Injured, the player can practice for two weeks but then must be waived or activated;
Option 2: After six weeks on Reserve/Injured, the player can be activated, waived, or begin unlimited practice. If practicing, then the player must count against the Developmental Squad of six.

No player is eligible for activation unless he has missed at least six regular season games. Each club will have five free re-activations for players placed on Reserve/Injured after the final cutdown. Any player placed on Reserve/Injured prior to or concurrent with the final cutdown on September 4 may not return to the club nor practice with the team that year. Clubs participating in postseason competition will be granted an additional re-activation for each postseason game, provided they have exhausted all previous activations. Players who were terminated via waivers from a club's Reserve/Injured List can be re-signed after the six-game requirement has been fulfilled but must clear procedural recall waivers to return to the same club's Active List. Players in the category of Reserve/Retired, Reserve/Did Not Report, or Reserve/Veteran Free Agent Asked to Re-sign, may not be reinstated during the period from 30 days before the end of the regular season through the postseason.

Developmental Squad

In 1989, each team also may establish a six-player Developmental Squad after the final cutdown to 45 active and two inactive players on September 4. Only rookie and first-year free agent players are eligible to be signed to a club's Developmental Squad. Compensation while on the Developmental Squad will be limited to a standard League-wide amount established for such squads. Each player will be bound exclusively to the club which signs him until that club chooses to terminate the contract. If a club signs a player on its Developmental Squad to its Active List, it must either use one of its five free activations or request procedural recall waivers. No player may be moved directly from a club's Active List to its Developmental Squad.

Trades

Unrestricted trading between the AFC and NFC is allowed in 1989 through October 17, after which trading of player contracts/rights will end until February 5, 1990.

Annual Active Player Limits

NFL

Year(s)	Limit
1985-89	45
1983-84	49
1982	45†–49
1978–81	45
1975–77	43
1974	47
1964–73	40
1963	37
1961–62	36
1960	38
1959	36
1957–58	35
1951–56	33
1949–50	32
1948	35
1947	35*–34
1945–46	33
1943–44	28
1940–42	33
1938–39	30
1936–37	25
1935	24
1930–34	20
1926–29	18
1925	16

†45 for first two games
*35 for first three games

AFL

Year(s)	Limit
1966–69	40
1965	38
1964	34
1962–63	33
1960–61	35

Tie-Breaking Procedures

The following procedures will be used to break standings ties for postseason playoffs and to determine regular-season schedules.

To Break a Tie Within a Division

If, at the end of the regular season, two or more clubs in the same division finish with identical won-lost-tied percentages, the following steps will be taken until a champion is determined.

Two Clubs

1. Head-to-head (best won-lost-tied percentage in games between the clubs).
2. Best won-lost-tied percentage in games played within the division.
3. Best won-lost-tied percentage in games played within the conference.
4. Best won-lost-tied percentage in common games, if applicable.
5. Best net points in division games.
6. Best net points in all games.
7. Strength of schedule.
8. Best net touchdowns in all games.
9. Coin toss

Three or More Clubs

(Note: If one team wins multiple-team tiebreaker to advance to playoff round, remaining teams revert to step 1 of applicable two-club format, i.e., either in division tiebreaker or Wild Card tiebreaker. If two teams in a multiple-team tie possess superior marks in a tiebreaking step, this pair of teams revert to top of applicable two-club format to break tie. One team advances to playoff round, while other returns to original group and step 1 of applicable tiebreaker).

1. Head-to-head (best won-lost-tied percentage in games among the clubs).
2. Best won-lost-tied percentage in games played within the division.
3. Best won-lost-tied percentage in games played within the conference.
4. Best won-lost-tied percentage in common games.
5. Best net points in division games.
6. Best net points in all games.
7. Strength of schedule.
8. Best net touchdowns in all games.
9. Coin toss.

To Break a Tie for the Wild Card Team

If it is necessary to break ties to determine the two Wild Card clubs from each conference, the following steps will be taken.

1. If the tied clubs are from the same division, apply division tiebreaker.
2. If the tied clubs are from different divisions, apply the following steps.

Two Clubs

1. Head-to-head, if applicable.
2. Best won-lost-tied percentage in games played within the conference.
3. Best won-lost-tied percentage in common games, minimum of four.
4. Best average net points in conference games.
5. Best net points in all games.
6. Strength of schedule.
7. Best net touchdowns in all games.
8. Coin toss.

Three or More Clubs

(Note: If one team wins multiple-team tiebreaker to advance to playoff round, remaining teams revert to step 1 of applicable two-club format, i.e., either in division tiebreaker or Wild Card tiebreaker. If two teams in a multiple-team tie possess superior marks in a tiebreaking step, this pair of teams revert to the top of the applicable two-club format to break tie. One team advances to playoff round, while other returns to original group and step 1 of applicable tiebreaker.)

1. Head-to-head sweep. (Applicable only if one club has defeated each of the others, or if one club has lost to each of the others.)
2. Best won-lost-tied percentage in games played within the conference.
3. Best won-lost-tied percentage in common games, minimum of four.
4. Best average net points in conference games.
5. Best net points in all games.
6. Strength of schedule.
7. Best net touchdowns in all games.
8. Coin toss.

Tie-Breaking Procedure for Selection Meeting

If two or more clubs are tied for selection order, the conventional strength of schedule tiebreaker will be applied, subject to the following exceptions for playoff teams.

1. The Super Bowl winner will be last and the Super Bowl loser will be next-to-last.
2. Any non-Super Bowl playoff team involved in a tie moves down in drafting priority as follows:
   A. Participation by a club in the playoffs without a victory adds one-half victory to the club's regular-season won-lost-tied record.
   B. For each victory in the playoffs, one full victory will be added to the club's regular-season won-lost-tied record.
3. Clubs with the best won-lost-tied records after these steps are applied will drop to their appropriate spots at the bottom of the tied segment. In no case will the above process move a club lower than the segment in which it was initially tied.
4. Tied clubs will alternate priority throughout the 12 rounds of the draft. In case of a tie involving three or more teams, the club with priority in the first round will drop to the bottom of the tied segment in the second round and move its way back to the top of the segment in each succeeding round.

Figuring the 1990 NFL Schedule

As soon as the final game of the 1989 NFL regular season (Cincinnati at Minnesota, December 25) has been completed, it will be possible to determine the 1990 opponents of the 28 teams.

Each 1990 team schedule is based on a "common opponent" formula initiated for the 1978 season and most recently modified in 1987. Under the common opponent format, the first- through fourth-place teams in a division play at least 12 of their 16 games the following season against common opponents, and the fifth-place team in the division plays at least 10 common opponent games. It is not a position scheduling format in which the strong play the strong and the weak play the weak.

For years the NFL had been seeking a more easily understood and balanced schedule that would provide both competitive equality and a variety of opponents. Under the old rotation scheduling system in effect from 1970–77, non-division opponents were determined by a pre-set formula. This often resulted in competitive imbalances.

With "common opponents" the basis for scheduling, a more competitive and equitable method of determining division champions and postseason playoff representatives has developed. Teams battling for a division title are playing at least 75 percent of their games against common opponents.

In 1987, NFL owners passed two by-law proposals designed to modify the common opponent scheduling format in the hopes of creating even more equity. The first, concerns pairings with non-division opponents:

Prior Year's Finish in Division	Pairings in Non-Division Games Within Conference	Previous Pairings 1978-86
1	1-1-2-3	1-1-4-4
2	1-2-2-4	2-2-3-3
3	1-3-3-4	2-2-3-3
4	2-3-4-4	1-1-4-4

The second bylaw change further specified that: "site locations (for the non-division games listed above) will be assigned so that, where possible by formula, teams do not play a second consecutive regular-season home or road game with an opponent." The formula to determine 1990 site locations will be used on the final day of the 1989 season when the division finishes have been determined.

The NFL also has used the same philosophy in the determination of site locations for interconference games (AFC vs. NFC), avoiding a team playing two consecutive home or road games with an opponent, where possible by formula.

Under the common opponent format, schedules of any NFL team are figured according to one of the following three formulas. (The reference point for the figuring is the team's final division standing. Ties for a position in divisions are broken according to the tie-breaking procedures outlined on page 13. The chart on the following page is included for use as you go through each step.)

A. First- through fourth-place teams in a five-team division (AFC East, AFC West, NFC East, NFC Central).

1. Home-and-home round-robin within the division (8 games).
2. One game each with the first- through fourth-place teams in a division of the other conference (4 games). In 1990, the AFC East will play the NFC East, the AFC Central will play the NFC West, and the AFC West will play the NFC Central.
3. The first-place team plays the first-place teams in the other divisions within the conference plus a second- and third-place team within the conference. The second-place team plays the second-place teams in the other divisions within the conference plus a first- and fourth-place team within the conference. The third-place team plays the third-place teams in the other divisions within the conference plus a first- and fourth-place team within the conference. The fourth-place team plays the fourth-place teams in the other divisions within the conference plus a second- and third-place team within the conference (4 games).

This completes the 16-game schedule.

B. First- through fourth-place teams in a four-team division (AFC Central, NFC West).

1. Home-and-home round-robin within the division (6 games).
2. One game with each of the fifth-place teams in the conference (2 games).
3. The same procedure that is listed in step A2 (4 games).
4. The same procedure that is listed in step A3 (4 games).

This completes the 16-game schedule.

C. The fifth-place teams in a division (AFC East, AFC West, NFC East, NFC Central).

1. Home-and-home round-robin within the division (8 games).
2. One game with each team in the four-team division of the conference (4 games).
3. A home-and-home with the other fifth-place team in the conference (2 games).
4. One game each with the fifth-place teams in the other conference (2 games).

This completes the 16-game schedule.

The 1990 Opponent Breakdown chart on the following page does not include the round-robin games within the division. Those are automatically scheduled on a home-and-away basis.

1989 NFL Standings

AFC

EAST AE

1
2
3
4
5

CENTRAL AC

1
2
3
4

WEST AW

1
2
3
4
5

NFC

EAST NE

1
2
3
4
5

WEST NW

1
2
3
4

CENTRAL NC

1
2
3
4
5

A Team's 1990 Schedule

Team Name

1990 Opponent Breakdown

(Certain game sites subject to change under NFL scheduling formulas.)

AE — AFC East

	Home	Away
AE1	AW1	AC1
	AW3	AC2
	NE2	NE1
	NE4	NE3
AE2	AW2	AC2
	AW1	AC4
	NE1	NE2
	NE3	NE4
AE3	AW3	AC3
	AW4	AC1
	NE2	NE1
	NE4	NE3
AE4	AW4	AC4
	AW2	AC3
	NE1	NE2
	NE3	NE4
AE5	AW5	AW5
	AC1	AC2
	AC3	AC4
	NE5	NC5

AC — AFC Central

	Home	Away
AC1	AE1	AW1
	AE3	AW2
	AW5	AE5
	NW2	NW1
	NW4	NW3
AC2	AE2	AW2
	AE1	AW4
	AE5	AW5
	NW1	NW2
	NW3	NW4
AC3	AE3	AW3
	AE4	AW1
	AW5	AE5
	NW2	NW1
	NW4	NW3
AC4	AE4	AW4
	AE2	AW3
	AE5	AW5
	NW1	NW2
	NW3	NW4

AW — AFC West

	Home	Away
AW1	AC1	AE1
	AC3	AE2
	NC2	NC1
	NC4	NC3
AW2	AC2	AE2
	AC1	AE4
	NC1	NC2
	NC3	NC4
AW3	AC3	AE3
	AC4	AE1
	NC2	NC1
	NC4	NC3
AW4	AC4	AE4
	AC2	AE3
	NC1	NC2
	NC3	NC4
AW5	AE5	AE5
	AC2	AC1
	AC4	AC3
	NC5	NE5

NE — NFC East

	Home	Away
NE1	NC1	NW1
	NC3	NW2
	AE1	AE2
	AE3	AE4
NE2	NC2	NW2
	NC1	NW4
	AE2	AE1
	AE4	AE3
NE3	NC3	NW3
	NC4	NW1
	AE1	AE2
	AE3	AE4
NE4	NC4	NW4
	NC2	NW3
	AE2	AE1
	AE4	AE3
NE5	NC5	NC5
	NW1	NW2
	NW3	NW4
	AW5	AE5

NC — NFC Central

	Home	Away
NC1	NW1	NE1
	NW3	NE2
	AW1	AW2
	AW3	AW4
NC2	NW2	NE2
	NW1	NE4
	AW2	AW1
	AW4	AW3
NC3	NW3	NE3
	NW4	NE1
	AW1	AW2
	AW3	AW4
NC4	NW4	NE4
	NW2	NE3
	AW2	AW1
	AW4	AW3
NC5	NE5	NE5
	NW2	NW1
	NW4	NW3
	AE5	AW5

NW — NFC West

	Home	Away
NW1	NE1	NC1
	NE3	NC2
	NC5	NE5
	AC1	AC2
	AC3	AC4
NW2	NE2	NC2
	NE1	NC4
	NE5	NC5
	AC2	AC1
	AC4	AC3
NW3	NE3	NC3
	NE4	NC1
	NC5	NE5
	AC1	AC2
	AC3	AC4
NW4	NE4	NC4
	NE2	NC3
	NE5	NC5
	AC2	AC1
	AC4	AC3

Instant Replay Approved for 1989

For the fourth consecutive season, NFL clubs have approved a limited system of Instant Replay on a one-year basis.

The system stays the same as in 1988. The Replay Official will be assigned a regular officiating crew and will attend crew meetings the day before each game.

The following table outlines the number of reversals and plays closely reviewed by instant replay in each of the previous three seasons.

	Games	Reversals	Plays Closely Reviewed
1986	224	38	374
1987	210	57	490
1988	224	53	537

In 1986, the system was approved by a 23-4-1 vote. In 1987, the vote was 21-7. In 1988, replay was cleared by a 23-5 margin. In 1989, the vote was 24-4.

The NFL has discussed Instant Replay in some degree or other since the early 1970s. The League experimented in 1976 and 1978 using two basic frameworks—an independent system using cameras, replay machines, and technicians separate from the network covering the games, and a "no-frills" approach using existing TV coverage.

In 1985, the NFL used the network feed of the nine nationally-televised preseason games to experiment with the basic system which later was adopted for 1986, 1987, and 1988. A total of 28 plays (17 confirmed call, 4 inconclusive, 1 reversed, and 6 no replay shown) were closely examined in the 1985 experiment.

Q—What is the objective of this system?

A—The clubs feel that on certain plays the telecast viewed by the general public should be used to correct an indisputable error. The system will be used to reverse an on-field decision only when the Replay Official has **indisputable visual evidence** available to him that warrants the change.

Q—Who will be involved?

A—The Replay Official (a former NFL or collegiate official) will be positioned in a sideline Replay Booth, which will house two TV monitors and two high-speed VCRs plus radio communications to the on-field officials. The Replay Official makes the decision although a Communicator (normally a member of the League Office staff) and a Technician also will be there to lend logistical help.

Q—Why is the system referred to as "limited" Instant Replay?

A—This system will concentrate on plays of **possession** or **touching** (e.g. fumbles, receptions, interceptions, muffs) and most plays governed by the **sidelines, goal lines, end lines,** and **line of scrimmage** (e.g. receiver or runner in or out of bounds, forward or backward passes, breaking the plane of the goal line). It also will be used to determine whether there are more than 11 men on the field.

Q—Why aren't most fouls included in this system?

A—It is recognized that in most circumstances the on-field officials have the best vantage points involving fouls. It is for this reason that Instant Replay **will not review** a list of the following 26 fouls:

1. Clipping
2. Encroachment and offsides
3. Grasp of facemask
4. False start
5. Defensive pass interference
6. Offensive pass interference
7. Offensive holding and illegal use of hands
8. Illegal batting or punching ball
9. Illegal block on free kick or scrimmage kick
10. Illegal crackback
11. Illegal motion
12. Illegal use of forearm or elbow
13. Illegal use of hands by defense
14. Illegally kicking ball
15. Illegally snapping ball
16. Intentional grounding
17. Member of punting team downfield early
18. Illegal formation
19. Palpably unfair act
20. Piling on
21. Roughing the passer
22. Running into/roughing kicker
23. Striking, kicking, or kneeing
24. Unnecessary roughness
25. Unsportsmanlike conduct
26. Use of helmet as a weapon

Q—Is the television network carrying the game part of the review process?

A—No. Although the Replay Official will be viewing the live network feed, there is no communication to television personnel as to which plays to show or not to show.

Q—What is the step-by-step procedure of a play review?

A—The Replay Official will view game action and a play will be replayed immediately on one of the two monitors, while the other one continues to record the live feed.

The Replay Official makes a determination if further study of the play is needed. If not, there is no contact with the field and play continues without interruption.

If the Replay Official believes an error may have been made the Umpire will be contacted via a headset.

The Replay Official will watch replay(s) on one or both monitors and complete his review within a reasonable period after the play is over.

The Replay Official will inform the Umpire of his decision, and the Referee will make the appropriate announcement on the wireless microphone.

NFL Passer Rating System

The NFL rates its forward passers for statistical purposes against a pre-fixed performance standard based on statistical achievements of all qualified pro passers since 1960. The system now being used replaced one that rated passers in relation to their position in a total group based on various criteria. The current system, which was adopted in 1973, removes inequities that existed in the former method and, at the same time, provides a means of comparing passing performances from one season to the next.

It is important to remember that the system is used to rate **passers,** not **quarterbacks.** Statistics do not reflect leadership, play-calling, and other intangible factors that go into making a successful professional quarterback. Four categories are used as a basis for compiling a rating:

—Percentage of touchdown passes per attempt
—Percentage of completions per attempt
—Percentage of interceptions per attempt
—Average yards gained per attempt

The base, or **average** standard, is 1.000. The bottom is .000. To earn a 2.000 rating, a passer must perform at exceptional levels, i.e., 70 percent in completions, 10 percent in touchdowns, 1.5 percent in interceptions, and 11 yards average gain per pass attempt. The **maximum** a passer can receive in any category is 2.375.

For example, to gain a 2.375 in completion percentage, a passer would have to complete 77.5 percent of his passes. The NFL record is 70.55 by Ken Anderson (Cincinnati, 1982). To gain 2.375 in percentage of interceptions, a passer would have to go the entire season without an interception. The 2.375 figure in average yards is 12.50, compared with the NFL record of 11.17 by Tommy O'Connell (Cleveland, 1957). To earn a 2.375 in percentage of touchdowns, a passer would have to achieve an 11.9. The record is 13.9 by Sid Luckman (Chicago, 1943).

In order to make the rating more understandable, the point rating is then converted into a scale of 100. For instance, if a passer completes 11 of 23 passes for 114 yards, with one touchdown and no interceptions, the four components would be:

—**Percentage of Completions**—11 of 23 is 47.8 percent. The point rating is 0.890.

—**Percentage of Touchdown Passes**—1 touchdown in 23 attempts works out to 4.3 percent for a rating of 0.860.

—**Percentage of Interceptions**—You can't do better than zero, so the passer receives a maximum rating of 2.375.

—**Average Yards Gained Per Attempt**—23 attempts divided into 114 yards equals 4.96 yards per attempt for a corresponding rating of 0.490.

The sum of the four components is 4.615, which converts to a rating of 76.9. In order for a passer to achieve 100, his points would have to total 6.000. In rare cases, where statistical performance has been superior, it is possible for a passer to go over 100. However, such an instance is rare. The leading passers each year were checked from 1932 when the NFL began keeping official statistics, and only nine passers in history have scored over 100 in the year they led the league in passing. The most recent passer to lead the league and score over 100 was Miami quarterback Dan Marino, who achieved a 108.9 rating in 1984. The highest-rated passer in a single season was Milt Plum, who had a 110.4 rating with Cleveland in 1960.

AFC ACTIVE STATISTICAL LEADERS

LEADING ACTIVE PASSERS, AMERICAN FOOTBALL CONFERENCE

1,000 or more attempts

	Yrs.	Att.	Comp.	Pct. Comp.	Yards	Avg. Gain	TD	Pct. TD	Had Int.	Pct. Int.	Rate Pts.
Dan Marino, Mia.	6	3100	1866	60.2	23856	7.70	196	6.3	103	3.3	91.5
Boomer Esiason, Cin.	5	1830	1038	56.7	14825	8.10	98	5.4	65	3.6	86.2
Dave Krieg, Sea.	9	2344	1358	57.9	17549	7.49	148	6.3	96	4.1	85.5
Ken O'Brien, N.Y.J.	7	1990	1183	59.4	14243	7.16	84	4.2	50	2.5	85.0
Bernie Kosar, Clev.	4	1427	831	58.2	10355	7.26	57	4.0	33	2.3	84.5
Jim Kelly, Buff.	3	1351	804	59.5	9771	7.23	56	4.1	45	3.3	81.8
Tony Eason, N.E.	6	1395	819	58.7	9971	7.15	57	4.1	44	3.2	81.3
John Elway, Den.	6	2654	1442	54.3	18144	6.84	102	3.8	96	3.6	73.6
Ron Jaworski, K.C.	14	4056	2151	53.0	27805	6.86	177	4.4	159	3.9	73.1
Warren Moon, Hou.	5	1977	1059	53.6	14669	7.42	78	3.9	85	4.3	72.9
Jay Schroeder, Raiders	4	1273	630	49.5	9284	7.29	52	4.1	50	3.9	71.0
Steve DeBerg, K.C.	11	3411	1922	56.3	22517	6.60	132	3.9	155	4.5	70.5
Steve Grogan, N.E.	14	3240	1696	52.3	24574	7.58	169	5.2	191	5.9	70.1
Mike Pagel, Clev.	7	1291	660	51.1	8263	6.40	42	3.3	51	4.0	65.7
Mark Malone, S.D.	9	1646	837	50.9	10162	6.17	60	3.6	81	4.9	61.8

TOP 10 ACTIVE RUSHERS, AFC

2,000 or more yards

	Yrs.	Att.	Yards	TD
1. Tony Dorsett, Den.	12	2936	12739	77
2. Eric Dickerson, Ind.	6	2136	9915	75
3. Marcus Allen, Raiders	7	1712	6982	61
4. Freeman McNeil, N.Y.J.	8	1525	6794	28
5. Curt Warner, Sea.	6	1455	6074	52
6. James Brooks, Cin.	8	1099	5104	35
7. Sammy Winder, Den.	7	1343	4956	35
8. Mike Rozier, Hou.	4	812	3083	25
9. Kevin Mack, Clev.	4	720	2989	25
Johnny Hector, N.Y.J.	6	697	2789	36
10. Herman Heard, K.C.	5	588	2478	13

Other Leading Rushers

Craig James, N.E.	5	585	2469	11
Mosi Tatupu, N.E.	11	585	2321	18
Gary Anderson, S.D.	4	548	2250	11
Steve Grogan, N.E.	14	432	2162	35

TOP 10 ACTIVE PASS RECEIVERS, AFC

200 or more receptions

	Yrs.	No.	Yards	TD
1. Steve Largent, Sea.	13	791	12686	97
2. Ozzie Newsome, Clev.	11	610	7416	44
3. James Lofton, Raiders	11	599	11085	54
4. Stanley Morgan, N.E.	12	506	9866	64
5. Todd Christensen, Raiders	10	461	5872	41
6. Wesley Walker, N.Y.J.	12	430	8217	71
7. Cris Collinsworth, Cin.	8	417	6698	36
8. Mickey Shuler, N.Y.J.	11	409	4497	37
9. Tony Dorsett, Den.	12	398	3554	13
10. Marcus Allen, Raiders	7	368	3470	16

Other Leading Receivers

Steve Watson, Den.	9	353	6112	36
Carlos Carson, K.C.	9	345	6265	32
Mark Clayton, Mia.	6	341	5554	54
Drew Hill, Hou.	9	310	5758	40
Doug Cosbie, Den.	10	300	3728	30
Mark Duper, Mia.	7	296	5495	41
Al Toon, N.Y.J.	4	292	3881	21
James Brooks, Cin.	8	278	2699	22
Stephone Paige, K.C.	6	259	4450	42
Bruce Hardy, Mia.	11	255	2453	25
Ray Butler, Clev.	9	239	3948	37
Matt Bouza, Ind.	8	234	3064	17
Andre Reed, Buff.	4	229	3096	22
Freeman McNeil, N.Y.J.	8	225	2211	11
Brian Brennan, Clev.	5	211	2966	16
Lionel James, S.D.	5	209	2278	10
Eddie Brown, Cin.	4	208	3787	24
Gerald Willhite, Den.	7	207	1767	5
Louis Lipps, Pitt.	5	203	3721	29
Willie Gault, L.A. Raiders	6	200	4042	29

TOP 10 ACTIVE SCORERS, AFC

250 or more points

	Yrs.	TD	FG	PAT	TP
1. Pat Leahy, N.Y.J.	15	0	241	467	1190
2. Chris Bahr, S.D.	13	0	224	461	1133
3. Nick Lowery, K.C.	10	0	201	304	907
4. Matt Bahr, Clev.	10	0	166	309	807
5. Gary Anderson, Pitt.	7	0	165	232	727
6. Rich Karlis, Den.	7	0	137	244	655
7. Norm Johnson, Sea.	7	0	121	273	636
8. Steve Largent, Sea.	13	98	0	1	589
9. Tony Dorsett, Den.	12	91	0	0	546
10. Marcus Allen, Raiders	7	78	0	0	468
Eric Dickerson, Ind.	6	78	0	0	468

Other Leading Scorers

Wesley Walker, N.Y.J.	12	71	0	0	428*
Tony Zendejas, Hou.	4	0	85	137	392
Stanley Morgan, N.E.	12	65	0	0	390
Curt Warner, Sea.	6	58	0	0	348
James Brooks, Cin.	8	57	0	0	342
Scott Norwood, Buff.	4	0	72	119	335
Mark Clayton, Mia.	6	55	0	0	330
James Lofton, Raiders	11	55	0	0	330
Fuad Reveiz, Mia.	4	0	53	161	320
Ozzie Newsome, Clev.	11	46	0	0	276
Dean Biasucci, Ind.	3	0	62	89	275
Sammy Winder, Den.	7	44	0	0	264
Todd Christensen, Raiders	10	42	0	0	252
Stephone Paige, K.C.	6	42	0	0	252

**total includes safety*

TOP 10 ACTIVE INTERCEPTORS, AFC

20 or more interceptions

	Yrs.	No.	Yards	TD
1. Mike Haynes, Raiders	13	46	688	2
2. Deron Cherry, K.C.	8	41	590	1
3. Raymond Clayborn, N.E.	12	35	555	1
4. Mike Harden, Den.	9	33	643	4
5. Dwayne Woodruff, Pitt.	9	30	522	3
6. Vann McElroy, Raiders	7	29	296	1
7. Roland James, N.E.	9	27	333	0
8. Hanford Dixon, Clev.	8	25	223	0
9. William Judson, Mia.	7	22	337	2
Albert Lewis, K.C.	6	22	195	0

Other Leading Interceptors

Fred Marion, N.E.	7	21	388	1
Johnnie Johnson, Sea.	9	21	372	4
Eugene Daniel, Ind.	5	21	167	1
Mike Richardson, Raiders	6	20	274	1
Bobby Watkins, Mia.	7	20	85	0

TOP 10 ACTIVE QUARTERBACK SACKERS, AFC

Official statistic since 1982

	No.
1. Jacob Green, Sea.	76
2. Andre Tippett, N.E.	72.5
3. Greg Townsend, Raiders	59
4. Al Baker, Clev.	55
Howie Long, Raiders	55
6. Rulon Jones, Den.	52.5
7. Bill Pickel, Raiders	48.5
Art Still, Buff.	48.5
9. Jeff Bryant, Sea.	45.5
10. Ezra Johnson, Ind.	44.5
Bruce Smith, Buff.	44.5

Other Leading Sackers

Lee Williams, S.D.	44
Keith Willis, Pitt.	40.5
Carl Hairston, Clev.	40

TOP 10 ACTIVE PUNT RETURNERS, AFC

40 or more punt returns

	Yrs.	No.	Yards	Avg.	TD
1. JoJo Townsell, N.Y.J.	4	77	907	11.8	2
2. Louis Lipps, Pitt.	5	103	1185	11.5	3
3. Irving Fryar, N.E.	5	164	1805	11.0	3
4. James Brooks, Cin.	8	52	565	10.9	0
5. Stanley Morgan, N.E.	12	92	960	10.4	1
Mike Haynes, Raiders	13	112	1168	10.4	2
7. Mike Martin, Cin.	6	125	1274	10.2	0
8. Gerald Willhite, Den.	7	101	1012	10.0	1
9. Lionel James, S.D.	5	124	1193	9.6	2
10. Roland James, N.E.	9	42	400	9.5	1

Other Leading Punt Returners

Gerald McNeil, Clev.	3	112	1049	9.4	1
Mark Clayton, Mia.	6	52	485	9.3	1
Tim Brown, Raiders	1	49	444	9.1	0
Paul Skansi, Sea.	6	95	858	9.0	0
Scott Schwedes, Mia.	2	48	433	9.0	0
Lew Barnes, K.C.	2	91	789	8.7	0
Rod Woodson, Pitt.	2	49	416	8.5	0
Nesby Glasgow, Sea.	10	80	651	8.1	1
Kenny Johnson, Hou.	9	91	732	8.0	0
Brian Brennan, Clev.	5	44	352	8.0	1
Bill Brooks, Ind.	3	43	292	6.8	0
Robb Riddick, Buff.	6	46	289	6.3	0

TOP 10 ACTIVE KICKOFF RETURNERS, AFC

40 or more kickoff returns

	Yrs.	No.	Yards	Avg.	TD
1. Raymond Clayborn, N.E.	12	57	1538	27.0	3
2. Tim Brown, Raiders	1	41	1098	26.8	1
3. Jamie Holland, S.D.	2	50	1220	24.4	1
4. Bobby Humphery, N.Y.J.	5	106	2560	24.2	2
5. Rod Woodson, Pitt.	2	50	1140	22.8	1
6. Nesby Glasgow, Sea.	10	84	1904	22.7	0
Carlos Carson, K.C.	9	57	1296	22.7	0
8. Albert Bentley, Ind.	4	120	2636	22.0	0
9. Mike Martin, Cin.	6	75	1643	21.9	0
10. Lorenzo Hampton, Mia.	4	79	1722	21.8	0
Ken Bell, Den.	3	74	1616	21.8	0

Other Leading Kickoff Returners

Barry Redden, S.D.	7	64	1390	21.7	0
JoJo Townsell, N.Y.J.	4	57	1237	21.7	1
Tim McGee, Cin.	3	58	1249	21.5	0
James Brooks, Cin.	8	118	2523	21.4	0
Steve Tasker, Buff.	4	40	857	21.4	0
Lionel James, S.D.	5	99	2094	21.2	0
Paul Palmer, K.C.	2	61	1287	21.1	2
Gerald McNeil, Clev.	3	60	1240	20.7	1
Dwight Stone, Pitt.	2	57	1178	20.7	1
Gary Anderson, S.D.	4	59	1217	20.6	1
Stanford Jennings, Cin.	5	81	1643	20.3	1
Robb Riddick, Buff.	6	63	1276	20.3	0
Leonard Harris, Hou.	3	41	828	20.2	0
Drew Hill, Hou.	9	172	3460	20.1	1
Allen Pinkett, Hou.	3	50	978	19.6	0

TOP 10 ACTIVE PUNTERS, AFC

50 or more punts

	Yrs.	No.	Avg.	LG
1. Rohn Stark, Ind.	7	514	44.3	72
2. Reggie Roby, Mia.	6	336	43.6	77
3. Ralf Mojsiejenko, S.D.	4	292	42.9	67
4. Mike Horan, Den.	5	313	42.1	75
5. Harry Newsome, Pitt.	4	293	41.5	64
6. Bryan Wagner, Clev.	2	115	41.2	71
7. Jeff Gossett, Raiders	7	431	40.9	64
8. Lee Johnson, Cin.	4	252	40.8	66
9. John Kidd, Buff.	5	381	40.7	67
10. Kelly Goodburn, K.C.	2	135	40.5	59

Other Leading Punters

Ruben Rodriguez, Sea.	2	117	40.5	68
Max Runager, K.C.	10	644	40.4	64
Scott Fulhage, Cin.	2	96	40.0	58
Joe Prokop, N.Y.J.	3	158	39.1	66
Greg Montgomery, Hou.	1	65	38.8	61
Jeff Feagles, N.E.	1	91	38.3	74

NFC ACTIVE STATISTICAL LEADERS

LEADING ACTIVE PASSERS, NATIONAL FOOTBALL CONFERENCE

1,000 or more attempts

	Yrs.	Att.	Comp.	Pct. Comp.	Yards	Avg. Gain	TD	Pct. TD	Had Int.	Pct. Int.	Rate Pts.
Joe Montana, S.F.	10	3673	2322	63.2	27533	7.50	190	5.2	99	2.7	92.0
Neil Lomax, Phx.	8	3153	1817	57.6	22771	7.22	136	4.3	90	2.9	82.7
Jim McMahon, Chi.	7	1513	874	57.8	11203	7.40	67	4.4	56	3.7	80.4
Bobby Hebert, N.O.	4	1032	582	56.4	6981	6.76	42	4.1	36	3.5	76.3
Wade Wilson, Minn.	7	1035	581	56.1	7612	7.35	45	4.3	45	4.3	75.9
Phil Simms, N.Y.G.	9	3253	1752	53.9	23174	7.12	142	4.4	123	3.8	75.4
Randall Cunningham, Phil.	4	1256	669	53.3	8533	6.79	56	4.5	43	3.4	75.4
Tommy Kramer, Minn.	12	3512	1934	55.1	23869	6.80	152	4.3	150	4.3	72.9
Eric Hipple, Det.	8	1528	823	53.9	10621	6.95	55	3.6	67	4.4	69.7
Doug Williams, Wash.	8	2414	1189	49.3	16413	6.80	99	4.1	90	3.7	69.6
Dave Wilson, N.O.	7	1039	551	53.0	6987	6.72	36	3.5	55	5.3	63.8
Randy Wright, G.B.	5	1119	602	53.8	7106	6.35	31	2.8	57	5.1	61.4

TOP 10 ACTIVE RUSHERS, NFC

2,000 or more yards

	Yrs.	Att.	Yards	TD
1. Ottis Anderson, N.Y.G.	10	1949	8294	55
2. Gerald Riggs, Wash.	7	1587	6631	48
3. James Wilder, T.B.	8	1505	5713	37
4. Roger Craig, S.F.	6	1274	5571	43
5. Joe Morris, N.Y.G.	7	1318	5296	48
6. Stump Mitchell, Phx.	8	943	4484	32
7. Darrin Nelson, Minn.	7	912	3892	16
8. Greg Bell, Rams	5	885	3658	35
9. James Jones, Det.	6	960	3452	23
10. Walter Abercrombie, Phil.	7	847	3357	22
Other Leading Rushers				
Herschel Walker, Dall.	3	721	3142	24
Rueben Mayes, N.O.	3	699	2898	16
Earnest Byner, Wash.	5	672	2713	23
Earl Ferrell, Phx.	7	536	2448	18

TOP 10 ACTIVE PASS RECEIVERS, NFC

200 or more receptions

	Yrs.	No.	Yards	TD
1. Art Monk, Wash.	9	576	7979	39
2. J.T. Smith, Phx.	11	464	5971	28
3. Roger Craig, S.F.	6	434	3768	15
4. Roy Green Phx.	10	425	6996	55
5. James Wilder, T.B.	8	394	3157	6
6. Mike Quick, Phil.	7	341	6101	58
7. Jimmie Giles, Phil.	12	334	4859	39
8. Ottis Anderson, N.Y.G.	10	319	2614	5
9. James Jones, Det.	6	285	2318	10
10. Henry Ellard, Rams	6	275	4361	28
Other Leading Receivers				
Steve Jordan, Minn.	7	274	3568	17
Jerry Rice, S.F.	4	264	4881	49
Gary Clark, Wash.	4	261	4149	26
John Spagnola, G.B.	9	261	2873	15
Pete Holohan, Rams	8	230	2713	10
Darrin Nelson, Minn.	7	225	2008	5
Tim Newsome Dall.	9	212	1966	11
Mark Bavaro, N.Y.G.	4	211	3051	20
Stump Mitchell, Phx.	8	208	1945	9
Don Warren, Wash.	10	205	2170	5
Earnest Byner Wash.	5	204	2034	8
Eric Martin, N.O.	4	201	3058	23

TOP 10 ACTIVE SCORERS, NFC

250 or more points

	Yrs.	TD	FG	PAT	TP
1. Eddie Murray, Det.	9	0	192	271	847
2. Morten Andersen, N.O.	7	0	151	203	656
3. Mike Lansford, Rams	7	0	120	222	582
4. Raul Allegre, N.Y.G.	6	0	108	144	468
5. Paul McFadden, Atl.	5	0	105	142	457
6. Kevin Butler, Chi.	4	0	93	152	431
7. Chuck Nelson, Minn.	5	0	63	175	364
8. Ottis Anderson, N.Y.G.	10	60	0	0	360
Al Del Greco, Phx.	5	0	66	162	360
10. Roger Craig, S.F.	6	58	0	0	348
Roy Green, Phx.	10	58	0	0	348
Mike Quick, Phil.	7	58	0	0	348
Other Leading Scorers					
Jerry Rice, S.F.	4	53	0	0	318
Donald Igwebuike, T.B.	4	0	72	101	317
Joe Morris, N.Y.G.	7	50	0	0	300
Gerald Riggs, Wash.	7	48	0	0	288
James Wilder, T.B.	8	43	0	0	258
Greg Bell, Rams	5	42	0	0	252
Stump Mitchell, Phx.	8	42	0	0	252

TOP 10 ACTIVE INTERCEPTORS, NFC

20 or more interceptions

	Yrs.	No.	Yards	TD
1. Dave Brown, G.B.	14	56	686	5
2. Everson Walls, Dall.	8	44	391	0
3. Ronnie Lott, S.F.	8	43	583	5
4. Michael Downs, Dall.	8	34	433	1
5. LeRoy Irvin, Rams	9	31	611	5
Dave Waymer, N.O.	9	31	329	0
7. Mark Lee, G.B.	9	28	239	0
8. Bobby Butler, Atl.	8	24	222	1
John Anderson, G.B.	11	24	166	1
10. Roynell Young, Phil.	9	23	106	0
Other Leading Interceptors				
Terry Kinard, N.Y.G.	6	22	439	1
Joey Browner, Minn.	6	20	195	2

TOP 10 ACTIVE QUARTERBACK SACKERS, NFC

Official statistic since 1982

	No.
1. Lawrence Taylor, N.Y.G.	89
2. Dexter Manley, Wash.	82
3. Richard Dent, Chi.	72
4. Reggie White, Phil.	70
5. Rickey Jackson, N.O.	65
6. Ed Jones, Dall.	56.5
7. Steve McMichael, Chi.	55.5
8. Dan Hampton, Chi.	55
9. Jim Jeffcoat, Dall.	51
Doug Martin, Minn.	51
Other Leading Sackers	
Curtis Greer, Minn.	50.5
Leonard Marshall, N.Y.G.	50.5
Charles Mann, Wash.	49.5

TOP 10 ACTIVE PUNT RETURNERS, NFC

40 or more punt returns

	Yrs.	No.	Yards	Avg.	TD
1. Mel Gray, Det.	3	49	657	13.4	1
2. John Taylor, S.F.	2	45	565	12.6	2
3. Vai Sikahema, Phx.	3	120	1413	11.8	3
4. Henry Ellard, Rams	6	129	1474	11.4	4
5. Bobby J. Edmonds, Det.	3	89	1010	11.3	1
6. Darrell Green, Wash.	6	48	532	11.1	0
7. J.T. Smith, Phx.	11	264	2730	10.3	4
8. Leo Lewis, Minn.	8	94	961	10.2	1
9. LeRoy Irvin, Rams	9	146	1450	9.9	4
10. Pete Mandley, Det.	5	143	1360	9.5	2
Don Griffin, S.F.	3	51	484	9.5	1
Other Leading Punt Returners					
Dennis McKinnon, Chi.	5	117	1104	9.4	3
Stump Mitchell, Phx.	8	156	1377	8.8	1
Kelvin Martin, Dall.	2	66	576	8.7	0
Bobby Futrell, T.B.	3	65	563	8.7	0
Ron Pitts, G.B.	3	50	436	8.7	2
Walter Stanley, G.B.	4	87	720	8.3	1
Phillip Epps, G.B.	7	100	819	8.2	1
Phil McConkey, N.Y.G.	5	213	1708	8.0	0
Eric Martin, N.O.	4	46	368	8.0	0
Willie Drewrey, T.B.	4	63	496	7.9	0
Evan Cooper, Atl.	5	101	763	7.6	0

TOP 10 ACTIVE KICKOFF RETURNERS, NFC

40 or more kickoff returns

	Yrs.	No.	Yards	Avg.	TD
1. Ron Brown, Rams	5	110	2694	24.5	4
2. Darrin Nelson, Minn.	7	85	1998	23.5	0
3. Dennis Gentry, Chi.	7	117	2741	23.4	3
Mel Gray, Det.	3	93	2172	23.4	1
5. Sylvester Stamps, T.B.	5	83	1934	23.3	1
6. Roy Green, Phx.	10	83	1917	23.1	1
7. Stump Mitchell, Phx.	8	177	4057	22.9	0
8. Vai Sikahema, Phx.	3	94	2083	22.2	0
9. Bobby J. Edmonds, Det.	3	101	2228	22.1	0
10. Willie Tullis, Det.	8	63	1384	22.0	1
Other Leading Kickoff Returners					
Darryl Clack, Dall.	3	80	1746	21.8	0
Gene Lang, Atl.	5	62	1335	21.5	0
Willie Drewrey, T.B.	4	60	1288	21.5	0
Gary Lee, Det.	2	50	1074	21.5	0
Del Rodgers, S.F.	4	82	1735	21.2	1
Donnie Elder, T.B.	3	59	1249	21.2	0
Stephen Starring, Det.	6	115	2389	20.8	0
Brent Fullwood, G.B.	2	45	931	20.7	0
Walter Stanley, G.B.	4	42	857	20.4	0
Randall Morris, Det.	5	84	1662	19.8	0
Herman Fontenot, G.B.	4	45	879	19.5	0
Jeff Smith, G.B.	4	77	1475	19.2	0
Phil McConkey, N.Y.G.	5	67	1284	19.2	0
Mark Lee, G.B.	9	45	859	19.1	0
Keith Griffin, Atl.	5	52	985	18.9	0
Evan Cooper, Atl.	5	43	790	18.4	0
Thomas Sanders, Chi.	4	56	1006	18.0	0

TOP 10 ACTIVE PUNTERS, NFC

50 or more punts

	Yrs.	No.	Avg.	LG
1. Sean Landeta, N.Y.G.	4	231	43.3	68
2. Rick Donnelly, Atl.	4	296	42.6	71
3. Rich Camarillo, Phx.	8	508	42.3	76
Jim Arnold, Det.	6	463	42.3	69
5. Maury Buford, G.B.	6	360	42.0	71
Brian Hansen, N.O.	5	363	42.0	66
7. Bucky Scribner, Minn.	4	258	41.4	70
8. Mike Saxon, Dall.	4	315	40.8	63
Dale Hatcher, Rams	4	296	40.8	67
10. Greg Horne, Phx.	2	122	40.6	66
Other Leading Punters				
John Teltschik, Phil.	3	288	40.2	70
Don Bracken, G.B.	4	238	39.9	65
Barry Helton, S.F.	1	78	39.3	53
Ray Criswell, Chi.	2	94	37.5	62

54th Annual NFL Draft, April 23-24, 1989

Atlanta Falcons (Drafted alternately 5-7-6)

1. Deion Sanders—5, DB, Florida State
   Shawn Collins—27, WR, Northern Arizona, from Cincinnati
2. Choice to Cincinnati
   Ralph Norwood—38, T, Louisiana State, from L.A. Raiders through Washington
3. Keith Jones—62, RB, Illinois
4. Choice to Cincinnati
5. Choice to Dallas through L.A. Raiders
6. Troy Sadowski—145, TE, Georgia
7. Undra Johnson—172, RB, West Virginia
8. Paul Singer—202, QB, Western Illinois
9. Chris Dunn—229, LB, Cal Poly-San Luis Obispo
10. Choice to Cincinnati
11. Greg Paterra—286, RB, Slippery Rock
12. Tony Bowick—313, NT, Tennessee-Chattanooga

Buffalo Bills (Drafted alternately 26-25)

1. Choice to L.A. Rams
2. Choice to L.A. Rams
3. Don Beebe—82, WR, Chadron, Neb.
4. John Kolesar—109, WR, Michigan
5. Michael Andrews—137, DB, Alcorn State
6. Sean Doctor—164, RB, Marshall
7. Brian Jordan—173, DB, Richmond, from Tampa Bay
   Chris Hale—193, DB, Southern California
8. Choice to Kansas City
9. Pat Rabold—249, DT, Wyoming
10. Carlo Cheattom—276, DB, Auburn
11. Richard Harvey—305, LB, Tulane
12. Derrell Marshall—332, T, Southern California

Chicago Bears (Drafted alternately 25-26)

1. Donnell Woolford—11, DB, Clemson, from L.A. Raiders
   Trace Armstrong—12, DE, Florida, from Washington
   Choice to Miami
2. John Roper—36, LB, Texas A&M, from Miami
   Dave Zawatson—54, T, California
3. Jerry Fontenot—65, G, Texas A&M, from Miami
   Choice to Philadelphia
4. Markus Paul—95, DB, Syracuse, from L.A. Raiders
   Choice to Washington through L.A. Raiders
5. Mark Green—130, RB, Notre Dame, from Philadelphia
   Greg Gilbert—136, LB, Alabama
6. Choice to New England through L.A. Raiders
7. Richard Brothers—189, DB, Arkansas, from Philadelphia
   Brent Snyder—192, QB, Utah State
8. Tony Woods—216, DT, Oklahoma, from Philadelphia
   Chris Dyko—221, T, Washington State
9. LaSalle Harper—243, LB, Arkansas, from Philadelphia
   Byron Sanders—248, RB, Northwestern
10. Todd Millikan—270, TE, Nebraska, from Philadelphia
    John Simpson—277, WR, Baylor
11. Joe Nelms—297, DT, California, from Philadelphia
    George Streeter—304, DB, Notre Dame
12. Freddy Weygand—330, WR, Auburn, from Philadelphia
    Anthony Phillips—333, G, Oklahoma

Cincinnati Bengals (Drafted 27th)

1. Choice to Atlanta
2. Eric Ball—35, RB, UCLA, from Atlanta
   Freddie Childress—55, G, Arkansas
3. Erik Wilhelm—83, QB, Oregon State
4. Kerry Owens—89, LB, Arkansas, from Atlanta
   Rob Woods—111, T, Arizona
5. Natu Tuatagaloa—138, DT, California
6. Craig Taylor—166, RB, West Virginia
7. Kendal Smith—194, WR, Utah State
8. Chris Chenault—222, LB, Kentucky
9. Richard Stephens—250, T, Tulsa
10. Cornell Holloway—256, DB, Pittsburgh, from Atlanta
    Bob Jean—278, QB, New Hampshire
11. Dana Wells—306, DT, Arizona
12. Scott Jones—334, T, Washington

Cleveland Browns (Drafted alternately 20-19-18-23-22-21)

1. Eric Metcalf—13, RB, Texas, from Denver
   Choice to Denver
2. Lawyer Tillman—31, WR, Auburn, from Green Bay
   Choice to Denver
3. Choice to Green Bay
4. Andrew Stewart—107, DE, Cincinnati
5. Kyle Kramer—114, DB, Bowling Green, from Green Bay
   Vernon Joines—116, WR, Maryland, from Kansas City
   Choice to Denver
6. Gary Wilkerson—160, DB, Penn State
7. Mike Graybill—187, T, Boston University
8. Rick Aeilts—214, TE, S.E. Missouri
9. Choice to Denver
10. John Buddenberg—274, T, Akron
11. Dan Plocki—301, K, Maryland
12. Marlon Brown—328, LB, Memphis State

Dallas Cowboys (Drafted 1st)

1. Troy Aikman—1, QB, UCLA
2. Steve Wisniewski—29, G, Penn State
   Daryl Johnston—39, RB, Syracuse, from Washington through L.A. Raiders
3. Mark Stepnoski—57, G, Pittsburgh
   Rhondy Weston—68, DE, Florida, from L.A. Raiders
4. Tony Tolbert—85, DE, Texas-El Paso
5. Keith Jennings—113, TE, Clemson
   Willis Crockett—119, LB, Georgia Tech, from Atlanta through L.A. Raiders
   Jeff Roth—125, DT, Florida, from Denver
6. Choice to L.A. Raiders
7. Kevin Peterson—168, LB, Northwestern
8. Charvez Foger—196, RB, Nevada-Reno
9. Tim Jackson—224, DB, Nebraska
10. Rod Carter—252, LB, Miami
11. Randy Shannon—280, LB, Miami
12. Scott Ankrom—308, WR, Texas Christian

Denver Broncos (Drafted 13th)

1. Choice to Cleveland
   Steve Atwater—20, DB, Arkansas, from Cleveland
2. Doug Widell—41, G, Boston College
   Warren Powers—47, DE, Maryland, from Cleveland
3. Darrell Hamilton—69, T, North Carolina
4. Richard McCullough—97, DE, Clemson
5. Choice to Dallas
   Darren Carrington—134, DB, Northern Arizona, from Cleveland
6. Anthony Stafford—152, WR, Oklahoma
7. Melvin Bratton—180, RB, Miami
8. Paul Green—208, TE, Southern California
9. Monte Smith—236, G, North Dakota
   Wayne Williams—241, RB, Florida, from Cleveland
10. Anthony Butts—264, DT, Mississippi State
11. Richard Shelton—292, DB, Liberty University
12. John Javis—320, WR, Howard

Detroit Lions (Drafted alternately 3-2)

1. Barry Sanders—3, RB, Oklahoma State
2. John Ford—30, WR, Virginia
3. Mike Utley—59, G, Washington State
4. Ray Crockett—86, DB, Baylor
5. Lawrence Pete—115, DT, Nebraska
6. Rodney Peete—141, QB, Southern California
7. Jerry Woods—170, DB, Northern Michigan
8. Chris Parker—197, DT, West Virginia
9. Derek MacCready—226, DE, Ohio State
10. Jason Phillips—253, WR, Houston
11. Keith Karpinski—282, LB, Penn State
12. James Cribbs—309, DE, Memphis State

Green Bay Packers (Drafted alternately 2-3)

1. Tony Mandarich—2, T, Michigan State
2. Choice to Cleveland
3. Matt Brock—58, DE, Oregon
   Anthony Dilweg—74, QB, Duke, from Cleveland
4. Jeff Graham—87, QB, Long Beach State
5. Choice to Cleveland
   Jeff Query—124, WR, Millikin, from Washington
   Vince Workman—127, RB, Ohio State, from New England through Cleveland
6. Chris Jacke—142, K, Texas-El Paso
7. Mark Hall—169, DE, S.W. Louisiana
8. Thomas King—198, DB, S.W. Louisiana
   Brian Shulman—206, P, Auburn, from Washington
9. Scott Kirby—225, T, Arizona State
10. Ben Jessie—254, DB, S.W. Texas State
11. Cedric Stallworth—281, DB, Georgia Tech
12. Stan Shiver—310, DB, Florida State

Houston Oilers (Drafted alternately 23-22-21-20-19-18)

1. David Williams—23, T, Florida
2. Scott Kozak—50, LB, Oregon
3. Bubba McDowell—77, DB, Miami
4. Rod Harris—104, WR, Texas A&M
5. Glenn Montgomery—131, NT, Houston
6. Bo Orlando—157, DB, West Virginia
7. Tracy Rogers—190, LB, Fresno State
8. Alvoid Mays—217, DB, West Virginia
9. Bob Mrosko—244, TE, Penn State
10. Tracy Johnson—271, RB, Clemson
11. Brian Smider—298, T, West Virginia
12. Chuck Hartlieb—325, QB, Iowa

Indianapolis Colts (Drafted alternately 15-17-16)

1. Choice to Seattle
   Andre Rison—22, WR, Michigan State, from Philadelphia
2. Choice to L.A. Rams
3. Mitchell Benson—72, DT, Texas Christian
4. Pat Tomberlin—99, G, Florida State
5. Choice to Washington
6. Quintus McDonald—155, LB, Penn State
7. Ivy Joe Hunter—182, RB, Kentucky
   Charles Washington—185, DB, Cameron, from N.Y. Giants
8. Kurt Larson—212, LB, Michigan State
9. William Mackall—239, WR, Tennessee-Martin
10. Jim Thompson—266, T, Auburn
11. Wayne Johnson—296, QB, Georgia
12. William DuBose—314, RB, South Carolina State, from Tampa Bay
    Steve Taylor—323, QB, Nebraska

Kansas City Chiefs (Drafted 4th)

1. Derrick Thomas—4, LB, Alabama
2. Mike Elkins—32, QB, Wake Forest
3. Naz Worthen—60, WR, North Carolina State
4. Stanley Petry—88, DB, Texas Christian
5. Choice to Cleveland
6. Robb Thomas—143, WR, Oregon State
7. Ron Sancho—171, LB, Louisiana State
8. Bryan Tobey—199, RB, Grambling
   Todd McNair—220, RB, Temple, from Buffalo
9. Jack Phillips—227, DB, Alcorn State
10. Rob McGovern—255, LB, Holy Cross
11. Marcus Turner—283, DB, UCLA
12. Bill Jones—311, RB, S.W. Texas State

Los Angeles Raiders (Drafted alternately 11-10-12)

1. Choice to Chicago
2. Choice to Atlanta through Washington
3. Choice to Dallas
4. Choice to Chicago
5. Choice to San Francisco
6. Jeff Francis—140, QB, Tennessee, from Dallas
   Choice to N.Y. Jets
   Doug Lloyd—156, RB, North Dakota State, from New England
7. Choice to New England
8. Derrick Gainer—205, RB, Florida A&M
9. Gary Gooden—235, DB, Indiana
10. Charles Jackson—262, DT, Jackson State
11. Choice to San Francisco
12. Choice to San Francisco

Los Angeles Rams (Drafted alternately 21-20-19-18-23-22)

1. Bill Hawkins—21, DE, Miami
   Cleveland Gary—26, RB, Miami, from Buffalo
2. Frank Stams—45, LB, Notre Dame, from Indianapolis
   Brian Smith—48, LB, Auburn
   Darryl Henley—53, DB, UCLA, from Buffalo
3. Kevin Robbins—75, T, Michigan State
4. Jeff Carlson—102, QB, Weber State
5. Alfred Jackson—135, WR, San Diego State
6. Thom Kaumeyer—148, DB, Oregon, from San Diego
   Mark Messner—161, LB, Michigan
7. George Bethune—188, LB, Alabama
8. Warren Wheat—215, T, Brigham Young
9. Vernon Kirk—242, TE, Pittsburgh
10. Mike Williams—269, WR, Northeastern
11. Choice to Tampa Bay
12. Choice to Tampa Bay

Miami Dolphins (Drafted alternately 9-8)

1. Sammie Smith—9, RB, Florida State
   Louis Oliver—25, DB, Florida, from Chicago
2. Choice to Chicago
3. Choice to Chicago
4. David Holmes—92, DB, Syracuse
5. Jeff Uhlenhake—121, C, Ohio State
6. Wes Pritchett—147, LB, Notre Dame
7. Jim Zdelar—176, T, Youngstown
8. Pete Stoyanovich—203, K, Indiana
9. Dana Batiste—232, LB, Texas A&M
10. Deval Glover—259, WR, Syracuse
    Greg Ross—275, NT, Memphis State, from Minnesota
11. Bert Weidner—288, DT, Kent State
12. J.B. Brown—315, DB, Maryland

Minnesota Vikings (Drafted 24th)

1. Choice to Pittsburgh
2. David Braxton—52, LB, Wake Forest
3. John Hunter—80, T, Brigham Young
4. Darryl Ingram—108, TE, California
5. Choice exercised in 1988 Supplemental Draft for Ryan Bethea, WR, South Carolina
6. Jeff Mickel—163, T, Eastern Washington
7. Benji Roland—191, DT, Auburn
8. Alex Stewart—219, DE, Cal State-Fullerton
9. Choice to New England
10. Choice to Miami
11. Brad Baxter—303, RB, Alabama State
12. Shawn Woodson—331, LB, James Madison
    Everett Ross—335, WR, Ohio State, from San Francisco through L.A. Raiders

New England Patriots (Drafted alternately 16-15-17)

1. Hart Lee Dykes—16, WR, Oklahoma State
2. Eric Coleman—43, DB, Wyoming
3. Marv Cook—63, TE, Iowa, from Tampa Bay
   Chris Gannon—73, DE, S.W. Louisiana
4. Maurice Hurst—96, DB, Southern University, from Washington
   Michael Timpson—100, WR, Penn State
5. Choice to Green Bay through Cleveland
6. Choice to L.A. Raiders
   Eric Mitchell—165, RB, Oklahoma, from Chicago through L.A. Raiders
7. Eric Lindstrom—178, LB, Boston College, from L.A. Raiders
   Choice to San Diego
8. Rodney Rice—210, DB, Brigham Young
   Tony Zackery—223, DB, Washington, from San Francisco through L.A. Raiders
9. Darron Norris—240, RB, Texas
   Curtis Wilson—247, C, Missouri, from Minnesota
10. Emanuel McNeil—267, DT, Tennessee-Martin
11. Tony Hinz—294, RB, Harvard
12. Aaron Chubb—324, LB, Georgia

New Orleans Saints (Drafted alternately 19-18-23-22-21-20)

1. Wayne Martin—19, DE, Arkansas
2. Robert Massey—46, DB, North Carolina Central
3. Kim Phillips—79, DB, North Texas State
4. Mike Mayes—106, DB, Louisiana State
5. Kevin Haverdink—133, T, Western Michigan
6. Floyd Turner—159, WR, N.W. Louisiana
7. David Griggs—186, LB, Virginia
8. Fred Hadley—213, WR, Mississippi State
9. Jerry Leggett—246, LB, Cal State-Fullerton
10. Joe Henderson—273, RB, Iowa State
11. Calvin Nicholson—300, DB, Oregon State
12. Mike Cadore—327, WR, Eastern Kentucky

New York Giants (Drafted alternately 18-23-22-21-20-19)

1. Brian Williams—18, G, Minnesota
2. Choice to San Diego
3. Bob Kratch—64, G, Iowa, from San Diego
   Greg Jackson—78, DB, Louisiana State
4. Lewis Tillman—93, RB, Jackson State, from San Diego
   Brad Henke—105, NT, Arizona
5. Dave Meggett—132, RB, Towson State
6. Howard Cross—158, TE, Alabama
7. Dave Popp—175, T, Eastern Illinois, from San Diego
   Choice to Indianapolis
8. Myron Guyton—218, DB, Eastern Kentucky
9. A.J. Greene—245, DB, Wake Forest
10. Rodney Lowe—272, DE, Mississippi
11. Jerome Rinehart—299, LB, Tennessee-Martin
12. Eric Smith—326, LB, UCLA

New York Jets (Drafted 14th)

1. Jeff Lageman—14, LB, Virginia
2. Dennis Byrd—42, DE, Tulsa
3. Joe Mott—70, LB, Iowa
4. Ron Stallworth—98, DE, Auburn
5. Tony Martin—126, WR, Mesa, Colo.
6. Marvin Washington—151, DE, Idaho, from L.A. Raiders
   Titus Dixon—153, WR, Troy State
7. Stevon Moore—181, DB, Mississippi
8. Anthony Brown—209, RB, West Virginia
9. Pat Marlatt—237, DT, West Virginia
10. Adam Bob—265, LB, Texas A&M
11. Artie Holmes—293, DB, Washington State
12. Willie Snead—321, WR, Florida

Philadelphia Eagles (Drafted alternately 22-21-20-19-18-23)

1. Choice to Indianapolis
2. Jessie Small—49, LB, Eastern Kentucky
3. Robert Drummond—76, RB, Syracuse
   Britt Hager—81, LB, Texas, from Chicago
4. Choice to Seattle
5. Choice to Chicago
6. Heath Sherman—162, RB, Texas A&I
7. Choice to Chicago
8. Choice to Chicago
9. Choice to Chicago
10. Choice to Chicago
11. Choice to Chicago
12. Choice to Chicago

Phoenix Cardinals (Drafted alternately 10-12-11)

1. Eric Hill—10, LB, Louisiana State
   Joe Wolf—17, G, Boston College, from Seattle
2. Walter Reeves—40, TE, Auburn
3. Mike Zandofsky—67, G, Washington
4. Jim Wahler—94, DT, UCLA
5. Richard Tardits—123, LB, Georgia
   David Edeen—128, DE, Wyoming, from Seattle
6. Jay Taylor—150, DB, San Jose State
7. Rickey Royal—177, DB, Sam Houston State
8. John Burch—207, RB, Tennessee-Martin
9. Kendall Trainor—234, K, Arkansas
10. Chris Becker—261, P, Texas Christian
11. Jeffrey Hunter—291, DE, Albany State, Ga.
12. Todd Nelson—318, G, Wisconsin

Pittsburgh Steelers (Drafted alternately 7-6-5)

1. Tim Worley—7, RB, Georgia
   Tom Ricketts—24, T, Pittsburgh, from Minnesota
2. Carnell Lake—34, DB, UCLA
3. Derek Hill—61, WR, Arizona
4. Jerrol Williams—91, LB, Purdue
5. David Arnold—118, DB, Michigan
6. Mark Stock—144, WR, Virginia Military
7. David Johnson—174, DB, Kentucky
8. Chris Asbeck—201, NT, Cincinnati
9. A.J. Jenkins—228, DE, Cal State-Fullerton
10. Jerry Olsavsky—258, LB, Pittsburgh
11. Brian Slater—285, WR, Washington
12. Carlton Haselrig—312, DE, Pittsburgh

San Diego Chargers (Drafted alternately 8-9)

1. Burt Grossman—8, DE, Pittsburgh
2. Courtney Hall—37, C, Rice
   Billy Joe Tolliver—51, QB, Texas Tech, from N.Y. Giants
3. Choice to N.Y. Giants
4. Choice to N.Y. Giants
5. Elliot Smith—120, DB, Alcorn State
6. Choice to L.A. Rams
7. Choice to N.Y. Giants
   Marion Butts—183, RB, Florida State, from New England
   Terrence Jones—195, QB, Tulane, from San Francisco
8. Dana Brinson—204, WR, Nebraska
9. Pat Davis—231, TE, Syracuse
10. Ricky Andrews—260, LB, Washington
11. Victor Floyd—287, RB, Florida State
12. Choice to Washington

San Francisco 49ers (Drafted 28th)

1. Keith DeLong—28, LB, Tennessee
2. Wesley Walls—56, TE, Mississippi
3. Keith Henderson—84, RB, Georgia
4. Mike Barber—112, WR, Marshall
5. Johnny Jackson—122, DB, Houston, from L.A. Raiders
   Choice to Washington through L.A. Raiders
6. Steve Hendrickson—167, LB, California
7. Choice to San Diego
8. Choice to New England through L.A. Raiders
9. Rudy Harmon—251, LB, Louisiana State
10. Andy Sinclair—279, C, Stanford
11. Jim Bell—289, RB, Boston College, from L.A. Raiders
    Norm McGee—307, WR, North Dakota
12. Antonio Goss—319, LB, North Carolina, from L.A. Raiders
    Choice to Minnesota through L.A. Raiders

Seattle Seahawks (Drafted alternately 17-16-15)

1. Andy Heck—15, T, Notre Dame, from Indianapolis
   Choice to Phoenix
2. Joe Tofflemire—44, C, Arizona
3. Elroy Harris—71, RB, Eastern Kentucky
4. Travis McNeal—101, TE, Tennessee-Chattanooga
   James Henry—103, DB, Southern Mississippi, from Philadelphia
5. Choice to Phoenix
6. Choice to Tampa Bay
7. Mike Nettles—184, DB, Memphis State
8. Marlin Williams—211, DE, Western Illinois
9. David Franks—238, G, Connecticut
10. Derrick Fenner—268, RB, North Carolina
11. Mike Baum—295, DE, Northwestern
12. R.J. Kors—322, DB, Long Beach State

Tampa Bay Buccaneers (Drafted alternately 6-5-7)

1. Broderick Thomas—6, LB, Nebraska
2. Danny Peebles—33, WR, North Carolina State
3. Choice to New England
4. Anthony Florence—90, DB, Bethune-Cookman
5. Jamie Lawson—117, RB, Nicholls State
6. Chris Mohr—146, P, Alabama
   Derrick Little—154, LB, South Carolina, from Seattle
7. Choice to Buffalo
8. Carl Bax—200, G, Missouri
9. Patrick Egu—230, RB, Nevada-Reno
10. Ty Granger—257, T, Clemson
11. Rod Mounts—284, G, Texas A&I
    Willie Griffin—290, DE, Nebraska, from Washington through L.A. Rams
    Herb Duncan—302, WR, Northern Arizona, from L.A. Rams
12. Choice to Indianapolis
    Terry Young—329, DB, Georgia Southern, from L.A. Rams

Washington Redskins (Drafted alternately 12-11-10)

1. Choice to Chicago
2. Choice to Dallas through L.A. Raiders
3. Tracy Rocker—66, DT, Auburn
4. Choice to New England
   Erik Affholter—110, WR, Southern California, from Chicago through L.A. Raiders
5. Choice to Green Bay
   Tim Smiley—129, DB, Arkansas State, from Indianapolis
   Lybrant Robinson—139, DE, Delaware State, from San Francisco through L.A. Raiders
6. A.J. Johnson—149, DB, S.W. Texas State
7. Kevin Hendrix—179, LB, South Carolina
8. Choice to Green Bay
9. Charles Darrington—233, TE, Kentucky
10. Mark Schlereth—263, C, Idaho
11. Choice to Tampa Bay through L.A. Rams
12. Jimmy Johnson—316, TE, Howard, from San Diego
    Joe Mickles—317, RB, Mississippi

Active Coaches' Career Records

Start of 1989 Season

Coach	Team(s)	Regular Season Yrs.	Won	Lost	Tied	Pct.	Postseason Won	Lost	Tied	Pct.	Career Won	Lost	Tied	Pct.
Don Shula	Baltimore Colts, Miami Dolphins	26	261	111	6	.698	16	13	0	.552	277	124	6	.673
Chuck Noll	Pittsburgh Steelers	20	168	125	1	.573	15	7	0	.682	183	132	1	.581
Chuck Knox	Los Angeles Rams, Buffalo Bills, Seattle Seahawks	16	148	89	1	.624	7	11	0	.389	155	100	1	.607
Joe Gibbs	Washington Redskins	8	81	39	0	.675	11	3	0	.786	92	42	0	.687
Mike Ditka	Chicago Bears	7	73	31	0	.702	5	4	0	.556	78	35	0	.690
Dan Reeves	Denver Broncos	8	74	45	1	.621	4	4	0	.500	78	49	1	.613
John Robinson	Los Angeles Rams	6	56	39	0	.589	2	5	0	.286	58	44	0	.569
Bill Parcells	New York Giants	6	52	42	1	.553	5	2	0	.714	57	44	1	.564
Marv Levy	Kansas City Chiefs, Buffalo Bills	8	52	59	0	.468	1	1	0	.500	53	60	0	.469
Joe Walton	New York Jets	6	49	45	1	.521	1	2	0	.333	50	47	1	.515
Raymond Berry	New England Patriots	5	43	28	0	.606	3	2	0	.600	46	30	0	.605
Marty Schottenheimer	Cleveland Browns, Kansas City Chiefs	5	44	27	0	.620	2	4	0	.333	46	31	0	.597
Sam Wyche	Cincinnati Bengals	5	41	38	0	.519	2	1	0	.667	43	39	0	.524
Ron Meyer	New England Patriots, Indianapolis Colts	6	39	28	0	.582	0	2	0	.000	39	30	0	.565
Ray Perkins	New York Giants, Tampa Bay Buccaneers	6	32	56	0	.364	1	1	0	.500	33	57	0	.367
Jerry Burns	Minnesota Vikings	3	28	19	0	.596	3	2	0	.600	31	21	0	.596
Marion Campbell	Atlanta Falcons, Philadelphia Eagles	8	31	71	1	.306	0	0	0	.000	31	71	1	.306
Jim Mora	New Orleans Saints	3	29	18	0	.617	0	1	0	.000	29	19	0	.604
Jerry Glanville	Houston Oilers	4	24	25	0	.490	2	2	0	.500	26	27	0	.491
Dan Henning	Atlanta Falcons, San Diego Chargers	4	22	41	1	.352	0	0	0	.000	22	41	1	.352
Buddy Ryan	Philadelphia Eagles	3	22	24	1	.479	0	1	0	.000	22	25	1	.469
Gene Stallings	Phoenix Cardinals	3	18	28	1	.394	0	0	0	.000	18	28	1	.394
Mike Shanahan	Los Angeles Raiders	1	7	9	0	.438	0	0	0	.000	7	9	0	.438
Lindy Infante	Green Bay Packers	1	4	12	0	.250	0	0	0	.000	4	12	0	.250
Wayne Fontes	Detroit Lions	1	2	3	0	.400	0	0	0	.000	2	3	0	.400
Bud Carson	Cleveland Browns	0	0	0	0	.000	0	0	0	.000	0	0	0	.000
Jimmy Johnson	Dallas Cowboys	0	0	0	0	.000	0	0	0	.000	0	0	0	.000
George Seifert	San Francisco 49ers	0	0	0	0	.000	0	0	0	.000	0	0	0	.000

Coaches With 100 Career Victories

Start of 1989 Season

Coach	Team(s)	Regular Season Yrs.	Won	Lost	Tied	Pct.	Postseason Won	Lost	Tied	Pct.	Career Won	Lost	Tied	Pct.
George Halas	Chicago Bears	40	319	148	31	.672	6	3	0	.667	325	151	31	.672
Don Shula	Baltimore Colts, Miami Dolphins	26	261	111	6	.698	16	13	0	.552	277	124	6	.673
Tom Landry	Dallas Cowboys	29	250	162	6	.605	20	16	0	.556	270	178	6	.601
Earl (Curly) Lambeau	Green Bay Packers, Chicago Cardinals, Washington Redskins	33	226	132	22	.624	3	2	0	.600	229	134	22	.623
Chuck Noll	Pittsburgh Steelers	20	168	125	1	.573	15	7	0	.682	183	132	1	.581
Paul Brown	Cleveland Browns, Cincinnati Bengals	21	166	100	6	.621	4	8	0	.333	170	108	6	.609
Bud Grant	Minnesota Vikings	18	158	96	5	.620	10	12	0	.455	168	108	5	.607
Chuck Knox	Los Angeles Rams, Buffalo Bills, Seattle Seahawks	16	148	89	1	.624	7	11	0	.389	155	100	1	.607
Steve Owen	New York Giants	23	151	100	17	.595	2	8	0	.200	153	108	17	.581
Hank Stram	Kansas City Chiefs, New Orleans Saints	17	131	97	10	.571	5	3	0	.625	136	100	10	.573
Weeb Ewbank	Baltimore Colts, New York Jets	20	130	129	7	.502	4	1	0	.800	134	130	7	.507
Sid Gillman	Los Angeles Rams, San Diego Chargers, Houston Oilers	18	122	99	7	.550	1	5	0	.167	123	104	7	.541
George Allen	Los Angeles Rams, Washington Redskins	12	116	47	5	.705	2	7	0	.222	118	54	5	.681
Don Coryell	St. Louis Cardinals, San Diego Chargers	14	111	83	1	.572	3	6	0	.333	114	89	1	.561
John Madden	Oakland Raiders	10	103	32	7	.750	9	7	0	.563	112	39	7	.731
Ray (Buddy) Parker	Chicago Cardinals, Detroit Lions, Pittsburgh Steelers	15	104	75	9	.577	3	1	0	.750	107	76	9	.581
Vince Lombardi	Green Bay Packers, Washington Redskins	10	96	34	6	.728	9	1	0	.900	105	35	6	.740
Bill Walsh	San Francisco 49ers	10	92	59	1	.609	10	4	0	.714	102	63	1	.617

Look for in 1989

Things that could happen in 1989:

• **Steve Largent,** Seattle, starts 1988 with 97 touchdown receptions, two short of Don Hutson's NFL record. Largent, who also has one rushing touchdown in his career, needs two more touchdowns to become only the seventh player to score 100 touchdowns in an NFL career.

• Largent's next 100-yard receiving game will be the forty-first of his career, and wi l tie him with Lance Alworth for second place on the all-time list. Don Maynard holds the NFL record of 50 such games.

• **Eric Dickerson,** Indianapolis, starts the season with 9,915 yards rushing in 90 games. He may break Jim Brown's record for the fewest games needed to reach 10,000 yards rushing. Brown reached that level in his ninety-eighth NFL game.

• Dickerson could become the first player in NFL history to gain 1,000 yards rushing for seven consecutive seasons. He shares the record of six straight 1,000-yard rushing seasons with Franco Harris and Walter Payton.

• Dickerson has 52 career 100-yard rushing games to rank behind only Jim Brown (58) and Payton (77).

• **Tony Dorsett,** Denver, has 2,936 rushing attempts, and needs only 14 more to pass Franco Harris (2,949) into second place on the all-time list; Payton holds the record with 3,838 carries.

• **Dan Marino,** Miami, and **Joe Montana,** San Francisco, each have passed for 3,000 or more yards in five different seasons, one short of the NFL record held by Dan Fouts.

• Marino has had 16 games in his six-year career in which he has thrown at least four touchdown passes. He is one short of the NFL record held by Johnny Unitas, who played for 18 seasons.

• Marino starts the season with 196 touchdown passes in 87 games. There have been 12 players in NFL history who have thrown 200 touchdown passes. Marino may break Unitas's record for the fewest games needed to reach 200 touchdown passes. Unitas reached that level in his 121st NFL game.

• Montana, who starts the season with 190 touchdown passes, may also reach the 200 plateau. He needs 25 scoring passes to break the San Francisco record of 214 established by John Brodie.

• **James Lofton,** Los Angeles Raiders, needs one reception to become the seventh player in NFL history with 600 receptions. **Art Monk,** Washington, needs 24 receptions to reach the 600 mark.

• **Stanley Morgan,** New England, needs 134 yards on receptions to become only the seventh player in NFL history to reach 10,000 career yards on receptions.

• **Cris Collinsworth,** Cincinnati, starts 1989 with 417 receptions for 6,698 yards. He needs four receptions and 409 yards to break the club records in those categories (420 catches, 7,106 yards), both held by Isaac Curtis.

• **Roy Green,** Phoenix, has 425 career receptions for 6,996 yards. He needs 56 catches and 923 yards to break the club records in those categories (480 and 7,918), both held by Jackie Smith.

• Green has scored 58 touchdowns. He needs three more to break the club record of 60, held by Sonny Randle.

• **Roger Craig,** San Francisco, needs four touchdowns to break the San Francisco record of 61 career touchdowns, held by Ken Willard.

• **Dave Brown,** Green Bay, has 56 career interceptions, and needs one to tie Bobby Boyd, Johnny Robinson, and Mel Blount for seventh place in NFL history. He needs two interceptions to tie Emmitt Thomas for sixth place.

• **Ronnie Lott,** San Francisco, has 43 career interceptions, and needs four to tie the San Francisco record of 47, held by Jimmy Johnson.

• **Everson Walls,** Dallas, has 44 interceptions, and needs eight more to tie the Dallas record of 52, held by Mel Renfro.

• **Reggie Williams,** Cincinnati, needs one recovery of an opponent's fumble to move past Carl Eller into third place in NFL history in that category. Williams and Eller have 23 apiece, and trail only Dick Butkus (25) and record-holder Jim Marshall (29).

• **LeRoy Irvin,** Los Angeles Rams, has scored 11 touchdowns on returns in his NFL career. The league record is 13, established by Lemar Parrish.

• If **Rulon Jones,** Denver, or **Steve McMichael,** Chicago, score a safety, either would tie the NFL record of four in a career; that record is shared by Ted Hendricks and Doug English.

• **Ron Brown,** Los Angeles Rams, has scored four touchdowns on kickoff returns in his career. That total is two short of the NFL record of six, shared by Ollie Matson, Gale Sayers, and Travis Williams.

• **J.T. Smith,** Phoenix, has a career total of 264 punt returns. He is 18 shy of the NFL record set by Billy Johnson.

• **Nick Lowery,** Kansas City, has kicked 17 field goals of 50 or more yards in his 10-year career. He needs one more to break the NFL record that he shares with Jan Stenerud, who played 19 seasons.

• Lowery has scored at least 100 points in six seasons. He needs one more such season to equal the NFL record of seven set by Stenerud.

• Lowery needs 93 points to reach 1,000 points in his career, a level previously reached by 14 players in NFL history.

• Lowery's streak of 172 consecutive extra points is the longest current streak in the NFL. If he makes his next 28, he will become the fifth NFL player to make 200 in a row. The others are: Tommy Davis (234), Jim Turner (221), Gary Anderson (202), and George Blanda (201).

• **Jim Breech,** Cincinnati, has scored at least one point in 137 consecutive games. He needs 15 more games to break the NFL record of 151, established by Fred Cox.

• **Mike Lansford,** Los Angeles Rams, has a career total of 120 field goals, and needs one more to break the club record that he currently shares with Bruce Gossett.

• **Scott Norwood,** Buffalo, has kicked 72 field goals. He needs three to break the Buffalo record of 74, held by John Leypoldt.

• Norwood needs 35 points to surpass John Leypoldt (369) as the Bills' all-time leading kick scorer. Norwood has 335 points.

• **Rich Karlis,** Denver, has a career total of 137 field goals. He is 14 shy of the club record of 151, established by Jim Turner.

• Karlis needs 88 points to pass Jim Turner and become the Broncos' all-time kick scoring leader. Karlis begins the season with 655 points compared to Turner's 742.

• **Tony Zendejas,** Houston, has 85 field goals in his four-year NFL career. He needs seven more to break the Houston record of 91, held by George Blanda.

• **Drew Hill,** Houston, has three 1,000-yard receiving seasons to tie Charley Hennigan for most in club history.

• **Carlos Carson,** Kansas City, needs 73 receptions to surpass Henry Marshall's club reception mark (416) and 1,042 yards to eclipse Otis Taylor's team receiving yardage total (7,306). Carson enters the season with 344 career catches for 6,265 yards.

• The sixth game of the regular season will mark Pittsburgh coach **Chuck Noll**'s 300th regular-season game. At that time, Noll will join George Halas (498), Tom Landry (418), Curly Lambeau (380), and Don Shula (378 entering 1989) as the only coaches in NFL history to coach 300 regular-season games.

• **Gary Anderson,** Pittsburgh, needs five points to break Roy Gerela's 12-year-old team record of 731 points. Anderson enters the season with 727 points.

• **Ed Jones,** Dallas, by suiting up for the 1989 season, will become the first player in Cowboys history to play in 15 seasons with the team. Jones also needs seven tackles to reach 1,000 for his career.

• **Chicago** will attempt to extend their streak of 64 consecutive victories when holding their opponents to 17 points-or-less.

• **Jim McMahon,** Chicago, needs 31 completions to surpass Sid Luckman's club record of 904. McMahon has 874 completions.

• **Andre Reed,** Buffalo, needs 68 receptions to become the Bills' all-time leading receiver with 297 catches. He currently ranks fifth behind Elbert Dubenion (296), Bob Chandler (295), Jerry Butler (278), and Frank Lewis (269). Reed has 229 receptions.

• **The Dolphins** as a team can extend their NFL-record of 12 consecutive games without allowing a sack, a span of 509 pass attempts. The streak dates back to the fourth game of the 1988 season.

THE AFC

BUFFALO BILLS

American Football Conference Eastern Division

Team Colors: Royal Blue, Scarlet Red, and White

One Bills Drive
Orchard Park, New York 14127
Telephone: (716) 648-1800

Club Officials

President: Ralph C. Wilson, Jr.
Executive Vice President: David N. Olsen
General Manager and Vice President-Administration: Bill Polian
Vice President-Head Coach: Marv Levy
Treasurer: Jeff Littmann
Assistant General Manager: Bill Munson
Director of Administration: Ed Stillwell
Director of College Scouting: John Butler
Director of Marketing/Sales: Jerry Foran
Director of Pro Personnel: Bob Ferguson
Director of Public/Community Relations: Denny Lynch
Director of Stadium Operations: Steve Champlin
Box Office Comptroller: June Foran
Manager of Media Relations: Scott Berchtold
Administrative Assistant: Jim Overdorf
Equipment Manager: Dave Hojnowski
Strength and Conditioning Coordinator: Rusty Jones
Trainers: Ed Abramoski, Bud Carpenter
Video Director: Henry Kunttu

Stadium: Rich Stadium • **Capacity:** 80,290
One Bills Drive
Orchard Park, New York 14127

Playing Surface: AstroTurf

Training Camp: Fredonia State University
Fredonia, New York 14063

1989 Schedule

Preseason

Aug. 13	at Cincinnati	8:00
Aug. 19	**New Orleans**	7:30
Aug. 26	vs. G.B. at Madison, Wis.	1:00
Sept. 1	vs. Atl. at Jacksonville, Fla.	8:00

Regular Season

Sept. 10	at Miami	4:00
Sept. 18	**Denver** (Monday)	9:00
Sept. 24	at Houston	12:00
Oct. 1	**New England**	1:00
Oct. 8	at Indianapolis	12:00
Oct. 16	**L.A. Rams** (Monday)	9:00
Oct. 22	**New York Jets**	1:00
Oct. 29	**Miami**	1:00
Nov. 5	at Atlanta	1:00
Nov. 12	**Indianapolis**	1:00
Nov. 19	at New England	1:00
Nov. 26	**Cincinnati**	1:00
Dec. 4	at Seattle (Monday)	6:00
Dec. 10	**New Orleans**	1:00
Dec. 17	at San Francisco	1:00
Dec. 23	at N.Y. Jets (Saturday)	12:30

Bills Coaching History

(180-242-8)

1960-61	Buster Ramsey	11-16-1
1962-65	Lou Saban	38-18-3
1966-68	Joe Collier*	13-17-1
1968	Harvey Johnson	1-10-1
1969-70	John Rauch	7-20-1
1971	Harvey Johnson	1-13-0
1972-76	Lou Saban**	32-29-1
1976-77	Jim Ringo	3-20-0
1978-82	Chuck Knox	38-38-0
1983-84	Kay Stephenson***	10-26-0
1985-86	Hank Bullough****	4-17-0
1986-88	Marv Levy	22-18-0

*Released after two games in 1968
**Resigned after five games in 1976
***Released after four games in 1985
****Released after nine games in 1986

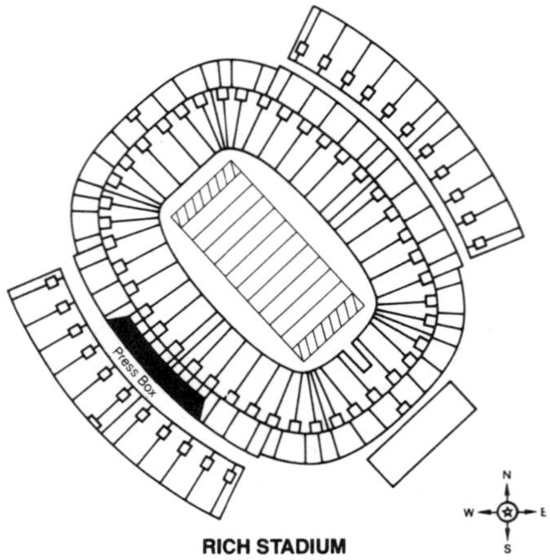

RICH STADIUM

Record Holders

Individual Records—Career

Category	Name	Performance
Rushing (Yds.)	O.J. Simpson, 1969-1977	10,183
Passing (Yds.)	Joe Ferguson, 1973-1984	27,590
Passing (TDs)	Joe Ferguson, 1973-1984	181
Receiving (No.)	Elbert Dubenion, 1960-67	296
Receiving (Yds.)	Elbert Dubenion, 1960-67	5,304
Interceptions	George (Butch) Byrd, 1964-1970	40
Punting (Avg.)	Paul Maguire, 1964-1970	42.1
Punt Return (Avg.)	Keith Moody, 1976-79	10.5
Kickoff Return (Avg.)	Wallace Francis, 1973-74	27.2
Field Goals	John Leypoldt, 1971-76	74
Touchdowns (Tot.)	O.J. Simpson, 1969-1977	70
Points	O.J. Simpson, 1969-1977	420

Individual Records—Single Season

Category	Name	Performance
Rushing (Yds.)	O.J. Simpson, 1973	2,003
Passing (Yds.)	Joe Ferguson, 1981	3,652
Passing (TDs)	Joe Ferguson, 1983	26
Receiving (No.)	Andre Reed, 1988	71
Receiving (Yds.)	Frank Lewis, 1981	1,244
Interceptions	Billy Atkins, 1961	10
	Tom Janik, 1967	10
Punting (Avg.)	Billy Atkins, 1961	44.5
Punt Return (Avg.)	Keith Moody, 1977	13.1
Kickoff Return (Avg.)	Ed Rutkowski, 1963	30.2
Field Goals	Scott Norwood, 1988	32
Touchdowns (Tot.)	O.J. Simpson, 1975	23
Points	O.J. Simpson, 1975	138

Individual Records—Single Game

Category	Name	Performance
Rushing (Yds.)	O.J. Simpson, 11-25-76	273
Passing (Yds.)	Joe Ferguson, 10-9-83	419
Passing (TDs)	Joe Ferguson, 9-23-79	5
	Joe Ferguson, 10-9-83	5
Receiving (No.)	Greg Bell, 9-8-85	13
Receiving (Yds.)	Jerry Butler, 9-23-79	255
Interceptions	Many times	3
	Last time by Jeff Nixon, 9-7-80	
Field Goals	Pete Gogolak, 12-5-65	5
	Scott Norwood, 9-25-88	5
Touchdowns (Tot.)	Cookie Gilchrist, 12-8-63	5
Points	Cookie Gilchrist, 12-8-63	30

1988 Team Record

Preseason (1-3)

Date	Result		Opponents
8/4	L	9-13	at Houston
8/13	L	13-24	Cincinnati
8/19	L	13-30	at Seattle
8/25	W	14- 7	vs. Tampa Bay at Nashville, Tenn.
		49-74	

Regular Season (12-4)

Date	Result		Opponents	Att.
9/4	W	13-10	Minnesota	76,783
9/11	W	9- 6	Miami	79,520
9/18	W	16-14	at New England	55,945
9/25	W	36-28	Pittsburgh	78,735
10/2	L	3-24	at Chicago	62,793
10/9	W	34-23	Indianapolis	76,018
10/17	W	37-14	at N.Y. Jets	70,218
10/23	W	23-20	New England	76,824
10/30	W	28- 0	Green Bay	79,176
11/6	W	13- 3	at Seattle	61,074
11/14	W	31- 6	at Miami	67,091
11/20	W	9- 6	N.Y. Jets (OT)	78,389
11/27	L	21-35	at Cincinnati	58,672
12/4	L	5-10	at Tampa Bay	49,498
12/11	W	37-21	L.A. Raiders	77,348
12/18	L	14-17	at Indianapolis	59,908

(OT) Overtime

Postseason (1-1)

Date	Result		Opponent	Att.
1/1	W	17-10	Houston	79,532
1/8	L	10-21	at Cincinnati	59,747

Score by Periods

Bills	71	83	81	91	3	—	329
Opponents	44	104	27	62	0	—	237

Attendance

Home 622,793 Away 485,199 Total 1,107,992
Single-game home record, 79,951 (9-7-86)
Single-season home record, 622,793 (1988)*
*NFL record

1988 Team Statistics

	Bills	Opp.
Total First Downs	313	299
Rushing	137	114
Passing	161	146
Penalty	15	39
Third Down: Made/Att.	88/207	69/192
Fourth Down: Made/Att.	9/13	6/17
Total Net Yards	5315	4578
Avg. Per Game	332.2	286.1
Total Plays	1012	971
Avg. Per Play	5.3	4.7
Net Yards Rushing	2133	1854
Avg. Per Game	133.3	115.9
Total Rushes	528	477
Net Yards Passing	3182	2724
Avg. Per Game	198.9	170.3
Sacked/Yards Lost	30/229	46/322
Gross Yards	3411	3046
Att./Completions	454/271	448/250
Completion Pct.	59.7	55.8
Had Intercepted	17	15
Punts/Avg.	62/39.5	75/39.7
Net Punting Avg.	35.3	34.5
Penalties/Yards Lost	109/824	90/713
Fumbles/Ball Lost	26/16	28/17
Touchdowns	33	29
Rushing	15	14
Passing	15	14
Returns	3	1
Avg. Time of Possession	29:54	30:06

1988 Individual Statistics

Scoring	TD R	TD P	TD Rt	PAT	FG	Saf	TP
Norwood	0	0	0	33/33	32/37	0	129
Riddick	12	1	1	0/0	0/0	0	84
Reed	0	6	0	0/0	0/0	0	36
Harmon	1	3	0	0/0	0/0	0	24
Rolle	0	2	0	0/0	0/0	0	12
Thomas	2	0	0	0/0	0/0	0	12
Burkett	0	1	0	0/0	0/0	0	6
F. Johnson	0	1	0	0/0	0/0	0	6
Kelso	0	0	1	0/0	0/0	0	6
Metzelaars	0	1	0	0/0	0/0	0	6
Seals	0	0	1	0/0	0/0	0	6
B. Smith	0	0	0	0/0	0/0	1	2
Bills	15	15	3	33/33	32/37	1	329
Opponents	14	14	1	27/29	12/24	0	237

Passing	Att.	Comp.	Yds.	Pct.	TD	Int.	Tkld.	Rate
Kelly	452	269	3380	59.5	15	17	30/229	78.2
Riddick	2	2	31	100.0	0	0	0/0	118.8
Bills	454	271	3411	59.7	15	17	30/229	78.5
Opponents	448	250	3046	55.8	14	15	46/322	73.4

Rushing	Att.	Yds.	Avg.	LG	TD
Thomas	207	881	4.3	37t	2
Riddick	111	438	3.9	21	12
Mueller	81	296	3.7	20	0
Harmon	57	212	3.7	32	1
Kelly	35	154	4.4	20	0
Byrum	28	91	3.3	11	0
Reed	6	64	10.7	36	0
Reich	3	−3	−1.0	−1	0
Bills	528	2133	4.0	37t	15
Opponents	477	1854	3.9	58t	14

Receiving	No.	Yds.	Avg.	LG	TD
Reed	71	968	13.6	65t	6
T. Johnson	37	514	13.9	49	0
Harmon	37	427	11.5	36	3
Metzelaars	33	438	13.3	35	1
Riddick	30	282	9.4	26	1
Burkett	23	354	15.4	34	1
Thomas	18	208	11.6	34	0
F. Johnson	9	170	18.9	66t	1
Mueller	8	42	5.3	17	0
Rolle	2	3	1.5	2t	2
Byrum	2	0	0.0	3	0
Kelly	1	5	5.0	5	0
Bills	271	3411	12.6	66t	15
Opponents	250	3046	12.2	63t	14

Interceptions	No.	Yds.	Avg.	LG	TD
Kelso	7	180	25.7	78t	1
Bennett	2	30	15.0	30	0
L. Smith, Phoe.-Buff.	2	29	14.5	15	0
L. Smith, Buff.	1	14	14.0	14	0
Cocroft	1	17	17.0	17	0
Davis	1	3	3.0	3	0
Bentley	1	0	0.0	0	0
Conlan	1	0	0.0	0	0
Odomes	1	0	0.0	0	0
Bills	15	244	16.3	78t	1
Opponents	17	202	11.9	40t	1

Punting	No.	Yds.	Avg.	In 20	LG
Kidd	62	2451	39.5	13	60
Bills	62	2451	39.5	13	60
Opponents	75	2977	39.7	21	64

Punt Returns	No.	FC	Yds.	Avg.	LG	TD
F. Johnson	16	3	72	4.5	16	0
Tucker	10	5	80	8.0	24	0
Bills	26	8	152	5.8	24	0
Opponents	36	10	222	6.2	18	0

Kickoff Returns	No.	Yds.	Avg.	LG	TD
Tucker	15	310	20.7	30	0
F. Johnson	14	250	17.9	24	0
Harmon	11	249	22.6	37	0
Riddick	6	100	16.7	23	0
Byrum	2	9	4.5	9	0
Pike	1	5	5.0	5	0
Rolle	1	12	12.0	12	0
Bills	50	935	18.7	37	0
Opponents	69	1117	16.2	30	0

Sacks	No.
B. Smith	11.0
Bennett	9.5
Still	6.0
Wright	5.0
Smerlas	4.0
Talley	2.5
Seals	2.0
Conlan	1.5
Radecic	1.5
Bentley	1.0
Garner	1.0
L. Smith	1.0
Bills	46.0
Opponents	30.0

1989 Draft Choices

Round	Name	Pos.	College
3.	Don Beebe	WR	Chadron, Neb.
4.	John Kolesar	WR	Michigan
5.	Michael Andrews	DB	Alcorn State
6.	Sean Doctor	RB	Marshall
7.	Brian Jordan	DB	Richmond
	Chris Hale	DB	Southern California
9.	Pat Rabold	DT	Wyoming
10.	Carlo Cheattom	DB	Auburn
11.	Richard Harvey	LB	Tulane
12.	Derrell Marshall	T	Southern California

Buffalo Bills 1989 Veteran Roster

No.	Name	Pos.	Ht.	Wt.	Birth-date	NFL Exp.	College	Hometown	How Acq.	'88 Games/ Starts
54	Bailey, Carlton	LB	6-2	240	12/15/64	2	North Carolina	Baltimore, Md.	D9-'88	6/0
75	Ballard, Howard	T	6-6	300	11/3/63	2	Alabama A&M	Ashland, Ala.	D11-'87	16/0
1	Bell, Albert	WR	6-0	170	4/23/64	2	Alabama	Los Angeles, Calif.	FA-'88	5/0*
55	Bennett, Cornelius	LB	6-2	235	8/25/66	3	Alabama	Birmingham, Ala.	T(Ind)-'87	16/16
50	Bentley, Ray	LB	6-2	235	11/25/60	4	Central Michigan	Grand Rapids, Mich.	FA-'86	16/16
81	Broughton, Walter	WR	5-10	180	10/20/62	3	Jacksonville State	Weaver, Ala.	FA-'86	1/0
85	Burkett, Chris	WR	6-4	210	8/21/62	5	Jackson State	Collins, Miss.	D2b-'85	11/8
29	†Burroughs, Derrick	CB	6-1	180	5/18/62	5	Memphis State	Mobile, Ala.	D1b-'85	14/13
61	Burton, Leonard	T	6-3	275	6/18/64	4	South Carolina	Memphis, Tenn.	D3-'86	16/4
58	Conlan, Shane	LB	6-3	235	4/3/64	3	Penn State	Frewsburg, N.Y.	D1-'87	13/13
79	Davis, John	C-T	6-4	304	8/22/65	3	Georgia Tech	Ellijay, Ga.	FA(Hou)-'89#	13/0*
23	Davis, Kenneth	RB	5-10	209	4/10/62	4	Texas Christian	Temple, Tex.	FA-'89	9/7*
21	Davis, Wayne	CB	5-11	180	7/17/63	5	Indiana State	Mt. Healthy, Ohio	T(SD)-'87	16/3
70	Devlin, Joe	T	6-5	280	2/23/54	13	Iowa	Frazer, Pa.	D2b-'76	16/16
45	Drane, Dwight	S	6-2	205	5/6/62	4	Oklahoma	Miami, Fla.	SD1-'84	16/4
53	Erlandson, Tom	LB	6-1	220	6/19/66	2	Washington	Denver, Colo.	D12b-'88	4/0
59	Frerotte, Mitch	T-G	6-3	275	3/30/65	2	Penn State	Kittanning, Pa.	FA-'89	0*
99	Garner, Hal	LB	6-4	235	1/18/62	4	Utah State	Logan, Utah	D3b-'85	12/1
8	†Gelbaugh, Stan	QB	6-3	207	12/4/62	3	Maryland	Carlisle, Pa.	FA-'88	0*
41	Guggemos, Neal	S	6-1	190	6/14/64	4	St. Thomas, Minn.	Winstead, Minn.	FA(NYG)-'89#	11/0*
49	Hagy, John	S	5-11	190	12/9/65	2	Texas	San Antonio, Tex.	D8a-'88	3/0
33	Harmon, Ronnie	RB	5-11	200	5/7/64	4	Iowa	Queens, N.Y.	D1a-'86	16/1
67	†Hull, Kent	C	6-4	275	1/13/61	4	Mississippi State	Greenwood, Miss.	FA-'86	16/16
47	Jackson, Kirby	CB	5-10	180	2/2/65	3	Mississippi State	Sturgis, Miss.	FA-'87	8/0
80	†Johnson, Flip	WR	5-10	185	7/13/63	2	McNeese State	Beaumont, Tex.	FA-'87	11/0
86	Johnson, Trumaine	WR	6-1	196	1/16/60	5	Grambling	Baker, La.	T(SD)-'87	16/10
12	Kelly, Jim	QB	6-3	218	2/14/60	4	Miami	East Brady, Pa.	D1b-'83	16/16
38	Kelso, Mark	S	5-11	185	7/23/63	4	William & Mary	Pittsburgh, Pa.	FA-'86	16/16
4	Kidd, John	P	6-3	208	8/22/61	6	Northwestern	Findlay, Ohio	D5-'84	16/0
28	Kinnebrew, Larry	RB	6-2	258	6/11/60	6	Tennessee State	Rome, Ga.	FA-'89	0*
63	Lingner, Adam	C	6-4	265	11/2/60	7	Illinois	Rock Island, Ill.	FA-'89	16/0*
84	McKeller, Keith	TE	6-6	245	7/9/64	2	Jacksonville State	Fairfield, Ala.	D9-'87	12/0
74	†Mesner, Bruce	NT	6-5	280	3/21/64	2	Maryland	Harrison, N.Y.	D8b-'87	0*
88	Metzelaars, Pete	TE	6-7	250	5/24/60	8	Wabash	Portage, Mich.	T(Sea)-'85	16/16
39	Mueller, Jamie	RB	6-1	225	10/4/64	3	Benedictine	Fairview Park, Ohio	D3b-'87	15/15
11	†Norwood, Scott	K	6-0	207	7/17/60	5	James Madison	Alexandria, Va.	FA-'85	16/0
37	Odomes, Nate	CB	5-10	188	8/25/65	3	Wisconsin	Columbus, Ga.	D2a-'87	16/16
94	†Pike, Mark	DE	6-4	272	12/27/63	3	Georgia Tech	Villa Hills, Ky.	D7b-'86	16/0
97	†Radecic, Scott	LB	6-3	242	6/14/62	6	Penn State	Pittsburgh, Pa.	W(KC)-'87	16/3
83	Reed, Andre	WR	6-0	190	1/29/64	5	Kutztown State	Allentown, Pa.	D4a-'85	15/14
14	Reich, Frank	QB	6-4	210	12/4/61	5	Maryland	Lebanon, Pa.	D3a-'85	3/0
62	Rentie, Caesar	T	6-3	291	11/10/64	2	Oklahoma	Hartshorne, Okla.	FA(Chi)-'89#	5/0*
40	Riddick, Robb	RB	6-0	195	4/26/57	8	Millersville State	Perkasie, Pa.	D9-'81	15/0
98	Ridgle, Elston	DE	6-6	270	8/24/63	2	Nevada-Reno	Woodland Hills, Calif.	FA-'88	0*
51	Ritcher, Jim	G	6-3	265	5/21/58	10	North Carolina State	Medina, Ohio	D1-'80	16/16
87	Rolle, Butch	TE	6-3	242	8/19/64	4	Michigan State	Hallandale, Fla.	D7c-'86	16/0
96	Seals, Leon	DE	6-4	265	1/30/64	3	Jackson State	Baton Rouge, La.	D4b-'87	16/5
76	Smerlas, Fred	NT	6-3	280	4/8/57	11	Boston College	Waltham, Mass.	D2a-'79	16/16
78	Smith, Bruce	DE	6-4	285	6/18/63	5	Virginia Tech	Norfolk, Va.	D1a-'85	12/12
46	Smith, Leonard	S	5-11	202	9/2/60	7	McNeese State	Baton Rouge, La.	T(Phx)-'88	16/15*
72	Still, Art	DE	6-7	255	12/5/55	12	Kentucky	Camden, N.J.	T(KC)-'88	15/15
64	Strenger, Rich	T	6-7	285	3/10/60	5	Michigan	Grafton, Wis.	FA-'88	0*
56	†Talley, Darryl	LB	6-4	235	7/10/60	7	West Virginia	Cleveland, Ohio	D2-'83	16/15
89	Tasker, Steve	WR-KR	5-9	185	4/10/62	5	Northwestern	Leoti, Kan.	W(Hou)-'86	14/0
34	Thomas, Thurman	RB	5-10	198	5/16/66	2	Oklahoma State	Missouri City, Tex.	D2-'88	15/15
22	Tucker, Erroll	KR-CB-S	5-8	170	7/6/64	2	Utah	Lynwood, Calif.	FA-'88	9/0
25	Tyrrell, Tim	RB	6-2	215	2/19/61	6	Northern Illinois	Hoffman Estates, Ill.	FA(Rams)-'89#	12/0*
65	Vogler, Tim	G	6-3	285	10/2/56	11	Ohio State	Covington, Ohio	FA-'79	10/10
73	Wolford, Will	T	6-5	280	5/18/64	4	Vanderbilt	Louisville, Ky.	D1b-'86	16/16
91	Wright, Jeff	NT	6-2	270	6/13/63	2	Central Missouri State	Lawrence, Kan.	D8b-'88	15/0
90	Young, Theo	TE	6-2	233	4/25/65	2	Arkansas	Newport, Ark.	FA-'89	0*

* Bell played 5 games with Green Bay in '88; J. Davis played 13 games with Houston; K. Davis played 9 games with Green Bay; Frerotte last active with Buffalo in '87; Gelbaugh active for 3 games but did not play; Guggemos played 11 games with N.Y. Giants; Kinnebrew last active with Cincinnati in '87; Lingner played 16 games with Kansas City; Mesner and Ridgle missed entire '88 season due to injury; Rentie played 5 games with Chicago; L. Smith played 3 games with Phoenix, 13 with Buffalo; Strenger last active with Detroit in '87; Tyrrell played 12 games with L.A. Rams; Young last active with Pittsburgh in '87.

† Option playout; subject to developments.

\# Plan B unconditional free agent.

Players lost through Plan B (5): RB Carl Byrum (Hou; 13 games in '88), CB-S Sherman Cocroft (TB; 13), T Dale Hellestrae (Raiders; 16), CB-S Martin Mayhew (Wash; 0), K Kirk Roach (GB; 0).

Also played with Bills in '88—LB Don Graham (10 games), CB-KR Roland Mitchell (3), DE Dean Prater (4), G Mark Traynowicz (4).

Coaching Staff

Head Coach
Marv Levy

Pro Career: Begins third full season as Bills head coach. Led Bills to a 12-4 record, the AFC East title, and a berth in the AFC Championship Game in 1988. In first full year in 1987, he led Bills to 7-8 record. Replaced Hank Bullough on November 3, 1986, and compiled a 2-5 record over final seven weeks of season. Previously served as head coach of the Kansas City Chiefs from 1978-82, producing a 31-42 mark. Levy began pro coaching career in 1969 as an assistant with the Philadelphia Eagles. He joined George Allen and the Los Angeles Rams as an assistant one year later and followed Allen to Washington, where he remained with the Redskins through the 1972 season when the Redskins played in Super Bowl VII. He was named head coach of the Montreal Alouettes (CFL) in 1973 and posted a 50-34-4 record and two Grey Cup victories (1974, 1977) in five seasons in Canada. After two seasons away from football, he became head coach of the Chicago Blitz of the USFL in 1984, the team's only year in existence. No pro playing experience. Career record: 53-60.

Background: Running back Coe College 1948-50. Coached at high school level for two years before returning to alma mater from 1953-55. Joined New Mexico staff in 1956 where he served as head coach in 1958-59. Head coach at California from 1960-63 before becoming head coach at William & Mary from 1964-68.

Personal: Born August 3, 1928, Chicago, Ill. Levy was Phi Beta Kappa at Coe College and earned master's degree in English history from Harvard. Marv and his wife, Dorothy, live in Orchard Park, N.Y.

Assistant Coaches

Tom Bresnahan, offensive line; born January 21, 1935, Springfield, Mass., lives in Hamburg, N.Y. Tackle Holy Cross 1953-55. No pro playing experience. College coach: Williams 1963-67, Columbia 1968-72, Navy 1973-80. Pro coach: Kansas City Chiefs 1981-82, New York Giants 1983-84, Phoenix Cardinals 1986-88, joined Bills in 1989.

Walt Corey, defensive coordinator, linebackers; born May 9, 1938, Latrobe, Pa., lives in West Seneca, N.Y. Defensive end Miami 1957-59. Pro linebacker Kansas City Chiefs 1960-66. College coach: Utah State 1967-69, Miami 1970-71. Pro coach: Kansas City Chiefs 1971-74, 1978-86, Cleveland Browns 1975-77, joined Bills in 1987.

Ted Cottrell, defensive line; born June 13, 1947, Chester, Pa., lives in Getzville, N.Y. Linebacker Delaware Valley College 1966-68. Pro linebacker Atlanta Falcons 1969-70, Winnipeg Blue Bombers (CFL) 1971. College coach: Rutgers 1973-80, 1983. Pro coach: Kansas City Chiefs 1981-82, New Jersey Generals (USFL) 1983-84, joined Bills in 1986.

Bruce DeHaven, special teams; born September 6, 1948, Trousdale, Kan., lives in East Aurora, N.Y. No college or pro playing experience. College coach: Kansas 1979-81, New Mexico State 1982. Pro coach: New Jersey Generals (USFL) 1983, Pittsburgh Maulers (USFL) 1984, Orlando Renegades (USFL) 1985, joined Bills in 1987.

Chuck Dickerson, special assistant to head coach; born August 1, 1937, Hammond, Ind., lives in Buffalo, N.Y. Defensive tackle Florida 1955-56, Illinois 1961. Pro defensive lineman Montreal Alouettes (CFL) 1962-64. College coach: Eastern Illinois 1967-70, 1981-82, Minnesota 1983. Pro coach: Toronto Rifles (Continental League) 1964-66, Chicago Fire (WFL) 1974-75, Toronto Argonauts (CFL) 1976-79, Memphis Showboats (USFL) 1984-86, joined Bills in 1987.

Rusty Jones, strength and conditioning; born August 14, 1953, Berwick, Maine, lives in Lakeview, N.Y. No college or pro playing experience. College coach: Springfield 1978-79. Pro coach: Pittsburgh Maulers (USFL) 1983-84, joined Bills in 1985.

Buffalo Bills 1989 First-Year Roster

Name	Pos.	Ht.	Wt.	Birth-date	College	Hometown	How Acq.
Andrews, Michael	CB-S	5-11	177	12/31/66	Alcorn State	Magnolia, Miss.	D5
Beebe, Don	WR	5-10	176	12/18/64	Chadron, Neb.	Sugar Grove, Ill.	D3
Cheattom, Kenneth	S-CB	5-11	189	3/18/67	Auburn	Sheffield, Ala.	D10
Doctor, Tom	LB	6-0	240	4/1/65	Canisius	Buffalo, N.Y.	FA
Doctor, Sean	RB	6-2	237	7/10/66	Marshall	Buffalo, N.Y.	D6
Driscoll, John (1)	T	6-5	285	9/4/64	New Hampshire	Fitchburg, Mass.	D12a-'88
Erlandson, Tom (1)	LB	6-1	220	6/19/66	Washington	Denver, Colo.	D12b-'88
Ford, Bernard (1)	WR	5-9	168	5/13/66	Central Florida	Cordele, Ga.	D3-'88
Hale, Chris	CB	5-7	161	1/4/66	Southern California	Monrovia, Calif.	D7b
Harvey, Richard	LB	6-2	227	11/11/66	Tulane	Pascagoula, Miss.	D11
Hickert, Paul	K	6-3	200	3/30/66	Murray State	Clearwater, Fla.	FA
Jordan, Brian	CB	6-1	205	3/29/67	Richmond	Baltimore, Md.	D7a
Kolesar, John	WR	5-10	187	4/14/67	Michigan	Westlake, Ohio	D4
Lockbaum, Gordon (1)	RB	5-11	200	11/16/65	Holy Cross	Glassboro, N.J.	FA
Marshall, Derrell	T	6-4	305	6/9/65	Southern California	Washington, D.C.	D12
Murray, Dan (1)	LB	6-1	240	10/20/66	East Stroudsburg	Vernon, N.J.	D6-'88
Rabold, Pat	NT	6-2	264	4/19/66	Wyoming	Glencoe, Ill.	D9
Wright, Bo (1)	RB	5-10	210	9/16/65	Alabama	Prichard, Ala.	D7b-'88

The term NFL Rookie is defined as a player who is in his first season of professional football and has not been on the roster of another professional football team for any regular-season or postseason games. A Rookie is designated by an "R" on NFL rosters. Players who have been active in another professional football league or players who have NFL experience, including either preseason training camp or being on an active roster for fewer than three regular-season or postseason games, are termed NFL First-Year Players. An NFL First-Year Player is designated by a "1" on NFL rosters. Thereafter, a player on an NFL active roster for at least three regular-season or postseason games is credited with an additional year of NFL playing experience.

NOTES

Chuck Lester, defensive assistant; born May 18, 1955, Chicago, Ill., lives in Orchard Park, N.Y. Linebacker Oklahoma 1974. No pro playing experience. College coach: Iowa State 1980-81, Oklahoma 1982-84. Pro scout: Kansas City Chiefs 1984-87. Pro coach: Joined Bills in 1987.

Ted Marchibroda, quarterbacks, passing-game coordinator; born March 15, 1931, Franklin, Pa., lives in East Aurora, N.Y. Quarterback St. Bonaventure 1950-51, Detroit 1952. Pro quarterback Pittsburgh Steelers 1953, 1955-56, Chicago Cardinals 1957. Pro coach: Washington Redskins 1961-65, 1971-74, Los Angeles Rams 1966-70, Baltimore Colts 1975-79 (head coach), Chicago Bears 1981, Detroit Lions 1982-83, Philadelphia Eagles 1984-85, joined Bills in 1987.

Nick Nicolau, receivers; born May 5, 1933, New York, N.Y., lives in Orchard Park, N.Y. Running back Southern Connecticut State 1957-59. No pro playing experience. College coach: Southern Connecticut 1960, Springfield 1961, Bridgeport 1962-69 (head coach 1965-69), Massachusetts 1970, Connecticut 1971-72, Kentucky 1973-75, Kent State 1976. Pro coach: Hamilton Tiger-Cats (CFL) 1977, Montreal Alouettes (CFL) 1978-79, New Orleans Saints 1980, Denver Broncos 1981-87, Los Angeles Raiders 1988, joined Bills in 1989.

Elijah Pitts, running backs; born February 3, 1938, Mayflower, Ark., lives in Orchard Park, N.Y. Running back Philander Smith 1957-60. Pro running back Green Bay Packers 1961-69, 1971, Los Angeles Rams 1970, Chicago Bears 1970, New Orleans Saints 1970. Pro coach: Los Angeles Rams 1974-77, Buffalo Bills 1978-80, Houston Oilers 1981-83, Hamilton Tiger-Cats (CFL) 1984, rejoined Bills in 1985.

Dick Roach, defensive backs; born August 23, 1937, Rapid City, S.D., lives in West Seneca, N.Y. Defensive back Black Hills State 1952-55. No pro playing experience. College coach: Montana State 1966-69, Oregon State 1970, Wyoming 1971-72, Fresno State 1973, Washington State 1974-75. Pro coach: Montreal Alouettes (CFL) 1976-77, Kansas City Chiefs 1978-80, New England Patriots 1981, Michigan Panthers (USFL) 1983-84, Tampa Bay Buccaneers 1985-86, joined Bills in 1987.

American Football Conference Central Division

Team Colors: Black, Orange, and White

200 Riverfront Stadium
Cincinnati, Ohio 45202
Telephone: (513) 621-3550

Club Officials

President: John Sawyer
General Manager: Paul E. Brown
Assistant General Manager: Michael Brown
Business Manager: Bill Connelly
Director of Public Relations: Allan Heim
Director of Player Personnel: Pete Brown
Accountant: Jay Reis
Ticket Manager: Paul Kelly
Consultant: John Murdough
Trainer: Marv Pollins
Equipment Manager: Tom Gray
Video Director: Al Davis

Stadium: Riverfront Stadium • **Capacity:** 59,755
200 Riverfront Stadium
Cincinnati, Ohio 45202

Playing Surface: AstroTurf-8

Training Camp: Wilmington College
Wilmington, Ohio 45177

1989 Schedule

Preseason

Aug. 13	**Buffalo**	8:00
Aug. 19	at Detroit	7:30
Aug. 28	at New Orleans	7:00
Sept. 1	at Minnesota	7:00

Regular Season

Sept. 10	at Chicago	12:00
Sept. 17	**Pittsburgh**	1:00
Sept. 25	**Cleveland** (Monday)	9:00
Oct. 1	at Kansas City	12:00
Oct. 8	at Pittsburgh	1:00
Oct. 15	**Miami**	1:00
Oct. 22	**Indianapolis**	1:00
Oct. 29	**Tampa Bay**	1:00
Nov. 5	at Los Angeles Raiders	1:00
Nov. 13	at Houston (Monday)	8:00
Nov. 19	**Detroit**	1:00
Nov. 26	at Buffalo	1:00
Dec. 3	at Cleveland	1:00
Dec. 10	**Seattle**	1:00
Dec. 17	**Houston**	1:00
Dec. 25	at Minnesota (Monday)	8:00

Bengals Coaching History

(158-159-1)

1968-75	Paul Brown	55-59-1
1976-78	Bill Johnson*	18-15-0
1978-79	Homer Rice	8-19-0
1980-83	Forrest Gregg	34-27-0
1984-88	Sam Wyche	43-39-0

*Resigned after five games in 1978

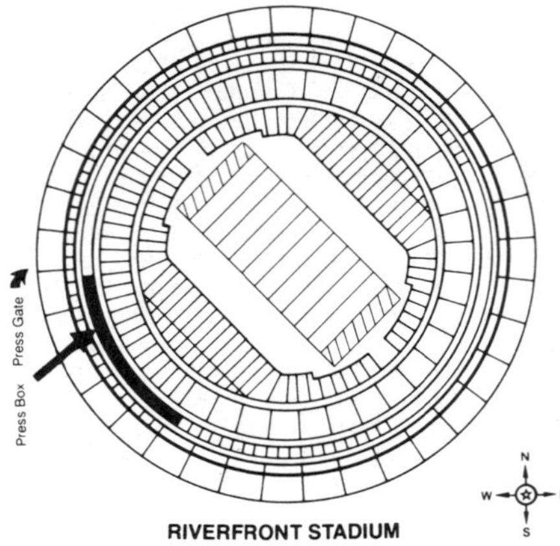

RIVERFRONT STADIUM

Record Holders

Individual Records—Career

Category	Name	Performance
Rushing (Yds.)	Pete Johnson, 1977-1983	5,421
Passing (Yds.)	Ken Anderson, 1971-1986	32,838
Passing (TDs)	Ken Anderson, 1971-1986	197
Receiving (No.)	Isaac Curtis, 1973-1984	420
Receiving (Yds.)	Isaac Curtis, 1973-1984	7,106
Interceptions (No.)	Ken Riley, 1969-1983	63
Punting (Avg.)	Dave Lewis, 1970-73	43.9
Punt Return (Avg.)	Mike Martin, 1983-87	10.4
Kickoff Return (Avg.)	Lemar Parrish, 1970-78	24.7
Field Goals	Jim Breech, 1980-87	143
Touchdowns (Tot.)	Pete Johnson, 1977-1983	70
Points	Jim Breech, 1981-87	713

Individual Records—Single Season

Category	Name	Performance
Rushing (Yds.)	James Brooks, 1986	1,087
Passing (Yds.)	Boomer Esiason, 1986	3,959
Passing (TDs)	Ken Anderson, 1981	29
Receiving (No.)	Dan Ross, 1981	71
Receiving (Yds.)	Eddie Brown, 1988	1,273
Interceptions	Ken Riley, 1976	9
Punting (Avg.)	Dave Lewis, 1970	46.2
Punt Return (Avg.)	Mike Martin, 1984	15.7
Kickoff Return (Avg.)	Lemar Parrish, 1980	30.2
Field Goals	Horst Muhlmann, 1972	27
Touchdowns (Tot.)	Pete Johnson, 1981	16
Points	Jim Breech, 1985	120

Individual Records—Single Game

Category	Name	Performance
Rushing (Yds.)	James Brooks, 12-7-86	163
Passing (Yds.)	Ken Anderson, 11-17-75	447
Passing (TDs)	Boomer Esiason, 12-21-86	5
Receiving (No.)	Many times	10
	Last time by Cris Collinsworth, 9-22-85	
Receiving (Yds.)	Cris Collinsworth, 10-2-83	216
	Eddie Brown, 11-6-88	216
Interceptions	Many times	3
	Last time by Ken Riley, 11-28-83	
Field Goals	Horst Muhlmann, 11-8-70	5
	Horst Muhlmann, 9-24-72	5
Touchdowns (Tot.)	Larry Kinnebrew, 10-28-84	4
Points	Larry Kinnebrew, 10-28-84	24

1988 Team Record

Preseason (4-1)

Date	Result		Opponents
7/30	W	14- 7	vs. L.A. Rams at Canton, Ohio
8/6	L	21-34	at Kansas City
8/13	W	24-13	at Buffalo
8/20	W	24- 7	Detroit
8/27	W	27-21	at New England
		110-82	

Regular Season (12-4)

Date	Result		Opponents	Att.
9/4	W	21-14	Phoenix	50,404
9/11	W	28-24	at Philadelphia	66,459
9/18	W	17-12	at Pittsburgh	56,647
9/25	W	24-17	Cleveland	54,943
10/2	W	45-21	at L.A. Raiders	42,594
10/9	W	36-19	N.Y. Jets	57,482
10/16	L	21-27	at New England	59,969
10/23	W	44-21	Houston	54,659
10/30	L	16-23	at Cleveland	79,147
11/6	W	42- 7	Pittsburgh	56,403
11/13	L	28-31	at Kansas City	34,614
11/20	W	38-24	at Dallas	37,865
11/27	W	35-21	Buffalo	58,672
12/4	W	27-10	San Diego	56,866
12/11	L	6-41	at Houston	50,269
12/17	W	20-17	Washington (OT)	52,157

(OT) Overtime

Postseason (2-1)

Date	Result		Opponent	Att.
12/31	W	21-13	Seattle	58,560
1/8	W	21-10	Buffalo	59,747
1/22	L	16-20	San Francisco	75,129

Score by Periods

Bengals	99	147	107	92	3	—	448
Opponents	67	79	95	88	0	—	329

Attendance

Home 441,586 Away 427,564 Total 869,150
Single-game home record, 60,284 (10-17-71)
Single-season home record, 441,586 (1988)

1988 Team Statistics

	Bengals	Opp.
Total First Downs	351	322
Rushing	159	126
Passing	165	177
Penalty	27	19
Third Down: Made/Att.	79/180	96/221
Fourth Down: Made/Att.	8/11	12/27
Total Net Yards	6057	5182
Avg. Per Game	378.6	323.9
Total Plays	985	1059
Avg. Per Play	6.1	4.9
Net Yards Rushing	2710	2048
Avg. Per Game	169.4	128.0
Total Rushes	563	493
Net Yards Passing	3347	3134
Avg. Per Game	209.2	195.9
Sacked/Yards Lost	30/245	42/374
Gross Yards	3592	3508
Att./Completions	392/225	524/283
Completion Pct.	57.4	54.0
Had Intercepted	14	22
Punts/Avg.	64/36.7	65/39.9
Net Punting Avg.	30.2	35.6
Penalties/Yards Lost	82/647	95/873
Fumbles/Ball Lost	28/13	28/14
Touchdowns	59	39
Rushing	27	18
Passing	28	19
Returns	4	2
Avg. Time of Possession	29:32	30:28

1988 Individual Statistics

Scoring	TD R	TD P	TD Rt	PAT	FG	Saf	TP
Woods	15	0	0	0/0	0/0	0	90
Breech	0	0	0	56/59	11/16	0	89
Brooks	8	6	0	0/0	0/0	0	84
Brown	0	9	0	0/0	0/0	0	54
McGee	0	6	0	0/0	0/0	0	36
Holman	0	3	0	0/0	0/0	0	18
Wilson	2	1	0	0/0	0/0	0	18
Jennings	1	0	1	0/0	0/0	0	12
Barker	0	0	1	0/0	0/0	0	6
Billups	0	0	1	0/0	0/0	0	6
Collinsworth	0	1	0	0/0	0/0	0	6
Esiason	1	0	0	0/0	0/0	0	6
Fulcher	0	0	1	0/0	0/0	0	6
Hillary	0	1	0	0/0	0/0	0	6
Martin	0	1	0	0/0	0/0	0	6
Johnson	0	0	0	0/0	1/2	0	3
Bengals	27	28	4	56/59	12/18	1	448
Opponents	18	19	2	38/39	17/24	3	329

Passing	Att.	Comp.	Yds.	Pct.	TD	Int.	Tkld.	Rate
Esiason	388	223	3572	57.5	28	14	30/245	97.4
Schonert	4	2	20	50.0	0	0	0/0	64.6
Bengals	392	225	3592	57.4	28	14	30/245	97.0
Opponents	524	283	3508	54.0	19	22	42/374	69.6

Rushing	Att.	Yds.	Avg.	LG	TD
Woods	203	1066	5.3	56	15
Brooks	182	931	5.1	51t	8
Wilson	112	398	3.6	19	2
Esiason	43	248	5.8	24	1
Jennings	17	47	2.8	9	1
Logan	2	10	5.0	9	0
Schonert	2	10	5.0	7	0
Norseth	1	5	5.0	5	0
Brown	1	−5	−5.0	−5	0
Bengals	563	2710	4.8	56	27
Opponents	493	2048	4.2	48	18

Receiving	No.	Yds.	Avg.	LG	TD
Brown	53	1273	24.0	86t	9
Holman	39	527	13.5	33	3
McGee	36	686	19.1	78t	6
Brooks	29	287	9.9	28t	6
Woods	21	199	9.5	25	0
Collinsworth	13	227	17.5	36	1
Wilson	9	110	12.2	28	1
Riggs	9	82	9.1	16	0
Hillary	5	76	15.2	31	1
Jennings	5	75	15.0	31	0
Martin	2	22	11.0	15t	1
Logan	2	20	10.0	17	0
Kattus	2	8	4.0	11	0
Bengals	225	3592	16.0	86t	28
Opponents	283	3508	12.4	65t	19

Interceptions	No.	Yds.	Avg.	LG	TD
Thomas	7	61	8.7	37	0
Fulcher	5	38	7.6	16t	1
Billups	4	47	11.8	29	0
Horton	3	13	4.3	11	0
Dixon	1	13	13.0	13	0
Wilcots	1	6	6.0	6	0
Zander	1	3	3.0	3	0
Bengals	22	181	8.2	37	1
Opponents	14	185	13.2	46	0

Punting	No.	Yds.	Avg.	In 20	LG
Johnson, Clev.-Cin.	31	1237	39.9	10	61
Johnson, Cin.	14	594	42.4	4	52
Fulhage	44	1672	38.0	13	53
Breech	3	64	21.3	1	30
Esiason	1	21	21.0	0	21
Bengals	64	2351	36.7	18	53
Opponents	65	2596	39.9	12	53

Punt Returns	No.	FC	Yds.	Avg.	LG	TD
Hillary	17	5	166	9.8	20	0
Brown	10	7	48	4.8	13	0
Martin	5	5	30	6.0	10	0
Bengals	32	17	244	7.6	20	0
Opponents	32	7	280	8.8	26	0

Kickoff Returns	No.	Yds.	Avg.	LG	TD
Jennings	32	684	21.4	98t	1
Hillary	12	195	16.3	24	0
Bussey	7	83	11.9	22	0
Logan	4	80	20.0	24	0
Brooks	1	−6	−6.0	−6	0
Dixon	1	18	18.0	18	0
Riggs*	0	0	—	0	0
Bengals	57	1054	18.5	98t	1
Opponents	61	1335	21.9	84	0

*one fair catch

Sacks	No.
Skow	9.5
Buck	6.0
Grant	5.0
Bussey	4.0
Barker	3.0
Krumrie	3.0
White	3.0
Williams	2.5
McClendon	2.0
Fulcher	1.5
Horton	1.0
Edwards	0.5
Bengals	42.0
Opponents	30.0

1989 Draft Choices

Round	Name	Pos.	College
2.	Eric Ball	RB	UCLA
	Freddie Childress	G	Arkansas
3.	Erik Wilhelm	QB	Oregon State
4.	Kerry Owens	LB	Arkansas
	Bob Woods	T	Arizona
5.	Natu Tuatagaloa	DT	California
6.	Craig Taylor	RB	West Virginia
7.	Kendal Smith	WR	Utah State
8.	Chris Chenault	LB	Kentucky
9.	Richard Stephens	T	Tulsa
10.	Cornell Holloway	DB	Pittsburgh
	Bob Jean	QB	New Hampshire
11.	Dana Wells	DT	Arizona
12.	Scott Jones	T	Washington

Cincinnati Bengals 1989 Veteran Roster

No.	Name	Pos.	Ht.	Wt.	Birth-date	NFL Exp.	College	Hometown	How Acq.	'88 Games/ Starts
35	Barber, Chris	S	6-0	187	1/15/64	2	North Carolina A&T	Winston-Salem, N.C.	FA-'87	0*
53	Barker, Leo	LB	6-2	227	11/7/59	6	New Mexico State	Cristobal, Panama	D7-'84	16/1
24	Billups, Lewis	CB	5-11	190	10/10/64	4	North Alabama	Fort Walton Beach, Fla.	D2-'86	16/16
74	†Blados, Brian	G	6-5	295	1/11/62	6	North Carolina	Arlington, Va.	D1b-'84	16/1
55	Brady, Ed	LB	6-2	235	6/17/60	6	Illinois	Morris, Ill.	D8-'84	16/0
3	Breech, Jim	K	5-6	161	4/11/56	11	California	Sacramento, Calif.	FA-'80	16/0
21	Brooks, James	RB	5-10	182	12/28/58	9	Auburn	Warner Robins, Ga.	T(SD)-'84	15/15
81	†Brown, Eddie	WR	6-0	185	12/17/62	5	Miami	Miami, Fla.	D1-'85	16/16
99	Buck, Jason	DE	6-5	265	7/27/63	3	Brigham Young	St. Anthony, Idaho	D1-'87	16/0
27	†Bussey, Barney	S	6-0	195	5/20/62	4	South Carolina	Lincolnton, Ga.	D5-'84	16/0
80	Collinsworth, Cris	WR	6-5	192	1/27/59	9	Florida	Titusville, Fla.	D2-'81	13/0
29	Dixon, Rickey	CB	5-11	177	12/26/66	2	Oklahoma	Dallas, Tex.	D1-'88	15/0
7	Esiason, Boomer	QB	6-5	225	4/17/61	6	Maryland	East Islip, N.Y.	D2-'84	16/16
33	Fulcher, David	S	6-3	228	9/28/64	4	Arizona State	Los Angeles, Calif.	D3b-'86	16/16
17	Fulhage, Scott	P	5-11	191	11/17/61	3	Kansas State	Beloit, Kan.	FA-'87	13/0
98	Grant, David	NT	6-4	277	9/17/65	2	West Virginia	Belleville, N.J.	D4-'88	16/0
71	Hammerstein, Mike	DE	6-4	270	3/29/63	3	Michigan	Wapakoneta, Ohio	D3a-'86	0*
89	Hillary, Ira	WR	5-11	190	11/13/62	3	South Carolina	Edgefield, S.C.	FA-'86	16/0
82	†Holman, Rodney	TE	6-3	238	4/20/60	8	Tulane	Ypsilanti, Mich.	D3-'82	16/16
37	Jackson, Robert	S	5-10	186	10/21/58	7	Central Michigan	Allendale, Mich.	FA-'89	0*
36	Jennings, Stanford	RB	6-1	205	3/12/62	6	Furman	Summerville, S.C.	D3-'84	16/1
11	Johnson, Lee	P	6-2	198	11/27/61	5	Brigham Young	Conroe, Tex.	FA-'88	15/0*
84	Kattus, Eric	TE	6-5	235	3/4/63	4	Michigan	Cincinnati, Ohio	D4-'86	4/0
58	Kelly, Joe	LB	6-2	231	12/11/64	4	Washington	Los Angeles, Calif.	D1-'86	16/15
42	Knapczyk, Ken	WR	6-0	185	4/21/63	2	Northern Iowa	Chicago, Ill.	FA-'88	0*
64	†Kozerski, Bruce	C-G	6-4	275	4/2/62	6	Holy Cross	Plains, Pa.	D9-'84	16/16
69	Krumrie, Tim	NT	6-2	268	5/20/60	7	Wisconsin	Eau Claire, Wis.	D10-'83	16/16
88	Martin, Mike	WR	5-10	186	11/18/60	7	Illinois	Washington, D.C.	D8-'83	4/0
72	McClendon, Skip	DE	6-7	275	4/9/64	3	Arizona State	Detroit, Mich.	D3-'87	16/16
85	McGee, Tim	WR	5-10	175	8/7/64	4	Tennessee	Cleveland, Ohio	D1a-'86	16/15
65	†Montoya, Max	G	6-5	275	5/12/56	11	UCLA	La Puente, Calif.	D7-'79	15/15
78	Muñoz, Anthony	T	6-6	278	8/19/58	10	Southern California	Ontario, Calif.	D1-'80	16/16
86	Parker, Carl	WR	6-2	201	2/5/65	2	Vanderbilt	Valdosta, Ga.	D12-'88	3/0
75	Reimers, Bruce	T	6-7	280	9/18/60	6	Iowa State	Humboldt, Iowa	D8-'84	16/16
87	Riggs, Jim	TE	6-5	245	9/29/63	3	Clemson	Laurinburg, N.C.	D4-'87	16/1
94	Romer, Rich	LB	6-3	214	2/27/66	2	Union College	East Greenbush, N.Y.	D7-'88	4/0
15	†Schonert, Turk	QB	6-1	196	1/15/57	10	Stanford	Placentia, Calif.	FA-'87	16/0
70	†Skow, Jim	DE	6-3	255	6/29/63	4	Nebraska	Omaha, Neb.	D3-'86	16/16
22	Thomas, Eric	CB	5-11	181	9/11/64	3	Tulane	Sacramento, Calif.	D2-'87	16/16
59	Walker, Kevin	LB	6-2	238	12/24/65	2	Maryland	West Milford, N.J.	D3-'88	3/0
63	Walter, Joe	T	6-6	290	6/18/63	5	Texas Tech	Dallas, Tex.	D7a-'85	16/16
51	†White, Leon	LB	6-3	245	10/4/63	4	Brigham Young	La Mesa, Calif.	D5-'86	16/16
41	Wilcots, Solomon	CB	5-11	185	10/9/64	3	Colorado	Rubidoux, Calif.	D8-'87	16/16
57	Williams, Reggie	LB	6-1	232	9/19/54	14	Dartmouth	Flint, Mich.	D3a-'76	16/16
30	Woods, Ickey	RB	6-2	232	2/28/66	2	Nevada-Las Vegas	Fresno, Calif.	D2-'88	16/10
91	†Zander, Carl	LB	6-2	235	3/23/63	5	Tennessee	Mendham, N.J.	D2-'85	16/16

* Barber, Hammerstein, and Knapczyk missed '88 season due to injury; Jackson last active with Cincinnati in '87; Johnson played 3 games with Cleveland, 12 with Cincinnati in '88.

† Option playout; subject to developments.

Plan B unconditional free agent.

Players lost through Plan B (9): S Ellis Dillahunt (Wash; 8 games in '88), T David Douglas (NE; 14), CB Ray Horton (Dall; 14), LB Emanuel King (Raiders; 7), RB Marc Logan (Mia; 9), NT Curtis Maxey (Wash; 3), QB Mike Norseth (Clev; 1), CB Daryl Smith (Minn; 7), T Dave Smith (KC; 14).

Also played with Bengals in '88—DE Eddie Edwards (11 games), LB Tim Inglis (4), RB Stanley Wilson (15).

COACHING STAFF

Head Coach
Sam Wyche

Pro Career: Led Cincinnati to AFC Central title with 12-4 regular-season record before coming within 34 seconds of defeating San Francisco (20-16 loss) in Super Bowl XXIII. Became the fifth head coach in Cincinnati history when he was named to lead the Bengals on December 28, 1983. Played quarterback with Bengals 1968-70, Washington Redskins 1971-73, Detroit Lions 1974-75, St. Louis Cardinals 1976, and Buffalo Bills 1977. Quarterback coach with San Francisco 49ers 1979-82. Career record: 43-39.

Background: Attended North Fulton High School in Atlanta and Furman University where he was the quarterback from 1962-65. Assistant coach at South Carolina in 1967. Head coach at Indiana University in 1983.

Personal: Born January 5, 1945, in Atlanta, Ga. Sam and his wife, Jane, have two children—Zak and Kerry. They live in Cincinnati.

Assistant Coaches

Jim Anderson, running backs; born March 27, 1948, Harrisburg, Pa., lives in Cincinnati. Linebacker-defensive end Cal Western (U.S. International) 1969-70. No pro playing experience. College coach: Cal Western 1970-71, Scottsdale Community College 1973, Nevada-Las Vegas 1974-75, Southern Methodist 1977-80, Stanford 1981-83. Pro coach: Joined Bengals in 1984.

Bruce Coslet, offensive coordinator; born August 5, 1946, Oakdale, Calif., lives in Cincinnati. Tight end Pacific 1965-67. Pro tight end Cincinnati Bengals 1969-76. Pro coach: San Francisco 49ers 1980, joined Bengals in 1981.

Bill Johnson, tight ends; born July 14, 1926, Tyler, Tex., lives in Cincinnati. Center Texas A&M 1944-46. Pro center San Francisco 49ers 1948-55. Pro coach: San Francisco 49ers 1956-67, Cincinnati Bengals 1968-78 (head coach 1976-78), Tampa Bay Buccaneers 1979-82, Detroit Lions 1983-84, rejoined Bengals in 1985.

Dick LeBeau, defensive coordinator-defensive backs; born September 9, 1937, London, Ohio, lives in Cincinnati. Halfback Ohio State 1957-59. Pro defensive back Detroit Lions 1959-72. Pro coach: Philadelphia Eagles 1973-75, Green Bay Packers 1976-79, joined Bengals in 1980.

Jim McNally, offensive line-running game; born December 13, 1943, Buffalo, N.Y., lives in Cincinnati. Guard Buffalo 1961-65. No pro playing experience. College coach: Buffalo 1966-69, Marshall 1973-75, Boston College 1976-78, Wake Forest 1979. Pro coach: Joined Bengals in 1980.

Dick Selcer, linebackers; born August 22, 1937, Cincinnati, Ohio, lives in Cincinnati. Running back Notre Dame 1955-58. No pro playing experience. College coach: Xavier, Ohio 1962-64, 1970-71 (head coach), Cincinnati 1965-66, Brown 1967-69, Wisconsin 1972-74, Kansas State 1975-77, Southwestern Louisiana 1978-80. Pro coach: Houston Oilers 1981-83, joined Bengals in 1984.

Mike Stock, special teams; born September 29, 1939, Barberton, Ohio, lives in Cincinnati. Fullback Northwestern 1958-60. No pro playing experience. College coach Northwestern 1961, Buffalo 1966-67, Navy 1968, Notre Dame 1969-75, 1983-86, Wisconsin 1976-77, Eastern Michigan 1978-82 (head coach). Pro coach: Joined Bengals in 1987.

Chuck Studley, linebackers; born January 17, 1929, Maywood, Ill., lives in Cincinnati. Guard Illinois 1949-51. No pro playing experience. College coach: Illinois 1955-59, Massachusetts 1960 (head coach), Cincinnati 1961-68 (head coach). Pro coach: Cincinnati Bengals 1969-78, San Francisco 49ers 1979-82, Houston Oilers 1983 (interim head coach for last 10 games), Miami Dolphins 1984-88, rejoined Bengals in 1989.

Kim Wood, strength; born July 12, 1945, Barrington, Ill., lives in Cincinnati. Running back Wisconsin 1965-68. No pro playing experience. Pro coach: Joined Bengals in 1975.

Cincinnati Bengals 1989 First-Year Roster

Name	Pos.	Ht.	Wt.	Birth-date	College	Hometown	How Acq.
Allen, Dennis	WR	6-0	185	7/7/63	Kansas State	Balch Springs, Tex.	FA
Ball, Eric	RB	6-1	215	7/1/66	UCLA	Ypsilanti, Mich.	D2
Carey, Richard	CB	5-8	171	5/6/68	Idaho	Seattle, Wash.	FA
Chenault, Chris	LB	6-2	246	11/19/65	Kentucky	Lexington, Ky.	D8
Childress, Freddie	G	6-4	350	9/17/66	Arkansas	West Helena, Ark.	D2a
Couch, Gary	WR	5-10	175	1/2/66	Minnesota	Minneapolis, Minn.	FA
D'Amico, Matt	LB	6-2	240	6/9/65	Maryland	Rockville, Md.	FA
Etze, Eric	K	5-10	207	6/13/66	Penn State	Winter Springs, Fla.	FA
Ferguson, Phil	DE	6-2	260	5/21/66	Furman	Greer, S.C.	FA
Gallery, James	K	6-1	205	9/15/61	Minnesota	Plymouth, Minn.	FA
Garrett, John	WR	5-11	180	3/2/65	Princeton	Monmouth Beach, N.J.	FA
Grimshaw, Brett	RB	5-9	229	2/1/66	Western Illinois	Burlington, Ill.	FA
Gruno, Tom	LB	6-1	237	2/17/66	Toledo	Massillon, Ohio	FA
Guerrero, John	T	6-3	329	12/13/65	Southern California	Oxnard, Calif.	FA
Harris, Franklin	TE	6-2	233	8/27/65	Northern Michigan	Garland, Tex.	FA
Harvey, Tony	WR	6-0	195	12/18/65	Kansas	Lawrence, Kan.	FA
Holifield, John (1)	RB	6-0	202	7/14/64	West Virginia	Romulus, Mich.	FA-'88
Holloway, Cornell	CB	5-11	185	1/30/66	Pittsburgh	Alliance, Ohio	D10
Howard, James	CB	6-0	185	4/5/66	Cal State-Fullerton	Paramount, Calif.	FA
Jacobs, Jeff	WR	6-1	193	9/10/64	Michigan State	Dallas, Tex.	FA
Jean, Bob	QB	6-2	210	3/18/66	New Hampshire	Newburyport, Mass.	D10a
Jetton, Paul (1)	G	6-4	288	10/6/64	Texas	Houston, Tex.	D6-'88
Jones, Scott	T	6-5	275	3/20/66	Washington	Port Angeles, Wash.	D12
McKinney, Al	RB	5-10	194	2/13/67	Cincinnati	Oberlin, Ohio	FA
Moyer, Ken	T	6-6	292	11/19/66	Toledo	Temperance, Mich.	FA
Owens, Kerry	LB	6-2	245	7/16/66	Arkansas	Roe, Ark.	D4
Rothwell, Mark	WR	5-11	185	8/23/65	Wisconsin-Stout	Madison, Wis.	FA
Shafer, Don	K	5-10	180	6/15/64	Southern California	Laguna Niguel, Calif.	FA
Simons, Kevin	G-T	6-3	288	4/25/67	Tennessee	Miami, Fla.	FA
Smith, Kendal	WR	5-10	182	11/23/65	Utah State	Redwood City, Calif.	D7
Stephens, Richard	T	6-7	309	11/1/65	Tulsa	Fenton, Mo.	D9
Stuart, Phil	T	6-5	305	11/25/65	Tennessee	Knoxville, Tenn.	FA
Tuatagaloa, Natu	NT	6-4	260	5/25/66	California	San Rafael, Calif.	D5
Taylor, Craig	RB	5-11	224	1/3/66	West Virginia	Linden, N.J.	D6
Vanderbilt, William	TE	6-4	235	1/27/66	Hope College	Holland, Mich.	FA
Vesling, Tim	K	6-0	185	11/20/64	Syracuse	Pittsford, N.Y.	FA
Washington, Carnell	NT	6-1	265	5/16/67	Temple	Chicago, Ill.	FA
Wells, Dana	NT	6-0	272	8/5/66	Arizona	Phoenix, Ariz.	D11
Wilhelm, Erik	QB	6-3	210	11/19/65	Oregon State	Lake Oswego, Ore.	D3
Woods, Rob	T	6-6	280	10/3/65	Arizona	Hampton, Va.	D4a

The term NFL Rookie is defined as a player who is in his first season of professional football and has not been on the roster of another professional football team for any regular-season or postseason games. A Rookie is designated by an "R" on NFL rosters. Players who have been active in another professional football league or players who have NFL experience, including either preseason training camp or being on an active roster for fewer than three regular-season or postseason games, are termed NFL First-Year Players. An NFL First-Year Player is designated by a "1" on NFL rosters. Thereafter, a player on an NFL active roster for at least three regular-season or postseason games is credited with an additional year of NFL playing experience.

NOTES

American Football Conference Central Division

Team Colors: Seal Brown, Orange, and White

Tower B
Cleveland Stadium
Cleveland, Ohio 44114
Telephone: (216) 696-5555

Club Officials

President and Owner: Arthur B. Modell
Executive Vice President/Legal and Administrative: Jim Bailey
Executive Vice President/Football Operations: Ernie Accorsi
Vice President/Public Relations: Kevin Byrne
Vice President/Finance: Mike Poplar
Vice President/Marketing: David Modell
Director of Player Relations: Ricky Feacher
Director of Marketing: David Modell
Director of Operations: John Lemmo
Director of Security: Ted Chappelle
Treasurer: Mike Srsen
Assistant Directors of Public Relations: Bob Eller, Francine Lubera
Player Personnel: Dom Anile, Tom Dimitroff, Gary Horton, Mike Lombardi
Head Trainer: Bill Tessendorf
Equipment Manager: Charley Cusick

Stadium: Cleveland Stadium • **Capacity:** 80,098
West 3rd Street
Cleveland, Ohio 44114

Playing Surface: Grass

Training Camp: Lakeland Community College
Mentor, Ohio 44060

1989 Schedule

Preseason

Aug. 6	vs. Phil. at London	1:00*
Aug. 12	at Detroit	7:30
Aug. 19	**Pittsburgh**	7:30
Aug. 26	at Phoenix	6:00
Sept. 2	**Tampa Bay**	7:00

*P.M. Eastern Time

Regular Season

Sept. 10	at Pittsburgh	4:00
Sept. 17	**New York Jets**	1:00
Sept. 25	at Cincinnati (Monday)	9:00
Oct. 1	**Denver**	1:00
Oct. 8	at Miami	1:00
Oct. 15	**Pittsburgh**	4:00
Oct. 23	**Chicago** (Monday)	9:00
Oct. 29	**Houston**	1:00
Nov. 5	at Tampa Bay	1:00
Nov. 12	at Seattle	1:00
Nov. 19	**Kansas City**	1:00
Nov. 23	at Detroit (Thanksgiving)	12:30
Dec. 3	**Cincinnati**	1:00
Dec. 10	at Indianapolis	4:00
Dec. 17	**Minnesota**	1:00
Dec. 23	at Houston (Saturday)	7:00

Browns Coaching History

(335-220-9)

1950-62	Paul Brown	115-49-5
1963-70	Blanton Collier	79-38-2
1971-74	Nick Skorich	30-26-2
1975-77	Forrest Gregg*	18-23-0
1977	Dick Modzelewski	0-1-0
1978-84	Sam Rutigliano**	47-52-0
1984-88	Marty Schottenheimer	46-31-0

*Resigned after 13 games in 1977
**Released after eight games in 1984

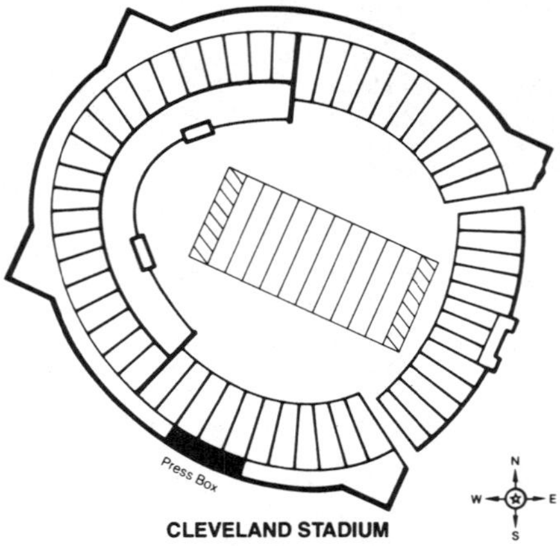

CLEVELAND STADIUM

Record Holders

Individual Records—Career

Category	Name	Performance
Rushing (Yds.)	Jim Brown, 1957-1965	12,312
Passing (Yds.)	Brian Sipe, 1974-1983	23,713
Passing (TDs)	Brian Sipe, 1974-1983	154
Receiving (No.)	Ozzie Newsome, 1978-1988	610
Receiving (Yds.)	Ozzie Newsome, 1978-1988	7,416
Interceptions	Thom Darden, 1972-74, 1976-1981	45
Punting (Avg.)	Horace Gillom, 1950-56	43.8
Punt Return (Avg.)	Greg Pruitt, 1973-1981	11.8
Kickoff Return (Avg.)	Greg Pruitt, 1973-1981	26.3
Field Goals	Lou Groza, 1950-59, 1961-67	234
Touchdowns (Tot.)	Jim Brown, 1957-1965	*126
Points	Lou Groza, 1950-59, 1961-67	1,349

Individual Records—Single Season

Category	Name	Performance
Rushing (Yds.)	Jim Brown, 1963	1,863
Passing (Yds.)	Brian Sipe, 1980	4,132
Passing (TDs)	Brian Sipe, 1980	30
Receiving (No.)	Ozzie Newsome, 1983	89
	Ozzie Newsome, 1984	89
Receiving (Yds.)	Paul Warfield, 1968	1,067
Interceptions	Thom Darden, 1978	10
Punting (Avg.)	Gary Collins, 1965	46.7
Punt Return (Avg.)	Leroy Kelly, 1965	15.6
Kickoff Return (Avg.)	Billy Reynolds, 1954	29.5
Field Goals	Matt Bahr, 1984	24
	Matt Bahr, 1988	24
Touchdowns (Tot.)	Jim Brown, 1965	21
Points	Jim Brown, 1965	126

Individual Records—Single Game

Category	Name	Performance
Rushing (Yds.)	Jim Brown, 11-24-57	237
	Jim Brown, 11-19-61	237
Passing (Yds.)	Bernie Kosar, 1-3-87	489
Passing (TDs)	Frank Ryan, 12-12-64	5
	Bill Nelsen, 11-2-69	5
	Brian Sipe, 10-7-79	5
Receiving (No.)	Ozzie Newsome, 10-14-84	14
Receiving (Yds.)	Ozzie Newsome, 10-14-84	191
Interceptions	Many times	3
	Last time by Frank Minnifield, 11-22-87	
Field Goals	Don Cockroft, 10-19-75	5
Touchdowns (Tot.)	Dub Jones, 11-25-51	*6
Points	Dub Jones, 11-25-51	36

*NFL Record

1988 Team Record

Preseason (3-1)

Date	Result		Opponents
8/6	W	13-10	Detroit
8/13	W	23- 3	at Tampa Bay
8/18	L	7-11	vs. N.Y. Jets at Montreal, Can.
8/26	W	17-13	N.Y. Giants
		60-37	

Regular Season (10-6)

Date	Result		Opponents	Att.
9/4	W	6- 3	at Kansas City	55,654
9/11	L	3-23	N.Y. Jets	74,434
9/19	W	23-17	Indianapolis	75,148
9/25	L	17-24	at Cincinnati	54,943
10/2	W	23- 9	at Pittsburgh	56,410
10/9	L	10-16	Seattle	78,605
10/16	W	19- 3	Philadelphia	78,787
10/23	W	29-21	at Phoenix	61,261
10/30	W	23-16	Cincinnati	79,147
11/7	L	17-24	at Houston	51,467
11/13	L	7-30	at Denver	75,806
11/20	W	27- 7	Pittsburgh	77,131
11/27	W	17-13	at Washington	51,604
12/4	W	24-21	Dallas	77,683
12/12	L	31-38	at Miami	61,884
12/18	W	28-23	Houston	74,610

Postseason (0-1)

Date	Result		Opponent	Att.
12/24	L	23-24	Houston	74,977

Score by Periods

Browns	46	81	63	114	0	—	304
Opponents	46	137	44	61	0	—	288

Attendance

Home 615,545 Away 469,029 Total 1,084,574
Single-game home record, 85,073 (9-21-70)
Single-season home record, 620,496 (1980)

1988 Team Statistics

	Browns	Opp.
Total First Downs	294	301
Rushing	93	114
Passing	177	162
Penalty	24	25
Third Down: Made/Att.	92/213	67/197
Fourth Down: Made/Att.	4/15	8/17
Total Net Yards	5011	4767
Avg. Per Game	313.2	297.9
Total Plays	1013	1009
Avg. Per Play	4.9	4.7
Net Yards Rushing	1575	1920
Avg. Per Game	98.4	120.0
Total Rushes	440	498
Net Yards Passing	3436	2847
Avg. Per Game	214.8	177.9
Sacked/Yards Lost	36/250	37/255
Gross Yards	3686	3102
Att./Completions	537/313	474/245
Completion Pct.	58.3	51.7
Had Intercepted	17	20
Punts/Avg.	67/38.5	69/39.4
Net Punting Avg.	33.0	32.4
Penalties/Yards Lost	110/875	100/789
Fumbles/Ball Lost	32/16	23/11
Touchdowns	33	30
Rushing	10	13
Passing	19	13
Returns	4	4
Avg. Time of Possession	30:50	29:10

1988 Individual Statistics

Scoring	TD R	TD P	TD Rt	PAT	FG	Saf	TP
Bahr	0	0	0	32/33	24/29	0	104
Langhorne	1	7	0	0/0	0/0	0	48
Byner	3	2	0	0/0	0/0	0	30
Mack	3	0	0	0/0	0/0	0	18
Slaughter	0	3	0	0/0	0/0	0	18
Fontenot	0	1	1	0/0	0/0	0	12
Manoa	2	0	0	0/0	0/0	0	12
Newsome	0	2	0	0/0	0/0	0	12
Bolden	0	1	0	0/0	0/0	0	6
Brennan	0	1	0	0/0	0/0	0	6
Kosar	1	0	0	0/0	0/0	0	6
Minnifield	0	0	1	0/0	0/0	0	6
Perry	0	0	1	0/0	0/0	0	6
Tennell	0	1	0	0/0	0/0	0	6
Washington	0	0	1	0/0	0/0	0	6
Weathers	0	1	0	0/0	0/0	0	6
Buchanan	0	0	0	0/0	0/0	1	2
Browns	10	19	4	32/33	24/29	1	304
Opponents	13	13	4	30/30	26/34	0	288

Passing	Att.	Comp.	Yds.	Pct.	TD	Int.	Tkld.	Rate
Kosar	259	156	1890	60.2	10	7	25/172	84.3
Pagel	134	71	736	53.0	3	4	1/9	64.1
Strock	91	55	736	60.4	6	5	4/26	85.2
Danielson	52	31	324	59.6	0	1	6/43	69.7
Fontenot	1	0	0	0.0	0	0	0/0	39.6
Browns	537	313	3686	58.3	19	17	36/250	77.9
Opponents	474	245	3102	51.7	13	20	37/255	64.0

Rushing	Att.	Yds.	Avg.	LG	TD
Byner	157	576	3.7	27t	3
Mack	123	485	3.9	65	3
Manoa	99	389	3.9	34	2
Fontenot	28	87	3.1	17	0
Langhorne	2	26	13.0	20t	1
Baker	3	19	6.3	13	0
Danielson	4	3	0.8	5	0
Pagel	4	1	0.3	5	0
Runager	1	0	0.0	0	0
Kosar	12	−1	−0.1	13	1
Strock	6	−2	−0.3	5	0
Bahr	1	−8	−8.0	−8	0
Browns	440	1575	3.6	65	10
Opponents	498	1920	3.9	41t	13

Receiving	No.	Yds.	Avg.	LG	TD
Byner	59	576	9.8	39t	2
Langhorne	57	780	13.7	77t	7
Brennan	46	579	12.6	33	1
Newsome	35	343	9.8	28	2
Slaughter	30	462	15.4	41	3
Weathers	29	436	15.0	49	1
Fontenot	19	170	8.9	15	1
Mack	11	87	7.9	25	0
Manoa	10	54	5.4	9	0
Tennell	9	88	9.8	26	1
McNeil	5	74	14.8	23	0
Young	2	34	17.0	25	0
Bolden	1	3	3.0	3t	1
Browns	313	3686	11.8	77t	19
Opponents	245	3102	12.7	54	13

Interceptions	No.	Yds.	Avg.	LG	TD
Wright	5	126	25.2	53	0
Minnifield	4	16	4.0	13	0
Washington	3	104	34.7	75t	1
M. Johnson	2	36	18.0	31	0
Dixon	2	24	12.0	24	0
Harper	2	13	6.5	8	0
E. Johnson	2	0	0.0	0	0
Browns	20	319	16.0	75t	1
Opponents	17	190	11.2	36t	2

Punting	No.	Yds.	Avg.	In 20	LG
Runager, S.F.-Clev.	49	1959	40.0	13	52
Runager, Clev.	48	1935	40.3	13	52
L. Johnson	17	643	37.8	6	61
Browns	67	2578	38.5	19	61
Opponents	69	2722	39.4	17	62

Punt Returns	No.	FC	Yds.	Avg.	LG	TD
McNeil	38	6	315	8.3	32	0
Weathers	2	0	10	5.0	9	0
Browns	40	6	325	8.1	32	0
Opponents	32	11	304	9.5	73t	1

Kickoff Returns	No.	Yds.	Avg.	LG	TD
Young	29	635	21.9	34	0
Fontenot	21	435	20.7	84	0
McNeil	2	38	19.0	22	0
Braggs	1	27	27.0	27	0
Perry	1	13	13.0	13	0
Tennell	1	11	11.0	11	0
Browns	55	1159	21.1	84	0
Opponents	58	973	16.8	29	0

Sacks	No.
Matthews	6.0
Perry	6.0
Buchanan	5.0
Grayson	5.0
Clancy	4.5
Hairston	3.0
E. Johnson	3.0
Harper	1.0
Hill	1.0
M. Jones	1.0
Washington	0.5
Browns	37.0
Opponents	36.0

1989 Draft Choices

Round	Name	Pos.	College
1.	Eric Metcalf	RB	Texas
2.	Lawyer Tillman	WR	Auburn
4.	Andrew Stewart	DE	Cincinnati
5.	Kyle Kramer	DB	Bowling Green
	Vernon Joines	WR	Maryland
6.	Gary Wilkerson	DB	Penn State
7.	Mike Graybill	T	Boston University
8.	Rick Aeilts	TE	S.E. Missouri
10.	John Buddenberg	T	Akron
11.	Dan Plocki	K	Maryland
12.	Marlon Brown	LB	Memphis State

Cleveland Browns 1989 Veteran Roster

No.	Name	Pos.	Ht.	Wt.	Birth-date	NFL Exp.	College	Hometown	How Acq.	'88 Games/ Starts
70	Aronson, Doug	G	6-3	290	8/14/64	2	San Diego State	San Francisco, Calif.	FA-'89	0*
9	Bahr, Matt	K	5-10	175	7/6/56	11	Penn State	Langhorne, Pa.	T(SF)-'81	16/0
60	Baker, Al	DE	6-6	280	12/9/56	12	Colorado State	Newark, N.J.	FA(Minn)-'89#	14/4*
43	†Baker, Tony	RB	5-10	180	6/11/64	3	East Carolina	High Point, N.C.	FA-'87	4/0
68	Banker, Ted	G	6-2	275	2/17/61	6	Southeast Missouri	Belleville, Ill.	FA(NYJ)-'89#	11/8*
97	Banks, Robert	DE	6-5	254	12/10/63	3	Notre Dame	Hampton, Va.	FA(Hou)-'89#	14/0*
64	Baugh, Tom	C	6-3	290	12/1/63	4	Southern Illinois	Brookfield, Ill.	FA(KC)-'89#	12/10*
93	Bennett, Charles	DE	6-6	280	2/9/63	2	Southwestern Louisiana	Alligator, Miss.	FA-'89	0*
24	Blaylock, Anthony	CB	5-11	190	2/21/65	2	Winston-Salem State	Raleigh, N.C.	D4-'88	12/0
77	Bolden, Rickey	T	6-4	280	9/8/61	6	Southern Methodist	Dallas, Tex.	D4a-'84	16/3
36	Braggs, Stephen	CB	5-10	180	8/29/65	3	Texas	Houston, Tex.	D6-'87	16/1
86	†Brennan, Brian	WR	5-9	178	2/15/62	6	Boston College	Bloomfield, Mich.	D4b-'84	16/1
72	Buchanan, Charles	DE	6-3	245	9/20/64	2	Tennessee State	Memphis, Tenn.	FA-'88	9/0
83	Butler, Ray	WR	6-3	203	6/28/56	10	Southern California	Sweeny, Tex.	FA(Sea)-'89#	12/1*
58	Charlton, Clifford	LB	6-3	240	2/16/65	2	Florida	Tallahassee, Fla.	D1-'88	16/1
25	Collins, Patrick	RB	5-9	188	8/4/66	2	Oklahoma	Tulsa, Okla.	FA(GB)-'89#	6/0*
17	Crawford, Derrick	WR	5-10	185	9/3/60	2	Memphis State	Memphis, Tenn.	FA-'89	0*
52	Dean, Kevin	LB	6-2	226	2/5/65	2	Texas Christian	Newton, Tex.	FA-'89	0*
29	†Dixon, Hanford	CB	5-11	195	12/25/58	9	Southern Mississippi	Theodore, Ala.	D1-'81	15/15
74	Farren, Paul	T-G	6-6	280	12/24/60	7	Boston University	Cohasset, Mass.	D12-'83	15/15
69	Fike, Dan	G	6-7	280	6/16/61	5	Florida	Pensacola, Fla.	FA-'85	16/16
30	Gash, Thane	S	6-0	200	9/1/65	2	East Tennessee State	Hendersonville, N.C.	D7-'88	16/1
39	Glenn, Kerry	CB	5-9	175	3/31/62	3	Minnesota	East St. Louis, Ill.	FA-'89	0*
56	Grayson, David	LB	6-2	230	2/27/64	3	Fresno State	San Diego, Calif.	FA-'87	16/14
78	Hairston, Carl	DE	6-2	280	12/15/52	14	Maryland-Eastern Shore	Martinsville, Va.	T(Phil)-'84	14/13
23	Harper, Mark	CB	5-9	185	11/5/61	4	Alcorn State	Memphis, Tenn.	FA-'86	13/1
35	†Hill, Will	S	6-0	200	3/5/63	2	Bishop College	Vero Beach, Fla.	FA-'87	16/1
51	Johnson, Eddie	LB	6-1	225	2/3/59	9	Louisville	Albany, Ga.	D7-'81	15/8
59	Johnson, Mike	LB	6-1	225	11/26/62	4	Virginia Tech	Hyattsville, Md.	SD1b-'84	16/16
95	†Jones, Marlon	DE	6-4	260	7/1/64	2	Central State, Ohio	Baltimore, Md.	FA-'87	16/1
66	Jones, Tony	T	6-5	280	5/24/66	2	Western Carolina	Royston, Ga.	FA-'88	4/0
19	Kosar, Bernie	QB	6-5	210	11/25/63	5	Miami	Boardman, Ohio	SD1-'85	9/9
55	Krauss, Barry	LB	6-3	255	3/17/57	11	Alabama	Pompano Beach, Fla.	FA(Ind)-'89#	16/15*
88	†Langhorne, Reggie	WR	6-2	200	4/7/63	5	Elizabeth City State	Carrollton, Va.	D7-'85	16/16
34	Mack, Kevin	RB	6-0	235	8/9/62	5	Clemson	Kings Mountain, N.C.	SD1-'84	11/11
42	Manoa, Tim	RB	6-1	227	8/9/64	3	Penn State	Pittsburgh, Pa.	D3a-'87	16/4
57	Matthews, Clay	LB	6-2	245	3/15/56	12	Southern California	New Trier, Ill.	D1a-'78	16/16
89	†McNeil, Gerald	WR-KR	5-7	147	3/27/62	4	Baylor	Killeen, Tex.	SD2-'84	16/0
31	Minnifield, Frank	CB	5-9	185	1/1/60	6	Louisville	Lexington, Ky.	FA-'84	15/15
82	Newsome, Ozzie	TE	6-2	232	3/16/56	12	Alabama	Leighton, Ala.	D1b-'78	16/14
7	Norseth, Mike	QB	6-2	200	8/22/64	3	Kansas	Crescenta Valley, Calif.	FA(Cin)-'89#	1/0*
28	t-Oliphant, Mike	RB	5-10	183	5/19/63	2	Puget Sound	Seattle, Wash.	T(Wash)-'89	8/0
10	†Pagel, Mike	QB	6-2	211	9/13/60	8	Arizona State	Phoenix, Ariz.	T(Ind)-'86	5/4
71	Perkins, Ray	DE	6-6	255	9/25/65	2	Virginia	Richmond, Va.	FA-'89	0*
92	Perry, Michael Dean	DE	6-0	285	8/27/65	2	Clemson	Aiken, S.C.	D2-'88	16/2
73	Rakoczy, Gregg	C	6-6	290	5/18/65	3	Miami	Medford Lakes, N.J.	D2-'87	16/16
63	†Risien, Cody	T	6-7	280	3/22/57	10	Texas A&M	Cypress, Tex.	D7-'79	16/16
99	Sims, Darryl	DE	6-3	290	7/23/61	5	Wisconsin	Bridgeport, Conn.	FA-'87	16/6
84	Slaughter, Webster	WR	6-1	170	10/19/64	4	San Diego State	Stockton, Calif.	D2-'86	8/8
12	Strock, Don	QB	6-5	220	11/27/50	16	Virginia Tech	Pottstown, Pa.	FA-'88	4/2
97	Strozier, Wilbur	TE	6-4	255	11/12/64	3	Georgia	Athens, Ga.	FA-'89	6/0*
81	Tennell, Derek	TE	6-5	245	2/12/64	3	UCLA	Los Angeles, Calif.	FA-'87	16/3
15	Wagner, Bryan	P	6-2	200	3/28/62	3	Cal State-Northridge	Chula Vista, Calif.	FA-'89	16/0*
50	Waiters, Van	LB	6-4	240	2/27/65	2	Indiana	Coral Gables, Fla.	D3-'88	16/0
48	Washington, Brian	S	6-0	210	9/10/65	2	Nebraska	Richmond, Va.	D10-'88	16/14
1	Woods, Chris	WR	5-11	190	7/19/62	2	Auburn	Birmingham, Ala.	FA(Raid)-'89#	2/0*
22	Wright, Felix	S	6-2	190	6/22/59	5	Drake	Carthage, Mo.	FA-'85	16/16

* Aronson last active with Cincinnati in '87; A. Baker played 14 games with Minnesota in '88; Banker played 11 games with N.Y. Jets; Banks played 14 games with Houston; Baugh played 12 games with Kansas City; Bennett last active with Miami in '87; Butler played 12 games with Seattle; Collins played 6 games with Green Bay; Crawford last active with San Francisco in '86; Dean last active with San Francisco in '87; Glenn last active with N.Y. Jets in '87; Krauss played 16 games with Indianapolis; Norseth played 1 game with Cincinnati; Perkins last active with Dallas in '87; Strozier played 6 games with San Diego; Wagner played 16 games with Chicago; Woods played 2 games with L.A. Raiders.

† Option playout; subject to developments.

Plan B unconditional free agent.

t- Browns traded for Oliphant (Washington).

Traded—Running back Earnest Byner to Washington, running back Herman Fontenot to Green Bay, linebacker Mike Junkin to Kansas City.

Players lost through Plan B (10): DE Sam Clancy (Ind; 16 games in '88), CB-S Danny Copeland (KC; 0), NT Bob Golic (Raiders; 16); K Jeff Jaeger (Raiders; 0), P Max Runager (KC; 13), TE Jeff Modesitt (Atl; 0), QB Steve Slayden (KC; active for 3 games but did not play), WR Clarence Weathers (Ind; 16), G Larry Williams (SD; 14), C Frank Winters (NYG; 16).

Also played with Browns in '88—QB Gary Danielson (2 games), TE Chris Dressel (active for 4 games but did not play), LB Anthony Griggs (5), T-G Darryl Haley (active for 1 game but did not play), P Lee Johnson (3), WR-KR Glen Young (15).

COACHING STAFF

Head Coach
Bud Carson

Pro Career: Begins first year as head coach of the Browns. Became seventh head coach of team on January 27, 1989. Entered pro coaching ranks as secondary coach of the Pittsburgh Steelers in 1972. Was defensive coordinator there from 1973-77, as Steelers won their first two Super Bowls (IX, X). Joined Los Angeles Rams as defensive coordinator from 1978-81, as Rams played in Super Bowl XIV. Defensive coordinator of Baltimore Colts (1982) and Kansas City Chiefs (1983). Was defensive coordinator of the New York Jets from 1985-88.

Background: Attended Freeport (Pa.) High School. Was an All-Southern defensive back at North Carolina for three seasons. Spent 30 months in the Marines following graduation. Began coaching career at North Carolina (1957-64) and spent one season (1965) at South Carolina. In 1966, he joined Georgia Tech's staff and succeeded Bobby Dodd as head coach the following year, where he compiled a 27-27 record in five years (1967-71). Was a volunteer coach at University of Kansas in 1984.

Personal: Born April 28, 1931, in Freeport, Pa. Bud and his wife, Linda, have four children, Dana, Cliff, Gary, and Cathy, and live in Moreland Hills, Ohio.

Assistant Coaches

Jed Hughes, secondary; born November 14, 1947, New York City, lives in Berea, Ohio. Tight end/split end Gettysburg College 1968-69. No pro playing experience. College coach: Stanford 1971-72, Michigan 1973-75, UCLA 1976-81. Pro coach: Minnesota Vikings 1982-83, Pittsburgh Steelers 1984-88, joined Browns in 1989.

Hal Hunter, offensive line; born June 3, 1934, Cannonsburg, Pa., lives in Berea, Ohio. Linebacker/guard Pittsburgh 1953-55. No pro playing experience. College coach: Richmond 1958-61, West Virginia 1962-63, Maryland 1964-65, Duke 1966-70, Kentucky 1971-72, Indiana 1973-76, California State (Pa.) 1977-80. Pro coach: Hamilton Tiger-Cats (CFL) 1981, Baltimore/Indianapolis Colts 1982-84 (interim head coach, final game in 1984), Pittsburgh Steelers 1985-88, joined Browns in 1989.

Paul Lanham, special teams coordinator; born July 31, 1930, Ripley, W. Va., lives in Berea, Ohio. Linebacker Glenville (W. Va.) State. No pro playing experience. College coach: Delaware 1960, Dayton 1961, Colorado State 1962-69, Arkansas 1970-71. Pro coach: St. Louis Cardinals 1972, Washington Redskins 1973-77, 1987-88, Los Angeles Rams 1978-82, Chicago Blitz/Arizona Wranglers (USFL) 1983-84, Detroit Lions 1985-86, joined Browns in 1989.

Richard Mann, receivers; born April 20, 1947, Aliquippa, Pa., lives in Strongsville, Ohio. Wide receiver Arizona State 1966-68. No pro playing experience. College coach: Arizona State 1974-79, Louisville 1980-81. Pro coach: Baltimore/Indianapolis Colts 1982-84, joined Browns in 1985.

Joe Popp, special assistant to the head coach; born September 29, 1931, Johnstown, Pa., lives in Berea, Ohio. Lineman Catawba College 1949-52. No pro playing experience. College coach North Carolina 1962-63, Wake Forest 1964-67, Georgia Tech 1968-72. Pro coach: Chicago Fire (WFL) 1974-75, joined Browns in 1989.

Dan Radakovich, defensive coordinator/linebackers; born November 27, 1935, Duquesne, Pa., lives in Berea, Ohio Center-linebacker Penn State 1954-56. No pro playing experience. College coach: Penn State 1960-69, Cincinnati 1970, Colorado 1972-73, North Carolina State 1982. Pro coach: Pittsburgh Steelers 1971, 1974-77, San Francisco 49ers 1978, Los Angeles Rams 1979-81, Denver Broncos 1983 Minnesota Vikings 1984, N.Y. Jets 1985-88, joined Browns in 1989.

Cleveland Browns 1989 First-Year Roster

Name	Pos.	Ht.	Wt.	Birth-date	College	Hometown	How Acq.
Aeilts, Rick	TE	6-5	245	12/13/65	S.E. Missouri State	Champaign, Ill.	D8
Birden, J.J.(1)	WR	5-9	160	6/16/65	Oregon	Portland, Ore.	D8-'88
Brown, Marlon	LB	6-4	221	6/30/62	Memphis State	Memphis, Tenn.	D12
Buddenberg, John	T	6-5	270	10/9/65	Akron	Bellaire, Ohio	D10
Fann, Donava	T	6-4	270	12/27/64	Bethune-Cookman	Jacksonville, Fla.	FA
Gibson, Tom (1)	NT-DE	6-7	250	12/20/63	Northern Arizona	Saugus, Calif.	FA
Graybill, Mike	T	6-7	265	10/14/66	Boston University	Hyattsville, Md.	D7
Grooms, Greg (1)	RB	6-2	195	10/16/64	Richmond	Richmond, Va.	FA
Guyton, Booker	WR	5-10	175	6/6/65	Pacific	Stockton, Calif.	FA
Hines, John (1)	DE	6-3	256	5/1/66	Alabama State	Opp, Ala.	FA
Jackson, Artis (1)	NT	6-5	280	9/9/65	Texas Tech	Dallas, Tex.	FA
Joines, Vernon	WR	6-1	190	6/20/65	Maryland	Baltimore, Md.	D5b
Jones, Fredrick (1)	LB	6-3	240	9/2/65	Florida State	Miami, Fla.	FA
Jones, Keith (1)	RB	5-10	182	2/5/66	Nebraska	Omaha, Neb.	FA
Jones, Lee (1)	DE	6-1	265	10/12/64	Nebraska	Omaha, Neb.	FA
Kramer, Kyle	S	6-2	175	1/12/67	Bowling Green	Kettering, Ohio	D5a
McGowan, Paul (1)	LB	6-0	230	1/13/66	Florida State	Winter Park, Fla.	FA
Metcalf, Eric	RB	5-9	180	1/23/68	Texas	Arlington, Va.	D1
Patton, Gary	RB	5-9	190	1/20/66	Eastern Michigan	Lorain, Ohio	FA
Pike, Chris (1)	NT-DE	6-8	301	1/13/64	Tulsa	Washington, D.C.	T(Phil)-'88
Plocki, Dan	K	5-7	177	11/17/66	Maryland	Pittsburgh, Pa.	D11
Smith, Vernice (1)	G-C	6-3	285	10/24/65	Florida A&M	Orlando, Fla.	FA
Solon, David (1)	T	6-6	285	2/15/66	St. Cloud State	Bloomington, Minn.	FA
Sorrells, Tyronne (1)	G	6-3	275	5/10/63	Georgia Tech	Buford, Ga.	FA
Stewart, Andrew	DE	6-4	256	11/20/65	Cincinnati	West Hempstead, N.Y.	D4
Stryzinski, Dan (1)	P	6-1	195	5/15/65	Indiana	Vincennes, Ind.	FA
Swarn, George (1)	RB	5-11	220	2/15/64	Miami, Ohio	Mansfield, Ohio	FA-'87
Talley, John (1)	TE	6-6	249	12/19/64	West Virginia	Cleveland, Ohio	FA
Teague, Pat (1)	LB	6-1	230	10/22/63	North Carolina State	Raleigh, N.C.	FA
Tillman, Lawyer	WR	6-4	227	5/20/66	Auburn	Mobile, Ala.	D2
Usher, Darryl (1)	WR-KR	5-8	170	1/3/65	Illinois	Los Angeles, Calif.	FA
Wilkerson, Gary	CB	6-0	181	10/11/65	Penn State	Sutherland, Va.	D6
Wilson, Teddy (1)	WR-KR	5-9	170	7/14/64	Central Florida	Zephyrhills, Fla.	FA

The term NFL Rookie is defined as a player who is in his first season of professional football and has not been on the roster of another professional football team for any regular-season or postseason games. A Rookie is designated by an "R" on NFL rosters. Players who have been active in another professional football league or players who have NFL experience, including either preseason training camp or being on an active roster for fewer than three regular-season or postseason games, are termed NFL First-Year Players. An NFL First-Year Player is designated by a "1" on NFL rosters. Thereafter, a player on an NFL active roster for at least three regular-season or postseason games is credited with an additional year of NFL playing experience.

NOTES

George Sefcik, running backs; born December 27, 1939, Cleveland, Ohio, lives in Westlake, Ohio. Halfback Notre Dame 1959-61. No pro playing experience. College coach: Notre Dame 1963-68, Kentucky 1969-72. Pro coach: Baltimore Colts 1973-74, Cleveland Browns 1975-77, Cincinnati Bengals 1979-83, Green Bay Packers 1984-87, Kansas City Chiefs 1988, rejoined Browns in 1989.

Lionel Taylor, special assistant-offense/tight ends; born August 15, 1936, Kansas City, Mo., lives in Berea, Ohio. Flanker New Mexico Highlands 1955-58. Pro wide receiver Chicago Bears 1959, Denver Broncos 1960-66, Houston Oilers 1967-68. College coach: Oregon State 1982-83, Texas Southern 1984-88 (head coach and athletic director). Pro coach: Pittsburgh Steelers 1970-76, Los Angeles Rams 1977-81, joined Browns in 1989.

John Teerlinck, defensive line; born April 9, 1951, Rochester, N.Y., lives in Berea, Ohio. Defensive lineman Western Illinois 1970-73. Pro defensive tackle San Diego Chargers 1974-76. College coach: Iowa Lakes J.C. 1977, Eastern Illinois 1978-79, Illinois 1980-82. Pro coach: Chicago/Arizona Blitz (USFL) 1983-84, joined Browns in 1989.

Marc Trestman, offensive coordinator/quarterbacks; born January 15, 1956, Minneapolis, Minn., lives in Strongsville, Ohio. Quarterback Minnesota 1975-77, Moorhead (Minn.) State 1978. Pro quarterback Minnesota Vikings 1979. College coach: Miami 1981-84. Pro coach: Minnesota Vikings 1985-86, Tampa Bay Buccaneers 1987, joined Browns in 1988.

American Football Conference Western Division

Team Colors: Orange, Royal Blue, and White

5700 Logan Street
Denver, Colorado 80216
Telephone: (303) 296-1982

Club Officials

President-Chief Executive Officer: Pat Bowlen
Vice President-Head Coach: Dan Reeves
General Manager: John Beake
Chief Financial Officer-Treasurer: Robert M. Hurley
Director of Administration: Sandy Waters
Director of Player Personnel: Reed Johnson
Director of Pro Personnel: Lide Huggins
Director of Media Relations: Jim Saccomano
Ticket Manager: Gail Stuckey
Director of Operations: Bill Harpole
Video Director: Rusty Nail
Director of Player and Community Relations: Charlie Lee
Equipment Manager: Dan Bill
Trainer: Steve Antonopulos

Stadium: Denver Mile High Stadium •
Capacity: 76,273
1900 West Eliot
Denver, Colorado 80204

Playing Surface: Grass (PAT)

Training Camp: University of Northern Colorado
Greeley, Colorado 80639

1989 Schedule

Preseason

Aug. 12	**Los Angeles Rams**	7:00
Aug. 19	at San Francisco	6:00
Aug. 26	**Dallas**	7:00
Sept. 2	at Indianapolis	7:30

Regular Season

Sept. 10	**Kansas City**	2:00
Sept. 18	at Buffalo (Monday)	9:00
Sept. 24	**Los Angeles Raiders**	2:00
Oct. 1	at Cleveland	1:00
Oct. 8	**San Diego**	2:00
Oct. 15	**Indianapolis**	2:00
Oct. 22	at Seattle	1:00
Oct. 29	**Philadelphia**	2:00
Nov. 5	**Pittsburgh**	2:00
Nov. 12	at Kansas City	12:00
Nov. 20	at Washington (Monday)	9:00
Nov. 26	**Seattle**	2:00
Dec. 3	at Los Angeles Raiders	1:00
Dec. 10	**New York Giants**	2:00
Dec. 16	at Phoenix (Saturday)	2:00
Dec. 24	at San Diego	1:00

Broncos Coaching History

(202-221-10)

1960-61	Frank Filchock	7-20-1
1962-64	Jack Faulkner*	9-22-1
1964-66	Mac Speedie**	6-19-1
1966	Ray Malavasi	4-8-0
1967-71	Lou Saban***	20-42-3
1971	Jerry Smith	2-3-0
1972-76	John Ralston	34-33-3
1977-80	Robert (Red) Miller	42-25-0
1981-88	Dan Reeves	78-49-1

*Released after four games in 1964
**Resigned after two games in 1966
***Resigned after nine games in 1971

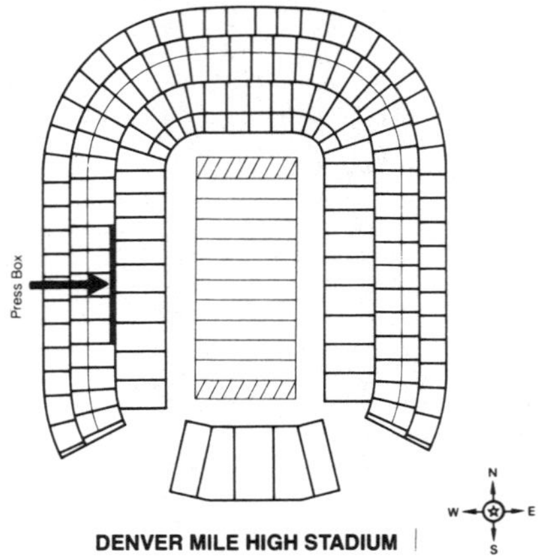

DENVER MILE HIGH STADIUM

Record Holders

Individual Records—Career

Category	Name	Performance
Rushing (Yds.)	Floyd Little, 1967-1975	6,323
Passing (Yds.)	John Elway, 1983-88	18,144
Passing (TDs)	John Elway, 1983-88	102
Receiving (No.)	Lionel Taylor, 1960-66	543
Receiving (Yds.)	Lionel Taylor, 1960-66	6,872
Interceptions	Steve Foley, 1976-1986	44
Punting (Avg.)	Jim Fraser, 1962-64	45.2
Punt Return (Avg.)	Rick Upchurch, 1975-1983	12.1
Kickoff Return (Avg.)	Abner Haynes, 1965-66	26.3
Field Goals	Jim Turner, 1971-79	151
Touchdowns (Tot.)	Floyd Little, 1967-1975	54
Points	Jim Turner, 1971-79	742

Individual Records—Single Season

Category	Name	Performance
Rushing (Yds.)	Otis Armstrong, 1974	1,407
Passing (Yds.)	John Elway, 1985	3,891
Passing (TDs)	Frank Tripucka, 1960	24
Receiving (No.)	Lionel Taylor, 1961	100
Receiving (Yds.)	Steve Watson, 1981	1,244
Interceptions	Goose Gonsoulin, 1960	11
Punting (Avg.)	Jim Fraser, 1963	46.1
Punt Return (Avg.)	Floyd Little, 1967	16.9
Kickoff Return (Avg.)	Bill Thompson, 1969	28.5
Field Goals	Gene Mingo, 1962	27
Touchdowns (Tot.)	Sammy Winder, 1986	14
Points	Gene Mingo, 1962	137

Individual Records—Single Game

Category	Name	Performance
Rushing (Yds.)	Otis Armstrong, 12-8-74	183
Passing (Yds.)	Frank Tripucka, 9-15-62	447
Passing (TDs)	Frank Tripucka, 10-28-62	5
	John Elway, 11-18-84	5
Receiving (No.)	Lionel Taylor, 11-29-64	13
	Bobby Anderson, 9-30-73	13
Receiving (Yds.)	Lionel Taylor, 11-27-60	199
Interceptions	Goose Gonsoulin, 9-18-60	*4
	Willie Brown, 11-15-64	*4
Field Goals	Gene Mingo, 10-6-63	5
	Rich Karlis, 11-20-83	5
Touchdowns (Tot.)	Many times	3
	Last time by Gerald Willhite, 11-16-86	
Points	Gene Mingo, 12-10-60	21

*NFL Record

1988 Team Record

Preseason (3-1)

Date	Result		Opponents
8/3	W	40-31	at L.A. Rams
8/13	W	34-24	San Francisco
8/19	L	13-16	at Miami (OT)
8/25	W	21-20	Indianapolis
		108-91	

Regular Season (8-8)

Date	Result		Opponents	Att.
9/4	L	14-21	Seattle	75,986
9/11	W	34- 3	San Diego	75,359
9/18	L	13-20	at Kansas City	63,268
9/26	L	27-30	L.A. Raiders (OT)	75,964
10/2	W	12- 0	at San Diego	55,763
10/9	W	16-13	at San Fran. (OT)	61,711
10/16	W	30-14	Atlanta	75,287
10/23	L	21-39	at Pittsburgh	49,811
10/31	L	23-55	at Indianapolis	60,544
11/6	W	17-11	Kansas City	74,227
11/13	W	30- 7	Cleveland	75,806
11/20	L	0-42	at New Orleans	68,075
11/27	W	35-24	L.A. Rams	74,141
12/4	L	20-21	at L.A. Raiders	65,561
12/11	L	14-42	at Seattle	62,838
12/17	W	21-10	New England	70,910

(OT) Overtime

Score by Periods

Broncos	43	127	64	90	3	—	327
Opponents	85	112	96	56	3	—	352

Attendance

Home 597,680 Away 487,571 Total 1,085,251
Single-game home record, 76,105 (1-4-87)
Single-season home record, 598,224 (1981)

1988 Team Statistics

	Broncos	Opp.
Total First Downs	338	316
Rushing	106	140
Passing	196	161
Penalty	36	15
Third Down: Made/Att.	85/210	81/214
Fourth Down: Made/Att.	4/13	9/18
Total Net Yards	5506	5471
Avg. Per Game	344.1	341.9
Total Plays	1077	1055
Avg. Per Play	5.1	5.2
Net Yards Rushing	1815	2538
Avg. Per Game	113.4	158.6
Total Rushes	464	552
Net Yards Passing	3691	2933
Avg. Per Game	230.7	183.3
Sacked/Yards Lost	32/250	36/235
Gross Yards	3941	3168
Att./Completions	581/324	467/262
Completion Pct.	55.8	56.1
Had Intercepted	22	16
Punts/Avg.	68/43.8	84/43.4
Net Punting Avg.	37.9	36.3
Penalties/Yards Lost	85/717	116/966
Fumbles/Ball Lost	34/12	23/13
Touchdowns	37	41
Rushing	13	21
Passing	24	18
Returns	0	2
Avg. Time of Possession	29:47	30:13

1988 Individual Statistics

Scoring	TD R	TD P	TD Rt	PAT	FG	Saf	TP
Karlis	0	0	0	36/37	23/36	0	105
Jackson	0	6	0	0/0	0/0	0	36
Sewell	1	5	0	0/0	0/0	0	36
Dorsett	5	0	0	0/0	0/0	0	30
V. Johnson	0	5	0	0/0	0/0	0	30
Winder	4	1	0	0/0	0/0	0	30
Kay	0	4	0	0/0	0/0	0	24
Mobley	0	2	0	0/0	0/0	0	12
Willhite	2	0	0	0/0	0/0	0	12
Elway	1	0	0	0/0	0/0	0	6
Nattiel	0	1	0	0/0	0/0	0	6
Broncos	13	24	0	36/37	23/36	0	327
Opponents	21	18	2	41/41	21/27	1	352

Passing	Att.	Comp.	Yds.	Pct.	TD	Int.	Tkld.	Rate
Elway	496	274	3309	55.2	17	19	30/237	71.4
Kubiak	69	43	497	62.3	5	3	2/13	90.1
Karcher	12	6	128	50.0	1	0	0/0	116.0
Dorsett	2	1	7	50.0	1	0	0/0	97.9
Nattiel	1	0	0	0.0	0	0	0/0	39.6
Sewell	1	0	0	0.0	0	0	0/0	39.6
Broncos	581	324	3941	55.8	24	22	32/250	74.8
Opponents	467	262	3168	56.1	18	16	36/235	75.7

Rushing	Att.	Yds.	Avg.	LG	TD
Dorsett	181	703	3.9	26	5
Winder	149	543	3.6	35	4
Elway	54	234	4.3	26	1
Sewell	32	135	4.2	26	1
Kubiak	17	65	3.8	15	0
Nattiel	5	51	10.2	29	0
Willhite	13	39	3.0	7	2
Bell	9	36	4.0	6	0
Thomas, Chi.-Den.	6	20	3.3	8	0
Thomas, Den.	1	0	0.0	0	0
Jackson	1	5	5.0	5	0
J. Johnson	1	3	3.0	3	0
V. Johnson	1	1	1.0	1	0
Broncos	464	1815	3.9	35	13
Opponents	552	2538	4.6	64t	21

Receiving	No.	Yds.	Avg.	LG	TD
V. Johnson	68	896	13.2	86	5
Jackson	46	852	18.5	63	6
Nattiel	46	574	12.5	74t	1
Sewell	38	507	13.3	68t	5
Kay	34	352	10.4	27	4
Willhite	32	238	7.4	15	0
Mobley	21	218	10.4	28	2
Winder	17	103	6.1	14	1
Dorsett	16	122	7.6	16	0
Massie	3	39	13.0	21	0
Graddy	1	30	30.0	30	0
J. Johnson	1	6	6.0	6	0
Kelly	1	4	4.0	4	0
Broncos	324	3941	12.2	86	24
Opponents	262	3168	12.1	55	18

Interceptions	No.	Yds.	Avg.	LG	TD
Harden	4	36	9.0	34	0
Castille	3	51	17.0	33	0
Robbins	2	66	33.0	39	0
Braxton	2	6	3.0	6	0
Dennison	1	29	29.0	29	0
Wilson	1	7	7.0	7	0
Fletcher	1	4	4.0	4	0
Bowyer	1	1	1.0	1	0
Haynes	1	0	0.0	0	0
Broncos	16	200	12.5	39	0
Opponents	22	344	15.6	86t	1

Punting	No.	Yds.	Avg.	In 20	LG
Horan	65	2861	44.0	19	70
Elway	3	117	39.0	2	40
Broncos	68	2978	43.8	21	70
Opponents	84	3643	43.4	20	68

Punt Returns	No.	FC	Yds.	Avg.	LG	TD
Nattiel	23	0	223	9.7	24	0
Clark	13	0	115	8.8	16	0
Willhite	13	2	90	6.9	12	0
Harden	2	2	14	7.0	14	0
Bell	1	0	4	4.0	4	0
J. Johnson	1	0	5	5.0	5	0
V. Johnson	0	1	0	—	0	0
Broncos	53	5	451	8.5	24	0
Opponents	33	4	364	11.0	66t	1

Kickoff Returns	No.	Yds.	Avg.	LG	TD
Bell	36	762	21.2	38	0
J. Johnson	14	292	20.9	34	0
Nattiel	6	124	20.7	25	0
Harden	1	9	9.0	9	0
Winder	1	11	11.0	11	0
Broncos	58	1198	20.7	38	0
Opponents	52	1035	19.9	40	0

Sacks	No.
Fletcher	9.0
Townsend	5.5
Jones	5.0
Ryan	3.5
Kragen	2.5
Robbins	2.0
Wilson	2.0
Bowyer	1.0
Braxton	1.0
Gilbert	1.0
Haynes	1.0
Mecklenburg	1.0
Smith	1.0
Dennison	0.5
Broncos	36.0
Opponents	32.0

1989 Draft Choices

Round	Name	Pos.	College
1.	Steve Atwater	DB	Arkansas
2.	Doug Widell	G	Boston College
	Warren Powers	DE	Maryland
3.	Darrell Hamilton	T	North Carolina
4.	Richard McCullough	DE	Clemson
5.	Darren Carrington	DB	Northern Arizona
6.	Anthony Stafford	WR	Oklahoma
7.	Mel Bratton	RB	Miami
8.	Paul Green	TE	Southern California
9.	Monte Smith	G	North Dakota
	Wayne Williams	RB	Florida
10.	Anthony Butts	DT	Mississippi State
11.	Richard Shelton	DB	Liberty
12.	John Javis	WR	Howard

Denver Broncos 1989 Veteran Roster

No.	Name	Pos.	Ht.	Wt.	Birth-date	NFL Exp.	College	Hometown	How Acq.	'88 Games/ Starts
35	Bell, Ken	RB	5-10	190	11/16/64	4	Boston College	Greenwich, Conn.	FA-'86	16/0
54	Bishop, Keith	C-G	6-3	265	3/10/57	9	Baylor	La Jolla, Calif.	D6-'80	16/10
68	Blair, Paul	T	6-4	280	8/3/63	3	Oklahoma State	Edmund, Okla.	FA(Chi)-'89#	0*
34	†Braxton, Tyrone	S	5-11	174	12/17/64	3	North Dakota State	Madison, Wis.	D12-'87	16/0
56	Brooks, Michael	LB	6-1	235	10/2/64	3	Louisiana State	Rustin, La.	D3-'87	16/4
64	Bryan, Billy	C	6-2	255	9/21/55	13	Duke	Burlington, N.C.	D4-'77	16/16
95	Bryan, Steve	NT	6-2	256	5/6/64	3	Oklahoma	Wagoner, Okla.	FA-'87	8/0
92	Carreker, Alphonso	DE	6-5	252	5/25/62	6	Florida State	Marietta, Ga.	FA(GB)-'89#	14/11*
28	Castille, Jeremiah	CB	5-10	175	1/15/61	7	Alabama	Columbus, Ga.	W(TB)-'87	16/15
63	Contz, Bill	T	6-5	270	5/12/61	7	Penn State	Belle Vernon, Pa.	FA(NO)-'89#	11/3*
86	Cosbie, Doug	TE	6-6	238	2/27/56	11	Santa Clara	Mountain View, Calif.	FA(Dall)-'89#	11/4*
58	Curtis, Scott	LB	6-1	227	12/26/64	2	New Hampshire	Lynnfield, Mass.	FA(Phil)-'89#	16/0*
55	Dennison, Rick	LB	6-3	220	6/22/58	8	Colorado State	Kalispel, Mont.	FA-'82	16/16
33	Dorsett, Tony	RB	5-11	189	4/7/54	13	Pittsburgh	Rochester, Pa.	T(Dall)-'88	16/13
7	Elway, John	QB	6-3	210	6/28/60	7	Stanford	Port Angeles, Wash.	T(Balt)-'83	15/15
73	†Fletcher, Simon	LB	6-5	240	2/18/62	5	Houston	Bay City, Tex.	D2b-'85	16/16
90	Gilbert, Freddie	DE	6-4	275	4/8/62	4	Georgia	Griffin, Ga.	SD1-'84	13/5
22	Goode, Kerry	RB	5-11	203	7/28/65	2	Alabama	Tampa, Fla.	FA(TB)-'89#	14/5*
37	Guidry, Kevin	CB	6-0	176	5/16/64	2	Louisiana State	Lake Charles, La.	D3-'88	14/0
31	Harden, Mike	S	6-1	192	2/16/59	10	Michigan	Memphis, Tenn.	D5a-'80	16/16
36	Haynes, Mark	CB	5-11	195	11/6/58	10	Colorado	Kansas City, Kan.	T(NYG)-'86	15/15
24	Henderson, Wymon	CB	5-9	181	12/15/61	3	Nevada-Las Vegas	North Miami Beach, Fla.	FA(Minn)-'89#	16/0*
78	†Hood, Winford	G	6-3	262	3/29/62	6	Georgia	Atlanta, Ga.	FA-'87	3/0
2	Horan, Mike	P	5-11	190	2/1/59	6	Long Beach State	Orange, Calif.	FA-'86	16/0
79	Humphries, Stefan	G	6-3	268	1/20/62	5	Michigan	Broward, Fla.	T(Chi)-'87	1/1
80	Jackson, Mark	WR	5-9	180	7/23/63	4	Purdue	Chicago, Ill.	D6b-'86	12/4
82	Johnson, Vance	WR	5-11	185	3/13/63	5	Arizona	Trenton, N.J.	D2a-'85	16/13
75	Jones, Rulon	DE	6-6	260	3/25/58	10	Utah State	Salt Lake City, Utah	D2-'80	16/0
66	Juriga, Jim	G-T	6-6	269	9/12/64	2	Illinois	Fort Wayne, Ind.	D4-'86	16/5
12	Karcher, Ken	QB	6-3	205	7/1/63	3	Tulane	Pittsburgh, Pa.	FA-'87	1/0
3	†Karlis, Rich	K	6-0	180	5/23/59	8	Cincinnati	Salem, Ohio	FA-'82	16/0
72	†Kartz, Keith	G-T	6-4	270	5/5/63	3	California	Las Vegas, Nev.	FA-'87	13/12
88	Kay, Clarence	TE	6-2	237	7/30/61	6	Georgia	Seneca, S.C.	D7-'84	14/14
87	Kelly, Pat	TE	6-6	252	10/29/65	2	Syracuse	Webster, N.Y.	D7a-'88	16/0
97	Klostermann, Bruce	LB	6-4	232	4/17/63	3	South Dakota State	Dubuque, Iowa	D8-'86	12/5
99	Knight, Shawn	NT-DE	6-6	288	6/4/64	3	Brigham Young	Provo, Utah	T(NO)-'88	14/0
71	Kragen, Greg	NT	6-3	265	3/4/62	5	Utah State	Chicago, Ill.	FA-'85	16/16
8	Kubiak, Gary	QB	6-0	192	8/15/61	7	Texas A&M	Houston, Tex.	D8-'83	16/1
76	Lanier, Ken	T	6-3	269	7/8/59	9	Florida State	Columbus, Ohio	D5-'81	16/16
59	Lucas, Tim	LB	6-3	230	4/3/61	3	California	Stockton, Calif.	FA-'87	16/0
85	Massie, Rick	WR	6-1	190	1/16/60	3	Kentucky	Paris, Ky.	FA-'87	4/0
77	Mecklenburg, Karl	LB	6-3	230	9/1/60	7	Minnesota	Edina, Minn.	D12-'83	9/9
89	†Mobley, Orson	TE	6-5	256	3/4/63	4	Salem College	Brooksville, Fla.	D6a-'86	16/9
51	Munford, Marc	LB	6-2	231	2/14/65	3	Nebraska	Lincoln, Neb.	D4-'87	7/0
84	Nattiel, Ricky	WR	5-9	180	1/25/66	3	Florida	Gainesville, Fla.	D1-'87	15/11
60	Perry, Gerald	T	6-6	305	11/12/64	2	Southern University	Columbia, S.C.	D2-'88	16/6
74	†Provence, Andrew	NT	6-3	270	3/8/61	6	South Carolina	Savannah, Ga.	T(Atl)-'88	0*
48	Robbins, Randy	S	6-2	189	9/14/62	6	Arizona	Casa Grande, Ariz.	D4-'84	16/5
57	†Ruether, Mike	C	6-4	275	9/20/62	4	Texas	Inglewood, Calif.	T(Phx)-'88	14/0
50	Ryan, Jim	LB	6-1	225	5/18/57	11	William & Mary	Bellmawr, N.J.	FA-'79	16/14
30	†Sewell, Steve	RB	6-3	210	4/2/63	5	Oklahoma	San Francisco, Calif.	D1-'85	16/3
49	Smith, Dennis	S	6-3	200	2/3/59	9	Southern California	Santa Monica, Calif.	D1-'81	11/11
70	Studdard, Dave	T	6-4	260	11/22/55	11	Texas	San Antonio, Tex.	FA-'79	11/4
61	Townsend, Andre	DE-NT	6-3	265	10/8/62	6	Mississippi	Chicago, Ill.	D2-'84	16/16
81	Watson, Steve	WR	6-4	195	5/28/57	10	Temple	Baltimore, Md.	FA-'79	0*
47	Willhite, Gerald	RB	5-10	200	5/30/59	8	San Jose State	Sacramento, Calif.	D1-'82	11/1
23	Winder, Sammy	RB	5-11	203	7/15/59	8	Southern Mississippi	Madison, Miss.	D5-'82	16/12
21	Woodberry, Dennis	CB	5-10	180	4/22/61	4	Southern Arkansas	Texarkana, Ark.	FA(Wash)-'89#	12/0*
83	Young, Mike	WR	6-1	183	2/21/62	5	UCLA	Hanford, Calif.	FA(Rams)-'89#	7/0*

* Blair last active with Chicago in '87; Carreker played 14 games for Green Bay in '88; Contz played 11 games with New Orleans; Cosbie played 11 games with Dallas; Curtis played 16 games with Philadelphia; Goode played 14 games with Tampa Bay; Henderson played 16 games with Minnesota; Provence and Watson missed '88 season due to injury; Woodberry played 12 games with Washington; Young played 7 games with L.A. Rams.

† Option playout; subject to developments.

Plan B unconditional free agent.

Retired—Steve Wilson, 10-year cornerback, 12 games in '88.

Players lost through Plan B (3): DE Walt Bowyer (KC; 16 games in '88), WR Sam Graddy (Raiders; 7), WR Jason Johnson (Pitt; 8).

Also played with Broncos in '88—S Kevin Clark (3 games), C-G Larry Lee (4), CB Bruce Plummer (8), RB Calvin Thomas (2).

Coaching Staff

Head Coach

Dan Reeves

Pro Career: Became ninth head coach in Broncos history on February 28, 1981, after spending entire pro career as both player and coach with Dallas Cowboys. His 1988 club went 8-8, finishing second in the AFC West. Reeves's Broncos won the AFC Western Division title and AFC championship in 1986 and 1987, the first AFC team to repeat as conference champion since 1978-79. Denver posted regular-season records of 10-4-1 (1987) and 11-5 (1986). Led Denver to an 11-5 record in 1985, barely missing a playoff berth. Guided Broncos to AFC West championship with a 13-3 record in 1984, and a 9-7 mark and playoff berth in 1983. His teams were 10-6 in 1981 and 2-7 in 1982. He joined the Cowboys as a free agent running back in 1965 and became a member of the coaching staff in 1970 when he undertook the dual role of player-coach for two seasons. Was Cowboys offensive backfield coach in 1972 and from 1974-76, and became offensive coordinator in 1977. Was an all-purpose running back during his eight seasons as a player, rushing for 1,990 yards and catching 129 passes for 1,693. Career record: 78-49-1.

Background: Quarterback at South Carolina from 1962-64. He was inducted into the school's Hall of Fame in 1978.

Personal: Born January 19, 1944, Rome, Ga. Dan and his wife, Pam, live in Denver and have three children—Dana, Laura, and Lee.

Assistant Coaches

Marvin Bass, special assistant; born August 28, 1919, Norfolk, Va., lives in Denver. Tackle William & Mary 1940-42. No pro playing experience. College coach: William & Mary 1944-48, 1950-51 (head coach), North Carolina 1949, 1953-55, South Carolina 1956-59, 1961-65, Georgia Tech 1960, Richmond 1973. Pro coach: Washington Redskins 1952, Montreal Beavers (Continental League) 1966-67, Montreal Alouettes (CFL) 1968, Buffalo Bills 1969-71, Birmingham Americans (WFL) 1974-75, joined Broncos in 1982.

Mo Forte, running backs; born March 1, 1947, Hannibal, Mo., lives in Denver. Running back Minnesota 1965-69. No pro playing experience. College coach: Minnesota 1970-75, Duke 1976-77, Michigan State 1978-79, Arizona State 1980-81, North Carolina A&T 1982-87 (head coach). Pro coach: Joined Broncos in 1988.

Chan Gailey, quarterbacks/wide receivers; born January 5, 1952, Americus, Ga., lives in Denver. Quarterback Florida 1971-74. No pro playing experience. College coach: Troy State 1976-77, 1983-84 (head coach), Air Force 1978-82. Pro coach: Joined Broncos in 1985.

George Henshaw, offensive line; born January 22, 1948, Richmond, Va., lives in Denver. Defensive tackle West Virginia 1967-69. No pro playing experience. College coach: West Virginia 1970-75, Florida State 1976-82, Alabama 1983-86, Tulsa 1987 (head coach). Pro coach: Joined Broncos in 1988.

Earl Leggett, defensive line; born May 5, 1933, Jacksonville, Fla., lives in Denver. Tackle Hinds J.C. 1953-54, Louisiana State 1955-56. Pro defensive tackle Chicago Bears 1957-65, Los Angeles Rams 1966, New Orleans Saints 1967-68. College coach: Nicholls State 1971, Texas Christian 1972-73. Pro coach: Southern California Sun (WFL) 1974-75, Seattle Seahawks 1976-77, San Francisco 49ers 1978, Los Angeles Raiders 1980-88, joined Broncos in 1989.

Pete Mangurian, tight ends/assistant offensive line; born June 17, 1955, Los Angeles, Calif., lives in Denver. Defensive lineman Louisiana State 1975-78. No pro playing experience. College coach: Southern Methodist 1979-80, New Mexico State 1981, Stanford 1982-83, Louisiana State 1984-87. Pro coach: Joined Broncos in 1988.

Denver Broncos 1989 First-Year Roster

Name	Pos.	Ht.	Wt.	Birth-date	College	Hometown	How Acq.
Alexander, Jeff	RB	6-0	232	1/15/65	Southern University	Baton Rouge, La.	FA-'88
Amend, David	G	6-4	274	5/18/65	Maryland	Baltimore, Md.	FA
Atwater, Steve	S	6-3	213	10/28/66	Arkansas	Chicago, Ill.	D1
Bratton, Melvin	RB	6-1	225	2/2/65	Miami	Miami, Fla.	D7
Butts, Anthony	DE	6-3	279	8/12/66	Mississippi State	Atlanta, Ga.	D10
Carrington, Darren	CB	6-1	189	10/10/66	Northern Arizona	Bronx, N.Y.	D5
Corrington, Kip (1)	S	6-0	175	4/12/65	Texas A&M	Ames, Iowa	T(Det)-'88
Ervin, Corris	CB	5-11	176	8/30/66	Central Florida	Vineland, N.J.	FA
Green, Paul	TE	6-2	223	10/8/66	Southern California	Fresno, Calif.	D8
Hamilton, Darrell	T	6-5	281	5/11/65	North Carolina	Washington, D.C.	D3
Javis, John	WR	5-10	181	5/14/67	Howard	Columbia, S.C.	D12
Marquez, Michael	RB	6-4	235	11/8/64	Colorado	Arvada, Colo.	FA
McCullough, Richard	DE	6-4	268	7/22/65	Clemson	Loris, S.C.	D4
Peterson, Blake	LB	6-3	249	5/14/66	Mesa, Colo.	Broomfield, Colo.	FA
Powers, Warren	DE	6-6	277	2/4/65	Maryland	Baltimore, Md.	D2b
Rule, Chris	QB	6-3	202	1/16/66	Colorado State	Englewood, Colo.	FA
Shelton, Richard	CB	5-10	180	1/2/66	Liberty	Marietta, Ga.	D11
Smith, Monte	G	6-4	261	4/24/67	North Dakota	Madison, Wis.	D9
Stafford, Anthony	WR	5-8	179	11/20/66	Oklahoma	St. Louis, Mo.	D6
Thornton, Randy (1)	LB	6-3	220	12/23/64	Houston	New Orleans, La.	FA-'88
Trip, Trint	NT	6-6	300	3/10/67	Minnesota	San Antonio, Tex.	FA
Ware, Reggie	RB	6-0	249	2/8/65	Auburn	Auburn, Ala.	FA
Wells, Kevin	C	6-5	285	4/21/66	San Diego State	Northglenn, Ohio	FA
White, Brian	T-G	6-4	275	11/13/64	Brigham Young	Jacksonville, Fla.	FA
Widell, Doug	G	6-4	282	9/23/66	Boston College	Hartford, Conn.	D2a
Williams, Wayne	RB	5-10	197	8/13/67	Florida	Daytona Beach, Fla.	D9b

The term NFL Rookie is defined as a player who is in his first season of professional football and has not been on the roster of another professional football team for any regular-season or postseason games. A Rookie is designated by an "R" on NFL rosters. Players who have been active in another professional football league or players who have NFL experience, including either preseason training camp or being on an active roster for fewer than three regular-season or postseason games, are termed NFL First-Year Players. An NFL First-Year Player is designated by a "1" on NFL rosters. Thereafter, a player on an NFL active roster for at least three regular-season or postseason games is credited with an additional year of NFL playing experience.

NOTES

Al Miller, strength and conditioning; born August 29, 1947, El Dorado, Ark., lives in Denver. Wide receiver Northeast Louisiana 1966-69. No pro playing experience. College coach: Northwestern Louisiana 1974-78, Mississippi State 1980, Northeast Louisiana 1981, Alabama 1982-84. Pro coach: Joined Broncos in 1985.

Mike Nolan, linebackers; born March 7, 1959, Baltimore, Md., lives in Denver. Safety Oregon 1977-80. No pro playing experience. College coach: Stanford 1982-83, Rice 1984-85, Louisiana State 1986. Pro coach: Joined Broncos in 1987.

Wade Phillips, defensive coordinator; born June 21, 1947, Orange, Tex., lives in Denver. Linebacker Houston 1966-68. No pro playing experience. College coach: Houston 1969, Oklahoma State 1973-74, Kansas 1975. Pro coach: Houston Oilers 1976-80, New Orleans Saints 1981-85 (head coach last four games of 1985), Philadelphia Eagles 1986-88, joined Broncos in 1989.

Harold Richardson, special teams; born September 27, 1944, Houston, Tex., lives in Denver. Tight end Southern Methodist 1964-67. No pro playing experience. College coach: Southern Methodist 1971-72, Oklahoma State 1973-76, Texas Christian 1977-78, North Texas State 1979-80, Colorado State 1986-88. Pro coach: New Orleans Saints 1981-85, joined Broncos in 1989.

Charlie Waters, defensive backs; born September 10, 1948, Miami, Fla., lives in Denver. Safety Clemson 1967-69. Pro safety Dallas Cowboys 1970-81. Pro coach: Joined Broncos in 1988.

American Football Conference Central Division

Team Colors: Columbia Blue, Scarlet, and White

6910 Fannin Street
Houston, Texas 77030
Telephone: (713) 797-9111

Club Officials

President: K. S. (Bud) Adams, Jr.
General Manager: Mike Holovak
Executive Assistant to President: Thomas S. Smith
Director of College Scouting: Dick Corrick
Executive Administrator: Lewis Mangum
Controller: Marilan Logan
Director of Media Relations: Chip Namias
Director of Marketing: Gregg Stengel
Executive Administrator: John Keith
Ticket Manager: Mike Mullis
Assistant Ticket Manager: Ralph Stolarski
Head Trainer: Brad Brown
Assistant Trainer: Don Moseley
Equipment Manager: Gordon Batty
Video Coordinator: Ken Sparacino

Stadium: Astrodome • **Capacity:** 61,000 (est.)
Loop 610, Kirby and Fannin Streets
Houston, Texas 77054

Playing Surface: AstroTurf-8

Training Camp: Blanco Hall
Southwest Texas State University
San Marcos, Texas 78666-4616

1989 Schedule

Preseason

Aug. 12	at Tampa Bay	7:00
Aug. 19	vs. Miami at Jacksonville	7:30
Aug. 26	vs. L.A. Raiders at Oakland	7:00
Sept. 2	at Dallas	8:00

Regular Season

Sept. 10	at Minnesota	3:00
Sept. 17	at San Diego	1:00
Sept. 24	**Buffalo**	12:00
Oct. 1	**Miami**	12:00
Oct. 8	at New England	1:00
Oct. 15	at Chicago	12:00
Oct. 22	**Pittsburgh**	12:00
Oct. 29	at Cleveland	1:00
Nov. 5	**Detroit**	12:00
Nov. 13	**Cincinnati** (Monday)	8:00
Nov. 19	**Los Angeles Raiders**	3:00
Nov. 26	at Kansas City	12:00
Dec. 3	at Pittsburgh	1:00
Dec. 10	**Tampa Bay**	12:00
Dec. 17	at Cincinnati	1:00
Dec. 23	**Cleveland** (Saturday)	7:00

Oilers Coaching History

(191-239-6)

1960-61	Lou Rymkus*	12-7-1
1961	Wally Lemm	10-0-0
1962-63	Frank (Pop) Ivy	17-12-0
1964	Sammy Baugh	4-10-0
1965	Hugh Taylor	4-10-0
1966-70	Wally Lemm	28-40-4
1971	Ed Hughes	4-9-1
1972-73	Bill Peterson**	1-18-0
1973-74	Sid Gillman	8-15-0
1975-80	O.A. (Bum) Phillips	59-38-0
1981-83	Ed Biles***	8-23-0
1983	Chuck Studley	2-8-0
1984-85	Hugh Campbell****	8-22-0
1985-88	Jerry Glanville	26-27-0

*Released after five games in 1961
**Released after five games in 1973
***Resigned after six games in 1983
****Released after 14 games in 1985

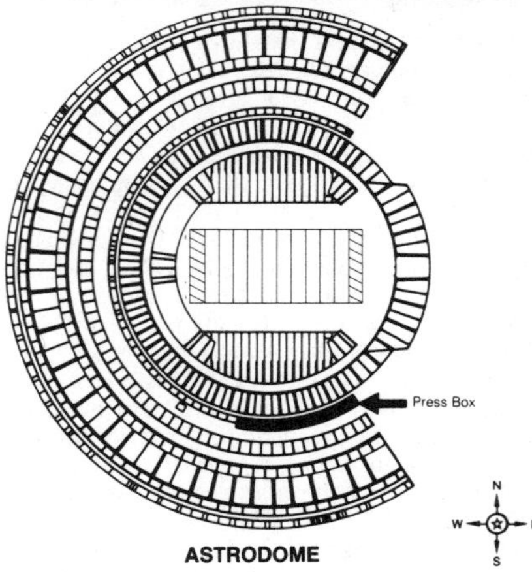

ASTRODOME

Record Holders

Individual Records—Career

Category	Name	Performance
Rushing (Yds.)	Earl Campbell, 1978-1984	8,574
Passing (Yds.)	George Blanda, 1960-66	19,149
Passing (TDs)	George Blanda, 1960-66	165
Receiving (No.)	Charley Hennigan, 1960-66	410
Receiving (Yds.)	Ken Burrough, 1971-1981	6,907
Interceptions	Jim Norton, 1960-68	45
Punting (Avg.)	Jim Norton, 1960-68	42.3
Punt Return (Avg.)	Billy Johnson, 1974-1980	13.2
Kickoff Return (Avg.)	Bobby Jancik, 1962-67	26.4
Field Goals	George Blanda, 1960-66	91
Touchdowns (Tot.)	Earl Campbell, 1978-1984	73
Points	George Blanda, 1960-66	596

Individual Records—Single Season

Category	Name	Performance
Rushing (Yds.)	Earl Campbell, 1980	1,934
Passing (Yds.)	Warren Moon, 1986	3,489
Passing (TDs)	George Blanda, 1961	36
Receiving (No.)	Charley Hennigan, 1964	101
Receiving (Yds.)	Charley Hennigan, 1961	*1,746
Interceptions	Fred Glick, 1963	12
	Mike Reinfeldt, 1979	12
Punting (Avg.)	Jim Norton, 1965	44.2
Punt Return (Avg.)	Billy Johnson, 1977	15.4
Kickoff Return (Avg.)	Ken Hall, 1960	31.2
Field Goals	Tony Zendejas, 1986	22
	Tony Zendejas, 1988	22
Touchdowns (Tot.)	Earl Campbell, 1979	19
Points	George Blanda, 1960	115

Individual Records—Single Game

Category	Name	Performance
Rushing (Yds.)	Billy Cannon, 12-10-61	216
Passing (Yds.)	George Blanda, 10-29-61	464
Passing (TDs)	George Blanda, 11-19-61	*7
Receiving (No.)	Charley Hennigan, 10-13-61	13
Receiving (Yds.)	Charley Hennigan, 10-13-61	272
Interceptions	Many times	3
	Last time by Willie Alexander, 11-14-71	
Field Goals	Skip Butler, 10-12-75	6
Touchdowns (Tot.)	Billy Cannon, 12-10-61	5
Points	Billy Cannon, 12-10-61	30

*NFL Record

1988 Team Record

Preseason (4-0)

Date	Result		Opponents
8/4	W	13- 9	Buffalo
8/13	W	27-14	vs. New Eng. at Memphis, Tenn.
8/20	W	20-17	at L.A. Rams (OT)
8/27	W	54-10	at Dallas
		114-50	

Regular Season (10-6)

Date	Result		Opponents	Att.
9/4	W	17-14	at Ind. (OT)	57,251
9/11	W	38-35	L.A. Raiders	46,050
9/18	L	3-45	at N.Y. Jets	64,683
9/25	W	31- 6	New England	38,646
10/2	L	23-32	at Philadelphia	64,692
10/9	W	7- 6	Kansas City	39,134
10/16	W	34-14	at Pittsburgh	52,229
10/23	L	21-44	at Cincinnati	54,659
10/30	W	41-17	Washington	48,781
11/7	W	24-17	Cleveland	51,467
11/13	L	24-27	at Seattle	60,446
11/20	W	38-20	Phoenix	43,843
11/24	W	25-17	at Dallas	50,845
12/4	L	34-37	Pittsburgh	47,791
12/11	W	41- 6	Cincinnati	50,269
12/18	L	23-28	at Cleveland	74,610

(OT) Overtime

Postseason (1-1)

Date	Result		Opponent	Att.
12/24	W	24-23	at Cleveland	74,977
1/1	L	10-17	at Buffalo	79,532

Score by Periods

Oilers	84	137	100	100	3	—	424
Opponents	85	112	71	97	0	—	365

Attendance

Home 365,981 Away 479,415 Total 845,396
Single-game home record, 55,452 (12-4-80)
Single-season home record, 400,156 (1980)

1988 Team Statistics

	Oilers	Opp.
Total First Downs	308	304
Rushing	141	94
Passing	148	170
Penalty	19	40
Third Down: Made/Att.	84/202	82/207
Fourth Down: Made/Att.	7/13	8/14
Total Net Yards	5205	4858
Avg. Per Game	325.3	303.6
Total Plays	1010	985
Avg. Per Play	5.2	4.9
Net Yards Rushing	2249	1592
Avg. Per Game	140.6	99.5
Total Rushes	558	431
Net Yards Passing	2956	3266
Avg. Per Game	184.8	204.1
Sacked/Yards Lost	24/210	42/353
Gross Yards	3166	3619
Att./Completions	428/218	512/281
Completion Pct.	50.9	54.9
Had Intercepted	18	22
Punts/Avg.	65/38.8	80/37.2
Net Punting Avg.	34.1	31.9
Penalties/Yards Lost	125/1150	118/947
Fumbles/Ball Lost	33/17	33/20
Touchdowns	51	46
Rushing	26	20
Passing	21	22
Returns	4	4
Avg. Time of Possession	31:11	28:49

1988 Individual Statistics

Scoring	TD R	TD P	TD Rt	PAT	FG	Saf	TP
Zendejas	0	0	0	48/50	22/34	0	114
Rozier	10	1	0	0/0	0/0	0	66
Hill	0	10	0	0/0	0/0	0	60
Pinkett	7	2	0	0/0	0/0	0	54
Givins	0	5	0	0/0	0/0	0	30
Moon	5	0	0	0/0	0/0	0	30
Highsmith	2	0	0	0/0	0/0	0	12
Brown	0	0	1	0/0	0/0	0	6
Bryant	0	0	1	0/0	0/0	0	6
Carlson	1	0	0	0/0	0/0	0	6
Dishman	0	0	1	0/0	0/0	0	6
Drewrey	0	1	0	0/0	0/0	0	6
Duncan	0	1	0	0/0	0/0	0	6
Jeffires	0	1	0	0/0	0/0	0	6
Pease	1	0	0	0/0	0/0	0	6
White	0	0	1	0/0	0/0	0	6
Fairs	0	0	0	0/0	0/0	1	2
Seale	0	0	0	0/0	0/0	1	2
Oilers	26	21	4	48/51	22/34	2	424
Opponents	20	22	4	43/46	14/18	2	365

Passing	Att.	Comp.	Yds.	Pct.	TD	Int.	Tkld.	Rate
Moon	294	160	2327	54.4	17	8	12/120	88.4
Carlson	112	52	775	46.4	4	6	10/72	59.2
Pease	22	6	64	27.3	0	4	2/18	0.0
Oilers	428	218	3166	50.9	21	18	24/210	74.2
Opponents	512	281	3619	54.9	22	22	42/353	73.7

Rushing	Att.	Yds.	Avg.	LG	TD
Rozier	251	1002	4.0	28	10
Pinkett	122	513	4.2	27	7
Highsmith	94	466	5.0	42	2
White	31	115	3.7	16	0
Moon	33	88	2.7	14	5
Carlson	12	36	3.0	10	1
Givins	4	26	6.5	10	0
Tillman	3	5	1.7	2	0
Pease	8	−2	−0.3	4t	1
Oilers	558	2249	4.0	42	26
Opponents	431	1592	3.7	44t	20

Receiving	No.	Yds.	Avg.	LG	TD
Hill	72	1141	15.8	57t	10
Givins	60	976	16.3	46	5
Duncan	22	302	13.7	36	1
Highsmith	12	131	10.9	28	0
Pinkett	12	114	9.5	51t	2
Drewrey	11	172	15.6	55	1
Rozier	11	99	9.0	18	1
Harris	10	136	13.6	42	0
Williams	6	46	7.7	10	0
Jeffires	2	49	24.5	42	1
Oilers	218	3166	14.5	57t	21
Opponents	281	3619	12.9	80t	22

Interceptions	No.	Yds.	Avg.	LG	TD
Donaldson	4	29	7.3	23	0
Bryant	3	56	18.7	36t	1
R. Johnson	3	0	0.0	0	0
Brown	2	48	24.0	44t	1
Lyles	2	3	1.5	3	0
K. Johnson	1	51	51.0	51	0
Seale	1	46	46.0	46	0
Allen	1	23	23.0	21	0
D. Smith	1	20	20.0	20	0
Fuller	1	9	9.0	9	0
Grimsley	1	9	9.0	9	0
Bostic	1	7	7.0	7	0
Byrd	1	1	1.0	1	0
Oilers	22	302	13.7	51	2
Opponents	18	289	16.1	73	1

Punting	No.	Yds.	Avg.	In 20	LG
Montgomery	65	2523	38.8	12	61
Oilers	65	2523	38.8	12	61
Opponents	80	2973	37.2	14	60

Punt Returns	No.	FC	Yds.	Avg.	LG	TD
K. Johnson	30	6	170	5.7	16	0
Duncan	4	2	47	11.8	26	0
Drewrey	2	2	8	4.0	8	0
Oilers	36	10	225	6.3	26	0
Opponents	35	9	206	5.9	18	0

Kickoff Returns	No.	Yds.	Avg.	LG	TD
Harris	34	678	19.9	56	0
White	8	196	24.5	90t	1
Pinkett	7	137	19.6	29	0
K. Johnson	6	157	26.2	56	0
Donaldson	1	5	5.0	5	0
Drewrey	1	10	10.0	10	0
Duncan	1	34	34.0	34	0
R. Johnson	1	2	2.0	2	0
Tillman	1	13	13.0	13	0
Oilers	60	1232	20.5	90t	1
Opponents	69	1362	19.7	92t	1

Sacks	No.
Childress	8.5
Fuller	8.5
Meads	8.0
S. Jones	7.5
D. Smith	3.0
Bostic	2.0
Lyles	1.5
Grimsley	1.0
Mikolas	1.0
Seale	1.0
Oilers	42.0
Opponents	24.0

1989 Draft Choices

Round	Name	Pos.	College
1.	David Williams	T	Florida
2.	Scott Kozak	LB	Oregon
3.	Bubba McDowell	DB	Miami
4.	Rod Harris	WR	Texas A&M
5.	Glenn Montgomery	NT	Houston
6.	Bo Orlando	DB	West Virginia
7.	Tracy Rogers	LB	Fresno State
8.	Alvoid Mays	DB	West Virginia
9.	Bob Mrosko	TE	Penn State
10.	Tracy Johnson	RB	Clemson
11.	Brian Smider	T	West Virginia
12.	Chuck Hartlieb	QB	Iowa

Houston Oilers 1989 Veteran Roster

No.	Name	Pos.	Ht.	Wt.	Birth-date	NFL Exp.	College	Hometown	How Acq.	'88 Games/ Starts
29	Allen, Patrick	CB	5-10	182	8/26/61	6	Utah State	Seattle, Wash.	D4b-'84	15/13
24	Brown, Steve	CB	5-11	192	3/20/60	7	Oregon	Sacramento, Calif.	D3c-'83	14/14
38	Bryant, Domingo	S	6-4	178	12/8/63	3	Texas A&M	Nacogdoches, Tex.	FA-'87	14/0
71	Byrd, Richard	NT	6-4	267	3/20/62	5	Southern Mississippi	Jackson, Miss.	D2b-'85	16/7
35	Byrum, Carl	RB	6-1	237	6/29/62	4	Mississippi Valley State	Southaven, Miss.	FA(Buff)-'89#	15/1*
14	Carlson, Cody	QB	6-3	199	11/5/63	3	Baylor	San Antonio, Tex.	D3-'87	6/5
79	Childress, Ray	DE	6-6	270	10/20/62	5	Texas A&M	Richardson, Tex.	D1a-'85	16/16
77	Davis, Bruce	T	6-6	315	6/21/56	11	UCLA	Indian Head, Md.	T(Raid)-'87	16/16
28	Dishman, Cris	CB	6-0	180	8/13/65	2	Purdue	Louisville, Ky.	D5a-'88	15/2
31	Donaldson, Jeff	S	6-0	190	4/19/62	6	Colorado	Fort Collins, Colo.	D9a-'84	16/16
80	†Duncan, Curtis	WR	5-11	185	1/26/65	3	Northwestern	Detroit, Mich.	D10-'87	16/0
51	Fairs, Eric	LB	6-3	240	2/17/64	4	Memphis State	Memphis, Tenn.	FA-'86	16/0
95	†Fuller, William	DE	6-3	269	3/8/62	4	North Carolina	Chesapeake, Va.	T(Rams)-'86	16/15
97	Garalczyk, Mark	NT-DE	6-6	275	8/12/64	3	Western Michigan	Fraser, Mich.	FA(NYJ)-'89#	14/0*
81	Givins, Ernest	WR	5-9	172	9/3/64	4	Louisville	St. Petersburg, Fla.	D2-'86	16/16
59	Grimsley, John	LB	6-2	238	2/25/62	6	Kentucky	Canton, Ohio	D6a-'84	16/16
83	Harris, Leonard	WR-KR	5-8	162	11/27/60	4	Texas Tech	McKinney, Tex.	FA-'87	16/0
32	Highsmith, Alonzo	RB	6-1	234	2/26/65	3	Miami	Miami, Fla.	D1a-'87	16/16
85	Hill, Drew	WR	5-9	175	10/5/56	10	Georgia Tech	Newnan, Ga.	T(Rams)-'85	16/16
76	Holle, Eric	NT	6-5	267	9/5/60	5	Texas	Austin, Tex.	FA-'89	0*
86	Jackson, Kenny	WR	5-11	180	2/15/62	6	Penn State	South River, N.J.	FA(Phil)-'89#	7/0*
84	Jeffires, Haywood	WR	6-2	198	12/12/64	2	North Carolina State	Greensboro, N.C.	D1b-'87	2/0
22	†Johnson, Kenny	S	5-10	175	1/7/58	10	Mississippi State	Moss Point, Miss.	FA-'87	13/0
23	†Johnson, Richard	CB	6-1	190	9/16/63	5	Wisconsin	Harvey, Ill.	D1-'85	16/3
27	Jones, Quintin	CB	5-11	193	7/28/66	2	Pittsburgh	Pompano Beach, Fla.	D2-'88	4/0
96	Jones, Sean	DE	6-7	273	12/19/62	6	Northeastern	Montclair, N.J.	T(Raid)-'88	16/0
93	Lyles, Robert	LB	6-1	230	3/21/61	6	Texas Christian	Los Angeles, Calif.	D5-'84	16/16
73	Maarleveld, J.D.	T	6-6	280	10/24/61	3	Maryland	Palisades, N.J.	FA-'89	0*
89	Magee, Calvin	TE	6-3	255	4/23/63	5	Southern University	New Orleans, La.	FA(TB)-'89#	13/3*
78	Maggs, Don	T-G	6-5	285	11/1/61	3	Tulane	Youngstown, Ohio	SD2-'84	16/0
74	Matthews, Bruce	G	6-5	293	8/8/61	7	Southern California	Arcadia, Calif.	D1-'83	16/16
91	Meads, Johnny	LB	6-2	235	6/25/61	6	Nicholls State	Napoleonville, La.	D3-'84	16/16
9	Montgomery, Greg	P	6-3	213	10/29/64	2	Michigan State	Red Bank, N.J.	D3-'88	16/16
50	Monger, Matt	LB	6-1	238	11/15/61	4	Oklahoma State	Miami, Okla.	FA(NYJ)-'89#	0*
1	Moon, Warren	QB	6-3	210	11/18/56	6	Washington	Los Angeles, Calif.	FA-'84	11/11
63	†Munchak, Mike	G	6-3	284	3/5/60	8	Penn State	Scranton, Pa.	D1-'82	16/16
52	Pennison, Jay	C	6-1	282	9/9/61	4	Nicholls State	Houma, La.	FA-'86	16/16
20	†Pinkett, Allen	RB	5-9	192	1/25/64	4	Notre Dame	Sterling, Va.	D3-'86	16/2
30	†Rozier, Mike	RB	5-10	213	3/1/61	5	Nebraska	Camden, N.J.	SD1-'84	15/14
98	Ruth, Mike	NT	6-2	275	6/25/64	3	Boston College	Fairview, Pa.	FA-'89	0*
69	Scotts, Colin	NT	6-6	265	4/26/63	2	Hawaii	Sydney, Australia	FA(Phx)-'89#	0*
53	Seale, Eugene	LB	5-10	240	6/3/64	3	Lamar	Jasper, Tex.	FA-'87	16/0
54	Smith, Al	LB	6-1	236	11/26/64	3	Utah State	Los Angeles, Calif.	D6a-'87	16/16
99	Smith, Doug	NT	6-5	282	6/13/59	5	Auburn	Bayboro, N.C.	D2a-'84	12/10
70	Steinkuhler, Dean	T	6-3	291	1/27/61	6	Nebraska	Burr, Neb.	D1-'84	16/16
75	Stroth, Vince	T	6-4	275	11/25/60	3	Brigham Young	San Jose, Calif.	W(Jets)-'88	6/0
88	Verhulst, Chris	TE	6-2	249	5/16/66	2	Chico State	San Ramon, Calif.	D5b-'88	1/0
44	White, Lorenzo	RB	5-11	209	4/12/66	2	Michigan State	Ft. Lauderdale, Fla.	D1-'88	11/0
66	Yarno, George	C-G	6-2	270	8/12/57	9	Washington State	Spokane, Wash.	FA(Atl)-'89#	16/5*
68	Young, Almon	G	6-3	285	7/3/62	2	Bethune-Cookman	Umatilla, Fla.	FA-'88	0*
7	†Zendejas, Tony	K	5-8	165	5/15/60	5	Nevada-Reno	Chino, Calif.	T(Wash)-'85	16/0

* Byrum played 15 games with Buffalo in '88; Garalczyk played 14 games with N.Y. Jets; Holle last active with Kansas City in '87; Jackson played 7 games with Philadelphia; Maarleveld last active with Tampa Bay in '87; Magee played 13 games with Tampa Bay; Monger last active with N.Y. Jets in '87; Ruth last active with New England in '87; Scotts last active with St. Louis in '87; Yarno played 16 games with Atlanta; Young missed '88 season due to injury.

† Option playout; subject to developments.

Plan B unconditional free agent.

Players lost through Plan B (15): DE Robert Banks (Clev; 14 games in '88), S Keith Bostic (Ind; 16), LB Toby Caston (Det; 16), LB Kurt Crain (GB; 0), T John Davis (Buff; 13), WR Willie Drewrey (TB; 14), LB Mark Dusbabek (Minn; 0), LB Walter Johnson (NO; 0), CB-S Audrey McMillian (Minn; 0), QB Brent Pease (Mia; 13), RB Spencer Tillman (SF; 16), C Dave Viaene (NE; 0), RB Ray Wallace (Pitt; 0), T Doug Williams (Sea; 0), TE Jamie Williams (SF; 16).

Also played with Oilers in '88—CB Calvin Loveall (3 games), NT Doug Mikolas (1).

COACHING STAFF

Head Coach,
Jerry Glanville

Pro Career: Named Houston's head coach on January 20, 1986, after serving as interim coach for last two games of 1985 season. Glanville was the Oilers' defensive coordinator in 1984-85, and has 25 years of coaching experience. He initially coached in the NFL for the Detroit Lions from 1974-76 as the special teams/defense coach. His next NFL position was with the Atlanta Falcons from 1977-82, first serving as defensive backfield/special teams coach before being elevated to defensive coordinator. In 1983, Glanville joined the Buffalo Bills as defensive backfield coach before assuming his duties with the Oilers. Career record: 26-27.

Background: Attended Montana State in 1960 before transferring to Northern Michigan, where he played linebacker from 1961-63. He coached in the Ohio high school system from 1964-66 before accepting an assistant coaching post at Western Kentucky in 1967. From 1968-73, he was an assistant at Georgia Tech, helping the Yellow Jackets to three bowl games.

Personal: Born October 14, 1941, in Detroit, Mich. Jerry and his wife, Brenda, live in Sugar Land, Tex., with their son, Justin.

Assistant Coaches

Kevin Gilbride, quarterbacks; born August 27, 1951, New Haven, Conn., lives in Missouri City, Tex. Quarterback/tight end Southern Connecticut State 1970-73. No pro playing experience. College coach: Idaho State 1974-75, Tufts 1976-77, American International 1978-79, Southern Connecticut State 1980-84, East Carolina 1987-88. Pro coach: Ottawa Roughriders (CFL) 1985-86, joined Oilers in 1989.

Kim Helton, offensive line; born July 28, 1948, Pensacola, Fla., lives in Sugar Land, Tex. Center Florida 1967-69. No pro playing experience. College coach: Florida 1972-78, Miami 1979-82. Pro coach: Tampa Bay Buccaneers 1983-86, joined Oilers in 1987.

Frank Novak, running backs; born May 18, 1938, Worcester, Mass., lives in Sugar Land, Tex. Quarterback Northern Michigan 1959-61. No pro playing experience. College coach: Northern Michigan 1966-72, East Carolina 1973, Virginia 1974-75, Western Illinois 1976-77, Holy Cross 1978-83, Massachusetts 1986, Missouri 1988. Pro coach: Oklahoma Outlaws (USFL) 1984, Birmingham Stallions (USFL) 1985, joined Oilers in 1989.

Floyd Reese, linebackers; born August 8, 1948, Springfield, Mo., lives in Sugar Land, Tex. Linebacker UCLA 1967-69. Pro defensive lineman Montreal Alouettes (CFL) 1970. College coach: UCLA 1971-73, Georgia Tech 1974. Pro coach: Detroit Lions 1975-77, San Francisco 49ers 1978, Minnesota Vikings 1979-85, joined Oilers in 1986.

Nick Saban, defensive backs; born October 31, 1951, Fairmont, W. Va., lives in Missouri City, Tex. Defensive back Kent State 1970-72. No pro playing experience. College coach: Kent State 1973-76, Syracuse 1977, West Virginia 1978-79, Ohio State 1980-81, Navy 1982, Michigan State 1983-87. Pro coach: Joined Oilers in 1988.

Ray Sherman, receivers; born November 27, 1951, Berkeley, Calif., lives in Missouri City, Tex. Wide receiver Laney, Calif., J.C. 1969-70, Fresno State 1971-72. Pro defensive back Green Bay Packers 1973. College coach: San Jose State 1974, California 1975, Michigan State 1976-77, Wake Forest 1978-80, California 1981, Purdue 1982-85, Georgia 1986-87. Pro coach: Joined Oilers in 1988.

Doug Shively, defensive line; born March 18, 1938, Lexington, Ky., lives in Sugar Land, Tex. End Kentucky 1955-58. No pro playing experience. College coach: Virginia Tech 1960-66, Kentucky 1967-70, Clemson 1971-72, North Carolina 1973. Pro coach: New Orleans Saints 1974-76, Atlanta Falcons 1977-82, Arizona Wranglers (USFL) 1983 (head coach), San Diego Chargers 1984, Tampa Bay Buccaneers 1985, joined Oilers in 1986.

Houston Oilers 1989 First-Year Roster

Name	Pos.	Ht.	Wt.	Birth-date	College	Hometown	How Acq.
Brantley, John	LB	6-2	245	10/23/65	Georgia	Wildwood, Fla.	FA
Courville, Vincent	WR	5-9	167	12/5/59	Rice	Galveston, Tex.	FA
Harris, Rod	WR-KR	5-10	183	11/14/66	Texas A&M	Dallas, Tex.	D4
Hartlieb, Chuck	QB	6-2	206	3/12/66	Iowa	Woodstock, Ill.	D12
Johnson, Tracy	RB	6-0	230	11/29/66	Clemson	Kannapolis, N.C.	D10
Keck, Wesley	RB	6-2	250	3/18/66	North Texas State	Nocona, Tex.	FA
Kozak, Scott	LB	6-3	226	11/28/65	Oregon	Colton, Ore.	D2
Mays, Alvoid	CB	5-10	217	7/10/65	West Virginia	Bradenton, Fla.	D8
McDowell, Bubba	S	6-1	195	11/4/66	Miami	Merritt Island, Fla.	D3
Montgomery, Glenn	NT	6-0	267	3/31/67	Houston	Gretna, La.	D5
Mrosko, Bob	TE	6-6	256	11/13/65	Penn State	Wickliffe, Ohio	D9
Orlando, Bo	CB	5-10	176	4/3/66	West Virginia	Berwick, Pa.	D6
Rogers, Tracy	LB	6-2	247	8/13/67	Fresno State	Taft, Calif.	D7
Royal, Tollie	LB	6-0	207	1/20/65	Sam Houston State	Gainesville, Fla.	FA
Smider, Brian	T	6-4	297	4/5/66	West Virginia	Pittsburgh, Pa.	D11
Vitale, John	G-C	6-1	274	12/28/65	Michigan	Warren, Mich.	FA
Williams, David	T	6-5	292	6/21/66	Florida	Lakeland, Fla.	D1

The term NFL Rookie is defined as a player who is in his first season of professional football and has not been on the roster of another professional football team for any regular-season or postseason games. A Rookie is designated by an "R" on NFL rosters. Players who have been active in another professional football league or players who have NFL experience, including either preseason training camp or being on an active roster for fewer than three regular-season or postseason games, are termed NFL First-Year Players. An NFL First-Year Player is designated by a "1" on NFL rosters. Thereafter, a player on an NFL active roster for at least three regular-season or postseason games is credited with an additional year of NFL playing experience.

NOTES

Richard Smith, special teams-tight ends; born October 17, 1955, Los Angeles, Calif., lives in Richmond, Tex. Offensive lineman Rio Hondo, Calif., J.C. 1975-76, Fresno State 1977-78. No pro playing experience. College coach: Rio Hondo, Calif., J.C. 1979-80, Cal State-Fullerton 1981-83, California 1984-86, Arizona 1987. Pro coach: Joined Oilers in 1988.

Steve Watterson, strength and rehabilitation; born November 27, 1956, Newport, R.I., lives in Sugar Land, Tex. University of Rhode Island. No college or pro playing experience. Pro coach: Philadelphia Eagles 1984-85 (assistant trainer), joined Oilers in 1986 (elevated to assistant coach in 1988).

INDIANAPOLIS COLTS

American Football Conference
Eastern Division

Team Colors: Royal Blue and White

P. O. Box 535000
Indianapolis, Indiana 46253
Telephone: (317) 297-2658

Club Officials

President-Treasurer: Robert Irsay
Vice President-General Manager: James Irsay
Vice President-General Counsel: Michael G. Chernoff
Assistant General Manager: Bob Terpening
Director of Player Personnel: Jack Bushofsky
Controller: Kurt Humphrey
Director of Operations: Pete Ward
Director of Public Relations: Craig Kelley
Ticket Manager: Larry Hall
Assistant Director of Public Relations: Keith Newton
Purchasing Administrator: David Filar
Equipment Manager: Jon Scott
Assistant Equipment Manager: Chris Matlock
Video Director: Marty Heckscher
Assistant Video Director: John Starliper
Head Trainer: Hunter Smith
Assistant Trainer: Dave Hammer
Team Physician and Orthopedic Surgeon: K. Donald Shelbourne
Orthopedic Surgeon: Arthur C. Rettig

Stadium: Hoosier Dome • **Capacity:** 60,127
100 South Capitol Avenue
Indianapolis, Indiana 46225

Playing Surface: AstroTurf

Training Camp: Anderson University
Anderson, Indiana 46011

1989 Schedule

Preseason

Aug. 12	at New Orleans	7:00
Aug. 19	at Green Bay	1:00
Aug. 26	**Tampa Bay**	7:30
Sept. 2	**Denver**	7:30

Regular Season

Sept. 10	**San Francisco**	12:00
Sept. 17	at Los Angeles Rams	1:00
Sept. 24	**Atlanta**	12:00
Oct. 1	at New York Jets	1:00
Oct. 8	**Buffalo**	12:00
Oct. 15	at Denver	2:00
Oct. 22	at Cincinnati	1:00
Oct. 29	**New England**	1:00
Nov. 5	at Miami	1:00
Nov. 12	at Buffalo	1:00
Nov. 19	**New York Jets**	8:00
Nov. 26	**San Diego**	1:00
Dec. 3	at New England	1:00
Dec. 10	**Cleveland**	4:00
Dec. 17	**Miami**	1:00
Dec. 24	at New Orleans	12:00

Colts Coaching History

Baltimore 1953-83
(260-251-7)

1953	Keith Molesworth	3-9-0
1954-62	Weeb Ewbank	61-52-1
1963-69	Don Shula	73-26-4
1970-72	Don McCafferty*	26-11-1
1972	John Sandusky	4-5-0
1973-74	Howard Schnellenberger**	4-13-0
1974	Joe Thomas	2-9-0
1975-79	Ted Marchibroda	41-36-0
1980-81	Mike McCormack	9-23-0
1982-84	Frank Kush***	11-28-1
1984	Hal Hunter	0-1-0
1985-86	Rod Dowhower****	5-24-0
1986-88	Ron Meyer	21-14-0

*Released after five games in 1972
**Released after three games in 1974
***Resigned after 15 games in 1984
****Released after 13 games in 1986

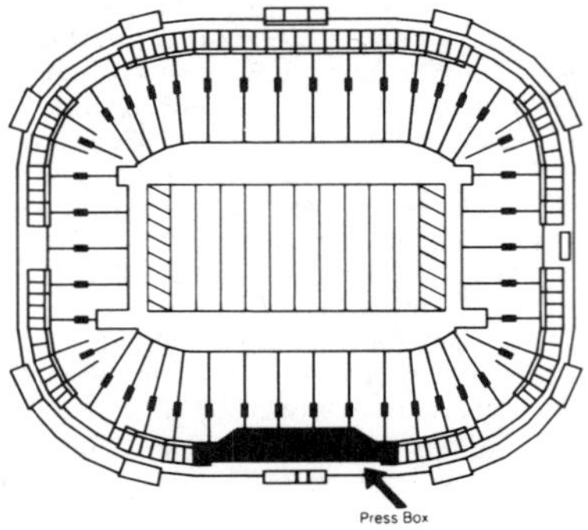

HOOSIER DOME

Record Holders

Individual Records—Career

Category	Name	Performance
Rushing (Yds.)	Lydell Mitchell, 1972-77	5,487
Passing (Yds.)	Johnny Unitas, 1956-1972	39,768
Passing (TDs)	Johnny Unitas, 1956-1972	287
Receiving (No.)	Raymond Berry, 1955-1967	631
Receiving (Yds.)	Raymond Berry, 1955-1967	9,275
Interceptions	Bob Boyd, 1960-68	57
Punting (Avg.)	Rohn Stark, 1982-88	44.3
Punt Return (Avg.)	Wendell Harris, 1964	12.6
Kickoff Return (Avg.)	Jim Duncan, 1969-1971	32.5
Field Goals	Lou Michaels, 1964-69	107
Touchdowns (Tot.)	Lenny Moore, 1956-1967	113
Points	Lenny Moore, 1956-1967	678

Individual Records—Single Season

Category	Name	Performance
Rushing (Yds.)	Eric Dickerson, 1988	1,659
Passing (Yds.)	Johnny Unitas, 1963	3,481
Passing (TDs)	Johnny Unitas, 1959	32
Receiving (No.)	Joe Washington, 1979	82
Receiving (Yds.)	Raymond Berry, 1960	1,298
Interceptions	Tom Keane, 1953	11
Punting (Avg.)	Rohn Stark, 1985	45.9
Punt Return (Avg.)	Wendell Harris, 1964	12.6
Kickoff Return (Avg.)	Jim Duncan, 1970	35.4
Field Goals	Raul Allegre, 1983	30
Touchdowns (Tot.)	Lenny Moore, 1964	20
Points	Lenny Moore, 1964	120

Individual Records—Single Game

Category	Name	Performance
Rushing (Yds.)	Norm Bulaich, 9-19-71	198
Passing (Yds.)	Johnny Unitas, 9-17-67	401
Passing (TDs)	Gary Cuozzo, 11-14-65	5
	Gary Hogeboom, 10-4-87	5
Receiving (No.)	Lydell Mitchell, 12-15-74	13
	Joe Washington, 9-2-79	13
Receiving (Yds.)	Raymond Berry, 11-10-57	224
Interceptions	Many times	3
	Last time by Leonard Coleman, 10-12-86	
Field Goals	Many times	5
	Last time by Dean Biasucci, 9-25-88	
Touchdowns (Tot.)	Many times	4
	Last time by Eric Dickerson, 10-31-88	
Points	Many times	24
	Last time by Eric Dickerson, 10-31-88	

1988 Team Record

Preseason (3-1)

Date	Result		Opponents
8/6	W	20- 7	at Tampa Bay
8/13	W	25-21	Green Bay
8/20	W	18- 6	New Orleans
8/25	L	20-21	at Denver
		83-55	

Regular Season (9-7)

Date	Result		Opponents	Att.
9/4	L	14-17	Houston (OT)	57,251
9/11	L	13-17	Chicago	60,503
9/19	L	17-23	at Cleveland	75,148
9/25	W	15-13	Miami	59,638
10/2	L	17-21	at New England	58,050
10/9	L	23-34	at Buffalo	76,018
10/16	W	35-31	Tampa Bay	53,135
10/23	W	16- 0	at San Diego	37,722
10/31	W	55-23	Denver	60,544
11/6	W	38-14	N.Y. Jets	59,233
11/13	W	20-13	at Green Bay	53,492
11/20	L	3-12	at Minnesota	58,342
11/27	W	24-21	New England	58,157
12/4	W	31-28	at Miami	45,236
12/10	L	16-34	at N.Y. Jets	46,284
12/18	W	17-14	Buffalo	59,908

(OT) Overtime

Score by Periods

Colts	77	135	61	81	0	—	354
Opponents	55	88	48	121	3	—	315

Attendance

Home 468,369 Away 450,292 Total 918,661
Single-game home record, 61,479 (11-13-83)
Single-season home record, 481,305 (1984)

1988 Team Statistics

	Colts	Opp.
Total First Downs	311	315
Rushing	153	109
Passing	130	184
Penalty	28	22
Third Down: Made/Att.	64/186	88/204
Fourth Down: Made/Att.	11/20	9/16
Total Net Yards	4870	5296
Avg. Per Game	304.4	331.0
Total Plays	982	1016
Avg. Per Play	5.0	5.2
Net Yards Rushing	2249	1694
Avg. Per Game	140.6	105.9
Total Rushes	545	447
Net Yards Passing	2621	3602
Avg. Per Game	163.8	225.1
Sacked/Yards Lost	34/244	30/201
Gross Yards	2865	3803
Att./Completions	403/222	539/321
Completion Pct.	55.1	59.6
Had Intercepted	22	15
Punts/Avg.	64/43.5	68/39.4
Net Punting Avg.	34.5	33.6
Penalties/Yards Lost	89/657	118/965
Fumbles/Ball Lost	20/8	32/20
Touchdowns	40	38
Rushing	23	14
Passing	15	21
Returns	2	3
Avg. Time of Possession	30:19	29:41

1988 Individual Statistics

Scoring	TD R	TD P	TD Rt	PAT	FG	Saf	TP
Biasucci	0	0	0	39/40	25/32	0	114
Dickerson	14	1	0	0/0	0/0	0	90
Verdin	0	4	1	0/0	0/0	0	30
Bouza	0	4	0	0/0	0/0	0	24
Bentley	2	1	0	0/0	0/0	0	18
Brooks	0	3	0	0/0	0/0	0	18
Chandler	3	0	0	0/0	0/0	0	18
Boyer	0	2	0	0/0	0/0	0	12
Turner	2	0	0	0/0	0/0	0	12
Daniel	0	0	1	0/0	0/0	0	6
Hogeboom	1	0	0	0/0	0/0	0	6
Wonsley	1	0	0	0/0	0/0	0	6
Colts	23	15	2	39/40	25/32	0	354
Opponents	14	21	3	36/38	17/25	0	315

Passing	Att.	Comp.	Yds.	Pct.	TD	Int.	Tkld.	Rate
Chandler	233	129	1619	55.4	8	12	18/128	67.2
Hogeboom	131	76	996	58.0	7	7	12/88	77.7
Trudeau	34	14	158	41.2	0	3	2/13	19.0
Turner	4	3	92	75.0	0	0	2/15	116.7
Bentley	1	0	0	0.0	0	0	0/0	39.6
Colts	403	222	2865	55.1	15	22	34/244	67.3
Opponents	539	321	3803	59.6	21	15	30/201	82.5

Rushing	Att.	Yds.	Avg.	LG	TD
Dickerson	388	1659	4.3	41t	14
Bentley	45	230	5.1	20	2
Chandler	46	139	3.0	29t	3
Verdin	8	77	9.6	44	0
Brooks	5	62	12.4	38	0
Wonsley	26	48	1.8	4	1
Turner	16	42	2.6	14	2
Hogeboom	11	−8	−0.7	6	1
Colts	545	2249	4.1	44	23
Opponents	447	1694	3.8	29	14

Receiving	No.	Yds.	Avg.	LG	TD
Brooks	54	867	16.1	53t	3
Dickerson	36	377	10.5	50t	1
Boyer	27	256	9.5	24t	2
Bentley	26	252	9.7	21	1
Beach	26	235	9.0	23	0
Bouza	25	342	13.7	28	4
Verdin	20	437	21.9	54	4
Bellini	5	64	12.8	25	0
Pruitt, Mia.-Ind.	2	38	19.0	19	0
Baldinger	1	37	37.0	37	0
Hinton	1	1	1.0	1	0
Donaldson	1	−3	−3.0	−3	0
Colts	222	2865	12.9	58	15
Opponents	321	3803	11.8	58	21

Interceptions	No.	Yds.	Avg.	LG	TD
Tullis	4	36	9.0	20	0
Prior	3	46	15.3	23	0
Bickett	3	7	2.3	7	0
Goode	2	53	26.5	35	0
Daniel	2	44	22.0	41t	1
Krauss	1	3	3.0	3	0
Colts	15	189	12.6	41t	1
Opponents	22	291	13.2	44t	1

Punting	No.	Yds.	Avg.	In 20	LG
Stark	64	2784	43.5	15	65
Colts	64	2784	43.5	15	65
Opponents	68	2677	39.4	25	74

Punt Returns	No.	FC	Yds.	Avg.	LG	TD
Verdin	22	7	239	10.9	73t	1
Brooks	3	0	15	5.0	8	0
Prior	1	5	0	0.0	0	0
Colts	26	12	254	9.8	73t	1
Opponents	37	3	418	11.3	59t	1

Kickoff Returns	No.	Yds.	Avg.	LG	TD
Bentley	39	775	19.9	40	0
Verdin	7	145	20.7	32	0
Banks	4	56	14.0	20	0
Beach	1	35	35.0	35	0
Wright	1	22	22.0	22	0
Colts	52	1033	19.9	40	0
Opponents	67	1480	22.1	95t	1

Sacks	No.
Hand	5.0
Bickett	3.5
Alston	3.0
Johnson	3.0
Thompson	3.0
Armstrong	2.0
Darby	2.0
Odom	2.0
Herrod	1.0
Prior	1.0
Swoope	1.0
Tullis	1.0
Wright	0.5
Colts	30.0
Opponents	34.0

1989 Draft Choices

Round	Name	Pos.	College
1.	Andre Rison	WR	Michigan State
3.	Mitchell Benson	DT	Texas Christian
4.	Pat Tomberlin	G	Florida State
6.	Quintus McDonald	LB	Penn State
7.	Ivy Joe Hunter	RB	Kentucky
	Charles Washington	DB	Cameron, Okla.
8.	Kurt Larson	LB	Michigan State
9.	William Mackall	WR	Tennessee-Martin
10.	Jim Thompson	T	Auburn
11.	Wayne Johnson	QB	Georgia
12.	William DuBose	RB	South Carolina St.
	Steve Taylor	QB	Nebraska

Indianapolis Colts 1989 Veteran Roster

No.	Name	Pos.	Ht.	Wt.	Birth-date	NFL Exp.	College	Hometown	How Acq.	'88 Games/ Starts
97	Alston, O'Brien	LB	6-6	241	12/21/65	2	Maryland	New Haven, Conn.	D10-'88	15/11
79	Armstrong, Harvey	NT	6-3	268	12/29/59	7	Southern Methodist	Houston, Tex.	FA-'86	16/1
62	†Baldinger, Brian	G	6-4	268	1/7/59	7	Duke	Massapequa Park, N.Y.	FA-'88	16/3
31	Ball, Michael	CB-S	6-0	211	8/5/64	2	Southern University	New Orleans, La.	D4-'88	16/0
86	Banks, Roy	WR	5-10	193	2/19/65	2	Eastern Illinois	Detroit, Mich.	D5-'87	14/0
81	†Beach, Pat	TE	6-4	252	12/28/59	7	Washington State	Pullman, Wash.	D6-'82	16/16
20	Bentley, Albert	RB	5-11	214	8/15/60	5	Miami	Immokalee, Fla.	SD2-'84	16/2
4	Biasucci, Dean	K	6-0	191	7/25/62	5	Western Carolina	Niagara Falls, N.Y.	FA-'86	16/0
50	Bickett, Duane	LB	6-5	243	12/1/62	5	Southern California	Los Angeles, Calif.	D1-'85	16/16
25	Bostic, Keith	S	6-1	223	1/17/61	7	Michigan	Ann Arbor, Mich.	FA(Hou)-'89#	16/16*
85	Bouza, Matt	WR	6-3	212	4/8/59	8	California	Sacramento, Calif.	FA-'82	15/5
84	Boyer, Mark	TE	6-4	242	9/16/62	5	Southern California	Huntington Beach, Calif.	D9-'85	16/13
88	†Brandes, John	TE	6-2	237	4/2/64	3	Cameron University	Fort Riley, Kan.	FA-'87	16/0
80	Brooks, Bill	WR	6-0	191	4/6/64	4	Boston University	Milton, Mass.	D4-'86	16/16
71	Call, Kevin	T	6-7	302	11/13/61	6	Colorado State	Boulder, Colo.	D5b-'84	8/4
17	Chandler, Chris	QB	6-4	215	10/12/65	2	Washington	Everett, Wash.	D3-'88	15/13
76	Clancy, Sam	DE	6-7	275	5/29/58	6	Pittsburgh	Pittsburgh, Pa.	FA(Clev)-'89#	16/12*
40	Clinkscales, Joey	WR	6-2	198	2/21/64	3	Tennessee	Asheville, N.C.	FA-'89	7/0*
38	Daniel, Eugene	CB	5-11	178	5/4/61	6	Louisiana State	Baton Rouge, La.	D8-'84	16/15
48	Dee, Donnie	TE	6-4	235	3/17/65	2	Tulsa	Kansas City, Mo.	D11-'88	13/0
29	Dickerson, Eric	RB	6-3	217	9/2/60	7	Southern Methodist	Sealy, Tex.	T(Rams)-'87	16/16
69	Dixon, Randy	G	6-3	293	3/12/65	3	Pittsburgh	Clewiston, Fla.	D4-'87	16/16
53	Donaldson, Ray	C	6-3	288	5/17/58	10	Georgia	Rome, Ga.	D2a-'80	16/16
74	Ehin, Chuck	NT	6-5	275	7/1/61	6	Brigham Young	Leyton, Utah	FA-'89	0*
67	Eisenhooth, Stan	T-G	6-5	275	7/8/63	2	Towson State	Wingate, Md.	FA(Sea)-'89#	13/0*
37	†Goode, Chris	CB	6-0	193	9/17/63	3	Alabama	Town Creek, Ala.	D10-'87	13/8
78	Hand, Jon	DE	6-7	298	11/13/63	4	Alabama	Sylacauga, Ala.	D1-'86	15/15
61	Hendley, Jim	C	6-4	265	10/25/64	2	Florida State	Valdosta, Ga.	FA-'89	0*
54	Herrod, Jeff	LB	6-0	237	7/29/66	2	Mississippi	Birmingham, Ala.	D9-'88	16/0
75	Hinton, Chris	T	6-4	295	7/31/61	7	Northwestern	Chicago, Ill.	T(Den)-'83	14/13
21	Holt, John	CB	5-10	179	5/14/59	9	West Texas State	Lawton, Okla.	T(TB)-'86	9/1
	Jackson, Earnest	RB	5-9	219	12/18/59	7	Texas A&M	Rosenberg, Tex.	FA-'89	12/6*
90	Johnson, Ezra	DE	6-4	250	10/2/55	13	Morris Brown	Shreveport, La.	FA-'88	10/1
63	Knight, Steve	T-G	6-4	295	3/13/62	2	Tennessee	Abingdon, Va.	FA-'89	0*
51	Kraynak, Rich	LB	6-1	225	1/20/61	6	Pittsburgh	Phoenixville, Pa.	FA-'89	0*
60	McQuaid, Dan	T-G	6-7	278	10/4/60	4	Nevada-Las Vegas	Sacramento, Calif.	W(Minn)-'88	1/0
28	Miller, Chuckie	CB	5-10	180	5/9/65	2	UCLA	Anniston, Ala.	D8-'87	3/1
41	Morrison, Tim	CB-S	6-1	200	4/3/63	3	North Carolina	Raeford, N.C.	FA-'89	0*
93	Odom, Cliff	LB	6-2	245	9/15/58	9	Texas-Arlington	Beaumont, Tex.	W(Raid)-'82	13/7
23	Plummer, Bruce	CB-S	6-1	197	9/1/64	3	Mississippi State	Bogalusa, La.	FA-'89	11/0*
39	†Prior, Mike	CB-S	6-0	200	11/14/63	4	Illinois State	Chicago Heights, Ill.	FA-'87	16/16
49	†Pruitt, James	WR	6-3	198	1/29/64	4	Cal State-Fullerton	Los Angeles, Calif.	W(Mia)-'88	1/0
72	Puzzuoli, Dave	NT	6-3	260	1/12/61	6	Pittsburgh	Stamford, Conn.	FA-'89	0*
14	Ramsey, Tom	QB	6-1	185	7/9/61	5	UCLA	Granada Hills, Calif.	FA-'89	7/1*
47	Robinson, Freddie	CB-S	6-1	191	2/1/64	3	Alabama	Mobile, Ala.	D6-'87	13/10
33	Rockins, Chris	CB-S	6-1	200	5/18/62	5	Oklahoma State	Sherman, Tex.	FA-'89	0*
3	Stark, Rohn	P	6-3	204	5/4/59	8	Florida State	Minneapolis, Minn.	D2b-'82	16/0
26	Swoope, Craig	CB-S	6-1	200	2/3/64	4	Illinois	Fort Pierce, Fla.	W(TB)-'87	11/4
27	Taylor, Keith	CB-S	5-11	193	12/21/64	2	Illinois	Pennsauken, N.J.	FA-'88	3/0
99	Thompson, Donnell	DE	6-4	275	10/27/58	9	North Carolina	Lumberton, N.C.	D1b-'81	16/16
10	Trudeau, Jack	QB	6-3	213	9/9/62	4	Illinois	Livermore, Calif.	D2-'86	2/2
12	Turner, Ricky	QB	6-0	190	5/14/62	2	Washington State	Harbor City, Calif.	FA-'88	4/0
64	†Utt, Ben	G	6-6	286	6/13/59	8	Georgia Tech	Vidalia, Ga.	FA-'82	16/16
83	†Verdin, Clarence	WR	5-8	160	6/14/63	4	Southwestern Louisiana	New Orleans, La.	T(Wash)-'88	16/11
57	Washington, Ronnie	LB	6-1	240	7/29/63	2	Northeast Louisiana	Monroe, La.	FA-'89	0*
87	Weathers, Clarence	WR	5-9	172	1/10/62	7	Delaware State	Fort Pierce, Fla.	FA(Clev)-'89#	16/6*
98	Willis, Mitch	NT-DE	6-8	285	3/16/62	5	Southern Methodist	Arlington, Tex.	FA(Atl)-'89#	11/0*
34	Wonsley, George	RB	5-10	219	11/23/60	6	Mississippi State	Moss Point, Miss.	D4b-'84	16/0
56	Young, Fredd	LB	6-1	233	11/14/61	6	New Mexico State	Dallas, Tex.	T(Sea)-'88	15/12

* Bostic played 16 games with Houston in '88; Clancy played 16 games with Cleveland; Clinkscales played 4 games with Pittsburgh, 3 with Tampa Bay; Ehin last active with San Diego in '87; Eisenhooth played 13 games with Seattle; Hendley last active with Atlanta in '87; Jackson played 12 games with Pittsburgh; Knight active for 1 game but did not play; Kraynak last active with Atlanta in '87; Morrison last active with Seattle in '87; Plummer played 8 games with Denver, 3 with Miami; Puzzuoli last active with Cleveland in '87; Ramsey played 7 games with New England; Rockins last active with Cleveland in '87; Washington last active with L.A. Raiders in '87; Weathers played 16 games with Cleveland; Willis played 2 games with L.A. Raiders, 9 with Atlanta.

† Option playout; subject to developments.

Plan B unconditional free agent.

Retired—Joe Klecko, 12-year nose tackle, 15 games in '88.

Players lost through Plan B (7): WR Mark Bellini (Phx; 15 games in '88), NT Byron Darby (Rams; 1), QB Gary Hogeboom (Phx; 9), LB Barry Krauss (Clev; 16), LB Orlando Lowry (KC; 16), T Joel Patten (SD; 16), CB Willie Tullis (Det; 16).

Also played with Colts in '88—K Jess Atkinson (1 game), K Kerry Brady (2), C Bob Brotzki (1), LB Johnie Cooks (2), RB Joe Cribbs (1), QB Bob Gagliano (2), T Chris Gambol (1), QB Bill Ransdell (active for 1 game but did not play), G Ron Solt (1), NT Don Thorp (1), CB-S Terry Wright (8).

COACHING STAFF

Head Coach, Ron Meyer

Pro Career: Named Colts' twelfth head coach on December 1, 1986. Led Colts to AFC Eastern Division championship in 1987 with a 9-6 record. Has won 21 of 35 games with the Colts. Served as head coach of New England Patriots from 1982-84. Compiled 18-15 regular-season record with one playoff game following the 1982 season. Career record: 39-30.

Background: Entered coaching ranks at Penn High School in Mishawauka, Indiana, in 1964. Joined staff at Purdue (where he played defensive back 1959-62) in 1965 in charge of the offensive backfield, receivers, and overall passing game. Remained at Purdue until becoming a scout with Dallas Cowboys for the 1971-72 seasons. Named head coach at Nevada-Las Vegas in 1973, directing the Rebels to a three-year 27-8 mark, including an undefeated (11-0) regular season in 1974 before losing in the national semifinals in the NCAA Division II playoffs. Named head coach at Southern Methodist in 1976, where he coached until 1981. The Mustangs had a 34-31-1 record during Meyer's tenure and won the Southwestern Conference championship his final year.

Personal: Born February 17, 1941, in Westerville, Ohio. Ron and his wife, Cindy, live in Indianapolis with their daughters Kathryn and Elizabeth. Ron's sons, Ron, Jr., and Ralph, reside in Dallas.

Assistant Coaches

Leon Burtnett, running backs; born May 30, 1943, Fresno, Calif., lives in Indianapolis. Fullback Southwestern (Kan.) University 1961-65. No pro playing experience. College coach: Montana State 1970, Washington State 1971, Wyoming 1972-73, San Jose State 1974-75, Michigan State 1976, Purdue 1977-86 (head coach 1982-86). Pro coach: Joined Colts in 1987.

George Catavolos, secondary; born May 8, 1945, Chicago, Ill., lives in Indianapolis. Defensive back Purdue 1964-66. No pro playing experience. College coach: Purdue 1967-68, 1971-76, Middle Tennessee State 1969, Louisville 1970, Kentucky 1977-81, Tennessee 1982-83. Pro coach: Joined Colts in 1984.

Milt Jackson, receivers; born October 16, 1943, Groesbeck, Tex., lives in Indianapolis. Defensive back Tulsa 1965-66. Pro defensive back San Francisco 49ers 1967. College coach: Oregon State 1973, Rice 1974, California 1975-76, Oregon 1977-78, UCLA 1979. Pro coach: San Francisco 49ers 1980-82, Buffalo Bills 1983-84, Philadelphia Eagles 1985, Houston Oilers 1986-88, joined Colts in 1989.

Larry Kennan, offensive coordinator; born June 13, 1944, Pomona, Calif., lives in Indianapolis. Quarterback LaVerne College 1962-65. College coach: Colorado 1969-72, Nevada-Las Vegas 1973-75, Southern Methodist 1976-78, Lamar 1979-81. Pro coach: Los Angeles Raiders 1982-87, Denver Broncos 1988, joined Colts in 1989.

Bill Muir, defensive coordinator; born October 26, 1942, Pittsburgh, Pa., lives in Indianapolis. Tackle Susquehanna 1962-64. No pro playing experience. College coach: Susquehanna 1965, Delaware Valley 1966-67, Rhode Island 1970-71, Idaho State 1972-73, Southern Methodist 1976-77. Pro coach: Orlando (Continental Football League) 1968-69, Houston-Shreveport Steamer (WFL) 1975, New England Patriots 1982-84, Detroit Lions 1985-88, joined Colts in 1989.

Dante Scarnecchia, offensive line; born February 15, 1948, Los Angeles, Calif., lives in Indianapolis. Center Taft, Calif., J.C. 1966-67, California Western 1968-69. No pro playing experience. College coach: California Western 1970-72, Iowa State 1973-74, Southern Methodist 1975-76, 1980-81, Pacific 1977-78, Northern Arizona 1979. Pro coach: New England Patriots 1982-88, joined Colts in 1989.

Indianapolis Colts 1989 First-Year Roster

Name	Pos.	Ht.	Wt.	Birth-date	College	Hometown	How Acq.
Baylor, John (1)	CB-S	6-0	195	3/5/65	Southern Mississippi	Meridian, Miss.	D6-'88
Benson, Mitchell	T	6-3	294	5/30/67	Texas Christian	Fort Worth, Tex.	D2
Brown, Phillip (1)	LB	6-2	230	5/30/64	Alabama	Birmingham, Ala.	FA
Carrier, Chris (1)	S	6-5	215	4/15/64	Louisiana State	Eunice, La.	FA
Crawford, Tim (1)	LB	6-4	250	12/17/62	Texas Tech	Houston, Tex.	FA
DuBose, William	RB	5-11	220	7/2/66	South Carolina State	Darlington, S.C.	D12
Hunter, Ivy Joe	RB	6-0	218	11/16/66	Kentucky	Gainesville, Fla.	D7a
Johnson, Wayne	QB	6-4	213	4/13/66	Georgia	Columbus, Ga.	D11
Larson, Kurt	LB	6-4	229	2/25/66	Michigan State	Waukesha, Wis.	D8
Mackall, William	WR	5-8	180	5/26/67	Tennessee-Martin	Panama City, Fla.	D9
McDonald, Quintus	LB	6-3	241	12/14/66	Penn State	Rockingham, N.C.	D6
Morgan, Weldon (1)	WR	6-2	207	7/10/63	S.W. Louisiana	New Orleans, La.	FA
Mulcahy, Philip (1)	NT-DE	6-4	285	11/6/64	Rhode Island	Worcester, Mass.	FA
Parker, Anthony	CB-S	5-10	176	2/11/66	Arizona State	Sylacauga, Ala.	FA
Rison, Andre	WR	5-10	185	3/18/67	Michigan State	Flint, Mich.	D1
Sam, Aaron (1)	RB	5-9	195	1/17/66	Central Florida	Orlando, Fla.	FA
Taylor, Steve	QB	5-11	206	1/7/67	Nebraska	Fresno, Calif.	D12b
Terry, Dewayne (1)	CB-S	6-1	190	7/16/66	Duke	Jacksonville, Fla.	FA
Thompson, Jim	T	6-7	268	5/18/66	Auburn	Enterprise, Ala.	D10
Tomberlin, Pat	T	6-2	299	1/29/66	Florida State	Jacksonville, Fla.	D4
Washington, Charles	CB-S	6-1	205	10/8/66	Cameron	Shreveport, La.	D7b

The term NFL Rookie is defined as a player who is in his first season of professional football and has not been on the roster of another professional football team for any regular-season or postseason games. A Rookie is designated by an "R" on NFL rosters. Players who have been active in another professional football league or players who have NFL experience, including either preseason training camp or being on an active roster for fewer than three regular-season or postseason games, are termed NFL First-Year Players. An NFL First-Year Player is designated by a "1" on NFL rosters. Thereafter, a player on an NFL active roster for at least three regular-season or postseason games is credited with an additional year of NFL playing experience.

NOTES

Brad Seely, special teams; born September 6, 1956, Vinton, Iowa, lives in Indianapolis. Tackle/guard South Dakota State 1974-77. No pro playing experience. College coach: Colorado State 1980, Southern Methodist 1981, North Carolina State 1982, Pacific 1983, Oklahoma State 1984-88. Pro coach: Joined Colts in 1989.

Rick Venturi, linebackers; born February 23, 1946, Taylorville, Ill., lives in Indianapolis. Quarterback Northwestern 1965-67. No pro playing experience. College coach: Northwestern 1968-72, 1978-80 (head coach), Purdue 1973-76, Illinois 1977. Pro coach: Joined Colts in 1982.

Tom Zupancic, strength and conditioning; born September 14, 1955, Indianapolis, lives in Indianapolis. Defensive tackle-offensive tackle Indiana Central 1975-78. No pro playing experience. Pro coach: Joined Colts in 1984.

American Football Conference Western Division

Team Colors: Red, Gold, and White

One Arrowhead Drive
Kansas City, Missouri 64129
Telephone: (816) 924-9300

Club Officials

Owner: Lamar Hunt
Chairman of the Board: Jack Steadman
President/General Manager and Chief Operating Officer: Carl Peterson
Executive Vice President of Administration: Tim Connolly
Assistant General Manager: Dennis Thum
Secretary: Jim Seigfreid
Executive Director of Marketing & Promotions: Mitch Wheeler
Director of Finance/Treasurer: Bob Tamasi
Director of Public Relations: Bob Moore
Director of Operations: Bill Dickerson
Director of Sales: Joel Finglass
Director of Development: Ken Blume
Player Personnel Director: Whitey Dovell
Assistant Director of Public Relations: Jim Carr
Promotions Coordinator: Amy Gillard
Community Relations Manager: Brenda Boatright
Ticket Manager: Phil Youtsey
Travel & Equipment Coordinator: Jon Phillips
Assistant Equipment Coordinator: Jeff Hiller
Trainer: Dave Kendall
Assistant Trainer: Bud Epps
Video Coordinator: Mike Dennis
Assistant Video Coordinator: Mike Kirk

Stadium: Arrowhead Stadium • **Capacity:** 78,067
One Arrowhead Drive
Kansas City, Missouri 64129

Playing Surface: AstroTurf-8

Training Camp: William Jewell College
Liberty, Missouri 64068

1989 Schedule

Preseason

Aug. 12	vs. Minn. at Memphis, Tenn.	7:30
Aug. 20	**New York Giants**	7:00
Aug. 27	at Chicago	7:00
Sept. 1	**New York Jets**	7:30

Regular Season

Sept. 10	at Denver	2:00
Sept. 17	**Los Angeles Raiders**	12:00
Sept. 24	at San Diego	1:00
Oct. 1	**Cincinnati**	12:00
Oct. 8	at Seattle	1:00
Oct. 15	at Los Angeles Raiders	1:00
Oct. 22	**Dallas**	12:00
Oct. 29	at Pittsburgh	1:00
Nov. 5	**Seattle**	12:00
Nov. 12	**Denver**	12:00
Nov. 19	at Cleveland	1:00
Nov. 26	**Houston**	12:00
Dec. 3	**Miami**	12:00
Dec. 10	at Green Bay	12:00
Dec. 17	**San Diego**	12:00
Dec. 24	at Miami	1:00

Chiefs Coaching History

Dallas Texans 1960-62
(210-208-11)

1960-74	Hank Stram	129-79-10
1975-77	Paul Wiggin*	11-24-0
1977	Tom Bettis	1-6-0
1978-82	Marv Levy	31-42-0
1983-86	John Mackovic	30-35-0
1987-88	Frank Gansz	8-22-1

*Released after seven games in 1977

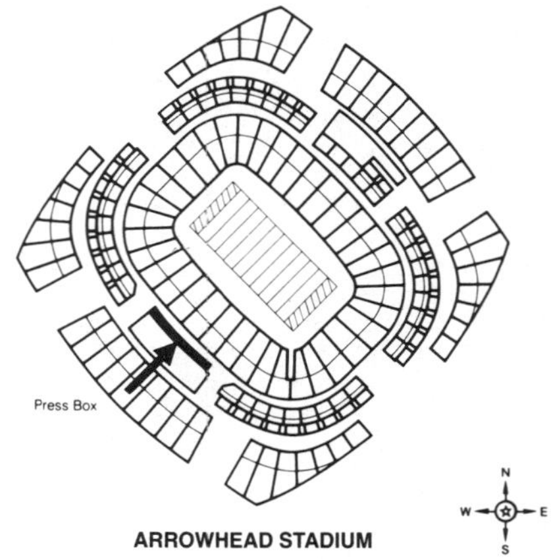

ARROWHEAD STADIUM

Record Holders

Individual Records—Career

Category	Name	Performance
Rushing (Yds.)	Ed Podolak, 1969-1977	4,451
Passing (Yds.)	Len Dawson, 1962-1975	28,507
Passing (TDs)	Len Dawson, 1962-1975	237
Receiving (No.)	Henry Marshall, 1976-1987	416
Receiving (Yds.)	Otis Taylor, 1965-1975	7,306
Interceptions	Emmitt Thomas, 1966-1978	58
Punting (Avg.)	Jerrel Wilson, 1963-1977	43.5
Punt Return (Avg.)	J.T. Smith, 1979-1984	10.6
Kickoff Return (Avg.)	Noland Smith, 1967-69	26.8
Field Goals	Jan Stenerud, 1967-1979	279
Touchdowns (Tot.)	Otis Taylor, 1965-1975	60
Points	Jan Stenerud, 1967-1979	1,231

Individual Records—Single Season

Category	Name	Performance
Rushing (Yds.)	Joe Delaney, 1981	1,121
Passing (Yds.)	Bill Kenney, 1983	4,348
Passing (TDs)	Len Dawson, 1964	30
Receiving (No.)	Carlos Carson, 1983	80
Receiving (Yds.)	Carlos Carson, 1983	1,351
Interceptions	Emmitt Thomas, 1974	12
Punting (Avg.)	Jerrel Wilson, 1965	46.0
Punt Return (Avg.)	Abner Haynes, 1960	15.4
Kickoff Return (Avg.)	Dave Grayson, 1962	29.7
Field Goals	Jan Stenerud, 1968	30
	Jan Stenerud, 1970	30
Touchdowns (Tot.)	Abner Haynes, 1962	19
Points	Jan Stenerud, 1968	129

Individual Records—Single Game

Category	Name	Performance
Rushing (Yds.)	Joe Delaney, 11-15-81	193
Passing (Yds.)	Len Dawson, 11-1-64	435
Passing (TDs)	Len Dawson, 11-1-64	6
Receiving (No.)	Ed Podolak, 10-7-73	12
Receiving (Yds.)	Stephone Paige, 12-22-85	*309
Interceptions	Bobby Ply, 12-16-62	*4
	Bobby Hunt, 12-4-64	*4
	Deron Cherry, 9-29-85	*4
Field Goals	Many times	5
	Last time by Nick Lowery, 11-13-88	
Touchdowns (Tot.)	Abner Haynes, 11-26-61	5
Points	Abner Haynes, 11-26-61	30

*NFL Record

1988 Team Record

Preseason (2-1-1)

Date	Result		Opponents
8/6	W	34-21	Cincinnati
8/13	W	27-13	at Atlanta
8/19	T	21-21	vs. Green Bay at Milwaukee (OT)
8/25	L	21-41	Phoenix
		103-96	

Regular Season (4-11-1)

Date	Result		Opponents	Att.
9/4	L	3- 6	Cleveland	55,654
9/11	L	10-31	at Seattle	61,512
9/18	W	20-13	Denver	63,268
9/25	L	23-24	San Diego	45,498
10/2	T	17-17	at N.Y. Jets (OT)	66,110
10/9	L	6- 7	at Houston	39,134
10/16	L	17-27	L.A. Raiders	77,078
10/23	L	6- 7	Detroit	66,926
10/30	L	10-17	at L.A. Raiders	36,103
11/6	L	11-17	at Denver	74,227
11/13	W	31-28	Cincinnati	34,614
11/20	W	27-24	Seattle	33,152
11/27	L	10-16	at Pittsburgh	42,057
12/4	W	38-34	N.Y. Jets	30,059
12/11	L	12-28	at N.Y. Giants	69,807
12/18	L	13-24	at San Diego	26,339

(OT) Overtime

Score by Periods

Chiefs	51	74	47	82	0	—	254
Opponents	77	118	52	73	0	—	320

Attendance

Home 406,249 Away 415,289 Total 821,538
Single-game home record, 82,094 (11-5-72)
Single-season home record, 509,291 (1972)

1988 Team Statistics

	Chiefs	Opp.
Total First Downs	289	318
Rushing	104	162
Passing	161	136
Penalty	24	20
Third Down: Made/Att.	88/224	94/209
Fourth Down: Made/Att.	12/18	6/13
Total Net Yards	4844	5026
Avg. Per Game	302.8	314.1
Total Plays	1019	1042
Avg. Per Play	4.8	4.8
Net Yards Rushing	1713	2592
Avg. Per Game	107.1	162.0
Total Rushes	448	609
Net Yards Passing	3131	2434
Avg. Per Game	195.7	152.1
Sacked/Yards Lost	43/353	23/157
Gross Yards	3484	2591
Att./Completions	528/282	410/214
Completion Pct.	53.4	52.2
Had Intercepted	21	18
Punts/Avg.	76/40.3	63/40.2
Net Punting Avg.	31.9	34.2
Penalties/Yards Lost	85/636	106/854
Fumbles/Ball Lost	21/12	30/13
Touchdowns	24	39
Rushing	8	23
Passing	16	12
Returns	0	4
Avg. Time of Possession	28:31	31:29

1988 Individual Statistics

Scoring	TD R	TD P	TD Rt	PAT	FG	Saf	TP
Lowery	0	0	0	23/23	27/32	0	104
Paige	0	7	0	0/0	0/0	0	42
Palmer	2	4	0	0/0	0/0	0	36
Carson	0	3	0	0/0	0/0	0	18
Okoye	3	0	0	0/0	0/0	0	18
Saxon	2	0	0	0/0	0/0	0	12
DeBerg	1	0	0	0/0	0/0	0	6
Harry	0	1	0	0/0	0/0	0	6
Hayes	0	1	0	0/0	0/0	0	6
C. Martin, Minn.-K.C.	0	0	1	0/0	0/0	0	6
Hackett	0	0	0	0/0	0/0	1	2
Lewis	0	0	0	0/0	0/0	1	2
Maas	0	0	0	0/0	0/0	1	2
Chiefs	8	16	0	23/24	27/32	3	254
Opponents	23	12	4	38/39	16/24	0	320

Passing	Att.	Comp.	Yds.	Pct.	TD	Int.	Tkld.	Rate
DeBerg	414	224	2935	54.1	16	16	30/246	73.5
Kenney	114	58	549	50.9	0	5	13/107	46.3
Chiefs	528	282	3484	53.4	16	21	43/353	67.6
Opponents	410	214	2591	52.2	12	18	23/157	63.4

Rushing	Att.	Yds.	Avg.	LG	TD
Okoye	105	473	4.5	48	3
Palmer	134	452	3.4	26t	2
Heard	106	438	4.1	20	0
Saxon	60	236	3.9	14	2
Moriarty	20	62	3.1	9	0
DeBerg	18	30	1.7	13	1
Goodburn	1	15	15.0	15	0
Kenney	2	4	2.0	2	0
Taylor	1	2	2.0	2	0
Carson	1	1	1.0	1	0
Chiefs	448	1713	3.8	48	8
Opponents	609	2592	4.3	36	23

Receiving	No.	Yds.	Avg.	LG	TD
Paige	61	902	14.8	49	7
Palmer	53	611	11.5	71t	4
Carson	46	711	15.5	80t	3
Harry	26	362	13.9	38	1
Hayes	22	233	10.6	25	1
Heard	20	198	9.9	32	0
Saxon	19	177	9.3	22	0
Roberts	10	104	10.4	20	0
Taylor	9	105	11.7	36	0
Okoye	8	51	6.4	12	0
Moriarty	6	40	6.7	12	0
Colbert	1	−3	−3.0	−3	0
Gamble	1	−7	−7.0	−7	0
Chiefs	282	3484	12.4	80t	16
Opponents	214	2591	12.1	42t	12

Interceptions	No.	Yds.	Avg.	LG	TD
Cherry	7	51	7.3	24	0
Burruss	2	57	28.5	32	0
J. Pearson	2	8	4.0	7	0
Hill	1	24	24.0	24	0
Lewis	1	19	19.0	19	0
Stensrud	1	5	5.0	5	0
Gamble	1	2	2.0	2	0
Cofield	1	0	0.0	0	0
Del Rio	1	0	0.0	0	0
Ross	1	0	0.0	0	0
Chiefs	18	166	9.2	32	0
Opponents	21	206	9.8	31	1

Punting	No.	Yds.	Avg.	In 20	LG
Goodburn	76	3059	40.3	10	59
Chiefs	76	3059	40.3	10	59
Opponents	63	2531	40.2	17	61

Punt Returns	No.	FC	Yds.	Avg.	LG	TD
Taylor	29	6	187	6.4	16	0
Hollis	3	0	28	9.3	15	0
Chiefs	32	6	215	6.7	16	0
Opponents	48	3	473	9.9	31	0

Kickoff Returns	No.	Yds.	Avg.	LG	TD
Palmer	23	364	15.8	23	0
Gamble	15	291	19.4	31	0
Hollis	6	106	17.7	28	0
Taylor	5	80	16.0	19	0
Ingram	2	16	8.0	9	0
Jenkins	2	12	6.0	12	0
Saxon	2	40	20.0	27	0
Porter	1	16	16.0	16	0
Chiefs	56	925	16.5	31	0
Opponents	57	1380	24.2	98t	2

Sacks	No.
Maas	4.0
Cofield	3.5
Hackett	3.0
Smith	2.5
Stensrud	2.5
Bell	2.0
Griffin	2.0
Snipes	2.0
Del Rio	1.0
C. Martin, Minn.-K.C.	1.0
Porter	0.5
Chiefs	23.0
Opponents	43.0

1989 Draft Choices

Round	Name	Pos.	College
1.	Derrick Thomas	LB	Alabama
2.	Mike Elkins	QB	Wake Forest
3.	Naz Worthen	WR	North Carolina St.
4.	Stanley Petry	DB	Texas Christian
6.	Robb Thomas	WR	Oregon State
7.	Ron Sancho	LB	Louisiana State
8.	Bryan Tobey	RB	Grambling
	Todd McNair	RB	Temple
9.	Jack Phillips	DB	Alcorn State
10.	Rob McGovern	LB	Holy Cross
11.	Marcus Turner	DB	UCLA
12.	Bill Jones	RB	S.W. Texas State

Kansas City Chiefs 1989 Veteran Roster

No.	Name	Pos.	Ht.	Wt.	Birth-date	NFL Exp.	College	Hometown	How Acq.	'88 Games/ Starts
61	Adickes, Mark	G	6-4	273	4/22/61	4	Baylor	Waco, Tex.	SD1-'84	10/10
32	Agee, Tommie	RB	6-0	218	2/22/64	2	Auburn	Maplesville, Ala.	FA(Sea)-'89#	16/0*
76	Alt, John	T	6-7	290	5/30/62	6	Iowa	Columbia Heights, Minn.	D1b-'84	14/13
54	Ashley, Walker Lee	LB	6-0	230	7/28/60	6	Penn State	Jersey City, N.J.	FA(Minn)-'89#	16/0*
77	†Baldinger, Rich	G-T	6-4	285	12/31/59	8	Wake Forest	Long Island, N.Y.	FA-'83	14/14
80	Barnes, Lew	WR-KR	5-8	163	12/27/62	3	Oregon	San Diego, Calif.	FA(Atl)-'89#	13/0*
99	†Bell, Mike	DE	6-4	260	8/30/57	9	Colorado State	Wichita, Kan.	D1a-'79	12/12
65	Bowyer, Walt	DE	6-4	260	9/8/60	5	Arizona State	Wilkinsburg, Pa.	FA(Den)-'89#	16/11*
34	Burruss, Lloyd	S	6-0	205	10/31/57	9	Maryland	Charlottesville, N.C.	D3c-'81	10/9
88	Carson, Carlos	WR	5-11	190	12/28/58	10	Louisiana State	Lake Worth, Fla.	D5a-'80	14/14
20	Cherry, Deron	S	5-11	203	9/12/59	9	Rutgers	Palmyra, N.J.	FA-'81	16/16
55	†Cooper, Louis	LB	6-2	245	8/5/63	5	Western Carolina	Marion, S.C.	FA-'85	11/4
17	DeBerg, Steve	QB	6-3	210	1/19/54	13	San Jose State	Anaheim, Calif.	T(TB)-'88	13/11
50	†Del Rio, Jack	LB	6-4	238	4/4/63	5	Southern California	Castro Valley, Calif.	T(NO)-'87	15/10
65	DiGiacomo, Curt	G-C	6-4	265	10/24/63	3	Arizona	Sacramento, Calif.	FA-'88	12/0
75	Eatman, Irv	T	6-7	294	1/1/61	4	UCLA	Dayton, Ohio	D8-'83	16/14
64	Feehery, Gerry	C	6-2	270	3/9/60	7	Syracuse	Springfield, Pa.	W(Phil)-'88	6/6
91	Gaines, Greg	LB	6-3	229	10/16/58	8	Tennessee	Hermitage, Tenn.	FA(Sea)-'89#	6/0*
22	Gamble, Kenny	RB	5-10	197	3/8/65	2	Colgate	Holyoke, Mass.	D10-'88	16/0
2	Goodburn, Kelly	P	6-2	198	4/14/62	3	Emporia State	Cherokee, Iowa	FA-'87	16/0
98	Griffin, Leonard	DE	6-4	270	9/22/62	4	Grambling	Lake Providence, La.	D3-'86	15/9
81	Griggs, Billy	TE	6-3	230	8/4/62	5	Virginia	Pennsauken, N.J.	FA(NYJ)-'89#	15/8*
56	Hackett, Dino	LB	6-3	228	6/28/64	4	Appalachian State	Greensboro, N.C.	D2-'86	13/13
86	†Harry, Emile	WR	5-11	176	4/5/63	3	Stanford	Los Angeles, Calif.	FA-'86	16/2
85	†Hayes, Jonathan	TE	6-5	239	8/11/62	5	Iowa	Pittsburgh, Pa.	D2-'85	16/9
44	Heard, Herman	RB	5-10	190	11/24/61	6	Southern Colorado	Denver, Colo.	D3-'84	12/5
23	†Hill, Greg	CB	6-1	202	2/12/61	7	Oklahoma State	Orange, Tex.	W(Hou)-'87	15/0
60	†Ingram, Byron	G	6-2	295	11/17/64	2	Eastern Kentucky	Lexington, Ky.	FA-'87	12/5
7	Jaworski, Ron	QB	6-1	205	3/23/51	15	Youngstown State	Lackawanna, N.Y.	FA(Mia)-'89#	16/0*
73	Jozwiak, Brian	G	6-5	293	6/20/63	4	West Virginia	Baltimore, Md.	D1-'86	3/1
9	†Kenney, Bill	QB	6-4	217	1/20/55	11	Northern Colorado	San Clemente, Calif.	FA-'79	16/5
29	†Lewis, Albert	CB	6-2	198	10/6/60	7	Grambling	Mansfield, La.	D3-'83	14/12
38	Loveall, Calvin	CB-S	5-9	180	7/23/62	2	Idaho	Kennewick, Wash.	FA(Atl)-'89#	11/0*
8	†Lowery, Nick	K	6-4	189	5/27/56	10	Dartmouth	Washington, D.C.	FA-'80	16/0
59	Lowry, Orlando	LB	6-4	236	8/14/61	5	Ohio State	Shaker Heights, Ohio	FA(Ind)-'89#	16/2*
72	Lutz, David	T	6-6	290	12/30/59	7	Georgia Tech	Peachland, N.C.	D2-'83	15/7
63	Maas, Bill	NT	6-5	268	3/2/62	6	Pittsburgh	Newton Square, Pa.	D1-'84	8/8
57	Martin, Chris	LB	6-2	231	12/19/60	7	Auburn	Huntsville, Ala.	W(Minn)-'88	15/0*
14	McManus, Danny	QB	6-0	200	6/17/65	2	Florida State	Dania, Fla.	D11-'88	0*
69	Meisner, Greg	NT	6-3	269	4/23/59	9	Pittsburgh	New Kensington, Pa.	FA(Rams)-'89#	12/1*
35	Okoye, Christian	RB	6-1	253	8/16/61	3	Azusa Pacific	Enugu, Nigeria	D2-'87	9/9
83	†Paige, Stephone	WR	6-2	185	10/15/61	7	Fresno State	Long Beach, Calif.	FA-'83	16/16
26	Palmer, Paul	RB-KR	5-9	181	10/14/64	3	Temple	Potomac, Md.	D1-'87	15/11
96	Pearson, Aaron	LB	6-0	240	8/22/64	4	Mississippi State	Gadsden, Ala.	D11-'86	16/10
24	Pearson, J.C.	CB	5-11	190	8/17/63	4	Washington	Oceanside, Calif.	FA-'86	16/6
27	Porter, Kevin	CB-S	5-10	215	4/11/66	2	Auburn	Atlanta, Ga.	D3-'88	15/7
87	Roberts, Alfredo	TE	6-3	250	3/1/65	2	Miami	Hollywood, Fla.	D8-'88	16/7
31	Ross, Kevin	CB	5-9	182	1/16/62	6	Temple	Paulsboro, N.J.	D7-'84	15/14
4	Runager, Max	P	6-1	189	3/24/56	11	South Carolina	Orangeburg, S.C.	FA(Clev)-'89#	14/0*
97	Saleaumua, Dan	NT	6-0	285	11/11/65	3	Arizona State	San Diego, Calif.	FA(Det)-'89#	16/0*
70	Sally, Jerome	NT	6-3	270	2/24/59	8	Missouri	Chicago, Ill.	FA-'88	3/2
21	Saxon, James	RB	5-11	215	3/23/66	2	San Jose State	Burton, S.C.	D6-'88	16/4
70	Smith, Dave	T	6-6	290	12/12/64	2	Southern Illinois	Lansing, Ill.	FA(Cin)-'89#	14/0*
90	Smith, Neil	DE	6-4	270	4/10/66	2	Nebraska	New Orleans, La.	D1-'88	13/7
52	Snipes, Angelo	LB	6-0	227	1/11/63	4	West Georgia	Atlanta, Ga.	FA-'87	15/8
67	†Stensrud, Mike	NT	6-5	280	2/19/56	11	Iowa State	Lake Mills, Ga.	FA-'88	13/5
53	Webster, Mike	C	6-2	260	3/18/52	16	Wisconsin	Tomahawk, Wis.	FA(Pitt)-'89	16/16*

* Agee played 16 games with Seattle in '88; Ashley played 16 games with Minnesota; Barnes played 13 games with Atlanta; Bowyer played 16 games with Denver; Gaines played 6 games with Seattle; B. Griggs played 15 games with N.Y. Jets; Jaworski played 16 games with Miami; Loveall played 4 games with Atlanta, 3 with Houston, 4 with Kansas City; Lowry played 16 games with Indianapolis; Martin played 9 games with Minnesota, 6 with Kansas City; McManus active for 7 games but did not play; Meisner played 12 games with L.A. Rams; Runager played 13 games with Cleveland, 1 with San Francisco; Saleaumua played 16 games with Detroit; D. Smith played 14 games with Cincinnati; Webster played 16 games with Pittsburgh.

† Option playout; subject to developments.

Plan B unconditional free agent.

Players lost through Plan B (13): NT-DE Gary Baldinger (Atl; 11 games in '88), C Tom Baugh (Clev; 12), LB Tim Cofield (NYJ; 16), WR Darrell Colbert (NO; 3), WR Stevie Hobbs (Wash; 0), LB Todd Howard (GB; 7), CB Sidney Johnson (TB; 13), WR Mike Johnson (NE; active for 1 game but did not play), DE Pete Koch (Raiders; 0), C Adam Lingner (Buff; 16), LB Troy Stedman (Pitt; 5), WR Kittrick Taylor (Atl; 16), DE-NT Don Thorp (Mia; 3).

Also played with Chiefs in '88—DE Dee Hardison (7 games), G James Harvey (1), LB Andy Hawkins (7), CB-S-KR David Hollis (2), RB-KR Keyvan Jenkins (2), TE Rod Jones (2), LB Jerry McCabe (3), DE-NT Ron McLean (6), RB Larry Moriarty (9).

COACHING STAFF

Head Coach, Marty Schottenheimer

Pro Career: Begins his first season as Chiefs' head coach after being named seventh head coach in franchise history on January 24, 1989. He was one of the most successful coaches in the NFL over the past four and a half years as head coach of the Cleveland Browns. In his four full seasons with the Browns, he produced four playoff berths, three AFC Central titles, two AFC Championship Game appearances, and consensus AFC coach of the year honors (1986). He has an impressive 32-15 regular-season record over the past three years, which stands as the best mark in the AFC over that span. His .620 regular-season winning percentage ranks sixth among active NFL coaches. He first joined the Browns in 1980 as defensive coordinator after serving as linebackers coach of the Detroit Lions from 1978-79. His first NFL coaching job came with the New York Giants, where he was linebackers coach and defensive coordinator from 1975-77. He served as assistant coach with the Portland Storm (WFL) in 1974. A seventh-round draft choice of the Buffalo Bills in 1965, he played linebacker with the Bills until 1968 and finished his pro playing career with the Boston Patriots in 1969-70. Career record: 46-31.

Background: All-America linebacker at University of Pittsburgh 1962-64. Following retirement from pro football, he worked as a real estate developer in both Miami and Denver from 1971-74.

Personal: Born September 23, 1943, Canonsburg, Pa. Marty and his wife, Patricia, live in Overland Park, Kan., and have one daughter, Kristen, and one son, Brian.

Assistant Coaches

Bruce Arians, running backs; born October 3, 1952, York, Pa., lives in Kansas City. Quarterback Virginia Tech 1971-74. No pro playing experience. College coach: Virginia Tech 1975-77, Mississippi State 1978-80, Alabama 1981-82, Temple 1983-88 (head coach). Pro coach: Joined Chiefs in 1989.

Russ Ball, assistant strength and conditioning; born August 28, 1959, Moberly, Mo., lives in Kansas City. Center Central Missouri State 1977-80. No pro playing experience. College coach: Missouri 1981-88. Pro coach: Joined Chiefs in 1989.

Bill Cowher, defensive coordinator-linebackers; born May 8, 1957, Pittsburgh, Pa., lives in Overland Park, Kan. Linebacker North Carolina State 1975-78. Pro linebacker Cleveland Browns 1980-82, Philadelphia Eagles 1983-84. Pro coach: Cleveland Browns 1985-88, joined Chiefs in 1989.

Tony Dungy, defensive backs; born October 6, 1955, Jackson, Mich., lives in Kansas City. Quarterback Minnesota 1973-76. Pro safety Pittsburgh Steelers 1977-78, San Francisco 49ers 1979. College coach: Minnesota 1980. Pro coach: Pittsburgh Steelers 1981-88, joined Chiefs in 1989.

Howard Mudd, offensive line; born February 10, 1942, Midland, Mich., lives in Kansas City. Guard Hillsdale 1961-63. Pro guard San Francisco 49ers 1964-69, Chicago Bears 1970-71. College coach: California 1972-73. Pro coach: San Diego Chargers 1974-76, San Francisco 49ers 1977, Seattle Seahawks 1978-82, Cleveland Browns 1983-88, joined Chiefs in 1989.

Joe Pendry, offensive coordinator-quarterbacks; born August 5, 1947, Matheny, W. Va., lives in Lakewood, Mo. Tight end West Virginia 1966-67. No pro playing experience. College coach: West Virginia 1967-74, 1976-77, Kansas State 1975, Pittsburgh 1978-79, Michigan State 1980-81. Pro coach: Philadelphia Stars (USFL) 1983, Pittsburgh Maulers (USFL) 1984 (head coach), Cleveland Browns 1985-88, joined Chiefs in 1989.

Tom Pratt, defensive line; born June 21, 1935, Edgerton, Wis., lives in Overland Park, Kan. Linebacker Miami 1957-59, Southern Mississippi 1960-62. No pro playing experience. Pro coach: Kansas City Chiefs 1963-77, New Orleans Saints 1978-80, Cleveland Browns 1981-88, rejoined Chiefs in 1989.

Kansas City Chiefs 1989 First-Year Roster

Name	Pos.	Ht.	Wt.	Birth-date	College	Hometown	How Acq.
Abdur-Ra'oof, Azizuddin (1)	WR	6-0	200	4/8/65	Maryland	Annapolis, Md.	D9-'88
Abraham, Gerald (1)	RB	5-10	207	7/4/65	Wyoming	Denver, Colo.	FA
Annexstad, Scott (1)	G	6-4	285	7/8/64	Mankato State	St. Peter, Minn.	FA
Chandler, Darren (1)	WR	5-9	165	3/29/66	Georgia Southern	Atlanta, Ga.	FA
Copeland, Danny (1)	S-CB	6-2	210	1/24/66	Eastern Kentucky	Thomasville, Ga.	FA
Elkins, Mike	QB	6-3	221	7/20/66	Wake Forest	Greensboro, N.C.	D2
Jones, Bill	RB	5-11	222	9/10/66	S.W. Texas State	Corsicana, Tex.	D12
Kelleher, Tom (1)	RB	6-0	230	8/24/65	Holy Cross	Vernon, Conn.	FA
Marshall, Willie (1)	WR	6-1	190	5/23/64	Temple	Columbus, N.J.	FA
McGovern, Rob	LB	6-2	222	10/1/66	Holy Cross	Oradell, N.J.	D10
McNair, Todd	RB	6-1	185	10/7/65	Temple	Pennsauken, N.J.	D8b
Petry, Stanley	CB	5-11	174	8/14/66	Texas Christian	Manuel, Tex.	D4
Phillips, Jack	S	6-0	201	5/23/66	Alcorn State	New Orleans, La.	D9
Phillips, Jon (1)	G	6-3	280	6/12/65	Oklahoma	Tulsa, Okla.	FA
Sancho, Ron	LB	6-2	230	6/21/65	Louisiana State	Avondale, La.	D7
Scully, Mike (1)	C-G	6-5	280	11/1/65	Illinois	Mt. Prospect, Ill.	FA
Slayden, Steve (1)	QB	6-1	185	1/22/66	Duke	Durham, N.C.	FA
Smith, Rod (1)	WR-KR	6-0	190	5/23/65	Nebraska	Mountain View, Calif.	FA
Standifer, Bob (1)	NT	6-5	267	6/3/63	Tenn.-Chattanooga	Chattanooga, Tenn.	FA
Tabor, Scott (1)	P	6-3	195	6/15/65	California	Lakeport, Calif.	FA
Thomas, Derrick	LB	6-3	234	1/1/67	Alabama	Miami, Fla.	D1
Thomas, Robb	WR	5-11	171	3/29/66	Oregon State	Corvallis, Ore.	D6
Tobey, Bryan	RB	6-1	250	4/7/65	Grambling	Hyannisport, Mass.	D8a
Turner, Marcus	CB	6-0	191	1/13/66	UCLA	Lakewood, Calif.	D11
Van Druten, Richard (1)	T	6-5	281	9/23/62	Abilene Christian	South Africa	FA-'88
Wolkow, Troy (1)	G	6-4	280	6/25/66	Minnesota	Lakeville, Minn.	FA
Worthen, Naz	WR	5-8	177	3/27/66	North Carolina State	Jacksonville, Fla.	D3

The term NFL Rookie is defined as a player who is in his first season of professional football and has not been on the roster of another professional football team for any regular-season or postseason games. A Rookie is designated by an "R" on NFL rosters. Players who have been active in another professional football league or players who have NFL experience, including either preseason training camp or being on an active roster for fewer than three regular-season or postseason games, are termed NFL First-Year Players. An NFL First-Year Player is designated by a "1" on NFL rosters. Thereafter, a player on an NFL active roster for at least three regular-season or postseason games is credited with an additional year of NFL playing experience.

NOTES

Dave Redding, strength and conditioning; born June 14, 1952, North Platte, Neb., lives in Kansas City. Defensive end Nebraska 1972-75. No pro playing experience. College coach: Nebraska 1976, Washington State 1977, Missouri 1978-81. Pro coach: Cleveland Browns 1982-88, joined Chiefs in 1989.

Al Saunders, receivers; born February 1, 1947, London, England, lives in Kansas City. Defensive back San Jose State 1966-68. No pro playing experience. College coach: Southern California 1970-71, Missouri 1972, Utah State 1973-75, California 1976-81. Tennessee 1982. Pro coach: San Diego Chargers 1983-88 (head coach 1986-88), joined Chiefs in 1989.

Kurt Schottenheimer, special teams; born October 1, 1949, McDonald, Pa., lives in Kansas City. Defensive back Miami 1969-70. No pro playing experience. College coach: William Patterson 1974, Michigan State 1978-82, Tulane 1983, Louisiana State 1984-85, Notre Dame 1986. Pro coach: Cleveland Browns 1987-88, joined Chiefs in 1989.

Darvin Wallis, special assistant-quality control; born February 14, 1949, Ft. Branch, Ind., lives in Overland Park, Kan. Defensive end Arizona 1970-71. No pro playing experience. College coach: Adams State 1976-77, Tulane 1978-79, Mississippi 1980-81. Pro coach: Cleveland Browns 1982-88, joined Chiefs in 1989.

American Football Conference Western Division

Team Colors: Silver and Black

332 Center Street
El Segundo, California 90245
Telephone: (213) 322-3451

Club Officials

President of the Managing General Partners: Al Davis
Executive Assistant: Al LoCasale
Player Personnel: Ron Wolf
Pro Football Scout: George Karras
Finance: Gary Huff
Senior Executive: John Herrera
Senior Administrator: Irv Kaze
Senior Administrator: Morris Bradshaw
Business Manager: Dave Houghton
Administrative Assistant: Mike Madden
Publications: Mike Taylor
Ticket Operations: Peter Eiges
Trainers: George Anderson, H. Rod Martin, Tod Sperber
Equipment Manager: Richard Romanski
Assistant Equipment Manager: Bob Romanski

Stadium: Los Angeles Memorial Coliseum • **Capacity:** 92,488
3911 South Figueroa Street
Los Angeles, California 90037

Playing Surface: Grass

Training Camp: Radisson Hotel
Oxnard, California 93030

1989 Schedule

Preseason

Aug. 12	**San Francisco**	6:00
Aug. 19	**Dallas**	6:00
Aug. 26	vs. Hou. at Oakland, Calif.	7:00
Sept. 2	**Chicago**	1:00

Regular Season

Sept. 10	**San Diego**	1:00
Sept. 17	at Kansas City	12:00
Sept. 24	at Denver	2:00
Oct. 1	**Seattle**	1:00
Oct. 9	at New York Jets (Monday)	9:00
Oct. 15	**Kansas City**	1:00
Oct. 22	at Philadelphia	1:00
Oct. 29	**Washington**	1:00
Nov. 5	**Cincinnati**	1:00
Nov. 12	at San Diego	5:00
Nov. 19	at Houston	3:00
Nov. 26	**New England**	1:00
Dec. 3	**Denver**	1:00
Dec. 10	**Phoenix**	1:00
Dec. 17	at Seattle	5:00
Dec. 24	at New York Giants	1:00

Raiders Coaching History

Oakland 1960-81
(277-163-11)

1960-61	Eddie Erdelatz*	6-10-0
1961-62	Marty Feldman**	2-15-0
1962	Red Conkright	1-8-0
1963-65	Al Davis	23-16-3
1966-68	John Rauch	35-10-1
1969-78	John Madden	112-39-7
1979-87	Tom Flores	91-56-0
1988	Mike Shanahan	7-9-0

*Released after two games in 1961
**Released after five games in 1962

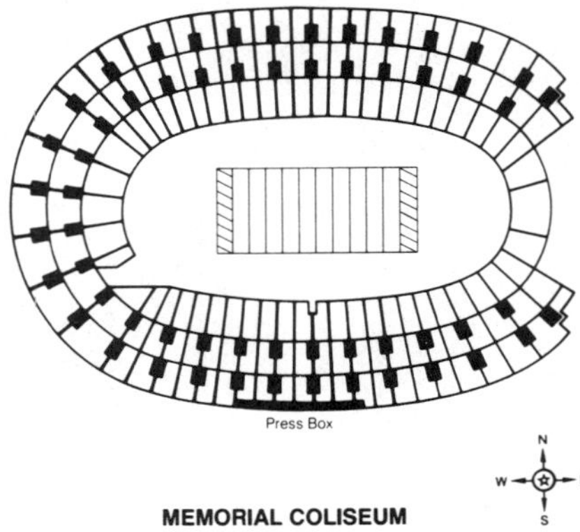

MEMORIAL COLISEUM

Record Holders

Individual Records—Career

Category	Name	Performance
Rushing (Yds.)	Marcus Allen, 1982-88	6,982
Passing (Yds.)	Ken Stabler, 1970-79	19,078
Passing (TDs)	Ken Stabler, 1970-79	150
Receiving (No.)	Fred Biletnikoff, 1965-1978	589
Receiving (Yds.)	Fred Biletnikoff, 1965-1978	8,974
Interceptions	Willie Brown, 1967-1978	39
	Lester Hayes, 1977-1986	39
Punting (Avg.)	Ray Guy, 1973-1986	42.5
Punt Return (Avg.)	Claude Gibson, 1963-65	12.6
Kickoff Return (Avg.)	Jack Larscheid, 1960-61	28.4
Field Goals	George Blanda, 1967-1975	156
Touchdowns (Tot.)	Marcus Allen, 1982-88	78
Points	George Blanda, 1967-1975	863

Individual Records—Single Season

Category	Name	Performance
Rushing (Yds.)	Marcus Allen, 1985	1,759
Passing (Yds.)	Ken Stabler, 1979	3,615
Passing (TDs)	Daryle Lamonica, 1969	34
Receiving (No.)	Todd Christensen, 1986	95
Receiving (Yds.)	Art Powell, 1964	1,361
Interceptions	Lester Hayes, 1980	13
Punting (Avg.)	Ray Guy, 1973	45.3
Punt Return (Avg.)	Claude Gibson, 1964	14.4
Kickoff Return (Avg.)	Harold Hart, 1975	30.5
Field Goals	George Blanda, 1973	23
Touchdowns (Tot.)	Marcus Allen, 1984	18
Points	George Blanda, 1968	117

Individual Records—Single Game

Category	Name	Performance
Rushing (Yds.)	Bo Jackson, 11-30-87	221
Passing (Yds.)	Cotton Davidson, 10-25-64	427
Passing (TDs)	Tom Flores, 12-22-63	6
	Daryle Lamonica, 10-19-69	6
Receiving (No.)	Dave Casper, 10-3-76	12
Receiving (Yds.)	Art Powell, 12-22-63	247
Interceptions	Many times	3
	Last time by Charles Phillips, 12-8-75	
Field Goals	Many times	4
	Last time by Chris Bahr, 10-6-85	
Touchdowns (Tot.)	Art Powell, 12-22-63	4
	Marcus Allen, 9-24-84	4
Points	Art Powell, 12-22-63	24
	Marcus Allen, 9-24-84	24

1988 Team Record

Preseason (1-3)

Date	Result		Opponents
8/6	L	10-24	at San Francisco
8/13	L	17-27	Dallas
8/20	L	27-45	Washington
8/26	W	37-22	at Chicago
		91-118	

Regular Season (7-9)

Date	Result		Opponents	Att.
9/4	W	24-13	San Diego	39,029
9/11	L	35-38	at Houston	46,050
9/18	L	17-22	L.A. Rams	84,870
9/26	W	30-27	at Denver (OT)	75,964
10/2	L	21-45	Cincinnati	42,594
10/9	L	14-24	Miami	50,751
10/16	W	27-17	at Kansas City	77,078
10/23	L	6-20	at New Orleans	66,249
10/30	W	17-10	Kansas City	36,103
11/6	W	13- 3	at San Diego	55,134
11/13	W	9- 3	at San Francisco	54,448
11/20	L	6-12	Atlanta	40,967
11/28	L	27-35	at Seattle	62,641
12/4	W	21-20	Denver	65,561
12/11	L	21-37	at Buffalo	77,348
12/18	L	37-43	Seattle	61,127

(OT) Overtime

Score by Periods

Raiders	56	91	68	107	3	—	325
Opponents	58	138	73	100	0	—	369

Attendance

Home 421,002 Away 514,912 Total 935,914
Single-game home record, 90,334 (1-1-84)
Single-season home record, 516,205 (1986)

1988 Team Statistics

	Raiders	Opp.
Total First Downs	283	310
Rushing	116	124
Passing	145	165
Penalty	22	21
Third Down: Made/Att.	71/220	88/232
Fourth Down: Made/Att.	10/18	8/11
Total Net Yards	4961	5379
Avg. Per Game	310.1	336.2
Total Plays	1035	1056
Avg. Per Play	4.8	5.1
Net Yards Rushing	1852	2208
Avg. Per Game	115.8	138.0
Total Rushes	493	533
Net Yards Passing	3109	3171
Avg. Per Game	194.3	198.2
Sacked/Yards Lost	46/394	40/300
Gross Yards	3503	3471
Att./Completions	496/219	483/265
Completion Pct.	44.2	54.9
Had Intercepted	20	17
Punts/Avg.	91/41.8	94/41.4
Net Punting Avg.	35.7	34.7
Penalties/Yards Lost	102/762	94/823
Fumbles/Ball Lost	33/13	31/17
Touchdowns	39	41
Rushing	15	17
Passing	21	23
Returns	3	1
Avg. Time of Possession	29:30	30:30

1988 Individual Statistics

Scoring	TD R	TD P	TD Rt	PAT	FG	Saf	TP
Bahr	0	0	0	37/39	18/29	0	91
Smith	3	6	0	0/0	0/0	0	54
Allen	7	1	0	0/0	0/0	0	48
T. Brown	1	5	1	0/0	0/0	0	42
Fernandez	0	4	0	0/0	0/0	0	24
Jackson	3	0	0	0/0	0/0	0	18
Gault	0	2	0	0/0	0/0	0	12
Junkin	0	2	0	0/0	0/0	0	12
Townsend	0	0	2	0/0	0/0	0	12
Schroeder	1	0	0	0/0	0/0	0	6
Strachan	0	1	0	0/0	0/0	0	6
Raiders	15	21	3	37/39	18/29	0	325
Opponents	17	23	1	40/41	27/29	1	369

Passing	Att.	Comp.	Yds.	Pct.	TD	Int.	Tkld.	Rate
Schroeder	256	113	1839	44.1	13	13	19/178	64.6
Beuerlein	238	105	1643	44.1	8	7	26/215	66.6
Allen	2	1	21	50.0	0	0	1/1	87.5
Raiders	496	219	3503	44.2	21	20	46/394	65.6
Opponents	483	265	3471	54.9	23	17	40/300	79.0

Rushing	Att.	Yds.	Avg.	LG	TD
Allen	223	831	3.7	32	7
Jackson	136	580	4.3	25	3
Smith	38	162	4.3	21	3
Schroeder	29	109	3.8	12	1
Mueller	17	60	3.5	13	0
T. Brown	14	50	3.6	12	1
Beuerlein	30	35	1.2	20	0
Strachan	4	12	3.0	5	0
Fernandez	1	9	9.0	9	0
Gault	1	4	4.0	4	0
Raiders	493	1852	3.8	32	15
Opponents	533	2208	4.1	73t	17

Receiving	No.	Yds.	Avg.	LG	TD
T. Brown	43	725	16.9	65t	5
Allen	34	303	8.9	30t	1
Fernandez	31	805	26.0	85t	4
Lofton	28	549	19.6	57	0
Smith	26	299	11.5	45t	6
Gault	16	392	24.5	57	2
Christensen	15	190	12.7	22	0
Jackson	9	79	8.8	27	0
Mueller	5	63	12.6	28	0
Parker	4	33	8.3	12	0
Junkin	4	25	6.3	9	2
Strachan	3	19	6.3	13t	1
Beuerlein	1	21	21.0	21	0
Raiders	219	3503	16.0	85t	21
Opponents	265	3471	13.1	86	23

Interceptions	No.	Yds.	Avg.	LG	TD
Haynes	3	30	10.0	30	0
McElroy	3	17	5.7	13	0
Price	2	18	9.0	18	0
Fellows	2	14	7.0	14	0
Anderson	2	−6	−3.0	2	0
Townsend	1	86	86.0	86t	1
Long	1	73	73.0	73	0
McKenzie	1	26	26.0	26	0
Lee	1	20	20.0	20	0
Washington	1	0	0.0	0	0
Raiders	17	278	16.4	86t	1
Opponents	20	219	11.0	48	0

Punting	No.	Yds.	Avg.	In 20	LG
Gossett	91	3804	41.8	27	58
Raiders	91	3804	41.8	27	58
Opponents	94	3889	41.4	22	70

Punt Returns	No.	FC	Yds.	Avg.	LG	TD
T. Brown	49	10	444	9.1	36	0
Adams	6	0	45	7.5	17	0
Raiders	55	10	489	8.9	36	0
Opponents	47	19	397	8.4	30	0

Kickoff Returns	No.	Yds.	Avg.	LG	TD
T. Brown	41	1098	26.8	97t	1
Adams	8	132	16.5	21	0
Mueller	5	97	19.4	25	0
Smith	3	46	15.3	16	0
Toran	2	0	0.0	0	0
Carter	1	14	14.0	14	0
Lee	1	0	0.0	0	0
Woods	1	20	20.0	20	0
Raiders	62	1407	22.7	97t	1
Opponents	61	1299	21.3	65	0

Sacks	No.
Townsend	11.5
Davis	5.5
Pickel	5.0
Wise	5.0
Long	3.0
Carter	2.0
Robinson	2.0
Toran	2.0
King	1.0
McKenzie	1.0
Millen	1.0
Taylor	1.0
Raiders	40.0
Opponents	46.0

1989 Draft Choices

Round	Name	Pos.	College
6.	Jeff Francis	QB	Tennessee
	Doug Lloyd	RB	North Dakota State
8.	Derrick Gainer	RB	Florida A&M
9.	Gary Gooden	DB	Indiana
10.	Charles Jackson	DT	Jackson State

Los Angeles Raiders 1989 Veteran Roster

No.	Name	Pos.	Ht.	Wt.	Birth-date	NFL Exp.	College	Hometown	How Acq.	'88 Games/ Starts
44	†Adams, Stefon	S	5-10	185	8/11/63	4	East Carolina	High Point, N.C.	D3-'85	14/0
32	Allen, Marcus	RB	6-2	205	3/26/60	8	Southern California	San Diego, Calif.	D1-'82	15/15
33	Anderson, Eddie	S	6-1	195	7/22/63	4	Fort Valley State	Warner Robins, Ga.	FA-'87	16/5
54	Benson, Tom	LB	6-2	240	9/6/61	6	Oklahoma	Ardmore, Tex.	FA(NE)-'89#	12/0*
7	Beuerlein, Steve	QB	6-2	205	3/7/65	2	Notre Dame	Fullerton, Calif.	D4-'87	10/8
64	Brown, Ron	LB	6-4	235	4/28/64	3	Southern California	Oroville, Calif.	FA-'88	16/0
81	Brown, Tim	WR-KR	6-0	195	7/22/66	2	Notre Dame	Dallas, Tex.	D1-'88	16/9
29	†Carter, Russell	S	6-2	200	2/10/62	6	Southern Methodist	Ardmore, Pa.	T(NYJ)-'88	15/12
46	Christensen, Todd	TE	6-3	230	8/3/56	11	Brigham Young	Eugene, Ore.	FA-'79	7/5
94	Costello, Joe	LB	6-3	240	6/1/60	4	Central Connecticut	New York, N.Y.	FA(Atl)-'89#	6/0*
47	Davis, Jeff	LB	6-0	230	1/26/60	7	Clemson	Greensboro, N.C.	FA-'89	0*
70	Davis, Scott	DE	6-7	270	8/7/65	2	Illinois	Plainfield, Ill.	D1-'88	15/2
11	Evans, Vince	QB	6-2	210	6/14/55	10	Southern California	Greensboro, N.C.	FA-'88	0*
86	Fernandez, Mervyn	WR	6-3	200	12/29/59	3	San Jose State	San Jose, Calif.	D10-'83	16/1
83	Gault, Willie	WR	6-1	180	9/5/60	7	Tennessee	Griffin, Ga.	T(Chi)-'88	15/6
63	†Gesek, John	G-C	6-5	275	2/18/63	3	Cal State-Sacramento	Danville, Calif.	D10-'87	12/6
79	Golic, Bob	DT	6-2	265	10/26/57	10	Notre Dame	Cleveland, Ohio	FA(Clev)-'89#	16/16*
6	†Gossett, Jeff	P	6-2	195	1/25/57	8	Eastern Illinois	Charleston, Ill.	T(Hou)-'88	16/0
85	Graddy, Sam	WR	5-10	165	2/10/64	3	Tennessee	Gaffney, S.C.	FA(Den)-'89#	7/0*
60	Graves, Rory	T	6-6	290	7/21/63	2	Ohio State	Decatur, Ga.	FA-'88	16/15
22	†Haynes, Mike	CB	6-2	190	7/1/53	14	Arizona State	Los Angeles, Calif.	T(NE)-'83	16/16
65	Hellestrae, Dale	G	6-5	285	7/11/62	4	Southern Methodist	Scottsdale, Ariz.	FA(Buff)-'89#	16/2*
88	Horton, Ethan	TE	6-4	235	12/19/62	3	North Carolina	Kannapolis, N.C.	FA-'89	0*
34	Jackson, Bo	RB	6-1	225	11/30/62	3	Auburn	Bessemer, Ala.	D7-'87	10/9
18	Jaeger, Jeff	K	5-11	185	11/26/64	2	Washington	Kent, Wash.	FA(Clev)-'89#	0*
87	Junkin, Trey	TE	6-2	230	1/23/61	7	Louisiana Tech	Winfield, La.	FA-'85	16/1
59	Kimmel, Jamie	LB	6-3	235	3/28/62	3	Syracuse	Conklin, N.Y.	D4-'85	0*
92	King, Emanuel	LB	6-4	250	8/15/63	5	Alabama	Leroy, Ala.	FA(Cin)-'89#	7/0*
52	King, Linden	LB	6-4	245	6/28/55	12	Colorado State	Colorado Springs, Colo.	FA-'86	14/13
74	Koch, Pete	DE	6-6	260	1/23/62	5	Maryland	Manhasset, N.Y.	FA(KC)-'89#	0*
69	Lee, Larry	G	6-2	270	9/10/59	9	UCLA	Dayton, Ohio	FA-'89	4/0*
40	†Lee, Zeph	S	6-3	205	6/17/63	3	Southern California	San Francisco, Calif.	D9-'86	8/1
51	Lewis, Bill	C	6-7	275	7/12/63	4	Nebraska	Sioux City, Iowa	D7-'86	14/14
80	Lofton, James	WR	6-3	190	7/5/56	12	Stanford	Los Angeles, Calif.	T(GB)-'87	16/16
75	Long, Howie	DE	6-5	265	1/6/60	9	Villanova	Charlestown, Mass.	D2-'81	7/6
26	McElroy, Vann	S	6-2	195	1/13/60	8	Baylor	Uvalde, Tex.	D3-'82	12/11
55	Millen, Matt	LB	6-2	250	3/12/58	10	Penn State	Hokendauqua, Pa.	D2-'80	16/16
72	Mosebar, Don	C-T	6-6	275	9/11/61	7	Southern California	Visalia, Calif.	D1-'83	13/13
42	Mueller, Vance	RB	6-0	215	5/5/64	4	Occidental	Jackson, Calif.	D4-'86	14/1
71	Pickel, Bill	DT	6-5	265	11/5/59	7	Rutgers	Brooklyn, N.Y.	D2-'83	16/16
20	Price, Dennis	CB	6-1	175	6/14/65	2	UCLA	Long Beach, Calif.	D5-'88	12/4
27	Richardson, Mike	CB	6-0	185	5/23/61	7	Arizona State	Compton, Calif.	FA(Chi)-'89#	16/15*
77	Riehm, Chris	G	6-6	280	4/14/61	3	Ohio State	Toledo, Ohio	FA-'86	8/4
57	†Robinson, Jerry	LB	6-2	230	12/18/56	11	UCLA	Santa Rosa, Calif.	T(Phil)-'85	15/15
13	Schroeder, Jay	QB	6-4	215	6/28/61	6	UCLA	Pacific Palisades, Calif.	T(Wash)-'88	9/8
58	Shipp, Jackie	LB	6-2	240	3/19/62	6	Oklahoma	Stillwater, Okla.	FA(Mia)-'89#	11/4*
35	Smith, Steve	RB	6-1	235	8/30/64	3	Penn State	Clinton, Md.	D3-'87	16/6
39	Strachan, Steve	RB	6-1	225	3/22/63	5	Boston College	Burlington, Mass.	D11-'85	16/0
96	Taylor, Malcolm	DT	6-6	280	6/20/60	6	Tennessee State	Crystal Springs, Miss.	FA-'87	15/3
30	Toran, Stacey	S	6-3	200	10/11/61	6	Notre Dame	Indianapolis, Ind.	D6-'84	12/4
93	Townsend, Greg	LB-DE	6-3	250	11/3/61	7	Texas Christian	Compton, Calif.	D4-'83	16/11
48	†Washington, Lionel	CB	6-0	185	10/21/60	7	Tulane	New Orleans, La.	T(StL)-'87	12/0
68	Wilkerson, Bruce	G-T	6-5	285	7/28/64	3	Tennessee	Philadelphia, Tenn.	D2-'87	16/16
50	Wilson, Otis	LB	6-2	225	9/15/57	9	Louisville	New York, N.Y.	FA(Chi)-'89#	0*
90	Wise, Mike	DE	6-7	270	6/5/64	3	California-Davis	Novato, Calif.	D4-'86	16/14
66	Wright, Steve	T	6-6	275	4/8/59	7	Northern Iowa	Wayzata, Minn.	FA-'88	15/3

* Benson played 12 games with New England in '88; Costello played 6 games with Atlanta; J. Davis last active with Tampa Bay in '87; Evans active for 6 games but did not play; Golic played 16 games with Cleveland; Graddy played 7 games with Denver; Hellestrae played 16 games with Buffalo; Horton last active with L.A. Raiders in '87; Jaeger last active with Cleveland in '87; Kimmel missed '88 season due to injury; E. King played 7 games with Cincinnati; Koch last active with Kansas City in '87; L. Lee played 4 games with Denver; Richardson played 16 games with Chicago; Shipp played 11 games with Miami; Wilson last active with Chicago in '87.

† Option playout; subject to developments.

\# Plan B unconditional free agent.

Players lost through Plan B (6): K Chris Bahr (SD; 16 games in '88), LB Reggie McKenzie (Phx; 16), RB Chris McLemore (Sea; 7), TE Andy Parker (SD; 16), RB Reggie Ware (Den; 0), WR Chris Woods (Clev; 2).

Also played with Raiders in '88—CB Ron Fellows (14 games), C Mike Freeman (2), S David Greenwood (2), G Charley Hannah (8), G Brian Holloway (2), T Jim Lachey (1), LB Rod Martin (16), LB Milt McColl (15), CB Terry McDaniel (2), LB Norwood Vann (1), C-T Dwight Wheeler (8), DT Mitch Willis (1).

COACHING STAFF

Head Coach, Mike Shanahan

Pro Career: Named eighth head coach in Raiders history on February 29, 1988. Had been NFL assistant coach previous four years with the Denver Broncos. Offensive coordinator with Broncos' AFC championship teams in 1986-87. Denver had 49-20-1 record during his four seasons there, winning three division titles and two conference championships. No pro playing experience. Career record: 7-9.

Background: Entered coaching ranks in 1973 as graduate assistant at Eastern Illinois University (where he had played quarterback). Joined staff at Oklahoma in 1975, working with running backs and receivers as Sooners won NCAA national championship. Served as offensive backfield coach at Northern Arizona in 1977. In 1978, was offensive coordinator at Eastern Illinois, helping guide team to NCAA Division II national championship. Offensive coordinator at Minnesota in 1979. Offensive coordinator at Florida 1980-83 as Gators built 32-15-1 record and played in bowl games in each of those four seasons. Served as assistant head coach at Florida in 1983 at age of 31. Had 77-29-3 record as college assistant coach.

Personal: Born August 24, 1952, in Oak Park, Ill. Mike and wife, Peggy, live in Palos Verdes, Calif., with their son Kyle and daughter Krystal.

Assistant Coaches

Dave Adolph, defensive coordinator; born June 6, 1937, Akron, Ohio, lives in El Segundo, Calif. Guard-linebacker Akron 1955-58. No pro playing experience. College coach: Akron 1963-64, Connecticut 1965-68, Kentucky 1969-72, Illinois 1973-76, Ohio State 1977-78. Pro coach: Cleveland Browns 1979-84, 1986-88, San Diego Chargers 1985, joined Raiders in 1989.

Fred Biletnikoff, wide receivers; born February 23, 1943, Erie, Pa., lives in El Segundo, Calif. Wide receiver Florida State 1962-64. Pro wide receiver Oakland Raiders 1965-78, Montreal Alouettes (CFL) 1980. College coach: Palomar, Calif., J.C. 1983, Diablo Valley, Calif., J.C. 1984, 1986. Pro coach: Oakland Invaders (USFL) 1985, Arizona Outlaws (USFL) 1986, Calgary Stampeders (CFL) 1987-88, joined Raiders in 1989.

John Dunn, strength and conditioning; born July 22, 1956, Great Barrington, Mass., lives in El Segundo, Calif. Guard Penn State 1975-77. No pro playing experience. College coach: Penn State 1978. Pro coach: Washington Redskins 1984-86, joined Raiders in 1987.

Alex Gibbs, assistant head coach; born February 11, 1941, Morganton, N.C., lives in El Segundo, Calif. Running back-defensive back Davidson 1959-63. No pro playing experience. College coach: Duke 1969-70, Kentucky 1971-72, West Virginia 1973-74, Ohio State 1975-78, Auburn 1979-81, Georgia 1982-83. Pro coach: Denver Broncos 1984-87, joined Raiders in 1988.

Sam Gruneisen, linebackers; born January 16, 1941, Louisville, Ky., lives in El Segundo, Calif. Tight end-linebacker-kicker Villanova 1959-61. Pro center San Diego Chargers 1962-72, Houston Oilers 1973. College coach: Grossmont, Calif., J.C. 1981, California 1982-83, San Jose State 1986. Pro coach: Los Angeles Express (USFL) 1984-85, joined Raiders in 1987.

Terry Robiskie, tight ends; born November 12, 1954, New Orleans, La., lives in Beverly Hills, Calif. Running back Louisiana State 1973-76. Pro running back Oakland Raiders 1977-79, Miami Dolphins 1980-81. Pro coach: Joined Raiders in 1982.

Pete Rodriguez, special teams; born July 25, 1940, Chicago, Ill., lives in El Segundo, Calif. Guard-linebacker Denver University 1959-60, Western State (Colo.) 1961-63. No pro playing experience. College coach: Western State (Colo.) 1964, Arizona 1968-69, Western Illinois 1970-73, 1979-82 (head coach), Florida State 1974-75, Iowa State 1976-78, Northern Iowa 1986. Pro coach: Michigan Panthers (USFL) 1983-84, Denver Gold (USFL) 1985, Jacksonville Bulls (USFL) 1986, Ottawa Rough Riders (CFL) 1987, joined Raiders in 1988.

Los Angeles Raiders 1989 First-Year Roster

Name	Pos.	Ht.	Wt.	Birth-date	College	Hometown	How Acq.
Alexander, Mike (1)	WR	6-3	195	3/19/65	Penn State	Piscataway, N.J.	D8-'88
Brown, Rex	CB	5-10	180	2/12/64	San Diego State	Huntington Beach, Calif.	FA
Burnham, Tim (1)	T	6-5	280	5/6/63	Washington	Anderson, Calif.	FA
Carter, Johnny (1)	DT	6-3	285	4/23/65	Grambling	New Orleans, La.	FA
Cormier, Joe (1)	LB	6-6	245	5/3/63	Southern California	Gardena, Calif.	FA
Crudup, Derrick (1)	S	6-2	210	2/15/65	Oklahoma	Delray Beach, Fla.	D7-'88
Dyal, Mike (1)	TE	6-2	240	5/20/66	Texas A&I	Kerrville, Tex.	FA-'88
Francis, Jeff	QB	6-4	215	7/7/66	Tennessee	Mt. Prospect, Ill.	D6a
Gainer, Derrick	RB	5-10	215	8/15/66	Florida A&M	Plant City, Fla.	D8
Gooden, Gary	WR-CB	6-0	170	12/10/67	Indiana	Brooklyn, N.Y.	D9-'88
Harrell, Newt (1)	G	6-5	295	9/17/64	West Texas State	Canyon, Tex.	D10-'88
Henry, Charles (1)	TE	6-4	230	4/18/64	Miami	St. Petersburg, Fla.	FA-'88
Jackson, Charles	DT	6-4	285	8/4/66	Jackson State	Miami, Fla.	D10
Land, Ben (1)	RB	6-0	195	7/3/65	Albany State	Donalsonville, Ga.	FA
Lloyd, Doug	RB	6-1	215	8/31/65	North Dakota State	Beaver Dam, Wis.	D6b
McDaniel, Terry (1)	CB	5-10	175	2/8/65	Tennessee	Saginaw, Mich.	D1-'88
Rother, Tim (1)	DT	6-7	275	9/28/65	Nebraska	Bellevue, Neb.	D4-'88
Snelson, Eric (1)	LB	6-3	240	7/20/65	Stanford	Antioch, Calif.	FA-'88
Wisniewski, Steve	G	6-4	280	4/7/67	Penn State	Houston, Tex.	T(Dall)
Zumwalt, Rich (1)	LB	6-3	230	5/19/65	Arizona State	Huntington Beach, Calif.	FA

The term NFL Rookie is defined as a player who is in his first season of professional football and has not been on the roster of another professional football team for any regular-season or postseason games. A Rookie is designated by an "R" on NFL rosters. Players who have been active in another professional football league or players who have NFL experience, including either preseason training camp or being on an active roster for fewer than three regular-season or postseason games, are termed NFL First-Year Players. An NFL First-Year Player is designated by a "1" on NFL rosters. Thereafter, a player on an NFL active roster for at least three regular-season or postseason games is credited with an additional year of NFL playing experience.

NOTES

Joe Scannella, offensive backfield; born May 22, 1932, Passaic, N.J., lives in El Segundo, Calif. Quarterback Lehigh 1947-50. Pro safety Saskatchewan Roughriders (CFL) 1951-52. College coach: Cornell 1960, C.W. Post 1963-68 (head coach 1964-68), Vermont 1970-71. Pro coach: Montreal Alouettes (CFL) 1969, 1978-81 (head coach), Oakland Raiders 1972-77, Cleveland Browns 1982-84, rejoined Raiders in 1987.

Art Shell, offensive line; born November 26, 1946, Charleston, S.C., lives in Rancho Palos Verdes, Calif. Tackle Maryland State 1965-67. Pro offensive tackle Oakland-Los Angeles Raiders 1968-82. Pro coach: Joined Raiders in 1983.

Jack Stanton, defensive backs; born June 6, 1938, Bridgeville, Pa., lives in El Segundo, Calif. Running back North Carolina State 1959-60. Pro running back Pittsburgh Steelers 1961, Toronto Argonauts (CFL) 1962-63. College coach: George Washington 1966, North Carolina State 1968-72, Florida State 1973, 1976-83, North Carolina 1974-75, Purdue 1986, New Mexico 1987-88. Pro coach: Atlanta Falcons 1984-85, joined Raiders in 1989.

Bill Urbanik, defensive line; born December 27, 1946, Donora, Pa., lives in El Segundo, Calif. Lineman Ohio State 1965-68. No pro playing experience. College coach: Marshall 1971-73, 1975, Northern Illinois 1976-78, Wake Forest 1979-83. Pro coach: Cincinnati Bengals 1984-88, joined Raiders in 1989.

Tom Walsh, quarterbacks; born April 16, 1949, Vallejo, Calif., lives in Manhattan Beach, Calif. UC-Santa Barbara 1971. No college or pro playing experience. College coach: University of San Diego 1972-76, U.S. International 1979, Murray State 1980, Cincinnati 1981. Pro coach: Joined Raiders in 1982.

American Football Conference Eastern Division

Team Colors: Aqua, Coral, and White

Joe Robbie Stadium
2269 N.W. 199th Street
Miami, Florida 33056
Telephone: (305) 620-5000

Club Officials

President: Joseph Robbie
Executive V.P./General Manager: J. Michael Robbie
V.P./Administration: Eddie J. Jones
V.P./Public Affairs: Tim Robbie
Head Coach: Don Shula
Director of Pro Scouting: Charley Winner
Director of Player Personnel: TBA
Director of Media Relations: Harvey Greene
Media Relations Assistants: Scott Stone, Fudge Browne
Director of Sales/Promotions: Dan Robbie
Marketing Director: David Evans
Director of Finance: William T. Duffy
Trainer: Bob Lundy
Equipment Manager: Bob Monica

Stadium: Joe Robbie Stadium • **Capacity:** 73,000
2269 N.W. 199th Street
Miami, Florida 33056

Playing Surface: Grass (PAT)

Training Camp: St. Thomas University
16400-D N.W. 32nd Avenue
Miami, Florida 33054

1989 Schedule

Preseason

Aug. 14	**Chicago**	8:00
Aug. 19	vs. Hou. at Jacksonville, Fla.	7:30
Aug. 25	at Washington	8:00
Sept. 2	**Philadelphia**	9:00

Regular Season

Sept. 10	**Buffalo**	4:00
Sept. 17	at New England	1:00
Sept. 24	**New York Jets**	4:00
Oct. 1	at Houston	12:00
Oct. 8	**Cleveland**	1:00
Oct. 15	at Cincinnati	1:00
Oct. 22	**Green Bay**	1:00
Oct. 29	at Buffalo	1:00
Nov. 5	**Indianapolis**	1:00
Nov. 12	at New York Jets	1:00
Nov. 19	at Dallas	12:00
Nov. 26	**Pittsburgh**	1:00
Dec. 3	at Kansas City	12:00
Dec. 10	**New England**	8:00
Dec. 17	at Indianapolis	1:00
Dec. 24	**Kansas City**	1:00

Dolphins Coaching History

(219-137-4)

1966-69	George Wilson	15-39-2
1970-88	Don Shula	204-98-2

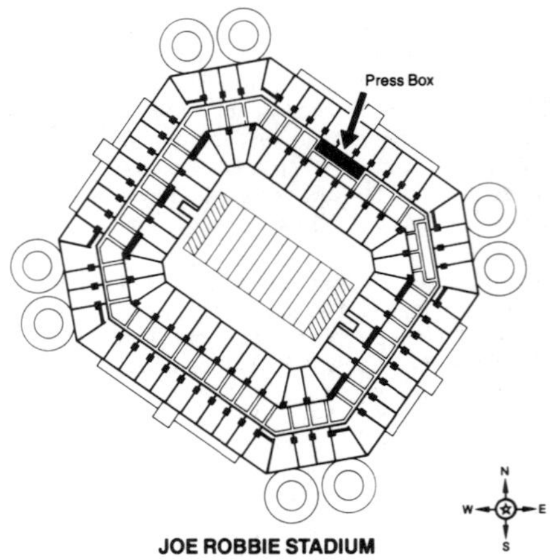

JOE ROBBIE STADIUM

Record Holders

Individual Records—Career

Category	Name	Performance
Rushing (Yds.)	Larry Csonka, 1968-1974, 1979	6,737
Passing (Yds.)	Bob Griese, 1967-1980	25,092
Passing (TDs)	Dan Marino, 1983-88	196
Receiving (No.)	Nat Moore, 1974-1986	510
Receiving (Yds.)	Nat Moore, 1974-1986	7,547
Interceptions	Jake Scott, 1970-75	35
Punting (Avg.)	Reggie Roby, 1983-88	43.6
Punt Return (Avg.)	Freddie Solomon, 1975-77	11.4
Kickoff Return (Avg.)	Mercury Morris, 1969-1975	26.5
Field Goals	Garo Yepremian, 1970-78	165
Touchdowns (Tot.)	Nat Moore, 1974-1986	75
Points	Garo Yepremian, 1970-78	830

Individual Records—Single Season

Category	Name	Performance
Rushing (Yds.)	Delvin Williams, 1978	1,258
Passing (Yds.)	Dan Marino, 1984	*5,084
Passing (TDs)	Dan Marino, 1984	*48
Receiving (No.)	Mark Clayton, 1988	86
Receiving (Yds.)	Mark Clayton, 1984	1,389
Interceptions	Dick Westmoreland, 1967	10
Punting (Avg.)	Reggie Roby, 1984	44.7
Punt Return (Avg.)	Freddie Solomon, 1975	12.3
Kickoff Return (Avg.)	Duriel Harris, 1976	32.9
Field Goals	Garo Yepremian, 1971	28
Touchdowns (Tot.)	Mark Clayton, 1984	18
Points	Garo Yepremian, 1971	117

Individual Records—Single Game

Category	Name	Performance
Rushing (Yds.)	Mercury Morris, 9-30-73	197
Passing (Yds.)	Dan Marino, 10-23-88	521
Passing (TDs)	Bob Griese, 11-24-77	6
	Dan Marino, 9-21-86	6
Receiving (No.)	Jim Jensen, 11-6-88	12
Receiving (Yds.)	Mark Duper, 11-10-85	217
Interceptions	Dick Anderson, 12-3-73	*4
Field Goals	Garo Yepremian, 9-26-71	5
Touchdowns (Tot.)	Paul Warfield, 12-15-73	4
Points	Paul Warfield, 12-15-73	24

*NFL Record

1988 Team Record

Preseason (2-3)

Date	Result		Opponents
7/31	W	27-21	vs. San Francisco at London, Eng.
8/6	L	17-20	at Chicago
8/13	L	10-27	Washington
8/19	W	16-13	Denver (OT)
8/26	L	17-24	at Minnesota
		87-105	

Regular Season (6-10)

Date	Result		Opponents	Att.
9/4	L	7-34	at Chicago	63,330
9/11	L	6- 9	at Buffalo	79,520
9/18	W	24-17	Green Bay	54,409
9/25	L	13-15	at Indianapolis	59,638
10/2	W	24- 7	Minnesota	59,867
10/9	W	24-14	at L.A. Raiders	50,751
10/16	W	31-28	San Diego	58,972
10/23	L	30-44	N.Y. Jets	68,292
10/30	W	17-14	at Tampa Bay	67,352
11/6	L	10-21	at New England	60,840
11/14	L	6-31	Buffalo	67,091
11/20	L	3- 6	New England	53,526
11/27	L	34-38	at N.Y. Jets	52,752
12/4	L	28-31	Indianapolis	45,236
12/12	W	38-31	Cleveland	61,884
12/18	L	24-40	at Pittsburgh	36,051

(OT) Overtime

Score by Periods

Dolphins	72	97	88	62	0	—	319
Opponents	51	159	69	101	0	—	380

Attendance

Home 469,277 Away 470,234 Total 939,511

Single-game home record, 68,292 (10-23-88; Joe Robbie Stadium)

Single-season home record, 469,277 (1988; Joe Robbie Stadium)

1988 Team Statistics

	Dolphins	Opp.
Total First Downs	321	359
Rushing	77	155
Passing	218	173
Penalty	26	31
Third Down: Made/Att.	71/184	101/207
Fourth Down: Made/Att.	7/16	6/13
Total Net Yards	5721	5781
Avg. Per Game	357.6	361.3
Total Plays	963	1072
Avg. Per Play	5.9	5.4
Net Yards Rushing	1205	2506
Avg. Per Game	75.3	156.6
Total Rushes	335	557
Net Yards Passing	4516	3275
Avg. Per Game	282.3	204.7
Sacked/Yards Lost	7/41	24/167
Gross Yards	4557	3442
Att./Completions	621/363	491/298
Completion Pct.	58.5	60.7
Had Intercepted	23	16
Punts/Avg.	64/43.0	58/41.8
Net Punting Avg.	35.3	35.0
Penalties/Yards Lost	99/845	103/734
Fumbles/Ball Lost	26/12	31/15
Touchdowns	41	45
Rushing	11	22
Passing	29	19
Returns	1	4
Avg. Time of Possession	27:02	32:58

1988 Individual Statistics

Scoring	TD R	TD P	TD Rt	PAT	FG	Saf	TP
Clayton	0	14	0	0/0	0/0	0	84
Hampton	9	3	0	0/0	0/0	0	72
Reveiz	0	0	0	31/32	8/12	0	55
Jensen	0	5	0	0/0	0/0	0	30
Edmunds	0	3	0	0/0	0/0	0	18
Franklin	0	0	0	6/7	4/11	0	18
Stradford	2	1	0	0/0	0/0	0	18
Banks	0	2	0	0/0	0/0	0	12
Duper	0	1	0	0/0	0/0	0	6
Hobley	0	0	1	0/0	0/0	0	6
Dolphins	11	29	1	37/41	12/23	0	319
Opponents	22	19	4	44/45	22/28	0	380

Passing	Att.	Comp.	Yds.	Pct.	TD	Int.	Tkld.	Rate
Marino	606	354	4434	58.4	28	23	6/31	80.8
Jaworski	14	9	123	64.3	1	0	1/10	116.1
Stradford	1	0	0	0.0	0	0	0/0	39.6
Dolphins	621	363	4557	58.5	29	23	7/41	81.5
Opponents	491	298	3442	60.7	19	16	24/167	81.2

Rushing	Att.	Yds.	Avg.	LG	TD
Hampton	117	414	3.5	33	9
Stradford	95	335	3.5	18	2
Davenport	55	273	5.0	64	0
Bennett	31	115	3.7	12	0
Jensen	10	68	6.8	23	0
Cribbs	5	21	4.2	11	0
Clayton	1	4	4.0	4	0
Edmunds	1	−8	−8.0	−8	0
Marino	20	−17	−0.9	6	0
Dolphins	335	1205	3.6	64	11
Opponents	557	2506	4.5	44	22

Receiving	No.	Yds.	Avg.	LG	TD
Clayton	86	1129	13.1	45t	14
Jensen	58	652	11.2	31	5
Stradford	56	426	7.6	36	1
Duper	39	626	16.1	56	1
Edmunds	33	575	17.4	80t	3
Davenport	30	282	9.4	27	0
Banks	23	430	18.7	55	2
Hampton	23	204	8.9	39t	3
Schwedes	6	130	21.7	42	0
Hardy	4	46	11.5	19	0
Pruitt	2	38	19.0	19	0
Bennett	2	16	8.0	12	0
Kinchen	1	3	3.0	3	0
Dolphins	363	4557	12.6	80t	29
Opponents	298	3442	11.6	47	19

Interceptions	No.	Yds.	Avg.	LG	TD
Williams	4	62	15.5	23	0
Judson	4	57	14.3	52	0
M. Brown	2	13	6.5	13	0
Offerdahl	2	2	1.0	2	0
Thomas	1	48	48.0	48	0
McNeal	1	23	23.0	23	0
Graf	1	14	14.0	14	0
Lankford	1	0	0.0	0	0
Dolphins	16	219	13.7	52	0
Opponents	23	399	17.3	78t	4

Punting	No.	Yds.	Avg.	In 20	LG
Roby	64	2754	43.0	18	64
Dolphins	64	2754	43.0	18	64
Opponents	58	2427	41.8	14	66

Punt Returns	No.	FC	Yds.	Avg.	LG	TD
Schwedes	24	7	230	9.6	36	0
Williams	3	3	29	9.7	14	0
Dolphins	27	10	259	9.6	36	0
Opponents	35	10	318	9.1	31	0

Kickoff Returns	No.	Yds.	Avg.	LG	TD
Cribbs	41	863	21.0	44	0
Hampton	9	216	24.0	37	0
Williams	8	159	19.9	27	0
Schwedes	3	49	16.3	25	0
Davenport	2	41	20.5	21	0
Edmunds	1	20	20.0	20	0
Hardy	1	17	17.0	17	0
Hill, G.B.-Mia.	1	1	1.0	1	0
Dolphins	65	1365	21.0	44	0
Opponents	53	1109	20.9	57	0

Sacks	No.
Turner	5.0
Sochia	4.5
Cline	4.0
Kumerow	3.0
Green	2.5
Bosa	2.0
Graf	1.0
Lankford	1.0
M. Brown	0.5
Offerdahl	0.5
Dolphins	24.0
Opponents	7.0

1989 Draft Choices

Round	Name	Pos.	College
1.	Sammie Smith	RB	Florida State
	Louis Oliver	DB	Florida
4.	David Holmes	DB	Syracuse
5.	Jeff Uhlenhake	C	Ohio State
6.	Wes Pritchett	LB	Notre Dame
7.	Jim Zdelar	T	Youngstown
8.	Pete Stoyanovich	K	Indiana
9.	Dana Batiste	LB	Texas A&M
10.	Deval Glover	WR	Syracuse
	Greg Ross	NT	Memphis State
11	Bert Weidner	DT	Kent State
12	J.B. Brown	DB	Maryland

Miami Dolphins 1989 Veteran Roster

No.	Name	Pos.	Ht.	Wt.	Birth-date	NFL Exp.	College	Hometown	How Acq.	'88 Games/ Starts
50	Ahrens, Dave	LB	6-4	245	12/5/58	9	Wisconsin	Oregon, Wis.	FA(Det)-'89#	8/0*
86	†Banks, Fred	WR	5-10	180	5/26/62	4	Liberty	Columbus, Ga.	FA-'87	11/2
34	Bennett, Woody	RB	6-2	244	3/24/55	11	Miami	York, Pa.	W(NYJ)-'80	16/7
97	Bosa, John	DE	6-4	273	1/10/64	3	Boston College	Keene, N.H.	D1-'87	6/6
43	Brown, Bud	S	6-0	193	4/19/61	6	Southern Mississippi	DeKalb, Miss.	D11-'84	16/3
51	†Brown, Mark	LB	6-2	238	7/18/61	7	Purdue	Inglewood, Calif.	D9-'83	13/12
59	Brudzinski, Bob	LB	6-4	235	1/1/55	13	Ohio State	Fremont, Ohio	T(Rams)-'81	16/0
77	Cheek, Louis	T	6-6	295	10/6/64	2	Texas A&M	Fairfield, Tex.	D8b-'88	15/0
60	Clark, Greg	LB	6-1	221	3/5/65	2	Arizona State	Torrance, Calif.	FA(Chi)-'89#	15/0*
83	Clayton, Mark	WR	5-9	184	4/8/61	7	Louisville	Indianapolis, Ind.	D8-'83	16/16
98	†Cline, Jackie	DE-NT	6-5	280	3/13/60	3	Alabama	McCalla, Ala.	W(Pitt)-'87	14/9
67	Conlin, Chris	G-C	6-3	280	6/7/65	2	Penn State	Glenside, Pa.	D5-'87	0*
20	Cribbs, Joe	RB	5-11	190	1/5/58	9	Auburn	Sulligent, Ala.	FA-'88	13/0*
91	Cross, Jeff	DE	6-4	270	3/25/66	2	Missouri	Blythe, Calif.	D9-'88	16/1
30	Davenport, Ron	RB	6-2	232	12/22/62	5	Louisville	Atlanta, Ga.	D6b-'85	16/5
65	Dellenbach, Jeff	C-T	6-5	280	2/14/63	5	Wisconsin	Wausau, Wis.	D4b-'85	16/16
74	Dennis, Mark	T	6-6	290	4/15/65	3	Illinois	Washington, Ill.	D8b-'87	13/7
85	Duper, Mark	WR	5-9	190	1/25/59	8	Northwestern Louisiana	Moreauville, La.	D2-'82	13/13
80	Edmunds, Ferrell	TE	6-6	248	4/16/65	2	Maryland	Danville, Va.	D3-'88	16/14
61	Foster, Roy	G	6-4	275	5/24/60	8	Southern California	Shawnee Mission, Kan.	D1-'82	15/15
53	Frye, David	LB	6-2	227	6/21/61	7	Purdue	Cincinnati, Ohio	FA-'86	8/0
58	Furjanic, Tony	LB	6-1	228	2/26/64	4	Notre Dame	Chicago, Ill.	FA-'88	6/0
48	Gage, Steve	S	6-3	210	5/10/64	3	Tulsa	Tulsa, Okla.	FA(Wash)-'89#	16/1*
62	Galbreath, Harry	G-C	6-1	275	1/1/65	2	Tennessee	Clarksville, Tenn.	D8a-'88	16/13
42	Gibson, Ernest	CB	5-10	185	10/3/61	6	Furman	Jacksonville, Fla.	FA(NE)-'89#	16/0*
79	Giesler, Jon	T	6-5	272	12/23/56	11	Michigan	Woodville, Ohio	D1-'79	13/9
99	Graf, Rick	LB	6-5	249	8/29/63	3	Wisconsin	Madison, Wis.	D2a-'87	16/16
55	Green, Hugh	LB	6-2	228	7/27/59	9	Pittsburgh	Natchez, Miss.	T(TB)-'85	16/16
27	†Hampton, Lorenzo	RB	5-11	208	3/12/62	5	Florida	Lake Wales, Fla.	D1-'85	16/10
84	Hardy, Bruce	TE	6-4	234	6/1/56	11	Arizona State	Bingham, Utah	D9-'78	2/2
29	Hobley, Liffort	S	6-0	202	5/12/62	4	Louisiana State	Shreveport, La.	FA-'87	16/13
11	Jensen, Jim	WR-RB	6-4	220	11/14/58	9	Boston University	Doylestown, Pa.	D11-'81	16/4
87	Johnson, Dan	TE	6-3	245	5/17/60	6	Iowa State	New Hope, Minn.	D7a-'82	0*
73	Johnson, Greg	G	6-4	295	12/19/64	2	Oklahoma	Moore, Okla.	D4-'88	2/0
49	Judson, William	CB	6-1	192	3/26/59	8	South Carolina State	Atlanta, Ga.	D8-'81	16/16
54	Junior, E.J.	LB	6-3	235	12/8/59	9	Alabama	Nashville, Tenn.	FA(Phx)-'89#	16/16*
88	Kinchen, Brian	TE	6-2	238	8/6/65	2	Louisiana State	Baton Rouge, La.	D12-'88	16/0
54	Kolic, Larry	LB	6-1	239	8/31/63	3	Ohio State	Smithville, Ohio	D7-'86	7/0
90	Kumerow, Eric	DE	6-7	260	4/17/65	2	Ohio State	Oak Park, Ill.	D1-'88	14/0
44	Lankford, Paul	CB	6-1	190	6/15/58	8	Penn State	Farmingdale, N.Y.	D3-'82	13/10
72	Lee, Ronnie	T	6-3	275	12/24/56	11	Baylor	Tyler, Tex.	T(Atl)-'84	16/16
25	Logan, Marc	RB	5-11	225	5/9/65	3	Kentucky	Lexington, Ky.	FA(Cin)-89#	9/0*
13	Marino, Dan	QB	6-4	222	9/15/61	7	Pittsburgh	Pittsburgh, Pa.	D1-'83	16/16
28	McNeal, Don	CB	6-0	193	5/6/58	9	Alabama	Atmore, Ala.	D1-'80	16/3
52	Nicolas, Scott	LB	6-3	230	8/7/60	7	Miami	Clearwater, Fla.	FA-'87	0*
56	Offerdahl, John	LB	6-3	237	8/17/64	4	Western Michigan	Fort Atkinson, Wis.	D2-'86	16/16
10	Pease, Brent	QB	6-2	200	10/8/64	3	Montana	Mountain Home, Idaho	FA(Hou)-'89#	13/0*
7	†Reveiz, Fuad	K	5-11	220	2/24/63	5	Tennessee	Miami, Fla.	D7-'85	11/0
4	†Roby, Reggie	P	6-2	242	7/30/61	7	Iowa	East Waterloo, Iowa	D6-'83	15/0
81	Schwedes, Scott	WR-KR	6-0	182	6/30/65	3	Syracuse	DeWitt, N.Y.	D2b-'87	16/1
70	Sochia, Brian	NT	6-3	275	7/21/61	7	Northwestern Oklahoma	Brasher Falls, N.Y.	FA-'86	16/16
57	Stephenson, Dwight	C	6-2	264	11/20/57	9	Alabama	Hampton, Va.	D2-'80	0*
23	Stradford, Troy	RB	5-9	192	9/11/64	3	Boston College	Linden, N.J.	D4-'87	15/6
45	Thomas, Rodney	CB	5-10	190	12/21/65	2	Brigham Young	Ontario, Calif.	D5-'88	12/1
96	Thorp, Don	DE	6-4	260	7/10/62	4	Illinois	Buffalo Grove, Ill.	FA(KC)-'89#	3/0*
76	†Toth, Tom	G	6-5	282	5/23/62	4	Western Michigan	Orland Park, Ill.	FA-'86	9/4
95	†Turner, T.J.	DE	6-4	280	5/16/63	4	Houston	Lufkin, Tex.	D3-'86	16/16
21	Watkins, Bobby	CB	5-10	184	5/31/60	8	Southwest Texas State	Dallas, Tex.	FA(Det)-'89#	16/0*
26	Williams, Jarvis	S	5-11	196	5/16/65	2	Florida	Palatka, Fla.	D2-'88	16/16

* Ahrens played 8 games with Detroit in '88; Clark played 15 games with Chicago; Conlin, D. Johnson, Nicolas, Scott, and Stephenson missed '88 season due to injury; Cribbs played 1 game with Indianapolis, 12 with Miami in '88; Gage played 16 games with Washington; Gibson played 16 games with New England; Junior played 16 games with Phoenix; Logan played 9 games with Cincinnati; Pease played 13 games with Houston; Thorp played 3 games with Kansas City; Watkins played 16 games with Detroit.

† Option playout; subject to developments.

\# Plan B unconditional free agent.

Retired—Glenn Blackwood, 9-year safety, 0 games in 88.

Players lost through Plan B (6): RB Tony Burse (Sea; 0 games in '88), QB Ron Jaworski (KC; 16), NT Mike Lambrecht (NYG; 8), CB-S Bruce Plummer (Ind; 3), LB Jackie Shipp (Raiders; 11), CB Reyna Thompson (NYG; 16).

Also played with Dolphins in '88—K Willie Beecher (active for 1 game but did not play), K Tony Franklin (5), LB Chris Gaines (4), DE Nate Hill (1), LB Ilia Jarostchuk (6), WR James Pruitt (11), LB Jackie Shipp (11), WR Jimmy Teal (active for 3 games but did not play).

COACHING STAFF

Head Coach, Don Shula

Pro Career: Begins his twenty-seventh season as an NFL head coach, and twentieth with the Dolphins. Miami has won or shared first place in the AFC East in 13 of his 19 years. Has most wins (277) among active NFL coaches and is second only to George Halas's 325. Captured back-to-back NFL championships, defeating Washington 14-7 in Super Bowl VII and Minnesota 24-7 in Super Bowl VIII. Lost to Dallas 24-3 in Super Bowl VI, to Washington 27-17 in Super Bowl XVII, and to San Francisco 38-16 in Super Bowl XIX. His 1972 17-0 club is the only team in NFL history to go undefeated throughout the regular season and postseason. Started his pro playing career with Cleveland Browns as defensive back in 1951. After two seasons with Browns, spent 1953-56 with Baltimore Colts and 1957 with Washington Redskins. Joined Detroit Lions as defensive coach in 1960 and was named head coach of the Colts in 1963. Baltimore had a 13-1 record in 1968 and captured NFL championship before losing to New York Jets in Super Bowl III. Career record: 277-124-6.

Background: Outstanding offensive player at John Carroll University in Cleveland before becoming defensive specialist as a pro. His alma mater gave him doctorate in humanities in May, 1973. Served as assistant coach at Virginia in 1958 and at Kentucky in 1959.

Personal: Born January 4, 1930, in Painesville, Ohio. Don and his wife, Dorothy, live in Miami Lakes, Fla., and have five children—David, Donna, Sharon, Annie, and Mike. David is Dallas's assistant head coach and Mike is an assistant coach with Tampa Bay.

Assistant Coaches

George Hill, linebackers; born April 28, 1933, Bay Village, Ohio, lives in Miami. Tackle-fullback Denison 1954-57. No pro playing experience. College coach: Findlay 1959, Denison 1960-64, Cornell 1965, Duke 1966-70, Ohio State 1971-78. Pro coach: Philadelphia Eagles 1979-84, Indianapolis Colts 1985-88, joined Dolphins in 1989.

Tom Olivadotti, defense; born September 22, 1945, Long Branch, N.J., lives in Cooper City, Fla. Defensive back-wide receiver Upsala 1963-66. No pro playing experience. College coach: Princeton 1975-77, Boston College 1978-79, Miami 1980-83. Pro coach: Cleveland Browns 1985-86, joined Dolphins in 1987.

Mel Phillips, defensive backs; born January 6, 1942, Shelby, N.C., lives in Miami Lakes, Fla. Defensive back-running back North Carolina A&T 1964-65. Pro defensive back San Francisco 49ers 1966-77. Pro coach: Detroit Lions 1980-84, joined Dolphins in 1985.

John Sandusky, assistant head coach-offense/offensive line; born December 28, 1925, Philadelphia, Pa., lives in Hollywood, Fla. Tackle Villanova 1946-49. Pro tackle Cleveland Browns 1950-55, Green Bay Packers 1956. College coach: Villanova 1957-58. Pro coach: Baltimore Colts 1959-72 (head coach 1972), Philadelphia Eagles 1973-75, joined Dolphins in 1976.

Larry Seiple, receivers; born February 14, 1945, Allentown, Pa., lives in Miami Lakes, Fla. Running back-receiver-punter Kentucky 1964-66. Pro punter-tight end-receiver-running back Miami Dolphins 1967-77. College coach: Miami 1978-79. Pro coach: Detroit Lions 1980-84, Tampa Bay Buccaneers 1985-86, joined Dolphins in 1988.

Dan Sekanovich, defensive line; born July 27, 1933, West Hazleton, Pa., lives in Cooper City, Fla. End Tennessee 1951-53. Pro defensive end Montreal Alouettes (CFL) 1954. College coach: Susquehanna 1961-63, Connecticut 1964-67, Pittsburgh 1968, Navy 1969-70, Kentucky 1971-72. Pro coach: Montreal Alouettes (CFL) 1973-76, New York Jets 1977-82, Atlanta Falcons 1983-85, joined Dolphins in 1986.

Miami Dolphins 1989 First-Year Roster

Name	Pos.	Ht.	Wt.	Birth-date	College	Hometown	How Acq.
Batisite, Dana	LB	6-0	225	3/22/66	Texas A&M	Spring, Tex.	D9
Brown, Andre	WR	6-3	203	8/21/66	Miami	Chicago, Ill.	FA
Brown, J.B.	CB	6-0	189	1/5/67	Maryland	Fort Washington, Md.	D12
Brown, Jerry	G	6-4	269	10/8/65	Utah State	Santa Rosa, Calif.	FA
Cartwright, Ricardo	WR	5-10	175	5/27/65	Florida A&M	Freeport, Bahamas	FA
Cooper, Jason (1)	TE	6-4	240	1/6/66	Duke	New Canaan, Conn.	FA
Davis, Billy	WR	5-10	175	11/5/65	Cincinnati	Berea, Ohio	FA
Fruhmorgan, John	G	6-4	295	9/28/65	Alabama	Tampa, Fla.	FA
Glover, Deval	WR	5-11	184	9/12/66	Syracuse	Troy, N.J.	D10a
Grant, African (1)	CB	6-0	198	8/2/65	Illinois	Englewood, N.J.	FA
Holmes, David	CB	6-1	191	7/8/66	Syracuse	Burlington, N.J.	D4
Holt, Glenn	WR	5-11	180	1/1/65	Western Kentucky	North Miami, Fla.	FA
McKinney, Reggie	RB	5-9	187	3/19/67	East Carolina	Dudley, N.C.	FA
Moon, L.B.	T	6-5	269	12/13/65	Texas A&M	Jenks, Okla.	FA
Nason, Scott	DE	6-5	265	5/20/66	Maine	Winthrop, Maine	FA
Oliver, Louis	S	6-2	225	3/9/66	Florida	Belle Glade, Fla.	D1b
Plaszek, Vince	NT	6-3	289	10/2/65	Washburn	West Seneca, N.Y.	FA
Pettyjohn, Barry (1)	T	6-5	280	3/29/64	Pittsburgh	Deer Park, Ohio	FA
Pritchett, Wes	LB	6-4	234	7/7/66	Notre Dame	Atlanta, Ga.	D6
Ross, Greg	DE	6-3	266	1/11/67	Memphis State	Tiptonville, Tenn.	D10b
Shapiro, John (1)	WR	6-3	198	2/11/65	Brown	Manhasset, N.Y.	FA
Smith, Sammie	RB	6-2	224	5/16/67	Florida State	Zellwood, Fla.	D1a
Staples, Greg	S	5-11	197	1/29/66	Auburn	Atmore, Ala.	FA
Stark, Chad (1)	RB	6-1	226	4/4/65	North Dakota State	Fargo, N.D.	FA
Starr, Eric (1)	RB	5-9	200	2/2/66	North Carolina	Ellenboro, N.C.	FA
Stoyanovich, Pete	K	5-10	178	4/28/67	Indiana	Dearborn Heights, Mich.	D8
Uhlenhake, Jeff	C	6-3	270	1/28/66	Ohio State	Newark, Ohio	D5
Vettrus, Tom	LB	6-3	235	12/3/66	Oregon State	Cascade Turner, Ore.	FA
Weber, Dave (1)	QB	6-3	224	6/23/65	Carroll	Menomonee Falls, Wis.	FA
Weidner, Bert	NT	6-3	261	1/20/66	Kent State	Eden, N.Y.	D11
Zdelar, Jim	T	6-5	288	5/24/66	Youngstown State	Youngstown, Ohio	D7

The term NFL Rookie is defined as a player who is in his first season of professional football and has not been on the roster of another professional football team for any regular-season or postseason games. A Rookie is designated by an "R" on NFL rosters. Players who have been active in another professional football league or players who have NFL experience, including either preseason training camp or being on an active roster for fewer than three regular-season or postseason games, are termed NFL First-Year Players. An NFL First-Year Player is designated by a "1" on NFL rosters. Thereafter, a player on an NFL active roster for at least three regular-season or postseason games is credited with an additional year of NFL playing experience.

NOTES

Gary Stevens, quarterbacks-passing game; born March 19, 1943, Cleveland, Ohio, lives in Kendall, Fla. Running back John Carroll 1963-65. No pro playing experience. College coach: Louisville 1971-74, Kent State 1975, West Virginia 1976-79, Miami 1980-88. Pro coach: Joined Dolphins in 1989.

Carl Taseff, offensive backs; born September 28, 1928, Cleveland, Ohio, lives in Miami. Back John Carroll 1947-50. Pro defensive back Cleveland Browns 1951, Baltimore Colts 1953-61, Philadelphia Eagles 1961, Buffalo Bills 1962. Pro coach: Boston Patriots 1964, Detroit Lions 1965-66, joined Dolphins in 1970.

Junior Wade, strength-conditioning; born February 2, 1947, Bath, S.C., lives in Miami. South Carolina State 1969. No college or pro playing experience. Pro coach: Joined Dolphins in 1975, coach since 1983.

Mike Westhoff, special teams-tight ends; born January 10, 1948, Pittsburgh, Pa., lives in Ft. Lauderdale, Fla. Center-linebacker Wichita State 1967-69. No pro playing experience. College coach: Indiana 1974-75, Dayton 1976, Indiana State 1977, Northwestern 1978-80, Texas Christian 1981. Pro coach: Baltimore/Indianapolis Colts 1982-84, Arizona Outlaws (USFL) 1985, joined Dolphins in 1986.

American Football Conference Eastern Division

Team Colors: Red, White, and Blue

Sullivan Stadium
Route 1
Foxboro, Massachusetts 02035
Telephone: (508) 543-7911

Club Officials

Chairman: Victor K. Kiam II
Vice Chairman: Francis W. Murray
President: William H. Sullivan, Jr.
Vice President: Francis J. (Bucko) Kilroy
General Manager: Patrick J. Sullivan
Vice President, Administration: Robert L. Durkin
Director of Player Development: Dick Steinberg
Director of Pro Scouting: Bill McPeak
Director of College Scouting: Joe Mendes
Executive Director of Player Personnel: Darryl Stingley
Personnel Scouts: Larry Cook, Charles Garcia, Mike Pollom, Pat Naughton, Ken Sternfeld, Bob Teahan
Director of Marketing/Public Relations: David J. Wintergrass
Director of Media Relations: Jim Greenidge
Assistant Media Relations: Jimmy Oldham
Box Office Manager: Frank Napoli
Trainer: Ron O'Neil
Equipment Manager: George Luongo
Video Manager: Ken Deininger

Stadium: Sullivan Stadium • **Capacity:** 60,794
Route 1
Foxboro, Massachusetts 02035

Playing Surface: SuperTurf

Training Camp: Bryant College
Route 7
Smithfield, Rhode Island 02917

1989 Schedule

Preseason

Aug. 12	**New York Giants**	7:00
Aug. 19	vs. Sea. at St. Louis, Mo.	8:00
Aug. 26	at Atlanta	7:30
Sept. 1	**Green Bay**	7:00

Regular Season

Sept. 10	at New York Jets	4:00
Sept. 17	**Miami**	1:00
Sept. 24	**Seattle**	1:00
Oct. 1	at Buffalo	1:00
Oct. 8	**Houston**	1:00
Oct. 15	at Atlanta	1:00
Oct. 22	at San Francisco	1:00
Oct. 29	at Indianapolis	1:00
Nov. 5	**New York Jets**	1:00
Nov. 12	**New Orleans**	1:00
Nov. 19	**Buffalo**	1:00
Nov. 26	at Los Angeles Raiders	1:00
Dec. 3	**Indianapolis**	1:00
Dec. 10	at Miami	8:00
Dec. 17	at Pittsburgh	1:00
Dec. 24	**Los Angeles Rams**	1:00

Patriots Coaching History

Boston 1960-70
(206-215-9)

1960-61	Lou Saban*	7-12-0
1961-68	Mike Holovak	53-47-9
1969-70	Clive Rush**	5-16-0
1970-72	John Mazur***	9-21-0
1972	Phil Bengtson	1-4-0
1973-78	Chuck Fairbanks****	46-41-0
1978	Hank Bullough-Ron Erhardt#	0-1-0
1979-81	Ron Erhardt	21-27-0
1982-84	Ron Meyer##	18-16-0
1984-88	Raymond Berry	46-30-0

*Released after five games in 1961
**Released after seven games in 1970
***Resigned after nine games in 1972
****Suspended for final regular season game in 1978
#Co-coaches
##Released after eight games in 1984

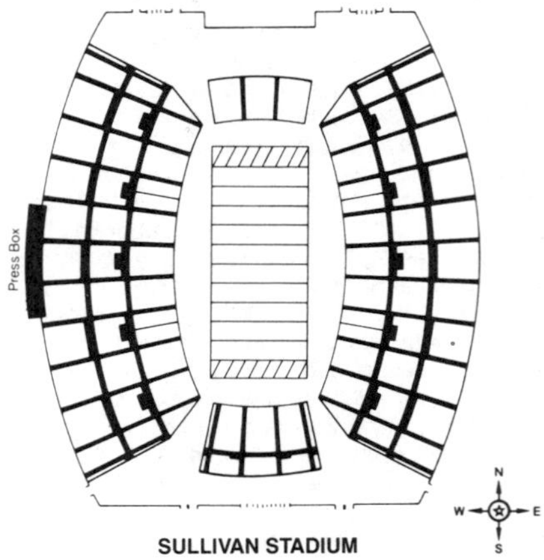

SULLIVAN STADIUM

Record Holders

Individual Records—Career

Category	Name	Performance
Rushing (Yds.)	Sam Cunningham, 1973-79, 1981-82	5,453
Passing (Yds.)	Steve Grogan, 1975-1988	24,574
Passing (TDs)	Steve Grogan, 1975-1988	169
Receiving (No.)	Stanley Morgan, 1977-1988	506
Receiving (Yds.)	Stanley Morgan, 1977-1988	9,866
Interceptions	Raymond Clayborn, 1977-1988	35
Punting (Avg.)	Rich Camarillo, 1981-87	42.6
Punt Return (Avg.)	Mack Herron, 1973-75	12.0
Kickoff Return (Avg.)	Horace Ivory, 1977-1981	27.6
Field Goals	Gino Cappelletti, 1960-1970	176
Touchdowns (Tot.)	Stanley Morgan, 1977-1988	65
Points	Gino Cappelletti, 1960-1970	1,130

Individual Records—Single Season

Category	Name	Performance
Rushing (Yds.)	Jim Nance, 1966	1,458
Passing (Yds.)	Vito (Babe) Parilli, 1964	3,465
Passing (TDs)	Vito (Babe) Parilli, 1964	31
Receiving (No.)	Stanley Morgan, 1986	84
Receiving (Yds.)	Stanley Morgan, 1986	1,491
Interceptions	Ron Hall, 1964	11
Punting (Avg.)	Rich Camarillo, 1983	44.6
Punt Return (Avg.)	Mack Herron, 1974	14.8
Kickoff Return (Avg.)	Raymond Clayborn, 1977	31.0
Field Goals	Tony Franklin, 1986	32
Touchdowns (Tot.)	Steve Grogan, 1976	13
	Stanley Morgan, 1979	13
Points	Gino Cappelletti, 1964	155

Individual Records—Single Game

Category	Name	Performance
Rushing (Yds.)	Tony Collins, 9-18-83	212
Passing (Yds.)	Tony Eason, 9-21-86	414
Passing (TDs)	Vito (Babe) Parilli, 11-15-64	5
	Vito (Babe) Parilli, 10-15-67	5
	Steve Grogan, 9-9-79	5
Receiving (No.)	Art Graham, 11-20-66	11
	Tony Collins, 11-29-87	11
Receiving (Yds.)	Stanley Morgan, 11-8-81	182
Interceptions	Many times	3
	Last time by Roland James, 10-23-83	
Field Goals	Gino Cappelletti, 10-4-64	6
Touchdowns (Tot.)	Many times	3
	Last time by Stanley Morgan, 9-21-86	
Points	Gino Cappelletti, 12-18-65	28

1988 Team Record

Preseason (1-3)

Date	Result		Opponents
8/6	L	30-34	Atlanta
8/13	L	14-27	vs. Houston at Memphis, Tenn.
8/20	W	24-21	at Philadelphia
8/26	L	21-27	Cincinnati
		89-109	

Regular Season (9-7)

Date	Result		Opponents	Att.
9/4	W	28- 3	N.Y. Jets	44,027
9/11	L	6-36	at Minnesota	55,545
9/18	L	14-16	Buffalo	55,945
9/25	L	6-31	at Houston	38,646
10/2	W	21-17	Indianapolis	58,050
10/9	L	3-45	at Green Bay	51,932
10/16	W	27-21	Cincinnati	59,969
10/23	L	20-23	at Buffalo	76,824
10/30	W	30- 7	Chicago	60,821
11/6	W	21-10	Miami	60,840
11/13	W	14-13	at N.Y. Jets	48,358
11/20	W	6- 3	at Miami	53,526
11/27	L	21-24	at Indianapolis	58,157
12/4	W	13- 7	Seattle	59,086
12/11	W	10- 7	Tampa Bay (OT)	39,889
12/17	L	10-21	at Denver	70,910

(OT) Overtime

Score by Periods

Patriots	49	87	50	61	3	—	250
Opponents	48	77	57	102	0	—	284

Attendance

Home 438,627 Away 453,898 Total 892,525
Single-game home record, 61,457 (12-5-71)
Single-season home record, 482,572 (1986)

1988 Team Statistics

	Patriots	Opp.
Total First Downs	264	272
Rushing	126	119
Passing	112	138
Penalty	26	15
Third Down: Made/Att.	79/219	58/199
Fourth Down: Made/Att.	9/14	9/18
Total Net Yards	4293	4681
Avg. Per Game	268.3	292.6
Total Plays	1000	961
Avg. Per Play	4.3	4.9
Net Yards Rushing	2120	2099
Avg. Per Game	132.5	131.2
Total Rushes	588	496
Net Yards Passing	2173	2582
Avg. Per Game	135.8	161.4
Sacked/Yards Lost	23/160	29/219
Gross Yards	2333	2801
Att./Completions	389/199	436/234
Completion Pct.	51.2	53.7
Had Intercepted	28	20
Punts/Avg.	91/38.3	86/42.2
Net Punting Avg.	34.1	35.5
Penalties/Yards Lost	87/665	108/858
Fumbles/Ball Lost	19/10	29/15
Touchdowns	31	33
Rushing	17	20
Passing	12	13
Returns	2	0
Avg. Time of Possession	31:04	28:56

1988 Individual Statistics

Scoring	TD R	TD P	TD Rt	PAT	FG	Saf	TP
Perryman	6	0	0	0/0	0/0	0	36
Staurovsky	0	0	0	14/15	7/11	0	35
Fryar	0	5	0	0/0	0/0	0	30
Stephens	4	0	1	0/0	0/0	0	30
Garcia	0	0	0	11/16	6/13	0	29
Morgan	0	4	0	0/0	0/0	0	24
Dawson	0	2	0	0/0	0/0	0	12
Dupard	2	0	0	0/0	0/0	0	12
Tatupu	2	0	0	0/0	0/0	0	12
Flutie	1	0	0	0/0	0/0	0	6
Grogan	1	0	0	0/0	0/0	0	6
C. James	1	0	0	0/0	0/0	0	6
Jones	0	1	0	0/0	0/0	0	6
Martin	0	0	1	0/0	0/0	0	6
Patriots	17	12	2	25/31	13/24	0	250
Opponents	20	13	0	33/33	17/26	1	284

Passing	Att.	Comp.	Yds.	Pct.	TD	Int.	Tkld.	Rate
Flutie	179	92	1150	51.4	8	10	11/65	63.3
Grogan	140	67	834	47.9	4	13	8/77	37.6
Eason	43	28	249	65.1	0	2	2/12	61.1
Ramsey	27	12	100	44.4	0	3	2/6	15.0
Patriots	389	199	2333	51.2	12	28	23/160	50.0
Opponents	436	234	2801	53.7	13	20	29/219	64.4

Rushing	Att.	Yds.	Avg.	LG	TD
Stephens	297	1168	3.9	52	4
Perryman	146	448	3.1	16	6
Flutie	38	179	4.7	16	1
Dupard	52	151	2.9	15	2
Tatupu	22	75	3.4	22	2
Allen	7	40	5.7	12	0
Eason	5	18	3.6	10	0
C. James	4	15	3.8	8t	1
Fryar	6	12	2.0	6	0
Grogan	6	12	2.0	6	1
Ramsey	3	8	2.7	9	0
Feagles	1	0	0.0	0	0
Morgan	1	−6	−6.0	−6	0
Patriots	588	2120	3.6	52	17
Opponents	496	2099	4.2	36	20

Receiving	No.	Yds.	Avg.	LG	TD
Dupard	34	232	6.8	15	0
Fryar	33	490	14.8	80t	5
Morgan	31	502	16.2	32	4
Jones	22	313	14.2	41t	1
Perryman	17	134	7.9	18	0
C. James	14	171	12.2	32	0
Stephens	14	98	7.0	17	0
Francis	11	161	14.6	51	0
Dawson	8	106	13.3	38	2
Tatupu	8	58	7.3	17	0
Martin	4	51	12.8	21	0
Scott	1	8	8.0	8	0
Johnson	1	5	5.0	5	0
Farrell	1	4	4.0	4	0
Patriots	199	2333	11.7	80t	12
Opponents	234	2801	12.0	51t	13

Interceptions	No.	Yds.	Avg.	LG	TD
Clayborn	4	65	16.3	31	0
Marion	4	47	11.8	22	0
R. James	4	30	7.5	22	0
McSwain	2	51	25.5	42	0
Rembert	2	10	5.0	6	0
Jordan	1	31	31.0	31	0
McGrew	1	6	6.0	6	0
Lippett	1	4	4.0	4	0
Bowman	1	0	0.0	0	0
Patriots	20	244	12.2	42	0
Opponents	28	286	10.2	40	0

Punting	No.	Yds.	Avg.	In 20	LG
Feagles	91	3482	38.3	24	74
Patriots	91	3482	38.3	24	74
Opponents	86	3633	42.2	19	70

Punt Returns	No.	FC	Yds.	Avg.	LG	TD
Fryar	38	8	398	10.5	30	0
Bowman	0	1	0	—	0	0
Patriots	38	9	398	10.5	30	0
Opponents	37	17	217	5.9	19	0

Kickoff Returns	No.	Yds.	Avg.	LG	TD
Martin	31	735	23.7	95t	1
Allen	18	391	21.7	30	0
Davis	6	106	17.7	24	0
Fryar	1	3	3.0	3	0
Tatupu	1	13	13.0	13	0
Patriots	57	1248	21.9	95t	1
Opponents	45	888	19.7	51	0

Sacks	No.
B. Williams	8.0
Tippett	7.0
Jordan	3.0
Rembert	3.0
Goad	2.0
McGrew	2.0
Veris	2.0
Hodge	1.0
Patriots	29.0
Opponents	23.0

1989 Draft Choices

Round	Name	Pos.	College
1.	Hart Lee Dykes	WR	Oklahoma State
2.	Eric Coleman	DB	Wyoming
3.	Marv Cook	TE	Iowa
	Chris Gannon	DE	S.W. Louisiana
4.	Maurice Hurst	DB	Southern Univ.
	Michael Timpson	WR	Penn State
6.	Eric Mitchel	RB	Oklahoma
7.	Eric Lindstrom	LB	Boston College
8.	Rodney Rice	DB	Brigham Young
	Tony Zackery	DB	Washington
9.	Darron Norris	RB	Texas
	Curtis Wilson	C	Missouri
10.	Emanuel McNeil	DT	Tennessee-Martin
11.	Tony Hinz	RB	Harvard
12.	Aaron Chubb	LB	Georgia

New England Patriots 1989 Veteran Roster

No.	Name	Pos.	Ht.	Wt.	Birth-date	NFL Exp.	College	Hometown	How Acq.	'88 Games/ Starts
39	Allen, Marvin	RB-KR	5-10	215	11/23/65	2	Tulane	Wichita Falls, Tex.	D11-'88	11/0
78	Armstrong, Bruce	T	6-4	284	9/7/65	3	Louisville	Miami, Fla.	D1-'87	16/16
68	†Baab, Mike	C	6-4	270	12/6/59	8	Texas	Euless, Tex.	T(Clev)-'88	15/12
28	†Bowman, Jim	S	6-2	210	10/26/63	5	Central Michigan	Cadillac, Mich.	D2b-'85	16/1
59	Brown, Vincent	LB	6-2	245	1/9/65	2	Mississippi Valley State	Decatur, Ga.	D2-'88	16/3
26	Clayborn, Raymond	CB	6-1	186	1/2/55	13	Texas	Ft. Worth, Tex.	D1a-'77	16/16
5	Davis, Greg	K	5-11	197	11/29/65	3	Citadel	Rome, Ga.	FA(Atl)-'89#	16/0*
87	Dawson, Lin	TE	6-3	240	6/24/59	8	North Carolina State	Kinston, N.C.	D8b-'81	6/6
67	Douglas, David	T	6-4	280	3/20/63	4	Tennessee	Evansville, Tenn.	FA(Cin)-'89#	14/0*
21	Dupard, Reggie	RB	5-11	205	10/30/63	4	Southern Methodist	New Orleans, La.	D1-'86	16/2
11	Eason, Tony	QB	6-4	212	10/8/59	7	Illinois	Walnut Grove, Calif.	D1-'83	2/2
66	†Fairchild, Paul	G-C	6-4	270	9/14/61	6	Kansas	Glidden, Iowa	D5-'84	16/3
62	†Farrell, Sean	G	6-3	260	5/25/60	8	Penn State	Westhampton, N.Y.	T(TB)-'87	15/15
6	Feagles, Jeff	P	6-0	198	3/7/66	2	Miami	Scottsdale, Ariz.	FA-'88	16/0
2	†Flutie, Doug	QB	5-10	175	10/23/62	4	Boston College	Natick, Mass.	T(Chi)-'87	11/9
81	Francis, Russ	TE	6-6	242	4/3/53	14	Oregon	Pleasant Hill, Ore.	FA-'87	12/8
80	†Fryar, Irving	WR-KR	6-0	200	9/28/62	6	Nebraska	Mt. Holly, N.J.	D1-'84	15/14
48	Gadbois, Dennis	WR	6-1	183	9/18/63	3	Boston University	Biddeford, Me.	FA-'87	2/0
72	Goad, Tim	NT	6-3	280	2/28/66	2	North Carolina	Claudville, Va.	D4a-'88	16/14
14	Grogan, Steve	QB	6-4	210	7/24/53	15	Kansas State	Ottawa, Kan.	D5a-'75	6/4
97	Hodge, Milford	NT-DE	6-3	278	3/11/61	4	Washington State	South San Francisco, Calif.	FA-'86	15/7
41	†Holmes, Darryl	S	6-2	190	9/6/64	3	Fort Valley State	Warner Robins, Ga.	FA-'87	16/0
32	James, Craig	RB	6-0	215	1/2/61	5	Southern Methodist	Houston, Tex.	D7-'83	6/0
39	James, Roland	S	6-2	191	2/18/58	10	Tennessee	Xenia, Ohio	D1a-'80	15/15
99	Jeter, Gary	DE	6-4	260	3/24/55	13	Southern California	Cleveland, Ohio	FA(Rams)-'89#	15/1*
85	Johnson, Steve	TE	6-6	245	6/22/65	2	Virginia Tech	Huntsville, Ala.	D6-'88	14/3
83	Jones, Cedric	WR	6-1	184	6/1/60	8	Duke	Weldon, N.C.	D3a-'82	16/2
18	Jones, Mike	WR	5-11	183	4/14/60	6	Tennessee State	Chattanooga, Tenn.	FA(KC)-'89#	0*
93	Jordan, Tim	LB	6-3	226	4/26/64	3	Wisconsin	Madison, Wis.	D4c-'87	16/6
42	Lippett, Ronnie	CB	5-11	180	12/10/60	7	Miami	Sebring, Fla.	D8-'83	15/15
31	†Marion, Fred	S	6-2	191	8/2/59	8	Miami	Gainesville, Fla.	D5-'82	16/16
82	Martin, Sammy	WR-KR	5-11	175	8/21/65	2	Louisiana State	New Orleans, La.	D4b-'88	16/0
64	Matich, Trevor	C	6-4	270	10/9/61	5	Brigham Young	Sacramento, Calif.	D1-'85	8/6
50	McGrew, Lawrence	LB	6-5	233	7/23/57	9	Southern California	Berkeley, Calif.	D2-'80	16/15
23	†McSwain, Rod	CB	6-1	198	1/28/62	6	Clemson	Caroleen, N.C.	T(Atl)-'84	16/1
86	Morgan, Stanley	WR	5-11	181	2/17/55	13	Tennessee	Easley, S.C.	D1b-'77	16/14
34	Perryman, Robert	RB	6-1	233	10/16/64	3	Michigan	Bourne, Mass.	D3-'87	16/16
76	Rehder, Tom	T	6-7	280	1/27/65	2	Notre Dame	Santa Maria, Calif.	D3-'88	16/0
52	Rembert, Johnny	LB	6-3	234	1/19/61	7	Clemson	Arcadia, Fla.	D4-'83	16/15
95	†Reynolds, Ed	LB	6-5	242	9/23/61	7	Virginia	Ridgeway, Va.	FA-'83	14/14
88	Scott, Willie	TE	6-4	245	2/13/59	9	South Carolina	Newberry, S.C.	T(KC)-'86	3/1
49	Sievers, Eric	TE	6-4	230	11/9/58	9	Maryland	Arlington, Va.	FA(Rams)-'89#	6/0*
77	†Sims, Kenneth	DE	6-5	271	10/31/59	7	Texas	Kosse, Tex.	D1a-'82	1/1
4	Staurovsky, Jason	K	5-9	170	3/23/63	3	Tulsa	Tulsa, Okla.	FA-'88	8/0
44	Stephens, John	RB	6-1	220	2/23/66	2	Northwestern Louisiana	Springhill, La.	D1-'88	16/14
30	Tatupu, Mosi	RB	6-0	227	4/26/55	12	Southern California	Honolulu, Hawaii	D8b-'78	16/0
56	Tippett, Andre	LB	6-3	241	12/27/59	8	Iowa	Newark, N.J.	D2b-'82	12/11
60	Veris, Garin	DE	6-4	255	2/27/63	5	Stanford	Chillicothe, Ohio	D2a-'85	11/9
73	†Villa, Danny	T	6-5	305	9/21/64	3	Arizona State	Nogales, Ariz.	D5a-'87	16/14
94	Ward, David	LB	6-2	232	3/10/64	2	Southern Arkansas	West Helena, Ark.	FA-'88	0*
96	†Williams, Brent	DE	6-3	278	10/23/64	4	Toledo	Flint, Mich.	D7b-'86	16/16
54	Williams, Ed	LB	6-4	244	9/8/61	5	Texas	Ector, Tex.	D2-'84	0*
15	Wilson, Marc	QB	6-6	205	2/15/57	9	Brigham Young	Seattle, Wash.	FA-'89	0*
61	Wooten, Ron	G	6-4	273	6/28/59	8	North Carolina	Kinston, N.C.	D6-'81	14/14

* Davis played 16 games with Atlanta in '88; Douglas played 14 games with Cincinnati; Jeter played 15 games with L.A. Rams; M. Jones active for 1 game with Kansas City in '88 but did not play; Sievers played 5 games with San Diego, 1 with L.A. Rams; Ward, E. Williams missed '88 season due to injury; Wilson last active with L.A. Raiders in '87.

† Option playout; subject to developments.

Plan B unconditional free agent.

Players lost through Plan B (6): LB Thomas Benson (Raiders; 12 games in '88), RB Elgin Davis (Pitt; 5), K Teddy Garcia (Phx; 16), CB Ernest Gibson (Mia; 16), DE-DT Tom Gibson (Clev; 0), LB Eric Naposki (Dall; 3), CB Eugene Profit (Wash; 1), WR Darryl Usher (Clev; 0), NT Toby Williams (GB; 15), G Troy Wolkow (KC; 0).

Also played with Patriots in '88—DE Edmund Nelson (12 games), QB Tom Ramsey (7).

COACHING STAFF

Head Coach, Raymond Berry

Pro Career: Has had winning record in each of his four full seasons with the Patriots. Last year, New England went 9-7. That follows the team going 8-7 in 1987 and 11-5 in both 1985 and 1986. In 1986, the Patriots won the AFC East title and then lost to Denver Broncos in divisional playoff game. The previous season saw the Patriots make Super Bowl XX after gaining entry into the playoffs as a wild-card team. New England reached the Super Bowl by winning three straight road playoff games, the only time it has been done in NFL history. Became ninth head coach in Patriots history when he was named to replace Ron Meyer on October 25, 1984, after the eighth game of the season. Played receiver for the Baltimore Colts 1955-67. Had 631 catches for 9,275 yards and 68 touchdowns in his playing career. His number of career receptions is presently fifth-best ever in the NFL, while his receiving yardage is eighth-best and his career touchdown catches fifteenth. Helped Colts to two world championships (1958 and 1959) and to NFL Championship Game (1964). Named all-pro three times (1958-60) and played in five Pro Bowl games. Led NFL in receiving 1958-60. Holds NFL Championship Game records for yardage (178) and receptions (12), set in 1958 sudden-death title game against New York Giants. Was inducted into Pro Football Hall of Fame on July 29, 1973, five years after his retirement. Was receivers coach with Dallas Cowboys in 1968-69, Detroit Lions 1973-75, Cleveland Browns 1976-77, and New England Patriots 1978-81. Career record: 46-30.

Background: Attended Paris (Tex.) High School, Schreiner (Tex.) Institute, and Southern Methodist 1951-54, where he played receiver. Receivers coach at Arkansas 1970-72.

Personal: Born February 27, 1933, in Corpus Christi, Tex. Raymond and his wife, Sally, live in Medfield, Mass., with their children—Mark, Suzanne, and Ashley.

Assistant Coaches

Don Blackmon, staff assistant; born March 14, 1958, Pompano Beach, Fla. lives in Norfolk, Mass. Linebacker Tulsa 1976-80. Pro linebacker New England Patriots 1981-87. Pro coach: Joined Patriots in 1988.

Jimmy Carr, defensive backs; born March 25, 1933, Kayford, W. Va., lives in North Attleboro, Mass. Running back-defensive back-linebacker Morris Harvey (now Univ. of Charleston, W. Va.) 1951-54. Pro running back-defensive back-linebacker Chicago Cardinals 1955-57, Montreal Alouettes (CFL) 1958, Philadelphia Eagles 1959-63, Washington Redskins 1964-65. Pro coach: Minnesota Vikings 1966-68, 1979-81, Chicago Bears 1969, 1973-74, Philadelphia Eagles 1970-72, Detroit Lions 1975-76, Buffalo Bills 1977, San Francisco 49ers 1978, Denver Gold (USFL) 1983-84, joined Patriots in 1985.

Bobby Grier, offensive backs-running game coordinator; born November 10, 1942, Detroit, Mich., lives in Holliston, Mass. Running back Iowa 1961-64. No pro playing experience. College coach: Eastern Michigan 1974-77, Boston College 1978-80. Pro coach: New England Patriots 1981. Moved to team's scouting department 1982-84. Rejoined Patriots coaching staff in 1985.

Ray Hamilton, assistant defensive line; born January 20, 1951, Omaha, Neb., lives in Sharon, Mass. Defensive tackle Oklahoma 1970-72. Nose tackle New England Patriots 1973-81. Pro coach: Joined Patriots in 1985.

Harold Jackson, receivers; born January 6, 1946, Quincy, Miss., lives in Milford, Mass. Wide receiver Jackson State 1964-67. Pro wide receiver Los Angeles Rams 1968, 1973-77, Philadelphia Eagles 1969-72, New England Patriots 1978-81, Seattle Seahawks 1983. Pro coach: Joined Patriots in 1985.

New England Patriots 1989 First-Year Roster

Name	Pos.	Ht.	Wt.	Birth-date	College	Hometown	How Acq.
Belli, Barry (1)	K	5-10	168	8/7/65	Fresno State	Bakersfield, Calif.	FA
Chubb, Aaron	LB	6-5	235	8/17/66	Georgia	Rockmart, Ga.	D12
Coleman, Eric	CB	6-0	190	12/27/66	Wyoming	Denver, Colo.	D2
Cook, Marv	TE	6-4	250	2/24/66	Iowa	West Branch, Iowa	D3a
Dykes, Hart Lee	WR	6-4	218	9/2/66	Oklahoma State	Bay City, Tex.	D1
Feggins, Howard (1)	CB	5-10	190	5/6/65	N.C.-Charlotte	South Hill, Va.	FA
Gannon, Chris	DE	6-6	265	1/20/66	S.W. Louisiana	Orange Park, Fla.	D3b
Hinz, Tony	RB	6-2	215	7/30/67	Harvard	Great Falls, Mont.	D11
Hurst, Maurice	CB	5-10	185	9/17/67	Southern University	New Orleans, La.	D4a
Kolodziey, Chris	K	6-1	195	2/26/65	Maryland	Ludlow, Mass.	FA
Lindstrom, Eric	LB	6-3	235	5/27/66	Boston College	Weymouth, Mass.	D7
McPhearson, Gerrick (1)	CB	5-9	173	5/31/66	Boston College	Towson, Md.	FA
McNeil, Emanuel	NT	6-3	285	6/9/67	Tennessee-Martin	Highland Springs, Va.	D10
Mitchel, Eric	RB	6-0	210	2/13/67	Oklahoma	Pine Bluff, Ark.	D6
Norris, Darron	RB	5-9	215	12/5/66	Texas	Oceanside, Calif.	D9a
Norton, Tim (1)	QB	6-3	205	4/28/64	Lewis & Clark	Oakland, Calif.	FA
Rice, Rodney	CB	5-8	180	6/18/66	Brigham Young	Atwater, Calif.	D8a
Robbins, Monte (1)	P	6-4	210	9/19/64	Michigan	Great Bend, Kan.	T(Wash)
Stallings, Robert (1)	TE	6-6	265	1/23/64	Southern Mississippi	Magnolia, Miss.	FA
Timpson, Michael	WR-KR	5-10	175	6/6/67	Penn State	Miami, Fla.	D4b
Viaene, David (1)	T	6-5	300	7/14/65	Minnesota-Duluth	Appleton, Wis.	FA
White, Kevin (1)	WR	5-11	203	6/30/65	South Carolina	Charlotte, N.C.	FA
White, Todd (1)	WR-KR	6-0	195	9/15/65	Cal State-Fullerton	Santa Monica, Calif.	FA
Wilkins, Peter (1)	LB	6-3	205	9/27/65	Idaho	Spokane, Wash.	FA
Wilson, Curtis	C	6-3	290	10/30/65	Missouri	Ponca City, Okla.	D9b
Zackery, Tony	CB	6-2	195	11/20/66	Washington	Seattle, Wash.	D8b

The term NFL Rookie is defined as a player who is in his first season of professional football and has not been on the roster of another professional football team for any regular-season or postseason games. A Rookie is designated by an "R" on NFL rosters. Players who have been active in another professional football league or players who have NFL experience, including either preseason training camp or being on an active roster for fewer than three regular-season or postseason games, are termed NFL First-Year Players. An NFL First-Year Player is designated by a "1" on NFL rosters. Thereafter, a player on an NFL active roster for at least three regular-season or postseason games is credited with an additional year of NFL playing experience.

NOTES

Eddie Khayat, defensive line; born September 14, 1935, Moss Point, Miss., lives in Milford, Mass. Offensive-defensive end Millsaps 1953, Perkinston J.C. 1954, Tulane 1955-56. Pro defensive end-defensive tackle Washington Redskins 1957, 1962-63, Philadelphia Eagles 1958-61, 1964-65, Boston Patriots 1966. Pro coach: New Orleans Saints 1967-70, Philadelphia Eagles 1971-72 (head coach), Detroit Lions 1973-74, 1982-84, Atlanta Falcons 1975-76, Baltimore Colts 1977-81, joined Patriots in 1985.

Guy Morriss, offensive line; born May 13, 1951, Colorado City, Tex., lives in Wrentham, Mass. Offensive guard Texas Christian 1970-72. Pro center Philadelphia Eagles 1973-83, New England Patriots 1984-87. Pro coach: Joined Patriots in 1988.

John Polonchek, special assistant to head coach; born January 1, 1928, in Granastrov, Czechoslovakia, lives in Norton, Mass. Running back-defensive back Michigan State 1947-49. No pro playing experience. College coach: Michigan State 1950, 1955-57, Colorado 1959-61. Pro coach: Oakland Raiders 1967-71, Green Bay Packers 1972-74, New England Patriots 1975-81, New Jersey Generals (USFL) 1982-83, Los Angeles Raiders 1984 (scout), rejoined Patriots in 1985.

Keith Rowen, special teams-tight ends; born September 2, 1952, New York, N.Y., lives in Foxboro, Mass. Offensive tackle Stanford 1972-74. No pro playing experience. College coach: Stanford 1975-76, Long Beach State 1977-78, Arizona 1979-82. Pro coach: Boston/New Orleans Breakers (USFL) 1983-84, Cleveland Browns 1984, Indianapolis Colts 1985-88, joined Patriots in 1989.

Don Shinnick, linebackers; born May 15, 1935, Kansas City, Mo., lives in Walpole, Mass. Guard-defensive back-running back-linebacker UCLA 1954-56. Pro linebacker Baltimore Colts 1957-69. College coach: Central Methodist College (head coach) 1979-81. Pro coach: Chicago Bears 1970-71, St. Louis Cardinals 1972, Oakland Raiders 1973-77, joined Patriots in 1985.

Richard Wood, quarterbacks; born February 2, 1936, Lanett, Ala., lives in Foxboro, Mass. Quarterback Auburn 1956-59. Pro quarterback Baltimore Colts 1960-61, San Diego Chargers 1962, Denver Broncos 1962, New York Jets 1963-64, Oakland Raiders 1965, Miami Dolphins 1966. College coach: Georgia 1967-68, Mississippi 1971-73, Auburn 1986. Pro coach: Oakland Raiders 1969-70, Cleveland Browns 1974, New Orleans Saints 1976-77, Atlanta Falcons 1978-82, Philadelphia Eagles 1983, Kansas City Chiefs 1987-88, joined Patriots in 1989.

American Football Conference
Eastern Division

Team Colors: Kelly Green and White

598 Madison Avenue
New York, New York 10022
Telephone: (212) 421-6600

Club Officials

Chairman of the Board: Leon Hess
President: Steve Gutman
Director of Player Personnel: Mike Hickey
Pro Personnel Director: Jim Royer
Talent Scouts: Joe Collins, Don Grammer, Sid Hall, Ron Nay, Marv Sunderland
Director of Public Relations: Frank Ramos
Assistant Director of Public Relations: Ron Cohen
Public Relations Assistant: Eileen Walker
Public Relations Assistant: Brooks Thomas
Director of Operations: Mike Kensil
Ticket Manager: Bob Parente
Video Director: Jim Pons
Trainer: Bob Reese
Assistant Trainers: Pepper Burruss, Joe Patten
Equipment Manager: Bill Hampton

Stadium: Giants Stadium • **Capacity:** 76,891
East Rutherford, New Jersey 07073

Playing Surface: AstroTurf

Training Center: 1000 Fulton Avenue
Hempstead, New York 11550
(516) 538-6600

1989 Schedule

Preseason

Aug. 12	vs. G.B. at Milwaukee	1:00
Aug. 20	vs. Phil. at Raleigh, N.C.	8:00
Aug. 26	at New York Giants	8:00
Sept. 1	at Kansas City	7:30

Regular Season

Sept. 10	**New England**	4:00
Sept. 17	at Cleveland	1:00
Sept. 24	at Miami	4:00
Oct. 1	**Indianapolis**	1:00
Oct. 9	**L.A. Raiders** (Monday)	9:00
Oct. 15	at New Orleans	3:00
Oct. 22	at Buffalo	1:00
Oct. 29	**San Francisco**	4:00
Nov. 5	at New England	1:00
Nov. 12	**Miami**	1:00
Nov. 19	at Indianapolis	8:00
Nov. 26	**Atlanta**	1:00
Dec. 3	at San Diego	1:00
Dec. 10	**Pittsburgh**	1:00
Dec. 17	at Los Angeles Rams	1:00
Dec. 23	**Buffalo** (Saturday)	12:30

Jets Coaching History

New York Titans 1960-62
(196-226-8)

1960-61	Sammy Baugh	14-14-0
1962	Clyde (Bulldog) Turner	5-9-0
1963-73	Weeb Ewbank	73-78-6
1974-75	Charley Winner*	9-14-0
1975	Ken Shipp	1-4-0
1976	Lou Holtz**	3-10-0
1976	Mike Holovak	0-1-0
1977-82	Walt Michaels	41-49-1
1983-88	Joe Walton	50-47-1

*Released after nine games in 1975
**Resigned after 13 games in 1976

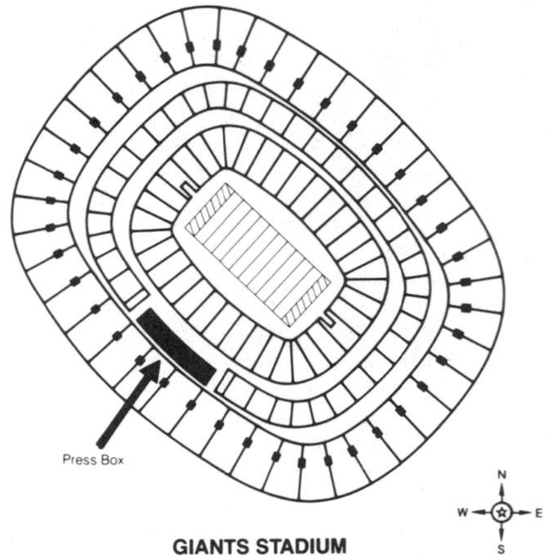

GIANTS STADIUM

Record Holders

Individual Records—Career

Category	Name	Performance
Rushing (Yds.)	Freeman McNeil,1981-88	6,794
Passing (Yds.)	Joe Namath, 1965-1976	27,057
Passing (TDs)	Joe Namath, 1965-1976	170
Receiving (No.)	Don Maynard, 1960-1972	627
Receiving (Yds.)	Don Maynard, 1960-1972	11,732
Interceptions	Bill Baird, 1963-69	34
Punting (Avg.)	Curley Johnson, 1961-68	42.8
Punt Return (Avg.)	Dick Christy, 1961-63	16.2
Kickoff Return (Avg.)	Bobby Humphery, 1984-88	24.2
Field Goals	Pat Leahy, 1974-1988	241
Touchdowns (Tot.)	Don Maynard, 1960-1972	88
Points	Pat Leahy, 1974-1988	1,190

Individual Records—Single Season

Category	Name	Performance
Rushing (Yds.)	Freeman McNeil, 1985	1,331
Passing (Yds.)	Joe Namath, 1967	4,007
Passing (TDs)	Al Dorow, 1960	26
	Joe Namath, 1967	26
Receiving (No.)	Al Toon, 1988	93
Receiving (Yds.)	Don Maynard, 1967	1,434
Interceptions	Dainard Paulson, 1964	12
Punting (Avg.)	Curley Johnson, 1965	45.3
Punt Return (Avg.)	Dick Christy, 1961	21.3
Kickoff Return (Avg.)	Bobby Humphery, 1984	30.7
Field Goals	Jim Turner, 1968	34
Touchdowns (Tot.)	Art Powell, 1960	14
	Don Maynard, 1965	14
	Emerson Boozer, 1972	14
Points	Jim Turner, 1968	145

Individual Records—Single Game

Category	Name	Performance
Rushing (Yds.)	Freeman McNeil, 9-15-85	192
Passing (Yds.)	Joe Namath, 9-24-72	496
Passing (TDs)	Joe Namath, 9-24-72	6
Receiving (No.)	Clark Gaines, 9-21-80	17
Receiving (Yds.)	Don Maynard, 11-17-68	228
Interceptions	Many times	3
	Last time by Erik McMillan, 10-23-88	
Field Goals	Jim Turner, 11-3-68	6
	Bobby Howfield, 12-3-72	6
Touchdowns (Tot.)	Wesley Walker, 9-21-86	4
Points	Jim Turner, 11-3-68	19
	Pat Leahy, 9-16-84	19

1988 Team Record

Preseason (1-3)

Date	Result		Opponents
8/6	L	12-23	at Philadelphia
8/13	L	21-24	at N.Y. Giants
8/18	W	11- 7	vs. Cleveland at Montreal, Can.
8/27	L	24-27	vs. Green Bay at Madison, Wis.
		68-81	

Regular Season (8-7-1)

Date	Result		Opponents	Att.
9/4	L	3-28	at New England	44,027
9/11	W	23- 3	at Cleveland	74,434
9/18	W	45- 3	Houston	64,683
9/25	W	17-10	at Detroit	29,250
10/2	T	17-17	Kansas City (OT)	66,110
10/9	L	19-36	at Cincinnati	57,482
10/17	L	14-37	Buffalo	70,218
10/23	W	44-30	at Miami	68,292
10/30	W	24-20	Pittsburgh	64,862
11/6	L	14-38	at Indianapolis	59,233
11/13	L	13-14	New England	48,358
11/20	L	6- 9	at Buffalo (OT)	78,389
11/27	W	38-34	Miami	52,752
12/4	L	34-38	at Kansas City	30,059
12/10	W	34-16	Indianapolis	46,284
12/18	W	27-21	N.Y. Giants	69,770

(OT) Overtime

Score by Periods

Jets	78	125	72	97	0	—	372
Opponents	86	64	104	97	3	—	354

Attendance

Home 483,037 Away 441,166 Total 924,203
Single-game home record, 74,975 (12-2-84)
Single-season home record, 541,832 (1985)

1988 Team Statistics

	Jets	Opp.
Total First Downs	331	310
Rushing	118	123
Passing	181	162
Penalty	32	25
Third Down: Made/Att.	97/233	87/214
Fourth Down: Made/Att.	7/17	11/21
Total Net Yards	5215	5633
Avg. Per Game	325.9	352.1
Total Plays	1094	1038
Avg. Per Play	4.8	5.4
Net Yards Rushing	2132	2124
Avg. Per Game	133.3	132.8
Total Rushes	514	517
Net Yards Passing	3083	3509
Avg. Per Game	192.7	219.3
Sacked/Yards Lost	42/291	45/314
Gross Yards	3374	3823
Att./Completions	538/299	476/244
Completion Pct.	55.6	51.3
Had Intercepted	11	24
Punts/Avg.	85/38.9	72/38.1
Net Punting Avg.	34.2	30.9
Penalties/Yards Lost	115/931	89/757
Fumbles/Ball Lost	32/16	35/16
Touchdowns	43	43
Rushing	19	15
Passing	20	28
Returns	4	0
Avg. Time of Possession	30:55	29:05

1988 Individual Statistics

Scoring	TD R	TD P	TD Rt	PAT	FG	Saf	TP
Leahy	0	0	0	43/43	23/28	0	112
Hector	10	0	0	0/0	0/0	0	60
McNeil	6	1	0	0/0	0/0	0	42
Walker	0	7	0	0/0	0/0	0	42
Shuler	0	5	0	0/0	0/0	0	30
Toon	0	5	0	0/0	0/0	0	30
Vick	3	0	0	0/0	0/0	0	18
McMillan	0	0	2	0/0	0/0	0	12
Sohn	0	2	0	0/0	0/0	0	12
Townsell	0	0	1	0/0	0/0	0	6
Zordich	0	0	1	0/0	0/0	0	6
Lyons	0	0	0	0/0	0/0	1	2
Jets	19	20	4	43/43	23/28	1	372
Opponents	15	28	0	36/43	20/30	0	354

Passing	Att.	Comp.	Yds.	Pct.	TD	Int.	Tkld.	Rate
O'Brien	424	236	2567	55.7	15	7	37/267	78.6
Ryan	113	63	807	55.8	5	4	5/24	78.3
Hector	1	0	0	0.0	0	0	0/0	39.6
Jets	538	299	3374	55.6	20	11	42/291	78.4
Opponents	476	244	3823	51.3	28	24	45/314	76.9

Rushing	Att.	Yds.	Avg.	LG	TD
McNeil	219	944	4.3	28	6
Hector	137	561	4.1	19	10
Vick	128	540	4.2	17	3
O'Brien	21	25	1.2	17	0
Ryan	5	22	4.4	15	0
Faaola	1	13	13.0	13	0
Walker	1	12	12.0	12	0
Leahy	1	10	10.0	10	0
Toon	1	5	5.0	5	0
Jets	514	2132	4.1	28	19
Opponents	517	2124	4.1	38	15

Receiving	No.	Yds.	Avg.	LG	TD
Toon	93	1067	11.5	42	5
Shuler	70	805	11.5	42t	5
McNeil	34	288	8.5	25	1
Walker	26	551	21.2	50t	7
Hector	26	237	9.1	30	0
Vick	19	120	6.3	17	0
Griggs	14	133	9.5	21	0
Sohn	7	66	9.4	17	2
Dunn	6	67	11.2	26	0
Townsell	4	40	10.0	19	0
Jets	299	3374	11.3	50t	20
Opponents	244	3823	15.7	80t	28

Interceptions	No.	Yds.	Avg.	LG	TD
McMillan	8	168	21.0	55t	2
Hasty	5	20	4.0	16	0
Booty	3	0	0.0	0	0
Howard	2	0	0.0	0	0
Miano	2	0	0.0	0	0
Zordich	1	35	35.0	35t	1
McArthur	1	3	3.0	3	0
Benson	1	2	2.0	2	0
Humphery	1	0	0.0	0	0
Jets	24	228	9.5	55t	3
Opponents	11	126	11.5	35	0

Punting	No.	Yds.	Avg.	In 20	LG
Prokop	85	3310	38.9	26	64
Jets	85	3310	38.9	26	64
Opponents	72	2742	38.1	13	66

Punt Returns	No.	FC	Yds.	Avg.	LG	TD
Townsell	35	9	409	11.7	59t	1
Sohn	3	1	9	3.0	5	0
Jets	38	10	418	11.0	59t	1
Opponents	34	9	201	5.9	24	0

Kickoff Returns	No.	Yds.	Avg.	LG	TD
Humphery	21	510	24.3	48	0
Townsell	31	601	19.4	40	0
Sohn	9	159	17.7	27	0
Harper	7	114	16.3	32	0
Faaola	2	9	4.5	7	0
Barber	1	11	11.0	11	0
Rose	1	0	0.0	0	0
Jets	72	1404	19.5	48	0
Opponents	70	1491	21.3	56	0

Sacks	No.
Lyons	7.5
Gastineau	7.0
Rose	5.0
Mersereau	4.5
Cole	3.0
Gordon	3.0
Benson	2.0
Humphery	2.0
McArthur	2.0
Nichols	1.5
Radachowsky	1.5
Baldwin	1.0
Frase	1.0
Hasty	1.0
Howard	1.0
Garalczyk	0.5
Miano	0.5
Jets	45.0
Opponents	42.0

1989 Draft Choices

Round	Name	Pos.	College
1.	Jeff Lageman	LB	Virginia
2.	Dennis Byrd	DE	Tulsa
3.	Joe Mott	LB	Iowa
4.	Ron Stallworth	DE	Auburn
5.	Tony Martin	WR	Mesa, Colo.
6.	Marvin Washington	DE	Idaho
	Titus Dixon	WR	Troy State
7.	Stevon Moore	DB	Mississippi
8.	Anthony Brown	RB	West Virginia
9.	Pat Marlatt	DT	West Virginia
10.	Adam Bob	LB	Texas A&M
11.	Artie Holmes	DB	Washington State
12.	Willie Snead	WR	Florida

New York Jets 1989 Veteran Roster

No.	Name	Pos.	Ht.	Wt.	Birth-date	NFL Exp.	College	Hometown	How Acq.	'88 Games/ Starts
60	Alexander, Dan	G	6-4	274	6/17/55	13	Louisiana State	Houston, Tex.	D8a-'77	14/13
46	Andrews, Mitch	TE	6-2	229	3/4/64	2	Louisiana State	Houma, La.	FA-'89	0*
23	Banks, Chuck	RB	6-0	225	1/4/64	3	West Virginia Tech	Baltimore, Md.	FA-'89	0*
31	Barber, Marion	RB	6-3	228	12/6/59	8	Minnesota	Detroit, Mich.	D2-'81	16/1
54	†Benson, Troy	LB	6-2	235	7/30/63	4	Pittsburgh	Altoona, Pa.	D5a-'85	16/16
64	Bingham, Guy	C-G	6-3	260	2/25/58	10	Montana	Aberdeen, Wash.	D10-'80	10/1
42	Booty, John	CB-S	6-0	179	10/9/65	2	Texas Christian	Carthage, Tex.	D10-'88	16/0
66	Cadigan, Dave	T-G	6-4	285	4/6/65	2	Southern California	Newport Beach, Calif.	D1-'88	5/4
59	Clifton, Kyle	LB	6-4	236	8/23/62	6	Texas Christian	Bridgeport, Tex.	D3-'84	16/15
56	Cofield, Tim	LB	6-2	242	5/18/63	4	Elizabeth City State	Murfreesboro, N.C.	FA(KC)-'89#	16/15*
62	Collier, Steve	T	6-7	330	4/19/63	2	Bethune-Cookman	Chicago, Ill.	FA(GB)-'89#	0*
61	Criswell, Jeff	T-G	6-7	284	3/7/64	3	Graceland	Sully, Iowa	FA-'88	15/12
63	Curtis, Bob	LB	6-2	235	10/23/64	2	Savannah State	Jacksonville, Fla.	W(Wash)-'88	0*
65	Dodge, Kirk	LB	6-1	233	6/4/62	4	Nevada-Las Vegas	Whittier, Calif.	FA-'89	0*
80	Dunn, K.D.	TE	6-2	237	4/28/63	5	Clemson	Decatur, Ga.	FA-'88	15/2
30	Faaola, Nuu	RB	5-11	220	1/15/64	4	Hawaii	Honolulu, Hawaii	D9-'86	16/0
91	Frase, Paul	DE	6-5	273	5/5/65	2	Syracuse	Barrington, N.H.	D6-'88	16/7
55	Gordon, Alex	LB	6-5	246	9/14/64	3	Cincinnati	Jacksonville, Fla.	D2-'87	13/12
79	Haight, Mike	G-T	6-4	281	10/6/62	4	Iowa	Dyersville, Iowa	D1-'86	14/9
84	Harper, Michael	WR-KR	5-10	180	5/11/61	4	Southern California	Kansas City, Mo.	FA-'86	10/0
40	Hasty, James	CB	6-0	200	5/23/65	2	Washington State	Seattle, Wash.	D3b-'88	15/15
34	†Hector, Johnny	RB	5-11	202	11/26/60	7	Texas A&M	New Iberia, La.	D2-'83	16/1
26	Holloway, Steve	TE	6-1	235	8/23/64	2	Tennessee State	Montgomery, Ala.	FA-'89	0*
28	Howard, Carl	CB-S	6-2	190	9/20/61	6	Rutgers	Irvington, N.J.	FA-'85	16/1
48	Humphery, Bobby	CB-KR	5-10	180	8/23/61	6	New Mexico State	Lubbock, Tex.	D9-'83	16/16
44	Johnson, James	LB	6-2	240	6/21/62	2	San Diego State	Lake Elsinore, Calif.	FA-'89	0*
23	Konecny, Mark	RB-KR	6-0	200	4/23/63	3	Alma College	Muskegon, Wis.	FA(Phil)-'89#	16/0*
5	Leahy, Pat	K	6-0	196	3/19/51	16	St. Louis	St. Louis, Mo.	FA-'74	16/0
93	Lyons, Marty	DE-DT	6-5	269	1/15/57	11	Alabama	St. Petersburg, Fla.	D1-'79	16/16
15	Mackey, Kyle	QB	6-3	216	3/2/63	3	East Texas State	Alpine, Tex.	FA-'88	0*
57	†McArthur, Kevin	LB	6-2	250	5/11/63	4	Lamar	Lake Charles, La.	FA-'86	16/16
68	†McElroy, Reggie	T	6-6	276	3/4/60	7	West Texas State	Beaumont, Tex.	D2-'82	16/16
22	McMillan, Erik	S	6-2	197	5/3/65	2	Missouri	Silver Spring, Md.	D3a-'88	13/13
24	McNeil, Freeman	RB	5-11	209	4/22/59	9	UCLA	Carson, Calif.	D1-'81	16/16
94	Mersereau, Scott	DT-DE	6-3	273	4/8/65	3	Southern Connecticut	Riverhead, N.Y.	FA-'87	16/15
36	†Miano, Rich	S	6-0	200	9/3/62	5	Hawaii	Honolulu, Hawaii	D6b-'85	16/16
46	Mitchell, Michael	CB	5-9	192	10/18/61	2	Howard Payne	Waco, Tex.	FA-'88	0*
77	Nichols, Gerald	DT-DE	6-2	267	2/10/64	3	Florida State	St. Louis, Mo.	D7-'87	16/2
7	†O'Brien, Ken	QB	6-4	200	11/27/60	7	California-Davis	Sacramento, Calif.	D1-'83	14/12
6	Prokop, Joe	P	6-2	224	7/7/60	4	Cal Poly-Pomona	White Bear Lake, Minn.	FA-'88	16/0
25	Radachowsky, George	S	5-11	190	9/7/62	5	Boston College	Danbury, Conn.	FA-'87	9/3
92	Rose, Ken	LB	6-1	204	6/9/62	3	Nevada-Las Vegas	Sacramento, Calif.	FA-'87	12/0
10	Ryan, Pat	QB	6-3	210	9/16/55	12	Tennessee	Oklahoma City, Okla.	D11-'78	16/4
75	Schreiber, Adam	C-G	6-4	277	2/20/62	6	Texas	Huntsville, Ala.	FA-'88	7/0
82	†Shuler, Mickey	TE	6-3	231	8/21/56	12	Penn State	Enola, Pa.	D3-'78	15/15
53	Sweeney, Jim	C-T-G	6-4	270	8/8/62	6	Pittsburgh	Pittsburgh, Pa.	D2a-'84	16/16
88	†Toon, Al	WR	6-4	205	4/30/63	5	Wisconsin	Newport News, Va.	D1-'85	15/15
83	†Townsell, JoJo	WR-KR	5-9	180	11/4/60	5	UCLA	Reno, Nev.	D3-'85	16/0
43	Vick, Roger	RB	6-3	228	8/11/64	3	Texas A&M	Tomball, Tex.	D1-'87	16/12
58	Walker, Jackie	LB	6-5	245	11/3/62	4	Jackson State	Monroe, La.	FA(TB)-'89#	16/0*
85	Walker, Wesley	WR	6-0	182	5/26/55	13	California	Carson, Calif.	D2-'77	16/10
33	Williams, Terry	CB	5-11	197	10/14/65	2	Bethune-Cookman	Homestead, Fla.	D2-'88	8/0
76	Withycombe, Mike	G-T	6-5	295	11/18/64	2	Fresno State	Lemoore, Calif.	D5-'88	6/1

* Andrews last active with Denver in '87; Banks last active with Indianapolis in '87; Cofield played 16 games with Kansas City in '88; Collier active for 1 game with Green Bay but did not play; Curtis last active with Washington in '87; Dodge last active with Denver in '87; Holloway last active with Tampa Bay in '87; Johnson last active with San Francisco in '87; Konecny played 16 games with Philadelphia; Mackey and Mitchell missed '88 season due to injury; Walker played 16 games with Tampa Bay.

† Option playout; subject to developments.

Plan B unconditional free agent.

Retired—Robin Cole, 12-year linebacker, 16 games in '88; Bob Crable, 7-year linebacker, missed '88 season due to injury; Mark Gastineau, 10-year defensive end, 7 games in '88; Kurt Sohn, 7-year wide receiver, 15 games in '88.

Players lost through Plan B (12): DE Tom Baldwin (Det; 16 games in '88), G Ted Banker (Clev; 11), LB Onzy Elam (Wash; 4), LB John Galvin (Minn; 16), DE Mark Garalczyk (Hou; 7), CB-S Kerry Glenn (Clev; 0), LB Don Graham (Wash; 0), TE Billy Griggs (KC; 15), WR Tracy Martin (Pitt; 0), LB Matt Monger (Hou; 0), G Ralph Tamm (Wash; 0), S Mike Zordich (Phx; 16).

Also played with Jets in '88— DE Barry Bennett (1 game), LB Steve Hammond (2), TE Keith Neubert (1), G Ron Tilton (active for 1 game but did not play).

COACHING STAFF

Head Coach, Joe Walton

Pro Career: Begins seventh year as head coach of the Jets. Entered pro coaching ranks as an assistant with the New York Giants in 1969-73. Joined the Washington Redskins' staff in 1974 and became the Redskins' offensive coordinator in 1978. Originally came to the Jets as the offensive coordinator in 1981. He played professionally for the Washington Redskins 1957-60 and the New York Giants 1961-63. Walton did some radio work before joining the Giants' staff as a scout in 1967-68. Career record: 50-47-1.

Background: Played tight end for the University of Pittsburgh 1953-56.

Personal: Born December 15, 1935, in Beaver Falls, Pa. Joe and his wife, Ginger, have three children—Jodi, Stacy, and Joseph, Jr. They live in Long Island.

Assistant Coaches

Zeke Bratkowski, quarterbacks; born October 20, 1931, Danville, Ill., lives in Long Island. Quarterback Georgia 1951-53. Pro quarterback Chicago Bears 1954, 1957-60, Los Angeles Rams 1961-63, Green Bay Packers 1963-68, 1971. Pro coach: Green Bay Packers 1969-70, 1975-81, Chicago Bears 1972-74, Baltimore-Indianapolis Colts 1982-84, joined Jets in 1985.

Ray Callahan, quality control; born April 28, 1933, Lebanon, Ky., lives in Long Island. Guard-linebacker Kentucky 1952-56. No pro playing experience. College coach: Kentucky 1963-67, Cincinnati 1968-72 (head coach 1969-72). Pro coach: Baltimore Colts 1973, Florida Blazers (WFL) 1974, Chicago Bears 1975-77, Washington Redskins 1978-80, Houston Oilers 1981-82, joined Jets in 1983.

Wally Chambers, defensive line; born May 15, 1951, Phenix City, Ala., lives in Long Island. Defensive lineman Eastern Kentucky 1969-72. Pro defensive lineman Chicago Bears 1973-77, Tampa Bay Buccaneers 1978-79. College coach: Northern Iowa 1983-84, East Carolina 1985-86, Temple 1987. Pro coach: Joined Jets in 1988.

Mike Faulkiner, secondary; born March 27, 1947, Cameron, W. Va., lives in Long Island. Quarterback-defensive back West Virginia Tech 1967-70. No pro playing experience. College coach: Eastern Illinois 1981. Pro coach: Toronto Argonauts (CFL) 1979, New York Giants 1980, Montreal Alouettes (CFL) 1982, joined Jets in 1983.

Bobby Hammond, running backs; born February 20, 1952, Orangeburg, S.C., lives in New York. Running back Morgan State 1973-75. Pro running back New York Giants 1976-79, Washington Redskins 1979-80. Pro coach: Joined Jets in 1983.

Ralph Hawkins, defensive coordinator; born May 4, 1935, Washington, D.C., lives in Long Island. Quarterback-defensive back Maryland 1953-55. No pro playing experience. College coach: Maryland 1959, 1967, Southern Methodist 1961, Kentucky 1962-65, Army 1966, Cincinnati 1968. Pro coach: Buffalo Bills 1969-71, 1981-82, Washington Redskins 1973-77, Baltimore Colts 1978, New York Giants 1979-80, Seattle Seahawks 1983-88, joined Jets in 1989.

Rod Humenuik, offensive line; born June 17, 1938, Detroit, Mich., lives in Long Island. Guard Southern California 1956-58. Pro guard Winnipeg Blue Bombers (CFL) 1960-62. College coach: Fullerton, Calif., J.C. 1964-65, Southern California 1966-70, Cal State-Northridge 1971-72 (head coach). Pro coach: Toronto Argonauts (CFL) 1973-74, Cleveland Browns 1975-82, Kansas City Chiefs 1983-84, New England 1985-88, joined Jets in 1989.

Rich Kotite, offensive coordinator-receivers; born October 13, 1942, Brooklyn, N.Y., lives in Staten Island. End Wagner 1963-65. Pro tight end New York Giants 1967, 1969-72, Pittsburgh Steelers 1968. College coach: Tennessee-Chattanooga 1973-76. Pro coach: New Orleans Saints 1977, Cleveland Browns 1978-82, joined Jets in 1983.

New York Jets 1989 First-Year Roster

Name	Pos.	Ht.	Wt.	Birth-date	College	Hometown	How Acq.
Amoia, Vince (1)	RB	5-10	210	3/30/63	Arizona State	Buffalo, N.Y.	FA
Beach, Sanjay (1)	WR	6-0	189	2/21/66	Colorado State	Chandler, Ariz.	FA
Bob, Adam	LB	6-2	240	10/30/67	Texas A&M	Lafayette, La.	D10
Brown, A.B.	RB	5-9	210	12/4/65	West Virginia	Salem, N.J.	D8
Bryant, Kevin (1)	CB	6-1	215	4/19/65	Delaware State	Passaic, N.J.	FA
Byrd, Dennis	DE	6-5	270	10/5/66	Tulsa	Mustang, Okla.	D2
Caldwell, Ralph (1)	LB	6-2	245	1/18/62	Indiana	Los Angeles, Calif.	FA
Davis, Jeff (1)	LB	6-2	230	1/19/66	Nevada-Reno	Reno, Nev.	FA
Dixon, Titus	WR-KR	5-6	152	6/15/66	Troy State	Clewiston, Fla.	D6b
Endre, Pete (1)	G	6-3	247	9/7/66	Indiana State	Mt. Prospect, Ill.	FA
Gloster, Keith	WR	5-11	174	12/30/64	Temple	Edgewood, N.J.	FA
Grabisna, Erwin (1)	DT	6-2	251	8/27/66	Case Western	Parma, Ohio	FA
Hammond, Darryl (1)	CB	6-1	206	9/24/66	Virginia	Tappahannock, Va.	FA
Hammond, Steve (1)	LB	6-4	225	2/5/60	Wake Forest	Merrick, N.Y.	FA
Harris, Gregg (1)	G	6-2	272	4/8/66	Wake Forest	Norfolk, Va.	FA
Hawkins, Roland (1)	WR	5-10	176	10/24/64	Oregon State	San Diego, Calif.	FA
Holmes, Artie (1)	S	5-11	205	4/27/66	Washington State	Rialto, Calif.	D11
Holmes, Carl	T	6-5	290	5/29/65	Temple	Philadelphia, Pa.	FA
Howard, Bryan (1)	G	6-4	271	1/11/64	Kansas	Woodland Hills, Calif.	FA
Jarvis, Ralph (1)	DE	6-4	252	6/1/65	Temple	Glen Mills, Pa.	FA
Jenkins, DeShon (1)	S	6-0	192	12/19/64	N.W. Louisiana	Jena, La.	FA
Jones, Chris (1)	WR	6-1	186	8/5/64	N.E. Louisiana	Lake Charles, La.	FA
Lageman, Jeff	LB	6-5	250	7/18/67	Virginia	Great Falls, Va.	D1
Lockley, Andre (1)	T	6-5	286	9/15/65	Tulane	Franklin, La.	FA
Marlatt, Pat	DT	6-5	270	5/3/66	West Virginia	Princeton, N.J.	D9
Martin, Tony	WR	6-0	180	9/5/65	Mesa, Colo.	Miami, Fla.	D5
Mason, Bob (1)	LB	6-1	256	9/3/65	Ithaca	Wakefield, Mass.	FA
McDowell, Willard (1)	DE	6-4	250	9/16/65	Norwich	Teaneck, N.J.	FA
Moore, Stevon	CB	5-11	205	2/9/67	Mississippi	Wiggins, Mich.	D7
Mott, Joe	LB	6-4	253	10/6/65	Iowa	Endicott, N.Y.	D3
Negrin, Rich (1)	G	6-2	266	5/29/66	Wagner	Edison, N.J.	FA
Neubert, Keith (1)	TE	6-5	250	9/13/64	Nebraska	Fort Atkinson, Wis.	D8-'88
Neubert, Steve	S	6-0	200	11/29/65	Morningside	Fort Atkinson, Wis.	FA
Newman, Teddy	LB	6-2	234	7/21/65	Kansas	Las Vegas, Nev.	FA
Oliver, Jeff (1)	G	6-3	274	7/28/65	Boston College	Delhi, N.Y.	FA
Pearson, Darryl (1)	WR	6-2	198	3/6/66	Alabama State	Silas, Ala.	FA
Possenti, Joe (1)	LB	6-3	235	7/20/65	Temple	Aston, Pa.	FA
Riley, Bobby (1)	WR	5-8	168	10/17/64	Oklahoma State	Stroud, Okla.	FA-'88
Schonyers, Toren (1)	LB	6-1	215	1/2/65	Temple	Burlington, N.J.	FA
Sellers, Danny	LB	6-2	230	6/12/65	Cincinnati	Cincinnati, Ohio	FA
Snead, Willie	WR	5-11	190	9/3/66	Florida	Belle Glade, Fla.	D12
Stallworth, Ron	DE	6-5	262	2/25/66	Auburn	Pensacola, Fla.	D4
Sterling, Rob (1)	S	5-11	195	2/11/66	Maine	Silver Spring, Md.	FA
Tanner, Randy (1)	WR	5-9	193	1/29/66	Southern California	La Puente, Calif.	FA
Washington, Marvin	DE	6-6	260	10/22/65	Idaho	Dallas, Tex.	D6a
Whitehurst, Clay (1)	WR	5-11	195	12/20/65	Alabama	Brentwood, Tenn.	FA
Wilkinson, Neal (1)	TE	6-4	230	10/2/64	James Madison	Alexandria, Va.	FA

The term NFL Rookie is defined as a player who is in his first season of professional football and has not been on the roster of another professional football team for any regular-season or postseason games. A Rookie is designated by an "R" on NFL rosters. Players who have been active in another professional football league or players who have NFL experience, including either preseason training camp or being on an active roster for fewer than three regular-season or postseason games, are termed NFL First-Year Players. An NFL First-Year Player is designated by a "1" on NFL rosters. Thereafter, a player on an NFL active roster for at least three regular-season or postseason games is credited with an additional year of NFL playing experience.

NOTES

Larry Pasquale, special teams; born April 21, 1941, Brooklyn, N.Y., lives in Long Island. Quarterback Bridgeport 1961-63. No pro playing experience. College coach: Slippery Rock State 1967, Boston University 1968, Navy 1969-70, Massachusetts 1971-75, Idaho State 1976. Pro coach: Montreal Alouettes (CFL) 1977-78, Detroit Lions 1979, joined Jets in 1980.

Jim Vechiarella, linebackers; born February 20, 1937, Youngstown, Ohio, lives in Long Island. Linebacker Youngstown State 1955-57. No pro playing experience. College coach: Youngstown State 1964-74, Southern Illinois 1976-77, Tulane 1978-80. Pro coach: Charlotte Hornets (WFL) 1975, Los Angeles Rams 1981-82, Kansas City Chiefs 1983-85, joined Jets in 1986.

American Football Conference Central Division

Team Colors: Black and Gold

Three Rivers Stadium
300 Stadium Circle
Pittsburgh, Pennsylvania 15212
Telephone: (412) 323-1200

Club Officials

President: Daniel M. Rooney
Vice President: John R. McGinley
Vice President: Arthur J. Rooney, Jr.
Director of Communications and Business: Joe Gordon
Controller: Ralph Meacham
Chief Negotiator: James A. Boston
Office Manager-Stadium: Dan Ferens
Public Relations Director: Dan Edwards
Publicity Director: Pat Hanlon
Director of Player Personnel: Dick Haley
Director of Pro Personnel and Development: Tom Donahoe
College Scouting Coordinator: Tom Modrak
Talent Scout-West: Bob Schmitz
Talent Scout-Midwest: Jesse Kaye
Director of Ticket Sales: Geraldine R. Glenn
Computer Director-Accounting: Jim Ellenberger
Trainers: Ralph Berlin, Francis Feld
Equipment Manager: Anthony Parisi

Stadium: Three Rivers Stadium • **Capacity:** 59,000
300 Stadium Circle
Pittsburgh, Pennsylvania 15212

Playing Surface: AstroTurf

Training Camp: St. Vincent College
Latrobe, Pennsylvania 15650

1989 Schedule

Preseason

Aug. 12	**Washington**	8:00
Aug. 19	at Cleveland	7:30
Aug. 26	at Philadelphia	7:30
Sept. 2	at New York Giants	8:00

Regular Season

Sept. 10	**Cleveland**	4:00
Sept. 17	at Cincinnati	1:00
Sept. 24	**Minnesota**	1:00
Oct. 1	at Detroit	1:00
Oct. 8	**Cincinnati**	1:00
Oct. 15	at Cleveland	4:00
Oct. 22	at Houston	12:00
Oct. 29	**Kansas City**	1:00
Nov. 5	at Denver	2:00
Nov. 12	**Chicago**	1:00
Nov. 19	**San Diego**	1:00
Nov. 26	at Miami	1:00
Dec. 3	**Houston**	1:00
Dec. 10	at New York Jets	1:00
Dec. 17	**New England**	1:00
Dec. 24	at Tampa Bay	1:00

Steelers Coaching History

Pittsburgh Pirates 1933-40
(344-387-20)

1933	Forrest (Jap) Douds	3-6-2
1934	Luby DiMelio	2-10-0
1935-36	Joe Bach	10-14-0
1937-39	Johnny Blood (McNally)*	6-19-0
1939-40	Walt Kiesling	3-13-3
1941	Bert Bell**	0-2-0
	Aldo (Buff) Donelli***	0-5-0
1941-44	Walt Kiesling****	13-20-2
1945	Jim Leonard	2-8-0
1946-47	Jock Sutherland	13-10-1
1948-51	Johnny Michelosen	20-26-2
1952-53	Joe Bach	11-13-0
1954-56	Walt Kiesling	14-22-0
1957-64	Raymond (Buddy) Parker	51-47-6
1965	Mike Nixon	2-12-0
1966-68	Bill Austin	11-28-3
1969-88	Chuck Noll	183-132-1

*Released after three games in 1939
**Resigned after two games in 1941
***Released after five games in 1941
****Co-coach with Earle (Greasy) Neale in Philadelphia-Pittsburgh merger in 1943 and with Phil Handler in Chicago Cardinals-Pittsburgh merger in 1944

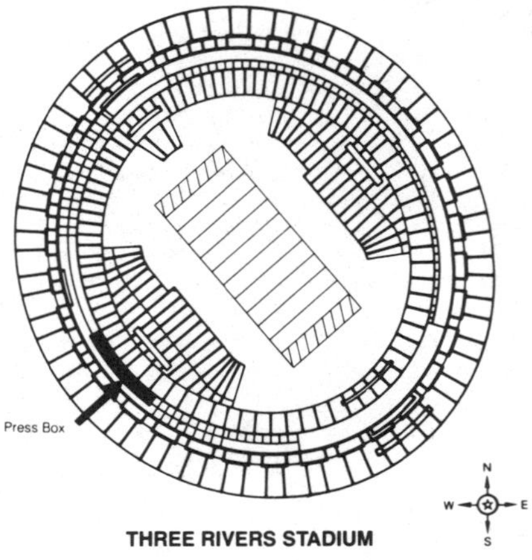

THREE RIVERS STADIUM

Record Holders

Individual Records—Career

Category	Name	Performance
Rushing (Yds.)	Franco Harris, 1972-1983	11,950
Passing (Yds.)	Terry Bradshaw, 1970-1983	27,989
Passing (TDs)	Terry Bradshaw, 1970-1983	212
Receiving (No.)	John Stallworth, 1974-1987	537
Receiving (Yds.)	John Stallworth, 1974-1987	8,723
Interceptions	Mel Blount, 1970-1983	57
Punting (Avg.)	Bobby Joe Green, 1960-61	45.7
Punt Return (Avg.)	Bobby Gage, 1949-1950	14.9
Kickoff Return (Avg.)	Lynn Chandnois, 1950-56	29.6
Field Goals	Gary Anderson, 1982-88	165
Touchdowns (Tot.)	Franco Harris, 1972-1983	100
Points	Roy Gerela, 1971-78	731

Individual Records—Single Season

Category	Name	Performance
Rushing (Yds.)	Franco Harris, 1975	1,246
Passing (Yds.)	Terry Bradshaw, 1979	3,724
Passing (TDs)	Terry Bradshaw, 1978	28
Receiving (No.)	John Stallworth, 1984	80
Receiving (Yds.)	John Stallworth, 1984	1,395
Interceptions	Mel Blount, 1975	11
Punting (Avg.)	Bobby Joe Green, 1961	47.0
Punt Return (Avg.)	Bobby Gage, 1949	16.0
Kickoff Return (Avg.)	Lynn Chandnois, 1952	35.2
Field Goals	Gary Anderson, 1985	33
Touchdowns (Tot.)	Louis Lipps, 1985	15
Points	Gary Anderson, 1985	139

Individual Records—Single Game

Category	Name	Performance
Rushing (Yds.)	John Fuqua, 12-20-70	218
Passing (Yds.)	Bobby Layne, 12-3-58	409
Passing (TDs)	Terry Bradshaw, 11-15-81	5
	Mark Malone, 9-8-85	5
Receiving (No.)	J.R. Wilburn, 10-22-67	12
Receiving (Yds.)	Buddy Dial, 10-22-61	235
Interceptions	Jack Butler, 12-13-53	*4
Field Goals	Gary Anderson, 10-23-88	6
Touchdowns (Tot.)	Ray Mathews, 10-17-54	4
	Roy Jefferson, 11-3-68	4
Points	Ray Mathews, 10-17-54	24
	Roy Jefferson, 11-3-68	24

*NFL Record

1988 Team Record

Preseason (3-1)

Date	Result		Opponents
8/5	W	44-31	at Washington
8/14	W	21-16	Philadelphia
8/20	L	17-28	at N.Y. Giants
8/27	W	31-28	at New Orleans
		113-103	

Regular Season (5-11)

Date	Result		Opponents	Att.
9/4	W	24-21	Dallas	56,813
9/11	L	29-30	at Washington	54,083
9/18	L	12-17	Cincinnati	56,647
9/25	L	28-36	at Buffalo	78,735
10/2	L	9-23	Cleveland	56,410
10/9	L	14-31	at Phoenix	53,278
10/16	L	14-34	Houston	52,229
10/23	W	39-21	Denver	49,811
10/30	L	20-24	at N.Y. Jets	64,862
11/6	L	7-42	at Cincinnati	56,403
11/13	L	26-27	Philadelphia	46,026
11/20	L	7-27	at Cleveland	77,131
11/27	W	16-10	Kansas City	42,057
12/4	W	37-34	at Houston	47,791
12/11	L	14-20	at San Diego	33,816
12/18	W	40-24	Miami	36,051

Score by Periods

Steelers	85	94	47	110	0	—	336
Opponents	64	138	103	116	0	—	421

Attendance

Home 396,044 Away 466,099 Total 862,143
Single-game home record, 59,541 (9-30-85)
Single-season home record, 462,567 (1983)

1988 Team Statistics

	Steelers	Opp.
Total First Downs	292	319
Rushing	120	110
Passing	150	181
Penalty	22	28
Third Down: Made/Att.	78/216	98/225
Fourth Down: Made/Att.	5/17	4/13
Total Net Yards	5204	5805
Avg. Per Game	325.3	362.8
Total Plays	1030	1067
Avg. Per Play	5.1	5.4
Net Yards Rushing	2228	1864
Avg. Per Game	139.3	116.5
Total Rushes	499	516
Net Yards Passing	2976	3941
Avg. Per Game	186.0	246.3
Sacked/Yards Lost	42/331	19/145
Gross Yards	3307	4086
Att./Completions	489/226	532/309
Completion Pct.	46.2	58.1
Had Intercepted	20	20
Punts/Avg.	71/41.5	67/40.7
Net Punting Avg.	32.8	35.0
Penalties/Yards Lost	99/803	79/705
Fumbles/Ball Lost	40/19	35/13
Touchdowns	36	49
Rushing	17	20
Passing	15	25
Returns	4	4
Avg. Time of Possession	28:31	31:29

1988 Individual Statistics

Scoring	TD R	TD P	TD Rt	PAT	FG	Saf	TP
Anderson	0	0	0	34/35	28/36	0	118
Brister	6	0	0	0/0	0/0	0	36
Hoge	3	3	0	0/0	0/0	0	36
Lipps	1	5	0	0/0	0/0	0	36
Carter	3	2	0	0/0	0/0	0	30
E. Jackson	3	0	0	0/0	0/0	0	18
Stone	0	1	1	0/0	0/0	0	12
Blackledge	1	0	0	0/0	0/0	0	6
Gothard	0	1	0	0/0	0/0	0	6
Jordan	0	0	1	0/0	0/0	0	6
Lockett	0	1	0	0/0	0/0	0	6
Thompson	0	1	0	0/0	0/0	0	6
W. Williams	0	1	0	0/0	0/0	0	6
Woodruff	0	0	1	0/0	0/0	0	6
Woodson	0	0	1	0/0	0/0	0	6
Steelers	17	15	4	34/36	28/36	1	336
Opponents	20	25	4	47/49	26/32	1	421

Passing	Att.	Comp.	Yds.	Pct.	TD	Int.	Tkld.	Rate
Brister	370	175	2634	47.3	11	14	36/292	65.3
Blackledge	79	38	494	48.1	2	3	4/25	60.8
Bono	35	10	110	28.6	1	2	1/8	25.9
Carter	3	2	56	66.7	0	0	0/0	109.7
Lipps	2	1	13	50.0	1	1	1/6	70.8
Steelers	489	226	3307	46.2	15	20	42/331	62.0
Opponents	532	309	4086	58.1	25	20	19/145	82.5

Rushing	Att.	Yds.	Avg.	LG	TD
Hoge	170	705	4.1	20	3
W. Williams	87	409	4.7	33	0
E. Jackson	74	315	4.3	29t	3
Carter	36	216	6.0	64t	3
Brister	45	209	4.6	20	6
Lipps	6	129	21.5	39t	1
Stone	40	127	3.2	11	0
Pollard	31	93	3.0	7	0
Blackledge	8	25	3.1	10	1
Newsome	2	0	0.0	0	0
Steelers	499	2228	4.5	64t	17
Opponents	516	1864	3.6	64	20

Receiving	No.	Yds.	Avg.	LG	TD
Lipps	50	973	19.5	89t	5
Hoge	50	487	9.7	40	3
Carter	32	363	11.3	33	2
Lockett	22	365	16.6	44	1
Thompson	16	370	23.1	50	1
Gothard	12	121	10.1	26	1
Stone	11	196	17.8	72t	1
W. Williams	11	66	6.0	21	1
Tr. Johnson	10	237	23.7	60	0
E. Jackson	9	84	9.3	24	0
Pollard	2	22	11.0	19	0
Hinnant	1	23	23.0	23	0
Steelers	226	3307	14.6	89t	15
Opponents	309	4086	13.2	86t	25

Interceptions	No.	Yds.	Avg.	LG	TD
Woodruff	4	109	27.3	78t	1
Woodson	4	98	24.5	29	0
Everett	3	31	10.3	29	0
Griffin	2	63	31.5	33	0
Jordan	1	28	28.0	28t	1
Carr	1	27	27.0	27	0
Gowdy	1	24	24.0	24	0
Hinkle	1	1	1.0	1	0
Little	1	0	0.0	0	0
Nickerson	1	0	0.0	0	0
Sanchez	1	0	0.0	0	0
Steelers	20	381	19.1	78t	2
Opponents	20	367	18.4	75t	1

Punting	No.	Yds.	Avg.	In 20	LG
Newsome	65	2950	45.4	9	62
Steelers	71	2950	41.5	9	62
Opponents	67	2726	40.7	16	63

Punt Returns	No.	FC	Yds.	Avg.	LG	TD
Woodson	33	6	281	8.5	28	0
Lipps	4	2	30	7.5	11	0
Sanchez	2	4	11	5.5	6	0
Steelers	39	12	322	8.3	28	0
Opponents	40	9	418	10.5	32	0

Kickoff Returns	No.	Yds.	Avg.	LG	TD
Woodson	37	850	23.0	92t	1
Stone	29	610	21.0	92t	1
Sanchez	4	71	17.8	19	0
Blankenship	1	5	5.0	5	0
Boyle	1	19	19.0	19	0
J. Jackson	1	10	10.0	10	0
W. Williams	1	10	10.0	10	0
Steelers	74	1575	21.3	92t	2
Opponents	63	1351	21.4	90t	1

Sacks	No.
Ti. Johnson	4.0
Carr	3.5
Nickerson	3.5
G. Williams	3.5
Jones	1.5
Reese	1.0
Hinkle	0.5
Lloyd	0.5
Thomas	0.5
Woodson	0.5
Steelers	19.0
Opponents	42.0

1989 Draft Choices

Round	Name	Pos.	College
1.	Tim Worley	RB	Georgia
	Tom Ricketts	T	Pittsburgh
2.	Carnell Lake	DB	UCLA
3.	Derek Hill	WR	Arizona
4.	Jerrol Williams	LB	Purdue
5.	David Arnold	DB	Michigan
6.	Mark Stock	WR	Virginia Military
7.	David Johnson	DB	Kentucky
8.	Chris Asbeck	NT	Cincinnati
9.	A.J. Jenkins	DE	Cal State-Fullerton
10.	Jerry Olsavsky	LB	Pittsburgh
11.	Brian Slater	WR	Washington
12.	Carlton Haselrig	DE	Pittsburgh

Pittsburgh Steelers 1989 Veteran Roster

No.	Name	Pos.	Ht.	Wt.	Birth-date	NFL Exp.	College	Hometown	How Acq.	'88 Games/ Starts
1	Anderson, Gary	K	5-11	175	7/16/59	8	Syracuse	Durban, South Africa	W(Buff)-'82	16/0
72	Aydelette, Buddy	T	6-4	262	8/19/56	3	Alabama	Mobile, Ala.	W(Minn)-'87	0*
14	Blackledge, Todd	QB	6-3	227	2/25/61	7	Penn State	Canton, Ohio	T(KC)-'88	3/3
60	Blankenship, Brian	G-C	6-1	275	4/7/63	3	Nebraska	Omaha, Neb.	FA-'87	13/12
6	Brister, Bubby	QB	6-3	205	8/15/62	4	Northeast Louisiana	Alexandria, La.	D3-'86	13/13
91	Carr, Gregg	LB	6-2	222	3/31/62	5	Auburn	Birmingham, Ala.	D6-'85	13/5
24	Carter, Rodney	RB	6-0	216	10/30/64	3	Purdue	Elizabeth, N.J.	D7-'86	14/1
40	Davis, Elgin	RB	5-10	192	10/23/65	3	Central Florida	Jacksonville, Fla.	FA-(NE)-'89#	5/0*
63	Dawson, Dermontti	G-C	6-2	271	6/17/65	2	Kentucky	Lexington, Ky.	D2-'88	8/5
27	Everett, Thomas	S	5-9	179	11/21/64	3	Baylor	Daingerfield, Tex.	D4-'87	14/12
68	Freeman, Lorenzo	NT	6-5	298	5/23/64	3	Pittsburgh	East Camden, N.J.	FA-'87	13/2
92	Gary, Keith	DE	6-3	268	9/14/59	7	Oklahoma	Fairfax, Va.	D1-'81	15/9
86	Gothard, Preston	TE	6-4	235	2/23/62	4	Alabama	Montgomery, Ala.	FA-'85	16/15
29	Gowdy, Cornell	S	6-1	202	10/2/63	4	Morgan State	Seat Pleasant, Md.	FA-'87	16/14
22	Griffin, Larry	CB	6-0	200	1/11/63	4	North Carolina	Chesapeake, Va.	FA-'87	15/3
35	Hall, Delton	CB-S	6-1	205	1/16/65	3	Clemson	Greensboro, N.C.	D2-'87	14/4
53	Hinkle, Bryan	LB	6-2	222	6/4/59	8	Oregon	Silverdale, Wash.	D6-'81	13/13
81	Hinnant, Mike	TE	6-3	258	9/8/66	2	Temple	Washington, D.C.	D8b-'88	16/1
33	Hoge, Merril	RB	6-2	226	1/26/65	3	Idaho State	Pocatello, Idaho	D10-'87	16/8
62	Ilkin, Tunch	T	6-3	266	9/23/57	10	Indiana State	Highland Park, Ill.	D6-'80	16/16
65	Jackson, John	T	6-6	282	1/4/65	2	Eastern Kentucky	Cincinnati, Ohio	D10-'88	16/0
88	Johnson, Jason	WR	5-11	180	11/8/65	2	Illinois State	Gary, Ind.	FA(Den)-'89#	8/0*
78	Johnson, Tim	DE-NT	6-3	261	1/29/65	3	Penn State	Sarasota, Fla.	D6-'87	15/12
85	†Johnson, Troy	WR	6-1	185	10/20/62	4	Southern University	Houma, La.	FA-'88	14/0
97	Jones, Aaron	DE-LB	6-5	257	12/18/66	2	Eastern Kentucky	Apopka, Fla.	D1-'88	15/12
55	Jordan, Darin	LB-DE	6-1	235	12/4/64	2	Northeastern	Stroughton, Mass.	D5a-'88	15/2
51	Lanza, Chuck	C	6-2	263	9/20/64	2	Notre Dame	Germantown, Tenn.	D3-'88	16/0
21	Lee, Greg	CB	6-1	207	1/15/65	2	Arkansas State	Pine Bluff, Ark.	FA-'88	16/0
83	†Lipps, Louis	WR-KR	5-10	190	8/9/62	6	Southern Mississippi	Reserve, La.	D1-'84	16/16
50	Little, David	LB	6-1	230	1/3/59	9	Florida	Miami, Fla.	D7-'81	16/14
95	Lloyd, Greg	LB	6-2	224	5/26/65	2	Fort Valley State	Fort Valley, Ga.	D6-'87	9/4
89	Lockett, Charles	WR	6-0	181	10/1/65	3	Long Beach State	Los Angeles, Calif.	D3-'87	16/5
74	†Long, Terry	G	5-11	275	7/21/59	6	East Carolina	Columbia, S.C.	D4-'84	12/11
19	Martin, Tracy	WR	6-3	205	12/4/64	2	North Dakota	Minneapolis, Minn.	FA(NYJ)-'89#	0*
84	Mularkey, Mike	TE	6-4	238	11/19/61	7	Florida	Ft. Lauderdale, Fla.	FA(Minn)-'89#	16/0*
18	Newsome, Harry	P	6-0	188	1/25/63	5	Wake Forest	Cheraw, S.C.	D8-'85	16/0
54	Nickerson, Hardy	LB	6-2	229	9/1/65	3	California	Los Angeles, Calif.	D5-'87	15/10
76	Putzier, Rollin	NT	6-4	281	12/10/65	2	Oregon	Coeur d'Alene, Idaho	FA-'88	5/0
64	Reese, Jerry	DE	6-2	267	7/11/64	2	Kentucky	Hopkinsville, Ky.	D5b-'88	15/0
23	Richard, Gary	CB-S	5-10	176	10/9/65	2	Pittsburgh	Denver, Colo.	FA(GB)-'89#	10/0*
79	Rienstra, John	G	6-5	268	3/22/63	4	Temple	Colorado Springs, Colo.	D1-'86	5/4
56	Smith, Vinson	LB	6-2	230	7/3/65	2	East Carolina	Statesville, N.C.	FA(Atl)-'89#	3/0*
94	Stedman, Troy	LB	6-3	243	5/19/65	2	Washburn	Cedar Falls, Iowa	FA(KC)-'89#	5/0*
20	Stone, Dwight	RB-KR	6-0	188	1/28/64	3	Middle Tennessee State	Florala, Ala.	FA-'87	16/6
90	Stowe, Tyronne	LB	6-1	236	5/30/65	3	Rutgers	Passaic, N.J.	FA-'88	10/4
43	Wallace, Ray	RB	6-0	230	12/3/63	3	Purdue	Indianapolis, Ind.	FA(Hou)-'89#	0*
98	Williams, Gerald	NT	6-3	262	9/3/63	4	Auburn	Lanett, Ala.	D2-'86	16/16
42	Williams, Warren	RB	6-0	202	7/29/65	2	Miami	Ft. Myers, Fla.	D6-'88	15/8
93	Willis, Keith	DE	6-1	263	7/29/59	7	Northeastern	Newark, N.J.	FA-'82	0*
73	†Wolfley, Craig	T-G	6-1	269	5/19/58	10	Syracuse	Buffalo, N.Y.	D5-'80	16/16
49	Woodruff, Dwayne	CB	6-0	198	2/18/57	10	Louisville	New Richmond, Ohio	D6-'79	14/13
26	Woodson, Rod	CB-KR	6-0	199	3/10/65	3	Purdue	Ft. Wayne, Ind.	D1-'87	16/16

* Aydelette, Wallace, and Willis missed '88 season due to injury; Davis played 5 games with New England in '88; Jason Johnson played 8 games with Denver; Martin played 12 games with N.Y. Jets; Mularkey played 16 games with Minnesota; Richard played 10 games with Green Bay; Smith played 3 games with Atlanta; Stedman played 5 games with Kansas City.

† Option playout; subject to developments.

Plan B unconditional free agent.

Players lost through Plan B (3): LB Anthony Henton (Sea; 16 games in '88), TE Jeff Markland (Mia; 1), C Mike Webster (KC; 16).

Also played with Steelers in '88—QB Steve Bono (2 games), T Jim Boyle (6), WR Joey Clinkscales (4), RB Earnest Jackson (12), RB Frank Pollard (10), CB-S Lupe Sanchez (16), DE Ben Thomas (8), WR Weegie Thompson (16).

COACHING STAFF

Head Coach, Chuck Noll

Pro Career: Became only NFL coach to win four Super Bowls when Steelers defeated Los Angeles Rams 31-19 in Super Bowl XIV. Put together 13 consecutive non-losing seasons and has guided Steelers into postseason play 11 of last 17 years. Led Pittsburgh to consecutive NFL championships twice (1974-75, 1978-79). With 183 career wins, is second among active NFL coaches behind Don Shula (277). Has tenth-highest winning percentage (.581) among active coaches and is fifth among the NFL's all-time winningest coaches with a 183-132-1 career record. Noll is one of only four coaches in NFL history to lead a team for 20 consecutive seasons—Curly Lambeau (29), Tom Landry (29), and Steve Owen (23) are the others. Played pro football as guard-linebacker for Cleveland Browns from 1953-59. At age 28, he started coaching career as defensive coach with Los Angeles (San Diego) Chargers in 1960. Left after 1965 season to become Shula's defensive backfield coach in Baltimore. Remained with Colts until taking over Pittsburgh reins as head coach in 1969. Career record: 183-132-1.

Background: Was an all-state star at Benedictine High in Cleveland. Captained the University of Dayton team, playing both tackle and linebacker. He was drafted by the Browns in 1953.

Personal: Born in Cleveland on January 5, 1932. He and his wife, Marianne, live in Pittsburgh and have one son—Chris.

Assistant Coaches

Ron Blackledge, offensive line; born April 15, 1938, Canton, Ohio, lives in Pittsburgh. Tight end-defensive end Bowling Green 1957-59. No pro playing experience. College coach: Ashland 1968-69, Cincinnati 1970-72, Kentucky 1973-75, Princeton 1976, Kent State 1977-81 (head coach 1979-81). Pro coach: Joined Steelers in 1982.

Dave Brazil, linebackers; born March 25, 1936, Detroit Mich., lives in Pittsburgh. No college or pro playing experience. College coach: Holy Cross 1968-69, Tulsa 1970-71, Eastern Michigan 1972-74, Boston College 1978-79, Kent State 1980-82. Pro coach: Detroit Wheel (WFL) 1975, Chicago Fire (WFL) 1976, Kansas City Chiefs 1984-88, joined Steelers in 1989.

John Fox, defensive backs; born February 8, 1955, Virginia Beach, Va., lives in Pittsburgh. Defensive back San Diego State 1975-77. No pro playing experience. College coach: U.S. International 1979, Boise State 1980, Long Beach State 1981, Utah 1982, Kansas 1983, 1985, Iowa State 1984, Pittsburgh 1986-88. Pro coach: Los Angeles Express (USFL) 1985, joined Steelers in 1989.

Joe Greene, defensive line; born September 24, 1946, Temple, Tex., lives in Pittsburgh. Defensive tackle North Texas State 1966-68. Pro defensive tackle Pittsburgh Steelers 1969-81. Inducted into Pro Football Hall of Fame in 1987. Pro coach: Joined Steelers in 1987.

Dick Hoak, offensive backfield; born December 8, 1939, Jeannette, Pa., lives in Greensburg, Pa. Halfback-quarterback Penn State 1958-60. Pro running back Pittsburgh Steelers 1961-70. Pro coach: Joined Steelers in 1972.

Jon Kolb, strength and conditioning coordinator; born August 30, 1947, Ponca City, Okla., lives in Pittsburgh. Center-linebacker Oklahoma State 1966-68. Pro tackle Pittsburgh Steelers 1969-81. Pro coach: Joined Steelers in 1982.

Tom Moore, offensive coordinator; born November 7, 1938, Owatonna, Minn., lives in Pittsburgh. Quarterback Iowa 1957-60. No pro playing experience. College coach: Iowa 1961-62, Dayton 1965-68, Wake Forest 1969, Georgia Tech 1970-71, Minnesota 1972-73, 1975-76. Pro coach: New York Stars (WFL) 1974, joined Steelers in 1977.

Dwain Painter, receivers; born February 13, 1942, Monroeville, Pa., lives in Pittsburgh. Quarterback-defensive back Rutgers 1961-64. No pro playing experience. College coach: San Jose State 1971-72, College of San Mateo 1973, Brigham Young 1974-75, UCLA 1976-78, Northern Arizona 1979-81 (head coach), Georgia Tech 1982-85, Texas 1986, Illinois 1987. Pro coach: Joined Steelers in 1988.

Rod Rust, defensive coordinator; born February 8, 1928, Webster City, Iowa, lives in Pittsburgh. Center-linebacker Iowa State 1947-49. No pro playing experience. College coach: New Mexico 1960-62, Stanford 1963-66, North Texas State 1967-72 (head coach). Pro coach: Montreal Alouettes (CFL) 1973-75, Philadelphia Eagles 1976-77, Kansas City Chiefs 1978-82, 1988, New England Patriots 1983-87, joined Steelers in 1989.

George Stewart, special teams; born December 29, 1958, Little Rock, Ark., lives in Pittsburgh. Guard Arkansas 1977-80. No pro playing experience. College coach: Minnesota 1984-85, Notre Dame 1986-88. Pro coach: Joined Steelers in 1989.

Pittsburgh Steelers 1989 First-Year Roster

Name	Pos.	Ht.	Wt.	Birth-date	College	Hometown	How Acq.
Arnold, David	CB-S	6-3	194	11/21/66	Michigan	Warren, Ohio	D5
Asbeck, Chris	NT	6-3	275	4/29/67	Cincinnati	Columbus, Ohio	D8
Haselrig, Carlton	NT	6-1	273	1/22/66	Pittsburgh-Johnstown	Johnstown, Pa.	D12
Hill, Derek	WR	6-1	189	11/4/67	Arizona	Carson, Calif.	D3
Jenkins, A.J.	DE	6-2	237	4/12/66	Cal State-Fullerton	Havelock, N.C.	D9
Johnson, Alvin	WR	5-10	185	11/22/65	Central Missouri State	Tulsa, Okla.	FA
Johnson, David	CB	6-0	190	7/14/66	Kentucky	Louisville, Ky.	D7
Kovach, Robert	G	6-3	275	6/7/66	West Virginia	New Castle, Pa.	FA
Lake, Carnell	S	6-1	204	7/15/67	UCLA	Inglewood, Calif.	D2
Nelson, Kevin	WR	5-9	183	1/16/66	Texas	Sugar Land, Tex.	FA
Olsavsky, Jerry	LB	6-1	217	3/29/67	Pittsburgh	Youngstown, Ohio	D10
O'Shea, Terence	TE	6-4	230	12/3/66	California, Pa.	Pittsburgh, Pa.	FA
Perkins, Nico	CB-S	6-0	208	3/27/67	Memphis State	Memphis, Tenn.	FA
Ricketts, Tom	T	6-5	295	11/2/65	Pittsburgh	Murrysville, Pa.	D1b
Slater, Brian	WR	6-4	199	5/15/66	Washington	Lake Stevens, Wash.	D11
Stock, Mark	WR	5-11	177	4/27/66	Virginia Military	Stone Mountain, Ga.	D6
Strom, Rick (1)	QB	6-2	210	3/11/65	Georgia Tech	Pittsburgh, Pa.	FA
Unga, Fine	RB	5-10	215	6/23/65	Weber State	Provo, Utah	FA
Williams, Jerrol	LB	6-5	235	7/5/67	Purdue	Las Vegas, Nev.	D4
Worley, Tim	RB	6-2	216	9/24/66	Georgia	Lumberton, N.C.	D1a

The term NFL Rookie is defined as a player who is in his first season of professional football and has not been on the roster of another professional football team for any regular-season or postseason games. A Rookie is designated by an "R" on NFL rosters. Players who have been active in another professional football league or players who have NFL experience, including either preseason training camp or being on an active roster for fewer than three regular-season or postseason games, are termed NFL First-Year Players. An NFL First-Year Player is designated by a "1" on NFL rosters. Thereafter, a player on an NFL active roster for at least three regular-season or postseason games is credited with an additional year of NFL playing experience.

NOTES

American Football Conference Western Division

Team Colors: Navy Blue, White, and Gold

San Diego Jack Murphy Stadium
P.O. Box 20666
San Diego, California 92120
Telephone: (619) 280-2111

Club Officials

Chairman of the Board/President: Alex G. Spanos
Vice Chairman: Dean A. Spanos
Director of Football Operations: Steve Ortmayer
Director of Administration: Jack E. Teele
Special Assistant to Chairman of the Board: Warren B. Jones, Jr.
Director of Player Personnel: Chet Franklin
Pro Scouting: Rudy Feldman
Director of College Scouting: Les Miller
Director of Public Relations: Rick Smith
Business Manager: Pat Curran
Director of Marketing: Rich Israel
Director of Ticket Operations: Joe Scott
Director of Community Relations: Bill Johnston
Public Relations Assistant: Rob Boulware
Chief Financial Officer: Jeremiah T. Murphy
Financial Officer: James T. Kesaris
Head Trainer: Larry Roberts
Equipment Manager: Sid Brooks

Stadium: San Diego Jack Murphy Stadium • **Capacity:** 60,750
9449 Friars Road
San Diego, California 92108

Playing Surface: Grass

Training Camp: University of California-San Diego
Third College
La Jolla, California 92037

1989 Schedule

Preseason

Aug. 13	**Dallas**	12:00
Aug. 19	at Chicago	8:00
Aug. 23	at San Francisco	6:00
Sept. 1	**Phoenix**	7:00

Regular Season

Sept. 10	at Los Angeles Raiders	1:00
Sept. 17	**Houston**	1:00
Sept. 24	**Kansas City**	1:00
Oct. 1	at Phoenix	1:00
Oct. 8	at Denver	2:00
Oct. 15	**Seattle**	1:00
Oct. 22	**New York Giants**	1:00
Oct. 29	at Seattle	1:00
Nov. 5	**Philadelphia**	1:00
Nov. 12	**Los Angeles Raiders**	5:00
Nov. 19	at Pittsburgh	1:00
Nov. 26	at Indianapolis	1:00
Dec. 3	**New York Jets**	1:00
Dec. 10	at Washington	1:00
Dec. 17	at Kansas City	12:00
Dec. 24	**Denver**	1:00

Chargers Coaching History

Los Angeles 1960
(214-207-11)

1960-69	Sid Gillman*	83-51-6
1969-70	Charlie Waller	9-7-3
1971	Sid Gillman**	4-6-0
1971-73	Harland Svare***	7-17-2
1973	Ron Waller	1-5-0
1974-78	Tommy Prothro****	21-39-0
1978-86	Don Coryell#	72-60-0
1986-88	Al Saunders	17-22-0

*Retired after nine games in 1969
**Resigned after 10 games in 1971
***Resigned after eight games in 1973
****Resigned after four games in 1978
#Resigned after eight games in 1986

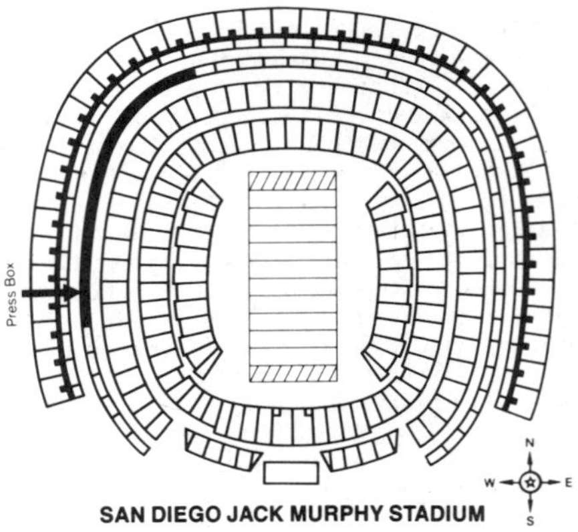

SAN DIEGO JACK MURPHY STADIUM

Record Holders

Individual Records—Career

Category	Name	Performance
Rushing (Yds.)	Paul Lowe, 1960-67	4,963
Passing (Yds.)	Dan Fouts, 1973-1987	43,040
Passing (TDs)	Dan Fouts, 1973-1987	254
Receiving (No.)	Charlie Joiner, 1976-1986	586
Receiving (Yds.)	Lance Alworth, 1962-1970	9,585
Interceptions	Dick Harris, 1960-65	29
Punting (Avg.)	Maury Buford, 1982-84	42.7
Punt Return (Avg.)	Leslie (Speedy) Duncan, 1964-1970	12.3
Kickoff Return (Avg.)	Leslie (Speedy) Duncan, 1964-1970	25.2
Field Goals	Rolf Benirschke, 1977-1986	146
Touchdowns	Lance Alworth, 1962-1970	83
Points	Rolf Benirschke, 1977-1986	766

Individual Records—Single Season

Category	Name	Performance
Rushing (Yds.)	Earnest Jackson, 1984	1,179
Passing (Yds.)	Dan Fouts, 1981	4,802
Passing (TDs)	Dan Fouts, 1981	33
Receiving (No.)	Kellen Winslow, 1980	89
Receiving (Yds.)	Lance Alworth, 1965	1,602
Interceptions	Charlie McNeil, 1961	9
Punting (Avg.)	Dennis Partee, 1969	44.6
Punt Return (Avg.)	Leslie (Speedy) Duncan, 1965	15.5
Kickoff Return (Avg.)	Keith Lincoln, 1962	28.4
Field Goals	Rolf Benirschke, 1980	24
Touchdowns	Chuck Muncie, 1981	19
Points	Rolf Benirschke, 1980	118

Individual Records—Single Game

Category	Name	Performance
Rushing (Yds.)	Gary Anderson, 12-18-88	217
Passing (Yds.)	Dan Fouts, 10-19-80	444
	Dan Fouts, 12-11-82	444
Passing (TDs)	Dan Fouts, 11-22-81	6
Receiving (No.)	Kellen Winslow, 10-7-84	15
Receiving (Yds.)	Wes Chandler, 12-20-82	260
Interceptions	Many times	3
	Last time by Pete Shaw, 11-2-80	
Field Goals	Many times	4
	Last time by Rolf Benirschke, 12-22-80	
Touchdowns (Tot.)	Kellen Winslow, 11-22-81	5
Points	Kellen Winslow, 11-22-81	30

1988 Team Record

Preseason (1-3)

Date	Result		Opponents
8/6	W	24-21	Dallas
8/13	L	6-27	at L.A. Rams
8/20	L	27-34	San Francisco
8/26	L	24-31	L.A. Rams
		81-113	

Regular Season (6-10)

Date	Result		Opponents	Att.
9/4	L	13-24	at L.A. Raiders	39,029
9/11	L	3-34	at Denver	75,359
9/18	W	17- 6	Seattle	44,449
9/25	W	24-23	at Kansas City	45,498
10/2	L	0-12	Denver	55,763
10/9	L	17-23	New Orleans	42,693
10/16	L	28-31	at Miami	58,972
10/23	L	0-16	Indianapolis	37,722
10/30	L	14-17	at Seattle	59,641
11/6	L	3-13	L.A. Raiders	55,134
11/13	W	10- 7	at Atlanta	26,329
11/20	W	38-24	at L.A. Rams	45,462
11/27	L	10-48	San Francisco	51,484
12/4	L	10-27	at Cincinnati	56,866
12/11	W	20-14	Pittsburgh	33,816
12/18	W	24-13	Kansas City	26,339

Score by Periods

Chargers	72	57	37	65	0	—	231
Opponents	69	105	57	101	0	—	332

Attendance

Home 347,400 Away 407,156 Total 754,556
Single-game home record, 61,880 (11-29-87)
Single-season home record, 415,626 (1985)

1988 Team Statistics

	Chargers	Opp.
Total First Downs	255	335
Rushing	115	135
Passing	116	173
Penalty	24	27
Third Down: Made/Att.	70/204	97/221
Fourth Down: Made/Att.	7/19	6/11
Total Net Yards	4429	5418
Avg. Per Game	276.8	338.6
Total Plays	937	1072
Avg. Per Play	4.7	5.1
Net Yards Rushing	2041	2133
Avg. Per Game	127.6	133.3
Total Rushes	438	521
Net Yards Passing	2388	3285
Avg. Per Game	149.3	205.3
Sacked/Yards Lost	31/240	34/240
Gross Yards	2628	3525
Att./Completions	468/241	517/274
Completion Pct.	51.5	53.0
Had Intercepted	20	16
Punts/Avg.	86/43.5	71/39.3
Net Punting Avg.	34.5	32.9
Penalties/Yards Lost	118/1039	74/619
Fumbles/Ball Lost	26/12	25/10
Touchdowns	27	38
Rushing	11	15
Passing	11	22
Returns	5	1
Avg. Time of Possession	28:22	31:38

1988 Individual Statistics

Scoring	TD R	TD P	TD Rt	PAT	FG	Saf	TP
Abbott	0	0	0	15/15	8/12	0	39
DeLine	0	0	0	12/12	6/8	0	30
Early	0	4	0	0/0	0/0	0	24
A. Miller	0	3	1	0/0	0/0	0	24
Malone	4	0	0	0/0	0/0	0	24
Anderson	3	0	0	0/0	0/0	0	18
Redden	3	0	0	0/0	0/0	0	18
Flutie	0	2	0	0/0	0/0	0	12
Holland	0	1	1	0/0	0/0	0	12
Adams	1	0	0	0/0	0/0	0	6
Bennett	0	0	1	0/0	0/0	0	6
Browner	0	0	1	0/0	0/0	0	6
James	0	1	0	0/0	0/0	0	6
Seale	0	0	1	0/0	0/0	0	6
Chargers	11	11	5	27/27	14/20	0	231
Opponents	15	22	1	36/38	22/36	1	332

Passing	Att.	Comp.	Yds.	Pct.	TD	Int.	Tkld.	Rate
Malone	272	147	1580	54.0	6	13	9/45	58.8
Laufenberg	144	69	778	47.9	4	5	18/155	59.3
Vlasic	52	25	270	48.1	1	2	3/32	54.2
James	0	0	0	—	0	0	1/8	0.0
Chargers	468	241	2628	51.5	11	20	31/240	58.4
Opponents	517	274	3525	53.0	22	16	34/240	75.9

Rushing	Att.	Yds.	Avg.	LG	TD
Anderson	225	1119	5.0	36	3
Spencer	44	215	4.9	24	0
Malone	37	169	4.6	36t	4
Adams	38	149	3.9	14	1
Laufenberg	31	120	3.9	23	0
James	23	105	4.6	23	0
Early	7	63	9.0	37	0
A. Miller	7	45	6.4	20	0
Redden	19	30	1.6	5t	3
Holland	3	19	6.3	10	0
Bernstine	2	7	3.5	5	0
Vlasic	2	0	0.0	0	0
Chargers	438	2041	4.7	37	11
Opponents	521	2133	4.1	37t	15

Receiving	No.	Yds.	Avg.	LG	TD
Holland	39	536	13.7	45	1
A. Miller	36	526	14.6	49	3
James	36	279	7.8	31	1
Anderson	32	182	5.7	20	0
Early	29	375	12.9	38t	4
Bernstine	29	340	11.7	59	0
Flutie	18	208	11.6	28	2
Cox	18	144	8.0	20	0
Jones, Wash.-S.D.	3	21	7.0	11	0
Jones, S.D.	1	11	11.0	11	0
Spencer	1	14	14.0	14	0
Redden	1	11	11.0	11	0
Sievers	1	2	2.0	2	0
Chargers	241	2628	10.9	59	11
Opponents	274	3525	12.9	96t	22

Interceptions	No.	Yds.	Avg.	LG	TD
Byrd	7	82	11.7	42	0
Browner	2	65	32.5	55t	1
Coleman	2	0	0.0	0	0
Bennett	1	21	21.0	21	0
Smith	1	9	9.0	9	0
Faucette	1	2	2.0	2	0
Glenn	1	0	0.0	0	0
Patterson	1	0	0.0	0	0
Chargers	16	179	11.2	55t	1
Opponents	20	307	15.4	44	0

Punting	No.	Yds.	Avg.	In 20	LG
Mojsiejenko	85	3745	44.1	22	62
Chargers	86	3745	43.5	22	62
Opponents	71	2792	39.3	16	65

Punt Returns	No.	FC	Yds.	Avg.	LG	TD
James	28	11	278	9.9	24	0
Flutie	7	5	36	5.1	10	0
Chargers	35	16	314	9.0	24	0
Opponents	56	5	558	10.0	36	0

Kickoff Returns	No.	Yds.	Avg.	LG	TD
Holland	31	810	26.1	94t	1
A. Miller	25	648	25.9	93t	1
Adams	1	13	13.0	13	0
Flutie	1	10	10.0	10	0
Jones	1	13	13.0	13	0
Spencer	1	16	16.0	16	0
Chargers	60	1510	25.2	94t	2
Opponents	47	1055	22.4	97t	1

Sacks	No.
Williams	11.0
O'Neal	4.0
Campbell	3.0
Hinkle	3.0
Keys	3.0
Browner	2.5
Phillips	2.0
Bayless	1.0
Glenn	1.0
P. Miller	1.0
Patterson	1.0
Smith	1.0
Wilson	0.5
Chargers	34.0
Opponents	31.0

1989 Draft Choices

Round	Name	Pos.	College
1.	Burt Grossman	DE	Pittsburgh
2.	Courtney Hall	C	Rice
	Billy Joe Tolliver	QB	Texas Tech
5.	Elliot Smith	DB	Alcorn State
7.	Marion Butts	RB	Florida State
	Terrence Jones	QB	Tulane
8.	Dana Brinson	WR	Nebraska
9.	Pat Davis	TE	Syracuse
10.	Ricky Andrews	LB	Washington
11.	Victor Floyd	RB	Florida State

San Diego Chargers 1989 Veteran Roster

No.	Name	Pos.	Ht.	Wt.	Birth-date	NFL Exp.	College	Hometown	How Acq.	'88 Games/ Starts
10	Abbott, Vince	K	5-11	206	5/31/59	3	Cal State-Fullerton	Santa Ana, Calif.	FA-'87	11/0
40	†Anderson, Gary	RB	6-0	181	4/18/61	5	Arkansas	Columbia, Mo.	D1b-'83	14/13
15	Archer, David	QB	6-2	208	2/15/62	6	Iowa State	Soda Springs, Idaho	FA-'89	1/0*
3	Bahr, Chris	K	5-10	170	2/3/53	14	Penn State	Langhorne, Pa.	FA(Raid)-'89#	16/0*
44	Bayless, Martin	S	6-2	200	11/11/62	6	Bowling Green	Dayton, Ohio	T(Buff)-'87	15/11
61	Behning, Mark	T	6-6	285	9/26/61	2	Nebraska	Denton, Tex.	FA-'89	0*
32	Bennett, Roy	CB	6-2	200	7/5/61	2	Jackson State	Birmingham, Ala.	FA-'87	16/2
82	Bernstine, Rod	TE	6-3	235	2/8/65	3	Texas A&M	Bryan, Tex.	D1-'87	14/13
58	Brandon, David	LB	6-4	225	2/9/65	3	Memphis State	Memphis, Tenn.	T(Buff)-'87	8/1
73	Brilz, Darrick	G-T	6-3	270	2/14/64	3	Oregon	Pinole, Calif.	W(Wash)-'88	14/0
57	†Browner, Keith	DE	6-6	260	1/24/62	5	Southern California	Atlanta, Ga.	FA-'88	16/15
22	Byrd, Gill	CB	5-11	196	2/20/61	7	San Jose State	San Francisco, Calif.	D1c-'83	16/16
95	Campbell, Joe	LB	6-3	242	12/28/66	2	New Mexico State	Tempe, Ariz.	D4a-'88	16/0
90	Caravello, Joe	TE	6-3	270	6/6/63	3	Tulane	El Segundo, Calif.	FA(Wash)-'89#	12/6*
71	Charles, Mike	NT	6-4	315	9/23/62	7	Syracuse	Newark, N.J.	W(TB)-'87	16/14
77	Clay, John	T	6-5	305	5/1/64	3	Missouri	St. Louis, Mo.	T(Raid)-'88	2/1
31	Coleman, Leonard	S	6-2	202	1/30/62	5	Vanderbilt	Lake Worth, Fla.	T(Ind)-'88	16/0
96	Collins, Jim	LB	6-2	233	6/11/58	8	Syracuse	Mendham, N.J.	FA(Rams)-'89#	4/4*
88	Cox, Arthur	TE	6-2	260	2/5/61	7	Texas Southern	Plant City, Fla.	FA-'88	16/16
6	DeLine, Steve	K	5-11	185	8/19/61	2	Colorado State	Englewood, Colo.	FA-'88	5/0
87	Early, Quinn	WR	6-0	190	4/13/65	2	Iowa	Great Neck, N.Y.	D3-'88	16/11
53	Faucette, Chuck	LB	6-3	238	10/17/63	2	Maryland	Willingboro, N.J.	FA-'87	8/8
51	Figaro, Cedric	LB	6-2	250	8/17/66	2	Notre Dame	Lafayette, La.	D6-'88	6/5
70	FitzPatrick, James	G-T	6-7	286	2/1/64	4	Southern California	Beaverton, Ore.	D1b-'86	11/0
89	Flutie, Darren	WR	5-10	185	11/18/66	2	Boston College	Natick, Mass.	FA-'88	16/0
25	Glenn, Vencie	S	6-0	187	10/26/64	4	Indiana State	Terre Haute, Ind.	T(NE)-'86	16/16
97	Hinkle, George	DE	6-5	269	3/17/65	2	Arizona	Pacific, Mo.	D11b-'88	3/1
86	†Holland, Jamie	WR	6-1	186	2/1/64	3	Ohio State	Wake Forest, N.C.	D7-'87	16/6
52	Jackson, Jeffery	LB	6-1	230	10/9/61	5	Auburn	Griffin, Ga.	FA-'87	14/1
26	†James, Lionel	RB	5-6	170	5/25/62	6	Auburn	Albany, Ga.	D5-'84	16/1
93	Keys, Tyrone	DE	6-7	275	10/24/60	7	Mississippi State	Jackson, Miss.	FA-'88	13/11
68	Kowalski, Gary	G-T	6-6	273	7/2/60	5	Boston College	Clinton, Conn.	T(Rams)-'85	2/2
24	Lyles, Lester	S	6-3	200	12/27/62	5	Virginia	Washington, D.C.	FA(Phx)-'89#	6/4*
62	Macek, Don	C	6-2	270	7/2/54	14	Boston College	Manchester, N.H.	D2-'76	5/5
16	†Malone, Mark	QB	6-4	222	11/22/58	10	Arizona State	El Cajon, Calif.	T(Pitt)-'88	12/8
60	McKnight, Dennis	C-G	6-3	270	9/12/59	8	Drake	Staten Island, N.Y.	FA-'82	16/16
83	Miller, Anthony	WR	5-11	180	4/15/65	2	Tennessee	Pasadena, Calif.	D1-'88	16/15
74	Miller, Brett	T	6-7	300	10/2/58	7	Iowa	Glendale, Calif.	FA(Atl)-'89#	15/4*
69	†Miller, Les	DE	6-7	285	3/1/65	3	Fort Hays State	Arkansas City, Kan.	FA-'87	13/0
48	Miller, Pat	S	6-1	210	6/24/64	2	Florida	Panama City, Fla.	FA-'87	8/3
2	Mojsiejenko, Ralf	P	6-3	212	1/28/63	5	Michigan State	Bridgman, Mich.	D4-'85	16/0
91	O'Neal, Leslie	DE	6-4	255	5/7/64	3	Oklahoma State	Little Rock, Ark.	D1a-'86	9/1
85	Parker, Andy	TE	6-5	245	9/8/61	6	Utah	Encinitas, Calif.	FA(Raid)-'89#	16/11*
78	Patten, Joel	T	6-7	307	2/7/58	4	Duke	Fairfax, Va.	FA(Ind)-'89#	16/13*
34	Patterson, Elvis	CB	5-11	198	10/21/60	6	Kansas	Houston, Tex.	FA-'87	14/6
75	†Phillips, Joe	DE	6-5	275	7/15/63	4	Southern Methodist	Vancouver, Wash.	FA-'87	16/16
50	†Plummer, Gary	LB	6-2	240	1/26/60	4	California	Fremont, Calif.	FA-'86	16/12
20	Redden, Barry	RB	5-10	219	7/21/60	8	Richmond	Sarasota, Fla.	T(Rams)-'87	8/2
65	Richards, David	T	6-4	301	4/11/66	2	UCLA	Dallas, Tex.	D4c-'88	16/16
66	Rosado, Dan	G-T	6-3	280	7/6/59	3	Northern Illinois	Canton, Ga.	FA-'87	12/11
30	Seale, Sam	CB	5-9	185	10/6/62	6	Western State, Colo.	Orange, N.J.	FA-'88	14/8
54	Smith, Billy Ray	LB	6-3	236	8/10/61	7	Arkansas	Plano, Tex.	D1a-'83	9/8
36	Smith, Timmy	RB	5-11	222	1/21/64	3	Texas Tech	Hobbs, N.M.	FA(Wash)-'89#	14/8*
43	Spencer, Tim	RB	6-1	227	12/10/60	5	Ohio State	St. Clairsville, Ohio	D11b-'83	16/1
47	Thomas, Johnny	CB	5-9	185	8/3/64	2	Baylor	Houston, Tex.	FA(Wash)-'89#	4/0*
76	Thompson, Broderick	G-T	6-4	290	8/14/60	4	Kansas	Cerritos, Calif.	FA-'87	16/16
13	Vlasic, Mark	QB	6-3	206	10/25/63	3	Iowa	Monaca, Pa.	D4-'87	2/2
67	Williams, Larry	G	6-5	290	7/3/63	4	Notre Dame	Santa Ana, Calif.	FA(Clev)-'89#	14/14*
99	Williams, Lee	DE	6-5	263	10/15/62	6	Bethune-Cookman	Ft. Lauderdale, Fla.	SD1-'84	16/16
72	Wilson, Karl	DE	6-4	268	9/10/64	3	Louisiana State	Baton Rouge, La.	D3-'87	13/2
59	Woodard, Ken	LB	6-1	220	1/22/60	8	Tuskegee Institute	Detroit, Mich.	FA-'88	8/0

* Archer played 1 game with Washington in '88; Bahr played 16 games with L.A. Raiders; Behning last active with Pittsburgh in '86; Caravello played 12 games with Washington; Collins played 4 games with L.A. Rams; Lyles played 6 games with Phoenix; B. Miller played 15 games with Atlanta; Parker played 16 games with L.A. Raiders; Patten played 16 games with Indianapolis; T. Smith played 14 games with Washington; Thomas played 4 games with Washington; Larry Williams played 14 games with Cleveland.

† Option playout; subject to developments.

Plan B unconditional free agent.

Retired—Steve Fuller, 8-year quarterback, no games in '88.

Players lost through Plan B (5): T Ken Dallafior (Det; 13 games in '88), T Chris Gambol (Det; 11), TE Anthony Jones (Dall; 4), LB Randy Kirk (Phx; 16), RB Kevin Scott (Dall; 1).

Also played with Chargers in '88—DE Keith Baldwin (6 games), S Jeff Dale (10), QB Babe Laufenberg (8), TE Eric Sievers (5), TE Wilbur Strozier (6).

COACHING STAFF

Head Coach, Dan Henning

Pro Career: Begins first season as San Diego's head coach. Named eighth head coach in Chargers' history February 9, 1989, replacing Al Saunders. Previously served as head coach of Atlanta Falcons from 1983-86, producing 22-41-1 record. Henning began his pro coaching career in 1972 as an assistant with Houston Oilers. Also was assistant with New York Jets 1976-78 and Miami Dolphins 1979-80. Served as assistant head coach with Washington Redskins 1981-82 and helped lead Washington to a Super Bowl victory following the 1982 season. Returned to Washington as receivers coach 1987-88. Played quarterback with Chargers 1964-67. Career record: 22-41-1.

Background: Played quarterback for William & Mary 1960-63. Began college coaching at Florida State 1968-70, 1974, and Virginia Tech 1971-73.

Personal: Born June 21, 1942, Bronx, N.Y. Attended St. Francis Prep in Brooklyn before attending William & Mary. Dan and his wife, Sandy, live in San Diego and have five children—Mary K., Patty, Danny, Terry, and Mike.

Assistant Coaches

Larry Beightol, offensive coordinator/offensive line; born November 21, 1942, Morrisdale, Pa., lives in San Diego. Guard-linebacker Catawba College 1961-63. No pro playing experience. College coach: William & Mary 1968-71, North Carolina State 1972-75, Auburn 1976, Arkansas 1977-78, 1980-82, Louisiana Tech 1979 (head coach), Missouri 1983-84. Pro coach: Atlanta Falcons 1985-86, Tampa Bay Buccaneers 1987-88, joined Chargers in 1989.

Gunther Cunningham, defensive line; born June 19, 1946, Munich, Germany, lives in San Diego. Linebacker Oregon 1965-67. No pro playing experience. College coach: Oregon 1969-71, Arkansas 1972, Stanford 1973-76, California 1977-80. Pro coach: Hamilton Tiger-Cats (CFL) 1981, Indianapolis Colts 1982-84, joined Chargers in 1985.

Mike Haluchak, linebackers; born November 28, 1949, Concord, Calif., lives in San Diego. Linebacker Southern California 1967-70. No pro playing experience. College coach: Southern California 1976-77, Cal State-Fullerton 1978, Pacific 1979-80, California 1981, North Carolina State 1982. Pro coach: Oakland Invaders (USFL) 1983-85, joined Chargers in 1986.

Bobby Jackson, running backs; born February 16, 1940, Forsyth, Ga., lives in San Diego. Linebacker-running back Samford (Ga.) 1959-62. No pro playing experience. College coach: Florida State 1965-69, Kansas State 1970-74, Louisville 1975-76, Tennessee 1977-82. Pro coach: Atlanta Falcons 1983-86, joined Chargers in 1987.

Charlie Joiner, receivers; born October 14, 1947, Many, La., lives in San Diego. Wide receiver Grambling 1965-68. Defensive back-wide receiver Houston Oilers 1969-72, Cincinnati Bengals 1972-75, San Diego Chargers 1976-86. Pro coach: Joined Chargers in 1987.

Ron Lynn, defensive coordinator; born December 6, 1944, Youngstown, Ohio, lives in San Diego. Quarterback-defensive back Mount Union (Ohio) 1963-65. No pro playing experience. College coach: Toledo 1966, Mount Union (Ohio) 1967-73, Kent State 1974-76, San Jose State 1977-78, Pacific 1979, California 1980-82. Pro coach: Oakland Invaders (USFL) 1983-85, joined Chargers in 1986.

Joe Madden, special teams; born March 5, 1935, Washington, D.C., lives in San Diego. Back Maryland 1954-56. No pro playing experience. College coach: Mississippi State 1962, Morehead State 1963, Wake Forest 1964-67, Iowa State 1968-71, Kansas State 1972, Pittsburgh 1973-76, Tennessee 1977-79. Pro coach: Detroit Lions 1980-84, Atlanta Falcons 1985-86, joined Chargers in 1989.

Ted Tollner, assistant head coach/quarterbacks; born May 29, 1940, San Francisco, Calif., lives in San Diego. Quarterback Cal Poly-SLO 1959-61. No pro playing experience. College coach: College of San Mateo 1971-72 (head coach), San Diego State 1973-80, Brigham Young 1981, Southern California 1982-86 (head coach 1983-86). Pro coach: Buffalo Bills 1987-88, joined Chargers in 1989.

San Diego Chargers 1989 First-Year Roster

Name	Pos.	Ht.	Wt.	Birth-date	College	Hometown	How Acq.
Andrews, Ricky	LB	6-2	236	4/14/66	Washington	Mililani, Hawaii	D10
Bedford, Brian (1)	TE	6-3	210	6/29/65	California	Sacramento, Calif.	T(Dall)-'88
Biggers, Kevin (1)	CB-S	5-11	188	5/6/62	Nebraska	Gardena, Calif.	FA
Brinson, Dana	WR	5-9	167	4/10/65	Nebraska	Valdosta, Ga.	D8
Butts, Marion	RB	6-1	248	8/1/66	Florida State	Sylvester, Ga.	D7a
Davis, Pat	TE	6-3	257	6/13/66	Syracuse	Trenton, N.J.	D9
Floyd, Eric (1)	T	6-5	300	10/28/65	Auburn	Rome, Ga.	FA
Floyd, Victor	RB	6-1	201	1/24/66	Florida State	Pensacola, Fla.	D11
Grossman, Burt	DE	6-6	270	4/10/67	Pittsburgh	Bala Cynwyn, Pa.	D1
Hall, Courtney	C	6-1	269	8/26/68	Rice	Wilmington, Calif.	D2a
Hobart, Kenneth (1)	S	6-0	214	1/27/61	Idaho	Kamiah, Idaho	FA
Hosea, Cedric (1)	RB	5-11	195	9/2/65	Tennessee-Martin	Pensacola, Fla.	FA
Howard, Joey (1)	T	6-5	285	9/14/65	Tennessee	Springfield, Ohio	D9-'88
Johnson, Leonard (1)	DE	6-6	260	5/17/63	Georgia Military	Garden City, Ga.	FA
Jones, Terrence	QB	6-1	208	6/18/66	Tulane	Lutcher, La.	D7b
Mattox, Marvin (1)	S	6-4	205	8/7/65	Kansas	Pomona, Calif.	FA
Scott, Michael (1)	G	6-4	275	4/29/65	Missouri	Florissant, Mo.	FA
Searels, Stacy (1)	C-G	6-5	281	5/19/65	Auburn	Trion, Ga.	D4b-'88
Smith, Elliot	CB-S	6-2	192	8/14/67	Alcorn State	Jackson, Miss.	D5
Tolliver, Billy Joe	QB	6-1	218	7/28/65	Texas Tech	Jamestown, N.D.	D2b
Washington, Ed (1)	DE	6-7	265	8/26/63	None	Los Angeles, Calif.	FA
Williams, Ronnie (1)	RB	6-3	225	1/19/66	Oklahoma State	Wichita Falls, Tex.	FA-'88

The term NFL Rookie is defined as a player who is in his first season of professional football and has not been on the roster of another professional football team for any regular-season or postseason games. A Rookie is designated by an "R" on NFL rosters. Players who have been active in another professional football league or players who have NFL experience, including either preseason training camp or being on an active roster for fewer than three regular-season or postseason games, are termed NFL First-Year Players. An NFL First-Year Player is designated by a "1" on NFL rosters. Thereafter, a player on an NFL active roster for at least three regular-season or postseason games is credited with an additional year of NFL playing experience.

NOTES

American Football Conference Western Division

Team Colors: Blue, Green, and Silver

11220 N.E. 53rd Street
Kirkland, Washington 98033
Telephone: (206) 827-9777

Club Officials

Owner: Ken Behring
President/General Manager: Tom Flores
Vice President/Assistant General Manager: Chuck Allen
Player Personnel Director: Mike Allman
Vice President/Public Relations: Gary Wright
Assistant Public Relations Director: Dave Neubert
Administrative Assistant: Sandy Gregory
Sales and Marketing Director: Reggie McKenzie
Business Manager: Mickey Loomis
Data Processing Director: Tom Monroe
Ticket Manager: James Nagaoka
Trainer: Jim Whitesel
Equipment Manager: Walt Loeffler

Stadium: Kingdome • **Capacity:** 64,984
201 South King Street
Seattle, Washington 98104

Playing Surface: AstroTurf

Training Camp: 11220 N.E. 53rd Street
Kirkland, Washington 98033

1989 Schedule

Preseason

Aug. 11	at Phoenix	7:30
Aug. 19	vs. N.E. at St. Louis, Mo.	8:00
Aug. 25	**Detroit**	7:30
Sept. 1	**San Francisco**	6:00

Regular Season

Sept. 10	at Philadelphia	4:00
Sept. 17	**Phoenix**	1:00
Sept. 24	at New England	1:00
Oct. 1	at Los Angeles Raiders	1:00
Oct. 8	**Kansas City**	1:00
Oct. 15	at San Diego	1:00
Oct. 22	**Denver**	1:00
Oct. 29	**San Diego**	1:00
Nov. 5	at Kansas City	12:00
Nov. 12	**Cleveland**	1:00
Nov. 19	at New York Giants	4:00
Nov. 26	at Denver	2:00
Dec. 4	**Buffalo** (Monday)	6:00
Dec. 10	at Cincinnati	1:00
Dec. 17	**Los Angeles Raiders**	5:00
Dec. 23	**Washington** (Saturday)	1:00

Seahawks Coaching History

(99-104-0)

1976-82	Jack Patera*	35-59-0
1982	Mike McCormack	4-3-0
1983-88	Chuck Knox	60-42-0

*Released after two games in 1982

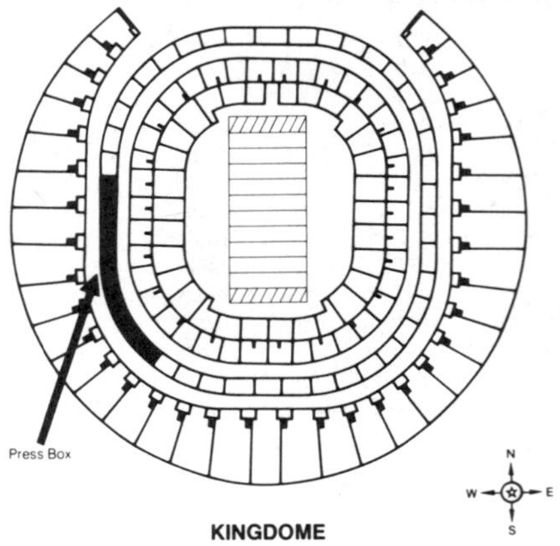

KINGDOME

Record Holders

Individual Records—Career

Category	Name	Performance
Rushing (Yds.)	Curt Warner, 1983-88	6,074
Passing (Yds.)	Jim Zorn, 1976-1984	20,042
Passing (TDs)	Dave Krieg, 1980-88	148
Receiving (No.)	Steve Largent, 1976-1988	*791
Receiving (Yds.)	Steve Largent, 1976-1988	*12,686
Interceptions	Dave Brown, 1976-1986	50
Punting (Avg.)	Herman Weaver, 1977-1980	40.0
Punt Return (Avg.)	Paul Johns, 1981-84	11.4
Kickoff Return (Avg.)	Zachary Dixon, 1983-84	23.4
Field Goals	Norm Johnson, 1982-88	121
Touchdowns (Tot.)	Steve Largent, 1976-1988	98
Points	Norm Johnson, 1982-88	636

Individual Records—Single Season

Category	Name	Performance
Rushing (Yds.)	Curt Warner, 1986	1,481
Passing (Yds.)	Dave Krieg, 1984	3,671
Passing (TDs)	Dave Krieg, 1984	32
Receiving (No.)	Steve Largent, 1985	79
Receiving (Yds.)	Steve Largent, 1985	1,287
Interceptions	John Harris, 1981	10
	Kenny Easley, 1984	10
Punting (Avg.)	Herman Weaver, 1980	41.8
Punt Return (Avg.)	Bobby Joe Edmonds, 1987	12.6
Kickoff Return (Avg.)	Al Hunter, 1978	24.1
Field Goals	Norm Johnson, 1986	22
	Norm Johnson, 1988	22
Touchdowns (Tot.)	David Sims, 1978	15
	Sherman Smith, 1979	15
Points	Norm Johnson, 1984	110

Individual Records—Single Game

Category	Name	Performance
Rushing (Yds.)	Curt Warner, 11-27-83	207
Passing (Yds.)	Dave Krieg, 11-20-83	418
Passing (TDs)	Dave Krieg, 12-2-84	5
	Dave Krieg, 9-15-85	5
	Dave Krieg, 11-28-88	5
Receiving (No.)	Steve Largent, 10-18-87	15
Receiving (Yds.)	Steve Largent, 10-18-87	261
Interceptions	Kenny Easley, 9-3-84	3
Field Goals	Norm Johnson, 9-20-87	5
	Norm Johnson, 12-18-88	5
Touchdowns (Tot.)	Daryl Turner, 9-15-85	4
	Curt Warner, 12-11-88	4
Points	Daryl Turner, 9-15-85	24
	Curt Warner, 12-11-88	24

*NFL Record

1988 Team Record

Preseason (3-1)

Date	Result		Opponents
8/4	W	21- 7	Phoenix
8/11	W	16-13	at Detroit (OT)
8/19	W	30-13	Buffalo
8/26	L	21-27	at San Francisco
		88-60	

Regular Season (9-7)

Date	Result		Opponents	Att.
9/4	W	21-14	at Denver	75,986
9/11	W	31-10	Kansas City	61,512
9/18	L	6-17	at San Diego	44,449
9/25	L	7-38	San Francisco	62,382
10/2	W	31-20	at Atlanta	28,619
10/9	W	16-10	at Cleveland	78,605
10/16	L	19-20	New Orleans	63,569
10/23	L	10-31	at L.A. Rams	57,033
10/30	W	17-14	San Diego	59,641
11/6	L	3-13	Buffalo	61,074
11/13	W	27-24	Houston	60,446
11/20	L	24-27	at Kansas City	33,152
11/28	W	35-27	L.A. Raiders	62,641
12/4	L	7-13	at New England	59,086
12/11	W	42-14	Denver	62,838
12/18	W	43-37	at L.A. Raiders	61,127

(OT) Overtime

Postseason (0-1)

Date	Result		Opponent	Att.
12/31	L	13-21	at Cincinnati	58,560

Score by Periods

Seahawks	58	124	83	74	0	—	339
Opponents	75	90	72	92	0	—	329

Attendance

Home 494,103 Away 438,057 Total 932,160
Single-game home record, 64,411 (12-15-84)
Single-season home record, 494,103 (1988)

1988 Team Statistics

	Seahawks	Opp.
Total First Downs	291	321
Rushing	125	134
Passing	139	171
Penalty	27	16
Third Down: Made/Att.	83/211	96/219
Fourth Down: Made/Att.	7/16	10/16
Total Net Yards	4842	5639
Avg. Per Game	302.6	352.4
Total Plays	983	1040
Avg. Per Play	4.9	5.4
Net Yards Rushing	2086	2286
Avg. Per Game	130.4	142.9
Total Rushes	517	509
Net Yards Passing	2756	3353
Avg. Per Game	172.3	209.6
Sacked/Yards Lost	29/223	30/265
Gross Yards	2979	3618
Att./Completions	437/245	501/280
Completion Pct.	56.1	55.9
Had Intercepted	20	22
Punts/Avg.	70/40.8	66/42.1
Net Punting Avg.	36.8	35.7
Penalties/Yards Lost	89/790	111/861
Fumbles/Ball Lost	29/14	31/18
Touchdowns	39	38
Rushing	14	14
Passing	22	21
Returns	3	3
Avg. Time of Possession	28:38	31:23

1988 Individual Statistics

Scoring	TD R	TD P	TD Rt	PAT	FG	Saf	TP
N. Johnson	0	0	0	39/39	22/28	0	105
Warner	10	2	0	0/0	0/0	0	72
Blades	0	8	0	0/0	0/0	0	48
Williams	4	3	0	0/0	0/0	0	42
Butler	0	4	0	0/0	0/0	0	24
Largent	0	2	0	0/0	0/0	0	12
Clark	0	1	0	0/0	0/0	0	6
Dean	0	0	1	0/0	0/0	0	6
Green	0	0	1	0/0	0/0	0	6
Skansi	0	1	0	0/0	0/0	0	6
Spagnola	0	1	0	0/0	0/0	0	6
Taylor	0	0	1	0/0	0/0	0	6
Seahawks	14	22	3	39/39	22/28	0	339
Opponents	14	21	3	38/38	21/32	0	329

Passing	Att.	Comp.	Yds.	Pct.	TD	Int.	Tkld.	Rate
Krieg	228	134	1741	58.8	18	8	12/92	94.6
Stouffer	173	98	1106	56.6	4	6	13/110	69.2
Kemp	35	13	132	37.1	0	5	3/21	9.2
Agee	1	0	0	0.0	0	1	0/0	0.0
Blades	0	0	0	—	0	0	1/0	0.0
Seahawks	437	245	2979	56.1	22	20	29/223	74.9
Opponents	501	280	3618	55.9	21	22	30/265	74.4

Rushing	Att.	Yds.	Avg.	LG	TD
Warner	266	1025	3.9	29	10
Williams	189	877	4.6	44t	4
Krieg	24	64	2.7	17	0
Kemp	6	51	8.5	21	0
Stouffer	19	27	1.4	17	0
Blades	5	24	4.8	12	0
Harmon	2	13	6.5	8	0
Morris	3	6	2.0	5	0
Agee	1	2	2.0	2	0
Rodriguez	1	0	0.0	0	0
Largent	1	−3	−3.0	−3	0
Seahawks	517	2086	4.0	44t	14
Opponents	509	2286	4.5	42	14

Receiving	No.	Yds.	Avg.	LG	TD
Williams	58	651	11.2	75t	3
Blades	40	682	17.1	55	8
Largent	39	645	16.5	46	2
Tice	29	244	8.4	26	0
Skansi	24	238	9.9	21	1
Warner	22	154	7.0	17	2
Butler	18	242	13.4	46t	4
Kane	6	32	5.3	9	0
Spagnola	5	40	8.0	16	1
Agee	3	31	10.3	13	0
Clark	1	20	20.0	20t	1
Seahawks	245	2979	12.2	75t	22
Opponents	280	3618	12.9	69t	21

Interceptions	No.	Yds.	Avg.	LG	TD
Moyer	6	79	13.2	34	0
Taylor	5	53	10.6	27t	1
Jenkins	3	41	13.7	21	0
Hollis	2	32	16.0	30	0
Glasgow	2	19	9.5	19	0
Dean	1	31	31.0	31	0
Comeaux	1	18	18.0	18	0
Miller	1	7	7.0	7	0
Robinson	1	0	0.0	0	0
Seahawks	22	280	12.7	34	1
Opponents	20	195	9.8	55t	1

Punting	No.	Yds.	Avg.	In 20	LG
Rodriguez	70	2858	40.8	14	68
Seahawks	70	2858	40.8	14	68
Opponents	66	2778	42.1	22	59

Punt Returns	No.	FC	Yds.	Avg.	LG	TD
Edmonds	35	8	340	9.7	41	0
Hollis, K.C.-Sea.	3	0	28	9.3	15	0
Glasgow	1	0	0	0.0	0	0
Hunter	1	0	0	0.0	0	0
Seahawks	37	8	340	9.2	41	0
Opponents	36	14	202	5.6	16	0

Kickoff Returns	No.	Yds.	Avg.	LG	TD
Edmonds	40	900	22.5	65	0
Hollis, K.C.-Sea.	13	261	20.1	35	0
Hollis, Sea.	7	155	22.1	35	0
Morris	11	218	19.8	30	0
Harmon	3	62	20.7	30	0
Tice	1	17	17.0	17	0
Seahawks	62	1352	21.8	65	0
Opponents	66	1207	18.3	95	0

Sacks	No.
Green	9.0
Woods	5.0
Bryant	3.5
Mitz	3.0
Wyman	2.5
Clarke	2.0
Nash	2.0
Harper	1.0
Robinson	1.0
Scholtz	1.0
Seahawks	30.0
Opponents	29.0

1989 Draft Choices

Round	Name	Pos.	College
1.	Andy Heck	T	Notre Dame
2.	Joe Tofflemire	C	Arizona
3.	Elroy Harris	RB	Eastern Kentucky
4.	Travis McNeal	TE	Tenn.-Chattanooga
	James Henry	DB	So. Mississippi
7.	Mike Nettles	CB	Memphis State
8.	Marlin Williams	DE	Western Illinois
9.	David Franks	G	Connecticut
10.	Derrick Fenner	RB	North Carolina
11.	Mike Baum	DE	Northwestern
12.	R.J. Kors	DB	Long Beach State

Seattle Seahawks 1989 Veteran Roster

No.	Name	Pos.	Ht.	Wt.	Birth-date	NFL Exp.	College	Hometown	How Acq.	'88 Games/ Starts
65	†Bailey, Edwin	G	6-4	273	5/15/59	9	South Carolina State	Savannah, Ga.	D5-'81	16/16
62	Barbay, Roland	NT	6-4	270	10/1/64	2	Louisiana State	New Orleans, La.	D7-'87	0*
89	Blades, Brian	WR	5-11	182	7/24/65	2	Miami	Ft. Lauderdale, Fla.	D2-'88	16/7
55	Bosworth, Brian	LB	6-2	248	3/9/65	3	Oklahoma	Irving, Tex.	D1-'88	10/10
77	Bryant, Jeff	DE	6-5	268	5/22/60	8	Clemson	Decatur, Ga.	D1-'82	16/12
35	Burse, Tony	RB	6-0	220	4/4/65	2	Middle Tennessee State	Lafayette, Ga.	FA(Mia)-'89#	0*
84	Clark, Louis	WR	6-0	193	7/3/64	3	Mississippi State	Shannon, Miss.	D10-'87	7/0
67	Clarke, Ken	NT	6-1	271	8/28/56	12	Syracuse	Boston, Mass.	FA-'88	16/1
53	†Comeaux, Darren	LB	6-1	227	4/15/60	8	Arizona State	San Diego, Calif.	W(SF)-'88	9/6
85	Embree, Jon	TE	6-2	230	10/15/65	2	Colorado	Wingate, Md.	FA(Rams)-'89#	12/0*
54	Feasel, Grant	C	6-7	277	6/28/60	5	Abilene Christian	Barstow, Calif.	FA-'87	16/2
22	Glasgow, Nesby	S	5-10	187	4/15/57	11	Washington	Gardena, Calif.	FA-'88	16/0
60	Godfrey, Chris	G	6-3	265	5/17/58	7	Michigan	Detroit, Mich.	FA-'88	9/2
79	Green, Jacob	DE	6-3	254	1/21/57	10	Texas A&M	Houston, Tex.	D1-'80	16/16
34	Harmon, Kevin	RB	6-0	190	10/26/65	2	Iowa	New York, N.Y.	D4-'88	5/0
29	Harper, Dwayne	CB	5-11	165	3/29/66	2	South Carolina State	Orangeburg, S.C.	D11b-'88	16/1
96	Henton, Anthony	LB	6-1	234	7/27/63	3	Troy State	Palos Verdes, Calif.	FA(Pitt)-'89#	16/4*
25	Hollis, David	S	5-11	180	7/4/65	3	Nevada-Las Vegas	Gardena, Calif.	FA-'88	6/0
23	Hunter, Patrick	CB	5-11	185	10/24/64	4	Nevada-Reno	San Francisco, Calif.	D3-'86	12/10
24	Jenkins, Melvin	CB	5-10	182	3/16/62	3	Cincinnati	Jackson, Miss.	FA-'87	16/16
26	Johnson, Johnnie	S	6-1	183	10/8/56	10	Texas	LaGrange, Tex.	FA(Rams)-'89#	16/16*
52	Johnson, M. L.	LB	6-3	229	1/24/64	3	Hawaii	Los Angeles, Calif.	D9-'87	16/1
9	†Johnson, Norm	K	6-2	197	5/31/60	8	UCLA	Garden Grove, Calif.	FA-'82	16/0
81	Kane, Tommy	WR	5-11	180	1/14/64	2	Syracuse	Montreal, Canada	D3-'88	9/0
15	†Kemp, Jeff	QB	6-0	198	7/11/59	9	Dartmouth	Bethesda, Md.	T(SF)-'87	11/1
17	Krieg, Dave	QB	6-1	192	10/20/58	10	Milton	Schofield, Wis.	FA-'80	9/9
80	†Largent, Steve	WR	5-11	191	9/28/54	14	Tulsa	Oklahoma City, Okla.	T(Hou)-'76	15/15
13	Mathison, Bruce	QB	6-3	205	4/25/59	5	Nebraska	Superior, Wis.	FA-'88	0*
70	†Mattes, Ron	T	6-6	302	8/8/63	4	Virginia	Shenandoah, Pa.	D7-'85	16/16
30	McLemore, Chris	RB	6-1	230	12/31/63	3	Arizona	Las Vegas, Nev.	FA(Raid)-'89#	7/0*
71	†Millard, Bryan	G	6-5	281	12/2/60	6	Texas	Dumas, Tex.	FA-'84	15/14
91	Miller, Darrin	LB	6-1	227	3/24/65	2	Tennessee	Flemington, N.J.	FA-'88	16/0
61	Mitz, Alonzo	DE	6-3	271	6/5/63	4	Florida	Fort Pierce, Fla.	D8-'86	16/4
21	Moyer, Paul	S	6-1	196	7/26/61	7	Arizona State	Villa Park, Calif.	FA-'83	16/16
72	†Nash, Joe	NT	6-2	269	10/11/60	8	Boston College	Dorchester, Mass.	FA-'82	16/16
88	Pattison, Mark	WR	6-2	191	12/13/61	4	Washington	Seattle, Wash.	FA(NO)-'89#	6/0*
97	Porter, Rufus	LB	6-1	207	5/18/65	2	Southern University	Baton Rouge, La.	FA-'88	16/0
41	†Robinson, Eugene	S	6-0	183	5/28/63	5	Colgate	Hartford, Conn.	FA-'85	16/16
5	Rodriguez, Ruben	P	6-2	214	3/3/65	3	Arizona	Woodlake, Calif.	D5b-'87	16/0
58	†Scholtz, Bruce	LB	6-6	241	9/26/58	8	Texas	Austin, Tex.	D2-'82	15/15
82	Skansi, Paul	WR	5-11	184	1/11/61	7	Washington	Gig Harbor, Wash.	FA-'85	16/1
11	Stouffer, Kelly	QB	6-3	210	7/6/64	2	Colorado State	Rushville, Neb.	T(Phx)-'88	8/6
20	†Taylor, Terry	CB	5-10	181	7/18/61	6	Southern Illinois	Youngstown, Ohio	D1-'84	14/8
64	Thomas, Kevin	C	6-2	268	7/27/64	2	Arizona State	Tucson, Ariz.	FA(TB)-'89#	10/0*
66	Traynowicz, Mark	C	6-5	280	11/20/62	5	Nebraska	Omaha, Neb.	FA(Phx)-'89#	9/0*
28	Warner, Curt	RB	5-11	205	3/18/61	6	Penn State	Pineville, W. Va.	D1-'83	16/16
98	Wilburn, Steve	DE	6-4	266	2/25/61	2	Illinois State	Chicago, Ill.	FA-'89	0*
68	Williams, Doug	T	6-6	295	10/1/62	3	Texas A&M	Cincinnati, Ohio	FA(Hou)-'89#	0*
32	Williams, John L.	RB	5-11	226	11/23/64	4	Florida	Palatka, Fla.	D1-'86	16/16
75	Wilson, Mike	T	6-5	274	5/28/55	12	Georgia	Gainesville, Ga.	T(Cin)-'86	16/16
57	†Woods, Tony	LB	6-4	244	9/11/65	3	Pittsburgh	Newark, N.J.	D1-'87	16/16
92	Wyman, David	LB	6-2	234	3/31/64	3	Stanford	Reno, Nev.	D2-'87	16/16

* Barbay and D. Williams missed '88 season due to injury; Burse active for 1 game with Miami but did not play; Embree played 12 games with L.A. Rams in '88; Henton played 16 games with Pittsburgh; J. Johnson played 16 games with L.A. Rams; Mathison inactive for 5 games with Seattle; McLemore played 7 games with L.A. Raiders; Pattison played 6 games with New Orleans; Thomas played 10 games with Tampa Bay; Traynowicz played 4 games with Buffalo, 5 with Phoenix; Wilburn last active with New England in '87.

† Option playout; subject to developments.

\# Plan B unconditional free agent.

Players lost through Plan B (8): RB Tommie Agee (KC; played 16 games in '88), C Blair Bush (GB; 16), WR Ray Butler (Clev; 11), KR Bobby Joe Edmonds (Det; 16), C Stan Eisenhooth (Ind; 13), LB Greg Gaines (KC; 6), TE John Spagnola (GB; 16), TE Mike Tice (Wash; 16).

Also played with Seahawks in '88—CB Lou Brock (1 game), G Tim Burnham (active for 1 game but did not play), S Vernon Dean (16), NT Roy Hart (active for 1 game but did not play), DE Doug Hollie (3), RB Randall Morris (9), G Alvin Powell (6), WR Jimmy Teal (2).

COACHING STAFF

Head Coach, Chuck Knox

Pro Career: Named head coach of Seahawks on January 26, 1983, after five seasons as head coach at Buffalo, where he led Bills to AFC East title in 1980. Led Los Angeles Rams to five straight NFC West titles before taking over Bills in 1978. Pro assistant with New York Jets 1963-66, coaching offensive line, before moving to Detroit in 1967. Served Lions in same capacity until named head coach of Rams in 1973. No pro playing experience. Career record: 155-100-1.

Background: Played tackle for Juniata College in Huntingdon, Pa., 1950-53. Was assistant coach at his alma mater in 1954, then spent 1955 season as line coach at Ellwood City High School in Pennsylvania. Moved to Wake Forest as an assistant coach in 1959-60, then Kentucky in 1961-62.

Personal: Born April 27, 1932, Sewickley, Pa. Chuck and his wife, Shirley, live in Bellevue, Wash., and have four children—Chris, Kathy, Colleen, and Chuck.

Assistant Coaches

John Becker, offensive coordinator-receivers; born February 16, 1943, Alexandria, Va., lives in Redmond, Wash. Cal State-Northridge 1965. No college or pro playing experience. College coach: UCLA 1970, New Mexico State 1971, New Mexico 1972-73, Los Angeles Valley J.C. (head coach) 1974-76, Oregon 1977-79. Pro coach: Philadelphia Eagles 1980-83, Buffalo Bills 1984, Indianapolis Colts 1985-88, joined Seahawks in 1989.

Tom Catlin, assistant head coach-defensive coordinator; born September 8, 1931, Ponca City, Okla., lives in Redmond, Wash. Center-linebacker Oklahoma 1950-52. Pro linebacker Cleveland Browns 1953-54, 1957-58, Philadelphia Eagles 1959. College coach: Army 1956. Pro coach: Dallas Texans-Kansas City Chiefs 1960-65, Los Angeles Rams 1966-77, Buffalo Bills 1978-82, joined Seahawks in 1983.

George Dyer, defensive line; born May 4, 1940, Alhambra, Calif., lives in Redmond, Wash. Center-linebacker U.C. Santa Barbara 1961-63. No pro playing experience. College coach: Humboldt State 1964-66, Coalinga, Calif., J.C. 1967 (head coach), Portland State 1968-71, Idaho 1972, San Jose State 1973, Michigan State 1977-79, Arizona State 1980-81. Pro coach: Winnipeg Blue Bombers (CFL) 1974-76, Buffalo Bills 1982, joined Seahawks in 1983.

Chick Harris, offensive backfield; born September 21, 1945, Durham, N.C., lives in Redmond, Wash. Running back Northern Arizona 1966-69. No pro playing experience. College coach: Colorado State 1970-72, Long Beach State 1973-74, Washington 1975-80. Pro coach: Buffalo Bills 1981-82, joined Seahawks in 1983.

Ken Meyer, quarterbacks; born July 14, 1926, Erie, Pa., lives in Bellevue, Wash. Quarterback Denison 1947-50. No pro playing experience. College coach: Denison 1952-57, Wake Forest 1958-59, Florida State 1960-62, Alabama 1963-67, Tulane 1981-82. Pro coach: San Francisco 49ers 1968, 1977 (head coach), New York Jets 1969-72, Los Angeles Rams 1973-76, Chicago Bears 1978-80, joined Seahawks in 1983.

Rod Perry, defensive backfield; born September 11, 1953, Fresno, Calif., lives in Kirkland, Wash. Defensive back Fresno City College and Colorado 1971-74. Pro cornerback Los Angeles Rams 1975-82, Cleveland Browns 1983-84. College coach: Columbia University 1985, Fresno City College 1986, Fresno State 1987-88. Pro coach: Joined Seahawks in 1989.

Russ Purnell, tight ends-assistant special teams; born June 12, 1948, Chicago, Ill., lives in Bellevue, Wash. Center Orange Coast, Calif., J.C. and Whittier College 1966-69. No pro playing experience. College coach: Whittier 1970-71, Southern California 1982-85. Pro coach: Joined Seahawks in 1986.

Kent Stephenson, offensive line; born February 4, 1942, Anita, Iowa, lives in Redmond, Wash. Guard-nose tackle Northern Iowa 1962-64. No pro playing experience. College coach: Wayne State 1965-68, North Dakota 1969-71, Southern Methodist 1972-73, Iowa 1974-76, Oklahoma State 1977-78, Kansas 1979-82. Pro coach: Michigan Panthers (USFL) 1983-84, joined Seahawks in 1985.

Rusty Tillman, special teams, assistant linebackers; born February 27, 1948, Beloit, Wis., lives in Bellevue, Wash. Linebacker Northern Arizona 1967-69. Pro linebacker Washington Redskins 1970-77. Pro coach: Joined Seahawks in 1979.

Joe Vitt, special assignments; born August 23, 1954, Camden, N.J., lives in Redmond, Wash. Linebacker Towson State 1973-75. No pro playing experience. Pro coach: Baltimore Colts 1979-81, joined Seahawks in 1982.

Seattle Seahawks 1989 First-Year Roster

Name	Pos.	Ht.	Wt.	Birth-date	College	Hometown	How Acq.
Baum, Mike	DE	6-6	270	5/20/66	Northwestern	Park Ridge, Ill.	D11
Cain, Joe (1)	LB	6-1	228	6/11/65	Oregon Tech	Compton, Calif.	FA
Des Rochers, Dave (1)	T	6-7	290	12/1/64	San Diego State	Glendora, Calif.	D12-'88
Fenner, Derrick	RB	6-3	235	4/6/67	North Carolina	Oxon Hill, Md.	D10
Floyd, Lucius (1)	RB	6-0	195	4/7/66	Nevada-Reno	Las Vegas, Nev.	FA
Franks, David	G	6-4	290	2/7/66	Connecticut	Waterbury, Conn.	D9
Galbreath, Neil (1)	CB	6-0	180	10/25/65	Central State, Okla.	Guthrie, Okla.	FA
Harris, Elroy	RB	5-9	218	8/8/66	Eastern Kentucky	Maitland, Fla.	D3
Hart, Roy (1)	NT	6-1	280	7/10/65	South Carolina	Tifton, Ga.	D6-'88
Heck, Andy	T	6-6	291	1/1/67	Notre Dame	Fairfax, Va.	D1
Henry, James	CB	5-9	190	10/24/65	Southern Mississippi	Poplarville, Miss.	D4b
Jefferson, James (1)	CB	6-1	195	11/18/63	Texas A&I	Kingsville, Tex.	FA
Kors, R.J.	S	6-0	195	6/27/66	Long Beach State	Woodland Hills, Calif.	D12
McCoy, Keith (1)	CB	5-11	177	11/27/64	Fresno State	Compton, Calif.	FA
McNeal, Travis	TE	6-3	239	1/10/67	Tenn.-Chattanooga	Birmingham, Ala.	D4a
Nettles, Mike	CB	5-10	188	8/23/67	Memphis State	Pensacola, Fla.	D7
Pearson, Pat (1)	G	6-4	272	3/2/65	Southern Mississippi	Huntsville, Ala.	FA
Peoples, Tim (1)	S	6-0	201	7/26/64	Washington	San Jose, Calif.	FA
Ramos, Mike	S	6-0	193	11/1/62	Washington	Missoula, Mont.	FA
Sandusky, Jim (1)	WR	5-10	182	9/9/61	San Diego State	Othello, Wash.	FA
Tofflemire, Joe	C	6-2	270	7/7/65	Arizona	Post Falls, Idaho	D2
Tyler, Robert (1)	TE	6-5	259	10/12/65	South Carolina State	Salley, N.C.	D8-'88
Weathers, Monte (1)	WR	5-8	165	1/20/66	Pittsburg State, Kan.	Riverton, Kan.	FA
Williams, Marlin	DE	6-3	253	4/12/65	Western Illinois	Tampa, Fla.	D8

The term NFL Rookie is defined as a player who is in his first season of professional football and has not been on the roster of another professional football team for any regular-season or postseason games. A Rookie is designated by an "R" on NFL rosters. Players who have been active in another professional football league or players who have NFL experience, including either preseason training camp or being on an active roster for fewer than three regular-season or postseason games, are termed NFL First-Year Players. An NFL First-Year Player is designated by a "1" on NFL rosters. Thereafter, a player on an NFL active roster for at least three regular-season or postseason games is credited with an additional year of NFL playing experience.

NOTES

THE NFC

ATLANTA FALCONS

National Football Conference Western Division

Team Colors: Red, Black, White, and Silver

Suwanee Road at I-85
Suwanee, Georgia 30174
Telephone: (404) 945-1111

Club Officials

Chairman of the Board: Rankin M. Smith, Sr.
President: Rankin Smith, Jr.
Executive Vice President: Taylor Smith
Vice President & Chief Financial Officer: Jim Hay
Director of College Player Personnel: Ken Herock
Director of Pro Scouting: Chuck Connor
Administrative Assistant: Danny Mock
Scouts: Charley Armey, Elbert Dubenion, Bill Groman, Joe Mack
Director of Marketing: Tommy Nobis
Director of Public Relations: Charlie Taylor
Asst. Director of Public Relations: Frank Kleha
Public Relations Assistant/Cheerleader Coordinator: Carol Breeding
Director of Ticket Operations: Jack Ragsdale
Assistant Director of Ticket Operations: Luci Bailey
Director of Video Operations: Tom Atcheson
Assistant Director of Video Operations: Andy Commer
Controller: Wallace Norman
Head Trainer: Jerry Rhea
Assistant Trainer: Billy Brooks
Equipment Manager: Whitey Zimmerman
Assistant Equipment Manager: Horace Daniel

Stadium: Atlanta-Fulton County Stadium • **Capacity:** 59,643
521 Capitol Avenue, S.W.
Atlanta, Georgia 30312

Playing Surface: Grass (PAT)

Training Camp: Suwanee Road at I-85
Suwanee, Georgia 30174

1989 Schedule

Preseason

Aug. 12	at Philadelphia	7:30
Aug. 19	at Tampa Bay	7:00
Aug. 26	**New England**	7:30
Sept. 1	vs. Buff. at Jacksonville, Fla.	8:00

Regular Season

Sept. 10	**Los Angeles Rams**	1:00
Sept. 17	**Dallas**	1:00
Sept. 24	at Indianapolis	12:00
Oct. 1	vs. Green Bay at Milwaukee	12:00
Oct. 8	at Los Angeles Rams	1:00
Oct. 15	**New England**	1:00
Oct. 22	at Phoenix	1:00
Oct. 29	at New Orleans	12:00
Nov. 5	**Buffalo**	1:00
Nov. 12	at San Francisco	1:00
Nov. 19	**New Orleans**	1:00
Nov. 26	at New York Jets	1:00
Dec. 3	**San Francisco**	1:00
Dec. 10	at Minnesota	12:00
Dec. 17	**Washington**	4:00
Dec. 24	**Detroit**	1:00

Falcons Coaching History

(127-208-5)

1966-68	Norb Hecker*	4-26-1
1968-74	Norm Van Brocklin**	37-49-3
1974-76	Marion Campbell***	6-19-0
1976	Pat Peppler	3-6-0
1977-82	Leeman Bennett	47-44-0
1983-86	Dan Henning	22-41-1
1987-88	Marion Campbell	8-23-0

*Released after three games in 1968
**Released after eight games in 1974
***Released after five games in 1976

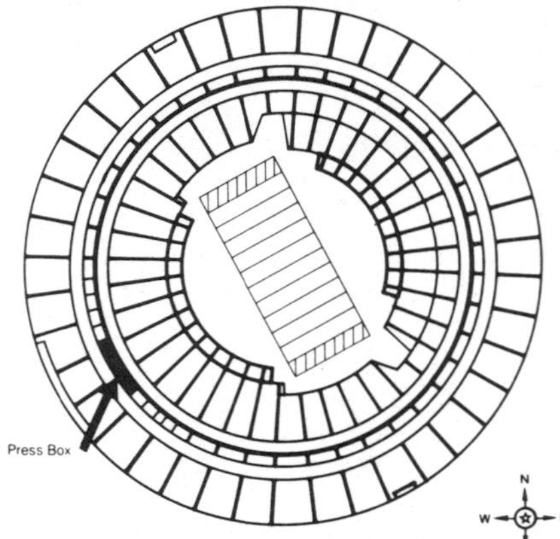

ATLANTA-FULTON COUNTY STADIUM

Record Holders

Individual Records—Career

Category	Name	Performance
Rushing (Yds.)	Gerald Riggs, 1982-88	6,631
Passing (Yds.)	Steve Bartkowski, 1975-1985	23,468
Passing (TDs)	Steve Bartkowski, 1975-1985	154
Receiving (No.)	Alfred Jenkins, 1975-1983	359
Receiving (Yds.)	Alfred Jenkins, 1975-1983	6,257
Interceptions	Rolland Lawrence, 1973-1980	39
Punting (Avg.)	Rick Donnelly, 1985-88	42.6
Punt Return (Avg.)	Al Dodd, 1973-74	11.8
Kickoff Return (Avg.)	Ron Smith, 1966-67	24.3
Field Goals	Mick Luckhurst, 1981-87	115
Touchdowns (Tot.)	Gerald Riggs, 1982-88	48
Points	Mick Luckhurst, 1981-87	558

Individual Records—Single Season

Category	Name	Performance
Rushing (Yds.)	Gerald Riggs, 1985	1,719
Passing (Yds.)	Steve Bartkowski, 1981	3,830
Passing (TDs)	Steve Bartkowski, 1980	31
Receiving (No.)	William Andrews, 1981	81
Receiving (Yds.)	Alfred Jenkins, 1981	1,358
Interceptions	Scott Case, 1988	10
Punting (Avg.)	Billy Lothridge, 1968	44.3
Punt Return (Avg.)	Gerald Tinker, 1974	13.9
Kickoff Return (Avg.)	Sylvester Stamps, 1987	27.5
Field Goals	Nick Mike-Mayer, 1973	26
Touchdowns (Tot.)	Alfred Jenkins, 1981	13
	Gerald Riggs, 1984	13
Points	Mick Luckhurst, 1981	114

Individual Records—Single Game

Category	Name	Performance
Rushing (Yds.)	Gerald Riggs, 9-2-84	202
Passing (Yds.)	Steve Bartkowski, 11-15-81	416
Passing (TDs)	Randy Johnson, 11-16-69	4
	Steve Bartkowski, 10-19-80	4
	Steve Bartkowski, 10-18-81	4
Receiving (No.)	William Andrews, 11-15-81	15
Receiving (Yds.)	Alfred Jackson, 12-2-84	193
Interceptions	Many times	2
	Last time by Scott Case, 11-27-88	
Field Goals	Nick Mike-Mayer, 11-4-73	5
	Tim Mazzetti, 10-30-78	5
Touchdowns (Tot.)	Many times	3
	Last time by Gerald Riggs, 11-17-85	
Points	Many times	18
	Last time by Gerald Riggs, 11-17-85	

1988 Team Record

Preseason (2-2)

Date	Result		Opponents
8/6	W	34-30	at New England
8/13	L	13-27	Kansas City
8/20	W	19-14	Tampa Bay
8/27	L	17-34	vs. Washington at Birmingham, Ala.
		83-105	

Regular Season (5-11)

Date	Result		Opponents	Att.
9/4	L	17-31	at Detroit	31,075
9/11	L	21-29	New Orleans	48,901
9/18	W	34-17	at San Francisco	60,168
9/25	L	20-26	at Dallas	39,702
10/2	L	20-31	Seattle	28,619
10/9	L	0-33	L.A. Rams	30,852
10/16	L	14-30	at Denver	75,287
10/23	L	16-23	N.Y. Giants	45,092
10/30	W	27-24	at Philadelphia	60,091
11/6	W	20- 0	Green Bay	29,952
11/13	L	7-10	San Diego	26,329
11/20	W	12- 6	at L.A. Raiders	40,967
11/27	W	17-10	Tampa Bay	14,020
12/4	L	3-13	San Francisco	44,048
12/11	L	7-22	at L.A. Rams	42,828
12/18	L	9-10	at New Orleans	60,566

Score by Periods

Falcons	33	82	45	84	0	—	244
Opponents	50	89	75	101	0	—	315

Attendance

Home 267,813 Away 410,684 Total 678,497
Single-game home record, 59,257 (10-30-77)
Single-season home record, 442,457 (1980)

1988 Team Statistics

	Falcons	Opp.
Total First Downs	257	312
Rushing	106	124
Passing	136	168
Penalty	15	20
Third Down: Made/Att.	89/239	86/214
Fourth Down: Made/Att.	6/8	5/10
Total Net Yards	4582	5692
Avg. Per Game	286.4	355.8
Total Plays	1002	1052
Avg. Per Play	4.6	5.4
Net Yards Rushing	2016	2319
Avg. Per Game	126.0	144.9
Total Rushes	478	518
Net Yards Passing	2566	3373
Avg. Per Game	160.4	210.8
Sacked/Yards Lost	43/348	30/211
Gross Yards	2914	3584
Att./Completions	481/250	504/281
Completion Pct.	52.0	55.8
Had Intercepted	19	24
Punts/Avg.	98/40.0	73/39.6
Net Punting Avg.	35.7	32.7
Penalties/Yards Lost	67/542	92/761
Fumbles/Ball Lost	29/18	29/14
Touchdowns	27	34
Rushing	11	14
Passing	13	17
Returns	3	3
Avg. Time of Possession	28:08	31:52

1988 Individual Statistics

Scoring	TD R	TD P	TD Rt	PAT	FG	Saf	TP
Davis	0	0	0	25/27	19/30	0	82
Settle	7	1	0	0/0	0/0	0	48
Haynes	0	4	0	0/0	0/0	0	24
Bailey	0	2	0	0/0	0/0	0	12
Dixon	0	2	0	0/0	0/0	0	12
Higdon	0	2	0	0/0	0/0	0	12
Dils	1	0	0	0/0	0/0	0	6
Gann	0	0	1	0/0	0/0	0	6
Griffin, Wash.-Atl.	0	1	0	0/0	0/0	0	6
Lang	0	1	0	0/0	0/0	0	6
C. Miller	1	0	0	0/0	0/0	0	6
Moore	0	0	1	0/0	0/0	0	6
Primus	1	0	0	0/0	0/0	0	6
Riggs	1	0	0	0/0	0/0	0	6
Tuggle	0	0	1	0/0	0/0	0	6
Whisenhunt	0	1	0	0/0	0/0	0	6
Falcons	11	13	3	25/27	19/30	0	244
Opponents	14	17	3	31/34	26/36	1	315

Passing	Att.	Comp.	Yds.	Pct.	TD	Int.	Tkld.	Rate
C. Miller	351	184	2133	52.4	11	12	24/207	67.3
Dils	99	49	566	49.5	2	5	15/112	52.8
Millen	31	17	215	54.8	0	2	4/29	49.8
Falcons	481	250	2914	52.0	13	19	43/348	63.2
Opponents	504	281	3584	55.8	17	24	30/211	69.6

Rushing	Att.	Yds.	Avg.	LG	TD
Settle	232	1024	4.4	62	7
Riggs	113	488	4.3	34	1
Lang	53	191	3.6	19	0
C. Miller	31	138	4.5	29	1
Primus	35	95	2.7	29t	1
Dixon	7	69	9.9	24	0
Griffin, Wash.-Atl.	6	23	3.8	9	0
Millen	1	7	7.0	7	0
Hester	1	3	3.0	3	0
Dils	2	1	0.5	1t	1
Stamps	3	0	0.0	3	0
Falcons	478	2016	4.2	62	11
Opponents	518	2319	4.5	44	14

Receiving	No.	Yds.	Avg.	LG	TD
Settle	68	570	8.4	27	1
Lang	37	398	10.8	50	1
Dixon	28	368	13.1	36	2
Riggs	22	171	7.8	30	0
Bailey	17	437	25.7	68t	2
Whisenhunt	16	174	10.9	25	1
Haynes	13	232	17.8	49t	4
Hester	12	176	14.7	41	0
Wilkins	11	134	12.2	33	0
Primus	8	42	5.3	8	0
Milling	5	66	13.2	34	0
Matthews	5	64	12.8	21	0
Stamps	5	22	4.4	7	0
Higdon	3	60	20.0	34t	2
Griffin, Wash.-Atl.	2	9	4.5	5	1
Falcons	250	2914	11.7	68t	13
Opponents	281	3584	12.8	68t	17

Interceptions	No.	Yds.	Avg.	LG	TD
Case	10	47	4.7	12	0
Moore	5	56	11.2	47t	1
Clark	4	40	10.0	21	0
Bruce	2	10	5.0	10	0
Gordon	2	10	5.0	7	0
Butler	1	22	22.0	22	0
Falcons	24	185	7.7	47t	1
Opponents	19	214	11.3	58	2

Punting	No.	Yds.	Avg.	In 20	LG
Donnelly	98	3920	40.0	27	61
Falcons	98	3920	40.0	27	61
Opponents	73	2893	39.6	21	56

Punt Returns	No.	FC	Yds.	Avg.	LG	TD
Barnes	34	8	307	9.0	68	0
Matthews	6	0	26	4.3	10	0
Cooper	2	1	10	5.0	10	0
Falcons	42	9	343	8.2	68	0
Opponents	51	23	297	5.8	31	0

Kickoff Returns	No.	Yds.	Avg.	LG	TD
Cooper	16	331	20.7	28	0
Gordon	14	209	14.9	32	0
Stamps	12	219	18.3	27	0
Barnes	6	142	23.7	36	0
Haynes	6	113	18.8	25	0
Griffin, Wash.-Atl.	3	45	15.0	24	0
Shelley	2	5	2.5	5	0
Dukes	1	13	13.0	13	0
Lang	1	12	12.0	12	0
Primus	1	13	13.0	13	0
Falcons	59	1057	17.9	36	0
Opponents	48	982	20.5	41	0

Sacks	No.
Bruce	6.0
Bryan	5.0
Cotton	5.0
Gann	4.0
Green	4.0
Casillas	2.0
Rade	2.0
Case	1.0
Gordon	1.0
Falcons	30.0
Opponents	43.0

1989 Draft Choices

Round	Name	Pos.	College
1.	Deion Sanders	DB	Florida State
	Shawn Collins	WR	Northern Arizona
2.	Ralph Norwood	T	Louisiana State
3.	Keith Jones	RB	Illinois
6.	Troy Sadowski	TE	Georgia
7.	Undra Johnson	RB	West Virginia
8.	Paul Singer	QB	Western Illinois
9.	Chris Dunn	LB	Cal Poly-SLO
11.	Greg Paterra	RB	Slippery Rock
12.	Tony Bowick	NT	Tenn.-Chattanooga

Atlanta Falcons 1989 Veteran Roster

No.	Name	Pos.	Ht.	Wt.	Birth-date	NFL Exp.	College	Hometown	How Acq.	'88 Games/ Starts
82	Bailey, Stacey	WR	6-0	157	2/10/60	8	San Jose State	San Rafael, Calif.	D3-'82	10/10
71	Baldinger, Gary	NT	6-3	265	10/4/63	4	Wake Forest	Philadelphia, Pa.	FA(KC)-'89#	11/4*
5	Benyola, George	K	5-10	185	9/17/64	2	Louisiana Tech	Rochester Hills, Mich.	FA-'89	0*
97	Boyle, Jim	T	6-5	285	7/27/62	3	Tulane	Cincinnati, Ohio	FA-'89	0*
63	Brotzki, Bob	T	6-5	275	12/24/62	4	Syracuse	Sandusky, Ohio	FA(Dall)-'89#	7/0*
98	Brown, Greg	DE	6-5	265	1/5/57	9	Kansas State	Washington, D.C.	T(Phil)-'87	16/1
93	Bruce, Aundray	LB	6-5	248	4/30/66	2	Auburn	Montgomery, Ala.	D1-'88	16/16
77	Bryan, Rick	DE	6-4	265	3/20/62	6	Oklahoma	Coweta, Okla.	D1-'84	16/15
23	Butler, Bobby	CB	5-11	175	5/28/59	9	Florida State	Delray Beach, Fla.	D1-'81	16/16
10	†Campbell, Scott	QB	6-0	195	4/15/62	5	Purdue	Hershey, Pa.	FA-'86	0*
68	Carlson, Mark	T	6-6	295	6/6/63	2	Southern Connecticut	Milford, Conn.	FA-'89	0*
25	Case, Scott	CB	6-0	178	5/17/62	6	Oklahoma	Edmond, Okla.	D2a-'84	16/15
75	Casillas, Tony	NT	6-3	280	10/26/63	4	Oklahoma	Norman, Okla.	D1a-'86	16/16
74	Clayton, Stan	T-G	6-3	265	1/31/65	2	Penn State	Cherry Hill, N.J.	D10-'88	2/2
20	Cooper, Evan	CB-S	5-11	194	6/28/62	6	Michigan	Miami, Fla.	FA-'88	9/0
51	Cotton, Marcus	LB	6-3	230	8/11/66	2	Southern California	Oakland, Calif.	D2-'88	11/5
	Craig, Paco	WR	5-10	170	2/2/65	2	UCLA	Riverside, Calif.	FA-'89	8/0*
22	Dimry, Charles	CB-S	6-0	175	1/31/66	2	Nevada-Las Vegas	San Diego, Calif.	D5-'88	16/1
86	Dixon, Floyd	WR	5-9	170	4/9/64	4	Stephen F. Austin	Beaumont, Tex.	D6a-'86	14/14
3	Donnelly, Rick	P	6-0	190	5/17/62	5	Wyoming	Long Island, N.Y.	FA-'85	16/0
64	†Dukes, Jamie	G	6-1	278	6/14/64	4	Florida State	Orlando, Fla.	FA-'86	12/5
48	Flowers, Kenny	RB	6-0	210	3/14/64	2	Clemson	Daytona Beach, Fla.	D2-'87	0*
79	†Fralic, Bill	G-T	6-5	280	10/31/62	5	Pittsburgh	Penn Hills, Pa.	D1-'85	14/14
76	†Gann, Mike	DE	6-5	275	10/19/63	5	Notre Dame	Lakewood, Colo.	D2-'85	16/16
41	†Gordon, Tim	S	6-0	188	5/7/65	3	Tulsa	Ardmore, Okla.	FA-'87	16/5
99	Green, Tim	LB	6-2	245	12/16/63	4	Syracuse	Liverpool, N.Y.	D1b-'86	10/5
26	Griffin, Keith	RB	5-8	185	10/26/61	6	Miami	Eastmoor, Ohio	FA-'88	8/0*
73	Harvey, James	G	6-3	265	11/27/65	2	Jackson State	New Orleans, La.	FA-'89	0*
81	Haynes, Michael	WR	6-0	180	12/24/65	2	Northern Arizona	New Orleans, La.	D7-'88	15/5
80	Heller, Ron	TE	6-3	235	9/18/63	3	Oregon State	Grass Valley, Calif.	FA(SF)-'89#	16/8*
89	Hester, Jessie	WR	5-11	170	1/21/63	5	Florida State	Belle Glade, Fla.	T(Raid)-'88	16/3
88	Higdon, Alex	TE	6-5	247	9/9/66	2	Ohio State	Cincinnati, Ohio	D3-'88	3/0
69	Hoover, Houston	T	6-2	285	6/2/65	2	Jackson State	Yazoo City, Miss.	D6-'88	15/12
78	Kenn, Mike	T	6-7	277	2/9/56	12	Michigan	Evanston, Ill.	D1-'78	16/16
33	†Lang, Gene	RB	5-10	206	3/15/62	6	Louisiana State	Pass Christian, Miss.	FA-'88	16/3
87	Lee, Danzell	TE	6-2	237	3/16/63	3	Lamar	Corsicana, Tex.	FA-'88	5/0
94	Martin, Charles	NT	6-4	280	8/31/59	6	Livingston	Canton, Ga.	FA-'88	16/0
6	McFadden, Paul	K	5-11	166	9/24/61	6	Youngstown State	Euclid, Ohio	FA(NYG)-'89#	12/0*
7	†Millen, Hugh	QB	6-5	216	11/22/63	2	Washington	Seattle, Wash.	FA-'88	3/0
12	Miller, Chris	QB	6-2	200	8/9/65	3	Oregon	Eugene, Ore.	D1-'87	13/13
84	Milling, James	WR	5-9	156	2/14/56	2	Maryland	Washington, D.C.	D11-'88	6/0
34	Moore, Robert	S	5-11	190	8/15/64	4	Northwestern Louisiana	Shreveport, La.	FA-'86	16/16
67	Oswald, Paul	G	6-4	275	4/9/64	2	Kansas	Topeka, Kan.	FA-'88	3/1
49	Primus, James	RB	5-11	196	5/18/64	2	UCLA	San Diego, Calif.	D9-'88	16/6
59	Rade, John	LB	6-1	240	8/31/60	7	Boise State	Sierra Vista, Ariz.	D8-'83	15/15
55	†Radloff, Wayne	C	6-5	277	5/17/61	5	Georgia	Winter Park, Fla.	FA-'85	10/10
95	Reid, Michael	LB	6-2	226	6/25/64	3	Wisconsin	Albany, Ga.	D7-'87	16/3
66	Robison, Tommy	G	6-4	290	11/17/61	2	Texas A&M	Portland, Tex.	FA(GB)-'89#	0*
61	†Scully, John	G	6-6	270	8/2/58	9	Notre Dame	Huntington, N.Y.	D4-'81	11/11
44	Settle, John	RB	5-9	207	6/2/65	3	Appalachian State	Ruffin, N.C.	FA-'87	16/13
37	Shelley, Elbert	S	5-11	180	12/24/64	3	Arkansas State	Trumann, Ark.	D11-'87	12/0
24	Taylor, Kitrick	WR-KR	5-10	190	7/22/64	2	Washington State	Claremont, Calif.	FA(KC)-'89#	16/0*
72	Thomas, John	T	6-4	290	3/6/64	2	Toledo	Cincinnati, Ohio	FA-'89	0*
58	†Tuggle, Jessie	LB	5-11	225	2/14/65	3	Valdosta State	Griffin, Ga.	FA-'87	16/8
54	†Williams, Joel	LB	6-1	227	12/13/56	11	Wisconsin-LaCrosse	Miami, Fla.	T(Phil)-'86	14/12

* Baldinger played 11 games with Kansas City in '88; Benyola last active with N.Y. Giants in '87; Boyle played 6 games with Pittsburgh; Brotzki played 7 games with Dallas; Campbell and Flowers missed '88 season due to injury; Carlson last active with Washington in '87; Craig played 8 games with Detroit; Griffin played 8 games with Washington; Harvey played 2 games with Kansas City; Heller played 16 games with San Francisco; McFadden played 12 games with N.Y. Giants; Robison last active with Green Bay in '87; Taylor played 16 games with Kansas City; Thomas last active with N.Y. Jets in '87.

† Option playout; subject to developments.

Plan B unconditional free agent.

Traded—Running back Gerald Riggs to Washington.

Players lost through Plan B (13): WR Lew Barnes (KC; 13 games in '88), QB Kerwin Bell (TB; active for 6 games but did not play), LB Philip Brown (Ind; 0), LB Joe Costello (Raiders; 6), K Greg Davis (NE; 16), CB-S Calvin Loveall (KC; 4), T Brett Miller (SD; 15), LB Vinson Smith (Pitt; 3), RB Sylvester Stamps (TB; 4), TE Ken Whisenhunt (Wash; 16), TE Gary Wilkins (GB; 14), NT Mitch Willis (Ind; 9), C George Yarno (Hou; 16).

Also played with Falcons in '88—RB Rick Badanjek (6 games), DE Reggie Camp (6), S Bret Clark (12), CB David Croudip (6), QB Steve Dils (7), CB Leander Knight (2), WR Aubrey Matthews (4).

COACHING STAFF

Head Coach and Director of Football Operations, Marion Campbell

Pro Career: Enters his third season as Falcons head coach after rejoining and serving as defensive coordinator in 1986. Served as an assistant coach with the Boston Patriots 1962-63, Minnesota Vikings 1964-66, Los Angeles Rams 1967-68, Atlanta Falcons 1969-76 (head coach 1974-76), Philadelphia Eagles 1977-85 (head coach 1983-85). Campbell was a defensive tackle with the San Francisco 49ers 1954-55 and Philadelphia Eagles 1956-61. Career record: 31-71-1.

Background: Campbell is serving as head coach with the Falcons for the second time. He's coached three NFL teams to number-one ranked defenses. He's been to an NFL championship as both a player and assistant coach. Campbell was an All-America defensive tackle at Georgia 1948-51.

Personal: Born May 25, 1929, Chester, S.C. Marion and his wife, June, live in Alpharetta, Ga., and have two children—Scott, 27, administrative assistant for the Falcons, and Alicia, 24.

Assistant Coaches

Tommy Brasher, defensive line; born December 30, 1940, El Dorado, Ark., lives in Dunwoody, Ga. Linebacker Arkansas 1961-63. No pro playing experience. College coach: Arkansas 1970, Virginia Tech 1971-73, Northeast Louisiana 1974, 1976, Southern Methodist 1977-81. Pro coach: Shreveport Steamer (WFL) 1975, New England Patriots 1982-84, Philadelphia Eagles 1985, joined Falcons in 1986.

Fred Bruney, assistant head coach/defense; born December 30, 1931, Martins Ferry, Ohio, lives in Atlanta. Back Ohio State 1949-52. Pro defensive back San Francisco 49ers 1953-56, Pittsburgh Steelers 1957, Washington Redskins 1958, Boston Patriots 1960-62. College coach: Ohio State 1959. Pro coach: Boston Patriots 1963, Philadelphia Eagles 1964-68, 1977-85, Atlanta Falcons 1969-76, rejoined Falcons in 1986.

Scott Campbell, administrative assistant, born August 16, 1961, Philadelphia, Pa., lives in Duluth, Ga. Tackle Georgia 1982-84. No pro playing experience. College coach: Auburn 1985-86. Pro coach: Joined Falcons in 1987.

Chuck Clausen, linebackers; born June 23, 1940, Anamosa, Iowa, lives in Roswell, Ga. Defensive lineman New Mexico 1961-63. No pro playing experience. College coach: William & Mary 1969-70, Ohio State 1971-75. Pro coach: Philadelphia Eagles 1976-85, joined Falcons in 1986.

Steve Crosby, running backs; born July 3, 1950, Great Bend, Kan., lives in Norcross, Ga. Running back Fort Hays (Kan.) State 1969-72. Pro running back New York Giants 1974-76. Pro coach: Miami Dolphins 1977-82, Atlanta Falcons 1983-84, Cleveland Browns 1985, rejoined Falcons in 1986.

Rod Dowhower, offensive coordinator; born April 15, 1943, Ord, Neb., lives in Dunwoody, Ga. Quarterback San Diego State 1963-64. No pro playing experience. College coach: San Diego State 1966-72, UCLA 1974-75, Boise State 1976, Stanford 1977-79 (head coach 1979). Pro coach: St. Louis Cardinals 1973, 1982-84, Denver Broncos 1980-81, Indianapolis Colts 1985-86 (head coach), joined Falcons in 1987.

Foge Fazio, special teams/tight ends; born February 22, 1939, Dawmont, W. Va., lives in Atlanta. Linebacker-center Pittsburgh 1957-60. Pro linebacker Boston Patriots 1961. College coach: Boston University 1967, Harvard 1968, Pittsburgh 1969-72, 1977-81 (head coach), Cincinnati 1973-76, Notre Dame 1986-87. Pro coach: Joined Falcons in 1988.

Jim Hanifan, assistant head coach/offense; born September 21, 1933, Compton, Calif., lives in Dunwoody, Ga. Tight end California 1952-54. Pro tight end Toronto Argonauts (CFL) 1955. College coach: Glendale, Calif., J.C. 1964-66, Utah 1967-70, California 1971-72, San Diego State 1972-73. Pro coach: St. Louis Cardinals 1974-85 (head coach 1980-85), joined Falcons in 1987.

Atlanta Falcons 1989 First-Year Roster

Name	Pos.	Ht.	Wt.	Birth-date	College	Hometown	How Acq.
Beckman, Brad (1)	TE	6-3	240	12/31/64	Nebraska-Omaha	Lincoln, Neb.	FA
Blount, Norris	CB	6-1	200	8/11/66	Baylor	Lubbock, Tex.	FA
Booker, Deon	RB	5-10	210	3/20/67	Louisville	St. Petersburg, Fla.	FA
Bowick, Tony	NT	6-2	265	10/3/66	Tenn.-Chattanooga	Slocumb, Ala.	D12
Bullitt, Steve (1)	LB	6-2	240	4/21/65	Texas A&M	El Paso, Tex.	FA
Chapman, Edward (1)	NT	6-3	272	4/5/64	Maryland	Philadelphia, Pa.	FA
Collins, Shawn	WR	6-2	207	2/20/67	Northern Arizona	San Diego, Calif.	D1b
Dunn, Chris	LB	6-3	230	2/1/66	Cal Poly-SLO	Whittier, Calif.	D9
Floyd, Norman (1)	S	6-1	205	2/10/66	South Carolina	Greenville, S.C.	FA
Frank, Garry (1)	G-C	6-2	280	12/20/64	Mississippi State	Berlin, Wis.	FA-'88
Gainer, Herb (1)	WR	6-2	195	8/25/65	Florida State	Sarasota, Fla.	FA
Harris, Greg (1)	WR-KR	5-9	157	12/30/65	Troy State	Valdosta, Ga.	FA
Hooper, Michael (1)	DE	6-3	270	10/7/65	San Diego State	Mountain View, Calif.	FA
Jackson, Ray (1)	CB	5-11	189	1/11/65	Ohio State	Akron, Ohio	FA
Johnson, Undra	RB	5-9	199	1/8/66	West Virginia	Ft. Lauderdale, Fla.	D7
Jones, Derwin (1)	NT-DE	6-4	275	9/6/64	Miami	Miami, Fla.	FA
Jones, Keith	RB	6-1	205	3/20/66	Illinois	Rock Hills, Mo.	D3
Jones, Robert (1)	S	6-1	205	6/22/65	Houston	Blanco, Tex.	FA
Metcalf, Maury	LB	6-2	240	2/2/66	Washington State	Sacramento, Calif.	FA
Millett, Mark	TE	6-3	235	3/5/66	S.W. Texas State	New Braunfels, Tex.	FA
Mira, George (1)	LB	6-0	235	6/13/65	Miami	Key West, Fla.	FA
Modesitt, Jeff (1)	TE	6-5	250	1/1/64	Delaware	Terre Haute, Ind.	FA
Murino, Louis (1)	G-T	6-6	301	1/14/66	Cal St.-Northridge	Downey, Calif.	FA
Norwood, Ralph	T	6-6	273	1/23/66	Louisiana State	Walker, La.	D2
Paterra, Greg	RB	5-11	211	5/12/67	Slippery Rock	McKeesport, Pa.	D11
Riley, Bob (1)	T	6-5	284	6/23/64	Indiana	Pittsburgh, Pa.	FA
Sadowski, Troy	TE	6-5	243	12/8/65	Georgia	Chamblee, Ga.	D6
Sanders, Deion	CB	6-0	187	8/9/67	Florida State	Ft. Myers, Fla.	D1a
Schmidt, Derek (1)	K	5-8	170	7/20/65	Florida State	Scotland	FA
Singer, Paul	QB	6-3	193	3/18/66	Western Illinois	Ft. Knox, Kan.	D8
Thaxton, Galand (1)	LB	6-1	238	10/23/64	Wyoming	Denver, Colo.	FA
Thomas, George (1)	WR	5-9	169	7/11/64	Nevada-Las Vegas	Indio, Calif.	D6a-'88
Whitaker, Danta (1)	TE	6-4	243	3/14/64	Mississippi Valley St.	Atlanta, Ga.	FA
Widmeyer, Kelly (1)	T	6-7	310	7/3/61	Weber State	Ogden, Utah	FA

The term NFL Rookie is defined as a player who is in his first season of professional football and has not been on the roster of another professional football team for any regular-season or postseason games. A Rookie is designated by an "R" on NFL rosters. Players who have been active in another professional football league or players who have NFL experience, including either preseason training camp or being on an active roster for fewer than three regular-season or postseason games, are termed NFL First-Year Players. An NFL First-Year Player is designated by a "1" on NFL rosters. Thereafter, a player on an NFL active roster for at least three regular-season or postseason games is credited with an additional year of NFL playing experience.

NOTES

Claude Humphrey, defensive assistant; born November 19, 1947, Memphis, Tenn., lives in Atlanta. Defensive end Tennessee State 1965-67. Pro defensive end Atlanta Falcons 1968-77, Philadelphia Eagles 1977-81. Pro coach: Philadelphia 1982, joined Falcons in 1987.

Tim Jorgensen, strength and conditioning; born April 21, 1955, St. Louis, Mo., lives in Snellville, Ga. Guard Southwest Missouri State 1974-76. No pro playing experience. College coach: Southwest Missouri State 1977-78, Alabama 1979, Louisiana State 1980-83. Pro coach: Philadelphia Eagles 1984-86, joined Falcons in 1987.

Jimmy Raye, receivers, born March 26, 1946, Fayetteville, N.C., lives in Suwanee, Ga. Quarterback Michigan State 1965-67. Pro defensive back Philadelphia Eagles 1969. College coach: Michigan State 1971-75, Wyoming 1976. Pro coach: San Francisco 49ers 1977, Detroit Lions 1978-79, Atlanta Falcons 1980-82, Los Angeles Rams 1983-84, Tampa Bay Buccaneers 1985-86, rejoined Falcons in 1987.

National Football Conference Central Division

Team Colors: Navy Blue, Orange, and White

Corporate Headquarters:
Halas Hall
250 North Washington
Lake Forest, Illinois 60045
Telephone: (312) 295-6600

Club Officials

Chairman of the Board: Edward W. McCaskey
President and Chief Executive Officer: Michael B. McCaskey
Secretary: Virginia H. McCaskey
Vice President-Player Personnel: Bill Tobin
Director of Administration: Tim LeFevour
Director of Community Involvement: Pat McCaskey
Director of Finance: Ted Phillips
Director of Marketing and Communications: Ken Valdiserri
Director of Public Relations: Bryan Harlan
Assistant Director of Public Relations: John Bostrom
Ticket Manager: Gary Christenson
Computer Systems: Greg Gershuny
Video Director: Mitch Friedman
Trainer: Fred Caito
Assistant Trainer: Brian McCaskey
Strength Coordinator: Clyde Emrich
Equipment Manager: Gary Haeger
Assistant Equipment Manager: Tony Medlin
Scouts: Jim Parmer, Rod Graves, Don King, Ken Geiger

Stadium: Soldier Field • **Capacity:** 66,949
425 McFetridge Place
Chicago, Illinois 60605

Playing Surface: Grass

Training Camp: Wisconsin-Platteville
Platteville, Wisconsin 53818

1989 Schedule

Preseason

Aug. 14	at Miami	8:00
Aug. 19	**San Diego**	6:00
Aug. 27	**Kansas City**	7:00
Sept. 2	at Los Angeles Raiders	1:00

Regular Season

Sept. 10	**Cincinnati**	12:00
Sept. 17	**Minnesota**	3:00
Sept. 24	at Detroit	1:00
Oct. 2	**Philadelphia** (Monday)	8:00
Oct. 8	at Tampa Bay	1:00
Oct. 15	**Houston**	12:00
Oct. 23	at Cleveland (Monday)	9:00
Oct. 29	**Los Angeles Rams**	12:00
Nov. 5	at Green Bay	12:00
Nov. 12	at Pittsburgh	1:00
Nov. 19	**Tampa Bay**	12:00
Nov. 26	at Washington	4:00
Dec. 3	at Minnesota	7:00
Dec. 10	**Detroit**	12:00
Dec. 17	**Green Bay**	12:00
Dec. 24	at San Francisco	1:00

Bears Coaching History

Decatur Staleys 1920
Chicago Staleys 1921
(545-342-42)

1920-29	George Halas	84-31-19
1930-32	Ralph Jones	24-10-7
1933-42	George Halas*	89-24-4
1942-45	Hunk Anderson-Luke Johnsos**	23-12-2
1946-55	George Halas	76-43-2
1956-57	John (Paddy) Driscoll	14-10-1
1958-67	George Halas	76-53-6
1968-71	Jim Dooley	20-36-0
1972-74	Abe Gibron	11-30-1
1975-77	Jack Pardee	20-23-0
1978-81	Neill Armstrong	30-35-0
1982-88	Mike Ditka	78-35-0

*Retired after six games to enter U.S. Navy
**Co-coaches

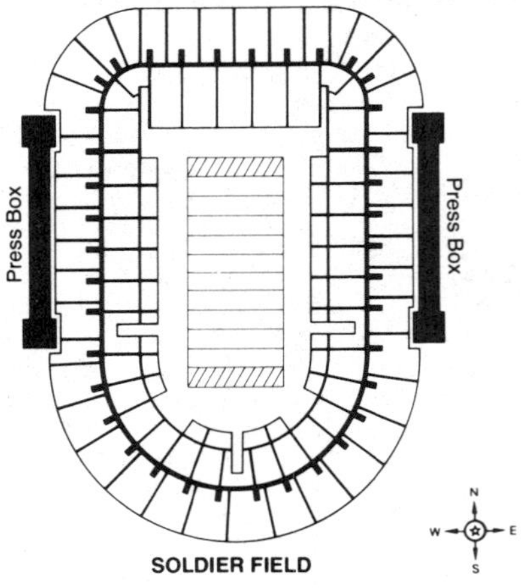

SOLDIER FIELD

Record Holders

Individual Records—Career

Category	Name	Performance
Rushing (Yds.)	Walter Payton, 1975-1987	*16,726
Passing (Yds.)	Sid Luckman, 1939-1950	14,686
Passing (TDs)	Sid Luckman, 1939-1950	137
Receiving (No.)	Walter Payton, 1975-1987	492
Receiving (Yds.)	Johnny Morris, 1958-1967	5,059
Interceptions	Gary Fencik, 1976-1987	38
Punting (Avg.)	George Gulyanics, 1947-1952	44.5
Punt Return (Avg.)	Ray (Scooter) McLean, 1940-47	14.8
Kickoff Return (Avg.)	Gale Sayers, 1965-1971	30.6
Field Goals	Bob Thomas, 1975-1984	128
Touchdowns (Tot.)	Walter Payton, 1975-1987	125
Points	Walter Payton, 1975-1987	750

Individual Records—Single Season

Category	Name	Performance
Rushing (Yds.)	Walter Payton, 1977	1,852
Passing (Yds.)	Bill Wade, 1962	3,172
Passing (TDs)	Sid Luckman, 1943	28
Receiving (No.)	Johnny Morris, 1964	93
Receiving (Yds.)	Johnny Morris, 1964	1,200
Interceptions	Roosevelt Taylor, 1963	9
Punting (Avg.)	Bobby Joe Green, 1963	46.5
Punt Return (Avg.)	Harry Clark, 1943	15.8
Kickoff Return (Avg.)	Gale Sayers, 1967	37.7
Field Goals	Kevin Butler, 1985	31
Touchdowns (Tot.)	Gale Sayers, 1965	**22
Points	Kevin Butler, 1985	**144

Individual Records—Single Game

Category	Name	Performance
Rushing (Yds.)	Walter Payton, 11-20-77	*275
Passing (Yds.)	Johnny Lujack, 12-11-49	468
Passing (TDs)	Sid Luckman, 11-14-43	*7
Receiving (No.)	Jim Keane, 10-23-49	14
Receiving (Yds.)	Harlon Hill, 10-31-54	214
Interceptions	Many times	3
	Last time by Ross Brupbacher, 12-12-76	
Field Goals	Roger LeClerc, 12-3-61	5
	Mac Percival, 10-20-68	5
Touchdowns (Tot.)	Gale Sayers, 12-12-65	*6
Points	Gale Sayers, 12-12-65	36

*NFL Record
**NFL Rookie Record

1988 Team Record

Preseason (1-3)

Date	Result		Opponents
8/6	W	20-17	Miami
8/14	L	21-28	vs. Minnesota at Goteborg, Sweden
8/22	L	9-17	at Dallas
8/26	L	22-37	L.A. Raiders
		72-99	

Regular Season (12-4)

Date	Result		Opponents	Att.
9/4	W	34- 7	Miami	63,330
9/11	W	17-13	at Indianapolis	60,503
9/18	L	7-31	Minnesota	63,990
9/25	W	24- 6	at Green Bay	56,492
10/2	W	24- 3	Buffalo	62,793
10/9	W	24- 7	at Detroit	64,526
10/16	W	17- 7	Dallas	64,759
10/24	W	10- 9	San Francisco	65,293
10/30	L	7-30	at New England	60,821
11/6	W	28-10	Tampa Bay	56,892
11/13	W	34-14	at Washington	52,418
11/20	W	27-15	at Tampa Bay	67,070
11/27	W	16- 0	Green Bay	62,026
12/5	L	3-23	at L.A. Rams	65,579
12/11	W	13-12	Detroit	55,010
12/19	L	27-28	at Minnesota	62,067

Postseason (1-1)

Date	Result		Opponent	Att.
12/31	W	20-12	Philadelphia	65,534
1/8	L	3-28	San Francisco	66,946

Score by Periods

Bears	77	131	42	62	0	—	312
Opponents	49	56	50	60	0	—	215

Attendance

Home 494,093 Away 489,476 Total 983,569
Single-game home record, 65,534 (12-31-88)
Single-season home record, 495,484 (1986)

1988 Team Statistics

	Bears	Opp.
Total First Downs	303	264
Rushing	137	76
Passing	134	158
Penalty	32	30
Third Down: Made/Att.	91/217	68/216
Fourth Down: Made/Att.	7/17	8/18
Total Net Yards	5317	4360
Avg. Per Game	332.3	272.5
Total Plays	1040	977
Avg. Per Play	5.1	4.5
Net Yards Rushing	2319	1326
Avg. Per Game	144.9	82.9
Total Rushes	555	389
Net Yards Passing	2998	3034
Avg. Per Game	187.4	189.6
Sacked/Yards Lost	24/175	43/365
Gross Yards	3173	3399
Att./Completions	461/248	545/245
Completion Pct.	53.8	45.0
Had Intercepted	15	26
Punts/Avg.	79/41.5	90/40.2
Net Punting Avg.	33.4	34.8
Penalties/Yards Lost	88/644	102/804
Fumbles/Ball Lost	37/19	17/9
Touchdowns	38	25
Rushing	25	5
Passing	13	18
Returns	0	2
Avg. Time of Possession	33:02	26:58

1988 Individual Statistics

Scoring	TD R	TD P	TD Rt	PAT	FG	Saf	TP
Butler	0	0	0	37/38	15/19	0	82
Anderson	12	0	0	0/0	0/0	0	72
Gentry	1	3	0	0/0	0/0	0	24
McKinnon	1	3	0	0/0	0/0	0	24
McMahon	4	0	0	0/0	0/0	0	24
Morris	0	4	0	0/0	0/0	0	24
Sanders	3	0	0	0/0	0/0	0	18
Moorehead	0	2	0	0/0	0/0	0	12
Suhey	2	0	0	0/0	0/0	0	12
Harbaugh	1	0	0	0/0	0/0	0	6
Muster	0	1	0	0/0	0/0	0	6
Tomczak	1	0	0	0/0	0/0	0	6
McMichael	0	0	0	0/0	0/0	1	2
Bears	25	13	0	37/38	15/19	1	312
Opponents	5	18	2	22/25	13/22	2	215

Passing	Att.	Comp.	Yds.	Pct.	TD	Int.	Tkld.	Rate
McMahon	192	114	1346	59.4	6	7	13/79	76.0
Tomczak	170	86	1310	50.6	7	6	5/47	75.4
Harbaugh	97	47	514	48.5	0	2	6/49	55.9
Anderson	1	0	0	0.0	0	0	0/0	39.6
Wagner	1	1	3	100.0	0	0	0/0	79.2
Bears	461	248	3173	53.8	13	15	24/175	71.4
Opponents	545	245	3399	45.0	18	26	43/365	56.7

Rushing	Att.	Yds.	Avg.	LG	TD
Anderson	249	1106	4.4	80t	12
Sanders	95	332	3.5	20t	3
Suhey	87	253	2.9	19	2
Muster	44	197	4.5	15	0
Harbaugh	19	110	5.8	19	1
McMahon	26	104	4.0	16	4
Gentry	7	86	12.3	58t	1
Morris	3	40	13.3	21	0
Tomczak	13	40	3.1	17	1
McKinnon	3	25	8.3	12	1
Thomas	5	20	4.0	8	0
Davis	1	3	3.0	3	0
Kozlowski	1	3	3.0	3	0
Wagner	2	0	0.0	0	0
Bears	555	2319	4.2	80t	25
Opponents	389	1326	3.4	32	5

Receiving	No.	Yds.	Avg.	LG	TD
McKinnon	45	704	15.6	76t	3
Anderson	39	371	9.5	36	0
Gentry	33	486	14.7	45	3
Morris	28	498	17.8	63t	4
Muster	21	236	11.2	40t	1
Suhey	20	154	7.7	29	0
Davis	15	220	14.7	36	0
Thornton	15	135	9.0	19	0
Moorehead	14	133	9.5	28	2
Sanders	9	94	10.4	39	0
Boso	6	50	8.3	15	0
Kozlowski	3	92	30.7	50	0
Bears	248	3173	12.8	76t	13
Opponents	245	3399	13.9	80t	18

Interceptions	No.	Yds.	Avg.	LG	TD
Jackson	8	94	11.8	46	0
Tate	4	35	8.8	17	0
Morrissey	3	13	4.3	13	0
Duerson	2	18	9.0	18	0
Richardson	2	15	7.5	15	0
Krumm	2	14	7.0	14	0
Rivera	2	0	0.0	0	0
Douglass	1	35	35.0	35	0
Singletary	1	13	13.0	13	0
Gayle	1	0	0.0	0	0
Bears	26	237	9.1	46	0
Opponents	15	175	11.7	94t	1

Punting	No.	Yds.	Avg.	In 20	LG
Wagner	79	3282	41.5	18	70
Bears	79	3282	41.5	18	70
Opponents	90	3622	40.2	29	62

Punt Returns	No.	FC	Yds.	Avg.	LG	TD
McKinnon	34	8	277	8.1	23	0
Davis	3	1	17	5.7	13	0
Kozlowski	1	0	0	0.0	0	0
Bears	38	9	294	7.7	23	0
Opponents	40	9	447	11.2	64	0

Kickoff Returns	No.	Yds.	Avg.	LG	TD
Gentry	27	578	21.4	51	0
Sanders	13	248	19.1	38	0
Muster	3	33	11.0	15	0
Kozlowski	2	37	18.5	24	0
Duerson*	0	0	—	0	0
Bears	45	896	19.9	51	0
Opponents	56	1130	20.2	51	0

*one fair catch

Sacks	No.
McMichael	11.5
Dent	10.5
Hampton	9.5
Harris	3.5
Chapura	2.0
Rivera	2.0
Duerson	1.0
Johnson	1.0
Singletary	1.0
Smith	1.0
Bears	43.0
Opponents	24.0

1989 Draft Choices

Round	Name	Pos.	College
1.	Donnell Woolford	DB	Clemson
	Trace Armstrong	DE	Florida
2.	John Roper	LB	Texas A&M
	Dave Zawatson	T	California
3.	Jerry Fontenot	G	Texas A&M
4.	Markus Paul	DB	Syracuse
5.	Mark Green	RB	Notre Dame
	Greg Gilbert	LB	Alabama
7.	Richard Brothers	DB	Arkansas
	Brent Snyder	QB	Utah State
8.	Tony Woods	DT	Oklahoma
	Chris Dyko	T	Washington State
9.	LaSalle Harper	LB	Arkansas
	Byron Sanders	RB	Northwestern
10.	Todd Millikan	TE	Nebraska
	John Simpson	WR	Baylor
11.	Joe Nelms	DT	California
	George Streeter	DB	Notre Dame
12.	Freddy Weygand	WR	Auburn
	Anthony Phillips	G	Oklahoma

Chicago Bears 1989 Veteran Roster

No.	Name	Pos.	Ht.	Wt.	Birth-date	NFL Exp.	College	Hometown	How Acq.	'88 Games/ Starts
54	†Adickes, John	C	6-3	264	6/29/64	3	Baylor	Kileen, Tex.	D6-'87	16/0
35	Anderson, Neal	RB	5-11	210	8/14/64	4	Florida	Graceville, Fla.	D1-'86	16/16
79	Becker, Kurt	G	6-5	269	12/22/58	8	Michigan	Aurora, Ill.	D6-'82	16/0
62	†Bortz, Mark	G	6-6	272	2/12/61	7	Iowa	Pardeeville, Wis.	D8-'83	16/16
86	Boso, Cap	TE	6-3	240	9/10/63	3	Illinois	Kansas City, Mo.	FA-'87	6/0
6	Butler, Kevin	K	6-1	204	7/24/62	5	Georgia	Atlanta, Ga.	D4-'85	16/0
94	†Chapura, Dick	DT	6-3	275	6/15/64	3	Missouri	Sarasota, Fla.	D10-'87	15/0
74	Covert, Jim	T	6-4	278	3/22/60	7	Pittsburgh	Conway, Pa.	D1-'83	9/8
82	Davis, Wendell	WR	5-11	188	1/3/66	2	Louisiana State	Shreveport, La.	D1b-'88	16/0
95	Dent, Richard	DE	6-5	268	12/13/60	7	Tennessee State	Atlanta, Ga.	D8-'83	13/12
37	Douglass, Maurice	CB-S	5-11	200	2/12/64	4	Kentucky	Trotwood, Ohio	D8-'86	15/9
22	†Duerson, Dave	S	6-1	212	11/28/60	7	Notre Dame	Muncie, Ind.	D3-'83	15/15
23	Gayle, Shaun	S	5-11	194	3/8/62	6	Ohio State	Hampton, Va.	D10-'84	4/4
29	Gentry, Dennis	WR	5-8	180	2/10/59	8	Baylor	Lubbock, Tex.	D4-'82	16/16
99	Hampton, Dan	DE	6-5	274	9/19/57	11	Arkansas	Oklahoma City, Okla.	D1-'79	16/16
4	Harbaugh, Jim	QB	6-3	204	12/23/63	3	Michigan	Kalamazoo, Mich.	D1-'87	10/2
63	Hilgenberg, Jay	C	6-3	260	3/21/60	9	Iowa	Iowa City, Iowa	FA-'81	16/16
24	Jackson, Vestee	CB	6-0	186	8/14/63	4	Washington	Fresno, Calif.	D2-'86	16/16
92	Johnson, Troy	LB	6-0	236	11/10/64	2	Oklahoma	Houston, Tex.	D5-'88	16/1
53	Jones, Dante	LB	6-1	236	3/23/65	2	Oklahoma	Dallas, Tex.	D2-'88	15/1
88	Kozlowski, Glen	WR	6-1	205	12/31/62	3	Brigham Young	Honolulu, Hawaii	D11-'86	16/0
44	Krumm, Todd	S	6-0	189	12/18/65	2	Michigan State	West Bloomfield, Mich.	FA-'88	15/0
43	Lynch, Lorenzo	CB-S	5-9	199	4/6/63	2	Cal State-Sacramento	Oakland, Calif.	FA-'88	9/0
85	McKinnon, Dennis	WR	6-1	177	8/22/61	6	Florida State	Quitman, Ga.	FA-'83	15/15
9	McMahon, Jim	QB	6-1	198	8/21/59	8	Brigham Young	Jersey City, N.J.	D1-'82	9/9
76	McMichael, Steve	DT	6-2	268	10/17/57	10	Texas	Houston, Tex.	FA-'81	16/16
84	Morris, Ron	WR	6-1	195	11/14/64	3	Southern Methodist	Cooper, Tex.	D2-'87	16/1
51	Morrissey, Jim	LB	6-3	227	12/24/62	5	Michigan State	Flint, Mich.	D11-'85	11/11
25	Muster, Brad	RB	6-3	231	4/11/65	2	Stanford	San Marin, Calif.	D1a-'88	16/0
72	†Perry, William	DT	6-2	320	12/16/62	5	Clemson	Aiken, S.C.	D1-'85	3/3
52	Pruitt, Mickey	LB-S	6-1	206	1/10/65	2	Colorado	Chicago, Ill.	FA-'88	14/3
59	Rivera, Ron	LB	6-3	240	1/7/62	6	California	Monterey, Calif.	D2-'84	16/16
20	Sanders, Thomas	RB	5-11	203	1/4/62	5	Texas A&M	Giddings, Tex.	D9-'85	16/0
75	Shannon, John	DT	6-3	269	1/18/65	2	Kentucky	Devon, Ky.	FA-'88	13/0
50	Singletary, Mike	LB	6-0	230	10/9/58	9	Baylor	Houston, Tex.	D2-'81	16/16
97	Smith, Sean	DT	6-4	290	3/27/65	3	Grambling	Bogalusa, La.	D4-'87	9/3
32	Stinson, Lemuel	CB-S	5-9	159	5/10/66	2	Texas Tech	Houston, Tex.	D6-'88	15/1
26	Suhey, Matt	RB	5-11	213	7/7/58	10	Penn State	State College, Pa.	D2-'80	16/16
49	Tate, David	CB-S	6-0	177	11/22/64	2	Colorado	Denver, Colo.	D8-'88	16/4
57	Thayer, Tom	G	6-4	270	8/16/61	5	Notre Dame	Joliet, Ill.	D4-'82	16/16
80	Thornton, James	TE	6-2	242	2/8/65	2	Cal State-Fullerton	Santa Rosa, Calif.	D4-'88	16/12
18	Tomczak, Mike	QB	6-1	198	10/23/62	5	Ohio State	Calumet City, Ill.	FA-'85	14/5
78	Van Horne, Keith	T	6-6	283	11/6/57	9	Southern California	Mt. Lebanon, Pa.	D1-'81	15/14
73	Wojciechowski, John	G	6-4	270	7/30/63	3	Michigan State	Detroit, Mich.	FA-'87	16/10

† Option playout; subject to developments.

Plan B unconditional free agent.

Retired—Emery Moorehead, 12-year tight end, 13 games in '88.

Players lost through Plan B (9): T Paul Blair (Den; 0 games in '88); LB Greg Clark (Mia; 15), DE Al Harris (Phil; 16), TE Brent Novoselsky (GB; 8), T Caesar Rentie (Buff; 5), CB Mike Richardson (Raiders; 16), RB Eric Starr (Mia; 0), P Bryan Wagner (Clev; 16), LB Otis Wilson (Raiders; 0).

Also played with Bears in '88—QB Ben Bennett (active for 2 games but did not play), S Greg Lasker (1), RB Calvin Thomas (1).

COACHING STAFF

Head Coach, Mike Ditka

Pro Career: Became tenth head coach of Bears on January 20, 1982, after serving nine years as an offensive assistant with Dallas. Led Bears to first Super Bowl title following 15-1 1985 season. Bears shut out New York Giants and Los Angeles Rams in playoffs before routing New England 46-10 in Super Bowl XX. Under Ditka, Chicago has won five consecutive NFC Central titles and has posted 12-4, 11-4 and 14-2 records the past three seasons. His 11-7 1984 record included a trip to NFC Championship Game at San Francisco (23-0 loss). The 49-year-old Ditka has won at least 10 games a season since 1984. Ditka is a 27-year veteran of the NFL as both a player and a coach. Had 12-year playing career as a tight end with Chicago (1961-66), Philadelphia (1967-68), and Dallas (1969-72). A first-round draft choice by Chicago in 1961, Ditka was NFL rookie of the year, all-NFL (1961-64), and played in five Pro Bowls (1962-66). He joined Cowboys coaching staff in 1973. In addition to working with Dallas special teams, Ditka coached Cowboys' receivers. During his NFL career, he has been in the playoffs 15 seasons and been a member of five NFC champions and three NFL champions. He became the first tight end to be inducted into the Pro Football Hall of Fame in July, 1988. Career record: 78-35.

Background: Played at Pittsburgh from 1958-60 and was a unanimous All-America his senior year. A two-way performer, he played both tight end and linebacker. He also was one of the nation's leading punters with a 40-plus-yard average over three years.

Personal: Born October 18, 1939, Carnegie, Pa. Mike and his wife, Diana, live in Bannockburn, Ill., and have four children—Michael, Mark, Megan, and Matt.

Assistant Coaches

Jim Dooley, research and quality control; born February 8, 1930, Stoutsville, Mo., lives in Chicago. End Miami 1949-51. Pro receiver Chicago Bears 1952-61. Pro coach: Chicago Bears 1962-71 (head coach 1968-71), Buffalo Bills 1972, rejoined Bears in 1981.

Ed Hughes, assistant to head coach; born October 23, 1927, Buffalo, N.Y., lives in Libertyville, Ill. Halfback Tulsa 1952-53. Pro defensive back Los Angeles Rams 1954-55, New York Giants 1956-58. Pro coach: Dallas Texans 1960-62, Denver Broncos 1963, Washington Redskins 1964-67, San Francisco 49ers 1968-70, Houston Oilers 1971 (head coach), St. Louis Cardinals 1972, Dallas Cowboys 1973-76, Detroit Lions 1977, New Orleans Saints 1978-80, Philadelphia Eagles 1981, joined Bears in 1982.

Steve Kazor, special teams/tight ends; born February 24, 1948, New Kensington, Pa., lives in Vernon Hills, Ill. Nose tackle Westminister College 1967-70. No pro playing experience. College coach: Emporia State 1973 (head coach), Texas-Arlington 1974, Colorado State 1975, Wyoming 1976, Texas 1976-78, Texas-El Paso 1979-80. Pro coach: Joined Bears in 1982.

Greg Landry, offensive coordinator; born December 18, 1946, Nashua, N.H., lives in Libertyville, Ill. Quarterback Massachusetts 1965-67. Pro quarterback Detroit Lions 1968-78, Baltimore Colts 1979-81, Chicago Blitz/Arizona Wranglers (USFL) 1983-84, Chicago Bears 1984. Pro coach: Cleveland Browns 1985, joined Bears in 1986.

Jim LaRue, defensive backfield; born August 11, 1925, Clinton, Okla., lives in Libertyville, Ill. Halfback Carson-Newman 1943, Duke 1944-45, Maryland 1947-49. No pro playing experience. College coach: Maryland 1950, Kansas State 1951-54, Houston 1955-56, Southern Methodist 1957-58, Arizona 1959-66 (head coach), Utah 1967-73, Wake Forest 1974-75. Pro coach: Buffalo Bills 1976-77, joined Bears in 1978.

Chicago Bears 1989 First-Year Roster

Name	Pos.	Ht.	Wt.	Birth-date	College	Hometown	How Acq.
Armstrong, Trace	DE	6-4	259	10/5/65	Florida	Birmingham, Ala.	D1b
Brothers, Richard	S	5-10	201	4/5/65	Arkansas	Houston, Tex.	D7a
Dyko, Chris	T	6-6	305	3/16/66	Washington State	University, Wash.	D8b
Fontenot, Jerry	G	6-3	272	11/21/66	Texas A&M	Lafayette, La.	D3
Gilbert, Greg	LB	6-1	216	6/20/67	Alabama	Decatur, Ala.	D5b
Green, Mark	RB	5-11	184	3/22/67	Notre Dame	Riverside, Calif.	D5a
Harper, LaSalle	LB	6-0	226	5/16/67	Arkansas	Houston, Tex.	D9a
Millikan, Todd	TE	6-2	238	1/24/66	Nebraska	Shenandoah, Iowa	D10a
Nelms, Joe	DT	6-4	262	5/21/65	California	San Francisco, Calif.	D11a
Paul, Markus	S	6-2	199	4/1/66	Syracuse	Kissimmee, Fla.	D4
Phillips, Anthony	G	6-0	275	7/6/66	Oklahoma	Tulsa, Okla.	D12b
Roper, John	LB	6-1	228	10/4/65	Texas A&M	Yates, Tex.	D2a
Sanders, Byron	RB	5-7	190	2/13/67	Northwestern	Wichita, Kan.	D9b
Simpson, John	WR	5-11	165	2/24/66	Baylor	Houston, Tex.	D10b
Snyder, Brent	QB	6-3	225	6/4/66	Utah State	Joliet, Ill.	D7b
Streeter, George	CB-S	6-1	217	3/28/67	Notre Dame	Chicago, Ill.	D11b
Weygand, Freddie	WR	5-11	187	6/17/66	Auburn	Gadsden, Ala.	D12a
Woods, Tony	DT	6-4	274	3/14/66	Oklahoma	Colorado Springs, Colo.	D8a
Woolford, Donnell	CB-S	5-9	187	1/6/66	Clemson	Fayetteville, N.C.	D1a
Zawatson, Dave	T	6-4	274	4/13/66	California	Concord, Calif.	D2b

The term NFL Rookie is defined as a player who is in his first season of professional football and has not been on the roster of another professional football team for any regular-season or postseason games. A Rookie is designated by an "R" on NFL rosters. Players who have been active in another professional football league or players who have NFL experience, including either preseason training camp or being on an active roster for fewer than three regular-season or postseason games, are termed NFL First-Year Players. An NFL First-Year Player is designated by a "1" on NFL rosters. Thereafter, a player on an NFL active roster for at least three regular-season or postseason games is credited with an additional year of NFL playing experience.

NOTES

John Levra, defensive line; born October 2, 1937, Arma, Kan., lives in Libertyville, Ill. Guard-linebacker Pittsburg (Kan.) State 1963-65. No pro playing experience. College coach: Stephen F. Austin 1971-74, Kansas 1975-78, North Texas State 1979. Pro coach: British Columbia Lions (CFL) 1980, New Orleans Saints 1981-85, joined Bears in 1986.

David McGinnis, linebackers; born August 7, 1951, Independence, Kan., lives in Lake Forest, Ill. Defensive back Texas Christian 1970-72. No pro playing experience. College coach: Texas Christian 1973-74, 1982, Missouri 1975-77, Indiana State 1978-81, Kansas State 1983-85. Pro coach: Joined Bears in 1986.

Johnny Roland, offensive backs; born May 21, 1943, Corpus Christi, Tex., lives in Vernon Hills, Ill. Running back Missouri 1963-65. Pro running back St. Louis Cardinals 1966-72, New York Giants 1973. College coach: Notre Dame 1975. Pro coach: Green Bay Packers 1974, Philadelphia Eagles 1976-78, joined Bears in 1983.

Dick Stanfel, offensive line; born July 20, 1927, San Francisco, Calif., lives in Libertyville, Ill. Guard San Francisco 1948-51. Pro guard Detroit Lions 1952-55, Washington Redskins 1956-58. College coach: Notre Dame 1959-62, California 1963. Pro coach: Philadelphia Eagles 1964-70, San Francisco 49ers 1971-75, New Orleans Saints 1976-80 (head coach, 4 games in 1980), joined Bears in 1981.

Vince Tobin, defensive coordinator; born September 29, 1943, in Burlington Junction, Mo., lives in Libertyville, Ill. Defensive back-running back Missouri 1961-64. No pro playing experience. College coach: Missouri 1967-76. Pro coach: British Columbia Lions (CFL) 1977-82, Philadelphia/Baltimore Stars (USFL) 1983-85, joined Bears in 1986.

National Football Conference
Eastern Division

Team Colors: Royal Blue, Metallic Silver Blue, and White

Cowboys Center
One Cowboys Parkway
Irving, Texas 75063
Telephone: (214) 556-9900

Club Officials

Owner/President/General Manager: Jerry Jones
Director of Player Personnel: Bob Ackles
Director of College Scouting: Dick Mansperger
Director of Pro Personnel: John Wooten
Director of Counseling Services: Larry Wansley
Controller: Jim Lancaster
Public Relations Directors: Greg Aiello, David Pelletier
Administrative Assistant: Bruce Mays
Ticket Manager: Steve Orsini
Trainers: Kevin O'Neill, Ken Locker, Don Cochren
Equipment Managers: Buck Buchanan, Jerry Fowler
Video Directors: Robert Blackwell, Kevin Wynn
Cheerleaders Director: Debbie Bond

Stadium: Texas Stadium • **Capacity:** 65,024
Irving, Texas 75062

Playing Surface: Texas Turf

Training Camp: California Lutheran University
Thousand Oaks, California 91360

1989 Schedule

Preseason

Aug. 13	at San Diego	12:00
Aug. 19	at Los Angeles Raiders	6:00
Aug. 26	at Denver	7:00
Sept. 2	**Houston**	8:00

Regular Season

Sept. 10	at New Orleans	12:00
Sept. 17	at Atlanta	1:00
Sept. 24	**Washington**	12:00
Oct. 1	**New York Giants**	3:00
Oct. 8	at Green Bay	12:00
Oct. 15	**San Francisco**	12:00
Oct. 22	at Kansas City	12:00
Oct. 29	**Phoenix**	12:00
Nov. 5	at Washington	8:00
Nov. 12	at Phoenix	2:00
Nov. 19	**Miami**	12:00
Nov. 23	**Philadelphia** (Thanksgiving)	3:00
Dec. 3	**Los Angeles Rams**	12:00
Dec. 10	at Philadelphia	1:00
Dec. 16	at N.Y. Giants (Saturday)	12:30
Dec. 24	**Green Bay**	12:00

Cowboys Coaching History

(270-178-6)

1960-88 Tom Landry 270-178-6

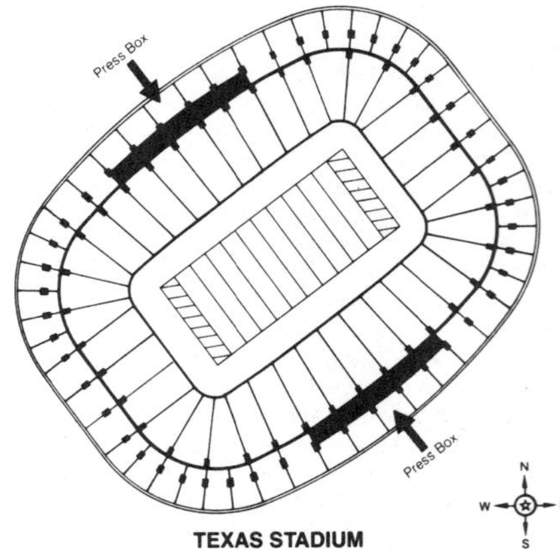

TEXAS STADIUM

Record Holders

Individual Records—Career

Category	Name	Performance
Rushing (Yds.)	Tony Dorsett, 1977-1987	12,036
Passing (Yds.)	Roger Staubach, 1969-1979	22,700
Passing (TDs)	Danny White, 1976-1988	155
Receiving (No.)	Drew Pearson, 1973-1983	489
Receiving (Yds.)	Tony Hill, 1977-1986	7,988
Interceptions	Mel Renfro, 1964-1977	52
Punting (Avg.)	Mike Saxon, 1985-88	40.8
Punt Return (Avg.)	Bob Hayes, 1965-1974	11.1
Kickoff Return (Avg.)	Mel Renfro, 1964-1977	26.4
Field Goals	Rafael Septien, 1978-1986	162
Touchdowns (Tot.)	Tony Dorsett, 1977-1987	86
Points	Rafael Septien, 1978-1986	874

Individual Records—Single Season

Category	Name	Performance
Rushing (Yds.)	Tony Dorsett, 1981	1,646
Passing (Yds.)	Danny White, 1983	3,980
Passing (TDs)	Danny White, 1983	29
Receiving (No.)	Herschel Walker, 1985	76
Receiving (Yds.)	Bob Hayes, 1966	1,232
Interceptions	Everson Walls, 1981	11
Punting (Avg.)	Sam Baker, 1962	45.4
Punt Return (Avg.)	Bob Hayes, 1968	20.8
Kickoff Return (Avg.)	Mel Renfro, 1965	30.0
Field Goals	Rafael Septien, 1981	27
Touchdowns (Tot.)	Dan Reeves, 1966	16
Points	Rafael Septien, 1983	123

Individual Records—Single Game

Category	Name	Performance
Rushing (Yds.)	Tony Dorsett, 12-4-77	206
Passing (Yds.)	Don Meredith, 11-10-63	460
Passing (TDs)	Many times	5
	Last time by Danny White, 10-30-83	
Receiving (No.)	Lance Rentzel, 11-19-67	13
Receiving (Yds.)	Bob Hayes, 11-13-66	246
Interceptions	Herb Adderley, 9-26-71	3
	Lee Roy Jordan, 11-4-73	3
	Dennis Thurman, 12-13-81	3
Field Goals	Roger Ruzek, 12-21-87	5
Touchdowns (Tot.)	Many times	4
	Last time by Duane Thomas, 12-18-71	
Points	Many times	24
	Last time by Duane Thomas, 12-18-71	

1988 Team Record

Preseason (2-2)

Date	Result		Opponents
8/6	L	21-24	at San Diego
8/13	W	27-17	at L.A. Raiders
8/22	W	17- 9	Chicago
8/27	L	10-54	Houston
		75-104	

Regular Season (3-13)

Date	Result		Opponents	Att.
9/4	L	21-24	at Pittsburgh	56,813
9/12	W	17-14	at Phoenix	67,139
9/18	L	10-12	N.Y. Giants	55,325
9/25	W	26-20	Atlanta	39,702
10/3	L	17-20	at New Orleans	68,474
10/9	L	17-35	Washington	63,325
10/16	L	7-17	at Chicago	64,759
10/23	L	23-24	at Philadelphia	66,309
10/30	L	10-16	Phoenix	42,196
11/6	L	21-29	at N.Y. Giants	75,826
11/13	L	3-43	Minnesota	57,830
11/20	L	24-38	Cincinnati	37,865
11/24	L	17-25	Houston	50,845
12/4	L	21-24	at Cleveland	77,683
12/11	W	24-17	at Washington	51,526
12/18	L	7-23	Philadelphia	46,131

Score by Periods

Cowboys	71	47	64	83	0	—	265
Opponents	80	125	74	102	0	—	381

Attendance

Home 393,219 Away 528,529 Total 921,748
Single-game home record, 80,259 (11-24-66)
Single-season home record, 511,541 (1981)

1988 Team Statistics

	Cowboys	Opp.
Total First Downs	311	297
Rushing	112	93
Passing	175	180
Penalty	24	24
Third Down: Made/Att.	84/217	89/226
Fourth Down: Made/Att.	7/16	4/11
Total Net Yards	5483	5414
Avg. Per Game	342.7	338.4
Total Plays	1059	1023
Avg. Per Play	5.2	5.3
Net Yards Rushing	1995	1858
Avg. Per Game	124.7	116.1
Total Rushes	469	454
Net Yards Passing	3488	3556
Avg. Per Game	218.0	222.3
Sacked/Yards Lost	35/239	46/327
Gross Yards	3727	3883
Att./Completions	555/307	523/264
Completion Pct.	55.3	50.5
Had Intercepted	27	10
Punts/Avg.	80/40.9	86/41.6
Net Punting Avg.	34.2	36.0
Penalties/Yards Lost	141/1148	92/772
Fumbles/Ball Lost	22/13	24/9
Touchdowns	32	44
Rushing	10	13
Passing	21	30
Returns	1	1
Avg. Time of Possession	30:41	29:19

1988 Individual Statistics

Scoring	TD R	TD P	TD Rt	PAT	FG	Saf	TP
Ruzek	0	0	0	27/27	12/22	0	63
Walker	5	2	0	0/0	0/0	0	42
Alexander	0	6	0	0/0	0/0	0	36
Irvin	0	5	0	0/0	0/0	0	30
Martin	0	3	0	0/0	0/0	0	18
Newsome	3	0	0	0/0	0/0	0	18
Folsom	0	2	0	0/0	0/0	0	12
Pelluer	2	0	0	0/0	0/0	0	12
Noonan	0	0	1	0/0	0/0	1	8
Zendejas	0	0	0	5/5	1/3	0	8
Chandler	0	1	0	0/0	0/0	0	6
Clack	0	1	0	0/0	0/0	0	6
Gay	0	1	0	0/0	0/0	0	6
Cowboys	10	21	1	32/32	13/25	1	265
Opponents	13	30	1	41/44	24/29	2	381

Passing	Att.	Comp.	Yds.	Pct.	TD	Int.	Tkld.	Rate
Pelluer	435	245	3139	56.3	17	19	21/112	73.9
Sweeney	78	33	314	42.3	3	5	9/80	40.2
D. White	42	29	274	69.0	1	3	5/47	65.0
Cowboys	555	307	3727	55.3	21	27	35/239	68.5
Opponents	523	264	3883	50.5	30	10	46/327	86.2

Rushing	Att.	Yds.	Avg.	LG	TD
Walker	361	1514	4.2	38	5
Pelluer	51	314	6.2	27	2
Newsome	32	75	2.3	8	3
Clack	11	54	4.9	17	0
Sweeney	6	34	5.7	10	0
Fowler	3	6	2.0	4	0
Irvin	1	2	2.0	2	0
Martin	4	−4	−1.0	11	0
Cowboys	469	1995	4.3	38	10
Opponents	454	1858	4.1	51t	13

Receiving	No.	Yds.	Avg.	LG	TD
Alexander	54	788	14.6	50t	6
Walker	53	505	9.5	50	2
Martin	49	622	12.7	35t	3
Irvin	32	654	20.4	61t	5
Newsome	30	236	7.9	32	0
Chandler	18	186	10.3	29	1
Clack	17	126	7.4	18	1
Gay	15	205	13.7	25	1
Cosbie	12	112	9.3	21	0
Fowler	10	64	6.4	13	0
Folsom	9	84	9.3	20	2
Edwards	5	93	18.6	27	0
Burbage	2	50	25.0	41	0
Newton	1	2	2.0	2	0
Cowboys	307	3727	12.1	61t	21
Opponents	264	3883	14.7	73t	30

Interceptions	No.	Yds.	Avg.	LG	TD
Williams	2	18	9.0	12	0
Downs	2	3	1.5	3	0
Walls	2	0	0.0	0	0
Francis	1	29	29.0	29	0
Noonan	1	17	17.0	17t	1
Bates	1	0	0.0	0	0
Hendrix	1	0	0.0	0	0
Cowboys	10	67	6.7	29	1
Opponents	27	314	11.6	66	0

Punting	No.	Yds.	Avg.	In 20	LG
Saxon	80	3271	40.9	24	55
Cowboys	80	3271	40.9	24	55
Opponents	86	3574	41.6	19	70

Punt Returns	No.	FC	Yds.	Avg.	LG	TD
Martin	44	15	360	8.2	21	0
Walls	1	0	0	0.0	0	0
Cowboys	45	15	360	8.0	21	0
Opponents	37	15	239	6.5	18	0

Kickoff Returns	No.	Yds.	Avg.	LG	TD
Burbage	20	448	22.4	53	0
Clack	32	690	21.6	40	0
Martin	12	210	17.5	31	0
Higgs	2	31	15.5	17	0
Smith	2	24	12.0	13	0
B. White	1	7	7.0	7	0
Cowboys	69	1410	20.4	53	0
Opponents	56	1060	18.9	44	0

Sacks	No.
Cobb	7.5
Noonan	7.5
Jones	7.0
Jeffcoat	6.5
Brooks	5.0
Walen	4.0
Albritton	2.0
Burton	2.0
R. White	1.5
Owens	1.0
Walls	1.0
Bates	0.5
Downs	0.5
Cowboys	46.0
Opponents	35.0

1989 Draft Choices

Round	Name	Pos.	College
1.	Troy Aikman	QB	UCLA
2.	Steve Wisniewski	G	Penn State
	Daryl Johnston	RB	Syracuse
3.	Mark Stepnoski	G	Pittsburgh
	Rhondy Weston	DE	Florida
4.	Tony Tolbert	DE	Texas-El Paso
5.	Keith Jennings	TE	Clemson
	Willis Crockett	LB	Georgia Tech
	Jeff Roth	DT	Florida
7.	Kevin Peterson	LB	Northwestern
8.	Charvez Foger	RB	Nevada-Reno
9.	Tim Jackson	DB	Nebraska
10.	Rod Carter	LB	Miami
11.	Randy Shannon	LB	Miami
12.	Scott Ankrom	WR	Texas Christian

Dallas Cowboys 1989 Veteran Roster

No.	Name	Pos.	Ht.	Wt.	Birth-date	NFL Exp.	College	Hometown	How Acq.	'88 Games/ Starts
36	Albritton, Vince	S	6-2	210	7/23/62	6	Washington	Oakland, Calif.	FA-'84	6/0
87	Alexander, Ray	WR	6-4	193	1/8/62	3	Florida A&M	Mobile, Ala.	FA-'87	16/11
82	Barksdale, Rod	WR	6-1	192	9/8/62	3	Arizona	Los Angeles, Calif.	T(Raid)-'87	0*
40	Bates, Bill	S	6-1	204	6/6/61	7	Tennessee	Knoxville, Tenn.	FA-'83	16/16
99	Brooks, Kevin	DT-DE	6-6	273	2/9/63	5	Michigan	Detroit, Mich.	D1-'85	15/14
27	Burbage, Cornell	CB-S	5-10	189	2/22/65	3	Kentucky	Lexington, Ky.	FA-'88	10/0
57	Burton, Ron	LB	6-1	245	5/2/64	3	North Carolina	Highland Springs, Va.	FA-'87	16/15
85	Chandler, Thornton	TE	6-5	245	11/27/63	4	Alabama	Jacksonville, Fla.	D6a-'86	16/12
42	Clack, Darryl	RB	5-10	218	10/29/63	4	Arizona State	Security, Colo.	D2-'86	15/0
59	Cobb, Garry	LB	6-2	233	3/16/57	11	Southern California	Stamford, Conn.	FA-'88	16/14
55	†Coyle, Eric	C	6-3	260	10/26/63	2	Colorado	Longmont, Colo.	FA(Wash)-'89#	0*
55	DeOssie, Steve	LB	6-2	245	11/22/62	6	Boston College	Roslindale, Mass.	D4-'84	16/1
26	Downs, Michael	S	6-3	204	6/9/59	9	Rice	Dallas, Tex.	FA-'81	16/16
81	Edwards, Kelvin	WR	6-2	204	7/19/64	4	Liberty	Eastpoint, Ga.	FA-'87	8/2
85	Folsom, Steve	TE	6-5	240	3/21/58	5	Utah	Santa Fe Springs, Calif.	FA-'87	16/4
46	Fowler, Todd	RB	6-3	221	6/9/62	6	Stephen F. Austin	Van, Tex.	SD1-'84	16/6
38	Francis, Ron	CB	5-9	201	4/7/64	3	Baylor	LaMarque, Tex.	D2-'87	13/2
80	Gay, Everett	WR	6-2	209	10/23/64	2	Texas	Houston, Tex.	D5-'87	16/0
66	Gogan, Kevin	T	6-7	306	11/2/64	3	Washington	Pacifica, Calif.	D8-'87	15/15
45	Hendrix, Manny	CB-S	5-10	178	10/20/64	4	Utah	Phoenix, Ariz.	FA-'86	16/0
20	†Horton, Ray	CB-S	5-11	190	4/12/60	7	Washington	Tacoma, Wash.	FA(Cin)-'89#	13/0*
52	Hurd, Jeff	LB	6-2	245	5/25/64	2	Kansas State	Kansas City, Mo.	FA-'87	0*
88	Irvin, Michael	WR	6-2	202	3/5/66	2	Miami	Fort Lauderdale, Fla.	D1-'88	14/10
53	Jax, Garth	LB	6-2	225	9/16/63	4	Florida State	Houston, Tex.	D11-'86	16/2
77	†Jeffcoat, Jim	DE	6-5	260	4/1/61	7	Arizona State	Cliffwood, N.J.	D1-'83	16/15
90	†Jones, Anthony	TE	6-3	248	5/16/60	6	Wichita State	Baltimore, Md.	FA(SD)-'89#	12/3*
72	Jones, Ed	DE	6-9	273	2/23/51	15	Tennessee State	Jackson, Tenn.	D1a-'74	16/16
68	†Ker, Crawford	G	6-3	285	5/5/62	5	Florida	Dunedin, Fla.	D3-'85	16/16
56	Lockhart, Eugene	LB	6-2	235	3/8/61	6	Houston	Crockett, Tex.	D6a-'84	16/16
83	Martin, Kelvin	WR	5-9	163	5/14/65	3	Boston College	Jacksonville, Fla.	D4-'87	16/7
20	Miller, Solomon	WR	6-3	176	12/6/64	3	Utah State	Los Angeles, Calif.	FA-'89	0*
58	Naposki, Eric	LB	6-2	230	12/20/66	2	Connecticut	Eastchester, N.Y.	FA(NE)-'89#	3/0*
30	Newsome, Timmy	RB	6-1	237	5/17/58	10	Winston-Salem State	Ahoskie, N.C.	D6-'80	9/8
67	Newton, Nate	G	6-3	317	12/20/61	4	Florida A&M	Orlando, Fla.	FA-'86	15/15
73	Noonan, Danny	DT	6-4	266	7/14/65	3	Nebraska	Lincoln, Neb.	D1-'87	16/16
51	Norton, Ken	LB	6-2	236	9/29/66	2	UCLA	Los Angeles, Calif.	D2-'88	3/0
31	Owens, Billy	S	6-1	207	12/2/65	2	Pittsburgh	Syracuse, N.Y.	D10-'88	16/0
16	†Pelluer, Steve	QB	6-4	208	7/29/62	6	Washington	Bellevue, Wash.	D5a-'84	16/14
60	Petersmark, Brett	T-G	6-4	275	3/5/64	2	Eastern Michigan	Redford, Mich.	FA-'89	0*
64	Rafferty, Tom	C	6-3	262	8/2/54	14	Penn State	Fayetteville, N.Y.	D4-'76	15/13
50	Rohrer, Jeff	LB	6-2	227	12/25/58	7	Yale	Manhattan Beach, Calif.	D2-'82	0*
9	Ruzek, Roger	K	6-1	195	12/17/60	3	Weber State	San Francisco, Calif.	FA-'87	14/0
39	Sargent, Broderick	RB	5-11	215	9/16/62	3	Baylor	Waxahachie, Tex.	FA-'89	0*
4	Saxon, Mike	P	6-3	188	7/10/62	5	San Diego State	Arcadia, Calif.	FA-'85	16/0
10	Secules, Scott	QB	6-3	219	11/8/64	2	Virginia	Centreville, Va.	D6-'88	0*
93	Sileo, Dan	DT	6-2	291	1/3/64	2	Miami	Stamford, Conn.	FA-'89	0*
79	Smith, Daryle	T	6-5	276	1/18/64	3	Tennessee	Knoxville, Tenn.	FA-'87	14/4
25	Tautalatasi, Junior	RB	5-11	208	3/24/63	4	Washington State	Alameda, Calif.	FA-'89	10/0*
63	Titensor, Glen	G	6-4	270	2/21/58	8	Brigham Young	Garden Grove, Calif.	D3-'81	10/1
71	Tuinei, Mark	C	6-5	283	3/31/60	7	Hawaii	Honolulu, Hawaii	FA-'83	5/4
95	Walen, Mark	DT-DE	6-5	267	3/10/63	3	UCLA	Burlingame, Calif.	D3-'86	15/2
34	Walker, Herschel	RB	6-1	223	3/3/62	4	Georgia	Wrightsville, Ga.	D5a-'85	16/16
24	Walls, Everson	CB	6-1	193	12/28/59	9	Grambling	Dallas, Tex.	FA-'81	16/16
65	White, Bob	C	6-5	273	4/9/63	3	Rhode Island	Lunenburg, Mass.	FA-'87	12/3
11	†White, Danny	QB	6-3	197	2/9/52	14	Arizona State	Mesa, Ariz.	D3a-'74	3/0
78	Widell, Dave	T	6-6	300	5/14/65	2	Boston College	Hartford, Conn.	D4-'88	14/9
23	Williams, Robert	CB	5-10	186	10/2/62	3	Baylor	Galveston, Tex.	FA-'87	16/14
76	Zimmerman, Jeff	G	6-3	313	1/10/65	2	Florida	Orlando, Fla.	D3-'87	1/0

* Barksdale, Hurd, and Rohrer missed '88 season due to injury; Coyle active for 1 game with Washington in '88 but did not play; Horton played 13 games with Cincinnati; A. Jones played 8 games with Washington, 4 with San Diego; Miller last active with Tampa Bay in '87; Naposki played 3 games with New England; Petersmark last active with Houston in '87; Sargent last active with St. Louis in '87; Secules active for 13 games but did not play; Sileo last active with Tampa Bay in '87; Tautalatasi played 10 games with Philadelphia.

† Option playout; subject to developments.

Plan B unconditional free agent.

Retired—Randy White, 14-year defensive tackle, 16 games in '88.

Players lost through Plan B (6): T Bob Brotzki (Atl; 10 games in '88), TE Doug Cosbie (Den; 11), RB Mark Higgs (Phil; 5), LB Garth Jax (Phx; 0), WR Mike Sherrard (SF; 0), QB Kevin Sweeney (SF; 3).

Also played with Cowboys in '88—LB Mike Hegman (active for 1 game but did not play), C Paul Oswald (1), LB Sean Scott (5), S Victor Scott (2), CB-S Charles Wright (3), K Luis Zendejas (2).

COACHING STAFF

Head Coach, Jimmy Johnson

Pro Career: Named second head coach in Cowboys history on February 25, 1989. He becomes the youngest head coach in the NFC. No pro playing experience.

Background: All-Southwest Conference defensive lineman on Arkansas's 1964 undefeated national championship team. Began coaching career in 1965 at Louisiana Tech. Moved on as an assistant at Wichita State 1967, Iowa State 1968-69, Oklahoma 1970-72, Arkansas 1973-76, and Pittsburgh 1977-78. Head coach at Oklahoma State from 1979-83. Compiled 52-9 (.853) record in five seasons as head coach at the University of Miami. Under Johnson, the Hurricanes won the national championship in 1987 and 34 of 36 games from 1986-88. Career collegiate record: 81-34-3.

Personal: Born July 16, 1943, Port Arthur, Tex. Jimmy and his wife, Linda Kay, live in Irving, Tex., and have two sons, Brent and Chad.

Assistant Coaches

Hubbard Alexander, wide receivers; born February 14, 1939, Winston-Salem, N.C., lives in Irving, Tex. Center Tennessee State 1958-61. No pro playing experience. College coach: Tennessee State 1962-63, Vanderbilt 1974-78, Miami 1979-88. Pro coach: Joined Cowboys in 1989.

Neill Armstrong, research and development; born March 9, 1926, Tishomingo, Okla., lives in Roanoke, Tex. End Oklahoma State 1943-46. Pro end-defensive back Philadelphia Eagles 1947-51, Winnipeg Blue Bombers (CFL) 1951, 1953-54. College coach: Oklahoma State 1955-61. Pro coach: Houston Oilers 1962-63, Edmonton Eskimos (CFL) 1964-69 (head coach), Minnesota Vikings 1970-77, Chicago Bears 1978-81 (head coach), joined Cowboys in 1982.

Joe Brodsky, running backs; born June 9, 1934, Miami, Fla., lives in Irving, Tex. Fullback/linebacker Florida 1953-56. No pro playing experience. College coach: Miami 1978-88. Pro coach: Joined Cowboys in 1989.

Dave Campo, defensive assistant; born July 18, 1947, New London, Conn., lives in Irving, Tex. Defensive back Central Connecticut State 1967-70. No pro playing experience. College coach: Central Connecticut State 1971-72, Albany State 1973, Bridgeport 1974, Pittsburgh 1975, Washington State 1976, Boise State 1977-79, Oregon State 1980, Weber State 1981-82, Iowa State 1983, Syracuse 1984-86, Miami 1987-88. Pro coach: Joined Cowboys in 1989.

Butch Davis, defensive line; born November 17, 1951, Tahlequah, Okla., lives in Irving, Tex. Defensive end Arkansas 1971-74. No pro playing experience. College coach: Oklahoma State 1979-83, Miami 1984-88. Pro coach: Joined Cowboys in 1989.

Alan Lowry, special teams; born November 21, 1950, Irving, Tex., lives in Roanoke, Tex. Defensive back-quarterback Texas 1970-72. No pro playing experience. College coach: Virginia Tech 1974, Wyoming 1975, Texas 1976-81. Pro coach: Joined Cowboys in 1982.

Dick Nolan, defensive backs; born March 26, 1932, Pittsburgh, Pa., lives in Roanoke, Tex. Offensive-defensive back Maryland 1951-53. Pro defensive back New York Giants 1954-57, 1959-61, St. Louis Cardinals 1958, Dallas 1962 (player-coach). Pro coach: Dallas Cowboys 1963-67, San Francisco 49ers 1968-75 (head coach), New Orleans Saints 1977-80 (head coach), Houston Oilers 1981, rejoined Cowboys in 1982.

Jerry Rhome, quarterbacks; born March 6, 1942, Dallas, Tex., lives in Irving, Tex. Quarterback Southern Methodist 1960-61, Tulsa 1963-64. Pro quarterback Dallas Cowboys 1965-68, Cleveland Browns 1969, Houston Oilers 1970, Los Angeles Rams 1971-72. College coach: Tulsa 1973-75. Pro coach: Seattle Seahawks 1976-82, Washington Redskins 1983-87, San Diego Chargers 1988, joined Cowboys in 1989.

Dallas Cowboys 1989 First-Year Roster

Name	Pos.	Ht.	Wt.	Birth-date	College	Hometown	How Acq.
Adams, Scott	T	6-5	275	9/28/66	Georgia	Lake City, Fla.	FA
Aikman, Troy	QB	6-3	220	11/21/66	UCLA	Henryetta, Okla.	D1
Ankrom, Scott	WR	6-1	200	1/4/66	Texas Christian	San Antonio, Tex.	D12
Brown, Eric	CB-S	5-11	177	4/12/67	Savannah State	Savannah, Ga.	FA
Carter, Rod	LB	6-1	228	10/10/66	Miami	Fort Lauderdale, Fla.	D10
Collins, Sam	DT-DE	6-6	260	3/16/67	Baylor	Lubbock, Tex.	FA
Crockett, Willis	LB	6-3	221	8/25/66	Georgia Tech	Douglas, Ga.	D5b
Crosby, Richard	WR	6-1	205	11/16/65	Grambling	Harvey, La.	FA
Daniels, Shawn	RB	5-11	238	9/3/66	Bowling Green	Montreal, Canada	FA
Davis, Reggie	WR	6-1	213	7/16/66	Texas Christian	Jasper, Tex.	FA
Dean, Kent (1)	TE	6-4	234	9/4/64	Kansas State	Derby, Kan.	FA
Duff, John	TE	6-6	222	7/31/67	New Mexico	Tustin, Calif.	FA
Farris, Ervin	RB	5-10	233	6/28/66	Texas Tech	Fort Worth, Tex.	FA
Foger, Charvez	RB	5-10	211	9/18/65	Nevada-Reno	Las Vegas, Nev.	D8
Ford, Darryl	LB	6-1	232	6/22/66	New Mexico State	Dallas, Tex.	FA
Hairston, Stacey	CB-S	5-9	170	8/16/67	Ohio Northern	Columbus, Ohio	FA
Hewitt, Paul	RB	5-7	195	4/30/67	San Diego State	Monrovia, Calif.	FA
Hooven, Owen (1)	T	6-8	302	8/11/66	Oregon State	Arcata, Calif.	D7-'88
Hutson, Mark (1)	G	6-3	289	8/29/66	Oklahoma	Fort Smith, Ark.	D3-'88
Jackson, Tim	CB-S	5-11	192	11/7/65	Nebraska	Dallas, Tex.	D9
James, Jeff (1)	WR	5-10	187	3/25/65	Stanford	Beverly Hills, Calif.	FA
Jennings, Keith	TE	6-4	241	5/19/66	Clemson	Summerville, S.C.	D5a
Johnson, Eddie	CB-S	5-9	169	8/4/67	Penn State	Pinehill, N.J.	FA
Johnston, Daryl	RB	6-2	237	2/10/66	Syracuse	Youngstown, N.Y.	D2
Kuiper, Ken	T	6-3	267	12/1/65	Washington State	Spokane, Wash.	FA
Manca, Massimo (1)	K	5-10	200	3/18/64	Penn State	Reno, Nev.	FA
Mazza, Vince (1)	P	6-3	225	11/5/63	Ashland College	Niagara Falls, N.Y.	FA
Moss, Zefross (1)	T	6-6	310	8/17/66	Alabama State	Tuscaloosa, Ala.	FA
Peterson, Kevin	LB	6-2	227	12/14/66	Northwestern	Evanston, Ill.	D7
Robinson, Robert	CB-S	5-10	181	11/27/67	South Carolina	Shelby, N.C.	FA
Roth, Jeff	DT	6-3	256	4/21/66	Florida	Seminole, Fla.	D5c
Scheller, Sean (1)	DE	6-5	250	9/27/65	Stanford	Edmonds, Wash.	FA
Seals, Mark	CB-S	6-0	201	1/31/67	Boston University	Syracuse, N.Y.	FA
Shannon, Randy	LB	6-0	224	2/24/66	Miami	Miami, Fla.	D11
Siglar, Ricky	T	6-6	295	6/14/66	San Jose State	Albuquerque, N.M.	FA
Stepnoski, Mark	G	6-2	269	1/20/67	Pittsburgh	Erie, Pa.	D3a
Thurman, Tyrone	WR	5-3	145	12/31/66	Texas Tech	Midland, Tex.	FA
Tippins, Ken	LB	6-1	226	7/22/66	Middle Tennessee St.	Adel, Ga.	FA
Tolbert, Tony	DE	6-6	245	12/29/67	Texas-El Paso	Englewood, N.J.	D4
Weston, Rhondy	DE	6-5	274	6/7/66	Florida	Belle Glade, Fla.	D3b

The term NFL Rookie is defined as a player who is in his first season of professional football and has not been on the roster of another professional football team for any regular-season or postseason games. A Rookie is designated by an "R" on NFL rosters. Players who have been active in another professional football league or players who have NFL experience, including either preseason training camp or being on an active roster for fewer than three regular-season or postseason games, are termed NFL First-Year Players. An NFL First-Year Player is designated by a "1" on NFL rosters. Thereafter, a player on an NFL active roster for at least three regular-season or postseason games is credited with an additional year of NFL playing experience.

NOTES

David Shula, assistant head coach/offensive coordinator; born May 28, 1959, Lexington, Ky., lives in Irving, Tex. Wide receiver Dartmouth 1978-80. Pro wide receiver Baltimore Colts 1981. Pro coach: Miami Dolphins 1982-88, joined Cowboys in 1989.

Dave Wannstedt, defensive coordinator/linebackers; born May 21, 1952, Pittsburgh, Pa., lives in Irving, Tex. Offensive tackle Pittsburgh 1970-73. No pro playing experience. College coach: Pittsburgh 1975-78, Oklahoma State 1979-82, Southern California 1983-85, Miami 1986-88. Pro coach: Joined Cowboys in 1989.

Bob Ward, conditioning; born July 4, 1933, Huntington Park, Calif., lives in Dallas. Fullback-quarterback Whitworth College 1952-54. Doctorate in physical education, Indiana University. No pro playing experience. College coach: Fullerton, Calif., J.C. (track) 1965-75. Pro coach: Joined Cowboys in 1975.

Tony Wise, offensive line; born December 28, 1951, Albany, N.Y., lives in Irving, Tex. Defensive back Ithaca College 1971-72. No pro playing experience. College coach: Albany State 1973, Bridgeport 1974, Central Connecticut State 1975, Washington State 1976, Pittsburgh 1977-78, Oklahoma State 1979-83, Syracuse 1984, Miami 1985-88. Pro coach: Joined Cowboys in 1989.

National Football Conference Central Division

Team Colors: Honolulu Blue and Silver

Pontiac Silverdome
1200 Featherstone Road — Box 4200
Pontiac, Michigan 48057
Telephone: (313) 335-4131

Club Officials

President-Owner: William Clay Ford
Executive Vice President-General Manager: Russell Thomas
Director of Football Operations-Head Coach: Wayne Fontes
Vice President/Finance: Charles Schmidt
Vice President/Player Personnel: Jerome R. Vainisi
Director of Player Personnel: Joe Bushofsky
Scouts: Dirk Dierking, Allen Hughes, Ron Hughes, Scott McEwen, Jim Owens, Jerry Neri, John Trump
Director of Public Relations: Bill Keenist
Director of Player Relations: Otis Canty
Accountant/Travel Coordinator: Tom Lesnau
Video Director: Steve Hermans
Director of Communications: Tim Pendell
Assistant Director of Public Relations: Arthur Triche
Ticket Manager: Fred Otto
Trainer: Kent Falb
Strength and Conditioning: Skip Allen
Equipment Manager: Dan Jaroshewich

Stadium: Pontiac Silverdome • **Capacity:** 80,500
1200 Featherstone Road
Pontiac, Michigan 48057

Playing Surface: AstroTurf

Training Camp: Oakland University
Rochester, Michigan 48063

1989 Schedule

Preseason

Aug. 12	**Cleveland**	7:30
Aug. 19	**Cincinnati**	7:30
Aug. 25	at Seattle	7:30
Sept. 2	at Los Angeles Rams	6:00

Regular Season

Sept. 10	**Phoenix**	1:00
Sept. 17	at New York Giants	4:00
Sept. 24	**Chicago**	1:00
Oct. 1	**Pittsburgh**	1:00
Oct. 8	at Minnesota	12:00
Oct. 15	at Tampa Bay	1:00
Oct. 22	**Minnesota**	1:00
Oct. 29	vs. Green Bay at Milwaukee	12:00
Nov. 5	at Houston	12:00
Nov. 12	**Green Bay**	1:00
Nov. 19	at Cincinnati	1:00
Nov. 23	**Cleveland** (Thanksgiving)	12:30
Dec. 3	**New Orleans**	1:00
Dec. 10	at Chicago	12:00
Dec. 17	**Tampa Bay**	1:00
Dec. 24	at Atlanta	1:00

Lions Coaching History

Portsmouth Spartans 1930-33 (368-379-32)

1930	Hal (Tubby) Griffen	5-6-3
1931-36	George (Potsy) Clark	49-20-6
1937-38	Earl (Dutch) Clark	14-8-0
1939	Elmer (Gus) Henderson	6-5-0
1940	George (Potsy) Clark	5-5-1
1941-42	Bill Edwards*	4-9-1
1942	John Karcis	0-8-0
1943-47	Charles (Gus) Dorais	20-31-2
1948-50	Alvin (Bo) McMillin	12-24-0
1951-56	Raymond (Buddy) Parker	50-24-2
1957-64	George Wilson	55-45-6
1965-66	Harry Gilmer	10-16-2
1967-72	Joe Schmidt	43-35-7
1973	Don McCafferty	6-7-1
1974-76	Rick Forzano**	15-17-0
1976-77	Tommy Hudspeth	11-13-0
1978-84	Monte Clark	43-63-1
1985-88	Darryl Rogers***	18-40-0
1988	Wayne Fontes	2-3-0

*Released after three games in 1942
**Resigned after four games in 1976
***Released after 11 games in 1988.

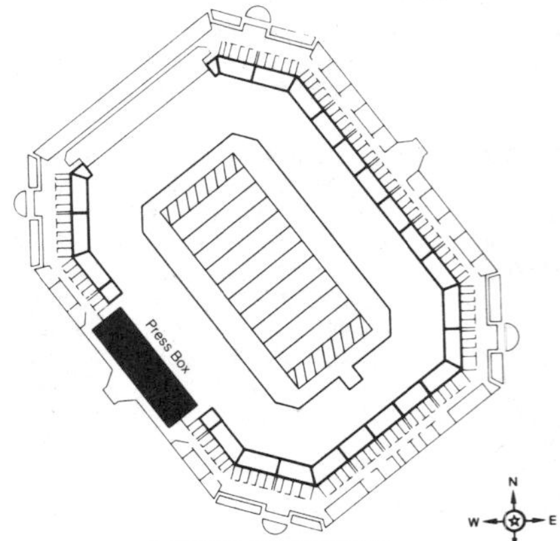

PONTIAC SILVERDOME

Record Holders

Individual Records—Career

Category	Name	Performance
Rushing (Yds.)	Billy Sims, 1980-84	5,106
Passing (Yds.)	Bobby Layne, 1950-58	15,710
Passing (TDs)	Bobby Layne, 1950-58	118
Receiving (No.)	Charlie Sanders, 1968-1977	336
Receiving (Yds.)	Gail Cogdill, 1960-68	5,220
Interceptions	Dick LeBeau, 1959-1972	62
Punting (Avg.)	Yale Lary, 1952-53, 1956-1964	44.3
Punt Return (Avg.)	Jack Christiansen, 1951-58	12.8
Kickoff Return (Avg.)	Pat Studstill, 1961-67	25.7
Field Goals	Eddie Murray, 1980-88	192
Touchdowns (Tot.)	Billy Sims, 1980-84	47
Points	Eddie Murray, 1980-88	857

Individual Records—Single Season

Category	Name	Performance
Rushing (Yds.)	Billy Sims, 1981	1,437
Passing (Yds.)	Gary Danielson, 1980	3,223
Passing (TDs)	Bobby Layne, 1951	26
Receiving (No.)	James Jones, 1984	77
Receiving (Yds.)	Pat Studstill, 1966	1,266
Interceptions	Don Doll, 1950	12
	Jack Christiansen, 1953	12
Punting (Avg.)	Yale Lary, 1963	48.9
Punt Return (Avg.)	Jack Christiansen, 1952	21.5
Kickoff Return (Avg.)	Tom Watkins, 1965	34.4
Field Goals	Eddie Murray, 1980	27
Touchdowns (Tot.)	Billy Sims, 1980	16
Points	Doak Walker, 1950	128

Individual Records—Single Game

Category	Name	Performance
Rushing (Yds.)	Bob Hoernschemeyer, 11-23-50	198
Passing (Yds.)	Bobby Layne, 11-5-50	374
Passing (TDs)	Gary Danielson, 12-9-78	5
Receiving (No.)	Cloyce Box, 12-3-50	12
	James Jones, 9-28-86	12
Receiving (Yds.)	Cloyce Box, 12-3-50	302
Interceptions	Don Doll, 10-23-49	*4
Field Goals	Garo Yepremian, 11-13-66	6
Touchdowns (Tot.)	Cloyce Box, 12-3-50	4
Points	Cloyce Box, 12-3-50	24

*NFL Record

1988 Team Record

Preseason (0-4)

Date	Result		Opponents
8/6	L	10-13	at Cleveland
8/11	L	13-16	Seattle (OT)
8/20	L	7-24	at Cincinnati
8/25	L	9-27	Philadelphia
		39-80	

Regular Season (4-12)

Date	Result		Opponents	Att.
9/4	W	31-17	Atlanta	31,075
9/11	L	10-17	at L.A. Rams	46,262
9/18	L	14-22	New Orleans	32,943
9/25	L	10-17	N.Y. Jets	29,250
10/2	L	13-20	at San Francisco	58,285
10/9	L	7-24	Chicago	64,526
10/16	L	10-30	at N.Y. Giants	74,813
10/23	W	7- 6	at Kansas City	66,926
10/30	L	10-13	N.Y. Giants (OT)	38,354
11/6	L	17-44	at Minnesota	55,573
11/13	L	20-23	Tampa Bay	25,956
11/20	W	19- 9	at Green Bay	44,327
11/24	L	0-23	Minnesota	46,379
12/4	W	30-14	Green Bay	28,124
12/11	L	12-13	at Chicago	55,010
12/18	L	10-21	at Tampa Bay	37,778

(OT) Overtime

Score by Periods

Lions	36	87	51	46	0	—	220
Opponents	34	93	78	105	3	—	313

Attendance

Home 296,607 Away 438,974 Total 735,581
Single-game home record, 80,444 (12-20-81)
Single-season home record, 622,593 (1980)

1988 Team Statistics

	Lions	Opp.
Total First Downs	226	334
Rushing	63	128
Passing	141	179
Penalty	22	27
Third Down: Made/Att.	73/217	99/217
Fourth Down: Made/Att.	7/12	4/10
Total Net Yards	3405	5316
Avg. Per Game	212.8	332.3
Total Plays	920	1071
Avg. Per Play	3.7	5.0
Net Yards Rushing	1243	2037
Avg. Per Game	77.7	127.3
Total Rushes	391	511
Net Yards Passing	2162	3279
Avg. Per Game	135.1	204.9
Sacked/Yards Lost	52/410	47/393
Gross Yards	2572	3672
Att./Completions	477/213	513/337
Completion Pct.	44.7	65.7
Had Intercepted	18	15
Punts/Avg.	97/42.4	74/39.4
Net Punting Avg.	35.9	31.7
Penalties/Yards Lost	94/804	106/869
Fumbles/Ball Lost	31/15	35/21
Touchdowns	23	34
Rushing	7	16
Passing	13	17
Returns	3	1
Avg. Time of Possession	27:27	32:33

1988 Individual Statistics

Scoring	TD R	TD P	TD Rt	PAT	FG	Saf	TP
Murray	0	0	0	22/23	20/21	0	82
James	5	2	0	0/0	0/0	0	42
Mandley	1	4	0	0/0	0/0	0	30
Chadwick	0	3	0	0/0	0/0	0	18
Bland	0	2	0	0/0	0/0	0	12
Jamison	0	0	2	0/0	0/0	0	12
Lee	0	1	0	0/0	0/0	0	6
Lewis	0	1	0	0/0	0/0	0	6
Mitchell	0	0	1	0/0	0/0	0	6
S. Williams	1	0	0	0/0	0/0	0	6
Lions	7	13	3	22/23	20/21	0	220
Opponents	16	17	1	32/34	25/29	1	313

Passing	Att.	Comp.	Yds.	Pct.	TD	Int.	Tkld.	Rate
Hilger	306	126	1558	41.2	7	12	31/251	48.9
Long	141	75	856	53.2	6	6	18/134	68.2
Hipple	27	12	158	44.4	0	0	3/25	63.5
Arnold	1	0	0	0.0	0	0	0/0	39.6
Jones	1	0	0	0.0	0	0	0/0	39.6
Witkowski	1	0	0	0.0	0	0	0/0	39.6
Lions	477	213	2572	44.7	13	18	52/410	55.1
Opponents	513	337	3672	65.7	17	15	47/393	85.5

Rushing	Att.	Yds.	Avg.	LG	TD
James	182	552	3.0	35	5
Jones	96	314	3.3	13	0
Paige	52	207	4.0	20	0
Mandley	6	44	7.3	21t	1
Painter	17	42	2.5	13	0
Hilger	18	27	1.5	11	0
Long	7	22	3.1	11	0
S. Williams	9	22	2.4	5	1
Morris, Sea.-Det.	3	6	2.0	5	0
Hipple	1	5	5.0	5	0
Bland	1	4	4.0	4	0
Woolfolk	1	4	4.0	4	0
Witkowski	1	0	0.0	0	0
Lions	391	1243	3.2	35	7
Opponents	511	2037	4.0	37	16

Receiving	No.	Yds.	Avg.	LG	TD
Mandley	44	617	14.0	56	4
James	39	382	9.8	39t	2
Jones	29	259	8.9	40	0
Lee	22	261	11.9	18	1
Bland	21	307	14.6	35	2
Chadwick	20	304	15.2	32	3
Carter	13	145	11.2	31	0
Paige	11	100	9.1	15	0
Starring, T.B.-Det.	8	164	20.5	53	0
Starring, Det.	5	89	17.8	40	0
S. Williams	3	46	15.3	32	0
Lewis	3	32	10.7	23	1
Craig	2	29	14.5	18	0
Painter	1	1	1.0	1	0
Lions	213	2572	12.1	56	13
Opponents	337	3672	10.9	51t	17

Interceptions	No.	Yds.	Avg.	LG	TD
Mitchell	3	107	35.7	90t	1
Jamison	3	56	18.7	52t	1
Griffin	2	31	15.5	31	0
Blades	2	12	6.0	7	0
Cherry	2	0	0.0	0	0
Holmes	1	32	32.0	32	0
J. Williams	1	5	5.0	5	0
McNorton	1	4	4.0	4	0
Lions	15	247	16.5	90t	2
Opponents	18	159	8.8	34	0

Punting	No.	Yds.	Avg.	In 20	LG
Arnold	97	4110	42.4	22	69
Lions	97	4110	42.4	22	69
Opponents	74	2915	39.4	18	67

Punt Returns	No.	FC	Yds.	Avg.	LG	TD
Mandley	37	7	287	7.8	25	0
Bland	5	1	59	11.8	24	0
Lions	42	8	346	8.2	25	0
Opponents	57	19	483	8.5	77t	1

Kickoff Returns	No.	Yds.	Avg.	LG	TD
Lee	18	355	19.7	39	0
Painter	17	347	20.4	32	0
Morris, Sea.-Det.	13	259	19.9	30	0
Morris, Det.	2	41	20.5	25	0
Bland	8	179	22.4	29	0
Starring	8	130	16.3	22	0
Woolfolk	4	99	24.8	46	0
Andolsek	1	3	3.0	3	0
Saleaumua	1	0	0.0	0	0
Lions	59	1154	19.6	46	0
Opponents	56	1076	19.2	41	0

Sacks	No.
Cofer	12.0
Ferguson	8.5
E. Williams	6.5
Jamison	5.5
Ball	2.0
Green	2.0
Saleaumua	2.0
Strauthers	2.0
J. Williams	2.0
Blades	1.0
Griffin	1.0
Lockett	1.0
Rogers	1.0
Gibson	0.5
Lions	47.0
Opponents	52.0

1989 Draft Choices

Round	Name	Pos.	College
1.	Barry Sanders	RB	Oklahoma State
2.	John Ford	WR	Virginia
3.	Mike Utley	G	Washington State
4.	Ray Crockett	DB	Baylor
5.	Lawrence Pete	DT	Nebraska
6.	Rodney Peete	QB	Southern California
7.	Jerry Woods	DB	Northern Michigan
8.	Chris Parker	DT	West Virginia
9.	Derek MacCready	DE	Ohio State
10.	Jason Phillips	WR	Houston
11.	Keith Karpinski	LB	Penn State
12.	James Cribbs	DE	Memphis State

Detroit Lions 1989 Veteran Roster

No.	Name	Pos.	Ht.	Wt.	Birth-date	NFL Exp.	College	Hometown	How Acq.	'88 Games/ Starts
65	Andolsek, Eric	G	6-2	277	8/22/66	2	Louisiana State	Thibodaux, La.	D5-'88	13/0
6	†Arnold, Jim	P	6-3	211	1/31/61	7	Vanderbilt	Dalton, Ga.	FA-'86	16/0
68	Baack, Steve	G	6-4	265	11/16/60	5	Oregon	John Day, Ore.	D3c-'84	0*
97	Baldwin, Steve	NT	6-4	270	5/13/61	5	Tulsa	Lansing, Ill.	FA(NYJ)-'89#	16/2*
93	Ball, Jerry	NT	6-1	292	12/15/64	3	Southern Methodist	Beaumont, Tex.	D3-'87	16/16
61	Barrows, Scott	G-C	6-3	280	3/31/63	4	West Virginia	Marietta, Ohio	FA-'86	16/1
25	Bernard, Karl	RB	5-11	205	10/12/64	2	Southwestern Louisiana	Baton Rouge, La.	FA-'87	0*
36	Blades, Bennie	CB-S	6-1	221	9/3/66	2	Miami	Ft. Lauderdale, Fla.	D1-'88	15/14
75	Brown, Lomas	T	6-4	275	3/30/63	5	Florida	Miami, Fla.	D1-'85	16/16
44	Carter, Pat	TE	6-4	250	8/1/66	2	Florida State	Sarasota, Fla.	D2b-'88	15/14
91	Caston, Toby	LB	6-1	240	7/17/65	3	Louisiana State	Monroe, La.	FA(Hou)-'89#	16/0*
89	Chadwick, Jeff	WR	6-3	190	12/16/60	7	Grand Valley State	Dearborn, Mich.	FA-'83	10/8
45	Cherry, Raphel	S	6-0	190	12/19/61	4	Hawaii	Little Rock, Ark.	FA-'87	16/3
2	Clark, Robert	WR	5-11	175	8/8/65	2	North Carolina Central	Richmond, Va.	FA(NO)-'89#	16/0*
55	†Cofer, Michael	LB	6-5	245	4/7/60	7	Tennessee	Knoxville, Tenn.	D3-'83	16/16
67	Dallafior, Ken	G	6-4	278	8/26/59	5	Minnesota	Madison Heights, Mich.	FA(SD)-'89#	13/13*
41	Edmonds, Bobby Joe	KR	5-11	186	9/26/64	4	Arkansas	St. Louis, Mo.	FA(Sea)-'89#	16/0*
77	Ferguson, Keith	DE	6-5	260	4/3/59	9	Ohio State	Miami, Fla.	W(SD)-'85	14/14
69	Gambol, Chris	T	6-6	303	9/4/64	2	Iowa	Oxford, Mich.	FA(SD)-'89#	11/0*
98	Gibson, Dennis	LB	6-2	240	2/8/64	3	Iowa State	Ankeny, Iowa	D8-'87	16/16
53	Glover, Kevin	C-G	6-2	275	6/17/63	5	Maryland	Upper Marlboro, Md.	D2-'85	16/16
23	Gray, Mel	RB-KR	5-9	166	3/16/61	4	Purdue	Williamsburg, Va.	FA(NO)-'89#	14/0*
62	Green, Curtis	DE-NT	6-3	270	6/3/57	9	Alabama State	Quincy, Fla.	D2-'81	11/0
34	Griffin, James	S	6-2	203	9/7/61	7	Middle Tennessee State	Camilla, Ga.	FA-'86	16/6
71	Hamilton, Steve	DE-NT	6-4	270	9/28/61	5	East Carolina	Williamsville, N.Y.	FA(Wash)-'89#	15/0*
12	Hilger, Rusty	QB	6-4	205	5/9/62	5	Oklahoma State	Oklahoma City, Okla.	FA-'88	11/9
17	†Hipple, Eric	QB	6-2	211	9/16/57	9	Utah State	Downey, Calif.	D4-'80	5/0
43	†Holmes, Jerry	CB	6-2	175	12/22/57	8	West Virginia	Hampton, Va.	FA-'88	16/16
33	James, Garry	RB	5-10	214	9/4/63	4	Louisiana State	Gretna, La.	D2-'86	16/16
58	†Jamison, George	LB	6-1	226	9/30/62	3	Cincinnati	Bridgeton, N.J.	SD2-'84	16/11
30	Jones, James	RB	6-2	230	3/21/61	7	Florida	Pompano Beach, Fla.	D1-'83	14/14
90	Jones, Victor	LB	6-2	245	10/19/66	2	Virginia Tech	Rockville, Md.	FA(TB)-'89#	8/0*
99	Kab, Vyto	TE	6-5	240	12/23/59	6	Penn State	Wayne, N.J.	FA-'87	0*
83	†Lee, Gary	WR-KR	6-1	201	2/12/65	3	Georgia Tech	Albany, Ga.	D12-'87	14/6
80	Lewis, Mark	TE	6-2	250	5/5/61	3	Texas A&M	Houston, Tex.	FA-'88	3/3
50	Lockett, Danny	LB	6-2	250	7/11/64	3	Arizona	Ft. Valley, Ga.	D6-'87	16/0
16	Long, Chuck	QB	6-4	221	2/18/63	4	Iowa	Wheaton, Ill.	D1-'86	7/7
82	Mandley, Pete	WR-KR	5-10	195	7/29/61	6	Northern Arizona	Mesa, Ariz.	D2-'84	15/14
29	†McNorton, Bruce	CB	5-11	175	2/28/59	8	Georgetown, Ky.	Daytona Beach, Fla.	D4-'82	16/16
74	Milinichik, Joe	G-T	6-5	275	3/30/63	3	North Carolina State	Macungie, Pa.	D3-'86	15/15
31	Mitchell, Devon	S	6-1	194	12/30/62	3	Iowa	Brooklyn, N.Y.	D4-'86	10/9
42	†Morris, Randall	RB	6-0	200	4/22/61	6	Tennessee	Long Beach, Calif.	FA-'88	13/0*
52	Mott, Steve	C	6-3	265	3/24/61	7	Alabama	New Orleans, La.	D5-'83	16/16
3	†Murray, Eddie	K	5-10	180	8/29/56	10	Tulane	Victoria, British Columbia	D7-'80	16/0
86	Nichols, Mark	WR	6-2	208	10/29/59	7	San Jose State	Bakersfield, Calif.	D1-'81	0*
49	†Paige, Tony	RB	5-10	235	10/14/62	6	Virginia Tech	Washington, D.C.	FA-'87	16/2
26	Painter, Carl	RB	5-9	185	5/10/64	2	Hampton Institute	Norfolk, Va.	D6-'88	12/0
51	Robinson, Shelton	LB	6-2	236	9/14/60	8	North Carolina	Pikeville, N.C.	T(Sea)-'86	12/0
60	Rogers, Reggie	DE	6-6	280	1/21/64	3	Washington	Sacramento, Calif.	D1-'87	5/2
47	Roundtree, Ray	WR	6-0	182	4/19/66	2	Penn State	Aiken, S.C.	D3-'88	4/0
84	Rubick, Rob	TE	6-3	234	9/27/60	8	Grand Valley State	Newberry, Mich.	D12b-'82	15/1
73	Salem, Harvey	T-G	6-6	285	1/15/61	7	California	El Cerrito, Calif.	T(Hou)-'86	16/16
64	†Sanders, Eric	T-G	6-7	280	10/22/58	9	Nevada-Reno	Reno, Nev.	W(Atl)-'86	16/0
72	Singer, Curt	T	6-5	279	11/4/61	3	Tennessee	Aliquippa, Pa.	FA-'88	3/0
54	Spielman, Chris	LB	6-0	247	10/11/65	2	Ohio State	Canton, Ohio	D2a-'88	16/16
81	Starring, Stephen	WR	5-10	172	7/30/61	7	McNeese State	Vinton, La.	FA-'88	12/0*
21	Tullis, Willie	CB	5-11	195	4/5/58	9	Troy State	Stafford, Tex.	FA(Ind)-'89#	16/9*
35	White, William	CB	5-10	191	2/19/66	2	Ohio State	Lima, Ohio	D4-'88	16/0
76	†Williams, Eric	DE	6-4	286	2/24/62	6	Washington State	Stockton, Calif.	D3a-'84	16/16
59	Williams, Jimmy	LB	6-3	230	11/15/60	8	Nebraska	Washington, D.C.	D1-'82	5/5
38	Williams, Scott	RB	6-2	234	7/21/62	4	Georgia	Charlotte, N.C.	FA-'86	11/0
21	Woolfolk, Butch	RB	6-1	212	3/1/60	8	Michigan	Westfield, N.J.	FA-'87	0*

* Baack, Bernard, and Woolfolk missed '88 season due to injury; Baldwin played 16 games with N.Y. Jets in '88; Caston played 16 games with Houston; Clark played 16 games with New Orleans; Dallafior played 13 games with San Diego; Edmonds played 16 games with Seattle; Gambol played 11 games with San Diego; Gray played 14 games with New Orleans; Hamilton played 15 games with Washington; V. Jones played 8 games with Tampa Bay; Kab last active with Detroit in '87; Morris played 10 games with Seattle, 3 with Detroit; Nichols last active with Detroit in '87; Starring played 6 games with Tampa Bay, 6 with Detroit; Tullis played 16 games with Indianapolis.

† Option playout; subject to developments.

\# Plan B unconditional free agent.

Players lost through Plan B (7): LB Dave Ahrens (Mia; 8 games in '88), WR Carl Bland (GB; 16), LB Paul Butcher (Phil; 16), DE Gary Hadd (Phx; 5), NT Dan Salaeumua (KC; 16), DE Thomas Strauthers (Minn; 10), CB-S Bobby Watkins (Mia; 16).

Also played with Lions in '88—CB-S Lou Brock (2 games), RB Jessie Clark (5), WR Paco Craig (8), QB John Witkowski (2).

COACHING STAFF

Head Coach, Wayne Fontes

Pro Career: Became Lions' seventeenth head coach and director of football operations on December 22, 1988, after serving five weeks as interim head coach. Fontes led the Lions to a 2-3 record during that span. He began his fourth season in Detroit as the team's defensive coordinator and secondary coach, following a nine-year stint with the Tampa Bay Buccaneers. A former defensive back with the New York Jets, Fontes advanced from secondary coach to defensive coordinator to assistant head coach of the Buccaneers during his years at Tampa Bay. As a player with the Jets (1962), his brief pro career was cut short by a broken leg, but Fontes still holds the club record for the longest interception return, an 83-yarder against Houston (12-15-62). Career record: 2-3-0.

Background: A former two-sport star (football and baseball) at Michigan State, Fontes earned all-Big Ten honors at defensive back for the Spartans. He earned his bachelor's degree in education and biological science and later earned his master's degree in administration, all from Michigan State. After directing the freshman team at Michigan State in 1965, Fontes became defensive backfield coach at Dayton in 1968. He also served in the same capacity at Iowa (1969-71) and Southern California (1972-75).

Personal: Born February 17, 1940, New Bedford, Mass. Fontes and his wife, Evelyn, live in Rochester Hills, Mich., and have three children: Mike, Scott, and Kim.

Assistant Coaches

Don Clemons, administrative assistant; born February 15, 1954, Newark, N.J., lives in Rochester, Mich. Defensive end Muehlenberg College 1973-76. No pro playing experience. College coach: Kutztown State 1977-78, New Mexico 1979, Arizona State 1980-84. Pro coach: Detroit Lions 1985-87, rejoined Lions in 1989.

Darrel "Mouse" Davis, offensive passing assistant; born September 6, 1932, Palouse, Wash., lives in Lake Orion, Mich. Quarterback Western Oregon State 1952-55. No pro playing experience. College coach: Portland State 1974-80 (head coach 1975-80). Pro coach: Toronto Argonauts (CFL) 1982-83, Houston Gamblers (USFL) 1984, Denver Gold (USFL) 1985, joined Lions in 1989.

Frank Gansz, special teams; born November 22, 1938, Altoona, Pa., lives in Auburn Hills, Mich. Center-linebacker Navy 1957-59. No pro playing experience. College coach: Air Force 1964, Colgate 1968, Navy 1969, Oklahoma State 1973, 1975, Army 1974, UCLA 1976-77. Pro coach: San Francisco 49ers 1978, Cincinnati Bengals 1979-80, Kansas City Chiefs 1981-82, 1986-88 (head coach 1987-88), joined Lions in 1989.

June Jones, quarterbacks, receivers; born February 19, 1953, Portland, Ore., lives in Lake Orion, Mich. Quarterback Hawaii 1973-74, Portland State 1975-76. Pro quarterback Atlanta Falcons 1977-81, Toronto Argonauts (CFL) 1982. College coach: Hawaii 1983. Pro coach: Toronto Argonauts (CFL) 1982, Houston Gamblers (USFL) 1984, Denver Gold (USFL) 1985, Houston Oilers 1987-88, joined Lions in 1989.

Dave Levy, running backs; born October 25, 1932, Carrollton, Mo., lives in Lake Orion, Mich. Guard UCLA 1952-53. No pro playing experience. College coach: UCLA 1954, Long Beach City College 1955, Southern California 1960-75. Pro coach: San Diego Chargers 1980-88, joined Lions in 1989.

Billie Matthews, defensive backs; born March 15, 1930, Houston, Tex., lives in Rochester, Mich. Quarterback Southern University 1948-51. No pro playing experience. College coach: Kansas 1970, UCLA 1971-78. Pro coach: San Francisco 49ers 1979-82, Philadelphia Eagles 1983-84, Indianapolis Colts 1985-86, Kansas City Chiefs 1987-88, joined Lions in 1989.

Detroit Lions 1989 First-Year Roster

Name	Pos.	Ht.	Wt.	Birth-date	College	Hometown	How Acq.
Alexander, Bruce	CB-S	5-9	170	9/17/65	Stephen F. Austin	Lufkin, Tex.	FA
Brown, Selwyn (1)	CB-S	5-10	204	9/28/65	Miami	St. Petersburg, Fla.	FA
Bryant, Willie (1)	CB-S	6-0	197	3/10/66	Louisiana State	Ft. Walton Beach, Fla.	FA
Byrne, Tom	QB	6-4	223	1/11/66	Notre Dame	Pacifica, Calif.	FA
Crockett, Ray	CB-S	5-9	178	1/5/67	Baylor	Duncanville, Tex.	D4
Cribbs, James	DE	6-3	269	7/10/66	Memphis State	Memphis, Tenn.	D12
Dixon, James	WR	5-8	181	2/2/67	Houston	Vernon, Tex.	FA
Ford, John	WR	6-1	204	7/31/66	Virginia	Belle Glade, Fla.	D2
Huge, Al (1)	NT	6-3	229	6/1/66	Hillsdale College	Northfield, Ohio	FA
Irvin, Todd (1)	T	6-5	288	2/1/65	Mississippi	Aberdeen, Miss.	FA
Johnson, Kelley (1)	WR	5-8	168	6/3/62	Colorado	Carlsbad, N.M.	FA
Johnson, Richard (1)	WR	5-6	185	10/19/61	Colorado	San Pedro, Calif.	FA
Karpinski, Keith	LB	6-2	255	10/12/66	Penn State	Hamtramck, Mich.	D11
Ketchum, Anthony (1)	WR	5-7	154	11/20/62	Houston	Needville, Tex.	FA
MacCready, Derek	DE	6-4	266	5/4/67	Ohio State	Montreal, Canada	D9
Martz, Robert (1)	NT-DE	6-7	250	2/19/65	Notre Dame	Bloomfield Hills, Mich.	FA
McCray, Mike	LB	6-1	237	6/23/65	Ohio State	Dayton, Ohio	FA
McDonald, Keith (1)	WR	5-7	159	11/7/63	San Jose State	Wilmington, Calif.	FA
Miller, John	S	6-1	192	6/22/66	Michigan State	Farmington, Mich.	FA
Mobley, Stacey (1)	WR	5-7	165	9/15/65	Jackson State	Port Orange, Fla.	FA
Murphy, Mark	NT	6-5	263	6/18/66	Boston College	New Castle, Pa.	FA
Parker, Chris	NT	6-4	285	6/9/66	West Virginia	Whitehall, Pa.	D8
Peete, Rodney	QB	6-0	195	3/16/66	Southern California	Tucson, Ariz.	D6
Pete, Lawrence	NT	6-0	286	1/18/66	Nebraska	Wichita, Kan.	D5
Phillips, Jason	WR	5-7	166	10/11/66	Houston	Houston, Tex.	D10
Phillips, John (1)	T-G	6-4	270	9/29/65	Clemson	Spruce Pine, N.C.	FA
Pizzo, Joseph (1)	QB	6-3	215	6/25/64	Mars Hill College	Quartz Hill, Calif.	FA
Powell, Jeff (1)	WR	5-9	186	5/27/63	Tennessee	Whites Creek, Tenn.	FA
Sanders, Barry	RB	5-8	203	7/16/68	Oklahoma State	Wichita, Kan.	D1
Sutkiewick, Rick	K	6-2	229	7/10/66	Michigan	Troy, Mich.	FA
Turner, Lonnie (1)	WR	5-7	164	8/31/60	Cal Poly-Pomona	Compton, Calif.	FA
Utley, Mike	G-T	6-6	288	12/20/65	Washington State	Seattle, Wash.	D3
Woods, Jerry	CB-S	5-9	187	2/13/66	Northern Michigan	Racine, Wis.	D7

The term NFL Rookie is defined as a player who is in his first season of professional football and has not been on the roster of another professional football team for any regular-season or postseason games. A Rookie is designated by an "R" on NFL rosters. Players who have been active in another professional football league or players who have NFL experience, including either preseason training camp or being on an active roster for fewer than three regular-season or postseason games, are termed NFL First-Year Players. An NFL First-Year Player is designated by a "1" on NFL rosters. Thereafter, a player on an NFL active roster for at least three regular-season or postseason games is credited with an additional year of NFL playing experience.

NOTES

Dick Modzelewski, defensive line; born January 16, 1931, West Natrona, Pa., lives in Rochester Hills, Mich. Tackle Maryland 1950-52. Pro defensive tackle Washington Redskins 1953-54, Pittsburgh Steelers 1955, New York Giants 1956-63, Cleveland Browns 1964-66. Pro coach: Cleveland Browns 1968-77, New York Giants 1978, Cincinnati Bengals 1979-83, Green Bay Packers 1984-87, joined Lions in 1988.

Mike Murphy, staff assistant, born September 25, 1944, New York, N.Y., lives in Rochester, Mich. Guard-linebacker Huron, S.D., College 1962-65. No pro playing experience. College coach: Vermont 1970-73, Idaho State 1974-76, Western Illinois 1977-78. Pro coach: Saskatchewan Roughriders (CFL) 1979-83, Chicago Blitz (USFL) 1984, joined Lions in 1985.

Herb Paterra, inside linebackers; born November 8, 1940, Glassport, Pa., lives in Rochester Hills, Mich. Offensive guard-linebacker Michigan State 1960-62. Pro linebacker Buffalo Bills 1963-64, Hamilton Tiger-Cats (CFL) 1965-68. College coach: Michigan State 1969-71, Wyoming 1972-74. Pro coach: Charlotte Hornets (WFL) 1975, Hamilton Tiger-Cats (CFL) 1978-79, Los Angeles Rams 1980-82, Edmonton Eskimos (CFL) 1983, Green Bay Packers 1984-85, Buffalo Bills 1986, Tampa Bay Buccaneers 1987-88, joined Lions in 1989.

Charlie Sanders, tight ends; born August 25, 1946, Greensboro, N.C., lives in Rochester, Mich. Tight end Minnesota 1966-67. Pro tight end Detroit Lions 1968-77. Pro coach: Joined Lions in 1989.

Jerry Wampfler, offensive line; born August 6, 1932, New Philadelphia, Ohio, lives in Lake Orion, Mich. Tackle Miami, Ohio 1951-54. No pro playing experience. College coach: Presbyterian 1955, Miami, Ohio 1963-65, Notre Dame 1966-69, Colorado State 1970-72 (head coach). Pro coach: Philadelphia Eagles 1973-75, 1979-83, Buffalo Bills 1976-77, New York Giants 1978, Green Bay Packers 1984-87, San Diego Chargers 1988, joined Lions in 1989.

Woody Widenhofer, defensive coordinator, outside linebackers; born January 20, 1943, Riverview, Mich., lives in Rochester Hills, Mich. Linebacker Missouri 1961-64. No pro playing experience. College coach: Michigan State 1969-70, Eastern Michigan 1971, Minnesota 1972, Missouri 1985-88 (head coach). Pro coach: Pittsburgh Steelers 1973-83, Oklahoma Outlaws (USFL) 1984 (head coach), joined Lions in 1989.

National Football Conference
Central Division

Team Colors: Dark Green, Gold, and White

1265 Lombardi Avenue
P.O. Box 10628
Green Bay, Wisconsin 54307-0628
Telephone: (414) 494-2351

Club Officials

Chairman of the Board: Robert J. Parins
President, CEO: Bob Harlan
Vice President: John Fabry
Secretary: Peter M. Platten III
Treasurer: Phil Hendrickson
Executive Vice President, Football Operations: Tom Braatz
Executive Director of Public Relations: Lee Remmel
Director of Marketing/Community Relations: Jeff Cieply
Assistant Director of Public Relations: Jeff Blumb
Green Bay Ticket Director: Mark Wagner
Milwaukee Ticket Director: Marge Paget
Accountant: Dick Blasczyk
Video Director: Al Treml
Trainer: Domenic Gentile
Equipment Manager: Bob Noel

Stadium: Lambeau Field • **Capacity:** 57,095
P.O. Box 10628
1265 Lombardi Avenue
Green Bay, Wisconsin 54307-0628

Milwaukee County Stadium •
Capacity: 56,051
Highway I-94
Milwaukee, Wisconsin 53214

Playing Surfaces: Grass

Training Camp: St. Norbert College
DePere, Wisconsin 54115

1989 Schedule

Preseason

Aug. 12	vs. N.Y. Jets at Milwaukee	1:00
Aug. 19	**Indianapolis**	1:00
Aug. 26	vs. Buffalo at Madison, Wis.	1:00
Sept. 1	at New England	7:00

Regular Season

Sept. 10	**Tampa Bay**	12:00
Sept. 17	**New Orleans**	12:00
Sept. 24	at Los Angeles Rams	1:00
Oct. 1	**Atlanta** at Milwaukee	12:00
Oct. 8	**Dallas**	12:00
Oct. 15	at Minnesota	12:00
Oct. 22	at Miami	1:00
Oct. 29	**Detroit** at Milwaukee	12:00
Nov. 5	**Chicago**	12:00
Nov. 12	at Detroit	1:00
Nov. 19	at San Francisco	1:00
Nov. 26	**Minnesota** at Milwaukee	12:00
Dec. 3	at Tampa Bay	1:00
Dec. 10	**Kansas City**	12:00
Dec. 17	at Chicago	12:00
Dec. 24	at Dallas	12:00

Packers Coaching History

(469-385-36)

1921-49	Earl (Curly) Lambeau	212-106-21
1950-53	Gene Ronzani*	14-31-1
1953	Hugh Devore- Ray (Scooter) McLean**	0-2-0
1954-57	Lisle Blackbourn	17-31-0
1958	Ray (Scooter) McLean	1-10-1
1959-67	Vince Lombardi	98-30-4
1968-70	Phil Bengtson	20-21-1
1971-74	Dan Devine	25-28-4
1975-83	Bart Starr	53-77-3
1984-87	Forrest Gregg	25-37-1
1988	Lindy Infante	4-12-0

*Released after 10 games in 1953
**Co-coaches

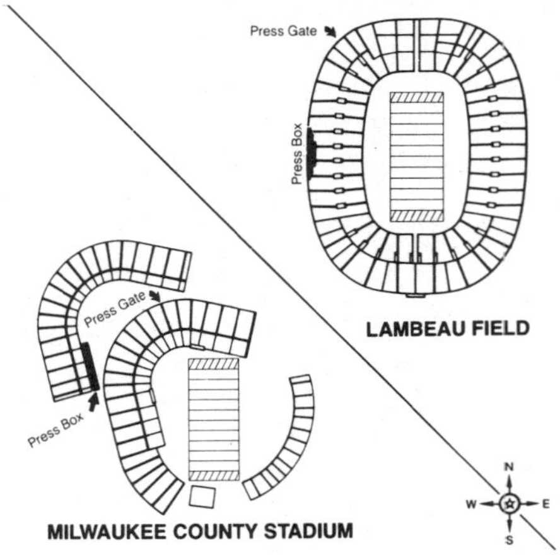

Record Holders

Individual Records—Career

Category	Name	Performance
Rushing (Yds.)	Jim Taylor, 1958-1966	8,207
Passing (Yds.)	Bart Starr, 1956-1971	23,718
Passing (TDs)	Bart Starr, 1956-1971	152
Receiving (No.)	James Lofton, 1978-1986	530
Receiving (Yds.)	James Lofton, 1978-1986	9,656
Interceptions	Bobby Dillon, 1952-59	52
Punting (Avg.)	Dick Deschaine, 1955-57	42.6
Punt Return (Avg.)	Billy Grimes, 1950-52	13.2
Kickoff Return (Avg.)	Travis Williams, 1967-1970	26.7
Field Goals	Chester Marcol, 1972-1980	120
Touchdowns (Tot.)	Don Hutson, 1935-1945	105
Points	Don Hutson, 1935-1945	823

Individual Records—Single Season

Category	Name	Performance
Rushing (Yds.)	Jim Taylor, 1962	1,407
Passing (Yds.)	Lynn Dickey, 1983	4,458
Passing (TDs)	Lynn Dickey, 1983	32
Receiving (No.)	Don Hutson, 1942	74
Receiving (Yds.)	James Lofton, 1984	1,361
Interceptions	Irv Comp, 1943	10
Punting (Avg.)	Jerry Norton, 1963	44.7
Punt Return (Avg.)	Billy Grimes, 1950	19.1
Kickoff Return (Avg.)	Travis Williams, 1967	41.1
Field Goals	Chester Marcol, 1972	33
Touchdowns (Tot.)	Jim Taylor, 1962	19
Points	Paul Hornung, 1960	*176

Individual Records—Single Game

Category	Name	Performance
Rushing (Yds.)	Jim Taylor, 12-3-61	186
Passing (Yds.)	Lynn Dickey, 10-12-80	418
Passing (TDs)	Many times Last time by Lynn Dickey, 9-4-83	5
Receiving (No.)	Don Hutson, 11-22-42	14
Receiving (Yds.)	Bill Howton, 10-21-56	257
Interceptions	Bobby Dillon, 11-26-53	*4
	Willie Buchanon, 9-24-78	*4
Field Goals	Many times Last time by Max Zendejas, 10-16-88	4
Touchdowns (Tot.)	Paul Hornung, 12-12-65	5
Points	Paul Hornung, 10-8-61	33

*NFL Record

1988 Team Record

Preseason (1-2-1)

Date	Result		Opponents
8/6	L	3-34	N.Y. Giants
8/13	L	21-25	at Indianapolis
8/19	T	21-21	vs. Kansas City at Milwaukee
8/27	W	27-24	vs. N.Y. Jets at Madison, Wis.
		72-104	

Regular Season (4-12)

Date	Result		Opponents	Att.
9/4	L	7-34	L.A. Rams	53,769
9/11	L	10-13	Tampa Bay	52,584
9/18	L	17-24	at Miami	54,409
9/25	L	6-24	Chicago	56,492
10/2	L	24-27	at Tampa Bay	40,003
10/9	W	45- 3	New England	51,932
10/16	W	34-14	at Minnesota	59,053
10/23	L	17-20	Washington	51,767
10/30	L	0-28	at Buffalo	79,176
11/6	L	0-20	at Atlanta	29,952
11/13	L	13-20	Indianapolis	53,492
11/20	L	9-19	Detroit	44,327
11/27	L	0-16	at Chicago	62,026
12/4	L	14-30	at Detroit	28,124
12/11	W	18- 6	Minnesota	48,892
12/18	W	26-17	at Phoenix	44,586

Score by Periods

Packers	58	58	47	77	0	—	240
Opponents	78	131	38	68	0	—	315

Attendance

Home 413,255 Away 397,329 Total 810,584
Single-game home record, 56,895 (11-3-85; Lambeau Field), 56,258 (9-28-80, Milwaukee County Stadium)
Single-season home record, 435,521 (1980)

1988 Team Statistics

	Packers	Opp.
Total First Downs	280	281
Rushing	78	130
Passing	175	136
Penalty	27	15
Third Down: Made/Att.	77/215	76/215
Fourth Down: Made/Att.	7/14	8/16
Total Net Yards	4664	4843
Avg. Per Game	291.5	302.7
Total Plays	1018	1018
Avg. Per Play	4.6	4.8
Net Yards Rushing	1379	2110
Avg. Per Game	86.2	131.9
Total Rushes	385	514
Net Yards Passing	3285	2733
Avg. Per Game	205.3	170.8
Sacked/Yards Lost	51/324	30/216
Gross Yards	3609	2949
Att./Completions	582/319	474/256
Completion Pct.	54.8	54.0
Had Intercepted	24	20
Punts/Avg.	86/38.2	76/37.6
Net Punting Avg.	31.8	33.6
Penalties/Yards Lost	94/785	112/903
Fumbles/Ball Lost	44/26	33/21
Touchdowns	29	34
Rushing	14	17
Passing	13	12
Returns	2	5
Avg. Time of Possession	29:16	30:44

1988 Individual Statistics

Scoring	TD R	TD P	TD Rt	PAT	FG	Saf	TP
Fullwood	7	1	0	0/0	0/0	0	48
Zendejas	0	0	0	17/19	9/16	0	44
Woodside	3	2	0	0/0	0/0	0	30
D. Dorsey, Phil.-G.B.	0	0	0	12/13	5/10	0	27
D. Dorsey, G.B.	0	0	0	3/4	1/3	0	6
West	0	3	0	0/0	0/0	0	18
Dawson, Phil.-G.B.	0	0	0	4/5	3/6	0	13
Dawson, G.B.	0	0	0	1/2	3/5	0	10
Matthews	0	2	0	0/0	0/0	0	12
Wright	2	0	0	0/0	0/0	0	12
Harris	0	0	1	0/0	0/0	2	10
Davis	1	0	0	0/0	0/0	0	6
Didier	0	1	0	0/0	0/0	0	6
Hackett	0	1	0	0/0	0/0	0	6
Majkowski	1	0	0	0/0	0/0	0	6
Mason	0	1	0	0/0	0/0	0	6
Pitts	0	0	1	0/0	0/0	0	6
Scott	0	1	0	0/0	0/0	0	6
Sharpe	0	1	0	0/0	0/0	0	6
Burrow	0	0	0	2/4	0/1	0	2
Packers	14	13	2	23/29	13/25	2	240
Opponents	17	12	5	34/34	25/35	1	315

Passing	Att.	Comp.	Yds.	Pct.	TD	Int.	Tkld.	Rate
Wright	244	141	1490	57.8	4	13	20/148	58.9
Majkowski	336	178	2119	53.0	9	11	31/176	67.8
Carruth	2	0	0	0.0	0	0	0/0	39.6
Packers	582	319	3609	54.8	13	24	51/324	63.9
Opponents	474	256	2949	54.0	12	20	30/216	63.9

Rushing	Att.	Yds.	Avg.	LG	TD
Fullwood	101	483	4.8	33t	7
Majkowski	47	225	4.8	24	1
Woodside	83	195	2.3	10	3
Mason	48	194	4.0	17	0
Davis	39	121	3.1	27	1
Carruth	49	114	2.3	14	0
Wright	8	43	5.4	19	2
Matthews	3	3	1.0	4	0
Collins	2	2	1.0	2	0
Stanley	1	1	1.0	1	0
Sharpe	4	−2	−0.5	5	0
Packers	385	1379	3.6	33t	14
Opponents	514	2110	4.1	80t	17

Receiving	No.	Yds.	Avg.	LG	TD
Sharpe	55	791	14.4	51	1
Kemp	48	620	12.9	36	0
Woodside	39	352	9.0	49t	2
West	30	276	9.2	35	3
Stanley	28	436	15.6	56	0
Carruth	24	211	8.8	31	0
Scott	20	275	13.8	41	1
Matthews, Atl.-G.B.	20	231	11.6	25	2
Matthews, G.B.	15	167	11.1	25	2
Fullwood	20	128	6.4	30t	1
Epps	11	99	9.0	25	0
Davis	11	81	7.4	11	0
Mason	8	84	10.5	39	1
Didier	5	37	7.4	15	1
Bolton	2	33	16.5	18	0
Collins	2	17	8.5	9	0
Hackett	1	2	2.0	2t	1
Packers	319	3609	11.3	56	13
Opponents	256	2949	11.5	46t	12

Interceptions	No.	Yds.	Avg.	LG	TD
Murphy	5	19	3.8	9	0
Cecil	4	56	14.0	33	0
Lee	3	37	12.3	27	0
Stills	3	29	9.7	17	0
D. Brown	3	27	9.0	15	0
Pitts	2	56	28.0	31	0
Packers	20	224	11.2	33	0
Opponents	24	386	16.1	90t	4

Punting	No.	Yds.	Avg.	In 20	LG
Bracken	85	3287	38.7	20	62
Packers	86	3287	38.2	20	62
Opponents	76	2859	37.6	22	69

Punt Returns	No.	FC	Yds.	Avg.	LG	TD
Stanley	12	3	52	4.3	15	0
Pitts	9	6	93	10.3	63t	1
Sharpe	9	7	48	5.3	14	0
Matthews, Atl.-G.B.	6	0	26	4.3	10	0
Jefferson	5	2	15	3.0	9	0
Packers	35	18	208	5.9	63t	1
Opponents	39	14	314	8.1	46	0

Kickoff Returns	No.	Yds.	Avg.	LG	TD
Fullwood	21	421	20.0	31	0
Woodside	19	343	18.1	29	0
Scott	12	207	17.3	27	0
Jefferson	4	116	29.0	46	0
Stanley	2	39	19.5	22	0
Hackett	1	9	9.0	9	0
Hill	1	1	1.0	1	0
Pitts	1	17	17.0	17	0
Sharpe	1	17	17.0	17	0
Stills	1	4	4.0	4	0
Winter	1	7	7.0	7	0
Packers	64	1181	18.5	46	0
Opponents	49	966	19.7	37	0

Sacks	No.
Harris	13.5
Winter	5.0
Patterson	4.0
R. Brown	1.5
Anderson	1.0
Dent	1.0
Greene	1.0
Stephen	1.0
Stills	1.0
Boyarsky	0.5
Noble	0.5
Packers	30.0
Opponents	51.0

1989 Draft Choices

Round	Name	Pos.	College
1.	Tony Mandarich	T	Michigan State
3.	Matt Brock	DE	Oregon
	Anthony Dilweg	QB	Duke
4.	Jeff Graham	QB	Long Beach State
5.	Jeff Query	WR	Millikin
	Vince Workman	RB	Ohio State
6.	Chris Jacke	K	Texas-El Paso
7.	Mark Hall	DE	S.W. Louisiana
8.	Thomas King	DB	S.W. Louisiana
	Brian Shulman	P	Auburn
9.	Scott Kirby	T	Arizona State
10.	Ben Jessie	DB	S.W. Texas State
11.	Cedric Stallworth	DB	Georgia Tech
12.	Stan Shiver	DB	Florida State

Green Bay Packers 1989 Veteran Roster

No.	Name	Pos.	Ht.	Wt.	Birth-date	NFL Exp.	College	Hometown	How Acq.	'88 Games/ Starts
59	Anderson, John	LB	6-3	228	2/14/56	12	Michigan	Waukesha, Wis.	D1b-'78	14/14
67	Ard, Billy	G	6-3	270	3/12/59	9	Wake Forest	Watchung, N.J.	FA(NYG)-'89#	16/16*
69	Bartlett, Doug	NT	6-2	257	5/22/63	2	Northern Illinois	Springfield, Ill.	FA(Phil)-'89#	10/0*
40	Bland, Carl	WR	5-11	182	8/17/61	6	Virginia Union	Richmond, Va.	FA(Det)-'89#	14/2*
82	Bolton, Scott	WR	6-0	188	1/4/65	2	Auburn	Theodore, Ala.	D12-'88	4/0
61	Boyarsky, Jerry	NT	6-3	290	5/15/59	8	Pittsburgh	Scranton, Pa.	FA-'87	2/2
17	Bracken, Don	P	6-1	211	2/16/62	5	Michigan	Thermopolis, Wyo.	FA-'85	16/0
32	Brown, Dave	CB-S	6-1	197	1/16/53	15	Michigan	Akron, Ohio	T(Sea)-'87	16/16
93	Brown, Robert	DE	6-2	267	5/21/60	8	Virginia Tech	Edenton, N.C.	D4-'82	16/16
51	Bush, Blair	C	6-3	272	11/25/56	12	Washington	Palos Verdes, Calif.	FA(Sea)-'89#	16/14*
63	Campen, James	C	6-3	270	6/11/64	3	Tulane	Sacramento, Calif.	FA(NO)-'89#	12/3*
58	Cannon, Mark	C	6-3	258	6/14/62	6	Texas-Arlington	Austin, Tex.	D11-'84	16/16
30	†Carruth, Paul Ott	RB	6-1	220	7/22/61	4	Alabama	McComb, Miss.	FA-'86	15/4
26	Cecil, Chuck	S	6-0	184	11/8/64	2	Arizona	San Diego, Calif.	D4b-'88	16/2
60	†Croston, David	T	6-5	280	11/10/63	2	Iowa	Sioux City, Iowa	D3a-'87	16/1
56	†Dent, Burnell	LB	6-1	236	3/16/63	4	Tulane	St. Rose, La.	D6-'86	10/3
80	Didier, Clint	TE	6-5	240	4/4/59	8	Portland State	Pasco, Wash.	FA-'88	15/0
99	Dorsey, John	LB	6-2	243	8/31/60	6	Connecticut	Leonardtown, Md.	D4-'84	16/6
85	†Epps, Phillip	WR	5-10	165	11/11/59	8	Texas Christian	Atlanta, Tex.	D12-'82	6/3
21	Fullwood, Brent	RB	5-11	209	10/10/63	3	Auburn	St. Cloud, Fla.	D1-'87	14/10
23	†Greene, Tiger	CB-S	6-0	194	2/15/62	5	Western Carolina	Hendersonville, N.C.	FA-'86	16/4
35	Haddix, Michael	RB	6-2	227	12/27/61	7	Mississippi State	Walnut, Miss.	FA(Phil)-'89#	16/3*
74	Haley, Darryl	T	6-5	265	2/16/61	7	Utah	Los Angeles, Calif.	FA-'88	13/0
65	Hallstrom, Ron	G	6-6	290	6/11/59	8	!owa	Moline, Ill.	D1-'82	16/16
41	Harris, Darryl	RB	5-10	178	2/20/66	2	Arizona State	Pomona, Calif.	FA(Minn)-'89#	14/0*
97	†Harris, Tim	LB	6-5	235	9/10/64	4	Memphis State	Birmingham, Ala.	D4a-'86	16/16
50	†Holland, Johnny	LB	6-2	221	3/11/65	3	Texas A&M	Hempstead, Tex.	D2-'87	13/13
25	Howard, Bobby	RB	6-0	220	6/1/64	3	Indiana	Pittsburgh, Pa.	FA(TB)-'89#	3/0*
53	Howard, Todd	LB	6-2	244	2/18/65	3	Texas A&M	Bryan, Tex.	FA(KC)-'89#	7/0*
24	Jakes, Van	CB-S	6-0	190	5/10/61	6	Kent State	Buffalo, N.Y.	FA(NO)-'89#	16/15*
81	Kemp, Perry	WR	5-11	170	12/31/61	3	California State, Pa.	Cannonsburg, Pa.	FA-'88	16/4
22	†Lee, Mark	CB-S	5-11	189	3/20/58	10	Washington	Hanford, Calif.	D2-'80	15/15
7	Majkowski, Don	QB	6-2	197	2/25/64	3	Virginia	Depew, N.Y.	D10-'87	13/9
34	Mason, Larry	RB	5-11	205	5/21/61	3	Troy State	McCall, Ala.	FA-'88	15/2
88	†Matthews, Aubrey	WR	5-7	165	9/15/62	4	Delta State	Moss Point, Miss.	FA-'88	7/2
98	Moore, Brent	LB	6-5	242	1/9/63	2	Southern California	Novato, Calif.	D9-'86	0*
57	Moran, Rich	C-G	6-2	275	3/19/62	5	San Diego State	Pleasanton, Calif.	D3-'85	16/16
37	†Murphy, Mark	S	6-2	201	4/22/58	8	West Liberty	Canton, Ohio	FA-'84	14/13
79	Nelson, Bob	NT	6-4	275	3/3/59	3	Miami	Baltimore, Md.	FA-'88	14/7
91	Noble, Brian	LB	6-3	252	9/6/62	5	Arizona State	Anaheim, Calif.	D5-'85	12/10
43	Novoselsky, Brent	TE	6-3	232	1/8/66	2	Pennsylvania	Skokie, Ill.	FA(Chi)-'89#	8/0*
96	Patterson, Shawn	NT-DE	6-5	261	4/6/65	2	Arizona State	Tempe, Ariz.	D2-'88	15/4
28	†Pitts, Ron	CB-S	5-10	175	10/14/62	4	UCLA	Orchard Park, N.Y.	FA-'88	14/1
75	†Ruettgers, Ken	T	6-5	280	8/20/62	5	Southern California	Bakersfield, Calif.	D1-'85	15/15
83	Scott, Patrick	WR	5-10	170	9/13/64	3	Grambling	Ringgold, La.	FA-'87	16/0
84	Sharpe, Sterling	WR-KR	5-11	202	4/6/65	2	South Carolina	Glenville, Ga.	D1-'88	16/16
19	Smith, Jeff	RB	5-9	205	3/22/62	5	Nebraska	Wichita, Kan.	FA(TB)-'89#	16/3*
89	Spagnola, John	TE	6-4	242	8/1/57	10	Yale	Bethlehem, Pa.	FA(Sea)-'89#	16/4*
87	†Stanley, Walter	WR-KR	5-9	179	11/5/62	5	Mesa, Colo.	Chicago, Ill.	D4-'85	7/7
54	†Stephen, Scott	LB	6-2	232	6/18/64	3	Arizona State	Los Angeles, Calif.	D3b-'87	8/0
29	†Stills, Ken	CB-S	5-10	186	9/6/63	5	Wisconsin	Oceanside, Calif.	D8-'85	14/13
49	Sutton, Mickey	CB	5-9	172	8/28/60	4	Montana	Union City, Calif.	FA(Rams)-'89#	15/0*
70	Uecker, Keith	G-T	6-5	284	6/29/60	7	Auburn	Hollywood, Fla.	W(Den)-'84	16/16
52	Weddington, Mike	LB	6-4	245	10/9/60	4	Oklahoma	Temple, Tex.	FA-'86	16/2
86	West, Ed	TE	6-1	243	8/2/61	6	Auburn	Leighton, Ala.	FA-'84	16/16
48	Wilkins, Gary	TE	6-2	235	11/23/63	3	Georgia Tech	West Palm Beach, Fla.	FA(Atl)-'89#	14/1*
90	Williams, Toby	NT	6-4	275	11/19/59	7	Nebraska	Washington, D.C.	FA(NE)-'89#	15/0*
68	Winter, Blaise	DE-NT	6-3	275	1/31/62	5	Syracuse	Blauvelt, N.Y.	T(SD)-'88	16/8
33	Woodside, Keith	RB	5-11	203	7/29/64	2	Texas A&M	Vidalia, La.	D3-'88	16/9
16	†Wright, Randy	QB	6-2	203	1/12/61	6	Wisconsin	St. Charles, Ill.	D6-'84	8/7

* Ard played 16 games with N.Y. Giants in '88; Bartlett played 10 games with Philadelphia; Bland played 14 games with Detroit; Bush played 16 games with Seattle; Campen played 12 games with New Orleans; Haddix played 16 games with Philadelphia; D. Harris played 14 games with Minnesota; B. Howard played 3 games with Tampa Bay; T. Howard played 7 games with Kansas City; Jakes played 16 games with New Orleans; Moore missed '88 season due to injury; Novoselsky played 8 games with Chicago; Smith played 16 games with Tampa Bay; Spagnola played 16 games with Seattle; Sutton played 15 games with L.A. Rams; Wilkins played 14 games with Atlanta; Williams played 15 games with New England.

† Option playout; subject to developments.

Plan B unconditional free agent.

Players lost through Plan B (8): DE Alphonso Carreker (Den; 14 games in '88), T Steve Collier (NYJ; active for 1 game but did not play), RB Pat Collins (Clev; 5), RB Kenneth Davis (Buff; 9), C Kani Kauahi (Phx; 16), CB-S Chris Mandeville (Wash; 0), CB Gary Richard (Pitt; 10), G Tommy Robison (Atl; 0).

Also played with Packers in '88—WR J.R. Ambrose (active for 1 game but did not play), WR Albert Bell (5), LB John Corker (2), K Dale Dawson (4), K Dean Dorsey (3), TE Joey Hackett (9), DE Nate Hill (3), T-G Tom Neville (2), LB Ron Simpkins (7), RB Lavale Thomas (1), K Max Zendejas (8).

COACHING STAFF

Head Coach, Lindy Infante

Pro Career: Named Packers' head coach on February 3, 1988, after serving as offensive coordinator of Cleveland Browns in 1986-87. In that two-year span the Browns won more games (22) than any other team in the AFC. Was previously head coach of the Jacksonville Bulls (USFL) in 1984-85, compiling a 15-21 record. Earlier had been quarterback/receivers coach of the Cincinnati Bengals in 1980-81 and offensive coordinator in 1982, helping Bengals gain Super Bowl XVI in 1981 and compile the best record in the NFL over the 1981-82 seasons (19-6). Began pro coaching career with Charlotte Hornets (WFL) in 1975, later moving into the NFL with the New York Giants in 1978. Career record: 4-12.

Background: Running back and defensive back at University of Florida (1960-62), winning second-team All-Southeastern Conference honors as senior, when he also was a team captain. Entered coaching at Miami High School (1965). College assistant at Florida 1966-71, Memphis State 1972-74, Tulane 1976, 1979.

Personal: Born May 27, 1940, in Miami, Fla. Attended Miami High School. He and his wife, Stephanie, live in Green Bay and have two sons, Brett, 17, and Brad, 16.

Assistant Coaches

Greg Blache, defensive line; born March 9, 1949, New Orleans, La., lives in Green Bay. No college or pro playing experience. College coach: Notre Dame 1973-75, 1981-83, Tulane 1976-80, Southern University 1986, Kansas 1987. Pro coach: Jacksonville Bulls (USFL) 1984-85, joined Packers in 1988.

Hank Bullough, defensive coordinator; born January 24, 1934, Scranton, Pa., lives in Green Bay. Offensive guard Michigan State 1952-54. Pro offensive guard Green Bay Packers 1955, 1958. College coach: Michigan State 1959-69. Pro coach: Baltimore Colts 1970-72, New England Patriots 1973-79, Cincinnati Bengals 1980-83, Pittsburgh Maulers (USFL) 1984-85, Buffalo Bills 1985-86 (compiled 4-17 record as head coach from October 1, 1985, through November 3, 1986), joined Packers in 1988.

Joe B. Clark, general offensive assistant; born December 22, 1932, Los Angeles, Calif., lives in Green Bay. Quarterback Santa Clara 1951-52. No pro playing experience. College coach: Wooster College 1958-59, Detroit 1960-64, Tulane 1965-70, Memphis State 1974, Nicholls State 1981-83, Southeastern Louisiana 1985, Southern University 1986. Pro coach: Charlotte Hornets (WFL) 1975, Jacksonville Bulls (USFL) 1984-85, joined Packers in 1988.

Charlie Davis, offensive line; born August 7, 1944, San Diego, Calif., lives in Green Bay. Linebacker San Diego City College 1961, UCLA 1962-64. No pro playing experience. College coach: San Francisco State 1967-70, Xavier 1971-73, Ball State 1974-75, Tulane 1976-80. Pro coach: Jacksonville Bulls (USFL) 1984-85, Cleveland Browns 1986-87, joined Packers in 1988.

Buddy Geis, receivers; born September 16, 1946, Altoona, Pa., lives in Green Bay. Running back Lock Haven State 1967-69. No pro playing experience. College coach: Arizona 1973-76, Tulane 1977-82, Memphis State 1986-87. Pro coach: Jacksonville Bulls (USFL) 1984-85, joined Packers in 1988.

Dick Jauron, defensive backfield; born October 7, 1950, Swampscott, Mass., lives in Green Bay. Defensive back Yale 1970-72. Pro defensive back Detroit Lions 1973-77, Cincinnati Bengals 1978-80. Pro coach: Buffalo Bills 1985, joined Packers in 1986.

Virgil Knight, strength-conditioning; born January 30, 1948, Clarksville, Ark., lives in Green Bay. Tight end Northeastern Oklahoma 1968-70. No pro playing experience. College coach: Arkansas Tech 1975-78, Florida 1979-80, Auburn 1981-83. Pro coach: Joined Packers in 1984.

Green Bay Packers 1989 First-Year Roster

Name	Pos.	Ht.	Wt.	Birth-date	College	Hometown	How Acq.
Affholter, Erik	WR-K	5-11	181	4/10/66	Southern California	Agoura, Calif.	T(Wash)
Ambrose, J.R. (1)	WR	6-0	185	4/19/64	Mississippi	Monroe, La.	FA-'88
Ariey, Mike (1)	T	6-5	285	3/12/64	San Diego State	Bakersfield, Calif.	FA
Armentrout, Joe (1)	RB	6-0	225	11/4/64	Wisconsin	Elgin, Ill.	FA-'88
Brady, Kerry (1)	K	6-1	215	8/27/63	Hawaii	Vancouver, Wash.	FA
Brock, Matt	DE	6-4	267	1/14/66	Oregon	San Diego, Calif.	D3a
Cooper, George (1)	RB	6-2	247	12/8/64	Ohio State	Wyandanch, N.Y.	FA
Dilweg, Anthony	QB	6-3	215	3/28/65	Duke	Bethesda, Md.	D3b
Flesher, Thomas (1)	DE	6-6	260	9/28/66	Weber State	Paradise, Calif.	FA
Hall, Mark	DE	6-4	285	8/21/65	S.W. Louisiana	Patterson, La.	D7
Jacke, Chris	K	6-0	197	3/12/66	Texas-El Paso	Richardson, Tex.	D6
Jessie, Ben	CB	6-0	205	8/3/66	S.W. Texas State	Corsicana, Tex.	D10
King, Thomas	S	6-1	190	3/31/66	S.W. Louisiana	Winnfield, La.	D8a
Kirby, Scott	T	6-6	284	8/7/66	Arizona State	Pinellas, Fla.	D9
Knapton, Jeff (1)	DE	6-5	260	8/28/66	Wyoming	Yuma, Colo.	FA
Mandarich, Tony	T	6-5	315	9/23/66	Michigan State	Oakville, Canada	D1
McGruder, Michael	CB-S	5-11	180	5/6/63	Kent State	Cleveland Hgts., Ohio	FA
Moore, Timothy (1)	LB	6-3	230	1/1/65	Michigan State	St. Johns, Mich.	FA
Query, Jeff	WR	5-11	165	3/7/67	Millikin	Forsyth, Ill.	D5a
Roach, Kirk (1)	K	6-1	217	11/8/66	Western Carolina	Doraville, Ga.	FA
Shiver, Stan	S	6-2	209	5/18/66	Florida State	Tifton, Ga.	D12
Shulman, Brian	P	5-10	184	4/20/66	Auburn	Brentwood, Tenn.	D8b
Stallworth, Cedric	CB	6-0	180	3/13/67	Georgia Tech	Decatur, Ga.	D11
Thomas, Lavale (1)	RB	6-0	205	12/12/63	Fresno State	Tulare, Calif.	FA-'87
Williams, Channing (1)	RB	5-10	221	2/22/64	Arizona State	Amarillo, Tex.	FA
Workman, Vince	RB	5-10	193	5/9/67	Ohio State	Dublin, Ohio	D5b
Zeno, Marc (1)	WR	6-3	202	5/21/65	Tulane	Lutcher, La.	FA

The term NFL Rookie is defined as a player who is in his first season of professional football and has not been on the roster of another professional football team for any regular-season or postseason games. A Rookie is designated by an "R" on NFL rosters. Players who have been active in another professional football league or players who have NFL experience, including either preseason training camp or being on an active roster for fewer than three regular-season or postseason games, are termed NFL First-Year Players. An NFL First-Year Player is designated by a "1" on NFL rosters. Thereafter, a player on an NFL active roster for at least three regular-season or postseason games is credited with an additional year of NFL playing experience.

NOTES

Dick Moseley, outside linebackers; born August 1, 1933, Detroit, Mich., lives in Green Bay. Running back-defensive back Eastern Michigan 1953-55. No pro playing experience. College coach: Eastern Michigan 1968-70, Wichita State 1971, Minnesota 1972-78, Colorado 1979-81. Pro coach: New Jersey Generals (USFL) 1982, Pittsburgh Maulers (USFL) 1983, Buffalo Bills 1984-85, Chicago Bruisers (Arena Football) 1987, joined Packers in 1988.

Willie Peete, offensive backfield; born July 14, 1937, Mesa, Ariz., lives in Green Bay. Tight end-defensive end Arizona 1956-59. No pro playing experience. College coach: Arizona 1960-62, 1971-82. Pro coach: Kansas City Chiefs 1983-86, joined Packers in 1987.

Howard Tippett, special teams; born September 23, 1938, Tallassee, Ala., lives in Green Bay. Quarterback/safety East Tennessee State 1956-58. No pro playing experience. College coach: Tulane 1963-65, West Virginia 1966, 1970-71, Houston 1967-69, Washington State 1976, UCLA 1980, Illinois 1987. Pro coach: Jacksonville Express (WFL) 1974-75, Tampa Bay Buccaneers 1981-86, joined Packers in 1988.

National Football Conference Western Division

Team Colors: Royal Blue, Gold, and White

Business Address:
2327 West Lincoln Avenue
Anaheim, California 92801

Ticket Office:
Anaheim Stadium
1900 State College Boulevard
Anaheim, California 92806
Telephone: (714) 535-7267
or (213) 585-5400

Club Officials

President: Georgia Frontiere
Executive Vice President: John Shaw
Vice President-Administration and General Counsel: Jay Zygmunt
Vice President-Media and Community Relations: Marshall Klein
Administrator, Football Operations: Jack Faulkner
Director of Operations: Dick Beam
Director of Player Personnel: John Math
Administrative Assistant/Consultant: Paul (Tank) Younger
Administration: Jack Youngblood
Director of Administration: Barbara Robinson
Director of Promotions/Sales: Pete Donovan
Director of Public Relations: John Oswald
Public Relations Assistant: Steve Miles
Trainers: George Menefee, Jim Anderson, Garrett Giemont, Blynn DeNiro
Equipment Managers: Don Hewitt, Todd Hewitt

Stadium: Anaheim Stadium • **Capacity:** 69,008
Anaheim, California 92806

Playing Surface: Grass

Training Camp: Cal State-Fullerton
Fullerton, California 92634

1989 Schedule

Preseason

Aug. 5	vs. San Francisco at Tokyo	10:00*
Aug. 12	at Denver	7:00
Aug. 21	**Phoenix**	8:00
Aug. 26	**Minnesota**	6:00
Sept. 2	**Detroit**	6:00

*P.M. Eastern Time

Regular Season

Sept. 10	at Atlanta	1:00
Sept. 17	**Indianapolis**	1:00
Sept. 24	**Green Bay**	1:00
Oct. 1	at San Francisco	1:00
Oct. 8	**Atlanta**	1:00
Oct. 16	at Buffalo (Monday)	9:00
Oct. 22	**New Orleans**	1:00
Oct. 29	at Chicago	12:00
Nov. 5	at Minnesota	12:00
Nov. 12	**New York Giants**	1:00
Nov. 19	**Phoenix**	1:00
Nov. 26	at New Orleans	7:00
Dec. 3	at Dallas	12:00
Dec. 11	**San Francisco** (Monday)	6:00
Dec. 17	**New York Jets**	1:00
Dec. 24	at New England	1:00

Rams Coaching History

Cleveland 1937-45 (375-306-20)

1937-38	Hugo Bezdek*	1-13-0
1938	Art Lewis	4-4-0
1939-42	Earl (Dutch) Clark	16-26-2
1944	Aldo (Buff) Donelli	4-6-0
1945-46	Adam Walsh	16-5-1
1947	Bob Snyder	6-6-0
1948-49	Clark Shaughnessy	14-8-3
1950-52	Joe Stydahar**	19-9-0
1952-54	Hamp Pool	23-11-2
1955-59	Sid Gillman	28-32-1
1960-62	Bob Waterfield***	9-24-1
1962-65	Harland Svare	14-31-3
1966-70	George Allen	49-19-4
1971-72	Tommy Prothro	14-12-2
1973-77	Chuck Knox	57-20-1
1978-82	Ray Malavasi	43-36-0
1983-88	John Robinson	58-44-0

*Released after three games in 1938
**Resigned after one game in 1952
***Resigned after eight games in 1962

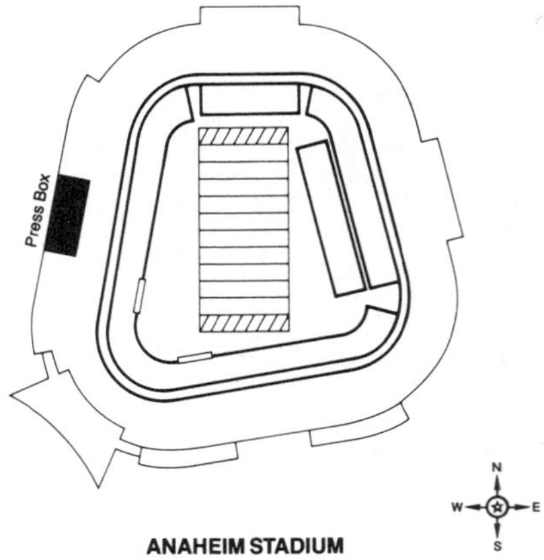

ANAHEIM STADIUM

Record Holders

Individual Records—Career

Category	Name	Performance
Rushing (Yds.)	Eric Dickerson, 1983-87	7,245
Passing (Yds.)	Roman Gabriel, 1962-1972	22,223
Passing (TDs)	Roman Gabriel, 1962-1972	154
Receiving (No.)	Tom Fears, 1948-1956	400
Receiving (Yds.)	Elroy (Crazylegs) Hirsch, 1949-1957	6,289
Interceptions	Ed Meador, 1959-1970	46
Punting (Avg.)	Danny Villanueva, 1960-64	44.2
Punt Return (Avg.)	Henry Ellard, 1983-88	12.1
Kickoff Return (Avg.)	Tom Wilson, 1956-1961	27.1
Field Goals	Bruce Gossett, 1964-69	120
	Mike Lansford, 1982-88	120
Touchdowns (Tot.)	Eric Dickerson, 1983-87	58
Points	Mike Lansford, 1982-88	582

Individual Records—Single Season

Category	Name	Performance
Rushing (Yds.)	Eric Dickerson, 1984	*2,105
Passing (Yds.)	Jim Everett, 1988	3,964
Passing (TDs)	Jim Everett, 1988	31
Receiving (No.)	Henry Ellard, 1988	86
Receiving (Yds.)	Elroy (Crazylegs) Hirsch, 1951	1,425
Interceptions	Dick (Night Train) Lane, 1952	*14
Punting (Avg.)	Danny Villanueva, 1962	45.5
Punt Return (Avg.)	Woodley Lewis, 1952	18.5
Kickoff Return (Avg.)	Verda (Vitamin T) Smith, 1950	33.7
Field Goals	David Ray, 1973	30
Touchdowns (Tot.)	Eric Dickerson, 1983	20
Points	David Ray, 1973	130

Individual Records—Single Game

Category	Name	Performance
Rushing (Yds.)	Eric Dickerson, 1-4-86	248
Passing (Yds.)	Norm Van Brocklin, 9-28-51	*554
Passing (TDs)	Many times	5
	Last time by Jim Everett, 9-25-88	
Receiving (No.)	Tom Fears, 12-3-50	*18
Receiving (Yds.)	Jim Benton, 11-22-45	303
Interceptions	Many times	3
	Last time by Pat Thomas, 10-7-79	
Field Goals	Bob Waterfield, 12-9-51	5
Touchdowns (Tot.)	Bob Shaw, 12-11-49	4
	Elroy (Crazylegs) Hirsch, 9-28-51	4
	Harold Jackson, 10-14-73	4
Points	Bob Shaw, 12-11-49	24
	Elroy (Crazylegs) Hirsch, 9-28-51	24
	Harold Jackson, 10-14-73	24

*NFL Record

1988 Team Record

Preseason (2-3)

Date	Result		Opponents
7/30	L	7-14	vs. Cincinnati at Canton, Ohio
8/3	L	31-40	Denver
8/13	W	27- 6	San Diego
8/20	L	17-20	Houston (OT)
8/26	W	31-24	at San Diego
		113-104	

Regular Season (10-6)

Date	Result		Opponents	Att.
9/4	W	34- 7	at Green Bay	53,769
9/11	W	17-10	Detroit	46,262
9/18	W	22-17	at L.A. Raiders	84,870
9/25	W	45-31	at N.Y. Giants	75,617
10/2	L	27-41	Phoenix	49,830
10/9	W	33- 0	at Atlanta	30,852
10/16	L	21-24	San Francisco	65,450
10/23	W	31-10	Seattle	57,033
10/30	W	12-10	at New Orleans	68,238
11/6	L	24-30	at Philadelphia	65,624
11/13	L	10-14	New Orleans	63,305
11/20	L	24-38	San Diego	45,462
11/27	L	24-35	at Denver	74,141
12/5	W	23- 3	Chicago	65,579
12/11	W	22- 7	Atlanta	42,828
12/18	W	38-16	at San Francisco	62,444

(OT) Overtime

Postseason (0-1)

Date	Result		Opponent	Att.
12/26	L	17-28	at Minnesota	57,666

Score by Periods

Rams	81	146	92	88	0	—	407
Opponents	37	94	76	86	0	—	293

Attendance

Home 435,749 Away 515,555 Total 951,304
Single-game home record, 102,368 (11-10-57; L.A. Coliseum), 67,037 (12-23-84; Anaheim Stadium)
Single-season home record, 519,175 (1973; L.A. Coliseum), 500,403 (1980; Anaheim Stadium)

1988 Team Statistics

	Rams	Opp.
Total First Downs	333	289
Rushing	114	100
Passing	203	166
Penalty	16	23
Third Down: Made/Att.	83/209	77/226
Fourth Down: Made/Att.	4/8	11/16
Total Net Yards	5808	4986
Avg. Per Game	363.0	311.6
Total Plays	1057	1041
Avg. Per Play	5.5	4.8
Net Yards Rushing	2003	1686
Avg. Per Game	125.2	105.4
Total Rushes	507	414
Net Yards Passing	3805	3300
Avg. Per Game	237.8	206.3
Sacked/Yards Lost	28/197	56/394
Gross Yards	4002	3694
Att./Completions	522/312	571/307
Completion Pct.	59.8	53.8
Had Intercepted	18	22
Punts/Avg.	76/39.5	93/39.9
Net Punting Avg.	34.2	33.9
Penalties/Yards Lost	78/587	111/937
Fumbles/Ball Lost	28/16	36/15
Touchdowns	48	35
Rushing	16	12
Passing	31	17
Returns	1	6
Avg. Time of Possession	31:09	28:51

1988 Individual Statistics

Scoring	TD R	TD P	TD Rt	PAT	FG	Saf	TP
Lansford	0	0	0	45/48	24/32	0	117
Bell	16	2	0	0/0	0/0	0	108
Ellard	0	10	0	0/0	0/0	0	60
D. Johnson	0	6	0	0/0	0/0	0	36
A. Cox	0	5	0	0/0	0/0	0	30
Holohan	0	3	0	0/0	0/0	0	18
McGee	0	3	0	0/0	0/0	0	18
Delpino	0	2	0	0/0	0/0	0	12
Gray	0	0	1	0/0	0/0	0	6
Greene	0	0	0	0/0	0/0	1	2
Rams	16	31	1	45/48	24/32	1	407
Opponents	12	17	6	35/35	16/23	0	293

Passing	Att.	Comp.	Yds.	Pct.	TD	Int.	Tkld.	Rate
Everett	517	308	3964	59.6	31	18	28/197	89.2
Herrmann	5	4	38	80.0	0	0	0/0	98.3
Rams	522	312	4002	59.8	31	18	28/197	89.3
Opponents	571	307	3694	53.8	17	22	56/394	67.7

Rushing	Att.	Yds.	Avg.	LG	TD
Bell	288	1212	4.2	44	16
White	88	323	3.7	13	0
Delpino	34	147	4.3	13	0
Green	35	117	3.3	13	0
Everett	34	104	3.1	19	0
McGee	22	69	3.1	12	0
Brown	3	24	8.0	13	0
Ellard	1	7	7.0	7	0
Guman	1	1	1.0	1	0
Herrmann	1	−1	−1.0	−1	0
Rams	507	2003	4.0	44	16
Opponents	414	1686	4.1	46t	12

Receiving	No.	Yds.	Avg.	LG	TD
Ellard	86	1414	16.4	68	10
Holohan	59	640	10.8	29	3
D. Johnson	42	350	8.3	23	6
Delpino	30	312	10.4	38	2
A. Cox	28	590	21.1	69t	5
Bell	24	124	5.2	20	2
McGee	16	117	7.3	16	3
Anderson	11	319	29.0	56	0
Green	6	57	9.5	19	0
White	6	36	6.0	18	0
Young	2	27	13.5	18	0
Brown	2	16	8.0	10	0
Sievers, S.D.-Rams	1	2	2.0	2	0
Rams	312	4002	12.8	69t	31
Opponents	307	3694	12.0	59	17

Interceptions	No.	Yds.	Avg.	LG	TD
J. Johnson	4	18	4.5	11	0
Gray	3	83	27.7	47t	1
Irvin	3	25	8.3	22	0
Stewart	2	61	30.5	43	0
Newman	2	27	13.5	27	0
Kelm	2	15	7.5	9	0
Meisner	1	20	20.0	20	0
Owens	1	11	11.0	11	0
Greene	1	10	10.0	10	0
Washington	1	7	7.0	7	0
Sutton	1	1	1.0	1	0
Jerue	1	0	0.0	0	0
Newsome	0	3	—	3	0
Rams	22	281	12.8	47t	1
Opponents	18	138	7.7	34	1

Punting	No.	Yds.	Avg.	In 20	LG
Hatcher	36	1424	39.6	13	54
Camarillo	40	1579	39.5	11	57
Rams	76	3003	39.5	24	57
Opponents	93	3714	39.9	21	61

Punt Returns	No.	FC	Yds.	Avg.	LG	TD
Hicks	25	0	144	5.8	13	0
Ellard	17	3	119	7.0	34	0
Sutton	3	6	52	17.3	46	0
J. Johnson	2	1	4	2.0	4	0
Gray	1	0	1	1.0	1	0
Irvin	1	1	2	2.0	2	0
Rams	49	11	322	6.6	46	0
Opponents	43	21	347	8.1	30	0

Kickoff Returns	No.	Yds.	Avg.	LG	TD
Brown	19	401	21.1	73	0
Green	17	345	20.3	44	0
Delpino	14	333	23.8	38	0
McDonald	3	34	11.3	22	0
Sutton	2	41	20.5	25	0
White	2	37	18.5	23	0
McGee	1	0	0.0	0	0
Stewart	1	0	0.0	0	0
Rams	59	1191	20.2	73	0
Opponents	81	1563	19.3	93t	1

Sacks	No.
Greene	16.5
Jeter	11.5
Wilcher	7.5
Owens	5.0
Miller	4.0
Strickland	4.0
Wright	2.0
Faryniarz	1.0
Meisner	1.0
Reed	1.0
Stewart	1.0
Stokes	1.0
Irvin	0.5
Rams	56.0
Opponents	28.0

1989 Draft Choices

Round	Name	Pos.	College
1.	Bill Hawkins	DE	Miami
	Cleveland Gary	RB	Miami
2.	Frank Stams	LB	Notre Dame
	Brian Smith	LB	Auburn
	Darryl Henley	DB	UCLA
3.	Kevin Robbins	T	Michigan State
4.	Jeff Carlson	QB	Weber State
5.	Alfred Jackson	WR	San Diego State
6.	Thom Kaumeyer	DB	Oregon
	Mark Messner	LB	Michigan
7.	George Bethune	LB	Alabama
8.	Warren Wheat	T	Brigham Young
9.	Vernon Kirk	TE	Pittsburgh
10.	Mike Williams	WR	Northeastern

Los Angeles Rams 1989 Veteran Roster

No.	Name	Pos.	Ht.	Wt.	Birth-date	NFL Exp.	College	Hometown	How Acq.	'88 Games/ Starts
83	Anderson, Willie	WR	6-0	169	3/7/65	2	UCLA	Paulsboro, N.J.	D2b-'88	16/10
42	†Bell, Greg	RB	5-10	210	8/1/62	6	Notre Dame	Columbus, Ohio	T(Buff)-'87	16/13
92	Brown, Richard	LB	6-3	240	9/21/65	2	San Diego State	Westminster, Calif.	FA-'89	0*
89	†Brown, Ron	WR	5-11	181	3/31/61	6	Arizona State	Baldwin Park, Calif.	T(Clev)-'84	7/0
84	Cox, Aaron	WR	5-9	174	3/13/65	2	Arizona State	Los Angeles, Calif.	D1b-'88	16/15
72	†Cox, Robert	T	6-5	270	12/30/63	3	UCLA	Dublin, Calif.	D6-'86	16/0
94	Darby, Byron	DE	6-4	260	6/4/60	7	Southern California	Los Angeles, Calif.	FA(Ind)-'89#	16/1*
57	Davis, Wayne	LB	6-1	213	3/10/64	3	Alabama	Gordo, Ala.	FA(Phx)-'89#	16/0*
39	Delpino, Robert	RB	6-0	205	11/2/65	2	Missouri	Dodge City, Kan.	D5a-'88	15/3
62	Diaz-Infante, David	C	6-2	280	3/31/64	2	San Jose State	San Jose, Calif.	FA-'89	0*
80	Ellard, Henry	WR	5-11	175	7/21/61	7	Fresno State	Fresno, Calif.	D2-'83	16/15
11	Everett, Jim	QB	6-5	212	1/3/63	4	Purdue	Albuquerque, N.M.	T(Hou)-'86	16/16
51	Faryniarz, Brett	LB	6-3	225	7/23/65	2	San Diego State	Sacramento, Calif.	FA-'88	15/0
25	Gray, Jerry	CB	6-0	185	12/2/62	5	Texas	Lubbock, Tex.	D1-'85	16/16
30	Green, Gaston	RB	5-10	189	8/8/66	2	UCLA	Gardena, Calif.	D1a-'88	10/0
91	Greene, Kevin	LB	6-3	238	7/31/62	5	Auburn	Granite City, Ill.	D5-'85	16/14
5	Hatcher, Dale	P	6-2	211	4/5/63	6	Clemson	Cheraw, S.C.	D3-'85	7/0
9	Herrmann, Mark	QB	6-4	186	1/9/59	9	Purdue	Carmel, Ind.	FA-'88	6/0
28	Hicks, Clifford	CB	5-10	188	8/18/64	3	Oregon	San Diego, Calif.	D3-'87	7/0
81	Holohan, Pete	TE	6-4	232	7/25/59	9	Notre Dame	Liverpool, N.Y.	T(SD)-'88	16/6
47	Irvin, LeRoy	CB	5-11	184	9/15/57	10	Kansas	Augusta, Ga.	D3-'80	16/16
59	Jerue, Mark	LB	6-3	234	1/15/60	7	Washington	Seattle, Wash.	T(Ind)-'83	12/11
86	Johnson, Damone	TE	6-4	230	3/2/62	4	Cal Poly-SLO	Santa Monica, Calif.	D6-'85	16/15
52	Kelm, Larry	LB	6-4	226	11/29/64	3	Texas A&M	Corpus Christi, Tex.	D4-'87	16/1
1	†Lansford, Mike	K	6-0	183	7/20/58	8	Washington	Arcadia, Calif.	FA-'82	16/0
67	†Love, Duval	G	6-3	280	6/24/63	5	UCLA	Fountain Valley, Calif.	D10-'85	15/15
90	McDonald, Mike	LB	6-1	235	6/22/58	5	Southern California	Burbank, Calif.	FA-'88	16/0
24	McGee, Buford	RB	6-0	206	8/16/60	6	Mississippi	Durant, Miss.	T(SD)-'87	16/10
98	Miller, Shawn	DE	6-4	255	3/14/61	6	Utah State	Ogden, Utah	FA-'84	16/16
66	Newberry, Tom	G	6-2	279	12/20/62	4	Wisconsin-LaCrosse	Onalaska, Wis.	D2-'86	16/16
26	Newman, Anthony	CB	6-0	199	11/25/65	2	Oregon	Beaverton, Ore.	D2a-'88	16/0
22	Newsome, Vince	S	6-1	183	1/22/61	7	Washington	Vacaville, Calif.	D4-'83	6/6
58	Owens, Mel	LB	6-2	224	12/7/58	9	Michigan	Detroit, Mich.	D1-'81	7/4
75	†Pankey, Irv	T	6-5	267	2/15/58	9	Penn State	Aberdeen, Pa.	D2-'80	16/16
93	Reed, Doug	DE	6-3	250	7/16/60	6	San Diego State	San Diego, Calif.	D4-'83	16/15
78	Slater, Jackie	T	6-4	275	5/27/54	14	Jackson State	Meridian, Miss.	D3-'76	16/16
61	†Slaton, Tony	C-G	6-3	265	4/12/61	6	Southern California	Merced, Calif.	FA-'84	15/1
56	Smith, Doug	C	6-3	260	11/25/56	12	Bowling Green	Columbus, Ohio	FA-'78	16/16
23	Stewart, Michael	S	5-11	195	7/12/65	3	Fresno State	Bakersfield, Calif.	D8-'87	16/10
53	Strickland, Fred	LB	6-2	224	8/15/66	2	Purdue	Lakeland, N.J.	D2c-'88	16/0
37	Washington, James	S	6-1	191	1/10/65	2	UCLA	Los Angeles, Calif.	D5b-'88	16/0
54	Wilcher, Mike	LB	6-3	240	3/20/60	7	North Carolina	Washington, D.C.	D2-'83	16/15
99	†Wright, Alvin	NT	6-2	256	2/5/61	4	Jacksonville State	Nedonee, Ala.	FA-'86	16/15

* Richard Brown last active with L.A. Rams in '87; Darby played 16 games with Indianapolis in '88; Davis played 16 games with Phoenix; Diaz-Infante last active with San Diego in '87.

† Option playout; subject to developments.

Plan B unconditional free agent.

Retired—Carl Ekern, 13-year linebacker, 16 games in '88; Mike Guman, 9-year running back, 1 game in '88; Charles White, 8-year running back, 12 games in '88.

Players lost through Plan B (12): LB Jim Collins (SD; 4 games in '88), TE Jon Embree (Sea; 12), DE Gary Jeter (NE; 15), S Johnnie Johnson (Sea; 16), RB Keith Jones (Clev; 0), NT Greg Meisner (KC; 12), G Mike Schad (Phil; 6), TE Eric Seivers (NE; 1), DE Fred Stokes (Wash; 5), CB Mickey Sutton (GB; 15), RB Tim Tyrrell (Buff; 12), WR Mike Young (Den; 8).

Also played with Rams in '88—P Rich Camarillo (9 games), S Frank Wattelet (2).

COACHING STAFF

Head Coach, John Robinson

Pro Career: Enters his seventh season as Rams head coach. Became winningest coach in club history last season (58 victories) after guiding team to its fifth playoff appearance in six seasons. Led Rams to a 10-6 record in 1988 and a playoff berth against Minnesota in the NFC Wild Card Game. Has won 10 or more games in five different seasons with Rams. Became seventeenth head coach in club history on February 14, 1983. Arrived with 23 years of coaching experience, including one on professional level with the Raiders in 1975. No pro playing experience. Career record: 58-44.

Background: Played end at Oregon 1955-58. Began coaching career with his alma mater from 1960-71. Became an assistant at Southern California from 1972-74. Returned as head coach in 1976 before resigning after the 1982 season. Compiled seven-year .819 winning percentage at Southern California with 67 wins, 14 losses, and 2 ties.

Personal: Born July 25, 1935, Chicago, Ill. John lives in Yorba Linda, Calif.

Assistant Coaches

Larry Brooks, assistant defensive line; born June 10, 1950, Prince George, Va., lives in Fountain Valley, Calif. Defensive tackle Virginia State 1968-71. Pro defensive tackle Los Angeles Rams 1972-82. Pro coach: Joined Rams in 1983.

Dick Coury, quarterbacks; born September 29, 1929, Athens, Ohio, lives in Anaheim, Calif. No college or pro playing experience. College coach: Southern California 1965-67, Cal State-Fullerton 1968-70 (head coach). Pro coach: Denver Broncos 1971-73, Portland Storm (WFL) 1974 (head coach), San Diego Chargers 1975, Philadelphia Eagles 1976-81, Boston/Portland Breakers (USFL) 1983-85 (head coach), joined Rams in 1986.

Artie Gigantino, special teams; born June 14, 1951, Edison, N.J., lives in Anaheim, Calif. Linebacker Bridgeport 1969-72. No pro playing experience. College coach: California 1973-78, Southern California 1979-86. Pro coach: Joined Rams in 1987.

Marv Goux, defensive line; born September 8, 1932, Santa Barbara, Calif., lives in Long Beach, Calif. Linebacker Southern California 1952, 1954-55. No pro playing experience. College coach: Southern California 1957-82. Pro coach: Joined Rams in 1983.

Gil Haskell, running backs; born September 24, 1943, San Francisco, Calif., lives in Diamond Bar, Calif. Defensive back San Francisco State 1961, 1963-65. No pro playing experience. College coach: Southern California 1978-82. Pro coach: Joined Rams in 1983.

Hudson Houck, offensive line; born January 7, 1943, Los Angeles, Calif., lives in Newport Beach, Calif. Center Southern California 1962-64. No pro playing experience. College coach: Southern California 1970-72, 1976-82, Stanford 1973-75. Pro coach: Joined Rams in 1983.

Steve Shafer, defensive backs; born December 8, 1940, Glendale, Calif., lives in Laguna Niguel, Calif. Quarterback-defensive back Utah State 1961-62. Pro defensive back British Columbia Lions (CFL) 1963-67. College coach: San Mateo, Calif., J.C. 1968-74 (head coach 1973-74), San Diego State 1975-82. Pro coach: Joined Rams in 1983.

Fritz Shurmur, defensive coordinator-inside linebackers; born July 15, 1932, Riverview, Mich., lives in Diamond Bar, Calif. Center Albion 1951-53. No pro playing experience. College coach: Albion 1956-61, Wyoming 1962-74 (head coach 1971-74). Pro coach: Detroit Lions 1975-77, New England Patriots 1978-81, joined Rams in 1982.

Norval Turner, tight ends-wide receivers; born May 17, 1952, Martinez, Calif., lives in Huntington Beach, Calif. Quarterback Oregon 1972-74. No pro playing experience. College coach: Oregon 1975, Southern California 1976-84. Pro coach: Joined Rams in 1985.

Los Angeles Rams 1989 First-Year Roster

Name	Pos.	Ht.	Wt.	Birth-date	College	Hometown	How Acq.
Bethune, George	LB	6-4	238	3/30/67	Alabama	Fort Walton Beach, Fla.	D7
Brock, Louis (1)	CB	5-11	172	5/8/64	Southern California	St. Louis, Mo.	FA
Brown, Henry (1)	NT	6-3	265	12/6/65	Florida	Fort Myers, Fla.	FA
Calvin, Richard (1)	RB	6-0	217	9/1/65	Washington State	Dallas, Tex.	FA
Carlson, Jeff	QB	6-3	215	5/23/66	Weber State	Cypress, Calif.	D4
Coauette, Greg	CB	6-3	205	10/29/64	Southern California	Burbank, Calif.	FA
Dominic, Steven (1)	DE	6-5	265	6/10/66	Cal State-Northridge	Covina, Calif.	FA
Doughty, Jim	LB	6-4	225	1/26/65	California-Davis	Reno, Nev.	FA
Farr, Mel	RB	6-0	223	8/12/66	UCLA	Birmingham, Mich.	FA
Gary, Cleveland	RB	6-0	226	5/4/66	Miami	Indiantown, Fla.	D1b
Harrison, Robert (1)	RB	6-2	220	8/31/63	Sacramento State	Eureka, Calif.	FA
Hawkins, Bill	DE	6-6	265	5/9/66	Miami	Miami, Fla.	D1a
Hawkins, Brian	WR	5-9	165	6/2/65	Oregon	Los Angeles, Calif.	FA
Henley, Darryl	CB	5-9	165	10/30/66	UCLA	LaVerne, Calif.	D2c
Henley, Thomas (1)	WR	5-10	180	7/28/65	Stanford	LaVerne, Calif.	FA
Jackson, Alfred	CB-S	6-0	177	7/10/67	San Diego State	Tulare, Calif.	D5
Johnson, Marco (1)	WR	5-9	171	9/4/65	Hawaii	Antelope Valley, Calif.	FA
Kaumeyer, Thom	S	5-11	187	3/17/67	Oregon	Cardiff, Calif.	D6a
Kirk, Vernon	TE	6-2	250	10/14/66	Pittsburgh	Donora, Pa.	D9
Lloyd, Andre	LB	6-1	240	6/29/65	Jackson State	Brookhaven, Miss.	FA
McCullough, Tyrone	WR	5-11	165	6/9/65	Long Beach State	Long Beach, Calif.	FA
McKee, Erik (1)	TE	6-4	245	4/2/65	Southern California	Wilmington, Calif.	FA
Messner, Mark	LB	6-2	256	12/29/65	Michigan	Detroit, Mich.	D6b
Mullin, R.C. (1)	T	6-6	300	6/28/65	S.W. Louisiana	Port Arthur, Tex.	D10-'88
Nunn, Clarence (1)	CB-S	5-11	175	12/29/64	San Diego State	Gardena, Calif.	FA
Parker, Chris	QB	6-1	190	12/19/64	Cal State-Northridge	Highland, Calif.	FA
Piel, Mike (1)	DE	6-4	263	9/21/65	Illinois	El Toro, Calif.	D3-'88
Robbins, Kevin	T	6-4	286	12/12/67	Michigan State	Washington, D.C.	D3
Salanoa, Thor (1)	LB	6-1	240	7/9/65	Brigham Young	Honolulu, Hawaii	FA
Sargent, Anthony	WR	5-9	172	12/1/66	Wyoming	Los Angeles, Calif.	FA
Schmidt, Mark (1)	T-G	6-5	275	12/10/65	UCLA	Claremont, Calif.	FA
Smith, Brian	LB	6-6	242	4/23/66	Auburn	Opelika, Ala.	D2b
Stams, Frank	LB	6-2	230	7/17/65	Notre Dame	Akron, Ohio	D2a
Taylor, Pernell	RB	5-11	228	1/8/65	Notre Dame	La Puente, Calif.	FA
Wheat, Warren	T	6-6	255	5/13/67	Brigham Young	Phoenix, Ariz.	D8
Williams, Mike	WR	5-10	177	10/9/66	Northeastern	Golden Bridge, N.Y.	D10

The term NFL Rookie is defined as a player who is in his first season of professional football and has not been on the roster of another professional football team for any regular-season or postseason games. A Rookie is designated by an "R" on NFL rosters. Players who have been active in another professional football league or players who have NFL experience, including either preseason training camp or being on an active roster for fewer than three regular-season or postseason games, are termed NFL First-Year Players. An NFL First-Year Player is designated by a "1" on NFL rosters. Thereafter, a player on an NFL active roster for at least three regular-season or postseason games is credited with an additional year of NFL playing experience.

NOTES

Fred Whittingham, outside linebackers; born February 4, 1942, Boston, Mass., lives in Santa Ana, Calif. Linebacker Cal Poly-SLO 1960-62. Pro linebacker Los Angeles Rams 1964, Philadelphia Eagles 1965-66, 1971, New Orleans Saints 1967-68, Dallas Cowboys 1969-70. College coach: Brigham Young 1973-81. Pro coach: Joined Rams in 1982.

Ernie Zampese, offensive coordinator; born March 12, 1936, Santa Barbara, Calif., lives in El Toro, Calif. Halfback Southern California 1956-58. No pro playing experience. College coach: Hancock, Calif., J.C. 1962-65, Cal Poly-SLO 1966, San Diego State 1967-75. Pro coach: San Diego Chargers 1976, 1979-86, New York Jets 1977-78 (scout), joined Rams in 1987.

National Football Conference Central Division

Team Colors: Purple, Gold, and White

9520 Viking Drive
Eden Prairie, Minnesota 55344
Telephone: (612) 828-6500

Club Officers

Chairman of the Board: John Skoglund
President: Wheelock Whitney
Senior Vice President: Jack Steele
Senior Vice President and Treasurer: Jaye F. Dyer
Secretary: Sheldon Kaplan
Executive Vice President: Mike Lynn

Club Officials

General Manager: Mike Lynn
Assistant G.M./Administration: Jeff Diamond
Assistant G.M./Football: Bob Hollway
Director of Finance: Harley Peterson
Ticket Manager: Harry Randolph
Director of Football Operations: Jerry Reichow
Director of Player Personnel: Frank Gilliam
Head Scout: Ralph Kohl
Assistant Head Scout: Don Deisch
Regional Scout: John Carson
Regional Scout: Conrad Cardano
Director of Public Relations: Merrill Swanson
Director of Communications and Community Relations: Kernal Buhler
Assistant Public Relations Director: Daniel Endy
Trainer: Fred Zamberletti
Equipment Manager: Dennis Ryan

Stadium: Hubert H. Humphrey Metrodome • **Capacity:** 63,000
500 11th Avenue So.
Minneapolis, Minnesota 55415

Playing Surface: AstroTurf

Training Camp: Mankato State University
Mankato, Minnesota 56001

1989 Schedule

Preseason

Aug. 12	vs. K.C. at Memphis, Tenn.	7:30
Aug. 21	**Washington**	7:00
Aug. 26	at Los Angeles Rams	6:00
Sept. 1	**Cincinnati**	7:00

Regular Season

Sept. 10	**Houston**	3:00
Sept. 17	at Chicago	3:00
Sept. 24	at Pittsburgh	1:00
Oct. 1	**Tampa Bay**	12:00
Oct. 8	**Detroit**	12:00
Oct. 15	**Green Bay**	12:00
Oct. 22	at Detroit	1:00
Oct. 30	at N.Y. Giants (Monday)	9:00
Nov. 5	**Los Angeles Rams**	12:00
Nov. 12	at Tampa Bay	1:00
Nov. 19	at Philadelphia	1:00
Nov. 26	vs. Green Bay at Milwaukee	12:00
Dec. 3	**Chicago**	7:00
Dec. 10	**Atlanta**	12:00
Dec. 17	at Cleveland	1:00
Dec. 25	**Cincinnati** (Monday)	8:00

Vikings Coaching History

(231-193-9)

1961-66	Norm Van Brocklin	29-51-4
1967-83	Bud Grant	161-99-5
1984	Les Steckel	3-13-0
1985	Bud Grant	7-9-0
1986-88	Jerry Burns	31-21-0

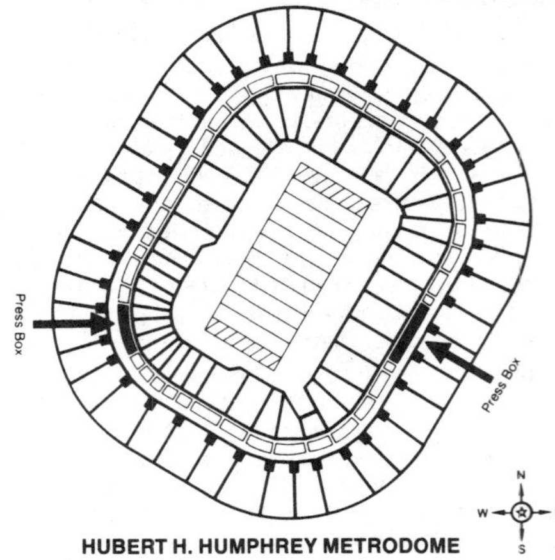

HUBERT H. HUMPHREY METRODOME

Record Holders

Individual Records—Career

Category	Name	Performance
Rushing (Yds.)	Chuck Foreman, 1973-79	5,879
Passing (Yds.)	Fran Tarkenton, 1961-66, 1972-78	33,098
Passing (TDs)	Fran Tarkenton, 1961-66, 1972-78	239
Receiving (No.)	Ahmad Rashad, 1976-1982	400
Receiving (Yds.)	Sammy White, 1976-1985	5,925
Interceptions	Paul Krause, 1968-1979	53
Punting (Avg.)	Bobby Walden, 1964-67	42.9
Punt Return (Avg.)	Leo Lewis, 1981-87	11.4
Kickoff Return (Avg.)	Bob Reed, 1962-63	27.1
Field Goals	Fred Cox, 1963-1977	282
Touchdowns (Tot.)	Bill Brown, 1962-1974	76
Points	Fred Cox, 1963-1977	1,365

Individual Records—Single Season

Category	Name	Performance
Rushing (Yds.)	Chuck Foreman, 1976	1,155
Passing (Yds.)	Tommy Kramer, 1981	3,912
Passing (TDs)	Tommy Kramer, 1981	26
Receiving (No.)	Rickey Young, 1978	88
Receiving (Yds.)	Anthony Carter, 1988	1,225
Interceptions	Paul Krause, 1975	10
Punting (Avg.)	Bobby Walden, 1964	46.4
Punt Return (Avg.)	Leo Lewis, 1987	12.5
Kickoff Return (Avg.)	John Gilliam, 1972	26.3
Field Goals	Fred Cox, 1970	30
Touchdowns (Tot.)	Chuck Foreman, 1975	22
Points	Chuck Foreman, 1975	132

Individual Records—Single Game

Category	Name	Performance
Rushing (Yds.)	Chuck Foreman, 10-24-76	200
Passing (Yds.)	Tommy Kramer, 11-2-86	490
Passing (TDs)	Joe Kapp, 9-28-69	*7
Receiving (No.)	Rickey Young, 12-16-79	15
Receiving (Yds.)	Sammy White, 11-7-76	210
Interceptions	Many times	3
	Last time by Willie Teal, 11-28-82	
Field Goals	Fred Cox, 9-23-73	5
	Jan Stenerud, 9-23-84	5
Touchdowns (Tot.)	Chuck Foreman, 12-20-75	4
	Ahmad Rashad, 9-2-79	4
Points	Chuck Foreman, 12-20-75	24
	Ahmad Rashad, 9-2-79	24

*NFL Record

1988 Team Record

Preseason (3-1)

Date	Result		Opponents
8/7	L	20-23	New Orleans
8/14	W	28-21	vs. Chicago at Goteborg, Sweden
8/21	W	19-16	at Phoenix (OT)
8/26	W	24-17	Miami
		91-77	

Regular Season (11-5)

Date	Result		Opponents	Att.
9/4	L	10-13	at Buffalo	76,783
9/11	W	36- 6	New England	55,545
9/18	W	31- 7	at Chicago	63,990
9/25	W	23-21	Philadelphia	56,012
10/2	L	7-24	at Miami	59,867
10/9	W	14-13	Tampa Bay	55,274
10/16	L	14-34	Green Bay	59,053
10/23	W	49-20	at Tampa Bay	48,020
10/30	L	21-24	at San Francisco	60,738
11/6	W	44-17	Detroit	55,573
11/13	W	43- 3	at Dallas	57,830
11/20	W	12- 3	Indianapolis	58,342
11/24	W	23- 0	at Detroit	46,379
12/4	W	45- 3	New Orleans	61,215
12/11	L	6-18	at Green Bay	48,892
12/19	W	28-27	Chicago	62,067

(OT) Overtime

Postseason (1-1)

Date	Result		Opponent	Att.
12/26	W	28-17	L.A. Rams	57,666
1/1	L	9-34	at San Francisco	61,848

Score by Periods

Vikings	82	132	91	101	0	— 406
Opponents	46	73	62	52	0	— 233

Attendance

Home 463,081 Away 462,499 Total 925,580
Single-game home record, 62,851 (10-19-86)
Single-season home record, 464,902 (1983)

1988 Team Statistics

	Vikings	Opp.
Total First Downs	318	243
Rushing	112	85
Passing	187	132
Penalty	19	26
Third Down: Made/Att.	83/222	59/203
Fourth Down: Made/Att.	8/17	3/7
Total Net Yards	5595	4091
Avg. Per Game	349.7	255.7
Total Plays	1068	952
Avg. Per Play	5.2	4.3
Net Yards Rushing	1806	1602
Avg. Per Game	112.9	100.1
Total Rushes	501	435
Net Yards Passing	3789	2489
Avg. Per Game	236.8	155.6
Sacked/Yards Lost	47/311	37/274
Gross Yards	4100	2763
Att./Completions	520/294	480/219
Completion Pct.	56.5	45.6
Had Intercepted	18	36
Punts/Avg.	86/39.4	96/42.3
Net Punting Avg.	32.6	35.1
Penalties/Yards Lost	118/998	91/753
Fumbles/Ball Lost	22/12	36/17
Touchdowns	49	24
Rushing	22	10
Passing	20	12
Returns	7	2
Avg. Time of Possession	31:05	28:55

1988 Individual Statistics

Scoring	TD R	TD P	TD Rt	PAT	FG	Saf	TP
C. Nelson	0	0	0	48/49	20/25	0	108
Anderson	7	1	0	0/0	0/0	0	48
Carter	0	6	0	0/0	0/0	0	36
Rice	6	0	0	0/0	0/0	0	36
Jones	0	5	0	0/0	0/0	0	30
Jordan	0	5	0	0/0	0/0	0	30
Fenney	3	0	0	0/0	0/0	0	18
Dozier	2	0	0	0/0	0/0	0	12
Lee	0	0	2	0/0	0/0	0	12
Wilson	2	0	0	0/0	0/0	0	12
Ashley	0	0	1	0/0	0/0	0	6
Edwards	0	0	1	0/0	0/0	0	6
Gustafson	0	1	0	0/0	0/0	0	6
D. Harris	1	0	0	0/0	0/0	0	6
Hilton	0	1	0	0/0	0/0	0	6
Lewis	0	1	0	0/0	0/0	0	6
C. Martin	0	0	1	0/0	0/0	0	6
D. Nelson	1	0	0	0/0	0/0	0	6
Solomon	0	0	1	0/0	0/0	0	6
Thomas	0	0	1	0/0	0/0	0	6
Holt	0	0	0	0/0	0/0	1	2
Vikings	22	20	7	48/49	20/25	2	406
Opponents	10	12	2	22/24	21/25	2	233

Passing	Att.	Comp.	Yds.	Pct.	TD	Int.	Tkld.	Rate
Wilson	332	204	2746	61.4	15	9	33/227	91.5
Kramer	173	83	1264	48.0	5	9	11/62	60.5
Gannon	15	7	90	46.7	0	0	3/22	66.0
Vikings	520	294	4100	56.5	20	18	47/311	80.4
Opponents	480	219	2763	45.6	12	36	37/274	41.2

Rushing	Att.	Yds.	Avg.	LG	TD
D. Nelson	112	380	3.4	27	1
Rice	110	322	2.9	24	6
Anderson	87	300	3.4	18	7
Fenney	55	271	4.9	28	3
Dozier	42	167	4.0	19t	2
D. Harris	34	151	4.4	34	1
Wilson	36	136	3.8	15	2
Carter	4	41	10.3	21	0
Gannon	4	29	7.3	15	0
Kramer	14	8	0.6	5	0
Jones	1	7	7.0	7	0
Scribner	1	0	0.0	0	0
Mularkey	1	−6	−6.0	−6	0
Vikings	501	1806	3.6	34	22
Opponents	435	1602	3.7	51t	10

Receiving	No.	Yds.	Avg.	LG	TD
Carter	72	1225	17.0	67t	6
Jordan	57	756	13.3	38	5
Jones	40	778	19.5	68t	5
Rice	30	279	9.3	38	0
Anderson	23	242	10.5	19	1
D. Nelson	16	105	6.6	27	0
Gustafson	15	231	15.4	47	1
Fenney	15	224	14.9	42	0
Lewis	11	141	12.8	46t	1
D. Harris	6	30	5.0	7	0
Dozier	5	49	9.8	20	0
Mularkey	3	39	13.0	19	0
Hilton	1	1	1.0	1t	1
Vikings	294	4100	13.9	68t	20
Opponents	219	2763	12.6	76t	12

Interceptions	No.	Yds.	Avg.	LG	TD
Lee	8	118	14.8	58t	2
Browner	5	29	5.8	18	0
Solomon	4	84	21.0	78t	1
Rutland	3	63	21.0	36	0
Fullington	3	57	19.0	40	0
Harris	3	46	15.3	27	0
Howard	3	16	5.3	10	0
Edwards	2	47	23.5	37t	1
Holt	2	15	7.5	15	0
Ashley	1	94	94.0	94t	1
Henderson	1	13	13.0	13	0
Thomas	1	7	7.0	7	0
Vikings	36	589	16.4	94t	5
Opponents	18	212	11.8	52t	1

Punting	No.	Yds.	Avg.	In 20	LG
Scribner	84	3387	40.3	23	55
Vikings	86	3387	39.4	23	55
Opponents	96	4059	42.3	15	62

Punt Returns	No.	FC	Yds.	Avg.	LG	TD
Lewis	58	19	550	9.5	64	0
Carter	1	1	3	3.0	3	0
Vikings	59	20	553	9.4	64	0
Opponents	39	13	405	10.4	40	0

Kickoff Returns	No.	Yds.	Avg.	LG	TD
D. Harris	39	833	21.4	30	0
D. Nelson	9	210	23.3	30	0
Dozier	5	105	21.0	27	0
Carter	1	0	0.0	0	0
Lewis	1	12	12.0	12	0
Rice	1	0	0.0	0	0
Vikings	56	1160	20.7	30	0
Opponents	81	1622	20.0	44	0

Sacks	No.
Doleman	8.0
Millard	8.0
Thomas	6.0
Baker	5.5
D. Martin	3.0
Solomon	2.5
Howard	1.0
C. Martin	1.0
Newton	1.0
Studwell	1.0
Vikings	37.0
Opponents	47.0

1989 Draft Choices

Round	Name	Pos.	College
2.	David Braxton	LB	Wake Forest
3.	John Hunter	T	Brigham Young
4.	Darryl Ingram	TE	California
6.	Jeff Mickel	T	East. Washington
7.	Benji Roland	DT	Auburn
8.	Alex Stewart	DE	Cal State-Fullerton
11.	Brad Baxter	RB	Alabama State
12.	Shawn Woodson	LB	James Madison
	Everett Ross	WR	Ohio State

Minnesota Vikings 1989 Veteran Roster

No.	Name	Pos.	Ht.	Wt.	Birth-date	NFL Exp.	College	Hometown	How Acq.	'88 Games/ Starts
89	Allen, Anthony	WR	5-11	182	6/29/59	4	Washington	Garfield, Wash.	FA(Wash)-'89#	14/0*
46	†Anderson, Alfred	RB	6-1	219	8/4/61	6	Baylor	Waco, Tex.	D3-'84	16/13
50	Berry, Ray	LB	6-2	230	10/28/63	3	Baylor	Abilene, Tex.	D2-'87	15/0
47	Browner, Joey	S	6-2	212	5/15/60	7	Southern California	Warren, Ohio	D1-'83	16/16
81	Carter, Anthony	WR	5-11	166	9/17/60	5	Michigan	Riviera Beach, Fla.	T(Mia)-'85	16/16
37	Curtis, Travis	S	5-10	180	9/27/65	2	West Virginia	Potomac, Md.	FA(Wash)-'89#	13/0*
56	Doleman, Chris	DE	6-5	250	10/16/61	5	Pittsburgh	York, Pa.	D1-'85	16/16
42	Dozier, D.J.	RB	6-0	198	9/21/65	3	Penn State	Virginia Beach, Va.	D1-'87	8/1
27	Edwards, Brad	S	6-1	198	2/22/66	2	South Carolina	Fayetteville, N.C.	D2-'88	16/6
31	Fenney, Rick	RB	6-1	240	12/7/64	3	Washington	Everett, Wash.	D8-'87	13/3
62	Foote, Chris	C	6-4	265	12/2/56	8	Southern California	Boulder, Colo.	T(NYG)-'87	16/5
29	Fullington, Darrell	S	6-1	183	4/17/64	2	Miami	New Smyrna Beach, Fla.	D5-'88	15/0
90	Galvin, John	LB	6-2	226	7/9/65	2	Boston College	Lowell, Mass.	FA(NYJ)-'89#	2/1*
16	Gannon, Rich	QB	6-3	197	12/20/65	3	Delaware	Philadelphia, Pa.	T(NE)-'87	3/0
74	Greer, Curtis	DE	6-4	258	11/10/58	9	Michigan	Detroit, Mich.	FA(Phx)-'89#	0*
80	Gustafson, Jim	WR	6-1	181	3/16/61	4	St. Thomas, Minn.	Minneapolis, Minn.	FA-'85	16/0
82	†Hilton, Carl	TE	6-3	232	2/28/64	4	Houston	Galveston, Tex.	D7-'86	8/0
30	Holt, Issiac	CB	6-1	197	10/4/62	5	Alcorn State	Birmingham, Ala.	D2-'85	13/9
51	Howard, David	LB	6-2	228	12/8/61	5	Long Beach State	Long Beach, Calif.	SD3-'84	16/16
72	Huffman, David	G	6-6	283	4/4/57	10	Notre Dame	Dallas, Tex.	FA-'85	2/1
76	Irwin, Tim	T	6-6	289	12/13/58	9	Tennessee	Knoxville, Tenn.	D3-'81	16/16
84	Jones, Hassan	WR	6-0	195	7/2/64	4	Florida State	Clearwater, Fla.	D5-'86	16/15
83	†Jordan, Steve	TE	6-3	236	1/10/61	9	Brown	Phoenix, Ariz.	D7-'82	16/16
69	Kalis, Todd	G	6-5	269	6/10/65	2	Arizona State	Phoenix, Ariz.	D4-'88	14/0
9	Kramer, Tommy	QB	6-2	207	3/7/55	13	Rice	San Antonio, Tex.	D1-'77	10/6
39	Lee, Carl	CB	5-11	184	4/6/61	7	Marshall	South Charleston, W. Va.	D7-'83	16/16
87	Lewis, Leo	WR	5-8	171	9/17/56	9	Missouri	Columbia, Mo.	FA-'81	16/1
63	Lowdermilk, Kirk	C	6-3	263	4/10/63	5	Ohio State	Salem, Ohio	D3a-'85	12/11
79	Martin, Doug	DE	6-3	270	5/22/57	10	Washington	Fairfield, Calif.	D1-'80	11/10
26	McMillian, Audrey	CB	6-0	190	8/13/62	4	Houston	Carthage, Tex.	FA(Hou)-'89#	0*
64	McDaniel, Randall	G	6-3	268	12/19/64	2	Arizona State	Avondale, Ariz.	D1-'88	16/15
57	t-Merriweather, Mike	LB	6-2	221	11/26/60	7	Pacific	Vallejo, Calif.	T(Pitt)-'89	0*
75	Millard, Keith	DT	6-6	260	3/18/62	5	Washington State	Pullman, Wash.	D1-'84	15/15
1	Nelson, Chuck	K	5-11	172	2/23/60	6	Washington	Seattle, Wash.	FA-'86	16/0
20	†Nelson, Darrin	RB	5-9	183	1/2/59	8	Stanford	Downey, Calif.	D1-'82	13/11
96	Newton, Tim	DT	6-0	283	3/23/63	5	Florida	Orlando, Fla.	D6b-'85	14/1
99	Noga, Al	DT	6-1	245	9/16/66	2	Hawaii	Honolulu, Hawaii	D3-'88	9/1
52	Rasmussen, Randy	C-G	6-1	254	9/27/60	6	Minnesota	Minneapolis, Minn.	FA-'87	7/0
36	†Rice, Allen	RB	5-10	203	4/5/62	6	Baylor	Houston, Tex.	D5-'84	16/4
60	Rodenhauser, Mark	C	6-5	252	6/1/61	2	Illinois State	Elmhurst, Ill.	FA(Chi)-'89#	0*
48	†Rutland, Reggie	S	6-1	195	6/20/64	3	Georgia Tech	East Point, Ga.	D4-'87	16/7
13	Scribner, Bucky	P	6-0	205	7/11/60	5	Kansas	Lawrence, Kan.	FA-'87	16/0
25	Smith, Daryl	CB	5-9	185	5/8/63	2	North Alabama	Opelika, Ala.	FA(Cin)-'89#	7/0*
54	†Solomon, Jesse	LB	6-0	235	11/4/63	4	Florida State	Madison, Fla.	D12-'86	16/16
94	Strauthers, Thomas	DE	6-4	265	4/6/61	5	Jackson State	Brookhaven, Miss.	FA(Det)-'89#	10/0*
55	†Studwell, Scott	LB	6-2	228	8/27/54	13	Illinois	Evansville, Ind.	D9-'77	16/16
97	Thomas, Henry	NT	6-2	268	1/12/65	3	Louisiana State	Houston, Tex.	D3-'87	15/15
11	Wilson, Wade	QB	6-3	208	2/1/59	9	East Texas State	Commerce, Tex.	D8-'81	14/10
65	Zimmerman, Gary	T	6-6	277	12/13/61	4	Oregon	Fullerton, Calif.	T(NYG)-'86	16/16

* Allen played 14 games with Washington in '88; Curtis played 12 games with Phoenix, 1 game with Washington; Galvin played 2 games with N.Y. Jets; Greer last active with St. Louis in '87; McMillian last active with Houston in '87; Merriweather last active with Pittsburgh in '87; Rodenhauser last active with Chicago in '87; Smith played 7 games with Cincinnati; Strauthers played 10 games with Detroit.

† Option playout; subject to developments.

\# Plan B unconditional free agent.

t- Vikings traded for Merriweather (Pittsburgh).

Retired—Barry Bennett, 10-year defensive end, 1 game in '88; William Gay, 11-year defensive end, 5 games in '88; Stafford Mays, 9-year defensive tackle, 3 games in '88.

Players lost through Plan B (8): LB Sam Anno (TB; 13 games in '88), LB Walker Lee Ashley (KC; 16), DE Al Baker (Clev; 14), CB-S Norman Floyd (Atl; 0), RB Darryl Harris (GB; 14), CB-S Wymon Henderson (Den; 16), TE Mike Mullarkey (Pitt; 16), G Terry Tausch (SF; 16).

Also played with Vikings in '88—TE Paul Coffman (8 games), S John Harris (13), G Mark McDonald (5), LB Chris Martin (9), T Dan McQuaid (3).

COACHING STAFF

Head Coach, Jerry Burns

Pro Career: Named fourth head coach in Vikings' history on January 6, 1986. Served as Vikings' assistant head coach and offensive coordinator under Bud Grant in 1985. Since his arrival in Minnesota as offensive coordinator in 1968, became known as an innovator and was credited with popularizing such changes as the one-back offense and short passing game. Has coached in six Super Bowls. Directed Vikings' offense in Super Bowls IV, VIII, IX, and XI, and coached defensive backs for Vince Lombardi on Green Bay's Super Bowl champions in Super Bowls I and II. No pro playing experience. Career record: 31-21.

Background: Quarterback at Michigan 1949-50. Began coaching career at Hawaii in 1951 as backfield coach for football team and head baseball coach. Moved to Whittier (Calif.) College in 1952 as backfield coach before returning to native Detroit in 1953 as head football coach at St. Mary's of Redford High School. Assistant coach at Iowa from 1954-60 before being named Hawkeyes head coach in 1961. Iowa was 16-27-2 in five seasons under Burns. He coached with the Packers in 1966-67 before joining the Vikings in 1968.

Personal: Born January 24, 1927, in Detroit, Mich. Graduated from Michigan with bachelor of science degree in physical education. Jerry and his wife, Marlyn, live in Eden Prairie, Minn., and have five children—Michael, Erin, Kelly, Kathy, and Kerry.

Assistant Coaches

Tom Batta, tight ends-special teams; born October 6, 1942, Youngstown, Ohio, lives in Bloomington, Minn. Offensive-defensive lineman Kent State 1961-63. No pro playing experience. College coach: Akron 1973, Colorado 1974-78, Kansas 1979-82, North Carolina State 1983. Pro coach: Joined Vikings in 1984.

Jerry Brown, receivers; born September 28, 1949, Kent, Ohio, lives in Eden Prairie, Minn. Defensive back Northwestern 1969-72. No pro playing experience. College coach: Eastern Illinois 1977-79, Cal State-Fullerton 1980-87. Pro coach: Joined Vikings in 1988.

John Brunner, running backs; born September 6, 1937, Perkasie, Pa., lives in Eden Prairie, Minn. Running back Maryland 1955-56, East Stroudsburg State 1958-59. No pro playing experience. College coach: Villanova 1967-69, Temple 1970-73, 1976-79, Princeton 1974-75. Pro coach: Detroit Lions 1980-82, Green Bay Packers 1983, Tampa Bay Buccaneers 1984, New England 1985-86 (scout), joined Vikings in 1987.

Pete Carroll, secondary; born September 15, 1951, San Francisco, Calif., lives in Bloomington, Minn. Defensive back Pacific 1969-72. No pro playing experience. College coach: Arkansas 1977, Iowa State 1978, Ohio State 1979, North Carolina State 1980-82, Pacific 1983. Pro coach: Buffalo Bills 1984, joined Vikings in 1985.

Monte Kiffin, linebackers; born February 29, 1940, Lexington, Neb., lives in Bloomington, Minn. Defensive end Nebraska 1961-63. Pro defensive end Winnipeg Blue Bombers (CFL) 1965-66. College coach: Nebraska 1966-76, Arkansas 1977-79, North Carolina State 1980-82 (head coach). Pro coach: Green Bay Packers 1983, Buffalo Bills 1984-85, joined Vikings in 1986.

John Michels, offensive line; born February 15, 1931, Philadelphia, Pa., lives in Bloomington, Minn. Guard Tennessee 1949-52. Pro guard Philadelphia Eagles 1953, 1956, Winnipeg Blue Bombers (CFL) 1957. College coach: Texas A&M 1958. Pro coach: Winnipeg Blue Bombers (CFL) 1959-66, joined Vikings in 1967.

Minnesota Vikings 1989 First-Year Roster

Name	Pos.	Ht.	Wt.	Birth-date	College	Hometown	How Acq.
Baxter, Brad	RB	6-1	231	5/5/67	Alabama State	Slocomb, Ala.	D11
Bethea, Ryan (1)	WR	6-3	206	3/26/67	South Carolina	Columbia, S.C.	SD5-'88
Braxton, David	LB	6-1	232	5/26/65	Wake Forest	Jacksonville, N.C.	D2
Dusbabek, Mark (1)	LB	6-3	238	6/23/64	Minnesota	Faribault, Minn.	FA
Fitzgerald, Jamie (1)	S	6-1	190	4/30/65	Idaho State	Spokane, Wash.	FA
Fuller, Joe	CB	5-11	180	9/25/64	Northern Iowa	Minneapolis, Minn.	FA
Galvin, John (1)	LB	6-3	226	7/9/65	Boston College	Lowell, Mass.	FA
Habib, Brian (1)	NT	6-6	271	12/2/64	Washington	Ellensburg, Wash.	D10-'88
Hunter, John	T	6-7	294	8/16/65	Brigham Young	North Bend, Ore.	D3
Ingram, Darryl	TE	6-2	228	5/2/66	California	Newhall, Calif.	D4
Mickel, Jeff	T	6-5	288	8/4/66	Eastern Washington	Edmonds, Wash.	D6
Roland, Benji	NT	6-2	270	4/4/67	Auburn	Eastman, Ga.	D7
Ross, Everett	WR	5-10	178	3/6/66	Ohio State	Columbus, Ohio	D12b
Stewart, Alex	DE	6-3	263	8/24/64	Cal State-Fullerton	Malverne, N.Y.	D8
Woodson, Shawn	LB	6-2	275	8/12/66	James Madison	Buckingham, Va.	D12a

The term NFL Rookie is defined as a player who is in his first season of professional football and has not been on the roster of another professional football team for any regular-season or postseason games. A Rookie is designated by an "R" on NFL rosters. Players who have been active in another professional football league or players who have NFL experience, including either preseason training camp or being on an active roster for fewer than three regular-season or postseason games, are termed NFL First-Year Players. An NFL First-Year Player is designated by a "1" on NFL rosters. Thereafter, a player on an NFL active roster for at least three regular-season or postseason games is credited with an additional year of NFL playing experience.

NOTES

Floyd Peters, defensive coordinator; born May 21, 1936, Council Bluffs, Iowa, lives in Bloomington, Minn. Defensive tackle-guard San Francisco State 1954-57. Pro defensive lineman Baltimore Colts 1958, Cleveland Browns 1959-62, Detroit Lions 1963, Philadelphia Eagles 1964-69, Washington Redskins 1970 (player/coach). Pro scout: Miami Dolphins 1971-73. Pro coach: New York Giants 1974-75, San Francisco 49ers 1976-77, Detroit Lions 1978-81, St. Louis Cardinals 1982-85, joined Vikings in 1986.

Dick Rehbein, assistant to offensive coordinator/passing game; born November 22, 1955, Green Bay, Wis., lives in Edina, Minn. Center Ripon 1973-77. No pro playing experience. Pro coach: Green Bay Packers 1979-83, Los Angeles Express (USFL) 1984, joined Vikings in 1984.

Bob Schnelker, offensive coordinator; born October 17, 1928, Galion, Ohio, lives in Eden Prairie, Minn. Tight end Bowling Green 1946-49. Pro tight end Cleveland Browns 1953, New York Giants 1954-59, Minnesota Vikings 1961, Pittsburgh Steelers 1961. Pro coach: Los Angeles Rams 1963-65, Green Bay Packers 1966-71, 1982-85, San Diego Chargers 1972-73, Miami Dolphins 1974, Kansas City Chiefs 1975-77, Detroit Lions 1978-81, joined Vikings in 1986.

Paul Wiggin, defensive line; born November 18, 1934, Modesto, Calif., lives in Eden Prairie, Minn. Offensive-defensive tackle Stanford 1953-56. Pro defensive end Cleveland Browns 1957-67. College coach: Stanford 1980-83 (head coach). Pro coach: San Francisco 49ers 1968-74, Kansas City Chiefs 1975-77 (head coach), New Orleans Saints 1978-79, joined Vikings in 1985.

National Football Conference Western Division

Team Colors: Old Gold, Black, and White

1500 Poydras Street
New Orleans, Louisiana 70112
Telephone: (504) 733-0255

Club Officials

Owner/General Partner: Tom Benson
President/General Manager: Jim Finks
Vice President/Administration: Jim Miller
Business Manager/Controller: Bruce Broussard
Director of Player Personnel: Bill Kuharich
Director of Marketing: Greg Suit
Assistant Director of Marketing: Bill Ferrante
Director of Media Relations: Rusty Kasmiersky
Assistant Director of Media Relations: Neal Gulkis
Director of Travel/Entertainment: Barra Birrcher
Player Personnel Scouts: Bill Baker, Hamp Cook, Hokie Gajan, Tom Marino, Carmen Piccone
Ticket Manager: Sandy King
Trainer: Dean Kleinschmidt
Equipment Manager: Dan Simmons
Video Director: Albert Aucoin

Stadium: Louisiana Superdome •
Capacity: 69,548
1500 Poydras Street
New Orleans, Louisiana 70112

Playing Surface: AstroTurf

Training Camp: University of Wisconsin-LaCrosse
LaCrosse, Wisconsin 54601

1989 Schedule

Preseason

Aug. 12	**Indianapolis**	7:00
Aug. 19	at Buffalo	7:30
Aug. 28	**Cincinnati**	7:00
Sept. 1	**Washington**	7:00

Regular Season

Sept. 10	**Dallas**	12:00
Sept. 17	at Green Bay	12:00
Sept. 24	at Tampa Bay	1:00
Oct. 1	**Washington**	12:00
Oct. 8	at San Francisco	1:00
Oct. 15	**New York Jets**	3:00
Oct. 22	at Los Angeles Rams	1:00
Oct. 29	**Atlanta**	12:00
Nov. 6	**San Francisco** (Monday)	8:00
Nov. 12	at New England	1:00
Nov. 19	at Atlanta	1:00
Nov. 26	**Los Angeles Rams**	7:00
Dec. 3	at Detroit	1:00
Dec. 10	at Buffalo	1:00
Dec. 18	**Philadelphia** (Monday)	8:00
Dec. 24	**Indianapolis**	12:00

Saints Coaching History

(112-206-5)

1967-70	Tom Fears*	13-34-2
1970-72	J.D. Roberts	7-25-3
1973-75	John North**	11-23-0
1975	Ernie Hefferle	1-7-0
1976-77	Hank Stram	7-21-0
1978-80	Dick Nolan***	15-29-0
1980	Dick Stanfel	1-3-0
1981-85	O.A. (Bum) Phillips****	27-42-0
1985	Wade Phillips	1-3-0
1986-88	Jim Mora	29-19-0

*Released after seven games in 1970
**Released after six games in 1975
***Released after 12 games in 1980
****Resigned after 12 games in 1985

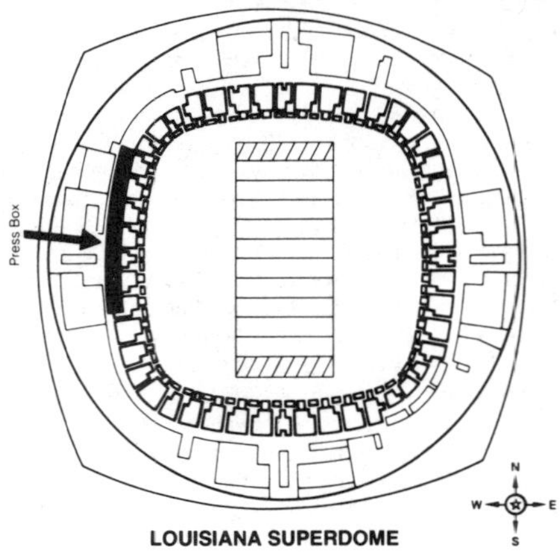

LOUISIANA SUPERDOME

Record Holders

Individual Records—Career

Category	Name	Performance
Rushing (Yds.)	George Rogers, 1981-84	4,267
Passing (Yds.)	Archie Manning, 1971-1982	21,734
Passing (TDs)	Archie Manning, 1971-1982	115
Receiving (No.)	Dan Abramowicz, 1967-1973	309
Receiving (Yds.)	Dan Abramowicz, 1967-1973	4,875
Interceptions	Tommy Myers, 1972-1982	36
Punting (Avg.)	Brian Hansen, 1984-88	42.0
Punt Return (Avg.)	Mel Gray, 1987	14.7
Kickoff Return (Avg.)	Walter Roberts, 1967	26.3
Field Goals	Morten Andersen, 1982-88	151
Touchdowns (Tot.)	Dan Abramowicz, 1967-1973	37
Points	Morten Andersen, 1982-88	656

Individual Records—Single Season

Category	Name	Performance
Rushing (Yds.)	George Rogers, 1981	1,674
Passing (Yds.)	Archie Manning, 1980	3,716
Passing (TDs)	Archie Manning, 1980	23
Receiving (No.)	Tony Galbreath, 1978	74
Receiving (Yds.)	Wes Chandler, 1979	1,069
Interceptions	Dave Whitsell, 1967	10
Punting (Avg.)	Brian Hansen, 1984	43.8
Punt Return (Avg.)	Mel Gray, 1987	14.7
Kickoff Return (Avg.)	Don Shy, 1969	27.9
Field Goals	Morten Andersen, 1985	31
Touchdowns (Tot.)	George Rogers, 1981	13
Points	Morten Andersen, 1987	121

Individual Records—Single Game

Category	Name	Performance
Rushing (Yds.)	George Rogers, 9-4-83	206
Passing (Yds.)	Archie Manning, 12-7-80	377
Passing (TDs)	Billy Kilmer, 11-2-69	6
Receiving (No.)	Tony Galbreath, 9-10-78	14
Receiving (Yds.)	Wes Chandler, 9-2-79	205
Interceptions	Tommy Myers, 9-3-78	3
	Dave Waymer, 10-6-85	3
	Reggie Sutton, 10-18-87	3
Field Goals	Morten Andersen, 12-1-85	5
	Morten Andersen, 11-15-87	5
Touchdowns (Tot.)	Many times	3
	Last time by Wayne Wilson, 1-2-83	
Points	Many times	18
	Last time by Wayne Wilson, 1-2-83	

1988 Team Record

Preseason (2-2)

Date	Result		Opponents
8/7	W	23-20	at Minnesota
8/12	W	33-28	at Phoenix
8/20	L	6-18	at Indianapolis
8/26	L	28-31	Pittsburgh
		90-97	

Regular Season (10-6)

Date	Result		Opponents	Att.
9/4	L	33-34	San Francisco	66,357
9/11	W	29-21	at Atlanta	48,901
9/18	W	22-14	at Detroit	32,943
9/25	W	13- 9	Tampa Bay	66,671
10/3	W	20-17	Dallas	68,474
10/9	W	23-17	at San Diego	42,693
10/16	W	20-19	at Seattle	63,569
10/23	W	20- 6	L.A. Raiders	66,249
10/30	L	10-12	L.A. Rams	68,238
11/6	L	24-27	at Washington	54,183
11/13	W	14-10	at L.A. Rams	63,305
11/20	W	42- 0	Denver	68,075
11/27	L	12-13	N.Y. Giants	66,526
12/4	L	3-45	at Minnesota	61,215
12/11	L	17-30	at San Francisco	62,977
12/18	W	10- 9	Atlanta	60,566

Score by Periods

Saints	64	93	101	54	0	—	312
Opponents	51	111	70	51	0	—	283

Attendance

Home 531,156 Away 429,786 Total 960,942
Single-game home record, 70,940 (11-4-79)
Single-season home record, 531,156 (1988)

1988 Team Statistics

	Saints	Opp.
Total First Downs	306	286
Rushing	108	97
Passing	179	167
Penalty	19	22
Third Down: Made/Att.	104/227	73/203
Fourth Down: Made/Att.	4/6	7/14
Total Net Yards	5131	5106
Avg. Per Game	320.7	319.1
Total Plays	1034	978
Avg. Per Play	5.0	5.2
Net Yards Rushing	2046	1779
Avg. Per Game	127.9	111.2
Total Rushes	512	442
Net Yards Passing	3085	3327
Avg. Per Game	192.8	207.9
Sacked/Yards Lost	24/171	31/252
Gross Yards	3256	3579
Att./Completions	498/286	505/277
Completion Pct.	57.4	54.9
Had Intercepted	16	17
Punts/Avg.	73/39.9	70/40.2
Net Punting Avg.	34.3	32.6
Penalties/Yards Lost	101/821	77/628
Fumbles/Ball Lost	29/16	27/15
Touchdowns	33	29
Rushing	9	7
Passing	21	19
Returns	3	3
Avg. Time of Possession	32:38	27:22

1988 Individual Statistics

Scoring	TD R	TD P	TD Rt	PAT	FG	Saf	TP
Andersen	0	0	0	32/33	26/36	0	110
Hill	0	7	0	0/0	0/0	0	42
Martin	0	7	0	0/0	0/0	0	42
Hilliard	5	1	0	0/0	0/0	0	36
Mayes	3	0	0	0/0	0/0	0	18
Clark	0	2	0	0/0	0/0	0	12
Perriman	0	2	0	0/0	0/0	0	12
Gray	0	0	1	0/0	0/0	0	6
Heyward	1	0	0	0/0	0/0	0	6
Jordan	0	0	1	0/0	0/0	0	6
Scales	0	1	0	0/0	0/0	0	6
Tice	0	1	0	0/0	0/0	0	6
Waymer	0	0	1	0/0	0/0	0	6
Jackson	0	0	0	0/0	0/0	1	2
Saints	9	21	3	32/33	26/36	2	312
Opponents	7	19	3	28/29	27/34	0	283

Passing	Att.	Comp.	Yds.	Pct.	TD	Int.	Tkld.	Rate
Hebert	478	280	3156	58.6	20	15	24/171	79.3
Wilson	16	5	73	31.3	0	1	0/0	21.1
Hilliard	2	1	27	50.0	1	0	0/0	135.4
Fourcade	1	0	0	0.0	0	0	0/0	39.6
Hill	1	0	0	0.0	0	0	0/0	39.6
Saints	498	286	3256	57.4	21	16	24/171	77.9
Opponents	505	277	3579	54.9	19	17	31/252	75.8

Rushing	Att.	Yds.	Avg.	LG	TD
Hilliard	204	823	4.0	36	5
Mayes	170	628	3.7	21	3
Heyward	74	355	4.8	73t	1
Jordan	19	115	6.1	44	0
Hebert	37	79	2.1	16	0
Perriman	3	17	5.7	17	0
Martin	2	12	6.0	9	0
Hansen	1	10	10.0	10	0
Hill	2	7	3.5	5	0
Saints	512	2046	4.0	73t	9
Opponents	442	1779	4.0	62	7

Receiving	No.	Yds.	Avg.	LG	TD
Martin	85	1083	12.7	40t	7
Hill	66	703	10.7	35	7
Hilliard	34	335	9.9	26	1
Tice	26	297	11.4	40	1
Clark	19	245	12.9	21t	2
Perriman	16	215	13.4	33	2
Heyward	13	105	8.1	18	0
Mayes	11	103	9.4	25	0
Jordan	5	70	14.0	25	0
Brenner	5	67	13.4	24	0
Scales	2	20	10.0	14	1
Hebert	2	0	0.0	2	0
Pattison	1	8	8.0	8	0
Benson	1	5	5.0	5	0
Saints	286	3256	11.4	40t	21
Opponents	277	3579	12.9	85t	19

Interceptions	No.	Yds.	Avg.	LG	TD
Atkins	4	42	10.5	40	0
Waymer	3	91	30.3	44	0
Jakes	3	61	20.3	39	0
Sutton	3	32	10.7	34	0
Johnson	1	34	34.0	34	0
Mack	1	19	19.0	19	0
Jackson	1	16	16.0	16	0
Cook	1	0	0.0	0	0
Saints	17	295	17.4	44	0
Opponents	16	226	14.1	78t	2

Punting	No.	Yds.	Avg.	In 20	LG
Hansen	72	2913	40.5	19	64
Saints	73	2913	39.9	19	64
Opponents	70	2815	40.2	15	56

Punt Returns	No.	FC	Yds.	Avg.	LG	TD
Gray	25	8	305	12.2	66t	1
Hill	10	4	108	10.8	31	0
Saints	35	12	413	11.8	66t	1
Opponents	39	16	248	6.4	17	0

Kickoff Returns	No.	Yds.	Avg.	LG	TD
Atkins	20	424	21.2	57	0
Gray	32	670	20.9	39	0
Mayes	7	132	18.9	33	0
Hilliard	6	111	18.5	30	0
Martin	3	32	10.7	18	0
Waymer	2	39	19.5	29	0
Saints	70	1408	20.1	57	0
Opponents	43	823	19.1	40	0

Sacks	No.
Jackson	7.0
Swilling	7.0
Geathers	3.5
Wilks	3.5
Gibson	2.0
Johnson	2.0
Kohlbrand	2.0
Elliott	1.0
Gregory	1.0
Mack	1.0
Warren	1.0
Saints	31.0
Opponents	24.0

1989 Draft Choices

Round	Name	Pos.	College
1.	Wayne Martin	DE	Arkansas
2.	Robert Massey	DB	No. Carolina Cent.
3.	Kim Phillips	DB	North Texas State
4.	Mike Mayes	DB	Louisiana State
5.	Kevin Haverdink	T	Western Michigan
6.	Floyd Turner	WR	N.W. Louisiana
7.	David Griggs	LB	Virginia
8.	Fred Hadley	WR	Mississippi State
9.	Jerry Leggett	LB	Cal State-Fullerton
10.	Joe Henderson	RB	Iowa State
11.	Calvin Nicholson	DB	Oregon State
12.	Mike Cadore	WR	Eastern Kentucky

New Orleans Saints 1989 Veteran Roster

No.	Name	Pos.	Ht.	Wt.	Birth-date	NFL Exp.	College	Hometown	How Acq.	'88 Games/ Starts
7	†Andersen, Morten	K	6-2	221	8/19/60	8	Michigan State	Indianapolis, Ind.	D4-'82	16/0
28	Atkins, Gene	CB-S	6-1	200	8/31/64	3	Florida A&M	Tallahassee, Fla.	D7-'87	16/6
76	Board, Dwaine	DE	6-5	248	11/29/56	10	North Carolina A&T	Rocky Mount, Va.	W(SF)-'88	4/0
85	Brenner, Hoby	TE	6-4	240	6/2/59	9	Southern California	Fullerton, Calif.	D3b-'81	10/8
67	Brock, Stan	T	6-6	292	6/8/58	10	Colorado	Beaverton, Ore.	D1-'80	7/7
75	Clark, Bruce	DE	6-3	275	3/31/58	8	Penn State	New Castle, Pa.	T(GB)-'82	16/2
	Colbert, Darrell	WR	5-10	174	11/16/64	3	Texas Southern	Beaumont, Tex.	FA(KC)-'89#	3/0*
41	Cook, Toi	S	5-11	188	12/3/64	3	Stanford	Canoga Park, Calif.	D8-'87	16/0
72	Dombrowski, Jim	T	6-5	298	10/19/63	4	Virginia	Williamsville, N.Y.	D1-'86	16/16
95	Dumbauld, Jonathan	DE	6-4	259	2/14/63	3	Kentucky	Troy, Ohio	FA-'88	1/0
63	†Edelman, Brad	G	6-6	270	9/3/60	8	Missouri	Creve Coeur, Mo.	D2-'82	14/13
52	Forde, Brian	LB	6-2	225	11/1/63	2	Washington State	Montreal, Canada	D7-'88	16/0
11	Fourcade, John	QB	6-1	208	10/11/60	3	Mississippi	Marrero, La.	FA-'87	1/0
97	†Geathers, James	DE	6-7	290	4/26/60	5	Wichita State	Georgetown, S.C.	D2-'84	16/6
27	†Gibson, Antonio	S	6-3	204	7/5/62	4	Cincinnati	Jackson, Miss.	FA-'86	10/10
77	†Gilbert, Daren	T	6-6	295	10/3/63	5	Cal State-Fullerton	Compton, Calif.	D2-'85	11/6
74	Gregory, Ted	NT	6-1	260	2/11/65	2	Syracuse	East Islip, N.Y.	T(Den)-'88	3/0
10	†Hansen, Brian	P	6-3	209	10/18/60	6	Sioux Falls	Hawarden, Iowa	D9-'84	16/0
92	Haynes, James	LB	6-2	233	8/9/60	6	Mississippi Valley State	Tallulah, La.	FA-'84	4/0
3	Hebert, Bobby	QB	6-4	215	8/19/60	5	Northwestern Louisiana	Cut Off, La.	FA-'85	16/16
34	Heyward, Craig	RB	5-11	251	9/26/66	2	Pittsburgh	Passaic, N.J.	D1-'88	11/8
61	†Hilgenberg, Joel	C-G	6-2	252	7/10/62	6	Iowa	Iowa City, Iowa	D4-'84	16/10
87	Hill, Lonzell	WR	5-11	189	9/25/65	3	Washington	Stockton, Calif.	D2-'87	16/15
21	†Hilliard, Dalton	RB	5-8	204	1/21/64	4	Louisiana State	Patterson, La.	D2-'86	16/9
57	Jackson, Rickey	LB	6-2	243	3/20/58	9	Pittsburgh	Pahokee, Fla.	D2-'81	16/16
53	Johnson, Vaughn	LB	6-3	235	3/24/62	4	North Carolina State	Morehead City, N.C.	SD1-'84	16/16
90	Johnson, Walter	LB	6-0	240	11/13/63	3	Louisiana Tech	Ferriday, La.	FA(Hou)-'89#	16/0*
93	Johnson, Will	LB	6-4	228	12/4/64	2	Northeast Louisiana	Monroe, La.	FA-'89	0*
23	Jordan, Buford	RB	6-0	223	6/26/62	4	McNeese State	Iota, La.	FA-'86	14/3
55	Kohlbrand, Joe	LB	6-4	242	3/18/63	5	Miami	Merritt Island, Fla.	D8-'85	16/2
60	Korte, Steve	C	6-2	260	1/15/60	7	Arkansas	Littleton, Colo.	D2-'83	16/16
24	†Mack, Milton	CB	5-11	182	9/20/63	3	Alcorn State	Jackson, Miss.	D5-'87	14/1
84	†Martin, Eric	WR	6-1	207	11/8/61	5	Louisiana State	Van Vleck, Tex.	D7-'85	16/16
39	Maxie, Brett	S	6-2	194	1/13/62	5	Texas Southern	Dallas, Tex.	FA-'85	16/16
36	Mayes, Rueben	RB	5-11	200	6/16/63	4	Washington State	N. Battleford, Saskatchewan	D3a-'86	16/9
51	Mills, Sam	LB	5-9	225	6/3/59	4	Montclair State	Long Branch, N.J.	FA-'86	16/16
80	Perriman, Brett	WR	5-9	175	10/10/65	2	Miami	Miami, Fla.	D2-'88	16/0
83	Scales, Greg	TE	6-4	253	5/9/66	2	Wake Forest	Winston-Salem, N.C.	D5a-'88	12/0
	Shepard, Derrick	WR	5-10	187	1/22/64	2	Oklahoma	Odessa, Tex.	FA(Wash)-'89#	5/0*
56	†Swilling, Pat	LB	6-3	242	10/25/64	4	Georgia Tech	Toccoa, Ga.	D3b-'87	15/14
69	Swoopes, Patrick	NT	6-4	280	3/4/64	2	Mississippi State	Bradshaw, Miss.	FA-'89	0*
82	Tice, John	TE	6-5	249	6/22/60	7	Maryland	Central Islip, N.Y.	D3a-'83	15/12
54	Toles, Alvin	LB	6-1	227	3/23/63	5	Tennessee	Forsythe, Ga.	D1-'85	11/0
65	Trapilo, Steve	G	6-5	281	9/20/64	3	Boston College	Milton, Mass.	D4-'87	9/9
78	Walker, Jeff	T	6-4	289	1/22/63	3	Memphis State	Olive Branch, Miss.	FA-'88	1/0
73	†Warren, Frank	DE	6-4	290	9/14/59	9	Auburn	Birmingham, Ala.	D3a-'81	16/12
44	Waymer, Dave	CB	6-1	188	7/1/58	10	Notre Dame	Charlotte, N.C.	D2-'80	16/9
94	†Wilks, Jim	DE	6-5	266	3/12/58	9	San Diego State	Pasadena, Calif.	D12-'81	16/16
18	Wilson, Dave	QB	6-3	206	4/27/59	8	Illinois	Anaheim, Calif.	SD1-'81	1/0

* Colbert played 3 games with Kansas City in '88; Walter Johnson played 16 games with Houston; Will Johnson last active with Chicago in '87; Shepard played 5 games with Washington; Swoopes last active with New Orleans in '87.

† Option playout; subject to developments.

\# Plan B unconditional free agent.

Players lost through Plan B (8): CB-S Michael Adams (Phx; 5 games in '88), C James Campen (GB; 3), RB Lydell Carr (Phx; 0), WR Robert Clark (Det; 16), T Bill Contz (Den; 11), KR Mel Gray (Det; 14), CB Van Jakes (GB; 16), WR Mark Pattison (Sea; 6).

Also played with Saints in '88—TE Cliff Benson (7 games), C Chuck Commiskey (6), NT Tony Elliott (14), CB Reggie Sutton (15), RB Barry Word (2).

COACHING STAFF

Head Coach, Jim Mora

Pro Career: Begins fourth year as NFL coach, after leading Saints to 10-6 record in 1988. Was named 1987 NFL coach of the year after leading Saints to a 12-4 record and the team's first playoff appearance. Came to New Orleans following a three-year career as the winningest coach in USFL history as head coach of the Philadelphia/Baltimore Stars. Directed Stars to championship game in each of his three seasons and won league championship in 1984 and 1985. He won USFL coach of the year honors following the 1984 season. Mora began his pro coaching career in 1978 as defensive line coach of the Seattle Seahawks. In 1982, he became defensive coordinator of the New England Patriots and played a vital role in the Patriots' march to the playoffs that year. No pro playing experience. Career record: 29-19.

Background: Played tight end and defensive end at Occidental College. Assistant coach at Occidental 1960-63 and head coach 1964-67. Linebacker coach at Stanford on a staff that included former Eagles head coach Dick Vermeil. Defensive assistant at Colorado 1968-73. Linebacker coach under Vermeil at UCLA 1974. Defensive coordinator at Washington 1975-77. Received bachelor's degree in physical education from Occidental in 1957. Also holds master's degree in education from Southern California.

Personal: Born May 24, 1935, in Glendale, Calif. Jim and his wife, Connie, live in Metairie, La., and have three sons—Michael, Stephen, and Jim, a defensive assistant for the San Diego Chargers.

Assistant Coaches

Paul Boudreau, offensive line; born December 30, 1949, Somerville, Mass., lives in Metairie, La. Guard Boston College 1971-73. No pro playing experience. College coach: Boston College 1974-76, Maine 1977-78, Dartmouth 1979-81, Navy 1983. Pro coach: Edmonton Eskimos (CFL) 1983-86, joined Saints in 1987.

Dom Capers, defensive backs; born August 7, 1950, Cambridge, Ohio, lives in Metairie, La. Defensive back Mount Union College 1968-71. No pro playing experience. College coach: Hawaii 1975-76, San Jose State 1977, California 1978-79, Tennessee 1980-81, Ohio State 1982-83. Pro coach: Philadelphia/Baltimore Stars (USFL) 1984-85, joined Saints in 1986.

Vic Fangio, outside linebackers; born August 22, 1958, Dunmore, Pa., lives in Destrehan, La. Defensive back East Stroudsburg 1976-78. No pro playing experience. College coach: North Carolina 1983. Pro coach: Philadelphia/Baltimore Stars (USFL) 1983-85, joined Saints in 1986.

Joe Marciano, tight ends-special teams; born February 10, 1954, Scranton, Pa., lives in Metairie, La. Quarterback Temple 1972-75. No pro playing experience. College coach: East Stroudsburg 1977, Rhode Island 1978-79, Villanova 1980, Penn State 1981, Temple 1982. Pro coach: Philadelphia/Baltimore Stars (USFL) 1983-85, joined Saints in 1986.

Russell Paternostro, strength and conditioning; born July 21, 1940, New Orleans, La., lives in Jefferson, La. San Diego State. No college or pro playing experience. Pro coach: Joined Saints in 1981.

John Pease, defensive line; born October 14, 1943, Pittsburgh, Pa., lives in Kenner, La. Wingback Utah 1963-64. No pro playing experience. College coach: Fullerton, Calif., J.C. 1970-73, Long Beach State 1974-76, Utah 1977, Washington 1978-83. Pro coach: Philadelphia/Baltimore Stars (USFL) 1983-85, joined Saints in 1986.

Steve Sidwell, defensive coordinator-inside linebackers; born August 30, 1944, Winfield, Kan., lives in Destrehan, La. Linebacker Colorado 1962-65. No pro playing experience. College coach: Colorado 1966-73, Nevada-Las Vegas 1974-75, Southern Methodist 1976-81. Pro coach: New England Patriots 1982-84, Indianapolis Colts 1985, joined Saints in 1986.

New Orleans Saints 1989 First-Year Roster

Name	Pos.	Ht.	Wt.	Birth-date	College	Hometown	How Acq.
Brown, Henry (1)	NT	6-3	262	1/27/65	Ohio State	Columbus, Ohio	FA
Cadore, Michael	WR	5-8	169	11/21/66	Eastern Kentucky	Titusville, Fla.	D12
Cooper, Richard (1)	NT	6-4	285	11/1/64	Tennessee	Memphis, Tenn.	FA
Curkendall, Pete (1)	NT	6-2	279	3/8/66	Penn State	Elmira, N.Y.	FA
Derby, Glenn (1)	T	6-6	290	6/7/64	Wisconsin	Oconomowoc, Wis.	D8-'88
Duhart, Tommy (1)	NT	6-3	281	11/29/64	S.E. Oklahoma	Belle Glade, Fla.	FA
Dunlap, Jerry (1)	CB	5-8	175	2/4/65	Youngstown State	Lorain, Ohio	FA
Griggs, David	LB	6-3	239	2/5/67	Virginia	Pennsauken, N.J.	D7
Hadley, Fred	WR	6-0	176	3/18/66	Mississippi State	Tupelo, Miss.	D8
Harvey, Stacy (1)	LB	6-4	245	3/8/65	Arizona State	Altadena, Calif.	FA
Haverdink, Kevin	T	6-5	285	10/20/65	Western Michigan	Hamilton, Mich.	D5
Henderson, Joe	RB	6-0	205	4/9/66	Iowa State	Chicago, Ill.	D10
Leggett, Jerry	LB	6-4	266	8/23/65	Cal State-Fullerton	Meridian, Miss.	D9
Martin, Wayne	DE	6-4	265	10/26/65	Arkansas	Cherry Valley, Ark.	D1
Massey, Robert	CB	5-10	182	2/17/67	N. Carolina Central	Charlotte, N.C.	D2
Mayes, Michael	CB	5-10	182	8/17/66	Louisiana State	DeRidder, La.	D4
Nicholson, Calvin	CB	5-9	183	7/9/67	Oregon State	Inglewood, Calif.	D11
Phillips, Kim	CB	5-9	188	10/28/66	North Texas State	New Boston, Tex.	D3
Simmons, Michael (1)	DE	6-4	269	11/14/65	Mississippi State	Eupora, Miss.	FA
Thompson, Bennie (1)	CB-S	6-0	200	2/10/63	Grambling	New Orleans, La.	FA
Turner, Floyd	WR	5-11	188	5/29/66	N.W. Louisiana	Mansfield, La.	D6
Winslow, George (1)	P	6-4	201	7/28/63	Villanova	Jenkintown, Pa.	FA
Wise, Deatrich (1)	NT	6-3	249	5/6/65	Jackson State	Evergreen, Ala.	FA

The term NFL Rookie is defined as a player who is in his first season of professional football and has not been on the roster of another professional football team for any regular-season or postseason games. A Rookie is designated by an "R" on NFL rosters. Players who have been active in another professional football league or players who have NFL experience, including either preseason training camp or being on an active roster for fewer than three regular-season or postseason games, are termed NFL First-Year Players. An NFL First-Year Player is designated by a "1" on NFL rosters. Thereafter, a player on an NFL active roster for at least three regular-season or postseason games is credited with an additional year of NFL playing experience.

NOTES

Jim Skipper, running backs; born January 23, 1949, Breaux Bridge, La., lives in Metairie, La. Defensive back Whittier College 1971-72. No pro playing experience. College coach: Cal Poly-Pomona 1974-76, San Jose State 1977-78, Pacific 1979, Oregon 1980-82. Pro coach: Philadelphia/Baltimore Stars (USFL) 1983-85, joined Saints in 1986.

Carl Smith, offensive coordinator-quarterbacks; born April 26, 1948, Wasco, Calif., lives in Metairie, La. Defensive back Cal Poly-SLO 1968-70. No pro playing experience. College coach: Cal Poly-SLO 1971, Colorado 1972-73, Southwestern Louisiana 1974-78, Lamar 1979-81, North Carolina State 1982. Pro coach: Philadelphia/Baltimore Stars (USFL) 1983-85, joined Saints in 1986.

Steve Walters, wide receivers; born June 16, 1948, Jonesboro, Ark., lives in Metairie, La. Quarterback-defensive back Arkansas 1967-70. No pro playing experience. College coach: Tampa 1973, Northeast Louisiana 1974-75, Morehead State 1976, Tulsa 1977-78, Memphis State 1979, Southern Methodist 1980-81, Alabama 1985. Pro coach: New England Patriots 1982-84, joined Saints in 1986.

National Football Conference Eastern Division

Team Colors: Blue, Red, and White

Giants Stadium
East Rutherford, New Jersey 07073
Telephone: (201) 935-8111

Club Officials

President: Wellington T. Mara
Vice President-Treasurer: Timothy J. Mara
Vice President-Secretary: Raymond J. Walsh
Vice President-General Manager: George Young
Assistant General Manager: Harry Hulmes
Controller: John Pasquali
Director of Player Personnel: Tom Boisture
Director of Pro Personnel: Tim Rooney
Director of Media Services: Ed Croke
Director of Promotions: Tom Power
Director of Special Projects: Victor Del Guercio
Box Office Treasurer: Jim Gleason
Trainer Emeritus: John Dziegiel
Head Trainer: Ronnie Barnes
Assistant Trainers: John Johnson, Mike Ryan
Equipment Manager: Ed Wagner, Jr.

Stadium: Giants Stadium • **Capacity:** 76,891
East Rutherford, New Jersey 07073

Playing Surface: AstroTurf

Training Camp: Fairleigh Dickinson-Madison
Florham Park, N.J. 07932

1989 Schedule

Preseason

Aug. 12	at New England	7:00
Aug. 20	at Kansas City	7:00
Aug. 26	**New York Jets**	8:00
Sept. 2	**Pittsburgh**	8:00

Regular Season

Sept. 11	at Washington (Monday)	9:00
Sept. 17	**Detroit**	4:00
Sept. 24	**Phoenix**	1:00
Oct. 1	at Dallas	3:00
Oct. 8	at Philadelphia	1:00
Oct. 15	**Washington**	1:00
Oct. 22	at San Diego	1:00
Oct. 30	**Minnesota** (Monday)	9:00
Nov. 5	at Phoenix	2:00
Nov. 12	at Los Angeles Rams	1:00
Nov. 19	**Seattle**	4:00
Nov. 27	at San Francisco (Monday)	6:00
Dec. 3	**Philadelphia**	1:00
Dec. 10	at Denver	2:00
Dec. 16	**Dallas** (Saturday)	12:30
Dec. 24	**Los Angeles Raiders**	1:00

Giants Coaching History

(452-382-32)

1925	Bob Folwell	8-4-0
1926	Joe Alexander	8-4-1
1927-28	Earl Potteiger	15-8-3
1929-30	LeRoy Andrews*	24-5-1
1930	Benny Friedman	2-0-0
1931-53	Steve Owen	153-108-17
1954-60	Jim Lee Howell	54-29-4
1961-68	Allie Sherman	57-54-4
1969-73	Alex Webster	29-40-1
1974-76	Bill Arnsparger**	7-28-0
1976-78	John McVay	14-23-0
1979-82	Ray Perkins	24-35-0
1983-88	Bill Parcells	57-44-1

*Released after 15 games in 1930
**Released after seven games in 1976

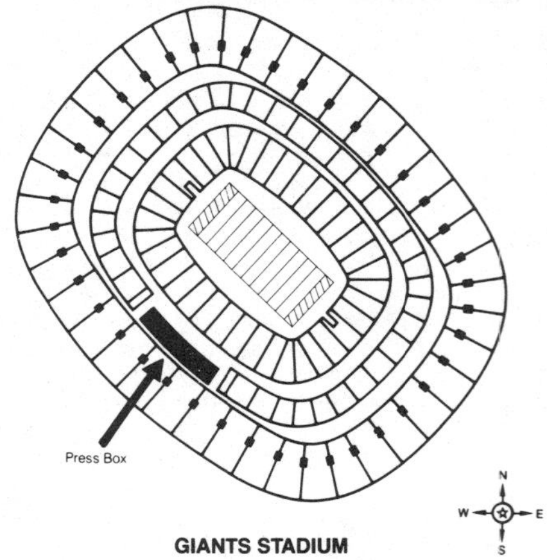

GIANTS STADIUM

Record Holders

Individual Records—Career

Category	Name	Performance
Rushing (Yds.)	Joe Morris, 1982-88	5,296
Passing (Yds.)	Phil Simms, 1979-1988	23,174
Passing (TDs)	Charlie Conerly, 1948-1961	173
Receiving (No.)	Joe Morrison, 1959-1972	395
Receiving (Yds.)	Frank Gifford, 1952-1960, 1962-64	5,434
Interceptions	Emlen Tunnell, 1948-1958	74
Punting (Avg.)	Don Chandler, 1956-1964	43.8
Punt Return (Avg.)	Bob Hammond, 1976-78	9.1
Kickoff Return (Avg.)	Rocky Thompson, 1971-72	27.2
Field Goals	Pete Gogolak, 1966-1974	126
Touchdowns (Tot.)	Frank Gifford, 1952-1960, 1962-64	78
Points	Pete Gogolak, 1966-1974	646

Individual Records—Single Season

Category	Name	Performance
Rushing (Yds.)	Joe Morris, 1986	1,516
Passing (Yds.)	Phil Simms, 1984	4,044
Passing (TDs)	Y.A. Tittle, 1963	36
Receiving (No.)	Earnest Gray, 1983	78
Receiving (Yds.)	Homer Jones, 1967	1,209
Interceptions	Otto Schnellbacher, 1951	11
	Jim Patton, 1958	11
Punting (Avg.)	Don Chandler, 1959	46.6
Punt Return (Avg.)	Merle Hapes, 1942	15.5
Kickoff Return (Avg.)	John Salscheider, 1949	31.6
Field Goals	Ali Haji-Sheikh, 1983	*35
Touchdowns (Tot.)	Joe Morris, 1985	21
Points	Ali Haji-Sheikh, 1983	127

Individual Records—Single Game

Category	Name	Performance
Rushing (Yds.)	Gene Roberts, 11-12-50	218
Passing (Yds.)	Phil Simms, 10-13-85	513
Passing (TDs)	Y.A. Tittle, 10-28-62	*7
Receiving (No.)	Mark Bavaro, 10-13-85	12
Receiving (Yds.)	Del Shofner, 10-28-62	269
Interceptions	Many times	3
	Last time by Terry Kinard, 9-27-87	
Field Goals	Joe Danelo, 10-18-81	6
Touchdowns (Tot.)	Ron Johnson, 10-2-72	4
	Earnest Gray, 9-7-80	4
Points	Ron Johnson, 10-2-72	24
	Earnest Gray, 9-7-80	24

*NFL Record

1988 Team Record

Preseason (3-1)

Date	Result		Opponents
8/6	W	34- 3	at Green Bay
8/13	W	24-21	N.Y. Jets
8/20	W	28-17	Pittsburgh
8/26	L	13-17	at Cleveland
		99-58	

Regular Season (10-6)

Date	Result		Opponents	Att.
9/5	W	27-20	Washington	76,417
9/11	L	17-20	San Francisco	75,943
9/18	W	12-10	at Dallas	55,325
9/25	L	31-45	L.A. Rams	75,617
10/2	W	24-23	at Washington	54,601
10/10	L	13-24	at Philadelphia	63,736
10/16	W	30-10	Detroit	74,813
10/23	W	23-16	at Atlanta	45,092
10/30	W	13-10	at Detroit (OT)	38,354
11/6	W	29-21	Dallas	75,826
11/13	L	17-24	at Phoenix	65,324
11/20	L	17-23	Philadelphia (OT)	43,621
11/27	W	13-12	at New Orleans	66,526
12/4	W	44- 7	Phoenix	73,438
12/11	W	28-12	Kansas City	69,807
12/18	L	21-27	at N.Y. Jets	69,770

(OT) Overtime

Score by Periods

Giants	59	83	95	119	3	—	359
Opponents	59	101	53	85	6	—	304

Attendance

Home 565,482 Away 458,728 Total 1,024,210
Single-game home record, 76,633 (1-11-87)
Single-season home record, 594,433 (1986)

1988 Team Statistics

	Giants	Opp.
Total First Downs	317	291
Rushing	123	95
Passing	168	177
Penalty	26	19
Third Down: Made/Att.	80/219	96/247
Fourth Down: Made/Att.	8/18	9/14
Total Net Yards	4955	5086
Avg. Per Game	309.7	317.9
Total Plays	1078	1072
Avg. Per Play	4.6	4.7
Net Yards Rushing	1689	1759
Avg. Per Game	105.6	109.9
Total Rushes	493	454
Net Yards Passing	3266	3327
Avg. Per Game	204.1	207.9
Sacked/Yards Lost	60/450	52/428
Gross Yards	3716	3755
Att./Completions	525/290	566/294
Completion Pct.	55.2	51.9
Had Intercepted	14	15
Punts/Avg.	81/39.9	93/39.8
Net Punting Avg.	33.7	34.2
Penalties/Yards Lost	88/660	116/902
Fumbles/Ball Lost	32/13	36/18
Touchdowns	41	33
Rushing	15	8
Passing	22	23
Returns	4	2
Avg. Time of Possession	29:24	30:36

1988 Individual Statistics

Scoring	TD R	TD P	TD Rt	PAT	FG	Saf	TP
McFadden	0	0	0	25/27	14/19	0	67
Anderson	8	0	0	0/0	0/0	0	48
Allegre	0	0	0	14/14	10/11	0	44
Baker	0	7	0	0/0	0/0	0	42
Morris	5	0	0	0/0	0/0	0	30
Bavaro	0	4	0	0/0	0/0	0	24
Manuel	0	4	0	0/0	0/0	0	24
Carthon	2	1	0	0/0	0/0	0	18
Robinson	0	3	0	0/0	0/0	0	18
Banks	0	0	1	0/0	0/0	0	6
Burt	0	0	1	0/0	0/0	0	6
Flynn	0	0	1	0/0	0/0	0	6
Ingram	0	1	0	0/0	0/0	0	6
P. Johnson	0	0	1	0/0	0/0	0	6
Mowatt	0	1	0	0/0	0/0	0	6
Turner	0	1	0	0/0	0/0	0	6
Collins	0	0	0	0/0	0/0	1	2
Giants	15	22	4	39/41	24/30	1	359
Opponents	8	23	2	31/32	25/33	0	304

Passing	Att.	Comp.	Yds.	Pct.	TD	Int.	Tkld.	Rate
Simms	479	263	3359	54.9	21	11	53/405	82.1
Hostetler	29	16	244	55.2	1	2	5/31	65.9
Rutledge	17	11	113	64.7	0	1	2/14	59.2
Giants	525	290	3716	55.2	22	14	60/450	80.5
Opponents	566	294	3755	51.9	23	15	52/428	75.5

Rushing	Att.	Yds.	Avg.	LG	TD
Morris	307	1083	3.5	27	5
Anderson	65	208	3.2	11	8
Simms	33	152	4.6	17	0
Carthon	46	146	3.2	8	2
Adams	29	76	2.6	15	0
Manuel	4	27	6.8	14	0
Rouson	1	1	1.0	1	0
Rutledge	3	−1	−0.3	0	0
Hostetler	5	−3	−0.6	0	0
Giants	493	1689	3.4	27	15
Opponents	454	1759	3.9	38	8

Receiving	No.	Yds.	Avg.	LG	TD
Manuel	65	1029	15.8	46	4
Bavaro	53	672	12.7	36	4
Baker	40	656	16.4	85t	7
Adams	27	174	6.4	19	0
Morris	22	166	7.5	24	0
Carthon	19	194	10.2	24	1
Mowatt	15	196	13.1	38t	1
Ingram	13	158	12.2	32	1
Turner	10	128	12.8	28t	1
Anderson	9	57	6.3	13	0
Robinson	7	143	20.4	62t	3
McConkey	5	72	14.4	28	0
Rouson	4	61	15.3	31	0
Hostetler	1	10	10.0	10	0
Giants	290	3716	12.8	85t	22
Opponents	294	3755	12.8	80t	23

Interceptions	No.	Yds.	Avg.	LG	TD
S. White	4	70	17.5	39	0
Kinard	3	46	15.3	39	0
Carson	2	66	33.0	66	0
P. Johnson	1	33	33.0	33t	1
A. White	1	29	29.0	29	0
Reasons	1	20	20.0	20	0
Banks	1	15	15.0	15t	1
Collins	1	13	13.0	13	0
Williams	1	0	0.0	0	0
Giants	15	292	19.5	66	2
Opponents	14	116	8.3	30	0

Punting	No.	Yds.	Avg.	In 20	LG
Buford	73	3012	41.3	13	66
Landeta	6	222	37.0	1	53
Giants	81	3234	39.9	14	66
Opponents	93	3697	39.8	26	66

Punt Returns	No.	FC	Yds.	Avg.	LG	TD
McConkey	40	25	313	7.8	35	0
Baker	5	0	34	6.8	11	0
Flynn	1	0	4	4.0	4	0
Kinard	1	0	8	8.0	8	0
Giants	47	25	359	7.6	35	0
Opponents	38	11	303	8.0	32	0

Kickoff Returns	No.	Yds.	Avg.	LG	TD
Guggemos	17	344	20.2	40	0
Hill	13	262	20.2	30	0
Ingram	8	129	16.1	27	0
Rouson	8	130	16.3	21	0
Haddix	6	123	20.5	24	0
Collins	4	67	16.8	26	0
S. White	3	62	20.7	26	0
McConkey	2	30	15.0	17	0
Beckman	1	7	7.0	7	0
Giants	62	1154	18.6	40	0
Opponents	73	1269	17.4	44	0

Sacks	No.
Taylor	15.5
Marshall	8.0
Martin	7.5
P. Johnson	4.0
Dorsey	3.5
Burt	3.0
Headen	3.0
Howard	3.0
Williams	2.0
Banks	1.5
Cooks	1.0
Giants	52.0
Opponents	60.0

1989 Draft Choices

Round	Name	Pos.	College
1.	Brian Williams	G	Minnesota
3.	Bob Kratch	G	Iowa
	Greg Jackson	DB	Louisiana State
4.	Lewis Tillman	RB	Jackson State
	Brad Henke	NT	Arizona
5.	Dave Meggett	RB	Towson State
6.	Howard Cross	TE	Alabama
7.	Dave Popp	T	Eastern Illinois
8.	Myron Guyton	DB	Eastern Kentucky
9.	A.J. Greene	DB	Wake Forest
10.	Rodney Lowe	DE	Mississippi
11.	Jerome Rinehart	LB	Tennessee-Martin
12.	Eric Smith	LB	UCLA

New York Giants 1989 Veteran Roster

No.	Name	Pos.	Ht.	Wt.	Birth-date	NFL Exp.	College	Hometown	How Acq.	'88 Games/ Starts
33	†Adams, George	RB	6-1	225	12/22/62	5	Kentucky	Lexington, Ky.	D1-'85	16/1
2	†Allegre, Raul	K	5-10	167	6/15/59	7	Texas	Torreon, Mexico	FA-'86	6/0
79	Althoff, Jim	NT	6-3	278	9/27/61	2	Winona State	McHenry, Ill.	FA-'89	0*
24	Anderson, Ottis	RB	6-2	225	11/19/57	11	Miami	West Palm Beach, Fla.	T(StL)-'86	16/0
85	Baker, Stephen	WR	5-8	160	8/30/64	3	Fresno State	San Antonio, Tex.	D3-'87	16/11
58	Banks, Carl	LB	6-4	235	8/29/62	6	Michigan State	Flint, Mich.	D1-'84	14/14
88	Baty, Greg	TE	6-5	240	8/24/64	3	Stanford	Sparta, N.J.	FA-'89	0*
89	Bavaro, Mark	TE	6-4	245	4/28/63	5	Notre Dame	Danvers, Mass.	D4-'85	16/15
64	Burt, Jim	NT	6-1	260	6/7/59	8	Miami	Orchard Park, N.Y.	FA-'81	16/11
44	Carthon, Maurice	RB	6-1	225	4/24/61	5	Arkansas State	Osceola, Ark.	FA-'85	16/14
25	Collins, Mark	CB	5-10	190	1/16/64	4	Cal State-Fullerton	San Bernardino, Calif.	D2-'86	11/11
98	Cooks, Johnie	LB	6-4	251	11/23/58	2	Mississippi State	Leland, Miss.	FA-'88	13/3
38	Cox, Greg	S	6-0	223	1/6/65	2	San Jose State	Niagara, N.Y.	FA(SF)-'89#	15/0*
77	Dorsey, Eric	DE	6-5	280	8/5/64	4	Notre Dame	McLean, Va.	D1-'86	16/16
76	Elliott, John	T	6-7	305	4/1/65	2	Michigan	Lake Ronkonkoma, N.Y.	D2-'88	16/5
28	Flynn, Tom	S	6-0	195	3/24/62	6	Pittsburgh	Verona, Pa.	FA-'87	16/0
37	Haddix, Wayne	CB	6-1	203	7/23/65	3	Liberty	Bolivar, Tenn.	FA-'87	7/0
48	Hill, Kenny	S	6-0	195	7/25/58	9	Yale	Oak Grove, La.	T(Raid)-'84	16/16
15	†Hostetler, Jeff	QB	6-3	212	4/22/61	6	West Virginia	Johnstown, Pa.	D3-'84	16/1
74	Howard, Erik	NT	6-4	268	11/12/64	4	Washington State	San Jose, Calif.	D2a-'86	16/5
82	Ingram, Mark	WR	5-10	188	8/23/65	3	Michigan State	Rockford, Ill.	D1-'87	7/4
68	Johnson, Damian	T	6-5	290	12/18/62	4	Kansas State	Great Bend, Kan.	FA-'86	6/6
52	†Johnson, Thomas	LB	6-3	248	7/29/64	4	Ohio State	Detroit, Mich.	D2b-'86	16/15
43	†Kinard, Terry	S	6-1	200	11/24/59	7	Clemson	Sumter, S.C.	D1-'83	16/16
90	Lambrecht, Mike	NT-DE	6-1	275	5/2/63	3	St. Cloud State	Watertown, Minn.	FA(Mia)-'89#	8/0*
5	Landeta, Sean	P	6-0	200	1/6/62	5	Towson State	Baltimore, Md.	FA-'85	1/0
86	†Manuel, Lionel	WR	5-11	180	4/13/62	6	Pacific	La Puente, Calif.	D7-'84	16/16
70	Marshall, Leonard	DE	6-3	285	10/22/61	7	Louisiana State	Franklin, La.	D2-'83	15/14
80	McConkey, Phil	WR	5-10	170	2/24/57	6	Navy	Buffalo, N.Y.	FA-'84	16/0
60	Moore, Eric	T	6-5	290	1/21/65	2	Indiana	Berkeley, Mo.	D1-'88	11/10
20	Morris, Joe	RB	5-7	195	9/15/60	8	Syracuse	Ayer, Mass.	D2-'82	16/15
84	†Mowatt, Zeke	TE	6-3	240	3/5/61	6	Florida State	Wauchula, Fla.	FA-'83	16/3
65	†Oates, Bart	C	6-3	265	12/16/58	5	Brigham Young	Albany, Ga.	FA-'85	16/16
55	†Reasons, Gary	LB	6-4	234	2/18/62	6	Northwestern Louisiana	Crowley, Tex.	D4a-'84	16/7
72	Riesenberg, Doug	T	6-5	275	7/22/65	3	California	Moscow, Idaho	D6a-'87	16/11
66	Roberts, William	T	6-5	280	8/5/62	5	Ohio State	Miami, Fla.	D1a-'84	16/13
81	Robinson, Stacy	WR	5-11	186	2/19/62	5	North Dakota State	St. Paul, Minn.	D2-'85	11/0
22	†Rouson, Lee	RB	6-1	222	10/18/62	5	Colorado	Greensboro, N.C.	D8-'85	16/0
17	Rutledge, Jeff	QB	6-1	195	1/22/57	11	Alabama	Birmingham, Ala.	T(Rams)-'82	1/0
51	Shaw, Rickey	LB	6-4	240	7/28/65	2	Oklahoma State	Fayetteville, N.C.	D4-'88	14/0
11	Simms, Phil	QB	6-3	214	11/3/56	11	Morehead State	Louisville, Ky.	D1-'79	15/15
56	Taylor, Lawrence	LB	6-3	243	2/4/59	9	North Carolina	Williamsburg, Va.	D1-'81	12/12
21	Thompson, Reyna	CB	6-0	193	8/28/63	4	Baylor	Dallas, Tex.	FA(Mia)-'89#	16/2*
83	Turner, Odessa	WR	6-3	205	10/12/64	3	Northwestern Louisiana	Monroe, La.	D4-'87	4/1
73	Washington, John	DE	6-4	275	2/2/63	4	Oklahoma State	Houston, Tex.	D3-'86	16/2
27	Welch, Herb	CB-S	5-11	180	1/12/61	5	UCLA	Downey, Calif.	D12-'85	0*
36	White, Adrian	S	6-0	200	4/6/64	3	Florida	Orange Park, Fla.	D2-'87	16/0
71	White, Robb	DE	6-4	270	5/26/65	2	South Dakota	Aberdeen, S.D.	FA-'88	1/0
39	White, Sheldon	CB-S	5-11	188	3/1/65	2	Miami, Ohio	Dayton, Ohio	D3-'88	16/5
23	Williams, Perry	CB	6-2	203	5/12/61	6	North Carolina State	Hamlet, N.C.	D7-'83	16/16
69	Winters, Frank	C	6-3	280	1/23/64	3	Western Illinois	Union City, N.J.	FA(Clev)-'89#	16/0*

* Althoff last active with Chicago in '87; Baty played 1 game with Phoenix in '88; Cox played 15 games with San Francisco in '88; Lambrecht played 8 games with Miami; Thompson played 16 games with Miami; Welch missed '88 season due to injury; Winters played 16 games with Cleveland.

† Option playout; subject to developments.

Plan B unconditional free agent.

Retired—Harry Carson, 13-year linebacker, 12 games in '88; George Martin, 14-year defensive end, 16 games in '88.

Players lost through Plan B (9): G Billy Ard (GB; 16 games in '88), T Mike Ariey (GB; 0), TE Brad Beckman (Atl; 9), DT Henry Brown (Rams; 0), P Maury Buford (GB; 15), S Neal Guggemos (Buff; 11), CB-S Sam Lilly (Phil; 0), K Paul McFadden (Atl; 10), TE Dante Whitaker (Atl; 0).

Also played with Giants in '88—C Joe Fields (13 games), LB Andy Headen (4), LB Byron Hunt (2), S Greg Lasker (4), T Karl Nelson (9), TE Tim Sherwin (3).

COACHING STAFF

Head Coach, Bill Parcells

Pro Career: Became twelfth head coach in New York Giants history on December 15, 1982. Parcells begins seventh campaign as head coach after spending two seasons as the Giants' defensive coordinator and linebacker coach. Led Giants to Super Bowl XXI victory over Denver 39-20 after Wild Card playoff berths in both 1984 and 1985. Started pro coaching career in 1980 as linebacker coach with New England Patriots. Career record: 57-44-1.

Background: Linebacker at Wichita State 1961-63. College assistant Hastings (Neb.) 1964, Wichita State 1965, Army 1966-69, Florida State 1970-72, Vanderbilt 1973-74, Texas Tech 1975-77, Air Force 1978 (head coach).

Personal: Born August 22, 1941, Englewood, N.J. Bill and his wife, Judy, live in Upper Saddle River, N.J., and have three daughters—Suzy, Jill, and Dallas.

Assistant Coaches

Bill Belichick, defensive coordinator/secondary; born April 16, 1952, Nashville, Tenn., lives in Chatham, N.J. Center-tight end Wesleyan 1972-74. No pro playing experience. Pro coach: Baltimore Colts 1975, Detroit Lions 1976-77, Denver Broncos 1978, joined Giants in 1979.

Tom Coughlin, receivers; born August 31, 1946, Waterloo, N.Y., lives in East Rutherford, N.J. Halfback Syracuse 1965-67. No pro playing experience. College coach: Rochester Tech 1969-73 (head coach), Syracuse 1974-80, Boston College 1981-83. Pro coach: Philadelphia Eagles 1984-85, Green Bay Packers 1986-87, joined Giants in 1988.

Romeo Crennell, special teams; born June 18, 1947, Lynchburg, Va., lives in Montvale, N.J. Defensive lineman Western Kentucky 1966-69. No pro playing experience. College coach: Western Kentucky 1970-74, Texas Tech 1975-77, Mississippi 1978-79, Georgia Tech 1980. Pro coach: Joined Giants in 1981.

Ron Erhardt, offensive coordinator; born February 27, 1932, Mandan, N.D., lives in Wykoff, N.J. Quarterback Jamestown (N.D.) College 1951-54. No pro playing experience. College coach: North Dakota State 1963-72 (head coach 1966-72). Pro coach: New England Patriots 1973-81 (head coach 1979-81), joined Giants in 1982.

Al Groh, linebackers; born July 13, 1944, New York City, lives in East Rutherford, N.J. Defensive end Virginia 1964-67. No pro playing experience. College coach: Army 1968-69, Virginia 1970-72, North Carolina 1973-77, Air Force 1978-79, Texas Tech 1980, Wake Forest (head coach) 1981-86, South Carolina 1988. Pro coach: Atlanta Falcons 1987, joined Giants in 1989.

Ray Handley, running backs; born October 8, 1944, Artesia, N.M., lives in West Orange, N.J. Running back Stanford 1963-65. No pro playing experience. College coach: Stanford 1967, 1971-74, 1979-83, Army 1968-69, Air Force 1975-78. Pro coach: Joined Giants in 1984.

Fred Hoaglin, offensive line; born January 28, 1944, Alliance, Ohio, lives in Sparta, N.J. Center Pittsburgh 1962-65. Pro center Cleveland Browns 1966-72, Baltimore Colts 1973, Houston Oilers 1974-75, Seattle Seahawks 1976. Pro coach: Detroit Lions 1978-84, joined Giants in 1985.

Lamar Leachman, defensive line; born August 7, 1934, Cartersville, Ga., lives in Ridgewood, N.J. Center-linebacker Tennessee 1952-55. No pro playing experience. College coach: Richmond 1966-67, Georgia Tech 1968-71, Memphis State 1972, South Carolina 1973. Pro coach: New York Stars (WFL) 1974, Toronto Argonauts (CFL) 1975-77, Montreal Alouettes (CFL) 1978-79, joined Giants in 1980.

Johnny Parker, strength and conditioning; born February 1, 1947, Greenville, S.C., lives in Montvale, N.J. Graduate of Mississippi, master's degree from Delta State University. No college or pro playing experience. College coach: South Carolina 1974-76, Indiana 1977-79, Louisiana State 1980, Mississippi 1981-83. Pro coach: Joined Giants in 1984.

New York Giants 1989 First-Year Roster

Name	Pos.	Ht.	Wt.	Birth-date	College	Hometown	How Acq.
Adams, Lish	LB	6-1	235	3/26/67	Sam Houston State	Jasper, Tex.	FA
Calvert, Derron	WR	6-0	170	8/6/65	Wilmington State	Cincinnati, Ohio	FA
Cole, Leon	DE	6-4	270	11/8/65	Texas A&M	East Orange, N.J.	FA
Cross, Howard	TE	6-5	245	8/8/67	Alabama	Huntsville, Ala.	D6
Fryar, Jeff	T	6-5	290	12/7/64	Indiana	Indianapolis, Ind.	FA
Green, A.J.	CB	5-8	167	6/24/66	Wake Forest	Hendersonville, N.C.	D9
Guyton, Myron	CB-S	6-1	205	8/26/67	Eastern Kentucky	Metcalf, Ga.	D8
Henke, Brad	NT	6-3	275	4/10/66	Arizona	Columbus, Neb.	D4a
Hooten, Mike	LB	6-4	240	11/1/65	Wake Forest	Raleigh, N.C.	FA
Howard, Stan (1)	WR	5-10	170	5/22/65	Murray State	Brooklyn, N.Y.	FA
Hudson, Dave	RB	6-0	228	4/28/66	Iowa	Ennis, Tex.	FA
Jackson, Greg	S	6-1	200	8/20/66	Louisiana State	Hialeah, Fla.	D3a
Kratch, Bob	G	6-3	288	1/6/66	Iowa	Mahwah, N.J.	D3
Kunkel, Greg (1)	T	6-5	290	12/9/64	Kentucky	Erlanger, Ky.	FA
Lowe, Rod	DE	6-5	260	12/2/67	Mississippi	Ft. Lauderdale, Fla.	D10
McCreary, Mike	LB	6-5	240	3/7/66	Toledo	Wooster, Ohio	FA
Meggett, David	RB	5-7	180	4/30/66	Towson State	Charleston, S.C.	D5
Miotke, Frank	WR	6-0	175	12/22/65	Grand Valley State	Dearborn, Mich.	FA
Pearcey, Tony	WR	6-2	180	3/2/66	Vanderbilt	Sarasota, Fla.	FA
Popp, Dave	T	6-5	285	10/30/66	Eastern Illinois	Arlington Heights, Ill.	D7
Rinehart, Jerome	DE	6-4	245	6/6/65	Tennessee-Martin	Norristown, Pa.	D11
Smith, Billy	P	5-11	193	9/30/66	Tenn.-Chattanooga	St. Louis, Mo.	FA
Smith, Eric	LB	6-3	235	3/31/66	UCLA	Oakland, Calif.	D12
Simpson, Tony (1)	RB	5-9	240	12/21/64	East Carolina	Elizabeth City, N.C.	FA
Tiebout, Dean	T	6-4	285	6/7/63	Western Kentucky	Bronx, N.Y.	FA
Tillman, Lewis	RB	6-0	195	4/16/66	Jackson State	Oklahoma City, Okla.	D4
Williams, Brian	G	6-5	300	6/8/66	Minnesota	Mt. Lebanon, Pa.	D1
Williams, Dayne	RB	6-0	230	5/10/66	Florida State	Leesburg, Fla.	FA

The term NFL Rookie is defined as a player who is in his first season of professional football and has not been on the roster of another professional football team for any regular-season or postseason games. A Rookie is designated by an "R" on NFL rosters. Players who have been active in another professional football league or players who have NFL experience, including either preseason training camp or being on an active roster for fewer than three regular-season or postseason games, are termed NFL First-Year Players. An NFL First-Year Player is designated by a "1" on NFL rosters. Thereafter, a player on an NFL active roster for at least three regular-season or postseason games is credited with an additional year of NFL playing experience.

NOTES

Mike Pope, tight ends; born March 15, 1942, Monroe, N.C., lives in River Vale, N.J. Quarterback Lenoir Rhyne 1962-64. No pro playing experience. College coach: Florida State 1970-74, Texas Tech 1975-77, Mississippi 1978-82. Pro coach: Joined Giants in 1983.

Mike Sweatman, assistant special teams; born October 23, 1946, Kansas City, Mo., lives in Wayne, N.J. Linebacker Kansas 1964-67. No pro playing experience. College coach: Kansas 1973-74, 1979-82, Tulsa 1977-78, Tennessee 1983. Pro coach: Minnesota Vikings 1984, joined Giants in 1985.

National Football Conference Eastern Division

Team Colors: Kelly Green, Silver, and White

Veterans Stadium
Broad Street and Pattison Avenue
Philadelphia, Pennsylvania 19148
Telephone: (215) 463-2500

Club Officials

Owner: Norman Braman
President-Chief Operating Officer: Harry Gamble
Vice President-Chief Financial Officer: Mimi Box
Vice President-Marketing and Development: Decker Uhlhorn
Vice President-Player Personnel: Bill Davis
Asst. to the President: George Azar, Patrick Forte
Director of Player Personnel: Joe Woolley
Scouts: Lou Blumling, King Hill, Tom Gamble
Director of Public Relations: Ron Howard
Asst. Director of Public Relations: Rich Burg
Associate Directors of Sales and Marketing: Jim Gallagher, Leslie Stephenson
Director of Administration: Vicki Chatley
Ticket Manager: Leo Carlin
Director of Penthouse Sales: Lou Scheinfeld
Asst. Director of Penthouse Sales: Ken Iman
Trainer: Otho Davis
Asst. Trainer: David Price
Player Relations Consultant: Lem Burnham, Ph.D.
Equipment Manager: Rusty Sweeney
Video Director: Mike Dougherty

Stadium: Veterans Stadium •
Capacity: 65,356
Broad Street and Pattison Avenue
Philadelphia, Pennsylvania 19148

Playing Surface: AstroTurf-8

Training Camp: West Chester University
West Chester, Pennsylvania 19382

1989 Schedule

Preseason

Aug. 6	vs. Cleveland at London	1:00*
Aug. 12	**Atlanta**	7:30
Aug. 20	vs. N.Y. Jets at Raleigh, N.C.	8:00
Aug. 26	**Pittsburgh**	7:30
Sept. 2	at Miami	9:00

*P.M. Eastern Time

Regular Season

Sept. 10	**Seattle**	4:00
Sept. 17	at Washington	1:00
Sept. 24	**San Francisco**	1:00
Oct. 2	at Chicago (Monday)	8:00
Oct. 8	**New York Giants**	1:00
Oct. 15	at Phoenix	1:00
Oct. 22	**Los Angeles Raiders**	1:00
Oct. 29	at Denver	2:00
Nov. 5	at San Diego	1:00
Nov. 12	**Washington**	1:00
Nov. 19	**Minnesota**	1:00
Nov. 23	at Dallas (Thanksgiving)	3:00
Dec. 3	at New York Giants	1:00
Dec. 10	**Dallas**	1:00
Dec. 18	at New Orleans (Monday)	8:00
Dec. 24	**Phoenix**	1:00

Eagles Coaching History

(312-401-24)

1933-35	Lud Wray	9-21-1
1936-40	Bert Bell	10-44-2
1941-50	Earle (Greasy) Neale*	66-44-5
1951	Alvin (Bo) McMillin**	2-0-0
1951	Wayne Millner	2-8-0
1952-55	Jim Trimble	25-20-3
1956-57	Hugh Devore	7-16-1
1958-60	Lawrence (Buck) Shaw	20-16-1
1961-63	Nick Skorich	15-24-3
1964-68	Joe Kuharich	28-41-1
1969-71	Jerry Williams***	7-22-2
1971-72	Ed Khayat	8-15-2
1973-75	Mike McCormack	16-25-1
1976-82	Dick Vermeil	57-51-0
1983-85	Marion Campbell****	17-29-1
1985	Fred Bruney	1-0-0
1986-88	Buddy Ryan	22-25-1

*Co-coach with Walt Kiesling in Philadelphia-Pittsburgh merger in 1943
**Retired after two games in 1951
***Released after three games in 1971
****Released after 15 games in 1985

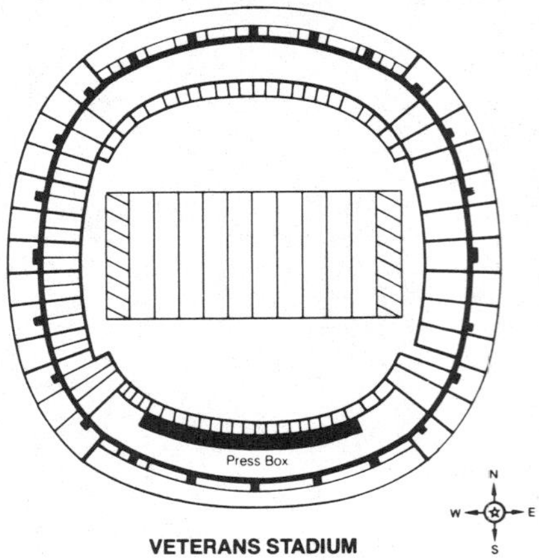

VETERANS STADIUM

Record Holders

Individual Records—Career

Category	Name	Performance
Rushing (Yds.)	Wilbert Montgomery, 1977-1984	6,538
Passing (Yds.)	Ron Jaworski, 1977-1986	26,963
Passing (TDs)	Ron Jaworski, 1977-1986	175
Receiving (No.)	Harold Carmichael, 1971-1983	589
Receiving (Yds.)	Harold Carmichael, 1971-1983	8,978
Interceptions	Bill Bradley, 1969-1976	34
Punting (Avg.)	Joe Muha, 1946-1950	42.9
Punt Return (Avg.)	Steve Van Buren, 1944-1951	13.9
Kickoff Return (Avg.)	Steve Van Buren, 1944-1951	26.7
Field Goals	Paul McFadden, 1984-87	91
Touchdowns (Tot.)	Harold Carmichael, 1971-1983	79
Points	Bobby Walston, 1951-1962	881

Individual Records—Single Season

Category	Name	Performance
Rushing (Yds.)	Wilbert Montgomery, 1979	1,512
Passing (Yds.)	Randall Cunningham, 1988	3,808
Passing (TDs)	Sonny Jurgensen, 1961	32
Receiving (No.)	Keith Jackson, 1988	81
Receiving (Yds.)	Mike Quick, 1983	1,409
Interceptions	Bill Bradley, 1971	11
Punting (Avg.)	Joe Muha, 1948	47.2
Punt Return (Avg.)	Steve Van Buren, 1944	15.3
Kickoff Return (Avg.)	Al Nelson, 1972	29.1
Field Goals	Paul McFadden, 1984	30
Touchdowns (Tot.)	Steve Van Buren, 1945	18
Points	Paul McFadden, 1984	116

Individual Records—Single Game

Category	Name	Performance
Rushing (Yds.)	Steve Van Buren, 11-27-49	205
Passing (Yds.)	Bobby Thomason, 11-18-53	437
Passing (TDs)	Adrian Burk, 10-17-54	*7
Receiving (No.)	Don Looney, 12-1-40	14
Receiving (Yds.)	Tommy McDonald, 12-10-60	237
Interceptions	Russ Craft, 9-24-50	*4
Field Goals	Tom Dempsey, 11-12-72	6
Touchdowns (Tot.)	Many times Last time by Wilbert Montgomery, 10-7-79	4
Points	Bobby Walston, 10-17-54	25

*NFL Record

1988 Team Record

Preseason (2-2)

Date	Result		Opponents
8/6	W	23-12	N.Y. Jets
8/14	L	16-21	at Pittsburgh
8/20	L	21-24	New England
8/25	W	27- 9	at Detroit
		87-66	

Regular Season (10-6)

Date	Result		Opponents	Att.
9/4	W	41-14	at Tampa Bay	43,502
9/11	L	24-28	Cincinnati	66,459
9/18	L	10-17	at Washington	53,920
9/25	L	21-23	at Minnesota	56,012
10/2	W	32-23	Houston	64,692
10/10	W	24-13	N.Y. Giants	63,736
10/16	L	3-19	at Cleveland	78,787
10/23	W	24-23	Dallas	66,309
10/30	L	24-27	Atlanta	60,091
11/6	W	30-24	L.A. Rams	65,624
11/13	W	27-26	at Pittsburgh	46,026
11/20	W	23-17	at N.Y. Giants (OT)	43,621
11/27	W	31-21	Phoenix	57,918
12/4	L	19-20	Washington	65,947
12/10	W	23-17	at Phoenix	54,832
12/18	W	23- 7	at Dallas	46,131

(OT) Overtime

Postseason (0-1)

Date	Result		Opponent	Att.
12/31	L	12-20	at Chicago	65,534

Score by Periods

Eagles	76	131	65	101	6	—	379
Opponents	111	47	73	88	0	—	319

Attendance

Home 510,776 Away 422,831 Total 933,607
Single-game home record, 72,111 (11-1-81)
Single-season home record, 557,325 (1980)

1988 Team Statistics

	Eagles	Opp.
Total First Downs	318	311
Rushing	105	85
Passing	179	199
Penalty	34	27
Third Down: Made/Att.	92/246	76/226
Fourth Down: Made/Att.	8/12	10/19
Total Net Yards	5430	5799
Avg. Per Game	339.4	362.4
Total Plays	1102	1086
Avg. Per Play	4.9	5.3
Net Yards Rushing	1945	1652
Avg. Per Game	121.6	103.3
Total Rushes	464	466
Net Yards Passing	3485	4147
Avg. Per Game	217.8	259.2
Sacked/Yards Lost	57/442	42/296
Gross Yards	3927	4443
Att./Completions	581/309	578/309
Completion Pct.	53.2	53.5
Had Intercepted	17	32
Punts/Avg.	104/39.7	85/37.8
Net Punting Avg.	34.3	32.4
Penalties/Yards Lost	115/907	115/897
Fumbles/Ball Lost	29/9	28/12
Touchdowns	44	37
Rushing	17	11
Passing	25	23
Returns	2	3
Avg. Time of Possession	31:09	28:51

1988 Individual Statistics

Scoring	TD R	TD P	TD Rt	PAT	FG	Saf	TP
Zendejas, Dall.-Phil.	0	0	0	35/36	20/27	0	95
Zendejas, Phil.	0	0	0	30/31	19/24	0	87
Byars	6	4	0	0/0	0/0	0	60
Carter	0	6	1	0/0	0/0	0	42
Cunningham	6	0	0	0/0	0/0	0	36
Kei. Jackson	0	6	0	0/0	0/0	0	36
Toney	4	1	0	0/0	0/0	0	30
Quick	0	4	0	0/0	0/0	0	24
Dorsey	0	0	0	9/9	4/7	0	21
Johnson	0	2	0	0/0	0/0	0	12
Simmons	0	0	1	0/0	0/0	1	8
Garrity	0	1	0	0/0	0/0	0	6
Giles	0	1	0	0/0	0/0	0	6
Hoage	1	0	0	0/0	0/0	0	6
Dawson	0	0	0	3/3	0/1	0	3
Jenkins	0	0	0	0/0	0/0	1	2
Eagles	17	25	2	42/43	23/32	2	379
Opponents	11	23	3	35/37	20/29	1	319

Passing	Att.	Comp.	Yds.	Pct.	TD	Int.	Tkld.	Rate
Cunningham	560	301	3808	53.8	24	16	57/442	77.6
Cavanaugh	16	7	101	43.8	1	1	0/0	59.6
Teltschik	3	1	18	33.3	0	0	0/0	54.9
Byars	2	0	0	0.0	0	0	0/0	39.6
Eagles	581	309	3927	53.2	25	17	57/442	76.7
Opponents	578	309	4443	53.5	23	32	42/296	68.9

Rushing	Att.	Yds.	Avg.	LG	TD
Cunningham	93	624	6.7	33t	6
Byars	152	517	3.4	52	6
Toney	139	502	3.6	20	4
Haddix	57	185	3.2	15	0
Hoage	1	38	38.0	38t	1
Teltschik	2	36	18.0	23	0
Tautalatasi	14	28	2.0	9	0
Abercrombie	5	14	2.8	5	0
Carter	1	1	1.0	1	0
Eagles	464	1945	4.2	52	17
Opponents	466	1652	3.5	65	11

Receiving	No.	Yds.	Avg.	LG	TD
Kei. Jackson	81	869	10.7	41	6
Byars	72	705	9.8	37t	4
Carter	39	761	19.5	80t	6
Toney	34	256	7.5	24	1
Quick	22	508	23.1	55t	4
Johnson	19	417	21.9	54	2
Garrity	17	208	12.2	20	1
Haddix	12	82	6.8	14	0
Giles	6	57	9.5	17	1
Tautalatasi	5	48	9.6	21	0
Konecny	1	18	18.0	18	0
Abercrombie	1	−2	−2.0	−2	0
Eagles	309	3927	12.7	80t	25
Opponents	309	4443	14.4	93t	23

Interceptions	No.	Yds.	Avg.	LG	TD
Hoage	8	116	14.5	38	0
Allen	5	76	15.2	21	0
Hopkins	5	21	4.2	11	0
Joyner	4	96	24.0	30	0
Frizzell	3	19	6.3	13	0
Waters	3	19	6.3	14	0
Young	2	5	2.5	5	0
Everett	1	0	0.0	0	0
Brown	1	−5	−5.0	−5	0
Bell	0	24	—	24	0
Eagles	32	371	11.6	38	0
Opponents	17	98	5.8	29	0

Punting	No.	Yds.	Avg.	In 20	LG
Cunningham	3	167	55.7	0	58
Teltschik	98	3958	40.4	28	70
Eagles	104	4125	39.7	28	70
Opponents	85	3209	37.8	17	56

Punt Returns	No.	FC	Yds.	Avg.	LG	TD
Konecny	33	25	233	7.1	24	0
Eagles	33	25	233	7.1	24	0
Opponents	47	27	393	8.4	68	0

Kickoff Returns	No.	Yds.	Avg.	LG	TD
Beals	34	625	18.4	32	0
Konecny	17	276	16.2	25	0
Abercrombie	5	87	17.4	31	0
Byars	2	20	10.0	14	0
Jenkins	1	20	20.0	20	0
Bartlett*	0	0	—	0	0
Eagles	59	1028	17.4	32	0
Opponents	63	1266	20.1	73	0

*one fair catch

Sacks	No.
White	18.0
Simmons	8.0
Brown	5.0
Joyner	3.5
Hoage	2.0
Pitts	1.5
Bartlett	1.0
Golic	1.0
Reichenbach	1.0
Bell	0.5
Waters	0.5
Eagles	42.0
Opponents	57.0

1989 Draft Choices

Round	Name	Pos.	College
2.	Jessie Small	LB	Eastern Kentucky
3.	Robert Drummond	RB	Syracuse
	Britt Hager	LB	Texas
6.	Heath Sherman	RB	Texas A&I

Philadelphia Eagles 1989 Veteran Roster

No.	Name	Pos.	Ht.	Wt.	Birth-date	NFL Exp.	College	Hometown	How Acq.	'88 Games/ Starts
32	Abercrombie, Walter	RB	6-0	210	9/26/59	8	Baylor	Waco, Tex.	FA-'88	5/0
72	Alexander, David	C-G	6-3	282	7/28/64	3	Tulsa	Broken Arrow, Okla.	D5-'87	16/12
21	Allen, Eric	CB	5-10	188	11/22/65	2	Arizona State	San Diego, Calif.	D2-'88	16/16
58	†Allert, Ty	LB	6-2	238	7/23/63	4	Texas	Rosenberg, Tex.	W(SD)-'87	10/0
87	Bailey, Eric	TE	6-5	245	5/12/63	2	Kansas State	Fort Worth, Tex.	FA-'87	0*
63	Baker, Ron	G	6-4	275	11/19/54	12	Oklahoma State	Emerson, Ind.	T(Balt)-'80	9/7
49	Bell, Todd	S	6-1	215	11/28/58	8	Ohio State	Middletown, Ohio	FA-'88	16/16
99	Brown, Jerome	DT	6-2	295	2/4/65	3	Miami	Brooksville, Fla.	D1-'87	16/15
51	Butcher, Paul	LB	6-0	230	11/8/63	4	Wayne State	Dearborn, Mich.	FA(Det)-'89#	16/0*
41	Byars, Keith	RB	6-1	238	10/14/63	4	Ohio State	Dayton, Ohio	D1-'86	16/16
80	Carter, Cris	WR	6-3	198	11/25/65	3	Ohio State	Middletown, Ohio	SD4-'87	16/16
6	Cavanaugh, Matt	QB	6-2	210	10/27/56	12	Pittsburgh	Youngstown, Ohio	T(SF)-'86	5/0
12	Cunningham, Randall	QB	6-4	203	3/27/63	5	Nevada-Las Vegas	Santa Barbara, Calif.	D2-'85	16/16
78	†Darwin, Matt	T	6-4	275	3/11/63	4	Texas A&M	Spring, Tex.	D4-'86	16/16
56	Evans, Byron	LB	6-2	235	2/23/64	3	Arizona	Phoenix, Ariz.	D4-'87	16/5
77	Evans, Donald	DE	6-2	258	3/14/64	2	Winston-Salem State	Kernsville, N.C.	FA-'88	5/0
42	Everett, Eric	CB	5-10	170	7/13/66	2	Texas Tech	Daingerfield, Tex.	D5-'88	16/1
33	†Frizzell, William	S	6-3	206	9/8/62	6	North Carolina Central	Greenville, N.C.	FA-'86	16/0
86	Garrity, Gregg	WR	5-10	175	11/24/60	7	Penn State	Bradford Woods, Pa.	W(Pitt)-'84	9/4
83	Giles, Jimmie	TE	6-3	245	11/8/54	13	Alcorn State	Greenville, Miss.	T(Det)-'87	16/1
90	†Golic, Mike	DT	6-5	275	12/12/62	4	Notre Dame	Cleveland, Ohio	FA-'87	12/1
95	Harris, Al	LB	6-5	265	12/31/56	10	Arizona State	Bangor, Me.	FA(Chi)-'89#	16/14*
73	Heller, Ron	T	6-6	280	8/25/62	6	Penn State	East Meadow, N.Y.	T(Sea)-'88	15/15
22	Higgs, Mark	RB	5-7	200	4/11/66	2	Kentucky	Owensboro, Ky.	FA(Dall)-'89#	5/0*
34	Hoage, Terry	S	6-3	201	4/11/62	6	Georgia	Huntsville, Tex.	FA-'86	16/0
84	Holloway, Derek	WR	5-8	162	1/17/61	3	Arkansas	Palmyra, N.J.	FA-'89	0*
48	Hopkins, Wes	S	6-1	215	9/26/61	6	Southern Methodist	Birmingham, Ala.	D2a-'83	16/16
88	Jackson, Keith	TE	6-2	250	4/19/65	2	Oklahoma	Little Rock, Ark.	D1-'88	16/15
46	Jenkins, Izel	CB	5-10	191	5/27/64	2	North Carolina State	Wilson, N.C.	D11-'88	16/0
53	†Jiles, Dwayne	LB	6-4	245	11/23/61	5	Texas Tech	Linden, Tex.	D5-'85	16/0
85	Johnson, Ron	WR	6-3	190	9/21/58	5	Long Beach State	Monterey, Calif.	FA-'88	10/4
59	Joyner, Seth	LB	6-2	248	11/18/64	4	Texas-El Paso	Spring Valley, N.Y.	D8-'86	16/16
97	Klingel, John	DE	6-3	270	12/21/63	3	Eastern Kentucky	Cardington, Ohio	FA-'87	16/0
89	Little, David	TE	6-2	230	4/18/61	6	Middle Tennessee State	Fresno, Calif.	FA-'85	10/0
74	†Pitts, Mike	DT	6-5	277	9/25/60	7	Alabama	Baltimore, Md.	T(Atl)-'87	16/16
82	†Quick, Mike	WR	6-2	195	5/14/59	8	North Carolina State	Richmond, N.C.	D1-'82	8/8
66	Reeves, Ken	T-G	6-5	270	10/4/61	5	Texas A&M	Pittsburg, Tex.	D6-'86	15/1
55	†Reichenbach, Mike	LB	6-2	235	9/14/61	6	East Stroudsburg	Bethlehem, Pa.	FA-'84	16/11
50	Rimington, Dave	C	6-3	285	5/22/60	7	Nebraska	Omaha, Neb.	FA-'88	16/16
79	Schad, Mike	G	6-5	290	10/2/63	2	Queen's College (Canada)	Bellville, Ontario	FA(Rams)-'89#	6/0*
96	Simmons, Clyde	DE	6-6	275	8/4/64	4	Western Carolina	Wilmington, N.C.	D9-'86	16/16
68	Singletary, Reggie	G-T	6-3	285	1/17/64	4	North Carolina State	Whiteville, N.C.	D12a-'86	16/9
65	Solt, Ron	G	6-3	288	5/19/62	5	Maryland	Wilkes-Barre, Pa.	T(Ind)-'88	1/0
61	Tamburello, Ben	G-C	6-3	278	9/9/64	2	Auburn	Birmingham, Ala.	D3-'87	16/4
10	Teltschik, John	P	6-2	210	3/8/64	4	Texas	Kerrville, Tex.	W(Chi)-'86	16/0
25	Toney, Anthony	RB	6-0	227	9/23/62	4	Texas A&M	Salinas, Calif.	D2a-'86	15/13
20	†Waters, Andre	S	5-11	199	3/10/62	6	Cheyney	Pahokee, Fla.	FA-'84	16/16
92	White, Reggie	DE	6-5	285	12/19/61	5	Tennessee	Chattanooga, Tenn.	SD1-'85	16/16
8	Zendejas, Luis	K	5-9	170	10/22/61	3	Arizona State	Chino, Calif.	FA-'88	14/0*

* Bailey missed '88 season due to injury; Butcher played 16 games with Detroit in '88; Harris played 16 games with Chicago; Higgs played 5 games with Dallas; Holloway last active with Tampa Bay in '87; Schad played 6 games with L.A. Rams; Zendejas played 2 games with Dallas, 12 with Philadelphia.

† Option playout; subject to developments.

Plan B unconditional free agent.

Players lost through Plan B (6): DT-DE Doug Bartlett (GB; 10 games in '88), LB Scott Curtis (Den; 16), RB Michael Haddix (GB; 16), WR Kenny Jackson (Hou; 7), RB-KR Mark Konecny (NYJ; 16), CB-S Rob Sterling (NYJ; 0).

Also played with Eagles in '88—WR-KR Shawn Beals (13 games), K Dale Dawson (1), K Dean Dorsey (3), DE Jonathan Dumbauld (1), G Adam Schreiber (6), RB Junior Tautalatasi (10), CB Roynell Young (15).

COACHING STAFF

Head Coach, Buddy Ryan

Pro Career: In 1988, Ryan's third season in Philadelphia, the Eagles won the NFC East with a 10-6 mark. Ryan was named head coach of the Eagles on January 29, 1986, after eight seasons as the defensive coordinator of the Chicago Bears. An NFL assistant coach for 18 years, Ryan has been on the staffs of three Super Bowl teams: Jets, 1968; Vikings, 1976; and Bears, 1985. He served as defensive line coach under Bud Grant with the Minnesota Vikings in 1976-77 before joining Chicago. From 1968-75, he was on the defensive staff of the New York Jets under coach Weeb Ewbank. In Ryan's eight seasons as defensive coordinator with Chicago, his defenses ranked among the NFL's top 10 six times. He devised the "46 defense" with its multiple variations of alignments and coverages. Career record: 22-25-1.

Background: Ryan was a four-year letterman at Oklahoma State from 1952-55 as an offensive guard. While serving in the U.S. Army in Korea, Ryan played on the Fourth Army championship team in Japan. He served as an assistant at the University of Buffalo from 1961-65, Vanderbilt 1966, and the University of the Pacific 1967. Ryan has a master's degree in education from Middle Tennessee State.

Personal: Born James Ryan on February 17, 1934, Frederick, Okla. Buddy and his wife, Joan, live in Cherry Hill, N.J., and have three sons: Jimmy, Jr., Rex, and Robert.

Assistant Coaches

Dave Atkins, offensive backfield; born May 18, 1949, Victoria, Tex., lives in Marlton, N.J. Running back Texas-El Paso 1970-72. Pro running back San Francisco 49ers 1973, Honolulu Hawaiians (WFL) 1974, San Diego Chargers 1975. College coach: Texas-El Paso 1979-80, San Diego State 1981-85. Pro coach: Joined Eagles in 1986.

Tom Bettis, defensive backs; born March 17, 1933, Chicago, Ill., lives in Marlton, N.J. Linebacker-guard Purdue 1952-54. Linebacker Green Bay Packers 1955-61, Pittsburgh Steelers 1962, Chicago Bears 1963. Pro coach: Chicago Bears 1964-65 (scout), Kansas City Chiefs 1966-77, 1988, St. Louis Cardinals 1978-84, Cleveland Browns 1985, Houston Oilers 1986-87, joined Eagles in 1989.

Jeff Fisher, defensive coordinator/linebackers; born February 25, 1958, Culver City, Calif., lives in Voorhees, N.J. Defensive back Southern California 1978-80. Pro defensive back-punt returner Chicago Bears 1981-85. Pro coach: Joined Eagles in 1986.

Dale Haupt, defensive line; born April 12, 1929, Manitowoc, Wis., lives in Cherry Hill, N.J. Defensive lineman-linebacker Wyoming 1950-53. No pro playing experience. College coach: Tennessee 1960-63, Iowa State 1964-65, Richmond 1966-71, North Carolina State 1972-76, Duke 1977. Pro coach: Chicago Bears 1978-85, joined Eagles in 1986.

Ronnie Jones, strength and conditioning/assistant linebackers; born October 17, 1955, Dumas, Tex., lives in Cherry Hill, N.J. Running back Northwestern State (Okla.) 1974-77. College coach: Northeastern State (Okla.) 1979-83, Tulsa 1984, Arizona State 1985-86. Pro coach: Joined Eagles in 1987.

Dan Neal, assistant offensive line; born August 30, 1949, Corbin, Ky., lives in Cherry Hill, N.J. Center Kentucky 1970-72. Pro center Baltimore Colts 1973-74, Chicago Bears 1975-83. Pro coach: Joined Eagles in 1986.

Ted Plumb, assistant head coach-offense; born August 20, 1939, Reno, Nev., lives in Cherry Hill, N.J. Wide receiver Baylor 1960-61. Pro wide receiver Buffalo Bills 1962. College coach: Cerritos, Calif., J.C. 1966-67, Texas Christian 1968-70, Tulsa 1971, Kansas 1972-73. Pro coach: New York Giants 1974-76, Atlanta Falcons 1977-79, Chicago Bears 1980-85, joined Eagles in 1986.

Philadelphia Eagles 1989 First-Year Roster

Name	Pos.	Ht.	Wt.	Birth-date	College	Hometown	How Acq.
Bailey, David	DE-LB	6-4	240	9/3/65	Oklahoma State	Stillwater, Okla.	FA
Berardelli, Paul	G-C	6-2	276	11/19/67	Villanova	Scranton, Pa.	FA
Cephus, Marvin (1)	WK-KR	5-10	173	3/10/65	Tulane	Houston, Tex.	FA
Czechowicz, Joe	WR	6-1	190	10/11/67	Ursinus	Philadelphia, Pa.	FA
Dial, Alan (1)	S	6-1	188	2/2/65	UCLA	Anniston, Ala.	FA
Donaway, Jim	G	6-2	282	6/23/67	Villanova	Union, N.J.	FA
Drummond, Robert	RB	6-1	205	6/21/67	Syracuse	Jamesville, N.Y.	D3a
Edwards, Kevin	CB-S	6-0	187	10/21/64	Virginia	Hackensack, N.J.	FA
Gabbard, Steve	T-G	6-4	275	7/19/66	Florida State	Charlotte, N.C.	FA
Gardenhire, Al	WR	6-0	175	10/20/66	Fresno State	Lynwood, Calif.	FA
Gerhart, Tom	S	6-0	205	6/4/65	Ohio	Lebanon, Pa.	FA
Gilliam, Melvin	CB-S	6-0	175	12/4/66	Oklahoma State	Tulsa, Okla.	FA
Hager, Britt	LB	6-1	222	2/20/66	Texas	Odessa, Tex.	D3b
Hess, William	CB-S-WR	5-9	172	2/6/66	West Chester	Orefield, Pa.	FA
Hunsaker, Brian	DT-DE	6-5	265	1/8/64	Utah	Logan, Utah	FA
Ivery, Thai (1)	WR-KR	6-1	188	8/26/64	Nevada-Reno	Albany, Calif.	FA
Jones, Tyrone	S	6-4	223	11/9/66	Arkansas State	Ruston, La.	FA
Kaufusi, Steve (1)	DE	6-4	274	10/17/63	Brigham Young	Salt Lake City, Utah	D12-'88
Lilly, Sammy (1)	CB-S	5-9	178	2/12/65	Georgia Tech	Augusta, Ga.	FA
Loving, James (1)	WR	5-9	183	6/22/66	Wyoming	Chicago, Ill.	FA
Mack, Gerald	CB-S	6-1	180	9/26/67	N. Carolina Central	Charlotte, N.C.	FA
Makor, Jao	K	5-11	195	5/12/63	Tennessee State	Antioch, Tenn.	FA
McPherson, Don (1)	QB	6-1	193	4/2/65	Syracuse	Hempstead, N.Y.	D6a-'88
Moten, Ron (1)	LB	6-1	237	9/15/64	Florida	Clearwater, Fla.	D6a-'87
Nash, Mitch	RB	5-9	195	12/3/66	Oklahoma State	Stillwater, Okla.	FA
Niemela, Al	QB	6-1	205	12/7/66	West Chester	New Providence, N.J.	FA
Patchan, Matt (1)	T	6-4	270	8/11/65	Miami	Penn Hills, Pa.	D3-'88
Perry, Scott	K	6-0	190	3/21/67	Moravian	Clarks Summit, Pa.	FA
Powell, Gerone	CB-S	6-0	196	2/2/66	Cheyney	Pahokee, Fla.	FA
Powers, Todd	RB	6-2	228	6/12/66	California	Youngstown, Ohio	FA
Rankin, Steve	DT-DE	6-3	288	3/18/66	Southern Mississippi	Albemarle, N.C.	FA
Salamone, Tom	P	6-0	205	2/22/67	Hofstra	North Caldwell, N.J.	FA
Sapolu, Saute	DT-DE	6-3	255	8/22/65	Arizona State	Long Beach, Calif.	FA
Schuster, Joe (1)	DT	6-4	270	12/30/64	Iowa	Faribault, Minn.	D10-'88
Sherman, Heath	RB	6-0	190	3/27/67	Texas A&I	El Campo, Tex.	D6
Singletary, Vantz	LB	6-0	244	11/23/65	Kansas State	Houston, Tex.	FA
Small, Jessie	LB	6-3	239	11/30/66	Eastern Kentucky	Boston, Ga.	D2
Williams, Bob (1)	TE	6-3	250	9/22/63	Penn State	Easton, Pa.	FA
Williams, Henry (1)	WR-KR	5-6	185	5/31/62	East Carolina	Memphis, Tenn.	FA

The term NFL Rookie is defined as a player who is in his first season of professional football and has not been on the roster of another professional football team for any regular-season or postseason games. A Rookie is designated by an "R" on NFL rosters. Players who have been active in another professional football league or players who have NFL experience, including either preseason training camp or being on an active roster for fewer than three regular-season or postseason games, are termed NFL First-Year Players. An NFL First-Year Player is designated by a "1" on NFL rosters. Thereafter, a player on an NFL active roster for at least three regular-season or postseason games is credited with an additional year of NFL playing experience.

NOTES

Al Roberts, special teams; born January 6, 1944, Fresno, Calif., lives in Marlton, N.J. Running back Washington 1964-65, Puget Sound 1967-68. No pro playing experience. College coach: Washington 1977-82, Purdue 1986, Wyoming 1987. Pro coach: Los Angeles Express (USFL) 1983-84, Houston Oilers 1984-85, joined Eagles in 1988.

Bill Walsh, offensive line; born September 8, 1927, Phillipsburg, N.J., lives in Marlton, N.J. Center Notre Dame 1945-48. Pro center Pittsburgh Steelers 1949-54. College coach: Notre Dame 1955-58, Kansas State 1959. Pro coach: Dallas Texans-Kansas City Chiefs 1960-74, Atlanta Falcons 1975-82, Houston Oilers 1983-86, joined Eagles in 1987.

Doug Scovill, quarterbacks; born July 1, 1927, Anacortes, Wash., lives in Voorhees, N.J. Quarterback Stockton, Calif., J.C. and Pacific 1948-51. No pro playing experience. College coach: San Mateo, Calif., J.C. 1958-62 (head coach), Navy 1963-65, Pacific 1966-69 (head coach), Brigham Young 1976-77, 1979-80, San Diego State 1981-85 (head coach). Pro coach: San Francisco 49ers 1970-75, Chicago Bears 1978, joined Eagles in 1986.

PHOENIX CARDINALS

National Football Conference Eastern Division

Team Colors: Cardinal Red, Black, and White

P.O. Box 888
Phoenix, Arizona 85001-0888
Telephone: (602) 967-1010

Club Officials

President: William V. Bidwill
Vice President/General Manager: Larry Wilson
Vice President/Administration: Curt Mosher
Vice President/Communications: Terry Bledsoe
Secretary and General Counsel: Thomas J. Guilfoil
Treasurer: Charley Schlegel
Counsel: Bob Wallace
Director of Pro Personnel: Erik Widmark
Director of Player Personnel: George Boone
Public Relations Director: Paul Jensen
Media Coordinator: Greg Gladysiewski
Director of Community Relations: Adele Harris
Director of Marketing: Joe Castor
Ticket Manager: Steve Walsh
Trainer: John Omohundro
Assistant Trainers: Jim Shearer, Jeff Herndon
Equipment Manager: Mark Ahlemeier
Assistant Equipment Manager: Steve Christensen

Stadium: Sun Devil Stadium • **Capacity:** 72,000
Fifth Street
Tempe, Arizona 85287

Playing Surface: Grass

Training Camp: Northern Arizona University
Flagstaff, Arizona 86011

1989 Schedule

Preseason

Aug. 11	**Seattle**	7:30
Aug. 21	at Los Angeles Rams	8:00
Aug. 26	**Cleveland**	6:00
Sept. 1	at San Diego	7:00

Regular Season

Sept. 10	at Detroit	1:00
Sept. 17	at Seattle	1:00
Sept. 24	at New York Giants	1:00
Oct. 1	**San Diego**	1:00
Oct. 8	at Washington	4:00
Oct. 15	**Philadelphia**	1:00
Oct. 22	**Atlanta**	1:00
Oct. 29	at Dallas	12:00
Nov. 5	**New York Giants**	2:00
Nov. 12	**Dallas**	2:00
Nov. 19	at Los Angeles Rams	1:00
Nov. 26	**Tampa Bay**	2:00
Dec. 3	**Washington**	2:00
Dec. 10	at Los Angeles Raiders	1:00
Dec. 16	**Denver** (Saturday)	2:00
Dec. 24	at Philadelphia	1:00

Cardinals Coaching History

Chicago 1920-59
St. Louis 1960-87
(361-471-39)

1920-22	John (Paddy) Driscoll	17-8-4
1923-24	Arnold Horween	13-8-1
1925-26	Norman Barry	16-8-2
1927	Guy Chamberlin	3-7-1
1928	Fred Gillies	1-5-0
1929	Dewey Scanlon	6-6-1
1930	Ernie Nevers	5-6-2
1931	LeRoy Andrews*	0-1-0
1931	Ernie Nevers	5-3-0
1932	Jack Chevigny	2-6-2
1933-34	Paul Schissler	6-15-1
1935-38	Milan Creighton	16-26-4
1939	Ernie Nevers	1-10-0
1940-42	Jimmy Conzelman	8-22-3
1943-45	Phil Handler**	1-29-0
1946-48	Jimmy Conzelman	27-10-0
1949	Phil Handler-Buddy Parker***	2-4-0
1949	Raymond (Buddy) Parker	4-1-1
1950-51	Earl (Curly) Lambeau****	7-15-0
1951	Phil Handler-Cecil Isbell#	1-1-0
1952	Joe Kuharich	4-8-0
1953-54	Joe Stydahar	3-20-1
1955-57	Ray Richards	14-21-1
1958-61	Frank (Pop) Ivy##	17-29-2
1961	Chuck Drulis-Ray Prochaska-Ray Willsey###	2-0-0
1962-65	Wally Lemm	27-26-3
1966-70	Charley Winner	35-30-5
1971-72	Bob Hollway	8-18-2
1973-77	Don Coryell	42-29-1
1978-79	Bud Wilkinson####	9-20-0
1979	Larry Wilson	2-1-0
1980-85	Jim Hanifan	39-50-1
1986-88	Gene Stallings	18-28-1

*Resigned after one game in 1931
**Co-coach with Walt Kiesling in Chicago Cardinals-Pittsburgh merger in 1944
***Co-coaches for first six games in 1949
****Resigned after 10 games in 1951
#Co-coaches
##Resigned after 12 games in 1961
###Co-coaches
####Released after 13 games in 1979

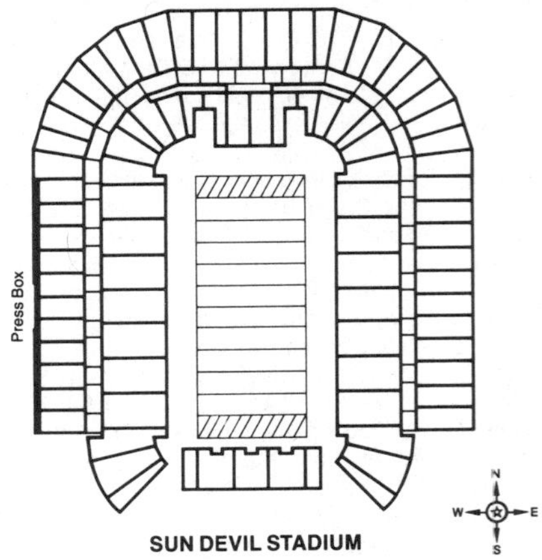

SUN DEVIL STADIUM

Record Holders

Individual Records—Career

Category	Name	Performance
Rushing (Yds.)	Ottis Anderson, 1979-1986	7,999
Passing (Yds.)	Jim Hart, 1966-1983	34,639
Passing (TDs)	Jim Hart, 1966-1983	209
Receiving (No.)	Jackie Smith, 1963-1977	480
Receiving (Yds.)	Jackie Smith, 1963-1977	7,918
Interceptions	Larry Wilson, 1960-1972	52
Punting (Avg.)	Jerry Norton, 1959-1961	44.9
Punt Return (Avg.)	Charley Trippi, 1947-1955	13.7
Kickoff Return (Avg.)	Ollie Matson, 1952, 1954-58	28.5
Field Goals	Jim Bakken, 1962-1978	282
Touchdowns (Tot.)	Sonny Randle, 1959-1966	60
Points	Jim Bakken, 1962-1978	1,380

Individual Records—Single Season

Category	Name	Performance
Rushing (Yds.)	Ottis Anderson, 1979	1,605
Passing (Yds.)	Neil Lomax, 1984	4,614
Passing (TDs)	Charley Johnson, 1963	28
	Neil Lomax, 1984	28
Receiving (No.)	J.T. Smith, 1987	91
Receiving (Yds.)	Roy Green, 1984	1,555
Interceptions	Bob Nussbaumer, 1949	12
Punting (Avg.)	Jerry Norton, 1960	45.6
Punt Return (Avg.)	John (Red) Cochran, 1949	20.9
Kickoff Return (Avg.)	Ollie Matson, 1958	35.5
Field Goals	Jim Bakken, 1967	27
Touchdowns (Tot.)	John David Crow, 1962	17
Points	Jim Bakken, 1967	117
	Neil O'Donoghue, 1984	117

Individual Records—Single Game

Category	Name	Performance
Rushing (Yds.)	John David Crow, 12-18-60	203
Passing (Yds.)	Neil Lomax, 12-16-84	468
Passing (TDs)	Jim Hardy, 10-2-50	6
	Charley Johnson, 9-26-65	6
	Charley Johnson, 11-2-69	6
Receiving (No.)	Sonny Randle, 11-4-62	16
Receiving (Yds.)	Sonny Randle, 11-4-62	256
Interceptions	Bob Nussbaumer, 11-13-49	*4
	Jerry Norton, 11-20-60	*4
Field Goals	Jim Bakken, 9-24-67	*7
Touchdowns (Tot.)	Ernie Nevers, 11-28-29	*6
Points	Ernie Nevers, 11-28-29	*40

*NFL Record

1988 Team Record

Preseason (1-3)

Date	Result		Opponents
8/4	L	7-21	at Seattle
8/12	L	28-33	New Orleans
8/21	L	16-19	Minnesota (OT)
8/25	W	41-21	Kansas City
		92-94	

Regular Season (7-9)

Date	Result		Opponents	Att.
9/4	L	14-21	at Cincinnati	50,404
9/12	L	14-17	Dallas	67,139
9/18	W	30-24	at Tampa Bay	35,034
9/25	W	30-21	Washington	61,973
10/2	W	41-27	at L.A. Rams	49,830
10/9	W	31-14	Pittsburgh	53,278
10/16	L	17-33	at Washington	54,402
10/23	L	21-29	Cleveland	61,261
10/30	W	16-10	at Dallas	42,196
11/6	W	24-23	San Francisco	64,544
11/13	W	24-17	N.Y. Giants	65,324
11/20	L	20-38	at Houston	43,843
11/27	L	21-31	at Philadelphia	57,918
12/4	L	7-44	at N.Y. Giants	73,438
12/10	L	17-23	Philadelphia	54,832
12/18	L	17-26	Green Bay	44,586

(OT) Overtime

Score by Periods

Cardinals	67	114	51	112	0	—	344
Opponents	101	106	84	107	0	—	398

Attendance

Home 472,937 Away 407,065 Total 880,002
Single-game home record, 67,139 (9-12-88)
Single-season home record, 472,937 (1988)

1988 Team Statistics

	Cardinals	Opp.
Total First Downs	336	301
Rushing	122	111
Passing	195	170
Penalty	19	20
Third Down: Made/Att.	92/230	75/210
Fourth Down: Made/Att.	12/20	5/10
Total Net Yards	5807	5169
Avg. Per Game	362.9	323.1
Total Plays	1102	1014
Avg. Per Play	5.3	5.1
Net Yards Rushing	2027	1925
Avg. Per Game	126.7	120.3
Total Rushes	480	467
Net Yards Passing	3780	3244
Avg. Per Game	236.3	202.8
Sacked/Yards Lost	60/411	39/295
Gross Yards	4191	3539
Att./Completions	562/322	508/264
Completion Pct.	57.3	52.0
Had Intercepted	19	16
Punts/Avg.	80/40.3	83/41.1
Net Punting Avg.	32.9	33.1
Penalties/Yards Lost	99/790	103/770
Fumbles/Ball Lost	34/16	27/13
Touchdowns	44	51
Rushing	15	19
Passing	26	30
Returns	3	2
Avg. Time of Possession	31:27	28:33

1988 Individual Statistics

Scoring	TD R	TD P	TD Rt	PAT	FG	Saf	TP
Del Greco	0	0	0	42/44	12/21	0	78
Ferrell	7	2	0	0/0	0/0	0	54
Green	0	7	0	0/0	0/0	0	42
S. Mitchell	4	1	0	0/0	0/0	0	30
J. Smith	0	5	0	0/0	0/0	0	30
Awalt	0	4	0	0/0	0/0	0	24
Novacek	0	4	0	0/0	0/0	0	24
E. Jones	0	3	0	0/0	0/0	0	18
Jordan	3	0	0	0/0	0/0	0	18
Junior	0	0	1	0/0	0/0	0	6
Lomax	1	0	0	0/0	0/0	0	6
Mack	0	0	1	0/0	0/0	0	6
Saddler	0	0	1	0/0	0/0	0	6
Harvey	0	0	0	0/0	0/0	1	2
Cardinals	15	26	3	42/44	12/21	1	344
Opponents	19	30	2	47/51	13/22	3	398

Passing	Att.	Comp.	Yds.	Pct.	TD	Int.	Tkld.	Rate
Lomax	443	255	3395	57.6	20	11	46/315	86.7
Stoudt	113	63	747	55.8	6	8	13/85	64.3
Tupa	6	4	49	66.7	0	0	1/11	91.7
Cardinals	562	322	4191	57.3	26	19	60/411	82.2
Opponents	508	264	3539	52.0	30	16	39/295	81.0

Rushing	Att.	Yds.	Avg.	LG	TD
Ferrell	202	924	4.6	47	7
S. Mitchell	164	726	4.4	47	4
Jordan	61	160	2.6	12	3
Stoudt	14	57	4.1	14	0
Lomax	17	55	3.2	13	1
Wolfley	9	43	4.8	20	0
Horne	3	20	6.7	20	0
J. Smith	1	15	15.0	15	0
Novacek	1	10	10.0	10	0
Del Greco	1	8	8.0	8	0
Jeffery	3	8	2.7	9	0
Green	4	1	0.3	18	0
Cardinals	480	2027	4.2	47	15
Opponents	467	1925	4.1	52	19

Receiving	No.	Yds.	Avg.	LG	TD
J. Smith	83	986	11.9	29	5
Green	68	1097	16.1	52	7
Awalt	39	454	11.6	52t	4
Novacek	38	569	15.0	42t	4
Ferrell	38	315	8.3	30	2
S. Mitchell	25	214	8.6	28	1
E. Jones	23	496	21.6	93t	3
Jordan	4	24	6.0	12	0
Wolfley	2	11	5.5	8	0
Moore	1	15	15.0	15	0
Holmes	1	10	10.0	10	0
Cardinals	322	4191	13.0	93t	26
Opponents	264	3539	13.4	61t	30

Interceptions	No.	Yds.	Avg.	LG	TD
Mack	3	33	11.0	12	0
Carter	3	0	0.0	0	0
McDonald	2	11	5.5	11	0
Lyles	2	0	0.0	0	0
Curtis	1	18	18.0	18	0
Le. Smith	1	15	15.0	15	0
Clasby	1	7	7.0	7	0
Junior	1	2	2.0	2	0
Young	1	2	2.0	2	0
R. Mitchell	1	0	0.0	0	0
Cardinals	16	88	5.5	18	0
Opponents	19	264	13.9	39	0

Punting	No.	Yds.	Avg.	In 20	LG
Horne	79	3228	40.9	16	66
Cardinals	80	3228	40.3	16	66
Opponents	83	3414	41.1	18	62

Punt Returns	No.	FC	Yds.	Avg.	LG	TD
Sikahema	33	8	341	10.3	28	0
J. Smith	17	2	119	7.0	15	0
Hunley	1	0	3	3.0	3	0
McAdoo	1	0	0	0.0	0	0
McDonald	0	1	0	—	0	0
Cardinals	52	11	463	8.9	28	0
Opponents	41	11	416	10.1	63t	1

Kickoff Returns	No.	Yds.	Avg.	LG	TD
Sikahema	23	475	20.7	39	0
McAdoo, T.B.-Phoe.	13	311	23.9	32	0
McAdoo, Phoe.	9	203	22.6	32	0
E. Jones	11	147	13.4	22	0
S. Mitchell	10	221	22.1	41	0
Clark	2	10	5.0	7	0
Ferrell	2	25	12.5	14	0
Jeffery	1	11	11.0	11	0
Phillips	1	4	4.0	4	0
Schillinger	1	10	10.0	10	0
Cardinals	60	1106	18.4	41	0
Opponents	65	1379	21.2	92t	1

Sacks	No.
Nunn	14.0
Harvey	6.0
Clasby	5.0
Alvord	2.0
Galloway	2.0
Junior	2.0
McDonald	2.0
Saddler	2.0
Bell	1.0
Curtis	1.0
Hunley	1.0
Noga	1.0
Cardinals	39.0
Opponents	60.0

1989 Draft Choices

Round	Name	Pos.	College
1.	Eric Hill	LB	Louisiana State
	Joe Wolf	G	Boston College
2.	Walter Reeves	TE	Auburn
3.	Mike Zandofsky	G	Washington
4.	Jim Wahler	DT	UCLA
5.	Richard Tardits	LB	Georgia
	David Edeen	DE	Wyoming
6.	Jay Taylor	DB	San Jose State
7.	Rickey Royal	DB	Sam Houston State
8.	John Burch	RB	Tennessee-Martin
9.	Kendall Trainor	K	Arkansas
10.	Chris Becker	P	Texas Christian
11.	Jeffrey Hunter	DE	Albany State, Ga.
12.	Todd Nelson	G	Wisconsin

Phoenix Cardinals 1989 Veteran Roster

No.	Name	Pos.	Ht.	Wt.	Birth-date	NFL Exp.	College	Hometown	How Acq.	'88 Games/ Starts
40	Adams, Michael	CB	5-10	195	4/5/64	3	Arkansas State	Cleveland, Miss.	FA(NO)-'89#	5/0*
60	Alvord, Steve	DT	6-4	272	10/2/64	3	Washington	Bellingham, Wash.	D8-'87	15/10
80	Awalt, Robert	TE	6-5	248	4/9/64	3	San Diego State	Sacramento, Calif.	D3a-'87	16/15
55	Bell, Anthony	LB	6-3	231	7/2/64	4	Michigan State	Miami, Fla.	D1-'86	16/16
82	Bellini, Mark	WR	5-11	185	1/19/64	3	Brigham Young	San Leandro, Calif.	FA(Ind)-'89#	15/0*
71	†Bostic, Joe	G	6-3	268	4/20/57	11	Clemson	Greensboro, N.C.	D3-'79	10/1
44	Brim, Michael	CB	6-0	186	1/23/66	2	Virginia Union	Danville, Va.	D4-'88	4/0
16	Camarillo, Rich	P	5-11	185	11/29/59	9	Washington	Pico Rivera, Calif.	FA-'89	9/0*
41	†Carter, Carl	CB	5-11	180	3/7/64	4	Texas Tech	Fort Worth, Tex.	D4-'86	16/16
34	Clark, Jessie	RB	6-0	233	1/3/60	7	Arkansas	Crossett, Ark.	FA-'88	4/0
79	Clasby, Bob	DT	6-5	260	9/28/60	4	Notre Dame	Milton, Mass.	FA-'86	16/16
94	Cooks, Rayford	DT	6-2	225	8/25/62	2	North Texas State	Houston, Tex.	FA-'89	0*
17	Del Greco, Al	K	5-10	191	3/2/62	6	Auburn	Coral Gables, Fla.	FA-'87	16/0
74	Dill, Scott	G	6-5	272	4/5/66	2	Memphis State	Birmingham, Ala.	D9-'88	13/0
31	Ferrell, Earl	RB	6-0	240	3/27/58	8	East Tennessee State	Halifax, Va.	D5-'82	16/16
65	†Galloway, David	DE	6-3	279	2/16/59	8	Florida	Brandon, Fla.	D2-'82	8/6
14	Garcia, Teddy	K	5-10	190	6/4/64	2	Northeast Louisiana	Lewisville, Tex.	FA(NE)-'89#	16/0*
81	Green, Roy	WR	6-0	195	6/30/57	11	Henderson State	Magnolia, Ark.	D1-'80	16/16
73	Hadd, Gary	DT	6-4	270	10/19/65	2	Minnesota	Burnsville, Minn.	FA(Det)-'89#	5/0*
56	Harvey, Ken	LB	6-2	225	5/6/65	2	California	Austin, Tex.	D1-'88	16/0
13	Hogeboom, Gary	QB	6-4	208	8/21/58	10	Central Michigan	Grand Rapids, Mich.	FA(Ind)-'89#	9/1*
83	Holmes, Don	WR	5-10	180	4/1/61	4	Mesa, Colo.	Grand Junction, Colo.	W(Ind)-'86	16/0
51	†Hunley, Ricky	LB	6-2	250	11/11/61	6	Arizona	Petersburg, Va.	T(Den)-'88	16/0
50	Jarostchuk, Ilia	LB	6-3	231	8/1/64	3	New Hampshire	Utica, N.Y.	FA-'89	6/0*
53	Jax, Garth	LB	6-2	222	9/16/63	4	Florida State	Houston, Tex.	FA(Dall)-'89#	16/2*
28	Jeffery, Tony	RB	5-11	208	7/8/64	2	Texas Christian	Gladewater, Tex.	D2-'88	3/0
86	Jones, Ernie	WR	5-11	186	12/15/64	2	Indiana	Elkhart, Ind.	D7-'88	16/0
59	Jones, Tyrone	LB	6-0	220	8/3/61	2	Southern University	St. Mary's, Ga.	FA-'88	1/0
32	Jordan, Tony	RB	6-2	220	5/5/65	2	Kansas State	Rochester, N.Y.	D5b-'88	9/2
57	Kauahi, Kani	C	6-2	273	9/6/59	7	Hawaii	Honolulu, Hawaii	FA(GB)-'89#	16/0*
70	Kennard, Derek	C-G	6-3	285	9/9/62	4	Nevada-Reno	Stockton, Calif.	SD2-'84	16/16
52	Kirk, Randy	LB	6-2	235	12/27/64	3	San Diego State	San Jose, Calif.	FA(SD)-'89#	16/0*
15	Lomax, Neil	QB	6-3	215	2/17/59	9	Portland State	Portland, Ore.	D2-'81	14/14
76	MacDonald, Mark	G-C	6-4	265	4/30/61	5	Boston College	West Roxbury, Mass.	FA-'88	1/0
47	Mack, Cedric	CB	6-0	194	9/14/60	7	Baylor	Freeport, Tex.	D2-'83	16/14
46	McDonald, Tim	CB-S	6-2	207	1/6/65	3	Southern California	Fresno, Calif.	D2-'87	16/15
54	McKenzie, Reggie	LB	6-1	235	2/8/63	5	Tennessee	Knoxville, Tenn.	FA(Raid)-'89	16/3*
95	McNanie, Sean	DE	6-5	270	9/9/61	7	San Diego State	Mundelein, Ill.	T(Buff)-'88	12/1
25	Mitchell, Roland	CB	5-11	180	3/15/64	3	Texas Tech	Bay City, Tex.	T(Buff)-'88	11/0
30	Mitchell, Stump	RB	5-9	188	3/15/59	9	Citadel	St. Mary's, Ga.	D9-'81	14/14
57	Noga, Niko	DE	6-1	235	3/2/62	6	Hawaii	Honolulu, Hawaii	D8-'84	16/16
85	†Novacek, Jay	TE	6-4	235	10/24/62	5	Wyoming	Gothenburg, Neb.	D6-'85	16/1
78	Nunn, Freddie Joe	DE	6-4	255	4/9/62	5	Mississippi	Louisville, Miss.	D1-'85	16/16
64	Peat, Todd	G	6-2	294	5/20/64	3	Northern Illinois	Champaign, Ill.	D11-'87	15/15
48	Phillips, Reggie	CB	5-10	175	12/29/60	5	Southern Methodist	Houston, Tex.	W(Chi)-'88	16/0
12	Prindle, Michael	K	5-9	163	11/12/63	2	Western Michigan	Grand Rapids, Mich.	FA-'89	0*
63	†Robbins, Tootie	T	6-5	302	6/2/58	8	East Carolina	Windsor, N.C.	D4-'82	15/15
72	Saddler, Rod	DE	6-5	276	9/26/65	3	Texas A&M	Atlanta, Ga.	D4-'87	16/15
87	Schillinger, Andy	WR	5-11	179	11/22/64	2	Miami, Ohio	Avon Lake, Ohio	D10-'88	3/0
67	†Sharpe, Luis	T	6-4	260	6/16/60	8	UCLA	Detroit, Mich.	D1-'82	16/16
36	Sikahema, Vai	RB-KR	5-9	191	8/29/62	4	Brigham Young	American Samoa	D10-'86	12/0
84	Smith, J.T.	WR	6-2	185	10/29/55	12	North Texas State	Leonard, Tex.	FA-'85	16/16
61	Smith, Lance	T-G	6-2	262	11/1/63	5	Louisiana State	Kannapolis, N.C.	D3-'85	16/16
19	Tupa, Tom	QB-P	6-4	220	9/6/66	2	Ohio State	Brecksville, Ohio	D3-'88	2/0
89	Walczak, Mark	TE	6-6	246	4/26/62	3	Arizona	Rochester, N.Y.	FA-'88	16/0
24	Wolfley, Ron	RB	6-0	222	10/14/62	5	West Virginia	Orchard Park, N.Y.	D4-'85	16/0
43	Young, Lonnie	S	6-1	182	7/18/63	5	Michigan State	Flint, Mich.	D12-'85	12/12
38	Zordich, Mike	S	5-11	207	10/12/63	3	Penn State	Youngstown, Ohio	FA(NYJ)-'89#	16/0*

* Adams played 5 games with New Orleans in '88; Bellini played 15 games with Indianapolis; Camarillo played 9 games with Rams; Cooks last active with Houston in '87; Garcia played 16 games with New England; Hadd played 5 games with Detroit; Hogeboom played 9 games with Indianapolis; Jarostchuk played 6 games with Miami; Jax played 16 games with Dallas; Kauahi played 16 games with Green Bay; Kirk played 16 games with San Diego; McKenzie played 16 games with Raiders; Prindle last active with Detroit in '87; Zordich played 16 games with N.Y. Jets.

† Option playout; subject to developments.

#Plan B unconditional free agent.

Players lost through Plan B (9): G-T Ray Brown (Wash; 15 games in '88), LB Wayne Davis (Rams; 16), DE Curtis Greer (Minn; 0), P Greg Horne (Wash; 16), LB E.J. Junior (Mia; 16), S Lester Lyles (SD; 6), T Mike Morris (Wash; 0); DE Colin Scotts (Hou; 0), G Mark Traynowicz (Sea; 5).

Also played with Cardinals in '88—TE Greg Baty (1 game), DT Mark Garalczyk (6), CB-S Greg Lasker (1), RB Derrick McAdoo (4), RB Ricky Moore (8), S Leonard Smith (3), QB Cliff Stoudt (16).

Coaching Staff

Head Coach, Gene Stallings

Pro Career: Named head coach on February 10, 1986. Became thirtieth head coach in the history of the franchise dating back to 1920. Defensive backfield coach with Dallas from 1972-85. No pro playing experience. Career record: 18-28-1.

Background: Played end at Texas A&M from 1954-57 and was All-Southwest Conference receiver at Texas A&M under Paul "Bear" Bryant and tri-captain on undefeated 1956 team. Coached in the collegiate ranks at Alabama 1958-64 and Texas A&M 1957, 1965-71 (head coach). Assistant under just two coaches in career: Bryant at Alabama, and Tom Landry at Dallas.

Personal: Born March 2, 1935, in Paris, Tex. Gene and his wife, Ruth Ann, live in Phoenix and have five children: Anna Lee, Laurie, John Mark, Jacklyn, and Martha Kate.

Assistant Coaches

Marv Braden, special teams; born January 25, 1938, Kansas City, Mo., lives in Phoenix. Linebacker Southwest Missouri State 1956-59. No pro playing experience. College coach: Parsons 1963-66, Northeast Missouri State 1967-68 (head coach), U.S. International 1969-72, Iowa State 1973, Southern Methodist 1974-75, Michigan State 1976. Pro coach: Denver Broncos 1977-80, San Diego Chargers 1981-85, joined Cardinals in 1986.

LeBaron Caruthers, strength and conditioning; born April 20, 1954, Nashville, Tenn., lives in Phoenix. Tackle East Carolina 1972-73. No pro playing experience. College coach: Auburn 1978-79, Southern Methodist 1980-81. Pro coach: New England Patriots 1982-84, joined Cardinals in 1986.

Jim Johnson, defensive line; born May 26, 1941, Maywood, Ill., lives in Phoenix. Quarterback Missouri 1959-62. Pro tight end Buffalo Bills 1963-64. College coach: Missouri Southern 1967-68 (head coach), Drake 1969-72, Indiana 1973-76, Notre Dame 1977-80. Pro coach: Oklahoma Outlaws (USFL) 1984, Jacksonville Bulls (USFL) 1985, joined Cardinals in 1986.

Hank Kuhlmann, running backs; born October 6, 1937, St. Louis, Mo., lives in Phoenix. Running back Missouri 1956-59. No pro playing experience. College coach: Missouri 1963-71, Notre Dame 1975-77. Pro coach: Green Bay Packers 1972-74, Chicago Bears 1978-82, Birmingham Stallions (USFL) 1983-85, joined Cardinals in 1986.

Leon McLaughlin, special assistant-quality control; born May 30, 1925, San Diego, Calif., lives in Phoenix. Center-linebacker UCLA 1946-49. Pro center Los Angeles Rams 1951-55. College coach: Washington State 1956, Stanford 1959-65, San Fernando Valley State 1969-70 (head coach). Pro coach: Pittsburgh Steelers 1966-68, Los Angeles Rams 1971-72, Detroit Lions 1973-74, Green Bay Packers 1975-76, New England Patriots 1977, joined Cardinals in 1978.

Mal Moore, receivers; born December 19, 1939, Dozier, Ala., lives in Phoenix. Quarterback-defensive back Alabama 1958-62. No pro playing experience. College coach: Montana State 1963, Alabama 1964-82, Notre Dame 1983-85. Pro coach: Joined Cardinals in 1986.

Joe Pascale, linebackers; born April 4, 1946, New York, N.Y., lives in Phoenix. Linebacker Connecticut 1963-66. No pro playing experience. College coach: Connecticut 1967-68, Rhode Island 1969-73, Idaho State 1974-76 (head coach 1976), Princeton 1977-79. Pro coach: Montreal Alouettes (CFL) 1980-81, Ottawa Rough Riders (CFL) 1982-83, New Jersey Generals (USFL) 1984-85, joined Cardinals in 1986.

Jim Shofner, offensive coordinator; born December 18, 1935, Grapevine, Tex., lives in Phoenix. Running back Texas Christian 1955-57. Pro defensive back Cleveland Browns 1958-63. College coach: Texas Christian 1964-66, 1974-76 (head coach). Pro coach: San Francisco 49ers 1967-73, 1977, Cleveland Browns 1978-80, Houston Oilers 1981-82, Dallas Cowboys 1983-85, joined Cardinals in 1986.

Mike Solari, offensive line; born January 16, 1955, Daly City, Calif., lives in Phoenix. Offensive lineman San Diego State 1975-76. No pro playing experience. College coach: Mira Vista, Calif., J.C. 1977-78, U.S. International 1979, Boise State 1980, Cincinnati 1981-82, Kansas 1983-85, Pittsburgh 1986. Pro coach: Dallas Cowboys 1987-88, joined Cardinals in 1989.

Dennis Thurman, defensive backs; born April 14, 1956, Los Angeles, Calif., lives in Phoenix. Safety Southern California 1974-77. Pro defensive back Dallas Cowboys 1978-85, St. Louis Cardinals 1986. Pro coach: Joined Cardinals in 1988.

Phoenix Cardinals 1989 First-Year Roster

Name	Pos.	Ht.	Wt.	Birth-date	College	Hometown	How Acq.
Becker, Chris	P	6-1	192	9/6/66	Texas Christian	Taylor, Tex.	D10
Brown, Kevin (1)	K	6-0	183	1/11/63	West Texas State	Canyon, Tex.	FA
Burch, John	RB	5-10	200	1/4/66	Tennessee-Martin	St. Augustine, Fla.	D8
Carr, Lydell (1)	RB	6-0	226	5/27/65	Oklahoma	Enid, Okla.	FA
Edeen, David	DE	6-4	254	5/23/66	Wyoming	Cheyenne, Wyo.	D5b
Hill, Eric	LB	6-1	248	11/14/66	Louisiana State	Galveston, Tex.	D1a
Hunter, Jeff	DE	6-4	263	4/12/66	Albany State, Ga.	Augusta, Ga.	D11
Knight, Ryan (1)	RB	6-0	209	3/16/66	Southern California	Riverside, Calif.	FA
Marshall, Warren (1)	RB	6-0	216	7/24/64	James Madison	High Point, N.C.	FA
Nelson, Todd	G	6-5	289	3/23/66	Wisconsin	Madison, Wis.	D12
Reed, Harvey (1)	RB	5-11	181	9/12/65	Howard	Miami, Fla.	FA
Reeves, Walter	TE	6-3	251	12/15/65	Auburn	Eufaula, Ala.	D2
Royal, Rickey	CB	5-9	187	7/26/66	Sam Houston State	Gainesville, Tex.	D7
Tardits, Richard	LB	6-2	220	7/30/65	Georgia	Biarritz, France	D5a
Taylor, Jay	CB	5-9	174	11/8/67	San Jose State	San Diego, Calif.	D6
Trainor, Kendall	K	6-1	202	7/8/67	Arkansas	Fredonia, Kan.	D9
Treadwell, David (1)	K	6-2	166	2/27/65	Clemson	Columbia, S.C.	FA
Wahler, Jim	DT	6-3	259	7/29/66	UCLA	San Jose, Calif.	D4
Wolf, Joe	G	6-5	279	12/28/66	Boston College	Allentown, Pa.	D1b
Zandofsky, Mike	G-T	6-2	297	11/30/65	Washington	Corvallis, Ore.	D3

The term NFL Rookie is defined as a player who is in his first season of professional football and has not been on the roster of another professional football team for any regular-season or postseason games. A Rookie is designated by an "R" on NFL rosters. Players who have been active in another professional football league or players who have NFL experience, including either preseason training camp or being on an active roster for fewer than three regular-season or postseason games, are termed NFL First-Year Players. An NFL First-Year Player is designated by a "1" on NFL rosters. Thereafter, a player on an NFL active roster for at least three regular-season or postseason games is credited with an additional year of NFL playing experience.

NOTES

SAN FRANCISCO 49ERS

National Football Conference Western Division

Team Colors: Forty Niners Gold and Scarlet

4949 Centennial Boulevard
Santa Clara, California 95054
Telephone: (408) 562-4949

Club Officials

Owner/President: Edward J. DeBartolo, Jr.
Executive Vice President-Football Operations: Bill Walsh
Executive Vice President-Front Office/ League Relations: Carmen Policy
Vice President-Football Administration: John McVay
Vice President-Business Operations & C.F.O: Keith Simon
Administrative Assistant: Norb Hecker
Director of Pro Scouting: Allan Webb
Director of College Scouting: Tony Razzano
Director of Public Relations: Jerry Walker
Director of Publications: Rodney Knox
Director of Marketing/Promotions: Laurie Welling
Coordinator of Football Operations: Neal Dahlen
Ticket Manager: Ken Dargel
Director of Stadium Operations: Murlan (Mo) Fowell
Video Director: Robert Yanagi
Trainer: Lindsy McLean
Equipment Manager: Bronco Hinek

Stadium: Candlestick Park • **Capacity:** 65,701
San Francisco, California 94124

Playing Surface: Grass

Training Camp: Sierra Community College
Rocklin, California 95677

1989 Schedule

Preseason

Aug. 5	vs. L.A. Rams at Tokyo	10:00*
Aug. 12	at Los Angeles Raiders	6:00
Aug. 19	**Denver**	6:00
Aug. 23	**San Diego**	6:00
Sept. 1	at Seattle	6:00

*P.M. Eastern Time

Regular Season

Sept. 10	at Indianapolis	12:00
Sept. 17	at Tampa Bay	4:00
Sept. 24	at Philadelphia	1:00
Oct. 1	**Los Angeles Rams**	1:00
Oct. 8	**New Orleans**	1:00
Oct. 15	at Dallas	12:00
Oct. 22	**New England**	1:00
Oct. 29	at New York Jets	4:00
Nov. 6	at New Orleans (Monday)	8:00
Nov. 12	**Atlanta**	1:00
Nov. 19	**Green Bay**	1:00
Nov. 27	**N.Y. Giants** (Monday)	6:00
Dec. 3	at Atlanta	1:00
Dec. 11	at L.A. Rams (Monday)	6:00
Dec. 17	**Buffalo**	1:00
Dec. 24	**Chicago**	1:00

49ers Coaching History

(282-263-13)

1950-54	Lawrence (Buck) Shaw	33-25-2
1955	Norman (Red) Strader	4-8-0
1956-58	Frankie Albert	19-17-1
1959-63	Howard (Red) Hickey*	27-27-1
1963-67	Jack Christiansen	26-38-3
1968-75	Dick Nolan	56-56-5
1976	Monte Clark	8-6-0
1977	Ken Meyer	5-9-0
1978	Pete McCulley**	1-8-0
1978	Fred O'Connor	1-6-0
1979-88	Bill Walsh	102-63-1

*Resigned after three games in 1963
**Released after nine games in 1978

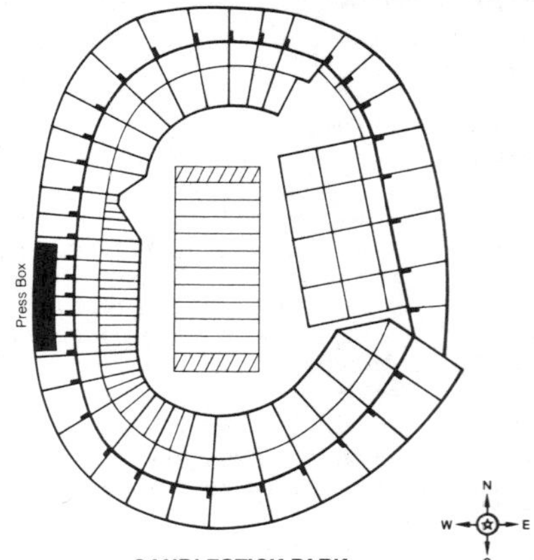

CANDLESTICK PARK

Record Holders

Individual Records—Career

Category	Name	Performance
Rushing (Yds.)	Joe Perry, 1950-1960, 1963	7,344
Passing (Yds.)	John Brodie, 1957-1973	31,548
Passing (TDs)	John Brodie, 1957-1973	214
Receiving (No.)	Dwight Clark, 1979-1987	506
Receiving (Yds.)	Dwight Clark, 1979-1987	6,750
Interceptions	Jimmy Johnson, 1961-1976	47
Punting (Avg.)	Tommy Davis, 1959-1969	44.7
Punt Return (Avg.)	Manfred Moore, 1974-75	14.7
Kickoff Return (Avg.)	Abe Woodson, 1958-1964	29.4
Field Goals	Ray Wersching, 1977-1987	190
Touchdowns (Tot.)	Ken Willard, 1965-1973	61
Points	Ray Wersching, 1977-1987	979

Individual Records—Single Season

Category	Name	Performance
Rushing (Yds.)	Roger Craig, 1988	1,502
Passing (Yds.)	Joe Montana, 1983	3,910
Passing (TDs)	Joe Montana, 1987	31
Receiving (No.)	Roger Craig, 1985	92
Receiving (Yds.)	Jerry Rice, 1986	1,570
Interceptions	Dave Baker, 1960	10
	Ronnie Lott, 1986	10
Punting (Avg.)	Tommy Davis, 1965	45.8
Punt Return (Avg.)	Dana McLemore, 1982	22.3
Kickoff Return (Avg.)	Joe Arenas, 1953	34.4
Field Goals	Mike Cofer, 1988	27
Touchdowns (Tot.)	Jerry Rice, 1987	23
Points	Jerry Rice, 1987	138

Individual Records—Single Game

Category	Name	Performance
Rushing (Yds.)	Delvin Williams, 10-31-76	194
Passing (Yds.)	Joe Montana, 11-17-86	441
Passing (TDs)	John Brodie, 11-23-65	5
	Steve Spurrier, 11-19-72	5
	Joe Montana, 10-6-85	5
Receiving (No.)	Many times	12
	Last time by Roger Craig, 12-1-86	
Receiving (Yds.)	Jerry Rice, 12-9-85	241
Interceptions	Dave Baker, 12-4-60	*4
Field Goals	Ray Wersching, 10-16-83	6
Touchdowns (Tot.)	Billy Kilmer, 10-15-61	4
Points	Gordy Soltau, 10-27-51	26

*NFL Record

1988 Team Record

Preseason (3-2)

Date	Result		Opponents
7/31	L	21-27	vs. Miami at London, Eng.
8/6	W	24-10	L.A. Raiders
8/13	L	24-34	at Denver
8/20	W	34-27	at San Diego
8/26	W	27-21	Seattle
		130-119	

Regular Season (10-6)

Date	Result		Opponents	Att.
9/4	W	34-33	at New Orleans	66,357
9/11	W	20-17	at N.Y. Giants	75,943
9/18	L	17-34	Atlanta	60,168
9/25	W	38- 7	at Seattle	62,382
10/2	W	20-13	Detroit	58,285
10/9	L	13-16	Denver (OT)	61,711
10/16	W	24-21	at L.A. Rams	65,450
10/24	L	9-10	at Chicago	65,293
10/30	W	24-21	Minnesota	60,738
11/6	L	23-24	at Phoenix	64,544
11/13	L	3- 9	L.A. Raiders	54,448
11/21	W	37-21	Washington	59,268
11/27	W	48-10	at San Diego	51,484
12/4	W	13- 3	at Atlanta	44,048
12/11	W	30-17	New Orleans	62,977
12/18	L	16-38	L.A. Rams	62,444

(OT) Overtime

Postseason (3-0)

Date	Result		Opponent	Att.
1/1	W	34- 9	Minnesota	61,848
1/8	W	28- 3	at Chicago	66,946
1/22	W	20-16	Cincinnati	75,129

Score by Periods

49ers	54	140	95	80	0	—	369
Opponents	31	92	77	91	3	—	294

Attendance

Home 480,039 Away 495,501 Total 975,540
Single-game home record, 63,509 (12-14-87)
Single-season home record, 480,039 (1988)

1988 Team Statistics

	49ers	Opp.
Total First Downs	326	277
Rushing	141	90
Passing	167	160
Penalty	18	27
Third Down: Made/Att.	94/225	88/225
Fourth Down: Made/Att.	5/10	6/16
Total Net Yards	5900	4575
Avg. Per Game	368.8	285.9
Total Plays	1076	1013
Avg. Per Play	5.5	4.5
Net Yards Rushing	2523	1588
Avg. Per Game	157.7	99.3
Total Rushes	527	441
Net Yards Passing	3377	2987
Avg. Per Game	211.1	186.7
Sacked/Yards Lost	47/298	42/297
Gross Yards	3675	3284
Att./Completions	502/293	530/292
Completion Pct.	58.4	55.1
Had Intercepted	14	22
Punts/Avg.	80/38.7	86/41.0
Net Punting Avg.	32.1	32.7
Penalties/Yards Lost	115/986	76/603
Fumbles/Ball Lost	27/12	30/16
Touchdowns	41	34
Rushing	18	8
Passing	21	25
Returns	2	1
Avg. Time of Possession	30:31	29:29

1988 Individual Statistics

Scoring	TD R	TD P	TD Rt	PAT	FG	Saf	TP
Cofer	0	0	0	40/41	27/38	0	121
Craig	9	1	0	0/0	0/0	0	60
Rice	1	9	0	0/0	0/0	0	60
Taylor	0	2	2	0/0	0/0	0	24
Frank	0	3	0	0/0	0/0	0	18
Montana	3	0	0	0/0	0/0	0	18
Wilson	0	3	0	0/0	0/0	0	18
DuBose	2	0	0	0/0	0/0	0	12
Jones	0	2	0	0/0	0/0	0	12
Rathman	2	0	0	0/0	0/0	0	12
McIntyre	0	1	0	0/0	0/0	0	6
Young	1	0	0	0/0	0/0	0	6
Haley	0	0	0	0/0	0/0	1	2
49ers	18	21	2	40/41	27/38	1	369
Opponents	8	25	1	34/34	18/24	1	294

Passing	Att.	Comp.	Yds.	Pct.	TD	Int.	Tkld.	Rate
Montana	397	238	2981	59.9	18	10	34/223	87.9
Young	101	54	680	53.5	3	3	13/75	72.2
Rice	3	1	14	33.3	0	1	0/0	9.7
Sydney	1	0	0	0.0	0	0	0/0	39.6
49ers	502	293	3675	58.4	21	14	47/298	83.5
Opponents	530	292	3284	55.1	25	22	42/297	72.2

Rushing	Att.	Yds.	Avg.	LG	TD
Craig	310	1502	4.8	46t	9
Rathman	102	427	4.2	26	2
Young	27	184	6.8	49t	1
Montana	38	132	3.5	15	3
DuBose	24	116	4.8	37t	2
Rice	13	107	8.2	29	1
Sydney	9	50	5.6	13	0
Flagler	3	5	1.7	4	0
Helton	1	0	0.0	0	0
49ers	527	2523	4.8	49t	18
Opponents	441	1588	3.6	36t	8

Receiving	No.	Yds.	Avg.	LG	TD
Craig	76	534	7.0	22	1
Rice	64	1306	20.4	96t	9
Rathman	42	382	9.1	24	0
Wilson	33	405	12.3	31	3
Frank	16	195	12.2	38	3
Taylor	14	325	23.2	73t	2
Heller	14	140	10.0	22	0
Greer	8	120	15.0	31	0
Jones	8	57	7.1	18t	2
DuBose	6	57	9.5	13	0
Flagler	4	72	18.0	57	0
Chandler	4	33	8.3	9	0
Sydney	2	18	9.0	9	0
McIntyre	1	17	17.0	17t	1
Nicholas	1	14	14.0	14	0
49ers	293	3675	12.5	96t	21
Opponents	292	3284	11.2	67t	25

Interceptions	No.	Yds.	Avg.	LG	TD
McKyer	7	11	1.6	7	0
Lott	5	59	11.8	44	0
Fuller	4	18	4.5	10	0
Holmoe	2	0	0.0	0	0
Wright	2	−2	−1.0	0	0
Turner	1	2	2.0	2	0
Carter	1	0	0.0	0	0
49ers	22	88	4.0	44	0
Opponents	14	185	13.2	47t	1

Punting	No.	Yds.	Avg.	In 20	LG
Helton	78	3069	39.3	22	53
Runager	1	24	24.0	0	24
49ers	80	3093	38.7	22	53
Opponents	86	3522	41.0	21	57

Punt Returns	No.	FC	Yds.	Avg.	LG	TD
Taylor	44	7	556	12.6	95t	2
Chandler	6	5	28	4.7	13	0
Griffin	4	3	28	7.0	10	0
49ers	54	15	612	11.3	95t	2
Opponents	47	10	426	9.1	41	0

Kickoff Returns	No.	Yds.	Avg.	LG	TD
DuBose	32	608	19.0	44	0
Taylor	12	225	18.8	29	0
Rodgers	6	98	16.3	24	0
Craig	2	32	16.0	17	0
Sydney	1	8	8.0	8	0
Thomas	1	5	5.0	5	0
Wilson	1	2	2.0	2	0
49ers	55	978	17.8	44	0
Opponents	73	1362	18.7	40	0

Sacks	No.
Haley	11.5
Carter	6.5
Roberts	6.0
Stubbs	6.0
Holt	5.0
Fagan	3.0
Ellison	1.0
Fuller	1.0
Griffin	1.0
Walter	1.0
49ers	42.0
Opponents	47.0

1989 Draft Choices

Round	Name	Pos.	College
1.	Keith DeLong	LB	Tennessee
2.	Wesley Walls	TE	Mississippi
3.	Keith Henderson	RB	Georgia
4.	Mike Barber	WR	Marshall
5.	Johnny Jackson	DB	Houston
6.	Steve Hendrickson	LB	California
9.	Rudy Harmon	LB	Louisiana State
10.	Andy Sinclair	C	Stanford
11.	Jim Bell	RB	Boston College
	Norm McGee	WR	North Dakota
12.	Antonio Goss	LB	North Carolina

San Francisco 49ers 1989 Veteran Roster

No.	Name	Pos.	Ht.	Wt.	Birth-date	NFL Exp.	College	Hometown	How Acq.	'88 Games/ Starts
79	Barton, Harris	T	6-4	280	4/19/64	3	North Carolina	Atlanta, Ga.	D1a-'87	16/16
65	†Bregel, Jeff	G	6-4	280	5/1/64	3	Southern California	Granada Hills, Calif.	D2-'87	13/0
31	Brooks, Chet	CB	5-11	191	1/1/66	2	Texas A&M	Dallas, Tex.	D11-'88	10/0
95	Carter, Michael	NT	6-2	285	10/29/60	6	Southern Methodist	Dallas, Tex.	D5a-'84	16/16
66	Cochran, Mark	T	6-5	285	5/6/63	2	Baylor	Waco, Tex.	FA-'88	0*
6	Cofer, Mike	K	6-1	190	2/19/62	2	North Carolina State	Charlotte, N.C.	FA-'88	16/0
69	Collie, Bruce	G-T	6-6	275	6/27/62	5	Texas-Arlington	San Antonio, Tex.	D5-'85	15/5
33	Craig, Roger	RB	6-0	224	7/10/60	7	Nebraska	Davenport, Iowa	D2-'83	16/15
25	DuBose, Doug	RB	5-11	190	3/14/64	2	Nebraska	Uncasville, Conn.	FA-'87	14/0
50	Ellison, Riki	LB	6-2	225	8/15/60	7	Southern California	Tucson, Ariz.	D5-'83	13/13
75	†Fagan, Kevin	DE	6-3	260	4/25/63	3	Miami	Lake Worth, Fla.	D4c-'86	14/14
55	†Fahnhorst, Jim	LB	6-4	230	11/8/58	6	Minnesota	St. Cloud, Minn.	FA-'84	16/3
32	Flagler, Terrence	RB	6-0	200	9/24/64	3	Clemson	New York, N.Y.	D1b-'87	3/0
49	Fuller, Jeff	S	6-2	216	8/8/62	6	Texas A&M	Dallas, Tex.	D5b-'84	16/16
83	Greer, Terry	WR	6-1	192	9/27/57	4	Alabama State	Santa Clara, Calif.	FA-'88	10/0
29	†Griffin, Don	CB	6-0	176	3/17/64	4	Middle Tennessee State	Pelham, Ga.	D6-'86	10/6
54	Hadley, Ron	LB	6-2	240	11/9/63	3	Washington	Edmonds, Wash.	FA-'87	3/0
94	Haley, Charles	LB-DE	6-5	230	1/6/64	4	James Madison	Campbell County, Va.	D4a-'86	16/14
9	Helton, Barry	P	6-3	205	1/2/66	2	Colorado	Simia, Colo.	D4-'88	15/0
46	Holmoe, Tom	S	6-2	195	3/17/60	6	Brigham Young	La Crescenta, Calif.	D4-'83	16/4
78	Holt, Pierce	NT	6-4	280	1/1/62	2	Angelo State	Houston, Tex.	D2b-'88	9/0
84	Jones, Brent	TE	6-4	230	2/12/63	3	Santa Clara	San Jose, Calif.	FA-'87	11/0
57	Kennedy, Sam	LB	6-3	235	7/10/64	2	San Jose State	Aptos, Calif.	FA-'86	16/0
67	Kugler, Pete	DE	6-4	255	3/9/59	7	Penn State	Cherry Hill, N.J.	FA-'86	6/1
42	Lott, Ronnie	S	6-0	200	5/8/59	9	Southern California	Rialto, Calif.	D1-'81	13/12
62	†McIntyre, Guy	G	6-3	265	2/17/61	6	Georgia	Thomasville, Ga.	D3-'84	16/12
22	†McKyer, Tim	CB	6-0	174	9/5/63	3	Texas-Arlington	Port Arthur, Tex.	D3b-'86	16/16
16	Montana, Joe	QB	6-2	195	6/11/56	11	Notre Dame	New Eagle, Pa.	D3-'79	14/13
20	†Nixon, Tory	CB	5-11	186	2/24/62	5	San Diego State	Eugene, Ore.	T(Wash)-'85	6/0
64	O'Connor, Paul	G	6-3	258	11/7/62	2	Miami	Miami, Fla.	FA-'88	0*
77	†Paris, Bubba	T	6-6	306	10/6/60	6	Michigan	Louisville, Ky.	D2-'82	16/1
15	Paye, John	QB	6-3	205	3/30/65	2	Stanford	Atherton, Calif.	D10-'87	0*
26	Pollard, Darryl	CB	5-11	187	5/11/65	3	Weber State	Foster City, Calif.	FA-'88	14/0
44	Rathman, Tom	RB	6-1	232	10/7/62	4	Nebraska	Grand Island, Neb.	D3a-'86	16/16
80	Rice, Jerry	WR	6-2	200	10/13/62	5	Mississippi Valley State	Crawford, Miss.	D1-'85	16/16
91	†Roberts, Larry	DE	6-3	275	6/2/63	4	Alabama	Dothan, Ala.	D2-'86	16/16
35	Rodgers, Del	RB-KR	5-10	203	6/22/60	5	Utah	Salinas, Calif.	FA-'88	1/0
53	Romanowski, Bill	LB	6-4	231	4/2/66	2	Boston College	Vernon, Conn.	D3-'88	16/8
61	Sapolu, Jessie	G-C	6-4	260	3/10/61	4	Hawaii	Honolulu, Hawaii	D11-'83	16/16
88	Sherrard, Mike	WR	6-2	187	6/21/63	2	UCLA	Los Angeles, Calif.	FA(Dall)-'89#	0*
72	Stover, Jeff	DE	6-5	275	5/22/58	8	Oregon	Corning, Calif.	FA-'82	7/0
96	Stubbs, Daniel	DE	6-4	260	1/3/65	2	Miami	Red Bank, N.J.	D2a-'88	16/1
24	Sydney, Harry	RB	6-0	217	6/26/59	3	Kansas	Fayetteville, N.C.	FA-'87	16/0
10	Sweeney, Kevin	QB	6-0	193	11/16/63	3	Fresno State	Fresno, Calif.	FA(Dall)-'89#	3/2*
66	Tausch, Terry	G	6-4	278	2/5/59	8	Texas	Plano, Tex.	FA(Minn)-'89#	16/16
82	Taylor, John	WR	6-1	185	3/31/62	3	Delaware State	Pennsauken, N.J.	D3c-'86	12/4
60	Thomas, Chuck	C	6-3	280	12/24/60	4	Oklahoma	Houston, Tex.	FA-'87	16/0
23	Tillman, Spencer	RB	5-11	206	4/21/64	3	Oklahoma	Houston, Tex.	FA(Hou)-'89#	16/0*
58	Turner, Keena	LB	6-2	222	10/22/58	10	Purdue	Chicago, Ill.	D2-'80	11/8
74	†Wallace, Steve	T	6-5	276	12/27/64	4	Auburn	Atlanta, Ga.	D4b-'86	16/15
99	†Walter, Michael	LB	6-3	238	11/30/60	7	Oregon	Eugene, Ore.	FA-'84	16/16
51	Washington, Chris	LB	6-4	240	3/6/62	7	Iowa State	Tampa, Fla.	FA(TB)-'89#	16/1*
81	Williams, Jamie	TE	6-4	245	2/25/60	7	Nebraska	Houston, Tex.	FA(Hou)-'89#	16/16*
85	Wilson, Mike	WR	6-3	215	12/19/58	9	Washington State	Los Angeles, Calif.	FA-'81	16/11
21	†Wright, Eric	CB	6-1	185	4/18/59	8	Missouri	St. Louis, Mo.	D2b-'81	15/10
8	Young, Steve	QB	6-2	200	10/11/61	5	Brigham Young	Salt Lake City, Utah	T(TB)-'87	11/3

* Cochran and O'Connor missed '88 season due to injury; Paye active for 3 games but did not play; Sherrard last active with Dallas in '86; Sweeney played 3 games with Dallas; Tillman played 16 games with Houston; Washington played 16 games with Tampa Bay; Williams played 16 games with Houston.

† Option playout; subject to developments.

\# Plan B unconditional free agent.

Retired—Randy Cross, 13-year guard-center, 16 games in '88; John Frank, 5-year tight end, 7 games in '88.

Players lost through Plan B (2): S Greg Cox (NYG; 15 games in '88), TE Ron Heller (Atl; 16).

Also played with 49ers in '88—RB Steve Bartalo (active for 1 game but did not play), DE Dwaine Board (3), WR Wes Chandler (4), NT Kevin Lilly (9), NT Doug Mikolas (1), WR Calvin Nicholas (7), P Max Runager (1), QB Todd Santos (active for 1 game but did not play).

COACHING STAFF

Head Coach, George Seifert

Pro Career: Named 49ers' head coach January 26, 1989, after serving as team's defensive coordinator since 1983. Joined 49ers as secondary coach in 1980. In only his second season in the pro ranks, San Francisco had the number-two defense in the NFL and a Super Bowl XVI title, despite three rookies starting in the defensive backfield. Finished 1987 with the top-ranked defense in the NFL and a 13-2 record. In 1988, San Francisco's defense ranked third en route to the Super Bowl XXIII title.

Background: Linebacker at University of Utah (1960-62). No pro playing experience. Served a six-month tour of duty with the U.S. Army following graduation from Utah. Returned to Utah as a graduate assistant in 1964. Named head coach at Westminster College in Salt Lake City in 1965. Assistant at Iowa 1966, Oregon 1967-71, and Stanford 1972-74. Left Stanford to become head coach at Cornell 1975-76. Joined Bill Walsh's staff at Stanford in 1977 and helped Cardinal to a two-year mark of 17-7, including victories in the Sun and Bluebonnet Bowls. Received B.A. in zoology from Utah in 1963 and masters in physical education in 1966.

Personal: Born January 22, 1940, in San Francisco, Calif. He and his wife, Linda, have two children—Eve and Jason—and live in Sunnyvale, Calif.

Assistant Coaches

Jerry Attaway, conditioning; born January 3, 1946, Susanville, Calif., lives in San Carlos, Calif. Defensive back Yuba, Calif., J.C. 1964-65, Cal-Davis 1967. No pro playing experience. College coach: Cal-Davis 1970-71, Idaho 1972-74, Utah State 1975-77, Southern California 1978-82. Pro coach: Joined 49ers in 1983.

Mike Holmgren, offensive coordinator/quarterbacks; born June 15, 1948, San Francisco, Calif., lives in San Jose, Calif. Quarterback Southern California 1966-69. No pro playing experience. College coach: San Francisco State 1981, Brigham Young 1982-85. Pro coach: Joined 49ers in 1986.

Al Lavan, running backs; born September 13, 1946, Pierce, Fla., lives in San Jose, Calif. Defensive back Colorado State 1965-67. Pro defensive back Philadelphia Eagles 1968, Atlanta Falcons 1969-70. College coach: Colorado State 1972, Louisville 1973, Iowa State 1974, Georgia Tech 1977-78, Stanford 1979. Pro coach: Atlanta Falcons 1975-76, Dallas Cowboys 1980-88, joined 49ers in 1989.

Sherman Lewis, receivers; born June 29, 1942, Louisville, Ky., lives in Sunnyvale, Calif. Running back Michigan State 1961-63. Pro running back Toronto Argonauts (CFL) 1964-65, New York Jets 1966. College coach: Michigan State 1969-82. Pro coach: Joined 49ers in 1983.

John Marshall, defensive line; born October 2, 1945, Arroyo Grande, Calif., lives in Santa Clara, Calif. Linebacker Washington State 1964. No pro playing experience. College coach: Oregon 1970-76, Southern California 1977-79. Pro coach: Green Bay Packers 1980-82, Atlanta Falcons 1983-85, Indianapolis Colts 1986-88, joined 49ers in 1989.

Bobb McKittrick, offensive line; born December 29, 1935, Baker, Ore., lives in San Mateo, Calif. Guard Oregon State 1955-57. No pro playing experience. College coach: Oregon State 1961-64, UCLA 1965-70. Pro coach: Los Angeles Rams 1971-72, San Diego Chargers 1974-78, joined 49ers in 1979.

Bill McPherson, defensive coordinator; born October 24, 1931, Santa Clara, Calif., lives in San Jose, Calif. Tackle Santa Clara 1950-52. No pro playing experience. College coach: Santa Clara 1963-74, UCLA 1975-77. Pro coach: Philadelphia Eagles 1978, joined 49ers in 1979.

Ray Rhodes, defensive backfield; born October 20, 1950, Mexia, Tex., lives in Fremont, Calif. Running back-wide receiver Texas Christian 1969-70, Tulsa 1972-73. Pro defensive back New York Giants 1974-79, San Francisco 49ers 1980. Pro coach: Joined 49ers in 1981.

Lynn Stiles, special teams/tight ends; born April 12, 1941, Kermit, Tex., lives in Sunnyvale, Calif. Guard Utah 1961-62. No pro playing experience. College coach: Utah 1963-65, Iowa 1966-70, UCLA 1971-75, San Jose State 1976-78 (head coach). Pro coach: Philadelphia Eagles 1979-85, joined 49ers in 1987.

Bob Zeman, linebackers; born February 22, 1937, Wheaton, Ill., lives in Santa Clara, Calif. Fullback/halfback Wisconsin 1957-59. Pro defensive back Los Angeles/San Diego Chargers 1960-61, 1965-66, Denver Broncos 1962-63. College coach: Northwestern 1968-69, Wisconsin 1970. Pro coach: Oakland Raiders 1971-77, 1984-86, Denver Broncos 1978-82, Buffalo Bills 1983, joined 49ers in 1989.

San Francisco 49ers 1989 First-Year Roster

Name	Pos.	Ht.	Wt.	Birth-date	College	Hometown	How Acq.
Bell, Jim	RB	6-0	205	6/24/65	Boston College	Madison, Conn.	D11a
Berg, Steve	DE	6-4	275	3/15/66	Gustavus Adolphus	Eden Prairie, Minn.	FA
Barber, Mike	WR	5-10	172	6/19/67	Marshall	Winfield, W. Va.	D4
Burman, Jon	T	6-6	300	6/17/66	Illinois	Carmel, Ind.	FA
Cannon, Willie	RB	6-1	212	9/28/64	Murray State	Murray, Ky.	FA
Clarkson, Larry	T	6-7	303	3/11/65	Montana	Abbotsford, Canada	FA
Cullity, Dave	T	6-7	275	6/15/64	Utah	Wooster, Ohio	FA
DeLong, Keith	LB	6-2	235	8/14/67	Tennessee	Knoxville, Tenn.	D1
Devine, Matt	LB	6-1	209	9/30/66	California-Davis	Davis, Calif.	FA
Evans, Vince	RB	5-11	225	9/8/63	North Carolina State	Fayetteville, N.C.	FA
Finch, Lonnie	CB	6-1	188	10/12/66	Oklahoma	Irving, Tex.	FA
Glasser, Jeff	DE	6-4	243	6/4/65	UCLA	Los Angeles, Calif.	FA
Goss, Antonio	LB	6-4	228	8/11/66	North Carolina	Randleman, N.C.	D12a
Haight, Dave	NT	6-2	279	4/11/66	Iowa	Dyersville, Iowa	FA
Harmon, Rudy	LB	6-1	230	10/6/65	Louisiana State	Beaumont, Tex.	D9
Harper, Glen	P	5-11	173	9/12/63	Washington State	Edmonton, Canada	FA
Harper, Robert	LB	6-2	242	10/6/65	Houston	Houston, Tex.	FA
Henderson, Keith	RB	6-1	220	8/4/66	Georgia	Cartersville, Ga.	D3
Hendrickson, Steve	LB	6-0	245	8/30/66	California	Napa, Calif.	D6
Hickerson, Eric	S	6-2	210	10/4/65	Indiana	New Albany, Ind.	FA
Hunter, John	LB	6-2	235	7/18/65	Bowling Green	Detroit, Mich.	FA
Jackson, Johnny	S	6-1	204	1/11/67	Houston	Harlingen, Tex.	D5a
Liggins, Guy	WR	6-2	200	6/4/66	San Jose State	San Jose, Calif.	FA
Malone, Art	CB	5-10	183	8/21/66	Washington	Ventura, Calif.	FA
Manu, Tika	DE	6-4	267	12/5/64	Utah	Salt Lake City, Utah	FA
McGee, Norm	WR	6-0	180	3/23/66	North Dakota	Milwaukee, Wis.	D11b
Morales, Marco	K	6-0	190	1/7/62	San Diego State	San Diego, Calif.	FA
O'Connor, Paul	G	6-3	258	11/7/62	Miami	Miami, Fla.	FA
Paye, John (1)	QB	6-3	205	3/30/65	Stanford	Atherton, Calif.	D10-'87
Sinclair, Andy	C	6-3	285	2/12/66	Stanford	Huntington Beach, Calif.	D10
Walls, Wesley	TE	6-5	246	2/26/66	Mississippi	Pontotic, Miss.	D2
Winfield, Earl	WR	6-0	185	8/8/61	North Carolina	Petersburg, Va.	FA
Wolfe, Mike	G	6-4	260	10/29/65	Oklahoma State	Miami, Okla.	FA

The term NFL Rookie is defined as a player who is in his first season of professional football and has not been on the roster of another professional football team for any regular-season or postseason games. A Rookie is designated by an "R" on NFL rosters. Players who have been active in another professional football league or players who have NFL experience, including either preseason training camp or being on an active roster for fewer than three regular-season or postseason games, are termed NFL First-Year Players. An NFL First-Year Player is designated by a "1" on NFL rosters. Thereafter, a player on an NFL active roster for at least three regular-season or postseason games is credited with an additional year of NFL playing experience.

NOTES

TAMPA BAY BUCCANEERS

National Football Conference Central Division

Team Colors: Florida Orange, White, and Red

One Buccaneer Place
Tampa, Florida 33607
Telephone: (813) 870-2700

Club Officials

Owner-President: Hugh F. Culverhouse
Vice President: Joy Culverhouse
Vice President-Head Coach: Ray Perkins
Vice President-Community Relations: Dr. Gay Culverhouse
Secretary-Treasurer: Ward Holland
Vice-President-Administration: Gen. William E. Klein
Assistant to the President: Phil Krueger
Director of Player Personnel: Jerry Angelo
Director of Pro Personnel: Ruston Webster
Director of Ticket Operations: Terry Wooten
Director of Public Relations: Rick Odioso
Director of Marketing & Advertising: Fred Doremus
Assistant Director-Media Relations: Mike McCall
Assistant Director-Special Events: Paul Royak
College Personnel: James Harris, Tom Heckert, Tim Ruskell, Jere Stripling
Controller: Joe Lucas
Trainer: Chris Smith
Assistant Trainer: Joe Joe Petrone
Equipment Manager: Frank Pupello
Assistant Equipment Manager: Carl Melchior
Video Director: Dave Levy
Assistant Video Director: Mike Perkins

Stadium: Tampa Stadium • **Capacity:** 74,315
North Dale Mabry
Tampa, Florida 33607

Playing Surface: Grass

Training Camp: University of Tampa
401 W. Kennedy Boulevard
Tampa, Florida 33606

1989 Schedule

Preseason

Aug. 12	**Houston**	7:00
Aug. 19	**Atlanta**	7:00
Aug. 26	at Indianapolis	7:30
Sept. 2	at Cleveland	7:00

Regular Season

Sept. 10	at Green Bay	12:00
Sept. 17	**San Francisco**	4:00
Sept. 24	**New Orleans**	1:00
Oct. 1	at Minnesota	12:00
Oct. 8	**Chicago**	1:00
Oct. 15	**Detroit**	1:00
Oct. 22	at Washington	1:00
Oct. 29	at Cincinnati	1:00
Nov. 5	**Cleveland**	1:00
Nov. 12	**Minnesota**	1:00
Nov. 19	at Chicago	12:00
Nov. 26	at Phoenix	2:00
Dec. 3	**Green Bay**	1:00
Dec. 10	at Houston	12:00
Dec. 17	at Detroit	1:00
Dec. 24	**Pittsburgh**	1:00

Buccaneers Coaching History

(58-141-1)

1976-84	John McKay	45-91-1
1985-86	Leeman Bennett	4-28-0
1987	Ray Perkins	9-22-0

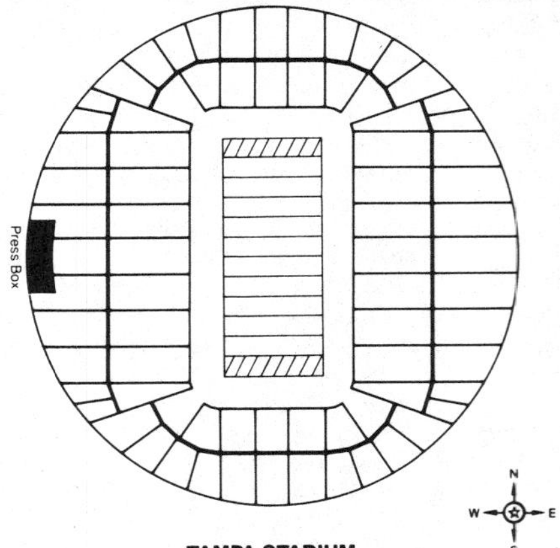

TAMPA STADIUM

Record Holders

Individual Records—Career

Category	Name	Performance
Rushing (Yds.)	James Wilder, 1981-88	5,713
Passing (Yds.)	Doug Williams, 1978-1982	12,648
Passing (TDs)	Doug Williams, 1978-1982	73
Receiving (No.)	James Wilder, 1981-88	394
Receiving (Yds.)	Kevin House, 1980-86	4,928
Interceptions	Cedric Brown, 1977-1984	29
Punting (Avg.)	Frank Garcia, 1983-87	41.1
Punt Return (Avg.)	Bobby Futrell, 1986-88	8.7
Kickoff Ret. (Avg.)	Donnie Elder, 1988	22.7
Field Goals	Donald Igwebuike, 1985-88	72
Touchdowns (Tot.)	James Wilder, 1981-88	43
Points	James Wilder, 1981-88	258

Individual Records—Single Season

Category	Name	Performance
Rushing (Yds.)	James Wilder, 1984	1,544
Passing (Yds.)	Doug Williams, 1981	3,563
Passing (TDs)	Doug Williams, 1980	20
Receiving (No.)	James Wilder, 1984	85
Receiving (Yds.)	Kevin House, 1981	1,176
Interceptions	Cedric Brown, 1981	9
Punting (Avg.)	Larry Swider, 1981	42.7
Punt Return (Avg.)	Bobby Futrell, 1988	10.5
Kickoff Return (Avg.)	Isaac Hagins, 1977	23.5
Field Goals	Donald Igwebuike, 1985	22
Touchdowns (Tot.)	James Wilder, 1984	13
Points	Donald Igwebuike, 1985	96

Individual Records—Single Game

Category	Name	Performance
Rushing (Yds.)	James Wilder, 11-6-83	219
Passing (Yds.)	Doug Williams, 11-16-80	486
Passing (TDs)	Steve DeBerg, 9-13-87	5
Receiving (No.)	James Wilder, 9-15-85	13
Receiving (Yds.)	Mark Carrier, 12-6-87	212
Interceptions	Many times	2
	Last time by Paul Tripoli, 10-4-87	
Field Goals	Bill Capece, 1-2-83	4
	Bill Capece, 10-30-83	4
	Donald Igwebuike, 11-24-85	4
Touchdowns	Jimmie Giles, 10-20-85	4
Points	Jimmie Giles, 10-20-85	24

1988 Team Record

Preseason (0-4)

Date	Result		Opponents
8/6	L	7-20	Indianapolis
8/13	L	3-23	Cleveland
8/20	L	14-19	at Atlanta
8/25	L	7-14	vs. Buffalo at Nashville, Tenn.
		31-76	

Regular Season (5-11)

Date	Result		Opponents	Att.
9/4	L	14-41	Philadelphia	43,502
9/11	W	13-10	at Green Bay	52,584
9/18	L	24-30	Phoenix	35,034
9/25	L	9-13	at New Orleans	66,671
10/2	W	27-24	Green Bay	40,003
10/9	L	13-14	at Minnesota	55,274
10/16	L	31-35	at Indianapolis	53,135
10/23	L	20-49	Minnesota	48,020
10/30	L	14-17	Miami	67,352
11/6	L	10-28	at Chicago	56,892
11/13	W	23-20	at Detroit	25,956
11/20	L	15-27	Chicago	67,070
11/27	L	10-17	at Atlanta	14,020
12/4	W	10- 5	Buffalo	49,498
12/11	L	7-10	at New Eng. (OT)	39,889
12/18	W	21-10	Detroit	37,778

(OT) Overtime

Score by Periods

Buccaneers	27	75	41	118	0	—	261
Opponents	105	93	95	54	3	—	350

Attendance

Home 388,257 Away 364,421 Total 752,678
Single-game home record, 72,033 (1-6-80)
Single-season home record, 545,980 (1979)

1988 Team Statistics

	Buccaneers	Opp.
Total First Downs	295	293
Rushing	91	104
Passing	173	169
Penalty	31	20
Third Down: Made/Att.	72/202	101/227
Fourth Down: Made/Att.	2/11	6/9
Total Net Yards	5061	5155
Avg. Per Game	316.3	322.2
Total Plays	998	1025
Avg. Per Play	5.1	5.0
Net Yards Rushing	1753	1551
Avg. Per Game	109.6	96.9
Total Rushes	452	478
Net Yards Passing	3308	3604
Avg. Per Game	206.8	225.3
Sacked/Yards Lost	34/300	20/140
Gross Yards	3608	3744
Att./Completions	512/253	527/304
Completion Pct.	49.4	57.7
Had Intercepted	36	21
Punts/Avg.	68/36.4	77/39.0
Net Punting Avg.	32.4	33.2
Penalties/Yards Lost	102/816	105/872
Fumbles/Ball Lost	27/16	29/12
Touchdowns	28	42
Rushing	11	21
Passing	16	19
Returns	1	2
Avg. Time of Possession	29:00	31:00

1988 Individual Statistics

Scoring	TD R	TD P	TD Rt	PAT	FG	Saf	TP
Igwebuike	0	0	0	21/21	19/25	0	78
Hill	0	9	0	0/0	0/0	0	54
Tate	7	1	0	0/0	0/0	0	48
Carrier	0	5	0	0/0	0/0	0	30
Carney	0	0	0	6/6	2/5	0	12
W. Howard	1	0	0	0/0	0/0	0	6
Murphy	0	0	1	0/0	0/0	0	6
Pillow	0	1	0	0/0	0/0	0	6
D. Smith	1	0	0	0/0	0/0	0	6
Testaverde	1	0	0	0/0	0/0	0	6
Wilder	1	0	0	0/0	0/0	0	6
Goode	0	0	0	0/0	0/0	1	2
Criswell	0	0	0	1/1	0/0	0	1
Buccaneers	11	16	1	28/28	21/30	1	261
Opponents	21	19	2	42/42	18/30	1	350

Passing	Att.	Comp.	Yds.	Pct.	TD	Int.	Tkld.	Rate
Testaverde	466	222	3240	47.6	13	35	33/292	48.8
Ferguson	46	31	368	67.4	3	1	1/8	104.3
Buccaneers	512	253	3608	49.4	16	36	34/300	53.7
Opponents	527	304	3744	57.7	19	21	20/140	75.2

Rushing	Att.	Yds.	Avg.	LG	TD
Tate	122	467	3.8	47t	7
W. Howard	115	452	3.9	29t	1
Wilder	86	343	4.0	19	1
Goode	63	231	3.7	22	0
Testaverde	28	138	4.9	24	1
J. Smith	20	87	4.4	23	0
D. Smith	13	46	3.5	15	1
Criswell	2	0	0.0	0	0
Ferguson	1	0	0.0	0	0
Hill	2	−11	−5.5	3	0
Buccaneers	452	1753	3.9	47t	11
Opponents	478	1551	3.2	48	21

Receiving	No.	Yds.	Avg.	LG	TD
Hill	58	1040	17.9	42t	9
Carrier	57	970	17.0	59t	5
Hall	39	555	14.2	37	0
J. Smith	16	134	8.4	22	0
Pillow	15	206	13.7	34	1
Wilder	15	124	8.3	24	0
D. Smith	12	138	11.5	25	0
W. Howard	11	97	8.8	16	0
Magee	9	103	11.4	25	0
Goode	7	68	9.7	22	0
G. Taylor	5	53	10.6	14	0
Tate	5	23	4.6	9	1
Starring	3	75	25.0	53	0
Parks	1	22	22.0	22	0
Buccaneers	253	3608	14.3	59t	16
Opponents	304	3744	12.3	56	19

Interceptions	No.	Yds.	Avg.	LG	TD
Hamilton	6	123	20.5	58	0
Reynolds	4	7	1.8	7	0
Elder	3	9	3.0	9	0
Robinson	2	28	14.0	28	0
Harris	2	26	13.0	24	0
Murphy	1	35	35.0	35t	1
Marve	1	29	29.0	29	0
Futrell	1	26	26.0	26	0
R. Jones	1	0	0.0	0	0
Buccaneers	21	283	13.5	58	1
Opponents	36	486	13.5	46	2

Punting	No.	Yds.	Avg.	In 20	LG
Criswell	68	2477	36.4	20	62
Buccaneers	68	2477	36.4	20	62
Opponents	77	3004	39.0	24	66

Punt Returns	No.	FC	Yds.	Avg.	LG	TD
Futrell	27	10	283	10.5	40	0
J. Smith	8	3	45	5.6	20	0
Elder	1	0	0	0.0	0	0
Buccaneers	36	13	328	9.1	40	0
Opponents	38	13	273	7.2	25	0

Kickoff Returns	No.	Yds.	Avg.	LG	TD
Elder	34	772	22.7	51	0
J. Smith	10	180	18.0	26	0
D. Smith	9	188	20.9	30	0
McAdoo	4	108	27.0	31	0
Pillow	3	38	12.7	17	0
Futrell	2	38	19.0	20	0
W. Howard	2	21	10.5	12	0
Buccaneers	64	1345	21.0	51	0
Opponents	52	1129	21.7	57	0

Sacks	No.
Holmes	4.0
Cannon	3.0
Davis	3.0
Jarvis	2.5
Goff	2.0
Lee	2.0
Marve	1.5
Murphy	1.0
Rolling	1.0
Buccaneers	20.0
Opponents	34.0

1989 Draft Choices

Round	Name	Pos.	College
1.	Broderick Thomas	LB	Nebraska
2.	Danny Peebles	WR	North Carolina St.
4.	Anthony Florence	DB	Bethune-Cookman
5.	Jamie Lawson	RB	Nicholls State
6.	Chris Mohr	P	Alabama
	Derrick Little	LB	South Carolina
8.	Carl Bax	G	Missouri
9.	Patrick Egu	RB	Nevada-Reno
10.	Ty Granger	T	Clemson
11.	Rod Mounts	G	Texas A&I
	Willie Griffin	DE	Nebraska
	Herb Duncan	WR	Northern Arizona
12.	Terry Young	DB	Georgia Southern

Tampa Bay Buccaneers 1989 Veteran Roster

No.	Name	Pos.	Ht.	Wt.	Birth-date	NFL Exp.	College	Hometown	How Acq.	'88 Games/ Starts
45	Anno, Sam	LB	6-2	230	1/26/65	3	Southern California	Santa Monica, Calif.	FA(Minn)-'89#	16/0*
11	Bell, Kerwin	QB	6-3	205	6/15/65	2	Florida	Mayo, Fla.	FA(Atl)-'89#	0*
69	Bruhin, John	G	6-3	280	12/9/64	2	Tennessee	Nashville, Tenn.	D4b-'88	16/6
78	Cannon, John	DE	6-5	260	7/30/60	8	William & Mary	Long Branch, N.J.	D3-'82	16/3
4	Carney, John	K	5-11	160	4/20/64	2	Notre Dame	Jupiter, Fla.	FA-'88	4/0
88	Carrier, Mark	WR	6-0	185	10/28/65	3	Nicholls State	Church Point, La.	D3-'87	16/16
21	Cocroft, Sherman	CB-S	6-1	190	8/29/61	5	San Jose State	Watsonville, Calif.	FA(Buff)-'89#	12/0*
53	Coleman, Sidney	LB	6-2	250	1/14/64	2	Southern Mississippi	Gulfport, Miss.	FA-'88	16/10
71	Cooper, Mark	T	6-5	280	2/14/60	7	Miami	Miami, Fla.	FA-'87	15/0
13	Criswell, Ray	P	6-0	195	8/16/63	3	Florida	Orange Park, Fla.	FA-'88	16/0
79	Davis, Reuben	DE	6-4	290	5/7/65	2	North Carolina	Greensboro, N.C.	D9-'88	16/13
87	Drewrey, Willie	WR	5-7	165	4/28/63	5	West Virginia	Columbus, N.J.	FA(Hou)-'89#	14/0*
40	Elder, Donnie	CB-S	5-9	175	12/13/63	5	Memphis State	Chattanooga, Tenn.	FA-'88	16/0
12	Ferguson, Joe	QB	6-1	190	4/23/50	17	Arkansas	Shreveport, La.	T(Ind)-'88	2/1
36	Futrell, Bobby	CB-S	5-11	190	8/4/62	4	Elizabeth City State	Ahoskie, N.C.	FA-'86	16/15
44	Gladman, Charles	RB	5-11	205	9/2/66	2	Pittsburgh	Akron, Ohio	FA-'89	0*
94	Goff, Robert	DE	6-3	270	10/2/65	2	Auburn	Bradenton, Fla.	D4a-'88	16/6
60	Grimes, Randy	C	6-4	275	7/20/60	7	Baylor	Tyler, Tex.	D2-'83	16/16
74	Gruber, Paul	T	6-5	290	2/24/65	2	Wisconsin	Prairie du Sac, Wis.	D1-'88	16/16
82	Hall, Ron	TE	6-4	245	3/15/64	3	Hawaii	Escondido, Calif.	D4b-'87	15/14
39	Hamilton, Harry	CB-S	6-0	195	11/29/62	6	Penn State	Wilkes-Barre, Pa.	FA-'88	16/16
20	Harris, Odie	CB-S	6-0	190	4/1/66	2	Sam Houston State	Bryan, Tex.	FA-'88	16/7
84	Hill, Bruce	WR	6-0	180	2/29/64	3	Arizona State	Lancaster, Calif.	D4c-'88	14/14
90	†Holmes, Ron	DE	6-4	265	8/26/63	5	Washington	Lacey, Wash.	D1-'85	10/10
43	Howard, William	RB	6-0	240	6/2/64	2	Tennessee	Lima, Ohio	D5-'88	15/9
1	†Igwebuike, Donald	K	5-9	185	12/27/60	5	Clemson	Anambra, Nigeria	D10-'85	12/0
95	†Jarvis, Curt	NT	6-2	265	1/28/65	2	Alabama	Gardendale, Ala.	D7a-'87	15/15
45	Johnson, Sidney	CB-S	5-9	175	3/7/65	2	California	Cerritos, Calif.	FA(KC)-'89#	13/0*
22	Jones, Rod	CB-S	6-0	185	3/31/64	4	Southern Methodist	Dallas, Tex.	D1b-'86	14/1
75	Kellin, Kevin	DE	6-5	270	11/16/59	4	Minnesota	Grand Rapids, Minn.	FA-'86	4/0
97	Lee, Shawn	NT	6-2	290	10/24/66	2	North Alabama	Brooklyn, N.Y.	D6-'88	15/0
68	Mallory, Rick	G	6-2	265	10/21/60	5	Washington	Renton, Wash.	D9-'84	16/16
99	Marve, Eugene	LB	6-2	240	8/14/60	8	Saginaw Valley State	Flint, Mich.	T(Buff)-'88	16/16
73	McHale, Tom	G	6-4	275	2/25/63	3	Cornell	Gaithersburg, Md.	FA-'87	10/0
58	Moss, Winston	LB	6-3	235	12/24/65	3	Miami	Miami, Fla.	D2b-'87	16/15
59	Murphy, Kevin	LB	6-2	235	9/8/63	4	Oklahoma	Plano, Tex.	D2-'86	16/16
57	Najarian, Pete	LB	6-2	230	12/22/63	2	Minnesota	Minneapolis, Minn.	FA-'88	1/0
85	Parks, Jeff	TE	6-4	240	9/14/64	4	Auburn	Gardendale, Ala.	FA-'88	3/1
80	Pillow, Frank	WR	5-10	170	3/11/65	2	Tennessee State	Nashville, Tenn.	D11-'88	15/0
54	†Randle, Ervin	LB	6-1	250	10/12/62	5	Baylor	Hearne, Tex.	D3-'85	9/6
29	Reynolds, Ricky	CB-S	5-11	190	1/19/65	3	Washington State	Sacramento, Calif.	D2a-'87	16/16
30	Robinson, Mark	CB-S	5-11	200	9/13/62	6	Penn State	Silver Spring, Md.	T(KC)-'88	9/9
55	Rolling, Henry	LB	6-2	225	9/8/65	2	Nevada-Reno	Henderson, Nev.	D5-'87	15/0
47	Smith, Don	RB-WR	5-11	195	10/30/63	2	Mississippi State	Hamilton, Miss.	D2-'87	10/3
93	Smith, Robert	DE	6-7	270	12/3/62	2	Grambling	Bogalusa, La.	FA-'89	0*
24	Stamps, Sylvester	RB	5-7	185	2/24/61	5	Jackson State	Vicksburg, Miss.	FA(Atl)-'89#	6/2*
70	†Swayne, Harry	DE	6-5	270	2/2/65	3	Rutgers	Philadelphia, Pa.	D7b-'87	10/1
34	Tate, Lars	RB	6-2	215	2/2/66	2	Georgia	Indianapolis, Ind.	D2-'88	15/5
72	Taylor, Rob	T	6-6	295	11/14/60	4	Northwestern	Fairmont, Ohio	FA-'86	16/16
14	Testaverde, Vinny	QB	6-5	215	11/13/63	3	Miami	Elmont, N.Y.	D1-'87	15/15
50	†Turk, Dan	G	6-4	260	6/25/62	4	Wisconsin	Milwaukee, Wis.	F(Pitt)-'87	12/10
33	Valentine, Ira	RB	6-1	220	6/4/63	2	Texas A&M	Marshall, Tex.	FA-'89	0*
32	Wilder, James	RB	6-3	225	5/12/58	9	Missouri	Sikeston, Mo.	D2-'82	7/7
46	Wonsley, Nathan	RB	5-9	185	12/2/63	2	Mississippi	Moss Point, Miss.	FA-'89	0*

* Anno played 16 games with Minnesota in '88; Bell active for 6 games with Atlanta but did not play; Cocroft played 12 games with Buffalo; Drewrey played 14 games with Houston; Gladman last active with Tampa Bay in '87; Johnson played 13 games with Kansas City; R. Smith last active with Minnesota in '85; Stamps played 6 games with Atlanta; Valentine last active with Houston in '87; Wonsley last active with Tampa Bay '86.

† Option playout; subject to developments.

Plan B unconditional free agent.

Players lost through Plan B (8): RB Kerry Goode (Den; 14 games in '88), RB Bobby Howard (GB; 1), LB Victor Jones (Det; 8), TE Calvin Magee (Hou; 13), RB Jeff Smith (GB; 16), C Kevin Thomas (Sea; 10), LB Jackie Walker (NYJ; 16), LB Chris Washington (SF; 16).

Also played with Buccaneers in '88—CB-S Selwyn Brown (4 games), WR Joey Clinkscales (3), CB-S Ray Isom (2), RB Derrick McAdoo (5), WR Stephen Starring (6), WR Gene Taylor (4).

COACHING STAFF

Head Coach, Ray Perkins

Pro Career: Named third head coach in Tampa Bay Buccaneers' history on December 31, 1986. Previous head coaching experience in the NFL came with New York Giants where he compiled a 24-35 record between 1979 and 1982. Perkins built the Giants into a playoff team by 1981, his third season. It marked the Giants' first playoff appearance in 18 years. Perkins worked five years as an assistant in the NFL, spending 1974-77 as receivers coach with New England Patriots and 1978 as offensive coordinator with San Diego Chargers. Drafted by the Baltimore Colts in the seventh round of the 1967 draft, and played five seasons there. Career record: 33-57.

Background: Bear Bryant's hand-picked successor at University of Alabama, where he compiled a 32-15-1 record between 1983-86, including three bowl game victories. College receiver at Alabama 1964-66 and All-America as a senior. College assistant at Mississippi State (1973).

Personal: Born November 6, 1941, in Mt. Olive, Mississippi. Ray and his wife, Carolyn, live in Tampa and have two sons—Tony and Mike.

Assistant Coaches

John Bobo, offensive line; born February 18, 1958, Alapaha, Ga., lives in Tampa. Tight end-defensive end Maryville 1976-79. No pro playing experience. College coach: Alabama 1985-86. Pro coach: Joined Buccaneers in 1987.

Louis Campbell, defensive assistant; born February 20, 1950, Crossett, Ark., lives in Tampa. Defensive back Arkansas 1970-72. No pro playing experience. College coach: Alabama 1973-76, 1980-83, Southern Methodist 1977-79, Oklahoma State 1984-88. Pro coach: Joined Buccaneers in 1989.

Sylvester Croom, running backs; born September 25, 1954, Tuscaloosa, Ala., lives in Tampa. Center Alabama 1971-74. Pro center New Orleans Saints 1975. College coach: Alabama 1976-86. Pro coach: Joined Buccaneers in 1987.

Mike DuBose, defensive line; born January 5, 1953, Opp, Ala., lives in Tampa. Defensive lineman Alabama 1971-73. No pro playing experience. College coach: Alabama 1974-75, 1983-86, Tennessee-Chattanooga 1980-81, Southern Mississippi 1982. Pro coach: Joined Buccaneers in 1987.

Doug Graber, defensive coordinator-secondary; born September 26, 1944, Detroit, Mich., lives in Clearwater, Fla. Defensive back Wayne State 1963-66. No pro playing experience. College coach: Michigan Tech 1969-71, Eastern Michigan 1972-75, Ball State 1976-77, Wisconsin 1978-81, Montana State 1982 (head coach). Pro coach: Kansas City Chiefs 1983-86, joined Buccaneers in 1987.

Kent Johnson, strength and conditioning; born February 21, 1956, Mexia, Tex., lives in Tampa. Defensive back Stephen F. Austin 1974-77. No pro playing experience. College coach: Northeast Louisiana 1979, Northwestern State (La.) 1980-81, Alabama 1983-86. Pro coach: Joined Buccaneers in 1987.

Joe Kines, outside linebackers; born July 13, 1944, Piedmont, Ala., lives in Tampa. Linebacker Jacksonville (Ala.) State 1963-65. No pro playing experience. College coach: Jacksonville State 1966, 1972-76, Clemson 1977-78, Florida 1979-84, Alabama 1985-86. Pro coach: Joined Buccaneers in 1987.

Mike Shula, offensive assistant; born June 3, 1965, Baltimore, Md., lives in Tampa. Quarterback Alabama 1984-86. Pro quarterback Tampa Bay 1987. Pro coach: Joined Buccaneers in 1988.

Rodney Stokes, special teams; born February 3, 1953, Brookhaven, Miss., lives in Tampa. Linebacker Delta State 1976-77. No pro playing experience. College coach: Alabama 1983-86. Pro coach: Joined Buccaneers in 1987.

Tampa Bay Buccaneers 1989 First-Year Roster

Name	Pos.	Ht.	Wt.	Birth-date	College	Hometown	How Acq.
Barney, Milton (1)	WR	5-9	160	12/23/63	Alcorn State	Gulfport, Miss.	FA
Bax, Carl	T-G	6-4	275	1/5/66	Missouri	St. Charles, Mo.	D8
Burdick, Shaun (1)	P	6-4	190	5/28/65	Cincinnati	Cincinnati, Ohio	FA
Casparriello, Peter (1)	TE	6-3	235	7/9/65	Boston College	Somerville, Mass.	FA
Chavous, Raymond (1)	NT-DE	6-4	300	6/2/65	Clemson	Aiken, S.C.	FA
Clapp, Tommy (1)	NT-DE	6-4	280	8/14/62	Louisiana State	New Orleans, La.	FA
Drew, Peter (1)	K	5-11	180	4/15/64	Troy State	Opelika, Ala.	FA
Duncan, Herb	WR	6-0	180	12/18/65	Northern Arizona	San Diego, Calif.	D11b
Egu, Patrick	RB	5-11	185	2/20/67	Nevada-Reno	Richmond, Calif.	D9
Florence, Anthony	CB-S	5-11	185	12/11/66	Bethune-Cookman	Delray Beach, Fla.	D4
Graham, Dan (1)	C	6-2	270	5/10/65	Northern Illinois	Wheaton, Ill.	FA
Granger, Ty	T-G	6-6	280	2/16/66	Clemson	Easley, S.C.	D10
Griffin, Willie	NT	6-3	300	3/24/66	Nebraska	Monrovia, Calif.	D11a
Harrison, Erick	WR	5-10	180	10/18/66	Tulsa	Bristow, Okla.	FA
Hegdale, Steve	T-G	6-5	295	10/24/65	Tulsa	McAlister, Tex.	FA
James, Michel (1)	WR	6-0	185	11/19/63	Washington State	Tacoma, Wash.	FA
Keyes, Bud (1)	QB	6-3	210	3/3/66	Wisconsin	Green Bay, Wis.	FA
Knighton, Billy (1)	P	6-1	190	3/5/64	Southern Mississippi	Montgomery, Ala.	FA
Lawson, Jamie	RB	5-10	245	10/2/65	Nicholls State	Raceland, La.	D5
Little, Derrick	LB	6-4	245	12/1/66	South Carolina	Athens, Ga.	D6a
Maloney, Donnie	RB	5-10	185	1/15/66	Tulsa	Chickasha, Okla.	FA
Marsh, Marvin (1)	RB	5-10	190	10/20/63	North Alabama	Gadsden, Ala.	FA
Massaro, Chuck	C	6-2	270	6/6/66	North Carolina State	Haddon Heights, N.J.	FA
Mitchell, Alvin	RB	6-0	235	8/20/64	Auburn	Venice, Calif.	FA
Mohr, Chris	P	6-4	215	5/11/66	Alabama	Thomson, Ga.	D6
Moody, Bill	RB	6-1	270	5/26/66	Memphis State	Humboldt, Tenn.	FA
Mounts, Rod	T-G	6-4	285	7/27/65	Texas A&I	Corpus Christi, Tex.	D11
Peebles, Danny	WR	5-11	170	4/30/66	North Carolina State	Raleigh, N.C.	D2
Phillips, Wendell (1)	CB-S	6-0	195	4/3/66	North Alabama	Leighton, Ala.	FA
Seals, Ray (1)	DE	6-3	245	6/17/65	None	Syracuse, N.Y.	FA
Simmonds, Mike (1)	G	6-4	290	8/12/64	Indiana State	Belleville, Ill.	D10-'87
Sowell, Brent (1)	T-G	6-5	285	3/27/63	Alabama	Clearwater, Fla.	FA
Thomas, Albert	CB-S	5-11	175	3/25/66	Tennessee State	Atlanta, Ga.	FA
Thomas, Broderick	LB	6-4	250	2/20/67	Nebraska	Houston, Tex.	D1
Waiters, Garey (1)	P	5-10	220	2/8/65	Jacksonville State	Akron, Ala.	FA
Young, Terry	CB-S	5-11	175	3/28/67	Georgia Southern	Savannah, Ga.	D12

The term NFL Rookie is defined as a player who is in his first season of professional football and has not been on the roster of another professional football team for any regular-season or postseason games. A Rookie is designated by an "R" on NFL rosters. Players who have been active in another professional football league or players who have NFL experience, including either preseason training camp or being on an active roster for fewer than three regular-season or postseason games, are termed NFL First-Year Players. An NFL First-Year Player is designated by a "1" on NFL rosters. Thereafter, a player on an NFL active roster for at least three regular-season or postseason games is credited with an additional year of NFL playing experience.

NOTES

Richard Williamson, receivers; born April 13, 1941, Fort Deposit, Ala., lives in Tampa. Receiver Alabama 1959-62. No pro playing experience. College coach: Alabama 1963-67, 1970-71, Arkansas 1968-69, 1972-74, Memphis State 1975-80 (head coach). Pro coach: Kansas City Chiefs 1983-86, joined Buccaneers in 1987.

National Football Conference Eastern Division

Team Colors: Burgundy and Gold

Redskin Park
P.O. Box 17247
Dulles International Airport
Washington, D.C. 20041
Telephone: (703) 471-9100

Club Officials

Chairman of the Board-Chief Operating Executive: Jack Kent Cooke
Executive Vice President: John Kent Cooke
Secretary: Robert N. Eisman
Controller: Doug Porter
Board of Directors: Jack Kent Cooke, John Kent Cooke, James Lacher, William A. Shea, Esq., The Honorable John W. Warner
General Manager: Charles Casserly
Assistant General Manager: Bobby Mitchell
Director of Player Personnel: Dick Daniels
Director of Pro Scouting: Kirk Mee
Scouts: Billy Devaney, George Saimes, Jerry Fauls, Chuck Banker
V.P.-Communications: Charlie Dayton
Director of Information: John C. Konoza
Director of Public Relations: Marty Hurney
Director of Marketing and Stadium Operations: Paul Denfeld
Director of Video: Donnie Schoenmann
Ticket Manager: Sue Barton
Head Trainer: Lamar (Bubba) Tyer
Asst. Trainers: Keoki Kamau, Al Bellamy
Equipment Manager: Jay Brunetti

Stadium: Robert F. Kennedy Stadium •
Capacity: 55,671
East Capitol Street
Washington, D.C. 20003

Playing Surface: Grass (PAT)

Training Camp: Dickinson College
Carlisle, Pennsylvania 17013

1989 Schedule

Preseason

Aug. 12	at Pittsburgh	8:00
Aug. 21	at Minnesota	7:00
Aug. 25	**Miami**	8:00
Sept. 1	at New Orleans	7:00

Regular Season

Sept. 11	**N.Y. Giants** (Monday)	9:00
Sept. 17	**Philadelphia**	1:00
Sept. 24	at Dallas	12:00
Oct. 1	at New Orleans	12:00
Oct. 8	**Phoenix**	4:00
Oct. 15	at New York Giants	1:00
Oct. 22	**Tampa Bay**	1:00
Oct. 29	at Los Angeles Raiders	1:00
Nov. 5	**Dallas**	8:00
Nov. 12	at Philadelphia	1:00
Nov. 20	**Denver** (Monday)	9:00
Nov. 26	**Chicago**	4:00
Dec. 3	at Phoenix	2:00
Dec. 10	**San Diego**	1:00
Dec. 17	at Atlanta	4:00
Dec. 23	at Seattle (Saturday)	1:00

Redskins Coaching History

Boston 1932-36
(398-342-26)

1932	Lud Wray	4-4-2
1933-34	William (Lone Star) Dietz	11-11-2
1935	Eddie Casey	2-8-1
1936-42	Ray Flaherty	56-23-3
1943	Arthur (Dutch) Bergman	7-4-1
1944-45	Dudley DeGroot	14-6-1
1946-48	Glen (Turk) Edwards	16-18-1
1949	John Whelchel*	3-3-1
1949-51	Herman Ball**	4-16-0
1951	Dick Todd	5-4-0
1952-53	Earl (Curly) Lambeau	10-13-1
1954-58	Joe Kuharich	26-32-2
1959-60	Mike Nixon	4-18-2
1961-65	Bill McPeak	21-46-3
1966-68	Otto Graham	17-22-3
1969	Vince Lombardi	7-5-2
1970	Bill Austin	6-8-0
1971-77	George Allen	69-35-1
1978-80	Jack Pardee	24-24-0
1981-88	Joe Gibbs	92-42-0

*Released after seven games in 1949
**Released after three games in 1951

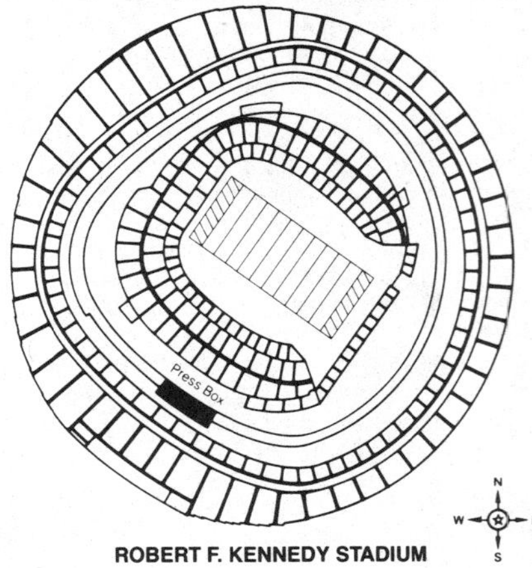

ROBERT F. KENNEDY STADIUM

Record Holders

Individual Records—Career

Category	Name	Performance
Rushing (Yds.)	John Riggins, 1976-79, 1981-85	7,472
Passing (Yds.)	Joe Theismann, 1974-1985	25,206
Passing (TDs)	Sonny Jurgensen, 1964-1974	209
Receiving (No.)	Charley Taylor, 1964-1977	649
Receiving (Yds.)	Charley Taylor, 1964-1977	9,140
Interceptions	Brig Owens, 1966-1977	36
Punting (Avg.)	Sammy Baugh, 1937-1952	45.1
Punt Return (Avg.)	Johnny Williams, 1952-53	12.8
Kickoff Return (Avg.)	Bobby Mitchell, 1962-68	28.5
Field Goals	Mark Moseley, 1974-1986	263
Touchdowns (Tot.)	Charley Taylor, 1964-1977	90
Points	Mark Moseley, 1974-1986	1,206

Individual Records—Single Season

Category	Name	Performance
Rushing (Yds.)	John Riggins, 1983	1,347
Passing (Yds.)	Jay Schroeder, 1986	4,109
Passing (TDs)	Sonny Jurgensen, 1967	31
Receiving (No.)	Art Monk, 1984	*106
Receiving (Yds.)	Bobby Mitchell, 1963	1,436
Interceptions	Dan Sandifer, 1948	13
Punting (Avg.)	Sammy Baugh, 1940	*51.4
Punt Return (Avg.)	Johnny Williams, 1952	15.3
Kickoff Return (Avg.)	Mike Nelms, 1981	29.7
Field Goals	Mark Moseley, 1983	33
Touchdowns (Tot.)	John Riggins, 1983	*24
Points	Mark Moseley, 1983	161

Individual Records—Single Game

Category	Name	Performance
Rushing (Yds.)	George Rogers, 12-21-85	206
Passing (Yds.)	Sammy Baugh, 10-31-43	446
Passing (TDs)	Sammy Baugh, 10-31-43	6
	Sammy Baugh, 11-23-47	6
Receiving (No.)	Art Monk, 12-15-85	13
	Kelvin Bryant, 12-7-86	13
Receiving (Yds.)	Anthony Allen, 10-4-87	255
Interceptions	Sammy Baugh, 11-14-43	*4
	Dan Sandifer, 10-31-48	*4
Field Goals	Many times	5
	Last time by Mark Moseley, 10-26-80	
Touchdowns (Tot.)	Dick James, 12-17-61	4
	Larry Brown, 12-4-73	4
Points	Dick James, 12-17-61	24
	Larry Brown, 12-4-73	24

*NFL Record

1988 Team Record

Preseason (3-1)

Date	Result		Opponents
8/5	L	31-44	Pittsburgh
8/13	W	27-10	at Miami
8/20	W	45-27	at L.A. Raiders
8/27	W	34-17	vs. Atlanta at Birmingham, Ala.
		137-98	

Regular Season (7-9)

Date	Result		Opponents	Att.
9/5	L	20-27	at N.Y. Giants	76,417
9/11	W	30-29	Pittsburgh	54,083
9/18	W	17-10	Philadelphia	53,920
9/25	L	21-30	at Phoenix	61,973
10/2	L	23-24	N.Y. Giants	54,601
10/9	W	35-17	at Dallas	63,325
10/16	W	33-17	Phoenix	54,402
10/23	W	20-17	at Green Bay	51,767
10/30	L	17-41	at Houston	48,781
11/6	W	27-24	New Orleans	54,183
11/13	L	14-34	Chicago	52,418
11/21	L	21-37	at San Francisco	59,268
11/27	L	13-17	Cleveland	51,604
12/4	W	20-19	at Philadelphia	65,947
12/11	L	17-24	Dallas	51,526
12/17	L	17-20	at Cincinnati (OT)	52,157

(OT) Overtime

Score by Periods

Redskins	86	79	89	91	0	—	345
Opponents	70	125	64	125	3	—	387

Attendance

Home 426,737 Away 479,635 Total 906,372
Single-game home record, 55,750 (11-10-85)
Single-season home record, 434,854 (1986)

1988 Team Statistics

	Redskins	Opp.
Total First Downs	307	294
Rushing	88	113
Passing	202	153
Penalty	17	28
Third Down: Made/Att.	97/223	75/201
Fourth Down: Made/Att.	10/16	4/10
Total Net Yards	5679	5184
Avg. Per Game	354.9	324.0
Total Plays	1053	982
Avg. Per Play	5.4	5.3
Net Yards Rushing	1543	1745
Avg. Per Game	96.4	109.1
Total Rushes	437	442
Net Yards Passing	4136	3439
Avg. Per Game	258.5	214.9
Sacked/Yards Lost	24/203	43/305
Gross Yards	4339	3744
Att./Completions	592/327	497/261
Completion Pct.	55.2	52.5
Had Intercepted	25	14
Punts/Avg.	67/38.2	79/39.4
Net Punting Avg.	29.8	34.2
Penalties/Yards Lost	96/817	91/711
Fumbles/Ball Lost	34/21	23/8
Touchdowns	41	46
Rushing	8	17
Passing	33	24
Returns	0	5
Avg. Time of Possession	30:57	29:03

1988 Individual Statistics

Scoring	TD R	TD P	TD Rt	PAT	FG	Saf	TP
Lohmiller	0	0	0	40/41	19/26	0	97
Sanders	0	12	0	0/0	0/0	0	72
Clark	0	7	0	0/0	0/0	0	42
Bryant	1	5	0	0/0	0/0	0	36
Monk	0	5	0	0/0	0/0	0	30
Smith	3	0	0	0/0	0/0	0	18
Morris	2	0	0	0/0	0/0	0	12
Orr	0	2	0	0/0	0/0	0	12
Allen	0	1	0	0/0	0/0	0	6
Griffin	0	1	0	0/0	0/0	0	6
Rypien	1	0	0	0/0	0/0	0	6
D. Williams	1	0	0	0/0	0/0	0	6
Caldwell	0	0	0	0/0	0/0	1	2
Redskins	8	33	0	40/41	19/26	1	345
Opponents	17	24	5	43/46	22/36	1	387

Passing	Att.	Comp.	Yds.	Pct.	TD	Int.	Tkld.	Rate
D. Williams	380	213	2609	56.1	15	12	10/88	77.4
Rypien	208	114	1730	54.8	18	13	14/115	85.2
Archer	2	0	0	0.0	0	0	0/0	39.6
G. Coleman	1	0	0	0.0	0	0	0/0	39.6
Monk	1	0	0	0.0	0	0	0/0	39.6
Redskins	592	327	4339	55.2	33	25	24/203	79.6
Opponents	497	261	3744	52.5	24	14	43/305	81.6

Rushing	Att.	Yds.	Avg.	LG	TD
Bryant	108	498	4.6	25	1
Smith	155	470	3.0	29	3
Morris	126	437	3.5	27t	2
Monk	7	46	6.6	23	0
Rypien	9	31	3.4	19t	1
Oliphant	8	30	3.8	20	0
Griffin	6	23	3.8	9	0
Sanders	2	14	7.0	7	0
Clark	2	6	3.0	4	0
Archer	3	1	0.3	4	0
D. Williams	9	0	0.0	4	1
G. Coleman	2	−13	−6.5	0	0
Redskins	437	1543	3.5	29	8
Opponents	442	1745	3.9	50t	17

Receiving	No.	Yds.	Avg.	LG	TD
Sanders	73	1148	15.7	55t	12
Monk	72	946	13.1	46t	5
Clark	59	892	15.1	60t	7
Bryant	42	447	10.6	47	5
McEwen	23	323	14.0	46	0
Oliphant	15	111	7.4	16	0
Warren	12	112	9.3	32	0
Orr	11	222	20.2	58	2
Smith	8	53	6.6	16	0
Allen	5	48	9.6	18	1
Caravello	2	15	7.5	8	0
Jones	2	10	5.0	9	0
Griffin	2	9	4.5	5	1
Morris	1	3	3.0	3	0
Redskins	327	4339	13.3	60t	33
Opponents	261	3744	14.3	80t	24

Interceptions	No.	Yds.	Avg.	LG	TD
Wilburn	4	24	6.0	14	0
Marshall	3	61	20.3	43	0
Walton	3	54	18.0	29	0
Bowles	1	20	20.0	20	0
Curtis, Phoe.-Wash.	1	18	18.0	18	0
Green	1	12	12.0	12	0
Davis	1	11	11.0	11	0
M. Coleman	1	11	11.0	11	0
Redskins	14	193	13.8	43	0
Opponents	25	271	10.8	40	0

Punting	No.	Yds.	Avg.	In 20	LG
Barnhardt	15	628	41.9	1	55
G. Coleman	39	1505	38.6	8	53
Cox	6	221	36.8	0	55
Lohmiller	6	208	34.7	1	42
Redskins	67	2562	38.2	10	55
Opponents	79	3116	39.4	21	54

Punt Returns	No.	FC	Yds.	Avg.	LG	TD
Shepard	12	2	104	8.7	23	0
Allen	10	2	62	6.2	14	0
Green	9	0	103	11.4	32	0
Clark	8	3	48	6.0	34	0
Oliphant	7	0	24	3.4	11	0
Johnson	3	1	26	8.7	15	0
Orr	2	0	10	5.0	10	0
Caldwell	1	0	0	0.0	0	0
Gage	0	1	0	—	0	0
Redskins	52	9	377	7.3	34	0
Opponents	39	7	448	11.5	95t	1

Kickoff Returns	No.	Yds.	Avg.	LG	TD
Morris	21	413	19.7	35	0
Sanders	19	362	19.1	31	0
Shepard	16	329	20.6	44	0
Oliphant	7	127	18.1	26	0
Gage	5	60	12.0	17	0
Griffin	3	45	15.0	24	0
Hamilton	1	7	7.0	7	0
Harbour	1	6	6.0	6	0
Orr	1	6	6.0	6	0
Redskins	74	1355	18.3	44	0
Opponents	61	1111	18.2	32	0

Sacks	No.
Manley	9.0
Mann	5.5
Caldwell	4.0
Grant	4.0
Marshall	4.0
Koch	3.5
M. Coleman	3.0
Hamel	2.0
Olkewicz	2.0
Butz	1.0
Curtis, Phoe.-Wash.	1.0
Green	1.0
Kaufman	1.0
Vaughn	1.0
Walton	1.0
Redskins	43.0
Opponents	24.0

1989 Draft Choices

Round	Name	Pos.	College
3.	Tracy Rocker	DT	Auburn
4.	Erik Affholter	WR	Southern California
5.	Tim Smiley	DB	Arkansas State
	Lybrant Robinson	DE	Delaware State
6.	A.J. Johnson	DB	S.W. Texas State
7.	Kevin Hendrix	LB	South Carolina
9.	Charles Darrington	TE	Kentucky
10.	Mark Schlereth	C	Idaho
12.	Jimmy Johnson	TE	Howard
	Joe Mickles	RB	Mississippi

Washington Redskins 1989 Veteran Roster

No.	Name	Pos.	Ht.	Wt.	Birth-date	NFL Exp.	College	Hometown	How Acq.	'88 Games/ Starts
14	Barnhardt, Tom	P	6-3	205	6/11/63	3	North Carolina	Salisbury, N.C.	FA-'88	4/0
80	Beals, Shawn	WR-KR	5-10	178	8/16/66	2	Idaho State	Pittsburgh, Calif.	FA(Phil)-'89#	13/0*
69	Benish, Dan	DT	6-5	275	11/21/60	6	Clemson	Youngstown, Ohio	FA-'87	0*
53	Bostic, Jeff	C	6-2	260	9/18/58	10	Clemson	Greensboro, N.C.	FA-'80	13/11
23	Bowles, Todd	S	6-2	203	11/18/63	4	Temple	Elizabeth, N.J.	FA-'86	16/16
29	Branch, Reggie	RB	5-11	235	10/22/62	4	East Carolina	Sanford, Fla.	FA-'86	7/0
67	Brown, Ray	G-T	6-5	280	12/12/62	4	Arkansas State	Marion, Ark.	FA(Phx)-'89#	15/1*
24	Bryant, Kelvin	RB	6-2	195	9/26/60	4	North Carolina	Tarboro, N.C.	FA-'86	10/4
21	t-Byner, Earnest	RB	5-10	215	9/15/62	6	East Carolina	Milledgeville, Ga.	T(Clev)-'89	16/16
50	Caldwell, Ravin	LB	6-3	229	8/4/63	3	Arkansas	Fort Smith, Ark.	D5-'86	16/1
84	†Clark, Gary	WR	5-9	173	5/1/63	5	James Madison	Dublin, Va.	FA-'85	16/13
51	Coleman, Monte	LB	6-2	230	11/4/57	11	Central Arkansas	Pine Bluff, Ark.	D11-'79	13/9
34	Davis, Brian	CB	6-2	190	8/31/63	3	Nebraska	Phoenix, Ariz.	D2a-'87	9/6
36	Dillahunt, Ellis	S	5-11	190	11/25/64	2	East Carolina	Jacksonville, N.C.	FA(Cin)-'89#	10/0*
92	Elam, Onzy	LB	6-2	225	12/1/64	3	Tennessee State	Miami, Fla.	FA(NYJ)-'89#	4/0*
54	Gouveia, Kurt	LB	6-1	227	9/14/64	3	Brigham Young	Waianae, Hawaii	D8-'86	16/0
57	Graham, Don	LB	6-2	244	1/31/64	2	Penn State	Pittsburgh, Pa.	FA(NYJ)-'89#	9/0*
77	Grant, Darryl	DT	6-1	275	11/22/59	9	Rice	San Antonio, Tex.	D9-'81	16/16
28	†Green, Darrell	CB	5-8	170	2/15/60	7	Texas A&I	Houston, Tex.	D1-'83	15/15
68	Grimm, Russ	G	6-3	275	5/2/59	9	Pittsburgh	Southmoreland, Pa.	D3-'81	5/4
78	†Hamel, Dean	DT	6-3	280	7/7/61	5	Tulsa	Warren, Mich.	D12-'85	16/0
59	Harbour, Dave	C	6-4	265	10/23/65	2	Illinois	Naperville, Ill.	FA-'88	15/0
4	Horne, Greg	P	6-0	188	11/22/64	3	Arkansas	Russellville, Ark.	FA(Phx)-'89#	16/0*
66	Jacoby, Joe	T	6-7	305	7/6/59	9	Louisville	Louisville, Ky.	FA-'81	16/13
55	Kaufman, Mel	LB	6-2	230	2/14/58	8	Cal Poly-SLO	Santa Monica, Calif.	FA-'81	11/6
74	Koch, Markus	DE	6-5	275	2/13/63	4	Boise State	Ontario, Canada	D2a-'85	11/6
79	Lachey, Jim	T	6-6	290	6/4/63	5	Ohio State	St. Henry, Ohio	T(Raid)-'88	15/14
8	Lohmiller, Chip	K	6-3	213	7/16/66	2	Minnesota	Springfield, Mo.	D2-'88	16/0
72	Manley, Dexter	DE	6-3	257	2/2/59	9	Oklahoma State	Houston, Tex.	D5-'81	16/13
71	Mann, Charles	DE	6-6	270	4/12/61	7	Nevada-Reno	Sacramento, Calif.	D3-'83	14/13
91	Manusky, Greg	LB	6-1	242	8/12/66	2	Colgate	Wyoming, Pa.	FA-'88	7/0
58	Marshall, Wilber	LB	6-1	230	4/18/62	6	Florida	Titusville, Fla.	FA-'88	16/16
96	Maxey, Curtis	DT	6-3	298	6/28/65	2	Grambling	Indianapolis, Ind.	FA(Cin)-'89#	3/0*
73	May, Mark	G-T	6-6	295	11/2/59	9	Pittsburgh	Oneonta, N.Y.	D1-'81	16/16
32	McEwen, Craig	RB	6-1	220	12/16/65	3	Utah	Queens, N.Y.	FA-'87	14/8
63	†McKenzie, Raleigh	C-G	6-2	270	2/8/63	5	Tennessee	Knoxville, Tenn.	D11-'85	16/14
81	†Monk, Art	WR	6-3	209	12/5/57	10	Syracuse	White Plains, N.Y.	D1-'80	16/13
22	Morris, Jamie	RB	5-7	188	6/6/65	2	Michigan	Ayer, Mass.	D4-'88	16/4
61	Morris, Mike	C-G	6-5	275	2/22/61	2	Northeast Missouri State	Centerville, Iowa	FA(Phx)-'89#	0*
52	Olkewicz, Neal	LB	6-0	230	1/30/57	11	Maryland	Phoenixville, Pa.	FA-'79	16/16
87	Orr, Terry	TE	6-3	227	9/27/61	4	Texas	Abilene, Tex.	D10-'85	16/3
48	Profit, Eugene	CB	5-10	175	11/11/64	3	Yale	Gardena, Calif.	FA(NE)-'89#	1/0*
39	t-Riggs, Gerald	RB	6-1	232	11/6/60	8	Arizona State	Las Vegas, Nev.	T(Atl)-'89	9/9*
11	Rypien, Mark	QB	6-4	234	10/2/62	2	Washington State	Spokane, Wash.	D6-'86	9/6
83	Sanders, Ricky	WR	5-11	180	8/30/62	4	Southwest Texas State	Temple, Tex.	T(NE)-'86	16/4
76	Simmons, Ed	T	6-5	280	12/31/63	3	Eastern Washington	Stockton, Calif.	D6b-'87	16/0
60	Stokes, Fred	DE	6-3	262	3/14/64	3	Georgia Southern	Vidalia, Ga.	FA(Rams)-'89	5/0*
86	Tice, Mike	TE	6-7	244	2/2/59	9	Maryland	Central Islip, N.Y.	FA(Sea)-'89#	16/16*
31	Vaughn, Clarence	S	6-0	202	7/17/64	3	Northern Illinois	Chicago, Ill.	D8-'87	14/0
40	Walton, Alvin	S	6-0	180	3/14/64	4	Kansas	Banning, Calif.	D3-'86	16/16
85	Warren, Don	TE	6-4	242	5/5/56	11	San Diego State	Covina, Calif.	D4-'79	14/14
82	Whisenhunt, Ken	TE	6-3	240	2/28/62	5	Georgia Tech	Augusta, Ga.	FA(Atl)-'89#	16/15*
45	Wilburn, Barry	CB	6-3	186	12/9/63	5	Mississippi	Memphis, Tenn.	D8-'85	10/10
17	Williams, Doug	QB	6-4	220	8/9/55	9	Grambling	Zachary, La.	T(TB)-'86	11/10

* Beals played 13 games with Philadelphia in '88 season; Benish and Hitchcock missed '88 season due to injury; Brown played 15 games with Phoenix; Dillahunt played 10 games with Cincinnati; Elam played 4 games with N.Y. Jets; Graham played 8 games with Buffalo, 1 with N.Y. Jets; Horne played 16 games with Phoenix; Maxey played 3 games with Cincinnati; M. Morris last active with Phoenix in '87; Profit played 1 game with New England; Stokes played 5 games with L.A. Rams; Tice played 16 games with Seattle; Whisenhunt played 16 games with Atlanta.

† Option playout; subject to developments.

Plan B unconditional free agent.

t- Redskins traded for Byner (Cleveland), Riggs (Atlanta).

Traded—RB Mike Oliphant to Cleveland.

Retired—Dave Butz, 15-year defensive tackle, 16 games in '88.

Players lost through Plan B (12): WR Anthony Allen (Minn; 14 games in '88), TE Joe Caravello (SD; 12), C Eric Coyle (Dall; active for 1 game but did not play), S Travis Curtis (Minn; 1), S Steve Gage (Wash; 16), DE-DT Steve Hamilton (Det; 15), LB Blake Peterson (Den; 0), WR Derrick Sheppard (NO; 5), RB Tim Smith (SD; 14), CB Johnny Thomas (SD; 4), CB-S Dennis Woodberry (Den; 12), WR Eric Yarber (SD; 0).

Also played with Redskins in '88—QB David Archer (1 game), P Greg Coleman (10), P Steve Cox (1), RB Keith Griffin (8), WR Billy Johnson (1), TE Anthony Jones (8), C Mike Scully (1).

COACHING STAFF

Head Coach, Joe Gibbs

Pro Career: Enters his ninth season as Redskins head coach. Needs eight victories to reach the 100-win plateau. Has led Redskins to two Super Bowl titles and three Super Bowl appearances during 1980's. Washington has appeared in postseason play five of last seven seasons under Gibbs. Named head coach on January 13, 1981, after spending eight years as an NFL assistant coach and nine seasons on the college level. Came to Redskins from San Diego Chargers, where he was offensive coordinator in 1979 and 1980. Prior to that, he was offensive coordinator for the Tampa Bay Buccaneers in 1978 and offensive backfield coach for the St. Louis Cardinals from 1973-77. While he was with San Diego, the Chargers won the AFC West title and led the NFL in passing two straight years. No pro playing experience. Career record: 92-42.

College: Played tight end, linebacker, and guard under Don Coryell at San Diego State in 1961 and 1962 after spending two years at Cerritos, Calif., J.C. 1959-60. Started college coaching career at San Diego State 1964-66, followed by Florida State 1967-68, Southern California 1969-70, and Arkansas 1971-72.

Personal: Born November 25, 1940, in Mocksville, N.C. Graduated from Santa Fe Springs, Calif., High School. Two-time national racquetball champion and ranked second in the over-35 category in 1978. He and his wife, Pat, live in Vienna, Va., and have two sons—J. D. and Coy.

Assistant Coaches

Don Breaux, running backs; born August 3, 1940, Jennings, La., lives in Centreville, Va. Quarterback McNeese State 1959-61. Pro quarterback Denver Broncos 1963, San Diego Chargers 1964-65. College coach: Florida State 1966-67, Arkansas 1968-71, 1977-80, Florida 1973-74, Texas 1975-76. Pro coach: Joined Redskins in 1981.

Joe Bugel, assistant head coach-offense; born March 10, 1940, Pittsburgh, Pa., lives in Oakton, Va. Guard Western Kentucky 1960-62. No pro playing experience. College coach: Western Kentucky 1964-68, Navy 1969-72, Iowa State 1973, Ohio State 1974. Pro coach: Detroit Lions 1975-76, Houston Oilers 1977-80, joined Redskins in 1981.

Jack Burns, quarterbacks; born January 3, 1949, Tampa, Fla., lives in Herndon, Va. Safety Florida 1967-71. No pro playing experience. College coach: Florida 1971-73, 1975, Louisville 1974, 1985-88, Texas 1976, Vanderbilt 1977-78, Auburn 1979-80. Pro scout: Tampa Bay Bandits (USFL) 1981-83. Pro coach: Joined Redskins in 1989.

Bobby DePaul, administrative assistant; born January 29, 1963, Cheverly, Md., lives in Bowie, Md. Linebacker Maryland 1982-83. No pro playing experience. College coach: Catholic University 1986-88. Pro coach: Joined Redskins in 1989.

Larry Peccatiello, defensive coordinator; born December 21, 1935, Newark, N.J., lives in Warrenton, Va. Receiver William & Mary 1955-58. No pro playing experience. College coach: William & Mary 1961-68, Navy 1969-70, Rice 1971. Pro coach: Houston Oilers 1972-75, Seattle Seahawks 1976-80, joined Redskins in 1981.

Richie Petitbon, assistant head coach-defense; born April 18, 1938, New Orleans, La., lives in Vienna, Va. Quarterback-defensive back Tulane 1955-58. Pro defensive back Chicago Bears 1959-67, Los Angeles Rams 1969-70, Washington Redskins 1971-73. Pro coach: Houston Oilers 1974-77, joined Redskins in 1978.

Dan Riley, conditioning; born October 19, 1949, Syracuse, N.Y., lives in Herndon, Va. No college or pro playing experience. College coach: Army 1973-76, Penn State 1977-81. Pro coach: Joined Redskins in 1982.

Washington Redskins 1989 First-Year Roster

Name	Pos.	Ht.	Wt.	Birth-date	College	Hometown	How Acq.
Bell, Grantis	WR-KR	5-8	155	8/11/66	West Virginia	Ft. Lauderdale, Fla.	FA
Bishop, Jim	C-G	6-4	285	2/15/67	Tulane	New Orleans, La.	FA
Bonner, Brian (1)	LB	6-1	225	10/9/65	Minnesota	Minneapolis, Minn.	FA-'88
Chipps, Dale (1)	WR	6-0	186	2/2/65	Towson State	Brandywine, Md.	FA-'88
Darrington, Charlie	TE	6-3	228	6/26/66	Kentucky	Tifton, Ga.	D9
Duckens, Mark (1)	DT	6-4	270	3/4/65	Arizona State	Wichita, Kan.	FA-'88
Friberg, Keith	LB	6-4	245	11/21/66	Syracuse	Staten Island, N.Y.	FA
Gordon, Cedric	WR	6-1	165	11/6/66	Ferris State	Ann Arbor, Mich.	FA
Graham, Jeff	QB	6-4	205	2/5/66	Long Beach State	Costa Mesa, Calif.	D4
Harry, Carl	WR-KR	5-9	168	10/26/67	Utah	Fountain Valley, Calif.	FA
Hendrix, Kevin	LB	6-3	266	1/21/66	South Carolina	Hickory, N.C.	D7
Hobbs, Stephen (1)	WR	5-11	190	11/14/65	North Alabama	Mendenhall, Miss.	FA
Humphries, Stan (1)	QB	6-2	223	4/14/65	N.E. Louisiana	Shreveport, La.	D6-'88
Johnson, A. J.	CB	5-8	176	6/22/67	S.W. Texas State	San Antonio, Tex.	D6
Johnson, Jimmie	TE	6-2	246	10/6/66	Howard	Augusta, Ga.	D12a
Mayhew, Martin (1)	CB	5-8	172	10/8/65	Florida State	Tallahassee, Fla.	FA
McGill, Darryl (1)	RB	5-10	210	3/28/66	Wake Forest	Durham, N.C.	D8-'88
Mehre, Harry	WR	6-0	177	2/15/66	William & Mary	Atlanta, Ga.	FA
Mickles, Joe	RB	5-10	210	12/25/65	Mississippi	Birmingham, Ala.	D12b
Mims, Carl (1)	CB	5-10	180	10/28/65	Sam Houston State	Gainesville, Tex.	D5-'88
Nunamacher, Jeff	G	6-2	285	9/10/65	Clemson	Somerville, N.J.	FA
Presbury, Robert	DE-DT	6-2	266	7/18/65	Delaware State	Edgewood, Md.	FA
Reaves, Willard (1)	RB	5-11	200	8/17/59	Northern Arizona	Flagstaff, Ariz.	FA-'88
Robinson, Lybrant	DE	6-4	250	8/31/64	Delaware State	Salisbury, Md.	D5b
Rocker, Tracy	DT	6-3	288	4/9/66	Auburn	Atlanta, Ga.	D3
Schlereth, Mark	C	6-3	265	1/25/66	Idaho	Anchorage, Alaska	D10
Smiley, Tim	S	6-0	190	5/11/66	Arkansas State	Wynne, Ark.	D5a
Smith, Dennis	T	6-6	290	9/9/65	Baylor	Waco, Tex.	FA
Tamm, Ralph (1)	G	6-3	285	3/11/66	West Chester State	Bensalem, Pa.	FA
Tuten, Richard (1)	P	6-2	218	1/5/65	Florida State	Ocala, Fla.	FA
Williams, Albert (1)	DE	6-5	243	6/17/65	James Madison	South Boston, Va.	FA

The term NFL Rookie is defined as a player who is in his first season of professional football and has not been on the roster of another professional football team for any regular-season or postseason games. A Rookie is designated by an "R" on NFL rosters. Players who have been active in another professional football league or players who have NFL experience, including either preseason training camp or being on an active roster for fewer than three regular-season or postseason games, are termed NFL First-Year Players. An NFL First-Year Player is designated by a "1" on NFL rosters. Thereafter, a player on an NFL active roster for at least three regular-season or postseason games is credited with an additional year of NFL playing experience.

NOTES

Wayne Sevier, special teams; born July 3, 1941, San Diego, Calif., lives in Warrenton, Va. Quarterback Chaffey, Calif., J.C. 1960, San Diego State 1961-62. No pro playing experience. College coach: California Western 1968-69. Pro coach: St. Louis Cardinals 1974-75, Atlanta Falcons 1976, San Diego Chargers 1979-80, 1987-88, Washington Redskins 1981-86, rejoined Redskins in 1989.

Warren Simmons, tight ends; born February 25, 1942, Poughkeepsie, N.Y., lives in Centreville, Va. Center San Diego State 1963-65. No pro playing experience. College coach: Cal State-Fullerton 1972-75, Cerritos, Calif., J.C. 1976-80. Pro coach: Joined Redskins in 1981.

Charley Taylor, wide receivers; born September 28, 1942, Grand Prairie, Tex., lives in Reston, Va. Running back Arizona State 1961-63. Pro running back-wide receiver Washington Redskins 1964-76. Pro coach: Joined Redskins in 1982.

Emmitt Thomas, defensive backs; born June 4, 1943, Angleton, Tex., lives in Reston, Va. Quarterback-wide receiver Bishop (Tex.) College 1963-65. Pro defensive back Kansas City Chiefs 1966-78. College coach: Central Missouri State 1979-80. Pro coach: St. Louis Cardinals 1981-85, joined Redskins in 1986.

LaVern Torgeson, defensive line; born February 28, 1929, LaCrosse, Wash., lives in Fairfax, Va. Center-linebacker Washington State 1948-50. Pro linebacker Detroit Lions 1951-54, Washington Redskins 1955-58. Pro coach: Washington Redskins 1959-61, 1971-77, Pittsburgh Steelers 1962-68, Los Angeles Rams 1969-70, 1978-80, rejoined Redskins in 1981.

1988 SEASON IN REVIEW

Trades

1988 Interconference Trades

Defensive end **Andrew Provence** from Atlanta to Denver for a draft choice (5/12).

Detroit traded the rights to defensive back **Kip Corrington** to Denver for a draft choice (5/13).

Defensive back **Tim Morrison** from Washington to Seattle for a draft choice (5/20).

Wide receiver **Wes Chandler** from San Diego to San Francisco for center **Fred Quillan** (6/2).

Running back **Tony Dorsett** from Dallas to Denver for a draft choice (6/6).

Defensive back **Bo Eason** from Houston to San Francisco for a draft choice (6/6).

Linebacker **Eugene Marve** from Buffalo to Tampa Bay for a draft choice (6/14).

Wide receiver **Brian Bedford** from Dallas to San Diego for a draft choice (6/29).

Linebacker **Milt McColl** from San Francisco to the Los Angeles Raiders for a draft choice (7/19).

Linebacker **Ricky Hunley** from Denver to Phoenix for center **Mike Ruether** (7/21).

Defensive back **Evan Cooper** from Philadelphia to Houston for a draft choice (7/23).

Defensive back **Elbert Foules** from Philadelphia to Houston for a draft choice (7/23).

Wide receiver **Willie Gault** from Chicago to the Los Angeles Raiders for draft choices (7/28).

Guard **Dan Remsberg** from Denver to Philadelphia for a draft choice (7/30).

Center **Carlos Scott** from Denver to Phoenix for a draft choice (8/2).

Guard/tackle **Curtis Rouse** from San Diego to Atlanta for a past consideration (8/4).

Wide receiver **Alphonso Williams** from San Diego to Tampa Bay for a draft choice (8/11).

Tight end **Tim Sherwin** from Indianapolis to the New York Giants for a draft choice (8/15).

Nose tackle **Tony Stephens** from New Orleans to New England for a draft choice (8/16).

Tight end **Bobby Micho** from Denver to Washington for a draft choice (8/17).

Wide receiver **Jessie Hester** from the Los Angeles Raiders to Atlanta for a draft choice (8/22).

Tackle **Ron Heller** from Seattle to Philadelphia for a draft choice (8/22).

Guard **Mark Traynowicz** from Buffalo to Philadelphia for a draft choice (8/23).

Defensive end **Sean McNanie** from Buffalo to Phoenix for a draft choice (8/23).

Wide receiver **Stephen Starring** from New England to Tampa Bay for a draft chioce (8/26).

Nose tackle **Shawn Knight** from New Orleans to Denver for nose tackle **Ted Gregory** (8/29).

Quarterback **Jay Schroeder** from Washington to the Los Angeles Raiders for tackle **Jim Lachey** and draft choices (9/7).

Defensive back **Leonard Smith** from Phoenix to Buffalo for defensive back **Roland Mitchell** and a draft choice (9/21).

Guard **Ron Solt** from Indianapolis to Philadelphia for draft choices (10/5).

Running back **Calvin Thomas** from Chicago to Denver for a draft choice (10/5).

1989 Interconference Trades

Denver's eleventh-round choice in 1989 from Chicago to Denver for a past consideration (2/11).

Pittsburgh linebacker **Mike Merriweather** to Minnesota for the Vikings' first-round choice in 1989. Pittsburgh selected tackle **Tom Ricketts** (Pittsburgh) (4/23).

Chicago's first-round choice in 1989 to Miami for the Dolphins' second- and third-round choices in 1989. Miami selected defensive back **Louis Oliver** (Florida). Chicago selected linebacker **John Roper** (Texas A&M) and guard **Jerry Fontenot** (Texas A&M) (4/23).

Cincinnati's first-round choice in 1989 to Atlanta for the Falcons' second-, fourth-, and tenth-round choices in 1989. Atlanta selected wide receiver **Shawn Collins** (Northern Arizona). Cincinnati selected running back **Eric Ball** (UCLA), linebacker **Kerry Owens** (Arkansas), and defensive back **Cornell Holloway** (Pittsburgh) (4/23).

Cleveland running back **Herman Fontenot** and the Browns' third-round choice in 1989, New England's fifth-round choice in 1989, and Cleveland's first-round choice in 1990 to Green Bay for the Packers' second- and fifth-round choices in 1989. Cleveland selected wide receiver **Lawyer Tillman** (Auburn) and defensive back **Kyle Kramer** (Bowling Green). Green Bay selected quarterback **Anthony Dilweg** (Duke) and running back **Vince Workman** (Ohio State) (4/23).

Dallas's rights to guard **Steve Wisniewski** (Penn State) and the Cowboys' sixth-round choice in 1989 to the Los Angeles Raiders for Washington's second-round choice, the Raiders' third-round choice, and Atlanta's fifth-round choice in 1989. Dallas selected running back **Daryl Johnston** (Syracuse), defensive end **Rhondy Weston** (Florida), and linebacker **Willis Crockett** (Georgia Tech). The Los Angeles Raiders selected quarterback **Jeff Francis** (Tennessee) (4/23).

The New York Giants' second-round choice in 1989 to San Diego for the Chargers' third-, fourth-, and seventh-round choices in 1989. San Diego selected quarterback **Billy Joe Tolliver** (Texas Tech). The New York Giants selected guard **Bob Kratch** (Iowa), running back **Lewis Tillman** (Jackson State), and tackle **David Popp** (Eastern Illinois) (4/23).

The Los Angeles Raiders' fourth-round choice in 1989 to Chicago for the Bears' fourth- and sixth-round choices in 1989. Chicago selected defensive back **Markus Paul** (Syracuse). The Raiders sent Chicago's fourth-round choice in 1989 to Washington as part of 1988 trade which sent quarterback **Jay Schroeder** from the Redskins to the Raiders. Washington selected wide receiver **Erik Affholter** (Southern California). The Raiders traded the Bears' sixth-round pick to the Patriots. (4/23).

Washington running back **Mike Oliphant** to Cleveland for running back **Earnest Byner** (4/23).

The Los Angeles Raiders' fifth-round choice in 1989 to San Francisco for the 49ers' fifth- and eighth-round choices in 1989. San Francisco selected defensive back **Johnny Jackson** (Houston). The Raiders sent San Francisco's fifth-round choice in 1989 to Washington as part of the 1988 trade which sent quarterback **Jay Schroeder** from the Redskins to the Raiders. Washington selected linebacker **Lybrant Robinson** (Delaware State) (4/23).

Indianapolis's fifth-round choice in 1989 to Washington for the Redskins' fourth- and eighth-round choices in 1990. Washington selected defensive back **Tim Smiley** (Arkansas State) (4/23).

The Los Angeles Raiders' eleventh-round choice in 1989 to San Francisco for the 49ers' twelfth-round choices in 1989 and 1990. San Francisco selected running back **Jim Bell** (Boston College). The Raiders traded San Francisco's twelfth-round choice in 1989 to Minnesota for the Vikings' eleventh-round choice in 1990 (4/24).

San Diego's twelfth-round choice in 1989 to Washington for the Redskins' twelfth-round choice in 1990. Washington selected tight end **Jimmy Johnson** (Howard) (4/24).

Minnesota's eleventh-round choice in 1990 to the Los Angeles Raiders for San Francisco's twelfth-round choice in 1989. Minnesota selected wide receiver **Everett Ross** (Ohio State) (4/24).

1988 AFC Trades

Defensive back **Russell Carter** from the New York Jets to the Los Angeles Raiders for a draft choice (5/20).

Defensive end **Art Still** from Kansas City to Buffalo for a draft choice (6/23).

Defensive back **Leonard Coleman** from Indianapolis to San Diego for a draft choice (7/8).

Tackle **Jim Lachey** from San Diego to the Los Angeles Raiders for tackle **John Clay** and a draft choice (8/1).

Wide receiver **Daryl Turner** from Seattle to Cleveland for a draft choice (8/2).

Punter **Jeff Gossett** from Houston to the Los Angeles Raiders for a past consideration (8/16).

Linebacker **Thomas Benson** from San Diego to New England for a draft choice (8/22).

Center **Mike Baab** from Cleveland to New England for a draft choice (8/29).

Linebacker **Anthony Griggs** from Cleveland to Indianapolis for a draft choice (8/30).

Linebacker **Fredd Young** from Seattle to Indianapolis for draft choices (9/9).

Running back **Napoleon McCallum** from the Los Angeles Raiders to San Diego for a past consideration (10/11).

1989 AFC Trades

The Los Angeles Raiders' third-round choice in 1989 and fourth-round choice in 1990 from San Diego to the Los Angeles Raiders for a past consideration (4/11).

Denver's first-round choice in 1989 to Cleveland for the Browns' first-, second-, fifth-, and ninth-round choices in 1989. Cleveland selected running back **Eric Metcalf** (Texas). Denver selected defensive back **Steve Atwater** (Arkansas), defensive end **Warren Powers** (Maryland), defensive back **Darren Carrington** (Northern Arizona), and running back **Wayne Williams** (Florida) (4/23).

Cleveland linebacker **Mike Junkin** to Kansas City for the Chiefs' fifth-round choice in 1989. Cleveland selected wide receiver **Vernon Joines** (Maryland) (4/23).

New England's sixth-round choice in 1989 to the Los Angeles Raiders for Chicago's sixth-round choice and San Francisco's eighth-round choice in 1989. The Raiders selected running back **Doug Lloyd** (North Dakota State). New England selected running back **Eric Mitchel** (Oklahoma) and defensive back **Tony Zackery** (Washington) (4/23).

1988 NFC Trade

San Francisco traded its rights to kicker **Tim Foley** to Atlanta for a draft choice (6/7).

1989 NFC Trades

Chicago's third-round choice in 1989 to Philadelphia for the Eagles' fifth-, seventh-, eighth-, ninth-, tenth-, eleventh-, and twelfth-round choices in 1989. Philadelphia selected linebacker **Britt Hager** (Texas). Chicago selected running back **Mark Green** (Notre Dame), defensive back **Richard Brothers** (Arkansas), defensive tackle **Tony Wood** (Oklahoma), linebacker **LaSalle Harper** (Arkansas), tight end **Todd Millikan** (Nebraska), defensive tackle **Joe Nelms** (California), and wide receiver **Fred Weygand** (Auburn) (4/21).

Washington's first-round choice in 1990 and the Los Angeles Raiders' second-round choice in 1989 to Atlanta for running back **Gerald Riggs** and the Falcons' fifth-round choice in 1990. Atlanta selected tackle **Ralph Norwood** (Louisiana State) (4/23).

Washington's rights to wide receiver **Erik Affholter** (Southern California) and the Redskins' fifth- and eighth-round choices in 1989 to Green Bay for the rights to quarterback **Jeff Graham** (Long Beach State). Green Bay selected wide receiver **Jeff Query** (Millikin) and punter **Brian Shulman** (Auburn) (4/23).

Tampa Bay's eighth-round choice in 1990 to the Los Angeles Rams for the Rams' eleventh- and twelfth-round choices and Washington's eleventh-round choice in 1989. Tampa Bay selected defensive end **Willie Griffin** (Nebraska), wide receiver **Herb Duncan** (Northern Arizona), and defensive back **Terry Young** (Georgia Southern) (4/24).

1988 PRESEASON STANDINGS

American Football Conference

Eastern Division

	W	L	T	Pct.	Pts.	OP
Indianapolis	3	1	0	.750	83	55
Miami**	2	3	0	.400	87	105
Buffalo	1	3	0	.250	49	74
New England	1	3	0	.250	89	109
N.Y. Jets	1	3	0	.250	68	81

Central Division

	W	L	T	Pct.	Pts.	OP
Houston	4	0	0	1.000	114	50
Cincinnati*	4	1	0	.800	110	82
Cleveland	3	1	0	.750	60	37
Pittsburgh	3	1	0	.750	113	103

Western Division

	W	L	T	Pct.	Pts.	OP
Denver	3	1	0	.750	108	91
Seattle	3	1	0	.750	88	60
Kansas City	2	1	1	.625	103	96
L.A. Raiders	1	3	0	.250	91	118
San Diego	1	3	0	.250	81	113

National Football Conference

Eastern Division

	W	L	T	Pct.	Pts.	OP
N.Y. Giants	3	1	0	.750	99	58
Washington	3	1	0	.750	137	98
Dallas	2	2	0	.500	75	104
Philadelphia	2	2	0	.500	87	66
Phoenix	1	3	0	.250	92	94

Central Division

	W	L	T	Pct.	Pts.	OP
Minnesota	3	1	0	.750	91	77
Green Bay	1	2	1	.375	72	104
Chicago	1	3	0	.250	72	99
Detroit	0	4	0	.000	39	80
Tampa Bay	0	4	0	.000	31	76

Western Division

	W	L	T	Pct.	Pts.	OP
San Fran.**	3	2	0	.600	130	119
Atlanta	2	2	0	.500	83	105
New Orleans	2	2	0	.500	90	97
L.A. Rams*	2	3	0	.400	113	104

*Includes Hall of Fame Game
**Includes American Bowl '88 in London, England

AFC Preseason Results—Team By Team

Eastern Division

Buffalo (1-3)

9	Houston	13
13	*Cincinnati	24
13	Seattle	30
14	Tampa Bay	7
49		74

Indianapolis (3-1)

20	Tampa Bay	7
25	*Green Bay	21
18	*New Orleans	6
20	Denver	21
83		55

Miami (2-3)

27	San Fran. (AB)	21
17	Chicago	20
10	*Washington	27
16	*Denver (OT)	13
17	Minnesota	24
87		105

New England (1-3)

30	*Atlanta	34
14	Houston	27
24	Philadelphia	21
21	*Cincinnati	27
89		109

N.Y. Jets (1-3)

12	Philadelphia	23
21	N.Y. Giants	24
11	Cleveland	7
24	Green Bay	27
68		81

Central Division

Cincinnati (4-1)

14	L.A. Rams (HOF)	7
21	Kansas City	34
24	Buffalo	13
24	*Detroit	7
27	New England	21
110		82

Cleveland (3-1)

13	*Detroit	10
23	Tampa Bay	3
7	N.Y. Jets	11
17	*N.Y. Giants	13
60		37

Houston (4-0)

13	*Buffalo	9
27	New England	14
20	L.A. Rams (OT)	17
54	Dallas	10
114		50

Pittsburgh (3-1)

44	Washington	31
21	*Philadelphia	16
17	N.Y. Giants	28
31	New Orleans	28
113		103

Western Division

Denver (3-1)

40	L.A. Rams	31
34	*San Francisco	24
13	Miami (OT)	16
21	*Indianapolis	20
108		91

Kansas City (2-1-1)

34	*Cincinnati	21
27	Atlanta	13
21	Green Bay (OT)	21
21	*Phoenix	41
103		96

L.A. Raiders (1-3)

10	San Francisco	24
17	*Dallas	27
27	*Washington	45
37	Chicago	22
91		118

San Diego (1-3)

24	*Dallas	21
6	L.A. Rams	27
27	*San Francisco	34
24	*L.A. Rams	31
81		113

Seattle (3-1)

21	*Phoenix	7
16	Detroit (OT)	13
30	*Buffalo	13
21	San Francisco	27
88		60

NFC Preseason Results—Team By Team

Eastern Division

Dallas (2-2)

21	San Diego	24
27	L.A. Raiders	17
17	*Chicago	9
10	*Houston	54
75		104

N.Y. Giants (3-1)

34	Green Bay	3
24	*N.Y. Jets	21
28	*Pittsburgh	17
13	Cleveland	17
99		58

Philadelphia (2-2)

23	*N.Y. Jets	12
16	Pittsburgh	21
21	*New England	24
27	Detroit	9
87		66

Phoenix (1-3)

7	Seattle	21
28	*New Orleans	33
16	*Minnesota (OT)	19
41	Kansas City	21
92		94

Washington (3-1)

31	*Pittsburgh	44
27	Miami	10
45	L.A. Raiders	27
34	Atlanta	17
137		98

Central Division

Chicago (1-3)

20	*Miami	17
21	Minnesota	28
9	Dallas	17
22	*L.A. Raiders	37
72		99

Detroit (0-4)

10	Cleveland	13
13	*Seattle (OT)	16
7	Cincinnati	24
9	*Philadelphia	27
39		80

Green Bay (1-2-1)

3	*N.Y. Giants	34
21	Indianapolis	25
21	*Kansas City (OT)	21
27	*N.Y. Jets	24
72		104

Minnesota (3-1)

20	*New Orleans	23
28	Chicago	21
19	Phoenix (OT)	16
24	*Miami	17
91		77

Tampa Bay (0-4)

7	*Indianapolis	20
3	*Cleveland	23
14	Atlanta	19
7	Buffalo	14
31		76

Western Division

Atlanta (2-2)

34	New England	30
13	*Kansas City	27
19	*Tampa Bay	14
17	Washington	34
83		105

L.A. Rams (2-3)

7	Cincinnati (HOF)	14
31	*Denver	40
27	*San Diego	6
17	*Houston (OT)	20
31	San Diego	24
113		104

New Orleans (2-2)

23	Minnesota	20
33	Phoenix	28
6	Indianapolis	18
28	*Pittsburgh	31
90		97

San Francisco (3-2)

21	Miami (AB)	27
24	*L.A. Raiders	10
24	Denver	34
34	San Diego	27
27	*Seattle	21
130		119

*denotes home game
(OT) denotes overtime
(HOF) denotes Hall of Fame Game
(AB) denotes American Bowl '88 Game

1988 NFL STANDINGS

American Football Conference

Eastern Division

	W	L	T	Pct.	Pts.	OP
Buffalo	12	4	0	.750	329	237
Indianapolis	9	7	0	.563	354	315
New England	9	7	0	.563	250	284
N.Y. Jets	8	7	1	.531	372	354
Miami	6	10	0	.375	319	380

Central Division

	W	L	T	Pct.	Pts.	OP
Cincinnati	12	4	0	.750	448	329
Cleveland*	10	6	0	.625	304	288
Houston*	10	6	0	.625	424	365
Pittsburgh	5	11	0	.313	336	421

Western Division

	W	L	T	Pct.	Pts.	OP
Seattle	9	7	0	.563	339	329
Denver	8	8	0	.500	327	352
L.A. Raiders	7	9	0	.438	325	369
San Diego	6	10	0	.375	231	332
Kansas City	4	11	1	.281	254	320

National Football Conference

Eastern Division

	W	L	T	Pct.	Pts.	OP
Philadelphia	10	6	0	.625	379	319
N.Y. Giants	10	6	0	.625	359	304
Washington	7	9	0	.438	345	387
Phoenix	7	9	0	.438	344	398
Dallas	3	13	0	.188	265	381

Central Division

	W	L	T	Pct.	Pts.	OP
Chicago	12	4	0	.750	312	215
Minnesota*	11	5	0	.688	406	233
Tampa Bay	5	11	0	.313	261	350
Detroit	4	12	0	.250	220	313
Green Bay	4	12	0	.250	240	315

Western Division

	W	L	T	Pct.	Pts.	OP
San Francisco	10	6	0	.625	369	294
L.A. Rams*	10	6	0	.625	407	293
New Orleans	10	6	0	.625	312	283
Atlanta	5	11	0	.313	244	315

**Wild Card qualifier for playoffs*

Indianapolis finished second in AFC East on basis of better record versus common opponents (7-5) over New England (6-6). Cleveland gained first AFC Wild Card position based on better division record (4-2) over Houston (3-3). Philadelphia finished first in NFC East on basis of head-to-head sweep over New York Giants. Washington finished third in NFC East on basis of better division record (4-4) over Phoenix (3-5). Detroit finished fourth in NFC Central on basis of head-to-head sweep over Green Bay. San Francisco finished first in NFC West based on better head-to-head record (3-1) over Los Angeles Rams (2-2) and New Orleans (1-3). Los Angeles Rams finished second in NFC West on basis of better division record (4-2) over New Orleans (3-3) and earned Wild Card position based on better conference record (8-4) over New York Giants (9-5) and New Orleans (6-6).

First-Round Playoffs

AFC .... Houston 24, Cleveland 23, December 24, at Cleveland
NFC .... Minnesota 28, Los Angeles Rams 17, December 26, at Minnesota

Divisional Playoffs

AFC .... Cincinnati 21, Seattle 13, December 31, at Cincinnati
Buffalo 17, Houston 10, January 1, at Buffalo
NFC .... Chicago 20, Philadelphia 12, December 31, at Chicago
San Francisco 34, Minnesota 9, January 1, at San Francisco

Championship Games

AFC .... Cincinnati 21, Buffalo 10, January 8, at Cincinnati
NFC .... San Francisco 28, Chicago 3, January 8, at Chicago
SUPER BOWL XXIII San Francisco 20, Cincinnati 16, January 22, at Joe Robbie Stadium, Miami, Florida
AFC-NFC PRO BOWL . NFC 34, AFC 3, January 29, at Aloha Stadium, Honolulu, Hawaii

AFC Season Records—Team by Team

BUFFALO (12-4)

13	*Minnesota	10
9	*Miami	6
16	at New England	14
36	*Pittsburgh	28
3	at Chicago	24
34	*Indianapolis	23
37	at N.Y. Jets	14
23	*New England	20
28	*Green Bay	0
13	at Seattle	3
31	at Miami	6
9	*N.Y. Jets (OT)	6
21	at Cincinnati	35
5	at Tampa Bay	10
37	*L.A. Raiders	21
14	at Indianapolis	17
329		237

CINCINNATI (12-4)

21	*Phoenix	14
28	at Philadelphia	24
17	at Pittsburgh	12
24	*Cleveland	17
45	at L.A. Raiders	21
36	*N.Y. Jets	19
21	at New England	27
44	*Houston	21
16	at Cleveland	23
42	*Pittsburgh	7
28	at Kansas City	31
38	at Dallas	24
35	*Buffalo	21
27	*San Diego	10
6	at Houston	41
20	*Washington (OT)	17
448		329

CLEVELAND (10-6)

6	at Kansas City	3
3	*N.Y. Jets	23
23	*Indianapolis	17
17	at Cincinnati	24
23	at Pittsburgh	9
10	*Seattle	16
19	*Philadelphia	3
29	at Phoenix	21
23	*Cincinnati	16
17	at Houston	24
7	at Denver	30
27	*Pittsburgh	7
17	at Washington	13
24	*Dallas	21
31	at Miami	38
28	*Houston	23
304		288

DENVER (8-8)

14	*Seattle	21
34	*San Diego	3
13	at Kansas City	20
27	*L.A. Raiders (OT)	30
12	at San Diego	0
16	at San Fran. (OT)	13
30	*Atlanta	14
21	at Pittsburgh	39
23	at Indianapolis	55
17	*Kansas City	11
30	*Cleveland	7
0	at New Orleans	42
35	*L.A. Rams	24
20	at L.A. Raiders	21
14	at Seattle	42
21	*New England	10
327		352

HOUSTON (10-6)

17	at Ind. (OT)	14
38	*L.A. Raiders	35
3	at N.Y. Jets	45
31	*New England	6
23	at Philadelphia	32
7	*Kansas City	6
34	at Pittsburgh	14
21	at Cincinnati	44
41	*Washington	17
24	*Cleveland	17
24	at Seattle	27
38	*Phoenix	20
25	at Dallas	17
34	*Pittsburgh	37
41	*Cincinnati	6
23	at Cleveland	28
424		365

INDIANAPOLIS (9-7)

14	*Houston (OT)	17
13	*Chicago	17
17	at Cleveland	23
15	*Miami	13
17	at New England	21
23	at Buffalo	34
35	*Tampa Bay	31
16	at San Diego	0
55	*Denver	23
38	*N.Y. Jets	14
20	at Green Bay	13
3	at Minnesota	12
24	*New England	21
31	at Miami	28
16	at N.Y. Jets	34
17	*Buffalo	14
354		315

KANSAS CITY (4-11-1)

3	*Cleveland	6
10	at Seattle	31
20	*Denver	13
23	*San Diego	24
17	at N.Y. Jets (OT)	17
6	at Houston	7
17	*L.A. Raiders	27
6	*Detroit	7
10	at L.A. Raiders	17
11	at Denver	17
31	*Cincinnati	28
27	*Seattle	24
10	at Pittsburgh	16
38	*N.Y. Jets	34
12	at N.Y. Giants	28
13	at San Diego	24
254		320

L.A. RAIDERS (7-9)

24	*San Diego	13
35	at Houston	38
17	*L.A. Rams	22
30	at Denver (OT)	27
21	*Cincinnati	45
14	*Miami	24
27	at Kansas City	17
6	at New Orleans	20
17	*Kansas City	10
13	at San Diego	3
9	at San Francisco	3
6	*Atlanta	12
27	at Seattle	35
21	*Denver	20
21	at Buffalo	37
37	*Seattle	43
325		369

MIAMI (6-10)

7	at Chicago	34
6	at Buffalo	9
24	*Green Bay	17
13	at Indianapolis	15
24	*Minnesota	7
24	at L.A. Raiders	14
31	*San Diego	28
30	*N.Y. Jets	44
17	at Tampa Bay	14
10	at New England	21
6	*Buffalo	31
3	*New England	6
34	at N.Y. Jets	38
28	*Indianapolis	31
38	*Cleveland	31
24	at Pittsburgh	40
319		380

NEW ENGLAND (9-7)

28	*N.Y. Jets	3
6	at Minnesota	36
14	*Buffalo	16
6	at Houston	31
21	*Indianapolis	17
3	at Green Bay	45
27	*Cincinnati	21
20	at Buffalo	23
30	*Chicago	7
21	*Miami	10
14	at N.Y. Jets	13
6	at Miami	3
21	at Indianapolis	24
13	*Seattle	7
10	*Tampa Bay (OT)	7
10	at Denver	21
250		284

N.Y. JETS (8-7-1)

3	at New England	28
23	at Cleveland	3
45	*Houston	3
17	at Detroit	10
17	*Kansas City (OT)	17
19	at Cincinnati	36
14	*Buffalo	37
44	at Miami	30
24	*Pittsburgh	20
14	at Indianapolis	38
13	*New England	14
6	at Buffalo (OT)	9
38	*Miami	34
34	at Kansas City	38
34	*Indianapolis	16
27	*N.Y. Giants	21
372		354

PITTSBURGH (5-11)

24	*Dallas	21
29	at Washington	30
12	*Cincinnati	17
28	at Buffalo	36
9	*Cleveland	23
14	at Phoenix	31
14	*Houston	34
39	*Denver	21
20	at N.Y. Jets	24
7	at Cincinnati	42
26	*Philadelphia	27
7	at Cleveland	27
16	*Kansas City	10
37	at Houston	34
14	at San Diego	20
40	*Miami	24
336		421

SAN DIEGO (6-10)

13	at L.A. Raiders	24
3	at Denver	34
17	*Seattle	6
24	at Kansas City	23
0	*Denver	12
17	*New Orleans	23
28	at Miami	31
0	*Indianapolis	16
14	at Seattle	17
3	*L.A. Raiders	13
10	at Atlanta	7
38	at L.A. Rams	24
10	*San Francisco	48
10	at Cincinnati	27
20	*Pittsburgh	14
24	*Kansas City	13
231		332

SEATTLE (9-7)

21	at Denver	14
31	*Kansas City	10
6	at San Diego	17
7	*San Francisco	38
31	at Atlanta	20
16	at Cleveland	10
19	*New Orleans	20
10	at L.A. Rams	31
17	*San Diego	14
3	*Buffalo	13
27	*Houston	24
24	at Kansas City	27
35	*L.A. Raiders	27
7	at New England	13
42	*Denver	14
43	at L.A. Raiders	37
339		329

** denotes home game*
(OT) denotes overtime

NFC Season Records—Team by Team

ATLANTA (5-11)

17	at Detroit	31
21	*New Orleans	29
34	at San Francisco	17
20	at Dallas	26
20	*Seattle	31
0	*L.A. Rams	33
14	at Denver	30
16	*N.Y. Giants	23
27	at Philadelphia	24
20	*Green Bay	0
7	*San Diego	10
12	at L.A. Raiders	6
17	*Tampa Bay	10
3	*San Francisco	13
7	at L.A. Rams	22
9	at New Orleans	10
244		315

CHICAGO (12-4)

34	*Miami	7
17	at Indianapolis	13
7	*Minnesota	31
24	at Green Bay	6
24	*Buffalo	3
24	at Detroit	7
17	*Dallas	7
10	*San Francisco	9
7	at New England	30
28	*Tampa Bay	10
34	at Washington	14
27	at Tampa Bay	15
16	*Green Bay	0
3	at L.A. Rams	23
13	*Detroit	12
27	at Minnesota	28
312		215

DALLAS (3-13)

21	at Pittsburgh	24
17	at Phoenix	14
10	*N.Y. Giants	12
26	*Atlanta	20
17	at New Orleans	20
17	*Washington	35
7	at Chicago	17
23	at Philadelphia	24
10	*Phoenix	16
21	at N.Y. Giants	29
3	*Minnesota	43
24	*Cincinnati	38
17	*Houston	25
21	at Cleveland	24
24	at Washington	17
7	*Philadelphia	23
265		381

DETROIT (4-12)

31	*Atlanta	17
10	at L.A. Rams	17
14	*New Orleans	22
10	*N.Y. Jets	17
13	at San Francisco	20
7	*Chicago	24
10	at N.Y. Giants	30
7	at Kansas City	6
10	*N.Y. Giants (OT)	13
17	at Minnesota	44
20	*Tampa Bay	23
19	at Green Bay	9
0	*Minnesota	23
30	*Green Bay	14
12	at Chicago	13
10	at Tampa Bay	21
220		313

GREEN BAY (4-12)

7	*L.A. Rams	34
10	*Tampa Bay	13
17	at Miami	24
6	*Chicago	24
24	at Tampa Bay	27
45	*New England	3
34	at Minnesota	14
17	*Washington	20
0	at Buffalo	28
0	at Atlanta	20
13	*Indianapolis	20
9	*Detroit	19
0	at Chicago	16
14	at Detroit	30
18	*Minnesota	6
26	at Phoenix	17
240		315

L.A. RAMS (10-6)

34	at Green Bay	7
17	*Detroit	10
22	at L.A. Raiders	17
45	at N.Y. Giants	31
27	*Phoenix	41
33	at Atlanta	0
21	*San Francisco	24
31	*Seattle	10
12	at New Orleans	10
24	at Philadelphia	30
10	*New Orleans	14
24	*San Diego	38
24	at Denver	35
23	*Chicago	3
22	*Atlanta	7
38	at San Francisco	16
407		293

MINNESOTA (11-5)

10	at Buffalo	13
36	*New England	6
31	at Chicago	7
23	*Philadelphia	21
7	at Miami	24
14	*Tampa Bay	13
14	*Green Bay	34
49	at Tampa Bay	20
21	at San Francisco	24
44	*Detroit	17
43	at Dallas	3
12	*Indianapolis	3
23	at Detroit	0
45	*New Orleans	3
6	at Green Bay	18
28	*Chicago	27
406		233

NEW ORLEANS (10-6)

33	*San Francisco	34
29	at Atlanta	21
22	at Detroit	14
13	*Tampa Bay	9
20	*Dallas	17
23	at San Diego	17
20	at Seattle	19
20	*L.A. Raiders	6
10	*L.A. Rams	12
24	at Washington	27
14	at L.A. Rams	10
42	*Denver	0
12	*N.Y. Giants	13
3	at Minnesota	45
17	at San Francisco	30
10	*Atlanta	9
312		283

N.Y. GIANTS (10-6)

27	*Washington	20
17	*San Francisco	20
12	at Dallas	10
31	*L.A. Rams	45
24	at Washington	23
13	at Philadelphia	24
30	*Detroit	10
23	at Atlanta	16
13	at Detroit (OT)	10
29	*Dallas	21
17	at Phoenix	24
17	*Philadelphia (OT)	23
13	at New Orleans	12
44	*Phoenix	7
28	*Kansas City	12
21	at N.Y. Jets	27
359		304

PHILADELPHIA (10-6)

41	at Tampa Bay	14
24	*Cincinnati	28
10	at Washington	17
21	at Minnesota	23
32	*Houston	23
24	*N.Y. Giants	13
3	at Cleveland	19
24	*Dallas	23
24	*Atlanta	27
30	*L.A. Rams	24
27	at Pittsburgh	26
23	at N.Y. Giants (OT)	17
31	*Phoenix	21
19	*Washington	20
23	at Phoenix	17
23	at Dallas	7
379		319

PHOENIX (7-9)

14	at Cincinnati	21
14	*Dallas	17
30	at Tampa Bay	24
30	*Washington	21
41	at L.A. Rams	27
31	*Pittsburgh	14
17	at Washington	33
21	*Cleveland	29
16	at Dallas	10
24	*San Francisco	23
24	*N.Y. Giants	17
20	at Houston	38
21	at Philadelphia	31
7	at N.Y. Giants	44
17	*Philadelphia	23
17	*Green Bay	26
344		398

SAN FRANCISCO (10-6)

34	at New Orleans	33
20	at N.Y. Giants	17
17	*Atlanta	34
38	at Seattle	7
20	*Detroit	13
13	*Denver (OT)	16
24	at L.A. Rams	21
9	at Chicago	10
24	*Minnesota	21
23	at Phoenix	24
3	*L.A. Raiders	9
37	*Washington	21
48	at San Diego	10
13	at Atlanta	3
30	*New Orleans	17
16	*L.A. Rams	38
369		294

TAMPA BAY (5-11)

14	*Philadelphia	41
13	at Green Bay	10
24	*Phoenix	30
9	at New Orleans	13
27	*Green Bay	24
13	at Minnesota	14
31	at Indianapolis	35
20	*Minnesota	49
14	*Miami	17
10	at Chicago	28
23	at Detroit	20
15	*Chicago	27
10	at Atlanta	17
10	*Buffalo	5
7	at New Eng. (OT)	10
21	*Detroit	10
261		350

WASHINGTON (7-9)

20	at N.Y. Giants	27
30	*Pittsburgh	29
17	*Philadelphia	10
21	at Phoenix	30
23	*N.Y. Giants	24
35	at Dallas	17
33	*Phoenix	17
20	at Green Bay	17
17	at Houston	41
27	*New Orleans	24
14	*Chicago	34
21	at San Francisco	37
13	*Cleveland	17
20	at Philadelphia	19
17	*Dallas	24
17	at Cincinnati (OT)	20
345		387

** denotes home game*
(OT) denotes overtime

Attendances as they appear in the following, and in the club-by-club sections starting on page 26, are turnstile counts and not paid attendance. Paid attendance totals are on page 202.

First Week Summaries

Standings

American Football Conference

Eastern Division

	W	L	T	Pct.	Pts.	OP
Buffalo	1	0	0	1.000	13	10
New England	1	0	0	1.000	28	3
Indianapolis	0	1	0	.000	14	17
Miami	0	1	0	.000	7	34
N.Y. Jets	0	1	0	.000	3	28
Central Division						
Cincinnati	1	0	0	1.000	21	14
Cleveland	1	0	0	1.000	6	3
Houston	1	0	0	1.000	17	14
Pittsburgh	1	0	0	1.000	24	21
Western Division						
L.A. Raiders	1	0	0	1.000	24	13
Seattle	1	0	0	1.000	21	14
Denver	0	1	0	.000	14	21
Kansas City	0	1	0	.000	3	6
San Diego	0	1	0	.000	13	24

National Football Conference

Eastern Division

	W	L	T	Pct.	Pts.	OP
N.Y. Giants	1	0	0	1.000	27	20
Philadelphia	1	0	0	1.000	41	14
Dallas	0	1	0	.000	21	24
Phoenix	0	1	0	.000	14	21
Washington	0	1	0	.000	20	27
Central Division						
Chicago	1	0	0	1.000	34	7
Detroit	1	0	0	1.000	31	17
Green Bay	0	1	0	.000	7	34
Minnesota	0	1	0	.000	10	13
Tampa Bay	0	1	0	.000	14	41
Western Division						
L.A. Rams	1	0	0	1.000	34	7
San Francisco	1	0	0	1.000	34	33
Atlanta	0	1	0	.000	17	31
New Orleans	0	1	0	.000	33	34

Sunday, September 4

Detroit 31, Atlanta 17—At Pontiac Silverdome, attendance 31,075. Chuck Long threw for two touchdowns and George Jamison returned a fumble for a score as the Lions defeated the Falcons. Long's seven-yard scoring pass to Pete Mandley and Eddie Murray's 37-yard field goal put Detroit ahead 10-3 at halftime. The Lions increased their lead to 24-3 in the third quarter on Garry James's one-yard scoring run and Jamison's four-yard fumble recovery return. Long's one-yard pass to Mark Lewis in the fourth quarter capped Detroit's scoring.

Atlanta	3	0	0	14	—	17
Detroit	0	10	14	7	—	31

Atl —FG Davis 19
Det —Mandley 7 pass from Long (Murray kick)
Det —FG Murray 37
Det —James 1 run (Murray kick)
Det —Jamison 4 fumble recovery return (Murray kick)
Atl —Higdon 9 pass from Miller (Davis kick)
Det —Lewis 1 pass from Long (Murray kick)
Atl —Settle 2 run (Davis kick)

Cleveland 6, Kansas City 3—At Arrowhead Stadium, attendance 55,654. Matt Bahr's 38-yard field goal with 25 seconds remaining helped the Browns defeat the Chiefs 6-3. Kansas City scored first on Nick Lowery's 33-yard field goal in the second quarter. Then Gary Danielson, who relieved injured Browns quarterback Bernie Kosar in the first quarter, led Cleveland on an 81-yard drive to set up Bahr's 19-yard field goal. The Browns' defense held the Chiefs to just nine first downs and 149 total yards.

Cleveland	0	3	0	3	—	6
Kansas City	0	3	0	0	—	3

KC —FG Lowery 33
Clev —FG Bahr 19
Clev —FG Bahr 38

Pittsburgh 24, Dallas 21—At Three Rivers Stadium, attendance 56,813. Earnest Jackson ran for two touchdowns and Bubby Brister scored on a one-yard run to lead the Steelers past the Cowboys. Jackson's 15-yard run and Gary Anderson's 32-yard field goal gave the Steelers a 10-7 halftime advantage. Pittsburgh increased its lead to 24-14 on Brister's one-yard bootleg and Jackson's 29-yard run. Cowboys quarterback Steve Pelluer's eight-yard pass to Ray Alexander narrowed the margin to 24-21. The victory was the Steelers' 100th win at Three Rivers Stadium.

Dallas	7	0	7	7	—	21
Pittsburgh	10	0	7	7	—	24

Dall —Newsome 3 run (Zendejas kick)
Pitt —Jackson 15 run (Anderson kick)
Pitt —FG Anderson 32
Pitt —Brister 1 run (Anderson kick)
Dall —Irvin 35 pass from Pelluer (Zendejas kick)
Pitt —Jackson 29 run (Anderson kick)
Dall —Alexander 8 pass from Pelluer (Zendejas kick)

Houston 17, Indianapolis 14—At Hoosier Dome, attendance 57,251. Tony Zendejas's 35-yard field goal 3:15 into overtime lifted the Oilers over the Colts. Houston's Steve Brown returned an interception 44 yards for a score in the final seconds of the first quarter to tie the game 7-7. Albert Bentley and Mike Rozier exchanged one-yard scoring runs to deadlock the game 14-14 at halftime. The teams played a scoreless second half, which led to the overtime. Indianapolis's Eric Dickerson rushed for 109 yards and had six receptions for 98 yards.

Houston	7	7	0	0	3	—	17
Indianapolis	7	7	0	0	0	—	14

Ind —Bouza 23 pass from Hogeboom (Biasucci kick)
Hou —Brown 44 interception return (Zendejas kick)
Ind —Bentley 1 run (Biasucci kick)
Hou —Rozier 1 run (Zendejas kick)
Hou —FG Zendejas 35

Los Angeles Rams 34, Green Bay 7—At Lambeau Field, attendance 53,460. Jim Everett threw two touchdown passes and Jerry Gray returned an interception for another score to power the Rams past the Packers. Los Angeles took a 7-0 lead when cornerback Anthony Newman recovered a fumble to set up Greg Bell's one-yard touchdown run. The Rams increased their lead to 21-0 at halftime on Everett's scoring passes to Bell (three yards) and Henry Ellard (11). Gray's 47-yard interception return for a touchdown and Mike Lansford's 33- and 29-yard field goals secured the win.

L.A. Rams	7	14	10	3	—	34
Green Bay	0	0	0	7	—	7

Rams —Bell 1 run (Lansford kick)
Rams —Bell 3 pass from Everett (Lansford kick)
Rams —Ellard 11 pass from Everett (Lansford kick)
Rams —FG Lansford 33
Rams —Gray 47 interception return (Lansford kick)
GB —West 17 pass from Majkowski (Zendejas kick)
Rams —FG Lansford 29

Chicago 34, Miami 7—At Soldier Field, attendance 63,330. Jim McMahon and Neal Anderson each ran for a pair of touchdowns as the Bears defeated the Dolphins. Anderson's two-yard touchdown run early in the first quarter was followed by Richard Dent's fumble recovery on the Dolphins' one-yard line to set up Anderson's second score. McMahon added scoring runs of one and two yards in the second quarter to put the game out of reach at halftime. The Chicago defense, which held Miami to 45 yards rushing, had a 45:32 to 14:28 time-of-possession advantage.

Miami	7	0	0	0	—	7
Chicago	14	14	0	6	—	34

Chi —Anderson 2 run (Butler kick)
Chi —Anderson 1 run (Butler kick)
Mia —Clayton 28 pass from Marino (Reveiz kick)
Chi —McMahon 1 run (Butler kick)
Chi —McMahon 2 run (Butler kick)
Chi —Sanders 20 run (kick blocked)

Buffalo 13, Minnesota 10—At Rich Stadium, attendance 76,783. Rookie Thurman Thomas ran for a touchdown and Scott Norwood kicked two field goals as the Bills upended the Vikings. Thomas, who rushed for 86 yards in his NFL regular season debut, had a five-yard scoring run in the first quarter. Norwood connected on field goals from 27 and 26 yards to complete Buffalo's scoring. Art Still accounted for three of the Bills' six sacks in his first game for Buffalo.

Minnesota	0	3	0	7	—	10
Buffalo	10	0	0	3	—	13

Buff —FG Norwood 27
Buff —Thomas 5 run (Norwood kick)
Minn —FG C. Nelson 30
Buff —FG Norwood 26
Minn —Rice 2 run (C. Nelson kick)

New England 28, New York Jets 3—At Sullivan Stadium, attendance 44,027. Steve Grogan connected with Irving Fryar on two touchdown passes as the Patriots defeated the Jets 28-7 to win their fifth straight season opener. New York took an early 3-0 lead on Pat Leahy's 29-yard field goal, but New England came back to take a 6-3 halftime lead on field goals of 39 and 24 yards by Teddy Garcia. Grogan fired scoring passes of 26 and 15 yards to Fryar, and Craig James added an eight-yard touchdown run in the fourth quarter to put the game out of reach.

N.Y. Jets	3	0	0	0	—	3
New England	3	3	10	12	—	28

NYJ —FG Leahy 29
NE —FG Garcia 39
NE —FG Garcia 24
NE —Fryar 26 pass from Grogan (Garcia kick)
NE —FG Garcia 47
NE —C. James 8 run (kick failed)
NE —Fryar 15 pass from Grogan (kick failed)

Philadelphia 41, Tampa Bay 14—At Tampa Stadium, attendance 43,502. Randall Cunningham threw two touchdown passes and ran for a third to lead the Eagles over the Buccaneers. Cunningham's scoring strikes to Mike Quick (37 yards) and Keith Jackson (eight), and Anthony Toney's two-yard run, put the Eagles ahead 21-0 at the end of the first quarter. Dean Dorsey's two field goals from 23 and 26 yards, and Cunningham's two-yard touchdown run, gave Philadelphia a 34-0 first-half lead. Tampa Bay's Vinny Testaverde threw for 324 yards, including touchdown passes to Bruce Hill (42 yards) and Mark Carrier (59). The Eagles' defense held the Buccaneers to just 43 yards rushing and registered five interceptions.

Philadelphia	21	13	7	0	—	41
Tampa Bay	0	0	14	0	—	14

Phil —Quick 37 pass from Cunningham (Dorsey kick)
Phil —Toney 2 run (Dorsey kick)
Phil —Jackson 8 pass from Cunningham (Dorsey kick)
Phil —FG Dorsey 23
Phil —FG Dorsey 26
Phil —Cunningham 2 run (Dorsey kick)
TB —Hill 42 pass from Testaverde (Igwebuike kick)
Phil —Hoage 38 run (Dorsey kick)
TB —Carrier 59 pass from Testaverde (Igwebuike kick)

Cincinnati 21, Phoenix 14—At Riverfront Stadium, attendance 50,404. Boomer Esiason threw for three touchdowns to highlight the Bengals' victory over the Cardinals. After a scoreless first quarter, Stump Mitchell put the Cardinals ahead 7-0 scoring on a four-yard pass from Neil Lomax. The Bengals answered with Esiason's 25-yard pass to James Brooks. Phoenix regained the lead but Esiason countered, this time on a 61-yard scoring pass to Eddie Brown, to tie the game 14-14. Mike Martin's 15-yard touchdown catch 3:45 into the fourth quarter proved to be decisive. Esiason, who completed 17 of 26 attempts for 271 yards, was named AFC offensive player of the week.

Phoenix	0	7	7	0	—	14
Cincinnati	0	7	7	7	—	21

Phx —Mitchell 4 pass from Lomax (Del Greco kick)
Cin —Brooks 25 pass from Esiason (Breech kick)
Phx —Green 29 pass from Lomax (Del Greco kick)
Cin —Brown 61 pass from Esiason (Breech kick)
Cin —Martin 15 pass from Esiason (Breech kick)

Los Angeles Raiders 24, San Diego 13—At Memorial Coliseum, attendance 39,029. Tim Brown returned his first NFL kickoff 97 yards for a touchdown as the Raiders defeated the Chargers to give Mike Shanahan a victory in his NFL head coaching debut. Los Angeles never trailed in the game after Marcus Allen scored on an 11-yard run midway through the second quarter. Chris Bahr kicked a 25-yard field goal in the fourth quarter and Allen added a one-yard run with 21 seconds remaining to finish the Raiders' scoring.

San Diego	0	3	3	7	—	13
L.A. Raiders	0	14	0	10	—	24

Raiders —Allen 11 run (Bahr kick)
SD —FG Abbott 23
Raiders —T. Brown 97 kickoff return (Bahr kick)
SD —FG Abbott 33
Raiders —FG Bahr 25
SD —Holland 24 pass from Laufenberg (Abbott kick)
Raiders —Allen 1 run (Bahr kick)

San Francisco 34, New Orleans 33—At Louisiana Superdome, attendance 69,145. Joe Montana threw three touchdown passes, including two to John Frank, as the 49ers edged the Saints. Trailing 17-10 in the third quarter, Montana completed scoring passes of 9 and 17 yards to Frank and 71 yards to Mike Wilson to give San Francisco a 31-17 lead. New Orleans rallied to cut the deficit to 31-26, but Michael Carter's fumble recovery in the fourth quarter set up Mike Cofer's decisive 32-yard field goal with 1:50 remaining.

San Francisco	7	3	21	3	—	34
New Orleans	7	10	0	16	—	33

SF —Craig 1 run (Cofer kick)
NO —Martin 2 pass from Hebert (Andersen kick)
NO —Clark 21 pass from Hebert (Andersen kick)
NO —FG Andersen 20
SF —FG Cofer 25
SF —Frank 9 pass from Montana (Cofer kick)
SF —Wilson 71 pass from Montana (Cofer kick)
SF —Frank 17 pass from Montana (Cofer kick)
NO —Hill 18 pass from Hebert (Andersen kick)
NO —Safety, Swilling tackled Young in end zone
SF —FG Cofer 32
NO —Perriman 15 pass from Hebert (Andersen kick)

Seattle 21, Denver 14—At Mile High Stadium, attendance 75,986. Dave Krieg fired two scoring passes in the third quarter to lead the Seahawks past the Broncos. With the score tied 7-7, Melvin Jenkins returned an interception 20 yards to set up Krieg's three-yard touchdown pass to Ray Butler. Later in the first quarter, Krieg found Curt Warner with a 14-yard touchdown pass to put Seattle ahead 21-7.

Seattle	0	7	14	0	—	21
Denver	0	7	0	7	—	14

Sea —Warner 5 run (N. Johnson kick)
Den —Mobley 1 pass from Elway (Karlis kick)
Sea —Butler 3 pass from Krieg (N. Johnson kick)
Sea —Warner 14 pass from Krieg (N. Johnson kick)
Den —Jackson 20 pass from Elway (Karlis kick)

Monday, September 5

New York Giants 27, Washington 20—At Giants Stadium, attendance 76,417. The New York Giants' defense scored two fourth-quarter touchdowns as the Super Bowl XXI champion Giants defeated the reigning Super Bowl XXII champion Redskins 27-20. With the score tied 13-13 in the fourth quarter, New York's Tom Flynn returned a blocked punt by Gary Reasons 27 yards for the go-ahead score. Less than three minutes later, Giants nose tackle Jim Burt returned a fumble 39 yards for a touchdown.

Washington	6	7	0	7	—	20
N.Y. Giants	0	3	10	14	—	27

Wash —FG Lohmiller 26
Wash —FG Lohmiller 25
Wash —Sanders 29 pass from Williams (Lohmiller kick)
NYG —FG Allegre 23
NYG —Morris 9 run (Allegre kick)
NYG —FG Allegre 32
NYG —Flynn 27 blocked punt return (Allegre kick)
NYG —Burt 39 fumble recovery return (Allegre kick)
Wash —Bryant 19 pass from Williams (Lohmiller kick)

Second Week Summaries

Standings

American Football Conference

Eastern Division	W	L	T	Pct.	Pts.	OP
Buffalo	2	0	0	1.000	22	16
New England	1	1	0	.500	34	39
N.Y. Jets	1	1	0	.500	26	31
Indianapolis	0	2	0	.000	27	34
Miami	0	2	0	.000	13	43
Central Division						
Cincinnati	2	0	0	1.000	49	38
Houston	2	0	0	1.000	55	49
Cleveland	1	1	0	.500	9	26
Pittsburgh	1	1	0	.500	53	51
Western Division						
Seattle	2	0	0	1.000	52	24
Denver	1	1	0	.500	48	24
L.A. Raiders	1	1	0	.500	59	51
Kansas City	0	2	0	.000	13	37
San Diego	0	2	0	.000	16	58

National Football Conference

Eastern Division	W	L	T	Pct.	Pts.	OP
Dallas	1	1	0	.500	38	38
N.Y. Giants	1	1	0	.500	44	40
Philadelphia	1	1	0	.500	65	42
Washington	1	1	0	.500	50	56
Phoenix	0	2	0	.000	28	38
Central Division						
Chicago	2	0	0	1.000	51	20
Detroit	1	1	0	.500	41	34
Minnesota	1	1	0	.500	46	19
Tampa Bay	1	1	0	.500	27	51
Green Bay	0	2	0	.000	17	47
Western Division						
L.A. Rams	2	0	0	1.000	51	17
San Francisco	2	0	0	1.000	54	50
New Orleans	1	1	0	.500	62	55
Atlanta	0	2	0	.000	38	60

Sunday, September 11

Chicago 17, Indianapolis 13—At Hoosier Dome, attendance 60,503. Jim McMahon threw one touchdown pass and Matt Suhey ran for another as the Bears defeated the Colts. McMahon hit Dennis Gentry for a 35-yard pass to open the scoring midway through the first quarter. Kevin Butler's 40-yard field goal as time ran out in the first half put the Bears ahead 10-6. Suhey's two-yard touchdown run in the fourth quarter capped the scoring. The Bears extended their streak to 26 games without allowing 100 yards rushing and held Colts quarterback Jack Trudeau to just four completions for 78 yards.

Chicago	7	3	0	7	—	17
Indianapolis	0	6	0	7	—	13

Chi —Gentry 35 pass from McMahon (Butler kick)
Ind —FG Biasucci 38
Ind —FG Biasucci 53
Chi —FG Butler 40
Ind —Dickerson 12 run (Biasucci kick)
Chi —Suhey 2 run (Butler kick)

Cincinnati 28, Philadelphia 24—At Veterans Stadium, attendance 66,459. Boomer Esiason completed 20 of 32 passes for 363 yards and four touchdowns as the Bengals rallied to defeat the Eagles. Esiason connected on touchdown passes of 78 yards to Tim McGee and 28 yards to James Brooks to tie the game 14-14 at halftime. After Esiason again found Brooks for a 15-yard scoring pass in the fourth quarter, Anthony Toney's one-yard touchdown run gave the Eagles a 24-21 advantage. Esiason rallied the Bengals again, capping a 15-play, 77-yard drive with a three-yard scoring pass to McGee for the win.

Cincinnati	7	7	0	14	—	28
Philadelphia	14	0	3	7	—	24

Phil —Toney 9 run (Dorsey kick)
Cin —McGee 78 pass from Esiason (Breech kick)
Phil —Jackson 15 pass from Cunningham (Dorsey kick)
Cin —Brooks 28 pass from Esiason (Breech kick)
Phil —FG Dorsey 34
Cin —Brooks 15 pass from Esiason (Breech kick)
Phil —Toney 1 run (Dorsey kick)
Cin —McGee 3 pass from Esiason (Breech kick)

Los Angeles Rams 17, Detroit 10—At Anaheim Stadium, attendance 46,262. Greg Bell gained 139 yards on 27 carries and one touchdown as the Rams topped the Lions. Bell's one-yard run for a score and Mike Lansford's 46-yard field goal tied the game 10-10 in the second quarter. Mike Wilcher's fumble recovery set up Jim Everett's four-yard scoring pass to Damone Johnson in the third quarter for the deciding score. Wilcher, who also had one-and-a-half sacks, was named NFC defensive player of the week.

Detroit	3	7	0	0	—	10
L.A. Rams	0	7	10	0	—	17

Det —FG Murray 30
Rams —Bell 1 run (Lansford kick)
Det —Lee 12 pass from Long (Murray kick)
Rams —FG Lansford 46
Rams —D. Johnson 4 pass from Everett (Lansford kick)

Seattle 31, Kansas City 10—At Arrowhead Stadium, attendance 61,512. Curt Warner ran for two touchdowns to help power the Seahawks past the Chiefs. Seattle put the game away early by exploding for 31 first-half points on Warner's one- and three-yard runs, Norm Johnson's 18-yard field goal, Dave Krieg's 17-yard pass to Brian Blades, and Jacob Green's fumble recovery in the end zone. The Seahawks' defense forced six turnovers, had six sacks, and held the Chiefs to 50 yards rushing. Green's three sacks and fumble recovery earned him AFC defensive player of the week honors.

Kansas City	3	0	0	7	—	10
Seattle	3	28	0	0	—	31

Sea —FG N. Johnson 18
KC —FG Lowery 27
Sea —Warner 1 run (N. Johnson kick)
Sea —Warner 3 run (N. Johnson kick)
Sea —Blades 17 pass from Krieg (N. Johnson kick)
Sea —Green recovered fumble in end zone (N. Johnson kick)
KC —Paige 15 pass from DeBerg (Lowery kick)

Houston 38, Los Angeles Raiders 35—At Astrodome, attendance 46,050. Allen Pinkett's six-yard touchdown run with 31 seconds remaining in the game lifted the Oilers over the Raiders. Trailing 28-24 in the fourth quarter, Cody Carlson (who replaced injured Oilers starting quarterback Warren Moon) threw a 12-yard touchdown pass to Ernest Givins to put Houston ahead 31-28, but Los Angeles regained the lead 35-31 as Marcus Allen ran one yard for a score. Pinkett also had touchdown runs of one and three yards in the first half.

L.A. Raiders	7	21	0	7	—	35
Houston	7	14	3	14	—	38

Raiders —Allen 1 run (Bahr kick)
Hou —Pinkett 3 run (Zendejas kick)
Raiders —Gault 42 pass from Beuerlein (Bahr kick)
Raiders —T. Brown 4 pass from Beuerlein (Bahr kick)
Hou —Pinkett 1 run (Zendejas kick)
Raiders —Smith 9 pass from Beuerlein (Bahr kick)
Hou —Hill 16 pass from Carlson (Zendejas kick)
Hou —FG Zendejas 19
Hou —Givins 12 pass from Carlson (Zendejas kick)
Raiders —Allen 1 run (Bahr kick)
Hou —Pinkett 6 run (Zendejas kick)

Buffalo 9, Miami 6—At Rich Stadium, attendance 79,529. Scott Norwood kicked three field goals, including a 28-yarder with 3:12 remaining in the game, to give the Bills a 9-6 win over the Dolphins. Fuad Reveiz's 31-yard field goal opened the scoring for Miami, but Norwood answered with a 41-yarder to tie the game 3-3 at halftime. Reveiz's 27-yard field goal gave the Dolphins a 6-3 lead, but Norwood retied the game 6-6 with a 35-yard kick early in the fourth quarter. Buffalo's Andre Reed caught eight passes for 122 yards.

Miami	3	0	3	0	—	6
Buffalo	0	3	0	6	—	9

Mia —FG Reveiz 31
Buff —FG Norwood 41
Mia —FG Reveiz 27
Buff —FG Norwood 35
Buff —FG Norwood 28

Minnesota 36, New England 6—At Metrodome, attendance 55,545. Tommy Kramer threw one touchdown pass and Darrin Nelson ran for another as the Vikings easily defeated the Patriots. Minnesota built a 24-6 first-half lead on scoring runs by Nelson (eight yards), Alfred Anderson (five), Chuck Nelson's 39-yard field goal, and Kramer's 29-yard pass to Anthony Carter. Minnesota's Issiac Holt tackled Patriots punter Jeff Feagles in the end zone for a safety for the only score in the third quarter. Nelson's 24-yard field goal and Darryl Harris's two-yard touchdown run completed the Vikings' scoring.

New England	3	3	0	0	—	6
Minnesota	10	14	2	10	—	36

Minn —D. Nelson 8 run (C. Nelson kick)
NE —FG Garcia 50
Minn —FG C. Nelson 39
Minn —Anderson 5 run (C. Nelson kick)
Minn —Carter 29 pass from Kramer (C. Nelson kick)
NE —FG Garcia 23
Minn —Safety, Holt tackled Feagles in end zone
Minn —FG C. Nelson 24
Minn —D. Harris 2 run (C. Nelson kick)

New Orleans 29, Atlanta 21—At Atlanta-Fulton County Stadium, attendance 48,901. Dalton Hilliard carried 16 times for 97 yards and one touchdown as the Saints defeated division-rival Atlanta. Down 14-6, New Orleans quarterback Bobby Hebert connected with Eric Martin on a 14-yard scoring pass to narrow the score to 14-12 at halftime. Hilliard's four-yard touchdown run in the fourth quarter completed the Saints' scoring. Morten Andersen added field goals of 41, 29, and 28 yards for New Orleans.

New Orleans	3	9	10	7	—	29
Atlanta	7	7	7	0	—	21

NO —FG Andersen 41
Atl —Whisenhunt 12 pass from Miller (Davis kick)
Atl —Higdon 34 pass from Miller (Davis kick)
NO —FG Andersen 29
NO —Martin 14 pass from Hebert (kick failed)
NO —FG Andersen 28
Atl —Settle 1 run (Davis kick)
NO —Mayes 17 run (Andersen kick)
NO —Hilliard 4 run (Andersen kick)

New York Jets 23, Cleveland 3—At Cleveland Stadium, attendance 74,434. Roger Vick ran for two fourth-quarter touchdowns to help the Jets defeat the Browns. New York led 9-3 in the fourth quarter on three Pat Leahy field goals (22, 23, and 29 yards) before Vick's touchdown runs from one and three yards. The Jets had a 37:47 to 22:13 time-of-possession advantage, while their defense held the Browns to 27 yards rushing.

N.Y. Jets	3	3	3	14	—	23
Cleveland	3	0	0	0	—	3

NYJ —FG Leahy 22
Clev —FG Bahr 47
NYJ —FG Leahy 29
NYJ —FG Leahy 23
NYJ —Vick 1 run (Leahy kick)
NYJ —Vick 3 run (Leahy kick)

Washington 30, Pittsburgh 29—At Robert F. Kennedy Stadium, attendance 54,083. Chip Lohmiller's 19-yard field goal with 12 seconds remaining completed the Redskins' comeback win over the Steelers. Trailing 19-10 in the second half, Jamie Morris's one-yard scoring run and Lohmiller's 46-yard kick gave Washington a 20-19 edge. The Steelers scored 10 unanswered points in the fourth quarter to regain the lead. Doug Williams's seven-yard scoring pass to Kelvin Bryant with 4:48 to play narrowed the deficit to 29-27 and put the Redskins in position to win the game with a field goal.

Pittsburgh	3	10	6	10	—	29
Washington	7	3	7	13	—	30

Pitt —FG Anderson 33
Wash —Clark 55 pass from Williams (Lohmiller kick)
Pitt —FG Anderson 24
Wash —FG Lohmiller 37
Pitt —Lipps 80 pass from Brister (Anderson kick)
Pitt —Brister 6 run (kick failed)
Wash —Morris 1 run (Lohmiller kick)
Wash —FG Lohmiller 46
Pitt —Stone 72 pass from Brister (Anderson kick)
Pitt —FG Anderson 43
Wash —Bryant 7 pass from Williams (Lohmiller kick)
Wash —FG Lohmiller 19

Denver 34, San Diego 3—At Mile High Stadium, attendance 75,359. John Elway threw two touchdown passes and Tony Dorsett ran for another as the Broncos overpowered the Chargers. Elway, who opened the scoring with a 44-yard touchdown pass to Mark Jackson, also completed a 24-yarder in the third quarter to Vance Johnson. Rich Karlis added field goals of 51 and 38 yards for Denver. Dorsett, who rushed for 113 yards on 23 carries, moved into third place on the NFL's all-time rushing list with 12,181 career yards, passing Franco Harris with 12,120.

San Diego	0	3	0	0	—	3
Denver	10	14	7	3	—	34

Den —Jackson 44 pass from Elway (Karlis kick)
Den —FG Karlis 51
Den —Willhite 1 run (Karlis kick)
SD —FG Abbott 20

Den —Dorsett 21 run (Karlis kick)
Den —Johnson 24 pass from Elway (Karlis kick)
Den —FG Karlis 38

San Francisco 20, New York Giants 17—At Giants Stadium, attendance 75,943. Joe Montana connected with Jerry Rice on a 78-yard touchdown pass with 42 seconds remaining to lift the 49ers over the Giants. San Francisco broke a 10-10 tie in the third quarter on Mike Cofer's 26-yard field goal, but New York recaptured the lead 17-13 on Phil Simms's 15-yard scoring pass to Lionel Manuel. Montana, who replaced Steve Young in the second half, completed 10 of 18 passes for 148 yards. Roger Craig ran for 110 yards on 18 carries and caught nine passes for 69 yards to earn NFC offensive player of the week honors.

San Francisco	0	10	3	7	—	20
N.Y. Giants	7	3	0	7	—	17

NYG —Manuel 12 pass from Simms (Allegre kick)
SF —FG Cofer 35
SF —DuBose 1 run (Cofer kick)
NYG —FG Allegre 36
SF —FG Cofer 26
NYG —Manuel 15 pass from Simms (Allegre kick)
SF —Rice 78 pass from Montana (Cofer kick)

Tampa Bay 13, Green Bay 10—At Lambeau Field, attendance 52,583. Donald Igwebuike kicked a 28-yard field goal on the final play of the game to help the Buccaneers down the Packers and end a nine-game losing streak. Green Bay held a 10-0 first-quarter lead, but Lars Tate's two-yard run and Igwebuike's 53-yard field goal brought Tampa Bay even 10-10 at halftime. It was Tampa Bay's first victory since November 1, 1987, when they defeated Green Bay 23-17 in Milwaukee.

Tampa Bay	0	10	0	3	—	13
Green Bay	10	0	0	0	—	10

GB —FG Zendejas 50
GB —Fullwood 30 pass from Wright (Zendejas kick)
TB —Tate 2 run (Igwebuike kick)
TB —FG Igwebuike 53
TB —FG Igwebuike 28

Monday, September 12

Dallas 17, Phoenix 14—At Sun Devil Stadium, attendance 67,139. Herschel Walker ran for a career-high 149 yards on 29 carries and one touchdown as Dallas defeated Phoenix in the Cardinals' regular-season opener at Sun Devil Stadium. Luis Zendejas kicked a 47-yard field goal and Walker scored on a three-yard run late in the second quarter to give the Cowboys a 10-7 halftime edge. Steve Pelluer added a one-yard scoring run in the fourth quarter to put the game away. Earl Ferrell caught a 16-yard touchdown pass from Neil Lomax for the Cardinals' first score in their new home.

Dallas	3	7	0	7	—	17
Phoenix	0	7	0	7	—	14

Dall —FG Zendejas 47
Phx —Ferrell 16 pass from Lomax (Del Greco kick)
Dall —Walker 3 run (Zendejas kick)
Dall —Pelluer 1 run (Zendejas kick)
Phx —Novacek 23 pass from Lomax (Del Greco kick)

Third Week Summaries

Standings

American Football Conference

Eastern Division

	W	L	T	Pct.	Pts.	OP
Buffalo	3	0	0	1.000	38	30
N.Y. Jets	2	1	0	.667	71	34
Miami	1	2	0	.333	37	60
New England	1	2	0	.333	48	55
Indianapolis	0	3	0	.000	44	57

Central Division

Cincinnati	3	0	0	1.000	66	50
Cleveland	2	1	0	.667	32	43
Houston	2	1	0	.667	58	94
Pittsburgh	1	2	0	.333	65	68

Western Division

Seattle	2	1	0	.667	58	41
Denver	1	2	0	.333	61	44
Kansas City	1	2	0	.333	33	50
L.A. Raiders	1	2	0	.333	76	73
San Diego	1	2	0	.333	33	64

National Football Conference

Eastern Division

	W	L	T	Pct.	Pts.	OP
N.Y. Giants	2	1	0	.667	56	50
Washington	2	1	0	.667	67	66
Dallas	1	2	0	.333	48	50
Philadelphia	1	2	0	.333	75	59
Phoenix	1	2	0	.333	58	62

Central Division

Chicago	2	1	0	.667	58	51
Minnesota	2	1	0	.667	77	26
Detroit	1	2	0	.333	55	56
Tampa Bay	1	2	0	.333	51	81
Green Bay	0	3	0	.000	34	71

Western Division

L.A. Rams	3	0	0	1.000	73	34
New Orleans	2	1	0	.667	84	69
San Francisco	2	1	0	.667	71	84
Atlanta	1	2	0	.333	72	77

Sunday, September 18

Atlanta 34, San Francisco 17—At Candlestick Park, attendance 60,168. The Falcons exploded for 21 points in the second quarter to defeat the 49ers for the first time since 1983. Gerald Riggs, who rushed 115 yards on 19 carries, had a three-yard touchdown run to open Atlanta's scoring. James Primus (29 yards) and Chris Miller (one) added touchdown runs to give the Falcons a 21-3 halftime advantage. Jeff Davis kicked field goals of 47 and 41 yards and Robert Moore returned an interception 47 yards to assure the victory. Joe Montana, who completed 32 of 48 passes for 343 yards, also had two touchdowns with three interceptions in the 49ers' losing cause.

Atlanta	0	21	3	10	—	34
San Francisco	3	0	7	7	—	17

SF —FG Cofer 38
Atl —Riggs 3 run (Davis kick)
Atl —Primus 29 run (Davis kick)
Atl —Miller 1 run (Davis kick)
Atl —FG Davis 47
SF —McIntyre 17 pass from Montana (Cofer kick)
Atl —Moore 47 interception return (Davis kick)
SF —Wilson 13 pass from Montana (Cofer kick)
Atl —FG Davis 41

Buffalo 16, New England 14—At Sullivan Stadium, attendance 55,945. Scott Norwood's 41-yard field goal with 11 seconds remaining helped the Bills snap an 11-game losing streak to the Patriots. Buffalo overcame a 14-3 halftime deficit on Norwood's 44-yard field goal and Jim Kelly's three-yard scoring pass to Robb Riddick. Riddick's touchdown was Buffalo's first touchdown in 11 quarters. Kelly led a drive from the Bills' 47-yard line with 1:50 remaining to set up Norwood's winning kick.

Buffalo	0	3	3	10	—	16
New England	0	14	0	0	—	14

Buff —FG Norwood 38
NE —Jones 41 pass from Grogan (Garcia kick)
NE —Morgan 19 pass from Grogan (Garcia kick)
Buff —FG Norwood 44
Buff —Riddick 3 pass from Kelly (Norwood kick)
Buff —FG Norwood 41

Cincinnati 17, Pittsburgh 12—At Three Rivers Stadium, attendance 56,647. Boomer Esiason threw two touchdown passes to help rally the Bengals over the Steelers. Cincinnati's defense forced six turnovers, including one in the second quarter which set up Esiason's 13-yard scoring pass to Stanley Wilson. Gary Anderson's 19-yard field goal early in the fourth quarter put Pittsburgh back in front 12-10, but Esiason found Eddie Brown with a 65-yard scoring bomb to secure the victory. Cincinnati's James Brooks led all rushers with 88 yards on 19 carries.

Cincinnati	0	7	3	7	—	17
Pittsburgh	2	0	7	3	—	12

Pitt —Safety, Montoya called for holding in end zone
Cin —Wilson 13 pass from Esiason (Breech kick)
Pitt —Lipps 9 pass from Brister (Anderson kick)
Cin —FG Breech 32
Pitt —FG Anderson 19
Cin —Brown 65 pass from Esiason (Breech kick)

Kansas City 20, Denver 13—At Arrowhead Stadium, attendance 63,268. Steve DeBerg, making his first start for the Chiefs, threw for 259 yards and two touchdowns to lead Kansas City over Denver. Nick Lowery's 50-yard field goal and DeBerg's six-yard touchdown pass to Carlos Carson tied the score 10-10 at halftime. DeBerg also threw a 14-yard scoring pass to Paul Palmer, and Lowery added a 29-yard field goal in the second half, while the Kansas City defense held the Broncos to only a field goal to assure the win.

Denver	3	7	0	3	—	13
Kansas City	3	7	7	3	—	20

KC —FG Lowery 50
Den —FG Karlis 23
KC —Carson 6 pass from DeBerg (Lowery kick)
Den —Dorsett 8 run (Karlis kick)
KC —Palmer 14 pass from DeBerg (Lowery kick)
Den —FG Karlis 42
KC —FG Lowery 29

Miami 24, Green Bay 17—At Joe Robbie Stadium, attendance 54,409. Dan Marino threw two first-half touchdown passes to lead the Dolphins past the Packers. Linebacker Rick Graf recovered a blocked punt to set up Lorenzo Hampton's two-yard scoring run and Marino hit Clayton for a 25-yard scoring pass in the first quarter to stake Miami to a 17-0 lead. Marino's four-yard touchdown pass to Ferrell Edmunds gave the Dolphins a 24-7 second-quarter lead. Marino, who completed 22 of 33 passes for 261 yards, became the forty-fifth NFL quarterback to throw for 20,000 yards.

Green Bay	0	14	3	0	—	17
Miami	17	7	0	0	—	24

Mia —FG Reveiz 29
Mia —Hampton 2 run (Reveiz kick)
Mia —Clayton 25 pass from Marino (Reveiz kick)
GB —Wright 1 run (Zendejas kick)
Mia —Edmunds 4 pass from Marino (Reveiz kick)
GB —Fullwood 1 run (Zendejas kick)
GB —FG Zendejas 36

New York Jets 45, Houston 3—At Giants Stadium, attendance 64,683. Wesley Walker caught six passes for 129 yards and three touchdowns as the Jets easily defeated the Oilers. Leading 14-3 in the second quarter, Jets quarterback Ken O'Brien finished off a 93-yard drive with a 50-yard scoring pass to Walker. O'Brien and Walker combined on a four-yard touchdown pass with 1:04 remaining in the first half for a 28-3 lead. Walker had a 23-yard scoring reception and Mike Zordich's 35-yard interception return for a touchdown in the fourth quarter completed the Jets' scoring. New York cornerback Bobby Humphery, who deflected six passes, made three tackles, and recovered a fumble, was named AFC defensive player of the week.

Houston	3	0	0	0	—	3
N.Y. Jets	14	14	3	14	—	45

Hou —FG Zendejas 30
NYJ —Sohn 8 pass from O'Brien (Leahy kick)
NYJ —McNeil 8 run (Leahy kick)
NYJ —Walker 50 pass from O'Brien (Leahy kick)
NYJ —Walker 4 pass from O'Brien (Leahy kick)
NYJ —FG Leahy 47
NYJ —Walker 23 pass from Ryan (Leahy kick)
NYJ —Zordich 35 interception return (Leahy kick)

Los Angeles Rams 22, Los Angeles Raiders 17—At Memorial Coliseum, attendance 84,870. Greg Bell rushed for 109 yards and one touchdown and the Rams' defense registered nine sacks to defeat the Raiders 22-17. The Rams led 10-3 at halftime on Bell's six-yard scoring run and Mike Lansford's 37-yard field goal. After the Raiders tied the score 10-10 in the third quarter, Kevin Greene sacked Steve Beuerlein in the end zone for a safety to give the Rams the lead for good, 12-10. Johnnie Johnson's interception led to Jim Everett's 54-yard scoring pass to Aaron Cox to put the game out of reach 22-10 with 2:13 remaining. Gary Jeter had five sacks and was named NFC defensive player of the week.

L.A. Rams	7	3	2	10	—	22
L.A. Raiders	0	3	7	7	—	17

Rams —Bell 6 run (Lansford kick)
Rams —FG Lansford 37
Raiders —FG Bahr 29
Raiders —Allen 30 pass from Beuerlein (Bahr kick)
Rams —Safety, Greene tackled Beuerlein in end zone
Rams —FG Lansford 46
Rams —Cox 54 pass from Everett (Lansford kick)
Raiders —T. Brown 49 pass from Beuerlein (Bahr kick)

Minnesota 31, Chicago 7—At Soldier Field, attendance 63,990. Tommy Kramer threw three scoring passes, including two to Anthony Carter, as the Vikings upended the Bears 31-7. Kramer combined with Carter on touchdown passes of 40 and 16 yards, and also hit Hassan Jones with a 19-yarder. Minnesota profited from five Chicago turnovers, including Chris Martin's third-quarter recovery of a fumbled punt return in the end zone for a touchdown. The Vikings' defense held the Bears to 70 yards rushing.

Minnesota	7	10	14	0	—	31
Chicago	7	0	0	0	—	7

Minn —Carter 40 pass from Kramer (C. Nelson kick)
Chi —Morris 11 pass from McMahon (Butler kick)
Minn —H. Jones 19 pass from Kramer (C. Nelson kick)
Minn —FG C. Nelson 31
Minn —C. Martin recovered fumbled punt in end zone (C. Nelson kick)
Minn —Carter 16 pass from Kramer (C. Nelson kick)

New Orleans 22, Detroit 14—At Pontiac Silverdome, attendance 32,943. The Saints scored 15 unanswered points in the second half to come from behind and defeat the Lions. New Orleans cut Detroit's lead to 14-12 in the third quarter, when Morten Andersen kicked a 37-yard field goal and Rickey Jackson tackled Chuck Long in the end zone for a safety. Dalton Hilliard ran four yards for the go-ahead score late in the third quarter after New Orleans stopped a fake punt attempt at the Detroit 12-yard line. Andersen kicked a 29-yard field goal in the fourth quarter to put the game out of reach.

New Orleans	0	7	12	3	—	22
Detroit	7	7	0	0	—	14

Det —Bland 9 pass from Long (Murray kick)
NO —Hill 29 pass from Hebert (Andersen kick)
Det —Bland 10 pass from Long (Murray kick)
NO —FG Andersen 37
NO —Safety, Jackson tackled Long in end zone
NO —Hilliard 4 run (Andersen kick)
NO —FG Andersen 29

New York Giants 12, Dallas 10—At Texas Stadium, attendance 55,325. Joe Morris ran for 107 yards and Lionel Manuel caught nine passes for 142 yards to lead the Giants over the Cowboys. Mark Collins tackled Darryl Clack in the end zone for a safety on the opening kickoff, and Raul Allegre kicked a 32-yard field goal to give New York a 5-3 halftime advantage. Manuel's nine-yard touchdown pass from Phil Simms in the third quarter proved decisive.

N.Y. Giants	5	0	7	0	—	12
Dallas	3	0	7	0	—	10

NYG — Safety, Collins tackled Clack in end zone
Dall — FG Ruzek 41
NYG — FG Allegre 32
NYG — Manuel 9 pass from Simms (Allegre kick)
Dall — Walker 27 pass from Pelluer (Ruzek kick)

Washington 17, Philadelphia 10—At Robert F. Kennedy Stadium, attendance 53,920. Timmy Smith ran for 107 yards and one touchdown as the Redskins downed the Eagles. Smith's 19-yard touchdown run in the first quarter, and Jamie Morris's 27-yard scoring run gave Washington a 14-3 halftime advantage. Randall Cunningham connected with Mike Quick for a 55-yard touchdown pass to narrow the margin in the fourth quarter, but the Eagles were unable to get any closer. The Redskins' defense had six sacks, including three by Markus Koch.

Philadelphia	0	3	0	7	— 10
Washington	14	0	3	0	— 17

Wash — Smith 19 run (Lohmiller kick)
Wash — Morris 27 run (Lohmiller kick)
Phil — FG Dorsey 23
Wash — FG Lohmiller 34
Phil — Quick 55 pass from Cunningham (Dorsey kick)

Phoenix 30, Tampa Bay 24—At Tampa Stadium, attendance 35,034. Cliff Stoudt threw a 42-yard scoring pass to Jay Novacek late in the fourth quarter to rally the Cardinals over the Buccaneers. Phoenix built a 20-3 lead in the first half on scoring runs of six yards by Stump Mitchell and one yard by Earl Ferrell, and Al Del Greco's 47- and 37-yard field goals. Tampa Bay edged ahead 24-23 midway through the final quarter, before Stoudt, who relieved starter Neil Lomax in the second half, connected with Novacek with 3:14 remaining for the win. Mitchell led all rushers with 110 yards on 18 carries.

Phoenix	13	7	3	7	— 30
Tampa Bay	0	3	7	14	— 24

Phx — FG Del Greco 47
Phx — Mitchell 6 run (Del Greco kick)
Phx — FG Del Greco 37
TB — FG Igwebuike 34
Phx — Ferrell 1 run (Del Greco kick)
TB — Hill 23 pass from Testaverde (Igwebuike kick)
Phx — FG Del Greco 23
TB — Wilder 5 run (Igwebuike kick)
TB — Tate 47 run (Igwebuike kick)
Phx — Novacek 42 pass from Stoudt (Del Greco kick)

San Diego 17, Seattle 6—At San Diego Jack Murphy Stadium, attendance 44,449. Gary Anderson rushed for 120 yards and one touchdown to help the Chargers beat Seattle and snap an eight-game losing streak. San Diego jumped to a 10-3 halftime lead on Keith Browner's 55-yard interception return and Vince Abbott's 48-yard field goal. Late in the fourth quarter, Chargers quarterback Babe Laufenberg led a 76-yard drive to set up Anderson's 25-yard touchdown run.

Seattle	0	3	0	3	— 6
San Diego	7	3	0	7	— 17

SD — Browner 55 interception return (Abbott kick)
SD — FG Abbott 48
Sea — FG Johnson 40
Sea — FG Johnson 42
SD — Anderson 25 run (Abbott kick)

Monday, September 19

Cleveland 23, Indianapolis 17—At Cleveland Stadium, attendance 75,148. Mike Pagel threw for 255 yards and two touchdowns and Matt Bahr kicked three field goals to lead the Browns over the Colts. Pagel, starting in his first game since 1985, completed a 14-yard pass to Ozzie Newsome to register Cleveland's first touchdown of the year. His 17-yard scoring pass to Webster Slaughter in the closing minutes of the first half gave the Browns a 17-10 halftime advantage. Bahr's field goals from 29 and 40 yards in the second half completed Cleveland's scoring. Clarence Verdin returned a punt 73 yards for a touchdown for the Colts' only second-half points. Eric Dickerson gained 117 yards on 22 carries for Indianapolis.

Indianapolis	3	7	0	7	— 17
Cleveland	7	10	3	3	— 23

Ind — FG Biasucci 30
Clev — Newsome 14 pass from Pagel (Bahr kick)
Clev — FG Bahr 21
Ind — Dickerson 41 run (Biasucci kick)
Clev — Slaughter 17 pass from Pagel (Bahr kick)
Clev — FG Bahr 29
Clev — FG Bahr 40
Ind — Verdin 73 punt return (Biasucci kick)

Fourth Week Summaries

Standings

American Football Conference

Eastern Division

	W	L	T	Pct.	Pts.	OP
Buffalo	4	0	0	1.000	74	58
N.Y. Jets	3	1	0	.750	88	44
Miami	1	3	0	.250	50	75
New England	1	3	0	.250	54	86
Indianapolis	1	3	0	.250	59	70

Central Division

Cincinnati	4	0	0	1.000	90	67
Houston	3	1	0	.750	89	100
Cleveland	2	2	0	.500	49	67
Pittsburgh	1	3	0	.250	93	104

Western Division

L.A. Raiders	2	2	0	.500	106	100
San Diego	2	2	0	.500	57	87
Seattle	2	2	0	.500	65	79
Denver	1	3	0	.250	88	74
Kansas City	1	3	0	.250	56	74

National Football Conference

Eastern Division

	W	L	T	Pct.	Pts.	OP
Dallas	2	2	0	.500	74	70
N.Y. Giants	2	2	0	.500	87	95
Phoenix	2	2	0	.500	88	83
Washington	2	2	0	.500	88	96
Philadelphia	1	3	0	.250	96	82

Central Division

Chicago	3	1	0	.750	82	57
Minnesota	3	1	0	.750	100	47
Detroit	1	3	0	.250	65	73
Tampa Bay	1	3	0	.250	60	94
Green Bay	0	4	0	.000	40	95

Western Division

L.A. Rams	4	0	0	1.000	118	65
New Orleans	3	1	0	.750	97	78
San Francisco	3	1	0	.750	109	91
Atlanta	1	3	0	.250	92	103

Sunday, September 25

Dallas 26, Atlanta 20—At Texas Stadium, attendance 39,702. Steve Pelluer connected with Ray Alexander on a 29-yard touchdown pass with 1:48 to play to rally the Cowboys over the Falcons. Dallas jumped to an early 14-0 lead, but a pair of Chris Miller scoring passes (68 yards to Stacey Bailey and 12 yards to Floyd Dixon) and Greg Davis's field goals from 43 and 24 yards put Atlanta ahead 20-14 in the third quarter. Danny Noonan's safety and Roger Ruzek's 25-yard field goal narrowed the margin to 20-19. Bill Bates's fumble recovery set up Pelluer's game-winning pass to Alexander. Bailey led all receivers with four catches for 169 yards.

Atlanta	7	10	3	0	— 20
Dallas	14	0	2	10	— 26

Dall — Noonan 17 interception return (Ruzek kick)
Dall — Walker 2 pass from Pelluer (Ruzek kick)
Atl — Bailey 68 pass from Miller (Davis kick)
Atl — Dixon 12 pass from Miller (Davis kick)
Atl — FG Davis 43
Atl — FG Davis 24
Dall — Safety, Noonan sacked Miller in end zone
Dall — FG Ruzek 25
Dall — Alexander 29 pass from Pelluer (Ruzek kick)

Chicago 24, Green Bay 6—At Lambeau Field, attendance 56,492. Neal Anderson carried 20 times for 105 yards and two touchdowns as the Bears downed the Packers. Chicago took a 17-6 halftime lead on Anderson's scoring runs from 45 and four yards and Kevin Butler's 35-yard field goal. Greg Clark recovered a fumbled punt to set up the Bears' final points on a five-yard scoring run by Thomas Sanders in the fourth quarter. Chicago's defense had five sacks, two interceptions, and held Green Bay to 34 yards rushing.

Chicago	0	17	0	7	— 24
Green Bay	6	0	0	0	— 6

GB — Fullwood 2 run (kick failed)
Chi — Anderson 45 run (Butler kick)
Chi — Anderson 4 run (Butler kick)
Chi — FG Butler 35
Chi — Sanders 5 run (Butler kick)

Cincinnati 24, Cleveland 17—At Riverfront Stadium, attendance 56,397. Rookie Ickey Woods ran for a pair of touchdowns in the second quarter to help the Bengals down the Browns. Cincinnati took a 24-10 halftime advantage on Lewis Billups's 26-yard fumble recovery return for a score, Woods's two one-yard touchdown runs, and Jim Breech's 34-yard field goal. The Bengals' Eddie Brown led all receivers with 127 yards on four receptions.

Cleveland	3	7	0	7	— 17
Cincinnati	7	17	0	0	— 24

Cin — Billups 26 fumble recovery return (Breech kick)
Clev — FG Bahr 27
Cin — FG Breech 34
Cin — Woods 1 run (Breech kick)
Clev — Brennan 11 pass from Pagel (Bahr kick)
Cin — Woods 1 run (Breech kick)
Clev — Mack 3 run (Bahr kick)

Los Angeles Rams 45, New York Giants 31—At Giants Stadium, attendance 75,617. Jim Everett completed a career-high five touchdown passes as the Rams outlasted the Giants. Los Angeles took a 28-10 halftime lead on Everett's touchdown passes to Pete Holohan (14 yards), Robert Delpino (5), and Aaron Cox (69), and Greg Bell's two-yard run. Everett also had a two-yard scoring pass to Bell in the third quarter and a 41-yarder to Henry Ellard in the fourth quarter. The Rams' defense had four sacks and held the Giants to 79 yards rushing.

L.A. Rams	7	21	7	10	— 45
N.Y. Giants	0	10	14	7	— 31

Rams — Holohan 14 pass from Everett (Lansford kick)
NYG — FG Allegre 34
Rams — Delpino 5 pass from Everett (Lansford kick)
Rams — Bell 2 run (Lansford kick)
Rams — A. Cox 69 pass from Everett (Lansford kick)
NYG — Ingram 9 pass from Simms (Allegre kick)
NYG — P. Johnson 33 interception return (Allegre kick)
Rams — Bell 2 pass from Everett (Lansford kick)
NYG — Morris 3 run (Allegre kick)
Rams — FG Lansford 41
Rams — Ellard 41 pass from Everett (Lansford kick)
NYG — Bavaro 16 pass from Simms (Allegre kick)

Indianapolis 15, Miami 13—At Hoosier Dome, attendance 59,638. Dean Biasucci kicked five field goals and Eric Dickerson rushed for 125 yards to lead the Colts past the Dolphins. Trailing 7-3 in the second quarter, Biasucci kicked field goals of 34, 41, and 51 yards to put Indianapolis ahead 12-7 at halftime. Biasucci's final field goal, a 25-yarder, capped a 91-yard drive in the fourth quarter. Dickerson moved into eighth place on the NFL career rushing list with 8,701 yards, surpassing Jim Taylor (8,597).

Miami	7	0	0	6	— 13
Indianapolis	3	9	0	3	— 15

Mia — Hampton 39 pass from Marino (Reveiz kick)
Ind — FG Biasucci 50
Ind — FG Biasucci 34
Ind — FG Biasucci 41
Ind — FG Biasucci 51
Ind — FG Biasucci 25
Mia — Stradford 8 pass from Marino (kick failed)

Houston 31, New England 6—At Astrodome, attendance 38,636. Allen Pinkett caught two touchdown passes and ran for another score as the Oilers dominated the Patriots. Mike Rozier's one-yard touchdown run and Cody Carlson's scoring completions of 51 and 22 yards to Pinkett gave Houston a commanding 21-6 third-quarter lead. Tony Zendejas's 49-yard field goal and Pinkett's one-yard run in the fourth quarter finished Houston's scoring. The Oilers' defense registered four sacks and had three interceptions.

New England	6	0	0	0	— 6
Houston	7	7	7	10	— 31

NE — Grogan 1 run (kick blocked)
Hou — Rozier 1 run (Zendejas kick)
Hou — Pinkett 51 pass from Carlson (Zendejas kick)
Hou — Pinkett 22 pass from Carlson (Zendejas kick)
Hou — FG Zendejas 49
Hou — Pinkett 1 run (Zendejas kick)

New York Jets 17, Detroit 10—At Pontiac Silverdome, attendance 29,250. Ken O'Brien threw for 253 yards and two touchdowns to help lead the Jets past the Lions. New York held a 10-3 halftime edge on Pat Leahy's 39-yard field goal and O'Brien's 10-yard scoring pass to Freeman McNeil. Detroit tied the game late in the third quarter on Garry James's one-yard run, but O'Brien's 26-yard touchdown pass to Wesley Walker with 5:21 to play in the fourth quarter proved decisive. O'Brien's string of consecutive passes without an interception ended at 211, the second-longest streak in NFL history, when Detroit safety Raphael Cherry picked off a pass in the third quarter.

N.Y. Jets	3	7	0	7	— 17
Detroit	3	0	7	0	— 10

NYJ — FG Leahy 39
Det — FG Murray 39
NYJ — McNeil 10 pass from O'Brien (Leahy kick)
Det — James 1 run (Murray kick)
NYJ — Walker 26 pass from O'Brien (Leahy kick)

Minnesota 23, Philadelphia 21—At Metrodome, attendance 56,012. Chuck Nelson's 32-yard field goal with 15 seconds remaining lifted the Vikings over the Eagles. Down 14-10, Wade Wilson scored on a three-yard run and Nelson kicked a 27-yard field goal to put Minnesota ahead 20-14 in the third quarter. Andre Waters's blocked punt set up Randall Cunningham's 13-yard scoring pass to Keith Jackson to give Philadelphia a 21-20 lead with 1:47 remaining. Tommy Kramer's 10-yard pass to Allen Rice on fourth down was the key play in the Vikings' decisive drive. Keith Millard registered four of Minnesota's eight sacks.

Philadelphia	0	14	0	7	— 21
Minnesota	10	0	7	6	— 23

Minn — Anderson 7 run (C. Nelson kick)
Minn — FG C. Nelson 21
Phil — Byars 1 run (Dawson kick)
Phil — Quick 22 pass from Cunningham (Dawson kick)
Minn — Wilson 3 run (C. Nelson kick)
Minn — FG C. Nelson 27
Phil — Jackson 13 pass from Cunningham (Dawson kick)
Minn — FG C. Nelson 32

Buffalo 36, Pittsburgh 28—At Rich Stadium, attendance 78,735. Robb Riddick ran for two touchdowns and Scott Norwood kicked five field goals to help the Bills defeat the Steelers. Buffalo held a 16-14 halftime edge on Jim Kelly's 26-yard pass to Chris Burkett and three Norwood field goals (from 38, 39, and 39 yards). The Bills increased their lead on Riddick's one-yard scoring plunge and his five-yard return of a blocked punt. Norwood's field goals from 48 and 49 yards in the fourth quarter gave him a Bills record of 12 consecutive field goals. Mark Kelso's second interception of the day with less than a minute to play sealed the Buffalo victory.

Pittsburgh	0	14	0	14	— 28
Buffalo	10	6	14	6	— 36

Buff — FG Norwood 38
Buff — Burkett 26 pass from Kelly (Norwood kick)
Pitt — Brister 1 run (Anderson kick)
Buff — FG Norwood 39
Pitt — W. Williams 5 pass from Brister (Anderson kick)
Buff — FG Norwood 39
Buff — Riddick 1 run (Norwood kick)
Buff — Riddick 5 blocked punt return (Norwood kick)
Buff — FG Norwood 48
Buff — FG Norwood 49
Pitt — Brister 1 run (Anderson kick)
Pitt — Thompson 42 pass from Brister (Anderson kick)

San Diego 24, Kansas City 23—At Arrowhead Stadium, attendance 45,498. Lionel James scored on a nine-yard pass from Babe Laufenberg with 52 seconds remaining as the Chargers squeaked by the Chiefs. San Diego jumped to a 14-0 first-quarter lead on Laufenberg's 38-yard pass to Quinn Early and Gary Anderson's 30-yard run. Kansas City rallied with 23 unanswered points to take a 23-14 third-quarter lead. Vince Abbott's 47-yard field goal midway through the fourth quarter narrowed the Chiefs' lead to 23-17. Laufenberg led a 61-yard, 13-play drive to set up James's winning reception.

San Diego	14	0	0	10	— 24
Kansas City	0	14	9	0	— 23

SD — Early 38 pass from Laufenberg (Abbott kick)
SD — Anderson 30 run (Abbott kick)
KC — Palmer 71 pass from DeBerg (Lowery kick)
KC — Paige 2 pass from DeBerg (Lowery kick)
KC — Palmer 6 pass from DeBerg (Lowery kick)
KC — Safety, Maas tackled Laufenberg in end zone
SD — FG Abbott 47
SD — James 9 pass from Laufenberg (Abbott kick)

San Francisco 38, Seattle 7—At Kingdome, attendance 62,382. Joe Montana threw four touchdown passes, including three to Jerry Rice, as the 49ers crushed the Seahawks. San Francisco took a 17-0 halftime advantage on Montana scoring passes of one yard to Rice and 13 yards to John Frank and Mike Cofer's 21-yard field goal. Rice, who had six receptions for 163 yards, also caught scoring passes of 69 and 60 yards in the third quarter to increase the 49ers' lead to 31-0. San Francisco maintained a 42:50 to 17:10 time-of-possession advantage.

San Francisco	7	10	14	7	— 38
Seattle	0	0	7	0	— 7

SF — Rice 1 pass from Montana (Cofer kick)
SF — Frank 13 pass from Montana (Cofer kick)
SF — FG Cofer 21
SF — Rice 69 pass from Montana (Cofer kick)
SF — Rice 60 pass from Montana (Cofer kick)
Sea — Butler 46 pass from Stouffer (N. Johnson kick)
SF — Wilson 16 pass from Young (Cofer kick)

New Orleans 13, Tampa Bay 9—At Louisiana Superdome, attendance 66,671. Bobby Hebert threw one touchdown pass and Morten Andersen kicked two field goals to help lead the Saints over the Buccaneers. Hebert capped a 70-yard, 12-play drive with a five-yard scoring pass to Lonzell Hill in the first quarter. Andersen's 28- and 41-yard field goals gave the Saints a 13-6 halftime advantage. Tampa Bay's Donald Igwebuike's third field goal of the day, a 35-yarder in the fourth quarter, provided the only score in the second half.

Tampa Bay	0	6	0	3	— 9
New Orleans	10	3	0	0	— 13

NO — L. Hill 5 pass from Hebert (Andersen kick)
NO — FG Andersen 28
TB — FG Igwebuike 25
NO — FG Andersen 41
TB — FG Igwebuike 35
TB — FG Igwebuike 35

Phoenix 30, Washington 21—At Sun Devil Stadium, attendance 61,973. Tony Jordan scored on two one-yard runs and Cedric Mack returned a fumble for a touchdown to give the Cardinals their first-ever home win in Sun Devil Stadium. Phoenix rallied from a 14-9 halftime deficit to take a 16-14 lead as Jordan ran one yard for a score. The Cardinals put the game out of reach when Neil Lomax connected with Roy Green on a 27-yard touchdown pass and Mack returned a fumble 45 yards for a score with 41 seconds remaining.

Washington	7	7	0	7	— 21
Phoenix	2	7	7	14	— 30

Wash — Monk 23 pass from Rypien (Lohmiller kick)
Phx — Safety, Harvey sacked Rypien in end zone
Phx — Jordan 1 run (Del Greco kick)
Wash — Sanders 18 pass from Rypien (Lohmiller kick)
Phx — Jordan 1 run (Del Greco kick)
Phx — Green 27 pass from Lomax (Del Greco kick)
Wash — Allen 2 pass from Rypien (Lohmiller kick)
Phx — Mack 45 fumble recovery return (Del Greco kick)

Monday, September 26

L.A. Raiders 30, Denver 27—At Mile High Stadium, attendance 75,964. Chris Bahr's 35-yard field goal with 2:25 remaining in overtime helped the Raiders defeat Denver and cap one of the greatest comebacks in their history. The Broncos exploded to a 24-0 first-half lead, but Jay Schroeder, making his first start for Los Angeles, threw two touchdown passes to Steve Smith (40 and 42 yards) in the third quarter to narrow the Broncos' lead to 24-14. Bahr's 28-yard field goal and Marcus Allen's four-yard run tied the game 24-24 in the fourth quarter. Denver's Rich Karlis kicked a 25-yard field goal with 3:01 to play to retake the lead, but Bahr's 44-yard field goal with four seconds remaining sent the game into overtime. Zeph Lee's 20-yard interception return set up Bahr's winning kick.

L.A. Raiders	0	0	14	13	3	— 30
Denver	7	17	0	3	0	— 27

Den — Dorsett 1 run (Karlis kick)
Den — Dorsett 1 run (Karlis kick)
Den — Sewell 7 pass from Elway (Karlis kick)
Den — FG Karlis 39
Raiders — Smith 40 pass from Schroeder (Bahr kick)
Raiders — Smith 42 pass from Schroeder (Bahr kick)
Raiders — FG Bahr 28
Raiders — Allen 4 run (Bahr kick)
Den — FG Karlis 25
Raiders — FG Bahr 44
Raiders — FG Bahr 35

Fifth Week Summaries

Standings

American Football Conference

Eastern Division

	W	L	T	Pct.	Pts.	OP
Buffalo	4	1	0	.800	77	82
N.Y. Jets	3	1	1	.700	105	61
Miami	2	3	0	.400	74	82
New England	2	3	0	.400	75	103
Indianapolis	1	4	0	.200	76	91

Central Division

	W	L	T	Pct.	Pts.	OP
Cincinnati	5	0	0	1.000	135	88
Cleveland	3	2	0	.600	72	76
Houston	3	2	0	.600	112	132
Pittsburgh	1	4	0	.200	102	127

Western Division

	W	L	T	Pct.	Pts.	OP
Seattle	3	2	0	.600	96	99
Denver	2	3	0	.400	100	74
L.A. Raiders	2	3	0	.400	127	145
San Diego	2	3	0	.400	57	99
Kansas City	1	3	1	.300	73	91

National Football Conference

Eastern Division

	W	L	T	Pct.	Pts.	OP
N.Y. Giants	3	2	0	.600	111	118
Phoenix	3	2	0	.600	129	110
Dallas	2	3	0	.400	91	90
Philadelphia	2	3	0	.400	128	105
Washington	2	3	0	.400	111	120

Central Division

	W	L	T	Pct.	Pts.	OP
Chicago	4	1	0	.800	106	60
Minnesota	3	2	0	.600	107	71
Tampa Bay	2	3	0	.400	87	118
Detroit	1	4	0	.200	78	93
Green Bay	0	5	0	.000	64	122

Western Division

	W	L	T	Pct.	Pts.	OP
L.A. Rams	4	1	0	.800	145	106
New Orleans	4	1	0	.800	117	95
San Francisco	4	1	0	.800	129	104
Atlanta	1	4	0	.200	112	134

Sunday, October 2

Chicago 24, Buffalo 3—At Soldier Field, attendance 62,793. Jim McMahon completed two touchdown passes as the Bears knocked the Bills from the ranks of the undefeated. Chicago put the game away by scoring 17 unanswered points in the second quarter on McMahon's scoring pass of 63 yards to Ron Morris, Kevin Butler's 22-yard field goal, and Dennis Gentry's 58-yard scoring run. The Bears' defense sacked Jim Kelly six times and held the Bills to zero rushing yards.

Buffalo	3	0	0	0	— 3
Chicago	7	17	0	0	— 24

Chi — Moorehead 4 pass from McMahon (Butler kick)
Buff — FG Norwood 28
Chi — Morris 63 pass from McMahon (Butler kick)
Chi — FG Butler 22
Chi — Gentry 58 run (Butler kick)

Cincinnati 45, Los Angeles Raiders 21—At Memorial Coliseum, attendance 42,594. Boomer Esiason passed for 332 yards and three touchdowns as the Bengals easily defeated the Raiders. Cincinnati took a commanding 24-7 halftime lead on Esiason's touchdown passes to Rodney Holman (14 yards) and Tim McGee (nine), Ickey Woods's three-yard scoring run, and Jim Breech's 28-yard field goal. The Bengals extended their lead to 38-7 in the third quarter on touchdown runs by Stanford Jennings (five yards) and Stanley Wilson (one). Esiason's third touchdown pass of the game traveled 15 yards to Ira Hillary in the fourth quarter. Jay Schroeder threw for 324 yards and a pair of touchdowns for the Raiders.

Cincinnati	3	21	14	7	— 45
L.A. Raiders	0	7	0	14	— 21

Cin — FG Breech 28
Cin — Holman 14 pass from Esiason (Breech kick)
Cin — Woods 3 run (Breech kick)
Raiders — T. Brown 65 pass from Schroeder (Bahr kick)
Cin — McGee 9 pass from Esiason (Breech kick)
Cin — Jennings 5 run (Breech kick)
Cin — S. Wilson 1 run (Breech kick)
Cin — Hillary 15 pass from Esiason (Breech kick)
Raiders — Schroeder 5 run (Bahr kick)
Raiders — Fernandez 24 pass from Schroeder (Bahr kick)

Cleveland 23, Pittsburgh 9—At Three Rivers Stadium, attendance 56,410. The Browns turned three of five second-half takeaways into scores to defeat the Steelers. Cleveland trailed 9-7 in the third quarter, but Eddie Johnson's fumble recovery set up Matt Bahr's 22-yard field goal to put the Browns ahead for good. Less than three minutes later, Johnson's interception set up another Bahr field goal (21 yards) to give the Browns a 13-9 edge. Pittsburgh's comeback attempt was thwarted when Cleveland rookie safety Brian Washington returned an interception 75 yards for a score. Bahr's 40-yard field goal capped the Browns' scoring.

Cleveland	0	7	6	10	— 23
Pittsburgh	6	3	0	0	— 9

Pitt — FG Anderson 49
Pitt — FG Anderson 35
Clev — Manoa 1 run (Bahr kick)
Pitt — FG Anderson 45
Clev — FG Bahr 22
Clev — FG Bahr 21
Clev — Washington 75 interception return (Bahr kick)
Clev — FG Bahr 40

Denver 12, San Diego 0—At San Diego Jack Murphy Stadium, attendance 55,763. Rich Karlis's four field goals were all the Broncos needed to defeat the Chargers. Denver took a 6-0 lead in the first quarter on Karlis's 30- and 43-yard field goals. John Elway led a 75-yard, 18-play drive to set up Karlis's 30-yard field goal in the third quarter, and his 28-yarder in the final period completed the scoring. Denver's defense held San Diego to 20 yards rushing and blocked Vince Abbott's 34-yard field-goal attempt in the first half to insure the Broncos' shutout.

Denver	6	0	3	3	— 12
San Diego	0	0	0	0	— 0

Den — FG Karlis 30
Den — FG Karlis 43
Den — FG Karlis 30
Den — FG Karlis 28

San Francisco 20, Detroit 13—At Candlestick Park, attendance 58,285. Jerry Rice ran for one touchdown and John Taylor returned a punt for another to help the 49ers defeat the Lions. After a scoreless first quarter, Rice capped a 68-yard drive with an 11-yard touchdown run. Taylor's 77-yard punt return for a score in the third quarter put San Francisco ahead 17-3. Mike Cofer completed the 49ers' scoring with two 29-yard field goals. Detroit's Pete Mandley, who caught an 11-yard touchdown pass from Chuck Long, led all receivers with 116 yards on seven receptions.

Detroit	0	3	3	7	— 13
San Francisco	0	10	7	3	— 20

SF — Rice 11 run (Cofer kick)
Det — FG Murray 24
SF — FG Cofer 29
SF — Taylor 77 punt return (Cofer kick)
Det — FG Murray 34
SF — FG Cofer 29
Det — Mandley 11 pass from Long (Murray kick)

Tampa Bay 27, Green Bay 24—At Tampa Stadium, attendance 40,003. Donald Igwebuike's 44-yard field goal with 12 seconds remaining lifted the Buccaneers over the winless Packers. Tampa Bay overcame a 24-10 fourth-quarter deficit with a one-yard touchdown run by Lars Tate and Vinny Testaverde's 19-yard touchdown pass to Bruce Hill. Kevin Murphy's 35-yard interception return for a score and Igwebuike's 45-yard field goal accounted for the Buccaneers' scoring in the first half.

Green Bay	3	7	7	7	— 24
Tampa Bay	0	10	0	17	— 27

GB — FG Zendejas 44
TB — FG Igwebuike 45
TB — Murphy 35 interception return (Igwebuike kick)
GB — West 14 pass from Wright (Zendejas kick)
GB — Fullwood 1 run (Zendejas kick)
TB — Tate 1 run (Igwebuike kick)
GB — Wright 1 run (Zendejas kick)
TB — Hill 19 pass from Testaverde (Igwebuike kick)
TB — FG Igwebuike 44

Philadelphia 32, Houston 23—At Veterans Stadium, attendance 64,692. Randall Cunningham threw two touchdown passes and rushed for another to lead the Eagles past the Oilers. Houston took a 16-0 first-quarter lead by blocking two punts for a safety and a touchdown and Cody Carlson's running one yard for a touchdown. Philadelphia rallied for 20 second-quarter points on Cunningham's scoring strikes to Cris Carter (38 yards) and Gregg Garrity (16), and two Luis Zendejas field goals (22 and 39 yards). Cunningham's 33-yard scoring run in the third quarter helped Philadelphia put the game away.

Houston	16	0	0	7	— 23
Philadelphia	0	20	9	3	— 32

Hou —Dishman 10 blocked punt return (T. Zendejas kick)
Hou —Safety, Fairs blocked punt out of end zone
Hou —Carlson 1 run (T. Zendejas kick)
Phil —FG L. Zendejas 22
Phil —Carter 38 pass from Cunningham (L. Zendejas kick)
Phil —Garrity 16 pass from Cunningham (L. Zendejas kick)
Phil —FG L. Zendejas 39
Phil —Cunningham 33 run (L. Zendejas kick)
Phil —Safety, Simmons tackled Carlson in end zone
Phil —FG L. Zendejas 41
Hou —Rozier 2 run (T. Zendejas kick)

New England 21, Indianapolis 17—At Sullivan Stadium, attendance 58,050. Doug Flutie's 13-yard touchdown run with 23 seconds remaining helped the Patriots snap a three-game losing streak. Flutie came off the bench in the fourth quarter and connected with Stanley Morgan for a 26-yard touchdown pass to break a 7-7 tie. Indianapolis answered with 10 points, but Flutie led a nine-play, 80-yard drive for the winning score. The Colts' Eric Dickerson rushed for 118 yards on 29 carries for his fourth 100-yard game in five weeks. Flutie was named AFC offensive player of the week for his performance.

Indianapolis	0	7	0	10	— 17
New England	0	7	0	14	— 21

NE —Perryman 1 run (Garcia kick)
Ind —Dickerson 1 run (Biasucci kick)
NE —Morgan 26 pass from Flutie (Garcia kick)
Ind —FG Biasucci 20
Ind —Brooks 48 pass from Chandler (Biasucci kick)
NE —Flutie 13 run (Garcia kick)

Kansas City 17, New York Jets 17—At Giants Stadium, attendance 66,110. The Chiefs and Jets played to only the twelfth tie since overtime play was introduced in 1974. New York led 17-3 in the fourth quarter on a pair of touchdown runs by Johnny Hector (four and one yards) and Pat Leahy's 23-yard field goal. Kansas City tied the game on Steve DeBerg's scoring passes of 80 yards to Carlos Carson and eight yards to Emile Harry with 51 seconds left in regulation. Carson finished with five receptions for 162 yards, while DeBerg completed 17 of 34 for 312 yards and two touchdowns. Freeman McNeil rushed for 154 yards on 22 carries, but fumbled at the Chiefs' 15-yard line with 38 seconds left in overtime.

Kansas City	0	0	3	14	0	— 17
N.Y. Jets	3	7	0	7	0	— 17

NYJ —FG Leahy 23
NYJ —Hector 4 run (Leahy kick)
KC —FG Lowery 34
NYJ —Hector 1 run (Leahy kick)
KC —Carson 80 pass from DeBerg (Lowery kick)
KC —Harry 8 pass from DeBerg (Lowery kick)

Miami 24, Minnesota 7—At Joe Robbie Stadium, attendance 59,867. Lorenzo Hampton caught a touchdown pass and ran for another as the Dolphins easily beat the Vikings. After a scoreless first quarter, Miami went ahead 17-0 at halftime on Fuad Reveiz's 38-yard field goal and Dan Marino touchdown passes to Jim Jensen (three yards) and Hampton (one). William Judson returned an interception 52 yards to set up Hampton's five-yard scoring run in the third quarter.

Minnesota	0	0	0	7	— 7
Miami	0	17	7	0	— 24

Mia —FG Reveiz 38
Mia —Jensen 3 pass from Marino (Reveiz kick)
Mia —Hampton 1 pass from Marino (Reveiz kick)
Mia —Hampton 5 run (Reveiz kick)
Minn —Lee 48 interception return (C. Nelson kick)

New York Giants 24, Washington Redskins 23—At Robert F. Kennedy Stadium, attendance 54,601. Odessa Turner caught eight passes for 103 yards and one touchdown as the Giants held off the Redskins. New York took a 17-9 halftime lead on scoring runs by Ottis Anderson (one yard) and Maurice Carthon (five) and Paul McFadden's 32-yard field goal. Phil Simms threw a 38-yard scoring strike to Turner in the third quarter to increase the Giants' lead to 24-9, but Mark Rypien countered with two touchdown passes to Ricky Sanders (49 and 21 yards) to narrow the deficit to 24-23. Washington had a chance to win the game, but Chip Lohmiller's 36-yard field goal try with 2:54 remaining sailed wide left.

N.Y. Giants	10	7	7	0	— 24
Washington	6	3	7	7	— 23

NYG —FG McFadden 32
Wash —Smith 1 run (kick failed)
NYG —Anderson 1 run (McFadden kick)
Wash —FG Lohmiller 30
NYG —Carthon 5 run (McFadden kick)
NYG —Turner 38 pass from Simms (McFadden kick)
Wash —Sanders 49 pass from Rypien (Lohmiller kick)
Wash —Sanders 21 pass from Rypien (Lohmiller kick)

Phoenix 41, Los Angeles Rams 27—At Anaheim Stadium, attendance 49,830. Neil Lomax completed 28 of 43 passes for 342 yards and two touchdowns as the Cardinals knocked the Rams from the ranks of the undefeated. Lomax's first-half scoring passes to Roy Green (33 yards) and Jay Novacek (eight), and Rod Saddler's 16-yard fumble recovery return for a score helped the Cardinals to a 24-14 halftime lead. Phoenix put the game away in the second half behind scoring runs by Earl Ferrell (seven yards) and Stump Mitchell (35) and Al Del Greco's field goals from 43 and 51 yards. Los Angeles's Greg Bell had scoring runs of five, four, and one yard, but, overall, the Rams were held to just 85 yards rushing. Jim Everett completed 25 of 33 passes for 300 yards and one touchdown.

Phoenix	10	14	3	14	— 41
L.A. Rams	7	7	6	7	— 27

Rams —Bell 5 run (Lansford kick)
Phx —R. Green 33 pass from Lomax (Del Greco kick)
Phx —FG Del Greco 43
Rams —Bell 4 run (Lansford kick)
Phx —Novacek 8 pass from Lomax (Del Greco kick)
Phx —Saddler 16 fumble recovery return (Del Greco kick)
Phx —FG Del Greco 51
Rams —D. Johnson 9 pass from Everett (kick failed)
Phx —Ferrell 7 run (Del Greco kick)
Phx —Mitchell 35 run (Del Greco kick)
Rams —Bell 1 run (Lansford kick)

Seattle 31, Atlanta 20—At Atlanta-Fulton County Stadium, attendance 28,619. John L. Williams scored on three one-yard touchdown runs to help the Seahawks end a two-game slide. Curt Warner's 12-yard touchdown run, Williams's first of three one-yard runs, and Norm Johnson's 44-yard field goal helped the Seahawks to a 17-3 halftime advantage. Williams's two scoring runs in the second half put the game out of reach. Warner led all rushers with 110 yards on 22 carries.

Seattle	7	10	7	7	— 31
Atlanta	3	0	10	7	— 20

Atl —FG Davis 32
Sea —Warner 12 run (N. Johnson kick)
Sea —Williams 1 run (N. Johnson kick)
Sea —FG N. Johnson 44
Atl —FG Davis 31
Atl —Bailey 45 pass from Dils (Davis kick)
Sea —Williams 1 run (N. Johnson kick)
Atl —Dils 1 run (Davis kick)
Sea —Williams 1 run (N. Johnson kick)

Monday, October 3

New Orleans 20, Dallas 17—At Louisiana Superdome, attendance 68,474. Morten Andersen kicked a 49-yard field goal as time expired to lift the Saints over the Cowboys. The Saints led 14-0 midway through the second quarter on Bobby Hebert's scoring strikes to Lonzell Hill (seven yards) and Brett Perriman (17). Steve Pelluer, who brought Dallas back in the third quarter to tie the score 14-14, connected on touchdown throws of 13 and 14 yards to Kelvin Martin. Andersen's 27-yard field goal was matched by the Cowboys' Roger Ruzek, who kicked a 39-yarder to tie the game with 2:24 remaining. Mel Grey's 39-yard kickoff return and Hebert's 26-yard pass to Perriman set up Andersen's winning kick.

Dallas	0	7	7	3	— 17
New Orleans	7	7	3	3	— 20

NO —Hill 7 pass from Hebert (Andersen kick)
NO —Perriman 17 pass from Hebert (Andersen kick)
Dall —K. Martin 13 pass from Pelluer (Ruzek kick)
Dall —K. Martin 14 pass from Pelluer (Ruzek kick)
NO —FG Andersen 27
Dall —FG Ruzek 39
NO —FG Andersen 49

Sixth Week Summaries

Standings

American Football Conference

Eastern Division

	W	L	T	Pct.	Pts.	OP
Buffalo	5	1	0	.833	111	105
N.Y. Jets	3	2	1	.583	124	97
Miami	3	3	0	.500	98	96
New England	2	4	0	.333	78	148
Indianapolis	1	5	0	.167	99	125

Central Division

Cincinnati	6	0	0	1.000	171	107
Houston	4	2	0	.667	119	138
Cleveland	3	3	0	.500	82	92
Pittsburgh	1	5	0	.167	116	158

Western Division

Seattle	4	2	0	.667	112	109
Denver	3	3	0	.500	116	87
L.A. Raiders	2	4	0	.333	141	169
San Diego	2	4	0	.333	74	122
Kansas City	1	4	1	.250	79	98

National Football Conference

Eastern Division

	W	L	T	Pct.	Pts.	OP
Phoenix	4	2	0	.667	160	124
N.Y. Giants	3	3	0	.500	124	142
Philadelphia	3	3	0	.500	152	118
Washington	3	3	0	.500	146	137
Dallas	2	4	0	.333	108	125

Central Division

Chicago	5	1	0	.833	130	67
Minnesota	4	2	0	.667	121	84
Tampa Bay	2	4	0	.333	100	132
Detroit	1	5	0	.167	85	117
Green Bay	1	5	0	.167	109	125

Western Division

L.A. Rams	5	1	0	.833	178	106
New Orleans	5	1	0	.833	140	112
San Francisco	4	2	0	.667	142	120
Atlanta	1	5	0	.167	112	167

Sunday, October 9

Chicago 24, Detroit 7—At Pontiac Silverdome, attendance 64,526. Dennis McKinnon and Ron Morris each caught touchdown passes to help the Bears defeat the Lions. Chicago opened a 17-0 first-half lead on Jim McMahon's 11-yard pass to McKinnon, Neal Anderson's one-yard run, and Kevin Butler's 37-yard field goal. Mike Tomczak relieved an injured McMahon in the second half and hit Morris with a 31-yard scoring strike to finish the Bears' scoring. Chicago's defense held the Lions to 42 yards rushing.

Chicago	7	10	0	7	— 24
Detroit	0	0	7	0	— 7

Chi —McKinnon 11 pass from McMahon (Butler kick)
Chi —Anderson 1 run (Butler kick)
Chi —FG Butler 37
Det —Mandley 7 pass from Hilger (Murray kick)
Chi —Morris 31 pass from Tomczak (Butler kick)

Denver 16, San Francisco 13—At Candlestick Park, attendance 61,711. Rich Karlis's 22-yard field goal with 6:49 remaining in overtime lifted the Broncos over the 49ers. Trailing 10-3 in the third quarter, Denver tied the score 13-13 on Karlis's 27-yard field goal and John Elway's eight-yard touchdown pass to Vance Johnson, which sent the game into overtime. Steve Wilson's interception set up Karlis's winning kick. The Broncos won the overtime toss but because of strong winds at Candlestick Park chose to kick off.

Denver	0	3	3	7	3	— 16
San Francisco	3	7	3	0	0	— 13

SF —FG Cofer 37
Den —FG Karlis 27
SF —Montana 6 run (Cofer kick)
Den —FG Karlis 27
SF —FG Cofer 27
Den —Johnson 8 pass from Elway (Karlis kick)
Den —FG Karlis 22

Buffalo 34, Indianapolis 23—At Rich Stadium, attendance 76,018. Jim Kelly completed three touchdown passes, including two to Andre Reed, to help lead the Bills over the Colts. Buffalo cut the Indianapolis lead to 17-7 at halftime on Kelly's 26-yard the scoring pass to Ronnie Harmon. The Bills took a 21-17 lead in the third quarter on Kelly's touchdown passes of 16 and 12 yards to Reed. Scott Norwood kicked two field goals (45 and 19 yards) and Robb Riddick ran one yard for a touchdown in the fourth quarter to put the game out of reach.

Indianapolis	10	7	3	3	— 23
Buffalo	0	7	14	13	— 34

Ind —FG Biasucci 31
Ind —Chandler 1 run (Biasucci kick)
Ind —Verdin 39 pass from Hogeboom (Biasucci kick)
Buff —Harmon 26 pass from Kelly (Norwood kick)
Buff —Reed 16 pass from Kelly (Norwood kick)
Ind —FG Biasucci 40
Buff —Reed 12 pass from Kelly (Norwood kick)
Ind —FG Biasucci 22
Buff —FG Norwood 45
Buff —FG Norwood 19
Buff —Riddick 1 run (Norwood kick)

Houston 7, Kansas City 6—At Astrodome, attendance 39,135. Brent Pease's four-yard touchdown run in the third quarter were all the points Houston needed as it rallied to beat the Chiefs. Kansas City led 6-0 at halftime on Nick Lowery's 28- and 51-yard field goals, but Pease came off the bench to lead a 63-yard drive for the winning score. Mike Rozier rushed for 141 yards on 27 carries.

Kansas City	3	3	0	0	— 6
Houston	0	0	7	0	— 7

KC —FG Lowery 28
KC —FG Lowery 51
Hou —Pease 4 run (Zendejas kick)

Los Angeles Rams 33, Atlanta 0—At Atlanta-Fulton County Stadium, attendance 30,852. Jim Everett passed for 234 yards and three touchdowns as the Rams shut out the Falcons. Los Angeles put the game away early by scoring 27 points in the first half on Everett's scoring passes to Henry Ellard (54 yards) and Buford McGee (four), Greg Bell's one-yard run, and Mike Lansford's 40- and 25-yard field goals. Bell carried 21 times for 155 yards. Kevin Greene, who accounted for three of the Rams' nine sacks, was named NFC defensive player of the week.

L.A. Rams	10	17	6	0	—	33
Atlanta	0	0	0	0	—	0

Rams — FG Lansford 40
Rams — Bell 1 run (Lansford kick)
Rams — FG Lansford 25
Rams — Ellard 54 pass from Everett (Lansford kick)
Rams — McGee 4 pass from Everett (Lansford kick)
Rams — Holohan 21 pass from Everett (kick failed)

Miami 24, Los Angeles Raiders 14—At Memorial Coliseum, attendance 50,751. The Dolphins scored two touchdowns within an 11-second span of the second quarter to snap a six-game losing streak against the Raiders. Miami broke a scoreless tie in the second quarter on Lorenzo Hampton's one-yard run, which capped an 11-play, 84-yard drive. The Raiders fumbled the ensuing kickoff, which Liffort Hobley returned 19 yards for a score. The Dolphins added 10 points to give them a commanding 24-0 lead at halftime on Fuad Reveiz's 45-yard field goal and Jim Jensen's 17-yard scoring reception from Dan Marino.

Miami	0	24	0	0	—	24
L.A. Raiders	0	0	7	7	—	14

Mia — Hampton 1 run (Reveiz kick)
Mia — Hobley 19 fumble recovery return (Reveiz kick)
Mia — FG Reveiz 45
Mia — Jensen 17 pass from Marino (Reveiz kick)
Raiders — Fernandez 7 pass from Schroeder (Bahr kick)
Raiders — Strachan 13 pass from Schroeder (Bahr kick)

Green Bay 45, New England 3—At Milwaukee County Stadium, attendance 51,932. Brent Fullwood ran for three touchdowns as the Packers crushed the Patriots for their first win of the season. Don Majkowski ran two yards for a score and threw a two-yard touchdown pass to Joey Hackett to help Green Bay to a 17-3 halftime lead. Fullwood, who rushed 14 times for 118 yards, had scoring runs of 7, 33, and 31 yards in the second half. Kenneth Davis ran eight yards for a touchdown with 2:59 to play to complete the Packers' onslaught.

New England	3	0	0	0	—	3
Green Bay	0	17	7	21	—	45

NE — FG Garcia 43
GB — FG Zendejas 25
GB — Majkowski 2 run (Zendejas kick)
GB — Hackett 2 pass from Majkowski (Zendejas kick)
GE — Fullwood 33 run (Zendejas kick)
GB — Fullwood 7 run (Zendejas kick)
GB — Fullwood 31 run (Zendejas kick)
GB — Davis 8 run (Zendejas kick)

New Orleans 23, San Diego 17—At San Diego Jack Murphy Stadium, attendance 42,693. Bobby Hebert completed two touchdown passes to lead the Saints to their fifth consecutive win by defeating the Chargers 23-17. New Orleans rebounded from a 14-0 first-quarter deficit on two Morten Andersen field goals (27 and 35 yards) and Hebert's 19-yard pass to Lonzell Hill. The Saints took the lead for good midway through the third quarter when Hebert hit Eric Martin on a 10-yard scoring pass. New Orleans's defense toughened in the second half, holding San Diego to one field goal.

New Orleans	0	13	7	3	—	23
San Diego	14	0	3	0	—	17

SD — Miller 47 pass from Laufenberg (Abbott kick)
SD — Bennett recovered blocked punt in end zone (Abbott kick)
NO — FG Andersen 27
NO — FG Andersen 35
NO — Hill 19 pass from Hebert (Andersen kick)
NO — Martin 10 pass from Hebert (Andersen kick)
SD — FG Abbott 35
NO — FG Andersen 34

Cincinnati 36, New York Jets 19—At Riverfront Stadium, attendance 57,482. Boomer Esiason threw three touchdown passes as the Bengals defeated the Jets to remain the NFL's only undefeated team. Esiason helped Cincinnati to a 19-12 halftime lead on touchdown passes of eight and 60 yards to Eddie Brown and 38 yards to Tim McGee. Rookie Ickey Woods, who rushed for 139 yards on 30 carries and had 5- and 17-yard scoring runs, was named AFC offensive player of the week.

N.Y. Jets	9	3	7	0	—	19
Cincinnati	6	13	7	10	—	36

NYJ — Safety, Lyons tackled Esiason in end zone
NYJ — Vick 1 run (Leahy kick)
Cin — Brown 60 pass from Esiason (kick failed)
Cin — Brown 8 pass from Esiason (kick blocked)
NYJ — FG Leahy 30
Cin — McGee 38 pass from Esiason (Breech kick)
NYJ — Toon 11 pass from O'Brien (Leahy kick)
Cin — Woods 5 run (Breech kick)
Cin — Woods 17 run (Breech kick)
Cin — FG Breech 25

Phoenix 31, Pittsburgh 14—At Sun Devil Stadium, attendance 53,278. Neil Lomax threw for 291 yards and three touchdowns to lead the Cardinals over the Steelers. Lomax connected with J.T. Smith on scoring strikes of three and 13 yards and hit Robert Awalt for a 32-yard touchdown pass. Tony Jordan added a one-yard scoring run for Phoenix. The Cardinals held Pittsburgh to 78 yards rushing and maintained a 37:51 to 22:09 time-of-possession advantage.

Pittsburgh	7	0	0	7	—	14
Phoenix	7	17	7	0	—	31

Phx — Awalt 32 pass from Lomax (Del Greco kick)
Pitt — Woodson 92 kickoff return (Anderson kick)
Phx — FG Del Greco 19
Phx — Jordan 1 run (Del Greco kick)
Phx — J.T. Smith 3 pass from Lomax (Del Greco kick)
Phx — J.T. Smith 13 pass from Lomax (Del Greco kick)
Pitt — Hoge 12 pass from Bono (Anderson kick)

Seattle 16, Cleveland 10—At Cleveland Stadium, attendance 78,605. Curt Warner ran for a touchdown and Norm Johnson kicked three field goals to lift the Seahawks over the Browns. Warner ran one yard for a touchdown in the first quarter to tie the game at 7-7. Defensive end Jeff Bryant blocked a Cleveland field-goal attempt to set up Johnson's first field goal, a 31-yarder. Johnson added a 38-yarder 2:10 before halftime to complete the Seahawks' first-half scoring.

Seattle	7	6	0	3	—	16
Cleveland	7	0	0	3	—	10

Clev — Mack 1 run (Bahr kick)
Sea — Warner 1 run (N. Johnson kick)
Sea — FG N. Johnson 31
Sea — FG N. Johnson 38
Sea — FG N. Johnson 22
Clev — FG Bahr 23

Minnesota 14, Tampa Bay 13—At Metrodome, attendance 55,274. Anthony Carter ran for one touchdown and set up another as the Vikings edged the Buccaneers. Carter, who had seven receptions for 82 yards, caught an 11-yard touchdown pass from Tommy Kramer to give Minnesota a 7-0 first-quarter lead. Tampa Bay came back to take a 10-7 halftime lead on Vinny Testaverde's 14-yard pass to Mark Carrier and Donald Igwebuike's 31-yard field goal. After the Vikings' David Howard recovered a fumble in the third quarter, Carter made a diving 11-yard reception to set up Allen Rice's one-yard scoring run.

Tampa Bay	0	10	0	3	—	13
Minnesota	7	0	7	0	—	14

Minn — Carter 11 pass from Kramer (C. Nelson kick)
TB — Carrier 14 pass from Testaverde (Igwebuike kick)
TB — FG Igwebuike 31
Minn — Rice 1 run (C. Nelson kick)
TB — FG Igwebuike 36

Washington 35, Dallas 17—At Texas Stadium, attendance 63,235. Mark Rypien completed three touchdown passes and ran for another as the Redskins defeated the Cowboys. Rypien had a hand in three first-half scores to give Washington a commanding 28-10 lead. He followed touchdown passes to Gary Clark (13 yards) and Kelvin Bryant (10) with his own 19-yard scoring run. Bryant, who rushed 23 times for 118 yards and had five receptions for 82 yards, ran for a nine-yard touchdown and caught a 24-yard pass from Rypien to complete the Redskins' scoring.

Washington	7	21	0	7	—	35
Dallas	7	3	0	7	—	17

Dall — Newsome 1 run (Ruzek kick)
Wash — Clark 13 pass from Rypien (Lohmiller kick)
Wash — Bryant 10 pass from Rypien (Lohmiller kick)
Dall — FG Ruzek 45
Wash — Bryant 9 run (Lohmiller kick)
Wash — Rypien 19 run (Lohmiller kick)
Dall — Martin 35 pass from Pelluer (Ruzek kick)
Wash — Bryant 24 pass from Rypien (Lohmiller kick)

Monday, October 10

Philadelphia 24, New York Giants 13—At Veterans Stadium, attendance 63,736. Randall Cunningham threw three touchdown passes to give the Eagles their first victory over the Giants since October 21, 1984. Cunningham gave Philadelphia a 14-3 halftime advantage on scoring passes to Jimmie Giles (four yards) and Keith Byars (five). New York narrowed the deficit to 17-10 early in the fourth quarter, but Cunningham's 80-yard scoring strike to Cris Carter with 1:48 to play sealed the victory. Cunningham, who was 31 of 41 for 369 yards, was named NFC offensive player of the week.

N.Y. Giants	3	0	3	7	—	13
Philadelphia	0	14	3	7	—	24

NYG — FG Allegre 47
Phil — Giles 4 pass from Cunningham (Zendejas kick)
Phil — Byars 5 pass from Cunningham (Zendejas kick)
Phil — FG Zendejas 37
NYG — FG Allegre 22
NYG — Mowatt 38 pass from Simms (Allegre kick)
Phil — Carter 80 pass from Cunningham (Zendejas kick)

Seventh Week Summaries

Standings

American Football Conference

Eastern Division

	W	L	T	Pct.	Pts.	OP
Buffalo	6	1	0	.857	148	119
Miami	4	3	0	.571	129	124
N.Y. Jets	3	3	1	.500	138	134
New England	3	4	0	.429	105	169
Indianapolis	2	5	0	.286	134	156
Central Division						
Cincinnati	6	1	0	.857	192	134
Houston	5	2	0	.714	153	152
Cleveland	4	3	0	.571	101	95
Pittsburgh	1	6	0	.143	130	192
Western Division						
Denver	4	3	0	.571	146	101
Seattle	4	3	0	.571	131	129
L.A. Raiders	3	4	0	.429	168	186
San Diego	2	5	0	.286	102	153
Kansas City	1	5	1	.214	96	125

National Football Conference

Eastern Division

	W	L	T	Pct.	Pts.	OP
N.Y. Giants	4	3	0	.571	154	152
Phoenix	4	3	0	.571	177	157
Washington	4	3	0	.571	179	154
Philadelphia	3	4	0	.429	155	137
Dallas	2	5	0	.286	115	142
Central Division						
Chicago	6	1	0	.857	147	74
Minnesota	4	3	0	.571	135	118
Green Bay	2	5	0	.286	143	139
Tampa Bay	2	5	0	.286	131	167
Detroit	1	6	0	.143	95	147
Western Division						
New Orleans	6	1	0	.857	160	131
L.A. Rams	5	2	0	.714	199	130
San Francisco	5	2	0	.714	166	141
Atlanta	1	6	0	.143	126	197

Sunday, October 16

Denver 30, Atlanta 14—At Mile High Stadium, attendance 75,287. Rich Karlis kicked three field goals and Gary Kubiak came off the bench to complete a fourth-quarter touchdown pass to lead the Broncos over the Falcons. With the score tied 7-7 in the third quarter, Sammy Winder scored on a one-yard run and Karlis kicked field goals of 47 and 41 yards to give Denver a 17-7 lead it never relinquished. Kubiak relieved John Elway in the third quarter and threw a 68-yard scoring bomb midway through the final period to Steve Sewell. Atlanta's John Settle led all rushers with 125 yards on 25 carries.

Atlanta	0	7	0	7	—	14
Denver	0	7	10	13	—	30

Den — Jackson 14 pass from Elway (Karlis kick)
Atl — Settle 1 run (Davis kick)
Den — Winder 1 run (Karlis kick)
Den — FG Karlis 47
Atl — Settle 1 pass from Dils (Davis kick)
Den — FG Karlis 41
Den — Sewell 68 pass from Kubiak (Karlis kick)
Den — FG Karlis 50

New England 27, Cincinnati 21—At Sullivan Stadium, attendance 59,969. Reggie Dupard had two second-half touchdown runs as the Patriots handed the Bengals their first loss of the season. New England took a 14-0 halftime lead on John Stephens's fumble recovery in the end zone and Mosi Tatupu's three-yard run that was set up by Tim Jordan's interception.

Cincinnati	0	0	14	7	—	21
New England	7	7	6	7	—	27

NE — Stephens fumble recovery in end zone (Garcia kick)
NE — Tatupu 3 run (Garcia kick)
NE — Dupard 3 run (kick failed)
Cin — Woods 1 run (Breech kick)
Cin — Brown 26 pass from Esiason (Breech kick)
NE — Dupard 10 run (Garcia kick)
Cin — Brown 16 pass from Esiason (Breech kick)

Chicago 17, Dallas 7—At Soldier Field, attendance 64,759. The Bears scored all the points they needed in the second quarter to defeat the Cowboys. After a scoreless first quarter, Dennis McKinnon's four-yard end-around touchdown capped an 80-yard drive. Chicago took a 17-0 halftime lead on Kevin Butler's 21-yard field goal and Jim McMahon's 39-yard touchdown pass to Ron Morris. The Bears' defense recorded five sacks and two interceptions. Danny White's 13-yard pass to Everett Gay with 5:07 remaining avoided a shutout.

Dallas	0	0	0	7	—	7
Chicago	0	17	0	0	—	17

Chi — McKinnon 4 run (Butler kick)
Chi — FG Butler 21
Chi — Morris 39 pass from McMahon (Butler kick)
Dall — Gay 13 pass from D. White (Ruzek kick)

New York Giants 30, Detroit 10—At Giants Stadium, attendance 74,813. Phil Simms threw two touchdown passes and Raul Allegre kicked three field goals as the Giants rallied to defeat the Lions. Trailing 10-7 in the third quarter, Simms completed a 51-yard touchdown pass to Stephen Baker for the go-ahead score. Allegre then converted field goals of 33, 48, and 25 yards to increase New York's lead to 23-10. Joe Morris's eight-yard run with 1:56 remaining finished the Giants' scoring.

Detroit	0	10	0	0 —	10
N.Y. Giants	0	7	16	7 —	30

NYG —Bavaro 6 pass from Simms (Allegre kick)
Det —James 39 pass from Hilger (Murray kick)
Det —FG Murray 32
NYG —Baker 51 pass from Simms (Allegre kick)
NYG —FG Allegre 33
NYG —FG Allegre 48
NYG —FG Allegre 25
NYG —Morris 8 run (Allegre kick)

Green Bay 34, Minnesota 14—At Metrodome, attendance 59,053. Max Zendejas kicked four field goals and Brent Fullwood ran for a touchdown to help the Packers defeat the Vikings. Green Bay opened a 16-7 halftime lead on scoring runs by Fullwood (two yards) and Keith Woodside (six), and Zendejas's 37-yard field goal. Packers linebacker Tim Harris, who tackled Wade Wilson in the end zone for a safety, then blocked and returned a punt 10 yards for a score, was named NFC defensive player of the week.

Green Bay	9	7	8	10 —	34
Minnesota	0	7	0	7 —	14

GB —Fullwood 2 run (kick failed)
GB —FG Zendejas 37
GB —Woodside 6 run (Zendejas kick)
Minn —Lewis 46 pass from Wilson (C. Nelson kick)
GB —FG Zendejas 22
GB —Safety, T. Harris tackled Wilson in end zone
GB —FG Zendejas 36
Minn —Rice 3 run (C. Nelson kick)
GB —FG Zendejas 45
GB —T. Harris 10 blocked punt return (Zendejas kick)

Houston 34, Pittsburgh 14—At Three Rivers Stadium, attendance 52,229. Warren Moon, playing for the first time in six weeks, threw two touchdown passes to lead the Oilers past the Steelers. Moon completed scoring passes to Ernest Givins (43 yards) and Drew Hill (24). Mike Rozier (two yards) and Allen Pinkett (one) added scoring runs. Pinkett's touchdown followed a blocked punt by Cris Dishman. Eugene Seale blocked a punt out of the end zone for a safety to help Houston to an 18-7 halftime advantage.

Houston	6	12	7	9 —	34
Pittsburgh	0	7	0	7 —	14

Hou —Rozier 2 run (pass failed)
Hou —FG Zendejas 50
Hou —Safety, Seale blocked punt out of end zone
Hou —Givins 43 pass from Moon (Zendejas kick)
Pitt —Lockett 9 pass from Blackledge (Anderson kick)
Hou —Pinkett 1 run (Zendejas kick)
Hou —FG Zendejas 27
Hou —Hill 24 pass from Moon (kick failed)
Pitt —Hoge 1 run (Anderson kick)

Los Angeles Raiders 27, Kansas City 17—At Arrowhead Stadium, attendance 77,078. Bo Jackson, making his NFL season debut, ran for 70 yards and a touchdown as the Raiders downed the Chiefs. Marcus Allen and Steve Smith each scored on a pair of one-yard runs to give Los Angeles a 14-7 halftime lead. Kansas City narrowed the margin to 14-10 in the third quarter on Nick Lowery's 43-yard field goal. Steve Beuerlein's four-yard pass to Trey Junkin and Jackson's one-yard run put the Raiders ahead to stay in the fourth quarter.

L.A. Raiders	7	7	0	13 —	27
Kansas City	0	7	0	10 —	17

Raiders —Allen 1 run (Bahr kick)
Raiders —S. Smith 1 run (Bahr kick)
KC —Palmer 48 pass from DeBerg (Lowery kick)
KC —FG Lowery 43
Raiders —Junkin 4 pass from Beuerlein (kick blocked)
Raiders —Jackson 1 run (Bahr kick)
KC —Paige 25 pass from DeBerg (Lowery kick)

New Orleans 20, Seattle 19—At Kingdome, attendance 63,569. Dave Waymer returned a blocked field-goal attempt 58 yards for a touchdown to help the Saints record their sixth straight victory. New Orleans took a 10-6 halftime lead on Bobby Hebert's 19-yard touchdown pass to Eric Martin and Morten Andersen's 23-yard field goal. Waymer's touchdown increased the Saints' lead to 17-13. Andersen's 31-yard field goal in the fourth quarter proved to be the game-winner.

New Orleans	0	10	7	3 —	20
Seattle	3	3	6	7 —	19

Sea —FG N. Johnson 22
NO —Martin 19 pass from Hebert (Andersen kick)
Sea —FG N. Johnson 47
NO —FG Andersen 23
Sea —FG N. Johnson 46
NO —Waymer 58 blocked field goal return (Andersen kick)
Sea —FG N. Johnson 42
NO —FG Andersen 31
Sea —Blades 3 pass from Stouffer (N. Johnson kick)

Cleveland 19, Philadelphia 3—At Cleveland Stadium, attendance 78,787. Don Strock, making his first NFL start since 1983, completed two touchdown passes and the Browns' defense registered nine sacks as Cleveland defeated Philadelphia 19-3. With the score tied 3-3 in the third quarter, Strock hit Webster Slaughter with a 15-yard scoring pass. Frank Minnifield's interception early in the fourth quarter set up Strock's second scoring strike, an 18-yarder to Reggie Langhorne. Matt Bahr added field goals of 24 and 37 yards for the Browns. Kevin Mack rushed 16 times for 100 yards.

Philadelphia	0	3	0	0 —	3
Cleveland	3	0	6	10 —	19

Clev —FG Bahr 24
Phil —FG Zendejas 39
Clev —Slaughter 15 pass from Strock (kick blocked)
Clev —FG Bahr 37
Clev —Langhorne 18 pass from Strock (Bahr kick)

Washington 33, Phoenix 17—At Robert F. Kennedy Stadium, attendance 54,402. Mark Rypien threw for 303 yards and four touchdowns as the Redskins defeated the Cardinals. Rypien's three first-half touchdown passes to Art Monk (19 and 46 yards) and Gary Clark (19) helped the Redskins to a 23-10 halftime lead. Rypien also completed a 60-yard scoring pass to Clark in the third quarter. Chip Lohmiller added a 20-yard field goal to finish the Redskins' scoring. Washington's defense had five sacks, including Ravin Caldwell's tackle of Neil Lomax in the end zone for a safety.

Phoenix	7	3	0	7 —	17
Washington	9	14	7	3 —	33

Phx —R. Green 23 pass from Lomax (Del Greco kick)
Wash —Safety, Caldwell tackled Lomax in end zone
Wash —Monk 19 pass from Rypien (Lohmiller kick)
Phx —FG Del Greco 38
Wash —Clark 19 pass from Rypien (Lohmiller kick)
Wash —Monk 46 pass from Rypien (Lohmiller kick)
Wash —Clark 60 pass from Rypien (Lohmiller kick)
Wash —FG Lohmiller 20
Phx —Novacek 41 pass from Lomax (Del Greco kick)

Miami 31, San Diego 28—At Joe Robbie Stadium, attendance 58,972. Dan Marino threw for 329 yards and a touchdown to lead the Dolphins past the Chargers. San Diego led 21-10 when Lorenzo Hampton scored on a pair of touchdown runs (one and two yards) to give the Dolphins a 24-21 lead in the fourth quarter. Marino hit Mark Duper with a 51-yard bomb to set up Troy Stradford's three-yard scoring run, which capped Miami's scoring. Marino also connected with Duper for a six-yard touchdown pass in the first quarter.

San Diego	7	14	7	0 —	28
Miami	7	3	7	14 —	31

SD —Early 15 pass from Malone (Abbott kick)
Mia —Duper 6 pass from Marino (Reveiz kick)
Mia —FG Reveiz 22
SD —Malone 1 run (Abbott kick)
SD —Flutie 21 pass from Malone (Abbott kick)
Mia —Hampton 2 run (Reveiz kick)
SD —Adams 1 run (Abbott kick)
Mia —Hampton 1 run (Reveiz kick)
Mia —Stradford 3 run (Reveiz kick)

San Francisco 24, Los Angeles Rams 21—At Anaheim Stadium, attendance 65,450. Roger Craig ran for a career-high 190 yards and three touchdowns to help the 49ers past the Rams. Craig's scoring runs of 46 and two yards in the first half gave San Francisco a 17-7 halftime lead. Jim Everett brought the Rams back in the third quarter with scoring passes to Henry Ellard (18 yards) and Buford McGee (eight). Craig's 16-yard touchdown run in the fourth quarter proved to be the game-winner. The victory gave the 49ers their eleventh straight road win, tying the NFL record set by the Los Angeles/San Diego Chargers in 1960-61.

San Francisco	7	10	0	7 —	24
L.A. Rams	7	0	14	0 —	21

SF —Craig 46 run (Cofer kick)
Rams —Cox 44 pass from Everett (Lansford kick)
SF —Craig 2 run (Cofer kick)
SF —FG Cofer 40
Rams —Ellard 18 pass from Everett (Lansford kick)
Rams —McGee 8 pass from Everett (Lansford kick)
SF —Craig 16 run (Cofer kick)

Indianapolis 35, Tampa Bay 31—At Hoosier Dome, attendance 53,135. Chris Chandler threw one touchdown pass and ran for another to highlight the Colts' victory over the Buccaneers. Eric Dickerson carried 27 times for 80 yards and scored on touchdown runs of one and 27 yards in the first half to help Indianapolis to a 21-10 halftime lead. Bill Brooks, who had seven receptions for 139 yards, caught a 28-yard touchdown pass from Chandler in the third quarter. Vinny Testaverde completed 25 of 42 passes for a career-high 469 yards and two touchdowns for Tampa Bay.

Tampa Bay	0	10	0	21 —	31
Indianapolis	7	14	14	0 —	35

Ind —Dickerson 1 run (Biasucci kick)
TB —FG Igwebuike 39
Ind —Dickerson 27 run (Biasucci kick)
TB —Hill 10 pass from Testaverde (Igwebuike kick)
Ind —Chandler 2 run (Biasucci kick)
Ind —Brooks 28 pass from Chandler (Biasucci kick)
Ind —E. Daniels 41 interception return (Biasucci kick)
TB —D. Smith 5 run (Igwebuike kick)
TB —Hill 16 pass from Testaverde (Igwebuike kick)
TB —Tate 1 run (Igwebuike kick)

Monday, October 17

Buffalo 37, New York Jets 14—At Giants Stadium, attendance 70,218. Jim Kelly threw for 302 yards and three touchdowns as the Bills defeated the Jets in their first Monday night football appearance since 1984. Andre Reed, who had seven catches for 132 yards, caught Kelly touchdown passes of 65 and 16 yards in the first half. Robb Riddick ran one yard for a score and Scott Norwood kicked a 30-yard field goal to give Buffalo a commanding 31-7 halftime lead. The Bills' defense recorded five sacks, including two-and-a-half by Bruce Smith.

Buffalo	17	14	3	3 —	37
N.Y. Jets	0	7	7	0 —	14

Buff —FG Norwood 30
Buff —Reed 65 pass from Kelly (Norwood kick)
Buff —F. Johnson 66 pass from Kelly (Norwood kick)
Buff —Riddick 1 run (Norwood kick)
NYJ —Hector 1 run (Leahy kick)
Buff —Reed 16 pass from Kelly (Norwood kick)
Buff —FG Norwood 34
NYJ —McMillan 40 interception return (Leahy kick)
Buff —FG Norwood 28

Eighth Week Summaries

Standings

American Football Conference

Eastern Division

	W	L	T	Pct.	Pts.	OP
Buffalo	7	1	0	.875	171	139
N.Y. Jets	4	3	1	.563	182	164
Miami	4	4	0	.500	159	168
Indianapolis	3	5	0	.375	150	156
New England	3	5	0	.375	125	192

Central Division

Cincinnati	7	1	0	.875	236	155
Cleveland	5	3	0	.625	130	116
Houston	5	3	0	.625	174	196
Pittsburgh	2	6	0	.333	169	213

Western Division

Denver	4	4	0	.500	167	140
Seattle	4	4	0	.500	141	160
L.A. Raiders	3	5	0	.375	174	206
San Diego	2	6	0	.333	102	169
Kansas City	1	6	1	.188	102	132

National Football Conference

Eastern Division

	W	L	T	Pct.	Pts.	OP
N.Y. Giants	5	3	0	.625	177	168
Washington	5	3	0	.625	199	171
Philadelphia	4	4	0	.500	179	160
Phoenix	4	4	0	.500	198	186
Dallas	2	6	0	.250	138	166

Central Division

Chicago	7	1	0	.875	157	83
Minnesota	5	3	0	.625	184	138
Detroit	2	6	0	.250	102	153
Green Bay	2	6	0	.250	160	159
Tampa Bay	2	6	0	.250	151	216

Western Division

New Orleans	7	1	0	.875	180	137
L.A. Rams	6	2	0	.750	230	140
San Francisco	5	3	0	.625	175	151
Atlanta	1	7	0	.125	142	220

Sunday, October 23

Cleveland 29, Phoenix 21—At Sun Devil Stadium, attendance 61,261. Bernie Kosar completed 25 of 43 passes for 314 yards and three touchdowns to lead the Browns over the Cardinals. Kosar threw a three-yard scoring pass to tackle-eligible Rickey Bolden and a 29-yard pass to Reggie Langhorne to help Cleveland take a 17-14 halftime lead. The Browns extended their lead in the second half on Kosar's 25-yard touchdown pass to Langhorne and Charles Buchanan's sack of Phoenix quarterback Cliff Stoudt in the end zone for a safety.

Cleveland	7	10	3	9 —	29
Phoenix	0	14	0	7 —	21

Clev —Bolden 3 pass from Kosar (Bahr kick)
Clev —Langhorne 29 pass from Kosar (Bahr kick)
Phx —Ferrell 2 run (Del Greco kick)
Phx —J. T. Smith 8 pass from Lomax (Del Greco kick)
Clev —FG Bahr 46
Clev —FG Bahr 23

Phx —Awalt 21 pass from Stoudt (Del Greco kick)
Clev —Langhorne 25 pass from Kosar (Bahr kick)
Clev —Safety, Buchanan sacked Stoudt in end zone

Philadelphia 24, Dallas 23—At Veterans Stadium, attendance 66,309. Randall Cunningham hit Anthony Toney on a two-yard touchdown pass with four seconds remaining as the Eagles rallied to defeat the Cowboys. Trailing 23-10 in the fourth quarter, Toney ran seven yards for a touchdown to cap a 99-yard drive and narrow the score to 23-17. Cunningham completed 26 of 53 for 298 yards and two touchdowns, while Dallas counterpart Steve Pelluer connected on 32 of 46 for 342 yards and one score.

Dallas	17	3	3	0	— 23
Philadelphia	0	7	3	14	— 24

Dall —Alexander 18 pass from Pelluer (Ruzek kick)
Dall —Newsome 1 run (Ruzek kick)
Dall —FG Ruzek 26
Dall —FG Ruzek 34
Phil —Byars 11 pass from Cunningham (Zendejas kick)
Phil —FG Zendejas 39
Dall —FG Ruzek 30
Phil —Toney 7 run (Zendejas kick)
Phil —Toney 2 pass from Cunningham (Zendejas kick)

Pittsburgh 39, Denver 21—At Mile High Stadium, attendance 49,811. Gary Anderson kicked a career-high six field goals and Rodney Carter scored a pair of touchdowns as the Steelers upended the Broncos. Pittsburgh jumped to a 27-0 lead at halftime on Carter's two scores (64-yard run and 10-yard reception), Todd Blackledge's one-yard run, and Anderson's 30- and 32-yard field goals. Anderson added field goals of 21, 37, 22, and 30 yards in the second half to give him 21 points, the most by a kicker in a game in 1988.

Denver	0	0	7	14	— 21
Pittsburgh	14	13	3	9	— 39

Pitt —Carter 64 run (Anderson kick)
Pitt —Blackledge 1 run (Anderson kick)
Pitt —FG Anderson 30
Pitt —Carter 10 pass from Blackledge (Anderson kick)
Pitt —FG Anderson 32
Den —Kay 17 pass from Kubiak (Karlis kick)
Pitt —FG Anderson 21
Pitt —FG Anderson 37
Pitt —FG Anderson 22
Den —Kay 14 pass from Kubiak (Karlis kick)
Den —Nattiel 74 pass from Karcher (Karlis kick)
Pitt —FG Anderson 30

Detroit 7, Kansas City 6—At Arrowhead Stadium, attendance 66,926. Rusty Hilger's 14-yard touchdown pass to Jeff Chadwick proved to be all the points the Lions needed to defeat the Chiefs. Nick Lowery kicked field goals of 38 and 43 yards for Kansas City. The Lions' defense registered four sacks and held the Chiefs to 61 yards rushing.

Detroit	0	7	0	0	— 7
Kansas City	0	3	3	0	— 6

KC —FG Lowery 38
Det —Chadwick 14 pass from Hilger (Murray kick)
KC —FG Lowery 43

Cincinnati 44, Houston 21—At Riverfront Stadium, attendance 54,659. James Brooks and Ickey Woods combined for five touchdowns as the Bengals crushed the Oilers. Cincinnati took an insurmountable 28-0 first-quarter lead on touchdown runs by Brooks (seven and nine yards) and Woods (one) and Leo Barker's 34-yard fumble return for a score. Brooks (18 yards) and Woods (one) added touchdown runs in the second half.

Houston	0	7	14	0	— 21
Cincinnati	28	0	7	9	— 44

Cin —Woods 1 run (Breech kick)
Cin —Brooks 7 run (Breech kick)
Cin —Brooks 9 run (Breech kick)
Cin —Barker 34 fumble recovery return (Breech kick)
Hou —Rozier 5 run (Zendejas kick)
Cin —Brooks 18 run (Breech kick)
Hou —Drewrey 10 pass from Moon (Zendejas kick)
Hou —Hill 15 pass from Moon (Zendejas kick)
Cin —Woods 1 run (Breech kick)
Cin —Safety, Moon fumbled out of end zone

Indianapolis 16, San Diego 0—At San Diego Jack Murphy Stadium, attendance 37,722. Dean Biasucci kicked three field goals and Eric Dickerson rushed for 169 yards as the Colts blanked the Chargers. Biasucci's field goals from 20 and 44 yards gave Indianapolis a 6-0 halftime lead. The Colts extended their lead to 16-0 in the second half on Biasucci's 51-yard field goal and Gary Hogeboom's 25-yard touchdown pass to Matt Bouza. Dickerson increased his career rushing total to 9,135 yards, the eighth player in NFL history to gain over 9,000 career yards.

Indianapolis	3	3	3	7	— 16
San Diego	0	0	0	0	— 0

Ind —FG Biasucci 20
Ind —FG Biasucci 44
Ind —FG Biasucci 51
Ind —Bouza 25 pass from Hogeboom (Biasucci kick)

New Orleans 20, Los Angeles Raiders 6—At Louisiana Superdome, attendance 66,249. Craig Heyward ran for 109 yards on 11 carries as the Saints won their seventh straight game. Trailing 6-3 in the third quarter, Heyward broke loose on a 73-yard touchdown run to give New Orleans a 10-6 edge. Dalton Hilliard's seven-yard touchdown run and Morten Andersen's 51- and 25-yard field goals completed the Saints' scoring.

L.A. Raiders	0	6	0	0	— 6
New Orleans	3	0	14	3	— 20

NO —FG Andersen 51
Raiders —Fernandez 85 pass from Schroeder (kick failed)
NO —Heyward 73 run (Andersen kick)
NO —Hilliard 7 run (Andersen kick)
NO —FG Andersen 25

Minnesota 49, Tampa Bay 20—At Tampa Stadium, attendance 48,020. Wade Wilson threw for 335 yards and three touchdowns as the Vikings exploded for 49 points against the Buccaneers. Wilson led Minnesota to a 28-10 first-half lead on a pair of four-yard scoring passes to Steve Jordan, a 26-yarder to Anthony Carter, and Rick Fenney's one-yard run. D. J. Dozier (two-yard run) and Allen Rice (four) also added scoring runs. Brad Edwards returned an interception 37 yards for a touchdown to finish the Vikings' scoring. Minnesota's defense had six interceptions and held Tampa Bay to 28 yards rushing.

Minnesota	7	21	7	14	— 49
Tampa Bay	10	0	3	7	— 20

TB —FG Igwebuike 18
Minn —Jordan 4 pass from Wilson (C. Nelson kick)
TB —Hill 8 pass from Testaverde (Igwebuike kick)
Minn —Fenney 1 run (C. Nelson kick)
Minn —Carter 26 pass from Wilson (C. Nelson kick)
Minn —Jordan 4 pass from Wilson (C. Nelson kick)
TB —FG Igwebuike 32
Minn —Edwards 37 interception return (C. Nelson kick)
Minn —Rice 4 run (C. Nelson kick)
TB —Tate 1 run (Igwebuike kick)
Minn —Dozier 2 run (C. Nelson kick)

Buffalo 23, New England 20—At Rich Stadium, attendance 76,824. Scott Norwood's 33-yard field goal with 13 seconds remaining in the game gave the Bills a 23-20 win over the Patriots. Jim Kelly's 10-yard touchdown pass to Pete Metzelaars broke a 13-13 tie in the third quarter. New England's Robert Perryman ran one yard for a touchdown to re-tie the game 20-20 midway through the fourth quarter. Patriots rookie John Stephens gained 134 yards on 25 carries and scored on an 11-yard run.

New England	7	6	0	7	— 20
Buffalo	7	6	7	3	— 23

NE —Fryar 12 pass from Flutie (Garcia kick)
Buff —Riddick 1 run (Norwood kick)
Buff —FG Norwood 30
NE —Stephens 11 run (kick failed)
Buff —FG Norwood 35
Buff —Metzelaars 10 pass from Kelly (Norwood kick)
NE —Perryman 1 run (Garcia kick)
Buff —FG Norwood 33

New York Giants 23, Atlanta 16—At Atlanta-Fulton County Stadium, attendance 45,092. The Giants' defense had two interceptions that set up two touchdowns as New York rallied for a 23-16 victory over the Falcons. Greg Davis's two field goals from 32 and 37 yards and John Settle's one-yard run gave Atlanta a 13-3 lead in the third quarter. New York rallied to tie the game 16-16 on two field goals by Paul McFadden and Ottis Anderson's one-yard run with 1:57 left that was set up by Harry Carson's interception. Carl Banks returned an interception 15 yards for a touchdown 23 seconds later for the win.

N.Y. Giants	0	3	3	17	— 23
Atlanta	3	7	3	3	— 16

Atl —FG Davis 32
NYG —FG McFadden 21
Atl —Settle 1 run (Davis kick)
Atl —FG Davis 37
NYG —FG McFadden 27
Atl —FG Davis 31
NYG —FG McFadden 45
NYG —Anderson 1 run (McFadden kick)
NYG —Banks 15 interception return (McFadden kick)

New York Jets 44, Miami 30—At Joe Robbie Stadium, attendance 68,292. Ken O'Brien threw three touchdown passes to power the Jets over the Dolphins. New York scored 24 unanswered points in the second quarter on O'Brien touchdown passes to Wesley Walker (35 yards) and Al Toon (six), rookie Erik McMillan's 55-yard interception return, and Pat Leahy's 28-yard field goal. Dan Marino completed 35 of 60 passes for 521 yards, the second-highest yardage total in NFL history to the Rams' Norm Van Brocklin's 554 yards against the New York Yanks in 1951. Marino completed three touchdown passes but also threw five interceptions.

N.Y. Jets	6	24	7	7	— 44
Miami	7	3	13	7	— 30

NYJ —FG Leahy 33
Mia —Clayton 45 pass from Marino (Franklin kick)
NYJ —FG Leahy 38
Mia —FG Franklin 36
NYJ —Walker 35 pass from O'Brien (Leahy kick)
NYJ —McMillan 55 interception return (Leahy kick)
NYJ —FG Leahy 28
NYJ —Toon 6 pass from O'Brien (Leahy kick)
Mia —Clayton 11 pass from Marino (Franklin kick)
NYJ —Sohn 13 pass from O'Brien (Leahy kick)
Mia —Jensen 2 pass from Marino (kick failed)
Mia —Stradford 1 run (Franklin kick)
NYJ —Hector 1 run (Leahy kick)

Los Angeles Rams 31, Seattle 10—At Anaheim Stadium, attendance 57,033. Jim Everett completed 20 of 27 passes for 311 yards and three touchdowns to help the Rams defeat the Seahawks. Everett, who completed scoring passes of 37 yards to Robert Delpino and one yard to Damone Johnson in the second quarter, also hit Aaron Cox for a 32-yard score in the third quarter. Los Angeles's defense had four interceptions, while the offense had a 34:12 to 25:48 time-of-possession advantage. Vernon Dean returned a blocked field goal 62 yards for Seattle's only touchdown.

Seattle	0	3	0	7	— 10
L.A. Rams	10	14	7	0	— 31

Rams —Bell 1 run (Lansford kick)
Rams —FG Lansford 39
Sea —FG N. Johnson 33
Rams —Delpino 37 pass from Everett (Lansford kick)
Rams —Johnson 1 pass from Everett (Lansford kick)
Rams —Cox 32 pass from Everett (Lansford kick)
Sea —Dean 62 blocked field goal return (N. Johnson kick)

Washington 20, Green Bay 17—At Milwaukee County Stadium, attendance 51,767. Doug Williams returned to action after missing five weeks from an appendectomy and threw two touchdown passes to lead the Redskins to a 20-17 comeback win over the Packers. Williams's 21-yard scoring pass to Art Monk gave Washington a 10-0 first-quarter lead. But Green Bay rallied to score the next 17 points and take a 17-10 third-quarter lead. Williams then found Kelvin Bryant on a 13-yard touchdown pass to tie the game 17-17. Chip Lohmiller's 20-yard field goal in the fourth quarter proved to be the decisive score.

Washington	10	0	7	3	— 20
Green Bay	7	3	7	0	— 17

Wash —FG Lohmiller 33
Wash —Monk 21 pass from Williams (Lohmiller kick)
GB —Woodside 49 pass from Majkowski (Zendejas kick)
GB —FG Zendejas 34
GB —Woodside 8 pass from Majkowski (Zendejas kick)
Wash —Bryant 13 pass from Williams (Lohmiller kick)
Wash —FG Lohmiller 20

Monday, October 24

Chicago 10, San Francisco 9—At Soldier Field, attendance 65,293. Jim McMahon ran one yard for a score and the Bears' defense recorded four sacks as Chicago edged San Francisco. The 49ers jumped to a 7-0 first-quarter lead on Jerry Rice's 23-yard scoring reception from Joe Montana. McMahon's quarterback keeper and Kevin Butler's 18-yard field goal put the Bears ahead at halftime 10-7. The 49ers scored their final points of the game when Larry Roberts and Charles Haley tackled McMahon in the end zone for a safety. The game marked the fifth straight time the Bears held an opponent to less than 10 points.

San Francisco	7	0	2	0	— 9
Chicago	0	10	0	0	— 10

SF —Rice 23 pass from Montana (Cofer kick)
Chi —McMahon 1 run (Butler kick)
Chi —FG Butler 18
SF —Safety, Roberts and Haley sacked McMahon in end zone

Ninth Week Summaries

Standings

American Football Conference

Eastern Division

	W	L	T	Pct.	Pts.	OP
Buffalo	8	1	0	.889	199	139
N.Y. Jets	5	3	1	.611	206	184
Miami	5	4	0	.556	176	182
Indianapolis	4	5	0	.444	205	179
New England	4	5	0	.444	155	199

Central Division

	W	L	T	Pct.	Pts.	OP
Cincinnati	7	2	0	.778	252	178
Cleveland	6	3	0	.667	153	132
Houston	6	3	0	.667	215	213
Pittsburgh	2	7	0	.222	189	237

Western Division

	W	L	T	Pct.	Pts.	OP
Seattle	5	4	0	.556	158	174
Denver	4	5	0	.444	190	195
L.A. Raiders	4	5	0	.444	191	216
San Diego	2	7	0	.222	116	186
Kansas City	1	7	1	.167	112	149

National Football Conference

Eastern Division

	W	L	T	Pct.	Pts.	OP
N.Y. Giants	6	3	0	.667	190	178
Phoenix	5	4	0	.556	214	196
Washington	5	4	0	.556	216	212

Philadelphia	4	5	0	.444	203	187
Dallas	2	7	0	.222	148	182

Central Division

Chicago	7	2	0	.778	164	113
Minnesota	5	4	0	.556	205	162
Detroit	2	7	0	.222	112	166
Green Bay	2	7	0	.222	160	187
Tampa Bay	2	7	0	.222	165	233

Western Division

L.A. Rams	7	2	0	.778	242	150
New Orleans	7	2	0	.778	190	149
San Francisco	6	3	0	.667	199	172
Atlanta	2	7	0	.222	169	244

Sunday, October 30

Atlanta 27, Philadelphia 24—At Veterans Stadium, attendance 65,244. Chris Miller's three touchdown passes helped the Falcons down the Eagles and snap a five-game losing streak. Miller threw scoring passes to Michael Haynes (19 yards) and Floyd Dixon (17), and Mike Gann returned a fumble 36 yards for a score to give Atlanta a 20-10 fourth-quarter lead. Philadelphia came back to go ahead 24-20 on Randall Cunningham's two scoring passes to Cris Carter. Miller found Haynes on a 49-yard touchdown pass for the game-winning score.

Atlanta	0	7	13	7	— 27
Philadelphia	3	7	0	14	— 24

Phil —FG Zendejas 28
Atl —Haynes 19 pass from C. Miller (Davis kick)
Phil —Byars 1 run (Zendejas kick)
Atl —Dixon 17 pass from Miller (kick blocked)
Atl —Gann 36 fumble recovery return (Davis kick)
Phil —Carter 4 pass from Cunningham (Zendejas kick)
Phil —Carter 50 pass from Cunningham (Zendejas kick)
Atl —Haynes 49 pass from Miller (Davis kick)

New England 30, Chicago 7—At Sullivan Stadium, attendance 60,821. Doug Flutie threw four touchdown passes, including two to tight end Lin Dawson, as the Patriots became the first team in six games to score more than nine points against the Bears. Flutie completed an 80-yard scoring bomb to Irving Fryar on the first play from scrimmage and then hit Dawson with scoring strikes of 13 and four yards to give New England a 20-7 halftime lead. Flutie connected with Stanley Morgan on a 26-yard touchdown pass in the fourth quarter to complete the scoring. Patriots rookie John Stephens gained 124 yards on 35 carries and became the first player in 31 games to rush for over 100 yards against the Bears.

Chicago	7	0	0	0	— 7
New England	6	14	3	7	— 30

NE —Fryar 80 pass from Flutie (kick blocked)
Chi —McMahon 1 run (Butler kick)
NE —Dawson 13 pass from Flutie (Staurovsky kick)
NE —Dawson 4 pass from Flutie (Staurovsky kick)
NE —FG Staurovsky 35
NE —Morgan 26 pass from Flutie (Staurovsky kick)

Cleveland 23, Cincinnati 16—At Cleveland Stadium, attendance 79,147. Herman Fontenot returned a blocked punt for a touchdown and ran back a kickoff 84 yards to set up another score as the Browns won their third straight over the Bengals. Cleveland held a 13-10 lead in the third quarter when Fontenot returned a blocked punt one yard for a touchdown to increase the Browns' lead to 20-10. Cleveland's Clarence Weathers led all receivers with a career-high seven catches for 140 yards. Cleveland's number-one ranked defense did not allow a touchdown by Cincinnati's top-ranked offense.

Cincinnati	0	10	3	3	— 16
Cleveland	3	7	10	3	— 23

Clev —FG Bahr 34
Cin —Fulcher 16 interception return (Breech kick)
Clev —Manoa 2 run (Bahr kick)
Cin —FG Breech 19
Clev —FG Bahr 39
Clev —Fontenot 1 blocked punt return (Bahr kick)
Cin —FG Breech 32
Clev —FG Bahr 29
Cin —FG Breech 22

Buffalo 28, Green Bay 0—At Rich Stadium, attendance 79,176. Buffalo's defense registered six sacks and forced four turnovers as the Bills shut out the Packers. Buffalo jumped to a 14-0 halftime lead on Robb Riddick's 2-yard run and Jim Kelly's one-yard scoring pass to Butch Rolle. Leading 14-0 in the third quarter, Mark Kelso returned an interception 78 yards for a touchdown and Leon Seals recovered a fumble and ran seven yards for another touchdown to complete the Bills' scoring.

Green Bay	0	0	0	0	— 0
Buffalo	7	7	7	7	— 28

Buff —Riddick 2 run (Norwood kick)
Buff —Rolle 1 pass from Kelly (Norwood kick)
Buff —Kelso 78 interception return (Norwood kick)
Buff —Seals 7 fumble recovery return (Norwood kick)

Los Angeles Raiders 17, Kansas City 10—At Memorial Coliseum, attendance 36,103. Bo Jackson and Marcus Allen each ran for touchdowns to help the Raiders over the Chiefs. Jackson ran 22 yards on Los Angeles's initial possession of the game. Kansas City tied the game 7-7 on Paul Palmer's three-yard run, but the Raiders drove 66 yards to set up Allen's one-yard score and take a 14-7 halftime lead. It was Allen's club-record seventy-eighth career touchdown. Chris Bahr added a 42-yard field goal in the fourth quarter to complete the Raiders' scoring.

Kansas City	0	7	0	3	— 10
L.A. Raiders	7	7	0	3	— 17

Raiders —Jackson 22 run (Bahr kick)
KC —Palmer 3 run (Lowery kick)
Raiders —Allen 1 run (Bahr kick)
Raiders —FG Bahr 42
KC —FG Lowery 45

Los Angeles Rams 12, New Orleans 10—At Louisiana Superdome, attendance 68,238. Mike Lansford kicked four field goals to account for all the Rams' points as Los Angeles snapped the Saints' seven-game winning streak. The Rams took a 6-0 halftime advantage on field goals of 37 and 18 yards by Lansford. New Orleans came back to take a 7-6 lead in the third quarter on Bobby Hebert's five-yard pass to Lonzell Hill. Lansford kicked a 47-yard field goal to regain the lead for Los Angeles. The Rams drove 52 yards to set up his final kick, a 30-yarder midway through the fourth quarter. Los Angeles's defense held New Orleans to 33 yards rushing. Eric Martin gained 132 yards on six catches for the Saints.

L.A. Rams	3	3	3	3	— 12
New Orleans	0	0	7	3	— 10

Rams —FG Lansford 37
Rams —FG Lansford 18
NO —Hill 5 pass from Hebert (Andersen kick)
Rams —FG Lansford 47
Rams —FG Lansford 30
NO —FG Andersen 33

Miami 17, Tampa Bay 14—At Tampa Stadium, attendance 67,352. Dan Marino and Mark Clayton combined for two touchdowns to help the Dolphins defeat the Buccaneers. After a scoreless first half, Marino fired scoring passes of five and eight yards to Clayton following fumble recoveries by T.J. Turner and Brian Sochia. Miami took a 17-0 third-quarter lead on Tony Franklin's 31-yard field goal that had been set up by Rick Graf's fumble recovery. Thirty-eight-year-old Joe Ferguson came off the bench to throw a pair of touchdown passes in the fourth quarter for Tampa Bay.

Miami	0	0	17	0	— 17
Tampa Bay	0	0	0	14	— 14

Mia —Clayton 5 pass from Marino (Franklin kick)
Mia —Clayton 8 pass from Marino (Franklin kick)
Mia —FG Franklin 31
TB —Tate 5 pass from Ferguson (Igwebuike kick)
TB —Hill 27 pass from Ferguson (Igwebuike kick)

San Francisco 24, Minnesota 21—At Candlestick Park, attendance 60,738. Steve Young's spectacular 49-yard touchdown run with 1:58 remaining gave the 49ers a 24-21 comeback win over the Vikings. Roger Craig's one-yard scoring run capped a 97-yard drive and gave San Francisco a 10-7 third-quarter lead. San Francisco took a 17-14 lead on Young's 73-yard touchdown bomb to John Taylor, but Minnesota countered with Rick Fenney's 12-yard scoring run to regain the lead 21-17.

Minnesota	0	7	7	7	— 21
San Francisco	0	3	14	7	— 24

Minn —W. Wilson 2 run (C. Nelson kick)
SF —FG Cofer 30
SF —Craig 1 run (Cofer kick)
Minn —Carter 67 pass from W. Wilson (C. Nelson kick)
SF —Taylor 73 pass from Young (Cofer kick)
Minn —Fenney 12 run (C. Nelson kick)
SF —Young 49 run (Cofer kick)

New York Giants 13, Detroit Lions 10—At Pontiac Silverdome, attendance 38,354. Paul McFadden's 33-yard field goal 1:13 into overtime helped the Giants beat the Lions. The Giants led 10-7 in the fourth quarter on McFadden's 42-yard field goal and Joe Morris's one-yard run. Eddie Murray's 37-yard field goal with 5:19 left in the quarter sent the game into overtime. Lawrence Taylor's fumble recovery on the Lions' 22-yard line set up McFadden's game-winning kick.

N.Y. Giants	0	3	7	0	3	— 13
Detroit	0	7	0	3	0	— 10

Det —Chadwick 15 pass from Hilger (Murray kick)
NYG —FG McFadden 42
NYG —Morris 1 run (McFadden kick)
Det —FG Murray 37
NYG —FG McFadden 33

Phoenix 16, Dallas 10—At Texas Stadium, attendance 42,196. Earl Ferrell's one-yard touchdown run with 50 seconds left in the game helped the Cardinals past the Cowboys. Trailing 10-0 in the fourth quarter, Phoenix's Al Del Greco kicked a 32-yard field goal and Ferrell caught a 14-yard touchdown pass from Neil Lomax to tie the game. Lomax completed a 42-yard pass to Ernie Jones to help set up Ferrell's winning run.

Phoenix	0	0	3	13	— 16
Dallas	0	0	10	0	— 10

Dall —FG Ruzek 39
Dall —Alexander 50 pass from Pelluer (Ruzek kick)
Phx —FG Del Greco 32
Phx —Ferrell 14 pass from Lomax (Del Greco kick)
Phx —Ferrell 1 run (kick failed)

New York Jets 24, Pittsburgh 20—At Giants Stadium, attendance 64,862. John Booty's fourth-quarter blocked punt set up Freeman McNeil's five-yard touchdown run to highlight the Jets' first-ever victory over the Steelers. Pittsburgh led 10-0 in the second quarter, but Pat Leahy's 41-yard field goal and Ken O'Brien's two-yard scoring pass to Mickey Shuler tied the game at halftime. Johnny Hector added a two-yard touchdown run for the Jets in the third quarter. New York's defense recorded six sacks and had two interceptions in defeating the Steelers for the first time in 10 tries.

Pittsburgh	10	0	0	10	— 20
N.Y. Jets	0	10	7	7	— 24

Pitt —FG Anderson 25
Pitt —Carter 24 pass from Brister (Anderson kick)
NYJ —FG Leahy 41
NYJ —Shuler 2 pass from O'Brien (Leahy kick)
NYJ —Hector 2 run (Leahy kick)
Pitt —FG Anderson 21
NYJ —McNeil 5 run (Leahy kick)
Pitt —Jackson 17 run (Anderson kick)

Seattle 17, San Diego 14—At Kingdome, attendance 59,641. Kelly Stouffer completed a six-yard touchdown pass to John L. Williams with 3:43 remaining as the Seahawks downed the Chargers. Seattle held a 10-0 lead at halftime on Norm Johnson's 26-yard field goal and Stouffer's 23-yard pass to Brian Blades. San Diego narrowed the score to 10-7 on Mark Malone's 11-yard touchdown pass to Anthony Miller. Stouffer's scoring pass to Williams sealed the win.

San Diego	0	0	0	14	— 14
Seattle	3	7	0	7	— 17

Sea —FG N. Johnson 26
Sea —Blades 23 pass from Stouffer (N. Johnson kick)
SD —A. Miller 11 pass from Malone (Abbott kick)
Sea —Williams 6 pass from Stouffer (N. Johnson kick)
SD —A. Miller 10 pass from Malone (Abbott kick)

Houston 41, Washington 17—At Astrodome, attendance 48,781. Warren Moon threw three touchdown passes to Drew Hill to highlight the Oilers' 41-17 victory over the Redskins. Moon hit Hill on scoring passes of 22 and 33 yards and also ran three yards for a touchdown to give Houston a 24-3 halftime advantage. Hill, who also scored on an 11-yard reception in the third quarter, recorded nine catches for 148 yards and was named AFC offensive player of the week. Houston's defense forced five turnovers, had three sacks, and held Washington to 29 yards rushing.

Washington	0	3	7	7	— 17
Houston	7	17	7	10	— 41

Hou —Hill 22 pass from Moon (Zendejas kick)
Wash —FG Lohmiller 46
Hou —Hill 33 pass from Moon (Zendejas kick)
Hou —Moon 3 run (Zendejas kick)
Hou —FG Zendejas 41
Wash —Smith 1 run (Lohmiller kick)
Hou —Hill 11 pass from Moon (Zendejas kick)
Hou —FG Zendejas 39
Hou —Pinkett 16 run (Zendejas kick)
Wash —Griffin 4 pass from Rypien (Lohmiller kick)

Monday, October 31

Indianapolis 55, Denver 23—At Hoosier Dome, attendance 60,544. Eric Dickerson ran for 159 yards and a club-record four touchdowns as the Colts crushed the Broncos on Halloween night. Dickerson's touchdown runs of 12, 11, and 1 yard helped Indianapolis to a 21-0 first-quarter lead. Dickerson's 41-yard run in the second quarter, plus scoring catches by Bill Brooks (53 yards) and Clarence Verdin (40) gave the Colts an insurmountable 45-10 halftime margin. Dean Biasucci kicked a 27-yard field goal and Albert Bentley ran four yards for a score in the fourth quarter to finish the onslaught. Indianapolis's defense registered three sacks and forced four turnovers. Dickerson passed the 1,000-yard rushing mark for an NFL-record-tying sixth consecutive season.

Denver	0	10	0	13	— 23
Indianapolis	21	24	3	7	— 55

Ind —Dickerson 12 run (Biasucci kick)
Ind —Dickerson 11 run (Biasucci kick)
Ind —Dickerson 1 run (Biasucci kick)
Ind —FG Biasucci 31
Ind —Dickerson 41 run (Biasucci kick)
Den —Sewell 2 pass from Elway (Karlis kick)
Ind —Brooks 53 pass from Hogeboom (Biasucci kick)
Den —FG Karlis 27
Ind —Verdin 40 pass from Chandler (Biasucci kick)
Ind —FG Biasucci 27
Ind —Bentley 4 run (Biasucci kick)
Den —V. Johnson 7 pass from Kubiak (kick failed)
Den —Sewell 48 pass from Kubiak (Karlis kick)

Tenth Week Summaries

Standings

American Football Conference

Eastern Division

	W	L	T	Pct.	Pts.	OP
Buffalo	9	1	0	.900	212	142
N.Y. Jets	5	4	1	.550	220	222

	W	L	T	Pct.	Pts.	OP
Indianapolis	5	5	0	.500	243	193
Miami	5	5	0	.500	186	203
New England	5	5	0	.500	176	209
Central Division						
Cincinnati	8	2	0	.800	294	185
Houston	7	3	0	.700	239	230
Cleveland	6	4	0	.600	170	156
Pittsburgh	2	8	0	.200	196	279
Western Division						
Denver	5	5	0	.500	207	206
L.A. Raiders	5	5	0	.500	204	219
Seattle	5	5	0	.500	161	187
San Diego	2	8	0	.200	119	199
Kansas City	1	8	1	.150	123	166

National Football Conference

Eastern Division

	W	L	T	Pct.	Pts.	OP
N.Y. Giants	7	3	0	.700	219	199
Phoenix	6	4	0	.600	238	219
Washington	6	4	0	.600	243	236
Philadelphia	5	5	0	.500	233	211
Dallas	2	8	0	.200	169	211
Central Division						
Chicago	8	2	0	.800	192	123
Minnesota	6	4	0	.600	249	179
Detroit	2	8	0	.200	129	210
Green Bay	2	8	0	.200	160	207
Tampa Bay	2	8	0	.200	175	261
Western Division						
L.A. Rams	7	3	0	.700	266	180
New Orleans	7	3	0	.700	214	176
San Francisco	6	4	0	.600	222	196
Atlanta	3	7	0	.300	189	244

Sunday, November 6

Buffalo 13, Seattle 3—At Kingdome, attendance 61,074. Robb Riddick scored the game's only touchdown and Scott Norwood kicked two field goals as the Bills defeated the Seahawks 13-3 to win their fifth straight game. With the game tied 3-3, Riddick ran one yard for a touchdown 1:57 before halftime. Buffalo put the game away in the fourth quarter when Ray Bentley recovered a fumble to set up Norwood's 23-yard field goal. The Bills' defense allowed only 145 total yards, while Buffalo's offense gained 336.

Buffalo	3	7	0	3	—	13
Seattle	0	3	0	0	—	3

Buff —FG Norwood 27
Sea —FG N. Johnson 41
Buff —Riddick 1 run (Norwood kick)
Buff —FG Norwood 23

New York Giants 29, Dallas 21—At Giants Stadium, attendance 75,826. Phil Simms completed two second-quarter touchdown passes to Stephen Baker to power the Giants over the Cowboys. New York took a 26-0 halftime lead on Paul McFadden's field goals from 37 and 50 yards, Ottis Anderson's one-yard touchdown run, and Simms's scoring passes of 22 and six yards to Baker. Dallas narrowed the lead to 26-21 in the second half when Kevin Sweeney relieved Steve Pelluer at quarterback and threw three touchdowns.

Dallas	0	0	7	14	—	21
N.Y. Giants	10	16	0	3	—	29

NYG —FG McFadden 37
NYG —Anderson 1 run (McFadden kick)
NYG —FG McFadden 50
NYG —Baker 22 pass from Simms (McFadden kick)
NYG —Baker 6 pass from Simms (kick failed)
Dall —Folsom 1 pass from Sweeney (Ruzek kick)
Dall —Irvin 9 pass from Sweeney (Ruzek kick)
NYG —FG McFadden 47
Dall —Alexander 2 pass from Sweeney (Ruzek kick)

Minnesota 44, Detroit 17—At Metrodome, attendance 55,573. Anthony Carter caught eight passes for 188 yards and Wade Wilson threw for a career-high 391 yards and two touchdowns as the Vikings dominated the Lions. Minnesota extended a 13-10 halftime lead when Wilson threw scoring passes to Steve Jordan (16 yards) and Jim Gustafson (10), and Rick Fenney and Allen Rice scored on runs of 20 and three yards, respectively. The Vikings outgained the Lions in total yards 553 to 89.

Detroit	0	10	7	0	—	17
Minnesota	7	6	10	21	—	44

Minn —Rice 3 run (C. Nelson kick)
Minn —Anderson 1 run (kick failed)
Det —FG Murray 48
Det —Jamison 52 interception return (Murray kick)
Minn —Jordan 16 pass from Wilson (C. Nelson kick)
Det —Mandley 8 pass from Hilger (Murray kick)
Minn —FG C. Nelson 18
Minn —Fenney 20 run (C. Nelson kick)
Minn —Gustafson 10 pass from Wilson (C. Nelson kick)
Minn —Rice 3 run (C. Nelson kick)

Atlanta 20, Green Bay 0—At Atlanta-Fulton County Stadium, attendance 29,952. Chris Miller threw a touchdown pass and Greg Davis kicked two field goals as the Falcons shut out the Packers to snap an eight-game home losing streak. Miller opened the scoring in the first quarter with a 45-yard touchdown pass to Gene Lang. Atlanta capitalized on seven Green Bay turnovers, including Robert Moore's five-yard interception return in the second period which led to John Settle's one-yard run. Davis's 52-yard field goal matched the club record and gave the Falcons a 17-0 halftime advantage. It was the Falcons' first shutout win since December 12, 1982, when they blanked the Saints 35-0.

Green Bay	0	0	0	0	—	0
Atlanta	7	10	0	3	—	20

Atl —Lang 45 pass from C. Miller (Davis kick)
Atl —Settle 1 run (Davis kick)
Atl —FG Davis 52
Atl —FG Davis 43

Denver 17, Kansas City 11—At Mile High Stadium, attendance 74,227. John Elway completed one touchdown pass and Sammy Winder ran for another to help the Broncos defeat the Chiefs and end a two-game losing streak. Denver jumped to a 14-5 halftime lead on Elway's six-yard pass to Vance Johnson and Winder's one-yard run. Rich Karlis's 42-yard field goal early in the fourth quarter secured the win. An interception by Mike Harden and a fumble recovery by Rick Dennison ended Kansas City scoring threats inside Denver's 10-yard line.

Kansas City	2	3	3	3	—	11
Denver	0	14	0	3	—	17

KC —Safety, Hackett tackled Dorsett in end zone
Den —Johnson 6 pass from Elway (Karlis kick)
Den —Winder 1 run (Karlis kick)
KC —FG Lowery 46
KC —FG Lowery 29
Den —FG Karlis 42
KC —FG Lowery 34

Philadelphia 30, Los Angeles Rams 24—At Veterans Stadium, attendance 66,469. Randall Cunningham threw three touchdown passes, including two to rookie tight end Keith Jackson, as the Eagles outlasted the Rams. Cunningham, who completed 22 of 39 for 323 yards, threw scoring passes of 22 and two yards to Jackson and 37 yards to Keith Byars to put the Eagles ahead 27-10 early in the fourth quarter. The Rams narrowed the margin to 30-24, but William Frizzell's interception at the Eagles' 7-yard line with 24 seconds remaining assured Philadelphia's victory.

L.A. Rams	3	7	0	14	—	24
Philadelphia	0	10	10	10	—	30

Rams —FG Lansford 22
Phil —FG Zendejas 23
Phil —Keith Jackson 22 pass from Cunningham (Zendejas kick)
Rams —Ellard 25 pass from Everett (Lansford kick)
Phil —Byars 37 pass from Cunningham (Zendejas kick)
Phil —FG Zendejas 50
Phil —Keith Jackson 2 pass from Cunningham (Zendejas kick)
Rams —Bell 1 run (Lansford kick)
Rams —McGee 14 pass from Everett (Lansford kick)
Phil —FG Zendejas 40

New England 21, Miami 10—At Sullivan Stadium, attendance 60,840. John Stephens ran for 104 yards and one touchdown to lead the Patriots past the Dolphins. New England took a 14-3 halftime lead on Robert Perryman's one-yard run and Doug Flutie's one-yard pass to Irving Fryar. Stephens, who recorded his third consecutive 100-yard rushing game, scored on a 13-yard run in the third quarter that gave the Patriots a commanding 21-3 advantage.

Miami	0	3	7	0	—	10
New England	0	14	7	0	—	21

NE —Perryman 1 run (Staurovsky kick)
Mia —FG Franklin 51
NE —Fryar 1 pass from Flutie (Staurovsky kick)
NE —Stephens 13 run (Staurovsky kick)
Mia —Edmunds 20 pass from Marino (Franklin kick)

Washington 27, New Orleans 24—At Robert F. Kennedy Stadium, attendance 54,183. Chip Lohmiller's 23-yard field goal with 47 seconds remaining lifted the Redskins over the Saints. Washington trailed New Orleans 24-17 in the fourth quarter, but Doug Williams capped a 94-yard drive with an eight-yard scoring pass to Ricky Sanders to tie the game. Williams then drove the Redskins 64 yards to set up Lohmiller's winning kick. New Orleans's Eric Martin caught 10 passes for 146 yards and a touchdown.

New Orleans	7	7	10	0	—	24
Washington	0	14	3	10	—	27

NO —Martin 2 pass from Hebert (Andersen kick)
Wash —G. Clark 1 pass from Williams (Lohmiller kick)
NO —R. Clark 18 pass from Hebert (Andersen kick)
Wash —Williams 1 run (Lohmiller kick)
Wash —FG Lohmiller 32
NO —Jordan 7 fumble recovery return (Andersen kick)
NO —FG Andersen 19
Wash —Sanders 8 pass from Williams (Lohmiller kick)
Wash —FG Lohmiller 23

Indianapolis 38, New York Jets 14—At Hoosier Dome, attendance 59,233. Chris Chandler completed one touchdown pass and ran for another as the Colts dominated the Jets. Johnny Hector ran for a pair of one-yard scores to give New York a 14-10 halftime edge. But Indianapolis exploded for 21 third-quarter points to take a 31-14 lead on Chandler's 44-yard pass to Clarence Verdin and scoring runs by Chandler (29 yards) and Eric Dickerson (two). The Colts' defense had three sacks and linebacker Duane Bickett had two interceptions as Indianapolis registered its fourth straight win for the first time in 11 seasons. Al Toon caught 13 passes for 106 yards for the Jets.

N.Y. Jets	0	14	0	0	—	14
Indianapolis	7	3	21	7	—	38

Ind —Hogeboom 2 run (Biasucci kick)
NYJ —Hector 1 run (Leahy kick)
NYJ —Hector 1 run (Leahy kick)
Ind —FG Biasucci 51
Ind —Verdin 44 pass from Chandler (Biasucci kick)
Ind —Chandler 29 run (Biasucci kick)
Ind —Dickerson 2 run (Biasucci kick)
Ind —Wonsley 3 run (Biasucci kick)

Cincinnati 42, Pittsburgh 7—At Riverfront Stadium, attendance 56,403. Boomer Esiason threw for 318 yards and three touchdowns as the Bengals crushed the Steelers. Cincinnati led 21-7 at halftime on Esiason's scoring passes of 86 yards to Eddie Brown and five yards to Tim McGee, and James Brooks's three-yard touchdown run. The Bengals continued to dominate in the second half as Brooks ran for two scores (two and nine yards). Brown, who also had a six-yard scoring reception in the third quarter and caught seven passes for a club-record 216 yards, was named AFC offensive player of the week. Rookie Ickey Woods gained 110 yards on 10 carries.

Pittsburgh	7	0	0	0	—	7
Cincinnati	14	7	14	7	—	42

Cin —Brown 86 pass from Esiason (Breech kick)
Pitt —Brister 9 run (Anderson kick)
Cin —McGee 5 pass from Esiason (Breech kick)
Cin —Brooks 3 run (Breech kick)
Cin —Brooks 2 run (Breech kick)
Cin —Brown 6 pass from Esiason (Breech kick)
Cin —Brooks 9 run (Breech kick)

Phoenix 24, San Francisco 23—At Sun Devil Stadium, attendance 64,544. Neil Lomax's nine-yard touchdown pass to Roy Green with three seconds remaining gave the Cardinals a 24-23 come-from-behind victory over the 49ers. San Francisco held a commanding 23-0 lead in the third quarter. Phoenix narrowed the score to 23-17 in the fourth quarter on Lomax scoring passes to Green (35 yards) and Ernie Jones (five), and Al Del Greco's 24-yard field goal. Lomax, who completed 25 of 41 passes for 323 yards, then directed a 66-yard drive to set up the nine-yard game-winning pass to Green. Roger Craig gained 162 yards rushing on 26 carries for the 49ers.

San Francisco	3	13	7	0	—	23
Phoenix	0	0	7	17	—	24

SF —FG Cofer 42
SF —Craig 3 run (Cofer kick)
SF —FG Cofer 27
SF —FG Cofer 30
SF —B. Jones 3 pass from Young (Cofer kick)
Phx —Green 35 pass from Lomax (Del Greco kick)
Phx —FG Del Greco 24
Phx —E. Jones 5 pass from Lomax (Del Greco kick)
Phx —Green 9 pass from Lomax (Del Greco kick)

Chicago 28, Tampa Bay 10—At Soldier Field, attendance 56,892. Mike Tomczak threw for 269 yards and two touchdowns to power the Bears over the Buccaneers. Thomas Sanders and Neal Anderson each scored on one-yard runs in the first half to give Chicago a 14-3 halftime lead. The Bears increased their lead to 28-3 when Tomczak completed touchdown passes to Dennis McKinnon (20 yards) and Emery Moorehead (two).

Tampa Bay	0	3	7	0	—	10
Chicago	0	14	14	0	—	28

TB —FG Igwebuike 45
Chi —Sanders 1 run (Butler kick)
Chi —Anderson 1 run (Butler kick)
Chi —McKinnon 20 pass from Tomczak (Butler kick)
Chi —Moorehead 2 pass from Tomczak (Butler kick)
TB —Hill 21 pass from Testaverde (Igwebuike kick)

Los Angeles Raiders 13, San Diego 3—At San Diego Jack Murphy Stadium, attendance 54,134. Steve Beuerlein's seven-yard touchdown pass to Trey Junkin were all the points the Raiders needed to hand the Chargers their sixth straight loss. Los Angeles snapped a 3-3 tie early in the fourth quarter when Beuerlein hit Junkin for the go-ahead score. Chris Bahr added field goals of 36 and 29 yards to complete Los Angeles's scoring. The Raiders outgained the Chargers in yards rushing 149 to 63.

L.A. Raiders	0	3	0	10	—	13
San Diego	3	0	0	0	—	3

SD —FG Abbott 40
Raiders —FG Bahr 36
Raiders —Junkin 7 pass from Beuerlein (Bahr kick)
Raiders —FG Bahr 29

Monday, November 7

Houston 24, Cleveland 17—At Astrodome, attendance 51,467. Alonzo Highsmith and Mike Rozier each ran for touchdowns to help the Oilers defeat the Browns. Highsmith's one-yard score gave Houston a 7-3 edge at halftime. Warren Moon completed an eight-yard touchdown pass to Ernest Givins and Rozier added a three-yard scoring run to increase the Oilers' advantage to 21-3 in the third period. Houston's defense held the Browns to 44 yards rushing, while the offense held a 35:58 to 24:02 time-of-possession advantage.

Cleveland	3	0	7	7	— 17
Houston	0	7	14	3	— 24

Clev — FG Bahr 40
Hou — Highsmith 1 run (Zendejas kick)
Hou — Givins 8 pass from Moon (Zendejas kick)
Hou — Rozier 3 run (Zendejas kick)
Clev — Langhorne 20 run (Bahr kick)
Clev — Newsome 4 pass from Kosar (Bahr kick)
Hou — FG Zendejas 47

Eleventh Week Summaries

Standings

American Football Conference

Eastern Division

	W	L	T	Pct.	Pts.	OP
Buffalo	10	1	0	.909	243	148
Indianapolis	6	5	0	.545	263	206
New England	6	5	0	.545	190	222
N.Y. Jets	5	5	1	.500	233	236
Miami	5	6	0	.455	192	234

Central Division

	W	L	T	Pct.	Pts.	OP
Cincinnati	8	3	0	.727	322	216
Houston	7	4	0	.636	263	257
Cleveland	6	5	0	.545	177	186
Pittsburgh	2	9	0	.182	222	206

Western Division

	W	L	T	Pct.	Pts.	OP
Denver	6	5	0	.545	237	213
L.A. Raiders	6	5	0	.545	213	222
Seattle	6	5	0	.545	188	211
San Diego	3	8	0	.273	129	206
Kansas City	2	8	1	.227	154	194

National Football Conference

Eastern Division

	W	L	T	Pct.	Pts.	OP
N.Y. Giants	7	4	0	.636	236	223
Phoenix	7	4	0	.636	262	236
Philadelphia	6	5	0	.545	260	237
Washington	6	5	0	.545	257	270
Dallas	2	9	0	.182	172	254

Central Division

	W	L	T	Pct.	Pts.	OP
Chicago	9	2	0	.818	226	137
Minnesota	7	4	0	.636	292	182
Tampa Bay	3	8	0	.273	198	281
Detroit	2	9	0	.182	149	233
Green Bay	2	9	0	.182	173	227

Western Division

	W	L	T	Pct.	Pts.	OP
New Orleans	8	3	0	.727	228	186
L.A. Rams	7	4	0	.636	276	194
San Francisco	6	5	0	.545	225	205
Atlanta	3	8	0	.273	196	254

Sunday, November 13

Chicago 34, Washington 14—At Robert F. Kennedy Stadium, attendance 52,418. Mike Tomczak threw one touchdown pass and ran for another to help the Bears defeat the Redskins. Chicago shut out Washington 20-0 in the first half as Tomczak (one-yard run) and Matt Suhey (three) scored and Kevin Butler kicked field goals of 32 and 24 yards. Chicago put the game away in the second half as Tomczak hit Dennis Gentry with a 22-yard pass and Neal Anderson ran 50 yards for a touchdown. The Bears' defense had five interceptions and three sacks.

Chicago	7	13	0	14	— 34
Washington	0	0	7	7	— 14

Chi — Tomczak 1 run (Butler kick)
Chi — Suhey 3 run (Butler kick)
Chi — FG Butler 32
Chi — FG Butler 24
Wash — Sanders 4 pass from Rypien (Lohmiller kick)
Chi — Gentry 22 pass from Tomczak (Butler kick)
Wash — Clark 3 pass from Rypien (Lohmiller kick)
Chi — Anderson 50 run (Butler kick)

Kansas City 31, Cincinnati 28—At Arrowhead Stadium, attendance 34,614. Nick Lowery's fifth field goal of the game, a 39-yarder with two seconds remaining, lifted the Chiefs over the Bengals. With Kansas City trailing 28-19 in the fourth quarter, Albert Lewis blocked a punt in the end zone for a safety and Christian Okoye ran one yard for a touchdown to tie the game 28-28 with 1:11 to play. Lewis's fumble recovery on Cincinnati's 28-yard line set up Lowery's winning kick.

Cincinnati	7	7	14	0	— 28
Kansas City	6	3	10	12	— 31

KC — FG Lowery 37
Cin — Woods 4 run (Breech kick)
KC — FG Lowery 35
KC — FG Lowery 23
Cin — Wilson 5 run (Breech kick)
Cin — Esiason 5 run (Breech kick)
KC — Paige 17 pass from DeBerg (Lowery kick)
Cin — Jennings 98 kickoff return (Breech kick)
KC — FG Lowery 47
KC — Safety, Lewis blocked punt out of end zone
KC — Okoye 1 run (Lowery kick)
KC — FG Lowery 39

Denver 30, Cleveland 7—At Mile High Stadium, attendance 75,806. John Elway completed two touchdown passes as the Broncos defeated the Browns for the tenth consecutive time. Denver exploded for 30 points in the first half on Elway's scoring passes to Orson Mobley (11 yards) and Steve Sewell (five), Gerald Willhite's one-yard run, and Rich Karlis's field goals from 18, 22, and 32 yards.

Cleveland	0	0	7	0	— 7
Denver	10	20	0	0	— 30

Den — FG Karlis 18
Den — Mobley 11 pass from Elway (Karlis kick)
Den — FG Karlis 22
Den — Willhite 1 run (Karlis kick)
Den — FG Karlis 32
Den — Sewell 5 pass from Elway (Karlis kick)
Clev — Byner 2 run (Bahr kick)

Seattle 27, Houston 24—At Kingdome, attendance 60,446. Norm Johnson kicked a 46-yard field goal with one second remaining to complete the Seahawks' comeback win over the Oilers. Seattle and Houston were deadlocked 17-17 entering the fourth quarter, when Warren Moon scored on an 11-yard keeper to give the Oilers a 24-17 lead. The Seahawks rallied to tie the game on John L. Williams's 44-yard run. Dave Krieg, playing in his first game in seven weeks because of injuries, drove Seattle 53 yards in 10 plays to set up Johnson's game-winning field goal. Williams gained 102 yards on 13 carries. Oilers wide receiver Drew Hill caught eight passes for 139 yards and a touchdown.

Houston	7	3	7	7	— 24
Seattle	7	3	7	10	— 27

Hou — Hill 57 pass from Moon (Zendejas kick)
Sea — Blades 23 pass from Krieg (N. Johnson kick)
Hou — FG Zendejas 52
Sea — FG N. Johnson 40
Hou — Pinkett 2 run (Zendejas kick)
Sea — Warner 3 run (N. Johnson kick)
Hou — Moon 11 run (Zendejas kick)
Sea — Williams 44 run (N. Johnson kick)
Sea — FG N. Johnson 46

Indianapolis 20, Green Bay 13—At Lambeau Field, attendance 53,492. Chris Chandler passed for two touchdowns and Dean Biasucci kicked two field goals as the Colts downed the Packers. Biasucci kicked field goals of 20 and 25 yards and Chandler hit Matt Bouza on a four-yard scoring pass to give Indianapolis a 13-3 halftime advantage. Chandler connected with Mark Boyer on a 24-yard pass midway through the third quarter to increase the Colts' lead to 20-3. Green Bay scored 10 points in the fourth quarter to cut the margin to 20-13, but Indianapolis's nose tackle Harvey Armstrong's pass deflection at the Colts' two-yard line on the last play of the game assured the victory.

Indianapolis	0	13	7	0	— 20
Green Bay	3	0	0	10	— 13

GB — FG Dawson 22
Ind — FG Biasucci 20
Ind — FG Biasucci 25
Ind — Bouza 4 pass from Chandler (Biasucci kick)
Ind — Boyer 24 pass from Chandler (Biasucci kick)
GB — FG Dawson 20
GB — Matthews 3 pass from Majkowski (Dawson kick)

Los Angeles Raiders 9, San Francisco 49ers 3—At Candlestick Park, attendance 54,448. Chris Bahr kicked three field goals to lead the Raiders to their third straight win. Bahr kicked 45- and 50-yard field goals in the third quarter and added a 19-yarder in the final period. The 49ers were held without a touchdown for the first time since their 49-3 loss to the New York Giants in the NFC Divisional Playoffs on January 4, 1987.

L.A. Raiders	0	0	6	3	— 9
San Francisco	0	3	0	0	— 3

SF — FG Cofer 44
Raiders — FG Bahr 45
Raiders — FG Bahr 50
Raiders — FG Bahr 19

New England 14, New York Jets 13—At Giants Stadium, attendance 48,358. John Stephens ran three yards for the clinching score midway through the final period, and the Patriots' defense forced three turnovers, en route to their first road win of the year. Larry McGrew's interception set up Doug Flutie's 19-yard scoring pass to Stanley Morgan to give New England a 7-3 lead 25 seconds into the third quarter. Stephens's touchdown run with 6:48 to play provided all the points the Patriots needed. Johnny Rembert had two fumble recoveries and a sack for New England.

New England	0	0	7	7	— 14
N.Y. Jets	0	3	3	7	— 13

NYJ — FG Leahy 47
NE — Morgan 19 pass from Flutie (Staurovsky kick)
NYJ — FG Leahy 48
NE — Stephens 3 run (Staurovsky kick)
NYJ — McNeil 6 run (Leahy kick)

New Orleans 14, Los Angeles Rams 10—At Anaheim Stadium, attendance 63,305. Dalton Hilliard and Rueben Mayes each had touchdown runs as the Saints defeated the Rams to gain sole possession of first place in the NFC Western Division. Hilliard ran four yards for a touchdown in the first quarter to cap an 87-yard drive. Mayes added a three-yard scoring run in the third quarter. Greg Bell ran one yard for a touchdown early in the fourth quarter to bring the Rams to within four points, but Gene Atkins's interception with 50 seconds remaining preserved the win.

New Orleans	0	7	7	0	— 14
L.A. Rams	0	3	0	7	— 10

NO — Hilliard 4 run (Andersen kick)
Rams — FG Lansford 23
NO — Mayes 3 run (Andersen kick)
Rams — Bell 1 run (Lansford kick)

Phoenix 24, New York Giants 17—At Sun Devil Stadium, attendance 65,324. Neil Lomax threw for 353 yards and two touchdowns as the Cardinals downed the Giants to move into a first-place tie with New York in the NFC Eastern Division. Lomax, who completed 25 of 35 passes, scored on a one-yard run and completed a seven-yard touchdown pass to Robert Awalt to help Phoenix to a 14-7 halftime lead. Lomax's 44-yard scoring pass to Roy Green capped an 85-yard drive to put the Cardinals ahead 21-7. Green caught nine passes for 176 yards and was named NFC offensive player of the week.

N.Y. Giants	0	7	0	10	— 17
Phoenix	14	0	0	10	— 24

Phx — Lomax 1 run (Del Greco kick)
Phx — Awalt 7 pass from Lomax (Del Greco kick)
NYG — Carthon 8 pass from Simms (McFadden kick)
Phx — Green 44 pass from Lomax (Del Greco kick)
NYG — Anderson 1 run (McFadden kick)
Phx — FG Del Greco 28
NYG — FG McFadden 40

Philadelphia 27, Pittsburgh 26—At Three Rivers Stadium, attendance 46,026. Luis Zendejas's 18-yard field goal with 1:15 left in the game gave the Eagles a 27-26 comeback win over the Steelers. Scoring runs by Keith Byars (one yard) and Randall Cunningham (seven) in the second quarter cut Pittsburgh's lead to 16-14. Zendejas's 34-yard field goal and Cunningham's 12-yard touchdown run put the Eagles ahead 24-23 early in the fourth quarter. Gary Anderson's 41-yard field goal with 3:06 left in the game helped the Steelers regain the lead 26-24. Cunningham's 41-yard completion to Cris Carter set up Zendejas's winning kick.

Philadelphia	0	14	3	10	— 27
Pittsburgh	10	6	7	3	— 26

Pitt — FG Anderson 52
Pitt — Hoge 13 pass from Lipps (Anderson kick)
Phil — Byars 1 run (Zendejas kick)
Pitt — FG Anderson 21
Phil — Cunningham 7 run (Zendejas kick)
Pitt — FG Anderson 29
Phil — FG Zendejas 34
Pitt — Lipps 89 pass from Brister (Anderson kick)
Phil — Cunningham 12 run (Zendejas kick)
Pitt — FG Anderson 41
Phil — FG Zendejas 18

San Diego 10, Atlanta 7—At Atlanta-Fulton County Stadium, attendance 26,326. Gary Anderson rushed for 145 yards on 24 carries to lead the Chargers over the Falcons, snapping San Diego's six-game losing streak. Vince Abbott's 23-yard field goal was all the scoring in the first half and gave San Diego a 3-0 lead. Barry Redden's game-winning five-yard scoring run with 4:32 to play was set up by Rod Bernstine's 57-yard reception. San Diego's defense held Atlanta to 57 yards rushing.

San Diego	0	3	0	7	— 10
Atlanta	0	0	0	7	— 7

SD — FG Abbott 23
SD — Redden 5 run (Abbott kick)
Atl — Haynes 22 pass from Miller (Davis kick)

Tampa Bay 23, Detroit 20—At Pontiac Silverdome, attendance 25,956. Donald Igwebuike kicked a 52-yard field goal with 10 seconds remaining in the game as the Buccaneers downed the Lions 23-20. Tampa Bay held a 20-13 lead with 2:10 to play on scoring runs by William Howard (29 yards) and Lars Tate (five), and Igwebuike field goals of 22 and 23 yards. Detroit tied the game 20-20 with 45 seconds remaining on Rusty Hilger's 19-yard pass to Garry James.

Tampa Bay	7	3	0	13	— 23
Detroit	10	0	0	10	— 20

Det — FG Murray 39
Det — James 1 run (Murray kick)
TB — Howard 29 run (Igwebuike kick)
TB — FG Igwebuike 23
Det — FG Murray 38
TB — Tate 5 run (Igwebuike kick)
TB — FG Igwebuike 22
Det — James 19 pass from Hilger (Murray kick)
TB — FG Igwebuike 52

Minnesota 43, Dallas 3—At Texas Stadium, attendance 57,830. Hassan Jones caught three passes for 132 yards and two touchdowns to help the Vikings easily defeat the Cowboys. Minnesota exploded for 17 first-quarter points on Wade Wilson's 26-yard pass to Jones, Henry Thomas's two-yard fumble return for a score, and Chuck Nelson's 39-yard field goal. The Vikings increased their lead by scoring 26 second-half points on Wilson's touchdown completions to Jones (64 yards) and Steve Jordan (three), D.J. Dozier's 19-yard run, Chuck Nelson's 27-yard field goal, and Al Baker's sack of Kevin Sweeney in the end zone for a safety. Roger Ruzek's second-quarter 50-yard field goal kept the Cowboys from being shut out.

Minnesota	17	0	17	9	— 43
Dallas	0	3	0	0	— 3

Minn —H. Jones 26 pass from Wilson (C. Nelson kick)
Minn —Thomas 2 fumble recovery return (C. Nelson kick)
Minn —FG C. Nelson 39
Dall —FG Ruzek 50
Minn —H. Jones 64 pass from Wilson (C. Nelson kick)
Minn —FG C. Nelson 27
Minn —Jordan 3 pass from Wilson (C. Nelson kick)
Minn —Dozier 19 run (C. Nelson kick)
Minn —Safety, Baker tackled Sweeney in end zone

Monday, November 14

Buffalo 31, Miami 6—At Joe Robbie Stadium, attendance 67,091. Robb Riddick and Ronnie Harmon each scored two touchdowns as the Bills handed the Dolphins their worst home loss since 1970. Buffalo opened up a 10-6 halftime lead on Jim Kelly's 16-yard scoring pass to Harmon and Scott Norwood's 30-yard field goal. Harmon added a six-yard run and Riddick rushed for two one-yard touchdowns in the second half to put the game away. The Bills' defense blanked the Dolphins over the last 30 minutes. Buffalo outgained Miami 416 yards to 257 and held the Dolphins to just 33 yards rushing.

Buffalo	7	3	14	7	— 31
Miami	0	6	0	0	— 6

Buff —Harmon 16 pass from Kelly (Norwood kick)
Buff —FG Norwood 30
Mia —Clayton 4 pass from Marino (kick failed)
Buff —Riddick 1 run (Norwood kick)
Buff —Harmon 6 run (Norwood kick)
Buff —Riddick 1 run (Norwood kick)

Twelfth Week Summaries

Standings

American Football Conference

Eastern Division

	W	L	T	Pct.	Pts.	OP
Buffalo	11	1	0	.917	252	154
New England	7	5	0	.583	196	225
Indianapolis	6	6	0	.500	266	218
N.Y. Jets	5	6	1	.458	239	245
Miami	5	7	0	.417	195	240
Central Division						
Cincinnati	9	3	0	.750	360	240
Houston	8	4	0	.667	301	277
Cleveland	7	5	0	.583	204	193
Pittsburgh	2	10	0	.167	229	333
Western Division						
Denver	6	6	0	.500	237	255
L.A. Raiders	6	6	0	.500	219	234
Seattle	6	6	0	.500	212	238
San Diego	4	8	0	.333	167	230
Kansas City	3	8	1	.292	181	218

National Football Conference

Eastern Division

	W	L	T	Pct.	Pts.	OP
N.Y. Giants	7	5	0	.583	253	246
Philadelphia	7	5	0	.583	283	254
Phoenix	7	5	0	.583	282	274
Washington	6	6	0	.500	278	307
Dallas	2	10	0	.167	196	292
Central Division						
Chicago	10	2	0	.833	253	152
Minnesota	8	4	0	.667	304	185
Detroit	3	9	0	.250	168	242
Tampa Bay	3	9	0	.250	213	308
Green Bay	2	10	0	.167	182	246
Western Division						
New Orleans	9	3	0	.750	270	186
L.A. Rams	7	5	0	.583	300	232
San Francisco	7	5	0	.583	262	226
Atlanta	4	8	0	.333	208	260

Sunday, November 20

Atlanta 12, Los Angeles Raiders 6—At Memorial Coliseum, attendance 40,967. John Settle's one-yard touchdown run in the fourth quarter lifted the Falcons over the Raiders. Greg Davis kicked field goals of 46 and 41 yards, but Chris Bahr answered with 42- and 31-yard field goals to tie the game 6-6 in the fourth quarter. Settle's game-winning run was set up by Aundray Bruce, who sacked Raiders quarterback Steve Beuerlein, then recovered his fumble and returned it 28 yards to the Raiders' 12-yard line. Bruce, who also had two sacks and an interception, was named NFC defensive player of the week.

Atlanta	0	3	3	6	— 12
L.A. Raiders	0	0	3	3	— 6

Atl —FG Davis 46
Atl —FG Davis 41
Raiders —FG Bahr 42
Raiders —FG Bahr 31
Atl —Settle 1 run (kick failed)

Chicago 27, Tampa Bay 15—At Tampa Stadium, attendance 67,070. Neal Anderson ran for two touchdowns and Mike Tomczak passed for another as the Bears defeated the Buccaneers for the twelfth consecutive time. Chicago took a 21-6 halftime lead on Anderson's one- and 17-yard scoring runs and Tomczak's 40-yard touchdown pass to Brad Muster. Keith Butler's field goals of 36 and 43 yards completed the Bears' scoring in the second half.

Chicago	14	7	0	6	— 27
Tampa Bay	3	3	0	9	— 15

Chi —Anderson 1 run (Butler kick)
Chi —Anderson 17 run (Butler kick)
TB —FG Igwebuike 27
Chi —Muster 40 pass from Tomczak (Butler kick)
TB —FG Igwebuike 23
TB —Safety, Goode tackled Wagner in end zone
Chi —FG Butler 36
Chi —FG Butler 43
TB —Pillow 7 pass from Ferguson (Criswell kick)

Cincinnati 38, Dallas 24—At Texas Stadium, attendance 37,865. Boomer Esiason threw three touchdown passes, including two to Rodney Holman, as the Bengals handed the Cowboys their eighth straight loss. Cincinnati jumped to a 24-3 halftime lead on Esiason touchdown passes to Holman (20 and five yards), James Brooks's 51-yard run, and Jim Breech's 41-yard field goal. Brooks, who rushed 16 times for 148 yards, also scored on a 13-yard pass from Esiason in the third quarter. Cincinnati's defense recorded six sacks. Herschel Walker gained 131 yards on 27 carries for the Cowboys.

Cincinnati	7	17	7	7	— 38
Dallas	3	0	7	14	— 24

Cin —Brooks 51 run (Breech kick)
Dall —FG Ruzek 44
Cin —Holman 20 pass from Esiason (Breech kick)
Cin —FG Breech 41
Cin —Holman 5 pass from Esiason (Breech kick)
Dall —Walker 11 run (Ruzek kick)
Cin —Brooks 13 pass from Esiason (Breech kick)
Cin —Woods 10 run (Breech kick)
Dall —Alexander 6 pass from Pelluer (Ruzek kick)
Dall —Chandler 1 pass from Pelluer (Ruzek kick)

New Orleans 42, Denver 0—At Louisiana Superdome, attendance 68,075. Bobby Hebert completed 20 of 23 passes for 193 yards and three touchdowns as the Saints shut out the Broncos. New Orleans opened a 21-0 first-half lead on Rueben Mayes's and Dalton Hilliard's two-yard runs and Eric Martin's 40-yard scoring reception from Hebert. Hebert also threw touchdown passes to John Tice (eight yards) and Martin (six). Mel Gray set a club record with a 66-yard punt return for a touchdown in the third quarter. Gray's return broke the previous record of 53 yards set by Charles Brown in 1968. The victory assured the Saints their second winning season in the club's 22-year history.

Denver	0	0	0	0	— 0
New Orleans	14	7	14	7	— 42

NO —Mayes 2 run (Andersen kick)
NO —Hilliard 2 run (Andersen kick)
NO —Martin 40 pass from Hebert (Andersen kick)
NO —Gray 66 punt return (Andersen kick)
NO —Tice 8 pass from Hebert (Andersen kick)
NO —Martin 6 pass from Hebert (Andersen kick)

Detroit 19, Green Bay 9—At Milwaukee County Stadium, attendance 44,327. Eddie Murray kicked four field goals and Scott Williams ran for a touchdown as the Lions were victorious in Detroit interim head coach Wayne Fontes's debut. Murray kicked field goals of 42, 37, and 19 yards to put Detroit ahead 9-0 at halftime. Williams's one-yard scoring run and Murray's 26-yard field goal in the fourth quarter completed the Lions' scoring.

Detroit	3	6	0	10	— 19
Green Bay	0	0	3	6	— 9

Det —FG Murray 42
Det —FG Murray 37
Det —FG Murray 19
GB —FG Dawson 32
Det —Williams 1 run (Murray kick)
Det —FG Murray 26
GB —Matthews 3 pass from Majkowski (kick failed)

Minnesota 12, Indianapolis 3—At Metrodome, attendance 58,342. Chuck Nelson kicked four field goals and the Minnesota defense held Eric Dickerson to 72 yards rushing to defeat the Colts 12-3. Nelson's field goals of 25 and 26 yards gave Minnesota a 6-0 halftime edge. He added 30- and 49-yarders in the second half to account for all the Vikings' scoring. Minnesota's victory snapped the Colts' five-game winning streak.

Indianapolis	0	0	0	3	— 3
Minnesota	0	6	3	3	— 12

Minn —FG C. Nelson 25
Minn —FG C. Nelson 26
Minn —FG C. Nelson 30
Ind —FG Biasucci 42
Minn —FG C. Nelson 49

Buffalo 9, New York Jets 6—At Rich Stadium, attendance 78,389. Scott Norwood kicked a 30-yard field goal 3:47 into overtime to help the Bills win their seventh consecutive game and clinch their first AFC East title since 1980. The only scoring in regulation time was Norwood's 25- and 26-yard field goals and Jets kicker Pat Leahy's 23- and 40-yard kicks. Derrick Burroughs's fumble recovery set up Norwood's winning kick.

N.Y. Jets	0	3	0	3	0	— 6
Buffalo	0	0	3	3	3	— 9

NYJ —FG Leahy 23
Buff —FG Norwood 25
Buff —FG Norwood 26
NYJ —FG Leahy 40
Buff —FG Norwood 30

Philadelphia 23, New York Giants 17—At Giants Stadium, attendance 43,621. Clyde Simmons returned a blocked field goal 15 yards for a touchdown in overtime as the Eagles downed the Giants. Phil Simms's scoring completions to Stacey Robinson (62 yards) and Stephen Baker (nine) put New York ahead 17-10 in the fourth quarter. But Cris Carter's fumble recovery in the end zone for a score with 4:28 to play sent the game into overtime. Luis Zendejas's 31-yard field-goal attempt was blocked by the Giants' Sheldon White and scooped up by Simmons for the winning score 6:10 into overtime.

Philadelphia	7	3	0	7	6	— 23
N.Y. Giants	7	3	7	0	0	— 17

Phil —Cunningham 1 run (Zendejas kick)
NYG —Robinson 62 pass from Simms (McFadden kick)
Phil —FG Zendejas 37
NYG —FG McFadden 21
NYG —Baker 9 pass from Simms (McFadden kick)
Phil —Carter fumble recovery in end zone (Zendejas kick)
Phil —Simmons 15 blocked field goal return (no kick attempted)

Houston 38, Phoenix 20—At Astrodome, attendance 43,843. Warren Moon completed three touchdown passes and ran for a fourth as the Oilers snapped the Cardinals' three-game winning streak. Houston took a commanding 24-7 halftime lead on scoring runs by Alonzo Highsmith (seven yards) and Moon (one), Tony Zendejas's 37-yard field goal, and Moon's 50-yard touchdown pass to Drew Hill. Ernest Givins had five receptions for 118 yards for the Oilers, while Hill caught five for 100. Linebacker Robert Lyles had two interceptions to set up 10 Houston points.

Phoenix	0	7	7	6	— 20
Houston	7	17	7	7	— 38

Hou —Highsmith 7 run (Zendejas kick)
Hou —FG Zendejas 37
Hou —Hill 50 pass from Moon (Zendejas kick)
Phx —Awalt 52 pass from Stoudt (Del Greco kick)
Hou —Moon 1 run (Zendejas kick)
Phx —J. T. Smith 4 pass from Stoudt (Del Greco kick)
Hou —Givins 30 pass from Moon (Zendejas kick)
Hou —Givins 13 pass from Moon (Zendejas kick)
Phx —Jones 14 pass from Stoudt (kick blocked)

Cleveland 27, Pittsburgh 7—At Cleveland Stadium, attendance 77,131. Bernie Kosar completed a career-long 77-yard scoring bomb to Reggie Langhorne in the third quarter to help the Browns defeat the Steelers for the sixth straight time. Cleveland took a 17-7 halftime lead on Kosar's two-yard touchdown pass to Derek Tennell, Frank Minnifield's 11-yard blocked punt return for a score, and Matt Bahr's 32-yard field goal. Cleveland's defense registered six sacks. Kosar's completion to Langhorne was the team's longest since Frank Pitts caught an 80-yarder from Mike Phipps against the New York Jets on December 17, 1972.

Pittsburgh	0	7	0	0	— 7
Cleveland	3	14	7	3	— 27

Clev —FG Bahr 32
Clev —Tennell 2 pass from Kosar (Bahr kick)
Clev —Minnifield 11 blocked punt return (Bahr kick)
Pitt —Carter 1 run (Anderson kick)
Clev —Langhorne 77 pass from Kosar (Bahr kick)
Clev —FG Bahr 34

San Diego 38, Los Angeles Rams 24—At Anaheim Stadium, attendance 45,462. Former Ram Barry Redden ran for two fourth-quarter touchdowns to give the Chargers a 38-24 win over Los Angeles. San Diego led 17-14 at the half on Anthony Miller's 93-yard kickoff return for a score, Mark Vlasic's four-yard scoring pass to Quinn Early, and Steve DeLine's 38-yard field goal. Keith Browner recovered a fumble in the third quarter and lateraled to Sam Seale, who ran 50 yards for a score to give San Diego a 24-14 advantage. Mark Malone replaced injured starter Vlasic in the third period and directed a pair of fourth-quarter scoring drives that resulted in two one-yard touchdown runs by Redden.

San Diego	14	3	7	14	— 38
L.A. Rams	7	7	0	10	— 24

SD —Early 4 pass from Vlasic (DeLine kick)
Rams —Holohan 4 pass from Everett (Lansford kick)
SD —A. Miller 93 kickoff return (DeLine kick)
SD —FG DeLine 38

Rams — Bell 12 run (Lansford kick)
SD — Seale 50 return of lateral from Browner (DeLine kick)
Rams — FG Lansford 20
SD — Redden 1 run (DeLine kick)
Rams — A. Cox 20 pass from Everett (Lansford kick)
SD — Redden 1 run (DeLine kick)

Kansas City 27, Seattle 24—At Arrowhead Stadium, attendance 33,152. Nick Lowery's 40-yard field goal with 46 seconds remaining lifted the Chiefs over the Seahawks. James Saxon and Christian Okoye each scored on two-yard runs to give Kansas City a 14-7 halftime lead. The Chiefs went ahead 24-14 on Lowery's 34-yard field goal and Steve DeBerg's one-yard bootleg. Seattle tied the game midway through the fourth quarter on Dave Krieg's 14-yard touchdown pass to Brian Blades. DeBerg led a 51-yard, 13-play drive to set up Lowery's winning kick. Stephone Paige had five receptions for 106 yards for the Chiefs.

Seattle	0	7	7	10	—	24
Kansas City	7	7	3	10	—	27

KC — Saxon 2 run (Lowery kick)
KC — Okoye 2 run (Lowery kick)
Sea — Butler 12 pass from Krieg (N. Johnson kick)
Sea — Taylor 27 interception return (N. Johnson kick)
KC — FG Lowery 34
KC — DeBerg 1 run (Lowery kick)
Sea — FG N. Johnson 32
Sea — Blades 14 pass from Krieg (N. Johnson kick)
KC — FG Lowery 40

New England 6, Miami 3—At Joe Robbie Stadium, attendance 53,526. Jason Staurovsky's two field goals provided all the scoring New England needed to help the Patriots register their seventh straight win over the Dolphins. The score was tied 3-3 at the half on field goals by Miami's Tony Franklin (27 yards) and Staurovsky (22). Staurovsky's 34-yard field goal in the third quarter proved decisive. The Patriots' John Stephens led all rushers with 20 carries for 88 yards. Johnny Rembert had nine solo tackles for New England.

New England	0	3	3	0	—	6
Miami	0	3	0	0	—	3

Mia — FG Franklin 27
NE — FG Staurovsky 22
NE — FG Staurovsky 34

Monday, November 21

San Francisco 37, Washington 21—At Candlestick Park, attendance 59,268. Joe Montana completed two touchdown passes and John Taylor returned a punt for another score as the 49ers easily defeated the Redskins. San Francisco jumped to a 23-7 halftime lead on Montana's 18-yard pass to Brent Jones, Taylor's 95-yard punt return, Tom Rathman's one-yard scoring run, and Mike Cofer's 52-yard field goal. Jerry Rice, who had three receptions for 105 yards, caught an 80-yarder from Montana in the fourth quarter. Bill Romanowski's fumble recovery in the fourth quarter set up Montana's four-yard touchdown run.

Washington	7	0	7	7	—	21
San Francisco	7	16	0	14	—	37

SF — Jones 18 pass from Montana (Cofer kick)
Wash — Sanders 15 pass from Williams (Lohmiller kick)
SF — FG Cofer 52
SF — Taylor 95 punt return (Cofer kick)
SF — Rathman 1 run (kick blocked)
Wash — Sanders 4 pass from Williams (Lohmiller kick)
SF — Montana 4 run (Cofer kick)
SF — Rice 80 pass from Montana (Cofer kick)
Wash — Monk 18 pass from Williams (Lohmiller kick)

Thirteenth Week Summaries

Standings

American Football Conference

Eastern Division	W	L	T	Pct.	Pts.	OP
Buffalo	11	2	0	.846	273	189
Indianapolis	7	6	0	.538	290	239
New England	7	6	0	.538	217	249
N.Y. Jets	6	6	1	.500	277	279
Miami	5	8	0	.385	229	278
Central Division						
Cincinnati	10	3	0	.769	395	261
Houston	9	4	0	.692	326	294
Cleveland	8	5	0	.615	221	206
Pittsburgh	3	10	0	.231	245	343
Western Division						
Denver	7	6	0	.538	272	279
Seattle	7	6	0	.538	247	265
L.A. Raiders	6	7	0	.462	246	269
San Diego	4	9	0	.308	177	278
Kansas City	3	9	1	.269	191	234

National Football Conference

Eastern Division	W	L	T	Pct.	Pts.	OP
N.Y. Giants	8	5	0	.615	266	258
Philadelphia	8	5	0	.615	314	275
Phoenix	7	6	0	.538	303	305
Washington	6	7	0	.462	291	324
Dallas	2	11	0	.154	213	317
Central Division						
Chicago	11	2	0	.846	269	152
Minnesota	9	4	0	.692	327	185
Detroit	3	10	0	.231	168	265
Tampa Bay	3	10	0	.231	223	325
Green Bay	2	11	0	.154	182	262
Western Division						
New Orleans	9	4	0	.692	282	199
San Francisco	8	5	0	.615	310	236
L.A. Rams	7	6	0	.538	324	267
Atlanta	5	8	0	.385	225	270

Thursday, November 24

Minnesota 23, Detroit 0—At Pontiac Silverdome, attendance 46,379. Alfred Anderson ran for two scores and Chuck Nelson kicked three field goals as the Vikings shut out the Lions. Minnesota opened the scoring in the second quarter as Wade Wilson led a 72-yard drive capped by Anderson's two-yard touchdown run. Anderson's one-yard scoring run and Nelson's 21- and 33-yard field goals put Minnesota ahead 20-0 at halftime. The Vikings held the Lions to 60 yards total offense and maintained a 44:57 to 15:03 time-of-possession advantage.

Minnesota	0	20	3	0	—	23
Detroit	0	0	0	0	—	0

Minn — Anderson 2 run (C. Nelson kick)
Minn — FG C. Nelson 21
Minn — Anderson 1 run (C. Nelson kick)
Minn — FG C. Nelson 33
Minn — FG C. Nelson 18

Houston 25, Dallas 17—At Texas Stadium, attendance 50,845. Tony Zendejas kicked four field goals to help the Oilers defeat the Cowboys and win the battle of Texas. With the score tied 10-10 in the third quarter, Steve Pelluer scored on a three-yard quarterback keeper to put Dallas ahead 17-10. Zendejas kicked a 49-yard field goal and Warren Moon hit Drew Hill for a five-yard scoring strike for the go-ahead scores. Zendejas added field goals from 47 and 22 yards to secure the victory.

Houston	0	10	3	12	—	25
Dallas	7	3	7	0	—	17

Dall — Walker 1 run (Ruzek kick)
Hou — FG Zendejas 28
Hou — Rozier 12 run (Zendejas kick)
Dall — FG Ruzek 29
Dall — Pelluer 3 run (Ruzek kick)
Hou — FG Zendejas 49
Hou — Hill 5 pass from Moon (kick failed)
Hou — FG Zendejas 47
Hou — FG Zendejas 22

Sunday, November 27

Cincinnati 35, Buffalo 21—At Riverfront Stadium, attendance 58,672. Ickey Woods ran for three touchdowns as the Bengals snapped the Bills' seven-game winning streak. Woods, who carried 26 times for 129 yards, scored on a two-yard run in the second quarter and added a one-yard scoring run and a second two-yarder in the second half. James Brooks ran three yards for a touchdown and caught a 13-yard scoring pass from Boomer Esiason.

Buffalo	0	7	7	7	—	21
Cincinnati	7	14	7	7	—	35

Cin — Brooks 3 run (Breech kick)
Cin — Brooks 13 pass from Esiason (Breech kick)
Cin — Woods 2 run (Breech kick)
Buff — Riddick 1 run (Norwood kick)
Cin — Woods 1 run (Breech kick)
Buff — Harmon 9 pass from Kelly (Norwood kick)
Buff — Riddick 1 run (Norwood kick)
Cin — Woods 2 run (Breech kick)

Cleveland 17, Washington 3—At Robert F. Kennedy Stadium, attendance 51,604. Ernest Byner ran 27 yards for a touchdown with 1:49 remaining to rally the Browns over the Redskins. Kevin Mack (22 carries for 116 yards) ran one yard for a touchdown to tie the game 10-10 in the fourth quarter. Chip Lohmiller's 40-yard field goal with 6:27 to play put Washington ahead 13-10. Mark Harper's interception with 41 seconds remaining sealed the Browns' victory.

Cleveland	0	3	0	14	—	17
Washington	0	0	10	3	—	13

Clev — FG Bahr 37
Wash — Clark 7 pass from Rypien (Lohmiller kick)
Wash — FG Lohmiller 21
Clev — Mack 1 run (Bahr kick)
Wash — FG Lohmiller 40
Clev — Byner 27 run (Bahr kick)

Chicago 16, Green Bay 0—At Soldier Field, attendance 62,026. Neal Anderson ran for 139 yards and scored two touchdowns as the Bears blanked the Packers to clinch a playoff berth. Anderson's second touchdown run, a career-long 80-yarder, gave Chicago a 14-0 third-quarter lead. Anderson also scored on a one-yard run in the first quarter.

Green Bay	0	0	0	0	—	0
Chicago	7	0	7	2	—	16

Chi — Anderson 1 run (Butler kick)
Chi — Anderson 80 run (Butler kick)
Chi — Safety, Majkowski stepped out of end zone

Pittsburgh 16, Kansas City 10—At Three Rivers Stadium, attendance 42,057. Gary Anderson kicked three field goals to help the Steelers over the Chiefs. Pittsburgh took a 6-0 first-quarter lead on Anderson's 23- and 20-yard field goals. Kansas City went ahead 7-6 in the second quarter on Steve DeBerg's four-yard pass to Stephone Paige. Merril Hoge's 10-yard run and Anderson's third field goal, a 22-yarder, sealed the win.

Kansas City	0	7	0	3	—	10
Pittsburgh	6	7	3	0	—	16

Pitt — FG Anderson 23
Pitt — FG Anderson 20
KC — Paige 4 pass from DeBerg (Lowery kick)
Pitt — Hoge 10 run (Anderson kick)
Pitt — FG Anderson 22
KC — FG Lowery 26

Denver 35, Los Angeles Rams 24—At Mile High Stadium, attendance 74,141. John Elway threw three touchdown passes, including two to Mark Jackson, as the Broncos outlasted the Rams. Elway completed a 39-yard pass to Jackson and scored on a one-yard run to help Denver take a 14-10 halftime lead. The Broncos took a 21-10 lead on their first play of the third quarter on Elway's 58-yard scoring pass to Jackson. Vance Johnson's 14-yard touchdown catch from Elway preceded running back Tony Dorsett's seven-yard touchdown pass to Sammy Winder in the fourth quarter. The Rams' Jim Everett completed 25 of 47 passes for 365 yards and two touchdowns.

L.A. Rams	7	3	7	7	—	24
Denver	0	14	21	0	—	35

Rams — Ellard 23 pass from Everett (Lansford kick)
Den — Jackson 39 pass from Elway (Karlis kick)
Rams — FG Lansford 23
Den — Elway 1 run (Karlis kick)
Den — Jackson 58 pass from Elway (Karlis kick)
Den — V. Johnson 14 pass from Elway (Karlis kick)
Den — Winder 7 pass from Dorsett (Karlis kick)
Rams — Ellard 54 pass from Everett (Lansford kick)
Rams — Bell 1 run (Lansford kick)

New York Jets 38, Miami 34—At Giants Stadium, attendance 52,752. Ken O'Brien completed two fourth-quarter touchdown passes to rally the Jets to a 38-34 win over the Dolphins. Miami's Dan Marino threw for 353 yards and five touchdowns, including two each to Fred Banks and Mark Clayton, to give the Dolphins a 34-24 lead entering the fourth quarter. O'Brien, who came off the bench to replace Pat Ryan (27 of 43 and 341 yards), connected on scoring passes of seven yards to Mickey Shuler and 18 yards to Wesley Walker for the victory. Clayton finished with 116 yards on seven receptions, while rookie tight end Ferrell Edmunds caught two for 117, including an 80-yard scoring pass.

Miami	7	7	20	0	—	34
N.Y. Jets	7	17	0	14	—	38

NYJ — Walker 8 pass from Ryan (Leahy kick)
Mia — Banks 10 pass from Marino (Reveiz kick)
NYJ — Shuler 14 pass from Ryan (Leahy kick)
NYJ — FG Leahy 29
Mia — Banks 37 pass from Marino (Reveiz kick)
NYJ — McNeil 3 run (Leahy kick)
Mia — Clayton 31 pass from Marino (Reveiz kick)
Mia — Clayton 25 pass from Marino (kick failed)
Mia — Edmunds 80 pass from Marino (Reveiz kick)
NYJ — Shuler 7 pass from O'Brien (Leahy kick)
NYJ — Walker 18 pass from O'Brien (Leahy kick)

Indianapolis 24, New England 21—At Hoosier Dome, attendance 58,157. Dean Biasucci's 28-yard field goal with 2:22 remaining gave the Colts a 24-21 win over the Patriots. Eric Dickerson ran for a pair of two-yard touchdowns to deadlock the score 14-14 at halftime. New England went ahead 21-14 in the fourth quarter on Mosi Tatupu's one-yard run. Indianapolis came right back on Chris Chandler's 18-yard scoring pass to Mark Boyer. Michael Ball's fumble recovery at the Patriots' 20-yard line set up Biasucci's winning kick.

New England	7	7	0	7	—	21
Indianapolis	7	7	0	10	—	24

NE — Martin 95 kickoff return (Staurovsky kick)
Ind — Dickerson 2 run (Biasucci kick)
NE — Perryman 1 run (Staurovsky kick)
Ind — Dickerson 2 run (Biasucci kick)
NE — Tatupu 1 run (Staurovsky kick)
Ind — Boyer 18 pass from Chandler (Biasucci kick)
Ind — FG Biasucci 28

Philadelphia 31, Phoenix 21—At Veterans Stadium, attendance 57,918. Ron Johnson caught two touchdown passes to lead the Eagles past the Cardinals. Philadelphia, who trailed 14-7 at halftime, retook the lead on Luis Zendejas's 28-yard field goal and Randall Cunningham's eight-yard touchdown pass to Cris Carter. The Eagles increased their lead on Matt Cavanaugh's nine-yard scoring pass to Johnson and Keith Byars's four-yard run. Johnson also had an 11-yard touchdown catch to open the scoring.

Phoenix	7	7	0	7	—	21
Philadelphia	7	0	17	7	—	31

Phil — Johnson 11 pass from Cunningham (Zendejas kick)
Phx — J. T. Smith 7 pass from Stoudt (Del Greco kick)
Phx — Ferrell 17 run (Del Greco kick)
Phil — FG Zendejas 28

Phil —Carter 8 pass from Cunningham (Zendejas kick)
Phil —Johnson 9 pass from Cavanaugh (Zendejas kick)
Phx —Ferrell 1 run (Del Greco kick)
Phx —Byars 4 run (Zendejas kick)

San Francisco 48, San Diego 10—At San Diego Jack Murphy Stadium, attendance 51,484. Joe Montana threw three touchdown passes, including a club-record 96-yarder to Jerry Rice, as the 49ers overpowered the Chargers. Rice, who caught six passes for 171 yards, also scored on a 41-yard reception in the third quarter. Roger Craig ran for two touchdowns from one and seven yards and scored a third on a two-yard pass from Montana.

San Francisco	7	17	14	10	— 48
San Diego	0	7	3	0	— 10

SF —Rice 96 pass from Montana (Cofer kick)
SF —Craig 1 run (Cofer kick)
SD —Malone 36 run (DeLine kick)
SF —Craig 2 pass from Montana (Cofer kick)
SF —FG Cofer 45
SF —Rice 41 pass from Montana (Cofer kick)
SD —FG DeLine 23
SF —Craig 7 run (Cofer kick)
SF —FG Cofer 32
SF —DuBose 37 run (Cofer kick)

Atlanta 17, Tampa Bay 10—At Atlanta-Fulton County Stadium, attendance 14,020. Chris Miller and Michael Haynes combined on a 37-yard fourth-quarter touchdown pass as the Falcons defeated the Buccaneers. Atlanta took a 10-0 halftime lead on Greg Davis's 40-yard field goal and John Settle's eight-yard run. Tampa Bay tied the game 10-10 on John Carney's 24-yard field goal and Lars Tate's two-yard run. Settle's 48-yard run helped set up Haynes's decisive score.

Tampa Bay	0	0	10	0	— 10
Atlanta	3	7	0	7	— 17

Atl —FG Davis 40
Atl —Settle 8 run (Davis kick)
TB —FG Carney 24
TB —Tate 2 run (Carney kick)
Atl —Haynes 37 pass from Miller (Davis kick)

New York Giants 13, New Orleans 12—At Louisiana Superdome, attendance 66,526. Paul McFadden's 35-yard field goal with 21 seconds remaining in the game lifted the Giants over the Saints. New York trailed 9-7 at halftime on Jeff Hostetler's 85-yard scoring bomb to Stephen Baker, but McFadden's 46-yard field goal early in the fourth quarter gave the Giants a 10-9 edge. Morten Andersen's fourth field goal of the game, a 45-yarder midway through the fourth quarter, gave New Orleans the lead. Jeff Rutledge, who replaced Jeff Hostetler in the second half, connected on a 33-yard pass to Baker to set up McFadden's game-winning kick.

N.Y. Giants	0	7	0	6	— 13
New Orleans	3	6	0	3	— 12

NO —FG Andersen 27
NO —FG Andersen 41
NYG —Baker 85 pass from Hostetler (McFadden kick)
NO —FG Andersen 26
NYG —FG McFadden 46
NO —FG Andersen 45
NYG —FG McFadden 35

Monday, November 28

Seattle 35, Los Angeles Raiders 27—At Kingdome, attendance 62,641. Dave Krieg completed 16 of 28 passes for 220 yards and five touchdowns as the Seahawks rallied to defeat the Raiders 35-27. Seattle led 21-20 at halftime on Krieg's scoring passes to Steve Largent (15 yards), Brian Blades (6), and Paul Skansi (11). Los Angeles went ahead 27-21 in the third quarter on Steve Smith's 4-yard run, but Krieg's fourth-quarter passes of seven yards to Curt Warner and 20 yards to Louis Clark put the game away. Warner led all rushers with 130 yards on 27 carries. John L. Williams added 105 yards on 17 rushes. Raiders rookie Tim Brown had 306 combined yards, including 114 on four receptions.

L.A. Raiders	14	6	7	0	— 27
Seattle	7	14	0	14	— 35

Sea —Largent 15 pass from Krieg (N. Johnson kick)
Raiders —Townsend fumble recovery in end zone (Bahr kick)
Raiders —T. Brown 49 pass from Beuerlein (Bahr kick)
Sea —Blades 6 pass from Krieg (N. Johnson kick)
Raiders —FG Bahr 46
Raiders —FG Bahr 46
Sea —Skansi 11 pass from Krieg (N. Johnson kick)
Raiders —S. Smith 4 run (Bahr kick)
Sea —Warner 7 pass from Krieg (N. Johnson kick)
Sea —Clark 20 pass from Krieg (N. Johnson kick)

Fourteenth Week Summaries

Standings

American Football Conference

Eastern Division

	W	L	T	Pct.	Pts.	OP
Buffalo	11	3	0	.786	278	199
Indianapolis	8	6	0	.571	321	267
New England	8	6	0	.571	230	256
N.Y. Jets	6	7	1	.464	311	317
Miami	5	9	0	.357	257	309

Central Division

	W	L	T	Pct.	Pts.	OP
Cincinnati	11	3	0	.786	422	271
Cleveland	9	5	0	.643	245	227
Houston	9	5	0	.643	360	331
Pittsburgh	4	10	0	.286	282	377

Western Division

	W	L	T	Pct.	Pts.	OP
Denver	7	7	0	.500	292	300
L.A. Raiders	7	7	0	.500	267	289
Seattle	7	7	0	.500	254	278
Kansas City	4	9	1	.321	229	268
San Diego	4	10	0	.286	187	305

National Football Conference

Eastern Division

	W	L	T	Pct.	Pts.	OP
N.Y. Giants	9	5	0	.643	310	265
Philadelphia	8	6	0	.571	333	295
Phoenix	7	7	0	.500	310	349
Washington	7	7	0	.500	311	343
Dallas	2	12	0	.143	234	341

Central Division

	W	L	T	Pct.	Pts.	OP
Chicago	11	3	0	.786	272	175
Minnesota	10	4	0	.714	372	188
Detroit	4	10	0	.286	198	279
Tampa Bay	4	10	0	.286	233	330
Green Bay	2	12	0	.143	196	292

Western Division

	W	L	T	Pct.	Pts.	OP
New Orleans	9	5	0	.643	285	244
San Francisco	9	5	0	.643	323	239
L.A. Rams	8	6	0	.571	347	270
Atlanta	5	9	0	.357	228	283

Sunday, December 4

Tampa Bay 10, Buffalo 5—At Tampa Stadium, attendance 49,498. Vinny Testaverde's four-yard touchdown run led the Buccaneers past the AFC Eastern Division champion Bills. Tampa Bay jumped to a 10-0 halftime lead on Testaverde's scoring run and John Carney's 29-yard field goal. Safety Mark Robinson's interception on the Buccaneers' 25-yard line in the final minutes of the game halted the Bills' final scoring threat. Tampa Bay held Buffalo to 39 yards rushing and had a 34:58 to 25:02 time-of-possession advantage.

Buffalo	0	0	2	3	— 5
Tampa Bay	0	10	0	0	— 10

TB —FG Carney 29
TB —Testaverde 4 run (Carney kick)
Buff —Safety, B. Smith tackled Testaverde in end zone
Buff —FG Norwood 30

Cleveland 24, Dallas 21—At Cleveland Stadium, attendance 77,683. Bernie Kosar threw for 308 yards and three touchdowns as the Browns handed the Cowboys their tenth straight loss. Trailing 14-10 in the third quarter, Kosar completed scoring passes of 14 yards to Herman Fontenot and 36 yards to Clarence Weathers just 1:51 later to put Cleveland ahead for good 24-14. Kosar also hit Reggie Langhorne on a 73-yard bomb in the first quarter. Cowboys running back Herschel Walker led all rushers with 134 yards on 25 carries.

Dallas	0	14	0	7	— 21
Cleveland	7	3	0	14	— 24

Clev —Langhorne 73 pass from Kosar (Bahr kick)
Dall —Clack 7 pass from Pelluer (Ruzek kick)
Clev —FG Bahr 25
Dall —Folsom 5 pass from Pelluer (Ruzek kick)
Clev —Fontenot 14 pass from Kosar (Bahr kick)
Clev —Weathers 36 pass from Kosar (Bahr kick)
Dall —Walker 4 run (Ruzek kick)

Los Angeles Raiders 21, Denver 20—At Memorial Coliseum, attendance 65,561. Raiders defensive end Greg Townsend returned an interception 86 yards for a score midway through the third quarter as the Raiders edged the Broncos. Los Angeles took a 14-0 halftime lead on Bo Jackson's four-yard touchdown run and Jay Schroeder's 45-yard scoring pass to Steve Smith. Townsend, who also had two sacks, was named AFC defensive player of the week. The win enabled the Raiders to move into a first-place tie in the AFC West with the Seahawks and Broncos. Denver's John Elway completed 29 of 49 passes for 324 yards and two touchdowns, including six for 138 to Mark Jackson.

Denver	0	0	13	7	— 20
L.A. Raiders	7	7	7	0	— 21

Raiders —B. Jackson 4 run (Bahr kick)
Raiders —S. Smith 45 pass from Schroeder (Bahr kick)
Raiders —Townsend 86 interception return (Bahr kick)
Den —FG Karlis 29
Den —FG Karlis 36
Den —Kay 6 pass from Elway (Karlis kick)
Den —Kay 4 pass from Elway (Karlis kick)

Detroit 30, Green Bay 14—At Pontiac Silverdome, attendance 28,124. Devon Mitchell returned an interception 90 yards for a touchdown to highlight the Lions' win over the Packers. Detroit jumped to a 27-0 halftime advantage on scoring runs by Pete Mandley (21 yards) and Garry James (two), two Eddie Murray field goals (26 and 23 yards), and Mitchell's interception return. Murray's 23-yard field goal in the fourth quarter completed the Lions' scoring.

Green Bay	0	0	0	14	— 14
Detroit	10	17	0	3	— 30

Det —FG Murray 26
Det —Mandley 21 run (Murray kick)
Det —FG Murray 23
Det —Mitchell 90 interception return (Murray kick)
Det —James 2 run (Murray kick)
GB —West 4 pass from Wright (Dorsey kick)
Det —FG Murray 23
GB —Sharpe 24 pass from Wright (Dorsey kick)

Indianapolis 31, Miami 28—At Joe Robbie Stadium, attendance 45,236. Eric Dickerson carried 31 times for 169 yards and a touchdown to lead the Colts over the Dolphins. Indianapolis took a 21-0 halftime lead on scoring runs by Dickerson (two yards) and Ricky Turner (one), and Chris Chandler's 19-yard pass to Clarence Verdin. Turner scored on another one-yard touchdown run late in the third quarter. Dean Biasucci's 47-yard field goal with 2:49 to play proved to be the game-winning points. The Colts held the Dolphins to 58 yards rushing while maintaining a 37:35 to 22:25 time-of-possession advantage.

Indianapolis	0	21	7	3	— 31
Miami	7	0	7	14	— 28

Mia —Hampton 1 run (Reveiz kick)
Ind —Turner 1 run (Biasucci kick)
Ind —Dickerson 2 run (Biasucci kick)
Ind —Verdin 19 pass from Chandler (Biasucci kick)
Mia —Clayton 27 pass from Marino (Reveiz kick)
Ind —Turner 1 run (Biasucci kick)
Mia —Jensen 1 pass from Marino (Reveiz kick)
Ind —FG Biasucci 47
Mia —Clayton 1 pass from Marino (Reveiz kick)

Minnesota 45, New Orleans 3—At Metrodome, attendance 61,215. Carl Lee and Jesse Solomon each returned interceptions for touchdowns as the Vikings easily defeated the Saints. Lee's interception return with 21 seconds remaining in the first half covered 58 yards. Solomon's 78-yard return for a score put Minnesota ahead 38-0 midway through the third quarter. Lee and Solomon were named NFC co-defensive players of the week. Wade Wilson threw for three touchdowns, including scoring passes of 15 and 68 yards to Hassan Jones. Minnesota extended its streak to 17 quarters without allowing a touchdown.

New Orleans	0	0	3	0	— 3
Minnesota	10	21	14	0	— 45

Minn —Anderson 1 run (C. Nelson kick)
Minn —FG C. Nelson 37
Minn —Hilton 1 pass from W. Wilson (C. Nelson kick)
Minn —Jones 15 pass from W. Wilson (C. Nelson kick)
Minn —Lee 58 interception return (C. Nelson kick)
Minn —Solomon 78 interception return (C. Nelson kick)
NO —FG Andersen 36
Minn —Jones 68 pass from W. Wilson (C. Nelson kick)

Kansas City 38, New York Jets 34—At Arrowhead Stadium, attendance 30,059. James Saxon's one-yard touchdown run with two seconds remaining in the game lifted the Chiefs over the Jets. Kansas City led 21-20 at the half on Steve DeBerg's touchdown passes to Carlos Carson (40 yards) and Stephone Paige (41 and 33). New York went ahead 34-24 in the fourth quarter, but Christian Okoye's one-yard scoring run narrowed the deficit to 34-31. Paige caught four passes for 113 yards for the Chiefs, while the Jets' Al Toon had five catches for 102 yards and a touchdown.

N.Y. Jets	10	10	7	7	— 34
Kansas City	14	7	0	17	— 38

KC —Carson 40 pass from DeBerg (Lowery kick)
KC —Paige 41 pass from DeBerg (Lowery kick)
NYJ —Shuler 42 pass from Ryan (Leahy kick)
NYJ —FG Leahy 33
KC —Paige 33 pass from DeBerg (Lowery kick)
NYJ —Toon 2 pass from Ryan (Leahy kick)
NYJ —FG Leahy 32
NYJ —Hector 6 run (Leahy kick)
KC —FG Lowery 21
NYJ —Hector 1 run (Leahy kick)
KC —Okoye 1 run (Lowery kick)
KC —Saxon 1 run (Lowery kick)

New York Giants 44, Phoenix 7—At Giants Stadium, attendance 73,439. Phil Simms returned to action and threw two touchdown passes to Stacey Robinson as the Giants downed the Cardinals to take sole possession of first place in the NFC East. New York led 17-7 at halftime on scoring passes from Simms to Robinson (14 and nine yards). Ottis Anderson ran for three one-yard scores in the second half and Joe Morris, who carried 32 times for 122 yards, added a four-yard touchdown run to complete the onslaught. The Giants' defense held the Cardinals to seven first downs and 158 yards total offense. Simms had missed the last two games with a knee injury.

Phoenix	0	7	0	0 —	7
N.Y. Giants	10	7	7	20 —	44

NYG —FG McFadden 21
NYG —Robinson 14 pass from Simms (McFadden kick)
NYG —Robinson 9 pass from Simms (McFadden kick)
Phx —Ferrell 4 run (Del Greco kick)
NYG —Anderson 1 run (McFadden kick)
NYG —Anderson 1 run (McFadden kick)
NYG —Morris 4 run (McFadden kick)
NYG —Anderson 1 run (kick failed)

Cincinnati 27, San Diego 10—At Riverfront Stadium, attendance 56,866. Ickey Woods ran for a career-high 141 yards and two touchdowns as the Bengals defeated the Chargers. Cincinnati went ahead 20-3 at halftime on scoring runs of four and 30 yards by Woods and Boomer Esiason's 23-yard scoring pass to Cris Collinsworth. Esiason also found James Brooks for a two-yard touchdown pass in the third quarter to finish the Bengals' scoring.

San Diego	3	0	7	0 —	10
Cincinnati	13	7	7	0 —	27

SD —FG DeLine 26
Cin —Woods 4 run (kick blocked)
Cin —Collinsworth 23 pass from Esiason (Breech kick)
Cin —Woods 30 run (Breech kick)
Cin —Brooks 2 pass from Esiason (Breech kick)
SD —Early 9 pass from Malone (DeLine kick)

San Francisco 13, Atlanta 3—At Atlanta-Fulton County Stadium, attendance 44,048. Joe Montana and Jerry Rice combined for the game's only touchdown in the second quarter on a 20-yard pass to lead the 49ers past the Falcons. Mike Cofer kicked field goals of 31 and 23 yards in the fourth quarter to finish San Francisco's scoring. The 49ers' defense limited Atlanta to 43 yards rushing. Roger Craig gained 103 yards on 23 carries to bring his season rushing total to 1,336, breaking San Francisco's club record of 1,262 set by Wendell Tyler in 1982.

San Francisco	0	7	0	6 —	13
Atlanta	0	0	0	3 —	3

SF —Rice 20 pass from Montana (Cofer kick)
Atl —FG Davis 21
SF —FG Cofer 31
SF —FG Cofer 23

New England 13, Seattle 7—At Sullivan Stadium, attendance 59,068. John Stephens rushed for 121 yards and the Patriots' defense held Seattle to 65 total yards and just two first downs en route to a 13-7 win. Jason Staurovsky kicked a pair of field goals (34 and 22 yards) in the second quarter, but Dave Krieg's 27-yard touchdown pass to Ray Butler early in the third period gave Seattle a 7-6 edge. Robert Perryman's one-yard scoring run midway through the third quarter sealed New England's victory.

Seattle	0	0	7	0 —	7
New England	0	6	7	0 —	13

NE —FG Staurovsky 34
NE —FG Staurovsky 22
Sea —Butler 27 pass from Krieg (N. Johnson kick)
NE —Perryman 1 run (Staurovsky kick)

Washington 20, Philadelphia 19—At Veterans Stadium, attendance 65,847. Chip Lohmiller's 44-yard field goal with one second remaining in the game lifted the Redskins over the Eagles. Philadelphia led 19-10 in the fourth quarter, but Doug Williams connected with Terry Orr on a two-yard scoring pass to cut the Eagles' lead to 19-17. Williams then directed a 15-play drive to set up Lohmiller's winning kick. Washington's Ricky Sanders, who caught 10 passes for 128 yards and a touchdown, was named NFC offensive player of the week.

Washington	7	0	3	10 —	20
Philadelphia	3	13	3	0 —	19

Phil —FG Zendejas 40
Wash —Sanders 16 pass from Rypien (Lohmiller kick)
Phil —Byars 2 run (Zendejas kick)
Phil —Byars 12 pass from Cunningham (kick failed)
Phil —FG Zendejas 19
Wash —FG Lohmiller 37
Wash —Orr 2 pass from Williams (Lohmiller kick)
Wash —FG Lohmiller 44

Pittsburgh 37, Houston 34—At Astrodome, attendance 47,471. Bubby Brister completed three touchdown passes as the Steelers rallied past the Oilers. Pittsburgh took a 17-13 halftime lead on Gary Anderson's 45-yard field goal, Dwight Stone's 92-yard kickoff return for a touchdown, and Brister's 80-yard scoring bomb to Louis Lipps. The Steelers increased their lead to 31-27 on Brister's 65-yard pass to Lipps and Merril Hoge's two-yard run, but Warren Moon's three-yard touchdown run with 1:30 remaining put the Oilers back on top 34-31. Brister hit Hoge for a 16-yard scoring strike with 20 seconds left in the game for the win. Brister, who completed 17 of 36 passes for 311 yards, was named AFC offensive player of the week. Lipps finished with 166 yards on four receptions.

Pittsburgh	3	14	7	13 —	37
Houston	0	13	14	7 —	34

Pitt —FG Anderson 45
Hou —FG Zendejas 36
Pitt —Stone 92 kickoff return (Anderson kick)
Hou —Rozier 6 pass from Moon (Zendejas kick)
Hou —FG Zendejas 41
Pitt —Lipps 80 pass from Brister (Anderson kick)
Pitt —Lipps 65 pass from Brister (Anderson kick)
Hou —White 90 kickoff return (Zendejas kick)
Hou —Moon 2 run (Zendejas kick)
Pitt —Hoge 2 run (Anderson kick)
Hou —Moon 3 run (Zendejas kick)
Pitt —Hoge 16 pass from Brister (kick failed)

Monday, December 5

Los Angeles Rams 23, Chicago 3—At Anaheim Stadium, attendance 65,579. Henry Ellard caught six passes for 132 yards and a touchdown to lead the Rams past the Bears. Los Angeles never trailed after Mike Lansford kicked field goals of 25 and 27 yards to give Los Angeles a 6-3 halftime lead. Jim Everett's 31-yard touchdown pass to Ellard capped a 66-yard, five-play drive in the third quarter and increased the Rams' lead to 13-3.

Chicago	0	3	0	0 —	3
L.A. Rams	3	3	7	10 —	23

Rams —FG Lansford 25
Rams —FG Lansford 27
Chi —FG Butler 39
Rams —Ellard 31 pass from Everett (Lansford kick)
Rams —Bell 1 run (Lansford kick)
Rams —FG Lansford 22

Fifteenth Week Summaries

Standings

American Football Conference

Eastern Division

	W	L	T	Pct.	Pts.	OP
Buffalo	12	3	0	.800	315	220
New England	9	6	0	.600	240	263
Indianapolis	8	7	0	.533	337	301
N.Y. Jets	7	7	1	.500	345	333
Miami	6	9	0	.400	295	340

Central Division

	W	L	T	Pct.	Pts.	OP
Cincinnati	11	4	0	.733	428	312
Houston	10	5	0	.667	401	337
Cleveland	9	6	0	.600	276	265
Pittsburgh	4	11	0	.267	296	397

Western Division

	W	L	T	Pct.	Pts.	OP
Seattle	8	7	0	.533	296	292
Denver	7	8	0	.467	306	342
L.A. Raiders	7	8	0	.467	288	326
San Diego	5	10	0	.333	207	319
Kansas City	4	10	1	.300	241	296

National Football Conference

Eastern Division

	W	L	T	Pct.	Pts.	OP
N.Y. Giants	10	5	0	.667	338	277
Philadelphia	9	6	0	.600	356	312
Phoenix	7	8	0	.467	327	372
Washington	7	8	0	.467	328	367
Dallas	3	12	0	.200	258	358

Central Division

	W	L	T	Pct.	Pts.	OP
Chicago	12	3	0	.800	285	187
Minnesota	10	5	0	.667	378	206
Detroit	4	11	0	.267	210	292
Tampa Bay	4	11	0	.267	240	340
Green Bay	3	12	0	.200	214	298

Western Division

	W	L	T	Pct.	Pts.	OP
San Francisco	10	5	0	.667	353	256
L.A. Rams	9	6	0	.600	369	277
New Orleans	9	6	0	.600	302	274
Atlanta	5	10	0	.333	235	305

Saturday, December 10

New York Jets 34, Indianapolis 16—At Giants Stadium, attendance 46,284. Freeman McNeil and Johnny Hector each ran for a touchdown as the Jets came back to defeat the Colts 34-16. New York exploded for 21 points in the third quarter on scoring runs by McNeil (one yard) and Hector (two), and Ken O'Brien's 33-yard scoring pass to Al Toon. Toon caught seven passes for 103 yards to give him 89 catches for the year, breaking his own club record of 85 in 1986. JoJo Townsell returned a punt 59 yards for a touchdown in the first quarter.

Indianapolis	6	7	3	0 —	16
N.Y. Jets	10	0	21	3 —	34

NYJ —FG Leahy 35
NYJ —Townsell 59 punt return (Leahy kick)
Ind —Dickerson 9 run (kick failed)
Ind —Dickerson 50 pass from Hogeboom (Biasucci kick)
NYJ —McNeil 1 run (Leahy kick)
NYJ —Hector 2 run (Leahy kick)
Ind —FG Biasucci 45
NYJ —Toon 33 pass from O'Brien (Leahy kick)
NYJ —FG Leahy 46

Philadelphia 23, Phoenix 17—At Veterans Stadium, attendance 54,832. Randall Cunningham threw for one touchdown and ran for another to help the Eagles defeat the Cardinals. Cunningham's 15-yard scoring run and 37-yard touchdown pass to Cris Carter, plus Keith Byars's four-yard touchdown run, gave Philadelphia a 21-0 first-quarter lead. The Cardinals came back to make the score 21-17 in the fourth quarter on Neil Lomax's 93-yard scoring bomb to Ernie Jones, E.J. Juniors' 36-yard fumble recovery for a touchdown, and Al Del Greco's 40-yard field goal. The Eagles' Izel Jenkins blocked a punt through the end zone for a safety to seal the victory.

Philadelphia	21	0	0	2 —	23
Phoenix	0	7	7	3 —	17

Phil —Cunningham 15 run (Zendejas kick)
Phil —Byars 4 run (Zendejas kick)
Phil —Carter 37 pass from Cunningham (Zendejas kick)
Phx —Jones 93 pass from Lomax (Del Greco kick)
Phx —Junior 36 fumble recovery return (Del Greco kick)
Phx —FG Del Greco 40
Phil —Safety, Jenkins blocked punt out of end zone

Sunday, December 11

Los Angeles Rams 22, Atlanta 7—At Anaheim Stadium, attendance 42,828. Jim Everett threw for 303 yards and a touchdown to help the Rams down the Falcons. Greg Bell's one-yard touchdown run and Everett's 28-yard scoring pass to Henry Ellard gave Los Angeles a 19-0 halftime lead. Pete Holohan had eight receptions for 126 yards for the Rams. Mike Lansford's three field goals (35, 36, and 32 yards) gave him 574 career points, breaking the club record of 573 set by Hall of Famer Bob Waterfield, who played with the team from 1946-1952.

Atlanta	0	0	0	7 —	7
L.A. Rams	3	16	3	0 —	22

Rams —FG Lansford 35
Rams —FG Lansford 36
Rams —Bell 1 run (Lansford kick)
Rams —Ellard 28 pass from Everett (kick failed)
Rams —FG Lansford 32
Atl —Tuggle 2 fumble recovery return (Davis kick)

Houston 41, Cincinnati 6—At Astrodome, attendance 50,269. Mike Rozier carried 22 times for 126 yards and three touchdowns as the Oilers crushed the Bengals. Houston took a 24-3 halftime lead on scoring runs by Rozier (15 and 13 yards), Warren Moon's 13-yard scoring pass to Curtis Duncan, and Tony Zendejas's 43-yard field goal. Rozier added a three-yard touchdown run in the fourth quarter. Eugene Seale returned an interception 46 yards to set up Moon's second scoring strike, a 33-yarder to Drew Hill, in the fourth quarter. The Bengals failed to score a touchdown for the first time this year.

Cincinnati	0	3	3	0 —	6
Houston	7	17	3	14 —	41

Hou —Rozier 13 run (Zendejas kick)
Hou —Rozier 15 run (Zendejas kick)
Cin —FG Breech 45
Hou —Duncan 13 pass from Moon (Zendejas kick)
Hou —FG Zendejas 43
Cin —FG Breech 27
Hou —FG Zendejas 48
Hou —Rozier 3 run (Zendejas kick)
Hou —Hill 33 pass from Moon (Zendejas kick)

Dallas 24, Washington 17—At Robert F. Kennedy Stadium, attendance 51,526. Steve Pelluer completed 21 of 36 passes for 333 yards and three touchdowns as the Cowboys snapped a 10-game losing streak by defeating the Redskins. Pelluer combined with Michael Irvin on scoring passes of 24 and 61 yards to help Dallas to a 17-3 third-quarter lead. Washington tied the game on Doug Williams's 40-yard scoring pass to Ricky Sanders and Mark Rypien's 50-yard touchdown pass to Terry Orr. The Cowboys went ahead to stay with 4:50 to play on Pelluer's 12-yard touchdown pass to Irvin. Irvin, who caught six passes for 149 yards, was named NFC offensive player of the week.

Dallas	3	7	7	7 —	24
Washington	3	0	14	0 —	17

Dall —FG Ruzek 22
Wash —FG Lohmiller 41
Dall —Irvin 24 pass from Pelluer (Ruzek kick)
Dall —Irvin 61 pass from Pelluer (Ruzek kick)
Wash —Sanders 40 pass from Williams (Lohmiller kick)
Wash —Orr 50 pass from Rypien (Lohmiller kick)
Dall —Irvin 12 pass from Pelluer (Ruzek kick)

Chicago 13, Detroit 12—At Soldier Field, attendance 55,010. Kevin Butler kicked a 32-yard field goal with four seconds remaining to help the Bears clinch their fifth straight NFC Central title. Chicago took a 10-6 lead on Butler's 35-yard field goal and Jim Harbaugh's four-yard touchdown run. Garry James's one-yard run gave Detroit a 12-10 lead in the fourth quarter. Harbaugh's 17-yard pass to Dennis McKinnon and 11-yarder to James Thornton set up Butler's winning field goal.

Detroit	0	3	3	6 —	12
Chicago	0	3	7	3 —	13

Chi —FG Butler 35
Det —FG Murray 25
Det —FG Murray 44
Chi —Harbaugh 4 run (Butler kick)
Det —James 1 run (kick blocked)
Chi —FG Butler 32

New York Giants 28, Kansas City 12—At Giants Stadium, attendance 69,809. Phil Simms threw two touchdown passes to Mark Bavaro as the Giants defeated the Chiefs to remain in playoff contention. New York built a 14-12 lead after three quarters on Simms's scoring passes of 12 and 24 yards to Bavaro. Ottis Anderson (two yards) and Maurice Carthon (five) added touchdown runs in the fourth quarter to put the game out of reach. Joe Morris gained 140 yards on 31 carries to help the Giants to their third straight win.

Kansas City	0	3	9	0	— 12
N.Y. Giants	7	0	7	14	— 28

NYG —Bavaro 12 pass from Simms (McFadden kick)
KC —FG Lowery 31
KC —FG Lowery 51
NYG —Bavaro 24 pass from Simms (McFadden kick)
KC —FG Lowery 46
KC —FG Lowery 41
NYG —Anderson 2 run (McFadden kick)
NYG —Carthon 5 run (McFadden kick)

Buffalo 37, Los Angeles Raiders 21—At Rich Stadium, attendance 77,348. Robb Riddick ran for two touchdowns and Scott Norwood kicked three field goals to help the Bills beat the Raiders. Buffalo built a 20-7 halftime lead on scoring runs by Riddick (one yard) and Thurman Thomas (37) and Norwood's pair of 30-yard field goals. The Bills increased their lead in the second half on Riddick's two-yard touchdown run and Jim Kelly's two-yard scoring pass to Butch Rolle. The Bills, who drew 77,348 despite eight-degree temperatures, established a home attendance record of 622,793 in eight games, the largest single-season in-house total in NFL history.

L.A. Raiders	7	0	7	7	— 21
Buffalo	7	13	7	10	— 37

Buff —Riddick 1 run (Norwood kick)
Raiders —Smith 1 run (Bahr kick)
Buff —Thomas 37 run (Norwood kick)
Buff —FG Norwood 30
Buff —FG Norwood 30
Buff —Riddick 2 run (Norwood kick)
Raiders —Brown 43 pass from Schroeder (Bahr kick)
Buff —Rolle 2 pass from Kelly (Norwood kick)
Raiders —Smith 6 pass from Schroeder (Bahr kick)
Buff —FG Norwood 22

Green Bay 18, Minnesota 10—At Lambeau Field, attendance 48,892. Don Majkowski's 11-yard touchdown pass to Patrick Scott helped the Packers defeat the Vikings and snap a seven-game losing streak. Green Bay led 10-3 at halftime on Keith Woodside's two-yard scoring run and Dean Dorsey's 20-yard field goal. Majkowski came off the bench in the second half and found Scott for the touchdown pass that put the Packers ahead 16-3. Tim Harris and Mike Weddington tackled Wade Wilson in the end zone for a safety to complete Green Bay's scoring. Perry Kemp had six receptions for 108 yards for the Packers.

Minnesota	0	3	0	3	— 6
Green Bay	7	3	6	2	— 18

GB —Woodside 2 run (Dorsey kick)
Minn —FG C. Nelson 38
GB —FG Dorsey 20
GB —Scott 11 pass from Majkowski (kick failed)
Minn —FG C. Nelson 37
GB —Safety, Weddington and Harris tackled Wilson in end zone

San Francisco 30, New Orleans 17—At Candlestick Park, attendance 62,977. Roger Craig ran for 115 yards and one touchdown as the 49ers downed the Saints to clinch a playoff berth for the sixth straight year. Scoring runs by Craig (one yard) and Joe Montana (two), and Montana's 68-yard touchdown pass to John Taylor, gave San Francisco a 21-10 halftime lead. Mike Cofer kicked field goals of 40, 47, and 19 yards in the second half to finish the 49ers' scoring.

New Orleans	3	7	7	0	— 17
San Francisco	0	21	3	6	— 30

NO —FG Andersen 38
SF —Craig 1 run (Cofer kick)
NO —Hill 27 pass from Hilliard (Andersen kick)
SF —Montana 2 run (Cofer kick)
SF —Taylor 68 pass from Montana (Cofer kick)
SF —FG Cofer 40
NO —Scales 6 pass from Hebert (Andersen kick)
SF —FG Cofer 47
SF —FG Cofer 19

San Diego 20, Pittsburgh 14—At San Diego Jack Murphy Stadium, attendance 33,816. Mark Malone threw one touchdown pass and ran for another to help the Chargers to a 20-14 win over his former team. Malone connected with Darren Flutie on a six-yard touchdown pass and then ran one yard for a score to give San Diego a 14-0 halftime lead. Steve DeLine's two field goals from 24 and 42 yards proved to be the game-winning points as Pittsburgh scored 14 points in the fourth quarter.

Pittsburgh	0	0	0	14	— 14
San Diego	0	14	0	6	— 20

SD —Flutie 6 pass from Malone (DeLine kick)
SD —Malone 1 run (DeLine kick)
SD —FG DeLine 24
Pitt —Gothard 3 pass from Brister (Anderson kick)
Pitt —Brister 3 run (Anderson kick)
SD —FG DeLine 42

New England 10, Tampa Bay 7—At Sullivan Stadium, attendance 39,889. Jason Staurovsky's 27-yard field goal 3:08 into overtime helped New England beat Tampa Bay and keep its playoff hopes alive. After a scoreless first half, Robert Perryman opened the Patriots' scoring with a six-yard run. The Buccaneers' Vinny Testaverde threw a 15-yard scoring pass to Mark Carrier that tied the game with 2:09 remaining. New England quarterback Tony Eason, making his first start since November 1, 1987, completed passes to Irving Fryar (21 yards) and Russ Francis (four) to help set up Staurovsky's winning kick. The victory marked the Patriots' first-ever win in 11 overtime games dating back to 1974.

Tampa Bay	0	0	0	7	0	— 7
New England	0	0	7	0	3	— 10

NE —Perryman 6 run (Staurovsky kick)
TB —Carrier 15 pass from Testaverde (Carney kick)
NE —FG Staurovsky 27

Seattle 42, Denver 14—At Kingdome, attendance 62,839. Curt Warner rushed for a team-record four touchdowns as the Seahawks moved into first place in the AFC West and eliminated the Broncos from the playoffs. Seattle took a commanding 28-7 halftime lead on Warner's pair of one-yard scoring runs and Dave Krieg's scoring passes to John L. Williams (14 yards) and John Spagnola (seven). Warner, who added scoring runs of 12 and 13 yards in the third quarter, gained 126 yards to give him 1,004 rushing yards for the season, his fourth 1,000-yard season in six years. Williams added 109 yards on 20 carries as Seattle rushed for 230 yards.

Denver	0	7	0	7	— 14
Seattle	7	21	14	0	— 42

Sea —Williams 14 pass from Krieg (N. Johnson kick)
Sea —Warner 1 run (N. Johnson kick)
Den —Jackson 15 pass from Elway (Karlis kick)
Sea —Warner 1 run (N. Johnson kick)
Sea —Spagnola 7 pass from Krieg (N. Johnson kick)
Sea —Warner 13 run (N. Johnson kick)
Sea —Warner 12 run (N. Johnson kick)
Den —Sewell 3 run (Karlis kick)

Monday, December 12

Miami 38, Cleveland 31—At Joe Robbie Stadium, attendance 61,884. Dan Marino completed 30 of 50 passes for 404 yards and four touchdowns as the Dolphins defeated the Browns to snap a five-game losing streak. Miami took a 31-17 fourth-quarter lead on scoring passes by Marino to Mark Clayton (nine and 11 yards), Jim Jensen (two), and Lorenzo Hampton (two). Don Strock, who came off the bench to relieve injured starting quarterback Bernie Kosar, rallied the Browns against his former team. He tied the game 31-31 with 59 seconds remaining on a pair of touchdown passes to Reggie Langhorne (three and two yards). Marino then completed a 46-yard pass to Fred Banks to set up Hampton's game-winning one-yard run with 34 seconds left. Banks (six catches for 118 yards) and Clayton (eight for 118) both topped 100 yards receiving. Marino was named AFC offensive player of the week for his performance.

Cleveland	0	10	7	14	— 31
Miami	0	17	7	14	— 38

Mia —Clayton 11 pass from Marino (Reveiz kick)
Clev —Byner 39 pass from Kosar (Bahr kick)
Clev —FG Bahr 33
Mia —Jensen 2 pass from Marino (Reveiz kick)
Mia —FG Reveiz 35
Mia —Hampton 2 pass from Marino (Reveiz kick)
Clev —Kosar 2 run (Bahr kick)
Mia —Clayton 9 pass from Marino (Reveiz kick)
Clev —Langhorne 3 pass from Strock (Bahr kick)
Clev —Langhorne 2 pass from Strock (Bahr kick)
Mia —Hampton 1 run (Reveiz kick)

Sixteenth Week Summaries

Standings

American Football Conference

Eastern Division

	W	L	T	Pct.	Pts.	OP
Buffalo*	12	4	0	.750	329	237
Indianapolis	9	7	0	.563	354	315
New England	9	7	0	.563	250	284
N.Y. Jets	8	7	1	.531	372	354
Miami	6	10	0	.375	319	380

Central Division

	W	L	T	Pct.	Pts.	OP
Cincinnati*	12	4	0	.750	448	329
Cleveland*	10	6	0	.625	304	288
Houston*	10	6	0	.625	424	365
Pittsburgh	5	11	0	.313	336	421

Western Division

	W	L	T	Pct.	Pts.	OP
Seattle*	9	7	0	.563	339	329
Denver	8	8	0	.500	327	352
L.A. Raiders	7	9	0	.438	325	369
San Diego	6	10	0	.375	231	332
Kansas City	4	11	1	.281	254	320

National Football Conference

Eastern Division

	W	L	T	Pct.	Pts.	OP
Philadelphia*	10	6	0	.625	379	319
N.Y. Giants	10	6	0	.625	359	304
Washington	7	9	0	.438	345	387
Phoenix	7	9	0	.438	344	398
Dallas	3	13	0	.188	265	381

Central Division

	W	L	T	Pct.	Pts.	OP
Chicago*	12	4	0	.750	312	215
Minnesota*	11	5	0	.688	406	233
Tampa Bay	5	11	0	.313	261	350
Detroit	4	12	0	.250	220	313
Green Bay	4	12	0	.250	240	315

Western Division

	W	L	T	Pct.	Pts.	OP
San Francisco*	10	6	0	.625	369	294
L.A. Rams*	10	6	0	.625	407	293
New Orleans	10	6	0	.625	312	283
Atlanta	5	11	0	.313	244	315

**Denotes playoff team*

Indianapolis second in AFC East because of better record vs. common opponents (7-5 vs. 6-6 by New England). Cleveland gained first AFC Wild Card position based on better division record (4-2 vs. 3-3 by Houston). Philadelphia first in NFC East because of head-to-head sweep of New York Giants. Washington third in NFC East because of better division record (4-4 vs. 3-5 by Phoenix). Detroit fourth in NFC Central because of head-to-head sweep of Green Bay. San Francisco first in NFC West based on winning percentage (3-1 vs. 2-2 by Los Angeles Rams, 1-3 by New Orleans). Los Angeles Rams second in NFC West based on better division record (4-2 vs. 3-3 by Saints) and earned Wild Card position based on better conference record (8-4 vs. 9-5 by Giants and 6-6 by Saints).

Saturday, December 17

Denver 21, New England 10—At Mile High Stadium, attendance 70,910. Sammy Winder ran for two touchdowns as the Broncos defeated the Patriots. Denver took a 14-10 halftime edge on scoring runs by Winder (one yard) and Tony Dorsett (five). Winder added a four-yard scoring run in the fourth quarter to seal the victory. Patriots running back John Stephens, who led all rushers with 130 yards, scored on a 23-yard run in the first period.

New England	7	3	0	0	— 10
Denver	7	7	0	7	— 21

NE —Stephens 23 run (Staurovsky kick)
Den —Winder 1 run (Karlis kick)
Den —Dorsett 5 run (Karlis kick)
NE —FG Staurovsky 32
Den —Winder 4 run (Karlis kick)

Cincinnati 20, Washington 17—At Riverfront Stadium, attendance 52,157. Jim Breech's 20-yard field goal 7:01 into overtime lifted the Bengals over the Redskins and enabled Cincinnati to capture its first AFC Central title since 1981. Washington got off to a 10-0 second-quarter advantage, but the Bengals came back to tie the game at halftime on Boomer Esiason's 17-yard scoring pass to Tim McGee and Lee Johnson's 50-yard field goal. After Washington took a 17-10 third-period lead, Esiason connected with Eddie Brown on a 69-yard scoring bomb to deadlock the game 17-17. Redskins kicker Chip Lohmiller missed a 29-yard field-goal attempt with five seconds remaining that would have won the game.

Washington	3	7	7	0	0	— 17
Cincinnati	0	10	0	7	3	— 20

Wash —FG Lohmiller 43
Wash —Clark 20 pass from Williams (Lohmiller kick)
Cin —FG Johnson 50
Cin —McGee 17 pass from Esiason (Breech kick)
Wash —Sanders 44 pass from Williams (Lohmiller kick)
Cin —Brown 69 pass from Esiason (Breech kick)
Cin —FG Breech 20

Sunday, December 18

New Orleans 10, Atlanta 9—At Louisiana Superdome, attendance 60,566. Morten Andersen kicked a 30-yard field goal with five seconds remaining to lift the Saints over the Falcons. Dalton Hilliard, who carried 25 times for 127 yards and caught six passes for 68 more, caught a 13-yard touchdown pass from Bobby Hebert in the first quarter. Atlanta took a 9-7 lead in the fourth quarter on Greg Davis's 39-yard field goal before Andersen's game-winning kick.

Atlanta	0	3	3	3	— 9
New Orleans	7	0	0	3	— 10

NO —Hilliard 13 pass from Hebert (Andersen kick)
Atl —FG Davis 27
Atl —FG Davis 43
Atl —FG Davis 39
NO —FG Andersen 30

Indianapolis 17, Buffalo 14—At Hoosier Dome, attendance 59,908. Gary Hogeboom, relieving injured Chris Chandler, threw two touchdown passes as the Colts rallied to defeat the Bills. Trailing 14-3 in the fourth quarter, Hogeboom completed a three-yard scoring pass to Matt Bouza and then found Albert Bentley for a seven-yard touchdown strike with 1:18 remaining in the game. Eric Dickerson rushed 36 times for 166 yards to total 1,659 yards and become the first Colts player to win the NFL rushing title since Alan Ameche (961) in 1955.

Buffalo	0	7	0	7	— 14
Indianapolis	3	0	0	14	— 17

Ind — FG Biasucci 52
Buff — Reed 23 pass from Kelly (Norwood kick)
Buff — Reed 6 pass from Kelly (Norwood kick)
Ind — Bouza 3 pass from Hogeboom (Biasucci kick)
Ind — Bentley 7 pass from Hogeboom (Biasucci kick)

Tampa Bay 21, Detroit 10—At Tampa Stadium, attendance 37,778. Vinny Testaverde threw three touchdown passes as the Buccaneers downed the Lions. Testaverde hit Bruce Hill and Mark Carrier for a pair of 31-yard scoring passes to give Tampa Bay a 14-0 halftime lead. Detroit scored 10 unanswered points in the third quarter to narrow the score to 14-10, but Carrier's 27-yard scoring reception assured the Buccaneers' win. Testaverde also threw three interceptions to give him a season total of 35, breaking the NFC record of 32 set by Fran Tarkenton in 1978.

Detroit	0	0	10	0	— 10
Tampa Bay	7	7	0	7	— 21

TB — Hill 31 pass from Testaverde (Carney kick)
TB — Carrier 31 pass from Testaverde (Carney kick)
Det — FG Murray 27
Det — Chadwick 19 pass from Hilger (Murray kick)
TB — Carrier 27 pass from Testaverde (Carney kick)

Green Bay 26, Phoenix 17—At Sun Devil Stadium, attendance 44,586. Don Majkowski completed two touchdown passes as the Packers handed the Cardinals their fifth straight loss. Green Bay held a 20-17 edge in the first half on Ron Pitts's 63-yard punt return for a touchdown, Keith Woodside's three-yard scoring run, and Majkowski's 10-yard pass to Larry Mason. Majkowski also connected with Clint Didier for a two-yard touchdown pass in the third quarter to provide the only scoring in the second half.

Green Bay	13	7	6	0	— 26
Phoenix	7	10	0	0	— 17

GB — Pitts 63 punt return (kick failed)
GB — Woodside 3 run (Burrow kick)
Phx — Mitchell 4 run (Del Greco kick)
Phx — FG Del Greco 20
Phx — Mitchell 12 run (Del Greco kick)
GB — Mason 10 pass from Majkowski (Burrow kick)
GB — Didier 2 pass from Majkowski (kick failed)

Cleveland 28, Houston 23—At Cleveland Stadium, attendance 74,610. Don Strock completed 25 of 42 passes for 326 yards and two touchdowns to rally the Browns over the Oilers. Cleveland trailed 23-7 in the third quarter, but Earnest Byner caught a two-yard pass from Strock and added a two-yard scoring run to narrow the score in the fourth quarter to 23-21. Webster Slaughter had six catches for 136 yards, including a 22-yard touchdown reception from Strock for the go-ahead score with 6:23 to play.

Houston	10	6	7	0	— 23
Cleveland	0	7	7	14	— 28

Hou — FG Zendejas 39
Hou — Bryant 36 interception return (Zendejas kick)
Clev — Perry 10 fumble recovery return (Bahr kick)
Hou — FG Zendejas 42
Hou — FG Zendejas 35
Hou — Jeffires 7 pass from Moon (Zendejas kick)
Clev — Byner 2 pass from Strock (Bahr kick)
Clev — Byner 2 run (Bahr kick)
Clev — Slaughter 22 pass from Strock (Bahr kick)

San Diego 24, Kansas City 13—At San Diego Jack Murphy Stadium, attendance 26,339. Gary Anderson carried 34 times for a club-record 217 yards and a touchdown as the Chargers downed the Chiefs. San Diego took a 17-13 halftime lead on scoring runs by Anderson (nine yards) and Mark Malone (five), and Steve DeLine's 45-yard field goal. Jamie Holland returned the opening kickoff of the second half 94 yards for a touchdown to complete San Diego's scoring. Anderson, who became San Diego's first 1,000-yard rusher since 1984 with 1,119 yards, broke Keith Lincoln's club record of 206 yards rushing, set against the Boston Patriots in the 1963 AFL Championship Game.

Kansas City	13	0	0	0	— 13
San Diego	10	7	7	0	— 24

KC — Palmer 26 run (Lowery kick)
SD — Anderson 9 run (DeLine kick)
KC — Paige 4 pass from DeBerg (kick failed)
SD — FG DeLine 45
SD — Malone 5 run (DeLine kick)
SD — Holland 94 kickoff return (DeLine kick)

Pittsburgh 40, Miami 24—At Three Rivers Stadium, attendance 36,051. Dwayne Woodruff and Darin Jordan each scored touchdowns on interception returns, and Warren Williams ran for 117 yards, to power the Steelers past the Dolphins. Pittsburgh took a 20-17 halftime lead on Woodruff's 78-yard interception return, Louis Lipps's 39-yard run for a touchdown, and Gary Anderson's field goals from 34 and 43 yards. The Steelers put the game away in the second half on Rodney Carter's one-yard touchdown run, Anderson's field goals from 22 and 34 yards, and Jordan's 28-yard interception return. The victory was Pittsburgh's third in the last four weeks. The Steelers rushed for 305 yards, the most ever given up by a Miami team.

Miami	10	7	0	7	— 24
Pittsburgh	7	13	7	13	— 40

Pitt — Woodruff 78 interception return (Anderson kick)
Mia — Hampton 4 run (Reveiz kick)
Mia — FG Reveiz 20
Pitt — Lipps 39 run (Anderson kick)
Mia — Hampton 1 run (Reveiz kick)
Pitt — FG Anderson 34
Pitt — FG Anderson 43
Pitt — Carter 1 run (Anderson kick)
Pitt — FG Anderson 34
Pitt — Jordan 28 interception return (Anderson kick)
Pitt — FG Anderson 22
Mia — Clayton 13 pass from Jaworski (Reveiz kick)

New York Jets 27, New York Giants 21—At Giants Stadium, attendance 69,770. Ken O'Brien threw two touchdown passes and Pat Leahy kicked two field goals as the Jets beat the Giants. The Jets opened a 13-7 halftime lead on O'Brien's five-yard pass to Mickey Shuler and a pair of Leahy field goals from 41 and 20 yards. After Freeman McNeil's six-yard run in the third quarter increased the Jets' lead to 20-7, Phil Simms completed a pair of nine-yard scoring passes to Stephen Baker and Lionel Manuel to put the Giants ahead 21-20. O'Brien found Al Toon for a five-yard touchdown pass with 37 seconds remaining for the win. Marty Lyons, who accounted for two of the Jets' season-high eight sacks, was named AFC defensive player of the week.

N.Y. Giants	0	7	7	7	— 21
N.Y. Jets	10	3	7	7	— 27

NYJ — FG Leahy 41
NYJ — Shuler 5 pass from O'Brien (Leahy kick)
NYJ — FG Leahy 20
NYG — Baker 5 pass from Simms (McFadden kick)
NYJ — McNeil 6 run (Leahy kick)
NYG — Baker 9 pass from Simms (McFadden kick)
NYG — Manuel 9 pass from Simms (McFadden kick)
NYJ — Toon 5 pass from O'Brien (Leahy kick)

Philadelphia 23, Dallas 7—At Texas Stadium, attendance 46,131. Randall Cunningham completed two touchdown passes as the Eagles downed the Cowboys to clinch their first NFC East title since 1980. Philadelphia jumped to a 10-7 halftime lead on Cunningham's 12-yard scoring pass to Keith Jackson and Luis Zendejas's 37-yard field goal. Cunningham's 15-yard touchdown pass to Mike Quick and Zendejas's pair of 27-yard field goals increased the Eagles' lead in the second half. Cowboys running back Herschel Walker set a club season record with 2,019 combined yards, surpassing Tony Dorsett's previous mark of 1,971 set in 1981.

Philadelphia	0	10	7	6	— 23
Dallas	7	0	0	0	— 7

Dall — Walker 1 run (Ruzek kick)
Phil — FG Zendejas 37
Phil — Jackson 12 pass from Cunningham (Zendejas kick)
Phil — Quick 15 pass from Cunningham (Zendejas kick)
Phil — FG Zendejas 27
Phil — FG Zendejas 27

Seattle 43, Los Angeles Raiders 37—At Memorial Coliseum, attendance 61,127. Dave Krieg threw for 410 yards and four touchdowns to lead the Seahawks over the Raiders and clinch their first AFC West title in the club's 13-year history. Krieg threw scoring passes of 35 yards to Steve Largent, 17 and 30 yards to Brian Blades, and 75 yards to John L. Williams. Seattle's Norm Johnson kicked five field goals from 39, 24, 40, 35, and 32 yards to tie his own club record. Krieg, who completed 19 of 32 passes, was named AFC offensive player of the week.

Seattle	14	9	14	6	— 43
L.A. Raiders	7	10	10	10	— 37

Raiders — T. Brown recovered fumble in end zone (Bahr kick)
Sea — Largent 35 pass from Krieg (N. Johnson kick)
Sea — Blades 17 pass from Krieg (N. Johnson kick)
Raiders — Gault 51 pass from Schroeder (Bahr kick)
Sea — FG N. Johnson 39
Raiders — FG Bahr 26
Sea — FG N. Johnson 24
Sea — FG N. Johnson 40
Sea — Blades 30 pass form Krieg (N. Johnson kick)
Raiders — FG Bahr 28
Sea — Williams 75 pass from Krieg (N. Johnson kick)
Raiders — S. Smith 4 pass from Schroeder (Bahr kick)
Sea — FG N. Johnson 35
Raiders — Fernandez 54 pass from Schroeder (Bahr kick)
Sea — FG N. Johnson 32
Raiders — FG Bahr 24

Los Angeles Rams 38, San Francisco 16—At Candlestick Park, attendance 62,444. Jim Everett passed for four touchdowns, including three to tight end Damone Johnson, as the Rams overpowered the 49ers to clinch an NFC Wild Card berth. Los Angeles exploded for 21 points in the second quarter on scoring passes from Everett to Johnson (16 yards) and Henry Ellard (nine), and Greg Bell's one-yard scoring run. Everett also hit Johnson for touchdowns of 11 and five yards in the second half to put the game away.

L.A. Rams	0	21	10	7	— 38
San Francisco	3	10	0	3	— 16

SF — FG Cofer 23
Rams — D. Johnson 16 pass from Everett (Lansford kick)
SF — Rathman 1 run (Cofer kick)
Rams — Ellard 9 pass from Everett (Lansford kick)
Rams — Bell 1 run (Lansford kick)
SF — FG Cofer 46
Rams — D. Johnson 11 pass from Everett (Lansford kick)
Rams — FG Lansford 49
Rams — D. Johnson 5 pass from Everett (Lansford kick)
SF — FG Cofer 36

Monday, December 19

Minnesota 28, Chicago 27—At Metrodome, attendance 62,067. Alfred Anderson scored two touchdowns and Walker Lee Ashley returned an interception 94 yards for a score to help the Vikings defeat the Bears. Minnesota took a 21-3 halftime lead on Wade Wilson's three-yard scoring pass to Steve Jordan and 18-yarder to Anderson, and Anderson's one-yard scoring run. Chicago scored 17 unanswered points to narrow the margin to 21-20 in the fourth quarter, but Ashley's interception proved decisive.

Chicago	0	3	14	10	— 27
Minnesota	7	14	0	7	— 28

Minn — Jordan 3 pass from Wilson (C. Nelson kick)
Minn — A. Anderson 1 run (C. Nelson kick)
Minn — A. Anderson 18 pass from Wilson (C. Nelson kick)
Chi — FG Butler 20
Chi — McKinnon 76 pass from Tomczak (Butler kick)
Chi — N. Anderson 51 run (Butler kick)
Chi — FG Butler 45
Minn — Ashley 94 interception return (C. Nelson kick)
Chi — Gentry 1 pass from Tomczak (Butler kick)

Seventeenth Week Summaries

Saturday, December 24, 1988
AFC First-Round Playoff Game

Houston 24, Cleveland 23—At Cleveland Stadium, attendance 74,977. The Oilers advanced to the AFC divisional round of the playoffs for the second straight year with a 24-23 win over the Browns. Allen Pinkett scored two touchdowns within a 15-second span of the second quarter, and Warren Moon rallied Houston with 10 fourth-quarter points for the win. Moon's 14-yard scoring pass to Pinkett seven seconds into the second quarter capped a 17-play, 91-yard drive and gave Houston a 7-3 lead. Nose tackle Richard Byrd recovered Don Strock's fumble on the Browns' next play from scrimmage, and Pinkett scored one play later on a 16-yard run for a 14-9 halftime lead. Mike Pagel replaced the injured Strock and completed a 14-yard touchdown pass to Webster Slaughter late in the third quarter for Cleveland's last lead of the day 16-14. Moon directed a 76-yard drive capped by Lorenzo White's one-yard run as Houston regained the lead 21-16. Richard Johnson's interception on the Browns' next possession led to Tony Zendejas's game-winning 49-yard field goal with 1:54 to play. Pinkett led all rushers with 82 yards on 14 carries, while Moon completed 16 of 26 passes for 213 yards and had three interceptions.

Houston	0	14	0	10	— 24
Cleveland	3	6	7	7	— 23

Clev — FG Bahr 33
Hou — Pinkett 14 pass from Moon (Zendejas kick)
Hou — Pinkett 16 run (Zendejas kick)
Clev — FG Bahr 26
Clev — FG Bahr 28
Clev — Slaughter 14 pass from Pagel (Bahr kick)
Hou — White 1 run (Zendejas kick)
Hou — FG Zendejas 49
Clev — Slaughter 2 pass from Pagel (Bahr kick)

Monday, December 26, 1988
NFC First-Round Playoff Game

Minnesota 28, Los Angeles Rams 17—At Metrodome, attendance 57,666. Minnesota's stingy defense set the tone for the Vikings' 28-17 victory over the Los Angeles Rams. Safety Joey Browner was credited with a pair of first-quarter interceptions that set up touchdowns within a space of 21 seconds. Browner's first interception was returned to Minnesota's 27-yard line and started a 73-yard touchdown drive culminated by running back Alfred Anderson's seven-yard touchdown run. On the first play of the Rams' next possession, Browner got his second interception of the day, returning it to Los Angeles's 17-yard line. On the Vikings' next play, running back Allen Rice ran the remaining yardage (17 yards) for the score. Minnesota quarterback Wade Wilson completed 17 of 28 passes for 253 yards, including a five-yard scoring toss to tight end Carl Hilton in the third period. Vikings wide receiver Anthony Carter caught four passes for 102 yards.

L.A. Rams	0	7	3	7	— 17
Minnesota	14	0	7	7	— 28

Minn —Anderson 7 run (C. Nelson kick)
Minn —Rice 17 run (C. Nelson kick)
Rams —D. Johnson 3 pass from Everett (Lansford kick)
Minn —Anderson 1 run (C. Nelson kick)
Rams —FG Lansford 43
Minn —Hilton 5 pass from Wilson (C. Nelson kick)
Rams —Holohan 11 pass from Everett (Lansford kick)

Eighteenth Week Summaries

Saturday, December 31, 1988
AFC Divisional Playoff Game

Cincinnati 21, Seattle 13—At Riverfront Stadium, attendance 58,560. The Bengals rushed for a season-high 254 yards and made three first-half touchdowns stand up as Cincinnati beat the Seahawks 21-13. The victory earned the Bengals their first trip to the AFC Championship Game since 1981. Rookie running back Ickey Woods carried 23 times for 126 yards and scored on a one-yard run to give Cincinnati a 21-0 halftime lead. A pair of three-yard touchdown runs by Stanley Wilson opened the Bengals' scoring and preceded Woods's score. James Brooks added 72 yards on 13 carries. Cincinnati's defense held Seattle to just 13 yards rushing the entire game and only 49 total yards in the first half. Seattle's John L. Williams caught 11 passes for 137 yards and one touchdown to help rally the Seahawks in the second half. Cincinnati kept the ball 34:51, including 20:07 of the first half.

Seattle	0	0	0	13	— 13
Cincinnati	7	14	0	0	— 21

Cin —Wilson 3 run (Breech kick)
Cin —Wilson 3 run (Breech kick)
Cin —Woods 1 run (Breech kick)
Sea —J. Williams 7 pass from Krieg (N. Johnson kick)
Sea —Krieg 1 run (kick failed)

Saturday, December 31, 1988
NFC Divisional Playoff Game

Chicago 20, Philadelphia 12—At Soldier Field, attendance 65,534. NFC Central Division champion Chicago advanced to its first NFC Championship Game since 1985 with a 20-12 win over NFC East titlist Philadelphia in a game played in fog during the second half. The Bears opened the scoring with a 64-yard touchdown pass from quarterback Mike Tomczak to wide receiver Dennis McKinnon 3:02 into the first period. The Eagles responded with a pair of Luis Zendejas field goals to narrow the margin to 7-6. Philadelphia moved the ball throughout the day but had trouble scoring touchdowns. The Eagles got inside the Bears' 25-yard line nine times, including five times inside the 11, but had only four field goals by game's end. Overall, Philadelphia compiled 430 yards total offense compared to Chicago's 341. Eagles quarterback Randall Cunningham completed 27 of 54 passes for 407 yards, although he was intercepted three times. Tomczak (10 of 20 for 172 yards, 1 touchdown with 3 interceptions) sustained a bruised left shoulder and was replaced by Jim McMahon. Running back Thomas Sanders led the Bears' rushing game with 94 yards on only eight carries.

Philadelphia	3	6	3	0	— 12
Chicago	7	10	0	3	— 20

Chi —McKinnon 64 pass from Tomczak (Butler kick)
Phil —FG Zendejas 42
Phil —FG Zendejas 29
Chi —Anderson 4 run (Butler kick)
Chi —FG Butler 46
Phil —FG Zendejas 30
Phil —FG Zendejas 35
Chi —FG Butler 27

Sunday, January 1, 1989
AFC Divisional Playoff Game

Buffalo 17, Houston 10—At Rich Stadium, attendance 79,532. Buffalo's special teams blocked a punt and a field goal, and the defense registered an interception and a fumble recovery in the fourth quarter, as the Bills advanced to their first-ever AFC Championship Game. Quarterback Jim Kelly completed a team-playoff record 19 of 33 passes for 244 yards with one interception. Rookie running back Thurman Thomas led all rushers with 75 yards on seven carries, including an 11-yard touchdown run that gave Buffalo a 14-3 lead in the third quarter. Robb Riddick's one-yard scoring run followed a blocked punt by safety Leonard Smith. Safety Mark Kelso intercepted a Warren Moon pass on the Oilers' second play of the fourth quarter. Derrick Burroughs's fumble recovery on Houston's next possession helped Buffalo preserve the win in their first-ever playoff game at Rich Stadium.

Houston	0	3	0	7	— 10
Buffalo	0	7	7	3	— 17

Buff —Riddick 1 run (Norwood kick)
Hou —FG Zendejas 35
Buff —Thomas 11 run (Norwood kick)
Buff —FG Norwood 27
Hou —Rozier 1 run (Zendejas kick)

Sunday, January 1, 1989
NFC Divisional Playoff Game

San Francisco 34, Minnesota 9—At Candlestick Park, attendance 61,848. NFC West champion San Francisco gained the right to seek its third NFC title of the decade, dominating Wild Card survivor Minnesota 34-9. The 49ers took a 21-3 halftime lead on three touchdown passes from quarterback Joe Montana to wide receiver Jerry Rice. Montana finished the game completing 16 of 27 passes for 178 yards and three touchdowns, including 11 of 14 for 111 yards and three scores in the first half. Rice finished with five catches for 61 yards and three touchdowns. The 49ers' defense shut down the Vikings by limiting Minnesota to 262 total yards. San Francisco had six sacks, including five in the first two periods. Defensive end Larry Roberts had 2½ sacks, followed by linebacker Charles Haley's 1½. 49ers safety Ronnie Lott had two interceptions. San Francisco rushed for 201 yards, including 135 on 21 carries by Roger Craig. Craig's total included an 80-yard touchdown run in the final period.

Minnesota	3	0	6	0	— 9
San Francisco	7	14	0	13	— 34

Minn —FG C. Nelson 47
SF —Rice 2 pass from Montana (Cofer kick)
SF —Rice 4 pass from Montana (Cofer kick)
SF —Rice 11 pass from Montana (Cofer kick)
Minn —Jones 5 pass from Wilson (kick failed)
SF —Craig 4 run (Cofer kick)
SF —Craig 80 run (kick failed)

Nineteenth Week Summaries

Sunday, January 8, 1989
AFC Championship Game

Cincinnati 21, Buffalo 10—At Riverfront Stadium, attendance 59,747. The AFC Central champion Cincinnati Bengals advanced to their second Super Bowl in the 1980s by defeating the Buffalo Bills 21-10. Rookie running back Ickey Woods gained 102 yards on 29 carries and scored two touchdowns to lead the Bengals' attack. Cincinnati ran the ball on 50 of 73 plays for 175 of its 249 total yards. Woods's first of two one-yard scoring runs, which followed an interception by cornerback Eric Thomas, gave Cincinnati a 7-0 lead late in the first quarter. After Buffalo tied the game 7-7 on Jim Kelly's nine-yard touchdown pass to Andre Reed, Bengals quarterback Boomer Esiason lofted a 10-yard scoring pass to running back James Brooks. A key play in the game came late in the third quarter. With the Bengals in punt formation and facing a fourth-and-four play on Buffalo's 33-yard line, backup quarterback Turk Schonert moved under center, took the snap, and handed off to Stanley Wilson, who gained six yards for a first down. Woods then followed with his second touchdown. The Bengals held the Bills to 181 total yards, the fewest allowed by a Sam Wyche-coached team, including minus-12 in the third quarter. Cincinnati yielded only 45 yards rushing for a two playoff game total of only 63 yards (18 against Seattle) and did not allow the Bills to convert a third-down play (zero for 10). Cincinnati's secondary intercepted three passes, including two of Kelly's first three passes. Safety David Fulcher's interception in the end zone with 8:07 to play sealed the win.

Buffalo	0	10	0	0	— 10
Cincinnati	7	7	0	7	— 21

Cin —Woods 1 run (Breech kick)
Buff —Reed 9 pass from Kelly (Norwood kick)
Cin —Brooks 10 pass from Esiason (Breech kick)
Buff —FG Norwood 39
Cin —Woods 1 run (Breech kick)

Sunday, January 8, 1989
NFC Championship Game

San Francisco 28, Chicago 3—At Soldier Field, attendance 66,946. NFC Western champion San Francisco earned the right to try for an unprecedented third Super Bowl championship during the 1980s by defeating NFC Central winner Chicago 28-3 in the NFC Championship Game. The victory marked the 49ers' first road playoff win since 1970. It also was the first NFC Championship Game win by the visiting team since 1979, when the Los Angeles Rams downed host Tampa Bay 9-0. In previous Super Bowl appearances, San Francisco downed Cincinnati 26-21 in Super Bowl XVI and Miami 38-16 in Game XIX. The 1988 NFC title game began in 17-degree temperature and a wind-chill of minus 26. The 49ers, who made the playoffs for the NFL's current best active streak of six straight seasons, took a 14-3 halftime lead on a pair of Joe Montana touchdown passes (61 and 27 yards) to wide receiver Jerry Rice, who also caught three touchdowns in San Francisco's 34-9 win over Minnesota in an NFC Divisional Playoff Game on January 1. San Francisco came right back after halftime with a 13-play, 78-yard touchdown drive capped by Montana's 5-yard scoring pass to tight end John Frank. The 49ers' final score came on fullback Tom Rathman's 4-yard run with 6:53 remaining. The 49ers' defense yielded Chicago only 267 yards and allowed the Bears inside San Francisco's 40-yard line only twice in the game. The Bears' longest play of the game was 18 yards.

San Francisco	7	7	7	7	— 28
Chicago	0	3	0	0	— 3

SF —Rice 61 pass from Montana (Cofer kick)
SF —Rice 27 pass from Montana (Cofer kick)
Chi —FG Butler 25
SF —Frank 5 pass from Montana (Cofer kick)
SF —Rathman 4 run (Cofer kick)

Twentieth Week Summary

Sunday, January 22, 1989
Super Bowl XXIII
Miami, Florida

San Francisco 20, Cincinnati 16—At Joe Robbie Stadium, attendance 75,129. NFC champion San Francisco captured its third Super Bowl of the 1980s by defeating AFC champion Cincinnati 20-16. The 49ers, who also won Super Bowls XVI and XIX, are the first NFC team to win three Super Bowls. Pittsburgh with four Super Bowl titles (IX, X, XIII, and XIV) and the Oakland/Los Angeles Raiders with three (XI, XV, and XVIII) lead AFC franchises. Even though San Francisco held an advantage in total net yards (454 to 229), the 49ers found themselves trailing the Bengals late in the game. With the score tied 13-13, Cincinnati took a 16-13 lead on Jim Breech's 40-yard field goal with 3:20 remaining. It was Breech's third field goal of the day and came after successful earlier attempts of 34 and 43 yards. The 49ers started their winning drive at their own 8-yard line. Over the next 11 plays, San Francisco covered 92 yards, with the decisive score coming on a 10-yard scoring pass from quarterback Joe Montana to wide receiver John Taylor with 34 seconds remaining. At halftime, the score was 3-3, which represented the first time in Super Bowl history the score was tied at intermission. After the teams traded third-period field goals, the Bengals jumped ahead 13-6 on Stanford Jennings's 93-yard kickoff return for a touchdown with 34 seconds remaining in the quarter. The 49ers didn't waste any time coming back as they covered 85 yards in four plays, concluding with Montana's 14-yard scoring pass to Rice 57 seconds into the final stanza. Rice was named the game's most valuable player after compiling 11 catches for a Super Bowl-record 215 yards. Montana completed 23 of 36 passes for a Super Bowl-record 357 yards and two touchdowns.

Cincinnati	0	3	10	3	— 16
San Francisco	3	0	3	14	— 20

SF —FG Cofer 41
Cin —FG Breech 34
Cin —FG Breech 43
SF —FG Cofer 32
Cin —Jennings 93 kickoff return (Breech kick)
SF —Rice 14 pass from Montana (Cofer kick)
Cin —FG Breech 40
SF —Taylor 10 pass from Montana (Cofer kick)

Twenty-First Week Summary

Sunday, January 29, 1989
AFC-NFC Pro Bowl
Honolulu, Hawaii

NFC 34, AFC 3—At Aloha Stadium, attendance 50,113. The NFC scored 34 unanswered points to snap a two-game losing streak to the AFC before the tenth straight sellout crowd in Honolulu's Aloha Stadium. Bills kicker Scott Norwood provided the AFC's only points on a 38-yard field goal 6:23 into the game. Touchdown runs by Dallas's Herschel Walker (four yards) and Atlanta's John Settle (one) gave the NFC a 14-3 halftime lead. Walker added a seven-yard scoring run, Saints kicker Morten Andersen kicked field goals of 27 and 51 yards, and Los Angeles Rams' wide receiver Henry Ellard caught an eight-yard scoring pass from Minnesota quarterback Wade Wilson in the second half to complete the scoring. Chicago running back Neal Anderson and Philadelphia quarterback Randall Cunningham, who were both appearing in their first Pro Bowl, also played major roles in the NFC's victory. Anderson rushed 13 times for 85 yards and had two receptions for 17. Cunningham, who was voted the game's outstanding player, rushed for 49 yards and completed 14 passes for 63 yards. The NFC, which had five takeaways, outgained the AFC 355 yards to 167 and held a time-of-possession advantage of 35:18 to 24:42. Houston quarterback Warren Moon completed 13 of 20 passes for 134 yards for the AFC. The win gave the NFC an 11-8 advantage in Pro Bowl games.

AFC	3	0	0	0	— 3
NFC	7	7	10	10	— 34

AFC —FG Norwood 38
NFC —Walker 4 run (Andersen kick)
NFC —Settle 1 run (Andersen kick)
NFC —FG Andersen 27
NFC —Walker 7 run (Andersen kick)
NFC —FG Andersen 51
NFC —Ellard 8 pass from Wilson (Andersen kick)

1988 Professional Football Awards

	NFL	AFC	NFC
Professional Football Writers of America			
Most Valuable Player	Boomer Esiason		
Rookie of the Year	John Stephens		
Coach of the Year		Sam Wyche	Mike Ditka
Associated Press			
Most Valuable Player	Boomer Esiason		
Offensive Player of the Year	Roger Craig		
Defensive Player of the Year	Mike Singletary		
Rookie of the Year—Offensive	John Stephens		
Rookie of the Year—Defensive	Erik McMillan		
Coach of the Year	Mike Ditka		
United Press International			
Offensive Player of the Year		Boomer Esiason	Roger Craig
Defensive Player of the Year		Bruce Smith & Cornelius Bennett	Mike Singletary
Coach of the Year		Marv Levy	Mike Ditka
The Sporting News			
Player of the Year	Boomer Esiason		
Rookie of the Year	Keith Jackson		
Coach of the Year	Marv Levy		
Football News			
Player of the Year		Boomer Esiason	Mike Singletary
Coach of the Year		Sam Wyche	Mike Ditka
Pro Football Weekly			
Offensive Player of the Year	Boomer Esiason		
Defensive Player of the Year	Mike Singletary		
Offensive Rookie of the Year	Keith Jackson		
Defensive Rookie of the Year	Erik McMillan		
Comeback Player of the Year	Greg Bell		
Football Digest			
Player of the Year	Boomer Esiason		
Offensive Rookie of the Year	Keith Jackson		
Defensive Rookie of the Year	Erik McMillan		
Coach of the Year	Mike Ditka		
Maxwell Club			
Player of the Year (Bert Bell Trophy)	Randall Cunningham		
Super Bowl XXIII Most Valuable Player (Selected by Sport Magazine)	Jerry Rice		
AFC-NFC Pro Bowl			
Player of the Game (Dan McGuire Award)	Randall Cunningham		

AFC-NFC Players of the Week:

	AFC Offense	AFC Defense	NFC Offense	NFC Defense
Week 1	QB Boomer Esiason, Cin.	DE Ray Childress, Hou.	RB Neal Anderson, Chi.	NT Michael Carter, SF
Week 2	RB Tony Dorsett, Den.	DE Jacob Green, Sea.	RB Roger Craig, SF	LB Michael Walter, SF
Week 3	QB Steve DeBerg, KC	CB Bobby Humphery, NYJ	RB Gerald Riggs, Atl.	DT Gary Jeter, Rams
Week 4	RB Allen Pinkett, Hou.	S Mark Kelso, Buff.	QB Joe Montana, SF	DE Ed Jones, Dall.
Week 5	QB Doug Flutie, NE	LB Mark Brown, Mia.	QB Neil Lomax, Phx.	DE Clyde Simmons, Phil.
Week 6	RB Ickey Woods, Cin.	LB Cornelius Bennett, Buff.	QB Randall Cunningham, Phil.	LB Kevin Greene, Rams
Week 7	QB Dan Marino, Mia.	S Fred Marion, NE	RB Roger Craig, SF	LB Tim Harris, GB
Week 8	RB Eric Dickerson, Ind.	LB Mike Johnson, Clev.	QB Wade Wilson, Minn.	LB Rickey Jackson, NO
Week 9	WR Drew Hill, Hou.	LB Cornelius Bennett, Buff.	QB Steve Young, SF	DE Freddie Joe Nunn, Phx.
Week 10	WR Eddie Brown, Cin.	LB Johnny Rembert, NE	QB Doug Williams, Wash.	DT Jerome Brown, Phil.
Week 11	RB Gary Anderson, SD	CB Albert Lewis, KC	WR Roy Green, Phx.	CB Vestee Jackson, Chi.
Week 12	RB James Brooks, Cin.	NT Fred Smerlas, Buff.	QB Bobby Hebert, NO	LB Aundray Bruce, Atl.
Week 13	QB John Elway, Den.	LB Duane Bickett, Ind.	WR Jerry Rice, SF	LB Lawrence Taylor, NYG
Week 14	QB Bubby Brister, Pitt.	DE Greg Townsend, Raiders	WR Ricky Sanders, Wash.	CB Carl Lee & LB Jesse Solomon, Minn.
Week 15	QB Dan Marino, Mia.	S Gill Byrd, SD	WR Michael Irvin, Dall.	CB Eric Wright, SF
Week 16	QB Dave Krieg, Sea.	DE Marty Lyons, NYJ	QB Jim Everett, Rams	DE Reggie White, Phil.

AFC-NFC Players of the Month:

	AFC Offense	AFC Defense	NFC Offense	NFC Defense
Sept.	QB Boomer Esiason, Cin.	CB Bobby Humphery, NYJ	QB Jim Everett, Rams	LB Rickey Jackson, NO
Oct.	QB Dan Marino, Mia.	LB Cornelius Bennett, Buff.	QB Neil Lomax, Phx.	LB Charles Haley, SF
Nov.	WR Drew Hill, Hou.	NT Tim Krumrie, Cin.	QB Randall Cunningham, Phil.	CB Scott Case, Atl.
Dec.	RB Eric Dickerson, Ind.	S Felix Wright, Clev.	WR Henry Ellard, Rams	DE Reggie White, Phil.

1988 ALL-PRO TEAMS

1988 PFWA All-Pro Team

Selected by the Professional Football Writers of America

Offense

Jerry Rice, San Francisco . . . . . Wide Receiver
Henry Ellard, Los Angeles Rams . . . . . Wide Receiver
Keith Jackson, Philadelphia . . . . . Tight End
Anthony Muñoz, Cincinnati . . . . . Tackle
Gary Zimmerman, Minnesota . . . . . Tackle
Bruce Matthews, Houston . . . . . Guard
Tom Newberry, Los Angeles Rams . . . . . Guard
Jay Hilgenberg, Chicago . . . . . Center
Boomer Esiason, Cincinnati . . . . . Quarterback
Roger Craig, San Francisco . . . . . Running Back
Eric Dickerson, Indianapolis . . . . . Running Back
Scott Norwood, Buffalo . . . . . Kicker
Tim Brown, Los Angeles Raiders . . . . . Kick Returner
John Taylor, San Francisco . . . . . Punt Returner

Defense

Reggie White, Philadelphia . . . . . Defensive End
Bruce Smith, Buffalo . . . . . Defensive End
Keith Millard, Minnesota . . . . . Defensive Tackle
Tim Krumrie, Cincinnati . . . . . Defensive Tackle
Lawrence Taylor, New York Giants . . . . . Outside Linebacker
Cornelius Bennett, Buffalo . . . . . Outside Linebacker
Shane Conlan, Buffalo . . . . . Inside Linebacker
Mike Singletary, Chicago . . . . . Inside Linebacker
Carl Lee, Minnesota . . . . . Cornerback
Frank Minnifield, Cleveland . . . . . Cornerback
Deron Cherry, Kansas City . . . . . Safety
Joey Browner, Minnesota . . . . . Safety
Mike Horan, Denver, & Jim Arnold, Detroit . . . . . Punter

1988 Associated Press All-Pro Team

Offense

Jerry Rice, San Francisco . . . . . Wide Receiver
Henry Ellard, Los Angeles Rams . . . . . Wide Receiver
Keith Jackson, Philadelphia . . . . . Tight End
Anthony Muñoz, Cincinnati . . . . . Tackle
Gary Zimmerman, Minnesota . . . . . Tackle
Bruce Matthews, Houston . . . . . Guard
Tom Newberry, Los Angeles Rams . . . . . Guard
Jay Hilgenberg, Chicago . . . . . Center
Boomer Esiason, Cincinnati . . . . . Quarterback
Eric Dickerson, Indianapolis . . . . . Running Back
Roger Craig, San Francisco . . . . . Running Back
Scott Norwood, Buffalo . . . . . Kicker

Defense

Reggie White, Philadelphia . . . . . Defensive End
Bruce Smith, Buffalo . . . . . Defensive End
Keith Millard, Minnesota . . . . . Defensive Tackle
Tim Krumrie, Cincinnati . . . . . Nose Tackle
Cornelius Bennett, Buffalo . . . . . Outside Linebacker
Lawrence Taylor, New York Giants . . . . . Outside Linebacker
Mike Singletary, Chicago . . . . . Inside Linebacker
Carl Lee, Minnesota . . . . . Cornerback
Frank Minnifield, Cleveland . . . . . Cornerback
Deron Cherry, Kansas City . . . . . Safety
Joey Browner, Minnesota . . . . . Safety
Mike Horan, Denver . . . . . Punter

1988 All-NFL Team

Selected by the Associated Press and Professional Football Writers of America

Offense

Jerry Rice, San Francisco (AP, PFWA) . . . . . Wide Receiver
Henry Ellard, Los Angeles Rams (AP, PFWA) . . . . . Wide Receiver
Keith Jackson, Philadelphia (AP, PFWA) . . . . . Tight End
Anthony Muñoz, Cincinnati (AP, PFWA) . . . . . Tackle
Gary Zimmerman, Minnesota (AP, PFWA) . . . . . Tackle
Bruce Matthews, Houston (AP, PFWA) . . . . . Guard
Tom Newberry, Los Angeles Rams (AP, PFWA) . . . . . Guard
Jay Hilgenberg, Chicago (AP, PFWA) . . . . . Center
Boomer Esiason, Cincinnati (AP, PFWA) . . . . . Quarterback
Roger Craig, San Francisco (AP, PFWA) . . . . . Running Back
Eric Dickerson, Indianapolis (AP, PFWA) . . . . . Running Back

Defense

Reggie White, Philadelphia (AP, PFWA) . . . . . Defensive End
Bruce Smith, Buffalo (AP, PFWA) . . . . . Defensive End
Keith Millard, Minnesota (AP, PFWA) . . . . . Defensive Tackle
Tim Krumrie, Cincinnati (AP, PFWA) . . . . . Defensive Tackle
Lawrence Taylor, New York Giants (AP, PFWA) . . . . . Outside Linebacker
Cornelius Bennett, Buffalo (AP, PFWA) . . . . . Outside Linebacker
Mike Singletary, Chicago (AP, PFWA) . . . . . Inside Linebacker
Shane Conlan, Buffalo (PFWA) . . . . . Inside Linebacker
Carl Lee, Minnesota (AP, PFWA) . . . . . Cornerback
Frank Minnifield, Cleveland (AP, PFWA) . . . . . Cornerback
Deron Cherry, Kansas City (AP, PFWA) . . . . . Safety
Joey Browner, Minnesota (AP, PFWA) . . . . . Safety

Specialists

Scott Norwood, Buffalo (AP, PFWA) . . . . . Kicker
Mike Horan, Denver (AP, PFWA) . . . . . Punter
Jim Arnold, Detroit (PFWA) . . . . . Punter
Tim Brown, Los Angeles Raiders (PFWA) . . . . . Kick Returner
John Taylor, San Francisco (PFWA) . . . . . Punt Returner

1988 UPI All-AFC Team

Selected by United Press International

Offense

Eddie Brown, Cincinnati . . . . . Wide Receiver
Al Toon, New York Jets . . . . . Wide Receiver
Mickey Shuler, New York Jets . . . . . Tight End
Anthony Muñoz, Cincinnati . . . . . Tackle
Bruce Armstrong, New England . . . . . Tackle
Bruce Matthews, Houston . . . . . Guard
Max Montoya, Cincinnati . . . . . Guard
Kent Hull, Buffalo . . . . . Center
Boomer Esiason, Cincinnati . . . . . Quarterback
Eric Dickerson, Indianapolis . . . . . Running Back
John Stephens, New England . . . . . Running Back
Scott Norwood, Buffalo . . . . . Kicker

Defense

Bruce Smith, Buffalo . . . . . Defensive End
Ray Childress, Houston . . . . . Defensive End
Fred Smerlas, Buffalo . . . . . Defensive Tackle
Cornelius Bennett, Buffalo . . . . . Outside Linebacker
Andre Tippett, New England . . . . . Outside Linebacker
Shane Conlan, Buffalo . . . . . Inside Linebacker
John Offerdahl, Miami . . . . . Inside Linebacker
Frank Minnifield, Cleveland . . . . . Cornerback
Albert Lewis, Kansas City . . . . . Cornerback
Deron Cherry, Kansas City . . . . . Safety
David Fulcher, Cincinnati . . . . . Safety
Mike Horan, Denver . . . . . Punter

1988 UPI All-NFC Team

Selected by United Press International

Offense

Jerry Rice, San Francisco	Wide Receiver
Henry Ellard, Los Angeles Rams	Wide Receiver
Keith Jackson, Philadelphia	Tight End
Gary Zimmerman, Minnesota	Tackle
Luis Sharpe, Phoenix	Tackle
Tom Newberry, Los Angeles Rams	Guard
Bill Fralic, Atlanta	Guard
Jay Hilgenberg, Chicago	Center
Randall Cunningham, Philadelphia	Quarterback
Herschel Walker, Dallas	Running Back
Roger Craig, San Francisco	Running Back
Morten Andersen, New Orleans	Kicker

Defense

Reggie White, Philadelphia	Defensive End
Richard Dent, Chicago	Defensive End
Dan Hampton, Chicago	Defensive Tackle
Lawrence Taylor, New York Giants	Outside Linebacker
Charles Haley, San Francisco	Outside Linebacker
Mike Singletary, Chicago	Inside Linebacker
Vaughan Johnson, New Orleans	Inside Linebacker
Carl Lee, Minnesota	Cornerback
Scott Case, Atlanta	Cornerback
Ronnie Lott, San Francisco	Safety
Joey Browner, Minnesota	Safety
Jim Arnold, Detroit	Punter

1988 PFWA All-Rookie Team

Selected by Professional Football Writers of America

Offense

Tim Brown, Los Angeles Raiders	Wide Receiver
Brian Blades, Seattle	Wide Receiver
Keith Jackson, Philadelphia	Tight End
Paul Gruber, Tampa Bay	Tackle
John Elliott, New York Giants	Tackle
Randall McDaniel, Minnesota	Guard
Eric Moore, New York Giants	Guard
No Selection	Center
Chris Chandler, Indianapolis	Quarterback
John Stephens, New England	Running Back
Ickey Woods, Cincinnati	Running Back
Chip Lohmiller, Washington	Kicker

Defense

Michael Dean Perry, Cleveland	Defensive End
Daniel Stubbs, San Francisco	Defensive End
Tim Goad, New England	Defensive Tackle
Pierce Holt, San Francisco	Defensive Tackle
Aundray Bruce, Atlanta	Outside Linebacker
O'Brien Alston, Indianapolis, and Bill Romanowski, San Francisco	Outside Linebacker
Sidney Coleman, Tampa Bay	Inside Linebacker
Chris Spielman, Detroit	Inside Linebacker
Eric Allen, Philadelphia	Cornerback
James Hasty, New York Jets	Cornerback
Bennie Blades, Detroit	Safety
Erik McMillan, New York Jets	Safety
Jeff Feagles, New England	Punter

1988 UPI All-Rookie Team

Selected by United Press International

Offense

Tim Brown, Los Angeles Raiders	Wide Receiver
Sterling Sharpe, Green Bay	Wide Receiver
Keith Jackson, Philadelphia	Tight End
Harry Galbreath, Miami	Lineman
Paul Gruber, Tampa Bay	Lineman
Randall McDaniel, Minnesota	Lineman
Gerald Perry, Denver	Lineman
David Richards, San Diego	Lineman
Chris Chandler, Indianapolis	Quarterback
John Stephens, New England	Running Back
Ickey Woods, Cincinnati	Running Back
Mike Cofer, San Francisco	Kicker

Defense

Michael Dean Perry, Cleveland	Defensive End
Daniel Stubbs, San Francisco	Defensive End
Tim Goad, New England	Defensive Tackle
Aundray Bruce, Atlanta	Outside Linebacker
Bill Romanowski, San Francisco	Outside Linebacker
Sidney Coleman, Tampa Bay	Inside Linebacker
Chris Spielman, Detroit	Inside Linebacker
Eric Allen, Philadelphia	Cornerback
James Hasty, New York Jets	Cornerback
Bennie Blades, Detroit	Safety
Erik McMillan, New York Jets	Safety
Jeff Feagles, New England	Punter

Ten Best Rushing Performances, 1988

	Attempts	Yards	TD
1. Gary Anderson San Diego vs. Kansas City, December 18	34	217	1
2. Roger Craig San Francisco vs. L.A. Rams, October 16	22	190	3
3. Gary Anderson San Diego vs. Pittsburgh, December 11	26	170	1
4. Eric Dickerson Indianapolis vs. San Diego, October 23	30	169	0
Eric Dickerson Indianapolis vs. Miami, December 4	31	169	1
6. Eric Dickerson Indianapolis vs. Buffalo, December 18	36	166	0
7. Roger Craig San Francisco vs. Phoenix, November 6	26	162	1
8. Eric Dickerson Indianapolis vs. Denver, October 31	21	159	4
9. Greg Bell L.A. Rams vs. Atlanta, October 9	21	155	1
10. Freeman McNeil N.Y. Jets vs. Kansas City, October 2	22	154	0

100-Yard Rushing Performances, 1988

First Week

Neal Anderson, Chicago	123 yards vs. Miami
Stump Mitchell, Phoenix	110 yards vs. Cincinnati
Eric Dickerson, Indianapolis	109 yards vs. Houston
Mike Rozier, Houston	100 yards vs. Indianapolis
Timmy Smith, Washington	100 yards vs. N.Y. Giants

Second Week

Herschel Walker, Dallas	149 yards vs. Phoenix
Greg Bell, L.A. Rams	139 yards vs. Detroit
Tony Dorsett, Denver	113 yards vs. San Diego
Roger Craig, San Francisco	110 yards vs. N.Y. Giants
John Settle, Atlanta	102 yards vs. New Orleans

Third Week

Gary Anderson, San Diego	120 yards vs. Seattle
Eric Dickerson, Indianapolis	117 yards vs. Cleveland
Gerald Riggs, Atlanta	115 yards vs. San Francisco
Stump Mitchell, Phoenix	110 yards vs. Tampa Bay
Greg Bell, L.A. Rams	109 yards vs. L.A. Raiders
Joe Morris, N.Y. Giants	107 yards vs. Dallas
Timmy Smith, Washington	107 yards vs. Philadelphia

Fourth Week

Gary Anderson, San Diego	131 yards vs. Kansas City
Eric Dickerson, Indianapolis	125 yards vs. Miami
Tony Dorsett, Denver	119 yards vs. L.A. Raiders
Greg Bell, L.A. Rams	112 yards vs. N.Y. Giants
Earl Ferrell, Phoenix	108 yards vs. Washington
Roger Craig, San Francisco	107 yards vs. Seattle
Neal Anderson, Chicago	105 yards vs. Green Bay

Fifth Week

Freeman McNeil, N.Y. Jets	154 yards vs. Kansas City
Herschel Walker, Dallas	124 yards vs. New Orleans
Eric Dickerson, Indianapolis	118 yards vs. New England
John Settle, Atlanta	115 yards vs. Seattle
Curt Warner, Seattle	110 yards vs. Atlanta

Sixth Week

Greg Bell, L.A. Rams	155 yards vs. Atlanta
Roger Craig, San Francisco	143 yards vs. Denver
Mike Rozier, Houston	141 yards vs. Kansas City
Ickey Woods, Cincinnati	139 yards vs. N.Y. Jets
Kelvin Bryant, Washington	118 yards vs. Dallas
Brent Fullwood, Green Bay	118 yards vs. New England
Sammy Winder, Denver	100 yards vs. San Francisco

Seventh Week

Roger Craig, San Francisco	190 yards vs. L.A. Rams
John Settle, Atlanta	125 yards vs. Denver
Kevin Mack, Cleveland	100 yards vs. Philadelphia

Eighth Week

Eric Dickerson, Indianapolis	169 yards vs. San Diego
Kelvin Bryant, Washington	140 yards vs. Green Bay
John Stephens, New England	134 yards vs. Buffalo
Earl Ferrell, Phoenix	110 yards vs. Cleveland
Craig Heyward, New Orleans	109 yards vs. L.A. Raiders
Rodney Carter, Pittsburgh	105 yards vs. Denver
Marcus Allen, L.A. Raiders	102 yards vs. New Orleans
James Brooks, Cincinnati	102 yards vs. Houston

Ninth Week

Eric Dickerson, Indianapolis	159 yards vs. Denver
John Stephens, New England	124 yards vs. Chicago
Thurman Thomas, Buffalo	116 yards vs. Green Bay
Earl Ferrell, Phoenix	110 yards vs. Dallas

Tenth Week

Roger Craig, San Francisco	162 yards vs. Phoenix
Ickey Woods, Cincinnati	110 yards vs. Pittsburgh
John Stephens, New England	104 yards vs. Miami

Eleventh Week

Gary Anderson, San Diego	145 yards vs. Atlanta
Lars Tate, Tampa Bay	106 yards vs. Detroit
Merril Hoge, Pittsburgh	102 yards vs. Philadelphia
Christian Okoye, Kansas City	102 yards vs. Cincinnati
John L. Williams, Seattle	102 yards vs. Houston

Twelfth Week

James Brooks, Cincinnati	148 yards vs. Dallas
Herschel Walker, Dallas	131 yards vs. Cincinnati
Rueben Mayes, New Orleans	115 yards vs. Denver
Robb Riddick, Buffalo	103 yards vs. N.Y. Jets

Thirteenth Week

Neal Anderson, Chicago	139 yards vs. Green Bay
Curt Warner, Seattle	130 yards vs. L.A. Raiders
Ickey Woods, Cincinnati	129 yards vs. Buffalo
Kevin Mack, Cleveland	116 yards vs. Washington
Greg Bell, L.A. Rams	112 yards vs. Denver
John L. Williams, Seattle	105 yards vs. L.A. Raiders

Fourteenth Week

Eric Dickerson, Indianapolis	169 yards vs. Miami
Ickey Woods, Cincinnati	141 yards vs. San Diego
Herschel Walker, Dallas	134 yards vs. Cleveland
Joe Morris, N.Y. Giants	122 yards vs. Phoenix
John Stephens, New England	121 yards vs. Seattle
Roger Craig, San Francisco	103 yards vs. Atlanta

Fifteenth Week

Gary Anderson, San Diego	170 yards vs. Pittsburgh
Joe Morris, N.Y. Giants	140 yards vs. Kansas City
Mike Rozier, Houston	126 yards vs. Cincinnati
Curt Warner, Seattle	126 yards vs. Denver
Roger Craig, San Francisco	115 yards vs. New Orleans
John L. Williams, Seattle	109 yards vs. Denver
Thurman Thomas, Buffalo	106 yards vs. L.A. Raiders
William Howard, Tampa Bay	101 yards vs. New England
Freeman McNeil, N.Y. Jets	100 yards vs. Indianapolis

Sixteenth Week

Gary Anderson, San Diego	217 yards vs. Kansas City
Eric Dickerson, Indianapolis	166 yards vs. Buffalo
Jamie Morris, Washington	152 yards vs. Cincinnati
John Stephens, New England	130 yards vs. Denver
Dalton Hilliard, New Orleans	127 yards vs. Atlanta
Neal Anderson, Chicago	122 yards vs. Minnesota
Warren Williams, Pittsburgh	117 yards vs. Miami
Ickey Woods, Cincinnati	115 yards vs. Washington

Times 100 or More (92)
Dickerson, 8; Craig, 7; G. Anderson, Bell, Stephens, Woods, 5; N. Anderson, Walker, 4; Ferrell, Morris, Rozier, Settle, Warner, J.L. Williams, 3; J. Brooks, Bryant, Dorsett, Mack, McNeil, S. Mitchell, T. Smith, Thomas, 2.

Ten Best Passing Yardage Performances, 1988

	Att.	Comp.	Yards	TD
1. Dan Marino Miami vs. N.Y. Jets, October 23	60	35	521	3
2 Vinny Testaverde Tampa Bay vs. Indianapolis, October 16	42	25	469	2
3. Doug Williams Washington vs. Pittsburgh, September 11	52	30	430	2
4. Dave Krieg Seattle vs. L.A. Raiders, December 18	32	19	410	4
5. Dan Marino Miami vs. Cleveland, December 12	50	30	404	4
6. Wade Wilson Minnesota vs. Detroit, November 6	35	28	391	2
7. Neil Lomax Phoenix vs. Philadelphia, December 10	50	29	384	1
8. Jim Everett L.A. Rams vs. Philadelphia, November 6	45	24	377	2
9. Steve Beuerlein L.A. Raiders vs. L.A. Rams, September 18	38	19	375	2
10. Kelly Stouffer Seattle vs. New Orleans, October 16	46	27	370	1

300-Yard Passing Performances, 1988

First Week	
Vinny Testaverde, Tampa Bay	324 yards vs. Philadelphia
Second Week	
Doug Williams, Washington	430 yards vs. Pittsburgh
Boomer Esiason, Cincinnati	363 yards vs. Philadelphia
Third Week	
Steve Beuerlein, L.A. Raiders	375 yards vs. L.A. Rams
Joe Montana, San Francisco	343 yards vs. Atlanta
Fourth Week	
Bubby Brister, Pittsburgh	330 yards vs. Buffalo
Phil Simms, N.Y. Giants	309 yards vs. L.A. Rams
Mark Rypien, Washington	303 yards vs. Phoenix
Joe Montana, San Francisco	302 yards vs. Seattle
Fifth Week	
Neil Lomax, Phoenix	342 yards vs. L.A. Rams
Boomer Esiason, Cincinnati	332 yards vs. L.A. Raiders
Jay Schroeder, L.A. Raiders	324 yards vs. Cincinnati
Randy Wright, Green Bay	321 yards vs. Tampa Bay
Steve DeBerg, Kansas City	312 yards vs. N.Y. Jets
Jim Everett, L.A. Rams	300 yards vs. Phoenix
Vinny Testaverde, Tampa Bay	300 yards vs. Green Bay
Sixth Week	
Randall Cunningham, Phil.	369 yards vs. N.Y. Giants
Phil Simms, N.Y. Giants	324 yards vs. Philadelphia
Jim Kelly, Buffalo	315 yards vs. Indianapolis
Seventh Week	
Vinny Testaverde, Tampa Bay	469 yards vs. Indianapolis
Kelly Stouffer, Seattle	370 yards vs. New Orleans
Neil Lomax, Phoenix	332 yards vs. Washington
Dan Marino, Miami	329 yards vs. San Diego
Phil Simms, N.Y. Giants	320 yards vs. Detroit
Mark Rypien, Washington	303 yards vs. Phoenix
Jim Kelly, Buffalo	302 yards vs. N.Y. Jets
Eighth Week	
Dan Marino, Miami	521 yards vs. N.Y. Jets
Steve Pelluer, Dallas	342 yards vs. Philadelphia
Wade Wilson, Minnesota	335 yards vs. Tampa Bay
Bernie Kosar, Cleveland	314 yards vs. Phoenix
Jim Everett, L.A. Rams	311 yards vs. Seattle
Ninth Week	
None	
Tenth Week	
Wade Wilson, Minnesota	391 yards vs. Detroit
Jim Everett, L.A. Rams	377 yards vs. Philadelphia
Dan Marino, Miami	359 yards vs. New England
Randall Cunningham, Phil.	323 yards vs. L.A. Rams
Neil Lomax, Phoenix	323 yards vs. San Francisco
Boomer Esiason, Cincinnati	318 yards vs. Pittsburgh
Vinny Testaverde, Tampa Bay	305 yards vs. Chicago
Eleventh Week	
Neil Lomax, Phoenix	353 yards vs. N.Y. Giants
Twelfth Week	
Don Majkowski, Green Bay	327 yards vs. Detroit
Thirteenth Week	
Jim Everett, L.A. Rams	365 yards vs. Denver
Dan Marino, Miami	353 yards vs. N.Y. Jets
Pat Ryan, N.Y. Jets	341 yards vs. Miami
Fourteenth Week	
John Elway, Denver	324 yards vs. L.A. Raiders
Bubby Brister, Pittsburgh	311 yards vs. Houston
Bernie Kosar, Cleveland	308 yards vs. Dallas
Dan Marino, Miami	304 yards vs. Indianapolis
Fifteenth Week	
Dan Marino, Miami	404 yards vs. Cleveland
Neil Lomax, Phoenix	384 yards vs. Philadelphia
Steve Pelluer, Dallas	333 yards vs. Washington
Jim Everett, L.A. Rams	303 yards vs. Atlanta
Sixteenth Week	
Dave Krieg, Seattle	410 yards vs. L.A. Raiders
Jay Schroeder, L.A. Raiders	354 yards vs. Seattle
Don Strock, Cleveland	326 yards vs. Houston

Times 300 or More (54)
Marino, 6; Everett, Lomax, 5: Testaverde, 4; Esiason, Simms, 3; Brister, Cunningham, Kelly, Kosar, Montana, Pelluer, Rypien, Schroeder, Wilson, 2.

Ten Best Receiving Yardage Performances, 1988

	Yards	No.	TD
1. Eddie Brown Cincinnati vs. Pittsburgh, November 6	216	7	2
2. Anthony Carter Minnesota vs. Detroit, November 6	188	8	0
3. Al Toon N.Y. Jets vs. Miami, November 27	181	14	0
4. John L. Williams Seattle vs. L.A. Raiders, December 18	180	7	1
5. Roy Green Phoenix vs. N.Y. Giants, November 13	176	9	1
6. Louis Lipps Pittsburgh vs. Philadelphia, November 13	171	6	1
Jerry Rice San Francisco vs. San Diego, November 27	171	6	2
8. Stacey Bailey Atlanta vs. Dallas, September 25	169	4	1
9. Henry Ellard L.A. Rams vs. Denver, November 27	167	11	2
10. Henry Ellard L.A. Rams vs. Philadelphia, November 6	166	7	1
Louis Lipps Pittsburgh vs. Houston, December 4	166	4	2
Ernie Jones Phoenix vs. Philadelphia, December 10	166	6	1

100-Yard Receiving Performances, 1988

(Number in parentheses is receptions.)

First Week
Bruce Hill, Tampa Bay — 157 yards (8) vs. Philadelphia
Eddie Brown, Cincinnati — 143 yards (6) vs. Phoenix

Second Week
Ricky Sanders, Washington — 145 yards (5) vs. Pittsburgh
Andre Reed, Buffalo — 122 yards (8) vs. Miami
Tim McGee, Cincinnati — 114 yards (4) vs. Philadelphia
Jerry Rice, San Francisco — 109 yards (4) vs. N.Y. Giants
Ernest Givins, Houston — 108 yards (9) vs. L.A. Raiders
Paul Palmer, Kansas City — 105 yards (8) vs. Seattle

Third Week
Jerry Rice, San Francisco — 163 yards (8) vs. Atlanta
Lionel Manuel, N.Y. Giants — 142 yards (9) vs. Dallas
James Lofton, L.A. Raiders — 130 yards (4) vs. L.A. Rams
Wesley Walker, N.Y. Jets — 129 yards (6) vs. Houston
Mike Quick, Philadelphia — 105 yards (4) vs. Washington
J.T. Smith, Phoenix — 103 yards (6) vs. Tampa Bay
Jay Novacek, Phoenix — 102 yards (5) vs. Tampa Bay

Fourth Week
Stacey Bailey, Atlanta — 169 yards (4) vs. Dallas
Jerry Rice, San Francisco — 163 yards (6) vs. Seattle
Sterling Sharpe, Green Bay — 137 yards (7) vs. Chicago
Vance Johnson, Denver — 134 yards (7) vs. L.A. Raiders
Eddie Brown, Cincinnati — 127 yards (4) vs. Cleveland
Paul Palmer, Kansas City — 122 yards (5) vs. San Diego
Steve Smith, L.A. Raiders — 122 yards (6) vs. Denver
Weegie Thompson, Pittsburgh — 118 yards (4) vs. Buffalo
Anthony Carter, Minnesota — 113 yards (6) vs. Philadelphia
Ray Alexander, Dallas — 107 yards (6) vs. Atlanta

Fifth Week
Carlos Carson, Kansas City — 162 yards (5) vs. N.Y. Jets
Mickey Shuler, N.Y. Jets — 152 yards (12) vs. Kansas City
Ricky Sanders, Washington — 141 yards (7) vs. N.Y. Giants
Pete Mandley, Detroit — 116 yards (7) vs. San Francisco
Walter Stanley, Green Bay — 107 yards (6) vs. Tampa Bay
Mervyn Fernandez, L.A. Raiders — 104 yards (4) vs. Cincinnati
Odessa Turner, N.Y. Giants — 103 yards (8) vs. Washington
Willie Gault, L.A. Raiders — 102 yards (4) vs. Cincinnati

Sixth Week
Cris Carter, Philadelphia — 162 yards (5) vs. N.Y. Giants
Mark Bavaro, N.Y. Giants — 148 yards (9) vs. Philadelphia
Henry Ellard, L.A. Rams — 134 yards (7) vs. Atlanta
Andre Reed, Buffalo — 124 yards (7) vs. Indianapolis
Roy Green, Phoenix — 119 yards (4) vs. Pittsburgh
James Lofton, L.A. Raiders — 113 yards (5) vs. Miami
Eddie Brown, Cincinnati — 103 yards (5) vs. N.Y. Jets

Seventh Week
Bruce Hill, Tampa Bay — 162 yards (7) vs. Indianapolis
Brian Blades, Seattle — 145 yards (8) vs. New Orleans
Bill Brooks, Indianapolis — 139 yards (7) vs. Tampa Bay
Andre Reed, Buffalo — 132 yards (7) vs. N.Y. Jets
Ron Hall, Tampa Bay — 121 yards (7) vs. Indianapolis
Mark Duper, Miami — 118 yards (7) vs. San Diego
Louis Lipps, Pittsburgh — 109 yards (8) vs. Houston
Ernest Givins, Houston — 104 yards (5) vs. Pittsburgh
Paul Palmer, Kansas City — 103 yards (5) vs. L.A. Raiders
Walter Stanley, Green Bay — 101 yards (5) vs. Minnesota

Eighth Week
Mervyn Fernandez, L.A. Raiders — 155 yards (4) vs. New Orleans
Mark Clayton, Miami — 153 yards (10) vs. N.Y. Jets
Mark Duper, Miami — 132 yards (6) vs. N.Y. Jets
Trumaine Johnson, Buffalo — 132 yards (6) vs. New England
Anthony Carter, Minnesota — 123 yards (6) vs. Tampa Bay
Ray Alexander, Dallas — 112 yards (8) vs. Philadelphia
Stephen Baker, N.Y. Giants — 104 yards (6) vs. Atlanta
Ricky Nattiel, Denver — 102 yards (3) vs. Pittsburgh
Henry Ellard, L.A. Rams — 101 yards (7) vs. Seattle

Ninth Week
Drew Hill, Houston — 148 yards (9) vs. Washington
Mark Carrier, Tampa Bay — 142 yards (9) vs. Miami
Clarence Weathers, Cleveland — 140 yards (7) vs. Cincinnati
Eric Martin, New Orleans — 132 yards (6) vs. L.A. Rams
Irving Fryar, New England — 122 yards (3) vs. Chicago
Bill Brooks, Indianapolis — 108 yards (3) vs. Denver

Tenth Week
Eddie Brown, Cincinnati — 216 yards (7) vs. Pittsburgh
Anthony Carter, Minnesota — 188 yards (8) vs. Detroit
Henry Ellard, L.A. Rams — 166 yards (7) vs. Philadelphia
Eric Martin, New Orleans — 146 yards (10) vs. Washington
Jim Jensen, Miami — 110 yards (12) vs. New England
Lionel Manuel, N.Y. Giants — 106 yards (5) vs. Dallas
Al Toon, N.Y. Jets — 106 yards (13) vs. Indianapolis
Ray Alexander, Dallas — 103 yards (8) vs. N.Y. Giants

Eleventh Week
Roy Green, Phoenix — 176 yards (9) vs. N.Y. Giants
Louis Lipps, Pittsburgh — 171 yards (6) vs. Philadelphia
Drew Hill, Houston — 139 yards (8) vs. Seattle
Hassan Jones, Minnesota — 132 yards (3) vs. Dallas
Craig McEwen, Washington — 120 yards (3) vs. Chicago
Dennis Gentry, Chicago — 116 yards (5) vs. Washington
John Settle, Atlanta — 106 yards (10) vs. San Diego

Twelfth Week
Sterling Sharpe, Green Bay — 124 yards (8) vs. Detroit
Ernest Givins, Houston — 118 yards (5) vs. Phoenix
J.T. Smith, Phoenix — 114 yards (10) vs. Houston
Eric Martin, New Orleans — 111 yards (8) vs. Denver
Stephone Paige, Kansas City — 106 yards (5) vs. Seattle
Jerry Rice, San Francisco — 105 yards (3) vs. Washington
Drew Hill, Houston — 100 yards (5) vs. Phoenix

Thirteenth Week
Al Toon, N.Y. Jets — 181 yards (14) vs. Miami
Jerry Rice, San Francisco — 171 yards (6) vs. San Diego
Henry Ellard, L.A. Rams — 167 yards (11) vs. Denver
Mark Jackson, Denver — 140 yards (6) vs. L.A. Rams
Stephen Baker, N.Y. Giants — 134 yards (3) vs. New Orleans
Ferrell Edmunds, Miami — 117 yards (2) vs. N.Y. Jets
Mark Clayton, Miami — 116 yards (6) vs. N.Y. Jets
Tim Brown, L.A. Raiders — 114 yards (4) vs. Seattle
Drew Hill, Houston — 113 yards (9) vs. Dallas

Fourteenth Week
Louis Lipps, Pittsburgh — 166 yards (4) vs. Houston
Mark Jackson, Denver — 145 yards (6) vs. L.A. Raiders
Henry Ellard, L.A. Rams — 132 yards (6) vs. Chicago
Ricky Sanders, Washington — 128 yards (10) vs. Philadelphia
Stephone Paige, Kansas City — 113 yards (4) vs. N.Y. Jets
Al Toon, N.Y. Jets — 102 yards (5) vs. Kansas City

Fifteenth Week

Ernie Jones, Phoenix	166 yards (6) vs. Philadelphia
Michael Irvin, Dallas	149 yards (6) vs. Washington
Mark Jackson, Denver	137 yards (7) vs. Seattle
Pete Holohan, L.A. Rams	126 yards (8) vs. Atlanta
Fred Banks, Miami	118 yards (6) vs. Cleveland
Perry Kemp, Green Bay	108 yards (6) vs. Minnesota
Mark Clayton, Miami	108 yards (8) vs. Cleveland
Terry Orr, Washington	104 yards (3) vs. Dallas
Art Monk, Washington	103 yards (7) vs. Dallas
Al Toon, N.Y. Jets	103 yards (7) vs. Indianapolis

Sixteenth Week

John L. Williams, Seattle	180 yards (7) vs. L.A. Raiders
Webster Slaughter, Cleveland	136 yards (6) vs. Houston
Brian Blades, Seattle	123 yards (4) vs. L.A. Raiders
Ricky Sanders, Washington	120 yards (6) vs. Cincinnati
Ernest Givins, Houston	119 yards (6) vs. Cleveland
Eddie Brown, Cincinnati	115 yards (2) vs. Washington
Mervyn Fernandez, L.A. Raiders	113 yards (4) vs. Seattle
Scott Schwedes, Miami	110 yards (4) vs. Pittsburgh
Willie Gault, L.A. Raiders	108 yards (2) vs. Seattle
Dennis McKinnon, Chicago	106 yards (4) vs. Minnesota

Times 100 or More (122)
E. Brown, Ellard, Rice, 5; Givins, Hill, Sanders, Toon, 4; Alexander, Carter, Clayton, Fernandez, M. Jackson, Lipps, E. Martin, Palmer, Reed, 3; Baker, Blades, B. Brooks, Duper, Gault, Green, Lofton, Manuel, Paige, Sharpe, J.T. Smith, Stanley, 2.

American Football Conference Offense

	Buff.	Cin.	Clev.	Den.	Hou.	Ind.	K.C.	Raid.	Mia.	N.E.	N.Y.J.	Pitt.	S.D.	Sea.
First Downs	313	351	294	338	308	311	289	283	321	264	331	292	255	291
Rushing	137	159	93	106	141	153	104	116	77	126	118	120	115	125
Passing	161	165	177	196	148	130	161	145	218	112	181	150	116	139
Penalty	15	27	24	36	19	28	24	22	26	26	32	22	24	27
Rushes	528	563	440	464	558	545	448	493	335	588	514	499	438	517
Net Yds. Gained	2133	2710	1575	1815	2249	2249	1713	1852	1205	2120	2132	2228	2041	2086
Avg. Gain	4.0	4.8	3.6	3.9	4.0	4.1	3.8	3.8	3.6	3.6	4.1	4.5	4.7	4.0
Avg. Yds. per Game	133.3	169.4	98.4	113.4	140.6	140.6	107.1	115.8	75.3	132.5	133.3	139.3	127.6	130.4
Passes Attempted	454	392	537	581	428	403	528	496	621	389	538	489	468	437
Completed	271	225	313	324	218	222	282	219	363	199	299	226	241	245
% Completed	59.7	57.4	58.3	55.8	50.9	55.1	53.4	44.2	58.5	51.2	55.6	46.2	51.5	56.1
Total Yds. Gained	3411	3592	3686	3941	3166	2865	3484	3503	4557	2333	3374	3307	2628	2979
Times Sacked	30	30	36	32	24	34	43	46	7	23	42	42	31	29
Yds. Lost	229	245	250	250	210	244	353	394	41	160	291	331	240	223
Net Yds. Gained	3182	3347	3436	3691	2956	2621	3131	3109	4516	2173	3083	2976	2388	2756
Avg. Yds. per Game	198.9	209.2	214.8	230.7	184.8	163.8	195.7	194.3	282.3	135.8	192.7	186.0	149.3	172.3
Net Yds. per Pass Play	6.57	7.93	6.00	6.02	6.54	6.00	5.48	5.74	7.19	5.27	5.32	5.60	4.79	5.91
Yds. Gained per Comp.	12.59	15.96	11.78	12.16	14.52	12.91	12.35	16.00	12.55	11.72	11.28	14.63	10.90	12.16
Combined Net Yds. Gained	5315	6057	5011	5506	5205	4870	4844	4961	5721	4293	5215	5204	4429	4842
% Total Yds. Rushing	40.1	44.7	31.4	33.0	43.2	46.2	35.4	37.3	21.1	49.4	40.9	42.8	46.1	43.1
% Total Yds. Passing	59.9	55.3	68.6	67.0	56.8	53.8	64.6	62.7	78.9	50.6	59.1	57.2	53.9	56.9
Avg. Yds. per Game	332.2	378.6	313.2	344.1	325.3	304.4	302.8	310.1	357.6	268.3	325.9	325.3	276.8	302.6
Ball Control Plays	1012	985	1013	1077	1010	982	1019	1035	963	1000	1094	1030	937	983
Avg. Yds. per Play	5.3	6.1	4.9	5.1	5.2	5.0	4.8	4.8	5.9	4.3	4.8	5.1	4.7	4.9
Avg. Time of Poss.	29:54	29:32	30:50	29:47	31:11	30:19	28:31	29:30	27:02	31:04	30:55	28:31	28:22	28:38
Third Down Efficiency	42.5	43.9	43.2	40.5	41.6	34.4	39.3	32.3	38.6	36.1	41.6	36.1	34.3	39.3
Had Intercepted	17	14	17	22	18	22	21	20	23	28	11	20	20	20
Yds. Opp. Returned	202	185	190	344	289	291	206	219	399	286	126	367	307	195
Ret. by Opp. for TD	1	0	2	1	1	1	1	0	4	0	0	1	0	1

	Buff.	Cin.	Clev.	Den.	Hou.	Ind.	K.C.	Raid.	Mia.	N.E.	N.Y.J.	Pitt.	S.D.	Sea.
Punts	62	64	67	68	65	64	76	91	64	91	85	71	86	70
Yds. Punted	2451	2351	2578	2978	2523	2784	3059	3804	2754	3482	3310	2950	3745	2858
Avg. Yds. per Punt	39.5	36.7	38.5	43.8	38.8	43.5	40.3	41.8	43.0	38.3	38.9	41.5	43.5	40.8
Punt Returns	26	32	40	53	36	26	32	55	27	38	38	39	35	37
Yds. Returned	152	244	325	451	225	254	215	489	259	398	418	322	314	340
Avg. Yds. per Return	5.8	7.6	8.1	8.5	6.3	9.8	6.7	8.9	9.6	10.5	11.0	8.3	9.0	9.2
Returned for TD	0	0	0	0	0	1	0	0	0	0	1	0	0	0
Kickoff Returns	50	57	55	58	60	52	56	62	65	57	72	74	60	62
Yds. Returned	935	1054	1159	1198	1232	1033	925	1407	1365	1248	1404	1575	1510	1352
Avg. Yds. per Return	18.7	18.5	21.1	20.7	20.5	19.9	16.5	22.7	21.0	21.9	19.5	21.3	25.2	21.8
Returned for TD	0	1	0	0	1	0	0	1	0	1	0	2	2	0
Fumbles	26	28	32	34	33	20	21	33	26	19	32	40	26	29
Lost	16	13	16	12	17	8	12	13	12	10	16	19	12	14
Out of Bounds	2	5	4	1	3	0	0	1	1	0	2	2	1	2
Own Rec. for TD	0	0	0	0	0	0	0	0	0	1	0	0	0	0
Opp. Rec. by	17	14	11	13	20	20	13	17	15	15	16	13	10	18
Opp. Rec. for TD	1	2	1	0	0	0	0	1	1	0	0	0	1	1
Penalties	109	82	110	85	125	89	85	102	99	87	115	99	118	89
Yds. Penalized	824	647	875	717	1150	657	636	762	845	665	931	803	1039	790
Total Points Scored	329	448	304	327	424	354	254	325	319	250	372	336	231	339
Total TDs	33	59	33	37	51	40	24	39	41	31	43	36	27	39
TDs Rushing	15	27	10	13	26	23	8	15	11	17	19	17	11	14
TDs Passing	15	28	19	24	21	15	16	21	29	12	20	15	11	22
TDs on Ret. and Rec.	3	4	4	0	4	2	0	3	1	2	4	4	5	3
Extra Points	33	56	32	36	48	39	23	37	37	25	43	34	27	39
Safeties	1	1	1	0	2	0	3	0	0	0	1	1	0	0
Field Goals Made	32	12	24	23	22	25	27	18	12	13	23	28	14	22
Field Goals Attempted	37	18	29	36	34	32	32	29	23	24	28	36	20	28
% Successful	86.5	66.7	82.8	63.9	64.7	78.1	84.4	62.1	52.2	54.2	82.1	77.8	70.0	78.6

American Football Conference Defense

	Buff.	Cin.	Clev.	Den.	Hou.	Ind.	K.C.	Raid.	Mia.	N.E.	N.Y.J.	Pitt.	S.D.	Sea.
First Downs	299	322	301	316	304	315	318	310	359	272	310	319	335	321
Rushing	114	126	114	140	94	109	162	124	155	119	123	110	135	134
Passing	146	177	162	161	170	184	136	165	173	138	162	181	173	171
Penalty	39	19	25	15	40	22	20	21	31	15	25	28	27	16
Rushes	477	493	498	552	431	447	609	533	557	496	517	516	521	509
Net Yds. Gained	1854	2048	1920	2538	1592	1694	2592	2208	2506	2099	2124	1864	2133	2286
Avg. Gain	3.9	4.2	3.9	4.6	3.7	3.8	4.3	4.1	4.5	4.2	4.1	3.6	4.1	4.5
Avg. Yds. per Game	115.9	128.0	120.0	158.6	99.5	105.9	162.0	138.0	156.6	131.2	132.8	116.5	133.3	142.9
Passes Attempted	448	524	474	467	512	539	410	483	491	436	476	532	517	501
Completed	250	283	245	262	281	321	214	265	298	234	244	309	274	280
% Completed	55.8	54.0	51.7	56.1	54.9	59.6	52.2	54.9	60.7	53.7	51.3	58.1	53.0	55.9
Total Yds. Gained	3046	3508	3102	3168	3619	3803	2591	3471	3442	2801	3823	4086	3525	3618
Times Sacked	46	42	37	36	42	30	23	40	24	29	45	19	34	30
Yds. Lost	322	374	255	235	353	201	157	300	167	219	314	145	240	265
Net Yds. Gained	2724	3134	2847	2933	3266	3602	2434	3171	3275	2582	3509	3941	3285	3353
Avg. Yds. per Game	170.3	195.9	177.9	183.3	204.1	225.1	152.1	198.2	204.7	161.4	219.3	246.3	205.3	209.6
Net Yds. per Pass Play	5.51	5.54	5.57	5.83	5.90	6.33	5.62	6.06	6.36	5.55	6.74	7.15	5.96	6.31
Yds. Gained per Comp.	12.18	12.40	12.66	12.09	12.88	11.85	12.11	13.10	11.55	11.97	15.67	13.22	12.86	12.92
Combined Net Yds. Gained	4578	5182	4767	5471	4858	5296	5026	5379	5781	4681	5633	5805	5418	5639
% Total Yds. Rushing	40.5	39.5	40.3	46.4	32.8	32.0	51.6	41.0	43.3	44.8	37.7	32.1	39.4	40.5
% Total Yds. Passing	59.5	60.5	59.7	53.6	67.2	68.0	48.4	59.0	56.7	55.2	62.3	67.9	60.6	59.5
Avg. Yds. per Game	286.1	323.9	297.9	341.9	303.6	331.0	314.1	336.2	361.3	292.6	352.1	362.8	338.6	352.4
Ball Control Plays	971	1059	1009	1055	985	1016	1042	1056	1072	961	1038	1067	1072	1040
Avg. Yds. per Play	4.7	4.9	4.7	5.2	4.9	5.2	4.8	5.1	5.4	4.9	5.4	5.4	5.1	5.4
Avg. Time of Poss.	30:06	30:28	29:10	30:13	28:49	29:41	31:29	30:30	32:58	28:56	29:05	31:29	31:38	31:23
Third Down Efficiency	35.9	43.4	34.0	37.9	39.6	43.1	45.0	37.9	48.8	29.1	40.7	43.6	43.9	43.8
Intercepted by	15	22	20	16	22	15	18	17	16	20	24	20	16	22
Yds. Returned by	244	181	319	200	302	189	166	278	219	244	228	381	179	280
Returned for TD	1	1	1	0	2	1	0	1	0	0	3	2	1	1
Punts	75	65	69	84	80	68	63	94	58	86	72	67	71	66
Yds. Punted	2977	2596	2722	3643	2973	2677	2531	3889	2427	3633	2742	2726	2792	2778
Avg. Yds. per Punt	39.7	39.9	39.4	43.4	37.2	39.4	40.2	41.4	41.8	42.2	38.1	40.7	39.3	42.1
Punt Returns	36	32	32	33	35	37	48	47	35	37	34	40	56	36
Yds. Returned	222	280	304	364	206	418	473	397	318	217	201	418	558	202
Avg. Yds. per Return	6.2	8.8	9.5	11.0	5.9	11.3	9.9	8.4	9.1	5.9	5.9	10.5	10.0	5.6
Returned for TD	0	0	1	1	0	1	0	0	0	0	0	0	0	0
Kickoff Returns	69	61	58	52	69	67	57	61	53	45	70	63	47	66
Yds. Returned	1117	1335	973	1035	1362	1480	1380	1299	1109	888	1491	1351	1055	1207
Avg. Yds. per Return	16.2	21.9	16.8	19.9	19.7	22.1	24.2	21.3	20.9	19.7	21.3	21.4	22.4	18.3
Returned for TD	0	0	0	0	1	1	2	0	0	0	0	1	1	0
Fumbles	28	28	23	23	33	32	30	31	31	29	35	35	25	31
Lost	17	14	11	13	20	20	13	17	15	15	16	13	10	18
Out of Bounds	0	3	1	0	2	1	1	0	3	1	4	2	1	0
Own Rec. for TD	0	1	0	0	0	0	0	0	0	0	0	0	0	0
Opp. Rec. by	16	13	16	12	17	8	12	13	12	10	16	19	12	14
Opp. Rec. for TD	0	0	1	0	2	0	1	1	0	0	0	0	0	1
Penalties	90	95	100	116	118	118	106	94	103	108	89	79	74	111
Yds. Penalized	713	873	789	966	947	965	854	823	734	858	757	705	619	861
Total Points Scored	237	329	288	352	365	315	320	369	380	284	354	421	332	329
Total TDs	29	39	30	41	46	38	39	41	45	33	43	49	38	38
TDs Rushing	14	18	13	21	20	14	23	17	22	20	15	20	15	14
TDs Passing	14	19	13	18	22	21	12	23	19	13	28	25	22	21
TDs on Ret. and Rec.	1	2	4	2	4	3	4	1	4	0	0	4	1	3
Extra Points	27	38	30	41	43	36	38	40	44	33	36	47	36	38
Safeties	0	3	0	1	2	0	0	1	0	1	0	1	1	0
Field Goals Made	12	17	26	21	14	17	16	27	22	17	20	26	22	21
Field Goals Attempted	24	24	34	27	18	25	24	29	28	26	30	32	36	32
% Successful	50.0	70.8	76.5	77.8	77.8	68.0	66.7	93.1	78.6	65.4	66.7	81.3	61.1	65.6

National Football Conference Offense

	Atl.	Chi.	Dall.	Det.	G.B.	Rams	Minn.	N.O.	N.Y.G.	Phil.	Phx.	S.F.	T.B.	Wash.
First Downs	257	303	311	226	280	333	318	306	317	318	336	326	295	307
Rushing	106	137	112	63	78	114	112	108	123	105	122	141	91	88
Passing	136	134	175	141	175	203	187	179	168	179	195	167	173	202
Penalty	15	32	24	22	27	16	19	19	26	34	19	18	31	17
Rushes	478	555	469	391	385	507	501	512	493	464	480	527	452	437
Net Yds. Gained	2016	2319	1995	1243	1379	2003	1806	2046	1689	1945	2027	2523	1753	1543
Avg. Gain	4.2	4.2	4.3	3.2	3.6	4.0	3.6	4.0	3.4	4.2	4.2	4.8	3.9	3.5
Avg. Yds. per Game	126.0	144.9	124.7	77.7	86.2	125.2	112.9	127.9	105.6	121.6	126.7	157.7	109.6	96.4
Passes Attempted	481	461	555	477	582	522	520	498	525	581	562	502	512	592
Completed	250	248	307	213	319	312	294	286	290	309	322	293	253	327
% Completed	52.0	53.8	55.3	44.7	54.8	59.8	56.5	57.4	55.2	53.2	57.3	58.4	49.4	55.2
Total Yds. Gained	2914	3173	3727	2572	3609	4002	4100	3256	3716	3927	4191	3675	3608	4339
Times Sacked	43	24	35	52	51	28	47	24	60	57	60	47	34	24
Yds. Lost	348	175	239	410	324	197	311	171	450	442	411	298	300	203
Net Yds. Gained	2566	2998	3488	2162	3285	3805	3789	3085	3266	3485	3780	3377	3308	4136
Avg. Yds. per Game	160.4	187.4	218.0	135.1	205.3	237.8	236.8	192.8	204.1	217.8	236.3	211.1	206.8	258.5
Net Yds. per Pass Play	4.90	6.18	5.91	4.09	5.19	6.92	6.68	5.91	5.58	5.46	6.08	6.15	6.06	6.71
Yds. Gained per Comp.	11.66	12.79	12.14	12.08	11.31	12.83	13.95	11.38	12.81	12.71	13.02	12.54	14.26	13.27
Combined Net Yds.	4582	5317	5483	3405	4664	5808	5595	5131	4955	5430	5807	5900	5061	5679
% Total Yds. Rushing	44.0	43.6	36.4	36.5	29.6	34.5	32.3	39.9	34.1	35.8	34.9	42.8	34.6	27.2
% Total Yds. Passing	56.0	56.4	63.6	63.5	70.4	65.5	67.7	60.1	65.9	64.2	65.1	57.2	65.4	72.8
Avg. Yds. per Game	286.4	332.3	342.7	212.8	291.5	363.0	349.7	320.7	309.7	339.4	362.9	368.8	316.3	354.9
Ball Control Plays	1002	1040	1059	920	1018	1057	1068	1034	1078	1102	1102	1076	998	1053
Avg. Yds. per Play	4.6	5.1	5.2	3.7	4.6	5.5	5.2	5.0	4.6	4.9	5.3	5.5	5.1	5.4
Avg. Time of Poss.	28:08	33:02	30:41	27:27	29:16	31:09	31:05	32:38	29:24	31:09	31:27	30:31	29:00	30:57
Third Down Efficiency	37.2	41.9	38.7	33.6	35.8	39.7	37.4	45.8	36.5	37.4	40.0	41.8	35.6	43.5
Had Intercepted	19	15	27	18	24	18	18	16	14	17	19	14	36	25
Yds. Opp. Returned	214	175	314	159	386	138	212	226	116	98	264	185	486	271
Ret. by Opp. for TD	2	1	0	0	4	1	1	2	0	0	0	1	2	0

	Atl.	Chi.	Dall.	Det.	G.B.	Rams	Minn.	N.O.	N.Y.G.	Phil.	Phx.	S.F.	T.B.	Wash.
Punts	98	79	80	97	86	76	86	73	81	104	80	80	68	67
Yds. Punted	3920	3282	3271	4110	3287	3003	3387	2913	3234	4125	3228	3093	2477	2562
Avg. Yds. per Punt	40.0	41.5	40.9	42.4	38.2	39.5	39.4	39.9	39.9	39.7	40.3	38.7	36.4	38.2
Punt Returns	42	38	45	42	35	49	59	35	47	33	52	54	36	52
Yds. Returned	343	294	360	346	208	322	553	413	359	233	463	612	328	377
Avg. Yds. per Return	8.2	7.7	8.0	8.2	5.9	6.6	9.4	11.8	7.6	7.1	8.9	11.3	9.1	7.3
Returned for TD	0	0	0	0	1	0	0	1	0	0	0	2	0	0
Kickoff Returns	59	45	69	59	64	59	56	70	62	59	60	55	64	74
Yds. Returned	1057	896	1410	1154	1181	1191	1160	1408	1154	1028	1106	978	1345	1355
Avg. Yds. per Return	17.9	19.9	20.4	19.6	18.5	20.2	20.7	20.1	18.6	17.4	18.4	17.8	21.0	18.3
Returned for TD	0	0	0	0	0	0	0	0	0	0	0	0	0	0
Fumbles	29	37	22	31	44	28	22	29	32	29	34	27	27	34
Lost	18	19	13	15	26	16	12	16	13	9	16	12	16	21
Out of Bounds	3	3	0	1	2	2	0	3	1	0	0	0	0	1
Own Rec. for TD	0	0	0	0	0	0	0	1	0	1	0	0	0	0
Opp. Rec. by	14	9	9	21	21	15	17	15	18	12	13	16	12	8
Opp. Rec. for TD	2	0	0	1	0	0	2	0	1	0	3	0	0	0
Penalties	67	88	141	94	94	78	118	101	88	115	99	115	102	96
Yds. Penalized	542	644	1148	804	785	587	998	821	660	907	790	986	816	817
Total Points Scored	244	312	265	220	240	407	406	312	359	379	344	369	261	345
Total TDs	27	38	32	23	29	48	49	33	41	44	44	41	28	41
TDs Rushing	11	25	10	7	14	16	22	9	15	17	15	18	11	8
TDs Passing	13	13	21	13	13	31	20	21	22	25	26	21	16	33
TDs on Ret. and Rec.	3	0	1	3	2	1	7	3	4	2	3	2	1	0
Extra Points	25	37	32	22	23	45	48	32	39	42	42	40	28	40
Safeties	0	1	1	0	2	1	2	2	1	2	1	1	1	1
Field Goals Made	19	15	13	20	13	24	20	26	24	23	12	27	21	19
Field Goals Attempted	30	19	25	21	25	32	25	36	30	32	21	38	30	26
% Successful	63.3	78.9	52.0	95.2	52.0	75.0	80.0	72.2	80.0	71.9	57.1	71.1	70.0	73.1

National Football Conference Defense

	Atl.	Chi.	Dall.	Det.	G.B.	Rams	Minn.	N.O.	N.Y.G.	Phil.	Phx.	S.F.	T.B.	Wash.
First Downs	312	264	297	334	281	289	243	286	291	311	301	277	293	294
Rushing	124	76	93	128	130	100	85	97	95	85	111	90	104	113
Passing	168	158	180	179	136	166	132	167	177	199	170	160	169	153
Penalty	20	30	24	27	15	23	26	22	19	27	20	27	20	28
Rushes	518	389	454	511	514	414	435	442	454	466	467	441	478	442
Net Yds. Gained	2319	1326	1858	2037	2110	1686	1602	1779	1759	1652	1925	1588	1551	1745
Avg. Gain	4.5	3.4	4.1	4.0	4.1	4.1	3.7	4.0	3.9	3.5	4.1	3.6	3.2	3.9
Avg. Yds. per Game	144.9	82.9	116.1	127.3	131.9	105.4	100.1	111.2	109.9	103.3	120.3	99.3	96.9	109.1
Passes Attempted	504	545	523	513	474	571	480	505	566	578	508	530	527	497
Completed	281	245	264	337	256	307	219	277	294	309	264	292	304	261
% Completed	55.8	45.0	50.5	65.7	54.0	53.8	45.6	54.9	51.9	53.5	52.0	55.1	57.7	52.5
Total Yds. Gained	3584	3399	3883	3672	2949	3694	2763	3579	3755	4443	3539	3284	3744	3744
Times Sacked	30	43	46	47	30	56	37	31	52	42	39	42	20	43
Yds. Lost	211	365	327	393	216	394	274	252	428	296	295	297	140	305
Net Yds. Gained	3373	3034	3556	3279	2733	3300	2489	3327	3327	4147	3244	2987	3604	3439
Avg. Yds. per Game	210.8	189.6	222.3	204.9	170.8	206.3	155.6	207.9	207.9	259.2	202.8	186.7	225.3	214.9
Net Yds. per Pass Play	6.32	5.16	6.25	5.86	5.42	5.26	4.81	6.21	5.38	6.69	5.93	5.22	6.59	6.37
Yds. Gained per Comp.	12.75	13.87	14.71	10.90	11.52	12.03	12.62	12.92	12.77	14.38	13.41	11.25	12.32	14.34
Combined Net Yds. Gained	5692	4360	5414	5316	4843	4986	4091	5106	5086	5799	5169	4575	5155	5184
% Total Yds. Rushing	40.7	30.4	34.3	38.3	43.6	33.8	39.2	34.8	34.6	28.5	37.2	34.7	30.1	33.7
% Total Yds. Passing	59.3	69.6	65.7	61.7	56.4	66.2	60.8	65.2	65.4	71.5	62.8	65.3	69.9	66.3
Avg. Yds. per Game	355.8	272.5	338.4	332.3	302.7	311.6	255.7	319.1	317.9	362.4	323.1	285.9	322.2	324.0
Ball Control Plays	1052	977	1023	1071	1018	1041	952	978	1072	1086	1014	1013	1025	982
Avg. Yds. per Play	5.4	4.5	5.3	5.0	4.8	4.8	4.3	5.2	4.7	5.3	5.1	4.5	5.0	5.3
Avg. Time of Poss.	31:52	26:58	29:19	32:33	30:44	28:51	28:55	27:22	30:36	28:51	28:33	29:29	31:00	29:03
Third Down Efficiency	40.2	31.5	39.4	45.6	35.3	34.1	29.1	36.0	38.9	33.6	35.7	39.1	44.5	37.3
Intercepted by	24	26	10	15	20	22	36	17	15	32	16	22	21	14
Yds. Returned by	185	237	67	247	224	281	589	295	292	371	88	88	283	193
Returned for TD	1	0	1	2	0	1	5	0	2	0	0	0	1	0

	Atl.	Chi.	Dall.	Det.	G.B.	Rams	Minn.	N.O.	N.Y.G.	Phil.	Phx.	S.F.	T.B.	Wash.
Punts	73	90	86	74	76	93	96	70	93	85	83	86	77	79
Yds. Punted	2893	3622	3574	2915	2859	3714	4059	2815	3697	3209	3414	3522	3004	3116
Avg. Yds. per Punt	39.6	40.2	41.6	39.4	37.6	39.9	42.3	40.2	39.8	37.8	41.1	41.0	39.0	39.4
Punt Returns	51	40	37	57	39	43	39	39	38	47	41	47	38	39
Yds. Returned	297	447	239	483	314	347	405	248	303	393	416	426	273	448
Avg. Yds. per Return	5.8	11.2	6.5	8.5	8.1	8.1	10.4	6.4	8.0	8.4	10.1	9.1	7.2	11.5
Returned for TD	0	0	0	1	0	0	0	0	0	0	1	0	0	1
Kickoff Returns	48	56	56	56	49	81	81	43	73	63	65	73	52	61
Yds. Returned	982	1130	1060	1076	966	1563	1622	823	1269	1266	1379	1362	1129	1111
Avg. Yds. per Return	20.5	20.2	18.9	19.2	19.7	19.3	20.0	19.1	17.4	20.1	21.2	18.7	21.7	18.2
Returned for TD	0	0	0	0	0	1	0	0	0	0	1	0	0	0
Fumbles	29	17	24	35	33	36	36	27	36	28	27	30	29	23
Lost	14	9	9	21	21	15	17	15	18	12	13	16	12	8
Out of Bounds	3	0	0	1	1	1	3	0	2	4	1	2	1	2
Own Rec. for TD	0	0	0	0	0	0	0	0	1	0	0	0	0	1
Opp. Rec. by	18	19	13	15	26	16	12	16	13	9	16	12	16	21
Opp. Rec. for TD	1	1	1	0	1	3	0	0	0	2	0	0	0	2
Penalties	92	102	92	106	112	111	91	77	116	115	103	76	105	91
Yds. Penalized	761	804	772	869	903	937	753	628	902	897	770	603	872	711
Total Points Scored	315	215	381	313	315	293	233	283	304	319	398	294	350	387
Total TDs	34	25	44	34	34	35	24	29	33	37	51	34	42	46
TDs Rushing	14	5	13	16	17	12	10	7	8	11	19	8	21	17
TDs Passing	17	18	30	17	12	17	12	19	23	23	30	25	19	24
TDs on Ret. and Rec.	3	2	1	1	5	6	2	3	2	3	2	1	2	5
Extra Points	31	22	41	32	34	35	22	28	31	35	47	34	42	43
Safeties	1	2	2	1	1	0	2	0	0	1	3	1	1	1
Field Goals Made	26	13	24	25	25	16	21	27	25	20	13	18	18	22
Field Goals Attempted	36	22	29	29	35	23	25	34	33	29	22	24	30	36
% Successful	72.2	59.1	82.8	86.2	71.4	69.6	84.0	79.4	75.8	69.0	59.1	75.0	60.0	61.1

AFC, NFC, and NFL Summary

	AFC Offense Total	AFC Offense Average	AFC Defense Total	AFC Defense Average	NFC Offense Total	NFC Offense Average	NFC Defense Total	NFC Defense Average	NFL Total	NFL Average
First Downs	4241	302.9	4401	314.4	4233	302.4	4073	290.9	8474	302.6
Rushing	1690	120.7	1759	125.6	1500	107.1	1431	102.2	3190	113.9
Passing	2199	157.1	2299	164.2	2414	172.4	2314	165.3	4613	164.8
Penalty	352	25.1	343	24.5	319	22.8	328	23.4	671	24.0
Rushes	6930	495.0	7156	511.1	6651	475.1	6425	458.9	13,581	485.0
Net Yds. Gained	28,108	2007.7	29,458	2104.1	26,287	1877.6	24,937	1781.2	54,395	1942.7
Avg. Gain	—	4.1	—	4.1	—	4.0	—	3.9	—	4.0
Avg. Yds. per Game	—	125.5	—	131.5	—	117.4	—	111.3	—	121.4
Passes Attempted	6761	482.9	6810	486.4	7370	526.4	7321	522.9	14,131	504.7
Completed	3647	260.5	3760	268.6	4023	287.4	3910	279.3	7670	273.9
% Completed	—	53.9	—	55.2	—	54.6	—	53.4	—	54.3
Total Yds. Gained	46,826	3344.7	47,603	3400.2	50,809	3629.2	50,032	3573.7	97,635	3487.0
Times Sacked	449	32.1	477	34.1	586	41.9	558	39.9	1035	37.0
Yds. Lost	3461	247.2	3547	253.4	4279	305.6	4193	299.5	7740	276.4
Net Yds. Gained	43,365	3097.5	44,056	3146.9	46,530	3323.6	45,839	3274.2	89,895	3210.5
Avg. Yds. per Game	—	193.6	—	196.7	—	207.7	—	204.6	—	200.7
Net Yds. per Pass Play	—	6.01	—	6.05	—	5.85	—	5.82	—	5.93
Yds. Gained per Comp.	—	12.84	—	12.66	—	12.63	—	12.80	—	12.73
Combined Net Yds. Gained	71,473	5105.2	73,514	5251.0	72,817	5201.2	70,776	5055.4	144,290	5153.2
% Total Yds. Rushing	—	39.3	—	40.1	—	36.1	—	35.2	—	37.7
% Total Yds. Passing	—	60.7	—	59.9	—	63.9	—	64.8	—	62.3
Avg. Yds. per Game	—	319.1	—	328.2	—	325.1	—	316.0	—	322.1
Ball Control Plays	14,140	1010.0	14,443	1031.6	14,607	1043.4	14,304	1021.7	28,747	1026.7
Avg. Yds. per Play	—	5.1	—	5.1	—	5.0	—	4.9	—	5.0
Third Down Efficiency	—	38.8	—	40.6	—	39.0	—	37.2	—	38.9

	AFC Offense Total	AFC Offense Average	AFC Defense Total	AFC Defense Average	NFC Offense Total	NFC Offense Average	NFC Defense Total	NFC Defense Average	NFL Total	NFL Average
Interceptions	263	18.8	273	19.5	290	20.7	280	20.0	553	19.8
Yds. Returned	3410	243.6	3606	257.6	3440	245.7	3244	231.7	6850	244.6
Returned for TD	14	1.0	13	0.9	13	0.9	14	1.0	27	1.0
Punts	1024	73.1	1018	72.7	1155	82.5	1161	82.9	2179	77.8
Yds. Punted	41,627	2973.4	41,106	2936.1	45,892	3278.0	46,413	3315.2	87,519	3125.7
Avg. Yds. per Punt	—	40.7	—	40.4	—	39.7	—	40.0	—	40.2
Punt Returns	514	36.7	538	38.4	619	44.2	595	42.5	1133	40.5
Yds. Returned	4406	314.7	4578	327.0	5211	372.2	5039	359.9	9617	343.5
Avg. Yds. per Return	—	8.6	—	8.5	—	8.4	—	8.5	—	8.5
Returned for TD	2	0.1	3	0.2	4	0.3	3	0.2	6	0.2
Kickoff Returns	840	60.0	838	59.9	855	61.1	857	61.2	1695	60.5
Yds. Returned	17,397	1242.6	17,082	1220.1	16,423	1173.1	16,738	1195.6	33,820	1207.9
Avg. Yds. per Return	—	20.7	—	20.4	—	19.2	—	19.5	—	20.0
Returned for TD	8	0.6	6	0.4	0	0.0	2	0.1	8	0.3
Fumbles	399	28.5	414	29.6	425	30.4	410	29.3	824	29.4
Lost	212	15.1	190	13.6	200	14.3	222	15.9	412	14.7
Out of Bounds	24	1.7	19	1.4	16	1.1	21	1.5	40	1.4
Own Rec. for TD	1	0.1	1	0.1	2	0.1	2	0.1	3	0.1
Opp. Rec.	212	15.1	190	13.6	200	14.3	222	15.9	412	14.7
Opp. Rec. for TD	8	0.6	6	0.4	9	0.6	11	0.8	17	0.6
Penalties	1394	99.6	1401	100.1	1396	99.7	1389	99.2	2790	99.6
Yds. Penalized	11,341	810.1	11,464	818.9	11,305	807.5	11,182	798.7	22,646	808.8
Total Points Scored	4612	329.4	4675	333.9	4463	318.8	4400	314.3	9075	324.1
Total TDs	533	38.1	549	39.2	518	37.0	502	35.9	1051	37.5
TDs Rushing	226	16.1	246	17.6	198	14.1	178	12.7	424	15.1
TDs Passing	268	19.1	270	19.3	288	20.6	286	20.4	556	19.9
TDs on Ret. and Rec.	39	2.8	33	2.4	32	2.3	38	2.7	71	2.5
Extra Points	509	36.4	527	37.6	495	35.4	477	34.1	1004	35.9
Safeties	10	0.7	10	0.7	16	1.1	16	1.1	26	0.9
Field Goals Made	295	21.1	278	19.9	276	19.7	293	20.9	571	20.4
Field Goals Attempted	406	29.0	389	27.8	390	27.9	407	29.1	796	28.4
% Successful	—	72.7	—	71.5	—	70.8	—	72.0	—	71.7

Club Leaders

	Offense	Defense
First Downs	Cin. 351	Minn. 243
Rushing	Cin. 159	Chi. 76
Passing	Mia. 218	Minn. 132
Penalty	Den. 36	Three with 15
Rushes	N.E. 588	Chi. 389
Net Yds. Gained	Cin. 2710	Chi. 1326
Avg. Gain	Cin. 4.8	T.B. 3.2
Passes Attempted	Mia. 621	K.C. 410
Completed	Mia. 363	K.C. 214
% Completed	Rams 59.8	Chi. 45.0
Total Yds. Gained	Mia. 4557	K.C. 2591
Times Sacked	Mia. 7	Rams 56
Yds. Lost	Mia. 41	N.Y.G. 428
Net Yds. Gained	Mia. 4516	K.C. 2434
Net Yds. per Pass Play	Cin. 7.93	Minn. 4.81
Yds. Gained per Comp.	Raiders 16.00	Det. 10.90
Combined Net Yds. Gained	Cin. 6057	Chi. 4360
% Total Yds. Rushing	N.E. 49.4	T.B. 30.1
% Total Yds. Passing	Mia. 78.9	K.C. 48.4
Ball Control Plays	Phil. & Phx. 1102	Minn. 952
Avg. Yds. per Play	Cin. 6.15	Minn. 4.30
Avg. Time of Poss.	Chi. 33:02	—
Third Down Efficiency	N.O. 45.8	Minn. 29.1
Interceptions	—	Minn. 36
Yds. Returned	—	Minn. 589
Returned for TD	—	Minn. 5
Punts	Phil. 104	—
Yds. Punted	Phil. 4125	—
Avg. Yds. per Punt	Den. 43.8	—
Punt Returns	Minn. 59	Cin. & Clev. 32
Yds. Returned	S.F. 612	N.Y.J. 201
Avg. Yds. per Return	N.O. 11.8	Sea. 5.6
Returned for TD	S.F. 2	—
Kickoff Returns	Pitt. & Wash. 74	N.O. 43
Yds. Returned	Pitt. 1575	N.O. 823
Avg. Yds. per Return	S.D. 25.2	Buff. 16.2
Returned for TD	Pitt. & S.D. 2	—
Total Points Scored	Cin. 448	Chi. 215
Total TDs	Cin. 59	Minn. 24
TDs Rushing	Cin. 27	Chi. 5
TDs Passing	Rams 31	Three with 12
TDs on Ret. and Rec.	Minn. 7	N.E. & N.Y.J. 0
Extra Points	Cin. 56	Chi. & Minn. 22
Safeties	K.C. 3	—
Field Goals Made	Buff. 32	Buff. 12
Field Goals Attempted	S.F. 38	Hou. 18
% Successful	Det. 95.2	Buff. 50.0

National Football League Club Rankings by Yards

	Offense			Defense		
Team	**Total**	**Rush**	**Pass**	**Total**	**Rush**	**Pass**
Atlanta	25	14	25	25	25	21
Buffalo	12	7	15	4	12	4
Chicago	11	3	20	2	*1	9
Cincinnati	*1	*1	11	15	18	10
Cleveland	18	24	9	6	15	6
Dallas	9	16	7	20	13	24
Denver	8	19	6	22	27	7
Detroit	28	27	28	18	17	15
Green Bay	24	26	13	7	20	5
Houston	14	4T	22	8	4	13
Indianapolis	21	4T	24	17	8	25
Kansas City	22	22	16	10	28	*1
Los Angeles Raiders	19	18	17	19	23	11
Los Angeles Rams	3	15	3	9	7	17
Miami	5	28	*1	26	26	14
Minnesota	7	20	4	*1	5	2
New England	27	9	27	5	19	3
New Orleans	16	11	18	12	11	18T
New York Giants	20	23	14	11	10	18T
New York Jets	13	8	19	23	21	23
Philadelphia	10	17	8	27	6	28
Phoenix	4	13	5	14	16	12
Pittsburgh	15	6	21	28	14	27
San Diego	26	12	26	21	22	16
San Francisco	2	2	10	3	3	8
Seattle	23	10	23	24	24	20
Tampa Bay	17	21	12	13	2	26
Washington	6	25	2	16	9	22

**—League leader*

T—Tied for position

AFC Takeaways/Giveaways

	Takeaways			Giveaways			
	Int.	**Fum.**	**Total**	**Int.**	**Fum.**	**Total**	**Net Diff.**
New York Jets	24	16	40	11	16	27	13
Cincinnati	22	14	36	14	13	27	9
Houston	22	20	42	18	17	35	7
Seattle	22	18	40	20	14	34	6
Indianapolis	15	20	35	22	8	30	5
Los Angeles Raiders	17	17	34	20	13	33	1
Buffalo	15	17	32	17	16	33	− 1
Cleveland	20	11	31	17	16	33	− 2
Kansas City	18	13	31	21	12	33	− 2
New England	20	15	35	28	10	38	− 3
Miami	16	15	31	23	12	35	− 4
Denver	16	13	29	22	12	34	− 5
Pittsburgh	20	13	33	20	19	39	− 6
San Diego	16	10	26	20	12	32	− 6

NFC Takeaways/Giveaways

	Takeaways			Giveaways			
	Int.	**Fum.**	**Total**	**Int.**	**Fum.**	**Total**	**Net Diff.**
Minnesota	36	17	53	18	12	30	23
Philadelphia	32	12	44	17	9	26	18
San Francisco	22	16	38	14	12	26	12
New York Giants	15	18	33	14	13	27	6
Detroit	15	21	36	18	15	33	3
Los Angeles Rams	22	15	37	18	16	34	3
Atlanta	24	14	38	19	18	37	1
Chicago	26	9	35	15	19	34	1
New Orleans	17	15	32	16	16	32	0
Phoenix	16	13	29	19	16	35	− 6
Green Bay	20	21	41	24	26	50	− 9
Tampa Bay	21	12	33	36	16	52	−19
Dallas	10	9	19	27	13	40	−21
Washington	14	8	22	25	21	46	−24

Scoring

Points
AFC: 129—Scott Norwood, Buffalo
NFC: 121—Mike Cofer, San Francisco

Touchdowns
NFC: 18—Greg Bell, L.A. Rams
AFC: 15—Eric Dickerson, Indianapolis
15—Ickey Woods, Cincinnati

Extra Points
AFC: 56—Jim Breech, Cincinnati
NFC: 48—Chuck Nelson, Minnesota

Field Goals
AFC: 32—Scott Norwood, Buffalo
NFC: 27—Mike Cofer, San Francisco

Field Goal Attempts
NFC: 38—Mike Cofer, San Francisco
AFC: 37—Scott Norwood, Buffalo

Longest Field Goal
AFC: 53—Dean Biasucci, Indianapolis vs. Chicago, September 11
NFC: 53—Donald Igwebuike, Tampa Bay at Green Bay, September 11

Most Points, Game
AFC: 24—Eric Dickerson, Indianapolis vs. Denver, October 31 (4 TD)
24—Curt Warner, Seattle vs. Denver, December 11 (4 TD)
NFC: 18—Jerry Rice, San Francisco at Seattle, September 25 (3 TD)
18—Greg Bell, L.A. Rams vs. Phoenix, October 2 (3 TD)
18—Kelvin Bryant, Washington at Dallas, October 9 (3 TD)
18—Brent Fullwood, Green Bay vs. New England, October 9 (3 TD)
18—Roger Craig, San Francisco at L.A. Rams, October 16 (3 TD)
18—Roger Craig, San Francisco at San Diego, November 27 (3 TD)
18—Ottis Anderson, N.Y. Giants vs. Phoenix, December 4 (3 TD)
18—Michael Irvin, Dallas at Washington, December 11 (3 TD)
18—Damone Johnson, L.A. Rams at San Francisco, December 18 (3 TD)

Team Leaders, Points
AFC: BUFFALO: 129, Scott Norwood; CINCINNATI: 90, Ickey Woods; CLEVELAND: 104, Matt Bahr; DENVER: 105, Rich Karlis; HOUSTON: 114, Tony Zendejas; INDIANAPOLIS: 114, Dean Biasucci; KANSAS CITY: 104, Nick Lowery; L.A. RAIDERS: 91, Chris Bahr; MIAMI: 84, Mark Clayton; NEW ENGLAND: 36, Bob Perryman; N.Y. JETS: 112, Pat Leahy; PITTSBURGH: 118, Gary Anderson; SAN DIEGO: 39, Vince Abbott; SEATTLE: 105, Norm Johnson.
NFC: ATLANTA: 82, Greg Davis; CHICAGO: 82, Kevin Butler; DALLAS: 63, Roger Ruzek; DETROIT: 82, Ed Murray; GREEN BAY: 48, Brent Fullwood; L.A. RAMS: 117, Mike Lansford; MINNESOTA: 108, Chuck Nelson; NEW ORLEANS: 110, Morten Andersen; N.Y. GIANTS: 67, Paul McFadden; PHILADELPHIA: 87, Luis Zendejas; PHOENIX: 78, Al Del Greco; SAN FRANCISCO: 121, Mike Cofer; TAMPA BAY: 78, Donald Igwebuike; WASHINGTON: 97, Chip Lohmiller.

Team Champions
AFC: 448—Cincinnati
NFC: 407—L.A. Rams

AFC Scoring—Team

	TD	TDR	TDP	TD Misc.	PAT	PAT Att.	FG	FG Att.	SAF	TP
Cincinnati	59	27	28	4	56	59	12	18	1	448
Houston	51	26	21	4	48	51	22	34	2	424
N.Y. Jets	43	19	20	4	43	43	23	28	1	372
Indianapolis	40	23	15	2	39	40	25	32	0	354
Seattle	39	14	22	3	39	39	22	28	0	339
Pittsburgh	36	17	15	4	34	36	28	36	1	336
Buffalo	33	15	15	3	33	33	32	37	1	329
Denver	37	13	24	0	36	37	23	36	0	327
L.A. Raiders	39	15	21	3	37	39	18	29	0	325
Miami	41	11	29	1	37	41	12	23	0	319
Cleveland	33	10	19	4	32	33	24	29	1	304
Kansas City	24	8	16	0	23	24	27	32	3	254
New England	31	17	12	2	25	31	13	24	0	250
San Diego	27	11	11	5	27	27	14	20	0	231
AFC Total	533	226	268	39	509	533	295	406	10	4612
AFC Average	38.1	16.1	19.1	2.8	36.4	38.1	21.1	29.0	0.7	329.4

NFC Scoring—Team

	TD	TDR	TDP	TD Misc.	PAT	PAT Att.	FG	FG Att.	SAF	TP
L.A. Rams	48	16	31	1	45	48	24	32	1	407
Minnesota	49	22	20	7	48	49	20	25	2	406
Philadelphia	44	17	25	2	42	43	23	32	2	379
San Francisco	41	18	21	2	40	41	27	38	1	369
N.Y. Giants	41	15	22	4	39	41	24	30	1	359
Washington	41	8	33	0	40	41	19	26	1	345
Phoenix	44	15	26	3	42	44	12	21	1	344
Chicago	38	25	13	0	37	38	15	19	1	312
New Orleans	33	9	21	3	32	33	26	36	2	312
Dallas	32	10	21	1	32	32	13	25	1	265
Tampa Bay	28	11	16	1	28	28	21	30	1	261
Atlanta	27	11	13	3	25	27	19	30	0	244
Green Bay	29	14	13	2	23	29	13	25	2	240
Detroit	23	7	13	3	22	23	20	21	0	220
NFC Total	518	198	288	32	495	517	276	390	16	4463
NFC Average	37.0	14.1	20.6	2.3	35.4	36.9	19.7	27.9	1.1	318.8
League Total	1051	424	556	71	1004	1050	571	796	26	9075
League Avg.	37.5	15.1	19.9	2.5	35.9	37.5	20.4	28.4	0.9	324.1

NFL Top 10 Scorers—Touchdowns

	TD	TDR	TDP	TD Misc.	TP
Bell, Greg, L.A. Rams	18	16	2	0	108
Dickerson, Eric, Indianapolis	15	14	1	0	90
Woods, Ickey, Cincinnati	15	15	0	0	90
Brooks, James, Cincinnati	14	8	6	0	84
Clayton, Mark, Miami	14	0	14	0	84
Riddick, Robb, Buffalo	14	12	1	1	84
Anderson, Neal, Chicago	12	12	0	0	72
Hampton, Lorenzo, Miami	12	9	3	0	72
Sanders, Ricky, Washington	12	0	12	0	72
Warner, Curt, Seattle	12	10	2	0	72

NFL Top 10 Scorers — Kicking

	PAT	PAT Att.	FG	FG Att.	TP
Norwood, Scott, Buffalo	33	33	32	37	129
Cofer, Mike, San Francisco	40	41	27	38	121
Anderson, Gary, Pittsburgh	34	35	28	36	118
Lansford, Mike, L.A. Rams	45	48	24	32	117
Biasucci, Dean, Indianapolis	39	40	25	32	114
Zendejas, Tony, Houston	48	50	22	34	114
Leahy, Pat, N.Y. Jets	43	43	23	28	112
Andersen, Morten, New Orleans	32	33	26	36	110
Nelson, Chuck, Minnesota	48	49	20	25	108
Johnson, Norm, Seattle	39	39	22	28	105
Karlis, Rich, Denver	36	37	23	36	105

AFC Scoring—Individual

Kickers	PAT	PAT Att.	FG	FG Att.	TP
Norwood, Scott, Buffalo	33	33	32	37	129
Anderson, Gary, Pittsburgh	34	35	28	36	118
Biasucci, Dean, Indianapolis	39	40	25	32	114
Zendejas, Tony, Houston	48	50	22	34	114
Leahy, Pat, N.Y. Jets	43	43	23	28	112
Johnson, Norm, Seattle	39	39	22	28	105
Karlis, Rich, Denver	36	37	23	36	105
Bahr, Matt, Cleveland	32	33	24	29	104
Lowery, Nick, Kansas City	23	23	27	32	104
Bahr, Chris, L.A. Raiders	37	39	18	29	91
Breech, Jim, Cincinnati	56	59	11	16	89
Reveiz, Fuad, Miami	31	32	8	12	55
Abbott, Vince, San Diego	15	15	8	12	39
Staurovsky, Jason, New England	14	15	7	11	35
DeLine, Steve, San Diego	12	12	6	8	30
Garcia, Teddy, New England	11	16	6	13	29
Franklin, Tony, Miami	6	7	4	11	18
Johnson, Lee, Cincinnati	0	0	1	2	3

Non-Kickers	TD	TDR	TDP	TD Misc.	TP
Dickerson, Eric, Indianapolis	15	14	1	0	90
Woods, Ickey, Cincinnati	15	15	0	0	90
Brooks, James, Cincinnati	14	8	6	0	84
Clayton, Mark, Miami	14	0	14	0	84
Riddick, Robb, Buffalo	14	12	1	1	84
Hampton, Lorenzo, Miami	12	9	3	0	72
Warner, Curt, Seattle	12	10	2	0	72
Rozier, Mike, Houston	11	10	1	0	66
Hector, Johnny, N.Y. Jets	10	10	0	0	60
Hill, Drew, Houston	10	0	10	0	60
Brown, Eddie, Cincinnati	9	0	9	0	54
Pinkett, Allen, Houston	9	7	2	0	54
Smith, Steve, L.A. Raiders	9	3	6	0	54
Allen, Marcus, L.A. Raiders	8	7	1	0	48
Blades, Brian, Seattle	8	0	8	0	48
Langhorne, Reggie, Cleveland	8	1	7	0	48
Brown, Tim, L.A. Raiders	7	1	5	1	42
McNeil, Freeman, N.Y. Jets	7	6	1	0	42
Paige, Stephone, Kansas City	7	0	7	0	42
Walker, Wesley, N.Y. Jets	7	0	7	0	42
Williams, John L., Seattle	7	4	3	0	42
Brister, Bubby, Pittsburgh	6	6	0	0	36
Hoge, Merril, Pittsburgh	6	3	3	0	36
Jackson, Mark, Denver	6	0	6	0	36
Lipps, Louis, Pittsburgh	6	1	5	0	36
McGee, Tim, Cincinnati	6	0	6	0	36
Palmer, Paul, Kansas City	6	2	4	0	36
Perryman, Bob, New England	6	6	0	0	36

	TD	TDR	TDP	TD Misc.	TP
Reed, Andre, Buffalo	6	0	6	0	36
Sewell, Steve, Denver	6	1	5	0	36
Byner, Earnest, Cleveland	5	3	2	0	30
Carter, Rodney, Pittsburgh	5	3	2	0	30
Dorsett, Tony, Denver	5	5	0	0	30
Fryar, Irving, New England	5	0	5	0	30
Givins, Ernest, Houston	5	0	5	0	30
Jensen, Jim, Miami	5	0	5	0	30
Johnson, Vance, Denver	5	0	5	0	30
Moon, Warren, Houston	5	5	0	0	30
Shuler, Mickey, N.Y. Jets	5	0	5	0	30
Stephens, John, New England	5	4	0	1	30
Toon, Al, N.Y. Jets	5	0	5	0	30
Verdin, Clarence, Indianapolis	5	0	4	1	30
Winder, Sammy, Denver	5	4	1	0	30
Bouza, Matt, Indianapolis	4	0	4	0	24
Butler, Raymond, Seattle	4	0	4	0	24
Early, Quinn, San Diego	4	0	4	0	24
Fernandez, Mervyn, L.A. Raiders	4	0	4	0	24
Harmon, Ronnie, Buffalo	4	1	3	0	24
Kay, Clarence, Denver	4	0	4	0	24
Malone, Mark, San Diego	4	4	0	0	24
Miller, Anthony, San Diego	4	0	3	1	24
Morgan, Stanley, New England	4	0	4	0	24
Anderson, Gary, San Diego	3	3	0	0	18
Bentley, Albert, Indianapolis	3	2	1	0	18
Brooks, Bill, Indianapolis	3	0	3	0	18
Carson, Carlos, Kansas City	3	0	3	0	18
Chandler, Chris, Indianapolis	3	3	0	0	18
Edmunds, Ferrell, Miami	3	0	3	0	18
Holman, Rodney, Cincinnati	3	0	3	0	18
Jackson, Bo, L.A. Raiders	3	3	0	0	18
Jackson, Earnest, Pittsburgh	3	3	0	0	18
Mack, Kevin, Cleveland	3	3	0	0	18
Okoye, Christian, Kansas City	3	3	0	0	18
Redden, Barry, San Diego	3	3	0	0	18
Slaughter, Webster, Cleveland	3	0	3	0	18
Stradford, Troy, Miami	3	2	1	0	18
Vick, Roger, N.Y. Jets	3	3	0	0	18
Wilson, Stanley, Cincinnati	3	2	1	0	18
Banks, Fred, Miami	2	0	2	0	12
Boyer, Mark, Indianapolis	2	0	2	0	12
Dawson, Lin, New England	2	0	2	0	12
Dupard, Reggie, New England	2	2	0	0	12
Flutie, Darren, San Diego	2	0	2	0	12
Fontenot, Herman, Cleveland	2	0	1	1	12
Gault, Willie, L.A. Raiders	2	0	2	0	12
Highsmith, Alonzo, Houston	2	2	0	0	12
Holland, Jamie, San Diego	2	0	1	1	12
Jennings, Stanford, Cincinnati	2	1	0	1	12
Junkin, Trey, L.A. Raiders	2	0	2	0	12
Largent, Steve, Seattle	2	0	2	0	12
Manoa, Tim, Cleveland	2	2	0	0	12
McMillan, Erik, N.Y. Jets	2	0	0	2	12
Mobley, Orson, Denver	2	0	2	0	12
Newsome, Ozzie, Cleveland	2	0	2	0	12
Rolle, Butch, Buffalo	2	0	2	0	12
Saxon, James, Kansas City	2	2	0	0	12
Sohn, Kurt, N.Y. Jets	2	0	2	0	12
Stone, Dwight, Pittsburgh	2	0	1	1	12
Tatupu, Mosi, New England	2	2	0	0	12
Thomas, Thurman, Buffalo	2	2	0	0	12
Townsend, Greg, L.A. Raiders	2	0	0	2	12
Turner, Ricky, Indianapolis	2	2	0	0	12
Willhite, Gerald, Denver	2	2	0	0	12
Adams, Curtis, San Diego	1	1	0	0	6
Barker, Leo, Cincinnati	1	0	0	1	6
Bennett, Roy, San Diego	1	0	0	1	6
Billups, Lewis, Cincinnati	1	0	0	1	6
Blackledge, Todd, Pittsburgh	1	1	0	0	6
Bolden, Rickey, Cleveland	1	0	1	0	6
Brennan, Brian, Cleveland	1	0	1	0	6
Brown, Steve, Houston	1	0	0	1	6
Browner, Keith, San Diego	1	0	0	1	6
Bryant, Domingo, Houston	1	0	0	1	6
Burkett, Chris, Buffalo	1	0	1	0	6
Carlson, Cody, Houston	1	1	0	0	6
Clark, Louis, Seattle	1	0	1	0	6
Collinsworth, Cris, Cincinnati	1	0	1	0	6
Daniel, Eugene, Indianapolis	1	0	0	1	6
Dean, Vernon, Seattle	1	0	0	1	6
DeBerg, Steve, Kansas City	1	1	0	0	6
Dishman, Cris, Houston	1	0	0	1	6
Drewrey, Willie, Houston	1	0	1	0	6
Duncan, Curtis, Houston	1	0	1	0	6
Duper, Mark, Miami	1	0	1	0	6
Elway, John, Denver	1	1	0	0	6
Esiason, Boomer, Cincinnati	1	1	0	0	6
Flutie, Doug, New England	1	1	0	0	6
Fulcher, David, Cincinnati	1	0	0	1	6
Gothard, Preston, Pittsburgh	1	0	1	0	6
Green, Jacob, Seattle	1	0	0	1	6
Grogan, Steve, New England	1	1	0	0	6
Harry, Emile, Kansas City	1	0	1	0	6
Hayes, Jonathan, Kansas City	1	0	1	0	6
Hillary, Ira, Cincinnati	1	0	1	0	6
Hobley, Liffort, Miami	1	0	0	1	6
Hogeboom, Gary, Indianapolis	1	1	0	0	6
James, Craig, New England	1	1	0	0	6
James, Lionel, San Diego	1	0	1	0	6
Jeffires, Haywood, Houston	1	0	1	0	6
Johnson, Flip, Buffalo	1	0	1	0	6
Jones, Cedric, New England	1	0	1	0	6
Jordan, Darin, Pittsburgh	1	0	0	1	6
Kelso, Mark, Buffalo	1	0	0	1	6
Kosar, Bernie, Cleveland	1	1	0	0	6
Lockett, Charles, Pittsburgh	1	0	1	0	6
Martin, Mike, Cincinnati	1	0	1	0	6
Martin, Sammy, New England	1	0	0	1	6
Metzelaars, Pete, Buffalo	1	0	1	0	6
Minnifield, Frank, Cleveland	1	0	0	1	6
Nattiel, Ricky, Denver	1	0	1	0	6
Pease, Brent, Houston	1	1	0	0	6
Perry, Michael Dean, Cleveland	1	0	0	1	6
Schroeder, Jay, L.A. Raiders	1	1	0	0	6
Seale, Sam, San Diego	1	0	0	1	6
Seals, Leon, Buffalo	1	0	0	1	6
Skansi, Paul, Seattle	1	0	1	0	6
Spagnola, John, Seattle	1	0	1	0	6
Strachan, Steve, L.A. Raiders	1	0	1	0	6
Taylor, Terry, Seattle	1	0	0	1	6
Tennell, Derek, Cleveland	1	0	1	0	6
Thompson, Weegie, Pittsburgh	1	0	1	0	6
Townsell, JoJo, N.Y. Jets	1	0	0	1	6
Washington, Brian, Cleveland	1	0	0	1	6
Weathers, Clarence, Cleveland	1	0	1	0	6
White, Lorenzo, Houston	1	0	0	1	6
Williams, Warren, Pittsburgh	1	0	1	0	6
Wonsley, George, Indianapolis	1	1	0	0	6
Woodruff, Dwayne, Pittsburgh	1	0	0	1	6
Woodson, Rod, Pittsburgh	1	0	0	1	6
Zordich, Mike, N.Y. Jets	1	0	0	1	6
Buchanan, Charles, Cleveland	0	0	0	0	*2
Fairs, Eric, Houston	0	0	0	0	*2
Hackett, Dino, Kansas City	0	0	0	0	*2
Lewis, Albert, Kansas City	0	0	0	0	*2
Lyons, Marty, N.Y. Jets	0	0	0	0	*2
Maas, Bill, Kansas City	0	0	0	0	*2
Seale, Eugene, Houston	0	0	0	0	*2
Smith, Bruce, Buffalo	0	0	0	0	*2

**indicates safety scored.*

NFC Scoring—Individual

Kickers	PAT	PAT Att.	FG	FG Att.	TP
Cofer, Mike, San Francisco	40	41	27	38	121
Lansford, Mike, L.A. Rams	45	48	24	32	117
Andersen, Morten, New Orleans	32	33	26	36	110
Nelson, Chuck, Minnesota	48	49	20	25	108
Lohmiller, Chip, Washington	40	41	19	26	97
Zendejas, Luis, Dallas-Philadelphia	35	36	20	27	95
Butler, Kevin, Chicago	37	38	15	19	82
Davis, Greg, Atlanta	25	27	19	30	82
Murray, Ed, Detroit	22	23	20	21	82
Del Greco, Al, Phoenix	42	44	12	21	78
Igwebuike, Donald, Tampa Bay	21	21	19	25	78
McFadden, Paul, N.Y. Giants	25	27	14	19	67
Ruzek, Roger, Dallas	27	27	12	22	63
Allegre, Raul, N.Y. Giants	14	14	10	11	44
Zendejas, Max, Green Bay	17	19	9	16	44
Dorsey, Dean, Philadelphia-Green Bay	12	13	5	10	27
Dawson, Dale, Philadelphia-Green Bay	4	5	3	6	13
Carney, John, Tampa Bay	6	6	2	5	12
Burrow, Curtis, Green Bay	2	4	0	1	2
Criswell, Ray, Tampa Bay	1	1	0	0	1

Non-Kickers	TD	TDR	TDP	TD Misc.	TP
Bell, Greg, L.A. Rams	18	16	2	0	108
Anderson, Neal, Chicago	12	12	0	0	72
Sanders, Ricky, Washington	12	0	12	0	72
Byars, Keith, Philadelphia	10	6	4	0	60
Craig, Roger, San Francisco	10	9	1	0	60
Ellard, Henry, L.A. Rams	10	0	10	0	60
Rice, Jerry, San Francisco	10	1	9	0	60
Ferrell, Earl, Phoenix	9	7	2	0	54
Hill, Bruce, Tampa Bay	9	0	9	0	54
Anderson, Alfred, Minnesota	8	7	1	0	48
Anderson, Ottis, N.Y. Giants	8	8	0	0	48
Fullwood, Brent, Green Bay	8	7	1	0	48
Settle, John, Atlanta	8	7	1	0	48
Tate, Lars, Tampa Bay	8	7	1	0	48
Baker, Stephen, N.Y. Giants	7	0	7	0	42
Carter, Cris, Philadelphia	7	0	6	1	42

Non-Kickers	TD	TDR	TDP	TD Misc.	TP
Clark, Gary, Washington	7	0	7	0	42
Green, Roy, Phoenix	7	0	7	0	42
Hill, Lonzell, New Orleans	7	0	7	0	42
James, Garry, Detroit	7	5	2	0	42
Martin, Eric, New Orleans	7	0	7	0	42
Walker, Herschel, Dallas	7	5	2	0	42
Alexander, Ray, Dallas	6	0	6	0	36
Bryant, Kelvin, Washington	6	1	5	0	36
Carter, Anthony, Minnesota	6	0	6	0	36
Cunningham, Randall, Philadelphia	6	6	0	0	36
Hilliard, Dalton, New Orleans	6	5	1	0	36
Jackson, Keith, Philadelphia	6	0	6	0	36
Johnson, Damone, L.A. Rams	6	0	6	0	36
Rice, Allen, Minnesota	6	6	0	0	36
Carrier, Mark, Tampa Bay	5	0	5	0	30
Cox, Aaron, L.A. Rams	5	0	5	0	30
Irvin, Michael, Dallas	5	0	5	0	30
Jones, Hassan, Minnesota	5	0	5	0	30
Jordan, Steve, Minnesota	5	0	5	0	30
Mandley, Pete, Detroit	5	1	4	0	30
Mitchell, Stump, Phoenix	5	4	1	0	30
Monk, Art, Washington	5	0	5	0	30
Morris, Joe, N.Y. Giants	5	5	0	0	30
Smith, J.T., Phoenix	5	0	5	0	30
Toney, Anthony, Philadelphia	5	4	1	0	30
Woodside, Keith, Green Bay	5	3	2	0	30
Awalt, Robert, Phoenix	4	0	4	0	24
Bavaro, Mark, N.Y. Giants	4	0	4	0	24
Gentry, Dennis, Chicago	4	1	3	0	24
Haynes, Michael, Atlanta	4	0	4	0	24
Manuel, Lionel, N.Y. Giants	4	0	4	0	24
McKinnon, Dennis, Chicago	4	1	3	0	24
McMahon, Jim, Chicago	4	4	0	0	24
Morris, Ron, Chicago	4	0	4	0	24
Novacek, Jay, Phoenix	4	0	4	0	24
Quick, Mike, Philadelphia	4	0	4	0	24
Taylor, John, San Francisco	4	0	2	2	24
Carthon, Maurice, N.Y. Giants	3	2	1	0	18
Chadwick, Jeff, Detroit	3	0	3	0	18
Fenney, Rick, Minnesota	3	3	0	0	18
Frank, John, San Francisco	3	0	3	0	18
Holohan, Pete, L.A. Rams	3	0	3	0	18
Jones, Ernie, Phoenix	3	0	3	0	18
Jordan, Tony, Phoenix	3	3	0	0	18
Martin, Kelvin, Dallas	3	0	3	0	18
Mayes, Rueben, New Orleans	3	3	0	0	18
McGee, Buford, L.A. Rams	3	0	3	0	18
Montana, Joe, San Francisco	3	3	0	0	18
Newsome, Tim, Dallas	3	3	0	0	18
Robinson, Stacy, N.Y. Giants	3	0	3	0	18
Sanders, Thomas, Chicago	3	3	0	0	18
Smith, Timmy, Washington	3	3	0	0	18
West, Ed, Green Bay	3	0	3	0	18
Wilson, Mike, San Francisco	3	0	3	0	18
Bailey, Stacey, Atlanta	2	0	2	0	12
Bland, Carl, Detroit	2	0	2	0	12
Clark, Robert, New Orleans	2	0	2	0	12
Delpino, Robert, L.A. Rams	2	0	2	0	12
Dixon, Floyd, Atlanta	2	0	2	0	12
Dozier, D.J., Minnesota	2	2	0	0	12
DuBose, Doug, San Francisco	2	2	0	0	12
Folsom, Steve, Dallas	2	0	2	0	12
Higdon, Alex, Atlanta	2	0	2	0	12
Jamison, George, Detroit	2	0	0	2	12
Johnson, Ron, Philadelphia	2	0	2	0	12
Jones, Brent, San Francisco	2	0	2	0	12
Lee, Carl, Minnesota	2	0	0	2	12
Matthews, Aubrey, Green Bay	2	0	2	0	12
Moorehead, Emery, Chicago	2	0	2	0	12
Morris, Jamie, Washington	2	2	0	0	12
Orr, Terry, Washington	2	0	2	0	12
Pelluer, Steve, Dallas	2	2	0	0	12
Perriman, Brett, New Orleans	2	0	2	0	12
Rathman, Tom, San Francisco	2	2	0	0	12
Suhey, Matt, Chicago	2	2	0	0	12
Wilson, Wade, Minnesota	2	2	0	0	12
Wright, Randy, Green Bay	2	2	0	0	12
Harris, Timothy, Green Bay	1	0	0	1	*10
Noonan, Danny, Dallas	1	0	0	1	*8
Simmons, Clyde, Philadelphia	1	0	0	1	*8
Allen, Anthony, Washington	1	0	1	0	6
Ashley, Walker Lee, Minnesota	1	0	0	1	6
Banks, Carl, N.Y. Giants	1	0	0	1	6
Burt, Jim, N.Y. Giants	1	0	0	1	6
Chandler, Thornton, Dallas	1	0	1	0	6
Clack, Darryl, Dallas	1	0	1	0	6
Davis, Kenneth, Green Bay	1	1	0	0	6
Didier, Clint, Green Bay	1	0	1	0	6
Dils, Steve, Atlanta	1	1	0	0	6
Edwards, Brad, Minnesota	1	0	0	1	6
Flynn, Tom, N.Y. Giants	1	0	0	1	6
Gann, Mike, Atlanta	1	0	0	1	6
Garrity, Gregg, Philadelphia	1	0	1	0	6
Gay, Everett, Dallas	1	0	1	0	6
Giles, Jimmie, Philadelphia	1	0	1	0	6
Gray, Jerry, L.A. Rams	1	0	0	1	6
Gray, Mel, New Orleans	1	0	0	1	6
Griffin, Keith, Washington	1	0	1	0	6
Gustafson, Jim, Minnesota	1	0	1	0	6
Hackett, Joey, Green Bay	1	0	1	0	6
Harbaugh, Jim, Chicago	1	1	0	0	6
Harris, Darryl, Minnesota	1	1	0	0	6
Heyward, Craig, New Orleans	1	1	0	0	6
Hilton, Carl, Minnesota	1	0	1	0	6
Hoage, Terry, Philadelphia	1	1	0	0	6
Howard, William, Tampa Bay	1	1	0	0	6
Ingram, Mark, N.Y. Giants	1	0	1	0	6
Johnson, Pepper, N.Y. Giants	1	0	0	1	6
Jordan, Buford, New Orleans	1	0	0	1	6
Junior, E.J., Phoenix	1	0	0	1	6
Lang, Gene, Atlanta	1	0	1	0	6
Lee, Gary, Detroit	1	0	1	0	6
Lewis, Leo, Minnesota	1	0	1	0	6
Lewis, Mark, Detroit	1	0	1	0	6
Lomax, Neil, Phoenix	1	1	0	0	6
Mack, Cedric, Phoenix	1	0	0	1	6
Majkowski, Don, Green Bay	1	1	0	0	6
Martin, Chris, Minnesota	1	0	0	1	6
Mason, Larry, Green Bay	1	0	1	0	6
McIntyre, Guy, San Francisco	1	0	1	0	6
Miller, Chris, Atlanta	1	1	0	0	6
Mitchell, Devon, Detroit	1	0	0	1	6
Moore, Robert, Atlanta	1	0	0	1	6
Mowatt, Zeke, N.Y. Giants	1	0	1	0	6
Murphy, Kevin, Tampa Bay	1	0	0	1	6
Muster, Brad, Chicago	1	0	1	0	6
Nelson, Darrin, Minnesota	1	1	0	0	6
Pillow, Frank, Tampa Bay	1	0	1	0	6
Pitts, Ron, Green Bay	1	0	0	1	6
Primus, James, Atlanta	1	1	0	0	6
Riggs, Gerald, Atlanta	1	1	0	0	6
Rypien, Mark, Washington	1	1	0	0	6
Saddler, Rod, Phoenix	1	0	0	1	6
Scales, Greg, New Orleans	1	0	1	0	6
Scott, Patrick, Green Bay	1	0	1	0	6
Sharpe, Sterling, Green Bay	1	0	1	0	6
Smith, Don, Tampa Bay	1	1	0	0	6
Solomon, Jesse, Minnesota	1	0	0	1	6
Testaverde, Vinny, Tampa Bay	1	1	0	0	6
Thomas, Henry, Minnesota	1	0	0	1	6
Tice, John, New Orleans	1	0	1	0	6
Tomczak, Mike, Chicago	1	1	0	0	6
Tuggle, Jessie, Atlanta	1	0	0	1	6
Turner, Odessa, N.Y. Giants	1	0	1	0	6
Waymer, Dave, New Orleans	1	0	0	1	6
Whisenhunt, Ken, Atlanta	1	0	1	0	6
Wilder, James, Tampa Bay	1	1	0	0	6
Williams, Doug, Washington	1	1	0	0	6
Williams, Scott, Detroit	1	1	0	0	6
Young, Steve, San Francisco	1	1	0	0	6
Caldwell, Ravin, Washington	0	0	0	0	*2
Collins, Mark, N.Y. Giants	0	0	0	0	*2
Goode, Kerry, Tampa Bay	0	0	0	0	*2
Greene, Kevin, L.A. Rams	0	0	0	0	*2
Haley, Charles, San Francisco	0	0	0	0	*2
Harvey, Ken, Phoenix	0	0	0	0	*2
Holt, Issiac, Minnesota	0	0	0	0	*2
Jackson, Rickey, New Orleans	0	0	0	0	*2
Jenkins, Izel, Philadelphia	0	0	0	0	*2
McMichael, Steve, Chicago	0	0	0	0	*2

**indicates safety scored.*

Field Goals

Best Percentage
NFC: .952—Ed Murray, Detroit
AFC: .865—Scott Norwood, Buffalo

Made
AFC: 32—Scott Norwood, Buffalo
NFC: 27—Mike Cofer, San Francisco

Attempts
NFC: 38—Mike Cofer, San Francisco
AFC: 37—Scott Norwood, Buffalo

Longest
AFC: 53—Dean Biasucci, Indianapolis
NFC: 53—Donald Igwebuike, Tampa Bay

Average Yards Made
AFC: 38.9—Tony Zendejas, Houston
NFC: 36.6—Max Zendejas, Green Bay

AFC Field Goals—Team

	Made	Att.	Pct.	Long
Buffalo	32	37	.865	49
Kansas City	27	32	.844	51
Cleveland	24	29	.828	47
N.Y. Jets	23	28	.821	48
Seattle	22	28	.786	47
Indianapolis	25	32	.781	53
Pittsburgh	28	36	.778	52
San Diego	14	20	.700	48
Cincinnati	12	18	.667	50
Houston	22	34	.647	52
Denver	23	36	.639	51
L.A. Raiders	18	29	.621	50
New England	13	24	.542	50
Miami	12	23	.522	51
AFC Totals	295	406	—	53
AFC Average	21.1	29.0	.727	—

NFC Field Goals—Team

	Made	Att.	Pct.	Long
Detroit	20	21	.952	48
Minnesota	20	25	.800	49
N.Y. Giants	24	30	.800	50
Chicago	15	19	.789	45
L.A. Rams	24	32	.750	49
Washington	19	26	.731	46
New Orleans	26	36	.722	51
Philadelphia	23	32	.719	50
San Francisco	27	38	.711	52
Tampa Bay	21	30	.700	53
Atlanta	19	30	.633	52
Phoenix	12	21	.571	51
Dallas	13	25	.520	50
Green Bay	13	25	.520	50
NFC Totals	276	390	—	53
NFC Average	19.7	27.9	.708	—
League Totals	571	796	—	53
League Average	20.4	28.4	.717	—

AFC Field Goals—Individual

	1-19	20-29	30-39	40-49	50 & Over	Totals	Avg. Yds. Att.	Avg. Yds. Made	Avg. Yds. Miss	Long
Norwood, Scott,	1-1	10-10	15-16	6-9	0-1	32-37	34.4	32.8	45.2	49
Buffalo	1.000	1.000	.938	.667	.000	.865				
Lowery, Nick,	0-0	7-8	9-11	8-10	3-3	27-32	37.3	37.1	38.8	51
Kansas City	—	.875	.818	.800	1.000	.844				
Bahr, Matt,	1-1	10-12	8-10	5-6	0-0	24-29	32.0	31.7	33.8	47
Cleveland	1.000	.833	.800	.833	—	.828				
Leahy, Pat,	0-0	9-9	7-8	7-10	0-1	23-28	35.5	33.7	43.4	48
N.Y. Jets	—	1.000	.875	.700	.000	.821				
Johnson, Norm,	1-1	4-4	7-9	10-14	0-0	22-28	36.5	35.5	40.3	47
Seattle	1.000	1.000	.778	.714	—	.786				
Biasucci, Dean,	0-0	8-8	5-6	6-10	6-8	25-32	39.2	36.7	48.0	53
Indianapolis	—	1.000	.833	.600	.750	.781				
Anderson, Gary,	1-1	11-11	9-10	6-12	1-2	28-36	35.1	31.6	47.6	52
Pittsburgh	1.000	1.000	.900	.500	.500	.778				
Breech, Jim,	1-1	5-5	3-4	2-5	0-1	11-16	33.4	29.5	41.8	45
Cincinnati	1.000	1.000	.750	.400	.000	.688				
Zendejas, Tony,	1-1	3-5	7-8	9-16	2-4	22-34	40.2	38.9	42.5	52
Houston	1.000	.600	.875	.563	.500	.647				
Karlis, Rich,	1-1	9-10	6-13	5-8	2-4	23-36	35.4	33.4	38.8	51
Denver	1.000	.900	.462	.625	.500	.639				
Bahr, Chris,	1-1	7-7	3-6	6-11	1-4	18-29	38.3	34.7	44.1	50
L.A. Raiders	1.000	1.000	.500	.545	.250	.621				
Non-Qualifiers (Less than 15 attempts)										
DeLine, Steve,	0-0	3-3	1-1	2-4	0-0	6-8	35.5	33.0	43.0	45
San Diego	—	1.000	1.000	.500	—	.750				
Abbott, Vince,	0-0	3-3	2-4	3-5	0-0	8-12	35.4	33.6	39.0	48
San Diego	—	1.000	.500	.600	—	.667				
Reveiz, Fuad,	0-0	4-4	3-4	1-2	0-2	8-12	36.4	30.9	47.5	45
Miami	—	1.000	.750	.500	.000	.667				
Staurovsky, Jason,	0-0	3-4	4-5	0-2	0-0	7-11	32.0	29.4	36.5	35
New England	—	.750	.800	.000	—	.636				
Johnson, Lee,	0-0	0-0	0-0	0-0	1-2	1-2	50.0	50.0	50.0	50
Cincinnati	—	—	—	—	.500	.500				
Garcia, Teddy,	0-0	2-3	1-3	2-5	1-2	6-13	38.8	37.7	39.9	50
New England	—	.667	.333	.400	.500	.462				
Franklin, Tony,	0-0	1-2	2-4	0-1	1-4	4-11	40.1	36.3	42.3	51
Miami	—	.500	.500	.000	.250	.364				
AFC Totals	8-8	99-108	92-122	78-130	18-38	295-406	36.4	34.2	42.1	53
	1.000	.917	.754	.600	.474	.727				
League Totals	21-22	193-216	190-246	139-242	28-70	571-796	36.0	33.6	41.9	53
	.955	.894	.772	.574	.400	.717				

NFC Field Goals—Individual

	1-19	20-29	30-39	40-49	50 & Over	Totals	Avg. Yds. Att.	Avg. Yds. Made	Avg. Yds. Miss	Long
Murray, Ed,	1-1	8-8	9-9	2-2	0-1	20-21	32.5	31.5	52.0	48
Detroit	1.000	1.000	1.000	1.000	.000	.952				
Nelson, Chuck,	2-3	7-7	10-10	1-5	0-0	20-25	32.1	30.4	38.8	49
Minnesota	.667	1.000	1.000	.200	—	.800				
Butler, Kevin,	1-1	4-4	7-8	3-6	0-0	15-19	33.8	31.9	40.8	45
Chicago	1.000	1.000	.875	.500	—	.789				
Igwebuike, Donald,	1-1	6-6	7-8	3-6	2-4	19-25	37.1	34.1	46.7	53
Tampa Bay	1.000	1.000	.875	.500	.500	.760				
Lansford, Mike,	1-1	9-12	8-10	6-8	0-1	24-32	33.3	32.6	35.5	49
L.A. Rams	1.000	.750	.800	.750	.000	.750				
Zendejas, Luis,	2-2	6-6	7-9	4-7	1-3	20-27	36.6	33.6	45.1	50
Dallas-Philadelphia	1.000	1.000	.778	.571	.333	.741				
McFadden, Paul,	0-0	4-4	4-6	5-6	1-3	14-19	38.7	35.5	47.6	50
N.Y. Giants	—	1.000	.667	.833	.333	.737				
Lohmiller, Chip,	1-1	6-8	5-7	7-10	0-0	19-26	34.0	33.0	36.7	46
Washington	1.000	.750	.714	.700	—	.731				
Andersen, Morten,	1-1	11-12	8-11	5-8	1-4	26-36	35.4	32.7	42.6	51
New Orleans	1.000	.917	.727	.625	.250	.722				
Cofer, Mike,	1-1	9-10	9-11	7-11	1-5	27-38	36.7	33.6	44.4	52
San Francisco	1.000	.900	.818	.636	.200	.711				
Davis, Greg,	1-1	3-4	6-9	8-12	1-4	19-30	37.9	36.3	40.8	52
Atlanta	1.000	.750	.667	.667	.250	.633				
Del Greco, Al,	1-1	4-6	3-3	3-9	1-2	12-21	37.1	33.5	41.9	51
Phoenix	1.000	.667	1.000	.333	.500	.571				

	1-19	20-29	30-39	40-49	50 & Over	Totals	Avg. Yds. Att.	Avg. Yds. Made	Avg. Yds. Miss	Long
Zendejas, Max,	0-0	2-3	4-5	2-6	1-2	9-16	38.6	36.6	41.1	50
Green Bay	—	.667	.800	.333	.500	.563				
Ruzek, Roger,	0-0	4-5	4-7	3-7	1-3	12-22	38.6	35.3	42.6	50
Dallas	—	.800	.571	.429	.333	.545				
Non-Qualifiers (Less than 15 attempts)										
Allegre, Raul,	0-0	3-3	5-6	2-2	0-0	10-11	33.7	33.2	39.0	48
N.Y. Giants	—	1.000	.833	1.000	—	.909				
Dawson, Dale,	0-0	2-3	1-2	0-1	0-0	3-6	29.5	24.7	34.3	32
Philadelphia-Green Bay	—	.667	.500	.000	—	.500				
Dorsey, Dean,	0-0	4-4	1-2	0-4	0-0	5-10	34.1	25.2	43.0	34
Philadelphia-Green Bay	—	1.000	.500	.000	—	.500				
Carney, John,	0-0	2-3	0-1	0-1	0-0	2-5	31.4	26.5	34.7	29
Tampa Bay	—	.667	.000	.000	—	.400				
Burrow, Curtis,	0-0	0-0	0-0	0-1	0-0	0-1	49.0	—	49.0	—
Green Bay	—	—	—	.000	—	.000				
NFC Totals	13-14	94-108	98-124	61-112	10-32	276-390	35.6	33.1	41.6	53
	.929	.870	.790	.545	.313	.708				
League Totals	21-22	193-216	190-246	139-242	28-70	571-796	36.0	33.6	41.9	53
	.955	.894	.772	.574	.400	.717				

Rushing

Individual Champions
- **AFC:** 1,659—Eric Dickerson, Indianapolis
- **NFC:** 1,514—Herschel Walker, Dallas

Attempts
- **AFC:** 388—Eric Dickerson, Indianapolis
- **NFC:** 361—Herschel Walker, Dallas

Most Attempts, Game
- **NFC:** 45—Jamie Morris, Washington at Cincinnati, December 17 (152 yards)
- **AFC:** 36—Eric Dickerson, Indianapolis vs. Buffalo, December 18 (166 yards)

Yards Per Attempt
- **AFC:** 5.3—Ickey Woods, Cincinnati
- **NFC:** 4.8—Roger Craig, San Francisco

Most Yards, Game
- **AFC:** 217—Gary Anderson, San Diego vs. Kansas City, December 18 (34 attempts)
- **NFC:** 190—Roger Craig, San Francisco at L.A. Rams, October 16 (22 attempts)

Longest
- **NFC:** 80—Neal Anderson, Chicago vs. Green Bay, November 27 (TD)
- **AFC:** 65—Kevin Mack, Cleveland vs. Philadelphia, October 16

Touchdowns
- **NFC:** 16—Greg Bell, L.A. Rams
- **AFC:** 15—Ickey Woods, Cincinnati

Team Leaders, Yards
- **AFC:** BUFFALO: 881, Thurman Thomas; CINCINNATI: 1,066, Ickey Woods; CLEVELAND: 576, Earnest Byner; DENVER: 703, Tony Dorsett; HOUSTON: 1,002, Mike Rozier; INDIANAPOLIS: 1,659, Eric Dickerson; KANSAS CITY: 473, Christian Okoye; L.A. RAIDERS: 831, Marcus Allen; MIAMI: 414, Lorenzo Hampton; NEW ENGLAND: 1,168, John Stephens; N.Y. JETS: 944, Freeman McNeil; PITTSBURGH: 705, Merril Hoge; SAN DIEGO: 1,119, Gary Anderson; SEATTLE: 1,025, Curt Warner.
- **NFC:** ATLANTA: 1,024, John Settle; CHICAGO: 1,106, Neal Anderson; DALLAS: 1,514, Herschel Walker; DETROIT: 552, Garry James; GREEN BAY: 483, Brent Fullwood; L.A. RAMS: 1,212, Greg Bell; MINNESOTA: 380, Darrin Nelson; NEW ORLEANS: 823, Dalton Hilliard; N.Y. GIANTS: 1,083, Joe Morris; PHILADELPHIA: 624, Randall Cunningham; PHOENIX: 924, Earl Ferrell; SAN FRANCISCO: 1,502, Roger Craig; TAMPA BAY: 467, Lars Tate; WASHINGTON: 498, Kelvin Bryant.

Team Champions
- **AFC:** 2,710—Cincinnati
- **NFC:** 2,523—San Francisco

AFC Rushing—Team

	Att.	Yards	Avg.	Long	TD
Cincinnati	563	2710	4.8	56	27
Houston	558	2249	4.0	42	26
Indianapolis	545	2249	4.1	44	23
Pittsburgh	499	2228	4.5	64t	17
Buffalo	528	2133	4.0	37t	15
N.Y. Jets	514	2132	4.1	28	19
New England	588	2120	3.6	52	17
Seattle	517	2086	4.0	44t	14
San Diego	438	2041	4.7	37	11
L.A. Raiders	493	1852	3.8	32	15
Denver	464	1815	3.9	35	13
Kansas City	448	1713	3.8	48	8
Cleveland	440	1575	3.6	65	10
Miami	335	1205	3.6	64	11
AFC Total	6,930	28,108	—	65	226
AFC Average	495.0	2007.7	4.1	—	16.1

NFC Rushing—Team

	Att.	Yards	Avg.	Long	TD
San Francisco	527	2523	4.8	49t	18
Chicago	555	2319	4.2	80t	25
New Orleans	512	2046	4.0	73t	9
Phoenix	480	2027	4.2	47	15
Atlanta	478	2016	4.2	62	11
L.A. Rams	507	2003	4.0	44	16
Dallas	469	1995	4.3	38	10
Philadelphia	464	1945	4.2	52	17
Minnesota	501	1806	3.6	34	22
Tampa Bay	452	1753	3.9	47t	11
N.Y. Giants	493	1689	3.4	27	15
Washington	437	1543	3.5	29	8
Green Bay	385	1379	3.6	33t	14
Detroit	391	1243	3.2	35	7
NFC Total	6,651	26,287	—	80t	198
NFC Average	475.1	1877.6	4.0	—	14.1
League Total	13,581	54,395	—	80t	424
League Average	485.0	1942.7	4.0	—	15.1

NFL Top 10 Rushers

	Att.	Yards	Avg.	Long	TD
Dickerson, Eric, Indianapolis	388	1659	4.3	41t	14
Walker, Herschel, Dallas	361	1514	4.2	38	5
Craig, Roger, San Francisco	310	1502	4.8	46t	9
Bell, Greg, L.A. Rams	288	1212	4.2	44	16
Stephens, John, New England	297	1168	3.9	52	4
Anderson, Gary, San Diego	225	1119	5.0	36	3
Anderson, Neal, Chicago	249	1106	4.4	80t	12
Morris, Joe, N.Y. Giants	307	1083	3.5	27	5
Woods, Ickey, Cincinnati	203	1066	5.3	56	15
Warner, Curt, Seattle	266	1025	3.9	29	10

AFC Rushing—Individual

	Att.	Yards	Avg.	Long	TD
Dickerson, Eric, Indianapolis	388	1659	4.3	41t	14
Stephens, John, New England	297	1168	3.9	52	4
Anderson, Gary, San Diego	225	1119	5.0	36	3
Woods, Ickey, Cincinnati	203	1066	5.3	56	15
Warner, Curt, Seattle	266	1025	3.9	29	10
Rozier, Mike, Houston	251	1002	4.0	28	10
McNeil, Freeman, N.Y. Jets	219	944	4.3	28	6
Brooks, James, Cincinnati	182	931	5.1	51t	8
Thomas, Thurman, Buffalo	207	881	4.3	37t	2
Williams, John L., Seattle	189	877	4.6	44t	4
Allen, Marcus, L.A. Raiders	223	831	3.7	32	7
Hoge, Merril, Pittsburgh	170	705	4.1	20	3
Dorsett, Tony, Denver	181	703	3.9	26	5
Jackson, Bo, L.A. Raiders	136	580	4.3	25	3
Byner, Earnest, Cleveland	157	576	3.7	27t	3
Hector, Johnny, N.Y. Jets	137	561	4.1	19	10
Winder, Sammy, Denver	149	543	3.6	35	4
Vick, Roger, N.Y. Jets	128	540	4.2	17	3
Pinkett, Allen, Houston	122	513	4.2	27	7
Mack, Kevin, Cleveland	123	485	3.9	65	3
Okoye, Christian, Kansas City	105	473	4.5	48	3
Highsmith, Alonzo, Houston	94	466	5.0	42	2
Palmer, Paul, Kansas City	134	452	3.4	26t	2
Perryman, Bob, New England	146	448	3.1	16	6
Heard, Herman, Kansas City	106	438	4.1	20	0
Riddick, Robb, Buffalo	111	438	3.9	21	12
Hampton, Lorenzo, Miami	117	414	3.5	33	9
Williams, Warren, Pittsburgh	87	409	4.7	33	0

	Att.	Yards	Avg.	Long	TD
Wilson, Stanley, Cincinnati	112	398	3.6	19	2
Manoa, Tim, Cleveland	99	389	3.9	34	2
Stradford, Troy, Miami	95	335	3.5	18	2
Jackson, Earnest, Pittsburgh	74	315	4.3	29t	3
Mueller, Jamie, Buffalo	81	296	3.7	20	0
Davenport, Ron, Miami	55	273	5.0	64	0
Esiason, Boomer, Cincinnati	43	248	5.8	24	1
Saxon, James, Kansas City	60	236	3.9	14	2
Elway, John, Denver	54	234	4.3	26	1
Bentley, Albert, Indianapolis	45	230	5.1	20	2
Carter, Rodney, Pittsburgh	36	216	6.0	64t	3
Spencer, Tim, San Diego	44	215	4.9	24	0
Harmon, Ronnie, Buffalo	57	212	3.7	32	1
Brister, Bubby, Pittsburgh	45	209	4.6	20	6
Flutie, Doug, New England	38	179	4.7	16	1
Malone, Mark, San Diego	37	169	4.6	36t	4
Smith, Steve, L.A. Raiders	38	162	4.3	21	3
Kelly, Jim, Buffalo	35	154	4.4	20	0
Dupard, Reggie, New England	52	151	2.9	15	2
Adams, Curtis, San Diego	38	149	3.9	14	1
Chandler, Chris, Indianapolis	46	139	3.0	29t	3
Sewell, Steve, Denver	32	135	4.2	26	1
Lipps, Louis, Pittsburgh	6	129	21.5	39t	1
Stone, Dwight, Pittsburgh	40	127	3.2	11	0
Laufenberg, Babe, San Diego	31	120	3.9	23	0
Bennett, Woody, Miami	31	115	3.7	12	0
White, Lorenzo, Houston	31	115	3.7	16	0
Schroeder, Jay, L.A. Raiders	29	109	3.8	12	1
James, Lionel, San Diego	23	105	4.6	23	0
Pollard, Frank, Pittsburgh	31	93	3.0	7	0
Byrum, Carl, Buffalo	28	91	3.3	11	0
Moon, Warren, Houston	33	88	2.7	14	5
Fontenot, Herman, Cleveland	28	87	3.1	17	0
Verdin, Clarence, Indianapolis	8	77	9.6	44	0
Tatupu, Mosi, New England	22	75	3.4	22	2
Jensen, Jim, Miami	10	68	6.8	23	0
Kubiak, Gary, Denver	17	65	3.8	15	0
Krieg, Dave, Seattle	24	64	2.7	17	0
Reed, Andre, Buffalo	6	64	10.7	36	0
Early, Quinn, San Diego	7	63	9.0	37	0
Brooks, Bill, Indianapolis	5	62	12.4	38	0
Moriarty, Larry, Kansas City	20	62	3.1	9	0
Mueller, Vance, L.A. Raiders	17	60	3.5	13	0
Kemp, Jeff, Seattle	6	51	8.5	21	0
Nattiel, Ricky, Denver	5	51	10.2	29	0
Brown, Tim, L.A. Raiders	14	50	3.6	12	1
Wonsley, George, Indianapolis	26	48	1.8	4	1
Jennings, Stanford, Cincinnati	17	47	2.8	9	1
Miller, Anthony, San Diego	7	45	6.4	20	0
Turner, Ricky, Indianapolis	16	42	2.6	14	2
Allen, Marvin, New England	7	40	5.7	12	0
Willhite, Gerald, Denver	13	39	3.0	7	2
Bell, Ken, Denver	9	36	4.0	6	0
Carlson, Cody, Houston	12	36	3.0	10	1
Beuerlein, Steve, L.A. Raiders	30	35	1.2	20	0
DeBerg, Steve, Kansas City	18	30	1.7	13	1
Redden, Barry, San Diego	19	30	1.6	5t	3
Stouffer, Kelly, Seattle	19	27	1.4	17	0
Givins, Ernest, Houston	4	26	6.5	10	0
Langhorne, Reggie, Cleveland	2	26	13.0	20t	1
Blackledge, Todd, Pittsburgh	8	25	3.1	10	1
O'Brien, Ken, N.Y. Jets	21	25	1.2	17	0
Blades, Brian, Seattle	5	24	4.8	12	0
Ryan, Pat, N.Y. Jets	5	22	4.4	15	0
Cribbs, Joe, Miami	5	21	4.2	11	0
Thomas, Calvin, Chicago-Denver	6	20	3.3	8	0
Baker, Tony, Cleveland	3	19	6.3	13	0
Holland, Jamie, San Diego	3	19	6.3	10	0
Eason, Tony, New England	5	18	3.6	10	0
Goodburn, Kelly, Kansas City	1	15	15.0	15	0
James, Craig, New England	4	15	3.8	8t	1
Faaola, Nuu, N.Y. Jets	1	13	13.0	13	0
Harmon, Kevin, Seattle	2	13	6.5	8	0
Fryar, Irving, New England	6	12	2.0	6	0
Grogan, Steve, New England	6	12	2.0	6	1
Strachan, Steve, L.A. Raiders	4	12	3.0	5	0
Walker, Wesley, N.Y. Jets	1	12	12.0	12	0
Leahy, Pat, N.Y. Jets	1	10	10.0	10	0
Logan, Marc, Cincinnati	2	10	5.0	9	0
Schonert, Turk, Cincinnati	2	10	5.0	7	0
Fernandez, Mervyn, L.A. Raiders	1	9	9.0	9	0
Ramsey, Tom, New England	3	8	2.7	9	0
Bernstine, Rod, San Diego	2	7	3.5	5	0
Morris, Randall, Seattle	3	6	2.0	5	0
Jackson, Mark, Denver	1	5	5.0	5	0
Norseth, Mike, Cincinnati	1	5	5.0	5	0
Tillman, Spencer, Houston	3	5	1.7	2	0
Toon, Al, N.Y. Jets	1	5	5.0	5	0
Clayton, Mark, Miami	1	4	4.0	4	0
Gault, Willie, L.A. Raiders	1	4	4.0	4	0
Kenney, Bill, Kansas City	2	4	2.0	2	0
Danielson, Gary, Cleveland	4	3	0.8	5	0
Johnson, Jason, Denver	1	3	3.0	3	0
Agee, Tommie, Seattle	1	2	2.0	2	0
Taylor, Kitrick, Kansas City	1	2	2.0	2	0
Carson, Carlos, Kansas City	1	1	1.0	1	0
Johnson, Vance, Denver	1	1	1.0	1	0
Pagel, Mike, Cleveland	4	1	0.3	5	0
Feagles, Jeff, New England	1	0	0.0	0	0
Newsome, Harry, Pittsburgh	2	0	0.0	0	0
Rodriguez, Ruben, Seattle	1	0	0.0	0	0
Runager, Max, Cleveland	1	0	0.0	0	0
Vlasic, Mark, San Diego	2	0	0.0	0	0
Kosar, Bernie, Cleveland	12	−1	−0.1	13	1
Pease, Brent, Houston	8	−2	−0.3	4t	1
Strock, Don, Cleveland	6	−2	−0.3	5	0
Largent, Steve, Seattle	1	−3	−3.0	−3	0
Reich, Frank, Buffalo	3	−3	−1.0	−1	0
Brown, Eddie, Cincinnati	1	−5	−5.0	−5	0
Morgan, Stanley, New England	1	−6	−6.0	−6	0
Bahr, Matt, Cleveland	1	−8	−8.0	−8	0
Edmunds, Ferrell, Miami	1	−8	−8.0	−8	0
Hogeboom, Gary, Indianapolis	11	−8	−0.7	6	1
Marino, Dan, Miami	20	−17	−0.9	6	0

t indicates touchdown.
Leader based on most yards gained.

NFC Rushing—Individual

	Att.	Yards	Avg.	Long	TD
Walker, Herschel, Dallas	361	1514	4.2	38	5
Craig, Roger, San Francisco	310	1502	4.8	46t	9
Bell, Greg, L.A. Rams	288	1212	4.2	44	16
Anderson, Neal, Chicago	249	1106	4.4	80t	12
Morris, Joe, N.Y. Giants	307	1083	3.5	27	5
Settle, John, Atlanta	232	1024	4.4	62	7
Ferrell, Earl, Phoenix	202	924	4.6	47	7
Hilliard, Dalton, New Orleans	204	823	4.0	36	5
Mitchell, Stump, Phoenix	164	726	4.4	47	4
Mayes, Rueben, New Orleans	170	628	3.7	21	3
Cunningham, Randall, Philadelphia	93	624	6.7	33t	6
James, Garry, Detroit	182	552	3.0	35	5
Byars, Keith, Philadelphia	152	517	3.4	52	6
Toney, Anthony, Philadelphia	139	502	3.6	20	4
Bryant, Kelvin, Washington	108	498	4.6	25	1
Riggs, Gerald, Atlanta	113	488	4.3	34	1
Fullwood, Brent, Green Bay	101	483	4.8	33t	7
Smith, Timmy, Washington	155	470	3.0	29	3
Tate, Lars, Tampa Bay	122	467	3.8	47t	7
Howard, William, Tampa Bay	115	452	3.9	29t	1
Morris, Jamie, Washington	126	437	3.5	27t	2
Rathman, Tom, San Francisco	102	427	4.2	26	2
Nelson, Darrin, Minnesota	112	380	3.4	27	1
Heyward, Craig, New Orleans	74	355	4.8	73t	1
Wilder, James, Tampa Bay	86	343	4.0	19	1
Sanders, Thomas, Chicago	95	332	3.5	20t	3
White, Charles, L.A. Rams	88	323	3.7	13	0
Rice, Allen, Minnesota	110	322	2.9	24	6
Jones, James, Detroit	96	314	3.3	13	0
Pelluer, Steve, Dallas	51	314	6.2	27	2
Anderson, Alfred, Minnesota	87	300	3.4	18	7
Fenney, Rick, Minnesota	55	271	4.9	28	3
Suhey, Matt, Chicago	87	253	2.9	19	2
Goode, Kerry, Tampa Bay	63	231	3.7	22	0
Majkowski, Don, Green Bay	47	225	4.8	24	1
Anderson, Ottis, N.Y. Giants	65	208	3.2	11	8
Paige, Tony, Detroit	52	207	4.0	20	0
Muster, Brad, Chicago	44	197	4.5	15	0
Woodside, Keith, Green Bay	83	195	2.3	10	3
Mason, Larry, Green Bay	48	194	4.0	17	0
Lang, Gene, Atlanta	53	191	3.6	19	0
Haddix, Michael, Philadelphia	57	185	3.2	15	0
Young, Steve, San Francisco	27	184	6.8	49t	1
Dozier, D.J., Minnesota	42	167	4.0	19t	2
Jordan, Tony, Phoenix	61	160	2.6	12	3
Simms, Phil, N.Y. Giants	33	152	4.6	17	0
Harris, Darryl, Minnesota	34	151	4.4	34	1
Delpino, Robert, L.A. Rams	34	147	4.3	13	0
Carthon, Maurice, N.Y. Giants	46	146	3.2	8	2
Miller, Chris, Atlanta	31	138	4.5	29	1
Testaverde, Vinny, Tampa Bay	28	138	4.9	24	1
Wilson, Wade, Minnesota	36	136	3.8	15	2
Montana, Joe, San Francisco	38	132	3.5	15	3
Davis, Kenneth, Green Bay	39	121	3.1	27	1
Green, Gaston, L.A. Rams	35	117	3.3	13	0
DuBose, Doug, San Francisco	24	116	4.8	37t	2
Jordan, Buford, New Orleans	19	115	6.1	44	0
Carruth, Paul Ott, Green Bay	49	114	2.3	14	0
Harbaugh, Jim, Chicago	19	110	5.8	19	1

	Att.	Yards	Avg.	Long	TD
Rice, Jerry, San Francisco	13	107	8.2	29	1
Everett, Jim, L.A. Rams	34	104	3.1	19	0
McMahon, Jim, Chicago	26	104	4.0	16	4
Primus, James, Atlanta	35	95	2.7	29t	1
Smith, Jeff, Tampa Bay	20	87	4.4	23	0
Gentry, Dennis, Chicago	7	86	12.3	58t	1
Hebert, Bobby, New Orleans	37	79	2.1	16	0
Adams, George, N.Y. Giants	29	76	2.6	15	0
Newsome, Tim, Dallas	32	75	2.3	8	3
Dixon, Floyd, Atlanta	7	69	9.9	24	0
McGee, Buford, L.A. Rams	22	69	3.1	12	0
Stoudt, Cliff, Phoenix	14	57	4.1	14	0
Lomax, Neil, Phoenix	17	55	3.2	13	1
Clack, Darryl, Dallas	11	54	4.9	17	0
Sydney, Harry, San Francisco	9	50	5.6	13	0
Monk, Art, Washington	7	46	6.6	23	0
Smith, Don, Tampa Bay	13	46	3.5	15	1
Mandley, Pete, Detroit	6	44	7.3	21t	1
Wolfley, Ron, Phoenix	9	43	4.8	20	0
Wright, Randy, Green Bay	8	43	5.4	19	2
Painter, Carl, Detroit	17	42	2.5	13	0
Carter, Anthony, Minnesota	4	41	10.3	21	0
Morris, Ron, Chicago	3	40	13.3	21	0
Tomczak, Mike, Chicago	13	40	3.1	17	1
Hoage, Terry, Philadelphia	1	38	38.0	38t	1
Teltschik, John, Philadelphia	2	36	18.0	23	0
Sweeney, Kevin, Dallas	6	34	5.7	10	0
Rypien, Mark, Washington	9	31	3.4	19t	1
Oliphant, Mike, Washington	8	30	3.8	20	0
Gannon, Rich, Minnesota	4	29	7.3	15	0
Tautalatasi, Junior, Philadelphia	14	28	2.0	9	0
Hilger, Rusty, Detroit	18	27	1.5	11	0
Manuel, Lionel, N.Y. Giants	4	27	6.8	14	0
McKinnon, Dennis, Chicago	3	25	8.3	12	1
Brown, Ron, L.A. Rams	3	24	8.0	13	0
Griffin, Keith, Washington	6	23	3.8	9	0
Long, Chuck, Detroit	7	22	3.1	11	0
Williams, Scott, Detroit	9	22	2.4	5	1
Horne, Greg, Phoenix	3	20	6.7	20	0
Perriman, Brett, New Orleans	3	17	5.7	17	0
Smith, J.T., Phoenix	1	15	15.0	15	0
Abercrombie, Walter, Philadelphia	5	14	2.8	5	0
Sanders, Ricky, Washington	2	14	7.0	7	0
Martin, Eric, New Orleans	2	12	6.0	9	0
Hansen, Brian, New Orleans	1	10	10.0	10	0
Novacek, Jay, Phoenix	1	10	10.0	10	0
Del Greco, Al, Phoenix	1	8	8.0	8	0
Jeffery, Tony, Phoenix	3	8	2.7	9	0
Kramer, Tommy, Minnesota	14	8	0.6	5	0
Ellard, Henry, L.A. Rams	1	7	7.0	7	0
Hill, Lonzell, New Orleans	2	7	3.5	5	0
Jones, Hassan, Minnesota	1	7	7.0	7	0
Millen, Hugh, Atlanta	1	7	7.0	7	0
Clark, Gary, Washington	2	6	3.0	4	0
Fowler, Todd, Dallas	3	6	2.0	4	0
Flagler, Terrence, San Francisco	3	5	1.7	4	0
Hipple, Eric, Detroit	1	5	5.0	5	0
Bland, Carl, Detroit	1	4	4.0	4	0
Woolfolk, Butch, Detroit	1	4	4.0	4	0
Davis, Wendell, Chicago	1	3	3.0	3	0
Hester, Jessie, Atlanta	1	3	3.0	3	0
Kozlowski, Glen, Chicago	1	3	3.0	3	0
Matthews, Aubrey, Green Bay	3	3	1.0	4	0
Collins, Patrick, Green Bay	2	2	1.0	2	0
Irvin, Michael, Dallas	1	2	2.0	2	0
Archer, David, Washington	3	1	0.3	4	0
Carter, Cris, Philadelphia	1	1	1.0	1	0
Dils, Steve, Atlanta	2	1	0.5	1t	1
Green, Roy, Phoenix	4	1	0.3	18	0
Guman, Mike, L.A. Rams	1	1	1.0	1	0
Rouson, Lee, N.Y. Giants	1	1	1.0	1	0
Stanley, Walter, Green Bay	1	1	1.0	1	0
Criswell, Ray, Tampa Bay	2	0	0.0	0	0
Ferguson, Joe, Tampa Bay	1	0	0.0	0	0
Helton, Barry, San Francisco	1	0	0.0	0	0
Scribner, Bucky, Minnesota	1	0	0.0	0	0
Stamps, Sylvester, Atlanta	3	0	0.0	3	0
Wagner, Bryan, Chicago	2	0	0.0	0	0
Williams, Doug, Washington	9	0	0.0	4	1
Witkowski, John, Detroit	1	0	0.0	0	0
Herrmann, Mark, L.A. Rams	1	−1	−1.0	−1	0
Rutledge, Jeff, N.Y. Giants	3	−1	−0.3	0	0
Sharpe, Sterling, Green Bay	4	−2	−0.5	5	0
Hostetler, Jeff, N.Y. Giants	5	−3	−0.6	0	0
Martin, Kelvin, Dallas	4	−4	−1.0	11	0
Mularkey, Mike, Minnesota	1	−6	−6.0	−6	0
Hill, Bruce, Tampa Bay	2	−11	−5.5	3	0
Coleman, Greg, Washington	2	−13	−6.5	0	0

t indicates touchdown.
Leader based on most yards gained.

Passing

Individual Champions (Rating Points)
AFC: 97.4—Boomer Esiason, Cincinnati
NFC: 91.5—Wade Wilson, Minnesota

Attempts
AFC: 606—Dan Marino, Miami
NFC: 560—Randall Cunningham, Philadelphia

Completions
AFC: 354—Dan Marino, Miami
NFC: 308—Jim Everett, L.A. Rams

Completion Percentage
NFC: 61.4—Wade Wilson, Minnesota
AFC: 60.2—Bernie Kosar, Cleveland

Yards
AFC: 4,434—Dan Marino, Miami
NFC: 3,964—Jim Everett, L.A. Rams

Most Yards, Game
AFC: 521—Dan Marino, Miami vs. N.Y. Jets, October 23 (60 attempts, 35 completions)
NFC: 469—Vinny Testaverde, Tampa Bay at Indianapolis, October 16 (42 attempts, 25 completions)

Longest
NFC: 96—Joe Montana (to Jerry Rice), San Francisco at San Diego, November 27 (TD)
AFC: 89—Bubby Brister (to Louis Lipps), Pittsburgh vs. Philadelphia, November 13 (TD)

Yards Per Attempt
AFC: 9.21—Boomer Esiason, Cincinnati
NFC: 8.27—Wade Wilson, Minnesota

Touchdown Passes
NFC: 31—Jim Everett, L.A. Rams
AFC: 28—Boomer Esiason, Cincinnati
28—Dan Marino, Miami

Most Touchdown Passes, Game
AFC: 5—Dave Krieg, Seattle vs. L.A. Raiders, November 28
5—Dan Marino, Miami at N.Y. Jets, November 27
NFC: 5—Jim Everett, L.A. Rams at N.Y. Giants, September 25

Lowest Interception Percentage
AFC: 1.7—Ken O'Brien, N.Y. Jets
NFC: 2.3—Phil Simms, N.Y. Giants

Team Champions
AFC: 4,516—Miami
NFC: 4,136—Washington

AFC Passing—Team

	Att.	Comp.	Pct. Comp.	Gross Yards	Tkd.	Yards Lost	Net Yards	TD	Pct. TD	Long	Int.	Pct. Int.	Avg. Yds. Att.	Avg. Yds. Comp.
Miami	621	363	58.5	4557	7	41	4516	29	4.7	80t	23	3.7	7.34	12.55
Denver	581	324	55.8	3941	32	250	3691	24	4.1	86	22	3.8	6.78	12.16
Cleveland	537	313	58.3	3686	36	250	3436	19	3.5	77t	17	3.2	6.86	11.78
Cincinnati	392	225	57.4	3592	30	245	3347	28	7.1	86t	14	3.6	9.16	15.96
Buffalo	454	271	59.7	3411	30	229	3182	15	3.3	66t	17	3.7	7.51	12.59
Kansas City	528	282	53.4	3484	43	353	3131	16	3.0	80t	21	4.0	6.60	12.35
L.A. Raiders	496	219	44.2	3503	46	394	3109	21	4.2	85t	20	4.0	7.06	16.00
N.Y. Jets	538	299	55.6	3374	42	291	3083	20	3.7	50t	11	2.0	6.27	11.28
Pittsburgh	489	226	46.2	3307	42	331	2976	15	3.1	89t	20	4.1	6.76	14.63
Houston	428	218	50.9	3166	24	210	2956	21	4.9	57t	18	4.2	7.40	14.52
Seattle	437	245	56.1	2979	29	223	2756	22	5.0	75t	20	4.6	6.82	12.16
Indianapolis	403	222	55.1	2865	34	244	2621	15	3.7	58	22	5.5	7.11	12.91
San Diego	468	241	51.5	2628	31	240	2388	11	2.4	59	20	4.3	5.62	10.90
New England	389	199	51.2	2333	23	160	2173	12	3.1	80t	28	7.2	6.00	11.72
AFC Total	6761	3647	—	46826	449	3461	43365	268	—	89t	273	—	—	—
AFC Average	482.9	260.5	53.9	3344.7	32.1	247.2	3097.5	19.1	4.0	—	19.5	4.0	6.93	12.84

NFC Passing—Team

	Att.	Comp.	Pct. Comp.	Gross Yards	Tkd.	Yards Lost	Net Yards	TD	Pct. TD	Long	Int.	Pct. Int.	Avg. Yds. Att.	Avg. Yds. Comp.
Washington	592	327	55.2	4339	24	203	4136	33	5.6	60t	25	4.2	7.33	13.27
L.A. Rams	522	312	59.8	4002	28	197	3805	31	5.9	69t	18	3.4	7.67	12.83
Minnesota	520	294	56.5	4100	47	311	3789	20	3.8	68t	18	3.5	7.88	13.95
Phoenix	562	322	57.3	4191	60	411	3780	26	4.6	93t	19	3.4	7.46	13.02
Dallas	555	307	55.3	3727	35	239	3488	21	3.8	61t	27	4.9	6.72	12.14
Philadelphia	581	309	53.2	3927	57	442	3485	25	4.3	80t	17	2.9	6.76	12.71
San Francisco	502	293	58.4	3675	47	298	3377	21	4.2	96t	14	2.8	7.32	12.54
Tampa Bay	512	253	49.4	3608	34	300	3308	16	3.1	59t	36	7.0	7.05	14.26
Green Bay	582	319	54.8	3609	51	324	3285	13	2.2	56	24	4.1	6.20	11.31
N.Y. Giants	525	290	55.2	3716	60	450	3266	22	4.2	85t	14	2.7	7.08	12.81
New Orleans	498	286	57.4	3256	24	171	3085	21	4.2	40t	16	3.2	6.54	11.38
Chicago	461	248	53.8	3173	24	175	2998	13	2.8	76t	15	3.3	6.88	12.79
Atlanta	481	250	52.0	2914	43	348	2566	13	2.7	68t	19	4.0	6.06	11.66
Detroit	477	213	44.7	2572	52	410	2162	13	2.7	56	18	3.8	5.39	12.08
NFC Total	7370	4023	—	50809	586	4279	46530	288	—	96t	280	—	—	—
NFC Average	526.4	287.4	54.6	3629.2	41.9	305.6	3323.6	20.6	3.9	—	20.0	3.8	6.89	12.63
League Total	14131	7670	—	97635	1035	7740	89895	556	—	96t	553	—	—	—
League Average	504.7	273.9	54.3	3487.0	37.0	276.4	3210.5	19.9	3.9	—	19.8	3.9	6.91	12.73

Leader based on net yards.

NFL Top 10 Individual Qualifiers

	Att.	Comp.	Pct. Comp.	Yards	Avg. Gain	TD	Pct. TD	Long	Int.	Pct. Int.	Rating Points
Esiason, Boomer, Cincinnati	388	223	57.5	3572	9.21	28	7.2	86t	14	3.6	97.4
Krieg, Dave, Seattle	228	134	58.8	1741	7.64	18	7.9	75t	8	3.5	94.6
Wilson, Wade, Minnesota	332	204	61.4	2746	8.27	15	4.5	68t	9	2.7	91.5
Everett, Jim, L.A. Rams	517	308	59.6	3964	7.67	31	6.0	69t	18	3.5	89.2
Moon, Warren, Houston	294	160	54.4	2327	7.91	17	5.8	57t	8	2.7	88.4
Montana, Joe, San Francisco	397	238	59.9	2981	7.51	18	4.5	96t	10	2.5	87.9
Lomax, Neil, Phoenix	443	255	57.6	3395	7.66	20	4.5	93t	11	2.5	86.7
Kosar, Bernie, Cleveland	259	156	60.2	1890	7.30	10	3.9	77t	7	2.7	84.3
Simms, Phil, N.Y. Giants	479	263	54.9	3359	7.01	21	4.4	62t	11	2.3	82.1
Marino, Dan, Miami	606	354	58.4	4434	7.32	28	4.6	80t	23	3.8	80.8

AFC Passing—Individual Qualifiers

	Att.	Comp.	Pct. Comp.	Yards	Avg. Gain	TD	Pct. TD	Long	Int.	Pct. Int.	Rating Points
Esiason, Boomer, Cincinnati	388	223	57.5	3572	9.21	28	7.2	86t	14	3.6	97.4
Krieg, Dave, Seattle	228	134	58.8	1741	7.64	18	7.9	75t	8	3.5	94.6
Moon, Warren, Houston	294	160	54.4	2327	7.91	17	5.8	57t	8	2.7	88.4
Kosar, Bernie, Cleveland	259	156	60.2	1890	7.30	10	3.9	77t	7	2.7	84.3
Marino, Dan, Miami	606	354	58.4	4434	7.32	28	4.6	80t	23	3.8	80.8
O'Brien, Ken, N.Y. Jets	424	236	55.7	2567	6.05	15	3.5	50t	7	1.7	78.6
Kelly, Jim, Buffalo	452	269	59.5	3380	7.48	15	3.3	66t	17	3.8	78.2
DeBerg, Steve, Kansas City	414	224	54.1	2935	7.09	16	3.9	80t	16	3.9	73.5
Elway, John, Denver	496	274	55.2	3309	6.67	17	3.4	86	19	3.8	71.4
Chandler, Chris, Indianapolis	233	129	55.4	1619	6.95	8	3.4	54	12	5.2	67.2
Beuerlein, Steve, L.A. Raiders	238	105	44.1	1643	6.90	8	3.4	57	7	2.9	66.6
Brister, Bubby, Pittsburgh	370	175	47.3	2634	7.12	11	3.0	89t	14	3.8	65.3
Schroeder, Jay, L.A. Raiders	256	113	44.1	1839	7.18	13	5.1	85t	13	5.1	64.6
Malone, Mark, San Diego	272	147	54.0	1580	5.81	6	2.2	59	13	4.8	58.8

Non-qualifiers	Att.	Comp.	Pct. Comp.	Yards	Avg. Gain	TD	Pct. TD	Long	Int.	Pct. Int.	Rating Points
Jaworski, Ron, Miami	14	9	64.3	123	8.79	1	7.1	22	0	0.0	116.1
Karcher, Ken, Denver	12	6	50.0	128	10.67	1	8.3	74t	0	0.0	116.0
Kubiak, Gary, Denver	69	43	62.3	497	7.20	5	7.2	68t	3	4.3	90.1
Strock, Don, Cleveland	91	55	60.4	736	8.09	6	6.6	41	5	5.5	85.2
Ryan, Pat, N.Y. Jets	113	63	55.8	807	7.14	5	4.4	42t	4	3.5	78.3
Hogeboom, Gary, Indianapolis	131	76	58.0	996	7.60	7	5.3	58	7	5.3	77.7
Danielson, Gary, Cleveland	52	31	59.6	324	6.23	0	0.0	26	1	1.9	69.7
Stouffer, Kelly, Seattle	173	98	56.6	1106	6.39	4	2.3	53	6	3.5	69.2
Pagel, Mike, Cleveland	134	71	53.0	736	5.49	3	2.2	28	4	3.0	64.1
Flutie, Doug, New England	179	92	51.4	1150	6.42	8	4.5	80t	10	5.6	63.3
Eason, Tony, New England	43	28	65.1	249	5.79	0	0.0	26	2	4.7	61.1
Blackledge, Todd, Pittsburgh	79	38	48.1	494	6.25	2	2.5	34	3	3.8	60.8
Laufenberg, Babe, San Diego	144	69	47.9	778	5.40	4	2.8	47t	5	3.5	59.3
Carlson, Cody, Houston	112	52	46.4	775	6.92	4	3.6	51t	6	5.4	59.2
Vlasic, Mark, San Diego	52	25	48.1	270	5.19	1	1.9	57	2	3.8	54.2
Kenney, Bill, Kansas City	114	58	50.9	549	4.82	0	0.0	25	5	4.4	46.3
Grogan, Steve, New England	140	67	47.9	834	5.96	4	2.9	41t	13	9.3	37.6
Bono, Steve, Pittsburgh	35	10	28.6	110	3.14	1	2.9	15	2	5.7	25.9
Trudeau, Jack, Indianapolis	34	14	41.2	158	4.65	0	0.0	48	3	8.8	19.0
Ramsey, Tom, New England	27	12	44.4	100	3.70	0	0.0	23	3	11.1	15.0
Kemp, Jeff, Seattle	35	13	37.1	132	3.77	0	0.0	19	5	14.3	9.2
Pease, Brent, Houston	22	6	27.3	64	2.91	0	0.0	21	4	18.2	0.0
Less than 10 attempts											
Agee, Tommie, Seattle	1	0	0.0	0	0.00	0	0.0	—	1	100.0	0.0
Allen, Marcus, L.A. Raiders	2	1	50.0	21	10.50	0	0.0	21	0	0.0	87.5
Bentley, Albert, Indianapolis	1	0	0.0	0	0.00	0	0.0	—	0	0.0	39.6
Blades, Brian, Seattle	0	0	—	0	—	0	—	—	0	—	0.0
Carter, Rodney, Pittsburgh	3	2	66.7	56	18.67	0	0.0	40	0	0.0	109.7
Dorsett, Tony, Denver	2	1	50.0	7	3.50	1	50.0	7t	0	0.0	97.9
Fontenot, Herman, Cleveland	1	0	0.0	0	0.00	0	0.0	—	0	0.0	39.6

	Att.	Comp.	Pct. Comp.	Yards	Avg. Gain	TD	Pct. TD	Long	Int.	Pct. Int.	Rating Points
Hector, Johnny, N.Y. Jets	1	0	0.0	0	0.00	0	0.0	—	0	0.0	39.6
James, Lionel, San Diego	0	0	—	0	—	0	—	—	0	—	0.0
Lipps, Louis, Pittsburgh	2	1	50.0	13	6.50	1	50.0	13t	1	50.0	70.8
Nattiel, Ricky, Denver	1	0	0.0	0	0.00	0	0.0	—	0	0.0	39.6
Riddick, Robb, Buffalo	2	2	100.0	31	15.50	0	0.0	26	0	0.0	118.8
Schonert, Turk, Cincinnati	4	2	50.0	20	5.00	0	0.0	17	0	0.0	64.6
Sewell, Steve, Denver	1	0	0.0	0	0.00	0	0.0	—	0	0.0	39.6
Stradford, Troy, Miami	1	0	0.0	0	0.00	0	0.0	—	0	0.0	39.6
Turner, Ricky, Indianapolis	4	3	75.0	92	23.00	0	0.0	37	0	0.0	116.7

t indicates touchdown.
Leader based on rating points, minimum 224 attempts.

NFC Passing — Individual Qualifiers

	Att.	Comp.	Pct. Comp.	Yards	Avg. Gain	TD	Pct. TD	Long	Int.	Pct. Int.	Rating Points
Wilson, Wade, Minnesota	332	204	61.4	2746	8.27	15	4.5	68t	9	2.7	91.5
Everett, Jim, L.A. Rams	517	308	59.6	3964	7.67	31	6.0	69t	18	3.5	89.2
Montana, Joe, San Francisco	397	238	59.9	2981	7.51	18	4.5	96t	10	2.5	87.9
Lomax, Neil, Phoenix	443	255	57.6	3395	7.66	20	4.5	93t	11	2.5	86.7
Simms, Phil, N.Y. Giants	479	263	54.9	3359	7.01	21	4.4	62t	11	2.3	82.1
Hebert, Bobby, New Orleans	478	280	58.6	3156	6.60	20	4.2	40t	15	3.1	79.3
Cunningham, Randall, Philadelphia	560	301	53.8	3808	6.80	24	4.3	80t	16	2.9	77.6
Williams, Doug, Washington	380	213	56.1	2609	6.87	15	3.9	58	12	3.2	77.4
Pelluer, Steve, Dallas	435	245	56.3	3139	7.22	17	3.9	61t	19	4.4	73.9
Majkowski, Don, Green Bay	336	178	53.0	2119	6.31	9	2.7	56	11	3.3	67.8
Miller, Chris, Atlanta	351	184	52.4	2133	6.08	11	3.1	68t	12	3.4	67.3
Wright, Randy, Green Bay	244	141	57.8	1490	6.11	4	1.6	51	13	5.3	58.9
Hilger, Rusty, Detroit	306	126	41.2	1558	5.09	7	2.3	56	12	3.9	48.9
Testaverde, Vinny, Tampa Bay	466	222	47.6	3240	6.95	13	2.8	59t	35	7.5	48.8

Non-qualifiers	Att.	Comp.	Pct. Comp.	Yards	Avg. Gain	TD	Pct. TD	Long	Int.	Pct. Int.	Rating Points
Ferguson, Joe, Tampa Bay	46	31	67.4	368	8.00	3	6.5	34	1	2.2	104.3
Rypien, Mark, Washington	208	114	54.8	1730	8.32	18	8.7	60t	13	6.3	85.2
McMahon, Jim, Chicago	192	114	59.4	1346	7.01	6	3.1	63t	7	3.6	76.0
Tomczak, Mike, Chicago	170	86	50.6	1310	7.71	7	4.1	76t	6	3.5	75.4
Young, Steve, San Francisco	101	54	53.5	680	6.73	3	3.0	73t	3	3.0	72.2
Long, Chuck, Detroit	141	75	53.2	856	6.07	6	4.3	40	6	4.3	68.2
Gannon, Rich, Minnesota	15	7	46.7	90	6.00	0	0.0	19	0	0.0	66.0
Hostetler, Jeff, N.Y. Giants	29	16	55.2	244	8.41	1	3.4	85t	2	6.9	65.9
White, Danny, Dallas	42	29	69.0	274	6.52	1	2.4	24	3	7.1	65.0
Stoudt, Cliff, Phoenix	113	63	55.8	747	6.61	6	5.3	52t	8	7.1	64.3
Hipple, Eric, Detroit	27	12	44.4	158	5.85	0	0.0	31	0	0.0	63.5
Kramer, Tommy, Minnesota	173	83	48.0	1264	7.31	5	2.9	47	9	5.2	60.5
Cavanaugh, Matt, Philadelphia	16	7	43.8	101	6.31	1	6.3	42	1	6.3	59.6
Rutledge, Jeff, N.Y. Giants	17	11	64.7	113	6.65	0	0.0	33	1	5.9	59.2
Harbaugh, Jim, Chicago	97	47	48.5	514	5.30	0	0.0	56	2	2.1	55.9
Dils, Steve, Atlanta	99	49	49.5	566	5.72	2	2.0	50	5	5.1	52.8
Millen, Hugh, Atlanta	31	17	54.8	215	6.94	0	0.0	38	2	6.5	49.8
Sweeney, Kevin, Dallas	78	33	42.3	314	4.03	3	3.8	28	5	6.4	40.2
Wilson, Dave, New Orleans	16	5	31.3	73	4.56	0	0.0	25	1	6.3	21.1
Less than 10 attempts											
Anderson, Neal, Chicago	1	0	0.0	0	0.00	0	0.0	—	0	0.0	39.6
Archer, David, Washington	2	0	0.0	0	0.00	0	0.0	—	0	0.0	39.6
Arnold, Jim, Detroit	1	0	0.0	0	0.00	0	0.0	—	0	0.0	39.6
Byars, Keith, Philadelphia	2	0	0.0	0	0.00	0	0.0	—	0	0.0	39.6
Carruth, Paul Ott, Green Bay	2	0	0.0	0	0.00	0	0.0	—	0	0.0	39.6
Coleman, Greg, Washington	1	0	0.0	0	0.00	0	0.0	—	0	0.0	39.6
Fourcade, John, New Orleans	1	0	0.0	0	0.00	0	0.0	—	0	0.0	39.6
Herrmann, Mark, L.A. Rams	5	4	80.0	38	7.60	0	0.0	15	0	0.0	98.3
Hill, Lonzell, New Orleans	1	0	0.0	0	0.00	0	0.0	—	0	0.0	39.6
Hilliard, Dalton, New Orleans	2	1	50.0	27	13.50	1	50.0	27t	0	0.0	135.4
Jones, James, Detroit	1	0	0.0	0	0.00	0	0.0	—	0	0.0	39.6
Monk, Art, Washington	1	0	0.0	0	0.00	0	0.0	—	0	0.0	39.6
Rice, Jerry, San Francisco	3	1	33.3	14	4.67	0	0.0	14	1	33.3	9.7
Sydney, Harry, San Francisco	1	0	0.0	0	0.00	0	0.0	—	0	0.0	39.6
Teltschik, John, Philadelphia	3	1	33.3	18	6.00	0	0.0	18	0	0.0	54.9
Tupa, Tom, Phoenix	6	4	66.7	49	8.17	0	0.0	22	0	0.0	91.7
Wagner, Bryan, Chicago	1	1	100.0	3	3.00	0	0.0	3	0	0.0	79.2
Witkowski, John, Detroit	1	0	0.0	0	0.00	0	0.0	—	0	0.0	39.6

t indicates touchdown.
Leader based on rating points, minimum 224 attempts.

Pass Receiving

Individual Champions

AFC: 93—Al Toon, N.Y. Jets

NFC: 86—Henry Ellard, L.A. Rams

Most Receptions, Game

AFC: 14—Al Toon, N.Y. Jets vs. Miami, November 27 (181 yards)

NFC: 11—Henry Ellard, L.A. Rams at Denver, November 27 (167 yards, 2 TD)

Yards

NFC: 1,414—Henry Ellard, L.A. Rams

AFC: 1,273—Eddie Brown, Cincinnati

Most Yards, Game

AFC: 216—Eddie Brown, Cincinnati vs. Pittsburgh, November 6 (7 receptions)

NFC: 188—Anthony Carter, Minnesota vs. Detroit, November 6 (8 receptions)

Yards Per Reception

AFC: 24.0—Eddie Brown, Cincinnati

NFC: 20.4—Michael Irvin, Dallas

Longest

NFC: 96—Jerry Rice (from Joe Montana) San Francisco at San Diego, November 27 (TD)

AFC: 89—Louis Lipps (from Bubby Brister) Pittsburgh vs. Philadelphia, November 13 (TD)

Touchdowns

AFC: 14—Mark Clayton, Miami

NFC: 12—Ricky Sanders, Washington

Team Leaders, Receptions

AFC: BUFFALO: 71, Andre Reed; CINCINNATI: 53, Eddie Brown; CLEVELAND: 59, Earnest Byner; DENVER: 68, Vance Johnson; HOUSTON: 72, Drew Hill; INDIANAPOLIS: 54, Bill Brooks; KANSAS CITY: 61, Stephone Paige; L.A. RAIDERS: 43, Tim Brown; MIAMI: 86, Mark Clayton; NEW ENGLAND: 34, Reggie Dupard; N.Y. JETS: 93, Al Toon; PITTSBURGH: 50, Merril Hoge, 50 Louis Lipps; SAN DIEGO: 39, Jamie Holland; SEATTLE: 58, John L. Williams.

NFC: ATLANTA: 68, John Settle; CHICAGO: 45, Dennis McKinnon; DALLAS: 54, Ray Alexander; DETROIT: 44, Pete Mandley; GREEN BAY: 55, Sterling Sharpe; L.A. RAMS: 86, Henry Ellard; MINNESOTA: 72, Anthony Carter; NEW ORLEANS: 85, Eric Martin; N.Y. GIANTS: 65, Lionel Manuel; PHILADELPHIA: 81, Keith Jackson; PHOENIX: 83, J.T. Smith; SAN FRANCISCO: 76, Roger Craig; TAMPA BAY: 58, Bruce Hill; WASHINGTON: 73, Ricky Sanders.

NFL Top 10 Pass Receivers

	No.	Yards	Avg.	Long	TD
Toon, Al, N.Y. Jets	93	1067	11.5	42	5
Ellard, Henry, L.A. Rams	86	1414	16.4	68	10
Clayton, Mark, Miami	86	1129	13.1	45t	14
Martin, Eric, New Orleans	85	1083	12.7	40t	7
Smith, J.T., Phoenix	83	986	11.9	29	5
Jackson, Keith, Philadelphia	81	869	10.7	41	6
Craig, Roger, San Francisco	76	534	7.0	22	1
Sanders, Ricky, Washington	73	1148	15.7	55t	12
Carter, Anthony, Minnesota	72	1225	17.0	67t	6
Hill, Drew, Houston	72	1141	15.8	57t	10
Monk, Art, Washington	72	946	13.1	46t	5
Byars, Keith, Philadelphia	72	705	9.8	37t	4

NFL Top 10 Pass Receivers By Yards

	Yards	No.	Avg.	Long	TD
Ellard, Henry, L.A. Rams	1414	86	16.4	68	10
Rice, Jerry, San Francisco	1306	64	20.4	96t	9
Brown, Eddie, Cincinnati	1273	53	24.0	86t	9
Carter, Anthony, Minnesota	1225	72	17.0	67t	6
Sanders, Ricky, Washington	1148	73	15.7	55t	12
Hill, Drew, Houston	1141	72	15.8	57t	10
Clayton, Mark, Miami	1129	86	13.1	45t	14
Green, Roy, Phoenix	1097	68	16.1	52	7
Martin, Eric, New Orleans	1083	85	12.7	40t	7
Toon, Al, N.Y. Jets	1067	93	11.5	42	5

AFC Pass Receiving—Individual

	No.	Yards	Avg.	Long	TD
Toon, Al, N.Y. Jets	93	1067	11.5	42	5
Clayton, Mark, Miami	86	1129	13.1	45t	14
Hill, Drew, Houston	72	1141	15.8	57t	10
Reed, Andre, Buffalo	71	968	13.6	65t	6
Shuler, Mickey, N.Y. Jets	70	805	11.5	42t	5
Johnson, Vance, Denver	68	896	13.2	86	5
Paige, Stephone, Kansas City	61	902	14.8	49	7
Givins, Ernest, Houston	60	976	16.3	46	5
Byner, Earnest, Cleveland	59	576	9.8	39t	2
Jensen, Jim, Miami	58	652	11.2	31	5
Williams, John L., Seattle	58	651	11.2	75t	3
Langhorne, Reggie, Cleveland	57	780	13.7	77t	7
Stradford, Troy, Miami	56	426	7.6	36	1
Brooks, Bill, Indianapolis	54	867	16.1	53t	3

	No.	Yards	Avg.	Long	TD
Brown, Eddie, Cincinnati	53	1273	24.0	86t	9
Palmer, Paul, Kansas City	53	611	11.5	71t	4
Lipps, Louis, Pittsburgh	50	973	19.5	89t	5
Hoge, Merril, Pittsburgh	50	487	9.7	40	3
Jackson, Mark, Denver	46	852	18.5	63	6
Carson, Carlos, Kansas City	46	711	15.5	80t	3
Brennan, Brian, Cleveland	46	579	12.6	33	1
Nattiel, Ricky, Denver	46	574	12.5	74t	1
Brown, Tim, L.A. Raiders	43	725	16.9	65t	5
Blades, Brian, Seattle	40	682	17.1	55	8
Largent, Steve, Seattle	39	645	16.5	46	2
Duper, Mark, Miami	39	626	16.1	56	1
Holland, Jamie, San Diego	39	536	13.7	45	1
Holman, Rodney, Cincinnati	39	527	13.5	33	3
Sewell, Steve, Denver	38	507	13.3	68t	5
Johnson, Trumaine, Buffalo	37	514	13.9	49	0
Harmon, Ronnie, Buffalo	37	427	11.5	36	3
McGee, Tim, Cincinnati	36	686	19.1	78t	6
Miller, Anthony, San Diego	36	526	14.6	49	3
Dickerson, Eric, Indianapolis	36	377	10.5	50t	1
James, Lionel, San Diego	36	279	7.8	31	1
Newsome, Ozzie, Cleveland	35	343	9.8	28	2
Kay, Clarence, Denver	34	352	10.4	27	4
Allen, Marcus, L.A. Raiders	34	303	8.9	30t	1
McNeil, Freeman, N.Y. Jets	34	288	8.5	25	1
Dupard, Reggie, New England	34	232	6.8	15	0
Edmunds, Ferrell, Miami	33	575	17.4	80t	3
Fryar, Irving, New England	33	490	14.8	80t	5
Metzelaars, Pete, Buffalo	33	438	13.3	35	1
Carter, Rodney, Pittsburgh	32	363	11.3	33	2
Willhite, Gerald, Denver	32	238	7.4	15	0
Anderson, Gary, San Diego	32	182	5.7	20	0
Fernandez, Mervyn, L.A. Raiders	31	805	26.0	85t	4
Morgan, Stanley, New England	31	502	16.2	32	4
Slaughter, Webster, Cleveland	30	462	15.4	41	3
Davenport, Ron, Miami	30	282	9.4	27	0
Riddick, Robb, Buffalo	30	282	9.4	26	1
Weathers, Clarence, Cleveland	29	436	15.0	49	1
Early, Quinn, San Diego	29	375	12.9	38t	4
Bernstine, Rod, San Diego	29	340	11.7	59	0
Brooks, James, Cincinnati	29	287	9.9	28t	6
Tice, Mike, Seattle	29	244	8.4	26	0
Lofton, James, L.A. Raiders	28	549	19.6	57	0
Boyer, Mark, Indianapolis	27	256	9.5	24t	2
Walker, Wesley, N.Y. Jets	26	551	21.2	50t	7
Harry, Emile, Kansas City	26	362	13.9	38	1
Smith, Steve, L.A. Raiders	26	299	11.5	45t	6
Bentley, Albert, Indianapolis	26	252	9.7	21	1
Hector, Johnny, N.Y. Jets	26	237	9.1	30	0
Beach, Pat, Indianapolis	26	235	9.0	23	0
Bouza, Matt, Indianapolis	25	342	13.7	28	4
Skansi, Paul, Seattle	24	238	9.9	21	1
Banks, Fred, Miami	23	430	18.7	55	2
Burkett, Chris, Buffalo	23	354	15.4	34	1
Hampton, Lorenzo, Miami	23	204	8.9	39t	3
Lockett, Charles, Pittsburgh	22	365	16.6	44	1
Jones, Cedric, New England	22	313	14.2	41t	1
Duncan, Curtis, Houston	22	302	13.7	36	1
Hayes, Jonathan, Kansas City	22	233	10.6	25	1
Warner, Curt, Seattle	22	154	7.0	17	2
Mobley, Orson, Denver	21	218	10.4	28	2
Woods, Ickey, Cincinnati	21	199	9.5	25	0
Verdin, Clarence, Indianapolis	20	437	21.9	54	4
Heard, Herman, Kansas City	20	198	9.9	32	0
Saxon, James, Kansas City	19	177	9.3	22	0
Fontenot, Herman, Cleveland	19	170	8.9	15	1
Vick, Roger, N.Y. Jets	19	120	6.3	17	0
Butler, Raymond, Seattle	18	242	13.4	46t	4
Flutie, Darren, San Diego	18	208	11.6	28	2
Thomas, Thurman, Buffalo	18	208	11.6	34	0
Cox, Arthur, San Diego	18	144	8.0	20	0
Perryman, Bob, New England	17	134	7.9	18	0
Winder, Sammy, Denver	17	103	6.1	14	1
Gault, Willie, L.A. Raiders	16	392	24.5	57	2
Thompson, Weegie, Pittsburgh	16	370	23.1	50	1
Dorsett, Tony, Denver	16	122	7.6	16	0
Christensen, Todd, L.A. Raiders	15	190	12.7	22	0
James, Craig, New England	14	171	12.2	32	0
Griggs, Billy, N.Y. Jets	14	133	9.5	21	0
Stephens, John, New England	14	98	7.0	17	0
Collinsworth, Cris, Cincinnati	13	227	17.5	36	1
Highsmith, Alonzo, Houston	12	131	10.9	28	0
Gothard, Preston, Pittsburgh	12	121	10.1	26	1
Pinkett, Allen, Houston	12	114	9.5	51t	2
Stone, Dwight, Pittsburgh	11	196	17.8	72t	1
Drewrey, Willie, Houston	11	172	15.6	55	1
Francis, Russ, New England	11	161	14.6	51	0
Rozier, Mike, Houston	11	99	9.0	18	1
Mack, Kevin, Cleveland	11	87	7.9	25	0

	No.	Yards	Avg.	Long	TD
Williams, Warren, Pittsburgh	11	66	6.0	21	1
Johnson, Troy, Pittsburgh	10	237	23.7	60	0
Harris, Leonard, Houston	10	136	13.6	42	0
Roberts, Alfredo, Kansas City	10	104	10.4	20	0
Manoa, Tim, Cleveland	10	54	5.4	9	0
Johnson, Flip, Buffalo	9	170	18.9	66t	1
Wilson, Stanley, Cincinnati	9	110	12.2	28	1
Taylor, Kitrick, Kansas City	9	105	11.7	36	0
Tennell, Derek, Cleveland	9	88	9.8	26	1
Jackson, Earnest, Pittsburgh	9	84	9.3	24	0
Riggs, Jim, Cincinnati	9	82	9.1	16	0
Jackson, Bo, L.A. Raiders	9	79	8.8	27	0
Dawson, Lin, New England	8	106	13.3	38	2
Tatupu, Mosi, New England	8	58	7.3	17	0
Okoye, Christian, Kansas City	8	51	6.4	12	0
Mueller, Jamie, Buffalo	8	42	5.3	17	0
Sohn, Kurt, N.Y. Jets	7	66	9.4	17	2
Schwedes, Scott, Miami	6	130	21.7	42	0
Dunn, K.D., N.Y. Jets	6	67	11.2	26	0
Williams, Jamie, Houston	6	46	7.7	10	0
Moriarty, Larry, Kansas City	6	40	6.7	12	0
Kane, Tommy, Seattle	6	32	5.3	9	0
Hillary, Ira, Cincinnati	5	76	15.2	31	1
Jennings, Stanford, Cincinnati	5	75	15.0	31	0
McNeil, Gerald, Cleveland	5	74	14.8	23	0
Bellini, Mark, Indianapolis	5	64	12.8	25	0
Mueller, Vance, L.A. Raiders	5	63	12.6	28	0
Spagnola, John, Seattle	5	40	8.0	16	1
Martin, Sammy, New England	4	51	12.8	21	0
Hardy, Bruce, Miami	4	46	11.5	19	0
Townsell, JoJo, N.Y. Jets	4	40	10.0	19	0
Parker, Andy, L.A. Raiders	4	33	8.3	12	0
Junkin, Trey, L.A. Raiders	4	25	6.3	9	2
Massie, Rick, Denver	3	39	13.0	21	0
Agee, Tommie, Seattle	3	31	10.3	13	0
Jones, Anthony, Washington-San Diego	3	21	7.0	11	0
Strachan, Steve, L.A. Raiders	3	19	6.3	13t	1
Jeffires, Haywood, Houston	2	49	24.5	42	1
Pruitt, James, Miami	2	38	19.0	19	0
Young, Glen, Cleveland	2	34	17.0	25	0
Martin, Mike, Cincinnati	2	22	11.0	15t	1
Pollard, Frank, Pittsburgh	2	22	11.0	19	0
Logan, Marc, Cincinnati	2	20	10.0	17	0
Bennett, Woody, Miami	2	16	8.0	12	0
Kattus, Eric, Cincinnati	2	8	4.0	11	0
Rolle, Butch, Buffalo	2	3	1.5	2t	2
Byrum, Carl, Buffalo	2	0	0.0	3	0
Baldinger, Brian, Indianapolis	1	37	37.0	37	0
Graddy, Sam, Denver	1	30	30.0	30	0
Hinnant, Mike, Pittsburgh	1	23	23.0	23	0
Beuerlein, Steve, L.A. Raiders	1	21	21.0	21	0
Clark, Louis, Seattle	1	20	20.0	20t	1
Spencer, Tim, San Diego	1	14	14.0	14	0
Redden, Barry, San Diego	1	11	11.0	11	0
Scott, Willie, New England	1	8	8.0	8	0
Johnson, Jason, Denver	1	6	6.0	6	0
Johnson, Steve, New England	1	5	5.0	5	0
Kelly, Jim, Buffalo	1	5	5.0	5	0
Farrell, Sean, New England	1	4	4.0	4	0
Kelly, Pat, Denver	1	4	4.0	4	0
Bolden, Rickey, Cleveland	1	3	3.0	3t	1
Kinchen, Brian, Miami	1	3	3.0	3	0
Sievers, Eric, San Diego	1	2	2.0	2	0
Hinton, Chris, Indianapolis	1	1	1.0	1	0
Colbert, Darrell, Kansas City	1	−3	−3.0	−3	0
Donaldson, Ray, Indianapolis	1	−3	−3.0	−3	0
Gamble, Kenny, Kansas City	1	−7	−7.0	−7	0

t indicates touchdown.
Leader based on most passes caught.

NFC Pass Receiving—Individual

	No.	Yards	Avg.	Long	TD
Ellard, Henry, L.A. Rams	86	1414	16.4	68	10
Martin, Eric, New Orleans	85	1083	12.7	40t	7
Smith, J.T., Phoenix	83	986	11.9	29	5
Jackson, Keith, Philadelphia	81	869	10.7	41	6
Craig, Roger, San Francisco	76	534	7.0	22	1
Sanders, Ricky, Washington	73	1148	15.7	55t	12
Carter, Anthony, Minnesota	72	1225	17.0	67t	6
Monk, Art, Washington	72	946	13.1	46t	5
Byars, Keith, Philadelphia	72	705	9.8	37t	4
Green, Roy, Phoenix	68	1097	16.1	52	7
Settle, John, Atlanta	68	570	8.4	27	1
Hill, Lonzell, New Orleans	66	703	10.7	35	7
Manuel, Lionel, N.Y. Giants	65	1029	15.8	46	4
Rice, Jerry, San Francisco	64	1306	20.4	96t	9
Clark, Gary, Washington	59	892	15.1	60t	7
Holohan, Pete, L.A. Rams	59	640	10.8	29	3
Hill, Bruce, Tampa Bay	58	1040	17.9	42t	9
Carrier, Mark, Tampa Bay	57	970	17.0	59t	5
Jordan, Steve, Minnesota	57	756	13.3	38	5
Sharpe, Sterling, Green Bay	55	791	14.4	51	1
Alexander, Ray, Dallas	54	788	14.6	50t	6
Bavaro, Mark, N.Y. Giants	53	672	12.7	36	4
Walker, Herschel, Dallas	53	505	9.5	50	2
Martin, Kelvin, Dallas	49	622	12.7	35t	3
Kemp, Perry, Green Bay	48	620	12.9	36	0
McKinnon, Dennis, Chicago	45	704	15.6	76t	3
Mandley, Pete, Detroit	44	617	14.0	56	4
Bryant, Kelvin, Washington	42	447	10.6	47	5
Rathman, Tom, San Francisco	42	382	9.1	24	0
Johnson, Damone, L.A. Rams	42	350	8.3	23	6
Jones, Hassan, Minnesota	40	778	19.5	68t	5
Baker, Stephen, N.Y. Giants	40	656	16.4	85t	7
Carter, Cris, Philadelphia	39	761	19.5	80t	6
Hall, Ron, Tampa Bay	39	555	14.2	37	0
Awalt, Robert, Phoenix	39	454	11.6	52t	4
James, Garry, Detroit	39	382	9.8	39t	2
Anderson, Neal, Chicago	39	371	9.5	36	0
Woodside, Keith, Green Bay	39	352	9.0	49t	2
Novacek, Jay, Phoenix	38	569	15.0	42t	4
Ferrell, Earl, Phoenix	38	315	8.3	30	2
Lang, Gene, Atlanta	37	398	10.8	50	1
Hilliard, Dalton, New Orleans	34	335	9.9	26	1
Toney, Anthony, Philadelphia	34	256	7.5	24	1
Gentry, Dennis, Chicago	33	486	14.7	45	3
Wilson, Mike, San Francisco	33	405	12.3	31	3
Irvin, Michael, Dallas	32	654	20.4	61t	5
Delpino, Robert, L.A. Rams	30	312	10.4	38	2
Rice, Allen, Minnesota	30	279	9.3	38	0
West, Ed, Green Bay	30	276	9.2	35	3
Newsome, Tim, Dallas	30	236	7.9	32	0
Jones, James, Detroit	29	259	8.9	40	0
Cox, Aaron, L.A. Rams	28	590	21.1	69t	5
Morris, Ron, Chicago	28	498	17.8	63t	4
Stanley, Walter, Green Bay	28	436	15.6	56	0
Dixon, Floyd, Atlanta	28	368	13.1	36	2
Adams, George, N.Y. Giants	27	174	6.4	19	0
Tice, John, New Orleans	26	297	11.4	40	1
Mitchell, Stump, Phoenix	25	214	8.6	28	1
Carruth, Paul Ott, Green Bay	24	211	8.8	31	0
Bell, Greg, L.A. Rams	24	124	5.2	20	2
Jones, Ernie, Phoenix	23	496	21.6	93t	3
McEwen, Craig, Washington	23	323	14.0	46	0
Anderson, Alfred, Minnesota	23	242	10.5	19	1
Quick, Mike, Philadelphia	22	508	23.1	55t	4
Lee, Gary, Detroit	22	261	11.9	18	1
Riggs, Gerald, Atlanta	22	171	7.8	30	0
Morris, Joe, N.Y. Giants	22	166	7.5	24	0
Bland, Carl, Detroit	21	307	14.6	35	2
Muster, Brad, Chicago	21	236	11.2	40t	1
Chadwick, Jeff, Detroit	20	304	15.2	32	3
Scott, Patrick, Green Bay	20	275	13.8	41	1
Matthews, Aubrey, Atlanta-Green Bay	20	231	11.6	25	2
Suhey, Matt, Chicago	20	154	7.7	29	0
Fullwood, Brent, Green Bay	20	128	6.4	30t	1
Johnson, Ron, Philadelphia	19	417	21.9	54	2
Clark, Robert, New Orleans	19	245	12.9	21t	2
Carthon, Maurice, N.Y. Giants	19	194	10.2	24	1
Chandler, Thornton, Dallas	18	186	10.3	29	1
Bailey, Stacey, Atlanta	17	437	25.7	68t	2
Garrity, Gregg, Philadelphia	17	208	12.2	20	1
Clack, Darryl, Dallas	17	126	7.4	18	1
Perriman, Brett, New Orleans	16	215	13.4	33	2
Frank, John, San Francisco	16	195	12.2	38	3
Whisenhunt, Ken, Atlanta	16	174	10.9	25	1
Smith, Jeff, Tampa Bay	16	134	8.4	22	0
McGee, Buford, L.A. Rams	16	117	7.3	16	3
Nelson, Darrin, Minnesota	16	105	6.6	27	0
Gustafson, Jim, Minnesota	15	231	15.4	47	1
Fenney, Rick, Minnesota	15	224	14.9	42	0
Davis, Wendell, Chicago	15	220	14.7	36	0
Pillow, Frank, Tampa Bay	15	206	13.7	34	1
Gay, Everett, Dallas	15	205	13.7	25	1
Mowatt, Zeke, N.Y. Giants	15	196	13.1	38t	1
Thornton, James, Chicago	15	135	9.0	19	0
Wilder, James, Tampa Bay	15	124	8.3	24	0
Oliphant, Mike, Washington	15	111	7.4	16	0
Taylor, John, San Francisco	14	325	23.2	73t	2
Heller, Ron, San Francisco	14	140	10.0	22	0
Moorehead, Emery, Chicago	14	133	9.5	28	2
Haynes, Michael, Atlanta	13	232	17.8	49t	4
Ingram, Mark, N.Y. Giants	13	158	12.2	32	1
Carter, Pat, Detroit	13	145	11.2	31	0
Heyward, Craig, New Orleans	13	105	8.1	18	0
Hester, Jessie, Atlanta	12	176	14.7	41	0
Smith, Don, Tampa Bay	12	138	11.5	25	0
Cosbie, Doug, Dallas	12	112	9.3	21	0

	No.	Yards	Avg.	Long	TD
Warren, Don, Washington	12	112	9.3	32	0
Haddix, Michael, Philadelphia	12	82	6.8	14	0
Anderson, Willie, L.A. Rams	11	319	29.0	56	0
Orr, Terry, Washington	11	222	20.2	58	2
Lewis, Leo, Minnesota	11	141	12.8	46t	1
Wilkins, Gary, Atlanta	11	134	12.2	33	0
Mayes, Rueben, New Orleans	11	103	9.4	25	0
Paige, Tony, Detroit	11	100	9.1	15	0
Epps, Phillip, Green Bay	11	99	9.0	25	0
Howard, William, Tampa Bay	11	97	8.8	16	0
Davis, Kenneth, Green Bay	11	81	7.4	11	0
Turner, Odessa, N.Y. Giants	10	128	12.8	28t	1
Fowler, Todd, Dallas	10	64	6.4	13	0
Magee, Calvin, Tampa Bay	9	103	11.4	25	0
Sanders, Thomas, Chicago	9	94	10.4	39	0
Folsom, Steve, Dallas	9	84	9.3	20	2
Anderson, Ottis, N.Y. Giants	9	57	6.3	13	0
Starring, Stephen, Tampa Bay-Detroit	8	164	20.5	53	0
Greer, Terry, San Francisco	8	120	15.0	31	0
Mason, Larry, Green Bay	8	84	10.5	39	1
Jones, Brent, San Francisco	8	57	7.1	18t	2
Smith, Timmy, Washington	8	53	6.6	16	0
Primus, James, Atlanta	8	42	5.3	8	0
Robinson, Stacy, N.Y. Giants	7	143	20.4	62t	3
Goode, Kerry, Tampa Bay	7	68	9.7	22	0
DuBose, Doug, San Francisco	6	57	9.5	13	0
Giles, Jimmie, Philadelphia	6	57	9.5	17	1
Green, Gaston, L.A. Rams	6	57	9.5	19	0
Boso, Cap, Chicago	6	50	8.3	15	0
White, Charles, L.A. Rams	6	36	6.0	18	0
Harris, Darryl, Minnesota	6	30	5.0	7	0
Edwards, Kelvin, Dallas	5	93	18.6	27	0
McConkey, Phil, N.Y. Giants	5	72	14.4	28	0
Jordan, Buford, New Orleans	5	70	14.0	25	0
Brenner, Hoby, New Orleans	5	67	13.4	24	0
Milling, James, Atlanta	5	66	13.2	34	0
Taylor, Gene, Tampa Bay	5	53	10.6	14	0
Dozier, D.J., Minnesota	5	49	9.8	20	0
Allen, Anthony, Washington	5	48	9.6	18	1
Tautalatasi, Junior, Philadelphia	5	48	9.6	21	0
Didier, Clint, Green Bay	5	37	7.4	15	1
Tate, Lars, Tampa Bay	5	23	4.6	9	1
Stamps, Sylvester, Atlanta	5	22	4.4	7	0
Flagler, Terrence, San Francisco	4	72	18.0	57	0
Rouson, Lee, N.Y. Giants	4	61	15.3	31	0
Chandler, Wes, San Francisco	4	33	8.3	9	0
Jordan, Tony, Phoenix	4	24	6.0	12	0
Kozlowski, Glen, Chicago	3	92	30.7	50	0
Higdon, Alex, Atlanta	3	60	20.0	34t	2
Williams, Scott, Detroit	3	46	15.3	32	0
Mularkey, Mike, Minnesota	3	39	13.0	19	0
Lewis, Mark, Detroit	3	32	10.7	23	1
Burbage, Cornell, Dallas	2	50	25.0	41	0
Bolton, Scott, Green Bay	2	33	16.5	18	0
Craig, Paco, Detroit	2	29	14.5	18	0
Young, Mike, L.A. Rams	2	27	13.5	18	0
Scales, Greg, New Orleans	2	20	10.0	14	1
Sydney, Harry, San Francisco	2	18	9.0	9	0
Collins, Patrick, Green Bay	2	17	8.5	9	0
Brown, Ron, L.A. Rams	2	16	8.0	10	0
Caravello, Joe, Washington	2	15	7.5	8	0
Wolfley, Ron, Phoenix	2	11	5.5	8	0
Griffin, Keith, Washington	2	9	4.5	5	1
Hebert, Bobby, New Orleans	2	0	0.0	2	0
Parks, Jeff, Tampa Bay	1	22	22.0	22	0
Konecny, Mark, Philadelphia	1	18	18.0	18	0
McIntyre, Guy, San Francisco	1	17	17.0	17t	1
Moore, Ricky, Phoenix	1	15	15.0	15	0
Nicholas, Calvin, San Francisco	1	14	14.0	14	0
Holmes, Don, Phoenix	1	10	10.0	10	0
Hostetler, Jeff, N.Y. Giants	1	10	10.0	10	0
Pattison, Mark, New Orleans	1	8	8.0	8	0
Benson, Cliff, New Orleans	1	5	5.0	5	0
Morris, Jamie, Washington	1	3	3.0	3	0
Hackett, Joey, Green Bay	1	2	2.0	2t	1
Newton, Nate, Dallas	1	2	2.0	2	0
Hilton, Carl, Minnesota	1	1	1.0	1t	1
Painter, Carl, Detroit	1	1	1.0	1	0
Abercrombie, Walter, Philadelphia	1	−2	−2.0	−2	0

t indicates touchdown.
Leader based on most passes caught.

Interceptions

Individual Champions
NFC: 10—Scott Case, Atlanta
AFC: 8—Erik McMillan, N.Y. Jets

Most Interceptions, Game
AFC: 3—Erik McMillan, N.Y. Jets at Miami, October 23
NFC: 2—By 16 players

Yards
AFC: 180—Mark Kelso, Buffalo
NFC: 123—Harry Hamilton, Tampa Bay

Longest
NFC: 94—Walker Lee Ashley, Minnesota vs. Chicago, December 19 (TD)
AFC: 86—Greg Townsend, L.A. Raiders vs. Denver, December 4 (TD)

Touchdowns
AFC: 2—Erik McMillan, N.Y. Jets
NFC: 2—Carl Lee, Minnesota

Team Leaders, Interceptions
AFC: BUFFALO: 7, Mark Kelso; CINCINNATI: 7, Eric Thomas; CLEVELAND: 5, Felix Wright; DENVER: 4, Mike Harden; HOUSTON: 4, Jeff Donaldson; INDIANAPOLIS: 4, Willie Tullis; KANSAS CITY: 7, Deron Cherry; L.A. RAIDERS: 3, Mike Haynes, Vann McElroy; MIAMI: 4, William Judson, Jarvis Williams; NEW ENGLAND: 4, Raymond Clayborn, Roland James, Fred Marion; N.Y. JETS: 8, Erik McMillan; PITTSBURGH: 4, Dwayne Woodruff, Rod Woodson; SAN DIEGO: 7, Gill Byrd; SEATTLE: 6, Paul Moyer.
NFC: ATLANTA: 10, Scott Case; CHICAGO: 8, Vestee Jackson; DALLAS: 2, Michael Downs, Everson Walls, Robert Williams; DETROIT: 3, George Jamison, Devon Mitchell; GREEN BAY: 5, Mark Murphy; L.A. RAMS: 4, Johnnie Johnson; MINNESOTA: 8, Carl Lee; NEW ORLEANS: 4, Gene Atkins; N.Y. GIANTS: 4, Sheldon White; PHILADELPHIA: 8, Terry Hoage; PHOENIX: 3, Carl Carter, Cedric Mack; SAN FRANCISCO: 7, Tim McKyer; TAMPA BAY: 6, Harry Hamilton; WASHINGTON: 4, Barry Wilburn.

Team Champions
NFC: 36—Minnesota
AFC: 24—N.Y. Jets

AFC Interceptions—Team

	No.	Yards	Avg.	Long	TD
N.Y. Jets	24	228	9.5	55t	3
Houston	22	302	13.7	51	2
Seattle	22	280	12.7	34	1
Cincinnati	22	181	8.2	37	1
Pittsburgh	20	381	19.1	78t	2
Cleveland	20	319	16.0	75t	1
New England	20	244	12.2	42	0
Kansas City	18	166	9.2	32	0
L.A. Raiders	17	278	16.4	86t	1
Miami	16	219	13.7	52	0
Denver	16	200	12.5	39	0
San Diego	16	179	11.2	55t	1
Buffalo	15	244	16.3	78t	1
Indianapolis	15	189	12.6	41t	1
AFC Total	263	3410	—	86t	14
AFC Average	18.8	243.6	13.0	—	1.0

NFC Interceptions—Team

	No.	Yards	Avg.	Long	TD
Minnesota	36	589	16.4	94t	5
Philadelphia	32	371	11.6	38	0
Chicago	26	237	9.1	46	0
Atlanta	24	185	7.7	47t	1
L.A. Rams	22	281	12.8	47t	1
San Francisco	22	88	4.0	44	0
Tampa Bay	21	283	13.5	58	1
Green Bay	20	224	11.2	33	0
New Orleans	17	295	17.4	44	0
Phoenix	16	88	5.5	18	0
N.Y. Giants	15	292	19.5	66	2
Detroit	15	247	16.5	90t	2
Washington	14	193	13.8	43	0
Dallas	10	67	6.7	29	1
NFC Total	290	3440	—	94t	13
NFC Average	20.7	245.7	11.9	—	0.9
League Total	553	6850	—	94t	27
League Average	19.8	244.6	12.4	—	1.0

NFL Top 10 Interceptors

	No.	Yards	Avg.	Long	TD
Case, Scott, Atlanta	10	47	4.7	12	0
McMillan, Erik, N.Y. Jets	8	168	21.0	55t	2
Lee, Carl, Minnesota	8	118	14.8	58t	2
Hoage, Terry, Philadelphia	8	116	14.5	38	0
Jackson, Vestee, Chicago	8	94	11.8	46	0
Kelso, Mark, Buffalo	7	180	25.7	78t	1
Byrd, Gill, San Diego	7	82	11.7	42	0
Thomas, Eric, Cincinnati	7	61	8.7	37	0
Cherry, Deron, Kansas City	7	51	7.3	24	0
McKyer, Tim, San Francisco	7	11	1.6	7	0

AFC Interceptions—Individual

	No.	Yards	Avg.	Long	TD
McMillan, Erik, N.Y. Jets	8	168	21.0	55t	2
Kelso, Mark, Buffalo	7	180	25.7	78t	1
Byrd, Gill, San Diego	7	82	11.7	42	0
Thomas, Eric, Cincinnati	7	61	8.7	37	0
Cherry, Deron, Kansas City	7	51	7.3	24	0
Moyer, Paul, Seattle	6	79	13.2	34	0
Wright, Felix, Cleveland	5	126	25.2	53	0
Taylor, Terry, Seattle	5	53	10.6	27t	1
Fulcher, David, Cincinnati	5	38	7.6	16t	1
Hasty, James, N.Y. Jets	5	20	4.0	16	0
Woodruff, Dwayne, Pittsburgh	4	109	27.3	78t	1
Woodson, Rod, Pittsburgh	4	98	24.5	29	0
Clayborn, Raymond, New England	4	65	16.3	31	0
Williams, Jarvis, Miami	4	62	15.5	23	0
Judson, William, Miami	4	57	14.3	52	0
Billups, Lewis, Cincinnati	4	47	11.8	29	0
Marion, Fred, New England	4	47	11.8	22	0
Harden, Mike, Denver	4	36	9.0	34	0
Tullis, Willie, Indianapolis	4	36	9.0	20	0
James, Roland, New England	4	30	7.5	22	0
Donaldson, Jeff, Houston	4	29	7.3	23	0
Minnifield, Frank, Cleveland	4	16	4.0	13	0
Washington, Brian, Cleveland	3	104	34.7	75t	1
Bryant, Domingo, Houston	3	56	18.7	36t	1
Castille, Jeremiah, Denver	3	51	17.0	33	0
Prior, Mike, Indianapolis	3	46	15.3	23	0
Jenkins, Mel, Seattle	3	41	13.7	21	0
Everett, Thomas, Pittsburgh	3	31	10.3	29	0
Haynes, Mike, L.A. Raiders	3	30	10.0	30	0
McElroy, Vann, L.A. Raiders	3	17	5.7	13	0
Horton, Ray, Cincinnati	3	13	4.3	11	0
Bickett, Duane, Indianapolis	3	7	2.3	7	0
Booty, John, N.Y. Jets	3	0	0.0	0	0
Johnson, Richard, Houston	3	0	0.0	0	0
Robbins, Randy, Denver	2	66	33.0	39	0
Browner, Keith, San Diego	2	65	32.5	55t	1
Griffin, Larry, Pittsburgh	2	63	31.5	33	0
Burruss, Lloyd, Kansas City	2	57	28.5	32	0
Goode, Chris, Indianapolis	2	53	26.5	35	0
McSwain, Rod, New England	2	51	25.5	42	0
Brown, Steve, Houston	2	48	24.0	44t	1
Daniel, Eugene, Indianapolis	2	44	22.0	41t	1
Johnson, Mike, Cleveland	2	36	18.0	31	0
Hollis, David, Seattle	2	32	16.0	30	0
Bennett, Cornelius, Buffalo	2	30	15.0	30	0
Smith, Leonard, Phoenix-Buffalo	2	29	14.5	15	0
Dixon, Hanford, Cleveland	2	24	12.0	24	0
Glasgow, Nesby, Seattle	2	19	9.5	19	0
Price, Dennis, L.A. Raiders	2	18	9.0	18	0
Fellows, Ron, L.A. Raiders	2	14	7.0	14	0
Brown, Mark, Miami	2	13	6.5	13	0
Harper, Mark, Cleveland	2	13	6.5	8	0
Rembert, Johnny, New England	2	10	5.0	6	0
Pearson, J.C., Kansas City	2	8	4.0	7	0
Braxton, Tyrone, Denver	2	6	3.0	6	0
Lyles, Robert, Houston	2	3	1.5	3	0
Offerdahl, John, Miami	2	2	1.0	2	0
Coleman, Leonard, San Diego	2	0	0.0	0	0
Howard, Carl, N.Y. Jets	2	0	0.0	0	0
Johnson, Eddie, Cleveland	2	0	0.0	0	0
Miano, Rich, N.Y. Jets	2	0	0.0	0	0
Anderson, Eddie, L.A. Raiders	2	−6	−3.0	2	0
Townsend, Greg, L.A. Raiders	1	86	86.0	86t	1
Long, Howie, L.A. Raiders	1	73	73.0	73	0
Johnson, Kenny, Houston	1	51	51.0	51	0
Thomas, Rodney, Miami	1	48	48.0	48	0
Seale, Eugene, Houston	1	46	46.0	46	0
Zordich, Mike, N.Y. Jets	1	35	35.0	35t	1
Dean, Vernon, Seattle	1	31	31.0	31	0
Jordan, Tim, New England	1	31	31.0	31	0
Dennison, Rick, Denver	1	29	29.0	29	0
Jordan, Darin, Pittsburgh	1	28	28.0	28t	1
Carr, Gregg, Pittsburgh	1	27	27.0	27	0
McKenzie, Reggie, L.A. Raiders	1	26	26.0	26	0
Gowdy, Cornell, Pittsburgh	1	24	24.0	24	0
Hill, Greg, Kansas City	1	24	24.0	24	0
Allen, Patrick, Houston	1	23	23.0	21	0
McNeal, Don, Miami	1	23	23.0	23	0
Bennett, Roy, San Diego	1	21	21.0	21	0
Lee, Zeph, L.A. Raiders	1	20	20.0	20	0
Smith, Doug, Houston	1	20	20.0	20	0
Lewis, Albert, Kansas City	1	19	19.0	19	0
Comeaux, Darren, Seattle	1	18	18.0	18	0
Cocroft, Sherman, Buffalo	1	17	17.0	17	0
Graf, Rick, Miami	1	14	14.0	14	0
Dixon, Rickey, Cincinnati	1	13	13.0	13	0
Fuller, William, Houston	1	9	9.0	9	0
Grimsley, John, Houston	1	9	9.0	9	0
Smith, Billy Ray, San Diego	1	9	9.0	9	0
Bostic, Keith, Houston	1	7	7.0	7	0
Miller, Darrin, Seattle	1	7	7.0	7	0
Wilson, Steve, Denver	1	7	7.0	7	0
McGrew, Larry, New England	1	6	6.0	6	0
Wilcots, Solomon, Cincinnati	1	6	6.0	6	0
Stensrud, Mike, Kansas City	1	5	5.0	5	0
Fletcher, Simon, Denver	1	4	4.0	4	0
Lippett, Ronnie, New England	1	4	4.0	4	0
Davis, Wayne, Buffalo	1	3	3.0	3	0
Krauss, Barry, Indianapolis	1	3	3.0	3	0
McArthur, Kevin, N.Y. Jets	1	3	3.0	3	0
Zander, Carl, Cincinnati	1	3	3.0	3	0
Benson, Troy, N.Y. Jets	1	2	2.0	2	0
Faucette, Chuck, San Diego	1	2	2.0	2	0
Gamble, Kenny, Kansas City	1	2	2.0	2	0
Bowyer, Walt, Denver	1	1	1.0	1	0
Byrd, Richard, Houston	1	1	1.0	1	0
Hinkle, Bryan, Pittsburgh	1	1	1.0	1	0
Bentley, Ray, Buffalo	1	0	0.0	0	0
Bowman, Jim, New England	1	0	0.0	0	0
Cofield, Tim, Kansas City	1	0	0.0	0	0
Conlan, Shane, Buffalo	1	0	0.0	0	0
Del Rio, Jack, Kansas City	1	0	0.0	0	0
Glenn, Vencie, San Diego	1	0	0.0	0	0
Haynes, Mark, Denver	1	0	0.0	0	0
Humphery, Bobby, N.Y. Jets	1	0	0.0	0	0
Lankford, Paul, Miami	1	0	0.0	0	0
Little, David, Pittsburgh	1	0	0.0	0	0
Nickerson, Hardy, Pittsburgh	1	0	0.0	0	0
Odomes, Nate, Buffalo	1	0	0.0	0	0
Patterson, Elvis, San Diego	1	0	0.0	0	0
Robinson, Eugene, Seattle	1	0	0.0	0	0
Ross, Kevin, Kansas City	1	0	0.0	0	0
Sanchez, Lupe, Pittsburgh	1	0	0.0	0	0
Washington, Lionel, L.A. Raiders	1	0	0.0	0	0

t indicates touchdown.
Leader based on most interceptions.

NFC Interceptions—Individual

	No.	Yards	Avg.	Long	TD
Case, Scott, Atlanta	10	47	4.7	12	0
Lee, Carl, Minnesota	8	118	14.8	58t	2
Hoage, Terry, Philadelphia	8	116	14.5	38	0
Jackson, Vestee, Chicago	8	94	11.8	46	0
McKyer, Tim, San Francisco	7	11	1.6	7	0
Hamilton, Harry, Tampa Bay	6	123	20.5	58	0
Allen, Eric, Philadelphia	5	76	15.2	21	0
Lott, Ronnie, San Francisco	5	59	11.8	44	0
Moore, Robert, Atlanta	5	56	11.2	47t	1
Browner, Joey, Minnesota	5	29	5.8	18	0
Hopkins, Wes, Philadelphia	5	21	4.2	11	0
Murphy, Mark, Green Bay	5	19	3.8	9	0
Joyner, Seth, Philadelphia	4	96	24.0	30	0
Solomon, Jesse, Minnesota	4	84	21.0	78t	1
White, Sheldon, N.Y. Giants	4	70	17.5	39	0
Cecil, Chuck, Green Bay	4	56	14.0	33	0
Atkins, Gene, New Orleans	4	42	10.5	40	0
Clark, Bret, Atlanta	4	40	10.0	21	0
Tate, David, Chicago	4	35	8.8	17	0
Wilburn, Barry, Washington	4	24	6.0	14	0
Fuller, Jeff, San Francisco	4	18	4.5	10	0
Johnson, Johnnie, L.A. Rams	4	18	4.5	11	0
Reynolds, Ricky, Tampa Bay	4	7	1.8	7	0
Mitchell, Devon, Detroit	3	107	35.7	90t	1
Waymer, Dave, New Orleans	3	91	30.3	44	0
Gray, Jerry, L.A. Rams	3	83	27.7	47t	1
Rutland, Reggie, Minnesota	3	63	21.0	36	0
Jakes, Van, New Orleans	3	61	20.3	39	0
Marshall, Wilber, Washington	3	61	20.3	43	0
Fullington, Darrell, Minnesota	3	57	19.0	40	0
Jamison, George, Detroit	3	56	18.7	52t	1
Walton, Alvin, Washington	3	54	18.0	29	0
Harris, John, Minnesota	3	46	15.3	27	0
Kinard, Terry, N.Y. Giants	3	46	15.3	39	0

	No.	Yards	Avg.	Long	TD
Lee, Mark, Green Bay	3	37	12.3	27	0
Mack, Cedric, Phoenix	3	33	11.0	12	0
Sutton, Reggie, New Orleans	3	32	10.7	34	0
Stills, Ken, Green Bay	3	29	9.7	17	0
Brown, Dave, Green Bay	3	27	9.0	15	0
Irvin, LeRoy, L.A. Rams	3	25	8.3	22	0
Frizzell, William, Philadelphia	3	19	6.3	13	0
Waters, Andre, Philadelphia	3	19	6.3	14	0
Howard, David, Minnesota	3	16	5.3	10	0
Morrissey, Jim, Chicago	3	13	4.3	13	0
Elder, Donnie, Tampa Bay	3	9	3.0	9	0
Carter, Carl, Phoenix	3	0	0.0	0	0
Carson, Harry, N.Y. Giants	2	66	33.0	66	0
Stewart, Michael. L.A. Rams	2	61	30.5	43	0
Pitts, Ron, Green Bay	2	56	28.0	31	0
Edwards, Brad, Minnesota	2	47	23.5	37t	1
Griffin, James, Detroit	2	31	15.5	31	0
Robinson, Mark, Tampa Bay	2	28	14.0	28	0
Newman, Anthony, L.A. Rams	2	27	13.5	27	0
Harris, Odie, Tampa Bay	2	26	13.0	24	0
Duerson, Dave, Chicago	2	18	9.0	18	0
Williams, Robert, Dallas	2	18	9.0	12	0
Holt, Issiac, Minnesota	2	15	7.5	15	0
Kelm, Larry, L.A. Rams	2	15	7.5	9	0
Richardson, Mike, Chicago	2	15	7.5	15	0
Krumm, Todd, Chicago	2	14	7.0	14	0
Blades, Bennie, Detroit	2	12	6.0	7	0
McDonald, Tim, Phoenix	2	11	5.5	11	0
Bruce, Aundray, Atlanta	2	10	5.0	10	0
Gordon, Tim, Atlanta	2	10	5.0	7	0
Young, Roynell, Philadelphia	2	5	2.5	5	0
Downs, Michael, Dallas	2	3	1.5	3	0
Cherry, Raphel, Detroit	2	0	0.0	0	0
Holmoe, Tom, San Francisco	2	0	0.0	0	0
Lyles, Lester, Phoenix	2	0	0.0	0	0
Rivera, Ron, Chicago	2	0	0.0	0	0
Walls, Everson, Dallas	2	0	0.0	0	0
Wright, Eric, San Francisco	2	−2	−1.0	0	0
Ashley, Walker Lee, Minnesota	1	94	94.0	94t	1
Douglass, Maurice, Chicago	1	35	35.0	35	0
Murphy, Kevin, Tampa Bay	1	35	35.0	35t	1
Johnson, Vaughan, New Orleans	1	34	34.0	34	0
Johnson, Pepper, N.Y. Giants	1	33	33.0	33t	1
Holmes, Jerry, Detroit	1	32	32.0	32	0
Francis, Ron, Dallas	1	29	29.0	29	0
Marve, Eugene, Tampa Bay	1	29	29.0	29	0
White, Adrian, N.Y. Giants	1	29	29.0	29	0
Futrell, Bobby, Tampa Bay	1	26	26.0	26	0
Butler, Bobby, Atlanta	1	22	22.0	22	0
Bowles, Todd, Washington	1	20	20.0	20	0
Meisner, Greg, L.A. Rams	1	20	20.0	20	0
Reasons, Gary, N.Y. Giants	1	20	20.0	20	0
Mack, Milton, New Orleans	1	19	19.0	19	0
Curtis, Travis, Phoenix	1	18	18.0	18	0
Noonan, Danny, Dallas	1	17	17.0	17t	1
Jackson, Rickey, New Orleans	1	16	16.0	16	0
Banks, Carl, N.Y. Giants	1	15	15.0	15t	1
Collins, Mark, N.Y. Giants	1	13	13.0	13	0
Henderson, Wymon, Minnesota	1	13	13.0	13	0
Singletary, Mike, Chicago	1	13	13.0	13	0
Green, Darrell, Washington	1	12	12.0	12	0
Coleman, Monte, Washington	1	11	11.0	11	0
Davis, Brian, Washington	1	11	11.0	11	0
Owens, Mel, L.A. Rams	1	11	11.0	11	0
Greene, Kevin, L.A. Rams	1	10	10.0	10	0
Clasby, Bob, Phoenix	1	7	7.0	7	0
Thomas, Henry, Minnesota	1	7	7.0	7	0
Washington, James, L.A. Rams	1	7	7.0	7	0
Williams, Jimmy, Detroit	1	5	5.0	5	0
McNorton, Bruce, Detroit	1	4	4.0	4	0
Junior, E. J., Phoenix	1	2	2.0	2	0
Turner, Keena, San Francisco	1	2	2.0	2	0
Young, Lonnie, Phoenix	1	2	2.0	2	0
Sutton, Mickey, L.A. Rams	1	1	1.0	1	0
Bates, Bill, Dallas	1	0	0.0	0	0
Carter, Michael, San Francisco	1	0	0.0	0	0
Cook, Toi, New Orleans	1	0	0.0	0	0
Everett, Eric, Philadelphia	1	0	0.0	0	0
Gayle, Shaun, Chicago	1	0	0.0	0	0
Hendrix, Manny, Dallas	1	0	0.0	0	0
Jerue, Mark, L.A. Rams	1	0	0.0	0	0
Jones, Rod, Tampa Bay	1	0	0.0	0	0
Mitchell, Roland, Phoenix	1	0	0.0	0	0
Williams, Perry, N.Y. Giants	1	0	0.0	0	0
Brown, Jerome, Philadelphia	1	−5	−5.0	−5	0
Bell, Todd, Philadelphia	0	24	—	24	0
Newsome, Vince, L.A. Rams	0	3	—	3	0

t indicates touchdown.
Leader based on most interceptions.

Punting

Individual Champions
AFC: 45.4—Harry Newsome, Pittsburgh
NFC: 42.4—Jim Arnold, Detroit

Net Average
AFC: 37.8—Mike Horan, Denver
NFC: 35.9—Jim Arnold, Detroit

Longest
AFC: 74—Jeff Feagles, New England vs. Indianapolis, October 2
NFC: 70—John Teltschik, Philadelphia vs. Dallas, October 23
70—Bryan Wagner, Chicago at New England, October 30

Most Punts
NFC: 98—Rick Donnelly, Atlanta
98—John Teltschik, Philadelphia
AFC: 91—Jeff Feagles, New England
91—Jeff Gossett, L.A. Raiders

Most Punts, Game
AFC: 10—Kelly Goodburn, Kansas City at N.Y. Jets, October 2
10—Rohn Stark, Indianapolis at New England, October 2
NFC: 11—Rick Donnelly, Atlanta at Philadelphia, October 30

Team Champions
AFC: 43.8—Denver
NFC: 42.4—Detroit

AFC Punting—Team

	Net Punts	Gross Yards	Long	Gross Avg.	TB	Blk.	Opp. Ret.	Ret. Yards	In 20	Net Avg.
Denver	68	2978	70	43.8	2	0	33	364	21	37.9
San Diego	86	3745	62	43.5	11	1	56	558	22	34.5
Indianapolis	64	2784	65	43.5	8	0	37	418	15	34.5
Miami	64	2754	64	43.0	9	0	35	318	18	35.3
L.A. Raiders	91	3804	58	41.8	8	0	47	397	27	35.7
Pittsburgh	71	2950	62	41.5	10	6	40	418	9	32.8
Seattle	70	2858	68	40.8	4	0	36	202	14	36.8
Kansas City	76	3059	59	40.3	8	0	48	473	10	31.9
Buffalo	62	2451	60	39.5	2	0	36	222	13	35.3
N.Y. Jets	85	3310	64	38.9	10	0	34	201	26	34.2
Houston	65	2523	61	38.8	5	0	35	206	12	34.1
Cleveland	67	2578	61	38.5	3	2	32	304	19	33.0
New England	91	3482	74	38.3	8	0	37	217	24	34.1
Cincinnati	64	2351	53	36.7	7	2	32	280	18	30.2
AFC Total	1,024	41,627	74	—	95	11	538	4,578	248	—
AFC Average	73.1	2,973.4	—	40.7	6.8	0.8	38.4	327.0	17.7	34.3

NFC Punting—Team

	Net Punts	Gross Yards	Long	Gross Avg.	TB	Blk.	Opp. Ret.	Ret. Yards	In 20	Net Avg.
Detroit	97	4110	69	42.4	7	0	57	483	22	35.9
Chicago	79	3282	70	41.5	10	0	40	447	18	33.4
Dallas	80	3271	55	40.9	15	0	37	239	24	34.2
Phoenix	80	3228	66	40.4	9	1	41	416	16	32.9
Atlanta	98	3920	61	40.0	6	0	51	297	27	35.7
N.Y. Giants	81	3234	66	39.9	10	2	38	303	14	33.7
New Orleans	73	2913	64	39.9	8	1	39	248	19	34.3
Philadelphia	104	4125	70	39.7	8	3	47	393	28	34.3
L.A. Rams	76	3003	57	39.5	3	0	43	347	24	34.2
Minnesota	86	3387	55	39.4	9	2	39	405	23	32.6
San Francisco	80	3093	53	38.7	5	1	47	426	22	32.1
Washington	67	2562	55	38.2	6	1	39	448	10	29.8
Green Bay	86	3287	62	38.2	12	1	39	314	20	31.8
Tampa Bay	68	2477	62	36.4	0	0	38	273	20	32.4
NFC Total	1,155	45,892	70	—	108	12	595	5,039	287	—
NFC Average	82.5	3,278.0	—	39.7	7.7	0.9	42.5	359.9	20.5	33.5
League Total	2,179	87,519	74	—	203	23	1,133	9,617	535	—
League Average	77.8	3,125.7	—	40.2	7.3	0.8	40.5	343.5	19.1	33.9

NFL Top 10 Punters

	Net Punts	Gross Yards	Long	Gross Avg.	Total Punts	TB	Blk.	Opp. Ret.	Ret. Yards	In 20	Net Avg.
Newsome, Harry, Pittsburgh	65	2950	62	45.4	71	10	6	40	418	9	32.8
Mojsiejenko, Ralf, San Diego	85	3745	62	44.1	86	11	1	56	558	22	34.5
Horan, Mike, Denver	65	2861	70	44.0	65	2	0	33	364	19	37.8
Stark, Rohn, Indianapolis	64	2784	65	43.5	64	8	0	37	418	15	34.5
Roby, Reggie, Miami	64	2754	64	43.0	64	9	0	35	318	18	35.3
Arnold, Jim, Detroit	97	4110	69	42.4	97	7	0	57	483	22	35.9
Gossett, Jeff, L.A. Raiders	91	3804	58	41.8	91	8	0	47	397	27	35.7
Wagner, Bryan, Chicago	79	3282	70	41.5	79	10	0	40	447	18	33.4

	Net Punts	Gross Yards	Long	Gross Avg.	Total Punts	TB	Blk.	Opp. Ret.	Ret. Yards	In 20	Net Avg.
Buford, Maury, N.Y. Giants	73	3012	66	41.3	75	10	2	36	296	13	33.5
Saxon, Mike, Dallas	80	3271	55	40.9	80	15	0	37	239	24	34.2

AFC Punting—Individual

	Net Punts	Gross Yards	Long	Gross Avg.	Total Punts	TB	Blk.	Opp. Ret.	Ret. Yards	In 20	Net Avg.
Newsome, Harry, Pittsburgh	65	2950	62	45.4	71	10	6	40	418	9	32.8
Mojsiejenko, Ralf, San Diego	85	3745	62	44.1	86	11	1	56	558	22	34.5
Horan, Mike, Denver	65	2861	70	44.0	65	2	0	33	364	19	37.8
Stark, Rohn, Indianapolis	64	2784	65	43.5	64	8	0	37	418	15	34.5
Roby, Reggie, Miami	64	2754	64	43.0	64	9	0	35	318	18	35.3
Gossett, Jeff, L.A. Raiders	91	3804	58	41.8	91	8	0	47	397	27	35.7
Rodriguez, Ruben, Seattle	70	2858	68	40.8	70	4	0	36	202	14	36.8
Goodburn, Kelly, Kansas City	76	3059	59	40.3	76	8	0	48	473	10	31.9
Runager, Max, San Francisco-Cleveland	49	1959	52	40.0	51	2	2	25	201	13	33.7
Kidd, John, Buffalo	62	2451	60	39.5	62	2	0	36	222	13	35.3
Prokop, Joe, N.Y. Jets	85	3310	64	38.9	85	10	0	34	201	26	34.2
Montgomery, Greg, Houston	65	2523	61	38.8	65	5	0	35	206	12	34.1
Feagles, Jeff, New England	91	3482	74	38.3	91	8	0	37	217	24	34.1
Fulhage, Scott, Cincinnati	44	1672	53	38.0	46	5	2	24	220	13	29.4
Non-Qualifiers											
Johnson, Lee, Cleveland-Cincinnati	31	1237	61	39.9	31	2	0	15	163	10	33.4
Breech, Jim, Cincinnati	3	64	30	21.3	3	1	0	0	0	1	14.7
Elway, John, Denver	3	117	40	39.0	3	0	0	0	0	2	39.0
Esiason, Boomer, Cincinnati	1	21	21	21.0	1	0	0	0	0	0	21.0

Leader based on gross average, minimum 40 punts.

NFC Punting—Individual

	Net Punts	Gross Yards	Long	Gross Avg.	Total Punts	TB	Blk.	Opp. Ret.	Ret. Yards	In 20	Net Avg.
Arnold, Jim, Detroit	97	4110	69	42.4	97	7	0	57	483	22	35.9
Wagner, Bryan, Chicago	79	3282	70	41.5	79	10	0	40	447	18	33.4
Buford, Maury, N.Y. Giants	73	3012	66	41.3	75	10	2	36	296	13	33.5
Saxon, Mike, Dallas	80	3271	55	40.9	80	15	0	37	239	24	34.2
Horne, Greg, Phoenix	79	3228	66	40.9	80	9	1	41	416	16	32.9
Hansen, Brian, New Orleans	72	2913	64	40.5	73	8	1	39	248	19	34.3
Teltschik, John, Philadelphia	98	3958	70	40.4	101	8	3	45	375	28	33.9
Scribner, Bucky, Minnesota	84	3387	55	40.3	86	9	2	39	405	23	32.6
Donnelly, Rick, Atlanta	98	3920	61	40.0	98	6	0	51	297	27	35.7
Camarillo, Rich, L.A. Rams	40	1579	57	39.5	40	2	0	26	145	11	34.8
Helton, Barry, San Francisco	78	3069	53	39.3	79	5	1	47	426	22	32.2
Bracken, Don, Green Bay	85	3287	62	38.7	86	12	1	39	314	20	31.8
Criswell, Ray, Tampa Bay	68	2477	62	36.4	68	0	0	38	273	20	32.4
Non-Qualifiers											
Coleman, Greg, Washington	39	1505	53	38.6	39	3	0	24	305	8	29.2
Hatcher, Dale, L.A. Rams	36	1424	54	39.6	36	1	0	17	202	13	33.4
Barnhardt, Tommy, Washington	15	628	55	41.9	15	2	0	9	74	1	34.3
Landeta, Sean, N.Y. Giants	6	222	53	37.0	6	0	0	2	7	1	35.8
Cox, Steve, Washington	6	221	55	36.8	7	1	1	3	44	0	22.4
Lohmiller, Chip, Washington	6	208	42	34.7	6	0	0	3	25	1	30.5
Cunningham, Randall, Washington	3	167	58	55.7	3	0	0	2	18	0	49.7

Leader based on gross average, minimum 40 punts.

Punt Returns

Individual Champions (Average)
NFC: 12.6—John Taylor, San Francisco
AFC: 11.7—JoJo Townsell, N.Y. Jets

Yards
NFC: 556—John Taylor, San Francisco
AFC: 444—Tim Brown, L.A. Raiders

Most Yards, Game
NFC: 113—John Taylor, San Francisco vs. Washington, November 21 (4 returns)
AFC: 110—JoJo Townsell, N.Y. Jets vs. Kansas City, October 2 (7 returns)

Longest
NFC: 95—John Taylor, San Francisco vs. Washington, November 21 (TD)
AFC: 73—Clarence Verdin, Indianapolis at Cleveland, September 19 (TD)

Most Returns
NFC: 58—Leo Lewis, Minnesota
AFC: 49—Tim Brown, L.A. Raiders

Most Returns, Game
AFC: 7—Ricky Nattiel, Denver vs. L.A. Raiders, September 26 (63 yards)
7—JoJo Townsell, N.Y. Jets vs. Kansas City, October 2 (110 yards)
7—Tim Brown, L.A. Raiders at San Diego, November 6 (102 yards)
NFC: 7—Dennis McKinnon, Chicago at Detroit, October 9 (63 yards)
7—Vai Sikahema, Phoenix vs. Pittsburgh, October 9 (57 yards)
7—J.T. Smith, Phoenix vs. San Francisco, November 6 (67 yards)

Fair Catches
NFC: 25—Mark Konecny, Philadelphia
25—Phil McConkey, N.Y. Giants
AFC: 11—Lionel James, San Diego

Touchdowns
NFC: 2—John Taylor, San Francisco
AFC: 1—JoJo Townsell, N.Y. Jets
1—Clarence Verdin, Indianapolis

Team Champions
NFC: 11.8—New Orleans
AFC: 11.0—N.Y. Jets

AFC Punt Returns—Team

	No.	FC	Yards	Avg.	Long	TD
N.Y. Jets	38	10	418	11.0	59t	1
New England	38	9	398	10.5	30	0
Indianapolis	26	12	254	9.8	73t	1
Miami	27	10	259	9.6	36	0
Seattle	37	8	340	9.2	41	0
San Diego	35	16	314	9.0	24	0
L.A. Raiders	55	10	489	8.9	36	0
Denver	53	5	451	8.5	24	0
Pittsburgh	39	12	322	8.3	28	0
Cleveland	40	6	325	8.1	32	0
Cincinnati	32	17	244	7.6	20	0
Kansas City	32	6	215	6.7	16	0
Houston	36	10	225	6.3	26	0
Buffalo	26	8	152	5.8	24	0
AFC Total	514	139	4,406	—	73t	2
AFC Average	36.7	9.9	314.7	8.6	—	0.1

NFC Punt Returns—Team

	No.	FC	Yards	Avg.	Long	TD
New Orleans	35	12	413	11.8	66t	1
San Francisco	54	15	612	11.3	95t	2
Minnesota	59	20	553	9.4	64	0
Tampa Bay	36	13	328	9.1	40	0
Phoenix	52	11	463	8.9	28	0
Detroit	42	8	346	8.2	25	0
Atlanta	42	9	343	8.2	68	0
Dallas	45	15	360	8.0	21	0
Chicago	38	9	294	7.7	23	0
N.Y. Giants	47	25	359	7.6	35	0
Washington	52	9	377	7.3	34	0
Philadelphia	33	25	233	7.1	24	0
L.A. Rams	49	11	322	6.6	46	0
Green Bay	35	18	208	5.9	63t	1
NFC Total	619	200	5211	—	95t	4
NFC Average	44.2	14.3	372.2	8.4	—	0.3
League Total	1,133	339	9617	—	95t	6
League Average	40.5	12.1	343.5	8.5	—	0.2

NFL Top 10 Punt Returners

	No.	FC	Yards	Avg.	Long	TD
Taylor, John, San Francisco	44	7	556	12.6	95t	2
Gray, Mel, New Orleans	25	8	305	12.2	66t	1
Townsell, JoJo, N.Y. Jets	35	9	409	11.7	59t	1
Verdin, Clarence, Indianapolis	22	7	239	10.9	73t	1
Fryar, Irving, New England	38	8	398	10.5	30	0
Futrell, Bobby, Tampa Bay	27	10	283	10.5	40	0
Sikahema, Vai, St. Louis	33	8	341	10.3	28	0
James, Lionel, San Diego	28	11	278	9.9	24	0
Edmonds, Bobby Joe, Seattle	35	8	340	9.7	41	0
Nattiel, Ricky, Denver	23	0	223	9.7	24	0

AFC Punt Returns—Individual

	No.	FC	Yards	Avg.	Long	TD
Townsell, JoJo, N.Y. Jets	35	9	409	11.7	59t	1
Verdin, Clarence, Indianapolis	22	7	239	10.9	73t	1
Fryar, Irving, New England	38	8	398	10.5	30	0
James, Lionel, San Diego	28	11	278	9.9	24	0
Edmonds, Bobby Joe, Seattle	35	8	340	9.7	41	0
Nattiel, Ricky, Denver	23	0	223	9.7	24	0
Schwedes, Scott, Miami	24	7	230	9.6	36	0
Brown, Tim, L.A. Raiders	49	10	444	9.1	36	0
Woodson, Rod, Pittsburgh	33	6	281	8.5	28	0
McNeil, Gerald, Cleveland	38	6	315	8.3	32	0
Taylor, Kitrick, Kansas City	29	6	187	6.4	16	0
Johnson, Kenny, Houston	30	6	170	5.7	16	0
Non-Qualifiers						
Hillary, Ira, Cincinnati	17	5	166	9.8	20	0
Johnson, Flip, Buffalo	16	3	72	4.5	16	0
Clark, Kevin, Denver	13	0	115	8.8	16	0
Willhite, Gerald, Denver	13	2	90	6.9	12	0
Tucker, Erroll, Buffalo	10	5	80	8.0	24	0
Brown, Eddie, Cincinnati	10	7	48	4.8	13	0
Flutie, Darren, San Diego	7	5	36	5.1	10	0
Adams, Stefon, L.A. Raiders	6	0	45	7.5	17	0
Martin, Mike, Cincinnati	5	5	30	6.0	10	0
Duncan, Curtis, Houston	4	2	47	11.8	26	0
Lipps, Louis, Pittsburgh	4	2	30	7.5	11	0
Williams, Jarvis, Miami	3	3	29	9.7	14	0
Hollis, David, Kansas City	3	0	28	9.3	15	0
Brooks, Bill, Indianapolis	3	0	15	5.0	8	0
Sohn, Kurt, N.Y. Jets	3	1	9	3.0	5	0
Harden, Mike, Denver	2	2	14	7.0	14	0
Sanchez, Lupe, Pittsburgh	2	4	11	5.5	6	0
Weathers, Clarence, Cleveland	2	0	10	5.0	9	0
Drewrey, Willie, Houston	2	2	8	4.0	8	0
Johnson, Jason, Denver	1	0	5	5.0	5	0
Bell, Ken, Denver	1	0	4	4.0	4	0
Glasgow, Nesby, Seattle	1	0	0	0.0	0	0
Hunter, Patrick, Seattle	1	0	0	0.0	0	0
Prior, Mike, Indianapolis	1	5	0	0.0	0	0
Bowman, Jim, New England	0	1	0	—	0	0
Johnson, Vance, Denver	0	1	0	—	0	0

t indicates touchdown.
Leader based on average return, minimum 20 returns.

NFC Punt Returns—Individual

	No.	FC	Yards	Avg.	Long	TD
Taylor, John, San Francisco	44	7	556	12.6	95t	2
Gray, Mel, New Orleans	25	8	305	12.2	66t	1
Futrell, Bobby, Tampa Bay	27	10	283	10.5	40	0
Sikahema, Vai, Phoenix	33	8	341	10.3	28	0
Lewis, Leo, Minnesota	58	19	550	9.5	64	0
Barnes, Lew, Atlanta	34	8	307	9.0	68	0
Martin, Kelvin, Dallas	44	15	360	8.2	21	0
McKinnon, Dennis, Chicago	34	8	277	8.1	23	0
McConkey, Phil, N.Y. Giants	40	25	313	7.8	35	0
Mandley, Pete, Detroit	37	7	287	7.8	25	0
Konecny, Mark, Philadelphia	33	25	233	7.1	24	0
Hicks, Cliff, L.A. Rams	25	0	144	5.8	13	0
Non-Qualifiers						
Ellard, Henry, L.A. Rams	17	3	119	7.0	34	0
Smith, J.T., Phoenix	17	2	119	7.0	15	0
Shepard, Derrick, Washington	12	2	104	8.7	23	0
Stanley, Walter, Green Bay	12	3	52	4.3	15	0
Hill, Lonzell, New Orleans	10	4	108	10.8	31	0
Allen, Anthony, Washington	10	2	62	6.2	14	0
Green, Darrell, Washington	9	0	103	11.4	32	0
Pitts, Ron, Green Bay	9	6	93	10.3	63t	1
Sharpe, Sterling, Green Bay	9	7	48	5.3	14	0
Clark, Gary, Washington	8	3	48	6.0	34	0
Smith, Jeff, Tampa Bay	8	3	45	5.6	20	0
Oliphant, Mike, Washington	7	0	24	3.4	11	0
Chandler, Wes, San Francisco	6	5	28	4.7	13	0
Matthews, Aubrey, Atlanta	6	0	26	4.3	10	0
Bland, Carl, Detroit	5	1	59	11.8	24	0
Baker, Stephen, N.Y. Giants	5	0	34	6.8	11	0
Jefferson, Norman, Green Bay	5	2	15	3.0	9	0
Griffin, Don, San Francisco	4	3	28	7.0	10	0
Sutton, Mickey, L.A. Rams	3	6	52	17.3	46	0
Johnson, Billy, Washington	3	1	26	8.7	15	0
Davis, Wendell, Chicago	3	1	17	5.7	13	0
Cooper, Evan, Atlanta	2	1	10	5.0	10	0
Orr, Terry, Washington	2	0	10	5.0	10	0
Johnson, Johnnie, L.A. Rams	2	1	4	2.0	4	0
Kinard, Terry, N.Y. Giants	1	0	8	8.0	8	0
Flynn, Tom, N.Y. Giants	1	0	4	4.0	4	0
Carter, Anthony, Minnesota	1	1	3	3.0	3	0
Hunley, Ricky, Phoenix	1	0	3	3.0	3	0
Irvin, LeRoy, L.A. Rams	1	1	2	2.0	2	0
Gray, Jerry, L.A. Rams	1	0	1	1.0	1	0
Caldwell, Ravin, Washington	1	0	0	0.0	0	0
Elder, Donnie, Tampa Bay	1	0	0	0.0	0	0
Kozlowski, Glen, Chicago	1	0	0	0.0	0	0
McAdoo, Derrick, Phoenix	1	0	0	0.0	0	0
Walls, Everson, Dallas	1	0	0	0.0	0	0
Gage, Steve, Washington	0	1	0	—	0	0
McDonald, Tim, Phoenix	0	1	0	—	0	0

t indicates touchdown.
Leader based on average return, minimum 20 returns.

Kickoff Returns

Individual Champions (Average)
AFC: 26.8—Tim Brown, L.A. Raiders
NFC: 22.7—Donnie Elder, Tampa Bay

Yards
AFC: 1,098—Tim Brown, L.A. Raiders
NFC: 833—Darryl Harris, Minnesota

Most Yards, Game
AFC: 192—Stanford Jennings, Cincinnati at Kansas City, November 13 (6 returns)
NFC: 154—Darryl Harris, Minnesota vs. Green Bay, October 16 (7 returns)
154—Dennis Gentry, Chicago at New England, October 30 (6 returns)

Longest
AFC: 98—Stanford Jennings, Cincinnati at Kansas City, November 13 (TD)
NFC: 73—Ron Brown, L.A. Rams at Philadelphia, November 6

Most Returns
AFC: 41—Tim Brown, L.A. Raiders
41—Joe Cribbs, Miami
NFC: 39—Darryl Harris, Minnesota

Most Returns, Game
AFC: 8—Joe Cribbs, Miami at Pittsburgh, December 18 (169 yards)
NFC: 7—Darryl Harris, Minnesota vs. Green Bay, October 16 (154 yards)

Touchdowns
AFC: 1—Tim Brown, L.A. Raiders
1—Jamie Holland, San Diego
1—Stanford Jennings, Cincinnati
1—Sammy Martin, New England
1—Anthony Miller, San Diego
1—Dwight Stone, Pittsburgh
1—Lorenzo White, Houston
1—Rod Woodson, Pittsburgh
NFC: None

Team Champions
AFC: 25.2—San Diego
NFC: 21.0—Tampa Bay

AFC Kickoff Returns—Team

	No.	Yards	Avg.	Long	TD
San Diego	60	1510	25.2	94t	2
L.A. Raiders	62	1407	22.7	97t	1
New England	57	1248	21.9	95t	1
Seattle	62	1352	21.8	65	0
Pittsburgh	74	1575	21.3	92t	2
Cleveland	55	1159	21.1	84	0
Miami	65	1365	21.0	44	0
Denver	58	1198	20.7	38	0
Houston	60	1232	20.5	90t	1
Indianapolis	52	1033	19.9	40	0
N.Y. Jets	72	1404	19.5	48	0
Buffalo	50	935	18.7	37	0
Cincinnati	57	1054	18.5	98t	1
Kansas City	56	925	16.5	31	0
AFC Total	840	17,397	—	98t	8
AFC Average	60.0	1,242.6	20.7	—	0.6

NFC Kickoff Returns—Team

	No.	Yards	Avg.	Long	TD
Tampa Bay	64	1345	21.0	51	0
Minnesota	56	1160	20.7	30	0
Dallas	69	1410	20.4	53	0

	No.	Yards	Avg.	Long	TD
L.A. Rams	59	1191	20.2	73	0
New Orleans	70	1408	20.1	57	0
Chicago	45	896	19.9	51	0
Detroit	59	1154	19.6	46	0
N.Y. Giants	62	1154	18.6	40	0
Green Bay	64	1181	18.5	46	0
Phoenix	60	1106	18.4	41	0
Washington	74	1355	18.3	44	0
Atlanta	59	1057	17.9	36	0
San Francisco	55	978	17.8	44	0
Philadelphia	59	1028	17.4	32	0
NFC Total	855	16,423	—	73	0
NFC Average	61.1	1,173.1	19.2	—	0.0
League Total	1,695	33,820	—	98t	8
League Average	60.5	1,207.9	20.0	—	0.3

NFL Top 10 Kickoff Returners

	No.	Yards	Avg.	Long	TD
Brown, Tim, L.A. Raiders	41	1098	26.8	97t	1
Holland, Jamie, San Diego	31	810	26.1	94t	1
Miller, Anthony, San Diego	25	648	25.9	93t	1
Humphery, Bobby, N.Y. Jets	21	510	24.3	48	0
Martin, Sammy, New England	31	735	23.7	95t	1
Woodson, Rod, Pittsburgh	37	850	23.0	92t	1
Elder, Donnie, Tampa Bay	34	772	22.7	51	0
Edmonds, Bobby Joe, Seattle	40	900	22.5	65	0
Burbage, Cornell, Dallas	20	448	22.4	53	0
Young, Glen, Cleveland	29	635	21.9	34	0

AFC Kickoff Returns—Individual

	No.	Yards	Avg.	Long	TD
Brown, Tim, L.A. Raiders	41	1098	26.8	97t	1
Holland, Jamie, San Diego	31	810	26.1	94t	1
Miller, Anthony, San Diego	25	648	25.9	93t	1
Humphery, Bobby, N.Y. Jets	21	510	24.3	48	0
Martin, Sammy, New England	31	735	23.7	95t	1
Woodson, Rod, Pittsburgh	37	850	23.0	92t	1
Edmonds, Bobby Joe, Seattle	40	900	22.5	65	0
Young, Glen, Cleveland	29	635	21.9	34	0
Jennings, Stanford, Cincinnati	32	684	21.4	98t	1
Bell, Ken, Denver	36	762	21.2	38	0
Cribbs, Joe, Miami	41	863	21.0	44	0
Stone, Dwight, Pittsburgh	29	610	21.0	92t	1
Fontenot, Herman, Cleveland	21	435	20.7	84	0
Bentley, Albert, Indianapolis	39	775	19.9	40	0
Harris, Leonard, Houston	34	678	19.9	56	0
Townsell, JoJo, N.Y. Jets	31	601	19.4	40	0
Palmer, Paul, Kansas City	23	364	15.8	23	0
Non-Qualifiers					
Allen, Marvin, New England	18	391	21.7	30	0
Tucker, Erroll, Buffalo	15	310	20.7	30	0
Gamble, Kenny, Kansas City	15	291	19.4	31	0
Johnson, Jason, Denver	14	292	20.9	34	0
Johnson, Flip, Buffalo	14	250	17.9	24	0
Hollis, David, Kansas City-Seattle	13	261	20.1	35	0
Hillary, Ira, Cincinnati	12	195	16.3	24	0
Harmon, Ronnie, Buffalo	11	249	22.6	37	0
Hampton, Lorenzo, Miami	9	216	24.0	37	0
Sohn, Kurt, N.Y. Jets	9	159	17.7	27	0
White, Lorenzo, Houston	8	196	24.5	90t	1
Williams, Jarvis, Miami	8	159	19.9	27	0
Adams, Stefon, L.A. Raiders	8	132	16.5	21	0
Verdin, Clarence, Indianapolis	7	145	20.7	32	0
Pinkett, Allen, Houston	7	137	19.6	29	0
Harper, Michael, N.Y. Jets	7	114	16.3	32	0
Bussey, Barney, Cincinnati	7	83	11.9	22	0
Johnson, Kenny, Houston	6	157	26.2	56	0
Nattiel, Ricky, Denver	6	124	20.7	25	0
Davis, Elgin, New England	6	106	17.7	24	0
Riddick, Robb, Buffalo	6	100	16.7	23	0
Mueller, Vance, L.A. Raiders	5	97	19.4	25	0
Taylor, Kitrick, Kansas City	5	80	16.0	19	0
Logan, Marc, Cincinnati	4	80	20.0	24	0
Sanchez, Lupe, Pittsburgh	4	71	17.8	19	0
Banks, Roy, Indianapolis	4	56	14.0	20	0
Harmon, Kevin, Seattle	3	62	20.7	30	0
Schwedes, Scott, Miami	3	49	16.3	25	0
Smith, Steve, L.A. Raiders	3	46	15.3	16	0
Davenport, Ron, Miami	2	41	20.5	21	0
Saxon, James, Kansas City	2	40	20.0	27	0
McNeil, Gerald, Cleveland	2	38	19.0	22	0
Ingram, Byron, Kansas City	2	16	8.0	9	0
Jenkins, Keyvan, Kansas City	2	12	6.0	12	0
Byrum, Carl, Buffalo	2	9	4.5	9	0
Faaola, Nuu, N.Y. Jets	2	9	4.5	7	0
Toran, Stacey, L.A. Raiders	2	0	0.0	0	0
Beach, Pat, Indianapolis	1	35	35.0	35	0
Duncan, Curtis, Houston	1	34	34.0	34	0
Braggs, Stephen, Cleveland	1	27	27.0	27	0
Wright, Terry, Indianapolis	1	22	22.0	22	0
Edmunds, Ferrell, Miami	1	20	20.0	20	0
Woods, Chris, L.A. Raiders	1	20	20.0	20	0
Boyle, Jim, Pittsburgh	1	19	19.0	19	0
Dixon, Rickey, Cincinnati	1	18	18.0	18	0
Hardy, Bruce, Miami	1	17	17.0	17	0
Tice, Mike, Seattle	1	17	17.0	17	0
Porter, Kevin, Kansas City	1	16	16.0	16	0
Spencer, Tim, San Diego	1	16	16.0	16	0
Carter, Russell, L.A. Raiders	1	14	14.0	14	0
Adams, Curtis, San Diego	1	13	13.0	13	0
Jones, Anthony, San Diego	1	13	13.0	13	0
Perry, Michael Dean, Cleveland	1	13	13.0	13	0
Tatupu, Mosi, New England	1	13	13.0	13	0
Tillman, Spencer, Houston	1	13	13.0	13	0
Rolle, Butch, Buffalo	1	12	12.0	12	0
Barber, Marion, N.Y. Jets	1	11	11.0	11	0
Tennell, Derek, Cleveland	1	11	11.0	11	0
Winder, Sammy, Denver	1	11	11.0	11	0
Drewrey, Willie, Houston	1	10	10.0	10	0
Flutie, Darren, San Diego	1	10	10.0	10	0
Jackson, John, Pittsburgh	1	10	10.0	10	0
Williams, Warren, Pittsburgh	1	10	10.0	10	0
Harden, Mike, Denver	1	9	9.0	9	0
Blankenship, Brian, Pittsburgh	1	5	5.0	5	0
Donaldson, Jeff, Houston	1	5	5.0	5	0
Pike, Mark, Buffalo	1	5	5.0	5	0
Fryar, Irving, New England	1	3	3.0	3	0
Johnson, Richard, Houston	1	2	2.0	2	0
Lee, Zeph, L.A. Raiders	1	0	0.0	0	0
Rose, Ken, N.Y. Jets	1	0	0.0	0	0
Brooks, James, Cincinnati	1	−6	−6.0	−6	0
Riggs, Jim, Cincinnati	0*	0	—	—	0

t indicates touchdown.
** indicates fair catch.*
Leader based on average return, minimum 20 returns.

NFC Kickoff Returns—Individual

	No.	Yards	Avg.	Long	TD
Elder, Donnie, Tampa Bay	34	772	22.7	51	0
Burbage, Cornell, Dallas	20	448	22.4	53	0
Clack, Darryl, Dallas	32	690	21.6	40	0
Harris, Darryl, Minnesota	39	833	21.4	30	0
Gentry, Dennis, Chicago	27	578	21.4	51	0
Atkins, Gene, New Orleans	20	424	21.2	57	0
Gray, Mel, New Orleans	32	670	20.9	39	0
Sikahema, Vai, Phoenix	23	475	20.7	39	0
Fullwood, Brent, Green Bay	21	421	20.0	31	0
Morris, Jamie, Washington	21	413	19.7	35	0
DuBose, Doug, San Francisco	32	608	19.0	44	0
Beals, Shawn, Philadelphia	34	625	18.4	32	0
Non-Qualifiers					
Brown, Ron, L.A. Rams	19	401	21.1	73	0
Sanders, Ricky, Washington	19	362	19.1	31	0
Woodside, Keith, Green Bay	19	343	18.1	29	0
Lee, Gary, Detroit	18	355	19.7	39	0
Painter, Carl, Detroit	17	347	20.4	32	0
Green, Gaston, L.A. Rams	17	345	20.3	44	0
Guggemos, Neal, N.Y. Giants	17	344	20.2	40	0
Konecny, Mark, Philadelphia	17	276	16.2	25	0
Cooper, Evan, Atlanta	16	331	20.7	28	0
Shepard, Derrick, Washington	16	329	20.6	44	0
Delpino, Robert, L.A. Rams	14	333	23.8	38	0
Gordon, Tim, Atlanta	14	209	14.9	32	0
McAdoo, Derrick, Tampa Bay-Phoenix	13	311	23.9	32	0
Hill, Kenny, N.Y. Giants	13	262	20.2	30	0
Morris, Randall, Seattle-Detroit	13	259	19.9	30	0
Sanders, Thomas, Chicago	13	248	19.1	38	0
Taylor, John, San Francisco	12	225	18.8	29	0
Stamps, Sylvester, Atlanta	12	219	18.3	27	0
Martin, Kelvin, Dallas	12	210	17.5	31	0
Scott, Patrick, Green Bay	12	207	17.3	27	0
Jones, Ernie, Phoenix	11	147	13.4	22	0
Mitchell, Stump, Phoenix	10	221	22.1	41	0
Smith, Jeff, Tampa Bay	10	180	18.0	26	0
Nelson, Darrin, Minnesota	9	210	23.3	30	0
Smith, Don, Tampa Bay	9	188	20.9	30	0
Bland, Carl, Detroit	8	179	22.4	29	0
Rouson, Lee, N.Y. Giants	8	130	16.3	21	0
Starring, Stephen, Detroit	8	130	16.3	22	0
Ingram, Mark, N.Y. Giants	8	129	16.1	27	0
Mayes, Rueben, New Orleans	7	132	18.9	33	0
Oliphant, Mike, Washington	7	127	18.1	26	0
Barnes, Lew, Atlanta	6	142	23.7	36	0

	No.	Yards	Avg.	Long	TD
Haddix, Wayne, N.Y. Giants	6	123	20.5	24	0
Haynes, Michael, Atlanta	6	113	18.8	25	0
Hilliard, Dalton, New Orleans	6	111	18.5	30	0
Rodgers, Del, San Francisco	6	98	16.3	24	0
Dozier, D.J., Minnesota	5	105	21.0	27	0
Abercrombie, Walter, Philadelphia	5	87	17.4	31	0
Gage, Steve, Washington	5	60	12.0	17	0
Jefferson, Norman, Green Bay	4	116	29.0	46	0
Woolfolk, Butch, Detroit	4	99	24.8	46	0
Collins, Mark, N.Y. Giants	4	67	16.8	26	0
White, Sheldon, N.Y. Giants	3	62	20.7	26	0
Griffin, Keith, Washington	3	45	15.0	24	0
Pillow, Frank, Tampa Bay	3	38	12.7	17	0
McDonald, Mike, L.A. Rams	3	34	11.3	22	0
Muster, Brad, Chicago	3	33	11.0	15	0
Martin, Eric, New Orleans	3	32	10.7	18	0
Sutton, Mickey, L.A. Rams	2	41	20.5	25	0
Stanley, Walter, Green Bay	2	39	19.5	22	0
Waymer, Dave, New Orleans	2	39	19.5	29	0
Futrell, Bobby, Tampa Bay	2	38	19.0	20	0
Kozlowski, Glen, Chicago	2	37	18.5	24	0
White, Charles, L.A. Rams	2	37	18.5	23	0
Craig, Roger, San Francisco	2	32	16.0	17	0
Higgs, Mark, Dallas	2	31	15.5	17	0
McConkey, Phil, N.Y. Giants	2	30	15.0	17	0
Ferrell, Earl, Phoenix	2	25	12.5	14	0
Smith, Daryle, Dallas	2	24	12.0	13	0
Howard, William, Tampa Bay	2	21	10.5	12	0
Byars, Keith, Philadelphia	2	20	10.0	14	0
Clark, Jessie, Phoenix	2	10	5.0	7	0
Shelley, Elbert, Atlanta	2	5	2.5	5	0
Jenkins, Izel, Philadelphia	1	20	20.0	20	0
Pitts, Ron, Green Bay	1	17	17.0	17	0
Sharpe, Sterling, Green Bay	1	17	17.0	17	0
Dukes, Jamie, Atlanta	1	13	13.0	13	0
Primus, James, Atlanta	1	13	13.0	13	0
Lang, Gene, Atlanta	1	12	12.0	12	0
Lewis, Leo, Minnesota	1	12	12.0	12	0
Jeffery, Tony, Phoenix	1	11	11.0	11	0
Schillinger, Andy, Phoenix	1	10	10.0	10	0
Hackett, Joey, Green Bay	1	9	9.0	9	0
Sydney, Harry, San Francisco	1*	8	8.0	8	0
Beckman, Brad, N.Y. Giants	1	7	7.0	7	0
Hamilton, Steve, Washington	1	7	7.0	7	0
White, Bob, Dallas	1	7	7.0	7	0
Winter, Blaise, Green Bay	1	7	7.0	7	0
Harbour, Dave, Washington	1	6	6.0	6	0
Orr, Terry, Washington	1	6	6.0	6	0
Thomas, Chuck, San Francisco	1	5	5.0	5	0
Phillips, Reggie, Phoenix	1	4	4.0	4	0
Stills, Ken, Green Bay	1	4	4.0	4	0
Andolsek, Eric, Detroit	1	3	3.0	3	0
Wilson, Mike, San Francisco	1	2	2.0	2	0
Hill, Nate, Green Bay	1	1	1.0	1	0
Carter, Anthony, Minnesota	1	0	0.0	0	0
McGee, Buford, L.A. Rams	1	0	0.0	0	0
Rice, Allen, Minnesota	1	0	0.0	0	0
Saleaumua, Dan, Detroit	1	0	0.0	0	0
Stewart, Michael, L.A. Rams	1	0	0.0	0	0
Bartlett, Doug, Philadelphia	0*	0	—	—	0
Duerson, Dave, Chicago	0*	0	—	—	0

t indicates touchdown.
** indicates fair catch.*
Leader based on average return, minimum 20 returns.

Fumbles

Most Fumbles
NFC: 12—Randall Cunningham, Philadelphia
AFC: 11—Ken O'Brien, N.Y. Jets

Most Fumbles, Game
AFC: 3—Ken O'Brien, N.Y. Jets at New England, September 4
3—Bubby Brister, Pittsburgh vs. Cincinnati, September 18
3—Dwight Stone, Pittsburgh vs. Cincinnati, September 18
3—Ken O'Brien, N.Y. Jets at Cincinnati, October 9
3—Warren Moon, Houston at Cincinnati, October 23
3—Mark Malone, San Diego at Seattle, October 30
NFC: 3—Norman Jefferson, Green Bay vs. L.A. Rams, September 4
3—Don Majkowski, Green Bay at Atlanta, November 6
3—Kevin Sweeney, Dallas vs. Minnesota, November 13

Own Fumbles Recovered
AFC: 7—Dan Marino, Miami
NFC: 6—Randall Cunningham, Philadelphia

Most Own Fumbles Recovered, Game
AFC: 2—Babe Laufenberg, San Diego at L.A. Raiders, September 4
2—Jay Schroeder, L.A. Raiders at Kansas City, October 16
2—Steve Strachan, L.A. Raiders at New Orleans, October 23
2—Anthony Muñoz, Cincinnati vs. Pittsburgh, November 6
2—Chris Chandler, Indianapolis at Minnesota, November 20
NFC: 2—Mark Konecny, Philadelphia vs. Atlanta, October 30
2—Don Majkowski, Green Bay at Buffalo, October 30
2—Neal Guggemos, N.Y. Giants vs. Dallas, November 6
2—Wade Wilson, Minnesota at Green Bay, December 11

Opponents' Fumbles Recovered
AFC: 7—Ray Childress, Houston
NFC: 4—Bennie Blades, Detroit
4—Ronnie Lott, San Francisco
4—Bruce McNorton, Detroit
4—Mark Murphy, Green Bay

Most Opponents' Fumbles Recovered, Game
AFC: 3—Ray Childress, Houston vs. Washington, October 30
NFC: 2—Joel Williams, Atlanta vs. New Orleans, September 11
2—Keena Turner, San Francisco at Phoenix, November 6
2—James Geathers, New Orleans vs. N.Y. Giants, November 27

Yards
AFC: 50—Mel Jenkins, Seattle
50—Sam Seale, San Diego
NFC: 45—Cedric Mack, Phoenix

Longest
AFC: 75—Keith Browner (25) to Sam Seale (50), San Diego at L.A. Rams, November 20 (TD)
50—Paul Moyer (0) to Melvin Jenkins (50), Seattle at L.A. Rams, October 23
NFC: 45—Cedric Mack, Phoenix vs. Washington, September 25 (TD)

AFC Fumbles—Team

	Fum.	Own Rec.	Fum. *O.B.	TD	Opp. Rec.	TD	Yds.	Tot. Rec.
New England	19	9	0	1	15	0	−5	24
Indianapolis	20	12	0	0	20	0	37	32
Kansas City	21	9	0	0	13	0	1	22
Buffalo	26	8	2	0	17	1	11	25
Miami	26	13	1	0	15	1	15	28
San Diego	26	13	1	0	10	1	37	23
Cincinnati	28	10	5	0	14	2	57	24
Seattle	29	13	2	0	18	1	−1	31
Cleveland	32	12	4	0	11	1	−28	23
N.Y. Jets	32	14	2	0	16	0	27	30
Houston	33	13	3	0	20	0	13	33
L.A. Raiders	33	19	1	0	17	1	24	36
Denver	34	21	1	0	13	0	−19	34
Pittsburgh	40	19	2	0	13	0	−12	32
AFC Total	399	185	24	1	212	8	157	397
AFC Average	28.5	13.2	1.7	0.1	15.1	0.6	11.2	28.4

NFC Fumbles—Team

	Fum.	Own Rec.	Fum. *O.B.	TD	Opp. Rec.	TD	Yds.	Tot. Rec.
Dallas	22	9	0	0	9	0	−3	18
Minnesota	22	10	0	0	17	2	44	27
San Francisco	27	15	0	0	16	0	−22	31
Tampa Bay	27	11	0	0	12	0	−44	23
L.A. Rams	28	10	2	0	15	0	15	25
Atlanta	29	8	3	0	14	2	91	22
New Orleans	29	10	3	1	15	0	14	25
Philadelphia	29	20	0	1	12	0	14	32
Detroit	31	15	1	0	21	1	5	36
N.Y. Giants	32	18	1	0	18	1	61	36
Phoenix	34	18	0	0	13	3	75	31
Washington	34	12	1	0	8	0	2	20
Chicago	37	15	3	0	9	0	−39	24
Green Bay	44	16	2	0	21	0	−28	37
NFC Total	425	187	16	2	200	9	185	387
NFC Average	30.4	13.4	1.1	0.1	14.3	0.6	13.2	27.6
League Total	824	372	40	3	412	17	342	784
League Average	29.4	13.3	1.4	0.1	14.7	0.6	12.2	28.0

**indicates fumbled out of bounds.*
Yards includes aborted plays, own recoveries, and opponents' recoveries.

AFC Fumbles—Individual

	Fum.	Own Rec.	Opp. Rec.	Yds.	Tot. Rec.
Adams, Curtis, San Diego	1	0	0	0	0
Adams, Stefon, L.A. Raiders	0	0	3	1	3
Agee, Tommie, Seattle	0	1	0	0	1
Allen, Marcus, L.A. Raiders	5	0	0	0	0
Allen, Marvin, New England	0	0	2	0	2
Allen, Patrick, Houston	0	0	1	7	1
Anderson, Gary, San Diego	5	3	0	0	3
Armstrong, Harvey, Indianapolis	0	0	2	0	2
Bailey, Edwin, Seattle	0	2	0	0	2
Baldinger, Brian, Indianapolis	0	1	0	0	1
Baldinger, Rich, Kansas City	0	1	0	0	1
Ball, Michael, Indianapolis	0	0	1	0	1
Barker, Leo, Cincinnati	0	0	1	34	1
Baugh, Tom, Kansas City	1	0	0	−9	0
Beach, Pat, Indianapolis	1	0	0	0	0
Bell, Ken, Denver	2	1	0	0	1
Bell, Mike, Kansas City	0	0	1	0	1
Bellini, Mark, Indianapolis	0	1	0	0	1
Bennett, Cornelius, Buffalo	0	0	3	0	3
Bennett, Woody, Miami	1	1	0	0	1

	Fum.	Own Rec.	Opp. Rec.	Yds.	Tot. Rec.
Benson, Troy, N.Y. Jets	0	0	1	0	1
Bentley, Albert, Indianapolis	2	0	0	0	0
Bentley, Ray, Buffalo	0	0	1	0	1
Beuerlein, Steve, L.A. Raiders	6	2	0	−1	2
Biasucci, Dean, Indianapolis	0	0	1	0	1
Bickett, Duane, Indianapolis	0	0	1	0	1
Billups, Lewis, Cincinnati	0	0	2	26	2
Bishop, Keith, Denver	1	0	0	−5	0
Blackledge, Todd, Pittsburgh	4	2	0	−2	2
Blades, Brian, Seattle	1	1	0	0	1
Blankenship, Brian, Pittsburgh	0	1	0	0	1
Booty, John, N.Y. Jets	0	0	2	0	2
Bostic, Keith, Houston	0	0	2	22	2
Bosworth, Brian, Seattle	0	0	1	0	1
Bouza, Matt, Indianapolis	0	1	0	0	1
Bowman, Jim, New England	0	1	0	0	1
Braxton, Tyrone, Denver	0	1	0	0	1
Brister, Bubby, Pittsburgh	8	2	0	0	2
Brooks, Bill, Indianapolis	1	2	0	0	2
Brooks, James, Cincinnati	1	0	0	0	0
Brown, Eddie, Cincinnati	1	1	0	0	1
Brown, Tim, L.A. Raiders	5	6	1	0	7
Browner, Keith, San Diego	0	0	1	25	1
Brudzinski, Bob, Miami	0	1	0	0	1
Bryan, Bill, Denver	0	1	0	0	1
Bryan, Steve, Denver	0	0	1	0	1
Bryant, Jeff, Seattle	0	0	2	0	2
Burroughs, Derrick, Buffalo	0	0	1	0	1
Bussey, Barney, Cincinnati	1	0	1	0	1
Byner, Earnest, Cleveland	5	2	0	0	2
Byrd, Gill, San Diego	1	0	0	0	0
Byrum, Carl, Buffalo	1	0	0	0	0
Cadigan, Dave, N.Y. Jets	0	1	0	0	1
Carlson, Cody, Houston	5	0	0	−12	0
Carter, Russell, L.A. Raiders	0	0	1	0	1
Chandler, Chris, Indianapolis	8	5	0	−6	5
Cherry, Deron, Kansas City	0	0	6	10	6
Childress, Ray, Houston	0	0	7	0	7
Christensen, Todd, L.A. Raiders	0	1	0	2	1
Clifton, Kyle, N.Y. Jets	0	0	2	6	2
Cocroft, Sherman, Buffalo	0	0	1	0	1
Cofield, Tim, Kansas City	0	0	1	0	1
Colbert, Darrell, Kansas City	1	1	0	0	1
Cole, Robin, N.Y. Jets	0	0	1	0	1
Coleman, Leonard, San Diego	0	0	1	0	1
Collinsworth, Cris, Cincinnati	1	0	0	0	0
Comeaux, Darren, Seattle	1	0	0	0	0
Conlan, Shane, Buffalo	0	0	1	0	1
Cribbs, Joe, Miami	1	0	0	0	0
Dallafior, Ken, San Diego	0	2	0	0	2
Danielson, Gary, Cleveland	1	0	0	−4	0
Davenport, Ron, Miami	1	0	0	0	0
Davis, Elgin, New England	1	0	0	0	0
Dean, Vernon, Seattle	0	0	1	0	1
DeBerg, Steve, Kansas City	1	0	0	0	0
Del Rio, Jack, Kansas City	0	1	0	0	1
Dellenbach, Jeff, Miami	1	0	0	−9	0
Dennison, Rick, Denver	0	0	3	0	3
Devlin, Joe, Buffalo	0	1	0	0	1
Dickerson, Eric, Indianapolis	5	1	0	0	1
Dishman, Cris, Houston	0	0	1	0	1
Dixon, Hanford, Cleveland	0	0	1	0	1
Dixon, Rickey, Cincinnati	0	0	1	−3	1
Donaldson, Jeff, Houston	0	0	2	0	2
Dorsett, Tony, Denver	6	1	0	0	1
Dupard, Reggie, New England	1	1	0	0	1
Early, Quinn, San Diego	1	0	0	0	0
Eason, Tony, New England	0	1	0	2	1
Edmonds, Bobby Joe, Seattle	2	1	0	0	1
Edmunds, Ferrell, Miami	4	0	0	0	0
Elway, John, Denver	7	5	0	−9	5
Esiason, Boomer, Cincinnati	5	4	0	0	4
Everett, Thomas, Pittsburgh	0	0	2	38	2
Fairs, Eric, Houston	0	0	1	0	1
Faucette, Chuck, San Diego	0	0	1	0	1
Feagles, Jeff, New England	0	1	0	0	1
Feasel, Grant, Seattle	1	1	3	−22	4
Fellows, Ron, L.A. Raiders	0	0	2	7	2
Fletcher, Simon, Denver	0	0	1	0	1
Flutie, Darren, San Diego	2	0	0	0	0
Flutie, Doug, New England	3	0	0	0	0
Fryar, Irving, New England	2	0	0	0	0
Fulcher, David, Cincinnati	1	0	0	0	0
Galvin, John, N.Y. Jets	0	0	1	0	1
Gamble, Kenny, Kansas City	1	0	0	0	0
Gastineau, Mark, N.Y. Jets	0	0	1	0	1
Gault, Willie, L.A. Raiders	1	0	0	0	0
Gesek, John, L.A. Raiders	1	0	0	0	0

	Fum.	Own Rec.	Opp. Rec.	Yds.	Tot. Rec.
Givins, Ernest, Houston	1	0	0	0	0
Glasgow, Nesby, Seattle	1	0	0	0	0
Glenn, Vencie, San Diego	0	0	2	0	2
Goode, Chris, Indianapolis	0	1	3	16	4
Gordon, Alex, N.Y. Jets	0	0	1	0	1
Gothard, Preston, Pittsburgh	0	1	0	0	1
Graf, Rick, Miami	0	0	3	5	3
Grant, David, Cincinnati	0	0	1	0	1
Graves, Rory, L.A. Raiders	0	1	0	0	1
Green, Hugh, Miami	0	0	1	5	1
Green, Jacob, Seattle	0	0	2	0	2
Griffin, Larry, Pittsburgh	1	0	1	0	1
Griggs, Billy, N.Y. Jets	1	1	0	0	1
Grimsley, John, Houston	0	0	1	0	1
Grogan, Steve, New England	2	1	0	0	1
Hackett, Dino, Kansas City	0	0	1	0	1
Hampton, Lorenzo, Miami	2	1	0	0	1
Hand, Jon, Indianapolis	0	0	1	0	1
Harden, Mike, Denver	1	1	0	0	1
Harmon, Ronnie, Buffalo	2	0	0	0	0
Harper, Dwayne, Seattle	0	0	1	0	1
Harper, Mark, Cleveland	0	0	1	0	1
Harris, Leonard, Houston	1	0	0	0	0
Hasty, James, N.Y. Jets	0	0	3	35	3
Hawkins, Andy, Kansas City	0	1	0	0	1
Haynes, Mike, L.A. Raiders	0	0	1	0	1
Heard, Herman, Kansas City	2	0	0	0	0
Hector, Johnny, N.Y. Jets	3	1	0	0	1
Highsmith, Alonzo, Houston	7	2	0	0	2
Hill, Will, Cleveland	0	0	1	0	1
Hinkle, Bryan, Pittsburgh	0	0	1	5	1
Hobley, Liffort, Miami	0	1	1	19	2
Hodge, Milford, New England	0	0	1	2	1
Hoge, Merril, Pittsburgh	8	6	0	0	6
Hogeboom, Gary, Indianapolis	2	0	0	0	0
Holland, Jamie, San Diego	1	0	0	0	0
Hollis, David, Kansas City	1	0	0	0	0
Holman, Rodney, Cincinnati	2	1	0	0	1
Holmes, Darryl, New England	0	0	1	0	1
Humphery, Bobby, N.Y. Jets	0	1	1	0	2
Hunter, Patrick, Seattle	1	0	0	0	0
Jackson, Bo, L.A. Raiders	5	2	0	0	2
Jackson, Earnest, Pittsburgh	3	0	0	0	0
Jackson, Mark, Denver	1	1	0	0	1
James, Lionel, San Diego	3	0	0	0	0
James, Roland, New England	0	0	1	0	1
Jenkins, Keyvan, Kansas City	1	0	0	0	0
Jenkins, Mel, Seattle	1	0	1	50	1
Jennings, Stanford, Cincinnati	1	0	0	0	0
Jensen, Jim, Miami	2	2	0	0	2
Johnson, Eddie, Cleveland	0	0	3	0	3
Johnson, Flip, Buffalo	1	0	0	0	0
Johnson, Jason, Denver	1	1	0	0	1
Johnson, Kenny, Houston	1	0	0	0	0
Johnson, Trumaine, Buffalo	1	0	0	0	0
Jones, Cedric, New England	1	0	0	0	0
Jordan, Darin, Pittsburgh	0	1	3	0	4
Jordan, Tim, New England	0	0	1	0	1
Judson, William, Miami	0	0	1	0	1
Kattus, Eric, Cincinnati	1	0	0	0	0
Kay, Clarence, Denver	1	0	0	0	0
Kelly, Jim, Buffalo	5	0	0	0	0
Kelly, Pat, Denver	1	0	0	0	0
Kenney, Bill, Kansas City	1	0	0	0	0
Keys, Tyrone, San Diego	0	0	1	2	1
Kirk, Randy, San Diego	0	1	0	0	1
Klecko, Joe, Indianapolis	0	0	1	0	1
Kosar, Bernie, Cleveland	0	2	0	0	2
Kragen, Greg, Denver	0	0	1	0	1
Krauss, Barry, Indianapolis	0	0	2	0	2
Krieg, Dave, Seattle	6	0	0	0	0
Krumrie, Tim, Cincinnati	0	0	3	0	3
Kubiak, Gary, Denver	3	3	0	−9	3
Langhorne, Reggie, Cleveland	3	1	0	0	1
Largent, Steve, Seattle	3	0	0	0	0
Laufenberg, Babe, San Diego	2	3	0	−10	3
Lewis, Albert, Kansas City	0	0	1	0	1
Lippett, Ronnie, New England	0	0	1	0	1
Lipps, Louis, Pittsburgh	2	0	0	0	0
Little, David, Pittsburgh	0	0	2	2	2
Lloyd, Greg, Pittsburgh	0	0	1	0	1
Lofton, James, L.A. Raiders	0	1	0	19	1
Logan, Marc, Cincinnati	1	0	0	0	0
Long, Terry, Pittsburgh	0	1	0	0	1
Lyles, Robert, Houston	0	0	2	5	2
Lyons, Marty, N.Y. Jets	0	1	1	0	2
Macek, Don, San Diego	1	0	0	0	0
Mack, Kevin, Cleveland	5	1	0	0	1

	Fum.	Own Rec.	Opp. Rec.	Yds.	Tot. Rec.
Malone, Mark, San Diego	6	1	0	−2	1
Manoa, Tim, Cleveland	4	0	0	0	0
Marino, Dan, Miami	10	7	1	−31	8
Marion, Fred, New England	0	0	2	16	2
Matthews, Clay, Cleveland	0	0	2	0	2
McElroy, Reggie, N.Y. Jets	0	1	0	0	1
McElroy, Vann, L.A. Raiders	0	0	1	0	1
McGee, Tim, Cincinnati	0	1	0	0	1
McMillan, Erik, N.Y. Jets	1	0	0	0	0
McNeal, Don, Miami	0	0	1	0	1
McNeil, Freeman, N.Y. Jets	3	0	0	0	0
McNeil, Gerald, Cleveland	3	1	0	0	1
Mersereau, Scott, N.Y. Jets	0	0	1	0	1
Metzelaars, Pete, Buffalo	0	1	0	0	1
Millen, Matt, L.A. Raiders	0	0	1	0	1
Miller, Anthony, San Diego	1	0	0	0	0
Miller, Darrin, Seattle	0	0	1	0	1
Mobley, Orson, Denver	1	1	0	0	1
Moon, Warren, Houston	8	4	0	−12	4
Morgan, Stanley, New England	1	1	0	0	1
Moyer, Paul, Seattle	0	0	2	0	2
Mueller, Jamie, Buffalo	2	1	0	0	1
Mueller, Vance, L.A. Raiders	1	0	1	0	1
Munchak, Mike, Houston	0	1	0	0	1
Muñoz, Anthony, Cincinnati	0	2	0	0	2
Nash, Joe, Seattle	0	0	1	0	1
Nattiel, Ricky, Denver	3	1	0	0	1
Newsome, Harry, Pittsburgh	0	1	0	0	1
Nickerson, Hardy, Pittsburgh	0	0	1	0	1
O'Brien, Ken, N.Y. Jets	11	5	0	−14	5
Odom, Cliff, Indianapolis	0	0	1	0	1
Offerdahl, John, Miami	0	0	1	0	1
Okoye, Christian, Kansas City	1	0	0	0	0
Pagel, Mike, Cleveland	0	1	0	0	1
Paige, Stephone, Kansas City	2	1	1	0	2
Palmer, Paul, Kansas City	7	1	0	0	1
Patterson, Elvis, San Diego	0	0	1	0	1
Pennison, Jay, Houston	1	1	0	0	1
Perry, Michael Dean, Cleveland	0	0	2	10	2
Perryman, Bob, New England	4	0	0	0	0
Pickel, Bill, L.A. Raiders	0	0	1	0	1
Pinkett, Allen, Houston	2	0	0	0	0
Pollard, Frank, Pittsburgh	1	0	0	0	0
Porter, Kevin, Kansas City	1	1	1	0	2
Porter, Rufus, Seattle	0	0	1	0	1
Prior, Mike, Indianapolis	1	0	1	12	1
Pruitt, James, Miami	1	0	0	0	0
Radecic, Scott, Buffalo	0	0	2	0	2
Rakoczy, Gregg, Cleveland	2	0	0	−16	0
Reed, Andre, Buffalo	1	0	0	0	0
Rembert, Johnny, New England	0	0	3	10	3
Richards, David, San Diego	0	1	0	0	1
Riddick, Robb, Buffalo	3	3	1	0	4
Rienstra, John, Pittsburgh	0	1	0	0	1
Riggs, Jim, Cincinnati	2	0	1	0	1
Robbins, Randy, Denver	1	1	1	0	2
Robinson, Jerry, L.A. Raiders	0	0	1	0	1
Rodriguez, Ruben, Seattle	1	1	0	0	1
Rosado, Dan, San Diego	1	1	0	−18	1
Rose, Ken, N.Y. Jets	0	1	0	0	1
Rozier, Mike, Houston	7	3	0	0	3
Runager, Max, Cleveland	1	1	0	−16	1
Ryan, Jim, Denver	0	0	1	0	1
Ryan, Pat, N.Y. Jets	1	0	0	0	0
Sally, Jerome, Kansas City	0	0	1	0	1
Sanchez, Lupe, Pittsburgh	0	0	1	0	1
Saxon, James, Kansas City	0	1	0	0	1
Schroeder, Jay, L.A. Raiders	6	3	0	−4	3
Schwedes, Scott, Miami	1	0	0	0	0
Seale, Sam, San Diego	0	0	2	50	2
Seals, Leon, Buffalo	0	0	3	7	3
Sewell, Steve, Denver	2	2	1	4	3
Shuler, Mickey, N.Y. Jets	1	2	0	0	2
Sims, Kenneth, New England	0	0	1	0	1
Slaughter, Webster, Cleveland	1	0	0	0	0
Smerlas, Fred, Buffalo	0	0	1	4	1
Smith, Al, Houston	0	0	1	0	1
Smith, Dennis, Denver	0	0	2	0	2
Smith, Doug, Houston	0	0	2	3	2
Smith, Steve, L.A. Raiders	1	1	0	0	1
Snipes, Angelo, Kansas City	0	1	0	0	1
Sochia, Brian, Miami	0	0	2	0	2
Sohn, Kurt, N.Y. Jets	0	0	1	0	1
Steinkuhler, Dean, Houston	0	2	0	0	2
Stephens, John, New England	3	3	0	4	3
Still, Art, Buffalo	0	0	1	0	1
Stone, Dwight, Pittsburgh	5	0	0	0	0
Stouffer, Kelly, Seattle	5	1	0	−17	1

	Fum.	Own Rec.	Opp. Rec.	Yds.	Tot. Rec.
Strachan, Steve, L.A. Raiders	2	2	1	0	3
Stradford, Troy, Miami	2	0	0	0	0
Strock, Don, Cleveland	4	2	0	−2	2
Swoope, Craig, Indianapolis	0	0	1	15	1
Talley, Darryl, Buffalo	0	0	1	0	1
Taylor, Kitrick, Kansas City	1	0	0	0	0
Thomas, Thurman, Buffalo	9	1	0	0	1
Thompson, Donnell, Indianapolis	0	0	2	0	2
Tice, Mike, Seattle	1	0	0	0	0
Toon, Al, N.Y. Jets	2	0	0	0	0
Townsell, JoJo, N.Y. Jets	3	0	0	0	0
Townsend, Andre, Denver	0	0	1	0	1
Townsend, Greg, L.A. Raiders	0	0	1	0	1
Tucker, Erroll, Buffalo	1	0	0	0	0
Tullis, Willie, Indianapolis	0	0	3	0	3
Turner, T.J., Miami	0	0	1	0	1
Veris, Garin, New England	0	0	1	0	1
Vick, Roger, N.Y. Jets	5	0	0	0	0
Villa, Danny, New England	1	0	0	−39	0
Vlasic, Mark, San Diego	1	1	0	−10	1
Walker, Wesley, N.Y. Jets	1	0	0	0	0
Warner, Curt, Seattle	5	1	0	−10	1
Weathers, Clarence, Cleveland	2	0	0	0	0
Webster, Mike, Pittsburgh	2	0	0	−58	0
White, Leon, Cincinnati	0	0	1	0	1
Wilcots, Solomon, Cincinnati	0	0	2	0	2
Willhite, Gerald, Denver	2	1	0	0	1
Williams, Brent, New England	0	0	1	0	1
Williams, Gerald, Pittsburgh	0	0	1	1	1
Williams, Jarvis, Miami	0	0	3	26	3
Williams, John L., Seattle	0	2	0	−2	2
Williams, Larry, Cleveland	0	1	0	0	1
Williams, Lee, San Diego	0	0	1	0	1
Williams, Warren, Pittsburgh	3	0	0	0	0
Wilson, Mike, Seattle	0	1	0	0	1
Wilson, Stanley, Cincinnati	3	0	0	0	0
Wilson, Steve, Denver	0	0	1	0	1
Winder, Sammy, Denver	1	0	0	0	0
Wise, Mike, L.A. Raiders	0	0	2	0	2
Wolford, Will, Buffalo	0	1	0	0	1
Woods, Ickey, Cincinnati	8	1	0	0	1
Woods, Tony, Seattle	0	1	0	0	1
Woodson, Rod, Pittsburgh	3	3	0	2	3
Wright, Felix, Cleveland	1	0	1	0	1
Wright, Jeff, Buffalo	0	0	1	0	1
Wyman, David, Seattle	0	0	2	0	2
Zander, Carl, Cincinnati	0	0	1	0	1

Yards include aborted plays, own recoveries, and opponents' recoveries.
Touchdowns: Leo Barker, Cincinnati; Lewis Billups, Cincinnati; Jacob Green, Seattle; Liffort Hobley, Miami; Michael Dean Perry, Cleveland; Sam Seale, San Diego; Leon Seals, Buffalo; John Stephens, New England; Greg Townsend, L.A. Raiders.
Includes both offensive and defensive recoveries for touchdowns.

NFC Fumbles—Individual

	Fum.	Own Rec.	Opp. Rec.	Yds.	Tot. Rec.
Adams, Michael, New Orleans	0	0	2	0	2
Adickes, John, Chicago	1	0	0	−13	0
Alexander, David, Philadelphia	0	1	0	0	1
Allen, Anthony, Washington	2	0	0	0	0
Allert, Ty, Philadelphia	0	0	1	0	1
Anderson, Alfred, Minnesota	3	0	0	0	0
Anderson, Neal, Chicago	8	2	0	0	2
Anderson, Ottis, N.Y. Giants	0	1	0	5	1
Atkins, Gene, New Orleans	1	1	1	0	2
Awalt, Robert, Phoenix	1	0	0	0	0
Baker, Stephen, N.Y. Giants	0	1	0	0	1
Barnes, Lew, Atlanta	4	0	0	0	0
Bates, Bill, Dallas	0	0	1	0	1
Bavaro, Mark, N.Y. Giants	1	0	0	0	0
Beals, Shawn, Philadelphia	1	1	0	0	1
Bell, Anthony, Phoenix	0	0	3	0	3
Bell, Greg, L.A. Rams	6	2	0	0	2
Bell, Todd, Philadelphia	0	0	2	0	2
Blades, Bennie, Detroit	0	0	4	22	4
Bland, Carl, Detroit	1	0	0	0	0
Bostic, Joe, Phoenix	0	1	0	0	1
Brown, Ron, L.A. Rams	1	0	0	0	0
Browner, Joey, Minnesota	0	0	2	9	2
Bruce, Aundray, Atlanta	0	0	1	0	1
Bryan, Rick, Atlanta	0	0	1	0	1
Bryant, Kelvin, Washington	3	1	0	0	1
Burbage, Cornell, Dallas	1	0	0	0	0
Burt, Jim, N.Y. Giants	0	0	2	39	2
Burton, Ron, Dallas	0	0	1	0	1
Butler, Bobby, Atlanta	0	0	3	29	3
Butz, Dave, Washington	0	0	1	0	1

	Fum.	Own Rec.	Opp. Rec.	Yds.	Tot. Rec.
Byars, Keith, Philadelphia	5	2	0	14	2
Cannon, John, Tampa Bay	0	0	1	0	1
Cannon, Mark, Green Bay	2	0	0	−31	0
Caravello, Joe, Washington	0	1	0	0	1
Carreker, Alphonso, Green Bay	0	0	1	0	1
Carrier, Mark, Tampa Bay	2	0	0	0	0
Carruth, Paul Ott, Green Bay	4	0	0	0	0
Carson, Harry, N.Y. Giants	0	0	2	12	2
Carter, Anthony, Minnesota	1	1	0	0	1
Carter, Cris, Philadelphia	0	1	0	0	1
Carthon, Maurice, N.Y. Giants	0	1	0	0	1
Casillas, Tony, Atlanta	0	0	1	0	1
Cecil, Chuck, Green Bay	0	0	1	0	1
Clark, Bret, Atlanta	1	0	1	12	1
Clark, Gary, Washington	2	0	0	0	0
Clark, Greg, Chicago	0	0	1	0	1
Clark, Robert, New Orleans	1	0	1	0	1
Cobb, Garry, Dallas	0	0	1	0	1
Cofer, Mike, Detroit	0	0	2	0	2
Coleman, Greg, Washington	1	1	0	−15	1
Coleman, Monte, Washington	0	0	1	9	1
Coleman, Sidney, Tampa Bay	0	0	1	0	1
Cooks, Johnie, N.Y. Giants	0	0	1	0	1
Cooper, Evan, Atlanta	1	0	0	0	0
Craig, Roger, San Francisco	8	2	0	0	2
Criswell, Ray, Tampa Bay	1	1	0	−31	1
Cross, Randy, San Francisco	0	1	0	0	1
Cunningham, Randall, Philadelphia	12	6	0	0	6
Darwin, Matt, Philadelphia	0	1	0	0	1
Davis, Wayne, Phoenix	0	0	1	0	1
Davis, Wendell, Chicago	2	1	0	0	1
Delpino, Robert, L.A. Rams	2	0	1	0	1
Dent, Burnell, Green Bay	0	0	1	0	1
Dent, Richard, Chicago	0	0	1	0	1
Didier, Clint, Green Bay	1	0	1	4	1
Dils, Steve, Atlanta	3	0	0	0	0
Dixon, Floyd, Atlanta	1	0	0	0	0
Dombrowski, Jim, New Orleans	0	1	0	0	1
Dorsey, Eric, N.Y. Giants	0	0	2	0	2
Douglass, Maurice, Chicago	1	1	2	0	3
Downs, Michael, Dallas	0	0	1	11	1
DuBose, Doug, San Francisco	2	1	1	0	2
Edwards, Kelvin, Dallas	1	1	0	0	1
Ekern, Carl, L.A. Rams	0	0	2	0	2
Elder, Donnie, Tampa Bay	1	1	0	6	1
Ellard, Henry, L.A. Rams	3	0	0	0	0
Elliott, John, N.Y. Giants	0	1	0	0	1
Evans, Byron, Philadelphia	0	0	2	0	2
Everett, Jim, L.A. Rams	7	0	0	−17	0
Ferguson, Joe, Tampa Bay	1	0	0	0	0
Ferrell, Earl, Phoenix	7	3	0	6	3
Flynn, Tom, N.Y. Giants	1	0	0	0	0
Frank, John, San Francisco	0	1	0	0	1
Fuller, Jeff, San Francisco	0	0	1	0	1
Fullington, Darrell, Minnesota	0	0	1	0	1
Fullwood, Brent, Green Bay	6	1	0	0	1
Futrell, Bobby, Tampa Bay	4	1	0	0	1
Galloway, David, Phoenix	0	0	1	0	1
Gann, Mike, Atlanta	0	0	2	36	2
Gay, Everett, Dallas	1	0	0	0	0
Geathers, James, New Orleans	0	0	3	0	3
Gentry, Dennis, Chicago	2	0	0	0	0
Gibson, Antonio, New Orleans	0	0	1	7	1
Gibson, Dennis, Detroit	0	0	1	0	1
Glover, Kevin, Detroit	0	2	0	0	2
Goff, Robert, Tampa Bay	0	0	3	0	3
Gordon, Tim, Atlanta	1	1	0	0	1
Grant, Darryl, Washington	0	0	1	0	1
Gray, Jerry, L.A. Rams	0	0	1	0	1
Gray, Mel, New Orleans	5	2	0	0	2
Green, Curtis, Detroit	0	0	1	0	1
Green, Darrell, Washington	1	1	0	0	1
Green, Gaston, L.A. Rams	1	3	0	0	3
Griffin, James, Detroit	0	0	1	7	1
Grimm, Russ, Washington	0	1	0	0	1
Gruber, Paul, Tampa Bay	0	2	0	0	2
Guggemos, Neal, N.Y. Giants	2	3	0	0	3
Haddix, Michael, Philadelphia	1	0	1	0	1
Haddix, Wayne, N.Y. Giants	1	0	0	0	0
Haley, Charles, San Francisco	0	0	2	0	2
Hamilton, Harry, Tampa Bay	1	0	2	0	2
Harbaugh, Jim, Chicago	1	0	0	−1	0
Harris, Al, Chicago	0	0	3	0	3
Harris, Darryl, Minnesota	1	0	0	−4	0
Harris, Odie, Tampa Bay	0	0	1	0	1
Haynes, James, New Orleans	0	1	0	0	1
Hebert, Bobby, New Orleans	9	1	0	0	1
Heller, Ron, Philadelphia	0	2	0	0	2
Helton, Barry, San Francisco	0	1	0	0	1
Henderson, Wymon, Minnesota	0	2	0	0	2
Hester, Jessie, Atlanta	1	0	0	0	0
Heyward, Craig, New Orleans	0	1	0	0	1
Hicks, Cliff, L.A. Rams	1	0	0	0	0
Hilgenberg, Jay, Chicago	1	1	0	−18	1
Hilger, Rusty, Detroit	7	5	0	−19	5
Hill, Bruce, Tampa Bay	2	1	0	0	1
Hill, Kenny, N.Y. Giants	2	1	0	0	1
Hill, Lonzell, New Orleans	3	0	0	0	0
Hilliard, Dalton, New Orleans	3	0	0	0	0
Holland, Johnny, Green Bay	0	0	1	0	1
Holohan, Pete, L.A. Rams	1	0	0	0	0
Holt, Pierce, San Francisco	0	0	1	0	1
Hoover, Houston, Atlanta	0	2	0	0	2
Hopkins, Wes, Philadelphia	0	0	1	0	1
Horne, Greg, Phoenix	2	2	0	−10	2
Hostetler, Jeff, N.Y. Giants	1	1	0	0	1
Howard, David, Minnesota	0	0	2	33	2
Howard, Erik, N.Y. Giants	0	0	2	0	2
Howard, William, Tampa Bay	2	0	0	0	0
Irvin, LeRoy, L.A. Rams	1	0	0	0	0
Jackson, Keith, Philadelphia	3	0	0	0	0
Jacoby, Joe, Washington	0	1	0	0	1
James, Garry, Detroit	3	0	0	0	0
Jamison, George, Detroit	0	0	3	4	3
Jax, Garth, Dallas	0	0	1	0	1
Jefferson, Norman, Green Bay	3	1	0	0	1
Johnson, Johnnie, L.A. Rams	1	1	2	0	3
Johnson, Pepper, N.Y. Giants	0	0	1	0	1
Jones, Ed, Dallas	0	0	2	0	2
Jones, Ernie, Phoenix	1	0	0	0	0
Jones, James, Detroit	2	0	0	0	0
Jordan, Buford, New Orleans	1	1	0	7	1
Jordan, Steve, Minnesota	2	0	0	0	0
Jordan, Tony, Phoenix	1	0	0	0	0
Joyner, Seth, Philadelphia	1	1	0	0	1
Junior, E.J., Phoenix	0	0	1	36	1
Kemp, Perry, Green Bay	3	0	0	0	0
Kennedy, Sam, San Francisco	0	1	1	0	2
Konecny, Mark, Philadelphia	3	2	0	0	2
Kozlowski, Glen, Chicago	1	0	0	0	0
Kramer, Tommy, Minnesota	3	0	0	−12	0
Lachey, Jim, Washington	0	1	0	0	1
Lang, Gene, Atlanta	3	0	0	0	0
Lee, Carl, Minnesota	0	0	1	0	1
Lee, Gary, Detroit	2	1	0	0	1
Lee, Mark, Green Bay	0	0	1	0	1
Lewis, Leo, Minnesota	2	0	0	0	0
Lockett, Danny, Detroit	0	1	0	0	1
Lomax, Neil, Phoenix	5	2	0	−9	2
Long, Chuck, Detroit	4	2	0	−3	2
Lott, Ronnie, San Francisco	0	0	4	3	4
Love, Duval, L.A. Rams	0	1	0	0	1
Loveall, Calvin, Atlanta	0	1	0	0	1
Mack, Cedric, Phoenix	0	0	1	45	1
Majkowski, Don, Green Bay	8	3	0	0	3
Mandley, Pete, Detroit	3	1	0	−2	1
Manuel, Lionel, N.Y. Giants	1	1	0	0	1
Martin, Chris, Minnesota	0	0	1	0	1
Martin, Eric, New Orleans	2	0	0	0	0
Martin, George, N.Y. Giants	0	0	2	4	2
Martin, Kelvin, Dallas	2	0	0	0	0
Matthews, Aubrey, Atlanta	2	0	0	0	0
Mayes, Rueben, New Orleans	1	0	0	0	0
McConkey, Phil, N.Y. Giants	2	0	0	0	0
McDonald, Mike, L.A. Rams	1	0	0	0	0
McDonald, Tim, Phoenix	0	0	1	9	1
McHale, Tom, Tampa Bay	1	0	0	−4	0
McKinnon, Dennis, Chicago	3	1	0	0	1
McMahon, Jim, Chicago	6	3	0	0	3
McMichael, Steve, Chicago	0	1	1	1	2
McNorton, Bruce, Detroit	0	0	4	36	4
Millard, Keith, Minnesota	0	0	2	5	2
Millen, Hugh, Atlanta	1	0	0	0	0
Miller, Chris, Atlanta	2	1	0	0	1
Mills, Sam, New Orleans	0	1	3	0	4
Mitchell, Stump, Phoenix	6	3	0	−3	3
Monk, Art, Washington	0	1	0	0	1
Montana, Joe, San Francisco	3	1	0	−3	1
Morris, Jamie, Washington	3	0	0	0	0
Morris, Joe, N.Y. Giants	7	1	0	0	1
Morrissey, Jim, Chicago	0	0	1	0	1
Mott, Steve, Detroit	3	0	0	−23	0
Mowatt, Zeke, N.Y. Giants	2	0	0	0	0
Murphy, Kevin, Tampa Bay	0	0	1	4	1
Murphy, Mark, Green Bay	0	0	4	0	4
Muster, Brad, Chicago	1	1	0	0	1

	Fum.	Own Rec.	Opp. Rec.	Yds.	Tot. Rec.
Nelson, Darrin, Minnesota	3	2	0	0	2
Newman, Anthony, L.A. Rams	0	0	1	0	1
Newsome, Tim, Dallas	1	1	0	0	1
Newsome, Vince, L.A. Rams	0	0	1	0	1
Newton, Tim, Minnesota	0	0	1	0	1
Noble, Brian, Green Bay	0	0	1	0	1
Norton, Ken, Dallas	0	0	1	0	1
Novacek, Jay, Phoenix	0	1	0	0	1
Nunn, Freddie Joe, Phoenix	0	0	2	8	2
Oates, Bart, N.Y. Giants	1	0	0	−10	0
Oliphant, Mike, Washington	2	1	0	0	1
Olkewicz, Neal, Washington	0	0	3	8	3
Orr, Terry, Washington	0	1	1	0	2
Owens, Mel, L.A. Rams	0	0	1	0	1
Paige, Tony, Detroit	1	0	0	0	0
Painter, Carl, Detroit	1	1	0	0	1
Pankey, Irv, L.A. Rams	0	1	0	0	1
Patterson, Shawn, Green Bay	0	0	1	0	1
Pelluer, Steve, Dallas	6	2	0	−18	2
Perriman, Brett, New Orleans	1	0	0	0	0
Pitts, Ron, Green Bay	1	2	2	0	4
Primus, James, Atlanta	0	1	0	0	1
Radloff, Wayne, Atlanta	0	1	0	0	1
Rathman, Tom, San Francisco	0	1	0	0	1
Reasons, Gary, N.Y. Giants	0	1	1	5	2
Reed, Doug, L.A. Rams	0	0	1	0	1
Reynolds, Ricky, Tampa Bay	0	2	0	0	2
Rice, Allen, Minnesota	1	1	0	0	1
Rice, Jerry, San Francisco	2	1	0	0	1
Riesenberg, Doug, N.Y. Giants	0	1	0	0	1
Riggs, Gerald, Atlanta	3	0	0	0	0
Rimington, Dave, Philadelphia	0	2	0	0	2
Rivera, Ron, Chicago	1	0	0	0	0
Roberts, William, N.Y. Giants	0	2	0	0	2
Rolling, Henry, Tampa Bay	0	1	1	0	2
Romanowski, Bill, San Francisco	0	0	1	0	1
Rouson, Lee, N.Y. Giants	2	2	0	0	2
Ruettgers, Ken, Green Bay	0	1	0	0	1
Rutland, Reggie, Minnesota	1	0	2	17	2
Rutledge, Jeff, N.Y. Giants	2	0	0	0	0
Rypien, Mark, Washington	6	0	0	0	0
Saddler, Rod, Phoenix	0	0	1	16	1
Saleaumua, Dan, Detroit	1	0	0	0	0
Salem, Harvey, Detroit	0	1	0	0	1
Sanders, Eric, Detroit	1	0	1	−17	1
Sanders, Thomas, Chicago	5	0	0	0	0
Scribner, Bucky, Minnesota	1	0	0	0	0
Settle, John, Atlanta	3	1	0	0	1
Sharpe, Sterling, Green Bay	3	1	0	0	1
Shaw, Ricky, N.Y. Giants	0	0	1	0	1
Shelley, Elbert, Atlanta	1	0	0	0	0
Shepard, Derrick, Washington	3	0	0	0	0
Sikahema, Vai, Phoenix	2	1	0	0	1
Simmons, Clyde, Philadelphia	0	0	3	0	3
Simms, Phil, N.Y. Giants	7	1	0	0	1
Singletary, Mike, Chicago	0	1	0	4	1
Smith, J. T., Phoenix	4	1	0	0	1
Smith, Timmy, Washington	4	1	0	0	1
Solomon, Jesse, Minnesota	0	0	2	3	2
Spielman, Chris, Detroit	0	0	1	0	1
Stamps, Sylvester, Atlanta	1	0	0	0	0
Stanley, Walter, Green Bay	3	1	0	0	1
Stewart, Michael, L.A. Rams	0	0	2	24	2
Stills, Ken, Green Bay	0	1	2	4	3
Stokes, Fred, L.A. Rams	0	1	1	0	2
Stoudt, Cliff, Phoenix	4	2	0	0	2
Strickland, Fred, L.A. Rams	0	1	1	0	2
Stubbs, Danny, San Francisco	0	0	1	0	1
Studwell, Scott, Minnesota	0	0	2	0	2
Suhey, Matt, Chicago	1	1	0	0	1
Sutton, Reggie, New Orleans	1	1	0	0	1
Sweeney, Kevin, Dallas	3	0	0	0	0
Swilling, Pat, New Orleans	0	0	1	0	1
Tate, Lars, Tampa Bay	2	0	0	0	0
Taylor, John, San Francisco	6	2	0	0	2
Taylor, Lawrence, N.Y. Giants	0	0	1	0	1
Teltschik, John, Philadelphia	1	1	0	0	1
Testaverde, Vinny, Tampa Bay	8	2	0	0	2
Thomas, Chuck, San Francisco	1	0	0	−12	0
Thomas, Henry, Minnesota	0	0	1	2	1
Thornton, James, Chicago	1	0	0	0	0
Tomczak, Mike, Chicago	1	0	0	−3	0
Toney, Anthony, Philadelphia	2	0	0	0	0
Tuggle, Jessie, Atlanta	0	0	1	2	1
Turk, Dan, Tampa Bay	1	0	1	−19	1
Turner, Keena, San Francisco	0	0	2	0	2
Uecker, Keith, Green Bay	0	1	1	0	2
Van Horne, Keith, Chicago	0	1	0	0	1
Wagner, Bryan, Chicago	1	1	0	−9	1
Walczak, Mark, Phoenix	1	1	0	−23	1
Walker, Herschel, Dallas	6	3	0	0	3
Walls, Everson, Dallas	1	0	1	4	1
Walter, Mike, San Francisco	0	1	1	0	2
Warren, Don, Washington	1	1	0	0	1
Warren, Frank, New Orleans	0	0	1	0	1
Washington, Chris, Tampa Bay	0	0	1	0	1
Waymer, Dave, New Orleans	1	0	1	0	1
Weddington, Mike, Green Bay	0	0	2	0	2
West, Ed, Green Bay	1	0	0	0	0
Whisenhunt, Ken, Atlanta	1	0	1	0	1
White, Charles, L.A. Rams	3	0	0	0	0
White, Reggie, Philadelphia	0	0	2	0	2
White, William, Detroit	0	0	1	0	1
Widell, Dave, Dallas	0	1	0	0	1
Wilburn, Barry, Washington	0	0	1	0	1
Wilcher, Mike, L.A. Rams	0	0	1	8	1
Wilder, James, Tampa Bay	1	0	0	0	0
Wilks, Jim, New Orleans	0	0	1	0	1
Williams, Doug, Washington	6	0	0	0	0
Williams, Jimmy, Detroit	0	0	1	0	1
Williams, Joel, Atlanta	0	0	3	12	3
Williams, Perry, N.Y. Giants	0	0	3	6	3
Williams, Robert, Dallas	0	1	0	0	1
Williams, Scott, Detroit	0	0	1	0	1
Wilson, Wade, Minnesota	4	4	0	−9	4
Winter, Blaise, Green Bay	0	0	2	0	2
Witkowski, John, Detroit	1	0	0	0	0
Wolfley, Ron, Phoenix	0	1	0	0	1
Woodside, Keith, Green Bay	3	1	0	0	1
Woolfolk, Butch, Detroit	1	1	0	0	1
Wright, Eric, San Francisco	0	0	1	0	1
Wright, Randy, Green Bay	6	3	0	−5	3
Young, Lonnie, Phoenix	0	0	2	0	2
Young, Steve, San Francisco	5	2	0	−10	2

Yards include aborted plays, own recoveries, and opponents' recoveries.

Touchdowns: Jim Burt, N.Y. Giants; Cris Carter, Philadelphia; Mike Gann, Atlanta; George Jamison, Detroit; Buford Jordan, New Orleans; E.J. Junior, Phoenix; Cedric Mack, Phoenix; Chris Martin, Minnesota; Rod Saddler, Phoenix; Henry Thomas, Minnesota; Jessie Tuggle, Atlanta.

Includes both offensive and defensive recoveries for touchdowns.

Sacks

Individual Champions

NFC: 18.0—Reggie White, Philadelphia
AFC: 11.5—Greg Townsend, L.A. Raiders

Most Sacks, Game

NFC: 5.0—Gary Jeter, L.A. Rams at L.A. Raiders, September 18
AFC: 3.0—Jacob Green, Seattle vs. Kansas City, September 11
3.0—Mark Gastineau, N.Y. Jets vs. Kansas City, October 2 (OT)
3.0—Lee Williams, San Diego vs. Denver, October 2
3.0—Marty Lyons, N.Y. Jets at Cincinnati, October 9
3.0—Charles Buchanan, Cleveland vs. Philadelphia, October 16
3.0—Lee Williams, San Diego at L.A. Rams, November 20
3.0—Ken Rose, N.Y. Jets vs. N.Y. Giants, December 18

Team Champions

NFC: 56—L.A. Rams
AFC: 46—Buffalo

AFC Sacks—Team

	Sacks	Yards
Buffalo	46	322
N.Y. Jets	45	314
Cincinnati	42	374
Houston	42	353
L.A. Raiders	40	300
Cleveland	37	255
Denver	36	235
San Diego	34	240
Seattle	30	265
Indianapolis	30	201
New England	29	219
Miami	24	167
Kansas City	23	157
Pittsburgh	19	145
AFC Total	477	3,547
AFC Average	34.1	253.4

NFC Sacks—Team

	Sacks	Yards
L.A. Rams	56	394
N.Y. Giants	52	428
Detroit	47	393
Dallas	46	327
Chicago	43	365
Washington	43	305
San Francisco	42	297
Philadelphia	42	296
Phoenix	39	295
Minnesota	37	274
New Orleans	31	252
Green Bay	30	216
Atlanta	30	211
Tampa Bay	20	140
NFC Total	558	4,193
NFC Average	39.9	299.5
League Total	1,035	7,740
League Average	37.0	276.4

NFL Top 10 Individual Leaders in Sacks

	Total
White, Reggie, Philadelphia	18.0
Green, Kevin, L.A. Rams	16.5
Taylor, Lawrence, N.Y. Giants	15.5
Nunn, Freddie Joe, Phoenix	14.0
Harris, Timothy, Green Bay	13.5
Cofer, Mike, Detroit	12.0
Haley, Charles, San Francisco	11.5
Jeter, Gary, L.A. Rams	11.5
McMichael, Steve, Chicago	11.5
Townsend, Greg, L.A. Raiders	11.5

AFC Sacks—Individual

Townsend, Greg, L.A. Raiders	11.5
Smith, Bruce, Buffalo	11.0
Williams, Lee, San Diego	11.0
Bennett, Cornelius, Buffalo	9.5
Skow, Jim, Cincinnati	9.5
Fletcher, Simon, Denver	9.0
Green, Jacob, Seattle	9.0
Childress, Ray, Houston	8.5
Fuller, William, Houston	8.5
Meads, Johnny, Houston	8.0
Williams, Brent, New England	8.0
Jones, Sean, Houston	7.5
Lyons, Marty, N.Y. Jets	7.5
Gastineau, Mark, N.Y. Jets	7.0
Tippett, Andre, New England	7.0
Buck, Jason, Cincinnati	6.0
Matthews, Clay, Cleveland	6.0
Perry, Michael Dean, Cleveland	6.0
Still, Art, Buffalo	6.0
Davis, Scott, L.A. Raiders	5.5
Townsend, Andre, Denver	5.5
Buchanan, Charles, Cleveland	5.0
Grant, David, Cincinnati	5.0
Grayson, Dave, Cleveland	5.0
Hand, Jon, Indianapolis	5.0
Jones, Rulon, Denver	5.0
Pickel, Bill, L.A. Raiders	5.0
Rose, Ken, N.Y. Jets	5.0
Turner, T. J., Miami	5.0
Wise, Mike, L.A. Raiders	5.0
Woods, Tony, Seattle	5.0
Wright, Jeff, Buffalo	5.0
Clancy, Sam, Cleveland	4.5
Mersereau, Scott, N.Y. Jets	4.5
Sochia, Brian, Miami	4.5
Bussey, Barney, Cincinnati	4.0
Cline, Jackie, Miami	4.0
Johnson, Tim, Pittsburgh	4.0
Maas, Bill, Kansas City	4.0
O'Neal, Leslie, San Diego	4.0
Smerlas, Fred, Buffalo	4.0
Bickett, Duane, Indianapolis	3.5
Bryant, Jeff, Seattle	3.5
Carr, Gregg, Pittsburgh	3.5
Cofield, Tim, Kansas City	3.5
Nickerson, Hardy, Pittsburgh	3.5
Ryan, Jim, Denver	3.5
Williams, Gerald, Pittsburgh	3.5
Alston, O'Brien, Indianapolis	3.0
Barker, Leo, Cincinnati	3.0
Campbell, Joe, San Diego	3.0
Cole, Robin, N.Y. Jets	3.0
Gordon, Alex, N.Y. Jets	3.0
Hackett, Dino, Kansas City	3.0
Hairston, Carl, Cleveland	3.0
Hinkle, George, San Diego	3.0
Johnson, Eddie, Cleveland	3.0
Johnson, Ezra, Indianapolis	3.0
Jordan, Tim, New England	3.0
Keys, Tyrone, San Diego	3.0
Krumrie, Tim, Cincinnati	3.0
Kumerow, Eric, Miami	3.0
Long, Howie, L.A. Raiders	3.0
Mitz, Alonzo, Seattle	3.0
Rembert, Johnny, New England	3.0
Smith, Doug, Houston	3.0
Thompson, Donnell, Indianapolis	3.0
White, Leon, Cincinnati	3.0
Browner, Keith, San Diego	2.5
Green, Hugh, Miami	2.5
Kragen, Greg, Denver	2.5
Smith, Neil, Kansas City	2.5
Stensrud, Mike, Kansas City	2.5
Talley, Darryl, Buffalo	2.5
Williams, Reggie, Cincinnati	2.5
Wyman, David, Seattle	2.5
Armstrong, Harvey, Indianapolis	2.0
Bell, Mike, Kansas City	2.0
Benson, Troy, N.Y. Jets	2.0
Bosa, John, Miami	2.0
Bostic, Keith, Houston	2.0
Carter, Russell, L.A. Raiders	2.0
Clarke, Ken, Seattle	2.0
Darby, Byron, Indianapolis	2.0
Goad, Tim, New England	2.0
Griffin, Leonard, Kansas City	2.0
Humphery, Bobby, N.Y. Jets	2.0
McArthur, Kevin, N.Y. Jets	2.0
McClendon, Skip, Cincinnati	2.0
McGrew, Larry, New England	2.0
Nash, Joe, Seattle	2.0
Odom, Cliff, Indianapolis	2.0
Phillips, Joe, San Diego	2.0
Robbins, Randy, Denver	2.0
Robinson, Jerry, L.A. Raiders	2.0
Seals, Leon, Buffalo	2.0
Snipes, Angelo, Kansas City	2.0
Toran, Stacey, L.A. Raiders	2.0
Veris, Garin, New England	2.0
Wilson, Steve, Denver	2.0
Conlan, Shane, Buffalo	1.5
Fulcher, David, Cincinnati	1.5
Jones, Aaron, Pittsburgh	1.5
Lyles, Robert, Houston	1.5
Nichols, Gerald, N.Y. Jets	1.5
Radachowsky, George, N.Y. Jets	1.5
Radecic, Scott, Buffalo	1.5
Baldwin, Tom, N.Y. Jets	1.0
Bayless, Martin, San Diego	1.0
Bentley, Ray, Buffalo	1.0
Bowyer, Walt, Denver	1.0
Braxton, Tyrone, Denver	1.0
Del Rio, Jack, Kansas City	1.0
Frase, Paul, N.Y. Jets	1.0
Garner, Hal, Buffalo	1.0
Gilbert, Freddie, Denver	1.0
Glenn, Vencie, San Diego	1.0
Graf, Rick, Miami	1.0
Grimsley, John, Houston	1.0
Harper, Dwayne, Seattle	1.0
Harper, Mark, Cleveland	1.0
Hasty, James, N.Y. Jets	1.0
Haynes, Mark, Denver	1.0
Herrod, Jeff, Indianapolis	1.0
Hill, Will, Cleveland	1.0
Hodge, Milford, New England	1.0
Horton, Ray, Cincinnati	1.0
Howard, Carl, N.Y. Jets	1.0
Jones, Marlon, Cleveland	1.0
King, Linden, L.A. Raiders	1.0
Lankford, Paul, Miami	1.0
McKenzie, Reggie, L.A. Raiders	1.0
Mecklenburg, Karl, Denver	1.0
Mikolas, Doug, Houston	1.0
Millen, Matt, L.A. Raiders	1.0
Miller, Pat, San Diego	1.0
Patterson, Elvis, San Diego	1.0
Prior, Mike, Indianapolis	1.0
Reese, Jerry, Pittsburgh	1.0
Robinson, Eugene, Seattle	1.0
Scholtz, Bruce, Seattle	1.0
Seale, Eugene, Houston	1.0
Smith, Billy Ray, San Diego	1.0
Smith, Dennis, Denver	1.0
Smith, Leonard, Buffalo	1.0
Swoope, Craig, Indianapolis	1.0
Taylor, Malcolm, L.A. Raiders	1.0
Tullis, Willie, Indianapolis	1.0
Brown, Mark, Miami	0.5
Dennison, Rick, Denver	0.5
Edwards, Eddie, Cincinnati	0.5
Garalczyk, Mark, N.Y. Jets	0.5
Hinkle, Bryan, Pittsburgh	0.5
Lloyd, Greg, Pittsburgh	0.5
Miano, Rich, N.Y. Jets	0.5
Offerdahl, John, Miami	0.5
Porter, Kevin, Kansas City	0.5
Thomas, Ben, Pittsburgh	0.5
Washington, Brian, Cleveland	0.5
Wilson, Karl, San Diego	0.5
Woodson, Rod, Pittsburgh	0.5
Wright, Terry, Indianapolis	0.5

NFC Sacks—Individual

White, Reggie, Philadelphia	18.0
Greene, Kevin, L.A. Rams	16.5
Taylor, Lawrence, N.Y. Giants	15.5
Nunn, Freddie Joe, Phoenix	14.0
Harris, Timothy, Green Bay	13.5
Cofer, Mike, Detroit	12.0
Haley, Charles, San Francisco	11.5
Jeter, Gary, L.A. Rams	11.5
McMichael, Steve, Chicago	11.5
Dent, Richard, Chicago	10.5
Hampton, Dan, Chicago	9.5
Manley, Dexter, Washington	9.0
Ferguson, Keith, Detroit	8.5
Doleman, Chris, Minnesota	8.0
Marshall, Leonard, N.Y. Giants	8.0
Millard, Keith, Minnesota	8.0
Simmons, Clyde, Philadelphia	8.0
Cobb, Garry, Dallas	7.5
Martin, George, N.Y. Giants	7.5
Noonan, Danny, Dallas	7.5
Wilcher, Mike, L.A. Rams	7.5
Jackson, Rickey, New Orleans	7.0
Jones, Ed, Dallas	7.0
Swilling, Pat, New Orleans	7.0
Carter, Michael, San Francisco	6.5
Jeffcoat, Jim, Dallas	6.5
Williams, Eric, Detroit	6.5
Bruce, Aundray, Atlanta	6.0
Harvey, Ken, Phoenix	6.0
Roberts, Larry, San Francisco	6.0
Stubbs, Danny, San Francisco	6.0
Thomas, Henry, Minnesota	6.0
Baker, Al, Minnesota	5.5
Jamison, George, Detroit	5.5
Mann, Charles, Washington	5.5
Brooks, Kevin, Dallas	5.0
Brown, Jerome, Philadelphia	5.0
Bryan, Rick, Atlanta	5.0
Clasby, Bob, Phoenix	5.0
Cotton, Marcus, Atlanta	5.0
Holt, Pierce, San Francisco	5.0
Owens, Mel, L.A. Rams	5.0
Winter, Blaise, Green Bay	5.0
Caldwell, Ravin, Washington	4.0
Gann, Mike, Atlanta	4.0
Grant, Darryl, Washington	4.0
Green, Tim, Atlanta	4.0
Holmes, Ron, Tampa Bay	4.0
Johnson, Pepper, N.Y. Giants	4.0
Marshall, Wilber, Washington	4.0
Miller, Shawn, L.A. Rams	4.0
Patterson, Shawn, Green Bay	4.0
Strickland, Fred, L.A. Rams	4.0
Walen, Mark, Dallas	4.0
Dorsey, Eric, N.Y. Giants	3.5
Geathers, James, New Orleans	3.5
Harris, Al, Chicago	3.5
Joyner, Seth, Philadelphia	3.5
Koch, Markus, Washington	3.5
Wilks, Jim, New Orleans	3.5
Burt, Jim, N.Y. Giants	3.0
Cannon, John, Tampa Bay	3.0
Coleman, Monte, Washington	3.0
Davis, Reuben, Tampa Bay	3.0
Fagan, Kevin, San Francisco	3.0
Headen, Andy, N.Y. Giants	3.0
Howard, Erik, N.Y. Giants	3.0
Martin, Doug, Minnesota	3.0
Jarvis, Curt, Tampa Bay	2.5
Solomon, Jesse, Minnesota	2.5
Albritton, Vince, Dallas	2.0
Alvord, Steve, Phoenix	2.0
Ball, Jerry, Detroit	2.0
Burton, Ron, Dallas	2.0
Casillas, Tony, Atlanta	2.0
Chapura, Dick, Chicago	2.0
Galloway, David, Phoenix	2.0
Gibson, Antonio, New Orleans	2.0
Goff, Robert, Tampa Bay	2.0
Green, Curtis, Detroit	2.0
Hamel, Dean, Washington	2.0
Hoage, Terry, Philadelphia	2.0
Johnson, Vaughan, New Orleans	2.0
Junior, E.J., Phoenix	2.0

Kohlbrand, Joe, New Orleans	2.0
Lee, Shawn, Tampa Bay	2.0
McDonald, Tim, Phoenix	2.0
Olkewicz, Neal, Washington	2.0
Rade, John, Atlanta	2.0
Rivera, Ron, Chicago	2.0
Saddler, Rod, Phoenix	2.0
Saleaumua, Dan, Detroit	2.0
Strauthers, Thomas, Detroit	2.0
Williams, Jimmy, Detroit	2.0
Williams, Perry, N.Y. Giants	2.0
Wright, Alvin, L.A. Rams	2.0
Banks, Carl, N.Y. Giants	1.5
Brown, Robert, Green Bay	1.5
Marve, Eugene, Tampa Bay	1.5
Pitts, Mike, Philadelphia	1.5
White, Randy, Dallas	1.5
Anderson, John, Green Bay	1.0
Bartlett, Doug, Philadelphia	1.0
Bell, Anthony, Phoenix	1.0
Blades, Bennie, Detroit	1.0
Butz, Dave, Washington	1.0
Case, Scott, Atlanta	1.0
Cooks, Johnie, N.Y. Giants	1.0
Curtis, Travis, Phoenix	1.0
Dent, Burnell, Green Bay	1.0
Duerson, Dave, Chicago	1.0
Elliott, Tony, New Orleans	1.0
Ellison, Riki, San Francisco	1.0
Faryniarz, Brett, L.A. Rams	1.0
Fuller, Jeff, San Francisco	1.0
Golic, Mike, Philadelphia	1.0
Gordon, Tim, Atlanta	1.0
Green, Darrell, Washington	1.0
Greene, Tiger, Green Bay	1.0
Gregory, Ted, New Orleans	1.0
Griffin, Don, San Francisco	1.0
Griffin, James, Detroit	1.0
Howard, David, Minnesota	1.0
Hunley, Ricky, Phoenix	1.0
Johnson, Troy, Chicago	1.0
Kaufman, Mel, Washington	1.0
Lockett, Danny, Detroit	1.0
Mack, Milton, New Orleans	1.0
Martin, Chris, Minnesota	1.0
Meisner, Greg, L.A. Rams	1.0
Murphy, Kevin, Tampa Bay	1.0
Newton, Tim, Minnesota	1.0
Noga, Niko, Phoenix	1.0
Owens, Billy, Dallas	1.0
Reed, Doug, L.A. Rams	1.0
Reichenbach, Mike, Philadelphia	1.0
Rogers, Reggie, Detroit	1.0
Rolling, Henry, Tampa Bay	1.0
Singletary, Mike, Chicago	1.0
Smith, Sean, Chicago	1.0
Stephen, Scott, Green Bay	1.0
Stewart, Michael, L.A. Rams	1.0
Stills, Ken, Green Bay	1.0
Stokes, Fred, L.A. Rams	1.0
Studwell, Scott, Minnesota	1.0
Vaughn, Clarence, Washington	1.0
Walls, Everson, Dallas	1.0
Walter, Mike, San Francisco	1.0
Walton, Alvin, Washington	1.0
Warren, Frank, New Orleans	1.0
Bates, Bill, Dallas	0.5
Bell, Todd, Philadelphia	0.5
Boyarsky, Jerry, Green Bay	0.5
Downs, Michael, Dallas	0.5
Gibson, Dennis, Detroit	0.5
Irvin, LeRoy, L.A. Rams	0.5
Noble, Brian, Green Bay	0.5
Waters, Andre, Philadelphia	0.5

1988 NFL Paid Attendance Breakdown

	Games	Attendance	Average
AFC Preseason	9	431,608	47,956
NFC Preseason	9	386,632	42,959
AFC-NFC Preseason, Interconference	40	2,008,021	50,201
NFL Preseason Total	**58**	**2,826,261**	**48,729**
AFC Regular Season	86	5,348,592	62,193
NFC Regular Season	86	5,037,684	58,578
AFC-NFC Regular Season, Interconference	52	3,153,572	60,646
NFL Regular Season Total	**224**	**13,539,848**	**60,446**
AFC First-Round Playoff	1		
(Houston-Cleveland)		75,896	
AFC Divisional Playoffs	2		
(Houston-Buffalo)		79,523	
(Seattle-Cincinnati)		59,501	
AFC Championship Game	1		
(Buffalo-Cincinnati)		60,003	
NFC First-Round Playoff	1		
(Los Angeles Rams-Minnesota)		61,204	
NFC Divisional Playoffs	2		
(Minnesota-San Francisco)		63,598	
(Philadelphia-Chicago)		66,442	
NFC Championship Game	1		
(San Francisco-Chicago)		66,908	
Super Bowl XXIII at Miami, Florida	1		
(Cincinnati-San Francisco)		75,129	
AFC-NFC Pro Bowl at Honolulu, Hawaii	1	50,113	
NFL Postseason Total	**10**	**658,317**	**65,832**
NFL All Games	**292**	**17,024,426**	**58,303**

One Million Plus Club

During the 1988 season, nine teams drew a combined home and away paid attendance of over 1 million. The Buffalo Bills, who had the second-highest paid home attendance in league history, drew an NFL-leading 1,138,881 fans in 1988.

Team	Total Paid Home Attendance	Total Paid Visiting Attendance	Total Paid Attendance
Buffalo	631,818	507,063	1,138,881
Cleveland	624,154	485,940	1,110,094
Denver	601,829	506,381	1,108,210
N.Y. Giants	607,650	479,652	1,087,302
N.Y. Jets	607,038	460,602	1,067,640
Miami	526,495	524,062	1,050,557
Chicago	528,426	499,836	1,028,262
San Francisco	508,189	509,776	1,017,965
Philadelphia	522,378	485,085	1,007,463

INSIDE THE NUMBERS

Eric Dickerson Nears 10,000 Yards Rushing

In his first six NFL seasons, Eric Dickerson has accumulated 9,915 yards rushing, the seventh-highest total in NFL history. Dickerson starts the 1989 season just 85 yards short of the 10,000-yard mark. He has played in 90 NFL games, and has 2,136 rushes.

Only six players in NFL history have rushed for 10,000 yards. They're listed here, along with their birthdates and the date that each reached 10,000 yards, with the numbers of games and carries required to reach that total. They are listed in the order of the fewest games required to reach 10,000 yards.

	First Season	Born	Date To Gain 10,000	Games To Gain 10,000	Rushes To Gain 10,000	Career Yards
Jim Brown	1957	2/17/36	11/1/64	98	*1,931	12,312
O.J. Simpson	1969	7/9/47	10/16/77	110	2,084	11,236
Walter Payton	1975	7/25/54	12/26/82	113	2,308	16,726
Tony Dorsett	1977	4/7/54	10/13/85	122	2,243	12,036
Franco Harris	1972	3/7/50	11/8/81	134	2,364	12,120
John Riggins	1971	8/4/49	10/14/84	156	2,555	11,352

*estimated

Dan Marino Nears 200 Touchdown Passes

In his first six NFL seasons, Dan Marino has thrown 196 touchdown passes. He is tied for fourteenth place in NFL history. Marino starts the 1989 season just four touchdown passes short of the 200 mark. He has played in 87 NFL games, and has 3,100 passes.

Only 12 players in NFL history have thrown 200 touchdown passes. They are listed here, along with their birthdates and the date that each reached 200 touchdown passes, with the numbers of games and passes required to reach that total. They are listed in the order of the fewest games required to reach 200 touchdown passes.

	First Season	Born	Date To Reach 200 TD	Games To Reach 200 TD	Passes To Reach 200 TD	Career TD Passes
Johnny Unitas	1956	5/7/33	10/31/65	121	*3,040	290
Fran Tarkenton	1961	2/3/40	11/29/70	137	*3,329	342
Dan Fouts	1973	6/10/51	11/18/84	143	4,245	254
John Hadl	1962	2/15/40	12/3/72	152	*3,558	244
Len Dawson	1957	6/20/35	10/18/71	153	*2,756	239
Sonny Jurgensen	1957	8/23/34	10/26/69	156	*3,239	255
Terry Bradshaw	1970	9/2/48	11/21/82	161	3,737	212
Y.A. Tittle	1950	10/24/26	12/15/63	164	*3,517	212
Roman Gabriel	1962	8/5/40	11/21/76	167	4,406	201
John Brodie	1957	8/14/35	12/19/71	180	*4,170	214
Jim Hart	1966	4/29/44	10/25/80	187	4,879	209
George Blanda	1949	9/17/27	9/10/66	202	*3,526	236

*estimated

Teams That Finished In First Place In Their Division the Season After Finishing in Last Place

Season	Team	Record	Previous Season
1967	Houston	9-4-1	*3-11
1968	Minnesota	8-6	3-8-3
1970	Cincinnati	8-6	4-9-1
1970	San Francisco	10-3-1	4-8-2
1972	Green Bay	10-4	4-8-2
1975	Baltimore	10-4	2-12
1979	Tampa Bay	10-6	5-11
1981	Cincinnati	12-4	6-10
1987	Indianapolis	9-6	3-13
1988	Cincinnati	12-4	4-11

*tied for last place

Records of NFL Teams in 1980s

AFC	W-L-T	Pct.	Division Titles	Playoff Berths	Postseason Record	Super Bowl Record
Miami	86-49-1	.636	4	5	6-5	0-2
Denver	82-53-1	.607	3	4	4-4	0-2
L.A. Raiders	81-55-0	.596	2	5	8-3	2-0
Cleveland	74-62-0	.544	4	6	2-6	0-0
Cincinnati	73-63-0	.537	2	3	4-3	0-2
New England	73-63-0	.537	1	3	3-3	0-1
Seattle	71-65-0	.522	1	4	3-4	0-0
N.Y. Jets	69-65-2	.515	0	4	3-4	0-0
Pittsburgh	68-68-0	.500	2	3	1-3	0-0
San Diego	66-70-0	.485	2	3	3-3	0-0
Buffalo	60-76-0	.441	2	3	2-3	0-0
Kansas City	58-77-1	.430	0	1	0-1	0-0
Houston	53-83-0	.390	0	3	2-3	0-0
Indianapolis	46-89-1	.342	1	1	0-1	0-0

NFC	W-L-T	Pct.	Division Titles	Playoff Berths	Postseason Record	Super Bowl Record
San Francisco	90-45-1	.665	6	7	10-4	3-0
Washington	87-49-0	.640	3	5	11-3	2-1
Chicago	86-50-0	.632	5	5	5-4	1-0
Dallas	78-58-0	.574	2	5	5-5	0-0
L.A. Rams	75-61-0	.551	1	6	2-6	0-0
N.Y. Giants	69-66-1	.511	1	4	6-3	1-0
Minnesota	67-69-0	.493	1	4	4-4	0-0
Philadelphia	65-69-2	.485	2	3	2-3	0-1
New Orleans	58-78-0	.426	0	1	0-1	0-0
Phoenix	57-77-2	.426	0	1	0-1	0-0
Green Bay	55-78-3	.415	0	1	1-1	0-0
Atlanta	54-81-1	.401	1	2	0-2	0-0
Detroit	54-81-1	.401	1	2	0-2	0-0
Tampa Bay	40-95-1	.298	1	2	0-2	0-0

Indianapolis totals include Baltimore, 1980-83
L.A. Raiders totals include Oakland, 1980-81
Phoenix totals include St. Louis, 1980-87

In 1982, due to players' strike, the divisional format was abandoned. (L.A. Raiders and Washington won regular-season conference titles, not included in "Division Titles" totals listed above. Sixteen teams were awarded playoff berths, included in totals listed above.)

Home Records Since 1980

AFC	W-L-T	Pct.	NFC	W-L-T	Pct.
Denver	52-17-0	.754	Chicago	50-18-0	.735
Miami	49-17-1	.739	Washington	48-19-0	.716
New England	44-24-0	.647	Dallas	44-24-0	.647
Pittsburgh	42-25-0	.627	San Francisco	43-25-0	.632
Seattle	43-26-0	.623	L.A. Rams	40-28-0	.588
Cincinnati	42-26-0	.618	Minnesota	40-29-0	.580
L.A. Raiders	42-26-0	.618	N.Y. Giants	39-30-0	.565
Cleveland	41-26-0	.612	Philadelphia	35-33-1	.514
Kansas City	38-29-0	.567	Detroit	33-34-1	.493
Buffalo	39-30-0	.565	Phoenix	32-34-1	.485
San Diego	37-30-0	.552	Green Bay	31-36-1	.463
N.Y. Jets	37-30-1	.551	New Orleans	30-38-0	.441
Houston	36-32-0	.529	Tampa Bay	27-40-1	.404
Indianapolis	23-44-1	.346	Atlanta	27-41-1	.399

Road Records Since 1980

AFC	W-L-T	Pct.	NFC	W-L-T	Pct.
L.A. Raiders	39-29-0	.574	San Francisco	47-20-1	.699
Miami	37-32-0	.536	Washington	39-30-0	.565
Cleveland	33-36-0	.478	Chicago	36-32-0	.529
N.Y. Jets	32-35-1	.478	L.A. Rams	35-33-0	.515
Cincinnati	31-37-0	.456	Dallas	34-34-0	.500
Denver	30-36-1	.455	N.Y. Giants	30-36-1	.455
New England	29-39-0	.426	Philadelphia	30-36-1	.455
San Diego	29-40-0	.420	New Orleans	28-40-0	.412
Seattle	28-39-0	.418	Atlanta	27-40-0	.403
Pittsburgh	26-43-0	.377	Minnesota	27-40-0	.403
Indianapolis	23-45-0	.338	Phoenix	25-43-1	.370
Buffalo	21-46-0	.313	Green Bay	24-42-2	.368
Kansas City	20-48-1	.297	Detroit	21-47-0	.309
Houston	17-51-0	.250	Tampa Bay	13-55-0	.191

Records by Months Since 1980

AFC	Sept. W-L-T	Oct. W-L-T	Nov. W-L-T	*Dec. W-L-T	Total W-L-T	Pct.
Miami	23-10	18-15-1	21-17	24- 7	86-49-1	.636
Denver	19-13-1	25- 9	22-15	16-16	82-53-1	.607
L.A. Raiders	21-12	20-14	21-16	19-13	81-55-0	.596
Cleveland	16-17	19-15	23-15	16-15	74-62-0	.544
Cincinnati	14-18	18-17	21-17	20-11	73-63-0	.537
New England	15-18	21-13	20-18	17-14	73-63-0	.537
Seattle	17-16	19-15	19-19	16-15	71-65-0	.522
N.Y. Jets	18-15	19-13-2	20-19	12-18	69-65-2	.515
Pittsburgh	16-16	18-17	20-18	14-17	68-68-0	.500
San Diego	18-15	11-23	21-17	16-15	66-70-0	.485
Buffalo	17-16	16-18	18-20	9-22	60-76-0	.441
Kansas City	16-17	14-19-1	11-27	17-14	58-77-1	.430
Houston	12-21	12-22	16-22	13-18	53-83-0	.390
Indianapolis	9-24	14-20	11-27	12-18-1	46-89-1	.342

NFC	Sept. W-L-T	Oct. W-L-T	Nov. W-L-T	*Dec. W-L-T	Total W-L-T	Pct.
San Francisco	22-11	21-12-1	23-14	24- 8	90-45-1	.665
Washington	17-16	22-12	25-14	23- 7	87-49-0	.640
Chicago	19-14	22-12	26-12	19-12	86-50-0	.632
Dallas	25- 8	19-15	21-18	13-17	78-58-0	.574
L.A. Rams	20-13	20-14	20-18	15-16	75-61-0	.551
N.Y. Giants	16-17	15-18-1	19-18	19-13	69-66-1	.511
Minnesota	21-12	13-21	20-19	13-17	67-69-0	.493
Philadelphia	15-18	21-13	17-20-1	12-18-1	65-69-2	.485
New Orleans	14-19	14-20	19-19	11-20	58-78-0	.426
Phoenix	12-21	15-18-1	16-23	14-15-1	57-77-2	.426
Green Bay	8-24-1	14-19-1	17-21	16-14-1	55-78-3	.415
Atlanta	16-17	11-22-1	16-22	11-20	54-81-1	.401
Detroit	15-18	14-20	15-23-1	10-20	54-81-1	.401
Tampa Bay	9-24	7-26-1	14-24	10-21	40-95-1	.298

Indianapolis totals include Baltimore, 1980-83
L.A. Raiders totals include Oakland, 1980-81
Phoenix totals include St. Louis, 1980-87
*Includes one game for each team played during January.

High and Low Single-Game Yardage Totals in 1980s

Most Total Yards, Game
661 San Diego vs. Cincinnati, Dec. 20, 1982
621 Cincinnati vs. N.Y. Jets, Dec. 21, 1986
597 N.Y. Jets vs. Miami, Nov. 27, 1988
594 Chicago vs. Green Bay, Dec. 7, 1980
593 San Diego vs. L.A. Raiders, Sept. 10, 1985 (OT)

Fewest Total Yards, Game
24 Chicago vs. Detroit, Nov. 22, 1981
57 New England vs. N.Y. Jets, Sept. 19, 1982
60 Detroit vs. Minnesota, Nov. 24, 1988
65 Tampa Bay vs. Green Bay, Dec. 1, 1985
65 Seattle vs. New England, Dec. 4, 1988

Most Yards Rushing, Game
356 L.A. Raiders vs. Seattle, Nov. 30, 1987
354 Dallas vs. Baltimore, Dec. 6, 1981
343 Pittsburgh vs. N.Y. Jets, Sept. 20, 1981
330 St. Louis vs. New Orleans, Oct. 5, 1980
330 Detroit vs. L.A. Rams, Sept. 7, 1980

Fewest Yards Rushing, Game
0 Buffalo vs. Chicago, Oct. 2, 1988
2 New England vs. New Orleans, Nov. 30, 1986
8 N.Y. Giants vs. L.A. Rams, Sept. 30, 1984
10 Philadelphia vs. N.Y. Giants, Nov. 20, 1983
12 Tampa Bay vs. Kansas City, Sept. 13, 1981

Most Yards Passing, Game
521 Miami vs. N.Y. Jets, Oct. 23, 1988
506 L.A. Rams vs. Chicago, Dec. 26, 1982
494 San Diego vs. Seattle, Sept. 15, 1985
486 San Diego vs. Cincinnati, Dec. 20, 1982
486 Tampa Bay vs. Minnesota, Nov. 16, 1980

Fewest Yards Passing, Game
−22 Atlanta vs. Chicago, Nov. 24, 1985
−20 Chicago vs. Detroit, Nov. 22, 1981
−13 Cincinnati vs. San Diego, Oct. 4, 1987
−12 St. Louis vs. Washington, Dec. 21, 1980
−4 Houston vs. Cincinnati, Oct. 4, 1981
−4 New England vs. N.Y. Jets, Sept. 19, 1982

NFL Individual Leaders From 1980 Through 1988

Points	Touchdowns	Field Goals
900, Nick Lowery	78, Marcus Allen	201, Nick Lowery
847, Ed Murray	78, Eric Dickerson	192, Ed Murray
833, Pat Leahy	67, Steve Largent	166, Pat Leahy
817, Chris Bahr	62, Walter Payton	165, Gary Anderson
802, Jim Breech	62, John Riggins	162, Chris Bahr
Rushes	**Rushing Yards**	**Rushing TDs**
2290, Walter Payton	9915, Eric Dickerson	75, Eric Dickerson
2188, Tony Dorsett	9800, Walter Payton	62, John Riggins
2136, Eric Dickerson	9300, Tony Dorsett	61, Marcus Allen
1712, Marcus Allen	7176, George Rogers	54, George Rogers
1692, George Rogers	6982, Marcus Allen	52, Tony Dorsett
		52, Curt Warner
Passes	**Completions**	**Passing Yards**
3650, Joe Montana	2309, Joe Montana	28,301, Dan Fouts
3599, Dan Fouts	2156, Dan Fouts	27,437, Joe Montana
3153, Neil Lomax	1866, Dan Marino	23,856, Dan Marino
3100, Dan Marino	1817, Neil Lomax	22,771, Neil Lomax
2988, Phil Simms	1618, Phil Simms	21,431, Phil Simms
TD Passes	**Receptions**	**Reception Yards**
196, Dan Marino	576, Art Monk	9299, James Lofton
189, Joe Montana	567, Steve Largent	8933, Steve Largent
172, Dan Fouts	517, Ozzie Newsome	7979, Art Monk
148, Dave Krieg	516, Kellen Winslow	7601, Stanley Morgan
136, Neil Lomax	499, James Lofton	7425, Wes Chandler
Receiving TDs	**Interceptions**	
66, Steve Largent	44, John Harris	
58, Mike Quick	44, Everson Walls	
55, Roy Green	43, Ronnie Lott	
55, Wesley Walker	41, Deron Cherry	
54, Mark Clayton	37, Donnie Shell	

Coaches in the 1980s

Highest Won-Lost Percentage (Minimum 50 Games)
.702 Mike Ditka, Chicago (73-31)
.675 Joe Gibbs, Washington (81-39)
.665 Bill Walsh, San Francisco (90-45-1)
.636 Don Shula, Miami (86-49-1)
.621 Dan Reeves, Denver (74-45-1)

Most Super Bowls Won
3 Bill Walsh, San Francisco
2 Tom Flores, L.A. Raiders
2 Joe Gibbs, Washington
1 Mike Ditka, Chicago
1 Bill Parcells, N.Y. Giants

NFL Home/Road Records, Past 5 Seasons

AFC

BUFFALO

	Total	Home	Road	Playoffs
1984	2-14	2-6	0-8	None
1985	2-14	2-6	0-8	None
1986	4-12	3-5	1-7	None
1987	7-8	4-4	3-4	None
1988	12-4	8-0	4-4	1-1*

*Lost AFC Championship Game

CINCINNATI

	Total	Home	Road	Playoffs
1984	8-8	5-3	3-5	None
1985	7-9	5-3	2-6	None
1986	10-6	6-2	4-4	None
1987	4-11	1-7	3-4	None
1988	12-4	8-0	4-4	2-1*

*Lost Super Bowl XXIII

CLEVELAND

	Total	Home	Road	Playoffs
1984	5-11	2-6	3-5	None
1985	8-8	5-3	3-5	0-1*
1986	12-4	6-2	6-2	1-1**
1987	10-5	5-2	5-3	1-1**
1988	10-6	6-2	4-4	0-1***

*Lost divisional playoff game
**Lost AFC Championship Game
***Lost first-round game

DENVER

	Total	Home	Road	Playoffs
1984	13-3	7-1	6-2	0-1*
1985	11-5	6-2	5-3	None
1986	11-5	7-1	4-4	2-1**
1987	10-4-1	7-1	3-3-1	2-1***
1988	8-8	6-2	2-6	None

*Lost divisional playoff game
**Lost Super Boxl XXI
***Lost Super Bowl XXII

HOUSTON

	Total	Home	Road	Playoffs
1984	3-13	2-6	1-7	None
1985	5-11	4-4	1-7	None
1986	5-11	4-4	1-7	None
1987	9-6	5-2	4-4	1-1*
1988	10-6	7-1	5-3	1-1*

*Lost divisional playoff game

INDIANAPOLIS

	Total	Home	Road	Playoffs
1984	4-12	2-6	2-6	None
1985	5-11	4-4	1-7	None
1986	3-13	1-7	2-6	None
1987	9-6	4-4	5-2	0-1*
1988	9-7	6-2	3-5	None

*Lost divisional playoff game

KANSAS CITY

	Total	Home	Road	Playoffs
1984	8-8	5-3	3-5	None
1985	6-10	5-3	1-7	None
1986	10-6	6-2	4-4	0-1*
1987	4-11	3-4	1-7	None
1988	4-11-1	4-4	0-7-1	None

*Lost first-round game

LOS ANGELES RAIDERS

	Total	Home	Road	Playoffs
1984	11-5	6-2	5-3	0-1*
1985	12-4	7-1	5-3	0-1**
1986	8-8	3-5	5-3	None
1987	5-10	3-5	2-5	None
1988	7-9	3-5	4-4	None

*Lost first-round game
**Lost divisional playoff game

MIAMI

	Total	Home	Road	Playoffs
1984	14-2	7-1	7-1	2-1*
1985	12-4	8-0	4-4	1-1**
1986	8-8	4-4	4-4	None
1987	8-7	4-3	4-4	None
1988	6-10	4-4	2-6	None

*Lost Super Bowl XIX
**Lost AFC Championship Game

NEW ENGLAND

	Total	Home	Road	Playoffs
1984	9-7	5-3	4-4	None
1985	11-5	7-1	4-4	3-1*
1986	11-5	4-4	7-1	0-1**
1987	8-7	5-3	3-4	None
1988	9-7	7-1	2-6	None

*Lost Super Bowl XX
**Lost divisional playoff game

NEW YORK JETS

	Total	Home	Road	Playoffs
1984	7-9	3-5	4-4	None
1985	11-5	7-1	4-4	0-1*
1986	10-6	5-3	5-3	1-1**
1987	6-9	4-4	2-5	None
1988	8-7-1	5-2-1	3-5	None

*Lost first-round game
**Lost divisional playoff game

PITTSBURGH

	Total	Home	Road	Playoffs
1984	9-7	6-2	3-5	1-1*
1985	7-9	5-3	2-6	None
1986	6-10	4-4	2-6	None
1987	8-7	4-3	4-4	None
1988	5-11	4-4	1-7	None

*Lost AFC Championship Game

SAN DIEGO

	Total	Home	Road	Playoffs
1984	7-9	4-4	3-5	None
1985	8-8	6-2	2-6	None
1986	4-12	2-6	2-6	None
1987	8-7	4-3	4-4	None
1988	6-10	3-5	3-5	None

SEATTLE

	Total	Home	Road	Playoffs
1984	12-4	7-1	5-3	1-1*
1985	8-8	5-3	3-5	None
1986	10-6	7-1	3-5	None
1987	9-6	6-2	3-4	0-1**
1988	9-7	5-3	4-4	0-1*

*Lost divisional playoff game
**Lost first-round game

NFC

ATLANTA

	Total	Home	Road	Playoffs
1984	4-12	2-6	2-6	None
1985	4-12	3-5	1-7	None
1986	7-8-1	2-5-1	5-3	None
1987	3-12	2-6	1-6	None
1988	5-11	2-6	3-5	None

CHICAGO

	Total	Home	Road	Playoffs
1984	10-6	6-2	4-4	1-1*
1985	15-1	8-0	7-1	3-0**
1986	14-2	7-1	7-1	0-1***
1987	11-4	6-2	5-2	0-1***
1988	12-4	7-1	5-3	1-1*

*Lost NFC Championship Game
**Won Super Bowl XX
***Lost divisional playoff game

DALLAS

	Total	Home	Road	Playoffs
1984	9-7	5-3	4-4	None
1985	10-6	7-1	3-5	0-1*
1986	7-9	3-5	4-4	None
1987	7-8	3-4	4-4	None
1988	3-13	1-7	2-6	None

*Lost divisional playoff game

DETROIT

	Total	Home	Road	Playoffs
1984	4-11-1	2-5-1	2-6	None
1985	7-9	6-2	1-7	None
1986	5-11	1-7	4-4	None
1987	4-11	1-6	3-5	None
1988	4-12	2-6	2-6	None

GREEN BAY

	Total	Home	Road	Playoffs
1984	8-8	5-3	3-5	None
1985	8-8	5-3	3-5	None
1986	4-12	1-7	3-5	None
1987	5-9-1	2-5-1	3-4	None
1988	4-12	2-6	2-6	None

LOS ANGELES RAMS

	Total	Home	Road	Playoffs
1984	10-6	5-3	5-3	0-1*
1985	11-5	6-2	5-3	1-1**
1986	10-6	6-2	4-4	0-1*
1987	6-9	3-4	3-5	None
1988	10-6	4-4	6-2	0-1*

*Lost first-round game
**Lost NFC Championship Game

MINNESOTA

	Total	Home	Road	Playoffs
1984	3-13	2-6	1-7	None
1985	7-9	4-4	3-5	None
1986	9-7	5-3	4-4	None
1987	8-7	5-3	3-4	2-1*
1988	11-5	7-1	4-4	1-1**

*Lost NFC Championship Game
**Lost divisional playoff game

NEW ORLEANS

	Total	Home	Road	Playoffs
1984	7-9	3-5	4-4	None
1985	5-11	3-5	2-6	None
1986	7-9	4-4	3-5	None
1987	12-3	6-1	6-2	0-1*
1988	10-6	5-3	5-3	None

*Lost first-round game

NEW YORK GIANTS

	Total	Home	Road	Playoffs
1984	9-7	6-2	3-5	1-1*
1985	10-6	6-2	4-4	1-1**
1986	14-2	8-0	6-2	3-0***
1987	6-9	5-3	1-6	None
1988	10-6	5-3	5-3	None

*Lost divisional playoff game
**Lost divisional playoff game
***Won Super Bowl XXI

PHILADELPHIA

	Total	Home	Road	Playoffs
1984	6-9-1	5-3	1-6-1	None
1985	7-9	4-4	3-5	None
1986	5-10-1	2-5-1	3-5	None
1987	7-8	4-4	3-4	None
1988	10-6	5-3	5-3	0-1*

*Lost divisional playoff game

PHOENIX
Includes St. Louis, 1984-87

	Total	Home	Road	Playoffs
1984	9-7	5-3	4-4	None
1985	5-11	4-4	1-7	None
1986	4-11-1	3-5	1-6-1	None
1987	7-8	4-3	3-5	None
1988	7-9	4-4	3-5	None

SAN FRANCISCO

	Total	Home	Road	Playoffs
1984	15-1	7-1	8-0	3-0*
1985	10-6	5-3	5-3	0-1**
1986	10-5-1	6-2	4-3-1	0-1***
1987	13-2	6-1	7-1	0-1***
1988	10-6	4-4	6-2	3-0#

*Won Super Bowl XIX
**Lost first-round game
***Lost divisional playoff game
#Won Super Bowl XXIII

TAMPA BAY

	Total	Home	Road	Playoffs
1984	6-10	6-2	0-8	None
1985	2-14	2-6	0-8	None
1986	2-14	1-7	1-7	None
1987	4-11	2-5	2-6	None
1988	5-11	3-5	2-6	None

WASHINGTON

	Total	Home	Road	Playoffs
1984	11-5	7-1	4-4	0-1*
1985	10-6	5-3	5-3	None
1986	12-4	7-1	5-3	2-1**
1987	11-4	6-1	5-3	3-0***
1988	7-9	4-4	3-5	None

*Lost divisional playoff game
**Lost NFC Championship Game
***Won Super Bowl XXII

Records for Each Current NFL Team for Most Points in a Game (Regular Season Only)

Note: When the record has been achieved more than once, only the most recent game is shown; summaries are listed in alphabetical order by conference. Bold face indicates team holding record.

BUFFALO BILLS
September 18, 1966, at Buffalo

Miami	3	7	0	14	— 24
Buffalo	21	27	3	7	— 58

TDs: Buff—Bobby Burnett 2, Butch Byrd 2, Jack Spikes 2, Bobby Crockett, Jack Kemp; Mia—Dave Kocourek, Bo Roberson, John Roderick. TD Passes: Buff—Jack Kemp, Daryle Lamonica; Mia—George Wilson 3. FGs: Buff—Booth Lusteg; Mia—Gene Mingo.

CINCINNATI BENGALS
December 17, 1972, at Houston

Cincinnati	3	13	17	28	— 61
Houston	3	7	0	7	— 17

TDs: Cin—Doug Dressler 3, Lemar Parrish 2, Ken Anderson, Neal Craig; Hou—Ken Burrough, Fred Willis. TD Passes: Cin—Ken Anderson; Hou—Kent Nix 2. FGs: Cin—Horst Muhlmann 4; Hou—Skip Butler.

CLEVELAND BROWNS
November 7, 1954, at Cleveland

Washington	0	3	0	0	— 3
Cleveland	13	14	21	14	— 62

TDs: Clev—Darrell Brewster 2, Mo Bassett, Ken Gorgal, Otto Graham, Dub Jones, Dante Lavelli, Curley Morrison. TD Passes: Clev—George Ratterman 3, Otto Graham. FGs: Clev—Lou Groza 2; Wash—Vic Janowicz.

DENVER BRONCOS
October 6, 1963, at Denver

San Diego	13	7	0	14	— 34
Denver	3	14	9	24	— 50

TDs: Den—Lionel Taylor 2, Goose Gonsoulin, Gene Prebola, Donnie Stone; SD—Keith Lincoln 2, Lance Alworth, Paul Lowe, Jacque MacKinnon. TD Passes: Den—John McCormick 3; SD—Tobin Rote 3, John Hadl 2. FGs: Den—Gene Mingo 5.

HOUSTON OILERS
October 14, 1962, at Houston

New York Titans	3	7	7	0	— 17
Houston	14	21	14	7	— 56

TDs: Hou—Bill Groman, 2, Bob McLeod 2, Dave Smith 2, Willard Dewveall, Charley Hennigan; NY—Dick Christy, Ed Cooke. TD Passes: Hou—George Blanda 6, Jacky Lee. FGs: NY—Bill Shockley.

INDIANAPOLIS COLTS
December 12, 1976, at Baltimore

Buffalo	3	3	7	7	— 20
Baltimore Colts	7	13	28	10	— 58

TDs: Balt—Roger Carr, Raymond Chester, Glenn Doughty, Roosevelt Leaks, Derrel Luce, Lydell Mitchell, Howard Stevens; Buff—Bob Chandler, O.J. Simpson. TD Passes: Balt—Bert Jones 3; Buff—Gary Marangi. FGs: Balt—Toni Linhart 3; Buff—George Jakowenko 2.

KANSAS CITY CHIEFS
September 7, 1963, at Denver

Kansas City	14	14	21	10	— 59
Denver	0	7	0	0	— 7

TDs: KC—Chris Burford 2, Frank Jackson 2, Dave Grayson, Abner Haynes, Sherrill Headrick, Curtis McClinton; Den—Lionel Taylor. TD Passes: KC—Len Dawson 4, Curtis McClinton; Den—Mickey Slaughter. FG: KC—Tommy Brooker.

LOS ANGELES RAIDERS
December 22, 1963, at Oakland

Houston	14	21	14	0	— 49
Oakland Raiders	7	28	7	10	— 52

TDs: Oak—Art Powell 4, Clem Daniels, Claude Gibson, Ken Herock; Hou—Willard Dewveall 2, Dave Smith 2, Charley Hennigan, Bob McLeod, Charley Tolar. TD Passes: Oak—Tom Flores 6; Hou—George Blanda 5. FG: Oak—Mike Mercer.

MIAMI DOLPHINS
November 24, 1977, at St. Louis

Miami	14	14	20	7	— 55
St. Louis	7	0	0	7	— 14

TDs: Mia—Nat Moore 3, Gary Davis, Duriel Harris, Leroy Harris, Benny Malone, Andre Tillman; StL—Ike Harris, Terry Metcalf. TD Passes: Mia—Bob Griese 6; StL—Jim Hart.

NEW ENGLAND PATRIOTS
September 9, 1979, at New England

New York Jets	3	0	0	0	— 3
New England	14	21	7	14	— 56

TDs: NE—Harold Jackson 3, Stanley Morgan 2, Allan Clark, Andy Johnson, Don Westbrook. TD Passes: NE—Steve Grogan 5, Tom Owen. FG: NYJ—Pat Leahy.

NEW YORK JETS
November 17, 1985, at New York

Tampa Bay	14	7	7	0	— 28
New York Jets	17	24	14	7	— 62

TDs: NYJ—Mickey Shuler 3, Johnny Hector 2, Tony Paige, Al Toon, Wesley Walker; TB—James Wilder 2, Kevin House, Calvin Magee. TD Passes: NYJ—Ken O'Brien 5; TB—Steve DeBerg 2. FGs: NYJ—Pat Leahy 2.

PITTSBURGH STEELERS
November 30, 1952, at Pittsburgh

New York Giants	0	0	7	0	— 7
Pittsburgh	14	14	7	28	— 63

TDs: Pitt—Lynn Chandnois 2, Dick Hensley 2, Jack Butler, George Hays, Ray Mathews, Ed Modzelewski, Elbie Nickel; NYG—Bill Stribling. TD Passes: Pitt—Jim Finks 4, Gary Kerkorian; NYG—Tom Landry.

SAN DIEGO CHARGERS
December 22, 1963, at San Diego

Denver	7	10	3	0	— 20
San Diego	10	16	10	22	— 58

TDs: SD—Paul Lowe 2, Chuck Allen, Bobby Jackson, Dave Kocourek, Keith Lincoln, Jacque MacKinnon; Den—Billy Joe, Donnie Stone. TD Passes: SD—John Hadl, Tobin Rote; Den—Don Breaux. FGs: SD—George Blair 3; Den—Gene Mingo 2.

SEATTLE SEAHAWKS
October 30, 1977, at Seattle

Buffalo	3	0	7	7	— 17
Seattle	14	28	7	7	— 56

TDs: Sea—Steve Largent 2, Duke Fergerson, Al Hunter, David Sims, Sherman Smith, Don Testerman, Jim Zorn; Buff—Joe Ferguson, John Kimbrough. TD Passes: Sea—Jim Zorn 4; Buff—Joe Ferguson. FG: Buff—Carson Long.

ATLANTA FALCONS
September 16, 1973, at New Orleans

Atlanta	0	24	21	17	—	62
New Orleans	0	0	7	0	—	7

TDs: Atl—Ken Burrow 2, Eddie Ray 2, Wes Chesson, Tom Hayes, Art Malone, Joe Profit; NO—Bill Butler. TD Passes: Atl—Dick Shiner 3, Bob Lee; NO—Archie Manning. FGs: Atl—Nick Mike-Mayer.

CHICAGO BEARS
December 7, 1980, at Chicago

Green Bay	0	7	0	0	—	7
Chicago	0	28	13	20	—	61

TDs: Chi—Walter Payton 3, Brian Baschnagel, Robin Earl, Roland Harper, Willie McClendon, Len Walterscheid, Rickey Watts; GB—James Lofton. TD Passes: Chi—Vince Evans 3; GB—Lynn Dickey.

DALLAS COWBOYS
October 12, 1980, at Dallas

San Francisco	0	7	0	7	—	14
Dallas	14	24	14	7	—	59

TDs: Dall—Drew Pearson 3, Ron Springs 2, Tony Dorsett, Billy Joe DuPree, Robert Newhouse; SF—Dwight Clark 2. TD Passes: Dall—Danny White 4; SF—Steve DeBerg 2. FG: Dall—Rafael Septien.

DETROIT LIONS
October 26, 1952, at Green Bay

Detroit	14	14	14	10	—	52
Green Bay	7	3	7	0	—	17

TDs: Det—Jug Girard 2, Bob Hoernschemeyer 2, Jack Christiansen, Jim Smith, Bill Swiacki; GB—Billy Howton, Jim Keane. TD Passes: Det—Bobby Layne 3; GB—Babe Parilli, Tobin Rote. FGs: Det—Pat Harder; GB—Bill Reichardt.

GREEN BAY PACKERS
October 7, 1945, at Milwaukee

Detroit	0	7	7	7	—	21
Green Bay	0	41	9	7	—	57

TDs: GB—Don Hutson 4, Charley Brock, Irv Comp, Ted Fritsch, Clyde Goodnight; Det—Chuck Fenenbock, John Greene, Bob Westfall. TD Passes: GB—Tex McKay 4, Lou Brock, Irv Comp; Det—Dave Ryan.

LOS ANGELES RAMS
October 22, 1950, at Los Angeles

Baltimore	13	0	7	7	—	27
Los Angeles	21	14	14	21	—	70

TDs: LA—Bob Boyd 2, Vitamin T. Smith 2, Tom Fears, Elroy (Crazylegs) Hirsch, Dick Hoerner, Ralph Pasquariello, Dan Towler, Bob Waterfield; Balt—Chet Mutryn 2, Adrian Burk, Billy Stone. TD Passes: LA—Norm Van Brocklin 2, Bob Waterfield 2, Glenn Davis; Balt—Adrian Burk 3.

MINNESOTA VIKINGS
October 18, 1970, at Minnesota

Dallas	3	3	0	7	—	13
Minnesota	14	20	17	3	—	54

TDs: Minn—Clint Jones 2, Ed Sharockman 2, John Beasley, Dave Osborn; Dall—Calvin Hill. TD Pass: Minn—Gary Cuozzo. FGs: Minn—Fred Cox 4; Dall—Mike Clark 2.

NEW ORLEANS SAINTS
November 21, 1976, at Seattle

New Orleans	3	17	28	3	—	51
Seattle	6	0	7	14	—	27

TDs: NO—Bobby Douglass 2, Tony Galbreath, Chuck Muncie, Tom Myers, Elex Price; Sea—Sherman Smith 2, Steve Largent, Jim Zorn. TD Pass: Sea—Bill Munson. FGs: NO—Rich Szaro 3.

NEW YORK GIANTS
November 26, 1972, at New York

Philadelphia	3	7	0	0	—	10
New York Giants	14	24	10	14	—	62

TDs: NYG—Don Herrmann 2, Ron Johnson 2, Bob Tucker 2, Randy Johnson; Phil—Harold Jackson. TD Passes: NYG—Norm Snead 3, Randy Johnson 2; Phil—John Reaves. FGs: NYG—Pete Gogolak 2; Phil—Tom Dempsey.

PHILADELPHIA EAGLES
November 6, 1934, at Philadelphia

Cincinnati Reds	0	0	0	0	—	0
Philadelphia	26	6	12	20	—	64

TDs: Phil—Joe Carter 3, Swede Hanson 3, Marvin Ellstrom, Roger Kirkman, Ed Matesic, Ed Storm. TD Passes: Phil—Ed Matesic 2, Albert Weiner 2, Marvin Elstrom.

ST. LOUIS CARDINALS
November 13, 1949, at New York

Chicago Cardinals	7	31	14	13	—	65
New York Bulldogs	7	0	6	7	—	20

TDs: Chi—Red Cochran 2, Pat Harder 2, Bill Dewell, Mel Kutner, Bob Ravensburg, Vic Schwall, Charlie Trippi; NY—Joe Golding, Frank Muehlheuser, Johnny Rauch. TD Passes: Chi—Paul Christman 3, Jim Hardy 3; NY—Bobby Layne. FG: Chi—Pat Harder.

SAN FRANCISCO 49ERS
September 19, 1965, at San Francisco

Chicago	3	0	0	21	—	24
San Francisco	0	24	21	7	—	52

TDs: SF—Bernie Casey 2, John David Crow, Charlie Krueger, Gary Lewis, Dave Parks, Ken Willard; Chi—Charlie Bivins 2, Andy Livingston. TD Passes: SF—John Brodie 4; Chi—Rudy Bukich 2. FGs: SF—Tommy Davis; Chi—Roger LeClerc.

TAMPA BAY BUCCANEERS
September 13, 1987, at Tampa Bay

Atlanta	0	3	0	7	—	10
Tampa Bay	14	13	7	14	—	48

TDs: TB—Gerald Carter 2, Cliff Austín, Steve Bartalo, Mark Carrier, Phil Freeman, Calvin Magee; Atl—Stacey Bailey. TD Passes: TB—Steve DeBerg 5; Atl—Scott Campbell. FG: Atl—Mick Luckhurst.

WASHINGTON REDSKINS
November 27, 1966, at Washington

New York Giants	0	14	14	13	—	41
Washington	13	21	14	24	—	72

TDs: Wash—A. D. Whitfield 3, Brig Owens 2, Charley Taylor 2, Rickie Harris, Joe Don Looney, Bobby Mitchell; NYG—Allen Jacobs, Homer Jones, Dan Lewis, Joe Morrison, Aaron Thomas, Gary Wood. TD Passes: Wash—Sonny Jurgensen 3; NYG—Gary Wood 2, Tom Kennedy. FG: Wash—Charlie Gogolak.

NFL Games In Which a Team Has Scored 60 or More Points

(Home team in capitals)

Regular Season

WASHINGTON 72, New York Giants 41	November 27, 1966
LOS ANGELES RAMS 70, Baltimore 27	October 22, 1950
Chicago Cardinals 65, NEW YORK BULLDOGS 20	November 13, 1949
LOS ANGELES RAMS 65, Detroit 24	October 29, 1950
PHILADELPHIA 64, Cincinnati 0	November 6, 1934
CHICAGO CARDINALS 63, New York Giants 35	October 17, 1948
AKRON 62, Oorang 0	October 29,1922
PITTSBURGH 62, New York Giants 7	November 30, 1952
CLEVELAND 62, New York Giants 14	December 6, 1953
CLEVELAND 62, Washington 3	November 7, 1954
NEW YORK GIANTS 62, Philadelphia 10	November 26, 1972
Atlanta 62, NEW ORLEANS 7	September 16, 1973
NEW YORK JETS 62, Tampa Bay 28	November 17, 1985
CHICAGO 61, San Francisco 20	December 12, 1965
Cincinnati 61, HOUSTON 17	December 17, 1972
CHICAGO 61, Green Bay 7	December 7, 1980
ROCK ISLAND 60, Evansville 0	October 15, 1922
CHICAGO CARDINALS 60, Rochester 0	October 7, 1923

Postseason

Chicago Bears 73, WASHINGTON 0	December 8, 1940

Youngest and Oldest Regular Starters in NFL in 1988

Minimum: 8 Games Started

Five Youngest Regular Starters

	Birthdate	Games Started	Position
Aaron Jones, Pittsburgh	12/18/66	12	DE
Craig Heyward, New Orleans	9/26/66	8	RB
Bennie Blades, Detroit	9/3/66	14	S
Pat Carter, Detroit	8/1/66	14	TE
Tim Brown, L.A. Raiders	7/22/66	9	WR

Five Oldest Regular Starters

	Birthdate	Games Started	Position
Dave Butz, Washington	6/23/50	16	DT
Ed Jones, Dallas	2/23/51	16	DE
Mike Webster, Pittsburgh	3/18/52	16	C
Carl Hairston, Cleveland	12/15/52	13	DE
Dave Brown, Green Bay	1/16/53	16	CB

Youngest and Oldest Regular Starters By Position

Minimum: 8 Games Started

	Youngest	Oldest
QB	10/12/65 Chris Chandler, Ind.	1/19/54 Steve DeBerg, K.C.
RB	9/26/66 Craig Heyward, N.O.	4/7/54 Tony Dorsett, Den.
WR	7/22/66 Tim Brown, Raiders	9/28/54 Steve Largent, Sea.
TE	8/1/66 Pat Carter, Det.	4/3/53 Russ Francis, N.E.
C	5/18/65 Gregg Rakoczy, Clev.	3/18/52 Mike Webster, Pitt.
G	6/2/65 Houston Hoover, Atl.	6/17/55 Dan Alexander, Jets
T	4/11/66 David Richards, S.D.	2/23/54 Joe Devlin, Buff.
DE	12/18/66 Aaron Jones, Pitt.	2/23/51 Ed Jones, Dall.
DT	2/28/66 Tim Goad, N.E.	6/23/50 Dave Butz, Wash.
LB	4/30/66 Aundray Bruce, Atl.	11/26/53 Harry Carson, Giants
CB	11/11/65 Eric Allen, Phil.	1/16/53 Dave Brown, G.B.
S	9/3/66 Bennie Blades, Det.	6/13/56 John Harris, Minn.

NFL's 70th Season by the Numbers

0 Number of touchdowns on kickoff returns by NFC teams last season.

2.25 Career rate of touchdown passes per game by Dan Marino, highest in NFL history.

2.51 Career rate of interceptions per 100 passes by Ken O'Brien, lowest rate by any quarterback in NFL history.

4 Great players of the past to be inducted into the Pro Football Hall of Fame on August 5: Mel Blount, Terry Bradshaw, Art Shell, and Willie Wood.

5 Consecutive seasons in which Chicago has won division title, longest current streak by any NFL team and two seasons shy of Rams' NFL record set from 1973 to 1979.

6 Consecutive seasons in which San Francisco has reached playoffs, longest active streak by any team and three seasons short of Dallas's NFL record set from 1975 to 1983.

7 Consecutive seasons that the Dolphins have allowed the fewest sacks in the NFL. No other team ever led for more than three years in succession.

8 Consecutive seasons earning selection to the Pro Bowl by Anthony Muñoz and Lawrence Taylor, the longest such streaks by any NFL players.

10 Consecutive seasons by Jerry Markbreit as referee of at least one postseason game, longest streak among current referees.

12 Total of tie games played in NFL in 14 seasons since sudden-death overtime was enacted for regular-season games.

17 Touchdowns scored by Tony Dorsett on Monday Night Football, the most by any player in history.

20 Postseason games won by Dallas Cowboys, most by any team in NFL history.

23 Opponents' fumbles recovered by Reggie Williams, the most by any active player.

50 Consecutive games in which Redskins have scored at least one touchdown, longest current streak in NFL.

64 Number of consecutive games won by Bears when they have held their opponents to 17 points-or-less.

78.2 Career field goal percentage of Morten Andersen, the best by any kicker (with 100 field goals) in NFL history.

85 Number of rushing yards needed by Eric Dickerson to reach 10,000.

92.0 Career pass rating by Joe Montana, highest in NFL history.

97 Steve Largent's career total of touchdown catches, two short of Don Hutson's NFL record.

137 Consecutive games by Jim Breech scoring at least one point, just 14 games shy of Fred Cox's NFL record.

167 Consecutive games with a reception by Steve Largent, an NFL record.

173 Consecutive extra points made by Nick Lowery, longest current streak in NFL.

178 Consecutive games by San Francisco without being shut out, longest streak by any NFL team.

261 Games won by Don Shula in regular-season play, just 58 short of George Halas's NFL record.

900 Points scored by Nick Lowery during 1980s, most by any player.

1950 Year of birth for Dave Butz, the oldest regular starter in the NFL last season.

Tony Dorsett's Career Rushing vs. Each Opponent

Opponent	Games	Rushes	Yards	Yards Per Rush	Yards Per Game	TD
Atlanta	4	57	295	5.2	73.8	1
Buffalo	2	45	187	4.2	93.5	0
Chicago	5	80	340	4.3	68.0	0
Cincinnati	2	37	183	4.9	91.5	0
Cleveland	4	63	289	4.6	72.3	2
Denver	2	34	112	3.3	56.0	0
Detroit	5	74	311	4.2	62.2	1
Green Bay	3	65	270	4.2	90.0	4
Houston	3	53	278	5.2	92.7	1
Indianapolis	4	75	448	6.0	112.0	0
Kansas City	3	38	187	4.9	62.3	3
L.A. Raiders	5	104	400	3.8	80.0	4
L.A. Rams	8	140	567	4.1	70.9	3
Miami	3	53	229	4.3	76.3	0
Minnesota	6	85	507	6.0	84.5	4
New England	5	64	351	5.5	70.2	2
New Orleans	5	90	464	5.2	92.8	4
N.Y. Giants	20	347	1389	4.0	69.5	8
N.Y. Jets	1	29	121	4.2	121.0	1
Philadelphia	21	348	1436	4.1	68.4	12
Phoenix	17	299	1487	5.0	87.5	11
Pittsburgh	5	79	313	4.0	62.6	2
San Diego	4	73	293	4.0	73.3	1
San Francisco	7	106	335	3.2	47.9	2
Seattle	5	73	315	4.3	63.0	5
Tampa Bay	4	69	292	4.2	73.0	0
Washington	20	356	1340	3.8	67.0	6
Totals	173	2936	12,739	4.3	73.6	77

Indianapolis totals include two games vs. Baltimore
L.A. Raiders totals include one game vs. Oakland
Phoenix totals include 17 games vs. St. Louis

Eric Dickerson's Career Rushing vs. Each Opponent

Opponent	Games	Rushes	Yards	Yards Per Rush	Yards Per Game	TD
Atlanta	8	157	772	4.9	96.5	9
Buffalo	4	97	376	3.9	94.0	1
Chicago	4	115	482	4.2	120.5	5
Cincinnati	1	22	89	4.0	89.0	1
Cleveland	4	83	355	4.3	88.8	2
Dallas	2	49	244	5.0	122.0	1
Denver	1	21	159	7.6	159.0	4
Detroit	2	54	329	6.1	164.5	4
Green Bay	4	95	426	4.5	106.5	2
Houston	4	105	609	5.8	152.3	4
Indianapolis	1	25	121	4.8	121.0	1
Kansas City	1	26	68	2.6	68.0	1
L.A. Raiders	1	25	98	3.9	98.0	0
Miami	5	133	673	5.1	134.6	4
Minnesota	3	73	217	3.0	72.3	1
New England	5	127	476	3.7	95.2	3
New Orleans	8	176	853	4.8	106.6	6
N.Y. Giants	3	77	312	4.1	104.0	1
N.Y. Jets	5	104	437	4.2	87.4	5
Philadelphia	2	45	161	3.6	80.5	0
Phoenix	3	79	525	6.6	175.0	4
Pittsburgh	1	23	49	2.1	49.0	0
San Diego	3	88	422	4.8	140.7	0
San Francisco	8	151	726	4.8	90.8	3
Seattle	1	31	150	4.8	150.0	3
Tampa Bay	5	143	749	5.2	149.8	10
Washington	1	12	37	3.1	37.0	0
Totals	90	2136	9915	4.6	110.2	75

Phoenix totals include three games vs. St. Louis

Marcus Allen's Career Rushing vs. Each Opponent

Opponent	Games	Rushes	Yards	Yards Per Rush	Yards Per Game	TD
Atlanta	3	47	230	4.9	76.7	1
Buffalo	3	52	173	3.3	57.7	2
Chicago	2	33	117	3.5	58.5	0
Cincinnati	4	67	235	3.5	58.8	2
Cleveland	3	47	172	3.7	57.3	0
Dallas	2	22	84	3.8	42.0	0
Denver	12	215	919	4.3	76.6	6
Detroit	2	39	135	3.5	67.5	1
Green Bay	2	53	217	4.1	108.5	2
Houston	3	60	247	4.1	82.3	3
Indianapolis	2	28	141	5.0	70.5	0
Kansas City	11	204	714	3.5	64.9	5
L.A. Rams	3	63	269	4.3	89.7	3
Miami	3	63	356	5.7	118.7	5
Minnesota	2	28	104	3.7	52.0	1
New England	2	37	139	3.8	69.5	1
New Orleans	2	48	209	4.4	104.5	2
N.Y. Giants	2	28	104	3.7	52.0	1
N.Y. Jets	1	20	76	3.8	76.0	2
Philadelphia	1	24	59	2.5	59.0	0
Phoenix	1	18	86	4.8	86.0	0
Pittsburgh	1	13	38	2.9	38.0	0
San Diego	12	244	1032	4.2	86.0	16
San Francisco	3	49	233	4.8	77.7	1
Seattle	13	187	789	4.2	60.7	7
Washington	2	23	104	4.5	52.0	0
Totals	97	1712	6982	4.1	72.0	61

Phoenix totals include one game vs. St. Louis

Curt Warner's Career Rushing vs. Each Opponent

Opponent	Games	Rushes	Yards	Yards Per Rush	Yards Per Game	TD
Atlanta	2	34	176	5.2	88.0	1
Buffalo	1	11	33	3.0	33.0	0
Chicago	1	17	75	4.4	75.0	2
Cincinnati	2	39	160	4.1	80.0	2
Cleveland	4	70	254	3.6	63.5	3
Dallas	2	34	144	4.2	72.0	2
Denver	10	213	1120	5.3	112.0	10

Opponent	Games	Rushes	Yards	Yards Per Rush	Yards Per Game	TD
Green Bay	1	25	123	4.9	123.0	1
Houston	1	18	72	4.0	72.0	1
Kansas City	10	181	763	4.2	76.3	7
L.A. Raiders	10	197	735	3.7	73.5	7
L.A. Rams	2	29	113	3.9	56.5	0
Minnesota	1	23	94	4.1	94.0	0
New England	4	75	304	4.1	76.0	2
New Orleans	2	34	73	2.1	36.5	1
N.Y. Giants	2	45	118	2.6	59.0	1
N.Y. Jets	4	54	242	4.5	60.5	3
Philadelphia	1	13	33	2.5	33.0	0
Phoenix	1	21	83	4.0	83.0	0
Pittsburgh	3	55	231	4.2	77.0	1
San Diego	9	208	911	4.4	101.2	7
San Francisco	2	28	77	2.8	38.5	0
Washington	2	31	140	4.5	70.0	1
Totals	75	1455	6074	4.2	81.0	52

Phoenix totals include one game vs. St. Louis

Roger Craig's Career Rushing vs. Each Opponent

Opponent	Games	Rushes	Yards	Yards Per Rush	Yards Per Game	TD
Atlanta	12	148	756	5.1	63.0	6
Buffalo	1	15	47	3.1	47.0	0
Chicago	4	36	145	4.0	36.3	0
Cincinnati	2	24	69	2.9	34.5	0
Cleveland	2	22	71	3.2	35.5	2
Dallas	2	23	125	5.4	62.5	1
Denver	2	48	260	5.4	130.0	0
Detroit	3	42	185	4.4	61.7	1
Green Bay	2	26	87	3.3	43.5	0
Houston	2	24	99	4.1	49.5	1
Indianapolis	1	2	22	11.0	22.0	0
Kansas City	1	15	55	3.7	55.0	1
L.A. Raiders	2	27	92	3.4	46.0	0
L.A. Rams	12	188	834	4.4	69.5	8
Miami	2	29	154	5.3	77.0	2
Minnesota	5	71	247	3.5	49.4	3
New England	2	34	140	4.1	70.0	1
New Orleans	12	151	644	4.3	53.7	5
N.Y. Giants	3	37	186	5.0	62.0	0
N.Y. Jets	2	25	112	4.5	56.0	2
Philadelphia	3	42	172	4.1	57.3	0
Phoenix	4	51	277	5.4	69.3	2
Pittsburgh	2	16	45	2.8	22.5	0
San Diego	1	17	87	5.1	87.0	2
Seattle	2	36	161	4.5	80.5	0
Tampa Bay	4	60	259	4.3	64.8	6
Washington	4	65	240	3.7	60.0	0
Totals	94	1274	5571	4.4	59.3	43

Phoenix totals include three games vs. St. Louis

Joe Montana's Career Passing vs. Each Opponent

Opponent	Games	Att.	Cmp.	Pct.	Yards	Avg. Gain	TD	Int.	Sacked
Atlanta	17	451	289	64.1	3147	6.98	25	14	23/169
Buffalo	2	64	43	67.2	381	5.95	2	0	6/46
Chicago	6	141	80	56.7	917	6.50	4	3	18/129
Cincinnati	3	115	71	61.7	738	6.42	7	5	7/60
Cleveland	3	103	71	68.9	818	7.94	6	4	5/40
Dallas	4	89	57	64.0	824	9.26	8	2	5/39
Denver	4	106	58	54.7	779	7.35	4	3	6/50
Detroit	5	120	74	61.7	713	5.94	2	2	9/55
Green Bay	3	67	49	73.1	528	7.88	2	1	3/21
Houston	3	107	75	70.1	846	7.91	7	3	3/13
Kansas City	2	69	43	62.3	488	7.07	2	2	3/16
L.A. Raiders	4	96	51	53.1	659	6.86	4	1	11/92
L.A Rams	19	549	354	64.5	4493	8.18	31	10	38/252
Miami	2	30	19	63.3	267	8.90	1	0	3/22
Minnesota	4	84	56	66.7	741	8.82	9	2	5/24
New England	3	86	53	61.6	613	7.13	5	2	6/39
New Orleans	17	405	245	60.5	2901	7.16	24	13	30/190
N.Y. Giants	6	148	93	62.8	991	6.70	6	3	5/31
N.Y. Jets	3	79	48	60.8	538	6.81	3	3	3/17
Philadelphia	2	20	10	50.0	118	5.90	0	1	1/9
Phoenix	6	141	95	67.4	1389	9.85	13	5	7/53
Pittsburgh	3	120	80	66.7	762	6.35	3	6	2/17
San Diego	3	68	45	66.2	627	9.22	6	2	2/13
Seattle	3	62	37	59.7	539	8.69	6	4	3/17
Tampa Bay	6	180	128	71.1	1364	7.58	5	3	6/45
Washington	5	173	98	56.6	1352	7.82	5	5	9/84
Totals	138	3673	2322	63.2	27,533	7.50	190	99	219/1543

L.A. Raiders totals include one game vs. Oakland
Phoenix totals include six games vs. St. Louis

Phil Simms's Career Passing vs. Each Opponent

Opponent	Games	Att.	Cmp.	Pct.	Yards	Avg. Gain	TD	Int.	Sacked
Atlanta	4	116	66	56.9	910	7.84	4	3	12/81
Chicago	1	28	15	53.6	181	6.46	1	0	8/53
Cincinnati	1	62	40	64.5	513	8.27	1	2	7/70
Cleveland	1	37	23	62.2	289	7.81	1	2	4/22
Dallas	16	435	214	49.2	3423	7.87	27	27	45/350
Denver	2	56	30	53.6	348	6.21	0	1	5/41
Detroit	2	68	45	66.2	547	8.04	2	0	10/71
Green Bay	5	156	97	62.2	1302	8.35	11	4	16/111
Houston	1	24	13	54.2	234	9.75	2	1	0/0
Indianapolis	1	14	7	50.0	67	4.79	1	4	3/19
Kansas City	3	82	42	51.2	587	7.16	5	5	7/52
L.A. Raiders	1	30	18	60.0	239	7.97	2	2	4/34
L.A. Rams	5	171	87	50.9	1115	6.52	6	5	20/160
Minnesota	1	38	25	65.8	310	8.16	1	2	2/17
New Orleans	5	155	90	58.1	1011	6.52	5	7	13/88
N.Y. Jets	4	135	78	57.8	928	6.87	5	2	21/167
Philadelphia	3	383	200	52.2	2778	7.25	15	12	38/296
Phoenix	14	413	207	50.1	2641	6.39	27	10	42/264
Pittsburgh	1	16	10	62.5	106	6.63	1	1	3/24
San Diego	2	66	32	48.5	435	6.59	1	3	6/58
San Francisco	5	178	104	58.4	1323	7.43	6	5	21/149
Seattle	2	52	26	50.0	293	5.63	2	5	8/52
Tampa Bay	6	177	101	57.1	960	5.42	5	5	17/189
Washington	13	361	182	50.4	2634	7.30	13	17	44/339
Totals	109	3253	1752	53.9	23,174	7.12	142	123	356/2707

Indianapolis totals include one game vs. Baltimore
Phoenix totals include 12 games vs. St. Louis

Dan Marino's Career Passing vs. Each Opponent

Opponent	Games	Att.	Cmp.	Pct.	Yards	Avg. Gain	TD	Int.	Sacked
Atlanta	1	40	20	50.0	303	7.58	2	4	0/0
Buffalo	11	370	242	65.4	2923	7.90	23	16	12/113
Cincinnati	2	70	44	62.9	479	6.84	4	0	4/30
Cleveland	2	89	52	58.4	699	7.85	6	4	0/0
Dallas	2	79	45	57.0	605	7.66	5	3	2/19
Denver	1	43	25	58.1	390	9.07	3	0	3/25
Detroit	1	44	23	52.3	247	5.61	2	2	1/8
Green Bay	2	77	52	67.5	606	7.87	7	3	1/5
Houston	4	111	67	60.4	895	8.06	8	5	2/9
Indianapolis	12	398	244	61.3	3242	8.15	24	5	8/57
Kansas City	1	35	23	65.7	258	7.37	2	1	0/0
L.A. Raiders	4	142	80	56.3	1021	7.19	10	5	5/49
L.A. Rams	2	84	54	64.3	682	8.12	7	2	1/4
Minnesota	1	37	20	54.1	264	7.14	2	3	0/0
New England	11	385	210	54.5	2423	6.29	16	18	7/64
New Orleans	2	63	39	61.9	391	6.21	4	1	1/6
N.Y. Jets	10	384	233	60.7	3240	8.44	31	13	12/72
Philadelphia	2	73	45	61.6	622	8.52	4	2	3/31
Phoenix	1	36	24	66.7	429	11.92	3	0	1/9
Pittsburgh	4	131	85	64.9	1030	7.86	7	8	0/0
San Diego	3	122	77	63.1	957	7.84	6	1	4/29
San Francisco	2	75	42	56.0	495	6.60	3	4	3/29
Tampa Bay	2	85	54	63.5	568	6.68	5	1	0/0
Washington	2	78	43	55.1	704	9.03	8	1	0/0
Totals	87	3100	1866	60.2	23,856	7.70	196	103	73/584

Indianapolis totals include two games vs. Baltimore
Phoenix totals include one game vs. St. Louis

John Elway's Career Passing vs. Each Opponent

Opponent	Games	Att.	Cmp.	Pct.	Yards	Avg. Gain	TD	Int.	Sacked
Atlanta	2	64	35	54.7	526	8.22	4	2	4/26
Buffalo	2	53	25	47.2	311	5.87	3	0	4/25
Chicago	3	53	27	50.9	388	7.32	3	3	3/25
Cincinnati	2	47	30	63.8	355	7.55	4	1	2/13
Cleveland	3	89	52	58.4	661	7.43	6	2	1/6
Dallas	1	24	12	50.0	200	8.33	3	0	1/2
Detroit	2	52	32	61.5	456	8.77	2	1	4/40
Green Bay	2	68	41	60.3	386	5.68	0	4	1/4
Houston	1	35	17	48.6	256	7.31	3	3	2/15
Indianapolis	4	128	64	50.0	848	6.63	4	1	13/103
Kansas City	10	318	166	52.2	1990	6.26	5	20	19/133
L.A. Raiders	10	289	159	55.0	1944	6.73	11	13	24/210
L.A. Rams	2	74	39	52.7	501	6.77	5	2	3/24
Miami	1	37	18	48.6	250	6.76	0	1	3/24
Minnesota	2	58	38	65.5	463	7.98	7	1	4/30
New England	4	140	75	53.6	917	6.55	6	4	6/35
New Orleans	2	79	46	58.2	519	6.57	4	2	4/35
N.Y. Giants	1	47	29	61.7	336	7.15	0	2	2/11
N.Y. Jets	1	28	13	46.4	145	5.18	0	1	5/27
Philadelphia	2	45	25	55.6	289	6.42	2	2	6/42
Pittsburgh	3	87	46	52.9	495	5.69	4	2	5/34
San Diego	11	353	194	55.0	2337	6.62	7	15	24/170
San Francisco	2	81	41	50.6	425	5.25	3	3	5/43

	Games	Att.	Cmp.	Pct.	Yards	Avg. Gain	TD	Int.	Sacked
Seattle	11	370	198	53.5	2864	7.74	15	11	24/191
Washington	1	35	20	57.1	282	8.06	1	0	3/23
Totals	85	2654	1442	54.3	18,144	6.84	102	96	172/1291

Indianapolis totals include two games vs. Baltimore

Boomer Esiason's Career Passing vs. Each Opponent

	Games	Att.	Cmp.	Pct.	Yards	Avg. Gain	TD	Int.	Sacked
Atlanta	2	32	15	46.9	168	5.25	0	0	2/0
Buffalo	4	80	49	61.3	704	8.80	5	2	4/39
Chicago	1	30	14	46.7	212	7.07	1	4	3/23
Cleveland	9	204	107	52.5	1424	6.98	3	6	15/119
Dallas	2	54	31	57.4	470	8.70	6	0	2/9
Denver	1	30	21	70.0	306	10.20	2	1	1/4
Detroit	1	27	13	48.1	167	6.19	0	1	1/0
Green Bay	1	24	15	62.5	207	8.63	3	0	3/24
Houston	9	275	159	57.8	2266	8.24	13	13	15/103
Indianapolis	1	26	17	65.4	236	9.08	2	0	2/20
Kansas City	3	107	61	57.0	788	7.36	4	2	4/49
L.A. Raiders	2	59	35	59.3	507	8.59	3	0	3/29
Miami	1	37	18	48.6	228	6.16	1	1	1/26
Minnesota	1	25	17	68.0	252	10.08	1	1	1/4
New England	4	124	66	53.2	967	7.80	7	6	4/36
New Orleans	2	43	18	41.9	171	3.98	2	2	6/58
N.Y. Giants	1	24	15	62.5	193	8.04	3	0	4/36
N.Y. Jets	5	117	65	55.6	1099	9.39	10	4	12/83
Philadelphia	1	32	20	62.5	363	11.34	4	1	1/10
Phoenix	2	38	24	63.2	356	9.37	4	1	3/22
Pittsburgh	9	257	153	59.5	2171	8.45	13	11	17/158
San Diego	2	63	36	57.1	498	7.90	5	2	7/57
San Francisco	1	29	14	48.3	180	6.21	1	1	3/16
Seattle	2	35	23	65.7	348	9.94	1	2	3/25
Washington	2	58	32	55.2	544	9.38	4	2	4/39
Totals	69	1830	1038	56.7	14,825	8.10	98	65	119/989

Phoenix totals include one game vs. St. Louis

Steve Largent's Career Receiving vs. Each Opponent

Opponent	Games	Rec.	Yards	Yards Per Rec.	Yards Per Game	TD
Atlanta	4	20	311	15.6	77.8	1
Buffalo	3	11	296	26.9	98.7	4
Chicago	5	22	349	15.9	69.8	2
Cincinnati	6	32	454	14.2	75.7	3
Cleveland	10	36	521	14.5	52.1	5
Dallas	4	14	180	12.9	45.0	2
Denver	23	95	1518	16.0	66.0	8
Detroit	4	29	502	17.3	125.5	6
Green Bay	5	26	419	16.1	83.8	2
Houston	5	15	300	20.0	60.0	3
Indianapolis	2	8	130	16.3	65.0	0
Kansas City	21	82	1255	15.3	59.8	5
L.A. Raiders	20	73	1207	16.5	60.4	10
L.A. Rams	4	12	141	11.8	35.3	0
Miami	2	3	41	13.7	20.5	1
Minnesota	4	13	172	13.2	43.0	2
New England	7	28	490	17.5	70.0	3
New Orleans	4	27	442	16.4	110.5	3
N.Y. Giants	5	19	237	12.5	47.4	2
N.Y. Jets	10	48	698	14.5	69.8	4
Philadelphia	3	16	264	16.5	88.0	2
Phoenix	2	13	241	18.5	120.5	3
Pittsburgh	7	28	508	18.1	72.6	4
San Diego	20	84	1374	16.4	68.7	16
San Francisco	4	16	311	19.4	77.8	1
Tampa Bay	2	7	93	13.3	46.5	2
Washington	4	14	232	16.6	58.0	3
Totals	190	791	12,686	16.0	66.8	97

Indianapolis totals include two games vs. Baltimore
L.A. Raiders totals include eight games vs. Oakland
Phoenix totals include two games vs. St. Louis

Steve Largent's Career Receiving By Passer

Passer	Rec.	Yards	Avg.	TD
Jim Zorn	455	7346	16.1	49
Dave Krieg	265	4219	15.9	37
Kelly Stouffer	19	269	14.2	0
Jeff Kemp	16	280	17.5	3
Gale Gilbert	14	234	16.7	2
Steve Myer	10	109	10.9	3
Bill Munson	6	84	14.0	1
Sam Adkins	5	102	20.4	1
David Sims	1	43	43.0	1
Totals	791	12,686	16.0	97

Steve Largent Milestones

Receptions

1st:	Sept. 12, 1976 vs. St. Louis	(1st game)
100th:	Sept. 17, 1978 vs. N.Y. Jets	(31st game)
200th:	Nov. 18, 1979 vs. New Orleans	(56th game)
300th:	Sept. 13, 1981 vs. Denver	(77th game)
400th:	Sept. 4, 1983 vs. Kansas City	(100th game)
500th:	Oct. 21, 1984 vs. Green Bay	(122nd game)
600th:	Nov. 17, 1985 vs. New England	(141st game)
700th:	Sept. 20, 1987 vs. Kansas City	(164th game)
751st:	Dec. 27, 1987 vs. Kansas City	(175th game)

Yards

1000th:	Oct. 30, 1977 vs. Buffalo	(20th game)
2000th:	Nov. 15, 1978 vs. Chicago	(38th game)
3000th:	Oct. 21, 1979 vs. Houston	(52nd game)
4000th:	Oct. 5, 1980 vs. Houston	(64th game)
5000th:	Sept. 20, 1981 vs. Oakland	(78th game)
6000th:	Dec. 20, 1981 vs. Cleveland	(91st game)
7000th:	Oct. 30, 1983 vs. L.A. Raiders	(107th game)
8000th:	Oct. 14, 1984 vs. Buffalo	(121st game)
9000th:	Sept. 23, 1985 vs. L.A. Rams	(133rd game)
10,000th:	Dec. 20, 1985 vs. Denver	(146th game)
11,000th:	Dec. 14, 1986 vs. San Diego	(161st game)
12,000th:	Dec. 27, 1987 vs. Kansas City	(175th game)

Touchdowns

1st:	Sept. 26, 1976 vs. San Francisco	(3rd game)
25th:	Oct. 21, 1979 vs. Houston	(52nd game)
50th:	Sept. 18, 1983 vs. San Diego	(102nd game)
75th:	Oct. 13, 1985 vs. Atlanta	(136th game)
97th:	Dec. 18, 1988 vs. L.A. Raiders	(190th game)

Steve Largent's Number of Games by Reception Total

15 receptions:	1 game	5 receptions:	24 games
12 receptions:	1 game	4 receptions:	37 games
9 receptions:	2 games	3 receptions:	32 games
8 receptions:	11 games	2 receptions:	30 games
7 receptions:	14 games	1 reception:	16 games
6 receptions:	20 games	0 receptions:	2 games*

*Oct. 9, 1977 vs. New England
Nov. 13, 1977 vs. N.Y. Jets

Starting Records of Active NFL Quarterbacks
Minimum: 10 starts

	W-L-T	Pct.
Mike Tomczak	15-3	.833
Jim McMahon	46-15	.754
Doug Flutie	8-3	.727
Don Strock	16-6	.727
Jay Schroeder	28-11	.718
Chris Chandler	9-4	.692
Joe Montana	75-36	.676
Danny White	62-30	.674
John Elway	54-28-1	.657
Bernie Kosar	30-17	.638
Dan Marino	54-31	.635
Wade Wilson	17-10	.630
Dave Krieg	50-30	.625
Bobby Hebert	23-14	.622
Jeff Kemp	13-8-1	.614
Pat Ryan	11-7	.611
Tony Eason	28-20	.583
Steve Grogan	72-53	.576
Phil Simms	60-46	.566
Boomer Esiason	35-27	.565
Jim Everett	18-14	.563
Turk Schonert	6-5	.545
Gary Hogeboom	13-11	.542
Ken O'Brien	31-27-1	.534
Randall Cunningham	19-17-1	.527
Todd Blackledge	14-13	.519
Jim Kelly	22-22	.500
Tommy Kramer	51-55	.481
Neil Lomax	47-52-2	.475
Doug Williams	37-41-1	.475
Cliff Stoudt	9-11	.450
Mark Malone	23-30	.434
Dan Majkowski	5-8-1	.393
Dave Wilson	12-19	.387
Warren Moon	26-42	.382
Steve Dils	10-17	.370
Rusty Hilger	5-9	.357
Mike Pagel	17-33-1	.343
Chris Miller	5-10	.333
Steve Pelluer	8-18	.308
Steve Young	7-18	.280
Steve DeBerg	24-66-1	.269
Bubby Brister	4-11	.267

	W-L-T	Pct.
Vinny Testaverde	5-14	.263
Jack Trudeau	5-16	.238
Randy Wright	7-25	.219
Chuck Long	4-17	.190
Mark Herrmann	2-9	.182

Individual NFL Leaders Over Last 2 Seasons, Last 3 Seasons, Last 4 Seasons

Last 2 Seasons	Last 3 Seasons	Last 4 Seasons
Points		
231, Morten Andersen	339, Morten Andersen	459, Morten Andersen
210, Dean Biasucci	300, Gary Anderson	439, Gary Anderson
206, Tony Zendejas	300, Rich Karlis	431, Kevin Butler
205, Gary Anderson	300, Tony Zendejas	410, Rich Karlis
204, Mike Lansford	298, Norm Johnson	410, Pat Leahy
Touchdowns		
33, Jerry Rice	49, Jerry Rice	53, Jerry Rice
22, Robb Riddick	35, Curt Warner	44, Eric Dickerson
22, Curt Warner	32, Eric Dickerson	44, Joe Morris
21, Mark Clayton	31, Mark Clayton	44, Curt Warner
21, Eric Dickerson	29, Johnny Hector	38, James Brooks
21, Johnny Hector	29, Herschel Walker	
Field Goals		
54, Morten Andersen	80, Morten Andersen	111, Morten Andersen
50, Gary Anderson	71, Gary Anderson	104, Gary Anderson
49, Dean Biasucci	65, Nick Lowery	93, Kevin Butler
46, Nick Lowery	64, Tony Zendejas	89, Nick Lowery
42, Scott Norwood	62, Dean Biasucci	85, Tony Zendejas
42, Tony Zendejas	62, Kevin Butler	
Rushes		
671, Eric Dickerson	1075, Eric Dickerson	1367, Eric Dickerson
570, Herschel Walker	841, Joe Morris	1135, Joe Morris
525, Roger Craig	819, Curt Warner	1110, Curt Warner
500, Joe Morris	729, Roger Craig	1056, Gerald Riggs
500, Curt Warner	721, Herschel Walker	1011, Marcus Allen
Rushing Yards		
2947, Eric Dickerson	4768, Eric Dickerson	6002, Eric Dickerson
2405, Herschel Walker	3491, Curt Warner	4593, Joe Morris
2317, Roger Craig	3257, Joe Morris	4585, Curt Warner
2010, Curt Warner	3147, Roger Craig	4409, Gerald Riggs
1959, Mike Rozier	3142, Herschel Walker	4197, Roger Craig
Rushing TDs		
21, Johnny Hector	31, Eric Dickerson	43, Eric Dickerson
20, Eric Dickerson	31, Curt Warner	43, Joe Morris
18, Curt Warner	29, Johnny Hector	39, Curt Warner
17, Robb Riddick	24, George Rogers	35, Johnny Hector
16, Greg Bell	24, Herschel Walker	31, George Rogers
Passes		
1050, Dan Marino	1673, Dan Marino	2240, Dan Marino
966, R. Cunningham	1410, John Elway	2015, John Elway
906, Neil Lomax	1351, Jim Kelly	1798, Neil Lomax
906, John Elway	1327, Neil Lomax	1787, Ken O'Brien
871, Jim Kelly	1299, Ken O'Brien	1728, Boomer Esiason
Completions		
617, Dan Marino	995, Dan Marino	1331, Dan Marino
530, Neil Lomax	804, Jim Kelly	1105, John Elway
524, R. Cunningham	778, John Elway	1067, Ken O'Brien
519, Jim Kelly	770, Neil Lomax	1035, Neil Lomax
504, Joe Montana	770, Ken O'Brien	998, Joe Montana
Passing Yards		
7679, Dan Marino	12,425, Dan Marino	16,562, Dan Marino
6893, Boomer Esiason	10,852, Boomer Esiason	14,295, Boomer Esiason
6782, Neil Lomax	9992, John Elway	13,883, John Elway
6594, R. Cunningham	9771, Jim Kelly	12,905, Phil Simms
6507, John Elway	9365, Neil Lomax	12,841, Ken O'Brien
TD Passes		
54, Dan Marino	98, Dan Marino	128, Dan Marino
49, Joe Montana	68, Boomer Esiason	95, Boomer Esiason
47, R. Cunningham	62, Dave Krieg	89, Dave Krieg
44, Boomer Esiason	59, Phil Simms	84, Joe Montana
44, Neil Lomax	57, Neil Lomax	81, Phil Simms
	57, Joe Montana	
Receptions		
174, J.T. Smith	254, J.T. Smith	315, Roger Craig
161, Al Toon	246, Al Toon	297, J.T. Smith
142, Roger Craig	223, Roger Craig	292, Al Toon
137, Henry Ellard	215, Jerry Rice	274, Art Monk
132, Mark Clayton	192, Mark Clayton	264, Jerry Rice
Reception Yards		
2384, Jerry Rice	3954, Jerry Rice	4881, Jerry Rice
2213, Henry Ellard	3242, Drew Hill	4411, Drew Hill
2147, Anthony Carter	3223, Gary Clark	4149, Gary Clark
2130, Drew Hill	3219, Al Toon	4051, Mark Clayton
2103, J.T. Smith	3117, J.T. Smith	3914, Steve Largent
Receiving TDs		
31, Jerry Rice	46, Jerry Rice	49, Jerry Rice
21, Mark Clayton	31, Mark Clayton	35, Mark Clayton
16, Drew Hill	24, Mike Quick	35, Mike Quick
15, Mike Quick	22, Stephone Paige	32, Stephone Paige
14, Gary Clark	21, Gary Clark	30, Drew Hill
14, Eric Martin	21, Drew Hill	
Interceptions		
13, Mark Kelso	20, Ronnie Lott	26, Deron Cherry
13, Barry Wilburn	19, Deron Cherry	26, Ronnie Lott
11, Joey Browner	17, Dave Waymer	23, Dave Waymer
11, Scott Case	15, Joey Browner	19, Scott Case
11, Carl Lee	15, Scott Case	19, Mike Harden
	15, Tim McKyer	19, Everson Walls
	15, Barry Wilburn	

NFL Team Leaders Over Last 2 Seasons, Last 3 Seasons, Last 4 Seasons

Last 2 Seasons	Last 3 Seasons	Last 4 Seasons
Highest Won-Lost Percentage		
.742, Chicago	.787, Chicago	.825, Chicago
.742, San Francisco	.713, San Francisco	.690, San Francisco
.710, New Orleans	.681, Cleveland	.643, Denver
.645, Cleveland	.638, N.Y. Giants	.635, Cleveland
.613, Three teams	.638, Washington	.635, N.Y. Giants
		.635, Washington
Most Points		
828, San Francisco	1202, San Francisco	1613, San Francisco
769, Houston	1142, Cincinnati	1583, Cincinnati
742, Minnesota	1140, Minnesota	1539, Miami
734, New Orleans	1111, Miami	1486, Minnesota
733, Cincinnati	1092, Washington	1476, Chicago
Most Total Yards		
11,887, San Francisco	17,969, San Francisco	23,889, San Francisco
11,434, Cincinnati	17,924, Cincinnati	23,824, Cincinnati
11,276, Washington	17,583, Miami	23,426, Miami
11,259, Miami	16,877, Washington	22,215, Washington
11,133, St. L./Phoenix	16,346, Denver	21,842, Denver
Most Rushing Yards		
4874, Cincinnati	7407, Cincinnati	9734, Chicago
4760, San Francisco	6973, Chicago	9590, Cincinnati
4392, Indianapolis	6746, San Francisco	8978, San Francisco
4372, Pittsburgh	6595, Pittsburgh	8772, Pittsburgh
4273, Chicago	6557, L.A. Rams	8614, L.A. Rams
Most Passing Yards		
8392, Miami	13,171, Miami	17,285, Miami
7631, Washington	11,500, Washington	14,911, San Francisco
7345, Denver	11,223, San Francisco	14,528, Denver
7127, San Francisco	10,883, Denver	14,318, San Diego
6891, Cleveland	10,635, Cleveland	14,315, Washington
Fewest Turnovers		
52, San Francisco	81, San Francisco	115, San Francisco
59, Cincinnati	86, Cleveland	122, Cleveland
60, New Orleans	88, Philadelphia	124, Cincinnati
61, N.Y. Jets	91, St.L./Phoenix	125, St.L./Phoenix
61, Philadelphia	92, Minnesota	127, N.Y. Jets
Fewest Points Allowed		
497, Chicago	684, Chicago	882, Chicago
527, Cleveland	794, San Francisco	1057, San Francisco
542, Buffalo	837, Cleveland	1131, Cleveland
547, San Francisco	841, Minnesota	1135, N.Y. Giants
553, Indianapolis	852, N.Y. Giants	1174, New England
Fewest Total Yards Allowed		
8575, Chicago	12,705, Chicago	16,840, Chicago
8670, San Francisco	13,550, San Francisco	18,741, San Francisco
8915, Minnesota	13,927, Minnesota	18,821, N.Y. Giants
9031, Cleveland	14,300, Cleveland	19,150, L.A. Raiders
9456, New Orleans	14,501, N.Y. Giants	19,258, Cleveland
Fewest Rushing Yards Allowed		
2639, Chicago	4202, Chicago	5521, Chicago
3199, San Francisco	4754, San Francisco	6286, N.Y. Giants
3295, Philadelphia	4804, N.Y. Giants	6437, San Francisco
3326, Minnesota	4888, New Orleans	6685, L.A. Rams
3329, New Orleans	5099, L.A. Rams	6963, Washington
Fewest Passing Yards Allowed		
5471, San Francisco	8503, Chicago	11,319, Chicago
5578, Buffalo	8656, Green Bay	11,718, New England
5589, Minnesota	8659, New England	11,782, Green Bay
5678, Cleveland	8796, San Francisco	11,972, L.A. Raiders
5681, New England	8805, Minnesota	12,046, Minnesota
Most Opponents' Turnovers		
92, Philadelphia	132, Minnesota	176, Minnesota
90, Minnesota	128, Philadelphia	164, New England
83, Green Bay	125, San Francisco	160, Chicago
80, Indianapolis	123, New Orleans	160, New Orleans
80, New Orleans	117, New England	160, Philadelphia
		160, San Francisco

Longest Streaks in NFL History

Games Played		
282	Jim Marshall	1960-79
240	Mick Tingelhoff	1962-78
234	Jim Bakken	1962-78
Games Scoring		
151	Fred Cox	1963-73
137	Jim Breech	1980-88 (current)
133	Garo Yepremian	1970-79
Games Scoring Touchdowns		
18	Lenny Moore	1963-65
14	O.J. Simpson	1975
13	John Riggins	1982-83
	Jerry Rice	1986-87
Extra Points		
234	Tommy Davis	1959-65
221	Jim Turner	1967-74
202	Gary Anderson	1983-88
Games Scoring Field Goals		
31	Fred Cox	1968-70
28	Jim Turner	1970-72
23	Morten Andersen	1986-88
Field Goals		
23	Mark Moseley	1981-82
22	Pat Leahy	1985-86
20	Garo Yepremian	1978-79
	Morten Andersen	1985-86
100-Yard Rushing Games		
11	Marcus Allen	1985-86
9	Walter Payton	1985
7	O.J. Simpson	1972-73
	Earl Campbell	1979
Games Rushing For Touchdowns		
13	John Riggins	1982-83
	George Rogers	1985-86
11	Lenny Moore	1963-64
9	Leroy Kelly	1968
Passes Completed		
22	Joe Montana	1987
20	Ken Anderson	1983
18	Steve DeBerg	1982
	Lynn Dickey	1983
	Joe Montana	1984
300-Yard Passing Games		
5	Joe Montana	1982
4	Dan Fouts	1979
	Bill Kenney	1983
Games Passing For Touchdowns		
47	Johnny Unitas	1956-60
30	Dan Marino	1985-87
28	Dave Krieg	1983-85
Passes Without Interception		
294	Bart Starr	1964-65
208	Milt Plum	1959-60
206	Roman Gabriel	1968-69
Games With Receptions		
167	Steve Largent	1977-88 (current)
143	Ozzie Newsome	1979-88 (current)
127	Harold Carmichael	1972-80
100-Yard Receiving Games		
7	Charley Hennigan	1961
	Bill Groman	1961
6	Raymond Berry	1960
	Pat Studstill	1966
5	Elroy (Crazylegs) Hirsch	1951
	Bob Boyd	1954
	Terry Barr	1963
	Lance Alworth	1966
Games With Touchdown Receptions		
13	Jerry Rice	1986-87
11	Elroy (Crazylegs) Hirsch	1950-51
	Buddy Dial	1959-60
9	Lance Alworth	1963
Games With Interceptions		
8	Tom Morrow	1962-63
7	Paul Krause	1964
	Larry Wilson	1966
	Ben Davis	1968
Punts Without A Block		
623	Dave Jennings	1976-83
619	Ray Guy	1979-86
578	Bobby Walden	1964-72

Records of Teams on Opening Day, 1933-88

AFC	W	L	T	Pct.	Longest W Strk.	Longest L Strk.	Current Streak
San Diego	18	11	0	.621	6	4	L-2
Denver	17	11	1	.607	3	4	L-1
L.A. Raiders	17	12	0	.586	5	5	W-2
Cleveland	22	17	0	.564	5	5	W-1
Indianapolis	20	16	0	.556	8	5	L-5
Houston	16	13	0	.552	4	3	W-4
Pittsburgh	27	23	4	.540	4	3	W-2
Cincinnati	11	10	0	.524	4	4	W-2
Kansas City	15	14	0	.517	5	4	L-1
New England	14	15	0	.483	5	3	W-5
Miami	10	12	1	.455	4	4	L-4
N.Y. Jets	13	16	0	.448	3	5	L-1
Buffalo	10	19	0	.345	3	5	W-1
Seattle	4	9	0	.308	3	8	W-1

NFC	W	L	T	Pct.	Longest W Strk.	Longest L Strk.	Current Streak
Dallas	22	6	1	.786	17	2	L-2
Minnesota	16	11	1	.593	4	2	L-1
N.Y. Giants	30	22	4	.577	3	3	W-1
Atlanta	13	10	0	.565	5	3	L-2
Chicago	31	24	1	.564	7	6	W-5
Detroit	30	24	2	.556	7	4	W-1
L.A. Rams	28	23	0	.549	5	6	W-1
Green Bay	28	25	3	.528	5	6	L-4
Washington	26	26	4	.500	6	5	L-1
San Francisco	17	21	1	.447	4	3	W-1
Phoenix	24	30	1	.444	6	6	L-1
Philadelphia	21	33	1	.389	5	9	W-1
Tampa Bay	4	9	0	.308	3	5	L-1
New Orleans	4	18	0	.182	1	6	L-1

Note: All tied games occurred prior to 1972, when calculation of ties as half-win, half-loss was begun.

Records of All NFL Teams for 1988 in Each Category of Games:

	Status at Halftime			Status After 3 Quarters		
AFC	**Leading**	**Tied**	**Trailing**	**Leading**	**Tied**	**Trailing**
Buffalo	7-1	2-0	3-3	9-1	1-0	2-3
Cincinnati	9-1	3-1	0-2	9-1	1-0	2-3
Cleveland	4-0	3-0	3-6	6-0	1-0	3-6
Denver	6-1	1-2	1-5	7-1	0-0	1-7
Houston	6-1	2-1	2-4	7-2	1-1	2-3
Indianapolis	6-2	1-2	2-3	7-0	1-2	1-5
Kansas City	2-1	1-2	1-8-1	2-1	0-1	2-9-1
L.A. Raiders	4-2	1-0	2-7	5-2	1-0	1-7
Miami	4-0	1-2	1-8	5-2	0-0	1-8
New England	5-1	3-2	1-4	8-1	1-1	0-5
N.Y. Jets	6-3-1	1-0	1-4	6-1-1	1-1	1-5
Pittsburgh	5-3	0-1	0-7	4-2	0-0	1-9
San Diego	5-2	1-1	0-7	5-1	0-1	1-8
Seattle	7-0	2-0	0-7	7-0	1-0	1-7
NFC	**Leading**	**Tied**	**Trailing**	**Leading**	**Tied**	**Trailing**
Atlanta	4-3	0-1	1-7	4-2	1-0	0-9
Chicago	11-0	1-0	0-4	12-0	0-0	0-4
Dallas	2-2	0-2	1-9	1-4	1-0	1-9
Detroit	4-4	0-2	0-6	4-0	0-2	0-10
Green Bay	4-0	0-3	0-9	4-1	0-2	0-9
L.A. Rams	9-0	0-1	1-5	10-1	0-0	0-5
Minnesota	9-1	0-0	2-4	11-0	0-0	0-5
New Orleans	6-2	0-1	4-3	10-2	0-0	0-4
N.Y. Giants	5-0	0-2	5-4	7-1	1-0	2-5
Philadelphia	5-3	2-2	3-1	7-2	0-0	3-4
Phoenix	4-1	1-1	2-7	5-0	0-1	2-8
San Francisco	7-3	1-0	2-3	9-2	0-0	1-4
Tampa Bay	2-1	3-2	0-8	2-0	2-1	1-10
Washington	3-2	2-1	2-6	3-2	1-2	3-5
Totals	151-40-1	32-32	40-151-1	176-32-1	15-15	32-176-1

Trailing at Halftime

	1981-88	1988 ONLY
Home Teams	171-489-3 (.260)	24-61-0 (.282)
Road Teams	155-706-3 (.181)	16-90-1 (.154)
All Teams	326-1195-6 (.215)	40-151-1 (.211)

Trailing After 3 Quarters

	1981-88	1988 ONLY
Home Teams	138-543-2 (.204)	17-69-0 (.198)
Road Teams	126-771-4 (.142)	15-107-1 (.126)
All Teams	264-1314-6 (.169)	32-176-1 (.156)

Oldest Individual Single-Season or Single-Game Records in NFL Record & Fact Book

Regular-Season Records That Have Not Been Surpassed or Tied

Most Points, Game—40, Ernie Nevers, Chi. Cardinals vs. Chi. Bears, Nov. 28, 1929 (6-td, 4-pat)

Most Touchdowns Rushing, Game—6, Ernie Nevers, Chi. Cardinals vs. Chi. Bears, Nov. 28, 1929

Highest Average Gain, Rushing, Season (Qualifiers)—9.94, Beattie Feathers, Chi. Bears, 1934 (101-1,004)

Highest Punting Average, Season (Qualifiers)—51.40, Sammy Baugh, Washington, 1940 (35-1,799)

Highest Punting Average, Game (minimum: 4 punts)—61.75, Bob Cifers, Detroit vs. Chi. Bears, Nov. 24, 1946 (4-247)

Highest Average Gain, Pass Receptions, Season (minimum: 24 receptions)—32.58, Don Currivan, Boston, 1947 (24-782)

Highest Average Gain, Passing, Game (minimum: 20 passes)—18.58, Sammy Baugh, Washington vs. Boston, Oct. 31, 1948 (24-446)

Most Touchdowns, Fumble Recoveries, Game—2, Fred (Dippy) Evans, Chi. Bears vs. Washington, Nov. 28, 1948

Most Yards Gained, Intercepted Passes, Rookie, Season—301, Don Doll, Detroit, 1949

Most Passes Had Intercepted, Game—8, Jim Hardy, Chi. Cardinals vs. Philadelphia, Sept. 24, 1950

Highest Average Gain, Rushing, Game (minimum: 10 attempts)—17.09, Marion Motley, Cleveland vs. Pittsburgh, Oct. 29, 1950 (11-188)

Most Yards Gained, Kickoff Returns, Game—294, Wally Triplett, Detroit vs. Los Angeles, Oct. 29, 1950

Highest Kickoff Return Average, Game (minimum: 3 returns)—73.50, Wally Triplett, Detroit vs. Los Angeles, Oct. 29, 1950 (4-294)

Most Pass Receptions, Game—18, Tom Fears, Los Angeles vs. Green Bay, Dec. 3, 1950

Highest Punt Return Average, Season (Qualifiers)—23.00, Herb Rich, Baltimore, 1950 (12-276)

Highest Punt Return Average, Rookie, Season (Qualifiers)—23.00, Herb Rich, Baltimore, 1950 (12-276)

Most Yards Passing, Game—554, Norm Van Brocklin, Los Angeles vs. N.Y. Yanks, Sept. 28, 1951

Most Touchdowns, Punt Returns, Rookie, Season—4, Jack Christiansen, Detroit, 1951

Most Interceptions By, Season—14, Dick (Night Train) Lane, Los Angeles, 1952

Most Interceptions By, Rookie, Season—14, Dick (Night Train) Lane, Los Angeles, 1952

Highest Average Gain, Passing, Season (Qualifiers)—11.17, Tommy O'Connell, Cleveland, 1957 (110-1,229)

Most Points, Season—176, Paul Hornung, Green Bay, 1960 (15-td, 41-pat, 15-fg)

Highest Pass Rating, Season—110.4, Milt Plum, Cleveland, 1960

Most Yards Gained, Pass Receptions, Rookie, Season—1,473, Bill Groman, Houston, 1960

Largest Trades in NFL History

(Based on number of players or draft choices involved)

15—March 26, 1953—T Mike McCormack, DT Don Colo, LB Tom Catlin, DB John Petitbon, and G Herschell Forester from Baltimore to Cleveland for DB Don Shula, DB Bert Rechichar, DB Carl Taseff, LB Ed Sharkey, E Gern Nagler, QB Harry Agganis, T Dick Batten, T Stu Sheets, G Art Spinney, and G Elmer Willhoite.

15—January 28, 1971—LB Marlin McKeever, first- and third-round choices in 1971, and third-, fourth-, fifth-, sixth-, and seventh-round choices in 1972 from Washington to the Los Angeles Rams for LB Maxie Baughan, LB Jack Pardee, LB Myron Pottios, RB Jeff Jordan, G John Wilbur, DT Diron Talbert, and a fifth-round choice in 1971.

12—June 13, 1952—Selection rights to Les Richter from the Dallas Texans to the Los Angeles Rams for RB Dick Hoerner, DB Tom Keane, DB George Sims, C Joe Reid, HB Billy Baggett, T Jack Halliday, FB Dick McKissack, LB Vic Vasicek, E Richard Wilkins, C Aubrey Phillips, and RB Dave Anderson.

10—March 23, 1959—Ollie Matson from the Chicago Cardinals to the Los Angeles Rams for T Frank Fuller, DE Glenn Holtzman, T Ken Panfil, DT Art Hauser, E John Tracey, FB Larry Hickman, HB Don Brown, the Rams' second-round choice in 1960, and a player to be delivered during the 1959 training camp.

10—October 31, 1987—RB Eric Dickerson from the Los Angeles Rams to Indianapolis. The rights to LB Cornelius Bennett from Indianapolis to Buffalo. Indianapolis running back Owen Gill and the Colts' first- and second-round choices in 1988 and second-round choice in 1989, plus Bills running back Greg Bell and Buffalo's first-round choice in 1988 and first- and second-round choices in 1989 to the Rams.

Retired Uniform Numbers in NFL

AFC

Buffalo:	None	
Cincinnati:	Bob Johnson	54
Cleveland:	Otto Graham	14
	Jim Brown	32
	Ernie Davis	45
	Don Fleming	46
	Lou Groza	76
Denver:	Frank Tripucka	18
	Floyd Little	44
Houston:	Earl Campbell	34
	Jim Norton	43
	Elvin Bethea	65
Indianapolis:	Johnny Unitas	19
	Buddy Young	22
	Lenny Moore	24
	Art Donovan	70
	Jim Parker	77
	Raymond Berry	82
	Gino Marchetti	89
Kansas City:	Len Dawson	16
	Abner Haynes	28
	Stone Johnson	33
	Mack Lee Hill	36
	Bobby Bell	78
Los Angeles Raiders:	None	
Miami:	Bob Griese	12
New England:	Gino Cappelletti	20
	Jim Hunt	79
	Bob Dee	89
New York Jets:	Joe Namath	12
	Don Maynard	13
Pittsburgh:	None	
San Diego:	Dan Fouts	14
Seattle:	"Fans/the twelfth man"	12

NFC

Atlanta:	Tommy Nobis	60
	Jeff Van Note	57
	William Andrews	31
Chicago:	Bronko Nagurski	3
	George McAfee	5
	Willie Galimore	28
	Walter Payton	34
	Brian Piccolo	41
	Sid Luckman	42
	Bill Hewitt	56
	Bill George	61
	Bulldog Turner	66
	Red Grange	77
Dallas:	None	
Detroit:	Dutch Clark	7
	Bobby Layne	22
	Doak Walker	37
	Joe Schmidt	56
	Chuck Hughes	85
	Charlie Sanders	88
Green Bay:	Tony Canadeo	3
	Don Hutson	14
	Bart Starr	15
	Ray Nitschke	66
Los Angeles Rams:	Bob Waterfield	7
	Merlin Olsen	74
Minnesota:	Fran Tarkenton	10
New Orleans:	Jim Taylor	31
	Doug Atkins	81
New York Giants:	Ray Flaherty	1
	Mel Hein	7
	Y.A. Tittle	14
	Al Blozis	32
	Joe Morrison	40
	Charlie Conerly	42
	Ken Strong	50
Philadelphia:	Steve Van Buren	15
	Tom Brookshier	40
	Pete Retzlaff	44
	Chuck Bednarik	60
	Al Wistert	70
St. Louis:	Larry Wilson	8
	Stan Mauldin	77
	J.V. Cain	88
	Marshall Goldberg	99
San Francisco:	John Brodie	12
	Joe Perry	34
	Jimmy Johnson	37
	Hugh McElhenny	39
	Charlie Krueger	70
	Leo Nomellini	73
	Dwight Clark	87
Tampa Bay:	Lee Roy Selmon	63
Washington:	Sammy Baugh	33

1988 NFL Score by Quarters

AFC Offense	1	2	3	4	OT	PTS
Cincinnati	99	147	107	92	3	448
Houston	84	137	100	100	3	424
N.Y. Jets	78	125	72	97	0	372
Indianapolis	77	135	61	81	0	354
Seattle	58	124	83	74	0	339
Pittsburgh	85	94	47	110	0	336
Buffalo	71	83	81	91	3	329
Denver	43	127	64	90	3	327
L.A. Raiders	56	91	68	107	3	325
Miami	72	97	88	62	0	319
Cleveland	46	81	63	114	0	304
Kansas City	51	74	47	82	0	254
New England	49	87	50	61	3	250
San Diego	72	57	37	65	0	231

NFC Offense	1	2	3	4	OT	PTS
L.A. Rams	81	146	92	88	0	407
Minnesota	82	132	91	101	0	406
Philadelphia	76	131	65	101	6	379
San Francisco	54	140	95	80	0	369
N.Y. Giants	59	83	95	119	3	359
Washington	86	79	89	91	0	345
Phoenix	67	114	51	112	0	344
Chicago	77	131	42	62	0	312
New Orleans	64	93	101	54	0	312
Dallas	71	47	64	83	0	265
Tampa Bay	27	75	41	118	0	261
Atlanta	33	82	45	84	0	244
Green Bay	58	58	47	77	0	240
Detroit	36	87	51	46	0	220

AFC Defense	1	2	3	4	OT	PTS
Buffalo	44	104	27	62	0	237
New England	48	77	57	102	0	284
Cleveland	46	137	44	61	0	288
Indianapolis	55	88	48	121	3	315
Kansas City	77	118	52	73	0	320
Cincinnati	67	79	95	88	0	329
Seattle	75	90	72	92	0	329
San Diego	69	105	57	101	0	332
Denver	85	112	96	56	3	352
N.Y. Jets	86	64	104	97	3	354
Houston	85	112	71	97	0	365
L.A. Raiders	58	138	73	100	0	369
Miami	51	159	69	101	0	380
Pittsburgh	64	138	103	116	0	421

NFC Defense	1	2	3	4	OT	PTS
Chicago	49	56	50	60	0	215
Minnesota	46	73	62	52	0	233
New Orleans	51	111	70	51	0	283
L.A. Rams	37	94	76	86	0	293
San Francisco	31	92	77	91	3	294
N.Y. Giants	59	101	53	85	6	304
Detroit	34	93	78	105	3	313
Atlanta	50	89	75	101	0	315
Green Bay	78	131	38	68	0	315
Philadelphia	111	47	73	88	0	319
Tampa Bay	105	93	95	54	3	350
Dallas	80	125	74	102	0	381
Washington	70	125	64	125	3	387
Phoenix	101	106	84	107	0	398

NFL TOTALS	1	2	3	4	OT	PTS
	1812	2857	1937	2442	27	9075

Team Leaders

Offense	Most Scored	Fewest Scored
1st Quarter	99, Cincinnati	27, Tampa Bay
2nd Quarter	147, Cincinnati	47, Atlanta
3rd Quarter	107, Cincinnati	37, San Diego
4th Quarter	119, N.Y. Giants	46, Detroit

Defense	Most Allowed	Fewest Allowed
1st Quarter	111, Philadelphia	31, San Fran.
2nd Quarter	159, Miami	47, Philadelphia
3rd Quarter	104, N.Y. Jets	27, Buffalo
4th Quarter	125, Washington	51, New Orleans

Greatest Comebacks in NFL History (Most Points Overcome To Win Game)

Regular-Season Games

From 28 points behind to win:
December 7, 1980, at San Francisco

New Orleans	14	21	0	0	0 — 35
San Francisco	0	7	14	14	3 — 38

NO —Harris 33 pass from Manning (Ricardo kick)
NO —Childs 21 pass from Manning (Ricardo kick)
NO —Holmes 1 run (Ricardo kick)
SF —Solomon 57 punt return (Wersching kick)
NO —Holmes 1 run (Ricardo kick)
NO —Harris 41 pass from Manning (Ricardo kick)
SF —Montana 1 run (Wersching kick)
SF —Clark 71 pass from Montana (Wersching kick)
SF —Solomon 14 pass from Montana (Wersching kick)
SF —Elliott 7 run (Wersching kick)
SF —FG Wersching 36

	N.O.	S.F.
First Downs	27	24
Total Yards	519	430
Yards Rushing	143	176
Yards Passing	376	254
Turnovers	3	0

From 25 points behind to win:
November 8, 1987, at St. Louis

Tampa Bay	7	7	14	0 — 28
St. Louis	0	3	0	28 — 31

TB —Carrier 5 pass from DeBerg (Igwebuike kick)
TB —Carter 3 pass from DeBerg (Igwebuike kick)
StL —FG Gallery 31
TB —Smith 34 pass from DeBerg (Igwebuike kick)
TB —Smith 3 run (Igwebuike kick)
StL —Awalt 4 pass from Lomax (Gallery kick)
StL —Noga 23 fumble recovery (Gallery kick)
StL —J. Smith 11 pass from Lomax (Gallery kick)
StL —J. Smith 17 pass from Lomax (Gallery kick)

	T.B.	St.L.
First Downs	26	26
Total Yards	377	415
Yards Rushing	83	137
Yards Passing	294	278
Turnovers	1	2

From 24 points behind to win:
October 27, 1946, at Washington

Philadelphia	0	0	14	14 — 28
Washington	10	14	0	0 — 24

Wash—Rosato 2 run (Poillon kick)
Wash—FG Poillon 28
Wash—Rosato 4 run (Poillon kick)
Wash—Lapka recovered fumble in end zone (Poillon kick)
Phil —Steele 1 run (Lio kick)
Phil —Pritchard 45 pass from Thompson (Lio kick)
Phil —Steinke 7 pass from Thompson (Lio kick)
Phil —Ferrante 30 pass from Thompson (Lio kick)

	Phil.	Wash.
First Downs	14	8
Total Yards	262	127
Yards Rushing	34	66
Yards Passing	228	61
Turnovers	6	3

From 24 points behind to win:
October 20, 1957, at Detroit

Baltimore	7	14	6	0 — 27
Detroit	0	3	7	21 — 31

Balt —Mutscheller 15 pass from Unitas (Rechichar kick)
Det —FG Martin 47
Balt —Moore 72 pass from Unitas (Rechichar kick)
Balt —Mutscheller 52 pass from Unitas (Rechichar kick)
Balt —Moore 4 pass from Unitas (kick failed)
Det —Junker 14 pass from Rote (Layne kick)
Det —Cassady 26 pass from Layne (Layne kick)
Det —Johnson 1 run (Layne kick)
Det —Cassady 29 pass from Layne (Layne kick)

	Balt.	Det.
First Downs	15	20
Total Yards	322	369
Yards Rushing	117	178
Yards Passing	205	191
Turnovers	6	4

From 24 points behind to win:
October 25, 1959, at Chicago

Philadelphia	0	0	21	7	— 28
Chi. Cardinals	7	10	7	0	— 24

Chi —Crow 10 pass from Roach (Conrad kick)
Chi —J. Hill 77 blocked field goal return (Conrad kick)
Chi —FG Conrad 15
Chi —Lane 37 interception return (Conrad kick)
Phil —Barnes 1 run (Walston kick)
Phil —McDonald 29 pass from Van Brocklin (Walston kick)
Phil —Barnes 2 run (Walston kick)
Phil —McDonald 22 pass from Van Brocklin (Walston kick)

	Phil.	Chi.
First Downs	22	14
Total Yards	399	313
Yards Rushing	168	163
Yards Passing	231	150
Turnovers	2	6

From 24 points behind to win:
October 23, 1960, at Denver

Boston	10	7	7	0	— 24
Denver	0	0	14	17	— 31

Bos —FG Cappelletti 12
Bos —Colclough 10 pass from Songin (Cappelletti kick)
Bos —Wells 6 pass from Songin (Cappelletti kick)
Bos —Miller 47 pass from Songin (Cappelletti kick)
Den—Carmichael 21 pass from Tripucka (Mingo kick)
Den—Jessup 19 pass from Tripucka (Mingo kick)
Den—Carmichael 35 lateral from Taylor, pass from Tripucka (Mingo kick)
Den—Taylor 8 pass from Tripucka (Mingo kick)
Den—FG Mingo 9

	Bos.	Den.
First Downs	19	16
Total Yards	434	326
Yards Rushing	211	65
Yards Passing	223	261
Turnovers	7	4

From 24 points behind to win:
December 15, 1974, at Miami

New England	21	3	0	3	— 27
Miami	0	17	7	10	— 34

NE —Hannah recovered fumble in end zone (J. Smith kick)
NE —Sanders 23 interception return (J. Smith kick)
NE —Herron 4 pass from Plunkett (J. Smith kick)
NE —FG J. Smith 46
Mia—Nottingham 1 run (Yepremian kick)
Mia—Baker 37 pass from Morrall (Yepremian kick)
Mia—FG Yepremian 28
Mia—Baker 46 pass from Morrall (Yepremian kick)
NE —FG J. Smith 34
Mia—Nottingham 2 run (Yepremian kick)
Mia—FG Yepremian 40

	N.E.	Mia.
First Downs	18	18
Total Yards	333	333
Yards Rushing	114	61
Yards Passing	219	272
Turnovers	3	4

From 24 points behind to win:
December 4, 1977, at Minnesota

San Francisco	0	10	14	3	— 27
Minnesota	0	0	7	21	— 28

SF —Delvin Williams 2 run (Wersching kick)
SF —FG Wersching 31
SF —Dave Williams 80 kickoff return (Wersching kick)
SF —Delvin Williams 5 run (Wersching kick)
Minn—McClanahan 15 pass from Lee (Cox kick)
Minn—Rashad 8 pass from Kramer (Cox kick)
Minn—Tucker 9 pass from Kramer (Cox kick)
SF —FG Wersching 31
Minn—S. White 69 pass from Kramer (Cox kick)

	S.F.	Minn.
First Downs	19	18
Total Yards	243	309
Yards Rushing	196	52
Yards Passing	47	257
Turnovers	2	5

From 24 points behind to win:
September 23, 1979, at Denver

Seattle	10	10	14	0	— 34
Denver	0	10	21	6	— 37

Sea—FG Herrera 28
Sea—Doornink 5 run (Herrera kick)
Den—FG Turner 27
Sea—Doornink 5 run (Herrera kick)
Den—Armstrong 2 run (Turner kick)
Sea—FG Herrera 22
Sea—McCullum 13 pass from Zorn (Herrera kick)
Sea—Smith 1 run (Herrera kick)
Den—Studdard 2 pass from Morton (Turner kick)
Den—Moses 11 pass from Morton (Turner kick)
Den—Upchurch 35 pass from Morton (Turner kick)
Den—Lytle 1 run (kick failed)

	Sea.	Den.
First Downs	22	23
Total Yards	350	344
Yards Rushing	153	90
Yards Passing	197	254
Turnovers	4	3

From 24 points behind to win:
September 23, 1979, at Cincinnati

Houston	0	10	17	0	3	— 30
Cincinnati	14	10	0	3	0	— 27

Cin —Johnson 1 run (Bahr kick)
Cin —Alexander 2 run (Bahr kick)
Cin —Johnson 1 run (Bahr kick)
Cin —FG Bahr 52
Hou—Burrough 35 pass from Pastorini (Fritsch kick)
Hou—FG Fritsch 33
Hou—Campbell 8 run (Fritsch kick)
Hou—Caster 22 pass from Pastorini (Fritsch kick)
Hou—FG Fritsch 47
Cin —FG Bahr 55
Hou—FG Fritsch 29

	Hou.	Cin.
First Downs	19	21
Total Yards	361	265
Yards Rushing	177	165
Yards Passing	184	100
Turnovers	3	2

From 24 points behind to win:
November 22, 1982, at Los Angeles

San Diego	10	14	0	0	— 24
L.A. Raiders	0	7	14	7	— 28

SD —FG Benirschke 19
SD —Scales 29 pass from Fouts (Benirschke kick)
SD —Muncie 2 run (Benirschke kick)
SD —Muncie 1 run (Benirschke kick)
Raiders—Christensen 1 pass from Plunkett (Bahr kick)
Raiders—Allen 3 run (Bahr kick)
Raiders—Allen 6 run (Bahr kick)
Raiders—Hawkins 1 run (Bahr kick)

	S.D.	Raiders
First Downs	26	23
Total Yards	411	326
Yards Rushing	72	181
Yards Passing	339	145
Turnovers	4	2

From 24 points behind to win:
September 26, 1988, at Denver

L.A. Raiders	0	0	14	13	3	— 30
Denver	7	17	0	3	0	— 27

Den —Dorsett 1 run (Karlis kick)
Den —Dorsett 1 run (Karlis kick)
Den —Sewell 7 pass from Elway (Karlis kick)
Den —FG Karlis 39
Raiders—Smith 40 pass from Schroeder (Bahr kick)
Raiders—Smith 42 pass from Schroeder (Bahr kick)
Raiders—FG Bahr 28
Raiders—Allen 4 run (Bahr kick)
Den —FG Karlis 25
Raiders—FG Bahr 44
Raiders—FG Bahr 35

	Raiders	Den.
First Downs	20	23
Total Yards	363	398
Yards Rushing	128	189
Yards Passing	235	209
Turnovers	1	5

Postseason Games

From 20 points behind to win:
Western Conference Playoff Game
December 22, 1957, at San Francisco

Detroit	0	7	14	10 — 31
San Francisco	14	10	3	0 — 27

SF —Owens 34 pass from Tittle (Soltau kick)
SF —McElhenny 47 pass from Tittle (Soltau kick)
Det—Junker 4 pass from Rote (Martin kick)
SF —Wilson 12 pass from Tittle (Soltau kick)
SF —FG Soltau 25
SF —FG Soltau 10
Det—Tracy 2 run (Martin kick)
Det—Tracy 58 run (Martin kick)
Det—Gedman 3 run (Martin kick)
Det—FG Martin 14

	Det.	S.F.
First Downs	22	20
Total Yards	324	351
Yards Rushing	129	127
Yards Passing	195	224
Turnovers	5	4

From 18 points behind to win:
NFC Divisional Playoff Game
December 23, 1972, at San Francisco

Dallas	3	10	0	17 — 30
San Francisco	7	14	7	0 — 28

SF —Washington 97 kickoff return (Gossett kick)
Dall —FG Fritsch 37
SF —Schreiber 1 run (Gossett kick)
SF —Schreiber 1 run (Gossett kick)
Dall —FG Fritsch 45
Dall —Alworth 28 pass from Morton (Fritsch kick)
SF —Schreiber 1 run (Gossett kick)
Dall —FG Fritsch 27
Dall —Parks 20 pass from Staubach (Fritsch kick)
Dall —Sellers 10 pass from Staubach (Fritsch kick)

	Dall.	S.F.
First Downs	22	13
Total Yards	402	255
Yards Rushing	165	105
Yards Passing	237	150
Turnovers	5	3

From 18 points behind to win:
AFC Divisional Playoff Game
January 4, 1986, at Miami

Cleveland	7	7	7	0 — 21
Miami	3	0	14	7 — 24

Mia —FG Reveiz 51
Clev—Newsome 16 pass from Kosar (Bahr kick)
Clev—Byner 21 run (Bahr kick)
Clev—Byner 66 run (Bahr kick)
Mia —Moore 6 pass from Marino (Reveiz kick)
Mia —Davenport 31 run (Reveiz kick)
Mia —Davenport 1 run (Reveiz kick)

	Clev.	Mia.
First Downs	17	20
Total Yards	313	330
Yards Rushing	251	92
Yards Passing	62	238
Turnovers	1	1

From 14 points behind to win:
NFC Divisional Playoff Game
January 3, 1981, at Philadelphia

Minnesota	7	7	2	0 — 16
Philadelphia	0	7	14	10 — 31

Minn —S. White 30 pass from Kramer (Danmeier kick)
Minn —Brown 1 run (Danmeier kick)
Phil —Carmichael 9 pass from Jaworski (Franklin kick)
Phil —Montgomery 8 run (Franklin kick)
Minn —Safety, Jaworski tackled in end zone by Martin and Blair
Phil —Montgomery 5 run (Franklin kick)
Phil —FG Franklin 33
Phil —Harrington 2 run (Franklin kick)

	Minn.	Phil.
First Downs	14	24
Total Yards	215	305
Yards Rushing	36	126
Yards Passing	179	179
Turnovers	8	3

From 14 points behind to win:
NFC Divisional Playoff Game
January 4, 1981, at Atlanta

Dallas	3	7	0	20 — 30
Atlanta	10	7	7	3 — 27

Atl —FG Mazzetti 38
Atl —Jenkins 60 pass from Bartkowski (Mazzetti kick)
Dall —FG Septien 38
Dall —DuPree 5 pass from D. White (Mazzetti kick)
Atl —Cain 1 run (Mazzetti kick)
Atl —Andrews 5 pass from Bartkowski (Mazzetti kick)
Dall —Newhouse 1 run (Septien kick)
Atl —FG Mazzetti 34
Dall —D. Pearson 14 pass from D. White (Septien kick)
Dall —D. Pearson 23 pass from D. White (pass failed)

	Dall.	Atl.
First Downs	22	18
Total Yards	422	371
Yards Rushing	112	86
Yards Passing	310	283
Turnovers	2	2

From 14 points behind to win:
NFC Divisional Playoff Game
January 10, 1988, at Chicago

Washington	0	14	7	0 — 21
Chicago	7	7	3	0 — 17

Chi —Thomas 2 run (Butler kick)
Chi —Morris 14 pass from McMahon (Butler kick)
Wash —Rogers 3 run (Haji-Sheikh kick)
Wash —Didier 18 pass from Williams (Haji-Sheikh kick)
Wash —Green 52 punt return (Haji-Sheikh kick)
Chi —FG Butler 25

	Wash.	Chi.
First Downs	17	15
Total Yards	272	280
Yards Rushing	72	110
Yards Passing	200	170
Turnovers	2	3

Records of NFL Divisions in Out-of-Division Games 1978–88

Since 1978, teams in a five-team division have been scheduled for eight games against out-of-division opponents; teams in a four-team division have been scheduled for 10 such games. These charts indicate the annual records for each division's teams in games against teams from other divisions:

NFC East

	W	L	T	Pct.	Pos.
1978	21	19	0	.525	2T
1979	23	17	0	.575	3
1980	19	21	0	.475	4
1981	26	14	0	.650	1
1982	13	6	0	.684	1
1983	23	17	0	.575	1
1984	24	15	1	.613	2
1985	22	18	0	.550	2
1986	23	17	0	.575	1T
1987	18	17	0	.514	3T
1988	17	23	0	.425	4
Totals	229	184	1	.554	2

NFC Central

	W	L	T	Pct.	Pos.
1978	16	24	0	.400	6
1979	14	26	0	.350	5
1980	16	24	0	.400	6
1981	18	22	0	.450	4T
1982	12	12	1	.500	3T
1983	15	25	0	.375	6
1984	11	28	1	.288	6
1985	19	21	0	.475	4
1986	14	26	0	.350	6
1987	14	24	1	.372	6
1988	16	24	0	.400	5
Totals	165	256	3	.393	6

NFC West

	W	L	T	Pct.	Pos.
1978	18	22	0	.450	5
1979	13	27	0	.325	6
1980	18	22	0	.450	5
1981	18	22	0	.450	4T
1982	7	15	0	.318	6
1983	22	18	0	.550	2T
1984	24	16	0	.600	3
1985	18	22	0	.450	5
1986	23	17	0	.575	1T
1987	23	15	0	.605	1
1988	23	17	0	.575	3
Totals	207	213	0	.493	4

AFC East

	W	L	T	Pct.	Pos.
1978	20	20	0	.500	4
1979	19	21	0	.475	4
1980	20	20	0	.500	3
1981	16	24	0	.400	6
1982	10	10	1	.500	3T
1983	22	18	0	.550	2T
1984	16	24	0	.400	4
1985	21	19	0	.475	3
1986	16	24	0	.400	5
1987	18	17	0	.514	3T
1988	24	15	1	.613	2
Totals	202	212	2	.488	5

AFC Central

	W	L	T	Pct.	Pos.
1978	24	16	0	.600	1
1979	24	16	0	.600	2
1980	25	15	0	.625	1
1981	20	20	0	.500	3
1982	10	10	0	.500	3T
1983	16	24	0	.400	5
1984	13	27	0	.325	5
1985	15	25	0	.375	6
1986	21	19	0	.525	4
1987	19	17	0	.528	2
1988	25	15	0	.625	1
Totals	212	204	0	.510	3

AFC West

	W	L	T	Pct.	Pos.
1978	21	19	0	.525	2T
1979	27	13	0	.675	1
1980	22	18	0	.550	2
1981	22	18	0	.550	2
1982	12	11	0	.522	2
1983	22	18	0	.550	2T
1984	31	9	0	.775	1
1985	25	15	0	.625	1
1986	23	17	0	.575	1T
1987	17	19	1	.473	5
1988	14	25	1	.363	6
Totals	236	182	2	.564	1

Composite Standings for 11 Seasons

	W	L	T	Pct.
AFC West	236	182	2	.564
NFC East	229	184	1	.554
AFC Central	212	204	0	.510
NFC West	207	213	0	.493
AFC East	202	212	2	.488
NFC Central	165	256	3	.393

Records of NFL Teams Since 1970 AFL-NFL Merger

AFC	W-L-T	Pct.	Division Titles	Playoff Berths	Post-season Record	Super Bowl Record
Miami	190- 88-2	.683	9	12	14-10	2-3
L.A. Raiders	181- 93-6	.659	8	12	16-9	3-0
Pittsburgh	167-112-1	.598	9	11	15-7	4-0
Denver	157-117-6	.570	5	7	6-7	0-3
Cincinnati	147-133-0	.525	4	6	4-6	0-2
Cleveland	146-132-2	.525	5	8	2-8	0-0
New England	139-141-0	.496	2	5	3-5	0-1
Seattle*	96-100-0	.490	1	4	3-4	0-0
San Diego	124-151-5	.451	3	4	3-4	0-0
N.Y. Jets	122-156-2	.439	0	4	3-4	0-0
Kansas City	118-156-6	.431	1	2	0-2	0-0
Indianapolis	119-159-2	.428	5	6	4-5	1-0
Houston	113-165-2	.406	0	5	6-5	0-0
Buffalo	111-167-2	.400	2	4	2-4	0-0

NFC	W-L-T	Pct.	Division Titles	Playoff Berths	Post-season Record	Super Bowl Record
Dallas	183- 97-0	.654	9	14	19-12	2-3
Washington	178-101-1	.638	4	10	13-8	2-2
L.A. Rams	173-103-4	.626	8	13	8-13	0-1
Minnesota	166-112-2	.596	9	12	11-12	0-3
San Francisco	150-127-3	.541	9	10	12-7	3-0
Chicago	146-133-1	.523	5	7	5-6	1-0
Phoenix	126-148-6	.460	2	3	0-3	0-0
Philadelphia	121-153-6	.442	2	5	3-5	0-1
Detroit	120-156-4	.435	1	3	0-3	0-0
N.Y. Giants	119-159-2	.429	1	4	6-3	1-0
Green Bay	112-160-8	.414	1	2	1-2	0-0
Atlanta	114-162-4	.413	1	3	1-3	0-0
New Orleans	100-176-4	.360	0	1	0-1	0-0
Tampa Bay*	57-138-1	.293	2	3	1-3	0-0

*entered NFL in 1976.

Indianapolis totals include Baltimore, 1970-83
L.A. Raiders totals include Oakland, 1970-81
Phoenix totals include St. Louis, 1970-87

Tie games before 1972 are not calculated in won-lost percentage.

In 1982, due to players' strike, the divisional format was abandoned. (L.A. Raiders and Washington won regular-season conference titles, not included in "Division Titles" totals listed above. Sixteen teams were awarded playoff berths, included in totals listed above.)

Longest Winning Streaks Since 1970

Regular-season games

16	Miami, 1971-73	(1 in 1971, 14 in 1972, 1 in 1973)
16	Miami, 1983-84	(5 in 1983, 11 in 1984)
14	Oakland, 1976-77	(10 in 1976, 4 in 1977)
13	Chicago, 1984-85	(1 in 1984, 12 in 1985)
13	Minnesota, 1974-75	(3 in 1974, 10 in 1975)
11	Pittsburgh, 1975	
11	Baltimore, 1975-76	(9 in 1975, 2 in 1976)
10	Miami, 1973	
10	Pittsburgh, 1976-77	(9 in 1976, 1 in 1977)
10	Denver, 1984	

NFL Playoff Appearances by Seasons

Team	Number of Seasons in Playoffs
Cleveland	21
Los Angeles Rams	21
New York Giants	20
Chicago	18
Dallas	18
Washington	16
Los Angeles Raiders	15
Minnesota	14
Green Bay	13
Miami	12
Pittsburgh	12
San Francisco	11
Indianapolis	11
Houston	10
Philadelphia	9
San Diego	9
Buffalo	8
Detroit	8
Denver	7
Cincinnati	6
Kansas City	6
New England	6
New York Jets	6
Phoenix	5
Seattle	4
Atlanta	3
Tampa Bay	3
New Orleans	1

Teams in Super Bowl Contention, 1978-88

	With 3 Weeks to Play	With 2 Weeks to Play	With 1 Week to Play
1988	21	18	15
1987	19	19	15
1986	19	17	14
1985	21	18	13
1984	18	14	13
1983	24	19	15
1982	20	17	12
1981	21	20	16
1980	20	14	12
1979	19	15	13
1978	20	17	12

Games Decided by 7 Points or Less and 3 Points or Less (1970-88)

	Games Decided by 7 Points or Less	Games Decided by 3 Points or Less
1970	58 of 182 (31.9%)	32 of 182 (17.6%)
1971	77 of 182 (42.3%)	34 of 182 (18.7%)
1972	71 of 182 (39.0%)	38 of 182 (20.9%)
1973	60 of 182 (32.9%)	28 of 182 (15.4%)
1974	91 of 182 (50.0%)	36 of 182 (19.8%)
1975	64 of 182 (35.1%)	35 of 182 (19.2%)
1976	72 of 196 (36.7%)	37 of 196 (18.9%)
1977	87 of 196 (44.3%)	35 of 196 (17.9%)
1978	108 of 224 (48.2%)	49 of 224 (21.9%)
1979	104 of 224 (46.4%)	51 of 224 (22.8%)
1980	108 of 224 (48.2%)	58 of 224 (25.9%)
1981	89 of 224 (39.7%)	59 of 224 (26.3%)
1982	60 of 126 (47.6%)	31 of 126 (24.6%)
1983	106 of 224 (47.3%)	54 of 224 (24.1%)
1984	96 of 224 (42.9%)	59 of 224 (26.3%)
1985	87 of 224 (38.8%)	38 of 224 (17.0%)
1986	106 of 224 (47.3%)	47 of 224 (21.0%)
1987	98 of 210 (46.7%)	40 of 210 (19.0%)
1988	113 of 224 (50.4%)	62 of 224 (27.7%)

1988 Records of Teams in Games Decided by 7 Points or Less and 3 Points or Less

AFC	7 Points or Less	3 Points or Less
Buffalo (12-4)	5-2	5-1
Cincinnati (12-4)	5-3	1-1
Cleveland (10-6)	6-4	2-0
Denver (8-8)	2-4	1-2
Houston (10-6)	4-3	3-2
Indianapolis (8-8)	6-4	4-1
Kansas City (4-11-1)	4-7-1	2-4-1
Los Angeles Raiders (7-9)	4-4	2-1
Miami (6-10)	4-5	2-4
New England (9-7)	6-3	3-3
New York Jets (8-7-1)	4-3-1	0-2-1
Pittsburgh (5-11)	3-5	2-2
San Diego (6-10)	3-3	2-2
Seattle (9-7)	5-3	2-2
NFC		
Atlanta (5-11)	3-4	1-2
Chicago (12-4)	3-1	2-1
Dallas (3-13)	3-6	1-5
Detroit (4-12)	1-6	1-3
Green Bay (4-12)	0-5	0-3
Los Angeles Rams (10-6)	3-3	1-1
Minnesota (11-5)	3-2	3-2
New Orleans (10-6)	6-4	3-4
New York Giants (10-6)	6-4	4-1
Philadelphia (10-6)	5-5	2-3
Phoenix (8-8)	4-3	1-1
San Francisco (10-6)	5-4	4-3
Tampa Bay (5-11)	4-7	3-3
Washington (7-9)	5-5	4-2

Super Bowl Champions Who Did Not Make Playoffs The Following Year

Washington—Super Bowl XXII champions did not make playoffs in 1988 season.

N.Y. Giants—Super Bowl XXI champions did not make playoffs in the 1987 season.

San Francisco—Super Bowl XVI champions did not make playoffs in the 1982 season.

Oakland—Super Bowl XV champions did not make playoffs in the 1981 season.

Pittsburgh—Super Bowl XIV champions did not make playoffs in the 1980 season.

Kansas City—Super Bowl IV champions did not make playoffs in the 1970 season.

Green Bay—Super Bowl II champions did not make playoffs in the 1968 season.

HISTORY

The Professional Football Hall of Fame is located in Canton, Ohio, site of the organizational meeting on September 17, 1920, from which the National Football League evolved. The NFL recognized Canton as the Hall of Fame site on April 27, 1961. Canton area individuals, foundations, and companies donated almost $400,000 in cash and services to provide funds for the construction of the original two-building complex, which was dedicated on September 7, 1963. The original Hall of Fame complex was almost doubled in size with the completion of a $620,000 expansion project that was dedicated on May 10, 1971. A second expansion project was completed on November 20, 1978. It now features four exhibition areas and a theater twice the size of the original one.

The Hall represents the sport of pro football in many ways—through four large and colorful exhibition galleries, in the twin enshrinement halls, with numerous fan-participation electronic devices, a research library, and an NFL gift shop.

In recent years, the Pro Football Hall of Fame has become an extremely popular tourist attraction. At the end of 1988, a total of 4,450,038 fans had visited the Pro Football Hall of Fame.

New members of the Pro Football Hall of Fame are elected annually by a 30-member National Board of Selectors, made up of media representatives from every league city, one at-large representative, and the president of the Pro Football Writers of America. Between four and seven new members are elected each year. An affirmative vote of approximately 80 percent is needed for election.

Any fan may nominate any eligible player or contributor simply by writing to the Pro Football Hall of Fame. Players must be retired five years to be eligible, while a coach need only to be retired with no time limit specified. Contributors (administrators, owners, *et al.*) may be elected while they are still active.

The charter class of 17 enshrinees was elected in 1963 and the honor roll now stands at 148 with the election of a four-man class in 1989. That class consists of Mel Blount, Terry Bradshaw, Art Shell, and Willie Wood.

Roster of Members

HERB ADDERLEY
Defensive back. 6-1, 200. Born in Philadelphia, Pennsylvania, June 8, 1939. Michigan State. Inducted in 1980. 1961-69 Green Bay Packers, 1970-72 Dallas Cowboys.

LANCE ALWORTH
Wide receiver. 6-0, 184. Born in Houston, Texas, August 3, 1940. Arkansas. Inducted in 1978. 1962-70 San Diego Chargers, 1971-72 Dallas Cowboys.

DOUG ATKINS
Defensive end. 6-8, 275. Born in Humboldt, Tennessee, May 8, 1930. Tennessee. Inducted in 1982. 1953-54 Cleveland Browns, 1955-66 Chicago Bears, 1967-69 New Orleans Saints.

MORRIS (RED) BADGRO
End. 6-0, 190. Born in Orilla, Washington, December 1, 1902. Southern California. Inducted in 1981. 1927 New York Yankees, 1930-35 New York Giants, 1936 Brooklyn Dodgers.

CLIFF BATTLES
Halfback. 6-1, 201. Born in Akron, Ohio, May 1, 1910. Died April 28, 1981. West Virginia Wesleyan. Inducted in 1968. 1932 Boston Braves, 1933-36 Boston Redskins, 1937 Washington Redskins.

SAMMY BAUGH
Quarterback. 6-2, 180. Born in Temple, Texas, March 17, 1914. Texas Christian. Inducted in 1963. 1937-52 Washington Redskins.

CHUCK BEDNARIK
Center-linebacker. 6-3, 230. Born in Bethlehem, Pennsylvania, May 1, 1925. Pennsylvania. Inducted in 1967. 1949-62 Philadelphia Eagles.

BERT BELL
Team owner. Commissioner. Born in Philadelphia, Pennsylvania, February 25, 1895. Died October 11, 1959. Pennsylvania. Inducted in 1963. 1933-40 Philadelphia Eagles, 1941-42 Pittsburgh Steelers, 1943 Phil-Pitt, 1944-46 Pittsburgh Steelers. Commissioner, 1946-59.

BOBBY BELL
Linebacker. 6-4, 225. Born in Shelby, North Carolina, June 17, 1940. Minnesota. Inducted in 1983. 1963-74 Kansas City Chiefs.

RAYMOND BERRY
End. 6-2, 187. Born in Corpus Christi, Texas, February 27, 1933. Southern Methodist. Inducted in 1973. 1955-67 Baltimore Colts.

CHARLES W. BIDWILL, SR.
Team owner. Born in Chicago, Illinois, September 16, 1895. Died April 19, 1947. Loyola of Chicago. Inducted in 1967. 1933-43 Chicago Cardinals, 1944 Card-Pitt, 1945-47 Chicago Cardinals.

FRED BILETNIKOFF
Wide receiver. 6-1, 190. Born in Erie, Pennsylvania, February 23, 1943. Florida State. Inducted in 1988. 1965-78 Oakland Raiders.

GEORGE BLANDA
Quarterback-kicker. 6-2, 215. Born in Youngwood, Pennsylvania, September 17, 1927. Kentucky. Inducted in 1981. 1949-58 Chicago Bears, 1950 Baltimore Colts, 1960-66 Houston Oilers, 1967-75 Oakland Raiders.

MEL BLOUNT
Cornerback. 6-3, 205. Born in Vidalia, Georgia, April 10, 1948. Southern University. Inducted in 1989. 1970-83 Pittsburgh Steelers.

TERRY BRADSHAW
Quarterback. 6-3, 210. Born in Shreveport, Louisiana, September 12, 1948. Louisiana Tech. Inducted in 1989. 1970-83 Pittsburgh Steelers.

JIM BROWN
Fullback. 6-2, 232. Born in St. Simons, Georgia, February 17, 1936. Syracuse. Inducted in 1971. 1957-65 Cleveland Browns.

PAUL BROWN
Coach. Born in Norwalk, Ohio, September 7, 1908. Miami, Ohio. Inducted in 1967. 1946-49 Cleveland Browns (AAFC), 1950-62 Cleveland Browns, 1968-75 Cincinnati Bengals.

ROOSEVELT BROWN
Tackle. 6-3, 255. Born in Charlottesville, Virginia, October 20, 1932. Morgan State. Inducted in 1975. 1953-65 New York Giants.

WILLIE BROWN
Defensive back. 6-1, 210. Born in Yazoo City, Mississippi, December 2, 1940. Grambling. Inducted in 1984. 1963-66 Denver Broncos, 1967-78 Oakland Raiders.

DICK BUTKUS
Linebacker. 6-3, 245. Born in Chicago, Illinois, December 9, 1942. Illinois. Inducted in 1979. 1965-73 Chicago Bears.

TONY CANADEO
Halfback. 5-11, 195. Born in Chicago, Illinois, May 5, 1919. Gonzaga. Inducted in 1974. 1941-44, 1946-52 Green Bay Packers.

JOE CARR
NFL president. Born in Columbus, Ohio, October 22, 1880. Died May 20, 1939. Did not attend college. Inducted in 1963. President, 1921-39 National Football League.

GUY CHAMBERLIN
End. Coach. 6-2, 210. Born in Blue Springs, Nebraska, January 16, 1894. Died April 4, 1967. Nebraska. Inducted in 1965. 1920 Decatur Staleys, 1921 Chicago Staleys, player-coach 1922-23 Canton Bulldogs, 1924 Cleveland Bulldogs, 1925-26 Frankford Yellow Jackets, 1927-28 Chicago Cardinals.

JACK CHRISTIANSEN
Defensive back. 6-1, 185. Born in Sublette, Kansas, December 20, 1928. Died June 29, 1986. Colorado State. Inducted in 1970. 1951-58 Detroit Lions.

EARL (DUTCH) CLARK
Quarterback. 6-0, 185. Born in Fowler, Colorado, October 11, 1906. Died August 5, 1978. Colorado College. Inducted in 1963. 1931-32 Portsmouth Spartans, 1934-38 Detroit Lions.

GEORGE CONNOR
Tackle-linebacker. 6-3, 240. Born in Chicago, Illinois, January 21, 1925. Holy Cross, Notre Dame. Inducted in 1975. 1948-55 Chicago Bears.

JIMMY CONZELMAN
Quarterback. Coach. Team owner. 6-0, 180. Born in St. Louis, Missouri, March 6, 1898. Died July 31, 1970. Washington, Missouri. Inducted in 1964. 1920 Decatur Staleys, 1921-22 Rock Island, Ill., Independents, 1923-24 Milwaukee Badgers; owner-coach, 1925-26 Detroit Panthers; player-coach 1927-29, coach 1930 Providence Steam Roller; coach, 1940-42 Chicago Cardinals, 1946-48 Chicago Cardinals.

LARRY CSONKA
Running back. 6-3, 235. Born in Stow, Ohio, December 25, 1946. Syracuse. Inducted in 1987. Miami Dolphins 1968-74, 1979, New York Giants 1976-78.

WILLIE DAVIS
Defensive end. 6-3, 245. Born in Lisbon, Louisiana, July 24, 1934. Grambling. Inducted in 1981. 1958-59 Cleveland Browns, 1960-69 Green Bay Packers.

LEN DAWSON
Quarterback. 6-0, 190. Born in Alliance, Ohio, June 20, 1935. Purdue. Inducted in 1987. Pittsburgh Steelers 1957-59, Cleveland Browns 1960-61, Dallas Texans 1962, Kansas City Chiefs 1963-75.

MIKE DITKA
Tight end. 6-3, 225. Born in Carnegie, Pennsylvania, October 18, 1939. Pittsburgh. Inducted in 1988. 1961-66 Chicago Bears, 1967-68 Philadelphia Eagles, 1969-72 Dallas Cowboys.

ART DONOVAN
Defensive tackle. 6-3, 265. Born in Bronx, New York, June 5, 1925. Boston College. Inducted in 1968. 1950 Baltimore Colts, 1951 New York Yanks, 1952 Dallas Texans, 1953-61 Baltimore Colts.

JOHN (PADDY) DRISCOLL
Quarterback. 5-11, 160. Born in Evanston, Illinois, January 11, 1896. Died June 29, 1968. Northwestern. Inducted in 1965. 1920 Decatur Staleys, 1920-25 Chicago Cardinals, 1926-29 Chicago Bears. Coach, 1956-57 Chicago Bears.

BILL DUDLEY
Halfback. 5-10, 176. Born in Bluefield, Virginia, December 24, 1921. Virginia. Inducted in 1966. 1942, 1945-46 Pittsburgh Steelers, 1947-49 Detroit Lions, 1950-51, 1953 Washington Redskins.

GLEN (TURK) EDWARDS
Tackle. 6-2, 260. Born in Mold, Washington, September 28, 1907. Died January 12, 1973. Washington State. Inducted in 1969. 1932 Boston Braves, 1933-36 Boston Redskins, 1937-40 Washington Redskins.

WEEB EWBANK
Coach. Born in Richmond, Indiana, May 6, 1907. Miami, Ohio. Inducted in 1978. 1954-62 Baltimore Colts, 1963-73 New York Jets.

TOM FEARS
End. 6-2, 215. Born in Los Angeles, California, December 3, 1923. Santa Clara, UCLA. Inducted in 1970. 1948-56 Los Angeles Rams.

RAY FLAHERTY
End. Coach. Born in Spokane, Washington, September 1, 1904. Gonzaga. Inducted in 1976. 1926 Los Angeles Wildcats (AFL), 1927-28 New York Yankees, 1928-29, 1931-35 New York Giants. Coach, 1936 Boston Redskins, 1937-42 Washington Redskins, 1946-48 New York Yankees (AAFC), 1949 Chicago Hornets (AAFC).

LEN FORD
End. 6-5, 260. Born in Washington,

D.C., February 18, 1926. Died March 14, 1972. Michigan. Inducted in 1976. 1948-49 Los Angeles Dons (AAFC), 1950-57 Cleveland Browns, 1958 Green Bay Packers.

DAN FORTMANN
Guard. 6-0, 207. Born in Pearl River, New York, April 11, 1916. Colgate. Inducted in 1965. 1936-43 Chicago Bears.

FRANK GATSKI
Center. 6-3, 240. Born in Farmington, West Virginia, March 13, 1922. Marshall, Auburn. Inducted in 1985. 1946-49 Cleveland Browns (AAFC), 1950-56 Cleveland Browns, 1957 Detroit Lions.

BILL GEORGE
Linebacker. 6-2, 230. Born in Waynesburg, Pennsylvania, October 27, 1930. Died September 30, 1982. Wake Forest. Inducted in 1974. 1952-65 Chicago Bears, 1966 Los Angeles Rams.

FRANK GIFFORD
Halfback. 6-1, 195. Born in Santa Monica, California, August 16, 1930. Southern California. Inducted in 1977. 1952-60, 1962-64 New York Giants.

SID GILLMAN
Coach. Born in Minneapolis, Minnesota, October 26, 1911. Ohio State. Inducted in 1983. 1955-59 Los Angeles Rams, 1960 Los Angeles Chargers, 1961-69 San Diego Chargers, 1973-74 Houston Oilers.

OTTO GRAHAM
Quarterback. 6-1, 195. Born in Waukegan, Illinois, December 6, 1921. Northwestern. Inducted in 1965. 1946-49 Cleveland Browns (AAFC), 1950-55 Cleveland Browns.

HAROLD (RED) GRANGE
Halfback. 6-0, 185. Born in Forksville, Pennsylvania, June 13, 1903. Illinois. Inducted in 1963. 1925 Chicago Bears, 1926 New York Yankees (AFL), 1927 New York Yankees, 1929-34 Chicago Bears.

JOE GREENE
Defensive tackle. 6-4, 260. Born in Temple, Texas, September 24, 1946. North Texas State. Inducted in 1987. 1969-81 Pittsburgh Steelers.

FORREST GREGG
Tackle. 6-4, 250. Born in Birthright, Texas, October 18, 1933. Southern Methodist. Inducted in 1977. 1956, 1958-70 Green Bay Packers, 1971 Dallas Cowboys.

LOU GROZA
Tackle-kicker. 6-3, 250. Born in Martin's Ferry, Ohio, January 25, 1924. Ohio State. Inducted in 1974. 1946-49 Cleveland Browns (AAFC), 1950-59, 1961-67 Cleveland Browns.

JOE GUYON
Halfback. 6-1, 180. Born in Mahnomen, Minnesota, November 26, 1892. Died November 27, 1971. Carlisle, Georgia Tech. Inducted in 1966. 1920 Canton Bulldogs, 1921 Cleveland Indians, 1922-23 Oorang Indians, 1924 Rock Island, Ill., Independents, 1924-25 Kansas City Cowboys, 1927 New York Giants.

GEORGE HALAS
End. Coach. Team owner. Born in Chicago, Illinois, February 2, 1895. Died October 31, 1983. Illinois. Inducted in 1963. 1920 Decatur Staleys, 1921 Chicago Staleys, 1922-29 Chicago Bears; coach, 1933-42, 1946-55, 1958-67 Chicago Bears.

JACK HAM
Linebacker. 6-1, 225. Born in Johnstown, Pennsylvania, December 23, 1948. Penn State. Inducted in 1988. 1971-82 Pittsburgh Steelers.

ED HEALEY
Tackle. 6-3, 220. Born in Indian Orchard, Massachusetts, December 28, 1894. Died December 9, 1978. Dartmouth. Inducted in 1964. 1920-22 Rock Island, Ill., Independents, 1922-27 Chicago Bears.

MEL HEIN
Center. 6-2, 225. Born in Redding, California, August 22, 1909. Washington State. Inducted in 1963. 1931-45 New York Giants.

WILBUR (PETE) HENRY
Tackle. 6-0, 250. Born in Mansfield, Ohio, October 31, 1897. Died February 7, 1952. Washington & Jefferson. Inducted in 1963. 1920-23, 1925-26 Canton Bulldogs, 1927 New York Giants, 1927-28 Pottsville Maroons.

ARNIE HERBER
Quarterback. 6-1, 200. Born in Green Bay, Wisconsin, April 2, 1910. Died October 14, 1969. Wisconsin, Regis College. Inducted in 1966. 1930-40 Green Bay Packers, 1944-45 New York Giants.

BILL HEWITT
End. 5-11, 191. Born in Bay City, Michigan, October 8, 1909. Died January 14, 1947. Michigan. Inducted in 1971. 1932-36 Chicago Bears, 1937-39 Philadelphia Eagles, 1943 Phil-Pitt.

CLARKE HINKLE
Fullback. 5-11, 201. Born in Toronto, Ohio, April 10, 1909. Died November 9, 1988. Bucknell. Inducted in 1964. 1932-41 Green Bay Packers.

ELROY (CRAZYLEGS) HIRSCH
Halfback-end. 6-2, 190. Born in Wausau, Wisconsin, June 17, 1923. Wisconsin, Michigan. Inducted in 1968. 1946-48 Chicago Rockets (AAFC), 1949-57 Los Angeles Rams.

PAUL HORNUNG
Halfback. 6-2, 220. Born in Louisville, Kentucky, December 23, 1935. Notre Dame. Inducted in 1986. 1957-62, 1964-66 Green Bay Packers.

KEN HOUSTON
Safety. 6-3, 198. Born in Lufkin, Texas, November 12, 1944. Prairie View A&M. Inducted in 1986. 1967-72 Houston Oilers, 1973-80 Washington Redskins.

CAL HUBBARD
Tackle. 6-5, 250. Born in Keytesville, Missouri, October 31, 1900. Died October 17, 1977. Centenary, Geneva. Inducted in 1963. 1927-28 New York Giants, 1929-33, 1935 Green Bay Packers, 1936 New York Giants, 1936 Pittsburgh Pirates.

SAM HUFF
Linebacker. 6-1, 230. Born in Morgantown, West Virginia, October 4, 1934. West Virginia. Inducted in 1982. 1956-63 New York Giants, 1964-67, 1969 Washington Redskins.

LAMAR HUNT
Team owner. Born in El Dorado, Arkansas, August 2, 1932. Southern Methodist. Inducted in 1972. 1960-62 Dallas Texans, 1963-88 Kansas City Chiefs.

DON HUTSON
End. 6-1, 180. Born in Pine Bluff, Arkansas, January 31, 1913. Alabama. Inducted in 1963. 1935-45 Green Bay Packers.

JOHN HENRY JOHNSON
Fullback. 6-2, 225. Born in Waterproof, Louisiana, November 24, 1929. St. Mary's, Arizona State. Inducted in 1987. San Francisco 49ers 1954-56, Detroit Lions 1957-59, Pittsburgh Steelers 1960-65, Houston Oilers 1966.

DAVID (DEACON) JONES
Defensive end. 6-5, 250. Born in Eatonville, Florida, December 9, 1938. Mississippi Vocational. Inducted in 1980. 1961-71 Los Angeles Rams, 1972-73 San Diego Chargers, 1974 Washington Redskins.

SONNY JURGENSEN
Quarterback. 6-0, 203. Born in Wilmington, North Carolina, August 23, 1934. Duke. Inducted in 1983. 1957-63 Philadelphia Eagles, 1964-74 Washington Redskins.

WALT KIESLING
Guard. Coach. 6-2, 245. Born in St. Paul, Minnesota, March 27, 1903. Died March 2, 1962. St. Thomas (Minnesota). Inducted in 1966. 1926-27 Duluth Eskimos, 1928 Pottsville Maroons, 1929-33 Chicago Cardinals, 1934 Chicago Bears, 1935-36 Green Bay Packers, 1937-38 Pittsburgh Pirates; coach, 1939-42 Pittsburgh Steelers; co-coach, 1943 Phil-Pitt, 1944 Card-Pitt; coach, 1954-56 Pittsburgh Steelers.

FRANK (BRUISER) KINARD
Tackle. 6-1, 210. Born in Pelahatchie, Mississippi, October 23, 1914. Died September 7, 1985. Mississippi. Inducted in 1971. 1938-44 Brooklyn Dodgers-Tigers, 1946-47 New York Yankees (AAFC).

EARL (CURLY) LAMBEAU
Coach. Born in Green Bay, Wisconsin, April 9, 1898. Died June 1, 1965. Notre Dame. Inducted in 1963. 1919-49 Green Bay Packers, 1950-51 Chicago Cardinals, 1952-53 Washington Redskins.

DICK (NIGHT TRAIN) LANE
Defensive back. 6-2, 210. Born in Austin, Texas, April 16, 1928. Scottsbluff Junior College. Inducted in 1974. 1952-53 Los Angeles Rams, 1954-59 Chicago Cardinals, 1960-65 Detroit Lions.

JIM LANGER
Center. 6-2, 255. Born in Little Falls, Minnesota, May 16, 1948. South Dakota State. Inducted in 1987. Miami Dolphins 1970-79, Minnesota Vikings 1980-81.

WILLIE LANIER
Linebacker. 6-1, 245. Born in Clover, Virginia, August 21, 1945. Morgan State. Inducted in 1986. 1967-77 Kansas City Chiefs.

YALE LARY
Defensive back-punter. 5-11, 189. Born in Fort Worth, Texas, November 24, 1930. Texas A&M. Inducted in 1979. 1952-53, 1956-64 Detroit Lions.

DANTE LAVELLI
End. 6-0, 199. Born in Hudson, Ohio, February 23, 1923. Ohio State. Inducted in 1975. 1946-49 Cleveland Browns (AAFC), 1950-56 Cleveland Browns.

BOBBY LAYNE
Quarterback. 6-2, 190. Born in Santa Anna, Texas, December 19, 1926. Died December 1, 1986. Texas. Inducted in 1967. 1948 Chicago Bears, 1949 New York Bulldogs, 1950-58 Detroit Lions, 1958-62 Pittsburgh Steelers.

ALPHONSE (TUFFY) LEEMANS
Fullback. 6-0, 200. Born in Superior, Wisconsin, November 12, 1912. Died January 19, 1979. George Washington. Inducted in 1978. 1936-43 New York Giants.

BOB LILLY
Defensive tackle. 6-5, 260. Born in Olney, Texas, July 26, 1939. Texas Christian. Inducted in 1980. 1961-74 Dallas Cowboys.

VINCE LOMBARDI
Coach. Born in Brooklyn, New York, June 11, 1913. Died September 3, 1970. Fordham. Inducted in 1971. 1959-67 Green Bay Packers, 1969 Washington Redskins.

SID LUCKMAN
Quarterback. 6-0, 195. Born in Brooklyn, New York, November 21, 1916. Columbia. Inducted in 1965. 1939-50 Chicago Bears.

ROY (LINK) LYMAN
Tackle. 6-2, 252. Born in Table Rock, Nebraska, November 30, 1898. Died December 16, 1972. Nebraska. Inducted in 1964. 1922-23, 1925 Canton Bulldogs, 1924 Cleveland Bulldogs, 1925 Frankford Yellow Jackets, 1926-28, 1930-31, 1933-34 Chicago Bears.

TIM MARA
Team owner. Born in New York, New York, July 29, 1887. Died February 17, 1959. Did not attend college. Inducted in 1963. 1925-59 New York Giants.

GINO MARCHETTI
Defensive end. 6-4, 245. Born in Smithers, West Virginia, January 2, 1927. San Francisco. Inducted in 1972. 1952 Dallas Texans, 1953-64, 1966 Baltimore Colts.

GEORGE PRESTON MARSHALL
Team owner. Born in Grafton, West Virginia, October 11, 1897. Died August 9, 1969. Randolph-Macon. Inducted in 1963. 1932 Boston Braves, 1933-36 Boston Redskins, 1937-69 Washington Redskins.

OLLIE MATSON
Halfback. 6-2, 220. Born in Trinity, Texas, May 1, 1930. San Francisco. Inducted in 1972. 1952, 1954-58 Chicago Cardinals, 1959-62 Los Angeles Rams, 1963 Detroit Lions, 1964-66 Philadelphia Eagles.

DON MAYNARD
Wide receiver. 6-1, 180. Born in Crosbyton, Texas, January 25, 1937. Texas Western. Inducted in 1987. New York Giants 1958, New York Titans 1960-62, New York Jets 1963-72, St. Louis Cardinals 1973.

GEORGE McAFEE
Halfback. 6-0, 177. Born in Ironton, Ohio, March 13, 1918. Duke. Inducted in 1966. 1940-41, 1945-50 Chicago Bears.

MIKE McCORMACK
Tackle. 6-4, 248. Born in Chicago, Illinois, June 21, 1930. Kansas. Inducted in 1984. 1951 New York Yanks, 1954-62 Cleveland Browns.

HUGH McELHENNY
Halfback. 6-1, 198. Born in Los Angeles, California, December 31, 1928. Washington. Inducted in 1970. 1952-60 San Francisco 49ers, 1961-62 Minnesota Vikings, 1963 New York Giants, 1964 Detroit Lions.

JOHNNY BLOOD (McNALLY)
Halfback. 6-0, 185. Born in New Richmond, Wisconsin, November 27, 1903. Died November 28, 1985. St. John's (Minnesota). Inducted in 1963. 1925-26 Milwaukee Badgers, 1926-27 Duluth Eskimos, 1928 Pottsville Maroons, 1929-33 Green Bay Packers, 1934 Pittsburgh Pirates, 1935-36 Green Bay Packers; player-coach, 1937-39 Pittsburgh Pirates.

MIKE MICHALSKE
Guard. 6-0, 209. Born in Cleveland, Ohio, April 24, 1903. Died October 26, 1983. Penn State. Inducted in 1964. 1926 New York Yankees (AFL), 1927-28 New York Yankees, 1929-35, 1937 Green Bay Packers.

WAYNE MILLNER
End. 6-0, 191. Born in Roxbury, Massachusetts, January 31, 1913. Died November 19, 1976. Notre Dame. Inducted in 1968. 1936 Boston Redskins, 1937-41, 1945 Washington Redskins.

BOBBY MITCHELL
Running back-wide receiver. 6-0, 195. Born in Hot Springs, Arkansas, June 6, 1935. Illinois. Inducted in 1983. 1958-61 Cleveland Browns, 1962-68 Washington Redskins.

RON MIX
Tackle. 6-4, 250. Born in Los Angeles, California, March 10, 1938. Southern California. Inducted in 1979. 1960 Los Angeles Chargers, 1961-69 San Diego Chargers, 1971 Oakland Raiders.

LENNY MOORE
Back. 6-1, 198. Born in Reading, Pennsylvania, November 25, 1933. Penn State. Inducted in 1975. 1956-67 Baltimore Colts.

MARION MOTLEY
Fullback. 6-1, 238. Born in Leesburg, Georgia, June 5, 1920. South Carolina State, Nevada. Inducted in 1968. 1946-49 Cleveland Browns (AAFC), 1950-53 Cleveland Browns, 1955 Pittsburgh Steelers.

GEORGE MUSSO
Guard-tackle. 6-2, 270. Born in Collinsville, Illinois. April 8, 1910. Millikin. Inducted in 1982. 1933-44 Chicago Bears.

BRONKO NAGURSKI
Fullback. 6-2, 225. Born in Rainy River, Ontario, Canada, November 3, 1908. Minnesota. Inducted in 1963. 1930-37, 1943 Chicago Bears.

JOE NAMATH
Quarterback. 6-2, 200. Born in Beaver Falls, Pennsylvania, May 31, 1943. Alabama. Inducted in 1985. 1965-76 New York Jets, 1977 Los Angeles Rams.

EARLE (GREASY) NEALE
Coach. Born in Parkersburg, West Virginia, November 5, 1891. Died November 2, 1973. West Virginia Wesleyan. Inducted in 1969. 1941-42, 1944-50 Philadelphia Eagles; co-coach, Phil-Pitt 1943.

ERNIE NEVERS
Fullback. 6-1, 205. Born in Willow River, Minnesota, June 11, 1903. Died May 3, 1976. Stanford. Inducted in 1963. 1926-27 Duluth Eskimos, 1929-31 Chicago Cardinals.

RAY NITSCHKE
Linebacker. 6-3, 235. Born in Elmwood Park, Illinois, December 29, 1936. Illinois. Inducted in 1978. 1958-72 Green Bay Packers.

LEO NOMELLINI
Defensive tackle. 6-3, 264. Born in Lucca, Italy, June 19, 1924. Minnesota. Inducted in 1969. 1950-63 San Francisco 49ers.

MERLIN OLSEN
Defensive tackle. 6-5, 270. Born in Logan, Utah, September 15, 1940. Utah State. Inducted in 1982. 1962-76 Los Angeles Rams.

JIM OTTO
Center. 6-2, 255. Born in Wausau, Wisconsin, January 5, 1938. Miami. Inducted in 1980. 1960-74 Oakland Raiders.

STEVE OWEN
Tackle. Coach. 6-0, 235. Born in Cleo Springs, Oklahoma, April 21, 1898. Died May 17, 1964. Phillips. Inducted in 1966. 1924-25 Kansas City Cowboys, 1926-30 New York Giants; coach, 1931-53 New York Giants.

ALAN PAGE
Defensive tackle. 6-4, 225. Born in Canton, Ohio, August 7, 1945. Inducted in 1988. 1967-78 Minnesota Vikings, 1978-81 Chicago Bears.

CLARENCE (ACE) PARKER
Quarterback. 5-11, 168. Born in Portsmouth, Virginia, May 17, 1912. Duke. Inducted in 1972. 1937-41 Brooklyn Dodgers, 1945 Boston Yanks, 1946 New York Yankees (AAFC).

JIM PARKER
Guard-tackle. 6-3, 273. Born in Macon, Georgia, April 3, 1934. Ohio State. Inducted in 1973. 1957-67 Baltimore Colts.

JOE PERRY
Fullback. 6-0, 200. Born in Stevens, Arkansas, January 27, 1927. Compton Junior College. Inducted in 1969. 1948-49 San Francisco 49ers (AAFC), 1950-60, 1963 San Francisco 49ers, 1961-62 Baltimore Colts.

PETE PIHOS
End. 6-1, 210. Born in Orlando, Florida, October 22, 1923. Indiana. Inducted in 1970. 1947-55 Philadelphia Eagles.

HUGH (SHORTY) RAY
Supervisor of officials 1938-56. Born in Highland Park, Illinois, September 21, 1884. Died September 16, 1956. Illinois. Inducted in 1966.

DAN REEVES
Team owner. Born in New York, New York, June 30, 1912. Died April 15, 1971. Georgetown. Inducted in 1967. 1941-45 Cleveland Rams, 1946-71 Los Angeles Rams.

JIM RINGO
Center. 6-1, 235. Born in Orange, New Jersey, November 21, 1931. Syracuse. Inducted in 1981. 1953-63 Green Bay Packers, 1964-67 Philadelphia Eagles.

ANDY ROBUSTELLI
Defensive end. 6-0, 230. Born in Stamford, Connecticut, December 6, 1925. Arnold College. Inducted in 1971. 1951-55 Los Angeles Rams, 1956-64 New York Giants.

ART ROONEY
Team owner. Born in Coulterville, Pennsylvania, January 27, 1901. Died August 25, 1988. Georgetown, Duquesne. Inducted in 1964. 1933-40 Pittsburgh Pirates, 1941-42, 1949-88 Pittsburgh Steelers, 1943 Phil-Pitt, 1944 Card-Pitt.

PETE ROZELLE
Commissioner. Born in South Gate, California, March 1, 1926. San Francisco. Inducted in 1985. Commissioner 1960-89.

GALE SAYERS
Running back. 6-0, 200. Born in Wichita, Kansas, May 30, 1943. Kansas. Inducted in 1977. 1965-71 Chicago Bears.

JOE SCHMIDT
Linebacker. 6-0, 222. Born in Pittsburgh, Pennsylvania, January 19, 1932. Pittsburgh. Inducted in 1973. 1953-65 Detroit Lions.

ART SHELL
Tackle. 6-5, 285. Born in Charleston, South Carolina, November 25, 1946. Maryland State-Eastern Shore. Inducted in 1989. 1968-81 Oakland Raiders, 1982 Los Angeles Raiders.

O.J. SIMPSON
Running back. 6-1, 212. Born in San Francisco, California, July 9, 1947. Southern California. Inducted in 1985. 1969-77 Buffalo Bills, 1978-79 San Francisco 49ers.

BART STARR
Quarterback. 6-1, 200. Born in Montgomery, Alabama, January 9, 1934. Alabama. Inducted in 1977. 1956-71 Green Bay Packers; coach, 1975-83 Green Bay Packers.

ROGER STAUBACH
Quarterback. 6-3, 202. Born in Cincinnati, Ohio, February 5, 1942. Navy. Inducted in 1985. 1969-79 Dallas Cowboys.

ERNIE STAUTNER
Defensive tackle. 6-2, 235. Born in Prinzing-by-Cham, Bavaria, Germany, April 20, 1925. Boston College. Inducted in 1969. 1950-63 Pittsburgh Steelers.

KEN STRONG
Halfback. 5-11, 210. Born in New Haven, Connecticut, August 6, 1906. Died October 5, 1979. New York University. Inducted in 1967. 1929-32 Staten Island Stapletons, 1933-35, 1939, 1944-47 New York Giants, 1936-37 New York Yanks (AFL).

JOE STYDAHAR
Tackle. 6-4, 230. Born in Kaylor, Pennsylvania, March 3, 1912. Died March 23, 1977. West Virginia. Inducted in 1967. 1936-42, 1945-46 Chicago Bears.

FRAN TARKENTON
Quarterback. 6-0, 185. Born in Richmond, Virginia, February 3, 1940. Georgia. Inducted in 1986. 1961-66, 1972-78 Minnesota Vikings, 1967-71 New York Giants.

CHARLEY TAYLOR
Running back-wide receiver. 6-3, 210. Born in Grand Prairie, Texas, September 28, 1941. Arizona State. Inducted in 1984. 1964-75, 1977 Washington Redskins.

JIM TAYLOR
Fullback. 6-0, 216. Born in Baton Rouge, Louisiana, September 20, 1935. Louisiana State. Inducted in 1976. 1958-66 Green Bay Packers, 1967 New Orleans Saints.

JIM THORPE
Halfback. 6-1, 190. Born in Prague, Oklahoma, May 28, 1888. Died March 28, 1953. Carlisle. Inducted in 1963. 1915-17, 1919-20, 1926 Canton Bulldogs, 1921 Cleveland Indians, 1922-23 Oorang Indians, 1924 Rock Island, Ill., Independents, 1925 New York Giants, 1928 Chicago Cardinals.

Y.A. TITTLE
Quarterback. 6-0, 200. Born in Marshall, Texas, October 24, 1926. Louisiana State. Inducted in 1971. 1948-49 Baltimore Colts (AAFC), 1950 Baltimore Colts, 1951-60 San Francisco 49ers, 1961-64 New York Giants.

GEORGE TRAFTON
Center. 6-2, 235. Born in Chicago, Illinois, December 6, 1896. Died September 5, 1971. Notre Dame. Inducted in 1964. 1920 Decatur Staleys, 1921 Chicago Staleys, 1922-32 Chicago Bears.

CHARLEY TRIPPI
Halfback. 6-0, 185. Born in Pittston, Pennsylvania, December 14, 1922. Georgia. Inducted in 1968. 1947-55 Chicago Cardinals.

EMLEN TUNNELL
Safety. 6-1, 200. Born in Bryn Mawr, Pennsylvania, March 29, 1925. Died July 23, 1975. Toledo, Iowa. Inducted in 1967. 1948-58 New York Giants, 1959-61 Green Bay Packers.

CLYDE (BULLDOG) TURNER
Center. 6-2, 235. Born in Sweetwater, Texas, November 10, 1919. Hardin-Simmons. Inducted in 1966. 1940-52 Chicago Bears.

JOHNNY UNITAS
Quarterback. 6-1, 195. Born in Pittsburgh, Pennsylvania, May 7, 1933. Louisville. Inducted in 1979. 1956-72 Baltimore Colts, 1973 San Diego Chargers.

GENE UPSHAW
Guard. 6-5, 255. Born in Robstown, Texas, August 15, 1945. Texas A & I. Inducted in 1987. Oakland Raiders 1967-81.

NORM VAN BROCKLIN
Quarterback. 6-1, 190. Born in Eagle Butte, South Dakota, March 15, 1926. Died May 2, 1983. Oregon. Inducted in 1971. 1949-57 Los Angeles Rams, 1958-60 Philadelphia Eagles.

STEVE VAN BUREN
Halfback. 6-1, 200. Born in La Ceiba, Honduras, December 28, 1920. Louisiana State. Inducted in 1965. 1944-51 Philadelphia Eagles.

DOAK WALKER
Halfback. 5-10, 172. Born in Dallas, Texas, January 1, 1927. Southern Methodist. Inducted in 1986. 1950-55 Detroit Lions.

PAUL WARFIELD
Wide receiver. 6-0, 188. Born in Warren, Ohio, November 28, 1942. Ohio State. Inducted in 1983. 1964-69, 1976-77 Cleveland Browns, 1970-74 Miami Dolphins.

BOB WATERFIELD
Quarterback. 6-2, 200. Born in Elmira, New York, July 26, 1920. Died March 25, 1983. UCLA. Inducted in 1965. 1945 Cleveland Rams, 1946-52 Los Angeles Rams.

ARNIE WEINMEISTER
Defensive tackle. 6-4, 235. Born in Rhein, Saskatchewan, Canada, March 23, 1923. Washington. Inducted in 1984. 1948-49 New York Yankees (AAFC), 1950-53 New York Giants.

BILL WILLIS
Guard. 6-2, 215. Born in Columbus, Ohio, October 5, 1921. Ohio State. Inducted in 1977. 1946-49 Cleveland Browns (AAFC), 1950-53 Cleveland Browns.

LARRY WILSON
Safety. 6-0, 190. Born in Rigby, Idaho, March 24, 1938. Utah. Inducted in 1978. 1960-72 St. Louis Cardinals.

ALEX WOJCIECHOWICZ
Center. 6-0, 235. Born in South River, New Jersey, August 12, 1915. Fordham. Inducted in 1968. 1938-46 Detroit Lions, 1946-50 Philadelphia Eagles.

WILLIE WOOD
Safety. 5-10, 190. Born in Washington, D.C., December 23, 1936. Southern California. Inducted in 1989. 1960-71 Green Bay Packers.

A CHRONOLOGY OF PROFESSIONAL FOOTBALL

1869 Rutgers and Princeton played a college soccer football game, the first ever, November 6. The game used modified London Football Association rules. During the next seven years, rugby gained favor with the major eastern schools over soccer, and modern football began to develop from rugby.
1876 At the Massasoit convention, the first rules for American football were written. Walter Camp, who would become known as "the father of American football," first became involved with the game.
1892 In an era in which football was a major attraction of local athletic clubs, an intense competition between two Pittsburgh-area clubs, the Allegheny Athletic Association (AAA) and the Pittsburgh Athletic Club (PAC), led to the making of the first professional football player. Former Yale All-America guard William (Pudge) Heffelfinger was paid $500 by the AAA to play in a game against the PAC, becoming the first person to be paid to play football, November 12. The AAA won the game 4-0 when Heffelfinger picked up a PAC fumble and ran 35 yards for a touchdown.
1893 The Pittsburgh Athletic Club signed one of its players, probably halfback Grant Dibert, to the first known pro football contract, which covered all of the PAC's games for the year.
1895 John Brallier became the first football player to openly turn pro, accepting $10 and expenses to play for the Latrobe YMCA against the Jeannette Athletic Club.
1896 The Allegheny Athletic Association team fielded the first completely professional team for its abbreviated two-game season.
1897 The Latrobe Athletic Association football team went entirely professional, becoming the first team to play a full season with only professionals.
1898 A touchdown was changed from four points to five.
1899 Chris O'Brien formed a neighborhood team, which played under the name the Morgan Athletic Club, on the south side of Chicago. The team later became known as the Normals, then the Racine (for a street in Chicago) Cardinals, the Chicago Cardinals, the St. Louis Cardinals, and, in 1988, the Phoenix Cardinals. The team remains the oldest continuing operation in pro football.
1900 William C. Temple took over the team payments for the Duquesne Country and Athletic Club, becoming the first known individual club owner.
1902 Baseball's Philadelphia Athletics, managed by Connie Mack, and the Philadelphia Phillies formed professional football teams, joining the Pittsburgh Stars in the first attempt at a pro football league, named the National Football League. The Athletics won the first night football game ever played, 39-0 over Kanaweola AC at Elmira, New York, November 21.

All three teams claimed the pro championship for the year, but the league president, Dave Berry, named the Stars the champions. Pitcher Rube Waddell was with the Athletics, and pitcher Christy Mathewson a fullback for Pittsburgh.

The first World Series of pro football, actually a five-team tournament, was played among a team made up of players from both the Athletics and the Phillies, but simply named "New York;" the New York Knickerbockers; the Syracuse AC; the Warlow AC; and the Orange (New Jersey) AC at New York's original Madison Square Garden. New York and Syracuse played the first indoor football game before 3,000, December 28. Syracuse, with Glen (Pop) Warner at guard, won 6-0 and went on to win the tournament.
1903 The Franklin (Pa.) Athletic Club won the second and last World Series of pro football over the Oreos AC of Asbury Park, New Jersey; the Watertown Red and Blacks; and the Orange AC.

Pro football was popularized in Ohio when the Massillon Tigers, a strong amateur team, hired four Pittsburgh pros to play in the season-ending game against Akron. At the same time, pro football declined in the Pittsburgh area, and the emphasis on the pro game moved west from Pennsylvania to Ohio.
1904 A field goal was changed from five points to four.

Ohio had at least seven pro teams, with Massillon winning the Ohio Independent Championship, that is, the pro title. Talk surfaced about forming a state-wide league to end spiraling salaries brought about by constant bidding for players and to write universal rules for the game. The feeble attempt to start the league failed.

Halfback Charles Follis signed a contract with the Shelby AC, making him the first-known black pro football player.
1905 The Canton AC, later to become known as the Bulldogs, became a professional team. Massillon again won the Ohio League championship.
1906 The forward pass was legalized. The first authenticated pass completion in a pro game came on October 27, when George (Peggy) Parratt of Massillon threw a completion to Dan (Bullet) Riley in a victory over a combined Benwood-Moundsville team.

Archrivals Canton and Massillon, the two best pro teams in America, played twice, with Canton winning the first game but Massillon winning the second and the Ohio League championship. A betting scandal and the financial disaster wrought upon the two clubs by paying huge salaries caused a temporary decline in interest in pro football in the two cities and, somewhat, through Ohio.
1909 A field goal dropped from four points to three.
1912 A touchdown was increased from five points to six.

Jack Cusack revived a strong pro team in Canton.
1913 Jim Thorpe, a former football and track star at the Carlisle Indian School (Pa.) and a double gold medal winner at the 1912 Olympics in Stockholm, played for the Pine Village Pros in Indiana.
1915 Massillon again fielded a major team, reviving the old rivalry with Canton. Cusack signed Thorpe to play for Canton for $250 a game.
1916 With Thorpe and former Carlisle teammate Pete Calac starring, Canton went 9-0-1, won the Ohio League championship, and was acclaimed the pro football champion.
1917 Despite an upset by Massillon, Canton again won the Ohio League championship.
1919 Canton again won the Ohio League championship, despite the team having been turned over from Cusack to Ralph Hay. Thorpe and Calac were joined in the backfield by Joe Guyon.

Earl (Curly) Lambeau and George Calhoun organized the Green Bay Packers. Lambeau's employer at the Indian Packing Company provided $500 for equipment and allowed the team to use the company field for practices. The Packers went 10-1.
1920 Pro football was in a state of confusion due to three major problems: dramatically rising salaries; players continually jumping from one team to another following the highest offer; and the use of college players still enrolled in school. A league in which all the members would follow the same rules seemed the answer. An organizational meeting, at which the Akron Pros, Canton Bulldogs, Cleveland Indians, and Dayton Triangles were represented, was held in Canton, Ohio, August 20. This meeting resulted in the formation of the American Professional Football Conference.

A second organizational meeting was held in Canton, September 17. The teams were from four states—Akron, Canton, Cleveland, and Dayton from Ohio; the Hammond Pros and Muncie Flyers from Indiana; the Rochester Jeffersons from New York; and the Rock Island Independents, Decatur Staleys, and Racine Cardinals from Illinois. The name of the league was changed to the American Professional Football Association. Hoping to capitalize on his fame, the members elected Thorpe president; Stanley Cofall of Cleveland was elected vice president. A membership fee of $100 per team was charged to give an appearance of respectability, but no team ever paid it. Scheduling was left up to the teams, and there was a wide variation both in the overall number of games played and in the number played against APFA member teams.

Four other teams—the Buffalo All-Americans, Chicago Tigers, Columbus Panhandles, and Detroit Heralds—joined the league sometime during the year. On September 26, the first game featuring an APFA team was played at Rock Island's Douglas Park. A crowd of 800 watched the Independents defeat the St. Paul Ideals 48-0. A week later, October 3, the first game matching two APFA teams was held. At Triangle Park, Dayton defeated Columbus 14-0, with Lou Partlow of Dayton scoring the first touchdown in a game between Association teams. The same day, Rock Island defeated Muncie 45-0.

By the beginning of December, most of the teams in the APFA had abandoned their hopes for a championship, and some of them, including the Chicago Tigers and the Detroit Heralds, had finished their seasons, disbanded, and had their franchises canceled by the Association. Four teams—Akron, Buffalo, Canton, and Decatur—still had championship aspirations, but a series of late-season games among them left Akron as the only undefeated team in the Association. At one of these games, Akron sold tackle Bob Nash to Buffalo for $300 and five percent of the gate receipts—the first APFA player deal.
1921 At the league meeting in Akron, April 30, the championship of the 1920 season was awarded to the Akron Pros. The APFA was reorganized, with Joe Carr of the Columbus Panhandles named president and Carl Storck of Dayton secretary-treasurer. Carr moved the Association's headquarters to Columbus, drafted a league constitution and by-laws, gave teams territorial rights, restricted player movements, developed membership criteria for the franchises, and issued standings for the first time, so that the APFA would have a clear champion.

The Association's membership increased to 22 teams, including the Green Bay Packers, who were awarded to John Clair of the Acme Packing Company.

Thorpe moved from Canton to the Cleveland Indians, but he was hurt early in the season and played very little.

A.E. Staley turned the Decatur Staleys over to player-coach George Halas, who moved the team to Cubs Park in Chicago. Staley paid Halas $5,000 to keep the name "Staleys" for one more year. Halas made halfback Ed (Dutch) Sternaman his partner.

The Staleys claimed the APFA championship with a 9-1-1 record, as did Buffalo at 9-1-2. Carr ruled in favor of the Staleys, giving Halas his first championship.
1922 After admitting the use of players who had college eligibility remaining during the 1921 season, Clair and the Green Bay management withdrew from the APFA, January 28. Curly Lambeau promised to obey league rules and then used $50 of his own money to buy back the franchise. Bad weather and low attendance plagued the Packers, and Lambeau went broke, but local merchants arranged a $2,500 loan for the club. A public non-profit corporation was set up to operate the team, with Lambeau as head coach and manager.

The American Professional Football Association changed its name to the National Football League, June 24. The Chicago Staleys became the Chicago Bears.

The NFL fielded 18 teams, including the new Oorang Indians of Marion, Ohio, an all-Indian team featuring Thorpe, Joe Guyon, and Pete Calac, and sponsored by the Oorang dog kennels.

Canton, led by player-coach Guy Chamberlin and tackles Link Lyman and Wilbur (Pete) Henry, emerged as the league's first true powerhouse, going 10-0-2.
1923 For the first time, all of the franchises considered to be part of the NFL fielded teams. Thorpe played first for Oorang, then for the Toledo Maroons. Against the Bears, Thorpe fumbled, and Halas picked up the ball and returned it 98 yards for a touchdown, a record that would last until 1972.

Canton had its second consecutive undefeated season, going 11-0-1 for the NFL title.

1924 The league had 18 franchises, including new ones in Kansas City, Kenosha, and Frankford, a section of Philadelphia. League champion Canton, successful on the field but not at the box office, was purchased by the owner of the Cleveland franchise, who kept the Canton franchise inactive, while using the best players for his Cleveland team, which he renamed the Bulldogs. Cleveland won the title with a 7-1-1 record.

1925 Five new franchises were admitted to the NFL—the New York Giants, who were awarded to Tim Mara and Billy Gibson for $500; the Detroit Panthers, featuring Jimmy Conzelman as owner, coach, and tailback; the Providence Steam Roller; a new Canton Bulldogs team; and the Pottsville Maroons, who had been perhaps the most successful independent pro team. The NFL established its first player limit, at 16 players.

Late in the season, the NFL made its greatest coup in gaining national recognition. Shortly after the University of Illinois season ended in November, All-America halfback Harold (Red) Grange signed a contract to play with the Chicago Bears. On Thanksgiving Day, a crowd of 36,000—the largest in pro football history—watched Grange and the Bears play the Chicago Cardinals to a scoreless tie at Wrigley Field. At the beginning of December, the Bears left on a barnstorming tour that saw them play eight games in 12 days, in St. Louis, Philadelphia, New York City, Washington, Boston, Pittsburgh, Detroit, and Chicago. A crowd of 73,000 watched the game against the Giants at the Polo Grounds, helping assure the future of the troubled NFL franchise in New York. The Bears then played nine more games in the South and West, including a game in Los Angeles, in which 75,000 fans watched them defeat the Los Angeles Tigers in the Los Angeles Memorial Coliseum.

Pottsville and the Chicago Cardinals were the top contenders for the league title, with Pottsville winning a late-season meeting 21-7. Pottsville scheduled a game against a team of former Notre Dame players for Shibe Park in Philadelphia. Frankford lodged a protest not only because the game was in Frankford's "protected territory," but because it was being played the same day as a Yellow Jackets home game. Carr gave three different notices forbidding Pottsville to play the game, but Pottsville played anyway, December 12. That day, Carr fined the club, suspended it from all rights and privileges (including the right to play for the NFL championship), and returned its franchise to the league. The Cardinals, who ended the season with the best record in the league, were named the 1925 champions.

1926 Grange's manager, C.C. Pyle, told the Bears that Grange wouldn't play for them unless he was paid a five-figure salary and given one-third ownership of the team. The Bears refused. Pyle leased Yankee Stadium in New York City, then petitioned for an NFL franchise. After he was refused, he started the first American Football League. It lasted one season and included Grange's New York Yankees and eight other teams. The AFL champion Philadelphia Quakers played a December game against the New York Giants, seventh in the NFL, and the Giants won 31-0. At the end of the season, the AFL folded.

Halas pushed through a rule that prohibited any team from signing a player whose college class had not graduated.

The NFL grew to 22 teams, including the Duluth Eskimos, who signed All-America fullback Ernie Nevers of Stanford, giving the league a gate attraction to rival Grange. The 15-member Eskimos, dubbed the "Iron Men of the North," played 29 exhibition and league games, 28 on the road, and Nevers played in all but 29 minutes of them.

Frankford edged the Bears for the championship, despite Halas having obtained John (Paddy) Driscoll from the Cardinals. On December 4, the Yellow Jackets scored in the final two minutes to defeat the Bears 7-6 and move ahead of them in the standings.

1927 At a special meeting in Cleveland, April 23, Carr decided to secure the NFL's future by eliminating the financially weaker teams and consolidating the quality players onto a limited number of more successful teams. The new-look NFL dropped to 12 teams, and the center of gravity of the league left the Midwest, where the NFL had started, and began to emerge in the large cities of the East. One of the new teams was Grange's New York Yankees, but Grange suffered a knee injury and the Yankees finished in the middle of the pack. The NFL championship was won by the cross-town rival New York Giants, who posted 10 shutouts in 13 games.

1928 Grange and Nevers both retired from pro football, and Duluth disbanded, as the NFL was reduced to only 10 teams. The Providence Steam Roller of Jimmy Conzelman and Pearce Johnson won the championship, playing in the Cycledrome, a 10,000-seat oval that had been built for bicycle races.

1929 Chris O'Brien sold the Chicago Cardinals to David Jones, July 27.

The NFL added a fourth official, the field judge, July 28.

Grange and Nevers returned to the NFL. Nevers scored six rushing touchdowns and four extra points as the Cardinals beat Grange's Bears 40-6, November 28. The 40 points set a record that remains the NFL's oldest.

Providence became the first NFL team to host a game at night under floodlights, against the Cardinals, November 3.

The Packers added back Johnny Blood (McNally), tackle Cal Hubbard, and guard Mike Michalske, and won their first NFL championship, edging the Giants, who featured quarterback Benny Friedman.

1930 Dayton, the last of the NFL's original franchises, was purchased by John Dwyer, moved to Brooklyn, and renamed the Dodgers. The Portsmouth, Ohio, Spartans entered the league.

The Packers edged the Giants for the title, but the most improved team was the Bears. Halas retired as a player and replaced himself as coach of the Bears with Ralph Jones, who refined the T-formation by introducing wide ends and a halfback in motion. Jones also introduced rookie All-America fullback-tackle Bronko Nagurski.

The Giants defeated a team of former Notre Dame players coached by Knute Rockne 22-0 before 55,000 at the Polo Grounds, December 14. The proceeds went to the New York Unemployment Fund to help those suffering because of the Great Depression, and the easy victory helped give the NFL credibility with the press and the public.

1931 The NFL decreased to 10 teams, and halfway through the season the Frankford franchise folded. Carr fined the Bears, Packers, and Portsmouth $1,000 each for using players whose college classes had not graduated.

The Packers won an unprecedented third consecutive title, beating out the Spartans, who were led by rookie backs Earl (Dutch) Clark and Glenn Presnell.

1932 George Preston Marshall, Vincent Bendix, Jay O'Brien, and M. Dorland Doyle were awarded a franchise for Boston, July 9. Despite the presence of two rookies—halfback Cliff Battles and tackle Glen (Turk) Edwards—the new team, named the Braves, lost money and Marshall was left as the sole owner at the end of the year.

NFL membership dropped to eight teams, the lowest in history. Official statistics were kept for the first time. The Bears and the Spartans finished the season in the first-ever tie for first place. After the season finale, the league office arranged for the first playoff game in NFL history. The game was moved indoors to Chicago Stadium because of bitter cold and heavy snow. The arena allowed only an 80-yard field that came right to the walls. The goal posts were moved from the end lines to the goal lines and, for safety, inbounds lines or hashmarks where the ball would be put in play were drawn 10 yards from the walls that butted against the sidelines. The Bears won 9-0, December 18, scoring the winning touchdown on a two-yard pass from Nagurski to Grange. The Spartans claimed Nagurski's pass was thrown from less than five yards behind the line of scrimmage, violating the existing passing rule, but the play stood.

1933 The NFL, which long had followed the rules of college football, made a number of significant changes from the college game for the first time and began to independently develop rules serving its needs and the style of play it preferred. The innovations from the 1932 championship game—inbounds line or hashmarks and goal posts on the goal lines—were adopted. Also the forward pass was legalized from anywhere behind the line of scrimmage, February 25.

Marshall and Halas pushed through a proposal that divided the NFL into two divisions, with the winners to meet in an annual championship game, July 8.

Three new franchises joined the league—the Pittsburgh Pirates of Art Rooney, the Philadelphia Eagles of Bert Bell and Lud Wray, and the Cincinnati Reds. The Staten Island Stapletons suspended operations for a year, but never returned to the league.

Halas bought out Sternaman, became sole owner of the Bears, and reinstated himself as head coach. Marshall changed the name of the Boston Braves to the Redskins. David Jones sold the Chicago Cardinals to Charles W. Bidwill.

In the first NFL Championship Game scheduled before the season, the Western Division champion Bears defeated the Eastern Division champion Giants 23-21 at Wrigley Field, December 17.

1934 G.A. (Dick) Richards purchased the Portsmouth Spartans, moved them to Detroit, and renamed them the Lions.

Professional football gained new prestige when the Bears were matched against the best college football players in the first Chicago College All-Star Game, August 31. The game ended in a scoreless tie before 79,432 at Soldier Field.

The Cincinnati Reds lost their first eight games, then were suspended from the league for defaulting on payments. The St. Louis Gunners, an independent team, joined the NFL by buying the Cincinnati franchise and went 1-2 the last three weeks.

Rookie Beattie Feathers of the Bears became the NFL's first 1,000-yard rusher, gaining 1,004 on 101 carries. The Thanksgiving Day game between the Bears and the Lions became the first NFL game broadcast nationally, with Graham McNamee the announcer for CBS radio.

In the championship game, on an extremely cold and icy day at the Polo Grounds, the Giants trailed the Bears 13-3 in the third quarter before changing to basketball shoes for better footing. The Giants won 30-13 in what has come to be known as the "Sneakers Game," December 9.

The player waiver rule was adopted, December 10.

1935 The NFL adopted Bert Bell's proposal to hold an annual draft of college players, to begin in 1936, with teams selecting in an inverse order of finish, May 19. The inbounds line or hashmarks were moved nearer the center of the field, 15 yards from the sidelines.

All-America end Don Hutson of Alabama joined Green Bay. The Lions defeated the Giants 26-7 in the NFL Championship Game, December 15.

1936 There were no franchise transactions for the first year since the formation of the NFL. It also was the first year in which all member teams played the same number of games.

The Eagles made University of Chicago halfback and Heisman Trophy winner Jay Berwanger the first player ever selected in the NFL draft, February 8. The Eagles traded his rights to the Bears, but Berwanger never played pro football. The first player selected to actually sign was the number-two pick, Riley Smith of Alabama, who was selected by Boston.

A rival league was formed, and it became the second to call itself the American Football League. The Boston Shamrocks were its champions.

Due to poor attendance, Marshall, the owner of the host team, moved the Championship Game from Boston to the Polo Grounds in New York. Green Bay defeated the Redskins 21-6, December 13.

1937 Homer Marshman was granted a Cleveland franchise, named the Rams, February 12. Marshall moved the Redskins to Washington, D.C., February 13. The Redskins signed TCU All-America tailback Sammy Baugh, who led them to a 28-21 victory over the Bears in the NFL Championship Game, December 12.

The Los Angeles Bulldogs had an 8-0 record to win the AFL title, but then the two-year-old league folded.

1938 At the suggestion of Halas, Hugh (Shorty) Ray became a technical advisor on rules and officiating to the NFL. A new rule called for a 15-yard penalty for roughing the passer.

Rookie Byron (Whizzer) White of the Pittsburgh Pirates led the NFL in rushing. The Giants defeated the Packers 23-17 for the NFL title, December 11.

Marshall, *Los Angeles Times* sports editor Bill Henry, and promoter Tom Gallery established the Pro Bowl game between the NFL champion and a team of pro all-stars.

1939 The New York Giants defeated the Pro All-Stars 13-10 in the first Pro Bowl, at Wrigley Field, Los Angeles, January 15.

Carr, NFL president since 1921, died in Columbus, May 20. Carl Storck was named acting president, May 25.

An NFL game was televised for the first time when NBC broadcast the Brooklyn Dodgers-Philadelphia Eagles game from Ebbets Field to the approximately 1,000 sets then in New York.

Green Bay defeated New York 27-0 in the NFL Championship Game, December 10 at Milwaukee. NFL attendance exceeded one million in a season for the first time, reaching 1,071,200.

1940 A six-team rival league, the third to call itself the American Football League, was formed, and the Columbus Bullies won its championship.

Halas's Bears, with additional coaching by Clark Shaughnessy of Stanford, defeated the Redskins 73-0 in the NFL Championship Game, December 8. The game, which was the most decisive victory in NFL history, popularized the Bears' T-formation with a man-in-motion. It was the first championship carried on network radio, broadcast by Red Barber to 120 stations of the Mutual Broadcasting System, which paid $2,500 for the rights.

Art Rooney sold the Pittsburgh franchise to Alexis Thompson, December 9, then bought part interest in the Philadelphia Eagles.

1941 Elmer Layden was named the first Commissioner of the NFL, March 1; Storck, the acting president, resigned, April 5. NFL headquarters were moved to Chicago.

Bell and Rooney traded the Eagles to Thompson for the Pirates, then renamed their new team the Steelers. Homer Marshman sold the Rams to Daniel F. Reeves and Fred Levy, Jr.

The league by-laws were revised to provide for playoffs in case there were ties in division races, and sudden-death overtimes in case a playoff game was tied after four quarters. An official *NFL Record Manual* was published for the first time.

Columbus again won the championship of the AFL, but the two-year-old league then folded.

The Bears and the Packers finished in a tie for the Western Division championship, setting up the first divisional playoff game in league history. The Bears won 33-14, then defeated the Giants 37-9 for the NFL championship, December 21.

1942 Players departing for service in World War II depleted the rosters of NFL teams. Halas left the Bears in midseason to join the Navy, and Luke Johnsos and Heartley (Hunk) Anderson served as co-coaches as the Bears went 11-0 in the regular season. The Redskins defeated the Bears 14-6 in the NFL Championship Game, December 13.

1943 The Cleveland Rams, with co-owners Reeves and Levy in the service, were granted permission to suspend operations for one season, April 6. Levy transferred his stock in the team to Reeves, April 16.

The NFL adopted free substitution, April 7. The league also made the wearing of helmets mandatory and approved a 10-game schedule for all teams.

Philadelphia and Pittsburgh were granted permission to merge for one season, June 19. The team, known as Phil-Pitt (and called the Steagles by fans), divided home games between the two cities, and Earle (Greasy) Neale of Philadelphia and Walt Kiesling of Pittsburgh served as co-coaches. The merger automatically dissolved the last day of the season, December 5.

Ted Collins was granted a franchise for Boston, to become active in 1944.

Sammy Baugh led the league in passing, punting, and interceptions. He led the Redskins to a tie with the Giants for the Eastern Division title, and then to a 28-0 victory in a divisional playoff game. The Bears beat the Redskins 41-21 in the NFL Championship Game, December 26.

1944 Collins, who had wanted a franchise in Yankee Stadium in New York, named his new team in Boston the Yanks. Cleveland resumed operations. The Brooklyn Dodgers changed their name to the Tigers.

Coaching from the bench was legalized, April 20.

The Cardinals and the Steelers were granted permission to merge for one year under the name Card-Pitt, April 21. Phil Handler of the Cardinals and Walt Kiesling of the Steelers served as co-coaches. The merger automatically dissolved the last day of the season, December 3.

In the NFL Championship Game, Green Bay defeated the New York Giants 14-7, December 17.

1945 The inbounds lines or hashmarks were moved from 15 yards away from the sidelines to nearer the center of the field—20 yards from the sidelines.

Brooklyn and Boston merged into a team that played home games in both cities and was known simply as "The Yanks." The team was coached by former Boston head coach Herb Kopf. In December, the Brooklyn franchise withdrew from the NFL to join the new All-America Football Conference; all the players on its active and reserve lists were assigned to The Yanks, who once again became the Boston Yanks.

Halas rejoined the Bears late in the season after service with the U.S. Navy. Although Halas took over much of the coaching duties, Anderson and Johnsos remained the coaches of record throughout the season.

Steve Van Buren of Philadelphia led the NFL in rushing, kickoff returns, and scoring.

After the Japanese surrendered ending World War II, a count showed that the NFL service roster, limited to men who had played in league games, totaled 638, 21 of whom had died in action.

Rookie quarterback Bob Waterfield led Cleveland to a 15-14 victory over Washington in the NFL Championship Game, December 16.

1946 The contract of Commissioner Layden was not renewed, and Bert Bell, the co-owner of the Steelers, replaced him, January 11. Bell moved the league headquarters from Chicago to the Philadelphia suburb of Bala Cynwyd.

Free substitution was withdrawn and substitutions were limited to no more than three men at a time. Forward passes were made automatically incomplete upon striking the goal posts, January 11.

The NFL took on a truly national appearance for the first time when Reeves was granted permission by the league to move his NFL champion Rams to Los Angeles.

The rival All-America Football Conference began play with eight teams. The Cleveland Browns, coached by Paul Brown, won the AAFC's first championship, defeating the New York Yankees 14-9.

Bill Dudley of the Steelers led the NFL in rushing, interceptions, and punt returns, and won the league's most valuable player award.

Backs Frank Filchock and Merle Hapes of the Giants were questioned about an attempt by a New York man to fix the championship game with the Bears. Bell suspended Hapes but allowed Filchock to play; he played well, but Chicago won 24-14, December 15.

1947 The NFL added a fifth official, the back judge.

A bonus choice was made for the first time in the NFL draft. One team each year would select the special choice before the first round began. The Chicago Bears won a lottery and the rights to the first choice and drafted back Bob Fenimore of Oklahoma A&M.

The Cleveland Browns again won the AAFC title, defeating the New York Yankees 14-3.

Charles Bidwill, Sr., owner of the Cardinals, died April 19, but his wife and sons retained ownership of the team. On December 28, the Cardinals won the NFL Championship Game 28-21 over the Philadelphia Eagles, who had beaten Pittsburgh 21-0 in a playoff.

1948 Plastic helmets were prohibited. A flexible artificial tee was permitted at the kickoff. Officials other than the referee were equipped with whistles, not horns, January 14.

Fred Mandel sold the Detroit Lions to a syndicate headed by D. Lyle Fife, January 15.

Halfback Fred Gehrke of the Los Angeles Rams painted horns on the Rams' helmets, the first modern helmet emblems in pro football.

The Cleveland Browns won their third straight championship in the AAFC, going 14-0 and then defeating the Buffalo Bills 49-7.

In a blizzard, the Eagles defeated the Cardinals 7-0 in the NFL Championship Game, December 19.

1949 Alexis Thompson sold the champion Eagles to a syndicate headed by James P. Clark, January 15. The Boston Yanks became the New York Bulldogs, sharing the Polo Grounds with the Giants.

Free substitution was adopted for one year, January 20.

The NFL had two 1,000-yard rushers in the same season for the first time—Steve Van Buren of Philadelphia and Tony Canadeo of Green Bay.

The AAFC played its season with a one-division, seven-team format. On December 9, Bell announced a merger agreement in which three AAFC franchises—Cleveland, San Francisco, and Baltimore—would join the NFL in 1950. The Browns won their fourth consecutive AAFC title, defeating the 49ers 21-7, December 11.

In a heavy rain, the Eagles defeated the Rams 14-0 in the NFL Championship Game, December 18.

1950 Unlimited free substitution was restored, opening the way for the era of two platoons and specialization in pro football, January 20.

Curly Lambeau, founder of the franchise and Green Bay's head coach since 1921, resigned under fire, February 1.

The name National Football League was restored after about three months as the National-American Football League. The American and National conferences were created to replace the Eastern and Western divisions, March 3.

The New York Bulldogs became the Yanks and divided the players of the former AAFC Yankees with the Giants. A special allocation draft was held in which the 13 teams drafted the remaining AAFC players, with special consideration for Baltimore, which received 15 choices compared to 10 for other teams.

The Los Angeles Rams became the first NFL team to have all of its games—both home and away—televised. The Washington Redskins followed the Rams in arranging to televise their games; other teams made deals to put selected games on television.

In the first game of the season, former AAFC champion Cleveland defeated NFL champion Philadelphia 35-10. For the first time, deadlocks occurred in both conferences and playoffs were necessary. The Browns defeated the Giants in the American and the Rams defeated the Bears in the National. Cleveland defeated Los Angeles 30-28 in the NFL Championship Game, December 24.

1951 The Pro Bowl game, dormant since 1942, was revived under a new format matching the all-stars of each conference at the Los Angeles Memorial Coliseum. The American Conference defeated the National Conference 28-27, January 14.

Abraham Watner returned the Baltimore franchise and its player contracts back to the NFL for $50,000. Baltimore's former players were made available for drafting at the same time as college players, January 18.

A rule was passed that no tackle, guard, or center would be eligible to catch a forward pass, January 18.

The Rams reversed their television policy and televised only road games.

The NFL Championship Game was televised coast-to-coast for the first time, December 23. The DuMont Network paid $75,000 for the rights to the game, in which the Rams defeated the Browns 24-17.

1952 Ted Collins sold the New York Yanks' franchise back to the NFL, January 19. A new franchise was awarded to a group in Dallas after it purchased the assets of the Yanks, January 24. The new Texans went 1-11, with the owners turning the franchise back to the league in midseason. For the last five games of the season, the commissioner's office operated the Texans as a road team, using Hershey, Pennsylvania, as a home base. At the end of the season the franchise was cancelled, the last time an NFL team failed.

The Pittsburgh Steelers abandoned the Single-Wing for the T-formation, the last pro team to do so.

The Detroit Lions won their first NFL championship in 17 years, defeating the Browns 17-7 in the title game, December 28.

1953 A Baltimore group headed by Carroll Rosenbloom was granted a franchise and was awarded the holdings of the defunct Dallas organization, January 23. The team, named the Colts, put together the largest trade in league history, acquiring 10 players from Cleveland in exchange for five.

The names of the American and National conferences were changed to the Eastern and Western conferences, January 24.

Jim Thorpe died, March 28.

Mickey McBride, founder of the Cleveland Browns, sold the franchise to a syndicate headed by Dave R. Jones, June 10.

The NFL policy of blacking out home games was upheld by Judge Allan K. Grim of the U.S. District Court in Philadelphia, November 12.

The Lions again defeated the Browns in the NFL Championship Game, winning 17-16, December 27.

1954 The Canadian Football League began a series of raids on NFL teams, signing quarterback Eddie LeBaron and defensive end Gene Brito of Washington and defensive tackle Arnie Weinmeister of the Giants, among others.

Fullback Joe Perry of the 49ers became the first player in league history to gain 1,000 yards rushing in consecutive seasons.

Cleveland defeated Detroit 56-10 in the NFL Championship Game, December 26.

1955 The sudden-death overtime rule was used for the first time in a preseason game between the Rams and Giants at Portland, Oregon, August 28. The Rams won 23-17 three minutes into overtime.

A rule change declared the ball dead immediately if the ball carrier touched the ground with any part of his body except his hands or feet while in the grasp of an opponent.

The NFL Players Association was founded.

The Baltimore Colts made an 80-cent phone call to Johnny Unitas and signed him as a free agent. Another quarterback, Otto Graham, played his last game as the Browns defeated the Rams 38-14 in the NFL Championship Game, December 26. Graham had quarterbacked the Browns to 10 championship-game appearances in 10 years.

NBC replaced DuMont as the network for the title game, paying a rights fee of $100,000.

1956 Grabbing an opponent's facemask (other than the ball carrier) was made illegal. Using radio receivers to communicate with players on the field was prohibited. A natural leather ball with white end stripes replaced the white ball with black stripes for night games.

The Giants moved from the Polo Grounds to Yankee Stadium.

Halas retired as coach of the Bears, and was replaced by Paddy Driscoll.

CBS became the first network to broadcast some NFL regular-season games to selected television markets across the nation.

The Giants routed the Bears 47-7 in the NFL Championship Game, December 30.

1957 Pete Rozelle was named general manager of the Rams. Anthony J. Morabito, founder and co-owner of the 49ers, died of a heart attack during a game against the Bears at Kezar Stadium, October 28. An NFL-record crowd of 102,368 saw the 49ers-Rams game at the Los Angeles Memorial Coliseum, November 10.

The Lions came from 20 points down to post a 31-27 playoff victory over the 49ers, December 22. Detroit defeated Cleveland 59-14 in the NFL Championship Game, December 29.

1958 The bonus selection in the draft was eliminated, January 29. The last selection was quarterback King Hill of Rice by the Chicago Cardinals.

Halas reinstated himself as coach of the Bears.

Jim Brown of Cleveland gained an NFL record 1,527 yards rushing. In a divisional playoff game, the Giants held Brown to eight yards and defeated Cleveland 10-0.

Baltimore, coached by Weeb Ewbank, defeated the Giants 23-17 in the first sudden-death overtime in an NFL Championship Game, December 28. The game ended when Colts fullback Alan Ameche scored on a one-yard touchdown run after 8:15 of overtime.

1959 Vince Lombardi was named head coach of the Green Bay Packers, January 28. Tim Mara, the co-founder of the Giants, died, February 17.

Lamar Hunt of Dallas announced his intentions to form a second pro football league. The first meeting was held in Chicago, August 14, and consisted of Hunt representing Dallas; Bob Howsam, Denver; K.S. (Bud) Adams, Houston; Barron Hilton, Los Angeles; Max Winter and Bill Boyer, Minneapolis; and Harry Wismer, New York City. They made plans to begin play in 1960.

The new league was named the American Football League, August 22. Buffalo, owned by Ralph Wilson, became the seventh franchise, October 28. Boston, owned by William H. Sullivan, became the eighth team, November 22. The first AFL draft, lasting 33 rounds, was held, November 22. Joe Foss was named AFL Commissioner, November 30. An additional draft of 20 rounds was held by the AFL, December 2.

NFL Commissioner Bert Bell died of a heart attack suffered at Franklin Field, Philadelphia, during the last two minutes of a game between the Eagles and the Steelers, October 11. Treasurer Austin Gunsel was named president in the office of the commissioner, October 14.

The Colts again defeated the Giants in the NFL Championship Game, 31-16, December 27.

1960 Pete Rozelle was elected NFL Commissioner as a compromise choice on the twenty-third ballot, January 26. Rozelle moved the league offices to New York City.

Hunt was elected AFL president for 1960, January 26. Minneapolis withdrew from the AFL, January 27, and the same ownership was given an NFL franchise for Minnesota (to start in 1961), January 28. Dallas received an NFL franchise for 1960, January 28. Oakland received an AFL franchise, January 30.

The AFL adopted the two-point option on points after touchdown, January 28. A "no-tampering" verbal pact, relative to players' contracts, was agreed to between the NFL and AFL, February 9.

The NFL owners voted to allow the transfer of the Chicago Cardinals to St. Louis, March 13.

The AFL signed a five-year television contract with ABC, June 9.

The Boston Patriots defeated the Buffalo Bills 28-7 before 16,000 at Buffalo in the first AFL preseason game, July 30. The Denver Broncos defeated the Patriots 13-10 before 21,597 at Boston in the first AFL regular-season game, September 9.

Philadelphia defeated Green Bay 17-13 in the NFL Championship Game, December 26.

1961 The Houston Oilers defeated the Los Angeles Chargers 24-16 before 32,183 in the first AFL Championship Game, January 1.

Detroit defeated Cleveland 17-16 in the first Playoff Bowl, or Bert Bell Benefit Bowl, between second-place teams in each conference in Miami, January 7.

End Willard Dewveall of the Bears played out his option and joined the Oilers, becoming the first player to deliberately move from one league to the other, January 14.

Ed McGah, Wayne Valley, and Robert Osborne bought out their partners in the ownership of the Raiders, January 17. The Chargers were transferred to San Diego, February 10. Dave R. Jones sold the Browns to a group headed by Arthur B. Modell, March 22. The Howsam brothers sold the Broncos to a group headed by Calvin Kunz and Gerry Phipps, May 26.

NBC was awarded a two-year contract for radio and television rights to the NFL Championship Game for $615,000 annually, $300,000 of which was to go directly into the NFL Player Benefit Plan, April 5.

Canton, Ohio, where the league that became the NFL was formed in 1920, was chosen as the site of the Pro Football Hall of Fame, April 27. Dick McCann, a former Redskins executive, was named executive director.

A bill legalizing single-network television contracts by professional sports leagues was introduced in Congress by Representative Emanuel Celler. It passed the House and Senate and was signed into law by President John F. Kennedy, September 30.

Houston defeated San Diego 10-3 for the AFL championship, December 24. Green Bay won its first NFL championship since 1944, defeating the New York Giants 37-0, December 31.

1962 The Western Division defeated the Eastern Division 47-27 in the first AFL All-Star Game, played before 20,973 in San Diego, January 7.

Both leagues prohibited grabbing any player's facemask. The AFL voted to make the scoreboard clock the official timer of the game.

The NFL entered into a single-network agreement with CBS for telecasting all regular-season games for $4,650,000 annually, January 10.

Judge Roszel Thompson of the U.S. District Court in Baltimore ruled against the AFL in its antitrust suit against the NFL, May 21. The AFL had charged the NFL with monopoly and conspiracy in areas of expansion, television, and player signings. The case lasted two and a half years, the trial two months.

McGah and Valley acquired controlling interest in the Raiders, May 24. The AFL assumed financial responsibility for the New York Titans, November 8. With Commissioner Rozelle as referee, Daniel F. Reeves regained the ownership of the Rams, outbidding his partners in sealed-envelope bidding for the team, November 27.

The Dallas Texans defeated the Oilers 20-17 for the AFL championship at Houston after 17 minutes, 54 seconds of overtime on a 25-yard field goal by Tommy Brooker, December 23. The game lasted a record 77 minutes, 54 seconds.

Judge Edward Weinfeld of the U.S. District Court in New York City upheld the legality of the NFL's television blackout within a 75-mile radius of home games and denied an injunction that would have forced the championship game between the Giants and the Packers to be televised in the New York City area, December 28. The Packers beat the Giants 16-7 for the NFL title, December 30.

1963 The Dallas Texans transferred to Kansas City, becoming the Chiefs, February 8. The New York Titans were sold to a five-man syndicate headed by David (Sonny) Werblin, March 28. Weeb Ewbank became the Titans' new head coach and the team's name was changed to the Jets, April 15. They began play in Shea Stadium.

NFL Properties, Inc., was founded to serve as the licensing arm of the NFL.

Rozelle indefinitely suspended Green Bay halfback Paul Hornung and Detroit defensive tackle Alex Karras for placing bets on their own teams and on other NFL games; he also fined five other Detroit players $2,000 each for betting on one game in which they did not participate, and the Detroit Lions Football Company $2,000 on each of two counts for failure to report information promptly and for lack of sideline supervision.

Paul Brown, head coach of the Browns since their inception, was fired and replaced by Blanton Collier. Don Shula replaced Weeb Ewbank as head coach of the Colts.

The AFL allowed the Jets and Raiders to select players from other franchises in hopes of giving the league more competitive balance, May 11.

NBC was awarded exclusive network broadcasting rights for the 1963 AFL Championship Game for $926,000, May 23.

The Pro Football Hall of Fame was dedicated at Canton, Ohio, September 7.

The U.S. Fourth Circuit Court of Appeals reaffirmed the lower court's finding for the NFL in the $10-million suit brought by the AFL, ending three and a half years of litigation, November 21.

Jim Brown of Cleveland rushed for an NFL single-season record 1,863 yards.

Boston defeated Buffalo 26-8 in the first divisional playoff game in AFL history, December 28. The Chargers defeated the Patriots in the AFL Championship Game, January 5.

The Bears defeated the Giants 14-10 in the NFL Championship Game, a record sixth and last title for Halas in his thirty-sixth season as the Bears' coach, December 29.

1964 The Chargers defeated the Patriots in the AFL Championship Game, January 5.

William Clay Ford, the Lions' president since 1961, purchased the team, January 10. A group representing the late James P. Clark sold the Eagles to a group headed by Jerry Wolman, January 21. Carroll Rosenbloom, the majority owner of the Colts since 1953, acquired complete ownership of the team, January 23.

CBS submitted the winning bid of $14.1 million per year for the NFL regular-season television rights for 1964 and 1965, January 24. CBS acquired the rights to the championship games for 1964 and 1965 for $1.8 million per game, April 17.

The AFL signed a five-year, $36-million television contract with NBC to begin with the 1965 season, assuring each team approximately $900,000 a year from television rights, January 29.

Hornung and Karras were reinstated by Rozelle, March 16.

Pete Gogolak of Cornell signed a contract with Buffalo, becoming the first soccer-style kicker in pro football.

Buffalo defeated San Diego 20-7 in the AFL Championship Game, December 26. Cleveland defeated Baltimore 27-0 in the NFL Championship Game, December 27.

1965 The NFL teams pledged not to sign college seniors until completion of all their games, including bowl games, and empowered the Commissioner to discipline the clubs up to as much as the loss of an entire draft list for a violation of the pledge, February 15.

The NFL added a sixth official, the line judge, February 19. The color of the officials' penalty flags was changed from white to bright gold, April 5.

Atlanta was awarded an NFL franchise for 1966, with Rankin Smith, Sr., as owner, June 30. Miami was awarded an AFL franchise for 1966, with Joe Robbie and Danny Thomas as owners, August 16.

Green Bay defeated Baltimore 13-10 in sudden-death overtime in a Western Conference playoff game. Don Chandler kicked a 25-yard field goal for the Packers after 13 minutes, 39 seconds of overtime, December 26. The Packers then defeated the Browns 23-12 in the NFL Championship Game, January 2.

In the AFL Championship Game, the Bills again defeated the Chargers, 23-0, December 26.

CBS acquired the rights to the NFL regular-season games in 1966 and 1967, with an option for 1968, for $18.8 million per year, December 29.

1966 The AFL-NFL war reached its peak, as the leagues spent a combined $7 million to sign their 1966 draft choices. The NFL signed 75 percent of its 232 draftees, the AFL 46 percent of its 181. Of the 111 common draft choices, 79 signed with the NFL, 28 with the AFL, and 4 went unsigned.

The rights to the 1966 and 1967 NFL Championship Games were sold to CBS for $2 million per game, February 14.

Foss resigned as AFL Commissioner, April 7. Al Davis, the head coach and general manager of the Raiders, was named to replace him, April 8.

Goal posts offset from the goal line, painted bright yellow, and with uprights 20 feet above the crossbar were made standard in the NFL, May 16.

A series of secret meetings regarding a possible AFL-NFL merger were held in the spring between Hunt of Kansas City and Tex Schramm of Dallas. Rozelle announced the merger, June 8. Under the agreement, the two leagues would combine to form an expanded league with 24 teams, to be increased to 26 to 1968 and to 28 by 1970 or soon thereafter. All existing franchises would be retained, and no franchises would be transferred outside their metropolitan areas. While maintaining separate schedules through 1969, the leagues agreed to play an annual AFL-NFL World Championship Game beginning in January, 1967, and to hold a combined draft, also beginning in 1967. Preseason games would be held between teams of each league starting in 1967. Official regular-season play would start in 1970 when the two leagues would officially merge to form one league with two conferences. Rozelle was named Commissioner of the expanded league setup.

Davis rejoined the Raiders, and Milt Woodard was named president of the AFL, July 25.

The St. Louis Cardinals moved into newly constructed Busch Memorial Stadium.

Barron Hilton sold the Chargers to a group headed by Eugene Klein and Sam Schulman, August 25.

Congress approved the AFL-NFL merger, passing legislation exempting the agreement itself from antitrust action, October 21.

New Orleans was awarded an NFL franchise to begin play in 1967, November 1. John Mecom, Jr., of Houston was designated majority stockholder and president of the franchise, December 15.

The NFL was realigned for the 1967-69 seasons into the Capitol and Century Divisions in the Eastern Conference and the Central and Coastal Divisions in the Western Conference, December 2. New Orleans and the New York Giants agreed to switch divisions in 1968 and return to the 1967 alignment in 1969.

The rights to the Super Bowl for four years were sold to CBS and NBC for $9.5 million, December 13.

1967 Green Bay earned the right to represent the NFL in the first AFL-NFL World Championship Game by defeating Dallas 34-27, January 1. The same day, Kansas City defeated Buffalo 31-7 to represent the AFL. The Packers defeated the Chiefs 35-10 before 61,946 fans at the Los Angeles Memorial Coliseum in the first game between AFL and NFL teams, January 15. The winning players' share for the Packers was $15,000 each, and the losing players' share for the Chiefs was $7,500 each. The game was televised by both CBS and NBC.

The "sling-shot" goal post and a six-foot-wide border around the field were made standard in the NFL, February 22.

Baltimore made Bubba Smith, a Michigan State defensive lineman, the first choice in the first combined AFL-NFL draft, March 14.

The AFL awarded a franchise to begin play in 1968 to Cincinnati, May 24. A group with Paul Brown as part owner, general manager, and head coach, was awarded the Cincinnati franchise, September 27.

Arthur B. Modell, the president of the Cleveland Browns, was elected president of the NFL, May 28.

An AFL team defeated an NFL team for the first time, when Denver beat Detroit 13-7 in a preseason game, August 5.

Green Bay defeated Dallas 21-17 for the NFL championship on a last-minute one-yard quarterback sneak by Bart Starr in 13-below-zero temperature at Green Bay, December 31. The same day, Oakland defeated Houston 40-7 for the AFL championship.

1968 Green Bay defeated Oakland 33-14 in Super Bowl II at Miami, January 14. The game had the first $3-million gate in pro football history.

Vince Lombardi resigned as head coach of the Packers, but remained as general manager, January 28.

Werblin sold his shares in the Jets to his partners Don Lillis, Leon Hess, Townsend Martin, and Phil Iselin, May 21. Lillis assumed the presidency of the club, but then died July 23. Iselin was appointed president, August 6.

Halas retired for the fourth and last time as head coach of the Bears, May 27.

The Oilers left Rice Stadium for the Astrodome and became the first NFL team to play its home games in a domed stadium.

The movie "Heidi" became a footnote in sports history when NBC didn't show the last 1:05 of the Jets-Raiders game in order to permit the children's special to begin on time. The Raiders scored two touchdowns in the last 42 seconds to win 43-32, November 17.

Ewbank became the first coach to win titles in both the NFL and AFL when his Jets defeated the Raiders 27-23 for the AFL championship, December 29. The same day, Baltimore defeated Cleveland 34-0.

1969 The AFL established a playoff format for the 1969 season, with the winner in one division playing the runner-up in the other, January 11.

An AFL team won the Super Bowl for the first time, as the Jets defeated the Colts 16-7 at Miami, January 12 in Super Bowl III. The title "Super Bowl" was recognized by the NFL for the first time.

Vince Lombardi became part owner, executive vice-president, and head coach of the Washington Redskins, Feb. 7.

Wolman sold the Eagles to Leonard Tose, May 1.

Baltimore, Cleveland, and Pittsburgh agreed to join the AFL teams to form the 13-team American Football Conference of the NFL in 1970, May 17. The NFL also agreed on a playoff format that would include one "wild-card" team per conference—the second-place team with the best record.

Monday Night Football was signed for 1970. ABC acquired the rights to televise 13 NFL regular-season Monday night games in 1970, 1971, and 1972.

George Preston Marshall, president emeritus of the Redskins, died at 72, August 9.

The NFL marked its fiftieth year by the wearing of a special patch by each of the 16 teams.

1970 Kansas City defeated Minnesota 23-7 in Super Bowl IV at New Orleans, January 11. The gross receipts of approximately $3.8 million were the largest ever for a one-day sports event.

Four-year television contracts, under which CBS would televise all NFC games and NBC all AFC games (except Monday night games) and the two would divide televising the Super Bowl and AFC-NFC Pro Bowl games, were announced, January 26.

Art Modell resigned as president of the NFL, March 12. Milt Woodard resigned as president of the AFL, March 13. Lamar Hunt was elected president of the AFC and George Halas was elected president of the NFC, March 19.

The merged 26-team league adopted rules changes putting names on the backs of players' jerseys, making a point after touchdown worth only one point, and making the scoreboard clock the official timing device of the game, March 18.

The Players Negotiating Committee and the NFL Players Association announced a four-year agreement guaranteeing approximately $4,535,000 annually to player pension and insurance benefits, August 3. The owners also agreed to contribute $250,000 annually to improve or implement items such as disability payments, widows' benefits, maternity benefits, and dental benefits. The agreement also provided for increased preseason game and per diem payments, averaging approximately $2.6 million annually.

The Pittsburgh Steelers moved into Three Rivers Stadium. The Cincinnati Bengals moved to Riverfront Stadium.

Lombardi died of cancer at 57, September 3.

Tom Dempsey of New Orleans kicked a game-winning NFL-record 63-yard field goal against Detroit, November 8.

1971 Baltimore defeated Dallas 16-13 on Jim O'Brien's 32-yard field goal with five seconds to go in Super Bowl V at Miami, January 17. The NBC telecast was viewed in an estimated 23,980,000 homes, the largest audience ever for a one-day sports event.

The NFC defeated the AFC 27-6 in the first AFC-NFC Pro Bowl at Los Angeles, January 24.

The Boston Patriots changed their name to the New England Patriots, March 25. Their new stadium, Schaefer Stadium, was dedicated in a 20-14 preseason victory over the Giants.

The Philadelphia Eagles left Franklin Field and played their games at the new Veterans Stadium.

The San Francisco 49ers left Kezar Stadium and moved their games to Candlestick Park.

Daniel F. Reeves, the president and general manager of the Rams, died at 58, April 15.

The Dallas Cowboys moved from

the Cotton Bowl into their new home, Texas Stadium, October 24.

Miami defeated Kansas City 27-24 in sudden-death overtime in an AFC Divisional Playoff Game, December 25. Garo Yepremian kicked a 37-yard field goal for the Dolphins after 22 minutes, 40 seconds of overtime, as the game lasted 82 minutes, 40 seconds overall, making it the longest game in history.

1972 Dallas defeated Miami 24-3 in Super Bowl VI at New Orleans, January 16. The CBS telecast was viewed in an estimated 27,450,000 homes, the top-rated one-day telecast ever.

The inbounds lines or hashmarks were moved nearer the center of the field, 23 yards, 1 foot, 9 inches from the sidelines, March 23. The method of determining won-lost percentage in standings changed. Tie games, previously not counted in the standings, were made equal to a half-game won and a half-game lost, May 24.

Robert Irsay purchased the Los Angeles Rams and transferred ownership of the club to Carroll Rosenbloom in exchange for the Baltimore Colts, July 13.

William V. Bidwill purchased the stock of his brother Charles (Stormy) Bidwill to become the sole owner of the St. Louis Cardinals, September 2.

The National District Attorneys Association endorsed the position of professional leagues in opposing proposed legalization of gambling in professional team sports, September 28.

Franco Harris's "Immaculate Reception" gave the Steelers their first postseason win ever, 13-7 over the Raiders, December 23.

1973 Rozelle announced that all Super Bowl VII tickets were sold and that the game would be telecast in Los Angeles, the site of the game, on an experimental basis, January 3.

Miami defeated Washington 14-7 in Super Bowl VII at Los Angeles, completing a 17-0 season, the first perfect-record regular-season and postseason mark in NFL history, January 14. The NBC telecast was viewed by approximately 75 million people.

The AFC defeated the NFC 33-28 in the Pro Bowl in Dallas, the first time since 1942 that the game was played outside Los Angeles, January 21.

A jersey numbering system was adopted, April 5: 1-19 for quarterbacks and specialists, 20-49 for running backs and defensive backs, 50-59 for centers and linebackers, 60-79 for defensive linemen and interior offensive linemen other than centers, and 80-89 for wide receivers and tight ends. Players who had been in the NFL in 1972 could continue to use old numbers.

NFL Charities, a non-profit organization, was created to derive an income from monies generated from NFL Properties' licensing of NFL trademarks and team names, June 26. NFL Charities was set up to support education and charitable activities and to supply economic support to persons formerly associated with professional football who were no longer able to support themselves.

Congress adopted experimental legislation (for three years) requiring any NFL game that had been declared a sellout 72 hours prior to kickoff to be made available for local televising, September 14. The legislation provided for an annual review to be made by the Federal Communications Commission.

The Buffalo Bills moved their home games from War Memorial Stadium to Rich Stadium in nearby Orchard Park. The Giants tied the Eagles 23-23 in the final game in Yankee Stadium, September 23. The Giants played the rest of their home games at the Yale Bowl in New Haven, Connecticut.

A rival league, the World Football League, was formed and was reported in operation, October 2. It had plans to start play in 1974.

O.J. Simpson of Buffalo became the first player to rush for more than 2,000 yards in a season, gaining 2,003.

1974 Miami defeated Minnesota 24-7 in Super Bowl VIII at Houston, the second consecutive Super Bowl championship for the Dolphins, January 13. The CBS telecast was viewed by approximately 75 million people.

Rozelle was given a 10-year contract effective January 1, 1973, February 27.

Tampa Bay was awarded a franchise to begin operation in 1976, April 24.

Sweeping rules changes were adopted to add action and tempo to games: one sudden-death overtime period was added for preseason and regular-season games; the goal posts were moved from the goal line to the end lines; kickoffs were moved from the 40- to the 35-yard line; after missed field goals from beyond the 20, the ball was to be returned to the line of scrimmage; restrictions were placed on members of the punting team to open up return possibilities; roll-blocking and cutting of wide receivers was eliminated; the extent of downfield contact a defender could have with an eligible receiver was restricted; the penalties for offensive holding, illegal use of the hands, and tripping were reduced from 15 to 10 yards; wide receivers blocking back toward the ball within three yards of the line of scrimmage were prevented from blocking below the waist, April 25.

The Toronto Northmen of the WFL signed Larry Csonka, Jim Kiick, and Paul Warfield of Miami, March 31.

Seattle was awarded an NFL franchise to begin play in 1976, June 4. Lloyd W. Nordstrom, president of the Seattle Seahawks, and Hugh Culverhouse, president of the Tampa Bay Buccaneers, signed franchise agreements, December 5.

The Birmingham Americans defeated the Florida Blazers 22-21 in the WFL World Bowl, winning the league championship, December 5.

1975 Pittsburgh defeated Minnesota 16-6 in Super Bowl IX at New Orleans, the Steelers' first championship since entering the NFL in 1933. The NBC telecast was viewed by approximately 78 million people.

The divisional winners with the highest won-loss percentage were made the home team for the divisional playoffs, and the surviving winners with the highest percentage made home teams for the championship games, June 26.

Referees were equipped with wireless microphones for all preseason, regular-season, and playoff games.

The Lions moved to the new Pontiac Silverdome. The Giants played their home games in Shea Stadium. The Saints moved into the Louisiana Superdome.

The World Football League folded, October 22.

1976 Pittsburgh defeated Dallas 21-17 in Super Bowl X in Miami. The Steelers joined Green Bay and Miami as the only teams to win two Super Bowls; the Cowboys became the first wild-card team to play in the Super Bowl. The CBS telecast was viewed by an estimated 80 million people, the largest television audience in history.

Lloyd Nordstrom, the president of the Seahawks, died at 66, January 20. His brother Elmer succeeded him as majority representative of the team.

The owners awarded Super Bowl XII, to be played on January 15, 1978, to New Orleans. They also adopted the use of two 30-second clocks for all games, visible to both players and fans to note the official time between the ready-for-play signal and snap of the ball, March 16.

A veteran player allocation was held to stock the Seattle and Tampa Bay franchises with 39 players each, March 30-31. In the college draft, Seattle and Tampa Bay each received eight extra choices, April 8-9.

The Giants moved into new Giants Stadium in East Rutherford, New Jersey.

The Steelers defeated the College All-Stars in a storm-shortened Chicago College All-Star Game, the last of the series, July 23. St. Louis defeated San Diego 20-10 in a preseason game before 38,000 in Korakuen Stadium, Tokyo, in the first NFL game outside of North America, August 16.

1977 Oakland defeated Minnesota 32-14 before a record crowd of 100,421 in Super Bowl XI at Pasadena, January 9. The paid attendance was a pro record 103,438. The NBC telecast was viewed by 81.9 million people, the largest ever to view a sports event. The victory was the fifth consecutive for the AFC in the Super Bowl.

The NFL Players Association and the NFL Management Council ratified a collective bargaining agreement extending until 1982, covering five football seasons while continuing the pension plan—including years 1974, 1975, and 1976—with contributions totaling more than $55 million. The total cost of the agreement was estimated at $107 million. The agreement called for a college draft at least through 1986; contained a no-strike, no-suit clause; established a 43-man active player limit; reduced pension vesting to four years; provided for increases in minimum salaries and preseason and postseason pay; improved insurance, medical, and dental benefits; modified previous practices in player movement and control; and reaffirmed the NFL Commissioner's disciplinary authority. Additionally, the agreement called for the NFL member clubs to make payments totaling $16 million the next 10 years to settle various legal disputes, February 25.

The San Francisco 49ers were sold to Edward J. DeBartolo, Jr., March 28.

A 16-game regular season, 4-game preseason was adopted to begin in 1978, March 29. A second wild card team was adopted for the playoffs beginning in 1978, with the wild card teams to play each other and the winners advancing to a round of eight postseason series.

The Seahawks were permanently aligned in the AFC Western Division and the Buccaneers in the NFC Central Division, March 31.

The owners awarded Super Bowl XIII, to be played on January 21, 1979, to Miami to be played in the Orange Bowl; Super Bowl XIV, to be played January 20, 1980, was awarded to Pasadena, to be played in the Rose Bowl, June 14.

Rules changes were adopted to open up the passing game and to cut down on injuries. Defenders were permitted to make contact with eligible receivers only once; the head slap was outlawed; offensive linemen were prohibited from thrusting their hands to an opponent's neck, face, or head; and wide receivers were prohibited from clipping, even in the legal clipping zone.

Rozelle negotiated contracts with the three television networks to televise all NFL regular-season and postseason games, plus selected preseason games, for four years beginning with the 1978 season. ABC was awarded yearly rights to 16 Monday night games, four prime-time games, the AFC-NFC Pro Bowl, and the Hall of Fame games. CBS received the rights to all NFC regular-season and postseason games (except those in the ABC package) and to Super Bowls XIV and XVI. NBC received the rights to all AFC regular-season and postseason games (except those in the ABC package) and to Super Bowls XIII and XV. Industry sources considered it the largest single television package ever negotiated, October.

Chicago's Walter Payton set a single-game rushing record with 275 yards (40 carries) against Minnesota, November 20.

1978 Dallas defeated Denver 27-10 in Super Bowl XII, held indoors for the first time, at the Louisiana Superdome in New Orleans, January 15. The CBS telecast was viewed by more than 102 million people, meaning the game was watched by more viewers than any other show of any kind in the history of television. Dallas's victory was the first for the NFC in six years.

According to a Louis Harris Sports Survey, 70 percent of the nation's sports fans said they followed football, compared to 54 percent who followed baseball. Football increased its lead as the country's favorite, 26 percent to 16 percent for baseball, January 19.

A seventh official, the side judge, was added to the officiating crew, March 14.

The NFL continued a trend toward opening up the game. Rules changes permitted a defender to maintain contact with a receiver within five yards of the line of scrimmage, but restricted contact beyond that point. The pass-blocking rule was interpreted to permit the extending of arms and open hands, March 17.

A study on the use of instant replay as an officiating aid was made during seven nationally televised preseason games.

The NFL played for the first time in Mexico City, with the Saints defeating the Eagles 14-7 in a preseason game, August 5.

Bolstered by the expansion of the

regular-season schedule from 14 to 16 weeks, NFL paid attendance exceeded 12 million (12,771,800) for the first time. The per-game average of 57,017 was the third-highest in league history and the most since 1973.

1979 Pittsburgh defeated Dallas 35-31 in Super Bowl XIII at Miami to become the first team ever to win three Super Bowls, January 21. The NBC telecast was viewed in 35,090,000 homes, by an estimated 96.6 million fans.

The owners awarded three future Super Bowl sites: Super Bowl XV to the Louisiana Superdome in New Orleans, to be played on January 25, 1981; Super Bowl XVI to the Pontiac Silverdome in Pontiac, Michigan, to be played on January 24, 1982; and Super Bowl XVII to Pasadena's Rose Bowl, to be played on January 30, 1983, March 13.

NFL rules changes emphasized additional player safety. The changes prohibited players on the receiving team from blocking below the waist during kickoffs, punts, and field-goal attempts; prohibited the wearing of torn or altered equipment and exposed pads that could be hazardous; extended the zone in which there could be no crackback blocks; and instructed officials to quickly whistle a play dead when a quarterback was clearly in the grasp of a tackler, March 16.

Rosenbloom, the president of the Rams, drowned at 72, April 2. His widow, Georgia, assumed control of the club.

1980 Pittsburgh defeated the Los Angeles Rams 31-19 in Super Bowl XIV at Pasadena to become the first team to win four Super Bowls, January 20. The game was viewed in a record 35,330,000 homes.

The AFC-NFC Pro Bowl, won 37-27 by the NFC, was played before 48,060 fans at Aloha Stadium in Honolulu, Hawaii. It was the first time in the 30-year history of the Pro Bowl that the game was played in a non-NFL city.

Rules changes placed greater restrictions on contact in the area of the head, neck, and face. Under the heading of "personal foul," players were prohibited from directly striking, swinging, or clubbing on the head, neck, or face. Starting in 1980, a penalty could be called for such contact whether or not the initial contact was made below the neck area.

CBS, with a record bid of $12 million, won the national radio rights to 26 NFL regular-season games and all 10 postseason games for the 1980-83 seasons.

The Los Angeles Rams moved their home games to Anaheim Stadium in nearby Orange County, California.

The Oakland Raiders joined the Los Angeles Coliseum Commission's antitrust suit against the NFL. The suit contended the league violated antitrust laws in declining to approve a proposed move by the Raiders from Oakland to Los Angeles.

NFL regular-season attendance of nearly 13.4 million set a record for the third year in a row. The average paid attendance for the 224-game 1980 regular season was 59,787, the highest in the league's 61-year history. NFL games in 1980 were played before 92.4 percent of total stadium capacity.

Television ratings in 1980 were the second-best in NFL history, trailing only the combined ratings of the 1976 season. All three networks posted gains, and NBC's 15.0 rating was its best ever. CBS and ABC had their best ratings since 1977, with 15.3 and 20.8 ratings, respectively. CBS Radio reported a record audience of 7 million for Monday night and special games.

1981 Oakland defeated Philadelphia 27-10 in Super Bowl XV at the Louisiana Superdome in New Orleans, to become the first wild card team to win a Super Bowl, January 25.

Edgar F. Kaiser, Jr., purchased the Denver Broncos from Gerald and Allan Phipps, February 26.

The owners adopted a disaster plan for re-stocking a team should the club be involved in a fatal accident, March 20.

The owners awarded Super Bowl XVIII to Tampa to be played in Tampa Stadium on January 22, 1984, June 3.

A CBS-New York Times poll showed that 48 percent of sports fans preferred football to 31 percent for baseball.

The NFL teams hosted 167 representatives from 44 predominantly black colleges during training camps for a total of 289 days. The program was adopted for renewal during each training camp period.

NFL regular-season attendance—13.6 million for an average of 60,745—set a record for the fourth year in a row. It also was the first time the per-game average exceeded 60,000. NFL games in 1981 were played before 93.8 percent of total stadium capacity.

ABC and CBS set all-time rating highs. ABC finished with a 21.7 rating and CBS with a 17.5 rating. NBC was down slightly to 13.9.

1982 San Francisco defeated Cincinnati 26-21 in Super Bowl XVI at the Pontiac Silverdome, in the first Super Bowl held in the North, January 24. The CBS telecast achieved the highest rating of any televised sports event ever, 49.1 with a 73.0 share. The game was viewed by a record 110.2 million fans. CBS Radio reported a record 14 million listeners for the game.

The NFL signed a five-year contract with the three television networks (ABC, CBS, and NBC) to televise all NFL regular-season and postseason games starting with the 1982 season.

The owners awarded the 1983, 1984, and 1985 AFC-NFC Pro Bowls to Honolulu's Aloha Stadium.

A jury ruled against the NFL in the antitrust trial brought by the Los Angeles Coliseum Commission and the Oakland Raiders, May 7. The verdict cleared the way for the Raiders to move to Los Angeles, where they defeated Green Bay 24-3 in their first preseason game, August 29.

The 1982 season was reduced from a 16-game schedule to 9 as the result of a 57-day players' strike. The strike was called by the NFLPA at 12:00 midnight on Monday, September 20, following the Green Bay at New York Giants game. Play resumed November 21-22 following ratification of the Collective Bargaining Agreement by NFL owners, November 17 in New York.

Under the Collective Bargaining Agreement, which was to run through the 1986 season, the NFL draft was extended through 1992 and the veteran free-agent system was left basically unchanged. A minimum salary schedule for years of experience was established; training camp and postseason pay were increased; players' medical, insurance, and retirement benefits were increased; and a severance-pay system was introduced to aid in career transition, a first in professional sports.

Despite the players' strike, the average paid attendance in 1982 was 58,472, the fifth-highest in league history.

The owners awarded the sites of two Super Bowls, December 14: Super Bowl XIX, to be played on January 25, 1985, to Stanford University Stadium in Palo Alto, California, with San Francisco as host team; and Super Bowl XX, to be played on January 26, 1986, to the Louisiana Superdome in New Orleans.

1983 Because of the shortened season, the NFL adopted a format of 16 teams competing in a Super Bowl Tournament for the 1982 playoffs. The NFC's number-one seed, Washington, defeated the AFC's number-two seed, Miami, 27-17 in Super Bowl XVII at the Rose Bowl in Pasadena, January 30. The Redskins' victory marked only the second time the NFC had won consecutive Super Bowls.

Super Bowl XVII was the second-highest rated live television program of all time, giving the NFL a sweep of the top 10 live programs in television history. The game was viewed in more than 40 million homes, the largest ever for a live telecast.

Halas, the owner of the Bears and the last surviving member of the NFL's second organizational meeting, died at 88, October 31.

1984 The Los Angeles Raiders defeated Washington 38-9 in Super Bowl XVIII at Tampa Stadium, January 22. The game achieved a 46.4 rating and 71.0 share.

An 11-man group headed by H.R. (Bum) Bright purchased the Dallas Cowboys from Clint Murchison, Jr., March 20. Club president Tex Schramm was designated as managing general partner.

Patrick Bowlen purchased a majority interest in the Denver Broncos from Edgar Kaiser, Jr., March 21.

The Colts relocated to Indianapolis, March 28. Their new home became the Hoosier Dome.

The owners awarded two Super Bowl sites at their May 23-25 meetings: Super Bowl XXI, to be played on January 25, 1987, to the Rose Bowl in Pasadena; and Super Bowl XXII, to be played on January 31, 1988, to San Diego Jack Murphy Stadium.

The New York Jets moved their home games to Giants Stadium in East Rutherford, New Jersey.

Alex G. Spanos purchased a majority interest in the San Diego Chargers from Eugene V. Klein, August 28.

Houston defeated Pittsburgh 23-20 to mark the one-hundredth overtime game in regular-season play since overtime was adopted in 1974, December 2.

On the field, many all-time records were set: Dan Marino of Miami passed for 5,084 yards and 48 touchdowns; Eric Dickerson of the Los Angeles Rams rushed for 2,105 yards; Art Monk of Washington caught 106 passes; and Walter Payton of Chicago broke Jim Brown's career rushing mark, finishing the season with 13,309 yards.

According to a CBS Sports/New York Times survey, 53 percent of the nation's sports fans said they most enjoyed watching football, compared to 18 percent for baseball, December 2-4.

NFL paid attendance exceeded 13 million for the fifth consecutive complete regular season when 13,398,112, an average of 59,813, attended games. The figure was the second-highest in league history. Teams averaged 42.4 points per game, the second-highest total since the 1970 merger.

1985 San Francisco defeated Miami 38-16 in Super Bowl XIX at Stanford Stadium in Palo Alto, California, January 20. The game was viewed on television by more people than any other live event in history. President Ronald Reagan, who took his second oath of office before tossing the coin for the game, was one of 115,936,000 viewers. The game drew a 46.4 rating and a 63.0 share. In addition, 6 million people watched the Super Bowl in the United Kingdom and a similar number in Italy. Super Bowl XIX had a direct economic impact of $113.5 million on the San Francisco Bay area.

NBC Radio and the NFL entered into a two-year agreement granting NBC the radio rights to a 37-game package in each of the 1985-86 seasons, March 6. The package included 27 regular-season games and 10 postseason games.

The owners awarded two Super Bowl sites at their annual meeting, March 10-15: Super Bowl XXIII, to be played on January 22, 1989, to the proposed Dolphins Stadium in Miami; and Super Bowl XXIV, to be played on January 28, 1990, to the Louisiana Superdome in New Orleans.

Norman Braman, in partnership with Edward Leibowitz, bought the Philadelphia Eagles from Leonard Tose, April 29.

Bruce Smith, a Virginia Tech defensive lineman selected by Buffalo, was the first player chosen in the fiftieth NFL draft, April 30.

A group headed by Tom Benson, Jr., was approved to purchase the New Orleans Saints from John W. Mecom, Jr., June 3.

The NFL owners adopted a resolution calling for a series of overseas preseason games, beginning in 1986, with one game to be played in England/Europe and/or one game in Japan each year. The game would be a fifth preseason game for the clubs involved and all arrangements and selection of the clubs would be under the control of the Commissioner, May 23.

The league-wide conversion to videotape from movie film for coaching study was approved.

Commissioner Rozelle was authorized to extend the commitment to Honolulu's Aloha Stadium for the AFC-NFC Pro Bowl for 1988, 1989, and 1990, October 15.

The NFL set a single-weekend paid attendance record when 902,657 tickets were sold for the weekend of October 27-28.

A Louis Harris poll in December revealed that pro football remained the sport most followed by Americans. Fifty-nine percent of those surveyed followed pro football, compared with 54 percent who followed baseball.

The Chicago-Miami Monday game had the highest rating, 29.6, and share, 46.0, of any prime-time game in NFL history, December 2. The game was viewed in more than 25 million homes.

The NFL showed a ratings increase on all three networks for the season, gaining 4 percent on NBC, 10 on CBS, and 16 on ABC.

1986 Chicago defeated New England 46-10 in Super Bowl XX at the Louisiana Superdome, January 26. The Patriots had earned the right to play the Bears by becoming the first wild card team to win three consecutive games on the road. The NBC telecast replaced the final episode of M*A*S*H as the most-viewed television program in history, with an audience of 127 million viewers, according to A.C. Nielsen figures. In addition to drawing a 48.3 rating and a 70 percent share in the United States, Super Bowl XX was televised to 59 foreign countries and beamed via satellite to the QE II. An estimated 300 million Chinese viewed a tape delay of the game in March. NBC Radio figures indicated an audience of 10 million for the game.

Super Bowl XX injected more than $100 million into the New Orleans-area economy, and fans spent $250 per day and a record $17.69 per person on game day.

The owners adopted limited use of instant replay as an officiating aid, prohibited players from wearing or otherwise displaying equipment, apparel, or other items that carry commercial names, names of organizations, or personal messages of any type, March 11.

After an 11-week trial, a jury in U.S. District Court in New York awarded the United States Football League one dollar in its $1.7 billion antitrust suit against the NFL. The jury rejected all of the USFL's television-related claims, which were the self-proclaimed "heart" of the USFL's case, July 29.

Chicago defeated Dallas 17-6 at Wembley Stadium in London in the first American Bowl. The game drew a sellout crowd of 82,699 and the NBC national telecast in this country produced a 12.4 rating and 36 percent share, making it the second-highest-rated daytime preseason game and highest daytime preseason television audience ever with 10,650,000 viewers, August 3.

Monday Night Football became the longest-running prime-time series in the history of the ABC network.

Instant replay was used to reverse two plays in 31 preseason games. During the regular season, 374 plays were closely reviewed by replay officials, leading to 38 reversals in 224 games. Eighteen plays were closely reviewed by instant replay in 10 postseason games with three reversals.

1987 The New York Giants defeated Denver 39-20 in Super Bowl XXI and captured their first NFL title since 1956. The game, played in Pasadena's Rose Bowl, drew a sellout crowd of 101,063. According to A.C. Nielsen figures, the CBS broadcast of the game was viewed in the U.S. on television by 122,640,000 people, making the telecast the second most-watched television show of all-time behind Super Bowl XX. The game was watched live or on tape in 55 foreign countries and NBC Radio's broadcast of the game was heard by a record 10.1 million people.

The NFL set an all-time paid attendance mark of 17,304,463 for all games, including preseason, regular-season, and postseason. Average regular-season game attendance (60,663) exceeded the 60,000 figure for only the second time in league history.

New three-year TV contracts with ABC, CBS, and NBC were announced for 1987-89 at the NFL annual meeting in Maui, Hawaii, March 15. Commissioner Rozelle and Broadcast Committee Chairman Art Modell also announced a three-year contract with ESPN to televise a miniseries of 13 prime-time games each season. The ESPN contract was the first with a cable network. However, NFL games on ESPN also were scheduled for regular television in the city of the visiting team and in the home city if the game was sold out 72 hours in advance.

Owners also voted to continue in effect for one year the instant replay system used during the 1986 season.

A special payment program was adopted to benefit nearly 1,000 former NFL players who participated in the League before the current Bert Bell NFL Pension Plan was created and made retroactive to the 1959 season. Players covered by the new program spent at least five years in the League and played all or part of their career prior to 1959. Each vested player would receive $60 per month for each year of service in the League for life.

Possible sites for Super Bowl XXV were reduced to five locations by the NFL Super Bowl XXV Site Selection Committee: Anaheim Stadium, Los Angeles Memorial Coliseum, Joe Robbie Stadium, San Diego Jack Murphy Stadium, and Tampa Stadium.

NFL and CBS Radio jointly announced agreement granting CBS the radio rights to a 40-game package in each of the next three NFL seasons, 1987-89, April 7.

NFL owners awarded Super Bowl XXV, to be played on January 27, 1991, to Tampa Stadium, May 20.

Over 400 former NFL players from the pre-1959 era received first payments from NFL owners, July 1.

The NFL's debut on ESPN produced the two highest-rated and most-watched sports programs in basic cable history. The Chicago at Miami game on August 16 drew an 8.9 rating in 3.81 million homes. Those records fell two weeks later when the Los Angeles Raiders at Dallas game achieved a 10.2 cable rating in 4.36 million homes.

Fifty-eight preseason games drew a record paid attendance of 3,116,870.

The 1987 season was reduced from a 16-game season to 15 as the result of a 24-day players' strike. The strike was called by the NFLPA on Tuesday, September 22, following the New England at New York Jets game. Games scheduled for the third weekend were cancelled but the games of weeks four, five, and six were played with replacement teams. Striking players returned for the seventh week of the season, October 25.

In a three-team deal involving 10 players and/or draft choices, the Los Angeles Rams traded running back Eric Dickerson to the Indianapolis Colts for six draft choices and two players. Buffalo obtained the rights to linebacker Cornelius Bennett from Indianapolis, sending Greg Bell and three draft choices to the Rams. The Colts added Owen Gill and three draft choices of their own to complete the deal with the Rams, October 31.

The Chicago at Minnesota game became the highest rated and most-watched sports program in basic cable history when it drew a 14.4 cable rating in 6.5 million homes, December 6.

Instant replay was used to reverse eight plays in 52 preseason games. During the strike-shortened 210-game regular season, 490 plays were closely reviewed by replay officials, leading to 57 reversals. Eighteen plays were closely reviewed by instant replay in 10 postseason games, with three reversals.

1988 Washington defeated Denver 42-10 in Super Bowl XXII to earn a second victory this decade in the NFL Championship Game. The game, played for the first time in San Diego Jack Murphy Stadium, drew a sellout crowd of 73,302. According to A. C. Nielsen figures, the ABC broadcast of the game was viewed in the U.S. on television by 115,000,000 people. The game was seen live or on tape in 60 foreign countries, including the People's Republic of China, and CBS's radio broadcast of the game was heard by 13.7 million people.

A total of 811 players shared in the postseason pool of $16.9 million, the most ever distributed in a single season.

In a unanimous 3-0 decision, the 2nd Circuit Court of Appeals in New York upheld the verdict of the jury that in July, 1986, had awarded the United States Football League one dollar in its $1.7 billion antitrust suit against the NFL. In a 91-page opinion, Judge Ralph K. Winter said the USFL sought "through court decree the success it failed to gain among football fans," March 10.

By a 23-5 margin, owners voted to continue the instant replay system for the third consecutive season with the Instant Replay Official to be assigned to a regular seven-man, on-the-field crew. At the NFL annual meeting in Phoenix, Arizona, a 45-second clock was also approved to replace the 30-second clock. For a normal sequence of plays, the interval between plays was changed to 45 seconds from the time the ball is signaled dead until it is snapped on the succeeding play.

NFL owners approved the transfer of the Cardinals' franchise from St. Louis to Phoenix; approved two Supplemental Drafts each year—one prior to training camp and one prior to the regular season; and voted to initiate an annual series of games in Japan/Asia as early as the 1989 preseason, March 14-18.

The NFL Annual Selection Meeting returned to a separate two-day format and for the first time originated on a Sunday. ESPN drew a 3.6 rating during their seven-hour coverage of the draft, which was viewed in 1.6 million homes, April 24-25.

Art Rooney, founder and owner of the Steelers, died at 87, August 25.

Paid and average attendance of 934,271 and 66,734 at 14 games on October 16-17 set single weekend records.

Commissioner Rozelle announced that two teams would play a preseason game as part of the American Bowl series on August 6, 1989, in the Korakuen Tokyo Dome in Japan, December 16.

NFL regular-season paid attendance of 13,535,335 and the average of 60,427 was the third highest all-time. Buffalo set an NFL team single-season, in-house attendance mark of 622,793.

1989 San Francisco defeated Cincinnati 20-16 in Super Bowl XXIII. The game, played for the first time at Joe Robbie Stadium in Miami, was attended by a sellout crowd of 75,129. NBC's telecast of the game was watched by an estimated 110,780,000 viewers, according to A.C. Nielsen, making it the sixth most-watched program in television history. The game was seen live or on tape in 60 foreign countries, including an estimated 300 million in China. The CBS Radio broadcast of the game was heard by 11.2 million people.

Commissioner Rozelle announced his retirement, pending the naming of a successor, March 22 at the NFL annual meeting at Palm Desert, California.

Following the announcement, AFC president Lamar Hunt and NFC president Wellington Mara announced the formation of a six-man search committee composed of Art Modell, Robert Parins, Dan Rooney, and Ralph Wilson. Hunt and Mara served as co-chairmen.

By a 24-4 margin, owners voted to continue the instant replay system for the fourth straight season. A strengthened policy regarding anabolic steroids and masking agents was announced by Commissioner Rozelle. NFL clubs called for strong disciplinary measures in cases of feigned injuries and adopted a joint proposal by the Long-Range Planning and Finance committees regarding player personnel rules, March 19-23.

Two hundred twenty-nine unconditional free agents signed with new teams under management's Plan B system, April 1.

Jerry Jones purchased a majority interest in the Dallas Cowboys from H.R. (Bum) Bright, April 18.

Tex Schramm was named president of the new Worldwide American Football League to work with a six-man committee of Dan Rooney, chairman; Norman Braman, Lamar Hunt, Victor Kiam, Mike Lynn, and Bill Walsh, April 18.

NFL and CBS Radio jointly announced agreement extending CBS's radio rights to an annual 40-game package through the 1994 season, April 18.

NFL owners awarded Super Bowl XXVI, to be played on January 26, 1992, to Minneapolis, May 24.

NFL COMMISSIONERS AND PRESIDENTS*

1920 . . . . Jim Thorpe, President
1921-39. . . . . Joe Carr, President
1939-41 . . . . . Carl Storck, President
1941-46 . . . . Elmer Layden, Commissioner
1946-59 . . . Bert Bell, Commissioner
1960-present. . . . . Pete Rozelle, Commissioner

*NFL treasurer Austin Gunsel served as president in the office of the commissioner following the death of Bert Bell (Oct. 11, 1959) until the election of Pete Rozelle (Jan. 26, 1960).

PAST STANDINGS

1988

American Conference

Eastern Division

	W	L	T	Pct.	Pts.	OP
Buffalo	12	4	0	.750	329	237
Indianapolis	9	7	0	.563	354	315
New England	9	7	0	.563	250	284
N.Y. Jets	8	7	1	.531	372	354
Miami	6	10	0	.375	319	380

Central Division

	W	L	T	Pct.	Pts.	OP
Cincinnati	12	4	0	.750	448	329
Cleveland*	10	6	0	.625	304	288
Houston*	10	6	0	.625	424	365
Pittsburgh	5	11	0	.313	336	421

Western Division

	W	L	T	Pct.	Pts.	OP
Seattle	9	7	0	.563	339	329
Denver	8	8	0	.500	327	352
L.A. Raiders	7	9	0	.438	325	369
San Diego	6	10	0	.375	231	332
Kansas City	4	11	1	.281	254	320

National Conference

Eastern Division

	W	L	T	Pct.	Pts.	OP
Philadelphia	10	6	0	.625	379	319
N.Y. Giants	10	6	0	.625	359	304
Washington	7	9	0	.438	345	387
Phoenix	7	9	0	.438	344	398
Dallas	3	13	0	.188	265	381

Central Division

	W	L	T	Pct.	Pts.	OP
Chicago	12	4	0	.750	312	215
Minnesota*	11	5	0	.688	406	233
Tampa Bay	5	11	0	.313	261	350
Detroit	4	12	0	.250	220	313
Green Bay	4	12	0	.250	240	315

Western Division

	W	L	T	Pct.	Pts.	OP
San Francisco	10	6	0	.625	369	294
L.A. Rams*	10	6	0	.625	407	293
New Orleans	10	6	0	.625	312	283
Atlanta	5	11	0	.313	244	315

**Wild Card qualifiers for playoffs*

Indianapolis finished second in AFC East on basis of better record versus common opponents (7-5) over New England (6-6). Cleveland gained first AFC Wild Card position based on better division record (4-2) over Houston (3-3). Philadelphia finished first in NFC East on basis of head-to-head sweep over New York Giants. Washington finished third in NFC East on basis of better division record (4-4) over Phoenix (3-5). Detroit finished fourth in NFC Central on basis of head-to-head sweep over Green Bay. San Francisco finished first in NFC West based on better head-to-head record (3-1) over Los Angeles Rams (2-2) and New Orleans (1-3). Los Angeles Rams finished second in NFC West on basis of better division record (4-2) over New Orleans (3-3) and earned Wild Card position based on better conference record (8-4) over New York Giants (9-5) and New Orleans (6-6).

First round playoff: Houston 24, CLEVELAND 23
Divisional playoffs: CINCINNATI 21, Seattle 13; BUFFALO 17, Houston 10
AFC championship: CINCINNATI 21, Buffalo 10
First round playoff: MINNESOTA 28, Los Angeles Rams 17
Divisional playoffs: CHICAGO 20, Philadelphia 12; SAN FRANCISCO 34, Minnesota 9
NFC championship: San Francisco 28, CHICAGO 3
Super Bowl XXIII: San Francisco (NFC) 20, Cincinnati (AFC) 16 at Joe Robbie Stadium, Miami, Florida

1987

American Conference

Eastern Division

	W	L	T	Pct.	Pts.	OP
Indianapolis	9	6	0	.600	300	238
New England	8	7	0	.533	320	293
Miami	8	7	0	.533	362	335
Buffalo	7	8	0	.467	270	305
N.Y. Jets	6	9	0	.400	334	360

Central Division

	W	L	T	Pct.	Pts.	OP
Cleveland	10	5	0	.667	390	239
Houston*	9	6	0	.600	345	349
Pittsburgh	8	7	0	.533	285	299
Cincinnati	4	11	0	.267	285	370

Western Division

	W	L	T	Pct.	Pts.	OP
Denver	10	4	1	.700	379	288
Seattle*	9	6	0	.600	371	314
San Diego	8	7	0	.533	253	317
L.A. Raiders	5	10	0	.333	301	289
Kansas City	4	11	0	.267	273	388

National Conference

Eastern Division

	W	L	T	Pct.	Pts.	OP
Washington	11	4	0	.733	379	285
Dallas	7	8	0	.467	340	348
St. Louis	7	8	0	.467	362	368
Philadelphia	7	8	0	.467	337	380
N.Y. Giants	6	9	0	.400	280	312

Central Division

	W	L	T	Pct.	Pts.	OP
Chicago	11	4	0	.733	356	282
Minnesota*	8	7	0	.533	336	335
Green Bay	5	9	1	.367	255	300
Tampa Bay	4	11	0	.267	286	360
Detroit	4	11	0	.267	269	384

Western Division

	W	L	T	Pct.	Pts.	OP
San Francisco	13	2	0	.867	459	253
New Orleans*	12	3	0	.800	422	283
L.A. Rams	6	9	0	.400	317	361
Atlanta	3	12	0	.200	205	436

**Wild Card qualifiers for playoffs*

Houston gained first AFC Wild Card position on better conference record (7-4) over Seattle (5-6).

First round playoff: HOUSTON 23, Seattle 20 (OT)
Divisional playoffs: CLEVELAND 38, Indianapolis 21
DENVER 34, Houston 10
AFC championship: DENVER 38, Cleveland 33
First round playoff: Minnesota 44, NEW ORLEANS 10
Divisional playoffs: Minnesota 36, SAN FRANCISCO 24
Washington 21, CHICAGO 17
NFC championship: WASHINGTON 17, Minnesota 10
Super Bowl XXII: Washington (NFC) 42, Denver (AFC) 10, at San Diego Jack Murphy Stadium, San Diego, Calif.

Note: 1987 regular season was reduced from 16 to 15 games for each team due to players' strike.

In the Past Standings section, home teams in playoff games are indicated by capital letters.

1986

American Conference

Eastern Division

	W	L	T	Pct.	Pts.	OP
New England	11	5	0	.688	412	307
N.Y. Jets*	10	6	0	.625	364	386
Miami	8	8	0	.500	430	405
Buffalo	4	12	0	.250	287	348
Indianapolis	3	13	0	.188	229	400

Central Division

	W	L	T	Pct.	Pts.	OP
Cleveland	12	4	0	.750	391	310
Cincinnati	10	6	0	.625	409	394
Pittsburgh	6	10	0	.375	307	336
Houston	5	11	0	.313	274	329

Western Division

	W	L	T	Pct.	Pts.	OP
Denver	11	5	0	.688	378	327
Kansas City*	10	6	0	.625	358	326
Seattle	10	6	0	.625	366	293
L.A. Raiders	8	8	0	.500	323	346
San Diego	4	12	0	.250	335	396

National Conference

Eastern Division

	W	L	T	Pct.	Pts.	OP
N.Y. Giants	14	2	0	.875	371	236
Washington*	12	4	0	.750	368	296
Dallas	7	9	0	.438	346	337
Philadelphia	5	10	1	.344	256	312
St. Louis	4	11	1	.281	218	351

Central Division

	W	L	T	Pct.	Pts.	OP
Chicago	14	2	0	.875	352	187
Minnesota	9	7	0	.563	398	273
Detroit	5	11	0	.313	277	326
Green Bay	4	12	0	.250	254	418
Tampa Bay	2	14	0	.125	239	473

Western Division

	W	L	T	Pct.	Pts.	OP
San Francisco	10	5	1	.656	374	247
L.A. Rams*	10	6	0	.625	309	267
Atlanta	7	8	1	.469	280	280
New Orleans	7	9	0	.438	288	287

**Wild Card qualifiers for playoffs*

New York Jets gained first AFC Wild Card position on better conference record (8-4) over Kansas City (9-5), Seattle (7-5), and Cincinnati (7-5). Kansas City gained second Wild Card based on better conference record (9-5) over Seattle (7-5) and Cincinnati (7-5).

First round playoff: NEW YORK JETS 35, Kansas City 15
Divisional playoffs: CLEVELAND 23, New York Jets 20 (OT)
DENVER 22, New England 17
AFC championship: Denver 23, CLEVELAND 20 (OT)
First round playoff: WASHINGTON 19, Los Angeles Rams 7
Divisional playoffs: Washington 27, CHICAGO 13
NEW YORK GIANTS 49, San Francisco 3
NFC championship: NEW YORK GIANTS 17, Washington 0
Super Bowl XXI: New York Giants (NFC) 39, Denver (AFC) 20, at Rose Bowl, Pasadena, Calif.

1985

American Conference

Eastern Division

	W	L	T	Pct.	Pts.	OP
Miami	12	4	0	.750	428	320
N.Y. Jets*	11	5	0	.688	393	264
New England*	11	5	0	.688	362	290
Indianapolis	5	11	0	.313	320	386
Buffalo	2	14	0	.125	200	381

Central Division

	W	L	T	Pct.	Pts.	OP
Cleveland	8	8	0	.500	287	294
Cincinnati	7	9	0	.438	441	437
Pittsburgh	7	9	0	.438	379	355
Houston	5	11	0	.313	284	412

Western Division

	W	L	T	Pct.	Pts.	OP
L.A. Raiders	12	4	0	.750	354	308
Denver	11	5	0	.688	380	329
Seattle	8	8	0	.500	349	303
San Diego	8	8	0	.500	467	435
Kansas City	6	10	0	.375	317	360

National Conference

Eastern Division

	W	L	T	Pct.	Pts.	OP
Dallas	10	6	0	.625	357	333
N.Y. Giants*	10	6	0	.625	399	283
Washington	10	6	0	.625	297	312
Philadelphia	7	9	0	.438	286	310
St. Louis	5	11	0	.313	278	414

Central Division

	W	L	T	Pct.	Pts.	OP
Chicago	15	1	0	.938	456	198
Green Bay	8	8	0	.500	337	355
Minnesota	7	9	0	.438	346	359
Detroit	7	9	0	.438	307	366
Tampa Bay	2	14	0	.125	294	448

Western Division

	W	L	T	Pct.	Pts.	OP
L.A. Rams	11	5	0	.688	340	277
San Francisco*	10	6	0	.625	411	263
New Orleans	5	11	0	.313	294	401
Atlanta	4	12	0	.250	282	452

**Wild Card qualifiers for playoffs*

New York Jets gained first AFC Wild Card position on better conference record (9-3) over New England (8-4) and Denver (8-4). New England gained second AFC Wild Card position based on better record vs. common opponents (4-2) than Denver (3-3). Dallas won NFC Eastern Division title based on better record (4-0) vs. New York Giants (1-3) and Washington (1-3). New York Giants gained first NFC Wild Card position based on better conference record (8-4) over San Francisco (7-5) and Washington (6-6). San Francisco gained second NFC Wild Card position based on head-to-head victory over Washington.

First round playoff: New England 26, NEW YORK JETS 14
Divisional playoffs: MIAMI 24, Cleveland 21;
New England 27, LOS ANGELES RAIDERS 20
AFC championship: New England 31, MIAMI 14
First round playoff: NEW YORK GIANTS 17, San Francisco 3
Divisional playoffs: LOS ANGELES RAMS 20, Dallas 0;
CHICAGO 21, New York Giants 0
NFC championship: CHICAGO 24, Los Angeles Rams 0
Super Bowl XX: Chicago (NFC) 46, New England (AFC) 10, at Louisiana Superdome, New Orleans, La.

1984

American Conference

Eastern Division

	W	L	T	Pct.	Pts.	OP
Miami	14	2	0	.875	513	298
New England	9	7	0	.563	362	352
N.Y. Jets	7	9	0	.438	332	364
Indianapolis	4	12	0	.250	239	414
Buffalo	2	14	0	.125	250	454

Central Division

	W	L	T	Pct.	Pts.	OP
Pittsburgh	9	7	0	.563	387	310
Cincinnati	8	8	0	.500	339	339
Cleveland	5	11	0	.313	250	297
Houston	3	13	0	.188	240	437

Western Division

	W	L	T	Pct.	Pts.	OP
Denver	13	3	0	.813	353	241
Seattle*	12	4	0	.750	418	282
L.A. Raiders*	11	5	0	.688	368	278
Kansas City	8	8	0	.500	314	324
San Diego	7	9	0	.438	394	413

National Conference

Eastern Division

	W	L	T	Pct.	Pts.	OP
Washington	11	5	0	.688	426	310
N.Y. Giants*	9	7	0	.563	299	301
St. Louis	9	7	0	.563	423	345
Dallas	9	7	0	.563	308	308
Philadelphia	6	9	1	.406	278	320

Central Division

	W	L	T	Pct.	Pts.	OP
Chicago	10	6	0	.625	325	248
Green Bay	8	8	0	.500	390	309
Tampa Bay	6	10	0	.375	335	380
Detroit	4	11	1	.281	283	408
Minnesota	3	13	0	.188	276	484

Western Division

	W	L	T	Pct.	Pts.	OP
San Francisco	15	1	0	.938	475	227
L.A. Rams*	10	6	0	.625	346	316
New Orleans	7	9	0	.438	298	361
Atlanta	4	12	0	.250	281	382

**Wild Card qualifiers for playoffs*

New York Giants clinched Wild Card berth based on 3-1 record vs. St. Louis's 2-2 and Dallas's 1-3. St. Louis finished ahead of Dallas based on better division record (5-3 to 3-5).

First round playoff: SEATTLE 13, Los Angeles Raiders 7
Divisional playoffs: MIAMI 31, Seattle 10; Pittsburgh 24, DENVER 17
AFC championship: MIAMI 45, Pittsburgh 28
First round playoff: New York Giants 16, LOS ANGELES RAMS 13
Divisional playoffs: SAN FRANCISCO 21, New York Giants 10; Chicago 23, WASHINGTON 19
NFC championship: SAN FRANCISCO 23, Chicago 0
Super Bowl XIX: San Francisco (NFC) 38, Miami (AFC) 16, at Stanford Stadium, Stanford, Calif.

1983

American Conference

Eastern Division

	W	L	T	Pct.	Pts.	OP
Miami	12	4	0	.750	389	250
New England	8	8	0	.500	274	289
Buffalo	8	8	0	.500	283	351
Baltimore	7	9	0	.438	264	354
N.Y. Jets	7	9	0	.438	313	331

Central Division

	W	L	T	Pct.	Pts.	OP
Pittsburgh	10	6	0	.625	355	303
Cleveland	9	7	0	.563	356	342
Cincinnati	7	9	0	.438	346	302
Houston	2	14	0	.125	288	460

Western Division

	W	L	T	Pct.	Pts.	OP
L.A. Raiders	12	4	0	.750	442	338
Seattle*	9	7	0	.563	403	397
Denver*	9	7	0	.563	302	327
San Diego	6	10	0	.375	358	462
Kansas City	6	10	0	.375	386	367

National Conference

Eastern Division

	W	L	T	Pct.	Pts.	OP
Washington	14	2	0	.875	541	332
Dallas*	12	4	0	.750	479	360
St. Louis	8	7	1	.531	374	428
Philadelphia	5	11	0	.313	233	322
N.Y. Giants	3	12	1	.219	267	347

Central Division

	W	L	T	Pct.	Pts.	OP
Detroit	9	7	0	.563	347	286
Green Bay	8	8	0	.500	429	439
Chicago	8	8	0	.500	311	301
Minnesota	8	8	0	.500	316	348
Tampa Bay	2	14	0	.125	241	380

Western Division

	W	L	T	Pct.	Pts.	OP
San Francisco	10	6	0	.625	432	293
L.A. Rams*	9	7	0	.563	361	344
New Orleans	8	8	0	.500	319	337
Atlanta	7	9	0	.438	370	389

**Wild Card qualifiers for playoffs*

Seattle and Denver gained Wild Card berths over Cleveland because of their victories over the Browns.

First round playoff: SEATTLE 31, Denver 7
Divisional playoffs: Seattle 27, MIAMI 20; LOS ANGELES RAIDERS 38, Pittsburgh 10
AFC championship: LOS ANGELES RAIDERS 30, Seattle 14
First round playoff: Los Angeles Rams 24, DALLAS 17
Divisional playoffs: SAN FRANCISCO 24, Detroit 23; WASHINGTON 51, L.A. Rams 7
NFC championship: WASHINGTON 24, San Francisco 21
Super Bowl XVIII: Los Angeles Raiders (AFC) 38, Washington (NFC) 9, at Tampa Stadium, Tampa, Fla.

1982

American Conference

	W	L	T	Pct.	Pts.	OP
L.A. Raiders	8	1	0	.889	260	200
Miami	7	2	0	.778	198	131
Cincinnati	7	2	0	.778	232	177
Pittsburgh	6	3	0	.667	204	146
San Diego	6	3	0	.667	288	221
N.Y. Jets	6	3	0	.667	245	166
New England	5	4	0	.556	143	157
Cleveland	4	5	0	.444	140	182
Buffalo	4	5	0	.444	150	154
Seattle	4	5	0	.444	127	147
Kansas City	3	6	0	.333	176	184
Denver	2	7	0	.222	148	226
Houston	1	8	0	.111	136	245
Baltimore	0	8	1	.056	113	236

National Conference

	W	L	T	Pct.	Pts.	OP
Washington	8	1	0	.889	190	128
Dallas	6	3	0	.667	226	145
Green Bay	5	3	1	.611	226	169
Minnesota	5	4	0	.556	187	198
Atlanta	5	4	0	.556	183	199
St. Louis	5	4	0	.556	135	170
Tampa Bay	5	4	0	.556	158	178
Detroit	4	5	0	.444	181	176
New Orleans	4	5	0	.444	129	160
N.Y. Giants	4	5	0	.444	164	160
San Francisco	3	6	0	.333	209	206
Chicago	3	6	0	.333	141	174
Philadelphia	3	6	0	.333	191	195
L.A. Rams	2	7	0	.222	200	250

As the result of a 57-day players' strike, the 1982 NFL regular season schedule was reduced from 16 weeks to 9. At the conclusion of the regular season, the NFL conducted a 16-team postseason Super Bowl Tournament. Eight teams from each conference were seeded 1-8 based on their records during the season.

Miami finished ahead of Cincinnati based on better conference record (6-1 to 6-2). Pittsburgh won common games tie-breaker with San Diego (3-1 to 2-1) after New York Jets were eliminated from three-way tie based on conference record (Pittsburgh and San Diego 5-3 vs. Jets 2-3). Cleveland finished ahead of Buffalo and Seattle based on better conference record (4-3 to 3-3 to 3-5). Minnesota (4-1), Atlanta (4-3), St. Louis (5-4), Tampa Bay (3-3) seeds were determined by best won-lost record in conference games. Detroit finished ahead of New Orleans and the New York Giants based on better conference record (4-4 to 3-5 to 3-5).

First round playoff: MIAMI 28, New England 13
LOS ANGELES RAIDERS 27, Cleveland 10
New York Jets 44, CINCINNATI 17
San Diego 31, PITTSBURGH 28
Second round playoff: New York Jets 17, LOS ANGELES RAIDERS 14
MIAMI 34, San Diego 13
AFC championship: MIAMI 14, New York Jets 0
First round playoff: WASHINGTON 31, Detroit 7
GREEN BAY 41, St. Louis 16
MINNESOTA 30, Atlanta 24
DALLAS 30, Tampa Bay 17
Second round playoff: WASHINGTON 21, Minnesota 7
DALLAS 37, Green Bay 26
NFC championship: WASHINGTON 31, Dallas 17
Super Bowl XVII: Washington (NFC) 27, Miami (AFC) 17, at Rose Bowl, Pasadena, Calif.

1981

American Conference

Eastern Division

	W	L	T	Pct.	Pts.	OP
Miami	11	4	1	.719	345	275
N.Y. Jets*	10	5	1	.656	355	287
Buffalo*	10	6	0	.625	311	276
Baltimore	2	14	0	.125	259	533
New England	2	14	0	.125	322	370

Central Division

	W	L	T	Pct.	Pts.	OP
Cincinnati	12	4	0	.750	421	304
Pittsburgh	8	8	0	.500	356	297
Houston	7	9	0	.438	281	355
Cleveland	5	11	0	.313	276	375

Western Division

	W	L	T	Pct.	Pts.	OP
San Diego	10	6	0	.625	478	390
Denver	10	6	0	.625	321	289
Kansas City	9	7	0	.563	343	290
Oakland	7	9	0	.438	273	343
Seattle	6	10	0	.375	322	388

National Conference

Eastern Division

	W	L	T	Pct.	Pts.	OP
Dallas	12	4	0	.750	367	277
Philadelphia*	10	6	0	.625	368	221
N.Y. Giants*	9	7	0	.563	295	257
Washington	8	8	0	.500	347	349
St. Louis	7	9	0	.438	315	408

Central Division

	W	L	T	Pct.	Pts.	OP
Tampa Bay	9	7	0	.563	315	268
Detroit	8	8	0	.500	397	322
Green Bay	8	8	0	.500	324	361
Minnesota	7	9	0	.438	325	369
Chicago	6	10	0	.375	253	324

Western Division

	W	L	T	Pct.	Pts.	OP
San Francisco	13	3	0	.813	357	250
Atlanta	7	9	0	.438	426	355
Los Angeles	6	10	0	.375	303	351
New Orleans	4	12	0	.250	207	378

**Wild Card qualifiers for playoffs*

San Diego won AFC Western title over Denver on the basis of a better division record (6-2 to 5-3). Buffalo won a Wild Card playoff berth over Denver as the result of a 9-7 victory in head-to-head competition.

First round playoff: Buffalo 31, NEW YORK JETS 27
Divisional playoffs: San Diego 41, MIAMI 38 (OT); CINCINNATI 28, Buffalo 21
AFC championship: CINCINNATI 27, San Diego 7
First round playoff: New York Giants 27, PHILADELPHIA 21
Divisional playoffs: DALLAS 38, Tampa Bay 0; SAN FRANCISCO 38, New York Giants 24
NFC championship: SAN FRANCISCO 28, Dallas 27
Super Bowl XVI: San Francisco (NFC) 26, Cincinnati (AFC) 21, at Silverdome, Pontiac, Mich

1980

American Conference

Eastern Division

	W	L	T	Pct.	Pts.	OP
Buffalo	11	5	0	.688	320	260
New England	10	6	0	.625	441	325
Miami	8	8	0	.500	266	305
Baltimore	7	9	0	.438	355	387
N.Y. Jets	4	12	0	.250	302	395

Central Division

	W	L	T	Pct.	Pts.	OP
Cleveland	11	5	0	.688	357	310
Houston*	11	5	0	.688	295	251
Pittsburgh	9	7	0	.563	352	313
Cincinnati	6	10	0	.375	244	312

Western Division

	W	L	T	Pct.	Pts.	OP
San Diego	11	5	0	.688	418	327
Oakland*	11	5	0	.688	364	306
Kansas City	8	8	0	.500	319	336
Denver	8	8	0	.500	310	323
Seattle	4	12	0	.250	291	408

National Conference

Eastern Division

	W	L	T	Pct.	Pts.	OP
Philadelphia	12	4	0	.750	384	222
Dallas*	12	4	0	.750	454	311
Washington	6	10	0	.375	261	293
St. Louis	5	11	0	.313	299	350
N.Y. Giants	4	12	0	.250	249	425

Central Division

	W	L	T	Pct.	Pts.	OP
Minnesota	9	7	0	.563	317	308
Detroit	9	7	0	.563	334	272
Chicago	7	9	0	.438	304	264
Tampa Bay	5	10	1	.344	271	341
Green Bay	5	10	1	.344	231	371

Western Division

	W	L	T	Pct.	Pts.	OP
Atlanta	12	4	0	.750	405	272
Los Angeles*	11	5	0	.688	424	289
San Francisco	6	10	0	.375	320	415
New Orleans	1	15	0	.063	291	487

**Wild Card qualifiers for playoffs*

Philadelphia won division title over Dallas on the basis of best net points in division games (plus 84 net points to plus 50). Minnesota won division title because of a better conference record than Detroit (8-4 to 9-5). Cleveland won division title because of a better conference record than Houston (8-4 to 7-5). San Diego won division title over Oakland on the basis of best net points in division games (plus 60 net points to plus 37).

First round playoff: OAKLAND 27, Houston 7
Divisional playoffs: SAN DIEGO 20, Buffalo 14; Oakland 14, CLEVELAND 12
AFC championship: Oakland 34, SAN DIEGO 27
First round playoff: DALLAS 34, Los Angeles 13
Divisional playoffs: PHILADELPHIA 31, Minnesota 16; Dallas 30, ATLANTA 27
NFC championship: PHILADELPHIA 20, Dallas 7
Super Bowl XV: Oakland (AFC) 27, Philadelphia (NFC) 10, at Louisiana Superdome, New Orleans, La.

1979

American Conference

Eastern Division

	W	L	T	Pct.	Pts.	OP
Miami	10	6	0	.625	341	257
New England	9	7	0	.563	411	326
N.Y. Jets	8	8	0	.500	337	383
Buffalo	7	9	0	.438	268	279
Baltimore	5	11	0	.313	271	351

Central Division

	W	L	T	Pct.	Pts.	OP
Pittsburgh	12	4	0	.750	416	262
Houston*	11	5	0	.688	362	331
Cleveland	9	7	0	.563	359	352
Cincinnati	4	12	0	.250	337	421

Western Division

	W	L	T	Pct.	Pts.	OP
San Diego	12	4	0	.750	411	246
Denver*	10	6	0	.625	289	262
Seattle	9	7	0	.563	378	372
Oakland	9	7	0	.563	365	337
Kansas City	7	9	0	.438	238	262

National Conference

Eastern Division

	W	L	T	Pct.	Pts.	OP
Dallas	11	5	0	.688	371	313
Philadelphia*	11	5	0	.688	339	282
Washington	10	6	0	.625	348	295
N.Y. Giants	6	10	0	.375	237	323
St. Louis	5	11	0	.313	307	358

Central Division

	W	L	T	Pct.	Pts.	OP
Tampa Bay	10	6	0	.625	273	237
Chicago*	10	6	0	.625	306	249
Minnesota	7	9	0	.438	259	337
Green Bay	5	11	0	.313	246	316
Detroit	2	14	0	.125	219	365

Western Division

	W	L	T	Pct.	Pts.	OP
Los Angeles	9	7	0	.563	323	309
New Orleans	8	8	0	.500	370	360
Atlanta	6	10	0	.375	300	388
San Francisco	2	14	0	.125	308	416

**Wild Card qualifiers for playoffs*

Dallas won division title because of a better conference record than Philadelphia (10-2 to 9-3). Tampa Bay won division title because of a better division record than Chicago (6-2 to 5-3). Chicago won a Wild Card berth over Washington on the basis of best net points in all games (plus 57 net points to plus 53).

First round playoff: HOUSTON 13, Denver 7
Divisional playoffs: Houston 17, SAN DIEGO 14; PITTSBURGH 34, Miami 14
AFC championship: PITTSBURGH 27, Houston 13
First round playoff: PHILADELPHIA 27, Chicago 17
Divisional playoffs: TAMPA BAY 24, Philadelphia 17; Los Angeles 21, DALLAS 19
NFC championship: Los Angeles 9, TAMPA BAY 0
Super Bowl XIV: Pittsburgh (AFC) 31, Los Angeles (NFC) 19, at Rose Bowl, Pasadena, Calif.

1978

American Conference

Eastern Division

	W	L	T	Pct.	Pts.	OP
New England	11	5	0	.688	358	286
Miami*	11	5	0	.688	372	254
N.Y. Jets	8	8	0	.500	359	364
Buffalo	5	11	0	.313	302	354
Baltimore	5	11	0	.313	239	421

Central Division

	W	L	T	Pct.	Pts.	OP
Pittsburgh	14	2	0	.875	356	195
Houston*	10	6	0	.625	283	298
Cleveland	8	8	0	.500	334	356
Cincinnati	4	12	0	.250	252	284

Western Division

	W	L	T	Pct.	Pts.	OP
Denver	10	6	0	.625	282	198
Oakland	9	7	0	.563	311	283
Seattle	9	7	0	.563	345	358
San Diego	9	7	0	.563	355	309
Kansas City	4	12	0	.250	243	327

National Conference

Eastern Division

	W	L	T	Pct.	Pts.	OP
Dallas	12	4	0	.750	384	208
Philadelphia*	9	7	0	.563	270	250
Washington	8	8	0	.500	273	283
St. Louis	6	10	0	.375	248	296
N.Y. Giants	6	10	0	.375	264	298

Central Division

	W	L	T	Pct.	Pts.	OP
Minnesota	8	7	1	.531	294	306
Green Bay	8	7	1	.531	249	269
Detroit	7	9	0	.438	290	300
Chicago	7	9	0	.438	253	274
Tampa Bay	5	11	0	.313	241	259

Western Division

	W	L	T	Pct.	Pts.	OP
Los Angeles	12	4	0	.750	316	245
Atlanta*	9	7	0	.563	240	290
New Orleans	7	9	0	.438	281	298
San Francisco	2	14	0	.125	219	350

**Wild Card qualifiers for playoffs*

New England won division title on the basis of a better division record than Miami (6-2 to 5-3). Minnesota won division title because of a better head-to-head record against Green Bay (1-0-1).

First round playoff: Houston 17, MIAMI 9
Divisional playoffs: Houston 31, NEW ENGLAND 14; PITTSBURGH 33, Denver 10
AFC championship: PITTSBURGH 34, Houston 5
First round playoff: ATLANTA 14, Philadelphia 13
Divisional playoffs: DALLAS 27, Atlanta 20; LOS ANGELES 34, Minnesota 10
NFC championship: Dallas 28, LOS ANGELES 0
Super Bowl XIII: Pittsburgh (AFC) 35, Dallas (NFC) 31, at Orange Bowl, Miami, Fla.

1977

American Conference

Eastern Division

	W	L	T	Pct.	Pts.	OP
Baltimore	10	4	0	.714	295	221
Miami	10	4	0	.714	313	197
New England	9	5	0	.643	278	217
N.Y. Jets	3	11	0	.214	191	300
Buffalo	3	11	0	.214	160	313

Central Division

	W	L	T	Pct.	Pts.	OP
Pittsburgh	9	5	0	.643	283	243
Houston	8	6	0	.571	299	230
Cincinnati	8	6	0	.571	238	235
Cleveland	6	8	0	.429	269	267

Western Division

	W	L	T	Pct.	Pts.	OP
Denver	12	2	0	.857	274	148
Oakland*	11	3	0	.786	351	230
San Diego	7	7	0	.500	222	205
Seattle	5	9	0	.357	282	373
Kansas City	2	12	0	.143	225	349

National Conference

Eastern Division

	W	L	T	Pct.	Pts.	OP
Dallas	12	2	0	.857	345	212
Washington	9	5	0	.643	196	189
St. Louis	7	7	0	.500	272	287
Philadelphia	5	9	0	.357	220	207
N.Y. Giants	5	9	0	.357	181	265

Central Division

	W	L	T	Pct.	Pts.	OP
Minnesota	9	5	0	.643	231	227
Chicago*	9	5	0	.643	255	253
Detroit	6	8	0	.429	183	252
Green Bay	4	10	0	.286	134	219
Tampa Bay	2	12	0	.143	103	223

Western Division

	W	L	T	Pct.	Pts.	OP
Los Angeles	10	4	0	.714	302	146
Atlanta	7	7	0	.500	179	129
San Francisco	5	9	0	.357	220	260
New Orleans	3	11	0	.214	232	336

**Wild Card qualifier for playoffs*

Baltimore won division title on the basis of a better conference record than Miami (9-3 to 8-4). Chicago won a Wild Card berth over Washington on the basis of best net points in conference games (plus 48 net points to plus 4).

Divisional playoffs: DENVER 34, Pittsburgh 21; Oakland 37, BALTIMORE 31 (OT)
AFC championship: DENVER 20, Oakland 17
Divisional playoffs: DALLAS 37, Chicago 7; Minnesota 14, LOS ANGELES 7
NFC championship: DALLAS 23, Minnesota 6
Super Bowl XII: Dallas (NFC) 27, Denver (AFC) 10, at Louisiana Superdome, New Orleans, La.

1976

American Conference

Eastern Division

	W	L	T	Pct.	Pts.	OP
Baltimore	11	3	0	.786	417	246
New England*	11	3	0	.786	376	236
Miami	6	8	0	.429	263	264
N.Y. Jets	3	11	0	.214	169	383
Buffalo	2	12	0	.143	245	363

Central Division

	W	L	T	Pct.	Pts.	OP
Pittsburgh	10	4	0	.714	342	138
Cincinnati	10	4	0	.714	335	210
Cleveland	9	5	0	.643	267	287
Houston	5	9	0	.357	222	273

Western Division

	W	L	T	Pct.	Pts.	OP
Oakland	13	1	0	.929	350	237
Denver	9	5	0	.643	315	206
San Diego	6	8	0	.429	248	285
Kansas City	5	9	0	.357	290	376
Tampa Bay	0	14	0	.000	125	412

National Conference

Eastern Division

	W	L	T	Pct.	Pts.	OP
Dallas	11	3	0	.786	296	194
Washington*	10	4	0	.714	291	217
St. Louis	10	4	0	.714	309	267
Philadelphia	4	10	0	.286	165	286
N.Y. Giants	3	11	0	.214	170	250

Central Division

	W	L	T	Pct.	Pts.	OP
Minnesota	11	2	1	.821	305	176
Chicago	7	7	0	.500	253	216
Detroit	6	8	0	.429	262	220
Green Bay	5	9	0	.357	218	299

Western Division

	W	L	T	Pct.	Pts.	OP
Los Angeles	10	3	1	.750	351	190
San Francisco	8	6	0	.571	270	190
Atlanta	4	10	0	.286	172	312
New Orleans	4	10	0	.286	253	346
Seattle	2	12	0	.143	229	429

**Wild Card qualifier for playoffs*

Baltimore won division title on the basis of a better division record than New England (7-1 to 6-2). Pittsburgh won division title because of a two-game sweep over Cincinnati. Washington won Wild Card berth over St. Louis because of a two-game sweep over Cardinals.

Divisional playoffs: OAKLAND 24, New England 21; Pittsburgh 40, BALTIMORE 14
AFC championship: OAKLAND 24, Pittsburgh 7
Divisional playoffs: MINNESOTA 35, Washington 20; Los Angeles 14, DALLAS 12
NFC championship: MINNESOTA 24, Los Angeles 13
Super Bowl XI: Oakland (AFC) 32, Minnesota (NFC) 14, at Rose Bowl, Pasadena, Calif.

1975

American Conference

Eastern Division

	W	L	T	Pct.	Pts.	OP
Baltimore	10	4	0	.714	395	269
Miami	10	4	0	.714	357	222
Buffalo	8	6	0	.571	420	355
New England	3	11	0	.214	258	358
N.Y. Jets	3	11	0	.214	258	433

Central Division

	W	L	T	Pct.	Pts.	OP
Pittsburgh	12	2	0	.857	373	162
Cincinnati*	11	3	0	.786	340	246
Houston	10	4	0	.714	293	226
Cleveland	3	11	0	.214	218	372

Western Division

	W	L	T	Pct.	Pts.	OP
Oakland	11	3	0	.786	375	255
Denver	6	8	0	.429	254	307
Kansas City	5	9	0	.357	282	341
San Diego	2	12	0	.143	189	345

National Conference

Eastern Division

	W	L	T	Pct.	Pts.	OP
St. Louis	11	3	0	.786	356	276
Dallas*	10	4	0	.714	350	268
Washington	8	6	0	.571	325	276
N.Y. Giants	5	9	0	.357	216	306
Philadelphia	4	10	0	.286	225	302

Central Division

	W	L	T	Pct.	Pts.	OP
Minnesota	12	2	0	.857	377	180
Detroit	7	7	0	.500	245	262
Chicago	4	10	0	.286	191	379
Green Bay	4	10	0	.286	226	285

Western Division

	W	L	T	Pct.	Pts.	OP
Los Angeles	12	2	0	.857	312	135
San Francisco	5	9	0	.357	255	286
Atlanta	4	10	0	.286	240	289
New Orleans	2	12	0	.143	165	360

*Wild Card qualifier for playoffs

Baltimore won division title on the basis of a two-game sweep over Miami.

Divisional playoffs: PITTSBURGH 28, Baltimore 10; OAKLAND 31, Cincinnati 28
AFC championship: PITTSBURGH 16, Oakland 10
Divisional playoffs: LOS ANGELES 35, St. Louis 23; Dallas 17, MINNESOTA 14
NFC championship: Dallas 37, LOS ANGELES 7
Super Bowl X: Pittsburgh (AFC) 21, Dallas (NFC) 17, at Orange Bowl, Miami, Fla.

1974

American Conference

Eastern Division

	W	L	T	Pct.	Pts.	OP
Miami	11	3	0	.786	327	216
Buffalo*	9	5	0	.643	264	244
New England	7	7	0	.500	348	289
N.Y. Jets	7	7	0	.500	279	300
Baltimore	2	12	0	.143	190	329

Central Division

	W	L	T	Pct.	Pts.	OP
Pittsburgh	10	3	1	.750	305	189
Cincinnati	7	7	0	.500	283	259
Houston	7	7	0	.500	236	282
Cleveland	4	10	0	.286	251	344

Western Division

	W	L	T	Pct.	Pts.	OP
Oakland	12	2	0	.857	355	228
Denver	7	6	1	.536	302	294
Kansas City	5	9	0	.357	233	293
San Diego	5	9	0	.357	212	285

National Conference

Eastern Division

	W	L	T	Pct.	Pts.	OP
St. Louis	10	4	0	.714	285	218
Washington*	10	4	0	.714	320	196
Dallas	8	6	0	.571	297	235
Philadelphia	7	7	0	.500	242	217
N.Y. Giants	2	12	0	.143	195	299

Central Division

	W	L	T	Pct.	Pts.	OP
Minnesota	10	4	0	.714	310	195
Detroit	7	7	0	.500	256	270
Green Bay	6	8	0	.429	210	206
Chicago	4	10	0	.286	152	279

Western Division

	W	L	T	Pct.	Pts.	OP
Los Angeles	10	4	0	.714	263	181
San Francisco	6	8	0	.429	226	236
New Orleans	5	9	0	.357	166	263
Atlanta	3	11	0	.214	111	271

*Wild Card qualifier for playoffs

St. Louis won division title because of a two-game sweep over Washington.

Divisional playoffs: OAKLAND 28, Miami 26; PITTSBURGH 32, Buffalo 14
AFC championship: Pittsburgh 24, OAKLAND 13
Divisional playoffs: MINNESOTA 30, St. Louis 14; LOS ANGELES 19, Washington 10
NFC championship: MINNESOTA 14, Los Angeles 10
Super Bowl IX: Pittsburgh (AFC) 16, Minnesota (NFC) 6, at Tulane Stadium, New Orleans, La

1973

American Conference

Eastern Division

	W	L	T	Pct.	Pts.	OP
Miami	12	2	0	.857	343	150
Buffalo	9	5	0	.643	259	230
New England	5	9	0	.357	258	300
Baltimore	4	10	0	.286	226	341
N.Y. Jets	4	10	0	.286	240	306

Central Division

	W	L	T	Pct.	Pts.	OP
Cincinnati	10	4	0	.714	286	231
Pittsburgh*	10	4	0	.714	347	210
Cleveland	7	5	2	.571	234	255
Houston	1	13	0	.071	199	447

Western Division

	W	L	T	Pct.	Pts.	OP
Oakland	9	4	1	.679	292	175
Denver	7	5	2	.571	354	296
Kansas City	7	5	2	.571	231	192
San Diego	2	11	1	.179	188	386

National Conference

Eastern Division

	W	L	T	Pct.	Pts.	OP
Dallas	10	4	0	.714	382	203
Washington*	10	4	0	.714	325	198
Philadelphia	5	8	1	.393	310	393
St. Louis	4	9	1	.321	286	365
N.Y. Giants	2	11	1	.179	226	362

Central Division

	W	L	T	Pct.	Pts.	OP
Minnesota	12	2	0	.857	296	168
Detroit	6	7	1	.464	271	247
Green Bay	5	7	2	.429	202	259
Chicago	3	11	0	.214	195	334

Western Division

	W	L	T	Pct.	Pts.	OP
Los Angeles	12	2	0	.857	388	178
Atlanta	9	5	0	.643	318	224
New Orleans	5	9	0	.357	163	312
San Francisco	5	9	0	.357	262	319

*Wild Card qualifier for playoffs

Cincinnati won division title on the basis of a better conference record than Pittsburgh (8-3 to 7-4). Dallas won division title on the basis of a better point differential vs. Washington (net 13 points).

Divisional playoffs: OAKLAND 33, Pittsburgh 14; MIAMI 34, Cincinnati 16
AFC championship: MIAMI 27, Oakland 10
Divisional playoffs: MINNESOTA 27, Washington 20; DALLAS 27, Los Angeles 16
NFC championship: Minnesota 27, DALLAS 10
Super Bowl VIII: Miami (AFC) 24, Minnesota (NFC) 7, at Rice Stadium, Houston, Tex.

1972

American Conference

Eastern Division

	W	L	T	Pct.	Pts.	OP
Miami	14	0	0	1.000	385	171
N.Y. Jets	7	7	0	.500	367	324
Baltimore	5	9	0	.357	235	252
Buffalo	4	9	1	.321	257	377
New England	3	11	0	.214	192	446

Central Division

	W	L	T	Pct.	Pts.	OP
Pittsburgh	11	3	0	.786	343	175
Cleveland*	10	4	0	.714	268	249
Cincinnati	8	6	0	.571	299	229
Houston	1	13	0	.071	164	380

Western Division

	W	L	T	Pct.	Pts.	OP
Oakland	10	3	1	.750	365	248
Kansas City	8	6	0	.571	287	254
Denver	5	9	0	.357	325	350
San Diego	4	9	1	.321	264	344

National Conference

Eastern Division

	W	L	T	Pct.	Pts.	OP
Washington	11	3	0	.786	336	218
Dallas*	10	4	0	.714	319	240
N.Y. Giants	8	6	0	.571	331	247
St. Louis	4	9	1	.321	193	303
Philadelphia	2	11	1	.179	145	352

Central Division

	W	L	T	Pct.	Pts.	OP
Green Bay	10	4	0	.714	304	226
Detroit	8	5	1	.607	339	290
Minnesota	7	7	0	.500	301	252
Chicago	4	9	1	.321	225	275

Western Division

	W	L	T	Pct.	Pts.	OP
San Francisco	8	5	1	.607	353	249
Atlanta	7	7	0	.500	269	274
Los Angeles	6	7	1	.464	291	286
New Orleans	2	11	1	.179	215	361

*Wild Card qualifier for playoffs

Divisional playoffs: PITTSBURGH 13, Oakland 7; MIAMI 20, Cleveland 14
AFC championship: Miami 21, PITTSBURGH 17
Divisional playoffs: Dallas 30, SAN FRANCISCO 28; WASHINGTON 16, Green Bay 3
NFC championship: WASHINGTON 26, Dallas 3
Super Bowl VII: Miami (AFC) 14, Washington (NFC) 7, at Memorial Coliseum, Los Angeles, Calif.

1971

American Conference

Eastern Division

	W	L	T	Pct.	Pts.	OP
Miami	10	3	1	.769	315	174
Baltimore*	10	4	0	.714	313	140
New England	6	8	0	.429	238	325
N.Y. Jets	6	8	0	.429	212	299
Buffalo	1	13	0	.071	184	394

Central Division

	W	L	T	Pct.	Pts.	OP
Cleveland	9	5	0	.643	285	273
Pittsburgh	6	8	0	.429	246	292
Houston	4	9	1	.308	251	330
Cincinnati	4	10	0	.286	284	265

Western Division

	W	L	T	Pct.	Pts.	OP
Kansas City	10	3	1	.769	302	208
Oakland	8	4	2	.667	344	278
San Diego	6	8	0	.429	311	341
Denver	4	9	1	.308	203	275

National Conference

Eastern Division

	W	L	T	Pct.	Pts.	OP
Dallas	11	3	0	.786	406	222
Washington*	9	4	1	.692	276	190
Philadelphia	6	7	1	.462	221	302
St. Louis	4	9	1	.308	231	279
N.Y. Giants	4	10	0	.286	228	362

Central Division

	W	L	T	Pct.	Pts.	OP
Minnesota	11	3	0	.786	245	139
Detroit	7	6	1	.538	341	286
Chicago	6	8	0	.429	185	276
Green Bay	4	8	2	.333	274	298

Western Division

	W	L	T	Pct.	Pts.	OP
San Francisco	9	5	0	.643	300	216
Los Angeles	8	5	1	.615	313	260
Atlanta	7	6	1	.538	274	277
New Orleans	4	8	2	.333	266	347

*Wild Card qualifier for playoffs

Divisional playoffs: Miami 27, KANSAS CITY 24 (OT); Baltimore 20, CLEVELAND 3
AFC championship: MIAMI 21, Baltimore 0
Divisional playoffs: Dallas 20, MINNESOTA 12; SAN FRANCISCO 24, Washington 20
NFC championship: DALLAS 14, San Francisco 3
Super Bowl VI: Dallas (NFC) 24, Miami (AFC) 3, at Tulane Stadium, New Orleans, La.

1970

American Conference

Eastern Division

	W	L	T	Pct.	Pts.	OP
Baltimore	11	2	1	.846	321	234
Miami*	10	4	0	.714	297	228
N.Y. Jets	4	10	0	.286	255	286
Buffalo	3	10	1	.231	204	337
Boston Patriots	2	12	0	.143	149	361

Central Division

	W	L	T	Pct.	Pts.	OP
Cincinnati	8	6	0	.571	312	255
Cleveland	7	7	0	.500	286	265
Pittsburgh	5	9	0	.357	210	272
Houston	3	10	1	.231	217	352

Western Division

	W	L	T	Pct.	Pts.	OP
Oakland	8	4	2	.667	300	293
Kansas City	7	5	2	.583	272	244
San Diego	5	6	3	.455	282	278
Denver	5	8	1	.385	253	264

National Conference

Eastern Division

	W	L	T	Pct.	Pts.	OP
Dallas	10	4	0	.714	299	221
N.Y. Giants	9	5	0	.643	301	270
St. Louis	8	5	1	.615	325	228
Washington	6	8	0	.429	297	314
Philadelphia	3	10	1	.231	241	332

Central Division

	W	L	T	Pct.	Pts.	OP
Minnesota	12	2	0	.857	335	143
Detroit*	10	4	0	.714	347	202
Chicago	6	8	0	.429	256	261
Green Bay	6	8	0	.429	196	293

Western Division

	W	L	T	Pct.	Pts.	OP
San Francisco	10	3	1	.769	352	267
Los Angeles	9	4	1	.692	325	202
Atlanta	4	8	2	.333	206	261
New Orleans	2	11	1	.154	172	347

*Wild Card qualifier for playoffs

Divisional playoffs: BALTIMORE 17, Cincinnati 0; OAKLAND 21, Miami 14
AFC championship: BALTIMORE 27, Oakland 17
Divisional playoffs: DALLAS 5, Detroit 0; San Francisco 17, MINNESOTA 14
NFC championship: Dallas 17, SAN FRANCISCO 10
Super Bowl V: Baltimore (AFC) 16, Dallas (NFC) 13, at Orange Bowl, Miami, Fla.

1969 NFL

Eastern Conference

Capitol Division

	W	L	T	Pct.	Pts.	OP
Dallas	11	2	1	.846	369	223
Washington	7	5	2	.583	307	319
New Orleans	5	9	0	.357	311	393
Philadelphia	4	9	1	.308	279	377

Century Division

	W	L	T	Pct.	Pts.	OP
Cleveland	10	3	1	.769	351	300
N.Y. Giants	6	8	0	.429	264	298
St. Louis	4	9	1	.308	314	389
Pittsburgh	1	13	0	.071	218	404

Western Conference

Coastal Division

	W	L	T	Pct.	Pts.	OP
Los Angeles	11	3	0	.786	320	243
Baltimore	8	5	1	.615	279	268
Atlanta	6	8	0	.429	276	268
San Francisco	4	8	2	.333	277	319

Central Division

	W	L	T	Pct.	Pts.	OP
Minnesota	12	2	0	.857	379	133
Detroit	9	4	1	.692	259	188
Green Bay	8	6	0	.571	269	221
Chicago	1	13	0	.071	210	339

Conference championships: Cleveland 38, DALLAS 14; MINNESOTA 23, Los Angeles 20
NFL championship: MINNESOTA 27, Cleveland 7
Super Bowl IV: Kansas City (AFL) 23, Minnesota (NFL) 7, at Tulane Stadium, New Orleans, La.

1969 AFL

Eastern Division

	W	L	T	Pct.	Pts.	OP
N.Y. Jets	10	4	0	.714	353	269
Houston	6	6	2	.500	278	279
Boston Patriots	4	10	0	.286	266	316
Buffalo	4	10	0	.286	230	359
Miami	3	10	1	.231	233	332

Western Division

	W	L	T	Pct.	Pts.	OP
Oakland	12	1	1	.923	377	242
Kansas City	11	3	0	.786	359	177
San Diego	8	6	0	.571	288	276
Denver	5	8	1	.385	297	344
Cincinnati	4	9	1	.308	280	367

Divisional Playoffs: Kansas City 13, N.Y. JETS 6; OAKLAND 56, Houston 7
AFL championship: Kansas City 17, OAKLAND 7

1968 NFL

Eastern Conference

Capitol Division

	W	L	T	Pct.	Pts.	OP
Dallas	12	2	0	.857	431	186
N.Y. Giants	7	7	0	.500	294	325
Washington	5	9	0	.357	249	358
Philadelphia	2	12	0	.143	202	351

Century Division

	W	L	T	Pct.	Pts.	OP
Cleveland	10	4	0	.714	394	273
St. Louis	9	4	1	.692	325	289
New Orleans	4	9	1	.308	246	327
Pittsburgh	2	11	1	.154	244	397

Western Conference

Coastal Division

	W	L	T	Pct.	Pts.	OP
Baltimore	13	1	0	.929	402	144
Los Angeles	10	3	1	.769	312	200
San Francisco	7	6	1	.538	303	310
Atlanta	2	12	0	.143	170	389

Central Division

	W	L	T	Pct.	Pts.	OP
Minnesota	8	6	0	.571	282	242
Chicago	7	7	0	.500	250	333
Green Bay	6	7	1	.462	281	227
Detroit	4	8	2	.333	207	241

Conference championships: CLEVELAND 31, Dallas 20; BALTIMORE 24, Minnesota 14
NFL championship: Baltimore 34, CLEVELAND 0
Super Bowl III: N.Y. Jets (AFL) 16, Baltimore (NFL) 7, at Orange Bowl, Miami, Fla.

1968 AFL

Eastern Division

	W	L	T	Pct.	Pts.	OP
N.Y. Jets	11	3	0	.786	419	280
Houston	7	7	0	.500	303	248
Miami	5	8	1	.385	276	355
Boston Patriots	4	10	0	.286	229	406
Buffalo	1	12	1	.077	199	367

Western Division

	W	L	T	Pct.	Pts.	OP
Oakland	12	2	0	.857	453	233
Kansas City	12	2	0	.857	371	170
San Diego	9	5	0	.643	382	310
Denver	5	9	0	.357	255	404
Cincinnati	3	11	0	.214	215	329

Western Division playoff: OAKLAND 41, Kansas City 6
AFL championship: N.Y. JETS 27, Oakland 23

1967 NFL

Eastern Conference

Capitol Division

	W	L	T	Pct.	Pts.	OP
Dallas	9	5	0	.643	342	268
Philadelphia	6	7	1	.462	351	409
Washington	5	6	3	.455	347	353
New Orleans	3	11	0	.214	233	379

Century Division

	W	L	T	Pct.	Pts.	OP
Cleveland	9	5	0	.643	334	297
N.Y. Giants	7	7	0	.500	369	379
St. Louis	6	7	1	.462	333	356
Pittsburgh	4	9	1	.308	281	320

Western Conference

Coastal Division

	W	L	T	Pct.	Pts.	OP
Los Angeles	11	1	2	.917	398	196
Baltimore	11	1	2	.917	394	198
San Francisco	7	7	0	.500	273	337
Atlanta	1	12	1	.077	175	422

Central Division

	W	L	T	Pct.	Pts.	OP
Green Bay	9	4	1	.692	332	209
Chicago	7	6	1	.538	239	218
Detroit	5	7	2	.417	260	259
Minnesota	3	8	3	.273	233	294

Los Angeles won division title on the basis of advantage in points (58-34) in two games vs. Baltimore.
Conference championships: DALLAS 52, Cleveland 14; GREEN BAY 28, Los Angeles 7
NFL championship: GREEN BAY 21, Dallas 17
Super Bowl II: Green Bay (NFL) 33, Oakland (AFL) 14, at Orange Bowl, Miami, Fla.

1967 AFL

Eastern Division

	W	L	T	Pct.	Pts.	OP
Houston	9	4	1	.692	258	199
N.Y. Jets	8	5	1	.615	371	329
Buffalo	4	10	0	.286	237	285
Miami	4	10	0	.286	219	407
Boston Patriots	3	10	1	.231	280	389

Western Division

	W	L	T	Pct.	Pts.	OP
Oakland	13	1	0	.929	468	233
Kansas City	9	5	0	.643	408	254
San Diego	8	5	1	.615	360	352
Denver	3	11	0	.214	256	409

AFL championship: OAKLAND 40, Houston 7

1966 NFL

Eastern Conference

	W	L	T	Pct.	Pts.	OP
Dallas	10	3	1	.769	445	239
Cleveland	9	5	0	.643	403	259
Philadelphia	9	5	0	.643	326	340
St. Louis	8	5	1	.615	264	265
Washington	7	7	0	.500	351	355
Pittsburgh	5	8	1	.385	316	347
Atlanta	3	11	0	.214	204	437
N.Y. Giants	1	12	1	.077	263	501

Western Conference

	W	L	T	Pct.	Pts.	OP
Green Bay	12	2	0	.857	335	163
Baltimore	9	5	0	.643	314	226
Los Angeles	8	6	0	.571	289	212
San Francisco	6	6	2	.500	320	325
Chicago	5	7	2	.417	234	272
Detroit	4	9	1	.308	206	317
Minnesota	4	9	1	.308	292	304

NFL championship: Green Bay 34, DALLAS 27
Super Bowl I: Green Bay (NFL) 35, Kansas City (AFL) 10, at Memorial Coliseum, Los Angeles, Calif.

1966 AFL

Eastern Division

	W	L	T	Pct.	Pts.	OP
Buffalo	9	4	1	.692	358	255
Boston Patriots	8	4	2	.677	315	283
N.Y. Jets	6	6	2	.500	322	312
Houston	3	11	0	.214	335	396
Miami	3	11	0	.214	213	362

Western Division

	W	L	T	Pct.	Pts.	OP
Kansas City	11	2	1	.846	448	276
Oakland	8	5	1	.615	315	288
San Diego	7	6	1	.538	335	284
Denver	4	10	0	.286	196	381

AFL championship: Kansas City 31, BUFFALO 7

1965 NFL

Eastern Conference

	W	L	T	Pct.	Pts.	OP
Cleveland	11	3	0	.786	363	325
Dallas	7	7	0	.500	325	280
N.Y. Giants	7	7	0	.500	270	338
Washington	6	8	0	.429	257	301
Philadelphia	5	9	0	.357	363	359
St. Louis	5	9	0	.357	296	309
Pittsburgh	2	12	0	.143	202	397

Western Conference

	W	L	T	Pct.	Pts.	OP
Green Bay	10	3	1	.769	316	224
Baltimore	10	3	1	.769	389	284
Chicago	9	5	0	.643	409	275
San Francisco	7	6	1	.538	421	402
Minnesota	7	7	0	.500	383	403
Detroit	6	7	1	.462	257	295
Los Angeles	4	10	0	.286	269	328

Western Conference playoff: GREEN BAY 13, Baltimore 10 (OT)
NFL championship: GREEN BAY 23, Cleveland 12

1965 AFL

Eastern Division

	W	L	T	Pct.	Pts.	OP
Buffalo	10	3	1	.769	313	226
N.Y. Jets	5	8	1	.385	285	303
Boston Patriots	4	8	2	.333	244	302
Houston	4	10	0	.286	298	429

Western Division

	W	L	T	Pct.	Pts.	OP
San Diego	9	2	3	.818	340	227
Oakland	8	5	1	.615	298	239
Kansas City	7	5	2	.583	322	285
Denver	4	10	0	.286	303	392

AFL championship: Buffalo 23, SAN DIEGO 0

1964 NFL

Eastern Conference

	W	L	T	Pct.	Pts.	OP
Cleveland	10	3	1	.769	415	293
St. Louis	9	3	2	.750	357	331
Philadelphia	6	8	0	.429	312	313
Washington	6	8	0	.429	307	305
Dallas	5	8	1	.385	250	289
Pittsburgh	5	9	0	.357	253	315
N.Y. Giants	2	10	2	.167	241	399

Western Conference

	W	L	T	Pct.	Pts.	OP
Baltimore	12	2	0	.857	428	225
Green Bay	8	5	1	.615	342	245
Minnesota	8	5	1	.615	355	296
Detroit	7	5	2	.583	280	260
Los Angeles	5	7	2	.417	283	339
Chicago	5	9	0	.357	260	379
San Francisco	4	10	0	.286	236	330

NFL championship: CLEVELAND 27, Baltimore 0

1964 AFL

Eastern Division

	W	L	T	Pct.	Pts.	OP
Buffalo	12	2	0	.857	400	242
Boston Patriots	10	3	1	.769	365	297
N.Y. Jets	5	8	1	.385	278	315
Houston	4	10	0	.286	310	355

Western Division

	W	L	T	Pct.	Pts.	OP
San Diego	8	5	1	.615	341	300
Kansas City	7	7	0	.500	366	306
Oakland	5	7	2	.417	303	350
Denver	2	11	1	.154	240	438

AFL championship: BUFFALO 20, San Diego 7

1963 NFL

Eastern Conference

	W	L	T	Pct.	Pts.	OP
N.Y. Giants	11	3	0	.786	448	280
Cleveland	10	4	0	.714	343	262
St. Louis	9	5	0	.643	341	283
Pittsburgh	7	4	3	.636	321	295
Dallas	4	10	0	.286	305	378
Washington	3	11	0	.214	279	398
Philadelphia	2	10	2	.167	242	381

Western Conference

	W	L	T	Pct.	Pts.	OP
Chicago	11	1	2	.917	301	144
Green Bay	11	2	1	.846	369	206
Baltimore	8	6	0	.571	316	285
Detroit	5	8	1	.385	326	265
Minnesota	5	8	1	.385	309	390
Los Angeles	5	9	0	.357	210	350
San Francisco	2	12	0	.143	198	391

NFL championship: CHICAGO 14, N.Y. Giants 10

1963 AFL

Eastern Division

	W	L	T	Pct.	Pts.	OP
Boston Patriots	7	6	1	.538	327	257
Buffalo	7	6	1	.538	304	291
Houston	6	8	0	.429	302	372
N.Y. Jets	5	8	1	.385	249	399

Western Division

	W	L	T	Pct.	Pts.	OP
San Diego	11	3	0	.786	399	256
Oakland	10	4	0	.714	363	288
Kansas City	5	7	2	.417	347	263
Denver	2	11	1	.154	301	473

Eastern Division playoff: Boston 26, BUFFALO 8
AFL championship: SAN DIEGO 51, Boston 10

1962 NFL

Eastern Conference

	W	L	T	Pct.	Pts.	OP
N.Y. Giants	12	2	0	.857	398	283
Pittsburgh	9	5	0	.643	312	363
Cleveland	7	6	1	.538	291	257
Washington	5	7	2	.417	305	376
Dallas Cowboys	5	8	1	.385	398	402
St. Louis	4	9	1	.308	287	361
Philadelphia	3	10	1	.231	282	356

Western Conference

	W	L	T	Pct.	Pts.	OP
Green Bay	13	1	0	.929	415	148
Detroit	11	3	0	.786	315	177
Chicago	9	5	0	.643	321	287
Baltimore	7	7	0	.500	293	288
San Francisco	6	8	0	.429	282	331
Minnesota	2	11	1	.154	254	410
Los Angeles	1	12	1	.077	220	334

NFL championship: Green Bay 16, N.Y. GIANTS 7

1962 AFL

Eastern Division

	W	L	T	Pct.	Pts.	OP
Houston	11	3	0	.786	387	270
Boston Patriots	9	4	1	.692	346	295
Buffalo	7	6	1	.538	309	272
N.Y. Titans	5	9	0	.357	278	423

Western Division

	W	L	T	Pct.	Pts.	OP
Dallas Texans	11	3	0	.786	389	233
Denver	7	7	0	.500	353	334
San Diego	4	10	0	.286	314	392
Oakland	1	13	0	.071	213	370

AFL championship: Dallas Texans 20, HOUSTON 17 (OT)

1961 NFL

Eastern Conference

	W	L	T	Pct.	Pts.	OP
N.Y. Giants	10	3	1	.769	368	220
Philadelphia	10	4	0	.714	361	297
Cleveland	8	5	1	.615	319	270
St. Louis	7	7	0	.500	279	267
Pittsburgh	6	8	0	.429	295	287
Dallas Cowboys	4	9	1	.308	236	380
Washington	1	12	1	.077	174	392

Western Conference

	W	L	T	Pct.	Pts.	OP
Green Bay	11	3	0	.786	391	223
Detroit	8	5	1	.615	270	258
Baltimore	8	6	0	.571	302	307
Chicago	8	6	0	.571	326	302
San Francisco	7	6	1	.538	346	272
Los Angeles	4	10	0	.286	263	333
Minnesota	3	11	0	.214	285	407

NFL championship: GREEN BAY 37, N.Y. Giants 0

1961 AFL

Eastern Division

	W	L	T	Pct.	Pts.	OP
Houston	10	3	1	.769	513	242
Boston Patriots	9	4	1	.692	413	313
N.Y. Titans	7	7	0	.500	301	390
Buffalo	6	8	0	.429	294	342

Western Division

	W	L	T	Pct.	Pts.	OP
San Diego	12	2	0	.857	396	219
Dallas Texans	6	8	0	.429	334	343
Denver	3	11	0	.214	251	432
Oakland	2	12	0	.143	237	458

AFL championship: Houston 10, SAN DIEGO 3

1960 NFL

Eastern Conference

	W	L	T	Pct.	Pts.	OP
Philadelphia	10	2	0	.833	321	246
Cleveland	8	3	1	.727	362	217
N.Y. Giants	6	4	2	.600	271	261
St. Louis	6	5	1	.545	288	230
Pittsburgh	5	6	1	.455	240	275
Washington	1	9	2	.100	178	309

Western Conference

	W	L	T	Pct.	Pts.	OP
Green Bay	8	4	0	.667	332	209
Detroit	7	5	0	.583	239	212
San Francisco	7	5	0	.583	208	205
Baltimore	6	6	0	.500	288	234
Chicago	5	6	1	.455	194	299
L.A. Rams	4	7	1	.364	265	297
Dallas Cowboys	0	11	1	.000	177	369

NFL championship: PHILADELPHIA 17, Green Bay 13

1960 AFL

Eastern Conference

	W	L	T	Pct.	Pts.	OP
Houston	10	4	0	.714	379	285
N.Y. Titans	7	7	0	.500	382	399
Buffalo	5	8	1	.385	296	303
Boston	5	9	0	.357	286	349

Western Conference

	W	L	T	Pct.	Pts.	OP
L.A. Chargers	10	4	0	.714	373	336
Dallas Texans	8	6	0	.571	362	253
Oakland	6	8	0	.429	319	388
Denver	4	9	1	.308	309	393

AFL championship: HOUSTON 24, L.A. Chargers 16

1959

Eastern Conference

	W	L	T	Pct.	Pts.	OP
N.Y. Giants	10	2	0	.833	284	170
Cleveland	7	5	0	.583	270	214
Philadelphia	7	5	0	.583	268	278
Pittsburgh	6	5	1	.545	257	216
Washington	3	9	0	.250	185	350
Chi. Cardinals	2	10	0	.167	234	324

Western Conference

	W	L	T	Pct.	Pts.	OP
Baltimore	9	3	0	.750	374	251
Chi. Bears	8	4	0	.667	252	196
Green Bay	7	5	0	.583	248	246
San Francisco	7	5	0	.583	255	237
Detroit	3	8	1	.273	203	275
Los Angeles	2	10	0	.167	242	315

NFL championship: BALTIMORE 31, N.Y. Giants 16

1958

Eastern Conference

	W	L	T	Pct.	Pts.	OP
N.Y. Giants	9	3	0	.750	246	183
Cleveland	9	3	0	.750	302	217
Pittsburgh	7	4	1	.636	261	230
Washington	4	7	1	.364	214	268
Chi. Cardinals	2	9	1	.182	261	356
Philadelphia	2	9	1	.182	235	306

Western Conference

	W	L	T	Pct.	Pts.	OP
Baltimore	9	3	0	.750	381	203
Chi. Bears	8	4	0	.667	298	230
Los Angeles	8	4	0	.667	344	278
San Francisco	6	6	0	.500	257	324
Detroit	4	7	1	.364	261	276
Green Bay	1	10	1	.091	193	382

Eastern Conference playoff: N.Y. GIANTS 10, Cleveland 0

NFL championship: Baltimore 23, N.Y. GIANTS 17 (OT)

1957

Eastern Conference

	W	L	T	Pct.	Pts.	OP
Cleveland	9	2	1	.818	269	172
N.Y. Giants	7	5	0	.583	254	211
Pittsburgh	6	6	0	.500	161	178
Washington	5	6	1	.455	251	230
Philadelphia	4	8	0	.333	173	230
Chi. Cardinals	3	9	0	.250	200	299

Western Conference

	W	L	T	Pct.	Pts.	OP
Detroit	8	4	0	.667	251	231
San Francisco	8	4	0	.667	260	264
Baltimore	7	5	0	.583	303	235
Los Angeles	6	6	0	.500	307	278
Chi. Bears	5	7	0	.417	203	211
Green Bay	3	9	0	.250	218	311

Western Conference playoff: Detroit 31, SAN FRANCISCO 27

NFL championship: DETROIT 59, Cleveland 14

1956

Eastern Conference

	W	L	T	Pct.	Pts.	OP
N.Y. Giants	8	3	1	.727	264	197
Chi. Cardinals	7	5	0	.583	240	182
Washington	6	6	0	.500	183	225
Cleveland	5	7	0	.417	167	177
Pittsburgh	5	7	0	.417	217	250
Philadelphia	3	8	1	.273	143	215

Western Conference

	W	L	T	Pct.	Pts.	OP
Chi. Bears	9	2	1	.818	363	246
Detroit	9	3	0	.750	300	188
San Francisco	5	6	1	.455	233	284
Baltimore	5	7	0	.417	270	322
Green Bay	4	8	0	.333	264	342
Los Angeles	4	8	0	.333	291	307

NFL championship: N.Y. GIANTS 47, Chi. Bears 7

1955

Eastern Conference

	W	L	T	Pct.	Pts.	OP
Cleveland	9	2	1	.818	349	218
Washington	8	4	0	.667	246	222
N.Y. Giants	6	5	1	.545	267	223
Chi. Cardinals	4	7	1	.364	224	252
Philadelphia	4	7	1	.364	248	231
Pittsburgh	4	8	0	.333	195	285

Western Conference

	W	L	T	Pct.	Pts.	OP
Los Angeles	8	3	1	.727	260	231
Chi. Bears	8	4	0	.667	294	251
Green Bay	6	6	0	.500	258	276
Baltimore	5	6	1	.455	214	239
San Francisco	4	8	0	.333	216	298
Detroit	3	9	0	.250	230	275

NFL championship: Cleveland 38, LOS ANGELES 14

1954

Eastern Conference

	W	L	T	Pct.	Pts.	OP
Cleveland	9	3	0	.750	336	162
Philadelphia	7	4	1	.636	284	230
N.Y. Giants	7	5	0	.583	293	184
Pittsburgh	5	7	0	.417	219	263
Washington	3	9	0	.250	207	432
Chi. Cardinals	2	10	0	.167	183	347

Western Conference

	W	L	T	Pct.	Pts.	OP
Detroit	9	2	1	.818	337	189
Chi. Bears	8	4	0	.667	301	279
San Francisco	7	4	1	.636	313	251
Los Angeles	6	5	1	.545	314	285
Green Bay	4	8	0	.333	234	251
Baltimore	3	9	0	.250	131	279

NFL championship: CLEVELAND 56, Detroit 10

1953

Eastern Conference

	W	L	T	Pct.	Pts.	OP
Cleveland	11	1	0	.917	348	162
Philadelphia	7	4	1	.636	352	215
Washington	6	5	1	.545	208	215
Pittsburgh	6	6	0	.500	211	263
N.Y. Giants	3	9	0	.250	179	277
Chi. Cardinals	1	10	1	.091	190	337

Western Conference

	W	L	T	Pct.	Pts.	OP
Detroit	10	2	0	.833	271	205
San Francisco	9	3	0	.750	372	237
Los Angeles	8	3	1	.727	366	236
Chi. Bears	3	8	1	.273	218	262
Baltimore	3	9	0	.250	182	350
Green Bay	2	9	1	.182	200	338

NFL championship: DETROIT 17, Cleveland 16

1952

American Conference

	W	L	T	Pct.	Pts.	OP
Cleveland	8	4	0	.667	310	213
N.Y. Giants	7	5	0	.583	234	231
Philadelphia	7	5	0	.583	252	271
Pittsburgh	5	7	0	.417	300	273
Chi. Cardinals	4	8	0	.333	172	221
Washington	4	8	0	.333	240	287

National Conference

	W	L	T	Pct.	Pts.	OP
Detroit	9	3	0	.750	344	192
Los Angeles	9	3	0	.750	349	234
San Francisco	7	5	0	.583	285	221
Green Bay	6	6	0	.500	295	312
Chi. Bears	5	7	0	.417	245	326
Dallas Texans	1	11	0	.083	182	427

National Conference playoff: DETROIT 31, Los Angeles 21

NFL championship: Detroit 17, CLEVELAND 7

1951

American Conference

	W	L	T	Pct.	Pts.	OP
Cleveland	11	1	0	.917	331	152
N.Y. Giants	9	2	1	.818	254	161
Washington	5	7	0	.417	183	296
Pittsburgh	4	7	1	.364	183	235
Philadelphia	4	8	0	.333	234	264
Chi. Cardinals	3	9	0	.250	210	287

National Conference

	W	L	T	Pct.	Pts.	OP
Los Angeles	8	4	0	.667	392	261
Detroit	7	4	1	.636	336	259
San Francisco	7	4	1	.636	255	205
Chi. Bears	7	5	0	.583	286	282
Green Bay	3	9	0	.250	254	375
N.Y. Yanks	1	9	2	.100	241	382

NFL championship: LOS ANGELES 24, Cleveland 17

1950

American Conference

	W	L	T	Pct.	Pts.	OP
Cleveland	10	2	0	.833	310	144
N.Y. Giants	10	2	0	.833	268	150
Philadelphia	6	6	0	.500	254	141
Pittsburgh	6	6	0	.500	180	195
Chi. Cardinals	5	7	0	.417	233	287
Washington	3	9	0	.250	232	326

National Conference

	W	L	T	Pct.	Pts.	OP
Los Angeles	9	3	0	.750	466	309
Chi. Bears	9	3	0	.750	279	207
N.Y. Yanks	7	5	0	.583	366	367
Detroit	6	6	0	.500	321	285
Green Bay	3	9	0	.250	244	406
San Francisco	3	9	0	.250	213	300
Baltimore	1	11	0	.083	213	462

American Conference playoff: CLEVELAND 8, N.Y. Giants 3

National Conference playoff: LOS ANGELES 24, Chi. Bears 14

NFL championship: CLEVELAND 30, Los Angeles 28

1949

Eastern Division

	W	L	T	Pct.	Pts.	OP
Philadelphia	11	1	0	.917	364	134
Pittsburgh	6	5	1	.545	224	214
N.Y. Giants	6	6	0	.500	287	298
Washington	4	7	1	.364	268	339
N.Y. Bulldogs	1	10	1	.091	153	365

Western Division

	W	L	T	Pct.	Pts.	OP
Los Angeles	8	2	2	.800	360	239
Chi. Bears	9	3	0	.750	332	218
Chi. Cardinals	6	5	1	.545	360	301
Detroit	4	8	0	.333	237	259
Green Bay	2	10	0	.167	114	329

NFL championship: Philadelphia 14, LOS ANGELES 0

1948

Eastern Division

	W	L	T	Pct.	Pts.	OP
Philadelphia	9	2	1	.818	376	156
Washington	7	5	0	.583	291	287
N.Y. Giants	4	8	0	.333	297	388
Pittsburgh	4	8	0	.333	200	243
Boston	3	9	0	.250	174	372

Western Division

	W	L	T	Pct.	Pts.	OP
Chi. Cardinals	11	1	0	.917	395	226
Chi. Bears	10	2	0	.833	375	151
Los Angeles	6	5	1	.545	327	269
Green Bay	3	9	0	.250	154	290
Detroit	2	10	0	.167	200	407

NFL championship: PHILADELPHIA 7, Chi. Cardinals 0

1947

Eastern Division

	W	L	T	Pct.	Pts.	OP
Philadelphia	8	4	0	.667	308	242
Pittsburgh	8	4	0	.667	240	259
Boston	4	7	1	.364	168	256
Washington	4	8	0	.333	295	367
N.Y. Giants	2	8	2	.200	190	309

Western Division

	W	L	T	Pct.	Pts.	OP
Chi. Cardinals	9	3	0	.750	306	231
Chi. Bears	8	4	0	.667	363	241
Green Bay	6	5	1	.545	274	210
Los Angeles	6	6	0	.500	259	214
Detroit	3	9	0	.250	231	305

Eastern Division playoff: Philadelphia 21, PITTSBURGH 0

NFL championship: CHI. CARDINALS 28, Philadelphia 21

1946

Eastern Division

	W	L	T	Pct.	Pts.	OP
N.Y. Giants	7	3	1	.700	236	162
Philadelphia	6	5	0	.545	231	220
Washington	5	5	1	.500	171	191
Pittsburgh	5	5	1	.500	136	117
Boston	2	8	1	.200	189	273

Western Division

	W	L	T	Pct.	Pts.	OP
Chi. Bears	8	2	1	.800	289	193
Los Angeles	6	4	1	.600	277	257
Green Bay	6	5	0	.545	148	158
Chi. Cardinals	6	5	0	.545	260	198
Detroit	1	10	0	.091	142	310

NFL championship: Chi. Bears 24, N.Y. GIANTS 14

1945

Eastern Division

	W	L	T	Pct.	Pts.	OP
Washington	8	2	0	.800	209	121
Philadelphia	7	3	0	.700	272	133
N.Y. Giants	3	6	1	.333	179	198
Boston	3	6	1	.333	123	211
Pittsburgh	2	8	0	.200	79	220

Western Division

	W	L	T	Pct.	Pts.	OP
Cleveland	9	1	0	.900	244	136
Detroit	7	3	0	.700	195	194
Green Bay	6	4	0	.600	258	173
Chi. Bears	3	7	0	.300	192	235
Chi. Cardinals	1	9	0	.100	98	228

NFL championship: CLEVELAND 15, Washington 14

1944

Eastern Division

	W	L	T	Pct.	Pts.	OP
N.Y. Giants	8	1	1	.889	206	75
Philadelphia	7	1	2	.875	267	131
Washington	6	3	1	.667	169	180
Boston	2	8	0	.200	82	233
Brooklyn	0	10	0	.000	69	166

Western Division

	W	L	T	Pct.	Pts.	OP
Green Bay	8	2	0	.800	238	141
Chi. Bears	6	3	1	.667	258	172
Detroit	6	3	1	.667	216	151
Cleveland	4	6	0	.400	188	224
Card-Pitt	0	10	0	.000	108	328

NFL championship: Green Bay 14, N.Y. GIANTS 7

1943

Eastern Division

	W	L	T	Pct.	Pts.	OP
Washington	6	3	1	.667	229	137
N.Y. Giants	6	3	1	.667	197	170
Phil-Pitt	5	4	1	.556	225	230
Brooklyn	2	8	0	.200	65	234

Western Division

	W	L	T	Pct.	Pts.	OP
Chi. Bears	8	1	1	.889	303	157
Green Bay	7	2	1	.778	264	172
Detroit	3	6	1	.333	178	218
Chi. Cardinals	0	10	0	.000	95	238

Eastern Division playoff: Washington 28, N.Y. GIANTS 0
NFL championship: CHI. BEARS 41, Washington 21

1942

Eastern Division

	W	L	T	Pct.	Pts.	OP
Washington	10	1	0	.909	227	102
Pittsburgh	7	4	0	.636	167	119
N.Y. Giants	5	5	1	.500	155	139
Brooklyn	3	8	0	.273	100	168
Philadelphia	2	9	0	.182	134	239

Western Division

	W	L	T	Pct.	Pts.	OP
Chi. Bears	11	0	0	1.000	376	84
Green Bay	8	2	1	.800	300	215
Cleveland	5	6	0	.455	150	207
Chi. Cardinals	3	8	0	.273	98	209
Detroit	0	11	0	.000	38	263

NFL championship: WASHINGTON 14, Chi. Bears 6

1941

Eastern Division

	W	L	T	Pct.	Pts.	OP
N.Y. Giants	8	3	0	.727	238	114
Brooklyn	7	4	0	.636	158	127
Washington	6	5	0	.545	176	174
Philadelphia	2	8	1	.200	119	218
Pittsburgh	1	9	1	.100	103	276

Western Division

	W	L	T	Pct.	Pts.	OP
Chi. Bears	10	1	0	.909	396	147
Green Bay	10	1	0	.909	258	120
Detroit	4	6	1	.400	121	195
Chi. Cardinals	3	7	1	.300	127	197
Cleveland	2	9	0	.182	116	244

Western Division playoff: CHI. BEARS 33, Green Bay 14
NFL championship: CHI. BEARS 37, N.Y. Giants 9

1940

Eastern Division

	W	L	T	Pct.	Pts.	OP
Washington	9	2	0	.818	245	142
Brooklyn	8	3	0	.727	186	120
N.Y. Giants	6	4	1	.600	131	133
Pittsburgh	2	7	2	.222	60	178
Philadelphia	1	10	0	.091	111	211

Western Division

	W	L	T	Pct.	Pts.	OP
Chi. Bears	8	3	0	.727	238	152
Green Bay	6	4	1	.600	238	155
Detroit	5	5	1	.500	138	153
Cleveland	4	6	1	.400	171	191
Chi. Cardinals	2	7	2	.222	139	222

NFL championship: Chi. Bears 73, WASHINGTON 0

1939

Eastern Division

	W	L	T	Pct.	Pts.	OP
N.Y. Giants	9	1	1	.900	168	85
Washington	8	2	1	.800	242	94
Brooklyn	4	6	1	.400	108	219
Philadelphia	1	9	1	.100	105	200
Pittsburgh	1	9	1	.100	114	216

Western Division

	W	L	T	Pct.	Pts.	OP
Green Bay	9	2	0	.818	233	153
Chi. Bears	8	3	0	.727	298	157
Detroit	6	5	0	.545	145	150
Cleveland	5	5	1	.500	195	164
Chi. Cardinals	1	10	0	.091	84	254

NFL championship: GREEN BAY 27, N.Y. Giants 0

1938

Eastern Division

	W	L	T	Pct.	Pts.	OP
N.Y. Giants	8	2	1	.800	194	79
Washington	6	3	2	.667	148	154
Brooklyn	4	4	3	.500	131	161
Philadelphia	5	6	0	.455	154	164
Pittsburgh	2	9	0	.182	79	169

Western Division

	W	L	T	Pct.	Pts.	OP
Green Bay	8	3	0	.727	223	118
Detroit	7	4	0	.636	119	108
Chi. Bears	6	5	0	.545	194	148
Cleveland	4	7	0	.364	131	215
Chi. Cardinals	2	9	0	.182	111	168

NFL championship: N.Y. GIANTS 23, Green Bay 17

1937

Eastern Division

	W	L	T	Pct.	Pts.	OP
Washington	8	3	0	.727	195	120
N.Y. Giants	6	3	2	.667	128	109
Pittsburgh	4	7	0	.364	122	145
Brooklyn	3	7	1	.300	82	174
Philadelphia	2	8	1	.200	86	177

Western Division

	W	L	T	Pct.	Pts.	OP
Chi. Bears	9	1	1	.900	201	100
Green Bay	7	4	0	.636	220	122
Detroit	7	4	0	.636	180	105
Chi. Cardinals	5	5	1	.500	135	165
Cleveland	1	10	0	.091	75	207

NFL championship: Washington 28, CHI. BEARS 21

1936

Eastern Division

	W	L	T	Pct.	Pts.	OP
Boston	7	5	0	.583	149	110
Pittsburgh	6	6	0	.500	98	187
N.Y. Giants	5	6	1	.455	115	163
Brooklyn	3	8	1	.273	92	161
Philadelphia	1	11	0	.083	51	206

Western Division

	W	L	T	Pct.	Pts.	OP
Green Bay	10	1	1	.909	248	118
Chi. Bears	9	3	0	.750	222	94
Detroit	8	4	0	.667	235	102
Chi. Cardinals	3	8	1	.273	74	143

NFL championship: Green Bay 21, Boston 6, at Polo Grounds, N.Y.

1935

Eastern Division

	W	L	T	Pct.	Pts.	OP
N. Y. Giants	9	3	0	.750	180	96
Brooklyn	5	6	1	.455	90	141
Pittsburgh	4	8	0	.333	100	209
Boston	2	8	1	.200	65	123
Philadelphia	2	9	0	.182	60	179

Western Division

	W	L	T	Pct.	Pts.	OP
Detroit	7	3	2	.700	191	111
Green Bay	8	4	0	.667	181	96
Chi. Bears	6	4	2	.600	192	106
Chi. Cardinals	6	4	2	.600	99	97

NFL championship: DETROIT 26, N.Y. Giants 7
One game between Boston and Philadelphia was canceled.

1934

Eastern Division

	W	L	T	Pct.	Pts.	OP
N.Y. Giants	8	5	0	.615	147	107
Boston	6	6	0	.500	107	94
Brooklyn	4	7	0	.364	61	153
Philadelphia	4	7	0	.364	127	85
Pittsburgh	2	10	0	.167	51	206

Western Division

	W	L	T	Pct.	Pts.	OP
Chi. Bears	13	0	0	1.000	286	86
Detroit	10	3	0	.769	238	59
Green Bay	7	6	0	.538	156	112
Chi. Cardinals	5	6	0	.455	80	84
St. Louis	1	2	0	.333	27	61
Cincinnati	0	8	0	.000	10	243

NFL championship: N.Y. GIANTS 30, Chi. Bears 13

1933

Eastern Division

	W	L	T	Pct.	Pts.	OP
N.Y. Giants	11	3	0	.786	244	101
Brooklyn	5	4	1	.556	93	54
Boston	5	5	2	.500	103	97
Philadelphia	3	5	1	.375	77	158
Pittsburgh	3	6	2	.333	67	208

Western Division

	W	L	T	Pct.	Pts.	OP
Chi. Bears	10	2	1	.833	133	82
Portsmouth	6	5	0	.545	128	87
Green Bay	5	7	1	.417	170	107
Cincinnati	3	6	1	.333	38	110
Chi. Cardinals	1	9	1	.100	52	101

NFL championship: CHI. BEARS 23, N.Y. Giants 21

1932

	W	L	T	Pct.
Chicago Bears	7	1	6	.875
Green Bay Packers	10	3	1	.769
Portsmouth Spartans	6	2	4	.750
Boston Braves	4	4	2	.500
New York Giants	4	6	2	.400
Brooklyn Dodgers	3	9	0	.250
Chicago Cardinals	2	6	2	.250
Staten Island Stapletons	2	7	3	.222

Chicago Bears and Portsmouth finished regularly scheduled games tied for first place. Bears won playoff game, which counted in standing, 9-0.

1931

	W	L	T	Pct.
Green Bay Packers	12	2	0	.857
Portsmouth Spartans	11	3	0	.786
Chicago Bears	8	5	0	.615
Chicago Cardinals	5	4	0	.556
New York Giants	7	6	1	.538
Providence Steam Roller	4	4	3	.500
Staten Island Stapletons	4	6	1	.400
Cleveland Indians	2	8	0	.200
Brooklyn Dodgers	2	12	0	.143
Frankford Yellow Jackets	1	6	1	.143

1930

	W	L	T	Pct.
Green Bay Packers	10	3	1	.769
New York Giants	13	4	0	.765
Chicago Bears	9	4	1	.692
Brooklyn Dodgers	7	4	1	.636
Providence Steam Roller	6	4	1	.600
Staten Island Stapletons	5	5	2	.500
Chicago Cardinals	5	6	2	.455
Portsmouth Spartans	5	6	3	.455
Frankford Yellow Jackets	4	13	1	.222
Minneapolis Red Jackets	1	7	1	.125
Newark Tornadoes	1	10	1	.091

1929

	W	L	T	Pct.
Green Bay Packers	12	0	1	1.000
New York Giants	13	1	1	.929
Frankford Yellow Jackets	9	4	5	.692
Chicago Cardinals	6	6	1	.500
Boston Bulldogs	4	4	0	.500
Orange Tornadoes	3	4	4	.429
Staten Island Stapletons	3	4	3	.429
Providence Steam Roller	4	6	2	.400
Chicago Bears	4	9	2	.308
Buffalo Bisons	1	7	1	.125
Minneapolis Red Jackets	1	9	0	.100
Dayton Triangles	0	6	0	.000

1928

	W	L	T	Pct.
Providence Steam Roller	8	1	2	.889
Frankford Yellow Jackets	11	3	2	.786
Detroit Wolverines	7	2	1	.778
Green Bay Packers	6	4	3	.600
Chicago Bears	7	5	1	.583
New York Giants	4	7	2	.364
New York Yankees	4	8	1	.333
Pottsville Maroons	2	8	0	.200
Chicago Cardinals	1	5	0	.167
Dayton Triangles	0	7	0	.000

1927

	W	L	T	Pct.
New York Giants	11	1	1	.917
Green Bay Packers	7	2	1	.778
Chicago Bears	9	3	2	.750
Cleveland Bulldogs	8	4	1	.667
Providence Steam Roller	8	5	1	.615
New York Yankees	7	8	1	.467
Frankford Yellow Jackets	6	9	3	.400
Pottsville Maroons	5	8	0	.385
Chicago Cardinals	3	7	1	.300
Dayton Triangles	1	6	1	.143
Duluth Eskimos	1	8	0	.111
Buffalo Bisons	0	5	0	.000

1926

	W	L	T	Pct.
Frankford Yellow Jackets	14	1	1	.933
Chicago Bears	12	1	3	.923
Pottsville Maroons	10	2	1	.833
Kansas City Cowboys	8	3	0	.727
Green Bay Packers	7	3	3	.700
Los Angeles Buccaneers	6	3	1	.667
New York Giants	8	4	1	.667
Duluth Eskimos	6	5	3	.545
Buffalo Rangers	4	4	2	.500
Chicago Cardinals	5	6	1	.455
Providence Steam Roller	5	7	1	.417
Detroit Panthers	4	6	2	.400
Hartford Blues	3	7	0	.300
Brooklyn Lions	3	8	0	.273
Milwaukee Badgers	2	7	0	.222
Akron Pros	1	4	3	.200
Dayton Triangles	1	4	1	.200
Racine Tornadoes	1	4	0	.200
Columbus Tigers	1	6	0	.143
Canton Bulldogs	1	9	3	.100
Hammond Pros	0	4	0	.000
Louisville Colonels	0	4	0	.000

1925

	W	L	T	Pct.
Chicago Cardinals	11	2	1	.846
Pottsville Maroons	10	2	0	.833
Detroit Panthers	8	2	2	.800
New York Giants	8	4	0	.667
Akron Indians	4	2	2	.667
Frankford Yellow Jackets	13	7	0	.650
Chicago Bears	9	5	3	.643
Rock Island Independents	5	3	3	.625
Green Bay Packers	8	5	0	.615
Providence Steam Roller	6	5	1	.545
Canton Bulldogs	4	4	0	.500
Cleveland Bulldogs	5	8	1	.385
Kansas City Cowboys	2	5	1	.286
Hammond Pros	1	4	0	.250
Buffalo Bisons	1	6	2	.143
Duluth Kelleys	0	3	0	.000
Rochester Jeffersons	0	6	1	.000
Milwaukee Badgers	0	6	0	.000
Dayton Triangles	0	7	1	.000
Columbus Tigers	0	9	0	.000

1924

	W	L	T	Pct.
Cleveland Bulldogs	7	1	1	.875
Chicago Bears	6	1	4	.857
Frankford Yellow Jackets	11	2	1	.846
Duluth Kelleys	5	1	0	.833
Rock Island Independents	6	2	2	.750
Green Bay Packers	7	4	0	.636
Racine Legion	4	3	3	.571
Chicago Cardinals	5	4	1	.556
Buffalo Bisons	6	5	0	.545
Columbus Tigers	4	4	0	.500
Hammond Pros	2	2	1	.500
Milwaukee Badgers	5	8	0	.385
Akron Indians	2	6	0	.333
Dayton Triangles	2	6	0	.333
Kansas City Blues	2	7	0	.222
Kenosha Maroons	0	5	1	.000
Minneapolis Marines	0	6	0	.000
Rochester Jeffersons	0	7	0	.000

1923

	W	L	T	Pct.
Canton Bulldogs	11	0	1	1.000
Chicago Bears	9	2	1	.818
Green Bay Packers	7	2	1	.778
Milwaukee Badgers	7	2	3	.778
Cleveland Indians	3	1	3	.750
Chicago Cardinals	8	4	0	.667
Duluth Kelleys	4	3	0	.571
Columbus Tigers	5	4	1	.556
Buffalo All-Americans	4	4	3	.500
Racine Legion	4	4	2	.500
Toledo Maroons	2	3	2	.400
Rock Island Independents	2	3	3	.400
Minneapolis Marines	2	5	2	.286
St. Louis All-Stars	1	4	2	.200
Hammond Pros	1	5	1	.167
Dayton Triangles	1	6	1	.143
Akron Indians	1	6	0	.143
Oorang Indians	1	10	0	.091
Rochester Jeffersons	0	2	0	.000
Louisville Brecks	0	3	0	.000

1922

	W	L	T	Pct.
Canton Bulldogs	10	0	2	1.000
Chicago Bears	9	3	0	.750
Chicago Cardinals	8	3	0	.727
Toledo Maroons	5	2	2	.714
Rock Island Independents	4	2	1	.667
Racine Legion	6	4	1	.600
Dayton Triangles	4	3	1	.571
Green Bay Packers	4	3	3	.571
Buffalo All-Americans	5	4	1	.556
Akron Pros	3	5	2	.375
Milwaukee Badgers	2	4	3	.333
Oorang Indians	2	6	0	.250
Minneapolis Marines	1	3	0	.250
Louisville Brecks	1	3	0	.250
Evansville Crimson Giants	0	3	0	.000
Rochester Jeffersons	0	4	1	.000
Hammond Pros	0	5	1	.000
Columbus Panhandles	0	7	0	.000

1921

	W	L	T	Pct.
Chicago Staleys	9	1	1	.900
Buffalo All-Americans	9	1	2	.900
Akron Pros	8	3	1	.727
Canton Bulldogs	5	2	3	.714
Rock Island Independents	4	2	1	.667
Evansville Crimson Giants	3	2	0	.600
Green Bay Packers	3	2	1	.600
Dayton Triangles	4	4	1	.500
Chicago Cardinals	3	3	2	.500
Rochester Jeffersons	2	3	0	.400
Cleveland Indians	3	5	0	.375
Washington Senators	1	2	0	.333
Cincinnati Celts	1	3	0	.250
Hammond Pros	1	3	1	.250
Minneapolis Marines	1	3	1	.250
Detroit Heralds	1	5	1	.167
Columbus Panhandles	1	8	0	.111
Tonawanda Kardex	0	1	0	.000
Muncie Flyers	0	2	0	.000
Louisville Brecks	0	2	0	.000
New York Giants	0	2	0	.000

1920

	W	L	T	Pct.
Akron Pros	8	0	3	1.000
Decatur Staleys	10	1	2	.909
Buffalo All-Americans	9	1	1	.900
Chicago Cardinals	6	2	2	.750
Rock Island Independents	6	2	2	.750
Dayton Triangles	5	2	2	.714
Rochester Jeffersons	6	3	2	.667
Canton Bulldogs	7	4	2	.636
Detroit Heralds	2	3	3	.400
Cleveland Tigers	2	4	2	.333
Chicago Tigers	2	5	1	.286
Hammond Pros	2	5	0	.286
Columbus Panhandles	2	6	2	.250
Muncie Flyers	0	1	0	.000

RS=REGULAR SEASON
PS=POSTSEASON

ATLANTA vs. BUFFALO
RS: Series tied, 2-2
1973—Bills, 17-6 (A)
1977—Bills, 3-0 (B)
1980—Falcons, 30-14 (B)
1983—Falcons, 31-14 (A)
(Points—Falcons 67, Bills 48)

ATLANTA vs. CHICAGO
RS: Falcons lead series, 9-6
1966—Bears, 23-6 (C)
1967—Bears, 23-14 (A)
1968—Falcons, 16-13 (C)
1969—Falcons, 48-31 (A)
1970—Bears, 23-14 (A)
1972—Falcons, 37-21 (C)
1973—Falcons, 46-6 (A)
1974—Falcons, 13-10 (A)
1976—Falcons, 10-0 (C)
1977—Falcons, 16-10 (C)
1978—Bears, 13-7 (C)
1980—Falcons, 28-17 (A)
1983—Falcons, 20-17 (C)
1985—Bears, 36-0 (C)
1986—Bears, 13-10 (A)
(Points—Falcons 285, Bears 256)

ATLANTA vs. CINCINNATI
RS: Bengals lead series, 5-1
1971—Falcons, 9-6 (C)
1975—Bengals, 21-14 (A)
1978—Bengals, 37-7 (C)
1981—Bengals, 30-28 (A)
1984—Bengals, 35-14 (C)
1987—Bengals, 16-10 (A)
(Points—Bengals 145, Falcons 82)

ATLANTA vs. CLEVELAND
RS: Browns lead series, 7-1
1966—Browns, 49-17 (A)
1968—Browns, 30-7 (C)
1971—Falcons, 31-14 (C)
1976—Browns, 20-17 (A)
1978—Browns, 24-16 (A)
1981—Browns, 28-17 (C)
1984—Browns, 23-7 (A)
1987—Browns, 38-3 (C)
(Points—Browns 226, Falcons 115)

ATLANTA vs. DALLAS
RS: Cowboys lead series, 7-3
PS: Cowboys lead series, 2-0
1966—Cowboys, 47-14 (A)
1967—Cowboys, 37-7 (D)
1969—Cowboys, 24-17 (A)
1970—Cowboys, 13-0 (D)
1974—Cowboys, 24-0 (A)
1976—Falcons, 17-10 (A)
1978—*Cowboys, 27-20 (D)
1980—*Cowboys, 30-27 (A)
1985—Cowboys, 24-10 (D)
1986—Falcons, 37-35 (D)
1987—Falcons, 21-10 (D)
1988—Cowboys, 26-20 (D)
(Points—Cowboys 307, Falcons 190)
**NFC Divisional Playoff*

ATLANTA vs. DENVER
RS: Broncos lead series, 4-3
1970—Broncos, 24-10 (D)
1972—Falcons, 23-20 (A)
1975—Falcons, 35-21 (A)
1979—Broncos, 20-17 (A) OT
1982—Falcons, 34-27 (D)
1985—Broncos, 44-28 (A)
1988—Broncos, 30-14 (D)
(Points—Broncos 186, Falcons 161)

ATLANTA vs. DETROIT
RS: Lions lead series, 14-5
1966—Lions, 28-10 (D)
1967—Lions, 24-3 (D)
1968—Lions, 24-7 (A)
1969—Lions, 27-21 (D)
1971—Lions, 41-38 (D)
1972—Lions, 26-23 (A)
1973—Lions, 31-6 (D)
1975—Lions, 17-14 (A)
1976—Lions, 24-10 (D)
1977—Falcons, 17-6 (A)
1978—Falcons, 14-0 (A)
1979—Lions, 24-23 (D)
1980—Falcons, 43-28 (A)
1983—Falcons, 30-14 (D)
1984—Lions, 27-24 (A) OT
1985—Lions, 28-27 (A)
1986—Falcons, 20-6 (D)
1987—Lions, 30-13 (A)
1988—Lions, 31-17 (D)
(Points—Lions 436, Falcons 360)

ATLANTA vs. GREEN BAY
RS: Packers lead series, 8-7
1966—Packers, 56-3 (Mil)
1967—Packers, 23-0 (Mil)
1968—Packers, 38-7 (A)
1969—Packers, 28-10 (GB)
1970—Packers, 27-24 (GB)
1971—Falcons, 28-21 (A)
1972—Falcons, 10-9 (Mil)
1974—Falcons, 10-3 (A)
1975—Packers, 22-13 (GB)
1976—Packers, 24-20 (A)
1979—Falcons, 25-7 (A)
1981—Falcons, 31-17 (GB)
1982—Packers, 38-7 (A)
1983—Falcons, 47-41 (A) OT
1988—Falcons, 20-0 (A)
(Points—Packers 354, Falcons 255)

ATLANTA vs. HOUSTON
RS: Falcons lead series, 4-2
1972—Falcons, 20-10 (A)
1976—Oilers, 20-14 (H)
1978—Falcons, 20-14 (A)
1981—Falcons, 31-27 (H)
1984—Falcons, 42-10 (A)
1987—Oilers, 37-33 (H)
(Points—Falcons 160, Oilers 118)

ATLANTA vs. *INDIANAPOLIS
RS: Colts lead series, 9-0
1966—Colts, 19-7 (A)
1967—Colts, 38-31 (B)
Colts, 49-7 (A)
1968—Colts, 28-20 (A)
Colts, 44-0 (B)
1969—Colts, 21-14 (A)
Colts, 13-6 (B)
1974—Colts, 17-7 (A)
1986—Colts, 28-23 (A)
(Points—Colts 257, Falcons 115)
**Franchise in Baltimore prior to 1984*

ATLANTA vs. KANSAS CITY
RS: Chiefs lead series, 2-0
1972—Chiefs, 17-14 (A)
1985—Chiefs, 38-10 (KC)
(Points—Chiefs 55, Falcons 24)

ATLANTA vs. *L.A. RAIDERS
RS: Raiders lead series, 4-2
1971—Falcons, 24-13 (A)
1975—Raiders, 37-34 (O) OT
1979—Raiders, 50-19 (O)
1982—Raiders, 38-14 (A)
1985—Raiders, 34-24 (A)
1988—Falcons, 12-6 (LA)
(Points—Raiders 178, Falcons 127)
**Franchise in Oakland prior to 1982*

ATLANTA vs. L.A. RAMS
RS: Rams lead series, 32-10-2
1966—Rams, 19-14 (A)
1967—Rams, 31-3 (A)
Rams, 20-3 (LA)
1968—Rams, 27-14 (LA)
Rams, 17-10 (A)
1969—Rams, 17-7 (LA)
Rams, 38-6 (A)
1970—Tie, 10-10 (LA)
Rams, 17-7 (A)
1971—Tie, 20-20 (LA)
Rams, 24-16 (A)
1972—Falcons, 31-3 (A)
Rams, 20-7 (LA)
1973—Rams, 31-0 (LA)
Falcons, 15-13 (A)
1974—Rams, 21-0 (LA)
Rams, 30-7 (A)
1975—Rams, 22-7 (LA)
Rams, 16-7 (A)
1976—Rams, 30-14 (A)
Rams, 59-0 (LA)
1977—Falcons, 17-6 (A)
Rams, 23-7 (LA)
1978—Rams, 10-0 (LA)
Falcons, 15-7 (A)
1979—Rams, 20-14 (LA)
Rams, 34-13 (A)
1980—Falcons, 13-10 (A)
Rams, 20-17 (LA) OT
1981—Rams, 37-35 (A)
Rams, 21-16 (LA)
1982—Falcons, 34-17 (A)
1983—Rams, 27-21 (LA)
Rams, 36-13 (A)
1984—Falcons, 30-28 (LA)
Rams, 24-10 (A)
1985—Rams, 17-6 (LA)
Falcons, 30-14 (A)
1986—Falcons, 26-14 (A)
Rams, 14-7 (LA)
1987—Falcons, 24-20 (A)
Rams, 33-0 (LA)
1988—Rams, 33-0 (A)
Rams, 22-7 (LA)
(Points—Rams 972, Falcons 553)

ATLANTA vs. MIAMI
RS: Dolphins lead series, 4-1
1970—Dolphins, 20-7 (A)
1974—Dolphins, 42-7 (M)
1980—Dolphins, 20-17 (A)
1983—Dolphins, 31-24 (M)
1986—Falcons, 20-14 (M)
(Points—Dolphins 127, Falcons 75)

ATLANTA vs. MINNESOTA
RS: Vikings lead series, 9-6
PS: Vikings lead series, 1-0
1966—Falcons, 20-13 (M)
1967—Falcons, 21-20 (A)
1968—Vikings, 47-7 (M)
1969—Falcons, 10-3 (A)
1970—Vikings, 37-7 (A)
1971—Vikings, 24-7 (M)
1973—Falcons, 20-14 (A)
1974—Vikings, 23-10 (M)
1975—Vikings, 38-0 (M)
1977—Vikings, 14-7 (A)
1980—Vikings, 24-23 (M)
1981—Falcons, 31-30 (A)
1982—*Vikings, 30-24 (M)
1984—Vikings, 27-20 (M)
1985—Falcons, 14-13 (A)
1987—Vikings, 24-13 (M)
(Points—Vikings 381, Falcons 234)
**NFC First Round Playoff*

ATLANTA vs. NEW ENGLAND
RS: Patriots lead series, 3-2
1972—Patriots, 21-20 (NE)
1977—Patriots, 16-10 (A)
1980—Falcons, 37-21 (NE)
1983—Falcons, 24-13 (A)
1986—Patriots, 25-17 (NE)
(Points—Falcons 108, Patriots 96)

ATLANTA vs. NEW ORLEANS
RS: Falcons lead series, 24-15
1967—Saints, 27-24 (NO)
1969—Falcons, 45-17 (A)
1970—Falcons, 14-3 (NO)
Falcons, 32-14 (A)
1971—Falcons, 28-6 (A)
Falcons, 24-20 (NO)
1972—Falcons, 21-14 (NO)
Falcons, 36-20 (A)
1973—Falcons, 62-7 (NO)
Falcons, 14-10 (A)
1974—Saints, 14-13 (NO)
Saints, 13-3 (A)
1975—Falcons, 14-7 (A)
Saints, 23-7 (NO)
1976—Saints, 30-0 (NO)
Falcons, 23-20 (A)
1977—Saints, 21-20 (NO)
Falcons, 35-7 (A)
1978—Falcons, 20-17 (NO)
Falcons, 20-17 (A)
1979—Falcons, 40-34 (NO) OT
Saints, 37-6 (A)
1980—Falcons, 41-14 (NO)
Falcons, 31-13 (A)
1981—Falcons, 27-0 (A)
Falcons, 41-10 (NO)
1982—Falcons, 35-0 (A)
Saints, 35-6 (NO)
1983—Saints, 19-17 (A)
Saints, 27-10 (NO)
1984—Falcons, 36-28 (NO)
Saints, 17-13 (A)
1985—Falcons, 31-24 (A)
Falcons, 16-10 (NO)
1986—Falcons, 31-10 (NO)
Saints, 14-9 (A)
1987—Saints, 38-0 (A)
1988—Saints, 29-21 (A)
Saints, 10-9 (NO)
(Points—Falcons 875, Saints 676)

ATLANTA vs. N.Y. GIANTS
RS: Series tied, 6-6
1966—Falcons, 27-16 (NY)
1968—Falcons, 24-21 (A)
1971—Giants, 21-17 (A)
1974—Falcons, 14-7 (New Haven)
1977—Falcons, 17-3 (A)
1978—Falcons, 23-20 (A)
1979—Giants, 24-3 (NY)
1981—Giants, 27-24 (A) OT
1982—Falcons, 16-14 (NY)
1983—Giants, 16-13 (A) OT
1984—Giants, 19-7 (A)
1988—Giants, 23-16 (A)
(Points—Giants 211, Falcons 201)

ATLANTA vs. N.Y. JETS
RS: Series tied, 2-2
1973—Falcons, 28-20 (NY)
1980—Jets, 14-7 (A)
1983—Falcons, 27-21 (NY)
1986—Jets, 28-14 (A)
(Points—Jets 83, Falcons 76)

ATLANTA vs. PHILADELPHIA
RS: Eagles lead series, 7-6-1
PS: Falcons lead series, 1-0
1966—Eagles, 23-10 (P)
1967—Eagles, 38-7 (A)
1969—Falcons, 27-3 (P)
1970—Tie, 13-13 (P)
1973—Falcons, 44-27 (P)
1976—Eagles, 14-13 (A)
1978—*Falcons, 14-13 (A)
1979—Falcons, 14-10 (P)
1980—Falcons, 20-17 (P)
1981—Eagles, 16-13 (P)
1983—Eagles, 28-24 (A)
1984—Falcons, 26-10 (A)
1985—Eagles, 23-17 (P) OT
1986—Eagles, 16-0 (A)
1988—Falcons, 27-24 (P)
(Points—Eagles 275, Falcons 269)
**NFC First Round Playoff*

ATLANTA vs. *PHOENIX
RS: Cardinals lead series, 7-4
1966—Falcons, 16-10 (A)
1968—Cardinals, 17-12 (StL)
1971—Cardinals, 26-9 (A)
1973—Cardinals, 32-10 (A)
1975—Cardinals, 23-20 (StL)
1978—Cardinals, 42-21 (StL)
1980—Falcons, 33-27 (StL) OT
1981—Falcons, 41-20 (A)
1982—Cardinals, 23-20 (A)
1986—Falcons, 33-13 (A)
1987—Cardinals, 34-21 (A)
(Points—Cardinals 267, Falcons 236)
**Franchise in St. Louis prior to 1988*

ATLANTA vs. PITTSBURGH
RS: Steelers lead series, 7-1
1966—Steelers, 57-33 (A)
1968—Steelers, 41-21 (A)
1970—Falcons, 27-16 (A)
1974—Steelers, 24-17 (P)
1978—Steelers, 31-7 (P)
1981—Steelers, 34-20 (A)
1984—Steelers, 35-10 (P)
1987—Steelers, 28-12 (A)
(Points—Steelers 266, Falcons 147)

ATLANTA vs. SAN DIEGO
RS: Falcons lead series, 2-1
1973—Falcons, 41-0 (SD)
1979—Falcons, 28-26 (SD)
1988—Chargers, 10-7 (A)
(Points—Falcons 76, Chargers 36)

ATLANTA vs. SAN FRANCISCO
RS: 49ers lead series, 25-18-1
1966—49ers, 44-7 (A)
1967—49ers, 38-7 (SF)
49ers, 34-28 (A)
1968—49ers, 28-13 (SF)
49ers, 14-12 (A)
1969—Falcons, 24-12 (A)
Falcons, 21-7 (SF)
1970—Falcons, 21-20 (A)
49ers, 24-20 (SF)
1971—Falcons, 20-17 (A)
49ers, 24-3 (SF)
1972—49ers, 49-14 (A)
49ers, 20-0 (SF)
1973—49ers, 13-9 (A)
Falcons, 17-3 (SF)
1974—49ers, 16-10 (A)
49ers, 27-0 (SF)
1975—Falcons, 17-3 (SF)
Falcons, 31-9 (A)
1976—49ers, 15-0 (SF)
Falcons, 21-16 (A)
1977—Falcons, 7-0 (SF)
49ers, 10-3 (A)
1978—Falcons, 20-17 (SF)
Falcons, 21-10 (A)
1979—49ers, 20-15 (SF)
Falcons, 31-21 (A)
1980—Falcons, 20-17 (SF)
Falcons, 35-10 (A)
1981—Falcons, 34-17 (A)
49ers, 17-14 (SF)
1982—Falcons, 17-7 (SF)
1983—49ers, 24-20 (SF)
Falcons, 28-24 (A)
1984—49ers, 14-5 (SF)
49ers, 35-17 (A)
1985—49ers, 35-16 (SF)
49ers, 38-17 (A)
1986—Tie, 10-10 (A) OT
49ers, 20-0 (SF)
1987—49ers, 25-17 (A)
49ers, 35-7 (SF)
1988—Falcons, 34-17 (SF)
49ers, 13-3 (A)
(Points—49ers 869, Falcons 686)

ATLANTA vs. SEATTLE
RS: Seahawks lead series, 4-0
1976—Seahawks, 30-13 (S)
1979—Seahawks, 31-28 (A)
1985—Seahawks, 30-26 (S)
1988—Seahawks, 31-20 (A)
(Points—Seahawks 122, Falcons 87)
ATLANTA vs. TAMPA BAY
RS: Series tied, 4-4
1977—Falcons, 17-0 (TB)
1978—Buccaneers, 14-9 (TB)
1979—Falcons, 17-14 (A)
1981—Buccaneers, 24-23 (TB)
1984—Buccaneers, 23-6 (TB)
1986—Falcons, 23-20 (TB) OT
1987—Buccaneers, 48-10 (TB)
1988—Falcons, 17-10 (A)
(Points—Buccaneers 153, Falcons 122)
ATLANTA vs. WASHINGTON
RS: Redskins lead series, 9-3-1
1966—Redskins, 33-20 (W)
1967—Tie, 20-20 (A)
1969—Redskins, 27-20 (W)
1972—Redskins, 24-13 (W)
1975—Redskins, 30-27 (A)
1977—Redskins, 10-6 (W)
1978—Falcons, 20-17 (A)
1979—Redskins, 16-7 (A)
1980—Falcons, 10-6 (A)
1983—Redskins, 37-21 (W)
1984—Redskins, 27-14 (W)
1985—Redskins, 44-10 (A)
1987—Falcons, 21-20 (A)
(Points—Redskins 311, Falcons 209)

BUFFALO vs. ATLANTA
RS: Series tied, 2-2;
See Atlanta vs. Buffalo
BUFFALO vs. CHICAGO
RS: Bears lead series, 3-1
1970—Bears, 31-13 (C)
1974—Bills, 16-6 (B)
1979—Bears, 7-0 (B)
1988—Bears, 24-3 (C)
(Points—Bears 68, Bills 32)
BUFFALO vs. CINCINNATI
RS: Bengals lead series, 9-5
PS: Bengals lead series, 2-0
1968—Bengals, 34-23 (C)
1969—Bills, 16-13 (B)
1970—Bengals, 43-14 (B)
1973—Bengals, 16-13 (B)
1975—Bengals, 33-24 (C)
1978—Bills, 5-0 (B)
1979—Bills, 51-24 (B)
1980—Bills, 14-0 (C)
1981—Bengals, 27-24 (C) OT
*Bengals, 28-21 (C)
1983—Bills, 10-6 (C)
1984—Bengals, 52-21 (C)
1985—Bengals, 23-17 (B)
1986—Bengals, 36-33 (C) OT
1988—Bengals, 35-21 (C)
**Bengals, 21-10 (C)
(Points—Bengals 391, Bills 317)
**AFC Divisional Playoff*
***AFC Championship*
BUFFALO vs. CLEVELAND
RS: Browns lead series, 7-2
1972—Browns, 27-10 (C)
1974—Bills, 15-10 (C)
1977—Browns, 27-16 (B)
1978—Browns, 41-20 (C)
1981—Bills, 22-13 (B)
1984—Browns, 13-10 (B)
1985—Browns, 17-7 (C)
1986—Browns, 21-17 (B)
1987—Browns, 27-21 (C)
(Points—Browns 196, Bills 138)
BUFFALO vs. DALLAS
RS: Cowboys lead series, 3-1
1971—Cowboys, 49-37 (B)
1976—Cowboys, 17-10 (D)
1981—Cowboys, 27-14 (D)
1984—Bills, 14-3 (B)
(Points—Cowboys 96, Bills 75)
BUFFALO vs. DENVER
RS: Bills lead series, 14-9-1
1960—Broncos, 27-21 (B)
Tie, 38-38 (D)
1961—Broncos, 22-10 (B)
Bills, 23-10 (D)
1962—Broncos, 23-20 (B)
Bills, 45-38 (D)
1963—Bills, 30-28 (D)
Bills, 27-17 (B)
1964—Bills, 30-13 (B)
Bills, 30-19 (D)
1965—Bills, 30-15 (D)
Bills, 31-13 (B)
1966—Bills, 38-21 (B)
1967—Bills, 17-16 (D)
Broncos, 21-20 (B)
1968—Broncos, 34-32 (D)
1969—Bills, 41-28 (B)
1970—Broncos, 25-10 (B)
1975—Bills, 38-14 (B)
1977—Broncos, 26-6 (D)
1979—Broncos, 19-16 (B)
1981—Bills, 9-7 (B)
1984—Broncos, 37-7 (B)
1987—Bills, 21-14 (B)
(Points—Bills 590, Broncos 525)
BUFFALO vs. DETROIT
RS: Series tied, 1-1-1
1972—Tie, 21-21 (B)
1976—Lions, 27-14 (D)
1979—Bills, 20-17 (D)
(Points—Lions 65, Bills 55)
BUFFALO vs. GREEN BAY
RS: Bills lead series, 3-1
1974—Bills, 27-7 (GB)
1979—Bills, 19-12 (B)
1982—Packers, 33-21 (Mil)
1988—Bills, 28-0 (B)
(Points—Bills 95, Packers 52)
BUFFALO vs. HOUSTON
RS: Oilers lead series, 18-10
PS: Bills lead series, 1-0
1960—Bills, 25-24 (B)
Oilers, 31-23 (H)
1961—Bills, 22-12 (H)
Oilers, 28-16 (B)
1962—Oilers, 28-23 (B)
Oilers, 17-14 (H)
1963—Oilers, 31-20 (B)
Oilers, 28-14 (H)
1964—Bills, 48-17 (H)
Bills, 24-10 (B)
1965—Oilers, 19-17 (B)
Bills, 29-18 (H)
1966—Bills, 27-20 (B)
Bills, 42-20 (H)
1967—Oilers, 20-3 (B)
Oilers, 10-3 (H)
1968—Oilers, 30-7 (B)
Oilers, 35-6 (H)
1969—Oilers, 17-3 (B)
Oilers, 28-14 (H)
1971—Oilers, 20-14 (B)
1974—Oilers, 21-9 (B)
1976—Oilers, 13-3 (B)
1978—Oilers, 17-10 (H)
1983—Bills, 30-13 (B)
1985—Bills, 20-0 (B)
1986—Oilers, 16-7 (H)
1987—Bills, 34-30 (B)
1988—*Bills, 17-10 (B)
(Points—Oilers 583, Bills 524)
**AFC Divisional Playoff*
BUFFALO vs. *INDIANAPOLIS
RS: Series tied, 18-18-1
1970—Tie, 17-17 (Balt)
Colts, 20-14 (Buff)
1971—Colts, 43-0 (Buff)
Colts, 24-0 (Balt)
1972—Colts, 17-0 (Buff)
Colts, 35-7 (Balt)
1973—Bills, 31-13 (Buff)
Bills, 24-17 (Balt)
1974—Bills, 27-14 (Balt)
Bills, 6-0 (Buff)
1975—Bills, 38-31 (Balt)
Colts, 42-35 (Buff)
1976—Colts, 31-13 (Buff)
Colts, 58-20 (Balt)
1977—Colts, 17-14 (Balt)
Colts, 31-13 (Buff)
1978—Bills, 24-17 (Buff)
Bills, 21-14 (Balt)
1979—Bills, 31-13 (Balt)
Colts, 14-13 (Buff)
1980—Colts, 17-12 (Buff)
Colts, 28-24 (Balt)
1981—Bills, 35-3 (Balt)
Bills, 23-17 (Buff)
1982—Bills, 20-0 (Buff)
1983—Bills, 28-23 (Buff)
Bills, 30-7 (Balt)
1984—Colts, 31-17 (I)
Bills, 21-15 (Buff)
1985—Colts, 49-17 (I)
Bills, 21-9 (Buff)
1986—Bills, 24-13 (Buff)
Colts, 24-14 (I)
1987—Colts, 47-6 (Buff)
Bills, 27-3 (I)
1988—Bills, 34-23 (Buff)
Colts, 17-14 (I)
(Points—Colts 794, Bills 715)
**Franchise in Baltimore prior to 1984*
BUFFALO vs. *KANSAS CITY
RS: Bills lead series, 15-11-1
PS: Chiefs lead series, 1-0
1960—Texans, 45-28 (B)
Texans, 24-7 (D)
1961—Bills, 27-24 (B)
Bills, 30-20 (D)
1962—Texans, 41-21 (D)
Bills, 23-14 (B)
1963—Tie, 27-27 (B)
Bills, 35-26 (KC)
1964—Bills, 34-17 (B)
Bills, 35-22 (KC)
1965—Bills, 23-7 (KC)
Bills, 34-25 (B)
1966—Chiefs, 42-20 (B)
Bills, 29-14 (KC)
**Chiefs, 31-7 (B)
1967—Chiefs, 23-13 (KC)
1968—Chiefs, 18-7 (B)
1969—Chiefs, 29-7 (B)
Chiefs, 22-19 (KC)
1971—Chiefs, 22-9 (KC)
1973—Bills, 23-14 (B)
1976—Bills, 50-17 (B)
1978—Bills, 28-13 (B)
Chiefs, 14-10 (KC)
1982—Bills, 14-9 (B)
1983—Bills, 14-9 (KC)
1986—Chiefs, 20-17 (B)
Bills, 17-14 (KC)
(Points—Chiefs 608, Bills 603)
**Franchise in Dallas prior to 1963 and known as Texans*
***AFL Championship*
BUFFALO vs. *L.A. RAIDERS
RS: Raiders lead series, 13-12
1960—Bills, 38-9 (B)
Raiders, 20-7 (O)
1961—Raiders, 31-22 (B)
Bills, 26-21 (O)
1962—Bills, 14-6 (B)
Bills, 10-6 (O)
1963—Raiders, 35-17 (O)
Bills, 12-0 (B)
1964—Bills, 23-20 (B)
Raiders, 16-13 (O)
1965—Bills, 17-12 (B)
Bills, 17-14 (O)
1966—Bills, 31-10 (O)
1967—Raiders, 24-20 (B)
Raiders, 28-21 (O)
1968—Raiders, 48-6 (B)
Raiders, 13-10 (O)
1969—Raiders, 50-21 (O)
1972—Raiders, 28-16 (O)
1974—Bills, 21-20 (B)
1977—Raiders, 34-13 (O)
1980—Bills, 24-7 (B)
1983—Raiders, 27-24 (B)
1987—Raiders, 34-21 (LA)
1988—Bills, 37-21 (B)
(Points—Raiders 534, Bills 481)
**Franchise in Oakland prior to 1982*
BUFFALO vs. L.A. RAMS
RS: Rams lead series, 3-1
1970—Rams, 19-0 (B)
1974—Rams, 19-14 (LA)
1980—Bills, 10-7 (B) OT
1983—Rams, 41-17 (LA)
(Points—Rams 86, Bills 41)
BUFFALO vs. MIAMI
RS: Dolphins lead series, 34-11-1
1966—Bills, 58-24 (B)
Bills, 29-0 (M)
1967—Bills, 35-13 (B)
Dolphins, 17-14 (M)
1968—Tie, 14-14 (M)
Dolphins, 21-17 (B)
1969—Dolphins, 24-6 (M)
Bills, 28-3 (B)
1970—Dolphins, 33-14 (B)
Dolphins, 45-7 (M)
1971—Dolphins, 29-14 (B)
Dolphins, 34-0 (M)
1972—Dolphins, 24-23 (M)
Dolphins, 30-16 (B)
1973—Dolphins, 27-6 (M)
Dolphins, 17-0 (B)
1974—Dolphins, 24-16 (B)
Dolphins, 35-28 (M)
1975—Dolphins, 35-30 (B)
Dolphins, 31-21 (M)
1976—Dolphins, 30-21 (B)
Dolphins, 45-27 (M)
1977—Dolphins, 13-0 (B)
Dolphins, 31-14 (M)
1978—Dolphins, 31-24 (M)
Dolphins, 25-24 (B)
1979—Dolphins, 9-7 (B)
Dolphins, 17-7 (M)
1980—Bills, 17-7 (B)
Dolphins, 17-14 (M)
1981—Bills, 31-21 (B)
Dolphins, 16-6 (M)
1982—Dolphins, 9-7 (B)
Dolphins, 27-10 (M)
1983—Dolphins, 12-0 (B)
Bills, 38-35 (M) OT
1984—Dolphins, 21-17 (B)
Dolphins, 38-7 (M)
1985—Dolphins, 23-14 (B)
Dolphins, 28-0 (M)
1986—Dolphins, 27-14 (M)
Dolphins, 34-24 (B)
1987—Bills, 34-31 (M) OT
Bills, 27-0 (B)
1988—Bills, 9-6 (B)
Bills, 31-6 (M)
(Points—Dolphins 1,039, Bills 800)
BUFFALO vs. MINNESOTA
RS: Vikings lead series, 4-2
1971—Vikings, 19-0 (M)
1975—Vikings, 35-13 (B)
1979—Vikings, 10-3 (M)
1982—Bills, 23-22 (B)
1985—Vikings, 27-20 (B)
1988—Bills, 13-10 (B)
(Points—Vikings 123, Bills 72)
BUFFALO vs. *NEW ENGLAND
RS: Patriots lead series, 31-25-1
PS: Patriots lead series, 1-0
1960—Bills, 13-0 (Bos)
Bills, 38-14 (Buff)
1961—Patriots, 23-21 (Buff)
Patriots, 52-21 (Bos)
1962—Tie, 28-28 (Buff)
Patriots, 21-10 (Bos)
1963—Bills, 28-21 (Buff)
Patriots, 17-7 (Bos)
**Patriots, 26-8 (Buff)
1964—Patriots, 36-28 (Buff)
Bills, 24-14 (Bos)
1965—Bills, 24-7 (Buff)
Bills, 23-7 (Bos)
1966—Patriots, 20-10 (Buff)
Patriots, 14-3 (Bos)
1967—Patriots, 23-0 (Buff)
Bills, 44-16 (Bos)
1968—Patriots, 16-7 (Buff)
Patriots, 23-6 (Bos)
1969—Bills, 23-16 (Buff)
Patriots, 35-21 (Bos)
1970—Bills, 45-10 (Bos)
Patriots, 14-10 (Buff)
1971—Patriots, 38-33 (NE)
Bills, 27-20 (Buff)
1972—Bills, 38-14 (Buff)
Bills, 27-24 (NE)
1973—Bills, 31-13 (NE)
Bills, 37-13 (Buff)
1974—Bills, 30-28 (Buff)
Bills, 29-28 (NE)
1975—Bills, 45-31 (Buff)
Bills, 34-14 (NE)
1976—Patriots, 26-22 (Buff)
Patriots, 20-10 (NE)
1977—Bills, 24-14 (NE)
Patriots, 20-7 (Buff)
1978—Patriots, 14-10 (Buff)
Patriots, 26-24 (NE)
1979—Patriots, 26-6 (Buff)
Bills, 16-13 (NE) OT
1980—Bills, 31-13 (Buff)
Patriots, 24-2 (NE)
1981—Bills, 20-17 (Buff)
Bills, 19-10 (NE)
1982—Patriots, 30-19 (NE)
1983—Patriots, 31-0 (Buff)
Patriots, 21-7 (NE)
1984—Patriots, 21-17 (Buff)
Patriots, 38-10 (NE)
1985—Patriots, 17-14 (Buff)
Patriots, 14-3 (NE)
1986—Patriots, 23-3 (Buff)
Patriots, 22-19 (NE)
1987—Patriots, 14-7 (NE)
Patriots, 13-7 (Buff)
1988—Bills, 16-14 (NE)
Bills, 23-20 (Buff)
(Points—Patriots 1,177, Bills 1,109)
**Franchise in Boston prior to 1971*
***Division Playoff*
BUFFALO vs. NEW ORLEANS
RS: Bills lead series, 2-1
1973—Saints, 13-0 (NO)
1980—Bills, 35-26 (NO)
1983—Bills, 27-21 (B)
(Points—Bills 62, Saints 60)
BUFFALO vs. N.Y. GIANTS
RS: Series tied, 2-2
1970—Giants, 20-6 (NY)
1975—Giants, 17-14 (B)
1978—Bills, 41-17 (B)
1987—Bills, 6-3 (B) OT
(Points—Bills 67, Giants 57)
BUFFALO vs. *N.Y. JETS
RS: Series tied, 28-28
PS: Bills lead series, 1-0
1960—Titans, 27-3 (NY)
Titans, 17-13 (B)

1961—Bills, 41-31 (B)
Titans, 21-14 (NY)
1962—Titans, 17-6 (B)
Bills, 20-3 (NY)
1963—Bills, 45-14 (B)
Bills, 19-10 (NY)
1964—Bills, 34-24 (B)
Bills, 20-7 (NY)
1965—Bills, 33-21 (B)
Jets, 14-12 (NY)
1966—Bills, 33-23 (NY)
Bills, 14-3 (B)
1967—Bills, 20-17 (B)
Jets, 20-10 (NY)
1968—Bills, 37-35 (B)
Jets, 25-21 (NY)
1969—Jets, 33-19 (B)
Jets, 16-6 (NY)
1970—Bills, 34-31 (B)
Bills, 10-6 (NY)
1971—Jets, 28-17 (NY)
Jets, 20-7 (B)
1972—Jets, 41-24 (B)
Jets, 41-3 (NY)
1973—Bills, 9-7 (B)
Bills, 34-14 (NY)
1974—Bills, 16-12 (B)
Jets, 20-10 (NY)
1975—Bills, 42-14 (B)
Bills, 24-23 (NY)
1976—Jets, 17-14 (NY)
Jets, 19-14 (B)
1977—Jets, 24-19 (B)
Bills, 14-10 (NY)
1978—Jets, 21-20 (B)
Jets, 45-14 (NY)
1979—Bills, 46-31 (B)
Bills, 14-12 (NY)
1980—Bills, 20-10 (B)
Bills, 31-24 (NY)
1981—Bills, 31-0 (B)
Jets, 33-14 (NY)
**Bills, 31-27 (NY)
1983—Jets, 34-10 (B)
Bills, 24-17 (NY)
1984—Jets, 28-26 (B)
Jets, 21-17 (NY)
1985—Jets, 42-3 (NY)
Jets, 27-7 (B)
1986—Jets, 28-24 (B)
Jets, 14-13 (NY)
1987—Jets, 31-28 (B)
Bills, 17-14 (NY)
1988—Bills, 37-14 (NY)
Bills, 9-6 (B) OT
(Points—Jets 1,184, Bills 1,147)
Jets known as Titans prior to 1963
***AFC First Round Playoff*

BUFFALO vs. PHILADELPHIA
RS: Eagles lead series, 4-1
1973—Bills, 27-26 (B)
1981—Eagles, 20-14 (B)
1984—Eagles, 27-17 (B)
1985—Eagles, 21-17 (P)
1987—Eagles, 17-7 (P)
(Points—Eagles 111, Bills 82)

BUFFALO vs. *PHOENIX
RS: Cardinals lead series, 3-2
1971—Cardinals, 28-23 (B)
1975—Bills, 32-14 (StL)
1981—Cardinals, 24-0 (StL)
1984—Cardinals, 37-7 (StL)
1986—Bills, 17-10 (B)
(Points—Cardinals 113, Bills 79)
Franchise in St. Louis prior to 1988

BUFFALO vs. PITTSBURGH
RS: Series tied, 5-5
PS: Steelers lead series, 1-0
1970—Steelers, 23-10 (P)
1972—Steelers, 38-21 (B)
1974—*Steelers, 32-14 (P)
1975—Bills, 30-21 (P)
1978—Steelers, 28-17 (B)
1979—Steelers, 28-0 (P)
1980—Bills, 28-13 (B)
1982—Bills, 13-0 (B)
1985—Steelers, 30-24 (P)
1986—Bills, 16-12 (B)
1988—Bills, 36-28 (B)
(Points—Steelers 253, Bills 209)
**AFC Divisional Playoff*

BUFFALO vs. *SAN DIEGO
RS: Chargers lead series, 16-7-2
PS: Bills lead series, 2-1
1960—Chargers, 24-10 (B)
Bills, 32-3 (LA)
1961—Chargers, 19-11 (B)
Chargers, 28-10 (SD)
1962—Bills, 35-10 (B)
Bills, 40-20 (SD)
1963—Chargers, 14-10 (SD)
Chargers, 23-13 (B)
1964—Bills, 30-3 (B)
Bills, 27-24 (SD)
**Bills, 20-7 (B)
1965—Chargers, 34-3 (B)
Tie, 20-20 (SD)
**Bills, 23-0 (SD)
1966—Chargers, 27-7 (SD)
Tie, 17-17 (B)
1967—Chargers, 37-17 (B)
1968—Chargers, 21-6 (B)
1969—Chargers, 45-6 (SD)
1971—Chargers, 20-3 (SD)
1973—Chargers, 34-7 (SD)
1976—Chargers, 34-13 (B)
1979—Chargers, 27-19 (SD)
1980—Bills, 26-24 (SD)
***Chargers, 20-14 (SD)
1981—Bills, 28-27 (SD)
1985—Chargers, 14-9 (B)
Chargers, 40-7 (SD)
(Points—Chargers 616, Bills 463)
Franchise in Los Angeles prior to 1961
***AFL Championship*
****AFC Divisional Playoff*

BUFFALO vs. SAN FRANCISCO
RS: Bills lead series, 2-1
1972—Bills, 27-20 (B)
1980—Bills, 18-13 (SF)
1983—49ers, 23-10 (B)
(Points—49ers 56, Bills 55)

BUFFALO vs. SEATTLE
RS: Seahawks lead series, 2-1
1977—Seahawks, 56-17 (S)
1984—Seahawks, 31-28 (S)
1988—Bills, 13-3 (S)
(Points—Seahawks 90, Bills 58)

BUFFALO vs. TAMPA BAY
RS: Buccaneers lead series, 4-1
1976—Bills, 14-9 (TB)
1978—Buccaneers, 31-10 (TB)
1982—Buccaneers, 24-23 (TB)
1986—Buccaneers, 34-28 (TB)
1988—Buccaneers, 10-5 (TB)
(Points—Buccaneers 108, Bills 80)

BUFFALO vs. WASHINGTON
RS: Redskins lead series, 3-2
1972—Bills, 24-17 (W)
1977—Redskins, 10-0 (B)
1981—Bills, 21-14 (B)
1984—Redskins, 41-14 (W)
1987—Redskins, 27-7 (B)
(Points—Redskins 109, Bills 66)

CHICAGO vs. ATLANTA
RS: Falcons lead series, 9-6;
See Atlanta vs. Chicago

CHICAGO vs. BUFFALO
RS: Bears lead series, 3-1;
See Buffalo vs. Chicago

CHICAGO vs. CINCINNATI
RS: Bengals lead series, 2-1
1972—Bengals, 13-3 (Chi)
1980—Bengals, 17-14 (Chi) OT
1986—Bears, 44-7 (Cin)
(Points—Bears 61, Bengals 37)

CHICAGO vs. CLEVELAND
RS: Browns lead series, 6-3
1951—Browns, 42-21 (Cle)
1954—Browns, 39-10 (Chi)
1960—Browns, 42-0 (Cle)
1961—Bears, 17-14 (Chi)
1967—Browns, 24-0 (Cle)
1969—Browns, 28-24 (Chi)
1972—Bears, 17-0 (Cle)
1980—Browns, 27-21 (Cle)
1986—Bears, 41-31 (Chi)
(Points—Browns 247, Bears 151)

CHICAGO vs. DALLAS
RS: Cowboys lead series, 7-6
PS: Cowboys lead series, 1-0
1960—Bears, 17-7 (C)
1962—Bears, 34-33 (D)
1964—Cowboys, 24-10 (C)
1968—Cowboys, 34-3 (C)
1971—Bears, 23-19 (C)
1973—Cowboys, 20-17 (C)
1976—Cowboys, 31-21 (D)
1977—*Cowboys, 37-7 (D)
1979—Cowboys, 24-20 (D)
1981—Cowboys, 10-9 (D)
1984—Cowboys, 23-14 (C)
1985—Bears, 44-0 (D)
1986—Bears, 24-10 (D)
1988—Bears, 17-7 (C)
(Points—Cowboys 279, Bears 260)
**NFC Divisional Playoff*

CHICAGO vs. DENVER
RS: Series tied, 4-4
1971—Broncos, 6-3 (D)
1973—Bears, 33-14 (D)
1976—Broncos, 28-14 (C)
1978—Broncos, 16-7 (D)
1981—Bears, 35-24 (C)
1983—Bears, 31-14 (C)
1984—Bears, 27-0 (C)
1987—Broncos, 31-29 (D)
(Points—Bears 179, Broncos 133)

CHICAGO vs. *DETROIT
RS: Bears lead series, 69-44-5
1930—Spartans, 7-6 (P)
Bears, 14-6 (C)
1931—Bears, 9-6 (C)
Spartans, 3-0 (P)
1932—Tie, 13-13 (C)
Tie, 7-7 (P)
Bears, 9-0 (C)
1933—Bears, 17-14 (C)
Bears, 17-7 (P)
1934—Bears, 19-16 (D)
Bears, 10-7 (C)
1935—Tie, 20-20 (C)
Lions, 14-2 (D)
1936—Bears, 12-10 (C)
Lions, 13-7 (D)
1937—Bears, 28-20 (C)
Bears, 13-0 (D)
1938—Lions, 13-7 (C)
Lions, 14-7 (D)
1939—Lions, 10-0 (C)
Bears, 23-13 (D)
1940—Bears, 7-0 (C)
Lions, 17-14 (D)
1941—Bears, 49-0 (C)
Bears, 24-7 (D)
1942—Bears, 16-0 (C)
Bears, 42-0 (D)
1943—Bears, 27-21 (D)
Bears, 35-14 (C)
1944—Tie, 21-21 (C)
Lions, 41-21 (D)
1945—Lions, 16-10 (D)
Lions, 35-28 (C)
1946—Bears, 42-6 (C)
Bears, 45-24 (D)
1947—Bears, 33-24 (C)
Bears, 34-14 (D)
1948—Bears, 28-0 (C)
Bears, 42-14 (D)
1949—Bears, 27-24 (C)
Bears, 28-7 (D)
1950—Bears, 35-21 (D)
Bears, 6-3 (C)
1951—Bears, 28-23 (D)
Lions, 41-28 (C)
1952—Bears, 24-23 (C)
Lions, 45-21 (D)
1953—Lions, 20-16 (C)
Lions, 13-7 (D)
1954—Lions, 48-23 (D)
Bears, 28-24 (C)
1955—Bears, 24-14 (D)
Bears, 21-20 (C)
1956—Lions, 42-10 (D)
Bears, 38-21 (C)
1957—Bears, 27-7 (D)
Lions, 21-13 (C)
1958—Bears, 20-7 (D)
Bears, 21-16 (C)
1959—Bears, 24-14 (D)
Bears, 25-14 (C)
1960—Bears, 28-7 (C)
Lions, 36-0 (D)
1961—Bears, 31-17 (D)
Lions, 16-15 (C)
1962—Lions, 11-3 (D)
Bears, 3-0 (C)
1963—Bears, 37-21 (D)
Bears, 24-14 (C)
1964—Lions, 10-0 (C)
Bears, 27-24 (D)
1965—Bears, 38-10 (C)
Bears, 17-10 (D)
1966—Lions, 14-3 (D)
Tie, 10-10 (C)
1967—Bears, 14-3 (C)
Bears, 27-13 (D)
1968—Lions, 42-0 (D)
Lions, 28-10 (C)
1969—Lions, 13-7 (D)
Lions, 20-3 (C)
1970—Lions, 28-14 (D)
Lions, 16-10 (C)
1971—Bears, 28-23 (D)
Lions, 28-3 (C)
1972—Lions, 38-24 (C)
Lions, 14-0 (D)
1973—Lions, 30-7 (C)
Lions, 40-7 (D)
1974—Bears, 17-9 (C)
Lions, 34-17 (D)
1975—Lions, 27-7 (D)
Bears, 25-21 (C)
1976—Bears, 10-3 (C)
Lions, 14-10 (D)
1977—Bears, 30-20 (C)
Bears, 31-14 (D)
1978—Bears, 19-0 (D)
Lions, 21-17 (C)
1979—Bears, 35-7 (C)
Lions, 20-0 (D)
1980—Bears, 24-7 (C)
Bears, 23-17 (D) OT
1981—Lions, 48-17 (D)
Lions, 23-7 (C)
1982—Lions, 17-10 (D)
Bears, 20-17 (C)
1983—Lions, 31-17 (D)
Lions, 38-17 (C)
1984—Bears, 16-14 (C)
Bears, 30-13 (D)
1985—Bears, 24-3 (C)
Bears, 37-17 (D)
1986—Bears, 13-7 (C)
Bears, 16-13 (D)
1987—Bears, 30-10 (C)
1988—Bears, 24-7 (D)
Bears, 13-12 (C)
(Points—Bears 2,198, Lions 1,955)
Franchise in Portsmouth prior to 1934 and known as the Spartans

***CHICAGO vs. GREEN BAY**
RS: Bears lead series, 75-55-6
PS: Bears lead series, 1-0
1921—Staleys, 20-0 (C)
1923—Bears, 3-0 (GB)
1924—Bears, 3-0 (C)
1925—Packers, 14-10 (GB)
Bears, 21-0 (C)
1926—Tie, 6-6 (GB)
Bears, 19-13 (C)
Tie, 3-3 (C)
1927—Bears, 7-6 (GB)
Bears, 14-6 (C)
1928—Tie, 12-12 (GB)
Packers, 16-6 (C)
Packers, 6-0 (C)
1929—Packers, 23-0 (GB)
Packers, 14-0 (C)
Packers, 25-0 (C)
1930—Packers, 7-0 (GB)
Packers, 13-12 (C)
Bears, 21-0 (C)
1931—Packers, 7-0 (GB)
Packers, 6-2 (C)
Bears, 7-6 (C)
1932—Tie, 0-0 (GB)
Packers, 2-0 (C)
Bears, 9-0 (C)
1933—Bears, 14-7 (GB)
Bears, 10-7 (C)
Bears, 7-6 (C)
1934—Bears, 24-10 (GB)
Bears, 27-14 (C)
1935—Packers, 7-0 (GB)
Packers, 17-14 (C)
1936—Bears, 30-3 (GB)
Packers, 21-10 (C)
1937—Bears, 14-2 (GB)
Packers, 24-14 (C)
1938—Bears, 2-0 (GB)
Packers, 24-17 (C)
1939—Packers, 21-16 (GB)
Bears, 30-27 (C)
1940—Bears, 41-10 (GB)
Bears, 14-7 (C)
1941—Bears, 25-17 (GB)
Packers, 16-14 (C)
**Bears, 33-14 (C)
1942—Bears, 44-28 (GB)
Bears, 38-7 (C)
1943—Tie, 21-21 (GB)
Bears, 21-7 (C)
1944—Packers, 42-28 (GB)
Bears, 21-0 (C)
1945—Packers, 31-21 (GB)
Bears, 28-24 (C)
1946—Bears, 30-7 (GB)
Bears, 10-7 (C)
1947—Packers, 29-20 (GB)
Bears, 20-17 (C)
1948—Bears, 45-7 (GB)
Bears, 7-6 (C)
1949—Bears, 17-0 (GB)
Bears, 24-3 (C)
1950—Packers, 31-21 (GB)
Bears, 28-14 (C)
1951—Bears, 31-20 (GB)
Bears, 24-13 (C)
1952—Bears, 24-14 (GB)
Packers, 41-28 (C)
1953—Bears, 17-13 (GB)
Tie, 21-21 (C)
1954—Bears, 10-3 (GB)
Bears, 28-23 (C)
1955—Packers, 24-3 (GB)
Bears, 52-31 (C)
1956—Bears, 37-21 (GB)
Bears, 38-14 (C)
1957—Packers, 21-17 (GB)
Bears, 21-14 (C)

1958—Bears, 34-20 (GB)
Bears, 24-10 (C)
1959—Packers, 9-6 (GB)
Bears, 28-17 (C)
1960—Bears, 17-14 (GB)
Packers, 41-13 (C)
1961—Packers, 24-0 (GB)
Packers, 31-28 (C)
1962—Packers, 49-0 (GB)
Packers, 38-7 (C)
1963—Bears, 10-3 (GB)
Bears, 26-7 (C)
1964—Packers, 23-12 (GB)
Packers, 17-3 (C)
1965—Packers, 23-14 (GB)
Bears, 31-10 (C)
1966—Packers, 17-0 (C)
Packers, 13-6 (GB)
1967—Packers, 13-10 (GB)
Packers, 17-13 (C)
1968—Bears, 13-10 (GB)
Packers, 28-27 (C)
1969—Packers, 17-0 (GB)
Packers, 21-3 (C)
1970—Packers, 20-19 (GB)
Bears, 35-17 (C)
1971—Packers, 17-14 (C)
Packers, 31-10 (GB)
1972—Packers, 20-17 (GB)
Packers, 23-17 (C)
1973—Bears, 31-17 (GB)
Packers, 21-0 (C)
1974—Bears, 10-9 (C)
Packers, 20-3 (Mil)
1975—Bears, 27-14 (C)
Packers, 28-7 (GB)
1976—Bears, 24-13 (C)
Bears, 16-10 (GB)
1977—Bears, 26-0 (GB)
Bears, 21-10 (C)
1978—Packers, 24-14 (GB)
Bears, 14-0 (C)
1979—Bears, 6-3 (C)
Bears, 15-14 (GB)
1980—Packers, 12-6 (GB) OT
Bears, 61-7 (C)
1981—Packers, 16-9 (C)
Packers, 21-17 (GB)
1983—Packers, 31-28 (GB)
Bears, 23-21 (C)
1984—Bears, 9-7 (GB)
Packers, 20-14 (C)
1985—Bears, 23-7 (C)
Bears, 16-10 (GB)
1986—Bears, 25-12 (GB)
Bears, 12-10 (C)
1987—Bears, 26-24 (GB)
Bears, 23-10 (C)
1988—Bears, 24-6 (GB)
Bears, 16-0 (C)
(Points—Bears 2,309, Packers 1,990)
Bears known as Staleys prior to 1922
***Division Playoff*

CHICAGO vs. HOUSTON
RS: Series tied, 2-2
1973—Bears, 35-14 (C)
1977—Oilers, 47-0 (H)
1980—Oilers, 10-6 (C)
1986—Bears, 20-7 (H)
(Points—Oilers 78, Bears 61)

CHICAGO vs. *INDIANAPOLIS
RS: Colts lead series, 21-15
1953—Colts, 13-9 (B)
Colts, 16-14 (C)
1954—Bears, 28-9 (C)
Bears, 28-13 (B)
1955—Colts, 23-17 (B)
Bears, 38-10 (C)
1956—Colts, 28-21 (B)
Bears, 58-27 (C)
1957—Colts, 21-10 (B)
Colts, 29-14 (C)
1958—Colts, 51-38 (B)
Colts, 17-0 (C)
1959—Bears, 26-21 (B)
Colts, 21-7 (C)
1960—Colts, 42-7 (B)
Colts, 24-20 (C)
1961—Bears, 24-10 (C)
Bears, 21-20 (B)
1962—Bears, 35-15 (C)
Bears, 57-0 (B)
1963—Bears, 10-3 (C)
Bears, 17-7 (B)
1964—Colts, 52-0 (B)
Colts, 40-24 (C)
1965—Colts, 26-21 (C)
Bears, 13-0 (B)
1966—Bears, 27-17 (C)
Colts, 21-16 (B)
1967—Colts, 24-3 (C)
1968—Colts, 28-7 (B)
1969—Colts, 24-21 (C)
1970—Colts, 21-20 (B)
1975—Colts, 35-7 (C)
1983—Colts, 22-19 (B) OT
1985—Bears, 17-10 (C)
1988—Bears, 17-13 (I)
(Points—Colts 753, Bears 711)
Franchise in Baltimore prior to 1984

CHICAGO vs. KANSAS CITY
RS: Bears lead series, 3-1
1973—Chiefs, 19-7 (KC)
1977—Bears, 28-27 (C)
1981—Bears, 16-13 (KC) OT
1987—Bears, 31-28 (C)
(Points—Chiefs 87, Bears 82)

CHICAGO vs. *L.A. RAIDERS
RS: Series tied, 3-3
1972—Raiders, 28-21 (O)
1976—Raiders, 28-27 (C)
1978—Raiders, 25-19 (C) OT
1981—Bears, 23-6 (O)
1984—Bears, 17-6 (C)
1987—Bears, 6-3 (LA)
(Points—Bears 113, Raiders 96)
Franchise in Oakland prior to 1982

CHICAGO vs. *L.A. RAMS
RS: Bears lead series, 42-28-3
PS: Series tied, 1-1
1937—Bears, 20-2 (Clev)
Bears, 15-7 (C)
1938—Rams, 14-7 (C)
Rams, 23-21 (Clev)
1939—Bears, 30-21 (Clev)
Bears, 35-21 (C)
1940—Bears, 21-14 (Clev)
Bears, 47-25 (C)
1941—Bears, 48-21 (Clev)
Bears, 31-13 (C)
1942—Bears, 21-7 (Clev)
Bears, 47-0 (C)
1944—Rams, 19-7 (Clev)
Bears, 28-21 (C)
1945—Rams, 17-0 (Clev)
Rams, 41-21 (C)
1946—Tie, 28-28 (C)
Bears, 27-21 (LA)
1947—Bears, 41-21 (LA)
Rams, 17-14 (C)
1948—Bears, 42-21 (C)
Bears, 21-6 (LA)
1949—Rams, 31-16 (C)
Rams, 27-24 (LA)
1950—Bears, 24-20 (LA)
Bears, 24-14 (C)
**Rams, 24-14 (LA)
1951—Rams, 42-17 (C)
1952—Rams, 31-7 (LA)
Rams, 40-24 (C)
1953—Rams, 38-24 (LA)
Bears, 24-21 (C)
1954—Rams, 42-38 (LA)
Bears, 24-13 (C)
1955—Bears, 31-20 (LA)
Bears, 24-3 (C)
1956—Bears, 35-24 (LA)
Bears, 30-21 (C)
1957—Bears, 34-26 (C)
Bears, 16-10 (LA)
1958—Bears, 31-10 (C)
Rams, 41-35 (LA)
1959—Rams, 28-21 (C)
Bears, 26-21 (LA)
1960—Bears, 34-27 (C)
Tie, 24-24 (LA)
1961—Bears, 21-17 (LA)
Bears, 28-24 (C)
1962—Bears, 27-23 (LA)
Bears, 30-14 (C)
1963—Bears, 52-14 (LA)
Bears, 6-0 (C)
1964—Bears, 38-17 (C)
Bears, 34-24 (LA)
1965—Rams, 30-28 (LA)
Bears, 31-6 (C)
1966—Rams, 31-17 (LA)
Bears, 17-10 (C)
1967—Rams, 28-17 (C)
1968—Bears, 17-16 (LA)
1969—Rams, 9-7 (C)
1971—Rams, 17-3 (LA)
1972—Tie, 13-13 (C)
1973—Rams, 26-0 (C)
1975—Rams, 38-10 (LA)
1976—Rams, 20-12 (LA)
1977—Bears, 24-23 (C)
1979—Bears, 27-23 (C)
1981—Rams, 24-7 (C)
1982—Bears, 34-26 (LA)
1983—Rams, 21-14 (LA)
1984—Rams, 29-13 (LA)
1985—***Bears, 24-0 (C)
1986—Rams, 20-17 (C)
1988—Rams, 23-3 (LA)
(Points—Bears 1,744, Rams 1,544)
Franchise in Cleveland prior to 1946
***Conference Playoff*
****NFC Championship*

CHICAGO vs. MIAMI
RS: Dolphins lead series, 4-1
1971—Dolphins, 34-3 (M)
1975—Dolphins, 46-13 (C)
1979—Dolphins, 31-16 (M)
1985—Dolphins, 38-24 (M)
1988—Bears, 34-7 (C)
(Points—Dolphins 156, Bears 90)

CHICAGO vs. MINNESOTA
RS: Vikings lead series, 28-25-2
1961—Vikings, 37-13 (M)
Bears, 52-35 (C)
1962—Bears, 13-0 (M)
Bears, 31-30 (C)
1963—Bears, 28-7 (M)
Tie, 17-17 (C)
1964—Bears, 34-28 (M)
Vikings, 41-14 (C)
1965—Bears, 45-37 (M)
Vikings, 24-17 (C)
1966—Bears, 13-10 (M)
Bears, 41-28 (C)
1967—Bears, 17-7 (M)
Tie, 10-10 (C)
1968—Bears, 27-17 (M)
Bears, 26-24 (C)
1969—Vikings, 31-0 (C)
Vikings, 31-14 (M)
1970—Vikings, 24-0 (C)
Vikings, 16-13 (M)
1971—Bears, 20-17 (M)
Vikings, 27-10 (C)
1972—Bears, 13-10 (C)
Vikings, 23-10 (M)
1973—Vikings, 22-13 (C)
Vikings, 31-13 (M)
1974—Vikings, 11-7 (M)
Vikings, 17-0 (C)
1975—Vikings, 28-3 (M)
Vikings, 13-9 (C)
1976—Vikings, 20-19 (M)
Bears, 14-13 (C)
1977—Vikings, 22-16 (M) OT
Bears, 10-7 (C)
1978—Vikings, 24-20 (C)
Vikings, 17-14 (M)
1979—Bears, 26-7 (C)
Vikings, 30-27 (M)
1980—Vikings, 34-14 (C)
Vikings, 13-7 (M)
1981—Vikings, 24-21 (M)
Bears, 10-9 (C)
1982—Vikings, 35-7 (M)
1983—Vikings, 23-14 (C)
Bears, 19-13 (M)
1984—Bears, 16-7 (C)
Bears, 34-3 (M)
1985—Bears, 33-24 (M)
Bears, 27-9 (C)
1986—Bears, 23-0 (C)
Vikings, 23-7 (M)
1987—Bears, 27-7 (C)
Bears, 30-24 (M)
1988—Vikings, 31-7 (C)
Vikings, 28-27 (M)
(Points—Vikings 1,100, Bears 992)

CHICAGO vs. NEW ENGLAND
RS: Patriots lead series, 3-2
PS: Bears lead series, 1-0
1973—Patriots, 13-10 (C)
1979—Patriots, 27-7 (C)
1982—Bears, 26-13 (C)
1985—Bears, 20-7 (C)
*Bears, 46-10 (New Orleans)
1988—Patriots, 30-7 (NE)
(Points—Bears 116, Patriots 110)
Super Bowl XX

CHICAGO vs. NEW ORLEANS
RS: Bears lead series, 7-5
1968—Bears, 23-17 (NO)
1970—Bears, 24-3 (NO)
1971—Bears, 35-14 (C)
1973—Saints, 21-16 (NO)
1974—Bears, 24-10 (C)
1975—Bears, 42-17 (NO)
1977—Saints, 42-24 (C)
1980—Bears, 22-3 (C)
1982—Saints, 10-0 (C)
1983—Saints, 34-31 (NO) OT
1984—Bears, 20-7 (C)
1987—Saints, 19-17 (C)
(Points—Bears 278, Saints 197)

CHICAGO vs. N.Y. GIANTS
RS: Bears lead series, 23-14-2
PS: Bears lead series, 5-2
1925—Bears, 19-7 (NY)
Giants, 9-0 (C)
1926—Bears, 7-0 (C)
1927—Giants, 13-7 (NY)
1928—Bears, 13-0 (C)
1929—Giants, 26-14 (C)
Giants, 34-0 (NY)
Giants, 14-9 (C)
1930—Giants, 12-0 (C)
Bears, 12-0 (NY)
1931—Bears, 6-0 (C)
Bears, 12-6 (NY)
Giants, 25-6 (C)
1932—Bears, 28-8 (NY)
Bears, 6-0 (C)
1933—Bears, 14-10 (C)
Giants, 3-0 (NY)
*Bears, 23-21 (C)
1934—Bears, 27-7 (C)
Bears, 10-9 (NY)
*Giants, 30-13 (NY)
1935—Bears, 20-3 (NY)
Giants, 3-0 (C)
1936—Bears, 25-7 (NY)
1937—Tie, 3-3 (NY)
1939—Giants, 16-13 (NY)
1940—Bears, 37-21 (NY)
1941—*Bears, 37-9 (C)
1942—Bears, 26-7 (NY)
1943—Bears, 56-7 (NY)
1946—Giants, 14-0 (NY)
*Bears, 24-14 (NY)
1948—Bears, 35-14 (C)
1949—Giants, 35-28 (NY)
1956—Tie, 17-17 (NY)
*Giants, 47-7 (NY)
1962—Giants, 26-24 (C)
1963—*Bears, 14-10 (C)
1965—Bears, 35-14 (NY)
1967—Bears, 34-7 (C)
1969—Giants, 28-24 (NY)
1970—Bears, 24-16 (NY)
1974—Bears, 16-13 (C)
1977—Bears, 12-9 (NY) OT
1985—**Bears, 21-0 (C)
1987—Bears, 34-19 (C)
(Points—Bears 792, Giants 593)
NFL Championship
***NFC Divisional Playoff*

CHICAGO vs. N.Y. JETS
RS: Bears lead series, 2-1
1974—Jets, 23-21 (C)
1979—Bears, 23-13 (C)
1985—Bears, 19-6 (NY)
(Points—Bears 63, Jets 42)

CHICAGO vs. PHILADELPHIA
RS: Bears lead series, 21-3-1
PS: Series tied, 1-1
1933—Tie, 3-3 (P)
1935—Bears, 39-0 (P)
1936—Bears, 17-0 (P)
Bears, 28-7 (P)
1938—Bears, 28-6 (P)
1939—Bears, 27-14 (C)
1941—Bears, 49-14 (P)
1942—Bears, 45-14 (C)
1944—Bears, 28-7 (P)
1946—Bears, 21-14 (C)
1947—Bears, 40-7 (C)
1948—Eagles, 12-7 (P)
1949—Bears, 38-21 (C)
1955—Bears, 17-10 (C)
1961—Eagles, 16-14 (P)
1963—Bears, 16-7 (C)
1968—Bears, 29-16 (P)
1970—Bears, 20-16 (C)
1972—Bears, 21-12 (P)
1975—Bears, 15-13 (C)
1979—*Eagles, 27-17 (P)
1980—Eagles, 17-14 (P)
1983—Bears, 7-6 (P)
Bears, 17-14 (C)
1986—Bears, 13-10 (C) OT
1987—Bears, 35-3 (P)
1988—**Bears, 20-12 (C)
(Points—Bears 625, Eagles 298)
NFC First Round Playoff
***NFC Divisional Playoff*

***CHICAGO vs. **PHOENIX**
RS: Bears lead series, 50-25-6
(NP denotes Normal Park;
Wr denotes Wrigley Field;
Co denotes Comiskey Park;
So denotes Soldier Field;
all Chicago)
1920—Cardinals, 7-6 (NP)
Staleys, 10-0 (Wr)
1921—Tie, 0-0 (Wr)
1922—Cardinals, 6-0 (Co)
Cardinals, 9-0 (Co)
1923—Bears, 3-0 (Wr)
1924—Bears, 6-0 (Wr)
Bears, 21-0 (Co)
1925—Cardinals, 9-0 (Co)
Tie, 0-0 (Wr)
1926—Bears, 16-0 (Wr)
Bears, 10-0 (So)
Tie, 0-0 (Wr)

1927—Bears, 9-0 (NP)
Cardinals, 3-0 (Wr)
1928—Bears, 15-0 (NP)
Bears, 34-0 (Wr)
1929—Tie, 0-0 (Wr)
Cardinals, 40-6 (Co)
1930—Bears, 32-6 (Co)
Bears, 6-0 (Wr)
1931—Bears, 26-13 (Wr)
Bears, 18-7 (Wr)
1932—Tie, 0-0 (Wr)
Bears, 34-0 (Wr)
1933—Bears, 12-9 (Wr)
Bears, 22-6 (Wr)
1934—Bears, 20-0 (Wr)
Bears, 17-6 (Wr)
1935—Tie, 7-7 (Wr)
Bears, 13-0 (Wr)
1936—Bears, 7-3 (Wr)
Cardinals, 14-7 (Wr)
1937—Bears, 16-7 (Wr)
Bears, 42-28 (Wr)
1938—Bears, 16-13 (So)
Bears, 34-28 (Wr)
1939—Bears, 44-7 (Wr)
Bears, 48-7 (Co)
1940—Cardinals, 21-7 (Co)
Bears, 31-23 (Wr)
1941—Bears, 53-7 (Wr)
Bears, 34-24 (Co)
1942—Bears, 41-14 (Wr)
Bears, 21-7 (Co)
1943—Bears, 20-0 (Wr)
Bears, 35-24 (Co)
1945—Cardinals, 16-7 (Wr)
Bears, 28-20 (Co)
1946—Bears, 34-17 (Co)
Cardinals, 35-28 (Wr)
1947—Cardinals, 31-7 (Co)
Cardinals, 30-21 (Wr)
1948—Bears, 28-17 (Co)
Cardinals, 24-21 (Wr)
1949—Bears, 17-7 (Co)
Bears, 52-21 (Wr)
1950—Bears, 27-6 (Wr)
Cardinals, 20-10 (Co)
1951—Cardinals, 28-14 (Co)
Cardinals, 24-14 (Wr)
1952—Cardinals, 21-10 (Co)
Bears, 10-7 (Wr)
1953—Cardinals, 24-17 (Wr)
1954—Bears, 29-7 (Co)
1955—Cardinals, 53-14 (Co)
1956—Bears, 10-3 (Wr)
1957—Bears, 14-6 (Co)
1958—Bears, 30-14 (Wr)
1959—Bears, 31-7 (So)
1965—Bears, 34-13 (Wr)
1966—Cardinals, 24-17 (StL)
1967—Bears, 30-3 (Wr)
1969—Cardinals, 20-17 (StL)
1972—Bears, 27-10 (StL)
1975—Cardinals, 34-20 (So)
1977—Cardinals, 16-13 (StL)
1978—Bears, 17-10 (So)
1979—Bears, 42-6 (So)
1982—Cardinals, 10-7 (So)
1984—Cardinals, 38-21 (StL)
(Points—Bears 1,517, Cardinals 977)
**Franchise in Decatur prior to 1921; Bears known as Staleys prior to 1922*
***Franchise in St. Louis prior to 1988 and in Chicago prior to 1960*

CHICAGO vs. *PITTSBURGH
RS: Bears lead series, 14-4-1
1934—Bears, 28-0 (P)
1935—Bears, 23-7 (P)
1936—Bears, 27-9 (P)
Bears, 26-6 (C)
1937—Bears, 7-0 (P)
1939—Bears, 32-0 (P)
1941—Bears, 34-7 (C)
1945—Bears, 28-7 (P)
1947—Bears, 49-7 (C)
1949—Bears, 30-21 (C)
1958—Steelers, 24-10 (P)
1959—Bears, 27-21 (C)
1963—Tie, 17-17 (P)
1967—Steelers, 41-13 (P)
1969—Bears, 38-7 (C)
1971—Bears, 17-15 (C)
1975—Steelers, 34-3 (P)
1980—Steelers, 38-3 (P)
1986—Bears, 13-10 (C) OT
(Points—Bears 425, Steelers 271)
**Steelers known as Pirates prior to 1941*

CHICAGO vs. SAN DIEGO
RS: Chargers lead series, 4-1
1970—Chargers, 20-7 (C)
1974—Chargers, 28-21 (SD)
1978—Chargers, 40-7 (SD)
1981—Bears, 20-17 (C) OT
1984—Chargers, 20-7 (SD)
(Points—Chargers 125, Bears 62)

CHICAGO vs. SAN FRANCISCO
RS: Bears lead series, 25-23-1
PS: 49ers lead series, 2-0
1950—Bears, 32-20 (SF)
Bears, 17-0 (C)
1951—Bears, 13-7 (C)
1952—49ers, 40-16 (C)
Bears, 20-17 (SF)
1953—49ers, 35-28 (C)
49ers, 24-14 (SF)
1954—49ers, 31-24 (C)
Bears, 31-27 (SF)
1955—49ers, 20-19 (C)
Bears, 34-23 (SF)
1956—Bears, 31-7 (C)
Bears, 38-21 (SF)
1957—49ers, 21-17 (C)
49ers, 21-17 (SF)
1958—Bears, 28-6 (C)
Bears, 27-14 (SF)
1959—49ers, 20-17 (SF)
Bears, 14-3 (C)
1960—Bears, 27-10 (C)
49ers, 25-7 (SF)
1961—Bears, 31-0 (C)
49ers, 41-31 (SF)
1962—Bears, 30-14 (SF)
49ers, 34-27 (C)
1963—49ers, 20-14 (SF)
Bears, 27-7 (C)
1964—49ers, 31-21 (SF)
Bears, 23-21 (C)
1965—49ers, 52-24 (SF)
Bears, 61-20 (C)
1966—Tie, 30-30 (C)
49ers, 41-14 (SF)
1967—Bears, 28-14 (SF)
1968—Bears, 27-19 (C)
1969—49ers, 42-21 (SF)
1970—49ers, 37-16 (C)
1971—49ers, 13-0 (SF)
1972—49ers, 34-21 (C)
1974—49ers, 34-0 (C)
1975—49ers, 31-3 (SF)
1976—Bears, 19-12 (SF)
1978—Bears, 16-13 (SF)
1979—Bears, 28-27 (SF)
1981—49ers, 28-17 (SF)
1983—Bears, 13-3 (C)
1984—*49ers, 23-0 (SF)
1985—Bears, 26-10 (SF)
1987—49ers, 41-0 (SF)
1988—Bears, 10-9 (C)
*49ers, 28-3 (C)
(Points—49ers 1,121, Bears 1,052)
**NFC Championship*

CHICAGO vs. SEATTLE
RS: Seahawks lead series, 4-1
1976—Bears, 34-7 (S)
1978—Seahawks, 31-29 (C)
1982—Seahawks, 20-14 (S)
1984—Seahawks, 38-9 (S)
1987—Seahawks, 34-21 (C)
(Points—Seahawks 130, Bears 107)

CHICAGO vs. TAMPA BAY
RS: Bears lead series, 18-4
1977—Bears, 10-0 (TB)
1978—Buccaneers, 33-19 (TB)
Bears, 14-3 (C)
1979—Buccaneers, 17-13 (C)
Bears, 14-0 (TB)
1980—Bears, 23-0 (C)
Bears, 14-13 (TB)
1981—Bears, 28-17 (C)
Buccaneers, 20-10 (TB)
1982—Buccaneers, 26-23 (TB) OT
1983—Bears, 17-10 (C)
Bears, 27-0 (TB)
1984—Bears, 34-14 (C)
Bears, 44-9 (TB)
1985—Bears, 38-28 (C)
Bears, 27-19 (TB)
1986—Bears, 23-3 (TB)
Bears, 48-14 (C)
1987—Bears, 20-3 (C)
Bears, 27-26 (TB)
1988—Bears, 28-10 (C)
Bears, 27-15 (TB)
(Points—Bears 528, Buccaneers 280)

CHICAGO vs. *WASHINGTON
RS: Bears lead series, 18-9-1
PS: Redskins lead series, 4-3
1932—Tie, 7-7 (B)
1933—Bears, 7-0 (C)
Redskins, 10-0 (B)
1934—Bears, 21-0 (B)
1935—Bears, 30-14 (B)
1936—Bears, 26-0 (B)
1937—**Redskins, 28-21 (C)
1938—Bears, 31-7 (C)
1940—Redskins, 7-3 (W)
**Bears, 73-0 (W)
1941—Bears, 35-21 (C)
1942—**Redskins, 14-6 (W)
1943—Redskins, 21-7 (W)
**Bears, 41-21 (C)
1945—Redskins, 28-21 (W)
1946—Bears, 24-20 (C)
1947—Bears, 56-20 (W)
1948—Bears, 48-13 (C)
1949—Bears, 31-21 (W)
1951—Bears, 27-0 (W)
1953—Bears, 27-24 (W)
1957—Redskins, 14-3 (C)
1964—Redskins, 27-20 (W)
1968—Redskins, 38-28 (C)
1971—Bears, 16-15 (C)
1974—Redskins, 42-0 (W)
1976—Bears, 33-7 (C)
1978—Bears, 14-10 (W)
1980—Bears, 35-21 (C)
1981—Redskins, 24-7 (C)
1984—***Bears, 23-19 (W)
1985—Bears, 45-10 (C)
1986—***Redskins, 27-13 (C)
1987—***Redskins, 21-17 (C)
1988—Bears, 34-14 (W)
(Points—Bears 830, Redskins 565)
**Franchise in Boston prior to 1937 and known as Braves prior to 1933*
***NFL Championship*
****NFC Divisional Playoff*

CINCINNATI vs. ATLANTA
RS: Bengals lead series, 5-1;
See Atlanta vs. Cincinnati

CINCINNATI vs. BUFFALO
RS: Bengals lead series, 9-5
PS: Bengals lead series, 2-0;
See Buffalo vs. Cincinnati

CINCINNATI vs. CHICAGO
RS: Bengals lead series, 2-1;
See Chicago vs. Cincinnati

CINCINNATI vs. CLEVELAND
RS: Browns lead series, 19-18
1970—Browns, 30-27 (Cle)
Bengals, 14-10 (Cin)
1971—Browns, 27-24 (Cin)
Browns, 31-27 (Cle)
1972—Browns, 27-6 (Cle)
Browns, 27-24 (Cin)
1973—Browns, 17-10 (Cle)
Bengals, 34-17 (Cin)
1974—Bengals, 33-7 (Cin)
Bengals, 34-24 (Cle)
1975—Bengals, 24-17 (Cin)
Browns, 35-23 (Cle)
1976—Bengals, 45-24 (Cle)
Bengals, 21-6 (Cin)
1977—Browns, 13-3 (Cin)
Bengals, 10-7 (Cle)
1978—Browns, 13-10 (Cle) OT
Bengals, 48-16 (Cin)
1979—Browns, 28-27 (Cle)
Bengals, 16-12 (Cin)
1980—Browns, 31-7 (Cle)
Browns, 27-24 (Cin)
1981—Browns, 20-17 (Cin)
Bengals, 41-21 (Cle)
1982—Bengals, 23-10 (Cin)
1983—Browns, 17-7 (Cle)
Bengals, 28-21 (Cin)
1984—Bengals, 12-9 (Cin)
Bengals, 20-17 (Cle) OT
1985—Bengals, 27-10 (Cin)
Browns, 24-6 (Cle)
1986—Bengals, 30-13 (Cle)
Browns, 34-3 (Cin)
1987—Browns, 34-0 (Cin)
Browns, 38-24 (Cle)
1988—Bengals, 24-17 (Cin)
Browns, 23-16 (Cle)
(Points—Bengals 769, Browns 754)

CINCINNATI vs. DALLAS
RS: Series tied, 2-2
1973—Cowboys, 38-10 (D)
1979—Cowboys, 38-13 (D)
1985—Bengals, 50-24 (C)
1988—Bengals, 38-24 (D)
(Points—Cowboys 124, Bengals 111)

CINCINNATI vs. DENVER
RS: Broncos lead series, 9-6
1968—Bengals, 24-10 (C)
Broncos, 10-7 (D)
1969—Broncos, 30-23 (C)
Broncos, 27-16 (D)
1971—Bengals, 24-10 (D)
1972—Bengals, 21-10 (C)
1973—Broncos, 28-10 (D)
1975—Bengals, 17-16 (D)
1976—Bengals, 17-7 (C)
1977—Broncos, 24-13 (C)
1979—Broncos, 10-0 (D)
1981—Bengals, 38-21 (C)
1983—Broncos, 24-17 (D)
1984—Broncos, 20-17 (D)
1986—Broncos, 34-28 (D)
(Points—Broncos 281, Bengals 272)

CINCINNATI vs. DETROIT
RS: Series tied, 2-2
1970—Lions, 38-3 (D)
1974—Lions, 23-19 (C)
1983—Bengals, 17-9 (C)
1986—Bengals, 24-17 (D)
(Points—Lions 87, Bengals 63)

CINCINNATI vs. GREEN BAY
RS: Bengals lead series, 4-2
1971—Packers, 20-17 (GB)
1976—Bengals, 28-7 (C)
1977—Bengals, 17-7 (Mil)
1980—Packers, 14-9 (GB)
1983—Bengals, 34-14 (C)
1986—Bengals, 34-28 (Mil)
(Points—Bengals 139, Packers 90)

CINCINNATI vs. HOUSTON
RS: Bengals lead series, 22-17-1
1968—Oilers, 27-17 (C)
1969—Tie, 31-31 (H)
1970—Oilers, 20-13 (C)
Bengals, 30-20 (H)
1971—Oilers, 10-6 (H)
Bengals, 28-13 (C)
1972—Bengals, 30-7 (C)
Bengals, 61-17 (H)
1973—Bengals, 24-10 (C)
Bengals, 27-24 (H)
1974—Oilers, 34-21 (C)
Oilers, 20-3 (H)
1975—Bengals, 21-19 (H)
Bengals, 23-19 (C)
1976—Bengals, 27-7 (H)
Bengals, 31-27 (C)
1977—Bengals, 13-10 (C) OT
Oilers, 21-16 (H)
1978—Bengals, 28-13 (C)
Oilers, 17-10 (H)
1979—Oilers, 30-27 (C) OT
Oilers, 42-21 (H)
1980—Oilers, 13-10 (C)
Oilers, 23-3 (H)
1981—Oilers, 17-10 (H)
Bengals, 34-21 (C)
1982—Bengals, 27-6 (C)
Bengals, 35-27 (H)
1983—Bengals, 55-14 (H)
Bengals, 38-10 (C)
1984—Bengals, 13-3 (C)
Bengals, 31-13 (H)
1985—Oilers, 44-27 (H)
Bengals, 45-27 (C)
1986—Bengals, 31-28 (C)
Oilers, 32-28 (H)
1987—Oilers, 31-29 (C)
Oilers, 21-17 (H)
1988—Bengals, 44-21 (C)
Oilers, 41-6 (H)
(Points—Bengals 991, Oilers 830)

CINCINNATI vs. *INDIANAPOLIS
RS: Bengals lead series, 5-4
PS: Colts lead series, 1-0
1970—**Colts, 17-0 (B)
1972—Colts, 20-19 (C)
1974—Bengals, 24-14 (B)
1976—Colts, 28-27 (B)
1979—Colts, 38-28 (B)
1980—Bengals, 34-33 (C)
1981—Bengals, 41-19 (B)
1982—Bengals, 20-17 (B)
1983—Colts, 34-31 (C)
1987—Bengals, 23-21 (I)
(Points—Bengals 247, Colts 241)
**Franchise in Baltimore prior to 1984*
***AFC Divisional Playoff*

CINCINNATI vs. KANSAS CITY
RS: Chiefs lead series, 10-8
1968—Chiefs, 13-3 (KC)
Chiefs, 16-9 (C)
1969—Bengals, 24-19 (C)
Chiefs, 42-22 (KC)
1970—Chiefs, 27-19 (C)
1972—Bengals, 23-16 (KC)
1973—Bengals, 14-6 (C)
1974—Bengals, 33-6 (C)
1976—Bengals, 27-24 (KC)
1977—Bengals, 27-7 (KC)
1978—Chiefs, 24-23 (C)
1979—Chiefs, 10-7 (C)
1980—Bengals, 20-6 (KC)
1983—Chiefs, 20-15 (KC)
1984—Chiefs, 27-22 (C)
1986—Chiefs, 24-14 (KC)
1987—Bengals, 30-27 (C) OT
1988—Chiefs, 31-28 (KC)
(Points—Bengals 360, Chiefs 345)

CINCINNATI vs. *L.A. RAIDERS
RS: Raiders lead series, 11-5
PS: Raiders lead series, 1-0
1968—Raiders, 31-10 (O)

Raiders, 34-0 (C)
1969—Bengals, 31-17 (C)
Raiders, 37-17 (O)
1970—Bengals, 31-21 (C)
1971—Raiders, 31-27 (O)
1972—Raiders, 20-14 (C)
1974—Raiders, 30-27 (O)
1975—Bengals, 14-10 (C)
**Raiders, 31-28 (O)
1976—Raiders, 35-20 (O)
1978—Raiders, 34-21 (C)
1980—Raiders, 28-17 (O)
1982—Bengals, 31-17 (C)
1983—Raiders, 20-10 (C)
1985—Raiders, 13-6 (LA)
1988—Bengals, 45-21 (LA)
(Points—Raiders 430, Bengals 349)
Franchise in Oakland prior to 1982
***AFC Divisional Playoff*

CINCINNATI vs. L.A. RAMS
RS: Bengals lead series, 3-2
1972—Rams, 15-12 (LA)
1976—Bengals, 20-12 (C)
1978—Bengals, 20-19 (LA)
1981—Bengals, 24-10 (C)
1984—Rams, 24-14 (C)
(Points—Bengals 90, Rams 80)

CINCINNATI vs. MIAMI
RS: Dolphins lead series, 7-3
PS: Dolphins lead series, 1-0
1968—Dolphins, 24-22 (C)
Bengals, 38-21 (M)
1969—Bengals, 27-21 (C)
1971—Dolphins, 23-13 (C)
1973—*Dolphins, 34-16 (M)
1974—Dolphins, 24-3 (M)
1977—Bengals, 23-17 (C)
1978—Dolphins, 21-0 (M)
1980—Dolphins, 17-16 (M)
1983—Dolphins, 38-14 (M)
1987—Dolphins, 20-14 (C)
(Points—Dolphins 260, Bengals 186)
**AFC Divisional Playoff*

CINCINNATI vs. MINNESOTA
RS: Bengals lead series, 3-2
1973—Bengals, 27-0 (C)
1977—Vikings, 42-10 (M)
1980—Bengals, 14-0 (C)
1983—Vikings, 20-14 (M)
1986—Bengals, 24-20 (C)
(Points—Bengals 89, Vikings 82)

CINCINNATI vs. *NEW ENGLAND
RS: Patriots lead series, 7-4
1968—Patriots, 33-14 (B)
1969—Patriots, 25-14 (C)
1970—Bengals, 45-7 (C)
1972—Bengals, 31-7 (NE)
1975—Bengals, 27-10 (C)
1978—Patriots, 10-3 (C)
1979—Patriots, 20-14 (C)
1984—Patriots, 20-14 (NE)
1985—Patriots, 34-23 (NE)
1986—Bengals, 31-7 (NE)
1988—Patriots, 27-21 (NE)
(Points—Bengals 237, Patriots 200)
**Franchise in Boston prior to 1971*

CINCINNATI vs. NEW ORLEANS
RS: Series tied, 3-3
1970—Bengals, 26-6 (C)
1975—Bengals, 21-0 (NO)
1978—Saints, 20-18 (C)
1981—Saints, 17-7 (NO)
1984—Bengals, 24-21 (NO)
1987—Saints, 41-24 (C)
(Points—Bengals 120, Saints 105)

CINCINNATI vs. N.Y. GIANTS
RS: Bengals lead series, 3-0
1972—Bengals, 13-10 (C)
1977—Bengals, 30-13 (C)
1985—Bengals, 35-30 (C)
(Points—Bengals 78, Giants 53)

CINCINNATI vs. N.Y. JETS
RS: Jets lead series, 7-5
PS: Jets lead series, 1-0
1968—Jets, 27-14 (NY)
1969—Jets, 21-7 (C)
Jets, 40-7 (NY)
1971—Jets, 35-21 (NY)
1973—Bengals, 20-14 (C)
1976—Bengals, 42-3 (NY)
1981—Bengals, 31-30 (NY)
1982—*Jets, 44-17 (C)
1984—Jets, 43-23 (NY)
1985—Jets, 29-20 (C)
1986—Bengals, 52-21 (C)
1987—Jets, 27-20 (NY)
1988—Bengals, 36-19 (C)
(Points—Jets 353, Bengals 310)
**AFC First Round Playoff*

CINCINNATI vs. PHILADELPHIA
RS: Bengals lead series, 5-0
1971—Bengals, 37-14 (C)
1975—Bengals, 31-0 (P)
1979—Bengals, 37-13 (C)
1982—Bengals, 18-14 (P)
1988—Bengals, 28-24 (P)
(Points—Bengals 151, Eagles 65)

CINCINNATI vs. *PHOENIX
RS: Bengals lead series, 3-1
1973—Bengals, 42-24 (C)
1979—Bengals, 34-28 (C)
1985—Cardinals, 41-27 (StL)
1988—Bengals, 21-14 (C)
(Points—Bengals 124, Cardinals 107)
**Franchise in St. Louis prior to 1988*

CINCINNATI vs. PITTSBURGH
RS: Steelers lead series, 20-17
1970—Steelers, 21-10 (P)
Bengals, 34-7 (C)
1971—Steelers, 21-10 (P)
Steelers, 21-13 (C)
1972—Bengals, 15-10 (C)
Steelers, 40-17 (P)
1973—Bengals, 19-7 (C)
Steelers, 20-13 (P)
1974—Bengals, 17-10 (C)
Steelers, 27-3 (P)
1975—Steelers, 30-24 (C)
Steelers, 35-14 (P)
1976—Steelers, 23-6 (P)
Steelers, 7-3 (C)
1977—Steelers, 20-14 (P)
Bengals, 17-10 (C)
1978—Steelers, 28-3 (C)
Steelers, 7-6 (P)
1979—Bengals, 34-10 (C)
Steelers, 37-17 (P)
1980—Bengals, 30-28 (C)
Bengals, 17-16 (P)
1981—Bengals, 34-7 (C)
Bengals, 17-10 (P)
1982—Steelers, 26-20 (P) OT
1983—Steelers, 24-14 (C)
Bengals, 23-10 (P)
1984—Steelers, 38-17 (P)
Bengals, 22-20 (C)
1985—Bengals, 37-24 (P)
Bengals, 26-21 (C)
1986—Bengals, 24-22 (C)
Steelers, 30-9 (P)
1987—Steelers, 23-20 (P)
Steelers, 30-16 (C)
1988—Bengals, 17-12 (P)
Bengals, 42-7 (C)
(Points—Steelers 739, Bengals 674)

CINCINNATI vs. SAN DIEGO
RS: Chargers lead series, 11-7
PS: Bengals lead series, 1-0
1968—Chargers, 29-13 (SD)
Chargers, 31-10 (C)
1969—Bengals, 34-20 (C)
Chargers, 21-14 (SD)
1970—Bengals, 17-14 (SD)
1971—Bengals, 31-0 (C)
1973—Bengals, 20-13 (SD)
1974—Chargers, 20-17 (C)
1975—Bengals, 47-17 (C)
1977—Chargers, 24-3 (SD)
1978—Chargers, 22-13 (SD)
1979—Chargers, 26-24 (C)
1980—Chargers, 31-14 (C)
1981—Bengals, 40-17 (SD)
*Bengals, 27-7 (C)
1982—Chargers, 50-34 (SD)
1985—Chargers, 44-41 (C)
1987—Chargers, 10-9 (C)
1988—Bengals, 27-10 (C)
(Points—Bengals 435, Chargers 406)
**AFC Championship*

CINCINNATI vs. SAN FRANCISCO
RS: 49ers lead series, 4-1
PS: 49ers lead series, 2-0
1974—Bengals, 21-3 (SF)
1978—49ers, 28-12 (SF)
1981—49ers, 21-3 (C)
*49ers, 26-21 (Detroit)
1984—49ers, 23-17 (SF)
1987—49ers, 27-26 (C)
1988—**49ers, 20-16 (Miami)
(Points—49ers 148, Bengals 116)
**Super Bowl XVI*
***Super Bowl XXIII*

CINCINNATI vs. SEATTLE
RS: Bengals lead series, 5-2
PS: Bengals lead series, 1-0
1977—Bengals, 42-20 (C)
1981—Bengals, 27-21 (C)
1982—Bengals, 24-10 (C)
1984—Seahawks, 26-6 (C)
1985—Seahawks, 28-24 (C)
1986—Bengals, 34-7 (C)
1987—Bengals, 17-10 (S)
1988—*Bengals, 21-13 (C)
(Points—Bengals 195, Seahawks 135)
**AFC Divisional Playoff*

CINCINNATI vs. TAMPA BAY
RS: Bengals lead series, 2-1
1976—Bengals, 21-0 (C)
1980—Buccaneers, 17-12 (C)
1983—Bengals, 23-17 (TB)
(Points—Bengals 56, Buccaneers 34)

CINCINNATI vs. WASHINGTON
RS: Redskins lead series, 3-2
1970—Redskins, 20-0 (W)
1974—Bengals, 28-17 (C)
1979—Redskins, 28-14 (W)
1985—Redskins, 27-24 (W)
1988—Bengals, 20-17 (C) OT
(Points—Redskins 109, Bengals 86)

CLEVELAND vs. ATLANTA
RS: Browns lead series, 7-1;
See Atlanta vs. Cleveland

CLEVELAND vs. BUFFALO
RS: Browns lead series, 7-2;
See Buffalo vs. Cleveland

CLEVELAND vs. CHICAGO
RS: Browns lead series, 6-3;
See Chicago vs. Cleveland

CLEVELAND vs. CINCINNATI
RS: Browns lead series, 19-18;
See Cincinnati vs. Cleveland

CLEVELAND vs. DALLAS
RS: Browns lead series, 14-8
PS: Browns lead series, 2-1
1960—Browns, 48-7 (D)
1961—Browns, 25-7 (C)
Browns, 38-17 (D)
1962—Browns, 19-10 (C)
Cowboys, 45-21 (D)
1963—Browns, 41-24 (D)
Browns, 27-17 (C)
1964—Browns, 27-6 (C)
Browns, 20-16 (D)
1965—Browns, 23-17 (C)
Browns, 24-17 (D)
1966—Browns, 30-21 (C)
Cowboys, 26-14 (D)
1967—Cowboys, 21-14 (C)
*Cowboys, 52-14 (D)
1968—Cowboys, 28-7 (C)
*Browns, 31-20 (C)
1969—Browns, 42-10 (C)
*Browns, 38-14 (D)
1970—Cowboys, 6-2 (C)
1974—Cowboys, 41-17 (D)
1979—Browns, 26-7 (C)
1982—Cowboys, 31-14 (D)
1985—Cowboys, 20-7 (D)
1988—Browns, 24-21 (C)
(Points—Browns 593, Cowboys 501)
**Conference Championship*

CLEVELAND vs. DENVER
RS: Broncos lead series, 9-3
PS: Broncos lead series, 2-0
1970—Browns, 27-13 (D)
1971—Broncos, 27-0 (C)
1972—Browns, 27-20 (D)
1974—Browns, 23-21 (C)
1975—Broncos, 16-15 (D)
1976—Broncos, 44-13 (D)
1978—Broncos, 19-7 (C)
1980—Broncos, 19-16 (C)
1981—Broncos, 23-20 (D) OT
1983—Broncos, 27-6 (D)
1984—Broncos, 24-14 (C)
1986—*Broncos, 23-20 (C) OT
1987—*Broncos, 38-33 (D)
1988—Broncos, 30-7 (D)
(Points—Broncos 344, Browns 228)
**AFC Championship*

CLEVELAND vs. DETROIT
RS: Lions lead series, 9-3
PS: Lions lead series, 3-1
1952—Lions, 17-6 (D)
*Lions, 17-7 (C)
1953—*Lions, 17-16 (D)
1954—Lions, 14-10 (C)
*Browns, 56-10 (C)
1957—Lions, 20-7 (D)
*Lions, 59-14 (D)
1958—Lions, 30-10 (C)
1963—Lions, 38-10 (D)
1964—Browns, 37-21 (C)
1967—Lions, 31-14 (D)
1969—Lions, 28-21 (C)
1970—Lions, 41-24 (C)
1975—Lions, 21-10 (D)
1983—Browns, 31-26 (D)
1986—Browns, 24-21 (C)
(Points—Lions 411, Browns 297)
**NFL Championship*

CLEVELAND vs. GREEN BAY
RS: Packers lead series, 7-5
PS: Packers lead series, 1-0
1953—Browns, 27-0 (Mil)
1955—Browns, 41-10 (C)
1956—Browns, 24-7 (Mil)
1961—Packers, 49-17 (C)
1964—Packers, 28-21 (Mil)
1965—*Packers, 23-12 (GB)
1966—Packers, 21-20 (C)
1967—Packers, 55-7 (Mil)
1969—Browns, 20-7 (C)
1972—Packers, 26-10 (C)
1980—Browns, 26-21 (C)
1983—Packers, 35-21 (Mil)
1986—Packers, 17-14 (C)
(Points—Packers 299, Browns 260)
**NFL Championship*

CLEVELAND vs. HOUSTON
RS: Browns lead series, 24-13
PS: Oilers lead series, 1-0
1970—Browns, 28-14 (C)
Browns, 21-10 (H)
1971—Browns, 31-0 (C)
Browns, 37-24 (H)
1972—Browns, 23-17 (H)
Browns, 20-0 (C)
1973—Browns, 42-13 (C)
Browns, 23-13 (H)
1974—Browns, 20-7 (C)
Oilers, 28-24 (H)
1975—Oilers, 40-10 (C)
Oilers, 21-10 (H)
1976—Browns, 21-7 (H)
Browns, 13-10 (C)
1977—Browns, 24-23 (H)
Oilers, 19-15 (C)
1978—Oilers, 16-13 (C)
Oilers, 14-10 (H)
1979—Oilers, 31-10 (H)
Browns, 14-7 (C)
1980—Oilers, 16-7 (C)
Browns, 17-14 (H)
1981—Oilers, 9-3 (C)
Oilers, 17-13 (H)
1982—Browns, 20-14 (H)
1983—Browns, 25-19 (C) OT
Oilers, 34-27 (H)
1984—Browns, 27-10 (C)
Browns, 27-20 (H)
1985—Browns, 21-6 (H)
Browns, 28-21 (C)
1986—Browns, 23-20 (H)
Browns, 13-10 (C) OT
1987—Oilers, 15-10 (C)
Browns, 40-7 (H)
1988—Oilers, 24-17 (H)
Browns, 28-23 (C)
*Oilers, 24-23 (C)
(Points—Browns 778, Oilers 617)
**AFC First Round Playoff*

CLEVELAND vs. *INDIANAPOLIS
RS: Browns lead series, 11-4
PS: Series tied, 2-2
1956—Colts, 21-7 (C)
1959—Browns, 38-31 (B)
1962—Colts, 36-14 (C)
1964—**Browns, 27-0 (C)
1968—Browns, 30-20 (B)
**Colts, 34-0 (C)
1971—Browns, 14-13 (B)
***Colts, 20-3 (C)
1973—Browns, 24-14 (C)
1975—Colts, 21-7 (B)
1978—Browns, 45-24 (B)
1979—Browns, 13-10 (C)
1980—Browns, 28-27 (B)
1981—Browns, 42-28 (C)
1983—Browns, 41-23 (C)
1986—Browns, 24-9 (I)
1987—Colts, 9-7 (C)
***Browns, 38-21 (C)
1988—Browns, 23-17 (C)
(Points—Browns 425, Colts 378)
**Franchise in Baltimore prior to 1984*
***NFL Championship*
****AFC Divisional Playoff*

CLEVELAND vs. KANSAS CITY
RS: Browns lead series, 6-5-1
1971—Chiefs, 13-7 (KC)
1972—Chiefs, 31-7 (C)
1973—Tie, 20-20 (KC)
1975—Browns, 40-14 (C)
1976—Chiefs, 39-14 (KC)
1977—Browns, 44-7 (C)
1978—Chiefs, 17-3 (KC)
1979—Browns, 27-24 (KC)
1980—Browns, 20-13 (C)
1984—Chiefs, 10-6 (KC)
1986—Browns, 20-7 (C)
1988—Browns, 6-3 (KC)
(Points—Browns 214, Chiefs 198)

CLEVELAND vs. *L.A. RAIDERS
RS: Raiders lead series, 8-2
PS: Raiders lead series, 2-0
1970—Raiders, 23-20 (O)
1971—Raiders, 34-20 (C)
1973—Browns, 7-3 (O)
1974—Raiders, 40-24 (C)

1975—Raiders, 38-17 (O)
1977—Raiders, 26-10 (C)
1979—Raiders, 19-14 (O)
1980—**Raiders, 14-12 (C)
1982—***Raiders, 27-10 (LA)
1985—Raiders, 21-20 (C)
1986—Raiders, 27-14 (LA)
1987—Browns, 24-17 (LA)
(Points—Raiders 289, Browns 192)
Franchise in Oakland prior to 1982
***AFC Divisional Playoff*
****AFC First Round Playoff*

CLEVELAND vs. L.A. RAMS
RS: Browns lead series, 7-6
PS: Browns lead series, 2-1
1950—*Browns, 30-28 (C)
1951—Browns, 38-23 (LA)
*Rams, 24-17 (LA)
1952—Browns, 37-7 (C)
1955—*Browns, 38-14 (LA)
1957—Browns, 45-31 (C)
1958—Browns, 30-27 (LA)
1963—Browns, 20-6 (C)
1965—Rams, 42-7 (LA)
1968—Rams, 24-6 (C)
1973—Rams, 30-17 (LA)
1977—Rams, 9-0 (C)
1978—Browns, 30-19 (C)
1981—Rams, 27-16 (LA)
1984—Rams, 20-17 (LA)
1987—Browns, 30-17 (C)
(Points—Browns 378, Rams 348)
**NFL Championship*

CLEVELAND vs. MIAMI
RS: Browns lead series, 4-2
PS: Dolphins lead series, 2-0
1970—Browns, 28-0 (M)
1972—*Dolphins, 20-14 (M)
1973—Dolphins, 17-9 (C)
1976—Browns, 17-13 (C)
1979—Browns, 30-24 (C) OT
1985—*Dolphins, 24-21 (M)
1986—Browns, 26-16 (C)
1988—Dolphins, 38-31 (M)
(Points—Browns 176, Dolphins 152)
**AFC Divisional Playoff*

CLEVELAND vs. MINNESOTA
RS: Vikings lead series, 6-2
PS: Vikings lead series, 1-0
1965—Vikings, 27-17 (C)
1967—Browns, 14-10 (C)
1969—Vikings, 51-3 (M)
*Vikings, 27-7 (M)
1973—Vikings, 26-3 (M)
1975—Vikings, 42-10 (C)
1980—Vikings, 28-23 (M)
1983—Vikings, 27-21 (C)
1986—Browns, 23-20 (M)
(Points—Vikings 258, Browns 121)
**NFL Championship*

CLEVELAND vs. NEW ENGLAND
RS: Browns lead series, 7-2
1971—Browns, 27-7 (C)
1974—Browns, 21-14 (NE)
1977—Browns, 30-27 (C) OT
1980—Patriots, 34-17 (NE)
1982—Browns, 10-7 (C)
1983—Browns, 30-0 (NE)
1984—Patriots, 17-16 (C)
1985—Browns, 24-20 (C)
1987—Browns, 20-10 (NE)
(Points—Browns 195, Patriots 136)

CLEVELAND vs. NEW ORLEANS
RS: Browns lead series, 8-2
1967—Browns, 42-7 (NO)
1968—Browns, 24-10 (NO)
Browns, 35-17 (C)
1969—Browns, 27-17 (NO)
1971—Browns, 21-17 (NO)
1975—Browns, 17-16 (C)
1978—Browns, 24-16 (NO)
1981—Browns, 20-17 (C)
1984—Saints, 16-14 (C)
1987—Saints, 28-21 (NO)
(Points—Browns 245, Saints 161)

CLEVELAND vs. N.Y. GIANTS
RS: Browns lead series, 25-15-2
PS: Series tied, 1-1
1950—Giants, 6-0 (C)
Giants, 17-13 (NY)
*Browns, 8-3 (C)
1951—Browns, 14-13 (C)
Browns, 10-0 (NY)
1952—Giants, 17-9 (C)
Giants, 37-34 (NY)
1953—Browns, 7-0 (NY)
Browns, 62-14 (C)
1954—Browns, 24-14 (C)
Browns, 16-7 (NY)
1955—Browns, 24-14 (C)
Tie, 35-35 (NY)
1956—Giants, 21-9 (C)
Browns, 24-7 (NY)
1957—Browns, 6-3 (C)
Browns, 34-28 (NY)
1958—Giants, 21-17 (C)
Giants, 13-10 (NY)
*Giants, 10-0 (NY)
1959—Giants, 10-6 (C)
Giants, 48-7 (NY)
1960—Giants, 17-13 (C)
Browns, 48-34 (NY)
1961—Giants, 37-21 (C)
Tie, 7-7 (NY)
1962—Browns, 17-7 (C)
Giants, 17-13 (NY)
1963—Browns, 35-24 (NY)
Giants, 33-6 (C)
1964—Browns, 42-20 (C)
Browns, 52-20 (NY)
1965—Browns, 38-14 (NY)
Browns, 34-21 (C)
1966—Browns, 28-7 (NY)
Browns, 49-40 (C)
1967—Giants, 38-34 (NY)
Browns, 24-14 (C)
1968—Browns, 45-10 (C)
1969—Browns, 28-17 (C)
Giants, 27-14 (NY)
1973—Browns, 12-10 (C)
1977—Browns, 21-7 (NY)
1985—Browns, 35-33 (NY)
(Points—Browns 985, Giants 792)
**Conference Playoff*

CLEVELAND vs. N.Y. JETS
RS: Browns lead series, 7-4
PS: Browns lead series, 1-0
1970—Browns, 31-21 (C)
1972—Browns, 26-10 (NY)
1976—Browns, 38-17 (C)
1978—Browns, 37-34 (C) OT
1979—Browns, 25-22 (NY) OT
1980—Browns, 17-14 (C)
1981—Jets, 14-13 (C)
1983—Browns, 10-7 (C)
1984—Jets, 24-20 (C)
1985—Jets, 37-10 (NY)
1986—*Browns, 23-20 (C) OT
1988—Jets, 23-3 (C)
(Points—Browns 253, Jets 243)
**AFC Divisional Playoff*

CLEVELAND vs. PHILADELPHIA
RS: Browns lead series, 30-11-1
1950—Browns, 35-10 (P)
Browns, 13-7 (C)
1951—Browns, 20-17 (C)
Browns, 24-9 (NY)
1952—Browns, 49-7 (P)
Eagles, 28-20 (C)
1953—Browns, 37-13 (C)
Eagles, 42-27 (P)
1954—Eagles, 28-10 (P)
Browns, 6-0 (C)
1955—Browns, 21-17 (C)
Eagles, 33-17 (P)
1956—Browns, 16-0 (P)
Browns, 17-14 (C)
1957—Browns, 24-7 (C)
Eagles, 17-7 (P)
1958—Browns, 28-14 (C)
Browns, 21-14 (P)
1959—Browns, 28-7 (C)
Browns, 28-21 (P)
1960—Browns, 41-24 (P)
Eagles, 31-29 (C)
1961—Eagles, 27-20 (P)
Browns, 45-24 (C)
1962—Eagles, 35-7 (P)
Tie, 14-14 (C)
1963—Browns, 37-7 (C)
Browns, 23-17 (P)
1964—Browns, 28-20 (P)
Browns, 38-24 (C)
1965—Browns, 35-17 (P)
Browns, 38-34 (C)
1966—Browns, 27-7 (C)
Eagles, 33-21 (P)
1967—Eagles, 28-24 (P)
1968—Browns, 47-13 (C)
1969—Browns, 27-20 (P)
1972—Browns, 27-17 (P)
1976—Browns, 24-3 (C)
1979—Browns, 24-19 (P)
1982—Eagles, 24-21 (C)
1988—Browns, 19-3 (C)
(Points—Browns 1,064, Eagles 746)

CLEVELAND vs. *PHOENIX
RS: Browns lead series, 31-10-3
1950—Browns, 34-24 (Cle)
Browns, 10-7 (Chi)
1951—Browns, 34-17 (Chi)
Browns, 49-28 (Cle)
1952—Browns, 28-13 (Cle)
Browns, 10-0 (Chi)
1953—Browns, 27-7 (Chi)
Browns, 27-16 (Cle)
1954—Browns, 31-7 (Cle)
Browns, 35-3 (Chi)
1955—Browns, 26-20 (Chi)
Browns, 35-24 (Cle)
1956—Cardinals, 9-7 (Chi)
Cardinals, 24-7 (Cle)
1957—Browns, 17-7 (Chi)
Browns, 31-0 (Cle)
1958—Browns, 35-28 (Cle)
Browns, 38-24 (Chi)
1959—Browns, 34-7 (Chi)
Browns, 17-7 (Cle)
1960—Browns, 28-27 (Cle)
Tie, 17-17 (StL)
1961—Browns, 20-17 (Cle)
Browns, 21-10 (StL)
1962—Browns, 34-7 (StL)
Browns, 38-14 (Cle)
1963—Cardinals, 20-14 (Cle)
Browns, 24-10 (StL)
1964—Tie, 33-33 (Cle)
Cardinals, 28-19 (StL)
1965—Cardinals, 49-13 (Cle)
Browns, 27-24 (StL)
1966—Cardinals, 34-28 (Cle)
Browns, 38-10 (StL)
1967—Browns, 20-16 (Cle)
Browns, 20-16 (StL)
1968—Cardinals, 27-21 (Cle)
Cardinals, 27-16 (StL)
1969—Tie, 21-21 (Cle)
Browns, 27-21 (StL)
1974—Cardinals, 29-7 (StL)
1979—Browns, 38-20 (StL)
1985—Cardinals, 27-24 (Cle) OT
1988—Browns, 29-21 (P)
(Points—Browns 1,109, Cardinals 797)
**Franchise in St. Louis prior to 1988, and in Chicago prior to 1960*

CLEVELAND vs. PITTSBURGH
RS: Browns lead series, 47-31
1950—Browns, 30-17 (P)
Browns, 45-7 (C)
1951—Browns, 17-0 (C)
Browns, 28-0 (P)
1952—Browns, 21-20 (P)
Browns, 29-28 (C)
1953—Browns, 34-16 (C)
Browns, 20-16 (P)
1954—Steelers, 55-27 (P)
Browns, 42-7 (C)
1955—Browns, 41-14 (C)
Browns, 30-7 (P)
1956—Browns, 14-10 (P)
Steelers, 24-16 (C)
1957—Browns, 23-12 (P)
Browns, 24-0 (C)
1958—Browns, 45-12 (P)
Browns, 27-10 (C)
1959—Steelers, 17-7 (P)
Steelers, 21-20 (C)
1960—Browns, 28-20 (C)
Steelers, 14-10 (P)
1961—Browns, 30-28 (P)
Steelers, 17-13 (C)
1962—Browns, 41-14 (P)
Browns, 35-14 (C)
1963—Browns, 35-23 (C)
Steelers, 9-7 (P)
1964—Steelers, 23-7 (C)
Browns, 30-17 (P)
1965—Browns, 24-19 (C)
Browns, 42-21 (P)
1966—Browns, 41-10 (C)
Steelers, 16-6 (P)
1967—Browns, 21-10 (C)
Browns, 34-14 (P)
1968—Browns, 31-24 (C)
Browns, 45-24 (P)
1969—Browns, 42-31 (C)
Browns, 24-3 (P)
1970—Browns, 15-7 (C)
Steelers, 28-9 (P)
1971—Browns, 27-17 (C)
Steelers, 26-9 (P)
1972—Browns, 26-24 (C)
Steelers, 30-0 (P)
1973—Steelers, 33-6 (P)
Browns, 21-16 (C)
1974—Steelers, 20-16 (P)
Steelers, 26-16 (C)
1975—Steelers, 42-6 (C)
Steelers, 31-17 (P)
1976—Steelers, 31-14 (P)
Browns, 18-16 (C)
1977—Steelers, 28-14 (C)
Steelers, 35-31 (P)
1978—Steelers, 15-9 (P) OT
Steelers, 34-14 (C)
1979—Steelers, 51-35 (C)
Steelers, 33-30 (P) OT
1980—Browns, 27-26 (C)
Steelers, 16-13 (P)
1981—Steelers, 13-7 (P)
Steelers, 32-10 (C)
1982—Browns, 10-9 (C)
Steelers, 37-21 (P)
1983—Steelers, 44-17 (P)
Browns, 30-17 (C)
1984—Browns, 20-10 (C)
Steelers, 23-20 (P)
1985—Browns, 17-7 (C)
Steelers, 10-9 (P)
1986—Browns, 27-24 (P)
Browns, 37-31 (C) OT
1987—Browns, 34-10 (C)
Browns, 19-13 (P)
1988—Browns, 23-9 (P)
Browns, 27-7 (C)
(Points—Browns 1,787, Steelers 1,525)

CLEVELAND vs. SAN DIEGO
RS: Chargers lead series, 6-5-1
1970—Chargers, 27-10 (C)
1972—Browns, 21-17 (SD)
1973—Tie, 16-16 (C)
1974—Chargers, 36-35 (SD)
1976—Browns, 21-17 (C)
1977—Chargers, 37-14 (SD)
1981—Chargers, 44-14 (C)
1982—Chargers, 30-13 (C)
1983—Browns, 30-24 (SD) OT
1985—Browns, 21-7 (SD)
1986—Browns, 47-17 (C)
1987—Chargers, 27-24 (SD) OT
(Points—Chargers 299, Browns 266)

CLEVELAND vs. SAN FRANCISCO
RS: Browns lead series, 8-5
1950—Browns, 34-14 (C)
1951—49ers, 24-10 (SF)
1953—Browns, 23-21 (C)
1955—Browns, 38-3 (SF)
1959—49ers, 21-20 (C)
1962—Browns, 13-10 (SF)
1968—Browns, 33-21 (SF)
1970—49ers, 34-31 (SF)
1974—Browns, 7-0 (C)
1978—Browns, 24-7 (C)
1981—Browns, 15-12 (SF)
1984—49ers, 41-7 (C)
1987—49ers, 38-24 (SF)
(Points—Browns 279, 49ers 246)

CLEVELAND vs. SEATTLE
RS: Seahawks lead series, 8-2
1977—Seahawks, 20-19 (S)
1978—Seahawks, 47-24 (S)
1979—Seahawks, 29-24 (C)
1980—Browns, 27-3 (S)
1981—Seahawks, 42-21 (S)
1982—Browns, 21-7 (S)
1983—Seahawks, 24-9 (C)
1984—Seahawks, 33-0 (S)
1985—Seahawks, 31-13 (S)
1988—Seahawks, 16-10 (C)
(Points—Seahawks 252, Browns 168)

CLEVELAND vs. TAMPA BAY
RS: Browns lead series, 3-0
1976—Browns, 24-7 (TB)
1980—Browns, 34-27 (TB)
1983—Browns, 20-0 (C)
(Points—Browns 78, Buccaneers 34)

CLEVELAND vs. WASHINGTON
RS: Browns lead series, 32-8-1
1950—Browns, 20-14 (C)
Browns, 45-21 (W)
1951—Browns, 45-0 (C)
1952—Browns, 19-15 (C)
Browns, 48-24 (W)
1953—Browns, 30-14 (W)
Browns, 27-3 (C)
1954—Browns, 62-3 (C)
Browns, 34-14 (W)
1955—Redskins, 27-17 (C)
Browns, 24-14 (W)
1956—Redskins, 20-9 (W)
Redskins, 20-17 (C)
1957—Browns, 21-17 (C)
Tie, 30-30 (W)
1958—Browns, 20-10 (W)
Browns, 21-14 (C)
1959—Browns, 34-7 (C)
Browns, 31-17 (W)
1960—Browns, 31-10 (W)
Browns, 27-16 (C)
1961—Browns, 31-7 (C)
Browns, 17-6 (W)
1962—Redskins, 17-16 (C)
Redskins, 17-9 (W)
1963—Browns, 37-14 (C)
Browns, 27-20 (W)
1964—Browns, 27-13 (W)
Browns, 34-24 (C)
1965—Browns, 17-7 (W)
Browns, 24-16 (C)
1966—Browns, 38-14 (W)
Browns, 14-3 (C)
1967—Browns, 42-37 (C)

1968—Browns, 24-21 (W)
1969—Browns, 27-23 (C)
1971—Browns, 20-13 (W)
1975—Redskins, 23-7 (C)
1979—Redskins, 13-9 (C)
1985—Redskins, 14-7 (C)
1988—Browns, 17-13 (W)
(Points—Browns 1,056, Redskins 625)

DALLAS vs. ATLANTA
RS: Cowboys lead series, 7-3
PS: Cowboys lead series, 2-0;
See Atlanta vs. Dallas
DALLAS vs. BUFFALO
RS: Cowboys lead series, 3-1;
See Buffalo vs. Dallas
DALLAS vs. CHICAGO
RS: Cowboys lead series, 7-6
PS: Cowboys lead series, 1-0;
See Chicago vs. Dallas
DALLAS vs. CINCINNATI
RS: Series tied, 2-2;
See Cincinnati vs. Dallas
DALLAS vs. CLEVELAND
RS: Browns lead series, 14-8
PS: Browns lead series, 2-1;
See Cleveland vs. Dallas
DALLAS vs. DENVER
RS: Series tied, 2-2
PS: Cowboys lead series, 1-0
1973—Cowboys, 22-10 (Den)
1977—Cowboys, 14-6 (Dal)
*Cowboys, 27-10 (New Orleans)
1980—Broncos, 41-20 (Den)
1986—Broncos, 29-14 (Den)
(Points—Cowboys 97, Broncos 96)
**Super Bowl XII*
DALLAS vs. DETROIT
RS: Cowboys lead series, 6-4
PS: Cowboys lead series, 1-0
1960—Lions, 23-14 (Det)
1963—Cowboys, 17-14 (Dal)
1968—Cowboys, 59-13 (Dal)
1970—*Cowboys, 5-0 (Dal)
1972—Cowboys, 28-24 (Dal)
1975—Cowboys, 36-10 (Det)
1977—Cowboys, 37-0 (Dal)
1981—Lions, 27-24 (Det)
1985—Lions, 26-21 (Det)
1986—Cowboys, 31-7 (Det)
1987—Lions, 27-17 (Det)
(Points—Cowboys 289, Lions 171)
**NFC Divisional Playoff*
DALLAS vs. GREEN BAY
RS: Packers lead series, 6-4
PS: Packers lead series, 2-1
1960—Packers, 41-7 (GB)
1964—Packers, 45-21 (D)
1965—Packers, 13-3 (Mil)
1966—*Packers, 34-27 (D)
1967—*Packers, 21-17 (GB)
1968—Packers, 28-17 (D)
1970—Cowboys, 16-3 (D)
1972—Packers, 16-13 (Mil)
1975—Packers, 19-17 (D)
1978—Cowboys, 42-14 (Mil)
1980—Cowboys, 28-7 (Mil)
1982—**Cowboys, 37-26 (D)
1984—Cowboys, 20-6 (D)
(Points—Packers 273, Cowboys 265)
**NFL Championship*
***NFC Second Round Playoff*
DALLAS vs. HOUSTON
RS: Cowboys lead series, 4-2
1970—Cowboys, 52-10 (D)
1974—Cowboys, 10-0 (H)
1979—Oilers, 30-24 (D)
1982—Cowboys, 37-7 (H)
1985—Cowboys, 17-10 (H)
1988—Oilers, 25-17 (D)
(Points—Cowboys 157, Oilers 82)
DALLAS vs. *INDIANAPOLIS
RS: Cowboys lead series, 6-2
PS: Colts lead series, 1-0
1960—Colts, 45-7 (D)
1967—Colts, 23-17 (B)
1969—Cowboys, 27-10 (D)
1970—**Colts, 16-13 (Miami)
1972—Cowboys, 21-0 (B)
1976—Cowboys, 30-27 (D)
1978—Cowboys, 38-0 (D)
1981—Cowboys, 37-13 (B)
1984—Cowboys, 22-3 (D)
(Points—Cowboys 212, Colts 137)
**Franchise in Baltimore prior to 1984*
***Super Bowl V*
DALLAS vs. KANSAS CITY
RS: Cowboys lead series, 2-1
1970—Cowboys, 27-16 (KC)
1975—Chiefs, 34-31 (D)
1983—Cowboys, 41-21 (D)
(Points—Cowboys 99, Chiefs 71)

DALLAS vs. *L.A. RAIDERS
RS: Raiders lead series, 3-1
1974—Raiders, 27-23 (O)
1980—Cowboys, 19-13 (O)
1983—Raiders, 40-38 (D)
1986—Raiders, 17-13 (D)
(Points—Raiders 97, Cowboys 93)
**Franchise in Oakland prior to 1982*
DALLAS vs. L.A. RAMS
RS: Series tied, 7-7
PS: Series tied, 4-4
1960—Rams, 38-13 (D)
1962—Cowboys, 27-17 (LA)
1967—Rams, 35-13 (D)
1969—Rams, 24-23 (LA)
1971—Cowboys, 28-21 (D)
1973—Rams, 37-31 (LA)
*Cowboys, 27-16 (D)
1975—Cowboys, 18-7 (D)
**Cowboys, 37-7 (LA)
1976—*Rams, 14-12 (D)
1978—Rams, 27-14 (LA)
**Cowboys, 28-0 (LA)
1979—Cowboys, 30-6 (D)
*Rams, 21-19 (D)
1980—Rams, 38-14 (LA)
***Cowboys, 34-13 (D)
1981—Cowboys, 29-17 (D)
1983—***Rams, 24-17 (D)
1984—Cowboys, 20-13 (LA)
1985—*Rams, 20-0 (LA)
1986—Rams, 29-10 (LA)
1987—Cowboys, 29-21 (LA)
(Points—Cowboys 473, Rams 445)
**NFC Divisional Playoff*
***NFC Championship*
****NFC First Round Playoff*
DALLAS vs. MIAMI
RS: Dolphins lead series, 4-1
PS: Cowboys lead series, 1-0
1971—*Cowboys, 24-3 (New Orleans)
1973—Dolphins, 14-7 (D)
1978—Dolphins, 23-16 (M)
1981—Cowboys, 28-27 (D)
1984—Dolphins, 28-21 (M)
1987—Dolphins, 20-14 (D)
(Points—Dolphins 115, Cowboys 110)
**Super Bowl VI*
DALLAS vs. MINNESOTA
RS: Cowboys lead series, 7-6
PS: Cowboys lead series, 3-1
1961—Cowboys, 21-7 (D)
Cowboys, 28-0 (M)
1966—Cowboys, 28-17 (D)
1968—Cowboys, 20-7 (M)
1970—Vikings, 54-13 (M)
1971—*Cowboys, 20-12 (M)
1973—**Vikings, 27-10 (D)
1974—Vikings, 23-21 (D)
1975—*Cowboys, 17-14 (M)
1977—Cowboys, 16-10 (M) OT
**Cowboys, 23-6 (D)
1978—Vikings, 21-10 (D)
1979—Cowboys, 36-20 (M)
1982—Vikings, 31-27 (M)
1983—Cowboys, 37-24 (M)
1987—Vikings, 44-38 (D) OT
1988—Vikings, 43-3 (D)
(Points—Cowboys 368, Vikings 360)
**NFC Divisional Playoff*
***NFC Championship*
DALLAS vs. NEW ENGLAND
RS: Cowboys lead series, 6-0
1971—Cowboys, 44-21 (D)
1975—Cowboys, 34-31 (NE)
1978—Cowboys, 17-10 (D)
1981—Cowboys, 35-21 (NE)
1984—Cowboys, 20-17 (D)
1987—Cowboys, 23-17 (NE) OT
(Points—Cowboys 173, Patriots 117)
DALLAS vs. NEW ORLEANS
RS: Cowboys lead series, 11-2
1967—Cowboys, 14-10 (D)
Cowboys, 27-10 (NO)
1968—Cowboys, 17-3 (NO)
1969—Cowboys, 21-17 (NO)
Cowboys, 33-17 (D)
1971—Saints, 24-14 (NO)
1973—Cowboys, 40-3 (D)
1976—Cowboys, 24-6 (NO)
1978—Cowboys, 27-7 (D)
1982—Cowboys, 21-7 (D)
1983—Cowboys, 21-20 (D)
1984—Cowboys, 30-27 (D) OT
1988—Saints, 20-17 (NO)
(Points—Cowboys 306, Saints 171)
DALLAS vs. N.Y. GIANTS
RS: Cowboys lead series, 35-16-2
1960—Tie, 31-31 (NY)
1961—Giants, 31-10 (D)
Cowboys, 17-16 (NY)
1962—Giants, 41-10 (D)
Giants, 41-31 (NY)
1963—Giants, 37-21 (NY)
Giants, 34-27 (D)
1964—Tie, 13-13 (D)
Cowboys, 31-21 (NY)
1965—Cowboys, 31-2 (D)
Cowboys, 38-20 (NY)
1966—Cowboys, 52-7 (D)
Cowboys, 17-7 (NY)
1967—Cowboys, 38-24 (D)
1968—Giants, 27-21 (D)
Cowboys, 28-10 (NY)
1969—Cowboys, 25-3 (D)
1970—Cowboys, 28-10 (D)
Giants, 23-20 (NY)
1971—Cowboys, 20-13 (D)
Cowboys, 42-14 (NY)
1972—Cowboys, 23-14 (NY)
Giants, 23-3 (D)
1973—Cowboys, 45-28 (D)
Cowboys, 23-10 (New Haven)
1974—Giants, 14-6 (D)
Cowboys, 21-7 (New Haven)
1975—Cowboys, 13-7 (NY)
Cowboys, 14-3 (D)
1976—Cowboys, 24-14 (NY)
Cowboys, 9-3 (D)
1977—Cowboys, 41-21 (D)
Cowboys, 24-10 (NY)
1978—Cowboys, 34-24 (NY)
Cowboys, 24-3 (D)
1979—Cowboys, 16-14 (NY)
Cowboys, 28-7 (D)
1980—Cowboys, 24-3 (D)
Giants, 38-35 (NY)
1981—Cowboys, 18-10 (D)
Giants, 13-10 (NY) OT
1983—Cowboys, 28-13 (D)
Cowboys, 38-20 (NY)
1984—Giants, 28-7 (NY)
Giants, 19-7 (D)
1985—Cowboys, 30-29 (NY)
Cowboys, 28-21 (D)
1986—Cowboys, 31-28 (D)
Giants, 17-14 (NY)
1987—Cowboys, 16-14 (NY)
Cowboys, 33-24 (D)
1988—Giants, 12-10 (D)
Giants, 29-21 (NY)
(Points—Cowboys 1,249, Giants 945)
DALLAS vs. N.Y. JETS
RS: Cowboys lead series, 4-0
1971—Cowboys, 52-10 (D)
1975—Cowboys, 31-21 (NY)
1978—Cowboys, 30-7 (NY)
1987—Cowboys, 38-24 (NY)
(Points—Cowboys 151, Jets 62)
DALLAS vs. PHILADELPHIA
RS: Cowboys lead series, 36-20
PS: Eagles lead series, 1-0
1960—Eagles, 27-25 (D)
1961—Eagles, 43-7 (D)
Eagles, 35-13 (P)
1962—Cowboys, 41-19 (D)
Eagles, 28-14 (P)
1963—Eagles, 24-21 (P)
Cowboys, 27-20 (D)
1964—Eagles, 17-14 (D)
Eagles, 24-14 (P)
1965—Eagles, 35-24 (D)
Cowboys, 21-19 (P)
1966—Cowboys, 56-7 (D)
Eagles, 24-23 (P)
1967—Eagles, 21-14 (P)
Cowboys, 38-17 (D)
1968—Cowboys, 45-13 (P)
Cowboys, 34-14 (D)
1969—Cowboys, 38-7 (P)
Cowboys, 49-14 (D)
1970—Cowboys, 17-7 (P)
Cowboys, 21-17 (D)
1971—Cowboys, 42-7 (P)
Cowboys, 20-7 (D)
1972—Cowboys, 28-6 (D)
Cowboys, 28-7 (P)
1973—Eagles, 30-16 (P)
Cowboys, 31-10 (D)
1974—Eagles, 13-10 (P)
Cowboys, 31-24 (D)
1975—Cowboys, 20-17 (P)
Cowboys, 27-17 (D)
1976—Cowboys, 27-7 (D)
Cowboys, 26-7 (P)
1977—Cowboys, 16-10 (P)
Cowboys, 24-14 (D)
1978—Cowboys, 14-7 (D)
Cowboys, 31-13 (P)
1979—Eagles, 31-21 (D)
Cowboys, 24-17 (P)
1980—Eagles, 17-10 (P)
Cowboys, 35-27 (D)
*Eagles, 20-7 (P)
1981—Cowboys, 17-14 (P)
Cowboys, 21-10 (D)
1982—Eagles, 24-20 (D)
1983—Cowboys, 37-7 (D)
Cowboys, 27-20 (P)
1984—Cowboys, 23-17 (D)
Cowboys, 26-10 (P)
1985—Eagles, 16-14 (P)
Cowboys, 34-17 (D)
1986—Cowboys, 17-14 (P)
Eagles, 23-21 (D)
1987—Cowboys, 41-22 (D)
Eagles, 37-20 (P)
1988—Eagles, 24-23 (P)
Eagles, 23-7 (D)
(Points—Cowboys 1,392, Eagles 1,018)
**NFC Championship*
DALLAS vs. *PHOENIX
RS: Cowboys lead series, 33-19-1
1960—Cardinals, 12-10 (StL)
1961—Cardinals, 31-17 (D)
Cardinals, 31-13 (StL)
1962—Cardinals, 28-24 (D)
Cardinals, 52-20 (StL)
1963—Cardinals, 34-7 (D)
Cowboys, 28-24 (StL)
1964—Cardinals, 16-6 (D)
Cowboys, 31-13 (StL)
1965—Cardinals, 20-13 (StL)
Cowboys, 27-13 (D)
1966—Tie, 10-10 (StL)
Cowboys, 31-17 (D)
1967—Cowboys, 46-21 (D)
1968—Cowboys, 27-10 (StL)
1969—Cowboys, 24-3 (D)
1970—Cardinals, 20-7 (StL)
Cardinals, 38-0 (D)
1971—Cowboys, 16-13 (StL)
Cowboys, 31-12 (D)
1972—Cowboys, 33-24 (D)
Cowboys, 27-6 (StL)
1973—Cowboys, 45-10 (D)
Cowboys, 30-3 (StL)
1974—Cardinals, 31-28 (StL)
Cowboys, 17-14 (D)
1975—Cowboys, 37-31 (D) OT
Cardinals, 31-17 (StL)
1976—Cardinals, 21-17 (StL)
Cowboys, 19-14 (D)
1977—Cowboys, 30-24 (StL)
Cardinals, 24-17 (D)
1978—Cowboys, 21-12 (D)
Cowboys, 24-21 (StL) OT
1979—Cowboys, 22-21 (StL)
Cowboys, 22-13 (D)
1980—Cowboys, 27-24 (StL)
Cowboys, 31-21 (D)
1981—Cowboys, 30-17 (D)
Cardinals, 20-17 (StL)
1982—Cowboys, 24-7 (StL)
1983—Cowboys, 34-17 (StL)
Cowboys, 35-17 (D)
1984—Cardinals, 31-20 (D)
Cowboys, 24-17 (StL)
1985—Cardinals, 21-10 (StL)
Cowboys, 35-17 (D)
1986—Cowboys, 31-7 (StL)
Cowboys, 37-6 (D)
1987—Cardinals, 24-13 (StL)
Cowboys, 21-16 (D)
1988—Cowboys, 17-14 (P)
Cardinals, 16-10 (D)
(Points—Cowboys 1,210, Cardinals 1,010)
**Franchise in St. Louis prior to 1988*
DALLAS vs. PITTSBURGH
RS: Series tied, 11-11
PS: Steelers lead series, 2-0
1960—Steelers, 35-28 (D)
1961—Cowboys, 27-24 (D)
Steelers, 37-7 (P)
1962—Steelers, 30-28 (D)
Cowboys, 42-27 (P)
1963—Steelers, 27-21 (P)
Steelers, 24-19 (D)
1964—Steelers, 23-17 (P)
Cowboys, 17-14 (D)
1965—Steelers, 22-13 (P)
Cowboys, 24-17 (D)
1966—Cowboys, 52-21 (D)
Cowboys, 20-7 (P)
1967—Cowboys, 24-21 (P)
1968—Cowboys, 28-7 (D)
1969—Cowboys, 10-7 (P)
1972—Cowboys, 17-13 (D)
1975—*Steelers, 21-17 (Miami)
1977—Steelers, 28-13 (P)
1978—**Steelers, 35-31 (Miami)
1979—Steelers, 14-3 (P)
1982—Steelers, 36-28 (D)
1985—Cowboys, 27-13 (D)
1988—Steelers, 24-21 (P)
(Points—Cowboys 534, Steelers 527)
**Super Bowl X*
***Super Bowl XIII*

DALLAS vs. SAN DIEGO
RS: Cowboys lead series, 3-1
1972—Cowboys, 34-28 (SD)
1980—Cowboys, 42-31 (D)
1983—Chargers, 24-23 (SD)
1986—Cowboys, 24-21 (SD)
(Points—Cowboys 123, Chargers 104)
DALLAS vs. SAN FRANCISCO
RS: 49ers lead series, 7-5-1
PS: Cowboys lead series, 3-1
1960—49ers, 26-14 (D)
1963—49ers, 31-24 (SF)
1965—Cowboys, 39-31 (D)
1967—49ers, 24-16 (SF)
1969—Tie, 24-24 (D)
1970—*Cowboys, 17-10 (SF)
1971—*Cowboys, 14-3 (D)
1972—49ers, 31-10 (D)
**Cowboys, 30-28 (SF)
1974—Cowboys, 20-14 (D)
1977—Cowboys, 42-35 (SF)
1979—Cowboys, 21-13 (SF)
1980—Cowboys, 59-14 (D)
1981—49ers, 45-14 (SF)
*49ers, 28-27 (SF)
1983—49ers, 42-17 (SF)
1985—49ers, 31-16 (SF)
(Points—49ers 430, Cowboys 404)
NFC Championship
**NFC Divisional Playoff*
DALLAS vs. SEATTLE
RS: Cowboys lead series, 3-1
1976—Cowboys, 28-13 (S)
1980—Cowboys, 51-7 (D)
1983—Cowboys, 35-10 (S)
1986—Seahawks, 31-14 (D)
(Points—Cowboys 128, Seahawks 61)
DALLAS vs. TAMPA BAY
RS: Cowboys lead series, 4-0
PS: Cowboys lead series, 2-0
1977—Cowboys, 23-7 (D)
1980—Cowboys, 28-17 (D)
1981—*Cowboys, 38-0 (D)
1982—Cowboys, 14-9 (D)
**Cowboys, 30-17 (D)
1983—Cowboys, 27-24 (D) OT
(Points—Cowboys 160, Buccaneers 74)
NFC Divisional Playoff
**NFC First Round Playoff*
DALLAS vs. WASHINGTON
RS: Cowboys lead series, 32-22-2
PS: Redskins lead series, 2-0
1960—Redskins, 26-14 (W)
1961—Tie, 28-28 (D)
Redskins, 34-24 (W)
1962—Tie, 35-35 (D)
Cowboys, 38-10 (W)
1963—Redskins, 21-17 (W)
Cowboys, 35-20 (D)
1964—Cowboys, 24-18 (D)
Redskins, 28-16 (W)
1965—Cowboys, 27-7 (D)
Redskins, 34-31 (W)
1966—Cowboys, 31-30 (W)
Redskins, 34-31 (D)
1967—Cowboys, 17-14 (W)
Redskins, 27-20 (D)
1968—Cowboys, 44-24 (W)
Cowboys, 29-20 (D)
1969—Cowboys, 41-28 (W)
Cowboys, 20-10 (D)
1970—Cowboys, 45-21 (W)
Cowboys, 34-0 (D)
1971—Redskins, 20-16 (D)
Cowboys, 13-0 (W)
1972—Redskins, 24-20 (W)
Cowboys, 34-24 (D)
*Redskins, 26-3 (W)
1973—Redskins, 14-7 (W)
Cowboys, 27-7 (D)
1974—Redskins, 28-21 (W)
Cowboys, 24-23 (D)
1975—Redskins, 30-24 (W) OT
Cowboys, 31-10 (D)
1976—Cowboys, 20-7 (W)
Redskins, 27-14 (D)
1977—Cowboys, 34-16 (D)
Cowboys, 14-7 (W)
1978—Redskins, 9-5 (W)
Cowboys, 37-10 (D)
1979—Redskins, 34-20 (W)
Cowboys, 35-34 (D)
1980—Cowboys, 17-3 (W)
Cowboys, 14-10 (D)
1981—Cowboys, 26-10 (W)
Cowboys, 24-10 (D)
1982—Cowboys, 24-10 (W)
*Redskins, 31-17 (W)
1983—Cowboys, 31-30 (W)
Redskins, 31-10 (D)
1984—Redskins, 34-14 (W)
Redskins, 30-28 (D)
1985—Cowboys, 44-14 (D)
Cowboys, 13-7 (W)
1986—Cowboys, 30-6 (D)
Redskins, 41-14 (W)
1987—Redskins, 13-7 (D)
Redskins, 24-20 (W)
1988—Redskins, 35-17 (D)
Cowboys, 24-17 (W)
(Points—Cowboys 1,374, Redskins 1,175)
NFC Championship

DENVER vs. ATLANTA
RS: Broncos lead series, 4-3;
See Atlanta vs. Denver
DENVER vs. BUFFALO
RS: Bills lead series, 14-9-1;
See Buffalo vs. Denver
DENVER vs. CHICAGO
RS: Series tied, 4-4;
See Chicago vs. Denver
DENVER vs. CINCINNATI
RS: Broncos lead series, 9-6;
See Cincinnati vs. Denver
DENVER vs. CLEVELAND
RS: Broncos lead series, 9-3
PS: Broncos lead series, 2-0;
See Cleveland vs. Denver
DENVER vs. DALLAS
RS: Series tied, 2-2
PS: Cowboys lead series, 1-0;
See Dallas vs. Denver
DENVER vs. DETROIT
RS: Broncos lead series, 4-2
1971—Lions, 24-20 (Den)
1974—Broncos, 31-27 (Det)
1978—Lions, 17-14 (Det)
1981—Broncos, 27-21 (Den)
1984—Broncos, 28-7 (Det)
1987—Broncos, 34-0 (Den)
(Points—Broncos 154, Lions 96)
DENVER vs. GREEN BAY
RS: Broncos lead series, 3-1-1
1971—Packers, 34-13 (Mil)
1975—Broncos, 23-13 (D)
1978—Broncos, 16-3 (D)
1984—Broncos, 17-14 (D)
1987—Tie, 17-17 (Mil) OT
(Points—Broncos 86, Packers 81)
DENVER vs. HOUSTON
RS: Oilers lead series, 18-10-1
PS: Series tied, 1-1
1960—Oilers, 45-25 (D)
Oilers, 20-10 (H)
1961—Oilers, 55-14 (D)
Oilers, 45-14 (H)
1962—Broncos, 20-10 (D)
Oilers, 34-17 (H)
1963—Oilers, 20-14 (H)
Oilers, 33-24 (D)
1964—Oilers, 38-17 (D)
Oilers, 34-15 (H)
1965—Broncos, 28-17 (D)
Broncos, 31-21 (H)
1966—Oilers, 45-7 (H)
Broncos, 40-38 (D)
1967—Oilers, 10-6 (H)
Oilers, 20-18 (D)
1968—Oilers, 38-17 (H)
1969—Oilers, 24-21 (H)
Tie, 20-20 (D)
1970—Oilers, 31-21 (H)
1972—Broncos, 30-17 (D)
1973—Broncos, 48-20 (H)
1974—Broncos, 37-14 (D)
1976—Oilers, 17-3 (H)
1977—Broncos, 24-14 (H)
1979—*Oilers, 13-7 (H)
1980—Oilers, 20-16 (D)
1983—Broncos, 26-14 (H)
1985—Broncos, 31-20 (D)
1987—Oilers, 40-10 (D)
**Broncos, 34-10 (D)
(Points—Oilers 797, Broncos 645)
AFC First Round Playoff
**AFC Divisional Playoff*
DENVER vs. *INDIANAPOLIS
RS: Broncos lead series, 6-2
1974—Broncos, 17-6 (B)
1977—Broncos, 27-13 (D)
1978—Colts, 7-6 (B)
1981—Broncos, 28-10 (D)
1983—Broncos, 17-10 (B)
Broncos, 21-19 (D)
1985—Broncos, 15-10 (I)
1988—Colts, 55-23 (I)
(Points—Broncos 154, Colts 130)
Franchise in Baltimore prior to 1984
DENVER vs. *KANSAS CITY
RS: Chiefs lead series, 35-22
1960—Texans, 17-14 (D)
Texans, 34-7 (Da)
1961—Texans, 19-12 (D)
Texans, 49-21 (Da)
1962—Texans, 24-3 (D)
Texans, 17-10 (Da)
1963—Chiefs, 59-7 (D)
Chiefs, 52-21 (KC)
1964—Broncos, 33-27 (D)
Chiefs, 49-39 (KC)
1965—Chiefs, 31-23 (D)
Chiefs, 45-35 (KC)
1966—Chiefs, 37-10 (KC)
Chiefs, 56-10 (D)
1967—Chiefs, 52-9 (KC)
Chiefs, 38-24 (D)
1968—Chiefs, 34-2 (KC)
Chiefs, 30-7 (D)
1969—Chiefs, 26-13 (D)
Chiefs, 31-17 (KC)
1970—Broncos, 26-13 (D)
Chiefs, 16-0 (KC)
1971—Chiefs, 16-3 (D)
Chiefs, 28-10 (KC)
1972—Chiefs, 45-24 (D)
Chiefs, 24-21 (KC)
1973—Chiefs, 16-14 (KC)
Broncos, 14-10 (D)
1974—Broncos, 17-14 (KC)
Chiefs, 42-34 (D)
1975—Broncos, 37-33 (D)
Chiefs, 26-13 (KC)
1976—Broncos, 35-26 (KC)
Broncos, 17-16 (D)
1977—Broncos, 23-7 (D)
Broncos, 14-7 (KC)
1978—Broncos, 23-17 (KC) OT
Broncos, 24-3 (D)
1979—Broncos, 24-10 (KC)
Broncos, 20-3 (D)
1980—Chiefs, 23-17 (D)
Chiefs, 31-14 (KC)
1981—Chiefs, 28-14 (KC)
Broncos, 16-13 (D)
1982—Chiefs, 37-16 (D)
1983—Broncos, 27-24 (D)
Chiefs, 48-17 (KC)
1984—Broncos, 21-0 (D)
Chiefs, 16-13 (KC)
1985—Broncos, 30-10 (KC)
Broncos, 14-13 (D)
1986—Broncos, 38-17 (D)
Chiefs, 37-10 (KC)
1987—Broncos, 26-17 (KC)
Broncos, 20-17 (D)
1988—Chiefs, 20-13 (KC)
Broncos, 17-11 (D)
(Points—Chiefs 1,461, Broncos 1,033)
Franchise in Dallas prior to 1963 and known as Texans
DENVER vs. *L.A. RAIDERS
RS: Raiders lead series, 38-17-2
PS: Broncos lead series, 1-0
1960—Broncos, 31-14 (D)
Raiders, 48-10 (O)
1961—Raiders, 33-19 (O)
Broncos, 27-24 (D)
1962—Broncos, 44-7 (D)
Broncos, 23-6 (O)
1963—Raiders, 26-10 (D)
Raiders, 35-31 (O)
1964—Raiders, 40-7 (O)
Tie, 20-20 (D)
1965—Raiders, 28-20 (D)
Raiders, 24-13 (O)
1966—Raiders, 17-3 (D)
Raiders, 28-10 (O)
1967—Raiders, 51-0 (O)
Raiders, 21-17 (D)
1968—Raiders, 43-7 (D)
Raiders, 33-27 (O)
1969—Raiders, 24-14 (D)
Raiders, 41-10 (O)
1970—Raiders, 35-23 (O)
Raiders, 24-19 (D)
1971—Raiders, 27-16 (D)
Raiders, 21-13 (O)
1972—Broncos, 30-23 (O)
Raiders, 37-20 (D)
1973—Tie, 23-23 (D)
Raiders, 21-17 (O)
1974—Raiders, 28-17 (D)
Broncos, 20-17 (O)
1975—Raiders, 42-17 (D)
Raiders, 17-10 (O)
1976—Raiders, 17-10 (D)
Raiders, 19-6 (O)
1977—Broncos, 30-7 (O)
Raiders, 24-14 (D)
**Broncos, 20-17 (D)
1978—Broncos, 14-6 (D)
Broncos, 21-6 (O)
1979—Raiders, 27-3 (O)
Raiders, 14-10 (D)
1980—Raiders, 9-3 (O)
Raiders, 24-21 (D)
1981—Broncos, 9-7 (D)
Broncos, 17-0 (O)
1982—Raiders, 27-10 (LA)
1983—Raiders, 22-7 (D)
Raiders, 22-20 (LA)
1984—Broncos, 16-13 (D)
Broncos, 22-19 (LA) OT
1985—Raiders, 31-28 (LA) OT
Raiders, 17-14 (D) OT
1986—Broncos, 38-36 (D)
Broncos, 21-10 (LA)
1987—Broncos, 30-14 (D)
Broncos, 23-17 (LA)
1988—Raiders, 30-27 (D) OT
Raiders, 21-20 (LA)
(Points—Raiders 1,334, Broncos 1,022)
Franchise in Oakland prior to 1982
**AFC Championship*
DENVER vs. L.A. RAMS
RS: Series tied, 3-3
1972—Broncos, 16-10 (LA)
1974—Rams, 17-10 (D)
1979—Rams, 13-9 (D)
1982—Broncos, 27-24 (LA)
1985—Rams, 20-16 (LA)
1988—Broncos, 35-24 (D)
(Points—Broncos 113, Rams 108)
DENVER vs. MIAMI
RS: Dolphins lead series, 5-2-1
1966—Dolphins, 24-7 (M)
Broncos, 17-7 (D)
1967—Dolphins, 35-21 (M)
1968—Broncos, 21-14 (D)
1969—Dolphins, 27-24 (M)
1971—Tie, 10-10 (D)
1975—Dolphins, 14-13 (M)
1985—Dolphins, 30-26 (D)
(Points—Dolphins 161, Broncos 139)
DENVER vs. MINNESOTA
RS: Vikings lead series, 3-2
1972—Vikings, 23-20 (D)
1978—Vikings, 12-9 (M) OT
1981—Broncos, 19-17 (D)
1984—Broncos, 42-21 (D)
1987—Vikings, 34-27 (M)
(Points—Broncos 117, Vikings 107)
DENVER vs. *NEW ENGLAND
RS: Broncos lead series, 14-12
PS: Broncos lead series, 1-0
1960—Broncos, 13-10 (B)
Broncos, 31-24 (D)
1961—Patriots, 45-17 (B)
Patriots, 28-24 (D)
1962—Patriots, 41-16 (B)
Patriots, 33-29 (D)
1963—Broncos, 14-10 (D)
Patriots, 40-21 (B)
1964—Patriots, 39-10 (D)
Patriots, 12-7 (B)
1965—Broncos, 27-10 (B)
Patriots, 28-20 (D)
1966—Patriots, 24-10 (D)
Broncos, 17-10 (B)
1967—Broncos, 26-21 (D)
1968—Patriots, 20-17 (D)
Broncos, 35-14 (B)
1969—Broncos, 35-7 (D)
1972—Broncos, 45-21 (D)
1976—Patriots, 38-14 (NE)
1979—Broncos, 45-10 (D)
1980—Patriots, 23-14 (NE)
1984—Broncos, 26-19 (D)
1986—Broncos, 27-20 (D)
**Broncos, 22-17 (D)
1987—Broncos, 31-20 (D)
1988—Broncos, 21-10 (D)
(Points—Broncos 614, Patriots 594)
Franchise in Boston prior to 1971
**AFC Divisional Playoff*
DENVER vs. NEW ORLEANS
RS: Broncos lead series, 4-1
1970—Broncos, 31-6 (NO)
1974—Broncos, 33-17 (D)
1979—Broncos, 10-3 (D)
1985—Broncos, 34-23 (D)
1988—Saints, 42-0 (NO)
(Points—Broncos 108, Saints 91)
DENVER vs. N.Y. GIANTS
RS: Series tied, 2-2
PS: Giants lead series, 1-0
1972—Giants, 29-17 (NY)
1976—Broncos, 14-13 (D)
1980—Broncos, 14-9 (NY)
1986—Giants, 19-16 (NY)
*Giants, 39-20 (Pasadena)
(Points—Giants 109, Broncos 81)
Super Bowl XXI
DENVER vs. *N.Y. JETS
RS: Jets lead series, 11-10-1
1960—Titans, 28-24 (NY)
Titans, 30-27 (D)
1961—Titans, 35-28 (NY)
Broncos, 27-10 (D)
1962—Broncos, 32-10 (NY)
Titans, 46-45 (D)

1963—Tie, 35-35 (NY)
Jets, 14-9 (D)
1964—Jets, 30-6 (NY)
Broncos, 20-16 (D)
1965—Broncos, 16-13 (D)
Jets, 45-10 (NY)
1966—Jets, 16-7 (D)
1967—Jets, 38-24 (D)
Broncos, 33-24 (NY)
1968—Broncos, 21-13 (NY)
1969—Broncos, 21-19 (D)
1973—Broncos, 40-28 (NY)
1976—Broncos, 46-3 (D)
1978—Jets, 31-28 (D)
1980—Broncos, 31-24 (D)
1986—Jets, 22-10 (NY)
(Points—Broncos 540, Jets 530)
Jets known as Titans prior to 1963

DENVER vs. PHILADELPHIA
RS: Eagles lead series, 3-2
1971—Eagles, 17-16 (P)
1975—Broncos, 25-10 (D)
1980—Eagles, 27-6 (P)
1983—Eagles, 13-10 (D)
1986—Broncos, 33-7 (P)
(Points—Broncos 90, Eagles 74)

DENVER vs. *PHOENIX
RS: Broncos lead series, 1-0-1
1973—Tie, 17-17 (StL)
1977—Broncos, 7-0 (D)
(Points—Broncos 24, Cardinals 17)
**Franchise in St. Louis prior to 1988*

DENVER vs. PITTSBURGH
RS: Broncos lead series, 7-4-1
PS: Steelers lead series, 2-1
1970—Broncos, 16-13 (D)
1971—Broncos, 22-10 (P)
1973—Broncos, 23-13 (P)
1974—Tie, 35-35 (D) OT
1975—Steelers, 20-9 (P)
1977—Broncos, 21-7 (D)
*Broncos, 34-21 (D)
1978—Steelers, 21-17 (D)
*Steelers, 33-10 (P)
1979—Steelers, 42-7 (P)
1983—Broncos, 14-10 (P)
1984—*Steelers, 24-17 (D)
1985—Broncos, 31-23 (P)
1986—Broncos, 21-10 (P)
1988—Steelers, 39-21 (P)
(Points—Steelers 321, Broncos 298)
**AFC Divisional Playoff*

DENVER vs. *SAN DIEGO
RS: Broncos lead series, 29-28-1
1960—Chargers, 23-19 (D)
Chargers, 41-33 (LA)
1961—Chargers, 37-0 (SD)
Chargers, 19-16 (D)
1962—Broncos, 30-21 (D)
Broncos, 23-20 (SD)
1963—Broncos, 50-34 (D)
Chargers, 58-20 (SD)
1964—Chargers, 42-14 (SD)
Chargers, 31-20 (D)
1965—Chargers, 34-31 (SD)
Chargers, 33-21 (D)
1966—Chargers, 24-17 (SD)
Broncos, 20-17 (D)
1967—Chargers, 38-21 (D)
Chargers, 24-20 (SD)
1968—Chargers, 55-24 (SD)
Chargers, 47-23 (D)
1969—Broncos, 13-0 (D)
Chargers, 45-24 (SD)
1970—Chargers, 24-21 (SD)
Tie, 17-17 (D)
1971—Broncos, 20-16 (D)
Chargers, 45-17 (SD)
1972—Chargers, 37-14 (SD)
Broncos, 38-13 (D)
1973—Broncos, 30-19 (D)
Broncos, 42-28 (SD)
1974—Broncos, 27-7 (D)
Chargers, 17-0 (SD)
1975—Broncos, 27-17 (SD)
Broncos, 13-10 (D) OT
1976—Broncos, 26-0 (D)
Broncos, 17-0 (SD)
1977—Broncos, 17-14 (SD)
Broncos, 17-9 (D)
1978—Broncos, 27-14 (D)
Chargers, 23-0 (SD)
1979—Broncos, 7-0 (D)
Chargers, 17-7 (SD)
1980—Chargers, 30-13 (D)
Broncos, 20-13 (SD)
1981—Broncos, 42-24 (D)
Chargers, 34-17 (SD)
1982—Chargers, 23-3 (D)
Chargers, 30-20 (SD)
1983—Broncos, 14-6 (D)
Chargers, 31-7 (SD)
1984—Broncos, 16-13 (SD)
Broncos, 16-13 (D)
1985—Chargers, 30-10 (SD)
Broncos, 30-24 (D) OT
1986—Broncos, 31-14 (SD)
Chargers, 9-3 (D)
1987—Broncos, 31-17 (SD)
Broncos, 24-0 (D)
1988—Broncos, 34-3 (D)
Broncos, 12-0 (SD)
(Points—Chargers 1,284, Broncos 1,166)
**Franchise in Los Angeles prior to 1961*

DENVER vs. SAN FRANCISCO
RS: Broncos lead series, 4-2
1970—49ers, 19-14 (SF)
1973—49ers, 36-34 (D)
1979—Broncos, 38-28 (SF)
1982—Broncos, 24-21 (D)
1985—Broncos, 17-16 (D)
1988—Broncos, 16-13 (SF) OT
(Points—Broncos 143, 49ers 133)

DENVER vs. SEATTLE
RS: Broncos lead series, 13-10
PS: Seahawks lead series, 1-0
1977—Broncos, 24-13 (S)
1978—Broncos, 28-7 (D)
Broncos, 20-17 (S) OT
1979—Broncos, 37-34 (D)
Seahawks, 28-23 (S)
1980—Broncos, 36-20 (D)
Broncos, 25-17 (S)
1981—Seahawks, 13-10 (S)
Broncos, 23-13 (D)
1982—Seahawks, 17-10 (D)
Seahawks, 13-11 (S)
1983—Seahawks, 27-19 (S)
Broncos, 38-27 (D)
*Seahawks, 31-7 (S)
1984—Seahawks, 27-24 (D)
Broncos, 31-14 (S)
1985—Broncos, 13-10 (D) OT
Broncos, 27-24 (S)
1986—Broncos, 20-13 (D)
Seahawks, 41-16 (S)
1987—Broncos, 40-17 (D)
Seahawks, 28-21 (S)
1988—Seahawks, 21-14 (D)
Seahawks, 42-14 (S)
(Points—Broncos 531, Seahawks 514)
**AFC First Round Playoff*

DENVER vs. TAMPA BAY
RS: Broncos lead series, 2-0
1976—Broncos, 48-13 (D)
1981—Broncos, 24-7 (TB)
(Points—Broncos 72, Buccaneers 20)

DENVER vs. WASHINGTON
RS: Series tied, 2-2
PS: Redskins lead series, 1-0
1970—Redskins, 19-3 (D)
1974—Redskins, 30-3 (W)
1980—Broncos, 20-17 (D)
1986—Broncos, 31-30 (D)
1987—*Redskins, 42-10 (San Diego)
(Points—Redskins 138, Broncos 67)
**Super Bowl XXII*

DETROIT vs. ATLANTA
RS: Lions lead series, 14-5;
See Atlanta vs. Detroit

DETROIT vs. BUFFALO
RS: Series tied, 1-1-1;
See Buffalo vs. Detroit

DETROIT vs. CHICAGO
RS: Bears lead series, 69-44-5;
See Chicago vs. Detroit

DETROIT vs. CINCINNATI
RS: Series tied, 2-2;
See Cincinnati vs. Detroit

DETROIT vs. CLEVELAND
RS: Lions lead series, 9-3
PS: Lions lead series, 3-1;
See Cleveland vs. Detroit

DETROIT vs. DALLAS
RS: Cowboys lead series, 6-4
PS: Cowboys lead series, 1-0;
See Dallas vs. Detroit

DETROIT vs. DENVER
RS: Broncos lead series, 4-2;
See Denver vs. Detroit

***DETROIT vs. GREEN BAY**
RS: Packers lead series, 59-51-7
1930—Packers, 47-13 (GB)
Tie, 6-6 (P)
1932—Packers, 15-10 (GB)
Spartans, 19-0 (P)
1933—Packers, 17-0 (GB)
Spartans, 7-0 (P)
1934—Lions, 3-0 (GB)
Packers, 3-0 (D)
1935—Packers, 13-9 (GB)
Packers, 31-7 (GB)
Lions, 20-10 (D)
1936—Packers, 20-18 (GB)
Packers, 26-17 (D)
1937—Packers, 26-6 (GB)
Packers, 14-13 (D)
1938—Lions, 17-7 (GB)
Packers, 28-7 (D)
1939—Packers, 26-7 (GB)
Packers, 12-7 (D)
1940—Lions, 23-14 (GB)
Packers, 50-7 (D)
1941—Packers, 23-0 (GB)
Packers, 24-7 (D)
1942—Packers, 38-7 (Mil)
Packers, 28-7 (D)
1943—Packers, 35-14 (GB)
Packers, 27-6 (D)
1944—Packers, 27-6 (GB)
Packers, 14-0 (D)
1945—Packers, 57-21 (Mil)
Lions, 14-3 (D)
1946—Packers, 10-7 (Mil)
Packers, 9-0 (D)
1947—Packers, 34-17 (GB)
Packers, 35-14 (D)
1948—Packers, 33-21 (GB)
Lions, 24-20 (D)
1949—Packers, 16-14 (GB)
Lions, 21-7 (D)
1950—Lions, 45-7 (GB)
Lions, 24-21 (D)
1951—Lions, 24-17 (GB)
Lions, 52-35 (D)
1952—Lions, 52-17 (GB)
Lions, 48-24 (D)
1953—Lions, 14-7 (GB)
Lions, 34-15 (D)
1954—Lions, 21-17 (GB)
Lions, 28-24 (D)
1955—Packers, 20-17 (GB)
Lions, 24-10 (D)
1956—Lions, 20-16 (GB)
Packers, 24-20 (D)
1957—Lions, 24-14 (GB)
Lions, 18-6 (D)
1958—Tie, 13-13 (GB)
Lions, 24-14 (D)
1959—Packers, 28-10 (GB)
Packers, 24-17 (D)
1960—Packers, 28-9 (GB)
Lions, 23-10 (D)
1961—Lions, 17-13 (Mil)
Packers, 17-9 (D)
1962—Packers, 9-7 (GB)
Lions, 26-14 (D)
1963—Packers, 31-10 (Mil)
Tie, 13-13 (D)
1964—Packers, 14-10 (D)
Packers, 30-7 (GB)
1965—Packers, 31-21 (D)
Lions, 12-7 (GB)
1966—Packers, 23-14 (GB)
Packers, 31-7 (D)
1967—Tie, 17-17 (GB)
Packers, 27-17 (D)
1968—Lions, 23-17 (GB)
Tie, 14-14 (D)
1969—Packers, 28-17 (D)
Lions, 16-10 (GB)
1970—Lions, 40-0 (GB)
Lions, 20-0 (D)
1971—Lions, 31-28 (D)
Tie, 14-14 (Mil)
1972—Packers, 24-23 (D)
Packers, 33-7 (GB)
1973—Tie, 13-13 (GB)
Lions, 34-0 (D)
1974—Packers, 21-19 (Mil)
Lions, 19-17 (D)
1975—Lions, 30-16 (Mil)
Lions, 13-10 (D)
1976—Packers, 24-14 (GB)
Lions, 27-6 (D)
1977—Lions, 10-6 (D)
Packers, 10-9 (GB)
1978—Packers, 13-7 (D)
Packers, 35-14 (Mil)
1979—Packers, 24-16 (Mil)
Packers, 18-13 (D)
1980—Lions, 29-7 (Mil)
Lions, 24-3 (D)
1981—Lions, 31-27 (D)
Packers, 31-17 (GB)
1982—Lions, 30-10 (GB)
Lions, 27-24 (D)
1983—Lions, 38-14 (D)
Lions, 23-20 (Mil) OT
1984—Packers, 41-9 (GB)
Lions, 31-28 (D)
1985—Packers, 43-10 (GB)
Packers, 26-23 (D)
1986—Lions, 21-14 (GB)
Packers, 44-40 (D)
1987—Lions, 19-16 (GB) OT
Packers, 34-33 (D)
1988—Lions, 19-9 (Mil)
Lions, 30-14 (D)
(Points—Packers 2,259, Lions 2,061)
**Franchise in Portsmouth prior to 1934 and known as the Spartans*

DETROIT vs. HOUSTON
RS: Series tied, 2-2
1971—Lions, 31-7 (H)
1975—Oilers, 24-8 (H)
1983—Oilers, 27-17 (H)
1986—Lions, 24-13 (D)
(Points—Lions 80, Oilers 71)

DETROIT vs. *INDIANAPOLIS
RS: Colts lead series, 17-16-2
1953—Lions, 27-17 (B)
Lions, 17-7 (D)
1954—Lions, 35-0 (D)
Lions, 27-3 (B)
1955—Colts, 28-13 (B)
Lions, 24-14 (D)
1956—Lions, 31-14 (B)
Lions, 27-3 (D)
1957—Colts, 34-14 (B)
Lions, 31-27 (D)
1958—Colts, 28-15 (B)
Colts, 40-14 (D)
1959—Colts, 21-9 (B)
Colts, 31-24 (D)
1960—Lions, 30-17 (D)
Lions, 20-15 (B)
1961—Lions, 16-15 (B)
Colts, 17-14 (D)
1962—Lions, 29-20 (B)
Lions, 21-14 (D)
1963—Colts, 25-21 (D)
Colts, 24-21 (B)
1964—Colts, 34-0 (D)
Lions, 31-14 (B)
1965—Colts, 31-7 (B)
Tie, 24-24 (D)
1966—Colts, 45-14 (B)
Lions, 20-14 (D)
1967—Colts, 41-7 (B)
1968—Colts, 27-10 (D)
1969—Tie, 17-17 (B)
1973—Colts, 29-27 (D)
1977—Lions, 13-10 (B)
1980—Colts, 10-9 (D)
1985—Colts, 14-6 (I)
(Points—Colts 724, Lions 665)
**Franchise in Baltimore prior to 1984*

DETROIT vs. KANSAS CITY
RS: Series tied, 3-3
1971—Lions, 32-21 (D)
1975—Chiefs, 24-21 (KC) OT
1980—Chiefs, 20-17 (KC)
1981—Lions, 27-10 (D)
1987—Chiefs, 27-20 (D)
1988—Lions, 7-6 (KC)
(Points—Lions 124, Chiefs 108)

DETROIT vs. *L.A. RAIDERS
RS: Raiders lead series, 4-2
1970—Lions, 28-14 (D)
1974—Raiders, 35-13 (O)
1978—Raiders, 29-17 (O)
1981—Lions, 16-0 (D)
1984—Raiders, 24-3 (D)
1987—Raiders, 27-7 (LA)
(Points—Raiders 129, Lions 84)
**Franchise in Oakland prior to 1982*

DETROIT vs. *L.A. RAMS
RS: Rams lead series, 39-33-1
PS: Lions lead series, 1-0
1937—Lions, 28-0 (C)
Lions, 27-7 (D)
1938—Rams, 21-17 (C)
Lions, 6-0 (D)
1939—Lions, 15-7 (D)
Rams, 14-3 (C)
1940—Lions, 6-0 (D)
Rams, 24-0 (C)
1941—Lions, 17-7 (D)
Lions, 14-0 (C)
1942—Rams, 14-0 (D)
Rams, 27-7 (C)
1944—Rams, 20-17 (D)
Lions, 26-14 (C)
1945—Rams, 28-21 (D)
1946—Rams, 35-14 (LA)
Rams, 41-20 (D)
1947—Rams, 27-13 (D)
Rams, 28-17 (LA)
1948—Rams, 44-7 (LA)
Rams, 34-27 (D)
1949—Rams, 27-24 (LA)
Rams, 21-10 (D)
1950—Rams, 30-28 (D)
Rams, 65-24 (LA)
1951—Rams, 27-21 (D)
Lions, 24-22 (LA)
1952—Lions, 17-14 (LA)
Lions, 24-16 (D)
**Lions, 31-21 (D)
1953—Rams, 31-19 (D)

Rams, 37-24 (LA)
1954—Lions, 21-3 (D)
Lions, 27-24 (LA)
1955—Rams, 17-10 (D)
Rams, 24-13 (LA)
1956—Lions, 24-21 (D)
Lions, 16-7 (LA)
1957—Lions, 10-7 (D)
Rams, 35-17 (LA)
1958—Rams, 42-28 (D)
Lions, 41-24 (LA)
1959—Lions, 17-7 (LA)
Lions, 23-17 (D)
1960—Rams, 48-35 (LA)
Lions, 12-10 (D)
1961—Lions, 14-13 (D)
Lions, 28-10 (LA)
1962—Lions, 13-10 (D)
Lions, 12-3 (LA)
1963—Lions, 23-2 (LA)
Rams, 28-21 (D)
1964—Tie, 17-17 (LA)
Lions, 37-17 (D)
1965—Lions, 20-0 (D)
Lions, 31-7 (LA)
1966—Rams, 14-7 (D)
Rams, 23-3 (LA)
1967—Rams, 31-7 (D)
1968—Rams, 10-7 (LA)
1969—Lions, 28-0 (D)
1970—Lions, 28-23 (LA)
1971—Rams, 21-13 (D)
1972—Lions, 34-17 (LA)
1974—Rams, 16-13 (LA)
1975—Rams, 20-0 (D)
1976—Rams, 20-17 (D)
1980—Lions, 41-20 (LA)
1981—Rams, 20-13 (LA)
1982—Lions, 19-14 (LA)
1983—Rams, 21-10 (LA)
1986—Rams, 14-10 (LA)
1987—Rams, 37-16 (D)
1988—Rams, 17-10 (LA)
(Points—Rams 1,434, Lions 1,334)
Franchise in Cleveland prior to 1946
***Conference Playoff*

DETROIT vs. MIAMI
RS: Dolphins lead series, 2-1
1973—Dolphins, 34-7 (M)
1979—Dolphins, 28-10 (D)
1985—Lions, 31-21 (D)
(Points—Dolphins 83, Lions 48)

DETROIT vs. MINNESOTA
RS: Vikings lead series, 35-18-2
1961—Lions, 37-10 (M)
Lions, 13-7 (D)
1962—Lions, 17-6 (M)
Lions, 37-23 (D)
1963—Lions, 28-10 (D)
Vikings, 34-31 (M)
1964—Lions, 24-20 (M)
Tie, 23-23 (D)
1965—Lions, 31-29 (M)
Vikings, 29-7 (D)
1966—Lions, 32-31 (M)
Vikings, 28-16 (D)
1967—Tie, 10-10 (M)
Lions, 14-3 (D)
1968—Vikings, 24-10 (M)
Vikings, 13-6 (D)
1969—Vikings, 24-10 (M)
Vikings, 27-0 (D)
1970—Vikings, 30-17 (D)
Vikings, 24-20 (M)
1971—Vikings, 16-13 (D)
Vikings, 29-10 (M)
1972—Vikings, 34-10 (D)
Vikings, 16-14 (M)
1973—Vikings, 23-9 (D)
Vikings, 28-7 (M)
1974—Vikings, 7-6 (D)
Lions, 20-16 (M)
1975—Vikings, 25-19 (M)
Lions, 17-10 (D)
1976—Vikings, 10-9 (D)
Vikings, 31-23 (M)
1977—Vikings, 14-7 (M)
Vikings, 30-21 (D)
1978—Vikings, 17-7 (M)
Lions, 45-14 (D)
1979—Vikings, 13-10 (D)
Vikings, 14-7 (M)
1980—Lions, 27-7 (D)
Vikings, 34-0 (M)
1981—Vikings, 26-24 (M)
Lions, 45-7 (D)
1982—Vikings, 34-31 (D)
1983—Vikings, 20-17 (M)
Lions, 13-2 (D)
1984—Vikings, 29-28 (D)
Lions, 16-14 (M)
1985—Vikings, 16-13 (M)
Lions, 41-21 (D)
1986—Lions, 13-10 (M)
Vikings, 24-10 (D)
1987—Vikings, 34-19 (M)
Vikings, 17-14 (D)
1988—Vikings, 44-17 (M)
Vikings, 23-0 (D)
(Points—Vikings 1,117, Lions 965)

DETROIT vs. NEW ENGLAND
RS: Series tied, 2-2
1971—Lions, 34-7 (NE)
1976—Lions, 30-10 (D)
1979—Patriots, 24-17 (NE)
1985—Patriots, 23-6 (NE)
(Points—Lions 87, Patriots 64)

DETROIT vs. NEW ORLEANS
RS: Saints lead series, 5-4-1
1968—Tie, 20-20 (D)
1970—Saints, 19-17 (NO)
1972—Lions, 27-14 (D)
1973—Saints, 20-13 (NO)
1974—Lions, 19-14 (D)
1976—Saints, 17-16 (NO)
1977—Lions, 23-19 (D)
1979—Saints, 17-7 (NO)
1980—Lions, 24-13 (D)
1988—Saints, 22-14 (D)
(Points—Lions 180, Saints 175)

***DETROIT vs. N.Y. GIANTS**
RS: Lions lead series, 17-13-1
PS: Lions lead series, 1-0
1930—Giants, 19-6 (P)
1931—Spartans, 14-6 (P)
Giants, 14-0 (NY)
1932—Spartans, 7-0 (P)
Spartans, 6-0 (NY)
1933—Spartans, 17-7 (P)
Giants, 13-10 (NY)
1934—Lions, 9-0 (D)
1935—**Lions, 26-7 (D)
1936—Giants, 14-7 (NY)
Lions, 38-0 (D)
1937—Lions, 17-0 (NY)
1939—Lions, 18-14 (D)
1941—Giants, 20-13 (NY)
1943—Tie, 0-0 (D)
1945—Giants, 35-14 (NY)
1947—Lions, 35-7 (D)
1949—Lions, 45-21 (NY)
1953—Lions, 27-16 (NY)
1955—Giants, 24-19 (D)
1958—Giants, 19-17 (D)
1962—Giants, 17-14 (NY)
1964—Lions, 26-3 (D)
1967—Lions, 30-7 (NY)
1969—Lions, 24-0 (D)
1972—Lions, 30-16 (D)
1974—Lions, 20-19 (D)
1976—Giants, 24-10 (NY)
1982—Giants, 13-6 (D)
1983—Lions, 15-9 (D)
1988—Giants, 30-10 (NY)
Giants, 13-10 (D) OT
(Points—Lions 540, Giants 387)
Franchise in Portsmouth prior to 1934 and known as the Spartans
***NFL Championship*

DETROIT vs. N.Y. JETS
RS: Jets lead series, 3-2
1972—Lions, 37-20 (D)
1979—Jets, 31-10 (NY)
1982—Jets, 28-13 (D)
1985—Lions, 31-20 (D)
1988—Jets, 17-10 (D)
(Points—Jets 116, Lions 101)

***DETROIT vs. PHILADELPHIA**
RS: Lions lead series, 12-9-2
1933—Spartans, 25-0 (P)
1934—Lions, 10-0 (P)
1935—Lions, 35-0 (D)
1936—Lions, 23-0 (P)
1938—Eagles, 21-7 (D)
1940—Lions, 21-0 (P)
1941—Lions, 21-17 (D)
1945—Lions, 28-24 (D)
1948—Eagles, 45-21 (P)
1949—Eagles, 22-14 (D)
1951—Lions, 28-10 (P)
1954—Tie, 13-13 (D)
1957—Lions, 27-16 (P)
1960—Eagles, 28-10 (P)
1961—Eagles, 27-24 (D)
1965—Lions, 35-28 (P)
1968—Eagles, 12-0 (D)
1971—Eagles, 23-20 (D)
1974—Eagles, 28-17 (P)
1977—Lions, 17-13 (D)
1979—Eagles, 44-7 (P)
1984—Tie, 23-23 (D) OT
1986—Lions, 13-11 (P)
(Points—Lions 439, Eagles 405)
Franchise in Portsmouth prior to 1934 and known as the Spartans

***DETROIT vs. **PHOENIX**
RS: Lions lead series, 25-15-5
1930—Tie, 0-0 (P)
Cardinals, 23-0 (C)
1931—Cardinals, 20-19 (C)
1932—Tie, 7-7 (P)
1933—Spartans, 7-6 (P)
1934—Lions, 6-0 (D)
Lions, 17-13 (C)
1935—Tie, 10-10 (D)
Lions, 7-6 (C)
1936—Lions, 39-0 (D)
Lions, 14-7 (C)
1937—Lions, 16-7 (C)
Lions, 16-7 (D)
1938—Lions, 10-0 (D)
Lions, 7-3 (C)
1939—Lions, 21-3 (D)
Lions, 17-3 (C)
1940—Tie, 0-0 (Buffalo)
Lions, 43-14 (C)
1941—Tie, 14-14 (C)
Lions, 21-3 (D)
1942—Cardinals, 13-0 (C)
Cardinals, 7-0 (D)
1943—Lions, 35-17 (D)
Lions, 7-0 (C)
1945—Lions, 10-0 (C)
Lions, 26-0 (D)
1946—Cardinals, 34-14 (C)
Cardinals, 36-14 (D)
1947—Cardinals, 45-21 (C)
Cardinals, 17-7 (D)
1948—Cardinals, 56-20 (C)
Cardinals, 28-14 (D)
1949—Lions, 24-7 (C)
Cardinals, 42-19 (D)
1959—Lions, 45-21 (D)
1961—Lions, 45-14 (StL)
1967—Cardinals, 38-28 (StL)
1969—Lions, 20-0 (D)
1970—Lions, 16-3 (D)
1973—Lions, 20-16 (StL)
1975—Cardinals, 24-13 (D)
1978—Cardinals, 21-14 (StL)
1980—Lions, 20-7 (D)
Cardinals, 24-23 (StL)
(Points—Lions 746, Cardinals 626)
Franchise in Portsmouth prior to 1934 and known as the Spartans
***Franchise in St. Louis prior to 1988 and in Chicago prior to 1960*

DETROIT vs. *PITTSBURGH
RS: Lions lead series, 13-9-1
1934—Lions, 40-7 (D)
1936—Lions, 28-3 (D)
1937—Lions, 7-3 (D)
1938—Lions, 16-7 (D)
1940—Pirates, 10-7 (D)
1942—Steelers, 35-7 (D)
1946—Lions, 17-7 (D)
1947—Steelers, 17-10 (P)
1948—Lions, 17-14 (D)
1949—Steelers, 14-7 (P)
1950—Lions, 10-7 (D)
1952—Lions, 31-6 (P)
1953—Lions, 38-21 (D)
1955—Lions, 31-28 (P)
1956—Lions, 45-7 (D)
1959—Tie, 10-10 (P)
1962—Lions, 45-7 (D)
1966—Steelers, 17-3 (P)
1967—Steelers, 24-14 (D)
1969—Steelers, 16-13 (P)
1973—Steelers, 24-10 (P)
1983—Lions, 45-3 (D)
1986—Steelers, 27-17 (P)
(Points—Lions 468, Steelers 314)
Steelers known as Pirates prior to 1941

DETROIT vs. SAN DIEGO
RS: Lions lead series, 3-2
1972—Lions, 34-20 (D)
1977—Lions, 20-0 (D)
1978—Lions, 31-14 (D)
1981—Chargers, 28-23 (SD)
1984—Chargers, 27-24 (SD)
(Points—Lions 132, Chargers 89)

DETROIT vs. SAN FRANCISCO
RS: Lions lead series, 25-23-1
PS: Series tied, 1-1
1950—Lions, 24-7 (D)
49ers, 28-27 (SF)
1951—49ers, 20-10 (D)
49ers, 21-17 (SF)
1952—49ers, 17-3 (SF)
49ers, 28-0 (D)
1953—Lions, 24-21 (D)
Lions, 14-10 (SF)
1954—49ers, 37-31 (SF)
Lions, 48-7 (D)
1955—49ers, 27-24 (D)
49ers, 38-21 (SF)
1956—Lions, 20-17 (D)
Lions, 17-13 (SF)
1957—49ers, 35-31 (SF)
Lions, 31-10 (D)
*Lions, 31-27 (SF)
1958—49ers, 24-21 (SF)
Lions, 35-21 (D)
1959—49ers, 34-13 (D)
49ers, 33-7 (SF)
1960—49ers, 14-10 (D)
Lions, 24-0 (SF)
1961—49ers, 49-0 (D)
Tie, 20-20 (SF)
1962—Lions, 45-24 (D)
Lions, 38-24 (SF)
1963—Lions, 26-3 (D)
Lions, 45-7 (SF)
1964—Lions, 26-17 (SF)
Lions, 24-7 (D)
1965—49ers, 27-21 (D)
49ers, 17-14 (SF)
1966—49ers, 27-24 (SF)
49ers, 41-14 (D)
1967—Lions, 45-3 (SF)
1968—49ers, 14-7 (D)
1969—Lions, 26-14 (SF)
1970—Lions, 28-7 (D)
1971—49ers, 31-27 (SF)
1973—Lions, 30-20 (D)
1974—Lions, 17-13 (D)
1975—Lions, 28-17 (SF)
1977—49ers, 28-7 (SF)
1978—Lions, 33-14 (D)
1980—Lions, 17-13 (D)
1981—Lions, 24-17 (D)
1983—**49ers, 24-23 (SF)
1984—49ers, 30-27 (D)
1985—Lions, 23-21 (D)
1988—49ers, 20-13 (SF)
(Points—Lions 1,155, 49ers 1,038)
Conference Playoff
***NFC Divisional Playoff*

DETROIT vs. SEATTLE
RS: Seahawks lead series, 3-1
1976—Lions, 41-14 (S)
1978—Seahawks, 28-16 (S)
1984—Seahawks, 38-17 (S)
1987—Seahawks, 37-14 (D)
(Points—Seahawks 117, Lions 88)

DETROIT vs. TAMPA BAY
RS: Series tied, 11-11
1977—Lions, 16-7 (D)
1978—Lions, 15-7 (TB)
Lions, 34-23 (D)
1979—Buccaneers, 31-16 (TB)
Buccaneers, 16-14 (D)
1980—Lions, 24-10 (TB)
Lions, 27-14 (D)
1981—Buccaneers, 28-10 (TB)
Buccaneers, 20-17 (D)
1982—Buccaneers, 23-21 (TB)
1983—Lions, 11-0 (TB)
Lions, 23-20 (D)
1984—Buccaneers, 21-17 (TB)
Lions, 13-7 (D) OT
1985—Lions, 30-9 (D)
Buccaneers, 19-16 (TB) OT
1986—Buccaneers, 24-20 (D)
Lions, 38-17 (TB)
1987—Buccaneers, 31-27 (D)
Lions, 20-10 (TB)
1988—Buccaneers, 23-20 (D)
Buccaneers, 21-10 (TB)
(Points—Lions 439, Buccaneers 381)

***DETROIT vs. **WASHINGTON**
RS: Redskins lead series, 19-8
PS: Redskins lead series, 1-0
1932—Spartans, 10-0 (P)
1933—Spartans, 13-0 (B)
1934—Lions, 24-0 (D)
1935—Lions, 17-7 (B)
Lions, 14-0 (D)
1938—Redskins, 7-5 (D)
1939—Redskins, 31-7 (W)
1940—Redskins, 20-14 (D)
1942—Redskins, 15-3 (D)
1943—Redskins, 42-20 (W)
1946—Redskins, 17-16 (W)
1947—Lions, 38-21 (D)
1948—Redskins, 46-21 (W)
1951—Lions, 35-17 (D)
1956—Redskins, 18-17 (W)
1965—Lions, 14-10 (D)
1968—Redskins, 14-3 (W)
1970—Redskins, 31-10 (W)
1973—Redskins, 20-0 (D)
1976—Redskins, 20-7 (W)
1978—Redskins, 21-19 (D)
1979—Redskins, 27-24 (D)
1981—Redskins, 33-31 (W)
1982—***Redskins, 31-7 (W)
1983—Redskins, 38-17 (W)
1984—Redskins, 28-14 (W)
1985—Redskins, 24-3 (W)

1987—Redskins, 20-13 (W)
(Points—Redskins 558, Lions 416)
*Franchise in Portsmouth prior to 1934 and known as the Spartans.
**Franchise in Boston prior to 1937
***NFC First Round Playoff

GREEN BAY vs. ATLANTA
RS: Packers lead series, 8-7;
See Atlanta vs. Green Bay
GREEN BAY vs. BUFFALO
RS: Bills lead series, 3-1;
See Buffalo vs. Green Bay
GREEN BAY vs. CHICAGO
RS: Bears lead series, 75-55-6
PS: Bears lead series, 1-0;
See Chicago vs. Green Bay
GREEN BAY vs. CINCINNATI
RS: Bengals lead series, 4-2;
See Cincinnati vs. Green Bay
GREEN BAY vs. CLEVELAND
RS: Packers lead series, 7-5
PS: Packers lead series, 1-0;
See Cleveland vs. Green Bay
GREEN BAY vs. DALLAS
RS: Packers lead series, 6-4
PS: Packers lead series, 2-1;
See Dallas vs. Green Bay
GREEN BAY vs. DENVER
RS: Broncos lead series, 3-1-1;
See Denver vs. Green Bay
GREEN BAY vs. DETROIT
RS: Packers lead series, 59-51-7;
See Detroit vs. Green Bay
GREEN BAY vs. HOUSTON
RS: Oilers lead series, 3-2
1972—Packers, 23-10 (H)
1977—Oilers, 16-10 (GB)
1980—Oilers, 22-3 (GB)
1983—Packers, 41-38 (H) OT
1986—Oilers, 31-3 (GB)
(Points—Oilers 117, Packers 80)
GREEN BAY vs. *INDIANAPOLIS
RS: Colts lead series, 18-17-1
PS: Packers lead series, 1-0
1953—Packers, 37-14 (GB)
Packers, 35-24 (B)
1954—Packers, 7-6 (B)
Packers, 24-13 (Mil)
1955—Colts, 24-20 (Mil)
Colts, 14-10 (B)
1956—Packers, 38-33 (Mil)
Colts, 28-21 (B)
1957—Colts, 45-17 (Mil)
Packers, 24-21 (B)
1958—Colts, 24-17 (Mil)
Colts, 56-0 (B)
1959—Colts, 38-21 (B)
Colts, 28-24 (Mil)
1960—Packers, 35-21 (GB)
Colts, 38-24 (B)
1961—Packers, 45-7 (GB)
Colts, 45-21 (B)
1962—Packers, 17-6 (B)
Packers, 17-13 (GB)
1963—Packers, 31-20 (GB)
Packers, 34-20 (B)
1964—Colts, 21-20 (GB)
Colts, 24-21 (B)
1965—Packers, 20-17 (Mil)
Packers, 42-27 (B)
**Packers, 13-10 (GB) OT
1966—Packers, 24-3 (Mil)
Packers, 14-10 (B)
1967—Colts, 13-10 (B)
1968—Colts, 16-3 (GB)
1969—Colts, 14-6 (B)
1970—Colts, 13-10 (Mil)
1974—Packers, 20-13 (B)
1982—Tie, 20-20 (B) OT
1985—Colts, 37-10 (I)
1988—Colts, 20-13 (GB)
(Points—Colts 796, Packers 765)
*Franchise in Baltimore prior to 1984
**Conference Playoff
GREEN BAY vs. KANSAS CITY
RS: Series tied, 1-1-1
PS: Packers lead series, 1-0
1966—*Packers, 35-10 (Los Angeles)
1973—Tie, 10-10 (Mil)
1977—Chiefs, 20-10 (KC)
1987—Packers, 23-3 (KC)
(Points—Packers 78, Chiefs 43)
*Super Bowl I
GREEN BAY vs. *L.A. RAIDERS
RS: Raiders lead series, 5-0
PS: Packers lead series, 1-0
1967—**Packers, 33-14 (Miami)
1972—Raiders, 20-14 (GB)
1976—Raiders, 18-14 (O)
1978—Raiders, 28-3 (GB)
1984—Raiders, 28-7 (LA)
1987—Raiders, 20-0 (GB)
(Points—Raiders 128, Packers 71)
*Franchise in Oakland prior to 1982
**Super Bowl II
GREEN BAY vs. *L.A. RAMS
RS: Rams lead series, 40-33-2
PS: Packers lead series, 1-0
1937—Packers, 35-10 (C)
Packers, 35-7 (GB)
1938—Packers, 26-17 (GB)
Packers, 28-7 (C)
1939—Rams, 27-24 (GB)
Packers, 7-6 (C)
1940—Packers, 31-14 (GB)
Tie, 13-13 (C)
1941—Packers, 24-7 (Mil)
Packers, 17-14 (C)
1942—Packers, 45-28 (GB)
Packers, 30-12 (C)
1944—Packers, 30-21 (GB)
Packers, 42-7 (C)
1945—Rams, 27-14 (GB)
Rams, 20-7 (C)
1946—Rams, 21-17 (Mil)
Rams, 38-17 (LA)
1947—Packers, 17-14 (Mil)
Packers, 30-10 (LA)
1948—Packers, 16-0 (GB)
Rams, 24-10 (LA)
1949—Rams, 48-7 (GB)
Rams, 35-7 (LA)
1950—Rams, 45-14 (Mil)
Rams, 51-14 (LA)
1951—Rams, 28-0 (Mil)
Rams, 42-14 (LA)
1952—Rams, 30-28 (Mil)
Rams, 45-27 (LA)
1953—Rams, 38-20 (Mil)
Rams, 33-17 (LA)
1954—Packers, 35-17 (Mil)
Rams, 35-27 (LA)
1955—Packers, 30-28 (Mil)
Rams, 31-17 (LA)
1956—Packers, 42-17 (Mil)
Rams, 49-21 (LA)
1957—Rams, 31-27 (Mil)
Rams, 42-17 (LA)
1958—Rams, 20-7 (GB)
Rams, 34-20 (LA)
1959—Rams, 45-6 (Mil)
Packers, 38-20 (LA)
1960—Rams, 33-31 (Mil)
Packers, 35-2 (LA)
1961—Packers, 35-17 (GB)
Packers, 24-17 (LA)
1962—Packers, 41-10 (Mil)
Packers, 20-17 (LA)
1963—Packers, 42-10 (GB)
Packers, 31-14 (LA)
1964—Rams, 27-17 (Mil)
Tie, 24-24 (LA)
1965—Packers, 6-3 (Mil)
Rams, 21-10 (LA)
1966—Packers, 24-13 (GB)
Packers, 27-23 (LA)
1967—Rams, 27-24 (LA)
**Packers, 28-7 (Mil)
1968—Rams, 16-14 (Mil)
1969—Rams, 34-21 (LA)
1970—Rams, 31-21 (GB)
1971—Rams, 30-13 (LA)
1973—Rams, 24-7 (LA)
1974—Packers, 17-6 (Mil)
1975—Rams, 22-5 (LA)
1977—Rams, 24-6 (Mil)
1978—Rams, 31-14 (LA)
1980—Rams, 51-21 (LA)
1981—Rams, 35-23 (LA)
1982—Packers, 35-23 (Mil)
1983—Packers, 27-24 (Mil)
1984—Packers, 31-6 (Mil)
1985—Rams, 34-17 (LA)
1988—Rams, 34-7 (GB)
(Points—Rams 1,817, Packers 1,648)
*Franchise in Cleveland prior to 1946
**Conference Championship
GREEN BAY vs. MIAMI
RS: Dolphins lead series, 5-0
1971—Dolphins, 27-6 (Mia)
1975—Dolphins, 31-7 (GB)
1979—Dolphins, 27-7 (Mia)
1985—Dolphins, 34-24 (GB)
1988—Dolphins, 24-17 (Mia)
(Points—Dolphins 143, Packers 61)
GREEN BAY vs. MINNESOTA
RS: Packers lead series, 28-26-1
1961—Packers, 33-7 (Minn)
Packers, 28-10 (Mil)
1962—Packers, 34-7 (GB)
Packers, 48-21 (Minn)
1963—Packers, 37-28 (Minn)
Packers, 28-7 (GB)
1964—Vikings, 24-23 (GB)
Packers, 42-13 (Minn)
1965—Packers, 38-13 (Minn)
Packers, 24-19 (GB)
1966—Vikings, 20-17 (GB)
Packers, 28-16 (Minn)
1967—Vikings, 10-7 (Mil)
Packers, 30-27 (Minn)
1968—Vikings, 26-13 (Mil)
Vikings, 14-10 (Minn)
1969—Vikings, 19-7 (Minn)
Vikings, 9-7 (Mil)
1970—Packers, 13-10 (Mil)
Vikings, 10-3 (Minn)
1971—Vikings, 24-13 (GB)
Vikings, 3-0 (Minn)
1972—Vikings, 27-13 (GB)
Packers, 23-7 (Minn)
1973—Vikings, 11-3 (Minn)
Vikings, 31-7 (GB)
1974—Vikings, 32-17 (GB)
Packers, 19-7 (Minn)
1975—Vikings, 28-17 (GB)
Vikings, 24-3 (Minn)
1976—Vikings, 17-10 (Mil)
Vikings, 20-9 (Minn)
1977—Vikings, 19-7 (Minn)
Vikings, 13-6 (GB)
1978—Vikings, 21-7 (Minn)
Tie, 10-10 (GB) OT
1979—Vikings, 27-21 (Minn) OT
Packers, 19-7 (Mil)
1980—Packers, 16-3 (GB)
Packers, 25-13 (Minn)
1981—Vikings, 30-13 (Mil)
Packers, 35-23 (Minn)
1982—Packers, 26-7 (Mil)
1983—Vikings, 20-17 (GB) OT
Packers, 29-21 (Minn)
1984—Packers, 45-17 (Mil)
Packers, 38-14 (Minn)
1985—Packers, 20-17 (Mil)
Packers, 27-17 (Minn)
1986—Vikings, 42-7 (Minn)
Vikings, 32-6 (GB)
1987—Packers, 23-16 (Minn)
Packers, 16-10 (Mil)
1988—Packers, 34-14 (Minn)
Packers, 18-6 (GB)
(Points—Packers 1,069, Vikings 940)
GREEN BAY vs. NEW ENGLAND
RS: Series tied, 2-2
1973—Patriots, 33-24 (NE)
1979—Packers, 27-14 (GB)
1985—Patriots, 26-20 (NE)
1988—Packers, 45-3 (Mil)
(Points—Packers 116, Patriots 76)
GREEN BAY vs. NEW ORLEANS
RS: Packers lead series, 10-4
1968—Packers, 29-7 (Mil)
1971—Saints, 29-21 (Mil)
1972—Packers, 30-20 (NO)
1973—Packers, 30-10 (Mil)
1975—Saints, 20-19 (NO)
1976—Packers, 32-27 (Mil)
1977—Packers, 24-20 (NO)
1978—Packers, 28-17 (Mil)
1979—Packers, 28-19 (Mil)
1981—Packers, 35-7 (NO)
1984—Packers, 23-13 (NO)
1985—Packers, 38-14 (Mil)
1986—Saints, 24-10 (NO)
1987—Saints, 33-24 (NO)
(Points—Packers 371, Saints 260)
GREEN BAY vs. N.Y. GIANTS
RS: Packers lead series, 21-19-2
PS: Packers lead series, 4-1
1928—Giants, 6-0 (GB)
Packers, 7-0 (NY)
1929—Packers, 20-6 (NY)
1930—Packers, 14-7 (GB)
Giants, 13-6 (NY)
1931—Packers, 27-7 (GB)
Packers, 14-10 (NY)
1932—Packers, 13-0 (GB)
Giants, 6-0 (NY)
1933—Giants, 10-7 (Mil)
Giants, 17-6 (NY)
1934—Packers, 20-6 (Mil)
Giants, 17-3 (NY)
1935—Packers, 16-7 (GB)
1936—Packers, 26-14 (NY)
1937—Giants, 10-0 (NY)
1938—Giants, 15-3 (NY)
*Giants, 23-17 (NY)
1939—*Packers, 27-0 (Mil)
1940—Giants, 7-3 (NY)
1942—Tie, 21-21 (NY)
1943—Packers, 35-21 (NY)
1944—Giants, 24-0 (NY)
*Packers, 14-7 (NY)
1945—Packers, 23-14 (NY)
1947—Tie, 24-24 (NY)
1948—Giants, 49-3 (Mil)
1949—Giants, 30-10 (GB)
1952—Packers, 17-3 (NY)
1957—Giants, 31-17 (GB)
1959—Giants, 20-3 (NY)
1961—Packers, 20-17 (Mil)
*Packers, 37-0 (GB)
1962—*Packers, 16-7 (NY)
1967—Packers, 48-21 (NY)
1969—Packers, 20-10 (Mil)
1971—Giants, 42-40 (GB)
1973—Packers, 16-14 (New Haven)
1975—Packers, 40-14 (Mil)
1980—Giants, 27-21 (NY)
1981—Packers, 27-14 (NY)
Packers, 26-24 (Mil)
1982—Packers, 27-19 (NY)
1983—Giants, 27-3 (NY)
1985—Packers, 23-20 (GB)
1986—Giants, 55-24 (NY)
1987—Giants, 20-10 (NY)
(Points—Packers 794, Giants 756)
*NFL Championship
GREEN BAY vs. N.Y. JETS
RS: Jets lead series, 4-1
1973—Packers, 23-7 (Mil)
1979—Jets, 27-22 (GB)
1981—Jets, 28-3 (NY)
1982—Jets, 15-13 (NY)
1985—Jets, 24-3 (Mil)
(Points—Jets 101, Packers 64)
GREEN BAY vs. PHILADELPHIA
RS: Packers lead series, 18-4
PS: Eagles lead series, 1-0
1933—Packers, 35-9 (GB)
Packers, 10-0 (P)
1934—Packers, 19-6 (GB)
1935—Packers, 13-6 (P)
1937—Packers, 37-7 (Mil)
1939—Packers, 23-16 (P)
1940—Packers, 27-20 (GB)
1942—Packers, 7-0 (P)
1946—Packers, 19-7 (P)
1947—Eagles, 28-14 (P)
1951—Packers, 37-24 (GB)
1952—Packers, 12-10 (Mil)
1954—Packers, 37-14 (P)
1958—Packers, 38-35 (GB)
1960—*Eagles, 17-13 (P)
1962—Packers, 49-0 (P)
1968—Packers, 30-13 (GB)
1970—Packers, 30-17 (Mil)
1974—Eagles, 36-14 (P)
1976—Packers, 28-13 (GB)
1978—Eagles, 10-3 (P)
1979—Eagles, 21-10 (GB)
1987—Packers, 16-10 (GB) OT
(Points—Packers 521, Eagles 319)
*NFL Championship
GREEN BAY vs. *PHOENIX
RS: Packers lead series, 38-21-4
PS: Packers lead series, 1-0
1921—Tie, 3-3 (C)
1922—Cardinals, 16-3 (C)
1924—Cardinals, 3-0 (C)
1925—Cardinals, 9-6 (C)
1926—Cardinals, 13-7 (GB)
Packers, 3-0 (C)
1927—Packers, 13-0 (GB)
Tie, 6-6 (C)
1928—Packers, 20-0 (GB)
1929—Packers, 9-2 (GB)
Packers, 7-6 (C)
Packers, 12-0 (C)
1930—Packers, 14-0 (GB)
Cardinals, 13-6 (C)
1931—Packers, 26-7 (GB)
Cardinals, 21-13 (C)
1932—Packers, 15-7 (GB)
Packers, 19-9 (C)
1933—Packers, 14-6 (C)
1934—Packers, 15-0 (GB)
Cardinals, 9-0 (Mil)
Cardinals, 6-0 (C)
1935—Cardinals, 7-6 (GB)
Cardinals, 3-0 (Mil)
Cardinals, 9-7 (C)
1936—Packers, 10-7 (GB)
Packers, 24-0 (Mil)
Tie, 0-0 (C)
1937—Cardinals, 14-7 (GB)
Packers, 34-13 (Mil)
1938—Packers, 28-7 (Mil)
Packers, 24-22 (Buffalo)
1939—Packers, 14-10 (GB)
Packers, 27-20 (Mil)
1940—Packers, 31-6 (Mil)
Packers, 28-7 (C)
1941—Packers, 14-13 (Mil)
Packers, 17-9 (GB)
1942—Packers, 17-13 (C)
Packers, 55-24 (GB)
1943—Packers, 28-7 (C)
Packers, 35-14 (Mil)
1945—Packers, 33-14 (GB)

1946—Packers, 19-7 (C)
Cardinals, 24-6 (GB)
1947—Cardinals, 14-10 (GB)
Cardinals, 21-20 (C)
1948—Cardinals, 17-7 (Mil)
Cardinals, 42-7 (C)
1949—Cardinals, 39-17 (Mil)
Cardinals, 41-21 (C)
1955—Packers, 31-14 (GB)
1956—Packers, 24-21 (C)
1962—Packers, 17-0 (Mil)
1963—Packers, 30-7 (StL)
1967—Packers, 31-23 (StL)
1969—Packers, 45-28 (GB)
1971—Tie, 16-16 (StL)
1973—Packers, 25-21 (GB)
1976—Cardinals, 29-0 (StL)
1982—**Packers, 41-16 (GB)
1984—Packers, 24-23 (GB)
1985—Cardinals, 43-28 (StL)
1988—Packers, 26-17 (P)
(Points—Packers 1,095, Cardinals 818)
Franchise in St. Louis prior to 1988, and in Chicago prior to 1960
**NFC First Round Playoff*

GREEN BAY vs. *PITTSBURGH
RS: Packers lead series, 16-11
1933—Packers, 47-0 (GB)
1935—Packers, 27-0 (GB)
Packers, 34-14 (P)
1936—Packers, 42-10 (Mil)
1938—Packers, 20-0 (GB)
1940—Packers, 24-3 (Mil)
1941—Packers, 54-7 (P)
1942—Packers, 24-21 (Mil)
1946—Packers, 17-7 (GB)
1947—Steelers, 18-17 (Mil)
1948—Steelers, 38-7 (P)
1949—Steelers, 30-7 (Mil)
1951—Packers, 35-33 (Mil)
Steelers, 28-7 (P)
1953—Steelers, 31-14 (P)
1954—Steelers, 21-20 (GB)
1957—Packers, 27-10 (P)
1960—Packers, 19-13 (P)
1963—Packers, 33-14 (Mil)
1965—Packers, 41-9 (P)
1967—Steelers, 24-17 (GB)
1969—Packers, 38-34 (P)
1970—Packers, 20-12 (P)
1975—Steelers, 16-13 (Mil)
1980—Steelers, 22-20 (P)
1983—Steelers, 25-21 (GB)
1986—Steelers, 27-3 (P)
(Points—Packers 648, Steelers 467)
Steelers known as Pirates prior to 1941

GREEN BAY vs. SAN DIEGO
RS: Packers lead series, 3-1
1970—Packers, 22-20 (SD)
1974—Packers, 34-0 (GB)
1978—Packers, 24-3 (SD)
1984—Chargers, 34-28 (GB)
(Points—Packers 108, Chargers 57)

GREEN BAY vs. SAN FRANCISCO
RS: 49ers lead series, 24-20-1
1950—Packers, 25-21 (GB)
49ers, 30-14 (SF)
1951—49ers, 31-19 (SF)
1952—49ers, 24-14 (SF)
1953—49ers, 37-7 (Mil)
49ers, 48-14 (SF)
1954—49ers, 23-17 (Mil)
49ers, 35-0 (SF)
1955—Packers, 27-21 (Mil)
Packers, 28-7 (SF)
1956—49ers, 17-16 (GB)
49ers, 38-20 (SF)
1957—49ers, 24-14 (Mil)
49ers, 27-20 (SF)
1958—49ers, 33-12 (Mil)
49ers, 48-21 (SF)
1959—Packers, 21-20 (GB)
Packers, 36-14 (SF)
1960—Packers, 41-14 (Mil)
Packers, 13-0 (SF)
1961—Packers, 30-10 (GB)
49ers, 22-21 (SF)
1962—Packers, 31-13 (Mil)
Packers, 31-21 (SF)
1963—Packers, 28-10 (Mil)
Packers, 21-17 (SF)
1964—Packers, 24-14 (Mil)
49ers, 24-14 (SF)
1965—Packers, 27-10 (GB)
Tie, 24-24 (SF)
1966—49ers, 21-20 (SF)
Packers, 20-7 (Mil)
1967—Packers, 13-0 (GB)
1968—49ers, 27-20 (SF)
1969—Packers, 14-7 (Mil)
1970—49ers, 26-10 (SF)
1972—Packers, 34-24 (Mil)
1973—49ers, 20-6 (SF)
1974—49ers, 7-6 (SF)
1976—49ers, 26-14 (GB)
1977—Packers, 16-14 (Mil)
1980—Packers, 23-16 (Mil)
1981—49ers, 13-3 (Mil)
1986—49ers, 31-17 (Mil)
1987—49ers, 23-12 (GB)
(Points—49ers 939, Packers 858)

GREEN BAY vs. SEATTLE
RS: Packers lead series, 3-2
1976—Packers, 27-20 (Mil)
1978—Packers, 45-28 (Mil)
1981—Packers, 34-24 (GB)
1984—Seahawks, 30-24 (Mil)
1987—Seahawks, 24-13 (S)
(Points—Packers 143, Seahawks 126)

GREEN BAY vs. TAMPA BAY
RS: Packers lead series, 10-9-1
1977—Packers, 13-0 (TB)
1978—Packers, 9-7 (GB)
Packers, 17-7 (TB)
1979—Buccaneers, 21-10 (GB)
Buccaneers, 21-3 (TB)
1980—Tie, 14-14 (TB) OT
Buccaneers, 20-17 (Mil)
1981—Buccaneers, 21-10 (GB)
Buccaneers, 37-3 (TB)
1983—Packers, 55-14 (GB)
Packers, 12-9 (TB) OT
1984—Buccaneers, 30-27 (TB) OT
Packers, 27-14 (GB)
1985—Packers, 21-0 (GB)
Packers, 20-17 (TB)
1986—Packers, 31-7 (Mil)
Packers, 21-7 (TB)
1987—Buccaneers, 23-17 (Mil)
1988—Buccaneers, 13-10 (GB)
Buccaneers, 27-24 (TB)
(Points—Packers 361, Buccaneers 309)

GREEN BAY vs. *WASHINGTON
RS: Packers lead series, 13-12-1
PS: Series tied, 1-1
1932—Packers, 21-0 (B)
1933—Tie, 7-7 (GB)
Redskins, 20-7 (B)
1934—Packers, 10-0 (B)
1936—Packers, 31-2 (GB)
Packers, 7-3 (B)
**Packers, 21-6 (New York)
1937—Redskins, 14-6 (W)
1939—Packers, 24-14 (Mil)
1941—Packers, 22-17 (W)
1943—Redskins, 33-7 (Mil)
1946—Packers, 20-7 (W)
1947—Packers, 27-10 (Mil)
1948—Redskins, 23-7 (Mil)
1949—Redskins, 30-0 (W)
1950—Packers, 35-21 (Mil)
1952—Packers, 35-20 (Mil)
1958—Redskins, 37-21 (W)
1959—Packers, 21-0 (GB)
1968—Packers, 27-7 (W)
1972—Redskins, 21-16 (W)
***Redskins, 16-3 (W)
1974—Redskins, 17-6 (GB)
1977—Redskins, 10-9 (W)
1979—Redskins, 38-21 (W)
1983—Packers, 48-47 (GB)
1986—Redskins, 16-7 (GB)
1988—Redskins, 20-17 (Mil)
(Points—Packers 483, Redskins 456)
Franchise in Boston prior to 1937 and known as Braves prior to 1933
**NFL Championship*
***NFC Divisional Playoff*

HOUSTON vs. ATLANTA
RS: Falcons lead series, 4-2;
See Atlanta vs. Houston

HOUSTON vs. BUFFALO
RS: Oilers lead series, 18-10
PS: Bills lead series, 1-0;
See Buffalo vs. Houston

HOUSTON vs. CHICAGO
RS: Series tied, 2-2;
See Chicago vs. Houston

HOUSTON vs. CINCINNATI
RS: Bengals lead series, 22-17-1;
See Cincinnati vs. Houston

HOUSTON vs. CLEVELAND
RS: Browns lead series, 24-13
PS: Oilers lead series, 1-0;
See Cleveland vs. Houston

HOUSTON vs. DALLAS
RS: Cowboys lead series, 4-2;
See Dallas vs. Houston

HOUSTON vs. DENVER
RS: Oilers lead series, 18-10-1
PS: Series tied, 1-1;
See Denver vs. Houston

HOUSTON vs. DETROIT
RS: Series tied, 2-2;
See Detroit vs. Houston

HOUSTON vs. GREEN BAY
RS: Oilers lead series, 3-2;
See Green Bay vs. Houston

HOUSTON vs. *INDIANAPOLIS
RS: Colts lead series, 6-5
1970—Colts, 24-20 (H)
1973—Oilers, 31-27 (B)
1976—Colts, 38-14 (B)
1979—Oilers, 28-16 (B)
1980—Oilers, 21-16 (H)
1983—Colts, 20-10 (B)
1984—Colts, 35-21 (H)
1985—Colts, 34-16 (I)
1986—Oilers, 31-17 (H)
1987—Colts, 51-27 (I)
1988—Oilers, 17-14 (I) OT
(Points—Colts 292, Oilers 236)
Franchise in Baltimore prior to 1984

HOUSTON vs. *KANSAS CITY
RS: Chiefs lead series, 20-13
PS: Chiefs lead series, 1-0
1960—Oilers, 20-10 (H)
Texans, 24-0 (D)
1961—Texans, 26-21 (D)
Oilers, 38-7 (H)
1962—Texans, 31-7 (H)
Oilers, 14-6 (D)
**Texans, 20-17 (H) OT
1963—Chiefs, 28-7 (KC)
Oilers, 28-7 (H)
1964—Chiefs, 28-7 (KC)
1964—Chiefs, 28-19 (H)
1965—Chiefs, 52-21 (KC)
Oilers, 38-36 (H)
1966—Chiefs, 48-23 (KC)
1967—Chiefs, 25-20 (H)
Oilers, 24-19 (KC)
1968—Chiefs, 26-21 (H)
Chiefs, 24-10 (KC)
1969—Chiefs, 24-0 (KC)
1970—Chiefs, 24-9 (KC)
1971—Chiefs, 20-16 (H)
1973—Chiefs, 38-14 (KC)
1974—Chiefs, 17-7 (H)
1975—Oilers, 17-13 (KC)
1977—Oilers, 34-20 (H)
1978—Oilers, 20-17 (KC)
1979—Oilers, 20-6 (H)
1980—Chiefs, 21-20 (KC)
1981—Chiefs, 23-10 (KC)
1983—Chiefs, 13-10 (H) OT
1984—Oilers, 17-16 (KC)
1985—Oilers, 23-20 (H)
1986—Chiefs, 27-13 (KC)
1988—Oilers, 7-6 (H)
(Points—Chiefs 750, Oilers 572)
Franchise in Dallas prior to 1963 and known as Texans
**AFL Championship*

HOUSTON vs. *L.A. RAIDERS
RS: Raiders lead series, 19-11
PS: Raiders lead series, 3-0
1960—Oilers, 37-22 (O)
Raiders, 14-13 (H)
1961—Oilers, 55-0 (H)
Oilers, 47-16 (O)
1962—Oilers, 28-20 (O)
Oilers, 32-17 (H)
1963—Raiders, 24-13 (H)
Raiders, 52-49 (O)
1964—Oilers, 42-28 (H)
Raiders, 20-10 (O)
1965—Raiders, 21-17 (O)
Raiders, 33-21 (H)
1966—Oilers, 31-0 (H)
Raiders, 38-23 (O)
1967—Raiders, 19-7 (H)
**Raiders, 40-7 (O)
1968—Raiders, 24-15 (H)
1969—Raiders, 21-17 (O)
***Raiders, 56-7 (O)
1971—Raiders, 41-21 (O)
1972—Raiders, 34-0 (H)
1973—Raiders, 17-6 (H)
1975—Oilers, 27-26 (O)
1976—Raiders, 14-13 (H)
1977—Raiders, 34-29 (O)
1978—Raiders, 21-17 (O)
1979—Oilers, 31-17 (H)
1980—****Raiders, 27-7 (O)
1981—Oilers, 17-16 (H)
1983—Raiders, 20-6 (LA)
1984—Raiders, 24-14 (H)
1986—Raiders, 28-17 (H)
1988—Oilers, 38-35 (H)
(Points—Raiders 819, Oilers 714)
Franchise in Oakland prior to 1982
**AFL Championship*
***Inter-Divisional Playoff*
****AFC First Round Playoff*

HOUSTON vs. L.A. RAMS
RS: Rams lead series, 3-2
1973—Rams, 31-26 (H)
1978—Rams, 10-6 (H)
1981—Oilers, 27-20 (LA)
1984—Rams, 27-16 (LA)
1987—Oilers, 20-16 (H)
(Points—Rams 104, Oilers 95)

HOUSTON vs. MIAMI
RS: Dolphins lead series, 10-9
PS: Oilers lead series, 1-0
1966—Dolphins, 20-13 (H)
Dolphins, 29-28 (M)
1967—Oilers, 17-14 (H)
Oilers, 41-10 (M)
1968—Oilers, 24-10 (M)
Dolphins, 24-7 (H)
1969—Oilers, 22-10 (H)
Oilers, 32-7 (M)
1970—Dolphins, 20-10 (H)
1972—Dolphins, 34-13 (M)
1975—Oilers, 20-19 (H)
1977—Dolphins, 27-7 (M)
1978—Oilers, 35-30 (H)
*Oilers, 17-9 (M)
1979—Oilers, 9-6 (M)
1981—Dolphins, 16-10 (H)
1983—Dolphins, 24-17 (H)
1984—Dolphins, 28-10 (M)
1985—Oilers, 26-23 (H)
1986—Dolphins, 28-7 (M)
(Points—Dolphins 388, Oilers 365)
AFC First Round Playoff

HOUSTON vs. MINNESOTA
RS: Series tied, 2-2
1974—Vikings, 51-10 (M)
1980—Oilers, 20-16 (H)
1983—Vikings, 34-14 (M)
1986—Oilers, 23-10 (H)
(Points—Vikings 111, Oilers 67)

HOUSTON vs. *NEW ENGLAND
RS: Patriots lead series, 15-13-1
PS: Oilers lead series, 1-0
1960—Oilers, 24-10 (B)
Oilers, 37-21 (H)
1961—Tie, 31-31 (B)
Oilers, 27-15 (H)
1962—Patriots, 34-21 (B)
Oilers, 21-17 (H)
1963—Patriots, 45-3 (B)
Patriots, 46-28 (H)
1964—Patriots, 25-24 (B)
Patriots, 34-17 (H)
1965—Oilers, 31-10 (H)
Patriots, 42-14 (B)
1966—Patriots, 27-21 (B)
Patriots, 38-14 (H)
1967—Patriots, 18-7 (B)
Oilers, 27-6 (H)
1968—Oilers, 16-0 (B)
Oilers, 45-17 (H)
1969—Patriots, 24-0 (B)
Oilers, 27-23 (H)
1971—Patriots, 28-20 (NE)
1973—Patriots, 32-0 (H)
1975—Oilers, 7-0 (NE)
1978—Oilers, 26-23 (NE)
**Oilers, 31-14 (NE)
1980—Oilers, 38-34 (H)
1981—Patriots, 38-10 (NE)
1982—Patriots, 29-21 (NE)
1987—Patriots, 21-7 (H)
1988—Oilers, 31-6 (H)
(Points—Patriots 708, Oilers 626)
Franchise in Boston prior to 1971
**AFC Divisional Playoff*

HOUSTON vs. NEW ORLEANS
RS: Saints lead series, 3-2-1
1971—Tie, 13-13 (H)
1976—Oilers, 31-26 (NO)
1978—Oilers, 17-12 (NO)
1981—Saints, 27-24 (H)
1984—Saints, 27-10 (H)
1987—Saints, 24-10 (NO)
(Points—Saints 129, Oilers 105)

HOUSTON vs. N.Y. GIANTS
RS: Giants lead series, 3-0
1973—Giants, 34-14 (NY)
1982—Giants, 17-14 (NY)
1985—Giants, 35-14 (H)
(Points—Giants 86, Oilers 42)

HOUSTON vs. *N.Y. JETS
RS: Oilers lead series, 15-11-1
1960—Oilers, 27-21 (H)
Oilers, 42-28 (NY)
1961—Oilers, 49-13 (H)
Oilers, 48-21 (NY)
1962—Oilers, 56-17 (H)
Oilers, 44-10 (NY)
1963—Jets, 24-17 (NY)
Oilers, 31-27 (H)
1964—Jets, 24-21 (NY)
Oilers, 33-17 (H)
1965—Oilers, 27-21 (H)
Jets, 41-14 (NY)
1966—Jets, 52-13 (NY)

Oilers, 24-0 (H)
1967—Tie, 28-28 (NY)
1968—Jets, 20-14 (H)
Jets, 26-7 (NY)
1969—Jets, 26-17 (NY)
Jets, 34-26 (H)
1972—Oilers, 26-20 (H)
1974—Oilers, 27-22 (NY)
1977—Oilers, 20-0 (H)
1979—Oilers, 27-24 (H) OT
1980—Jets, 31-28 (NY) OT
1981—Jets, 33-17 (NY)
1984—Oilers, 31-20 (H)
1988—Jets, 45-3 (NY)
(Points—Oilers 717, Jets 645)
*Jets known as Titans prior to 1963

HOUSTON vs. PHILADELPHIA
RS: Eagles lead series, 4-0
1972—Eagles, 18-17 (H)
1979—Eagles, 26-20 (H)
1982—Eagles, 35-14 (P)
1988—Eagles, 32-23 (P)
(Points—Eagles 111, Oilers 74)

HOUSTON vs. *PHOENIX
RS: Cardinals lead series, 3-2
1970—Cardinals, 44-0 (StL)
1974—Cardinals, 31-27 (H)
1979—Cardinals, 24-17 (H)
1985—Oilers, 20-10 (StL)
1988—Oilers, 38-20 (H)
(Points—Cardinals 129, Oilers 102)
*Franchise in St. Louis prior to 1988

HOUSTON vs. PITTSBURGH
RS: Steelers lead series, 25-12
PS: Steelers lead series, 2-0
1970—Oilers, 19-7 (P)
Steelers, 7-3 (H)
1971—Steelers, 23-16 (P)
Oilers, 29-3 (H)
1972—Steelers, 24-7 (P)
Steelers, 9-3 (H)
1973—Steelers, 36-7 (H)
Steelers, 33-7 (P)
1974—Steelers, 13-7 (H)
Oilers, 13-10 (P)
1975—Steelers, 24-17 (P)
Steelers, 32-9 (H)
1976—Steelers, 32-16 (P)
Steelers, 21-0 (H)
1977—Oilers, 27-10 (H)
Steelers, 27-10 (P)
1978—Oilers, 24-17 (P)
Steelers, 13-3 (H)
*Steelers, 34-5 (P)
1979—Steelers, 38-7 (P)
Oilers, 20-17 (H)
*Steelers, 27-13 (P)
1980—Steelers, 31-17 (P)
Oilers, 6-0 (H)
1981—Steelers, 26-13 (P)
Oilers, 21-20 (H)
1982—Steelers, 24-10 (H)
1983—Steelers, 40-28 (H)
Steelers, 17-10 (P)
1984—Steelers, 35-7 (P)
Oilers, 23-20 (H) OT
1985—Steelers, 20-0 (P)
Steelers, 30-7 (H)
1986—Steelers, 22-16 (H) OT
Steelers, 21-10 (P)
1987—Oilers, 23-3 (P)
Oilers, 24-16 (H)
1988—Oilers, 34-14 (P)
Steelers, 37-34 (H)
(Points—Steelers 833, Oilers 545)
*AFC Championship

HOUSTON vs. *SAN DIEGO
RS: Chargers lead series, 17-10-1
PS: Oilers lead series, 3-0
1960—Oilers, 38-28 (H)
Chargers, 24-21 (LA)
**Oilers, 24-16 (H)
1961—Chargers, 34-24 (SD)
Oilers, 33-13 (H)
**Oilers, 10-3 (SD)
1962—Oilers, 42-17 (SD)
Oilers, 33-27 (H)
1963—Chargers, 27-0 (SD)
Chargers 20-14 (H)
1964—Chargers, 27-21 (SD)
Chargers, 20-17 (H)
1965—Chargers, 31-14 (SD)
Chargers, 37-26 (H)
1966—Chargers, 28-22 (H)
1967—Chargers, 13-3 (SD)
Oilers, 24-17 (H)
1968—Chargers, 30-14 (SD)
1969—Chargers, 21-17 (H)
1970—Tie, 31-31 (SD)
1971—Oilers, 49-33 (H)
1972—Chargers, 34-20 (SD)
1974—Oilers, 21-14 (H)
1975—Oilers, 33-17 (H)
1976—Chargers, 30-27 (SD)
1978—Chargers, 45-24 (H)
1979—***Oilers, 17-14 (SD)
1984—Chargers, 31-14 (SD)
1985—Oilers, 37-35 (H)
1986—Chargers, 27-0 (SD)
1987—Oilers, 33-18 (H)
(Points—Chargers 762, Oilers 703)
*Franchise in Los Angeles prior to 1961
**AFL Championship
***AFC Divisional Playoff

HOUSTON vs. SAN FRANCISCO
RS: 49ers lead series, 4-2
1970—49ers, 30-20 (H)
1975—Oilers, 27-13 (SF)
1978—Oilers, 20-19 (H)
1981—49ers, 28-6 (SF)
1984—49ers, 34-21 (H)
1987—49ers, 27-20 (SF)
(Points—49ers 151, Oilers 114)

HOUSTON vs. SEATTLE
RS: Series tied, 3-3
PS: Oilers lead series, 1-0
1977—Oilers, 22-10 (S)
1979—Seahawks, 34-14 (S)
1980—Seahawks, 26-7 (H)
1981—Oilers, 35-17 (H)
1982—Oilers, 23-21 (H)
1987—*Oilers, 23-20 (H) OT
1988—Seahawks, 27-24 (S)
(Points—Seahawks 155, Oilers 148)
*AFC First Round Playoffs

HOUSTON vs. TAMPA BAY
RS: Oilers lead series, 2-1
1976—Oilers, 20-0 (H)
1980—Oilers, 20-14 (H)
1983—Buccaneers, 33-24 (TB)
(Points—Oilers 64, Buccaneers 47)

HOUSTON vs. WASHINGTON
RS: Oilers lead series, 3-2
1971—Redskins, 22-13 (W)
1975—Oilers, 13-10 (H)
1979—Oilers, 29-27 (W)
1985—Redskins, 16-13 (W)
1988—Oilers, 41-17 (H)
(Points—Oilers 109, Redskins 92)

INDIANAPOLIS vs. ATLANTA
RS: Colts lead series, 9-0;
See Atlanta vs. Indianapolis

INDIANAPOLIS vs. BUFFALO
RS: Series tied, 18-18-1;
See Buffalo vs. Indianapolis

INDIANAPOLIS vs. CHICAGO
RS: Colts lead series, 21-15;
See Chicago vs. Indianapolis

INDIANAPOLIS vs. CINCINNATI
RS: Bengals lead series, 5-4
PS: Colts lead series, 1-0;
See Cincinnati vs. Indianapolis

INDIANAPOLIS vs. CLEVELAND
RS: Browns lead series, 11-4
PS: Series tied, 2-2;
See Cleveland vs. Indianapolis

INDIANAPOLIS vs. DALLAS
RS: Cowboys lead series, 6-2
PS: Colts lead series, 1-0;
See Dallas vs. Indianapolis

INDIANAPOLIS vs. DENVER
RS: Broncos lead series, 6-2;
See Denver vs. Indianapolis

INDIANAPOLIS vs. DETROIT
RS: Colts lead series, 17-16-2;
See Detroit vs. Indianapolis

INDIANAPOLIS vs. GREEN BAY
RS: Colts lead series, 18-17-1
PS: Packers lead series, 1-0;
See Green Bay vs. Indianapolis

INDIANAPOLIS vs. HOUSTON
RS: Colts lead series, 6-5;
See Houston vs. Indianapolis

***INDIANAPOLIS vs. KANSAS CITY**
RS: Chiefs lead series, 6-3
1970—Chiefs, 44-24 (B)
1972—Chiefs, 24-10 (KC)
1975—Colts, 28-14 (B)
1977—Colts, 17-6 (KC)
1979—Chiefs, 14-0 (KC)
Chiefs, 10-7 (B)
1980—Colts, 31-24 (KC)
Chiefs, 38-28 (B)
1985—Chiefs, 20-7 (KC)
(Points—Chiefs 194, Colts 152)
*Franchise in Baltimore prior to 1984

***INDIANAPOLIS vs **L.A. RAIDERS**
RS: Raiders lead series, 3-2
PS: Series tied, 1-1
1970—***Colts, 27-17 (B)
1971—Colts, 37-14 (O)
1973—Raiders, 34-21 (B)
1975—Raiders, 31-20 (B)
1977—****Raiders, 37-31 (B) OT
1984—Raiders, 21-7 (LA)
1986—Colts, 30-24 (LA)
(Points—Raiders 178, Colts 173)
*Franchise in Baltimore prior to 1984
**Franchise in Oakland prior to 1982
***AFC Championship
****AFC Divisional Playoff

***INDIANAPOLIS vs. L.A. RAMS**
RS: Colts lead series, 20-15-2
1953—Rams, 21-13 (B)
Rams, 45-2 (LA)
1954—Rams, 48-0 (B)
Colts, 22-21 (LA)
1955—Tie, 17-17 (B)
Rams, 20-14 (LA)
1956—Colts, 56-21 (B)
Rams, 31-7 (LA)
1957—Colts, 31-14 (B)
Rams, 37-21 (LA)
1958—Colts, 34-7 (B)
Rams, 30-28 (LA)
1959—Colts, 35-21 (B)
Colts, 45-26 (LA)
1960—Colts, 31-17 (B)
Rams, 10-3 (LA)
1961—Colts, 27-24 (B)
Rams, 34-17 (LA)
1962—Colts, 30-27 (B)
Colts, 14-2 (LA)
1963—Rams, 17-16 (LA)
Colts, 19-16 (B)
1964—Colts, 35-20 (B)
Colts, 24-7 (LA)
1965—Colts, 35-20 (B)
Colts, 20-17 (LA)
1966—Colts, 17-3 (LA)
Rams, 23-7 (B)
1967—Tie, 24-24 (B)
Rams, 34-10 (LA)
1968—Colts, 27-10 (B)
Colts, 28-24 (LA)
1969—Rams, 27-20 (B)
Colts, 13-7 (LA)
1971—Colts, 24-17 (B)
1975—Rams, 24-13 (LA)
1986—Rams, 24-7 (I)
(Points—Rams 787, Colts 786)
*Franchise in Baltimore prior to 1984

***INDIANAPOLIS vs. MIAMI**
RS: Dolphins lead series, 26-12
PS: Dolphins lead series, 1-0
1970—Colts, 35-0 (B)
Dolphins, 34-17 (M)
1971—Dolphins, 17-14 (M)
Colts, 14-3 (B)
**Dolphins, 21-0 (M)
1972—Dolphins, 23-0 (B)
Dolphins, 16-0 (M)
1973—Dolphins, 44-0 (M)
Colts, 16-3 (B)
1974—Dolphins, 17-7 (M)
Dolphins, 17-16 (B)
1975—Colts, 33-17 (M)
Colts, 10-7 (B) OT
1976—Colts, 28-14 (B)
Colts, 17-16 (M)
1977—Colts, 45-28 (B)
Dolphins, 17-6 (M)
1978—Dolphins, 42-0 (B)
Dolphins, 26-8 (M)
1979—Dolphins, 19-0 (M)
Dolphins, 28-24 (B)
1980—Colts, 30-17 (M)
Dolphins, 24-14 (B)
1981—Dolphins, 31-28 (B)
Dolphins, 27-10 (M)
1982—Dolphins, 24-20 (M)
Dolphins, 34-7 (B)
1983—Dolphins, 21-7 (B)
Dolphins, 37-0 (M)
1984—Dolphins, 44-7 (M)
Dolphins, 35-17 (I)
1985—Dolphins, 30-13 (M)
Dolphins, 34-20 (I)
1986—Dolphins, 30-10 (M)
Dolphins, 17-13 (I)
1987—Dolphins, 23-10 (I)
Colts, 40-21 (M)
1988—Colts, 15-13 (I)
Colts, 31-28 (M)
(Points—Dolphins 899, Colts 582)
*Franchise in Baltimore prior to 1984
**AFC Championship

***INDIANAPOLIS vs. MINNESOTA**
RS: Colts lead series, 11-6-1
PS: Colts lead series, 1-0
1961—Colts, 34-33 (B)
Vikings, 28-20 (M)
1962—Colts, 34-7 (M)
Colts, 42-17 (B)
1963—Colts, 37-34 (M)
Colts, 41-10 (B)
1964—Vikings, 34-24 (M)
Colts, 17-14 (B)
1965—Colts, 35-16 (B)
Colts, 41-21 (M)
1966—Colts, 38-23 (M)
Colts, 20-17 (B)
1967—Tie, 20-20 (M)
1968—Colts, 21-9 (B)
**Colts, 24-14 (B)
1969—Vikings, 52-14 (M)
1971—Vikings, 10-3 (M)
1982—Vikings, 13-10 (M)
1988—Vikings, 12-3 (M)
(Points—Colts 478, Vikings 384)
*Franchise in Baltimore prior to 1984
**Conference Championship

***INDIANAPOLIS vs. **NEW ENGLAND**
RS: Patriots lead series, 20-17
1970—Colts, 14-6 (Bos)
Colts, 27-3 (Balt)
1971—Colts, 23-3 (NE)
Patriots, 21-17 (Balt)
1972—Colts, 24-17 (NE)
Colts, 31-0 (Balt)
1973—Patriots, 24-16 (NE)
Colts, 18-13 (Balt)
1974—Patriots, 42-3 (NE)
Patriots, 27-17 (Balt)
1975—Patriots, 21-10 (NE)
Colts, 34-21 (Balt)
1976—Colts, 27-13 (NE)
Patriots, 21-14 (Balt)
1977—Patriots, 17-3 (NE)
Colts, 30-24 (Balt)
1978—Colts, 34-27 (NE)
Patriots, 35-14 (Balt)
1979—Colts, 31-26 (Balt)
Patriots, 50-21 (NE)
1980—Patriots, 37-21 (Balt)
Patriots, 47-21 (NE)
1981—Colts, 29-28 (NE)
Colts, 23-21 (Balt)
1982—Patriots, 24-13 (Balt)
1983—Colts, 29-23 (NE) OT
Colts, 12-7 (B)
1984—Patriots, 50-17 (I)
Patriots, 16-10 (NE)
1985—Patriots, 34-15 (NE)
Patriots, 38-31 (I)
1986—Patriots, 33-3 (NE)
Patriots, 30-21 (I)
1987—Colts, 30-16 (I)
Patriots, 24-0 (NE)
1988—Patriots, 21-17 (NE)
Colts, 24-21 (I)
(Points—Patriots 881, Colts 724)
*Franchise in Baltimore prior to 1984
**Franchise in Boston prior to 1971

***INDIANAPOLIS vs. NEW ORLEANS**
RS: Colts lead series, 3-1
1967—Colts, 30-10 (B)
1969—Colts, 30-10 (NO)
1973—Colts, 14-10 (B)
1986—Saints, 17-14 (I)
(Points—Colts 88, Saints 47)
*Franchise in Baltimore prior to 1984

***INDIANAPOLIS vs. N.Y. GIANTS**
RS: Colts lead series, 5-3
PS: Colts lead series, 2-0
1954—Colts, 20-14 (B)
1955—Giants, 17-7 (NY)
1958—Giants, 24-21 (NY)
**Colts, 23-17 (NY) OT
1959—**Colts, 31-16 (B)
1963—Giants, 37-28 (B)
1968—Colts, 26-0 (NY)
1971—Colts, 31-7 (NY)
1975—Colts, 21-0 (NY)
1979—Colts, 31-7 (NY)
(Points—Colts 239, Giants 139)
*Franchise in Baltimore prior to 1984
**NFL Championship

***INDIANAPOLIS vs. N.Y. JETS**
RS: Colts lead series, 19-18
PS: Jets lead series, 1-0
1968—**Jets 16-7 (Miami)
1970—Colts, 29-22 (NY)
Colts, 35-20 (B)
1971—Colts, 22-0 (B)
Colts, 14-13 (NY)
1972—Jets, 44-34 (B)
Jets, 24-20 (NY)
1973—Jets, 34-10 (B)
Jets, 20-17 (NY)
1974—Colts, 35-20 (NY)
Jets, 45-38 (B)
1975—Colts, 45-28 (NY)
Colts, 52-19 (B)
1976—Colts, 20-0 (NY)
Colts, 33-16 (B)
1977—Colts, 20-12 (NY)
Colts, 33-12 (B)
1978—Jets, 33-10 (B)
Jets, 24-16 (NY)
1979—Colts, 10-8 (B)

Jets, 30-17 (NY)
1980—Colts, 17-14 (NY)
Colts, 35-21 (B)
1981—Jets, 41-14 (B)
Jets, 25-0 (NY)
1982—Jets, 37-0 (NY)
1983—Colts, 17-14 (NY)
Jets, 10-6 (B)
1984—Jets, 23-14 (I)
Colts, 9-5 (NY)
1985—Jets, 25-20 (NY)
Jets, 35-17 (I)
1986—Jets, 26-7 (I)
Jets, 31-16 (NY)
1987—Colts, 6-0 (I)
Colts, 19-14 (NY)
1988—Colts, 38-14 (I)
Jets, 34-16 (NY)
(Points—Jets 809, Colts 768)
*Franchise in Baltimore prior to 1984
**Super Bowl III

*INDIANAPOLIS vs. PHILADELPHIA
RS: Series tied, 5-5
1953—Eagles, 45-14 (P)
1965—Colts, 34-24 (B)
1967—Colts, 38-6 (P)
1969—Colts, 24-20 (B)
1970—Colts, 29-10 (B)
1974—Eagles, 30-10 (P)
1978—Eagles, 17-14 (B)
1981—Eagles, 38-13 (P)
1983—Colts, 22-21 (P)
1984—Eagles, 16-7 (P)
(Points—Eagles 227, Colts 205)
*Franchise in Baltimore prior to 1984

*INDIANAPOLIS vs. **PHOENIX
RS: Cardinals lead series, 5-4
1961—Colts, 16-0 (B)
1964—Colts, 47-27 (B)
1968—Colts, 27-0 (B)
1972—Cardinals, 10-3 (B)
1976—Cardinals, 24-17 (StL)
1978—Colts, 30-17 (StL)
1980—Cardinals, 17-10 (B)
1981—Cardinals, 35-24 (B)
1984—Cardinals, 34-33 (I)
(Points—Colts 207, Cardinals 164)
*Franchise in Baltimore prior to 1984
**Franchise in St. Louis prior to 1988

*INDIANAPOLIS vs. PITTSBURGH
RS: Steelers lead series, 8-4
PS: Steelers lead series, 2-0
1957—Steelers, 19-13 (B)
1968—Colts, 41-7 (P)
1971—Colts, 34-21 (B)
1974—Steelers, 30-0 (B)
1975—**Steelers, 28-10 (P)
1976—**Steelers, 40-14 (B)
1977—Colts, 31-21 (B)
1978—Steelers, 35-13 (P)
1979—Steelers, 17-13 (P)
1980—Steelers, 20-17 (B)
1983—Steelers, 24-13 (B)
1984—Colts, 17-16 (I)
1985—Steelers, 45-3 (P)
1987—Steelers, 21-7 (P)
(Points—Steelers 344, Colts 226)
*Franchise in Baltimore prior to 1984
**AFC Divisional Playoff

*INDIANAPOLIS vs. SAN DIEGO
RS: Chargers lead series, 6-4
1970—Colts, 16-14 (SD)
1972—Chargers, 23-20 (B)
1976—Colts, 37-21 (SD)
1981—Chargers, 43-14 (B)
1982—Chargers, 44-26 (SD)
1984—Chargers, 38-10 (I)
1986—Chargers, 17-3 (I)
1987—Chargers, 16-13 (I)
Colts, 20-7 (SD)
1988—Colts, 16-0 (SD)
(Points—Chargers 223, Colts 175)
*Franchise in Baltimore prior to 1984

*INDIANAPOLIS vs. SAN FRANCISCO
RS: Colts lead series, 21-15
1953—49ers, 38-21 (B)
49ers, 45-14 (SF)
1954—Colts, 17-13 (B)
49ers, 10-7 (SF)
1955—Colts, 26-14 (B)
49ers, 35-24 (SF)
1956—49ers, 20-17 (B)
49ers, 30-17 (SF)
1957—Colts, 27-21 (B)
49ers, 17-13 (SF)
1958—Colts, 35-27 (B)
49ers, 21-12 (SF)
1959—Colts, 45-14 (B)
Colts, 34-14 (SF)
1960—49ers, 30-22 (B)
49ers, 34-10 (SF)
1961—Colts, 20-17 (B)
Colts, 27-24 (SF)
1962—49ers, 21-13 (B)
Colts, 22-3 (SF)
1963—Colts, 20-14 (SF)
Colts, 20-3 (B)
1964—Colts, 37-7 (B)
Colts, 14-3 (SF)
1965—Colts, 27-24 (B)
Colts, 34-28 (SF)
1966—Colts, 36-14 (B)
Colts, 30-14 (SF)
1967—Colts, 41-7 (B)
Colts, 26-9 (SF)
1968—Colts, 27-10 (B)
Colts, 42-14 (SF)
1969—49ers, 24-21 (B)
49ers, 20-17 (SF)
1972—49ers, 24-21 (SF)
1986—49ers, 35-14 (SF)
(Points—Colts 850, 49ers 698)
*Franchise in Baltimore prior to 1984

*INDIANAPOLIS vs. SEATTLE
RS: Colts lead series, 2-0
1977—Colts, 29-14 (S)
1978—Colts, 17-14 (S)
(Points—Colts 46, Seahawks 28)
*Franchise in Baltimore prior to 1984

*INDIANAPOLIS vs. TAMPA BAY
RS: Colts lead series, 4-1
1976—Colts, 42-17 (B)
1979—Buccaneers, 29-26 (B) OT
1985—Colts, 31-23 (TB)
1987—Colts, 24-6 (I)
1988—Colts, 35-31 (I)
(Points—Colts 158, Buccaneers 106)
*Franchise in Baltimore prior to 1984

*INDIANAPOLIS vs. WASHINGTON
RS: Colts lead series, 15-6
1953—Colts, 27-17 (B)
1954—Redskins, 24-21 (W)
1955—Redskins, 14-13 (B)
1956—Colts, 19-17 (B)
1957—Colts, 21-17 (W)
1958—Colts, 35-10 (B)
1959—Redskins, 27-24 (W)
1960—Colts, 20-0 (B)
1961—Colts, 27-6 (W)
1962—Colts, 34-21 (B)
1963—Colts, 36-20 (W)
1964—Colts, 45-17 (B)
1965—Colts, 38-7 (W)
1966—Colts, 37-10 (B)
1967—Colts, 17-13 (W)
1969—Colts, 41-17 (B)
1973—Redskins, 22-14 (W)
1977—Colts, 10-3 (B)
1978—Colts, 21-17 (B)
1981—Redskins, 38-14 (W)
1984—Redskins, 35-7 (I)
(Points—Colts 521, Redskins 352)
*Franchise in Baltimore prior to 1984

KANSAS CITY vs. ATLANTA
RS: Chiefs lead series, 2-0;
See Atlanta vs. Kansas City

KANSAS CITY vs. BUFFALO
RS: Bills lead series, 15-11-1
PS: Chiefs lead series, 1-0;
See Buffalo vs. Kansas City

KANSAS CITY vs. CHICAGO
RS: Bears lead series, 3-1;
See Chicago vs. Kansas City

KANSAS CITY vs. CINCINNATI
RS: Chiefs lead series, 10-8;
See Cincinnati vs. Kansas City

KANSAS CITY vs. CLEVELAND
RS: Browns lead series, 6-5-1;
See Cleveland vs. Kansas City

KANSAS CITY vs. DALLAS
RS: Cowboys lead series, 2-1;
See Dallas vs. Kansas City

KANSAS CITY vs. DENVER
RS: Chiefs lead series, 35-22;
See Denver vs. Kansas City

KANSAS CITY vs. DETROIT
RS: Series tied, 3-3;
See Detroit vs. Kansas City

KANSAS CITY vs. GREEN BAY
RS: Series tied, 1-1-1
PS: Packers lead series, 1-0;
See Green Bay vs. Kansas City

KANSAS CITY vs. HOUSTON
RS: Chiefs lead series, 20-13
PS: Chiefs lead series, 1-0;
See Houston vs. Kansas City

KANSAS CITY vs. INDIANAPOLIS
RS: Chiefs lead series, 6-3;
See Indianapolis vs. Kansas City

*KANSAS CITY vs. **L.A. RAIDERS
RS: Raiders lead series, 33-22-2
PS: Series tied, 1-1
1960—Texans, 34-16 (O)
Raiders, 20-19 (D)
1961—Texans, 42-35 (O)
Texans, 43-11 (D)
1962—Texans, 26-16 (O)
Texans, 35-7 (D)
1963—Raiders, 10-7 (O)
Raiders, 22-7 (KC)
1964—Chiefs, 21-9 (O)
Chiefs, 42-7 (KC)
1965—Raiders, 37-10 (O)
Chiefs, 14-7 (KC)
1966—Chiefs, 32-10 (O)
Raiders, 34-13 (KC)
1967—Raiders, 23-21 (O)
Raiders, 44-22 (KC)
1968—Chiefs, 24-10 (KC)
Raiders, 38-21 (O)
***Raiders, 41-6 (O)
1969—Raiders, 27-24 (KC)
Raiders, 10-6 (O)
****Chiefs, 17-7 (O)
1970—Tie, 17-17 (KC)
Raiders, 20-6 (O)
1971—Tie, 20-20 (O)
Chiefs, 16-14 (KC)
1972—Chiefs, 27-14 (KC)
Raiders, 26-3 (O)
1973—Chiefs, 16-3 (KC)
Raiders, 37-7 (O)
1974—Raiders, 27-7 (O)
Raiders, 7-6 (KC)
1975—Chiefs, 42-10 (KC)
Raiders, 28-20 (O)
1976—Raiders, 24-21 (KC)
Raiders, 21-10 (O)
1977—Raiders, 37-28 (KC)
Raiders, 21-20 (O)
1978—Raiders, 28-6 (O)
Raiders, 20-10 (KC)
1979—Chiefs, 35-7 (KC)
Chiefs, 24-21 (O)
1980—Raiders, 27-14 (KC)
Chiefs, 31-17 (O)
1981—Chiefs, 27-0 (KC)
Chiefs, 28-17 (O)
1982—Raiders, 21-16 (KC)
1983—Raiders, 21-20 (LA)
Raiders, 28-20 (KC)
1984—Raiders, 22-20 (KC)
Raiders, 17-7 (LA)
1985—Chiefs, 36-20 (KC)
Raiders, 19-10 (LA)
1986—Raiders, 24-17 (KC)
Chiefs, 20-17 (LA)
1987—Raiders, 35-17 (LA)
Chiefs, 16-10 (KC)
1988—Raiders, 27-17 (KC)
Raiders, 17-10 (LA)
(Points—Raiders 1,182, Chiefs 1,153)
*Franchise in Dallas prior to 1963 and known as Texans
**Franchise in Oakland prior to 1982
***Division Playoff
****AFL Championship

KANSAS CITY vs. L.A. RAMS
RS: Rams lead series, 3-0
1973—Rams, 23-13 (KC)
1982—Rams, 20-14 (LA)
1985—Rams, 16-0 (KC)
(Points—Rams 59, Chiefs 27)

KANSAS CITY vs. MIAMI
RS: Chiefs lead series, 7-6
PS: Dolphins lead series, 1-0
1966—Chiefs, 34-16 (KC)
Chiefs, 19-18 (M)
1967—Chiefs, 24-0 (M)
Chiefs, 41-0 (KC)
1968—Chiefs, 48-3 (M)
1969—Chiefs, 17-10 (KC)
1971—*Dolphins, 27-24 (KC) OT
1972—Dolphins, 20-10 (KC)
1974—Dolphins, 9-3 (M)
1976—Chiefs, 20-17 (M) OT
1981—Dolphins, 17-7 (KC)
1983—Dolphins, 14-6 (M)
1985—Dolphins, 31-0 (M)
1987—Dolphins, 42-0 (M)
(Points—Chiefs 253, Dolphins 224)
*AFC Divisional Playoff

KANSAS CITY vs. MINNESOTA
RS: Vikings lead series, 2-1
PS: Chiefs lead series, 1-0
1969—*Chiefs, 23-7 (New Orleans)
1970—Vikings, 27-10 (M)
1974—Vikings, 35-15 (KC)
1981—Chiefs, 10-6 (M)
(Points—Vikings 75, Chiefs 58)
*Super Bowl IV

*KANSAS CITY vs. **NEW ENGLAND
RS: Chiefs lead series, 11-7-3
1960—Patriots, 42-14 (B)
Texans, 34-0 (D)
1961—Patriots, 18-17 (D)
Patriots, 28-21 (B)
1962—Texans, 42-28 (D)
Texans, 27-7 (B)
1963—Tie, 24-24 (B)
Chiefs, 35-3 (KC)
1964—Patriots, 24-7 (B)
Patriots, 31-24 (KC)
1965—Chiefs, 27-17 (KC)
Tie, 10-10 (B)
1966—Chiefs, 43-24 (B)
Tie, 27-27 (KC)
1967—Chiefs, 33-10 (B)
1968—Chiefs, 31-17 (KC)
1969—Chiefs, 31-0 (B)
1970—Chiefs, 23-10 (KC)
1973—Chiefs, 10-7 (NE)
1977—Patriots, 21-17 (NE)
1981—Patriots, 33-17 (NE)
(Points—Chiefs 514, Patriots 381)
*Franchise located in Dallas prior to 1963 and known as Texans
**Franchise in Boston prior to 1971

KANSAS CITY vs. NEW ORLEANS
RS: Series tied, 2-2
1972—Chiefs, 20-17 (NO)
1976—Saints, 27-17 (KC)
1982—Saints, 27-17 (NO)
1985—Chiefs, 47-27 (NO)
(Points—Chiefs 101, Saints 98)

KANSAS CITY vs. N.Y. GIANTS
RS: Giants lead series, 5-1
1974—Giants, 33-27 (KC)
1978—Giants, 26-10 (NY)
1979—Giants, 21-17 (KC)
1983—Chiefs, 38-17 (KC)
1984—Giants, 28-27 (NY)
1988—Giants, 28-12 (NY)
(Points—Giants 153, Chiefs 131)

*KANSAS CITY vs. **N.Y. JETS
RS: Chiefs lead series, 13-12-1
PS: Series tied, 1-1
1960—Titans, 37-35 (D)
Titans, 41-35 (NY)
1961—Titans, 28-7 (NY)
Texans, 35-24 (D)
1962—Texans, 20-17 (D)
Texans, 52-31 (NY)
1963—Jets, 17-0 (NY)
Chiefs, 48-0 (KC)
1964—Jets, 27-14 (NY)
Chiefs, 24-7 (KC)
1965—Chiefs, 14-10 (NY)
Jets, 13-10 (KC)
1966—Chiefs, 32-24 (NY)
1967—Chiefs, 42-18 (KC)
Chiefs, 21-7 (NY)
1968—Jets, 20-19 (KC)
1969—Chiefs, 34-16 (NY)
***Chiefs, 13-6 (NY)
1971—Jets, 13-10 (NY)
1974—Chiefs, 24-16 (KC)
1975—Jets, 30-24 (KC)
1982—Chiefs, 37-13 (KC)
1984—Jets, 17-16 (KC)
Jets, 28-7 (NY)
1986—****Jets, 35-15 (NY)
1987—Jets, 16-9 (KC)
1988—Tie, 17-17 (NY)
Chiefs, 38-34 (KC)
(Points—Chiefs 652, Jets 562)
*Franchise in Dallas prior to 1963 and known as Texans
**Jets known as Titans prior to 1963
***Inter-Divisional Playoff
****AFC First Round Playoff

KANSAS CITY vs. PHILADELPHIA
RS: Eagles lead series, 1-0
1972—Eagles, 21-20 (KC)

KANSAS CITY vs. *PHOENIX
RS: Chiefs lead series, 3-1-1
1970—Tie, 6-6 (KC)
1974—Chiefs, 17-13 (StL)
1980—Chiefs, 21-13 (StL)
1983—Chiefs, 38-14 (KC)
1986—Cardinals, 23-14 (StL)
(Points—Chiefs 96, Cardinals 69)
*Franchise in St. Louis prior to 1988

KANSAS CITY vs. PITTSBURGH
RS: Steelers lead series, 11-5
1970—Chiefs, 31-14 (P)
1971—Chiefs, 38-16 (KC)
1972—Steelers, 16-7 (P)
1974—Steelers, 34-24 (KC)
1975—Steelers, 28-3 (P)
1976—Steelers, 45-0 (KC)
1978—Steelers, 27-24 (P)
1979—Steelers, 30-3 (KC)
1980—Steelers, 21-16 (P)
1981—Chiefs, 37-33 (P)
1982—Steelers, 35-14 (P)
1984—Chiefs, 37-27 (P)
1985—Steelers, 36-28 (KC)
1986—Chiefs, 24-19 (P)
1987—Steelers, 17-16 (KC)
1988—Steelers, 16-10 (P)

(Points—Steelers 414, Chiefs 312)
***KANSAS CITY vs. **SAN DIEGO**
RS: Chargers lead series, 29-27-1
1960—Chargers, 21-20 (LA)
Texans, 17-0 (D)
1961—Chargers, 26-10 (D)
Chargers, 24-14 (SD)
1962—Chargers, 32-28 (SD)
Texans, 26-17 (D)
1963—Chargers, 24-10 (SD)
Chargers, 38-17 (KC)
1964—Chargers, 28-14 (KC)
Chiefs, 49-6 (SD)
1965—Tie, 10-10 (SD)
Chiefs, 31-7 (KC)
1966—Chiefs, 24-14 (KC)
Chiefs, 27-17 (SD)
1967—Chargers, 45-31 (SD)
Chargers, 17-16 (KC)
1968—Chiefs, 27-20 (KC)
Chiefs, 40-3 (SD)
1969—Chiefs, 27-9 (SD)
Chiefs, 27-3 (KC)
1970—Chiefs, 26-14 (KC)
Chargers, 31-13 (SD)
1971—Chargers, 21-14 (SD)
Chiefs, 31-10 (KC)
1972—Chiefs, 26-14 (SD)
Chargers, 27-17 (KC)
1973—Chiefs, 19-0 (SD)
Chiefs, 33-6 (KC)
1974—Chiefs, 24-14 (SD)
Chargers, 14-7 (KC)
1975—Chiefs, 12-10 (SD)
Chargers, 28-20 (KC)
1976—Chargers, 30-16 (KC)
Chiefs, 23-20 (SD)
1977—Chargers, 23-7 (KC)
Chiefs, 21-16 (SD)
1978—Chargers, 29-23 (SD) OT
Chiefs, 23-0 (KC)
1979—Chargers, 20-14 (KC)
Chargers, 28-7 (SD)
1980—Chargers, 24-7 (KC)
Chargers, 20-7 (SD)
1981—Chargers, 42-31 (KC)
Chargers, 22-20 (SD)
1982—Chiefs, 19-12 (KC)
1983—Chargers, 17-14 (KC)
Chargers, 41-38 (SD)
1984—Chiefs, 31-13 (KC)
Chiefs, 42-21 (SD)
1985—Chargers, 31-20 (SD)
Chiefs, 38-34 (KC)
1986—Chiefs, 42-41 (KC)
Chiefs, 24-23 (SD)
1987—Chiefs, 20-13 (KC)
Chargers, 42-21 (SD)
1988—Chargers, 24-23 (KC)
Chargers, 24-13 (SD)
(Points—Chiefs 1,251, Chargers 1,160)
**Franchise in Dallas prior to 1963 and known as Texans*
***Franchise in Los Angeles prior to 1961*
KANSAS CITY vs. SAN FRANCISCO
RS: 49ers lead series, 3-1
1971—Chiefs, 26-17 (SF)
1975—49ers, 20-3 (KC)
1982—49ers, 26-13 (KC)
1985—49ers, 31-3 (SF)
(Points—49ers 94, Chiefs 45)
KANSAS CITY vs. SEATTLE
RS: Chiefs lead series, 11-10
1977—Seahawks, 34-31 (KC)
1978—Seahawks, 13-10 (KC)
Seahawks, 23-19 (S)
1979—Chiefs, 24-6 (S)
Chiefs, 37-21 (KC)
1980—Seahawks, 17-16 (KC)
Chiefs, 31-30 (S)
1981—Chiefs, 20-14 (S)
Chiefs, 40-13 (KC)
1983—Chiefs, 17-13 (KC)
Seahawks, 51-48 (S) OT
1984—Seahawks, 45-0 (S)
Chiefs, 34-7 (KC)
1985—Chiefs, 28-7 (KC)
Seahawks, 24-6 (S)
1986—Seahawks, 23-17 (S)
Chiefs, 27-7 (KC)
1987—Seahawks, 43-14 (S)
Chiefs, 41-20 (KC)
1988—Seahawks, 31-10 (S)
Chiefs, 27-24 (KC)
(Points—Chiefs 497, Seahawks 466)
KANSAS CITY vs. TAMPA BAY
RS: Chiefs lead series, 4-2
1976—Chiefs, 28-19 (TB)
1978—Buccaneers, 30-13 (KC)
1979—Buccaneers, 3-0 (TB)
1981—Chiefs, 19-10 (KC)
1984—Chiefs, 24-20 (KC)
1986—Chiefs, 27-20 (KC)
(Points—Chiefs 111, Buccaneers 102)
KANSAS CITY vs. WASHINGTON
RS: Chiefs lead series, 2-1
1971—Chiefs, 27-20 (KC)
1976—Chiefs, 33-30 (W)
1983—Redskins, 27-12 (W)
(Points—Redskins 77, Chiefs 72)

L.A. RAIDERS vs. ATLANTA
RS: Raiders lead series, 4-2;
See Atlanta vs. L.A. Raiders
L.A. RAIDERS vs. BUFFALO
RS: Raiders lead series, 13-12;
See Buffalo vs. L.A. Raiders
L.A. RAIDERS vs. CHICAGO
RS: Series tied, 3-3;
See Chicago vs. L.A. Raiders
L.A. RAIDERS vs. CINCINNATI
RS: Raiders lead series, 11-5
PS: Raiders lead series, 1-0;
See Cincinnati vs. L.A. Raiders
L.A. RAIDERS vs. CLEVELAND
RS: Raiders lead series, 8-2
PS: Raiders lead series, 2-0;
See Cleveland vs. L.A. Raiders
L.A. RAIDERS vs. DALLAS
RS: Raiders lead series, 3-1;
See Dallas vs. L.A. Raiders
L.A. RAIDERS vs. DENVER
RS: Raiders lead series, 38-17-2
PS: Broncos lead series, 1-0;
See Denver vs. L.A. Raiders
L.A. RAIDERS vs. DETROIT
RS: Raiders lead series, 4-2;
See Detroit vs. L.A. Raiders
L.A. RAIDERS vs. GREEN BAY
RS: Raiders lead series, 5-0
PS: Packers lead series, 1-0;
See Green Bay vs. L.A. Raiders
L.A. RAIDERS vs. HOUSTON
RS: Raiders lead series, 19-11
PS: Raiders lead series, 3-0;
See Houston vs. L.A. Raiders
L.A. RAIDERS vs. INDIANAPOLIS
RS: Raiders lead series, 3-2
PS: Series tied, 1-1;
See Indianapolis vs. L.A. Raiders
L.A. RAIDERS vs. KANSAS CITY
RS: Raiders lead series, 33-22-2
PS: Series tied, 1-1;
See Kansas City vs. L.A. Raiders
***L.A. RAIDERS vs. L.A. RAMS**
RS: Raiders lead series, 4-2
1972—Raiders, 45-17 (O)
1977—Rams, 20-14 (LA)
1979—Raiders, 24-17 (LA)
1982—Raiders, 37-31 (LA Raiders)
1985—Raiders, 16-6 (LA Rams)
1988—Rams, 22-17 (LA Raiders)
(Points—Raiders 153, Rams 113)
**Franchise in Oakland prior to 1982*
***L.A. RAIDERS vs. MIAMI**
RS: Raiders lead series, 13-3-1
PS: Raiders lead series, 2-1
1966—Raiders, 23-14 (M)
Raiders, 21-10 (O)
1967—Raiders, 31-17 (O)
1968—Raiders, 47-21 (M)
1969—Raiders, 20-17 (O)
Tie, 20-20 (M)
1970—Dolphins, 20-13 (M)
**Raiders, 21-14 (O)
1973—Raiders, 12-7 (O)
***Dolphins, 27-10 (M)
1974—**Raiders, 28-26 (O)
1975—Raiders, 31-21 (M)
1978—Dolphins, 23-6 (M)
1979—Raiders, 13-3 (O)
1980—Raiders, 16-10 (O)
1981—Raiders, 33-17 (M)
1983—Raiders, 27-14 (LA)
1984—Raiders, 45-34 (M)
1986—Raiders, 30-28 (M)
1988—Dolphins, 24-14 (LA)
(Points—Raiders 461, Dolphins 367)
**Franchise in Oakland prior to 1982*
***AFC Divisional Playoff*
****AFC Championship*
***L.A. RAIDERS vs. MINNESOTA**
RS: Raiders lead series, 4-2
PS: Raiders lead series, 1-0
1973—Vikings, 24-16 (M)
1976—**Raiders, 32-14 (Pasadena)
1977—Raiders, 35-13 (O)
1978—Raiders, 27-20 (O)
1981—Raiders, 36-10 (M)
1984—Raiders, 23-20 (LA)
1987—Vikings, 31-20 (M)
(Points—Raiders 189, Vikings 132)
**Franchise in Oakland prior to 1982*
***Super Bowl XI*
***L.A. RAIDERS vs. **NEW ENGLAND**
RS: Patriots lead series, 12-11-1
PS: Series tied, 1-1
1960—Raiders, 27-14 (O)
Patriots, 34-28 (B)
1961—Patriots, 20-17 (B)
Patriots, 35-21 (O)
1962—Patriots, 26-16 (B)
Raiders, 20-0 (O)
1963—Patriots, 20-14 (O)
Patriots, 20-14 (B)
1964—Patriots, 17-14 (O)
Tie, 43-43 (B)
1965—Raiders, 24-10 (B)
Raiders, 30-21 (O)
1966—Patriots, 24-21 (B)
1967—Raiders, 35-7 (O)
Raiders, 48-14 (B)
1968—Raiders, 41-10 (O)
1969—Raiders, 38-23 (B)
1971—Patriots, 20-6 (NE)
1974—Raiders, 41-26 (O)
1976—Patriots, 48-17 (NE)
***Raiders, 24-21 (O)
1978—Patriots, 21-14 (O)
1981—Raiders, 27-17 (O)
1985—Raiders, 35-20 (NE)
***Patriots, 27-20 (LA)
1987—Patriots, 26-23 (NE)
(Points—Raiders 658, Patriots 564)
**Franchise in Oakland prior to 1982*
***Franchise in Boston prior to 1971*
****AFC Divisional Playoff*
***L.A. RAIDERS vs. NEW ORLEANS**
RS: Raiders lead series, 3-1-1
1971—Tie, 21-21 (NO)
1975—Raiders, 48-10 (O)
1979—Raiders, 42-35 (NO)
1985—Raiders, 23-13 (LA)
1988—Saints, 20-6 (NO)
(Points—Raiders 140, Saints 99)
**Franchise in Oakland prior to 1982*
***L.A. RAIDERS vs. N.Y. GIANTS**
RS: Raiders lead series, 3-1
1973—Raiders, 42-0 (O)
1980—Raiders, 33-17 (NY)
1983—Raiders, 27-12 (LA)
1986—Giants, 14-9 (LA)
(Points—Raiders 111, Giants 43)
**Franchise in Oakland prior to 1982*
***L.A. RAIDERS vs. **N.Y. JETS**
RS: Raiders lead series, 12-9-2
PS: Jets lead series, 2-0
1960—Raiders, 28-27 (NY)
Titans, 31-28 (O)
1961—Titans, 14-6 (O)
Titans, 23-12 (NY)
1962—Titans, 28-17 (O)
Titans, 31-21 (NY)
1963—Jets, 10-7 (NY)
Raiders, 49-26 (O)
1964—Jets, 35-13 (NY)
Raiders, 35-26 (O)
1965—Tie, 24-24 (NY)
Raiders, 24-14 (O)
1966—Raiders, 24-21 (NY)
Tie, 28-28 (O)
1967—Jets, 27-14 (NY)
Raiders, 38-29 (O)
1968—Raiders, 43-32 (O)
***Jets, 27-23 (NY)
1969—Raiders, 27-14 (NY)
1970—Raiders, 14-13 (NY)
1972—Raiders, 24-16 (O)
1977—Raiders, 28-27 (NY)
1979—Jets, 28-19 (NY)
1982—****Jets, 17-14 (LA)
1985—Raiders, 31-0 (LA)
(Points—Raiders 591, Jets 568)
**Franchise in Oakland prior to 1982*
***Jets known as Titans prior to 1963*
****AFL Championship*
*****AFC Second Round Playoff*
***L.A. RAIDERS vs. PHILADELPHIA**
RS: Series tied, 2-2
PS: Raiders lead series, 1-0
1971—Raiders, 34-10 (O)
1976—Raiders, 26-7 (P)
1980—Eagles, 10-7 (P)
**Raiders, 27-10 (NO)
1986—Eagles, 33-27 (LA) OT
(Points—Raiders 121, Eagles 70)
**Franchise in Oakland prior to 1982*
***Super Bowl XV*
***L.A. RAIDERS vs. **PHOENIX**
RS: Series tied, 1-1
1973—Raiders, 17-10 (StL)
1983—Cardinals, 34-24 (LA)
(Points—Cardinals 44, Raiders 41)
**Franchise in Oakland prior to 1982*
***Franchise in St. Louis prior to 1988*
***L.A. RAIDERS vs. PITTSBURGH**
RS: Raiders lead series, 6-3
PS: Series tied, 3-3
1970—Raiders, 31-14 (O)
1972—Steelers, 34-28 (P)
**Steelers, 13-7 (P)
1973—Steelers, 17-9 (O)
**Raiders, 33-14 (O)
1974—Raiders, 17-0 (P)
***Steelers, 24-13 (O)
1975—***Steelers, 16-10 (P)
1976—Raiders, 31-28 (O)
***Raiders, 24-7 (O)
1977—Raiders, 16-7 (P)
1980—Raiders, 45-34 (P)
1981—Raiders, 30-27 (O)
1983—**Raiders, 38-10 (LA)
1984—Steelers, 13-7 (LA)
(Points—Raiders 339, Steelers 258)
**Franchise in Oakland prior to 1982*
***AFC Divisional Playoff*
****AFC Championship*
***L.A. RAIDERS vs. **SAN DIEGO**
RS: Raiders lead series, 36-20-2
PS: Raiders lead series, 1-0
1960—Chargers, 52-28 (LA)
Chargers, 41-17 (O)
1961—Chargers, 44-0 (SD)
Chargers, 41-10 (O)
1962—Chargers, 42-33 (O)
Chargers, 31-21 (SD)
1963—Raiders, 34-33 (SD)
Raiders, 41-27 (O)
1964—Chargers, 31-17 (O)
Raiders, 21-20 (SD)
1965—Chargers, 17-6 (O)
Chargers, 24-14 (SD)
1966—Chargers, 29-20 (O)
Raiders, 41-19 (SD)
1967—Raiders, 51-10 (O)
Raiders, 41-21 (SD)
1968—Chargers, 23-14 (O)
Raiders, 34-27 (SD)
1969—Raiders, 24-12 (SD)
Raiders, 21-16 (O)
1970—Tie, 27-27 (SD)
Raiders, 20-17 (O)
1971—Raiders, 34-0 (SD)
Raiders, 34-33 (O)
1972—Tie, 17-17 (O)
Raiders, 21-19 (SD)
1973—Raiders, 27-17 (SD)
Raiders, 31-3 (O)
1974—Raiders, 14-10 (SD)
Raiders, 17-10 (O)
1975—Raiders, 6-0 (SD)
Raiders, 25-0 (O)
1976—Raiders, 27-17 (SD)
Raiders, 24-0 (O)
1977—Raiders, 24-0 (O)
Chargers, 12-7 (SD)
1978—Raiders, 21-20 (SD)
Chargers, 27-23 (O)
1979—Chargers, 30-10 (SD)
Raiders, 45-22 (O)
1980—Chargers, 30-24 (SD) OT
Raiders, 38-24 (O)
***Raiders, 34-27 (SD)
1981—Chargers, 55-21 (O)
Chargers, 23-10 (SD)
1982—Raiders, 28-24 (LA)
Raiders, 41-34 (SD)
1983—Raiders, 42-10 (SD)
Raiders, 30-14 (LA)
1984—Raiders, 33-30 (LA)
Raiders, 44-37 (SD)
1985—Raiders, 34-21 (LA)
Chargers, 40-34 (SD) OT
1986—Raiders, 17-13 (LA)
Raiders, 37-31 (SD) OT
1987—Chargers, 23-17 (LA)
Chargers, 16-14 (SD)
1988—Raiders, 24-13 (LA)
Raiders, 13-3 (SD)
(Points—Raiders 1,477, Chargers 1,309)
**Franchise in Oakland prior to 1982*
***Franchise in Los Angeles prior to 1961*
****AFC Championship*
***L.A. RAIDERS vs. SAN FRANCISCO**
RS: Raiders lead series, 4-2
1970—49ers, 38-7 (O)
1974—Raiders, 35-24 (SF)
1979—Raiders, 23-10 (O)
1982—Raiders, 23-17 (SF)
1985—49ers, 34-10 (LA)
1988—Raiders, 9-3 (SF)
(Points—49ers 126, Raiders 107)
**Franchise in Oakland prior to 1982*
***L.A. RAIDERS vs. SEATTLE**
RS: Seahawks lead series, 12-10
PS: Series tied, 1-1
1977—Raiders, 44-7 (O)
1978—Seahawks, 27-7 (S)
Seahawks, 17-16 (O)
1979—Seahawks, 27-10 (S)
Seahawks, 29-24 (O)
1980—Raiders, 33-14 (O)

Raiders, 19-17 (S)
1981—Raiders, 20-10 (O)
Raiders, 32-31 (S)
1982—Raiders, 28-23 (LA)
1983—Seahawks, 38-36 (S)
Seahawks, 34-21 (LA)
**Raiders, 30-14 (LA)
1984—Raiders, 28-14 (LA)
Seahawks, 17-14 (S)
***Seahawks, 13-7 (S)
1985—Seahawks, 33-3 (S)
Raiders, 13-3 (LA)
1986—Raiders, 14-10 (LA)
Seahawks, 37-0 (S)
1987—Seahawks, 35-13 (LA)
Raiders, 37-14 (S)
1988—Seahawks, 35-27 (S)
Seahawks, 43-37 (LA)
(Points—Seahawks 542, Raiders 513)
Franchise in Oakland prior to 1982
***AFC Championship*
****AFC First Round Playoff*

***L.A. RAIDERS vs. TAMPA BAY**
RS: Raiders lead series, 2-0
1976—Raiders, 49-16 (O)
1981—Raiders, 18-16 (O)
(Points—Raiders 67, Buccaneers 32)
Franchise in Oakland prior to 1982

***L.A. RAIDERS vs. WASHINGTON**
RS: Raiders lead series, 3-2
PS: Raiders lead series, 1-0
1970—Raiders, 34-20 (O)
1975—Raiders, 26-23 (W) OT
1980—Raiders, 24-21 (O)
1983—Redskins, 37-35 (W)
**Raiders, 38-9 (Tampa)
1986—Redskins, 10-6 (W)
(Points—Raiders 163, Redskins 120)
Franchise in Oakland prior to 1982
***Super Bowl XVIII*

L.A. RAMS vs. ATLANTA
RS: Rams lead series, 32-10-2;
See Atlanta vs. L.A. Rams

L.A. RAMS vs. BUFFALO
RS: Rams lead series, 3-1;
See Buffalo vs. L.A. Rams

L.A. RAMS vs. CHICAGO
RS: Bears lead series, 42-28-3
PS: Series tied, 1-1;
See Chicago vs. L.A. Rams

L.A. RAMS vs. CINCINNATI
RS: Bengals lead series, 3-2;
See Cincinnati vs. L.A. Rams

L.A. RAMS vs. CLEVELAND
RS: Browns lead series, 7-6
PS: Browns lead series, 2-1;
See Cleveland vs. L.A. Rams

L.A. RAMS vs. DALLAS
RS: Series tied, 7-7
PS: Series tied, 4-4;
See Dallas vs. L.A. Rams

L.A. RAMS vs. DENVER
RS: Series tied, 3-3;
See Denver vs. L.A. Rams

L.A. RAMS vs. DETROIT
RS: Rams lead series, 39-33-1
PS: Lions lead series, 1-0;
See Detroit vs. L.A. Rams

L.A. RAMS vs. GREEN BAY
RS: Rams lead series, 40-33-2
PS: Packers lead series, 1-0;
See Green Bay vs. L.A. Rams

L.A. RAMS vs. HOUSTON
RS: Rams lead series, 3-2;
See Houston vs. L.A. Rams

L.A. RAMS vs. INDIANAPOLIS
RS: Colts lead series, 20-15-2;
See Indianapolis vs. L.A. Rams

L.A. RAMS vs. KANSAS CITY
RS: Rams lead series, 3-0;
See Kansas City vs. L.A. Rams

L.A. RAMS VS. L.A. RAIDERS
RS: Raiders lead series, 4-2;
See L.A. Raiders vs. L.A. Rams

L.A. RAMS vs. MIAMI
RS: Dolphins lead series, 4-1
1971—Dolphins, 20-14 (LA)
1976—Rams, 31-28 (M)
1980—Dolphins, 35-14 (LA)
1983—Dolphins, 30-14 (M)
1986—Dolphins 37-31 (LA) OT
(Points—Dolphins 150, Rams 104)

L.A. RAMS vs. MINNESOTA
RS: Vikings lead series, 12-11-2
PS: Vikings lead series, 5-1
1961—Rams, 31-17 (LA)
Vikings, 42-21 (M)
1962—Vikings, 38-14 (LA)
Tie, 24-24 (M)
1963—Rams, 27-24 (LA)
Vikings, 21-13 (M)
1964—Rams, 22-13 (LA)
Vikings, 34-13 (M)
1965—Vikings, 38-35 (LA)
Vikings, 24-13 (M)
1966—Vikings, 35-7 (M)
Rams, 21-6 (LA)
1967—Rams, 39-3 (LA)
1968—Rams, 31-3 (M)
1969—Vikings, 20-13 (LA)
*Vikings, 23-20 (M)
1970—Vikings, 13-3 (M)
1972—Vikings, 45-41 (LA)
1973—Vikings, 10-9 (M)
1974—Rams, 20-17 (LA)
**Vikings, 14-10 (M)
1976—Tie, 10-10 (M) OT
**Vikings, 24-13 (M)
1977—Rams, 35-3 (LA)
***Vikings, 14-7 (LA)
1978—Rams, 34-17 (M)
***Rams, 34-10 (LA)
1979—Rams, 27-21 (LA) OT
1985—Rams, 13-10 (LA)
1987—Vikings, 21-16 (LA)
1988—****Vikings, 28-17 (M)
(Points—Rams 633, Vikings 622)
**Conference Championship*
***NFC Championship*
****NFC Divisional Playoff*
*****NFC First Round Playoff*

L.A. RAMS vs. NEW ENGLAND
RS: Patriots lead series, 3-1
1974—Patriots, 20-14 (NE)
1980—Rams, 17-14 (NE)
1983—Patriots, 21-7 (LA)
1986—Patriots, 30-28 (LA)
(Points—Patriots 85, Rams 66)

L.A. RAMS vs. NEW ORLEANS
RS: Rams lead series, 25-13
1967—Rams, 27-13 (NO)
1969—Rams, 36-17 (LA)
1970—Rams, 30-17 (NO)
Rams, 34-16 (LA)
1971—Saints, 24-20 (NO)
Rams, 45-28 (LA)
1972—Rams, 34-14 (LA)
Saints, 19-16 (NO)
1973—Rams, 29-7 (LA)
Rams, 24-13 (NO)
1974—Rams, 24-0 (LA)
Saints, 20-7 (NO)
1975—Rams, 38-14 (LA)
Rams, 14-7 (NO)
1976—Rams, 16-10 (NO)
Rams, 33-14 (LA)
1977—Rams, 14-7 (LA)
Saints, 27-26 (NO)
1978—Rams, 26-20 (NO)
Saints, 10-3 (LA)
1979—Rams, 35-17 (NO)
Saints, 29-14 (LA)
1980—Rams, 45-31 (LA)
Rams, 27-7 (NO)
1981—Saints, 23-17 (NO)
Saints, 21-13 (LA)
1983—Rams, 30-27 (LA)
Rams, 26-24 (NO)
1984—Rams, 28-10 (NO)
Rams, 34-21 (LA)
1985—Rams, 28-10 (LA)
Saints, 29-3 (NO)
1986—Saints, 6-0 (NO)
Rams, 26-13 (LA)
1987—Saints, 37-10 (NO)
Saints, 31-14 (LA)
1988—Rams, 12-10 (NO)
Saints, 14-10 (LA)
(Points—Rams 868, Saints 657)

***L.A. RAMS vs. N.Y. GIANTS**
RS: Rams lead series, 17-7
PS: Giants lead series, 1-0
1938—Giants, 28-0 (NY)
1940—Rams, 13-0 (NY)
1941—Giants, 49-14 (NY)
1945—Rams, 21-17 (NY)
1946—Rams, 31-21 (NY)
1947—Rams, 34-10 (LA)
1948—Rams, 52-37 (NY)
1953—Rams, 21-7 (LA)
1954—Rams, 17-16 (NY)
1959—Giants, 23-21 (LA)
1961—Giants, 24-14 (NY)
1966—Rams, 55-14 (LA)
1968—Rams, 24-21 (LA)
1970—Rams, 31-3 (NY)
1973—Rams, 40-6 (LA)
1976—Rams, 24-10 (LA)
1978—Rams, 20-17 (NY)
1979—Giants, 20-14 (LA)
1980—Rams, 28-7 (NY)
1981—Giants, 10-7 (NY)
1983—Rams, 16-6 (NY)
1984—Rams, 33-12 (LA)
**Giants, 16-13 (LA)
1985—Giants, 24-19 (NY)
1988—Rams, 45-31 (NY)
(Points—Rams 607, Giants 429)
Franchise in Cleveland prior to 1946
***NFC First Round Playoff*

L.A. RAMS vs. N.Y. JETS
RS: Rams lead series, 3-2
1970—Jets, 31-20 (LA)
1974—Rams, 20-13 (NY)
1980—Rams, 38-13 (LA)
1983—Jets, 27-24 (NY) OT
1986—Rams, 17-3 (NY)
(Points—Rams 119, Jets 87)

***L.A. RAMS vs. PHILADELPHIA**
RS: Rams lead series, 15-10-1
PS: Eagles lead series, 1-0
1937—Rams, 21-3 (P)
1939—Rams, 35-13 (Colorado Springs)
1940—Rams, 21-13 (C)
1942—Rams, 24-14 (Akron)
1944—Eagles, 26-13 (P)
1945—Eagles, 28-14 (P)
1946—Eagles, 25-14 (LA)
1947—Eagles, 14-7 (P)
1948—Tie, 28-28 (LA)
1949—Eagles, 38-14 (P)
**Eagles, 14-0 (LA)
1950—Eagles, 56-20 (P)
1955—Rams, 23-21 (P)
1956—Rams, 27-7 (LA)
1957—Rams, 17-13 (LA)
1959—Eagles, 23-20 (P)
1964—Rams, 20-10 (LA)
1967—Rams, 33-17 (LA)
1969—Rams, 23-17 (P)
1972—Rams, 34-3 (P)
1975—Rams, 42-3 (P)
1977—Rams, 20-0 (LA)
1978—Rams, 16-14 (P)
1983—Eagles, 13-9 (P)
1985—Rams, 17-6 (P)
1986—Eagles, 34-20 (P)
1988—Eagles, 30-24 (P)
(Points—Rams 556, Eagles 483)
Franchise in Cleveland prior to 1946
***NFL Championship*

***L.A. RAMS vs. **PHOENIX**
RS: Rams lead series, 21-16-2
PS: Rams lead series, 1-0
1937—Cardinals, 6-0 (Clev)
Cardinals, 13-7 (Chi)
1938—Cardinals, 7-6 (Clev)
Cardinals, 31-17 (Chi)
1939—Rams, 24-0 (Chi)
Rams, 14-0 (Clev)
1940—Rams, 26-14 (Clev)
Cardinals, 17-7 (Chi)
1941—Rams, 10-6 (Clev)
Cardinals, 7-0 (Chi)
1942—Cardinals, 7-0 (Chi)
Rams, 7-3 (Clev)
1945—Rams, 21-0 (Clev)
Rams, 35-21 (Chi)
1946—Cardinals, 34-10 (Chi)
Rams, 17-14 (LA)
1947—Rams, 27-7 (LA)
Cardinals, 17-10 (Chi)
1948—Cardinals, 27-22 (LA)
Cardinals, 27-24 (Chi)
1949—Tie, 28-28 (Chi)
Cardinals, 31-27 (LA)
1951—Rams, 45-21 (LA)
1953—Tie, 24-24 (Chi)
1954—Rams, 28-17 (LA)
1958—Rams, 20-14 (Chi)
1960—Cardinals, 43-21 (LA)
1965—Rams, 27-3 (StL)
1968—Rams, 24-13 (StL)
1970—Rams, 34-13 (LA)
1972—Cardinals, 24-14 (StL)
1975—***Rams, 35-23 (LA)
1976—Cardinals, 30-28 (LA)
1979—Rams, 21-0 (LA)
1980—Rams, 21-13 (StL)
1984—Rams, 16-13 (StL)
1985—Rams, 46-14 (LA)
1986—Rams, 16-10 (StL)
1987—Rams, 27-24 (StL)
1988—Cardinals, 41-27 (LA)
(Points—Rams 813, Cardinals 657)
Franchise in Cleveland prior to 1946
***Franchise in St. Louis prior to 1988 and in Chicago prior to 1960*
****NFC Divisional Playoff*

***L.A. RAMS vs. **PITTSBURGH**
RS: Rams lead series, 13-3-2
PS: Steelers lead series, 1-0
1938—Rams, 13-7 (New Orleans)
1939—Tie, 14-14 (C)
1941—Rams, 17-14 (Akron)
1947—Rams, 48-7 (P)
1948—Rams, 31-14 (LA)
1949—Tie, 7-7 (P)
1952—Rams, 28-14 (LA)
1955—Rams, 27-26 (LA)
1956—Steelers, 30-13 (P)
1961—Rams, 24-14 (LA)
1964—Rams, 26-14 (P)
1968—Rams, 45-10 (LA)
1971—Rams, 23-14 (P)
1975—Rams, 10-3 (LA)
1978—Rams, 10-7 (LA)
1979—***Steelers, 31-19 (Pasadena)
1981—Steelers, 24-0 (P)
1984—Steelers, 24-14 (P)
1987—Rams, 31-21 (LA)
(Points—Rams 400, Steelers 295)
Franchise in Cleveland prior to 1946
***Steelers known as Pirates prior to 1941*
****Super Bowl XIV*

L.A. RAMS vs. SAN DIEGO
RS: Series tied, 2-2
1970—Rams, 37-10 (LA)
1975—Rams, 13-10 (SD) OT
1979—Chargers, 40-16 (LA)
1988—Chargers, 38-24 (LA)
(Points—Chargers 98, Rams 90)

L.A. RAMS vs. SAN FRANCISCO
RS: Rams lead series, 46-30-2
1950—Rams, 35-14 (SF)
Rams, 28-21 (LA)
1951—49ers, 44-17 (SF)
Rams, 23-16 (LA)
1952—Rams, 35-9 (LA)
Rams, 34-21 (SF)
1953—49ers, 31-30 (SF)
49ers, 31-27 (LA)
1954—Tie, 24-24 (LA)
Rams, 42-34 (SF)
1955—Rams, 23-14 (SF)
Rams, 27-14 (LA)
1956—49ers, 33-30 (SF)
Rams, 30-6 (LA)
1957—49ers, 23-20 (SF)
Rams, 37-24 (LA)
1958—Rams, 33-3 (SF)
Rams, 56-7 (LA)
1959—49ers, 34-0 (SF)
49ers, 24-16 (LA)
1960—49ers, 13-9 (SF)
49ers, 23-7 (LA)
1961—49ers, 35-0 (SF)
Rams, 17-7 (LA)
1962—Rams, 28-14 (SF)
49ers, 24-17 (LA)
1963—Rams, 28-21 (LA)
Rams, 21-17 (SF)
1964—Rams, 42-14 (LA)
49ers, 28-7 (SF)
1965—49ers, 45-21 (LA)
49ers, 30-27 (SF)
1966—Rams, 34-3 (LA)
49ers, 21-13 (SF)
1967—49ers, 27-24 (LA)
Rams, 17-7 (SF)
1968—Rams, 24-10 (LA)
Tie, 20-20 (SF)
1969—Rams, 27-21 (SF)
Rams, 41-30 (LA)
1970—49ers, 20-6 (LA)
Rams, 30-13 (SF)
1971—Rams, 20-13 (SF)
Rams, 17-6 (LA)
1972—Rams, 31-7 (LA)
Rams, 26-16 (SF)
1973—Rams, 40-20 (SF)
Rams, 31-13 (LA)
1974—Rams, 37-14 (LA)
Rams, 15-13 (SF)
1975—Rams, 23-14 (SF)
49ers, 24-23 (LA)
1976—49ers, 16-0 (LA)
Rams, 23-3 (SF)
1977—Rams, 34-14 (LA)
Rams, 23-10 (SF)
1978—Rams, 27-10 (LA)
Rams, 31-28 (SF)
1979—Rams, 27-24 (LA)
Rams, 26-20 (SF)
1980—Rams, 48-26 (LA)
Rams, 31-17 (SF)
1981—49ers, 20-17 (SF)
49ers, 33-31 (LA)
1982—49ers, 30-24 (LA)
Rams, 21-20 (SF)
1983—Rams, 10-7 (SF)
49ers, 45-35 (LA)
1984—49ers, 33-0 (LA)
49ers, 19-16 (SF)
1985—49ers, 28-14 (LA)
Rams, 27-20 (SF)
1986—Rams, 16-13 (LA)
49ers, 24-14 (SF)
1987—49ers, 31-10 (LA)
49ers, 48-0 (SF)
1988—49ers, 24-21 (LA)

Rams, 38-16 (SF)
(Points—Rams 1,854, 49ers 1,589)
L.A. RAMS vs. SEATTLE
RS: Rams lead series, 4-0
1976—Rams, 45-6 (LA)
1979—Rams, 24-0 (S)
1985—Rams, 35-24 (S)
1988—Rams, 31-10 (LA)
(Points—Rams 135, Seahawks 40)
L.A. RAMS vs. TAMPA BAY
RS: Rams lead series, 6-2
PS: Rams lead series, 1-0
1977—Rams, 31-0 (LA)
1978—Rams, 26-23 (LA)
1979—Buccaneers, 21-6 (TB)
*Rams, 9-0 (TB)
1980—Buccaneers, 10-9 (TB)
1984—Rams, 34-33 (TB)
1985—Rams, 31-27 (TB)
1986—Rams, 26-20 (LA) OT
1987—Rams, 35-3 (LA)
(Points—Rams 207, Buccaneers 137)
**NFC Championship*
***L.A. RAMS vs. WASHINGTON**
RS: Redskins lead series, 13-4-1
PS: Series tied, 2-2
1937—Redskins, 16-7 (C)
1938—Redskins, 37-13 (W)
1941—Redskins, 17-13 (W)
1942—Redskins, 33-14 (W)
1944—Redskins, 14-10 (W)
1945—**Rams, 15-14 (C)
1948—Rams, 41-13 (W)
1949—Rams, 53-27 (LA)
1951—Redskins, 31-21 (W)
1962—Redskins, 20-14 (W)
1963—Redskins, 37-14 (LA)
1967—Tie, 28-28 (LA)
1969—Rams, 24-13 (W)
1971—Redskins, 38-24 (LA)
1974—Redskins, 23-17 (LA)
***Rams, 19-10 (LA)
1977—Redskins, 17-14 (W)
1981—Redskins, 30-7 (LA)
1983—Redskins, 42-20 (LA)
***Redskins, 51-7 (W)
1986—****Redskins, 19-7 (W)
1987—Rams, 30-26 (W)
(Points—Redskins 556, Rams 412)
**Franchise in Cleveland prior to 1946*
***NFL Championship*
****NFC Divisional Playoff*
*****NFC First Round Playoff*

MIAMI vs. ATLANTA
RS: Dolphins lead series, 4-1;
See Atlanta vs. Miami
MIAMI vs. BUFFALO
RS: Dolphins lead series, 34-11-1;
See Buffalo vs. Miami
MIAMI vs. CHICAGO
RS: Dolphins lead series, 4-1;
See Chicago vs. Miami
MIAMI vs. CINCINNATI
RS: Dolphins lead series, 7-3
PS: Dolphins lead series, 1-0;
See Cincinnati vs. Miami
MIAMI vs. CLEVELAND
RS: Browns lead series, 4-2
PS: Dolphins lead series, 2-0;
See Cleveland vs. Miami
MIAMI vs. DALLAS
RS: Dolphins lead series, 4-1
PS: Cowboys lead series, 1-0;
See Dallas vs. Miami
MIAMI vs. DENVER
RS: Dolphins lead series, 5-2-1;
See Denver vs. Miami
MIAMI vs. DETROIT
RS: Dolphins lead series, 2-1;
See Detroit vs. Miami
MIAMI vs. GREEN BAY
RS: Dolphins lead series, 5-0;
See Green Bay vs. Miami
MIAMI vs. HOUSTON
RS: Dolphins lead series, 10-9
PS: Oilers lead series, 1-0;
See Houston vs. Miami
MIAMI vs. INDIANAPOLIS
RS: Dolphins lead series, 26-12
PS: Dolphins lead series, 1-0;
See Indianapolis vs. Miami
MIAMI vs. KANSAS CITY
RS: Chiefs lead series, 7-6
PS: Dolphins lead series, 1-0;
See Kansas City vs. Miami
MIAMI vs. L.A. RAIDERS
RS: Raiders lead series, 13-3-1
PS: Raiders lead series, 2-1;
See L.A. Raiders vs. Miami
MIAMI vs. L.A. RAMS
RS: Dolphins lead series, 4-1;
See L.A. Rams vs. Miami
MIAMI vs. MINNESOTA
RS: Dolphins lead series, 4-1
PS: Dolphins lead series, 1-0
1972—Dolphins, 16-14 (Minn)
1973—*Dolphins, 24-7 (Houston)
1976—Vikings, 29-7 (Mia)
1979—Dolphins, 27-12 (Minn)
1982—Dolphins, 22-14 (Mia)
1988—Dolphins, 24-7 (Mia)
(Points—Dolphins 120, Vikings 83)
**Super Bowl VIII*
MIAMI vs. *NEW ENGLAND
RS: Dolphins lead series, 24-20
PS: Series tied, 1-1
1966—Patriots, 20-14 (M)
1967—Patriots, 41-10 (B)
Dolphins, 41-32 (M)
1968—Dolphins, 34-10 (B)
Dolphins, 38-7 (M)
1969—Dolphins, 17-16 (B)
Patriots, 38-23 (Tampa)
1970—Patriots, 27-14 (B)
Dolphins, 37-20 (M)
1971—Dolphins, 41-3 (M)
Patriots, 34-13 (NE)
1972—Dolphins, 52-0 (M)
Dolphins, 37-21 (NE)
1973—Dolphins, 44-23 (M)
Dolphins, 30-14 (NE)
1974—Patriots, 34-24 (NE)
Dolphins, 34-27 (M)
1975—Dolphins, 22-14 (NE)
Dolphins, 20-7 (M)
1976—Patriots, 30-14 (NE)
Dolphins, 10-3 (M)
1977—Dolphins, 17-5 (M)
Patriots, 14-10 (NE)
1978—Patriots, 33-24 (NE)
Dolphins, 23-3 (M)
1979—Patriots, 28-13 (NE)
Dolphins, 39-24 (M)
1980—Patriots, 34-0 (NE)
Dolphins, 16-13 (M) OT
1981—Dolphins, 30-27 (NE) OT
Dolphins, 24-14 (M)
1982—Patriots, 3-0 (NE)
**Dolphins, 28-13 (M)
1983—Dolphins, 34-24 (M)
Patriots, 17-6 (NE)
1984—Dolphins, 28-7 (M)
Dolphins, 44-24 (NE)
1985—Patriots, 17-13 (NE)
Dolphins, 30-27 (M)
***Patriots, 31-14 (M)
1986—Patriots, 34-7 (NE)
Patriots, 34-27 (M)
1987—Patriots, 28-21 (NE)
Patriots, 24-10 (M)
1988—Patriots, 21-10 (NE)
Patriots, 6-3 (M)
(Points—Dolphins 1,040, Patriots 926)
**Franchise in Boston prior to 1971*
***AFC First Round Playoff*
****AFC Championship*
MIAMI vs. NEW ORLEANS
RS: Dolphins lead series, 4-1
1970—Dolphins, 21-10 (M)
1974—Dolphins, 21-0 (NO)
1980—Dolphins, 21-16 (M)
1983—Saints, 17-7 (NO)
1986—Dolphins, 31-27 (NO)
(Points—Dolphins 101, Saints 70)
MIAMI vs. N.Y. GIANTS
RS: Dolphins lead series, 1-0
1972—Dolphins, 23-13 (NY)
MIAMI vs. N.Y. JETS
RS: Dolphins lead series, 23-22-1
PS: Dolphins lead series, 1-0
1966—Jets, 19-14 (M)
Jets, 30-13 (NY)
1967—Jets, 29-7 (NY)
Jets, 33-14 (M)
1968—Jets, 35-17 (NY)
Jets, 31-7 (M)
1969—Jets, 34-31 (NY)
Jets, 27-9 (M)
1970—Dolphins, 20-6 (NY)
Dolphins, 16-10 (M)
1971—Jets, 14-10 (M)
Dolphins, 30-14 (NY)
1972—Dolphins, 27-17 (NY)
Dolphins, 28-24 (M)
1973—Dolphins, 31-3 (M)
Dolphins, 24-14 (NY)
1974—Dolphins, 21-17 (M)
Jets, 17-14 (NY)
1975—Dolphins, 43-0 (NY)
Dolphins, 27-7 (M)
1976—Dolphins, 16-0 (M)
Dolphins, 27-7 (NY)
1977—Dolphins, 21-17 (M)
Dolphins, 14-10 (NY)
1978—Jets, 33-20 (NY)
Jets, 24-13 (M)
1979—Jets, 33-27 (NY)
Jets, 27-24 (M)
1980—Jets, 17-14 (NY)
Jets, 24-17 (M)
1981—Tie, 28-28 (M) OT
Jets, 16-15 (NY)
1982—Dolphins, 45-28 (NY)
Dolphins, 20-19 (M)
*Dolphins, 14-0 (M)
1983—Dolphins, 32-14 (NY)
Dolphins, 34-14 (M)
1984—Dolphins, 31-17 (NY)
Dolphins, 28-17 (M)
1985—Jets, 23-7 (NY)
Dolphins, 21-17 (M)
1986—Jets, 51-45 (NY) OT
Dolphins, 45-3 (M)
1987—Jets, 37-31 (NY) OT
Dolphins, 37-28 (M)
1988—Jets, 44-30 (M)
Jets, 38-34 (NY)
(Points—Dolphins 1,093, Jets 967)
**AFC Championship*
MIAMI vs. PHILADELPHIA
RS: Dolphins lead series, 4-2
1970—Eagles, 24-17 (P)
1975—Dolphins, 24-16 (M)
1978—Eagles, 17-3 (P)
1981—Dolphins, 13-10 (M)
1984—Dolphins, 24-23 (M)
1987—Dolphins, 28-10 (P)
(Points—Dolphins 109, Eagles 100)
MIAMI vs. *PHOENIX
RS: Dolphins lead series, 5-0
1972—Dolphins, 31-10 (M)
1977—Dolphins, 55-14 (StL)
1978—Dolphins, 24-10 (M)
1981—Dolphins, 20-7 (StL)
1984—Dolphins, 36-28 (StL)
(Points—Dolphins 166, Cardinals 69)
**Franchise in St. Louis prior to 1988*
MIAMI vs. PITTSBURGH
RS: Dolphins lead series, 6-3
PS: Dolphins lead series, 2-1
1971—Dolphins, 24-21 (M)
1972—*Dolphins, 21-17 (P)
1973—Dolphins, 30-26 (M)
1976—Steelers, 14-3 (P)
1979—**Steelers, 34-14 (P)
1980—Steelers, 23-10 (P)
1981—Dolphins, 30-10 (M)
1984—Dolphins, 31-7 (P)
*Dolphins, 45-28 (M)
1985—Dolphins, 24-20 (M)
1987—Dolphins, 35-24 (M)
1988—Steelers, 40-24 (P)
(Points—Dolphins 291, Steelers 264)
**AFC Championship*
***AFC Divisional Playoff*
MIAMI vs. SAN DIEGO
RS: Chargers lead series, 8-5
PS: Series tied, 1-1
1966—Chargers, 44-10 (SD)
1967—Chargers, 24-0 (SD)
Dolphins, 41-24 (M)
1968—Chargers, 34-28 (SD)
1969—Chargers, 21-14 (M)
1972—Dolphins, 24-10 (M)
1974—Dolphins, 28-21 (SD)
1977—Chargers, 14-13 (M)
1978—Dolphins, 28-21 (SD)
1980—Chargers, 27-24 (M) OT
1981—*Chargers, 41-38 (M) OT
1982—**Dolphins, 34-13 (M)
1984—Chargers, 34-28 (SD) OT
1986—Chargers, 50-28 (SD)
1988—Dolphins, 31-28 (M)
(Points—Chargers 406, Dolphins 369)
**AFC Divisional Playoff*
***AFC Second Round Playoff*
MIAMI vs. SAN FRANCISCO
RS: Dolphins lead series, 4-1
PS: 49ers lead series, 1-0
1973—Dolphins, 21-13 (M)
1977—Dolphins, 19-15 (SF)
1980—Dolphins, 17-13 (M)
1983—Dolphins, 20-17 (SF)
1984—*49ers, 38-16 (Stanford)
1986—49ers, 31-16 (M)
(Points—49ers 127, Dolphins 109)
**Super Bowl XIX*
MIAMI vs. SEATTLE
RS: Dolphins lead series, 2-1
PS: Series tied, 1-1
1977—Dolphins, 31-13 (M)
1979—Dolphins, 19-10 (M)
1983—*Seahawks, 27-20 (M)
1984—*Dolphins, 31-10 (M)
1987—Seahawks, 24-20 (S)
(Points—Dolphins 121, Seahawks 84)
**AFC Divisional Playoff*
MIAMI vs. TAMPA BAY
RS: Dolphins lead series, 3-1
1976—Dolphins, 23-20 (TB)
1982—Buccaneers, 23-17 (TB)
1985—Dolphins, 41-38 (M)
1988—Dolphins, 17-14 (TB)
(Points—Dolphins 98, Buccaneers 95)
MIAMI vs. WASHINGTON
RS: Dolphins lead series, 4-1
PS: Series tied, 1-1
1972—*Dolphins, 14-7 (Los Angeles)
1974—Redskins, 20-17 (W)
1978—Dolphins, 16-0 (W)
1981—Dolphins, 13-10 (M)
1982—**Redskins, 27-17 (Pasadena)
1984—Dolphins, 35-17 (W)
1987—Dolphins, 23-21 (M)
(Points—Dolphins 135, Redskins 102)
**Super Bowl VII*
***Super Bowl XVII*

MINNESOTA vs. ATLANTA
RS: Vikings lead series, 9-6
PS: Vikings lead series, 1-0;
See Atlanta vs. Minnesota
MINNESOTA vs. BUFFALO
RS: Vikings lead series, 4-2;
See Buffalo vs. Minnesota
MINNESOTA vs. CHICAGO
RS: Vikings lead series, 28-25-2;
See Chicago vs. Minnesota
MINNESOTA vs. CINCINNATI
RS: Bengals lead series, 3-2;
See Cincinnati vs. Minnesota
MINNESOTA vs. CLEVELAND
RS: Vikings lead series, 6-2
PS: Vikings lead series, 1-0;
See Cleveland vs. Minnesota
MINNESOTA vs. DALLAS
RS: Cowboys lead series, 7-6
PS: Cowboys lead series, 3-1;
See Dallas vs. Minnesota
MINNESOTA vs. DENVER
RS: Vikings lead series, 3-2;
See Denver vs. Minnesota
MINNESOTA vs. DETROIT
RS: Vikings lead series, 35-18-2;
See Detroit vs. Minnesota
MINNESOTA vs. GREEN BAY
RS: Packers lead series, 28-26-1;
See Green Bay vs. Minnesota
MINNESOTA vs. HOUSTON
RS: Series tied, 2-2;
See Houston vs. Minnesota
MINNESOTA vs. INDIANAPOLIS
RS: Colts lead series, 11-6-1
PS: Colts lead series, 1-0;
See Indianapolis vs. Minnesota
MINNESOTA vs. KANSAS CITY
RS: Vikings lead series, 2-1
PS: Chiefs lead series, 1-0;
See Kansas City vs. Minnesota
MINNESOTA vs. L.A. RAIDERS
RS: Raiders lead series, 4-2
PS: Raiders lead series, 1-0;
See L.A. Raiders vs. Minnesota
MINNESOTA vs. L.A. RAMS
RS: Vikings lead series, 12-11-2
PS: Vikings lead series, 5-1;
See L.A. Rams vs. Minnesota
MINNESOTA vs. MIAMI
RS: Dolphins lead series, 4-1
PS: Dolphins lead series, 1-0;
See Miami vs. Minnesota
MINNESOTA vs. *NEW ENGLAND
RS: Series tied, 2-2
1970—Vikings, 35-14 (B)
1974—Patriots, 17-14 (M)
1979—Patriots, 27-23 (NE)
1988—Vikings, 36-6 (M)
(Points—Vikings 108, Patriots 64)
**Franchise in Boston prior to 1971*
MINNESOTA vs. NEW ORLEANS
RS: Vikings lead series, 10-4
PS: Vikings lead series, 1-0
1968—Saints, 20-17 (NO)
1970—Vikings, 26-0 (M)
1971—Vikings, 23-10 (NO)
1972—Vikings, 37-6 (M)
1974—Vikings, 29-9 (M)
1975—Vikings, 20-7 (NO)
1976—Vikings, 40-9 (NO)
1978—Saints, 31-24 (NO)
1980—Vikings, 23-20 (NO)
1981—Vikings, 20-10 (M)
1983—Saints, 17-16 (NO)
1985—Saints, 30-23 (M)
1986—Vikings, 33-17 (M)
1987—*Vikings, 44-10 (NO)
1988—Vikings, 45-3 (M)
(Points—Vikings 420, Saints 199)
**NFC First Round Playoff*

MINNESOTA vs. N.Y. GIANTS
RS: Vikings lead series, 6-2
1964—Vikings, 30-21 (NY)
1965—Vikings, 40-14 (M)
1967—Vikings, 27-24 (M)
1969—Giants, 24-23 (NY)
1971—Vikings, 17-10 (NY)
1973—Vikings, 31-7 (New Haven)
1976—Vikings, 24-7 (M)
1986—Giants, 22-20 (M)
(Points—Vikings 212, Giants 129)
MINNESOTA vs. N.Y. JETS
RS: Jets lead series, 3-1
1970—Jets, 20-10 (NY)
1975—Vikings, 29-21 (M)
1979—Jets, 14-7 (NY)
1982—Jets 42-14 (M)
(Points—Jets 97, Vikings 60)
MINNESOTA vs. PHILADELPHIA
RS: Vikings lead series, 10-3
PS: Eagles lead series, 1-0
1962—Vikings, 31-21 (M)
1963—Vikings, 34-13 (P)
1968—Vikings, 24-17 (P)
1971—Vikings, 13-0 (P)
1973—Vikings, 28-21 (M)
1976—Vikings, 31-12 (P)
1978—Vikings, 28-27 (M)
1980—Eagles, 42-7 (M)
*Eagles, 31-16 (P)
1981—Vikings, 35-23 (M)
1984—Eagles, 19-17 (P)
1985—Vikings, 28-23 (P)
Eagles, 37-35 (M)
1988—Vikings, 23-21 (M)
(Points—Vikings 350, Eagles 307)
**NFC Divisional Playoff*
MINNESOTA vs. *PHOENIX
RS: Cardinals lead series, 7-2
PS: Vikings lead series, 1-0
1963—Cardinals, 56-14 (M)
1967—Cardinals, 34-24 (M)
1969—Vikings, 27-10 (StL)
1972—Cardinals, 19-17 (M)
1974—Vikings, 28-24 (StL)
**Vikings, 30-14 (M)
1977—Cardinals, 27-7 (M)
1979—Cardinals, 37-7 (StL)
1981—Cardinals, 30-17 (StL)
1983—Cardinals, 41-31 (StL)
(Points—Cardinals 292, Vikings 202)
**Franchise in St. Louis prior to 1988*
***NFC Divisional Playoff*
MINNESOTA vs. PITTSBURGH
RS: Vikings lead series, 6-3
PS: Steelers lead series, 1-0
1962—Steelers, 39-31 (P)
1964—Vikings, 30-10 (M)
1967—Vikings, 41-27 (P)
1969—Vikings, 52-14 (M)
1972—Steelers, 23-10 (P)
1974—*Steelers, 16-6 (New Orleans)
1976—Vikings, 17-6 (M)
1980—Steelers, 23-17 (M)
1983—Vikings, 17-14 (P)
1986—Vikings, 31-7 (M)
(Points—Vikings 252, Steelers 179)
**Super Bowl IX*
MINNESOTA vs. SAN DIEGO
RS: Series tied, 3-3
1971—Chargers, 30-14 (SD)
1975—Vikings, 28-13 (M)
1978—Chargers, 13-7 (M)
1981—Vikings, 33-31 (SD)
1984—Chargers, 42-13 (M)
1985—Vikings, 21-17 (M)
(Points—Chargers 146, Vikings 116)
MINNESOTA vs. SAN FRANCISCO
RS: Vikings lead series, 14-12-1
PS: 49ers lead series, 2-1
1961—49ers, 38-24 (M)
49ers, 38-28 (SF)
1962—49ers, 21-7 (SF)
49ers, 35-12 (M)
1963—Vikings, 24-20 (SF)
Vikings, 45-14 (M)
1964—Vikings, 27-22 (SF)
Vikings, 24-7 (M)
1965—Vikings, 42-41 (SF)
49ers, 45-24 (M)
1966—Tie, 20-20 (SF)
Vikings, 28-3 (SF)
1967—49ers, 27-21 (M)
1968—Vikings, 30-20 (SF)
1969—Vikings, 10-7 (M)
1970—*49ers, 17-14 (M)
1971—49ers, 13-9 (M)
1972—49ers, 20-17 (SF)
1973—Vikings, 17-13 (SF)
1975—Vikings, 27-17 (M)
1976—49ers, 20-16 (SF)
1977—Vikings, 28-27 (M)
1979—Vikings, 28-22 (M)
1983—49ers, 48-17 (M)
1984—49ers, 51-7 (SF)
1985—Vikings, 28-21 (M)
1986—Vikings, 27-24 (SF) OT
1987—*Vikings, 36-24 (SF)
1988—49ers, 24-21 (SF)
*49ers, 34-9 (SF)
(Points—49ers 733, Vikings 667)
**NFC Divisional Playoff*
MINNESOTA vs. SEATTLE
RS: Seahawks lead series, 3-1
1976—Vikings, 27-21 (M)
1978—Seahawks, 29-28 (S)
1984—Seahawks, 20-12 (M)
1987—Seahawks, 28-17 (S)
(Points—Seahawks 98, Vikings 84)
MINNESOTA vs. TAMPA BAY
RS: Vikings lead series, 16-6
1977—Vikings, 9-3 (TB)
1978—Buccaneers, 16-10 (M)
Vikings, 24-7 (TB)
1979—Buccaneers, 12-10 (M)
Vikings, 23-22 (TB)
1980—Vikings, 38-30 (M)
Vikings, 21-10 (TB)
1981—Buccaneers, 21-13 (TB)
Vikings, 25-10 (M)
1982—Vikings, 17-10 (M)
1983—Vikings, 19-16 (TB) OT
Buccaneers, 17-12 (M)
1984—Buccaneers, 35-31 (TB)
Vikings, 27-24 (M)
1985—Vikings, 31-16 (TB)
Vikings, 26-7 (M)
1986—Vikings, 23-10 (TB)
Vikings, 45-13 (M)
1987—Buccaneers, 20-10 (TB)
Vikings, 23-17 (M)
1988—Vikings, 14-13 (M)
Vikings, 49-20 (TB)
(Points—Vikings 500, Buccaneers 349)
MINNESOTA vs. WASHINGTON
RS: Redskins lead series, 5-3
PS: Series tied, 2-2
1968—Vikings, 27-14 (M)
1970—Vikings, 19-10 (W)
1972—Redskins, 24-21 (M)
1973—*Vikings, 27-20 (M)
1975—Redskins, 31-30 (W)
1976—*Vikings, 35-20 (M)
1980—Vikings, 39-14 (W)
1982—**Redskins, 21-7 (W)
1984—Redskins, 31-17 (M)
1986—Redskins, 44-38 (W) OT
1987—Redskins, 27-24 (M) OT
***Redskins, 17-10 (W)
(Points—Vikings 294, Redskins 273)
**NFC Divisional Playoff*
***NFC Second Round Playoff*
****NFC Championship*

NEW ENGLAND vs. ATLANTA
RS: Patriots lead series, 3-2;
See Atlanta vs. New England
NEW ENGLAND vs. BUFFALO
RS: Patriots lead series, 31-25-1
PS: Patriots lead series, 1-0;
See Buffalo vs. New England
NEW ENGLAND vs. CHICAGO
RS: Patriots lead series, 3-2
PS: Bears lead series, 1-0;
See Chicago vs. New England
NEW ENGLAND vs. CINCINNATI
RS: Patriots lead series, 7-4;
See Cincinnati vs. New England
NEW ENGLAND vs. CLEVELAND
RS: Browns lead series, 7-2;
See Cleveland vs. New England
NEW ENGLAND vs. DALLAS
RS: Cowboys lead series, 6-0;
See Dallas vs. New England
NEW ENGLAND vs. DENVER
RS: Broncos lead series, 14-12
PS: Broncos lead series, 1-0;
See Denver vs. New England
NEW ENGLAND vs. DETROIT
RS: Series tied, 2-2;
See Detroit vs. New England
NEW ENGLAND vs. GREEN BAY
RS: Series tied, 2-2;
See Green Bay vs. New England
NEW ENGLAND vs. HOUSTON
RS: Patriots lead series, 15-13-1
PS: Oilers lead series, 1-0;
See Houston vs. New England
NEW ENGLAND vs. INDIANAPOLIS
RS: Patriots lead series, 20-17;
See Indianapolis vs. New England
NEW ENGLAND vs. KANSAS CITY
RS: Chiefs lead series, 11-7-3;
See Kansas City vs. New England
NEW ENGLAND vs. L.A. RAIDERS
RS: Patriots lead series, 12-11-1
PS: Series tied, 1-1;
See L.A. Raiders vs. New England
NEW ENGLAND vs. L.A. RAMS
RS: Patriots lead series, 3-1;
See L.A. Rams vs. New England
NEW ENGLAND vs. MIAMI
RS: Dolphins lead series, 24-20
PS: Series tied, 1-1;
See Miami vs. New England
NEW ENGLAND vs. MINNESOTA
RS: Series tied, 2-2;
See Minnesota vs. New England
NEW ENGLAND vs. NEW ORLEANS
RS: Patriots lead series, 5-0
1972—Patriots, 17-10 (NO)
1976—Patriots, 27-6 (NE)
1980—Patriots, 38-27 (NO)
1983—Patriots, 7-0 (NE)
1986—Patriots, 21-20 (NO)
(Points—Patriots 110, Saints 63)
***NEW ENGLAND vs. N.Y. GIANTS**
RS: Giants lead series, 2-1
1970—Giants, 16-0 (B)
1974—Patriots, 28-20 (New Haven)
1987—Giants, 17-10 (NY)
(Points—Giants 53, Patriots 38)
**Franchise in Boston prior to 1971*
***NEW ENGLAND vs. **N.Y. JETS**
RS: Jets lead series, 31-25-1
PS: Patriots lead series, 1-0
1960—Patriots, 28-24 (NY)
Patriots, 38-21 (B)
1961—Titans, 21-20 (B)
Titans, 37-30 (NY)
1962—Patriots, 43-14 (NY)
Patriots, 24-17 (B)
1963—Patriots, 38-14 (B)
Jets, 31-24 (NY)
1964—Patriots, 26-10 (B)
Jets, 35-14 (NY)
1965—Jets, 30-20 (B)
Patriots, 27-23 (NY)
1966—Tie, 24-24 (B)
Jets, 38-28 (NY)
1967—Jets, 30-23 (NY)
Jets, 29-24 (B)
1968—Jets, 47-31 (Birmingham)
Jets, 48-14 (NY)
1969—Jets, 23-14 (B)
Jets, 23-17 (NY)
1970—Jets, 31-21 (B)
Jets, 17-3 (NY)
1971—Patriots, 20-0 (NE)
Jets, 13-6 (NY)
1972—Jets, 41-13 (NE)
Jets, 34-10 (NY)
1973—Jets, 9-7 (NE)
Jets, 33-13 (NY)
1974—Patriots, 24-0 (NY)
Jets, 21-16 (NE)
1975—Jets, 36-7 (NY)
Jets, 30-28 (NE)
1976—Patriots, 41-7 (NE)
Patriots, 38-24 (NY)
1977—Jets, 30-27 (NY)
Patriots, 24-13 (NE)
1978—Patriots, 55-21 (NE)
Patriots, 19-17 (NY)
1979—Patriots, 56-3 (NE)
Jets, 27-26 (NY)
1980—Patriots, 21-11 (NY)
Patriots, 34-21 (NE)
1981—Jets, 28-24 (NY)
Jets, 17-6 (NE)
1982—Jets, 31-7 (NE)
1983—Patriots, 23-13 (NE)
Jets, 26-3 (NY)
1984—Patriots, 28-21 (NY)
Patriots, 30-20 (NE)
1985—Patriots, 20-13 (NE)
Jets, 16-13 (NY) OT
***Patriots, 26-14 (NY)
1986—Patriots, 20-6 (NY)
Jets, 31-24 (NE)
1987—Jets, 43-24 (NY)
Patriots, 42-20 (NE)
1988—Patriots, 28-3 (NE)
Patriots, 14-13 (NY)
(Points—Patriots 1,348, Jets 1,293)
**Franchise in Boston prior to 1971*
***Jets known as Titans prior to 1963*
****AFC First Round Playoff*
NEW ENGLAND vs. PHILADELPHIA
RS: Eagles lead series, 4-2
1973—Eagles, 24-23 (P)
1977—Patriots, 14-6 (NE)
1978—Patriots, 24-14 (NE)
1981—Eagles, 13-3 (P)
1984—Eagles, 27-17 (P)
1987—Eagles, 34-31 (NE) OT
(Points—Eagles 118, Patriots 112)
***NEW ENGLAND vs. **PHOENIX**
RS: Cardinals lead series, 4-1
1970—Cardinals, 31-0 (StL)
1975—Cardinals, 24-17 (StL)
1978—Patriots, 16-6 (StL)
1981—Cardinals, 27-20 (NE)
1984—Cardinals, 33-10 (NE)
(Points—Cardinals 121, Patriots 63)
**Franchise in Boston prior to 1971*
***Franchise in St. Louis prior to 1988*
NEW ENGLAND vs. PITTSBURGH
RS: Steelers lead series, 5-3
1972—Steelers, 33-3 (P)
1974—Steelers, 21-17 (NE)
1976—Patriots, 30-27 (P)
1979—Steelers, 16-13 (NE) OT
1981—Steelers, 27-21 (P) OT
1982—Steelers, 37-14 (P)
1983—Patriots, 28-23 (P)
1986—Patriots, 34-0 (P)
(Points—Steelers 184, Patriots 160)
***NEW ENGLAND vs. **SAN DIEGO**
RS: Patriots lead series, 13-11-2
PS: Chargers lead series, 1-0
1960—Patriots, 35-0 (LA)
Chargers, 45-16 (B)
1961—Chargers, 38-27 (B)
Patriots, 41-0 (SD)
1962—Patriots, 24-20 (B)
Patriots, 20-14 (SD)
1963—Chargers, 17-13 (SD)
Chargers, 7-6 (B)
***Chargers, 51-10 (SD)
1964—Patriots, 33-28 (SD)
Chargers, 26-17 (B)
1965—Tie, 10-10 (B)
Patriots, 22-6 (SD)
1966—Chargers, 24-0 (SD)
Patriots, 35-17 (B)
1967—Chargers, 28-14 (SD)
Tie, 31-31 (SD)
1968—Chargers, 27-17 (B)
1969—Chargers, 13-10 (B)
Chargers, 28-18 (SD)
1970—Chargers, 16-14 (B)
1973—Patriots, 30-14 (NE)
1975—Patriots, 33-19 (SD)
1977—Patriots, 24-20 (SD)
1978—Patriots, 28-23 (NE)
1979—Patriots, 27-21 (NE)
1983—Patriots, 37-21 (NE)
(Points—Patriots 592, Chargers 564)
**Franchise in Boston prior to 1971*
***Franchise in Los Angeles prior to 1961*
****AFL Championship*
NEW ENGLAND vs. SAN FRANCISCO
RS: 49ers lead series, 4-1
1971—49ers, 27-10 (SF)
1975—Patriots, 24-16 (NE)
1980—49ers, 21-17 (SF)
1983—49ers, 33-13 (NE)
1986—49ers, 29-24 (NE)
(Points—49ers 126, Patriots 88)
NEW ENGLAND vs. SEATTLE
RS: Patriots lead series, 6-2
1977—Patriots, 31-0 (NE)
1980—Patriots, 37-31 (S)
1982—Patriots, 16-0 (S)
1983—Seahawks, 24-6 (S)
1984—Patriots, 38-23 (NE)
1985—Patriots, 20-13 (S)
1986—Seahawks, 38-31 (NE)
1988—Patriots, 13-7 (NE)
(Points—Patriots 192, Seahawks 136)
NEW ENGLAND vs. TAMPA BAY
RS: Patriots lead series, 3-0
1976—Patriots, 31-14 (TB)
1985—Patriots, 32-14 (TB)
1988—Patriots, 10-7 (NE) OT
(Points—Patriots 73, Buccaneers 35)
NEW ENGLAND vs. WASHINGTON
RS: Redskins lead series, 3-1
1972—Patriots, 24-23 (NE)
1978—Redskins, 16-14 (NE)
1981—Redskins, 24-22 (W)
1984—Redskins, 26-10 (NE)
(Points—Redskins 89, Patriots 70)

NEW ORLEANS vs. ATLANTA
RS: Falcons lead series, 24-15;
See Atlanta vs. New Orleans
NEW ORLEANS vs. BUFFALO
RS: Bills lead series, 2-1;
See Buffalo vs. New Orleans
NEW ORLEANS vs. CHICAGO
RS: Bears lead series, 7-5;
See Chicago vs. New Orleans
NEW ORLEANS vs. CINCINNATI
RS: Series tied, 3-3;
See Cincinnati vs. New Orleans
NEW ORLEANS vs. CLEVELAND
RS: Browns lead series, 8-2;
See Cleveland vs. New Orleans
NEW ORLEANS vs. DALLAS
RS: Cowboys lead series, 11-2;

See Dallas vs. New Orleans
NEW ORLEANS vs. DENVER
RS: Broncos lead series, 4-1;
See Denver vs. New Orleans
NEW ORLEANS vs. DETROIT
RS: Saints lead series, 5-4-1;
See Detroit vs. New Orleans
NEW ORLEANS vs. GREEN BAY
RS: Packers lead series, 10-4;
See Green Bay vs. New Orleans
NEW ORLEANS vs. HOUSTON
RS: Saints lead series, 3-2-1;
See Houston vs. New Orleans
NEW ORLEANS vs. INDIANAPOLIS
RS: Colts lead series, 3-1;
See Indianapolis vs. New Orleans
NEW ORLEANS vs. KANSAS CITY
RS: Series tied, 2-2;
See Kansas City vs. New Orleans
NEW ORLEANS vs. L.A. RAIDERS
RS: Raiders lead series, 3-1-1;
See L.A. Raiders vs. New Orleans
NEW ORLEANS vs. L.A. RAMS
RS: Rams lead series, 25-13;
See L.A. Rams vs. New Orleans
NEW ORLEANS vs. MIAMI
RS: Dolphins lead series, 4-1;
See Miami vs. New Orleans
NEW ORLEANS vs. MINNESOTA
RS: Vikings lead series, 10-4
PS: Vikings lead series, 1-0;
See Minnesota vs. New Orleans
NEW ORLEANS vs. NEW ENGLAND
RS: Patriots lead series, 5-0;
See New England vs. New Orleans
NEW ORLEANS vs. N.Y. GIANTS
RS: Giants lead series, 8-6
1967—Giants, 27-21 (NY)
1968—Giants, 38-21 (NY)
1969—Saints, 25-24 (NY)
1970—Saints, 14-10 (NO)
1972—Giants, 45-21 (NY)
1975—Giants, 28-14 (NY)
1978—Saints, 28-17 (NO)
1979—Saints, 24-14 (NO)
1981—Giants, 20-7 (NY)
1984—Saints, 10-3 (NY)
1985—Giants, 21-13 (NO)
1986—Giants, 20-17 (NY)
1987—Saints, 23-14 (NO)
1988—Giants, 13-12 (NO)
(Points—Giants 294, Saints 250)
NEW ORLEANS vs. N.Y. JETS
RS: Jets lead series, 4-1
1972—Jets, 18-17 (NY)
1977—Jets, 16-13 (NO)
1980—Saints, 21-20 (NY)
1983—Jets, 31-28 (NO)
1986—Jets, 28-23 (NY)
(Points—Jets 113, Saints 102)
NEW ORLEANS vs. PHILADELPHIA
RS: Eagles lead series, 9-6
1967—Saints, 31-24 (NO)
Eagles, 48-21 (P)
1968—Eagles, 29-17 (P)
1969—Eagles, 13-10 (P)
Saints, 26-17 (NO)
1972—Saints, 21-3 (NO)
1974—Saints, 14-10 (NO)
1977—Eagles, 28-7 (P)
1978—Eagles, 24-17 (NO)
1979—Eagles, 26-14 (NO)
1980—Eagles, 34-21 (NO)
1981—Eagles, 31-14 (NO)
1983—Saints, 20-17 (P) OT
1985—Saints, 23-21 (NO)
1987—Eagles, 27-17 (P)
(Points—Eagles 352, Saints 273)
NEW ORLEANS vs. *PHOENIX
RS: Cardinals lead series, 10-5
1967—Cardinals, 31-20 (StL)
1968—Cardinals, 21-20 (NO)
Cardinals, 31-17 (StL)
1969—Saints, 51-42 (StL)
1970—Cardinals, 24-17 (StL)
1974—Saints, 14-0 (NO)
1977—Cardinals, 49-31 (StL)
1980—Cardinals, 40-7 (NO)
1981—Cardinals, 30-3 (StL)
1982—Cardinals, 21-7 (NO)
1983—Saints, 28-17 (NO)
1984—Saints, 34-24 (NO)
1985—Cardinals, 28-16 (StL)
1986—Saints, 16-7 (StL)
1987—Cardinals, 24-19 (StL)
(Points—Cardinals 389, Saints 300)
**Franchise in St. Louis prior to 1988*
NEW ORLEANS vs. PITTSBURGH
RS: Saints lead series, 5-4
1967—Steelers, 14-10 (NO)
1968—Saints, 16-12 (P)
Saints, 24-14 (NO)
1969—Saints, 27-24 (NO)
1974—Steelers, 28-7 (NO)
1978—Steelers, 20-14 (P)
1981—Steelers, 20-6 (NO)
1984—Saints, 27-24 (NO)
1987—Saints, 20-16 (P)
(Points—Steelers 172, Saints 151)
NEW ORLEANS vs. SAN DIEGO
RS: Chargers lead series, 3-1
1973—Chargers, 17-14 (SD)
1977—Chargers, 14-0 (NO)
1979—Chargers, 35-0 (NO)
1988—Saints, 23-17 (SD)
(Points—Chargers 83, Saints 37)
NEW ORLEANS vs. SAN FRANCISCO
RS: 49ers lead series, 26-11-2
1967—49ers, 27-13 (SF)
1969—Saints, 43-38 (NO)
1970—Tie, 20-20 (SF)
49ers, 38-27 (NO)
1971—49ers, 38-20 (NO)
Saints, 26-20 (SF)
1972—49ers, 37-2 (NO)
Tie, 20-20 (SF)
1973—49ers, 40-0 (SF)
Saints, 16-10 (NO)
1974—49ers, 17-13 (NO)
49ers, 35-21 (SF)
1975—49ers, 35-21 (SF)
49ers, 16-6 (NO)
1976—49ers, 33-3 (SF)
49ers, 27-7 (NO)
1977—49ers, 10-7 (NO) OT
49ers, 20-17 (SF)
1978—Saints, 14-7 (SF)
Saints, 24-13 (NO)
1979—Saints, 30-21 (SF)
Saints, 31-20 (NO)
1980—49ers, 26-23 (NO)
49ers, 38-35 (SF) OT
1981—49ers, 21-14 (SF)
49ers, 21-17 (NO)
1982—Saints, 23-20 (SF)
1983—49ers, 32-13 (NO)
49ers, 27-0 (SF)
1984—49ers, 30-20 (SF)
49ers, 35-3 (NO)
1985—Saints, 20-17 (SF)
49ers, 31-19 (NO)
1986—49ers, 26-17 (SF)
Saints, 23-10 (NO)
1987—49ers, 24-22 (NO)
Saints, 26-24 (SF)
1988—49ers, 34-33 (NO)
49ers, 30-17 (SF)
(Points—49ers 988, Saints 706)
NEW ORLEANS vs. SEATTLE
RS: Series tied, 2-2
1976—Saints, 51-27 (S)
1979—Seahawks, 38-24 (S)
1985—Seahawks, 27-3 (NO)
1988—Saints, 20-19 (S)
(Points—Seahawks 111, Saints 98)
NEW ORLEANS vs. TAMPA BAY
RS: Saints lead series, 8-3
1977—Buccaneers, 33-14 (NO)
1978—Saints, 17-10 (TB)
1979—Saints, 42-14 (TB)
1981—Buccaneers, 31-14 (NO)
1982—Buccaneers, 13-10 (NO)
1983—Saints, 24-21 (TB)
1984—Saints, 17-13 (NO)
1985—Saints, 20-13 (NO)
1986—Saints, 38-7 (NO)
1987—Saints, 44-34 (NO)
1988—Saints, 13-9 (NO)
(Points—Saints 253, Buccaneers 198)
NEW ORLEANS vs. WASHINGTON
RS: Redskins lead series, 9-4
1967—Redskins, 30-10 (NO)
Saints, 30-14 (W)
1968—Saints, 37-17 (NO)
1969—Redskins, 26-20 (NO)
Redskins, 17-14 (W)
1971—Redskins, 24-14 (W)
1973—Saints, 19-3 (NO)
1975—Redskins, 41-3 (W)
1979—Saints, 14-10 (W)
1980—Redskins, 22-14 (W)
1982—Redskins, 27-10 (NO)
1986—Redskins, 14-6 (NO)
1988—Redskins, 27-24 (W)
(Points—Redskins 272, Saints 215)

N.Y. GIANTS vs. ATLANTA
RS: Series tied, 6-6;
See Atlanta vs. N.Y. Giants
N.Y. GIANTS vs. BUFFALO
RS: Series tied, 2-2;
See Buffalo vs. N.Y. Giants
N.Y. GIANTS vs. CHICAGO
RS: Bears lead series, 23-14-2
PS: Bears lead series, 5-2;
See Chicago vs. N.Y. Giants
N.Y. GIANTS vs. CINCINNATI
RS: Bengals lead series, 3-0;
See Cincinnati vs. N.Y. Giants
N.Y. GIANTS vs. CLEVELAND
RS: Browns lead series, 25-15-2
PS: Series tied, 1-1;
See Cleveland vs. N.Y. Giants
N.Y. GIANTS vs. DALLAS
RS: Cowboys lead series, 35-16-2;
See Dallas vs. N.Y. Giants
N.Y. GIANTS vs. DENVER
RS: Series tied, 2-2
PS: Giants lead series, 1-0;
See Denver vs. N.Y. Giants
N.Y. GIANTS vs. DETROIT
RS: Lions lead series, 17-13-1
PS: Lions lead series, 1-0;
See Detroit vs. N.Y. Giants
N.Y. GIANTS vs. GREEN BAY
RS: Packers lead series, 21-19-2
PS: Packers lead series, 4-1;
See Green Bay vs. N.Y. Giants
N.Y. GIANTS vs. HOUSTON
RS: Giants lead series, 3-0;
See Houston vs. N.Y. Giants
N.Y. GIANTS vs. INDIANAPOLIS
RS: Colts lead series, 5-3
PS: Colts lead series, 2-0;
See Indianapolis vs. N.Y. Giants
N.Y. GIANTS vs. KANSAS CITY
RS: Giants lead series, 5-1;
See Kansas City vs. N.Y. Giants
N.Y. GIANTS vs. L.A. RAIDERS
RS: Raiders lead series, 3-1;
See L.A. Raiders vs. N.Y. Giants
N.Y. GIANTS vs. L.A. RAMS
RS: Rams lead series, 17-7
PS: Giants lead series, 1-0;
See L.A. Rams vs. N.Y. Giants
N.Y. GIANTS vs. MIAMI
RS: Dolphins lead series, 1-0;
See Miami vs. N.Y. Giants
N.Y. GIANTS vs. MINNESOTA
RS: Vikings lead series, 6-2;
See Minnesota vs. N.Y. Giants
N.Y. GIANTS vs. NEW ENGLAND
RS: Giants lead series, 2-1;
See New England vs. N.Y. Giants
N.Y. GIANTS vs. NEW ORLEANS
RS: Giants lead series, 8-6;
See New Orleans vs. N.Y. Giants
N.Y. GIANTS vs. N.Y. JETS
RS: Series tied, 3-3
1970—Giants, 22-10 (NYJ)
1974—Jets, 26-20 (New Haven) OT
1981—Jets, 26-7 (NYG)
1984—Giants, 20-10 (NYJ)
1987—Giants, 20-7 (NYG)
1988—Jets, 27-21 (NYJ)
(Points—Giants 110, Jets 106)
N.Y. GIANTS vs. PHILADELPHIA
RS: Giants lead series, 59-47-2
PS: Giants lead series, 1-0
1933—Giants, 56-0 (NY)
Giants, 20-14 (P)
1934—Giants, 17-0 (NY)
Eagles, 6-0 (P)
1935—Giants, 10-0 (NY)
Giants, 21-14 (P)
1936—Eagles, 10-7 (P)
Giants, 21-17 (NY)
1937—Giants, 16-7 (P)
Giants, 21-0 (NY)
1938—Eagles, 14-10 (P)
Giants, 17-7 (NY)
1939—Giants, 13-3 (P)
Giants, 27-10 (NY)
1940—Giants, 20-14 (P)
Giants, 17-7 (NY)
1941—Giants, 24-0 (P)
Giants, 16-0 (NY)
1942—Giants, 35-17 (NY)
Giants, 14-0 (P)
1944—Eagles, 24-17 (NY)
Tie, 21-21 (P)
1945—Eagles, 38-17 (P)
Giants, 28-21 (NY)
1946—Eagles, 24-14 (P)
Giants, 45-17 (NY)
1947—Eagles, 23-0 (P)
Eagles, 41-24 (NY)
1948—Eagles, 45-0 (P)
Eagles, 35-14 (NY)
1949—Eagles, 24-3 (NY)
Eagles, 17-3 (P)
1950—Giants, 7-3 (NY)
Giants, 9-7 (P)
1951—Giants, 26-24 (NY)
Giants, 23-7 (P)
1952—Giants, 31-7 (P)
Eagles, 14-10 (NY)
1953—Eagles, 30-7 (P)
Giants, 37-28 (NY)
1954—Giants, 27-14 (NY)
Eagles, 29-14 (P)
1955—Eagles, 27-17 (P)
Giants, 31-7 (NY)
1956—Giants, 20-3 (NY)
Giants, 21-7 (P)
1957—Giants, 24-20 (P)
Giants, 13-0 (NY)
1958—Eagles, 27-24 (P)
Giants, 24-10 (NY)
1959—Eagles, 49-21 (P)
Giants, 24-7 (NY)
1960—Eagles, 17-10 (NY)
Eagles, 31-23 (P)
1961—Giants, 38-21 (NY)
Giants, 28-24 (P)
1962—Giants, 29-13 (P)
Giants, 19-14 (NY)
1963—Giants, 37-14 (P)
Giants, 42-14 (NY)
1964—Eagles, 38-7 (P)
Eagles, 23-17 (NY)
1965—Giants, 16-14 (P)
Giants, 35-27 (NY)
1966—Eagles, 35-17 (P)
Eagles, 31-3 (NY)
1967—Giants, 44-7 (NY)
1968—Giants, 34-25 (P)
Giants, 7-6 (NY)
1969—Eagles, 23-20 (NY)
1970—Giants, 30-23 (NY)
Eagles, 23-20 (P)
1971—Eagles, 23-7 (P)
Eagles, 41-28 (NY)
1972—Giants, 27-12 (P)
Giants, 62-10 (NY)
1973—Tie, 23-23 (NY)
Eagles, 20-16 (P)
1974—Eagles, 35-7 (P)
Eagles, 20-7 (New Haven)
1975—Giants, 23-14 (P)
Eagles, 13-10 (NY)
1976—Eagles, 20-7 (P)
Eagles, 10-0 (NY)
1977—Eagles, 28-10 (NY)
Eagles, 17-14 (P)
1978—Eagles, 19-17 (NY)
Eagles, 20-3 (P)
1979—Eagles, 23-17 (P)
Eagles, 17-13 (NY)
1980—Eagles, 35-3 (P)
Eagles, 31-16 (NY)
1981—Eagles, 24-10 (NY)
Giants, 20-10 (P)
*Giants, 27-21 (P)
1982—Giants, 23-7 (NY)
Giants, 26-24 (P)
1983—Eagles, 17-13 (NY)
Giants, 23-0 (P)
1984—Giants, 28-27 (NY)
Eagles, 24-10 (P)
1985—Giants, 21-0 (NY)
Giants, 16-10 (P) OT
1986—Giants, 35-3 (NY)
Giants, 17-14 (P)
1987—Giants, 20-17 (P)
Giants, 23-20 (NY) OT
1988—Eagles, 24-13 (P)
Eagles, 23-17 (NY) OT
(Points—Giants 2,106, Eagles 1,909)
**NFC First Round Playoff*
N.Y. GIANTS vs. *PHOENIX
RS: Giants lead series, 57-33-2
1926—Giants, 20-0 (NY)
1927—Giants, 28-7 (NY)
1929—Giants, 24-21 (NY)
1930—Giants, 25-12 (NY)
Giants, 13-7 (C)
1935—Cardinals, 14-13 (NY)
1936—Giants, 14-6 (NY)
1938—Giants, 6-0 (NY)
1939—Giants, 17-7 (NY)
1941—Cardinals, 10-7 (NY)
1942—Giants, 21-7 (NY)
1943—Giants, 24-13 (NY)
1946—Giants, 28-24 (NY)
1947—Giants, 35-31 (NY)
1948—Cardinals, 63-35 (NY)
1949—Giants, 41-38 (C)
1950—Cardinals, 17-3 (C)
Giants, 51-21 (NY)
1951—Giants, 28-17 (NY)
Giants, 10-0 (C)
1952—Cardinals, 24-23 (NY)
Giants, 28-6 (C)
1953—Giants, 21-7 (NY)
Giants, 23-20 (C)
1954—Giants, 41-10 (C)
Giants, 31-17 (NY)
1955—Cardinals, 28-17 (C)
Giants, 10-0 (NY)
1956—Cardinals, 35-27 (C)
Giants, 23-10 (NY)

1957—Giants, 27-14 (NY)
Giants, 28-21 (C)
1958—Giants, 37-7 (Buffalo)
Cardinals, 23-6 (NY)
1959—Giants, 9-3 (NY)
Giants, 30-20 (Minn)
1960—Giants, 35-14 (StL)
Cardinals, 20-13 (NY)
1961—Cardinals, 21-10 (NY)
Giants, 24-9 (StL)
1962—Giants, 31-14 (StL)
Giants, 31-28 (NY)
1963—Giants, 38-21 (StL)
Cardinals, 24-17 (NY)
1964—Giants, 34-17 (NY)
Tie, 10-10 (StL)
1965—Giants, 14-10 (NY)
Giants, 28-15 (StL)
1966—Cardinals, 24-19 (StL)
Cardinals, 20-17 (NY)
1967—Giants, 37-20 (StL)
Giants, 37-14 (NY)
1968—Cardinals, 28-21 (NY)
1969—Cardinals, 42-17 (StL)
Giants, 49-6 (NY)
1970—Giants, 35-17 (NY)
Giants, 34-17 (StL)
1971—Giants, 21-20 (StL)
Cardinals, 24-7 (NY)
1972—Giants, 27-21 (NY)
Giants, 13-7 (StL)
1973—Cardinals, 35-27 (StL)
Giants, 24-13 (New Haven)
1974—Cardinals, 23-21 (New Haven)
Cardinals, 26-14 (StL)
1975—Cardinals, 26-14 (StL)
Cardinals, 20-13 (NY)
1976—Cardinals, 27-21 (StL)
Cardinals, 17-14 (NY)
1977—Cardinals, 28-0 (StL)
Giants, 27-7 (NY)
1978—Cardinals, 20-10 (StL)
Giants, 17-0 (NY)
1979—Cardinals, 27-14 (NY)
Cardinals, 29-20 (StL)
1980—Giants, 41-35 (StL)
Cardinals, 23-7 (NY)
1981—Giants, 34-14 (NY)
Giants, 20-10 (StL)
1982—Cardinals, 24-21 (StL)
1983—Tie, 20-20 (StL) OT
Cardinals, 10-6 (NY)
1984—Giants, 16-10 (NY)
Cardinals, 31-21 (StL)
1985—Giants, 27-17 (NY)
Giants, 34-3 (StL)
1986—Giants, 13-6 (StL)
Giants, 27-7 (NY)
1987—Giants, 30-7 (NY)
Cardinals, 27-24 (StL)
1988—Cardinals, 24-17 (P)
Giants, 44-7 (NY)
(Points—Giants 2,081, Cardinals 1,596)
Franchise in St. Louis prior to 1988 and in Chicago prior to 1960

N.Y. GIANTS vs. *PITTSBURGH
RS: Giants lead series, 41-26-3
1933—Giants, 23-2 (P)
Giants, 27-3 (NY)
1934—Giants, 14-12 (P)
Giants, 17-7 (NY)
1935—Giants, 42-7 (P)
Giants, 13-0 (NY)
1936—Pirates, 10-7 (P)
1937—Giants, 10-7 (P)
Giants, 17-0 (NY)
1938—Giants, 27-14 (P)
Pirates, 13-10 (NY)
1939—Giants, 14-7 (P)
Giants, 23-7 (NY)
1940—Tie, 10-10 (P)
Giants, 12-0 (NY)
1941—Giants, 37-10 (P)
Giants, 28-7 (NY)
1942—Steelers, 13-10 (P)
Steelers, 17-9 (NY)
1945—Giants, 34-6 (P)
Steelers, 21-7 (NY)
1946—Giants, 17-14 (P)
Giants, 7-0 (NY)
1947—Steelers, 38-21 (NY)
Steelers, 24-7 (P)
1948—Giants, 34-27 (NY)
Steelers, 38-28 (P)
1949—Steelers, 28-7 (P)
Steelers, 21-17 (NY)
1950—Giants, 18-7 (P)
Steelers, 17-6 (NY)
1951—Tie, 13-13 (P)
Giants, 14-0 (NY)
1952—Steelers, 63-7 (P)
1953—Steelers, 24-14 (P)
Steelers, 14-10 (NY)
1954—Giants, 30-6 (P)
Giants, 24-3 (NY)
1955—Steelers, 30-23 (P)
1956—Steelers, 19-17 (NY)
1956—Giants, 38-10 (NY)
Giants, 17-14 (P)
1957—Giants, 35-0 (NY)
Steelers, 21-10 (P)
1958—Giants, 17-6 (NY)
Steelers, 31-10 (P)
1959—Giants, 21-16 (P)
Steelers, 14-9 (NY)
1960—Giants, 19-17 (P)
Giants, 27-24 (NY)
1961—Giants, 17-14 (P)
Giants, 42-21 (NY)
1962—Giants, 31-27 (P)
Steelers, 20-17 (NY)
1963—Steelers, 31-0 (P)
Giants, 33-17 (NY)
1964—Steelers, 27-24 (P)
Steelers, 44-17 (NY)
1965—Giants, 23-13 (P)
Giants, 35-10 (NY)
1966—Tie, 34-34 (P)
Steelers, 47-28 (NY)
1967—Giants, 27-24 (P)
Giants, 28-20 (NY)
1968—Giants, 34-20 (P)
1969—Giants, 10-7 (NY)
Giants, 21-17 (P)
1971—Steelers, 17-13 (P)
1976—Steelers, 27-0 (NY)
1985—Giants, 28-10 (NY)
(Points—Giants 1,370, Steelers 1,159)
Steelers known as Pirates prior to 1941

N.Y. GIANTS vs. SAN DIEGO
RS: Giants lead series, 3-2
1971—Giants, 35-17 (NY)
1975—Giants, 35-24 (NY)
1980—Chargers, 44-7 (SD)
1983—Chargers, 41-34 (NY)
1986—Giants, 20-7 (NY)
(Points—Chargers 133, Giants 131)

N.Y. GIANTS vs. SAN FRANCISCO
RS: Giants lead series, 10-7
PS: Series tied, 2-2
1952—Giants, 23-14 (NY)
1956—Giants, 38-21 (SF)
1957—49ers, 27-17 (NY)
1960—Giants, 21-19 (SF)
1963—Giants, 48-14 (NY)
1968—49ers, 26-10 (NY)
1972—Giants, 23-17 (SF)
1975—Giants, 26-23 (SF)
1977—Giants, 20-17 (NY)
1978—Giants, 27-10 (NY)
1979—Giants, 32-16 (NY)
1980—49ers, 12-0 (SF)
1981—49ers, 17-10 (SF)
*49ers, 38-24 (SF)
1984—49ers, 31-10 (NY)
*49ers, 21-10 (SF)
1985—**Giants, 17-3 (NY)
1986—Giants, 21-17 (SF)
*Giants, 49-3 (NY)
1987—49ers, 41-21 (NY)
1988—49ers, 20-17 (NY)
(Points—Giants 464, 49ers 407)
**NFC Divisional Playoff*
***NFC First Round Playoff*

N.Y. GIANTS vs. SEATTLE
RS: Giants lead series, 3-2
1976—Giants, 28-16 (NY)
1980—Giants, 27-21 (S)
1981—Giants, 32-0 (S)
1983—Seahawks, 17-12 (NY)
1986—Seahawks, 17-12 (S)
(Points—Giants 111, Seahawks 71)

N.Y. GIANTS vs. TAMPA BAY
RS: Giants lead series, 6-3
1977—Giants, 10-0 (TB)
1978—Giants, 19-13 (TB)
Giants, 17-14 (NY)
1979—Giants, 17-14 (NY)
Buccaneers, 31-3 (TB)
1980—Buccaneers, 30-13 (TB)
1984—Giants, 17-14 (NY)
Buccaneers, 20-17 (TB)
1985—Giants, 22-20 (NY)
(Points—Buccaneers 156, Giants 135)

N.Y. GIANTS vs. *WASHINGTON
RS: Giants lead series, 62-47-3
PS: Series tied, 1-1
1932—Braves, 14-6 (B)
Tie, 0-0 (NY)
1933—Redskins, 21-20 (B)
Giants, 7-0 (NY)
1934—Giants, 16-13 (B)
Giants, 3-0 (NY)
1935—Giants, 20-12 (B)
Giants, 17-6 (NY)
1936—Giants, 7-0 (B)
Redskins, 14-0 (NY)
1937—Redskins, 13-3 (W)
Redskins, 49-14 (NY)
1938—Giants, 10-7 (W)
Giants, 36-0 (NY)
1939—Tie, 0-0 (W)
Giants, 9-7 (NY)
1940—Redskins, 21-7 (W)
Giants, 21-7 (NY)
1941—Giants, 17-10 (W)
Giants, 20-13 (NY)
1942—Giants, 14-7 (W)
Redskins, 14-7 (NY)
1943—Giants, 14-10 (NY)
Giants, 31-7 (W)
**Redskins, 28-0 (NY)
1944—Giants, 16-13 (NY)
Giants, 31-0 (W)
1945—Redskins, 24-14 (NY)
Redskins, 17-0 (W)
1946—Redskins, 24-14 (W)
Giants, 31-0 (NY)
1947—Redskins, 28-20 (W)
Giants, 35-10 (NY)
1948—Redskins, 41-10 (W)
Redskins, 28-21 (NY)
1949—Giants, 45-35 (W)
Giants, 23-7 (NY)
1950—Giants, 21-17 (W)
Giants, 24-21 (NY)
1951—Giants, 35-14 (W)
Giants, 28-14 (NY)
1952—Giants, 14-10 (W)
Redskins, 27-17 (NY)
1953—Redskins, 13-9 (W)
Redskins, 24-21 (NY)
1954—Giants, 51-21 (W)
Giants, 24-7 (NY)
1955—Giants, 35-7 (NY)
Giants, 27-20 (W)
1956—Redskins, 33-7 (W)
Giants, 28-14 (NY)
1957—Giants, 24-20 (W)
Redskins, 31-14 (NY)
1958—Giants, 21-14 (W)
Giants, 30-0 (NY)
1959—Giants, 45-14 (NY)
Giants, 24-10 (W)
1960—Tie, 24-24 (NY)
Giants, 17-3 (W)
1961—Giants, 24-21 (W)
Giants, 53-0 (NY)
1962—Giants, 49-34 (NY)
Giants, 42-24 (NY)
1963—Giants, 24-14 (W)
Giants, 44-14 (NY)
1964—Giants, 13-10 (NY)
Redskins, 36-21 (W)
1965—Redskins, 23-7 (NY)
Giants, 27-10 (W)
1966—Giants, 13-10 (NY)
Redskins, 72-41 (W)
1967—Redskins, 38-34 (W)
1968—Giants, 48-21 (NY)
Giants, 13-10 (W)
1969—Redskins, 20-14 (W)
1970—Giants, 35-33 (NY)
Giants, 27-24 (W)
1971—Redskins, 30-3 (NY)
Redskins, 23-7 (W)
1972—Redskins, 23-16 (NY)
Redskins, 27-13 (W)
1973—Redskins, 21-3 (New Haven)
Redskins, 27-24 (W)
1974—Redskins, 13-10 (New Haven)
Redskins, 24-3 (W)
1975—Redskins, 49-13 (W)
Redskins, 21-13 (NY)
1976—Redskins, 19-17 (W)
Giants, 12-9 (NY)
1977—Giants, 20-17 (NY)
Giants, 17-6 (W)
1978—Giants, 17-6 (NY)
Redskins, 16-13 (W) OT
1979—Redskins, 27-0 (W)
Giants, 14-6 (NY)
1980—Redskins, 23-21 (NY)
Redskins, 16-13 (W)
1981—Giants, 17-7 (W)
Redskins, 30-27 (NY) OT
1982—Redskins, 27-17 (NY)
Redskins, 15-14 (W)
1983—Redskins, 33-17 (NY)
Redskins, 31-22 (W)
1984—Redskins, 30-14 (W)
Giants, 37-13 (NY)
1985—Giants, 17-3 (NY)
Redskins, 23-21 (W)
1986—Giants, 27-20 (NY)
Giants, 24-14 (W)
***Giants, 17-0 (NY)
1987—Redskins, 38-12 (NY)
Redskins, 23-19 (W)
1988—Giants, 27-20 (NY)
Giants, 24-23 (W)
(Points—Giants 2,230, Redskins 2,025)
**Franchise in Boston prior to 1937 and known as Braves prior to 1933*
***Division Playoff*
****NFC Championship*

N.Y. JETS vs. ATLANTA
RS: Series tied, 2-2;
See Atlanta vs. N.Y. Jets
N.Y. JETS vs. BUFFALO
RS: Series tied, 28-28
PS: Bills lead series, 1-0;
See Buffalo vs. N.Y. Jets
N.Y. JETS vs. CHICAGO
RS: Bears lead series, 2-1;
See Chicago vs. N.Y. Jets
N.Y. JETS vs. CINCINNATI
RS: Jets lead series, 7-5
PS: Jets lead series, 1-0;
See Cincinnati vs. N.Y. Jets
N.Y. JETS vs. CLEVELAND
RS: Browns lead series, 7-4
PS: Browns lead series, 1-0;
See Cleveland vs. N.Y. Jets
N.Y. JETS vs. DALLAS
RS: Cowboys lead series, 4-0;
See Dallas vs. N.Y. Jets
N.Y. JETS vs. DENVER
RS: Jets lead series, 11-10-1;
See Denver vs. N.Y. Jets
N.Y. JETS vs. DETROIT
RS: Jets lead series, 3-2;
See Detroit vs. N.Y. Jets
N.Y. JETS vs. GREEN BAY
RS: Jets lead series, 4-1;
See Green Bay vs. N.Y. Jets
N.Y. JETS vs. HOUSTON
RS: Oilers lead series, 15-11-1;
See Houston vs. N.Y. Jets
N.Y. JETS vs. INDIANAPOLIS
RS: Colts lead series, 19-18
PS: Jets lead series, 1-0;
See Indianapolis vs. N.Y. Jets
N.Y. JETS vs. KANSAS CITY
RS: Chiefs lead series, 13-12-1
PS: Series tied, 1-1;
See Kansas City vs. N.Y. Jets
N.Y. JETS vs. L.A. RAIDERS
RS: Raiders lead series, 12-9-2
PS: Jets lead series, 2-0;
See L.A. Raiders vs. N.Y. Jets
N.Y. JETS vs. L.A. RAMS
RS: Rams lead series, 3-2;
See L.A. Rams vs. N.Y. Jets
N.Y. JETS vs. MIAMI
RS: Dolphins lead series, 23-22-1
PS: Dolphins lead series, 1-0;
See Miami vs. N.Y. Jets
N.Y. JETS vs. MINNESOTA
RS: Jets lead series, 3-1;
See Minnesota vs. N.Y. Jets
N.Y. JETS vs. NEW ENGLAND
RS: Jets lead series, 31-25-1
PS: Patriots lead series, 1-0;
See New England vs. N.Y. Jets
N.Y. JETS vs. NEW ORLEANS
RS: Jets lead series, 4-1;
See New Orleans vs. N.Y. Jets
N.Y. JETS vs. N.Y. GIANTS
RS: Series tied, 3-3;
See N.Y. Giants vs. N.Y. Jets
N.Y. JETS vs. PHILADELPHIA
RS: Eagles lead series, 4-0
1973—Eagles, 24-23 (P)
1977—Eagles, 27-0 (P)
1978—Eagles, 17-9 (P)
1987—Eagles, 38-27 (NY)
(Points—Eagles 106, Jets 59)
N.Y. JETS vs. *PHOENIX
RS: Cardinals lead series, 2-1
1971—Cardinals, 17-10 (StL)
1975—Cardinals 37-6 (NY)
1978—Jets, 23-10 (NY)
(Points—Cardinals 64, Jets 39)
**Franchise in St. Louis prior to 1988*
N.Y. JETS vs. PITTSBURGH
RS: Steelers lead series, 9-1
1970—Steelers, 21-17 (P)
1973—Steelers, 26-14 (P)
1975—Steelers, 20-7 (NY)
1977—Steelers, 23-20 (NY)
1978—Steelers, 28-17 (NY)
1981—Steelers, 38-10 (P)
1983—Steelers, 34-7 (NY)
1984—Steelers, 23-17 (NY)
1986—Steelers, 45-24 (NY)
1988—Jets, 24-20 (NY)
(Points—Steelers 278, Jets 157)
***N.Y. JETS vs. **SAN DIEGO**
RS: Chargers lead series, 14-7-1
1960—Chargers, 21-7 (NY)

Chargers, 50-43 (LA)
1961—Chargers, 25-10 (NY)
Chargers, 48-13 (SD)
1962—Chargers, 40-14 (SD)
Titans, 23-3 (NY)
1963—Chargers, 24-20 (SD)
Chargers, 53-7 (NY)
1964—Tie, 17-17 (NY)
Chargers, 38-3 (SD)
1965—Chargers, 34-9 (NY)
Chargers, 38-7 (SD)
1966—Jets, 17-16 (NY)
Chargers, 42-27 (SD)
1967—Jets, 42-31 (SD)
1968—Jets, 23-20 (NY)
Jets, 37-15 (SD)
1969—Chargers, 34-27 (SD)
1971—Chargers, 49-21 (SD)
1974—Jets, 27-14 (NY)
1975—Chargers, 24-16 (SD)
1983—Jets, 41-29 (SD)
(Points—Chargers 665, Jets 451)
Jets known as Titans prior to 1963
***Franchise in Los Angeles prior to 1961*

N.Y. JETS vs. SAN FRANCISCO
RS: 49ers lead series, 4-1
1971—49ers, 24-21 (NY)
1976—49ers, 17-6 (SF)
1980—49ers, 37-27 (NY)
1983—Jets, 27-13 (SF)
1986—49ers, 24-10 (SF)
(Points—49ers 115, Jets 91)

N.Y. JETS vs. SEATTLE
RS: Seahawks lead series, 7-3
1977—Seahawks, 17-0 (NY)
1978—Seahawks, 24-17 (NY)
1979—Seahawks, 30-7 (S)
1980—Seahawks, 27-17 (NY)
1981—Seahawks, 19-3 (NY)
Seahawks, 27-23 (S)
1983—Seahawks, 17-10 (NY)
1985—Jets, 17-14 (NY)
1986—Jets, 38-7 (S)
1987—Jets, 30-14 (NY)
(Points—Seahawks 196, Jets 162)

N.Y. JETS vs. TAMPA BAY
RS: Jets lead series, 3-1
1976—Jets, 34-0 (NY)
1982—Jets, 32-17 (NY)
1984—Buccaneers, 41-21 (TB)
1985—Jets, 62-28 (NY)
(Points—Jets 149, Buccaneers 86)

N.Y. JETS vs. WASHINGTON
RS: Redskins lead series, 4-0
1972—Redskins, 35-17 (NY)
1976—Redskins, 37-16 (NY)
1978—Redskins, 23-3 (W)
1987—Redskins, 17-16 (W)
(Points—Redskins 112, Jets 52)

PHILADELPHIA vs. ATLANTA
RS: Eagles lead series, 7-6-1
PS: Falcons lead series, 1-0;
See Atlanta vs. Philadelphia

PHILADELPHIA vs. BUFFALO
RS: Eagles lead series, 4-1;
See Buffalo vs. Philadelphia

PHILADELPHIA vs. CHICAGO
RS: Bears lead series, 21-3-1
PS: Series tied, 1-1;
See Chicago vs. Philadelphia

PHILADELPHIA vs. CINCINNATI
RS: Bengals lead series, 5-0;
See Cincinnati vs. Philadelphia

PHILADELPHIA vs. CLEVELAND
RS: Browns lead series, 30-11-1;
See Cleveland vs. Philadelphia

PHILADELPHIA vs. DALLAS
RS: Cowboys lead series, 36-20
PS: Eagles lead series, 1-0;
See Dallas vs. Philadelphia

PHILADELPHIA vs. DENVER
RS: Eagles lead series, 3-2;
See Denver vs. Philadelphia

PHILADELPHIA vs. DETROIT
RS: Lions lead series, 12-9-2;
See Detroit vs. Philadelphia

PHILADELPHIA vs. GREEN BAY
RS: Packers lead series, 18-4
PS: Eagles lead series, 1-0;
See Green Bay vs. Philadelphia

PHILADELPHIA vs. HOUSTON
RS: Eagles lead series, 4-0;
See Houston vs. Philadelphia

PHILADELPHIA vs. INDIANAPOLIS
RS: Series tied, 5-5;
See Indianapolis vs. Philadelphia

PHILADELPHIA vs. KANSAS CITY
RS: Eagles lead series, 1-0;
See Kansas City vs. Philadelphia

PHILADELPHIA vs. L.A. RAIDERS
RS: Series tied, 2-2
PS: Raiders lead series, 1-0;
See L.A. Raiders vs. Philadelphia

PHILADELPHIA vs. L.A. RAMS
RS: Rams lead series, 15-10-1
PS: Eagles lead series, 1-0;
See L.A. Rams vs. Philadelphia

PHILADELPHIA vs. MIAMI
RS: Dolphins lead series, 4-2;
See Miami vs. Philadelphia

PHILADELPHIA vs. MINNESOTA
RS: Vikings lead series, 10-3
PS: Eagles lead series, 1-0;
See Minnesota vs. Philadelphia

PHILADELPHIA vs. NEW ENGLAND
RS: Eagles lead series, 4-2;
See New England vs. Philadelphia

PHILADELPHIA vs. NEW ORLEANS
RS: Eagles lead series, 9-6;
See New Orleans vs. Philadelphia

PHILADELPHIA vs. N.Y. GIANTS
RS: Giants lead series, 59-47-2
PS: Giants lead series, 1-0;
See N.Y. Giants vs. Philadelphia

PHILADELPHIA vs. N.Y. JETS
RS: Eagles lead series, 4-0;
See N.Y. Jets vs. Philadelphia

PHILADELPHIA vs. *PHOENIX
RS: Cardinals lead series, 41-36-5
PS: Series tied, 1-1
1935—Cardinals, 12-3 (C)
1936—Cardinals, 13-0 (C)
1937—Tie, 6-6 (P)
1938—Eagles, 7-0 (Erie, Pa.)
1941—Eagles, 21-14 (P)
1945—Eagles, 21-6 (P)
1947—Cardinals, 45-21 (P)
**Cardinals, 28-21 (C)
1948—Cardinals, 21-14 (C)
**Eagles, 7-0 (P)
1949—Eagles, 28-3 (P)
1950—Eagles, 45-7 (C)
Cardinals, 14-10 (P)
1951—Eagles, 17-14 (C)
1952—Eagles, 10-7 (P)
Cardinals, 28-22 (C)
1953—Eagles, 56-17 (C)
Eagles, 38-0 (P)
1954—Eagles, 35-16 (C)
Eagles, 30-14 (P)
1955—Tie, 24-24 (C)
Eagles, 27-3 (P)
1956—Cardinals, 20-6 (P)
Cardinals, 28-17 (C)
1957—Eagles, 38-21 (C)
Cardinals, 31-27 (P)
1958—Tie, 21-21 (C)
Eagles, 49-21 (P)
1959—Eagles, 28-24 (Minn)
Eagles, 27-17 (P)
1960—Eagles, 31-27 (P)
Eagles, 20-6 (StL)
1961—Cardinals, 30-27 (P)
Eagles, 20-7 (StL)
1962—Cardinals, 27-21 (P)
Cardinals, 45-35 (StL)
1963—Cardinals, 28-24 (P)
Cardinals, 38-14 (StL)
1964—Cardinals, 38-13 (P)
Cardinals, 36-34 (StL)
1965—Eagles, 34-27 (P)
Eagles, 28-24 (StL)
1966—Cardinals, 16-13 (StL)
Cardinals, 41-10 (P)
1967—Cardinals, 48-14 (StL)
1968—Cardinals, 45-17 (P)
1969—Eagles, 34-30 (StL)
1970—Cardinals, 35-20 (P)
Cardinals, 23-14 (StL)
1971—Eagles, 37-20 (StL)
Eagles, 19-7 (P)
1972—Tie, 6-6 (P)
Cardinals, 24-23 (StL)
1973—Cardinals, 34-23 (P)
Eagles, 27-24 (StL)
1974—Cardinals, 7-3 (StL)
Cardinals, 13-3 (P)
1975—Cardinals, 31-20 (StL)
Cardinals, 24-23 (P)
1976—Cardinals, 33-14 (StL)
Cardinals, 17-14 (P)
1977—Cardinals, 21-17 (P)
Cardinals, 21-16 (StL)
1978—Cardinals, 16-10 (P)
Eagles, 14-10 (StL)
1979—Eagles, 24-20 (StL)
Eagles, 16-13 (P)
1980—Cardinals, 24-14 (StL)
Eagles, 17-3 (P)
1981—Eagles, 52-10 (StL)
Eagles, 38-0 (P)
1982—Cardinals, 23-20 (P)
1983—Cardinals, 14-11 (P)
Cardinals, 31-7 (StL)
1984—Cardinals, 34-14 (P)
Cardinals, 17-16 (StL)
1985—Eagles, 30-7 (P)
Eagles, 24-14 (StL)
1986—Cardinals, 13-10 (StL)
Tie, 10-10 (P) OT
1987—Eagles, 28-23 (StL)
Cardinals, 31-19 (P)
1988—Eagles, 31-21 (P)
Eagles, 23-17 (Phoe)
(Points—Eagles 1,772, Cardinals 1,679)
**Franchise in St. Louis prior to 1988 and in Chicago prior to 1960*
***NFL Championship*

PHILADELPHIA vs. *PITTSBURGH
RS: Eagles lead series, 42-25-3
PS: Eagles lead series, 1-0
1933—Eagles, 25-6 (Phila)
1934—Eagles, 17-0 (Pitt)
Pirates, 9-7 (Phila)
1935—Pirates, 17-7 (Phila)
Eagles, 17-6 (Pitt)
1936—Pirates, 17-0 (Pitt)
Pirates, 6-0 (Johnstown, Pa.)
1937—Pirates, 27-14 (Pitt)
Pirates, 16-7 (Pitt)
1938—Eagles, 27-7 (Buffalo)
Eagles, 14-7 (Charleston, W. Va.)
1939—Eagles, 17-14 (Phila)
Pirates, 24-12 (Pitt)
1940—Pirates, 7-3 (Pitt)
Eagles, 7-0 (Phila)
1941—Eagles, 10-7 (Pitt)
Tie, 7-7 (Phila)
1942—Eagles, 24-14 (Pitt)
Steelers, 14-0 (Phila)
1945—Eagles, 45-3 (Pitt)
Eagles, 30-6 (Phila)
1946—Steelers, 10-7 (Pitt)
Eagles, 10-7 (Phila)
1947—Steelers, 35-24 (Pitt)
Eagles, 21-0 (Phila)
**Eagles, 21-0 (Pitt)
1948—Eagles, 34-7 (Pitt)
Eagles, 17-0 (Phila)
1949—Eagles, 38-7 (Pitt)
Eagles, 34-17 (Phila)
1950—Eagles, 17-10 (Pitt)
Steelers, 9-7 (Phila)
1951—Eagles, 34-13 (Pitt)
Steelers, 17-13 (Phila)
1952—Eagles, 31-25 (Pitt)
Eagles, 26-21 (Phila)
1953—Eagles, 23-17 (Phila)
Eagles, 35-7 (Pitt)
1954—Eagles, 24-22 (Phila)
Steelers, 17-7 (Pitt)
1955—Steelers, 13-7 (Pitt)
Eagles, 24-0 (Phila)
1956—Eagles, 35-21 (Pitt)
Eagles, 14-7 (Phila)
1957—Steelers, 6-0 (Pitt)
Eagles, 7-6 (Phila)
1958—Steelers, 24-3 (Pitt)
Steelers, 31-24 (Phila)
1959—Eagles, 28-24 (Phila)
Steelers, 31-0 (Pitt)
1960—Eagles, 34-7 (Phila)
Steelers, 27-21 (Pitt)
1961—Eagles, 21-16 (Phila)
Eagles, 35-24 (Pitt)
1962—Steelers, 13-7 (Pitt)
Steelers, 26-17 (Phila)
1963—Tie, 21-21 (Phila)
Tie, 20-20 (Pitt)
1964—Eagles, 21-7 (Phila)
Eagles, 34-10 (Pitt)
1965—Steelers, 20-14 (Phila)
Eagles, 47-13 (Pitt)
1966—Eagles, 31-14 (Pitt)
Eagles, 27-23 (Phila)
1967—Eagles, 34-24 (Phila)
1968—Steelers, 6-3 (Pitt)
1969—Eagles, 41-27 (Phila)
1970—Eagles, 30-20 (Phila)
1974—Steelers, 27-0 (Pitt)
1979—Eagles, 17-14 (Phila)
1988—Eagles, 27-26 (Pitt)
(Points—Eagles 1,357, Steelers 993)
**Steelers known as Pirates prior to 1941*
***Division Playoff*

PHILADELPHIA vs. SAN DIEGO
RS: Series tied, 2-2
1974—Eagles, 13-7 (SD)
1980—Chargers, 22-21 (SD)
1985—Chargers, 20-14 (SD)
1986—Eagles, 23-7 (P)
(Points—Eagles 71, Chargers 56)

PHILADELPHIA vs. SAN FRANCISCO
RS: 49ers lead series, 10-4-1
1951—Eagles, 21-14 (P)
1953—49ers, 31-21 (SF)
1956—Tie, 10-10 (P)
1958—49ers, 30-24 (P)
1959—49ers, 24-14 (SF)
1964—49ers, 28-24 (P)
1966—Eagles, 35-34 (SF)
1967—49ers, 28-27 (P)
1969—49ers, 14-13 (SF)
1971—49ers, 31-3 (P)
1973—49ers, 38-28 (SF)
1975—Eagles, 27-17 (P)
1983—Eagles, 22-17 (SF)
1984—49ers, 21-9 (P)
1985—49ers, 24-13 (SF)
(Points—49ers 361, Eagles 291)

PHILADELPHIA vs. SEATTLE
RS: Eagles lead series, 2-1
1976—Eagles, 27-10 (P)
1980—Eagles, 27-20 (S)
1986—Seahawks, 24-20 (S)
(Points—Eagles 74, Seahawks 54)

PHILADELPHIA vs. TAMPA BAY
RS: Eagles lead series, 3-0
PS: Buccaneers lead series, 1-0
1977—Eagles, 13-3 (P)
1979—*Buccaneers, 24-17 (TB)
1981—Eagles, 20-10 (P)
1988—Eagles, 41-14 (TB)
(Points—Eagles 91, Buccaneers 51)
**NFC Divisional Playoff*

PHILADELPHIA vs. *WASHINGTON
RS: Redskins lead series, 62-40-5
1934—Redskins, 6-0 (B)
Redskins, 14-7 (P)
1935—Eagles, 7-6 (B)
1936—Redskins, 26-3 (P)
Redskins, 17-7 (B)
1937—Eagles, 14-0 (W)
Redskins, 10-7 (P)
1938—Redskins, 26-23 (P)
Redskins, 20-14 (W)
1939—Redskins, 7-0 (P)
Redskins, 7-6 (W)
1940—Redskins, 34-17 (P)
Redskins, 13-6 (W)
1941—Redskins, 21-17 (P)
Redskins, 20-14 (W)
1942—Redskins, 14-10 (P)
Redskins, 30-27 (W)
1944—Tie, 31-31 (P)
Eagles, 37-7 (W)
1945—Redskins, 24-14 (W)
Eagles, 16-0 (P)
1946—Eagles, 28-24 (W)
Redskins, 27-10 (P)
1947—Eagles, 45-42 (P)
Eagles, 38-14 (W)
1948—Eagles, 45-0 (W)
Eagles, 42-21 (P)
1949—Eagles, 49-14 (P)
Eagles, 44-21 (W)
1950—Eagles, 35-3 (P)
Eagles, 33-0 (W)
1951—Redskins, 27-23 (P)
Eagles, 35-21 (W)
1952—Eagles, 38-20 (P)
Redskins, 27-21 (W)
1953—Tie, 21-21 (P)
Redskins, 10-0 (W)
1954—Eagles, 49-21 (W)
Eagles, 41-33 (P)
1955—Redskins, 31-30 (P)
Redskins, 34-21 (W)
1956—Eagles, 13-9 (P)
Redskins, 19-17 (W)
1957—Eagles, 21-12 (P)
Redskins, 42-7 (W)
1958—Redskins, 24-14 (P)
Redskins, 20-0 (W)
1959—Eagles, 30-23 (P)
Eagles, 34-14 (W)
1960—Eagles, 19-13 (P)
Eagles, 38-28 (W)
1961—Eagles, 14-7 (P)
Eagles, 27-24 (W)
1962—Redskins, 27-21 (P)
Eagles, 37-14 (W)
1963—Eagles, 37-24 (W)
Redskins, 13-10 (P)
1964—Redskins, 35-20 (W)
Redskins, 21-10 (P)
1965—Redskins, 23-21 (W)
Eagles, 21-14 (P)
1966—Redskins, 27-13 (P)
Eagles, 37-28 (W)
1967—Eagles, 35-24 (P)
Tie, 35-35 (W)
1968—Redskins, 17-14 (W)
Redskins, 16-10 (P)
1969—Tie, 28-28 (W)
Redskins, 34-29 (P)
1970—Redskins, 33-21 (P)
Redskins, 24-6 (W)
1971—Tie, 7-7 (W)
Redskins, 20-13 (P)
1972—Redskins, 14-0 (W)

Redskins, 23-7 (P)
1973—Redskins, 28-7 (P)
Redskins, 38-20 (W)
1974—Redskins, 27-20 (P)
Redskins, 26-7 (W)
1975—Eagles, 26-10 (P)
Eagles, 26-3 (W)
1976—Redskins, 20-17 (P) OT
Redskins, 24-0 (W)
1977—Redskins, 23-17 (W)
Redskins, 17-14 (P)
1978—Redskins, 35-30 (W)
Eagles, 17-10 (P)
1979—Eagles, 28-17 (P)
Redskins, 17-7 (W)
1980—Eagles, 24-14 (P)
Eagles, 24-0 (W)
1981—Eagles, 36-13 (P)
Redskins, 15-13 (W)
1982—Redskins, 37-34 (P) OT
Redskins, 13-9 (W)
1983—Redskins, 23-13 (P)
Redskins, 28-24 (W)
1984—Redskins, 20-0 (W)
Eagles, 16-10 (P)
1985—Eagles, 19-6 (W)
Redskins, 17-12 (P)
1986—Redskins, 41-14 (W)
Redskins, 21-14 (P)
1987—Redskins, 34-24 (W)
Eagles, 31-27 (P)
1988—Redskins, 17-10 (W)
Redskins, 20-19 (P)
(Points—Eagles 2,163, Redskins 2,131)
Franchise in Boston prior to 1937

PHOENIX vs. ATLANTA
RS: Cardinals lead series, 7-4;
See Atlanta vs. Phoenix
PHOENIX vs. BUFFALO
RS: Cardinals lead series, 3-2;
See Buffalo vs. Phoenix
PHOENIX vs. CHICAGO
RS: Bears lead series, 50-25-6;
See Chicago vs. Phoenix
PHOENIX vs. CINCINNATI
RS: Bengals lead series, 3-1;
See Cincinnati vs. Phoenix
PHOENIX vs. CLEVELAND
RS: Browns lead series, 31-10-3;
See Cleveland vs. Phoenix
PHOENIX vs. DALLAS
RS: Cowboys lead series, 33-19-1;
See Dallas vs. Phoenix
PHOENIX vs. DENVER
RS: Broncos lead series, 1-0-1;
See Denver vs. Phoenix
PHOENIX vs. DETROIT
RS: Lions lead series, 25-15-5;
See Detroit vs. Phoenix
PHOENIX vs. GREEN BAY
RS: Packers lead series, 38-21-4
PS: Packers lead series, 1-0;
See Green Bay vs. Phoenix
PHOENIX vs. HOUSTON
RS: Cardinals lead series, 3-2;
See Houston vs. Phoenix
PHOENIX vs. INDIANAPOLIS
RS: Cardinals lead series, 5-4;
See Indianapolis vs. Phoenix
PHOENIX vs. KANSAS CITY
RS: Chiefs lead series, 3-1-1;
See Kansas City vs. Phoenix
PHOENIX vs. L.A. RAIDERS
RS: Series tied, 1-1;
See L.A. Raiders vs. Phoenix
PHOENIX vs. L.A. RAMS
RS: Rams lead series, 21-16-2
PS: Rams lead series, 1-0;
See L.A. Rams vs. Phoenix
PHOENIX vs. MIAMI
RS: Dolphins lead series, 5-0;
See Miami vs. Phoenix
PHOENIX vs. MINNESOTA
RS: Cardinals lead series, 7-2
PS: Vikings lead series, 1-0;
See Minnesota vs. Phoenix
PHOENIX vs. NEW ENGLAND
RS: Cardinals lead series, 4-1;
See New England vs. Phoenix
PHOENIX vs. NEW ORLEANS
RS: Cardinals lead series, 10-5;
See New Orleans vs. Phoenix
PHOENIX vs. N.Y. GIANTS
RS: Giants lead series, 57-33-2;
See N.Y. Giants vs. Phoenix
PHOENIX vs. N.Y. JETS
RS: Cardinals lead series, 2-1;
See N.Y. Jets vs. Phoenix
PHOENIX vs. PHILADELPHIA
RS: Cardinals lead series, 41-36-5
PS: Series tied, 1-1;
See Philadelphia vs. Phoenix

***PHOENIX vs. **PITTSBURGH**
RS: Steelers lead series, 29-21-3
1933—Pirates, 14-13 (C)
1935—Pirates, 17-13 (P)
1936—Cardinals, 14-6 (C)
1937—Cardinals, 13-7 (P)
1939—Cardinals, 10-0 (P)
1940—Tie, 7-7 (P)
1942—Steelers, 19-3 (P)
1945—Steelers, 23-0 (P)
1946—Steelers, 14-7 (P)
1948—Cardinals, 24-7 (P)
1950—Steelers, 28-17 (C)
Steelers, 28-7 (P)
1951—Steelers, 28-14 (C)
1952—Steelers, 34-28 (C)
Steelers, 17-14 (P)
1953—Steelers, 31-28 (P)
Steelers, 21-17 (C)
1954—Cardinals, 17-14 (C)
Steelers, 20-17 (P)
1955—Steelers, 14-7 (P)
Cardinals, 27-13 (C)
1956—Steelers, 14-7 (P)
Cardinals, 38-27 (C)
1957—Steelers, 29-20 (P)
Steelers, 27-2 (C)
1958—Steelers, 27-20 (C)
Steelers, 38-21 (P)
1959—Cardinals, 45-24 (C)
Steelers, 35-20 (P)
1960—Steelers, 27-14 (P)
Cardinals, 38-7 (StL)
1961—Steelers, 30-27 (P)
Cardinals, 20-0 (StL)
1962—Steelers, 26-17 (StL)
Steelers, 19-7 (P)
1963—Steelers, 23-10 (P)
Cardinals, 24-23 (StL)
1964—Cardinals, 34-30 (StL)
Cardinals, 21-20 (P)
1965—Cardinals, 20-7 (P)
Cardinals, 21-17 (P)
1966—Steelers, 30-9 (P)
Cardinals, 6-3 (StL)
1967—Cardinals, 28-14 (P)
Tie, 14-14 (StL)
1968—Tie, 28-28 (StL)
Cardinals, 20-10 (P)
1969—Cardinals, 27-14 (P)
Cardinals, 47-10 (StL)
1972—Steelers, 25-19 (StL)
1979—Steelers, 24-21 (StL)
1985—Steelers, 23-10 (P)
1988—Cardinals, 31-14 (Phoe)
(Points—Steelers 1,021, Cardinals 983)
*Franchise in St. Louis prior to 1988
and in Chicago prior to 1960*
***Steelers known as Pirates prior to 1941*
***PHOENIX vs. SAN DIEGO**
RS: Chargers lead series, 3-1
1971—Chargers, 20-17 (SD)
1976—Chargers, 43-24 (SD)
1983—Cardinals, 44-14 (StL)
1987—Chargers, 28-24 (SD)
(Points—Cardinals 109, Chargers 105)
Franchise in St. Louis prior to 1988
***PHOENIX vs. SAN FRANCISCO**
RS: Series tied, 8-8
1951—Cardinals, 27-21 (SF)
1957—Cardinals, 20-10 (SF)
1962—49ers, 24-17 (StL)
1964—Cardinals, 23-13 (SF)
1968—49ers, 35-17 (SF)
1971—49ers, 26-14 (StL)
1974—Cardinals, 34-9 (SF)
1976—Cardinals, 23-20 (StL) OT
1978—Cardinals, 16-10 (SF)
1979—Cardinals, 13-10 (StL)
1980—49ers, 24-21 (SF) OT
1982—49ers, 31-20 (StL)
1983—49ers, 42-27 (StL)
1986—49ers, 43-17 (SF)
1987—49ers, 34-28 (SF)
1988—Cardinals, 24-23 (P)
(Points—49ers 375, Cardinals 341)
*Franchise in St. Louis prior to 1988
and in Chicago prior to 1960*
***PHOENIX vs. SEATTLE**
RS: Cardinals lead series, 2-0
1976—Cardinals, 30-24 (S)
1983—Cardinals, 33-28 (StL)
(Points—Cardinals 63, Seahawks 52)
Franchise in St. Louis prior to 1988
***PHOENIX vs. TAMPA BAY**
RS: Cardinals lead series, 6-3
1977—Buccaneers, 17-7 (TB)
1981—Buccaneers, 20-10 (TB)
1983—Cardinals, 34-27 (TB)
1985—Buccaneers, 16-0 (TB)
1986—Cardinals, 30-19 (TB)
Cardinals, 21-17 (StL)
1987—Cardinals, 31-28 (StL)
Cardinals, 31-14 (TB)
1988—Cardinals, 30-24 (TB)
(Points—Cardinals 194, Buccaneers 182)
Franchise in St. Louis prior to 1988
***PHOENIX vs. **WASHINGTON**
RS: Redskins lead series, 54-33-2;
1932—Cardinals, 9-0 (B)
Braves, 8-6 (C)
1933—Redskins, 10-0 (C)
Tie, 0-0 (B)
1934—Redskins, 9-0 (B)
1935—Cardinals, 6-0 (B)
1936—Redskins, 13-10 (B)
1937—Cardinals, 21-14 (W)
1939—Redskins, 28-7 (W)
1940—Redskins, 28-21 (W)
1942—Redskins, 28-0 (W)
1943—Redskins, 13-7 (W)
1945—Redskins, 24-21 (W)
1947—Redskins, 45-21 (W)
1949—Cardinals, 38-7 (C)
1950—Cardinals, 38-28 (W)
1951—Redskins, 7-3 (C)
Redskins, 20-17 (W)
1952—Redskins, 23-7 (C)
Cardinals, 17-6 (W)
1953—Redskins, 24-13 (C)
Redskins, 28-17 (W)
1954—Cardinals, 38-16 (C)
Redskins, 37-20 (W)
1955—Cardinals, 24-10 (W)
Redskins, 31-0 (C)
1956—Cardinals, 31-3 (W)
Redskins, 17-14 (C)
1957—Redskins, 37-14 (C)
Cardinals, 44-14 (W)
1958—Cardinals, 37-10 (C)
Redskins, 45-31 (W)
1959—Cardinals, 49-21 (C)
Redskins, 23-14 (W)
1960—Cardinals, 44-7 (StL)
Cardinals, 26-14 (W)
1961—Cardinals, 24-0 (W)
Cardinals, 38-24 (StL)
1962—Redskins, 24-14 (W)
Tie, 17-17 (StL)
1963—Cardinals, 21-7 (W)
Cardinals, 24-20 (StL)
1964—Cardinals, 23-17 (W)
Cardinals, 38-24 (StL)
1965—Cardinals, 37-16 (W)
Redskins, 24-20 (StL)
1966—Cardinals, 23-7 (StL)
Redskins, 26-20 (W)
1967—Cardinals, 27-21 (W)
1968—Cardinals, 41-14 (StL)
1969—Redskins, 33-17 (W)
1970—Cardinals, 27-17 (StL)
Redskins, 28-27 (W)
1971—Redskins, 24-17 (StL)
Redskins, 20-0 (W)
1972—Redskins, 24-10 (W)
Redskins, 33-3 (StL)
1973—Cardinals, 34-27 (StL)
Redskins, 31-13 (W)
1974—Cardinals, 17-10 (W)
Cardinals, 23-20 (StL)
1975—Redskins, 27-17 (W)
Cardinals, 20-17 (StL) OT
1976—Redskins, 20-10 (W)
Redskins, 16-10 (StL)
1977—Redskins, 24-14 (W)
Redskins, 26-20 (StL)
1978—Redskins, 28-10 (StL)
Cardinals, 27-17 (W)
1979—Redskins, 17-7 (StL)
Redskins, 30-28 (W)
1980—Redskins, 23-0 (W)
Redskins, 31-7 (StL)
1981—Cardinals, 40-30 (StL)
Redskins, 42-21 (W)
1982—Redskins, 12-7 (StL)
Redskins, 28-0 (W)
1983—Redskins, 38-14 (StL)
Redskins, 45-7 (W)
1984—Cardinals, 26-24 (StL)
Redskins, 29-27 (W)
1985—Redskins, 27-10 (W)
Redskins, 27-16 (StL)
1986—Redskins, 28-21 (W)
Redskins, 20-17 (StL)
1987—Redskins, 28-21 (W)
Redskins, 34-17 (StL)
1988—Cardinals, 30-21 (P)
Redskins, 33-17 (W)
(Points—Redskins 1,898, Cardinals 1,681)
*Franchise in St. Louis prior to 1988
and in Chicago prior to 1960*
***Franchise in Boston prior to 1937 and
known as Braves prior to 1933*

PITTSBURGH vs. ATLANTA
RS: Steelers lead series, 7-1;
See Atlanta vs. Pittsburgh
PITTSBURGH vs. BUFFALO
RS: Series tied, 5-5
PS: Steelers lead series, 1-0;
See Buffalo vs. Pittsburgh
PITTSBURGH vs. CHICAGO
RS: Bears lead series, 14-4-1;
See Chicago vs. Pittsburgh
PITTSBURGH vs. CINCINNATI
RS: Steelers lead series, 20-17;
See Cincinnati vs. Pittsburgh
PITTSBURGH vs. CLEVELAND
RS: Browns lead series, 47-31;
See Cleveland vs. Pittsburgh
PITTSBURGH vs. DALLAS
RS: Series tied, 11-11
PS: Steelers lead series, 2-0;
See Dallas vs. Pittsburgh
PITTSBURGH vs. DENVER
RS: Broncos lead series, 7-4-1
PS: Steelers lead series, 2-1;
See Denver vs. Pittsburgh
PITTSBURGH vs. DETROIT
RS: Lions lead series, 13-9-1;
See Detroit vs. Pittsburgh
PITTSBURGH vs. GREEN BAY
RS: Packers lead series, 16-11;
See Green Bay vs. Pittsburgh
PITTSBURGH vs. HOUSTON
RS: Steelers lead series, 25-12
PS: Steelers lead series, 2-0;
See Houston vs. Pittsburgh
PITTSBURGH vs. INDIANAPOLIS
RS: Steelers lead series, 8-4
PS: Steelers lead series, 2-0;
See Indianapolis vs. Pittsburgh
PITTSBURGH vs. KANSAS CITY
RS: Steelers lead series, 11-5;
See Kansas City vs. Pittsburgh
PITTSBURGH vs. L.A. RAIDERS
RS: Raiders lead series, 6-3
PS: Series tied, 3-3;
See L.A. Raiders vs. Pittsburgh
PITTSBURGH vs. L.A. RAMS
RS: Rams lead series, 13-3-2
PS: Steelers lead series, 1-0;
See L.A. Rams vs. Pittsburgh
PITTSBURGH vs. MIAMI
RS: Dolphins lead series, 6-3
PS: Dolphins lead series, 2-1;
See Miami vs. Pittsburgh
PITTSBURGH vs. MINNESOTA
RS: Vikings lead series, 6-3
PS: Steelers lead series, 1-0;
See Minnesota vs. Pittsburgh
PITTSBURGH vs. NEW ENGLAND
RS: Steelers lead series, 5-3;
See New England vs. Pittsburgh
PITTSBURGH vs. NEW ORLEANS
RS: Saints lead series, 5-4;
See New Orleans vs. Pittsburgh
PITTSBURGH vs. N.Y. GIANTS
RS: Giants lead series, 41-26-3;
See N.Y. Giants vs. Pittsburgh
PITTSBURGH vs. N.Y. JETS
RS: Steelers lead series, 9-1;
See N.Y. Jets vs. Pittsburgh
PITTSBURGH vs. PHILADELPHIA
RS: Eagles lead series, 42-25-3
PS: Eagles lead series, 1-0;
See Philadelphia vs. Pittsburgh
PITTSBURGH vs. PHOENIX
RS: Steelers lead series, 29-21-3;
See Phoenix vs. Pittsburgh
PITTSBURGH vs. SAN DIEGO
RS: Steelers lead series, 9-4
PS: Chargers lead series, 1-0
1971—Steelers, 21-17 (P)
1972—Steelers, 24-2 (SD)
1973—Steelers, 38-21 (P)
1975—Steelers, 37-0 (SD)
1976—Steelers, 23-0 (P)
1977—Steelers, 10-9 (SD)
1979—Chargers, 35-7 (SD)
1980—Chargers, 26-17 (SD)
1982—*Chargers, 31-28 (P)
1983—Steelers, 26-3 (P)
1984—Steelers, 52-24 (P)
1985—Chargers, 54-44 (SD)
1987—Steelers, 20-16 (SD)
1988—Chargers, 20-14 (SD)
(Points—Steelers 361, Chargers 258)
AFC First Round Playoff
PITTSBURGH vs. SAN FRANCISCO
RS: Steelers lead series, 7-6
1951—49ers, 28-24 (P)
1952—Steelers, 24-7 (SF)
1954—49ers, 31-3 (SF)
1958—49ers, 23-20 (SF)
1961—Steelers, 20-10 (P)
1965—49ers, 27-17 (SF)
1968—49ers, 45-28 (P)
1973—Steelers, 37-14 (SF)

1977—Steelers, 27-0 (P)
1978—Steelers, 24-7 (SF)
1981—49ers, 17-14 (P)
1984—Steelers, 20-17 (SF)
1987—Steelers, 30-17 (P)
(Points—Steelers 288, 49ers 243)
PITTSBURGH vs. SEATTLE
RS: Steelers lead series, 4-3
1977—Steelers, 30-20 (P)
1978—Steelers, 21-10 (P)
1981—Seahawks, 24-21 (S)
1982—Seahawks, 16-0 (S)
1983—Steelers, 27-21 (S)
1986—Seahawks, 30-0 (S)
1987—Steelers, 13-9 (P)
(Points—Seahawks 130, Steelers 112)
PITTSBURGH vs. TAMPA BAY
RS: Steelers lead series, 3-0
1976—Steelers, 42-0 (P)
1980—Steelers, 24-21 (TB)
1983—Steelers, 17-12 (P)
(Points—Steelers 83, Buccaneers 33)
***PITTSBURGH vs. **WASHINGTON**
RS: Redskins lead series, 41-27-3
1933—Redskins, 21-6 (P)
Pirates, 16-14 (B)
1934—Redskins, 7-0 (P)
Redskins, 39-0 (B)
1935—Pirates, 6-0 (P)
Redskins, 13-3 (B)
1936—Pirates, 10-0 (P)
Redskins, 30-0 (B)
1937—Redskins, 34-20 (W)
Pirates, 21-13 (P)
1938—Redskins, 7-0 (P)
Redskins, 15-0 (W)
1939—Redskins, 44-14 (W)
Redskins, 21-14 (P)
1940—Redskins, 40-10 (P)
Redskins, 37-10 (W)
1941—Redskins, 24-20 (P)
Redskins, 23-3 (W)
1942—Redskins, 28-14 (W)
Redskins, 14-0 (P)
1945—Redskins, 14-0 (P)
Redskins, 24-0 (W)
1946—Tie, 14-14 (W)
Steelers, 14-7 (P)
1947—Redskins, 27-26 (W)
Steelers, 21-14 (P)
1948—Redskins, 17-14 (W)
Steelers, 10-7 (P)
1949—Redskins, 27-14 (P)
Redskins, 27-14 (W)
1950—Steelers, 26-7 (W)
Redskins, 24-7 (P)
1951—Redskins, 22-7 (P)
Steelers, 20-10 (W)
1952—Redskins, 28-24 (P)
Steelers, 24-23 (W)
1953—Redskins, 17-9 (P)
Steelers, 14-13 (W)
1954—Steelers, 37-7 (P)
Redskins, 17-14 (W)
1955—Redskins, 23-14 (P)
Redskins, 28-17 (W)
1956—Steelers, 30-13 (P)
Steelers, 23-0 (W)
1957—Steelers, 28-7 (P)
Redskins, 10-3 (W)
1958—Steelers, 24-16 (P)
Tie, 14-14 (W)
1959—Redskins, 23-17 (P)
Steelers, 27-6 (W)
1960—Tie, 27-27 (W)
Steelers, 22-10 (P)
1961—Steelers, 20-0 (P)
Steelers, 30-14 (P)
1962—Steelers, 23-21 (P)
Steelers, 27-24 (W)
1963—Steelers, 38-27 (P)
Steelers, 34-28 (W)
1964—Redskins, 30-0 (P)
Steelers, 14-7 (W)
1965—Redskins, 31-3 (P)
Redskins, 35-14 (W)
1966—Redskins, 33-27 (P)
Redskins, 24-10 (W)
1967—Redskins, 15-10 (P)
1968—Redskins, 16-13 (W)
1969—Redskins, 14-7 (P)
1973—Steelers, 21-16 (P)
1979—Steelers, 38-7 (P)
1985—Redskins, 30-23 (P)
1988—Redskins, 30-29 (W)
(Points—Redskins 1,349, Steelers 1,103)
**Steelers known as Pirates prior to 1941*
***Franchise in Boston prior to 1937*

SAN DIEGO vs. ATLANTA
RS: Falcons lead series, 2-1;
See Atlanta vs. San Diego
SAN DIEGO vs. BUFFALO
RS: Chargers lead series, 16-7-2
PS: Bills lead series, 2-1;
See Buffalo vs. San Diego
SAN DIEGO vs. CHICAGO
RS: Chargers lead series, 4-1;
See Chicago vs. San Diego
SAN DIEGO vs. CINCINNATI
RS: Chargers lead series, 11-7
PS: Bengals lead series, 1-0;
See Cincinnati vs. San Diego
SAN DIEGO vs. CLEVELAND
RS: Chargers lead series, 6-5-1;
See Cleveland vs. San Diego
SAN DIEGO vs. DALLAS
RS: Cowboys lead series, 3-1;
See Dallas vs. San Diego
SAN DIEGO vs. DENVER
RS: Broncos lead series, 29-28-1;
See Denver vs. San Diego
SAN DIEGO vs. DETROIT
RS: Lions lead series, 3-2;
See Detroit vs. San Diego
SAN DIEGO vs. GREEN BAY
RS: Packers lead series, 3-1;
See Green Bay vs. San Diego
SAN DIEGO vs. HOUSTON
RS: Chargers lead series, 17-10-1
PS: Oilers lead series, 3-0;
See Houston vs. San Diego
SAN DIEGO vs. INDIANAPOLIS
RS: Chargers lead series, 6-4;
See Indianapolis vs. San Diego
SAN DIEGO vs. KANSAS CITY
RS: Chargers lead series, 29-27-1;
See Kansas City vs. San Diego
SAN DIEGO vs. L.A. RAIDERS
RS: Raiders lead series, 36-20-2
PS: Raiders lead series, 1-0;
See L.A. Raiders vs. San Diego
SAN DIEGO vs. L.A. RAMS
RS: Series tied, 2-2;
See L.A. Rams vs. San Diego
SAN DIEGO vs. MIAMI
RS: Chargers lead series, 8-5
PS: Series tied, 1-1;
See Miami vs. San Diego
SAN DIEGO vs. MINNESOTA
RS: Series tied, 3-3;
See Minnesota vs. San Diego
SAN DIEGO vs. NEW ENGLAND
RS: Patriots lead series, 13-11-2
PS: Chargers lead series, 1-0;
See New England vs. San Diego
SAN DIEGO vs. NEW ORLEANS
RS: Chargers lead series, 3-1;
See New Orleans vs. San Diego
SAN DIEGO vs. N.Y. GIANTS
RS: Giants lead series, 3-2;
See N.Y. Giants vs. San Diego
SAN DIEGO vs. N.Y. JETS
RS: Chargers lead series, 14-7-1;
See N.Y. Jets vs. San Diego
SAN DIEGO vs. PHILADELPHIA
RS: Series tied, 2-2;
See Philadelphia vs. San Diego
SAN DIEGO vs. PHOENIX
RS: Chargers lead series, 3-1;
See Phoenix vs. San Diego
SAN DIEGO vs. PITTSBURGH
RS: Steelers lead series, 9-4
PS: Chargers lead series, 1-0;
See Pittsburgh vs. San Diego
SAN DIEGO vs. SAN FRANCISCO
RS: Chargers lead series, 3-2
1972—49ers, 34-3 (SF)
1976—Chargers, 13-7 (SD) OT
1979—Chargers, 31-9 (SD)
1982—Chargers, 41-37 (SF)
1988—49ers, 48-10 (SD)
(Points—49ers 135, Chargers 98)
SAN DIEGO vs. SEATTLE
RS: Series tied, 10-10
1977—Chargers, 30-28 (S)
1978—Chargers, 24-20 (S)
Chargers, 37-10 (SD)
1979—Chargers, 33-16 (S)
Chargers, 20-10 (SD)
1980—Chargers, 34-13 (S)
Chargers, 21-14 (SD)
1981—Chargers, 24-10 (SD)
Seahawks, 44-23 (S)
1983—Seahawks, 34-31 (S)
Chargers, 28-21 (SD)
1984—Seahawks, 31-17 (S)
Seahawks, 24-0 (SD)
1985—Seahawks, 49-35 (SD)
Seahawks, 26-21 (S)
1986—Seahawks, 33-7 (S)
Seahawks, 34-24 (SD)
1987—Seahawks, 34-3 (S)
1988—Chargers, 17-6 (SD)
Seahawks, 17-14 (S)
(Points—Seahawks 474, Chargers 443)
SAN DIEGO vs. TAMPA BAY
RS: Chargers lead series, 3-0
1976—Chargers, 23-0 (TB)
1981—Chargers, 24-23 (TB)
1987—Chargers, 17-13 (TB)
(Points—Chargers 64, Buccaneers 36)
SAN DIEGO vs. WASHINGTON
RS: Redskins lead series, 4-0
1973—Redskins, 38-0 (W)
1980—Redskins, 40-17 (W)
1983—Redskins, 27-24 (SD)
1986—Redskins, 30-27 (SD)
(Points—Redskins 135, Chargers 68)

SAN FRANCISCO vs. ATLANTA
RS: 49ers lead series, 25-18-1;
See Atlanta vs. San Francisco
SAN FRANCISCO vs. BUFFALO
RS: Bills lead series, 2-1;
See Buffalo vs. San Francisco
SAN FRANCISCO vs. CHICAGO
RS: Bears lead series, 25-23-1
PS: 49ers lead series, 2-0;
See Chicago vs. San Francisco
SAN FRANCISCO vs. CINCINNATI
RS: 49ers lead series, 4-1
PS: 49ers lead series, 2-0;
See Cincinnati vs. San Francisco
SAN FRANCISCO vs. CLEVELAND
RS: Browns lead series, 8-5;
See Cleveland vs. San Francisco
SAN FRANCISCO vs. DALLAS
RS: 49ers lead series, 7-5-1
PS: Cowboys lead series, 3-1;
See Dallas vs. San Francisco
SAN FRANCISCO vs. DENVER
RS: Broncos lead series, 4-2;
See Denver vs. San Francisco
SAN FRANCISCO vs. DETROIT
RS: Lions lead series, 25-23-1
PS: Series tied, 1-1;
See Detroit vs. San Francisco
SAN FRANCISCO vs. GREEN BAY
RS: 49ers lead series, 24-20-1;
See Green Bay vs. San Francisco
SAN FRANCISCO vs. HOUSTON
RS: 49ers lead series, 4-2;
See Houston vs. San Francisco
SAN FRANCISCO vs. INDIANAPOLIS
RS: Colts lead series, 21-15;
See Indianapolis vs. San Francisco
SAN FRANCISCO vs. KANSAS CITY
RS: 49ers lead series, 3-1;
See Kansas City vs. San Francisco
SAN FRANCISCO vs. L.A RAIDERS
RS: Raiders lead series, 4-2;
See L.A. Raiders vs. San Francisco
SAN FRANCISCO vs. L.A. RAMS
RS: Rams lead series, 46-30-2;
See L.A. Rams vs. San Francisco
SAN FRANCISCO vs. MIAMI
RS: Dolphins lead series, 4-1
PS: 49ers lead series, 1-0;
See Miami vs. San Francisco
SAN FRANCISCO vs. MINNESOTA
RS: Vikings lead series, 14-12-1
PS: 49ers lead series, 2-1;
See Minnesota vs. San Francisco
SAN FRANCISCO vs. NEW ENGLAND
RS: 49ers lead series, 4-1;
See New England vs. San Francisco
SAN FRANCISCO vs. NEW ORLEANS
RS: 49ers lead series, 26-11-2;
See New Orleans vs. San Francisco
SAN FRANCISCO vs. N.Y. GIANTS
RS: Giants lead series, 10-7
PS: Series tied, 2-2;
See N.Y. Giants vs. San Francisco
SAN FRANCISCO vs. N.Y. JETS
RS: 49ers lead series, 4-1;
See N.Y. Jets vs. San Francisco
SAN FRANCISCO vs. PHILADELPHIA
RS: 49ers lead series, 10-4-1;
See Philadelphia vs. San Francisco
SAN FRANCISCO vs. PHOENIX
RS: Series tied, 8-8;
See Phoenix vs. San Francisco
SAN FRANCISCO vs. PITTSBURGH
RS: Steelers lead series, 7-6;
See Pittsburgh vs. San Francisco
SAN FRANCISCO vs. SAN DIEGO
RS: Chargers lead series, 3-2;
See San Diego vs. San Francisco
SAN FRANCISCO vs. SEATTLE
RS: 49ers lead series, 3-1
1976—49ers, 37-21 (S)
1979—Seahawks, 35-24 (SF)
1985—49ers, 19-6 (SF)
1988—49ers, 38-7 (S)
(Points—49ers 118, Seahawks 69)
SAN FRANCISCO vs. TAMPA BAY
RS: 49ers lead series, 7-1
1977—49ers, 20-10 (SF)
1978—49ers, 6-3 (SF)
1979—49ers, 23-7 (SF)
1980—Buccaneers, 24-23 (SF)
1983—49ers, 35-21 (SF)
1984—49ers, 24-17 (SF)
1986—49ers, 31-7 (TB)
1987—49ers, 24-10 (TB)
(Points—49ers 186, Buccaneers 99)
SAN FRANCISCO vs. WASHINGTON
RS: 49ers lead series, 8-6-1
PS: Series tied, 1-1
1952—49ers, 23-17 (W)
1954—49ers, 41-7 (SF)
1955—Redskins, 7-0 (W)
1961—49ers, 35-3 (SF)
1967—Redskins, 31-28 (W)
1969—Tie, 17-17 (SF)
1970—49ers, 26-17 (SF)
1971—*49ers, 24-20 (SF)
1973—Redskins, 33-9 (W)
1976—Redskins, 24-21 (SF)
1978—Redskins, 38-20 (W)
1981—49ers, 30-17 (W)
1983—**Redskins, 24-21 (W)
1984—49ers, 37-31 (SF)
1985—49ers, 35-8 (W)
1986—Redskins, 14-6 (W)
1988—49ers, 37-21 (SF)
(Points—49ers 410, Redskins 329)
**NFC Divisional Playoff*
***NFC Championship*

SEATTLE vs. ATLANTA
RS: Seahawks lead series, 4-0;
See Atlanta vs. Seattle
SEATTLE vs. BUFFALO
RS: Seahawks lead series, 2-1;
See Buffalo vs. Seattle
SEATTLE vs. CHICAGO
RS: Seahawks lead series, 4-1;
See Chicago vs. Seattle
SEATTLE vs. CINCINNATI
RS: Bengals lead series, 5-2
PS: Bengals lead series, 1-0;
See Cincinnati vs. Seattle
SEATTLE vs. CLEVELAND
RS: Seahawks lead series, 8-2;
See Cleveland vs. Seattle
SEATTLE vs. DALLAS
RS: Cowboys lead series, 3-1;
See Dallas vs. Seattle
SEATTLE vs. DENVER
RS: Broncos lead series, 13-10
PS: Seahawks lead series, 1-0;
See Denver vs. Seattle
SEATTLE vs. DETROIT
RS: Seahawks lead series, 3-1;
See Detroit vs. Seattle
SEATTLE vs. GREEN BAY
RS: Packers lead series, 3-2;
See Green Bay vs. Seattle
SEATTLE vs. HOUSTON
RS: Series tied, 3-3
PS: Oilers lead series, 1-0;
See Houston vs. Seattle
SEATTLE vs. INDIANAPOLIS
RS: Colts lead series, 2-0;
See Indianapolis vs. Seattle
SEATTLE vs. KANSAS CITY
RS: Chiefs lead series, 11-10;
See Kansas City vs. Seattle
SEATTLE vs. L.A. RAIDERS
RS: Seahawks lead series, 12-10
PS: Series tied, 1-1;
See L.A. Raiders vs. Seattle
SEATTLE vs. L.A. RAMS
RS: Rams lead series, 4-0;
See L.A. Rams vs. Seattle
SEATTLE vs. MIAMI
RS: Dolphins lead series, 2-1
PS: Series tied, 1-1;
See Miami vs. Seattle
SEATTLE vs. MINNESOTA
RS: Seahawks lead series, 3-1;
See Minnesota vs. Seattle
SEATTLE vs. NEW ENGLAND
RS: Patriots lead series, 6-2;
See New England vs. Seattle
SEATTLE vs. NEW ORLEANS
RS: Series tied, 2-2;
See New Orleans vs. Seattle
SEATTLE vs. N.Y. GIANTS
RS: Giants lead series, 3-2;
See N.Y. Giants vs. Seattle
SEATTLE vs. N.Y. JETS
RS: Seahawks lead series, 7-3;
See N.Y. Jets vs. Seattle
SEATTLE vs. PHILADELPHIA
RS: Eagles lead series, 2-1;
See Philadelphia vs. Seattle
SEATTLE vs. PHOENIX
Cardinals lead series, 2-0;

See Phoenix vs. Seattle
SEATTLE vs. PITTSBURGH
RS: Steelers lead series, 4-3;
See Pittsburgh vs. Seattle
SEATTLE vs. SAN DIEGO
RS: Series tied, 10-10;
See San Diego vs. Seattle
SEATTLE vs. SAN FRANCISCO
RS: 49ers lead series, 3-1;
See San Francisco vs. Seattle
SEATTLE vs. TAMPA BAY
RS: Seahawks lead series, 2-0
1976—Seahawks, 13-10 (TB)
1977—Seahawks, 30-23 (S)
(Points—Seahawks 43, Buccaneers 33)
SEATTLE vs. WASHINGTON
RS: Redskins lead series, 3-1
1976—Redskins, 31-7 (W)
1980—Seahawks, 14-0 (W)
1983—Redskins, 27-17 (S)
1986—Redskins, 19-14 (W)
(Points—Redskins 77, Seahawks 52)

TAMPA BAY vs. ATLANTA
RS: Series tied, 4-4;
See Atlanta vs. Tampa Bay
TAMPA BAY vs. BUFFALO
RS: Buccaneers lead series, 4-1;
See Buffalo vs. Tampa Bay
TAMPA BAY vs. CHICAGO
RS: Bears lead series, 18-4;
See Chicago vs. Tampa Bay
TAMPA BAY vs. CINCINNATI
RS: Bengals lead series, 2-1;
See Cincinnati vs. Tampa Bay
TAMPA BAY vs. CLEVELAND
RS: Browns lead series, 3-0;
See Cleveland vs. Tampa Bay
TAMPA BAY vs. DALLAS
RS: Cowboys lead series, 4-0
PS: Cowboys lead series, 2-0;
See Dallas vs. Tampa Bay
TAMPA BAY vs. DENVER
RS: Broncos lead series, 2-0;
See Denver vs. Tampa Bay
TAMPA BAY vs. DETROIT
RS: Series tied, 11-11;
See Detroit vs. Tampa Bay
TAMPA BAY vs. GREEN BAY
RS: Packers lead series, 10-9-1;
See Green Bay vs. Tampa Bay
TAMPA BAY vs. HOUSTON
RS: Oilers lead series, 2-1;
See Houston vs. Tampa Bay
TAMPA BAY vs. INDIANAPOLIS
RS: Colts lead series, 4-1;
See Indianapolis vs. Tampa Bay
TAMPA BAY vs. KANSAS CITY
RS: Chiefs lead series, 4-2;
See Kansas City vs. Tampa Bay
TAMPA BAY vs. L.A RAIDERS
RS: Raiders lead series, 2-0;
See L.A. Raiders vs. Tampa Bay
TAMPA BAY vs. L.A. RAMS
RS: Rams lead series, 6-2
PS: Rams lead series, 1-0;
See L.A. Rams vs. Tampa Bay
TAMPA BAY vs. MIAMI
RS: Dolphins lead series, 3-1;
See Miami vs. Tampa Bay
TAMPA BAY vs. MINNESOTA
RS: Vikings lead series, 16-6;
See Minnesota vs. Tampa Bay
TAMPA BAY vs. NEW ENGLAND
RS: Patriots lead series, 3-0;
See New England vs. Tampa Bay
TAMPA BAY vs. NEW ORLEANS
RS: Saints lead series, 8-3;
See New Orleans vs. Tampa Bay
TAMPA BAY vs. N.Y. GIANTS
RS: Giants lead series, 6-3;
See N.Y. Giants vs. Tampa Bay
TAMPA BAY vs. N.Y. JETS
RS: Jets lead series, 3-1;
See N.Y. Jets vs. Tampa Bay
TAMPA BAY vs. PHILADELPHIA
RS: Eagles lead series, 3-0
PS: Buccaneers lead series, 1-0;
See Philadelphia vs. Tampa Bay
TAMPA BAY vs. PHOENIX
RS: Cardinals lead series, 6-3
See Phoenix vs. Tampa Bay
TAMPA BAY vs. PITTSBURGH
RS: Steelers lead series, 3-0;
See Pittsburgh vs. Tampa Bay
TAMPA BAY vs. SAN DIEGO
RS: Chargers lead series, 3-0;
See San Diego vs. Tampa Bay
TAMPA BAY vs. SAN FRANCISCO
RS: 49ers lead series, 7-1;
See San Francisco vs. Tampa Bay
TAMPA BAY vs. SEATTLE
RS: Seahawks lead series, 2-0;
See Seattle vs. Tampa Bay
TAMPA BAY vs. WASHINGTON
RS: Redskins lead series, 2-0
1977—Redskins, 10-0 (TB)
1982—Redskins, 21-13 (TB)
(Points—Redskins 31, Buccaneers 13)

WASHINGTON vs. ATLANTA
RS: Redskins lead series, 9-3-1;
See Atlanta vs. Washington
WASHINGTON vs. BUFFALO
RS: Redskins lead series, 3-2;
See Buffalo vs. Washington
WASHINGTON vs. CHICAGO
RS: Bears lead series, 18-9-1
PS: Redskins lead series, 4-3;
See Chicago vs. Washington
WASHINGTON vs. CINCINNATI
RS: Redskins lead series, 3-2;
See Cincinnati vs. Washington
WASHINGTON vs. CLEVELAND
RS: Browns lead series, 32-8-1;
See Cleveland vs. Washington
WASHINGTON vs. DALLAS
RS: Cowboys lead series, 32-22-2
PS: Redskins lead series, 2-0;
See Dallas vs. Washington
WASHINGTON vs. DENVER
RS: Series tied, 2-2
PS: Redskins lead series, 1-0;
See Denver vs. Washington
WASHINGTON vs. DETROIT
RS: Redskins lead series, 19-8
PS: Redskins lead series, 1-0;
See Detroit vs. Washington
WASHINGTON vs. GREEN BAY
RS: Packers lead series, 13-12-1
PS: Series tied, 1-1;
See Green Bay vs. Washington
WASHINGTON vs. HOUSTON
RS: Oilers lead series, 3-2;
See Houston vs. Washington
WASHINGTON vs. INDIANAPOLIS
RS: Colts lead series, 15-6;
See Indianapolis vs. Washington
WASHINGTON vs. KANSAS CITY
RS: Chiefs lead series, 2-1;
See Kansas City vs. Washington
WASHINGTON vs. L.A. RAIDERS
RS: Raiders lead series, 3-2
PS: Raiders lead series, 1-0;
See L.A. Raiders vs. Washington
WASHINGTON vs. L.A. RAMS
RS: Redskins lead series, 13-4-1
PS: Series tied, 2-2;
See L.A. Rams vs. Washington
WASHINGTON vs. MIAMI
RS: Dolphins lead series, 4-1
PS: Series tied, 1-1;
See Miami vs. Washington
WASHINGTON vs. MINNESOTA
RS: Redskins lead series, 5-3
PS: Series tied, 2-2;
See Minnesota vs. Washington
WASHINGTON vs. NEW ENGLAND
RS: Redskins lead series, 3-1;
See New England vs. Washington
WASHINGTON vs. NEW ORLEANS
RS: Redskins lead series, 9-4;
See New Orleans vs. Washington
WASHINGTON vs. N.Y. GIANTS
RS: Redskins lead series, 62-47-3
PS: Series tied, 1-1;
See N.Y. Giants vs. Washington
WASHINGTON vs. N.Y. JETS
RS: Redskins lead series, 4-0;
See N.Y. Jets vs. Washington
WASHINGTON vs. PHILADELPHIA
RS: Redskins lead series, 62-40-5;
See Philadelphia vs. Washington
WASHINGTON vs. PHOENIX
RS: Redskins lead series, 54-33-2;
See Phoenix vs. Washington
WASHINGTON vs. PITTSBURGH
RS: Redskins lead series, 41-27-3;
See Pittsburgh vs. Washington
WASHINGTON vs. SAN DIEGO
RS: Redskins lead series, 4-0;
See San Diego vs. Washington
WASHINGTON vs. SAN FRANCISCO
RS: 49ers lead series, 8-6-1
PS: Series tied, 1-1;
See San Francisco vs. Washington
WASHINGTON vs. SEATTLE
RS: Redskins lead series, 3-1;
See Seattle vs. Washington
WASHINGTON vs. TAMPA BAY
RS: Redskins lead series, 2-0;
See Tampa Bay vs. Washington

SUPER BOWL SUMMARIES

Results

Season	Date	Winner (Share)	Loser (Share)	Score	Site	Attendance
XXIII	1-22-89	San Francisco ($36,000)	Cincinnati ($18,000)	20-16	Miami	75,129
XXII	1-31-88	Washington ($36,000)	Denver ($18,000)	42-10	San Diego	73,302
XXI	1-25-87	N.Y. Giants ($36,000)	Denver ($18,000)	39-20	Pasadena	101,063
XX	1-26-86	Chicago ($36,000)	New England ($18,000)	46-10	New Orleans	73,818
XIX	1-20-85	San Francisco ($36,000)	Miami ($18,000)	38-16	Stanford	84,059
XVIII	1-22-84	L.A. Raiders ($36,000)	Washington ($18,000)	38-9	Tampa	72,920
XVII	1-30-83	Washington ($36,000)	Miami ($18,000)	27-17	Pasadena	103,667
XVI	1-24-82	San Francisco ($18,000)	Cincinnati ($9,000)	26-21	Pontiac	81,270
XV	1-25-81	Oakland ($18,000)	Philadelphia ($9,000)	27-10	New Orleans	76,135
XIV	1-20-80	Pittsburgh ($18,000)	Los Angeles ($9,000)	31-19	Pasadena	103,985
XIII	1-21-79	Pittsburgh ($18,000)	Dallas ($9,000)	35-31	Miami	79,484
XII	1-15-78	Dallas ($18,000)	Denver ($9,000)	27-10	New Orleans	75,583
XI	1-9-77	Oakland ($15,000)	Minnesota ($7,500)	32-14	Pasadena	103,438
X	1-18-76	Pittsburgh ($15,000)	Dallas ($7,500)	21-17	Miami	80,187
IX	1-12-75	Pittsburgh ($15,000)	Minnesota ($7,500)	16-6	New Orleans	80,997
VIII	1-13-74	Miami ($15,000)	Minnesota ($7,500)	24-7	Houston	71,882
VII	1-14-73	Miami ($15,000)	Washington ($7,500)	14-7	Los Angeles	90,182
VI	1-16-72	Dallas ($15,000)	Miami ($7,500)	24-3	New Orleans	81,023
V	1-17-71	Baltimore ($15,000)	Dallas ($7,500)	16-13	Miami	79,204
IV	1-11-70	Kansas City ($15,000)	Minnesota ($7,500)	23-7	New Orleans	80,562
III	1-12-69	N.Y. Jets ($15,000)	Baltimore ($7,500)	16-7	Miami	75,389
II	1-14-68	Green Bay ($15,000)	Oakland ($7,500)	33-14	Miami	75,546
I	1-15-67	Green Bay ($15,000)	Kansas City ($7,500)	35-10	Los Angeles	61,946

Super Bowl Composite Standings

	W	L	Pct.	Pts.	OP
Pittsburgh Steelers	4	0	1.000	103	73
San Francisco 49ers	3	0	1.000	84	53
Green Bay Packers	2	0	1.000	68	24
Chicago Bears	1	0	1.000	46	10
New York Giants	1	0	1.000	39	20
New York Jets	1	0	1.000	16	7
Oakland/L.A. Raiders	3	1	.750	111	66
Washington Redskins	2	2	.500	85	79
Baltimore Colts	1	1	.500	23	29
Kansas City Chiefs	1	1	.500	33	42
Dallas Cowboys	2	3	.400	112	85
Miami Dolphins	2	3	.400	74	103
Los Angeles Rams	0	1	.000	19	31
New England Patriots	0	1	.000	10	46
Philadelphia Eagles	0	1	.000	10	27
Cincinnati Bengals	0	2	.000	37	46
Denver Broncos	0	3	.000	40	108
Minnesota Vikings	0	4	.000	34	95

Past Super Bowl Most Valuable Players

(Selected by Sport Magazine)

Super Bowl I — QB Bart Starr, Green Bay
Super Bowl II — QB Bart Starr, Green Bay
Super Bowl III — QB Joe Namath, New York Jets
Super Bowl IV — QB Len Dawson, Kansas City
Super Bowl V — LB Chuck Howley, Dallas
Super Bowl VI — QB Roger Staubach, Dallas
Super Bowl VII — S Jake Scott, Miami
Super Bowl VIII — RB Larry Csonka, Miami
Super Bowl IX — RB Franco Harris, Pittsburgh
Super Bowl X — WR Lynn Swann, Pittsburgh
Super Bowl XI — WR Fred Biletnikoff, Oakland
Super Bowl XII — DT Randy White and DE Harvey Martin, Dallas
Super Bowl XIII — QB Terry Bradshaw, Pittsburgh
Super Bowl XIV — QB Terry Bradshaw, Pittsburgh
Super Bowl XV — QB Jim Plunkett, Oakland
Super Bowl XVI — QB Joe Montana, San Francisco
Super Bowl XVII — RB John Riggins, Washington
Super Bowl XVIII — RB Marcus Allen, Los Angeles Raiders
Super Bowl XIX — QB Joe Montana, San Francisco
Super Bowl XX — DE Richard Dent, Chicago
Super Bowl XXI — QB Phil Simms, New York Giants
Super Bowl XXII — QB Doug Williams, Washington
Super Bowl XXIII — WR Jerry Rice, San Francisco

Super Bowl XXIII

Joe Robbie Stadium, Miami, Florida — January 22, 1989

Attendance: 75,129

SAN FRANCISCO 20, CINCINNATI 16—NFC champion San Francisco captured its third Super Bowl of the 1980s by defeating AFC champion Cincinnati 20-16. The 49ers, who also won Super Bowls XVI and XIX, are the first NFC team to win three Super Bowls. Pittsburgh with four Super Bowl titles (IX, X, XIII, and XIV) and the Oakland/Los Angeles Raiders with three (XI, XV, and XVIII) lead AFC franchises. Even though San Francisco held an advantage in total net yards (454 to 229), the 49ers found themselves trailing the Bengals late in the game. With the score tied 13-13, Cincinnati took a 16-13 lead on Jim Breech's 40-yard field goal with 3:20 remaining. It was Breech's third field goal of the day and came after successful earlier attempts of 34 and 43 yards. The 49ers started their winning drive at their own 8-yard line. Over the next 11 plays, San Francisco covered 92 yards with the decisive score coming on a 10-yard pass from quarterback Joe Montana to wide receiver John Taylor with 34 seconds remaining. At halftime, the score was 3-3, which represented the first time in Super Bowl history the score was tied at intermission. After the teams traded third-period field goals, the Bengals jumped ahead 13-6 on Stanford Jennings's 93-yard kickoff return for a touchdown with 34 seconds remaining in the quarter. The 49ers didn't waste any time coming back as they covered 85 yards in four plays, concluding with Montana's 14-yard scoring pass to Rice 57 seconds into the final stanza. Rice was named the game's most valuable player after compiling 11 catches for a Super Bowl record 215 yards. Montana completed 23 of 36 passes for a Super Bowl record 357 yards and two touchdowns.

Cincinnati (16)	Offense	San Francisco (20)
Tim McGee	WR	John Taylor
Anthony Muñoz	LT	Steve Wallace
Bruce Reimers	LG	Jessie Sapolu
Bruce Kozerski	C	Randy Cross
Max Montoya	RG	Guy McIntyre
Brian Blados	RT	Harris Barton
Rodney Holman	TE	John Frank
Eddie Brown	WR	Jerry Rice
Boomer Esiason	QB	Joe Montana
James Brooks	RB	Roger Craig
Ickey Woods	RB	Tom Rathman
	Defense	
Jim Skow	LE	Larry Roberts
Tim Krumrie	NT	Michael Carter
Jason Buck	RE	Kevin Fagan
Leon White	LOLB	Charles Haley
Carl Zander	LILB	Jim Fahnhorst
Joe Kelly	RILB	Michael Walter
Reggie Williams	ROLB	Keena Turner
Lewis Billups	LCB	Tim McKyer
Eric Thomas	RCB	Don Griffin
David Fulcher	SS	Jeff Fuller
Solomon Wilcots	FS	Ronnie Lott

Substitutions

Cincinnati—Offense: K—Jim Breech. P—Lee Johnson. QB—Turk Schonert. RB—Stanford Jennings, Marc Logan. WR—Cris Collinsworth, Ira Hillary, Carl Parker. TE—Jim Riggs. G—Jim Rourke. T—Dave Smith. Defense: E—Eddie Edwards, Skip McClendon. T—David Grant. LB—Leo Barker, Ed Brady, Emanuel King. CB—Rickey Dixon, Ray Horton, Daryl Smith. S—Barney Bussey. DNP: QB—Mike Norseth.

San Francisco—Offense: K—Mike Cofer. P—Barry Helton. RB—Del Rodgers, Harry Sydney. WR—Terry Greer, Mike Wilson. TE—Ron Heller, Brent Jones. C—Chuck Thomas. G—Bruce Collie. T—Bubba Paris. Defense: E—Pierce Holt, Pete Kugler, Jeff Stover, Danny Stubbs. LB—Riki Ellison, Sam Kennedy, Bill Romanowski. CB—Darryl Pollard, Eric Wright. S—Greg Cox, Tom Holmoe. DNP: QB—Steve Young.

Officials

Referee—Jerry Seeman. Umpire—Gordon Wells. Line Judge—Bob Beeks. Head Linesman—Jerry Bergman. Back Judge—Paul Baetz. Field Judge—Bobby Skelton. Side Judge—Gary Lane.

Scoring

Cincinnati	0	3	10	3	— 16
San Francisco	3	0	3	14	— 20

SF —FG Cofer 41
Cin—FG Breech 34
Cin—FG Breech 43
SF —FG Cofer 32
Cin—Jennings 93 kickoff return (Breech kick)
SF —Rice 14 pass from Montana (Cofer kick)
Cin—FG Breech 40
SF —Taylor 10 pass from Montana (Cofer kick)

Team Statistics

	Cincinnati	S.F.
Total First Downs	13	23
First Downs Rushing	7	6
First Downs Passing	6	16
First Downs Penalty	0	1
Total Net Yardage	229	451
Total Offensive Plays	58	67
Average Gain per Offensive Play	3.9	6.8
Rushes	28	27
Yards Gained Rushing (net)	106	112
Average Yards per Rush	3.8	4.1
Passes Attempted	25	36
Passes Completed	11	23
Had Intercepted	1	0
Tackled Attempting to Pass	5	4
Yards Lost Attempting to Pass	21	18
Yards Gained Passing (net)	123	339
Punts	5	4
Average Distance	44.2	37.0
Punt Returns	2	3
Punt Return Yardage	5	56
Kickoff Returns	3	5
Kickoff Return Yardage	132	77
Interception Return Yardage	0	0
Total Return Yardage	137	133
Fumbles	1	4
Own Fumbles Recovered	1	3
Opponents Fumbles Recovered	1	0
Penalties	7	4
Yards Penalized	65	32
Total Points Scored	16	20
Touchdowns Rushing	0	0
Touchdowns Passing	0	2
Touchdowns Returns	1	0
Extra Points	1	2
Field Goals	3	2
Field Goals Attempted	3	4
Safeties	0	0
Third Down Efficiency	4/13	4/13
Fourth Down Efficiency	0/1	0/0
Time of Possession	32:43	27:17

Individual Statistics

Rushing

Cincinnati	No.	Yds.	LG	TD
Woods	20	79	10	0
Brooks	6	24	11	0
Jennings	1	3	3	0
Esiason	1	0	0	0
San Francisco	**No.**	**Yds.**	**LG**	**TD**
Craig	17	71	13	0
Rathman	5	23	11	0
Montana	4	13	11	0
Rice	1	5	5	0

Passing

Cin.	Att.	Comp.	Yds.	TD	Int.
Esiason	25	11	144	0	1
San Fran.	**Att.**	**Comp.**	**Yds.**	**TD**	**Int.**
Montana	36	23	357	2	0

Receiving

Cincinnati	No.	Yds.	LG	TD
Brown	4	44	17	0
Collinsworth	3	40	23	0
McGee	2	23	18	0
Brooks	1	20	20	0
Hillary	1	17	17	0
San Fran.	**No.**	**Yds.**	**LG**	**TD**
Rice	11	215	44	1
Craig	8	101	40	0
Frank	2	15	8	0
Rathman	1	16	16	0
Taylor	1	10	10t	1

Interceptions

Cincinnati	No.	Yds.	LG	TD
None				
San Fran.	**No.**	**Yds.**	**LG**	**TD**
Romanowski	1	0	0	0

Punting

Cincinnati	No.	Avg.	LG	Blk.
Johnson	5	44.2	63	0
San Fran.	**No.**	**Avg.**	**LG**	**Blk.**
Helton	4	37.0	55	0

Punt Returns

Cincinnati	No.	FC	Yds.	LG	TD
Horton	1	0	5	5	0
Hillary	1	0	0	0	0
San Fran.	**No.**	**FC**	**Yds.**	**LG**	**TD**
Taylor	3	1	56	45	0

Kickoff Returns

Cincinnati	No.	Yds.	LG	TD
Jennings	2	117	93t	1
Brooks	1	15	15	0
San Fran.	**No.**	**Yds.**	**LG**	**TD**
Rodgers	3	53	22	0
Taylor	1	13	13	0
Sydney	1	11	11	0

Super Bowl XXII

San Diego Jack Murphy Stadium, San Diego, California — January 31, 1988
Attendance: 73,302

WASHINGTON 42, DENVER 10—NFC champion Washington won Super Bowl XXII and its second NFL championship of the 1980s with a 42-10 decision over AFC champion Denver. The Redskins, who also won Super Bowl XVII, enjoyed a record-setting second quarter en route to the victory. The Broncos broke in front 10-0 when quarterback John Elway threw a 56-yard touchdown pass to wide receiver Ricky Nattiel on the Broncos' first play from scrimmage. Following a Washington punt, Denver's Rich Karlis kicked a 24-yard field goal to cap a seven-play, 61-yard scoring drive. The Redskins then erupted for 35 points on five straight possessions in the second period and coasted thereafter. The 35 points established an NFL postseason mark for most points scored in a period, bettering the previous total of 21 by San Francisco in Super Bowl XIX and Chicago in Super Bowl XX. Redskins quarterback Doug Williams led the second-period explosion by throwing a Super Bowl record-tying four touchdown passes, including 80- and 50-yarders to wide receiver Ricky Sanders, a 27-yarder to wide receiver Gary Clark, and an 8-yarder to tight end Clint Didier. Washington scored five touchdowns in 18 plays with total time of possession of only 5:47. Overall, Williams completed 18 of 29 passes for 340 yards and was named the game's most valuable player. His pass-yardage total eclipsed the previous Super Bowl record of 331 yards by Joe Montana of San Francisco in Super Bowl XIX. Sanders ended with 193 yards on eight catches, breaking the previous Super Bowl yardage record of 161 yards by Lynn Swann of Pittsburgh in Game X. Rookie running back Timmy Smith was the game's leading rusher with 22 carries for a Super Bowl record 204 yards, breaking the previous mark of 191 yards by Marcus Allen of the Raiders in Game XVIII. Smith also scored twice on runs of 58 and 4 yards. Washington's six touchdowns and 602 total yards gained also set Super Bowl records. Redskins cornerback Barry Wilburn had two of the team's three interceptions, and free safety Alvin Walton had two of Washington's five sacks.

Washington (NFC)	0	35	0	7	— 42
Denver (AFC)	10	0	0	0	— 10

Den —Nattiel 56 pass from Elway (Karlis kick)
Den —FG Karlis 24
Wash—Sanders 80 pass from Williams (Haji-Sheikh kick)
Wash—Clark 27 pass from Williams (Haji-Sheikh kick)
Wash—Smith 58 run (Haji-Sheikh kick)
Wash—Sanders 50 pass from Williams (Haji-Sheikh kick)
Wash—Didier 8 pass from Williams (Haji-Sheikh kick)
Wash—Smith 4 run (Haji-Sheikh kick)

Super Bowl XXI

Rose Bowl, Pasadena, California — January 25, 1987
Attendance: 101,063

NEW YORK GIANTS 39, DENVER 20—The NFC champion New York Giants captured their first NFL title since 1956 when they downed the AFC champion Denver Broncos, 39-20, in Super Bowl XXI. The victory marked the NFC's fifth NFL title in the past six seasons. The Broncos, behind the passing of quarterback John Elway, who was 13 of 20 for 187 yards in the first half, held a 10-9 lead at intermission, the narrowest halftime margin in Super Bowl history. Denver's Rich Karlis opened the scoring with a Super Bowl record-tying 48-yard field goal. New York drove 78 yards in nine plays on the next series to take a 7-3 lead on quarterback Phil Simms's six-yard touchdown pass to tight end Zeke Mowatt. The Broncos came right back with a 58-yard scoring drive on six plays capped by Elway's four-yard touchdown run. The only scoring in the second period was the sack of Elway in the end zone by defensive end George Martin for a New York safety. The Giants produced a key defensive stand early in the second quarter when the Broncos had a first down at the New York one-yard line, but failed to score on three running plays and Karlis's 23-yard missed field-goal attempt. The Giants took command of the game in the third period en route to a 30-point second half, the most ever scored in one half of Super Bowl play. New York took the lead for good on tight end Mark Bavaro's 13-yard touchdown catch 4:52 into the third period. The nine-play, 63-yard scoring drive included the successful conversion of a fourth down and one play on the New York 46-yard line. Denver was limited to only two net yards on 10 offensive plays in the third period. Simms set Super Bowl records for most consecutive completions (10) and highest completion percentage (88 percent on 22 completions in 25 attempts). He also passed for 268 yards and three touchdowns and was named the game's most valuable player. New York running back Joe Morris was the game's leading rusher with 20 carries for 67 yards. Denver wide receiver Vance Johnson led all receivers with five catches for 121 yards. The Giants defeated their three playoff opponents by a cumulative total of 82 points (New York 105, opponents 23), the largest such margin by a Super Bowl winner.

Denver (AFC)	10	0	0	10	— 20
N.Y. Giants (NFC)	7	2	17	13	— 39

Den —FG Karlis 48
NYG—Mowatt 6 pass from Simms (Allegre kick)
Den —Elway 4 run (Karlis kick)
NYG—Safety, Martin tackled Elway in end zone
NYG—Bavaro 13 pass from Simms (Allegre kick)
NYG—FG Allegre 21
NYG—Morris 1 run (Allegre kick)
NYG—McConkey 6 pass from Simms (Allegre kick)
Den —FG Karlis 28
NYG—Anderson 2 run (kick failed)
Den —V. Johnson 47 pass from Elway (Karlis kick)

Super Bowl XX

Louisiana Superdome, New Orleans, Louisiana — January 26, 1986

Attendance: 73,818

CHICAGO 46, NEW ENGLAND 10—The NFC champion Chicago Bears, seeking their first NFL title since 1963, scored a Super Bowl-record 46 points in downing AFC champion New England 46-10 in Super Bowl XX. The previous record for most points in a Super Bowl was 38, shared by San Francisco in XIX and the Los Angeles Raiders in XVIII. The Bears' league-leading defense tied the Super Bowl record for sacks (7) and limited the Patriots to a record-low seven yards rushing. New England took the quickest lead in Super Bowl history when Tony Franklin kicked a 36-yard field goal with 1:19 elapsed in the first period. The score came about because of Larry McGrew's fumble recovery at the Chicago 19-yard line. However, the Bears rebounded for a 23-3 first-half lead, while building a yardage advantage of 236 total yards to New England's minus 19. Running back Matt Suhey rushed eight times for 37 yards, including an 11-yard touchdown run, and caught one pass for 24 yards in the first half. After the Patriots first drive of the second half ended with a punt to the Bears' 4-yard line, Chicago marched 96 yards in nine plays with quarterback Jim McMahon's one-yard scoring run capping the drive. McMahon became the first quarterback in Super Bowl history to rush for a pair of touchdowns. The Bears completed their scoring via a 28-yard interception return by reserve cornerback Reggie Phillips, a one-yard run by defensive tackle/fullback William Perry, and a safety when defensive end Henry Waechter tackled Patriots quarterback Steve Grogan in the end zone. Bears defensive end Richard Dent became the fourth defender to be named the game's most valuable player after contributing 1½ sacks. The Bears' victory margin of 36 points was the largest in Super Bowl history, bettering the previous mark of 29 by the Los Angeles Raiders when they topped Washington 38-9 in Game XVIII. McMahon completed 12 of 20 passes for 256 yards before leaving the game in the fourth period with a wrist injury. The NFL's all-time leading rusher, Bears running back Walter Payton, carried 22 times for 61 yards. Wide receiver Willie Gault caught four passes for 129 yards, the fourth-most receiving yards in a Super Bowl. Chicago coach Mike Ditka became the second man (Tom Flores of Raiders was the other) who played in a Super Bowl and coached a team to a victory in the game.

Chicago (NFC)	13	10	21	2	— 46
New England (AFC)	3	0	0	7	— 10

NE—FG Franklin 36
Chi—FG Butler 28
Chi—FG Butler 24
Chi—Suhey 11 run (Butler kick)
Chi—McMahon 2 run (Butler kick)
Chi—FG Butler 24
Chi—McMahon 1 run (Butler kick)
Chi—Phillips 28 interception return (Butler kick)
Chi—Perry 1 run (Butler kick)
NE—Fryar 8 pass from Grogan (Franklin kick)
Chi—Safety, Waechter tackled Grogan in end zone

Super Bowl XIX

Stanford Stadium, Stanford, California — January 20, 1985

Attendance: 84,059

SAN FRANCISCO 38, MIAMI 16—The San Francisco 49ers captured their second Super Bowl title with a dominating offense and a defense that tamed Miami's explosive passing attack. The Dolphins held a 10-7 lead at the end of the first period, which represented the most points scored by two teams in an opening quarter of a Super Bowl. However, the 49ers used excellent field position in the second period to build a 28-16 halftime lead. Running back Roger Craig set a Super Bowl record by scoring three touchdowns on pass receptions of 8 and 16 yards and a run of 2 yards. San Francisco's Joe Montana was voted the game's most valuable player. He joined Green Bay's Bart Starr and Pittsburgh's Terry Bradshaw as the only two-time Super Bowl most valuable players. Montana completed 24 of 35 passes for a Super Bowl-record 331 yards and three touchdowns, and rushed five times for 59 yards, including a six-yard touchdown. Craig had 58 yards on 15 carries and caught seven passes for 77 yards. Wendell Tyler rushed 13 times for 65 yards and had four catches for 70 yards. Dwight Clark had six receptions for 77 yards, while Russ Francis had five for 60. San Francisco's 537 total net yards bettered the previous Super Bowl record of 429 yards by Oakland in Super Bowl XI. The 49ers also held a time of possession advantage over the Dolphins of 37:11 to 22:49.

Miami (AFC)	10	6	0	0	— 16
San Francisco (NFC)	7	21	10	0	— 38

Mia—FG von Schamann 37
SF—Monroe 33 pass from Montana (Wersching kick)
Mia—D. Johnson 2 pass from Marino (von Schamann kick)
SF—Craig 8 pass from Montana (Wersching kick)
SF—Montana 6 run (Wersching kick)
SF—Craig 2 run (Wersching kick)
Mia—FG von Schamann 31
Mia—FG von Schamann 30
SF—FG Wersching 27
SF—Craig 16 pass from Montana (Wersching kick)

Super Bowl XVIII

Tampa Stadium, Tampa, Florida — January 22, 1984

Attendance: 72,920

LOS ANGELES RAIDERS 38, WASHINGTON 9—The Los Angeles Raiders dominated the Washington Redskins from the beginning in Super Bowl XVIII and achieved the most lopsided victory in Super Bowl history, surpassing Green Bay's 35-10 win over Kansas City in Super Bowl I. The Raiders took a 7-0 lead 4:52 into the game when Derrick Jensen blocked a Jeff Hayes punt and recovered it in the end zone for a touchdown. With 9:14 remaining in the first half, Raiders quarterback Jim Plunkett threw a 12-yard touchdown pass to wide receiver Cliff Branch to complete a three-play, 65-yard drive. Washington cut the Raiders' lead to 14-3 on a 24-yard field goal by Mark Moseley. With seven seconds left in the first half, Raiders linebacker Jack Squirek intercepted a Joe Theismann pass at the Redskins' 5-yard line and ran it in for a touchdown to give Los Angeles a 21-3 halftime lead. In the third period, running back Marcus Allen, who rushed for a Super Bowl record 191 yards on 20 carries, increased the Raiders' lead to 35-3 on touchdown runs of 5 and 74 yards, the latter erasing the previous Super Bowl record of 58 yards set by Baltimore's Tom Matte in Game III. Allen was named the game's most valuable player. The victory over Washington raised Raiders coach Tom Flores' playoff record to 8-1, including a 27-10 win against Philadelphia in Super Bowl XV. The 38 points scored by the Raiders was the highest total by a Super Bowl team. The previous high was 35 points by Green Bay in Game I.

Washington (NFC)	0	3	6	0	— 9
L.A. Raiders (AFC)	7	14	14	3	— 38

Raiders—Jensen recovered blocked punt in end zone (Bahr kick)
Raiders—Branch 12 pass from Plunkett (Bahr kick)
Wash—FG Moseley 24
Raiders—Squirek 5 interception return (Bahr kick)
Wash—Riggins 1 run (kick blocked)
Raiders—Allen 5 run (Bahr kick)
Raiders—Allen 74 run (Bahr kick)
Raiders—FG Bahr 21

Super Bowl XVII

Rose Bowl, Pasadena, California — January 30, 1983

Attendance: 103,667

WASHINGTON 27, MIAMI 17—Fullback John Riggins's Super Bowl record 166 yards on 38 carries sparked Washington to a 27-17 victory over AFC champion Miami. It was Riggins's fourth straight 100-yard rushing game during the playoffs, also a record. The win marked Washington's first NFL title since 1942, and was only the second time in Super Bowl history NFC teams scored consecutive victories (Green Bay did it in Super Bowls I and II and San Francisco won Super Bowl XVI). The Redskins, under second-year head coach Joe Gibbs, used a balanced offense that accounted for 400 total yards (a Super Bowl record 276 yards rushing and 124 passing), second in Super Bowl history to 429 yards by Oakland in Super Bowl XI. The Dolphins built a 17-10 halftime lead on a 76-yard touchdown pass from quarterback David Woodley to wide receiver Jimmy Cefalo 6:49 into the first period, a 20-yard field goal by Uwe von Schamann with 6:00 left in the half, and a Super Bowl record 98-yard kickoff return by Fulton Walker with 1:38 remaining. Washington had tied the score at 10-10 with 1:51 left on a four-yard touchdown pass from Joe Theismann to wide receiver Alvin Garrett. Mark Moseley started the Redskins' scoring with a 31-yard field goal late in the first period, and added a 20-yarder midway through the third period to cut the Dolphins' lead to 17-13. Riggins, who was voted the game's most valuable player, gave Washington its first lead of the game with 10:01 left when he ran 43 yards off left tackle for a touchdown on a fourth-and-one situation. Wide receiver Charlie Brown caught a six-yard scoring pass from Theismann with 1:55 left to complete the scoring. The Dolphins managed only 176 yards (142 in first half). Theismann completed 15 of 23 passes for 143 yards, two touchdowns, and had two interceptions. For Miami, Woodley was 4 of 14 for 97 yards, with one touchdown, and one interception. Don Strock was 0 for 3 in relief.

Miami (AFC)	7	10	0	0	— 17
Washington (NFC)	0	10	3	14	— 27

Mia—Cefalo 76 pass from Woodley (von Schamann kick)
Wash—FG Moseley 31
Mia—FG von Schamann 20
Wash—Garrett 4 pass from Theismann (Moseley kick)
Mia—Walker 98 kickoff return (von Schamann kick)
Wash—FG Moseley 20
Wash—Riggins 43 run (Moseley kick)
Wash—Brown 6 pass from Theismann (Moseley kick)

Super Bowl XVI

Pontiac Silverdome, Pontiac, Michigan — January 24, 1982

Attendance: 81,270

SAN FRANCISCO 26, CINCINNATI 21—Ray Wersching's Super Bowl record-tying four field goals and Joe Montana's controlled passing helped lift the San Francisco 49ers to their first NFL championship with a 26-21 victory over Cincinnati. The 49ers built a game-record 20-0 halftime lead via Montana's one-yard touchdown run, which capped an 11-play, 68-yard drive; fullback Earl Cooper's 11-yard scoring pass from Montana, which climaxed a Super Bowl record 92-yard drive on 12 plays; and Wersching's 22- and 26-yard field goals. The Bengals rebounded in the second half, closing the gap to 20-14 on quarterback Ken Anderson's five-yard run and Dan Ross's four-yard reception from Anderson, who established Super Bowl passing records for completions (25) and completion percentage (73.5 percent on 25 of 34). Wersching added early fourth-period field goals of 40 and 23 yards to increase the 49ers' lead to 26-14. The Bengals managed to score on an Anderson-to-Ross three-yard pass with only 16 seconds remaining. Ross set a Super Bowl record with 11 receptions for 104 yards. Montana, the game's most valuable player, completed 14 of 22 passes for 157 yards. Cincinnati compiled 356 yards to San Francisco's 275, which marked the first time in Super Bowl history that the team that gained the most yards from scrimmage lost the game.

San Francisco (NFC)	7	13	0	6	— 26
Cincinnati (AFC)	0	0	7	14	— 21

SF —Montana 1 run (Wersching kick)
SF —Cooper 11 pass from Montana (Wersching kick)
SF —FG Wersching 22
SF —FG Wersching 26
Cin—Anderson 5 run (Breech kick)
Cin—Ross 4 pass from Anderson (Breech kick)
SF —FG Wersching 40
SF —FG Wersching 23
Cin—Ross 3 pass from Anderson (Breech kick)

Super Bowl XV

Louisiana Superdome, New Orleans, Louisiana January 25, 1981
Attendance: 76,135

OAKLAND 27, PHILADELPHIA 10—Jim Plunkett threw three touchdown passes, including an 80-yarder to Kenny King, as the Raiders became the first wild card team to win the Super Bowl. Plunkett's touchdown bomb to King—the longest play in Super Bowl history—gave Oakland a decisive 14-0 lead with nine seconds left in the first period. Linebacker Rod Martin had set up Oakland's first touchdown, a two-yard reception by Cliff Branch, with a 16-yard interception return to the Eagles' 32 yard line. The Eagles never recovered from that early deficit, managing only a Tony Franklin field goal (30 yards) and an eight-yard touchdown pass from Ron Jaworski to Keith Krepfle the rest of the game. Plunkett, who became a starter in the sixth game of the season, completed 13 of 21 for 261 yards and was named the game's most valuable player. Oakland won 9 of 11 games with Plunkett starting, but that was good enough only for second place in the AFC West, although they tied division winner San Diego with an 11-5 record. The Raiders, who had previously won Super Bowl XI over Minnesota, had to win three playoff games to get to the championship game. Oakland defeated Houston 27-7 at home followed by road victories over Cleveland, 14-12 and San Diego, 34-27. Oakland's Mark van Eeghen was the game's leading rusher with 80 yards on 19 carries. Philadelphia's Wilbert Montgomery led all receivers with six receptions for 91 yards. Branch had five for 67 and Harold Carmichael of Philadelphia five for 83. Martin finished the game with three interceptions, a Super Bowl record.

Oakland (AFC)	14	0	10	3	— 27
Philadelphia (NFC)	0	3	0	7	— 10

Oak—Branch 2 pass from Plunkett (Bahr kick)
Oak—King 80 pass from Plunkett (Bahr kick)
Phil —FG Franklin 30
Oak—Branch 29 pass from Plunkett (Bahr kick)
Oak—FG Bahr 46
Phil —Krepfle 8 pass from Jaworski (Franklin kick)
Oak—FG Bahr 35

Super Bowl XIV

Rose Bowl, Pasadena, California January 20, 1980
Attendance: 103,985

PITTSBURGH 31, LOS ANGELES 19—Terry Bradshaw completed 14 of 21 passes for 309 yards and set two passing records as the Steelers became the first team to win four Super Bowls. Despite three interceptions by the Rams, Bradshaw kept his poise and brought the Steelers from behind twice in the second half. Trailing 13-10 at halftime, Pittsburgh went ahead 17-13 when Bradshaw hit Lynn Swann with a 47-yard touchdown pass after 2:48 of the third quarter. On the Rams' next possession Vince Ferragamo, who completed 15 of 25 passes for 212 yards, responded with a 50-yard pass to Billy Waddy that moved Los Angeles from its own 26 to the Steelers' 24. On the following play, Lawrence McCutcheon connected with Ron Smith on a halfback option pass that gave the Rams a 19-17 lead. On Pittsburgh's initial possession of the final period, Bradshaw lofted a 73-yard scoring pass to John Stallworth to put the Steelers in front to stay, 24-19. Franco Harris scored on a one-yard run later in the quarter to seal the verdict. A 45-yard pass from Bradshaw to Stallworth was the key play in the drive to Harris's score. Bradshaw, the game's most valuable player for the second straight year, set career Super Bowl records for most touchdown passes (nine) and most passing yards (932). Larry Anderson gave the Steelers excellent field position throughout the game with five kickoff returns for a record 162 yards.

Los Angeles (NFC)	7	6	6	0	— 19
Pittsburgh (AFC)	3	7	7	14	— 31

Pitt—FG Bahr 41
LA —Bryant 1 run (Corral kick)
Pitt—Harris 1 run (Bahr kick)
LA —FG Corral 31
LA —FG Corral 45
Pitt—Swann 47 pass from Bradshaw (Bahr kick)
LA —Smith 24 pass from McCutcheon (kick failed)
Pitt—Stallworth 73 pass from Bradshaw (Bahr kick)
Pitt—Harris 1 run (Bahr kick)

Super Bowl XIII

Orange Bowl, Miami, Florida January 21, 1979
Attendance: 79,484

PITTSBURGH 35, DALLAS 31—Terry Bradshaw threw a record four touchdown passes to lead the Steelers to victory. The Steelers became the first team to win three Super Bowls, mostly because of Bradshaw's accurate arm. Bradshaw, voted the game's most valuable player, completed 17 of 30 passes for 318 yards, a personal high. Four of those passes went for touchdowns—two to John Stallworth and the third, with 26 seconds remaining in the second period, to Rocky Bleier for a 21-14 halftime lead. The Cowboys scored twice before intermission on Roger Staubach's 39-yard pass to Tony Hill and a 37-yard run by linebacker Mike Hegman, who stole the ball from Bradshaw. The Steelers broke open the contest with two touchdowns in a span of 19 seconds midway through the final period. Franco Harris rambled 22 yards up the middle to give the Steelers a 28-17 lead with 7:10 left. Pittsburgh got the ball right back when Randy White fumbled the kickoff and Dennis Winston recovered for the Steelers. On first down, Bradshaw fired his fourth touchdown pass, an 18-yarder to Lynn Swann to boost the Steelers' lead to 35-17 with 6:51 to play. The Cowboys refused to let the Steelers run away with the contest. Staubach connected with Billy Joe DuPree on a seven-yard scoring pass with 2:23 left. Then the Cowboys recovered an onside kick and Staubach took them in for another score, passing four yards to Butch Johnson with 22 seconds remaining. Bleier recovered another onside kick with 17 seconds left to seal the victory for the Steelers.

Pittsburgh (AFC)	7	14	0	14	— 35
Dallas (NFC)	7	7	3	14	— 31

Pitt —Stallworth 28 pass from Bradshaw (Gerela kick)
Dall—Hill 39 pass from Staubach (Septien kick)
Dall—Hegman 37 fumble recovery return (Septien kick)
Pitt —Stallworth 75 pass from Bradshaw (Gerela kick)
Pitt —Bleier 7 pass from Bradshaw (Gerela kick)
Dall—FG Septien 27
Pitt —Harris 22 run (Gerela kick)
Pitt —Swann 18 pass from Bradshaw (Gerela kick)
Dall—DuPree 7 pass from Staubach (Septien kick)
Dall—B. Johnson 4 pass from Staubach (Septien kick)

Super Bowl XII

Louisiana Superdome, New Orleans, Louisiana January 15, 1978
Attendance: 75,583

DALLAS 27, DENVER 10—The Cowboys evened their Super Bowl record at 2-2 by defeating Denver before a sellout crowd of 75,583, plus 102,010,000 television viewers, the largest audience ever to watch a sporting event. Dallas converted two interceptions into 10 points and Efren Herrera added a 35-yard field goal for a 13-0 halftime advantage. In the third period Craig Morton engineered a drive to the Cowboys' 30 and Jim Turner's 47-yard field goal made the score 13-3. After an exchange of punts, Butch Johnson made a spectacular diving catch in the end zone to complete a 45-yard pass from Roger Staubach and put the Cowboys ahead 20-3. Following Rick Upchurch's 67-yard kickoff return, Norris Weese guided the Broncos to a touchdown to cut the Dallas lead to 20-10. Dallas clinched the victory when running back Robert Newhouse threw a 29-yard touchdown pass to Golden Richards with 7:04 remaining in the game. It was the first pass thrown by Newhouse since 1975. Harvey Martin and Randy White, who were named co-most valuable players, led the Cowboys' defense, which recovered four fumbles and intercepted four passes.

Dallas (NFC)	10	3	7	7	— 27
Denver (AFC)	0	0	10	0	— 10

Dall—Dorsett 3 run (Herrera kick)
Dall—FG Herrera 35
Dall—FG Herrera 43
Den—FG Turner 47
Dall—Johnson 45 pass from Staubach (Herrera kick)
Den—Lytle 1 run (Turner kick)
Dall—Richards 29 pass from Newhouse (Herrera kick)

Super Bowl XI

Rose Bowl, Pasadena, California January 9, 1977
Attendance: 103,438

OAKLAND 32, MINNESOTA 14—The Raiders won their first NFL championship before a record Super Bowl crowd plus 81 million television viewers, the largest audience ever to watch a sporting event. The Raiders gained a record-breaking 429 yards, including running back Clarence Davis's 137 yards rushing. Wide receiver Fred Biletnikoff made four key receptions, which earned him the game's most valuable player trophy. Oakland scored on three successive possessions in the second quarter to build a 16-0 halftime lead. Errol Mann's 24-yard field goal opened the scoring, then the AFC champions put together drives of 64 and 35 yards, scoring on a one-yard pass from Ken Stabler to Dave Casper and a one-yard run by Pete Banaszak. The Raiders increased their lead to 19-0 on a 40-yard field goal in the third quarter, but Minnesota responded with a 12-play, 58-yard drive late in the period, with Fran Tarkenton passing eight yards to wide receiver Sammy White to cut the deficit to 19-7. Two fourth-quarter interceptions clinched the title for the Raiders. One set up Banaszak's second touchdown run, the other resulted in cornerback Willie Brown's Super Bowl record 75-yard interception return.

Oakland (AFC)	0	16	3	13	— 32
Minnesota (NFC)	0	0	7	7	— 14

Oak —FG Mann 24
Oak —Casper 1 pass from Stabler (Mann kick)
Oak —Banaszak 1 run (kick failed)
Oak —FG Mann 40
Minn—S. White 8 pass from Tarkenton (Cox kick)
Oak —Banaszak 2 run (Mann kick)
Oak —Brown 75 interception return (kick failed)
Minn—Voigt 13 pass from Lee (Cox kick)

Super Bowl X

Orange Bowl, Miami, Florida — January 18, 1976

Attendance: 80,187

PITTSBURGH 21, DALLAS 17—The Steelers won the Super Bowl for the second year in a row on Terry Bradshaw's 64-yard touchdown pass to Lynn Swann and an aggressive defense that snuffed out a late rally by the Cowboys with an end-zone interception on the final play of the game. In the fourth quarter, Pittsburgh ran on fourth down and gave up the ball on the Cowboys' 39 with 1:22 to play. Roger Staubach ran and passed for two first downs but his last desperation pass was picked off by Glen Edwards. Dallas's scoring was the result of two touchdown passes by Staubach, one to Drew Pearson for 29 yards and the other to Percy Howard for 34 yards. Toni Fritsch had a 36-yard field goal. The Steelers scored on two touchdown passes by Bradshaw, one to Randy Grossman for seven yards and the long bomb to Swann. Roy Gerela had 36- and 18-yard field goals. Reggie Harrison blocked a punt through the end zone for a safety. Swann set a Super Bowl record by gaining 161 yards on his four receptions.

Dallas (NFC)	7	3	0	7	— 17
Pittsburgh (AFC)	7	0	0	14	— 21

Dall—D. Pearson 29 pass from Staubach (Fritsch kick)
Pitt —Grossman 7 pass from Bradshaw (Gerela kick)
Dall—FG Fritsch 36
Pitt —Safety, Harrison blocked Hoopes's punt through end zone
Pitt —FG Gerela 36
Pitt —FG Gerela 18
Pitt —Swann 64 pass from Bradshaw (kick failed)
Dall—P. Howard 34 pass from Staubach (Fritsch kick)

Super Bowl IX

Tulane Stadium, New Orleans, Louisiana — January 12, 1975

Attendance: 80,997

PITTSBURGH 16, MINNESOTA 6—AFC champion Pittsburgh, in its initial Super Bowl appearance, and NFC champion Minnesota, making a third bid for its first Super Bowl title, struggled through a first half in which the only score was produced by the Steelers' defense when Dwight White downed Vikings' quarterback Fran Tarkenton in the end zone for a safety 7:49 into the second period. The Steelers forced another break and took advantage on the second half kickoff when Minnesota's Bill Brown fumbled and Marv Kellum recovered for Pittsburgh on the Vikings' 30. After Rocky Bleier failed to gain on first down, Franco Harris carried three consecutive times for 24 yards, a loss of 3, and a 12-yard touchdown and a 9-0 lead. Though its offense was completely stymied by Pittsburgh's defense, Minnesota managed to move into a threatening position after 4:27 of the final period when Matt Blair blocked Bobby Walden's punt and Terry Brown recovered the ball in the end zone for a touchdown. Fred Cox's kick failed and the Steelers led 9-6. Pittsburgh wasted no time putting the victory away. The Steelers took the ensuing kickoff and marched 66 yards in 11 plays, climaxed by Terry Bradshaw's four-yard scoring pass to Larry Brown with 3:31 left. Pittsburgh's defense permitted Minnesota only 119 yards total offense, including a Super Bowl low of 17 yards rushing. The Steelers, meanwhile, gained 333 yards, including Harris's record 158 yards on 34 carries.

Pittsburgh (AFC)	0	2	7	7	— 16
Minnesota (NFC)	0	0	0	6	— 6

Pitt —Safety, White downed Tarkenton in end zone
Pitt —Harris 12 run (Gerela kick)
Minn—T. Brown recovered blocked punt in end zone (kick failed)
Pitt —L. Brown 4 pass from Bradshaw (Gerela kick)

Super Bowl VIII

Rice Stadium, Houston, Texas — January 13, 1974

Attendance: 71,882

MIAMI 24, MINNESOTA 7—The defending NFL champion Dolphins, representing the AFC for the third straight year, scored the first two times they had possession on marches of 62 and 56 yards in the first period while the Miami defense limited the Vikings to only seven plays. Larry Csonka climaxed the initial 10-play drive with a five-yard touchdown bolt through right guard after 5:27 had elapsed. Four plays later, Miami began another 10-play scoring drive, which ended with Jim Kiick bursting one yard through the middle for another touchdown after 13:38 of the period. Garo Yepremian added a 28-yard field goal midway in the second period for a 17-0 Miami lead. Minnesota then drove from its 20 to a second-and-two situation on the Miami 7 yard line with 1:18 left in the half. But on two plays, Miami limited Oscar Reed to one yard. On fourth-and-one from the 6, Reed went over right tackle, but Dolphins middle linebacker Nick Buoniconti jarred the ball loose and Jake Scott recovered for Miami to halt the Minnesota threat. The Vikings were unable to muster enough offense in the second half to threaten the Dolphins. Csonka rushed 33 times for a Super Bowl record 145 yards. Bob Griese of Miami completed six of seven passes for 73 yards.

Minnesota (NFC)	0	0	0	7	— 7
Miami (AFC)	14	3	7	0	— 24

Mia —Csonka 5 run (Yepremian kick)
Mia —Kiick 1 run (Yepremian kick)
Mia —FG Yepremian 28
Mia —Csonka 2 run (Yepremian kick)
Minn—Tarkenton 4 run (Cox kick)

Super Bowl VII

Memorial Coliseum, Los Angeles, California — January 14, 1973

Attendance: 90,182

MIAMI 14, WASHINGTON 7—The Dolphins played virtually perfect football in the first half as their defense permitted the Redskins to cross midfield only once and their offense turned good field position into two touchdowns. On its third possession, Miami opened its first scoring drive from the Dolphins' 37 yard line. An 18-yard pass from Bob Griese to Paul Warfield preceded by three plays Griese's 28-yard touchdown pass to Howard Twilley. After Washington moved from its 17 to the Miami 48 with two minutes remaining in the first half, Dolphins linebacker Nick Buoniconti intercepted a Billy Kilmer pass at the Miami 41 and returned it to the Washington 27. Jim Kiick ran for three yards, Larry Csonka for three, Griese passed to Jim Mandich for 19, and Kiick gained one to the 1 yard line. With 18 seconds left until intermission, Kiick scored from the 1. Washington's only touchdown came with 7:07 left in the game and resulted from a misplayed field goal attempt and fumble by Garo Yepremian, with the Redskins' Mike Bass picking the ball out of the air and running 49 yards for the score. Jake Scott returned his second interception from three yards deep in the end zone to the Redskins' 48-yard line with just over five minutes to play, ending Washington's best scoring opportunity of the second half. Scott was voted the game's most valuable player.

Miami (AFC)	7	7	0	0	— 14
Washington (NFC)	0	0	0	7	— 7

Mia —Twilley 28 pass from Griese (Yepremian kick)
Mia —Kiick 1 run (Yepremian kick)
Wash—Bass 49 fumble recovery return (Knight kick)

Super Bowl VI

Tulane Stadium, New Orleans, Louisiana — January 16, 1972

Attendance: 81,023

DALLAS 24, MIAMI 3—The Cowboys rushed for a record 252 yards and their defense limited the Dolphins to a low of 185 yards while not permitting a touchdown for the first time in Super Bowl history. Dallas converted Chuck Howley's recovery of Larry Csonka's first fumble of the season into a 3-0 advantage and led at halftime 10-3. After Dallas received the second-half kickoff, Duane Thomas led a 71-yard march in eight plays for a 17-3 margin. Howley intercepted Bob Griese's pass at the 50 and returned it to the Miami 9 early in the fourth period, and three plays later Roger Staubach passed seven yards to Mike Ditka for the final touchdown. Thomas rushed for 95 yards and Walt Garrison gained 74. Staubach, voted the game's most valuable player, completed 12 of 19 passes for 119 yards and two touchdowns.

Dallas (NFC)	3	7	7	7	— 24
Miami (AFC)	0	3	0	0	— 3

Dall—FG Clark 9
Dall—Alworth 7 pass from Staubach (Clark kick)
Mia—FG Yepremian 31
Dall—D. Thomas 3 run (Clark kick)
Dall—Ditka 7 pass from Staubach (Clark kick)

Super Bowl V

Orange Bowl, Miami, Florida — January 17, 1971

Attendance: 79,204

BALTIMORE 16, DALLAS 13—A 32-yard field goal by first-year kicker Jim O'Brien brought the Baltimore Colts a victory over the Dallas Cowboys in the final five seconds of Super Bowl V. The game between the champions of the AFC and NFC was played on artificial turf for the first time. Dallas led 13-6 at the half but interceptions by Rick Volk and Mike Curtis set up a Baltimore touchdown and O'Brien's decisive kick in the fourth period. Earl Morrall relieved an injured Johnny Unitas late in the first half, although Unitas completed the Colts' only scoring pass. It caromed off receiver Eddie Hinton's fingertips, off Dallas defensive back Mel Renfro, and finally settled into the grasp of John Mackey, who went 45 yards to score on a 75-yard play.

Baltimore (AFC)	0	6	0	10	— 16
Dallas (NFC)	3	10	0	0	— 13

Dall—FG Clark 14
Dall—FG Clark 30
Balt—Mackey 75 pass from Unitas (kick blocked)
Dall—Thomas 7 pass from Morton (Clark kick)
Balt—Nowatzke 2 run (O'Brien kick)
Balt—FG O'Brien 32

Super Bowl IV

Tulane Stadium, New Orleans, Louisiana — January 11, 1970

Attendance: 80,562

KANSAS CITY 23, MINNESOTA 7—The AFL squared the Super Bowl at two games apiece with the NFL, building a 16-0 halftime lead behind Len Dawson's superb quarterbacking and a powerful defense. Dawson, the fourth consecutive quarterback to be chosen the Super Bowl's top player, called an almost flawless game, completing 12 of 17 passes and hitting Otis Taylor on a 46-yard play for the final Chiefs touchdown. The Kansas City defense limited Minnesota's strong rushing game to 67 yards and had three interceptions and two fumble recoveries. The crowd of 80,562 set a Super Bowl record, as did the gross receipts of $3,817,872.69.

Minnesota (NFL)	0	0	7	0	— 7
Kansas City (AFL)	3	13	7	0	— 23

KC —FG Stenerud 48
KC —FG Stenerud 32

KC —FG Stenerud 25
KC —Garrett 5 run (Stenerud kick)
Minn—Osborn 4 run (Cox kick)
KC —Taylor 46 pass from Dawson (Stenerud kick)

Super Bowl III

Orange Bowl, Miami, Florida January 12, 1969
Attendance: 75,389

NEW YORK JETS 16, BALTIMORE 7—Jets quarterback Joe Namath "guaranteed" victory on the Thursday before the game, then went out and led the AFL to its first Super Bowl victory over a Baltimore team that had lost only once in 16 games all season. Namath, chosen the outstanding player, completed 17 of 28 passes for 206 yards and directed a steady attack that dominated the NFL champions after the Jets' defense had intercepted Colts quarterback Earl Morrall three times in the first half. The Jets had 337 total yards, including 121 yards rushing by Matt Snell. Johnny Unitas, who had missed most of the season with a sore elbow, came off the bench and led Baltimore to its only touchdown late in the fourth quarter after New York led 16-0.

New York Jets (AFL)	0	7	6	3	— 16
Baltimore (NFL)	0	0	0	7	— 7

NYJ—Snell 4 run (Turner kick)
NYJ—FG Turner 32
NYJ—FG Turner 30
NYJ—FG Turner 9
Balt—Hill 1 run (Michaels kick)

Super Bowl II

Orange Bowl, Miami, Florida January 14, 1968
Attendance: 75,546

GREEN BAY 33, OAKLAND 14—Green Bay, after winning its third consecutive NFL championship, won the Super Bowl title for the second straight year 33-14 over the AFL champion Raiders in a game that drew the first $3-million gate in football history. Bart Starr again was chosen the game's most valuable player as he completed 13 of 24 passes for 202 yards and one touchdown and directed a Packers attack that was in control all the way after building a 16-7 halftime lead. Don Chandler kicked four field goals and all-pro cornerback Herb Adderley capped the Green Bay scoring with a 60-yard run with an interception. The game marked the last for Vince Lombardi as Packers coach, ending nine years at Green Bay in which he won six Western Conference championships, five NFL championships, and two Super Bowls.

Green Bay (NFL)	3	13	10	7	— 33
Oakland (AFL)	0	7	0	7	— 14

GB —FG Chandler 39
GB —FG Chandler 20
GB —Dowler 62 pass from Starr (Chandler kick)
Oak—Miller 23 pass from Lamonica (Blanda kick)
GB —FG Chandler 43
GB —Anderson 2 run (Chandler kick)
GB —FG Chandler 31
GB —Adderley 60 interception return (Chandler kick)
Oak—Miller 23 pass from Lamonica (Blanda kick)

Super Bowl I

Memorial Coliseum, Los Angeles, California January 15, 1967
Attendance: 61,946

GREEN BAY 35, KANSAS CITY 10—The Green Bay Packers opened the Super Bowl series by defeating Kansas City's American Football League champions 35-10 behind the passing of Bart Starr, the receiving of Max McGee, and a key interception by all-pro safety Willie Wood. Green Bay broke open the game with three second-half touchdowns, the first of which was set up by Wood's 40-yard return of an interception to the Chiefs' 5 yard line. McGee, filling in for ailing Boyd Dowler after having caught only three passes all season, caught seven from Starr for 138 yards and two touchdowns. Elijah Pitts ran for two other scores. The Chiefs' 10 points came in the second quarter, the only touchdown on a seven-yard pass from Len Dawson to Curtis McClinton. Starr completed 16 of 23 passes for 250 yards and two touchdowns and was chosen the most valuable player. The Packers collected $15,000 per man and the Chiefs $7,500—the largest single-game shares in the history of team sports.

Kansas City (AFL)	0	10	0	0	— 10
Green Bay (NFL)	7	7	14	7	— 35

GB—McGee 37 pass from Starr (Chandler kick)
KC—McClinton 7 pass from Dawson (Mercer kick)
GB—Taylor 14 run (Chandler kick)
KC—FG Mercer 31
GB—Pitts 5 run (Chandler kick)
GB—McGee 13 pass from Starr (Chandler kick)
GB—Pitts 1 run (Chandler kick)

AFC Championship Game

Includes AFL Championship Games (1960-69)

Results

Season	Date	Winner (Share)	Loser (Share)	Score	Site	Attendance
1988	Jan. 8	Cincinnati ($18,000)	Buffalo ($18,000)	21-10	Cincinnati	59,747
1987	Jan. 17	Denver ($18,000)	Cleveland ($18,000)	38-33	Denver	76,197
1986	Jan. 11	Denver ($18,000)	Cleveland ($18,000)	23-20*	Cleveland	79,973
1985	Jan. 12	New England ($18,000)	Miami ($18,000)	31-14	Miami	75,662
1984	Jan. 6	Miami ($18,000)	Pittsburgh ($18,000)	45-28	Miami	76,029
1983	Jan. 8	L.A. Raiders ($18,000)	Seattle ($18,000)	30-14	Los Angeles	91,445
1982	Jan. 23	Miami ($18,000)	N.Y. Jets ($18,000)	14-0	Miami	67,396
1981	Jan. 10	Cincinnati ($9,000)	San Diego ($9,000)	27-7	Cincinnati	46,302
1980	Jan. 11	Oakland ($9,000)	San Diego ($9,000)	34-27	San Diego	52,675
1979	Jan. 6	Pittsburgh ($9,000)	Houston ($9,000)	27-13	Pittsburgh	50,475
1978	Jan. 7	Pittsburgh ($9,000)	Houston ($9,000)	34-5	Pittsburgh	50,725
1977	Jan. 1	Denver ($9,000)	Oakland ($9,000)	20-17	Denver	75,044
1976	Dec. 26	Oakland ($8,500)	Pittsburgh ($5,500)	24-7	Oakland	53,821
1975	Jan. 4	Pittsburgh ($8,500)	Oakland ($5,500)	16-10	Pittsburgh	50,609
1974	Dec. 29	Pittsburgh ($8,500)	Oakland ($5,500)	24-13	Oakland	53,800
1973	Dec. 30	Miami ($8,500)	Oakland ($5,500)	27-10	Miami	79,325
1972	Dec. 31	Miami ($8,500)	Pittsburgh ($5,500)	21-17	Pittsburgh	50,845
1971	Jan. 2	Miami ($8,500)	Baltimore ($5,500)	21-0	Miami	76,622
1970	Jan. 3	Baltimore ($8,500)	Oakland ($5,500)	27-17	Baltimore	54,799
1969	Jan. 4	Kansas City ($7,755)	Oakland ($6,252)	17-7	Oakland	53,564
1968	Dec. 29	N.Y. Jets ($7,007)	Oakland ($5,349)	27-23	New York	62,627
1967	Dec. 31	Oakland ($6,321)	Houston ($4,996)	40-7	Oakland	53,330
1966	Jan. 1	Kansas City ($5,309)	Buffalo ($3,799)	31-7	Buffalo	42,080
1965	Dec. 26	Buffalo ($5,189)	San Diego ($3,447)	23-0	San Diego	30,361
1964	Dec. 26	Buffalo ($2,668)	San Diego ($1,738)	20-7	Buffalo	40,242
1963	Jan. 5	San Diego ($2,498)	Boston ($1,596)	51-10	San Diego	30,127
1962	Dec. 23	Dallas ($2,206)	Houston ($1,471)	20-17*	Houston	37,981
1961	Dec. 24	Houston ($1,792)	San Diego ($1,111)	10-3	San Diego	29,556
1960	Jan. 1	Houston ($1,025)	L.A. Chargers ($718)	24-16	Houston	32,183

**Sudden death overtime.*

AFC Championship Game Composite Standings

	W	L	Pct.	Pts.	OP
Denver Broncos	3	0	1.000	81	70
Kansas City Chiefs*	3	0	1.000	68	31
Cincinnati Bengals	2	0	1.000	48	17
Miami Dolphins	5	1	.833	142	86
Pittsburgh Steelers	4	3	.571	153	131
Baltimore Colts	1	1	.500	27	38
Buffalo Bills	2	2	.500	60	59
New England Patriots**	1	1	.500	41	65
New York Jets	1	1	.500	27	37
Oakland/L.A. Raiders	4	7	.364	225	213
Houston Oilers	2	4	.333	76	140
San Diego Chargers***	1	6	.143	111	148
Seattle Seahawks	0	1	.000	14	30
Cleveland Browns	0	2	.000	53	61

**One game played when franchise was in Dallas (Texans). (Won 20-17)*
***One game played when franchise was in Boston. (Lost 51-10)*
****One game played when franchise was in Los Angeles. (Lost 24-16)*

1988 American Football Conference Championship Game

Riverfront Stadium, Cincinnati, Ohio — January 8, 1989

Attendance: 59,747

CINCINNATI 21, BUFFALO 10—The AFC Central champion Cincinnati Bengals advanced to their second Super Bowl in the 1980s by defeating the Buffalo Bills 21-10. Rookie running back Ickey Woods gained 102 yards on 29 carries and scored two touchdowns to lead the Bengals' ground attack. Cincinnati ran the ball on 50 of 73 plays for 175 of its 249 total yards. Woods's first of two one-yard scoring runs, which followed an interception by cornerback Eric Thomas, gave Cincinnati a 7-0 lead late in the first quarter. After Buffalo tied the game 7-7 on Jim Kelly's nine-yard touchdown pass to Andre Reed, Bengals quarterback Boomer Esiason lofted a 10-yard scoring pass to running back James Brooks. A key play in the game came late in the third quarter. With the Bengals in punt formation and facing a fourth-and-four play on the Buffalo 33-yard line, backup quarterback Turk Schonert moved under center, took the snap, and handed off to Stanley Wilson who gained six yards for a first down. Woods then followed with his second touchdown. The Bengals held the Bills to 181 total yards, the fewest allowed by a Sam Wyche-coached team, including minus-12 in the third quarter. Cincinnati yielded only 45 yards rushing for a two playoff game total of only 63 yards (18 against Seattle) and did not allow the Bills to convert a third-down play (zero for 10). Cincinnati's secondary intercepted three passes, including two of Buffalo quarterback Jim Kelly's first three passes. Safety David Fulcher's interception in the end zone with 8:07 to play sealed the win.

Buffalo (10)	Offense	Cincinnati (21)
Trumaine Johnson	WR	Tim McGee
Will Wolford	LT	Anthony Muñoz
Jim Ritcher	LG	Bruce Reimers
Kent Hull	C	Bruce Kozerski
Dale Hellestrae	RG	Max Montoya
Joe Devlin	RT	Brian Blados
Pete Metzelaars	TE	Rodney Holman
Andre Reed	WR	Eddie Brown
Jim Kelly	QB	Boomer Esiason
Thurman Thomas	RB	James Brooks
Jamie Mueller	RB	Ickey Woods
	Defense	
Art Still	LE	Jim Skow
Fred Smerlas	NT	Tim Krumrie
Bruce Smith	RE	Jason Buck
Darryl Talley	LOLB	Leon White
Shane Conlan	LILB	Carl Zander
Ray Bentley	RILB	Joe Kelly
Cornelius Bennett	ROLB	Reggie Williams
Derrick Burroughs	LCB	Lewis Billups
Nate Odomes	RCB	Eric Thomas
Leonard Smith	SS	David Fulcher
Mark Kelso	FS	Solomon Wilcots

Substitutions

Buffalo—Offense: K—Scott Norwood. P—John Kidd. RB—Carl Byrum, Ronnie Harmon, Robb Riddick. WR—Chris Burkett, Steve Tasker. TE—Butch Rolle. KR—Erroll Tucker. T—Howard Ballard, Len Burton. Defense: E—Mark Pike, Leon Seals. T—Jeff Wright. LB—Carlton Bailey, Hal Garner, Scott Radecic. CB—Sherman Cocroft, Wayne Davis, Kirby Jackson. S—Dwight Drane. DNP: QB—Frank Reich. WR—Flip Johnson.

Cincinnati—Offense: K—Jim Breech. P—Lee Johnson. QB—Turk Schonert. RB—Stanford Jennings, Stanley Wilson. WR—Cris Collinsworth, Ira Hillary, Carl Parker. TE—James Riggs. T—David Douglas, David Smith. Defense: E—Curtis Maxey, Skip McClendon. T—David Grant. LB—Leo Barker, Ed Bradley, Emanuel King. CB—Ray Horton, Daryl Smith. S—Barney Bussey, Rickey Dixon. DNP: QB—Mike Norseth. T—Jim Rourke.

Officials

Referee—Gene Barth. Umpire—Ed Fiffick. Line Judge—Ron Blum. Head Linesman—Earnie Frantz. Back Judge—Paul Baetz. Field Judge—Bob Lewis. Side Judge—Bill Quinby.

Scoring

Buffalo	0	10	0	0	— 10
Cincinnati	7	7	0	7	— 21

Cin — Woods 1 run (Breech kick)
Buff — Reed pass 9 from Kelly (Norwood kick)
Cin — Brooks 10 pass from Esiason (Breech kick)
Buff — FG Norwood 39
Cin — Woods 1 run (Breech kick)

Team Statistics

	Buffalo	Cincinnati
Total First Downs	10	23
First Downs Rushing	2	15
First Downs Passing	8	5
First Downs Penalty	0	3
Total Net Yardage	181	249
Total Offensive Plays	50	73
Average Gain per Offensive Play	3.6	3.1
Rushes	17	50
Yards Gained Rushing (net)	45	175
Average Yards per Rush	2.6	3.5
Passes Attempted	30	20
Passes Completed	14	11
Had Intercepted	3	2
Tackled Attempting to Pass	3	3
Yards Lost Attempting to Pass	27	20
Yards Gained Passing (net)	136	74
Punts	6	6
Average Distance	45.1	36.8
Punt Returns	1	3
Punt Return Yardage	2	24
Kickoff Returns	3	3
Kickoff Return Yardage	57	30
Interception Return Yardage	25	23
Total Return Yardage	84	77
Fumbles	0	2
Own Fumbles Recovered	0	2
Opponents Fumbles Recovered	0	0
Penalties	5	4
Yards Penalized	50	45
Total Points Scored	10	21
Touchdowns Rushing	0	2
Touchdowns Passing	1	1
Touchdowns Returns	0	0
Extra Points	1	3
Field Goals	1	0
Field Goals Attempted	2	0
Safeties	0	0
Third Down Efficiency	0/10	7/15
Fourth Down Efficiency	0/1	1/1
Time of Possession	20:31	39:29

Individual Statistics

Rushing

Buffalo	**No.**	**Yds.**	**LG**	**TD**
Mueller	8	21	13	0
Kelly	2	10	5	0
Thomas	4	6	2	0
Riddick	1	4	4	0
Byrum	1	3	3	0
Harmon	1	1	1	0
Cincinnati	**No.**	**Yds.**	**LG**	**TD**
Wods	29	102	16	2
Wilson	5	29	9	0
Esiason	7	26	29	0
Jennings	2	12	8	0
Brooks	7	6	5	0
Holman	4	38	21	0
Brooks	2	21	11	1
Riggs	2	16	13	0
McGee	2	14	8	0
Collinsworth	1	5	5	0

Passing

Buffalo	**Att.**	**Comp.**	**Yds.**	**TD**	**Int.**
Kelly	30	14	163	1	3
Cincinnati	**Att.**	**Comp.**	**Yds.**	**TD**	**Int.**
Esiason	20	11	94	1	2

Receiving

Buffalo	**No.**	**Yds.**	**LG**	**TD**
Reed	5	55	18	1
Riddick	3	28	14	0
Harmon	3	18	9	0
T. Johnson	2	48	26	0
Metzelaars	1	14	14	0

Interceptions

Buffalo	**No.**	**Yds.**	**LG**	**TD**
Kelso	1	25	25	0
Bentley	1	0	0	0
Cincinnati	**No.**	**Yds.**	**LG**	**TD**
Thomas	1	26	26	0
Fulcher	1	0	0	0
Billups	1	−3	−3	0

Punting

Buffalo	**No.**	**Avg.**	**LG**	**Blk.**
Kidd	6	45.1	50	0
Cincinnati	**No.**	**Avg.**	**LG**	**Blk.**
Johnson	6	36.8	58	0

Punt Returns

Buffalo	**No.**	**FC**	**Yds.**	**LG**	**TD**
Tucker	1	1	2	2	0
Cincinnati	**No.**	**FC**	**Yds.**	**LG**	**TD**
Hillary	2	0	24	15	0
Dixon	1	0	0	0	0

Kickoff Returns

Buffalo	**No.**	**Yds.**	**LG**	**TD**
Harmon	2	45	23	0
Tucker	1	12	12	0
Cincinnati	**No.**	**Yds.**	**LG**	**TD**
Hillary	2	11	11	0
Jennings	1	19	19	0

NFC Championship Game

Includes NFL Championship Games (1933-69)

Results

Season	Date	Winner (Share)	Loser (Share)	Score	Site	Attendance
1988	Jan. 8	San Francisco ($18,000)	Chicago ($18,000)	28-3	Chicago	66,946
1987	Jan. 17	Washington ($18,000)	Minnesota ($18,000)	17-10	Washington	55,212
1986	Jan. 11	New York Giants ($18,000)	Washington ($18,000)	17-0	New York	76,891
1985	Jan. 12	Chicago ($18,000)	L.A. Rams ($18,000)	24-0	Chicago	66,030
1984	Jan. 6	San Francisco ($18,000)	Chicago ($18,000)	23-0	San Francisco	61,336
1983	Jan. 8	Washington ($18,000)	San Francisco ($18,000)	24-21	Washington	55,363
1982	Jan. 22	Washington ($18,000)	Dallas ($18,000)	31-17	Washington	55,045
1981	Jan. 10	San Francisco ($9,000)	Dallas ($9,000)	28-27	San Francisco	60,525
1980	Jan. 11	Philadelphia ($9,000)	Dallas ($9,000)	20-7	Philadelphia	71,522
1979	Jan. 6	Los Angeles ($9,000)	Tampa Bay ($9,000)	9-0	Tampa Bay	72,033
1978	Jan. 7	Dallas ($9,000)	Los Angeles ($9,000)	28-0	Los Angeles	71,086
1977	Jan. 1	Dallas ($9,000)	Minnesota ($9,000)	23-6	Dallas	64,293
1976	Dec. 26	Minnesota ($8,500)	Los Angeles ($5,500)	24-13	Minnesota	48,379
1975	Jan. 4	Dallas ($8,500)	Los Angeles ($5,500)	37-7	Los Angeles	88,919
1974	Dec. 29	Minnesota ($8,500)	Los Angeles ($5,500)	14-10	Minnesota	48,444
1973	Dec. 30	Minnesota ($8,500)	Dallas ($5,500)	27-10	Dallas	64,422
1972	Dec. 31	Washington ($8,500)	Dallas ($5,500)	26-3	Washington	53,129
1971	Jan. 2	Dallas ($8,500)	San Francisco ($5,500)	14-3	Dallas	63,409
1970	Jan. 3	Dallas ($8,500)	San Francisco ($5,500)	17-10	San Francisco	59,364
1969	Jan. 4	Minnesota ($7,930)	Cleveland ($5,118)	27-7	Minnesota	46,503
1968	Dec. 29	Baltimore ($9,306)	Cleveland ($5,963)	34-0	Cleveland	78,410
1967	Dec. 31	Green Bay ($7,950)	Dallas ($5,299)	21-17	Green Bay	50,861
1966	Jan. 1	Green Bay ($9,813)	Dallas ($6,527)	34-27	Dallas	74,152
1965	Jan. 2	Green Bay ($7,819)	Cleveland ($5,288)	23-12	Green Bay	50,777
1964	Dec. 27	Cleveland ($8,052)	Baltimore ($5,571)	27-0	Cleveland	79,544
1963	Dec. 29	Chicago ($5,899)	New York ($4,218)	14-10	Chicago	45,801
1962	Dec. 30	Green Bay ($5,888)	New York ($4,166)	16-7	New York	64,892
1961	Dec. 31	Green Bay ($5,195)	New York ($3,339)	37-0	Green Bay	39,029
1960	Dec. 26	Philadelphia ($5,116)	Green Bay ($3,105)	17-13	Philadelphia	67,325
1959	Dec. 27	Baltimore ($4,674)	New York ($3,083)	31-16	Baltimore	57,545
1958	Dec. 28	Baltimore ($4,718)	New York ($3,111)	23-17*	New York	64,185
1957	Dec. 29	Detroit ($4,295)	Cleveland ($2,750)	59-14	Detroit	55,263
1956	Dec. 30	New York ($3,779)	Chi. Bears ($2,485)	47-7	New York	56,836
1955	Dec. 26	Cleveland ($3,508)	Los Angeles ($2,316)	38-14	Los Angeles	85,693
1954	Dec. 26	Cleveland ($2,478)	Detroit ($1,585)	56-10	Cleveland	43,827
1953	Dec. 27	Detroit ($2,424)	Cleveland ($1,654)	17-16	Detroit	54,577
1952	Dec. 28	Detroit ($2,274)	Cleveland ($1,712)	17-7	Cleveland	50,934
1951	Dec. 23	Los Angeles ($2,108)	Cleveland ($1,483)	24-17	Los Angeles	57,522

1950	Dec. 24	Cleveland ($1,113)	Los Angeles ($686)	30-28	Cleveland	29,751
1949	Dec. 18	Philadelphia ($1,094)	Los Angeles ($739)	14-0	Los Angeles	27,980
1948	Dec. 19	Philadelphia ($1,540)	Chi. Cardinals ($874)	7-0	Philadelphia	36,309
1947	Dec. 28	Chi. Cardinals ($1,132)	Philadelphia ($754)	28-21	Chicago	30,759
1946	Dec. 15	Chi. Bears ($1,975)	New York ($1,295)	24-14	New York	58,346
1945	Dec. 16	Cleveland ($1,469)	Washington ($902)	15-14	Cleveland	32,178
1944	Dec. 17	Green Bay ($1,449)	New York ($814)	14-7	New York	46,016
1943	Dec. 26	Chi. Bears ($1,146)	Washington ($765)	41-21	Chicago	34,320
1942	Dec. 13	Washington ($965)	Chi. Bears ($637)	14-6	Washington	36,006
1941	Dec. 21	Chi. Bears ($430)	New York ($288)	37-9	Chicago	13,341
1940	Dec. 8	Chi. Bears ($873)	Washington ($606)	73-0	Washington	36,034
1939	Dec. 10	Green Bay ($703.97)	New York ($455.57)	27-0	Milwaukee	32,279
1938	Dec. 11	New York ($504.45)	Green Bay ($368.81)	23-17	New York	48,120
1937	Dec. 12	Washington ($225.90)	Chi. Bears ($127.78)	28-21	Chicago	15,870
1936	Dec. 13	Green Bay ($250)	Boston ($180)	21-6	New York	29,545
1935	Dec. 15	Detroit ($313.35)	New York ($200.20)	26-7	Detroit	15,000
1934	Dec. 9	New York ($621)	Chi. Bears ($414.02)	30-13	New York	35,059
1933	Dec. 17	Chi. Bears ($210.34)	New York ($140.22)	23-21	Chicago	26,000

**Sudden death overtime.*

NFC Championship Game Composite Standings

	W	L	Pct.	Pts.	OP
Green Bay Packers	8	2	.800	223	116
Philadelphia Eagles	4	1	.800	79	48
Baltimore Colts	3	1	.750	88	60
Detroit Lions*	4	2	.667	129	109
Minnesota Vikings	4	2	.667	108	80
Washington Redskins**	6	5	.545	181	245
Chicago Bears	7	6	.536	286	245
Phoenix Cardinals***	1	1	.500	28	28
San Francisco 49ers	3	3	.500	113	85
Dallas Cowboys	5	7	.417	227	213
Cleveland Browns	4	7	.364	224	253
Los Angeles Rams****	3	8	.273	120	240
New York Giants	4	11	.267	225	309
Tampa Bay Buccaneers	0	1	.000	0	9

**One game played when franchise was in Portsmouth. (Lost 9-0)*
***One game played when franchise was in Boston. (Lost 21-6)*
****Both games played when franchise was in Chicago. (Won 28-21, lost 7-0)*
*****One game played when franchise was in Cleveland. (Won 15-14)*

1988 National Football Conference Championship Game

Soldier Field, Chicago, Illinois — January 8, 1989 — Attendance: 66,946

SAN FRANCISCO 49ERS 28, CHICAGO BEARS 3—NFC Western champion San Francisco earned the right to try for an unprecedented third Super Bowl championship during the 1980s by defeating NFC Central titlist Chicago 28-3 in the NFC Championship Game. The victory marked the 49ers' first road playoff win since 1970. It was also the first NFC Championship Game win by the visiting team since 1979 when the Los Angeles Rams downed host Tampa Bay 9-0. In previous Super Bowl appearances, San Francisco downed Cincinnati 26-21 in Super Bowl XVI and Miami 38-16 in Game XIX. The 1988 NFC title game began in 17-degree temperature and a wind-chill of minus 26. The 49ers, who made the playoffs for the NFL's current best active streak of six straight seasons, took a 14-3 halftime lead on a pair of Joe Montana touchdown passes (61 and 27 yards) to wide receiver Jerry Rice, who had caught three touchdowns in San Francisco's 34-9 win over Minnesota in an NFC Divisional Playoff Game on January 1. San Francisco came right back after halftime with a 13-play, 78-yard touchdown drive capped by Montana's 5-yard scoring pass to tight end John Frank. The 49ers' final score came on fullback Tom Rathman's 4-yard run with 6:53 remaining. The 49ers' defense yielded Chicago only 267 yards and allowed the Bears inside the San Francisco 40-yard line only twice in the game. The Bears' longest play of the game was 18 yards. San Francisco played near-flawlessly with no penalties and only one lost fumble.

San Francisco (28)	Offense	Chicago (3)
Jerry Rice	WR	Dennis Gentry
Steve Wallace	LT	Jim Covert
Jesse Sapolu	LG	Mark Bortz
Randy Cross	C	Jay Hilgenberg
Guy McIntyre	RG	Tom Thayer
Harris Barton	RT	Keith Van Horne
Brent Jones	TE	Jim Thornton
John Taylor	WR	Dennis McKinnon
Joe Montana	QB	Jim McMahon
John Frank	TE-RB	Neal Anderson
Roger Craig	RB	Matt Suhey

	Defense	
Larry Roberts	LE	Al Harris
Michael Carter	NT-LT	Steve McMichael
Kevin Fagan	RE-RT	Dan Hampton
Charles Haley	LOLB-RE	Sean Smith
Jim Fahnhorst	LILB-LLB	Ron Rivera
Michael Walter	RILB-MLB	Mike Singletary
Keena Turner	ROLB-RLB	Jim Morrissey
Tim McKyer	LCB	Mike Richardson
Don Griffin	RCB	Vestee Jackson
Jeff Fuller	SS	Dave Duerson
Ronnie Lott	FS	Maurice Douglass

Substitutions

San Francisco—Offense: K—Mike Cofer. P—Barry Helton. QB—Steve Young. RB—Terrence Flagler, Tom Rathman, Del Rodgers, Harry Sydney. WR—Terry Greer, Mike Wilson. TE—Ron Heller. C—Chuck Thomas. T—Bubba Paris. Defense: E—Pierce Holt, Pete Kugler, Daniel Stubbs. G—Bruce Collie. LB—Ron Hadley, Sam Kennedy, Bill Romanowski. CB—Darryl Pollard. S—Greg Cox, Tom Holmoe. DNP: CB—Eric Wright.
Chicago—Offense: K—Kevin Butler. P—Bryan Wagner. QB—Mike Tomczak. RB—Brad Muster, Thomas Sanders. WR—Wendell Davis, Glen Kozlowski, Ron Morris. TE—Emery Moorehead. C—John Adickes. G—Kurt Becker. Defense: T—Dick Chapura, John Shannon. LB—Greg Clark, Troy Johnson, Dante Jones, Mickey Pruitt. S—Todd Krumm, Lorenzo Lynch. CB—Lemuel Stinson, David Tate. DNP: QB—Jim Harbaugh, T—John Wojciechowski.

Officials

Referee—Bob McElwee. Umpire—Bob Boylston. Line Judge—Jack Johnson. Head Linesman—Leo Miles. Back Judge—Banks Williams. Field Judge—Pat Mallette. Side Judge—Tom Fincken.

Scoring

San Francisco	7	7	7	7	— 28
Chicago	0	3	0	0	— 3

SF —Rice 61 pass from Montana (Cofer kick)
SF —Rice 27 pass from Montana (Cofer kick)
Chi—FG Butler 25
SF —Frank 5 pass from Montana (Cofer kick)
SF —Rathman 4 run (Cofer kick)

Team Statistics

	San Francisco	Chicago
Total First Downs	21	15
First Downs Rushing	9	8
First Downs Passing	12	7
First Downs Penalty	0	0
Total Net Yardage	406	267
Total Offensive Plays	66	66
Average Gain per Offensive Play	6.2	4.0
Rushes	37	25
Yards Gained Rushing (net)	138	91
Average Yards per Rush	3.7	3.6
Passes Attempted	27	41
Passes Completed	17	20
Had Intercepted	0	1
Tackled Attempting to Pass	2	0
Yards Lost Attempting to Pass	20	0
Yards Gained Passing (net)	268	176
Punts	6	7
Average Distance	34.5	31.4
Punt Returns	4	1
Punt Return Yardage	24	1
Kickoff Returns	2	5
Kickoff Return Yardage	36	89
Interception Return Yardage	0	0

Total Return Yardage	60	90
Fumbles	1	2
Own Fumbles Recovered	0	1
Opponents Fumbles Recovered	1	1
Penalties	0	3
Yards Penalized	0	35
Total Points Scored	28	3
Touchdowns Rushing	1	0
Touchdowns Passing	3	0
Touchdowns Returns	0	0
Extra Points	4	0
Field Goals	0	1
Field Goals Attempted	0	1
Safeties	0	0
Third Down Efficiency	9/15	4/14
Fourth Down Efficiency	0/0	1/2
Time of Possession	31:03	28:57

Individual Statistics

Rushing

San Francisco	No.	Yds.	LG	TD
Craig	18	68	11	0
Rathman	10	36	12	1
Montana	3	12	7	0
Sydney	2	12	8	0
Flagler	3	7	6	0
Rice	1	3	3	0
Chicago	**No.**	**Yds.**	**LG**	**TD**
Anderson	14	59	16	0
Sanders	7	22	14	0
McMahon	1	9	9	0
Suhey	1	3	3	0
Muster	1	2	2	0
McKinnon	1	−4	−4	0

Passing

San Fran.	Att.	Comp.	Yds.	TD	Int.
Montana	27	17	288	3	0
Chicago	**Att.**	**Comp.**	**Yds.**	**TD**	**Int.**
McMahon	29	14	121	0	1
Tomczak	12	6	55	0	0

Receiving

San Fran.	No.	Yds.	LG	TD
Rice	5	133	61t	2
Rathman	5	51	22	0
Taylor	3	51	32	0
Craig	2	33	23	0
Frank	2	20	15	1
Chicago	**No.**	**Yds.**	**LG**	**TD**
Anderson	5	31	13	0
Thornton	4	52	18	0
McKinnon	4	32	13	0
Morris	2	25	18	0
Suhey	2	8	4	0
Sanders	1	12	12	0
Muster	1	9	9	0
Gentry	1	7	7	0

Interceptions

San Fran.	No.	Yds.	LG	TD
Fuller	1	0	0	0
Chicago				
None				

Punting

San Fran.	No.	Avg.	LG	Blk.
Helton	6	34.5	55	0
Chicago	**No.**	**Avg.**	**LG**	**Blk.**
Wagner	7	31.4	48	0

Punt Returns

San Fran.	No.	FC	Yds.	LG	TD
Taylor	4	0	24	11	0
Chicago	**No.**	**FC**	**Yds.**	**LG**	**TD**
McKinnon	1	0	1	1	0

Kickoff Returns

San Fran.	No.	Yds.	LG	TD
Taylor	1	22	22	0
Sydney	1	14	14	0
Chicago	**No.**	**Yds.**	**LG**	**TD**
Sanders	2	31	19	0
Muster	1	21	21	0
Gentry	1	19	19	0
Stinson	1	18	18	0

AFC Divisional Playoffs

Includes Second-Round Playoff Games (1982), AFC Inter-Divisional Games (1969), and special playoff games to break ties for AFL Division Championships (1963, 1968)

Results

Season	Date	Winner (Share)	Loser (Share)	Score	Site	Attendance
1988	Jan. 1	Buffalo ($10,000)	Houston ($10,000)	17-10	Buffalo	79,532
	Dec. 31	Cincinnati ($10,000)	Seattle ($10,000)	21-13	Cincinnati	58,560
1987	Jan. 10	Denver ($10,000)	Houston ($10,000)	34-10	Denver	75,440
	Jan. 9	Cleveland ($10,000)	Indianapolis ($10,000)	38-21	Cleveland	79,372
1986	Jan. 4	Denver ($10,000)	New England ($10,000)	22-17	Denver	75,262
	Jan. 3	Cleveland ($10,000)	N.Y. Jets ($10,000)	23-20*	Cleveland	79,720
1985	Jan. 5	New England ($10,000)	L.A. Raiders ($10,000)	27-20	Los Angeles	87,163
	Jan. 4	Miami ($10,000)	Cleveland ($10,000)	24-21	Miami	74,667
1984	Dec. 30	Pittsburgh ($10,000)	Denver ($10,000)	24-17	Denver	74,981
	Dec. 29	Miami ($10,000)	Seattle ($10,000)	31-10	Miami	73,469
1983	Jan. 1	L.A. Raiders ($10,000)	Pittsburgh ($10,000)	38-10	Los Angeles	90,380
	Dec. 31	Seattle ($10,000)	Miami ($10,000)	27-20	Miami	74,136
1982	Jan. 16	Miami ($10,000)	San Diego ($10,000)	34-13	Miami	71,383
	Jan. 15	N.Y. Jets ($10,000)	L.A. Raiders ($10,000)	17-14	Los Angeles	90,038
1981	Jan. 3	Cincinnati ($5,000)	Buffalo ($5,000)	28-21	Cincinnati	55,420
	Jan. 2	San Diego ($5,000)	Miami ($5,000)	41-38*	Miami	73,735
1980	Jan. 4	Oakland ($5,000)	Cleveland ($5,000)	14-12	Cleveland	78,245
	Jan. 3	San Diego ($5,000)	Buffalo ($5,000)	20-14	San Diego	52,253
1979	Dec. 30	Pittsburgh ($5,000)	Miami ($5,000)	34-14	Pittsburgh	50,214
	Dec. 29	Houston ($5,000)	San Diego ($5,000)	17-14	San Diego	51,192
1978	Dec. 31	Houston ($5,000)	New England ($5,000)	31-14	New England	60,735
	Dec. 30	Pittsburgh ($5,000)	Denver ($5,000)	33-10	Pittsburgh	50,230
1977	Dec. 24	Oakland ($5,000)	Baltimore ($5,000)	37-31	Baltimore	59,925
	Dec. 24	Denver ($5,000)	Pittsburgh ($5,000)	34-21	Denver	75,059
1976	Dec. 19	Pittsburgh ($)	Baltimore ($)	40-14	Baltimore	59,296
	Dec. 18	Oakland ($)	New England ($)	24-21	Oakland	53,050
1975	Dec. 28	Oakland ($)	Cincinnati ($)	31-28	Oakland	53,030
	Dec. 27	Pittsburgh ($)	Baltimore ($)	28-10	Pittsburgh	49,557
1974	Dec. 22	Pittsburgh ($)	Buffalo ($)	32-14	Pittsburgh	49,841
	Dec. 21	Oakland ($)	Miami ($)	28-26	Oakland	53,023
1973	Dec. 23	Miami ($)	Cincinnati ($)	34-16	Miami	78,928
	Dec. 22	Oakland ($)	Pittsburgh ($)	33-14	Oakland	52,646
1972	Dec. 24	Miami ($)	Cleveland ($)	20-14	Miami	78,916
	Dec. 23	Pittsburgh ($)	Oakland ($)	13-7	Pittsburgh	50,327
1971	Dec. 26	Baltimore ($)	Cleveland ($)	20-3	Cleveland	70,734
	Dec. 25	Miami ($)	Kansas City ($)	27-24*	Kansas City	45,822
1970	Dec. 27	Oakland ($)	Miami ($)	21-14	Oakland	52,594
	Dec. 26	Baltimore ($)	Cincinnati ($)	17-0	Baltimore	49,694
1969	Dec. 21	Oakland ($)	Houston ($)	56-7	Oakland	53,539
	Dec. 20	Kansas City ($)	N.Y. Jets ($)	13-6	New York	62,977
1968	Dec. 22	Oakland ($)	Kansas City ($)	41-6	Oakland	53,605
1963	Dec. 28	Boston ($)	Buffalo ($)	26-8	Buffalo	33,044

**Sudden Death Overtime.*

$ Players received 1/14 of annual salary for playoff appearances.

1988 AFC Divisional Playoffs

Riverfront Stadium, Cincinnati, Ohio — December 31, 1988
Attendance: 58,560

Cincinnati 21, Seattle 13—The Bengals rushed for a season-high 254 yards and made three first-half touchdowns stand up as Cincinnati beat the Seahawks 21-13. The victory earned the Bengals their first trip to the AFC Championship Game since 1981. Rookie running back Ickey Woods carried 23 times for 126 yards and scored on a one-yard run to give Cincinnati a 21-0 halftime lead. A pair of three-yard touchdown runs by Stanley Wilson opened the Bengals' scoring and preceded Woods's score. James Brooks added 72 yards on 13 carries. Cincinnati's defense held Seattle to just 18 yards rushing the entire game and only 49 total yards in the first half. Seattle's John L. Williams caught 11 passes for 137 yards and one touchdown to help rally the Seahawks in the second half. Cincinnati kept the ball 34:51, including 20:07 of the first half.

Seattle	0	0	0	13	—13
Cincinnati	7	14	0	0	—21

Cin —Wilson 3 run (Breech kick)
Cin —Wilson 3 run (Breech kick)
Cin —Woods 1 run (Breech kick)
Sea—Williams 7 pass from Krieg (N. Johnson kick)
Sea—Krieg 1 run (kick failed)

Rich Stadium, Orchard Park, New York — January 1, 1989
Attendance: 79,532

Buffalo 17, Houston 10—Buffalo's special teams blocked a punt and a field goal, and the defense registered an interception and a fumble recovery in the fourth quarter, as the Bills advanced to their first-ever AFC Championship Game. Quarterback Jim Kelly completed a team playoff-record 19 of 33 passes for 244 yards with one interception. Rookie running back Thurman Thomas led all rushers with 75 yards on seven carries, including an 11-yard touchdown run for a 14-3 lead in the third quarter. Robb Riddick's one-yard scoring run followed a blocked punt by safety Leonard Smith. Safety Mark Kelso intercepted a Warren Moon pass on the Oilers' second play of the fourth quarter. Derrick Burroughs's fumble recovery on Houston's next possession helped Buffalo preserve the win in their first-ever playoff game at Rich Stadium.

Houston	0	3	0	7	—10
Buffalo	0	7	7	3	—17

Buff—Riddick 1 run (Norwood kick)
Hou—FG Zendejas 35
Buff—Thomas 11 run (Norwood kick)
Buff—FG Norwood 27
Hou—Rozier 1 run (Zenedjas kick)

NFC Divisional Playoffs

Includes Second-Round Playoff Games (1982), NFL Conference Championship Games (1967-69), and special playoff games to break ties for NFL Division or Conference Championships (1941, 1943, 1947, 1950, 1952, 1957, 1958, 1965)

Results

Season	Date	Winner (Share)	Loser (Share)	Score	Site	Attendance
1988	Jan. 1	San Francisco ($10,000)	Minnesota ($10,000)	34-9	San Francisco	61,848
	Dec. 31	Chicago ($10,000)	Philadelphia ($10,000)	20-12	Chicago	65,534
1987	Jan. 10	Washington ($10,000)	Chicago ($10,000)	21-17	Chicago	65,268
	Jan. 9	Minnesota ($10,000)	San Francisco ($10,000)	36-24	San Francisco	63,008
1986	Jan. 4	N.Y. Giants ($10,000)	San Francisco ($10,000)	49-3	East Rutherford	75,691
	Jan. 3	Washington ($10,000)	Chicago ($10,000)	27-13	Chicago	65,524
1985	Jan. 5	Chicago ($10,000)	N.Y. Giants ($10,000)	21-0	Chicago	65,670
	Jan. 4	L.A. Rams ($10,000)	Dallas ($10,000)	20-0	Anaheim	66,581
1984	Dec. 30	Chicago ($10,000)	Washington ($10,000)	23-19	Washington	55,431
	Dec. 29	San Francisco ($10,000)	N.Y. Giants ($10,000)	21-10	San Francisco	60,303
1983	Jan. 1	Washington ($10,000)	L.A. Rams ($10,000)	51-7	Washington	54,440
	Dec. 31	San Francisco ($10,000)	Detroit ($10,000)	24-23	San Francisco	59,979
1982	Jan. 16	Dallas ($10,000)	Green Bay ($10,000)	37-26	Dallas	63,972
	Jan. 15	Washington ($10,000)	Minnesota ($10,000)	21-7	Washington	54,593
1981	Jan. 3	San Francisco ($5,000)	N.Y. Giants ($5,000)	38-24	San Francisco	58,360
	Jan. 2	Dallas ($5,000)	Tampa Bay ($5,000)	38-0	Dallas	64,848
1980	Jan. 4	Dallas ($5,000)	Atlanta ($5,000)	30-27	Atlanta	59,793
	Jan. 3	Philadelphia ($5,000)	Minnesota ($5,000)	31-16	Philadelphia	70,178
1979	Dec. 30	Los Angeles ($5,000)	Dallas ($5,000)	21-19	Dallas	64,792
	Dec. 29	Tampa Bay ($5,000)	Philadelphia ($5,000)	24-17	Tampa Bay	71,402
1978	Dec. 31	Los Angeles ($5,000)	Minnesota ($5,000)	34-10	Los Angeles	70,436
	Dec. 30	Dallas ($5,000)	Atlanta ($5,000)	27-20	Dallas	63,406
1977	Dec. 26	Dallas ($5,000)	Chicago ($5,000)	37-7	Dallas	63,260
	Dec. 26	Minnesota ($5,000)	Los Angeles ($5,000)	14-7	Los Angeles	70,203
1976	Dec. 19	Los Angeles ($)	Dallas ($)	14-12	Dallas	63,283
	Dec. 18	Minnesota ($)	Washington ($)	35-20	Minnesota	47,466
1975	Dec. 28	Dallas ($)	Minnesota ($)	17-14	Minnesota	48,050
	Dec. 27	Los Angeles ($)	St. Louis ($)	35-23	Los Angeles	73,459
1974	Dec. 22	Los Angeles ($)	Washington ($)	19-10	Los Angeles	77,925
	Dec. 21	Minnesota ($)	St. Louis ($)	30-14	Minnesota	48,150
1973	Dec. 23	Dallas ($)	Los Angeles ($)	27-16	Dallas	63,272
	Dec. 22	Minnesota ($)	Washington ($)	27-20	Minnesota	48,040
1972	Dec. 24	Washington ($)	Green Bay ($)	16-3	Washington	52,321
	Dec. 23	Dallas ($)	San Francisco ($)	30-28	San Francisco	59,746
1971	Dec. 26	San Francisco ($)	Washington ($)	24-20	San Francisco	45,327
	Dec. 25	Dallas ($)	Minnesota ($)	20-12	Minnesota	47,307
1970	Dec. 27	San Francisco ($)	Minnesota ($)	17-14	Minnesota	45,103
	Dec. 26	Dallas ($)	Detroit ($)	5-0	Dallas	69,613
1969	Dec. 28	Cleveland ($)	Dallas ($)	38-14	Dallas	69,321
	Dec. 27	Minnesota ($)	Los Angeles ($)	23-20	Minnesota	47,900
1968	Dec. 22	Baltimore ($)	Minnesota ($)	24-14	Baltimore	60,238
	Dec. 21	Cleveland ($)	Dallas ($)	31-20	Cleveland	81,497
1967	Dec. 24	Dallas ($)	Cleveland ($)	52-14	Dallas	70,786
	Dec. 23	Green Bay ($)	Los Angeles ($)	28-7	Milwaukee	49,861
1965	Dec. 26	Green Bay ($)	Baltimore ($)	13-10*	Green Bay	50,484
1958	Dec. 21	N.Y. Giants (#)	Cleveland (#)	10-0	New York	61,274
1957	Dec. 22	Detroit (#)	San Francisco (#)	31-27	San Francisco	60,118
1952	Dec. 21	Detroit (#)	Los Angeles (#)	31-21	Detroit	47,645
1950	Dec. 17	Los Angeles (#)	Chicago Bears (#)	24-14	Los Angeles	83,501
	Dec. 17	Cleveland (#)	N.Y. Giants (#)	8-3	Cleveland	33,054
1947	Dec. 21	Philadelphia (#)	Pittsburgh (#)	21-0	Pittsburgh	35,729
1943	Dec. 19	Washington (+)	N.Y. Giants (+)	28-0	New York	42,800
1941	Dec. 14	Chicago Bears (+)	Green Bay (+)	33-14	Chicago	43,425

**Sudden Death Overtime.*
$ Players received 1/14 of annual salary for playoff appearances.
 # Players received 1/12 of annual salary for playoff appearances.
+ Players received 1/10 of annual salary for playoff appearances.

1988 NFC Divisional Playoffs

Soldier Field, Chicago, Illinois December 31, 1988
Attendance: 65,534

Chicago 20, Philadelphia 12—NFC Central Division champion Chicago advanced to its first NFC Championship Game since 1985 with a 20-12 win over NFC East titlist Philadelphia in a game played in fog during the second half. The Bears opened the scoring with a 64-yard touchdown pass from quarterback Mike Tomczak to wide receiver Dennis McKinnon 3:02 into the first period. The Eagles responded with a pair of Luis Zendejas field goals to narrow the margin to 7-6. Philadelphia moved the ball throughout the day but had trouble scoring touchdowns. The Eagles got inside the Bears' 25-yard line nine times, including five times inside the 11, but had only four field goals by game's end. Overall, Philadelphia compiled 430 yards total offense compared to Chicago's 341. Eagles quarterback Randall Cunningham completed 27 of 54 passes for 407 yards, although he was intercepted three times. Tomczak (10 of 20 for 172 yards, 1 touchdown, with 3 interceptions) sustained a bruised left shoulder and was replaced by Jim McMahon. Running back Thomas Sanders led the Bears' rushing game with 94 yards on only eight carries.

Philadelphia	3	6	3	0	— 12
Chicago	7	10	0	3	— 20

Chi —McKinnon 64 pass from Tomczak (Butler kick)
Phil—FG Zendejas 42
Phil—FG Zendejas 29
Chi —Anderson 4 run (Butler kick)
Chi —FG Butler 46
Phil—FG Zendejas 30
Phil—FG Zendejas 35
Chi —FG Butler 27

Candlestick Park, San Francisco, California January 1, 1989
Attendance: 61,848

San Francisco 34, Minnesota 9—NFC West champion San Francisco gained the right to seek its third NFC title of the decade, dominating Wild Card survivor Minnesota 34-9. The 49ers took a 21-3 halftime lead on three touchdown passes from quarterback Joe Montana to wide receiver Jerry Rice. Montana finished the game completing 16 of 27 for 178 yards and three touchdowns, including 11 of 14 for 111 yards and three scores in the first half. Rice finished with five catches for 61 yards and three touchdowns. The 49ers' defense shut down the Vikings by limiting Minnesota to 262 total yards. San Francisco had six sacks, including five in the first two periods. Defensive end Larry Roberts had 2½ sacks followed by linebacker Charles Haley's 1½. 49ers safety Ronnie Lott also had two interceptions. San Francisco rushed for 201 yards, including 135 on 21 carries by Roger Craig. Craig's total included an 80-yard touchdown run in the final period.

Minnesota	3	0	6	0	— 9
San Francisco	7	14	0	13	— 34

Minn – FG C. Nelson 47
SF – Rice 2 pass from Montana (Cofer kick)
SF – Rice 4 pass from Montana (Cofer kick)
SF – Rice 11 pass from Montana (Cofer kick)
Minn – Jones 5 pass from Wilson (kick failed)
SF – Craig 4 run (Cofer kick)
SF – Craig 80 run (kick failed)

AFC First-Round Playoff Games

Results

Season	Date	Winner (Share)	Loser (Share)	Score	Site	Attendance
1988	Dec. 26	Houston ($6,000)	Cleveland ($6,000)	24-23	Cleveland	75,896
1987	Jan. 3	Houston ($6,000)	Seattle ($6,000)	23-20*	Houston	50,519
1986	Dec. 28	N.Y. Jets ($6,000)	Kansas City ($6,000)	35-15	East Rutherford	75,210
1985	Dec. 28	New England ($6,000)	N.Y. Jets ($6,000)	26-14	East Rutherford	75,945
1984	Dec. 22	Seattle ($6,000)	L.A. Raiders ($6,000)	13-7	Seattle	62,049
1983	Dec. 24	Seattle ($6,000)	Denver ($6,000)	31-7	Seattle	64,275
1982	Jan. 9	N.Y. Jets ($6,000)	Cincinnati ($6,000)	44-17	Cincinnati	57,560
	Jan. 9	San Diego ($6,000)	Pittsburgh ($6,000)	31-28	Pittsburgh	53,546
	Jan. 8	L.A. Raiders ($6,000)	Cleveland ($6,000)	27-10	Los Angeles	56,555
	Jan. 8	Miami ($6,000)	New England ($6,000)	28-13	Miami	68,842
1981	Dec. 27	Buffalo ($3,000)	N.Y. Jets ($3,000)	31-27	New York	57,050
1980	Dec. 28	Oakland ($3,000)	Houston ($3,000)	27-7	Oakland	53,333
1979	Dec. 23	Houston ($3,000)	Denver ($3,000)	13-7	Houston	48,776
1978	Dec. 24	Houston ($3,000)	Miami ($3,000)	17-9	Miami	72,445

**Sudden death overtime.*

1988 AFC First-Round Playoff Game

Cleveland Stadium, Cleveland, Ohio December 24, 1988
Attendance: 74,977

Houston 24, Cleveland 23—The Oilers advanced to the AFC divisional round of the playoffs for the second straight year with a 24-23 win over the Browns. Allen Pinkett scored two touchdowns within a 15-second span of the second quarter and Warren Moon rallied Houston with 10 fourth-quarter points for the win. Moon's 14-yard scoring pass to Pinkett seven seconds into the second quarter capped a 17-play, 91-yard drive and gave Houston a 7-3 lead. Nose tackle Richard Byrd recovered Don Strock's fumble on the Browns' next play from scrimmage and Pinkett scored one play later on a 16-yard run for a 14-9 halftime lead. Mike Pagel replaced the injured Strock and completed a 14-yard touchdown pass to Webster Slaughter late in the third quarter for Cleveland's last lead of the day 16-14. Moon directed a 76-yard drive capped by Lorenzo White's one-yard run as Houston regained the lead 21-16. Richard Johnson's interception on the Browns' next possession led to Tony Zendejas's game-winning 49-yard field goal with 1:54 to play. Pinkett led all rushers with 82 yards on 14 carries, while Moon completed 16 of 26 passes for 213 yards with three interceptions.

Houston	0	14	0	10	— 24
Cleveland	3	6	7	7	— 23

Clev—FG Bahr 33
Hou—Pinkett 14 pass from Moon (Zendejas kick)
Hou—Pinkett 16 run (Zendejas kick)
Clev—FG Bahr 26
Clev—FG Bahr 28
Clev—Slaughter 14 pass from Pagel (Bahr kick)
Hou—White 1 run (Zendejas kick)
Hou—FG Zendejas 49
Clev—Slaughter 2 pass from Pagel (Bahr kick)

NFC First-Round Playoff Games

Results

Season	Date	Winner (Share)	Loser (Share)	Score	Site	Attendance
1988	Dec. 26	Minnesota ($6,000)	L.A. Rams ($6,000)	28-17	Minnesota	61,204
1987	Jan. 3	Minnesota ($6,000)	New Orleans ($6,000)	44-10	New Orleans	68,546
1986	Dec. 28	Washington ($6,000)	L.A. Rams ($6,000)	19-7	Washington	54,567
1985	Dec. 29	N.Y. Giants ($6,000)	San Francisco ($6,000)	17-3	East Rutherford	75,131
1984	Dec. 23	N.Y. Giants ($6,000)	L.A. Rams ($6,000)	16-3	Anaheim	67,037
1983	Dec. 26	L.A. Rams ($6,000)	Dallas ($6,000)	24-17	Dallas	62,118
1982	Jan. 9	Dallas ($6,000)	Tampa Bay ($6,000)	30-17	Dallas	65,042
	Jan. 9	Minnesota ($6,000)	Atlanta ($6,000)	30-24	Minnesota	60,560
	Jan. 8	Green Bay ($6,000)	St. Louis ($6,000)	41-16	Green Bay	54,282
	Jan. 8	Washington ($6,000)	Detroit ($6,000)	31-7	Washington	55,045
1981	Dec. 27	N.Y. Giants ($3,000)	Philadelphia ($3,000)	27-21	Philadelphia	71,611
1980	Dec. 28	Dallas ($3,000)	Los Angeles ($3,000)	34-13	Dallas	63,052
1979	Dec. 23	Philadelphia ($3,000)	Chicago ($3,000)	27-17	Philadelphia	69,397
1978	Dec. 24	Atlanta ($3,000)	Philadelphia ($3,000)	14-13	Atlanta	59,403

1988 NFC First-Round Playoff Game

Metrodome, Minneapolis, Minnesota December 26, 1988
Attendance: 61,204

Minnesota 28, Los Angeles Rams 17—Minnesota's stingy defense set the tone for the Vikings' 28-17 victory over the Los Angeles Rams. Safety Joey Browner was credited with a pair of first-quarter interceptions that set up touchdowns within a space of 21 seconds. Browner's first interception was returned to Minnesota's 27-yard line and started a 73-yard touchdown drive culminated by running back Alfred Anderson's 7-yard touchdown run. On the first play of the Rams' next possession, Browner got his second interception of the day, returning it to the Los Angeles 17-yard line. On the Vikings' next play, running back Allen Rice ran the remaining yardage (17 yards) for the score. Minnesota quarterback Wade Wilson completed 17 of 28 passes for 253 yards, including a five-yard touchdown toss to tight end Carl Hilton in the third period. Vikings wide receiver Anthony Carter caught four passes for 102 yards.

L.A. Rams	0	7	3	7	— 17
Minnesota	14	0	7	7	— 28

Minn —Anderson 7 run (C. Nelson kick)
Minn —Rice 17 run (C. Nelson kick)
Rams—D. Johnson 3 pass from Everett (Lansford kick)
Minn —Anderson 1 run (C. Nelson kick)
Rams—FG Lansford 43
Minn —Hilton 5 pass from Wilson (C. Nelson kick)
Rams—Holohan 11 pass from Everett (Lansford kick)

AFC-NFC Pro Bowl At A Glance (1971-1989)

NFC leads series, 11-8

Results

Year	Date	Winner (Share)	Loser (Share)	Score	Site	Attendance
1989	Jan. 29	NFC ($10,000)	AFC ($5,000)	34-3	Honolulu	50,113
1988	Feb. 7	AFC ($10,000)	NFC ($5,000)	15-6	Honolulu	50,113
1987	Feb. 1	AFC ($10,000)	NFC ($5,000)	10-6	Honolulu	50,101
1986	Feb. 2	NFC ($10,000)	AFC ($5,000)	28-24	Honolulu	50,101
1985	Jan. 27	AFC ($10,000)	NFC ($5,000)	22-14	Honolulu	50,385
1984	Jan. 29	NFC ($10,000)	AFC ($5,000)	45-3	Honolulu	50,445
1983	Feb. 6	NFC ($10,000)	AFC ($5,000)	20-19	Honolulu	49,883
1982	Jan. 31	AFC ($5,000)	NFC ($2,500)	16-13	Honolulu	50,402
1981	Feb. 1	NFC ($5,000)	AFC ($2,500)	21-7	Honolulu	50,360
1980	Jan. 27	NFC ($5,000)	AFC ($2,500)	37-27	Honolulu	49,800
1979	Jan. 29	NFC ($5,000)	AFC ($2,500)	13-7	Los Angeles	46,281
1978	Jan. 23	NFC ($5,000)	AFC ($2,500)	14-13	Tampa	51,337
1977	Jan. 17	AFC ($2,000)	NFC ($1,500)	24-14	Seattle	64,752
1976	Jan. 26	NFC ($2,000)	AFC ($1,500)	23-20	New Orleans	30,546
1975	Jan. 20	NFC ($2,000)	AFC ($1,500)	17-10	Miami	26,484
1974	Jan. 20	AFC ($2,000)	NFC ($1,500)	15-13	Kansas City	66,918
1973	Jan. 21	AFC ($2,000)	NFC ($1,500)	33-28	Irving	37,091
1972	Jan. 23	AFC ($2,000)	NFC ($1,500)	26-13	Los Angeles	53,647
1971	Jan. 24	NFC ($2,000)	AFC ($1,500)	27-6	Los Angeles	48,222

1989 AFC-NFC Pro Bowl

Aloha Stadium, Honolulu, Hawaii — January 29, 1989

Attendance: 50,113

NFC 34, AFC 3—The NFC scored 34 unanswered points to snap a two-game losing streak to the AFC before the tenth straight sellout crowd in Honolulu's Aloha Stadium. Bills kicker Scott Norwood provided the AFC's only points on a 38-yard field goal 6:23 into the game. Touchdown runs by Dallas's Herschel Walker (four yards) and Atlanta's John Settle (one) brought the NFC a 14-3 half-time lead. Walker added a seven-yard scoring run, the Saints' Morten Andersen kicked field goals of 27 and 51 yards, and Los Angeles Rams' wide receiver Henry Ellard caught an eight-yard scoring pass from Minnesota quarterback Wade Wilson in the second half to complete the scoring. Chicago running back Neal Anderson and Philadelphia quarterback Randall Cunningham, who were both appearing in their first Pro Bowl, also played major roles in the NFC's victory. Anderson rushed 13 times for 85 yards and had two receptions for 17. Cunningham, who was voted the game's outstanding player, completed 10 of 14 passes for 63 yards and rushed for 49 yards. The NFC, which had five takeaways, outgained the AFC 355 yards to 167 and held a time-of-possession advantage of 35:18 to 24:42. Houston quarterback Warren Moon completed 13 of 20 passes for 134 yards for the AFC. The win gave the NFC an 11-8 advantage in Pro Bowl games.

AFC (3)	Offense	NFC (34)
Al Toon (N.Y. Jets)	WR	Henry Ellard (L.A. Rams)
Anthony Muñoz (Cincinnati)	LT	Gary Zimmerman (Minnesota)
Bruce Matthews (Houston)	LG	Tom Newberry (L.A. Rams)
Ray Donaldson (Indianapolis)	C	Jay Hilgenberg (Chicago)
Max Montoya (Cincinnati)	RG	Mark May (Washington)
Chris Hinton (Indianapolis)	RT	Jackie Slater (L.A. Rams)
Mickey Shuler (N.Y. Jets)	TE	Keith Jackson (Philadelphia)
Eddie Brown (Cincinnati)	WR	Anthony Carter (Minnesota)
Warren Moon (Houston)	QB	Randall Cunningham (Philadelphia)
Eric Dickerson (Indianapolis)	RB	Roger Craig (San Francisco)
John Stephens (New England)	RB	Herschel Walker (Dallas)
	Defense	
Lee Williams (San Diego)	LE	Reggie White (Philadelphia)
Fred Smerlas (Buffalo)	NT	Keith Millard (Minnesota)
Bruce Smith (Buffalo)	RE	Chris Doleman (Minnesota)
Andre Tippett (New England)	LOLB	Lawrence Taylor (N.Y. Giants)
Matt Millen (L.A. Raiders)	LILB	Sam Mills (New Orleans)
Johnny Rembert (New England)	RILB	Mike Singletary (Chicago)
Cornelius Bennett (Buffalo)	ROLB	Mike Cofer (Detroit)
Frank Minnifield (Cleveland)	LCB	Carl Lee (Minnesota)
Hanford Dixon (Cleveland)	RCB	Jerry Gray (L.A. Rams)
David Fulcher (Cincinnati)	SS	Joey Browner (Minnesota)
Deron Cherry (Kansas City)	FS	Ronnie Lott (San Francisco)

Substitutions

AFC—Offense: K—Scott Norwood (Buffalo). P—Mike Horan (Denver). QB—Dave Krieg (Seattle). RB—Mike Rozier (Houston), James Brooks (Cincinnati). WR—Mark Clayton (Miami), Andre Reed (Buffalo). TE—Rodney Holman (Cincinnati). KR—Tim Brown (L.A. Raiders). C—Kent Hull (Buffalo). G—Mike Munchak (Houston). T—Tunch Ilkin (Pittsburgh). Defense: E—Ray Childress (Houston). T—Brian Sochia (Miami). LB—John Grimsley (Houston), Clay Matthews (Cleveland). CB—Eric Thomas (Cincinnati). S—Erik McMillan (N.Y. Jets), ST—Rufus Porter (Seattle). DNP: LB—Shane Conlan (Buffalo).

NFC—Offense: K—Morten Andersen (New Orleans). P—Jim Arnold (Detroit). QB—Wade Wilson (Minnesota). RB—Neal Anderson (Chicago), John Settle (Atlanta). WR—Eric Martin (New Orleans), J.T. Smith (Phoenix). TE—Steve Jordan (Minnesota). KR—John Taylor (San Francisco). C—Doug Smith (L.A. Rams). G—Mark Bortz (Chicago). T—Luis Sharpe (Phoenix). Defense: E—Charles Mann (Washington). T—Michael Carter (San Francisco). LB—Charles Haley (San Francisco), Scott Studwell (Minnesota). CB—Scott Case (Atlanta). S—Dave Duerson (Chicago), Terry Kinard (N.Y. Giants). ST—Ron Wolfley (Phoenix).

Head Coaches

NFC—Mike Ditka (Chicago)
AFC—Marv Levy (Buffalo)

Officials

Referee—Ben Dreith. Umpire—Dave Hamilton. Line Judge—Dick McKenzie. Head Linesman—Tom Barnes. Back Judge—Bruce Maurer. Field Judge—Don Dorkowski. Side Judge—Dick Creed.

Scoring

AFC	3	0	0	0	— 3
NFC	7	7	10	10	— 34

AFC—FG Norwood 38
NFC—Walker 4 run (Andersen kick)
NFC—Settle 1 run (Andersen kick)
NFC—FG Andersen 27
NFC—Walker 7 run (Andersen kick)
NFC—FG Andersen 51
NFC—Ellard 8 pass from Wilson (Andersen kick)

Team Statistics

	AFC	NFC
Total First Downs	12	22
First Downs Rushing	4	11
First Downs Passing	8	10
First Downs Penalty	0	1
Total Net Yardage	167	355
Total Offensive Plays	55	66
Average Gain per Offensive Play	3.0	5.4
Rushes	15	40
Yards Gained Rushing (net)	70	216
Average Yards per Rush	4.7	5.4
Passes Attempted	34	24
Passes Completed	16	16
Passes Had Intercepted	2	1
Tackled Attempting to Pass	6	2
Yards Lost Attempting to Pass	58	15
Yards Gained Passing (net)	97	139
Punts	5	0
Average Distance	43.2	—
Punt Returns	0	3
Punt Return Yardage	0	30
Kickoff Returns	4	2
Kickoff Return Yardage	82	42
Interception Return Yardage	0	68
Total Return Yardage	82	140
Fumbles	0	3
Own Fumbles Recovered	0	2
Opponents Fumbles Recovered	1	0
Penalties	7	1
Yards Penalized	30	5
Total Points Scored	3	34
Touchdowns	0	4
Touchdowns Rushing	0	3

	AFC	NFC
Touchdowns Passing	0	1
Touchdowns Returns	0	0
Extra Points	0	4
Field Goals	1	2
Field Goals Attempted	1	2
Safeties	0	0
Third Down Efficiency	7/14	6/11
Fourth Down Efficiency	0/1	2/3
Time of Possession	24:42	35:18

Individual Statistics

Rushing

AFC	No.	Yds.	LG	TD
Dickerson	7	25	7	0
Brooks	2	24	15	0
Stephens	2	17	11	0
Moon	1	4	4	0
Krieg	1	2	2	0
E. Brown	1	−1	−1	0
Rozier	1	−1	−1	0
NFC	**No.**	**Yds.**	**LG**	**TD**
Anderson	13	85	25	0
Cunningham	2	49	32	0
Settle	11	29	5	1
Walker	6	22	7t	2
Wilson	2	15	15	0
Craig	3	11	7	0
A. Carter	1	9	9	0
Ellard	1	4	4	0
J.T. Smith	1	−8	−8	0

Passing

AFC	Att.	Comp.	Yds.	TD	Int.
Moon	20	13	134	0	1
Krieg	14	3	21	0	1
NFC	**Att.**	**Comp.**	**Yds.**	**TD**	**Int.**
Cunningham	14	9	83	0	0
Wilson	10	7	71	1	1

Receiving

AFC	No.	Yds.	LG	TD
Reed	5	42	11	0
Clayton	3	36	15	0
Toon	2	42	34	0
Brooks	2	16	9	0
Stephens	2	0	0	0
T. Brown	1	13	13	0
Dickerson	1	6	6	0

NFC	No.	Yds.	LG	TD
Jackson	4	26	9	0
J.T. Smith	2	30	19	0
Jordan	2	23	14	0
Ellard	2	21	13	1
Craig	2	19	10	0
Anderson	2	17	16	0
A. Carter	1	9	9	0
Martin	1	9	9	0

Interceptions

AFC	No.	Yds.	LG	TD
Thomas	1	0	0	0
NFC	**No.**	**Yds.**	**LG**	**TD**
Kinard	1	34	34	0
Lott	1	34	34	0

Punting

AFC	No.	Avg.	LG	Blk.
Horan	5	43.2	48	0
NFC				
None				

Punt Returns

AFC	No.	FC	Yds.	LG	TD
None					
NFC	**No.**	**FC**	**Yds.**	**LG**	**TD**
J. Taylor	3	1	30	24	0

Kickoff Returns

AFC	No.	Yds.	LG	TD
T. Brown	3	63	25	0
E. Brown	1	19	19	0
NFC	**No.**	**Yds.**	**LG**	**TD**
J. Taylor	1	26	26	0
Ellard	1	16	16	0

1988 AFC-NFC Pro Bowl

Aloha Stadium, Honolulu, Hawaii — February 7, 1988

Attendance: 50,113

AFC 15, NFC 6—Led by a tenacious pass rush, the AFC defeated the NFC for the second consecutive year, 15-6, before the fifth straight sellout crowd in Honolulu's Aloha Stadium. Buffalo quarterback Jim Kelly scored the game's lone touchdown on a one-yard run for a 7-6 halftime lead. Colts kicker Dean Biasucci added field goals from 37 and 30 yards to complete the AFC's scoring. Saints kicker Morten Andersen had 25- and 36-yard field goals to account for the NFC's points. AFC defenders held the NFC to 213 yards and recorded eight sacks. Bills defensive end Bruce Smith, who had five tackles and two sacks, was voted the game's outstanding player. Oilers running back Mike Rozier led all rushers with 49 yards on nine carries. Jets wide receiver Al Toon had five receptions for 75 yards. The AFC generated 341 yards total offense and held a time-of-possession advantage of 34:14 to 25:46. By winning, the AFC cut the NFC's lead in the Pro Bowl series to 10-8.

NFC	0	6	0	0	— 6
AFC	0	7	6	2	— 15

NFC—FG Andersen 25
AFC—Kelly 1 run (Biasucci kick)
NFC—FG Andersen 36
AFC—FG Biasucci 37
AFC—FG Biasucci 30
AFC—Safety, Montana forced out of end zone

1987 AFC-NFC Pro Bowl

Aloha Stadium, Honolulu, Hawaii — February 1, 1987

Attendance: 50,101

AFC 10, NFC 6—The AFC defeated the NFC, 10-6, in the lowest-scoring game in AFC-NFC Pro Bowl history. The AFC took a 10-0 halftime lead on Broncos quarterback John Elway's 10-yard touchdown pass to Raiders tight end Todd Christensen and Patriots kicker Tony Franklin's 26-yard field goal. The AFC defense made the lead stand up by forcing the NFC to settle for a pair of field goals from 38 and 19 yards by Saints kicker Morten Andersen after the NFC had first downs at the AFC 31-, 7-, 16-, 15-, 5-, and 7-yard lines. Both AFC scores were set up by fumble recoveries by Seahawks linebacker Fredd Young and Dolphins linebacker John Offerdahl, respectively. Eagles defensive end Reggie White, who tied a Pro Bowl record with four sacks and also contributed seven solo tackles, was voted the game's outstanding player. The AFC victory cut the NFC's lead in the Pro Bowl series to 10-7.

AFC	7	3	0	0	— 10
NFC	0	0	3	3	— 6

AFC—Christensen 10 pass from Elway (Franklin kick)
AFC—FG Franklin 26
NFC—FG Andersen 38
NFC—FG Andersen 19

1986 AFC-NFC Pro Bowl

Aloha Stadium, Honolulu, Hawaii — February 2, 1986

Attendance: 50,101

NFC 28, AFC 24—New York Giants quarterback Phil Simms brought the NFC back from a 24-7 halftime deficit to a 28-24 win over the AFC. Simms, who completed 15 of 27 passes for 212 yards and three touchdowns, was named the most valuable player of the game. The AFC had taken its first-half lead behind a two-yard run by Los Angeles Raiders running back Marcus Allen, who also threw a 51-yard scoring pass to San Diego wide receiver Wes Chandler, an 11-yard touchdown catch by Pittsburgh wide receiver Louis Lipps, and a 34-yard field goal by Steelers kicker Gary Anderson. Minnesota's Joey Browner accounted for the NFC's only score before halftime with a 48-yard touchdown interception return. After intermission, the NFC blanked the AFC while scoring three touchdowns via a 15-yard catch by Washington wide receiver Art Monk, a 2-yard reception by Dallas tight end Doug Cosbie, and a 15-yard catch by Tampa Bay tight end Jimmie Giles with 2:47 remaining in the game. The victory gave the NFC a 10-6 Pro Bowl record vs. the AFC.

NFC	0	7	7	14	— 28
AFC	7	17	0	0	— 24

AFC—Allen 2 run (Anderson kick)
NFC—Browner 48 interception return (Andersen kick)
AFC—Chandler 51 pass from Allen (Anderson kick)
AFC—FG Anderson 34
AFC—Lipps 11 pass from O'Brien (Anderson kick)
NFC—Monk 15 pass from Simms (Andersen kick)
NFC—Cosbie 2 pass from Simms (Andersen kick)
NFC—Giles 15 pass from Simms (Andersen kick)

1985 AFC-NFC Pro Bowl

Aloha Stadium, Honolulu, Hawaii — January 27, 1985

Attendance: 50,385

AFC 22, NFC 14—Defensive end Art Still of the Kansas City Chiefs recovered a fumble and returned it 83 yards for a touchdown to clinch the AFC's victory over the NFC. Still's touchdown came in the fourth period with the AFC trailing 14-12 and was one of several outstanding defensive plays in a Pro Bowl dominated by two record-breaking defenses. Both teams combined for a Pro Bowl-record 17 sacks, including four by New York Jets defensive end Mark Gastineau, who was named the game's outstanding player. The AFC's first score came on a safety when Gastineau tackled running back Eric Dickerson of the Los Angeles Rams in the end zone. The AFC's second score, a six-yard pass from Miami's Dan Marino to Los Angeles Raiders running back Marcus Allen, was set up by a partial block of a punt by Seahawks linebacker Fredd Young. The NFC led the series 9-6, since it started in 1971.

AFC	0	9	0	13	— 22
NFC	0	0	7	7	— 14

AFC—Safety, Gastineau tackled Dickerson in end zone
AFC—Allen 6 pass from Marino (Johnson kick)
NFC—Lofton 13 pass from Montana (Stenerud kick)
NFC—Payton 1 run (Stenerud kick)
AFC—FG Johnson 33
AFC—Still 83 fumble recovery return (Johnson kick)
AFC—FG Johnson 22

1984 AFC-NFC Pro Bowl

Aloha Stadium, Honolulu, Hawaii — January 29, 1984

Attendance: 50,445

NFC 45, AFC 3—The NFC won its sixth Pro Bowl in the last seven seasons, 45-3 over the AFC. The NFC was led by the passing of most valuable player Joe Theismann of Washington, who completed 21 of 27 passes for 242 yards and three touchdowns. Theismann set Pro Bowl records for completions and touchdown passes. The NFC established Pro Bowl marks for most points scored and fewest points allowed. Running back William Andrews of Atlanta had six carries for 43 yards and caught four passes for 49 yards, including scoring receptions of 16 and 2 yards. Los Angeles Rams rookie Eric Dickerson gained 46 yards on 11 carries, including a 14-yard touchdown run, and had 45 yards on five catches. Rams safety Nolan Cromwell had a 44-yard interception return for a touchdown early in the third period to give the NFC a commanding 24-3 lead. Green Bay wide receiver James Lofton caught an eight-yard touchdown pass, while tight end teammate Paul Coffman had a six-yard scoring catch.

NFC	3	14	14	14	— 45
AFC	0	3	0	0	— 3

NFC—FG Haji-Sheikh 23
NFC—Andrews 16 pass from Theismann (Haji-Sheikh kick)
NFC—Andrews 2 pass from Montana (Haji-Sheikh kick)
AFC—FG Anderson 43
NFC—Cromwell 44 interception return (Haji-Sheikh kick)
NFC—Lofton 8 pass from Theismann (Haji-Sheikh kick)
NFC—Coffman 6 pass from Theismann (Haji-Sheikh kick)
NFC—Dickerson 14 run (Haji-Sheikh kick)

1983 AFC-NFC Pro Bowl

Aloha Stadium, Honolulu, Hawaii — February 6, 1983

Attendance: 49,883

NFC 20, AFC 19—Danny White threw an 11-yard touchdown pass to John Jefferson with 35 seconds remaining to give the NFC a 20-19 victory over the AFC. White, who completed 14 of 26 passes for 162 yards, kept the winning 65-yard drive alive with a 14-yard completion to Jefferson on a fourth-and-seven play at the AFC 25. The AFC was ahead 12-10 at halftime and increased the lead to 19-10 in the third period, when Marcus Allen scored on a one-yard run. Dan Fouts, who attempted 30 passes, set Pro Bowl records for most completions (17) and yards (274). John Stallworth was the AFC's leading receiver with seven catches for 67 yards. William Andrews topped the NFC with five receptions for 48 yards. Fouts and Jefferson were voted co-winners of the player of the game award.

AFC	9	3	7	0	— 19
NFC	0	10	0	10	— 20

AFC—Walker 34 pass from Fouts (Benirschke kick)
AFC—Safety, Still tackled Theismann in end zone
NFC—Andrews 3 run (Moseley kick)
NFC—FG Moseley 35
AFC—FG Benirschke 29
AFC—Allen 1 run (Benirschke kick)
NFC—FG Moseley 41
NFC—Jefferson 11 pass from D. White (Moseley kick)

1982 AFC-NFC Pro Bowl

Aloha Stadium, Honolulu, Hawaii — January 31, 1982

Attendance: 50,402

AFC 16, NFC 13—Nick Lowery kicked a 23-yard field goal with three seconds remaining to give the AFC a 16-13 victory over the NFC. Lowery's kick climaxed a 69-yard drive directed by quarterback Dan Fouts. The NFC gained a 13-13 tie with 2:43 to go when Tony Dorsett ran four yards for a touchdown. In the drive to the game-winning field goal, Fouts completed three passes, including a 23-yarder to San Diego teammate Kellen Winslow that put the ball on the NFC's 5-yard line. Two plays later, Lowery kicked the field goal. Winslow, who caught six passes for 86 yards, was named co-player of the game along with NFC defensive end Lee Roy Selmon.

NFC	0	6	0	7	— 13
AFC	0	0	13	3	— 16

NFC—Giles 4 pass from Montana (kick blocked)
AFC—Muncie 2 run (kick failed)
AFC—Campbell 1 run (Lowery kick)
NFC—Dorsett 4 run (Septien kick)
AFC—FG Lowery 23

1981 AFC-NFC Pro Bowl

Aloha Stadium, Honolulu, Hawaii — February 1, 1981

Attendance: 50,360

NFC 21, AFC 7—Ed Murray kicked four field goals and Steve Bartkowski fired a 55-yard scoring pass to Alfred Jenkins to lead the NFC to its fourth straight victory over the AFC and a 7-4 edge in the series. Murray was named the game's most valuable player and missed tying Garo Yepremian's Pro Bowl record of five field goals when a 37-yard attempt hit the crossbar with 22 seconds remaining. The AFC's only score came on a nine-yard pass from Brian Sipe to Stanley Morgan in the second period. Bartkowski completed 9 of 21 passes for 173 yards, while Sipe connected on 10 of 15 for 142 yards. Ottis Anderson led all rushers with 70 yards on 10 carries. Earl Campbell, the NFL's leading rusher in 1980, was limited to 24 yards on eight attempts.

AFC	0	7	0	0	— 7
NFC	3	6	0	12	— 21

NFC—FG Murray 31
AFC—Morgan 9 pass from Sipe (J. Smith kick)
NFC—FG Murray 31
NFC—FG Murray 34
NFC—Jenkins 55 pass from Bartkowski (Murray kick)
NFC—FG Murray 36
NFC—Safety (Team)

1980 AFC-NFC Pro Bowl

Aloha Stadium, Honolulu, Hawaii — January 27, 1980

Attendance: 49,800

NFC 37, AFC 27—Running back Chuck Muncie ran for two touchdowns and threw a 25-yard option pass for another score to give the NFC its third consecutive victory over the AFC. Muncie, who was selected the game's most valuable player, snapped a 3-3 tie on a one-yard touchdown run at 1:41 of the second quarter, then scored on an 11-yard run in the fourth quarter for the NFC's final touchdown. Two scoring records were set in the game—37 points by the NFC, eclipsing the 33 by the AFC in 1973, and the 64 points by both teams, surpassing the 61 scored in 1973.

NFC	3	20	7	7	— 37
AFC	3	7	10	7	— 27

NFC—FG Moseley 37
AFC—FG Fritsch 19
NFC—Muncie 1 run (Moseley kick)
AFC—Pruitt 1 pass from Bradshaw (Fritsch kick)
NFC—D. Hill 13 pass from Manning (kick failed)
NFC—T. Hill 25 pass from Muncie (Moseley kick)
NFC—Henry 86 punt return (Moseley kick)
AFC—Campbell 2 run (Fritsch kick)
AFC—FG Fritsch 29
NFC—Muncie 11 run (Moseley kick)
AFC—Campbell 1 run (Fritsch kick)

1979 AFC-NFC Pro Bowl

Memorial Coliseum, Los Angeles, California — January 29, 1979

Attendance: 46,281

NFC 13, AFC 7—Roger Staubach completed 9 of 15 passes for 125 yards, including the winning touchdown on a 19-yard strike to Dallas Cowboys teammate Tony Hill in the third period. The winning drive began at the AFC's 45 yard line after a shanked punt. Staubach hit Ahmad Rashad with passes of 15 and 17 yards to set up Hill's decisive catch. The victory gave the NFC a 5-4 advantage in Pro Bowl games. Rashad, who accounted for 89 yards on five receptions, was named the player of the game. The AFC led 7-6 at halftime on Bob Griese's eight-yard scoring toss to Steve Largent late in the second quarter. Largent finished the game with five receptions for 75 yards. The NFC scored first as Archie Manning marched his team 70 yards in 11 plays, capped by Wilbert Montgomery's two-yard touchdown run. The AFC's Earl Campbell was the game's leading rusher with 66 yards on 12 carries.

AFC	0	7	0	0	— 7
NFC	0	6	7	0	— 13

NFC—Montgomery 2 run (kick failed)
AFC—Largent 8 pass from Griese (Yepremian kick)
NFC—T. Hill 19 pass from Staubach (Corral kick)

1978 AFC-NFC Pro Bowl

Tampa Stadium, Tampa, Florida — January 23, 1978

Attendance: 51,337

NFC 14, AFC 13—Walter Payton, the NFL's leading rusher in 1977, sparked a second-half comeback to give the NFC a 14-13 win and tie the series between the two conferences at four victories each. Payton, who was the game's most valuable player, gained 77 yards on 13 carries and scored the tying touchdown on a one-yard burst with 7:37 left in the game. Efren Herrera kicked the winning extra point. The AFC dominated the first half of the game, taking a 13-0 lead on field goals of 21 and 39 yards by Toni Linhart and a 10-yard touchdown pass from Ken Stabler to Oakland teammate Cliff Branch. On the NFC's first possession of the second half, Pat Haden put together the first touchdown drive after Eddie Brown returned Ray Guy's punt to the AFC 46-yard line. Haden connected on all four of his passes on that drive, finally hitting Terry Metcalf with a four-yard scoring toss. The NFC continued to rally and, with Jim Hart at quarterback, moved 63 yards in 12 plays for the go-ahead score. During the winning drive, Hart completed five of six passes for 38 yards and Payton picked up 20 more on the ground.

AFC	3	10	0	0	— 13
NFC	0	0	7	7	— 14

AFC—FG Linhart 21
AFC—Branch 10 pass from Stabler (Linhart kick)
AFC—FG Linhart 39
NFC—Metcalf 4 pass from Haden (Herrera kick)
NFC—Payton 1 run (Herrera kick)

1977 AFC-NFC Pro Bowl

Kingdome, Seattle, Washington — January 17, 1977

Attendance: 64,752

AFC 24, NFC 14—O. J. Simpson's three-yard touchdown burst at 7:03 of the first quarter gave the AFC a lead it would not surrender, the victory breaking a two-game NFC win streak and giving the American Conference stars a 4-3 series lead. The AFC took a 17-7 lead midway through the second period on the first of two Ken Anderson touchdown passes, a 12-yarder to Charlie Joiner. But the NFC mounted a 73-yard drive capped by Lawrence McCutcheon's one-yard touchdown plunge to pull within three of the AFC, 17-14, at the half. Following a scoreless third quarter, player of the game Mel Blount thwarted a possible NFC score when he intercepted Jim Hart's pass in the end zone. Less than three minutes later, Blount again picked off a Hart pass, returning it 16 yards to the NFC 27. That set up Anderson's 27-yard touchdown strike to Cliff Branch for the final score.

NFC	0	14	0	0	— 14
AFC	10	7	0	7	— 24

AFC—Simpson 3 run (Linhart kick)
AFC—FG Linhart 31
NFC—Thomas 15 run (Bakken kick)
AFC—Joiner 12 pass from Anderson (Linhart kick)
NFC—McCutcheon 1 run (Bakken kick)
AFC—Branch 27 pass from Anderson (Linhart kick)

1976 AFC-NFC Pro Bowl

Superdome, New Orleans, Louisiana — January 26, 1976

Attendance: 30,546

NFC 23, AFC 20—Mike Boryla, a late substitute who did not enter the game until 5:39 remained, lifted the National Football Conference to a 23-20 victory over the American Football Conference with two touchdown passes in the final minutes. It was the second straight NFC win, squaring the series at 3-3. Until Boryla started firing the ball the AFC was in control, leading 13-0 at the half. Boryla entered the game after Billy Johnson had raced 90 yards with a punt to make the score 20-9 in favor of the AFC. He floated a 14-yard pass to Terry Metcalf and later fired an eight-yarder to Mel Gray for the winner.

AFC	0	13	0	7	— 20
NFC	0	0	9	14	— 23

AFC—FG Stenerud 20
AFC—FG Stenerud 35
AFC—Burrough 64 pass from Pastorini (Stenerud kick)
NFC—FG Bakken 42
NFC—Foreman 4 pass from Hart (kick blocked)
AFC—Johnson 90 punt return (Stenerud kick)
NFC—Metcalf 14 pass from Boryla (Bakken kick)
NFC—Gray 8 pass from Boryla (Bakken kick)

1975 AFC-NFC Pro Bowl

Orange Bowl, Miami, Florida — January 20, 1975
Attendance: 26,484

NFC 17, AFC 10—Los Angeles quarterback James Harris, who took over the NFC offense after Jim Hart of St. Louis suffered a laceration above his right eye in the second period, threw a pair of touchdown passes early in the fourth period to pace the NFC to its second victory in the five-game Pro Bowl series. The NFC win snapped a three-game AFC victory string. Harris, who was named the player of the game, connected with St. Louis's Mel Gray for an eight-yard touchdown 2:03 into the final period. One minute and 24 seconds later, following a recovery by Washington's Ken Houston of a fumble by Franco Harris of Pittsburgh, Harris tossed another eight-yard scoring pass to Washington's Charley Taylor for the decisive points.

NFC	0	3	0	14	— 17
AFC	0	0	10	0	— 10

NFC—FG Marcol 33
AFC—Warfield 32 pass from Griese (Gerela kick)
AFC—FG Gerela 33
NFC—Gray 8 pass from J. Harris (Marcol kick)
NFC—Taylor 8 pass from J. Harris (Marcol kick)

1974 AFC-NFC Pro Bowl

Arrowhead Stadium, Kansas City, Missouri — January 20, 1974
Attendance: 66,918

AFC 15, NFC 13—Miami's Garo Yepremian kicked his fifth consecutive field goal without a miss from the 42-yard line with 21 seconds remaining to give the AFC its third straight victory since the NFC won the inaugural game following the 1970 season. The field goal by Yepremian, who was voted the game's outstanding player, offset a 21-yard field goal by Atlanta's Nick Mike-Mayer that had given the NFC a 13-12 advantage with 1:41 remaining. The only touchdown in the game was scored by the NFC on a 14-yard pass from Philadelphia's Roman Gabriel to Lawrence McCutcheon of the Los Angeles Rams.

NFC	0	10	0	3	— 13
AFC	3	3	3	6	— 15

AFC—FG Yepremian 16
NFC—FG Mike-Mayer 27
NFC—McCutcheon 14 pass from Gabriel (Mike-Mayer kick)
AFC—FG Yepremian 37
AFC—FG Yepremian 27
AFC—FG Yepremian 41
NFC—FG Mike-Mayer 21
AFC—FG Yepremian 42

1973 AFC-NFC Pro Bowl

Texas Stadium, Irving, Texas — January 21, 1973
Attendance: 37,091

AFC 33, NFC 28—Paced by the rushing and receiving of player of the game O.J. Simpson, the AFC erased a 14-0 first period deficit and built a commanding 33-14 lead midway through the fourth period before the NFC managed two touchdowns in the final minute of play. Simpson rushed for 112 yards and caught three passes for 58 more to gain unanimous recognition in the balloting for player of the game. John Brockington scored three touchdowns for the NFC.

AFC	0	10	10	13	— 33
NFC	14	0	0	14	— 28

NFC—Brockington 1 run (Marcol kick)
NFC—Brockington 3 pass from Kilmer (Marcol kick)
AFC—Simpson 7 run (Gerela kick)
AFC—FG Gerela 18
AFC—FG Gerela 22
AFC—Hubbard 11 run (Gerela kick)
AFC—O. Taylor 5 pass from Lamonica (kick failed)
AFC—Bell 12 interception return (Gerela kick)
NFC—Brockington 1 run (Marcol kick)
NFC—Kwalick 12 pass from Snead (Marcol kick)

1972 AFC-NFC Pro Bowl

Memorial Coliseum, Los Angeles, California — January 23, 1972
Attendance: 53,647

AFC 26, NFC 13—Four field goals by Jan Stenerud of Kansas City, including a 6-6 tie-breaker from 48 yards, helped lift the AFC from a 6-0 deficit to a 19-6 advantage early in the fourth period. The AFC defense picked off three interceptions. Stenerud was selected as the outstanding offensive player and his Kansas City teammate, linebacker Willie Lanier, was the game's outstanding defensive player.

AFC	0	3	13	10	— 26
NFC	0	6	0	7	— 13

NFC—Grim 50 pass from Landry (kick failed)
AFC—FG Stenerud 25
AFC—FG Stenerud 23
AFC—FG Stenerud 48
AFC—Morin 5 pass from Dawson (Stenerud kick)
AFC—FG Stenerud 42
NFC—V. Washington 2 run (Knight kick)
AFC—F. Little 6 run (Stenerud kick)

1971 AFC-NFC Pro Bowl

Memorial Coliseum, Los Angeles, California — January 24, 1971
Attendance: 48,222

NFC 27, AFC 6—Mel Renfro of Dallas broke open the first meeting between the American Football Conference and National Football Conference all-star teams as he returned a pair of punts 82 and 56 yards for touchdowns in the final period to provide the NFC with a 27-6 victory over the AFC. Renfro was voted the game's outstanding back and linebacker Fred Carr of Green Bay the outstanding lineman.

AFC	0	3	3	0	— 6
NFC	0	3	10	14	— 27

AFC—FG Stenerud 37
NFC—FG Cox 13
NFC—Osborn 23 pass from Brodie (Cox kick)
NFC—FG Cox 35
AFC—FG Stenerud 16
NFC—Renfro 82 punt return (Cox kick)
NFC—Renfro 56 punt return (Cox kick)

Pro Bowl All-Time Results

Date	Result	Site (attendance)	Honored players
Jan. 15, 1939	New York Giants 13, Pro All-Stars 10	Wrigley Field, Los Angeles (20,000)	
Jan. 14, 1940	Green Bay 16, NFL All-Stars 7	Gilmore Stadium, Los Angeles (18,000)	
Dec. 29, 1940	Chicago Bears 28, NFL All-Stars 14	Gilmore Stadium, Los Angeles (21,624)	
Jan. 4, 1942	Chicago Bears 35, NFL All-Stars 24	Polo Grounds, New York (17,725)	
Dec. 27, 1942	NFL All-Stars 17, Washington 14	Shibe Park, Philadelphia (18,671)	
Jan. 14, 1951	American Conf. 28, National Conf. 27	Los Angeles Memorial Coliseum (53,676)	Otto Graham, Cleveland, player of the game
Jan. 12, 1952	National Conf. 30, American Conf. 13	Los Angeles Memorial Coliseum (19,400)	Dan Towler, Los Angeles, player of the game
Jan. 10, 1953	National Conf. 27, American Conf. 7	Los Angeles Memorial Coliseum (34,208)	Don Doll, Detroit, player of the game
Jan. 17, 1954	East 20, West 9	Los Angeles Memorial Coliseum (44,214)	Chuck Bednarik, Philadelphia, player of the game
Jan. 16, 1955	West 26, East 19	Los Angeles Memorial Coliseum (43,972)	Billy Wilson, San Francisco, player of the game
Jan. 15, 1956	East 31, West 30	Los Angeles Memorial Coliseum (37,867)	Ollie Matson, Chi. Cardinals, player of the game
Jan. 13, 1957	West 19, East 10	Los Angeles Memorial Coliseum (44,177)	Bert Rechichar, Baltimore, outstanding back Ernie Stautner, Pittsburgh, outstanding lineman
Jan. 12, 1958	West 26, East 7	Los Angeles Memorial Coliseum (66,634)	Hugh McElhenny, San Francisco, outstanding back Gene Brito, Washington, outstanding lineman
Jan. 11, 1959	East 28, West 21	Los Angeles Memorial Coliseum (72,250)	Frank Gifford, N.Y. Giants, outstanding back Doug Atkins, Chi. Bears, outstanding lineman
Jan. 17, 1960	West 38, East 21	Los Angeles Memorial Coliseum (56,876)	Johnny Unitas, Baltimore, outstanding back Gene (Big Daddy) Lipscomb, Baltimore, outstanding lineman
Jan. 15, 1961	West 35, East 31	Los Angeles Memorial Coliseum (62,971)	Johnny Unitas, Baltimore, outstanding back Sam Huff, N.Y. Giants, outstanding lineman
Jan. 7, 1962	AFL West 47, East 27	Balboa Stadium, San Diego (20,973)	Cotton Davidson, Dallas Texans, player of the game
Jan. 14, 1962	NFL West 31, East 30	Los Angeles Memorial Coliseum (57,409)	Jim Brown, Cleveland, outstanding back Henry Jordan, Green Bay, outstanding lineman
Jan. 13, 1963	AFL West 21, East 14	Balboa Stadium, San Diego (27,641)	Curtis McClinton, Dallas Texans, outstanding offensive player Earl Faison, San Diego, outstanding defensive player
Jan. 13, 1963	NFL East 30, West 20	Los Angeles Memorial Coliseum (61,374)	Jim Brown, Cleveland, outstanding back Gene (Big Daddy) Lipscomb, Pittsburgh, outstanding lineman
Jan. 12, 1964	NFL West 31, East 17	Los Angeles Memorial Coliseum (67,242)	Johnny Unitas, Baltimore, player of the game Gino Marchetti, Baltimore, outstanding lineman
Jan. 19, 1964	AFL West 27, East 24	Balboa Stadium, San Diego (20,016)	Keith Lincoln, San Diego, outstanding offensive player Archie Matsos, Oakland, outstanding defensive player
Jan. 10, 1965	NFL West 34, East 14	Los Angeles Memorial Coliseum (60,598)	Fran Tarkenton, Minnesota, outstanding back Terry Barr, Detroit, outstanding lineman
Jan. 16, 1965	AFL West 38, East 14	Jeppesen Stadium, Houston (15,446)	Keith Lincoln, San Diego, outstanding offensive player Willie Brown, Denver, outstanding defensive player
Jan. 15, 1966	AFL All-Stars 30, Buffalo 19	Rice Stadium, Houston (35,572)	Joe Namath, N.Y. Jets, most valuable player, offense Frank Buncom, San Diego, most valuable player, defense
Jan. 15, 1966	NFL East 36, West 7	Los Angeles Memorial Coliseum (60,124)	Jim Brown, Cleveland, outstanding back Dale Meinert, St. Louis, outstanding lineman
Jan. 21, 1967	AFL East 30, West 23	Oakland-Alameda County Coliseum (18,876)	Babe Parilli, Boston, outstanding offensive player Verlon Biggs, N.Y. Jets, outstanding defensive player
Jan. 22, 1967	NFL East 20, West 10	Los Angeles Memorial Coliseum (15,062)	Gale Sayers, Chicago, outstanding back Floyd Peters, Philadelphia, outstanding lineman
Jan. 21, 1968	AFL East 25, West 24	Gator Bowl, Jacksonville, Fla. (40,103)	Joe Namath and Don Maynard, N.Y. Jets, out. off. players Leslie (Speedy) Duncan, San Diego, out. def. player
Jan. 21, 1968	NFL West 38, East 20	Los Angeles Memorial Coliseum (53,289)	Gale Sayers, Chicago, outstanding back Dave Robinson, Green Bay, outstanding lineman
Jan. 19, 1969	AFL West 38, East 25	Gator Bowl, Jacksonville, Fla. (41,058)	Len Dawson, Kansas City, outstanding offensive player George Webster, Houston, outstanding defensive player
Jan. 19, 1969	NFL West 10, East 7	Los Angeles Memorial Coliseum (32,050)	Roman Gabriel, Los Angeles, outstanding back Merlin Olsen, Los Angeles, outstanding lineman
Jan. 17, 1970	AFL West 26, East 3	Astrodome, Houston (30,170)	John Hadl, San Diego, player of the game
Jan. 18, 1970	NFL West 16, East 13	Los Angeles Memorial Coliseum (57,786)	Gale Sayers, Chicago, outstanding back George Andrie, Dallas, outstanding lineman
Jan. 24, 1971	NFC 27, AFC 6	Los Angeles Memorial Coliseum (48,222)	Mel Renfro, Dallas, outstanding back Fred Carr, Green Bay, outstanding lineman
Jan. 23, 1972	AFC 26, NFC 13	Los Angeles Memorial Coliseum (53,647)	Jan Stenerud, Kansas City, outstanding offensive player Willie Lanier, Kansas City, outstanding defensive player
Jan. 21, 1973	AFC 33, NFC 28	Texas Stadium, Irving (37,091)	O.J. Simpson, Buffalo, player of the game
Jan. 20, 1974	AFC 15, NFC 13	Arrowhead Stadium, Kansas City (66,918)	Garo Yepremian, Miami, player of the game
Jan. 20, 1975	NFC 17, AFC 10	Orange Bowl, Miami (26,484)	James Harris, Los Angeles, player of the game
Jan. 26, 1976	NFC 23, AFC 20	Louisiana Superdome, New Orleans (30,546)	Billy Johnson, Houston, player of the game
Jan. 17, 1977	AFC 24, NFC 14	Kingdome, Seattle (64,752)	Mel Blount, Pittsburgh, player of the game
Jan. 23, 1978	NFC 14, AFC 13	Tampa Stadium (51,337)	Walter Payton, Chicago, player of the game
Jan. 29, 1979	NFC 13, AFC 7	Los Angeles Memorial Coliseum (46,281)	Ahmad Rashad, Minnesota, player of the game
Jan. 27, 1980	NFC 37, AFC 27	Aloha Stadium, Honolulu (49,800)	Chuck Muncie, New Orleans, player of the game
Feb. 1, 1981	NFC 21, AFC 7	Aloha Stadium, Honolulu (50,360)	Eddie Murray, Detroit, player of the game
Jan. 31, 1982	AFC 16, NFC 13	Aloha Stadium, Honolulu (50,402)	Kellen Winslow, San Diego, and Lee Roy Selmon, Tampa Bay, players of the game
Feb. 6, 1983	NFC 20, AFC 19	Aloha Stadium, Honolulu (49,883)	Dan Fouts, San Diego, and John Jefferson, Green Bay, players of the game
Jan. 29, 1984	NFC 45, AFC 3	Aloha Stadium, Honolulu (50,445)	Joe Theismann, Washington, player of the game
Jan. 27, 1985	AFC 22, NFC 14	Aloha Stadium, Honolulu (50,385)	Mark Gastineau, N.Y. Jets, player of the game
Feb. 2, 1986	NFC 28, AFC 24	Aloha Stadium, Honolulu (50,101)	Phil Simms, N.Y. Giants, player of the game
Feb. 1, 1987	AFC 10, NFC 6	Aloha Stadium, Honolulu (50,101)	Reggie White, Philadelphia, player of the game
Feb. 7, 1988	AFC 15, NFC 6	Aloha Stadium, Honolulu (50,113)	Bruce Smith, Buffalo, player of the game
Jan. 29, 1989	NFC 34, AFC 3	Aloha Stadium, Honolulu (50,113)	Randall Cunningham, Philadelphia, player of the game

AFC VS. NFC (REGULAR SEASON), 1970-1988

	1970	1971	1972	1973	1974	1975	1976	1977	1978	1979	1980	1981	1982	1983	1984	1985	1986	1987	1988	Totals
Miami	2-1	3-0	3-0	3-0	2-1	3-0	0-2	2-0	3-1	4-0	4-0	3-1	1-1	3-1	4-0	3-1	2-2	3-0	3-1	51-12
L.A. Raiders	1-2	1-1-1	3-0	2-1	3-0	3-0	3-0	1-1	4-0	4-0	2-2	2-2	3-0	2-2	3-1	3-1	1-3	2-2	1-3	44-21-1
Cincinnati	1-2	1-2	2-1	2-1	2-1	3-0	2-0	2-1	2-2	2-2	2-2	2-2	1-0	3-1	2-2	2-2	3-1	1-2	4-0	39-24
Pittsburgh	0-3	1-2	2-1	3-0	3-0	2-1	1-1	2-0	3-1	3-1	4-0	3-1	1-0	2-2	3-1	1-3	2-2	2-2	1-3	39-24
Denver	2-2	1-3	1-3	0-3-1	2-2	2-1	2-0	1-1	2-2	3-1	3-1	3-1	2-1	0-2	3-1	3-1	3-1	2-1-1	3-1	38-28-2
Seattle								1-0	3-1	3-1	1-3	0-2	1-0	1-3	4-0	2-2	3-1	4-0	1-3	24-16
New England	0-3	0-3	3-0	2-1	3-0	1-2	1-1	2-0	2-2	3-1	1-3	0-4	0-1	2-2	0-4	3-1	3-1	0-3	2-2	28-34
Cleveland	0-3	2-1	1-2	1-2	1-2	1-3	2-0	1-1	4-0	3-1	3-1	3-1	0-2	2-2	1-3	1-3	2-2	2-2	4-0	34-31
San Diego	1-2	2-1	0-3	1-2	1-2	0-3	2-0	1-1	2-2	3-1	2-2	2-2	1-0	2-2	4-0	1-1	0-4	2-0	2-2	29-30
Indianapolis	3-0	2-1	0-3	2-1	1-2	2-1	0-2	1-1	2-2	1-1	1-1	0-4	0-1-1	2-0	0-4	3-1	1-3	1-0	2-2	24-30-1
N.Y. Jets	2-1	0-3	1-2	0-3	2-1	0-3	0-2	1-1	1-3	3-1	1-3	2-0	4-0	3-1	0-2	2-2	2-2	0-4	2-0	26-34
Kansas City	0-2-1	2-1	2-1	1-1-1	1-2	2-1	1-1	1-1	0-2	0-2	2-0	2-2	0-3	2-2	1-1	2-2	1-1	1-2	0-2	21-29-2
Houston	0-3	0-2-1	0-3	0-3	0-3	3-0	2-0	2-0	2-2	2-2	4-0	1-3	0-3	1-3	0-4	1-3	2-2	2-2	3-1	25-39-1
Buffalo	0-3	0-3	2-0-1	2-1	2-1	1-2	0-2	1-1	1-1	2-2	3-1	1-3	1-2	1-3	1-3	0-2	1-1	1-2	2-2	22-35-1
Tampa Bay							0-1													0-1
TOTALS	12-27-1	15-23-2	20-19-1	19-19-2	23-17	23-17	16-12	19-9	31-21	36-16	33-19	24-28	15-14-1	26-26	26-26	27-25	26-26	23-22-1	30-22	444-388-8

NFC VS. AFC (REGULAR SEASON), 1970-1988

	1970	1971	1972	1973	1974	1975	1976	1977	1978	1979	1980	1981	1982	1983	1984	1985	1986	1987	1988	Totals
Dallas	3-0	3-0	3-0	2-1	2-1	2-1	2-0	1-1	3-1	1-3	3-1	4-0	2-1	2-2	2-2	3-1	1-3	2-1	0-4	41-23
Philadelphia	2-1	1-2	2-1	2-1	2-1	0-3	0-2	1-1	3-1	2-2	3-1	3-1	2-1	1-1	3-1	1-1	2-2	3-1	2-2	35-26
Washington	2-1	1-2	1-2	2-1	2-1	1-2	1-1	1-1	2-2	2-2	1-3	2-2		4-0	3-1	4-0	3-1	2-1	1-3	35-26
L.A. Rams	2-1	1-2	1-2	3-0	3-1	3-0	1-1	2-0	2-2	2-2	2-2	1-3	1-2	1-3	3-1	3-1	2-2	1-2	2-2	36-29
San Francisco	4-0	2-1	2-1	1-2	0-3	1-2	1-1	0-2	1-3	0-4	2-2	3-1	1-3	2-2	3-1	3-1	4-0	3-1	2-2	35-32
Minnesota	2-1	2-1	1-2	2-1	2-1	4-0	2-0	1-1	1-3	1-3	1-3	1-3	1-3	4-0	0-4	2-0	1-3	2-1	2-2	32-32
Phoenix	2-0-1	2-1	1-2	0-2-1	2-1	2-1	1-1	0-2	0-4	1-3	1-1	3-1		3-1	3-1	2-2	1-1	0-1	1-3	25-28-2
N.Y. Giants	3-0	1-2	1-2	1-2	1-2	2-1	0-2	0-2	1-1	1-1	1-3	1-1	1-0	0-4	2-0	2-2	3-1	2-1	1-1	24-28
Chicago	1-2	1-2	1-2	2-2	0-3	0-3	0-2	1-1	0-4	2-2	0-4	4-0	1-1	1-1	2-2	3-1	4-0	2-2	3-1	28-35
Detroit	3-0	4-0	2-0-1	0-3	1-2	1-2	2-0	2-0	2-2	0-4	0-2	2-2	0-1	1-3	0-4	2-2	1-3	0-4	1-1	24-35-1
Green Bay	2-1	2-1	2-1	1-1-1	2-1	0-3	0-2	0-3	2-2	1-3	1-3	1-1	1-1-1	2-2	0-4	0-4	1-3	1-2-1	1-3	20-41-3
New Orleans	0-3	0-1-2	0-3	1-2	0-3	0-3	1-2	0-2	1-3	0-4	1-3	2-2	1-0	1-3	3-1	0-4	1-3	4-0	4-0	20-42-2
Tampa Bay								0-1	2-0	2-0	1-3	0-4	2-1	1-3	1-1	0-4	1-1	0-2	1-3	11-23
Atlanta	1-2	3-0	2-2	2-1	0-3	1-2	0-2	0-2	1-3	1-3	2-2	1-3	1-1	3-1	1-3	0-4	1-3	0-4	1-3	21-44
Seattle							1-0													1-0
TOTALS	27-12-1	23-15-2	19-20-1	19-19-2	17-23	17-23	12-16	9-19	21-31	16-36	19-33	28-24	14-15-1	26-26	26-26	25-27	26-26	22-23-1	22-30	388-444-8

Regular Season Interconference Records, 1970-1988

American Football Conference

Eastern Division	W	L	T	Pct.
Miami	51	12	0	.810
New England	28	34	0	.452
Indianapolis	24	30	1	.445
New York Jets	26	34	0	.433
Buffalo	22	35	1	.388
Central Division				
Cincinnati	39	24	0	.619
Pittsburgh	39	24	0	.619
Cleveland	34	31	0	.523
Houston	25	39	1	.392
Western Division				
Los Angeles Raiders	44	21	1	.674
Seattle	24	16	0	.600
Denver	38	28	2	.574
San Diego	29	30	0	.492
Kansas City	21	29	2	.423

National Football Conference

Eastern Division	W	L	T	Pct.
Dallas	41	23	0	.641
Philadelphia	35	26	0	.574
Washington	35	26	0	.574
Phoenix	25	28	2	.473
New York Giants	24	28	0	.462
Central Division				
Minnesota	32	32	0	.500
Chicago	28	35	0	.444
Detroit	24	35	1	.408
Green Bay	20	41	3	.336
Tampa Bay	11	23	0	.324
Western Division				
Los Angeles Rams	36	29	0	.554
San Francisco	35	32	0	.522
New Orleans	20	42	2	.328
Atlanta	21	44	0	.323

Interconference Victories, 1970-1988

Regular Season	AFC	NFC	Tie	Preseason	AFC	NFC	Tie
1970	12	27	1	1970	21	28	1
1971	15	23	2	1971	28	28	3
1972	20	19	1	1972	27	25	4
1973	19	19	2	1973	23	35	2
1974	23	17	0	1974	35	25	0
1975	23	17	0	1975	30	26	1
1976	16	12	0	1976	30	31	0
1977	19	9	0	1977	38	25	0
1978	31	21	0	1978	20	19	0
1979	36	16	0	1979	25	18	0
1980	33	19	0	1980	22	20	1
1981	24	28	0	1981	18	19	0
1982	15	14	1	1982	25	16	0
1983	26	26	0	1983	15	24	0
1984	26	26	0	1984	16	19	0
1985	27	25	0	1985	10	22	1
1986	26	26	0	1986	22	17	0
1987	23	22	1	1987	22	22	0
1988	30	22	0	1988	23	16	1
Total	444	388	8	Total	450	435	14

1988 Interconference Games (Home Team in capital letters)

AFC 30, NFC 22

AFC Victories

PITTSBURGH 24, Dallas 21
BUFFALO 13, Minnesota 10
CINCINNATI 21, Phoenix 14
Cincinnati 28, PHILADELPHIA 24
MIAMI 24, Green Bay 17
New York Jets 17, DETROIT 10
MIAMI 24, Minnesota 7
Seattle 31, ATLANTA 20
Denver 16, SAN FRANCISCO 13
DENVER 30, Atlanta 14
CLEVELAND 19, Philadelphia 3
INDIANAPOLIS 35, Tampa Bay 31
Cleveland 29, PHOENIX 21
NEW ENGLAND 30, Chicago 7
BUFFALO 28, Green Bay 0
Miami 17, TAMPA BAY 14
HOUSTON 41, Washington 17
Indianapolis 20, GREEN BAY 13
Los Angeles Raiders 9, SAN FRANCISCO 3
San Diego 10, ATLANTA 7
Cincinnati 38, DALLAS 24
HOUSTON 38, Phoenix 20
San Diego 38, LOS ANGELES RAMS 24
Houston 25, DALLAS 17
Cleveland 17, WASHINGTON 13
DENVER 35, Los Angeles Rams 24
CLEVELAND 24, Dallas 21
NEW ENGLAND 10, Tampa Bay 7
CINCINNATI 20, Washington 17
NEW YORK JETS 27, New York Giants 21

NFC Victories

CHICAGO 34, Miami 7
Chicago 17, INDIANAPOLIS 13
MINNESOTA 36, New England 6
WASHINGTON 30, Pittsburgh 29
Los Angeles Rams 22, LOS ANGELES RAIDERS 17
San Francisco 38, SEATTLE 7
CHICAGO 24, Buffalo 3
PHILADELPHIA 32, Houston 23
GREEN BAY 45, New England 3
New Orleans 23, SAN DIEGO 17
PHOENIX 31, Pittsburgh 14
Detroit 7, KANSAS CITY 6
New Orleans 20, SEATTLE 19
NEW ORLEANS 20, Los Angeles Raiders 6
LOS ANGELES RAMS 31, Seattle 10
Philadelphia 27, PITTSBURGH 26
Atlanta 12, LOS ANGELES RAIDERS 6
NEW ORLEANS 42, Denver 0
MINNESOTA 12, Indianapolis 3
San Francisco 48, SAN DIEGO 10
TAMPA BAY 10, Buffalo 5
NEW YORK GIANTS 28, Kansas City 12

Monday Night Football, 1970–1988

(Home Team in capitals, games listed in chronological order.)

1988
NEW YORK GIANTS 27, Washington 20
Dallas 17, PHOENIX 14
CLEVELAND 23, Indianapolis 17
Los Angeles Raiders 30, DENVER 27 (OT)
NEW ORLEANS 20, Dallas 17
PHILADELPHIA 24, New York Giants 13
Buffalo 37, NEW YORK JETS 14
CHICAGO 10, San Francisco 9
INDIANAPOLIS 55, Denver 23
HOUSTON 24, Cleveland 17
Buffalo 31, MIAMI 6
SAN FRANCISCO 37, Washington 21
SEATTLE 35, Los Angeles Raiders 27
LOS ANGELES RAMS 23, Chicago 3
MIAMI 38, Cleveland 31
MINNESOTA 28, Chicago 27

1987
CHICAGO 34, New York Giants 19
NEW YORK JETS 43, New England 24
San Francisco 41, NEW YORK GIANTS 21
DENVER 30, Los Angeles Raiders 14
Washington 13, DALLAS 7
CLEVELAND 30, Los Angeles Rams 17
MINNESOTA 34, Denver 27
DALLAS 33, New York Giants 24
NEW YORK JETS 30, Seattle 14
DENVER 31, Chicago 29
Los Angeles Rams 30, WASHINGTON 26
Los Angeles Raiders 37, SEATTLE 14
MIAMI 37, New York Jets 28
SAN FRANCISCO 41, Chicago 0
Dallas 29, LOS ANGELES RAMS 21
New England 24, MIAMI 10

1986
DALLAS 31, New York Giants 28
Denver 21, PITTSBURGH 10
Chicago 25, GREEN BAY 12
Dallas 31, ST. LOUIS 7
SEATTLE 33, San Diego 7
CINCINNATI 24, Pittsburgh 22
NEW YORK JETS 22, Denver 10
NEW YORK GIANTS 27, Washington 20
Los Angeles Rams 20, CHICAGO 17
CLEVELAND 26, Miami 16
WASHINGTON 14, San Francisco 6
MIAMI 45, New York Jets 3
New York Giants 21, SAN FRANCISCO 17
SEATTLE 37, Los Angeles Raiders 0
Chicago 16, DETROIT 13
New England 34, MIAMI 27

1985
DALLAS 44, Washington 14
CLEVELAND 17, Pittsburgh 7
Los Angeles Rams 35, SEATTLE 24
Cincinnati 37, PITTSBURGH 24
WASHINGTON 27, St. Louis 10
NEW YORK JETS 23, Miami 7
CHICAGO 23, Green Bay 7
LOS ANGELES RAIDERS 34, San Diego 21
ST. LOUIS 21, Dallas 10
DENVER 17, San Francisco 16
WASHINGTON 23, New York Giants 21
SAN FRANCISCO 19, Seattle 6
MIAMI 30, Chicago 24
Los Angeles Rams 27, SAN FRANCISCO 20
MIAMI 30, New England 27
L.A. Raiders 16, L.A. RAMS 6

1984
Dallas 20, LOS ANGELES RAMS 13
SAN FRANCISCO 37, Washington 31
Miami 21, BUFFALO 17
LOS ANGELES RAIDERS 33, San Diego 30
PITTSBURGH 38, Cincinnati 17
San Francisco 31, NEW YORK GIANTS 10
DENVER 17, Green Bay 14
Los Angeles Rams 24, ATLANTA 10
Seattle 24, SAN DIEGO 0
WASHINGTON 27, Atlanta 14
SEATTLE 17, Los Angeles Raiders 14
NEW ORLEANS 27, Pittsburgh 24
MIAMI 28, New York Jets 17
SAN DIEGO 20, Chicago 7
Los Angeles Raiders 24, DETROIT 3
MIAMI 28, Dallas 21

1983
Dallas 31, WASHINGTON 30
San Diego 17, KANSAS CITY 14
LOS ANGELES RAIDERS 27, Miami 14
NEW YORK GIANTS 27, Green Bay 3
New York Jets 34, BUFFALO 10
Pittsburgh 24, CINCINNATI 14
GREEN BAY 48, Washington 47
ST. LOUIS 20, New York Giants 20 (OT)
Washington 27, SAN DIEGO 24
DETROIT 15, New York Giants 9
Los Angeles Rams 36, ATLANTA 13
New York Jets 31, NEW ORLEANS 28
MIAMI 38, Cincinnati 14
DETROIT 13, Minnesota 2
Green Bay 12, TAMPA BAY 9 (OT)
SAN FRANCISCO 42, Dallas 17

1982
Pittsburgh 36, DALLAS 28
Green Bay 27, NEW YORK GIANTS 19
LOS ANGELES RAIDERS 28, San Diego 24
TAMPA BAY 23, Miami 17
New York Jets 28, DETROIT 13
Dallas 37, HOUSTON 7
SAN DIEGO 50, Cincinnati 34
MIAMI 27, Buffalo 10
MINNESOTA 31, Dallas 27

1981
San Diego 44, CLEVELAND 14
Oakland 36, MINNESOTA 10
Dallas 35, NEW ENGLAND 21
Los Angeles 24, CHICAGO 7
PHILADELPHIA 16, Atlanta 13
BUFFALO 31, Miami 21
DETROIT 48, Chicago 17
PITTSBURGH 26, Houston 13
DENVER 19, Minnesota 17
DALLAS 27, Buffalo 14
SEATTLE 44, San Diego 23
ATLANTA 31, Minnesota 30
MIAMI 13, Philadelphia 10
OAKLAND 30, Pittsburgh 27
LOS ANGELES 21, Atlanta 16
SAN DIEGO 23, Oakland 10

1980
Dallas 17, WASHINGTON 3
Houston 16, CLEVELAND 7
PHILADELPHIA 35, New York Giants 3
NEW ENGLAND 23, Denver 14
CHICAGO 23, Tampa Bay 0
DENVER 20, Washington 17
Oakland 45, PITTSBURGH 34
NEW YORK JETS 17, Miami 14
CLEVELAND 27, Chicago 21
HOUSTON 38, New England 34
Oakland 19, SEATTLE 17
Los Angeles 27, NEW ORLEANS 7
OAKLAND 9, Denver 3
MIAMI 16, New England 13 (OT)
LOS ANGELES 38, Dallas 14
SAN DIEGO 26, Pittsburgh 17

1979
Pittsburgh 16, NEW ENGLAND 13 (OT)
Atlanta 14, PHILADELPHIA 10
WASHINGTON 27, New York Giants 0
CLEVELAND 26, Dallas 7
GREEN BAY 27, New England 14
OAKLAND 13, Miami 3
NEW YORK JETS 14, Minnesota 7
PITTSBURGH 42, Denver 7
Seattle 31, ATLANTA 28
Houston 9, MIAMI 6
Philadelphia 31, DALLAS 21
LOS ANGELES 20, Atlanta 14
SEATTLE 30, New York Jets 7
Oakland 42, NEW ORLEANS 35
HOUSTON 20, Pittsburgh 17
SAN DIEGO 17, Denver 7

1978
DALLAS 38, Baltimore 0
MINNESOTA 12, Denver 9 (OT)
Baltimore 34, NEW ENGLAND 27
Minnesota 24, CHICAGO 20
WASHINGTON 9, Dallas 5
MIAMI 21, Cincinnati 0
DENVER 16, Chicago 7
Houston 24, PITTSBURGH 17
ATLANTA 15, Los Angeles 7
BALTIMORE 21, Washington 17
Oakland 34, CINCINNATI 21
HOUSTON 35, Miami 30
Pittsburgh 24, SAN FRANCISCO 7
SAN DIEGO 40, Chicago 7
Cincinnati 20, LOS ANGELES 19
MIAMI 23, New England 3

1977
PITTSBURGH 27, San Francisco 0
CLEVELAND 30, New England 27 (OT)
Oakland 37, KANSAS CITY 28
CHICAGO 24, Los Angeles 23
PITTSBURGH 20, Cincinnati 14
LOS ANGELES 35, Minnesota 3
ST. LOUIS 28, New York Giants 0
BALTIMORE 10, Washington 3
St. Louis 24, DALLAS 17
WASHINGTON 10, Green Bay 9
OAKLAND 34, Buffalo 13
MIAMI 17, Baltimore 6
Dallas 42, SAN FRANCISCO 35

1976
Miami 30, BUFFALO 21
Oakland 24, KANSAS CITY 21
Washington 20, PHILADELPHIA 17 (OT)
MINNESOTA 17, Pittsburgh 6
San Francisco 16, LOS ANGELES 0
NEW ENGLAND 41, New York Jets 7
WASHINGTON 20, St. Louis 10
BALTIMORE 38, Houston 14
CINCINNATI 20, Los Angeles 12
DALLAS 17, Buffalo 10
Baltimore 17, MIAMI 16
SAN FRANCISCO 20, Minnesota 16
OAKLAND 35, Cincinnati 20

1975
Oakland 31, MIAMI 21
DENVER 23, Green Bay 13
Dallas 36, DETROIT 10
WASHINGTON 27, St. Louis 17
New York Giants 17, BUFFALO 14
Minnesota 13, CHICAGO 9
Los Angeles 42, PHILADELPHIA 3
Kansas City 34, DALLAS 31
CINCINNATI 33, Buffalo 24
Pittsburgh 32, HOUSTON 9
MIAMI 20, New England 7
OAKLAND 17, Denver 10

1974
BUFFALO 21, Oakland 20
PHILADELPHIA 13, Dallas 10
WASHINGTON 30, Denver 3
MIAMI 21, New York Jets 17
DETROIT 17, San Francisco 13
CHICAGO 10, Green Bay 9
PITTSBURGH 24, Atlanta 17
Los Angeles 15, SAN FRANCISCO 13
Minnesota 28, ST. LOUIS 24
Kansas City 42, DENVER 34
Pittsburgh 28, NEW ORLEANS 7
MIAMI 24, Cincinnati 3
Washington 23, LOS ANGELES 17

1973
GREEN BAY 23, New York Jets 7
DALLAS 40, New Orleans 3
DETROIT 31, Atlanta 6
WASHINGTON 14, Dallas 7
Miami 17, CLEVELAND 9
DENVER 23, Oakland 23
BUFFALO 23, Kansas City 14
PITTSBURGH 21, Washington 16
KANSAS CITY 19, Chicago 7
ATLANTA 20, Minnesota 14
SAN FRANCISCO 20, Green Bay 6
MIAMI 30, Pittsburgh 26
LOS ANGELES 40, New York Giants 6

1972
Washington 24, MINNESOTA 21
Kansas City 20, NEW ORLEANS 17
New York Giants 27, PHILADELPHIA 12
Oakland 34, HOUSTON 0
Green Bay 24, DETROIT 23
CHICAGO 13, Minnesota 10
DALLAS 28, Detroit 24
Baltimore 24, NEW ENGLAND 17
Cleveland 21, SAN DIEGO 17
WASHINGTON 24, Atlanta 13
MIAMI 31, St. Louis 10
Los Angeles 26, SAN FRANCISCO 16
OAKLAND 24, New York Jets 16

1971
Minnesota 16, DETROIT 13
ST. LOUIS 17, New York Jets 10
Oakland 34, CLEVELAND 20
DALLAS 20, New York Giants 13
KANSAS CITY 38, Pittsburgh 16
MINNESOTA 10, Baltimore 3
GREEN BAY 14, Detroit 14
BALTIMORE 24, Los Angeles 17
SAN DIEGO 20, St. Louis 17
ATLANTA 28, Green Bay 21
MIAMI 34, Chicago 3
Kansas City 26, SAN FRANCISCO 17
Washington 38, LOS ANGELES 24

1970
CLEVELAND 31, New York Jets 21
Kansas City 44, BALTIMORE 24
DETROIT 28, Chicago 14
Green Bay 22, SAN DIEGO 20
OAKLAND 34, Washington 20
MINNESOTA 13, Los Angeles 3
PITTSBURGH 21, Cincinnati 10
Baltimore 13, GREEN BAY 10
St. Louis 38, DALLAS 0
PHILADELPHIA 23, New York Giants 20
Miami 20, ATLANTA 7
Cleveland 21, HOUSTON 10
Detroit 28, LOS ANGELES 23

Monday Night Won-Lost Records, 1970-1988

	Total	1988	1987	1986	1985	1984	1983	1982	1981	1980	1979	1978	1977	1976	1975	1974	1973	1972	1971	1970
Buffalo	5-9	2-0				0-1	0-1	0-1	1-1				0-1	0-2	0-2	1-0	1-0			
Cincinnati	5-10			1-0	1-0	0-1	0-2	0-1				1-2	0-1	1-1	1-0	0-1				0-1
Cleveland	10-6	1-2	1-0	1-0	1-0				0-1	1-1	1-0		1-0				0-1	1-0	0-1	2-0
Denver	9-12-1	0-2	2-1	1-1	1-0	1-0			1-0	1-2	0-2	1-1			1-1	0-2	0-0-1			
Houston	7-6	1-0						0-1	0-1	2-0	2-0	2-0		0-1	0-1			0-1		0-1
Indianapolis	9-5	1-1										2-1	1-1	2-0				1-0	1-1	1-1
Kansas City	7-4						0-1						0-1	0-1	1-0	1-0	1-1	1-0	2-0	1-0
L.A. Raiders	26-6-1	1-1	1-1	0-1	2-0	2-1	1-0	1-0	2-1	3-0	2-0	1-0	2-0	2-0	2-0	0-1	0-0-1	2-0	1-0	1-0
Miami	24-14	1-1	1-1	1-2	2-1	3-0	1-1	1-1	1-1	1-1	0-2	2-1	1-0	1-1	1-1	2-0	2-0	1-0	1-0	1-0
New England	4-12		1-1	1-0	0-1				0-1	1-2	0-2	0-2	0-1	1-0	0-1			0-1		
New York Jets	9-12	0-1	2-1	1-1	1-0	0-1	2-0	1-0		1-0	1-1			0-1	0-1	0-1	0-1	0-1	0-1	0-1
Pittsburgh	14-13			0-2	0-2	1-1	1-0	1-0	1-1	0-2	2-1	1-1	2-0	0-1	1-0	2-0	1-1		0-1	1-0
San Diego	10-9			0-1	0-1	1-2	1-1	1-1	2-1	1-0	1-0	1-0			1-0			0-1	1-0	0-1
Seattle	8-5	1-0	0-2	2-0	0-2	2-0			1-0	0-1	2-0									
Atlanta	5-11					0-2	0-1		1-2		1-2	1-0				0-1	1-1	0-1	1-0	0-1
Chicago	9-17	1-2	1-2	2-1	1-1	0-1			0-2	1-1		0-3	1-0		0-1	1-0	0-1	1-0	0-1	0-1
Dallas	19-16	1-1	2-1	2-0	1-1	1-1	1-1	1-2	2-0	1-1	0-2	1-1	1-1	1-0	1-1	0-1	1-1	1-0	1-0	0-1
Detroit	7-7-1			0-1		0-1	2-0	0-1	1-0						0-1	1-0	1-0	0-2	0-1-1	2-0
Green Bay	7-10-1			0-1	0-1	0-1	2-1	1-0			1-0		0-1		0-1	0-1	1-1	1-0	0-1-1	1-1
L.A. Rams	17-14	1-0	1-2	1-0	2-1	1-1	1-0		2-0	2-0	1-0	0-2	1-1	0-2	1-0	1-1	1-0	1-0	0-2	0-2
Minnesota	11-10	1-0	1-0				0-1	1-0	0-3		0-1	2-0	0-1	1-1	1-0	1-0	0-1	0-2	2-0	1-0
New Orleans	2-6	1-0				1-0	0-1			0-1	0-1					0-1	0-1	0-1		
New York Giants	6-15-1	1-1	0-3	2-1	0-1	0-1	1-1-1	0-1		0-1	0-1		0-1		1-0		0-1	1-0	0-1	0-1
Philadelphia	6-5	1-0							1-1	1-0	1-1			0-1	0-1	1-0		0-1		1-0
Phoenix	5-8-1	0-1		0-1	1-1		0-0-1					2-0	0-1	0-1	0-1		0-1	1-1	1-0	
San Francisco	10-12	1-1	2-0	0-2	1-2	2-0	1-0					0-1	0-2	2-0		0-2	1-0	0-1	0-1	
Tampa Bay	1-2						0-1	1-0		0-1										
Washington	18-14	0-2	1-1	1-1	2-1	1-1	1-2			0-2	1-0	1-1	1-1	2-0	1-0	2-0	1-1	2-0	1-0	0-1

Monday Night Syndrome

1988

1988

Of the 15 winning teams:
6 won the next week
9 lost the next week
0 tied the next week

Of the 15 losing teams:
11 won the next week
4 lost the next week
0 tied the next week

Of the 30 NFL teams:
17 won the next week
13 lost the next week
0 tied the next week

1970-1988

Of the 259 winning teams:
145 won the next week
111 lost the next week
3 tied the next week

Of the 259 losing teams:
137 won the next week
121 lost the next week
1 tied the next week

Of the 6 tying teams:
5 won the next week
1 lost the next week
0 tied the next week

Of the 524 NFL teams:
287 won the next week
233 lost the next week
4 tied the next week

Thursday-Sunday Night Football, 1974-1988

(Home Team in capitals, games listed in chronological order.)

1988
HOUSTON 41, Washington 17 (Sun.)
Los Angeles Raiders 13, SAN DIEGO 3 (Sun.)
Minnesota 34, DALLAS 3 (Sun.)
New England 6, MIAMI 3 (Sun.)
New York Giants 13, NEW ORLEANS 12 (Sun.)
Pittsburgh 37, HOUSTON 34 (Sun.)
SEATTLE 42, Denver 14 (Sun.)
Los Angeles Rams 38, SAN FRANCISCO 16 (Sun.)

1987
NEW YORK GIANTS 17, New England 10 (Sun.)
SAN DIEGO 16, Los Angeles Raiders 14 (Sun.)
Miami 20, DALLAS 14 (Sun.)
SAN FRANCISCO 38, Cleveland 24 (Sun.)
Chicago 30, MINNESOTA 24 (Sun.)
SEATTLE 28, Denver 21 (Sun.)
MIAMI 23, Washington 21 (Sun.)
SAN FRANCISCO 48, Los Angeles Rams 0 (Sun.)

1986
New England 20, NEW YORK JETS 6 (Thur.)
Cincinnati 30, CLEVELAND 13 (Thur.)
Los Angeles Raiders 37, SAN DIEGO 31 (OT) (Thur.)
LOS ANGELES RAMS 29, Dallas 10 (Sun.)
SAN FRANCISCO 24, Los Angeles Rams 14 (Fri.)

1985
KANSAS CITY 36, Los Angeles Raiders 20 (Thur.)
Chicago 33, MINNESOTA 24 (Thur.)
Dallas 30, NEW YORK GIANTS 29 (Sun.)
SAN DIEGO 54, Pittsburgh 44 (Sun.)
Denver 27, SEATTLE 24 (Fri.)

1984
Pittsburgh 23, NEW YORK JETS 17 (Thur.)
Denver 24, CLEVELAND 14 (Sun.)
DALLAS 30, New Orleans 27 (Sun.)
Washington 31, MINNESOTA 17 (Thur.)
SAN FRANCISCO 19, Los Angeles Rams 16 (Fri.)

1983
San Francisco 48, MINNESOTA 17 (Thur.)
CLEVELAND 17, Cincinnati 7 (Thur.)
Los Angeles Raiders 40, DALLAS 38 (Sun.)
Los Angeles Raiders 42, SAN DIEGO 10 (Thur.)
MIAMI 34, New York Jets 14 (Fri.)

1982
BUFFALO 23, Minnesota 22 (Thur.)
SAN FRANCISCO 30, Los Angeles Rams 24 (Thur.)
ATLANTA 17, San Francisco 7 (Sun.)

1981
MIAMI 30, Pittsburgh 10 (Thur.)
Philadelphia 20, BUFFALO 14 (Thur.)
DALLAS 29, Los Angeles 17 (Sun.)
HOUSTON 17, Cleveland 13 (Thur.)

1980
TAMPA BAY 10, Los Angeles 9 (Thur.)
DALLAS 42, San Diego 31 (Sun.)
San Diego 27, MIAMI 24 (OT) (Thur.)
HOUSTON 6, Pittsburgh 0 (Thur.)

1979
Los Angeles 13, DENVER 9 (Thur.)
DALLAS 30, Los Angeles 6 (Sun.)
OAKLAND 45, San Diego 22 (Thur.)
MIAMI 39, New England 24 (Thur.)

1978
New England 21, OAKLAND 14 (Sun.)
Minnesota 21, DALLAS 10 (Thur.)
LOS ANGELES 10, Pittsburgh 7 (Sun.)
Denver 21, OAKLAND 6 (Sun.)

1977
Minnesota 30, DETROIT 21 (Sat.)

1976
Los Angeles 20, DETROIT 17 (Sat.)

1975
LOS ANGELES 10, Pittsburgh 3 (Sat.)

1974
OAKLAND 27, Dallas 23 (Sat.)

History of Overtime Games

Preseason

Aug. 28, 1955	Los Angeles 23, New York Giants 17, at Portland, Oregon
Aug. 24, 1962	Denver 27, Dallas Texans 24, at Fort Worth, Texas
Aug. 10, 1974	San Diego 20, New York Jets 14, at San Diego
Aug. 17, 1974	Pittsburgh 33, Philadelphia 30, at Philadelphia
Aug. 17, 1974	Dallas 19, Houston 13, at Dallas
Aug. 17, 1974	Cincinnati 13, Atlanta 7, at Atlanta
Sept. 6, 1974	Buffalo 23, New York Giants 17, at Buffalo
Aug. 9, 1975	Baltimore 23, Denver 20, at Denver
Aug. 30, 1975	New England 20, Green Bay 17, at Milwaukee
Sept. 13, 1975	Minnesota 14, San Diego 14, at San Diego
Aug. 1, 1976	New England 13, New York Giants 7, at New England
Aug. 2, 1976	Kansas City 9, Houston 3, at Kansas City
Aug. 20, 1976	New Orleans 26, Baltimore 20, at Baltimore
Sept. 4, 1976	Dallas 26, Houston 20, at Dallas
Aug. 13, 1977	Seattle 23, Dallas 17, at Seattle
Aug. 28, 1977	New England 13, Pittsburgh 10, at New England
Aug. 28, 1977	New York Giants 24, Buffalo 21, at East Rutherford, N.J.
Aug. 2, 1979	Seattle 12, Minnesota 9, at Minnesota
Aug. 4, 1979	Los Angeles 20, Oakland 14, at Los Angeles
Aug. 24, 1979	Denver 20, New England 17, at Denver
Aug. 23, 1980	Tampa Bay 20, Cincinnati 14, at Tampa Bay
Aug. 5, 1981	San Francisco 27, Seattle 24, at Seattle
Aug. 29, 1981	New Orleans 20, Detroit 17, at New Orleans
Aug. 28, 1982	Miami 17, Kansas City 17, at Kansas City
Sept. 3, 1982	Miami 16, New York Giants 13, at Miami
Aug. 6, 1983	L.A. Raiders 26, San Francisco 23, at Los Angeles
Aug. 6, 1983	Atlanta 13, Washington 10, at Atlanta
Aug. 13, 1983	St. Louis 27, Chicago 24, at St. Louis
Aug. 18, 1983	New York Jets 20, Cincinnati 17, at Cincinnati
Aug. 27, 1983	Chicago 20, Kansas City 17, at Chicago
Aug. 11, 1984	Pittsburgh 20, Philadelphia 17, at Pittsburgh
Aug. 9, 1985	Buffalo 10, Detroit 10, at Pontiac, Mich.
Aug. 10, 1985	Minnesota 16, Miami 13, at Miami
Aug. 17, 1985	Dallas 27, San Diego 24, at San Diego
Aug. 24, 1985	N.Y. Giants 34, N.Y. Jets 31, at East Rutherford, N.J.
Aug. 15, 1986	Washington 27, Pittsburgh 24, at Washington
Aug. 15, 1986	Detroit 30, Seattle 27, at Detroit
Aug. 23, 1986	Los Angeles Rams 20, San Diego 17, at Anaheim
Aug. 30, 1986	Minnesota 23, Indianapolis 20, at Indianapolis
Aug. 23, 1987	Philadelphia 19, New England 13, at New England
Sept. 5, 1987	Cleveland 30, Green Bay 24, at Milwaukee
Sept. 6, 1987	Kansas City 13, St. Louis 10, at Memphis, Tenn.
Aug. 11, 1988	Seattle 16, Detroit 13, at Detroit
Aug. 19, 1988	Miami 16, Denver 13, at Miami
Aug. 20, 1988	Houston 20, Los Angeles Rams 17, at Anaheim
Aug. 21, 1988	Minnesota 19, Phoenix 16, at Phoenix

Regular Season

Sept. 22, 1974—Pittsburgh 35, Denver 35, at Denver; Steelers win toss. Gilliam's pass intercepted and returned by Rowser to Denver's 42. Turner misses 41-yard field goal. Walden punts and Greer returns to Broncos' 39. Van Heusen punts and Edwards returns to Steelers' 16. Game ends with Steelers on own 26.

Nov. 10, 1974—New York Jets 26, New York Giants 20, at New Haven, Conn.; Giants win toss. Gogolak misses 42-yard field goal. Namath passes to Boozer for five yards and touchdown at 6:53.

Sept. 28, 1975—Dallas 37, St. Louis 31, at Dallas; Cardinals win toss. Hart's pass intercepted and returned by Jordan to Cardinals' 37. Staubach passes to DuPree for three yards and touchdown at 7:53.

Oct. 12, 1975—Los Angeles 13, San Diego 10, at San Diego; Chargers win toss. Partee punts to Rams' 14. Dempsey kicks 22-yard field goal at 9:27.

Nov. 2, 1975—Washington 30, Dallas 24, at Washington; Cowboys win toss. Staubach's pass intercepted and returned by Houston to Cowboys' 35. Kilmer runs one yard for touchdown at 6:34.

Nov. 16, 1975—St. Louis 20, Washington 17, at St. Louis; Cardinals win toss. Bakken kicks 37-yard field goal at 7:00.

Nov. 23, 1975—Kansas City 24, Detroit 21, at Kansas City; Lions win toss. Chiefs take over on downs at own 38. Stenerud kicks 26-yard field goal at 6:44.

Nov. 23, 1975—Oakland 26, Washington 23, at Washington; Redskins win toss. Bragg punts to Raiders' 42. Blanda kicks 27-yard field goal at 7:13.

Nov. 30, 1975—Denver 13, San Diego 10, at Denver; Broncos win toss. Turner kicks 25-yard field goal at 4:13.

Nov. 30, 1975—Oakland 37, Atlanta 34, at Oakland; Falcons win toss. James punts to Raiders' 16. Guy punts and Herron returns to Falcons' 41. Nick Mike-Mayer misses 45-yard field goal. Guy punts into Falcons' end zone. James punts to Raiders' 39. Blanda kicks 36-yard field goal at 15:00.

Dec. 14, 1975—Baltimore 10, Miami 7, at Baltimore; Dolphins win toss. Seiple punts to Colts' 4. Linhart kicks 31-yard field goal at 12:44.

Sept. 19, 1976—Minnesota 10, Los Angeles 10, at Minnesota; Vikings win toss. Tarkenton's pass intercepted by Monte Jackson and returned to Minnesota 16. Allen blocks Dempsey's 30-yard field goal attempt, ball rolls into end zone for touchback. Clabo punts and Scribner returns to Rams' 20. Rusty Jackson punts to Vikings' 35. Tarkenton's pass intercepted by Kay at Rams' 1, no return. Game ends with Rams on own 3.

***Sept. 27, 1976—Washington 20, Philadelphia 17,** at Philadelphia; Eagles win toss. Jones punts and E. Brown loses one yard on return to Redskins' 40. Bragg punts 51 yards into end zone for touchback. Jones punts and E. Brown returns to Redskins' 42. Bragg punts and Marshall returns to Eagles' 41. Boryla's pass intercepted by Dusek at Redskins' 37, no return. Bragg punts and Bradley returns. Philadelphia holding penalty moves ball back to Eagles' 8. Boryla pass intercepted by E. Brown and returned to Eagles' 22. Moseley kicks 29-yard field goal at 12:49.

Oct. 17, 1976—Kansas City 20, Miami 17, at Miami; Chiefs win toss. Wilson punts into end zone for touchback. Bulaich fumbles into Kansas City end zone, Collier recovers for touchback. Stenerud kicks 34-yard field goal at 14:48.

Oct. 31, 1976—St. Louis 23, San Francisco 20, at St. Louis; Cardinals win toss. Joyce punts and Leonard fumbles on return, Jones recovers at 49ers' 43. Bakken kicks 21-yard field goal at 6:42.

Dec. 5, 1976—San Diego 13, San Francisco 7, at San Diego; Chargers win toss. Morris runs 13 yards for touchdown at 5:12.

Sept. 18, 1977—Dallas 16, Minnesota 10, at Minnesota; Vikings win toss. Dallas starts on Vikings' 47 after a punt early in the overtime period. Staubach scores seven plays later on a four-yard run at 6:14.

***Sept. 26, 1977—Cleveland 30, New England 27,** at Cleveland; Browns win toss. Sipe throws a 22-yard pass to Logan at Patriots' 19. Cockroft kicks 35-yard field goal at 4:45.

Oct. 16, 1977—Minnesota 22, Chicago 16, at Minnesota; Bears win toss. Parsons punts 53 yards to Vikings' 18. Minnesota drives to Bears' 11. On a first-and-10, Vikings fake a field goal and holder Krause hits Voigt with a touchdown pass at 6:45.

Oct. 30, 1977—Cincinnati 13, Houston 10, at Cincinnati; Bengals win toss. Bahr kicks a 22-yard field goal at 5:51.

Nov. 13, 1977—San Francisco 10, New Orleans 7, at New Orleans; Saints win toss. Saints fail to move ball and Blanchard punts to 49ers' 41. Wersching kicks a 33-yard field goal at 6:33.

Dec. 18, 1977—Chicago 12, New York Giants 9, at East Rutherford, N.J.; Giants win toss. The ball changes hands eight times before Thomas kicks a 28-yard field goal at 14:51.

Sept. 10, 1978—Cleveland 13, Cincinnati 10, at Cleveland; Browns win toss. Collins returns kickoff 41 yards to Browns' 47. Cockroft kicks 27-yard field goal at 4:30.

***Sept. 11, 1978—Minnesota 12, Denver 9,** at Minnesota; Vikings win toss. Danmeier kicks 44-yard field goal at 2:56.

Sept. 24, 1978—Pittsburgh 15, Cleveland 9, at Pittsburgh; Steelers win toss. Cunningham scores on a 37-yard "gadget" pass from Bradshaw at 3:43. Steelers start winning drive on their 21.

Sept. 24, 1978—Denver 23, Kansas City 17, at Kansas City; Broncos win toss. Dilts punts to Kansas City. Chiefs advance to Broncos' 40 where Reed fails to make first down on fourth-and-one situation. Broncos march downfield. Preston scores two-yard touchdown at 10:28.

Oct. 1, 1978—Oakland 25, Chicago 19, at Chicago; Bears win toss. Both teams punt on first possession. On Chicago's second offensive series, Colzie intercepts Avellini's pass and returns it to Bears' 3. Three plays later, Whittington runs two yards for a touchdown at 5:19.

Oct. 15, 1978—Dallas 24, St. Louis 21, at St. Louis; Cowboys win toss. Dallas drives from its 23 into field goal range. Septien kicks 27-yard field goal at 3:28.

Oct. 29, 1978—Denver 20, Seattle 17, at Seattle; Broncos win toss. Ball changes hands four times before Turner kicks 18-yard field goal at 12:59.

Nov. 12, 1978—San Diego 29, Kansas City 23, at San Diego; Chiefs win toss. Fouts hits Jefferson for decisive 14-yard touchdown pass on the last play (15:00) of overtime period.

Nov. 12, 1978—Washington 16, New York Giants 13, at Washington; Redskins win toss. Moseley kicks winning 45-yard field goal at 8:32 after missing first down field goal attempt of 35 yards at 4:50.

Nov. 26, 1978—Green Bay 10, Minnesota 10, at Green Bay; Packers win toss. Both teams have possession of the ball four times.

Dec. 9, 1978—Cleveland 37, New York Jets 34, at Cleveland; Browns win toss. Cockroft kicks 22-yard field goal at 3:07.

Sept. 2, 1979—Atlanta 40, New Orleans 34, at New Orleans; Falcons win toss. Bartkowski's pass intercepted by Myers and returned to Falcons' 46. Erxleben punts to Falcons' 4. James punts to Chandler on Saints' 43. Erxleben punts and Ryckman returns to Falcons' 28. James punts and Chandler returns to Saints' 36. Erxleben retrieves punt snap on Saints' 1 and attempts pass. Mayberry intercepts and returns six yards for touchdown at 8:22.

Sept. 2, 1979—Cleveland 25, New York Jets 22, at New York; Jets win toss. Leahy's 43-yard field goal attempt goes wide right at 4:41. Evans's punt blocked by Dykes is recovered by Newton. Ramsey punts into end zone for touchback. Evans punts and Harper returns to Jets' 24. Robinson's pass intercepted by Davis and returned 33 yards to Jets' 31. Cockroft kicks 27-yard field goal at 14:45.

***Sept. 3, 1979—Pittsburgh 16, New England 13,** at Foxboro; Patriots win toss. Hare punts to Swann at Steelers' 31. Bahr kicks 41-yard field goal at 5:10.

Sept. 9, 1979—Tampa Bay 29, Baltimore 26, at Baltimore; Colts win toss. Landry fumbles, recovered by Kollar at Colts' 14. O'Donoghue kicks 31-yard, first-down field goal at 1:41.

Sept. 16, 1979—Denver 20, Atlanta 17, at Atlanta; Broncos win toss. Broncos march 65 yards to Falcons' 7. Turner kicks 24-yard field goal at 6:15.

Sept. 23, 1979—Houston 30, Cincinnati 27, at Cincinnati; Oilers win toss. Parsley punts and Lusby returns to Bengals' 33. Bahr's 32-yard field goal attempt is wide right at 8:05. Parsley's punt downed on Bengals' 5. McInally punts and Ellender returns to Bengals' 42. Fritsch's third down, 29-yard field goal attempt hits left upright and bounces through at 14:28.

Sept. 23, 1979—Minnesota 27, Green Bay 21, at Minnesota; Vikings win toss. Kramer throws 50-yard touchdown pass to Rashad at 3:18.

Oct. 28, 1979—Houston 27, New York Jets 24, at Houston; Oilers win toss. Oilers march 58 yards to Jets' 18. Fritsch kicks 35-yard field goal at 5:10.

Nov. 18, 1979—Cleveland 30, Miami 24, at Cleveland; Browns win toss. Sipe passes 39 yards to Rucker for touchdown at 1:59.

Nov. 25, 1979—Pittsburgh 33, Cleveland 30, at Pittsburgh; Browns win toss. Sipe's pass intercepted by Blount on Steelers' 4. Bradshaw pass intercepted by Bolton on Browns' 12. Evans punts and Bell returns to Steelers' 17. Bahr kicks 37-yard field goal at 14:51.

Nov. 25, 1979—Buffalo 16, New England 13, at Foxboro; Patriots win toss. Hare's punt downed on Bills' 38. Jackson punts and Morgan returns to Patriots' 20. Grogan's pass intercepted by Haslett and returned to Bills' 42. Ferguson's 51-yard pass to Butler sets up N. Mike-Mayer's 29-yard field goal at 9:15.

Dec. 2, 1979—Los Angeles 27, Minnesota 21, at Los Angeles; Rams win toss. Clark punts and Miller returns to Vikings' 25. Kramer's pass intercepted by Brown and returned to Rams' 40. Cromwell, holding for 22-yard field goal attempt, runs around left end untouched for winning score at 6:53.

Sept. 7, 1980—Green Bay 12, Chicago 6, at Green Bay; Bears win toss. Parsons punts and Nixon returns 16 yards. Five plays later, Marcol returns own blocked field goal attempt 24 yards for touchdown at 6:00.

Sept. 14, 1980—San Diego 30, Oakland 24, at San Diego; Raiders win toss. Pastorini's first-down pass intercepted by Edwards. Millen intercepts Fouts' first-down pass and returns to San Diego 46. Bahr's 50-yard field goal attempt partially blocked by Williams and recovered on Chargers' 32. Eight plays later, Fouts throws 24-yard touchdown pass to Jefferson at 8:09.

Sept. 14, 1980—San Francisco 24, St. Louis 21, at San Francisco; Cardinals win toss. Swider punts and Robinson returns to 49ers' 32. San Francisco drives 52 yards to St. Louis 16, where Wersching kicks 33-yard field goal at 4:12.

Oct. 12, 1980—Green Bay 14, Tampa Bay 14, at Tampa Bay; Packers win toss. Teams trade punts twice. Lee returns second Tampa Bay punt to Green Bay 42. Dickey completes three passes to Buccaneers' 18, where Birney's 36-yard field goal attempt is wide right as time expires.

Nov. 9, 1980—Atlanta 33, St. Louis 27, at St. Louis; Falcons win toss. Strong runs 21 yards for touchdown at 4:20.

#**Nov. 20, 1980—San Diego 27, Miami 24,** at Miami; Chargers win toss. Partridge punts into end zone, Dolphins take over on their own 20. Woodley's pass for Nathan intercepted by Lowe and returned 28 yards to Dolphins' 12. Benirschke kicks 28-yard field goal at 7:14.

Nov. 23, 1980—New York Jets 31, Houston 28, at New York; Jets win toss. Leahy kicks 38-yard field goal at 3:58.

Nov. 27, 1980—Chicago 23, Detroit 17, at Detroit; Bears win toss. Williams returns kickoff 95 yards for touchdown at 0:21.

Dec. 7, 1980—Buffalo 10, Los Angeles 7, at Buffalo; Rams win toss. Corral punts and Hooks returns to Bills' 34. Ferguson's 30-yard pass to Lewis sets up N. Mike-Mayer's 30-yard field goal at 5:14.

Dec. 7, 1980—San Francisco 38, New Orleans 35, at San Francisco; Saints win toss. Erxleben's punt downed by Hardy on 49ers' 27. Wersching kicks 36-yard field goal at 7:40.

*__Dec. 8, 1980—Miami 16, New England 13,__ at Miami; Dolphins win toss. Von Schamann kicks 23-yard field goal at 3:20.

Dec. 14, 1980—Cincinnati 17, Chicago 14, at Chicago; Bengals win toss. Breech kicks 28-yard field goal at 4:23.

Dec. 21, 1980—Los Angeles 20, Atlanta 17, at Los Angeles; Rams win toss. Corral's punt downed at Rams' 37. James punts into end zone for touchback. Corral's punt downed on Falcons' 17. Bartkowski fumbles when hit by Harris, recovered by Delaney. Corral kicks 23-yard field goal on first play of possession at 7:00.

Sept. 27, 1981—Cincinnati 27, Buffalo 24, at Cincinnati; Bills win toss. Cater punts into end zone for touchback. Bengals drive to the Bills' 10 where Breech kicks 28-yard field goal at 9:33.

Sept. 27, 1981—Pittsburgh 27, New England 21, at Pittsburgh; Patriots win toss. Hubach punts and Smith returns five yards to midfield. Four plays later Bradshaw throws 24-yard touchdown pass to Swann at 3:19.

Oct. 4, 1981—Miami 28, New York Jets 28, at Miami; Jets win toss. Teams trade punts twice. Leahy's 48-yard field goal attempt is wide right as time expires.

Oct. 25, 1981—New York Giants 27, Atlanta 24, at Atlanta; Giants win toss. Jennings' punt goes out of bounds at New York 47. Bright returns Atlanta punt to Giants' 14. Woerner fair catches punt at own 28. Andrews fumbles on first play, recovered by Van Pelt. Danelo kicks 40-yard field goal four plays later at 9:20.

Oct. 25, 1981—Chicago 20, San Diego 17, at Chicago; Bears win toss. Teams trade punts. Bears' second punt returned by Brooks to Chargers' 33. Fouts pass intercepted by Fencik and returned 32 yards to San Diego 27. Roveto kicks 27-yard field goal seven plays later at 9:30.

Nov. 8, 1981—Chicago 16, Kansas City 13, at Kansas City; Bears win toss. Teams trade punts. Kansas City takes over on downs on its own 38. Fuller's fumble recovered by Harris on Chicago 36. Roveto's 37-yard field goal wide, but Chiefs penalized for leverage. Roveto's 22-yard field goal attempt three plays later is good at 13:07.

Nov. 8, 1981—Denver 23, Cleveland 20, at Denver; Browns win toss. D. Smith recovers Hill's fumble at Denver 48. Morton's 33-yard pass to Upchurch and six-yard run by Preston set up Steinfort's 30-yard field goal at 4:10.

Nov. 8, 1981—Miami 30, New England 27, at New England; Dolphins win toss. Orosz punts and Morgan returns six yards to New England 26. Grogan's pass intercepted by Brudzinski who returns 19 yards to Patriots' 26. Von Schamann kicks 30-yard field goal on first down at 7:09.

Nov. 15, 1981—Washington 30, New York Giants 27, at New York; Giants win toss. Nelms returns Giants' punt 26 yards to New York 47. Five plays later Moseley kicks 48-yard field goal at 3:44.

Dec. 20, 1981—New York Giants 13, Dallas 10, at New York; Cowboys win toss and kick off. Jennings punts to Dallas 40. Taylor recovers Dorsett's fumble on second down. Danelo's 33-yard field goal attempt hits right upright and bounces back. White's pass for Pearson intercepted by Hunt and returned seven yards to Dallas 24. Four plays later Danelo kicks 35-yard field goal at 6:19.

Sept. 12, 1982—Washington 37, Philadelphia 34, at Philadelphia; Redskins win toss. Theismann completes five passes for 63 yards to set up Moseley's 26-yard field goal at 4:47.

Sept. 19, 1982—Pittsburgh 26, Cincinnati 20, at Pittsburgh; Bengals win toss. Anderson's pass intended for Kreider intercepted by Woodruff and returned 30 yards to Cincinnati 2. Bradshaw completes two-yard touchdown pass to Stallworth on first down at 1:08.

Dec. 19, 1982—Baltimore 20, Green Bay 20, at Baltimore; Packers win toss. K. Anderson intercepts Dickey's first-down pass and returns to Packers' 42. Miller's 44-yard field goal attempt blocked by G. Lewis. Teams trade punts before Stenerud's 47-yard field goal attempt is wide right. Teams trade punts again before time expires in Colts possession.

Jan. 2, 1983—Tampa Bay 26, Chicago 23, at Tampa Bay; Bears win toss. Parsons punts to T. Bell at Buccaneers' 40. Capece kicks 33-yard field goal at 3:14.

Sept. 4, 1983—Baltimore 29, New England 23, at New England; Patriots win toss. Cooks runs 52 yards with fumble recovery three plays into overtime at 0:30.

Sept. 4, 1983—Green Bay 41, Houston 38, at Houston; Packers win toss. Stenerud kicks 42-yard field goal at 5:55.

Sept. 11, 1983—New York Giants 16, Atlanta 13, at Atlanta; Giants win toss. Dennis returns kickoff 54 yards to Atlanta 41. Haji-Sheikh kicks 30-yard field goal at 3:38.

Sept. 18, 1983—New Orleans 34, Chicago 31, at New Orleans; Bears win toss. Parsons punts and Groth returns five yards to New Orleans 34. Stabler pass intercepted by Schmidt at Chicago 47. Parsons punt downed by Gentry at New Orleans 2. Stabler gains 36 yards in four passes; Wilson 38 in six carries. Andersen kicks 41-yard field goal at 10:57.

Sept. 18, 1983—Minnesota 19, Tampa Bay 16, at Tampa; Vikings win toss. Coleman punts and Bell returns eight yards to Tampa Bay 47. Capece's 33-yard field goal attempt sails wide at 7:26. Dils and Young combine for 48-yard gain to Tampa Bay 27. Ricardo kicks 42-yard field goal at 9:27.

Sept. 25, 1983—Baltimore 22, Chicago 19, at Baltimore; Colts win toss. Allegre kicks 33-yard field goal nine plays later at 4:51.

Sept. 25, 1983—Cleveland 30, San Diego 24, at San Diego; Browns win toss. Walker returns kickoff 33 yards to Cleveland 37. Sipe completes 48-yard touchdown pass to Holt four plays later at 1:53.

Sept. 25, 1983—New York Jets 27, Los Angeles Rams 24, at New York; Jets win toss. Ramsey punts to Irvin who returns to 25 but penalty puts Rams on own 13. Holmes 30-yard interception return sets up Leahy's 26-yard field goal at 3:22.

Oct. 9, 1983—Buffalo 38, Miami 35, at Miami; Dolphins win toss. Von Schamann's 52-yard field goal attempt goes wide at 12:36. Cater punts to Clayton who loses 11 to own 13. Von Schamann's 43-yard field goal attempt sails wide at 5:15. Danelo kicks 36-yard field goal nine plays later at 13:58.

Oct. 9, 1983—Dallas 27, Tampa Bay 24, at Dallas; Cowboys win toss. Septien's 51-yard field goal attempt goes wide but Buccaneers penalized for roughing kicker. Septien kicks 42-yard field goal at 4:38.

Oct. 23, 1983—Kansas City 13, Houston 10, at Houston; Chiefs win toss. Lowery kicks 41-yard field goal 13 plays later at 7:41.

Oct. 23, 1983—Minnesota 20, Green Bay 17, at Green Bay; Packers win toss. Scribner's punt downed on Vikings' 42. Ricardo kicks 32-yard field goal eight plays later at 5:05.

*__Oct. 24, 1983—New York Giants 20, St. Louis 20,__ at St. Louis; Cardinals win toss. Teams trade punts before O'Donoghue's 44-yard field goal attempt is wide left. Jennings' punt returned by Bird to St. Louis 21. Lomax pass intercepted by Haynes who loses six yards to New York 33. Jennings' punt downed on St. Louis 17. O'Donoghue's 19-yard field goal attempt is wide right. Rutledge's pass intercepted by L. Washington who returns 25 yards to New York 25. O'Donoghue's 42-yard field goal attempt is wide right. Rutledge's pass intercepted by W. Smith at St. Louis 33 to end game.

Oct. 30, 1983—Cleveland 25, Houston 19, at Cleveland; Oilers win toss. Teams trade punts. Nielsen's pass intercepted by Whitwell who returns to Houston 20. Green runs 20 yards for touchdown on first down at 6:34.

Nov. 20, 1983—Detroit 23, Green Bay 20, at Milwaukee; Packers win toss. Scribner punts and Jenkins returns 14 yards to Green Bay 45. Murray's 33-yard field goal attempt is wide left at 9:32. Whitehurst's pass intercepted by Watkins and returned to Green Bay 27. Murray kicks 37-yard field goal four plays later at 8:30.

Nov. 27, 1983—Atlanta 47, Green Bay 41, at Atlanta; Packers win toss. K. Johnson returns interception 31 yards for touchdown at 2:13.

Nov. 27, 1983—Seattle 51, Kansas City 48, at Seattle; Seahawks win toss. Dixon's 47-yard kickoff return sets up N. Johnson's 42-yard field goal at 1:36.

Dec. 11, 1983—New Orleans 20, Philadelphia 17, at Philadelphia; Eagles win toss. Runager punts to Groth who fair catches on New Orleans 32. Stabler completes two passes for 36 yards to Goodlow to set up Andersen's 50-yard field goal at 5:30.

*__Dec. 12, 1983—Green Bay 12, Tampa Bay 9,__ at Tampa; Packers win toss. Stenerud kicks 23-yard field goal 11 plays later at 4:07.

Sept. 9, 1984—Detroit 27, Atlanta 24, at Atlanta; Lions win toss. Murray kicks 48-yard field goal nine plays later at 5:06.

Sept. 30, 1984—Tampa Bay 30, Green Bay 27, at Tampa; Packers win toss. Scribner punts 44 yards to Tampa Bay 2. Epps returns Garcia's punt three yards to Green Bay 27. Scribner's punt downed on Buccaneers' 33. Ariri kicks 46-yard field goal 11 plays later at 10:32.

Oct. 14, 1984—Detroit 13, Tampa Bay 7, at Detroit; Buccaneers win toss. Tampa Bay drives to Lions' 39 before Wilder fumbles. Five plays later Danielson hits Thompson with 37-yard touchdown pass at 4:34.

Oct. 21, 1984—Dallas 30, New Orleans 27, at Dallas; Cowboys win toss. Septien kicks 41-yard field goal eight plays later at 3:42.

Oct. 28, 1984—Denver 22, Los Angeles Raiders 19, at Los Angeles; Raiders win toss. Hawkins fumble recovered by Foley at Denver 7. Teams trade punts. Karlis' 42-yard field goal attempt is wide left. Teams trade punts. Wilson pass intercepted by R. Jackson at Los Angeles 45, returned 23 yards to Los Angeles 22. Karlis kicks 35-yard field goal two plays later at 15:00.

Nov. 4, 1984—Philadelphia 23, Detroit 23, at Detroit; Lions win toss. Lions drive to Eagles' 3 in eight plays. Murray's 21-yard field goal attempt hits right upright and bounces back. Jaworski's pass intercepted by Watkins at Detroit 5. Teams trade punts. Cooper returns Black's punt five yards to Eagles' 14. Time expires four plays later with Eagles on own 21.

Nov. 18, 1984—San Diego 34, Miami 28, at San Diego; Chargers win toss. McGee scores eight plays later on a 25-yard run at 3:17.

Dec. 2, 1984—Cincinnati 20, Cleveland 17, at Cleveland; Browns win toss. Simmons returns Cox's punt 30 yards to Cleveland 35. Breech kicks 35-yard field goal seven plays later at 4:34.

Dec. 2, 1984—Houston 23, Pittsburgh 20, at Houston; Oilers win toss. Cooper kicks 30-yard field goal 16 plays later at 5:53.

Sept. 8, 1985—St. Louis 27, Cleveland 24, at Cleveland; Cardinals win toss. O'Donoghue kicks 35-yard field goal nine plays later at 5:27.

Sept. 29, 1985—New York Giants 16, Philadelphia 10, at Philadelphia; Eagles win toss. Jaworski's pass tipped by Quick and intercepted by Patterson who returns 29 yards for touchdown at 0:55.

Oct. 20, 1985—Denver 13, Seattle 10, at Denver; Seahawks win toss. Teams trade punts twice. Krieg's pass intercepted by Hunter and returned to Seahawks' 15. Karlis kicks 24-yard field goal four plays later at 9:19.

Nov. 10, 1985—Philadelphia 23, Atlanta 17, at Philadelphia; Falcons win toss. Donnelly's 62-yard punt goes out of bounds at Eagles' 1. Jaworski completes 99-yard touchdown pass to Quick two plays later at 1:49.

Nov. 10, 1985—San Diego 40, Los Angeles Raiders 34, at San Diego; Chargers win toss. James scores on 17-yard run seven plays later at 3:44.

Nov. 17, 1985—Denver 30, San Diego 24, at Denver; Chargers win toss. Thomas' 40-yard field goal attempt blocked by Smith and returned 60 yards by Wright for touchdown at 4:45.

Nov. 24, 1985—New York Jets 16, New England 13, at New York; Jets win toss. Teams trade punts twice. Patriots' second punt returned 46 yards by Sohn to Patriots' 15. Leahy kicks 32-yard field goal one play later at 10:05.

Nov. 24, 1985—Tampa Bay 19, Detroit 16, at Tampa; Lions win toss. Teams trade punts. Lions' punt downed on Buccaneers' 38. Igwebuike kicks 24-yard field goal 11 plays later at 12:31.

Nov. 24, 1985—Los Angeles Raiders 31, Denver 28, at Los Angeles; Raiders win toss. Bahr kicks 32-yard field goal six plays later at 2:42.

Dec. 8, 1985—Los Angeles Raiders 17, Denver 14, at Denver; Broncos win toss. Teams trade punts twice. Elway's fumble recovered by Townsend at Broncos' 8. Bahr kicks 26-yard field goal one play later at 4:55.

Sept. 14, 1986—Chicago 13, Philadelphia 10, at Chicago; Eagles win toss. Crawford's fumble of kickoff recovered by Jackson at Eagles' 35. Butler kicks 23-yard field goal 10 plays later at 5:56.

Sept. 14, 1986—Cincinnati 36, Buffalo 33, at Cincinnati; Bills win toss. Zander intercepts Kelly's first-down pass and returns it to Bills' 17. Breech kicks 20-yard field goal two plays later at 0:56.

Sept. 21, 1986—New York Jets 51, Miami 45, at New York; Jets win toss. O'Brien completes 43-yard touchdown pass to Walker five plays later at 2:35.

Sept. 28, 1986—Pittsburgh 22, Houston 16, at Houston; Oilers win toss. Johnson's punt returned 41 yards by Woods to Oilers' 15. Abercrombie scores on three-yard run three plays later at 2:35.

Sept. 28, 1986—Atlanta 23, Tampa Bay 20, at Tampa; Falcons win toss. Teams trade punts. Luckhurst kicks 34-yard field goal 10 plays later at 12:35.

Oct. 5, 1986—Los Angeles Rams 26, Tampa Bay 20, at Anaheim; Rams win toss. Dickerson scores four plays later on 42-yard run at 2:16.

Oct. 12, 1986—Minnesota 27, San Francisco 24, at San Francisco; Vikings win toss. C. Nelson kicks 28-yard field goal nine plays later at 4:27.

Oct. 19, 1986—San Francisco 10, Atlanta 10, at Atlanta; Falcons win toss. Teams trade punts twice. Donnelly punts to 49ers' 27. The following play Wilson recovers Rice's fumble at 49ers' 46 as time expires.

Nov. 2, 1986—Washington 44, Minnesota 38, at Washington; Redskins win toss. Schroeder completes 38-yard touchdown pass to Clark four plays later at 1:46.

Nov. 20, 1986—Los Angeles Raiders 37, San Diego 31, at San Diego; Raiders win toss. Teams trade punts. Allen scores five plays later on 28-yard run at 8:33.

Nov. 23, 1986—Cleveland 37, Pittsburgh 31, at Cleveland; Browns win toss. Teams trade punts. Six plays later Kosar hits Slaughter with 36-yard touchdown pass at 6:37.

Nov. 30, 1986—Chicago 13, Pittsburgh 10, at Chicago; Bears win toss and kick off. Newsome's punt returned by Barnes to Chicago 49. Butler kicks 42-yard field goal five plays later at 3:55.

Nov. 30, 1986—Philadelphia 33, Los Angeles Raiders 27, at Los Angeles; Eagles win toss. Teams trade punts. Long recovers Cunningham's fumble at Philadelphia 42. Waters returns Allen's fumble 81 yards to Los Angeles 4. Cunningham scores on one-yard run two plays later at 6:53.

Nov. 30, 1986—Cleveland 13, Houston 10, at Cleveland; Oilers win toss and kick off. Gossett punts to Houston 39. Luck's pass intercepted by Minnifield at Cleveland 21. Gossett punts to Houston 34. Luck's pass intercepted by Minnifield at Cleveland 43 who returns 20 yards to Houston 37. Moseley kicks 29-yard field goal nine plays later at 14:44.

Dec. 7, 1986—St. Louis 10, Philadelphia 10, at Philadelphia; Cardinals win toss. White blocks Schubert's 40-yard field goal attempt. Teams trade punts. McFadden's 43-yard field goal attempt is wide left. Schubert's 37-yard field goal attempt is wide right. Cavanaugh's pass intercepted by Carter and returned to Eagles' 48 to end game.

Dec. 14, 1986—Miami 37, Los Angeles Rams 31, at Anaheim; Dolphins win toss. Marino completes 20-yard touchdown pass to Duper six plays later at 3:04.

Sept. 20, 1987—Denver 17, Green Bay 17, at Green Bay; Packers win toss. Del Greco's 47-yard field goal attempt is short. Teams trade punts. Elway intercepted by Noble who returns 10 yards to Green Bay 34. Davis fumbles on next play and Smith recovers. Two plays later, Karlis's 40-yard field goal attempt is wide left. Time expires two plays later with Packers on own 23.

Oct. 11, 1987—Detroit 19, Green Bay 16, at Green Bay; Lions win toss. Prindle's 42-yard field goal attempt is wide left. Packers punt downed on Detroit 17. Prindle kicks 31-yard field goal 16 plays later at 12:26.

Oct. 18, 1987—New York Jets 37, Miami 31, at New York; Jets win toss. Teams trade punts. Ryan intercepted by Hooper at Jets' 47 who returns 11 yards. Mackey intercepted by Haslett at Jets' 37 who returns 9 yards. Jets punt. Mackey intercepted by Radachowsky who returns 45 yards to Miami 24. Ryan completes eight-yard touchdown pass to Hunter five plays later at 14:26.

Oct. 18, 1987—Green Bay 16, Philadelphia 10, at Green Bay; Packers win toss. Hargrove scores on seven-yard run 10 plays later at 5:04.

Oct. 18, 1987—Buffalo 6, New York Giants 3, at Buffalo; Bills win toss. Schlopy's 28-yard field goal attempt is wide left. Teams trade punts. Rutledge intercepted by Clark who returns 23 yards to Buffalo 40. Schlopy kicks 27-yard field goal nine plays later at 14:41.

Oct. 25, 1987—Buffalo 34, Miami 31, at Miami; Bills win toss. Norwood kicks 27-yard field goal seven plays later at 4:12.

Nov. 1, 1987—San Diego 27, Cleveland 24, at San Diego; Browns win toss. Kosar intercepted by Glenn who returns 20 yards to Browns' 25. Abbott kicks 33-yard field goal three plays later at 2:16.

Nov. 15, 1987—Dallas 23, New England 17, at New England; Cowboys win toss. Walker scores on 60-yard run four plays later at 1:50.

Nov. 26, 1987—Minnesota 44, Dallas 38, at Dallas; Vikings win toss. Coleman's punt downed by Hilton at Cowboys' 37. White intercepted by Studwell who returns 12 yards to Vikings' 37. D. Nelson scores on 24-yard run seven plays later at 7:51.

Nov. 29, 1987—Philadelphia 34, New England 31, at New England; Patriots win toss. Ramsey intercepted by Joyner who returns 29 yards to Eagles' 32. Fryar fair catches Teltschik's punt at Patriots' 13. Franklin's 46-yard field goal attempt is short. McFadden's 39-yard field goal attempt is wide left. Tatupu fumbles on next play and Cobb recovers. McFadden kicks 38-yard field goal four plays later at 12:16.

Dec. 6, 1987—New York Giants 23, Philadelphia 20, at New York; Giants win toss and kick off. Teams trade punts twice. Teltschik's punt is returned 16 yards by McConkey to Eagles' 33. Three plays later, Allegre's 50-yard field goal attempt is blocked by Joyner and returned 25 yards by Hoage to Eagles' 30. McConkey returns Teltschik's punt four yards to Giants' 44. Allegre kicks 28-yard field goal four plays later at 10:42.

Dec. 6, 1987—Cincinnati 30, Kansas City 27, at Cincinnati; Bengals win toss. Teams trade punts. Breech kicks 32-yard field goal 16 plays later at 9:44.

Dec. 26, 1987—Washington 27, Minnesota 24, at Minnesota; Redskins win toss. Haji-Sheikh kicks 26-yard field goal six plays later at 2:09.

Sept. 4, 1988—Houston 17, Indianapolis 14, at Indianapolis; Colts win toss. Dickerson fumble recovered by Odom who returns six yards to Colts' 42. Zendejas kicks 35-yard field goal six plays later at 3:51.

***Sept. 26, 1988—Los Angeles Raiders 30, Denver 27,** at Denver; Broncos win toss. Teams trade punts twice. Elway intercepted by Lee who returns 20 yards to Broncos' 31. Bahr kicks 35-yard field goal four plays later at 12:35.

Oct. 2, 1988—New York Jets 17, Kansas City 17, at New York; Chiefs win toss. Chiefs punt goes into end zone for touchback. Leahy's 44-yard field goal attempt is wide right. Chiefs punt is returned by Townsell to Jets' 26. Burruss recovers McNeil's fumble at Chiefs' 11. DeBerg intercepted by Humphery at Jets' 49. Three plays later, time expires.

Oct. 9, 1988—Denver 16, San Francisco 13, at San Francisco; Broncos win toss and kick off. Young intercepted by Haynes at Broncos' 32. Denver punt downed at 49ers' 5. Young intercepted by Wilson who returns seven yards to 49ers' 5. Karlis kicks 22-yard field goal two plays later at 8:11.

Oct. 30, 1988—New York Giants 13, Detroit 10, at Detroit; Lions win toss. James's fumble recovered by Taylor at Lions' 22. Three plays later, McFadden kicks 33-yard field goal at 1:13.

Nov. 20, 1988—Buffalo 9, New York Jets 6, at Buffalo; Jets win toss. Vick's fumble recovered by Bennett at Bills' 32. Norwood kicks 30-yard field goal five plays later at 3:47.

Nov. 20, 1988—Philadelphia 23, New York Giants 17, at New York; Eagles win toss. Philadelphia's punt goes into end zone for touchback. Hostetler intercepted by Hoage who returns 11 yards to Giants' 41. Six plays later, Zendejas's 30-yard field-goal attempt is blocked and ball is recovered behind line of scrimmage by Eagles' Simmons, who runs 15 yards for touchdown at 3:09.

Dec. 11, 1988—New England 10, Tampa Bay 7, at New England; Buccaneers win toss and kick off. Staurovsky kicks 27-yard field goal six plays later at 3:08.

Dec. 17, 1988—Cincinnati 20, Washington 17, at Cincinnati; Bengals win toss. Cincinnati's punt returned by Oliphant to Redskins' 16. Grant recovers Williams's fumble at Redskins' 17. Breech kicks 20-yard field goal three plays later at 7:01.

*indicates Monday night game
#indicates Thursday night game

Postseason

Dec. 28, 1958—Baltimore 23, New York Giants 17, at New York; Giants win toss. Maynard returns kickoff to Giants' 20. Chandler punts and Taseff returns one yard to Colts' 20. Colts win at 8:15 on a one-yard run by Ameche.

Dec. 23, 1962—Dallas Texans 20, Houston Oilers 17, at Houston; Texans win toss and kick off. Jancik returns kickoff to Oilers' 33. Norton punts and Jackson makes fair catch on Texans' 22. Wilson punts and Jancik makes fair catch on Oilers' 45. Robinson intercepts Blanda's pass and returns 13 yards to Oilers' 47. Wilson's punt rolls dead at Oilers' 12. Hull intercepts Blanda's pass and returns 23 yards to midfield. Texans win at 17:54 on a 25-yard field goal by Brooker.

Dec. 26, 1965—Green Bay 13, Baltimore 10, at Green Bay; Packers win toss. Moore returns kickoff to Packers' 22. Chandler punts and Haymond returns nine yards to Colts' 41. Gilburg punts and Wood makes fair catch at Packers' 21. Chandler punts and Haymond returns one yard to Colts' 41. Michaels misses 47-yard field goal. Packers win at 13:39 on 25-yard field goal by Chandler.

Dec. 25, 1971—Miami 27, Kansas City 24, at Kansas City; Chiefs win toss. Podolak, after a lateral from Buchanan, returns kickoff to Chiefs' 46. Stenerud's 42-yard field goal is blocked. Seiple punts and Podolak makes fair catch at Chiefs' 17. Wilson punts and Scott returns 18 yards to Dolphins' 39. Yepremian misses 62-yard field goal. Scott intercepts Dawson's pass and returns 13 yards to Dolphins' 46. Seiple punts and Podolak loses one yard to Chiefs' 15. Wilson punts and Scott makes fair catch on Dolphins' 30. Dolphins win at 22:40 on a 37-yard field goal by Yepremian.

Dec. 24, 1977—Oakland 37, Baltimore 31, at Baltimore; Colts win toss. Raiders start on own 42 following a punt late in the first overtime. Oakland works way into a threatening position on Stabler's 19-yard pass to Branch at Colts' 26. Four plays later, on the second play of the second overtime, Stabler hits Casper with a 10-yard touchdown pass at 15:43.

Jan. 2, 1982—San Diego 41, Miami 38, at Miami; Chargers win toss. San Diego drives from its 13 to Miami 8. On second-and-goal, Benirschke misses 27-yard field goal attempt wide left at 9:15. Miami has the ball twice and San Diego twice more before the Dolphins get their third possession. Miami drives from the San Diego 46 to Chargers' 17 and on fourth-and-two, von Schamann's 34-yard field goal attempt is blocked by San Diego's Winslow after 11:27. Fouts then completes four of five passes, including a 29-yarder to Joiner that puts the ball on Dolphins' 10. On first down, Benirschke kicks a 20-yard field goal at 13:52. San Diego's winning drive covered 74 yards in six plays.

Jan. 3, 1987—Cleveland 23, New York Jets 20, at Cleveland; Jets win toss. Jets' punt downed at Browns' 26. Moseley's 23-yard field goal attempt is wide right. Teams trade punts. Jets' second punt downed at Browns' 31. First overtime period expires eight plays later with Browns in possession at Jets' 42. Moseley kicks 27-yard field goal four plays into second overtime at 17:02.

Jan. 11, 1987—Denver 23, Cleveland 20, at Cleveland; Browns win toss. Broncos hold Browns on four downs. Browns' punt returned four yards to Denver's 25. Elway completes 22- and 28-yard passes to set up Karlis's 33-yard field goal nine plays into drive at 5:38.

Jan. 3, 1988—Houston 23, Seattle 20, at Houston. Seahawks win toss. Rodriguez punts to K. Johnson who returns one yard to Houston 15. Zendejas kicks 32-yard field goal 12 plays later at 8:05.

NFL Postseason Overtime Games (By Length of Game)

Dec. 25, 1971	Miami 27, KANSAS CITY 24	82:40
Dec. 23, 1962	Dallas Texans 20, HOUSTON 17	77:54
Jan. 3, 1987	CLEVELAND 23, New York Jets 20	77:02
Dec. 24, 1977	Oakland 37, BALTIMORE 31	75:43
Jan. 2, 1982	San Diego 41, MIAMI 38	73:52
Dec. 26, 1965	GREEN BAY 13, Baltimore 10	73:39
Dec. 28, 1958	Baltimore 23, N.Y. GIANTS 17	68:15
Jan. 3, 1988	HOUSTON 23, Seattle 20	68:05
Jan. 11, 1987	Denver 23, CLEVELAND 20	65:38

Home team in CAPS

Overtime Won-Lost Records, 1974-1988 (Regular Season)

	W	L	T
Atlanta	4	7	1
Buffalo	6	2	0
Chicago	6	7	0
Cincinnati	7	3	0
Cleveland	9	6	0
Dallas	6	3	0
Denver	9	4	2
Detroit	4	4	1
Green Bay	4	6	4
Houston	4	7	0
Indianapolis	3	2	1
Kansas City	3	5	1
Los Angeles Raiders	7	4	0
Los Angeles Rams	4	3	1
Miami	3	9	1
Minnesota	7	4	2
New England	1	10	0
New Orleans	2	4	0
New York Giants	6	6	1
New York Jets	6	4	2
Philadelphia	4	7	2
Phoenix	3	4	2
Pittsburgh	6	3	1
San Diego	7	6	0
San Francisco	3	4	1
Seattle	1	2	0
Tampa Bay	4	7	1
Washington	7	3	0

Overtime Games By Year (Regular Season)

1988- 9	1980-13
1987-13	1979-12
1986-16	1978-11
1985-10	1977- 6
1984- 9	1976- 5
1983-19	1975- 9
1982- 4	1974- 2
1981-10	

Overtime Game Summary—1974-1988

There have been 148 overtime games in regular-season play since the rule was adopted in 1974. The breakdown follows:

103 times both teams had at least one possession (70%)

- 44 times the team which won the coin toss drove for winning score (29 FG, 15 TD) (30%)
- 75 times the team which won the coin toss won the game (51%)
- 61 times the team which lost the coin toss won the game (41%)
- 93 games were decided by a field goal (63%)
- 43 games were decided by a touchdown (29%)
- 12 games ended tied (8%). Last time: New York Jets 17, Kansas City 17; 10/2/88
- 72 times the home team won the game (49%)
- 64 times the visiting team won the game (43%)

Most Overtime Games, Season

5 Green Bay Packers, 1983

4 Denver Broncos, 1985

3 By many teams, last time: Green Bay Packers, New England Patriots, Philadelphia Eagles, 1987

Longest Consecutive Game Streaks Without Overtime (current)

71 games New Orleans Saints (last OT game, 10/21/84 vs. Dallas)

56 games Seattle Seahawks (last OT game, 10/25/85 vs. Denver)

40 games Atlanta Falcons (last OT game, 10/19/86 vs. San Francisco)

Shortest Overtime Games

0:21 Chicago 23, Detroit 17; 11/27/80—Initial overtime kickoff return for a touchdown.

0:30 Baltimore 29, New England 23; 9/4/83

0:55 New York Giants 16, Philadelphia 10; 9/29/85

Longest Overtime Games (All Postseason Games)

22:40 Miami 27, Kansas City 24; 12/25/71

17:54 Dallas Texans 20, Houston 17; 12/23/62

17:02 Cleveland 23, New York Jets 20; 1/3/87

There have been nine postseason overtime games dating back to 1958. In all cases, both teams had at least one possession. Last postseason overtime: Houston 23, Seattle 20; 1/3/88.

Overtime Scoring Summary

93 were decided by a field goal

17 were decided by a touchdown pass

16 were decided by a touchdown run

- 3 were decided by interceptions (Atlanta 40, New Orleans 34, 9/2/79; Atlanta 47, Green Bay 41, 11/27/83; New York Giants 16, Philadelphia 10; 9/29/85)
- 1 was decided by a kickoff return (Chicago 23, Detroit 17; 11/27/80)
- 1 was decided by a fumble recovery (Baltimore 29, New England 23; 9/4/83)
- 1 was decided on a fake field goal/touchdown run (Los Angeles Rams 27, Minnesota 21; 12/2/79)
- 1 was decided on a fake field goal/touchdown pass (Minnesota 22, Chicago 16; 10/16/77)
- 1 was decided on a blocked field goal (Denver 30, San Diego 24; 11/17/85)
- 1 was decided on a blocked field goal/recovery by kicker (Green Bay 12, Chicago 6; 9/7/80)
- 1 was decided on a blocked field goal/recovery by kicking team (Philadelphia 23, New York Giants 17; 11/20/88)

12 ended tied

Overtime Records

Longest Touchdown Pass

99 Yards—Ron Jaworski to Mike Quick, Philadelphia 23, Atlanta 17 (11/10/85)
50 Yards—Tommy Kramer to Ahmad Rashad, Minnesota 27, Green Bay 21 (9/23/79)
48 Yards—Brian Sipe to Harry Holt, Cleveland 30, San Diego 24 (9/23/83)

Longest Touchdown Run

60 Yards—Herschel Walker, Dallas 23, New England 17 (11/15/87)
42 Yards—Eric Dickerson, Los Angeles Rams 26, Tampa Bay 20 (10/5/86)
28 Yards—Marcus Allen, Los Angeles Raiders 37, San Diego 31 (11/20/86)

Longest Field Goal

50 Yards—Morten Andersen, New Orleans 20, Philadelphia 17 (12/11/83)
48 Yards—Eddie Murray, Detroit 27, Atlanta 24 (9/9/84);
Mark Moseley, Washington 30, New York Giants 27 (11/15/81)
46 Yards—Obed Ariri, Tampa Bay 30, Green Bay 27 (9/30/84)

Longest Touchdown Plays

99 Yards—(Pass) Ron Jaworski to Mike Quick, Philadelphia 23, Atlanta 17 (11/10/85)
60 Yards—(Blocked field goal return) Louis Wright, Denver 30, San Diego 24 (11/17/85)
(Run) Herschel Walker, Dallas 23, New England 17 (11/15/87)
52 Yards—(Fumble recovery) Johnie Cooks, Baltimore 29, New England 23 (9/4/83)

Chicago All-Star Game

Pro teams won 31, lost 9, and tied 2. The game was discontinued after 1976.

Year	Date	Winner	Loser	Attendance
1976*	July 23	Pittsburgh 24	All-Stars 0	52,895
1975	Aug. 1	Pittsburgh 21	All-Stars 14	54,103
1974		No game was played		
1973	July 27	Miami 14	All-Stars 3	54,103
1972	July 28	Dallas 20	All-Stars 7	54,162
1971	July 30	Baltimore 24	All-Stars 17	52,289
1970	July 31	Kansas City 24	All-Stars 3	69,940
1969	Aug. 1	N.Y. Jets 26	All-Stars 24	74,208
1968	Aug. 2	Green Bay 34	All-Stars 17	69,917
1967	Aug. 4	Green Bay 27	All-Stars 0	70,934
1966	Aug. 5	Green Bay 38	All-Stars 0	72,000
1965	Aug. 6	Cleveland 24	All-Stars 16	68,000
1964	Aug. 7	Chicago 28	All-Stars 17	65,000
1963	Aug. 2	All-Stars 20	Green Bay 17	65,000
1962	Aug. 3	Green Bay 42	All-Stars 20	65,000
1961	Aug. 4	Philadelphia 28	All-Stars 14	66,000
1960	Aug. 12	Baltimore 32	All-Stars 7	70,000
1959	Aug. 14	Baltimore 29	All-Stars 0	70,000
1958	Aug. 15	All-Stars 35	Detroit 19	70,000
1957	Aug. 9	N.Y. Giants 22	All-Stars 12	75,000
1956	Aug. 10	Cleveland 26	All-Stars 0	75,000
1955	Aug. 12	All-Stars 30	Cleveland 27	75,000
1954	Aug. 13	Detroit 31	All-Stars 6	93,470
1953	Aug. 14	Detroit 24	All-Stars 10	93,818
1952	Aug. 15	Los Angeles 10	All-Stars 7	88,316
1951	Aug. 17	Cleveland 33	All-Stars 0	92,180
1950	Aug. 11	All-Stars 17	Philadelphia 7	88,885
1949	Aug. 12	Philadelphia 38	All-Stars 0	93,780
1948	Aug. 20	Chi. Cardinals 28	All-Stars 0	101,220
1947	Aug. 22	All-Stars 16	Chi. Bears 0	105,840
1946	Aug. 23	All-Stars 16	Los Angeles 0	97,380
1945	Aug. 30	Green Bay 19	All-Stars 7	92,753
1944	Aug. 30	Chi. Bears 24	All-Stars 21	48,769
1943	Aug. 25	All-Stars 27	Washington 7	48,471
1942	Aug. 28	Chi. Bears 21	All-Stars 0	101,100
1941	Aug. 28	Chi. Bears 37	All-Stars 13	98,203
1940	Aug. 29	Green Bay 45	All-Stars 28	84,567
1939	Aug. 30	N.Y. Giants 9	All-Stars 0	81,456
1938	Aug. 31	All-Stars 28	Washington 16	74,250
1937	Sept. 1	All-Stars 6	Green Bay 0	84,560
1936	Sept. 3	All-Stars 7	Detroit 7 (tie)	76,000
1935	Aug. 29	Chi. Bears 5	All-Stars 0	77,450
1934	Aug. 31	Chi. Bears 0	All-Stars 0 (tie)	79,432

*Game shortened due to thunderstorms.

NFL Playoff Bowl

Western Conference won 8, Eastern Conference won 2. All games played at Miami's Orange Bowl.

1970	Los Angeles Rams 31, Dallas Cowboys 0
1969	Dallas Cowboys 17, Minnesota Vikings 13
1968	Los Angeles Rams 30, Cleveland Browns 6
1967	Baltimore Colts 20, Philadelphia Eagles 14
1966	Baltimore Colts 35, Dallas Cowboys 3
1965	St. Louis Cardinals 24, Green Bay Packers 17
1964	Green Bay Packers 40, Cleveland Browns 23
1963	Detroit Lions 17, Pittsburgh Steelers 10
1962	Detroit Lions 28, Philadelphia Eagles 10
1961	Detroit Lions 17, Cleveland Browns 16

Pro Football Hall of Fame Game

1962	New York Giants 21, St. Louis Cardinals 21
1963	Pittsburgh Steelers 16, Cleveland Browns 7
1964	Baltimore Colts 48, Pittsburgh Steelers 17
1965	Washington Redskins 20, Detroit Lions 3
1966	No game
1967	Philadelphia Eagles 28, Cleveland Browns 13
1968	Chicago Bears 30, Dallas Cowboys 24
1969	Green Bay Packers 38, Atlanta Falcons 24
1970	New Orleans Saints 14, Minnesota Vikings 13
1971	Los Angeles Rams (NFC) 17, Houston Oilers (AFC) 6
1972	Kansas City Chiefs (AFC) 23, New York Giants (NFC) 17
1973	San Francisco 49ers (NFC) 20, New England Patriots (AFC) 7
1974	St. Louis Cardinals (NFC) 21, Buffalo Bills (AFC) 13
1975	Washington Redskins (NFC) 17, Cincinnati Bengals (AFC) 9
1976	Denver Broncos (AFC) 10, Detroit Lions (NFC) 7
1977	Chicago Bears (NFC) 20, New York Jets (AFC) 6
1978	Philadelphia Eagles (NFC) 17, Miami Dolphins (AFC) 3
1979	Oakland Raiders (AFC) 20, Dallas Cowboys (NFC) 13
1980*	San Diego Chargers (AFC) 0, Green Bay Packers (NFC) 0
1981	Cleveland Browns (AFC) 24, Atlanta Falcons (NFC) 10
1982	Minnesota Vikings (NFC) 30, Baltimore Colts (AFC) 14
1983	Pittsburgh Steelers (AFC) 27, New Orleans Saints (NFC) 14
1984	Seattle Seahawks (AFC) 38, Tampa Bay Buccaneers (NFC) 0
1985	New York Giants (NFC) 21, Houston Oilers (AFC) 20
1986	New England Patriots (AFC) 21, St. Louis Cardinals (NFC) 16
1987	San Francisco 49ers (NFC) 20, Kansas City Chiefs (AFC) 7
1988	Cincinnati Bengals (AFC) 14, Los Angeles Rams (NFC) 7

*Game called with 5:29 remaining due to severe thunder & lightning.

NFL International Games

Date	Site	Teams
Aug. 12, 1950	Ottawa, Canada	N.Y. Giants 20, Ottawa Roughriders 6
Aug. 11, 1951	Ottawa, Canada	N.Y. Giants 38, Ottawa Roughriders 6
Aug. 5, 1959	Toronto, Canada	Chi. Cardinals 55, Tor. Argonauts 26
Aug. 6, 1960	Toronto, Canada	Pittsburgh 43, Toronto Argonauts 16
Aug. 15, 1960	Toronto, Canada	Chicago Bears 16, N.Y. Giants 7
Aug. 2, 1961	Toronto, Canada	St. Louis 36, Toronto Argonauts 7
Aug. 5, 1961	Montreal, Canada	Chi. Bears 34, Montreal Allouettes 16
Aug. 8, 1961	Hamilton, Canada	Hamilton Tiger-Cats 38, Buffalo 21
Aug. 11, 1969	Montreal, Canada	Pittsburgh 17, N.Y. Giants 13
Aug. 25, 1969	Montreal, Canada	Detroit 22, Boston Patriots 9
Aug. 16, 1976	Tokyo, Japan	St. Louis 20, San Diego 10
Aug. 5, 1978	Mexico City, Mexico	New Orleans 14, Philadelphia 7
Aug. 6, 1983	London, England	Minnesota 28, St. Louis 10
Aug. 3, 1986	London, England	Chicago Bears 17, Dallas 6
Aug. 9, 1987	London, England	Los Angeles Rams 28, Denver 27
July 31, 1988	London, England	Miami 27, San Francisco 21
Aug. 14, 1988	Goteborg, Sweden	Minnesota 28, Chicago 21
Aug. 18, 1988	Montreal, Canada	N.Y. Jets 11, Cleveland 7

NFL Paid Attendance

Year	Regular Season	Average	Postseason	Super Bowl
1988	13,539,848 (224 games)	60,446	658,317 (10)	75,129
1987*	11,406,166 (210 games)	54,315	656,977 (10)	73,302
1986	13,588,551 (224 games)	60,663	734,002 (10)	101,063
1985	13,345,047 (224 games)	59,567	710,768 (10)	73,818
1984	13,398,112 (224 games)	59,813	665,194 (10)	84,059
1983	13,277,222 (224 games)	59,273	675,513 (10)	72,932
1982**	7,367,438 (126 games)	58,472	1,033,153 (16)	103,667
1981	13,606,990 (224 games)	60,745	637,763 (10)	81,270
1980	13,392,230 (224 games)	59,787	624,430 (10)	75,500
1979	13,182,039 (224 games)	58,848	630,326 (10)	103,985
1978	12,771,800 (224 games)	57,017	624,388 (10)	79,641
1977	11,018,632 (196 games)	56,218	534,925 (8)	75,804
1976	11,070,543 (196 games)	56,482	492,884 (8)	103,438
1975	10,213,193 (182 games)	56,116	475,919 (8)	80,187
1974	10,236,322 (182 games)	56,244	438,664 (8)	80,997
1973	10,730,933 (182 games)	58,961	525,433 (8)	71,882
1972	10,445,827 (182 games)	57,395	483,345 (8)	90,182
1971	10,076,035 (182 games)	55,363	483,891 (8)	81,023
1970	9,533,333 (182 games)	52,381	458,493 (8)	79,204
1969	6,096,127 (112 games) NFL	54,430	162,279 (3)	80,562
	2,843,373 (70 games) AFL	40,620	167,088 (3)	
1968	5,882,313 (112 games) NFL	52,521	215,902 (3)	75,377
	2,635,004 (70 games) AFL	37,643	114,438 (2)	
1967	5,938,924 (112 games) NFL	53,026	166,208 (3)	75,546
	2,295,697 (63 games) AFL	36,439	53,330 (1)	
1966	5,337,044 (105 games) NFL	50,829	74,152 (1)	61,946†
	2,160,369 (63 games) AFL	34,291	42,080 (1)	
1965	4,634,021 (98 games) NFL	47,286	100,304 (2)	
	1,782,384 (56 games) AFL	31,828	30,361 (1)	
1964	4,563,049 (98 games) NFL	46,562	79,544 (1)	
	1,447,875 (56 games) AFL	25,855	40,242 (1)	
1963	4,163,643 (98 games) NFL	42,486	45,801 (1)	
	1,208,697 (56 games) AFL	21,584	63,171 (2)	
1962	4,003,421 (98 games) NFL	40,851	64,892 (1)	
	1,147,302 (56 games) AFL	20,487	37,981 (1)	
1961	3,986,159 (98 games) NFL	40,675	39,029 (1)	
	1,002,657 (56 games) AFL	17,904	29,556 (1)	
1960	3,128,296 (78 games) NFL	40,106	67,325 (1)	
	926,156 (56 games) AFL	16,538	32,183 (1)	
1959	3,140,000 (72 games)	43,617	57,545 (1)	
1958	3,006,124 (72 games)	41,752	123,659 (2)	
1957	2,836,318 (72 games)	39,393	119,579 (2)	
1956	2,551,263 (72 games)	35,434	56,836 (1)	
1955	2,521,836 (72 games)	35,026	85,693 (1)	
1954	2,190,571 (72 games)	30,425	43,827 (1)	
1953	2,164,585 (72 games)	30,064	54,577 (1)	
1952	2,052,126 (72 games)	28,502	97,507 (2)	
1951	1,913,019 (72 games)	26,570	57,522 (1)	
1950	1,977,753 (78 games)	25,356	136,647 (3)	
1949	1,391,735 (60 games)	23,196	27,980 (1)	
1948	1,525,243 (60 games)	25,421	36,309 (1)	
1947	1,837,437 (60 games)	30,624	66,268 (2)	
1946	1,732,135 (55 games)	31,493	58,346 (1)	
1945	1,270,401 (50 games)	25,408	32,178 (1)	
1944	1,019,649 (50 games)	20,393	46,016 (1)	
1943	969,128 (40 games)	24,228	71,315 (2)	
1942	887,920 (55 games)	16,144	36,006 (1)	
1941	1,108,615 (55 games)	20,157	55,870 (2)	
1940	1,063,025 (55 games)	19,328	36,034 (1)	
1939	1,071,200 (55 games)	19,476	32,279 (1)	
1938	937,197 (55 games)	17,040	48,120 (1)	
1937	963,039 (55 games)	17,510	15,878 (1)	
1936	816,007 (54 games)	15,111	29,545 (1)	
1935	638,178 (53 games)	12,041	15,000 (1)	
1934	492,684 (60 games)	8,211	35,059 (1)	

*Players 24-day strike reduced 224-game schedule to 210 games.
**Players 57-day strike reduced 224-game schedule to 126 games.
†Only Super Bowl that did not sell out.

NFL's 10 Biggest Attendance Weekends

(Paid Count)

Weekend	Games	Attendance
October 16-17, 1988	14	934,211
October 27-28, 1985	14	902,128
October 12-13, 1980	14	898,223
September 23-24, 1984	14	894,402
November 11-12, 1979	14	890,972
September 16, 19-20, 1983	14	886,323
September 11-12, 1988	14	885,815
November 20, 23-24, 1980	14	885,601
November 9-10, 1986	14	882,762
September 12-13, 1982	14	882,042

NFL's 10 Highest Scoring Weekends

Point Total	Date	Weekend
761	October 16-17, 1983	7th
736	October 25-26, 1987	7th
732	November 9-10, 1980	10th
725	November 24, 27-28, 1983	13th
711	November 26, 29-30, 1987	12th
710	November 28, December 1-2, 1985	13th
696	October 2-3, 1983	5th
676	September 21-22, 1980	3rd
675	October 23-24, 1983	8th
675	December 19-22, 1986	16th

Top 10 Televised Sports Events

(Based on A.C. Nielsen Figures)

Program	Date	Network	Share	Rating
Super Bowl XVI	1/24/82	CBS	73.0	49.1
Super Bowl XVII	1/30/83	NBC	69.0	48.6
Super Bowl XX	1/26/86	NBC	70.0	48.3
Super Bowl XII	1/15/78	CBS	67.0	47.2
Super Bowl XIII	1/21/79	NBC	74.0	47.1
Super Bowl XVIII	1/22/84	CBS	71.0	46.4
Super Bowl XIX	1/20/85	ABC	63.0	46.4
Super Bowl XIV	1/20/80	CBS	67.0	46.3
Super Bowl XXI	1/25/87	CBS	66.0	45.8
Super Bowl XI	1/9/77	NBC	73.0	44.4

Ten Most Watched TV Programs & Estimated Total Number of Viewers

(Based on A.C. Nielsen Figures)

Program	Date	Network	*Total Viewers
Super Bowl XX	Jan. 26, 1986	NBC	127,000,000
Super Bowl XXI	Jan. 25, 1987	CBS	122,640,000
M*A*S*H (Special)	Feb. 28, 1983	CBS	121,624,000
Super Bowl XIX	Jan. 20, 1985	ABC	115,936,000
Super Bowl XXII	Jan. 31, 1988	ABC	115,000,000
Super Bowl XXIII	Jan. 22, 1989	NBC	110,800,000
Super Bowl XVI	Jan. 24, 1982	CBS	110,230,000
Super Bowl XVII	Jan. 30, 1983	NBC	109,040,000
Super Bowl XII	Jan. 15, 1978	CBS	102,010,000
Roots, Part 8	Jan. 30, 1977	ABC	98,706,000

*Watched some portion of the broadcast

NUMBER-ONE DRAFT CHOICES

Season	Team	Player	Position	College
1989	Dallas	Troy Aikman	QB	UCLA
1988	Atlanta	Aundray Bruce	LB	Auburn
1987	Tampa Bay	Vinny Testaverde	QB	Miami
1986	Tampa Bay	Bo Jackson	RB	Auburn
1985	Buffalo	Bruce Smith	DE	Virginia Tech
1984	New England	Irving Fryar	WR	Nebraska
1983	Baltimore	John Elway	QB	Stanford
1982	New England	Kenneth Sims	DT	Texas
1981	New Orleans	George Rogers	RB	South Carolina
1980	Detroit	Billy Sims	RB	Oklahoma
1979	Buffalo	Tom Cousineau	LB	Ohio State
1978	Houston	Earl Campbell	RB	Texas
1977	Tampa Bay	Ricky Bell	RB	Southern California
1976	Tampa Bay	Lee Roy Selmon	DE	Oklahoma
1975	Atlanta	Steve Bartkowski	QB	California
1974	Dallas	Ed Jones	DE	Tennessee State
1973	Houston	John Matuszak	DE	Tampa
1972	Buffalo	Walt Patulski	DE	Notre Dame
1971	New England	Jim Plunkett	QB	Stanford
1970	Pittsburgh	Terry Bradshaw	QB	Louisiana Tech
1969	Buffalo (AFL)	O.J. Simpson	RB	Southern California
1968	Minnesota	Ron Yary	T	Southern California
1967	Baltimore	Bubba Smith	DT	Michigan State
1966	Atlanta	Tommy Nobis	LB	Texas
	Miami (AFL)	Jim Grabowski	RB	Illinois
1965	New York Giants	Tucker Frederickson	RB	Auburn
	Houston (AFL)	Lawrence Elkins	E	Baylor
1964	San Francisco	Dave Parks	E	Texas Tech
	Boston (AFL)	Jack Concannon	QB	Boston College
1963	Los Angeles	Terry Baker	QB	Oregon State
	Kansas City (AFL)	Buck Buchanan	DT	Grambling
1962	Washington	Ernie Davis	RB	Syracuse
	Oakland (AFL)	Roman Gabriel	QB	North Carolina State
1961	Minnesota	Tommy Mason	RB	Tulane
	Buffalo (AFL)	Ken Rice	G	Auburn
1960	Los Angeles	Billy Cannon	RB	Louisiana State
	(AFL had no formal first pick)			
1959	Green Bay	Randy Duncan	QB	Iowa
1958	Chicago Cardinals	King Hill	QB	Rice
1957	Green Bay	Paul Hornung	HB	Notre Dame
1956	Pittsburgh	Gary Glick	DB	Colorado A&M
1955	Baltimore	George Shaw	QB	Oregon
1954	Cleveland	Bobby Garrett	QB	Stanford
1953	San Francisco	Harry Babcock	E	Georgia
1952	Los Angeles	Bill Wade	QB	Vanderbilt
1951	New York Giants	Kyle Rote	HB	Southern Methodist
1950	Detroit	Leon Hart	E	Notre Dame
1949	Philadelphia	Chuck Bednarik	C	Pennsylvania
1948	Washington	Harry Gilmer	QB	Alabama
1947	Chicago Bears	Bob Fenimore	HB	Oklahoma A&M
1946	Boston	Frank Dancewicz	QB	Notre Dame
1945	Chicago Cardinals	Charley Trippi	HB	Georgia
1944	Boston	Angelo Bertelli	QB	Notre Dame
1943	Detroit	Frank Sinkwich	HB	Georgia
1942	Pittsburgh	Bill Dudley	HB	Virginia
1941	Chicago Bears	Tom Harmon	HB	Michigan
1940	Chicago Cardinals	George Cafego	HB	Tennessee
1939	Chicago Cardinals	Ki Aldrich	C	Texas Christian
1938	Cleveland	Corbett Davis	FB	Indiana
1937	Philadelphia	Sam Francis	FB	Nebraska
1936	Philadelphia	Jay Berwanger	HB	Chicago

Note: From 1947 through 1958, the first selection in the draft was a Bonus pick, awarded to the winner of a random draw. That club, in turn, forfeited its last-round draft choice. The winner of the Bonus choice was eliminated from future draws. The system was abolished after 1958, by which time all clubs had received a Bonus choice.

If club had no first-round selection, first player drafted is listed with round in parentheses.

Atlanta Falcons

Year	Player, College, Position
1966	Tommy Nobis, Texas, LB
	Randy Johnson, Texas A&I, QB
1967	Leo Carroll, San Diego State, DE (2)
1968	Claude Humphrey, Tennessee State, DE
1969	George Kunz, Notre Dame, T
1970	John Small, Citadel, LB
1971	Joe Profit, Northeast Louisiana, RB
1972	Clarence Ellis, Notre Dame, DB
1973	Greg Marx, Notre Dame, DT (2)
1974	Gerald Tinker, Kent State, WR (2)
1975	Steve Bartkowski, California, QB
1976	Bubba Bean, Texas A&M, RB
1977	Warren Bryant, Kentucky, T
	Wilson Faumuina, San Jose State, DT
1978	Mike Kenn, Michigan, T
1979	Don Smith, Miami, DE
1980	Junior Miller, Nebraska, TE
1981	Bobby Butler, Florida State, DB
1982	Gerald Riggs, Arizona State, RB
1983	Mike Pitts, Alabama, DE
1984	Rick Bryan, Oklahoma, DT
1985	Bill Fralic, Pittsburgh, T
1986	Tony Casillas, Oklahoma, NT
	Tim Green, Syracuse, LB
1987	Chris Miller, Oregon, QB
1988	Aundray Bruce, Auburn, LB
1989	Deion Sanders, Florida State, DB
	Shawn Collins, Northern Arizona, WR

Buffalo Bills

Year	Player, College, Position
1960	Richie Lucas, Penn State, QB
1961	Ken Rice, Auburn, T
1962	Ernie Davis, Syracuse, RB
1963	Dave Behrman, Michigan State, C
1964	Carl Eller, Minnesota, DE
1965	Jim Davidson, Ohio State, T
1966	Mike Dennis, Mississippi, RB
1967	John Pitts, Arizona State, S
1968	Haven Moses, San Diego State, WR
1969	O.J. Simpson, Southern California, RB
1970	Al Cowlings, Southern California, DE
1971	J. D. Hill, Arizona State, WR
1972	Walt Patulski, Notre Dame, DE
1973	Paul Seymour, Michigan, TE
	Joe DeLamielleure, Michigan State, G
1974	Reuben Gant, Oklahoma State, TE
1975	Tom Ruud, Nebraska, LB
1976	Mario Clark, Oregon, DB
1977	Phil Dokes, Oklahoma State, DT
1978	Terry Miller, Oklahoma State, RB
1979	Tom Cousineau, Ohio State, LB
	Jerry Butler, Clemson, WR
1980	Jim Ritcher, North Carolina State, C
1981	Booker Moore, Penn State, RB
1982	Perry Tuttle, Clemson, WR
1983	Tony Hunter, Notre Dame, TE
	Jim Kelly, Miami, QB
1984	Greg Bell, Notre Dame, RB
1985	Bruce Smith, Virginia Tech, DE
	Derrick Burroughs, Memphis State, DB
1986	Ronnie Harmon, Iowa, RB
	Will Wolford, Vanderbilt, T
1987	Shane Conlan, Penn State, LB
1988	Thurman Thomas, Oklahoma State, RB (2)
1989	Don Beebe, Chadron, Neb., WR (3)

Chicago Bears

Year	Player, College, Position
1936	Joe Stydahar, West Virginia, T
1937	Les McDonald, Nebraska, E
1938	Joe Gray, Oregon State, B
1939	Sid Luckman, Columbia, QB
	Bill Osmanski, Holy Cross, B
1940	Clyde (Bulldog) Turner, Hardin-Simmons, C
1941	Tom Harmon, Michigan, B
1942	Frankie Albert, Stanford, B
1943	Bob Steber, Missouri, B
1944	Ray Evans, Kansas, B
1945	Don Lund, Michigan, B
1946	Johnny Lujack, Notre Dame, QB
1947	Bob Fenimore, Oklahoma State, B
	Don Kindt, Wisconsin, B
1948	Bobby Layne, Texas, QB
	Max Bumgardner, Texas, E
1949	Dick Harris, Texas, C
1950	Chuck Hunsinger, Florida, B
	Fred Morrison, Ohio State, B
1951	Bob Williams, Notre Dame, B
	Billy Stone, Bradley, B
	Gene Schroeder, Virginia, E
1952	Jim Dooley, Miami, B
1953	Billy Anderson, Compton (Calif.) J.C., B
1954	Stan Wallace, Illinois, B
1955	Ron Drzewiecki, Marquette, B
1956	Menan (Tex) Schriewer, Texas, E
1957	Earl Leggett, Louisiana State, T
1958	Chuck Howley, West Virginia, G
1959	Don Clark, Ohio State, B
1960	Roger Davis, Syracuse, G
1961	Mike Ditka, Pittsburgh, E
1962	Ronnie Bull, Baylor, RB
1963	Dave Behrman, Michigan State, C
1964	Dick Evey, Tennessee, DT
1965	Dick Butkus, Illinois, LB
	Gale Sayers, Kansas, RB
	Steve DeLong, Tennessee, T
1966	George Rice, Louisiana State, DT
1967	Loyd Phillips, Arkansas, DE
1968	Mike Hull, Southern California, RB
1969	Rufus Mayes, Ohio State, T
1970	George Farmer, UCLA, WR (3)
1971	Joe Moore, Missouri, RB
1972	Lionel Antoine, Southern Illinois, T
	Craig Clemons, Iowa, DB
1973	Wally Chambers, Eastern Kentucky, DE
1974	Waymond Bryant, Tennessee State, LB
	Dave Gallagher, Michigan, DT
1975	Walter Payton, Jackson State, RB
1976	Dennis Lick, Wisconsin, T
1977	Ted Albrecht, California, T
1978	Brad Shearer, Texas, DT (3)
1979	Dan Hampton, Arkansas, DT
	Al Harris, Arizona State, DE
1980	Otis Wilson, Louisville, LB
1981	Keith Van Horne, Southern California, T
1982	Jim McMahon, Brigham Young, QB
1983	Jim Covert, Pittsburgh, T
	Willie Gault, Tennessee, WR
1984	Wilber Marshall, Florida, LB
1985	William Perry, Clemson, DT
1986	Neal Anderson, Florida, RB
1987	Jim Harbaugh, Michigan, QB
1988	Brad Muster, Stanford, RB
	Wendell Davis, Louisiana State, WR
1989	Donnell Woolford, Clemson, DB
	Trace Armstrong, Florida, DE

Cincinnati Bengals

Year	Player, College, Position
1968	Bob Johnson, Tennessee, C
1969	Greg Cook, Cincinnati, QB
1970	Mike Reid, Penn State, DT
1971	Vernon Holland, Tennessee State, T
1972	Sherman White, California, DE
1973	Isaac Curtis, San Diego State, WR
1974	Bill Kollar, Montana State, DT
1975	Glenn Cameron, Florida, LB
1976	Billy Brooks, Oklahoma, WR
	Archie Griffin, Ohio State, RB
1977	Eddie Edwards, Miami, DT
	Wilson Whitley, Houston, DT
	Mike Cobb, Michigan State, TE
1978	Ross Browner, Notre Dame, DT
	Blair Bush, Washington, C
1979	Jack Thompson, Washington State, QB
	Charles Alexander, Louisiana State, RB
1980	Anthony Muñoz, Southern California, T
1981	David Verser, Kansas, WR
1982	Glen Collins, Mississippi State, DE
1983	Dave Rimington, Nebraska, C
1984	Ricky Hunley, Arizona, LB
	Pete Koch, Maryland, DE
	Brian Blados, North Carolina, T
1985	Eddie Brown, Miami, WR
	Emanuel King, Alabama, LB
1986	Joe Kelly, Washington, LB
	Tim McGee, Tennessee, WR
1987	Jason Buck, Brigham Young, DE
1988	Rickey Dixon, Oklahoma, DB
1989	Eric Ball, UCLA, RB (2)

Cleveland Browns

Year	Player, College, Position
1950	Ken Carpenter, Oregon State, B
1951	Ken Konz, Louisiana State, B
1952	Bert Rechichar, Tennessee, DB
	Harry Agganis, Boston U., QB
1953	Doug Atkins, Tennessee, DE
1954	Bobby Garrett, Stanford, QB
	John Bauer, Illinois, G
1955	Kurt Burris, Oklahoma, C
1956	Preston Carpenter, Arkansas, B
1957	Jim Brown, Syracuse, RB
1958	Jim Shofner, Texas Christian, DB
1959	Rich Kreitling, Illinois, DE
1960	Jim Houston, Ohio State, DE
1961	Bobby Crespino, Mississippi, TE
1962	Gary Collins, Maryland, WR
	Leroy Jackson, Western Illinois, RB
1963	Tom Hutchinson, Kentucky, WR
1964	Paul Warfield, Ohio State, WR
1965	James Garcia, Purdue, T (2)
1966	Milt Morin, Massachusetts, TE
1967	Bob Matheson, Duke, LB
1968	Marvin Upshaw, Trinity, Tex., DT-DE
1969	Ron Johnson, Michigan, RB
1970	Mike Phipps, Purdue, QB
	Bob McKay, Texas, T
1971	Clarence Scott, Kansas State, CB
1972	Thom Darden, Michigan, DB
1973	Steve Holden, Arizona State, WR
	Pete Adams, Southern California, T
1974	Billy Corbett, Johnson C. Smith, T (2)
1975	Mack Mitchell, Houston, DE
1976	Mike Pruitt, Purdue, RB
1977	Robert Jackson, Texas A&M, LB
1978	Clay Matthews, Southern California, LB
	Ozzie Newsome, Alabama, TE
1979	Willis Adams, Houston, WR
1980	Charles White, Southern California, RB
1981	Hanford Dixon, Southern Mississippi, DB
1982	Chip Banks, Southern California, LB
1983	Ron Brown, Arizona State, WR (2)
1984	Don Rogers, UCLA, DB
1985	Greg Allen, Florida State, RB (2)
1986	Webster Slaughter, San Diego State, WR (2)
1987	Mike Junkin, Duke, LB
1988	Clifford Charlton, Florida, LB
1989	Eric Metcalf, Texas, RB

Dallas Cowboys

Year	Player, College, Position
1960	None
1961	Bob Lilly, Texas Christian, DT
1962	Sonny Gibbs, Texas Christian, QB (2)
1963	Lee Roy Jordan, Alabama, LB
1964	Scott Appleton, Texas, DT
1965	Craig Morton, California, QB
1966	John Niland, Iowa, G
1967	Phil Clark, Northwestern, DB (3)
1968	Dennis Homan, Alabama, WR
1969	Calvin Hill, Yale, RB
1970	Duane Thomas, West Texas State, RB
1971	Tody Smith, Southern California, DE
1972	Bill Thomas, Boston College, RB
1973	Billy Joe DuPree, Michigan State, TE
1974	Ed (Too Tall) Jones, Tennessee State, DE
	Charley Young, North Carolina State, RB
1975	Randy White, Maryland, LB
	Thomas Henderson, Langston, LB
1976	Aaron Kyle, Wyoming, DB
1977	Tony Dorsett, Pittsburgh, RB
1978	Larry Bethea, Michigan State, DE

1979 Robert Shaw, Tennessee, C
1980 Bill Roe, Colorado, LB (3)
1981 Howard Richards, Missouri, T
1982 Rod Hill, Kentucky State, DB
1983 Jim Jeffcoat, Arizona State, DE
1984 Billy Cannon, Jr., Texas A&M, LB
1985 Kevin Brooks, Michigan, DE
1986 Mike Sherrard, UCLA, WR
1987 Danny Noonan, Nebraska, DT
1988 Michael Irvin, Miami, WR
1989 Troy Aikman, UCLA, QB

Denver Broncos

Year	Player, College, Position
1960	Roger LeClerc, Trinity, Conn., C
1961	Bob Gaiters, New Mexico State, RB
1962	Merlin Olsen, Utah State, DT
1963	Kermit Alexander, UCLA, CB
1964	Bob Brown, Nebraska, T
1965	Dick Butkus, Illinois, LB (2)
1966	Jerry Shay, Purdue, DT
1967	Floyd Little, Syracuse, RB
1968	Curley Culp, Arizona State, DE (2)
1969	Grady Cavness, Texas-El Paso, DB (2)
1970	Bob Anderson, Colorado, RB
1971	Marv Montgomery, Southern California, T
1972	Riley Odoms, Houston, TE
1973	Otis Armstrong, Purdue, RB
1974	Randy Gradishar, Ohio State, LB
1975	Louis Wright, San Jose State, DB
1976	Tom Glassic, Virginia, G
1977	Steve Schindler, Boston College, G
1978	Don Latimer, Miami, DT
1979	Kelvin Clark, Nebraska, T
1980	Rulon Jones, Utah State, DE (2)
1981	Dennis Smith, Southern California, DB
1982	Gerald Willhite, San Jose State, RB
1983	Chris Hinton, Northwestern, G
1984	Andre Townsend, Mississippi, DE (2)
1985	Steve Sewell, Oklahoma, RB
1986	Jim Juriga, Illinois, T (4)
1987	Ricky Nattiel, Florida, WR
1988	Ted Gregory, Syracuse, NT
1989	Steve Atwater, Arkansas, DB

Detroit Lions

Year	Player, College, Position
1936	Sid Wagner, Michigan State, G
1937	Lloyd Cardwell, Nebraska, B
1938	Alex Wojciechowicz, Fordham, C
1939	John Pingel, Michigan State, B
1940	Doyle Nave, Southern California, B
1941	Jim Thomason, Texas A&M, B
1942	Bob Westfall, Michigan, B
1943	Frank Sinkwich, Georgia, B
1944	Otto Graham, Northwestern, B
1945	Frank Szymanski, Notre Dame, C
1946	Bill Dellastatious, Missouri, B
1947	Glenn Davis, Army, B
1948	Y.A. Tittle, Louisiana State, B
1949	John Rauch, Georgia, B
1950	Leon Hart, Notre Dame, E
	Joe Watson, Rice, C
1951	Dick Stanfel, San Francisco, G (2)
1952	Yale Lary, Texas A&M, B (3)
1953	Harley Sewell, Texas, G
1954	Dick Chapman, Rice, T
1955	Dave Middleton, Auburn, B
1956	Hopalong Cassady, Ohio State, B
1957	Bill Glass, Baylor, G
1958	Alex Karras, Iowa, T
1959	Nick Pietrosante, Notre Dame, B
1960	John Robinson, Louisiana State, S
1961	Danny LaRose, Missouri, T (2)
1962	John Hadl, Kansas, QB
1963	Daryl Sanders, Ohio State, T
1964	Pete Beathard, Southern California, QB
1965	Tom Nowatzke, Indiana, RB
1966	Nick Eddy, Notre Dame, RB (2)
1967	Mel Farr, UCLA, RB
1968	Greg Landry, Massachusetts, QB
	Earl McCullouch, Southern California, WR
1969	Altie Taylor, Utah State, RB (2)
1970	Steve Owens, Oklahoma, RB
1971	Bob Bell, Cincinnati, DT
1972	Herb Orvis, Colorado, DE
1973	Ernie Price, Texas A&I, DE
1974	Ed O'Neil, Penn State, LB
1975	Lynn Boden, South Dakota State, G
1976	James Hunter, Grambling, DB
	Lawrence Gaines, Wyoming, RB
1977	Walt Williams, New Mexico State, DB (2)
1978	Luther Bradley, Notre Dame, DB
1979	Keith Dorney, Penn State, T
1980	Billy Sims, Oklahoma, RB
1981	Mark Nichols, San Jose State, WR
1982	Jimmy Williams, Nebraska, LB
1983	James Jones, Florida, RB
1984	David Lewis, California, TE
1985	Lomas Brown, Florida, T
1986	Chuck Long, Iowa, QB
1987	Reggie Rogers, Washington, DE
1988	Bennie Blades, Miami, DB
1989	Barry Sanders, Oklahoma State, RB

Green Bay Packers

Year	Player, College, Position
1936	Russ Letlow, San Francisco, G
1937	Eddie Jankowski, Wisconsin, B
1938	Cecil Isbell, Purdue, B
1939	Larry Buhler, Minnesota, B
1940	Harold Van Every, Minnesota, B
1941	George Paskvan, Wisconsin, B
1942	Urban Odson, Minnesota, T
1943	Dick Wildung, Minnesota, T
1944	Merv Pregulman, Michigan, G
1945	Walt Schlinkman, Texas Tech, B
1946	Johnny (Strike) Strzykalski, Marquette, B
1947	Ernie Case, UCLA, B
1948	Earl (Jug) Girard, Wisconsin, B
1949	Stan Heath, Nevada, B
1950	Clayton Tonnemaker, Minnesota, C
1951	Bob Gain, Kentucky, T
1952	Babe Parilli, Kentucky, QB
1953	Al Carmichael, Southern California, B
1954	Art Hunter, Notre Dame, T
	Veryl Switzer, Kansas State, B
1955	Tom Bettis, Purdue, G
1956	Jack Losch, Miami, B
1957	Paul Hornung, Notre Dame, B
	Ron Kramer, Michigan, E
1958	Dan Currie, Michigan State, C
1959	Randy Duncan, Iowa, B
1960	Tom Moore, Vanderbilt, RB
1961	Herb Adderley, Michigan State, CB
1962	Earl Gros, Louisiana State, RB
1963	Dave Robinson, Penn State, LB
1964	Lloyd Voss, Nebraska, DT
1965	Donny Anderson, Texas Tech, RB
	Lawrence Elkins, Baylor, E
1966	Jim Grabowski, Illinois, RB
	Gale Gillingham, Minnesota, T
1967	Bob Hyland, Boston College, C
	Don Horn, San Diego State, QB
1968	Fred Carr, Texas-El Paso, LB
	Bill Lueck, Arizona, G
1969	Rich Moore, Villanova, DT
1970	Mike McCoy, Notre Dame, DT
	Rich McGeorge, Elon, TE
1971	John Brockington, Ohio State, RB
1972	Willie Buchanon, San Diego State, DB
	Jerry Tagge, Nebraska, QB
1973	Barry Smith, Florida State, WR
1974	Barty Smith, Richmond, RB
1975	Bill Bain, Southern California, G (2)
1976	Mark Koncar, Colorado, T
1977	Mike Butler, Kansas, DE
	Ezra Johnson, Morris Brown, DE
1978	James Lofton, Stanford, WR
	John Anderson, Michigan, LB
1979	Eddie Lee Ivery, Georgia Tech, RB
1980	Bruce Clark, Penn State, DE
	George Cumby, Oklahoma, LB
1981	Rich Campbell, California, QB
1982	Ron Hallstrom, Iowa, G
1983	Tim Lewis, Pittsburgh, DB
1984	Alphonso Carreker, Florida State, DE
1985	Ken Ruettgers, Southern California, T
1986	Kenneth Davis, Texas Christian, RB (2)
1987	Brent Fullwood, Auburn, RB
1988	Sterling Sharpe, South Carolina, WR
1989	Tony Mandarich, Michigan State, T

Houston Oilers

Year	Player, College, Position
1960	Billy Cannon, Louisiana State, RB
1961	Mike Ditka, Pittsburgh, E
1962	Ray Jacobs, Howard Payne, DT
1963	Danny Brabham, Arkansas, LB
1964	Scott Appleton, Texas, DT
1965	Lawrence Elkins, Baylor, WR
1966	Tommy Nobis, Texas, LB
1967	George Webster, Michigan State, LB
	Tom Regner, Notre Dame, G
1968	Mac Haik, Mississippi, WR (2)
1969	Ron Pritchard, Arizona State, LB
1970	Doug Wilkerson, N. Carolina Central, G
1971	Dan Pastorini, Santa Clara, QB
1972	Greg Sampson, Stanford, DE
1973	John Matuszak, Tampa, DE
	George Amundson, Iowa State, RB
1974	Steve Manstedt, Nebraska, LB (4)
1975	Robert Brazile, Jackson State, LB
	Don Hardeman, Texas A&I, RB
1976	Mike Barber, Louisiana Tech, TE (2)
1977	Morris Towns, Missouri, T
1978	Earl Campbell, Texas, RB
1979	Mike Stensrud, Iowa State, DE (2)
1980	Angelo Fields, Michigan State, T (2)
1981	Michael Holston, Morgan State, WR (3)
1982	Mike Munchak, Penn State, G
1983	Bruce Matthews, Southern California, T
1984	Dean Steinkuhler, Nebraska, T
1985	Ray Childress, Texas A&M, DE
	Richard Johnson, Wisconsin, DB
1986	Jim Everett, Purdue, QB
1987	Alonzo Highsmith, Miami, RB
	Haywood Jeffires, North Carolina St., WR
1988	Lorenzo White, Michigan State, RB
1989	David Williams, Florida, T

Indianapolis Colts

Year	Player, College, Position
1953	Billy Vessels, Oklahoma, B
1954	Cotton Davidson, Baylor, B
1955	George Shaw, Oregon, B
	Alan Ameche, Wisconsin, FB
1956	Lenny Moore, Penn State, B
1957	Jim Parker, Ohio State, G
1958	Lenny Lyles, Louisville, B
1959	Jackie Burkett, Auburn, C
1960	Ron Mix, Southern California, T
1961	Tom Matte, Ohio State, RB
1962	Wendell Harris, Louisiana State, S
1963	Bob Vogel, Ohio State, T
1964	Marv Woodson, Indiana, CB
1965	Mike Curtis, Duke, LB
1966	Sam Ball, Kentucky, T
1967	Bubba Smith, Michigan State, DT
	Jim Detwiler, Michigan, RB
1968	John Williams, Minnesota G
1969	Eddie Hinton, Oklahoma, WR
1970	orman Bulaich, Texas Christian, RB
1971	Don McCauley, North Carolina, RB
	Leonard Dunlap, North Texas State, DB
1972	Tom Drougas, Oregon, T
1973	Bert Jones, Louisiana State, QB
	Joe Ehrmann, DT, Syracuse
1974	John Dutton, Nebraska, DE
	Roger Carr, Louisiana Tech, WR
1975	Ken Huff, North Carolina, G
1976	Ken Novak, Purdue, DT
1977	Randy Burke, Kentucky, WR
1978	Reese McCall, Auburn, TE
1979	Barry Krauss, Alabama, LB
1980	Curtis Dickey, Texas A&M, RB
	Derrick Hatchett, Texas, DB
1981	Randy McMillan, Pittsburgh, RB
	Donnell Thompson, North Carolina, DT
1982	Johnie Cooks, Mississippi State, LB
	Art Schlichter, Ohio State, QB
1983	John Elway, Stanford, QB
1984	Leonard Coleman, Vanderbilt, DB
	Ron Solt, Maryland, G
1985	Duane Bickett, Southern California, LB
1986	Jon Hand, Alabama, DE
1987	Cornelius Bennett, Alabama, LB
1988	Chris Chandler, Washington, QB (3)
1989	Andre Rison, Michigan State, WR

Kansas City Chiefs

Year Player, College, Position

1960 Don Meredith, Southern Methodist, QB
1961 E.J. Holub, Texas Tech, C
1962 Ronnie Bull, Baylor, RB
1963 Buck Buchanan, Grambling, DT
Ed Budde, Michigan State, G
1964 Pete Beathard, Southern California, QB
1965 Gale Sayers, Kansas, RB
1966 Aaron Brown, Minnesota, DE
1967 Gene Trosch, Miami, DE-DT
1968 Mo Moorman, Texas A&M, G
George Daney, Texas-El Paso, G
1969 Jim Marsalis, Tennessee State, CB
1970 Sid Smith, Southern California, T
1971 Elmo Wright, Houston, WR
1972 Jeff Kinney, Nebraska, RB
1973 Gary Butler, Rice, TE (2)
1974 Woody Green, Arizona State, RB
1975 Elmore Stephens, Kentucky, TE (2)
1976 Rod Walters, Iowa, G
1977 Gary Green, Baylor, DB
1978 Art Still, Kentucky, DE
1979 Mike Bell, Colorado State, DE
Steve Fuller, Clemson, QB
1980 Brad Budde, Southern California, G
1981 Willie Scott, South Carolina, TE
1982 Anthony Hancock, Tennessee, WR
1983 Todd Blackledge, Penn State, QB
1984 Bil! Maas, Pittsburgh, DT
John Alt, Iowa, T
1985 Ethan Horton, North Carolina, RB
1986 Brian Jozwiak, West Virginia, T
1987 Paul Palmer, Temple, RB
1988 Neil Smith, Nebraska, DE
1989 Derrick Thomas, Alabama, LB

Los Angeles Raiders

Year Player, College, Position

1960 Dale Hackbart, Wisconsin, CB
1961 Joe Rutgens, Illinois, DT
1962 Roman Gabriel, North Carolina State, QB
1963 George Wilson, Alabama, RB (6)
1964 Tony Lorick, Arizona State, RB
1965 Harry Schuh, Memphis State, T
1966 Rodger Bird, Kentucky, S
1967 Gene Upshaw, Texas A&I, G
1968 Eldridge Dickey, Tennessee State, QB
1969 Art Thoms, Syracuse, DT
1970 Raymond Chester, Morgan State, TE
1971 Jack Tatum, Ohio State, S
1972 Mike Siani, Villanova, WR
1973 Ray Guy, Southern Mississippi, K-P
1974 Henry Lawrence, Florida A&M, T
1975 Neal Colzie, Ohio State, DB
1976 Charles Philyaw, Texas Southern, DT (2)
1977 Mike Davis, Colorado, DB (2)
1978 Dave Browning, Washington, DE (2)
1979 Willie Jones, Florida State, DE (2)
1980 Marc Wilson, Brigham Young, QB
1981 Ted Watts, Texas Tech, DB
Curt Marsh, Washington, T
1982 Marcus Allen, Southern California, RB
1983 Don Mosebar, Southern California, T
1984 Sean Jones, Northeastern, DE (2)
1985 Jessie Hester, Florida State, WR
1986 Bob Buczkowski, Pittsburgh, DE
1987 John Clay, Missouri, T
1988 Tim Brown, Notre Dame, WR
Terry McDaniel, Tennessee, DB
Scott Davis, Illinois, DE
1989 Jeff Francis, Tennessee, QB (6)

Los Angeles Rams

Year Player, College, Position

1937 Johnny Drake, Purdue, B
1938 Corbett Davis, Indiana, B
1939 Parker Hall, Mississippi, B
1940 Ollie Cordill, Rice, B
1941 Rudy Mucha, Washington, C
1942 Jack Wilson, Baylor, B
1943 Mike Holovak, Boston College, B
1944 Tony Butkovich, Illinois, B
1945 Elroy (Crazylegs) Hirsch, Wisconsin, B
1946 Emil Sitko, Notre Dame, B
1947 Herman Wedemeyer, St. Mary's, Calif., B
1948 Tom Keane, West Virginia, B (2)
1949 Bobby Thomason, Virginia Military, B
1950 Ralph Pasquariello, Villanova, B
Stan West, Oklahoma, G
1951 Bud McFadin, Texas, G
1952 Bill Wade, Vanderbilt, QB
Bob Carey, Michigan State, E
1953 Donn Moomaw, UCLA, C
Ed Barker, Washington State, E
1954 Ed Beatty, Cincinnati, C
1955 Larry Morris, Georgia Tech, C
1956 Joe Marconi, West Virginia, B
Charles Horton, Vanderbilt, B
1957 Jon Arnett, Southern California, B
Del Shofner, Baylor, E
1958 Lou Michaels, Kentucky, T
Jim Phillips, Auburn, E
1959 Dick Bass, Pacific, B
Paul Dickson, Baylor, T
1960 Billy Cannon, Louisiana State, RB
1961 Marlin McKeever, Southern California, E-LB
1962 Roman Gabriel, North Carolina State, QB
Merlin Olsen, Utah State, DT
1963 Terry Baker, Oregon State, QB
Rufus Guthrie, Georgia Tech, G
1964 Bill Munson, Utah State, QB
1965 Clancy Williams, Washington State, CB
1966 Tom Mack, Michigan, G
1967 Willie Ellison, Texas Southern, RB (2)
1968 Gary Beban, UCLA, QB (2)
1969 Larry Smith, Florida, RB
Jim Seymour, Notre Dame, WR
Bob Klein, Southern California, TE
1970 Jack Reynolds, Tennessee, LB
1971 Isiah Robertson, Southern, LB
Jack Youngblood, Florida, DE
1972 Jim Bertelsen, Texas, RB (2)
1973 Cullen Bryant, Colorado, DB (2)
1974 John Cappelletti, Penn State, RB
1975 Mike Fanning, Notre Dame, DT
Dennis Harrah, Miami, T
Doug France, Ohio State, T
1976 Kevin McLain, Colorado State, LB
1977 Bob Brudzinski, Ohio State, LB
1978 Elvis Peacock, Oklahoma, RB
1979 George Andrews, Nebraska, LB
Kent Hill, Georgia Tech, T
1980 Johnnie Johnson, Texas, DB
1981 Mel Owens, Michigan, LB
1982 Barry Redden, Richmond, RB
1983 Eric Dickerson, Southern Methodist, RB
1984 Hal Stephens, East Carolina, DE (5)
1985 Jerry Gray, Texas, DB
1986 Mike Schad, Queen's University, Canada, T
1987 Donald Evans, Winston-Salem, DE (2)
1988 Gaston Green, UCLA, RB
Aaron Cox, Arizona State, WR
1989 Bill Hawkins, Miami, DE
Cleveland Gary, Miami, RB

Miami Dolphins

Year Player, College, Position

1966 Jim Grabowski, Illinois, RB
Rick Norton, Kentucky, QB
1967 Bob Griese, Purdue, QB
1968 Larry Csonka, Syracuse, RB
Doug Crusan, Indiana, T
1969 Bill Stanfill, Georgia, DE
1970 Jim Mandich, Michigan, TE (2)
1971 Otto Stowe, Iowa State, WR (2)
1972 Mike Kadish, Notre Dame, DT
1973 Chuck Bradley, Oregon, C (2)
1974 Donald Reese, Jackson State, DE
1975 Darryl Carlton, Tampa, T
1976 Larry Gordon, Arizona State, LB
Kim Bokamper, San Jose State, LB
1977 A.J. Duhe, Louisiana State, DT
1978 Guy Benjamin, Stanford, QB (2)
1979 Jon Giesler, Michigan, T
1980 Don McNeal, Alabama, DB
1981 David Overstreet, Oklahoma, RB
1982 Roy Foster, Southern California, G
1983 Dan Marino, Pittsburgh, QB
1984 Jackie Shipp, Oklahoma, LB
1985 Lorenzo Hampton, Florida, RB
1986 John Offerdahl, Western Michigan, LB (2)
1987 John Bosa, Boston College, DE
1988 Eric Kumerow, Ohio State, DE
1989 Sammie Smith, Florida State, RB
Louis Oliver, Florida, DB

Minnesota Vikings

Year Player, College, Position

1961 Tommy Mason, Tulane, RB
1962 Bill Miller, Miami, WR (3)
1963 Jim Dunaway, Mississippi, T
1964 Carl Eller, Minnesota, DE
1965 Jack Snow, Notre Dame, WR
1966 Jerry Shay, Purdue, DT
1967 Clint Jones, Michigan State, RB
Gene Washington, Michigan State, WR
Alan Page, Notre Dame, DT
1968 Ron Yary, Southern California, T
1969 Ed White, California, G (2)
1970 John Ward, Oklahoma State, DT
1971 Leo Hayden, Ohio State, RB
1972 Jeff Siemon, Stanford, LB
1973 Chuck Foreman, Miami, RB
1974 Fred McNeill, UCLA, LB
Steve Riley, Southern California, T
1975 Mark Mullaney, Colorado State, DE
1976 James White, Oklahoma State, DT
1977 Tommy Kramer, Rice, QB
1978 Randy Holloway, Pittsburgh, DE
1979 Ted Brown, North Carolina State, RB
1980 Doug Martin, Washington, DT
1981 Mardye McDole, Mississippi State, WR (2)
1982 Darrin Nelson, Stanford, RB
1983 Joey Browner, Southern California, DB
1984 Keith Millard, Washington State, DE
1985 Chris Doleman, Pittsburgh, LB
1986 Gerald Robinson, Auburn, DE
1987 D.J. Dozier, Penn State, RB
1988 Randall McDaniel, Arizona State, G
1989 David Braxton, Wake Forest, LB (2)

New England Patriots

Year Player, College, Position

1960 Ron Burton, Northwestern, RB
1961 Tommy Mason, Tulane, RB
1962 Gary Collins, Maryland, WR
1963 Art Graham, Boston College, WR
1964 Jack Concannon, Boston College, QB
1965 Jerry Rush, Michigan State, DE
1966 Karl Singer, Purdue, T
1967 John Charles, Purdue, S
1968 Dennis Byrd, North Carolina State, DE
1969 Ron Sellers, Florida State, WR
1970 Phil Olsen, Utah State, DE
1971 Jim Plunkett, Stanford, QB
1972 Tom Reynolds, San Diego State, WR (2)
1973 John Hannah, Alabama, G
Sam Cunningham, Southern California, RB
Darryl Stingley, Purdue, WR
1974 Steve Corbett, Boston College, G (2)
1975 Russ Francis, Oregon, TE
1976 Mike Haynes, Arizona State, DB
Pete Brock, Colorado, C
Tim Fox, Ohio State, DB
1977 Raymond Clayborn, Texas, DB
Stanley Morgan, Tennessee, WR
1978 Bob Cryder, Alabama, G
1979 Rick Sanford, South Carolina, DB
1980 Roland James, Tennessee, DB
Vagas Ferguson, Notre Dame, RB
1981 Brian Holloway, Stanford, T
1982 Kenneth Sims, Texas, DT
Lester Williams, Miami, DT
1983 Tony Eason, Illinois, QB
1984 Irving Fryar, Nebraska, WR
1985 Trevor Matich, Brigham Young, C
1986 Reggie Dupard, Southern Methodist, RB
1987 Bruce Armstrong, Louisville, T
1988 John Stephens, Northwestern St., La., RB
1989 Hart Lee Dykes, Oklahoma State, WR

New Orleans Saints

Year Player, College, Position

1967 Les Kelley, Alabama, RB
1968 Kevin Hardy, Notre Dame, DE
1969 John Shinners, Xavier, G
1970 Ken Burrough, Texas Southern, WR
1971 Archie Manning, Mississippi, QB
1972 Royce Smith, Georgia, G

1973	Derland Moore, Oklahoma, DE (2)
1974	Rick Middleton, Ohio State, LB
1975	Larry Burton, Purdue, WR
	Kurt Schumacher, Ohio State, T
1976	Chuck Muncie, California, RB
1977	Joe Campbell, Maryland, DE
1978	Wes Chandler, Florida, WR
1979	Russell Erxleben, Texas, P-K
1980	Stan Brock, Colorado, T
1981	George Rogers, South Carolina, RB
1982	Lindsay Scott, Georgia, WR
1983	Steve Korte, Arkansas, G (2)
1984	James Geathers, Wichita State, DE
1985	Alvin Toles, Tennessee, LB
1986	Jim Dombrowski, Virginia, T
1987	Shawn Knight, Brigham Young, DT
1988	Craig Heyward, Pittsburgh, RB
1989	Wayne Martin, Arkansas, DE

New York Giants

Year	Player, College, Position
1936	Art Lewis, Ohio U., T
1937	Ed Widseth, Minnesota, T
1938	George Karamatic, Gonzaga, B
1939	Walt Neilson, Arizona, B
1940	Grenville Lansdell, Southern California, B
1941	George Franck, Minnesota, B
1942	Merle Hapes, Mississippi, B
1943	Steve Filipowicz, Fordham, B
1944	Billy Hillenbrand, Indiana, B
1945	Elmer Barbour, Wake Forest, B
1946	George Connor, Notre Dame, T
1947	Vic Schwall, Northwestern, B
1948	Tony Minisi, Pennsylvania, B
1949	Paul Page, Southern Methodist, B
1950	Travis Tidwell, Auburn, B
1951	Kyle Rote, Southern Methodist, B
	Jim Spavital, Oklahoma A&M, B
1952	Frank Gifford, Southern California, B
1953	Bobby Marlow, Alabama, B
1954	Ken Buck, Pacific, C (2)
1955	Joe Heap, Notre Dame, B
1956	Henry Moore, Arkansas, B (2)
1957	Sam DeLuca, South Carolina, T (2)
1958	Phil King, Vanderbilt, B
1959	Lee Grosscup, Utah, B
1960	Lou Cordileone, Clemson, G
1961	Bruce Tarbox, Syracuse, G (2)
1962	Jerry Hillebrand, Colorado, LB
1963	Frank Lasky, Florida, T (2)
1964	Joe Don Looney, Oklahoma, RB
1965	Tucker Frederickson, Auburn, RB
1966	Francis Peay, Missouri, T
1967	Louis Thompson, Alabama, DT (4)
1968	Dick Buzin, Penn State, T (2)
1969	Fred Dryer, San Diego State, DE
1970	Jim Files, Oklahoma, LB
1971	Rocky Thompson, West Texas State, WR
1972	Eldridge Small, Texas A&I, DB
	Larry Jacobson, Nebraska, DE
1973	Brad Van Pelt, Michigan State, LB (2)
1974	John Hicks, Ohio State, G
1975	Al Simpson, Colorado State, T (2)
1976	Troy Archer, Colorado, DE
1977	Gary Jeter, Southern California, DT
1978	Gordon King, Stanford, T
1979	Phil Simms, Morehead State, QB
1980	Mark Haynes, Colorado, DB
1981	Lawrence Taylor, North Carolina, LB
1982	Butch Woolfolk, Michigan, RB
1983	Terry Kinard, Clemson, DB
1984	Carl Banks, Michigan State, LB
	William Roberts, Ohio State, T
1985	George Adams, Kentucky, RB
1986	Eric Dorsey, Notre Dame, DE
1987	Mark Ingram, Michigan State, WR
1988	Eric Moore, Indiana, T
1989	Brian Williams, Minnesota, G

New York Jets

Year	Player, College, Position
1960	George Izo, Notre Dame, QB
1961	Tom Brown, Minnesota, G
1962	Sandy Stephens, Minnesota, QB
1963	Jerry Stovall, Louisiana State, S
1964	Matt Snell, Ohio State, RB
1965	Joe Namath, Alabama, QB
	Tom Nowatzke, Indiana, RB
1966	Bill Yearby, Michigan, DT
1967	Paul Seiler, Notre Dame, T
1968	Lee White, Weber State, RB
1969	Dave Foley, Ohio State, T
1970	Steve Tannen, Florida, CB
1971	John Riggins, Kansas, RB
1972	Jerome Barkum, Jackson State, WR
	Mike Taylor, Michigan, LB
1973	Burgess Owens, Miami, DB
1974	Carl Barzilauskas, Indiana, DT
1975	Anthony Davis, Southern California, RB (2)
1976	Richard Todd, Alabama, QB
1977	Marvin Powell, Southern California, T
1978	Chris Ward, Ohio State, T
1979	Marty Lyons, Alabama, DE
1980	Johnny (Lam) Jones, Texas, WR
1981	Freeman McNeil, UCLA, RB
1982	Bob Crable, Notre Dame, LB
1983	Ken O'Brien, Cal-Davis, QB
1984	Russell Carter, Southern Methodist, DB
	Ron Faurot, Arkansas, DE
1985	Al Toon, Wisconsin, WR
1986	Mike Haight, Iowa, T
1987	Roger Vick, Texas A&M, RB
1988	Dave Cadigan, Southern California, T
1989	Jeff Lageman, Virginia, LB

Philadelphia Eagles

Year	Player, College, Position
1936	Jay Berwanger, Chicago, B
1937	Sam Francis, Nebraska, B
1938	Jim McDonald, Ohio State, B
1939	Davey O'Brien, Texas Christian, B
1940	George McAfee, Duke, B
1941	Art Jones, Richmond, B (2)
1942	Pete Kmetovic, Stanford, B
1943	Joe Muha, Virginia Military, B
1944	Steve Van Buren, Louisiana State, B
1945	John Yonaker, Notre Dame, E
1946	Leo Riggs, Southern California, B
1947	Neill Armstrong, Oklahoma A&M, E
1948	Clyde (Smackover) Scott, Arkansas, B
1949	Chuck Bednarik, Pennsylvania, C
	Frank Tripucka, Notre Dame, B
1950	Harry (Bud) Grant, Minnesota, E
1951	Ebert Van Buren, Louisiana State, B
	Chet Mutryn, Xavier, B
1952	Johnny Bright, Drake, B
1953	Al Conway, Army, B (2)
1954	Neil Worden, Notre Dame, B
1955	Dick Bielski, Maryland, B
1956	Bob Pellegrini, Maryland, C
1957	Clarence Peaks, Michigan State, B
1958	Walt Kowalczyk, Michigan State, B
1959	J.D. Smith, Rice, T (2)
1960	Ron Burton, Northwestern, RB
1961	Art Baker, Syracuse, RB
1962	Pete Case, Georgia, G (2)
1963	Ed Budde, Michigan State, G
1964	Bob Brown, Nebraska, T
1965	Ray Rissmiller, Georgia, T (2)
1966	Randy Beisler, Indiana, DE
1967	Harry Jones, Arkansas, RB
1968	Tim Rossovich, Southern California, DE
1969	Leroy Keyes, Purdue, RB
1970	Steve Zabel, Oklahoma, TE
1971	Richard Harris, Grambling, DE
1972	John Reaves, Florida, QB
1973	Jerry Sisemore, Texas, T
	Charle Young, Southern California, TE
1974	Mitch Sutton, Kansas, DT (3)
1975	Bill Capraun, Miami, T (7)
1976	Mike Smith, Florida, DE (4)
1977	Skip Sharp, Kansas, DB (5)
1978	Reggie Wilkes, Georgia Tech, LB (3)
1979	Jerry Robinson, UCLA, LB
1980	Roynell Young, Alcorn State, DB
1981	Leonard Mitchell, Houston, DE
1982	Mike Quick, North Carolina State, WR
1983	Michael Haddix, Mississippi State, RB
1984	Kenny Jackson, Penn State, WR
1985	Kevin Allen, Indiana, T
1986	Keith Byars, Ohio State, RB
1987	Jerome Brown, Miami, DT
1988	Keith Jackson, Oklahoma, TE
1989	Jessie Small, Eastern Kentucky, LB (2)

Phoenix Cardinals

Year	Player, College, Position
1936	Jim Lawrence, Texas Christian, B
1937	Ray Buivid, Marquette, B
1938	Jack Robbins, Arkansas, B
1939	Charles (Ki) Aldrich, Texas Christian, C
1940	George Cafego, Tennessee, B
1941	John Kimbrough, Texas A&M, B
1942	Steve Lach, Duke, B
1943	Glenn Dobbs, Tulsa, B
1944	Pat Harder, Wisconsin, B
1945	Charley Trippi, Georgia, B
1946	Dub Jones, Louisiana State, B
1947	DeWitt (Tex) Coulter, Army, T
1948	Jim Spavital, Oklahoma A&M, B
1949	Bill Fischer, Notre Dame, G
1950	Jack Jennings, Ohio State, T (2)
1951	Jerry Groom, Notre Dame, C
1952	Ollie Matson, San Francisco, B
1953	Johnny Olszewski, California, B
1954	Lamar McHan, Arkansas, B
1955	Max Boydston, Oklahoma, E
1956	Joe Childress, Auburn, B
1957	Jerry Tubbs, Oklahoma, C
1958	King Hill, Rice, B
	John David Crow, Texas A&M, B
1959	Bill Stacy, Mississippi State, B
1960	George Izo, Notre Dame, QB
1961	Ken Rice, Auburn, T
1962	Fate Echols, Northwestern, DT
	Irv Goode, Kentucky, C
1963	Jerry Stovall, Louisiana State, S
	Don Brumm, Purdue, DE
1964	Ken Kortas, Louisville, DT
1965	Joe Namath, Alabama, QB
1966	Carl McAdams, Oklahoma, LB
1967	Dave Williams, Washington, WR
1968	MacArthur Lane, Utah State, RB
1969	Roger Wehrli, Missouri, DB
1970	Larry Stegent, Texas A&M, RB
1971	Norm Thompson, Utah, CB
1972	Bobby Moore, Oregon, RB-WR
1973	Dave Butz, Purdue, DT
1974	J.V. Cain, Colorado, TE
1975	Tim Gray, Texas A&M, DB
1976	Mike Dawson, Arizona, DT
1977	Steve Pisarkiewicz, Missouri, QB
1978	Steve Little, Arkansas, K
	Ken Greene, Washington State, DB
1979	Ottis Anderson, Miami, RB
1980	Curtis Greer, Michigan, DE
1981	E. J. Junior, Alabama, LB
1982	Luis Sharpe, UCLA, T
1983	Leonard Smith, McNeese State, DB
1984	Clyde Duncan, Tennessee, WR
1985	Freddie Joe Nunn, Mississippi, LB
1986	Anthony Bell, Michigan State, LB
1987	Kelly Stouffer, Colorado State, QB
1988	Ken Harvey, California, LB
1989	Eric Hill, Louisiana State, LB
	Joe Wolf, Boston College, G

Pittsburgh Steelers

Year	Player, College, Position
1936	Bill Shakespeare, Notre Dame, B
1937	Mike Basrak, Duquesne, C
1938	Byron (Whizzer) White, Colorado, B
1939	Bill Patterson, Baylor, B (3)
1940	Kay Eakin, Arkansas, B
1941	Chet Gladchuk, Boston College, C (2)
1942	Bill Dudley, Virginia, B
1943	Bill Daley, Minnesota, B
1944	Johnny Podesto, St. Mary's, Calif., B
1945	Paul Duhart, Florida, B
1946	Felix (Doc) Blanchard, Army, B
1947	Hub Bechtol, Texas, E
1948	Dan Edwards, Georgia, E
1949	Bobby Gage, Clemson, B
1950	Lynn Chandnois, Michigan State, B
1951	Butch Avinger, Alabama, B
1952	Ed Modzelewski, Maryland, B
1953	Ted Marchibroda, St. Bonaventure, B
1954	Johnny Lattner, Notre Dame, B
1955	Frank Varrichione, Notre Dame, T
1956	Gary Glick, Colorado A&M, B
	Art Davis, Mississippi State, B
1957	Len Dawson, Purdue, B

1958	Larry Krutko, West Virginia, B (2)
1959	Tom Barnett, Purdue, B (8)
1960	Jack Spikes, Texas Christian, RB
1961	Myron Pottios, Notre Dame, LB (2)
1962	Bob Ferguson, Ohio State, RB
1963	Frank Atkinson, Stanford, T (8)
1964	Paul Martha, Pittsburgh, S
1965	Roy Jefferson, Utah, WR (2)
1966	Dick Leftridge, West Virginia, RB
1967	Don Shy, San Diego State, RB (2)
1968	Mike Taylor, Southern California, T
1969	Joe Greene, North Texas State, DT
1970	Terry Bradshaw, Louisiana Tech, QB
1971	Frank Lewis, Grambling, WR
1972	Franco Harris, Penn State, RB
1973	J.T. Thomas, Florida State, DB
1974	Lynn Swann, Southern California, WR
1975	Dave Brown, Michigan, DB
1976	Bennie Cunningham, Clemson, TE
1977	Robin Cole, New Mexico, LB
1978	Ron Johnson, Eastern Michigan, DB
1979	Greg Hawthorne, Baylor, RB
1980	Mark Malone, Arizona State, QB
1981	Keith Gary, Oklahoma, DE
1982	Walter Abercrombie, Baylor, RB
1983	Gabriel Rivera, Texas Tech, DT
1984	Louis Lipps, Southern Mississippi, WR
1985	Darryl Sims, Wisconsin, DE
1986	John Rienstra, Temple, G
1987	Rod Woodson, Purdue, DB
1988	Aaron Jones, Eastern Kentucky, DE
1989	Tim Worley, Georgia, RB
	Tom Ricketts, Pittsburgh, T

San Diego Chargers

Year	Player, College, Position
1960	Monty Stickles, Notre Dame, E
1961	Earl Faison, Indiana, DE
1962	Bob Ferguson, Ohio State, RB
1963	Walt Sweeney, Syracuse, G
1964	Ted Davis, Georgia Tech, LB
1965	Steve DeLong, Tennessee, DE
1966	Don Davis, Cal State-Los Angeles, DT
1967	Ron Billingsley, Wyoming, DE
1968	Russ Washington, Missouri, DT
	Jimmy Hill, Texas A&I, DB
1969	Marty Domres, Columbia, QB
	Bob Babich, Miami, Ohio, LB
1970	Walker Gillette, Richmond, WR
1971	Leon Burns, Long Beach State, RB
1972	Pete Lazetich, Stanford, DE (2)
1973	Johnny Rodgers, Nebraska, WR
1974	Bo Matthews, Colorado, RB
	Don Goode, Kansas, LB
1975	Gary Johnson, Grambling, DT
	Mike Williams, Louisiana State, DB
1976	Joe Washington, Oklahoma, RB
1977	Bob Rush, Memphis State, C
1978	John Jefferson, Arizona State, WR
1979	Kellen Winslow, Missouri, TE
1980	Ed Luther, San Jose State, QB (4)
1981	James Brooks, Auburn, RB
1982	Hollis Hall, Clemson, DB (7)
1983	Billy Ray Smith, Arkansas, LB
	Gary Anderson, Arkansas, WR
	Gill Byrd, San Jose State, DB
1984	Mossy Cade, Texas, DB
1985	Jim Lachey, Ohio State, G
1986	Leslie O'Neal, Oklahoma State, DE
	James FitzPatrick, Southern California, T
1987	Rod Bernstine, Texas A&M, TE
1988	Anthony Miller, Tennessee, WR
1989	Burt Grossman, Pittsburgh, DE

San Francisco 49ers

Year	Player, College, Position
1950	Leo Nomellini, Minnesota, T
1951	Y.A. Tittle, Louisiana State, B
1952	Hugh McElhenny, Washington, B
1953	Harry Babcock, Georgia, E
	Tom Stolhandske, Texas, E
1954	Bernie Faloney, Maryland, B
1955	Dickie Moegle, Rice, B
1956	Earl Morrall, Michigan State, B
1957	John Brodie, Stanford, B
1958	Jim Pace, Michigan, B
	Charlie Krueger, Texas A&M, T
1959	Dave Baker, Oklahoma, B
	Dan James, Ohio State, C
1960	Monty Stickles, Notre Dame, E
1961	Jimmy Johnson, UCLA, CB
	Bernie Casey, Bowling Green, WR
	Bill Kilmer, UCLA, QB
1962	Lance Alworth, Arkansas, WR
1963	Kermit Alexander, UCLA, CB
1964	Dave Parks, Texas Tech, WR
1965	Ken Willard, North Carolina, RB
	George Donnelly, Illinois, DB
1966	Stan Hindman, Mississippi, DE
1967	Steve Spurrier, Florida, QB
	Cas Banaszek, Northwestern, T
1968	Forrest Blue, Auburn, C
1969	Ted Kwalick, Penn State, TE
	Gene Washington, Stanford, WR
1970	Cedrick Hardman, North Texas State, DE
	Bruce Taylor, Boston U., DB
1971	Tim Anderson, Ohio State, DB
1972	Terry Beasley, Auburn, WR
1973	Mike Holmes, Texas Southern, DB
1974	Wilbur Jackson, Alabama, RB
	Bill Sandifer, UCLA, DT
1975	Jimmy Webb, Mississippi State, DT
1976	Randy Cross, UCLA, C (2)
1977	Elmo Boyd, Eastern Kentucky, WR (3)
1978	Ken MacAfee, Notre Dame, TE
	Dan Bunz, Cal State-Long Beach, LB
1979	James Owens, UCLA, WR (2)
1980	Earl Cooper, Rice, RB
	Jim Stuckey, Clemson, DT
1981	Ronnie Lott, Southern California, DB
1982	Bubba Paris, Michigan, T (2)
1983	Roger Craig, Nebraska, RB (2)
1984	Todd Shell, Brigham Young, LB
1985	Jerry Rice, Mississippi Valley State, WR
1986	Larry Roberts, Alabama, DE (2)
1987	Harris Barton, North Carolina, T
	Terrence Flagler, Clemson, RB
1988	Danny Stubbs, Miami, DE (2)
1989	Keith DeLong, Tennessee, LB

Seattle Seahawks

Year	Player, College, Position
1976	Steve Niehaus, Notre Dame, DT
1977	Steve August, Tulsa, G
1978	Keith Simpson, Memphis State, DB
1979	Manu Tuiasosopo, UCLA, DT
1980	Jacob Green, Texas A&M, DE
1981	Ken Easley, UCLA, DB
1982	Jeff Bryant, Clemson, DE
1983	Curt Warner, Penn State, RB
1984	Terry Taylor, Southern Illinois, DB
1985	Owen Gill, Iowa, RB (2)
1986	John L. Williams, Florida, RB
1987	Tony Woods, Pittsburgh, LB
1988	Brian Blades, Miami, WR (2)
1989	Andy Heck, Notre Dame, T

Tampa Bay Buccaneers

Year	Player, College, Position
1976	Lee Roy Selmon, Oklahoma, DT
1977	Ricky Bell, Southern California, RB
1978	Doug Williams, Grambling, QB
1979	Greg Roberts, Oklahoma, G (2)
1980	Ray Snell, Wisconsin, G
1981	Hugh Green, Pittsburgh, LB
1982	Sean Farrell, Penn State, G
1983	Randy Grimes, Baylor, C (2)
1984	Keith Browner, Southern California, LB (2)
1985	Ron Holmes, Washington, DE
1986	Bo Jackson, Auburn, RB
	Roderick Jones, Southern Methodist, DB
1987	Vinny Testaverde, Miami, QB
1988	Paul Gruber, Wisconsin, T
1989	Broderick Thomas, Nebraska, LB

Washington Redskins

Year	Player, College, Position
1936	Riley Smith, Alabama, B
1937	Sammy Baugh, Texas Christian, B
1938	Andy Farkas, Detroit, B
1939	I.B. Hale, Texas Christian, T
1940	Ed Boell, New York U., B
1941	Forest Evashevski, Michigan, B
1942	Orban (Spec) Sanders, Texas, B
1943	Jack Jenkins, Missouri, B
1944	Mike Micka, Colgate, B
1945	Jim Hardy, Southern California, B
1946	Cal Rossi, UCLA, B*
1947	Cal Rossi, UCLA, B
1948	Harry Gilmer, Alabama, B
	Lowell Tew, Alabama, B
1949	Rob Goode, Texas A&M, B
1950	George Thomas, Oklahoma, B
1951	Leon Heath, Oklahoma, B
1952	Larry Isbell, Baylor, B
1953	Jack Scarbath, Maryland, B
1954	Steve Meilinger, Kentucky, E
1955	Ralph Guglielmi, Notre Dame, B
1956	Ed Vereb, Maryland, B
1957	Don Bosseler, Miami, B
1958	Mike Sommer, George Washington, B (2)
1959	Don Allard, Boston College, B
1960	Richie Lucas, Penn State, QB
1961	Norman Snead, Wake Forest, QB
	Joe Rutgens, Illinois, DT
1962	Ernie Davis, Syracuse, RB
1963	Pat Richter, Wisconsin, TE
1964	Charley Taylor, Arizona State, RB-WR
1965	Bob Breitenstein, Tulsa, T (2)
1966	Charlie Gogolak, Princeton, K
1967	Ray McDonald, Idaho, RB
1968	Jim Smith, Oregon, DB
1969	Eugene Epps, Texas-El Paso, DB (2)
1970	Bill Brundige, Colorado, DT (2)
1971	Cotton Speyrer, Texas, WR (2)
1972	Moses Denson, Maryland State, RB (8)
1973	Charles Cantrell, Lamar, G (5)
1974	Jon Keyworth, Colorado, TE (6)
1975	Mike Thomas, Nevada-Las Vegas, RB (6)
1976	Mike Hughes, Baylor, G (5)
1977	Duncan McColl, Stanford, DE (4)
1978	Tony Green, Florida, RB (6)
1979	Don Warren, San Diego State, TE (4)
1980	Art Monk, Syracuse, WR
1981	Mark May, Pittsburgh, T
1982	Vernon Dean, San Diego State, DB (2)
1983	Darrell Green, Texas A&I, DB
1984	Bob Slater, Oklahoma, DT (2)
1985	Tory Nixon, San Diego State, DB (2)
1986	Markus Koch, Boise State, DE (2)
1987	Brian Davis, Nebraska, DB (2)
1988	Chip Lohmiller, Minnesota, K (2)
1989	Tracy Rocker, Auburn, DT (3)

Choice lost due to ineligibility.

RECORDS

Compiled by Elias Sports Bureau

The following records reflect all available official information on the National Football League from its formation in 1920 to date. Also included are all applicable records from the American Football League, 1960-69.

Individual Records

Service

Most Seasons

26 George Blanda, Chi. Bears, 1949, 1950-58; Baltimore, 1950; Houston, 1960-66; Oakland, 1967-75
21 Earl Morrall, San Francisco, 1956; Pittsburgh, 1957-58; Detroit, 1958-64; N.Y. Giants, 1965-67; Baltimore, 1968-71; Miami, 1972-76
20 Jim Marshall, Cleveland, 1960; Minnesota, 1961-79

Most Seasons, One Club

19 Jim Marshall, Minnesota, 1961-79
18 Jim Hart, St. Louis, 1966-83
Jeff Van Note, Atlanta, 1969-86
17 Lou Groza, Cleveland, 1950-59, 1961-67
Johnny Unitas, Baltimore, 1956-72
John Brodie, San Francisco, 1957-73
Jim Bakken, St. Louis, 1962-78
Mick Tingelhoff, Minnesota, 1962-78

Most Games Played, Career

340 George Blanda, Chi. Bears, 1949, 1950-58; Baltimore, 1950; Houston, 1960-66; Oakland, 1967-75
282 Jim Marshall, Cleveland, 1960; Minnesota, 1961-79
263 Jan Stenerud, Kansas City, 1967-79; Green Bay, 1980-83; Minnesota, 1984-85

Most Consecutive Games Played, Career

282 Jim Marshall, Cleveland, 1960; Minnesota, 1961-79
240 Mick Tingelhoff, Minnesota, 1962-78
234 Jim Bakken, St. Louis, 1962-78

Most Seasons, Coach

40 George Halas, Chi. Bears, 1920-29, 1933-42, 1946-55, 1958-67
33 Earl (Curly) Lambeau, Green Bay, 1921-49; Chi. Cardinals, 1950-51; Washington, 1952-53
29 Tom Landry, Dallas, 1960-88

Scoring

Most Seasons Leading League

5 Don Hutson, Green Bay, 1940-44
Gino Cappelletti, Boston, 1961, 1963-66
3 Earl (Dutch) Clark, Portsmouth, 1932; Detroit, 1935-36
Pat Harder, Chi. Cardinals, 1947-49
Paul Hornung, Green Bay, 1959-61
2 Jack Manders, Chi. Bears, 1934, 1937
Gordy Soltau, San Francisco, 1952-53
Doak Walker, Detroit, 1950, 1955
Gene Mingo, Denver, 1960, 1962
Jim Turner, N.Y. Jets, 1968-69
Fred Cox, Minnesota, 1969-70
Chester Marcol, Green Bay, 1972, 1974
John Smith, New England, 1979-80

Most Consecutive Seasons Leading League

5 Don Hutson, Green Bay, 1940-44
4 Gino Cappelletti, Boston, 1963-66
3 Pat Harder, Chi. Cardinals, 1947-49
Paul Hornung, Green Bay, 1959-61

Points

Most Points, Career

2,002 George Blanda, Chi. Bears, 1949, 1950-58; Baltimore, 1950; Houston, 1960-66; Oakland, 1967-75 (9-td, 943-pat, 335-fg)
1,699 Jan Stenerud, Kansas City, 1967-79; Green Bay, 1980-83; Minnesota, 1984-85 (580-pat, 373-fg)
1,439 Jim Turner, N.Y. Jets, 1964-70; Denver, 1971-79 (1-td, 521-pat, 304-fg)

Most Points, Season

176 Paul Hornung, Green Bay, 1960 (15-td, 41-pat, 15-fg)
161 Mark Moseley, Washington, 1983 (62-pat, 33-fg)
155 Gino Cappelletti, Boston, 1964 (7-td, 38-pat, 25-fg)

Most Points, No Touchdowns, Season

161 Mark Moseley, Washington, 1983 (62-pat, 33-fg)
145 Jim Turner, N.Y. Jets, 1968 (43-pat, 34-fg)
144 Kevin Butler, Chicago, 1985 (51-pat, 31-fg)

Most Seasons, 100 or More Points

7 Jan Stenerud, Kansas City, 1967-71; Green Bay, 1981, 1983
6 Gino Cappelletti, Boston, 1961-66
George Blanda, Houston, 1960-61; Oakland, 1967-69, 1973
Bruce Gossett, Los Angeles, 1966-67, 1969; San Francisco, 1970-71, 1973
Nick Lowery, Kansas City, 1981, 1983-86, 1988
5 Lou Michaels, Pittsburgh, 1962; Baltimore, 1964-65, 1967-68
Tony Franklin, Philadelphia, 1979, 1981; New England, 1984-86

Most Points, Rookie, Season

144 Kevin Butler, Chicago, 1985 (51-pat, 31-fg)
132 Gale Sayers, Chicago, 1965 (22-td)
128 Doak Walker, Detroit, 1950 (11-td, 38-pat, 8-fg)
Cookie Gilchrist, Buffalo, 1962 (15-td, 14-pat, 8-fg)
Chester Marcol, Green Bay, 1972 (29-pat, 33-fg)

Most Points, Game

40 Ernie Nevers, Chi. Cardinals vs. Chi. Bears, Nov. 28, 1929 (6-td, 4-pat)
36 Dub Jones, Cleveland vs. Chi. Bears, Nov. 25, 1951 (6-td)
Gale Sayers, Chicago vs. San Francisco, Dec. 12, 1965 (6-td)
33 Paul Hornung, Green Bay vs. Baltimore, Oct. 8, 1961 (4-td, 6-pat, 1-fg)

Most Consecutive Games Scoring

151 Fred Cox, Minnesota, 1963-73
137 Jim Breech, Oakland, 1979; Cincinnati, 1980-88 (current)
133 Garo Yepremian, Miami, 1970-78; New Orleans, 1979

Touchdowns

Most Seasons Leading League

8 Don Hutson, Green Bay, 1935-38, 1941-44
3 Jim Brown, Cleveland, 1958-59, 1963
Lance Alworth, San Diego, 1964-66
2 By many players

Most Consecutive Seasons Leading League

4 Don Hutson, Green Bay, 1935-38, 1941-44
3 Lance Alworth, San Diego, 1964-66
2 By many players

Most Touchdowns, Career

126 Jim Brown, Cleveland, 1957-65 (106-r, 20-p)
125 Walter Payton, Chicago, 1975-87 (110-r, 15-p)
116 John Riggins, N.Y. Jets, 1971-75; Washington, 1976-79, 1981-85 (104-r, 12-p)

Most Touchdowns, Season

24 John Riggins, Washington, 1983 (24-r)
23 O.J. Simpson, Buffalo, 1975 (16-r, 7-p)
Jerry Rice, San Francisco, 1987 (1-r, 22-p)
22 Gale Sayers, Chicago, 1965 (14-r, 6-p, 2-ret)
Chuck Foreman, Minnesota, 1975 (13-r, 9-p)

Most Touchdowns, Rookie, Season

22 Gale Sayers, Chicago, 1965 (14-r, 6-p, 2-ret)
20 Eric Dickerson, L.A. Rams, 1983 (18-r, 2-p)
16 Billy Sims, Detroit, 1980 (13-r, 3-p)

Most Touchdowns, Game

6 Ernie Nevers, Chi. Cardinals vs. Chi. Bears, Nov. 28, 1929 (6-r)
Dub Jones, Cleveland vs. Chi. Bears, Nov. 25, 1951 (4-r, 2-p)
Gale Sayers, Chicago vs. San Francisco, Dec. 12, 1965 (4-r, 1-p, 1-ret)
5 Bob Shaw, Chi. Cardinals vs. Baltimore, Oct. 2, 1950 (5-p)
Jim Brown, Cleveland vs. Baltimore, Nov. 1, 1959 (5-r)
Abner Haynes, Dall. Texans vs. Oakland, Nov. 26, 1961 (4-r, 1-p)
Billy Cannon, Houston vs. N.Y. Titans, Dec. 10, 1961 (3-r, 2-p)
Cookie Gilchrist, Buffalo vs. N.Y. Jets, Dec. 8, 1963 (5-r)
Paul Hornung, Green Bay vs. Baltimore, Dec. 12, 1965 (3-r, 2-p)
Kellen Winslow, San Diego vs. Oakland, Nov. 22, 1981 (5-p)
4 By many players

Most Consecutive Games Scoring Touchdowns

18 Lenny Moore, Baltimore, 1963-65
14 O.J. Simpson, Buffalo, 1975
13 John Riggins, Washington, 1982-83
Jerry Rice, San Francisco, 1986-87

Points After Touchdown

Most Seasons Leading League

8 George Blanda, Chi. Bears, 1956; Houston, 1961-62; Oakland, 1967-69, 1972, 1974
4 Bob Waterfield, Cleveland, 1945; Los Angeles, 1946, 1950, 1952
3 Earl (Dutch) Clark, Portsmouth, 1932; Detroit, 1935-36
Jack Manders, Chi. Bears, 1933-35
Don Hutson, Green Bay, 1941-42, 1945

Most Points After Touchdown Attempted, Career

959 George Blanda, Chi. Bears, 1949, 1950-58; Baltimore, 1950; Houston, 1960-66; Oakland, 1967-75
657 Lou Groza, Cleveland, 1950-59, 1961-67
601 Jan Stenerud, Kansas City, 1967-79; Green Bay, 1980-83; Minnesota, 1984-85

Most Points After Touchdown Attempted, Season

70 Uwe von Schamann, Miami, 1984
65 George Blanda, Houston, 1961
63 Mark Moseley, Washington, 1983

Most Points After Touchdown Attempted, Game

10 Charlie Gogolak, Washington vs. N.Y. Giants, Nov. 27, 1966
9 Pat Harder, Chi. Cardinals vs. N.Y. Giants, Oct. 17, 1948; vs. N.Y. Bulldogs, Nov. 13, 1949
Bob Waterfield, Los Angeles vs. Baltimore, Oct. 22, 1950
Bob Thomas, Chicago vs. Green Bay, Dec. 7, 1980
8 By many players

Most Points After Touchdown, Career

943 George Blanda, Chi. Bears, 1949, 1950-58; Baltimore, 1950; Houston, 1960-66; Oakland, 1967-75
641 Lou Groza, Cleveland, 1950-59, 1961-67
580 Jan Stenerud, Kansas City, 1967-79; Green Bay, 1980-83; Minnesota, 1984-85

Most Points After Touchdown, Season

66 Uwe von Schamann, Miami, 1984
64 George Blanda, Houston, 1961
62 Mark Moseley, Washington, 1983

Most Points After Touchdown, Game

9 Pat Harder, Chi. Cardinals vs. N.Y. Giants, Oct. 17, 1948
Bob Waterfield, Los Angeles vs. Baltimore, Oct. 22, 1950
Charlie Gogolak, Washington vs. N.Y. Giants, Nov. 27, 1966
8 By many players

Most Consecutive Points After Touchdown

234 Tommy Davis, San Francisco, 1959-65
221 Jim Turner, N.Y. Jets, 1967-70; Denver, 1971-74
202 Gary Anderson, Pittsburgh, 1983-88

Highest Points After Touchdown Percentage, Career (200 points after touchdown)

99.43 Tommy Davis, San Francisco, 1959-69 (350-348)
99.35 Nick Lowery, New England, 1978; Kansas City, 1980-88 (306-304)
99.15 Gary Anderson, Pittsburgh, 1982-88 (234-232)

Most Points After Touchdown, No Misses, Season

56 Danny Villanueva, Dallas, 1966
Ray Wersching, San Francisco, 1984
54 Mike Clark, Dallas, 1968
George Blanda, Oakland, 1968
53 Pat Harder, Chi. Cardinals, 1948

Most Points After Touchdown, No Misses, Game

9 Pat Harder, Chi. Cardinals vs. N.Y. Giants, Oct. 17, 1948
Bob Waterfield, Los Angeles vs. Baltimore, Oct. 22, 1950
8 By many players

Field Goals

Most Seasons Leading League

5 Lou Groza, Cleveland, 1950, 1952-54, 1957
4 Jack Manders, Chi. Bears, 1933-34, 1936-37
Ward Cuff, N.Y. Giants, 1938-39, 1943; Green Bay, 1947
Mark Moseley, Washington, 1976-77, 1979, 1982
3 Bob Waterfield, Los Angeles, 1947, 1949, 1951
Gino Cappelletti, Boston, 1961, 1963-64
Fred Cox, Minnesota, 1965, 1969-70
Jan Stenerud, Kansas City, 1967, 1970, 1975

Most Consecutive Seasons Leading League

3 Lou Groza, Cleveland, 1952-54
2 By many players

Most Field Goals Attempted, Career

638 George Blanda, Chi. Bears, 1949, 1950-58; Baltimore, 1950; Houston, 1960-66; Oakland, 1967-75
558 Jan Stenerud, Kansas City, 1967-79; Green Bay, 1980-83; Minnesota, 1984-85
488 Jim Turner, N.Y. Jets, 1964-70; Denver, 1971-79

Most Field Goals Attempted, Season

49 Bruce Gossett, Los Angeles, 1966
Curt Knight, Washington, 1971
48 Chester Marcol, Green Bay, 1972
47 Jim Turner, N.Y. Jets, 1969
David Ray, Los Angeles, 1973
Mark Moseley, Washington, 1983

Most Field Goals Attempted, Game

9 Jim Bakken, St. Louis vs. Pittsburgh, Sept. 24, 1967
8 Lou Michaels, Pittsburgh vs. St. Louis, Dec. 2, 1962
Garo Yepremian, Detroit vs. Minnesota, Nov. 13, 1966
Jim Turner, N.Y. Jets vs. Buffalo, Nov. 3, 1968
7 By many players

Most Field Goals, Career

373 Jan Stenerud, Kansas City, 1967-79; Green Bay, 1980-83; Minnesota, 1984-85
335 George Blanda, Chi. Bears, 1949, 1950-58; Baltimore, 1950; Houston, 1960-66; Oakland, 1967-75
304 Jim Turner, N.Y. Jets, 1964-70; Denver, 1971-79

Most Field Goals, Season

35 Ali Haji-Sheikh, N.Y. Giants, 1983
34 Jim Turner, N.Y. Jets, 1968
33 Chester Marcol, Green Bay, 1972
Mark Moseley, Washington, 1983
Gary Anderson, Pittsburgh, 1985

Most Field Goals, Rookie, Season

35 Ali Haji-Sheikh, N.Y. Giants, 1983
33 Chester Marcol, Green Bay, 1972
31 Kevin Butler, Chicago, 1985

Most Field Goals, Game

7 Jim Bakken, St. Louis vs. Pittsburgh, Sept. 24, 1967
6 Gino Cappelletti, Boston vs. Denver, Oct. 4, 1964
Garo Yepremian, Detroit vs. Minnesota, Nov. 13, 1966
Jim Turner, N.Y. Jets vs. Buffalo, Nov. 3, 1968
Tom Dempsey, Philadelphia vs. Houston, Nov. 12, 1972
Bobby Howfield, N.Y. Jets vs. New Orleans, Dec. 3, 1972
Jim Bakken, St. Louis vs. Atlanta, Dec. 9, 1973
Joe Danelo, N.Y. Giants vs. Seattle, Oct. 18, 1981
Ray Wersching, San Francisco vs. New Orleans, Oct. 16, 1983
Gary Anderson, Pittsburgh vs. Denver, Oct. 23, 1988
5 By many players

Most Field Goals, One Quarter

4 Garo Yepremian, Detroit vs. Minnesota, Nov. 13, 1966 (second quarter)
Curt Knight, Washington vs. N.Y. Giants, Nov. 15, 1970 (second quarter)
Roger Ruzek, Dallas vs. N.Y. Giants, Nov. 2, 1987 (fourth quarter)
3 By many players

Most Consecutive Games Scoring Field Goals

31 Fred Cox, Minnesota, 1968-70
28 Jim Turner, N.Y. Jets, 1970; Denver, 1971-72
23 Morten Andersen, New Orleans, 1986-88

Most Consecutive Field Goals

23 Mark Moseley, Washington, 1981-82
22 Pat Leahy, N.Y. Jets, 1985-86
20 Garo Yepremian, Miami, 1978; New Orleans, 1979
Morten Andersen, New Orleans, 1985-86

Longest Field Goal

63 Tom Dempsey, New Orleans vs. Detroit, Nov. 8, 1970
60 Steve Cox, Cleveland vs. Cincinnati, Oct. 21, 1984
59 Tony Franklin, Philadelphia vs. Dallas, Nov. 12, 1979

Highest Field Goal Percentage, Career (100 field goals)

78.24 Morten Andersen, New Orleans, 1982-88 (193-151)
77.91 Nick Lowery, New England, 1978; Kansas City, 1980-88 (258-201)
77.83 Gary Anderson, Pittsburgh, 1982-88 (212-165)

Highest Field Goal Percentage, Season (Qualifiers)

95.24 Mark Moseley, Washington, 1982 (21-20)
Ed Murray, Detroit, 1988 (21-20)
91.67 Jan Stenerud, Green Bay, 1981 (24-22)
88.89 Nick Lowery, Kansas City, 1985 (27-24)
Dean Biasucci, Indianapolis, 1987 (27-24)

Most Field Goals, No Misses, Game

6 Gino Cappelletti, Boston vs. Denver, Oct. 4, 1964
Joe Danelo, N.Y. Giants vs. Seattle, Oct. 18, 1981
Ray Wersching, San Francisco vs. New Orleans, Oct. 16, 1983
Gary Anderson, Pittsburgh vs. Denver, Oct. 23, 1988
5 Roger LeClerc, Chicago vs. Detroit, Dec. 3, 1961
Lou Michaels, Baltimore vs. San Francisco, Sept. 25, 1966
Mac Percival, Chicago vs. Philadelphia, Oct. 20, 1968
Roy Gerela, Houston vs. Miami, Sept. 28, 1969
Jan Stenerud, Kansas City vs. Buffalo, Nov. 2, 1969; vs. Buffalo, Dec. 7, 1969; Minnesota vs. Detroit, Sept. 23, 1984
Horst Muhlmann, Cincinnati vs. Buffalo, Nov. 8, 1970; vs. Pittsburgh, Sept. 24, 1972
Bruce Gossett, San Francisco vs. Denver, Sept. 23, 1973
Nick Mike-Mayer, Atlanta vs. Los Angeles, Nov. 4, 1973
Curt Knight, Washington vs. Baltimore, Nov. 18, 1973
Tim Mazzetti, Atlanta vs. Los Angeles, Oct. 30, 1978
Ed Murray, Detroit vs. Green Bay, Sept. 14, 1980
Rich Karlis, Denver vs. Seattle, Nov. 20, 1983
Pat Leahy, N.Y. Jets vs. Cincinnati, Sept. 16, 1984
Nick Lowery, Kansas City vs. L.A. Raiders, Sept. 12, 1985; vs. Cincinnati, Nov. 13, 1988
Eric Schubert, N.Y. Giants vs. Tampa Bay, Nov. 3, 1985
Gary Anderson, Pittsburgh vs. Kansas City, Nov. 10, 1985
Morten Andersen, New Orleans vs. L.A. Rams, Dec. 1, 1985
Roger Ruzek, Dallas vs. L.A. Rams, Dec. 21, 1987
Scott Norwood, Buffalo vs. Pittsburgh, Sept. 25, 1988
Norm Johnson, Seattle vs. L.A. Raiders, Dec. 18, 1988

Most Field Goals, 50 or More Yards, Career

17 Jan Stenerud, Kansas City, 1967-79; Green Bay, 1980-83; Minnesota, 1984-85
Nick Lowery, New England, 1978; Kansas City, 1980-88
13 Ed Murray, Detroit, 1980-88
Morten Andersen, New Orleans, 1982-88
12 Tom Dempsey, New Orleans, 1969-70; Philadelphia, 1971-74; Los Angeles, 1975-76; Houston, 1977; Buffalo, 1978-79
Mark Moseley, Philadelphia, 1970; Houston, 1971-72; Washington, 1974-86; Cleveland, 1986
Chris Bahr, Cincinnati, 1976-79; Oakland, 1980-81; L.A. Raiders, 1982-88

Most Field Goals, 50 or More Yards, Season

6 Dean Biasucci, Indianapolis, 1988
5 Fred Steinfort, Denver, 1980
Norm Johnson, Seattle, 1986
4 Horst Muhlmann, Cincinnati, 1970
Mark Moseley, Washington, 1977
Nick Lowery, Kansas City, 1980
Raul Allegre, Baltimore, 1983

Most Field Goals, 50 or More Yards, Game

2 Jim Martin, Detroit vs. Baltimore, Oct. 23, 1960
Tom Dempsey, New Orleans vs. Los Angeles, Dec. 6, 1970
Chris Bahr, Cincinnati vs. Houston, Sept. 23, 1979
Nick Lowery, Kansas City vs. Seattle, Sept. 14, 1980; vs. New Orleans, Sept. 8, 1985; vs. Detroit, Nov. 26, 1987
Mark Moseley, Washington vs. New Orleans, Oct. 26, 1980
Fred Steinfort, Denver vs. Seattle, Dec. 21, 1980
Mick Luckhurst, Atlanta vs. Denver, Dec. 5, 1982; vs. L.A. Rams, Oct. 7, 1984
Morten Andersen, New Orleans vs. Philadelphia, Dec. 11, 1983
Paul McFadden, Philadelphia vs. Detroit, Nov. 4, 1984
Pat Leahy, N.Y. Jets vs. New England, Oct. 20, 1985
Tony Zendejas, Houston vs. San Diego, Nov. 24, 1985
Norm Johnson, Seattle vs. L.A. Raiders, Dec. 8, 1986
Raul Allegre, N.Y. Giants vs. Philadelphia, Nov. 15, 1987
Dean Biasucci, Indianapolis vs. Miami, Sept. 25, 1988

Safeties

Most Safeties, Career

4 Ted Hendricks, Baltimore, 1969-73; Green Bay, 1974; Oakland, 1975-81; L.A. Raiders, 1982-83
Doug English, Detroit, 1975-79, 1981-85
3 Bill McPeak, Pittsburgh, 1949-57
Charlie Krueger, San Francisco, 1959-73
Ernie Stautner, Pittsburgh, 1950-63
Jim Katcavage, N.Y. Giants, 1956-68
Roger Brown, Detroit, 1960-66; Los Angeles, 1967-69
Bruce Maher, Detroit, 1960-67; N.Y. Giants, 1968-69
Ron McDole, St. Louis, 1961; Houston, 1962; Buffalo, 1963-70; Washington, 1971-78
Alan Page, Minnesota, 1967-78; Chicago, 1979-81
Lyle Alzado, Denver, 1971-78; Cleveland, 1979-81; L.A. Raiders, 1982-85
Rulon Jones, Denver, 1980-88
Steve McMichael, New England, 1980; Chicago, 1981-88
2 By many players

Most Safeties, Season

2 Tom Nash, Green Bay, 1932
Roger Brown, Detroit, 1962
Ron McDole, Buffalo, 1964
Alan Page, Minnesota, 1971
Fred Dryer, Los Angeles, 1973
Benny Barnes, Dallas, 1973
James Young, Houston, 1977
Tom Hannon, Minnesota, 1981
Doug English, Detroit, 1983
Don Blackmon, New England, 1985
Timothy Harris, Green Bay, 1988

Most Safeties, Game

2 Fred Dryer, Los Angeles vs. Green Bay, Oct. 21, 1973

Rushing

Most Seasons Leading League

8 Jim Brown, Cleveland, 1957-61, 1963-65
4 Steve Van Buren, Philadelphia, 1945, 1947-49
O.J. Simpson, Buffalo, 1972-73, 1975-76
Eric Dickerson, L.A. Rams, 1983-84, 1986; Indianapolis, 1988
3 Earl Campbell, Houston, 1978-80

Most Consecutive Seasons Leading League

5 Jim Brown, Cleveland, 1957-61
3 Steve Van Buren, Philadelphia, 1947-49
Jim Brown, Cleveland, 1963-65
Earl Campbell, Houston, 1978-80
2 Bill Paschal, N.Y. Giants, 1943-44
Joe Perry, San Francisco, 1953-54
Jim Nance, Boston, 1966-67
Leroy Kelly, Cleveland, 1967-68
O.J. Simpson, Buffalo, 1972-73; 1975-76
Eric Dickerson, L.A. Rams, 1983-84

Attempts

Most Seasons Leading League

6 Jim Brown, Cleveland, 1958-59, 1961, 1963-65
4 Steve Van Buren, Philadelphia, 1947-50
Walter Payton, Chicago, 1976-79
3 Cookie Gilchrist, Buffalo, 1963-64; Denver, 1965
Jim Nance, Boston, 1966-67, 1969
O. J. Simpson, Buffalo, 1973-75
Eric Dickerson, L.A. Rams, 1983, 1986; Indianapolis, 1988

Most Consecutive Seasons Leading League

4 Steve Van Buren, Philadelphia, 1947-50
Walter Payton, Chicago, 1976-79
3 Jim Brown, Cleveland, 1963-65
Cookie Gilchrist, Buffalo, 1963-64; Denver, 1965
O.J. Simpson, Buffalo, 1973-75
2 By many players

Most Attempts, Career

3,838 Walter Payton, Chicago, 1975-87
2,949 Franco Harris, Pittsburgh, 1972-83; Seattle, 1984
2,936 Tony Dorsett, Dallas, 1977-87; Denver, 1988

Most Attempts, Season

407 James Wilder, Tampa Bay, 1984
404 Eric Dickerson, L.A. Rams, 1986
397 Gerald Riggs, Atlanta, 1985

Most Attempts, Rookie, Season

390 Eric Dickerson, L.A. Rams, 1983
378 George Rogers, New Orleans, 1981
335 Curt Warner, Seattle, 1983

Most Attempts, Game

45 Jamie Morris, Washington vs. Cincinnati, Dec. 17, 1988 (OT)
43 Butch Woolfolk, N.Y. Giants vs. Philadelphia, Nov. 20, 1983
James Wilder, Tampa Bay vs. Green Bay, Sept. 30, 1984 (OT)
42 James Wilder, Tampa Bay vs. Pittsburgh, Oct. 30, 1983

Yards Gained

Most Yards Gained, Career

16,726 Walter Payton, Chicago, 1975-87
12,739 Tony Dorsett, Dallas, 1977-87; Denver, 1988
12,312 Jim Brown, Cleveland, 1957-65

Most Seasons, 1,000 or More Yards Rushing

10 Walter Payton, Chicago, 1976-81, 1983-86
8 Franco Harris, Pittsburgh, 1972, 1974-79, 1983
Tony Dorsett, Dallas, 1977-81, 1983-85
7 Jim Brown, Cleveland, 1958-61, 1963-65

Most Consecutive Seasons, 1,000 or More Yards Rushing

6 Franco Harris, Pittsburgh, 1974-79
Walter Payton, Chicago, 1976-81
Eric Dickerson, L.A. Rams, 1983-86; L.A. Rams-Indianapolis, 1987; Indianapolis, 1988
5 Jim Taylor, Green Bay, 1960-64
O.J. Simpson, Buffalo, 1972-76
Tony Dorsett, Dallas, 1977-81
4 Jim Brown, Cleveland, 1958-61
Earl Campbell, Houston, 1978-81
Walter Payton, Chicago, 1983-86

Most Yards Gained, Season

2,105 Eric Dickerson, L.A. Rams, 1984
2,003 O.J. Simpson, Buffalo, 1973
1,934 Earl Campbell, Houston, 1980

Most Yards Gained, Rookie, Season

1,808 Eric Dickerson, L.A. Rams, 1983
1,674 George Rogers, New Orleans, 1981
1,605 Ottis Anderson, St. Louis, 1979

Most Yards Gained, Game

275 Walter Payton, Chicago vs. Minnesota, Nov. 20, 1977
273 O.J. Simpson, Buffalo vs. Detroit, Nov. 25, 1976
250 O.J. Simpson, Buffalo vs. New England, Sept. 16, 1973

Most Games, 200 or More Yards Rushing, Career

6 O.J. Simpson, Buffalo, 1969-77; San Francisco, 1978-79
4 Jim Brown, Cleveland, 1957-65
Earl Campbell, Houston, 1978-84; New Orleans, 1984-85
3 Eric Dickerson, L.A. Rams, 1983-87; Indianapolis, 1987-88

Most Games, 200 or More Yards Rushing, Season

4 Earl Campbell, Houston, 1980
3 O.J. Simpson, Buffalo, 1973
2 Jim Brown, Cleveland, 1963
O.J. Simpson, Buffalo, 1976
Walter Payton, Chicago, 1977
Eric Dickerson, L.A. Rams, 1984

Most Consecutive Games, 200 or More Yards Rushing

2 O.J. Simpson, Buffalo, 1973, 1976
Earl Campbell, Houston, 1980

Most Games, 100 or More Yards Rushing, Career

77 Walter Payton, Chicago, 1975-87
58 Jim Brown, Cleveland, 1957-65
52 Eric Dickerson, L.A. Rams, 1983-87; Indianapolis, 1987-88

Most Games, 100 or More Yards Rushing, Season

12 Eric Dickerson, L.A. Rams, 1984
11 O.J. Simpson, Buffalo, 1973
Earl Campbell, Houston, 1979
Marcus Allen, L.A. Raiders, 1985
Eric Dickerson, L.A. Rams, 1986
10 Walter Payton, Chicago, 1977, 1985
Earl Campbell, Houston, 1980

Most Consecutive Games, 100 or More Yards Rushing

11 Marcus Allen, L.A. Raiders, 1985-86
9 Walter Payton, Chicago, 1985
7 O.J. Simpson, Buffalo, 1972-73
Earl Campbell, Houston, 1979

Longest Run From Scrimmage

99 Tony Dorsett, Dallas vs. Minnesota, Jan. 3, 1983 (TD)
97 Andy Uram, Green Bay vs. Chi. Cardinals, Oct. 8, 1939 (TD)
Bob Gage, Pittsburgh vs. Chi. Bears, Dec. 4, 1949 (TD)
96 Jim Spavital, Baltimore vs. Green Bay, Nov. 5, 1950 (TD)
Bob Hoernschemeyer, Detroit vs. N.Y. Yanks, Nov. 23, 1950 (TD)

Average Gain

Highest Average Gain, Career (700 attempts)

5.22 Jim Brown, Cleveland, 1957-65 (2,359-12,312)
5.14 Eugene (Mercury) Morris, Miami, 1969-75; San Diego, 1976 (804-4,133)
5.00 Gale Sayers, Chicago, 1965-71 (991-4,956)

Highest Average Gain, Season (Qualifiers)

9.94 Beattie Feathers, Chi. Bears, 1934 (101-1,004)
6.87 Bobby Douglass, Chicago, 1972 (141-968)
6.78 Dan Towler, Los Angeles, 1951 (126-854)

Highest Average Gain, Game (10 attempts)

17.09 Marion Motley, Cleveland vs. Pittsburgh, Oct. 29, 1950 (11-188)
16.70 Bill Grimes, Green Bay vs. N.Y. Yanks, Oct. 8, 1950 (10-167)
16.57 Bobby Mitchell, Cleveland vs. Washington, Nov. 15, 1959 (14-232)

Touchdowns

Most Seasons Leading League

5 Jim Brown, Cleveland, 1957-59, 1963, 1965
4 Steve Van Buren, Philadelphia, 1945, 1947-49
3 Abner Haynes, Dall. Texans, 1960-62
Cookie Gilchrist, Buffalo, 1962-64
Paul Lowe, L.A. Chargers, 1960; San Diego, 1961, 1965
Leroy Kelly, Cleveland, 1966-68

Most Consecutive Seasons Leading League

3 Steve Van Buren, Philadelphia, 1947-49
Jim Brown, Cleveland, 1957-59
Abner Haynes, Dall. Texans, 1960-62
Cookie Gilchrist, Buffalo, 1962-64
Leroy Kelly, Cleveland, 1966-68

Most Touchdowns, Career

110 Walter Payton, Chicago, 1975-87
106 Jim Brown, Cleveland, 1957-65
104 John Riggins, N.Y. Jets, 1971-75; Washington, 1976-79, 1981-85

Most Touchdowns, Season

24 John Riggins, Washington, 1983
21 Joe Morris, N.Y. Giants, 1985
19 Jim Taylor, Green Bay, 1962
Earl Campbell, Houston, 1979
Chuck Muncie, San Diego, 1981

Most Touchdowns, Rookie, Season

18 Eric Dickerson, L.A. Rams, 1983
15 Ickey Woods, Cincinnati, 1988
14 Gale Sayers, Chicago, 1965

Most Touchdowns, Game

6 Ernie Nevers, Chi. Cardinals vs. Chi. Bears, Nov. 28, 1929
5 Jim Brown, Cleveland vs. Baltimore, Nov. 1, 1959
Cookie Gilchrist, Buffalo vs. N.Y. Jets, Dec. 8, 1963
4 By many players

Most Consecutive Games Rushing for Touchdowns

13 John Riggins, Washington, 1982-83
George Rogers, Washington, 1985-86
11 Lenny Moore, Baltimore, 1963-64
9 Leroy Kelly, Cleveland, 1968

Passing

Most Seasons Leading League

6 Sammy Baugh, Washington, 1937, 1940, 1943, 1945, 1947, 1949
4 Len Dawson, Dall. Texans; 1962; Kansas City, 1964, 1966, 1968
Roger Staubach, Dallas, 1971, 1973, 1978-79
Ken Anderson, Cincinnati, 1974-75, 1981-82
3 Arnie Herber, Green Bay, 1932, 1934, 1936
Norm Van Brocklin, Los Angeles, 1950, 1952, 1954
Bart Starr, Green Bay, 1962, 1964, 1966

Most Consecutive Seasons Leading League

2 Cecil Isbell, Green Bay, 1941-42
Milt Plum, Cleveland, 1960-61
Ken Anderson, Cincinnati, 1974-75, 1981-82
Roger Staubach, Dallas, 1978-79

Pass Rating

Highest Pass Rating, Career (1,500 attempts)

92.0 Joe Montana, San Francisco, 1979-88
91.5 Dan Marino, Miami, 1983-88
86.2 Boomer Esiason, Cincinnati, 1984-88

Highest Pass Rating, Season (Qualifiers)

110.4 Milt Plum, Cleveland, 1960
109.9 Sammy Baugh, Washington, 1945
108.9 Dan Marino, Miami, 1984

Highest Pass Rating, Rookie, Season (Qualifiers)

96.0 Dan Marino, Miami, 1983
88.2 Greg Cook, Cincinnati, 1969
84.0 Charlie Conerly, N.Y. Giants, 1948

Attempts

Most Seasons Leading League

4 Sammy Baugh, Washington, 1937, 1943, 1947-48
Johnny Unitas, Baltimore, 1957, 1959-61
George Blanda, Chi. Bears, 1953; Houston, 1963-65
3 Arnie Herber, Green Bay, 1932, 1934, 1936
Sonny Jurgensen, Washington, 1966-67, 1969
Dan Marino, Miami, 1984, 1986, 1988
2 By many players

Most Consecutive Seasons Leading League

3 Johnny Unitas, Baltimore, 1959-61
George Blanda, Houston, 1963-65
2 By many players

Most Passes Attempted, Career

6,467 Fran Tarkenton, Minnesota, 1961-66, 1972-78; N.Y. Giants, 1967-71
5,604 Dan Fouts, San Diego, 1973-87
5,186 Johnny Unitas, Baltimore, 1956-72; San Diego, 1973

Most Passes Attempted, Season
623 Dan Marino, Miami, 1986
609 Dan Fouts, San Diego, 1981
606 Dan Marino, Miami, 1988
Most Passes Attempted, Rookie, Season
439 Jim Zorn, Seattle, 1976
417 Jack Trudeau, Indianapolis, 1986
375 Norm Snead, Washington, 1961
Most Passes Attempted, Game
68 George Blanda, Houston vs. Buffalo, Nov. 1, 1964
62 Joe Namath, N.Y. Jets vs. Baltimore, Oct. 18, 1970
Steve Dils, Minnesota vs. Tampa Bay, Sept. 5, 1981
Phil Simms, N.Y. Giants vs. Cincinnati, Oct. 13, 1985
61 Tommy Kramer, Minnesota vs. New England, Dec. 16, 1979
Neil Lomax, St. Louis vs. San Diego, Sept. 20, 1987

Completions
Most Seasons Leading League
5 Sammy Baugh, Washington, 1937, 1943, 1945, 1947-48
4 George Blanda, Chi. Bears, 1953; Houston, 1963-65
Sonny Jurgensen, Philadelphia, 1961; Washington, 1966-67, 1969
Dan Marino, Miami, 1984-86, 1988
3 Arnie Herber, Green Bay, 1932, 1934, 1936
Johnny Unitas, Baltimore, 1959-60, 1963
John Brodie, San Francisco, 1965, 1968, 1970
Fran Tarkenton, Minnesota, 1975-76, 1978
Most Consecutive Seasons Leading League
3 George Blanda, Houston, 1963-65
Dan Marino, Miami, 1984-86
2 By many players
Most Passes Completed, Career
3,686 Fran Tarkenton, Minnesota, 1961-66, 1972-78; N.Y. Giants, 1967-71
3,297 Dan Fouts, San Diego, 1973-87
2,830 Johnny Unitas, Baltimore, 1956-72; San Diego, 1973
Most Passes Completed, Season
378 Dan Marino, Miami, 1986
362 Dan Marino, Miami, 1984
360 Dan Fouts, San Diego, 1981
Most Passes Completed, Rookie, Season
208 Jim Zorn, Seattle, 1976
204 Jack Trudeau, Indianapolis, 1986
183 Jeff Komlo, Detroit, 1979
Most Passes Completed, Game
42 Richard Todd, N.Y. Jets vs. San Francisco, Sept. 21, 1980
40 Ken Anderson, Cincinnati vs. San Diego, Dec. 20, 1982
Phil Simms, N.Y. Giants vs. Cincinnati, Oct. 13, 1985
39 Dan Marino, Miami vs. Buffalo, Nov. 16, 1986
Most Consecutive Passes Completed
22 Joe Montana, San Francisco vs. Cleveland (5), Nov. 29, 1987; vs. Green Bay (17), Dec. 6, 1987
20 Ken Anderson, Cincinnati vs. Houston, Jan. 2, 1983
18 Steve DeBerg, Denver vs. L.A. Rams (17), Dec. 12, 1982; vs. Kansas City (1), Dec. 19, 1982
Lynn Dickey, Green Bay vs. Houston, Sept. 4, 1983
Joe Montana, San Francisco vs. L.A. Rams (13), Oct. 28, 1984; vs. Cincinnati (5), Nov. 4, 1984

Completion Percentage
Most Seasons Leading League
8 Len Dawson, Dall. Texans, 1962; Kansas City, 1964-69, 1975
7 Sammy Baugh, Washington, 1940, 1942-43, 1945, 1947-49
4 Bart Starr, Green Bay, 1962, 1966, 1968-69
Joe Montana, San Francisco, 1980-81, 1985, 1987
Most Consecutive Seasons Leading League
6 Len Dawson, Kansas City, 1964-69
3 Sammy Baugh, Washington, 1947-49
Otto Graham, Cleveland, 1953-55
Milt Plum, Cleveland, 1959-61
2 By many players
Highest Completion Percentage, Career (1,500 attempts)
63.22 Joe Montana, San Francisco, 1979-88 (3,673-2,322)
60.19 Dan Marino, Miami, 1983-88 (3,100-1,866)
59.85 Ken Stabler, Oakland, 1970-79; Houston, 1980-81; New Orleans, 1982-84 (3,793-2,270)
Highest Completion Percentage, Season (Qualifiers)
70.55 Ken Anderson, Cincinnati, 1982 (309-218)
70.33 Sammy Baugh, Washington, 1945 (182-128)
67.29 Steve Bartkowski, Atlanta, 1984 (269-181)
Highest Completion Percentage, Rookie, Season (Qualifiers)
58.45 Dan Marino, Miami, 1983 (296-173)
57.14 Jim McMahon, Chicago, 1982 (269-181)
56.07 Fran Tarkenton, Minnesota, 1961 (280-157)
Highest Completion Percentage, Game (20 attempts)
90.91 Ken Anderson, Cincinnati vs. Pittsburgh, Nov. 10, 1974 (22-20)
90.48 Lynn Dickey, Green Bay vs. New Orleans, Dec. 13, 1981 (21-19)
87.50 Danny White, Dallas vs. Philadelphia, Nov. 6, 1983 (24-21)

Yards Gained
Most Seasons Leading League
5 Sonny Jurgensen, Philadelphia, 1961-62; Washington, 1966-67, 1969
4 Sammy Baugh, Washington, 1937, 1940, 1947-48
Johnny Unitas, Baltimore, 1957, 1959-60, 1963
Dan Fouts, San Diego, 1979-82
Dan Marino, Miami, 1984-86, 1988
3 Arnie Herber, Green Bay, 1932, 1934, 1936
Sid Luckman, Chi. Bears, 1943, 1945-46
John Brodie, San Francisco, 1965, 1968, 1970
John Hadl, San Diego, 1965, 1968, 1971
Joe Namath, N.Y. Jets, 1966-67, 1972
Most Consecutive Seasons Leading League
4 Dan Fouts, San Diego, 1979-82
3 Dan Marino, Miami, 1984-86
2 By many players

Most Yards Gained, Career
47,003 Fran Tarkenton, Minnesota, 1961-66, 1972-78; N.Y. Giants, 1967-71
43,040 Dan Fouts, San Diego, 1973-87
40,239 Johnny Unitas, Baltimore, 1956-72; San Diego, 1973
Most Seasons, 3,000 or More Yards Passing
6 Dan Fouts, San Diego, 1979-81, 1984-86
5 Sonny Jurgensen, Philadelphia, 1961-62; Washington, 1966-67, 1969
Tommy Kramer, Minnesota, 1979-81, 1985-86
Joe Montana, San Francisco, 1981, 1983-85, 1987
Dan Marino, Miami, 1984-88
4 Brian Sipe, Cleveland, 1979-81, 1983
Ron Jaworski, Philadelphia, 1980-81, 1983, 1985
Danny White, Dallas, 1980-81, 1983, 1985
John Elway, Denver, 1985-88
Boomer Esiason, Cincinnati, 1985-88
Neil Lomax, St. Louis, 1984-85, 1987; Phoenix, 1988
Phil Simms, N.Y. Giants, 1984-86, 1988
Most Yards Gained, Season
5,084 Dan Marino, Miami, 1984
4,802 Dan Fouts, San Diego, 1981
4,746 Dan Marino, Miami, 1986
Most Yards Gained, Rookie, Season
2,571 Jim Zorn, Seattle, 1976
2,507 Dennis Shaw, Buffalo, 1970
2,337 Norm Snead, Washington, 1961
Most Yards Gained, Game
554 Norm Van Brocklin, Los Angeles vs. N.Y. Yanks, Sept. 28, 1951
521 Dan Marino, Miami vs. N.Y. Jets, Oct. 23, 1988
513 Phil Simms, N.Y. Giants vs. Cincinnati, Oct. 13, 1985
Most Games, 400 or More Yards Passing, Career
9 Dan Marino, Miami, 1983-88
6 Dan Fouts, San Diego, 1973-87
5 Sonny Jurgensen, Philadelphia, 1957-63; Washington, 1964-74
Most Games, 400 or More Yards Passing, Season
4 Dan Marino, Miami, 1984
3 Dan Marino, Miami, 1986
2 George Blanda, Houston, 1961
Sonny Jurgensen, Philadelphia, 1961
Joe Namath, N.Y. Jets, 1972
Dan Fouts, San Diego, 1982, 1985
Phil Simms, N.Y. Giants, 1985
Ken O'Brien, N.Y. Jets, 1986
Bernie Kosar, Cleveland, 1986
Dan Marino, Miami, 1988
Most Consecutive Games, 400 or More Yards Passing
2 Dan Fouts, San Diego, 1982
Dan Marino, Miami, 1984
Phil Simms, N.Y. Giants, 1985
Most Games, 300 or More Yards Passing, Career
51 Dan Fouts, San Diego, 1973-87
32 Dan Marino, Miami, 1983-88
26 Johnny Unitas, Baltimore, 1956-72; San Diego, 1973
Joe Montana, San Francisco, 1979-88
Most Games, 300 or More Yards Passing, Season
9 Dan Marino, Miami, 1984
8 Dan Fouts, San Diego, 1980
7 Dan Fouts, San Diego, 1981, 1985
Bill Kenney, Kansas City, 1983
Neil Lomax, St. Louis, 1984
Most Consecutive Games, 300 or More Yards Passing, Season
5 Joe Montana, San Francisco, 1982
4 Dan Fouts, San Diego, 1979
Bill Kenney, Kansas City, 1983
3 By many players
Longest Pass Completion (All TDs except as noted)
99 Frank Filchock (to Farkas), Washington vs. Pittsburgh, Oct. 15, 1939
George Izo (to Mitchell), Washington vs. Cleveland, Sept. 15, 1963
Karl Sweetan (to Studstill), Detroit vs. Baltimore, Oct. 16, 1966
Sonny Jurgensen (to Allen), Washington vs. Chicago, Sept. 15, 1968
Jim Plunkett (to Branch), L.A. Raiders vs. Washington, Oct. 2, 1983
Ron Jaworski (to Quick), Philadelphia vs. Atlanta, Nov. 10, 1985
98 Doug Russell (to Tinsley), Chi. Cardinals vs. Cleveland, Nov. 27, 1938
Ogden Compton (to Lane), Chi. Cardinals vs. Green Bay, Nov. 13, 1955
Bill Wade (to Farrington), Chicago Bears vs. Detroit, Oct. 8, 1961
Jacky Lee (to Dewveall), Houston vs. San Diego, Nov. 25, 1962
Earl Morrall (to Jones), N.Y. Giants vs. Pittsburgh, Sept. 11, 1966
Jim Hart (to Moore), St. Louis vs. Los Angeles, Dec. 10, 1972 (no TD)
97 Pat Coffee (to Tinsley), Chi. Cardinals vs. Chi. Bears, Dec. 5, 1937
Bobby Layne (to Box), Detroit vs. Green Bay, Nov. 26, 1953
George Shaw (to Tarr), Denver vs. Boston, Sept. 21, 1962

Average Gain
Most Seasons Leading League
7 Sid Luckman, Chi. Bears, 1939-43, 1946-47
3 Arnie Herber, Green Bay, 1932, 1934, 1936
Norm Van Brocklin, Los Angeles, 1950, 1952, 1954
Len Dawson, Dall. Texans, 1962; Kansas City, 1966, 1968
Bart Starr, Green Bay, 1966-68
Most Consecutive Seasons Leading League
5 Sid Luckman, Chi. Bears, 1939-43
3 Bart Starr, Green Bay, 1966-68
2 Bernie Masterson, Chi. Bears, 1937-38
Sid Luckman, Chi. Bears, 1946-47
Johnny Unitas, Baltimore, 1964-65
Terry Bradshaw, Pittsburgh, 1977-78
Steve Grogan, New England, 1980-81
Highest Average Gain, Career (1,500 attempts)
8.63 Otto Graham, Cleveland, 1950-55 (1,565-13,499)
8.42 Sid Luckman, Chi. Bears, 1939-50 (1,744-14,686)
8.16 Norm Van Brocklin, Los Angeles, 1949-57; Philadelphia, 1958-60 (2,895-23,611)
Highest Average Gain, Season (Qualifiers)
11.17 Tommy O'Connell, Cleveland, 1957 (110-1,229)
10.86 Sid Luckman, Chi. Bears, 1943 (202-2,194)

10.55 Otto Graham, Cleveland, 1953 (258-2,722)

Highest Average Gain, Rookie, Season (Qualifiers)

9.411 Greg Cook, Cincinnati, 1969 (197-1,854)
9.409 Bob Waterfield, Cleveland, 1945 (171-1,609)
8.36 Zeke Bratkowski, Chi. Bears, 1954 (130-1,087)

Highest Average Gain, Game (20 attempts)

18.58 Sammy Baugh, Washington vs. Boston, Oct. 31, 1948 (24-446)
18.50 Johnny Unitas, Baltimore vs. Atlanta, Nov. 12, 1967 (20-370)
17.71 Joe Namath, N.Y. Jets vs. Baltimore, Sept. 24, 1972 (28-496)

Touchdowns

Most Seasons Leading League

4 Johnny Unitas, Baltimore, 1957-60
Len Dawson, Dall. Texans, 1962; Kansas City, 1963, 1965-66
3 Arnie Herber, Green Bay, 1932, 1934, 1936
Sid Luckman, Chi. Bears, 1943, 1945-46
Y.A. Tittle, San Francisco, 1955; N.Y. Giants, 1962-63
Dan Marino, Miami, 1984-86
2 By many players

Most Consecutive Seasons Leading League

4 Johnny Unitas, Baltimore, 1957-60
3 Dan Marino, Miami, 1984-86
2 By many players

Most Touchdown Passes, Career

342 Fran Tarkenton, Minnesota, 1961-66, 1972-78; N.Y. Giants, 1967-71
290 Johnny Unitas, Baltimore, 1956-72: San Diego, 1973
255 Sonny Jurgensen, Philadelphia, 1957-63; Washington, 1964-74

Most Touchdown Passes, Season

48 Dan Marino, Miami, 1984
44 Dan Marino, Miami, 1986
36 George Blanda, Houston, 1961
Y.A. Tittle, N.Y. Giants, 1963

Most Touchdown Passes, Rookie, Season

22 Charlie Conerly, N.Y. Giants, 1948
20 Dan Marino, Miami, 1983
19 Jim Plunkett, New England, 1971

Most Touchdown Passes, Game

7 Sid Luckman, Chi. Bears vs. N.Y. Giants, Nov. 14, 1943
Adrian Burk, Philadelphia vs. Washington, Oct. 17, 1954
George Blanda, Houston vs. N.Y. Titans, Nov. 19, 1961
Y.A. Tittle, N.Y. Giants vs. Washington, Oct. 28, 1962
Joe Kapp, Minnesota vs. Baltimore, Sept. 28, 1969
6 By many players. Last time: Tommy Kramer, Minnesota vs. Green Bay, Sept. 28, 1986

Most Games, Four or More Touchdown Passes, Career

17 Johnny Unitas, Baltimore, 1956-72; San Diego, 1973
16 Dan Marino, Miami, 1983-88
13 George Blanda, Chi. Bears, 1949, 1950-58; Baltimore, 1950; Houston, 1960-66; Oakland, 1967-75

Most Games, Four or More Touchdown Passes, Season

6 Dan Marino, Miami, 1984
5 Dan Marino, Miami, 1986
4 George Blanda, Houston, 1961
Vince Ferragamo, Los Angeles, 1980

Most Consecutive Games, Four or More Touchdown Passes

4 Dan Marino, Miami, 1984
2 By many players

Most Consecutive Games, Touchdown Passes

47 Johnny Unitas, Baltimore, 1956-60
30 Dan Marino, Miami, 1985-87
28 Dave Krieg, Seattle, 1983-85

Had Intercepted

Most Consecutive Passes Attempted, None Intercepted

294 Bart Starr, Green Bay, 1964-65
208 Milt Plum, Cleveland, 1959-60
206 Roman Gabriel, Los Angeles, 1968-69

Most Passes Had Intercepted, Career

277 George Blanda, Chi. Bears, 1949, 1950-58; Baltimore, 1950; Houston, 1960-66; Oakland, 1967-75
268 John Hadl, San Diego, 1962-72; Los Angeles, 1973-74; Green Bay, 1974-75; Houston, 1976-77
266 Fran Tarkenton, Minnesota, 1961-66, 1972-78; N.Y. Giants, 1967-71

Most Passes Had Intercepted, Season

42 George Blanda, Houston, 1962
34 Frank Tripucka, Denver, 1960
32 John Hadl, San Diego, 1968
Fran Tarkenton, Minnesota, 1978

Most Passes Had Intercepted, Game

8 Jim Hardy, Chi. Cardinals vs. Philadelphia, Sept. 24, 1950
7 Parker Hall, Cleveland vs. Green Bay, Nov. 8, 1942
Frank Sinkwich, Detroit vs. Green Bay, Oct. 24, 1943
Bob Waterfield, Los Angeles vs. Green Bay, Oct. 17, 1948
Zeke Bratkowski, Chicago vs. Baltimore, Oct. 2, 1960
Tommy Wade, Pittsburgh vs. Philadelphia, Dec. 12, 1965
Ken Stabler, Oakland vs. Denver, Oct. 16, 1977
Steve DeBerg, Tampa Bay vs. San Francisco, Sept. 7, 1986
6 By many players

Most Attempts, No Interceptions, Game

57 Joe Montana, San Francisco vs. Atlanta, Oct. 6, 1985
54 Dan Marino, Miami vs. Buffalo, Nov. 16, 1986
51 Scott Brunner, N.Y. Giants vs. St. Louis, Dec. 26, 1982

Lowest Percentage, Passes Had Intercepted

Most Seasons Leading League, Lowest Percentage, Passes Had Intercepted

5 Sammy Baugh, Washington, 1940, 1942, 1944-45, 1947
3 Charlie Conerly, N.Y. Giants, 1950, 1956, 1959
Bart Starr, Green Bay, 1962, 1964, 1966
Roger Staubach, Dallas, 1971, 1977, 1979
Ken Anderson, Cincinnati, 1972, 1981-82
Ken O'Brien, N.Y. Jets, 1985, 1987-88
2 By many players

Lowest Percentage, Passes Had Intercepted, Career (1,500 attempts)

2.51 Ken O'Brien, N.Y. Jets, 1983-88 (1,990-50)
2.70 Joe Montana, San Francisco, 1979-88 (3,673-99)
2.85 Neil Lomax, St. Louis, 1981-87; Phoenix, 1988 (3,153-90)

Lowest Percentage, Passes Had Intercepted, Season (Qualifiers)

0.66 Joe Ferguson, Buffalo, 1976 (151-1)
1.16 Steve Bartkowski, Atlanta, 1983 (432-5)
1.20 Bart Starr, Green Bay, 1966 (251-3)

Lowest Percentage, Passes Had Intercepted, Rookie, Season (Qualifiers)

2.03 Dan Marino, Miami, 1983 (296-6)
2.10 Gary Wood, N.Y. Giants, 1964 (143-3)
2.82 Bernie Kosar, Cleveland, 1985 (248-7)

Times Sacked

Times Sacked has been compiled since 1963.

Most Times Sacked, Career

483 Fran Tarkenton, Minnesota, 1961-66, 1972-78; N.Y. Giants, 1967-71
405 Craig Morton, Dallas, 1965-74; N.Y. Giants, 1974-76; Denver, 1977-82
398 Ken Anderson, Cincinnati, 1971-86

Most Times Sacked, Season

72 Randall Cunningham, Philadelphia, 1986
62 Ken O'Brien, N.Y. Jets, 1985
61 Neil Lomax, St. Louis, 1985

Most Times Sacked, Game

12 Bert Jones, Baltimore vs. St. Louis, Oct. 26, 1980
Warren Moon, Houston vs. Dallas, Sept. 29, 1985
11 Charley Johnson, St. Louis vs. N.Y. Giants, Nov. 1, 1964
Bart Starr, Green Bay vs. Detroit, Nov. 7, 1965
Jack Kemp, Buffalo vs. Oakland, Oct. 15, 1967
Bob Berry, Atlanta vs. St. Louis, Nov. 24, 1968
Greg Landry, Detroit vs. Dallas, Oct. 6, 1975
Ron Jaworski, Philadelphia vs. St. Louis, Dec. 18, 1983
Paul McDonald, Cleveland vs. Kansas City, Sept. 30, 1984
Archie Manning, Minnesota vs. Chicago, Oct. 28, 1984
Steve Pelluer, Dallas vs. San Diego, Nov. 16, 1986
Randall Cunningham, Philadelphia vs. L.A. Raiders, Nov. 30, 1986 (OT)
David Norrie, N.Y. Jets vs. Dallas, Oct. 4, 1987
10 By many players

Pass Receiving

Most Seasons Leading League

8 Don Hutson, Green Bay, 1936-37, 1939, 1941-45
5 Lionel Taylor, Denver, 1960-63, 1965
3 Tom Fears, Los Angeles, 1948-50
Pete Pihos, Philadelphia, 1953-55
Billy Wilson, San Francisco, 1954, 1956-57
Raymond Berry, Baltimore, 1958-60
Lance Alworth, San Diego, 1966, 1968-69

Most Consecutive Seasons Leading League

5 Don Hutson, Green Bay, 1941-45
4 Lionel Taylor, Denver, 1960-63
3 Tom Fears, Los Angeles, 1948-50
Pete Pihos, Philadelphia, 1953-55
Raymond Berry, Baltimore, 1958-60

Most Pass Receptions, Career

791 Steve Largent, Seattle, 1976-88
750 Charlie Joiner, Houston, 1969-72; Cincinnati, 1972-75; San Diego, 1976-86
649 Charley Taylor, Washington, 1964-75, 1977

Most Seasons, 50 or More Pass Receptions

10 Steve Largent, Seattle, 1976, 1978-81, 1983-87
7 Raymond Berry, Baltimore, 1958-62, 1965-66
Art Powell, N.Y. Titans, 1960-62; Oakland, 1963-66
Lance Alworth, San Diego, 1963-69
Charley Taylor, Washington, 1964, 1966-67, 1969, 1973-75
Charlie Joiner, San Diego, 1976, 1979-81, 1983-85
Wes Chandler, New Orleans, 1979-80; New Orleans-San Diego, 1981; San Diego, 1983-86
Dwight Clark, San Francisco, 1980-86
James Lofton, Green Bay, 1979-81, 1983-86
Kellen Winslow, San Diego, 1980-84, 1986-87
6 Lionel Taylor, Denver, 1960-65
Bobby Mitchell, Washington, 1962-67
Ahmad Rashad, Minnesota, 1976-81
Ozzie Newsome, Cleveland, 1979-81, 1983-85
Art Monk, Washington, 1980-81, 1984-86, 1988

Most Pass Receptions, Season

106 Art Monk, Washington, 1984
101 Charley Hennigan, Houston, 1964
100 Lionel Taylor, Denver, 1961

Most Pass Receptions, Rookie, Season

83 Earl Cooper, San Francisco, 1980
81 Keith Jackson, Philadelphia, 1988
72 Bill Groman, Houston, 1960

Most Pass Receptions, Game

18 Tom Fears, Los Angeles vs. Green Bay, Dec. 3, 1950
17 Clark Gaines, N.Y. Jets vs. San Francisco, Sept. 21, 1980
16 Sonny Randle, St. Louis vs. N.Y. Giants, Nov. 4, 1962

Most Consecutive Games, Pass Receptions

167 Steve Largent, Seattle, 1977-88 (current)
143 Ozzie Newsome, Cleveland, 1979-88 (current)
127 Harold Carmichael, Philadelphia, 1972-80

Yards Gained

Most Seasons Leading League

7 Don Hutson, Green Bay, 1936, 1938-39, 1941-44
3 Raymond Berry, Baltimore, 1957, 1959-60
Lance Alworth, San Diego, 1965-66, 1968
2 By many players

Most Consecutive Seasons Leading League

4 Don Hutson, Green Bay, 1941-44
2 By many players

Most Yards Gained, Career

12,686 Steve Largent, Seattle, 1976-88

12,146 Charlie Joiner, Houston, 1969-72; Cincinnati, 1972-75; San Diego, 1976-86
11,834 Don Maynard, N.Y. Giants, 1958; N.Y. Jets, 1960-72; St. Louis, 1973

Most Seasons, 1,000 or More Yards, Pass Receiving
8 Steve Largent, Seattle, 1978-81, 1983-86
7 Lance Alworth, San Diego, 1963-69
5 Art Powell, N.Y. Titans, 1960, 1962; Oakland, 1963-64, 1966
Don Maynard, N.Y. Jets, 1960, 1962, 1965, 1967-68
James Lofton, Green Bay, 1980-81, 1983-85

Most Yards Gained, Season
1,746 Charley Hennigan, Houston, 1961
1,602 Lance Alworth, San Diego, 1965
1,570 Jerry Rice, San Francisco, 1986

Most Yards Gained, Rookie, Season
1,473 Bill Groman, Houston, 1960
1,231 Bill Howton, Green Bay, 1952
1,131 Bill Brooks, Indianapolis, 1986

Most Yards Gained, Game
309 Stephone Paige, Kansas City vs. San Diego, Dec. 22, 1985
303 Jim Benton, Cleveland vs. Detroit, Nov. 22, 1945
302 Cloyce Box, Detroit vs. Baltimore, Dec. 3, 1950

Most Games, 200 or More Yards Pass Receiving, Career
5 Lance Alworth, San Diego, 1962-70; Dallas, 1971-72
4 Don Hutson, Green Bay, 1935-45
Charley Hennigan, Houston, 1960-66
3 Don Maynard, N.Y. Giants, 1958; N.Y. Jets, 1960-72; St. Louis, 1973
Wes Chandler, New Orleans, 1978-81; San Diego, 1981-87; San Francisco, 1988

Most Games, 200 or More Yards Pass Receiving, Season
3 Charley Hennigan, Houston, 1961
2 Don Hutson, Green Bay, 1942
Gene Roberts, N.Y. Giants, 1949
Lance Alworth, San Diego, 1963
Don Maynard, N.Y. Jets, 1968

Most Games, 100 or More Yards Pass Receiving, Career
50 Don Maynard, N.Y. Giants, 1958; N.Y. Jets, 1960-72; St. Louis, 1973
41 Lance Alworth, San Diego, 1962-70; Dallas, 1971-72
40 Steve Largent, Seattle, 1976-88

Most Games, 100 or More Yards Pass Receiving, Season
10 Charley Hennigan, Houston, 1961
9 Elroy (Crazylegs) Hirsch, Los Angeles, 1951
Bill Groman, Houston, 1960
Lance Alworth, San Diego, 1965
Don Maynard, N.Y. Jets, 1967
Stanley Morgan, New England, 1986
8 Charley Hennigan, Houston, 1964
Lance Alworth, San Diego, 1967
Mark Duper, Miami, 1986

Most Consecutive Games, 100 or More Yards Pass Receiving
7 Charley Hennigan, Houston, 1961
Bill Groman, Houston, 1961
6 Raymond Berry, Baltimore, 1960
Pat Studstill, Detroit, 1966
5 Elroy (Crazylegs) Hirsch, Los Angeles, 1951
Bob Boyd, Los Angeles, 1954
Terry Barr, Detroit, 1963
Lance Alworth, San Diego, 1966

Longest Pass Reception (All TDs except as noted)
99 Andy Farkas (from Filchock), Washington vs. Pittsburgh, Oct. 15, 1939
Bobby Mitchell (from Izo), Washington vs. Cleveland, Sept. 15, 1963
Pat Studstill (from Sweetan), Detroit vs. Baltimore, Oct. 16, 1966
Gerry Allen (from Jurgensen), Washington vs. Chicago, Sept. 15, 1968
Cliff Branch (from Plunkett), L.A. Raiders vs. Washington, Oct. 2, 1983
Mike Quick (from Jaworski), Philadelphia vs. Atlanta, Nov. 10, 1985
98 Gaynell Tinsley (from Russell), Chi. Cardinals vs. Cleveland, Nov. 17, 1938
Dick (Night Train) Lane (from Compton), Chi. Cardinals vs. Green Bay, Nov. 13, 1955
John Farrington (from Wade), Chicago vs. Detroit, Oct. 8, 1961
Willard Dewveall (from Lee), Houston vs. San Diego, Nov. 25, 1962
Homer Jones (from Morrall), N.Y. Giants vs. Pittsburgh, Sept. 11, 1966
Bobby Moore (from Hart), St. Louis vs. Los Angeles, Dec. 10, 1972 (no TD)
97 Gaynell Tinsley (from Coffee), Chi. Cardinals vs. Chi. Bears, Dec. 5, 1937
Cloyce Box (from Layne), Detroit vs. Green Bay, Nov. 26, 1953
Jerry Tarr (from Shaw), Denver vs. Boston, Sept. 21, 1962

Average Gain

Highest Average Gain, Career (200 receptions)
22.26 Homer Jones, N.Y. Giants, 1964-69; Cleveland, 1970 (224-4,986)
20.82 Buddy Dial, Pittsburgh, 1959-63; Dallas, 1964-66 (261-5,436)
20.24 Harlon Hill, Chi. Bears, 1954-61; Pittsburgh, 1962; Detroit, 1962 (233-4,717)

Highest Average Gain, Season (24 receptions)
32.58 Don Currivan, Boston, 1947 (24-782)
31.44 Bucky Pope, Los Angeles, 1964 (25-786)
28.60 Bobby Duckworth, San Diego, 1984 (25-715)

Highest Average Gain, Game (3 receptions)
60.67 Bill Groman, Houston vs. Denver, Nov. 20, 1960 (3-182)
Homer Jones, N.Y. Giants vs. Washington, Dec. 12, 1965 (3-182)
60.33 Don Currivan, Boston vs. Washington, Nov. 30, 1947 (3-181)
59.67 Bobby Duckworth, San Diego vs. Chicago, Dec. 3, 1984 (3-179)

Touchdowns

Most Seasons Leading League
9 Don Hutson, Green Bay, 1935-38, 1940-44
3 Lance Alworth, San Diego, 1964-66
2 By many players

Most Consecutive Seasons Leading League
5 Don Hutson, Green Bay, 1940-44
4 Don Hutson, Green Bay, 1935-38
3 Lance Alworth, San Diego, 1964-66

Most Touchdowns, Career
99 Don Hutson, Green Bay, 1935-45
97 Steve Largent, Seattle, 1976-88
88 Don Maynard, N.Y. Giants, 1958; N.Y. Jets, 1960-72; St. Louis, 1973

Most Touchdowns, Season
22 Jerry Rice, San Francisco, 1987
18 Mark Clayton, Miami, 1984
17 Don Hutson, Green Bay, 1942
Elroy (Crazylegs) Hirsch, Los Angeles, 1951
Bill Groman, Houston, 1961

Most Touchdowns, Rookie, Season
13 Bill Howton, Green Bay, 1952
John Jefferson, San Diego, 1979
12 Harlon Hill, Chi. Bears, 1954
Bill Groman, Houston, 1960
Mike Ditka, Chicago, 1961
Bob Hayes, Dallas, 1965
10 Bill Swiacki, N.Y. Giants, 1948
Bucky Pope, Los Angeles, 1964
Sammy White, Minnesota, 1976
Daryl Turner, Seattle, 1984

Most Touchdowns, Game
5 Bob Shaw, Chi. Cardinals vs. Baltimore, Oct. 2, 1950
Kellen Winslow, San Diego vs. Oakland, Nov. 22, 1981
4 By many players. Last time: Wesley Walker, N.Y. Jets vs. Miami, Sept. 21, 1986 (OT)

Most Consecutive Games, Touchdowns
13 Jerry Rice, San Francisco, 1986-87
11 Elroy (Crazylegs) Hirsch, Los Angeles, 1950-51
Buddy Dial, Pittsburgh, 1959-60
9 Lance Alworth, San Diego, 1963

Interceptions By

Most Seasons Leading League
3 Everson Walls, Dallas, 1981-82, 1985
2 Dick (Night Train) Lane, Los Angeles, 1952; Chi. Cardinals, 1954
Jack Christiansen, Detroit, 1953, 1957
Milt Davis, Baltimore, 1957, 1959
Dick Lynch, N.Y. Giants, 1961, 1963
Johnny Robinson, Kansas City, 1966, 1970
Bill Bradley, Philadelphia, 1971-72
Emmitt Thomas, Kansas City, 1969, 1974

Most Interceptions By, Career
81 Paul Krause, Washington, 1964-67; Minnesota, 1968-79
79 Emlen Tunnell, N.Y. Giants, 1948-58; Green Bay, 1959-61
68 Dick (Night Train) Lane, Los Angeles, 1952-53; Chi. Cardinals, 1954-59; Detroit, 1960-65

Most Interceptions By, Season
14 Dick (Night Train) Lane, Los Angeles, 1952
13 Dan Sandifer, Washington, 1948
Orban (Spec) Sanders, N.Y. Yanks, 1950
Lester Hayes, Oakland, 1980
12 By nine players

Most Interceptions By, Rookie, Season
14 Dick (Night Train) Lane, Los Angeles, 1952
13 Dan Sandifer, Washington, 1948
12 Woodley Lewis, Los Angeles, 1950
Paul Krause, Washington, 1964

Most Interceptions By, Game
4 Sammy Baugh, Washington vs. Detroit, Nov. 14, 1943
Dan Sandifer, Washington vs. Boston, Oct. 31, 1948
Don Doll, Detroit vs. Chi. Cardinals, Oct. 23, 1949
Bob Nussbaumer, Chi. Cardinals vs. N.Y. Bulldogs, Nov. 13, 1949
Russ Craft, Philadelphia vs. Chi. Cardinals, Sept. 24, 1950
Bobby Dillon, Green Bay vs. Detroit, Nov. 26, 1953
Jack Butler, Pittsburgh vs. Washington, Dec. 13, 1953
Austin (Goose) Gonsoulin, Denver vs. Buffalo, Sept. 18, 1960
Jerry Norton, St. Louis vs. Washington, Nov. 20, 1960; vs. Pittsburgh, Nov. 26, 1961
Dave Baker, San Francisco vs. L.A. Rams, Dec. 4, 1960
Bobby Ply, Dall. Texans vs. San Diego, Dec. 16, 1962
Bobby Hunt, Kansas City vs. Houston, Oct. 4, 1964
Willie Brown, Denver vs. N.Y. Jets, Nov. 15, 1964
Dick Anderson, Miami vs. Pittsburgh, Dec. 3, 1973
Willie Buchanon, Green Bay vs. San Diego, Sept. 24, 1978
Deron Cherry, Kansas City vs. Seattle, Sept. 29, 1985

Most Consecutive Games, Passes Intercepted By
8 Tom Morrow, Oakland, 1962-63
7 Paul Krause, Washington, 1964
Larry Wilson, St. Louis, 1966
Ben Davis, Cleveland, 1968
6 Dick (Night Train) Lane, Chi. Cardinals, 1954-55
Will Sherman, Los Angeles, 1954-55
Jim Shofner, Cleveland, 1960
Paul Krause, Minnesota, 1968
Willie Williams, N.Y. Giants, 1968
Kermit Alexander, San Francisco, 1968-69
Mel Blount, Pittsburgh, 1975
Eric Harris, Kansas City, 1980
Lester Hayes, Oakland, 1980
Barry Wilburn, Washington, 1987

Yards Gained

Most Seasons Leading League
2 Dick (Night Train) Lane, Los Angeles, 1952; Chi. Cardinals, 1954
Herb Adderley, Green Bay, 1965, 1969
Dick Anderson, Miami, 1968, 1970

Most Yards Gained, Career
1,282 Emlen Tunnell, N.Y. Giants, 1948-58; Green Bay, 1959-61
1,207 Dick (Night Train) Lane, Los Angeles, 1952-53; Chi. Cardinals, 1954-59; Detroit, 1960-65
1,185 Paul Krause, Washington, 1964-67; Minnesota, 1968-79

Most Yards Gained, Season
349 Charlie McNeil, San Diego, 1961
301 Don Doll, Detroit, 1949
298 Dick (Night Train) Lane, Los Angeles, 1952

Most Yards Gained, Rookie, Season
301 Don Doll, Detroit, 1949
298 Dick (Night Train) Lane, Los Angeles, 1952

275 Woodley Lewis, Los Angeles, 1950

Most Yards Gained, Game

177 Charlie McNeil, San Diego vs. Houston, Sept. 24, 1961
167 Dick Jauron, Detroit vs. Chicago, Nov. 18, 1973
151 Tom Myers, New Orleans vs. Minnesota, Sept. 3, 1978
Mike Haynes, L.A. Raiders vs. Miami, Dec. 2, 1984

Longest Return (All TDs)

103 Vencie Glenn, San Diego vs. Denver, Nov. 29, 1987
102 Bob Smith, Detroit vs. Chi. Bears, Nov. 24, 1949
Erich Barnes, N.Y. Giants vs. Dall. Cowboys, Oct. 15, 1961
Gary Barbaro, Kansas City vs. Seattle, Dec. 11, 1977
Louis Breeden, Cincinnati vs. San Diego, Nov. 8, 1981
101 Richie Petitbon, Chicago vs Los Angeles, Dec. 9, 1962
Henry Carr, N.Y. Giants vs. Los Angeles, Nov. 13, 1966
Tony Greene, Buffalo vs. Kansas City, Oct. 3, 1976
Tom Pridemore, Atlanta vs. San Francisco, Sept. 20, 1981

Touchdowns

Most Touchdowns, Career

9 Ken Houston, Houston, 1967-72; Washington, 1973-80
7 Herb Adderley, Green Bay, 1961-69; Dallas, 1970-72
Erich Barnes, Chi. Bears, 1958-60; N.Y. Giants, 1961-64; Cleveland, 1965-70
Lem Barney, Detroit, 1967-77
6 Tom Janik, Denver, 1963-64; Buffalo, 1965-68; Boston, 1969-70; New England, 1971
Miller Farr, Denver, 1965; San Diego, 1965-66; Houston, 1967-69; St. Louis, 1970-72; Detroit, 1973
Bobby Bell, Kansas City, 1963-74

Most Touchdowns, Season

4 Ken Houston, Houston, 1971
Jim Kearney, Kansas City, 1972
3 Dick Harris, San Diego, 1961
Dick Lynch, N.Y. Giants, 1963
Herb Adderley, Green Bay, 1965
Lem Barney, Detroit, 1967
Miller Farr, Houston, 1967
Monte Jackson, Los Angeles, 1976
Rod Perry, Los Angeles, 1978
Ronnie Lott, San Francisco, 1981
Lloyd Burruss, Kansas City, 1986
2 By many players

Most Touchdowns, Rookie, Season

3 Lem Barney, Detroit, 1967
Ronnie Lott, San Francisco, 1981
2 By many players

Most Touchdowns, Game

2 Bill Blackburn, Chi. Cardinals vs. Boston, Oct. 24, 1948
Dan Sandifer, Washington vs. Boston, Oct. 31, 1948
Bob Franklin, Cleveland vs. Chicago, Dec. 11, 1960
Bill Stacy, St. Louis vs. Dall. Cowboys, Nov. 5, 1961
Jerry Norton, St. Louis vs. Pittsburgh, Nov. 26, 1961
Miller Farr, Houston vs. Buffalo, Dec. 7, 1968
Ken Houston, Houston vs. San Diego, Dec. 19, 1971
Jim Kearney, Kansas City vs. Denver, Oct. 1, 1972
Lemar Parrish, Cincinnati vs. Houston, Dec. 17, 1972
Dick Anderson, Miami vs. Pittsburgh, Dec. 3, 1973
Prentice McCray, New England vs. N.Y. Jets, Nov. 21, 1976
Kenny Johnson, Atlanta vs. Green Bay, Nov. 27, 1983 (OT)
Mike Kozlowski, Miami vs. N.Y. Jets, Dec. 16, 1983
Dave Brown, Seattle vs. Kansas City, Nov. 4, 1984
Lloyd Burruss, Kansas City vs. San Diego, Oct. 19, 1986

Punting

Most Seasons Leading League

4 Sammy Baugh, Washington, 1940-43
Jerrel Wilson, Kansas City, 1965, 1968, 1972-73
3 Yale Lary, Detroit, 1959, 1961, 1963
Jim Fraser, Denver, 1962-64
Ray Guy, Oakland, 1974-75, 1977
Rohn Stark, Baltimore, 1983; Indianapolis, 1985-86
2 By many players

Most Consecutive Seasons Leading League

4 Sammy Baugh, Washington, 1940-43
3 Jim Fraser, Denver, 1962-64
2 By many players

Punts

Most Punts, Career

1,154 Dave Jennings, N.Y. Giants, 1974-84; N.Y. Jets, 1985-87
1,083 John James, Atlanta, 1972-81; Detroit, 1982, Houston, 1982-84
1,072 Jerrel Wilson, Kansas City, 1963-77; New England, 1978

Most Punts, Season

114 Bob Parsons, Chicago, 1981
109 John James, Atlanta, 1978
108 John Teltschik, Philadelphia, 1986

Most Punts, Rookie, Season

108 John Teltschik, Philadelphia, 1986
99 Lewis Colbert, Kansas City, 1986
96 Mike Connell, San Francisco, 1978
Chris Norman, Denver, 1984

Most Punts, Game

15 John Teltschik, Philadelphia vs. N.Y. Giants, Dec. 6, 1987 (OT)
14 Dick Nesbitt, Chi. Cardinals vs. Chi. Bears, Nov. 30, 1933
Keith Molesworth, Chi. Bears vs. Green Bay, Dec. 10, 1933
Sammy Baugh, Washington vs. Philadelphia, Nov. 5, 1939
Carl Kinscherf, N.Y. Giants vs. Detroit, Nov. 7, 1943
George Taliaferro, N.Y. Yanks vs. Los Angeles, Sept. 28, 1951
12 Parker Hall, Cleveland vs. Green Bay, Nov. 26, 1939
Beryl Clark, Chi. Cardinals vs. Detroit, Sept. 15, 1940
Len Barnum, Philadelphia vs. Washington, Oct. 4, 1942
Horace Gillom, Cleveland vs. Philadelphia, Dec. 3, 1950
Adrian Burk, Philadelphia vs. Green Bay, Nov. 2, 1952; vs. N.Y. Giants, Dec. 12, 1954
Bob Scarpitto, Denver vs. Oakland, Sept. 10, 1967
Bill Van Heusen, Denver vs. Cincinnati, Oct. 6, 1968
Tom Blanchard, New Orleans vs. Minnesota, Nov. 16, 1975
Rusty Jackson, Los Angeles vs. San Francisco, Nov. 21, 1976
Wilbur Summers, Detroit vs. San Francisco, Oct. 23, 1977
John James, Atlanta vs. Washington, Dec. 10, 1978
Luke Prestridge, Denver vs. Buffalo, Oct. 25, 1981
Greg Coleman, Minnesota vs. Green Bay, Nov. 21, 1982

Longest Punt

98 Steve O'Neal, N.Y. Jets vs. Denver, Sept. 21, 1969
94 Joe Lintzenich, Chi. Bears vs. N.Y. Giants, Nov. 16, 1931
90 Don Chandler, Green Bay vs. San Francisco, Oct. 10, 1965

Average Yardage

Highest Average, Punting, Career (300 punts)

45.10 Sammy Baugh, Washington, 1937-52 (338-15,245)
44.68 Tommy Davis, San Francisco, 1959-69 (511-22,833)
44.34 Rohn Stark, Baltimore, 1982-83; Indianapolis, 1984-88 (514-22,791)

Highest Average, Punting, Season (Qualifiers)

51.40 Sammy Baugh, Washington, 1940 (35-1,799)
48.94 Yale Lary, Detroit, 1963 (35-1,713)
48.73 Sammy Baugh, Washington, 1941 (30-1,462)

Highest Average, Punting, Rookie, Season (Qualifiers)

46.40 Bobby Walden, Minnesota, 1964 (72-3,341)
46.22 Dave Lewis, Cincinnati, 1970 (79-3,651)
45.92 Frank Sinkwich, Detroit, 1943 (12-551)

Highest Average, Punting, Game (4 punts)

61.75 Bob Cifers, Detroit vs. Chi. Bears, Nov. 24, 1946 (4-247)
61.60 Roy McKay, Green Bay vs. Chi. Cardinals, Oct. 28, 1945 (5-308)
59.40 Sammy Baugh, Washington vs. Detroit, Oct. 27, 1940 (5-297)

Punts Had Blocked

Most Consecutive Punts, None Blocked

623 Dave Jennings, N.Y. Giants, 1976-83
619 Ray Guy, Oakland, 1979-81; L.A. Raiders, 1982-86
578 Bobby Walden, Minnesota, 1964-67; Pittsburgh, 1968-72

Most Punts Had Blocked, Career

14 Herman Weaver, Detroit, 1970-76; Seattle, 1977-80
12 Jerrel Wilson, Kansas City, 1963-77; New England, 1978
Tom Blanchard, N.Y. Giants, 1971-73; New Orleans, 1974-78; Tampa Bay, 1979-81
11 David Lee, Baltimore, 1966-78

Most Punts Had Blocked, Season

6 Harry Newsome, Pittsburgh, 1988
3 By many players

Punt Returns

Most Seasons Leading League

3 Les (Speedy) Duncan, San Diego, 1965-66; Washington, 1971
Rick Upchurch, Denver, 1976, 1978, 1982
2 Dick Christy, N.Y. Titans, 1961-62
Claude Gibson, Oakland, 1963-64
Billy Johnson, Houston, 1975, 1977

Punt Returns

Most Punt Returns, Career

282 Billy Johnson, Houston, 1974-80; Atlanta, 1982-87; Washington, 1988
264 J. T. Smith, Washington, 1978; Kansas City, 1978-84; St. Louis, 1985-87; Phoenix, 1988
258 Emlen Tunnell, N.Y. Giants, 1948-58; Green Bay, 1959-61

Most Punt Returns, Season

70 Danny Reece, Tampa Bay, 1979
62 Fulton Walker, Miami-L.A. Raiders, 1985
58 J. T. Smith, Kansas City, 1979
Greg Pruitt, L.A. Raiders, 1983
Leo Lewis, Minnesota, 1988

Most Punt Returns, Rookie, Season

57 Lew Barnes, Chicago, 1986
54 James Jones, Dallas, 1980
53 Louis Lipps, Pittsburgh, 1984

Most Punt Returns, Game

11 Eddie Brown, Washington vs. Tampa Bay, Oct. 9, 1977
10 Theo Bell, Pittsburgh vs. Buffalo, Dec. 16, 1979
Mike Nelms, Washington vs. New Orleans, Dec. 26, 1982
9 Rodger Bird, Oakland vs. Denver, Sept. 10, 1967
Ralph McGill, San Francisco vs. Atlanta, Oct. 29, 1972
Ed Podolak, Kansas City vs. San Diego, Nov. 10, 1974
Anthony Leonard, San Francisco vs. New Orleans, Oct. 17, 1976
Butch Johnson, Dallas vs. Buffalo, Nov. 15, 1976
Larry Marshall, Philadelphia vs. Tampa Bay, Sept. 18, 1977
Nesby Glasgow, Baltimore vs. Kansas City, Sept. 2, 1979
Mike Nelms, Washington vs. St. Louis, Dec. 21, 1980
Leon Bright, N.Y. Giants vs. Philadelphia, Dec. 11, 1982
Pete Shaw, N.Y. Giants vs. Philadelphia, Nov. 20, 1983
Cleotha Montgomery, L.A. Raiders vs. Detroit, Dec. 10, 1984
Phil McConkey, N.Y. Giants vs. Philadelphia, Dec. 6, 1987 (OT)

Fair Catches

Most Fair Catches, Season

25 Mark Konecny, Philadelphia, 1988
Phil McConkey, N.Y. Giants, 1988
24 Ken Graham, San Diego, 1969
22 Lem Barney, Detroit, 1976

Most Fair Catches, Game

7 Lem Barney, Detroit vs. Chicago, Nov. 21, 1976
Bobby Morse, Philadelphia vs. Buffalo, Dec. 27, 1987
6 Jake Scott, Miami vs. Buffalo, Dec. 20, 1970
Greg Pruitt, L.A. Raiders vs. Seattle, Oct. 7, 1984
5 By many players

Yards Gained

Most Seasons Leading League

3 Alvin Haymond, Baltimore, 1965-66; Los Angeles, 1969

2 Bill Dudley, Pittsburgh, 1942, 1946
Emlen Tunnell, N.Y. Giants, 1951-52
Dick Christy, N.Y. Titans, 1961-62
Claude Gibson, Oakland, 1963-64
Rodger Bird, Oakland, 1966-67
J. T. Smith, Kansas City, 1979-80
Vai Sikahema, St. Louis, 1986-87

Most Yards Gained, Career
3,317 Billy Johnson, Houston, 1974-80; Atlanta, 1982-87; Washington, 1988
3,008 Rick Upchurch, Denver, 1975-83
2,730 J. T. Smith, Washington, 1978; Kansas City, 1978-84; St. Louis, 1985-87; Phoenix, 1988

Most Yards Gained, Season
692 Fulton Walker, Miami-L.A. Raiders, 1985
666 Greg Pruitt, L.A. Raiders, 1983
656 Louis Lipps, Pittsburgh, 1984

Most Yards Gained, Rookie, Season
656 Louis Lipps, Pittsburgh, 1984
655 Neal Colzie, Oakland, 1975
608 Mike Haynes, New England, 1976

Most Yards Gained, Game
207 LeRoy Irvin, Los Angeles vs. Atlanta, Oct. 11, 1981
205 George Atkinson, Oakland vs. Buffalo, Sept. 15, 1968
184 Tom Watkins, Detroit vs. San Francisco, Oct. 6, 1963

Longest Punt Return (All TDs)
98 Gil LeFebvre, Cincinnati vs. Brooklyn, Dec. 3, 1933
Charlie West, Minnesota vs. Washington, Nov. 3, 1968
Dennis Morgan, Dallas vs. St. Louis, Oct. 13, 1974
97 Greg Pruitt, L.A. Raiders vs. Washington, Oct. 2, 1983
96 Bill Dudley, Washington vs. Pittsburgh, Dec. 3, 1950

Average Yardage
Highest Average, Career (75 returns)
12.78 George McAfee, Chi. Bears, 1940-41, 1945-50 (112-1,431)
12.75 Jack Christiansen, Detroit, 1951-58 (85-1,084)
12.55 Claude Gibson, San Diego, 1961-62; Oakland, 1963-65 (110-1,381)

Highest Average, Season (Qualifiers)
23.00 Herb Rich, Baltimore, 1950 (12-276)
21.47 Jack Christiansen, Detroit, 1952 (15-322)
21.28 Dick Christy, N.Y. Titans, 1961 (18-383)

Highest Average, Rookie, Season (Qualifiers)
23.00 Herb Rich, Baltimore, 1950 (12-276)
20.88 Jerry Davis, Chi. Cardinals, 1948 (16-334)
20.73 Frank Sinkwich, Detroit, 1943 (11-228)

Highest Average, Game (3 returns)
47.67 Chuck Latourette, St. Louis vs. New Orleans, Sept. 29, 1968 (3-143)
47.33 Johnny Roland, St. Louis vs. Philadelphia, Oct. 2, 1966 (3-142)
45.67 Dick Christy, N.Y. Titans vs. Denver, Sept. 24, 1961 (3-137)

Touchdowns
Most Touchdowns, Career
8 Jack Christiansen, Detroit, 1951-58
Rick Upchurch, Denver, 1975-83
6 Billy Johnson, Houston, 1974-80; Atlanta, 1982-87; Washington, 1988
5 Emlen Tunnell, N.Y. Giants, 1948-58; Green Bay, 1959-61

Most Touchdowns, Season
4 Jack Christiansen, Detroit, 1951
Rick Upchurch, Denver, 1976
3 Emlen Tunnell, N.Y. Giants, 1951
Billy Johnson, Houston, 1975
LeRoy Irvin, Los Angeles, 1981
2 By many players

Most Touchdowns, Rookie, Season
4 Jack Christiansen, Detroit, 1951
2 By six players

Most Touchdowns, Game
2 Jack Christiansen, Detroit vs. Los Angeles, Oct. 14, 1951; vs. Green Bay, Nov. 22, 1951
Dick Christy, N.Y. Titans vs. Denver, Sept. 24, 1961
Rick Upchurch, Denver vs. Cleveland, Sept. 26, 1976
LeRoy Irvin, Los Angeles vs. Atlanta, Oct. 11, 1981
Vai Sikahema, St. Louis vs. Tampa Bay, Dec. 21, 1986

Kickoff Returns
Most Seasons Leading League
3 Abe Woodson, San Francisco, 1959, 1962-63
2 Lynn Chandnois, Pittsburgh, 1951-52
Bobby Jancik, Houston, 1962-63
Travis Williams, Green Bay, 1967; Los Angeles, 1971

Kickoff Returns
Most Kickoff Returns, Career
275 Ron Smith, Chicago, 1965, 1970-72; Atlanta, 1966-67; Los Angeles, 1968-69; San Diego, 1973; Oakland, 1974
243 Bruce Harper, N.Y. Jets, 1977-84
194 Steve Odom, Green Bay, 1974-79; N.Y. Giants, 1979

Most Kickoff Returns, Season
60 Drew Hill, Los Angeles, 1981
55 Bruce Harper, N.Y. Jets, 1978, 1979
David Turner, Cincinnati, 1979
Stump Mitchell, St. Louis, 1981
53 Eddie Payton, Minnesota, 1980
Buster Rhymes, Minnesota, 1985

Most Kickoff Returns, Rookie, Season
55 Stump Mitchell, St. Louis, 1981
53 Buster Rhymes, Minnesota, 1985
50 Nesby Glasgow, Baltimore, 1979
Dino Hall, Cleveland, 1979

Most Kickoff Returns, Game
9 Noland Smith, Kansas City vs. Oakland, Nov. 23, 1967
Dino Hall, Cleveland vs. Pittsburgh, Oct. 7, 1979
Paul Palmer, Kansas City vs. Seattle, Sept. 20, 1987
8 George Taliaferro, N.Y. Yanks vs. N.Y. Giants, Dec. 3, 1950
Bobby Jancik, Houston vs. Boston, Dec. 8, 1963; vs. Oakland, Dec. 22, 1963
Mel Renfro, Dallas vs. Green Bay, Nov. 29, 1964
Willie Porter, Boston vs. N.Y. Jets, Sept. 22, 1968
Keith Moody, Buffalo vs. Seattle, Oct. 30, 1977
Brian Baschnagel, Chicago vs. Houston, Nov. 6, 1977
Bruce Harper, N.Y. Jets vs. New England, Oct. 29, 1978; vs. New England, Sept. 9, 1979
Dino Hall, Cleveland vs. Pittsburgh, Nov. 25, 1979
Terry Metcalf, Washington vs. St. Louis, Sept. 20, 1981
Harlan Huckleby, Green Bay vs. Washington, Oct. 17, 1983
Gary Ellerson, Green Bay vs. St. Louis, Sept. 29, 1985
Bobby Humphery, N.Y. Jets vs. Cincinnati, Dec. 21, 1986
Bobby Joe Edmonds, Seattle vs. L.A. Raiders, Nov. 30, 1987
Joe Cribbs, Miami vs. Pittsburgh, Dec. 18, 1988
7 By many players

Yards Gained
Most Seasons Leading League
3 Bruce Harper, N.Y. Jets, 1977-79
2 Marshall Goldberg, Chi. Cardinals, 1941-42
Woodley Lewis, Los Angeles, 1953-54
Al Carmichael, Green Bay, 1956-57
Timmy Brown, Philadelphia, 1961, 1963
Bobby Jancik, Houston, 1963, 1966
Ron Smith, Atlanta, 1966-67

Most Yards Gained, Career
6,922 Ron Smith, Chicago, 1965, 1970-72; Atlanta, 1966-67; Los Angeles, 1968-69; San Diego, 1973; Oakland, 1974
5,538 Abe Woodson, San Francisco, 1958-64; St. Louis, 1965-66
5,407 Bruce Harper, N.Y. Jets, 1977-84

Most Yards Gained, Season
1,345 Buster Rhymes, Minnesota, 1985
1,317 Bobby Jancik, Houston, 1963
1,314 Dave Hampton, Green Bay, 1971

Most Yards Gained, Rookie, Season
1,345 Buster Rhymes, Minnesota, 1985
1,292 Stump Mitchell, St. Louis, 1981
1,245 Odell Barry, Denver, 1964

Most Yards Gained, Game
294 Wally Triplett, Detroit vs. Los Angeles, Oct. 29, 1950
247 Timmy Brown, Philadelphia vs. Dallas, Nov. 6, 1966
244 Noland Smith, Kansas City vs. San Diego, Oct. 15, 1967

Longest Kickoff Return (All TDs)
106 Al Carmichael, Green Bay vs. Chi. Bears, Oct. 7, 1956
Noland Smith, Kansas City vs. Denver, Dec. 17, 1967
Roy Green, St. Louis vs. Dallas, Oct. 21, 1979
105 Frank Seno, Chi. Cardinals vs. N.Y. Giants, Oct. 20, 1946
Ollie Matson, Chi. Cardinals vs. Washington, Oct. 14, 1956
Abe Woodson, San Francisco vs. Los Angeles, Nov. 8, 1959
Timmy Brown, Philadelphia vs. Cleveland, Sept. 17, 1961
Jon Arnett, Los Angeles vs. Detroit, Oct. 29, 1961
Eugene (Mercury) Morris, Miami vs. Cincinnati, Sept. 14, 1969
Travis Williams, Los Angeles vs. New Orleans, Dec. 5, 1971
104 By many players

Average Yardage
Highest Average, Career (75 returns)
30.56 Gale Sayers, Chicago, 1965-71 (91-2,781)
29.57 Lynn Chandnois, Pittsburgh, 1950-56 (92-2,720)
28.69 Abe Woodson, San Francisco, 1958-64; St. Louis, 1965-66 (193-5,538)

Highest Average, Season (Qualifiers)
41.06 Travis Williams, Green Bay, 1967 (18-739)
37.69 Gale Sayers, Chicago, 1967 (16-603)
35.50 Ollie Matson, Chi. Cardinals, 1958 (14-497)

Highest Average, Rookie, Season (Qualifiers)
41.06 Travis Williams, Green Bay, 1967 (18-739)
33.08 Tom Moore, Green Bay, 1960 (12-397)
32.88 Duriel Harris, Miami, 1976 (17-559)

Highest Average, Game (3 returns)
73.50 Wally Triplett, Detroit vs. Los Angeles, Oct. 29, 1950 (4-294)
67.33 Lenny Lyles, San Francisco vs. Baltimore, Dec. 18, 1960 (3-202)
65.33 Ken Hall, Houston vs. N.Y. Titans, Oct. 23, 1960 (3-196)

Touchdowns
Most Touchdowns, Career
6 Ollie Matson, Chi. Cardinals, 1952, 1954-58; L.A. Rams, 1959-62; Detroit, 1963; Philadelphia, 1964
Gale Sayers, Chicago, 1965-71
Travis Williams, Green Bay, 1967-70; Los Angeles, 1971
5 Bobby Mitchell, Cleveland, 1958-61; Washington, 1962-68
Abe Woodson, San Francisco, 1958-64; St. Louis, 1965-66
Timmy Brown, Green Bay, 1959; Philadelphia, 1960-67; Baltimore, 1968
4 Cecil Turner, Chicago, 1968-73
Ron Brown, L.A. Rams, 1984-88

Most Touchdowns, Season
4 Travis Williams, Green Bay, 1967
Cecil Turner, Chicago, 1970
3 Verda (Vitamin T) Smith, Los Angeles, 1950
Abe Woodson, San Francisco, 1963
Gale Sayers, Chicago, 1967
Raymond Clayborn, New England, 1977
Ron Brown, L.A. Rams, 1985
2 By many players

Most Touchdowns, Rookie, Season
4 Travis Williams, Green Bay, 1967
3 Raymond Clayborn, New England, 1977
2 By seven players

Most Touchdowns, Game
2 Timmy Brown, Philadelphia vs. Dallas, Nov. 6, 1966
Travis Williams, Green Bay vs. Cleveland, Nov. 12, 1967
Ron Brown, L.A. Rams vs. Green Bay, Nov. 24, 1985

Combined Kick Returns

Most Combined Kick Returns, Career

510 Ron Smith, Chicago, 1965, 1970-72; Atlanta, 1966-67; Los Angeles, 1968-69; San Diego, 1973; Oakland, 1974 (p-235, k-275)
426 Bruce Harper, N.Y. Jets, 1977-84 (p-183, k-243)
423 Alvin Haymond, Baltimore, 1964-67; Philadelphia, 1968; Los Angeles, 1969-71; Washington, 1972; Houston, 1973 (p-253, k-170)

Most Combined Kick Returns, Season

100 Larry Jones, Washington, 1975 (p-53, k-47)
97 Stump Mitchell, St. Louis, 1981 (p-42, k-55)
94 Nesby Glasgow, Baltimore, 1979 (p-44, k-50)

Most Combined Kick Returns, Game

13 Stump Mitchell, St. Louis vs. Atlanta, Oct. 18, 1981 (p-6, k-7)
12 Mel Renfro, Dallas vs. Green Bay, Nov. 29, 1964 (p-4, k-8)
Larry Jones, Washington vs. Dallas, Dec. 13, 1975 (p-6, k-6)
Eddie Brown, Washington vs. Tampa Bay, Oct. 9, 1977 (p-11, k-1)
Nesby Glasgow, Baltimore vs. Denver, Sept. 2, 1979 (p-9, k-3)
11 By many players

Yards Gained

Most Yards Returned, Career

8,710 Ron Smith, Chicago, 1965, 1970-72; Atlanta, 1966-67; Los Angeles, 1968-69; San Diego, 1973; Oakland, 1974 (p-1,788, k-6,922)
7,191 Bruce Harper, N.Y. Jets, 1977-84 (p-1,784, k-5,407)
6,740 Les (Speedy) Duncan, San Diego, 1964-70; Washington, 1971-74 (p-2,201, k-4,539)

Most Yards Returned, Season

1,737 Stump Mitchell, St. Louis, 1981 (p-445, k-1,292)
1,658 Bruce Harper, N.Y. Jets, 1978 (p-378, k-1,280)
1,591 Mike Nelms, Washington, 1981 (p-492, k-1,099)

Most Yards Returned, Game

294 Wally Triplett, Detroit vs. Los Angeles, Oct. 29, 1950 (k-294)
Woodley Lewis, Los Angeles vs. Detroit, Oct. 18, 1953 (p-120, k-174)
289 Eddie Payton, Detroit vs. Minnesota, Dec. 17, 1977 (p-105, k-184)
282 Les (Speedy) Duncan, San Diego vs. N.Y. Jets, Nov. 24, 1968 (p-102, k-180)

Touchdowns

Most Touchdowns, Career

9 Ollie Matson, Chi. Cardinals, 1952, 1954-58; Los Angeles, 1959-62; Detroit, 1963; Philadelphia, 1964-66 (p-3, k-6)
8 Jack Christiansen, Detroit, 1951-58 (p-8)
Bobby Mitchell, Cleveland, 1958-61; Washington, 1962-68 (p-3, k-5)
Gale Sayers, Chicago, 1965-71 (p-2, k-6)
Rick Upchurch, Denver, 1975-83 (p-8)
Billy Johnson, Houston, 1974-80; Atlanta, 1982-87; Washington, 1988 (p-6, k-2)
7 Abe Woodson, San Francisco, 1958-64; St. Louis, 1965-66 (p-2, k-5)

Most Touchdowns, Season

4 Jack Christiansen, Detroit, 1951 (p-4)
Emlen Tunnell, N.Y. Giants, 1951 (p-3, k-1)
Gale Sayers, Chicago, 1967 (p-1, k-3)
Travis Williams, Green Bay, 1967 (k-4)
Cecil Turner, Chicago, 1970 (k-4)
Billy Johnson, Houston, 1975 (p-3, k-1)
Rick Upchurch, Denver, 1976 (p-4)
3 Verda (Vitamin T) Smith, Los Angeles, 1950 (k-3)
Abe Woodson, San Francisco, 1963 (k-3)
Raymond Clayborn, New England, 1977 (k-3)
Billy Johnson, Houston, 1977 (p-2, k-1)
LeRoy Irvin, Los Angeles, 1981 (p-3)
Ron Brown, L.A. Rams, 1985 (k-3)
2 By many players

Most Touchdowns, Game

2 Jack Christiansen, Detroit vs. Los Angeles, Oct. 14, 1951 (p-2); vs. Green Bay, Nov. 22, 1951 (p-2)
Jim Patton, N.Y. Giants vs. Washington, Oct. 30, 1955 (p-1, k-1)
Bobby Mitchell, Cleveland vs. Philadelphia, Nov. 23, 1958 (p-1, k-1)
Dick Christy, N.Y. Titans vs. Denver, Sept. 24, 1961 (p-2)
Al Frazier, Denver vs. Boston, Dec. 3, 1961 (p-1, k-1)
Timmy Brown, Philadelphia vs. Dallas, Nov. 6, 1966 (k-2)
Travis Williams, Green Bay vs. Cleveland, Nov. 12, 1967 (k-2); vs. Pittsburgh, Nov. 2, 1969 (p-1, k-1)
Gale Sayers, Chicago vs. San Francisco, Dec. 3, 1967 (p-1, k-1)
Rick Upchurch, Denver vs. Cleveland, Sept. 26, 1976 (p-2)
Eddie Payton, Detroit vs. Minnesota, Dec. 17, 1977 (p-1, k-1)
LeRoy Irvin, Los Angeles vs. Atlanta, Oct. 11, 1981 (p-2)
Ron Brown, L.A. Rams vs. Green Bay, Nov. 24, 1985 (k-2)
Vai Sikahema, St. Louis vs. Tampa Bay, Dec. 21, 1986 (p-2)

Fumbles

Most Fumbles, Career

106 Dan Fouts, San Diego, 1973-87
105 Roman Gabriel, Los Angeles, 1962-72; Philadelphia, 1973-77
95 Johnny Unitas, Baltimore, 1956-72; San Diego, 1973

Most Fumbles, Season

17 Dan Pastorini, Houston, 1973
Warren Moon, Houston, 1984
16 Don Meredith, Dallas, 1964
Joe Cribbs, Buffalo, 1980
Steve Fuller, Kansas City, 1980
Paul McDonald, Cleveland, 1984
Phil Simms, N.Y. Giants, 1985
15 Paul Christman, Chi. Cardinals, 1946
Sammy Baugh, Washington, 1947
Sam Etcheverry, St. Louis, 1961
Len Dawson, Kansas City, 1964
Terry Metcalf, St. Louis, 1976
Steve DeBerg, Tampa Bay, 1984

Most Fumbles, Game

7 Len Dawson, Kansas City vs. San Diego, Nov. 15, 1964
6 Sam Etcheverry, St. Louis vs. N.Y. Giants, Sept, 17, 1961
5 Paul Christman, Chi. Cardinals vs. Green Bay, Nov. 10, 1946
Charlie Conerly, N.Y. Giants vs. San Francisco, Dec. 1, 1957
Jack Kemp, Buffalo vs. Houston, Oct. 29, 1967
Roman Gabriel, Philadelphia vs. Oakland, Nov. 21, 1976
Randall Cunningham, Philadelphia vs. L.A. Raiders, Nov. 30, 1986 (OT)
Willie Totten, Buffalo vs. Indianapolis, Oct. 4, 1987
Dave Walter, Cincinnati vs. Seattle, Oct. 11, 1987

Fumbles Recovered

Most Fumbles Recovered, Career, Own and Opponents'

43 Fran Tarkenton, Minnesota, 1961-66, 1972-78; N.Y. Giants, 1967-71 (43 own)
38 Jack Kemp, Pittsburgh, 1957; L.A. Chargers, 1960; San Diego, 1961-62; Buffalo, 1962-67, 1969 (38 own)
Dan Fouts, San Diego, 1973-87 (37 own, 1 opp)
37 Roman Gabriel, Los Angeles, 1962-72; Philadelphia, 1973-77 (37 own)

Most Fumbles Recovered, Season, Own and Opponents'

9 Don Hultz, Minnesota, 1963 (9 opp)
8 Paul Christman, Chi. Cardinals, 1945 (8 own)
Joe Schmidt, Detroit, 1955 (8 opp)
Bill Butler, Minnesota, 1963 (8 own)
Kermit Alexander, San Francisco, 1965 (4 own, 4 opp)
Jack Lambert, Pittsburgh, 1976 (1 own, 7 opp)
Danny White, Dallas, 1981 (8 own)
Dan Marino, Miami, 1988 (7 own, 1 opp)
7 By many players

Most Fumbles Recovered, Game, Own and Opponents'

4 Otto Graham, Cleveland vs. N.Y. Giants, Oct. 25, 1953 (4 own)
Sam Etcheverry, St. Louis vs. N.Y. Giants, Sept. 17, 1961 (4 own)
Roman Gabriel, Los Angeles vs. San Francisco, Oct. 12, 1969 (4 own)
Joe Ferguson, Buffalo vs. Miami, Sept. 18, 1977 (4 own)
Randall Cunningham, Philadelphia vs. L.A. Raiders, Nov. 30, 1986 (OT) (4 own)
3 By many players

Own Fumbles Recovered

Most Own Fumbles Recovered, Career

43 Fran Tarkenton, Minnesota, 1961-66, 1972-78; N.Y. Giants, 1967-71
38 Jack Kemp, Pittsburgh, 1957; L.A. Chargers, 1960; San Diego, 1961-62; Buffalo, 1962-67, 1969
37 Roman Gabriel, Los Angeles, 1962-72; Philadelphia, 1973-77
Dan Fouts, San Diego, 1973-87

Most Own Fumbles Recovered, Season

8 Paul Christman, Chi. Cardinals, 1945
Bill Butler, Minnesota, 1963
Danny White, Dallas, 1981
7 Sammy Baugh, Washington, 1947
Tommy Thompson, Philadelphia, 1947
John Roach, St. Louis, 1960
Jack Larscheid, Oakland, 1960
Gary Huff, Chicago, 1974
Terry Metcalf, St. Louis, 1974
Joe Ferguson, Buffalo, 1977
Fran Tarkenton, Minnesota, 1978
Greg Pruitt, L.A. Raiders, 1983
Warren Moon, Houston, 1984
Dan Marino, Miami, 1988
6 By many players

Most Own Fumbles Recovered, Game

4 Otto Graham, Cleveland vs. N.Y. Giants, Oct. 25, 1953
Sam Etcheverry, St. Louis vs. N.Y. Giants, Sept. 17, 1961
Roman Gabriel, Los Angeles vs. San Francisco, Oct. 12, 1969
Joe Ferguson, Buffalo vs. Miami, Sept. 18, 1977
Randall Cunningham, Philadelphia vs. L.A. Raiders, Nov. 30, 1986 (OT)
3 By many players

Opponents' Fumbles Recovered

Most Opponents' Fumbles Recovered, Career

29 Jim Marshall, Cleveland, 1960; Minnesota, 1961-79
25 Dick Butkus, Chicago, 1965-73
23 Carl Eller, Minnesota, 1964-78; Seattle, 1979
Reggie Williams, Cincinnati, 1976-88

Most Opponents' Fumbles Recovered, Season

9 Don Hultz, Minnesota, 1963
8 Joe Schmidt, Detroit, 1955
7 Alan Page, Minnesota, 1970
Jack Lambert, Pittsburgh, 1976
Ray Childress, Houston, 1988

Most Opponents' Fumbles Recovered, Game

3 Corwin Clatt, Chi. Cardinals vs. Detroit, Nov. 6, 1949
Vic Sears, Philadelphia vs. Green Bay, Nov. 2, 1952
Ed Beatty, San Francisco vs. Los Angeles, Oct. 7, 1956
Ron Carroll, Houston vs. Cincinnati, Oct. 27, 1974
Maurice Spencer, New Orleans vs. Atlanta, Oct. 10, 1976
Steve Nelson, New England vs. Philadelphia, Oct. 8, 1978
Charles Jackson, Kansas City vs. Pittsburgh, Sept. 6, 1981
Willie Buchanon, San Diego vs. Denver, Sept. 27, 1981
Joey Browner, Minnesota vs. San Francisco, Sept. 8, 1985
Ray Childress, Houston vs. Washington, Oct. 30, 1988
2 By many players

Yards Returning Fumbles

Longest Fumble Run (All TDs)

104 Jack Tatum, Oakland vs. Green Bay, Sept. 24, 1972 (opp)
98 George Halas, Chi. Bears vs. Oorang Indians, Marion, Ohio, Nov. 4, 1923 (opp)
97 Chuck Howley, Dallas vs. Atlanta, Oct. 2, 1966 (opp)

Touchdowns

Most Touchdowns, Career (Total)

4 Bill Thompson, Denver, 1969-81
3 Ralph Heywood, Detroit, 1947-48; Boston, 1948; N.Y. Bulldogs, 1949
Leo Sugar, Chi. Cardinals, 1954-59; St. Louis, 1960; Philadelphia, 1961; Detroit, 1962
Bud McFadin, Los Angeles, 1952-56; Denver, 1960-63; Houston, 1964-65
Doug Cline, Houston, 1960-66; San Diego, 1966
Bob Lilly, Dall. Cowboys, 1961-74

Chris Hanburger, Washington, 1965-78
Lemar Parrish, Cincinnati, 1970-77; Washington, 1978-81; Buffalo, 1982
Paul Krause, Washington, 1964-67; Minnesota, 1968-79
Brad Dusek, Washington, 1974-81
David Logan, Tampa Bay, 1979-86; Green Bay, 1987
Thomas Howard, Kansas City, 1977-83; St. Louis, 1984-85
2 By many players

Most Touchdowns, Season (Total)
2 Harold McPhail, Boston, 1934
Harry Ebding, Detroit, 1937
John Morelli, Boston, 1944
Frank Maznicki, Boston, 1947
Fred (Dippy) Evans, Chi. Bears, 1948
Ralph Heywood, Boston, 1948
Art Tait, N.Y. Yanks, 1951
John Dwyer, Los Angeles, 1952
Leo Sugar, Chi. Cardinals, 1957
Doug Cline, Houston, 1961
Jim Bradshaw, Pittsburgh, 1964
Royce Berry, Cincinnati, 1970
Ahmad Rashad, Buffalo, 1974
Tim Gray, Kansas City, 1977
Charles Phillips, Oakland, 1978
Kenny Johnson, Atlanta, 1981
George Martin, N.Y. Giants, 1981
Del Rodgers, Green Bay, 1982
Mike Douglass, Green Bay, 1983
Shelton Robinson, Seattle, 1983

Most Touchdowns, Career (Own recovered)
2 Ken Kavanaugh, Chi. Bears, 1940-41, 1945-50
Mike Ditka, Chicago, 1961-66; Philadelphia, 1967-68; Dallas, 1969-72
Gail Cogdill, Detroit, 1960-68; Baltimore, 1968; Atlanta, 1969-70
Ahmad Rashad, St. Louis, 1972-73; Buffalo, 1974; Minnesota, 1976-82
Jim Mitchell, Atlanta, 1969-79
Drew Pearson, Dallas, 1973-83
Del Rodgers, Green Bay, 1982, 1984; San Francisco, 1987-88

Most Touchdowns, Season (Own recovered)
2 Ahmad Rashad, Buffalo, 1974
Del Rodgers, Green Bay, 1982
1 By many players

Most Touchdowns, Career (Opponents' recovered)
3 Leo Sugar, Chi. Cardinals, 1954-59; St. Louis, 1960; Philadelphia, 1961; Detroit, 1962
Doug Cline, Houston, 1960-66; San Diego, 1966
Bud McFadin, Los Angeles, 1952-56; Denver, 1960-63; Houston, 1964-65
Bob Lilly, Dall. Cowboys, 1961-74
Chris Hanburger, Washington, 1965-78
Paul Krause, Washington, 1964-67; Minnesota, 1968-79
Lemar Parrish, Cincinnati, 1970-77; Washington, 1978-81; Buffalo, 1982
Bill Thompson, Denver, 1969-81
Brad Dusek, Washington, 1974-81
David Logan, Tampa Bay, 1979-86; Green Bay, 1987
Thomas Howard, Kansas City, 1977-83; St. Louis, 1984-85
2 By many players

Most Touchdowns, Season (Opponents' recovered)
2 Harold McPhail, Boston, 1934
Harry Ebding, Detroit, 1937
John Morelli, Boston, 1944
Frank Maznicki, Boston, 1947
Fred (Dippy) Evans, Chi. Bears, 1948
Ralph Heywood, Boston, 1948
Art Tait, N.Y. Yanks, 1951
John Dwyer, Los Angeles, 1952
Leo Sugar, Chi. Cardinals, 1957
Doug Cline, Houston, 1961
Jim Bradshaw, Pittsburgh, 1964
Royce Berry, Cincinnati, 1970
Tim Gray, Kansas City, 1977
Charles Phillips, Oakland, 1978
Kenny Johnson, Atlanta, 1981
George Martin, N.Y. Giants, 1981
Mike Douglass, Green Bay, 1983
Shelton Robinson, Seattle, 1983

Most Touchdowns, Game (Opponents' recovered)
2 Fred (Dippy) Evans, Chi. Bears vs. Washington, Nov. 28, 1948

Combined Net Yards Gained

Rushing, receiving, interception returns, punt returns, kickoff returns, and fumble returns

Most Seasons Leading League
5 Jim Brown, Cleveland, 1958-61, 1964
3 Cliff Battles, Boston, 1932-33; Washington, 1937
Gale Sayers, Chicago, 1965-67
Eric Dickerson, L.A. Rams, 1983-84, 1986
2 By many players

Most Consecutive Seasons Leading League
4 Jim Brown, Cleveland, 1958-61
3 Gale Sayers, Chicago, 1965-67
2 Cliff Battles, Boston, 1932-33
Charley Trippi, Chi. Cardinals, 1948-49
Timmy Brown, Philadelphia, 1962-63
Floyd Little, Denver, 1967-68
James Brooks, San Diego, 1981-82
Eric Dickerson, L.A. Rams, 1983-84

Attempts

Most Attempts, Career
4,368 Walter Payton, Chicago, 1975-87
3,351 Tony Dorsett, Dallas, 1977-87; Denver, 1988
3,281 Franco Harris, Pittsburgh, 1972-83; Seattle, 1984

Most Attempts, Season
496 James Wilder, Tampa Bay, 1984
449 Marcus Allen, L.A. Raiders, 1985
442 Eric Dickerson, L.A. Rams, 1983

Most Attempts, Rookie, Season
442 Eric Dickerson, L.A. Rams, 1983
395 George Rogers, New Orleans, 1981
390 Joe Cribbs, Buffalo, 1980

Most Attempts, Game
48 James Wilder, Tampa Bay vs. Pittsburgh, Oct. 30, 1983
47 James Wilder, Tampa Bay vs. Green Bay, Sept. 30, 1984 (OT)
46 Gerald Riggs, Atlanta vs. L.A. Rams, Nov. 17, 1985

Yards Gained

Most Yards Gained, Career
21,803 Walter Payton, Chicago, 1975-87
16,326 Tony Dorsett, Dallas, 1977-87; Denver, 1988
15,459 Jim Brown, Cleveland, 1957-65

Most Yards Gained, Season
2,535 Lionel James, San Diego, 1985
2,462 Terry Metcalf, St. Louis, 1975
2,444 Mack Herron, New England, 1974

Most Yards Gained, Rookie, Season
2,317 Tim Brown, L.A. Raiders, 1988
2,272 Gale Sayers, Chicago, 1965
2,212 Eric Dickerson, L.A. Rams, 1983

Most Yards Gained, Game
373 Billy Cannon, Houston vs. N.Y. Titans, Dec. 10, 1961
345 Lionel James, San Diego vs. L.A. Raiders, Nov. 10, 1985 (OT)
341 Timmy Brown, Philadelphia vs. St. Louis, Dec. 16, 1962

Sacks

Sacks have been compiled since 1982.

Most Sacks, Career
89 Lawrence Taylor, N.Y. Giants, 1982-88
82 Dexter Manley, Washington, 1982-88
76 Jacob Green, Seattle, 1982-88

Most Sacks, Season
22 Mark Gastineau, N.Y. Jets, 1984
21 Reggie White, Philadelphia, 1987
20.5 Lawrence Taylor, N.Y. Giants, 1986

Most Sacks, Game
6 Fred Dean, San Francisco vs. New Orleans, Nov. 13, 1983
5.5 William Gay, Detroit vs. Tampa Bay, Sept. 4, 1983
5 Howie Long, L.A. Raiders vs. Washington, Oct. 2, 1983
Randy Holloway, Minnesota vs. Atlanta, Sept. 16, 1984
Jim Jeffcoat, Dallas vs. Washington, Nov. 10, 1985
Leslie O'Neal, San Diego vs. Dallas, Nov. 16, 1986
Gary Jeter, L.A. Rams vs. L.A. Raiders, Sept. 18, 1988

Miscellaneous

Longest Return of Missed Field Goal (All TDs)
101 Al Nelson, Philadelphia vs. Dallas, Sept. 26, 1971
100 Al Nelson, Philadelphia vs. Cleveland, Dec. 11, 1966
Ken Ellis, Green Bay vs. N.Y. Giants, Sept. 19, 1971
99 Jerry Williams, Los Angeles vs. Green Bay, Dec. 16, 1951
Carl Taseff, Baltimore vs. Los Angeles, Dec. 12, 1959
Timmy Brown, Philadelphia vs. St. Louis, Sept. 16, 1962

Team Records

Championships

Most Seasons League Champion
11 Green Bay, 1929-31, 1936, 1939, 1944, 1961-62, 1965-67
9 Chi. Bears, 1921, 1932-33, 1940-41, 1943, 1946, 1963, 1985
5 N.Y. Giants, 1927, 1934, 1938, 1956, 1986

Most Consecutive Seasons League Champion
3 Green Bay, 1929-31, 1965-67
2 Canton, 1922-23
Chi. Bears, 1932-33, 1940-41
Philadelphia, 1948-49
Detroit, 1952-53
Cleveland, 1954-55
Baltimore, 1958-59
Houston, 1960-61
Green Bay, 1961-62
Buffalo, 1964-65
Miami, 1972-73
Pittsburgh, 1974-75, 1978-79

Most Times Finishing First, Regular Season (Since 1933)
17 Clev. Browns, 1950-55, 1957, 1964-65, 1967-69, 1971, 1980, 1985-87
15 Clev./L.A. Rams, 1945, 1949-51, 1955, 1967, 1969, 1973-79, 1985
N.Y. Giants, 1933-35, 1938-39, 1941, 1944, 1946, 1956, 1958-59, 1961-63, 1986
Chi. Bears, 1933-34, 1937, 1940-43, 1946, 1956, 1963, 1984-88
13 Dallas, 1966-71, 1973, 1976-79, 1981, 1985

Most Consecutive Times Finishing First, Regular Season (Since 1933)
7 Los Angeles, 1973-79
6 Cleveland, 1950-55
Dallas, 1966-71
Minnesota, 1973-78
Pittsburgh, 1974-79
5 Oakland, 1972-76
Chicago, 1984-88

Games Won

Most Consecutive Games Won (Incl. postseason games)
18 Chi. Bears, 1933-34, 1941-42
Miami, 1972-73
17 Oakland, 1976-77
14 Washington, 1942-43

Most Consecutive Games Won (Regular season)
17 Chi. Bears, 1933-34
16 Chi. Bears, 1941-42
Miami, 1971-73; 1983-84
15 L.A. Chargers/San Diego, 1960-61

Most Consecutive Games Without Defeat (Incl. postseason games)
25 Canton, 1921-23 (won 22, tied 3)
23 Green Bay, 1928-30 (won 21, tied 2)
18 Chi. Bears, 1933-34 (won 18); 1941-42 (won 18)
Miami, 1972-73 (won 18)

Most Consecutive Games Without Defeat (Regular season)
25 Canton, 1921-23 (won 22, tied 3)
24 Chi. Bears, 1941-43 (won 23, tied 1)
23 Green Bay, 1928-30 (won 21, tied 2)

Most Games Won, Season (Incl. postseason games)
18 San Francisco, 1984
Chicago, 1985
17 Miami, 1972
Pittsburgh, 1978
N.Y. Giants, 1986
16 Oakland, 1976
San Francisco, 1981
Washington, 1983
Miami, 1984

Most Games Won, Season (Since 1932)
15 San Francisco, 1984
Chicago, 1985
14 Miami, 1972, 1984
Pittsburgh, 1978
Washington, 1983
Chicago, 1986
N.Y. Giants, 1986
13 Chi. Bears, 1934
Green Bay, 1962
Oakland, 1967, 1976
Baltimore, 1968
San Francisco, 1981, 1987
Denver, 1984

Most Consecutive Games Won, Season (Incl. postseason games)
17 Miami, 1972
13 Chi. Bears, 1934
Oakland, 1976
12 Minnesota, 1969
San Francisco, 1984
Chicago, 1985
N.Y. Giants, 1986

Most Consecutive Games Won, Season
14 Miami, 1972
13 Chi. Bears, 1934
12 Minnesota, 1969
Chicago, 1985

Most Consecutive Games Won, Start of Season
14 Miami, 1972, entire season
13 Chi. Bears, 1934, entire season
12 Chicago, 1985

Most Consecutive Games Won, End of Season
14 Miami, 1972, entire season
13 Chi. Bears, 1934, entire season
11 Chi. Bears, 1942, entire season
Cleveland, 1951

Most Consecutive Games Without Defeat, Season (Incl. postseason games)
17 Miami, 1972
13 Chi. Bears, 1926, 1934
Green Bay, 1929
Baltimore, 1967
Oakland, 1976
12 Canton, 1922, 1923
Minnesota, 1969
San Francisco, 1984
Chicago, 1985
N.Y. Giants, 1986

Most Consecutive Games Without Defeat, Season
14 Miami, 1972
13 Chi. Bears, 1926, 1934
Green Bay, 1929
Baltimore, 1967
12 Canton, 1922, 1923
Minnesota, 1969
Chicago, 1985

Most Consecutive Games Without Defeat, Start of Season
14 Miami, 1972, entire season
13 Chi. Bears, 1926, 1934, entire seasons
Green Bay, 1929, entire season
Baltimore, 1967
12 Canton, 1922, 1923, entire seasons
Chicago, 1985

Most Consecutive Games Without Defeat, End of Season
14 Miami, 1972, entire season
13 Green Bay, 1929, entire season
Chi. Bears, 1934, entire season
12 Canton, 1922, 1923, entire seasons

Most Consecutive Home Games Won
27 Miami, 1971-74
20 Green Bay, 1929-32
18 Oakland, 1968-70
Dallas, 1979-81

Most Consecutive Home Games Without Defeat
30 Green Bay, 1928-33 (won 27, tied 3)
27 Miami, 1971-74 (won 27)
18 Chi. Bears, 1932-35 (won 17, tied 1); 1941-44 (won 17, tied 1)
Oakland, 1968-70 (won 18)
Dallas, 1979-81 (won 18)

Most Consecutive Road Games Won
11 L.A. Chargers/San Diego, 1960-61
San Francisco, 1987-88
10 Chi. Bears, 1941-42
Dallas, 1968-69
New Orleans, 1987-88
9 Chi. Bears, 1933-34
Kansas City, 1966-67
Oakland, 1967-68, 1974-75, 1976-77
Pittsburgh, 1974-75
Washington, 1981-83
San Francisco, 1983-84

Most Consecutive Road Games Without Defeat
13 Chi. Bears, 1941-43 (won 12, tied 1)
12 Green Bay, 1928-30 (won 10, tied 2)
11 L.A. Chargers/San Diego, 1960-61 (won 11)
Los Angeles, 1966-68 (won 10, tied 1)
San Francisco, 1987-88 (won 11)

Most Shutout Games Won or Tied, Season (Since 1932)
7 Chi. Bears, 1932 (won 4, tied 3)
Green Bay, 1932 (won 6, tied 1)
Detroit, 1934 (won 7)
5 Chi. Cardinals, 1934 (won 5)
N.Y. Giants, 1944 (won 5)
Pittsburgh, 1976 (won 5)
4 By many teams

Most Consecutive Shutout Games Won or Tied (Since 1932)
7 Detroit, 1934 (won 7)
3 Chi. Bears, 1932 (tied 3)
Green Bay, 1932 (won 3)
New York, 1935 (won 3)
St. Louis, 1970 (won 3)
Pittsburgh, 1976 (won 3)
2 By many teams

Games Lost

Most Consecutive Games Lost
26 Tampa Bay, 1976-77
19 Chi. Cardinals, 1942-43, 1945
Oakland, 1961-62
18 Houston, 1972-73

Most Consecutive Games Without Victory
26 Tampa Bay, 1976-77 (lost 26)
23 Washington, 1960-61 (lost 20, tied 3)

Most Games Lost, Season (Since 1932)
15 New Orleans, 1980
14 Tampa Bay, 1976, 1983, 1985, 1986
San Francisco, 1978, 1979
Detroit, 1979
Baltimore, 1981
New England, 1981
Houston, 1983
Buffalo, 1984, 1985
13 Oakland, 1962
Chicago, 1969
Pittsburgh, 1969
Buffalo, 1971
Houston, 1972, 1973, 1984
Minnesota, 1984
Indianapolis, 1986
Dallas, 1988

Most Consecutive Games Lost, Season
14 Tampa Bay, 1976
New Orleans, 1980
Baltimore, 1981
13 Oakland, 1962
Indianapolis, 1986
12 Tampa Bay, 1977

Most Consecutive Games Lost, Start of Season
14 Tampa Bay, 1976, entire season
New Orleans, 1980
13 Oakland, 1962
Indianapolis, 1986
12 Tampa Bay, 1977

Most Consecutive Games Lost, End of Season
14 Tampa Bay, 1976, entire season
13 Pittsburgh, 1969
11 Philadelphia, 1936
Detroit, 1942, entire season
Houston, 1972

Most Consecutive Games Without Victory, Season
14 Tampa Bay, 1976, entire season
New Orleans, 1980
Baltimore, 1981
13 Washington, 1961
Oakland, 1962
Indianapolis, 1986
12 Dall. Cowboys, 1960, entire season
Tampa Bay, 1977

Most Consecutive Games Without Victory, Start of Season
14 Tampa Bay, 1976, entire season
New Orleans, 1980
13 Washington, 1961
Oakland, 1962
Indianapolis, 1986
12 Dall. Cowboys, 1960, entire season
Tampa Bay, 1977

Most Consecutive Games Without Victory, End of Season
14 Tampa Bay, 1976, entire season
13 Pittsburgh, 1969
12 Dall. Cowboys, 1960, entire season

Most Consecutive Home Games Lost
13 Houston, 1972-73
Tampa Bay, 1976-77
11 Oakland, 1961-62
Los Angeles, 1961-63
10 Pittsburgh, 1937-39
Washington, 1960-61

N.Y. Giants, 1973-75
New Orleans, 1979-80

Most Consecutive Home Games Without Victory
13 Houston, 1972-73 (lost 13)
Tampa Bay, 1976-77 (lost 13)
12 Philadelphia, 1936-38 (lost 11, tied 1)
11 Washington, 1960-61 (lost 10, tied 1)
Oakland, 1961-62 (lost 11)
Los Angeles, 1961-63 (lost 11)

Most Consecutive Road Games Lost
23 Houston, 1981-84
22 Buffalo, 1983-86
19 Tampa Bay, 1983-85

Most Consecutive Road Games Without Victory
23 Houston, 1981-84 (lost 23)
22 Buffalo, 1983-86 (lost 22)
19 Tampa Bay, 1983-85 (lost 19)

Most Shutout Games Lost or Tied, Season (Since 1932)
6 Cincinnati, 1934 (lost 6)
Pittsburgh, 1934 (lost 6)
Philadelphia, 1936 (lost 6)
Tampa Bay, 1977 (lost 6)
5 Boston, 1932 (lost 4, tied 1), 1933 (lost 4, tied 1)
N.Y. Giants, 1932 (lost 4, tied 1)
Cincinnati, 1933 (lost 4, tied 1)
Brooklyn, 1934 (lost 5), 1942 (lost 5)
Detroit, 1942 (lost 5)
Tampa Bay, 1976 (lost 5)
4 By many teams

Most Consecutive Shutout Games Lost or Tied (Since 1932)
6 Brooklyn, 1942-43 (lost 6)
4 Chi. Bears, 1932 (lost 1, tied 3)
Philadelphia, 1936 (lost 4)
3 Chi. Cardinals, 1934 (lost 3), 1938 (lost 3)
Brooklyn, 1935 (lost 3), 1937 (lost 3)
Oakland, 1981 (lost 3)

Tie Games

Most Tie Games, Season
6 Chi. Bears, 1932
5 Frankford, 1929
4 Chi. Bears, 1924
Orange, 1929
Portsmouth, 1932

Most Consecutive Tie Games
3 Chi. Bears, 1932
2 By many teams

Scoring

Most Seasons Leading League
9 Chi. Bears, 1934-35, 1939, 1941-43, 1946-47, 1956
6 Green Bay, 1932, 1936-38, 1961-62
L.A. Rams, 1950-52, 1957, 1967, 1973
5 Oakland, 1967-69, 1974, 1977
Dall. Cowboys, 1966, 1968, 1971, 1978, 1980
San Diego, 1963, 1965, 1981-82, 1985

Most Consecutive Seasons Leading League
3 Green Bay, 1936-38
Chi. Bears, 1941-43
Los Angeles, 1950-52
Oakland, 1967-69

Points

Most Points, Season
541 Washington, 1983
513 Houston, 1961
Miami, 1984
479 Dallas, 1983

Fewest Points, Season (Since 1932)
37 Cincinnati/St. Louis, 1934
38 Cincinnati, 1933
Detroit, 1942
51 Pittsburgh, 1934
Philadelphia, 1936

Most Points, Game
72 Washington vs. N.Y. Giants, Nov. 27, 1966
70 Los Angeles vs. Baltimore, Oct. 22, 1950
65 Chi. Cardinals vs. N.Y. Bulldogs, Nov. 13, 1949
Los Angeles vs. Detroit, Oct. 29, 1950

Most Points, Both Teams, Game
113 Washington (72) vs. N.Y. Giants (41), Nov. 27, 1966
101 Oakland (52) vs. Houston (49), Dec. 22, 1963
99 Seattle (51) vs. Kansas City (48), Nov. 27, 1983 (OT)

Fewest Points, Both Teams, Game
0 In many games. Last time: N.Y. Giants vs. Detroit, Nov. 7, 1943

Most Points, Shutout Victory, Game
64 Philadelphia vs. Cincinnati, Nov. 6, 1934
62 Akron vs. Oorang, Oct. 29, 1922
60 Rock Island vs. Evansville, Oct. 15, 1922
Chi. Cardinals vs. Rochester, Oct. 7, 1923

Fewest Points, Shutout Victory, Game
2 Green Bay vs. Chi. Bears, Oct. 16, 1932
Chi. Bears vs. Green Bay, Sept. 18, 1938

Most Points Overcome to Win Game
28 San Francisco vs. New Orleans, Dec. 7, 1980 (OT) (trailed 7-35, won 38-35)
25 St. Louis vs. Tampa Bay, Nov. 8, 1987 (trailed 3-28, won 31-28)
24 Philadelphia vs. Washington, Oct. 27, 1946 (trailed 0-24, won 28-24)
Detroit vs. Baltimore, Oct. 20, 1957 (trailed 3-27, won 31-27)
Philadelphia vs. Chi. Cardinals, Oct. 25, 1959 (trailed 0-24, won 28-24)
Denver vs. Boston, Oct. 23, 1960 (trailed 0-24, won 31-24)
Miami vs. New England, Dec. 15, 1974 (trailed 0-24, won 34-27)
Minnesota vs. San Francisco, Dec. 4, 1977 (trailed 0-24, won 28-27)
Denver vs. Seattle, Sept. 23, 1979 (trailed 10-34, won 37-34)
Houston vs. Cincinnati, Sept. 23, 1979 (OT) (trailed 0-24, won 30-27)
L.A. Raiders vs. San Diego, Nov. 22, 1982 (trailed 0-24, won 28-24)
L.A. Raiders vs. Denver, Sept. 26, 1988 (OT) (trailed 0-24, won 30-27)

Most Points Overcome to Tie Game
31 Denver vs. Buffalo, Nov. 27, 1960 (trailed 7-38, tied 38-38)
28 Los Angeles vs. Philadelphia, Oct. 3, 1948 (trailed 0-28, tied 28-28)

Most Points, Each Half
1st: 49 Green Bay vs. Tampa Bay, Oct. 2, 1983
48 Buffalo vs. Miami, Sept. 18, 1966
45 Green Bay vs. Cleveland, Nov. 12, 1967
Indianapolis vs. Denver, Oct. 31, 1988
2nd: 49 Chi. Bears vs. Philadelphia, Nov. 30, 1941
48 Chi. Cardinals vs. Baltimore, Oct. 2, 1950
N.Y. Giants vs. Baltimore, Nov. 19, 1950

Most Points, Both Teams, Each Half
1st: 70 Houston (35) vs. Oakland (35), Dec. 22, 1963
2nd: 65 Washington (38) vs. N.Y. Giants (27), Nov. 27, 1966

Most Points, One Quarter
41 Green Bay vs. Detroit, Oct. 7, 1945 (second quarter)
Los Angeles vs. Detroit, Oct. 29, 1950 (third quarter)
37 Los Angeles vs. Green Bay, Sept. 21, 1980 (second quarter)
35 Chi. Cardinals vs. Boston, Oct. 24, 1948 (third quarter)
Green Bay vs. Cleveland, Nov. 12, 1967 (first quarter); vs. Tampa Bay, Oct. 2, 1983 (second quarter)

Most Points, Both Teams, One Quarter
49 Oakland (28) vs. Houston (21), Dec. 22, 1963 (second quarter)
48 Green Bay (41) vs. Detroit (7), Oct. 7, 1945 (second quarter)
Los Angeles (41) vs. Detroit (7), Oct. 29, 1950 (third quarter)
47 St. Louis (27) vs. Philadelphia (20), Dec. 13, 1964 (second quarter)

Most Points, Each Quarter
1st: 35 Green Bay vs. Cleveland, Nov. 12, 1967
2nd: 41 Green Bay vs. Detroit, Oct. 7, 1945
3rd: 41 Los Angeles vs. Detroit, Oct. 29, 1950
4th: 31 Oakland vs. Denver, Dec. 17, 1960; vs. San Diego, Dec. 8, 1963
Atlanta vs. Green Bay, Sept. 13, 1981

Most Points, Both Teams, Each Quarter
1st: 42 Green Bay (35) vs. Cleveland (7), Nov. 12, 1967
2nd: 49 Oakland (28) vs. Houston (21), Dec. 22, 1963
3rd: 48 Los Angeles (41) vs. Detroit (7), Oct. 29, 1950
4th: 42 Chi. Cardinals (28) vs. Philadelphia (14), Dec. 7, 1947
Green Bay (28) vs. Chi. Bears (14), Nov. 6, 1955
N.Y. Jets (28) vs. Boston (14), Oct. 27, 1968
Pittsburgh (21) vs. Cleveland (21), Oct. 18, 1969

Most Consecutive Games Scoring
274 Cleveland, 1950-71
218 Dallas, 1970-85
217 Oakland, 1966-81

Touchdowns

Most Seasons Leading League, Touchdowns
13 Chi. Bears, 1932, 1934-35, 1939, 1941-44, 1946-48, 1956, 1965
7 Dall. Cowboys, 1966, 1968, 1971, 1973, 1977-78, 1980
6 Oakland, 1967-69, 1972, 1974, 1977
San Diego, 1963, 1965, 1979, 1981-82, 1985

Most Consecutive Seasons Leading League, Touchdowns
4 Chi. Bears, 1941-44
Los Angeles, 1949-52
3 Chi. Bears, 1946-48
Baltimore, 1957-59
Oakland, 1967-69
2 By many teams

Most Touchdowns, Season
70 Miami, 1984
66 Houston, 1961
64 Los Angeles, 1950

Fewest Touchdowns, Season (Since 1932)
3 Cincinnati, 1933
4 Cincinnati/St. Louis, 1934
5 Detroit, 1942

Most Touchdowns, Game
10 Philadelphia vs. Cincinnati, Nov. 6, 1934
Los Angeles vs. Baltimore, Oct. 22, 1950
Washington vs. N.Y. Giants, Nov. 27, 1966
9 Chi. Cardinals vs. Rochester, Oct. 7, 1923; vs. N.Y. Giants, Oct. 17, 1948; vs. N.Y. Bulldogs, Nov. 13, 1949
Los Angeles vs. Detroit, Oct. 29, 1950
Pittsburgh vs. N.Y. Giants, Nov. 30, 1952
Chicago vs. San Francisco, Dec. 12, 1965; vs. Green Bay, Dec. 7, 1980
8 By many teams.

Most Touchdowns, Both Teams, Game
16 Washington (10) vs. N.Y. Giants (6), Nov. 27, 1966
14 Chi. Cardinals (9) vs. N.Y. Giants (5), Oct. 17, 1948
Los Angeles (10) vs. Baltimore (4), Oct. 22, 1950
Houston (7) vs. Oakland (7), Dec. 22, 1963
13 New Orleans (7) vs. St. Louis (6), Nov. 2, 1969
Kansas City (7) vs. Seattle (6), Nov. 27, 1983 (OT)
San Diego (8) vs. Pittsburgh (5), Dec. 8, 1985
N.Y. Jets (7) vs. Miami (6), Sept. 21, 1986 (OT)

Most Consecutive Games Scoring Touchdowns
166 Cleveland, 1957-69
97 Oakland, 1966-73
96 Kansas City, 1963-70

Points After Touchdown

Most Points After Touchdown, Season
66 Miami, 1984
65 Houston, 1961
62 Washington, 1983

Fewest Points After Touchdown, Season
2 Chi. Cardinals, 1933
3 Cincinnati, 1933
Pittsburgh, 1934
4 Cincinnati/St. Louis, 1934

Most Points After Touchdown, Game
10 Los Angeles vs. Baltimore, Oct. 22, 1950
9 Chi. Cardinals vs. N.Y. Giants, Oct. 17, 1948
Pittsburgh vs. N.Y. Giants, Nov. 30, 1952
Washington vs. N.Y. Giants, Nov. 27, 1966
8 By many teams

Most Points After Touchdown, Both Teams, Game
14 Chi. Cardinals (9) vs. N.Y. Giants (5), Oct. 17, 1948
Houston (7) vs. Oakland (7), Dec. 22, 1963
Washington (9) vs. N.Y. Giants (5), Nov. 27, 1966
13 Los Angeles (10) vs. Baltimore (3), Oct. 22, 1950
12 In many games

Field Goals

Most Seasons Leading League, Field Goals
11 Green Bay, 1935-36, 1940-43, 1946-47, 1955, 1972, 1974
7 Washington, 1945, 1956, 1971, 1976-77, 1979, 1982
N.Y. Giants, 1933, 1937, 1939, 1941, 1944, 1959, 1983
5 Portsmouth/Detroit, 1932-33, 1937-38, 1980

Most Consecutive Seasons Leading League, Field Goals
4 Green Bay, 1940-43
3 Cleveland, 1952-54
2 By many teams

Most Field Goals Attempted, Season
49 Los Angeles, 1966
Washington, 1971
48 Green Bay, 1972
47 N.Y. Jets, 1969
Los Angeles, 1973
Washington, 1983

Fewest Field Goals Attempted, Season (Since 1938)
0 Chi. Bears, 1944
2 Cleveland, 1939
Card-Pitt, 1944
Boston, 1946
Chi. Bears, 1947
3 Chi. Bears, 1945
Cleveland, 1945

Most Field Goals Attempted, Game
9 St. Louis vs. Pittsburgh, Sept. 24, 1967
8 Pittsburgh vs. St. Louis, Dec. 2, 1962
Detroit vs. Minnesota, Nov. 13, 1966
N.Y. Jets vs. Buffalo, Nov. 3, 1968
7 By many teams

Most Field Goals Attempted, Both Teams, Game
11 St. Louis (6) vs. Pittsburgh (5), Nov. 13, 1966
Washington (6) vs. Chicago (5), Nov. 14, 1971
Green Bay (6) vs. Detroit (5), Sept. 29, 1974
Washington (6) vs. N.Y. Giants (5), Nov. 14, 1976
10 Denver (5) vs. Boston (5), Nov. 11, 1962
Boston (7) vs. San Diego (3), Sept. 20, 1964
Buffalo (7) vs. Houston (3), Dec. 5, 1965
St. Louis (7) vs. Atlanta (3), Dec. 11, 1966
Boston (7) vs. Buffalo (3), Sept. 24, 1967
Detroit (7) vs. Minnesota (3), Sept. 20, 1971
Washington (7) vs. Houston (3), Oct. 10, 1971
Green Bay (5) vs. St. Louis (5), Dec. 5, 1971
Kansas City (7) vs. Buffalo (3), Dec. 19, 1971
Kansas City (5) vs. San Diego (5), Oct. 29, 1972
Minnesota (6) vs. Chicago (4), Sept. 23, 1973
Cleveland (7) vs. Denver (3), Oct. 19, 1975
Cleveland (5) vs. Denver (5), Oct. 5, 1980
9 In many games

Most Field Goals, Season
35 N.Y. Giants, 1983
34 N.Y. Jets, 1968
33 Green Bay, 1972
Washington, 1983
Pittsburgh, 1985
New Orleans, 1987

Fewest Field Goals, Season (Since 1932)
0 Boston, 1932, 1935
Chi. Cardinals, 1932, 1945
Green Bay, 1932, 1944
N.Y. Giants, 1932
Brooklyn, 1944
Card-Pitt, 1944
Chi. Bears, 1944, 1947
Boston, 1946
Baltimore, 1950
Dallas, 1952

Most Field Goals, Game
7 St. Louis vs. Pittsburgh, Sept. 24, 1967
6 Boston vs. Denver, Oct. 4, 1964
Detroit vs. Minnesota, Nov. 13, 1966
N.Y. Jets vs. Buffalo, Nov. 3, 1968; vs. New Orleans, Dec. 3, 1972
Philadelphia vs. Houston, Nov. 12, 1972
St. Louis vs. Atlanta, Dec. 9, 1973
N.Y. Giants vs. Seattle, Oct. 18, 1981
San Francisco vs. New Orleans, Oct. 16, 1983
Pittsburgh vs. Denver, Oct. 23, 1988
5 By many teams

Most Field Goals, Both Teams, Game
8 Cleveland (4) vs. St. Louis (4), Sept. 20, 1964
Chicago (5) vs. Philadelphia (3), Oct. 20, 1968
Washington (5) vs. Chicago (3), Nov. 14, 1971
Kansas City (5) vs. Buffalo (3), Dec. 19, 1971
Detroit (4) vs. Green Bay (4), Sept. 29, 1974
Cleveland (5) vs. Denver (3), Oct. 19, 1975
New England (4) vs. San Diego (4), Nov. 9, 1975
San Francisco (6) vs. New Orleans (2), Oct. 16, 1983
Seattle (5) vs. L.A. Raiders (3), Dec. 18, 1988
7 In many games

Most Consecutive Games Scoring Field Goals
31 Minnesota, 1968-70
21 San Francisco, 1970-72
New Orleans, 1987-88
20 Los Angeles, 1970-71
Miami, 1970-72

Safeties

Most Safeties, Season
4 Detroit, 1962
3 Green Bay, 1932, 1975
Pittsburgh, 1947
N.Y. Yanks, 1950
Detroit, 1960
St. Louis, 1960
Buffalo, 1964
Minnesota, 1965, 1981
Cleveland, 1970
L.A. Rams, 1973, 1984
Houston, 1977
Dallas, 1981
Oakland, 1981
Chicago, 1985
Kansas City, 1988
2 By many teams

Most Safeties, Game
3 L.A. Rams vs. N.Y. Giants, Sept. 30, 1984
2 Cincinnati vs. Chi. Cardinals, Nov. 19, 1933
Detroit vs. Brooklyn, Dec. 1, 1935
N.Y. Giants vs. Pittsburgh, Sept. 17, 1950; vs. Washington, Nov. 5, 1961
Chicago vs. Pittsburgh, Nov. 9, 1969
Dallas vs. Philadelphia, Nov. 19, 1972
Los Angeles vs. Green Bay, Oct. 21, 1973
Oakland vs. San Diego, Oct. 26, 1975
Denver vs. Seattle, Jan. 2, 1983
New Orleans vs. Cleveland, Sept. 13, 1987
Buffalo vs. Denver, Nov. 8, 1987

Most Safeties, Both Teams, Game
3 L.A. Rams (3) vs. N.Y. Giants (0), Sept. 30, 1984
2 Chi. Bears (1) vs. San Francisco (1), Oct. 19, 1952
Cincinnati (1) vs. Los Angeles (1), Oct. 22, 1972
Atlanta (1) vs. Detroit (1), Oct. 5, 1980
Houston (1) vs. Philadelphia (1), Oct. 2, 1988
(Also see previous record)

First Downs

Most Seasons Leading League
9 Chi. Bears, 1935, 1939, 1941, 1943, 1945, 1947-49, 1955
7 San Diego, 1965, 1969, 1980-83, 1985
6 L.A. Rams, 1946, 1950-51, 1954, 1957, 1973

Most Consecutive Seasons Leading League
4 San Diego, 1980-83
3 Chi. Bears, 1947-49
2 By many teams

Most First Downs, Season
387 Miami, 1984
380 San Diego, 1985
379 San Diego, 1981

Fewest First Downs, Season
51 Cincinnati, 1933
64 Pittsburgh, 1935
67 Philadelphia, 1937

Most First Downs, Game
39 N.Y. Jets vs. Miami, Nov. 27, 1988
38 Los Angeles vs. N.Y. Giants, Nov. 13, 1966
37 Green Bay vs. Philadelphia, Nov. 11, 1962

Fewest First Downs, Game
0 N.Y. Giants vs. Green Bay, Oct. 1, 1933; vs. Washington, Sept. 27, 1942
Pittsburgh vs. Boston, Oct. 29, 1933
Philadelphia vs. Detroit, Sept. 20, 1935
Denver vs. Houston, Sept. 3, 1966

Most First Downs, Both Teams, Game
62 San Diego (32) vs. Seattle (30), Sept. 15, 1985
59 Miami (31) vs. Buffalo (28), Oct. 9, 1983 (OT)
Seattle (33) vs. Kansas City (26), Nov. 27, 1983 (OT)
N.Y. Jets (32) vs. Miami (27), Sept. 21, 1986 (OT)
N.Y. Jets (39) vs. Miami (20), Nov. 27, 1988
58 Los Angeles (30) vs. Chi. Bears (28), Oct. 24, 1954
Denver (34) vs. Kansas City (24), Nov. 18, 1974
Atlanta (35) vs. New Orleans (23), Sept. 2, 1979 (OT)
Pittsburgh (36) vs. Cleveland (22), Nov. 25, 1979 (OT)
San Diego (34) vs. Miami (24), Nov. 18, 1984 (OT)
Cincinnati (32) vs. San Diego (26), Sept. 22, 1985

Fewest First Downs, Both Teams, Game
5 N.Y. Giants (0) vs. Green Bay (5), Oct. 1, 1933

Most First Downs, Rushing, Season
181 New England, 1978
177 Los Angeles, 1973
176 Chicago, 1985

Fewest First Downs, Rushing, Season
36 Cleveland, 1942
Boston, 1944
39 Brooklyn, 1943
40 Philadelphia, 1940
Detroit, 1945

Most First Downs, Rushing, Game
25 Philadelphia vs. Washington, Dec. 2, 1951
21 Cleveland vs. Philadelphia, Dec. 13, 1959
Los Angeles vs. New Orleans, Nov. 25, 1973
Pittsburgh vs. Kansas City, Nov. 7, 1976
New England vs. Denver, Nov. 28, 1976
Oakland vs. Green Bay, Sept. 17, 1978
20 By eight teams

Fewest First Downs, Rushing, Game
0 By many teams. Last times: Cleveland vs. Dallas, Dec. 4, 1988; Seattle vs. New England, Dec. 4, 1988

Most First Downs, Passing, Season
259 San Diego, 1985
250 Miami, 1986
244 San Diego, 1980

Fewest First Downs, Passing, Season
18 Pittsburgh, 1941
23 Brooklyn, 1942
N.Y. Giants, 1944
24 N.Y. Giants, 1943

Most First Downs, Passing, Game
29 N.Y. Giants vs. Cincinnati, Oct. 13, 1985
27 San Diego vs. Seattle, Sept. 15, 1985
26 Miami vs. Cleveland, Dec. 12, 1988

Fewest First Downs, Passing, Game
0 By many teams. Last time: Houston vs. Kansas City, Oct. 9, 1988

Most First Downs, Penalty, Season
42 Chicago, 1987
41 Denver, 1986
39 Seattle, 1978

Fewest First Downs, Penalty, Season
2 Brooklyn, 1940
4 Chi. Cardinals, 1940
N.Y. Giants, 1942, 1944
Washington, 1944
Cleveland, 1952
Kansas City, 1969
5 Brooklyn, 1939
Chi. Bears, 1939
Detroit, 1953
Los Angeles, 1953
Houston, 1982

Most First Downs, Penalty, Game
11 Denver vs. Houston, Oct. 6, 1985
9 Chi. Bears vs. Cleveland, Nov. 25, 1951
Baltimore vs. Pittsburgh, Oct. 30, 1977
N.Y. Jets vs. Houston, Sept. 18, 1988
8 Philadelphia vs. Detroit, Dec. 2, 1979
Cincinnati vs. N.Y. Jets, Oct. 6, 1985
Buffalo vs. Houston, Sept. 20, 1987

Fewest First Downs, Penalty, Game
0 By many teams

Net Yards Gained Rushing and Passing

Most Seasons Leading League
12 Chi. Bears, 1932, 1934-35, 1939, 1941-44, 1947, 1949, 1955-56
7 San Diego, 1963, 1965, 1980-83, 1985
6 L.A. Rams, 1946, 1950-51, 1954, 1957, 1973
Baltimore, 1958-60, 1964, 1967, 1976
Dall. Cowboys, 1966, 1968-69, 1971, 1974, 1977

Most Consecutive Seasons Leading League
4 Chi. Bears, 1941-44
San Diego, 1980-83
3 Baltimore, 1958-60
Houston, 1960-62
Oakland, 1968-70
2 By many teams

Most Yards Gained, Season
6,936 Miami, 1984
6,744 San Diego, 1981
6,535 San Diego, 1985

Fewest Yards Gained, Season
1,150 Cincinnati, 1933
1,443 Chi. Cardinals, 1934
1,486 Chi. Cardinals, 1933

Most Yards Gained, Game
735 Los Angeles vs. N.Y. Yanks, Sept. 28, 1951
683 Pittsburgh vs. Chi. Cardinals, Dec. 13, 1958
682 Chi. Bears vs. N.Y. Giants, Nov. 14, 1943

Fewest Yards Gained, Game
−7 Seattle vs. Los Angeles, Nov. 4, 1979
−5 Denver vs. Oakland, Sept. 10, 1967
14 Chi. Cardinals vs. Detroit, Sept. 15, 1940

Most Yards Gained, Both Teams, Game
1,133 Los Angeles (636) vs. N.Y. Yanks (497), Nov. 19, 1950
1,102 San Diego (661) vs. Cincinnati (441), Dec. 20, 1982
1,087 St. Louis (589) vs. Philadelphia (498), Dec. 16, 1962

Fewest Yards Gained, Both Teams, Game
30 Chi. Cardinals (14) vs. Detroit (16), Sept. 15, 1940

Most Consecutive Games, 400 or More Yards Gained
11 San Diego, 1982-83
6 Houston, 1961-62
San Diego, 1981
San Francisco, 1987
5 Chi. Bears, 1947, 1955
Los Angeles, 1950
Philadelphia, 1953
Oakland, 1968
New England, 1981
Cincinnati, 1986

Most Consecutive Games, 300 or More Yards Gained
29 Los Angeles, 1949-51
26 Miami, 1983-85
20 Chi. Bears, 1948-50

Rushing

Most Seasons Leading League
16 Chi. Bears, 1932, 1934-35, 1939-42, 1951, 1955-56, 1968, 1977, 1983-86
6 Cleveland, 1958-59, 1963, 1965-67
5 Buffalo, 1962, 1964, 1973, 1975, 1982

Most Consecutive Seasons Leading League
4 Chi. Bears, 1939-42, 1983-86
3 Detroit, 1936-38
San Francisco, 1952-54
Cleveland, 1965-67
2 By many teams

Most Rushing Attempts, Season
681 Oakland, 1977
674 Chicago, 1984
671 New England, 1978

Fewest Rushing Attempts, Season
211 Philadelphia, 1982
219 San Francisco, 1982
225 Houston, 1982

Most Rushing Attempts, Game
72 Chi. Bears vs. Brooklyn, Oct. 20, 1935
70 Chi. Cardinals vs. Green Bay, Dec. 5, 1948
69 Chi. Cardinals vs. Green Bay, Dec. 6, 1936
Kansas City vs. Cincinnati, Sept. 3, 1978

Fewest Rushing Attempts, Game
6 Chi. Cardinals vs. Boston, Oct. 29, 1933
7 Oakland vs. Buffalo, Oct. 15, 1963
Houston vs. N.Y. Giants, Dec. 8, 1985
8 Denver vs. Oakland, Dec. 17, 1960
Buffalo vs. St. Louis, Sept. 9, 1984

Most Rushing Attempts, Both Teams, Game
108 Chi. Cardinals (70) vs. Green Bay (38), Dec. 5, 1948
105 Oakland (62) vs. Atlanta (43), Nov. 30, 1975 (OT)
103 Kansas City (53) vs. San Diego (50), Nov. 12, 1978 (OT)

Fewest Rushing Attempts, Both Teams, Game
36 Cincinnati (16) vs. Chi. Bears (20), Sept. 30, 1934
37 Atlanta (18) vs. San Francisco (19), Oct. 6, 1985
38 N.Y. Jets (13) vs. Buffalo (25), Nov. 8, 1964

Yards Gained

Most Yards Gained Rushing, Season
3,165 New England, 1978
3,088 Buffalo, 1973
2,986 Kansas City, 1978

Fewest Yards Gained Rushing, Season
298 Philadelphia, 1940
467 Detroit, 1946
471 Boston, 1944

Most Yards Gained Rushing, Game
426 Detroit vs. Pittsburgh, Nov. 4, 1934
423 N.Y. Giants vs. Baltimore, Nov. 19, 1950
420 Boston vs. N.Y. Giants, Oct. 8, 1933

Fewest Yards Gained Rushing, Game
−53 Detroit vs. Chi. Cardinals, Oct. 17, 1943
−36 Philadelphia vs. Chi. Bears, Nov. 19, 1939
−33 Phil-Pitt vs. Brooklyn, Oct. 2, 1943

Most Yards Gained Rushing, Both Teams, Game
595 Los Angeles (371) vs. N.Y. Yanks (224), Nov. 18, 1951
574 Chi. Bears (396) vs. Pittsburgh (178), Oct. 10, 1934
557 Chi. Bears (406) vs. Green Bay (151), Nov. 6, 1955

Fewest Yards Gained Rushing, Both Teams, Game
−15 Detroit (−53) vs. Chi. Cardinals (38), Oct. 17, 1943
4 Detroit (−10) vs. Chi. Cardinals (14), Sept. 15, 1940
63 Chi. Cardinals (−1) vs. N.Y. Giants (64), Oct. 18, 1953

Average Gain

Highest Average Gain, Rushing, Season
5.74 Cleveland, 1963
5.65 San Francisco, 1954
5.56 San Diego, 1963

Lowest Average Gain, Rushing, Season
0.94 Philadelphia, 1940
1.45 Boston, 1944
1.55 Pittsburgh, 1935

Touchdowns

Most Touchdowns, Rushing, Season
36 Green Bay, 1962
33 Pittsburgh, 1976
30 Chi. Bears, 1941
New England, 1978
Washington, 1983

Fewest Touchdowns, Rushing, Season
1 Brooklyn, 1934
2 Chi. Cardinals, 1933
Cincinnati, 1933
Pittsburgh, 1934, 1940
Philadelphia, 1935, 1936, 1937, 1938, 1972
3 By many teams

Most Touchdowns, Rushing, Game
7 Los Angeles vs. Atlanta, Dec. 4, 1976
6 By many teams

Most Touchdowns, Rushing, Both Teams, Game
8 Los Angeles (6) vs. N.Y. Yanks (2), Nov. 18, 1951
Cleveland (6) vs. Los Angeles (2), Nov. 24, 1957
7 In many games

Passing

Attempts

Most Passes Attempted, Season
709 Minnesota, 1981
662 San Diego, 1984
645 Miami, 1986

Fewest Passes Attempted, Season
102 Cincinnati, 1933
106 Boston, 1933
120 Detroit, 1937

Most Passes Attempted, Game
68 Houston vs. Buffalo, Nov 1, 1964
65 San Diego vs. Kansas City, Oct. 19, 1986
63 Minnesota vs. Tampa Bay, Sept. 5, 1981

Fewest Passes Attempted, Game
0 Green Bay vs. Portsmouth, Oct. 8, 1933
Detroit vs. Cleveland, Sept. 10, 1937
Pittsburgh vs. Brooklyn, Nov. 16, 1941; vs. Los Angeles, Nov. 13, 1949
Cleveland vs. Philadelphia, Dec. 3, 1950

Most Passes Attempted, Both Teams, Game
104 Miami (55) vs. N.Y. Jets (49), Oct. 18, 1987 (OT)
102 San Francisco (57) vs. Atlanta (45), Oct. 6, 1985
100 Tampa Bay (54) vs. Kansas City (46), Oct. 28, 1984
San Francisco (60) vs. Washington (40), Nov. 17, 1986

Fewest Passes Attempted, Both Teams, Game
4 Chi. Cardinals (1) vs. Detroit (3), Nov. 3, 1935
Detroit (0) vs. Cleveland (4), Sept. 10, 1937
6 Chi. Cardinals (2) vs. Detroit (4), Sept. 15, 1940
8 Brooklyn (2) vs. Philadelphia (6), Oct. 1, 1939

Completions

Most Passes Completed, Season
401 San Diego, 1984
392 Miami, 1986
386 San Diego, 1985

Fewest Passes Completed, Season
25 Cincinnati, 1933
33 Boston, 1933
34 Chi. Cardinals, 1934
Detroit, 1934

Most Passes Completed, Game
42 N.Y. Jets vs. San Francisco, Sept. 21, 1980
40 Cincinnati vs. San Diego, Dec. 20, 1982
Dallas vs. Detroit, Sept. 15, 1985
N.Y. Giants vs. Cincinnati, Oct. 13, 1985
39 Miami vs. Buffalo, Nov. 16, 1986

Fewest Passes Completed, Game
0 By many teams. Last time: Buffalo vs. N.Y. Jets, Sept. 29, 1974

Most Passes Completed, Both Teams, Game
68 San Francisco (37) vs. Atlanta (31), Oct. 6, 1985
66 Cincinnati (40) vs. San Diego (26), Dec. 20, 1982
65 San Diego (33) vs. San Francisco (32), Dec. 11, 1982
San Diego (37) vs. Miami (28), Nov. 18, 1984 (OT)

Fewest Passes Completed, Both Teams, Game
1 Chi. Cardinals (0) vs. Philadelphia (1), Nov. 8, 1936
Detroit (0) vs. Cleveland (1), Sept. 10, 1937
Chi. Cardinals (0) vs. Detroit (1), Sept. 15, 1940
Brooklyn (0) vs. Pittsburgh (1), Nov. 29, 1942
2 Chi. Cardinals (0) vs. Detroit (2), Nov. 3, 1935
Buffalo (0) vs. N.Y. Jets (2), Sept. 29, 1974
3 Brooklyn (1) vs. Philadelphia (2), Oct. 1, 1939

Yards Gained

Most Seasons Leading League, Passing Yardage
10 San Diego, 1965, 1968, 1971, 1978-83, 1985
8 Chi. Bears, 1932, 1939, 1941, 1943, 1945, 1949, 1954, 1964
7 Washington, 1938, 1940, 1944, 1947-48, 1967, 1974

Most Consecutive Seasons Leading League, Passing Yardage
6 San Diego, 1978-83
4 Green Bay, 1934-37
3 Miami, 1986-88

Most Yards Gained, Passing, Season
5,018 Miami, 1984
4,870 San Diego, 1985
4,779 Miami, 1986

Fewest Yards Gained, Passing, Season
302 Chi. Cardinals, 1934
357 Cincinnati, 1933
459 Boston, 1934

Most Yards Gained, Passing, Game
554 Los Angeles vs. N.Y. Yanks, Sept. 28, 1951
530 Minnesota vs. Baltimore, Sept. 28, 1969
521 Miami vs. N.Y. Jets, Oct. 23, 1988

Fewest Yards Gained, Passing, Game
−53 Denver vs. Oakland, Sept. 10, 1967
−52 Cincinnati vs. Houston, Oct. 31, 1971
−39 Atlanta vs. San Francisco, Oct. 23, 1976

Most Yards Gained, Passing, Both Teams, Game
884 N.Y. Jets (449) vs. Miami (435), Sept. 21, 1986 (OT)
883 San Diego (486) vs. Cincinnati (397), Dec. 20, 1982
849 Minnesota (471) vs. Washington (378), Nov. 2, 1986 (OT)

Fewest Yards Gained, Passing, Both Teams, Game
−11 Green Bay (−10) vs. Dallas (−1), Oct. 24, 1965
1 Chi. Cardinals (0) vs. Philadelphia (1), Nov. 8, 1936
7 Brooklyn (0) vs. Pittsburgh (7), Nov. 29, 1942

Times Sacked

Most Seasons Leading League, Fewest Times Sacked
8 Miami, 1973, 1982-88
4 San Diego, 1963-64, 1967-68
San Francisco, 1964-65, 1970-71
3 N.Y. Jets, 1965-66, 1968
Houston, 1961-62, 1978
St. Louis, 1974-76

Most Consecutive Seasons Leading League, Fewest Times Sacked
7 Miami, 1982-88
3 St. Louis, 1974-76
2 By many teams

Most Times Sacked, Season
104 Philadelphia, 1986
72 Philadelphia, 1987
70 Atlanta, 1968

Fewest Times Sacked, Season
7 Miami, 1988
8 San Francisco, 1970
St. Louis, 1975
9 N.Y. Jets, 1966

Most Times Sacked, Game
12 Pittsburgh vs. Dallas, Nov. 20, 1966
Baltimore vs. St. Louis, Oct. 26, 1980
Detroit vs. Chicago, Dec. 16, 1984
Houston vs. Dallas, Sept. 29, 1985
11 St. Louis vs. N.Y. Giants, Nov. 1, 1964
Los Angeles vs. Baltimore, Nov. 22, 1964
Denver vs. Buffalo, Dec. 13, 1964; vs. Oakland, Nov. 5, 1967
Green Bay vs. Detroit, Nov. 7, 1965
Buffalo vs. Oakland, Oct. 15, 1967
Atlanta vs. St. Louis, Nov. 24, 1968; vs. Cleveland, Nov. 18, 1984
Detroit vs. Dallas, Oct. 6, 1975
Philadelphia vs. St. Louis, Dec. 18, 1983; vs. Detroit, Nov. 16, 1986; vs. L.A. Raiders, Nov. 30, 1986 (OT); vs. Chicago, Oct. 4, 1987
Cleveland vs. Kansas City, Sept. 30, 1984
Minnesota vs. Chicago, Oct. 28, 1984
Dallas vs. San Diego, Nov. 16, 1986
L.A. Raiders vs. Seattle, Dec. 8, 1986
N.Y. Jets vs. Dallas, Oct. 4, 1987
10 By many teams

Most Times Sacked, Both Teams, Game
18 Green Bay (10) vs. San Diego (8), Sept. 24, 1978
17 Buffalo (10) vs. N.Y. Titans (7), Nov. 23, 1961
Pittsburgh (12) vs. Dallas (5), Nov. 20, 1966
Atlanta (9) vs. Philadelphia (8), Dec. 16, 1984
Philadelphia (11) vs. L.A. Raiders (6), Nov. 30, 1986 (OT)
16 Los Angeles (11) vs. Baltimore (5), Nov. 22, 1964
Buffalo (11) vs. Oakland (5), Oct. 15, 1967

Completion Percentage

Most Seasons Leading League, Completion Percentage
11 Washington, 1937, 1939-40, 1942-45, 1947-48, 1969-70
7 Green Bay, 1936, 1941, 1961-62, 1964, 1966, 1968
San Francisco, 1952, 1957-58, 1965, 1981, 1983, 1987
6 Cleveland, 1951, 1953-55, 1959-60
Dall. Texans/Kansas City, 1962, 1964, 1966-69

Most Consecutive Seasons Leading League, Completion Percentage
4 Washington, 1942-45
Kansas City, 1966-69
3 Cleveland, 1953-55
2 By many teams

Highest Completion Percentage, Season
70.645 Cincinnati, 1982 (310-219)
64.271 San Francisco, 1987 (501-322)
64.266 Oakland, 1976 (361-232)

Lowest Completion Percentage, Season
22.9 Philadelphia, 1936 (170-39)
24.5 Cincinnati, 1933 (102-25)
25.0 Pittsburgh, 1941 (168-42)

Touchdowns

Most Touchdowns, Passing, Season
49 Miami, 1984
48 Houston, 1961
46 Miami, 1986

Fewest Touchdowns, Passing, Season
0 Cincinnati, 1933
Pittsburgh, 1945
1 Boston, 1932, 1933
Chi. Cardinals, 1934
Cincinnati/St. Louis, 1934
Detroit, 1942
2 Chi. Cardinals, 1932, 1935
Stapleton, 1932
Brooklyn, 1936
Pittsburgh, 1942

Most Touchdowns, Passing, Game
7 Chi. Bears vs. N.Y. Giants, Nov. 14, 1943
Philadelphia vs. Washington, Oct. 17, 1954
Houston vs. N.Y. Titans, Nov. 19, 1961; vs. N.Y. Titans, Oct. 14, 1962
N.Y. Giants vs. Washington, Oct. 28, 1962
Minnesota vs. Baltimore, Sept. 28, 1969
San Diego vs. Oakland, Nov. 22, 1981
6 By many teams.

Most Touchdowns, Passing, Both Teams, Game
12 New Orleans (6) vs. St. Louis (6), Nov. 2, 1969
11 N.Y. Giants (7) vs. Washington (4), Oct. 28, 1962
Oakland (6) vs. Houston (5), Dec. 22, 1963
10 Miami (6) vs. N.Y. Jets (4), Sept. 21, 1986 (OT)

Passes Had Intercepted

Most Passes Had Intercepted, Season
48 Houston, 1962
45 Denver, 1961
41 Card-Pitt, 1944

Fewest Passes Had Intercepted, Season
5 Cleveland, 1960
Green Bay, 1966
6 Green Bay, 1964
St. Louis, 1982
7 Los Angeles, 1969

Most Passes Had Intercepted, Game
9 Detroit vs. Green Bay, Oct. 24, 1943
Pittsburgh vs. Philadelphia, Dec. 12, 1965
8 Green Bay vs. N.Y. Giants, Nov. 21, 1948
Chi. Cardinals vs. Philadelphia, Sept. 24, 1950
N.Y. Yanks vs. N.Y. Giants, Dec. 16, 1951
Denver vs. Houston, Dec. 2, 1962

Chi. Bears vs. Detroit, Sept. 22, 1968
Baltimore vs. N.Y. Jets, Sept. 23, 1973
7 By many teams. Last time: Green Bay vs. New Orleans, Sept. 14, 1986

Most Passes Had Intercepted, Both Teams, Game
13 Denver (8) vs. Houston (5), Dec. 2, 1962
11 Philadelphia (7) vs. Boston (4), Nov. 3, 1935
Boston (6) vs. Pittsburgh (5), Dec. 1, 1935
Cleveland (7) vs. Green Bay (4), Oct. 30, 1938
Green Bay (7) vs. Detroit (4), Oct. 20, 1940
Detroit (7) vs. Chi. Bears (4), Nov. 22, 1942
Detroit (7) vs. Cleveland (4), Nov. 26, 1944
Chi. Cardinals (8) vs. Philadelphia (3), Sept. 24, 1950
Washington (7) vs. N.Y. Giants (4), Dec. 8, 1963
Pittsburgh (9) vs. Philadelphia (2), Dec 12, 1965
10 In many games

Punting

Most Seasons Leading League (Average Distance)
7 Denver, 1962-64, 1966-67, 1982, 1988
6 Washington, 1940-43, 1945, 1958
Kansas City, 1968, 1971-73, 1979, 1984
4 L.A. Rams, 1946, 1949, 1955-56
Baltimore/Indianapolis, 1966, 1969, 1983, 1985

Most Consecutive Seasons Leading League (Average Distance)
4 Washington, 1940-43
3 Cleveland, 1950-52
Denver, 1962-64
Kansas City, 1971-73

Most Punts, Season
114 Chicago, 1981
113 Boston, 1934
Brooklyn, 1934
112 Boston, 1935

Fewest Punts, Season
23 San Diego, 1982
31 Cincinnati, 1982
32 Chi. Bears, 1941

Most Punts, Game
17 Chi. Bears vs. Green Bay, Oct. 22, 1933
Cincinnati vs. Pittsburgh, Oct. 22, 1933
16 Cincinnati vs. Portsmouth, Sept. 17, 1933
Chi. Cardinals vs. Chi. Bears, Nov. 30, 1933; vs. Detroit, Sept. 15, 1940

Fewest Punts, Game
0 By many teams. Last time: Washington vs. Cincinnati, Dec. 17, 1988 (OT)

Most Punts, Both Teams, Game
31 Chi. Bears (17) vs. Green Bay (14), Oct. 22, 1933
Cincinnati (17), vs. Pittsburgh (14), Oct. 22, 1933
29 Chi. Cardinals (15) vs. Cincinnati (14), Nov. 12, 1933
Chi. Cardinals (16) vs. Chi. Bears (13), Nov. 30, 1933
Chi. Cardinals (16) vs. Detroit (13), Sept. 15, 1940

Fewest Punts, Both Teams, Game
1 Dall. Cowboys (0) vs. Cleveland (1), Dec. 3, 1961
Chicago (0) vs. Detroit (1), Oct. 1, 1972
San Francisco (0) vs. N.Y. Giants (1), Oct. 15, 1972
Green Bay (0) vs. Buffalo (1), Dec. 5, 1982
Miami (0) vs. Buffalo (1), Oct. 12, 1986
2 In many games

Average Yardage

Highest Average Distance, Punting, Season
47.6 Detroit, 1961 (56-2,664)
47.0 Pittsburgh, 1961 (73-3,431)
46.9 Pittsburgh, 1953 (80-3,752)

Lowest Average Distance, Punting, Season
32.7 Card-Pitt, 1944 (60-1,964)
33.8 Cincinnati, 1986 (59-1,996)
33.9 Detroit, 1969 (74-2,510)

Punt Returns

Most Seasons Leading League (Average Return)
8 Detroit, 1943-45, 1951-52, 1962, 1966, 1969
7 Chi. Cardinals/St. Louis, 1948-49, 1955-56, 1959, 1986-87
5 Cleveland, 1958, 1960, 1964-65, 1967
Green Bay, 1950, 1953-54, 1961, 1972
Dall. Texans/Kansas City, 1960, 1968, 1970, 1979-80

Most Consecutive Seasons Leading League (Average Return)
3 Detroit, 1943-45
2 By many teams

Most Punt Returns, Season
71 Pittsburgh, 1976
Tampa Bay, 1979
L.A. Raiders, 1985
67 Pittsburgh, 1974
Los Angeles, 1978
L.A. Raiders, 1984
65 San Francisco, 1976

Fewest Punt Returns, Season
12 Baltimore, 1981
San Diego, 1982
14 Los Angeles, 1961
Philadelphia, 1962
Baltimore, 1982
15 Houston, 1960
Washington, 1960
Oakland, 1961
N.Y. Giants, 1969
Philadelphia, 1973
Kansas City, 1982

Most Punt Returns, Game
12 Philadelphia vs. Cleveland, Dec. 3, 1950
11 Chi. Bears vs. Chi. Cardinals, Oct. 8, 1950
Washington vs. Tampa Bay, Oct. 9, 1977
10 Philadelphia vs. N.Y. Giants, Nov. 26, 1950
Philadelphia vs. Tampa Bay, Sept. 18, 1977
Pittsburgh vs. Buffalo, Dec. 16, 1979
Washington vs. New Orleans, Dec. 26, 1982

Most Punt Returns, Both Teams, Game
17 Philadelphia (12) vs. Cleveland (5), Dec. 3, 1950
16 N.Y. Giants (9) vs. Philadelphia (7), Dec. 12, 1954
Washington (11) vs. Tampa Bay (5), Oct. 9, 1977
15 Detroit (8) vs. Cleveland (7), Sept. 27, 1942
Los Angeles (8) vs. Baltimore (7), Nov. 27, 1966
Pittsburgh (8) vs. Houston (7), Dec. 1, 1974
Philadelphia (10) vs. Tampa Bay (5), Sept. 18, 1977
Baltimore (9) vs. Kansas City (6), Sept. 2, 1979
Washington (10) vs. New Orleans (5), Dec. 26, 1982
L.A. Raiders (8) vs. Cleveland (7), Nov. 16, 1986

Fair Catches

Most Fair Catches, Season
34 Baltimore, 1971
32 San Diego, 1969
30 St. Louis, 1967
Minnesota, 1971

Fewest Fair Catches, Season
0 San Diego, 1975
New England, 1976
Tampa Bay, 1976
Pittsburgh, 1977
Dallas, 1982
1 Cleveland, 1974
San Francisco, 1975
Kansas City, 1976
St. Louis, 1976, 1982
San Diego, 1976
L.A. Rams, 1982
Tampa Bay, 1982
2 By many teams

Most Fair Catches, Game
7 Minnesota vs. Dallas, Sept. 25, 1966
Detroit vs. Chicago, Nov. 21, 1976
Philadelphia vs. Buffalo, Dec. 27, 1987
6 By many teams

Yards Gained

Most Yards, Punt Returns, Season
785 L.A. Raiders, 1985
781 Chi. Bears, 1948
774 Pittsburgh, 1974

Fewest Yards, Punt Returns, Season
27 St. Louis, 1965
35 N.Y. Giants, 1965
37 New England, 1972

Most Yards, Punt Returns, Game
231 Detroit vs. San Francisco, Oct. 6, 1963
225 Oakland vs. Buffalo, Sept. 15, 1968
219 Los Angeles vs. Atlanta, Oct. 11, 1981

Most Yards, Punt Returns, Both Teams, Game
282 Los Angeles (219) vs. Atlanta (63), Oct. 11, 1981
245 Detroit (231) vs. San Francisco (14), Oct. 6, 1963
244 Oakland (225) vs. Buffalo (19), Sept. 15, 1968

Average Yards Returning Punts

Highest Average, Punt Returns, Season
20.2 Chi. Bears, 1941 (27-546)
19.1 Chi. Cardinals, 1948 (35-669)
18.2 Chi. Cardinals, 1949 (30-546)

Lowest Average, Punt Returns, Season
1.2 St. Louis, 1965 (23-27)
1.5 N.Y. Giants, 1965 (24-35)
1.7 Washington, 1970 (27-45)

Touchdowns Returning Punts

Most Touchdowns, Punt Returns, Season
5 Chi. Cardinals, 1959
4 Chi. Cardinals, 1948
Detroit, 1951
N.Y. Giants, 1951
Denver, 1976
3 Washington, 1941
Detroit, 1952
Pittsburgh, 1952
Houston, 1975
Los Angeles, 1981

Most Touchdowns, Punt Returns, Game
2 Detroit vs. Los Angeles, Oct. 14, 1951; vs. Green Bay, Nov. 22, 1951
Chi. Cardinals vs. Pittsburgh, Nov. 1, 1959; vs. N.Y. Giants, Nov. 22, 1959
N.Y. Titans vs. Denver, Sept. 24, 1961
Denver vs. Cleveland, Sept. 26, 1976
Los Angeles vs. Atlanta, Oct. 11, 1981
St. Louis vs. Tampa Bay, Dec. 21, 1986

Most Touchdowns, Punt Returns, Both Teams, Game
2 Philadelphia (1) vs. Washington (1), Nov. 9, 1952
Kansas City (1) vs. Buffalo (1), Sept. 11, 1966
Baltimore (1) vs. New England (1), Nov. 18, 1979
L.A. Raiders (1) vs. Philadelphia (1), Nov. 30, 1986 (OT)
(Also see previous record)

Kickoff Returns

Most Seasons Leading League (Average Return)
7 Washington, 1942, 1947, 1962-63, 1973-74, 1981
6 Chicago Bears, 1943, 1948, 1958, 1966, 1972, 1985
5 N.Y. Giants, 1944, 1946, 1949, 1951, 1953

Most Consecutive Seasons Leading League (Average Return)
3 Denver, 1965-67
2 By many teams
Most Kickoff Returns, Season
88 New Orleans, 1980
86 Minnesota, 1984
84 Baltimore, 1981
Fewest Kickoff Returns, Season
17 N.Y. Giants, 1944
20 N.Y. Giants, 1941, 1943
Chi. Bears, 1942
23 Washington, 1942
Most Kickoff Returns, Game
12 N.Y. Giants vs. Washington, Nov. 27, 1966
10 By many teams
Most Kickoff Returns, Both Teams, Game
19 N.Y. Giants (12) vs. Washington (7), Nov. 27, 1966
18 Houston (10) vs. Oakland (8), Dec. 22, 1963
17 Washington (9) vs. Green Bay (8), Oct. 17, 1983
San Diego (9) vs. Pittsburgh (8), Dec. 8, 1985
Detroit (9) vs. Green Bay (8), Nov. 27, 1986
L.A. Raiders (9) vs. Seattle (8), Dec. 18, 1988

Yards Gained
Most Yards, Kickoff Returns, Season
1,973 New Orleans, 1980
1,824 Houston, 1963
1,801 Denver, 1963
Fewest Yards, Kickoff Returns, Season
282 N.Y. Giants, 1940
381 Green Bay, 1940
424 Chicago, 1963
Most Yards, Kickoff Returns, Game
362 Detroit vs. Los Angeles, Oct. 29, 1950
304 Chi. Bears vs. Green Bay, Nov. 9, 1952
295 Denver vs. Boston, Oct. 4, 1964
Most Yards, Kickoff Returns, Both Teams, Game
560 Detroit (362) vs. Los Angeles (198), Oct. 29, 1950
453 Washington (236) vs. Philadelphia (217), Sept. 28, 1947
447 N.Y. Giants (236) vs. Cleveland (211), Dec. 4, 1966

Average Yardage
Highest Average, Kickoff Returns, Season
29.4 Chicago, 1972 (52-1,528)
28.9 Pittsburgh, 1952 (39-1,128)
28.2 Washington, 1962 (61-1,720)
Lowest Average, Kickoff Returns, Season
16.3 Chicago, 1963 (26-424)
16.4 Chicago, 1983 (58-953)
16.5 San Diego, 1961 (39-642)

Touchdowns
Most Touchdowns, Kickoff Returns, Season
4 Green Bay, 1967
Chicago, 1970
3 L.A. Rams, 1950, 1985
Chi. Cardinals, 1954
San Francisco, 1963
Denver, 1966
Chicago, 1967
New England, 1977
2 By many teams
Most Touchdowns, Kickoff Returns, Game
2 Chi. Bears vs. Green Bay, Sept. 22, 1940; vs. Green Bay, Nov. 9, 1952
Philadelphia vs. Dallas, Nov. 6, 1966
Green Bay vs. Cleveland, Nov. 12, 1967
L.A. Rams vs. Green Bay, Nov. 24, 1985
Most Touchdowns, Kickoff Returns, Both Teams, Game
2 Washington (1) vs. Philadelphia (1), Nov. 1, 1942
Washington (1) vs. Philadelphia (1), Sept. 28, 1947
Los Angeles (1) vs. Detroit (1), Oct. 29, 1950
N.Y. Yanks (1) vs. N.Y. Giants (1), Nov. 4, 1951 (consecutive)
Baltimore (1) vs. Chi. Bears (1), Oct. 4, 1958
Buffalo (1) vs. Boston (1), Nov. 3, 1962
Pittsburgh (1) vs. Dallas (1), Oct. 30, 1966
St. Louis (1) vs. Washington (1), Sept. 23, 1973 (consecutive)
Atlanta (1) vs. San Francisco (1), Dec. 20, 1987 (consecutive)
Houston (1) vs. Pittsburgh (1), Dec. 4, 1988
(Also see previous record)

Fumbles
Most Fumbles, Season
56 Chi. Bears, 1938
San Francisco, 1978
54 Philadelphia, 1946
51 New England, 1973
Fewest Fumbles, Season
8 Cleveland, 1959
11 Green Bay, 1944
12 Brooklyn, 1934
Detroit, 1943
Cincinnati, 1982
Minnesota, 1982
Most Fumbles, Game
10 Phil-Pitt vs. New York, Oct. 9, 1943
Detroit vs. Minnesota, Nov. 12, 1967
Kansas City vs. Houston, Oct. 12, 1969
San Francisco vs. Detroit, Dec. 17, 1978
9 Philadelphia vs. Green Bay, Oct. 13, 1946
Kansas City vs. San Diego, Nov. 15, 1964
N.Y. Giants vs. Buffalo, Oct. 20, 1975
St. Louis vs. Washington, Oct. 25, 1976
San Diego vs. Green Bay, Sept. 24, 1978
Pittsburgh vs. Cincinnati, Oct. 14, 1979
Cleveland vs. Seattle, Dec. 20, 1981
8 By many teams. Last time: Tampa Bay vs. New York Jets, Dec. 12, 1982
Most Fumbles, Both Teams, Game
14 Chi. Bears (7) vs. Cleveland (7), Nov. 24, 1940
St. Louis (8) vs. N.Y. Giants (6), Sept. 17, 1961
Kansas City (10) vs. Houston (4), Oct. 12, 1969
13 Washington (8) vs. Pittsburgh (5), Nov. 14, 1937
Philadelphia (7) vs. Boston (6), Dec. 8, 1946
N.Y. Giants (7) vs. Washington (6), Nov. 5, 1950
Kansas City (9) vs. San Diego (4), Nov. 15, 1964
Buffalo (7) vs. Denver (6), Dec. 13, 1964
N.Y. Jets (7) vs. Houston (6), Sept. 12, 1965
Houston (8) vs. Pittsburgh (5), Dec. 9, 1973
St. Louis (9) vs. Washington (4), Oct. 25, 1976
Cleveland (9) vs. Seattle (4), Dec. 20, 1981
Green Bay (7) vs. Detroit (6), Oct. 6, 1985
12 In many games

Fumbles Lost
Most Fumbles Lost, Season
36 Chi. Cardinals, 1959
31 Green Bay, 1952
29 Chi. Cardinals, 1946
Pittsburgh, 1950
Fewest Fumbles Lost, Season
3 Philadelphia, 1938
Minnesota, 1980
4 San Francisco, 1960
Kansas City, 1982
5 Chi. Cardinals, 1943
Detroit, 1943
N.Y. Giants, 1943
Cleveland, 1959
Minnesota, 1982
Most Fumbles Lost, Game
8 St. Louis vs. Washington, Oct. 25, 1976
7 Cincinnati vs. Buffalo, Nov. 30, 1969
Cleveland vs. Seattle, Dec. 20, 1981
6 By many teams. Last time: L.A. Rams vs. New England, Dec. 11, 1983

Fumbles Recovered
Most Fumbles Recovered, Season, Own and Opponents'
58 Minnesota, 1963 (27 own, 31 opp)
51 Chi. Bears, 1938 (37 own, 14 opp)
San Francisco, 1978 (24 own, 27 opp)
50 Philadelphia, 1987 (23 own, 27 opp)
Fewest Fumbles Recovered, Season, Own and Opponents'
9 San Francisco, 1982 (5 own, 4 opp)
11 Cincinnati, 1982 (5 own, 6 opp)
13 Baltimore, 1967 (5 own, 8 opp)
N.Y. Jets, 1967 (7 own, 6 opp)
Philadelphia, 1968 (6 own, 7 opp)
Miami, 1973 (5 own, 8 opp)
Chicago, 1982 (6 own, 7 opp)
Denver, 1982 (6 own, 7 opp)
Miami, 1982 (5 own, 8 opp)
N.Y. Giants, 1982 (7 own, 6 opp)
Most Fumbles Recovered, Game, Own and Opponents'
10 Denver vs. Buffalo, Dec. 13, 1964 (5 own, 5 opp)
Pittsburgh vs. Houston, Dec. 9, 1973 (5 own, 5 opp)
Washington vs. St. Louis, Oct. 25, 1976 (2 own, 8 opp)
9 St. Louis vs. N.Y. Giants, Sept. 17, 1961 (6 own, 3 opp)
Houston vs. Cincinnati, Oct. 27, 1974 (4 own, 5 opp)
Kansas City vs. Dallas, Nov. 10, 1975 (4 own, 5 opp)
Green Bay vs. Detroit, Oct. 6, 1985 (5 own, 4 opp)
8 By many teams
Most Own Fumbles Recovered, Season
37 Chi. Bears, 1938
28 Pittsburgh, 1987
27 Philadelphia, 1946
Minnesota, 1963
Fewest Own Fumbles Recovered, Season
2 Washington, 1958
3 Detroit, 1956
Cleveland, 1959
Houston, 1982
4 By many teams
Most Opponents' Fumbles Recovered, Season
31 Minnesota, 1963
29 Cleveland, 1951
28 Green Bay, 1946
Houston, 1977
Seattle, 1983
Fewest Opponents' Fumbles Recovered, Season
3 Los Angeles, 1974
4 Philadelphia, 1944
San Francisco, 1982
5 Baltimore, 1982
Most Opponents' Fumbles Recovered, Game
8 Washington vs. St. Louis, Oct. 25, 1976
7 Buffalo vs. Cincinnati, Nov. 30, 1969
Seattle vs. Cleveland, Dec. 20, 1981
6 By many teams. Last time: New England vs. L.A. Rams, Dec. 11, 1983

Touchdowns
Most Touchdowns, Fumbles Recovered, Season, Own and Opponents'
5 Chi. Bears, 1942 (1 own, 4 opp)
Los Angeles, 1952 (1 own, 4 opp)
San Francisco, 1965 (1 own, 4 opp)
Oakland, 1978 (2 own, 3 opp)
4 Chi. Bears, 1948 (1 own, 3 opp)
Boston, 1948 (4 opp)

Denver, 1979 (1 own, 3 opp), 1984 (4 opp)
Atlanta, 1981 (1 own, 3 opp)
St. Louis, 1987 (4 opp)
3 By many teams

Most Touchdowns, Own Fumbles Recovered, Season
2 Chi. Bears, 1953
New England, 1973
Buffalo, 1974
Denver, 1975
Oakland, 1978
Green Bay, 1982
New Orleans, 1983
Cleveland, 1986

Most Touchdowns, Opponents' Fumbles Recovered, Season
4 Detroit, 1937
Chi. Bears, 1942
Boston, 1948
Los Angeles, 1952
San Francisco, 1965
Denver, 1984
St. Louis, 1987
3 By many teams

Most Touchdowns, Fumbles Recovered, Game, Own and Opponents'
2 Detroit vs. Cleveland, Nov. 7, 1937 (2 opp); vs. Green Bay, Sept. 17, 1950 (1 own, 1 opp); vs. Chi. Cardinals, Dec. 6, 1959 (1 own, 1 opp); vs. Minnesota, Dec. 9, 1962 (1 own, 1 opp)
Philadelphia vs. New York, Sept. 25, 1938 (2 opp); vs. St. Louis, Nov. 21, 1971 (1 own, 1 opp)
Chi. Bears vs. Washington, Nov. 28, 1948 (2 opp)
N.Y. Giants vs. Pittsburgh, Sept. 17, 1950 (2 opp); vs. Green Bay, Sept. 19, 1971 (2 opp)
Cleveland vs. Dall. Cowboys, Dec. 3, 1961 (2 opp); vs. N.Y. Giants, Oct. 25, 1964 (2 opp)
Green Bay vs. Dallas, Nov. 26, 1964 (2 opp)
San Francisco vs. Detroit, Nov. 14, 1965 (2 opp)
Oakland vs. Buffalo, Dec. 24, 1967 (2 opp)
Washington vs. San Diego, Sept. 16, 1973 (2 opp); vs. Minnesota, Nov. 29, 1984 (1 own, 1 opp)
New Orleans vs. San Francisco, Oct. 19, 1975 (2 opp)
Cincinnati vs. Pittsburgh, Oct. 14, 1979 (2 opp)
Atlanta vs. Detroit, Oct. 5, 1980 (2 opp)
Kansas City vs. Oakland, Oct. 5, 1980 (2 opp)
New England vs. Baltimore, Nov. 23, 1980 (2 opp)
Denver vs. Green Bay, Oct. 15, 1984 (2 opp)
Miami vs. Kansas City, Oct. 11, 1987 (2 opp)
St. Louis vs. New Orleans, Oct. 11, 1987 (2 opp)

Most Touchdowns, Own Fumbles Recovered, Game
1 By many teams

Most Touchdowns, Opponents' Fumbles Recovered, Game
2 Detroit vs. Cleveland, Nov. 7, 1937
Philadelphia vs. N.Y. Giants, Sept. 25, 1938
Chi. Bears vs. Washington, Nov. 28, 1948
N.Y. Giants vs. Pittsburgh, Sept. 17, 1950; vs. Green Bay, Sept. 19, 1971
Cleveland vs. Dall. Cowboys, Dec. 3, 1961; vs. N.Y. Giants, Oct. 25, 1964
Green Bay vs. Dallas, Nov. 26, 1964
San Francisco vs. Detroit, Nov. 14, 1965
Oakland vs. Buffalo, Dec. 24, 1967
Washington vs. San Diego, Sept. 16, 1973
New Orleans vs. San Francisco, Oct. 19, 1975
Cincinnati vs. Pittsburgh, Oct. 14, 1979
Atlanta vs. Detroit, Oct. 5, 1980
Kansas City vs. Oakland, Oct. 5, 1980
New England vs. Baltimore, Nov. 23, 1980
Denver vs. Green Bay, Oct. 15, 1984
Miami vs. Kansas City, Oct. 11, 1987
St. Louis vs. New Orleans, Oct. 11, 1987

Turnovers

(Number of times losing the ball on interceptions and fumbles.)

Most Turnovers, Season
63 San Francisco, 1978
58 Chi. Bears, 1947
Pittsburgh, 1950
N.Y. Giants, 1983
57 Green Bay, 1950
Houston, 1962, 1963
Pittsburgh, 1965

Fewest Turnovers, Season
12 Kansas City, 1982
14 N.Y. Giants, 1943
Cleveland, 1959
16 San Francisco, 1960
Cincinnati, 1982
St. Louis, 1982
Washington, 1982

Most Turnovers, Game
12 Detroit vs. Chi. Bears, Nov. 22, 1942
Chi. Cardinals vs. Philadelphia, Sept. 24, 1950
Pittsburgh vs. Philadelphia, Dec. 12, 1965
11 San Diego vs. Green Bay, Sept. 24, 1978
10 Washington vs. N.Y. Giants, Dec. 4, 1938; vs. N.Y. Giants, Dec. 8, 1963
Pittsburgh vs. Green Bay, Nov. 23, 1941
Detroit vs. Green Bay, Oct. 24, 1943; vs. Denver, Oct. 7, 1984
Chi. Cardinals vs. Green Bay, Nov. 10, 1946; vs. N.Y. Giants, Nov. 2, 1952
Minnesota vs. Detroit, Dec. 9, 1962
Houston vs. Oakland, Sept. 7, 1963
Chicago vs. Detroit, Sept. 22, 1968
St. Louis vs. Washington, Oct. 25, 1976
N.Y. Jets vs. New England, Nov. 21, 1976
San Francisco vs. Dallas, Oct. 12, 1980
Cleveland vs. Seattle, Dec. 20, 1981

Most Turnovers, Both Teams, Game
17 Detroit (12) vs. Chi. Bears (5), Nov. 22, 1942
Boston (9) vs. Philadelphia (8), Dec. 8, 1946
16 Chi. Cardinals (12) vs. Philadelphia (4), Sept. 24, 1950
Chi. Cardinals (8) vs. Chi. Bears (8), Dec. 7, 1958
Minnesota (10) vs. Detroit (6), Dec. 9, 1962
Houston (9) vs. Kansas City (7), Oct. 12, 1969
15 Philadelphia (8) vs. Chi. Cardinals (7), Oct. 3, 1954
Denver (9) vs. Houston (6), Dec. 2, 1962
Washington (10) vs. N.Y. Giants (5), Dec. 8, 1963
St. Louis (9) vs. Kansas City (6), Oct. 2, 1983

Penalties

Most Seasons Leading League, Fewest Penalties
11 Miami, 1968, 1976-84, 1986
9 Pittsburgh, 1946-47, 1950-52, 1954, 1963, 1965, 1968
5 Green Bay, 1955-56, 1966-67, 1974
Boston/New England, 1962, 1964-65, 1973, 1987

Most Consecutive Seasons Leading League, Fewest Penalties
9 Miami, 1976-84
3 Pittsburgh, 1950-52
2 By many teams

Most Seasons Leading League, Most Penalties
16 Chi. Bears, 1941-44, 1946-49, 1951, 1959-61, 1963, 1965, 1968, 1976
7 Oakland/L.A. Raiders, 1963, 1966, 1968-69, 1975, 1982, 1984
6 L.A. Rams, 1950, 1952, 1962, 1969, 1978, 1980

Most Consecutive Seasons Leading League, Most Penalties
4 Chi. Bears, 1941-44, 1946-49
3 Chi. Cardinals, 1954-56
Chi. Bears, 1959-61

Fewest Penalties, Season
19 Detroit, 1937
21 Boston, 1935
24 Philadelphia, 1936

Most Penalties, Season
144 Buffalo, 1983
143 L.A. Raiders, 1984
141 Dallas, 1988

Fewest Penalties, Game
0 By many teams. Last time: San Francisco vs. New Orleans, Dec. 11, 1988

Most Penalties, Game
22 Brooklyn vs. Green Bay, Sept. 17, 1944
Chi. Bears vs. Philadelphia, Nov. 26, 1944
21 Cleveland vs. Chi. Bears, Nov. 25, 1951
20 Tampa Bay vs. Seattle, Oct. 17, 1976

Fewest Penalties, Both Teams, Game
0 Brooklyn vs. Pittsburgh, Oct. 28, 1934
Brooklyn vs. Boston, Sept. 28, 1936
Cleveland vs. Chi. Bears, Oct. 9, 1938
Pittsburgh vs. Philadelphia, Nov. 10, 1940

Most Penalties, Both Teams, Game
37 Cleveland (21) vs. Chi. Bears (16), Nov. 25, 1951
35 Tampa Bay (20) vs. Seattle (15), Oct. 17, 1976
33 Brooklyn (22) vs. Green Bay (11), Sept. 17, 1944

Yards Penalized

Most Seasons Leading League, Fewest Yards Penalized
11 Miami, 1967-68, 1973, 1977-84
8 Boston/Washington, 1935, 1953-54, 1956-58, 1970, 1985
7 Pittsburgh, 1946-47, 1950, 1952, 1962, 1965, 1968

Most Consecutive Seasons Leading League, Fewest Yards Penalized
8 Miami, 1977-84
3 Washington, 1956-58
Boston, 1964-66
2 By many teams

Most Seasons Leading League, Most Yards Penalized
15 Chi. Bears, 1935, 1937, 1939-44, 1946-47, 1949, 1951, 1961-62, 1968
7 Oakland/L.A. Raiders, 1963-64, 1968-69, 1975, 1982, 1984
6 Buffalo, 1962, 1967, 1970, 1972, 1981, 1983

Most Consecutive Seasons Leading League, Most Yards Penalized
6 Chi. Bears, 1939-44
3 Cleveland, 1976-78
2 By many teams

Fewest Yards Penalized, Season
139 Detroit, 1937
146 Philadelphia, 1937
159 Philadelphia, 1936

Most Yards Penalized, Season
1,274 Oakland, 1969
1,239 Baltimore, 1979
1,209 L.A. Raiders, 1984

Fewest Yards Penalized, Game
0 By many teams. Last time: San Francisco vs. New Orleans, Dec. 11, 1988

Most Yards Penalized, Game
209 Cleveland vs. Chi. Bears, Nov. 25, 1951
190 Tampa Bay vs. Seattle, Oct. 17, 1976
189 Houston vs. Buffalo, Oct. 31, 1965

Fewest Yards Penalized, Both Teams, Game
0 Brooklyn vs. Pittsburgh, Oct. 28, 1934
Brooklyn vs. Boston, Sept. 28, 1936
Cleveland vs. Chi. Bears, Oct. 9, 1938
Pittsburgh vs. Philadelphia, Nov. 10, 1940

Most Yards Penalized, Both Teams, Game
374 Cleveland (209) vs. Chi. Bears (165), Nov. 25, 1951
310 Tampa Bay (190) vs. Seattle (120), Oct. 17, 1976
309 Green Bay (184) vs. Boston (125), Oct. 21, 1945

Defense

Scoring

Most Seasons Leading League, Fewest Points Allowed
9 Chi. Bears, 1932, 1936-37, 1942, 1948, 1963, 1985-86, 1988
8 N.Y. Giants, 1935, 1938-39, 1941, 1944, 1958-59, 1961
6 Cleveland, 1951, 1953-57

Most Consecutive Seasons Leading League, Fewest Points Allowed
5 Cleveland, 1953-57
3 Buffalo, 1964-66
Minnesota, 1969-71
2 By many teams

Fewest Points Allowed, Season (Since 1932)
44 Chi. Bears, 1932
54 Brooklyn, 1933
59 Detroit, 1934

Most Points Allowed, Season
533 Baltimore, 1981
501 N.Y. Giants, 1966
487 New Orleans, 1980

Fewest Touchdowns Allowed, Season (Since 1932)
6 Chi. Bears, 1932
Brooklyn, 1933
7 Detroit, 1934
8 Green Bay, 1932

Most Touchdowns Allowed, Season
68 Baltimore, 1981
66 N.Y. Giants, 1966
63 Baltimore, 1950

First Downs

Fewest First Downs Allowed Season
77 Detroit, 1935
79 Boston, 1935
82 Washington, 1937

Most First Downs Allowed, Season
406 Baltimore, 1981
371 Seattle, 1981
366 Green Bay, 1983

Fewest First Downs Allowed, Rushing, Season
35 Chi. Bears, 1942
40 Green Bay, 1939
41 Brooklyn, 1944

Most First Downs Allowed, Rushing, Season
179 Detroit, 1985
178 New Orleans, 1980
175 Seattle, 1981

Fewest First Downs Allowed, Passing, Season
33 Chi. Bears, 1943
34 Pittsburgh, 1941
Washington, 1943
35 Detroit, 1940
Philadelphia, 1940, 1944

Most First Downs Allowed, Passing, Season
218 San Diego, 1985
216 San Diego, 1981
N.Y. Jets, 1986
214 Baltimore, 1981

Fewest First Downs Allowed, Penalty, Season
1 Boston, 1944
3 Philadelphia, 1940
Pittsburgh, 1945
Washington, 1957
4 Cleveland, 1940
Green Bay, 1943
N.Y. Giants, 1943

Most First Downs Allowed, Penalty, Season
48 Houston, 1985
46 Houston, 1986
43 L.A. Raiders, 1984

Net Yards Allowed Rushing and Passing

Most Seasons Leading League, Fewest Yards Allowed
8 Chi. Bears, 1942-43, 1948, 1958, 1963, 1984-86
6 N.Y. Giants, 1938, 1940-41, 1951, 1956, 1959
5 Boston/Washington, 1935-37, 1939, 1946
Philadelphia, 1944-45, 1949, 1953, 1981

Most Consecutive Seasons Leading League, Fewest Yards Allowed
3 Boston/Washington, 1935-37
Chicago, 1984-86
2 By many teams

Fewest Yards Allowed, Season
1,539 Chi. Cardinals, 1934
1,703 Chi. Bears, 1942
1,789 Brooklyn, 1933

Most Yards Allowed, Season
6,793 Baltimore, 1981
6,403 Green Bay, 1983
6,352 Minnesota, 1984

Rushing

Most Seasons Leading League, Fewest Yards Allowed
10 Chi. Bears, 1937, 1939, 1942, 1946, 1949, 1963, 1984-85, 1987-88
7 Detroit, 1938, 1950, 1952, 1962, 1970, 1980-81
6 Dallas, 1966-69, 1972, 1978

Most Consecutive Seasons Leading League, Fewest Yards Allowed
4 Dallas, 1966-69
2 By many teams

Fewest Yards Allowed, Rushing, Season
519 Chi. Bears, 1942
558 Philadelphia, 1944
762 Pittsburgh, 1982

Most Yards Allowed, Rushing, Season
3,228 Buffalo, 1978
3,106 New Orleans, 1980
3,010 Baltimore, 1978

Fewest Touchdowns Allowed, Rushing, Season
2 Detroit, 1934
Dallas, 1968
Minnesota, 1971
3 By many teams

Most Touchdowns Allowed, Rushing, Season
36 Oakland, 1961
31 N.Y. Giants, 1980
Tampa Bay, 1986
30 Baltimore, 1981

Passing

Most Seasons Leading League, Fewest Yards Allowed
8 Green Bay, 1947-48, 1962, 1964-68
7 Washington, 1939, 1942, 1945, 1952-53, 1980, 1985
6 Chi. Bears, 1938, 1943-44, 1958, 1960, 1963

Most Consecutive Seasons Leading League, Fewest Yards Allowed
5 Green Bay, 1964-68
2 By many teams

Fewest Yards Allowed, Passing, Season
545 Philadelphia, 1934
558 Portsmouth, 1933
585 Chi. Cardinals, 1934

Most Yards Allowed, Passing, Season
4,389 N.Y. Jets, 1986
4,311 San Diego, 1981
4,293 San Diego, 1985

Fewest Touchdowns Allowed, Passing, Season
1 Portsmouth, 1932
Philadelphia, 1934
2 Brooklyn, 1933
Chi. Bears, 1934
3 Chi. Bears, 1932, 1936
Green Bay, 1932, 1934
N.Y. Giants, 1939, 1944

Most Touchdowns Allowed, Passing, Season
40 Denver, 1963
38 St. Louis, 1969
37 Washington, 1961
Baltimore, 1981

Sacks

Most Seasons Leading League
5 Oakland/L.A. Raiders, 1966-68, 1982, 1986
4 Boston/New England, 1961, 1963, 1977, 1979
Dallas, 1966, 1968-69, 1978
3 Dallas/Kansas City, 1960, 1965, 1969
San Francisco, 1967, 1972, 1976
L.A. Rams, 1968, 1970, 1988

Most Consecutive Seasons Leading League
3 Oakland, 1966-68
2 Dallas, 1968-69

Most Sacks, Season
72 Chicago, 1984
70 Chicago, 1987
68 N.Y. Giants, 1985

Fewest Sacks, Season
11 Baltimore, 1982
12 Buffalo, 1982
13 Baltimore, 1981

Most Sacks, Game
12 Dallas vs. Pittsburgh, Nov. 20, 1966; vs. Houston, Sept. 29, 1985
St. Louis vs. Baltimore, Oct. 26, 1980
Chicago vs. Detroit, Dec. 16, 1984
11 N.Y. Giants vs. St. Louis, Nov. 1, 1964
Baltimore vs. Los Angeles, Nov. 22, 1964
Buffalo vs. Denver, Dec. 13, 1964
Detroit vs. Green Bay, Nov. 7, 1965; vs. Philadelphia, Nov. 16, 1986
Oakland vs. Buffalo, Oct. 15, 1967; vs. Denver, Nov. 5, 1967
St. Louis vs. Atlanta, Nov. 24, 1968; vs. Philadelphia, Dec. 18, 1983
Dallas vs. Detroit, Oct. 6, 1975; vs. N.Y. Jets, Oct. 4, 1987
Kansas City vs. Cleveland, Sept. 30, 1984
Chicago vs. Minnesota, Oct. 28, 1984; vs. Philadelphia, Oct. 4, 1987
Cleveland vs. Atlanta, Nov. 18, 1984
San Diego vs. Dallas, Nov. 16, 1986
L.A. Raiders vs. Philadelphia, Nov. 30, 1986 (OT)
Seattle vs. L.A. Raiders, Dec. 8, 1986
10 By many teams

Most Opponents Yards Lost Attempting to Pass, Season
666 Oakland, 1967
583 Chicago, 1984
573 San Francisco, 1976

Fewest Opponents Yards Lost Attempting to Pass, Season
75 Green Bay, 1956
77 N.Y. Bulldogs, 1949
78 Green Bay, 1958

Interceptions By

Most Seasons Leading League
9 N.Y. Giants, 1933, 1937-39, 1944, 1948, 1951, 1954, 1961
8 Green Bay, 1940, 1942-43, 1947, 1955, 1957, 1962, 1965
7 Chi. Bears, 1935-36, 1941-42, 1946, 1963, 1985

Most Consecutive Seasons Leading League
5 Kansas City, 1966-70
3 N.Y. Giants, 1937-39
2 By many teams

Most Passes Intercepted By, Season
49 San Diego, 1961
42 Green Bay, 1943
41 N.Y. Giants, 1951

Fewest Passes Intercepted By, Season
3 Houston, 1982
5 Baltimore, 1982
6 Houston, 1972
St. Louis, 1982

Most Passes Intercepted By, Game
9 Green Bay vs. Detroit, Oct. 24, 1943
Philadelphia vs. Pittsburgh, Dec. 12, 1965
8 N.Y. Giants vs. Green Bay, Nov. 21, 1948; vs. N.Y. Yanks, Dec. 16, 1951
Philadelphia vs. Chi. Cardinals, Sept. 24, 1950
Houston vs. Denver, Dec. 2, 1962
Detroit vs. Chicago, Sept. 22, 1968
N.Y. Jets vs. Baltimore, Sept. 23, 1973
7 By many teams. Last time: New Orleans vs. Green Bay, Sept. 14, 1986
Most Consecutive Games, One or More Interceptions By
46 L.A. Chargers/San Diego, 1960-63
37 Detroit, 1960-63
36 Boston, 1944-47
Washington, 1962-65
Most Yards Returning Interceptions, Season
929 San Diego, 1961
712 Los Angeles, 1952
697 Seattle, 1984
Fewest Yards Returning Interceptions, Season
5 Los Angeles, 1959
42 Philadelphia, 1982
47 Houston, 1982
Most Yards Returning Interceptions, Game
325 Seattle vs. Kansas City, Nov. 4, 1984
314 Los Angeles vs. San Francisco, Oct. 18, 1964
245 Houston vs. N.Y. Jets, Oct. 15, 1967
Most Touchdowns, Returning Interceptions, Season
9 San Diego, 1961
7 Seattle, 1984
6 Cleveland, 1960
Green Bay, 1966
Detroit, 1967
Houston, 1967
Most Touchdowns Returning Interceptions, Game
4 Seattle vs. Kansas City, Nov. 4, 1984
3 Baltimore vs. Green Bay, Nov. 5, 1950
Cleveland vs. Chicago, Dec. 11, 1960
Philadelphia vs. Pittsburgh, Dec. 12, 1965
Baltimore vs. Pittsburgh, Sept. 29, 1968
Buffalo vs. N.Y. Jets, Sept. 29, 1968
Houston vs. San Diego, Dec. 19, 1971
Cincinnati vs. Houston, Dec. 17, 1972
Tampa Bay vs. New Orleans, Dec. 11, 1977
2 By many teams
Most Touchdowns Returning Interceptions, Both Teams, Game
4 Philadelphia (3) vs. Pittsburgh (1), Dec. 12, 1965
Seattle (4) vs. Kansas City (0), Nov. 4, 1984
3 Los Angeles (2) vs. Detroit (1), Nov. 1, 1953
Cleveland (2) vs. N.Y. Giants (1), Dec. 18, 1960
Pittsburgh (2) vs. Cincinnati (1), Oct. 10, 1983
Kansas City (2) vs. San Diego (1), Oct. 19, 1986
(Also see previous record)

Punt Returns
Fewest Opponents Punt Returns, Season
7 Washington, 1962
San Diego, 1982
10 Buffalo, 1982
11 Boston, 1962
Most Opponents Punt Returns, Season
71 Tampa Bay, 1976, 1977
69 N.Y. Giants, 1953
68 Cleveland, 1974
Fewest Yards Allowed, Punt Returns, Season
22 Green Bay, 1967
34 Washington, 1962
39 Cleveland, 1959
Washington, 1972
Most Yards Allowed, Punt Returns, Season
932 Green Bay, 1949
913 Boston, 1947
906 New Orleans, 1974
Lowest Average Allowed, Punt Returns, Season
1.20 Chi. Cardinals, 1954 (46-55)
1.22 Cleveland, 1959 (32-39)
1.55 Chi. Cardinals, 1953 (44-68)
Highest Average Allowed, Punt Returns, Season
18.6 Green Bay, 1949 (50-932)
18.0 Cleveland, 1977 (31-558)
17.9 Boston, 1960 (20-357)
Most Touchdowns Allowed, Punt Returns, Season
4 New York, 1959
3 Green Bay, 1949
Chi. Cardinals, 1951
Los Angeles, 1951
Washington, 1952
Dallas, 1952
Pittsburgh, 1959
N.Y. Jets, 1968
Cleveland, 1977
Atlanta, 1986
Tampa Bay, 1986
2 By many teams

Kickoff Returns
Fewest Opponents Kickoff Returns, Season
10 Brooklyn, 1943
15 Detroit, 1942
Brooklyn, 1944
18 Cleveland, 1941
Boston, 1944
Most Opponents Kickoff Returns, Season
91 Washington, 1983
89 New England, 1980
88 San Diego, 1981
Fewest Yards Allowed, Kickoff Returns, Season
225 Brooklyn, 1943
293 Brooklyn, 1944
361 Seattle, 1982
Most Yards Allowed, Kickoff Returns, Season
2,045 Kansas City, 1966
1,827 Chicago, 1985
1,816 N.Y. Giants, 1963
Lowest Average Allowed, Kickoff Returns, Season
14.3 Cleveland, 1980 (71-1,018)
15.0 Seattle, 1982 (24-361)
15.8 Buffalo, 1987 (43-679)
Highest Average Allowed, Kickoff Returns, Season
29.5 N.Y. Jets, 1972 (47-1,386)
29.4 Los Angeles, 1950 (48-1,411)
29.1 New England, 1971 (49-1,427)
Most Touchdowns Allowed, Kickoff Returns, Season
3 Minnesota, 1963, 1970
Dallas, 1966
Detroit, 1980
Pittsburgh, 1986
2 By many teams

Fumbles
Fewest Opponents Fumbles, Season
11 Cleveland, 1956
Baltimore, 1982
13 Los Angeles, 1956
Chicago, 1960
Cleveland, 1963, 1965
Detroit, 1967
San Diego, 1969
14 Baltimore, 1970
Oakland, 1975
Buffalo, 1982
St. Louis, 1982
San Francisco, 1982
Most Opponents Fumbles, Season
50 Minnesota, 1963
San Francisco, 1978
48 N.Y. Giants, 1980
N.Y. Jets, 1986
47 N.Y. Giants, 1977
Seattle, 1984

Turnovers
(Number of times losing the ball on interceptions and fumbles.)
Fewest Opponents Turnovers, Season
11 Baltimore, 1982
13 San Francisco, 1982
15 St. Louis, 1982
Most Opponents Turnovers, Season
66 San Diego, 1961
63 Seattle, 1984
61 Washington, 1983
Most Opponents Turnovers, Game
12 Chi. Bears vs. Detroit, Nov. 22, 1942
Philadelphia vs. Chi. Cardinals, Sept. 24, 1950; vs. Pittsburgh, Dec. 12, 1965
11 Green Bay vs. San Diego, Sept. 24, 1978
10 N.Y. Giants vs. Washington, Dec. 4, 1938; vs. Chi. Cardinals, Nov. 2, 1952; vs. Washington, Dec. 8, 1963
Green Bay vs. Pittsburgh, Nov. 23, 1941; vs. Detroit, Oct. 24, 1943; vs. Chi. Cardinals, Nov. 10, 1946
Detroit vs. Minnesota, Dec. 9, 1962; vs. Chicago, Sept. 22, 1968
Oakland vs. Houston, Sept. 7, 1963
Washington vs. St. Louis, Oct. 25, 1976
New England vs. N.Y. Jets, Nov. 21, 1976
Dallas vs. San Francisco, Oct. 12, 1980
Seattle vs. Cleveland, Dec. 20, 1981
Denver vs. Detroit, Oct. 7, 1984

1,000 Yards Rushing in a Season

Year	Player, Team	Att.	Yards	Avg.	Long	TD
1988	Eric Dickerson, Indianapolis[6]	388	1,659	4.3	41	14
	Herschel Walker, Dallas	361	1,514	4.2	38	5
	Roger Craig, San Francisco[2]	310	1,502	4.8	46	9
	Greg Bell, L.A. Rams[2]	288	1,212	4.2	44	16
	*John Stephens, New England	297	1,168	3.9	52	4
	Gary Anderson, San Diego	225	1,119	5.0	36	3
	Neal Anderson, Chicago	249	1,106	4.4	80	12
	Joe Morris, N.Y. Giants[3]	307	1,083	3.5	27	5
	Ickey Woods, Cincinnati	203	1,066	5.3	56	15
	Curt Warner, Seattle[4]	266	1,025	3.9	29	10
	John Settle, Atlanta	232	1,024	4.4	62	7
	Mike Rozier, Houston	251	1,002	4.0	28	10
1987	Charles White, L.A. Rams	324	1,374	4.2	58	11
	Eric Dickerson, L.A. Rams-Indianapolis[5]	283	1,288	4.6	57	6
1986	Eric Dickerson, L.A. Rams[4]	404	1,821	4.5	42	11
	Joe Morris, N.Y. Giants[2]	341	1,516	4.4	54	14
	Curt Warner, Seattle[3]	319	1,481	4.6	60	13
	*Rueben Mayes, New Orleans	286	1,353	4.7	50	8
	Walter Payton, Chicago[10]	321	1,333	4.2	41	8
	Gerald Riggs, Atlanta[3]	343	1,327	3.9	31	9
	George Rogers, Washington[4]	303	1,203	4.0	42	18
	James Brooks, Cincinnati	205	1,087	5.3	56	5
1985	Marcus Allen, L.A. Raiders[3]	390	1,759	4.6	61	11
	Gerald Riggs, Atlanta[2]	397	1,719	4.3	50	10
	Walter Payton, Chicago[9]	324	1,551	4.8	40	9
	Joe Morris, N.Y. Giants	294	1,336	4.5	65	21
	Freeman McNeil, N.Y. Jets[2]	294	1,331	4.5	69	3
	Tony Dorsett, Dallas[8]	305	1,307	4.3	60	7
	James Wilder, Tampa Bay[2]	365	1,300	3.6	28	10
	Eric Dickerson, L.A. Rams[3]	292	1,234	4.2	43	12
	Craig James, New England	263	1,227	4.7	65	5
	*Kevin Mack, Cleveland	222	1,104	5.0	61	7
	Curt Warner, Seattle[2]	291	1,094	3.8	38	8
	George Rogers, Washington[3]	231	1,093	4.7	35	7
	Roger Craig, San Francisco	214	1,050	4.9	62	9
	Earnest Jackson, Philadelphia[2]	282	1,028	3.6	59	5
	Stump Mitchell, St. Louis	183	1,006	5.5	64	7
	Earnest Byner, Cleveland	244	1,002	4.1	36	8
1984	Eric Dickerson, L.A. Rams[2]	379	2,105	5.6	66	14
	Walter Payton, Chicago[8]	381	1,684	4.4	72	11
	James Wilder, Tampa Bay	407	1,544	3.8	37	13
	Gerald Riggs, Atlanta	353	1,486	4.2	57	13
	Wendell Tyler, San Francisco[3]	246	1,262	5.1	40	7
	John Riggins, Washington[5]	327	1,239	3.8	24	14
	Tony Dorsett, Dallas[7]	302	1,189	3.9	31	6
	Earnest Jackson, San Diego	296	1,179	4.0	32	8
	Ottis Anderson, St. Louis[5]	289	1,174	4.1	24	6
	Marcus Allen, L.A. Raiders[2]	275	1,168	4.2	52	13
	Sammy Winder, Denver	296	1,153	3.9	24	4
	*Greg Bell, Buffalo	262	1,100	4.2	85	7
	Freeman McNeil, N.Y. Jets	229	1,070	4.7	53	5
1983	*Eric Dickerson, L.A. Rams	390	1,808	4.6	85	18
	William Andrews, Atlanta[4]	331	1,567	4.7	27	7
	*Curt Warner, Seattle	335	1,449	4.3	60	13
	Walter Payton, Chicago[7]	314	1,421	4.5	49	6
	John Riggins, Washington[4]	375	1,347	3.6	44	24
	Tony Dorsett, Dallas[6]	289	1,321	4.6	77	8
	Earl Campbell, Houston[5]	322	1,301	4.0	42	12
	Ottis Anderson, St. Louis[4]	296	1,270	4.3	43	5
	Mike Pruitt, Cleveland[4]	293	1,184	4.0	27	10
	George Rogers, New Orleans[2]	256	1,144	4.5	76	5
	Joe Cribbs, Buffalo[3]	263	1,131	4.3	45	3
	Curtis Dickey, Baltimore	254	1,122	4.4	56	4
	Tony Collins, New England	219	1,049	4.8	50	10
	Billy Sims, Detroit[3]	220	1,040	4.7	41	7
	Marcus Allen, L.A. Raiders	266	1,014	3.8	19	9
	Franco Harris, Pittsburgh[8]	279	1,007	3.6	19	5
1981	*George Rogers, New Orleans	378	1,674	4.4	79	13
	Tony Dorsett, Dallas[5]	342	1,646	4.8	75	4
	Billy Sims, Detroit[2]	296	1,437	4.9	51	13
	Wilbert Montgomery, Philadelphia[3]	286	1,402	4.9	41	8
	Ottis Anderson, St. Louis[3]	328	1,376	4.2	28	9
	Earl Campbell, Houston[4]	361	1,376	3.8	43	10
	William Andrews, Atlanta[3]	289	1,301	4.5	29	10
	Walter Payton, Chicago[6]	339	1,222	3.6	39	6
	Chuck Muncie, San Diego[2]	251	1,144	4.6	73	19
	*Joe Delaney, Kansas City	234	1,121	4.8	82	3
	Mike Pruitt, Cleveland[3]	247	1,103	4.5	21	7
	Joe Cribbs, Buffalo[2]	257	1,097	4.3	35	3
	Pete Johnson, Cincinnati	274	1,077	3.9	39	12
	Wendell Tyler, Los Angeles[2]	260	1,074	4.1	69	12
	Ted Brown, Minnesota	274	1,063	3.9	34	6
1980	Earl Campbell, Houston[3]	373	1,934	5.2	55	13
	Walter Payton, Chicago[5]	317	1,460	4.6	69	6
	Ottis Anderson, St. Louis[2]	301	1,352	4.5	52	9
	William Andrews, Atlanta[2]	265	1,308	4.9	33	4
	*Billy Sims, Detroit	313	1,303	4.2	52	13
	Tony Dorsett, Dallas[4]	278	1,185	4.3	56	11
	*Joe Cribbs, Buffalo	306	1,185	3.9	48	11
	Mike Pruitt, Cleveland[2]	249	1,034	4.2	56	6
1979	Earl Campbell, Houston[2]	368	1,697	4.6	61	19
	Walter Payton, Chicago[4]	369	1,610	4.4	43	14
	*Ottis Anderson, St. Louis	331	1,605	4.8	76	8
	Wilbert Montgomery, Philadelphia[2]	338	1,512	4.5	62	9
	Mike Pruitt, Cleveland	264	1,294	4.9	77	9
	Ricky Bell, Tampa Bay	283	1,263	4.5	49	7
	Chuck Muncie, New Orleans	238	1,198	5.0	69	11
	Franco Harris, Pittsburgh[7]	267	1,186	4.4	71	11
	John Riggins, Washington[3]	260	1,153	4.4	66	9
	Wendell Tyler, Los Angeles	218	1,109	5.1	63	9
	Tony Dorsett, Dallas[3]	250	1,107	4.4	41	6
	*William Andrews, Atlanta	239	1,023	4.3	23	3
1978	*Earl Campbell, Houston	302	1,450	4.8	81	13
	Walter Payton, Chicago[3]	333	1,395	4.2	76	11
	Tony Dorsett, Dallas[2]	290	1,325	4.6	63	7
	Delvin Williams, Miami[2]	272	1,258	4.6	58	8
	Wilbert Montgomery, Philadelphia	259	1,220	4.7	47	9
	Terdell Middleton, Green Bay	284	1,116	3.9	76	11
	Franco Harris, Pittsburgh[6]	310	1,082	3.5	37	8
	Mark van Eeghen, Oakland[3]	270	1,080	4.0	34	9
	*Terry Miller, Buffalo	238	1,060	4.5	60	7
	Tony Reed, Kansas City	206	1,053	5.1	62	5
	John Riggins, Washington[2]	248	1,014	4.1	31	5
1977	Walter Payton, Chicago[2]	339	1,852	5.5	73	14
	Mark van Eeghen, Oakland[2]	324	1,273	3.9	27	7
	Lawrence McCutcheon, Los Angeles[4]	294	1,238	4.2	48	7
	Franco Harris, Pittsburgh[5]	300	1,162	3.9	61	11
	Lydell Mitchell, Baltimore[3]	301	1,159	3.9	64	3
	Chuck Foreman, Minnesota[3]	270	1,112	4.1	51	6
	Greg Pruitt, Cleveland[3]	236	1,086	4.6	78	3
	Sam Cunningham, New England	270	1,015	3.8	31	4
	*Tony Dorsett, Dallas	208	1,007	4.8	84	12
1976	O.J. Simpson, Buffalo[5]	290	1,503	5.2	75	8
	Walter Payton, Chicago	311	1,390	4.5	60	13
	Delvin Williams, San Francisco	248	1,203	4.9	80	7
	Lydell Mitchell, Baltimore[2]	289	1,200	4.2	43	5
	Lawrence McCutcheon, Los Angeles[3]	291	1,168	4.0	40	9
	Chuck Foreman, Minnesota[2]	278	1,155	4.2	46	13
	Franco Harris, Pittsburgh[4]	289	1,128	3.9	30	14
	Mike Thomas, Washington	254	1,101	4.3	28	5
	Rocky Bleier, Pittsburgh	220	1,036	4.7	28	5
	Mark van Eeghen, Oakland	233	1,012	4.3	21	3
	Otis Armstrong, Denver[2]	247	1,008	4.1	31	5
	Greg Pruitt, Cleveland[2]	209	1,000	4.8	64	4
1975	O.J. Simpson, Buffalo[4]	329	1,817	5.5	88	16
	Franco Harris, Pittsburgh[3]	262	1,246	4.8	36	10
	Lydell Mitchell, Baltimore	289	1,193	4.1	70	11
	Jim Otis, St. Louis	269	1,076	4.0	30	5
	Chuck Foreman, Minnesota	280	1,070	3.8	31	13
	Greg Pruitt, Cleveland	217	1,067	4.9	50	8
	John Riggins, N.Y. Jets	238	1,005	4.2	42	8
	Dave Hampton, Atlanta	250	1,002	4.0	22	5
1974	Otis Armstrong, Denver	263	1,407	5.3	43	9
	*Don Woods, San Diego	227	1,162	5.1	56	7
	O.J. Simpson, Buffalo[3]	270	1,125	4.2	41	3
	Lawrence McCutcheon, Los Angeles[2]	236	1,109	4.7	23	3
	Franco Harris, Pittsburgh[2]	208	1,006	4.8	54	5
1973	O.J. Simpson, Buffalo[2]	332	2,003	6.0	80	12
	John Brockington, Green Bay[3]	265	1,144	4.3	53	3
	Calvin Hill, Dallas[2]	273	1,142	4.2	21	6
	Lawrence McCutcheon, Los Angeles	210	1,097	5.2	37	2
	Larry Csonka, Miami[3]	219	1,003	4.6	25	5
1972	O.J. Simpson, Buffalo	292	1,251	4.3	94	6
	Larry Brown, Washington[2]	285	1,216	4.3	38	8
	Ron Johnson, N.Y. Giants[2]	298	1,182	4.0	35	9
	Larry Csonka, Miami[2]	213	1,117	5.2	45	6
	Marv Hubbard, Oakland	219	1,100	5.0	39	4
	*Franco Harris, Pittsburgh	188	1,055	5.6	75	10
	Calvin Hill, Dallas	245	1,036	4.2	26	6
	Mike Garrett, San Diego[2]	272	1,031	3.8	41	6
	John Brockington, Green Bay[2]	274	1,027	3.7	30	8
	Eugene (Mercury) Morris, Miami	190	1,000	5.3	33	12
1971	Floyd Little, Denver	284	1,133	4.0	40	6
	*John Brockington, Green Bay	216	1,105	5.1	52	4
	Larry Csonka, Miami	195	1,051	5.4	28	7
	Steve Owens, Detroit	246	1,035	4.2	23	8
	Willie Ellison, Los Angeles	211	1,000	4.7	80	4
1970	Larry Brown, Washington	237	1,125	4.7	75	5
	Ron Johnson, N.Y. Giants	263	1,027	3.9	68	8
1969	Gale Sayers, Chicago[2]	236	1,032	4.4	28	8
1968	Leroy Kelly, Cleveland[3]	248	1,239	5.0	65	16
	*Paul Robinson, Cincinnati	238	1,023	4.3	87	8
1967	Jim Nance, Boston[2]	269	1,216	4.5	53	7
	Leroy Kelly, Cleveland[2]	235	1,205	5.1	42	11
	Hoyle Granger, Houston	236	1,194	5.1	67	6
	Mike Garrett, Kansas City	236	1,087	4.6	58	9
1966	Jim Nance, Boston	299	1,458	4.9	65	11
	Gale Sayers, Chicago	229	1,231	5.4	58	8
	Leroy Kelly, Cleveland	209	1,141	5.5	70	15
	Dick Bass, Los Angeles[2]	248	1,090	4.4	50	8
1965	Jim Brown, Cleveland[7]	289	1,544	5.3	67	17
	Paul Lowe, San Diego[2]	222	1,121	5.0	59	7
1964	Jim Brown, Cleveland[6]	280	1,446	5.2	71	7
	Jim Taylor, Green Bay[5]	235	1,169	5.0	84	12
	John Henry Johnson, Pittsburgh[2]	235	1,048	4.5	45	7
1963	Jim Brown, Cleveland[5]	291	1,863	6.4	80	12
	Clem Daniels, Oakland	215	1,099	5.1	74	3
	Jim Taylor, Green Bay[4]	248	1,018	4.1	40	9
	Paul Lowe, San Diego	177	1,010	5.7	66	8
1962	Jim Taylor, Green Bay[3]	272	1,474	5.4	51	19
	John Henry Johnson, Pittsburgh	251	1,141	4.5	40	7
	*Cookie Gilchrist, Buffalo	214	1,096	5.1	44	13
	Abner Haynes, Dall. Texans	221	1,049	4.7	71	13
	Dick Bass, Los Angeles	196	1,033	5.3	57	6
	Charlie Tolar, Houston	244	1,012	4.1	25	7

1961	Jim Brown, Cleveland[4]	305	1,408	4.6	38	8
	Jim Taylor, Green Bay[2]	243	1,307	5.4	53	15
1960	Jim Brown, Cleveland[3]	215	1,257	5.8	71	9
	Jim Taylor, Green Bay	230	1,101	4.8	32	11
	John David Crow, St. Louis	183	1,071	5.9	57	6
1959	Jim Brown, Cleveland[2]	290	1,329	4.6	70	14
	J. D. Smith, San Francisco	207	1,036	5.0	73	10
1958	Jim Brown, Cleveland	257	1,527	5.9	65	17
1956	Rick Casares, Chi. Bears	234	1,126	4.8	68	12
1954	Joe Perry, San Francisco[2]	173	1,049	6.1	58	8
1953	Joe Perry, San Francisco	192	1,018	5.3	51	10
1949	Steve Van Buren, Philadelphia[2]	263	1,146	4.4	41	11
	Tony Canadeo, Green Bay	208	1,052	5.1	54	4
1947	Steve Van Buren, Philadelphia	217	1,008	4.6	45	13
1934	*Beattie Feathers, Chi. Bears	101	1,004	9.9	82	8

**First year in the league.*

200 Yards Rushing in a Game

Date	Player, Team, Opponent	Att.	Yards	TD
Dec. 18, 1988	Gary Anderson, San Diego vs. Kansas City	34	217	1
Nov. 30, 1987	*Bo Jackson, L.A. Raiders vs. Seattle	18	221	2
Nov. 15, 1987	Charles White, L.A. Rams vs. St. Louis	34	213	1
Dec. 7, 1986	Rueben Mayes, New Orleans vs. Miami	28	203	2
Oct. 5, 1986	Eric Dickerson, L.A. Rams vs. Tampa Bay (OT)	30	207	2
Dec. 21, 1985	George Rogers, Washington vs. St. Louis	34	206	1
Dec. 21, 1985	Joe Morris, N.Y. Giants vs. Pittsburgh	36	202	3
Dec. 9, 1984	Eric Dickerson, L.A. Rams vs. Houston	27	215	2
Nov. 18, 1984	*Greg Bell, Buffalo vs. Dallas	27	206	1
Nov. 4, 1984	Eric Dickerson, L.A. Rams vs. St. Louis	21	208	0
Sept. 2, 1984	Gerald Riggs, Atlanta vs. New Orleans	35	202	2
Nov. 27, 1983	*Curt Warner, Seattle vs. Kansas City (OT)	32	207	3
Nov. 6, 1983	James Wilder, Tampa Bay vs. Minnesota	31	219	1
Sept. 18, 1983	Tony Collins, New England vs. N.Y. Jets	23	212	3
Sept. 4, 1983	George Rogers, New Orleans vs. St. Louis	24	206	2
Dec. 21, 1980	Earl Campbell, Houston vs. Minnesota	29	203	1
Nov. 16, 1980	Earl Campbell, Houston vs. Chicago	31	206	0
Oct. 26, 1980	Earl Campbell, Houston vs. Cincinnati	27	202	2
Oct. 19, 1980	Earl Campbell, Houston vs. Tampa Bay	33	203	0
Nov. 26, 1978	*Terry Miller, Buffalo vs. N.Y. Giants	21	208	2
Dec. 4, 1977	*Tony Dorsett, Dallas vs. Philadelphia	23	206	2
Nov. 20, 1977	Walter Payton, Chicago vs. Minnesota	40	275	1
Oct. 30, 1977	Walter Payton, Chicago vs. Green Bay	23	205	2
Dec. 5, 1976	O.J. Simpson, Buffalo vs. Miami	24	203	1
Nov. 25, 1976	O.J. Simpson, Buffalo vs. Detroit	29	273	2
Oct. 24, 1976	Chuck Foreman, Minnesota vs. Philadelphia	28	200	2
Dec. 14, 1975	Greg Pruitt, Cleveland vs. Kansas City	26	214	3
Sept. 28, 1975	O.J. Simpson, Buffalo vs. Pittsburgh	28	227	1
Dec. 16, 1973	O.J. Simpson, Buffalo vs. N.Y. Jets	34	200	1
Dec. 9, 1973	O.J. Simpson, Buffalo vs. New England	22	219	1
Sept. 16, 1973	O.J. Simpson, Buffalo vs. New England	29	250	2
Dec. 5, 1971	Willie Ellison, Los Angeles vs. New Orleans	26	247	1
Dec. 20, 1970	John (Frenchy) Fuqua, Pittsburgh vs. Philadelphia	20	218	2
Nov. 3, 1968	Gale Sayers, Chicago vs. Green Bay	24	205	0
Oct. 30, 1966	Jim Nance, Boston vs. Oakland	38	208	2
Oct. 10, 1964	John Henry Johnson, Pittsburgh vs. Cleveland	30	200	3
Dec. 8, 1963	Cookie Gilchrist, Buffalo vs. N.Y. Jets	36	243	5
Nov. 3, 1963	Jim Brown, Cleveland vs. Philadelphia	28	223	1
Oct. 20, 1963	Clem Daniels, Oakland vs. N.Y. Jets	27	200	2
Sept. 22, 1963	Jim Brown, Cleveland vs. Dallas	20	232	2
Dec. 10, 1961	Billy Cannon, Houston vs. N.Y. Titans	25	216	3
Nov. 19, 1961	Jim Brown, Cleveland vs. Philadelphia	34	237	4
Dec. 18, 1960	John David Crow, St. Louis vs. Pittsburgh	24	203	0
Nov. 15, 1959	Bobby Mitchell, Cleveland vs. Washington	14	232	3
Nov. 24, 1957	*Jim Brown, Cleveland vs. Los Angeles	31	237	4
Dec. 16, 1956	*Tom Wilson, Los Angeles vs. Green Bay	23	223	0
Nov. 22, 1953	Dan Towler, Los Angeles vs. Baltimore	14	205	1
Nov. 12, 1950	Gene Roberts, N.Y. Giants vs. Chi. Cardinals	26	218	2
Nov. 27, 1949	Steve Van Buren, Philadelphia vs. Pittsburgh	27	205	0
Oct. 8, 1933	Cliff Battles, Boston vs. N.Y. Giants	16	215	1

**First year in the league.*

Times 200 or More

50 times by 35 players . . . Simpson 6; Brown, Campbell 4; Dickerson 3; Payton, Rogers 2.

4,000 Yards Passing in a Season

Year	Player, Team	Att.	Comp.	Pct.	Yards	TD	Int.
1988	Dan Marino, Miami[4]	606	354	58.4	4,434	28	23
1986	Dan Marino, Miami[3]	623	378	60.7	4,746	44	23
	Jay Schroeder, Washington	541	276	51.0	4,109	22	22
1985	Dan Marino, Miami[2]	567	336	59.3	4,137	30	21
1984	Dan Marino, Miami	564	362	64.2	5,084	48	17
	Neil Lomax, St. Louis	560	345	61.6	4,614	28	16
	Phil Simms, N.Y. Giants	533	286	53.7	4,044	22	18
1983	Lynn Dickey, Green Bay	484	289	59.7	4,458	32	29
	Bill Kenney, Kansas City	603	346	57.4	4,348	24	18
1981	Dan Fouts, San Diego[3]	609	360	59.1	4,802	33	17
1980	Dan Fouts, San Diego[2]	589	348	59.1	4,715	30	24
	Brian Sipe, Cleveland	554	337	60.8	4,132	30	14
1979	Dan Fouts, San Diego	530	332	62.6	4,082	24	24
1967	Joe Namath, N.Y. Jets	491	258	52.5	4,007	26	28

400 Yards Passing in a Game

Date	Player, Team, Opponent	Att.	Comp.	Yards	TD
Dec. 18, 1988	Dave Krieg, Seattle at L.A. Raiders	32	19	410	4
Dec. 12, 1988	Dan Marino, Miami vs. Cleveland	50	30	404	4
Oct. 23, 1988	Dan Marino, Miami vs. N.Y. Jets	60	35	521	3
Oct. 16, 1988	Vinny Testaverde, Tampa Bay at Indianapolis	42	25	469	2
Sept. 11, 1988	Doug Williams, Washington vs. Pittsburgh	52	30	430	2
Nov. 29, 1987	Tom Ramsey, New England vs. Philadelphia	53	34	402	3
Nov. 22, 1987	Boomer Esiason, Cincinnati vs. Pittsburgh	53	30	409	0
Sept. 20, 1987	Neil Lomax, St. Louis vs. San Diego	61	32	457	3
Dec. 21, 1986	Boomer Esiason, Cincinnati vs. N.Y. Jets	30	23	425	5
Dec. 14, 1986	Dan Marino, Miami vs. L.A. Rams (OT)	46	29	403	5
Nov. 23, 1986	Bernie Kosar, Cleveland vs. Pittsburgh (OT)	46	28	414	2
Nov. 17, 1986	Joe Montana, San Francisco vs. Washington	60	33	441	0
Nov. 16, 1986	Dan Marino, Miami vs. Buffalo	54	39	404	4
Nov. 10, 1986	Bernie Kosar, Cleveland vs. Miami	50	32	401	0
Nov. 2, 1986	Tommy Kramer, Minnesota vs. Washington (OT)	35	20	490	4
Nov. 2, 1986	Ken O'Brien, N.Y. Jets vs. Seattle	32	26	431	4
Oct. 27, 1986	Jay Schroeder, Washington vs. N.Y. Giants	40	22	420	1
Oct. 12, 1986	Steve Grogan, New England vs. N.Y. Jets	42	23	401	3
Sept. 21, 1986	Ken O'Brien, N.Y. Jets vs. Miami (OT)	43	29	479	4
Sept. 21, 1986	Dan Marino, Miami vs. N.Y. Jets (OT)	50	30	448	6
Sept. 21, 1986	Tony Eason, New England vs. Seattle	45	26	414	3
Dec. 20, 1985	John Elway, Denver vs. Seattle	42	24	432	1
Nov. 10, 1985	Dan Fouts, San Diego vs. L.A. Raiders (OT)	41	26	436	4
Oct. 13, 1985	Phil Simms, N.Y. Giants vs. Cincinnati	62	40	513	1
Oct. 13, 1985	Dave Krieg, Seattle vs. Atlanta	51	33	405	4
Oct. 6, 1985	Phil Simms, N.Y. Giants vs. Dallas	36	18	432	3
Oct. 6, 1985	Joe Montana, San Francisco vs. Atlanta	57	37	429	5
Sept. 19, 1985	Tommy Kramer, Minnesota vs. Chicago	55	28	436	3
Sept. 15, 1985	Dan Fouts, San Diego vs. Seattle	43	29	440	4
Dec. 16, 1984	Neil Lomax, St. Louis vs. Washington	46	37	468	2
Dec. 9, 1984	Dan Marino, Miami vs. Indianapolis	41	29	404	4
Dec. 2, 1984	Dan Marino, Miami vs. L.A. Raiders	57	35	470	4
Nov. 25, 1984	Dave Krieg, Seattle vs. Denver	44	30	406	3
Nov. 4, 1984	Dan Marino, Miami vs. N.Y. Jets	42	23	422	2
Oct. 21, 1984	Dan Fouts, San Diego vs. L.A. Raiders	45	24	410	3
Sept. 30, 1984	Dan Marino, Miami vs. St. Louis	36	24	429	3
Sept. 2, 1984	Phil Simms, N.Y. Giants vs. Philadelphia	30	23	409	4
Dec. 11, 1983	Bill Kenney, Kansas City vs. San Diego	41	31	411	4
Nov. 20, 1983	Dave Krieg, Seattle vs. Denver	42	31	418	3
Oct. 9, 1983	Joe Ferguson, Buffalo vs. Miami (OT)	55	38	419	5
Oct. 2, 1983	Joe Theismann, Washington vs. L.A. Raiders	39	23	417	3
Sept. 25, 1983	Richard Todd, N.Y. Jets vs. L.A. Rams (OT)	50	37	446	2
Dec. 26, 1982	Vince Ferragamo, L.A. Rams vs. Chicago	46	30	509	3
Dec. 20, 1982	Dan Fouts, San Diego vs. Cincinnati	40	25	435	1
Dec. 20, 1982	Ken Anderson, Cincinnati vs. San Diego	56	40	416	2
Dec. 11, 1982	Dan Fouts, San Diego vs. San Francisco	48	33	444	5
Nov. 21, 1982	Joe Montana, San Francisco vs. St. Louis	39	26	408	3
Nov. 15, 1981	Steve Bartkowski, Atlanta vs. Pittsburgh	50	33	416	2
Oct. 25, 1981	Brian Sipe, Cleveland vs. Baltimore	41	30	444	4
Oct. 25, 1981	David Woodley, Miami vs. Dallas	37	21	408	3
Oct. 11, 1981	Tommy Kramer, Minnesota vs. San Diego	43	27	444	4
Dec. 14, 1980	Tommy Kramer, Minnesota vs. Cleveland	49	38	456	4
Nov. 16, 1980	Doug Williams, Tampa Bay vs. Minnesota	55	30	486	4
Oct. 19, 1980	Dan Fouts, San Diego vs. N.Y. Giants	41	26	444	3
Oct. 12, 1980	Lynn Dickey, Green Bay vs. Tampa Bay (OT)	51	35	418	1
Sept. 21, 1980	Richard Todd, N.Y. Jets vs. San Francisco	60	42	447	3
Oct. 3, 1976	James Harris, Los Angeles vs. Miami	29	17	436	2
Nov. 17, 1975	Ken Anderson, Cincinnati vs. Buffalo	46	30	447	2
Nov. 18, 1974	Charley Johnson, Denver vs. Kansas City	42	28	445	2
Dec. 11, 1972	Joe Namath, N.Y. Jets vs. Oakland	46	25	403	1
Sept. 24, 1972	Joe Namath, N.Y. Jets vs. Baltimore	28	15	496	6
Dec. 21, 1969	Don Horn, Green Bay vs. St. Louis	31	22	410	5
Sept. 28, 1969	Joe Kapp, Minnesota vs. Baltimore	43	28	449	7
Sept. 9, 1968	Pete Beathard, Houston vs. Kansas City	48	23	413	2
Nov. 26, 1967	Sonny Jurgensen, Washington vs. Cleveland	50	32	418	3
Oct. 1, 1967	Joe Namath, N.Y. Jets vs. Miami	39	23	415	3
Sept. 17, 1967	Johnny Unitas, Baltimore vs. Atlanta	32	22	401	2
Nov. 13, 1966	Don Meredith, Dallas vs. Washington	29	21	406	2
Nov. 28, 1965	Sonny Jurgensen, Washington vs. Dallas	43	26	411	3
Oct. 24, 1965	Fran Tarkenton, Minnesota vs. San Francisco	35	21	407	3
Nov. 1, 1964	Len Dawson, Kansas City vs. Denver	38	23	435	6
Oct. 25, 1964	Cotton Davidson, Oakland vs. Denver	36	23	427	5
Oct. 16, 1964	Babe Parilli, Boston vs. Oakland	47	25	422	4
Dec. 22, 1963	Tom Flores, Oakland vs. Houston	29	17	407	6
Nov. 17, 1963	Norm Snead, Washington vs. Pittsburgh	40	23	424	2
Nov. 10, 1963	Don Meredith, Dallas vs. San Francisco	48	30	460	3
Oct. 13, 1963	Charley Johnson, St. Louis vs. Pittsburgh	41	20	428	2
Dec. 16, 1962	Sonny Jurgensen, Philadelphia vs. St. Louis	34	15	419	5
Nov. 18, 1962	Bill Wade, Chicago vs. Dall. Cowboys	46	28	466	2
Oct. 28, 1962	Y.A. Tittle, N.Y. Giants vs. Washington	39	27	505	7
Sept. 15, 1962	Frank Tripucka, Denver vs. Buffalo	56	29	447	2
Dec. 17, 1961	Sonny Jurgensen, Philadelphia vs. Detroit	42	27	403	3
Nov. 19, 1961	George Blanda, Houston vs. N.Y. Titans	32	20	418	7
Oct. 29, 1961	George Blanda, Houston vs. Buffalo	32	18	464	4
Oct. 29, 1961	Sonny Jurgensen, Philadelphia vs. Washington	41	27	436	3
Oct. 13, 1961	Jacky Lee, Houston vs. Boston	41	27	457	2
Dec. 13, 1958	Bobby Layne, Pittsburgh vs. Chi. Cardinals	49	23	409	2
Nov. 8, 1953	Bobby Thomason, Philadelphia vs. N.Y. Giants	44	22	437	4
Oct. 4, 1952	Otto Graham, Cleveland vs. Pittsburgh	49	21	401	3
Sept. 28, 1951	Norm Van Brocklin, Los Angeles vs. N.Y. Yanks	41	27	554	5
Dec. 11, 1949	Johnny Lujack, Chi. Bears vs. Chi. Cardinals	39	24	468	6
Oct. 31, 1948	Sammy Baugh, Washington vs. Boston	24	17	446	4
Oct. 31, 1948	Jim Hardy, Los Angeles vs. Chi. Cardinals	53	28	406	3
Nov. 14, 1943	Sid Luckman, Chi. Bears vs. N.Y. Giants	32	21	433	7

Times 400 or More

94 times by 55 players . . . Marino 9; Fouts 6; Jurgensen 5; Kramer, Krieg 4; Montana, Namath, Simms 3; Anderson, Blanda, Esiason, Johnson, Kosar, Lomax, Meredith, O'Brien, Todd, Williams 2.

1,000 Yards Pass Receiving in a Season

Year	Player, Team	No.	Yards	Avg.	Long	TD
1988	Henry Ellard, L.A. Rams	86	1,414	16.4	68	10
	Jerry Rice, San Francisco[3]	64	1,306	20.4	96	9
	Eddie Brown, Cincinnati	53	1,273	24.0	86	9
	Anthony Carter, Minnesota	72	1,225	17.0	67	6
	Ricky Sanders, Washington	73	1,148	15.7	55	12
	Drew Hill, Houston[3]	72	1,141	15.8	57	10
	Mark Clayton, Miami[3]	86	1,129	13.1	45	14
	Roy Green, Phoenix[3]	68	1,097	16.1	52	7
	Eric Martin, New Orleans	85	1,083	12.7	40	7
	Al Toon, N.Y. Jets[2]	93	1,067	11.5	42	5
	Bruce Hill, Tampa Bay	58	1,040	17.9	42	9
	Lionel Manuel, N.Y. Giants	65	1,029	15.8	46	4
1987	J.T. Smith, St. Louis[2]	91	1,117	12.3	38	8
	Jerry Rice, San Francisco[2]	65	1,078	16.6	57	22
	Gary Clark, Washington[2]	56	1,066	19.0	84	7
	Carlos Carson, Kansas City[3]	55	1,044	19.0	81	7
1986	Jerry Rice, San Francisco	86	1,570	18.3	66	15
	Stanley Morgan, New England[3]	84	1,491	17.8	44	10
	Mark Duper, Miami[3]	67	1,313	19.6	85	11
	Gary Clark, Washington	74	1,265	17.1	55	7
	Al Toon, N.Y. Jets	85	1,176	13.8	62	8
	Todd Christensen, L.A. Raiders[3]	95	1,153	12.1	35	8
	Mark Clayton, Miami[2]	60	1,150	19.2	68	10
	*Bill Brooks, Indianapolis	65	1,131	17.4	84	8
	Drew Hill, Houston[2]	65	1,112	17.1	81	5
	Steve Largent, Seattle[8]	70	1,070	15.3	38	9
	Art Monk, Washington[3]	73	1,068	14.6	69	4
	*Earnest Givins, Houston	61	1,062	17.4	60	3
	Cris Collinsworth, Cincinnati[4]	62	1,024	16.5	46	10
	Wesley Walker, N.Y. Jets[2]	49	1,016	20.7	83	12
	J.T. Smith, St. Louis	80	1,014	12.7	45	6
	Mark Bavaro, N.Y. Giants	66	1,001	15.2	41	4
1985	Steve Largent, Seattle[7]	79	1,287	16.3	43	6
	Mike Quick, Philadelphia[3]	73	1,247	17.1	99	11
	Art Monk, Washington[2]	91	1,226	13.5	53	2
	Wes Chandler, San Diego[4]	67	1,199	17.9	75	10
	Drew Hill, Houston	64	1,169	18.3	57	9
	James Lofton, Green Bay[5]	69	1,153	16.7	56	4
	Louis Lipps, Pittsburgh	59	1,134	19.2	51	12
	Cris Collinsworth, Cincinnati[3]	65	1,125	17.3	71	5
	Tony Hill, Dallas[3]	74	1,113	15.0	53	7
	Lionel James, San Diego	86	1,027	11.9	67	6
	Roger Craig, San Francisco	92	1,016	11.0	73	6
1984	Roy Green, St. Louis[2]	78	1,555	19.9	83	12
	John Stallworth, Pittsburgh[3]	80	1,395	17.4	51	11
	Mark Clayton, Miami	73	1,389	19.0	65	18
	Art Monk, Washington	106	1,372	12.9	72	7
	James Lofton, Green Bay[4]	62	1,361	22.0	79	7
	Mark Duper, Miami[2]	71	1,306	18.4	80	8
	Steve Watson, Denver[3]	69	1,170	17.0	73	7
	Steve Largent, Seattle[6]	74	1,164	15.7	65	12
	Tim Smith, Houston[2]	69	1,141	16.5	75	4
	Stacey Bailey, Atlanta	67	1,138	17.0	61	6
	Carlos Carson, Kansas City[2]	57	1,078	18.9	57	4
	Mike Quick, Philadelphia[2]	61	1,052	17.2	90	9
	Todd Christensen, L.A. Raiders[2]	80	1,007	12.6	38	7
	Kevin House, Tampa Bay[2]	76	1,005	13.2	55	5
	Ozzie Newsome, Cleveland[2]	89	1,001	11.2	52	5
1983	Mike Quick, Philadelphia	69	1,409	20.4	83	13
	Carlos Carson, Kansas City	80	1,351	16.9	50	7
	James Lofton, Green Bay[3]	58	1,300	22.4	74	8
	Todd Christensen, L.A. Raiders	92	1,247	13.6	45	12
	Roy Green, St. Louis	78	1,227	15.7	71	14
	Charlie Brown, Washington	78	1,225	15.7	75	8
	Tim Smith, Houston	83	1,176	14.2	47	6
	Kellen Winslow, San Diego[3]	88	1,172	13.3	46	8
	Earnest Gray, N.Y. Giants	78	1,139	14.6	62	5
	Steve Watson, Denver[2]	59	1,133	19.2	78	5
	Cris Collinsworth, Cincinnati[2]	66	1,130	17.1	63	5
	Steve Largent, Seattle[5]	72	1,074	14.9	46	11
	Mark Duper, Miami	51	1,003	19.7	85	10
1982	Wes Chandler, San Diego[3]	49	1,032	21.1	66	9
1981	Alfred Jenkins, Atlanta[2]	70	1,358	19.4	67	13
	James Lofton, Green Bay[2]	71	1,294	18.2	75	8
	Frank Lewis, Buffalo[2]	70	1,244	17.8	33	4
	Steve Watson, Denver	60	1,244	20.7	95	13
	Steve Largent, Seattle[4]	75	1,224	16.3	57	9
	Charlie Joiner, San Diego[4]	70	1,188	17.0	57	7
	Kevin House, Tampa Bay	56	1,176	21.0	84	9
	Wes Chandler, N.O.-San Diego[2]	69	1,142	16.6	51	6
	Dwight Clark, San Francisco	85	1,105	13.0	78	4
	John Stallworth, Pittsburgh[2]	63	1,098	17.4	55	5
	Kellen Winslow, San Diego[2]	88	1,075	12.2	67	10
	Pat Tilley, St. Louis	66	1,040	15.8	75	3
	Stanley Morgan, New England[2]	44	1,029	23.4	76	6
	Harold Carmichael, Philadelphia[3]	61	1,028	16.9	85	6
	Freddie Scott, Detroit	53	1,022	19.3	48	5
	*Cris Collinsworth, Cincinnati	67	1,009	15.1	74	8
	Joe Senser, Minnesota	79	1,004	12.7	53	8
	Ozzie Newsome, Cleveland	69	1,002	14.5	62	6
	Sammy White, Minnesota	66	1,001	15.2	53	3
1980	John Jefferson, San Diego[3]	82	1,340	16.3	58	13
	Kellen Winslow, San Diego	89	1,290	14.5	65	9
	James Lofton, Green Bay	71	1,226	17.3	47	4
	Charlie Joiner, San Diego[3]	71	1,132	15.9	51	4
	Ahmad Rashad, Minnesota[2]	69	1,095	15.9	76	5
	Steve Largent, Seattle[3]	66	1,064	16.1	67	6
	Tony Hill, Dallas[2]	60	1,055	17.6	58	8
	Alfred Jenkins, Atlanta	57	1,026	18.0	57	6
1979	Steve Largent, Seattle[2]	66	1,237	18.7	55	9
	John Stallworth, Pittsburgh	70	1,183	16.9	65	8
	Ahmad Rashad, Minnesota	80	1,156	14.5	52	9
	John Jefferson, San Diego[2]	61	1,090	17.9	65	10
	Frank Lewis, Buffalo	54	1,082	20.0	55	2
	Wes Chandler, New Orleans	65	1,069	16.4	85	6
	Tony Hill, Dallas	60	1,062	17.7	75	10
	Drew Pearson, Dallas[2]	55	1,026	18.7	56	8
	Wallace Francis, Atlanta	74	1,013	13.7	42	8
	Harold Jackson, New England[3]	45	1,013	22.5	59	7
	Charlie Joiner, San Diego[2]	72	1,008	14.0	39	4
	Stanley Morgan, New England	44	1,002	22.8	63	12
1978	Wesley Walker, N.Y. Jets	48	1,169	24.4	77	8
	Steve Largent, Seattle	71	1,168	16.5	57	8
	Harold Carmichael, Philadelphia[2]	55	1,072	19.5	56	8
	*John Jefferson, San Diego	56	1,001	17.9	46	13
1976	Roger Carr, Baltimore	43	1,112	25.9	79	11
	Cliff Branch, Oakland[2]	46	1,111	24.2	88	12
	Charlie Joiner, San Diego	50	1,056	21.1	81	7
1975	Ken Burrough, Houston	53	1,063	20.1	77	8
1974	Cliff Branch, Oakland	60	1,092	18.2	67	13
	Drew Pearson, Dallas	62	1,087	17.5	50	2
1973	Harold Carmichael, Philadelphia	67	1,116	16.7	73	9
1972	Harold Jackson, Philadelphia[2]	62	1,048	16.9	77	4
	John Gilliam, Minnesota	47	1,035	22.0	66	7
1971	Otis Taylor, Kansas City[2]	57	1,110	19.5	82	7
1970	Gene Washington, San Francisco	53	1,100	20.8	79	12
	Marlin Briscoe, Buffalo	57	1,036	18.2	48	8
	Dick Gordon, Chicago	71	1,026	14.5	69	13
	Gary Garrison, San Diego[2]	44	1,006	22.9	67	12
1969	Warren Wells, Oakland[2]	47	1,260	26.8	80	14
	Harold Jackson, Philadelphia	65	1,116	17.2	65	9
	Roy Jefferson, Pittsburgh[2]	67	1,079	16.1	63	9
	Dan Abramowicz, New Orleans	73	1,015	13.9	49	7
	Lance Alworth, San Diego[7]	64	1,003	15.7	76	4
1968	Lance Alworth, San Diego[6]	68	1,312	19.3	80	10
	Don Maynard, N.Y. Jets[5]	57	1,297	22.8	87	10
	George Sauer, N.Y. Jets[3]	66	1,141	17.3	43	3
	Warren Wells, Oakland	53	1,137	21.5	94	11
	Gary Garrison, San Diego	52	1,103	21.2	84	10
	Roy Jefferson, Pittsburgh	58	1,074	18.5	62	11
	Paul Warfield, Cleveland	50	1,067	21.3	65	12
	Homer Jones, N.Y. Giants[3]	45	1,057	23.5	84	7
	Fred Biletnikoff, Oakland	61	1,037	17.0	82	6
	Lance Rentzel, Dallas	54	1,009	18.7	65	6
1967	Don Maynard, N.Y. Jets[4]	71	1,434	20.2	75	10
	Ben Hawkins, Philadelphia	59	1,265	21.4	87	10
	Homer Jones, N.Y. Giants[2]	49	1,209	24.7	70	13
	Jackie Smith, St. Louis	56	1,205	21.5	76	9
	George Sauer, N.Y. Jets[2]	75	1,189	15.9	61	6
	Lance Alworth, San Diego[5]	52	1,010	19.4	71	9
1966	Lance Alworth, San Diego[4]	73	1,383	18.9	78	13
	Otis Taylor, Kansas City	58	1,297	22.4	89	8
	Pat Studstill, Detroit	67	1,266	18.9	99	5
	Bob Hayes, Dallas[2]	64	1,232	19.3	95	13
	Charlie Frazier, Houston	57	1,129	19.8	79	12
	Charley Taylor, Washington	72	1,119	15.5	86	12
	George Sauer, N.Y. Jets	63	1,081	17.2	77	5
	Homer Jones, N.Y. Giants	48	1,044	21.8	98	8
	Art Powell, Oakland[5]	53	1,026	19.4	46	11
1965	Lance Alworth, San Diego[3]	69	1,602	23.2	85	14
	Dave Parks, San Francisco	80	1,344	16.8	53	12
	Don Maynard, N.Y. Jets[3]	68	1,218	17.9	56	14
	Pete Retzlaff, Philadelphia	66	1,190	18.0	78	10
	Lionel Taylor, Denver[4]	85	1,131	13.3	63	6
	Tommy McDonald, Los Angeles[3]	67	1,036	15.5	51	9
	*Bob Hayes, Dallas	46	1,003	21.8	82	12
1964	Charley Hennigan, Houston[3]	101	1,546	15.3	53	8
	Art Powell, Oakland[4]	76	1,361	17.9	77	11
	Lance Alworth, San Diego[2]	61	1,235	20.2	82	13
	Johnny Morris, Chicago	93	1,200	12.9	63	10
	Elbert Dubenion, Buffalo	42	1,139	27.1	72	10
	Terry Barr, Detroit[2]	57	1,030	18.1	58	9
1963	Bobby Mitchell, Washington[2]	69	1,436	20.8	99	7
	Art Powell, Oakland[3]	73	1,304	17.9	85	16
	Buddy Dial, Pittsburgh[2]	60	1,295	21.6	83	9
	Lance Alworth, San Diego	61	1,205	19.8	85	11
	Del Shofner, N.Y. Giants[4]	64	1,181	18.5	70	9
	Lionel Taylor, Denver[3]	78	1,101	14.1	72	10
	Terry Barr, Detroit	66	1,086	16.5	75	13
	Charley Hennigan, Houston[2]	61	1,051	17.2	83	10
	Sonny Randle, St. Louis[2]	51	1,014	19.9	68	12
	Bake Turner, N.Y. Jets	71	1,009	14.2	53	6
1962	Bobby Mitchell, Washington	72	1,384	19.2	81	11
	Sonny Randle, St. Louis	63	1,158	18.4	86	7
	Tommy McDonald, Philadelphia[2]	58	1,146	19.8	60	10
	Del Shofner, N.Y. Giants[3]	53	1,133	21.4	69	12
	Art Powell, N.Y. Titans[2]	64	1,130	17.7	80	8
	Frank Clarke, Dall. Cowboys	47	1,043	22.2	66	14
	Don Maynard, N.Y. Titans[2]	56	1,041	18.6	86	8
1961	Charley Hennigan, Houston	82	1,746	21.3	80	12
	Lionel Taylor, Denver[2]	100	1,176	11.8	52	4
	Bill Groman, Houston[2]	50	1,175	23.5	80	17
	Tommy McDonald, Philadelphia	64	1,144	17.9	66	13
	Del Shofner, N.Y. Giants[2]	68	1,125	16.5	46	11
	Jim Phillips, Los Angeles	78	1,092	14.0	69	5
	*Mike Ditka, Chicago	56	1,076	19.2	76	12
	Dave Kocourek, San Diego	55	1,055	19.2	76	4
	Buddy Dial, Pittsburgh	53	1,047	19.8	88	12
	R.C. Owens, San Francisco	55	1,032	18.8	54	5
1960	*Bill Groman, Houston	72	1,473	20.5	92	12
	Raymond Berry, Baltimore	74	1,298	17.5	70	10

	Don Maynard, N.Y. Titans	72	1,265	17.6	65	6
	Lionel Taylor, Denver	92	1,235	13.4	80	12
	Art Powell, N.Y. Titans	69	1,167	16.9	76	14
1958	Del Shofner, Los Angeles	51	1,097	21.5	92	8
1956	Bill Howton, Green Bay[2]	55	1,188	21.6	66	12
	Harlon Hill, Chi. Bears[2]	47	1,128	24.0	79	11
1954	Bob Boyd, Los Angeles	53	1,212	22.9	80	6
	*Harlon Hill, Chi. Bears	45	1,124	25.0	76	12
1953	Pete Pihos, Philadelphia	63	1,049	16.7	59	10
1952	*Bill Howton, Green Bay	53	1,231	23.2	90	13
1951	Elroy (Crazylegs) Hirsch, Los Angeles	66	1,495	22.7	91	17
1950	Tom Fears, Los Angeles[2]	84	1,116	13.3	53	7
	Cloyce Box, Detroit	50	1,009	20.2	82	11
1949	Bob Mann, Detroit	66	1,014	15.4	64	4
	Tom Fears, Los Angeles	77	1,013	13.2	51	9
1945	Jim Benton, Cleveland	45	1,067	23.7	84	8
1942	Don Hutson, Green Bay	74	1,211	16.4	73	17

First year in the league.

250 Yards Pass Receiving in a Game

Date	Player, Team, Opponent	No.	Yards	TD
Oct. 18, 1987	Steve Largent, Seattle vs. Detroit	15	261	3
Oct. 4, 1987	*Anthony Allen, Washington vs. St. Louis	7	255	3
Dec. 22, 1985	Stephone Paige, Kansas City vs. San Diego	8	309	2
Dec. 20, 1982	Wes Chandler, San Diego vs. Cincinnati	10	260	2
Sept. 23, 1979	*Jerry Butler, Buffalo vs. N.Y. Jets	10	255	4
Nov. 4, 1962	Sonny Randle, St. Louis vs. N.Y. Giants	16	256	1
Oct. 28, 1962	Del Shofner, N.Y. Giants vs. Washington	11	269	1
Oct. 13, 1961	Charley Hennigan, Houston vs. Boston	13	272	1
Oct. 21, 1956	Billy Howton, Green Bay vs. Los Angeles	7	257	2
Dec. 3, 1950	Cloyce Box, Detroit vs. Baltimore	12	302	4
Nov. 22, 1945	Jim Benton, Cleveland vs. Detroit	10	303	1

First year in the league.

2,000 Combined Net Yards Gained in a Season

Year	Player, Team	Rushing Att.-Yds.	Pass Rec.	Punt Ret.	Kickoff Ret.	Fum. Runs	Total Yds.
1988	*Tim Brown, L.A. Raiders	14-50	43-725	49-444	41-1,098	7-0	147-2,317
	Roger Craig, San Fran.	310-1,502	76-534	0-0	0-0	2-0	386-2,036
	Eric Dickerson, Indianapolis	388-1,659	36-377	0-0	0-0	1-0	425-2,036
1986	Eric Dickerson, L.A. Rams	404-1,821	26-205	0-0	0-0	2-0	432-2,026
	Gary Anderson, San Diego	127-442	80-871	25-227	24-482	2-0	258-2,022
1985	Lionel James, San Diego	105-516	86-1,027	25-213	36-779	1-0	253-2,535
	Marcus Allen, L.A. Raiders	380-1,759	67-555	0-0	0-0	2-(−6)	449-2,308
	Roger Craig, San Fran.	214-1,050	92-1,016	0-0	0-0	0-0	306-2,066
	Walter Payton, Chicago	324-1,551	49-483	0-0	0-0	1-0	374-2,034
1984	Eric Dickerson, L.A. Rams	379-2,105	21-139	0-0	0-0	4-15	404-2,259
	James Wilder, Tampa Bay	407-1,544	85-685	0-0	0-0	4-0	496-2,229
	Walter Payton, Chicago	381-1,684	45-368	0-0	0-0	1-0	427-2,052
1983	*Eric Dickerson, L.A. Rams	390-1,808	51-404	0-0	0-0	1-0	442-2,212
	William Andrews, Atlanta	331-1,567	59-609	0-0	0-0	2-0	392-2,176
	Walter Payton, Chicago	314-1,421	53-607	0-0	0-0	2-0	369-2,028
1981	*James Brooks, San Diego	109-525	46-329	22-290	40-949	2-0	219-2,093
	William Andrews, Atlanta	289-1,301	81-735	0-0	0-0	0-0	370-2,036
1980	Bruce Harper, N.Y. Jets	45-126	50-634	28-242	49-1,070	3-0	175-2,072
1979	Wilbert Montgomery, Phil.	338-1,512	41-494	0-0	1-6	2-0	382-2,012
1978	Bruce Harper, N.Y. Jets	58-303	13-196	30-378	55-1,280	1-0	157-2,157
1977	Walter Payton, Chicago	339-1,852	27-269	0-0	2-95	5-0	373-2,216
	Terry Metcalf, St. Louis	149-739	34-403	14-108	32-772	1-0	230-2,022
1975	Terry Metcalf, St. Louis	165-816	43-378	23-285	35-960	2-23	268-2,462
	O.J. Simpson, Buffalo	329-1,817	28-426	0-0	0-0	1-0	358-2,243
1974	Mack Herron, New England	231-824	38-474	35-517	28-629	3-0	335-2,444
	Otis Armstrong, Denver	263-1,407	38-405	0-0	16-386	1-0	318-2,198
	Terry Metcalf, St. Louis	152-718	50-377	26-340	20-623	7-0	255-2,058
1973	O.J. Simpson, Buffalo	332-2,003	6-70	0-0	0-0	0-0	338-2,073
1966	Gale Sayers, Chicago	229-1,231	34-447	6-44	23-718	3-0	295-2,440
	Leroy Kelly, Cleveland	209-1,141	32-366	13-104	19-403	0-0	273-2,014
1965	*Gale Sayers, Chicago	166-867	29-507	16-238	21-660	4-0	236-2,272
1963	Timmy Brown, Philadelphia	192-841	36-487	16-152	33-945	2-3	279-2,428
	Jim Brown, Cleveland	291-1,863	24-268	0-0	0-0	0-0	315-2,131
1962	Timmy Brown, Philadelphia	137-545	52-849	6-81	30-831	4-0	229-2,306
	Dick Christy, N.Y. Titans	114-535	62-538	15-250	38-824	2-0	231-2,147
1961	Billy Cannon, Houston	200-948	43-586	9-70	18-439	2-0	272-2,043
1960	*Abner Haynes, Dall. Texans	156-875	55-576	14-215	19-434	4-0	248-2,100

First year in the league.

300 Combined Net Yards Gained in a Game

Date	Player, Team, Opponent	No.	Yards	TD
Nov. 28, 1988	Tim Brown, L.A. Raiders vs. San Diego	12	306	1
Dec. 22, 1985	Stephone Paige, Kansas City vs. San Diego	8	309	2
Nov. 10, 1985	Lionel James, San Diego vs. L.A. Raiders (OT)	23	345	0
Sept. 22, 1985	Lionel James, San Diego vs. Cincinnati	20	316	2
Dec. 21, 1975	Walter Payton, Chicago vs. New Orleans	32	300	1
Nov. 23, 1975	Greg Pruitt, Cleveland vs. Cincinnati	28	304	2
Nov. 1, 1970	Eugene (Mercury) Morris, Miami vs. Baltimore	17	302	0
Oct. 4, 1970	O. J. Simpson, Buffalo vs. N.Y. Jets	26	303	2
Dec. 6, 1969	Jerry LeVias, Houston vs. N.Y. Jets	18	329	1
Nov. 2, 1969	Travis Williams, Green Bay vs. Pittsburgh	11	314	3
Dec. 18, 1966	Gale Sayers, Chicago vs. Minnesota	20	339	2
Dec. 12, 1965	Gale Sayers, Chicago vs. San Francisco	17	336	6
Nov. 17, 1963	Gary Ballman, Pittsburgh vs. Washington	12	320	2
Dec. 16, 1962	Timmy Brown, Philadelphia vs. St. Louis	19	341	2
Dec. 10, 1961	Billy Cannon, Houston vs. N.Y. Titans	32	373	5
Nov 19, 1961	Jim Brown, Cleveland vs. Philadelphia	38	313	4
Dec. 3, 1950	Cloyce Box, Detroit vs. Baltimore	13	302	4
Oct. 29, 1950	Wally Triplett, Detroit vs. Los Angeles	11	331	1
Nov. 22, 1945	Jim Benton, Cleveland vs. Detroit	10	303	1

Top 20 Scorers

Player	Years	TD	FG	PAT	TP
George Blanda	26	9	335	943	2,002
Jan Stenerud	19	0	373	580	1,699
Jim Turner	16	1	304	521	1,439
Mark Moseley	16	0	300	482	1,382
Jim Bakken	17	0	282	534	1,380
Fred Cox	15	0	282	519	1,365
Lou Groza	17	1	234	641	1,349
Pat Leahy	15	0	241	467	1,190
Chris Bahr	13	0	224	461	1,133
Gino Cappelletti	11	42	176	350	1,130
Ray Wersching	15	0	222	456	1,122
Don Cockroft	13	0	216	432	1,080
Garo Yepremian	14	0	210	444	1,074
Bruce Gossett	11	0	219	374	1,031
Sam Baker	15	2	179	428	977
Rafael Septien	10	0	180	420	960
Lou Michaels	13	1	187	386	955
Nick Lowery	10	0	201	304	907
Roy Gerela	11	0	184	351	903
Bobby Walston	12	46	80	365	881

Cappelletti's total includes four two-point conversions.
Michaels's total includes one safety.

Top 20 Touchdown Scorers

Player	Years	Rush	Pass Rec.	Returns	Total TD
Jim Brown	9	106	20	0	126
Walter Payton	13	110	15	0	125
John Riggins	14	104	12	0	116
Lenny Moore	12	63	48	2	113
Don Hutson	11	3	99	3	105
Franco Harris	13	91	9	0	100
Steve Largent	13	1	97	0	98
Jim Taylor	10	83	10	0	93
Tony Dorsett	12	77	13	1	91
Bobby Mitchell	11	18	65	8	91
Leroy Kelly	10	74	13	3	90
Charley Taylor	13	11	79	0	90
Don Maynard	15	0	88	0	88
Lance Alworth	11	2	85	0	87
Paul Warfield	13	1	85	0	86
Tommy McDonald	12	0	84	1	85
Pete Johnson	8	76	6	0	82
Art Powell	10	0	81	1	82
Harold Carmichael	14	0	79	0	79
Marcus Allen	7	61	16	1	78
Eric Dickerson	6	75	3	0	78
Frank Gifford	12	34	43	1	78

Top 20 Rushers

Player	Years	Att.	Yards	Avg.	Long	TD
Walter Payton	13	3,838	16,726	4.4	76	110
Tony Dorsett	12	2,936	12,739	4.3	99	77
Jim Brown	9	2,359	12,312	5.2	80	106
Franco Harris	13	2,949	12,120	4.1	75	91
John Riggins	14	2,916	11,352	3.9	66	104
O.J. Simpson	11	2,404	11,236	4.7	94	61
Eric Dickerson	6	2,136	9,915	4.6	85	75
Earl Campbell	8	2,187	9,407	4.3	81	74
Jim Taylor	10	1,941	8,597	4.4	84	83
Joe Perry	14	1,737	8,378	4.8	78	53
Ottis Anderson	10	1,949	8,294	4.3	76	55
Larry Csonka	11	1,891	8,081	4.3	54	64
Mike Pruitt	11	1,844	7,378	4.0	77	51
Leroy Kelly	10	1,727	7,274	4.2	70	74
George Rogers	7	1,692	7,176	4.2	79	54
Marcus Allen	7	1,712	6,982	4.1	61	61
John Henry Johnson	13	1,571	6,803	4.3	87	48
Freeman McNeil	8	1,525	6,794	4.5	69	28
Wilbert Montgomery	9	1,540	6,789	4.4	90	45
Chuck Muncie	9	1,561	6,702	4.3	73	71

Top 20 Passers

Player	Years	Att.	Comp.	Pct. Comp.	Yards	TD	Pct. TD	Int.	Pct. Int.	Avg. Gain	Rating
Joe Montana	10	3,673	2,322	63.2	27,533	190	5.2	99	2.7	7.50	92.0
Dan Marino	6	3,100	1,866	60.2	23,856	196	6.3	103	3.3	7.70	91.5
Boomer Esiason	5	1,830	1,038	56.7	14,825	98	5.4	65	3.6	8.10	86.2
Dave Krieg	9	2,344	1,358	57.9	17,549	148	6.3	96	4.1	7.49	85.5
Ken O'Brien	5	1,990	1,183	59.4	14,243	84	4.2	50	2.5	7.16	85.0
Roger Staubach	11	2,958	1,685	57.0	22,700	153	5.2	109	3.7	7.67	83.4
Neil Lomax	8	3,153	1,817	57.6	22,771	136	4.3	90	2.9	7.22	82.7
Sonny Jurgensen	18	4,262	2,433	57.1	32,224	255	6.0	189	4.4	7.56	82.6
Len Dawson	19	3,741	2,136	57.1	28,711	239	6.4	183	4.9	7.67	82.6
Ken Anderson	16	4,475	2,654	59.3	32,838	197	4.4	160	3.6	7.34	81.9
Danny White	13	2,950	1,761	59.7	21,959	155	5.3	132	4.5	7.44	81.7
Bart Starr	16	3,149	1,808	57.4	24,718	152	4.8	138	4.4	7.85	80.5
Jim McMahon	7	1,513	874	57.8	11,203	67	4.4	56	3.7	7.40	80.4
Fran Tarkenton	18	6,467	3,686	57.0	47,003	342	5.3	266	4.1	7.27	80.4
Dan Fouts	15	5,604	3,297	58.8	43,040	254	4.5	242	4.3	7.68	80.2
Bert Jones	10	2,551	1,430	56.1	18,190	124	4.9	101	4.0	7.13	78.2
Johnny Unitas	18	5,186	2,830	54.6	40,239	290	5.6	253	4.9	7.76	78.2
Otto Graham	6	1,565	872	55.7	13,499	88	5.6	94	6.0	8.63	78.2
Frank Ryan	13	2,133	1,090	51.1	16,042	149	7.0	111	5.2	7.52	77.6
Joe Theismann	12	3,602	2,044	56.7	25,206	160	4.4	138	3.8	7.00	77.4

1,500 or more attempts. The passing ratings are based on performance standards established for completion percentage, interception percentage, touchdown percentage, and average gain. Passers are allocated points according to how their marks compare with those standards.

Top 20 Pass Receivers

Player	Years	No.	Yards	Avg.	Long	TD
Steve Largent	13	791	12,686	16.0	74	97
Charlie Joiner	18	750	12,146	16.2	87	65
Charley Taylor	13	649	9,110	14.0	88	79
Don Maynard	15	633	11,834	18.7	87	88
Raymond Berry	13	631	9,275	14.7	70	68
Ozzie Newsome	11	610	7,416	12.2	74	44
James Lofton	11	599	11,085	18.5	74	54
Harold Carmichael	14	590	8,985	15.2	85	79
Fred Biletnikoff	14	589	8,974	15.2	82	76
Harold Jackson	16	579	10,372	17.9	79	76
Art Monk	9	576	7,979	13.9	79	39
Lionel Taylor	10	567	7,195	12.7	80	45
Wes Chandler	11	559	8,966	16.0	85	56
Lance Alworth	11	542	10,266	18.9	85	85
Kellen Winslow	9	541	6,741	12.5	67	45
John Stallworth	14	537	8,723	16.2	74	63
Bobby Mitchell	11	521	7,954	15.3	99	65
Nat Moore	13	510	7,546	14.8	79	74
Dwight Clark	9	506	6,750	13.3	80	48
Stanley Morgan	12	506	9,866	19.5	76	64

Top 20 Interceptors

Player	Years	No.	Yards	Avg.	Long	TD
Paul Krause	16	81	1,185	14.6	81	3
Emlen Tunnell	14	79	1,282	16.2	55	4
Dick (Night Train) Lane	14	68	1,207	17.8	80	5
Ken Riley	15	65	596	9.2	66	5
Dick LeBeau	13	62	762	12.3	70	3
Emmitt Thomas	13	58	937	16.2	73	5
Bobby Boyd	9	57	994	17.4	74	4
Johnny Robinson	12	57	741	13.0	57	1
Mel Blount	14	57	736	12.9	52	2
Lem Barney	11	56	1,077	19.2	71	7
Dave Brown	14	56	686	12.3	90	5
Pat Fischer	17	56	941	16.8	69	4
Willie Brown	16	54	472	8.7	45	2
Bobby Dillon	8	52	976	18.8	61	5
Jack Butler	9	52	826	15.9	52	4
Larry Wilson	13	52	800	15.4	96	5
Jim Patton	12	52	712	13.7	51	2
Mel Renfro	14	52	626	12.0	90	3
Bobby Bryant	13	51	749	14.7	56	3
Donnie Shell	14	51	490	9.6	67	2

Top 20 Punters

Player	Years	No.	Yards	Avg.	Long	Blk.
Sammy Baugh	16	338	15,245	45.1	85	9
Tommy Davis	11	511	22,833	44.7	82	2
Rohn Stark	7	514	22,791	44.3	72	4
Yale Lary	11	503	22,279	44.3	74	4
Horace Gillom	7	385	16,872	43.8	80	5
Jerry Norton	11	358	15,671	43.8	78	2
Reggie Roby	6	336	14,647	43.6	77	1
Don Chandler	12	660	28,678	43.5	90	4
Jerrel Wilson	16	1,072	46,139	43.0	72	12
Norm Van Brocklin	12	523	22,413	42.9	72	3
Danny Villanueva	8	488	20,862	42.8	68	2
Bobby Joe Green	14	970	41,317	42.6	75	3
Sam Baker	15	703	29,938	42.6	72	2
Ray Guy	14	1,049	44,493	42.4	74	3
Bob Waterfield	8	315	13,367	42.4	88	5
Rich Camarillo	8	508	21,501	42.3	76	4
Curley Johnson	10	559	23,651	42.3	73	6
Jim Arnold	6	463	19,584	42.3	69	3
Mike Horan	5	313	13,189	42.1	75	2
Jim Norton	9	522	21,961	42.1	79	7

300 or more punts.

Top 20 Punt Returners

Player	Years	No.	Yards	Avg.	Long	TD
George McAfee	8	112	1,431	12.8	74	2
Jack Christiansen	8	85	1,084	12.8	89	8
Claude Gibson	5	110	1,381	12.6	85	3
Bill Dudley	9	124	1,515	12.2	96	3
Rick Upchurch	9	248	3,008	12.1	92	8
JoJo Townsell	4	77	907	11.8	91	2
Vai Sikahema	3	120	1,413	11.8	76	3
Billy Johnson	14	282	3,317	11.8	87	6
Mack Herron	3	84	982	11.7	66	0
Billy Thompson	13	157	1,814	11.6	60	0
Louis Lipps	5	103	1,185	11.5	76	3
Henry Ellard	6	129	1,474	11.4	83	4
Bobby Joe Edmonds	3	89	1,010	11.3	75	1
Bosh Pritchard	6	95	1,072	11.3	81	2
Rodger Bird	3	94	1,063	11.3	78	0
Bob Hayes	11	104	1,158	11.1	90	3
Terry Metcalf	6	84	936	11.1	69	1
Floyd Little	9	81	893	11.0	72	2
Irving Fryar	5	164	1,805	11.0	85	3
Les (Speedy) Duncan	11	202	2,201	10.9	95	4

75 or more returns.

Top 20 Kickoff Returners

Player	Years	No.	Yards	Avg.	Long	TD
Gale Sayers	7	91	2,781	30.6	103	6
Lynn Chandnois	7	92	2,720	29.6	93	3
Abe Woodson	9	193	5,538	28.7	105	5
Claude (Buddy) Young	6	90	2,514	27.9	104	2
Travis Williams	5	102	2,801	27.5	105	6
Joe Arenas	7	139	3,798	27.3	96	1
Clarence Davis	8	79	2,140	27.1	76	0
Lenny Lyles	12	81	2,161	26.7	103	3
Steve Van Buren	8	76	2,030	26.7	98	3
Bobby Jancik	6	158	4,185	26.5	61	0
Eugene (Mercury) Morris	8	111	2,947	26.5	105	3
Bobby Mitchell	11	102	2,690	26.4	98	5
Mel Renfro	14	85	2,246	26.4	100	2
Ollie Matson	14	143	3,746	26.2	105	6
Alvin Haymond	10	170	4,438	26.1	98	2
Noland Smith	3	82	2,137	26.1	106	1
Tim Brown	10	184	4,781	26.0	105	5
Al Nelson	9	101	2,625	26.0	78	0
Vic Washington	6	129	3,341	25.9	98	1
Dave Hampton	8	113	2,923	25.9	101	3

75 or more returns.

Top 20 Combined Yards Gained

	Years	Tot.	Rush.	Rec.	Int. Ret.	Punt Ret.	Kickoff Ret.	Fumble Ret.
Walter Payton	13	21,803	16,726	4,538	0	0	539	0
Tony Dorsett	12	16,326	12,739	3,554	0	0	0	33
Jim Brown	9	15,459	12,312	2,499	0	0	648	0
Franco Harris	13	14,622	12,120	2,287	0	0	233	−18
O.J. Simpson	11	14,368	11,236	2,142	0	0	990	0
Bobby Mitchell	11	14,078	2,735	7,954	0	699	2,690	0
John Riggins	14	13,435	11,352	2,090	0	0	0	−7
Greg Pruitt	12	13,262	5,672	3,069	0	2,007	2,514	0
Steve Largent	13	12,993	83	12,686	0	68	156	0
Ollie Matson	14	12,884	5,173	3,285	51	595	3,746	34
Tim Brown	10	12,684	3,862	3,399	0	639	4,781	3
Lenny Moore	12	12,451	5,174	6,039	0	56	1,180	2
Don Maynard	15	12,379	70	11,834	0	132	343	0
Charlie Joiner	18	12,367	22	12,146	0	0	194	5
Leroy Kelly	10	12,330	7,274	2,281	0	990	1,784	1
Floyd Little	9	12,173	6,323	2,418	0	893	2,523	16
Abner Haynes	8	12,065	4,630	3,535	0	875	3,025	0
Stump Mitchell	8	11,860	4,484	1,945	0	1,377	4,057	−3
Bruce Harper	8	11,429	1,829	2,409	0	1,784	5,407	0
Hugh McElhenny	13	11,375	5,281	3,247	0	920	1,921	6

YEARLY STATISTICAL LEADERS

Annual Scoring Leaders

Year	Player, Team	TD	FG	PAT	TP
1988	Scott Norwood, Buffalo, AFC	0	32	33	129
	Mike Cofer, San Francisco, NFC	0	27	40	121
1987	Jerry Rice, San Francisco, NFC	23	0	0	138
	Jim Breech, Cincinnati, AFC	0	24	25	97
1986	Tony Franklin, New England, AFC	0	32	44	140
	Kevin Butler, Chicago, NFC	0	28	36	120
1985	*Kevin Butler, Chicago, NFC	0	31	51	144
	Gary Anderson, Pittsburgh, AFC	0	33	40	139
1984	Ray Wersching, San Francisco, NFC	0	25	56	131
	Gary Anderson, Pittsburgh, AFC	0	24	45	117
1983	Mark Moseley, Washington, NFC	0	33	62	161
	Gary Anderson, Pittsburgh, AFC	0	27	38	119
1982	*Marcus Allen, L.A. Raiders, AFC	14	0	0	84
	Wendell Tyler, L.A. Rams, NFC	13	0	0	78
1981	Ed Murray, Detroit, NFC	0	25	46	121
	Rafael Septien, Dallas, NFC	0	27	40	121
	Jim Breech, Cincinnati, AFC	0	22	49	115
	Nick Lowery, Kansas City, AFC	0	26	37	115
1980	John Smith, New England, AFC	0	26	51	129
	*Ed Murray, Detroit, NFC	0	27	35	116
1979	John Smith, New England, AFC	0	23	46	115
	Mark Moseley, Washington, NFC	0	25	39	114
1978	*Frank Corral, Los Angeles, NFC	0	29	31	118
	Pat Leahy, N.Y. Jets, AFC	0	22	41	107
1977	Errol Mann, Oakland, AFC	0	20	39	99
	Walter Payton, Chicago, NFC	16	0	0	96
1976	Toni Linhart, Baltimore, AFC	0	20	49	109
	Mark Moseley, Washington, NFC	0	22	31	97
1975	O.J. Simpson, Buffalo, AFC	23	0	0	138
	Chuck Foreman, Minnesota, NFC	22	0	0	132
1974	Chester Marcol, Green Bay, NFC	0	25	19	94
	Roy Gerela, Pittsburgh, AFC	0	20	33	93
1973	David Ray, Los Angeles, NFC	0	30	40	130
	Roy Gerela, Pittsburgh, AFC	0	29	36	123
1972	*Chester Marcol, Green Bay, NFC	0	33	29	128
	Bobby Howfield, N.Y. Jets, AFC	0	27	40	121
1971	Garo Yepremian, Miami, AFC	0	28	33	117
	Curt Knight, Washington, NFC	0	29	27	114
1970	Fred Cox, Minnesota, NFC	0	30	35	125
	Jan Stenerud, Kansas City, AFC	0	30	26	116
1969	Jim Turner, N.Y. Jets, AFL	0	32	33	129
	Fred Cox, Minnesota, NFL	0	26	43	121
1968	Jim Turner, N.Y. Jets, AFL	0	34	43	145
	Leroy Kelly, Cleveland, NFL	20	0	0	120
1967	Jim Bakken, St. Louis, NFL	0	27	36	117
	George Blanda, Oakland, AFL	0	20	56	116
1966	Gino Cappelletti, Boston, AFL	6	16	35	119
	Bruce Gossett, Los Angeles, NFL	0	28	29	113
1965	*Gale Sayers, Chicago, NFL	22	0	0	132
	Gino Cappelletti, Boston, AFL	9	17	27	132
1964	Gino Cappelletti, Boston, AFL	7	25	36	#155
	Lenny Moore, Baltimore, NFL	20	0	0	120
1963	Gino Cappelletti, Boston, AFL	2	22	35	113
	Don Chandler, N.Y. Giants, NFL	0	18	52	106
1962	Gene Mingo, Denver, AFL	4	27	32	137
	Jim Taylor, Green Bay, NFL	19	0	0	114
1961	Gino Cappelletti, Boston, AFL	8	17	48	147
	Paul Hornung, Green Bay, NFL	10	15	41	146
1960	Paul Hornung, Green Bay, NFL	15	15	41	176
	*Gene Mingo, Denver, AFL	6	18	33	123
1959	Paul Hornung, Green Bay	7	7	31	94
1958	Jim Brown, Cleveland	18	0	0	108
1957	Sam Baker, Washington	1	14	29	77
	Lou Groza, Cleveland	0	15	32	77
1956	Bobby Layne, Detroit	5	12	33	99
1955	Doak Walker, Detroit	7	9	27	96
1954	Bobby Walston, Philadelphia	11	4	36	114
1953	Gordy Soltau, San Francisco	6	10	48	114
1952	Gordy Soltau, San Francisco	7	6	34	94
1951	Elroy (Crazylegs) Hirsch, Los Angeles	17	0	0	102
1950	*Doak Walker, Detroit	11	8	38	128
1949	Pat Harder, Chi. Cardinals	8	3	45	102
	Gene Roberts, N.Y. Giants	17	0	0	102
1948	Pat Harder, Chi. Cardinals	6	7	53	110
1947	Pat Harder, Chi. Cardinals	7	7	39	102
1946	Ted Fritsch, Green Bay	10	9	13	100
1945	Steve Van Buren, Philadelphia	18	0	2	110
1944	Don Hutson, Green Bay	9	0	31	85
1943	Don Hutson, Green Bay	12	3	36	117
1942	Don Hutson, Green Bay	17	1	33	138
1941	Don Hutson, Green Bay	12	1	20	95
1940	Don Hutson, Green Bay	7	0	15	57
1939	Andy Farkas, Washington	11	0	2	68
1938	Clarke Hinkle, Green Bay	7	3	7	58
1937	Jack Manders, Chi. Bears	5	8	15	69
1936	Earl (Dutch) Clark, Detroit	7	4	19	73
1935	Earl (Dutch) Clark, Detroit	6	1	16	55
1934	Jack Manders, Chi. Bears	3	10	31	79
1933	Ken Strong, N.Y. Giants	6	5	13	64
	Glenn Presnell, Portsmouth	6	6	10	64
1932	Earl (Dutch) Clark, Portsmouth	6	3	10	55

**First year in the league.*
#Cappelletti's total includes a two-point conversion.

Annual Leaders—Most Field Goals Made

Year	Player, Team	Att.	Made	Pct.
1988	Scott Norwood, Buffalo, AFC	37	32	86.5
	Mike Cofer, San Francisco, NFC	38	27	71.1
1987	Morten Andersen, New Orleans, NFC	36	28	77.8
	Dean Biasucci, Indianapolis, AFC	27	24	88.9
	Jim Breech, Cincinnati, AFC	30	24	80.0
1986	Tony Franklin, New England, AFC	41	32	78.0
	Kevin Butler, Chicago, NFC	41	28	68.3
1985	Gary Anderson, Pittsburgh, AFC	42	33	78.6
	Morten Andersen, New Orleans, NFC	35	31	88.6
	*Kevin Butler, Chicago, NFC	37	31	83.8
1984	*Paul McFadden, Philadelphia, NFC	37	30	81.1
	Gary Anderson, Pittsburgh, AFC	32	24	75.0
	Matt Bahr, Cleveland, AFC	32	24	75.0
1983	*Ali Haji-Sheikh, N.Y. Giants, NFC	42	35	83.3
	*Raul Allegre, Baltimore, AFC	35	30	85.7
1982	Mark Moseley, Washington, NFC	21	20	95.2
	Nick Lowery, Kansas City, AFC	24	19	79.2
1981	Rafael Septien, Dallas, NFC	35	27	77.1
	Nick Lowery, Kansas City, AFC	36	26	72.2
1980	*Ed Murray, Detroit, NFC	42	27	64.3
	John Smith, New England, AFC	34	26	76.5
	Fred Steinfort, Denver, AFC	34	26	76.5
1979	Mark Moseley, Washington, NFC	33	25	75.8
	John Smith, New England, AFC	33	23	69.7
1978	*Frank Corral, Los Angeles, NFC	43	29	67.4
	Pat Leahy, N.Y. Jets, AFC	30	22	73.3
1977	Mark Moseley, Washington, NFC	37	21	56.8
	Errol Mann, Oakland, AFC	28	20	71.4
1976	Mark Moseley, Washington, NFC	34	22	64.7
	Jan Stenerud, Kansas City, AFC	38	21	55.3
1975	Jan Stenerud, Kansas City, AFC	32	22	68.8
	Toni Fritsch, Dallas, NFC	35	22	62.9
1974	Chester Marcol, Green Bay, NFC	39	25	64.1
	Roy Gerela, Pittsburgh, AFC	29	20	69.0
1973	David Ray, Los Angeles, NFC	47	30	63.8
	Roy Gerela, Pittsburgh, AFC	43	29	67.4
1972	*Chester Marcol, Green Bay, NFC	48	33	68.8
	Roy Gerela, Pittsburgh, AFC	41	28	68.3
1971	Curt Knight, Washington, NFC	49	29	59.2
	Garo Yepremian, Miami, AFC	40	28	70.0
1970	Jan Stenerud, Kansas City, AFC	42	30	71.4
	Fred Cox, Minnesota, NFC	46	30	65.2
1969	Jim Turner, N.Y. Jets, AFL	47	32	68.1
	Fred Cox, Minnesota, NFL	37	26	70.3
1968	Jim Turner, N.Y. Jets, AFL	46	34	73.9
	Mac Percival, Chicago, NFL	36	25	69.4
1967	Jim Bakken, St. Louis, NFL	39	27	69.2
	Jan Stenerud, Kansas City, AFL	36	21	58.3
1966	Bruce Gossett, Los Angeles, NFL	49	28	57.1
	Mike Mercer, Oakland-Kansas City, AFL	30	21	70.0
1965	Pete Gogolak, Buffalo, AFL	46	28	60.9
	Fred Cox, Minnesota, NFL	35	23	65.7
1964	Jim Bakken, St. Louis, NFL	38	25	65.8
	Gino Cappelletti, Boston, AFL	39	25	64.1
1963	Jim Martin, Baltimore, NFL	39	24	61.5
	Gino Cappelletti, Boston, AFL	38	22	57.9
1962	Gene Mingo, Denver, AFL	39	27	69.2
	Lou Michaels, Pittsburgh, NFL	42	26	61.9
1961	Steve Myhra, Baltimore, NFL	39	21	53.8
	Gino Cappelletti, Boston, AFL	32	17	53.1
1960	Tommy Davis, San Francisco, NFL	32	19	59.4
	*Gene Mingo, Denver, AFL	28	18	64.3
1959	Pat Summerall, New York Giants	29	20	69.0
1958	Paige Cothren, Los Angeles	25	14	56.0
	*Tom Miner, Pittsburgh	28	14	50.0
1957	Lou Groza, Cleveland	22	15	68.2
1956	Sam Baker, Washington	25	17	68.0
1955	Fred Cone, Green Bay	24	16	66.7
1954	Lou Groza, Cleveland	24	16	66.7
1953	Lou Groza, Cleveland	26	23	88.5
1952	Lou Groza, Cleveland	33	19	57.6
1951	Bob Waterfield, Los Angeles	23	13	56.5
1950	*Lou Groza, Cleveland	19	13	68.4
1949	Cliff Patton, Philadelphia	18	9	50.0
	Bob Waterfield, Los Angeles	16	9	56.3
1948	Cliff Patton, Philadelphia	12	8	66.7
1947	Ward Cuff, Green Bay	16	7	43.8
	Pat Harder, Chi. Cardinals	10	7	70.0
	Bob Waterfield, Los Angeles	16	7	43.8
1946	Ted Fritsch, Green Bay	17	9	52.9
1945	Joe Aguirre, Washington	13	7	53.8
1944	Ken Strong, N.Y. Giants	12	6	50.0
1943	Ward Cuff, N.Y. Giants	9	3	33.3
	Don Hutson, Green Bay	5	3	60.0
1942	Bill Daddio, Chi. Cardinals	10	5	50.0
1941	Clarke Hinkle, Green Bay	14	6	42.9
1940	Clarke Hinkle, Green Bay	14	9	64.3
1939	Ward Cuff, N.Y. Giants	16	7	43.8
1938	Ward Cuff, N.Y. Giants	9	5	55.6
	Ralph Kercheval, Brooklyn	13	5	38.5
1937	Jack Manders, Chi. Bears		8	
1936	Jack Manders, Chi. Bears		7	
	Armand Niccolai, Pittsburgh		7	
1935	Armand Niccolai, Pittsburgh		6	
	Bill Smith, Chi. Cardinals		6	
1934	Jack Manders, Chi. Bears		10	

1933	*Jack Manders, Chi. Bears	6
	Glenn Presnell, Portsmouth	6
1932	Earl (Dutch) Clark, Portsmouth	3

First year in the league.

Annual Rushing Leaders

Year	Player, Team	Att.	Yards	Avg.	TD
1988	Eric Dickerson, Indianapolis, AFC	388	1,659	4.3	14
	Herschel Walker, Dallas, NFC	361	1,514	4.2	5
1987	Charles White, L.A. Rams, NFC	324	1,374	4.2	11
	Eric Dickerson, Indianapolis, AFC	223	1,011	4.5	5
1986	Eric Dickerson, L.A. Rams, NFC	404	1,821	4.5	11
	Curt Warner, Seattle, AFC	319	1,481	4.6	13
1985	Marcus Allen, L.A. Raiders, AFC	380	1,759	4.6	11
	Gerald Riggs, Atlanta, NFC	397	1,719	4.3	10
1984	Eric Dickerson, L.A. Rams, NFC	379	2,105	5.6	14
	Earnest Jackson, San Diego, AFC	296	1,179	4.0	8
1983	*Eric Dickerson, L.A. Rams, NFC	390	1,808	4.6	18
	*Curt Warner, Seattle, AFC	335	1,449	4.3	13
1982	Freeman McNeil, N.Y. Jets, AFC	151	786	5.2	6
	Tony Dorsett, Dallas, NFC	177	745	4.2	5
1981	*George Rogers, New Orleans, NFC	378	1,674	4.4	13
	Earl Campbell, Houston, AFC	361	1,376	3.8	10
1980	Earl Campbell, Houston, AFC	373	1,934	5.2	13
	Walter Payton, Chicago, NFC	317	1,460	4.6	6
1979	Earl Campbell, Houston, AFC	368	1,697	4.6	19
	Walter Payton, Chicago, NFC	369	1,610	4.4	14
1978	*Earl Campbell, Houston, AFC	302	1,450	4.8	13
	Walter Payton, Chicago, NFC	333	1,395	4.2	11
1977	Walter Payton, Chicago, NFC	339	1,852	5.5	14
	Mark van Eeghen, Oakland, AFC	324	1,273	3.9	7
1976	O.J. Simpson, Buffalo, AFC	290	1,503	5.2	8
	Walter Payton, Chicago, NFC	311	1,390	4.5	13
1975	O.J. Simpson, Buffalo, AFC	329	1,817	5.5	16
	Jim Otis, St. Louis, NFC	269	1,076	4.0	5
1974	Otis Armstrong, Denver, AFC	263	1,407	5.3	9
	Lawrence McCutcheon, Los Angeles, NFC	236	1,109	4.7	3
1973	O.J. Simpson, Buffalo, AFC	332	2,003	6.0	12
	John Brockington, Green Bay, NFC	265	1,144	4.3	3
1972	O.J. Simpson, Buffalo, AFC	292	1,251	4.3	6
	Larry Brown, Washington, NFC	285	1,216	4.3	8
1971	Floyd Little, Denver, AFC	284	1,133	4.0	6
	*John Brockington, Green Bay, NFC	216	1,105	5.1	4
1970	Larry Brown, Washington, NFC	237	1,125	4.7	5
	Floyd Little, Denver, AFC	209	901	4.3	3
1969	Gale Sayers, Chicago, NFL	236	1,032	4.4	8
	Dickie Post, San Diego, AFL	182	873	4.8	6
1968	Leroy Kelly, Cleveland, NFL	248	1,239	5.0	16
	*Paul Robinson, Cincinnati, AFL	238	1,023	4.3	8
1967	Jim Nance, Boston, AFL	269	1,216	4.5	7
	Leroy Kelly, Cleveland, NFL	235	1,205	5.1	11
1966	Jim Nance, Boston, AFL	299	1,458	4.9	11
	Gale Sayers, Chicago, NFL	229	1,231	5.4	8
1965	Jim Brown, Cleveland, NFL	289	1,544	5.3	17
	Paul Lowe, San Diego, AFL	222	1,121	5.0	7
1964	Jim Brown, Cleveland, NFL	280	1,446	5.2	7
	Cookie Gilchrist, Buffalo, AFL	230	981	4.3	6
1963	Jim Brown, Cleveland, NFL	291	1,863	6.4	12
	Clem Daniels, Oakland, AFL	215	1,099	5.1	3
1962	Jim Taylor, Green Bay, NFL	272	1,474	5.4	19
	*Cookie Gilchrist, Buffalo, AFL	214	1,096	5.1	13
1961	Jim Brown, Cleveland, NFL	305	1,408	4.6	8
	Billy Cannon, Houston, AFL	200	948	4.7	6
1960	Jim Brown, Cleveland, NFL	215	1,257	5.8	9
	*Abner Haynes, Dall. Texans, AFL	156	875	5.6	9
1959	Jim Brown, Cleveland	290	1,329	4.6	14
1958	Jim Brown, Cleveland	257	1,527	5.9	17
1957	*Jim Brown, Cleveland	202	942	4.7	9
1956	Rick Casares, Chi. Bears	234	1,126	4.8	12
1955	*Alan Ameche, Baltimore	213	961	4.5	9
1954	Joe Perry, San Francisco	173	1,049	6.1	8
1953	Joe Perry, San Francisco	192	1,018	5.3	10
1952	Dan Towler, Los Angeles	156	894	5.7	10
1951	Eddie Price, N.Y. Giants	271	971	3.6	7
1950	*Marion Motley, Cleveland	140	810	5.8	3
1949	Steve Van Buren, Philadelphia	263	1,146	4.4	11
1948	Steve Van Buren, Philadelphia	201	945	4.7	10
1947	Steve Van Buren, Philadelphia	217	1,008	4.6	13
1946	Bill Dudley, Pittsburgh	146	604	4.1	3
1945	Steve Van Buren, Philadelphia	143	832	5.8	15
1944	Bill Paschal, N.Y. Giants	196	737	3.8	9
1943	*Bill Paschal, N.Y. Giants	147	572	3.9	10
1942	*Bill Dudley, Pittsburgh	162	696	4.3	5
1941	Clarence (Pug) Manders, Brooklyn	111	486	4.4	5
1940	Byron (Whizzer) White, Detroit	146	514	3.5	5
1939	*Bill Osmanski, Chicago	121	699	5.8	7
1938	*Byron (Whizzer) White, Pittsburgh	152	567	3.7	4
1937	Cliff Battles, Washington	216	874	4.0	5
1936	*Alphonse (Tuffy) Leemans, N.Y. Giants	206	830	4.0	2
1935	Doug Russell, Chi. Cardinals	140	499	3.6	0
1934	*Beattie Feathers, Chi. Bears	101	1,004	9.9	8
1933	Jim Musick, Boston	173	809	4.7	5
1932	*Cliff Battles, Boston	148	576	3.9	3

First year in the league.

Annual Passing Leaders

Year	Player, Team	Att.	Comp.	Yards	TD	Int.
1988	Boomer Esiason, Cincinnati, AFC	388	223	3,572	28	14
	Wade Wilson, Minnesota, NFC	332	204	2,746	15	9
1987	Joe Montana, San Francisco, NFC	398	266	3,054	31	13
	Bernie Kosar, Cleveland, AFC	389	241	3,033	22	9
1986	Tommy Kramer, Minnesota, NFC	372	208	3,000	24	10
	Dan Marino, Miami, AFC	623	378	4,746	44	23
1985	Ken O'Brien, N.Y. Jets, AFC	488	297	3,888	25	8
	Joe Montana, San Francisco, NFC	494	303	3,653	27	13
1984	Dan Marino, Miami, AFC	564	362	5,084	48	17
	Joe Montana, San Francisco, NFC	432	279	3,630	28	10
1983	Steve Bartkowski, Atlanta, NFC	432	274	3,167	22	5
	*Dan Marino, Miami, AFC	296	173	2,210	20	6
1982	Ken Anderson, Cincinnati, AFC	309	218	2,495	12	9
	Joe Theismann, Washington, NFC	252	161	2,033	13	9
1981	Ken Anderson, Cincinnati, AFC	479	300	3,754	29	10
	Joe Montana, San Francisco, NFC	488	311	3,565	19	12
1980	Brian Sipe, Cleveland, AFC	554	337	4,132	30	14
	Ron Jaworski, Philadelphia, NFC	451	257	3,529	27	12
1979	Roger Staubach, Dallas, NFC	461	267	3,586	27	11
	Dan Fouts, San Diego, AFC	530	332	4,082	24	24
1978	Roger Staubach, Dallas, NFC	413	231	3,190	25	16
	Terry Bradshaw, Pittsburgh, AFC	368	207	2,915	28	20
1977	Bob Griese, Miami, AFC	307	180	2,252	22	13
	Roger Staubach, Dallas, NFC	361	210	2,620	18	9
1976	Ken Stabler, Oakland, AFC	291	194	2,737	27	17
	James Harris, Los Angeles, NFC	158	91	1,460	8	6
1975	Ken Anderson, Cincinnati, AFC	377	228	3,169	21	11
	Fran Tarkenton, Minnesota, NFC	425	273	2,994	25	13
1974	Ken Anderson, Cincinnati, AFC	328	213	2,667	18	10
	Sonny Jurgensen, Washington, NFC	167	107	1,185	11	5
1973	Roger Staubach, Dallas, NFC	286	179	2,428	23	15
	Ken Stabler, Oakland, AFC	260	163	1,997	14	10
1972	Norm Snead, N.Y. Giants, NFC	325	196	2,307	17	12
	Earl Morrall, Miami, AFC	150	83	1,360	11	7
1971	Roger Staubach, Dallas, NFC	211	126	1,882	15	4
	Bob Griese, Miami, AFC	263	145	2,089	19	9
1970	John Brodie, San Francisco, NFC	378	223	2,941	24	10
	Daryle Lamonica, Oakland, AFC	356	179	2,516	22	15
1969	Sonny Jurgensen, Washington, NFL	442	274	3,102	22	15
	*Greg Cook, Cincinnati, AFL	197	106	1,854	15	11
1968	Len Dawson, Kansas City, AFL	224	131	2,109	17	9
	Earl Morrall, Baltimore, NFL	317	182	2,909	26	17
1967	Sonny Jurgensen, Washington, NFL	508	288	3,747	31	16
	Daryle Lamonica, Oakland, AFL	425	220	3,228	30	20
1966	Bart Starr, Green Bay, NFL	251	156	2,257	14	3
	Len Dawson, Kansas City, AFL	284	159	2,527	26	10
1965	Rudy Bukich, Chicago, NFL	312	176	2,641	20	9
	John Hadl, San Diego, AFL	348	174	2,798	20	21
1964	Len Dawson, Kansas City, AFL	354	199	2,879	30	18
	Bart Starr, Green Bay, NFL	272	163	2,144	15	4
1963	Y.A. Tittle, N.Y. Giants, NFL	367	221	3,145	36	14
	Tobin Rote, San Diego, AFL	286	170	2,510	20	17
1962	Len Dawson, Dall. Texans, AFL	310	189	2,759	29	17
	Bart Starr, Green Bay, NFL	285	178	2,438	12	9
1961	George Blanda, Houston, AFL	362	187	3,330	36	22
	Milt Plum, Cleveland, NFL	302	177	2,416	18	10
1960	Milt Plum, Cleveland, NFL	250	151	2,297	21	5
	Jack Kemp, L.A. Chargers, AFL	406	211	3,018	20	25
1959	Charlie Conerly, N.Y. Giants	194	113	1,706	14	4
1958	Eddie LeBaron, Washington	145	79	1,365	11	10
1957	Tommy O'Connell, Cleveland	110	63	1,229	9	8
1956	Ed Brown, Chi. Bears	168	96	1,667	11	12
1955	Otto Graham, Cleveland	185	98	1,721	15	8
1954	Norm Van Brocklin, Los Angeles	260	139	2,637	13	21
1953	Otto Graham, Cleveland	258	167	2,722	11	9
1952	Norm Van Brocklin, Los Angeles	205	113	1,736	14	17
1951	Bob Waterfield, Los Angeles	176	88	1,566	13	10
1950	Norm Van Brocklin, Los Angeles	233	127	2,061	18	14
1949	Sammy Baugh, Washington	255	145	1,903	18	14
1948	Tommy Thompson, Philadelphia	246	141	1,965	25	11
1947	Sammy Baugh, Washington	354	210	2,938	25	15
1946	Bob Waterfield, Los Angeles	251	127	1,747	18	17
1945	Sammy Baugh, Washington	182	128	1,669	11	4
	Sid Luckman, Chi. Bears	217	117	1,725	14	10
1944	Frank Filchock, Washington	147	84	1,139	13	9
1943	Sammy Baugh, Washington	239	133	1,754	23	19
1942	Cecil Isbell, Green Bay	268	146	2,021	24	14
1941	Cecil Isbell, Green Bay	206	117	1,479	15	11
1940	Sammy Baugh, Washington	177	111	1,367	12	10
1939	*Parker Hall, Cleveland	208	106	1,227	9	13
1938	Ed Danowski, N.Y. Giants	129	70	848	7	8
1937	*Sammy Baugh, Washington	171	81	1,127	8	14
1936	Arnie Herber, Green Bay	173	77	1,239	11	13
1935	Ed Danowski, N.Y. Giants	113	57	794	10	9
1934	Arnie Herber, Green Bay	115	42	799	8	12
1933	*Harry Newman, N.Y. Giants	136	53	973	11	17
1932	Arnie Herber, Green Bay	101	37	639	9	9

First year in the league.

Annual Pass Receiving Leaders

Year	Player, Team	No.	Yards	Avg.	TD
1988	Al Toon, N.Y. Jets, AFC	93	1,067	11.5	5
	Henry Ellard, L.A. Rams, NFC	86	1,414	16.4	10
1987	J.T. Smith, St. Louis, NFC	91	1,117	12.3	8
	Al Toon, N.Y. Jets, AFC	68	976	14.4	5
1986	Todd Christensen, L.A. Raiders, AFC	95	1,153	12.1	8
	Jerry Rice, San Francisco, NFC	86	1,570	18.3	15
1985	Roger Craig, San Francisco, NFC	92	1,016	11.0	6
	Lionel James, San Diego, AFC	86	1,027	11.9	6
1984	Art Monk, Washington, NFC	106	1,372	12.9	7
	Ozzie Newsome, Cleveland, AFC	89	1,001	11.2	5
1983	Todd Christensen, L.A. Raiders, AFC	92	1,247	13.6	12
	Roy Green, St. Louis, NFC	78	1,227	15.7	14
	Charlie Brown, Washington, NFC	78	1,225	15.7	8
	Earnest Gray, N.Y. Giants, NFC	78	1,139	14.6	5
1982	Dwight Clark, San Francisco, NFC	60	913	15.2	5
	Kellen Winslow, San Diego, AFC	54	721	13.4	6

1981	Kellen Winslow, San Diego, AFC	88	1,075	12.2	10
	Dwight Clark, San Francisco, NFC	85	1,105	13.0	4
1980	Kellen Winslow, San Diego, AFC	89	1,290	14.5	9
	*Earl Cooper, San Francisco, NFC	83	567	6.8	4
1979	Joe Washington, Baltimore, AFC	82	750	9.1	3
	Ahmad Rashad, Minnesota, NFC	80	1,156	14.5	9
1978	Rickey Young, Minnesota, NFC	88	704	8.0	5
	Steve Largent, Seattle, AFC	71	1,168	16.5	8
1977	Lydell Mitchell, Baltimore, AFC	71	620	8.7	4
	Ahmad Rashad, Minnesota, NFC	51	681	13.4	2
1976	MacArthur Lane, Kansas City, AFC	66	686	10.4	1
	Drew Pearson, Dallas, NFC	58	806	13.9	6
1975	Chuck Foreman, Minnesota, NFC	73	691	9.5	9
	Reggie Rucker, Cleveland, AFC	60	770	12.8	3
	Lydell Mitchell, Baltimore, AFC	60	544	9.1	4
1974	Lydell Mitchell, Baltimore, AFC	72	544	7.6	2
	Charles Young, Philadelphia, NFC	63	696	11.0	3
1973	Harold Carmichael, Philadelphia, NFC	67	1,116	16.7	9
	Fred Willis, Houston, AFC	57	371	6.5	1
1972	Harold Jackson, Philadelphia, NFC	62	1,048	16.9	4
	Fred Biletnikoff, Oakland, AFC	58	802	13.8	7
1971	Fred Biletnikoff, Oakland, AFC	61	929	15.2	9
	Bob Tucker, N.Y. Giants, NFC	59	791	13.4	4
1970	Dick Gordon, Chicago, NFC	71	1,026	14.5	13
	Marlin Briscoe, Buffalo, AFC	57	1,036	18.2	8
1969	Dan Abramowicz, New Orleans, NFL	73	1,015	13.9	7
	Lance Alworth, San Diego, AFL	64	1,003	15.7	4
1968	Clifton McNeil, San Francisco, NFL	71	994	14.0	7
	Lance Alworth, San Diego, AFL	68	1,312	19.3	10
1967	George Sauer, N.Y. Jets, AFL	75	1,189	15.9	6
	Charley Taylor, Washington, NFL	70	990	14.1	9
1966	Lance Alworth, San Diego, AFL	73	1,383	18.9	13
	Charley Taylor, Washington, NFL	72	1,119	15.5	12
1965	Lionel Taylor, Denver, AFL	85	1,131	13.3	6
	Dave Parks, San Francisco, NFL	80	1,344	16.8	12
1964	Charley Hennigan, Houston, AFL	101	1,546	15.3	8
	Johnny Morris, Chicago, NFL	93	1,200	12.9	10
1963	Lionel Taylor, Denver, AFL	78	1,101	14.1	10
	Bobby Joe Conrad, St. Louis, NFL	73	967	13.2	10
1962	Lionel Taylor, Denver, AFL	77	908	11.8	4
	Bobby Mitchell, Washington, NFL	72	1,384	19.2	11
1961	Lionel Taylor, Denver, AFL	100	1,176	11.8	4
	Jim (Red) Phillips, Los Angeles, NFL	78	1,092	14.0	5
1960	Lionel Taylor, Denver, AFL	92	1,235	13.4	12
	Raymond Berry, Baltimore, NFL	74	1,298	17.5	10
1959	Raymond Berry, Baltimore	66	959	14.5	14
1958	Raymond Berry, Baltimore	56	794	14.2	9
	Pete Retzlaff, Philadelphia	56	766	13.7	2
1957	Billy Wilson, San Francisco	52	757	14.6	6
1956	Billy Wilson, San Francisco	60	889	14.8	5
1955	Pete Pihos, Philadelphia	62	864	13.9	7
1954	Pete Pihos, Philadelphia	60	872	14.5	10
	Billy Wilson, San Francisco	60	830	13.8	5
1953	Pete Pihos, Philadelphia	63	1,049	16.7	10
1952	Mac Speedie, Cleveland	62	911	14.7	5
1951	Elroy (Crazylegs) Hirsch, Los Angeles	66	1,495	22.7	17
1950	Tom Fears, Los Angeles	84	1,116	13.3	7
1949	Tom Fears, Los Angeles	77	1,013	13.2	9
1948	*Tom Fears, Los Angeles	51	698	13.7	4
1947	Jim Keane, Chi. Bears	64	910	14.2	10
1946	Jim Benton, Los Angeles	63	981	15.6	6
1945	Don Hutson, Green Bay	47	834	17.7	9
1944	Don Hutson, Green Bay	58	866	14.9	9
1943	Don Hutson, Green Bay	47	776	16.5	11
1942	Don Hutson, Green Bay	74	1,211	16.4	17
1941	Don Hutson, Green Bay	58	738	12.7	10
1940	*Don Looney, Philadelphia	58	707	12.2	4
1939	Don Hutson, Green Bay	34	846	24.9	6
1938	Gaynell Tinsley, Chi. Cardinals	41	516	12.6	1
1937	Don Hutson, Green Bay	41	552	13.5	7
1936	Don Hutson, Green Bay	34	536	15.8	8
1935	*Tod Goodwin, N.Y. Giants	26	432	16.6	4
1934	Joe Carter, Philadelphia	16	238	14.9	4
	Morris (Red) Badgro, N.Y. Giants	16	206	12.9	1
1933	John (Shipwreck) Kelly, Brooklyn	22	246	11.2	3
1932	Ray Flaherty, N.Y. Giants	21	350	16.7	3

**First year in the league.*

Annual Interception Leaders

Year	Player, Team	No.	Yards	TD
1988	Scott Case, Atlanta, NFC	10	47	0
	Erik McMillan, N.Y. Jets, AFC	8	168	2
1987	Barry Wilburn, Washington, NFC	9	135	1
	Mike Prior, Indianapolis, AFC	6	57	0
	Mark Kelso, Buffalo, AFC	6	25	0
	Keith Bostic, Houston, AFC	6	−14	0
1986	Ronnie Lott, San Francisco, NFC	10	134	1
	Deron Cherry, Kansas City, AFC	9	150	0
1985	Everson Walls, Dallas, NFC	9	31	0
	Albert Lewis, Kansas City, AFC	8	59	0
	Eugene Daniel, Indianapolis, AFC	8	53	0
1984	Ken Easley, Seattle, AFC	10	126	2
	*Tom Flynn, Green Bay, NFC	9	106	0
1983	Mark Murphy, Washington, NFC	9	127	0
	Ken Riley, Cincinnati, AFC	8	89	2
	Vann McElroy, L.A. Raiders, AFC	8	68	0
1982	Everson Walls, Dallas, NFC	7	61	0
	Ken Riley, Cincinnati, AFC	5	88	1
	Bobby Jackson, N.Y. Jets, AFC	5	84	1
	Dwayne Woodruff, Pittsburgh, AFC	5	53	0
	Donnie Shell, Pittsburgh, AFC	5	27	0
1981	*Everson Walls, Dallas, NFC	11	133	0
	John Harris, Seattle, AFC	10	155	2
1980	Lester Hayes, Oakland, AFC	13	273	1
	Nolan Cromwell, Los Angeles, NFC	8	140	1
1979	Mike Reinfeldt, Houston, AFC	12	205	0
	Lemar Parrish, Washington, NFC	9	65	0
1978	Thom Darden, Cleveland, AFC	10	200	0
	Ken Stone, St. Louis, NFC	9	139	0
	Willie Buchanon, Green Bay, NFC	9	93	1
1977	Lyle Blackwood, Baltimore, AFC	10	163	0
	Rolland Lawrence, Atlanta, NFC	7	138	0
1976	Monte Jackson, Los Angeles, NFC	10	173	3
	Ken Riley, Cincinnati, AFC	9	141	1
1975	Mel Blount, Pittsburgh, AFC	11	121	0
	Paul Krause, Minnesota, NFC	10	201	0
1974	Emmitt Thomas, Kansas City, AFC	12	214	2
	Ray Brown, Atlanta, NFC	8	164	1
1973	Dick Anderson, Miami, AFC	8	163	2
	Mike Wagner, Pittsburgh, AFC	8	134	0
	Bobby Bryant, Minnesota, NFC	7	105	1
1972	Bill Bradley, Philadelphia, NFC	9	73	0
	Mike Sensibaugh, Kansas City, AFC	8	65	0
1971	Bill Bradley, Philadelphia, NFC	11	248	0
	Ken Houston, Houston, AFC	9	220	4
1970	Johnny Robinson, Kansas City, AFC	10	155	0
	Dick LeBeau, Detroit, NFC	9	96	0
1969	Mel Renfro, Dallas, NFL	10	118	0
	Emmitt Thomas, Kansas City, AFL	9	146	1
1968	Dave Grayson, Oakland, AFL	10	195	1
	Willie Williams, N.Y. Giants, NFL	10	103	0
1967	Miller Farr, Houston, AFL	10	264	3
	*Lem Barney, Detroit, NFL	10	232	3
	Tom Janik, Buffalo, AFL	10	222	2
	Dave Whitsell, New Orleans, NFL	10	178	2
	Dick Westmoreland, Miami, AFL	10	127	1
1966	Larry Wilson, St. Louis, NFL	10	180	2
	Johnny Robinson, Kansas City, AFL	10	136	1
	Bobby Hunt, Kansas City, AFL	10	113	0
1965	W.K. Hicks, Houston, AFL	9	156	0
	Bobby Boyd, Baltimore, NFL	9	78	1
1964	Dainard Paulson, N.Y. Jets, AFL	12	157	1
	*Paul Krause, Washington, NFL	12	140	1
1963	Fred Glick, Houston, AFL	12	180	1
	Dick Lynch, N.Y. Giants, NFL	9	251	3
	Roosevelt Taylor, Chicago, NFL	9	172	1
1962	Lee Riley, N.Y. Titans, AFL	11	122	0
	Willie Wood, Green Bay, NFL	9	132	0
1961	Billy Atkins, Buffalo, AFL	10	158	0
	Dick Lynch, N.Y. Giants, NFL	9	60	0
1960	*Austin (Goose) Gonsoulin, Denver, AFL	11	98	0
	Dave Baker, San Francisco, NFL	10	96	0
	Jerry Norton, St. Louis, NFL	10	96	0
1959	Dean Derby, Pittsburgh	7	127	0
	Milt Davis, Baltimore	7	119	1
	Don Shinnick, Baltimore	7	70	0
1958	Jim Patton, N.Y. Giants	11	183	0
1957	*Milt Davis, Baltimore	10	219	2
	Jack Christiansen, Detroit	10	137	1
	Jack Butler, Pittsburgh	10	85	0
1956	Lindon Crow, Chi. Cardinals	11	170	0
1955	Will Sherman, Los Angeles	11	101	0
1954	Dick (Night Train) Lane, Chi. Cardinals	10	181	0
1953	Jack Christiansen, Detroit	12	238	1
1952	*Dick (Night Train) Lane, Los Angeles	14	298	2
1951	Otto Schnellbacher, N.Y. Giants	11	194	2
1950	*Orban (Spec) Sanders, N.Y. Yanks	13	199	0
1949	Bob Nussbaumer, Chi. Cardinals	12	157	0
1948	*Dan Sandifer, Washington	13	258	2
1947	Frank Reagan, N.Y. Giants	10	203	0
	Frank Seno, Boston	10	100	0
1946	Bill Dudley, Pittsburgh	10	242	1
1945	Roy Zimmerman, Philadelphia	7	90	0
1944	*Howard Livingston, N.Y. Giants	9	172	1
1943	Sammy Baugh, Washington	11	112	0
1942	Clyde (Bulldog) Turner, Chi. Bears	8	96	1
1941	Marshall Goldberg, Chi. Cardinals	7	54	0
	*Art Jones, Pittsburgh	7	35	0
1940	Clarence (Ace) Parker, Brooklyn	6	146	1
	Kent Ryan, Detroit	6	65	0
	Don Hutson, Green Bay	6	24	0

**First year in the league.*

Annual Punting Leaders

Year	Player, Team	No.	Avg.	Long
1988	Harry Newsome, Pittsburgh, AFC	65	45.4	62
	Jim Arnold, Detroit, NFC	97	42.4	69
1987	Rick Donnelly, Atlanta, NFC	61	44.0	62
	Ralf Mojsiejenko, San Diego, AFC	67	42.9	57
1986	Rohn Stark, Indianapolis, AFC	76	45.2	63
	Sean Landeta, N.Y. Giants, NFC	79	44.8	61
1985	Rohn Stark, Indianapolis, AFC	78	45.9	68
	*Rick Donnelly, Atlanta, NFC	59	43.6	68
1984	Jim Arnold, Kansas City, AFC	98	44.9	63
	*Brian Hansen, New Orleans, NFC	69	43.8	66
1983	Rohn Stark, Baltimore, AFC	91	45.3	68
	*Frank Garcia, Tampa Bay, NFC	95	42.2	64
1982	Luke Prestridge, Denver, AFC	45	45.0	65
	Carl Birdsong, St. Louis, NFC	54	43.8	65
1981	Pat McInally, Cincinnati, AFC	72	45.4	62
	Tom Skladany, Detroit, NFC	64	43.5	74
1980	Dave Jennings, N.Y. Giants, NFC	94	44.8	63
	Luke Prestridge, Denver, AFC	70	43.9	57
1979	*Bob Grupp, Kansas City, AFC	89	43.6	74

	Dave Jennings, N.Y. Giants, NFC	104	42.7	72
1978	Pat McInally, Cincinnati, AFC	91	43.1	65
	*Tom Skladany, Detroit, NFC	86	42.5	63
1977	Ray Guy, Oakland, AFC	59	43.3	74
	Tom Blanchard, New Orleans, NFC	82	42.4	66
1976	Marv Bateman, Buffalo, AFC	86	42.8	78
	John James, Atlanta, NFC	101	42.1	67
1975	Ray Guy, Oakland, AFC	68	43.8	64
	Herman Weaver, Detroit, NFC	80	42.0	61
1974	Ray Guy, Oakland, AFC	74	42.2	66
	Tom Blanchard, New Orleans, NFC	88	42.1	71
1973	Jerrel Wilson, Kansas City, AFC	80	45.5	68
	*Tom Wittum, San Francisco, NFC	79	43.7	62
1972	Jerrel Wilson, Kansas City, AFC	66	44.8	69
	Dave Chapple, Los Angeles, NFC	53	44.2	70
1971	Dave Lewis, Cincinnati, AFC	72	44.8	56
	Tom McNeill, Philadelphia, NFC	73	42.0	64
1970	*Dave Lewis, Cincinnati, AFC	79	46.2	63
	*Julian Fagan, New Orleans, NFC	77	42.5	64
1969	David Lee, Baltimore, NFL	57	45.3	66
	Dennis Partee, San Diego, AFL	71	44.6	62
1968	Jerrel Wilson, Kansas City, AFL	63	45.1	70
	Billy Lothridge, Atlanta, NFL	75	44.3	70
1967	Bob Scarpitto, Denver, AFL	105	44.9	73
	Billy Lothridge, Atlanta, NFL	87	43.7	62
1966	Bob Scarpitto, Denver, AFL	76	45.8	70
	*David Lee, Baltimore, NFL	49	45.6	64
1965	Gary Collins, Cleveland, NFL	65	46.7	71
	Jerrel Wilson, Kansas City, AFL	69	45.4	64
1964	*Bobby Walden, Minnesota, NFL	72	46.4	73
	Jim Fraser, Denver, AFL	73	44.2	67
1963	Yale Lary, Detroit, NFL	35	48.9	73
	Jim Fraser, Denver, AFL	81	44.4	66
1962	Tommy Davis, San Francisco, NFL	48	45.6	82
	Jim Fraser, Denver, AFL	55	43.6	75
1961	Yale Lary, Detroit, NFL	52	48.4	71
	Billy Atkins, Buffalo, AFL	85	44.5	70
1960	Jerry Norton, St. Louis, NFL	39	45.6	62
	*Paul Maguire, L.A. Chargers, AFL	43	40.5	61
1959	Yale Lary, Detroit	45	47.1	67
1958	Sam Baker, Washington	48	45.4	64
1957	Don Chandler, N.Y. Giants	60	44.6	61
1956	Norm Van Brocklin, Los Angeles	48	43.1	72
1955	Norm Van Brocklin, Los Angeles	60	44.6	61
1954	Pat Brady, Pittsburgh	66	43.2	72
1953	Pat Brady, Pittsburgh	80	46.9	64
1952	Horace Gillom, Cleveland	61	45.7	73
1951	Horace Gillom, Cleveland	73	45.5	66
1950	*Fred (Curly) Morrison, Chi. Bears	57	43.3	65
1949	*Mike Boyda, N.Y. Bulldogs	56	44.2	61
1948	Joe Muha, Philadelphia	57	47.3	82
1947	Jack Jacobs, Green Bay	57	43.5	74
1946	Roy McKay, Green Bay	64	42.7	64
1945	Roy McKay, Green Bay	44	41.2	73
1944	Frank Sinkwich, Detroit	45	41.0	73
1943	Sammy Baugh, Washington	50	45.9	81
1942	Sammy Baugh, Washington	37	48.2	74
1941	Sammy Baugh, Washington	30	48.7	75
1940	Sammy Baugh, Washington	35	51.4	85
1939	*Parker Hall, Cleveland	58	40.8	80

First year in the league.

Annual Punt Return Leaders

Year	Player, Team	No.	Yards	Avg.	Long	TD
1988	John Taylor, San Francisco, NFC	44	556	12.6	95	2
	JoJo Townsell, N.Y. Jets, AFC	35	409	11.7	59	1
1987	Mel Gray, New Orleans, NFC	24	352	14.7	80	0
	Bobby Joe Edmonds, Seattle, AFC	20	251	12.6	40	0
1986	*Bobby Joe Edmonds, Seattle, AFC	34	419	12.3	75	1
	*Vai Sikahema, St. Louis, NFC	43	522	12.1	71	2
1985	Irving Fryar, New England, AFC	37	520	14.1	85	2
	Henry Ellard, L.A. Rams, NFC	37	501	13.5	80	1
1984	Mike Martin, Cincinnati, AFC	24	376	15.7	55	0
	Henry Ellard, L.A. Rams, NFC	30	403	13.4	83	2
1983	*Henry Ellard, L.A. Rams, NFC	16	217	13.6	72	1
	Kirk Springs, N.Y. Jets, AFC	23	287	12.5	76	1
1982	Rick Upchurch, Denver, AFC	15	242	16.1	78	2
	Billy Johnson, Atlanta, NFC	24	273	11.4	71	0
1981	LeRoy Irvin, Los Angeles, NFC	46	615	13.4	84	3
	*James Brooks, San Diego, AFC	22	290	13.2	42	0
1980	J. T. Smith, Kansas City, AFC	40	581	14.5	75	2
	*Kenny Johnson, Atlanta, NFC	23	281	12.2	56	0
1979	John Sciarra, Philadelphia, NFC	16	182	11.4	38	0
	*Tony Nathan, Miami, AFC	28	306	10.9	86	1
1978	Rick Upchurch, Denver, AFC	36	493	13.7	75	1
	Jackie Wallace, Los Angeles, NFC	52	618	11.9	58	0
1977	Billy Johnson, Houston, AFC	35	539	15.4	87	2
	Larry Marshall, Philadelphia, NFC	46	489	10.6	48	0
1976	Rick Upchurch, Denver, AFC	39	536	13.7	92	4
	Eddie Brown, Washington, NFC	48	646	13.5	71	1
1975	Billy Johnson, Houston, AFC	40	612	15.3	83	3
	Terry Metcalf, St. Louis, NFC	23	285	12.4	69	1
1974	Lemar Parrish, Cincinnati, AFC	18	338	18.8	90	2
	Dick Jauron, Detroit, NFC	17	286	16.8	58	0
1973	Bruce Taylor, San Francisco, NFC	15	207	13.8	61	0
	Ron Smith, San Diego, AFC	27	352	13.0	84	2
1972	*Ken Ellis, Green Bay, NFC	14	215	15.4	80	1
	Chris Farasopoulos, N.Y. Jets, AFC	17	179	10.5	65	1
1971	Les (Speedy) Duncan, Washington, NFC	22	233	10.6	33	0
	Leroy Kelly, Cleveland, AFC	30	292	9.7	74	0
1970	Ed Podolak, Kansas City, AFC	23	311	13.5	60	0
	*Bruce Taylor, San Francisco, NFC	43	516	12.0	76	0

1969	Alvin Haymond, Los Angeles, NFL	33	435	13.2	52	0
	*Bill Thompson, Denver, AFL	25	288	11.5	40	0
1968	Bob Hayes, Dallas, NFL	15	312	20.8	90	2
	Noland Smith, Kansas City, AFL	18	270	15.0	80	1
1967	Floyd Little, Denver, AFL	16	270	16.9	72	1
	Ben Davis, Cleveland, NFL	18	229	12.7	52	1
1966	Les (Speedy) Duncan, San Diego, AFL	18	238	13.2	81	1
	Johnny Roland, St. Louis, NFL	20	221	11.1	86	1
1965	Leroy Kelly, Cleveland, NFL	17	265	15.6	67	2
	Les (Speedy) Duncan, San Diego, AFL	30	464	15.5	66	2
1964	Bobby Jancik, Houston, AFL	12	220	18.3	82	1
	Tommy Watkins, Detroit, NFL	16	238	14.9	68	2
1963	Dick James, Washington, NFL	16	214	13.4	39	0
	Claude (Hoot) Gibson, Oakland, AFL	26	307	11.8	85	2
1962	Dick Christy, N.Y. Titans, AFL	15	250	16.7	73	2
	Pat Studstill, Detroit, NFL	29	457	15.8	44	0
1961	Dick Christy, N.Y. Titans, AFL	18	383	21.3	70	2
	Willie Wood, Green Bay, NFL	14	225	16.1	72	2
1960	*Abner Haynes, Dall. Texans, AFL	14	215	15.4	46	0
	Abe Woodson, San Francisco, NFL	13	174	13.4	48	0
1959	Johnny Morris, Chi. Bears	14	171	12.2	78	1
1958	Jon Arnett, Los Angeles	18	223	12.4	58	0
1957	Bert Zagers, Washington	14	217	15.5	76	2
1956	Ken Konz, Cleveland	13	187	14.4	65	1
1955	Ollie Matson, Chi. Cardinals	13	245	18.8	78	2
1954	*Veryl Switzer, Green Bay	24	306	12.8	93	1
1953	Charley Trippi, Chi. Cardinals	21	239	11.4	38	0
1952	Jack Christiansen, Detroit	15	322	21.5	79	2
1951	Claude (Buddy) Young, N.Y. Yanks	12	231	19.3	79	1
1950	*Herb Rich, Baltimore	12	276	23.0	86	1
1949	Verda (Vitamin T) Smith, Los Angeles	27	427	15.8	85	1
1948	George McAfee, Chi. Bears	30	417	13.9	60	1
1947	*Walt Slater, Pittsburgh	28	435	15.5	33	0
1946	Bill Dudley, Pittsburgh	27	385	14.3	52	0
1945	*Dave Ryan, Detroit	15	220	14.7	56	0
1944	*Steve Van Buren, Philadelphia	15	230	15.3	55	1
1943	Andy Farkas, Washington	15	168	11.2	33	0
1942	Merlyn Condit, Brooklyn	21	210	10.0	23	0
1941	Byron (Whizzer) White, Detroit	19	262	13.8	64	0

First year in the league.

Annual Kickoff Return Leaders

Year	Player, Team	No.	Yards	Avg.	Long	TD
1988	Tim Brown, L.A. Raiders, AFC	41	1,098	26.8	97	1
	Donnie Elder, Tampa Bay, NFC	34	772	22.7	51	0
1987	Sylvester Stamps, Atlanta, NFC	24	660	27.5	97	1
	Paul Palmer, Kansas City, AFC	38	923	24.3	95	2
1986	Dennis Gentry, Chicago, NFC	20	576	28.8	91	1
	*Lupe Sanchez, Pittsburgh, AFC	25	591	23.6	64	0
1985	Ron Brown, L.A. Rams, NFC	28	918	32.8	98	3
	Glen Young, Cleveland, AFC	35	898	25.7	63	0
1984	*Bobby Humphery, N.Y. Jets, AFC	22	675	30.7	97	1
	Barry Redden, L.A. Rams, NFC	23	530	23.0	40	0
1983	Fulton Walker, Miami, AFC	36	962	26.7	78	0
	Darrin Nelson, Minnesota, NFC	18	445	24.7	50	0
1982	*Mike Mosley, Buffalo, AFC	18	487	27.1	66	0
	Alvin Hall, Detroit, NFC	16	426	26.6	96	1
1981	Mike Nelms, Washington, NFC	37	1,099	29.7	84	0
	Carl Roaches, Houston, AFC	28	769	27.5	96	1
1980	Horace Ivory, New England, AFC	36	992	27.6	98	1
	Rich Mauti, New Orleans, NFC	31	798	25.7	52	0
1979	Larry Brunson, Oakland, AFC	17	441	25.9	89	0
	*Jimmy Edwards, Minnesota, NFC	44	1,103	25.1	83	0
1978	Steve Odom, Green Bay, NFC	25	677	27.1	95	1
	*Keith Wright, Cleveland, AFC	30	789	26.3	86	0
1977	*Raymond Clayborn, New England, AFC	28	869	31.0	101	3
	*Wilbert Montgomery, Philadelphia, NFC	23	619	26.9	99	1
1976	*Duriel Harris, Miami, AFC	17	559	32.9	69	0
	Cullen Bryant, Los Angeles, NFC	16	459	28.7	90	1
1975	*Walter Payton, Chicago, NFC	14	444	31.7	70	0
	Harold Hart, Oakland, AFC	17	518	30.5	102	1
1974	Terry Metcalf, St. Louis, NFC	20	623	31.2	94	1
	Greg Pruitt, Cleveland, AFC	22	606	27.5	88	1
1973	Carl Garrett, Chicago, NFC	16	486	30.4	67	0
	*Wallace Francis, Buffalo, AFC	23	687	29.9	101	2
1972	Ron Smith, Chicago, NFC	30	924	30.8	94	1
	*Bruce Laird, Baltimore, AFC	29	843	29.1	73	0
1971	Travis Williams, Los Angeles, NFC	25	743	29.7	105	1
	Eugene (Mercury) Morris, Miami, AFC	15	423	28.2	94	1
1970	Jim Duncan, Baltimore, AFC	20	707	35.4	99	1
	Cecil Turner, Chicago, NFC	23	752	32.7	96	4
1969	Bobby Williams, Detroit, NFL	17	563	33.1	96	1
	*Bill Thompson, Denver, AFL	18	513	28.5	63	0
1968	Preston Pearson, Baltimore, NFL	15	527	35.1	102	2
	*George Atkinson, Oakland, AFL	32	802	25.1	60	0
1967	*Travis Williams, Green Bay, NFL	18	739	41.1	104	4
	*Zeke Moore, Houston, AFL	14	405	28.9	92	1
1966	Gale Sayers, Chicago, NFL	23	718	31.2	93	2
	*Goldie Sellers, Denver, AFL	19	541	28.5	100	2
1965	Tommy Watkins, Detroit, NFL	17	584	34.4	94	0
	Abner Haynes, Denver, AFL	34	901	26.5	60	0
1964	*Clarence Childs, N.Y. Giants, NFL	34	987	29.0	100	1
	Bo Roberson, Oakland, AFL	36	975	27.1	59	0
1963	Abe Woodson, San Francisco, NFL	29	935	32.2	103	3
	Bobby Jancik, Houston, AFL	45	1,317	29.3	53	0
1962	Abe Woodson, San Francisco, NFL	37	1,157	31.3	79	0
	*Bobby Jancik, Houston, AFL	24	826	30.3	61	0
1961	Dick Bass, Los Angeles, NFL	23	698	30.3	64	0
	*Dave Grayson, Dall. Texans, AFL	16	453	28.3	73	0
1960	*Tom Moore, Green Bay, NFL	12	397	33.1	84	0
	Ken Hall, Houston, AFL	19	594	31.3	104	1
1959	Abe Woodson, San Francisco	13	382	29.4	105	1
1958	Ollie Matson, Chi. Cardinals	14	497	35.5	101	2

1957	*Jon Arnett, Los Angeles	18	504	28.0	98	1
1956	*Tom Wilson, Los Angeles	15	477	31.8	103	1
1955	Al Carmichael, Green Bay	14	418	29.9	100	1
1954	Billy Reynolds, Cleveland	14	413	29.5	51	0
1953	Joe Arenas, San Francisco	16	551	34.4	82	0
1952	Lynn Chandnois, Pittsburgh	17	599	35.2	93	2
1951	Lynn Chandnois, Pittsburgh	12	390	32.5	55	0
1950	Verda (Vitamin T) Smith, Los Angeles	22	742	33.7	97	3
1949	*Don Doll, Detroit	21	536	25.5	56	0
1948	*Joe Scott, N.Y. Giants	20	569	28.5	99	1
1947	Eddie Saenz, Washington	29	797	27.5	94	2
1946	Abe Karnofsky, Boston	21	599	28.5	97	1
1945	Steve Van Buren, Philadelphia	13	373	28.7	98	1
1944	Bob Thurbon, Card.-Pitt	12	291	24.3	55	0
1943	Ken Heineman, Brooklyn	16	444	27.8	69	0
1942	Marshall Goldberg, Chi. Cardinals	15	393	26.2	95	1
1941	Marshall Goldberg, Chi. Cardinals	12	290	24.2	41	0

**First year in the league.*

Points Scored

Year	Team	Points
1988	Cincinnati, AFC	448
	L.A. Rams, NFC	407
1987	San Francisco, NFC	459
	Cleveland, AFC	390
1986	Miami, AFC	430
	Minnesota, NFC	398
1985	San Diego, AFC	467
	Chicago, NFC	456
1984	Miami, AFC	513
	San Francisco, NFC	475
1983	Washington, NFC	541
	L.A. Raiders, AFC	442
1982	San Diego, AFC	288
	Dallas, NFC	226
	Green Bay, NFC	226
1981	San Diego, AFC	478
	Atlanta, NFC	426
1980	Dallas, NFC	454
	New England, AFC	441
1979	Pittsburgh, AFC	416
	Dallas, NFC	371
1978	Dallas, NFC	384
	Miami, AFC	372
1977	Oakland, AFC	351
	Dallas, NFC	345
1976	Baltimore, AFC	417
	Los Angeles, NFC	351
1975	Buffalo, AFC	420
	Minnesota, NFC	377
1974	Oakland, AFC	355
	Washington, NFC	320
1973	Los Angeles, NFC	388
	Denver, AFC	354
1972	Miami, AFC	385
	San Francisco, NFC	353
1971	Dallas, NFC	406
	Oakland, AFC	344
1970	San Francisco, NFC	352
	Baltimore, AFC	321
1969	Minnesota, NFL	379
	Oakland, AFL	377
1968	Oakland, AFL	453
	Dallas, NFL	431
1967	Oakland, AFL	468
	Los Angeles, NFL	398
1966	Kansas City, AFL	448
	Dallas, NFL	445
1965	San Francisco, NFL	421
	San Diego, AFL	340
1964	Baltimore, NFL	428
	Buffalo, AFL	400
1963	N.Y. Giants, NFL	448
	San Diego, AFL	399
1962	Green Bay, NFL	415
	Dall. Texans, AFL	389
1961	Houston, AFL	513
	Green Bay, NFL	391
1960	N.Y. Titans, AFL	382
	Cleveland, NFL	362
1959	Baltimore	374
1958	Baltimore	381
1957	Los Angeles	307
1956	Chi. Bears	363
1955	Cleveland	349
1954	Detroit	337
1953	San Francisco	372
1952	Los Angeles	349
1951	Los Angeles	392
1950	Los Angeles	466
1949	Philadelphia	364
1948	Chi. Cardinals	395
1947	Chi. Bears	363
1946	Chi. Bears	289
1945	Philadelphia	272
1944	Philadelphia	267
1943	Chi. Bears	303
1942	Chi. Bears	376
1941	Chi. Bears	396
1940	Washington	245
1939	Chi. Bears	298
1938	Green Bay	223
1937	Green Bay	220
1936	Green Bay	248
1935	Chi. Bears	192
1934	Chi. Bears	286
1933	N.Y. Giants	244
1932	Green Bay	152

Total Yards Gained

Year	Team	Yards
1988	Cincinnati, AFC	6,057
	San Francisco, NFC	5,900
1987	San Francisco, NFC	5,987
	Denver, AFC	5,624
1986	Cincinnati, AFC	6,490
	San Francisco, NFC	6,082
1985	San Diego, AFC	6,535
	San Francisco, NFC	5,920
1984	Miami, AFC	6,936
	San Francisco, NFC	6,366
1983	San Diego, AFC	6,197
	Green Bay, NFC	6,172
1982	San Diego, AFC	4,048
	San Francisco, NFC	3,242
1981	San Diego, AFC	6,744
	Detroit, NFC	5,933
1980	San Diego, AFC	6,410
	Los Angeles, NFC	6,006
1979	Pittsburgh, AFC	6,258
	Dallas, NFC	5,968
1978	New England, AFC	5,965
	Dallas, NFC	5,959
1977	Dallas, NFC	4,812
	Oakland, AFC	4,736
1976	Baltimore, AFC	5,236
	St. Louis, NFC	5,136
1975	Buffalo, AFC	5,467
	Dallas, NFC	5,025
1974	Dallas, NFC	4,983
	Oakland, AFC	4,718
1973	Los Angeles, NFC	4,906
	Oakland, AFC	4,773
1972	Miami, AFC	5,036
	N.Y. Giants, NFC	4,483
1971	Dallas, NFC	5,035
	San Diego, AFC	4,738
1970	Oakland, AFC	4,829
	San Francisco, NFC	4,503
1969	Dallas, NFL	5,122
	Oakland, AFL	5,036
1968	Oakland, AFL	5,696
	Dallas, NFL	5,117
1967	N.Y. Jets, AFL	5,152
	Baltimore, NFL	5,008
1966	Dallas, NFL	5,145
	Kansas City, AFL	5,114
1965	San Francisco, NFL	5,270
	San Diego, AFL	5,188
1964	Buffalo, AFL	5,206
	Baltimore, NFL	4,779
1963	San Diego, AFL	5,153
	N.Y. Giants, NFL	5,024
1962	N.Y. Giants, NFL	5,005
	Houston, AFL	4,971
1961	Houston, AFL	6,288
	Philadelphia, NFL	5,112
1960	Houston, AFL	4,936
	Baltimore, NFL	4,245
1959	Baltimore	4,458
1958	Baltimore	4,539
1957	Los Angeles	4,143
1956	Chi. Bears	4,537
1955	Chi. Bears	4,316
1954	Los Angeles	5,187
1953	Philadelphia	4,811
1952	Cleveland	4,352
1951	Los Angeles	5,506
1950	Los Angeles	5,420
1949	Chi. Bears	4,873
1948	Chi. Cardinals	4,705
1947	Chi. Bears	5,053
1946	Los Angeles	3,793
1945	Washington	3,549
1944	Chi. Bears	3,239
1943	Chi. Bears	4,045
1942	Chi. Bears	3,900
1941	Chi. Bears	4,265
1940	Green Bay	3,400
1939	Chi. Bears	3,988
1938	Green Bay	3,037
1937	Green Bay	3,201
1936	Detroit	3,703
1935	Chi. Bears	3,454
1934	Chi. Bears	3,900
1933	N.Y. Giants	2,973
1932	Chi. Bears	2,755

Yards Rushing

Year	Team	Yards
1988	Cincinnati, AFC	2,710
	San Francisco, NFC	2,523
1987	San Francisco, NFC	2,237
	L.A. Raiders, AFC	2,197
1986	Chicago, NFC	2,700
	Cincinnati, AFC	2,533
1985	Chicago, NFC	2,761
	Indianapolis, AFC	2,439
1984	Chicago, NFC	2,974
	N.Y. Jets, AFC	2,189
1983	Chicago, NFC	2,727
	Baltimore, AFC	2,695
1982	Buffalo, AFC	1,371
	Dallas, NFC	1,313
1981	Detroit, NFC	2,795
	Kansas City, AFC	2,633
1980	Los Angeles, NFC	2,799
	Houston, AFC	2,635
1979	N.Y. Jets, AFC	2,646
	St. Louis, NFC	2,582
1978	New England, AFC	3,165
	Dallas, NFC	2,783
1977	Chicago, NFC	2,811
	Oakland, AFC	2,627
1976	Pittsburgh, AFC	2,971
	Los Angeles, NFC	2,528
1975	Buffalo, AFC	2,974
	Dallas, NFC	2,432
1974	Dallas, NFC	2,454
	Pittsburgh, AFC	2,417
1973	Buffalo, AFC	3,088
	Los Angeles, NFC	2,925
1972	Miami, AFC	2,960
	Chicago, NFC	2,360
1971	Miami, AFC	2,429
	Detroit, NFC	2,376
1970	Dallas, NFC	2,300
	Miami, AFC	2,082
1969	Dallas, NFL	2,276
	Kansas City, AFL	2,220
1968	Chicago, NFL	2,377
	Kansas City, AFL	2,227
1967	Cleveland, NFL	2,139
	Houston, AFL	2,122
1966	Kansas City, AFL	2,274
	Cleveland, NFL	2,166
1965	Cleveland, NFL	2,331
	San Diego, AFL	2,085
1964	Green Bay, NFL	2,276
	Buffalo, AFL	2,040
1963	Cleveland, NFL	2,639
	San Diego, AFL	2,203
1962	Buffalo, AFL	2,480
	Green Bay, NFL	2,460
1961	Green Bay, NFL	2,350
	Dall. Texans, AFL	2,189
1960	St. Louis, NFL	2,356
	Oakland, AFL	2,056
1959	Cleveland	2,149
1958	Cleveland	2,526
1957	Los Angeles	2,142
1956	Chi. Bears	2,468
1955	Chi. Bears	2,388
1954	San Francisco	2,498
1953	San Francisco	2,230
1952	San Francisco	1,905
1951	Chi. Bears	2,408
1950	N.Y. Giants	2,336
1949	Philadelphia	2,607
1948	Chi. Cardinals	2,560
1947	Los Angeles	2,171
1946	Green Bay	1,765
1945	Cleveland	1,714
1944	Philadelphia	1,661
1943	Phil-Pitt	1,730
1942	Chi. Bears	1,881
1941	Chi. Bears	2,263
1940	Chi. Bears	1,818
1939	Chi. Bears	2,043
1938	Detroit	1,893
1937	Detroit	2,074
1936	Detroit	2,885
1935	Chi. Bears	2,096
1934	Chi. Bears	2,847
1933	Boston	2,260
1932	Chi. Bears	1,770

Yards Passing

Leadership in this category has been based on net yards since 1952.

Year	Team	Yards
1988	Miami, AFC	4,516
	Washington, NFC	4,136
1987	Miami, AFC	3,876
	San Francisco, NFC	3,750
1986	Miami, AFC	4,779
	San Francisco, NFC	4,096
1985	San Diego, AFC	4,870
	Dallas, NFC	3,861
1984	Miami, AFC	5,018
	St. Louis, NFC	4,257
1983	San Diego, AFC	4,661
	Green Bay, NFC	4,365
1982	San Diego, AFC	2,927
	San Francisco, NFC	2,502
1981	San Diego, AFC	4,739
	Minnesota, NFC	4,333
1980	San Diego, AFC	4,531
	Minnesota, NFC	3,688
1979	San Diego, AFC	3,915
	San Francisco, NFC	3,641
1978	San Diego, AFC	3,375
	Minnesota, NFC	3,243
1977	Buffalo, AFC	2,530
	St. Louis, NFC	2,499
1976	Baltimore, AFC	2,933
	Minnesota, NFC	2,855
1975	Cincinnati, AFC	3,241
	Washington, NFC	2,917
1974	Washington, NFC	2,978
	Cincinnati, AFC	2,804
1973	Philadelphia, NFC	2,998
	Denver, AFC	2,519
1972	N.Y. Jets, AFC	2,777
	San Francisco, NFC	2,735
1971	San Diego, AFC	3,134
	Dallas, NFC	2,786
1970	San Francisco, NFC	2,923
	Oakland, AFC	2,865
1969	Oakland, AFL	3,271
	San Francisco, NFL	3,158
1968	San Diego, AFL	3,623
	Dallas, NFL	3,026
1967	N.Y. Jets, AFL	3,845
	Washington, NFL	3,730
1966	N.Y. Jets, AFL	3,464
	Dallas, NFL	3,023
1965	San Francisco, NFL	3,487
	San Diego, AFL	3,103
1964	Houston, AFL	3,527
	Chicago, NFL	2,841
1963	Baltimore, NFL	3,296
	Houston, AFL	3,222
1962	Denver, AFL	3,404
	Philadelphia, NFL	3,385
1961	Houston, AFL	4,392
	Philadelphia, NFL	3,605
1960	Houston, AFL	3,203
	Baltimore, NFL	2,956
1959	Baltimore	2,753
1958	Pittsburgh	2,752
1957	Baltimore	2,388
1956	Los Angeles	2,419
1955	Philadelphia	2,472
1954	Chi. Bears	3,104
1953	Philadelphia	3,089
1952	Cleveland	2,566
1951	Los Angeles	3,296
1950	Los Angeles	3,709
1949	Chi. Bears	3,055
1948	Washington	2,861
1947	Washington	3,336
1946	Los Angeles	2,080
1945	Chi. Bears	1,857
1944	Washington	2,021
1943	Chi. Bears	2,310
1942	Green Bay	2,407
1941	Chi. Bears	2,002
1940	Washington	1,887
1939	Chi. Bears	1,965
1938	Washington	1,536
1937	Green Bay	1,398
1936	Green Bay	1,629
1935	Green Bay	1,449
1934	Green Bay	1,165
1933	N.Y. Giants	1,348
1932	Chi. Bears	1,013

Fewest Points Allowed

Year	Team	Points
1988	Chicago, NFC	215
	Buffalo, AFC	237
1987	Indianapolis, AFC	238
	San Francisco, NFC	253
1986	Chicago, NFC	187
	Seattle, AFC	293
1985	Chicago, NFC	198
	N.Y. Jets, AFC	264
1984	San Francisco, NFC	227

	Denver, AFC	241
1983	Miami, AFC	250
	Detroit, NFC	286
1982	Washington, NFC	128
	Miami, AFC	131
1981	Philadelphia, NFC	221
	Miami, AFC	275
1980	Philadelphia, NFC	222
	Houston, AFC	251
1979	Tampa Bay, NFC	237
	San Diego, AFC	246
1978	Pittsburgh, AFC	195
	Dallas, NFC	208
1977	Atlanta, NFC	129
	Denver, AFC	148
1976	Pittsburgh, AFC	138
	Minnesota, NFC	176
1975	Los Angeles, NFC	135
	Pittsburgh, AFC	162
1974	Los Angeles, NFC	181
	Pittsburgh, AFC	189
1973	Miami, AFC	150
	Minnesota, NFC	168
1972	Miami, AFC	171
	Washington, NFC	218
1971	Minnesota, NFC	139
	Baltimore, AFC	140
1970	Minnesota, NFC	143
	Miami, AFC	228
1969	Minnesota, NFL	133
	Kansas City, AFL	177
1968	Baltimore, NFL	144
	Kansas City, AFL	170
1967	Los Angeles, NFL	196
	Houston, AFL	199
1966	Green Bay, NFL	163
	Buffalo, AFL	255
1965	Green Bay, NFL	224
	Buffalo, AFL	226
1964	Baltimore, NFL	225
	Buffalo, AFL	242
1963	Chicago, NFL	144
	San Diego, AFL	255
1962	Green Bay, NFL	148
	Dall. Texans, AFL	233
1961	San Diego, AFL	219
	N.Y. Giants, NFL	220
1960	San Francisco, NFL	205
	Dall. Texans, AFL	253
1959	N.Y. Giants	170
1958	N.Y. Giants	183
1957	Cleveland	172
1956	Cleveland	177
1955	Cleveland	218
1954	Cleveland	162
1953	Cleveland	162
1952	Detroit	192
1951	Cleveland	152
1950	Philadelphia	141
1949	Philadelphia	134
1948	Chi. Bears	151
1947	Green Bay	210
1946	Pittsburgh	117
1945	Washington	121
1944	N.Y. Giants	75
1943	Washington	137
1942	Chi. Bears	84
1941	N.Y. Giants	114
1940	Brooklyn	120
1939	N.Y. Giants	85
1938	N.Y. Giants	79
1937	Chi. Bears	100
1936	Chi. Bears	94
1935	Green Bay	96
	N.Y. Giants	96
1934	Detroit	59
1933	Brooklyn	54
1932	Chi. Bears	44

Fewest Total Yards Allowed

Year	Team	Yards
1988	Minnesota, NFC	4,091
	Buffalo, AFC	4,578
1987	San Francisco, NFC	4,095
	Cleveland, AFC	4,264
1986	Chicago, NFC	4,130
	L.A. Raiders, AFC	4,804
1985	Chicago, NFC	4,135
	L.A. Raiders, AFC	4,603
1984	Chicago, NFC	3,863
	Cleveland, AFC	4,641
1983	Cincinnati, AFC	4,327
	New Orleans, NFC	4,691
1982	Miami, AFC	2,312
	Tampa Bay, NFC	2,442
1981	Philadelphia, NFC	4,447
	N.Y. Jets, AFC	4,871
1980	Buffalo, AFC	4,101
	Philadelphia, NFC	4,443
1979	Tampa Bay, NFC	3,949
	Pittsburgh, AFC	4,270
1978	Los Angeles, NFC	3,893
	Pittsburgh, AFC	4,168
1977	Dallas, NFC	3,213
	New England, AFC	3,638
1976	Pittsburgh, AFC	3,323
	San Francisco, NFC	3,562
1975	Minnesota, NFC	3,153
	Oakland, AFC	3,629
1974	Pittsburgh, AFC	3,074
	Washington, NFC	3,285
1973	Los Angeles, NFC	2,951
	Oakland, AFC	3,160
1972	Miami, AFC	3,297
	Green Bay, NFC	3,474
1971	Baltimore, AFC	2,852
	Minnesota, NFC	3,406
1970	Minnesota, NFC	2,803
	N.Y. Jets, AFC	3,655
1969	Minnesota, NFL	2,720
	Kansas City, AFL	3,163
1968	Los Angeles, NFL	3,118
	N.Y. Jets, AFL	3,363
1967	Oakland, AFL	3,294
	Green Bay, NFL	3,300
1966	St. Louis, NFL	3,492
	Oakland, AFL	3,910
1965	San Diego, AFL	3,262
	Detroit, NFL	3,557
1964	Green Bay, NFL	3,179
	Buffalo, AFL	3,878
1963	Chicago, NFL	3,176
	Boston, AFL	3,834
1962	Detroit, NFL	3,217
	Dall. Texans, AFL	3,951
1961	San Diego, AFL	3,726
	Baltimore, NFL	3,782
1960	St. Louis, NFL	3,029
	Buffalo, AFL	3,866
1959	N.Y. Giants	2,843
1958	Chi. Bears	3,066
1957	Pittsburgh	2,791
1956	N.Y. Giants	3,081
1955	Cleveland	2,841
1954	Cleveland	2,658
1953	Philadelphia	2,998
1952	Cleveland	3,075
1951	N.Y. Giants	3,250
1950	Cleveland	3,154
1949	Philadelphia	2,831
1948	Chi. Bears	2,931
1947	Green Bay	3,396
1946	Washington	2,451
1945	Philadelphia	2,073
1944	Philadelphia	1,943
1943	Chi. Bears	2,262
1942	Chi. Bears	1,703
1941	N.Y. Giants	2,368
1940	N.Y. Giants	2,219
1939	Washington	2,116
1938	N.Y. Giants	2,029
1937	Washington	2,123
1936	Boston	2,181
1935	Boston	1,996
1934	Chi. Cardinals	1,539
1933	Brooklyn	1,789

Fewest Yards Rushing Allowed

Year	Team	Yards
1988	Chicago, NFC	1,326
	Houston, AFC	1,592
1987	Chicago, NFC	1,413
	Cleveland, AFC	1,433
1986	N.Y. Giants, NFC	1,284
	Denver, AFC	1,651
1985	Chicago, NFC	1,319
	N.Y. Jets, AFC	1,516
1984	Chicago, NFC	1,377
	Pittsburgh, AFC	1,617
1983	Washington, NFC	1,289
	Cincinnati, AFC	1,499
1982	Pittsburgh, AFC	762
	Detroit, NFC	854
1981	Detroit, NFC	1,623
	Kansas City, AFC	1,747
1980	Detroit, NFC	1,599
	Cincinnati, AFC	1,680
1979	Denver, AFC	1,693
	Tampa Bay, NFC	1,873
1978	Dallas, NFC	1,721
	Pittsburgh, AFC	1,774
1977	Denver, AFC	1,531
	Dallas, NFC	1,651
1976	Pittsburgh, AFC	1,457
	Los Angeles, NFC	1,564
1975	Minnesota, NFC	1,532
	Houston, AFC	1,680
1974	Los Angeles, NFC	1,302
	New England, AFC	1,587
1973	Los Angeles, NFC	1,270
	Oakland, AFC	1,470
1972	Dallas, NFC	1,515
	Miami, AFC	1,548
1971	Baltimore, AFC	1,113
	Dallas, NFC	1,144
1970	Detroit, NFC	1,152
	N.Y. Jets, AFC	1,283
1969	Dallas, NFL	1,050
	Kansas City, AFL	1,091
1968	Dallas, NFL	1,195
	N.Y. Jets, AFL	1,195
1967	Dallas, NFL	1,081
	Oakland, AFL	1,129
1966	Buffalo, AFL	1,051
	Dallas, NFL	1,176
1965	San Diego, AFL	1,094
	Los Angeles, NFL	1,409
1964	Buffalo, AFL	913
	Los Angeles, NFL	1,501
1963	Boston, AFL	1,107
	Chicago, NFL	1,442
1962	Detroit, NFL	1,231
	Dall. Texans, AFL	1,250
1961	Boston, AFL	1,041
	Pittsburgh, NFL	1,463
1960	St. Louis, NFL	1,212
	Dall. Texans, AFL	1,338
1959	N.Y. Giants	1,261
1958	Baltimore	1,291
1957	Baltimore	1,174
1956	N.Y. Giants	1,443
1955	Cleveland	1,189
1954	Cleveland	1,050
1953	Philadelphia	1,117
1952	Detroit	1,145
1951	N.Y. Giants	913
1950	Detroit	1,367
1949	Chi. Bears	1,196
1948	Philadelphia	1,209
1947	Philadelphia	1,329
1946	Chi. Bears	1,060
1945	Philadelphia	817
1944	Philadelphia	558
1943	Phil-Pitt	793
1942	Chi. Bears	519
1941	Washington	1,042
1940	N.Y. Giants	977
1939	Chi. Bears	812
1938	Detroit	1,081
1937	Chi. Bears	933
1936	Boston	1,148
1935	Boston	998
1934	Chi. Cardinals	954
1933	Brooklyn	964

Fewest Yards Passing Allowed

Leadership in this category has been based on net yards since 1952.

Year	Team	Yards
1988	Kansas City, AFC	2,434
	Minnesota, NFC	2,489
1987	San Francisco, NFC	2,484
	L.A. Raiders, AFC	2,727
1986	St. Louis, NFC	2,637
	New England, AFC	2,978
1985	Washington, NFC	2,746
	Pittsburgh, AFC	2,783
1984	New Orleans, NFC	2,453
	Cleveland, AFC	2,696
1983	New Orleans, NFC	2,691
	Cincinnati, AFC	2,828
1982	Miami, AFC	1,027
	Tampa Bay, NFC	1,384
1981	Philadelphia, NFC	2,696
	Buffalo, AFC	2,870
1980	Washington, NFC	2,171
	Buffalo, AFC	2,282
1979	Tampa Bay, NFC	2,076
	Buffalo, AFC	2,530
1978	Buffalo, AFC	1,960
	Los Angeles, NFC	2,048
1977	Atlanta, NFC	1,384
	San Diego, AFC	1,725
1976	Minnesota, NFC	1,575
	Cincinnati, AFC	1,758
1975	Minnesota, NFC	1,621
	Cincinnati, AFC	1,729
1974	Pittsburgh, AFC	1,466
	Atlanta, NFC	1,572
1973	Miami, AFC	1,290
	Atlanta, NFC	1,430
1972	Minnesota, NFC	1,699
	Cleveland, AFC	1,736
1971	Atlanta, NFC	1,638
	Baltimore, AFC	1,739
1970	Minnesota, NFC	1,438
	Kansas City, AFC	2,010
1969	Minnesota, NFL	1,631
	Kansas City, AFL	2,072
1968	Houston, AFL	1,671
	Green Bay, NFL	1,796
1967	Green Bay, NFL	1,377
	Buffalo, AFL	1,825
1966	Green Bay, NFL	1,959
	Oakland, AFL	2,118
1965	Green Bay, NFL	1,981
	San Diego, AFL	2,168
1964	Green Bay, NFL	1,647
	San Diego, AFL	2,518
1963	Chicago, NFL	1,734
	Oakland, AFL	2,589
1962	Green Bay, NFL	1,746
	Oakland, AFL	2,306
1961	Baltimore, NFL	1,913
	San Diego, AFL	2,363
1960	Chicago, NFL	1,388
	Buffalo, AFL	2,124
1959	N.Y. Giants	1,582
1958	Chi. Bears	1,769
1957	Cleveland	1,300
1956	Cleveland	1,103
1955	Pittsburgh	1,295
1954	Cleveland	1,608
1953	Washington	1,751
1952	Washington	1,580
1951	Pittsburgh	1,687
1950	Cleveland	1,581
1949	Philadelphia	1,607
1948	Green Bay	1,626
1947	Green Bay	1,790
1946	Pittsburgh	939
1945	Washington	1,121
1944	Chi. Bears	1,052
1943	Chi. Bears	980
1942	Washington	1,093
1941	Pittsburgh	1,168
1940	Philadelphia	1,012
1939	Washington	1,116
1938	Chi. Bears	897
1937	Detroit	804
1936	Philadelphia	853
1935	Chi. Cardinals	793
1934	Philadelphia	545
1933	Portsmouth	558

SUPER BOWL RECORDS

Compiled by Elias Sports Bureau

1967: Super Bowl I	1975: Super Bowl IX	1983: Super Bowl XVII
1968: Super Bowl II	1976: Super Bowl X	1984: Super Bowl XVIII
1969: Super Bowl III	1977: Super Bowl XI	1985: Super Bowl XIX
1970: Super Bowl IV	1978: Super Bowl XII	1986: Super Bowl XX
1971: Super Bowl V	1979: Super Bowl XIII	1987: Super Bowl XXI
1972: Super Bowl VI	1980: Super Bowl XIV	1988: Super Bowl XXII
1973: Super Bowl VII	1981: Super Bowl XV	1989: Super Bowl XXIII
1974: Super Bowl VIII	1982: Super Bowl XVI	

Individual Records

Service

Most Games

5 Marv Fleming, Green Bay, 1967-68; Miami, 1972-74
Larry Cole, Dallas, 1971-72, 1976, 1978-79
Cliff Harris, Dallas, 1971-72, 1976, 1978-79
D. D. Lewis, Dallas, 1971-72, 1976, 1978-79
Preston Pearson, Baltimore, 1969; Pittsburgh, 1975; Dallas, 1976, 1978-79
Charlie Waters, Dallas, 1971-72, 1976, 1978-79
Rayfield Wright, Dallas, 1971-72, 1976, 1978-79
4 By many players

Most Games, Winning Team

4 By many players

Most Games, Coach

6 Don Shula, Baltimore, 1969; Miami, 1972-74, 1983, 1985
5 Tom Landry, Dallas, 1971-72, 1976, 1978-79
4 Bud Grant, Minnesota, 1970, 1974-75, 1977
Chuck Noll, Pittsburgh, 1975-76, 1979-80

Most Games, Winning Team, Coach

4 Chuck Noll, Pittsburgh, 1975-76, 1979-80
3 Bill Walsh, San Francisco, 1982, 1985, 1989
2 Vince Lombardi, Green Bay, 1967-68
Tom Landry, Dallas, 1972, 1978
Don Shula, Miami, 1973-74
Tom Flores, Oakland, 1981; L.A. Raiders, 1984
Joe Gibbs, Washington, 1983, 1988

Most Games, Losing Team, Coach

4 Bud Grant, Minnesota, 1970, 1974-75, 1977
Don Shula, Baltimore, 1969; Miami, 1972, 1983, 1985
3 Tom Landry, Dallas, 1971, 1976, 1979
2 Dan Reeves, Denver, 1987-88

Scoring

Points

Most Points, Career

24 Franco Harris, Pittsburgh, 4 games (4-td)
22 Ray Wersching, San Francisco, 2 games (7-pat, 5-fg)
20 Don Chandler, Green Bay, 2 games (8-pat, 4-fg)

Most Points, Game

18 Roger Craig, San Francisco vs. Miami, 1985 (3-td)
15 Don Chandler, Green Bay vs. Oakland, 1968 (3-pat, 4-fg)
14 Ray Wersching, San Francisco vs. Cincinnati, 1982 (2-pat, 4-fg)
Kevin Butler, Chicago vs. New England, 1986 (5-pat, 3-fg)

Touchdowns

Most Touchdowns, Career

4 Franco Harris, Pittsburgh, 4 games (4-r)
3 John Stallworth, Pittsburgh, 4 games (3-p)
Lynn Swann, Pittsburgh, 4 games (3-p)
Cliff Branch, Oakland-L.A. Raiders, 3 games (3-p)
Roger Craig, San Francisco, 2 games (1-r, 2-p)
2 By many players

Most Touchdowns, Game

3 Roger Craig, San Francisco vs. Miami, 1985 (1-r, 2-p)
2 Max McGee, Green Bay vs. Kansas City, 1967 (2-p)
Elijah Pitts, Green Bay vs. Kansas City, 1967 (2-r)
Bill Miller, Oakland vs. Green Bay, 1968 (2-p)
Larry Csonka, Miami vs. Minnesota, 1974 (2-r)
Pete Banaszak, Oakland vs. Minnesota, 1977 (2-r)
John Stallworth, Pittsburgh vs. Dallas, 1979 (2-p)
Franco Harris, Pittsburgh vs. Los Angeles, 1980 (2-r)
Cliff Branch, Oakland vs. Philadelphia, 1981 (2-p)
Dan Ross, Cincinnati vs. San Francisco, 1982 (2-p)
Marcus Allen, L.A. Raiders vs. Washington, 1984 (2-r)
Jim McMahon, Chicago vs. New England, 1986 (2-r)
Ricky Sanders, Washington vs. Denver, 1988 (2-p)
Timmy Smith, Washington vs. Denver, 1988 (2-r)

Points After Touchdown

Most Points After Touchdown, Career

8 Don Chandler, Green Bay, 2 games (8 att)
Roy Gerela, Pittsburgh, 3 games (9 att)
Chris Bahr, Oakland-L.A. Raiders, 2 games (8 att)
7 Ray Wersching, San Francisco, 2 games (7 att)
6 Ali Haji-Sheikh, Washington, 1 game (6 att)

Most Points After Touchdown, Game

6 Ali Haji-Sheikh, Washington vs. Denver, 1988 (6 att)
5 Don Chandler, Green Bay vs. Kansas City, 1967 (5 att)
Roy Gerela, Pittsburgh vs. Dallas, 1979 (5 att)
Chris Bahr, L.A. Raiders vs. Washington, 1984 (5 att)
Ray Wersching, San Francisco vs. Miami, 1985 (5 att)
Kevin Butler, Chicago vs. New England, 1986 (5 att)
4 Rafael Septien, Dallas vs. Pittsburgh, 1979 (4 att)
Matt Bahr, Pittsburgh vs. Los Angeles, 1980 (4 att)
Raul Allegre, N.Y. Giants vs. Denver, 1987 (5 att)

Field Goals

Field Goals Attempted, Career

7 Roy Gerela, Pittsburgh, 3 games
6 Jim Turner, N.Y. Jets-Denver, 2 games
Rich Karlis, Denver, 2 games
5 Efren Herrera, Dallas, 1 game
Ray Wersching, San Francisco, 2 games

Most Field Goals Attempted, Game

5 Jim Turner, N.Y. Jets vs. Baltimore, 1969
Efren Herrera, Dallas vs. Denver, 1978
4 Don Chandler, Green Bay vs. Oakland, 1968
Roy Gerela, Pittsburgh vs. Dallas, 1976
Ray Wersching, San Francisco vs. Cincinnati, 1982
Rich Karlis, Denver vs. N.Y. Giants, 1987
Mike Cofer, San Francisco vs. Cincinnati, 1989

Most Field Goals, Career

5 Ray Wersching, San Francisco, 2 games (5 att)
4 Don Chandler, Green Bay, 2 games (4 att)
Jim Turner, N.Y. Jets-Denver, 2 games (6 att)
Uwe von Schamann, Miami, 2 games (4 att)
3 Mike Clark, Dallas, 2 games (3 att)
Jan Stenerud, Kansas City, 1 game (3 att)
Chris Bahr, Oakland-L.A. Raiders, 2 games (4 att)
Mark Moseley, Washington, 2 games (4 att)
Kevin Butler, Chicago, 1 game (3 att)
Rich Karlis, Denver, 2 games (6 att)
Jim Breech, Cincinnati, 2 games (3 att)

Most Field Goals, Game

4 Don Chandler, Green Bay vs. Oakland, 1968
Ray Wersching, San Francisco vs. Cincinnati, 1982
3 Jim Turner, N.Y. Jets vs. Baltimore, 1969
Jan Stenerud, Kansas City vs. Minnesota, 1970
Uwe von Schamann, Miami vs. San Francisco, 1985
Kevin Butler, Chicago vs. New England, 1986
Jim Breech, Cincinnati vs. San Francisco, 1989

Longest Field Goal

48 Jan Stenerud, Kansas City vs. Minnesota, 1970
Rich Karlis, Denver vs. N.Y. Giants, 1987
47 Jim Turner, Denver vs. Dallas, 1978
46 Chris Bahr, Oakland vs. Philadelphia, 1981

Safeties

Most Safeties, Game

1 Dwight White, Pittsburgh vs. Minnesota, 1975
Reggie Harrison, Pittsburgh vs. Dallas, 1976
Henry Waechter, Chicago vs. New England, 1986
George Martin, N.Y. Giants vs. Denver, 1987

Rushing

Attempts

Most Attempts, Career

101 Franco Harris, Pittsburgh, 4 games
64 John Riggins, Washington, 2 games
57 Larry Csonka, Miami, 3 games

Most Attempts, Game

38 John Riggins, Washington vs. Miami, 1983
34 Franco Harris, Pittsburgh vs. Minnesota, 1975
33 Larry Csonka, Miami vs. Minnesota, 1974

Yards Gained

Most Yards Gained, Career

354 Franco Harris, Pittsburgh, 4 games
297 Larry Csonka, Miami, 3 games
230 John Riggins, Washington, 2 games

Most Yards Gained, Game

204 Timmy Smith, Washington vs. Denver, 1988
191 Marcus Allen, L.A. Raiders vs. Washington, 1984
166 John Riggins, Washington vs. Miami, 1983

Longest Run From Scrimmage

74 Marcus Allen, L.A. Raiders vs. Washington, 1984 (TD)
58 Tom Matte, Baltimore vs. N.Y. Jets, 1969
Timmy Smith, Washington vs. Denver, 1988 (TD)
49 Larry Csonka, Miami vs. Washington, 1973

Average Gain

Highest Average Gain, Career (20 attempts)

9.6 Marcus Allen, L.A. Raiders, 1 game (20-191)
9.3 Timmy Smith, Washington, 1 game (22-204)
5.3 Walt Garrison, Dallas, 2 games (26-139)

Highest Average Gain, Game (10 attempts)

10.5 Tom Matte, Baltimore vs. N.Y. Jets, 1969 (11-116)
9.6 Marcus Allen, L.A. Raiders vs. Washington, 1984 (20-191)
9.3 Timmy Smith, Washington vs. Denver, 1988 (22-204)

Touchdowns

Most Touchdowns, Career

4 Franco Harris, Pittsburgh, 4 games
2 Elijah Pitts, Green Bay, 1 game
Jim Kiick, Miami, 3 games
Larry Csonka, Miami, 3 games
Pete Banaszak, Oakland, 2 games
Marcus Allen, L.A. Raiders, 1 game
John Riggins, Washington, 2 games
Jim McMahon, Chicago, 1 game
Timmy Smith, Washington, 1 game

Most Touchdowns, Game

2 Elijah Pitts, Green Bay vs. Kansas City, 1967
Larry Csonka, Miami vs. Minnesota, 1974

Pete Banaszak, Oakland vs. Minnesota, 1977
Franco Harris, Pittsburgh vs. Los Angeles, 1980
Marcus Allen, L.A. Raiders vs. Washington, 1984
Jim McMahon, Chicago vs. New England, 1986
Timmy Smith, Washington vs. Denver, 1988

Passing

Attempts

Most Passes Attempted, Career
98 Roger Staubach, Dallas, 4 games
93 Joe Montana, San Francisco, 3 games
89 Fran Tarkenton, Minnesota, 3 games

Most Passes Attempted, Game
50 Dan Marino, Miami vs. San Francisco, 1985
38 Ron Jaworski, Philadelphia vs. Oakland, 1981
John Elway, Denver vs. Washington, 1988
37 John Elway, Denver vs. N.Y. Giants, 1987

Completions

Most Passes Completed, Career
61 Roger Staubach, Dallas, 4 games
Joe Montana, San Francisco, 3 games
49 Terry Bradshaw, Pittsburgh, 4 games
46 Fran Tarkenton, Minnesota, 3 games

Most Passes Completed, Game
29 Dan Marino, Miami vs. San Francisco, 1985
25 Ken Anderson, Cincinnati vs. San Francisco, 1982
24 Joe Montana, San Francisco vs. Miami, 1985

Most Consecutive Completions, Game
10 Phil Simms, N.Y. Giants vs. Denver, 1987
8 Len Dawson, Kansas City vs. Green Bay, 1967
Joe Theismann, Washington vs. Miami, 1983

Completion Percentage

Highest Completion Percentage, Career (40 attempts)
65.6 Joe Montana, San Francisco, 3 games (93-61)
63.6 Len Dawson, Kansas City, 2 games (44-28)
63.4 Bob Griese, Miami, 3 games (41-26)

Highest Completion Percentage, Game (20 attempts)
88.0 Phil Simms, N.Y. Giants vs. Denver, 1987 (25-22)
73.5 Ken Anderson, Cincinnati vs. San Francisco, 1982 (34-25)
69.6 Bart Starr, Green Bay vs. Kansas City, 1967 (23-16)

Yards Gained

Most Yards Gained, Career
932 Terry Bradshaw, Pittsburgh, 4 games
845 Joe Montana, San Francisco, 3 games
734 Roger Staubach, Dallas, 4 games

Most Yards Gained, Game
357 Joe Montana, San Francisco vs. Cincinnati, 1989
340 Doug Williams, Washington vs. Denver, 1988
331 Joe Montana, San Francisco vs. Miami, 1985

Longest Pass Completion
80 Jim Plunkett (to King), Oakland vs. Philadelphia, 1981 (TD)
Doug Williams (to Sanders), Washington vs. Denver, 1988 (TD)
76 David Woodley (to Cefalo), Miami vs. Washington, 1983 (TD)
75 Johnny Unitas (to Mackey), Baltimore vs. Dallas, 1971 (TD)
Terry Bradshaw (to Stallworth), Pittsburgh vs. Dallas, 1979 (TD)

Average Gain

Highest Average Gain, Career (40 attempts)
11.10 Terry Bradshaw, Pittsburgh, 4 games (84-932)
9.62 Bart Starr, Green Bay, 2 games (47-452)
9.41 Jim Plunkett, Oakland-L.A. Raiders, 2 games (46-433)

Highest Average Gain, Game (20 attempts)
14.71 Terry Bradshaw, Pittsburgh vs. Los Angeles, 1980 (21-309)
12.80 Jim McMahon, Chicago vs. New England, 1986 (20-256)
12.43 Jim Plunkett, Oakland vs. Philadelphia, 1981 (21-261)

Touchdowns

Most Touchdown Passes, Career
9 Terry Bradshaw, Pittsburgh, 4 games
8 Roger Staubach, Dallas, 4 games
6 Joe Montana, San Francisco, 3 games

Most Touchdown Passes, Game
4 Terry Bradshaw, Pittsburgh vs. Dallas, 1979
Doug Williams, Washington vs. Denver, 1988
3 Roger Staubach, Dallas vs. Pittsburgh, 1979
Jim Plunkett, Oakland vs. Philadelphia, 1981
Joe Montana, San Francisco vs. Miami, 1985
Phil Simms, N.Y. Giants vs. Denver, 1987
2 By many players

Had Intercepted

Lowest Percentage, Passes Had Intercepted, Career (40 attempts)
0.00 Jim Plunkett, Oakland-L.A. Raiders, 2 games (46-0)
Joe Montana, San Francisco, 3 games (93-0)
2.13 Bart Starr, Green Bay, 2 games (47-1)
4.08 Roger Staubach, Dallas, 4 games (98-4)

Most Attempts, Without Interception, Game
36 Joe Montana, San Francisco vs. Cincinnati, 1989
35 Joe Montana, San Francisco vs. Miami, 1985
28 Joe Namath, N.Y. Jets vs. Baltimore, 1969

Most Passes Had Intercepted, Career
7 Craig Morton, Dallas-Denver, 2 games
6 Fran Tarkenton, Minnesota, 3 games
4 Earl Morrall, Baltimore-Miami, 4 games
Roger Staubach, Dallas, 4 games
Terry Bradshaw, Pittsburgh, 4 games
Joe Theismann, Washington, 2 games
John Elway, Denver, 2 games

Most Passes Had Intercepted, Game
4 Craig Morton, Denver vs. Dallas, 1978
3 By eight players

Pass Receiving

Receptions

Most Receptions, Career
16 Lynn Swann, Pittsburgh, 4 games
15 Chuck Foreman, Minnesota, 3 games
Roger Craig, San Francisco, 2 games
14 Cliff Branch, Oakland-L.A. Raiders, 3 games

Most Receptions, Game
11 Dan Ross, Cincinnati vs. San Francisco, 1982
Jerry Rice, San Francisco vs. Cincinnati, 1989
10 Tony Nathan, Miami vs. San Francisco, 1985
9 Ricky Sanders, Washington vs. Denver, 1988

Yards Gained

Most Yards Gained, Career
364 Lynn Swann, Pittsburgh, 4 games
268 John Stallworth, Pittsburgh, 4 games
215 Jerry Rice, San Francisco, 1 game

Most Yards Gained, Game
215 Jerry Rice, San Francisco vs. Cincinnati, 1989
193 Ricky Sanders, Washington vs. Denver, 1988
161 Lynn Swann, Pittsburgh vs. Dallas, 1976

Longest Reception
80 Kenny King (from Plunkett), Oakland vs. Philadelphia, 1981 (TD)
Ricky Sanders (from Williams), Washington vs. Denver, 1988 (TD)
76 Jimmy Cefalo (from Woodley), Miami vs. Washington, 1983 (TD)
75 John Mackey (from Unitas), Baltimore vs. Dallas, 1971 (TD)
John Stallworth (from Bradshaw), Pittsburgh vs. Dallas, 1979 (TD)

Average Gain

Highest Average Gain, Career (8 receptions)
24.4 John Stallworth, Pittsburgh, 4 games (11-268)
22.8 Lynn Swann, Pittsburgh, 4 games (16-364)
21.4 Ricky Sanders, Washington, 1 game (9-193)

Highest Average Gain, Game (3 receptions)
40.33 John Stallworth, Pittsburgh vs. Los Angeles, 1980 (3-121)
40.25 Lynn Swann, Pittsburgh vs. Dallas, 1979 (4-161)
38.33 John Stallworth, Pittsburgh vs. Dallas, 1979 (3-115)

Touchdowns

Most Touchdowns, Career
3 John Stallworth, Pittsburgh, 4 games
Lynn Swann, Pittsburgh, 4 games
Cliff Branch, Oakland-L.A. Raiders, 3 games
2 Max McGee, Green Bay, 2 games
Bill Miller, Oakland, 1 game
Butch Johnson, Dallas, 2 games
Dan Ross, Cincinnati, 1 game
Roger Craig, San Francisco, 2 games
Ricky Sanders, Washington, 1 game

Most Touchdowns, Game
2 Max McGee, Green Bay vs. Kansas City, 1967
Bill Miller, Oakland vs. Green Bay, 1968
John Stallworth, Pittsburgh vs. Dallas, 1979
Cliff Branch, Oakland vs. Philadelphia, 1981
Dan Ross, Cincinnati vs. San Francisco, 1982
Roger Craig, San Francisco vs. Miami, 1985
Ricky Sanders, Washington vs. Denver, 1988

Interceptions By

Most Interceptions By, Career
3 Chuck Howley, Dallas, 2 games
Rod Martin, Oakland-L.A. Raiders, 2 games
2 Randy Beverly, N.Y. Jets, 1 game
Jake Scott, Miami, 3 games
Mike Wagner, Pittsburgh, 3 games
Mel Blount, Pittsburgh, 4 games
Eric Wright, San Francisco, 3 games
Barry Wilburn, Washington, 1 game

Most Interceptions By, Game
3 Rod Martin, Oakland vs. Philadelphia, 1981
2 Randy Beverly, N.Y. Jets vs. Baltimore, 1969
Chuck Howley, Dallas vs. Baltimore, 1971
Jake Scott, Miami vs. Washington, 1973
Barry Wilburn, Washington vs. Denver, 1988

Yards Gained

Most Yards Gained, Career
75 Willie Brown, Oakland, 2 games
63 Chuck Howley, Dallas, 2 games
Jake Scott, Miami, 3 games
60 Herb Adderley, Green Bay-Dallas, 4 games

Most Yards Gained, Game
75 Willie Brown, Oakland vs. Minnesota, 1977
63 Jake Scott, Miami vs. Washington, 1973
60 Herb Adderley, Green Bay vs. Oakland, 1968

Longest Return
75 Willie Brown, Oakland vs. Minnesota, 1977 (TD)
60 Herb Adderley, Green Bay vs. Oakland, 1968 (TD)
55 Jake Scott, Miami vs. Washington, 1973

Touchdowns

Most Touchdowns, Game
1 Herb Adderley, Green Bay vs. Oakland, 1968
Willie Brown, Oakland vs. Minnesota, 1977
Jack Squirek, L.A. Raiders vs. Washington, 1984
Reggie Phillips, Chicago vs. New England, 1986

Punting

Most Punts, Career

17 Mike Eischeid, Oakland-Minnesota, 3 games
15 Larry Seiple, Miami, 3 games
14 Ron Widby, Dallas, 2 games
Ray Guy, Oakland-L.A. Raiders, 3 games

Most Punts, Game

9 Ron Widby, Dallas vs. Baltimore, 1971
7 By eight players

Longest Punt

63 Lee Johnson, Cincinnati vs. San Francisco, 1989
62 Rich Camarillo, New England vs. Chicago, 1986
61 Jerrel Wilson, Kansas City vs. Green Bay, 1967

Average Yardage

Highest Average, Punting, Career (10 punts)

46.5 Jerrel Wilson, Kansas City, 2 games (11-511)
41.9 Ray Guy, Oakland-L.A. Raiders, 3 games (14-587)
41.3 Larry Seiple, Miami, 3 games (15-620)

Highest Average, Punting, Game (4 punts)

48.5 Jerrel Wilson, Kansas City vs. Minnesota, 1970 (4-194)
46.3 Jim Miller, San Francisco vs. Cincinnati, 1982 (4-185)
45.3 Jerrel Wilson, Kansas City vs. Green Bay, 1967 (7-317)

Punt Returns

Most Punt Returns, Career

6 Willie Wood, Green Bay, 2 games
Jake Scott, Miami, 3 games
Theo Bell, Pittsburgh, 2 games
Mike Nelms, Washington, 1 game
5 Dana McLemore, San Francisco, 1 game
4 By seven players

Most Punt Returns, Game

6 Mike Nelms, Washington vs. Miami, 1983
5 Willie Wood, Green Bay vs. Oakland, 1968
Dana McLemore, San Francisco vs. Miami, 1985
4 By six players

Most Fair Catches, Game

3 Ron Gardin, Baltimore vs. Dallas, 1971
Golden Richards, Dallas vs. Pittsburgh, 1976
Greg Pruitt, L.A. Raiders vs. Washington, 1984

Yards Gained

Most Yards Gained, Career

56 John Taylor, San Francisco, 1 game
52 Mike Nelms, Washington, 1 game
51 Dana McLemore, San Francisco, 1 game

Most Yards Gained, Game

56 John Taylor, San Francisco vs. Cincinnati, 1989
52 Mike Nelms, Washington vs. Miami, 1983
51 Dana McLemore, San Francisco vs. Miami, 1985

Longest Return

45 John Taylor, San Francisco vs. Cincinnati, 1989
34 Darrell Green, Washington vs. L.A. Raiders, 1984
31 Willie Wood, Green Bay vs. Oakland, 1968

Average Yardage

Highest Average, Career (4 returns)

10.8 Neal Colzie, Oakland, 1 game (4-43)
10.2 Dana McLemore, San Francisco, 1 game (5-51)
8.8 Mike Fuller, Cincinnati, 1 game (4-35)

Highest Average, Game (3 returns)

18.7 John Taylor, San Francisco vs. Cincinnati, 1989 (3-56)
11.3 Lynn Swann, Pittsburgh vs. Minnesota, 1975 (3-34)
10.8 Neal Colzie, Oakland vs. Minnesota, 1977 (4-43)

Touchdowns

Most Touchdowns, Game

None

Kickoff Returns

Most Kickoff Returns, Career

8 Larry Anderson, Pittsburgh, 2 games
Fulton Walker, Miami, 2 games
Ken Bell, Denver, 2 games
7 Preston Pearson, Baltimore-Pittsburgh-Dallas, 5 games
Stephen Starring, New England, 1 game
6 Eugene (Mercury) Morris, Miami, 3 games

Most Kickoff Returns, Game

7 Stephen Starring, New England vs. Chicago, 1986
5 Larry Anderson, Pittsburgh vs. Los Angeles, 1980
Billy Campfield, Philadelphia vs. Oakland, 1981
David Verser, Cincinnati vs. San Francisco, 1982
Alvin Garrett, Washington vs. L.A. Raiders, 1984
Ken Bell, Denver vs. Washington, 1988

Yards Gained

Most Yards Gained, Career

283 Fulton Walker, Miami, 2 games
207 Larry Anderson, Pittsburgh, 2 games
153 Stephen Starring, New England, 1 game

Most Yards Gained, Game

190 Fulton Walker, Miami vs. Washington, 1983
162 Larry Anderson, Pittsburgh vs. Los Angeles, 1980
153 Stephen Starring, New England vs. Chicago, 1986

Longest Return

98 Fulton Walker, Miami vs. Washington, 1983 (TD)
93 Stanford Jennings, Cincinnati vs. San Francisco, 1989 (TD)
67 Rick Upchurch, Denver vs. Dallas, 1978

Average Yardage

Highest Average, Career (4 returns)

35.4 Fulton Walker, Miami, 2 games (8-283)
25.9 Larry Anderson, Pittsburgh, 2 games (8-207)
22.5 Jim Duncan, Baltimore, 1 game (4-90)

Highest Average, Game (3 returns)

47.5 Fulton Walker, Miami vs. Washington, 1983 (4-190)
32.4 Larry Anderson, Pittsburgh vs. Los Angeles, 1980 (5-162)
31.3 Rick Upchurch, Denver vs. Dallas, 1978 (3-94)

Touchdowns

Most Touchdowns, Game

1 Fulton Walker, Miami vs. Washington, 1983
Stanford Jennings, Cincinnati vs. San Francisco, 1989

Fumbles

Most Fumbles, Career

5 Roger Staubach, Dallas, 4 games
3 Franco Harris, Pittsburgh, 4 games
Terry Bradshaw, Pittsburgh, 4 games
2 By six players

Most Fumbles, Game

3 Roger Staubach, Dallas vs. Pittsburgh, 1976
2 Franco Harris, Pittsburgh vs. Minnesota, 1975
Butch Johnson, Dallas vs. Denver, 1978
Terry Bradshaw, Pittsburgh vs. Dallas, 1979
Joe Montana, San Francisco vs. Cincinnati, 1989

Recoveries

Most Fumbles Recovered, Career

2 Jake Scott, Miami, 3 games (1 own, 1 opp)
Fran Tarkenton, Minnesota, 3 games (2 own)
Franco Harris, Pittsburgh, 4 games (2 own)
Roger Staubach, Dallas, 4 games (2 own)
Bobby Walden, Pittsburgh, 2 games (2 own)
John Fitzgerald, Dallas, 4 games (2 own)
Randy Hughes, Dallas, 3 games (2 opp)
Butch Johnson, Dallas, 2 games (2 own)
Mike Singletary, Chicago, 1 game (2 opp)

Most Fumbles Recovered, Game

2 Jake Scott, Miami vs. Minnesota, 1974 (1 own, 1 opp)
Roger Staubach, Dallas vs. Pittsburgh, 1976 (2 own)
Randy Hughes, Dallas vs. Denver, 1978 (2 opp)
Butch Johnson, Dallas vs. Denver, 1978 (2 own)
Mike Singletary, Chicago vs. New England, 1986 (2 opp)

Yards Gained

Most Yards Gained, Game

49 Mike Bass, Washington vs. Miami, 1973 (opp)
37 Mike Hegman, Dallas vs. Pittsburgh, 1979 (opp)
21 Randy Hughes, Dallas vs. Denver, 1978 (opp)

Longest Return

49 Mike Bass, Washington vs. Miami, 1973 (TD)
37 Mike Hegman, Dallas vs. Pittsburgh, 1979 (TD)
19 Randy Hughes, Dallas vs. Denver, 1978

Touchdowns

Most Touchdowns, Game

1 Mike Bass, Washington vs. Miami, 1973 (opp 49 yds)
Mike Hegman, Dallas vs. Pittsburgh, 1979 (opp 37 yds)

Combined Net Yards Gained

Attempts

Most Attempts, Career

108 Franco Harris, Pittsburgh, 4 games
66 John Riggins, Washington, 2 games
60 Larry Csonka, Miami, 3 games

Most Attempts, Game

39 John Riggins, Washington vs. Miami, 1983
35 Franco Harris, Pittsburgh vs. Minnesota, 1975
34 Matt Snell, N.Y. Jets vs. Baltimore, 1969

Yards Gained

Most Yards Gained, Career

468 Franco Harris, Pittsburgh, 4 games
391 Lynn Swann, Pittsburgh, 4 games
314 Larry Csonka, Miami, 3 games

Most Yards Gained, Game

239 Ricky Sanders, Washington vs. Denver, 1988
220 Jerry Rice, San Francisco vs. Cincinnati, 1989
213 Timmy Smith, Washington vs. Denver, 1988

Sacks

Sacks have been compiled since 1983.

Most Sacks, Game

2 Dwaine Board, San Francisco vs. Miami, 1985
Dennis Owens, New England vs. Chicago, 1986
Otis Wilson, Chicago vs. New England, 1986
Leonard Marshall, N.Y. Giants vs. Denver, 1987
Alvin Walton, Washington vs. Denver, 1988
Charles Haley, San Francisco vs. Cincinnati, 1989

Team Records

Games, Victories, Defeats

Most Games

5 Dallas, 1971-72, 1976, 1978-79
Miami, 1972-74, 1983, 1985
4 Minnesota, 1970, 1974-75, 1977
Pittsburgh, 1975-76, 1979-80

Oakland/L.A. Raiders, 1968, 1977, 1981, 1984
Washington, 1973, 1983-84, 1988
3 Denver, 1978, 1987-88
San Francisco, 1982, 1985, 1989

Most Consecutive Games
3 Miami, 1972-74
2 Green Bay, 1967-68
Dallas, 1971-72
Minnesota, 1974-75
Pittsburgh, 1975-76, 1979-80
Washington, 1983-84
Denver, 1987-88

Most Games Won
4 Pittsburgh, 1975-76, 1979-80
3 Oakland/L.A. Raiders, 1977, 1981, 1984
San Francisco, 1982, 1985, 1989
2 Green Bay, 1967-68
Miami, 1973-74
Dallas, 1972, 1978
Washington, 1983, 1988

Most Consecutive Games Won
2 Green Bay, 1967-68
Miami, 1973-74
Pittsburgh, 1975-76, 1979-80

Most Games Lost
4 Minnesota, 1970, 1974-75, 1977
3 Dallas, 1971, 1976, 1979
Miami, 1972, 1983, 1985
Denver, 1978, 1987-88
2 Washington, 1973, 1984
Cincinnati, 1982, 1989

Most Consecutive Games Lost
2 Minnesota, 1974-75
Denver, 1987-88

Scoring

Most Points, Game
46 Chicago vs. New England, 1986
42 Washington vs. Denver, 1988
39 N.Y. Giants vs. Denver, 1987

Fewest Points, Game
3 Miami vs. Dallas, 1972
6 Minnesota vs. Pittsburgh, 1975
7 By four teams

Most Points, Both Teams, Game
66 Pittsburgh (35) vs. Dallas (31), 1979
59 N.Y. Giants (39) vs. Denver (20), 1987
56 Chicago (46) vs. New England (10), 1986

Fewest Points, Both Teams, Game
21 Washington (7) vs. Miami (14), 1973
22 Minnesota (6) vs. Pittsburgh (16), 1975
23 Baltimore (7) vs. N.Y. Jets (16), 1969

Largest Margin of Victory, Game
36 Chicago vs. New England, 1986 (46-10)
32 Washington vs. Denver, 1988 (42-10)
29 L.A. Raiders vs. Washington, 1984 (38-9)

Most Points, Each Half
1st: 35 Washington vs. Denver, 1988
2nd: 30 N.Y. Giants vs. Denver, 1987

Most Points, Each Quarter
1st: 14 Miami vs. Minnesota, 1974
Oakland vs. Philadelphia, 1981
2nd: 35 Washington vs. Denver, 1988
3rd: 21 Chicago vs. New England, 1986
4th: 14 Pittsburgh vs. Dallas, 1976; vs. Dallas, 1979; vs. Los Angeles, 1980
Dallas vs. Pittsburgh, 1979
Cincinnati vs. San Francisco, 1982
Washington vs. Miami, 1983
San Francisco vs. Cincinnati, 1989

Most Points, Both Teams, Each Half
1st: 45 Washington (35) vs. Denver (10), 1988
2nd: 40 N.Y. Giants (30) vs. Denver (10), 1987

Fewest Points, Both Teams, Each Half
1st: 2 Minnesota (0) vs. Pittsburgh (2), 1975
2nd: 7 Miami (0) vs. Washington (7), 1973
Denver (0) vs. Washington (7), 1988

Most Points, Both Teams, Each Quarter
1st: 17 Miami (10) vs. San Francisco (7), 1985
Denver (10) vs. N.Y. Giants (7), 1987
2nd: 35 Washington (35) vs. Denver (0), 1988
3rd: 21 Chicago (21) vs. New England (0), 1986
4th: 28 Dallas (14) vs. Pittsburgh (14), 1979

Touchdowns

Most Touchdowns, Game
6 Washington vs. Denver, 1988
5 Green Bay vs. Kansas City, 1967
Pittsburgh vs. Dallas, 1979
L.A. Raiders vs. Washington, 1984
San Francisco vs. Miami, 1985
Chicago vs. New England, 1986
N.Y. Giants vs. Denver, 1987
4 Oakland vs. Minnesota, 1977
Dallas vs. Pittsburgh, 1979
Pittsburgh vs. Los Angeles, 1980

Fewest Touchdowns, Game
0 Miami vs. Dallas, 1972
1 By 15 teams

Most Touchdowns, Both Teams, Game
9 Pittsburgh (5) vs. Dallas (4), 1979
7 N.Y. Giants (5) vs. Denver (2), 1987
Washington (6) vs. Denver (1), 1988
6 Green Bay (5) vs. Kansas City (1), 1967
Oakland (4) vs. Minnesota (2), 1977
Pittsburgh (4) vs. Los Angeles (2), 1980
L.A. Raiders (5) vs. Washington (1), 1984
San Francisco (5) vs. Miami (1), 1985
Chicago (5) vs. New England (1), 1986

Fewest Touchdowns, Both Teams, Game
2 Baltimore (1) vs. N.Y. Jets (1), 1969
3 In six games

Points After Touchdown

Most Points After Touchdown, Game
6 Washington vs. Denver, 1988
5 Green Bay vs. Kansas City, 1967
Pittsburgh vs. Dallas, 1979
L.A. Raiders vs. Washington, 1984
San Francisco vs. Miami, 1985
Chicago vs. New England, 1986
4 Dallas vs. Pittsburgh, 1979
Pittsburgh vs. Los Angeles, 1980
N.Y. Giants vs. Denver, 1987

Most Points After Touchdown, Both Teams, Game
9 Pittsburgh (5) vs. Dallas (4), 1979
7 Washington (6) vs. Denver (1), 1988
6 Green Bay (5) vs. Kansas City (1), 1967
San Francisco (5) vs. Miami (1), 1985
Chicago (5) vs. New England (1), 1986
N.Y. Giants (4) vs. Denver (2), 1987

Fewest Points After Touchdown, Both Teams, Game
2 Baltimore (1) vs. N.Y. Jets (1), 1969
Baltimore (1) vs. Dallas (1), 1971
Minnesota (0) vs. Pittsburgh (2), 1975

Field Goals

Most Field Goals Attempted, Game
5 N.Y. Jets vs. Baltimore, 1969
Dallas vs. Denver, 1978
4 Green Bay vs. Oakland, 1968
Pittsburgh vs. Dallas, 1976
San Francisco vs. Cincinnati, 1982; 1989
Denver vs. N.Y. Giants, 1987

Most Field Goals Attempted, Both Teams, Game
7 N.Y. Jets (5) vs. Baltimore (2), 1969
San Francisco (4) vs. Cincinnati (3), 1989
6 Dallas (5) vs. Denver (1), 1978
5 Green Bay (4) vs. Oakland (1), 1968
Pittsburgh (4) vs. Dallas (1), 1976
Oakland (3) vs. Philadelphia (2), 1981
Denver (4) vs. N.Y. Giants (1), 1987

Fewest Field Goals Attempted, Both Teams, Game
1 Minnesota (0) vs. Miami (1), 1974
2 Green Bay (0) vs. Kansas City (2), 1967
Miami (1) vs. Washington (1), 1973
Dallas (1) vs. Pittsburgh (1), 1979

Most Field Goals, Game
4 Green Bay vs. Oakland, 1968
San Francisco vs. Cincinnati, 1982
3 N.Y. Jets vs. Baltimore, 1969
Kansas City vs. Minnesota, 1970
Miami vs. San Francisco, 1985
Chicago vs. New England, 1986
Cincinnati vs. San Francisco, 1989

Most Field Goals, Both Teams, Game
5 Cincinnati (3) vs. San Francisco (2), 1989
4 Green Bay (4) vs. Oakland (0), 1968
San Francisco (4) vs. Cincinnati (0), 1982
Miami (3) vs. San Francisco (1), 1985
Chicago (3) vs. New England (1), 1986
3 In eight games

Fewest Field Goals, Both Teams, Game
0 Miami vs. Washington, 1973
Pittsburgh vs. Minnesota, 1975
1 Green Bay (0) vs. Kansas City (1), 1967
Minnesota (0) vs. Miami (1), 1974
Pittsburgh (0) vs. Dallas (1), 1979
Washington (0) vs. Denver (1), 1988

Safeties

Most Safeties, Game
1 Pittsburgh vs. Minnesota, 1975; vs. Dallas, 1976
Chicago vs. New England, 1986
N.Y. Giants vs. Denver, 1987

First Downs

Most First Downs, Game
31 San Francisco vs. Miami, 1985
25 Washington vs. Denver, 1988
24 Cincinnati vs. San Francisco, 1982
Washington vs. Miami, 1983
N.Y. Giants vs. Denver, 1987

Fewest First Downs, Game
9 Minnesota vs. Pittsburgh, 1975
Miami vs. Washington, 1983
10 Dallas vs. Baltimore, 1971
Miami vs. Dallas, 1972
11 Denver vs. Dallas, 1978

Most First Downs, Both Teams, Game
50 San Francisco (31) vs. Miami (19), 1985
47 N.Y. Giants (24) vs. Denver (23), 1987
44 Cincinnati (24) vs. San Francisco (20), 1982

Fewest First Downs, Both Teams, Game
24 Dallas (10) vs. Baltimore (14), 1971
26 Minnesota (9) vs. Pittsburgh (17), 1975
27 Pittsburgh (13) vs. Dallas (14), 1976

Rushing
Most First Downs, Rushing, Game
16 San Francisco vs. Miami, 1985
15 Dallas vs. Miami, 1972
14 Washington vs. Miami, 1983
Fewest First Downs, Rushing, Game
1 New England vs. Chicago, 1986
2 Minnesota vs. Kansas City, 1970; vs. Pittsburgh, 1975; vs. Oakland, 1977
Pittsburgh vs. Dallas, 1979
Miami vs. San Francisco, 1985
3 Miami vs. Dallas, 1972
Philadelphia vs. Oakland, 1981
Most First Downs, Rushing, Both Teams, Game
21 Washington (14) vs. Miami (7), 1983
19 Washington (13) vs. Denver (6), 1988
18 Dallas (15) vs. Miami (3), 1972
Miami (13) vs. Minnesota (5), 1974
San Francisco (16) vs. Miami (2), 1985
Fewest First Downs, Rushing, Both Teams, Game
8 Baltimore (4) vs. Dallas (4), 1971
Pittsburgh (2) vs. Dallas (6), 1979
9 Philadelphia (3) vs. Oakland (6), 1981
10 Minnesota (2) vs. Kansas City (8), 1970

Passing
Most First Downs, Passing, Game
17 Miami vs. San Francisco, 1985
16 Denver vs. N.Y. Giants, 1987
San Francisco vs. Cincinnati, 1989
15 Minnesota vs. Oakland, 1977
Pittsburgh vs. Dallas, 1979
San Francisco vs. Miami, 1985
Fewest First Downs, Passing, Game
1 Denver vs. Dallas, 1978
2 Miami vs. Washington, 1983
4 Miami vs. Minnesota, 1974
Most First Downs, Passing, Both Teams, Game
32 Miami (17) vs. San Francisco (15), 1985
29 Denver (16) vs. N.Y. Giants (13), 1987
28 Pittsburgh (15) vs. Dallas (13), 1979
Fewest First Downs, Passing, Both Teams, Game
9 Denver (1) vs. Dallas (8), 1978
10 Minnesota (5) vs. Pittsburgh (5), 1975
11 Dallas (5) vs. Baltimore (6), 1971
Miami (2) vs. Washington (9), 1983

Penalty
Most First Downs, Penalty, Game
4 Baltimore vs. Dallas, 1971
Miami vs. Minnesota, 1974
Cincinnati vs. San Francisco, 1982
3 Kansas City vs. Minnesota, 1970
Minnesota vs. Oakland, 1977
Most First Downs, Penalty, Both Teams, Game
6 Cincinnati (4) vs. San Francisco (2), 1982
5 Baltimore (4) vs. Dallas (1), 1971
Miami (4) vs. Minnesota (1), 1974
4 Kansas City (3) vs. Minnesota (1), 1970
Fewest First Downs, Penalty, Both Teams, Game
0 Dallas vs. Miami, 1972
Miami vs. Washington, 1973
Dallas vs. Pittsburgh, 1976
Miami vs. San Francisco, 1985
1 Green Bay (0) vs. Kansas City (1), 1967
Miami (0) vs. Washington (1), 1983
Cincinnati (0) vs. San Francisco (1), 1989

Net Yards Gained Rushing and Passing
Most Yards Gained, Game
602 Washington vs. Denver, 1988
537 San Francisco vs. Miami, 1985
451 San Francisco vs. Cincinnati, 1989
Fewest Yards Gained, Game
119 Minnesota vs. Pittsburgh, 1975
123 New England vs. Chicago, 1986
156 Denver vs. Dallas, 1978
Most Yards Gained, Both Teams, Game
929 Washington (602) vs. Denver (327), 1988
851 San Francisco (537) vs. Miami (314), 1985
782 Oakland (429) vs. Minnesota (353), 1977
Fewest Yards Gained, Both Teams, Game
452 Minnesota (119) vs. Pittsburgh (333), 1975
481 Washington (228) vs. Miami (253), 1973
Denver (156) vs. Dallas (325), 1978
497 Minnesota (238) vs. Miami (259), 1974

Rushing
Attempts
Most Attempts, Game
57 Pittsburgh vs. Minnesota, 1975
53 Miami vs. Minnesota, 1974
52 Oakland vs. Minnesota, 1977
Washington vs. Miami, 1983
Fewest Attempts, Game
9 Miami vs. San Francisco, 1985
11 New England vs. Chicago, 1986
17 Denver vs. Washington, 1988

Most Attempts, Both Teams, Game
81 Washington (52) vs. Miami (29), 1983
78 Pittsburgh (57) vs. Minnesota (21), 1975
Oakland (52) vs. Minnesota (26), 1977
77 Miami (53) vs. Minnesota (24), 1974
Pittsburgh (46) vs. Dallas (31), 1976
Fewest Attempts, Both Teams, Game
49 Miami (9) vs. San Francisco (40), 1985
52 Kansas City (19) vs. Green Bay (33), 1967
55 San Francisco (27) vs. Cincinnati (28), 1989

Yards Gained
Most Yards Gained, Game
280 Washington vs. Denver, 1988
276 Washington vs. Miami, 1983
266 Oakland vs. Minnesota, 1977
Fewest Yards Gained, Game
7 New England vs. Chicago, 1986
17 Minnesota vs. Pittsburgh, 1975
25 Miami vs. San Francisco, 1985
Most Yards Gained, Both Teams, Game
377 Washington (280) vs. Denver (97), 1988
372 Washington (276) vs. Miami (96), 1983
337 Oakland (266) vs. Minnesota (71), 1977
Fewest Yards Gained, Both Teams, Game
171 Baltimore (69) vs. Dallas (102), 1971
174 New England (7) vs. Chicago (167), 1986
186 Philadelphia (69) vs. Oakland (117), 1981

Average Gain
Highest Average Gain, Game
7.00 L.A. Raiders vs. Washington, 1984 (33-231)
Washington vs. Denver, 1988 (40-280)
6.22 Baltimore vs. N.Y. Jets, 1969 (23-143)
5.71 Denver vs. Washington, 1988 (17-97)
Lowest Average Gain, Game
0.64 New England vs. Chicago, 1986 (11-7)
0.81 Minnesota vs. Pittsburgh, 1975 (21-17)
2.23 Baltimore vs. Dallas, 1971 (31-69)

Touchdowns
Most Touchdowns, Game
4 Chicago vs. New England, 1986
3 Green Bay vs. Kansas City, 1967
Miami vs. Minnesota, 1974
2 Oakland vs. Minnesota, 1977
Pittsburgh vs. Los Angeles, 1980
L.A. Raiders vs. Washington, 1984
San Francisco vs. Miami, 1985
N.Y. Giants vs. Denver, 1987
Washington vs. Denver, 1988
Fewest Touchdowns, Game
0 By 17 teams
Most Touchdowns, Both Teams, Game
4 Miami (3) vs. Minnesota (1), 1974
Chicago (4) vs. New England (0), 1986
3 Green Bay (3) vs. Kansas City (0), 1967
Pittsburgh (2) vs. Los Angeles (1), 1980
L.A. Raiders (2) vs. Washington (1), 1984
N.Y. Giants (2) vs. Denver (1), 1987
Fewest Touchdowns, Both Teams, Game
0 Pittsburgh vs. Dallas, 1976
Oakland vs. Philadelphia, 1981
Cincinnati vs. San Francisco, 1989
1 In seven games

Passing
Attempts
Most Passes Attempted, Game
50 Miami vs. San Francisco, 1985
44 Minnesota vs. Oakland, 1977
41 Baltimore vs. N.Y. Jets, 1969
Denver vs. N.Y. Giants, 1987
Fewest Passes Attempted, Game
7 Miami vs. Minnesota, 1974
11 Miami vs. Washington, 1973
14 Pittsburgh vs. Minnesota, 1975
Most Passes Attempted, Both Teams, Game
85 Miami (50) vs. San Francisco (35), 1985
70 Baltimore (41) vs. N.Y. Jets (29), 1969
69 Denver (39) vs. Washington (30), 1988
Fewest Passes Attempted, Both Teams, Game
35 Miami (7) vs. Minnesota (28), 1974
39 Miami (11) vs. Washington (28), 1973
40 Pittsburgh (14) vs. Minnesota (26), 1975
Miami (17) vs. Washington (23), 1983

Completions
Most Passes Completed, Game
29 Miami vs. San Francisco, 1985
26 Denver vs. N.Y. Giants, 1987
25 Cincinnati vs. San Francisco, 1982
Fewest Passes Completed, Game
4 Miami vs. Washington, 1983
6 Miami vs. Minnesota, 1974
8 Miami vs. Washington, 1973
Denver vs. Dallas, 1978
Most Passes Completed, Both Teams, Game
53 Miami (29) vs. San Francisco (24), 1985
48 Denver (26) vs. N.Y. Giants (22), 1987
39 Cincinnati (25) vs. San Francisco (14), 1982

Fewest Passes Completed, Both Teams, Game
19 Miami (4) vs. Washington (15), 1983
20 Pittsburgh (9) vs. Minnesota (11), 1975
22 Miami (8) vs. Washington (14), 1973

Completion Percentage
Highest Completion Percentage, Game (20 attempts)
88.0 N.Y. Giants vs. Denver, 1987 (25-22)
73.5 Cincinnati vs. San Francisco, 1982 (34-25)
68.6 San Francisco vs. Miami, 1985 (35-24)
Lowest Completion Percentage, Game (20 attempts)
32.0 Denver vs. Dallas, 1978 (25-8)
38.5 Denver vs. Washington, 1988 (39-15)
41.5 Baltimore vs. N.Y. Jets, 1969 (41-17)

Yards Gained
Most Yards Gained, Game
339 San Francisco vs. Cincinnati, 1989
326 San Francisco vs. Miami, 1985
322 Washington vs. Denver, 1988
Fewest Yards Gained, Game
35 Denver vs. Dallas, 1978
63 Miami vs. Minnesota, 1974
69 Miami vs. Washington, 1973
Most Yards Gained, Both Teams, Game
615 San Francisco (326) vs. Miami (289), 1985
583 Denver (320) vs. N.Y. Giants (263), 1987
552 Washington (322) vs. Denver (230), 1988
Fewest Yards Gained, Both Teams, Game
156 Miami (69) vs. Washington (87), 1973
186 Pittsburgh (84) vs. Minnesota (102), 1975
205 Dallas (100) vs. Miami (105), 1972

Times Sacked
Most Times Sacked, Game
7 Dallas vs. Pittsburgh, 1976
New England vs. Chicago, 1986
6 Kansas City vs. Green Bay, 1967
Washington vs. L.A. Raiders, 1984
5 Dallas vs. Denver, 1978; vs. Pittsburgh, 1979
Cincinnati vs. San Francisco, 1982; 1989
Denver vs. Washington, 1988
Fewest Times Sacked, Game
0 Baltimore vs. N.Y. Jets, 1969; vs. Dallas, 1971
Minnesota vs. Pittsburgh, 1975
Pittsburgh vs. Los Angeles, 1980
Philadelphia vs. Oakland, 1981
1 By eight teams
Most Times Sacked, Both Teams, Game
10 New England (7) vs. Chicago (3), 1986
9 Kansas City (6) vs. Green Bay (3), 1967
Dallas (7) vs. Pittsburgh (2), 1976
Dallas (5) vs. Denver (4), 1978
Dallas (5) vs. Pittsburgh (4), 1979
Cincinnati (5) vs. San Francisco (4), 1989
8 Washington (6) vs. L.A. Raiders (2), 1984
Fewest Times Sacked, Both Teams, Game
1 Philadelphia (0) vs. Oakland (1), 1981
2 Baltimore (0) vs. N.Y. Jets (2), 1969
Baltimore (0) vs. Dallas (2), 1971
Minnesota (0) vs. Pittsburgh (2), 1975
3 In three games

Touchdowns
Most Touchdowns, Game
4 Pittsburgh vs. Dallas, 1979
Washington vs. Denver, 1988
3 Dallas vs. Pittsburgh, 1979
Oakland vs. Philadelphia, 1981
San Francisco vs. Miami, 1985
N.Y. Giants vs. Denver, 1987
2 By 11 teams
Fewest Touchdowns, Game
0 By 12 teams
Most Touchdowns, Both Teams, Game
7 Pittsburgh (4) vs. Dallas (3), 1979
5 Washington (4) vs. Denver (1), 1988
4 Dallas (2) vs. Pittsburgh (2), 1976
Oakland (3) vs. Philadelphia (1), 1981
San Francisco (3) vs. Miami (1), 1985
N.Y. Giants (3) vs. Denver (1), 1987
Fewest Touchdowns, Both Teams, Game
0 N.Y. Jets vs. Baltimore, 1969
Miami vs. Minnesota, 1974
1 In five games

Interceptions By
Most Interceptions By, Game
4 N.Y. Jets vs. Baltimore, 1969
Dallas vs. Denver, 1978
3 By nine teams
Most Interceptions By, Both Teams, Game
6 Baltimore (3) vs. Dallas (3), 1971
4 In six games
Fewest Interceptions By, Both Teams, Game
1 Oakland (0) vs. Green Bay (1), 1968
Miami (0) vs. Dallas (1), 1972
Minnesota (0) vs. Miami (1), 1974
N.Y. Giants (0) vs. Denver (1), 1987
San Francisco (1) vs. Cincinnati (0), 1989

Yards Gained
Most Yards Gained, Game
95 Miami vs. Washington, 1973
91 Oakland vs. Minnesota, 1977
89 Pittsburgh vs. Dallas, 1976
Most Yards Gained, Both Teams, Game
95 Miami (95) vs. Washington (0), 1973
91 Oakland (91) vs. Minnesota (0), 1977
89 Pittsburgh (89) vs. Dallas (0), 1976

Touchdowns
Most Touchdowns, Game
1 Green Bay vs. Oakland, 1968
Oakland vs. Minnesota, 1977
L.A. Raiders vs. Washington, 1984
Chicago vs. New England, 1986

Punting
Most Punts, Game
9 Dallas vs. Baltimore, 1971
8 Washington vs. L.A. Raiders, 1984
7 By seven teams
Fewest Punts, Game
2 Pittsburgh vs. Los Angeles, 1980
Denver vs. N.Y. Giants, 1987
3 By nine teams
Most Punts, Both Teams, Game
15 Washington (8) vs. L.A. Raiders (7), 1984
13 Dallas (9) vs. Baltimore (4), 1971
Pittsburgh (7) vs. Minnesota (6), 1975
12 In three games
Fewest Punts, Both Teams, Game
5 Denver (2) vs. N.Y. Giants (3), 1987
6 Oakland (3) vs. Philadelphia (3), 1981
7 In four games

Average Yardage
Highest Average, Game (4 punts)
48.50 Kansas City vs. Minnesota, 1970 (4-194)
46.25 San Francisco vs. Cincinnati, 1982 (4-185)
45.29 Kansas City vs. Green Bay, 1967 (7-317)
Lowest Average, Game (4 punts)
31.20 Washington vs. Miami, 1973 (5-156)
32.38 Washington vs. L.A. Raiders, 1984 (8-259)
32.40 Oakland vs. Minnesota, 1977 (5-162)

Punt Returns
Most Punt Returns, Game
6 Washington vs. Miami, 1983
5 By five teams
Fewest Punt Returns, Game
0 Minnesota vs. Miami, 1974
1 By 11 teams
Most Punt Returns, Both Teams, Game
9 Pittsburgh (5) vs. Minnesota (4), 1975
8 Green Bay (5) vs. Oakland (3), 1968
Baltimore (5) vs. Dallas (3), 1971
Washington (6) vs. Miami (2), 1983
7 Green Bay (4) vs. Kansas City (3), 1967
Oakland (4) vs. Minnesota (3), 1977
San Francisco (5) vs. Miami (2), 1985
Fewest Punt Returns, Both Teams, Game
2 Dallas (1) vs. Miami (1), 1972
Denver (1) vs. N.Y. Giants (1), 1987
3 Kansas City (1) vs. Minnesota (2), 1970
Minnesota (0) vs. Miami (3), 1974
Washington (1) vs. Denver (2), 1988
4 L.A. Raiders (2) vs. Washington (2), 1984
Chicago (2) vs. New England (2), 1986

Yards Gained
Most Yards Gained, Game
56 San Francisco vs. Cincinnati, 1989
52 Washington vs. Miami, 1983
51 San Francisco vs. Miami, 1985
Fewest Yards Gained, Game
−1 Dallas vs. Miami, 1972
0 By five teams
Most Yards Gained, Both Teams, Game
74 Washington (52) vs. Miami (22), 1983
66 San Francisco (51) vs. Miami (15), 1985
61 San Francisco (56) vs. Cincinnati (5), 1989
Fewest Yards Gained, Both Teams, Game
13 Miami (4) vs. Washington (9), 1973
18 Kansas City (0) vs. Minnesota (18), 1970
Washington (0) vs. Denver (18), 1988
20 Dallas (−1) vs. Miami (21), 1972
Minnesota (0) vs. Miami (20), 1974

Average Return
Highest Average, Game (3 returns)
18.7 San Francisco vs. Cincinnati, 1989 (3-56)
10.8 Oakland vs. Minnesota, 1977 (4-43)
10.2 San Francisco vs. Miami, 1985 (5-51)

Touchdowns
Most Touchdowns, Game
None

Kickoff Returns

Most Kickoff Returns, Game

7 Oakland vs. Green Bay, 1968
Minnesota vs. Oakland, 1977
Cincinnati vs. San Francisco, 1982
Washington vs. L.A. Raiders, 1984
Miami vs. San Francisco, 1985
New England vs. Chicago, 1986
6 By six teams

Fewest Kickoff Returns, Game

1 N.Y. Jets vs. Baltimore, 1969
L.A. Raiders vs. Washington, 1984
2 By six teams

Most Kickoff Returns, Both Teams, Game

11 Los Angeles (6) vs. Pittsburgh (5), 1980
Miami (7) vs. San Francisco (4), 1985
New England (7) vs. Chicago (4), 1986
10 Oakland (7) vs. Green Bay (3), 1968
9 In eight games

Fewest Kickoff Returns, Both Teams, Game

5 N.Y. Jets (1) vs. Baltimore (4), 1969
Miami (2) vs. Washington (3), 1973
6 In three games

Yards Gained

Most Yards Gained, Game

222 Miami vs. Washington, 1983
173 Denver vs. Dallas, 1978
162 Pittsburgh vs. Los Angeles, 1980

Fewest Yards Gained, Game

17 L.A. Raiders vs. Washington, 1984
25 N.Y. Jets vs. Baltimore, 1969
32 Pittsburgh vs. Minnesota, 1975

Most Yards Gained, Both Teams, Game

279 Miami (222) vs. Washington (57), 1983
231 Pittsburgh (162) vs. Los Angeles (79), 1980
224 Denver (173) vs. Dallas (51), 1978

Fewest Yards Gained, Both Teams, Game

78 Miami (33) vs. Washington (45), 1973
82 Pittsburgh (32) vs. Minnesota (50), 1975
92 San Francisco (40) vs. Cincinnati (52), 1982

Average Gain

Highest Average, Game (3 returns)

44.0 Cincinnati vs. San Francisco, 1989 (3-132)
37.0 Miami vs. Washington, 1983 (6-222)
32.4 Pittsburgh vs. Los Angeles, 1980 (5-162)

Touchdowns

Most Touchdowns, Game

1 Miami vs. Washington, 1983
Cincinnati vs. San Francisco, 1989

Penalties

Most Penalties, Game

12 Dallas vs. Denver, 1978
10 Dallas vs. Baltimore, 1971
9 Dallas vs. Pittsburgh, 1979

Fewest Penalties, Game

0 Miami vs. Dallas, 1972
Pittsburgh vs. Dallas, 1976
1 Green Bay vs. Oakland, 1968
Miami vs. Minnesota, 1974; vs. San Francisco, 1985
2 By four teams

Most Penalties, Both Teams, Game

20 Dallas (12) vs. Denver (8), 1978
16 Cincinnati (8) vs. San Francisco (8), 1982
14 Dallas (10) vs. Baltimore (4), 1971
Dallas (9) vs. Pittsburgh (5), 1979

Fewest Penalties, Both Teams, Game

2 Pittsburgh (0) vs. Dallas (2), 1976
3 Miami (0) vs. Dallas (3), 1972
Miami (1) vs. San Francisco (2), 1985
5 Green Bay (1) vs. Oakland (4), 1968

Yards Penalized

Most Yards Penalized, Game

133 Dallas vs. Baltimore, 1971
122 Pittsburgh vs. Minnesota, 1975
94 Dallas vs. Denver, 1978

Fewest Yards Penalized, Game

0 Miami vs. Dallas, 1972
Pittsburgh vs. Dallas, 1976
4 Miami vs. Minnesota, 1974
10 Miami vs. San Francisco, 1985
San Francisco vs. Miami, 1985

Most Yards Penalized, Both Teams, Game

164 Dallas (133) vs. Baltimore (31), 1971
154 Dallas (94) vs. Denver (60), 1978
140 Pittsburgh (122) vs. Minnesota (18), 1975

Fewest Yards Penalized, Both Teams, Game

15 Miami (0) vs. Dallas (15), 1972
20 Pittsburgh (0) vs. Dallas (20), 1976
Miami (10) vs. San Francisco (10), 1985
43 Green Bay (12) vs. Oakland (31), 1968

Fumbles

Most Fumbles, Game

6 Dallas vs. Denver, 1978
5 Baltimore vs. Dallas, 1971
4 By five teams

Fewest Fumbles, Game

0 By eight teams

Most Fumbles, Both Teams, Game

10 Dallas (6) vs. Denver (4), 1978
8 Dallas (4) vs. Pittsburgh (4), 1976
7 Pittsburgh (4) vs. Minnesota (3), 1975
New England (4) vs. Chicago (3), 1986

Fewest Fumbles, Both Teams, Game

0 Los Angeles vs. Pittsburgh, 1980
1 Oakland (0) vs. Minnesota (1), 1977
Oakland (0) vs. Philadelphia (1), 1981
Denver (0) vs. Washington (1), 1988
2 In four games

Most Fumbles Lost, Game

4 Baltimore vs. Dallas, 1971
Denver vs. Dallas, 1978
New England vs. Chicago, 1986
2 In many games

Most Fumbles Lost, Both Teams, Game

6 Denver (4) vs. Dallas (2), 1978
New England (4) vs. Chicago (2), 1986
5 Baltimore (4) vs. Dallas (1), 1971
4 Minnesota (2) vs. Pittsburgh (2), 1975
Dallas (2) vs. Pittsburgh (2), 1979

Fewest Fumbles Lost, Both Teams, Game

0 Green Bay vs. Kansas City, 1967
Dallas vs. Pittsburgh, 1976
Los Angeles vs. Pittsburgh, 1980
Denver vs. N.Y. Giants, 1987
Denver vs. Washington, 1988
1 Washington (0) vs. Miami (1), 1973
Miami (0) vs. Minnesota (1), 1974
Oakland (0) vs. Minnesota (1), 1977
Oakland (0) vs. Philadelphia (1), 1981
Washington (0) vs. Miami (1), 1983
Cincinnati (0) vs. San Francisco (1), 1989
2 In four games

Most Fumbles Recovered, Game

8 Dallas vs. Denver, 1978 (4 own, 4 opp)
5 Chicago vs. New England, 1986 (1 own, 4 opp)
4 Pittsburgh vs. Minnesota, 1975 (2 own, 2 opp)
Dallas vs. Pittsburgh, 1976 (4 own)

Turnovers

(Number of times losing the ball on interceptions and fumbles.)

Most Turnovers, Game

8 Denver vs. Dallas, 1978
7 Baltimore vs. Dallas, 1971
6 New England vs. Chicago, 1986

Fewest Turnovers, Game

0 Green Bay vs. Oakland, 1968
Miami vs. Minnesota, 1974
Pittsburgh vs. Dallas, 1976
Oakland vs. Minnesota, 1977; vs. Philadelphia, 1981
N.Y. Giants vs. Denver, 1987
1 By many teams

Most Turnovers, Both Teams, Game

11 Baltimore (7) vs. Dallas (4), 1971
10 Denver (8) vs. Dallas (2), 1978
8 New England (6) vs. Chicago (2), 1986

Fewest Turnovers, Both Teams, Game

1 N.Y. Giants (0) vs. Denver (1), 1987
2 Green Bay (1) vs. Kansas City (1), 1967
Miami (0) vs. Minnesota (2), 1974
Cincinnati (1) vs. San Francisco (1), 1989
3 Green Bay (0) vs. Oakland (3), 1968
Pittsburgh (0) vs. Dallas (3), 1976
Oakland (0) vs. Minnesota (3), 1977

POSTSEASON GAME RECORDS

Compiled by Elias Sports Bureau

Throughout this all-time postseason record section, the following abbreviations are used to indicate various levels of postseason games:

SB	Super Bowl (1966 to date)
AFC	AFC Championship Game (1970 to date) or AFL Championship Game (1960-69)
NFC	NFC Championship Game (1970 to date) or NFL Championship Game (1933-69)
AFC-D	AFC Divisional Playoff Game (1970 to date), AFC Second-Round Playoff Game (1982), AFL Inter-Divisional Playoff Game (1969), or special playoff game to break tie for AFL Division Championship (1963, 1968)
NFC-D	NFC Divisional Playoff Game (1970 to date), NFC Second-Round Playoff Game (1982), NFL Conference Championship Game (1967-69), or special playoff game to break tie for NFL Division or Conference Championship (1941, 1943, 1947, 1950, 1952, 1957, 1958, 1965)
AFC-FR	AFC First-Round Playoff Game (1978 to date)
NFC-FR	NFC First-Round Playoff Game (1978 to date)

Year references are to the season following which the postseason game occurred, even if the game was played in the next calendar year.

Postseason Game Composite Standings

	W	L	Pct.	Pts.	OP
Green Bay Packers	13	5	.722	416	259
Pittsburgh Steelers	15	8	.652	533	447
Los Angeles Raiders*	19	12	.613	761	535
Detroit Lions	6	4	.600	221	208
San Francisco 49ers	12	8	.600	440	401
Miami Dolphins	14	10	.583	535	468
Washington Redskins**	16	12	.571	569	523
Dallas Cowboys	20	16	.556	805	640
Kansas City Chiefs***	5	4	.556	159	182
Philadelphia Eagles	7	6	.538	231	193
Chicago Bears	12	11	.522	497	436
Houston Oilers	8	8	.500	235	361
Indianapolis Colts****	8	8	.500	285	300
New York Jets	5	5	.500	206	183
Minnesota Vikings	13	14	.481	505	529
Denver Broncos	6	7	.462	252	327
Seattle Seahawks	3	4	.429	128	139
Buffalo Bills	4	6	.400	165	202
Cincinnati Bengals	4	6	.400	195	223
New England Patriots†	4	6	.400	195	258
New York Giants	10	16	.385	430	485
Los Angeles Rams††	11	19	.367	458	647
Cleveland Browns	9	17	.346	512	583
San Diego Chargers†††	4	8	.333	230	279
Atlanta Falcons	1	3	.250	85	100
Tampa Bay Buccaneers	1	3	.250	41	94
Phoenix Cardinals††††	1	4	.200	81	134
New Orleans Saints	0	1	.000	10	44

**24 games played when franchise was in Oakland (won 15, lost 9, 587 points scored, 435 points allowed).*
***One game played when franchise was in Boston (lost 21-6).*
****One game played when franchise was Dallas Texans (lost 20-17).*
*****15 games played when franchise was in Baltimore (won 8, lost 7, 264 points scored, 262 points allowed).*
†Two games played when franchise was in Boston (won 26-8, lost 51-10).
††One game played when franchise was in Cleveland (won 15-14).
†††One game played when franchise was in Los Angeles (lost 24-16).
††††Two games played when franchise was in Chicago (won 28-21, lost 7-0), three games played when franchise was in St. Louis (lost 30-14, lost 35-23, lost 41-16).

Individual Records

Service

Most Games, Career
27 D. D. Lewis, Dallas (SB-5, NFC-9, NFC-D 12, NFC-FR 1)
26 Larry Cole, Dallas (SB-5, NFC-8, NFC-D-12, NFC-FR 1)
25 Charlie Waters, Dallas (SB-5, NFC-9, NFC-D 10, NFC-FR 1)

Scoring

Points

Most Points, Career
115 George Blanda, Chi. Bears-Houston-Oakland, 19 games (49-pat, 22-fg)
102 Franco Harris, Pittsburgh, 19 games (17-td)
95 Rafael Septien, L.A. Rams-Dallas, 15 games (41-pat, 18-fg)

Most Points, Game
19 Pat Harder, NFC-D: Detroit vs. Los Angeles, 1952 (2-td, 4-pat, 1-fg)
Paul Hornung, NFC: Green Bay vs. N.Y. Giants, 1961 (1-td, 4-pat, 3-fg)
18 By 16 players

Touchdowns

Most Touchdowns, Career
17 Franco Harris, Pittsburgh, 19 games (16-r, 1-p)
12 John Riggins, Washington, 9 games (12-r)
John Stallworth, Pittsburgh, 18 games (12-p)
10 Fred Biletnikoff, Oakland, 19 games (10-p)
Larry Csonka, Miami, 12 games (9-r, 1-p)
Tony Dorsett, Dallas, 17 games (9-r, 1-p)
Marcus Allen, L.A. Raiders, 7 games (8-r, 2-p)

Most Touchdowns, Game
3 Andy Farkas, NFC-D: Washington vs. N.Y. Giants, 1943 (3-r)
Tom Fears, NFC-D: Los Angeles vs. Chi. Bears, 1950 (3-p)
Otto Graham, NFC: Cleveland vs. Detroit, 1954 (3-r)
Gary Collins, NFC: Cleveland vs. Baltimore, 1964 (3-p)
Craig Baynham, NFC-D: Dallas vs. Cleveland, 1967 (2-r, 1-p)
Fred Biletnikoff, AFC-D: Oakland vs. Kansas City, 1968 (3-p)
Tom Matte, NFC: Baltimore vs. Cleveland, 1968 (3-r)
Larry Schreiber, NFC-D: San Francisco vs. Dallas, 1972 (3-r)
Larry Csonka, AFC: Miami vs. Oakland, 1973 (3-r)
Franco Harris, AFC-D: Pittsburgh vs. Buffalo, 1974 (3-r)
Preston Pearson, NFC: Dallas vs. Los Angeles, 1975 (3-p)
Dave Casper, AFC-D: Oakland vs. Baltimore, 1977 (OT) (3-p)
Alvin Garrett, NFC-FR: Washington vs. Detroit, 1982 (3-p)
John Riggins, NFC-D: Washington vs. L.A. Rams, 1983 (3-r)
Roger Craig, SB: San Francisco vs. Miami, 1984 (1-r, 2-p)
Jerry Rice, NFC-D: San Francisco vs. Minnesota, 1988 (3-p)

Most Consecutive Games Scoring Touchdowns
8 John Stallworth, Pittsburgh, 1978-83
7 John Riggins, Washington, 1982-84
Marcus Allen, L.A. Raiders, 1982-85 (current)
5 Duane Thomas, Dallas, 1970-71
Franco Harris, Pittsburgh, 1974-75
Franco Harris, Pittsburgh, 1977-79

Points After Touchdown

Most Points After Touchdown, Career
49 George Blanda, Chi. Bears-Houston-Oakland, 19 games (49 att)
41 Rafael Septien, L.A. Rams-Dallas, 15 games (41 att)
38 Fred Cox, Minnesota, 18 games (40 att)

Most Points After Touchdown, Game
8 Lou Groza, NFC: Cleveland vs. Detroit, 1954 (8 att)
Jim Martin, NFC: Detroit vs. Cleveland, 1957 (8 att)
George Blanda, AFC-D: Oakland vs. Houston, 1969 (8 att)
7 Danny Villanueva, NFC-D: Dallas vs. Cleveland, 1967 (7 att)
Raul Allegre, NFC-D: N.Y. Giants vs. San Francisco, 1986
6 George Blair, AFC: San Diego vs. Boston, 1963 (6 att)
Mark Moseley, NFC-D: Washington vs. L.A. Rams, 1983 (6 att)
Uwe von Schamann, AFC: Miami vs. Pittsburgh, 1984 (6 att)
Ali Haji-Sheikh, SB: Washington vs. Denver, 1987 (6 att)

Most Points After Touchdown, No Misses, Career
49 George Blanda, Chi. Bears-Houston-Oakland, 19 games
41 Rafael Septien, L.A. Rams-Dallas, 14 games
33 Chris Bahr, Oakland-L.A. Raiders, 11 games

Field Goals

Most Field Goals Attempted, Career
39 George Blanda, Chi. Bears-Houston-Oakland, 19 games
31 Mark Moseley, Washington-Cleveland, 11 games
27 Roy Gerela, Houston-Pittsburgh, 15 games

Most Field Goals Attempted, Game
6 George Blanda, AFC: Oakland vs. Houston, 1967
David Ray, NFC-D: Los Angeles vs. Dallas, 1973
Mark Moseley, AFC-D: Cleveland vs. N.Y. Jets, 1986 (OT)
5 Jerry Kramer, NFC: Green Bay vs. N.Y. Giants, 1962
Gino Cappelletti, AFC-D: Boston vs. Buffalo, 1963
Pete Gogolak, AFC: Buffalo vs. San Diego, 1965
Jan Stenerud, AFC-D: Kansas City vs. N.Y. Jets, 1969
George Blanda, AFC-D: Oakland vs. Pittsburgh, 1973
Ed Murray, NFC-D: Detroit vs. San Francisco, 1983
Mark Moseley, NFC: Washington vs. San Francisco, 1983
Tony Franklin, AFC-FR: New England vs. N.Y. Jets, 1985
Tony Zendejas, AFC-FR: Houston vs. Seattle, 1987 (OT)
Chuck Nelson, NFC-D: Minnesota vs. San Francisco, 1987
Luis Zendejas, NFC-D: Philadelphia vs. Chicago, 1988
4 By many players

Most Field Goals, Career
22 George Blanda, Chi. Bears-Houston-Oakland, 19 games
20 Toni Fritsch, Dallas-Houston, 14 games
18 Rafael Septien, L.A. Rams-Dallas, 15 games

Most Field Goals, Game
5 Chuck Nelson, NFC-D: Minnesota vs. San Francisco, 1987
4 Gino Cappelletti, AFC-D: Boston vs. Buffalo, 1963
George Blanda, AFC: Oakland vs. Houston, 1967
Don Chandler, SB: Green Bay vs. Oakland, 1967
Curt Knight, NFC: Washington vs. Dallas, 1972
George Blanda, AFC-D: Oakland vs. Pittsburgh, 1973
Ray Wersching, SB: San Francisco vs. Cincinnati, 1981
Tony Franklin, AFC-FR: New England vs. N.Y. Jets, 1985
Jess Atkinson, NFC-FR: Washington vs. L.A. Rams, 1986
Luis Zendejas, NFC-D: Philadelphia vs. Chicago, 1988
3 By many players

Most Consecutive Field Goals
15 Rafael Septien, Dallas, 1978-82
9 Chuck Nelson, Minnesota, 1987
8 Tony Fritsch, Houston, 1978-79

Longest Field Goal
54 Ed Murray, NFC-D: Detroit vs. San Francisco, 1983
52 Lou Groza, NFC: Cleveland vs. Los Angeles, 1951
Curt Knight, NFC-D: Washington vs. Minnesota, 1973
Matt Bahr, AFC-FR: Cleveland vs. L.A. Raiders, 1982
51 Fuad Reveiz, AFC-D: Miami vs. Cleveland, 1985

Highest Field Goal Percentage, Career (10 field goals)
90.9 Chuck Nelson, Minnesota, 5 games (11-10)
85.7 Rafael Septien, L.A. Rams-Dallas, 15 games (21-18)
80.0 Toni Fritsch, Dallas-Houston, 14 games (25-20)

Safeties

Most Safeties, Game

1 Bill Willis, NFC-D: Cleveland vs. N.Y. Giants, 1950
Carl Eller, NFC-D: Minnesota vs. Los Angeles, 1969
George Andrie, NFC-D: Dallas vs. Detroit, 1970
Alan Page, NFC-D: Minnesota vs. Dallas, 1971
Dwight White, SB: Pittsburgh vs. Minnesota, 1974
Reggie Harrison, SB: Pittsburgh vs. Dallas, 1975
Jim Jensen, NFC-D: Dallas vs. Los Angeles, 1976
Ted Washington, AFC: Houston vs. Pittsburgh, 1978
Randy White, NFC-D: Dallas vs. Los Angeles, 1979
Henry Waechter, SB: Chicago vs. New England, 1985
Rulon Jones, AFC-FR: Denver vs. New England, 1986
George Martin, SB: N.Y. Giants vs. Denver, 1986
D.D. Hoggard, AFC: Cleveland vs. Denver, 1987

Rushing

Attempts

Most Attempts, Career

400 Franco Harris, Pittsburgh, 19 games
302 Tony Dorsett, Dallas, 17 games
251 John Riggins, Washington, 9 games

Most Attempts, Game

38 Ricky Bell, NFC-D: Tampa Bay vs. Philadelphia, 1979
John Riggins, SB: Washington vs. Miami, 1982
37 Lawrence McCutcheon, NFC-D: Los Angeles vs. St. Louis, 1975
John Riggins, NFC-D: Washington vs. Minnesota, 1982
36 John Riggins, NFC: Washington vs. Dallas, 1982
John Riggins, NFC: Washington vs. San Francisco, 1983

Yards Gained

Most Yards Gained, Career

1,556 Franco Harris, Pittsburgh, 19 games
1,383 Tony Dorsett, Dallas, 17 games
996 John Riggins, Washington, 9 games

Most Yards Gained, Game

248 Eric Dickerson, NFC-D: L.A. Rams vs. Dallas, 1985
206 Keith Lincoln, AFC: San Diego vs. Boston, 1963
204 Timmy Smith, SB: Washington vs. Denver, 1987

Most Games, 100 or More Yards Rushing, Career

6 John Riggins, Washington, 9 games
5 Franco Harris, Pittsburgh, 19 games
4 Larry Csonka, Miami, 12 games
Chuck Foreman, Minnesota, 13 games
Marcus Allen, L.A. Raiders, 7 games

Most Consecutive Games, 100 or More Yards Rushing

6 John Riggins, Washington, 1982-83
3 Larry Csonka, Miami, 1973-74
Franco Harris, Pittsburgh, 1974-75
Marcus Allen, L.A. Raiders, 1983

Longest Run From Scrimmage

80 Roger Craig, NFC-D: San Francisco vs. Minnesota, 1988 (TD)
74 Marcus Allen, SB: L.A. Raiders vs. Washington, 1983 (TD)
71 Hugh McElhenny, NFC-D: San Francisco vs. Detroit, 1957
James Lofton, NFC-D: Green Bay vs. Dallas, 1982 (TD)

Average Gain

Highest Average Gain, Career (50 attempts)

6.71 Timmy Smith, Washington, 3 games (51-342)
6.67 Paul Lowe, L.A. Chargers-San Diego, 5 games (57-380)
6.46 Earnest Byner, Cleveland, 5 games (63-407)

Highest Average Gain, Game (10 attempts)

15.90 Elmer Angsman, NFC: Chi. Cardinals vs. Philadelphia, 1947 (10-159)
15.85 Keith Lincoln, AFC: San Diego vs. Boston, 1963 (13-206)
10.90 Bill Osmanski, NFC: Chi. Bears vs. Washington, 1940 (10-109)

Touchdowns

Most Touchdowns, Career

16 Franco Harris, Pittsburgh, 19 games
12 John Riggins, Washington, 9 games
9 Larry Csonka, Miami, 12 games
Tony Dorsett, Dallas, 17 games

Most Touchdowns, Game

3 Andy Farkas, NFC-D: Washington vs. N.Y. Giants, 1943
Otto Graham, NFC: Cleveland vs. Detroit, 1954
Tom Matte, NFC: Baltimore vs. Cleveland, 1968
Larry Schreiber, NFC-D: San Francisco vs. Dallas, 1972
Larry Csonka, AFC: Miami vs. Oakland, 1973
Franco Harris, AFC-D: Pittsburgh vs. Buffalo, 1974
John Riggins, NFC-D: Washington vs. L.A. Rams, 1983

Most Consecutive Games Rushing for Touchdowns

7 John Riggins, Washington, 1982-84
5 Franco Harris, Pittsburgh, 1974-75
Franco Harris, Pittsburgh, 1977-79
3 By many players

Passing

Pass Rating

Highest Pass Rating, Career (100 attempts)

104.8 Bart Starr, Green Bay, 10 games
93.3 Ken Anderson, Cincinnati, 6 games
91.4 Joe Theismann, Washington, 10 games

Attempts

Most Passes Attempted, Career

456 Terry Bradshaw, Pittsburgh, 19 games
453 Joe Montana, San Francisco, 14 games
410 Roger Staubach, Dallas, 20 games

Most Passes Attempted, Game

64 Bernie Kosar, AFC-D: Cleveland vs. N.Y. Jets, 1986 (OT)
54 Randall Cunningham, NFC-D: Philadelphia vs. Chicago, 1988
53 Dan Fouts, AFC-D: San Diego vs. Miami, 1981 (OT)
Danny White, NFC-FR: Dallas vs. L.A. Rams, 1983

Completions

Most Passes Completed, Career

270 Joe Montana, San Francisco, 14 games
261 Terry Bradshaw, Pittsburgh, 19 games
223 Roger Staubach, Dallas, 20 games

Most Passes Completed, Game

33 Dan Fouts, AFC-D: San Diego vs. Miami, 1981 (OT)
Bernie Kosar, AFC-D: Cleveland vs. N.Y. Jets, 1986 (OT)
32 Neil Lomax, NFC-FR: St. Louis vs. Green Bay, 1982
Danny White, NFC-FR: Dallas vs. L.A. Rams, 1983
29 Don Strock, AFC-D: Miami vs. San Diego, 1981 (OT)
Dan Marino, SB: Miami vs. San Francisco, 1984

Completion Percentage

Highest Completion Percentage, Career (100 attempts)

66.3 Ken Anderson, Cincinnati, 6 games (166-110)
61.2 Dan Pastorini, Houston, 5 games (116-71)
61.0 Bart Starr, Green Bay, 10 games (213-130)

Highest Completion Percentage, Game (15 completions)

88.0 Phil Simms, SB: N.Y. Giants vs. Denver, 1986 (25-22)
84.2 David Woodley, AFC-FR: Miami vs. New England, 1982 (19-16)
78.9 Norm Van Brocklin, NFC-D: Los Angeles vs. Detroit, 1952 (19-15)

Yards Gained

Most Yards Gained, Career

3,833 Terry Bradshaw, Pittsburgh, 19 games
3,494 Joe Montana, San Francisco, 14 games
2,791 Roger Staubach, Dallas, 20 games

Most Yards Gained, Game

489 Bernie Kosar, AFC-D: Cleveland vs. N.Y. Jets, 1986 (OT)
433 Dan Fouts, AFC-D: San Diego vs. Miami, 1981 (OT)
421 Dan Marino, AFC: Miami vs. Pittsburgh, 1984

Most Games, 300 or More Yards Passing, Career

5 Dan Fouts, San Diego, 7 games
Joe Montana, San Francisco, 14 games
3 Terry Bradshaw, Pittsburgh, 19 games
Danny White, Dallas, 17 games
Dan Marino, Miami, 4 games
2 Daryle Lamonica, Buffalo-Oakland, 13 games
Ken Anderson, Cincinnati, 6 games
Bernie Kosar, Cleveland, 5 games

Most Consecutive Games, 300 or More Yards Passing

4 Dan Fouts, San Diego, 1979-81
2 Daryle Lamonica, Oakland, 1968
Ken Anderson, Cincinnati, 1981-82
Terry Bradshaw, Pittsburgh, 1979-82
Joe Montana, San Francisco, 1983-84
Dan Marino, Miami, 1984

Longest Pass Completion

93 Daryle Lamonica (to Dubenion), AFC-D: Buffalo vs. Boston, 1963 (TD)
88 George Blanda (to Cannon), AFC: Houston vs. L.A. Chargers, 1960 (TD)
86 Don Meredith (to Hayes), NFC-D: Dallas vs. Cleveland, 1967 (TD)

Average Gain

Highest Average Gain, Career (100 attempts)

8.45 Joe Theismann, Washington, 10 games (211-1,782)
8.43 Jim Plunkett, Oakland-L.A. Raiders, 10 games (272-2,293)
8.41 Terry Bradshaw, Pittsburgh, 19 games (456-3,833)

Highest Average Gain, Game (20 attempts)

14.71 Terry Bradshaw, SB: Pittsburgh vs. Los Angeles, 1979 (21-309)
13.33 Bob Waterfield, NFC-D: Los Angeles vs. Chi. Bears, 1950 (21-280)
13.16 Dan Marino, AFC: Miami vs. Pittsburgh, 1984 (32-421)

Touchdowns

Most Touchdown Passes, Career

30 Terry Bradshaw, Pittsburgh, 19 games
25 Joe Montana, San Francisco, 14 games
24 Roger Staubach, Dallas, 20 games

Most Touchdown Passes, Game

6 Daryle Lamonica, AFC-D: Oakland vs. Houston, 1969
5 Sid Luckman, NFC: Chi. Bears vs. Washington, 1943
Daryle Lamonica, AFC-D: Oakland vs. Kansas City, 1968
4 Otto Graham, NFC: Cleveland vs. Los Angeles, 1950
Tobin Rote, NFC: Detroit vs. Cleveland, 1957
Bart Starr, NFC: Green Bay vs. Dallas, 1966
Ken Stabler, AFC-D: Oakland vs. Miami, 1974
Roger Staubach, NFC: Dallas vs. Los Angeles, 1975
Terry Bradshaw, SB: Pittsburgh vs. Dallas, 1978
Don Strock, AFC-D: Miami vs. San Diego, 1981 (OT)
Lynn Dickey, NFC-FR: Green Bay vs. St. Louis, 1982
Dan Marino, AFC: Miami vs. Pittsburgh, 1984
Doug Williams, SB: Washington vs. Denver, 1987

Most Consecutive Games, Touchdown Passes

10 Ken Stabler, Oakland, 1973-77
8 Terry Bradshaw, Pittsburgh, 1977-82
Joe Montana, San Francisco, 1981-84
7 John Elway, Denver, 1984-87 (current)

Had Intercepted

Lowest Percentage, Passes Had Intercepted, Career (100 attempts)

1.41 Bart Starr, Green Bay, 10 games (213-3)
1.51 Phil Simms, N.Y. Giants, 7 games (199-3)
1.89 Jay Schroeder, Washington, 6 games (106-2)

Most Attempts Without Interception, Game

47 Daryle Lamonica, AFC: Oakland vs. N.Y. Jets, 1968
42 Dan Fouts, AFC-FR: San Diego vs. Pittsburgh, 1982
39 Daryle Lamonica, AFC-D: Oakland vs. Kansas City, 1968
Ron Jaworski, NFC-D: Philadelphia vs. Tampa Bay, 1979
Tommy Kramer, NFC-D: Minnesota vs. Washington, 1982

Most Passes Had Intercepted, Career

26 Terry Bradshaw, Pittsburgh, 19 games
19 Roger Staubach, Dallas, 20 games

17 George Blanda, Chi. Bears-Houston-Oakland, 19 games
Fran Tarkenton, Minnesota, 11 games

Most Passes Had Intercepted, Game
6 Frank Filchock, NFC: N.Y. Giants vs. Chi. Bears, 1946
Bobby Layne, NFC: Detroit vs. Cleveland, 1954
Norm Van Brocklin, NFC: Los Angeles vs. Cleveland, 1955
5 Frank Filchock, NFC: Washington vs. Chi. Bears, 1940
George Blanda, AFC: Houston vs. San Diego, 1961
George Blanda, AFC: Houston vs. Dall. Texans, 1962 (OT)
Y.A. Tittle, NFC: N.Y. Giants vs. Chicago, 1963
Mike Phipps, AFC-D: Cleveland vs. Miami, 1972
Dan Pastorini, AFC: Houston vs. Pittsburgh, 1978
Dan Fouts, AFC-D: San Diego vs. Houston, 1979
Tommy Kramer, NFC-D: Minnesota vs. Philadelphia, 1980
Dan Fouts, AFC-D: San Diego vs. Miami, 1982
Richard Todd, AFC: N.Y. Jets vs Miami, 1982
Gary Danielson, NFC-D: Detroit vs. San Francisco, 1983
4 By many players

Pass Receiving

Receptions

Most Receptions, Career
73 Cliff Branch, Oakland-L.A. Raiders, 22 games
70 Fred Biletnikoff, Oakland, 19 games
67 Drew Pearson, Dallas, 22 games

Most Receptions, Game
13 Kellen Winslow, AFC-D: San Diego vs. Miami, 1981 (OT)
12 Raymond Berry, NFC: Baltimore vs. N.Y. Giants, 1958
11 Dante Lavelli, NFC: Cleveland vs. Los Angeles, 1950
Dan Ross, SB: Cincinnati vs. San Francisco, 1981
Franco Harris, AFC-FR: Pittsburgh vs. San Diego, 1982
Steve Watson, AFC-D: Denver vs. Pittsburgh, 1984
John L. Williams, AFC-D: Seattle vs. Cincinnati, 1988
Jerry Rice, SB: San Francisco vs. Cincinnati, 1988

Most Consecutive Games, Pass Receptions
22 Drew Pearson, Dallas, 1973-83
18 Paul Warfield, Cleveland-Miami, 1964-74
Cliff Branch, Oakland-L.A. Raiders, 1974-83
17 John Stallworth, Pittsburgh, 1974-84

Yards Gained

Most Yards Gained, Career
1,289 Cliff Branch, Oakland-L.A. Raiders, 22 games
1,167 Fred Biletnikoff, Oakland, 19 games
1,121 Paul Warfield, Cleveland-Miami, 18 games

Most Yards Gained, Game
227 Anthony Carter, NFC-D: Minnesota vs. San Francisco, 1987
215 Jerry Rice, SB: San Francisco vs. Cincinnati, 1988
198 Tom Fears, NFC-D: Los Angeles vs. Chi. Bears, 1950

Most Games, 100 or More Yards Receiving, Career
5 John Stallworth, Pittsburgh, 18 games
4 Fred Biletnikoff, Oakland, 19 games
Dwight Clark, San Francisco, 7 games
3 Tom Fears, L.A. Rams, 6 games
Cliff Branch, Oakland-L.A. Raiders, 22 games
Tony Nathan, Miami, 10 games

Most Consecutive Games, 100 or More Yards Receiving, Career
3 Tom Fears, Los Angeles, 1950-51
2 Lenny Moore, Baltimore, 1958-59
Fred Biletnikoff, Oakland, 1968
Paul Warfield, Miami, 1971
Charlie Joiner, San Diego, 1981
Dwight Clark, San Francisco, 1981
Cris Collinsworth, Cincinnati, 1981-82
John Stallworth, Pittsburgh, 1979-82
Wesley Walker, N.Y. Jets, 1982
Charlie Brown, Washington, 1983
Steve Largent, Seattle, 1984-87
Jerry Rice, San Francisco, 1988 (current)

Longest Reception
93 Elbert Dubenion (from Lamonica), AFC-D: Buffalo vs. Boston, 1963 (TD)
88 Billy Cannon (from Blanda), AFC: Houston vs. L.A. Chargers, 1960 (TD)
86 Bob Hayes (from Meredith), NFC: Dallas vs. Cleveland, 1967 (TD)

Average Gain

Highest Average Gain, Career (20 receptions)
22.8 Harold Jackson, L.A. Rams-New England-Minnesota-Seattle, 14 games (24-548)
20.7 Charlie Brown, Washington, 8 games (31-643)
20.5 Frank Lewis, Pittsburgh-Buffalo, 12 games (27-553)

Highest Average Gain, Game (3 receptions)
46.3 Harold Jackson, NFC: Los Angeles vs. Minnesota, 1974 (3-139)
42.7 Billy Cannon, AFC: Houston vs. L.A. Chargers, 1960 (3-128)
42.0 Lenny Moore, NFC: Baltimore vs. N.Y. Giants, 1959 (3-126)

Touchdowns

Most Touchdowns, Career
12 John Stallworth, Pittsburgh, 18 games
10 Fred Biletnikoff, Oakland, 19 games
9 Lynn Swann, Pittsburgh, 16 games

Most Touchdowns, Game
3 Tom Fears, NFC-D: Los Angeles vs. Chi. Bears, 1950
Gary Collins, NFC: Cleveland vs. Baltimore, 1964
Fred Biletnikoff, AFC-D: Oakland vs. Kansas City, 1968
Preston Pearson, NFC: Dallas vs. Los Angeles, 1975
Dave Casper, AFC-D: Oakland vs. Baltimore, 1977 (OT)
Alvin Garrett, NFC-FR: Washington vs. Detroit, 1982
Jerry Rice, NFC-D: San Francisco vs. Minnesota, 1988

Most Consecutive Games, Touchdown Passes Caught
8 John Stallworth, Pittsburgh, 1978-83
4 Lynn Swann, Pittsburgh, 1978-79
Harold Carmichael, Philadelphia, 1978-80

Fred Solomon, San Francisco, 1983-84
3 By many players

Interceptions By

Most Interceptions, Career
9 Charlie Waters, Dallas, 25 games
Bill Simpson, Los Angeles-Buffalo, 11 games
8 Lester Hayes, Oakland-L.A. Raiders, 13 games
7 Willie Brown, Oakland, 17 games
Dennis Thurman, Dallas, 14 games

Most Interceptions, Game
4 Vernon Perry, AFC-D: Houston vs. San Diego, 1979
3 Joe Laws, NFC: Green Bay vs. N.Y. Giants, 1944
Charlie Waters, NFC-D: Dallas vs. Chicago, 1977
Rod Martin, SB: Oakland vs. Philadelphia, 1980
Dennis Thurman, NFC-D: Dallas vs. Green Bay, 1982
A.J. Duhe, AFC: Miami vs. N.Y. Jets, 1982
2 By many players

Most Consecutive Games, Interceptions
3 Warren Lahr, Cleveland, 1950-51
Ken Gorgal, Cleveland, 1950-53
Joe Schmidt, Detroit, 1954-57
Emmitt Thomas, Kansas City, 1969
Mel Renfro, Dallas, 1970
Rick Volk, Baltimore, 1970-71
Mike Wagner, Pittsburgh, 1975-76
Randy Hughes, Dallas, 1977-78
Vernon Perry, Houston, 1979-80
Lester Hayes, Oakland, 1980
Gerald Small, Miami, 1982
Lester Hayes, L.A. Raiders, 1982-83
Fred Marion, New England, 1985
John Harris, Seattle-Minnesota, 1984-87

Yards Gained

Most Yards Gained, Career
196 Willie Brown, Oakland, 17 games
151 Glen Edwards, Pittsburgh-San Diego, 17 games
149 Bill Simpson, Los Angeles-Buffalo, 11 games
LeRoy Irvin, L.A. Rams, 7 games

Most Yards Gained, Game
98 Darrol Ray, AFC-FR: N.Y. Jets vs. Cincinnati, 1982
94 LeRoy Irvin, NFC-FR: L.A. Rams vs. Dallas, 1983
88 Walt Sumner, NFC-D: Cleveland vs. Dallas, 1969

Longest Return
98 Darrol Ray, AFC-FR: N.Y. Jets vs. Cincinnati, 1982 (TD)
94 LeRoy Irvin, NFC-FR: L.A. Rams vs. Dallas, 1983
88 Walt Sumner, NFC-D: Cleveland vs. Dallas, 1969 (TD)

Touchdowns

Most Touchdowns, Career
3 Willie Brown, Oakland, 17 games
2 Lester Hayes, Oakland-L.A. Raiders, 13 games

Most Touchdowns, Game
1 By 43 players

Punting

Most Punts, Career
111 Ray Guy, Oakland-L.A. Raiders, 22 games
84 Danny White, Dallas, 18 games
73 Mike Eischeid, Oakland-Minnesota, 14 games

Most Punts, Game
14 Dave Jennings, AFC-D: N.Y. Jets vs. Cleveland, 1986 (OT)
12 David Lee, AFC-D: Baltimore vs. Oakland, 1977 (OT)
11 Ken Strong, NFC: N.Y. Giants vs. Chi. Bears, 1933
Jim Norton, AFC: Houston vs. Oakland, 1967
Dale Hatcher, NFC: L.A. Rams vs. Chicago, 1985

Longest Punt
76 Ed Danowski, NFC: N.Y. Giants vs. Detroit, 1935
72 Charlie Conerly, NFC-D: N.Y. Giants vs. Cleveland, 1950
71 Ray Guy, AFC: Oakland vs. San Diego, 1980

Average Yardage

Highest Average, Career (20 punts)
44.5 Rich Camarillo, New England, 6 games (35-1,559)
43.4 Jerrel Wilson, Kansas City-New England, 8 games (43-1,866)
43.1 Don Chandler, N.Y. Giants-Green Bay, 14 games (53-2,282)

Highest Average, Game (4 punts)
56.0 Ray Guy, AFC: Oakland vs. San Diego, 1980 (4-224)
52.5 Sammy Baugh, NFC: Washington vs. Chi. Bears, 1942 (6-315)
51.4 John Hadl, AFC: San Diego vs. Buffalo, 1965 (5-257)

Punt Returns

Most Punt Returns, Career
25 Theo Bell, Pittsburgh-Tampa Bay, 10 games
19 Willie Wood, Green Bay, 10 games
Butch Johnson, Dallas-Denver, 18 games
Phil McConkey, N.Y. Giants, 5 games
18 Neal Colzie, Oakland-Miami-Tampa Bay, 10 games
Gerald McNeil, Cleveland, 5 games

Most Punt Returns, Game
7 Ron Gardin, AFC-D: Baltimore vs. Cincinnati, 1970
Carl Roaches, AFC-FR: Houston vs. Oakland, 1980
Gerald McNeil, AFC-D: Cleveland vs. N.Y. Jets, 1986 (OT)
Phil McConkey, NFC-D: N.Y. Giants vs. San Francisco, 1986
6 George McAfee, NFC-D: Chi. Bears vs. Los Angeles, 1950
Eddie Brown, NFC-D: Washington vs. Minnesota, 1976
Theo Bell, AFC: Pittsburgh vs. Houston, 1978
Eddie Brown, NFC: Los Angeles vs. Tampa Bay, 1979
John Sciarra, NFC: Philadelphia vs. Dallas, 1980
Kurt Sohn, AFC: N.Y. Jets vs. Miami, 1982

Mike Nelms, SB: Washington vs. Miami, 1982
Anthony Carter, NFC-FR: Minnesota vs. New Orleans, 1987
5 By many players

Yards Gained

Most Yards Gained, Career
237 Anthony Carter, Minnesota, 5 games
221 Neal Colzie, Oakland-Miami-Tampa Bay, 10 games
208 Butch Johnson, Dallas-Denver, 18 games

Most Yards Gained, Game
143 Anthony Carter, NFC-FR: Minnesota vs. New Orleans, 1987
141 Bob Hayes, NFC-D: Dallas vs. Cleveland, 1967
102 Charley Trippi, NFC: Chi. Cardinals vs. Philadelphia, 1947

Longest Return
84 Anthony Carter, NFC-FR: Minnesota vs. New Orleans, 1987 (TD)
81 Hugh Gallarneau, NFC-D: Chi. Bears vs. Green Bay, 1941 (TD)
79 Bosh Pritchard, NFC-D: Philadelphia vs. Pittsburgh, 1947 (TD)

Average Yardage

Highest Average, Career (10 returns)
15.8 Anthony Carter, Minnesota, 5 games (15-237)
12.6 Bob Hayes, Dallas, 15 games (12-151)
12.4 Mike Fuller, San Diego-Cincinnati, 7 games (13-161)

Highest Average Gain, Game (3 returns)
47.0 Bob Hayes, NFC-D: Dallas vs. Cleveland, 1967 (3-141)
29.0 George (Butch) Byrd, AFC: Buffalo vs. San Diego, 1965 (3-87)
25.3 Bosh Pritchard, NFC-D: Philadelphia vs. Pittsburgh, 1947 (4-101)

Touchdowns

Most Touchdowns
1 Hugh Gallarneau, NFC-D: Chicago Bears vs. Green Bay, 1941
Bosh Pritchard, NFC-D: Philadelphia vs. Pittsburgh, 1947
Charley Trippi, NFC: Chicago Cardinals vs. Philadelphia, 1947
Verda (Vitamin T) Smith, NFC-D: Los Angeles vs. Detroit, 1952
George (Butch) Byrd, AFC: Buffalo vs. San Diego, 1965
Golden Richards, NFC: Dallas vs. Minnesota, 1973
Wes Chandler, AFC-D: San Diego vs. Miami, 1981 (OT)
Shaun Gayle, NFC-D: Chicago vs. N.Y. Giants, 1985
Anthony Carter, NFC-FR: Minnesota vs. New Orleans, 1987
Darrell Green, NFC-D: Washington vs. Chicago, 1987

Kickoff Returns

Most Kickoff Returns, Career
29 Fulton Walker, Miami-L.A. Raiders, 10 games
19 Preston Pearson, Baltimore-Pittsburgh-Dallas, 22 games
18 Charlie West, Minnesota, 9 games

Most Kickoff Returns, Game
7 Don Bingham, NFC: Chi. Bears vs. N.Y. Giants, 1956
Reggie Brown, NFC-FR: Atlanta vs. Minnesota, 1982
David Verser, AFC-FR: Cincinnati vs. N.Y. Jets, 1982
Del Rodgers, NFC-D: Green Bay vs. Dallas, 1982
Henry Ellard, NFC-D: L.A. Rams vs. Washington, 1983
Stephen Starring, SB: New England vs. Chicago, 1985
6 Wallace Francis, AFC-D: Buffalo vs. Pittsburgh, 1974
Eddie Brown, NFC-D: Washington vs. Minnesota, 1976
Eddie Payton, NFC-D: Minnesota vs. Philadelphia, 1980
Alvin Hall, NFC-FR: Detroit vs. Washington, 1982
Fulton Walker, AFC-D: Miami vs. Seattle, 1983
Johnny Hector, AFC-FR: N.Y. Jets vs. New England, 1985
Lorenzo Hampton, AFC: Miami vs. New England, 1985
Albert Bentley, AFC-D: Indianapolis vs. Cleveland, 1987
5 By many players

Yards Gained

Most Yards Gained, Career
677 Fulton Walker, Miami-L.A. Raiders, 10 games
481 Carl Garrett, Oakland, 5 games
458 Cullen Bryant, L.A. Rams-Seattle, 19 games

Most Yards Gained, Game
190 Fulton Walker, SB: Miami vs. Washington, 1982
170 Les (Speedy) Duncan, NFC-D: Washington vs. San Francisco, 1971
169 Carl Garrett, AFC-D: Oakland vs. Baltimore, 1977 (OT)

Longest Return
98 Fulton Walker, SB: Miami vs. Washington, 1982 (TD)
97 Vic Washington, NFC-D: San Francisco vs. Dallas, 1972 (TD)
93 Stanford Jennings, SB: Cincinnati vs. San Francisco, 1988 (TD)

Average Yardage

Highest Average, Career (10 returns)
30.1 Carl Garrett, Oakland, 5 games (16-481)
27.9 George Atkinson, Oakland, 16 games (12-335)
25.3 Dennis Gentry, Chicago, 9 games (14-354)

Highest Average, Game (3 returns)
56.7 Les (Speedy) Duncan, NFC-D: Washington vs. San Francisco, 1971 (3-170)
51.3 Ed Podolak, AFC-D: Kansas City vs. Miami, 1971 (OT) (3-154)
49.0 Les (Speedy) Duncan, AFC: San Diego vs. Buffalo, 1964 (3-147)

Touchdowns

Most Touchdowns
1 Vic Washington, NFC-D: San Francisco vs. Dallas, 1972
Nat Moore, AFC-D: Miami vs. Oakland, 1974
Marshall Johnson, AFC-D: Baltimore vs. Oakland, 1977 (OT)
Fulton Walker, SB: Miami vs. Washington, 1982
Stanford Jennings, SB: Cincinnati vs. San Francisco, 1988

Fumbles

Most Fumbles, Career
13 Tony Dorsett, Dallas, 17 games
10 Franco Harris, Pittsburgh, 19 games
Terry Bradshaw, Pittsburgh, 19 games
Roger Staubach, Dallas, 20 games
9 Chuck Foreman, Minnesota, 13 games

Most Fumbles, Game
4 Brian Sipe, AFC-D: Cleveland vs. Oakland, 1980
3 Y.A. Tittle, NFC-D: San Francisco vs. Detroit, 1957
Bill Nelsen, AFC-D: Cleveland vs. Baltimore, 1972
Chuck Foreman, NFC: Minnesota vs. Los Angeles, 1974
Lawrence McCutcheon, NFC-D: Los Angeles vs. St. Louis, 1975
Roger Staubach, SB: Dallas vs. Pittsburgh, 1975
Terry Bradshaw, AFC: Pittsburgh vs. Houston, 1978
Earl Campbell, AFC: Houston vs. Pittsburgh, 1978
Franco Harris, AFC: Pittsburgh vs. Houston, 1978
Chuck Muncie, AFC: San Diego vs. Cincinnati, 1981
Andra Franklin, AFC-FR: Miami vs. New England, 1982
Eric Dickerson, NFC-FR: L.A. Rams vs. Washington, 1986
2 By many players

Recoveries

Most Own Fumbles Recovered, Career
5 Roger Staubach, Dallas, 20 games
4 Fran Tarkenton, Minnesota, 11 games
3 Alex Webster, N.Y. Giants, 7 games
Don Meredith, Dallas, 4 games
Franco Harris, Pittsburgh, 19 games
Gerry Mullins, Pittsburgh, 18 games
Ron Jaworski, Los Angeles-Philadelphia, 10 games
Lyle Blackwood, Cincinnati-Baltimore-Miami, 14 games
Joe Montana, San Francisco, 14 games

Most Opponents' Fumbles Recovered, Career
4 Cliff Harris, Dallas, 21 games
Harvey Martin, Dallas, 22 games
Ted Hendricks, Baltimore-Oakland-L.A. Raiders, 21 games
3 Paul Krause, Minnesota, 19 games
Jack Lambert, Pittsburgh, 18 games
Fred Dryer, Los Angeles, 14 games
Charlie Waters, Dallas, 25 games
Jack Ham, Pittsburgh, 16 games
Mike Hegman, Dallas, 16 games
Tom Jackson, Denver, 10 games
Mike Singletary, Chicago, 9 games
Monte Coleman, Washington, 14 games
Darryl Grant, Washington, 14 games
Alvin Walton, Washington, 6 games
2 By many players

Most Fumbles Recovered, Game, Own and Opponents'
3 Jack Lambert, AFC: Pittsburgh vs. Oakland, 1975 (3 opp)
Ron Jaworski, NFC-FR: Philadelphia vs. N.Y. Giants, 1981 (3 own)
2 By many players

Yards Gained

Longest Return
93 Andy Russell, AFC-D: Pittsburgh vs. Baltimore, 1975 (opp, TD)
60 Mike Curtis, NFC-D: Baltimore vs. Minnesota, 1968 (opp, TD)
Hugh Green, NFC-FR: Tampa Bay vs. Dallas, 1982 (opp, TD)
52 Wilber Marshall, NFC: Chicago vs. L.A. Rams, 1985 (opp, TD)

Touchdowns

Most Touchdowns
1 By 22 players

Combined Net Yards Gained

Rushing, receiving, interception returns, punt returns, kickoff returns, and fumble returns.

Attempts

Most Attempts, Career
454 Franco Harris, Pittsburgh, 19 games
350 Tony Dorsett, Dallas, 17 games
275 Chuck Foreman, Minnesota, 13 games

Most Attempts, Game
40 Lawrence McCutcheon, NFC-D: Los Angeles vs. St. Louis, 1975
39 John Riggins, SB: Washington vs. Miami, 1982
38 Ricky Bell, NFC-D: Tampa Bay vs. Philadelphia, 1979
Rob Carpenter, NFC-FR: N.Y. Giants vs. Philadelphia, 1981

Yards Gained

Most Yards Gained, Career
2,060 Franco Harris, Pittsburgh, 19 games
1,786 Tony Dorsett, Dallas, 17 games
1,307 Chuck Foreman, Minnesota, 13 games

Most Yards Gained, Game
350 Ed Podolak, AFC-D: Kansas City vs. Miami, 1971 (OT)
329 Keith Lincoln, AFC: San Diego vs. Boston, 1963
285 Bob Hayes, NFC-D: Dallas vs. Cleveland, 1967

Sacks

Sacks have been compiled since 1982

Most Sacks, Career
10.5 Richard Dent, Chicago, 7 games
8 Dexter Manley, Washington, 14 games
7.5 Mark Gastineau, N.Y. Jets, 6 games

Most Sacks, Game
3.5 Rich Milot, NFC-D: Washington vs. Chicago, 1984
Richard Dent, NFC-D: Chicago vs. N.Y. Giants, 1985
3 Richard Dent, NFC-D: Chicago vs. Washington, 1984
Garin Veris, AFC-FR: New England vs. N.Y. Jets, 1985
Gary Jeter, NFC-D: L.A. Rams vs. Dallas, 1985
Carl Hairston, AFC-D: Cleveland vs. N.Y. Jets, 1986 (OT)
Charles Mann, NFC-D: Washington vs. Chicago, 1987
Kevin Greene, NFC-FR: L.A. Rams vs. Minnesota, 1988
2.5 Lyle Alzado, AFC-D: L.A. Raiders vs. Pittsburgh, 1983
Jacob Green, AFC-FR: Seattle vs. L.A. Raiders, 1984
Larry Roberts, NFC-D: San Francisco vs. Minnesota, 1988

Team Records

Games, Victories, Defeats

Most Seasons Participating in Postseason Games
21 Cleveland/L.A. Rams, 1945, 1949-52, 1955, 1967, 1969, 1973-80, 1983-86, 1988
Cleveland, 1950-55, 1957-58, 1964-65, 1967-69, 1971-72, 1980, 1982, 1985-88
20 N.Y. Giants, 1933-35, 1938-39, 1941, 1943-44, 1946, 1950, 1956, 1958-59, 1961-63, 1981, 1984-86
18 Dallas, 1966-73, 1975-83, 1985
Chicago, 1933-34, 1937, 1940-43, 1946, 1950, 1956, 1963, 1977, 1979, 1984-88

Most Consecutive Seasons Participating in Postseason Games
9 Dallas, 1975-83
8 Dallas, 1966-73
Pittsburgh, 1972-79
Los Angeles, 1973-80
6 Cleveland, 1950-55
Oakland, 1972-77
Minnesota, 1973-78
San Francisco, 1983-88

Most Games
36 Dallas, 1966-73, 1975-83, 1985
31 Oakland/L. A. Raiders, 1967-70, 1973-77, 1980, 1982-85
30 Cleveland/L.A. Rams, 1945, 1949-52, 1955, 1967, 1969, 1973-80, 1983-86, 1988

Most Games Won
20 Dallas, 1967, 1970-73, 1975, 1977-78, 1980-82
19 Oakland/L. A. Raiders, 1967-70, 1973-77, 1980, 1982-83
16 Washington, 1937, 1942-43, 1972, 1982-83, 1986-87

Most Consecutive Games Won
9 Green Bay, 1961-62, 1965-67
7 Pittsburgh, 1974-76
6 Miami, 1972-73
Pittsburgh, 1978-79
Washington, 1982-83

Most Games Lost
19 L.A. Rams, 1949-50, 1952, 1955, 1967, 1969, 1973-80, 1983-86, 1988
17 Cleveland, 1951-53, 1957-58, 1965, 1967-69, 1971-72, 1980, 1982, 1985-88
16 Dallas, 1966-70, 1972-73, 1975-76, 1978-83, 1985
N. Y. Giants, 1933, 1935, 1939, 1941, 1943-44, 1946, 1950, 1958-59, 1961-63, 1981, 1984-85

Most Consecutive Games Lost
6 N.Y. Giants, 1939, 1941, 1943-44, 1946, 1950
Cleveland, 1969, 1971-72, 1980, 1982, 1985
5 N.Y. Giants, 1958-59, 1961-63
Los Angeles, 1952, 1955, 1967, 1969, 1973
Denver, 1977-79, 1983-84
Baltimore/Indianapolis, 1971, 1975-77, 1987 (current)
4 Washington, 1972-74, 1976
Miami, 1974, 1978-79, 1981
Chi. Cardinals/St. Louis, 1948, 1974-75, 1982 (current)
Boston/New England, 1963, 1976, 1978, 1982

Scoring

Most Points, Game
73 NFC: Chi. Bears vs. Washington, 1940
59 NFC: Detroit vs. Cleveland, 1957
56 NFC: Cleveland vs. Detroit, 1954
AFC-D: Oakland vs. Houston, 1969

Most Points, Both Teams, Game
79 AFC-D: San Diego (41) vs. Miami (38), 1981 (OT)
73 NFC: Chi. Bears (73) vs. Washington (0), 1940
NFC: Detroit (59) vs. Cleveland (14), 1957
AFC: Miami (45) vs. Pittsburgh (28), 1984
71 AFC: Denver (38) vs. Cleveland (33), 1987

Fewest Points, Both Teams, Game
5 NFC-D: Detroit (0) vs. Dallas (5), 1970
7 NFC: Chi. Cardinals (0) vs. Philadelphia (7), 1948
9 NFC: Tampa Bay (0) vs. Los Angeles (9), 1979

Largest Margin of Victory, Game
73 NFC: Chi. Bears vs. Washington, 1940 (73-0)
49 AFC-D: Oakland vs. Houston, 1969 (56-7)
46 NFC: Cleveland vs. Detroit, 1954 (56-10)
NFC-D: N.Y. Giants vs. San Francisco, 1986 (49-3)

Most Points, Shutout Victory, Game
73 NFC: Chi. Bears vs. Washington, 1940
38 NFC-D: Dallas vs. Tampa Bay, 1981
37 NFC: Green Bay vs. N.Y. Giants, 1961

Most Points Overcome to Win Game
20 NFC-D: Detroit vs. San Francisco, 1957 (trailed 7-27, won 31-27)
18 NFC-D: Dallas vs. San Francisco, 1972 (trailed 3-21, won 30-28)
AFC-D: Miami vs. Cleveland, 1985 (trailed 3-21, won 24-21)
14 NFC-D: Philadelphia vs. Minnesota, 1980 (trailed 0-14, won 31-16)
NFC-D: Dallas vs. Atlanta, 1980 (trailed 10-24, won 30-27)
NFC-D: Washington vs. Chicago, 1987 (trailed 0-14, won 21-17)

Most Points, Each Half
1st: 38 NFC-D: Washington vs. L.A. Rams, 1983
35 NFC: Cleveland vs. Detroit, 1954
AFC-D: Oakland vs. Houston, 1969
SB: Washington vs. Denver, 1987
34 NFC: N. Y. Giants vs. Chi. Bears, 1956
2nd: 45 NFC: Chi. Bears vs. Washington, 1940
30 SB: N.Y. Giants vs. Denver, 1986
AFC: Cleveland vs. Denver, 1987
28 NFC: Chi. Bears vs. N. Y. Giants, 1941
NFC: Detroit vs. Cleveland, 1957
NFC-D: Dallas vs. Cleveland, 1967
NFC-D: Dallas vs. Tampa Bay, 1981

Most Points, Each Quarter
1st: 28 AFC-D: Oakland vs. Houston, 1969
24 AFC-D: San Diego vs. Miami, 1981 (OT)
21 NFC: Chi. Bears vs. Washington, 1940
AFC: San Diego vs. Boston, 1963
AFC-D: Oakland vs. Kansas City, 1968
AFC: Oakland vs. San Diego, 1980
2nd: 35 SB: Washington vs. Denver, 1987
26 AFC-D: Pittsburgh vs. Buffalo, 1974
24 NFC-D: Chi. Bears vs. Green Bay, 1941
NFC: Green Bay vs. N. Y. Giants, 1961
3rd: 26 NFC: Chi. Bears vs. Washington, 1940
21 NFC-D: Dallas vs. Cleveland, 1967
NFC-D: Dallas vs. Tampa Bay, 1981
AFC-D: L.A. Raiders vs. Pittsburgh, 1983
SB: Chicago vs. New England, 1985
NFC-D: N.Y. Giants vs. San Francisco, 1986
AFC: Cleveland vs. Denver, 1987
17 NFC: Cleveland vs. Baltimore, 1964
NFC-D: Dallas vs. Chicago, 1977
SB: N.Y. Giants vs. Denver, 1986
4th 27 NFC: N.Y. Giants vs. Chi. Bears, 1934
24 NFC: Baltimore vs. N. Y. Giants, 1959
21 AFC: Pittsburgh vs. Oakland, 1974
NFC: Dallas vs. Los Angeles, 1978
AFC-FR: N. Y. Jets vs. Cincinnati, 1982
NFC: San Francisco vs. Washington, 1983
OT: 6 NFC: Baltimore vs. N.Y. Giants, 1958
AFC-D: Oakland vs. Baltimore, 1977

Touchdowns

Most Touchdowns, Game
11 NFC: Chi. Bears vs. Washington, 1940
8 NFC: Cleveland vs. Detroit, 1954
NFC: Detroit vs. Cleveland, 1957
AFC-D: Oakland vs. Houston, 1969
7 AFC: San Diego vs. Boston, 1963
NFC-D: Dallas vs. Cleveland, 1967
NFC-D: N.Y. Giants vs. San Francisco, 1986

Most Touchdowns, Both Teams, Game
11 NFC: Chi. Bears (11) vs. Washington (0), 1940
10 NFC: Detroit (8) vs. Cleveland (2), 1957
AFC-D: Miami (5) vs. San Diego (5), 1981 (OT)
AFC: Miami (6) vs. Pittsburgh (4), 1984
9 NFC: Chi. Bears (6) vs. Washington (3), 1943
NFC: Cleveland (8) vs. Detroit (1), 1954
NFC-D: Dallas (7) vs. Cleveland (2), 1967
AFC-D: Oakland (8) vs. Houston (1), 1969
AFC-D: Oakland (5) vs. Baltimore (4), 1977 (OT)
SB: Pittsburgh (5) vs. Dallas (4), 1978
AFC: Denver (5) vs. Cleveland (4), 1987

Fewest Touchdowns, Both Teams, Game
0 NFC-D: N.Y. Giants vs. Cleveland, 1950
NFC-D: Dallas vs. Detroit, 1970
NFC: Los Angeles vs. Tampa Bay, 1979
1 NFC: Chi. Cardinals (0) vs. Philadelphia (1), 1948
AFC: San Diego (0) vs. Houston (1), 1961
AFC-D: N. Y. Jets (0) vs. Kansas City (1), 1969
NFC-D: Green Bay (0) vs. Washington (1), 1972
2 In many games

Points After Touchdown

Most Points After Touchdown, Game
8 NFC: Cleveland vs. Detroit, 1954
NFC: Detroit vs. Cleveland, 1957
AFC-D: Oakland vs. Houston, 1969
7 NFC: Chi. Bears vs. Washington, 1940
NFC-D: Dallas vs. Cleveland, 1967
NFC-D: N.Y. Giants vs. San Francisco, 1986
6 AFC: San Diego vs. Boston, 1963
NFC-D: Washington vs. L.A. Rams, 1983
AFC: Miami vs. Pittsburgh, 1984

Most Points After Touchdown, Both Teams, Game
10 NFC: Detroit (8) vs. Cleveland (2), 1957
AFC-D: Miami (5) vs. San Diego (5), 1981 (OT)
AFC: Miami (6) vs. Pittsburgh (4), 1984
9 NFC: Cleveland (8) vs. Detroit (1), 1954
NFC-D: Dallas (7) vs. Cleveland (2), 1967
AFC-D: Oakland (8) vs. Houston (1), 1969
AFC: Denver (5) vs. Cleveland (4), 1987
8 In many games

Fewest Points After Touchdown, Both Teams, Game
0 NFC-D: N.Y. Giants vs. Cleveland, 1950
NFC-D: Dallas vs. Detroit, 1970
NFC: Los Angeles vs. Tampa Bay, 1979

Field Goals

Most Field Goals, Game
5 NFC-D: Minnesota vs. San Francisco, 1987
4 AFC-D: Boston vs. Buffalo, 1963
AFC: Oakland vs. Houston, 1967
SB: Green Bay vs. Oakland, 1967
NFC: Washington vs. Dallas, 1972
AFC-D: Oakland vs. Pittsburgh, 1973
SB: San Francisco vs. Cincinnati, 1981
AFC-FR: New England vs. N.Y. Jets, 1985
NFC-FR: Washington vs. L.A. Rams, 1986
NFC-D: Philadelphia vs. Chicago, 1988
3 By many teams

Most Field Goals, Both Teams, Game
6 NFC-D: Minnesota (5) vs. San Francisco (1), 1987
NFC-D: Philadelphia (4) vs. Chicago (2), 1988
5 NFC: Green Bay (3) vs. Cleveland (2), 1965
AFC: Oakland (3) vs. N.Y. Jets (2), 1968
NFC: Washington (4) vs. Dallas (1), 1972
AFC-D: Cincinnati (3) vs. Miami (2), 1973
NFC-D: Los Angeles (3) vs. Dallas (2), 1973

NFC-D: Dallas (3) vs. Green Bay (2), 1982
NFC-FR: N.Y. Giants (3) vs. L.A. Rams (2), 1984
AFC-D: Cleveland (3) vs. N.Y. Jets (2), 1986 (OT)
AFC: Denver (3) vs. Cleveland (2), 1986 (OT)
AFC-FR: Houston (3) vs. Seattle (2), 1987 (OT)
SB: Cincinnati (3) vs. San Francisco (2), 1988
4 In many games

Most Field Goals Attempted, Game
6 AFC: Oakland vs. Houston, 1967
NFC-D: Los Angeles vs. Dallas, 1973
AFC-D: Cleveland vs. N.Y. Jets, 1986 (OT)
5 By many teams

Most Field Goals Attempted, Both Teams, Game
9 NFC-D: Philadelphia (5) vs. Chicago (4), 1988
8 NFC-D: Los Angeles (6) vs. Dallas (2), 1973
NFC-D: Detroit (5) vs. San Francisco (3), 1983
AFC-D: Cleveland (6) vs. N.Y. Jets (2), 1986 (OT)
NFC-D: Minnesota (5) vs. San Francisco (3), 1987
7 In many games

Safeties
Most Safeties, Game
1 By 17 teams

First Downs
Most First Downs, Game
34 AFC-D: San Diego vs. Miami, 1981 (OT)
33 AFC-D: Cleveland vs. N.Y. Jets, 1986 (OT)
31 SB: San Francisco vs. Miami, 1984

Fewest First Downs, Game
6 NFC: N.Y. Giants vs. Green Bay, 1961
7 NFC: Green Bay vs. Boston, 1936
NFC-D: Pittsburgh vs. Philadelphia, 1947
NFC: Chi. Cardinals vs. Philadelphia, 1948
NFC: Los Angeles vs. Philadelphia, 1949
NFC-D: Cleveland vs. N. Y. Giants, 1958
AFC-D: Cincinnati vs. Baltimore, 1970
NFC-D: Detroit vs. Dallas, 1970
8 By many teams

Most First Downs, Both Teams, Game
59 AFC-D: San Diego (34) vs. Miami (25), 1981 (OT)
55 AFC-FR: San Diego (29) vs. Pittsburgh (26), 1982
50 AFC: Oakland (28) vs. Baltimore (22), 1977 (OT)
NFC-FR: St. Louis (28) vs. Green Bay (22), 1982
AFC-FR: N. Y. Jets (27) vs. Cincinnati (23), 1982
AFC: Miami (28) vs. Pittsburgh (22), 1984
SB: San Francisco (31) vs. Miami (19), 1984

Fewest First Downs, Both Teams, Game
15 NFC: Green Bay (7) vs. Boston (8), 1936
19 NFC: N. Y. Giants (9) vs. Green Bay (10), 1939
NFC: Washington (9) vs. Chi. Bears (10), 1942
20 NFC-D: Cleveland (9) vs. N. Y. Giants (11), 1950

Rushing
Most First Downs, Rushing, Game
19 NFC-FR: Dallas vs. Los Angeles, 1980
18 AFC-D: Miami vs. Cincinnati, 1973
AFC-D: Pittsburgh vs. Buffalo, 1974
17 AFC-D: Cincinnati vs. Seattle, 1988

Fewest First Downs, Rushing, Game
0 NFC: Los Angeles vs. Philadelphia, 1949
AFC-D: Buffalo vs. Boston, 1963
AFC: Oakland vs. Pittsburgh, 1974
NFC-FR: New Orleans vs. Minnesota, 1987
1 NFC: N. Y. Giants vs. Green Bay, 1961
AFC-D: Houston vs. Oakland, 1969
NFC: Los Angeles vs. Dallas, 1975
AFC-FR: Cleveland vs. L. A. Raiders, 1982
NFC-D: N.Y. Giants vs. Chicago, 1985
SB: New England vs. Chicago, 1985
AFC-FR: Seattle vs. Houston, 1987 (OT)
NFC-D: Philadelphia vs. Chicago, 1988
AFC-D: Seattle vs. Cincinnati, 1988
2 By many teams

Most First Downs, Rushing, Both Teams, Game
25 NFC-FR: Dallas (19) vs. Los Angeles (6), 1980
23 NFC: Cleveland (15) vs. Detroit (8), 1952
AFC-D: Miami (18) vs. Cincinnati (5), 1973
AFC-D: Pittsburgh (18) vs. Buffalo (5), 1974
22 AFC: Miami (18) vs. Oakland (4), 1973
AFC-D: Buffalo (11) vs. Cincinnati (11), 1981
AFC-D: L.A. Raiders (13) vs. Pittsburgh (9), 1983

Fewest First Downs, Rushing, Both Teams, Game
5 AFC-D: Buffalo (0) vs. Boston (5), 1963
6 NFC: Green Bay (2) vs. Boston (4), 1936
NFC-D: Baltimore (2) vs. Minnesota (4), 1968
AFC-D: Houston (1) vs. Oakland (5), 1969
7 NFC-D: Washington (2) vs. N. Y. Giants (5), 1943
NFC: Baltimore (3) vs. N. Y. Giants (4), 1959
NFC: Washington (3) vs. Dallas (4), 1972
AFC-FR: N. Y. Jets (3) vs. Buffalo (4), 1981

Passing
Most First Downs, Passing, Game
21 AFC-D: Miami vs. San Diego, 1981 (OT)
AFC-D: San Diego vs. Miami, 1981 (OT)
AFC-D: Cleveland vs. N.Y. Jets, 1986 (OT)
NFC-D: Philadelphia vs. Chicago, 1988
20 NFC-FR: Dallas vs. L.A. Rams, 1983
19 NFC-FR: St. Louis vs. Green Bay, 1982
NFC-FR: Dallas vs. Tampa Bay, 1982
AFC-FR: Pittsburgh vs. San Diego, 1982
AFC-FR: San Diego vs. Pittsburgh, 1982
NFC: Dallas vs. Washington, 1982

Fewest First Downs, Passing, Game
0 NFC: Philadelphia vs. Chi. Cardinals, 1948
1 NFC-D: N. Y. Giants vs. Washington, 1943
NFC: Cleveland vs. Detroit, 1953
SB: Denver vs. Dallas, 1977
2 By many teams

Most First Downs, Passing, Both Teams, Game
42 AFC-D: Miami (21) vs. San Diego (21), 1981 (OT)
38 AFC-FR: Pittsburgh (19) vs. San Diego (19), 1982
32 NFC-FR: St. Louis (19) vs. Green Bay (13), 1982
AFC: Miami (18) vs. Pittsburgh (14), 1984
SB: Miami (17) vs. San Francisco (15), 1984

Fewest First Downs, Passing, Both Teams, Game
2 NFC: Philadelphia (0) vs. Chi. Cardinals (2), 1948
4 NFC-D: Cleveland (2) vs. N. Y. Giants (2), 1950
5 NFC: Detroit (2) vs. N. Y. Giants (3), 1935
NFC: Green Bay (2) vs. N. Y. Giants (3), 1939

Penalty
Most First Downs, Penalty, Game
7 AFC-D: New England vs. Oakland, 1976
6 AFC-D: Cleveland vs. N.Y. Jets, 1986 (OT)
5 AFC-FR: Cleveland vs. L. A. Raiders, 1982

Most First Downs, Penalty, Both Teams, Game
9 AFC-D: New England (7) vs. Oakland (2), 1976
8 NFC-FR: Atlanta (4) vs. Minnesota (4), 1982
7 AFC-D: Baltimore (4) vs. Oakland (3), 1977 (OT)

Net Yards Gained Rushing and Passing
Most Yards Gained, Game
610 AFC: San Diego vs. Boston, 1963
602 SB: Washington vs. Denver, 1987
569 AFC: Miami vs. Pittsburgh, 1984

Fewest Yards Gained, Game
86 NFC-D: Cleveland vs. N.Y. Giants, 1958
99 NFC: Chi. Cardinals vs. Philadelphia, 1948
114 NFC-D: N.Y. Giants vs. Washington, 1943

Most Yards Gained, Both Teams, Game
1,036 AFC-D: San Diego (564) vs. Miami (472), 1981 (OT)
1,024 AFC: Miami (569) vs. Pittsburgh (455), 1984
929 SB: Washington (602) vs. Denver (327), 1987

Fewest Yards Gained, Both Teams, Game
331 NFC: Chi. Cardinals (99) vs. Philadelphia (232), 1948
332 NFC-D: N.Y. Giants (150) vs. Cleveland (182), 1950
336 NFC: Boston (116) vs. Green Bay (220), 1936

Rushing
Attempts
Most Attempts, Game
65 NFC: Detroit vs. N.Y. Giants, 1935
61 NFC: Philadelphia vs. Los Angeles, 1949
59 AFC: New England vs. Miami, 1985

Fewest Attempts, Game
9 SB: Miami vs. San Francisco, 1984
11 SB: New England vs. Chicago, 1985
AFC-FR: Seattle vs. Houston, 1987 (OT)
12 AFC-D: Buffalo vs. Boston, 1963

Most Attempts, Both Teams, Game
109 NFC: Detroit (65) vs. N.Y. Giants (44), 1935
97 AFC-D: Baltimore (50) vs. Oakland (47), 1977 (OT)
91 NFC: Philadelphia (57) vs. Chi. Cardinals (34), 1948

Fewest Attempts, Both Teams, Game
45 AFC-FR: N.Y. Jets (22) vs. Buffalo (23), 1981
46 AFC: Buffalo (13) vs. Kansas City (33), 1966
48 AFC-D: Buffalo (12) vs. Boston (36), 1963
AFC: Boston (16) vs. San Diego (32), 1963

Yards Gained
Most Yards Gained, Game
382 NFC: Chi. Bears vs. Washington, 1940
338 NFC-FR: Dallas vs. Los Angeles, 1980
318 AFC: San Diego vs. Boston, 1963

Fewest Yards Gained, Game
7 AFC-D: Buffalo vs. Boston, 1963
SB: New England vs. Chicago, 1985
17 SB: Minnesota vs. Pittsburgh, 1974
18 AFC-D: Seattle vs. Cincinnati, 1988

Most Yards Gained, Both Teams, Game
430 NFC-FR: Dallas (338) vs. Los Angeles (92), 1980
426 NFC: Cleveland (227) vs. Detroit (199), 1952
404 NFC: Chi. Bears (382) vs. Washington (22), 1940

Fewest Yards Gained, Both Teams, Game
90 AFC-D: Buffalo (7) vs. Boston (83), 1963
106 NFC: Boston (39) vs. Green Bay (67), 1936
128 NFC-FR: Philadelphia (53) vs. Atlanta (75), 1978

Average Gain
Highest Average Gain, Game
9.94 AFC: San Diego vs. Boston, 1963 (32-318)
9.29 NFC-D: Green Bay vs. Dallas, 1982 (17-158)
7.35 NFC-FR: Dallas vs. Los Angeles, 1980 (46-338)

Lowest Average Gain, Game
0.58 AFC-D: Buffalo vs. Boston, 1963 (12-7)
0.64 SB: New England vs. Chicago, 1985 (11-7)
0.81 SB: Minnesota vs. Pittsburgh, 1974 (21-17)

Touchdowns
Most Touchdowns, Game
7 NFC: Chi. Bears vs. Washington, 1940
5 NFC: Cleveland vs. Detroit, 1954

4 NFC: Detroit vs. N.Y. Giants, 1935
AFC: San Diego vs. Boston, 1963
NFC-D: Dallas vs. Cleveland, 1967
NFC: Baltimore vs. Cleveland, 1968
NFC-FR: Dallas vs. Los Angeles, 1980
AFC-D: L.A. Raiders vs. Pittsburgh, 1983
SB: Chicago vs. New England, 1985

Most Touchdowns, Both Teams, Game
7 NFC: Chi. Bears (7) vs. Washington (0), 1940
6 NFC: Cleveland (5) vs. Detroit (1), 1954
5 NFC: Chi. Cardinals (3) vs. Philadelphia (2), 1947
AFC: San Diego (4) vs. Boston (1), 1963
AFC-D: Cincinnati (3) vs. Buffalo (2), 1981

Passing

Attempts

Most Attempts, Game
65 AFC-D: Cleveland vs. N.Y. Jets, 1986 (OT)
55 NFC-D: Philadelphia vs. Chicago, 1988
54 AFC-D: San Diego vs. Miami, 1981 (OT)

Fewest Attempts, Game
5 NFC: Detroit vs. N.Y. Giants, 1935
6 AFC: Miami vs. Oakland, 1973
7 SB: Miami vs. Minnesota, 1973

Most Attempts, Both Teams, Game
102 AFC-D: San Diego (54) vs. Miami (48), 1981 (OT)
96 AFC: N.Y. Jets (49) vs. Oakland (47), 1968
95 AFC-D: Cleveland (65) vs. N.Y. Jets (30), 1986 (OT)

Fewest Attempts, Both Teams, Game
18 NFC: Detroit (5) vs. N.Y. Giants (13), 1935
21 NFC: Chi. Bears (7) vs. N.Y. Giants (14), 1933
23 NFC: Chi. Cardinals (11) vs. Philadelphia (12), 1948

Completions

Most Completions, Game
34 AFC-D: Cleveland vs. N.Y. Jets, 1986 (OT)
33 AFC-D: San Diego vs. Miami, 1981 (OT)
32 NFC-FR: St. Louis vs. Green Bay, 1982
NFC-FR: Dallas vs. L.A. Rams, 1983

Fewest Completions, Game
2 NFC: Detroit vs. N.Y. Giants, 1935
NFC: Philadelphia vs. Chi. Cardinals, 1948
3 NFC: N.Y. Giants vs. Chi. Bears, 1941
NFC: Green Bay vs. N.Y. Giants, 1944
NFC: Chi. Cardinals vs. Philadelphia, 1947
NFC: Chi. Cardinals vs. Philadelphia, 1948
NFC-D: Cleveland vs. N.Y. Giants, 1950
NFC-D: N.Y. Giants vs. Cleveland, 1950
NFC: Cleveland vs. Detroit, 1953
AFC: Miami vs. Oakland, 1973
4 NFC-D: Dallas vs. Detroit, 1970
AFC: Miami vs. Baltimore, 1971
SB: Miami vs. Washington, 1982
AFC-FR: Seattle vs. L.A. Raiders, 1984

Most Completions, Both Teams, Game
64 AFC-D: San Diego (33) vs. Miami (31), 1981 (OT)
55 AFC-FR: Pittsburgh (28) vs. San Diego (27), 1982
53 SB: Miami (29) vs. San Francisco (24), 1984

Fewest Completions, Both Teams, Game
5 NFC: Philadelphia (2) vs. Chi. Cardinals (3), 1948
6 NFC: Detroit (2) vs. N.Y. Giants (4), 1935
NFC-D: Cleveland (3) vs. N.Y. Giants (3), 1950
11 NFC: Green Bay (3) vs. N.Y. Giants (8), 1944
NFC-D: Dallas (4) vs. Detroit (7), 1970

Completion Percentage

Highest Completion Percentage, Game (20 attempts)
88.0 SB: N.Y. Giants vs. Denver, 1986 (25-22)
80.0 NFC-D: Washington vs. L.A Rams, 1983 (25-20)
79.2 AFC-D: Pittsburgh vs. Baltimore, 1976 (24-19)

Lowest Completion Percentage, Game (20 attempts)
18.5 NFC: Tampa Bay vs. Los Angeles, 1979 (27-5)
20.0 NFC-D: N.Y. Giants vs. Washington, 1943 (20-4)
25.8 NFC: Chi. Bears vs. Washington, 1937 (31-8)

Yards Gained

Most Yards Gained, Game
483 AFC-D: Cleveland vs. N.Y. Jets, 1986 (OT)
435 AFC: Miami vs. Pittsburgh, 1984
415 AFC-D: San Diego vs. Miami, 1981 (OT)

Fewest Yards Gained, Game
3 NFC: Chi. Cardinals vs. Philadelphia, 1948
7 NFC: Philadelphia vs. Chi. Cardinals, 1948
9 NFC-D: N.Y. Giants vs. Cleveland, 1950
NFC: Cleveland vs. Detroit, 1953

Most Yards Gained, Both Teams, Game
809 AFC-D: San Diego (415) vs. Miami (394), 1981 (OT)
747 AFC: Miami (435) vs. Pittsburgh (312), 1984
666 AFC-D: Cleveland (483) vs. N.Y. Jets (183), 1986 (OT)

Fewest Yards Gained, Both Teams, Game
10 NFC: Chi. Cardinals (3) vs. Philadelphia (7), 1948
38 NFC-D: N.Y. Giants (9) vs. Cleveland (29), 1950
102 NFC-D: Dallas (22) vs. Detroit (80), 1970

Times Sacked

Most Times Sacked, Game
9 AFC: Kansas City vs. Buffalo, 1966
NFC: Chicago vs. San Francisco, 1984
AFC-D: N.Y. Jets vs. Cleveland, 1986 (OT)
8 NFC: Green Bay vs. Dallas, 1967
NFC: Minnesota vs. Washington, 1987
7 NFC-D: Dallas vs. Los Angeles, 1973
SB: Dallas vs. Pittsburgh, 1975
AFC-FR: Houston vs. Oakland, 1980
NFC-D: Washington vs. Chicago, 1984
SB: New England vs. Chicago, 1985

Most Times Sacked, Both Teams, Game
13 AFC: Kansas City (9) vs. Buffalo (4), 1966
AFC-D: N.Y. Jets (9) vs. Cleveland (4), 1986 (OT)
12 NFC-D: Dallas (7) vs. Los Angeles (5), 1973
NFC-D: Washington (7) vs. Chicago (5), 1984
NFC: Chicago (9) vs. San Francisco (3), 1984
10 AFC-FR: Houston (7) vs. Oakland (3), 1980
NFC-D: N.Y. Giants (6) vs. San Francisco (4), 1984
SB: New England (7) vs. Chicago (3), 1985

Fewest Times Sacked, Both Teams, Game
0 AFC-D: Buffalo vs. Pittsburgh, 1974
AFC-FR: Pittsburgh vs. San Diego, 1982
1 In many games

Touchdowns

Most Touchdowns, Game
6 AFC-D: Oakland vs. Houston, 1969
5 NFC: Chi. Bears vs. Washington, 1943
NFC: Detroit vs. Cleveland, 1957
AFC-D: Oakland vs. Kansas City, 1968
4 NFC: Cleveland vs. Los Angeles, 1950
NFC: Green Bay vs. Dallas, 1966
AFC-D: Oakland vs. Miami, 1974
NFC: Dallas vs. Los Angeles, 1975
SB: Pittsburgh vs. Dallas, 1978
AFC-D: Miami vs. San Diego, 1981 (OT)
NFC-FR: Green Bay vs. St. Louis, 1982
AFC: Miami vs. Pittsburgh, 1984
NFC-D: N.Y. Giants vs. San Francisco, 1986
SB: Washington vs. Denver, 1987

Most Touchdowns, Both Teams, Game
7 NFC: Chi. Bears (5) vs. Washington (2), 1943
AFC-D: Oakland (6) vs. Houston (1), 1969
SB: Pittsburgh (4) vs. Dallas (3), 1978
AFC-D: Miami (4) vs. San Diego (3), 1981 (OT)
AFC: Miami (4) vs. Pittsburgh (3), 1984
6 NFC-FR: Green Bay (4) vs. St. Louis (2), 1982
AFC: Cleveland (3) vs. Denver (3), 1987
5 In many games

Interceptions By

Most Interceptions By, Game
8 NFC: Chi. Bears vs. Washington, 1940
7 NFC: Cleveland vs. Los Angeles, 1955
6 NFC: Green Bay vs. N.Y. Giants, 1939
NFC: Chi. Bears vs. N.Y. Giants, 1946
NFC: Cleveland vs. Detroit, 1954
AFC: San Diego vs. Houston, 1961

Most Interceptions By, Both Teams, Game
10 NFC: Cleveland (7) vs. Los Angeles (3), 1955
AFC: San Diego (6) vs. Houston (4), 1961
9 NFC: Green Bay (6) vs. N.Y. Giants (3), 1939
8 NFC: Chi. Bears (8) vs. Washington (0), 1940
NFC: Chi. Bears (6) vs. N.Y. Giants (2), 1946
NFC: Cleveland (6) vs. Detroit (2), 1954
AFC-FR: Buffalo (4) vs. N.Y. Jets (4), 1981
AFC: Miami (5) vs. N.Y. Jets (3), 1982

Yards Gained

Most Yards Gained, Game
138 AFC-FR: N.Y. Jets vs. Cincinnati, 1982
136 AFC: Dall. Texans vs. Houston, 1962 (OT)
130 NFC-D: Los Angeles vs. St. Louis, 1975

Most Yards Gained, Both Teams, Game
156 NFC: Green Bay (123) vs. N.Y. Giants (33), 1939
149 NFC: Cleveland (103) vs. Los Angeles (46), 1955
141 AFC-FR: Buffalo (79) vs. N.Y. Jets (62), 1981

Touchdowns

Most Touchdowns, Game
3 NFC: Chi. Bears vs. Washington, 1940
2 NFC-D: Los Angeles vs. St. Louis, 1975
1 In many games

Punting

Most Punts, Game
14 AFC-D: N.Y. Jets vs. Cleveland, 1986 (OT)
13 NFC: N.Y. Giants vs. Chi. Bears, 1933
AFC-D: Baltimore vs. Oakland, 1977 (OT)
11 AFC: Houston vs. Oakland, 1967
AFC-D: Houston vs. Oakland, 1969
NFC: L.A. Rams vs. Chicago, 1985

Fewest Punts, Game
0 NFC-FR: St. Louis vs. Green Bay, 1982
AFC-FR: N.Y. Jets vs. Cincinnati, 1982
1 NFC-D: Cleveland vs. Dallas, 1969
AFC: Miami vs. Oakland, 1973
AFC-D: Oakland vs. Cincinnati, 1975
AFC-D: Pittsburgh vs. Baltimore, 1976
AFC: Pittsburgh vs. Houston, 1978
NFC-FR: Green Bay vs. St. Louis, 1982
AFC-FR: Miami vs. New England, 1982
AFC-FR: San Diego vs. Pittsburgh, 1982
AFC-D: Cleveland vs. Indianapolis, 1987
2 In many games

Most Punts, Both Teams, Game
23 NFC: N.Y. Giants (13) vs. Chi. Bears (10), 1933
22 AFC-D: N.Y. Jets (14) vs. Cleveland (8), 1986 (OT)

21 AFC-D: Baltimore (13) vs. Oakland (8), 1977 (OT)
NFC: L.A. Rams (11) vs. Chicago (10), 1985

Fewest Punts, Both Teams, Game
1 NFC-FR: St. Louis (0) vs. Green Bay (1), 1982
2 AFC-FR: N.Y. Jets (0) vs. Cincinnati (2), 1982
3 AFC: Miami (1) vs. Oakland (2), 1973
AFC-FR: San Diego (1) vs. Pittsburgh (2), 1982

Average Yardage
Highest Average, Punting, Game (4 punts)
56.0 AFC: Oakland vs. San Diego, 1980
52.5 NFC: Washington vs. Chi. Bears, 1942
51.3 AFC: Pittsburgh vs. Miami, 1972

Lowest Average, Punting, Game (4 punts)
24.9 NFC: Washington vs. Chi. Bears, 1937
25.5 NFC: Green Bay vs. N.Y. Giants, 1962
27.8 AFC-D: San Diego vs. Buffalo, 1980

Punt Returns
Most Punt Returns, Game
8 NFC: Green Bay vs. N.Y. Giants, 1944
7 By eight teams

Most Punt Returns, Both Teams, Game
13 AFC-FR: Houston (7) vs. Oakland (6), 1980
11 NFC: Green Bay (8) vs. N.Y. Giants (3), 1944
NFC-D: Green Bay (6) vs. Baltimore (5), 1965
10 In many games

Fewest Punt Returns, Both Teams, Game
0 NFC: Chi. Bears vs. N.Y. Giants, 1941
AFC: Boston vs. San Diego, 1963
NFC-FR: Green Bay vs. St. Louis, 1982
1 AFC: Miami (0) vs. Pittsburgh (1), 1972
AFC: Cincinnati (0) vs. San Diego (1), 1981
AFC-FR: Cincinnati (0) vs. N.Y. Jets (1), 1982
AFC-FR: San Diego (0) vs. Pittsburgh (1), 1982
NFC-D: Minnesota (0) vs. Washington (1), 1982
AFC: Seattle (0) vs. L.A. Raiders (1), 1983
2 In many games

Yards Gained
Most Yards Gained, Game
155 NFC-D: Dallas vs. Cleveland, 1967
150 NFC: Chi. Cardinals vs. Philadelphia, 1947
143 NFC-FR: Minnesota vs. New Orleans, 1987

Fewest Yards Gained, Game
−10 NFC: Green Bay vs. Cleveland, 1965
−9 NFC: Dallas vs. Green Bay, 1966
AFC-D: Kansas City vs. Oakland, 1968
−5 AFC-D: Miami vs. Oakland, 1970
NFC-D: San Francisco vs. Dallas, 1972
NFC: Dallas vs. Washington, 1972

Most Yards Gained, Both Teams, Game
166 NFC-D: Dallas (155) vs. Cleveland (11), 1967
160 NFC: Chi. Cardinals (150) vs. Philadelphia (10), 1947
146 NFC-D: Philadelphia (112) vs. Pittsburgh (34), 1947

Fewest Yards Gained, Both Teams, Game
−9 NFC: Dallas (−9) vs. Green Bay (0), 1966
−6 AFC-D: Miami (−5) vs. Oakland (−1), 1970
−3 NFC-D: San Francisco (−5) vs. Dallas (2), 1972

Touchdowns
Most Touchdowns, Game
1 By 10 teams

Kickoff Returns
Most Kickoff Returns, Game
10 NFC-D: L.A. Rams vs. Washington, 1983
9 NFC: Chi. Bears vs. N.Y. Giants, 1956
AFC: Boston vs. San Diego, 1963
AFC: Houston vs. Oakland, 1967
8 By many teams

Most Kickoff Returns, Both Teams, Game
13 NFC-D: Green Bay (7) vs. Dallas (6), 1982
12 AFC: Boston (9) vs. San Diego (3), 1963
NFC: Dallas (6) vs. Green Bay (6), 1966
AFC-D: Baltimore (6) vs. Oakland (6), 1977 (OT)
AFC: Oakland (6) vs. San Diego (6), 1980
AFC-D: Miami (6) vs. San Diego (6), 1981 (OT)
NFC-D: N.Y. Giants (7) vs. San Francisco (5), 1981
AFC-FR: Cincinnati (8) vs. N.Y. Jets (4), 1982
NFC-D: L.A. Rams (10) vs. Washington (2), 1983
11 In many games

Fewest Kickoff Returns, Both Teams, Game
1 NFC: Green Bay (0) vs. Boston (1), 1936
2 NFC-D: Los Angeles (0) vs. Chi. Bears (2), 1950
AFC: Houston (0) vs. San Diego (2), 1961
AFC-D: Oakland (1) vs. Pittsburgh (1), 1972
AFC-D: N.Y. Jets (0) vs. L.A. Raiders (2), 1982
AFC: Miami (1) vs. N.Y. Jets (1), 1982
NFC: N.Y. Giants (0) vs. Washington (2), 1986
3 In many games

Yards Gained
Most Yards Gained, Game
225 NFC: Washington vs. Chi. Bears, 1940
222 SB: Miami vs. Washington, 1982
215 AFC: Houston vs. Oakland, 1967

Most Yards Gained, Both Teams, Game
379 AFC-D: Baltimore (193) vs. Oakland (186), 1977 (OT)
321 NFC-D: Dallas (173) vs. Green Bay (148), 1982
318 AFC-D: Miami (183) vs. Oakland (135), 1974

Fewest Yards Gained, Both Teams, Game
15 NFC: N.Y. Giants (0) vs. Washington (15), 1986
31 NFC-D: Los Angeles (0) vs. Chi. Bears (31), 1950
32 NFC: Green Bay (0) vs. Boston (32), 1936

Touchdowns
Most Touchdowns, Game
1 NFC-D: San Francisco vs. Dallas, 1972
AFC-D: Miami vs. Oakland, 1974
AFC-D: Baltimore vs. Oakland, 1977 (OT)
SB: Miami vs. Washington, 1982
SB: Cincinnati vs. San Francisco, 1988

Penalties
Most Penalties, Game
14 AFC-FR: Oakland vs. Houston, 1980
NFC-D: San Francisco vs. N.Y. Giants, 1981
13 AFC-FR: Houston vs. Cleveland, 1988
12 NFC-D: Chi. Bears vs. Green Bay, 1941
AFC-D: Pittsburgh vs. Baltimore, 1976
SB: Dallas vs. Denver, 1977
AFC-FR: N.Y. Jets vs. Cincinnati, 1982

Fewest Penalties, Game
0 NFC: Philadelphia vs. Green Bay, 1960
NFC-D: Detroit vs. Dallas, 1970
AFC-D: Miami vs. Oakland, 1970
SB: Miami vs. Dallas, 1971
NFC-D: Washington vs. Minnesota, 1973
SB: Pittsburgh vs. Dallas, 1975
NFC: San Francisco vs. Chicago, 1988
1 By many teams

Most Penalties, Both Teams, Game
22 AFC-FR: Oakland (14) vs. Houston (8), 1980
NFC-D: San Francisco (14) vs. N.Y. Giants (8), 1981
AFC-FR: Houston (13) vs. Cleveland (9), 1988
21 AFC-D: Oakland (11) vs. New England (10), 1976
20 SB: Dallas (12) vs. Denver (8), 1977

Fewest Penalties, Both Teams, Game
2 NFC: Washington (1) vs. Chi. Bears (1), 1937
NFC-D: Washington (0) vs. Minnesota (2), 1973
SB: Pittsburgh (0) vs. Dallas (2), 1975
3 AFC: Miami (1) vs. Baltimore (2), 1971
NFC: San Francisco (1) vs. Dallas (2), 1971
SB: Miami (0) vs. Dallas (3), 1971
AFC-D: Pittsburgh (1) vs. Oakland (2), 1972
AFC-D: Miami (1) vs. Cincinnati (2), 1973
SB: Miami (1) vs. San Francisco (2), 1984
NFC: San Francisco (0) vs. Chicago (3), 1988
4 NFC-D: Cleveland (2) vs. Dallas (2), 1967
NFC-D: Minnesota (1) vs. San Francisco (3), 1970
AFC-D: Miami (0) vs. Oakland (4), 1970
NFC-D: Dallas (2) vs. Minnesota (2), 1971

Yards Penalized
Most Yards Penalized, Game
145 NFC-D: San Francisco vs. N.Y. Giants, 1981
133 SB: Dallas vs. Baltimore, 1970
128 NFC-D: Chi. Bears vs. Green Bay, 1941

Fewest Yards Penalized, Game
0 By seven teams

Most Yards Penalized, Both Teams, Game
206 NFC-D: San Francisco (145) vs. N.Y. Giants (61), 1981
193 AFC-FR: Houston (118) vs. Cleveland (75), 1988
192 AFC-D: Denver (104) vs. Pittsburgh (88), 1978

Fewest Yards Penalized, Both Teams, Game
9 NFC-D: Washington (0) vs. Minnesota (9), 1973
15 SB: Miami (0) vs. Dallas (15), 1971
20 NFC: Washington (5) vs. Chi. Bears (15), 1937
AFC-D: Pittsburgh (5) vs. Oakland (15), 1972
SB: Pittsburgh (0) vs. Dallas (20), 1975
Miami (10) vs. San Francisco (10), 1984

Fumbles
Most Fumbles, Game
6 By nine teams

Most Fumbles, Both Teams, Game
12 AFC: Houston (6) vs. Pittsburgh (6), 1978
10 NFC: Chi. Bears (5) vs. N.Y. Giants (5), 1934
SB: Dallas (6) vs. Denver (4), 1977
9 NFC-D: San Francisco (6) vs. Detroit (3), 1957
NFC-D: San Francisco (5) vs. Dallas (4), 1972
NFC: Dallas (5) vs. Philadelphia (4), 1980

Most Fumbles Lost, Game
4 NFC: N.Y. Giants vs. Baltimore, 1958 (OT)
AFC: Kansas City vs. Oakland, 1969
SB: Baltimore vs. Dallas, 1970
AFC: Pittsburgh vs. Oakland, 1975
SB: Denver vs. Dallas, 1977
AFC: Houston vs. Pittsburgh, 1978
AFC: Miami vs. New England, 1985
SB: New England vs. Chicago, 1985
NFC-FR: L.A. Rams vs. Washington, 1986
3 By many teams

Fewest Fumbles, Both Teams, Game
0 NFC: Green Bay vs. Cleveland, 1965
AFC: Buffalo vs. San Diego, 1965
AFC-D: Oakland vs. Miami, 1974
AFC-D: Houston vs. San Diego, 1979
NFC-D: Dallas vs. Los Angeles, 1979
SB: Los Angeles vs. Pittsburgh, 1979
AFC-D: Buffalo vs. Cincinnati, 1981
AFC-D: Cleveland vs. N.Y. Jets, 1986 (OT)

AFC-D: Denver vs. New England, 1986
SB: Denver vs. N.Y. Giants, 1986
1 In many games

Recoveries

Most Total Fumbles Recovered, Game
8 SB: Dallas vs. Denver, 1977 (4 own, 4 opp)
7 NFC: Chi. Bears vs. N.Y. Giants, 1934 (5 own, 2 opp)
NFC-D: San Francisco vs. Detroit, 1957 (4 own, 3 opp)
NFC-D: San Francisco vs. Dallas, 1972 (4 own, 3 opp)
AFC: Pittsburgh vs. Houston, 1978 (3 own, 4 opp)
6 AFC: Houston vs. San Diego, 1961 (4 own, 2 opp)
AFC-D: Cleveland vs. Baltimore, 1971 (4 own, 2 opp)
AFC-D: Cleveland vs. Oakland, 1980 (5 own, 1 opp)
NFC: Philadelphia vs. Dallas, 1980 (3 own, 3 opp)

Most Own Fumbles Recovered, Game
5 NFC: Chi. Bears vs. N.Y. Giants, 1934
AFC-D: Cleveland vs. Oakland, 1980
4 By many teams

Turnovers

(Numbers of times losing the ball on interceptions and fumbles.)

Most Turnovers, Game
9 NFC: Washington vs. Chi. Bears, 1940
NFC: Detroit vs. Cleveland, 1954
AFC: Houston vs. Pittsburgh, 1978
8 NFC: N.Y. Giants vs. Chi. Bears, 1946
NFC: Los Angeles vs. Cleveland, 1955
NFC: Cleveland vs. Detroit, 1957
SB: Denver vs. Dallas, 1977
NFC-D: Minnesota vs. Philadelphia, 1980
7 AFC: Houston vs. San Diego, 1961
SB: Baltimore vs. Dallas, 1970
AFC: Pittsburgh vs. Oakland, 1975
NFC-D: Chicago vs. Dallas, 1977
NFC: Los Angeles vs. Dallas, 1978
AFC-D: San Diego vs. Miami, 1982

Fewest Turnovers, Game
0 By many teams

Most Turnovers, Both Teams, Game
14 AFC: Houston (9) vs. Pittsburgh (5), 1978
13 NFC: Detroit (9) vs. Cleveland (4), 1954
AFC: Houston (7) vs. San Diego (6), 1961
12 AFC: Pittsburgh (7) vs. Oakland (5), 1975

Fewest Turnovers, Both Teams, Game
1 AFC-D: Baltimore (0) vs. Cincinnati (1), 1970
AFC-D: Pittsburgh (0) vs. Buffalo (1), 1974
AFC: Oakland (0) vs. Pittsburgh (1), 1976
NFC-D: Minnesota (0) vs. Washington (1), 1982
NFC-D: Chicago (0) vs. N.Y. Giants (1), 1985
SB: N.Y. Giants (0) vs. Denver (1), 1986
NFC: Washington (0) vs. Minnesota (1), 1987
2 In many games

Compiled by Elias Sports Bureau

Individual Records

Service

Most Games

9 *Ken Houston, Houston, 1971-73; Washington, 1974-79
Joe Greene, Pittsburgh, 1971-77, 1979-80
Jack Lambert, Pittsburgh, 1976-84
Walter Payton, Chicago, 1977-81, 1984-87
Harry Carson, N.Y. Giants, 1979-80, 1982-88
Mike Webster, Pittsburgh, 1979-86, 1988
8 Tom Mack, Los Angeles, 1971-76, 1978-79
*Franco Harris, Pittsburgh, 1973-76, 1978-81
Lemar Parrish, Cincinnati, 1971-72, 1975-77; Washington, 1978, 1980-81
Art Shell, Oakland, 1973-79, 1981
Ted Hendricks, Baltimore, 1972-74; Green Bay, 1975; Oakland, 1981-82; L.A. Raiders, 1983-84
*John Hannah, New England, 1977, 1979-83, 1985-86
*Randy White, Dallas, 1978, 1980-86
*Mike Haynes, New England, 1978-81, 1983; L.A. Raiders, 1985-87
Lawrence Taylor, N.Y. Giants, 1982-89
7 Ron Yary, Minnesota, 1972-78
Elvin Bethea, Houston, 1972-76, 1979-80
Roger Wehrli, St. Louis, 1971-72, 1975-78, 1980
Jack Youngblood, Los Angeles, 1974-80
Ray Guy, Oakland, 1974-79, 1981
Robert Brazile, Houston, 1977-83
Randy Gradishar, Denver, 1976, 1978-80, 1982-84
James Lofton, Green Bay, 1979, 1981-86
Ronnie Lott, San Francisco, 1982-85, 1987-89
*Anthony Muñoz, Cincinnati, 1982-87, 1989
*Also selected, but did not play, in one additional game

Scoring

Points

Most Points, Career

30 Jan Stenerud, Kansas City, 1971-72, 1976; Green Bay, 1985 (6-pat, 8-fg)
26 Morten Andersen, New Orleans, 1986-89 (8-pat, 6-fg)
18 John Brockington, Green Bay, 1972-74 (3-td)
Earl Campbell, Houston, 1979-82, 1984 (3-td)
Chuck Muncie, New Orleans, 1980; San Diego, 1982-83 (3-td)
William Andrews, Atlanta, 1981-84 (3-td)
Marcus Allen, L.A. Raiders, 1983, 1985-86, 1988 (3-td)

Most Points, Game

18 John Brockington, Green Bay, 1973 (3-td)
15 Garo Yepremian, Miami, 1974 (5-fg)
14 Jan Stenerud, Kansas City, 1972 (2-pat, 4-fg)

Touchdowns

Most Touchdowns, Career

3 John Brockington, Green Bay, 1972-74 (2-r, 1-p)
Earl Campbell, Houston, 1979-82, 1984 (3-r)
Chuck Muncie, New Orleans, 1980; San Diego, 1982-83 (3-r)
William Andrews, Atlanta, 1981-84 (1-r, 2-p)
Marcus Allen, L.A. Raiders, 1983, 1985-86, 1988 (2-r, 1-p)
2 By 11 players

Most Touchdowns, Game

3 John Brockington, Green Bay, 1973 (2-r, 1-p)
2 Mel Renfro, Dallas, 1971 (2-ret)
Earl Campbell, Houston, 1980 (2-r)
Chuck Muncie, New Orleans, 1980 (2-r)
William Andrews, Atlanta, 1984 (2-p)
Herschel Walker, Dallas, 1989 (2-r)

Points After Touchdown

Most Points After Touchdown, Career

8 Morten Andersen, New Orleans, 1986-89
6 Chester Marcol, Green Bay, 1973, 1975 (6 att)
Mark Moseley, Washington, 1980, 1983 (7 att)
Ali Haji-Sheikh, N.Y. Giants, 1984 (6 att)
Jan Stenerud, Kansas City, 1971-72, 1976; Green Bay, 1985 (6 att)

Most Points After Touchdown, Game

6 Ali Haji-Sheikh, N.Y. Giants, 1984 (6 att)
4 Chester Marcol, Green Bay, 1973 (4 att)
Mark Moseley, Washington, 1980 (5 att)
Morten Andersen, New Orleans, 1986 (4 att); 1989 (4 att)

Field Goals

Most Field Goals Attempted, Career

15 Jan Stenerud, Kansas City, 1971-72, 1976; Green Bay, 1985
8 Morten Andersen, New Orleans, 1986-89
7 Garo Yepremian, Miami, 1974, 1979
Mark Moseley, Washington, 1980, 1983

Most Field Goals Attempted, Game

6 Jan Stenerud, Kansas City, 1972
Ed Murray, Detroit, 1981
Mark Moseley, Washington, 1983
5 Garo Yepremian, Miami, 1974
4 Jan Stenerud, Kansas City, 1976

Most Field Goals, Career

8 Jan Stenerud, Kansas City, 1971-72, 1976; Green Bay, 1985
6 Morten Andersen, New Orleans, 1986-89
5 Garo Yepremian, Miami, 1974, 1979

Most Field Goals, Game

5 Garo Yepremian, Miami, 1974 (5 att)
4 Jan Stenerud, Kansas City, 1972 (6 att)
Ed Murray, Detroit, 1981 (6 att)
2 By many players

Longest Field Goal

51 Morten Andersen, New Orleans, 1989
48 Jan Stenerud, Kansas City, 1972
43 Gary Anderson, Pittsburgh, 1984

Safeties

Most Safeties, Game

1 Art Still, Kansas City, 1983
Mark Gastineau, N.Y. Jets, 1985

Rushing

Attempts

Most Attempts, Career

81 Walter Payton, Chicago, 1977-81, 1984-87
68 O.J. Simpson, Buffalo, 1973-77
48 Eric Dickerson, L.A. Rams, 1984-85, 1987; Indianapolis, 1988-89

Most Attempts, Game

19 O.J. Simpson, Buffalo, 1974
17 Marv Hubbard, Oakland, 1974
16 O.J. Simpson, Buffalo, 1973
Marcus Allen, L.A. Raiders, 1986

Yards Gained

Most Yards Gained, Career

368 Walter Payton, Chicago, 1977-81, 1984-87
356 O.J. Simpson, Buffalo, 1973-77
220 Earl Campbell, Houston, 1979-82, 1984

Most Yards Gained, Game

112 O. J. Simpson, Buffalo, 1973
104 Marv Hubbard, Oakland, 1974
85 Neal Anderson, Chicago, 1989

Longest Run From Scrimmage

41 Lawrence McCutcheon, Los Angeles, 1976
32 Randall Cunningham, Philadelphia, 1989
30 O.J. Simpson, Buffalo, 1975

Average Gain

Highest Average Gain, Career (20 attempts)

5.81 Marv Hubbard, Oakland, 1972-74 (36-209)
5.71 Wilbert Montgomery, Philadelphia, 1979-80 (21-120)
5.36 Larry Csonka, Miami, 1971-72, 1975 (22-118)

Highest Average Gain, Game (10 attempts)

7.00 O.J. Simpson, Buffalo, 1973 (16-112)
Ottis Anderson, St. Louis, 1981 (10-70)
6.91 Walter Payton, Chicago, 1985 (11-76)
6.90 Earl Campbell, Houston, 1980 (10-69)

Touchdowns

Most Touchdowns, Career

3 Earl Campbell, Houston, 1979-82, 1984
Chuck Muncie, New Orleans, 1980; San Diego, 1982-83
2 John Brockington, Green Bay, 1972-74
O.J. Simpson, Buffalo, 1973-77
Walter Payton, Chicago, 1977-81, 1984-87
Marcus Allen, L.A. Raiders, 1983, 1985-86, 1988
Herschel Walker, Dallas, 1988-89

Most Touchdowns, Game

2 John Brockington, Green Bay, 1973
Earl Campbell, Houston, 1980
Chuck Muncie, New Orleans, 1980
Herschel Walker, Dallas, 1989

Passing

Attempts

Most Attempts, Career

120 Dan Fouts, San Diego, 1980-84, 1986
88 Bob Griese, Miami, 1971-72, 1974-75, 1977, 1979
57 Joe Montana, San Francisco, 1982, 1984-85, 1988

Most Attempts, Game

32 Bill Kenney, Kansas City, 1984
30 Dan Fouts, San Diego, 1983
28 Jim Hart, St. Louis, 1976

Completions

Most Completions, Career

63 Dan Fouts, San Diego, 1980-84, 1986
44 Bob Griese, Miami, 1971-72, 1974-75, 1977, 1979
33 Ken Anderson, Cincinnati, 1976-77, 1982-83

Most Completions, Game

21 Joe Theismann, Washington, 1984
17 Dan Fouts, San Diego, 1983
16 Dan Fouts, San Diego, 1986

Completion Percentage

Highest Completion Percentage, Career (40 attempts)

68.9 Joe Theismann, Washington, 1983-84 (45-31)
58.9 Ken Anderson, Cincinnati, 1976-77, 1982-83 (56-33)
52.5 Dan Fouts, San Diego, 1980-84, 1986 (120-63)

Highest Completion Percentage, Game (10 attempts)

90.0 Archie Manning, New Orleans, 1980 (10-9)
77.8 Joe Theismann, Washington, 1984 (27-21)
71.4 Joe Montana, San Francisco, 1985 (14-10)

Yards Gained
Most Yards Gained, Career
890 Dan Fouts, San Diego, 1980-84, 1986
554 Bob Griese, Miami, 1971-72, 1974-75, 1977, 1979
398 Ken Anderson, Cincinnati, 1976-77, 1982-83
Most Yards Gained, Game
274 Dan Fouts, San Diego, 1983
242 Joe Theismann, Washington, 1984
212 Phil Simms, N.Y. Giants, 1986
Longest Completion
64 Dan Pastorini, Houston (to Burrough, Houston), 1976 (TD)
57 James Harris, Los Angeles (to Gray, St. Louis), 1975
Ken Anderson, Cincinnati (to G. Pruitt, Cleveland), 1977
56 Dan Marino, Miami (to Allen, L.A. Raiders), 1985

Average Gain
Highest Average Gain, Career (40 attempts)
7.64 Joe Theismann, Washington, 1983-84 (45-344)
7.42 Dan Fouts, San Diego, 1980-84, 1986 (120-890)
7.11 Ken Anderson, Cincinnati, 1976-77, 1982-83 (56-398)
Highest Average Gain, Game (10 attempts)
11.40 Ken Anderson, Cincinnati, 1977 (10-114)
11.20 Archie Manning, New Orleans, 1980 (10-112)
11.09 Greg Landry, Detroit, 1972 (11-122)

Touchdowns
Most Touchdowns, Career
3 Joe Theismann, Washington, 1983-84
Joe Montana, San Francisco, 1982, 1984-85, 1988
Phil Simms, N.Y. Giants, 1986
2 James Harris, Los Angeles, 1975
Mike Boryla, Philadelphia, 1976
Ken Anderson, Cincinnati, 1976-77, 1982-83
Most Touchdowns, Game
3 Joe Theismann, Washington, 1984
Phil Simms, N.Y. Giants, 1986
2 James Harris, Los Angeles, 1975
Mike Boryla, Philadelphia, 1976
Ken Anderson, Cincinnati, 1977

Had Intercepted
Most Passes Had Intercepted, Career
8 Dan Fouts, San Diego, 1980-84, 1986
6 Jim Hart, St. Louis, 1975-78
5 Ken Stabler, Oakland, 1974-75, 1978
Most Passes Had Intercepted, Game
5 Jim Hart, St. Louis, 1977
4 Ken Stabler, Oakland, 1974
3 Dan Fouts, San Diego, 1986
Most Attempts, Without Interception, Game
27 Joe Theismann, Washington, 1984
Phil Simms, N.Y. Giants, 1986
26 John Brodie, San Francisco, 1971
Danny White, Dallas, 1983
21 Roman Gabriel, Philadelphia, 1974
Dan Marino, Miami, 1985

Percentage, Passes Had Intercepted
Lowest Percentage, Passes Had Intercepted, Career (40 attempts)
0.00 Joe Theismann, Washington, 1983-84 (45-0)
3.41 Bob Griese, Miami, 1971-72, 1974-75, 1977, 1979 (88-3)
5.36 Ken Anderson, Cincinnati, 1976-77, 1982-83 (56-3)

Pass Receiving
Receptions
Most Receptions, Career
18 Walter Payton, Chicago, 1977-81, 1984-87
17 Steve Largent, Seattle, 1979, 1982, 1985-88
14 John Stallworth, Pittsburgh, 1980, 1983, 1985
James Lofton, Green Bay, 1979, 1981-86
Marcus Allen, L.A. Raiders, 1983, 1985-86, 1988
Most Receptions, Game
8 Steve Largent, Seattle, 1986
7 John Stallworth, Pittsburgh, 1983
6 John Stallworth, Pittsburgh, 1980
Kellen Winslow, San Diego, 1982

Yards Gained
Most Yards Gained, Career
236 Steve Largent, Seattle, 1979, 1982, 1985-88
226 Wes Chandler, New Orleans, 1980; San Diego, 1983-84, 1986
206 James Lofton, Green Bay, 1979, 1981-86
Most Yards Gained, Game
114 Wes Chandler, San Diego, 1986
96 Ken Burrough, Houston, 1976
91 Alfred Jenkins, Atlanta, 1981
Longest Reception
64 Ken Burrough, Houston (from Pastorini, Houston), 1976 (TD)
57 Mel Gray, St. Louis (from Harris, Los Angeles), 1975
Greg Pruitt, Cleveland (from Anderson, Cincinnati), 1977
56 Marcus Allen, L.A. Raiders (from Marino, Miami), 1985

Touchdowns
Most Touchdowns, Career
2 Mel Gray, St. Louis, 1975-78
Cliff Branch, Oakland, 1975-78
Terry Metcalf, St. Louis, 1975-76, 1978
Tony Hill, Dallas, 1979-80, 1986
William Andrews, Atlanta, 1981-84
James Lofton, Green Bay, 1979, 1981-86
Jimmie Giles, Tampa Bay, 1981-83, 1986
Most Touchdowns, Game
2 William Andrews, Atlanta, 1984

Interceptions By
Most Interceptions, Career
4 Everson Walls, Dallas, 1982-84, 1986
3 Ken Houston, Houston, 1971-73; Washington, 1974-79
Jack Lambert, Pittsburgh, 1976-84
Ted Hendricks, Baltimore, 1972-74; Green Bay, 1975; Oakland, 1981-82; L.A. Raiders, 1983-84
Mike Haynes, New England, 1978-81, 1983; L.A. Raiders, 1985-87
2 By six players
Most Interceptions By, Game
2 Mel Blount, Pittsburgh, 1977
Everson Walls, Dallas, 1982, 1983
LeRoy Irvin, L.A. Rams, 1986

Yards Gained
Most Yards Gained, Career
77 Ted Hendricks, Baltimore, 1972-74; Green Bay, 1975; Oakland, 1981-82; L.A. Raiders, 1983-84
48 Joey Browner, Minnesota, 1986-89
44 Nolan Cromwell, L.A. Rams, 1981-84
Most Yards Gained, Game
65 Ted Hendricks, Baltimore, 1973
48 Joey Browner, Minnesota, 1986
44 Nolan Cromwell, L.A. Rams, 1984
Longest Gain
65 Ted Hendricks, Baltimore, 1973
48 Joey Browner, Minnesota, 1986 (TD)
44 Nolan Cromwell, L.A. Rams, 1984 (TD)

Touchdowns
Most Touchdowns, Game
1 Bobby Bell, Kansas City, 1973
Nolan Cromwell, L.A. Rams, 1984
Joey Browner, Minnesota, 1986

Punting
Most Punts, Career
33 Ray Guy, Oakland, 1974-79, 1981
19 Dave Jennings, N.Y. Giants, 1979-81, 1983
16 Jerrel Wilson, Kansas City, 1971-73
Tom Wittum, San Francisco, 1974-75
Most Punts, Game
10 Reggie Roby, Miami, 1985
9 Tom Wittum, San Francisco, 1974
Rohn Stark, Indianapolis, 1987
8 Jerrel Wilson, Kansas City, 1971
Tom Skladany, Detroit, 1982
Longest Punt
64 Tom Wittum, San Francisco, 1974
61 Reggie Roby, Miami, 1985
60 Ron Widby, Dallas, 1972

Average Yardage
Highest Average, Career (10 punts)
45.25 Jerrel Wilson, Kansas City, 1971-73 (16-724)
44.64 Ray Guy, Oakland, 1974-79, 1981 (33-1,473)
44.63 Tom Wittum, San Francisco, 1974-75 (16-714)
Highest Average, Game (4 punts)
49.57 Jim Arnold, Detroit, 1988 (7-347)
49.00 Ray Guy, Oakland, 1974 (4-196)
47.75 Bob Grupp, Kansas City, 1980 (4-191)

Punt Returns
Most Punt Returns, Career
13 Rick Upchurch, Denver, 1977, 1979-80, 1983
11 Vai Sikahema, St. Louis, 1987-88
10 Mike Nelms, Washington, 1981-83
Most Punt Returns, Game
7 Vai Sikahema, St. Louis, 1987
6 Henry Ellard, L.A. Rams, 1985
Gerald McNeil, Cleveland, 1988
5 Rick Upchurch, Denver, 1980
Mike Nelms, Washington, 1981
Carl Roaches, Houston, 1982
Most Fair Catches, Game
2 Jerry Logan, Baltimore, 1971
Dick Anderson, Miami, 1974
Henry Ellard, L.A. Rams, 1985

Yards Gained
Most Yards Gained, Career
183 Billy Johnson, Houston, 1976, 1978; Atlanta, 1984
138 Rick Upchurch, Denver, 1977, 1979-80, 1983
119 Mike Nelms, Washington, 1981-83
Most Yards Gained, Game
159 Billy Johnson, Houston, 1976
138 Mel Renfro, Dallas, 1971
117 Wally Henry, Philadelphia, 1980
Longest Punt Return
90 Billy Johnson, Houston, 1976 (TD)
86 Wally Henry, Philadelphia, 1980 (TD)
82 Mel Renfro, Dallas, 1971 (TD)

Touchdowns
Most Touchdowns, Game
2 Mel Renfro, Dallas, 1971
1 Billy Johnson, Houston, 1976
Wally Henry, Philadelphia, 1980

Kickoff Returns

Most Kickoff Returns, Career

10 Rick Upchurch, Denver, 1977, 1979-80, 1983
Greg Pruitt, Cleveland, 1974-75, 1977-78; L.A. Raiders, 1984
8 Mike Nelms, Washington, 1981-83
6 Terry Metcalf, St. Louis, 1975-76, 1978
Vai Sikahema, St. Louis, 1987-88

Most Kickoff Returns, Game

6 Greg Pruitt, L.A. Raiders, 1984
5 Les (Speedy) Duncan, Washington, 1972
Ron Smith, Chicago, 1973
Herb Mul-Key, Washington, 1974
4 By six players

Yards Gained

Most Yards Gained, Career

309 Greg Pruitt, Cleveland, 1974-75, 1977-78; L.A. Raiders, 1984
222 Rick Upchurch, Denver, 1977, 1979-80, 1983
175 Les (Speedy) Duncan, Washington, 1972

Most Yards Gained, Game

192 Greg Pruitt, L.A. Raiders, 1984
175 Les (Speedy) Duncan, Washington, 1972
152 Ron Smith, Chicago, 1973

Longest Kickoff Return

62 Greg Pruitt, L.A. Raiders, 1984
61 Eugene (Mercury) Morris, Miami, 1972
55 Ron Smith, Chicago, 1973

Touchdowns

Most Touchdowns, Game

None

Fumbles

Most Fumbles, Career

6 Dan Fouts, San Diego, 1980-84, 1986
4 Lawrence McCutcheon, Los Angeles, 1974-78
Franco Harris, Pittsburgh, 1973-76, 1978-81
Jay Schroeder, Washington, 1987
Vai Sikahema, St. Louis, 1987-88
3 O.J. Simpson, Buffalo, 1973-77
William Andrews, Atlanta, 1981-84
Joe Montana, San Francisco, 1982, 1984-85, 1988
Walter Payton, Chicago, 1977-81, 1984-87
Neil Lomax, St. Louis, 1985, 1988

Most Fumbles, Game

4 Jay Schroeder, Washington, 1987
3 Dan Fouts, San Diego, 1982
Vai Sikahema, St. Louis, 1987
2 By 11 players

Recoveries

Most Fumbles Recovered, Career

3 Harold Jackson, Philadelphia, 1973; Los Angeles, 1974, 1976, 1978 (3-own)
Dan Fouts, San Diego, 1980-84, 1986 (3-own)
Randy White, Dallas, 1978, 1980-86 (3-opp)
2 By many players

Most Fumbles Recovered, Game

2 Dick Anderson, Miami, 1974 (1-own, 1-opp)
Harold Jackson, Los Angeles, 1974 (2-own)
Dan Fouts, San Diego, 1982 (2-own)

Yardage

Longest Fumble Return

83 Art Still, Kansas City, 1985 (TD, opp)
51 Phil Villapiano, Oakland, 1974 (opp)
37 Sam Mills, New Orleans, 1988 (opp)

Touchdowns

Most Touchdowns, Game

1 Art Still, Kansas City, 1985

Sacks

Sacks have been compiled since 1983.

Most Sacks, Career

7 Mark Gastineau, N.Y. Jets, 1983-86
Reggie White, Philadelphia, 1987-89
6 Howie Long, L.A. Raiders, 1984-88

Most Sacks, Game

4 Mark Gastineau, N.Y. Jets, 1985
Reggie White, Philadelphia, 1987
3 Richard Dent, Chicago, 1985
2 By many players

Team Records

Scoring

Most Points, Game

45 NFC, 1984

Fewest Points, Game

3 AFC, 1984, 1989

Most Points, Both Teams, Game

64 NFC (37) vs. AFC (27), 1980

Fewest Points, Both Teams, Game

16 NFC (6) vs. AFC (10), 1987

Touchdowns

Most Touchdowns, Game

6 NFC, 1984

Fewest Touchdowns, Game

0 AFC, 1971, 1974, 1984, 1989
NFC, 1987, 1988

Most Touchdowns, Both Teams, Game

8 AFC (4) vs. NFC (4), 1973
NFC (5) vs. AFC (3), 1980

Fewest Touchdowns, Both Teams, Game

1 AFC (0) vs. NFC (1), 1974
NFC (0) vs. AFC (1), 1987
NFC (0) vs. AFC (1), 1988

Points After Touchdown

Most Points After Touchdown, Game

6 NFC, 1984

Most Points After Touchdown, Both Teams, Game

7 NFC (4) vs. AFC (3), 1973
NFC (4) vs. AFC (3), 1980
NFC (4) vs. AFC (3), 1986

Field Goals

Most Field Goals Attempted, Game

6 AFC, 1972
NFC, 1981, 1983

Most Field Goals Attempted, Both Teams, Game

9 NFC (6) vs. AFC (3), 1983

Most Field Goals, Game

5 AFC, 1974

Most Field Goals, Both Teams, Game

7 AFC (5) vs. NFC (2), 1974

Net Yards Gained Rushing And Passing

Most Yards Gained, Game

466 AFC, 1983

Fewest Yards Gained, Game

146 AFC, 1971

Most Yards Gained, Both Teams, Game

811 AFC (466) vs. NFC (345), 1983

Fewest Yards Gained, Both Teams, Game

424 AFC (202) vs. NFC (222), 1987

Rushing

Attempts

Most Attempts, Game

50 AFC, 1974

Fewest Attempts, Game

15 AFC, 1989

Most Attempts, Both Teams, Game

80 AFC (50) vs. NFC (30), 1974

Fewest Attempts, Both Teams, Game

54 AFC (27) vs. NFC (27), 1983
AFC (18) vs. NFC (36), 1984

Yards Gained

Most Yards Gained, Game

224 NFC, 1976

Fewest Yards Gained, Game

64 NFC, 1974

Most Yards Gained, Both Teams, Game

425 NFC (224) vs. AFC (201), 1976

Fewest Yards Gained, Both Teams, Game

178 AFC (66) vs. NFC (112), 1971

Touchdowns

Most Touchdowns, Game

3 NFC, 1989

Most Touchdowns, Both Teams, Game

4 AFC (2) vs. NFC (2), 1973
AFC (2) vs. NFC (2), 1980

Passing

Attempts

Most Attempts, Game

50 AFC, 1983

Fewest Attempts, Game

17 NFC, 1972

Most Attempts, Both Teams, Game

94 AFC (50) vs. NFC (44), 1983

Fewest Attempts, Both Teams, Game

42 NFC (17) vs. AFC (25), 1972

Completions

Most Completions, Game

31 AFC, 1983

Fewest Completions, Game

7 NFC, 1972, 1982

Most Completions, Both Teams, Game

55 AFC (31) vs. NFC (24), 1983

Fewest Completions, Both Teams, Game

18 NFC (7) vs. AFC (11), 1972

Yards Gained

Most Yards Gained, Game

387 AFC, 1983

Fewest Yards Gained, Game

42 NFC, 1982

Most Yards Gained, Both Teams, Game

608 AFC (387) vs. NFC (221), 1983

Fewest Yards Gained, Both Teams, Game

215 NFC (89) vs. AFC (126), 1972

Times Sacked

Most Times Sacked, Game

9 NFC, 1985

Fewest Times Sacked, Game

0 NFC, 1971

Most Times Sacked, Both Teams, Game
17 NFC (9) vs. AFC (8), 1985
Fewest Times Sacked, Both Teams, Game
4 AFC (2) vs. NFC (2), 1978

Touchdowns
Most Touchdowns, Game
4 NFC, 1984
Most Touchdowns, Both Teams, Game
5 NFC (3) vs. AFC (2), 1986

Interceptions By
Most Interceptions By, Game
6 AFC, 1977
Most Interceptions By, Both Teams, Game
7 AFC (6) vs. NFC (1), 1977

Yards Gained
Most Yards Gained, Game
78 NFC, 1986
Most Yards Gained, Both Teams, Game
99 NFC (64) vs. AFC (35), 1975

Touchdowns
Most Touchdowns, Game
1 AFC, 1973
NFC, 1984, 1986

Punting
Most Punts, Game
10 AFC, 1985
Fewest Punts, Game
0 NFC, 1989
Most Punts, Both Teams, Game
16 AFC (10) vs. NFC (6), 1985
Fewest Punts, Both Teams, Game
5 NFC (0) vs. AFC (5), 1989

Average Yardage
Highest Average, Game
49.57 NFC, 1988 (7-347)

Punt Returns
Most Punt Returns, Game
7 NFC, 1985, 1987
Fewest Punt Returns, Game
0 AFC, 1984, 1989
Most Punt Returns, Both Teams, Game
11 NFC (7) vs. AFC (4), 1985
Fewest Punt Returns, Both Teams, Game
3 AFC (0) vs. NFC (3), 1984
AFC (0) vs. NFC (3), 1989

Yards Gained
Most Yards Gained, Game
177 AFC, 1976
Fewest Yards Gained, Game
0 AFC, 1984, 1989
Most Yards Gained, Both Teams, Game
263 AFC (177) vs. NFC (86), 1976
Fewest Yards Gained, Both Teams, Game
16 AFC (0) vs. NFC (16), 1984

Touchdowns
Most Touchdowns, Game
2 NFC, 1971

Kickoff Returns
Most Kickoff Returns, Game
7 AFC, 1984
Fewest Kickoff Returns, Game
1 NFC, 1971, 1984
AFC, 1988
Most Kickoff Returns, Both Teams, Game
10 AFC (5) vs. NFC (5), 1976
AFC (5) vs. NFC (5), 1986
Fewest Kickoff Returns, Both Teams, Game
5 NFC (2) vs. AFC (3), 1979
AFC (1) vs. NFC (4), 1988

Yards Gained
Most Yards Gained, Game
215 AFC, 1984
Fewest Yards Gained, Game
6 NFC, 1971
Most Yards Gained, Both Teams, Game
293 NFC (200) vs. AFC (93), 1972
Fewest Yards Gained, Both Teams, Game
99 NFC (48) vs. AFC (51), 1987

Touchdowns
Most Touchdowns, Game
None

Fumbles
Most Fumbles, Game
10 NFC, 1974
Most Fumbles, Both Teams, Game
15 NFC (10) vs. AFC (5), 1974

Recoveries
Most Fumbles Recovered, Game
10 NFC, 1974 (6 own, 4 opp)
Most Fumbles Lost, Game
4 AFC, 1974, 1988

Yards Gained
Most Yards Gained, Game
87 AFC, 1985

Touchdowns
Most Touchdowns, Game
1 AFC, 1985

Turnovers
(Number of times losing the ball on interceptions and fumbles.)
Most Turnovers, Game
8 AFC, 1974
Fewest Turnovers, Game
1 AFC, 1972, 1976, 1978, 1979, 1985, 1987
NFC, 1976, 1980, 1983
Most Turnovers, Both Teams, Game
12 AFC (8) vs. NFC (4), 1974
Fewest Turnovers, Both Teams, Game
2 AFC (1) vs. NFC (1), 1976

RULES

1989 NFL Roster of Officials

Art McNally, Supervisor of Officials
Jack Reader, Assistant Supervisor of Officials
Joe Gardi, Assistant Supervisor of Officials
Tony Veteri, Assistant Supervisor of Officials

No.	Name	Position	College
25	Alderton, John	Line Judge	Portland State
115	Ancich, Hendi	Umpire	Harbor College
81	Anderson, Dave	Head Linesman	Salem College
34	Austin, Gerald	Side Judge	Western Carolina
22	Baetz, Paul	Back Judge	Heidelberg
116	Baker, Bob	Line Judge	East Texas State
26	Baltz, Mark	Head Linesman	Ohio University
55	Barnes, Tom	Head Linesman	Minnesota
14	Barth, Gene	Referee	St. Louis
56	Baynes, Ron	Line Judge	Auburn
59	Beeks, Bob	Line Judge	Lincoln
17	Bergman, Jerry	Head Linesman	Duquesne
83	Blum, Ron	Line Judge	Marin College
110	Botchan, Ron	Umpire	Occidental
101	Boylston, Bob	Umpire	Alabama
39	Carlsen, Don	Line Judge	Cal State-Chico
63	Carollo, Bill	Side Judge	Wisconsin
43	Cashion, Red	Referee	Texas A&M
24	Clymer, Roy	Back Judge	New Mexico State
65	Coleman, Walt	Line Judge	Arkansas
27	Conway, Al	Umpire	Army
71	Coukart, Ed	Umpire	Northwestern
61	Creed, Dick	Side Judge	Louisville
75	Daopoulos, Jim	Back Judge	Kentucky
78	Demmas, Art	Umpire	Vanderbilt
45	DeSouza, Ron	Line Judge	Morgan State
74	Dodez, Ray	Line Judge	Wooster
31	Dolack, Dick	Field Judge	Ferris State
6	Dooley, Tom	Referee	VMI
113	Dorkowski, Don	Field Judge	Cal St.-Los Angeles
102	Douglas, Merrill	Side Judge	Utah
12	Dreith, Ben	Referee	Colorado State
57	Fiffick, Ed	Umpire	Marquette
47	Fincken, Tom	Side Judge	Kansas State
111	Frantz, Earnie	Head Linesman	No College
62	Gandy, Duwayne	Side Judge	Tulsa
50	Gereb, Neil	Umpire	California
72	Gierke, Terry	Head Linesman	Portland State
15	Glass, Bama	Line Judge	Colorado
23	Grier, Johnny	Referee	D.C. Teachers
40	Haggerty, Pat	Referee	Colorado State
96	Hakes, Don	Field Judge	Bradley
104	Hamer, Dale	Referee	California, Pa., Univ.
42	Hamilton, Dave	Umpire	Utah
44	Hampton, Donnie	Field Judge	Georgia
105	Hantak, Dick	Referee	S.E. Missouri
66	Hawk, Dave	Side Judge	Southern Methodist
112	Haynes, Joe	Line Judge	Alcorn State
16	Jackson, Doyle	Side Judge	Central Arkansas
54	Johnson, Jack	Line Judge	Pacific Lutheran
114	Johnson, Tom	Head Linesman	Miami, Ohio
97	Jones, Nathan	Side Judge	Lewis & Clark
60	Jorgensen, Dick	Referee	Wisconsin
106	Jury, Al	Back Judge	San Bernardino Valley
107	Kearney, Jim	Back Judge	Pennsylvania
67	Keck, John	Umpire	Cornell College
108	Kemp, Stan	Side Judge	Michigan
86	Kukar, Bernie	Field Judge	St. John's
120	Lane, Gary	Side Judge	Missouri
18	Lewis, Bob	Field Judge	No College
49	Look, Dean	Back Judge	Michigan State
90	Mace, Gil	Side Judge	Westminster
82	Mallette, Pat	Field Judge	Nebraska
9	Markbreit, Jerry	Referee	Illinois
38	Maurer, Bruce	Back Judge	Ohio State
48	McCarter, Gordon	Referee	Western Reserve
95	McElwee, Bob	Referee	Navy
41	McKenzie, Dick	Line Judge	Ashland
76	Merrifield, Ed	Field Judge	Missouri
35	Miles, Leo	Head Linesman	Virginia State
80	Millis, Tim	Back Judge	Millsaps
117	Montgomery, Ben	Umpire	Morehouse
36	Moore, Bob	Back Judge	Dayton
88	Moss, Dave	Umpire	Dartmouth
20	Nemmers, Larry	Side Judge	Upper Iowa
51	Orem, Dale	Line Judge	Louisville
77	Orr, Don	Field Judge	Vanderbilt
64	Parry, Dave	Side Judge	Wabash
10	Phares, Ron	Head Linesman	Virginia Tech
79	Pointer, Aaron	Head Linesman	Pacific Lutheran
92	Poole, Jim	Back Judge	San Diego State
58	Quinby, Bill	Side Judge	Iowa State
5	Quirk, Jim	Line Judge	Delaware
53	Reynolds, Bill	Line Judge	West Chester State
68	Richard, Louis	Back Judge	S.W. Louisiana
30	Riggs, Dennis	Umpire	Bellarmine
121	Rivers, Sanford	Head Linesman	Youngstown State
46	Robison, John	Field Judge	Utah
33	Roe, Howard	Referee	Wichita State
122	Schmitz, Bill	Field Judge	Colorado State
70	Seeman, Jerry	Referee	Winona State
109	Semon, Sid	Head Linesman	So. California
118	Sifferman, Tom	Back Judge	Seattle
73	Skelton, Bobby	Field Judge	Alabama
29	Slavin, Howard	Side Judge	So. California
119	Spitler, Ron	Field Judge	Panhandle State
91	Stanley, Bill	Field Judge	Redlands
103	Stuart, Rex	Umpire	Appalachian State
37	Toler, Burl	Head Linesman	San Francisco
52	Tompkins, Ben	Back Judge	Texas
4	Toole, Doug	Back Judge	Utah State
32	Tunney, Jim	Referee	Occidental
93	Vaughan, Jack	Field Judge	Mississippi State
100	Wagner, Bob	Umpire	Penn State
28	Wedge, Don	Back Judge	Ohio Wesleyan
87	Weidner, Paul	Head Linesman	Cincinnati
89	Wells, Gordon	Umpire	Occidental
123	White, Tom	Head Linesman	Temple
99	Williams, Banks	Back Judge	Houston
8	Williams, Dale	Head Linesman	Cal St.-Northridge
84	Wortman, Bob	Field Judge	Findlay
11	Wyant, Fred	Referee	West Virginia

1989 NFL Replay Officials

L.T. Bonner—25 years officiating experience including 10 years in Big Ten, three in USFL. First year as Replay Official.

Gaylord Bryan—Officiated 24 years in Pac 10; worked seven Bowl games; officiated in USFL. First year as Replay Official.

Mark Burns—Worked in League office for seven years; five in Officiating Department; game observer since 1986. Third year as Replay Official.

Royal Cathcart—16 years as NFL Line Judge and Side Judge. Former NFL player. Third year as Replay Official.

Bill Fette—25 years as Field Judge in Pac 10; worked three Rose Bowls. Second year as Replay Official.

Jack Fette—23 years as NFL Line Judge; officiated in Super Bowls V, VIII, X, XII, and XXII. Second year as Replay Official.

Fritz Graf—24 years as NFL Field Judge; game observer since 1984. Officiated in Super Bowls V, VIII, XV, and XVIII. Fourth year as Replay Official.

Chuck Heberling—22 years as NFL Referee and Line Judge. Fourth year as Replay Official.

Dave Kamanski—25 years as NCAA Official; Pac 10 referee for 20 years; worked three Rose Bowls, three East/West Shrine Games, and three Japan Bowls. Second year as Replay Official.

Tom Kelleher—28 years as NFL Back Judge. Officiated in Super Bowls IV, VII, XI, XV, and XIX. Second year as Replay Official.

Grover Klemmer—19 years as NFL Side Judge and Back Judge. Third year as Replay Official.

Cal Lepore—15 years as NFL Head Linesman and Referee. Officiated in Super Bowl III. Fourth year as Replay Official.

Bill Parkinson—Officiated 35 years primarily in ECAC and Major Independent Collegiate Conference. Officiated in USFL three years. First year as Replay Official.

Al Sabato—20 years as NFL Head Linesman. Game observer since 1982. Officiated in Super Bowls I and VI. Fourth year as Replay Official.

George Sladky—17 years as NCAA Official; nine years in Big 10, eight years with Southwest Conference. Worked six Bowl games. Third year as Replay Official.

Bill Swanson—21 years as NFL Back Judge. Officiated in Super Bowls XI an XVI. Fourth year as Replay Official.

Numerical Roster

No.	Name	Position
4	Doug Toole	BJ
5	Jim Quirk	LJ
6	Tom Dooley	R
8	Dale Williams	HL
9	Jerry Markbreit	R
10	Ron Phares	HL
11	Fred Wyant	R
12	Ben Dreith	R
14	Gene Barth	R
15	Bama Glass	LJ
16	Doyle Jackson	SJ
17	Jerry Bergman	HL
18	Bob Lewis	FJ
20	Larry Nemmers	SJ
22	Paul Baetz	BJ
23	Johnny Grier	R
24	Roy Clymer	BJ
25	John Alderton	LJ
26	Mark Baltz	HL
27	Al Conway	U
28	Don Wedge	BJ
29	Howard Slavin	SJ
30	Dennis Riggs	U
31	Dick Dolack	FJ
32	Jim Tunney	R
33	Howard Roe	R
34	Gerald Austin	SJ
35	Leo Miles	HL
36	Bob Moore	BJ
37	Burl Toler	HL
38	Bruce Maurer	BJ
39	Don Carlsen	LJ
40	Pat Haggerty	R
41	Dick McKenzie	LJ
42	Dave Hamilton	U
43	Red Cashion	R
44	Donnie Hampton	FJ
45	Ron DeSouza	LJ
46	John Robison	FJ
47	Tom Fincken	SJ
48	Gordon McCarter	R
49	Dean Look	BJ
50	Neil Gereb	U
51	Dale Orem	LJ
52	Ben Tompkins	BJ
53	Bill Reynolds	LJ
54	Jack Johnson	LJ
55	Tom Barnes	HL
56	Ron Baynes	LJ
57	Ed Fiffick	U
58	Bill Quinby	SJ
59	Bob Beeks	LJ
60	Dick Jorgensen	R
61	Dick Creed	SJ
62	Duwayne Gandy	SJ
63	Bill Carollo	SJ
64	Dave Parry	SJ
65	Walt Coleman	LJ
66	Dave Hawk	SJ
67	John Keck	U
68	Louis Richard	BJ
70	Jerry Seeman	R
71	Ed Coukart	U
72	Terry Gierke	HL
73	Bobby Skelton	FJ
74	Ray Dodez	LJ
75	Jim Daopoulos	BJ
76	Ed Merrifield	FJ
77	Don Orr	FJ
78	Art Demmas	U
79	Aaron Pointer	HL
80	Tim Millis	BJ
81	Dave Anderson	HL
82	Pat Mallette	FJ
83	Ron Blum	LJ
84	Bob Wortman	FJ
86	Bernie Kukar	FJ
87	Paul Weidner	HL
88	Dave Moss	U
89	Gordon Wells	U
90	Gil Mace	SJ
91	Bill Stanley	FJ
92	Jim Poole	BJ
93	Jack Vaughan	FJ
95	Bob McElwee	R
96	Don Hakes	FJ
97	Nathan Jones	SJ
99	Banks Williams	BJ
100	Bob Wagner	U
101	Bob Boylston	U
102	Merrill Douglas	SJ
103	Rex Stuart	U
104	Dale Hamer	R
105	Dick Hantak	R
106	Al Jury	BJ
107	Jim Kearney	BJ
108	Stan Kemp	SJ
109	Sid Semon	HL
110	Ron Botchan	U
111	Earnie Frantz	HL
112	Joe Haynes	LJ
113	Don Dorkowski	FJ
114	Tom Johnson	HL
115	Hendi Ancich	U
116	Bob Baker	LJ
117	Ben Montgomery	U
118	Tom Sifferman	BJ
119	Ron Spitler	FJ
120	Gary Lane	SJ
121	Sanford Rivers	HL
122	Bill Schmitz	FJ
123	Tom White	HL

1989 Officials at a Glance

Referees

Gene Barth, No. **14,** St. Louis, president, oil company, 19th year.
Red Cashion, No. **43,** Texas A&M, chairman of the board, insurance company, 18th year.
Tom Dooley, No. **6,** VMI, general contractor, 12th year.
Ben Dreith, No. **12,** Colorado State, high school teacher, 30th year.
Johnny Grier, No. **23,** D.C. Teachers, planning engineer, 9th year.
Pat Haggerty, No. **40,** Colorado State, retired teacher, 25th year.
Dale Hamer, No. **104,** California (Pa.) University, vice-president, leasing and finance, 12th year.
Dick Hantak, No. **105,** S.E. Missouri, educator, 12th year.
Dick Jorgensen, No. **60,** Wisconsin, bank president, 22nd year.
Jerry Markbreit, No. **9,** Illinois, trade and barter manager, 14th year.
Gordon McCarter, No. **48,** Western Reserve, regional sales manager, 23rd year.
Bob McElwee, No. **95,** U.S. Naval Academy, owner, construction company, 14th year.
Howard Roe, No. **33,** Wichita State, director of corporate insurance/administration, 6th year.
Jerry Seeman, No. **70,** Winona State, district school administrator, 15th year.
Jim Tunney, No. **32,** Occidental, president of motivation company and professional speaker, 30th year.
Fred Wyant, No. **11,** West Virginia, life insurance company, investment management, former NFL player, 24th year.

Umpires

Hendi Ancich, No. **115,** Harbor, longshoreman, 8th year.
Ron Botchan, No. **110,** Occidental, college professor, former AFL player, 10th year.
Bob Boylston, No. **101,** Alabama, stockbroker, 12th year.
Al Conway, No. **27,** Army, vice-president, manufacturing, 21st year.
Ed Coukart, No. **71,** Northwestern, senior vice-president, bank, 1st year.
Art Demmas, No. **78,** Vanderbilt, vice-president, institutional investments, 22nd year.
Ed Fiffick, No. **57,** Marquette, podiatric physician, 11th year.
Neil Gereb, No. **50,** California, project manager, aircraft company, 9th year.
Dave Hamilton, No. **42,** Utah, assistant executive director, 15th year.
John Keck, No. **67,** Cornell, petroleum distributor, 18th year.
Ben Montgomery, No. **117,** Morehouse, school administrator, 8th year.
Dave Moss, No. **88,** Dartmouth, financial counselor, 10th year.
Dennis Riggs, No. **30,** Bellarmine, vice-president, seminary, 2nd year.
Rex Stuart, No. **103,** Appalachian State, insurance agent, 6th year.
Bob Wagner, No. **100,** Penn State, executive director, 5th year.
Gordon Wells, No. **89,** Occidental, chairman, college physical education department, 18th year.

Head Linesmen

Dave Anderson, No. **81,** Salem, insurance executive, 6th year.
Mark Baltz, No. **26,** Ohio University, manufacturer's representative, 1st year.
Tom Barnes, No. **55,** Minnesota, manufacturer's representative, 4th year.
Jerry Bergman, No. **17,** Duquesne, executive director, pension fund, 24th year.
Earnie Frantz, No. **111,** vice-president and manager, land title company, 9th year.
Terry Gierke, No. **72,** Portland State, real estate broker, 9th year.
Tom Johnson, No. **114,** Miami, Ohio, teacher, 8th year.
Leo Miles, No. **35,** Virginia State, retired university athletic director, former NFL player, 21st year.
Ron Phares, No. **10,** Virginia Tech, vice-president, general contracting firm, 5th year.
Aaron Pointer, No. **79,** Pacific Lutheran, recreation specialist, 3rd year.
Sanford Rivers, No. **121,** Youngstown State, assistant vice-president, 1st year.
Sid Semon, No. **109,** Southern California, chairman, physical education department, 12th year.
Burl Toler, No. **37,** San Francisco, director of personnel, San Francisco Community College District, 25th year.
Paul Weidner, No. **87,** Cincinnati, marketing manager, 4th year.
Tom White, No. **123,** Temple, president, athletic manufacturing, 1st year.
Dale Williams, No. **8,** Cal State-Northridge, coordinator, athletic officials, 10th year.

Line Judges

John Alderton, No. **25,** Portland State, vice-president, insurance, 1st year.
Bob Baker, No. **116,** East Texas State, teacher, counselor, 3rd year.
Ron Baynes, No. **56,** Auburn, high school administrator, coach, 3rd year.
Bob Beeks, No. **59,** Lincoln, retired law enforcement officer, 22nd year.
Ron Blum, No. **83,** Marin College, P.G.A. golf professional, 5th year.
Don Carlsen, No. **39,** Cal State-Chico, budget analyst, controller, 1st year.
Walt Coleman, No. **65,** Arkansas, president, dairy company, 1st year.
Ron DeSouza, No. **45,** Morgan State, vice-president, administration, 10th year.
Ray Dodez, No. **74,** Wooster, communications consultant, 22nd year.
Bama Glass, No. **15,** Colorado, owner and manager, retail sales, 11th year.
Joe Haynes, No. **112,** Alcorn State, deputy superintendent, public schools, 6th year.
Jack Johnson, No. **54,** Pacific Lutheran, president, sports promotions, 14th year.
Dick McKenzie, No. **41,** Ashland, school treasurer, 12th year.
Dale Orem, No. **51,** Louisville, mayor, 10th year.
Jim Quirk, No. **5,** Delaware, vice-president, international sales, 2nd year.
Bill Reynolds, No. **53,** West Chester State, teacher and athletic director, 15th year.

Back Judges

Paul Baetz, No. **22,** Heidelberg, financial consultant, 12th year.
Roy Clymer, No. **24,** New Mexico State, district manager, gas company, 10th year.
Jim Daopoulos, No. **75,** Kentucky, mortgage broker, 1st year.
Al Jury, No. **106,** San Bernardino Valley, state traffic officer, 12th year.
Jim Kearney, No. **107,** Pennsylvania, marketing manager, 12th year.
Dean Look, No. **49,** Michigan State, vice-president, instrument maker, former AFL player, 17th year.
Bruce Maurer, No. **38,** Ohio State, administrator/associate director, recreational sports, 3rd year.
Tim Millis, No. **80,** Millsaps, consultant, financial investigation, 1st year.
Bob Moore, No. **36,** Dayton, attorney, 6th year.
Jim Poole, No. **92,** San Diego State, professor, college physical education, 15th year.
Louis Richard, No. **68,** Southwestern Louisiana, sales manager, 4th year.
Tom Sifferman, No. **118,** Seattle, manufacturer's representative, 4th year.
Ben Tompkins, No. **52,** Texas, attorney, 19th year.
Doug Toole, No. **4,** Utah State, physical therapist, orthopedic and sports medicine, 2nd year.
Don Wedge, No. **28,** Ohio Wesleyan, executive account manager, industrial real estate, 18th year.
Banks Williams, No. **99,** Houston, vice-president-sales, concrete company, 12th year.

Side Judges

Gerald Austin, No. **34,** Western Carolina, associate superintendent, county schools, 8th year.
Bill Carollo, No. **63,** Wisconsin, account executive, 1st year.
Richard Creed, No. **61,** Louisville, manager, real estate, 12th year.
Merrill Douglas, No. **102,** Utah, deputy sheriff, former NFL player, 9th year.
Tom Fincken, No. **47,** Emporia State, educator, 6th year.
Duwayne Gandy, No. **62,** Tulsa, regional sales manager, educational publishing, 9th year.
Dave Hawk, No. **66,** Southern Methodist, owner, warehousing company, 18th year.
Doyle Jackson, No. **16,** Central Arkansas, high school teacher, department chairman, 2nd year.
Nate Jones, No. **97,** Lewis and Clark, high school principal, 13th year.
Stan Kemp, No. **108,** Michigan, vice-president, insurance executive, 4th year.
Gary Lane, No. **120,** Missouri, divisional marketing manager, former NFL player, 8th year.
Gil Mace, No. **90,** Westminster, national account manager, 16th year.
Larry Nemmers, No. **20,** Upper Iowa, high school principal, 5th year.
Dave Parry, No. **64,** Wabash, high school athletic director, 15th year.
Bill Quinby, No. **58,** Iowa, director, career counseling, 12th year.
Howard Slavin, No. **29,** Southern California, attorney, 3rd year.

Field Judges

Dick Dolack, No. **31,** Ferris State, pharmacist, 24th year.
Don Dorkowski, No. **113,** Los Angeles State College, high school director, health and safety, 4th year.
Don Hakes, No. **96,** Bradley, high school teacher, 13th year.
Donnie Hampton, No. **44,** Georgia, president, mortgage company, 2nd year.
Bernie Kukar, No. **86,** St. John's, owner/director, summer camp for boys, 6th year.
Bob Lewis, No. **18,** retired U.S. government specialist, 14th year.
Pat Mallette, No. **82,** Nebraska, real estate broker, 21st year.
Ed Merrifield, No. **76,** Missouri, sales representative, 15th year.
Don Orr, No. **77,** Vanderbilt, mechanical contractor, 19th year.
John Robison, No. **46,** Utah, high school counselor and coach, 2nd year.
Bill Schmitz, No. **122,** Colorado State, sales manager, 1st year.
Bobby Skelton, No. **73,** Alabama, industrial representative, 5th year.
Ron Spitler, No. **119,** Panhandle State, owner, service center, 8th year.
Bill Stanley, No. **91,** Redlands, college dean, athletic director, 16th year.
Jack Vaughan, No. **93,** Mississippi State, financial services, 14th year.
Bob Wortman, No. **84,** Findlay, supervisor, college basketball officials, 24th year.

1

TOUCHDOWN, FIELD GOAL, or SUCCESSFUL TRY
Both arms extended above head.

2

SAFETY
Palms together above head.

3

FIRST DOWN
Arm pointed toward defensive team's goal.

4

CROWD NOISE, DEAD BALL or NEUTRAL ZONE ESTABLISHED
One arm above head with an open hand.
With fist closed: **Fourth Down.**

5

BALL ILLEGALLY TOUCHED, KICKED, OR BATTED
Fingertips tap both shoulders.

6

TIME OUT
Hands crisscrossed above head.
Same signal followed by placing one hand on top of cap: **Referee's Time Out.**
Same signal followed by arm swung at side: **Touchback.**

7

NO TIME OUT or TIME IN WITH WHISTLE
Full arm circled to simulate moving clock.

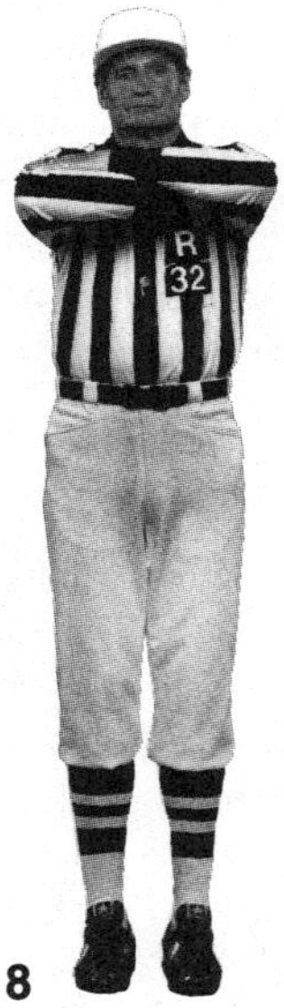

8

DELAY OF GAME, ILLEGAL SUBSTITUTION, or EXCESS TIME OUT
Folded arms.

9

FALSE START, ILLEGAL SHIFT, ILLEGAL PROCEDURE, ILLEGAL FORMATION, or KICKOFF OR SAFETY KICK OUT OF BOUNDS
Forearms rotated over and over in front of body.

10

PERSONAL FOUL
One wrist striking the other above head.
Same signal followed by swinging leg: **Running Into or Roughing Kicker.**
Same signal followed by raised arm swinging forward: **Running Into or Roughing Passer.**
Same signal followed by hand striking back of calf: **Clipping**

11

HOLDING
Grasping one wrist, the fist clenched, in front of chest.

12

ILLEGAL USE OF HANDS, ARMS, OR BODY
Grasping one wrist, the hand open and facing forward, in front of chest.

13

PENALTY REFUSED, INCOMPLETE PASS, PLAY OVER, or MISSED GOAL
Hands shifted in horizontal plane.

14

PASS JUGGLED INBOUNDS AND CAUGHT OUT OF BOUNDS
Hands up and down in front of chest (following incomplete pass signal).

15

ILLEGAL FORWARD PASS
One hand waved behind back followed by loss of down signal (23).

16

INTENTIONAL GROUNDING OF PASS
Parallel arms waved in a diagonal plane across body. Followed by loss of down signal (23).

17

INTERFERENCE WITH FORWARD PASS or FAIR CATCH
Hands open and extended forward from shoulders with hands vertical.

18

INVALID FAIR CATCH SIGNAL
One hand waved above head.

19

INELIGIBLE RECEIVER OR INELIGIBLE MEMBER OF KICKING TEAM DOWNFIELD
Right hand touching top of cap.

20

ILLEGAL CONTACT
One open hand extended forward

21

OFFSIDE or ENCROACHING
Hands on hips.

22

ILLEGAL MOTION AT SNAP
Horizontal arc with one hand.

23

LOSS OF DOWN
Both hands held behind head.

24

CRAWLING, INTERLOCKING INTERFERENCE, PUSHING, or HELPING RUNNER
Pushing movement of hands to front with arms downward.

25

TOUCHING A FORWARD PASS OR SCRIMMAGE KICK
Diagonal motion of one hand across another.

26

UNSPORTSMANLIKE CONDUCT
Arms outstretched, palms down. (Same signal means continuous action fouls are disregarded.) Chop block.

27

ILLEGAL CUT or BLOCKING BELOW THE WAIST
Hand striking front of thigh preceded by personal foul signal (10).

28

ILLEGAL CRACKBACK
Strike of an open right hand against the right mid thigh preceded by personal foul signal (10).

29

PLAYER DISQUALIFIED
Ejection signal.

30

TRIPPING
Repeated action of right foot in back of left heel.

31

UNCATCHABLE FORWARD PASS
Palm of right hand held parallel to ground above head and moved back and forth.

NFL Digest of Rules

This Digest of Rules of the National Football League has been prepared to aid players, fans, and members of the press, radio, and television media in their understanding of the game.

It is not meant to be a substitute for the official rule book. In any case of conflict between these explanations and the official rules, the rules always have precedence.

In order to make it easier to coordinate the information in this digest the topics discussed generally follow the order of the rule book.

Officials' Jurisdictions, Positions, and Duties

Referee—General oversight and control of game. Gives signals for all fouls and is final authority for rule interpretations. Takes a position in backfield 10 to 12 yards behind line of scrimmage, favors right side (if quarterback is right-handed passer). Determines legality of snap, observes deep back(s) for legal motion. On running play, observes quarterback during and after handoff, remains with him until action has cleared away, then proceeds downfield, checking on runner and contact behind him. When runner is downed, Referee determines forward progress from wing official and if necessary, adjusts final position of ball.

On pass plays, drops back as quarterback begins to fade back, picks up legality of blocks by near linemen. Changes to complete concentration on quarterback as defenders approach. Primarily responsible to rule on possible roughing action on passer and if ball becomes loose, rules whether ball is free on a fumble or dead on an incomplete pass.

During kicking situations, Referee has primary responsibility to rule on kicker's actions and whether or not any subsequent contact by a defender is legal.

Umpire—Primary responsibility to rule on players' equipment, as well as their conduct and actions on scrimmage line. Lines up approximately four to five yards downfield, varying position from in front of weakside tackle to strongside guard. Looks for possible false start by offensive linemen. Observes legality of contact by both offensive linemen while blocking and by defensive players while they attempt to ward off blockers. Is prepared to call rule infractions if they occur on offense or defense. Moves forward to line of scrimmage when pass play develops in order to insure that interior linemen do not move illegally downfield. If offensive linemen indicate screen pass is to be attempted, Umpire shifts his attention toward screen side, picks up potential receiver in order to insure that he will legally be permitted to run his pattern and continues to rule on action of blockers. Umpire is to assist in ruling on incomplete or trapped passes when ball is thrown overhead or short.

Head Linesman—Primarily responsible for ruling on offside, encroachment, and actions pertaining to scrimmage line prior to or at snap. Keys on closest setback on his side of the field. On pass plays, Linesman is responsible to clear this receiver approximately seven yards downfield as he moves to a point five yards beyond the line. Linesman's secondary responsibility is to rule on any illegal action taken by defenders on any delay receiver moving downfield. Has full responsibility for ruling on sideline plays on his side, e.g., pass receiver or runner in or out of bounds. Together with Referee, Linesman is responsible for keeping track of number of downs and is in charge of mechanics of his chain crew in connection with its duties.

Linesman must be prepared to assist in determining forward progress by a runner on play directed toward middle or into his side zone. He, in turn, is to signal Referee or Umpire what forward point ball has reached. Linesman is also responsible to rule on legality of action involving any receiver who approaches his side zone. He is to call pass interference when the infraction occurs and is to rule on legality of blockers and defenders on plays involving ball carriers, whether it is entirely a running play, a combination pass and run, or a play involving a kick.

Line Judge—Straddles line of scrimmage on side of field opposite Linesman. Keeps time of game as a backup for clock operator. Along with Linesman is responsible for offside, encroachment, and actions pertaining to scrimmage line prior to or at snap. Line Judge keys on closest setback on his side of field. Line Judge is to observe his receiver until he moves at least seven yards downfield. He then moves toward backfield side, being especially alert to rule on any back in motion and on flight of ball when pass is made (he must rule whether forward or backward). Line Judge has primary responsibility to rule whether or not passer is behind or beyond line of scrimmage when pass is made. He also assists in observing actions by blockers and defenders who are on his side of field. After pass is thrown, Line Judge directs attention toward activities that occur in back of Umpire. During punting situations, Line Judge remains at line of scrimmage to be sure that only the end men move downfield until kick has been made. He also rules whether or not the kick crossed line and then observes action by members of the kicking team who are moving downfield to cover the kick.

Back Judge—Operates on same side of field as Line Judge, 17 yards deep. Keys on wide receiver on his side. Concentrates on path of end or back, observing legality of his potential block(s) or of actions taken against him. Is prepared to rule from deep position on holding or illegal use of hands by end or back or on defensive infractions committed by player guarding him. Has primary responsibility to make decisions involving sideline on his side of field, e.g., pass receiver or runner in or out of bounds.

Back Judge makes decisions involving catching, recovery, or illegal touching of a loose ball beyond line of scrimmage; rules on plays involving pass receiver, including legality of catch or pass interference; assists in covering actions of runner, including blocks by teammates and that of defenders; calls clipping on punt returns; and, together with Field Judge, rules whether or not field goal attempts are successful.

Side Judge—Operates on same side of field as Linesman, 17 yards deep. Keys on wide receiver on his side. Concentrates on path of end or back, observing legality of his potential block(s) or of actions taken against him. Is prepared to rule from deep position on holding or illegal use of hands by end or back or on defensive infractions committed by player guarding him. Has primary responsibility to make decisions involving sideline on his side of field, e.g., pass receiver or runner in or out of bounds.

Side Judge makes decisions involving catching, recovery, or illegal touching of a loose ball beyond line of scrimmage; rules on plays involving pass receiver, including legality of catch or pass interference; assists in covering actions of runner, including blocks by teammates and that of defenders; and calls clipping on punt returns.

Field Judge—Takes a position 25 yards downfield. In general, favors the tight end's side of field. Keys on tight end, concentrates on his path and observes legality of tight end's potential block(s) or of actions taken against him. Is prepared to rule from deep position on holding or illegal use of hands by end or back or on defensive infractions committed by player guarding him.

Field Judge times interval between plays on 45/30-second clock plus intermission between two periods of each half; makes decisions involving catching, recovery, or illegal touching of a loose ball beyond line of scrimmage; is responsible to rule on plays involving end line; calls pass interference, fair catch infractions, and clipping on kick returns; and, together with Back Judge, rules whether or not field goals and conversions are successful.

Definitions

1. **Chucking:** Warding off an opponent who is in front of a defender by contacting him with a quick extension of arm or arms, followed by the return of arm(s) to a flexed position, thereby breaking the original contact.
2. **Clipping:** Throwing the body across the back of an opponent's leg or hitting him from the back below the waist while moving up from behind unless the opponent is a runner or the action is in close line play.
3. **Close Line Play:** The area between the positions normally occupied by the offensive tackles, extending three yards on each side of the line of scrimmage.
4. **Crackback:** Eligible receivers who take or move to a position more than two yards outside the tackle may not block an opponent below the waist if they then move back inside to block.
5. **Dead Ball:** Ball not in play.
6. **Double Foul:** A foul by each team during the same down.
7. **Down:** The period of action that starts when the ball is put in play and ends when it is dead.
8. **Encroachment:** When a player enters the neutral zone and makes contact with an opponent before the ball is snapped.
9. **Fair Catch:** An unhindered catch of a kick by a member of the receiving team who must raise one arm a full length above his head while the kick is in flight.
10. **Foul:** Any violation of a playing rule.
11. **Free Kick:** A kickoff, kick after a safety, or kick after a fair catch. It may be a placekick, dropkick, or punt, except a punt may not be used on a kickoff.
12. **Fumble:** The loss of possession of the ball.
13. **Impetus:** The action of a player that gives momentum to the ball.
14. **Live Ball:** A ball legally free kicked or snapped. It continues in play until the down ends.
15. **Loose Ball:** A live ball not in possession of any player.
16. **Muff:** The touching of a loose ball by a player in an unsuccessful attempt to obtain possession.
17. **Neutral Zone:** The space the length of a ball between the two scrimmage lines. The offensive team and defensive team must remain behind their end of the ball.
    Exception: The offensive player who snaps the ball.
18. **Offside:** A player is offside when any part of his body is beyond his scrimmage or free kick line when the ball is snapped.
19. **Own Goal:** The goal a team is guarding.
20. **Pocket Area:** Applies from a point two yards outside of either offensive tackle and includes the tight end if he drops off the line of scrimmage to pass protect. Pocket extends longitudinally behind the line back to offensive team's own end line.
21. **Possession:** When a player controls the ball throughout the act of clearly touching both feet, or any other part of his body other than his hand(s), to the ground inbounds.
22. **Punt:** A kick made when a player drops the ball and kicks it while it is in flight.
23. **Safety:** The situation in which the ball is dead on or behind a team's own goal if the impetus comes from a player on that team. Two points are scored for the opposing team.
24. **Shift:** The movement of two or more offensive players at the same time before the snap.
25. **Striking:** The act of swinging, clubbing, or propelling the arm or forearm in contacting an opponent.
26. **Sudden Death:** The continuation of a tied game into sudden death overtime in which the team scoring first (by safety, field goal, or touchdown) wins.
27. **Touchback:** When a ball is dead on or behind a team's own goal line, provided the impetus came from an opponent and provided it is not a touchdown or a missed field goal.
28. **Touchdown:** When any part of the ball, legally in possession of a player inbounds, is on, above, or over the opponent's goal line, provided it is not a touchback.
29. **Unsportsmanlike Conduct:** Any act contrary to the generally understood principles of sportsmanship.

Summary of Penalties

Automatic First Down

1. Awarded to offensive team on all defensive fouls with these exceptions:
   (a) Offside.
   (b) Encroachment.
   (c) Delay of game.
   (d) Illegal substitution.
   (e) Excessive time out(s).
   (f) Incidental grasp of facemask.
   (g) Prolonged, excessive or premeditated celebrations by individual players or groups of players.
   (h) Running into the kicker.

Loss of Down (No yardage)

1. Second forward pass behind the line.
2. Forward pass strikes ground, goal post, or crossbar.
3. Forward pass goes out of bounds.
4. Forward pass is first touched by eligible receiver who has gone out of bounds and returned.
5. Forward pass touches or is caught by an ineligible receiver on or behind line.
6. Forward pass thrown from behind line of scrimmage after ball once crossed the line.

Five Yards

1. Crawling.
2. Defensive holding or illegal use of hands (automatic first down).
3. Delay of game.
4. Encroachment.
5. Too many time outs.
6. False start.
7. Illegal formation.
8. Illegal shift.
9. Illegal motion.
10. Illegal substitution.
11. First onside kickoff out of bounds between goal lines and not touched.
12. Invalid fair catch signal.
13. More than 11 players on the field at snap for either team.
14. Less than seven men on offensive line at snap.
15. Offside.
16. Failure to pause one second after shift or huddle.
17. Running into kicker.
18. More than one man in motion at snap.
19. Grasping facemask of opponent.
20. Player out of bounds at snap.
21. Ineligible member(s) of kicking team going beyond line of scrimmage before ball is kicked.
22. Illegal return.
23. Failure to report change of eligibility.
24. Prolonged, excessive or premeditated celebrations by individual players or groups of players.
25. Loss of team time out(s) or five-yard penalty on the defense for excessive crowd noise.

10 Yards

1. Offensive pass interference.
2. Ineligible player downfield during passing down.
3. Holding, illegal use of hands, arms or body by offense.
4. Tripping by a member of either team.
5. Helping the runner.
6. Illegal batting or punching a loose ball.
7. Deliberately kicking a loose ball.

15 Yards

1. Chop block.
2. Clipping below the waist.
3. Fair catch interference.
4. Illegal crackback block by offense.
5. Piling on (automatic first down).
6. Roughing the kicker (automatic first down).
7. Roughing the passer (automatic first down).
8. Twisting, turning, or pulling an opponent by the facemask.
9. Unnecessary roughness.
10. Unsportsmanlike conduct.
11. Delay of game at start of either half.
12. Illegal blocking below the waist.
13. A tackler using his helmet to butt, spear, or ram an opponent.
14. Any player who uses the top of his helmet unnecessarily.
15. A punter, placekicker or holder who simulates being roughed by a defensive player.
16. A defender who takes a running start from beyond the line of scrimmage in an attempt to block a field goal or point after touchdown.

Five Yards and Loss of Down

1. Forward pass thrown from beyond line of scrimmage.

10 Yards and Loss of Down

1. Intentional grounding of forward pass (safety if passer is in own end zone). If foul occurs more than 10 yards behind line, play results in loss of down at spot of foul.

15 Yards and Loss of Coin Toss Option

1. Team's late arrival on the field prior to scheduled kickoff.

15 Yards (and disqualification if flagrant)

1. Striking opponent with fist.
2. Kicking or kneeing opponent.
3. Striking opponent on head or neck with forearm, elbow, or hands whether or not the initial contact is made below the neck area.
4. Roughing kicker.
5. Roughing passer.
6. Malicious unnecessary roughness.
7. Unsportsmanlike conduct.
8. Palpably unfair act. (Distance penalty determined by the Referee after consultation with other officials.)

15 Yards and Automatic Disqualification

1. Using a helmet that is not worn as a weapon.

Suspension From Game

1. Illegal equipment. (Player may return after one down when legally equipped.)

Touchdown

1. When Referee determines a palpably unfair act deprived a team of a touchdown. (Example: Player comes off bench and tackles runner apparently en route to touchdown.)

Field

1. Sidelines and end lines are out of bounds. The goal line is actually in the end zone. A player with the ball in his possession scores when the ball is on, above, or over the goal line.
2. The field is rimmed by a white border, a minimum six feet wide, along the sidelines. All of this is out of bounds.
3. The hashmarks (inbound lines) are 70 feet, 9 inches from each sideline.
4. Goal posts must be single-standard type, offset from the end line and painted bright gold. The goal posts must be 18 feet, 6 inches wide and the top face of the crossbar must be 10 feet above the ground. Vertical posts extend at least 30 feet above the crossbar. A ribbon 4 inches by 42 inches long is to be attached to the top of each post. The actual goal is the plane extending indefinitely above the crossbar and between the outer edges of the posts.
5. The field is 360 feet long and 160 feet wide. The end zones are 30 feet deep. The line used in try-for-point plays is two yards out from the goal line.
6. Chain crew members and ball boys must be uniformly identifiable.
7. All clubs must use standardized sideline markers. Pylons must be used for goal line and end line markings.
8. End zone markings and club identification at 50 yard line must be approved by the Commissioner to avoid any confusion as to delineation of goal lines, sidelines, and end lines.

Ball

1. The home club must have 24 balls available for testing by the Referee one hour before game time. In case of bad weather, a playable ball is to be substituted on request of the offensive team captain.

Coin Toss

1. The toss of coin will take place within three minutes of kickoff in center of field. The toss will be called by the visiting captain. The winner may choose one of two privileges and the loser gets the other:
   (a) Receive or kick
   (b) Goal his team will defend
2. Immediately prior to the start of the second half, the captains of both teams must inform the officials of their respective choices. The loser of the original coin toss gets first choice.

Timing

1. The stadium clock is official. In case it stops or is operating incorrectly, the Line Judge takes over the official timing on the field.
2. Each period is 15 minutes. The intermission between the periods is two minutes. Halftime is 15 minutes, unless otherwise specified.
3. On charged team time outs, the Field Judge starts watch and blows whistle after 1 minute 50 seconds, unless television does not utilize the time for commercial. In this case the length of the time out is reduced to 40 seconds.
4. Referee may allow two minutes for injured player and three minutes for equipment repair.
5. Each team is allowed three time outs each half.
6. Time between plays will be 45 seconds from the end of a given play until the snap of the ball for the next play, or a 30-second interval after certain administrative stoppages and game delays.
7. Clock will start running when ball is snapped following all changes of team possession.
8. Consecutive team time outs can be taken by opposing teams but the length of the second time out will be reduced to 40 seconds.
9. When, in the judgment of the Referee, the level of crowd noise prevents the offense from hearing its signals, he can institute a series of procedures which can result in a loss of team time outs or a five-yard penalty against the defensive team.

Sudden Death

1. The sudden death system of determining the winner shall prevail when score is tied at the end of the regulation playing time of all NFL games. The team scoring first during overtime play shall be the winner and the game automatically ends upon any score (by safety, field goal, or touchdown) or when a score is awarded by Referee for a palpably unfair act.
2. At the end of regulation time the Referee will immediately toss coin at center of field in accordance with rules pertaining to the usual pregame toss. The captain of the visiting team will call the toss.
3. Following a three-minute intermission after the end of the regulation game, play will be continued in 15-minute periods or until there is a score. There is a two-minute intermission between subsequent periods. The teams

change goals at the start of each period. Each team has three time outs and general provisions for play in the last two minutes of a half shall prevail. Disqualified players are not allowed to return.

Exception: In preseason and regular season games there shall be a maximum of 15 minutes of sudden death with two time outs instead of three. General provisions for play in the last two minutes of a half will be in force.

Timing in Final Two Minutes of Each Half

1. On kickoff, clock does not start until the ball has been legally touched by player of either team in the field of play. (In all other cases, clock starts with kickoff.)
2. A team cannot "buy" an excess time out for a penalty. However, a fourth time out is allowed without penalty for an injured player, who must be removed immediately. A fifth time out or more is allowed for an injury and a five-yard penalty is assessed if the clock was running. Additionally, if the clock was running and the score is tied or the team in possession is losing, the ball cannot be put in play for at least 10 seconds on the fourth or more time out. The half or game can end while those 10 seconds are run off on the clock.
3. If the defensive team is behind in the score and commits a foul when it has no time outs left in the final 30 seconds of either half, the offensive team can decline the penalty for the foul and have the time on the clock expire.
4. Fouls that occur in the last five minutes of the fourth quarter as well as the last two minutes of the first half will result in the clock starting on the snap.

Try-for-Point

1. After a touchdown, the scoring team is allowed a try-for-point during one scrimmage down. The ball may be spotted anywhere between the inbounds lines, two or more yards from the goal line. The successful conversion counts one point, whether by run, kick, or pass.
2. The defensive team never can score on a try-for-point. As soon as defense gets possession, or kick is blocked, ball is dead.
3. Any distance penalty for fouls committed by the defense that prevent the try from being attempted can be enforced on the succeeding kickoff. Any foul committed on a successful try will result in a distance penalty being assessed on the ensuing kickoff.
4. Only the fumbling player may advance a fumble during a try-for-point.

Players-Substitutions

1. Each team is permitted 11 men on the field at the snap.
2. Unlimited substitution is permitted. However, players may enter the field only when the ball is dead. Players who have been substituted for are not permitted to linger on the field. Such lingering will be interpreted as unsportsmanlike conduct.
3. Players leaving the game must be out of bounds on their own side, clearing the field between the end lines, before a snap or free kick. If player crosses end line leaving field, it is delay of game (five-yard penalty).
4. Substitutes who remain in the game must move onto the field as far as the inside of the field numerals before moving to a wide position.

Kickoff

1. The kickoff shall be from the kicking team's 35 yard line at the start of each half and after a field goal and try-for-point. A kickoff is one type of free kick.
2. Either a one-, two-, or three-inch tee may be used (no tee permitted for field goal or try-for-point plays). The ball is put in play by a placekick or dropkick.
3. If kickoff clears the opponent's goal posts it is not a field goal.
4. A kickoff is illegal unless it travels 10 yards OR is touched by the receiving team. Once the ball is touched by the receiving team it is a free ball. Receivers may recover and advance. Kicking team may recover but NOT advance UNLESS receiver had possession and lost the ball.
5. When a kickoff goes out of bounds between the goal lines without being touched by the receiving team, the ball belongs to the receivers 30 yards from the spot of the kick or at the out-of-bounds spot unless the ball went out-of-bounds the first time an onside kick was attempted. In this case the kicking team is to be penalized five yards and the ball must be kicked again.
6. When a kickoff goes out of bounds between the goal lines and is touched last by receiving team, it is receiver's ball at out-of-bounds spot.

Free Kick

1. In addition to a kickoff, the other free kicks are a kick after a safety and a kick after a fair catch. In both cases, a dropkick, placekick, or punt may be used (a punt may not be used on a kickoff).
2. On a free kick after a fair catch, captain of receiving team has the option to put ball in play by punt, dropkick, or placekick without a tee, or by snap. If the placekick or dropkick goes between the uprights a field goal is scored.
3. On a free kick after a safety, the team scored upon puts ball in play by a punt, dropkick, or placekick without tee. No score can be made on a free kick following a safety, even if a series of penalties places team in position. (A field goal can be scored only on a play from scrimmage or a free kick after a fair catch.)

Field Goal

1. All field goals attempted and missed from scrimmage line beyond the 20 yard line will result in the defensive team taking possession of the ball at the scrimmage line. On any field goal attempted and missed from scrimmage line inside the 20 yard line, ball will revert to defensive team at the 20 yard line.

Safety

1. The important factor in a safety is impetus. Two points are scored for the opposing team when the ball is dead on or behind a team's own goal line if the impetus came from a player on that team.

Examples of Safety:

(a) Blocked punt goes out of kicking team's end zone. Impetus was provided by punting team. The block only changes direction of ball, not impetus.
(b) Ball carrier retreats from field of play into his own end zone and is downed. Ball carrier provides impetus.
(c) Offensive team commits a foul and spot of enforcement is behind its own goal line.
(d) Player on receiving team muffs punt and, trying to get ball, forces or illegally kicks it into end zone where he or a teammate recovers. He has given new impetus to the ball.

Examples of Non-Safety:

(a) Player intercepts a pass with both feet inbounds in the field of play and his momentum carries him into his own end zone. Ball is put in play at spot of interception.
(b) Player intercepts a pass in his own end zone and is downed. Impetus came from passing team, not from defense. (Touchback)
(c) Player passes from behind his own goal line. Opponent bats down ball in end zone. (Incomplete pass)

Measuring

1. The forward point of the ball is used when measuring.

Position of Players at Snap

1. Offensive team must have at least seven players on line.
2. Offensive players, not on line, must be at least one yard back at snap. (**Exception:** player who takes snap.)
3. No interior lineman may move after taking or simulating a three-point stance.
4. No player of either team may invade neutral zone before snap.
5. No player of offensive team may charge or move, after assuming set position, in such manner as to lead defense to believe snap has started.
6. If a player changes his eligibility, the Referee must alert the defensive captain after player has reported to him.
7. All players of offensive team must be stationary at snap, except one back who may be in motion parallel to scrimmage line or backward (not forward).
8. After a shift or huddle all players on offensive team must come to an absolute stop for at least one second with no movement of hands, feet, head, or swaying of body.
9. Quarterbacks can be called for a false start penalty (five yards) if their actions are judged to be an obvious attempt to draw an opponent offside.

Use of Hands, Arms, and Body

1. No player on offense may assist a runner except by blocking for him. There shall be no interlocking interference.
2. A runner may ward off opponents with his hands and arms but no other player on offense may use hands or arms to obstruct an opponent by grasping with hands, pushing, or encircling any part of his body during a block. Hands (open or closed) can be thrust forward to initially contact an opponent on or outside the opponent's frame, but the blocker must work to bring his hands on or inside the frame.
   Note: Pass blocking: Hand(s) thrust forward that slip outside the body of the defender will be legal if blocker worked to bring them back inside. Hand(s) or arm(s) that encircle a defender—i.e., hook an opponent—is to be considered illegal and officials are to call a foul for holding.
   Blocker cannot use his hands or arms to push from behind, hang onto, or encircle an opponent in a manner that restricts his movement as the play develops.
3. Hands cannot be thrust forward above the frame to contact an opponent on the neck, face or head.
   Note: The frame is defined as the part of the opponent's body below the neck that is presented to the blocker.
4. A defensive player may not tackle or hold an opponent other than a runner. Otherwise, he may use his hands, arms, or body only:
   (a) To defend or protect himself against an obstructing opponent.
   Exception: An eligible receiver is considered to be an obstructing opponent ONLY to a point five yards beyond the line of scrimmage unless the player who receives the snap clearly demonstrates no further intention to pass the ball. Within this five-yard zone, a defensive player may make contact with an eligible receiver that may be maintained as long as it is continuous and unbroken. The defensive player cannot use his hands or arms to push from behind, hang onto, or encircle an eligible receiver in a manner that restricts movement as the play develops. Beyond this five-yard limitation, a defender may use his hands or arms ONLY to defend or protect himself against impending contact caused by a receiver. In such reaction, the defender may not contact a receiver who attempts to take a path to evade him.
   (b) To push or pull opponent out of the way on line of scrimmage.
   (c) In actual attempt to get at or tackle runner.
   (d) To push or pull opponent out of the way in a legal attempt to recover a loose ball.
   (e) During a legal block on an opponent who is not an eligible pass receiver.
   (f) When legally blocking an eligible pass receiver above the waist.
   Exception: Eligible receivers lined up within two yards of the tackle, whether on or immediately behind the line, may be blocked below the waist at or behind the line of scrimmage. NO eligible receiver may be blocked below the waist after he goes beyond the line.
   Note: Once the quarterback hands off or pitches the ball to a back, or if the quarterback leaves the pocket area, the restrictions on the defensive team relative to the offensive receivers will end, provided the ball is not in the air.

5. A defensive player must not contact an opponent above the shoulders with the palm of his hand except to ward him off on the line. This exception is permitted only if it is not a repeated act against the same opponent during any one contact. In all other cases the palms may be used on head, neck, or face only to ward off or push an opponent in legal attempt to get at the ball.
6. Any offensive player who pretends to possess the ball or to whom a teammate pretends to give the ball may be tackled provided he is crossing his scrimmage line between the ends of a normal tight offensive line.
7. An offensive player who lines up more than two yards outside his own tackle or a player who, at the snap, is in a backfield position and subsequently takes a position more than two yards outside a tackle may not clip an opponent anywhere nor may he contact an opponent below the waist if the blocker is moving toward the ball and if contact is made within an area five yards on either side of the line.
8. A player of either team may block at any time provided it is not pass interference, fair catch interference, or unnecessary roughness.
9. A player may not bat or punch:
   (a) A loose ball (in field of play) toward his opponent's goal line or in any direction in either end zone.
   (b) A ball in player possession or attempt to get possession.
   Exception: A forward or backward pass may be batted, tipped, or deflected in any direction at any time by either the offense or the defense.
   Note: A pass in flight that is controlled or caught may only be thrown backward.
10. No player may deliberately kick any ball except as a punt, dropkick, or placekick.

Forward Pass

1. A forward pass may be touched or caught by any eligible receiver. All members of the defensive team are eligible. Eligible receivers on the offensive team are players on either end of line (other than center, guard, or tackle) or players at least one yard behind the line at the snap. A T-formation quarterback is not eligible to receive a forward pass during a play from scrimmage.
   Exception: T-formation quarterback becomes eligible if pass is previously touched by an eligible receiver.
2. An offensive team may make only one forward pass during each play from scrimmage (Loss of down).
3. The passer must be behind his line of scrimmage (Loss of down and five yards, enforced from the spot of pass).
4. Any eligible offensive player may catch a forward pass. If a pass is touched by one offensive player and touched or caught by a second eligible offensive player, pass completion is legal. Further, all offensive players become eligible once a pass is touched by an eligible receiver or any defensive player.
5. The rules concerning a forward pass and ineligible receivers:
   (a) If ball is touched accidentally by an ineligible receiver on or behind his line: loss of down.
   (b) If ineligible receiver is illegally downfield: loss of 10 yards.
   (c) If touched or caught (intentionally or accidentally) by ineligible receiver beyond the line: loss of 10 yards or loss of down.
6. The player who first controls and continues to maintain control of a pass will be awarded the ball even though his opponent later establishes joint control of the ball.
7. Any forward pass becomes incomplete and ball is dead if:
   (a) Pass hits the ground or goes out of bounds.
   (b) Hits the goal post or the crossbar of either team.
   (c) Is caught by offensive player after touching ineligible receiver.
   (d) An illegal pass is caught by the passer.
8. A forward pass is complete when a receiver clearly touches the ground with both feet inbounds while in possession of the ball. If a receiver would have landed inbounds with both feet but is carried or pushed out of bounds while maintaining possession of the ball, pass is complete at the out-of-bounds spot.
9. If an eligible receiver goes out of bounds accidentally or is forced out by a defender and returns to catch a pass, the play is regarded as a pass caught out of bounds. (Loss of down, no yardage.)
10. On a fourth down pass—when the offensive team is inside the opposition's 20 yard line—an incomplete pass results in a loss of down at the line of scrimmage.
11. If a personal foul is committed by the defense prior to the completion of a pass, the penalty is 15 yards from the spot where ball becomes dead.
12. If a personal foul is committed by the offense prior to the completion of a pass, the penalty is 15 yards from the previous line of scrimmage.

Intentional Grounding of Forward Pass

1. Intentional grounding of a forward pass is a foul: loss of down and 10 yards from previous spot if passer is in the field of play or loss of down at the spot of the foul if it occurs more than 10 yards behind the line or safety if passer is in his own end zone when ball is released.
2. It is considered intentional grounding of a forward pass when the ball strikes the ground after the passer throws, tosses, or lobs the ball to prevent a loss of yards by his team.
3. It is not intentional grounding when the defensive rushers have not put sufficient pressure on the passer to prevent him, for strategic purposes, from throwing the ball downfield in a natural and effective motion even though there is no apparent chance of completion.

Protection of Passer

1. By interpretation, a pass begins when the passer—with possession of ball—starts to bring his hand forward. If ball strikes ground after this action has begun, play is ruled an incomplete pass. If passer loses control of ball prior to his bringing his hand forward, play is ruled a fumble.
2. No defensive player may run into a passer of a legal forward pass after the ball has left his hand (15 yards). The Referee must determine whether opponent had a reasonable chance to stop his momentum during an attempt to block the pass or tackle the passer while he still had the ball.
3. No defensive player who has an unrestricted path to the quarterback may hit him flagrantly in the area of the knee(s) when approaching in any direction.
4. Officials are to blow the play dead as soon as the quarterback is clearly in the grasp and control of any tackler.

Pass Interference

1. There shall be no interference with a forward pass thrown from behind the line. The restriction for the passing team starts with the snap. The restriction on the defensive team starts when the ball leaves the passer's hand. Both restrictions end when the ball is touched by anyone.
2. The penalty for defensive pass interference is an automatic first down at the spot of the foul. If interference is in the end zone, it is first down for the offense on the defense's 1 yard line. If previous spot was inside the defense's 1 yard line, penalty is half the distance to the goal line.
3. The penalty for offensive pass interference is 10 yards from the previous spot.
4. It is pass interference by either team when any player movement beyond the offensive line significantly hinders the progress of an eligible player or such player's opportunity to catch the ball during a legal forward pass. When players are competing for position to make a play on the ball, any contact by hands, arms or body shall be considered incidental unless prohibited. Prohibited conduct shall be when a player physically restricts or impedes the opponent in such a manner that is visually evident and materially affects the opponent's opportunity to gain position or retain his position to catch the ball. If a player has gained position, he shall not be considered to have impeded or restricted his opponent in a prohibited manner if all of his actions are a bona fide effort to go to and catch the ball. Provided an eligible player is not interfered with in such a manner, the following exceptions to pass interference will prevail:
   (a) If neither player is looking for the ball and there is incidental contact in the act of moving to the ball that does not materially affect the route of an eligible player, there is no interference. If there is any question whether the incidental contact materially affects the route, the ruling shall be no interference.
   Note: Inadvertent tripping is not a foul in this situation.
   (b) Any eligible player looking for and intent on playing the ball who initiates contact, however severe, while attempting to move to the spot of completion or interception will not be called for interference.
   (c) Any eligible player who makes contact, however severe, with one or more eligible players while looking for and making a genuine attempt to catch or bat a reachable ball, will not be called for interference.
   (d) It must be remembered that defensive players have as much right to the ball as offensive eligible receivers.
   (e) Pass interference by the defense is not to be called when the forward pass is clearly uncatchable.
   (f) Note: There is no defensive pass interference behind the line.

Backward Pass

1. Any pass not forward is regarded as a backward pass or lateral. A pass parallel to the line is a backward pass. A runner may pass backward at any time. Any player on either team may catch the pass or recover the ball after it touches the ground.
2. A backward pass that strikes the ground can be recovered and advanced by offensive team.
3. A backward pass that strikes the ground can be recovered but cannot be advanced by the defensive team.
4. A backward pass caught in the air can be advanced by the defensive team.

Fumble

1. The distinction between a fumble and a muff should be kept in mind in considering rules about fumbles. A fumble is the loss of possession of the ball. A muff is the touching of a loose ball by a player in an unsuccessful attempt to obtain possession.
2. A fumble may be advanced by any player on either team regardless of whether recovered before or after ball hits the ground.
3. A fumble that goes forward and out of bounds will return to the fumbling team at the spot of the fumble unless the ball goes out of bounds in the opponent's end zone. In this case, the defensive team is to take possession at the spot of the fumble.
4. If an offensive player fumbles anywhere on the field during a fourth down play, or if a player fumbles on any down after the two-minute warning in a half, only the fumbling player is permitted to recover and/or advance the ball. If recovered by any other offensive player, the ball is dead at the spot of the fumble unless it is recovered behind the spot of the fumble. In that case, ball is dead at spot of recovery. Any defensive player may recover and/or advance any fumble.
   Exception: The fourth-down fumble rule does not apply if a player touches, but does not possess, a direct snap from center, i.e., a snap in flight as opposed to a hand-to-hand exchange.

Kicks From Scrimmage

1. Any punt or missed field goal that touches a goal post is dead.
2. During a kick from scrimmage, only the end men, as eligible receivers on the line of scrimmage at the time of the snap, are permitted to go beyond the line before the ball is kicked.

Exception: An eligible receiver who, at the snap, is aligned or in motion behind the line and more than one yard outside the end man on his side of the line, clearly making him the outside receiver, REPLACES that end man as the player eligible to go downfield after the snap. All other members of the kicking team must remain at the line of scrimmage until the ball has been kicked.

3. Any punt that is blocked and does not cross the line of scrimmage can be recovered and advanced by either team. However, if offensive team recovers it must make the yardage necessary for its first down to retain possession if punt was on fourth down.
4. The kicking team may never advance its own kick even though legal recovery is made beyond the line of scrimmage. Possession only.
5. A member of the receiving team may not run into or rough a kicker who kicks from behind his line unless contact is:
   (a) Incidental to and after he had touched ball in flight.
   (b) Caused by kicker's own motions.
   (c) Occurs during a quick kick, or a kick made after a run, or after kicker recovers a loose ball. Ball is loose when kicker muffs snap or snap hits ground.
   (d) Defender is blocked into kicker.
   The penalty for running into the kicker is 5 yards. For roughing the kicker: 15 yards, an automatic first down and disqualification if flagrant.
6. If a member of the kicking team attempting to down the ball on or inside opponent's 5 yard line carries the ball into the end zone, it is a touchback.
7. Fouls during a punt are enforced from the previous spot (line of scrimmage). **Exception:** Illegal touching, illegal fair catch, invalid fair catch signal, and fouls by the receiving team during loose ball after ball is kicked.
8. While the ball is in the air or rolling on the ground following a punt or field goal attempt and receiving team commits a foul before gaining possession, receiving team will retain possession and will be penalized for its foul.
9. It will be illegal for a defensive player to jump or stand on any player, or be picked up by a teammate or to use a hand or hands on a teammate to gain additional height in an attempt to block a kick (Penalty 15 yards, unsportsmanlike conduct).
10. A punted ball remains a kicked ball until it is declared dead or in possession of either team.
11. Any member of the punting team may down the ball anywhere in the field of play. However, it is illegal touching (Official's time out and receiver's ball at spot of illegal touching). This foul does not offset any foul by receivers during the down.
12. Defensive team may advance all kicks from scrimmage (including unsuccessful field goal) whether or not ball crosses defensive team's goal line. Rules pertaining to kicks from scrimmage apply until defensive team gains possession.

Fair Catch

1. The member of the receiving team must raise one arm a full length above his head and wave it from side to side while kick is in flight. (Failure to give proper sign: receivers' ball five yards behind spot of signal.) **Note:** It is legal for the receiver to shield his eyes from the sun by raising one hand no higher than the helmet.
2. No opponent may interfere with the fair catcher, the ball, or his path to the ball. Penalty: 15 yards from spot of foul and fair catch is awarded.
3. A player who signals for a fair catch is not required to catch the ball. However, if a player signals for a fair catch, he may not block or initiate contact with any player on the kicking team until the ball touches a player. Penalty: snap 15 yards behind spot of foul.
4. If ball hits ground or is touched by member of kicking team in flight, fair catch signal is off and all rules for a kicked ball apply.
5. Any undue advance by a fair catch receiver is delay of game. No specific distance is specified for "undue advance" as ball is dead at spot of catch. If player comes to a reasonable stop, no penalty. For violation, five yards.
6. If time expires while ball is in play and a fair catch is awarded, receiving team may choose to extend the period with one free kick down. However, placekicker may not use tee.

Foul on Last Play of Half or Game

1. On a foul by defense on last play of half or game, the down is replayed if penalty is accepted.
2. On a foul by the offense on last play of half or game, the down is not replayed and the play in which the foul is committed is nullified. Exception: Fair catch interference, foul following change of possession, illegal touching. No score by offense counts.
3. On double foul on last play of half or game, down is replayed.

Spot of Enforcement of Foul

1. There are four basic spots at which a penalty for a foul is enforced:
   (a) Spot of foul: The spot where the foul is committed.
   (b) Previous spot: The spot where the ball was put in play.
   (c) Spot of snap, pass, fumble, return kick, or free kick: The spot where the act connected with the foul occurred.
   (d) Succeeding spot: The spot where the ball next would be put in play if no distance penalty were to be enforced.
   Exception: If foul occurs after a touchdown and before the whistle for a try-for-point, succeeding spot is spot of next kickoff.
2. All fouls committed by offensive team behind the line of scrimmage and in the field of play shall be penalized from the previous spot.
3. When spot of enforcement for fouls involving defensive holding or illegal use of hands by the defense is behind the line of scrimmage, any penalty yardage to be assessed on that play shall be measured from the line if the foul occurred beyond the line.

Double Foul

1. If there is a double foul during a down in which there is a change of possession, the team last gaining possession may keep the ball unless its foul was committed prior to the change of possession.
2. If double foul occurs after a change of possession, the defensive team retains the ball at the spot of its foul or dead ball spot.
3. If one of the fouls of a double foul involves disqualification, that player must be removed, but no penalty yardage is to be assessed.
4. If the kickers foul during a punt before possession changes and the receivers foul after possession changes, penalties will be offset and the down is replayed.

Penalty Enforced on Following Kickoff

1. When a team scores by touchdown, field goal, extra point, or safety and either team commits a personal foul, unsportsmanlike conduct, or obvious unfair act during the down, the penalty will be assessed on the following kickoff.

Procedures to Terminate or Temporarily Delay Completion of a Game

The National Football League holds to the position that all games should be played to their conclusion. However, if in the opinion of appropriate League authorities, it is impossible to begin or continue a game due to an emergency, or a game is deemed to be imminently threatened by any such emergency—e.g., severely inclement weather, lightning, flooding, power failure, interference by spectators, or other non-participants—then the following procedures will serve as guidelines for the Commissioner and/or his duly appointed representatives. The Commissioner will have the power to review the circumstances of each emergency and to adjust the following procedures in whatever manner he deems appropriate. If, in the Commissioner's opinion, it is reasonable to project that the resumption of an interrupted game would not change its ultimate result, he will be empowered to terminate the game.

1. The League employees vested with the authority to define emergencies under these procedures are the Commissioner, his representatives, and the game referee. In cases where neither the Commissioner nor his representatives are present, the referee shall have sole authority but he must make every effort to contact the Commissioner or representative for consultation. In all cases of significant delay, the League authorities will consult with the management of the participating clubs.
2. If, due to an emergency, a regular-season or postseason game is not started at its scheduled time and cannot be played at any later time that same day, the game, nevertheless, must be played on a subsequent date to be determined by the Commissioner.
3. If there is deemed to be a threat of an emergency (e.g., incoming tropical storm) that may occur during the playing of a game, the starting time of such game will not be moved to an earlier time unless there is clearly sufficient time to make an orderly change.
4. If an interrupted regular-season or postseason game cannot be completed on the same day, such game will be rescheduled by the Commissioner and resumed at that point.
5. In instances which require the Commissioner to reschedule a regular-season game, he will make every effort to set the game for no later than two days after its originally scheduled date, and if possible, at its original site. If unable to do so, he will schedule it at the nearest available facility. If it is impossible to schedule the game within two days after its original date, the Commissioner will attempt to schedule it on the Tuesday of the next calendar week in which the two involved clubs play other clubs no earlier than Sunday.
6. If an emergency interrupts a postseason game and such game cannot be resumed on that same date, the Commissioner will make every effort to arrange for its completion as soon as possible. If unable to schedule the game at the same site, he will select an appropriate alternate site. He will terminate the game short of completion only if in his judgment the continuation of the game would not be normally expected to alter the ultimate outcome.
7. In all instances where a game is resumed after interruption, the resumption will begin at the point at which the game was interrupted. The referee will call time out when it is necessary to declare an emergency interruption, and he will make a record of the team possessing the ball, position of the ball on the field, down, distance, time remaining in the period, and any other pertinent information required for an efficient and equitable resumption of play.

Note: In recent history, only two games, both preseason, have been terminated. In 1976, the Chicago College All-Star game was terminated due to thunderstorms with the Steelers leading the All-Stars 24-0, and the 1980 Pro Football Hall of Fame Game at Canton, Ohio, was called with 5:29 remaining due to severe thunder and lightning with the Chargers and Packers tied 0-0.

NOTES

NOTES

NOTES

NOTES

NOTES

NOTES